THE
EXPOSITOR'S
BIBLE
COMMENTARY

THE EXPOSITOR'S BIBLE COMMENTARY

in Thirteen Volumes

When complete, the Expositor's Bible Commentary will include the following volumes:

To see which titles are available, visit www.zondervan.com.

THE
EXPOSITOR'S
BIBLE
COMMENTARY

REVISED EDITION

Numbers to Ruth

Tremper Longman III & David E. Garland

General Editors

ZONDERVAN ACADEMIC

Numbers–Ruth
Numbers — copyright © 2012 by Ronald B. Allen
Deuteronomy — copyright © 2012 by Michael A. Grisanti
Joshua — copyright © 2012 by Hélène Dallaire
Judges — copyright © 2012 by Mark J. Boda
Ruth — copyright © 2012 by George M. Schwab

Requests for information should be addressed to:

Zondervan, 3900 *Sparks Dr. SE, Grand Rapids, Michigan 49546*

Library of Congress Cataloging-in-Publication Data

The expositor's Bible commentary / [general editors], Tremper Longman III and David E. Garland. — Rev.
     p. cm.
    Includes bibliographical references.
    ISBN 978-0-310-23494-4
    1. Bible. N.T. — Commentaries. I. Longman, Tremper. II. Garland, David E.
  BS2341.53.E96 2005
  220.7 — dc22
                                      2005006281

Interior design: Tracey Walker

Printed in the United States of America

20 21 22 23 24 25 26 27 28 29 30 31 32 33 34 35 /TRM/ 25 24 23 22 21 20 19 18 17 16 15 14 13 12 11 10 9 8 7 6 5

CONTENTS

CONTRIBUTORS TO VOLUME TWO

Numbers: **Ronald B. Allen** (Th.D., Dallas Theological Seminary) is senior professor of Bible exposition at Dallas Theological Seminary, Dallas, Texas.

Deuteronomy: **Michael A. Grisanti** (Ph.D., Dallas Theological Seminary) is professor of Old Testament at The Master's Seminary, Sun Valley, California. He has written numerous journal and periodical articles and assisted in various editorial projects, including contributions to *The New International Dictionary of Old Testament Theology and Exegesis* (Zondervan, 1997) and *Eerdmans Dictionary of the Bible.*

Joshua: **Hélène Dallaire** (Ph.D., Hebrew Union College) is Associate Professor of Old Testament at Denver Seminary in Denver, Colorado. She served for five years on the faculty of Hebrew Union and is currently on the design team of the Communicative Hebrew Learning and Teaching project (CoHeLeT).

Judges: **Mark J. Boda** (Ph.D., University of Cambridge) is professor of Old Testament at McMaster Divinity College in Hamilton, Ontario, Canada. He is the author of *Haggai, Zechariah* in the NIV Application Commentary series (Zondervan, 2004) and *Praying the Tradition.*

Ruth: **George M. Schwab** (Ph.D., Westminster Theological Seminary) is associate professor of Old Testament at Erskine Theological Seminary in Due West, South Carolina.

General editor: **Tremper Longman III** (Ph.D., Yale University) is Robert H. Gundry professor of biblical studies at Westmont College in Santa Barbara, California.

General editor: **David E. Garland** (Ph.D., Southern Baptist Theological Seminary) is associate dean of academic affairs and William M. Hinson professor of Christian Scriptures at George W. Truett Seminary, Baylor University, in Waco, Texas.

PREFACE

Frank Gaebelein wrote the following in the preface to the original Expositor's Bible Commentary (which first appeared in 1979): "The title of this work defines its purpose. Written primarily by expositors for expositors, it aims to provide preachers, teachers, and students of the Bible with a new and comprehensive commentary on the books of the Old and New Testaments." Those volumes achieved that purpose admirably. The original EBC was exceptionally well received and had an enormous impact on the life of the church. It has served as the mainstay of countless pastors and students who could not afford an extensive library on each book of the Bible but who wanted solid guidance from scholars committed to the authority of the Holy Scriptures.

Gaebelein also wrote, "A commentary that will continue to be useful through the years should handle contemporary trends in biblical studies in such a way as to avoid becoming outdated when critical fashions change." This revision continues the EBC's exalted purpose and stands on the shoulders of the expositors of the first edition, but it seeks to maintain the usefulness of the commentary by interacting with new discoveries and academic discussions. While the primary goal of this commentary is to elucidate the text and not to provide a guide to the scholarly literature about the text, the commentators critically engage recent academic discussion and provide updated bibliographies so that pastors, teachers, and students can keep abreast of modern scholarship.

Some of the commentaries in the EBC have been revised by the original author or in conjunction with a younger colleague. In other cases, scholars have been commissioned to offer fresh commentaries because the original author had passed on or wanted to pass on the baton to the next generation of evangelical scholars. Today, with commentaries on a single book of the Old and New Testaments often extending into multiple volumes, the need for a comprehensive yet succinct commentary that guides one to the gist of the text's meaning is even more pressing. The new EBC seeks to fill this need.

The theological stance of this commentary series remains unchanged: the authors are committed to the divine inspiration, complete trustworthiness, and full authority of the Bible. The commentators have demonstrated proficiency in the biblical book that is their specialty, as well as commitment to the church and the pastoral dimension of biblical interpretation. They also represent the geographical and confessional diversity that characterized the first contributors.

The commentaries adhere to the same chief principle of grammatico-historical interpretation that drove the first edition. In the foreword to the inaugural issue of the journal *New Testament Studies* in 1954, Matthew Black warned that "the danger in the present is that theology, with its head too high in the clouds, may end by falling into the pit of an unhistorical and uncritical dogmatism. Into any new theological undertaking must be brought all that was best in the old ideal of sound learning, scrupulous attention to philology, text and history." The dangers that Black warned against over fifty years ago have not vanished. Indeed, new dangers arise in a secular, consumerist culture that finds it more acceptable to use God's name in exclamations than in prayer and that encourages insipid theologies that hang in the wind and shift to tickle the ears and to meet the latest fancy. Only a solid biblical foundation can fend off these fads.

The Bible was not written for our information but for our transformation. It is not a quarry to find stones with which to batter others but to find the rock on which to build the church. It does not invite us simply to speak of God but to hear God and to confess that his Son, Jesus Christ, is Lord to the glory of God the Father (Php 2:10). It also calls us to obey his commandments (Mt 28:20). It is not a self-interpreting text, however. Interpretation of the Holy Scriptures requires sound learning and regard for history, language, and text. Exegetes must interpret not only the primary documents but all that has a bearing, direct or indirect, on the grammar and syntax, historical context, transmission, and translation of these writings.

The translation used in this commentary remains the New International Version (North American edition), but all of the commentators work from the original languages (Hebrew and Greek) and draw on other translations when deemed useful. The format is also very similar to the original EBC, while the design is extensively updated with a view to enhanced ease of use for the reader. Each commentary section begins with an introduction (printed in a single-column format) that provides the reader with the background necessary to understand the Bible book. Almost all introductions include a short bibliography and an outline. The Bible text is divided into primary units that are often explained in an "Overview" section that precedes commentary on specific verses. The complete text of the New International Version is provided for quick reference, and an extensive "Commentary" section (printed in a double-column format) follows the reproducing of the text. When the Hebrew or Greek text is cited in the commentary section, a phonetic system of transliteration and translation is used. The "Notes" section (printed in a single-column format) provides a specialized discussion of key words or concepts, as well as helpful resource information. The original languages and their transliterations will appear in this section. Finally, on occasion, expanded thoughts can be found in a "Reflections" section (printed in a double-column format) that follows the Notes section.

One additional feature is worth mentioning. Throughout this volume, wherever specific biblical words are discussed, the Goodrick-Kohlenberger (GK) numbers have been added. These numbers, which appear in the *Strongest NIV Exhaustive Concordance* and other reference tools, are based on the numbering system developed by Edward Goodrick and John Kohlenberger III and provide a system similar but superior to the Strong's numbering system.

The editors wish to thank all of the contributors for their hard work and commitment to this project. We also deeply appreciate the labor and skill of the staff at Zondervan. It is a joy to work with them — in particular Jack Kuhatschek, Stan Gundry, Katya Covrett, Dirk Buursma, and Verlyn Verbrugge. In addition, we acknowledge with thanks the work of Connie Gundry Tappy as copy editor.

We all fervently desire that these commentaries will result not only in a deeper intellectual grasp of the Word of God but also in hearts that more profoundly love and obey the God who reveals himself to us in its pages.

David E. Garland, associate dean for academic affairs and
William M. Hinson professor of Christian Scriptures, George W.
Truett Theological Seminary at Baylor University

Tremper Longman III, Robert H. Gundry professor of biblical
studies, Westmont College

ABBREVIATIONS

Bible Texts, Versions, Etc.

ASV	American Standard Version	NET	New English Translation (www. netbible.com)
AT	*The Complete Bible: An American Translation* (NT: E. J. Goodspeed)	NETS	New English Translation of the Septuagint
Barclay	*The New Testament, A New Translation*	NIV	New International Version
Beck	*New Testament in Language of Today*	NJB	New Jerusalem Bible
		NJPS	New Jewish Publication Society
BHK	*Biblia Hebraica Kittel*	NKJV	New King James Version
BHS	*Biblia Hebraica Stuttgartensia*	NLT	New Living Translation
CEV	Contemporary English Version	Norlie	*New Testament in Modern English*
CSB	Christian Standard Bible	NRSV	New Revised Standard Version
ESV	English Standard Version	Phillips	*New Testament in Modern English,* J. B. Phillips
GNB	Good News Bible (see also TEV)		
GWT	God's Word Translation	REB	Revised English Bible
JB	Jerusalem Bible	Rieu	*Penguin Bible*
KJV	King James Version	RSV	Revised Standard Version
Knox	*Holy Bible: A Translation from the Latin Vulgate*	RV	Revised Version
		Tanakh	Tanakh, a Jewish translation of the Hebrew Bible
MLB	Modern Language Bible		
Moffatt	*A New Translation of the Bible,* James Moffatt	TCNT	Twentieth Century New Testament
Montgomery	*Centenary Translation of the New Testament in Modern English*	TEV	Today's English Version
		TNIV	Today's New International Version
NA[27]	*Novum Testamentum Graece,* Nestle-Aland, 27th ed.	UBS[4]	*The Greek New Testament,* United Bible Societies, 4th ed.
NAB	New American Bible		
NASB	New American Standard Bible	Weymouth	*New Testament in Modern Speech,* R. F. Weymouth
NCV	New Century Version		
NEB	New English Bible	Williams	*The New Testament in the Language of the People,* C. B. Williams

Old Testament, New Testament, Apocrypha

Ge	Genesis	Mt	Matthew
Ex	Exodus	Mk	Mark
Lev	Leviticus	Lk	Luke
Nu	Numbers	Jn	John
Dt	Deuteronomy	Ac	Acts
Jos	Joshua	Ro	Romans
Jdg	Judges	1–2Co	1–2 Corinthians
Ru	Ruth	Gal	Galatians
1–2Sa	1–2 Samuel	Eph	Ephesians
1–2 Kgdms	1–2 Kingdoms (LXX)	Php	Philippians
1–2Ki	1–2 Kings	Col	Colossians
3–4 Kgdms	3–4 Kingdoms (LXX)	1–2Th	1–2 Thessalonians
1–2Ch	1–2 Chronicles	1–2Ti	1–2 Timothy
Ezr	Ezra	Tit	Titus
Ne	Nehemiah	Phm	Philemon
Est	Esther	Heb	Hebrews
Job	Job	Jas	James
Ps/Pss	Psalm/Psalms	1–2Pe	1–2 Peter
Pr	Proverbs	1–2–3Jn	1–2–3 John
Ecc	Ecclesiastes	Jude	Jude
SS	Song of Songs	Rev	Revelation
Isa	Isaiah	Add Esth	Additions to Esther
Jer	Jeremiah	Add Dan	Additions to Daniel
La	Lamentations	Bar	Baruch
Eze	Ezekiel	Bel	Bel and the Dragon
Da	Daniel	Ep Jer	Epistle of Jeremiah
Hos	Hosea	1–2 Esd	1–2 Esdras
Joel	Joel	1–2 Macc	1–2 Maccabees
Am	Amos	3–4 Macc	3–4 Maccabees
Ob	Obadiah	Jdt	Judith
Jnh	Jonah	Pr Azar	Prayer of Azariah
Mic	Micah	Pr Man	Prayer of Manasseh
Na	Nahum	Ps 151	Psalm 151
Hab	Habakkuk	Sir	Sirach/Ecclesiasticus
Zep	Zephaniah	Sus	Susanna
Hag	Haggai	Tob	Tobit
Zec	Zechariah	Wis	Wisdom of Solomon
Mal	Malachi		

Dead Sea Scrolls and Related Texts

CD	Cairo Genizah copy of the *Damascus Document*	4QpPs	*Pesher Psalms* (texts from Qumran)
DSS	Dead Sea Scrolls	4Q44 (4QDt*q*)	Deuteronomy (texts from Qumran)
1QapGen	*Genesis Apocryphon* (texts from Qumran)	4Q174	*Florilegium* (texts from Qumran)
1QH	*Hôdāyōt* or *Thanksgiving Hymns* (texts from Qumran)	4Q252	*Commentary on Genesis A*, formerly *Patriarchal Blessings* (texts from Qumran)
1QIsa	Isaiah (texts from Qumran)		
1QM	*Milḥāmāh* or *War Scroll* (texts from Qumran)	4Q394	*Miqṣat Maʿaśê ha-Torah*ᵃ (texts from Qumran)
1QpHab	Pesher Habakkuk (texts from Qumran)	4Q400 = 407	*Songs of the Sabbath Sacrifice* (texts from Qumran)
1QS	*Serek hayyaḥad* or *Rule of the Community* (texts from Qumran)	4Q502	*Ritual of Marriage* (texts from Qumran)
1QSa	*Rule of the Congregation* (texts from Qumran)	4Q521	*Messianic Apocalypse* (texts from Qumran)
1QpMic	*Pesher Micah* (texts from Qumran)	4Q525	*Beatitudes* (texts from Qumran)
		11QPsᵃ	*Psalms Scroll*ᵃ
4QpNa	*Pesher Nahum* (texts from Qumran)	11Q13	*Melchizedek* (texts from Qumran)

Other Ancient Texts

ʾAbot R. Nat.	*ʾAbot of Rabbi Nathan*	Ant.	*Jewish Antiquities* (Josephus)
Abraham	*On the Life of Abraham* (Philo)	Ant. rom.	*Antiquitates romanae* (Dionysius of Halicarnassus)
Ad.	*Adelphi* (Terence)		
Aeth.	*Aethiopica* (Heliodorus)	1 Apol.	*First Apology* (Justin Martyr)
Ag.	*Agamemnon* (Aeschylus)	Apol.	*Apologia* (Plato, Tertullian)
Ag. Ap.	*Against Apion* (Josephus)	Apos. Con.	*Apostolic Constitutions*
Agr.	*De Lege agraria* (Cicero)	Ascen. Isa.	*Ascension of Isaiah*
Alc.	*Alcibiades* (Plutarch)	As. Mos.	*Assumption of Moses*
Alex.	*Alexander the False Prophet* (Lucian)	Att.	*Epistulae ad Atticum* (Cicero)
		b. ʿAbod. Zar.	ʿAbodah Zarah (Babylonian Talmud)
Amic.	*De amicitia* (Cicero)		
An.	*De anima* (Tertullian)	2–4 Bar.	*2–4 Baruch*
Anab.	*Anabasis* (Xenophon)	b. ʿArak	ʿArakin (Babylonian Talmud)
Ann.	*Annales* (Tacitus)	b. B. Bat.	*Bava Batra* (Babylonian Talmud)
Ant.	*Antigone* (Sophocles)		

b. B. Qam.	*Baba Qamma* (Babylonian Talmud)	*Comm. Matt.*	*Commentarium in evangelium Matthaei* (Origen)
b. Ber.	*Berakhot* (Babylonian Talmud)	*Corrept.*	*De correptione et gratia* (Augustine)
b. Hag.	*Hagigah* (Babylonian Talmud)	*Cyr.*	*Cyropaedia* (Xenophon)
b. Hor.	*Horayot* (Babylonian Talmud)	*Decal.*	*De decalogo* (Philo)
b. Ker.	*Kerithot* (Babylonian Talmud)	*Decl.*	*Declamationes* (Quintilian)
b. Ketub.	*Ketubbot* (Babylonian Talmud)	*Def. orac.*	*De defectu oraculorum* (Plutarch)
b. Meg.	*Megillah* (Babylonian Talmud)	*Deipn.*	*Deipnosophistae* (Athenaeus)
b. Menaḥ.	*Menaḥot* (Babylonian Talmud)	*Deut. Rab.*	*Deuteronomy Rabbah*
b. Moᶜed Qat.	*Moᶜed Qatan* (Babylonian Talmud)	*Dial.*	*Dialogus cum Tryphone* (Justin Martyr)
b. Ned.	*Nedarim* (Babylonian Talmud)	*Diatr.*	*Diatribai* (Epictetus)
b. Nez.	*Neziqin* (Babylonian Talmud)	*Did.*	*Didache*
b. Pesaḥ.	*Pesaḥim* (Babylonian Talmud)	*Disc.*	*Discourses* (Epictetus)
b. Roš Haš.	*b. Roš Haššanah* (Babylonian Talmud)	*Doctr. chr.*	*De doctrina christiana* (Augustine)
		Dom.	*Domitianus* (Suetonius)
b. Šabb.	*Šabbat* (Babylonian Talmud)	*Ebr.*	*De ebrietate* (Philo)
b. Sanh.	*Sanhedrin* (Babylonian Talmud)	*E Delph.*	*De E apud Delphos* (Plutarch)
b. Šebu.	*Shevuᶜot* (Babylonian Talmud)	*1–2 En.*	*1–2 Enoch*
b. Soṭah	*Soṭah* (Babylonian Talmud)	*Ench.*	*Enchiridion* (Epictetus)
b. Taᶜan.	*Taᶜanit* (Babylonian Talmud)	*Ep.*	*Epistulae morales* (Seneca)
b. Yebam.	*Yebamot* (Babylonian Talmud)	*Eph.*	*To the Ephesians* (Ignatius)
b. Yoma	*Yoma* (Babylonian Talmud)	*Epist.*	*Epistulae* (Jerome, Pliny, Hippocrates)
Bapt.	*De baptismo* (Tertullian)		
Barn.	*Barnabas*	*Ep. Tra.*	*Epistulae ad Trajanum* (Pliny)
Ben.	*De beneficiis* (Seneca)	*Eth. nic.*	*Ethica nichomachea* (Aristotle)
Bibl.	*Bibliotheca* (Photius)	*Exod. Rab.*	*Exodus Rabbah*
Bibl. hist.	*Bibliotheca historica* (Diodorus Siculus)	*Fam.*	*Epistulae ad familiares* (Cicero)
		Fid. Grat.	*De fide ad Gratianum* (Ambrose)
Bride	*Advice to the Bride and Groom* (Plutarch)	*Flacc.*	*In Flaccum* (Philo)
		Flight	*On Flight and Finding* (Philo)
Cels.	*Contra Celsum* (Origen)	*Fr. Prov.*	*Fragmenta in Proverbia* (Hippolytus)
Cic.	*Cicero* (Plutarch)		
Claud.	*Divus Claudius* (Suetonius)	*Gen. Rab.*	*Genesis Rabbah*
1–2 Clem.	*1–2 Clement*	*Geogr.*	*Geographica* (Strabo)
Comm. Dan.	*Commentarium in Danielem* (Hippolytus)	*Gorg.*	*Gorgias* (Plato)
		Haer.	*Adversus Haereses* (Irenaeus)
Comm. Jo.	*Commentarii in evangelium Joannis* (Origen)	*Heir*	*Who Is the Heir?* (Philo)
		Hell.	*Hellenica* (Xenophon)

Hist.	*Historicus* (Polybius, Cassius Dio, Thucydides)	*m. Naz.*	*Nazir* (Mishnah)
Hist.	*Historiae* (Herodotus, Tacitus)	*m. Ned.*	*Nedarim* (Mishnah)
Hist. eccl.	*History of the Church* (Eusebius)	*m. Nid.*	*Niddah* (Mishnah)
Hist. Rome	*The History of Rome* (Livy)	*m. Pesaḥ.*	*Pesaḥim* (Mishnah)
Hom. Acts	*Homilies on Acts* (John Chrysostom)	*m. Šabb.*	*Šabbat* (Mishnah)
Hom. Col.	*Homilies on Colossians* (John Chrysostom)	*m. Sanh.*	*Sanhedrin* (Mishnah)
Hom. Jo.	*Homilies on John* (John Chrysostom)	*m. Šeqal.*	*Šeqalim* (Mishnah)
Hom. Josh.	*Homilies on Joshua* (Origen)	*m. Taʿan.*	*Taʿanit* (Mishnah)
Hom. Phil.	*Homilies on Philippians* (John Chrysostom)	*m. Tamid*	*Tamid* (Mishnah)
Hom. Rom.	*Homilies on Romans* (John Chrysostom)	*m. Ṭehar.*	*Ṭeharot* (Mishnah)
Hom. 1 Tim.	*Homilies on 1 Timothy* (John Chrysostom)	*Magn.*	*To the Magnesians* (Ignatius)
		Mand.	*Mandate* (Shepherd of Hermas)
Hom. 2 Tim.	*Homilies on 2 Timothy* (John Chrysostom)	*Marc.*	*Adversus Marcionem* (Tertullian)
		Mem.	*Memorabilia* (Xenophon)
Hom. Tit.	*Homilies on Titus* (John Chrysostom)	*Midr. Ps.*	*Midrash on Psalms*
		Migr.	*De migratione Abrahami* (Philo)
Hypoth.	*Hypothetica* (Philo)	*Mor.*	*Moralia* (Plutarch)
Inst.	*Institutio oratoria* (Quintilian)	*Moses*	*On the Life of Moses* (Philo)
Jos. Asen.	*Joseph and Aseneth*	*Nat.*	*Naturalis historia* (Pliny)
Joseph	*On the Life of Joseph* (Philo)	*Num. Rab.*	*Numbers Rabbah*
Jub.	*Jubilees*	*Onir.*	*Onirocritica* (Artemidorus)
J.W.	*Jewish War* (Josephus)	*Or.*	*Orationes* (Demosthenes)
Lam. Rab.	*Lamentations Rabbah*	*Or.*	*Orationes* (Dio Chrysostom)
L.A.E.	*Life of Adam and Eve*	*Paed.*	*Paedagogus* (Clement of Alexandria)
Leg.	*Legum allegoriae* (Philo)		
Legat.	*Legatio ad Gaium* (Philo)	*Peregr.*	*The Passing of Peregrinus* (Lucian)
Let. Aris.	*Letter of Aristeas*	*Pesiq. Rab.*	*Pesiqta Rabbati*
Lev. Rab.	*Leviticus Rabbah*	*Pesiq. Rab Kah.*	*Pesiqta of Rab Kahana*
Liv. Pro.	*Lives of the Prophets*	*Phaed.*	*Phaedo* (Plato)
m. Bek.	*Bekhorot* (Mishnah)	*Phil.*	*To the Philippians* (Polycarp)
m. Bik.	*Bikkurim* (Mishnah)	*Phld.*	*To the Philadelphians* (Ignatius)
m. Giṭ.	*Giṭṭin* (Mishnah)	*Phorm.*	*Phormio* (Terence)
m. Mak.	*Makkot* (Mishnah)	*Planc.*	*Pro Plancio* (Cicero)
m. Mid.	*Middot* (Mishnah)	*Plant.*	*De plantatione* (Philo)
		Pol.	*Politica* (Aristotle)
		Pol.	*To Polycarp* (Ignatius)
		Posterity	*On the Posterity of Cain* (Origen)
		Praescr.	*De praescriptione haereticorum* (Tertullian)
		Princ.	*De principiis* (Origen)

Prom.	Prometheus vinctus (Aeschylus)	Stat.	Ad populum Antiochenum de statuis
Pss. Sol.	Psalms of Solomon		(John Chrysostom)
Pud.	De pudicitia (Tertullian)	Strom.	Stromata (Clement of Alexandria)
Pyth.	Pythionikai (Pindar)	T. Ash.	Testament of Asher
Pyth. orac.	De Pythiae oraculis (Plutarch)	T. Dan	Testament of Dan
Quaest. conv.	Quaestionum convivialium libri IX	T. Gad	Testament of Gad
	(Plutarch)	T. Naph.	Testament of Naphtali
Quint. fratr.	Epistulae ad Quintum fratrem	Tg. Neof.	Targum Neofiti
	(Cicero)	Tg. Onq.	Targum Onqelos
Rab. Perd.	Pro Rabirio Perduellionis Reo	Tg. Ps.-J.	Targum Pseudo-Jonathan
	(Cicero)	Theaet.	Theaetetus (Plato)
Resp.	Respublica (Plato)	t. Ḥul.	Ḥullin (Tosefta)
Rewards	On Rewards and Punishments	T. Jos.	Testament of Joseph
	(Philo)	T. Jud.	Testament of Judah
Rhet.	Rhetorica (Aristotle)	T. Levi	Testament of Levi
Rhet.	Volumina rhetorica (Philodemus)	T. Mos.	Testament of Moses
Rom.	To the Romans (Ignatius)	T. Naph.	Testament of Naphtali
Rosc. com.	Pro Roscio comoedo (Cicero)	Trall.	To the Trallians (Ignatius)
Sacrifices	On the Sacrifices of Cain and Abel	T. Reu.	Testament of Reuben
	(Philo)	Tusc.	Tusculanae disputationes (Cicero)
Sat.	Satirae (Horace, Juvenal)	Verr.	In Verrem (Cicero)
Sera	De sera numinis vindicta (Plutarch)	Virt.	De virtutibus (Philo)
Serm.	Sermones (Augustine)	Vis.	Visions (Shepherd of Hermas)
Sib. Or.	Sibylline Oracles	Vit. Apoll.	Vita Apollonii (Philostratus)
Sim.	Similitudes (Shepherd of Hermas)	Vit. beat.	De vita beata (Seneca)
Smyrn.	To the Smyrnaeans (Ignatius)	Vit. soph.	Vitae sophistarum (Philostratus)
S. ʿOlam Rab.	Seder ʿOlam Rabbah	y. ʿAbod. Zar.	ʿAbodah Zarah (Jerusalem
Somn.	De somniis (Philo)		Talmud)
Spec.	De specialibus legibus (Philo)	y. Ḥag.	Ḥagigah (Jerusalem Talmud)
		y. Šabb.	Šabbat (Jerusalem Talmud)

Journals, Periodicals, Reference Works, Series

AASOR	Annual of the American Schools of Oriental Research	ABRL	Anchor Bible Reference Library
		ABW	Archaeology in the Biblical World
AB	Anchor Bible	ACCS	Ancient Christian Commentary
ABD	Anchor Bible Dictionary		on Scripture
ABR	Australian Biblical Review	ACNT	Augsburg Commentaries on the
AbrN	Abr-Nahrain		New Testament

AcT	*Acta theologica*	*BASOR*	*Bulletin of the American Schools of Oriental Research*
AEHL	*Archaeological Encyclopedia of the Holy Land* (3rd ed.)	BBB	Bonner biblische Beiträge
AHw	*Akkadisches Handwörterbuch*	*BBR*	*Bulletin for Biblical Research*
AIs	*Ancient Israel,* by Roland de Vaux	BDAG	Bauer, Danker, Arndt, and Gingrich (3d ed.). *Greek-English Lexicon of the New Testament and Other Early Christian Literature*
AJBI	*Annual of the Japanese Biblical Institute*		
AJSL	*American Journal of Semitic Languages and Literature*	BDB	Brown, Driver, and Briggs. *A Hebrew and English Lexicon of the Old Testament*
AnBib	Analecta biblica		
ANEP	*The Ancient Near East in Pictures Relating to the Old Testament*	BDF	Blass, Debrunner, and Funk. *A Greek Grammar of the New Testament and Other Early Christian Literature*
ANET	*Ancient Near Eastern Texts Relating to the Old Testament*		
ANF	*Ante-Nicene Fathers*		
AnOr	Analecta orientalia	*BEB*	*Baker Encyclopedia of the Bible*
ANRW	*Aufstieg und Niedergang der römischen Welt*	BECNT	Baker Exegetical Commentary on the New Testament
AOAT	Alter Orient und Altes Testament	*Ber*	*Berytus*
AR	*Archiv für Religionswissenschaft*	BETL	Bibliotheca ephemeridum theologicarum lovaniensium
ARM	Archives royales de Mari		
ASORMS	American Schools of Oriental Research Monograph Series	BGU	*Aegyptische Urkunden aus den Königlichen Staatlichen Museen zu Berlin, Griechische Urkunden*
ASTI	*Annual of the Swedish Theological Institute*		
AThR	*Anglican Theological Review*	*BHRG*	*Biblical Hebrew Reference Grammar,* ed. C. Van Der Merwe, J. A. Naudé, and J. H. Kroeze
ATLA	American Theological Library Association		
AuOr	Aula orientalis	*BI*	*Biblical Illustrator*
AUSDDS	Andrews University Seminary Doctoral Dissertation Series	*Bib*	*Biblica*
		BibInt	*Biblical Interpretation*
AUSS	*Andrews University Seminary Studies*	BibOr	Biblica et orientalia
		BibS(N)	Biblische Studien (Neukirchen)
BA	*Biblical Archaeologist*	*Bijdr*	*Bijdragen: Tijdschrit voor filosofie en theologie*
BAGD	Bauer, Arndt, Gingrich, and Danker (2nd ed.). *Greek-English Lexicon of the New Testament and Other Early Christian Literature*	BIS	Biblical Interpretation Studies
		BJRL	*Bulletin of the John Rylands University Library of Manchester*
		BJS	Brown Judaic Studies
BAR	*Biblical Archaeology Review*	BKAT	Biblischer Kommentar, Altes Testament

BN	*Biblische Notizen*	*CTR*	*Criswell Theological Review*
BR	*Biblical Research*	*DCH*	*Dictionary of Classical Hebrew*
BRev	*Bible Review*	*DDD*	*Dictionary of Deities and Demons in the Bible*
BSac	*Bibliotheca sacra*		
BSC	Bible Student's Commentary	DJD	Discoveries in the Judean Desert
BST	The Bible Speaks Today	*DRev*	*Downside Review*
BT	*The Bible Translator*	*DukeDivR*	*Duke Divinity Review*
BTB	*Biblical Theology Bulletin*	EA	El-Amarna tablets
BWANT	Beiträge zur Wissenschaft zum Alter und Neuen Testament	EBC	Expositor's Bible Commentary
		EBib	*Études bibliques*
BZ	*Biblische Zeitschrift*	ECC	Eerdmans Critical Commentary
BZAW	Beihefte zur Zeitschrift für die alttestamentliche Wissenschaft	*EcR*	*Ecumenical Review*
		EDNT	*Exegetical Dictionary of the New Testament*
BZNW	Beihefte zur Zeitschrift für die neutestamentliche Wissenschaft		
		EgT	*Eglise et théologie*
CAD	*Assyrian Dictionary of the Oriental Institute of the University of Chicago*	EGT	Expositor's Greek Testament
		EncJud	*Encyclopedia Judaica*
		ErIsr	*Eretz-Israel*
CAH	Cambridge Ancient History	ESCJ	Etudes sur le christianisme et le judaisme (Studies in Christianity and Judaism)
CahRB	Cahiers de la Revue biblique		
CBC	Cambridge Bible Commentary		
CBQ	*Catholic Biblical Quarterly*	*EstBib*	*Estudios bíblicos*
CBQMS	Catholic Biblical Quarterly Monograph Series	*ETL*	*Ephemerides theologicae lovanienses*
		ETS	Evangelical Theological Society
CGTC	Cambridge Greek Testament Commentary	*EuroJTh*	*European Journal of Theology*
		EvJ	*Evangelical Journal*
CH	*Church History*	*EvQ*	*Evangelical Quarterly*
ChrT	*Christianity Today*	*EvT*	*Evangelische Theologie*
CIG	*Corpus inscriptionum graecarum*	*ExAud*	*Ex auditu*
CIL	*Corpus inscriptionum latinarum*	*Exeg*	*Exegetica*
CJT	*Canadian Journal of Theology*	*ExpTim*	*Expository Times*
ConBNT	Coniectanea biblica: New Testament Series	FF	Foundations and Facets
		FRLANT	Forschungen zur Religion und Literatur des Alten und Neuen Testaments
ConBOT	Coniectanea biblica: Old Testament Series		
COS	*The Context of Scripture*	GBS	Guides to Biblical Scholarship
CTJ	*Calvin Theological Journal*	GKC	*Genesius' Hebrew Grammar*
CTM	*Concordia Theological Monthly*	*GNS*	*Good News Studies*
CTQ	*Concordia Theological Quarterly*	*GR*	*Greece and Rome*

Grammar	*A Grammar of the Greek New Testament; in the Light of Historical Research* (A. T. Robertson)	*IDBSup*	*Interpreter's Dictionary of the Bible: Supplement*
GRBS	*Greek, Roman, and Byzantine Studies*	*IEJ*	*Israel Exploration Journal*
GTJ	*Grace Theological Journal*	*IJT*	*Indian Journal of Theology*
HALOT	Koehler, Baumgartner, and Stamm. *The Hebrew and Aramaic Lexicon of the Old Testament*	*Imm*	*Immanuel*
		Int	*Interpretation*
		ISBE	*International Standard Bible Ency- clopedia*, 2d ed.
HAR	*Hebrew Annual Review*	*IVPBBC*	IVP Bible Background Commentary
HAT	Handbuch zum Alten Testament		
HBD	*HarperCollins Bible Dictionary*	*IVPNTC*	IVP New Testament Commen- tary
HBT	*Horizons in Biblical Theology*		
Herm	Hermeneia commentary series	*JAAR*	*Journal of the American Academy of Religion*
HeyJ	*Heythrop Journal*		
HNT	Handbuch zum Neuen Testa- ment	JAARSup	JAAR Supplement Series
		JANESCU	*Journal of the Ancient Near Eastern Society of Columbia University*
HNTC	Harper's New Testament Com- mentaries	*JAOS*	*Journal of the American Oriental Society*
Hor	*Horizons*		
HS	*Hebrew Studies*	JAOSSup	Journal of the American Oriental Society Supplement Series
HSM	Harvard Semitic Monographs	*JBL*	*Journal of Biblical Literature*
HSS	Harvard Semitic Studies	*JBMW*	*Journal for Biblical Manhood and Womanhood*
HTKNT	Herders theologischer Kommen- tar zum Neuen Testament		
		JBQ	*Jewish Biblical Quaterly*
HTR	*Harvard Theological Review*	*JBR*	*Journal of Bible and Religion*
HTS	Harvard Theological Studies	*JCS*	*Journal of Cuneiform Studies*
HUBP	Hebrew Union Bible Project	*Jeev*	*Jeevadhara*
HUCA	*Hebrew Union College Annual*	*JE*	*Jewish Encyclopedia*
IB	*Interpreter's Bible*	*JETS*	*Journal of the Evangelical Theologi- cal Society*
IBC	Interpretation: A Bible Com- mentary for Teaching and Preaching		
		JJS	*Journal of Jewish Studies*
		JNES	*Journal of Near Eastern Studies*
IBHS	*An Introduction to Biblical Hebrew Syntax* (Waltke and O'Connor)	*JNSL*	*Journal of Northwest Semitic Languages*
IBS	*Irish Biblical Studies*	*JPOS*	*Journal of the Palestine Oriental Society*
ICC	International Critical Commentary		
		JQR	*Jewish Quarterly Review*
IDB	*Interpreter's Dictionary of the Bible*	*JRS*	*Journal of Roman Studies*

JSNT	*Journal for the Study of the New Testament*	MM	Moulton and Milligan. *The Vocabulary of the Greek Testament*
JSNTSup	JSNT Supplement Series	*MSJ*	*The Master's Seminary Journal*
JSOT	*Journal for the Study of the Old Testament*	NAC	New American Commentary
		NBC	*New Bible Commentary*, rev. ed.
JSOTSup	JSOT Supplement Series	*NBD*	*New Bible Dictionary*, 2d ed.
JSP	*Journal for the Study of the Pseudepigrapha*	NCB	New Century Bible
		NCBC	New Century Bible Commentary
JSS	*Journal of Semitic Studies*		
JSSEA	*Journal of the Society for the Study of Egyptian Antiquities*	*Neot*	*Neotestamentica*
		NETS	*A New English Translation of the Septuagint and Other Greek Translations Traditionally Included under That Title* (Oxford, 2007)
JTC	*Journal for Theology and the Church*		
JTS	*Journal of Theological Studies*		
Joüon	P. Joüon, *Grammar of Biblical Hebrew*, trans. and revised by T. Muroaka		
		NewDocs	*New Documents Illustrating Early Christianity*
K&D	Keil and Delitzsch, *Biblical Commentary on the Old Testament*	NIBC	New International Biblical Commentary
KB	Koehler-Baumgartner, *Hebräisches und Aramäisches Lexicon zum Alten Testament* (first or second edition; third edition is *HALOT*)	NICNT	New International Commentary on the New Testament
		NICOT	New International Commentary on the Old Testament
		NIDNTT	*New International Dictionary of New Testament Theology*
KEK	Kritisch-exegetischer Kommentar über das Neue Testament	*NIDOTTE*	*New International Dictionary of Old Testament Theology and Exegesis*
KHAT	Kurgefasstes exegetisches Handbuch zum Alten Testament		
KTU	*Die keilalphabetischen Texte aus Ugarit*	NIGTC	New International Greek Testament Commentary
L&N	Louw and Nida. *Greek-English Lexicon of the New Testament: Based on Semantic Domains*	NIVAC	NIV Application Commentary
		NIVSB	Zondervan NIV Study Bible
		Notes	*Notes on Translation*
LCC	Library of Christian Classics	*NovT*	*Novum Testamentum*
LCL	Loeb Classical Library	NovTSup	Novum Testamentum Supplements
LEC	Library of Early Christianity		
LS	*Louvain Studies*	*NPNF*	*Nicene and Post-Nicene Fathers*
LSJ	Liddell, Scott, and Jones. *A Greek-English Lexicon*	NTC	New Testament Commentary (Baker)
LTP	*Laval théologique et philosophique*	NTD	Das Neue Testament Deutsch
		NTG	New Testament Guides

NTS	*New Testament Studies*	SBB	Stuttgarter biblische Beiträge
NTT	New Testament Theology	*SBJT*	*Southern Baptist Journal of*
NTTS	New Testament Tools and		*Theology*
	Studies	SBLDS	Society of Biblical Literature
OBO	Orbis biblicus et orientalis		Dissertation Series
OBT	Overtures to Biblical Theology	*SBLSP*	*Society of Biblical Literature Semi-*
OJRS	*Ohio Journal of Religious Studies*		*nar Papers*
OLA	Orientalia lovaniensia analecta	SBLWAW	Society of Biblical Literature
Or	*Orientalia* (NS)		Writings from the Ancient World
OTE	Old Testament Essays	*SBT*	*Studies in Biblical Theology*
OTG	Old Testament Guides	*ScEccl*	*Sciences ecclésiastiques*
OTL	Old Testament Library	*ScEs*	*Science et esprit*
OTS	Old Testament Studies	ScrHier	Scripta hierosolymitana
OtSt	*Oudtestamentische Studien*	*SE*	*Studia evangelica*
PEGLMBS	*Proceedings, Eastern Great Lakes*	SEG	Supplementum epigraphicum
	and Midwest Bible Societies		graecum
PEQ	*Palestine Exploration Quarterly*	*Sem*	*Semitica*
PG	Patrologia graeca	SJLA	Studies in Judaism of Late
PL	Patrologia latina		Antiquity
PNTC	Pillar New Testament	*SJOT*	*Scandinavian Journal of the Old*
	Commentary		*Testament*
Presb	*Presbyterion*	*SJT*	*Scottish Journal of Theology*
PresR	*Presbyterian Review*	SNT	Studien zum Neuen Testament
PRSt	*Perspectives in Religious Studies*	SNTSMS	Society for New Testament
PTMS	Pittsburgh Theological Mono-		Studies Monograph Series
	graph Series	SNTSU	Studien zum Neuen Testament
PTR	*Princeton Theological Review*		und seiner Umwelt
RB	*Revue biblique*	SP	Sacra pagina
RBibLit	*Review of Biblical Literature*	*SR*	*Studies in Religion*
RefJ	*Reformed Journal*	*ST*	*Studia theologica*
RelSRev	*Religious Studies Review*	Str-B	Strack, H. L., and P. Billerbeck,
ResQ	*Restoration Quarterly*		*Kommentar zum Neuen Testament*
RevExp	*Review and Expositor*		*aus Talmud und Midrasch*
RevQ	*Revue de Qumran*	*StudBT*	*Studia biblica et theologica*
RevScRel	*Revue des sciences religieuses*	SUNT	Studien zur Umwelt des Neuen
RHPR	*Revue d'histoire et de philosophie*		Testaments
	religieuses	*SVF*	*Stoicorum veterum fragmenta*
RTR	*Reformed Theological Review*	SVT	Studia in Veteris Testamenti
SAOC	Studies in Ancient Oriental	*SwJT*	*Southwestern Journal of Theology*
	Civilizations	*TA*	*Tel Aviv*

TBD	*Tyndale Bible Dictionary*	*TZ*	*Theologische Zeitschrift*
TBT	*The Bible Today*	UBD	*Unger's Bible Dictionary*
TDNT	Kittel and Friedrich. *Theological Dictionary of the New Testament*	UF	*Ugarit-Forschungen*
		UT	*Ugaritic Textbook*
TDOT	Botterweck and Ringgren. *Theological Dictionary of the Old Testament*	VE	*Vox evangelica*
		VT	*Vetus Testamentum*
		VTSup	Supplements to Vetus Testamentum
TF	*Theologische Forschung*		
THAT	*Theologisches Handwörterbuch zum Alten Testament*	WBC	Word Biblical Commentary
		WBE	*Wycliffe Bible Encyclopedia*
Them	*Themelios*	WEC	Wycliffe Exegetical Commentary
ThEv	*Theologia Evangelica*	WMANT	Wissenschaftliche Monographien zum Alten und Neuen Testament
THKNT	Theologischer Handkommentar zum Neuen Testament		
ThTo	*Theology Today*	*WTJ*	*Westminster Theological Journal*
TJ	*Trinity Journal*	WUNT	Wissenschaftliche Untersuchungen zum Neuen Testament
TLNT	*Theological Lexicon of the New Testament*		
		YCS	*Yale Classical Studies*
TLOT	*Theological Lexicon of the Old Testament*	*ZAH*	*Zeitschrift für Althebräistik*
		ZAW	*Zeitschrift für die alttestamentliche Wissenschaft*
TNTC	Tyndale New Testament Commentaries		
		ZNW	*Zeitschrift für die neutestamentliche Wissenschaft und die Kunde der älterern Kirche*
TOTC	Tyndale Old Testament Commentaries		
TQ	*Theologische Quartalschrift*	ZPEB	*Zondervan Pictorial Encyclopedia of the Bible*
TS	*Theological Studies*		
TWOT	*Theological Wordbook of the Old Testament*	*ZWT*	*Zeitschrift für wissenschaftliche Theologie*
TynBul	*Tyndale Bulletin*		

General

AD	*anno Domini* (in the year of [our] Lord)	ca.	*circa* (around, about, approximately)
Akkad.	Akkadian	cf.	*confer*, compare
Arab.	Arabic	ch(s).	chapter(s)
Aram.	Aramaic	d.	died
BC	before Christ	diss.	dissertation
		ed(s).	editor(s), edited by, edition

e.g.	*exempli gratia*, for example	n.d.	no date
esp.	especially	NS	New Series
et al.	*et alii*, and others	NT	New Testament
EV	English versions of the Bible	OT	Old Testament
f(f).	and the following one(s)	p(p).	page(s)
fig.	figuratively	par.	parallel (indicates textual
frg.	fragment		parallels)
Gk.	Greek	para.	paragraph
GK	Goodrick & Kohlenberger num-	repr.	reprinted
	bering system	rev.	revised
Heb.	Hebrew	Samar.	Samaritan Pentateuch
ibid.	*ibidem*, in the same place	s.v.	*sub verbo*, under the word
i.e.	*id est*, that is	Syr.	Syriac
JPS	Jewish Publication Society	Tg.	Targum
Lat.	Latin	TR	Textus Receptus (Greek text of
lit.	literally		the KJV translation)
LXX	Septuagint (the Greek OT)	trans.	translator, translated by
MS(S)	manuscript(s)	v(v).	verse(s)
MT	Masoretic Text of the OT	vs.	versus
n(n).	note(s)	Vul.	Vulgate

NUMBERS

RONALD B. ALLEN

Introduction

1. BACKGROUND

Commentators on the book of Numbers tend to begin with a survey of the problems this book presents and even express a sense of ennui concerning the matter of the numbers in the book. At the beginning of his sterling work, Raymond Brown admits, "Numbers might not score a high rating in a 'favourite book of the Bible' competition."[1] Nonetheless, we begin where Arnold M. Goldberg concludes. In his summary he asserts the importance of the book of Numbers to *Heilsgeschichte*, the "salvation history" of the people of God.[2] Going beyond him we contend that the book of Numbers is sublime. It forms an essential link in that forward-directedness from Adam to Jesus. In the most unusual of ways, it heightens our appreciation of and response to the person of Yahweh. For Christians this book is rewarding, for in it we find ourselves

---

1. Raymond Brown, *The Message of Numbers—Journey to the Promised Land* (BST; ed. H. A. Motyer; Downers Grove, Ill.: InterVarsity Press, 1984), 14. It is evident throughout his commentary that this situation is one that Brown, former principal of Spurgeon's College in London, wishes to change—and change mightily.
2. Arnold Goldberg, *Das Buch Numeri* (Die Welt der Bible; Dusseldorf: Patmos, 1970), 136. He goes on, "For the Christian reader, this book is first of all an epoch of *Heilsgeschichte*, an epoch of that history that moves forward from Adam the fallen man to Jesus." (Note that all translations from German, French, and Dutch sources are my own, unless otherwise noted.)

confronting in new ways the meaning of our salvation in Jesus Christ. He who is the goal of all history is the goal of the book of Numbers.[3]

God has time; the wilderness has sand. In this aphorism we find the heart of the book of Numbers. All true biblical understanding is based on a solid conviction of the overwhelming grace of God (see Ex 34:5–7). When the people of Israel whom God had redeemed, those whom he had delivered from Egypt and made alive in him—when these people rebelled against him in the wilderness, when they said "No" to action and "No thanks" to his leadership, they risked destruction. But God, who is rich in mercy, did not annihilate them. He did not make an end of them. Rather, he allowed his erring people to live out the rest of their lives in the wilderness—for God has time. And he allowed their children to bury them—for the wilderness has sand.

Then, to the next generation the challenge was to be given: Would they like their parents say "No" to God? Or would they follow him as he would lead them into the land of promise? Well, God has time and the wilderness has sand. If the second generation behaved as their mothers and fathers had, then they too would be buried in the sands of the wilderness. But one day there would be a generation that would rise up and follow God, follow him all the way to Canaan. This idea is the heart of the book of Numbers. It describes how God chastened in wrath his disobedient people, while he waited for their children to accept the challenge of his gracious gift in leading them to Canaan.

Worship is an emphasis in the book of Numbers that has not been given sufficient attention. It is generally known that the book contains important materials for the worship patterns of Israel. Documentary-critical scholars, for example, are convinced that much of the book is the work of priests, so pervasive are "priestly" elements in this book.[4] But it is not just that the book of Numbers *contains* worship materials such as the celebrated Aaronic Benediction (Nu 6) or instructions about Passover (Nu 9). In the end we may discover that the pulse of the book is worship; the book of Numbers may be viewed as a worship document. It *was* a text for the worship of God by Moses and those who aligned themselves with him. By God's grace it may become a book of worship for us as well.

However, before the book of Numbers will become a book of worship for us, we will find it to be a book of trouble. The introduction to this book is longer than some in this series because of the (sometimes baffling) problems it presents to the modern reader.

The book of Numbers yields significant rewards for the patient reader. In a day marked by pop art, quick fixes, and fast foods, the book of Numbers is troublesome. It simply does not appeal to the person who is unwilling to invest time and energy in the study of Scripture. The modern reader will be discouraged first just by the name of the book. "Numbers" seems to be a particularly inappropriate title for a part of the revelation of God. The title seems as interesting as a book named, for example, "Telephone Directory." A suspicion of increasing dullness may settle in long before the reader finishes the first chapter. By the fifth

---

3. This sentiment is that of Johann Christian Konrad von Hoffmann (1810–77), the scholar who gave the term *Heilsgeschichte* its classic, precritical definition. See the sympathetic exposition of von Hoffmann's contribution to biblical theology by Hans-Joachim Kraus, *Die biblische Theologie: Ihre Geschichte und Problematik* (Neukirchen-Vluyn: Neukirchener, 1970), 247–53.

4. They term the book the work of P; more on this topic later.

chapter he or she may have dropped out altogether. Numbers is not "fast food" literature! Indeed, some wonder whether it is any kind of literature at all. Ashley notes, "The Book of Numbers will never replace the Psalms at the heart of Christian devotion nor the Gospel of John and the Epistle to the Romans at the heart of Christian theology, nor should it." But he continues, "The book of Numbers tells a story."[5] The story is the thing, for the chief actor is God.

Once a reader braves these murky waters, she or he will discover that there are four major problems to face in the book of Numbers: (1) its seeming lack of coherence as a book, (2) the dizzying variety of its contents, (3) the problematic large numbers of the tribes of Israel, and (4) the fascinating but confusing story of Balaam (Nu 22–24). These factors may combine to arrest the interest of even the most pious readers.[6]

In the nonevangelical, critical study of the Bible—the schools of European, British, and American biblical scholarship that have pursued "J-E-D-P source criticism" in the Pentateuch, or some of the more recent forms of redaction criticism—the book of Numbers has provided a fruitful source for analysis. The book is something of a "garden of flowers," each to be plucked, placed in a different vase, and then labeled according to critical ideas of source criticism. Many of the commentaries on the book of Numbers attempt to trace several supposed sources in the varied materials in the book. Surprisingly, a commentary on the book of Numbers published by a major evangelical house is one of the most critical of all. Philip J. Budd's commentary is marked by an aggressive appeal to source criticism and a theology that appears to be Unitarian in nature. He is entirely negative concerning the historical value of the book of Numbers. Budd writes, "The book appears to lack the kind of information the historian of the second millenium [*sic*] requires."[7] In view of these difficulties, then, it is not surprising that many Bible readers do not come to the book of Numbers with noticeable enthusiasm.

This commentary seeks to provide a modest reason for a reassessment of the book of Numbers as an important contribution to the Torah, as an integral part of Holy Scripture, and as a necessary component in the building of a balanced and informed biblical theology. It also endeavors to rescue this book for worshiping believers. We need to rediscover reverence, recital, and reality as elements of our worship today.

2. THE BOOK OF NUMBERS AS SCRIPTURE

For those who take the concepts of Scripture and canon seriously, the book of Numbers may take on increasing significance. Evangelical Christian theologians have long announced the conviction that the Scriptures are the result of the outbreathing of God, or "inspiration." Indeed, we stand or fall on this

---

5. Timothy R. Ashley, *The Book of Numbers* (NICOT; Grand Rapids: Eerdmans, 1990), ix.

6. The history of the study of the book of Numbers only exacerbates the problem. For the most part evangelicals have not found a great interest in this book. The comparison is unfair, perhaps; but a check of the computer catalog in a theological library will confirm a suspicion that may arise in a casual search of a Christian bookstore: there are few independent works on the book of Numbers. Most commentaries (including this one) have been published as part of a larger series that covers each of the books of the Bible. This said, three major commentaries on Numbers by evangelical writers have been published since the first edition of the present work; these works are by Timothy R. Ashley (NICOT), R. Dennis Cole (NAC), and R. K. Harrison (WEC).

7. Philip J. Budd, *Numbers* (WBC 5; Waco, Tex.: Word, 1984), xxvi. Note that "millenium" may be a British spelling for the American "millennium."

conviction. There are churches, denominations, Bible schools, seminaries, and even scholarly societies that hold together on the basic premise of the inspiration of Scripture and its concomitant inerrancy. One of the texts cited repeatedly to buttress this point of view is 2 Timothy 3:16: "All Scripture is God-breathed." These words are used at times as a prooftext for the divine origin of the Bible—not an inconsiderable issue!

But as important as they are, these words are not the principal assertion of Paul in this well-known passage. They are the assumption. Paul argues that *since* Timothy knows that the Scriptures are the outbreathing of God himself, therefore he—and we—should regard them as eminently worthwhile. The Holy Scriptures, which have the ability to make one wise to salvation (2Ti 3:15) and are the product of the outbreathing of God (3:16a), are profitable for "teaching, rebuking, correcting and training in righteousness" (3:16b). Indeed, they are the means for the full equipping of the Christian for doing every good work of God (3:17).

Furthermore, the "holy Scriptures" (2Ti 3:15) and "all Scripture" (3:16) to which these verses directly refer comprise the Hebrew Scriptures, or what is commonly known today as the "Old Testament." To be sure, by extension the designations in 2 Timothy include the NT writings, but these are not the passage's principal concern. At the time Paul was writing, the NT was not complete, and many believers did not have access to what was written. The Scriptures that Timothy had studied from his earliest youth were not the writings of Paul or the gospels. Timothy was a student of Moses, Isaiah, and David—particularly of Moses. In classical Jewish thought, the Scriptures are first the books of Torah, followed by the Prophets and the Writings. (An emphasis on Torah at the expense of the rest of the OT developed in Judaism following the Council of Jamnia in AD 90.)

Thus the principal teaching of this classic NT passage on inspiration focuses on the role of the Torah in Christian living. Moreover, Paul's familiar command to "preach the Word" (2Ti 4:2) continues the postulate of 2 Timothy 3:16–17 (the chapter division notwithstanding). Interestingly, numerous theologians and preachers who from these verses make much of the importance of the inspiration of Scripture fail to recognize the importance of the Torah as the foundational document of biblical faith. The logic of the passage sounds as follows:

> Since the Scriptures make you wise to salvation, continue in them as you have from your youth. Since they are the outbreathing of God, these Scriptures are eminently useful for teaching, rebuking, correcting, and training in righteousness. Indeed, they may equip the person of God for every good work. So preach the Word, a task that begins with the preaching of Torah.

When one discovers the significance of the book of Numbers as a creditable unit in the unfolding of the whole of Scripture, its material becomes essential to building a biblical theology. This commentary proceeds along these lines. Even though the title "Numbers" seems uninspiring, and despite those aspects of the book that the modern reader may consider to be less than scintillating, this book of Torah can make one wise to salvation and is useful for teaching, rebuking, correcting, and training in righteousness. The book of Numbers is an essential part of the Holy Scriptures of God. God's people dare not ignore its teachings.

3. THE BOOK OF NUMBERS AS TORAH

The book of Numbers is not only a part of Scripture and, hence, inspired, inerrant, and relevant for doctrine, guidance, and instruction in righteous living; it is also an essential part of the Torah, the Pentateuch of Moses. While many acknowledge the foundational nature of the Torah to the development of Scripture, it would seem that there is rarely a serious consideration of its contributions as authoritative and informing Scripture in the practical outworking of evangelical theology.[8] Aside from a few celebrated texts on creation and the fall, selections dealing with the names and ascriptions of deity, and passages presenting the basic ideas of covenant, the Torah is generally neglected. True, passages are chosen from time to time to illustrate truths already affirmed in the NT, but rarely do theologians build theological propositions solidly on Torah truth. Frequently a few passages that are regarded as messianic are selected for study.[9] But the rest of the text seems to be regarded as just "filler." Genesis, understandably, is read more than the rest of the books of the Torah; Numbers, however, is read very little for basic theology.

Yet the Bible only holds together insofar as it is seen as an organic development from the beginning forward. The books of the Torah are like the full-bud stage of a rose: the entire flower is present—everything the flower will become—but not all of its inner beauty is visible. The Prophets and the Writings are akin to the opening of the rose. They do not so much present new truth as develop and clarify truth that has been already expressed in the books of the Torah.[10]

In the teaching of Jesus we find the rose of Scripture, as it were, in the full-bloom stage. His words reveal more fully than ever what God has meant from the beginning in his revelation. In a sense we may say that the teaching of Jesus is the full blossom of Torah truth. The letters in the NT are akin to the rose in the full-blown stage. In this stage of the flower, the bloom is still intact, but the petals are opened to their fullest extent. In this stage much attention is given to the fine detail of a given petal, but there is a danger in losing a sense of the form and contours of the flower.

To begin a study of Scripture in the NT letters poses the danger of proceeding on the basis of a great deal that is not known. Since the texture of Scripture is so detailed, the balance of teaching the whole of Scripture on a given topic may be lost. This issue is particularly problematic among those evangelicals who believe that only the letters are "church truth," and that the OT is truly "old," connected only with the Hebrew people in the past but not really of any real value to God's people today. Equally disastrous is for

8. Certainly we do not suggest that all have neglected the teachings of the Torah as informing evangelical faith. A number of evangelical scholars have written spirited presentations of numerous biblical themes from the Pentateuch. These writers include, among others, Walter C. Kaiser Jr., Meredith G. Kline, G. Herbert Livingston, Eugene H. Merrill, Allen P. Ross, John H. Sailhamer, Elmer B. Smick, Willem A. VanGemeren, Bruce K. Waltke, Ronald F. Youngblood, and others. My point is that these writers and others notwithstanding, the broad teachings of the Torah as important contributions to biblical faith for evangelical churches are still waiting to be discovered by many scholars.

9. In E. W. Hengstenberg's significant, classic study of messianic texts in Hebrew Scripture, he considered only one passage in the book of Numbers—Numbers 24:17–19, Balaam's fourth oracle. This work, by a formidable defender of orthodox faith in turbulent times of growing rationalism in Europe, was published first in German in 1828. A second, greatly expanded edition was published in 1854–57. Presently, a fine, abridged edition in English (with a foreword by Walter C. Kaiser Jr.) is *The Christology of the Old Testament and a Commentary on the Messianic Predictions* (trans. Reuel Keith; abridg. Thomas Kerchever Arnold; repr., Grand Rapids: Kregel, 1970). What was Hengstenberg's conclusion respecting Balaam's "star and scepter" prophecy respecting messianic prophecy? It is negative! In section 91 he concludes: "There is, then, no sufficient reason for referring this prophecy to the Messiah" (p. 36).

10. This concept of Scripture as an "opening rose" is developed considerably further in Ronald B. Allen, *Grace, Always Grace* (Grand Rapids: Kregel, forthcoming).

the reader to view the Bible as a "flat book" (Walter C. Kaiser's phrase), devoid of development whatsoever. This view sees the book of Genesis and the book of John as presenting the same theological ideas with the same precision and on the same level. These "gospelizers" of the Torah inadvertently make the early books irrelevant; for if the Torah teaches precisely, and on the same level, what the Gospels teach, then the Torah is not needed. It is merely quaintly redundant.

This commentary proceeds on the premise that the Torah is foundational to the entirety of Scripture, that the rest of the Bible cannot be understood correctly apart from a solid basis in Torah. Further, this commentary also proceeds on the theses that the book of Numbers is truly a "book,"[11] that it has a sense of coherence, and that its problematic use of large numbers is capable of solution. Indeed, the numbers when viewed correctly may become its glory!

4. TEXT

The Hebrew text (the MT) of the book of Numbers is relatively free of difficulty. Since the Torah was especially revered in ancient times, its transmission seems to be cleaner than that of many other biblical books. Periodically in the commentary that follows, attention will be given to special textual difficulties, particularly in the poetic sections; and comparisons will be made with the Samaritan recension and the LXX. A few times I will suggest emendations of the MT, new meanings for disputed words, or unusual meanings to more common words. I observe (perhaps with some surprise) that the presence of many numbers in the two census lists (Nu 1–4; 26) do not betray corruption in the process of transmission; thus, those who resort to the solution of the problem of the large numbers by suggesting textual corruption have to assume that such problems are very ancient (pre-Masoretic). The Hebrew text used throughout the commentary is *BHS*.

5. HISTORICAL BACKGROUND AND PURPOSE

The book of Numbers, the fourth book of the Pentateuch, is traditionally ascribed to Moses. The name of the book in the English versions comes from the LXX (the Greek translation of the Hebrew Bible), through the Vulgate (Latin), and is based on the census lists that are found in chs. 1–4 and 26. The Greek name for the book, an attempt to describe the prominence of the numerical listings of the tribes of Israel, is *Arithmoi*. The Latin translation in the Vulgate is *Numeri*, the basis for the title "Numbers" in standard English translations.

Eusebius mentions that Jewish designations for the book include the Hebrew phrase *sēper mispārîm* ("The Book of Numbers"). More commonly, however, we think of two other Hebrew names for the book. One comes from the first word of Numbers 1:1, *wayᵉdabbēr* ("And [Yahweh] spoke [to Moses]"). This term is significant in that it is a characteristic phrasing that marks section after section in this Torah scroll as the revelation of the Lord to Moses. An even more descriptive Hebrew name for the book is taken from the

---

11. There are some approaches to the book of Numbers that see it as merely a convenient section of the whole, with due allowance for the number of columns of text handily maintained in a scroll. In these approaches, there is no real sense of a "book."

fourth word in verse 1, *b^emidbar* ("In the Desert," or "In the Wilderness").[12] This name is generally regarded as more descriptive of its contents. The book is set in the thirty-eight-year period of Israel's experience in the Wilderness of Sinai following the exodus from Egypt. Hence "In the Wilderness" seems to be a particularly apt description of its contents. This term is not only fitting for the experience of Israel in this part of her early history, but it is also a metaphor for the condition of judgment that fell on the people who refused to enter the land of rest. We will argue, however, that the word "Numbers" really is the superior title for the book as a whole—and that *it is in its numbers* that the book has significant power.

This book contains much material that is similar to the books of Exodus and Leviticus in terms of legislation for the people and particularly material dealing with the rights and regulations of the Levites and the priests. The dramatic narrative of the book is most significant. It is in the book of Numbers that we read of the murmuring and rebellions of the people of God against his grace and their subsequent judgment. Those whom God had redeemed from slavery in Egypt and those to whom he had displayed his grace at Mount Sinai responded with indifference, ingratitude, and repeated acts of rebellion. The community of the redeemed was punished by the Lord by being forbidden to enter the Promised Land. They were made to live out their lives in the Wilderness of Sinai; only their children would enjoy the promise that was originally to be theirs.

Since Numbers presents this story of rebellion, there is a sense in which the book stands in the middle of the salvation experience of the people of God. The generation that was delivered from slavery in Egypt did not continue to respond to the Lord with faith and gratitude. Instead, they forfeited their part in the Land of Promise. Only their children would experience the blessing of conquest, and they would experience it only if they demonstrated a daring faithfulness their parents had not. Again, God has time and the wilderness has sand. The book covers a span of thirty-eight years, from the first day of the first month of the second year of the exodus (Nu 7:1; Ex 40:2, 17; cf. the first day of the second month, Nu 1:1) until the first day of the eleventh month of the fortieth year (Dt 1:3). The whole of the wilderness period is usually called "forty years" (as in Nu 14:33).

Provisionally, we may state that the original recipients of the book were the people of Israel in the second generation from the exodus awaiting the command of God to cross the Jordan to conquer the land of Canaan. The book describes the affairs of the people of the first generation, but its teaching was for their sons and daughters, who were now mature and were about to enter Canaan.

We may also venture the purpose of the book in this manner:

- to compel obedience to Yahweh by members of the new community by reminding them of the wrath of God on their parents because of their breach of covenant,
- to encourage them to trust in the ongoing promises of their Lord as they follow him into their heritage in Canaan, and
- to provoke them to the worship of God and to the enjoyment of their salvation.

---

12. The traditional rendering of *midbar* (GK 4497) as "desert" may lead the modern reader to think of expanses of sand dunes such as an image of the Sahara presents. The "wilderness" was not hospitable, but neither was it as bleak an area as the term "desert" may convey.

The book also carries an implied threat: If the sons and daughters behave as their parents had done, then they will suffer the same fate—burial in the wilderness. Their children (the third generation) may be the ones to enter the land. Thus the book that describes the "Wilderness Years" is designed to encourage spiritual confidence on the part of the people who are about to leave the wilderness as well as to encourage later generations. Despite its sorry record of blemish, betrayal, and benighted living among the covenantal people, the book of Numbers as a whole portrays a confident life of faith in the fear of Yahweh. Furthermore, this confident living, this spiritual triumphalism, becomes a major element in the worship of Yahweh.

6. AUTHORSHIP AND DATE

As noted above, the book of Numbers, at least in its core, has traditionally been ascribed to Moses, the great prophet of God. This position has much to commend it.

1. The statements concerning the writing activity of Moses found here and elsewhere in the Pentateuch (e.g., Nu 33:1–2; cf. Ex 17:14; 24:4; 34:27 et al.).
2. The Pentateuch appears as a unity and comes, in some manner, from one great master writer.
3. The excellent training of Moses in the princely educational system was designed to produce, among other leaders, the very pharaohs of Egypt—an education that would have prepared Moses for this great literary task (see the report of the Jewish tradition in the preaching of Stephen; Ac 7:22).
4. Moses was the principal human protagonist in the record of the deliverance and wilderness experiences of Israel in its formative years, thus making him the logical choice as the recorder of those events.
5. Various NT citations speak of Moses as the one responsible for the books of the Torah (e.g., Mt 19:8; Jn 5:46–47; Ro 10:5; et al.).[13]

Many modern scholars of the Bible proceed from other lines of inquiry to argue that Moses was not the author of Numbers (either in its final form or basic core) or, for that matter, of any of the books of the

---

13. Standard evangelical introductions to the OT detail these points and others. The reader is encouraged to review the arguments in his *Survey of Old Testament Introduction*. After a long, productive life, Dr. Archer died in 2004. His volume has had a lustrous history; the first edition was published in 1964, the second in 1974. In its third edition (1994), Archer observed concerning Moses: "It seems absolutely incredible that he would have committed none of his records to writing (as even twentieth-century critics contend), when he had the grandest and most significant matters to record which are to be found in all of human literature" (*SOTI*-1994, 125). The conclusion of Dillard and Longman is the following: "In the final analysis, it is possible to affirm the substantial Mosaic authorship of the Pentateuch in line with the occasional internal evidence and the strong external testimony, while allowing for earlier sources as well as later glosses and elaboration" (*Introduction to the Old Testament*, 47).

In the first edition of their Old Testament survey (*OTS*-1982), William Sanford LaSor, David Allan Hubbard, and Frederic Wm. Bush concluded: "Although it is unlikely that Moses wrote the Pentateuch *as it exists in its final form*, the connectedness and uniformity of the evidence certainly affirms that he is the originator, instigator, and the most important figure in the stream of literary activity that produced it" (ibid., 63 [emphasis theirs]). In the second edition (*OTS*-1996), these authors affirm some role of Moses in the "production and formation" of the Pentateuch, but something less than describing him as its author: "Hence Moses' role in the production of the Pentateuch must be affirmed as highly formative, although it is unlikely that Moses wrote the Pentateuch *as it exists in its final form*" (ibid., 9 [emphasis theirs]).

Pentateuch. These critical scholars[14] believe that at most only a few seed-thoughts of the Pentateuch really go back to the man Moses,[15] that Jewish tradition (uncritically adopted by Christian tradition) oversimplified the matter by ascribing the writing of these books to their ancient hero Moses, and that the process of the writing of the book of Numbers was exceedingly complex, the book's being comprised primarily of Priestly source materials ("P"),[16] as well as some materials from the Yahwist ("J") and the Elohist ("E").

The classic statement on the book of Numbers in this regard was given by George Buchanan Gray more than one hundred years ago (1903):

---

14. By the term "critical scholars," I refer to those who to some degree follow the "assured results of [higher] criticism" usually associated with the Graf–Kuenen–Wellhausen school of Documentary Hypothesis, or to more modern scholars who follow various schemes of redaction criticism and who distance themselves from the concept of divine inspiration of the Bible. The phrase "critical scholars," to be sure, is not a helpful term; it is far too vague. Archer chose to use the terms "Documentarian Critics" (SOTI-1996, 268) and "the School of Negative Criticism" (ibid., 112). Numerous critical theories respecting Pentateuchal origins have come into play since Wellhausen's "triumph." Moreover, not all critical scholars are as "critical" as others. Some display a robust faith in God and a lively interest in the theology of the text, even when they criticize its origin and unity. Numerous conservative scholars are "critical" in the sense that they bring the text under a literary and critical purview but with different results from the standard documentarian scholar. Some evangelicals tend to gather all critical scholars in the same pouch and then to dismiss them entirely. Along the way we may even speak in judgment of their faith in God, a judgment we should not make apart from a clear denial on the part of such a scholar. Actually, we all owe a debt of a sort to these critical scholars. They have been marked by a rugged determination to observe details in the text that others might tend to ignore; they have forced those who are more conservative writers to think through issues more deeply rather than to read the text with a simplistic naiveté. In our responses to some of their more egregious opinions, we may have come nearer truth concerning the origin of Scripture than we might have done had there never been these attacks on the integrity of Scripture. The one common element that marks those whom I designate "critical scholars" is their lack of interest in, or denial of, inspiration and its corollary, inerrancy. Critical scholars may even seem to come to the text with a bias against inspiration and inerrancy; the text comes under their judgment and acumen. The ideal stance of the conservative, evangelical (I suggest, the "reverent") scholar is that while he or she reads the text with attention to detail and is forced to deal with ambiguities, astringencies, and abnormalities, nonetheless such a reader comes to the text from the vantage of faith in the inerrancy of the Word of God. Finally, the "reverent scholar" (who may use some critical tools) stands not *over* the text but *under* its authority. Rather than the scholar's being critical of the text, the text is critical of him or her, as it is of all faithful readers.

15. Actually, the most critical of these scholars cast doubt on whether Moses ever existed. Noordtzij reports that E. Meyer in 1906 argued that the question as to whether Moses was historical or mythological is not meaningful for historical research; that Holscher in 1922 affirmed Moses was not a historical person; that Wellhausen viewed Moses as a postulate, not a person, and that the man Moses left nothing positive behind; that G. Beer presented Moses as a finder of springs and a snake charmer; that the most R. Kittel could say of the historicity of the man Moses is suggestive but that his existence is only proven on the basis of a historical postulate: the founding of the nation demands an individual who plays a key role (see A. Noordtzij, *Numbers* (BSC; transl. Ed. van der Maas [Grand Rapids: Zondervan, 1983], 9).

16. Generally, critical scholars, following the lead of Wellhausen, regard the Priestly portions of the Pentateuch ("P") as postexilic. Wellhausen and his followers considered the tabernacle and its traditions to be a backward projection to Mosaic times from the latest period in biblical history. More recently there has been a movement, led particularly by some Jewish scholars, to date P in preexilic times. See David R. Hildenbrand, "A Summary of Recent Findings in Support of an Early Date for the So-Called Priestly Material of the Pentateuch," *JETS* 29 (June 1986): 129–38.

Judged even by itself, Numbers supplies abundant evidence that it is not the work of Moses, or even of a contemporary of the events described. Not only is Moses referred to throughout in the 3rd person, and, in one passage in particular, in terms that have always occasioned difficulties to those who assumed the Mosaic authorship, but the repetitions, the divergent and contradictory accounts of the same matter, the marked differences of style in different parts, the impossible numbers, and many other features of the book, prove clearly that Numbers is not the work of one who was contemporary with the events described, or familiar with the conditions presupposed.[17]

The "one passage in particular" that was so bothersome to Gray—and indeed even to many readers who are more favorably predisposed to Mosaic authorship—is 12:3: "Now Moses was a very humble man, more humble than anyone else on the face of the earth." The presumption of many readers is that this is the last possible statement a truly humble man would write about himself. For many documentary-critical readers, this verse is the last nail in the coffin of the question of the Mosaic authorship of the book. (But see the newer view of the meaning of this verse in the present commentary below.)

Gray then turned to 33:2, which seems to be a clear statement of Mosaic authorship: "At the LORD's command Moses recorded the stages in their journey." Even this verse gets turned on its head as Gray writes:

> In one passage only (33:2) does the book lay any claim to the authority of Moses for its statements; that passage is closely related to others (P) which are clearly of far later origin than the age of Moses, and consequently the Mosaic *authorship* even of this particular passage cannot be seriously considered. [18](emphasis his)

The negative-critical assessment of the contribution of the historical Moses to the writing of the book of Numbers presented with such confidence by Gray near the beginning of the last century has been carried on with little waning of enthusiasm by critical scholars throughout the decades that have followed. We may cite just a few examples.

Otto Eissfeldt approached the first books of the Bible not as the Pentateuch (Genesis through Deuteronomy) but as the Hexateuch (Genesis through Joshua) and argued that these books have connections as well with the books of Kings. He also presented his discovery of a new stratum in these books, a stratum he called "L" (Lay). The materials earlier attributed to "J" (the Yahwist) he believed to be in fact a combining of two sources, "L" and "J," and in doing so he followed suggestions from H. Gunkel and R. Smend. In his major work, after eighty-eight pages of dense prose, he then had much of the German text of the first six books of the Bible printed in columnar form under four headings: L, J, E, and P. (In the case of the book of Deuteronomy, he included only chs. 31–34, since he regarded the balance as D.) A non-documentarian who pages through the book may find that the results are simply astonishing.

Where large blocks of material are assigned to one source, Eissfeldt simply summarizes. Hence Numbers 1:1–10:10 is assigned to P, so that text is not printed out in its column. In other cases in his partitioning of the book of Numbers, Eissfeldt asserts considerable interplay of putative sources, usually with paragraphs

---

17. George Buchanan Gray, *Introduction to the Massoretico-Criticial Edition of the Hebrew Bible* (ICC; Edinburgh: T&T Clark, 1903), xxix–xxx.

18. Ibid., xxx.

printed as blocks in the "correct column." But at Numbers 14:1, he divides phrases in this one verse among three sources (P, E, J), and in verse 2, he assigns all the verse to P except for the words "all Israel," which are assigned (alone!) to E.[19]

Not many people are going to plow through the convoluted columns of Eissfeldt's tome. To ease the chore for the curious modern reader, a new book has made the task of distinguishing sources far simpler—by printing the text of the Pentateuch with varied colors and fonts. Thus in *The Bible with Sources Revealed*, J is represented with a light green font, E with a bold green font, P with a blue font, RJE (portions where the Redactor combined J and E, a task achieved sometime following the destruction of Samaria in 722 BC) with a green font with a background screen, R (for Redactor, the work of the final editor) with a blue font with a background screen. No fewer than three colors are used to distinguish putative layers of D (Deuteronomy), and Genesis 14 bears the distinction of having its own colored font (blue italic) to indicate an independent source, the chapter revealing none of the traits of J or E or P.[20]

Otto Kaiser, former professor of Old Testament at the University of Marburg, published his widely used *Old Testament Introduction* (in German) in 1969; the English translation was published in 1975.[21] This book contains no section on the book of Numbers or, for that matter, on the books of Genesis, Exodus, or Leviticus. Kaiser approaches the content of these four books ("the Tetrateuch") with only slight modifications of the literary-critical stance of Karl Heinrich Graf, Abraham Kuenen, and Julius Wellhausen. With (characteristic) German assurance of his position, Kaiser writes:

> The documentary hypothesis ... has proved well suited to solve the problem of the involved narrative, and so performed not only a literary task, but one which is at the same time decisive for our knowledge of the sources for the history and theology of Israel. The sources have been by and large distinguished correctly ... [and] they have been set, at least relatively correctly, in the context of the history of Israel, and so provide the framework for the history of its faith.[22]

Thus Kaiser's treatment pays no attention to the five books of Moses; instead his chapters are titled:

(7) The Growth of the Pentateuchal Narrative at the Pre-Literary Stage
(8) The Yahwistic History
(9) The Elohistic History
(10) The Priestly Writing
(11) Deuteronomy[23]

---

19. Otto Eissfeldt, *Hexateuch-Synopse: Die Erzählung der fünf Bücher Mose und des Buches Josua mit dem Anfange des Richterbuches* (Darmstadt: Wissenschaftliche, 1962), 169*.
20. Richard Elliott Friedman, *The Bible with Sources Revealed: A New View into the Five Books of Moses* (San Francisco: HarperSanFrancisco, 2003). The author concedes that there was an attempt at a "Polychrome Bible" (1903) but that modern printing techniques made the production of the 2003 version possible (ibid., 5).
21. Otto Kaiser, *Introduction to the Old Testament: A Presentation of Its Results and Problems* (trans. John Sturdy; Gütersloh: Gütersloher Verlagshaus Gerd Mohn, 1969; repr., Minneapolis: Augsburg, 1975).
22. Ibid., 44.
23. Ibid., vii.

Another major figure of modern German critical scholarship writing in the mid-twentieth century was Martin Noth. He minced no words in his negative evaluation of the unity of the book of Numbers and the role of Moses in its composition:

> There can be no question of the unity of the book of Numbers, nor of its originating from the hand of a single author. This is already clear from the confusion and lack of order in its contents. It is also clear from the juxtaposition of quite varied styles and methods of presentation, as well as from the repeated confrontation of factually contradictory concepts in one and the same situation. It is also clear, finally, from the relationship of secondary dependence which can sometimes be established between one section and another. These facts are so self-evident that the assertion of the disunity of the book does not require exhaustive proof.[24]

Near the end of the twentieth century, we have yet another, only slightly less dogmatic assertion. Budd states with approval:

> The confidence of these earlier analysts is not often shared by more recent investigators, particularly in matters of detail, but there remains a very wide measure of agreement as to the identity and extent of the priestly material (P). In the book of Numbers there is very general acceptance of a total priestly contribution in the following chapters—1–9, 15, 17–19, 26–31, 33–36—and of a substantial influence in 10, 13–14, 16, 20, 25, 32. The only chapters lacking such influence would appear to be 11–12, 21–24.[25]

Many of the arguments given by these scholars may be countered by evidence from within the Bible and from what we now know concerning patterns of writing in the ancient world that run directly counter to the basic postulates of standard critical theory.[26] But the most telling distinction between nonevangelical scholars and evangelical scholars is one's starting point. When a person begins with the postulate of the divine inspiration of Scripture and of its concomitant inerrancy, that person reads the data of Scripture quite differently from the manner of one who does not begin with a belief in the inspiration, authority, and inerrancy of Scripture.

I believe it is prudent to make the following points:

(1) Gray and others notwithstanding, Moses certainly wrote the travel itinerary of the book (see 33:2), as explicitly stated by Scripture. Gray's rejection of the statement, based on an appeal to prior late-dating of the putative Priestly document, is simply nothing more than an example of special pleading. He argues that Moses cannot have been the author because the book does not assert his authorship; and in the one verse where the book does assert that Moses wrote a section, Gray dismisses that datum for other reasons. With this approach one can deny just about anything.

---

24. Martin Noth, *Numbers: A Commentary* (OTL; trans. James D. Martin; Philadelphia: Westminster, 1968), 4.

25. See Budd (*Numbers*, xviii–xix), who goes on to state why P must be dated to the exilic or early postexilic periods. As to the chapters that escape assignment to P, they are consigned to JE (xxii). Further, the classic critical dating of J in about 850 BC is now lowered by Budd considerably. He argues (xxiv) that the Yahwist was a member of the court of King Josiah, that is, a contemporary of Jeremiah in the last part of the seventh century BC.

26. This point was made by Kenneth A. Kitchen, *Ancient Orient and Old Testament* (Downers Grove, Ill.: InterVarsity Press, 1966). He argues that if biblical scholars in the late nineteenth century had truly been aware of the mounting evidence of actual historical and literary materials from the ancient Near East, they would not have developed their specious and factually unfounded theory of the documentary composition of the Pentateuch. The facts, he avers, were against them.

(2) Moses is portrayed as the central character of the book (with the exception of chs. 22–24, which feature Balaam). This factor makes it probable that, *if Moses was a historical figure*, Moses was the source of the materials. Employing the third person allows the writer to use his name repeatedly. The third-person format in the book is a factor that we observe; but this seeming peculiarity may be just a matter of taste and style, not necessarily the betrayal of the hand of another author.

(3) Moses is the person the book repeatedly emphasizes as the one who received the words of Yahweh. Among the most characteristic phrases in the book are the statements speaking of the revelation of Yahweh to Moses (e.g., 1:1: "The Lord spoke to Moses in the Tent of Meeting"). Maarsingh writes, "Over and over we hear such expressions as 'the Lord spoke to Moses,' 'the Lord commanded Moses,' and 'according to the word of the Lord.' In the book of Numbers alone these expressions, almost always addressed to Moses, occur 139 times."[27] If a person other than Moses wrote the book of Numbers, and if the book relates genuine revelation of God to Moses, then that writer would have had to have been quite dependent on Moses for his material. One may, of course, decide that the relevance of these words to the real person of Moses is inconsequential. Some believe the phrasing, "And the Lord said to Moses," serves merely to introduce a new topic but has neither historical, revelatory significance nor any personal reference to the Moses of history. It is suggested that later writers, desiring to present their material as authoritative, would have used these formulaic words as a matter of course.[28] But it is also possible, and is the belief of many, that these words may indeed report Moses' reception of the word of God.[29]

When one argues for the Mosaic composition of the book of Numbers, it is not necessary to claim that the book came from his hand complete and finalized. With reference to Moses, we may style the book of Numbers, "The Memoirs of Moses in the Wilderness." The varied styles and the seeming inconsistencies of the book may have been produced in part by its occasional nature in the lifetime of Moses. Further, this book may have received some additions following the lifetime of Moses, though this material may also

---

27. B. Maarsingh, *Numbers: A Practical Commentary* (transl. John Vriend; Grand Rapids: Eerdmans, 1987), 5.

28. A twist on this issue is presented in the "Temple Scroll" (one of the Dead Sea Scrolls) from Qumran, believed to have been written in the second half of the second century BC. In that scroll Moses is regarded as the principal means of revelation, but the speaker is generally God in the first person. This observation is notable where the scroll quotes from Numbers 30:3–16. In this passage, which the MT says was given by Yahweh to Moses, the Temple Scroll cites it as God speaking in the first person. This factor leads Jacob Milgrom to conclude, "There can be no doubt that the Dead Sea sectarians regarded the Temple Scroll as quintessential Tora, the true word of God" ("The Temple Scroll," *BA* 41/3 [September 1978]: 119). So here is the curiosity: Critical scholars have an almost genetic predisposition to disbelieve assertions of Mosaic authorship of the books of Torah in the Hebrew canon; but, given a novel work from a questionable source *outside canon*, the statements of authorship and significance are taken at face value. As we say in Brooklyn, "Go figure!"

29. G. Herbert Livingston writes: "The concept that God prompted men to speak and/or write the content of the Scripture without negating the humanness of the people involved, without destroying the authenticity of the Word spoken or written, without polluting the purity of motive of the men involved, is valid. Such a concept would be far superior to claims that God did not speak directly to any man, that humanity is of necessity given to falsehood, the distortion of truth, or that historical facts have been twisted by religious or other inferior motives" (*The Pentateuch in Its Cultural Environment* [2nd ed.; Grand Rapids: Baker, 1987], 274). In his chapter "The Manuscripts and Mosaic Authorship" (ibid., 207–75), Livingston presents many positive concepts as alternatives to standard critical positions.

have reached back to the time of Moses. Thus some of what we may regard as later insertions may be just as ancient, having been written by a contemporary of Moses, as the larger framework into which they are placed. The insertions may have been added to the book as a whole, under the direction of the Holy Spirit at a later time, or the book may have been compiled by another hand using Mosaic material. This would also explain the inclusion of the Balaam story.

Further, if we accept the possibility of insertions and additions to Numbers or that the book is a compilation from a period later than Moses, we would still accept them as a part of the Holy Spirit's ongoing work on his Word. We certainly confront instances of this ongoing work in the book of Psalms. Numerous psalms have later editorial (sometimes musical) additions; and some psalms are later constructions of various parts of earlier poems. Yet the "reverent critical reader" of the Psalms still speaks of the product as the work of the Spirit of God through various hands.[30] The additions and insertions from a later time—if that is what they are—are still Scripture. They are a part of the Word of God as we have received it; the additions and insertions also comprise a part of the Hebrew-Christian canon. The proper stance for the reader who has sought to determine these factors is not in judgment but in acknowledgment, not in superior knowledge but in reverent submission.

When we examine the text of Numbers, we conclude that it is possible that some portions of the book were additions from later periods of Israel's history.[31] For example, the supposed protestation of the humility of Moses (12:3) would hardly be convincing if it came from his own mouth, as Gray and countless others have observed.[32] One section in Numbers 14 seems to be oddly placed within the larger chapter. There is

---

30. I refer here to musical notations, such as the famous "Selah"; to various musical notations in the superscriptions; to the clearly editorial addition to Psalm 72 (v.20); to psalms such as 108, which is an anthology of parts of Psalms 57 and 60; and the like. I have written on these items in Ronald B. Allen, *And I Will Praise Him: A Guide to Worship in the Psalms* (repr., Grand Rapids: Kregel, 1999). My point is that the work of the Spirit of God did not stop on the frets of the harp of David; the work of the Spirit seems to have extended to the singers and custodians who shaped the music of earlier times for continuing use in temple worship. Evangelical scholarship has been too long at an impasse; in our acts of rejecting critical theories that argue against any unity of a text or authenticity of a unit, we may have pressed too strongly for too tight a view of the composition of certain sections of Hebrew Scriptures based on the (presumed) model of a NT letter, rather than sought to understand some of the dynamics that actually seem to have functioned in earlier biblical times.

31. Noordtzij (*Numbers*, 12–16), for example, is an antagonist of the Wellhausen school and its methods. But he observes, "Like the other parts of the Pentateuch, Numbers does not constitute a literary unit in that its various elements do not date from the same time period." He then proceeds to list a number of texts that he feels come from a later period. His listing may not be correct (perhaps it is too limited or too broad); but the questions he raises are valid ones. Again, he raises them for reasons different from those the standard critical approach suggests; yet it is likely that if the standard critical approach had not brought its assaults on the text, neither would a reverent scholar such as Noordtzij have asked his questions. Unlike the critical scholars he brings under critical scrutiny, Noordtzij concludes that "for the most part the contents of Numbers ... can be explained without any difficulty on the basis of the situation as it existed during Moses' time."

32. However, see the commentary on this verse for an alternative explanation. The translation of this troubling verse of Moses' vaunted humility may be something different from what is commonly supposed. In the commentary, following the suggestion of Cleon Rogers, I suggest a rendering of this verse that greatly relieves its difficulty respecting the issue of Mosaic authorship; more importantly, it advances the story line.

a medieval tradition that Numbers 10:35–36 formed a part of the (suppressed) book of Eldad and Medad (see Note). Numbers 14:26–35 seems to be a "layer" with respect to 14:20–25 (see comments). Numbers 18:21–24 may appear to have something of a retrospective element (see comments). A more likely example of an addition to the book in my judgment is the passage in Numbers 15 describing the incident of the man caught in violation of the Sabbath rest (vv.32–36). Notice the way this section begins: "While the Israelites were in the wilderness" (v.32). This is similar to other biblical accounts that were written long after the events they portray. Compare, for example, the opening words of the book of Ruth: "In the days when the judges ruled" (Ru 1:1). The words in Numbers 15:32 appear to take the reader back to an earlier age;[33] they seem to be surprising in a book whose setting from the beginning was "in the wilderness" (see 1:1).

Equally difficult in Numbers is the origin of the Balaam story (chs. 22–24). As observed in the commentary, great speculation centers on the possible ways that this story complex could have come to Israel and become a part of the book of Numbers. Since Moses was not a participant in these events, their origin as Scripture is problematic. (Although the pericope is about Balaam and Barak, it is definitely an Israelite document. A good analogy would be the book of Job, whose author we do not know and whose main characters are people outside the covenantal community.) It is not my purpose to list all the passages in Numbers that may have been later additions, but we may pose the possibility of later additions.

If we are willing to admit even one sentence (12:3), one pericope (15:32–36), or one section (chs. 22–25) as a possible addition to the book at a later time than that of Moses, then we should be willing to examine each pericope with the question as to whether it, too, may be a possible later addition.[34] We will not conclude with the critical scholar that the entirety of the book came from a later time, but neither should we insist that every word and every verse necessarily came from the pen of Moses. Evangelicals have usually been pressed so hard by documentary-critical scholars who deny any part of the book as coming from Moses that the former have tended to claim too much for Moses. My desire is to be ruggedly, radically biblical, no matter where that may lead us.[35]

We may conclude, however, that it is reasonable to assume that the essential content of Numbers did come from Moses, the servant of the Lord. His name is cited repeatedly in the book; he was the principal human protagonist in the book; and he was the one with the training, opportunity, motivation, and opportunity to produce the book. It is almost axiomatic to observe that God brings good out of even the most grim, the most dismal situations. We may reckon that one of the good things that came out of the ghastly waste of life and energy of the condemned, rebellious first generation of the Hebrew people was the opportunity the wilderness experience afforded to Moses, prince and prophet of God, to write the books associated with his name.

An interesting use of the principal story line of Numbers is found in the message of the judge Jephthah to the Ammonites (Jdg 11:15–27). The basic plot and many of the details of Numbers were well known by

---

33. Again, see comments.
34. Perhaps I should add that we should also be willing to face each verse, each pericope, and each section as though it *is* part of the original work of Moses. Bias can work two ways. The critical bias of one scholar may be offset by the conservative bias of another.
35. A point made by LaSor, Hubbard, and Bush (*OTS*-1982, 62).

this Hebrew judge and were used by him with the facility of a Stephen of a much later day. The knowledge of these events during the chaotic period of the judges suggests that at least part of the basic story line of Numbers was known in Jephthah's day; thus, it is not unreasonable to suggest that the framework of the book was written before the period of the judges — something explained in the traditional belief in the Mosaic authorship of the book. The best suggestion for the time the book reached finished form seems to be during the united monarchy. Much later (and against critical thought), some of the cultural and geographical issues of the book become moot and arcane. So I believe the finished form[36] of Numbers may have come as early as the time of Samuel, but certainly by the age of Solomon.[37]

7. UNITY AND ORGANIZATION

Numbers is not easy to analyze or outline to show its inner structure. The contents are remarkably varied, and the arrangement of materials seems problematic. It is difficult to know how to divide the book; some even despair of thinking that the thirty-six chapters really form a "book," seeing no real independent unity within the book of Numbers. Goldberg, for example, says that Numbers was never a self-standing literary work; its existence as a "book" was always as just a part of the larger Pentateuch.[38] Rendtorff begins his discussion of Numbers in this vein: "Of all the books in the Pentateuch, the Book of Numbers is the hardest to survey. It contains a great deal of material of a markedly varied kind and gives the impression of being very heterogeneous. It is even difficult to decide how to divide it."[39]

While we all are aware of the ancient Jewish and Christian designation that speaks of "the Five Books of Moses," or the Pentateuch, some scholars believe that this arrangement is not apt. Of the five "books" in that section of the Bible, Numbers is considered by many to be the least clearly a "book." We expect a book to have a beginning, middle, and end, as is true of Genesis and Deuteronomy and, perhaps to a lesser degree, Exodus and Leviticus. But many feel that the book of Numbers has no real beginning, no clear ending, and only a muddled middle.

Readers tend to find the opening chapters of Numbers to be merely a continuation of the situation of Israel in the region of Sinai that begins in Exodus 19, a situation that includes the extensive materials in the book of Leviticus. The last chapters of Numbers present Israel in the plains of Moab, which is the

---

36. I propose the term "finished form" as preferable to "final form," as the latter wording may not admit even the smallest of scribal activities.

37. These are the conclusions of R. K. Harrison (*IOT*, 622). More recently Harrison argued strongly for the unity of the book and its early (Mosaic) composition, based in part on his view of the work of literate administrators among the tribes of Israel. Later called *sōperîm* (but see Ex 5:16–19, the "foremen"; in Nu 1:16–18 Moses has given certain men supervisory status), these "scribes or annalists made a fundamental contribution to Hebrew culture by helping to establish their successors as among the best historiographers in the ancient Near East, as contrasted with the propagandist activities of their counterparts in such countries as Egypt and Assyria" (R. K. Harrison, *Numbers* [WEC; Chicago: Moody Press, 1990], 16).

38. Goldberg, *Das Buch Numeri*, 11. The issues are complex. We do not know that the book of Numbers ever existed apart from the larger unity of the Pentateuch, but I believe that it does have a compelling literary unity that makes it a "self-standing book."

39. Rolf Rendtorff, *The Old Testament: An Introduction* (trans. John Bowden; Philadelphia: Fortress, 1986), 147.

staging area for Deuteronomy. In between are a few connecting passages describing the misadventures of Israel in the region of Kadesh. In all this narrative, many believe there is just a miscellany of varied accounts. Indeed, some commentators present the material of Numbers as a collection of disconnected parts of other books in the Torah.

An example of the disconnected-collection approach is afforded by Gray.[40] He suggests that the materials of Exodus, Leviticus, and Numbers would be far better regrouped into these sections:

1. The Exodus from Egypt to Sinai (Ex 1–18)
2. At Sinai (Ex 19–Nu 10:10, including the book of Leviticus)
3. From Sinai to the Jordan (Nu 10:11–36:13)[41]

Noth also speaks strongly against the literary integrity of Numbers: "We can scarcely speak of a special significance peculiar to the book of Numbers. It has its significance within the framework and context of the greater Pentateuch [as a] whole."[42]

Thus some feel that the "book" of Numbers may exist merely to allow the (presumably) sacred or mystical number five to be used in the seminal section of the Bible, i.e., the Torah, and the arrangement of the material in the book may be rather inadequate. In fact, we have no solid information that the number *five* had a mystical or sacred sense apart from the fact that the Torah is in five parts. Eissfeldt, for example, suggests that the fivefold division of the books of the Torah is secondary in nature, that it arises from a desire to divide the larger complex into five manageable parts of approximately equal size.[43]

The seeming appearance of Numbers to lack a literary sense of coherence as a "book" is compounded by the sense that the materials in it seem to present themselves in a nearly incoherent variety. The book contains numerous lists of names and numbers, involved genealogies, dramatic historical narratives, arcane rites of purification and ritual sacrifice, lists of sites visited in the wanderings of Israel, lovely poetry, the quintessential blessing of Yahweh on his people, impassioned personal encounters, rather dull and prosaic documents on priestly duties, engaging flashes of personality conflicts, stories of intrigue and betrayal, accounts of robust heroism and daring faith, tedious descriptions of detail in ritual, some hymn fragments, quotations from other ancient books, exultant praises to Yahweh, and—most surprisingly—exalted poetic prophecies providing a blessing of Israel from a pagan mantic prophet who has fallen under the "spell" of Yahweh, God of Israel. With all this discordant material in view, it is difficult to imagine a biblical category of writing (except perhaps apocalyptic—yet even there see 24:23–24) that does not find some part or

---

40. Gray, *Numbers*, xxiv.

41. Noordtzij, *Numbers*, 5 is of a similar opinion. He writes, "Therefore the division of the Pentateuch into five books has, where Numbers is concerned, ignored the clear intention of the author, since 1:1–10:10 is a continuation of Leviticus and 33:50–36:13 forms an introduction to Deuteronomy."

42. Noth, *Numbers*, 11. *Within the Pentateuch*, however, Noth affirms that the book of Numbers is "indispensable," but he sees no independent significance of the "book" of Numbers.

43. Otto Eissfeldt, *The Old Testament: An Introduction* (trans. P. Ackroyd; Oxford: Blackwell, 1965), 256–57. Further, there must have been a practical issue of dealing with the size of biblical scrolls. Scroll capacity issues may have demanded some divisions of materials.

other in this book. In all this variety one searches for meaning and coherence. What is it, we wonder, that holds the book together?

So we turn to the question of the nature of the "book" of Numbers. The standard approach to the study of a book of the Bible begins with an attempt to discover the author's intended structure. On the basis of this structure, one may develop an outline and begin to see how the parts relate to the whole. Organizing principles of a book of the Bible may be one of several types. Some books are arranged along chronological lines; some along geographical lines; some along thematic lines; some along logical lines of deductive reasoning. Some books present a narrative flow (tell a story); others argue ideas.

The problem with Numbers is that it does not seem to follow any of these several lines of development. There is some attention to the issues of chronology in the book. But the chapters that have chronological notes are not given in sequence, and some of the chronological notes are only partial. We do not seem to be helped in our quest for a sense of meaning in Numbers by examining the chronological notices. There are several notices of time, but they are incomplete and are not arranged in a strict order:

1:1 — On the first day of the second month of the second year of the exodus; this follows the erection of the tabernacle by one month (see Ex 40:2, 17)

7:1 — On the first day of the first month of the second year of the exodus; the day of the completion of the tabernacle (see Ex 40:2, 17)

9:1 — In the first month of the second year of the exodus; a notice that precedes ch. 1

9:15 — On the day the tabernacle was set up; agreeing with 7:1

10:11 — On the twentieth day of the second month of the second year of the exodus, that is, following the events described in 1:1

20:1 — In the first month. The year is not given, but a comparison of 20:22–29 with 33:38 leads to the conclusion that this date is in the fortieth year of the exodus, that is, thirty-eight years after the events of the earlier chapters.

We are appreciative of these few dates, for without them we would make several errors in our understanding of Numbers. But these few dates are scarcely sufficient for rendering a scheme for the order and structure of the book as a whole. In fact, the larger period of Israel's experience in the wilderness is passed over with scarcely a comment—a strange phenomenon if chronology was the binding glue for the book. Noordtzij observes:

> The thirty-eight years of Israel's wanderings, punishment for their refusal to enter Canaan from Kadesh (ch. 14), thus fall between the first five and the sixth dates. Of this period we are only told of the rebellion of Korah, Dathan, and Abiram (ch. 16), the budding of Aaron's staff (ch. 17), and Moses' sin (20:7–12). The school of Wellhausen concluded from the paucity of information that the author knew little or nothing about those years; but this ignores the fact that the Old Testament does not give us a history of Israel, but rather a history of God's revelation. Periods during which little or nothing happened that would be important for a knowledge of that history are simply passed over in silence.[44]

---

44. Noordtzij, *Numbers,* 6.

The problem we face in attempting to discover the principal framework for the arrangement of Numbers is exacerbated when we survey the ways that scholars have attempted to arrange the larger sections of the book in a major structural outline. Many scholars tend to look at Numbers in terms of three large units based on geographical considerations. The book begins, as we have noted, with Israel encamped in the Wilderness of Sinai (1:1). A common break is proffered to come after 10:10, where the people move from Sinai to make their way to Kadesh (10:11). Third, the people are suddenly in the region of Moab, across from Jericho, some thirty-eight years later in ch. 22. However, the precise division between these second and third sections is generally debated.

Here we may survey some examples of standard outlines of the book to make the issue plain. Gray's outline of Numbers is in three parts:[45]

(1) Numbers 1:1−10:10 (plus 10:29−32)
  Scene: The Desert of Sinai
  Period: nineteen days
(2) Numbers 10:11−21:9
  Scene: North of Sinai, west of the Arabah
  Period: thirty-seven (or, in round numbers, forty) years
(3) Numbers 21:10−36:13
  Scene: East of the Arabah (Jordan valley)
  Period: Not more than five months

There are two unusual factors in his outline. The first is the reminder that Moses' invitation to his brother-in-law Hobab to accompany Israel on their journey must have preceded their leaving Sinai; hence the inclusion of 10:29−32 in the first section. The other is his singular marking of the second/third division at 21:9/21:10, which speaks of the Hebrews beginning their journey to Moab.

A more common example of a three-part structure to the book of Numbers is given by Unger in his popular Bible dictionary:

(1) Departure from Sinai (1:1−10:10)
(2) From Sinai to Moab (10:11−21:35)
(3) Plains of Moab (22:2−36:13)[46]

Rendtorff has a slightly more complex three-part outline:

(1) Part of the Sinai pericope, which begins with Exodus 19:21; primarily regulations about the cult
  (1:1−10:10)
(2) The stay of the Israelites in the desert, connected with Exodus 15:22−18:27 (10:11−20:13)

---

45. Gray, *Numbers*, xxvi−xxix.
46. Merrill F. Unger, *Unger's Bible Dictionary* (3rd ed.; Chicago: Moody Press, 1966), 799. Notice that 22:1 is curiously omitted; perhaps he intended to include it with the second section. Many writers put their principal break between the second and third major blocks of Numbers at this point.

(3) The occupation of Transjordan (some make the break only within or at the end of ch. 21). Passages in 33:50–56 and others display a marked Deuteronomistic stamp (20:14–36:13).[47]

Again, Rendtorff's approach has a geographical break in the latter part of the book, but he is not sure where to place it (20:13/14, or somewhere within or at the end of ch. 21).

Here is an outline of the book of Numbers that has four parts by inserting a subdivision of the initial march of Israel from Sinai to Paran (10:11–12:16):

(1) Organization Prior to Leaving Sinai (1:1–10:10)
(2) Israel on the March — Sinai to Paran (10:11–12:16)
(3) The Murmurings in the Desert of Paran (13:1–21:35)
(4) Israel Encamped in the Plains of Moab (22:1–36:13).[48]

Here is an outline that has five parts, the standard three geographical divisions coupled to two units of journeys:

(1) Israel in the Desert of Sinai (1:1–10:10)
(2) From Sinai to Kadesh (10:11–12:16)
(3) In the Kadesh area (13:1–20:21)
(4) Detour to avoid Edom (20:22–21:35)
(5) Israel in the plains of Moab (22:1–36:13).[49]

Here is an outline with five parts as well, but observe that the divisions do not match the one just noted:

(1) Preparations for Travel (1:1–10:10)
(2) The Journey to Kadesh Barnea (10:11–14:45)
(3) The Journey to the Plains of Moab (15:1–22:1)
(4) The Moabites and Balaam (22:2–25:18)
(5) Final Preparations for Entering Canaan (chs. 26–36).[50]

Finally, here is one of the most satisfactory of the standard, geographically based outlines. The presentation I give shows the subordinate relationship of the journey motifs to the stationary sections:

47. Rendtorff, *The Old Testament: An Introduction*, 147–49.
48. John Joseph Owens, "Numbers," in *Leviticus–Ruth* (Broadman Bible Commentary 2; ed. Clifton J. Allen; Nashville: Nelson, 1999), 80–82. Earlier in his work, Owens, 75, suggests a threefold geographical division:

1. At Sinai. Preparations are made for the journey of unknown duration (1:1–10:10)

2. From Sinai to the Desert of Paran (10:11–20:29)

3. The approach east of the Dead Sea (21:1–36:13)

49. John B. Taylor, "The Five Books," in *Eerdmans' Handbook to the Bible* (ed. David and Pat Alexander; Grand Rapids: Eerdmans, 1973), 185–94.
50. Eugene H. Merrill, "Numbers," in *The Bible Knowledge Commentary — Old Testament* (ed. John F. Walvoord and Roy B. Zuck; Wheaton, Ill.: Victor, 1985), 215–16.

(1) At Sinai: Preparations for departure (1:1–10:10)

    —Journey from Sinai to Kadesh (10:11–12:16)

(2) At Kadesh in the Desert of Paran (13:1–20:13)

    —Journey from Kadesh to the plains of Moab (20:14–22:1)

(3) On the plains of Moab (22:2–32:42)

    —Miscellaneous matters (33:1–36:13).[51]

This sampling of outlines for the book of Numbers shows a tendency to group its materials along geographical lines in three broad categories, with occasional resorts to transitional elements. But these outlines also show the difficulty that scholars have in coming to a consensus in this endeavor. While there is a general agreement that the first section ends in 10:10, there is little agreement on the ending of the second section of the book. Childs writes:

> However, the problem of determining the structure from the geographical indicators appears most clearly in the division of 21:9. From a literary perspective a major division at this point is far from obvious. Moreover, Noth ends his second section at 20:13 before the beginning of the conquest traditions, and de Vaux sets the break at 22:1 when Israel encamped on the plains of Moab beyond the Jordan at Jericho. This disagreement confirms the impression that there are no clear indications within the text of how the editors wished to divide the material at this juncture. For this reason, although geographical features are significant, their importance in establishing a structure should not be exaggerated. The biblical editors seem less concerned with this literary problem than are modern commentators.[52]

This uncertainty leaves us somewhat uncomfortable. There are two principal difficulties with the standard approach to outlining the book of Numbers geographically. First, as Childs observes, the details of the text are not sufficiently clear (and have little scholarly consensus) to make these divisions convincing. Second, the threefold division of the book on geographical terms only adds to the sense that the "book" of Numbers is not really a book at all, only a strange cluster of varied chapters that really belong to the larger unity of the Pentateuch. Again we hear the words of those scholars from Gray to Budd that suggest the "book" of Numbers really has no independent unity or independent significance.

The problem with this general approach to Numbers is that it leaves the book dependent on both Exodus and Deuteronomy and somewhat derivative of both. Some writers are so taken with this notion that they have developed the idea of a "tri-teuch" instead of a "pentateuch." They assert the independent existence of the books of Genesis and Deuteronomy but lump Exodus–Leviticus–Numbers together, principally on geographical grounds.

---

51. LaSor, Hubbard, and Bush, *OTS*-1982, 164–65. The enumerating of the elements and the partial indenting are my own representation of their prose description. (These writers present a similar scheme in the later edition, *OTS*-1996, 100–101.)

52. Brevard S. Childs, *Introduction to the Old Testament as Scripture* (Philadelphia: Fortress, 1979), 195. Perhaps this idea of uncertainty explains the fact that Maarsingh gives no outline at all in his commentary on the book of Numbers. The commentary is based on comments on each of ninety-five sections with no attempt at all to relate these sections to larger units. See the table of contents in Maarsingh, *Numbers,* iii–v.

Dennis T. Olson was one of the first to break from this tradition of the geographical approach and to develop the view that Numbers is an independent book with a convincing structural integrity of its own. He presented his patterns first in his doctoral dissertation and subsequently in his commentary on Numbers.[53] The book of Numbers assuredly has its place in the larger Torah, but it is truly a book on its own merits with a coherent beginning, middle, and end. He observes, as we have done, that "the central problem in the interpretation of the book of Numbers ... is the failure to detect a convincing and meaningful structure for the book."[54] The direction of Olson's work is simply stunning. In my reading he is the first to break through the morass of scholarship that treats the "book" of Numbers as merely a convention and not a true book, a weak sister in the Pentateuch.

The genius of Olson's approach is that once he has stated it, the reader says, "Of course!" And one wonders why no one has approached the book in this way before Olson. Most of the treatments we have surveyed are somewhat at a loss to explain the chronological abnormalities in the book. Why does it begin "out of order," with the events of the second month of the second year of the exodus (1:1) rather than with the events of the first month (7:1; 9:1, 15)? Rashi (AD 1040–1105), cited by Noordtzij,[55] thought this was the case so the book could begin on a positive note rather than on something that reflected negatively on Israel. Yet there is really nothing negative in the events of chs. 7 and 9. Furthermore, the tendency of many readers is to rush through the numbers to get to the heart of the book. The importance of the "numbers" in Numbers has simply not been understood. Since the book of Numbers begins with the "numbers," so shall we.

Olson argues that the two census lists in the book are its framing principle; these lists serve as "the overarching literary and theological structure of the book of Numbers."[56] The first census, of course, describes the first generation of Hebrews who left Egypt in the exodus. The second census describes the second generation of Hebrews who left Egypt. The first generation of Hebrews rebelled against Yahweh; they were consigned to living out their lives in the wilderness. The second generation was given the opportunity by God to recapture the promises first given to their parents, to move into the Land of Promise, and to receive their proper inheritance. Olson characterizes this pattern as "the death of the old and the birth of the new."

Olson begins with the census lists in chs. 1 and 26. Olson finds these chapters to be essentially important in establishing the correct approach to the book. Indeed, the book of Numbers is a *biped* rather than a *triped*. The first major unit concerns the experiences of the first generation of the exodus and their failure

---

53. See Dennis T. Olson, *The Death of the Old and the Birth of the New: The Framework of the Book of Numbers and the Pentateuch* (BJS; Chico, Calif.: Scholars, 1985); *Numbers* (Interpretation; Louisville, Ky.: John Knox, 1996). Actually, Elmer Smick anticipated Olson in several aspects in his commentary on "Numbers" in *Wycliffe Bible Commentary* (ed. C. F. Pfeiffer and E. F. Harrison; Chicago: Moody Press, 1962). Smick's outline has three major sections: (1) Part one: Israel in the desert (1:1–21:35 [+22:1]); (2) Part two: Foreign intrigue against Israel (22:2–25:18); (3) Part three: Preparation for entering the land (26:1–36:13). Smick presents the Balaam story as a hinge between the two larger sections, each of which begins with a census. Still, Olson's work stands on its own, not only in the outline he presents, but also in the theology he derives from this outline.

54. Olson, *The Death of the Old*, 31.

55. Noordtzij, *Numbers*, 6.

56. Olson, *The Death of the Old*, 81.

to act in obedience to the Lord to claim their inheritance in the land of Canaan. Hence the text moves resolutely to a presentation of the word of God for the second generation. The "famous" division at 10:11 turns out to be subordinate to the principal division markers that center on the numbers of the tribes (chs. 1, 26). The reason for the second census list is because the first census listing became irrelevant for the new generation. The first listing was of their parents. The new listing was for the people of their own day.

This observation led Olson to propose an outline that has two unequal sections, 1:1–25:18 and 26:1–36:13. In the first section the focus is on the first generation of the people of God in their march in the wilderness; the second section presents the new generation being prepared to enter the Promised Land. In the first section there are two major subdivisions: the preparation for the march (1:1–10:36), a subsection that presents the hope of conquest in a positive manner, followed by the cycle of rebellion (11:1–25:18), in which there is a mixture of texts of hope and failure. The second section has two "parts" as well, one stated and *the other implied*. It is in his "implied subsection" that the genius of Olson's approach may be seen. The stated subsection (26:1–36:13) is the preparation for the people to enter the land, a section that roughly parallels the first part of the book and is positive in nature. The book ends in an implied question: Will the new generation be faithful to God, or will they rebel as their parents did? We may paraphrase, "God has time and the wilderness has sand."

Here is a modification of Olson's basic structural outline,[57] which I shall follow in my commentary (references in the outline being tied to the commentary):

I. The Experience of the First Generation in the Wilderness (1:1–25:18)
   A. The Preparation for the Triumphal March to the Promised Land (1:1–10:36)
      1. Setting Apart the People (1:1–10:10)
      2. Setting Forth the People (10:11–36)
   B. The Rebellion and Judgment of a Fearful People (11:1–25:18)
      1. A Cycle of Rebellion and Atonement and the Record of Death (11:1–20:29)
      2. A Climax of Rebellion and Hope and the End of Their Dying (21:1–25:18)
II. The Prospects for the Second Generation to Enter the Promised Land (26:1–36:13)
   A. The Preparation for the Triumphal March to the Promised Land, the Second Generation (26:1–32:42)
   B. A Review of the First Generation's Journey, and Words of Warning and Encouragement to the Second Generation (33:1–56)
   C. An Anticipation of the Promised Land (34:1–36:13)
   D. [The Prospects for the Second Generation Are for Good, but the Warning from the Experience of the First Generation Must Not Be Forgotten]

---

57. His wording may be superior; see his outline (*Death of the Old*, 118–20) plus the commentary that follows (ibid., 120–24). Olson's two headings are: "Part One—The Death of the Old Generation, Numbers 1–25" and "Part Two—The Rise of the New Generation on the Edge of the Promised Land, Numbers 26–36." See now Olson, *Numbers*, ix–xi, 3–7. I am very pleased to see that Dillard and Longman follow Olson's approach as well (*AIOT*, 86–87).

8. THEOLOGICAL THEMES

The Old and the New

The simplest summary of the theology of Numbers is found in the slogan of Olson that we have referred to above: "the death of the old and the birth of the new." Numbers presents the concept of the chastening wrath of God on his own disobedient people. Yet in his wrath Yahweh remembered mercy; a new generation would arise to inherit the land. The association of the Lord's wrath and mercy, the coupling of his anger and his love—no matter how strange it may seem to us—these are marked features of the teaching of the Torah and the Prophets.[58]

An entire generation that had formed a holy community; a people related to God by the sovereignty of grace and the cultic rites of the sacrifice of Passover; a nation delivered from its formidable foes by the direct intervention of God's powerful right hand in the exodus from Egypt; a community entrusted with his Torah, graced with his word, and allowed to participate in his holy worship—this people lost their right to enjoy the Promised Land, their true heritage in the Lord. Of all the nations of the earth, the word of God had come only to the descendants of Jacob (see Ps 147:19–20). Of all the nations of the earth, the right hand of the Lord had reached out only to them in their deliverance (see Dt 4:32–34). Of all the peoples of the earth, only they were the family of God (see Dt 7:7–10). But even on them his heavy hand had fallen.

Because of their rebellion against God's grace and disbelief in his power to deliver them to the uttermost, the people of Israel were in breach of covenant. Those who were caught in the breach comprised an entire generation (all persons over the age of twenty), including women and men, mighty and lowly, godly and profane. Miriam and Aaron, yes, and even Moses, the great prophet and servant of the Lord, were not exempt from God's wrath when they disobeyed him or resisted his will (see esp. 20:1–13).

The fourth book of the Pentateuch thus presents a sobering, chilling reality. The God who had entered into covenant with Abraham (Ge 12), who had delivered his people from bondage in the exodus (Ex 14–15), who had revealed his holiness and the means to approach his grace through celebrative and sacrificial worship (Lev 1–7)—this same Yahweh was also a God of wrath and a consuming fire. His wrath extended to his errant children as well as to the enemy nations of Egypt and Canaan.

God's wrath, as von Rad writes, is *his* wrath, not the supposed wrath of the law. God's wrath is a mark of his sovereignty—and a memorial of his grace:

> Certainly, the Old Testament tells of many judgments which overtook the disobedient nation. But who was their author? Was it the Law? It was God himself acting on Israel, and not a legal system of salvation which worked out according to a prearranged plan. In particular, it was God himself who always remained Lord even over Israel's sin, and whose judgments even the preexilic prophets—and their successors even more clearly than they—represented as being at the same time evidence of his faithfulness to his chosen people. None of these

---

58. See S. Erlandsson, "The Wrath of YHWH," *TynBul* 23 (1972): 111–16. He writes, "Anger seems to be an essential element of YHWH's love which is inseparably connected with His holiness and His justice" (115).

judgments brings irrevocable rejection. The Lord never failed to accompany his faithful people, and he always took them back.[59]

That even Moses would come under the wrath of God is stunning! Chapter 20, which records the error of Moses, begins with the notice of the death of Miriam (v.1) and concludes with the record of the death of Aaron (vv.22–29). Here was the passing of the noblest of the leadership of the people, the old guard. Those whom God had used to establish the nation were dying before the nation came into its land. Miriam, who had led the joyful singing at the day of redemption (Ex 15), would not live to sing a song of praise to the Lord in Canaan. Aaron, who for a generation had led the people in worship by means of the sacrifice of untold numbers of animals, would not be allowed to offer a tiny pigeon in the Promised Land. And Moses, hoary old man that he was—having led a life difficult to rival in the service of God, save only by Jesus—Moses, who had spoken the words of God from the holy mount of Sinai, would see the Promised Land only from a promontory in Moab.

Questions no doubt came to a people who had experienced such greatness at the hand of God and now sensed such ignominy: Has God indeed finished with us? Is he done with the nation as a whole? Are the glorious promises God gave to our fathers and mothers just a thing of the past? Have we no hope?

Balaam

In one of the most remarkable sections of the Bible, the Lord worked providentially and directly to proclaim his continued faithfulness to his people, despite their continuing unfaithfulness. This section is the comic account of the pagan diviner Balaam (Nu 22–24). Here the God of laughter brings a smile to his people to encourage them in the prospects of their new hope, even as the older persons among them were still dying. God's promises would still be realized, they now came to believe—realized in themselves!

In Balaam we have the pagan counterpart to Moses the man of God. This idea has become clearer in a recent archaeological discovery of texts bearing Balaam's name at Deir 'Allah in Jordan. The discovery of these prophetic texts in Aramaic (dated variously from the mid-eighth through the sixth centuries BC) shows how famous Balaam was in the ancient Near East even centuries after his death.[60] Balaam was an internationally known prophet, a diviner who was expert in examining the entrails of animals and in watching the movement of birds to discover the will of the gods. He thought that the Lord God of Israel

---

59. Gerhard von Rad, *The Theology of Israel's Prophetic Traditions* (vol. 2 of *Old Testament Theology*; trans. D. M. G. Stalker; New York: Harper & Row, 1965), 406.

60. See Jacob Hoftijzer, "The Prophet Balaam in a 6th-Century Aramaic Inscription," *BA* 39, 1 (March 1976): 11–17. The dating of these inscriptions ranges widely. J. Naveh dated the find in the eighth century ("The Date of the Deir 'Allah Inscriptions in Aramaic Script," *IEJ* 17 [1967]: 256–58); Frank Moore Cross Jr., dated it in the seventh century ("Notes on the Ammonite Inscription from Tell Sīrān," *BASOR* 212 [1973]: 12–15). The fact that the prophecy was written on a wall seems to indicate that it was an important historical example of the oracles of this diviner that might be preserved for posterity. Stephen A. Kaufman observes that the texts of these inscriptions "remain enticingly obscure," that perhaps we need the powers of a Balaam to help banish the darkness ("Review Article: The Aramaic Texts from Deir 'Alla," *BASOR* 239 [Summer 1980]: 71–74). Dennis Cole (*Numbers* [NAC 3B; Nashville: Broadman & Holman, 2000], 367–70) presents reconstructions and translations of these texts.

was like any other deity whom he imagined he might manipulate by mantic acts. But from the early part of the narrative, when he first encountered the true God in visions, and in the hilarious narrative of the journey on the donkey (ch. 22), Balaam began to learn what for him was a strange, bizarre, even incomprehensible lesson: An encounter with the *true* God was fundamentally different from anything he had ever known. But then he had never known Yahweh!

When at the instigation of Balak, king of Moab, Balaam finally began to utter his curse on the nation of Israel, the pagan mantic found his mouth unable to express the least of the contempt he desired to declare. Instead, from his mouth, and at the loss of his honorarium (!), came the loveliest of blessings on Israel and the most ferocious of curses on the enemies roundabout (chs. 23–24). Balak was furious! And Israel, who later heard this account, rollicked joyfully with the laughter of God.

In his seven prophetic oracles, Balaam proclaimed God's great grace for his people, his grace revealed in his blessing: "I have received a command to bless; he has blessed, and I cannot change it" (23:20).

It is the blessing of God on Israel that is the heart of the book of Numbers and the heart of the Torah. This reminder of the blessing of God in the most unusual circumstances of the oracles of Balaam leads us to the celebrative and joyful aspects of the book. Zdeněk Soušek writes:

> The Balaam pericope is a weighty component of the message concerning the salvation work of Yahweh. The superiority of Yahweh over all his foes is there demonstrated. The incident is a mighty comfort to the threat and quaking in the presence of wicked powers and is an eloquent testimony that no annihilator, no destroyer, no death has the last word—but Yahweh, who intervenes entirely unexpectedly to save his community, to open to it new horizons and to give to it new hope.[61]

Soušek is not the only scholar deeply impressed with the importance of the Balaam story in biblical theology. Moriarty writes:

> Textual difficulties disregarded, few sections in the Pentateuch are more important theologically than this remarkable narrative. In a real sense the Balaam story may be said to summarize the revelation of God's purpose as it was communicated to Moses.[62]

God's blessing on Israel rests in his sovereign will. The immediate enjoyment of God's blessing will ever be dependent on the faithfulness of his people. But the ultimate realization of God's blessing is sure—because of the character of God, which is incapable of change:

God is not a man, that he should lie,
    nor a son of man, that he should change his mind.
Does he speak and then not act?
    Does he promise and not fulfill? (Nu 23:19)

---

61. Zdeněk Soušek, "Bileam und seine Eselin: Exegetischetheologische Bemerkungen zu Numbers 22," *Communio Viatorum* 10 (1967): 185. (Translations given in this commentary from German, French, and Dutch writings are mine, unless otherwise noted.)

62. Frederick L. Moriarty, "Numbers," in *Jerome Biblical Commentary* (ed. Raymond E. Brown, Joseph A. Fitzmyer, and Roland E. Murphy; 2 vols. [Englewood Cliffs, NJ: Prentice-Hall, 1968], 1:95.

Most remarkably, this untoward, alien man Balaam—who stood at enmity with Israel and was no friend of God—was given a prophetic vision of the coming of a Victor-King, a Deliverer who is the Promised One, even Messiah Yeshua:

> I see him, but not now;
>> I behold him, but not near.
> A star will come out of Jacob;
>> a scepter will rise out of Israel.
> He will crush the foreheads of Moab,
>> the skulls of all the sons of Sheth. (Nu 24:17)

The story of Balaam the pagan mantic has its sorry side, however. What he was unable to do by means of the negative prophetic word, the curse viewed as a word of power, he did by means of seduction and deception. The events of Numbers 25 are sometimes thought to be just more in the long recital of the sins of Israel against God, followed by yet another outburst of God's anger against his sinning people. In a sense, however, the rebellion in Numbers 25 is the spiritual nadir of the book. And Balaam was at the heart of it, though we do not discover so until ch. 31.

At the instigation of Balaam, Midianite women (Moabite enemies of Israel) seduced leading figures of Israel to join them in the worship of their god, the manifestation of Baal at Peor. The worship of Baal employed some of the same terminology as the worship of the Lord. Perhaps some of the people went to the pagan sacrificial feasts in innocence. But the terms carried different meanings in the two religions. Instead of celebrating the wonder of knowing God and being his people of all the peoples of the earth, the worship of Baal moved from feasting and drinking to the most debased of sexual orgies. It is not unlikely, though some have overstated the case, that hallucinogenic drugs were involved. Certainly the rites became a frenzy of sexual activity. As the people easily succumbed to Egyptian-styled pagan rites at Sinai while Moses was speaking with God (see Ex 32, where the golden calf was similar to the Egyptian bull-god Apis), so now they had their first taste of the seductive religion of Canaan in the sexually oriented worship of Baal and his consorts.

At one unbelievable moment the frenzy broke into the camp of Israel and extended to the very entrance of the tabernacle of God (see commentary). One prince of Israel brazenly copulated with a woman, likely a Midianite priestess of the Baal cult, in boldest daring, in the very proximity of the place for the worship of the Lord. As they gyrated one against the other in their primeval dance in celebration of Baal, in profanation of the holy that is nearly unspeakable, Phinehas, a great hero of faith, thrust a spear through both of them. The blade pierced through the back of the man and into the belly of the woman. A grandson of Aaron, Phinehas showed himself of all the men present to be a hero. His zeal for Yahweh was like the very zeal of God himself, and it reminds us of the zeal of the Promised One (Pss 2; 110). Phinehas typifies the strong sword of Jesus (Rev 19:11–16). Moreover, his action stemmed the plague that had broken out in the camp. This was the last plague; it was the end of the dying of the older generation. Now they were all gone.

Then two things transpired. First, Yahweh established his covenant of peace with Phinehas. In addition to the great covenant God established with Israel through Moses on Mount Sinai (beginning in Ex 19), we are accustomed to think of the earlier covenant of God with Abraham (Ge 15) and the later covenant of God with David (2Sa 7). We also look forward in the Hebrew Scriptures to the establishment of the new covenant (Jer 31). In the book of Numbers we discover another of God's gracious covenants, his covenant with Phinehas (Nu 25). This covenant with God's priest was as important for true worship as was the covenant God established with David for the true royal house. Second, through the action of Phinehas "atonement was made for Israel" (25:13). The holy relationship of God and people was reestablished.

Worship

The book of Numbers has a great deal to contribute to the theology of worship. The NT concept that in worship all should be done in an orderly and fitting manner (1Co 14:40) finds its basis in the book of Numbers. Not only do we learn of order and procedure, we also learn of pageantry and procession, festival and fasting, demanded sacrifices and freewill offerings, restrictions and blessings. Other special features of the book include the provisions for the Nazirite vow (6:1–21), the beauty of the Aaronic Benediction (6:22–27), and the repetitive, lengthy record of the dedication offerings given by the elders of each tribe (ch. 7), the lengthy repetitions emphasizing the solemnity of the event and the magnanimity of the people in their gratitude to God the Deliverer. But the most prominent feature of all is blessing. The words God gave to Aaron and to his sons (hence words vouchsafed to Phinehas) are words whereby God showed his desire to bestow blessing on his people — his desire that they sense the smile of his face (see the comments on 6:23–27).

Thus, it is in the book of Numbers that the ongoing purposes of God for his covenantal people are reaffirmed. Despite his judgment on the first generation of those he redeemed from Egypt, his murmuring people, God was still determined to bring the new generation into the Land of Promise and realization.

From this observation it follows that the entire book of Numbers is a pointing back to failure and an addressing forward of the possibility of success. But in all there is warning. "God has time and the wilderness has sand." The second generation had to act — but the expectation was that they would. Yes, the first generation failed; no, the new generation did not have to fail. Yes, there were repeated instances reported of the rebellions of the first generation (chs. 1–25); but as yet there had been none, not one, reported of the second generation (chs. 26–33). The first generation was one of the dead and the dying; but there is not one death mentioned in the latter section of the book (chs. 26–33).

The fortunes of the people were not the result of time and tide, of chance and happenstance, of the fickle wills of capricious deities. The people could make their own fortune, for the eternal God had given them carte blanche. If they would respond in faithfulness and in wholehearted obedience, there was no promise he had given that would not be fulfilled. If they behaved as their parents had done, then there might have to be another forty years of waiting it out in the wilderness — and the wilderness has sand.

God has time! He is not in a hurry. Finally he would have a generation of people like Joshua and Caleb who would focus on him entirely and not be intimidated by the walls of cities and the stature of their men, or be swayed by the sniveling words of the weak and the cowardly. The book of Numbers is the call to a robust faith in the Lord. And for people of such faith, there is no end of blessing.

Numbers

What seems to be the most embarrassing element of the book — the numbers that seem impossibly inflated for a small nation at the beginning of its existence — are its crown and glory. These numbers are a mark of God's blessing. They are a fulfillment of his covenant. They anticipate numbers of peoples who will be like the stars of the heavens, the sand of the seashore.

The numbers in each of the census takings, the old and the new (Nu 1; 46), add up to more than six hundred thousand fighting men, an immense army under the banners of the Lord. These numbers lead us to extrapolate a population that may extend to 2.5 or 3 million persons—perhaps even more. The numbers lead us to think in superlatives. They remind us of God's grace, they point to his mercy, and they anticipate his glory. These numbers have a theological meaning. They are used for effect, not simple bombast.

Poor old Balaam thought he had the "number" of the people of Israel. He found that he could not number their dust (see comments on 23:10)! It was God who had Israel's number! And their number was their destiny. Their number was their full complement. This truth, too, Balaam saw. He looked down from his height and saw their expanse, and what he saw was only the fringe of their habitation; he saw that their dwelling was apart from all nations (23:9).

The number of the people had grown from a small figure to an immense number in an amazingly brief period of time. But their number at present was only a cipher compared to their number in God's future for them. The numbers in the book of Numbers are also part of its theology. The numbers extol the glory of God in his people.

Numbers includes more than numerical listings of the tribes. This book records events of lasting significance for Israel and for the inheritors of blessing in God's church. God did display his wrath even against his errant people; but his grace was renewed as surely as is the dawn.

9. THE PROBLEM OF THE LARGE NUMBERS

The exceedingly high numbers of the able-bodied men over the age of twenty conscripted into the armies of Israel (chs. 1 and 26) are troublesome, to say the least. The numbers of soldiers in each list total in excess of six hundred thousand (603,550 in 1:46; 601,730 in 26:51). These numbers of men mustered for warfare demand a total population estimated to be at least 2.5 million. Indeed, perhaps a population of nearly five million might be required to supply a conscripted army of six hundred thousand able-bodied men over twenty years old. Such numbers seem to be exceedingly (impossibly?) large for the times, the locale, the wilderness sojourn, and in comparison to what we now judge to have been the numbers of the inhabitants of the land of Canaan whom the Israelites would set out to conquer.

We may observe that problems with large numbers in historical studies are not limited to biblical texts. Just as an example, we may think about the ideas of the numbers of indigenous peoples in the Americas on the eve of European contact. Schweikart and Allen deal with this issue in the excursus, "Did Columbus Kill Most of the Indians?" They document a vast array of conjectures of the numbers of native peoples in the Americas (and the numbers that may have been killed as a result of European contact).[63] In an extensive bibliography on the subject, they cite "the best" review of the literature as the work of John D. Daniels, "The Indian Population of North America in 1492."[64] The difference between this debate and that relating

63. See Larry Schweikart and Michael Allen, *A Patriot's History of the United States: From Columbus's Great Discovery to the War on Terror* (New York: Penguin/Sentinel, 2004), 7–10.
64. John D. Daniels, "The Indian Population of North America in 1492," *William & Mary Quarterly* (April 1999): 298–320.

to the book of Numbers is significant; in the latter case we are dealing with inspired Scripture, not with estimates and guesses from older sources.

Many faithful readers of the Bible have taken these large numbers at face value and without question.[65] Frankly, I am sympathetic with them, and elsewhere I have written in support of this point of view.[66] Some commentators have gone to considerable length to work out the mathematical possibilities of these numbers in terms of birthrate statistics, the logistics of crossing the Red Sea in one night, dwelling in the wilderness, marching in the order of the tribes, massing on the eastern shore of the Jordan River, population density probabilities, and the issues relating to conquering the Promised Land. None of the early modern conservative commentators worked so hard on these issues as C. F. Keil.[67]

Yet the more that modern scholars study such attempts to make these large numbers manageable in the constraints of what we now know about the social-geographical context of the Late Bronze Age, the more difficult these issues become. Frankly, we begin to wonder whether we are not engaging in special pleading. At issue is not a lack of belief in miracles, as is sometimes assumed; for numerous reverent or conservative scholars have been attracted to one or more options concerning the nature of these large numbers. The work of God with his people was miraculous throughout the wilderness experience, no matter how many or how few they might have been. These approaches are based on an attempt to find what is believed to be a more realistically accurate number for the peoples of Israel at this time.

The first-time visitor to the nation of Israel faces a number of shocking realizations. None is more striking than the observation of how very small the country is. It is astonishingly small![68] When one looks about a bit, there often comes a sudden realization: the numbers in the book of Numbers are simply impossibly large. *The land is just not extensive enough to make sense for numbers this large in an age so long ago.*

---

65. In fact, it has been my experience when teaching on these ideas in church adult education classes and in the theological academy that many people who have a broad knowledge of the Bible have never considered the numbers of these chapters to be problematic; the concepts of an army of six hundred thousand and a consequent population of 2.5 million (or more) in this account are often just considered to be a part of the routine data from the OT story—data to be believed, not questioned.

66. I refer to the notes I authored for the book of Numbers in *The NIV Study Bible*, Introduction: Special Problem, and note on 1:46.

67. C. F. Keil and F. Delitzsch, *The Pentateuch* (Biblical Commentary on the Old Testament; trans. James Martin; repr. Grand Rapids: Eerdmans, n.d.), 2:46–47; 3:4–15. Keil (3:5–6, n. 2) correctly attributed God's miraculous provision of manna as the principal support for the nutrition of the people, but the question may be raised as to the dietary support for the animals of the peoples of Israel. Regarding the meeting of this need, Keil asserted, "the peninsula of Sinai yielded much more subsistence in ancient times than is to be found there at present." The question, of course, is whether such an assertion is anecdotal, wishful thinking, or capable of demonstration by modern methods of research of ancient climatic and growth patterns in what today is a rather desolate, barren region.

68. The traditional habitation area, north to south ("from Dan to Beersheba"), stretches a distance of only 150 miles; the distance from the Mediterranean Sea to the Jordan River averages about thirty miles. See Ronald B. Allen, "The Land of Israel," in *Israel—The Land and the People: An Evangelical Affirmation of God's Promises* (ed. H. Wayne House; Grand Rapids: Kregel, 1998), 17–33.

Corruption in Transmission

Various suggestions have been made to solve the problem of the large numbers. Some have argued that these numbers may have been corrupted in transmission. The general faithfulness of the textual transmission of the Hebrew Bible (and the Greek NT) is truly marvelous.[69] At the same time, in neither testament was this process perfect. We have certain examples of the corruption of numbers in parallel passages in the historical literature. An event described in 2 Samuel 10:18 speaks of seven hundred chariots, but the parallel text in 1 Chronicles 19:18 reads seven thousand. First Samuel 13:1 lacks the number altogether for the age of Saul: "Saul was ... years old." The number of people who died in the final plague of Numbers is listed as twenty-four thousand (25:9), but 1 Corinthians 10:8 gives twenty-three thousand for the same event.

Thus, it is possible for one to argue that the numbers of the census lists in Numbers 1 and 26 have suffered problems in scribal transmission; however, the apparatus of *BHS* does not betray notices of textual difficulties in the numbers in these two chapters. Moreover, if error in textual transmission is suggested as the explanation for these large numbers, it would not be the isolated addition of a digit here or the dropping of a hundred there. For textual transmission difficulties to be of any "help" in a significant reduction of numbers in these census lists, scribal errata would have to be massive in scope. The entire list has to be in error. Again, the textual record does not betray any discussion of such problems. It almost takes more faith to believe in textual-transmission problems in these lists than it does to work out the logistics of the numbers as they presently stand.

A Later Period or a Fabrication

Some critical scholars have suggested that the large numbers in the census lists in Numbers 1 and 26 are actually projections backward from the time of David. This proposal by the nineteenth-century German scholar Dillmann helped to preserve the numbers, but much was lost in terms of the integrity of Torah.[70] Others (more critical) simply dismissed the numbers as fictional—as indeed is the tendency today for many scholars to hold most of the OT story line as fabrication.[71] Budd, for instance, holds nothing back:

---

69. See S. K. Soderlund, "Text and Manuscripts of the Old Testament" (*ISBE*[2] 4:798–814). His assessment of the MT is impressive: "The phenomenon of the MT is unique in the field of biblical textual criticism. No other stream of scribal transmission, in neither the OT nor NT manifests such remarkable uniformity. Intense study of the MT MSS since the late eighteenth century has shown that only a limited number of consonantal variants of substance can be found in the entire tradition. When this observation is seen to hold true not only for the principal MSS of the ben Asher tradition but also for the numerous text specimens of the Cairo Genizah antedating those MSS, the phenomenon is truly extraordinary and bears witness to a genuinely conservative and cautious scribal tradition" (ibid., 811).

70. August Dillmann, *Die Bücher Numeri, Deuteronomium und Josua* (KHAT; 2nd ed.; Leipzig: S. Hirzel, 1886), 7. See also William Foxwell Albright, *From the Stone Age to Christianity* (2nd ed.; New York: Doubleday, 1957), 253; Albright first developed this idea in an article, "The Administrative Districts of Israel and Judah," *JPOS* 5 (1925): 20–25. Harrison remarked on two flaws in Albright's proposal—on its own grounds. First, the tribe of Simeon was in the process of being amalgamated into the tribe of Judah by the time of David; it had no real independent status in the early monarchy. But the number given for Simeon in Numbers 1:23 (59,300) makes it one of the largest of the tribes in the census. Second, this number is really too large even for the time of David! See Harrison, *Numbers*, 43.

71. See, e.g., Gray, *Numbers*, 13.

"The historical difficulties in accepting the figure as it stands are insuperable."[72] In his own approach, Budd posits a back-reading from a postexilic time based on haggadic speculation. He suggests that the tabernacle tax of 301,775 shekels in Exodus 38:25–28, at one-half shekel per person, gave rise to the idea of 603,550 men liable for the tax; therefore, the numbers in Numbers 1 and 26 arose not from any misunderstanding "but from haggadic contemplation of the priestly Tabernacle, and from what was doubtless a post-exilic level of Temple tax."[73]

Different Meanings

The Bible student who does not have skills in reading biblical Hebrew may be surprised to learn that numbers in the Hebrew Bible are presented not in numerical characters but in words. Thus the sum for the fighting men of the tribe of Reuben in 1:21 does not appear in the MT as in English versions (46,500); rather, the numbers are words, written out in a laborious but serviceable pattern. Here are the words in transliteration: *šiššâ wᵉʾarbāʿîm ʾelep waḥᵃmēš mēʾôt*, "six and [plus] forty thousand and [plus] five hundreds," woodenly expressed.[74]

Considerable focus has been given to the word *ʾelep* (GK 547), translated "thousand" in these lists. Many scholars have felt that this word for "thousand" might have a different meaning here than the usual numerical idea. The issue is made more complex in that there may be three homonyms (words

---

72. Budd, *Numbers*, 6. Consider this dour view of Budd (xxvi):

Our investigations have proceeded on the assumption that the book of Numbers is a complex accumulation of tradition, and not a simply factual account of Israel's journey from Sinai to the border of the land. This assumption is rooted in the findings of literary and historical criticism, and has been shown to be justified at every stage of the enquiry. The book of Numbers lacks many of the essential data that the modern historian requires—a clear witness to the use of sources close to or contemporary with the period described, in the form of annals, chronicles, inscriptions, and a firm backbone of dates which can be worked in with the known history of the second half of the second millenium [*sic*] BC. The question must necessarily be raised as to what value if any the book has to the historian of the second millenium. In general the prospects are not very promising. The book appears to lack the kind of information the historian of the second millenium requires.

The issues of "biblical minimalism" are the focus of two books by the "moderate" scholar, William G. Dever: *What Did the Biblical Writers Know and When Did They Know It?: What Archaeology Can Tell Us About the Reality of Ancient Israel* (Grand Rapids: Eerdmans, 2001) and *Who Were the Early Israelites and Where Did They Come From?* (Grand Rapids: Eerdmans, 2003). More conservative responses to minimalism may be found today in Kenneth A. Kitchen, *On the Reliability of the Old Testament* (Grand Rapids: Eerdmans, 2003), and Iain Provan, V. Phillips Long, and Tremper Longman III, *A Biblical History of Israel* (Louisville, Ky.: Westminster John Knox, 2003).

73. Budd, *Numbers*, 8–9. Walter C. Kaiser Jr. also makes much of the tabernacle tax issue in Exodus 38:25–27, but to the opposite point of Budd! Kaiser's view is that the precise numbers in this passage fit nicely with the large numbers in the census lists in Numbers 1 and 26. He writes, "All attempts to whittle down this number [which argues for a total population of over two million people] ... fail to meet the standard of consistency with other contexts" (*A History of Israel: From the Bronze Age through the Jewish Wars* [Nashville: Broadman & Holman, 1998], 102).

74. Further, there are no notes in the apparatus of *BHS* to suggest that any of these words has a history of scribal variation. We do not know whether numerical characters or some form of ciphers were used in an earlier period, or whether the use of words, as here, was the case from the first writing of the text.

with the same spelling) that could be confused, either in ancient times or today. One Hebrew word *ʾelep* certainly means "thousand" and is correctly so translated. But another Hebrew word *ʾelep* is a graphic term derived from pastoral language that was used to number herds.[75] As one would look out over many cattle, one might speak in approximate terms of animals numbering *ʾelep* ("a thousand"). Thus the word "thousands" may be a simple statement of approximation: There were "thousands" of persons in each tribe.

In some biblical passages the Hebrew word for "thousand" (*ʾelep*) is a technical term for a company of men that may or may not equal one thousand (e.g., Nu 31:5; Jos 22:14 ["a family division"]; 1Sa 23:23 ["clans"]).[76] One might argue that the term *ʾelep* has lost all sense of a specific numerical value and means simply a "troop." Each tribe might be composed of thirty to seventy troops, and the total of the fighting men for these troops would number in the hundreds. This would mean that for Reuben, instead of an actual count of forty-six thousand five hundred men (Nu 1:21), there were perhaps forty-six troops with five hundred fighting men; for Simeon, instead of fifty-nine thousand three hundred men (Nu 1:23), there were fifty-nine troops with three hundred fighting men, etc. This would yield a total of 589 troops and some 5,550 fighting men, with each troop having about nine or ten men. This is the preferred conclusion of Noth.[77]

The problem with this approach, however, is that in Numbers 1:44–46 the numbers are totaled in such a way as to regard the term *ʾelep* as one more than 999. Regarding the word *ʾelep* as a rough approximation only works where approximation appears to be the intent (see, e.g., 1Sa 4:10, where Israel had thirty thousand foot soldiers defeated by the Philistines, the number in this passage doubtless giving merely an approximation of the number of soldiers who were defeated).

Others have observed that the term *ʾelep* ("thousand") is close in spelling to the word *ʾallûp* (BDB, 49b; *HALOT* 1:54), a term meaning "chieftain" or "commander" elsewhere in the Bible.[78] In Genesis 36:15–43, this word is used for the chieftains of Edom. Sir Flinders Petrie argued in 1923 that the term *ʾelep* may mean a family unit, family members living in one tent—perhaps a "clan." One solution, then, for the large numbers in these lists may be found in this confusion of the word for "thousand" and that for "chieftain" or "clan." In this way the figure fifty-three thousand four hundred (of Asher in 26:47) might mean "fifty-three units (chiefs, clans) and four hundred men." The figure thirty-two thousand two hundred (of Manasseh in 1:35) would mean "thirty-two units (chiefs, clans) and two hundred men." Such a procedure would give a greatly reduced total for the whole population.

But this procedure would also be at variance with the fact that the biblical text adds the "thousands" in the same way that it adds the "hundreds" for the large total. The numbers joined to *ʾelep* and to the

---

75. In fact, some uses of Hebrew *ʾelep* indicate animals such as cattle (see, e.g., Pr 14:4, *bᵉʾên ʾᵃlāpîm*, "where there are no oxen"). In Ugaritic, *alp* means "ox" (see Gordon, *UT*, Gl. 200; cf. *HALOT* 1:59), termed I אֶלֶף (*ʾelep* I). *HALOT* (ibid.) terms *ʾelep* = "thousand" as II אֶלֶף (*ʾelep* II). See also P. P. Jenson, "544 אלף," *NIDOTTE*, 1:415–16.

76. This meaning for *ʾelep* is termed III אֶלֶף (*ʾelep* III; *HALOT* I:59–60), "a group of a thousand, a clan," as in 1 Samuel 10:19, *lᵉšibṭêkem ûlᵉʾalpêkem* ("by your tribes and clans").

77. Noth, *Numbers*, 22–23.

78. The Hebrew word II אַלּוּף (*ʾallûp* II, "chief of a thousand"; *HALOT* 1:54) is related to the Ugaritic *ulp* (voc. *ullupu*), "chief." See also Gordon H. Johnston, "477 אלוף," *NIDOTTE*, 1:406–10.

hundreds are linked in Hebrew by the simple "and" (w^e), which normally suggests that they should be added together. This approach would presuppose that the early meaning of the word *ʾelep* (or *ʾallûp*) as "chief" or "clan" was not understood by later editors, who mistakenly added these words as numbers to the hundreds. Such an approach leads to a greatly reduced number for the fighting men and the total population of Israel than is usually assumed. The totals for the twelve tribes in this approach would be 5,550 men and 598 "chiefs."[79] With the additional numbers required for women and children, the population of the community would be reduced dramatically to about fifteen thousand to eighteen thousand, rather than the two million or more required by the traditional understanding of these numbers.[80]

This sort of speculation, however, presents its own new difficulties, which may be as hard to solve as the problem of the larger numbers. First, the proportion of "chiefs" to fighting men seems top-heavy (forty-six "chiefs" for five hundred men in Reuben; fifty-nine "chiefs" for three hundred men in Simeon; etc.). This is a high percentage of officers to fighting men in any army. Second, the totals in 1:46 and 2:32 do not sustain this distinction in the meaning of the term *ʾelep*. The ancients were able to add figures in the same manner as we do, and they seem to have added the numbers for the twelve tribes without any distinction for the hundreds and the thousands as different types of groupings. They carried the figures for the hundreds into the column for the thousands, as any school child might.[81]

---

79. Kitchen (*Reliability*, 265) cites this example with approval, among other similar attempts at a solution. The number 598 corrects a misunderstanding of scribes who added two columns that should not have been added. That is, the 598 clans formed one column, and the 5,550 fighting men formed the second. Adding "pomegranates and dates" (!), the "5" from the "thousands" column of the fighting men was mistakenly added to the 598 in the "clans" column, thereby leading to the false aggregate of 603[598 + 5], 550. Thus the original intent was to portray 598 clans or tents, some 5,550 fighting men, and a total population of perhaps 20,000 people. By mistakenly mixing numbers from two disparate columns, some scribe made the astonishingly glaring error of a sum that causes one's head to reel!

80. Provan, Long, and Longman (*Biblical History*, 130–31) cite the work of C. J. Humphreys, who centers on Numbers 3:46 (see my treatment below) and works the figures for a total of about five thousand males and a total population of twenty thousand (see "The Large Number of People in the Exodus from Egypt: Decoding Mathematically the Very Large Numbers in Numbers 1 and 26," *VT* 48 (1998): 196–213. See also J. Milgrom, "On Decoding Very Large Numbers," *VT* 49 (1999): 131–32; R. Heinzerling, "On the Interpretation of the Census Lists by C. J. Humphreys and G. E. Mendenhall," *VT* 50 (2000): 250–52; and Humphrey's response in "The Numbers in the Exodus from Egypt: A Further Appraisal," *VT* 50 (2000): 322–28. (These several articles are cited in *Biblical History*, 333, n. 95).

81. While mathematical functions described in the Bible include addition (Ge 5:3–31), subtraction (Ge 18:28–33), multiplication (Lev 25:8), and division (Nu 31:27–30), some of the neighbors of Israel had greatly advanced mathematical calculations. The ancient Egyptians used mathematical concepts in their extraordinary building projects. The Sumerians and later peoples of Mesopotamia had both decimal and sexagesimal (based on the number sixty) systems, and they demonstrated basic and more advanced concepts of mathematics (even geometry and algebra). See B. C. Birch, "Number," *ISBE*[2], 3:556–57. Birch is sympathetic to patterns of reduction of the numbers in the census lists in Numbers by some means similar to those mentioned in the text above (ibid., 557–58).

A variation on the above approach is given by Noordtzij,[82] who states that we cannot translate the term *ʾelep* as "thousand" but only by an *X*, as we no longer know how large it was. He concludes that the total complement of the army of Israel in Numbers 1:46 should not be read 603,550, but 603 *X* + 550 men.[83]

Dual Meanings

John Wenham has a more complex solution to the problem of these large numbers. He believes that the term *ʾelep* is used in two distinct ways in these lists, one to indicate "armed men" and the other to indicate "thousands." Along the way scribes seemed to have confused the two meanings and simply added both terms as though they were "thousands." Wenham says the numbers for the tribe of Simeon, given as fifty-nine thousand three hundred (Nu 1:22), were originally intended to mean something like this:

fifty-seven armed men and twenty-three hundreds of units.
But this came to be written:
fifty-seven *ʾlp* and two *ʾlp*, three hundreds.
He summarizes:

Not realizing that *ʾlp* in one case meant "armed man" and in the other "thousand," this was tidied up to read 59,300. When these figures are carefully decoded, a remarkably clear picture of the whole military organization emerges. The total fighting force is some 18,000 which would probably mean a figure of about 72,000 for the whole migration.[84]

Many would regard a total of fewer than one hundred thousand people to be a satisfactory number for the Hebrew population in terms of these factors: (1) the former slave status in Egypt, (2) the gravely difficult conditions for provision of such a large population in the wilderness, and (3) the fright of the people occasioned by the smallness of their numbers against the fortified cities of Canaan. Further, there are some texts in the Torah that suggest the population of the Hebrew nation was rather small. For example, Deuteronomy 7:7 states that the Lord's affection was set on Israel not because they were more numerous than other peoples, "for you were the fewest of all peoples" (but see below).

---

82. Noordtzij, *Numbers*, 27.
83. Noordtzij's translator, Ed van der Maas, observes that Noordtzij does not gain very much by this approach. He runs into trouble along three lines: (1) squaring with the totals that the text presents (1:46; 2:32; 26:51, plus Ex 38:25–28); (2) dealing adequately with the shekels paid as atonement money in Exodus 38:25–26, where one-half shekel was paid for each of the Israelites (100 talents and 1,775 shekels; as 1 talent = 3,000 shekels, the 100 talents comprise 300,000 talents; when this sum is added to 1,775, the total is 301,775 shekels, precisely one-half shekel for each of the 603,350 men of the census); and (3) if *ʾelep* is less than 1,000, it cannot be less than 751 (an absurdity!), for the number of the Kohathites was 2 *ʾelep* and 750 (Nu 4:36); if the *ʾelep* were less than 750 men, then one could subtract an *ʾelep* and simply add it to the 750 men. If the *ʾelep* is 751, then there is only a 25 percent reduction of the total number, a sum still presenting innumerable problems. See the translator's footnote, *Numbers*, 27, n. 1.
84. John Wenham, "The Large Numbers of the Old Testament," in *Eerdmans Handbook to the Bible*, 192. He adds that the figures for the Levites seem to have an extra zero. When that is dropped, the Levites become a standardized tribe of 2,200 males.

Yet in this case, as in the former ones, the totals of 1:46 and 2:32 would have had to be regarded as errors of understanding by later scribes of an unusual, complex, and otherwise nonattested use of the word *ʾelep*. Those who believe strongly in the reliability of the text of Scripture have difficulty in approaches such as these, for these ideas seem to allow or to suggest the possibility of actual errors in the text of Scripture. There are later insertions in the Bible that most scholars, including inerrantists, regard as mistakes. The "three witnesses" text of 1 John 5:7–8 is a classic example. Yet the textual evidence is clear in that instance; no Greek texts from before the sixteenth century have this reading. There is, however, no known textual suspicion of the integrity of Numbers 1:46.

It may be observed that the type of reduction suggested by Wenham for the numbers in Numbers 1 and 2 will not solve other problems of "large numbers" in the book but will only compound them.[85] What, for example, is to be done with the totals for the tribe of Levi, namely, twenty-two thousand males from one month old and upward (3:39)? Surely here one could not speak of twenty-one chiefs and one thousand men (chiefs from one month old and upward?). Yet if the figure of twenty-two thousand males is maintained for this tribe, it would be unusually lopsided with respect to the revised numbers of a population of sixty to seventy-five thousand members. There is in fact a rather strong consistency in the totals given in the Bible for the large numbers of Numbers 1:46 (see Ex 12:37; 38:26; Nu 2:32; 11:21; 26:51). Suggestions for changes in Numbers 1 and 2 would demand a wholesale revision of numerous other texts and would assume a methodological path of basic misunderstanding in various points of Scripture.

Further, the uses of numbers of peoples who are said to have died in various plagues do not accord with a smaller population suggested by modern scholars. One example only is the destruction of twenty-four thousand in the plague at Baal Peor (Nu 25:9). Would this number be read as twenty-three chiefs and thirteen hundred fighting men? Not likely, especially when at least one woman was included with the men among the slain (see vv. 9, 18). Yet twenty-four thousand would be nearly a third of the entire population on the basis of revisionary theories. (However, see the commentary on ch. 25.)

For a number of reasons, many conservative writers conclude that despite the clever and interesting suggestions made by some scholars to reduce significantly what appear to be impossibly large numbers in these chapters—and despite their own sense of uneasiness about these large numbers—it appears to be prudent to stay with the large numbers of the census figures of Numbers 1 and 26.[86]

Further, the words "fewest of all peoples" of Deuteronomy 7:7 may be either an example of the use of hyperbole for effect, or perhaps a reference not to the population of Israel at the time of the exodus but at

---

85. One estimation of Wenham's approach was summarized: "The case to reduce the numbers as recorded in the text of Numbers is thoroughly—but in my view unconvincingly—discussed by Gordon J. Wenham in his fine commentary" (Gordon J. Keddie, *According to the Promise: The Message of the Book of Numbers* [Welwyn Commentary Series; Durham, Engl.: Evangelical, 1992], 216, n. 1 on ch. 1). That makes one wonder what he might say concerning my approach, below.

86. Harrison (*Numbers*, 47), for example, summarizes: "From these brief comments it will be apparent that there are difficulties with the large numbers both here and elsewhere in the OT that cannot be resolved without further information"; Ashley (*Numbers*, 66) writes: "In short, we lack the materials in the text to solve this problem. When all is said and done one must admit that the answer is elusive"; and Olson (*The Death of the Old*, 14) writes: "In any case the high numbers in the census lists are difficult to reconcile historically."

the time of God's choice of her in one man (Abram) and in the subsequent family of seventy that made its way to Egypt at the beginning of the sojourn. (Yet see further on 1:46 for another interpretation.)

Symbolic Meanings

Options have been presented that regard these large numbers as symbolic figures rather than strictly mathematical items. One possibility for the meaning of the large numbers may lie in gematria, a rhetorical-symbolical use of numbers for effect. The Hebrew people gave numerical values to letters, basically following the order of the alphabet. In this case *aleph* = 1; *beth* = 2; *gimel* = 3; etc. One suggestion is that in using this scheme, one discovers that the numerical equivalent for the Hebrew letters in the phrase, "people [children] of Israel" ($b^e n\hat{e}$-$yi\acute{s}r\bar{a}^{\,>}\bar{e}l$), works out to 603, the number of the thousands of Israel ($b = 2 + n = 50 + y = 10 + y = 10 + \acute{s} = 300 + r = 200 + \,^{>} = 1 + l = 30$ for a grand total of 603).[87] Less convincing are the attempts to discover the gematria underlying the number 550.[88] Nor is there any convincing gematria presented to explain the 601,000 in Israel in the census of Numbers 26.[89] Further, there is no pattern alleged to explain the seemingly random numbers for each of the tribes leading to the grand sum of 603,550.

Some believe that legitimate examples of gematria are found in the Bible.[90] One may be found in the book of Proverbs. The second large section of the book, "the proverbs of Solomon" (Pr 10:1–22:16) has precisely 375 proverbs, the numerical equivalent for the consonants in the name of Solomon (שְׁלֹמֹה [$\check{s}^e l\hat{o}m\bar{o}h$]—$\check{s}$ = 300; l = 30; m = 40; h = 5). Scholars question, however, whether the gematria concept was known as early as the time of Moses—and if it was known, would it have been used in Numbers?

One more observation many have made about the numbers in these census lists is that while they are rounded off, they appear to be random in nature.[91] Olson has observed, however, that the impression of randomness is not really accurate. Both of the sums approximate six hundred thousand. This is the product of 12 x 50,000. In other words, the twelve tribes have an average of fifty thousand members in the army. Further, in each list there are six tribes that have fewer than fifty thousasnd men and six that have greater than fifty thousand. Moreover, the tribe of Judah has the largest number in both lists, a mark of its superiority (over Reuben!) in the wilderness experience. Olson nicely concludes that the number, as it presently stands, "appears to express the gracious extent of God's blessing of Israel in multiplying Israel's descendants to such large numbers and strength."

An even more complicated explanation has been advanced by M. Barnouin, where the numerical totals for each tribe are said to be symbolic of the numeric equivalents of certain astronomical periods.

---

87. The pattern is not as obvious as it might seem. The first *yod* (י) is actually not a consonant; it is a "vowel-letter," an aid to the lengthening (and signing) of the vowel *ṣērê* (viz. ֵ = *ê*). We may observe that this formula works only if the *ṣērê-yod* combination that ends the word $b^e n\hat{e}$ is given the *consonantal* equivalent of "y = 10"; otherwise the total is only 593.
88. See Budd, *Numbers*, 7 (for development).
89. See Noordtzij, *Numbers*, 24.
90. Joseph A. Romero, for example, argues for a gematria on the number of fish caught in John 21:11; the precise number 153 is equal to the Hebrew letters forming the words "the children of God" ("Gematria and John 21:11—the Children of God," *JBL* 97 [1978]: 163–64). One wonders, however, how many phrases he tried out before settling on this one.
91. Olson, *Numbers*, 79.

For example, the number of the men of Benjamin (thirty-five thousand four hundred; Nu 1:37) is one hundred times a short lunar year (354 days). Other numbers are said to be compounds of the periods of various planets (Mercury, Venus, Mars, Jupiter, and Saturn) in differing combinations.[92] This point of view seems to be faulted seriously both in its complexity and in its unexpectedness in a literature that seems to bear no clues of this type of hidden significance.

It appears to me that comparing the tribes of Israel to astral and planetary bodies would be a precarious venture, given the antipathy of the (orthodox) faith of Israel to these ideas. We proceed on the basis of divine revelation in Torah, not fanciful human speculation. It is possible, of course, that such procedures might be used in a subtle polemic against Babylonian religion, but it would seem that this would only be appropriate in the context of a clash with the Babylonian world. This type of argument might carry more weight for one who argues for an exilic provenance for the book of Numbers (which provenance Barnouin, the proponent of this theory, indeed suggests).

We may observe as a preliminary conclusion that while the problems of the large numbers have not been solved satisfactorily today — or at least that the solutions that have been suggested have not seemed to have won large appeal — the Bible does point to a remarkable increase of the descendants of Jacob within the four centuries of their sojourn in Egypt (see Ex 1:7–12), and that these high numbers, with all of their problems, point to the great role of providence and miracle in God's dealings with his people during their life in the wilderness.

10. THE LARGE NUMBERS—TOWARD A SOLUTION

The Problem

The principal problem is one of suitability. To put it bluntly, the numbers of the conscripted soldiers in the tribes of Israel stated and implied in this book just seem to be far too large to be historically credible. If the numbers of the men who were mustered for war from the age of twenty and up actually add up to over six hundred thousand, then the total populace would have had to be at least two million individuals — perhaps considerably more. This number does not seem large for a nation in our own crowded day, but it seems an almost impossibly large sum for the totals of the nation of Israel in ancient times at the very beginning of its existence. They were a fugitive people who fled Egypt, crossed the seabed in one night, gathered at a mountain at Mount Sinai, and then lived for a generation in the wilderness before finally entering Canaan.

Perhaps some perspective is in order. The city near which I live for part of the year is moderately sized by modern standards. The population of the city of Portland, Oregon, is in excess of half a million. When

---

92. This is the work of M. Barnouin, "Les recensements du livre des Nombres et l'astronomie babylonienne," *VT* 27 (1977): 280–303; it is discussed by Gordon Wenham (*Numbers: An Introduction and Commentary* [TOTC; Downers Grove, IL: InterVarsity Press, 1981], 64–66). Wenham seems to be somewhat open to Barnouin's approach but uses (British?) understatement in evaluating its convincing quality. In another article Barnouin suggests that the original number of the men mustered for war was but six thousand, the later total of six hundred thousand being a multiplication by one hundred ("Remarques sur les tableaux numeriques du livre des Nombres," *RB* 76 [1969]: 351–64). I am also open to multiplication (see below) but regard a total of six thousand to be too few.

the surrounding cities and towns that make up the metropolitan area are added, the number increases to 1.3 million. Now this is a lot of people. When I look around the area where I live, I see wide-ranging territories, massive structures, and large areas of single-family homes that are built to house and provide for this populace.[93] But if the numbers of Numbers 1 and 26 are correct, I have to imagine a population twice the size of the metropolitan area in which I live and then view that vast number of people living their lives in the Wilderness of Sinai for a period of forty years. I know that scholars have attempted to explain exactly how such numbers can be accounted for. Keil, for example, even worked out the mathematics for the crossing of the Red Sea by a population of this size. Yet I have to ask whether it is reasonable to have to account for these large numbers in this manner.

Here is another comparison. The estimate for the population of modern state of Israel is 5.5 million. This present population of Israel is roughly twice the size of the number of Hebrews who approached from the wilderness with great fear to conquer the land. The population of modern Israel is mixed between scattered rural settlements, small towns, and three large cities. As we look at the modern cities with their sprawling size and multistoried buildings, we wonder how the ancient farmlands, towns, and walled cities might have accommodated such numbers. Further, one's breath is taken away when the ideas of water, sewage, food supply—the practical matters of living—come into play. Since the testimony of the wicked Hebrew spies (tribal agents) was an exaggerated report of the size of the cities, their towering walls, and hulking men—all the stuff of fear—the implication at the least is that the Canaanite population was significantly larger and more powerful than the approaching Hebrew populace (see, e.g., the refrain of proportion: "to drive out before you nations greater and stronger than you," Dt 4:38; 7:1). The more we think of these numbers, the more they boggle our minds.

What do we know of the population of Canaan in the biblical period? Numerous attempts have been made to estimate populations at various periods. More recent scientific estimations of the population of Canaan during the Iron Age reduce greatly earlier estimates of several million. Israeli archaeologist Yigal Shiloh suggests the combined population of Judah and Israel in the eighth century BC to be about nine hundred thousand.[94] Since we may presume that the population of Canaan was considerably more dense in the eighth century BC under Hebrew settlement than in the fifteenth century BC during Canaanite times, it is most difficult to imagine an invading force of Hebrews that numbered several million to have much sense of need to trust in the Lord for the conquest of the land. By sheer numbers they would simply overwhelm the native population.

Other issues are not as difficult. The observation is sometimes raised that in Exodus 1:15 there were just two midwives, Shiphrah and Puah. This would certainly mean they were very overworked women for a nation so large! Actually, this is a nonissue. It does not matter how large or how small the nation of Israel

---

93. I certainly do not mean to suggest that peoples in ancient times lived in similar structures and territories as people in modern, Western cities. But a view of a modern city gives at least a sense of the enormity of what we mean when we say, perhaps a little glibly, that the people of Israel numbered in the millions at the beginning of their history as a nation.

94. Yigal Shiloh, "The Population of Iron Age Palestine in the Light of a Sample Analysis of Urban Plans, Areas, and Population Density," *BASOR* 239 (Summer 1980): 32.

was; two midwives were insufficient in all cases. Thus these two women are celebrated for their faith, but they were the leaders of, not the whole of, the guild of midwives.

Another well-worn issue has to do with the allegedly impossible growth of the people from seventy persons to more than two million in just four centuries. There have been commentators who have worked out the mathematics of this increase and have stated that such an increase, while grandly dramatic, is not beyond the possibility of human reproduction—particularly when that reproductive capacity is enhanced and blessed by the Lord in fulfillment of his promise to make his people many, though they began with so few.

In fact, Scripture assures us that the growth of the population of the Hebrew people was a dramatic outworking of God's grace, a fulfillment of his promise. The narrative of growth in Exodus 1:7 is emphatic. Three verbs along with complementary adverbs and rhetorical flourish exult in the work of God in their dramatic growth: "but the Israelites were fruitful and multiplied greatly and became exceedingly numerous, so that the land was filled with them." This unprecedented growth of the nation was in fulfillment of numerous promises of God to the fathers (see Ge 17:2, 6; 22:17; 26:4; 28:14; 35:11; 48:4). Moses was able to use the patriarchal phrase of abundance as he recounted his experience as their leader: "The LORD your God has increased your numbers so that today you are as many as the stars in the sky" (Dt 1:10; cf. Ex 32:13).[95]

Yet there are counter-indications to this immense size of the population that are also well known. Some writers point to the rhetorical underplaying of the size of the nation in Deuteronomy 7:7, where the numbers of the Hebrews are greatly minimized: "for you were the fewest of all peoples." This is a rhetorical use of language, but its effect will be in proportion to the sense of the people, "Yes, we were few compared to other great nations."

Another counter-indication has to do with the sheer logistics of two million people or more crossing the Red Sea in one night, coupled with their organization and provision in the wilderness for a generation. Now all this is certainly possible within the wonder of the work of the Lord. We have no doubt of God's ability to provide for two million or two billion persons, if that were his pleasure. But we still wonder at these large numbers in terms of the lands and cities of the ancient world. Were the cities of ancient Canaan (most of which were smaller than thirty acres in size) in the Late Bronze Age sufficiently large to be a formidable threat to the millions of Hebrews who were about to descend on them from the wilderness? Would the ten tribal agents (the "spies") have been so fearful of the residents of the land if they represented a people so large in numbers? And could the land of Canaan have absorbed such a huge company in biblical

---

95. In his commentary on Numbers, my friend and beloved former student R. Dennis Cole (*Numbers*, 81–82) does me the honor of quoting at some length my presentation on this issue from the first edition of *EBC*. He notes (correctly), "the number of stars visible to the naked human eye on a clear night is approximately seventeen thousand, and thus even sixty thousand far exceeds that expectation" (ibid., 82, n. 39). To this point I make two observations: (1) the comparison to the stars in God's promise for the increase of the descendants of Abraham is sustained in Torah and beyond (Ge 22:17; 26:4; Ex 32:13; Dt 1:10; 10:22; 28:62; cf. 1Ch 27:23; Ne 9:23; Jer 33:22; cf. Heb 11:12), and (2) when the conditions are right (the night very dark and the sky very clear), one may see not only the "standard glory" of some seventeen thousand stars, but also the unbelievable wonder of the visible portion of the Milky Way galaxy, with its "billions and billions and billions" of stars (à la the late astronomer Carl Sagan).

times, right at the beginning of Israel's experience? We do not doubt that the population of Israel under her great kings David and Solomon might have numbered upwards of one million. But we pause at the thought of more than twice that many persons right at the beginning of her history.

So there we have it: The numbers of the book of Numbers are just too large!

A Suggestion

For the above reasons, I suggest for consideration the possibility that the large numbers in the census lists in the book of Numbers are deliberately and purposefully exaggerated as a rhetorical device to bring glory to God, bring derision to enemies, and point forward to the fulfillment of God's promise to the fathers that their descendants would be innumerable as the stars.

We know of indisputable examples of the rhetorical use of numbers in the Torah; see, for example "thousands of myriads" in Genesis 24:60 (the blessing on Rebekah by her family) and "myriads of thousands" in Numbers 10:36 (the words of blessing in the "Battle Song of Moses"—see commentary and Note on Nu 10:36). Here are these vibrant phrases:

לְאַלְפֵי רְבָבָה (l^eʾalpê r^ebābâ, "for thousands of myriads")

רִבְבוֹת אַלְפֵי יִשְׂרָאֵל (rib^ebôt ʾalpê yiśrāʾēl, "the countless thousands of Israel")

It appears possible to me that the figures given in the two census lists for the army of Israel may be a magnification by a factor of ten. An army of about sixty thousand men would fit what we know of the criteria of the region and the times. John Wenham's reduction to eighteen thousand (see above) seems to be too small a figure and is based on too complex a solution to be convincing. Similarly, Barnouin's reduction by the factor of one hundred and Petrie's and Noth's proposals leave much too small a figure and are based on an extraordinarily complex and alien system. We desire a solution that is both simple in concept and yet provides a sufficiently large population to be the fulfillment of promise, but not so large as to be seemingly impossible.

The suggestion of a rhetorical exaggeration by a factor of ten has much to commend it. It is a simple answer that does not demand convolutions in numbers that other suggestions require. It takes into account the "round" number nature of each integer. It fits in nicely with the approximation of six hundred thousand as a multiple of 50,000 x 12, the number of the tribes. It results in an army in excess of sixty thousand men, with a total population of about two hundred fifty to three hundred thousand. This sum seems to fit the requirements of the social, geographical, and political realities without diminishing at all the sense of the miraculous and providential care of God.

An army of sixty thousand is not an insignificant force, but it was likely smaller than the combined armies of the city-states of Canaan at the time. In this way the peoples of Israel must have seemed to be a "swarm" as they lived in Egypt, but they were still "the smallest of nations" when ranked with great world powers. This smaller number accords with the large (but not supernatural!) force the Egyptian pharaoh sent in pursuit of them to the Red Sea. Six hundred chariots (Ex 14:7) is a considerable force and would surely be a death threat against the unorganized people of Israel. This approach also allows for the drama of the conquest of the book of Judges, where battles were won by the armies of Israel in league with Yahweh, their Great Warrior. This smaller number also fits the Hebrews' failure to occupy the full land also detailed in Judges. In addition, it accords well with the famous Mernepthah stele, which records Israel as among the peoples of Canaan during that pharaoh's raid, aptly dated to the period of the judges. A population of several million would have made more of an impression on Pharaoh Mernepthah!

Perhaps the strongest textual support for this magnification of the numbers of the people by a factor of ten is found in the text describing the redemption of the firstborn sons of the families of Israel (Nu 3:40–51). The number of firstborn sons above the age of one month was calculated to be 22,273 (Nu 3:43). In a section of the book in which all the other sums appear to be rounded, this is *the only figure that is specific to the digit*. Further, it is far too small a sum to represent a population in the millions (see commentary in loc.). Such would require that each family in Israel would have had to produce upwards of fifty children—a number "unbearable" (pun intended!).[96] But the quantity 22,273 (which is also a number in Numbers!) would work admirably with a population one tenth the common conclusion—that is, two hundred fifty thousand persons. In this case, live births—and surviving children—would be more in the range of five per family.

Unknown to me at the time I was writing the first edition of this commentary, then-doctoral student David M. Fouts was working on his dissertation on large numbers in the OT, particularly in the records of the monarchy. Fouts's work includes discussions of population density studies in ancient Israel and the methodologies used to determine these concepts. His conclusions, drawn especially on Akkadian records, indicate a widespread use of what he calls "the ancient Near Eastern literary convention of numerical hyperbole in military contexts," often with a factor of ten (or sixty in cultures where the sexagesimal system prevailed).[97] Needless to say, Fouts's research has been enormously encouraging to me![98]

Again, this smaller number does not diminish the miraculous aspect of God's work in causing the growth of the Hebrew people in Egypt.[99] It possibly enhances it, for we confront now a cluster of miracles that we may embrace readily rather than shun from some sense of embarrassment, as some do! The supernatural increase of the people in Egypt, the crossing of the Red Sea in one night, the gathering of the people at Mount Sinai, their daily provision in the wilderness, their entry into the Promised Land—all was miraculous! Only the Lord could so provide for this vast number of people in this manner; and mark it well, a population of over a quarter million is indeed vast. But now we can envision a series of miracles that better fits the geography, the topography, and the times. The "myth" of the exodus becomes the history of redemption.

---

96. Wenham, *Numbers*, 61; Cole, *Numbers*, 78–79. These estimations are mind-boggling!

97. David M. Fouts, "The Use of Large Numbers in the Old Testament with Particular Emphasis on the Use of *'elep*" (Th.D. diss., Dallas Theological Seminary, 1992); see also his "A Defense of the Hyperbolic Interpretation of Large Numbers in the Old Testament," *JETS* 40 (1997): 377–87, and "The Incredible Numbers of the Hebrew Kings," in *Giving the Sense: Understanding and Using Old Testament Historical Texts* (ed. David M. Howard Jr. and Michael A. Grisanti; Grand Rapids: Kregel, 2003), 283–99.

98. This "fix" is certainly not a "slam dunk." An impartial reader of both my ideas and those of Fouts could easily object, "But does this 'fix' not create a false impression?" The answer is not easy, for it may. And certainly it has done so in the minds of modern readers. But it is possible that in ancient times the rhetorical hyperbole of numbers in military contexts was such a "given" that it would occasion little confusion.

99. Unbelieving rationalism undermines the whole notion of the irruption of God in the lives of his people. *Rationalism* as an antitheistic point of view is to be contrasted with the role of *reason* in biblical interpretation. A view that is more reasonable but does not attempt to diminish the miraculous should not be brashly charged with the ugly notion of rationalism.

Furthermore, now we can also deal with the large numbers not as problem words but as power words. The deliberate exaggeration was not for misrepresentation or for simple bombast. This rhetorical use of numbers (see above) was a mark of faith in the Lord, who had provided great increase to a family of seventy persons and who one day would make his people as the stars in number. One day they would truly be innumerable—except to him, who counts them all and knows their names! These "embarrassing numbers" should be seen as not embarrassing at all. These numbers celebrate Yahweh. They are numbers of worship! I envision these texts being read in worship celebrations. The studied units, with their formulaic structure and power numbers, would evoke pride of patriotism, sense of belonging, and—most important—the celebration of the Lord.[100]

John Wenham may offer a historical parallel that serves as an explanation for this magnification of the numbers by ten, although he applies it only to the tribe of Levi. He writes that there is now a solution to the mystery of Plato's Atlantis. Plato received his information on this civilization from Egyptian priests. What they gave him was a detailed account of the Minoan culture. But they had inflated the population by a factor of ten. Plato could not locate such an immense population in the Mediterranean. Instead he placed it in the Atlantic and removed the date to remote antiquity.[101]

It appears to me that the numbers of the census are real figures. They are treated like real integers; there is no confusion of hundreds and thousands. Here are numbers that are internally consistent and coherent.

---

100. The principal objection that may come to the position I advance is the observation that the number 603,550 is in general agreement with the similarly large number in the second census in 26:51 (601,730); and it is in accord with other statements in the Torah of a population of about six hundred thousand men (see again Ex 12:37; 38:26). We may observe that the same deliberate rhetorical function occurs in the second census. In fact, it is even more important that the new generation was regarded with the same significance as the first. The words of Balaam (Nu 23:10) emphasize the "mystique" of the immense numbers of Israel. But what to him was but "mystique" was to Moses nothing less than the power of God.

Kaiser has concern for any view that seeks to reduce the gross numbers because of his attention to the parallel numbers in Exodus, particularly with reference to the tabernacle tax. "All attempts to whittle down this number ... fail to meet the standard of consistency with other contexts" (*A History of Israel*, 102).

As to the numbers in Exodus, they must be based on the numbers in the census lists of Numbers 1:46; that is, the interpretation of the numbers in the book of Numbers has priority over the interpretation of these same numbers in Exodus as there was no census taken before that given in Numbers. This approach means that the interpretation we derive in Numbers will work as well for the round figure of six hundred thousand in Exodus 12:37. Exodus 38:26 is more difficult because of the specific numbers used for weights (vv.25–31). Yet if the pattern of six hundred thousand (strictly 603,550) is established as the power number for Israel, then the payment of the redemption price would be rhetorically inflated to fit the established number. The "truth" of the passage is that there was the exact payment of one-half shekel for each of the numbered men in the census, whatever that exact number might have been. The one problem remaining is the payment of the half-shekel in Exodus 38:25–26. This 100 talents + 1,775 shekels form the one number that does not easily arise from a purposeful tenfold increase. I suggest, with some temerity, that the numbers in this passage may have been inserted into the text of Exodus on the basis of the census of Numbers 1–4. The number 603,550 in Exodus 38:25 is certainly based on the census total in Numbers 1:44. That is, once the factor of a tenfold magnification was established in Numbers, then the payment of the redemption price, to be consistent, would be presented in such a way as to agree with this larger number.

101. Wenham, "Large Numbers," 192.

Yet I propose that for rhetorical reasons they may have been deliberately magnified by a factor of ten. The promise was that the people would number as the stars. Six hundred thousand must have seemed like an "astronomical" number in these early biblical times. Certainly the "real" number of sixty thousand men was large, particularly for the wilderness sojourn. But the sixty thousand would still not be an overwhelming force for the task ahead—that of conquering the peoples of the land, who were seven in number and far more numerous than Israel. To have any success in their task, this army would need to have the help of the Lord along every step of their path. From the abortive battle with the Amalekites in the first generation (Nu 14:44–45), to their decisive victories over Arad (21:1–3) and the small kingdoms of Sihon and Og a generation later (21:21–31), these numbers fit the situation. Here now is a seasoned army of approximately sixty thousand men, ready to march across the (dry bed of the) Jordan River and to take the ancient city of Jericho as the firstfruits of conquest in the land—an offering to Yahweh.

This number of about sixty thousand fits the requirements of both a great (miraculous) growth and a manageable size for the time and place of their habitation. The use of deliberate exaggeration by a factor of ten may be regarded as a *celebration of the work of the Lord*. We have not taken seriously enough the formulaic nature of the chapters that give the numbers of the tribes. Not only does this make "neat" record keeping; there is also within these sections a sense of the sublime, of the orderly presentation of an offering of joy to God. These census lists that some moderns find frightfully dull may well have been conceived by their author as a joyful offering of praise to God. And may we not think that God takes pleasure in these words still?

This rhetorical use of numbers is also a *prophetic symbol* (a type!) of the numbers yet to come! One day the people of God will be astral-like—they will be innumerable, uncountable to all but him who knows the number and name of every star (Ps 147:4)!

The obvious objection one may bring, that people do not use numbers in this way today, is not overwhelming. We know that in ancient times numbers were used with deliberate exaggeration for rhetorical effect. One needs only to think of the ancient Sumerian king list to find an example that long predates the time of Moses. In this list the reigns of kings from remote antiquity were vastly exaggerated. We believe this was for the rhetorical function of indicating their tremendous importance.[102]

An even more common use of rhetorical language is in battle braggadocio and mottoes of heroes:

Saul has slain his thousands,
    and David his tens of thousands. (1 Sam 18:7)[103]

---

102. We may also find rhetorical uses of numbers in the genealogies of Genesis. Dwight Wayne Young has developed several considerations that help explain the immense numbers used in the lives of the antediluvians. He contends that the attribution of extraordinary length of life was a rhetorical device to elevate these thirty patriarchs to an elite circle in the Pentateuch ("The Incredible Life Spans of the Antediluvian Patriarchs," *JNESCU* 47 [1988]: 123–29).

103. Some may ask, "But is not this simply poetic license?" And I would respond, "Of course!" Battle braggadocio is indeed poetic license—a rhetorical use of language. Notice especially Saul's response: "'They have credited David with tens of thousands,' he thought, 'but me with only thousands'" (v.8). More modern examples of rhetorical numbers are used by politicians and (dare we say it) some evangelists! It is also fascinating to see that the praise of David is an inflation of Saul's praise *by a factor of ten*. David had in fact not killed thousands, not even hundreds. He had killed just one enemy. But when the enemy was of the size and threat factor of Goliath, well, the singers of songs from the villages knew what to do! For their new hero they magnified by ten the praise they had previously accorded to their king.

I am aware that some may regard the concept of "rhetorical use of numbers" as a departure from "literal interpretation." But that is not necessarily the case. A departure from literal interpretation would be to spiritualize the numbers, to find some mystical significance in them that was never really intended, or to pretend to some bizarre meaning imported from another environment. Without evidence in the text, Barnouin's approach, using Babylonian astrological symbolism, appears to me to be spiritualizing the text.

Literal interpretation of numbers includes understandings that extend from mathematical exactitude, through general approximation, to literary license. The only demand of literal interpretation (better, "normal" interpretation) is that the reader ought to seek to find the use he or she believes the text itself presents and demands. It is an abuse of literal interpretation to insist that the way we use numbers in our digital and pocket-calculator age is the way that biblical persons did in fact use numbers in their day.

In summary, the book of Numbers is just that! It is a book that uses numbers to celebrate the work of the Lord! And in these numbers is his praise.

11. BIBLIOGRAPHY

Albright, William. "The Oracles of Balaam." *Journal of Biblical Literature* 43 (1944): 207–33.

Allen, Ronald B. "The Theology of the Balaam Oracles." Pages 79–119 in *Tradition and Testament: Essays in Honor of Charles Lee Feinberg*. Edited by John S. Feinberg and Paul D. Feinberg. Chicago: Moody Press, 1981.

Allen, Ronald B., and Craig H. Allen, *The Wonder of Worship: A New Understanding of the Worship Experience*. Nashville: Nelson, 2003.

Budd, Philip J. *Numbers*. Word Biblical Commentary 5. Edited by David A. Hubbard and Glenn W. Barker. Waco, Tex.: Word, 1984.

Cole, R. Dennis. *Numbers*. The New American Commentary 3B. Edited by E. Ray Clendenen. Nashville: Broadman & Holman, 2000.

Dever, William G. *What Did the Biblical Writers Know & When Did They Know It?: What Archaeology Can Tell Us about the Reality of Ancient Israel*. Grand Rapids: Eerdmans, 2001.

———. *Who Were the Early Israelites and Where Did They Come From?* Grand Rapids: Eerdmans, 2003.

Ginsburg, Christian D. *Introduction to the Massoretico-Critical Edition of the Hebrew Bible*. 1897. Repr., New York: KTAV, 1966.

Goldberg, Arnold M. *Das Buch Numeri*. Die Welt der Bibel. Dusseldorf: Patmos, 1970.

Gray, George Buchanan. *A Critical and Exegetical Commentary on Numbers*. International Critical Commentary. Edinburgh: T&T Clark, 1903.

Greenstone, Julius H. *Numbers, With Commentary*. The Holy Scriptures. Philadelphia: The Jewish Publication Society of America, 5699/1939.

Harrison, R. K. *Numbers*. The Wycliffe Exegetical Commentary. Edited by Kenneth L. Barker. Chicago: Moody Press, 1990.

Hirsch, Samson Raphael. *The Pentateuch Translated and Explained*. Vol. 4, *Numbers*. Translated by Isaac Levy. London: Isaac Levy, 1964.

Howard, David M. Jr., and Michael A. Grisanti, eds. *Giving the Sense: Understanding and Using Old Testament Historical Texts*. Grand Rapids: Kregel, 2003.

Keil, C. F., and F. Delitzsch. *The Pentateuch*. Vol. 3 of *Biblical Commentary on the Old Testament*. Translated by James Martin. Repr., Grand Rapids: Eerdmans, n.d.

Kitchen, Kenneth. *On the Reliability of the Old Testament*. Grand Rapids: Eerdmans, 2003.

———. *Poetry of Ancient Egypt*. Documenta Mundi: Aegyptiaca 1; Jonsered, Sweden: Paul Åströms, 1999.

Merrill, Eugene H. "Numbers." In *The Bible Knowledge Commentary — Old Testament*. Edited by John F. Walvoord and Roy B. Zuck. Wheaton, Ill.: Victor/SP, 1985.

Milgrom, Jacob. *Numbers*. The JPS Torah Commentary. Edited by Nahum M. Sarna and Chaim Potok. Philadelphia: Jewish Publication Society, 1990.

Noordtzij, A. *Numbers*. Bible Student's Commentary. Translated by Ed van der Maas. Grand Rapids: Zondervan, 1983.

Noth, Martin. *Numbers: A Commentary*. The Old Testament Library. Translated by James D. Martin. Philadelphia: Westminster, 1968.

Olson, Dennis T. *The Death of the Old and the Birth of the New: The Framework of the Book of Numbers and the Pentateuch*. Brown Judaic Studies. Chico, Calif.: Scholars, 1985.

Von Rad, Gerhard. *Old Testament Theology*. 2 vols. Translated by D. M. G. Stalker. San Francisco: HarperCollins, 1962.

Wenham, Gordon J. *Numbers: An Introduction and Commentary*. Downers Grove, Ill: InterVarsity Press, 1981.

Williams, Ronald J. *Hebrew Syntax: An Outline*. 2nd ed. Toronto: University of Toronto Press, 1976.

12. OUTLINE

Text and Exposition

OVERVIEW

Two types of response are possible for the modern reader who first glances at ch. 1 of the book of Numbers. One is ennui, a sense of boredom. First the reader is told about the command of the Lord for Moses and Aaron to take a military census of Israel. This sounds rather unpromising. Then the reader is assaulted by a list of unfamiliar, compound Hebrew names (1:5–15), names that are a threat to any but the most self-assured Scripture reader. As though this were not enough, the reader then finds twelve two-verse paragraphs that are identical in wording except for the name of the tribe and the sum of its people (1:20–43).

Worse, the paragraphs all center on numbers. The first chapter of the book teems with numbers; everywhere we turn we read number after number. No wonder the book has come down to us in English with a singularly uninspiring title! Who but a mathematician could rise with joy to a book called "Numbers"?

But these same features may bring another response, especially for the reader who approaches tasks with curiosity. This is the response of intrigue, interest, and even wonderment. Surely the Torah was not written to bore the reader—ancient or modern! The listing of names was never meant simply to test the skills of a reader, nor could the repetitions merely have been designed to test a person's resolve to continue reading—no matter what! There must be significance in these names, numbers, and repetition.

Further, we soon discover that the tedious repetition in ch. 1 is not unique to the book. The repeti-

tion of ch. 7 similarly seeks to undermine whatever appreciation we might try to muster up for the values underlying such repetitious language.

Thus the expectations of the modern reader in approaching this text are irrelevant to a valid evaluation of the purpose and nature of the book. As with any book of Scripture—indeed, any book of intrinsic merit—the book of Numbers must be read on its own grounds. The Bible sets its own agenda; the materials of Scripture take their own shape. That its interests and methods may be different from our own is beside the point. If this book is to be received by the modern reader with the integrity and demands of Scripture as a significant part of the divine outbreathing (2Ti 3:16)—the fourth portion of the Torah, the book of Moses—then we must set bias aside, avoid negative prejudgments, escape first impressions, and come to the book as it is.

The best approach toward any obtuse or "difficult" portion of Scripture is to pepper it with questions. In the case at hand we might ask: Why would the ancient sages feel it important to include the names of each tribal representative? Why was it believed impressive to list the number of men from each tribe in such a formal manner, requiring the measure of repetition as 1:20–43 presents? What are the values suggested by these repeated paragraphs? Is it possible that in this alien aesthetic form these verses of repeated phraseology are not to be regarded as tiresome at all but something of dignity, solemnity, and even beauty? Is there perhaps an impressive nature to these paragraphs that speaks of the pride of each tribe?

Indeed, the repetitions are likely instructive as to the power of God and his faithfulness to his promises. That reader who first turned his face away from these pages with disdain may have turned away from something that is intended to bring praise to God and confidence among his people. It becomes our point of view that these numbers, in their highly stylized environments, are a matter of *celebration of the faithfulness of Yahweh to his covenantal people*. So as we come to these numbers and words, let us come to them on their own terms to see what in them is impressive — and what in them is instructive for us.

I. THE EXPERIENCE OF THE FIRST GENERATION IN THE WILDERNESS (1:1–25:18)

OVERVIEW

An explanation is given in the Introduction (Unity and Organization) for the unusual outline this commentary presents. Following the lead of Dennis T. Olson, I see the macrostructure of the book of Numbers as a bifid of unequal parts. The two censuses (chs. 1–4, 26) are the keys to our understanding the structure of the book. The first census (chs. 1–4) concerns the first generation of the exodus community; the second census (ch. 26) focuses on the experiences of the second generation, the people to whom this book is primarily directed. The first generation of the redeemed was prepared for triumph but ended in disaster. The second generation now has an opportunity for greatness — if only the people will learn from the failures of their fathers and mothers the absolute necessity of robust faithfulness to Yahweh despite all obstacles.

A. The Preparation for the Triumphal March to the Promised Land (1:1–10:36)

OVERVIEW

The record of the experiences of the first generation is presented in two broad parts. Chapters 1–10 record the story of their preparation for triumph; chs. 11–25 follow with the sorry record of repeated acts of rebellion and unbelief, punctuated by bursts of God's wrath and instances of his grace.

1. Setting Apart the People (1:1–10:10)

OVERVIEW

As the book as a whole presents itself as a bifid of unequal parts, so chs. 1–10 also form a bifid of unequal sections: 1:1–10:10 records the meticulous preparation of the people for their triumphal march into Canaan; 10:11–36 describes their first steps under the leadership of Moses.

a. The Census of the First Generation (1:1–4:49)

i. *The muster (1:1–54)*

(a) The command of the Lord (1:1–4)

¹The LORD spoke to Moses in the Tent of Meeting in the Desert of Sinai on the first day of the second month of the second year after the Israelites came out of Egypt. He said: ²"Take a census of the whole Israelite community by their clans and families, listing every man by name, one by one. ³You and Aaron are to number by their divisions all the men in Israel twenty years old or more who are able to serve in the army. ⁴One man from each tribe, each the head of his family, is to help you.

COMMENTARY

1 Each phrase of verse 1 is significant for our study; we need to move slowly here. One of the most pervasive emphases in the book of Numbers is that Yahweh spoke to Moses, and through Moses, to Israel. From the opening words of the book (1:1) to its closing words (36:13), this concept is stated over 150 times and in more than twenty ways. One Hebrew name for the book of Numbers is *way^e dabbēr* ("and [Yahweh] spoke"), the first word in the Hebrew text. This name is highly appropriate, given the strong emphasis on God's revelation to Moses in Numbers.

The opening words set the stage for the chapter and, indeed, for the entire book. The phrase, "the LORD [Yahweh] spoke to Moses," presents a point of view that will be repeated (and restated) almost to the point of tedium throughout this book. Yet it is just such a phrase that is so important to the self-attestation of the divine origin of Numbers. The phrasing announces the record of a divine disclosure of the eternal God to his servant Moses, and from Moses a faithful transmission to the people of God. This type of phrase does not satisfy our curiosity as

to how Moses heard the word of God, whether as the articulated words of a human voice; a mystical inner sensation, perhaps a clearly articulated cluster of words in his mind; or some vague mental image. This phrase merely presents the source and reception of communication. Numbers 12:6–8 is the major text describing the Lord's use of Moses as his prophet. This section will indicate something of the special manner of the divine disclosure to Moses, but the phrasing that is most characteristic merely states the most important point: Yahweh spoke to Moses.

That the subject of the verb "spoke" is Yahweh points to his initiation and, by that measure, to his grace. The fact that God speaks at all to anyone is evidence of his mercy, that he continued to speak to Moses throughout his leadership of the people of God is a mystery, and that he spoke to Moses with the intent that others would read these words throughout the centuries is a marvel. The repetition of phrases such as this throughout the Torah serves for emphasis. We are to be duly impressed with the fact that the Lord is the Great Communicator, that of his own volition he reached out to Moses to convey to him the divine word and to relate through him to the nation the divine will. Other gods are mute. Other gods are silent. Other gods are no God at all. But the God of Scripture, the Lord of covenant—Yahweh, God of Israel—speaks! What he desires more than anything else is a people who will hear him, who will take joy in obeying him, and who will bring him pleasure by their response.

The second phrase of v.1 (NIV) centers on the place of God's speaking to Moses: "in the Tent of Meeting" (*be'ōhel mô'ēd*); this phrase follows "in the Desert of Sinai" in the Hebrew construction). There are other terms and phrases used for this tent in Numbers. It is called "the tabernacle" (*hammiškān*; vv.50, 51) and "the tabernacle of the Testimony" (*miškan hā'ēdut*; vv.50, 53). The expression "the Tent of Meeting" speaks of the revelatory and communion aspect of the tent. The term "tabernacle" by itself points to the temporary and transitory nature of the tent; it was a moveable and portable shrine, specially designed for the worship of God by a people on the move. The expression "the tabernacle of the Testimony" suggests the covenantal significa- tion of the tent; within were the symbols of the presence of the Lord among his people, his guaran- tees of continuing relationship.

Critical scholarship has confounded the issue by suggesting that these several terms refer to differ- ent tents, or that they are telltale pointers to dif- ferent strata in the tortured path (in their view) of the composition of the Torah. But this approach is unnecessary; it seems preferable to read these several terms as correlative, stylistic variants used for effect to describe various realities of the central focus of God's relationship with his people in the wilder- ness—the tent of his presence.

The more common Hebrew name for the book of Numbers is *be'midbar* ("In the Wilderness"), the fifth word in the Hebrew text. God spoke to Moses

in the Tent of Meeting during the lengthy period that Israel spent in the Desert of Sinai. The wilder- ness setting is pervasive in Numbers. Recall from the introduction, "God has time, and the wilderness has sand."

The book begins with the leadership of Israel's following faithfully the commands of the Lord and the people's being mustered together for war against the cities of Canaan in anticipation of a great conquest of the Land of Promise. But because of the perfidy of the people, that great event of con- quest—the realization of the promise of God to the fathers and mothers of Israel—was denied for a generation. Instead, in judgment for doubt and for casting the worst possible accusations against God about their deliverance—that their "wives and children will be taken as plunder" (14:3)—the entire populace over the age of twenty would spend the rest of their natural days in the wilderness. Only Joshua and Caleb, because of their exceptional, unswerving faith in the face of their timid compa- triots, would enter the land.

As it turned out, Miriam and Aaron—and even Moses—died in the wilderness. The expression "in the wilderness" is rich in its meaning and associa- tions. It is not just descriptive of a physical feature of topography; it is also a metaphor for the experi- ence of the people of Israel described in this book. One day their descendants would enter the land, but this book is the record of the experience of the people "in the Desert of Sinai."

This first verse also gives a specific temporal notice for the command of God to take a census of the nation—a date that is precise and detailed: "on the first day of the second month of the sec- ond year after the Israelites came out of Egypt." The book of Numbers begins thirteen months after the great exodus. The people had spent the previous year in the region of Mount Sinai receiving the law, erecting the tabernacle, and becoming a people.

Now they were to be mustered as a military force and formed into a cohesive nation to provide the basis for an orderly march. The events of Numbers cover a period of thirty-eight years and nine or ten months, i.e., the period of Israel's wilderness wanderings. The second month in the Hebrew calendar corresponds roughly to our April. Later, when Israel was established in Canaan, this second month would be the month of general harvest between the Feast of Firstfruits and Pentecost or Weeks, seven weeks following Passover. That Israel was being numbered during a time that later would be associated with the harvesting of crops would probably not have been lost on the later readers of this book.

This pattern of dating events from the exodus signified the centrality of the exodus in the experience of God's people. Time would now be measured from their leaving Egypt. The wording is not unlike the Christian reckoning of time as "BC" ("Before Christ") and "AD" ("Anno Domini," meaning "in the Year of our Lord"). Time, for Israel, had its beginning with the exodus, just as time for the Christian has its beginning and meaning with the salvation provided in the Savior, Jesus. The exodus was God's great act of deliverance of his people from bondage; the story of the exodus is the gospel in the OT.

Another example of dating from the exodus is found in 1 Kings 6:1, where the beginning of the building of the temple of Solomon is dated in the four-hundred-eightieth year of Israel's exodus from Egypt. Whether this date is an exact figure (i.e., one year more than four hundred seventy-nine years) or, as is sometimes suggested, a round number suggesting twelve generations (i.e., 12 x 40—the approximation of a generation), the point is still sure: the dating of Israel's experience with God begins with the exodus from Egypt (see Notes).

Gordon J. Wenham, 56, observes that the materials of the book of Numbers are not arranged strictly in chronological order (also, see Introduction: Unity and Organization). The descriptions of 7:1-9:15 belong to the first two weeks of the first month of the second year of the exodus (cf. Ex 40:2; Nu 9:1), whereas the census and related affairs of Numbers 1-6 begin on the first day of the second month (see, again, 1:1). The concern of the writer was thematic rather than strictly chronological; it was literary rather than pedantic. The issues of the numbering of the people and the ordering of the camp were believed to be foundational to the understanding readers would need for the stories of offerings, worship, and Passover in chs. 7-9. Moreover, as noted in the introduction, Olson has shown the book of Numbers to be a biped, each section beginning with a census (chs. 1-4; 26; see Notes). The deliberate changing of chronology of the materials of the book is a signal to the reader that chronology is not nearly as important as the fact of the census.

The dating of the exodus itself remains a deeply debated issue among biblical scholars, both moderate and conservative. (More liberal scholars—sometimes called "minimalists"—do not regard the exodus as a historical event; for them the issue is moot.) Archaeological evidence has been adduced for both an early thirteenth-century date (the "late date view") as well as a mid-fifteenth-century date (the "early date view"). Kenneth A. Kitchen has argued ably for the thirteenth-century date (*Ancient Orient and Old Testament* [Downers Grove, Ill.: InterVarsity Press, 1966], 57-75; see now his *Reliability*, 241-74). Gleason L. Archer Jr., however, has argued vigorously for the fifteenth-century date for the exodus (see his introductory article on "The Chronology of the Old Testament" in *EBC*[1], 1:366-67). Such a pattern would suggest that the events of the book of Numbers extended thirty-eight years into the second half of the fifteenth century BC (see Notes).

2 The Hebrew verbs *śĕʾû* ("take"; v.2) and *tipqĕdû* ("number"; v.3; see Notes) are in the plural, indicating that Moses and Aaron were to complete this task together (see v.3, "you and Aaron"), but the primary responsibility for the task lay with Moses. The purpose of this census was to form a military roster, not a social, political, or taxation document, as some modern interpreters have suggested. There are other reasons for the census however: (1) to demonstrate to the people the extent of God's faithfulness in fulfilling the provisions of the Abrahamic covenant in multiplying the physical descendants of Abraham (Ge 12:2; 15:5; 17:4–6; 22:17), (2) to provide a clear sense of family and clan identity for the individual, and (3) to provide the means for an orderly march of the people to their new home in Canaan.

There is a remarkable specificity in the numbering process, moving from the broadest groupings to the individual. These Hebrew phrasings are "clans," "families," "names," and "every male by their heads." This stylistic device, common in Hebrew prose, moves from the most general to the specific, thus giving a sense of the totality of a task and the enormity of carrying it out. We find the same type of approach in the words that came to Abram describing the associations he must leave as he was to set out on his journey of faith with the Lord: "your country," "your people," "your father's household" (Ge 12:1; order as in the MT). Similarly, in the story of the binding of Isaac Abraham was told to take his "son," his "only son," whom "he loves," "even Isaac" (Ge 22:2; order as in the MT).

3 The words of verse 3 also point clearly to the principal military purpose of the census: those males who were over the age of twenty and who were able to serve in the army. This type of phrase occurs fourteen times in ch. 1 and again in 26:2.

Readers who are bothered by the military nature of the census prefer to view it as an early experiment in sociology. The wording of the MT is so patently military in nature, however, that this escape simply does not seem to be possible. The point of the census was to prepare the armies of Israel for their triumphal war of conquest against the peoples of Canaan. In fulfillment of the promise Yahweh made to father Abraham (Ge 15:16–21), the descendants of those who went to Egypt were to return with great possessions and would then be given the land inhabited by numerous nations and ethnic groups. Evil pervaded those nations and groups; the sins of the Amorites had now reached full measure (cf. Ge 15:16). The campaign of conquest was soon to begin.

Our knowledge of the end of the story makes this a sad record to read: all the peoples who were numbered for military duty in this chapter—every one of them save only Joshua and Caleb—died without ever experiencing God's war of conquest. It is true that some participated in the abortive engagement with the Amalekites following their rebellion against the Lord (14:44–45), but this was not a glorious war of victory. It was an ignoble rout! Victory would come only to their children, a generation removed. Hence this listing, intended by God to be a roster of soldiers, a table of heroes, a memorial of victors, became instead a memorial of those who were to die in the wilderness without ever experiencing God's greater purpose in their lives.

There was another mustering of soldiers for war at the end of the wilderness period (ch. 26). The men in that account were entirely different persons from those listed in ch. 1. Except for Joshua and Caleb, all those in ch. 1 died in the wilderness between slavery and liberty, between cursing and blessing, between there and here, with hopes dashed and desires never fulfilled. All died in the dry, barren wilderness, though God had intended for them the enjoyment of the good life in the good land and his gracious hand. But in the new roster of Numbers 26 there was a new generation, a new beginning, a new hope. It was "the death of the old and the birth of the new" (cf. Olson's title; see Introduction).

4 By having a representative from each tribe assist Moses and Aaron, not only would the task be made somewhat more manageable, but also all would regard the resultant count as legitimate. No tribe would have reason to suggest that it was under- or overrepresented in the census, since a worthy man from each tribe was a partner with Moses and Aaron in accomplishing the task. Election observers in our own day fill a similar role.

NOTES

1 The wording of the first verse of Numbers, when compared with the wording of the last verse (36:13), fits well with the concept that Numbers is an independent "book" within the larger collection of the fivefold book, the Pentateuch. This is a point argued well by Olson, 46–49. He also ties the book of Numbers to the תּוֹלְדוֹת (*tôlᵉdôt*, "generations, family histories") formula of Genesis (cf. Ge 2:4a; 5:1; et al.; see Nu 3:1 and Notes). This wording provides the overarching structure for the entirety of the Pentateuch (Olson, 83–114; also in Dennis Olson, *Numbers* [Interpretation; Louisville, Ky.: John Knox, 1996], 3–7); cf. comments on 3:1.

לְצֵאתָם מֵאֶרֶץ מִצְרָיִם (*lᵉṣēʾtām mēʾereṣ miṣrayim*, "their leaving the land of Egypt") is not simply a slogan; the miraculous departure of the people of Israel from Egypt, the exodus, is the fundamental act in their history. A recent presentation for the "early date" ca. 1446 BC (or even a bit earlier) is made by William H. Shea, "The Date of the Exodus," in Howard and Grisanti, eds., *Giving the Sense*, 236–55. Conservative scholars who support the "late date" (ca. 1290 BC) include LaSor, Hubbard, and Bush, in *OTS–1996*, 59–60, and Kitchen, *Reliability*, 307–10. Conservative scholars continue to debate the dating of the exodus. The position taken in this commentary is based on the "early date" chronology. However, the greater issue these days is not *when* the exodus took place, but *whether* it ever happened. William G. Dever (*What Did the Biblical Writers Know?* 2001; *Who Were the Early Israelites?* 2003), not known as an evangelical writer, nevertheless has been in the forefront in the engagement of those scholars (sometimes called "minimalists") who deny most of the historicity of the OT story. Recent evangelical works that challenge minimalists include those by Kitchen (*Reliability*) and Raymond B. Dillard and Tremper Longman III (*AIOT*).

3 תִּפְקְדוּ (*tipqᵉdû*, "number") is a use of the significant Hebrew verb פָּקַד (*pāqad*, "to attend to, visit, muster"; GK 7212) that at times describes Yahweh's "visiting" his people, either in great grace (e.g., Ge 21:1) or in horrific judgment (e.g., Hos 1:4). In Numbers it is used with the idea of "passing in review, mustering, numbering."

4 The Hebrew expression אִישׁ אִישׁ לַמַּטֶּה (*ʾîš ʾîš lammaṭṭeh*, lit., "man, man for the tribe") is distributive: "one man from each tribe"; see Williams, *Hebrew Syntax*, sec. 15; cf. Nu 9:10; 14:34).

(b) The names of the men (1:5–16)

⁵These are the names of the men who are to assist you:
from Reuben, Elizur son of Shedeur;
⁶from Simeon, Shelumiel son of Zurishaddai;
⁷from Judah, Nahshon son of Amminadab;
⁸from Issachar, Nethanel son of Zuar;
⁹from Zebulun, Eliab son of Helon;
¹⁰from the sons of Joseph:
   from Ephraim, Elishama son of Ammihud;
   from Manasseh, Gamaliel son of Pedahzur;
¹¹from Benjamin, Abidan son of Gideoni;
¹²from Dan, Ahiezer son of Ammishaddai;
¹³from Asher, Pagiel son of Ocran;
¹⁴from Gad, Eliasaph son of Deuel;
¹⁵from Naphtali, Ahira son of Enan."
¹⁶These were the men appointed from the community, the leaders of their ancestral tribes. They were the heads of the clans of Israel.

COMMENTARY

5–15 The names of these luminaries occur again in chs. 2, 7, and 10; as noted above, more is the sadness as the list of those who would die in the wilderness is given three times! Most of these names are theophoric; that is, they are built by compounding one of the designations for God into a name that is a significant banner of faith in the person and work of God. The antiquity of this list of names is revealed by the fact that many are built on the names El (*ʾēl*, "God"), *Shaddai* (*šadday*, traditionally translated "Almighty"), *Ammi* (*ʿammî*, "My Kinsman"), *Zur* (*ṣûr*, "Rock") and *Ab* (*ʾab*, "Father"). (See also the list naming the leaders of Levitical families in 3:24, 30, 35, where the same patterns are in play.) At a later time in Israel's history, we would expect many names to be based on the covenantal name *Yahweh* because of the revelation of this name and its significance (see Ex 2:23–3:15; 34:1–8).

The paucity of names based on *Yahweh* (e.g., names beginning with "Jeho-" or ending in "-jah" or "-iah") in this list may be a significant argument for the antiquity of this text (see Notes). Whereas the name *Yahweh* was available for name-building in the period before the exodus, it did not come into greater use until after the revelation of a new significance of that name in Yahweh's revelational encounter with Moses and the subsequent teaching of these truths to the populace of Israel. Here are the names and suggested probable meanings (in order of their listing):

Elizur (ʾĕlîṣûr, "[My] God Is a Rock") son of Shedeur (šᵉdêʾûr, "Shaddai Is a Flame"), chief of Reuben (v.5);

Shelumiel (šᵉlumîʾēl, "[My] Peace Is God") son of Zurishaddai (ṣûrîšadday, "[My] Rock Is Shaddai"), chief of Simeon (v.6);

Nahshon (naḥšôn, "Serpentine") son of Amminadab (ʿammînādāb, "[My] Kinsman [God] Is Noble"), chief of Judah (v.7);

Nethanel (nᵉtanʾēl, "God Has Given") son of Zuar (ṣûʿār, "Little One"), chief of Issachar (v.8);

Eliab (ʾĕlîʾāb, "[My] God Is Father") son of Helon (ḥēlōn, "Rampart-like" [?]), chief of Zebulun (v.9);

Elishama (ʾĕlîšāmāʿ, "[My] God Has Heard") son of Ammihud (ʿammîhûd, "[My] Kinsman [God] Is Majesty"), chief of Ephraim (v.10);

Gamaliel (gamlîʾēl, "Reward of God") son of Pedahzur (pᵉdâṣûr, "The Rock [God] Has Ransomed"), chief of Manasseh (v.10);

Abidan (ʾăbîdān, "[My] Father [God] Is Judge") son of Gideoni (gidʿōnî, "My Hewer"), chief of Benjamin (v.11);

Ahiezer (ʾăḥîʿezer, "[My] Brother [God] Is Help") son of Ammishaddai (ʿammîšadday, "[My] Kinsman [God] Is Shaddai"), chief of Dan (v.12);

Pagiel (pagʿîʾēl, "Encountered by God") son of Ocran (ʿokrān, "Troubled") chief of Asher (v.13);

Eliasaph (ʾĕlyāsāp, "God has Added") son of Deuel (dᵉʿûʾēl, "Know God!"), chief of Gad (v.14; see Note at 2:14);

Ahira (ʾăḥîraʿ, "My Brother Is Evil") son of Enan (ʿēnān, "Seeing"), chief of Naphtali (v.15).

Noth, 13–19, argues that the source for this material is the putative P (late in the fifth century BC) because of the schematic nature and orderliness of presentation, but that the name lists that P used in his record must have come from a very early period in Israel's experience (at least from a pre-Davidic period). His admission of the antiquity of the names is in fact something that may slightly undermine his approach to the writing of this text.

16 The Hebrew adjective underlying the phrase "the men appointed" (qārîʾ, singular) is a technical term for representatives used only here and in 26:9. Verse 16 is legal, formal, and precise in tone. Three phrases are used to give sanction to each of these leaders. Levi is not represented in this list (see 1:47).

NOTES

5 On the problems and precarious nature of attempting to discover the precise meaning of Hebrew names, see comments on 13:4–15. The meaning we may adduce for a biblical name is a bit tenuous, as the meaning cannot be determined by context in the same manner as with other nouns and verbs. Most of the suggested translations given here are from BDB. The argument for the antiquity of the list, based on the phenomenon of the patterns of formation, is significant because it is "substructural." That is, if these lists were fraudulent concoctions from a later period (as critical scholars allege), the tendency would have been for the forger to use nominal patterns of the period of the writing—unless, of course, the creative forger knew that by using antique patterns of names he (she?) would fool later (modern?) readers!

16 The Hebrew word נָשִׂיא (*nāśîʾ*, "leader"; GK 5954) speaks of one who is "lifted up" or "selected." The noun is derived from the verb נָשָׂא (*nāśāʾ*, "to lift up"; GK 5951). The vowel pattern of this noun is the same as that for the word "prophet," נָבִיא (*nābîʾ*). It presents a passive infix.

(c) The summary of the census (1:17–19)

> [17]Moses and Aaron took these men whose names had been given, [18]and they called the whole community together on the first day of the second month. The people indicated their ancestry by their clans and families, and the men twenty years old or more were listed by name, one by one, [19]as the LORD commanded Moses. And so he counted them in the Desert of Sinai:

COMMENTARY

17 This verse indicates the leadership of Moses and Aaron in the task, as it does their obedience to the command of Yahweh. This chapter is marked by a studied triumphalism. Numbering the tribes and mustering the army were sacred functions that prepared the people for their war of conquest under the right hand of God, who was their Warrior (see Ex 15:3, "The LORD is a warrior").

18 The expression "twenty years or more" is taken by Gershon Brin ("The Formulae 'From … and Onward/Upward,'" *JBL* 99 [1980]: 161–71)

to indicate generational identity; i.e., one who was under the age of twenty was still regarded as a member of his father's house, while one over the age of twenty was an individual who was morally and civilly responsible.

19 Hebrew prose often gives a summary statement and follows with details that explicate the summary. This verse is that summary, and verses 20–43 present the details. Genesis 1:1 may be viewed as a similar summary statement, the details being given in the rest of the chapter.

(d) The listings of the census by each tribe (1:20–43)

> [20]From the descendants of Reuben the firstborn son of Israel:
> All the men twenty years old or more who were able to serve in the army were listed by name, one by one, according to the records of their clans and families. [21]The number from the tribe of Reuben was 46,500.
> [22]From the descendants of Simeon:
> All the men twenty years old or more who were able to serve in the army were counted and listed by name, one by one, according to the records of their clans and families. [23]The number from the tribe of Simeon was 59,300.

²⁴From the descendants of Gad:

All the men twenty years old or more who were able to serve in the army were listed by name, according to the records of their clans and families. ²⁵The number from the tribe of Gad was 45,650.

²⁶From the descendants of Judah:

All the men twenty years old or more who were able to serve in the army were listed by name, according to the records of their clans and families. ²⁷The number from the tribe of Judah was 74,600.

²⁸From the descendants of Issachar:

All the men twenty years old or more who were able to serve in the army were listed by name, according to the records of their clans and families. ²⁹The number from the tribe of Issachar was 54,400.

³⁰From the descendants of Zebulun:

All the men twenty years old or more who were able to serve in the army were listed by name, according to the records of their clans and families. ³¹The number from the tribe of Zebulun was 57,400.

³²From the sons of Joseph:

From the descendants of Ephraim:

All the men twenty years old or more who were able to serve in the army were listed by name, according to the records of their clans and families. ³³The number from the tribe of Ephraim was 40,500.

³⁴From the descendants of Manasseh:

All the men twenty years old or more who were able to serve in the army were listed by name, according to the records of their clans and families. ³⁵The number from the tribe of Manasseh was 32,200.

³⁶From the descendants of Benjamin:

All the men twenty years old or more who were able to serve in the army were listed by name, according to the records of their clans and families. ³⁷The number from the tribe of Benjamin was 35,400.

³⁸From the descendants of Dan:

All the men twenty years old or more who were able to serve in the army were listed by name, according to the records of their clans and families. ³⁹The number from the tribe of Dan was 62,700.

⁴⁰From the descendants of Asher:

All the men twenty years old or more who were able to serve in the army were listed by name, according to the records of their clans and families. ⁴¹The number from the tribe of Asher was 41,500.

> ⁴²From the descendants of Naphtali:
>
> All the men twenty years old or more who were able to serve in the army were listed by name, according to the records of their clans and families. ⁴³The number from the tribe of Naphtali was 53,400.

COMMENTARY

20–43 For each tribe there are two verses in repetitive, formulaic structure giving: (1) the name of the tribe, (2) the specifics of those numbered, (3) the name of the tribe restated, and (4) the total enumerated for that tribe.

Certainly one of the most difficult issues in the book of Numbers concerns the large numbers of these lists. Noth, 21, places the issue darkly: "The main problem of the section 1.20–46 consists in the figures that are given. Their size, as is generally recognized, lies outside the sphere of what is historically acceptable. In no sense do they bear even a tolerable relationship to what we otherwise know of the strength of military conscription in the ancient East."

More recently Budd, 6, concurs, "The central difficulty here is the impossibly large numbers of fighting men recorded. The historical difficulties in accepting the figure as it stands are insuperable." More conservative writers concur. Here is an assessment by LaSor, Hubbard, and Bush (*OTS*–1996, 105):

> Most cities that have been excavated [in Israel] cover sites of a few acres that could have housed a few thousand people at the most. At no time would Palestine [Israel] have had more than a few dozen towns of any significant size. Every bit of available evidence, biblical, extrabiblical, and archaeological, seems to discourage interpreting the numbers literally.

That the numbers for each of the tribes are rounded may be seen in that each unit is rounded to the hundreds (but Gad to the fifties [1:25]).

A peculiarity in the numbers that leads some to believe they may be symbolic is that the hundreds are grouped between two hundred and seven hundred; there are no hundreds in zeros, one hundreds, eight hundreds, or nine hundreds. Yet whatever we may make of these factors, we may observe that the same numbers are given for each tribe in ch. 2, where there are four triads of tribes with consistent use of numbers, sums, and grand totals. Further, the total might have been rounded to six hundred thousand but was not (see 1:46; 2:32).

In this chapter the Hebrew word translated "thousand" (*ʾelep*) is clearly taken to mean one thousand for the total to be achieved in verse 46. Varied suggestions have been made (such as that by Noth) that demand the totals arose only in a later period in which there was confusion about the unusual meaning of the term *ʾelep* in this section. But that appears to be an attempt to play the game from two sides. The passage cannot have come from a later time (as is believed by documentarians; this is a "P text"!), and yet contain a misuse of the word *ʾelep*—at the time of the writing. (See the extensive treatment of this term in the Introduction: The Problem of the Large Numbers).

Because the descendants of Levi were excluded from the census (see on v.47), the descendants of Joseph are listed according to the families of his two sons, Ephraim (vv.32–33) and Manasseh (vv.34–35). In this way, the traditional tribal number of twelve is maintained, and Joseph is given the "double portion" of the ranking heir of Jacob (cf. Ge 49:22–26; Dt 33:13–17). Second Kings 2:9 is also to be understood in this manner; Elisha was not asking Elijah that he might have double the power of his master or that he might do double the number of miracles of his mentor. Rather, of all the sons of the prophets who might wish to be regarded as the proper heir of Elijah, Elisha desired that honor for himself. The phrase "a double portion of your spirit" suggests the honor of the privileged son who would receive a double share of the inheritance of the father.

(e) The summary of the census (1:44–46)

44These were the men counted by Moses and Aaron and the twelve leaders of Israel, each one representing his family. **45**All the Israelites twenty years old or more who were able to serve in Israel's army were counted according to their families. **46**The total number was 603,550.

COMMENTARY

44–46 As noted in the introduction, there appears to be no textual difficulty in the Hebrew tradition in the soundness of this large number (or the integers used to achieve it) for the census of the fighting men of Israel. The number 603,550 is the proper sum of the twelve components listed in verses 21–43. And there is no convincing unusual meaning suggested for the word "one thousand" (ʾelep).

The mathematics of these numbers is accurate and complex. It is complex in that the totals are reached in two ways: (1) a linear listing of twelve units (1:20–43), with the total given (1:46); (2) four sets of triads, each with a subtotal, and then the grand total (2:3–32), which equals the total in 1:46. These numbers are also consistent with the figures in Exodus 12:37–38 ("about six hundred thousand men on foot, besides women and children") and in Exodus 38:26 (603,550 men of twenty years old or more). Furthermore, they relate well to the figures of the second census in Numbers 26:51 (601,730 men) at the beginning of the new generation. This large number of men conscripted for the army suggests a population for the entire community in excess (perhaps considerably) of two million people.

There are at least three implications we may draw from this immense number: (1) Moses was responsible for this immense number of people in the most difficult of circumstances, the management task God gave to Moses being exceedingly demanding; (2) the demands on God's providence (and overt miracle) were immense during the generation of wilderness sojourn; and (3) in the end, all those people who were numbered, along with the women and the other males not counted—all of them, excepting only Joshua and Caleb, would die in the wilderness because of their collective act of unbelief in the power of God and their lack of trust in his faithfulness to his promise.

Another concept related to these large numbers concerns the wonders in the fulfillment of the particular blessing of God in the unusual growth of the people of the family of Jacob in Egypt. Exodus 1:7 describes in five Hebrew phrases the stunning growth of the Hebrew people in Egypt during the four centuries of their sojourn. So numerous had the Hebrew people become that they were regarded as a threat to the security of Egypt (Ex 1:9–10, 20). Israel's numerical growth from the seventy who entered Egypt (Ex 1:5) was an evidence of God's great blessing and his faithfulness to his covenant with Abraham (Ge 12:2; 15:5; 17:4–6; 22:17). The growth of the nation was God's benediction on them. As we are troubled with the immensity of the numbers, we should not neglect to reflect on this benediction the numbers present and respond to the Lord in gratitude.

It is not necessary to magnify difficulty in order to praise God. As we return to the difficulty of these numbers, we find ourselves concluding with most critical scholars and many conservative scholars that these numbers cannot be what they first appear to be. Yet because of the manner in which they are added together, we may find ourselves uncomfortable with those suggestions that speak of earlier understandings that the later scribes forgot. To speak of their adding hundreds and "thousands" as an "understandable error" is a troubling expression. Understandable error is still error.

So we return to the position suggested in the Introduction: The Problem of the Large Numbers. We may treat these numbers as "real" numbers (better, "common numbers"), even as the text appears to present them. The hundreds were added to the thousands as in all such sums. But these numbers (in terms of their addition) are numbers that were used for effect. I suggest there is a deliberate exaggeration, a rhetorical device used to give praise to God and hope to his people, of the sums for each tribe and hence for the total. By deliberately magnifying these numbers by a common factor (ten, the number of the digits), the writer was able to use them as

"power words." That is, the ancients who were the recipients of these words knew what we may have forgotten, that numbers may be used for purposes other than merely reporting data.

By deliberately exaggerating the numbers of the fighting men of the tribes of Israel, the point achieved was a type of "believers' braggadocio!" The nation that had been crafted by God within the context of slavery and servitude was now a power to be reckoned with among the great powers of the ancient world. More, God had promised that the descendants of Abraham would outnumber the stars, would be more numerous than grains of sand on the shore of the sea. The unprecedented growth of the nation fulfilled numerous promises of God to the fathers (see Ge 17:2, 6; 22:17; 26:4; 28:14; 35:11; 48:4). Moses was able to use the patriarchal phrase of abundance as he recounted his experience as their leader: "The Lord your God has increased your numbers so that today you are as many as the stars in the sky" (Dt 1:10; cf. Ex 32:13).

Moreover, the greatly inflated numbers promise greater things to come. One day, families of all nations will find their blessing in the same God who brought blessing to Abraham. One day the Seed of Abraham will be the Savior of the world. *Big numbers at the beginning are a promise of even bigger numbers at the end!* If numbers have ever been used for propaganda (!), here, it appears, is a biblical precedent for the exaggeration of numbers in praise of God.

We may ask: What is the role of deception in all this? The answer is simple, even if it may not be convincing to some. None of those who first read these words would have been deceived. All would have known that these "power numbers" far outstripped the acutal facts of the day. The appearance of deception arises only when the conventions of using numbers in these manners are forgotten.

Here is an example of the "proper role" of archaeology as it relates to the Bible. When surveys of excavated sites in the little land of Israel present city mounds (tells) that are measured in acres instead of in tens of miles squared, when actual house plans are surveyed within these city mounds and extrapolations are made of the numerical possibilities these ancient plots present — well, then, these and other considerations gel together to help one come to a reappraisal of the actual facts of the case. In the process we are in a discovery of the "original meaning" of the biblical text. For the "original meaning" does not just come in a parsing

of verbs or a word study of nouns or a syntactical study of a clause — original meaning also includes the manner in which the ancient writers used these verbs, nouns, and clauses — *and numbers*.

Here is the clincher: *how they used numbers was their concern!* It is not up to modern readers to sit in judgment; our task is merely to understand, to appreciate, and then to begin to share with the ancients their joy in these exquisite numbers! Hence, in the alchemy of the mind in one's new appreciation of numbers, we join them in *their* celebration.

(f) The reason for the exclusion of the Levites (1:47–54)

[47]The families of the tribe of Levi, however, were not counted along with the others. [48]The LORD had said to Moses: [49]"You must not count the tribe of Levi or include them in the census of the other Israelites. [50]Instead, appoint the Levites to be in charge of the tabernacle of the Testimony — over all its furnishings and everything belonging to it. They are to carry the tabernacle and all its furnishings; they are to take care of it and encamp around it. [51]Whenever the tabernacle is to move, the Levites are to take it down, and whenever the tabernacle is to be set up, the Levites shall do it. Anyone else who goes near it shall be put to death. [52]The Israelites are to set up their tents by divisions, each man in his own camp under his own standard. [53]The Levites, however, are to set up their tents around the tabernacle of the Testimony so that wrath will not fall on the Israelite community. The Levites are to be responsible for the care of the tabernacle of the Testimony."
[54]The Israelites did all this just as the LORD commanded Moses.

COMMENTARY

47–49 The Levites, because of their sacral tasks, were excluded from this military listing; they were to be engaged in the ceremonies and maintenance of the tabernacle. Chapter 3 discusses their families, numbers, and functions.

50 As in Exodus 38:21, the sanctuary is here called "the tabernacle of the Testimony." The "Testimony" refers to the Ten Words (Ten Commandments) written on stone tablets (Ex 31:18; 32:15; 34:29). These tablets were placed in the ark (Ex 25:16, 21; 40:20), leading to the phrase "the ark of the Testimony" (Ex 25:22; 26:33–34; et al.). In Psalm 19:7[8] the Hebrew term ʿēdût ("testimony"; "statutes," NIV) is used for the word of God in a more general sense but still with the background of the Ten Words of Exodus.

51-52 The Hebrew word *hazzār*, rendered "anyone else" (v.51), is often translated "stranger, alien, foreigner" (as in Isa 1:7; Hos 7:9). Thus a non-Levitical Israelite was considered an alien to the religious duties of the tabernacle (see Ex 29:33; 30:33; Lev 22:12). The punishment of death is reiterated in Numbers 3:10, 38; 18:7 and was enacted by divine fiat in 16:31-33 (see 1Sa 6:19). The sense of the Divine Presence was both blessing and cursing in the camp: blessing for those who had a proper sense of awe and wonder of the nearness of deity, and cursing for those who had no sense of place, no respect for the Divine Presence.

53 The tents of the Levites are detailed in 3:21-38. The encampment of the Levites around the tabernacle was a protective hedge against trespassing by the laity (non-Levites) to keep them from incurring the wrath of God. The dwelling of the Levites around the central shrine was a measure of God's grace and a reminder of his presence.

54 In view of Israel's great disobedience in the later chapters of Numbers, these words of initial compliance to God's word have a special poignancy. Israel began so well, then failed so terribly; her experience remains a potent lesson to all people of faith who follow them. Ending well is the desire. Most racers get off the blocks reasonably well, but the winner is only certified as such at the end of the course.

ii. The placement of the tribes (2:1-34)

OVERVIEW

Chapter 2 has a symmetrically arranged structure (see Introduction: Outline). The details of this chapter are presented in studied orderliness as a literary exhibit of the physical symmetry expected of the peoples who would be encamped around the central shrine. As in the case of ch. 1, the details of this chapter seem to reflect the joy of the writer in knowing the relation each tribe has to the whole, each individual to the tribe, and the nation to the central shrine—and how all relate to the Lord Yahweh. Thus in some manner this chapter is another means of bringing glory to God. The book of Numbers should be read as *a book of the worship of Yahweh*! There is an element of pride, joy, and expectation in the seemingly routine matters of this chapter. Here was the place of encampment for each tribe in proximity to the Divine Presence, and from these camps the people would set out under the hand of God to enter the Land of Promise and take possession in his power. The chapter should be read with expectation that the conquest will be as orderly and purposeful as the place of camping in the wilderness.

There is a sense in which the orderliness of these early chapters of Numbers is akin to the orderliness of Genesis 1. As God has created the heavens and the earth and all that fills them with order, beauty, purpose, and wonder, so he constituted his people with order, beauty, purpose, and wonder. And as the heavens and earth may "praise" God in their responses to his commands (Ps 147:13-18), so the peoples of God may praise him in their responses to his commands (Ps 147:19-20). Indeed, his people must praise him.

Critical scholars respond to the orderliness and symmetry of this text in quite another manner. N. H. Snaith (*Leviticus and Numbers* [NCB; Greenwood, SC: Attic, 1967], 186), for example, regards the whole chapter "as an idealistic reconstruction to fit in with later religious ideas." For such writers, the very beauty of the text becomes its downfall. For ourselves, let the beauty of the text be its strength and lead us to be reflective of the beauty of the Lord in the midst of his people.

(a) Summary command (2:1–2)

> ¹The Lord said to Moses and Aaron: ²"The Israelites are to camp around the Tent of Meeting some distance from it, each man under his standard with the banners of his family."

COMMENTARY

1 The standard pattern of formal Hebrew prose is followed in this chapter. First there is an announcement of the topic, and then come the details of that topic in an orderly presentation, followed finally by a summary of the whole. This type of organization must have been satisfying to the ancient writers by its giving a sense of wholeness, direction, and orderliness to an account. As in the case of ch. 1, material of this sort may fail to excite the modern reader. Yet if one pauses to think of the order and structure of the text, the underlying significance of the passage may be realized more easily. God is about to bring to pass a great marvel with his people, but it only will occur as they are rightly related to him and to one another.

The relatedness of the people round about the central shrine was the essence of their meaning as a people. Apart from this order, the Hebrews would have remained a disorganized group, nearly a mob — large, disorganized, unruly, and bound for disaster. With this pattern and the discipline and devotion it implied, there was the opportunity for grand victory. The order of the chapter is a promise of the fulfillment of the working of God in their midst. That Israel in fact did fail God is the sadder story, for he had given to them the means for full success.

This chapter begins with the announcement of the revelation of the Lord to Moses and Aaron (using the Hebrew verb *dābar* in the Hiphil, "to speak"). The more usual phrasing in the Torah is "And Yahweh spoke to Moses, saying," as in 1:1. Here the words "and Aaron" are added, as in 4:1, 17; 14:26; 16:20; 19:1. A similar phrase (with a different Heb. verb, *ʿāmar*, "to say": "And the Lord said to Moses and Aaron") is found in 20:12, 23. The reference to Aaron along with his illustrious brother in this chapter indicates the strong focus on the shrine of God's presence in the center of the camp. Aaron, as will be detailed in ch. 3, had the principal task of maintaining the purity, order, and organization of the work respecting the central shrine.

2 The Hebrew word order of verse 2 stresses the role of the individual in the context of the community; each one was to know his or her exact position within the camp. A more literal translation, following the studied order of the Hebrew original, follows:

> Each by his standard,
> > by the banners of their fathers' house,
> the Israelites will encamp;
> > in a circuit some way off from the Tent of Meeting
> they will encamp.

The repetition of the verb "will encamp" is for stately stress. Here was the meaning of the individual in Israel, and here was the significance of his family.

The people of Israel were a community that had their essential meaning in relationship to God and to one another. But ever in the community was the continuing stress on the individual to know where one belonged in the larger group. Corporate solidarity in ancient Israel was a reality of daily life, but the individual was also very important. The words interplay in these texts: each individual/the people // the people/each individual.

The text stresses not just the relationship each person and each tribe was to have to the central shrine but also that no one was to approach the shrine too casually. The dwelling of the tribes was in a circuit about the shrine but at some distance from it. The Hebrew word *minneged* means "some way off" or "from a distance." These words build on 1:52–53 and the protective grace of God, demanding a sufficient distance to serve as a protective barrier from any untoward approach to the shrine of the Divine Presence. The warning was to prevent the judgment of God that such an approach might provoke. Gerhard von Rad, 2:374–78, writes that all true knowledge of God begins with the assertion of his hiddenness. Too casual an approach betrayed too minimal a reverence.

Here we sense anew a recurring theme in the Torah: God's holiness may not be forgotten by his people, but his grace is protective for them. His desire was not to destroy the unwary but to protect such from their own folly—and to demonstrate the wonder of his person in the midst of their camp.

God could have maintained "distance" between himself and the people, thus rendering the warning unnecessary. Then no one would be in danger of harm. The true believer, however, so caught up with the wonder of knowing that the God of the whole universe was present in some mysterious way in the midst of the encampment of the people of the new Israel, would seek to learn to live with the mystery of God's awesome presence. The fright of danger could be lost in the sense of the proximity of his glory and the nearness of his grace.

Each tribe had its banner and each triad (group of three) of tribes had its standard. Jewish tradition suggests that the tribal banners corresponded in color to the twelve stones in the breastpiece of the high priest (Ex 28:15–21). Further, this tradition holds that the standard of the triad led by Judah had the figure of a lion, that of Reuben the figure of a man, that of Ephraim the figure of an ox, and that of Dan the figure of an eagle (see the four living creatures described in Eze 1:10; cf. Rev 4:7). These traditions are late, however, and difficult to substantiate; Torah does not describe the nature or designs of the banners of Numbers 2 (see KD 3:17).

(b) Details of execution (2:3–33)

(i) Eastern encampment (2:3–9)

OVERVIEW

In ch. 1 the nation was mustered and the genealogical relationships clarified. In ch. 2 the nation was set in structural order; further, the line of march and the place of encampment were established. The numbers of ch. 1 are given in new patterns of arrangement—four sets of triads—

but they are the same numbers. The repetition of these grand sums of each tribe is a further reflection of the grace of God in their increase during their sojourn in Egypt. The numbers in chs. 1 and 2 are in agreement; if one offers ways to change the seemingly clear sense of the numbers in ch. 1, then that person also has to deal with the repetitions in this chapter. The same leaders of ch. 1 figure again here and also in 10:14–28. The listing of their names is a matter of significant honor; it is also a matter of sadness. These names were not forgotten in Israel, but their lives were lost in the wilderness, far from the land of God's gracious promise.

---

³On the east, toward the sunrise, the divisions of the camp of Judah are to encamp under their standard. The leader of the people of Judah is Nahshon son of Amminadab. ⁴His division numbers 74,600.

⁵The tribe of Issachar will camp next to them. The leader of the people of Issachar is Nethanel son of Zuar. ⁶His division numbers 54,400.

⁷The tribe of Zebulun will be next. The leader of the people of Zebulun is Eliab son of Helon. ⁸His division numbers 57,400.

⁹All the men assigned to the camp of Judah, according to their divisions, number 186,400. They will set out first.

COMMENTARY

3–9 Judah, Issachar, and Zebulun were the fourth, fifth, and sixth of the six sons born to Jacob by Leah. It is somewhat surprising to have these three tribes first in the order of march since Reuben is regularly remembered as Jacob's firstborn son (1:20). However, because of the perfidy of the three older brothers (Reuben, Simeon, and Levi; see Ge 49:3–7), Judah was ascendant and was granted pride of place among his brothers (49:8). Judah became scion of the royal line in which the Messiah would be born (49:10; Ru 4:18–21; Mt 1:1–16).

Further, the placement on the east was significant in Israel's thought. East is the place of the rising of the sun, the source of hope and sustenance. Westward was the sea. Israel's traditional stance was with its back to the ocean and the descent of the sun. The ancient Hebrew people were not a seafaring folk like the Phoenicians and the Egyptians. For Israel the place of pride was on the east; hence there we find the triad of tribes headed by Judah, Jacob's fourth son, the father of the royal house that leads to King Messiah.

(ii) Southern encampment (2:10–16)

---

¹⁰On the south will be the divisions of the camp of Reuben under their standard. The leader of the people of Reuben is Elizur son of Shedeur. ¹¹His division numbers 46,500.

> [12]The tribe of Simeon will camp next to them. The leader of the people of Simeon is Shelumiel son of Zurishaddai. [13]His division numbers 59,300.
>
> [14]The tribe of Gad will be next. The leader of the people of Gad is Eliasaph son of Deuel. [15]His division numbers 45,650.
>
> [16]All the men assigned to the camp of Reuben, according to their divisions, number 151,450. They will set out second.

COMMENTARY

10–16 Reuben, Jacob's firstborn son, led the second triad, on the south. As one's stance in facing eastward has the south on the right hand, there was a secondary honor given to the tribes associated with Reuben. He was joined by Simeon, the second son of Jacob by Leah. Levi, Leah's third son, was not included with the divisions of the congregation but was reserved the special function of the service of the tabernacle and the guarding of the precinct from the untoward actions of the rest of the community (see v. 17 and ch. 3). This triad is completed by Gad, the first son of Leah's maidservant, Zilpah.

NOTE

14 There is a well-known textual difficulty in 1:14 and 2:14 respecting the name דְּעוּאֵל ($d^{ec}\hat{u}\bar{e}l$, "Deuel"). The MT actually reads רְעוּאֵל ($r^{ec}\hat{u}\bar{e}l$, "Reuel") here in 2:14 but has "Deuel" in 1:14 and in 7:42. The Hebrew letters *dalet* ד (*d*) and *resh* ר (*r*) were confused at times by scribes because of their similarity in form. See the NIV's margin on Genesis 10:4, where a similar problem is presented by the name Rodanim versus Dodanim. Other MSS of the MT, along with the versions, read "Deuel" here in 2:14, which reading I suspect is the superior one.

(iii) Tent and the Levites (2:17)

> [17]Then the Tent of Meeting and the camp of the Levites will set out in the middle of the camps. They will set out in the same order as they encamp, each in his own place under his standard.

COMMENTARY

17 The tent here is the tabernacle—the great Tent of Meeting in the center of the encampment. This was representative of Yahweh's presence within the heart of the camp. It is a change from Exodus

33:7–11. Then Moses' personal tent (see Note) was without the camp, and Moses would go outside the camp to seek the word of God. Here the tent is within the camp, and all Israel was positioned around it. Earlier, the Lord would "come down" from time to time; here he was continually in their midst.

There is a sense here of the progressive manifestation of the presence of God in the midst of the people. First he was on the mountain of Sinai; then he came to the tent outside the camp; then he indwelt the tent in the midst of the camp. One day he would reveal himself through the incarnation in the midst of his people (Jn 1:1–18); and, on a day still to come, there will be an even greater realization of the presence of the person of God dwelling in the midst of his people in the new Jerusalem (Rev 21:1–4). The story of the Bible is largely the story of the progressive revelation of God among his people (*Heilsgeschichte*—"the history of salvation," in the "good sense") and the progressive preparation of a people to be fit to live in his presence.

This verse relates not only to the manner of encampment but especially to the manner of their march. On the line of march the triads of Judah and Reuben would lead the community; next would come the tabernacle with the attendant protective hedge of Levites (see 1:53); then would come the triads of Ephraim and Dan. In this way there was not only the sense of the indwelling presence of God in the midst of the people, there was also the sense that the people in their families and tribes were protecting before and behind the shrine of his presence.

NOTE

17 Some critical scholars have made much of the position of the tent within or without the camp as a means of distinguishing putative sources (JE, the tent without the camp as a source of revelation; P, the tent within the camp as a place of worship). Yet James Orr (*The Problem of the Old Testament Considered with reference to Recent Criticism* [New York: Scribner's Sons, 1906], 165–70) showed long ago that the texts agree that it was God's intention that the regular placement of the tent was to be within the camp, both for revelation and for worship.

(iv) Western encampment (2:18–24)

[18]On the west will be the divisions of the camp of Ephraim under their standard. The leader of the people of Ephraim is Elishama son of Ammihud. [19]His division numbers 40,500.
[20]The tribe of Manasseh will be next to them. The leader of the people of Manasseh is Gamaliel son of Pedahzur. [21]His division numbers 32,200.
[22]The tribe of Benjamin will be next. The leader of the people of Benjamin is Abidan son of Gideoni. [23]His division numbers 35,400.
[24]All the men assigned to the camp of Ephraim, according to their divisions, number 108,100. They will set out third.

COMMENTARY

18–24 The tribes descended from Rachel were on the west. Joseph's two sons, Manasseh and Ephraim, received a special blessing from their grandfather Jacob; but in the process the younger son, Ephraim, was given precedence over Manasseh (Ge 48:5–20). Here, true to Jacob's words, Ephraim was ahead of Manasseh. Benjamin came last—the lastborn son of Jacob, Joseph's younger brother, on whom the aged father doted after the presumed death of Joseph.

(v) Northern encampment (2:25–31)

²⁵On the north will be the divisions of the camp of Dan, under their standard. The leader of the people of Dan is Ahiezer son of Ammishaddai. ²⁶His division numbers 62,700.
²⁷The tribe of Asher will camp next to them. The leader of the people of Asher is Pagiel son of Ocran. ²⁸His division numbers 41,500.
²⁹The tribe of Naphtali will be next. The leader of the people of Naphtali is Ahira son of Enan. ³⁰His division numbers 53,400.
³¹All the men assigned to the camp of Dan number 157,600. They will set out last, under their standards.

COMMENTARY

25–31 Dan was the first son of Bilhah, the maidservant of Rachel. Asher was the second son of Zilpah, the maidservant of Leah. Naphtali was the second son of Bilhah. These, then, are secondary tribes and are positioned on the northern side of the shrine of the presence, as it were, on the left hand. Here again we need to read these texts with the values of the people who first experienced them. Our orientation tends to be to the north, but Israel's orientation was to the east. In the final settlement of the land, these three tribes situated to the north of the shrine actually settled in the northern sections of the land of Canaan.

(vi) Summary totals (2:32–33)

³²These are the Israelites, counted according to their families. All those in the camps, by their divisions, number 603,550. ³³The Levites, however, were not counted along with the other Israelites, as the LORD commanded Moses.

COMMENTARY

32–33 These verses conform to and summarize 1:44–53. The total number is the same as in 1:46 (see Introduction), and the distinction of the Levites is maintained (see comments on 1:47–53). The arrangement of the numbers of the tribes in triads (each with subtotals, as well as the grand total for the whole) signifies the concept of stability in these large numbers in the text. Suggestions to reduce the numbers to obtain a "more manageable" portrait should be presented with due care for all the citations, not just a few. Kitchen's suggestions, for example, may be seen as an effective way to lower the gross numbers drastically; but his approach does not appear to manage subsidiary numbers (see Introduction: The Problem of the Large Numbers).

(c) Summary conclusion (2:34)

³⁴So the Israelites did everything the LORD commanded Moses; that is the way they encamped under their standards, and that is the way they set out, each with his clan and family.

COMMENTARY

34 As in 1:54, these words of absolute compliance contrast with Israel's later folly. This verse also speaks of significant order—a major accomplishment for a people so numerous, so recently enslaved, and more recently a mob in disarray. The text speaks well of the administrative leadership of Moses, God's reluctant prophet, and of the work done by the twelve worthies who were the leaders of each tribe. Certainly the text points to the mercy of God and his blessing on the people. It may have been the beauty of the order of this plan of encampment that led the unlikely prophet Balaam to say, "How beautiful are your tents, O Jacob, / your dwelling places, O Israel!" (Nu 24:5).

Fittingly, Balaam's words—the gasp of an outsider—became among the most treasured in the community. Cyrus Gordon wrote of them, "They have remained the most cherished passages in Scripture throughout Synagogue history" (*Before the Bible: The Common Background of Greek and Hebrew Civilizations* [London: Collins, 1962], 41). In receiving praise from the outsider Balaam, the order and beauty of the camp must continue to stir the heart of the faithful to exhibit even more robust praise. Again the book of Numbers, despite our initial misgivings, is a book of worship.

NOTE

34 The diagram of the camp (with an eastern orientation!) would look like this:

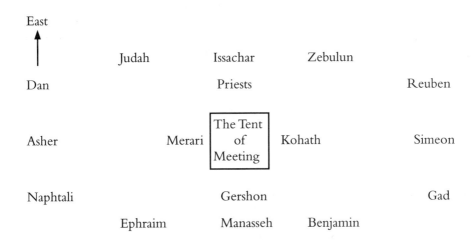

East

Judah   Issachar   Zebulun

Dan   Priests   Reuben

Asher   Merari   The Tent of Meeting   Kohath   Simeon

Naphtali   Gershon   Gad

Ephraim   Manasseh   Benjamin

iii. The placement and the numbers of the Levites and firstborn of Israel (3:1–51)

OVERVIEW

The notion of order continues to lace itself unabatedly through this chapter. When the reader slows down to the pace of the text, he or she begins to discover something of the beauty and dignity of these chapters. True, no one would confuse these texts with great literature (but there *are* texts of sublime artistry in the book; see the Balaam cycle, 22:2–24:25). Dillard and Longman (*AIOT*, 87) write, "The book of Numbers is not among the literary high points of the Old Testament." There is nothing in these texts about story, characterization, emotive depth, or literary finesse. These chapters are neither psalm nor proverb, neither oracle nor epic.

This is not to say, however, that these early chapters of Numbers are not written well—for indeed they are. They have about them a stately grace, a dignity, and a sense of presence. When the modern reader attempts to envision the magnitude of the task the Lord gave to Moses to bring order to an immense number of people who were so recently slaves and now so newly free, the resulting sensation the reader may feel is one of overwhelming burden. But these chapters do not speak of burden at all. There is about them a sense of calm control—the control of God himself. In these chapters is an implied call to order in our own lives and affairs—a call that may cut some of us deeply who have grown accustomed to the disaster of disorder.

Not only is each chapter marked by order, but so also is the placement of these several chapters in the book. The first chapter of Numbers records the organization of the nation of Israel along the lines of family, clan, and tribe, with leaders for each tribe and the totals of the fighting men for each of the tribes. Chapter 2 shows how the various tribes are arranged around the central shrine in their encampments. In the midst of the tribes was the shrine, and about the shrine were the priestly and Levitical families who served as a protective hedge for the laity (non-Levites) and as the authorized personnel admitted to handle sacred things on behalf of the people. In ch. 3 we draw closer to the center and observe the families and their numbers who made up these cultic personnel.

(a) The family of Aaron and Moses (3:1–4)

[1]This is the account of the family of Aaron and Moses at the time the LORD talked with Moses on Mount Sinai.
[2]The names of the sons of Aaron were Nadab the firstborn and Abihu, Eleazar and Ithamar. [3]Those were the names of Aaron's sons, the anointed priests, who were ordained to serve as priests. [4]Nadab and Abihu, however, fell dead before the LORD when they made an offering with unauthorized fire before him in the Desert of Sinai. They had no sons; so only Eleazar and Ithamar served as priests during the lifetime of their father Aaron.

COMMENTARY

1–2 At first blush the wording "the family of Aaron and Moses" (v.1) seems out of order because of the normal placing of Moses before Aaron. But the emphasis is correct: it is the family of Aaron that is about to be described (see v.2). The genealogy of Exodus 6:16–20 (cf. 1Ch 6:1–3) suggests that Aaron and Moses were the (immediate) sons of Amram and Jochebed. However, it is likely that portrayal of this picture is incomplete (a common practice among the writers of these lists in the Bible, and one that must be kept in mind in reading all biblical genealogies, including those of Genesis and Matthew). Amram and his wife-aunt Jochebed were likely more remote ancestors of Aaron and Moses.

At the time of the exodus, there were numerous descendants of Amram, as we learn in this chapter (v.27). Moses' and Aaron's sister, Miriam, was the oldest of the three siblings. It was she who kept watch over the infant Moses when he was placed in his boat in the reeds of the Nile (Ex 2:4). Aaron was three years older than Moses (Ex 7:7). Aaron's wife was Elisheba, the daughter of Amminadab and sister of Nahshon (prince of the tribe of Judah; see Nu 1:7; 2:3), and the mother of the four sons noted in this chapter (see Ex 6:23).

Olson, 98–114, has remarked on the singular importance of the Hebrew term *tôlᵉdôt*("generations"; "account of the family," NIV; GK 9352) in verse 1. He regards the phrase "these are the generations of Aaron and Moses" to be the principal link that ties the books of the Pentateuch together. This use of the word *tôlᵉdôt* harks back to the eleven times it is used in the book of Genesis (see Notes). He states (108):

> For the first time after the formative events of the exodus deliverance and the revelation on Mount Sinai, the people of Israel are organized into a holy people on the march under the leadership of Aaron and Moses with the priests and Levites at the center of the camp. A whole new chapter has opened in the life of the people of Israel, and this new beginning is marked by the *tôlᵉdôt* formula.

Then Olson, 114, presents the structure of the books of Genesis through Numbers based on the term *tôlᵉdōt* (presented below with slight alteration).

I. Genesis: The first generations of God's people to whom the promises were made, and the *tôlᵉdōt* of each succeeding generation up to the *tôlᵉdōt* of Jacob

II. Exodus: The first generation of God's people who experienced the exodus out of Egypt and God's revelation at Mount Sinai; the *tôlᵉdōt* of Jacob

III. Leviticus: Further instructions to the generations of the exodus and Sinai; the *tôlᵉdōt* of Jacob continued

IV. Numbers: The death of the old generation and the birth of the new

   A. The continuation of the *tôlᵉdot* of Jacob and the introduction of the *tôlᵉdōt* of Aaron and Moses (Nu 1–25)

   B. The continuation of the *tôlᵉdōt* of Jacob and the *tôlᵉdōt* of Aaron and Moses into a new generation (Nu 26–36)

3 Exodus 28:41 records God's command to Moses to anoint his brother, Aaron, and his sons as priests of Yahweh (see Ex 30:30; Lev 8:30). This solemn act gave recognition to a special consecration to the Lord and a particular knowledge on their part that they were no longer ordinary — they were now special to God. Olive oil was used commonly to anoint prophets (1Ki 19:16) and kings (1Sa 16:13) for special service to God; but apparently so was the oil of the ancient persimmon (called "balsam" by Greek writers). There is a report of a discovery of a Herodian jug still containing once-fragrant oil of the type used to anoint the kings of Judah. It was found buried in one of the Qumran caves in 1988. In this case the fragrance of the ancient oil came from the (now extinct) ancient persimmon (cf. Joel Brinkley, "Ancient Balm for Anointing Kings Found," *New York Times Service* [Feb. 16, 1989]).

Inanimate objects could be anointed as well, for example, the stone at Bethel (Ge 28:18) and the altar of the tabernacle (Ex 29:36). The general Hebrew term meaning "anointed one" (*māšîaḥ*; GK 5417) became in time the specific term for the Messiah (Christ). While many individuals may be anointed (and be a "messiah"), it is Jesus alone who is *the* Messiah, the Anointed One, who fulfills all God's covenantal promises.

This anointing led naturally to being ordained. The Hebrew idiom "who were ordained" literally reads, "to fill the hand" (*ᵃšer-millēᵓ yādām lᵉkahēn*, "those whom — he filled their hands — as priest"; see also Ex 29:9; 32:29). The act was an investing of authority, a consecration, and a setting apart. The hands of the anointed ones were filled with an awesome sense of the presence of the divine mystery. These were men of moment, servants of God.

4 For the primary story of Nadab and Abihu, see Leviticus 10:1–2. The accentuation of Numbers 3:2 indicates that Aaron may still have been grieving for his firstborn son, Nadab. The accents lead to the following punctuation: "Now these are the names of the sons of Aaron: the firstborn, Nadab; also Abihu, Eleazar, and Ithamar." Hirsch, 23, observes, "It is as if the report pauses painfully over Nadab, then lingers on Abihu and then quickly adds Eleazar and Ithamar." Nadab is given double "honor" in this wording; he is identified as the firstborn, and the accents set his name off from those of his brothers. It is for these reasons that the mysterious report of the sin of Nadab and Abihu is so trenchant to us — and remained so to Aaron!

"Unauthorized fire" translates a Hebrew expression (*ᵓēš zārâ*, "strange fire, alien fire") — a term that seems deliberately obscure. It is as though the narrator found the concept to be distasteful. This is not unlike the reserve of the Torah in detailing the nuances of the notorious scandal of the behavior of the "sons of God" in Genesis 6:1–4. The essential issue here is that Nadab and Abihu were using fire that the Lord had not commanded (Lev 10:1). The pain of the account is strengthened by its brevity and mystery. We are left at a loss to explain their motivation, just as we do not know the precise form of their error. Were they rebellious or presumptuous? Were they careless or ignorant? Or was their sin some combination of these and other things? The prohibition of wine and beer to the priests in their priestly service, directed in the subsequent text (Lev 10:8–11), may lead us to infer that these sons of Aaron had committed their offense against God while in a drunken state.

Verse 4 states the matter of the death of these errant priests of the Lord succinctly: "[They] fell dead before the Lord." Leviticus 10:2 specifies more fully: "So fire came out from the presence of the Lord and consumed them, and they died before the Lord." This wording suggests that Yahweh may have used a bolt of lightning; the same seems to be the case of the fire from Yahweh that consumed the offering and the altar of Elijah on Mount Carmel (1Ki 18:38). There is tragic poetic justice that these wicked priests who used unauthorized fire in the worship of the Lord were themselves destroyed by fire from his presence.

Nadab's and Abihu's fate was made even sadder, from a cultural point of view, in that they did not leave sons to continue their names among the priestly rolls in Israel. When they died, their story was over. Each time they are mentioned in the Bible, it is with sadness (cf. Nu 26:61; 1Ch 24:2). It was also the mercy of God that Aaron had two other sons who were not involved in the perfidy of their brothers. Hence the Aaronic priestly line was extended through the two younger sons, Eleazar and Ithamar (see 1Ch 24:1–4), who continued to minister throughout the lifetime of Aaron.

NOTES

1 תּוֹלְדֹת (tôlᵉdôt, "the account of" or "family histories") is used as the organizing principle of the book of Genesis, where it occurs ten times—at the beginning of each main section (2:4; 5:1; 6:9; 10:1; 11:10, 27; 25:12, 19; 36:1 [with a repetition for emphasis at 36:9]; 37:2).

3 הַמְּשֻׁחִים (hammᵉšuḥîm, "the anointed ones," a plural old Qal passive participle) is related to the verb מָשַׁח (māšaḥ, "to anoint, consecrate"); see Notes at 7:1; 18:8.

4 On the idea of regarding things too casually, Western Christians may learn lessons from emerging Christian communities in non-Western lands. In a preaching and teaching ministry in Thailand, I found that there were printed cards given to American ministers requesting that they not place their Bibles on the floor. "It is a holy book," the gentle reminder said.

REFLECTION

All the commands for obedience on the part of the priests beginning in Leviticus 8:1 leave us unprepared for the rash disobedience of the older sons of Aaron. The story is shocking. It is marked by the pathos of a father forbidden to grieve over the death of his sons (Lev 10:3–7). The lesson was starkly evident: proximity to the holiness of God placed tremendous demands of righteousness, exactitude, and obedience on his priests. For all time the deaths of Aaron's newly consecrated sons should warn God's ministers of the awesome seriousness of their tasks (see also 1Sa 2:12–17, 22–25, 27–36; 3:11–14; 4:1–11). The most common reports of failure we hear of God's ministers in our own day are of their malfeasance, indolence, greed, lust, and abuse of power. Tragically the lessons of the past are forgotten with frightful ease. The spiritual descendants of Nadab and Abihu continue to occupy the ranks of the "ministers" of God.

The reference to Nadab and Abihu serves another purpose: it sets the tone for the seriousness of the priestly and Levitical duties this chapter presents. If a person who had no right to be in the proximity of the central shrine, or near its holy

things, happened to come near, that person might die. This warning is given repeatedly (Nu 1:51, 53; 2:2, "some distance from it"). A person who came near without authorization was like a stranger, an alien; such a person had no right to approach and might lose his or her life by doing so. But those whose proper place *was* in the proximity of holy things and near the holy shrine were themselves under warning. They were also to take care, for opportunity for sin was enhanced by their familiarity with holy things.

It is ever this way. Some preachers tend to tell jokes about the Bible, to use the Lord's name casually, to speak light-heartedly of the institutions of the Lord. Often devout laypeople have a higher sense of reverence for the things of God than those whose job it is to handle those things reverently but who deal with them routinely (see Notes).

(b) The duties for the Levites (3:5–10)

⁵The LORD said to Moses, ⁶"Bring the tribe of Levi and present them to Aaron the priest to assist him. ⁷They are to perform duties for him and for the whole community at the Tent of Meeting by doing the work of the tabernacle. ⁸They are to take care of all the furnishings of the Tent of Meeting, fulfilling the obligations of the Israelites by doing the work of the tabernacle. ⁹Give the Levites to Aaron and his sons; they are the Israelites who are to be given wholly to him. ¹⁰Appoint Aaron and his sons to serve as priests; anyone else who approaches the sanctuary must be put to death."

COMMENTARY

5–8 These commands are not followed by a report of obedience, as were those in chs. 1 and 2, but further details are given in ch. 8. Clear distinctions are made here between the priestly house (the sons of Aaron) and the Levites. The latter were to be aids to the priests. The Levites served not only

Aaron but also the entire nation in the process (vv.7–8). The Levites come out from among the nation; they were a part of the nation but were now distinct.

Interestingly, Moses is addressed in verse 5. He was responsible for the nation as a whole and, hence, for the faithful obedience of the Levites in their service of the priestly house of Aaron. Moreover, the tribe of the Levites was to be "brought near" (v.6) — terminology for approaching the Divine Presence. Only Moses had an open invitation to draw near to God in a direct manner. Now he is presented with the task of drawing these other ministers near to their work before the Lord. This work consisted of service to Aaron and the guarding of the ministry relating to him and the whole congregation (v.7). Moreover, they were responsible for the tasks of moving the furnishings of the tabernacle at times when the camp would be on the move (v.8).

The key to the work of the Levites during times when the camp was not on the move may be in the words "perform duties for him" (v.7). The Hebrew phrase combines both verb and noun from the same root (*wᵉšomrû ʾet-mišmartô*), a common form of emphasis in Hebrew rhetorical style. The basic meaning of the Hebrew verb *šāmar* is "to keep watch, guard." Hence, as Wenham, 70, suggests, the Levites apparently had two tasks: to guard the holy things from affront by foolish people, and to care for the holy things when the people were on the move.

9 The Levites were subsidiary to the priests, as is made clear by the wording of this verse. The verse begins with a directive form of the verb "to give" (*nātan*), then uses an expression made emphatic by repetition (*nᵉtûnim nᵉtûnim*, "given given" ("wholly given," NIV), an idiom for totality (Williams, *Hebrew Syntax*, sec. 16). Despite the textual difficulty in this passage (see Note), the issue here is service to Aaron (and through him to the Lord); in 8:16 it is to the Lord.

10 The warning of the death penalty of 1:51 is repeated. The Hebrew term *hazzār* is, literally, "the strange one" ("anyone else," NIV), anyone lacking authorization. Service at the tabernacle could be performed only at the express command of God.

There is a special poignancy in this verse as it follows the paragraph reminding us of the deaths of Aaron's sons. They were authorized persons and used unauthorized means. If the sons of Aaron were put to death at the commencement of their duties, how dare an unauthorized person even think to trespass (see 3:38; 18:7)? Wenham, 70, suggests that the Levites were those who were authorized to carry out the death penalty, to keep the wrath of God against untoward offenders of his majesty and holiness from breaking out against the entire camp. Numbers 25:7–8 presents a powerful example of this stricture. But there the protagonist was not a Levite but a priest, Phinehas, son of Eleazar. Perhaps the Levites in that occasion were so lax that Phinehas decided he had to work quickly himself or there would not be time to quell the evil that was right before the tent (see ch. 25).

NOTE

9 לוֹ (*lô*, "to him") is the reading in our text, but some MSS of the MT, Samaritan recension, and LXX read לִי (*lî*, "to me"), as in 8:16. It appears that here the issue is service to Aaron; in 8:16 service is respecting the Lord.

(c) The separation of the Levites (3:11–13)

¹¹The Lᴏʀᴅ also said to Moses, ¹²"I have taken the Levites from among the Israelites in place of the first male offspring of every Israelite woman. The Levites are mine, ¹³for all the firstborn are mine. When I struck down all the firstborn in Egypt, I set apart for myself every firstborn in Israel, whether man or animal. They are to be mine. I am the Lᴏʀᴅ."

COMMENTARY

11–13 The Hebrew word *taḥat* ("in place of"; v.12) serves as a clear example of substitution in the Hebrew Scriptures (cf. Ge 22:13: "a ram ... instead of his son"; cf. also Mt 20:28).

The MT has a grand emphasis on Yahweh as he speaks of himself and his work in these verses. The text uses the word "mine" (*lî*, "for myself") four times in vv.12–13; in addition, note the emphatic "I" at the beginning of v.12, the concluding "I am the Lᴏʀᴅ," and three verbs constructed with the first person pronoun ("I have taken," "I struck down," and "I set apart"). Again we are told that the

Levites were from among the people of Israel but were now designated to be the exclusive property of Yahweh (see Ex 13:2).

The last phrase of this section, "I am the Lᴏʀᴅ," is a characteristic punctuation in the legislative portions of the Torah. These words add authority, significance, and weight to the text. This phrase is a reminder of both what has been revealed about his blessed person and work and what he has shown himself to be in relation to his people. The phrase points to him and to his people in relationship to him, but it does so as a divine punctuation of the text.

(d) The census of the Levites (3:14–39)

(i) The principals (3:14–20)

¹⁴The Lᴏʀᴅ said to Moses in the Desert of Sinai, ¹⁵"Count the Levites by their families and clans. Count every male a month old or more." ¹⁶So Moses counted them, as he was commanded by the word of the Lᴏʀᴅ.

¹⁷These were the names of the sons of Levi:
Gershon, Kohath and Merari.
¹⁸These were the names of the Gershonite clans:
Libni and Shimei.
¹⁹The Kohathite clans:
Amram, Izhar, Hebron and Uzziel.

²⁰The Merarite clans:
Mahli and Mushi.
These were the Levite clans, according to their families.

COMMENTARY

14–20 The enumerating of the Levites corresponds to that of the other tribes in chs. 1–2, but this roster was to be done of males from the age of one month rather than twenty years. The Levites were not being mustered for war but for special service in the sacral precincts of the Lord. They were distinct from the rest of the tribes in several aspects: (1) they had their service in and about the holy things and the holy place of God; (2) they were not numbered among the tribes but were to be distributed among them; (3) they were numbered differently from the other tribes; (4) they were not the fighting men of Israel but her ministers, subject to the leadership of the priests; and (5) they had certain restrictions of behavior and manner that marked their office as distinct from the rest of the people.

The obedience of Moses to the commands of God in these early texts of Numbers is explicit and total. These records of his obedience will serve to display the incongruity of his terrible lapse as described in 20:1–13. Also in 3:14–16 we have one of many texts in Numbers that speaks of the revelation of the word of God to his servant Moses. Those who minimize the role of Moses do so in the face of abundant, direct textual assertions to the contrary.

(ii) Gershon (3:21–26)

²¹To Gershon belonged the clans of the Libnites and Shimeites; these were the Gershonite clans. ²²The number of all the males a month old or more who were counted was 7,500. ²³The Gershonite clans were to camp on the west, behind the tabernacle. ²⁴The leader of the families of the Gershonites was Eliasaph son of Lael. ²⁵At the Tent of Meeting the Gershonites were responsible for the care of the tabernacle and tent, its coverings, the curtain at the entrance to the Tent of Meeting, ²⁶the curtains of the courtyard, the curtain at the entrance to the courtyard surrounding the tabernacle and altar, and the ropes — and everything related to their use.

COMMENTARY

21–26 The words of 1:53 — "their tents around the tabernacle of the Testimony" — are detailed by the four paragraphs in verses 21–38 (all describing Levitical families):

Gershon to the west (vv.21–26);
Kohath to the south (vv.27–32);
Merari to the north (vv.33–37);
Moses and Aaron and sons to the east (v.38).

In the laic (non-Levitical) tribes, the list begins with the most favored:

Judah on the east (2:3);
Reuben on the south (2:10);
Ephraim on the west (2:18);
Dan on the north (2:25).

In the Levitical clans, the listing moves up to the most favored, as noted above. The leaders of the Levitical houses correspond to the leaders of the laic tribes (see 1:5–15). As in the case of the names of the other tribal leaders, these names are theophoric (built on compounds of terms for God). Also, as in the names listed in 1:5–15, these names show formations with the same building blocks, but not with the divine name Yahweh.

Eliasaph (ʾelyāsāp, "[My] God Has Added") son of Lael (lāʾēl, "Belonging to God") (3:24)

Elizaphan (ʾelîṣāpān, "[My] God Has Protected") son of Uzziel (ʿuzzîʾēl, "My Strength Is God") (3:30)

Zuriel (ṣûrîʾēl, "My Rock Is God") son of Abihail (ʾăbîḥāyil, "My Father [God] Is Might") (3:35)

Under the leadership of Eliasaph, the clan of Gershon was to camp on the west side of the tabernacle (v.23), that is, away from its entrance. Their particular charge was the structure itself: the tent, its coverings, and the varied curtains and ropes. This was a significant charge for the people of the house of Gershon, whose male members over the age of one month numbered seventy-five hundred.

There were three curtains or covering screens of the tabernacle: (1) one at the gate of the court (v.26; 4:26); (2) a second at the entrance of the tent (vv.25, 31; 4:25); (3) and a third dividing off the Most Holy Place within the tent (4:5).

(iii) Kohath (3:27–32)

27To Kohath belonged the clans of the Amramites, Izharites, Hebronites and Uzzielites; these were the Kohathite clans. 28The number of all the males a month old or more was 8,600. The Kohathites were responsible for the care of the sanctuary. 29The Kohathite clans were to camp on the south side of the tabernacle. 30The leader of the families of the Kohathite clans was Elizaphan son of Uzziel. 31They were responsible for the care of the ark, the table, the lampstand, the altars, the articles of the sanctuary used in ministering, the curtain, and everything related to their use. 32The chief leader of the Levites was Eleazar son of Aaron, the priest. He was appointed over those who were responsible for the care of the sanctuary.

COMMENTARY

27–32 The Kohathites under the leadership of Elizaphan were to encamp on the southern side of the sanctuary. This clan, the largest of the Levitical families, had particular concerns for the care of the principal furnishings of the tabernacle, including the ark, the table, the lamps, and the altars, along with many implements of their service. Aaron's son Eleazar, "the chief leader" (*ûnᵉśîʾ nᵉśîʾê hallēwî*, lit., "the leader of the leaders of the Levite[s]"; v.32), was placed over this group of Levites, probably because of the inordinately sensitive nature of their work.

The term "Amramites" (v.27) reminds us of the family of Aaron and Moses. Aaron was an Amramite (see Ex 6:20). The presence of the family of the Amramites suggests that Amram was not the immediate father of Aaron, Miriam, and Moses but a notable ancestor. Hence Aaron and Moses were from the family of Kohath, of the tribe of Levi. The Kohathites were responsible for the care of the most holy things (4:4–18).

The total number of Levites given in v.39 is 22,000, which is 300 fewer than the total of 7,500 Gershonites (v.22), 8,600 Kohathites (v.28), and 6,200 Merarites (v.34), together totaling 22,300. Many scholars believe that there has been a textual corruption in the number in v.28, that the correct number of the Kohathites is 8,300 (as in the LXX). Because the totals of all other numbers in these chapters of Numbers are consistent, it is reasonable to assume a dysfunction in textual transmission in this instance. But the fact that there is a textual difficulty with a number here cannot be projected back to the numbers of ch. 1 as a way to evade the problems of the large numbers. For textual corruption to have been a factor, it would have to have happened on a scale unprecedented in the Bible. In this instance we have the proverbial exception that proves the rule.

(iv) Merari (3:33–37)

³³To Merari belonged the clans of the Mahlites and the Mushites; these were the Merarite clans. ³⁴The number of all the males a month old or more who were counted was 6,200. ³⁵The leader of the families of the Merarite clans was Zuriel son of Abihail; they were to camp on the north side of the tabernacle. ³⁶The Merarites were appointed to take care of the frames of the tabernacle, its crossbars, posts, bases, all its equipment, and everything related to their use, ³⁷as well as the posts of the surrounding courtyard with their bases, tent pegs and ropes.

COMMENTARY

33–37 The house of Merari, encamped on the northern side of the tabernacle, was led by Zuriel and numbered 6,200 males from the age of one month. Their particular charge was the care of the frames, posts, bases, and crossbars of the tent, as well as all auxiliary materials. It is fitting that this clan of Levites was stationed on the north, as their work was not nearly as glamorous as that of the other two companies of Levites. There was a consistency in that this house of the Levites was on the same side of the tent as the triad of tribes led by Dan.

(v) Moses and Aaron (3:38)

³⁸Moses and Aaron and his sons were to camp to the east of the tabernacle, toward the sunrise, in front of the Tent of Meeting. They were responsible for the care of the sanctuary on behalf of the Israelites. Anyone else who approached the sanctuary was to be put to death.

COMMENTARY

38 Moses and Aaron had the most honored location, as we would expect. They guarded the entrance to the Tent of Meeting, and they did so facing the sun. There is a sense in which the opening of the tent best faces the east, for this was the direction of the encampment of the people. Later, when Solomon built the holy temple in Jerusalem, its entrance also faced eastward. The morning sun would shine first on the entrance of the Holy Place, as a symbol of the life-giving light of God, thus illumining the location of his presence.

Moses and Aaron were not placed in the posture of arrogance on the eastern side of the tabernacle; they were placed there for a representational ministry ("on behalf of the Israelites"). Theirs was an exclusive work but beneficent to the community. Service in the tabernacle was an act of mercy, a means for the people to come before God. Yet it was marked by severity—all had to be done in God's way! God receives the worship of his people only because of his mercy. The sovereignty of God was evident in his limitations on the means to approach him. The "stranger" (*hazzār*, "anyone else," NIV) could be a better man or woman, more pious and devout than a given descendant of Aaron; yet he or she would still face death in the case of actions based on presumption. The warning of death to the "stranger" is found four times in the book (see 1:51; 3:10, 38; 18:7).

(vi) The sum (3:39)

³⁹The total number of Levites counted at the LORD's command by Moses and Aaron according to their clans, including every male a month old or more, was 22,000.

COMMENTARY

39 Concerning the grand sum of 22,000 Levites, we observe first of all that this is a bit small compared with the numbers given for the other tribes in ch. 1. (There is consistency, however, when this number is compared to the 23,000 Levites in the second census; see 26:62.) The sum is particularly small when we realize that the 22,000 included all males in the tribe of Levi who were over the age of one month rather than over the age of twenty years, as in the other tribes.

The single, most difficult issue in the numbers of the tribes is the relative fewness of Levites compared to the other tribes. This case remains true however we interpret the meaning of these numbers. If we suggest that the numbers of the other tribes were deliberately inflated by a factor of ten (see Introduction), then the totals for Reuben would be 4,650 and for Simeon 5,930 from the age of twenty and upward. The smallest of the laic tribes would be Benjamin at 3,400; the largest Judah, with 7,400. If we assume that the numbers for the tribe of Levi are similarly inflated, they would number 2,200—again a small number with respect to the other tribes. If we were to regard the number for the tribe of Levi as the only noninflated figure of the tribes of Israel, then the 22,000 males over the age of one month would suggest a tribe that was large—indeed, they would become the largest tribe of all.

Even with the priest-centeredness of the book of Numbers, we would be surprised to find a number this large in proportion to the whole for the tribe of Levi. The smaller figure, then, of 2,200 seems the more reasonable. John Wenham suggests the number (22,000) of the tribe of Levi is likely inflated by a factor of ten (see Introduction). This number, too, would have been rhetorically exaggerated as a *power number* (see Introduction for a description of this concept).

NOTE

39 The word וְאַהֲרֹן (*wĕ'ahărōn*, "and Aaron") has a dot or point (*puncta extraordinarius*) over each letter of the word, thus indicating doubt on the part of ancient scribes as to the inclusion of Aaron's name in this verse. This word is one of fifteen words in MT marked with these superior dots; three of the other examples are in Numbers (9:10; 21:30; 29:15). The presence of these dots over a questionable word (or a letter of a word) the scribes were loath to drop completely shows the level of care and concern for the minutiae of the text by the Jewish scholars through the ages. The word "Aaron" is lacking in numerous Hebrew MSS of 3:39 as well as in the Samaritan recension and the Syriac, but it is included in the LXX. It may have been included here because of the presence of the name "Aaron" at the beginning of the chapter and in 4:1. The great authority on minutiae of MT was the nineteenth-century Hebrew Christian scholar Christian D. Ginsburg, whose book *Introduction to the Massoretico-Critical Edition of the Hebrew Bible* was first published in 1897. He explains the issue here as a scribal dispute as to whether Moses alone was to number the Levites (as 3:14–16 might suggest), or whether Moses was to be joined by Aaron in doing so (as in 4:41, 45–46; cf. 1:3–4; ibid., 328–29).

(e) The census and redemption of the firstborn (3:40–51)

(i) The census (3:40–43)

40The LORD said to Moses, "Count all the firstborn Israelite males who are a month old or more and make a list of their names. **41**Take the Levites for me in place of all the firstborn of the Israelites, and the livestock of the Levites in place of all the firstborn of the livestock of the Israelites. I am the LORD."

42So Moses counted all the firstborn of the Israelites, as the LORD commanded him. 43The total number of firstborn males a month old or more, listed by name, was 22,273.

COMMENTARY

40–43 This pivotal passage centers on the concept of redemption of the firstborn in Israel. This first paragraph may be judged to be the most significant passage in Numbers with respect to our understanding of the issue of how numbers are used in the census lists.

The basic teaching is that the male Levites over the age of one month were to be regarded by Yahweh as "belonging to him" as the payment of redemption for the firstborn of the nation. The firstborn of animals were to be sacrificed to the Lord, but God never countenanced the sacrifice of persons on his altars. Hence a substitution was made. A male Levite was regarded as a substitution for the firstborn member of a family in a non-Levitical tribe. Notice that the firstborn of the livestock were also included in the substitutionary arrangement: Levite for firstborn of Israel, and Levite's livestock for firstborn livestock of Israel.

God's command is specific in this text (v.40). There was to be a count of a discrete populace grouping, and the name of each individual was to be written down ("make a list"; cf. 1:2). The number of kol-becôr zākār ("all the firstborn males") of the Hebrew families came to 22,273 (v.43). *This number stands out from all the other numbers in these three chapters.* All the other numbers are rounded, including the total number of the Levites, 22,000. The number here is specific to the final digit. Yet this specific number of the firstborn of Israel is related to the rounded number of the Levites

to provide a surplus of 273 firstborn males, for whom a redemption price had to be made (v.46).

As the number of firstborn Israelite males exceeded the number of the Levites by 273 (v.43), the remainder had to be redeemed by the payment of five shekels each (v.47; see 27:6). A question presents itself as to why the rounded number of the Levites (22,000) is posed against a specific number of the firstborn of Israel (22,273). Perhaps the rounded number was in accordance with the rounded numbers of the other tribes. This disparity in types of numbers allows the text to bear a significant lesson on redemption.

The number of the firstborn sons of Israel (22,273) is patently much too small for a population that is usually regarded to have been 2.5 million. Each mother would have had to give live births in excess of fifty children even to approach this grand sum! The disparity of this number of firstborn sons (22,273) to the "high" sums (2.5 million) is, frankly, impossible to sustain. This number appears to be *the key* for the problem of the large numbers in the book.

This number of firstborn sons would accord very well for a population of about 250,000 (one-tenth of the sum of the common view). Again, it is the only number in the series that is not rounded off—it stands out as a specific sum. This number presents the best opportunity for finding a means to reduce the huge sum of ch. 1.

Conservative writers who strive to defend the sense of the integrity of the Bible have had to find a way to deal with this surprisingly small number. The great nineteenth-century expositor C. F. Keil (3:9–11) proposed a solution for the seeming disparity. He argued that the 22,273 firstborn of Israel were those born *since* the time of the exodus, all the firstborn of Israel *at the time* of the exodus having already been sanctified to the Lord at the Passover (Ex 12:22–23). But this solution presents its own problem, "since nowhere is that allegedly distinct group assigned any special service of the Lord" (*NIV Study Bible*, note on 3:43). It also suggests some special pleading. There is no indication in the text that these firstborn were born after the exodus. Nor would it have been likely that anyone would have thought that this number of the firstborn of Israel was restricted to those born since the exodus—except in an attempt to deal with the (implausibly) large numbers of the population indicated in ch. 1 (see Notes).

With some temerity I suggest the following possibility, a proposal of an alternative way of thinking of these numbers. In this passage, we confront two difficulties: one concerns the disparity of a mere 22,273 firstborn sons in a population of several million; the other concerns the subtraction of a rounded number (22,000) from a specific number (22,273) and then making much of the difference between the two. Keil's proposal was based on the postulate that the numbers of the conscripted troops of Israel were "ordinary numbers," as were these two disputed numbers of 22,273 firstborn and 22,000 Levites of a certain age. Hence he had to deal with the unusually small number of firstborn sons of Israel for a population so very large. My suggestion is that the unexpectedly small number of the firstborn is an impressive clue to the size of the population as a whole and that there may be two

different uses of numbers in this passage, specific and rhetorical. Although we normally do not use numbers in this way today, that fact is beside the point. Neither would we subtract a rounded number (22,000) from a specific number (22,273)—and then make a major point of the remainder (273). Yet this is precisely what this passage does!

My proposal, then, is that Moses here presents a comparison of numbers of different sorts. The one number is specific and exact (22,273); the other is rounded, inflated, rhetorical (22,000). The number of the firstborn of Israel (22,273) is a specific, concrete number of the firstborn of all the families of Israel in the first generation. This is the surest figure for calculating the numbers of the whole community; the extrapolation of 250,000 is considered fitting for this number of firstborn persons. Against this specific figure (22,273) is pitted a rhetorical figure (22,000, the number of Levites of a certain age) in order to provide an analogy of redemption. The "surplus" of these two discordant types of figures (one specific, concrete; one inflated, rounded off) affords the opportunity to deal with the problem of a surplus.

The payment of a redemption price of five sanctuary shekels per individual teaches us that every individual needs to be accounted for, *no matter how* these numbers are used. That is, there is the possibility that the point of the passage is not the numbers per se but *that which the numbers represent*—the importance of paying the redemption price for each individual firstborn person in the young nation as a symbol of the redemption of each individual in the nation. The theology of the exodus demands that the nation as a whole be under the blood of the Passover, that the nation as a whole was rescued from Egypt, and that the nation as a whole was a part of the new community in relation to Yahweh. In the attention given to the 273 supernumeraries, there is a focus on the individuals who make up the nation. Certainly we are not interested in making any numerical symbolism of the number 273. The number is not as important as the issue the number represents: corporate solidarity and the importance of the individual are twin realities in the new community of Israel.

NOTES

41 The words אֲנִי יהוה (*ʾanî yhwh*, "I am the LORD") add solemnity and emphasis. The phrase is intrusive in the original—startling and surprising, having the force: "Listen to ME!" What is being commanded conforms to God's character, as expressed in his covenantal name, *Yahweh*.

43 The number 22,273, representing the firstborn sons among all the families of Israel is, as noted above, far too small for the 2.5 million people that conservative writers have sought to uphold, based on (good) convictions of inspiration and accuracy of the Word of God. One of the problems posed by the large numbers of people in this traditional standpoint is the idea of this massive populace—along with herds and flocks—living in the wilderness for a generation. We know about God's provision of manna, but what were the provisions for the animals? I so admire Keil because of his clear desire to honor God's Word. But he did engage in special pleading by suggesting that the conditions of the Sinai Peninsula "yielded much more subsistence in ancient times than is to be found there at present." Such "paleo-agricultural" concepts—even if true—could not have been known in the late nineteenth century, when he wrote these words. At best, his assertion appears to be well-intentioned wishful thinking.

(ii) The redemption (3:44–51)

> **44**The LORD also said to Moses, **45**"Take the Levites in place of all the firstborn of Israel, and the livestock of the Levites in place of their livestock. The Levites are to be mine. I am the LORD. **46**To redeem the 273 firstborn Israelites who exceed the number of the Levites, **47**collect five shekels for each one, according to the sanctuary shekel, which weighs twenty gerahs. **48**Give the money for the redemption of the additional Israelites to Aaron and his sons."
>
> **49**So Moses collected the redemption money from those who exceeded the number redeemed by the Levites. **50**From the firstborn of the Israelites he collected silver weighing 1,365 shekels, according to the sanctuary shekel. **51**Moses gave the redemption money to Aaron and his sons, as he was commanded by the word of the LORD.

COMMENTARY

44–51 To make up for the number of the firstborn Israelites beyond the number of the Levites, a special tax of five shekels (the price of a slave for a boy under the age of five; see 27:6) was to be paid for each of the 273 supernumeraries (see Note). This payment is a redemption price according to the heavier sanctuary shekel. That silver was then paid to Aaron and his sons, as commanded by the Lord so that the full complement of the firstborn sons of the community might all be redeemed together.

The redemption of the firstborn was a marvelous expression of God's grace. Never since the story of the binding of Isaac (Ge 22) had God demanded the firstborn son of any of his people be slain as a sacrifice to his majesty. Nor did God demand that his people enslave themselves to him (cf. Ro 12:1–2). Nevertheless, the firstborn sons were the special possession of the Lord. God did not demand the life of these sons; such would be abhorrent to the Hebrew faith. God did not demand their enslavement; such would be a slight on his mercy. But he did demand their redemption—and provided the means for bringing it to pass.

We suspect the community paid the redemption price; it is possible that the families of those judged to be the supernumeraries may have had to pay this tax themselves. The resultant weight of the silver payment collected (1,365 shekels, v.50) is given as a statement of the impressive nature of the transaction and a witness to its accuracy (5 x 273). The pattern was one Levite for each firstborn, five shekels for each child beyond the number of the Levites. In this way each firstborn was accounted for in God's plan of redemption.

Christians cannot help but turn their thoughts to the NT and the Savior who has redeemed his people—not by the payment of silver and gold, but with his own precious blood. And so we have been redeemed.

NOTE

47 In חֲמֵשֶׁת חֲמֵשֶׁת (*ḥᵃmēšet ḥᵃmēšet*, "five, five"), the duplication of the word is for distribution: "five from each," as in Williams, *Hebrew Syntax*, sec. 15. Compare 29:15, "one tenth, one tenth."

שְׁקָלִים (*šᵉqālîm*, "shekels"; GK 9203) is a problematic word, as the modern reader likely assumes that coins are in view here, as would be the case when monetary units are mentioned in the NT. In fact, coins did not come into use until the Persian period (the sixth century BC). All references to "shekels" in early OT narratives are actually describing "weighed" amounts of (precious) metals. The basic meaning of שֶׁקֶל (*šeqel*) is "weight." See David Hendin's definitive work, *Guide to Biblical Coins* (4th ed.; New York: Amphora, 2001), 57–70 ("A Time before Coins"), with values by Herbert Kreindler; see also the photographic examples of ancient shekel weights on Plate 1 in the appendix.

iv. The numbers of the Levites in tabernacle service (4:1–49)

OVERVIEW

The sense of order and organization already observed in Numbers comes to its finest point in this chapter. Again we observe that the standard pattern in Hebrew prose is a movement from the general to the specific, from the broad to the particular. Chapters 1–4 follow this concept nicely. Chapter 1 presents the leaders and the numbers of the soldiers conscripted from each tribe; ch. 2

shows how each of the tribes is related to group-ings surrounding the Tent of Meeting; ch. 3 gives the census of the Levitical males from one month and older and a listing of the Levites by their fami-lies; and ch. 4 presents the census of the Levites from twenty-five to fifty years of age and the work each family was to do. The chapters have moved from the nation as a whole to the particular fami-lies of the one tribe that has responsibility to main-tain the symbols of Israel's worship of the Lord. Each chapter gets more specific, narrower in focus, with the central emphasis on the worship of the Lord at the Tent of Meeting.

Another standard feature of Hebrew prose is to give a topic sentence, detail the particulars relating to that topic, and then conclude with a summary of the completion of the intended action. Genesis 1:1–2:3 is written in this way: 1:1 gives the topical sentence on creation, 1:2–31 details the creative actions of God, and 2:1–3 (or, better, 2:1–4a) sum-marizes God's creative work. We find a variation on this same pattern nicely displayed in Numbers 4. In this case there is not a topical sentence but an extended command (vv.1–33) followed by a report of its execution (vv.34–45) and a summary (vv.46–49).

(a) The command for the census and a description of duties (4:1–33)

(i) The family of Kohath (4:1–20)

¹The Lord said to Moses and Aaron: ²"Take a census of the Kohathite branch of the Levites by their clans and families. ³Count all the men from thirty to fifty years of age who come to serve in the work in the Tent of Meeting.

⁴"This is the work of the Kohathites in the Tent of Meeting: the care of the most holy things. ⁵When the camp is to move, Aaron and his sons are to go in and take down the shielding curtain and cover the ark of the Testimony with it. ⁶Then they are to cover this with hides of sea cows, spread a cloth of solid blue over that and put the poles in place.

⁷"Over the table of the Presence they are to spread a blue cloth and put on it the plates, dishes and bowls, and the jars for drink offerings; the bread that is continually there is to remain on it. ⁸Over these they are to spread a scarlet cloth, cover that with hides of sea cows and put its poles in place.

⁹"They are to take a blue cloth and cover the lampstand that is for light, together with its lamps, its wick trimmers and trays, and all its jars for the oil used to supply it. ¹⁰Then they are to wrap it and all its accessories in a covering of hides of sea cows and put it on a carrying frame.

¹¹"Over the gold altar they are to spread a blue cloth and cover that with hides of sea cows and put its poles in place.

¹²"They are to take all the articles used for ministering in the sanctuary, wrap them in a blue cloth, cover that with hides of sea cows and put them on a carrying frame.

¹³"They are to remove the ashes from the bronze altar and spread a purple cloth over it. ¹⁴Then they are to place on it all the utensils used for ministering at the altar, including the firepans, meat forks, shovels and sprinkling bowls. Over it they are to spread a covering of hides of sea cows and put its poles in place.

¹⁵"After Aaron and his sons have finished covering the holy furnishings and all the holy articles, and when the camp is ready to move, the Kohathites are to come to do the carrying. But they must not touch the holy things or they will die. The Kohathites are to carry those things that are in the Tent of Meeting.

¹⁶"Eleazar son of Aaron, the priest, is to have charge of the oil for the light, the fragrant incense, the regular grain offering and the anointing oil. He is to be in charge of the entire tabernacle and everything in it, including its holy furnishings and articles."

¹⁷The LORD said to Moses and Aaron, ¹⁸"See that the Kohathite tribal clans are not cut off from the Levites. ¹⁹So that they may live and not die when they come near the most holy things, do this for them: Aaron and his sons are to go into the sanctuary and assign to each man his work and what he is to carry. ²⁰But the Kohathites must not go in to look at the holy things, even for a moment, or they will die."

COMMENTARY

1 When the sons of Levi are mentioned in 3:17, their order is Gershon, Kohath, and Merari; this order also informs the structure of the balance of ch. 3: Gershonites (vv.21–26), Kohathites (vv.27–32), and Merarites (vv.33–37). The same order is given in the familial records of Jacob (Ge 46:11), Moses and Aaron (Ex 6:16), and the Levitites (1Ch 6:1, 16).

2 The order of the list of sons in the Bible is not necessarily that of birth order; but the consistent pattern Gershon, Kohath, and Merari suggests that birth order is intended. This makes the order of the Levitical families in Numbers 4 somewhat unexpected, as the families of Kohath (the presumed second son) are mentioned first (vv.2–20), then the families of Gershon (vv.21–28), and finally the families of Merari (vv.29–33). The same pattern is recapitulated in the numberings listed at the end of the chapter (vv.34–45).

The reason for this elevation of the second son over his older brother seems to be based on the sovereign selection of the Lord and the favored work he gave this family in proximity to the holiest things. Furthermore, this reflects a recurring pattern in the OT: the surprising elevation of a lesser son over his older brother. These are examples of the grace of God that reaches out in sovereign selection, bringing blessing to whom he wishes to bring blessing, elevating whom he desires to elevate, for reasons of his own will. The pattern is found repeatedly in the Pentateuch and the subsequent historical narrative (Isaac over Ishmael, Jacob over Esau, Joseph over Reuben, Moses over Aaron, Saul and David over their respective brothers). It almost would seem that the standard place of ascendancy in God's program was to be the second, or the younger, son!

3 The census in this chapter is distinct from that of ch. 3. Here the census is of all males from "thirty to fifty years of age." In ch. 3 the census listed all males over the age of one month (v.15). The present chapter lists those Levites who are of the age to serve in the tabernacle. Of the 22,000 Levite males mentioned in 3:39, there are 8,580 of service age (v.48). If these numbers are to be reduced by a factor of ten (see comment on 3:39), then the corresponding numbers would be 2,200 and 858. From 8:24 we learn that the beginning age for service is twenty-five; perhaps the first five years are something of an apprenticeship.

Critical scholars seize on "contradictions" such as these as markers of confusion in the development of the putative P source. J. Alberto Soggin, for example (*Introduction to the Old Testament* [trans. John Bowden; Philadelphia: Westminster, 1976], 140), cites the contrasting ages for the Levites and differing offerings in similar texts and then concludes: "Even at the heart of P we have contradictions, duplicates and interpolations of compositions which clearly show signs of being of autonomous origin." Yet there are other ways of dealing with the difficulties of these texts.

Along with the negative conclusions these approaches bring to the text in terms of its veracity are the damaging attitudes these approaches yield with respect to the artistry and beauty of the text. When a writer begins with P and then decides that P is made of numerous conflicting elements, which now become new centers of research, the sense of the whole of the text is lost. Variety of expression is not seen as stylistic creativity but as an indication of fracture; disagreements of parallel passages are not amenable to harmonization in the whole but are necessary components of a theory of the discovery of supposed parts. The result is the loss of Scripture — the loss as the authoritative Word of God as the living sword, sharp and active, as a beautiful expression of the person of God.

4–5 The paragraphs detailing the work of the Kohathites in their care of the most holy things (v.4) come to the modern reader as truly from another time. The attention to care and detail for holy things is, lamentably, a lost art. Even though the primary care of these holy things was given to the Kohathites, they were forbidden to touch them (v.15) — or even to look on them (v.20) — lest they die. These strictures are stunning. As the holy angels who surround the throne of the Divine Presence shield their faces and feet from his presence (cf. Isa 6:1–3), so the Kohathites were to shield themselves from too familiar an approach to the holiest of things (v.5), for the most holy things symbolize the presence of the most holy God.

All the work of the Kohathites was to be supervised strictly by Aaron and his sons; only the priests themselves were able to touch and look on the unveiled holy things. We presume that even they had to be extremely careful in this regard; the memory of the story of Nadab and Abihu still rings in our ears (see 3:2–4).

Several impressions emerge from the reading of this section:

(1) *The sense of planning, order, and execution.* Nothing in the holy things of God was to be left to chance or to improvisation. None of the sacred persons who ministered in his presence was to be unprepared or untaught. All the preparation suggests a rigorous training schedule before actual work would be done by a given priest. As noted above, this call for preparation may account for the distinction of twenty-five years of age in 8:24 and thirty years in 4:3. That intervening five-year period was presumably a time of intense internship.

(2) *The sheer quantity and variety of the holy things.* At times we have an impression of a crude, primitive nature of the worship patterns of ancient Israel, especially in the earliest periods. Yet if these texts adequately reflect the times of Moses, as a natural

reading suggests, then the worship implements from the time of Moses were many and varied—and, we suspect, quite precious.

(3) *The use of color, texture, and layers.* Each of the covering curtains must have been impressive in color, texture, and design; but the variety of the coverings and their several uses speak of a legitimate enjoyment of luxury in worship and a celebration of the presence of God. The solid blue cloth, the scarlet cloth, the blue cloth, the gold altar, the bronze altar, the purple cloth, plus numerous hides, skins, and other cloths all present a wondrous delight in serving in the presence of God.

(4) *The mobility and transportability of the tabernacle.* A further impression is the sense we have that everything was movable. The tent was designed to be set up and taken down; it was a temporary abode.

(5) *The sense of hierarchy among the workers, along with an affirmation of the sense of dignity of purpose and the importance of work in one's life.* Each individual was given a task to do (see v.33). Some tasks were more elegant than others, but every task had to be done.

6–15 Translators have had difficulty in identifying the precise nature of the "hides of sea cows" (i.e., the outer covering of the ark) and some of the other items of holy furniture. The Hebrew word rendered "sea cow" (*taḥaš*) is similar to the Arabic term for the dolphin; hence, porpoise-hide or hide of sea cows seems correct.

The use of dramatic colors in the elements of holy worship in Israel has led to speculation as to the symbolic interpretation each color represents; however, the fact that colors were emphasized at all may be more significant for some modern readers, who may tend to have a dour view of worship in ancient Israel and perhaps an unimaginative appreciation of color in their own worship tradition.

The manner of the transport of the holy things was by foot, with the six packages of holy things suspended between carriers by poles (see vv.6, 8, 11, 14) or kept on a carrier frame (vv.10, 12). The sad story of Uzzah, who attempted to keep the ark of the covenant from tumbling to the earth when David was having it brought to the city of Jerusalem (2Sa 6:6–7), was an unwitting test of the profound significance of these words.

16 The special functions of the high priest are specified in this section both as delimitation and as mercy to the other sacral persons. The priest had certain duties peculiar to his office that no one else might ever do. But in God's mercy he did provide a person who could draw near to the most holy things on behalf of the people. Were the high priest unable to attend to the holy things, there could be no worship from any of the community. Hence his welfare ought to have been the concern of the people, for theirs was certainly tied to him.

17–20 The final section relating to the Kohathites in this portion concerns their ongoing service before the Lord in the context of God's people. But it also presents a significant warning: any improper approach toward, touch of, or glance at the sacred things would mean death.

As in other instances of this sort, the underlying reason on God's part may well have been mercy. It is through his mercy that God made himself known to anyone; through his continuing mercy he did not take the lives of more persons because of their wickedness; and through his condescending mercy he presented himself in their midst. The revelation of God's word brought with it demands, some of which seem harsh and difficult. But God was near. Some demands seem so judgmental; yet God has not destroyed all. Some seem to be so threatening; yet God by his mercy allowed some sense of his presence to remain known in the camp. His manifestation was based on his mercy; his strictures allowed his mercy to continue to be realized.

NOTE

16 הַמִּשְׁחָה (*hāmmišḥâ*, "the anointing oil") is a word related to the verb מָשַׁח (*māšaḥ*, "to smear, anoint"); see the similar word מָשְׁחָה (*mošḥâ*, "consecrated portion") in 18:8 (see Note).

(ii) The family of Gershon (4:21–28)

²¹The Lᴏʀᴅ said to Moses, ²²"Take a census also of the Gershonites by their families and clans. ²³Count all the men from thirty to fifty years of age who come to serve in the work at the Tent of Meeting.

²⁴"This is the service of the Gershonite clans as they work and carry burdens: ²⁵They are to carry the curtains of the tabernacle, the Tent of Meeting, its covering and the outer covering of hides of sea cows, the curtains for the entrance to the Tent of Meeting, ²⁶the curtains of the courtyard surrounding the tabernacle and altar, the curtain for the entrance, the ropes and all the equipment used in its service. The Gershonites are to do all that needs to be done with these things. ²⁷All their service, whether carrying or doing other work, is to be done under the direction of Aaron and his sons. You shall assign to them as their responsibility all they are to carry. ²⁸This is the service of the Gershonite clans at the Tent of Meeting. Their duties are to be under the direction of Ithamar son of Aaron, the priest.

COMMENTARY

21–28 What we term "typical Hebrew stylistics" are displayed in this chapter, with its repetition and restatement—the very literary devices that classical criticism has taken in a wrong-headed direction. Repetition and restatement in the prose sections of the Bible may have a similar effect on the reader as the use of parallelism in the poetic portions. We are in an alien aesthetic when we come to passages such as this. Before arrogantly dismissing them, we should learn to understand their underlying values. Then we will be better able to appreciate these values.

The Gershonites cared for the outer curtains and hides of the tabernacle. They and the Merarites were permitted to touch the things they were responsible for; the men of Kohath were not to touch or even look at the things of the Most Holy Place. But the Gershonites and the Merarites were not to do their work alone. Even with them Aaron was to be the chief responsible agent, but he was able to delegate some of that responsibility to his son Ithamar (v.28).

(iii) The family of Merari (4:29–33)

²⁹"Count the Merarites by their clans and families. ³⁰Count all the men from thirty to fifty years of age who come to serve in the work at the Tent of Meeting. ³¹This is their duty

as they perform service at the Tent of Meeting: to carry the frames of the tabernacle, its crossbars, posts and bases, [32]as well as the posts of the surrounding courtyard with their bases, tent pegs, ropes, all their equipment and everything related to their use. Assign to each man the specific things he is to carry. [33]This is the service of the Merarite clans as they work at the Tent of Meeting under the direction of Ithamar son of Aaron, the priest."

COMMENTARY

29-33 Similar phrasing to the two other family units graces this section, with instructions that the family of Merari was to have their principal work with the frames, crossbars, posts, bases, pegs, ropes, and other equipment. Their work was as important as that of any other family group; for without it the more desirable, prestigious work of the tabernacle could not have been done. Hence the Merarites could take an interest even in the placing of a post, a peg, or a rope, not because each of these items is a distinct, suitable "type of Christ," but because the worship of God could not proceed—nor could the camp move out—unless these people were doing their holy work.

(b) A description of the census (4:34-45)

[34]Moses, Aaron and the leaders of the community counted the Kohathites by their clans and families. [35]All the men from thirty to fifty years of age who came to serve in the work in the Tent of Meeting, [36]counted by clans, were 2,750. [37]This was the total of all those in the Kohathite clans who served in the Tent of Meeting. Moses and Aaron counted them according to the LORD's command through Moses.

[38]The Gershonites were counted by their clans and families. [39]All the men from thirty to fifty years of age who came to serve in the work at the Tent of Meeting, [40]counted by their clans and families, were 2,630. [41]This was the total of those in the Gershonite clans who served at the Tent of Meeting. Moses and Aaron counted them according to the LORD's command.

[42]The Merarites were counted by their clans and families. [43]All the men from thirty to fifty years of age who came to serve in the work at the Tent of Meeting, [44]counted by their clans, were 3,200. [45]This was the total of those in the Merarite clans. Moses and Aaron counted them according to the LORD's command through Moses.

COMMENTARY

34-45 The most notable thing in the census of the Levitical families in this section is the use of numbers. The numbers still appear to be rounded; but since the numbers are smaller than the numbers in ch. 1, the rounding is done to the tens: 2,750 from Kohath, 2,630 from Gershon, and 3,200 from Merari.

(c) A summary of the census and the work of Moses in the census (4:46–49)

⁴⁶So Moses, Aaron and the leaders of Israel counted all the Levites by their clans and families. ⁴⁷All the men from thirty to fifty years of age who came to do the work of serving and carrying the Tent of Meeting ⁴⁸numbered 8,580. ⁴⁹At the LORD's command through Moses, each was assigned his work and told what to carry.
Thus they were counted, as the LORD commanded Moses.

COMMENTARY

46–49 Here we find the seemingly routine use of a summary text in which notice is given of compliance on the part of the leaders. Further, the total number of the men from the three Levitical families from the age of thirty to fifty who worked in and about the Tent of Meeting was 8,580. The addition of the three addends could be displayed as follows: 2,750 + 2,630 + 3,200 = 8,580—the total number of Levites who were mustered for the service of God in the Tent of Meeting. Again, if the theory of a tenfold inflation of these figures is presumed, then the

numbers may be reduced to 275 + 263 + 320 = 858. In either case, the addition is the same.

These summary texts give a sense of completion to the unit. Hebrew style seems to allow the reader to enjoy a sense of "going full circle." When the summary of actions of obedience is given as here, there is a sense in which the reader may derive satisfaction. When there is no summary, no record of final action, then questions arise: What is the point? Where is the obedience? What is the basic meaning?

b. Diverse Commands and Rituals in Preparation for the Triumphal March (5:1–10:10)

i. The test for purity and the law of jealousy (5:1–31)

OVERVIEW

The ordering, numbering, and structuring of the camp was completed at the end of ch. 4. Men of military age have been mustered for service (ch. 1); the secular tribes have been arranged around the central shrine (ch. 2); the Levites have been numbered, arranged around the inner core of the shrine (ch. 3) and given their appropriate duties in the management of the holy things

(ch. 4). The next six and one half chapters present various commands for ritual purity within the camp—all necessary to the final preparations for the movement of the people through the wilderness and their journey on to their new home in the land of Canaan. This new stage—the setting forth of the holy people on their triumphal march—begins in 10:11.

The information in ch. 5 is especially interesting and is marked by symmetry of the chapter and its elements. There are three issues in this chapter: (1) a command of the Lord for expelling from the camp those who are ritually defiled (vv.1–4); (2) a command of the Lord for restitution for offenses against another person within the camp (vv.5–10); and (3) a command of the Lord for a ritual procedure in cases of marital jealousy (vv.11–31). Each section begins in precisely the same way and develops in a similar manner (though of uneven length): (1) an introductory monocolon with the command of the Lord to Moses (see vv.1, 5, 11); (2) a subordinate command for Moses to speak the command to the people (see vv.2a, 6a, 12a); (3) the substance of the command and its application in the life of the people (see vv.2b–3, 6b–8, 12b–28); (4) a concluding section on the command (see vv.4, 10, 29–31).

The introductory commands of the Lord to Moses (vv.1, 5, 11) are not to be read merely as stylistic devices to introduce a new subject, though this is one function of this phrasing. Reverent readers find in the wording, "And the LORD spoke to Moses, saying …," a recurring emphasis on the divine origin of these texts and a repeated emphasis that Yahweh has taken the initiative in communicating his word to his people through his servant Moses. There are some passages and narratives that were provoked by the inquiry of the people, and the response of the Lord is forthcoming (see, e.g., the story of the daughters of Zelophehad, ch. 27). But the customary pattern in Torah is the initiation of God in his gracious self-disclosure and in the presentation of his will for the good of his people.

Further, the subordinate commands for Moses to relate the word of the Lord to the people (vv.2a, 6a, 12a) present three aspects of the divine communication: (1) Moses is the prophet of Yahweh, the great *nābîʾ*—one who was called by God and who spoke for him; (2) the commands of God were to be disseminated throughout the community, not reserved for Moses or some elite few in an inner circle; and (3) the words of God were to be presented to the people as authoritative commands, not just as divine suggestions ("command the Israelites," v.2a; "speak to the Israelites," v.6a; "speak to the Israelites and say to them," v.12a).

(a) The expulsion of the impure from the camp (5:1–4)

¹The LORD said to Moses, ²"Command the Israelites to send away from the camp anyone who has an infectious skin disease or a discharge of any kind, or who is ceremonially unclean because of a dead body. ³Send away male and female alike; send them outside the camp so they will not defile their camp, where I dwell among them." ⁴The Israelites did this; they sent them outside the camp. They did just as the LORD had instructed Moses.

COMMENTARY

1–2 In biblical times, skin diseases, especially open sores, were among the three prominent factors (along with oozing discharges and contact with dead bodies) that rendered a person unclean. Such persons were regarded as unfit to be in the community and were potential contaminants of the tabernacle and the pure worship of the Lord. They were to be excluded from the community during the period of their malady. This brief paragraph uses the verb *šalaḥ* ("to send away, expel") no fewer than four times in vv.1–4. The emphasis on this strong verb points to the seriousness of the situation: such people must be expelled.

The OT concept of "uncleanness" is hard for the modern, Western reader to understand. We may think of the idea of "unclean" as meaning "dirty" or "soiled." In Scripture, the idea of "unclean" has more to do with being "unfit, unsuitable"—unfit in the realm of the purity of the rule of God. Aspects of uncleanness were not left in the arena of the abstract or theoretical; the focus was on tangible issues such as clearly evident skin diseases. It is implied that the priests were the agents for dismissing the unclean from the congregation—and agents for readmitting the cleansed.

The Hebrew word for "skin disease" (*ṣārûaʿ*, Qal passive participle from *ṣāraʿ*; GK 7665; v.2) has traditionally been translated "leper, one struck with leprosy." A view commonly held today is that this word was not used in the Bible to describe what we know as leprosy, usually termed "Hansen's disease" (but see Note). John Wilkinson has described the biblical data in clinical terms ("Leprosy and Leviticus: The Problem of Description and Identification," *SJT* 30 [1984]: 153–69). The verb *ṣāraʿ* and the corresponding noun *ṣāraʿat* (used esp. in Lev 13) do not seem to describe one specific disease but a number of complex disorders of the skin, including swellings, eruptions, spots, and itches (see Lev 13:2). These disorders are further described in terms of five secondary features: change of skin color, change of hair color, infiltration of the skin, extension or spread in the skin, and ulceration of the skin.

Some modern interpreters have attempted to give precise identifications of these various diseases. E. V. Hulse ("The Nature of Biblical 'Leprosy' and

the Use of Alternative Medical Terms in Modern Translations of the Bible," *PEQ* 107 [1975]: 87–105) suggests that some of the diseases indicated in Leviticus 13 and Numbers 5 include psoriasis, favus, leucoderma, and various types of eczema. While Hulse is likely correct in his general lines of identification, the issue of these texts does not appear to be the precise diagnosis of disease so much as the observation of certain symptoms of disease.

Wilkinson suggests that the priests of the period were not required to identify a specific disease, only a manifestation of a serious disorder. Leviticus 13 gives a diagnostic flow chart in which certain physical manifestations, not the underlying disease, were signs for the priests to rule as to whether or not a person was ritually unclean and hence not permitted to remain in the camp of Israel during the period of skin inflammation. The issue in skin disease was similar to that of the identification of animals that were clean or unclean according to the dietary laws of Israel (see Lev 11). Again, the principal issue in that chapter is not the precise identification of genus and phylum but, with reference to the animals, an observation of digestive habits and an examination of the hoof.

Even the NIV's translation in these passages—"an infectious skin disease"—may be too specific. It is not clearly indicated that the offending skin disease was infectious, for some of the diseases that might cause the disorders described in Leviticus 13 (e.g., psoriasis) are not infectious. A preferable, nonspecific translation of the noun *ṣāraʿat* and the passive forms of the verb *ṣāraʿ* is "[to suffer] a serious skin disorder." Incidentally, the broad range of meaning for the Hebrew term translated "a serious skin disorder" may carry over into the NT (Greek) words as well. "Leprosy" appears to be too specific a translation in either testament and has been misleading for many readers and unfortunate for many who suffer from Hansen's disease today (but see

Notes). We may also observe that this text presents the basis in the book of Numbers for an application in the life of Miriam (see ch. 12).

The second issue rendering a person ritually unclean in v.2 is a discharge of any kind (see Lev 15:2). The Hebrew term *zāb* (GK 2307) is used in four ways in Scripture: (1) of the flowing of water from the rock (Ps 78:20); (2) of the land flowing with milk and honey (Ex 3:8); (3) of one pining away from hunger (La 4:9); and (4) of an uncontrolled discharge of fluid from a man (Lev 15:2) or a woman (v.25). These discharges were primarily from the sexual organs and were chronic in nature. Again, these matters were tangible. The people who suffered from these maladies became living object lessons to the whole camp of the necessity for all people to be "clean" in their approach to God.

In ancient Israel, the third factor rendering a person unclean, and hence to be excluded from the camp, was contact with a dead body. The ultimate, tangible sign of uncleanness was the corpse. Processes of decay and disease in dead flesh were evident to all. Physical contact with a corpse was a sure mark of uncleanness (and possibly a source of [infection, though such would not have been known by the people of the time)]; normal contacts with others in the community of those who had become unclean would have to be curtailed until proper cleansing had been made (see comment on 6:6).

3 The modern reader should be impressed with the fact that the various disorders that rendered one unclean—and hence to be expelled from the camp—affected male and female alike. The concepts of clean and unclean cut across gender lines. Women were excluded along with men, and women might be released from exclusion along with men.

The essential issue in all laws of purity in Israel was not magic or health or superstition; the great reality was the presence of Yahweh in the camp—there can be no uncleanness where he dwells. The last words of v.3 are dramatic in their presentation: "I am dwelling in their midst" (see Notes).

4 Verse 4 presents the full compliance of Israel to this law when it was initiated. As in 1:54; 2:34; 3:16, 42, 51; 4:49, this section ends with a report of the obedience of the people and of Moses to the commands of God. It is with sadness we will recall these reports at later times in Israel's experience, when she learned the pattern of failure to obey the Lord's commands.

NOTES

2 צָרוּעַ (*ṣārûaʿ*, a Qal passive participle of the denominative verb צָרַע [*ṣāraʿ*], "to be struck with leprosy, be leprous"; used as a substantive, "one struck with leprosy, a leper"; GK 7665) and צָרַעַת (*ṣāraʿat*, "leprosy") are generally regarded today as generic terms for skin disease, not terms specifically to be identified with leprosy (Hansen's disease). However, R. K. Harrison focused specially on medical issues in his studies of OT issues. He believed that leprosy *is* indicated by these terms. He writes (101):

> According to epidemiological and other studies, there is little doubt that Hansen's disease, caused by the tiny organism *Mycobacterium leprae*, was known and feared in Palestine by at least the time of Amos (ca. 760 BC). The dread disease may be the one referred to in a cuneiform tablet from the Old Babylonian period (ca. 2250–1175 BC), but this cannot be demonstrated with certainty. If the *ukhedu* disease of the Ebers medical papyrus from ancient Egypt (ca. 2300 BC) was a form of clinical leprosy, which is certainly possible, then the disease would be well known in Egypt by 1500 BC.

Despite claims by some modern doctors and theological writers that the *ṣāraʿat* of Leviticus 13 in its malignant form could not possibly have been Hansen's disease, there are in fact striking correspondences between it and the malignant form of *ṣāraʿat* described in Leviticus. Those who deny such an identification have failed to suggest a plausible clinical alternative.

See also Harrison's work on this term in the following sources: "Leprosy," *ISBE*[2], 3:103–6; "Leprosy," *IDB*, 3:111–13; "Leprosy," *NIDNTT*, 2:463–66.

Allen P. Ross argues that there are more serious biblical issues than the exact taxonomy of the disease(s) indicated by the Hebrew word: "Any exposition must begin with the intended meaning of the passage in its context. In this case the expositor must look at these diseases as part of the contamination of a fallen world" (*Holiness to the LORD: A Guide to the Exposition of the Book of Leviticus* [Grand Rapids: Baker, 2002], 278).

3 אֲנִי שֹׁכֵן בְּתוֹכָם (*ʾanî šōkēn bᵉtôkām*, "I am dwelling in their midst") marks the loveliest of ideas — the fact that the living God condescended to make his presence known in the midst of his people. The verb שָׁכַן (*šākan*, "to settle down, abide"; GK 8905) is here a participle describing an ongoing, gracious action of Yahweh. This verb is particularly associated with its nominal complement, מִשְׁכָּן (*miškān*, "dwelling place, tabernacle"), as God's presence was "centered" in the great tent, particularly in and over the Most Holy Place. See especially Exodus 40:34–35, which exults: the "glory of the LORD filled the tabernacle [הַמִּשְׁכָּן, *hammiškān*)] ... the cloud had settled [שָׁכַן, *šākan*)] upon it." These words would give rise to the term "Shekinah," the idea of God's abiding presence among his people. See also Numbers 9:15–23.

It is a fascinating congruence that the NT (Greek) term in John 1:14 that describes the dwelling of Christ amid his people (σκηνόω, *skēnoō*, "to dwell"; GK *5012*) has the same consonants (*s-k-n*) as the Hebrew verb שָׁכַן (*šākan*). This Greek verb is also used of the future dwelling of God with people (see Rev 21:3) — a gracious action that harks back to the tabernacle and then goes so far beyond that historic experience of Israel in the wilderness. See Ronald B. Allen, "Affirming Right-of-Way on Ancient Paths," *BSac* 153 (January–March 1996): 3–11.

4 In his healing ministries, Jesus reached out to meet the physical needs of all manner of people, "healing every disease and sickness among the people" (Mt 4:23), including the types of maladies described in this passage. He healed lepers (Mk 1:40–43) and a woman with a discharge (Mk 5:25–34), and he reached out to, touched, and raised (!) the dead (Mk 5:35–43; Lk 7:11–17). He healed women as well as men, the poor and the broken, thus fulfilling the prophecy of Messiah promised by Isaiah 61:1–2a (see Lk 4:16–20).

REFLECTION

When we think through the issues of vv. 1–4, we discover mercy. We may observe, in view of the dramatic phrase, "I am dwelling in their midst," that the essential reason for the importance of "uncleanness" in the camp was the indwelling presence of the Lord. His commands that the unclean be expelled from the camp were, essentially, expressions of his mercy: (1) the polluting presence of the unclean may make others unclean, thus spreading the problem; (2) the continuing presence of the unclean within the camp may demand God's judgment; and (3) the pervasive spread of uncleanness in the camp may demand that the Lord withdraw his own presence. It was Yahweh's lavish mercy that allowed him to abide with his people at all; it was his continuing desire to express that mercy that prompted the expulsion of the unclean from the camp.

For these reasons Christians are impressed with the fact that the Lord Jesus extended the mercy of God dramatically, in that he reached out to meet the needs of persons who had become unclean from each of the three stipulations of this text (see Note on v.4). Furthermore, following the wording of v.3, "male and female alike," we see that Jesus in his ministry reached out both to women and to men who were ritually unclean. In these deeds of mercy, the Lord acted as healer and as priest; he cleansed their diseases and then declared them pure.

(b) Restitution for personal wrongs (5:5–10)

OVERVIEW

Another issue that led to impurity in the camp was an unresolved personal injury. This type of evil would have been harder to diagnose than the mysterious skin disorders or fluid discharges of the earlier section. While the skin disorders and contact with dead bodies might lead to exclusion from the ritual of the worship of God in the community, social disorders would equally disrupt the cohesion of the people. These are examples of the OT concept sometimes described as "corporate solidarity" (see, e.g., the story of the sin of Achan in Jos 7). The health and effectiveness of the whole community depended on the health and effectiveness of the individuals within the community. There was an inner flow of continuity between the concepts of the community and the individual in these texts.

> [5]The LORD said to Moses, [6]"Say to the Israelites: 'When a man or woman wrongs another in any way and so is unfaithful to the LORD, that person is guilty [7]and must confess the sin he has committed. He must make full restitution for his wrong, add one fifth to it and give it all to the person he has wronged. [8]But if that person has no close relative to whom restitution can be made for the wrong, the restitution belongs to the LORD and must be given to the priest, along with the ram with which atonement is made for him. [9]All the sacred contributions the Israelites bring to a priest will belong to him. [10]Each man's sacred gifts are his own, but what he gives to the priest will belong to the priest.'"

COMMENTARY

5–7 In this situation one person within the camp has wronged another. The connection of vv.5–10 (personal wrongs) to the first paragraph (ritual uncleanness) may be one of moving from the outward and visible to the inward and more secret faults that would mar the purity of the community. Those with evident marks of uncleanness were to be expelled for the duration of their malady. But more insidious were those people who had overtly sinned against others in the community and who thought they might continue to function as though there were no real wrong.

A casual reader of the English versions may notice the consistent use of masculine pronouns and assume that this is yet another text dealing with the religious and moral obligations of the male believer under the provisions of Torah. Yet the section clearly begins with the words, "when a man or a *woman*" (ʾîš ʾô-ʾiššâ, emphasis added; v.6; see also at 6:2). The point is that the worship of God was for women and for men. The obligations of repentance were for men and for women. Women are also sinners. Women are also significant. It is important that the woman reader see herself in these words just as the male reader does.

The particulars of the text demanded a procedure for restitution in the case of unspecified personal wrongs. Of first importance was the recognition that such wrongs were not slight offenses between people only; in fact, they were acts of treachery against Yahweh, the Great Suzerain. The expression "and so is unfaithful to the LORD" may be more strongly rendered, "to commit a serious act of treachery against Yahweh." As David was later to confess, his principal sin was not against Uriah or Bathsheba or his family or his nation—though he had sinned against them all. He said, "I have sinned against the LORD" (2Sa 12:13; Ps 51:4 [6 Heb]).

The steps in the ritual for restitution included (1) a condition of guilt—the person was guilty (v.6), and this guilt excluded that person from active participation in the community as surely as a serious skin disease or contact with a dead body did; (2) a public confession of that sin (v.7a)—presumably in the precincts of the sacred shrine, before witnesses and priests; (3) full restitution plus one fifth to the one wronged (see Lev 22:14; 27:11–13, 31); (4) a sacrifice to the Lord of a ram as an offering for atonement.

8 Each of these steps is enumerated in Leviticus 6:1–7 in the initial presentation of the law of defrauding. However, Numbers 5 has an additional provision. What if a person had defrauded someone but that person was no longer living and had no living relative to whom restitution might be paid? Verse 8 adds the next proviso: (5) the payment of restitution was to be made to the priest when there was no suitable relative to whom such payment might otherwise be made. In this way the debt was paid fully, no matter who of the injured family had survived. The term for "close relative" is gōʾēl, often translated "kinsman-redeemer" (e.g., Ru 4:3; see Note).

9–10 Finally, a note is added that the offerings presented to the priests truly belonged to the priests. It was not a sham that was then withdrawn secretly after a public presentation.

Again, the intent of this law on defrauding is clear in the context of this chapter: purity among the people was essential for their successful journey through the wilderness and their eventual triumph over the inhabitants of the land. Just as the physically impure needed to be expelled from the camp, so those attitudes and jealousies one might have against another of a petty or serious nature also needed to be dealt with equitably for the camp to remain pure.

NOTE

8 גֹּאֵל (gōʾēl, "close relative"; GK 1457) is a word especially significant in the book of Ruth. It was the duty of the male relative of a deceased person who left a childless widow to redeem her from childlessness through marriage; such a one was called "redeemer" (from גָּאַל, gāʾal, "to redeem"; *HALOT*, 1:169). In an unpublished paper, Donald A. Glenn of Dallas Theological Seminary argued that the fundamental meaning of the term גֹּאֵל (gōʾēl) is "protector of family rights." This meaning is especially fitting in Numbers 5:8, a situation describing the one "who receives restitution for a wrong" (*HALOT*, 1:169).

(c) The law of jealousy (5:11–31)

OVERVIEW

Yet another element that would lead to impurity within the camp was undetected marital infidelity. The law concerning jealousy is best read in the context and flow of the two earlier laws in this chapter. As a diseased person who was ritually unclean would compromise the entire camp and so had to be expelled during the time of his or her disease (5:1–4), and as an unrequited wrong would bring trouble between people who were within the camp as surely as would be brought by one with disease of the skin (5:5–10), so the unexposed but treacherous act of marital infidelity also would bring harm to the camp as a whole. Acts of marital infidelity were not regarded as peccadilloes in Israel; to be unfaithful to one's spouse was to be unfaithful to one's God. The following text has its harsh side; there is also mercy in it, as we will discover.

(i) The seed of jealousy (5:11–15)

¹¹Then the LORD said to Moses, ¹²"Speak to the Israelites and say to them: 'If a man's wife goes astray and is unfaithful to him ¹³by sleeping with another man, and this is hidden from her husband and her impurity is undetected (since there is no witness against her and she has not been caught in the act), ¹⁴and if feelings of jealousy come over her husband and he suspects his wife and she is impure — or if he is jealous and suspects her even though she is not impure — ¹⁵then he is to take his wife to the priest. He must also take an offering of a tenth of an ephah of barley flour on her behalf. He must not pour oil on it or put incense on it, because it is a grain offering for jealousy, a reminder offering to draw attention to guilt.

COMMENTARY

11–13 Again, the connection with the preceding two paragraphs seems to be a progression from the more open and obvious to the more personal and hidden sins. Issues of purity were established with the physical marks (vv.1–4), expanded to interpersonal relationships (vv.5–10), and then extended into the most intimate of relationships, that of the marriage bed of a man and woman (vv.11–31). A test for marital fidelity was far harder to prove than a test for a skin disorder; hence the larger part of the chapter is given over to this most sensitive of issues.

The provisions of this law have connections (and discontinuities) with other laws in the ancient Near East. The Code of Hammurabi (ca. 1727 BC) has a pair of laws that we may compare with our text (*ANET*, 171):

CH 131: If a seignior's wife was accused by her husband, but she was not caught while lying with another man, she shall make affirmation by god and return to her house.

CH 132: If the finger was pointed at the wife of a seignior because of another man, but she has not been caught while lying with the other man, she shall throw herself into the river for the sake of her husband.

These laws from ancient Babylon deal with two types of accusation. The second law suggests community knowledge of infidelity, but the woman had not been caught "in the act." The presumed unfaithful woman was to undergo the ordeal of trial by death by flinging herself into the "sacred" Euphrates River. If she were guilty, it was presumed she would drown; if innocent, she would survive the ordeal and would be able to return to her husband with no attachment of guilt (see G. R. Driver and John C. Miles, *The Babylonian Laws* [Oxford: Clarendon, 1952], 2:283–84). The first law is closer to the biblical example in Numbers 5:11–31. In this case the husband had only a private suspicion of his wife's infidelity. She was to present herself in a temple for a solemn oath and might then return to her home.

This text has an implied possibility of failure to affirm (or survive the false affirmation of) this oath. The Akkadian text does not say how that failure might be recognized, but the parallel Hebrew text suggests one possibility. We may find in this type of law both an affirmation of the importance of marital fidelity in the ancient world — even in Babylon! — as well as a measure of protection for a woman under false accusation. Without limiting

legislation such as this, presumably the husband might have done her physical harm — or even killed her — on the sole basis of private feelings of jealousy, real or imagined. A function of law in the ancient Near East was to limit private acts of vengeance and retribution while maintaining propriety and civil order. The fascinating aspect of comparing this text from the Code of Hammurabi with Numbers 5 lies in the paucity of information concerning the oath ceremony in the Babylonian temple compared to the unusual richness of the text in Scripture.

14–15 The husband's "feelings of jealousy" (v.14) may have been provoked on the basis of good cause and the issue needed to be faced; the concern was not just for the bruised feelings of the husband but was ultimately based on the reality of God's dwelling among his people (v.3). Yet the chapter has a strong and serious thrust to it that is designed to prevent a childish, self-centered charge of unfaithfulness. As in Babylonian law, this text was not to be used as a pretext by a capricious, petty, or malevolent husband to badger a good woman. Everything about the text speaks of seriousness, intention, and the presence of the Lord in the process.

The use of the word "impure" (*niṭmāʾâ*, a third feminine singular Niphal perfect from *ṭāmēʾ*, "to be, become unclean"; v.14) shows the subject matter of this chapter is of a piece — the purity of the camp of the people whom God indwells is the burden of the text. Further, the religious nature of the text is seen in the presentation of the woman under accusation to the priest (v.15). The actions presented in this chapter seem to be severe and harsh. Perhaps we should imagine the consequences on a woman justly or falsely charged with adultery by an angry husband in a context in which there was no provision for her guilt or innocence to be demonstrated. That she was taken to the priest is finally to be seen as an act of mercy.

This chapter provides abundant insight into the role of ritual in ancient Near Eastern thinking, practices remote to the Western reader but more common among certain Eastern and (especially) African peoples. The text is of special interest to those who search for what they believe to be remnants of primitive rites within the books of Moses. Each element of the ritual is charged with meaning, though we may not understand all the meaning today. Yet we need to take our lead from the text, not from supposed African or even ancient Near Eastern parallels. This passage is not an ordeal of death; the Hebrew woman did not cast herself into the sacred river or drink a magic potion. She presented herself before the Lord and his priest for vindication or condemnation; the results would be seen in the future in her own body (see below).

The gravity of the ritual for a suspected unfaithful wife shows that Torah regards marital infidelity most seriously. Such was not just a concern of a jealous husband; the entire community was affected by this breach of faith. Hence the judgment was in the context of the community. Our contemporary attitudes that suggest sexual infidelity is a minor, personal matter are far removed from the teaching of Scripture.

This celebrated text is subject to much discussion during these days in which the issues of women and men continue to be debated within the circle of faith. With respect to women, this text may be viewed constructively and sympathetically or negatively and angrily. The negative, angry approach tends to focus on the obvious inequities inherent in the situation. The husband of a woman might shame her publicly and force her to a rigorous, demeaning religious trial merely on the (unfounded) suspicion of a misdeed on her part, that of marital faithlessness. She may have presented no evidence whatsoever; merely the thought on the part of the husband was sufficient

to bring her to trial. Further, there is no mention whatsoever of the guilt, trial, and judgment of the man with whom this woman is supposed to have been involved—all the weight of guilt, shame, trial, and judgment rested on the shoulders of the woman under accusation. Again, the accusation was by her husband, a presentation suggestive of intense marital discord.

There is, however, another manner of approach to this and similar passages. The alternative approach, as noted even with reference to the Babylonian law, is to suggest the passage actually presents a timely limitation on an angry, suspicious husband—a protection of the wife from his abusive hand. Were there not such a provision as in this text in a male-dominated culture, we may suppose that an angry, suspicious husband might have lashed out against his wife without any sure reason for his angry suspicions, harmed her physically and mentally, and even taken her life. Certainly there have been men throughout history who have behaved in just this manner. But God reaches out through Moses and the gift of the Torah—and with the precedent of ancient Near Eastern law!—and provided a means of escape for a woman under suspicion of unfaithfulness by a jealous husband. The trial she was taken to was not a kangaroo court; it was in the precincts of the tabernacle, under the jurisdiction of the priests, in concert with a solemn sacrifice—she placed herself under the hand of Yahweh. (This entire picture assumes that the principals in the tabernacle [and later the temple] were godly people who gladly followed Torah. In much of Israel's history, these ideals were rarely realized.)

The woman who had been brought to such a place would not take this issue lightly. Public humiliation, shame, anger at her spouse, and exposure before priests and people were all terrifying prospects. But then neither would her husband take these issues lightly. For he was not just spreading rumors or digging at his wife in the privacy of their home; he, too, was coming before Yahweh, and he, too, might be judged. Hence the better approach to this text is not to think along the lines of primitive magic or of rampant male dominance. It is rather another expression of God's mercy toward women, so often abused by prideful men, particularly in antiquity. Here was a means of escape from suspicion and evasion of punishment.

If the woman was indeed guilty of unfaithfulness, the husband was vindicated. His vindication was important—not just to relieve the pique he might be feeling, but for the sense of the ongoing stability of the family. If a woman was unfaithful to her husband, she might be carrying the child of another man; and the rights of inheritance in a tribe/clan/family setting might become hopelessly enmeshed in the complexities of family relationships that are common in modern society (and soap operas) but unusual in earlier days.

But if the woman was indeed innocent, her husband would have his reasons for jealousy alleviated. Again, this is a limitation on his jealous nature. Most men, we suspect, would be very careful before pressing the issue. The results could be disastrous for themselves.

NOTE

14–15 The idea that these laws in Torah are ameliorative in the larger social and cultural setting of the ancient Near East is also presented by William J. Webb, *Slaves, Women & Homosexuals: Exploring the Hermeneutics of Cultural Analysis* (Downers Grove, Ill.: InterVarsity, 2001). He writes (79), "Neither in Israel nor in other ancient Near Eastern countries was there a reciprocal ordeal for the wife to impose upon the husband suspected of adultery. Thus a clear gender inequality existed in Israel and its broader environment. However, the fact that Israel had the more civil and less-easily-abused approach to the matter yields a sense of quiet reduction in patriarchal powers compared to its foreign context. The suspected adulteress is simply turned over to Yahweh in an oath and temple ritual."

(ii) The curse of the oath (5:16–22)

[16]"The priest shall bring her and have her stand before the Lord. [17]Then he shall take some holy water in a clay jar and put some dust from the tabernacle floor into the water. [18]After the priest has had the woman stand before the Lord, he shall loosen her hair and place in her hands the reminder offering, the grain offering for jealousy, while he himself holds the bitter water that brings a curse. [19]Then the priest shall put the woman under oath and say to her, "If no other man has slept with you and you have not gone astray and become impure while married to your husband, may this bitter water that brings a curse not harm you. [20]But if you have gone astray while married to your husband and you have defiled yourself by sleeping with a man other than your husband"— [21]here the priest is to

put the woman under this curse of the oath —"may the LORD cause your people to curse and denounce you when he causes your thigh to waste away and your abdomen to swell. ²²May this water that brings a curse enter your body so that your abdomen swells and your thigh wastes away.'"

"'Then the woman is to say, "Amen. So be it."

COMMENTARY

16 The central phrasing of this text is that the priest would have the woman stand before the Lord. The repetition in v.18 is for emphasis. These phrases demand that we distance ourselves from the approach of some interpreters who suggest that this passage is merely an adventure in magic and potions or psychology and manipulation. The biblical phrasing demands a theological understanding of the woman's judgment. Further, that she is brought before the Lord helps again to demonstrate the concept of purity and the proper connection of this law with the two earlier laws of the chapter.

17–18 Admittedly, the wording of v.17 (cf. v.23) seems like what we might imagine a magical rite to be. Taking holy water, adding dust, and mixing a doubtful drink seems to be worlds away from things we understand. Many interpreters assume that adding the dust from the floor to the holy water is what made that water "bitter" (v.18). Yet that assumption is unlikely. A small amount of soil from the floor of the tabernacle was not likely to make the water taste "bitter." Rather, we should concentrate on the holiness of the place; hence we think of the extension of holiness to the very ground on which the tabernacle was placed. Holy dust was added to holy water not to change the taste but to emphasize the holiness of the matter.

In v.18 the woman was made to loosen her hair. This act may be a sign of openness on her part. In the solemn place in which she found herself, with holy priests and holy drinks, the tendency for this woman might be to shrink away, to cover herself with her garments. She was not to do so, however. She was to be presented in a manner of openness before Yahweh. This loosening of the hair would be for the guilty woman an expectation of judgment and mourning (see Lev 13:45; 21:10). For the innocent wife, who had nothing to fear but the demonstration of the glory of the Lord, the loosening of her hair might be a strengthening act of feminine personhood in the Holy Place.

The terminology of bitter water's bringing a curse is problematic. The Hebrew phrase (see Note) could also be translated, "the curse-bringing water of bitterness." It is not that the water was bitter tasting but that this water had the potential of bearing with it a bitter curse. That this potion was neither simply a tool of magic nor merely a psychological device to determine stress is to be seen in the repeated emphasis on the role of the Lord in the proceedings (vv.16, 18, 21, 25). That is, the verdict of the woman was precipitated by her physiological and psychological responses to the bitter water, but the judgment was from the Lord. The bitterness of the water was potential, not actual; the cursing associated with the water was also potential, not essential. The water was holy, set apart for specific function in the worship of God. But it was not necessarily of a bad taste. Again, the phrase may be rendered in a somewhat expansive manner: "the water that may result in bitterness and provoke a profound curse."

19–20 The priest presents two possibilities. First, the woman might be truly innocent (v.19). In this case his specific prayer to the Lord was that the water with the potential of bitterness not bring harm to her. The priest's words to the innocent woman assured her of no harm from the bitter water. Second, if she were truly guilty of the deed that her husband suspected (v.20), then the full onus of the curse-bearing waters would come to her, enter her body, descend through her intestines, and be the physical means the Lord would use to produce a physical change in her body.

21–22 Verse 21 describes the physical change: "your thigh to waste away and your abdomen to swell." The NIV's margin has "causes you to have a miscarrying womb and barrenness." The figurative language here (and in vv.22, 27) speaks of the woman's loss of capacity for childbearing (and, if pregnant at the time of her judgment, her miscarriage of the child). This meaning becomes clear in the opposite case (v.28), in the determination of the fate of a woman wrongly charged: "she will be cleared of guilt and will be able to have children." For a woman in the ancient Near East to be denied the ability to bear children was a personal loss of inestimable proportion. In that culture, it was in bearing children that a woman's significance was realized. Barrenness was a grievous punishment indeed!

We reject, then, those interpretations that suggest the woman who was guilty would drop dead following her drinking of the potion. Rather, like the woman in the Babylonian text, she might return to her home to await the outcome of the oath. If she were innocent of infidelity, she should count on bearing children. This means, of course, that she would return to her husband's embrace. If she were guilty of infidelity but not caught in the act, she would suffer debilitating physical symptoms that would prohibit successful pregnancies. Again, this development also presumes that she returned to the embrace of her husband. She would then bear her guilt in her body and the inner chambers of her heart. In either case the woman was to hear the words of the curse, in the midst of the solemn precincts, and then bring that potential curse on herself by saying to the Lord and his priest, "Amen. So be it" (v.22). The double "Amen" (lit. Heb.) would be her signal that she understood the issues and was in agreement with the judgment — or would escape from judgment — that would come into her body.

NOTE

18 מֵי הַמָּרִים הַמְאָרֲרִים (*mê hammārîm hamʾārᵃrîm*, "the bitter, curse-bringing waters") forms a strong, ominous phrase. The verbal form is אָרַר (*ʾārar*, "to curse," here a Piel masculine plural participle; GK 826), used as descriptive of the "bitter waters." The Piel of this verb means "to produce a curse on." Compare the expressions in 8:7, מֵי חַטָּאת (*mê ḥaṭṭāʾt*, lit., "water of sin," meaning, "water that purifies from sin"), and in 19:9, מֵי נִדָּה (*mê niddâ*, "water of cleansing," for purification from sin).

(iii) The bitter waters (5:23–28)

²³"The priest is to write these curses on a scroll and then wash them off into the bitter water. ²⁴He shall have the woman drink the bitter water that brings a curse, and this water will enter her and cause bitter suffering. ²⁵The priest is to take from her hands the grain offering for jealousy, wave it before the LORD and bring it to the altar. ²⁶The priest is then to take a handful of the grain offering as a memorial offering and burn it on the altar; after that, he is to have the woman drink the water. ²⁷If she has defiled herself and been unfaithful to her husband, then when she is made to drink the water that brings a curse, it will go into her and cause bitter suffering; her abdomen will swell and her thigh waste away, and she will become accursed among her people. ²⁸If, however, the woman has not defiled herself and is free from impurity, she will be cleared of guilt and will be able to have children.

COMMENTARY

23–28 The language of this section is somewhat repetitive of the earlier paragraphs. These repetitive and similar wordings have prompted critical scholars to posit varied textual strata inelegantly pieced together. The tendency today, however, is to view the text as a whole. In this approach the repetitions and similar phrasings are marks of literary purpose and structure (see, e.g., Michael Fishbane, "Accusations of Adultery: A Study of Law and Scribal Practice in Numbers 5:11–31," *HUCA* 45 [1974]: 25–45; Herbert Chanan Brichto, "The Case of the Sota and a Reconsideration of Biblical 'Law,'" *HUCA* 46 [1975]: 55–70; and esp. Tikva Frymer-Kensky, "The Strange Case of the Suspected Sotah [Numbers V 11–31]," *VT* 34 [1984]: 11–26).

Verses 23–28 give the final step in the procedure. After the words of cursing had been announced, the priest would write them on a scroll (or perhaps a wooden tablet) and then blot the letters off into the water. The woman was not only to hear the words, but in a dramatic, figurative sense she was to drink them. In this way the awful sense of taking the curse into one's own body was realized. The bitterness of the waters, again, was not in their taste but in the potential they bore in their association with the curse attendant to them.

The NIV suggests the very drinking of the water would cause suffering: "this water will enter her and cause bitter suffering" (v.24). This phrase may also be read in a more benign manner: "and the waters that cause curses shall enter her for bitterness." The bitterness was not in taste, convulsions, or physical shock but in the latent sense of the potential judgment on her body of childlessness. "Bitterness" is a most appropriate term for just this potential judgment. The innocent woman would not suffer the bitterness of the water, for she was innocent of the curses associated with it.

(iv) The summary of the law of jealousy (5:29–31)

> [29]"'This, then, is the law of jealousy when a woman goes astray and defiles herself while married to her husband, [30]or when feelings of jealousy come over a man because he suspects his wife. The priest is to have her stand before the LORD and is to apply this entire law to her. [31]The husband will be innocent of any wrongdoing, but the woman will bear the consequences of her sin.'"

COMMENTARY

29–31 The summary statement of this law is put in terms of the woman who has been justly accused by her husband. Again, in this summary statement there is repetition and recapitulation of dominant themes from the involved legislation—typical devices of the writers of biblical prose. The section ends ominously, as the chapter began. The chapter's cohesion comes from its addressing of instances relating to the maintaining of purity within the camp. The importance of marital fidelity in this passage should not be lost on modern readers in a time in which such ideas are thought by so many to be quaint but irrelevant. Numerous NT texts may be cited (esp. 1Co 5) supporting God's reaffirmation of the prohibition given in the seventh commandment: You are not to commit adultery.

ii. The vow of the Nazirite and the Aaronic benediction (6:1–27)

OVERVIEW

Numbers 6 continues the theme of the purification of the people of the new nation in two disparate manners. First is the presentation for the opportunity for an individual to make an extraordinary vow of religious devotion as a distinctive way of showing one's separation to the Lord for a limited period of time. The chapter then provides the regular manner in which the priests were to invoke the blessing of the Lord on the entire community. The text thus moves from the particular to the general, from the unusual to the regular. In this way the issue of special relationship with God is presented in a comprehensive manner.

(a) The vow of the Nazirite (6:1–21)

The special, unusual vow of the Nazirite is the first focus of the chapter.

(i) The basic prohibition against wine (6:1–4)

> [1]The LORD said to Moses, [2]"Speak to the Israelites and say to them: 'If a man or woman wants to make a special vow, a vow of separation to the LORD as a Nazirite, [3]he must

abstain from wine and other fermented drink and must not drink vinegar made from wine or from other fermented drink. He must not drink grape juice or eat grapes or raisins. ⁴As long as he is a Nazirite, he must not eat anything that comes from the grapevine, not even the seeds or skins.

COMMENTARY

1–2 When one thinks of the term "Nazirite," the name Samson may come to mind (Jdg 13–16). But it turns out that his situation did not reflect the normal meaning of the Nazirite vow (and, as is well known, he did not keep the vows well at all!). Neither is it generally known that these vows of special devotion to God could be made by a woman as well as a man. Many simply assume that the religious vows of the Nazirite were intended for males only. However, this text expressly begins, "If a man or woman" (Heb. ʾîš ʾô-ʾiššâ; see also 5:6). Thus, women were not precluded from this vow (contra the pronominal renderings in most English versions; but see 30:1–16, which speaks of the differences between other vows of men and women).

The Hebrew text uses an unusually strong verb in describing the vow of the Nazirite in the phrasing "wants to make a special vow." The verb pālāʾ (GK 7098) in the Hiphil means "to make a hard, difficult vow" (cf. 15:3, 8, where this verb in the Piel means "to complete a special, difficult vow"). This verb in the Niphal is used extensively throughout the Bible with God as subject and is often rendered by words of wonder or amazement (cf. Ex 3:20, "the wonders that I will perform"; Ps 118:23, "it is marvelous in our eyes"). In our passage, as in Leviticus 27:2, the Hiphil is used of an extraordinary vow of a devotee of Yahweh. This vow, then, does not describe a routine matter or even an expected act of devotion one might make from time to time. This vow was an act of unusual devotion to God, based

perhaps on an intense desire to demonstrate to the Lord one's utter separation to him.

The term "Nazirite," a transliteration of the Hebrew nāzîr (GK 5687), describes the person who has marked out a specific period for personal separation or consecration, a special time for unusual devotion to God. This text speaks of a restricted period of time for the Nazirite vow, though some persons took the vow for a lifetime. The word Nazirite is sometimes confused with Nazarene, the word used to describe Jesus as coming from his hometown, Nazareth (see Mt 2:23; Mk 14:67; 16:6; Ac 24:5; see Note).

In discussions of the Nazirite, attention is usually given to the prohibitions demanded on the person who took this vow. Yet more important is the positive "separation to Yahweh" afforded by the vow (vv.2, 8). It is on this aspect that the text lays its primary stress; the prohibitions were means of achieving the sense of separation. The Nazirite vow was not just an act of superior self-discipline, an achieving of spiritual prowess; it was to be regarded as a supreme act of total devotion to the person and work of the Lord that would override certain normal and expected patterns of behavior.

The person who made pledges for a particular time of special devotion to the Lord as a nāzîr had to face three demanding limitations: (1) absolute abstinence from all produce of the vine, (2) total forswearing of trimming of (and likely all caring for) the hair, and (3) utter separation from contamination by any contact with a dead body. Thus three areas of life were regulated for the Nazirite during the period of his vow: diet (ordinary pleasure), appearance (ordinary care), and associations (ordinary obligation). Every Israelite was under regulations in these general areas, but for the Nazirite each of these regulations was heightened.

Leviticus 11 details the dietary restrictions for the nation as an act of daily holiness (the practice of being distinct, separate). For the Nazirite one major clean food was prohibited during the course of one's vow. This chapter is not a tract against the drinking of wine by spiritual people; rather, it concerns a specific aspect of the expected (good!) diet that was voluntarily foresworn for a period of time as a physical reminder of the duty of devotion to God. After the period of the consecration was over, wine (along with all other grape products) was permitted again (v.20). An analogy may be found in the practice of some Christians of foregoing certain good foods during the period of Lent to prod spiritual devotion to Christ in the special period of remembrance of his sufferings.

3–4 The first paragraph contains prohibitions concerning the produce of the vine. All intoxicating drinks (as indicated by the hendiadys formed by the Hebrew words sometimes translated "wine and strong drink," meaning "all intoxicants") and everything associated with them were prohibited to the Nazirite during the period of the vow. The term "fermented drink" (v.3) is *šēkār* ("beer"; GK 8911), a word often used in association with "wine" (*yayin*), as here, and often found in texts condemning drunkenness (see 1Sa 1:15; Pr 20:1; Isa 5:11, 22; 28:7; 56:12; Mic 2:11). But this word is also used in other texts describing the normal, moderate drinking (along with wine) that was to become a part of the expected, common food of the people of Israel when they would enter the land, but which

they had not had the opportunity to enjoy during the wilderness experience (see Dt 29:6), as well as for sacral meals enhanced with wine and fermented drinks in the true worship of God (see Nu 28:7; Dt 14:26).

Further, *šēkār* could be used in the drink offering (Nu 28:7) in the worship of the Lord. Since we know that *yayin* is the fermented product of the vine, we now conclude that *šēkār* is the fermented product of the field, i.e., beer (see KB, 972). Again, the usual association with this word is drunkenness, but this association is not a necessary one. The Nazirite was to abstain from both wine and beer and from everything associated with the wine grape (v.3).

Verse 3 prohibits the Nazirite from partaking of anything that comes from the grapevine—not just the fermented beverages but also even the vinegar (*ḥōmeṣ*) that results when such products sour. Moreover, the prohibition included fresh grape juice, grapes either fresh or dried, and even the seed and skin of the grape. It appears to be the case that the forbidding of all products of the grapevine was a way of saying that the person undertaking the vow was not to have even a remote association with wine. The Hebrew words translated by the NIV as "seeds and skins" are uncertain in meaning, but they refer to the most insignificant products of the vine. The prohibition could not have been more inclusive. The Nazirite was not even "to smell the cork," as it were.

I conclude, therefore, that here the basic issue for the person under the solemn, difficult vow of the *nāzîr* was abstaining from all use of the grape and vine as a disavowal of "*ordinary pleasure*." That is, for the period of time of her or his vow, wine—and everything associated with it—was now off limits, as wine symbolized pleasure (see Ps 104:15, "[Yahweh makes] wine that gladdens the heart of man").

NOTE

2 The Hebrew term נָזִיר (*nāzîr*, "consecrated one, devotee, Nazirite") has two other uses in the OT besides the person who takes the special vow intended in this chapter; these other uses help us to understand its special meaning here. Joseph is called a *nāzîr* in the blessings of Jacob on his sons (recorded in Ge 49). Joseph was given the chief blessing of his father. He was regarded as a *nāzîr*, in the sense of "a prince, a consecrated person": "Let all these [blessings] rest on the head of Joseph, / on the brow of *the prince* among his brothers" (נְזִיר אֶחָיו, *nᵉzîr ʾeḥāyw*; Ge 49:26).

The word is also used of "untended" vines וְאֶת־עִנְּבֵי נְזִירֶךָ (*wᵉʾet-ʿinnᵉbê nᵉzîrekā*, "and the grape [vines] of your non-tending") during the time of the sabbatical year (Lev 25:5, 11). Presumably these vines are termed *nāzîr* because they were not tended or trimmed, just as the Nazirite was not to trim his or her hair during the period of special vow. Thus a *nāzîr* was a person who was specially consecrated to Yahweh and who was marked out as distinct by his or her lack of ordinary personal care.

The word "Nazirite" is often confused with the term "Nazarene," used in the NT to describe Jesus in terms of his Galilean hometown, Nazareth (see Mt 2:23). However, the spelling of this town name in Hebrew is distinct from the verbal root of the *nāzîr*. Nazareth is not spelled with a "z" (Heb. *zayin*) but with an explosive "ts" (Heb. *tsade* [*ṣādê*]). "Nazirite" and "Nazarene" are not related. Following the lead of Bargil Pixner (*With Jesus through Galilee: According to the Fifth Gospel* [trans. Christo Botha and Dom David Fisher; Rosh Pina, Israel: Corozin, 1992], 14–19), I believe the term "Nazarene" is best understood as a fulfillment of the prophecy of Isaiah 11:1, "from his roots a Branch [נֵצֶר, *neṣer*] will bear fruit." See Ronald B. Allen, "Does Anything Good Come from Nazareth?" *Kindred Spirit* 23/9 (Winter 1999): 2–3, 11.

(ii) Basic prohibitions concerning hair and dead bodies (6:5–8)

> ⁵"'During the entire period of his vow of separation no razor may be used on his head. He must be holy until the period of his separation to the LORD is over; he must let the hair of his head grow long. ⁶Throughout the period of his separation to the LORD he must not go near a dead body. ⁷Even if his own father or mother or brother or sister dies, he must not make himself ceremonially unclean on account of them, because the symbol of his separation to God is on his head. ⁸Throughout the period of his separation he is consecrated to the LORD.

COMMENTARY

5 A second voluntary prohibition for the Nazirite was the normal and expected trimming of the hair. During the period of one's Nazirite vow, the hair was not to be trimmed at all (see Jdg 13:5 for the beginning of the account of Samson, a lifelong *nāzîr*). The unexpectedly long hair of a (long-term) Nazirite man would be a physical mark of his vow of special "separation" (*nezer*, from the same root as the term "Nazirite"; GK 5694) to the Lord; as distinctive, say, as the habit of a monk or a nun. It would be misleading to call these persons the "monks and nuns" of Israel, however, as they were not required to be celibate.

Since most persons would not take long-term vows as Nazirites, it is difficult to appreciate the prohibition of going without a hair trim for a significant period of time. I suspect that getting one's hair trimmed in biblical times would not come more often than once per month in any event. Further, since women in most cultures wear their hair longer than men do, one wonders what the issue would be for a female *nāzîr* not getting her hair trimmed in a month's time. So I propose that we should take our lead from the extensive comments concerning wine in vv.1–4. In that case, not only was the drinking of wine and beer prohibited—one could not even touch a grape leaf. So it seems likely that the prohibition concerning the hair would go beyond just the trimming of it. I propose that the expected understanding (contextually) would include forgoing the ordinary care of one's hair. And that would be particularly impressive for a woman—and not a small thing even for a man.

We may presume that the Nazirite woman might not only have let her hair grow long but may also have allowed it to remain relatively unkempt (cf., again, the use of *nāzîr* regarding untended vines in Lev 25:5, 11), or perhaps she would let it hang loose as opposed to putting it up. Otherwise, it is difficult to see how the (unusually) long hair of a woman would be a distinctive sign of her period of vow. The Nazirite was to be "holy" (v.5); the untrimmed (and perhaps unkempt) hair would be a special mark of one who was so set apart. (Leviticus 21:5 prohibited the priests of Israel from certain types of shaving of the head or the beard, presumably in

imitation of pagan mantic practices.) The Nazirite was not to trim his or her hair. Compare as well the shaving of the entire body of the Levite at the time of his initial consecration in the service of the Lord in the holy tabernacle (8:7). The paragraph ends with the primary issue of the Nazirite relationship: he or she was consecrated to the Lord (6:8). Such a person was to abstain from *ordinary personal care*.

6–8 The third prohibition for the Nazirite concerned physical contact with dead bodies (see comment on 5:2 for general contamination by contact with dead bodies). For the Nazirite the prohibition extended even to the deceased within his own family (v.7). The listing of family members who might die during the time of one's vow makes this text particularly piquant; the prohibition stings the soul. In this way the general commands become intense; here a person faced heart-rending decisions not to behave normally in times of great grief because of a prior decision based on a desire for a time of intense consecration to the Lord.

No one making a Nazirite vow would be able to know for certain what the personal demands might be in this regard during the time period of the vow. Even a priest was expected to care for the dead body of a close relative (Lev 21:1–3). But the Nazirite could not care for such a body, no matter how beloved the person might have been, or he or she would bring personal contamination. This was a prohibition of *ordinary obligation*.

The vow of the Nazirite was most serious indeed! The prohibition of ingesting wine and grapes meant that one would forswear *ordinary pleasure*. That of caring for one's hair was a prohibition of *ordinary care*. That of contact with dead bodies was a prohibition of *ordinary obligation*. And during this period one was to have an extraordinary focus on the person of God. Notice, however, that the Nazirite vow does not proscribe sexual activity, as is commonly assumed.

(iii) The specific prohibition concerning accidental death (6:9–12)

9"'If someone dies suddenly in his presence, thus defiling the hair he has dedicated, he must shave his head on the day of his cleansing — the seventh day. 10Then on the eighth day he must bring two doves or two young pigeons to the priest at the entrance to the Tent of Meeting. 11The priest is to offer one as a sin offering and the other as a burnt offering to make atonement for him because he sinned by being in the presence of the dead body. That same day he is to consecrate his head. 12He must dedicate himself to the LORD for the period of his separation and must bring a year-old male lamb as a guilt offering. The previous days do not count, because he became defiled during his separation.

COMMENTARY

9–12 This paragraph makes the demands of the male or female Nazirite (see again v.2) even more severe, as it speaks of the accidental death of a person in the proximity of the one under vow (v.9). In this case the accidental death made the Nazirite unclean, guilty of sin before the Lord. The basic provisions of the Nazirite vow concerned areas where he or she was able to make conscious decisions. This section deals with the unexpected, unplanned events of daily living. The particularity of the hair, the *nezer* ("dedicated"; v.9), is the special focus of the person's contamination. This dedicated hair was to be shaved on the seventh day of the Nazirite's rite of purification. (The shaving of one's head would be particularly difficult if the *nāzîr* were a woman!)

Then, following obligatory offerings of birds (the less expensive offerings) for sin (v.8) and burnt offerings and a lamb (the more expensive) for guilt, the person would rededicate him- or herself to the Lord for the period of time that had originally been planned (v.11); the time spent up to that point would no longer count (v.12) because of the contamination, no matter how inadvertent. No wonder this vow is termed a "hard vow" (*pālā*, "wants to make a special vow"; v.2); no wonder that all vows to the Lord were to be made with great caution (Pr 20:25). The terrible tragedy of the life of Samson was that he never took his vows to God seriously until the end of his sorry life.

(iv) The ritual for the completion of the vow (6:13–20)

13"'Now this is the law for the Nazirite when the period of his separation is over. He is to be brought to the entrance to the Tent of Meeting. 14There he is to present his offerings to the LORD: a year-old male lamb without defect for a burnt offering, a year-old ewe lamb without defect for a sin offering, a ram without defect for a fellowship offering, 15together

with their grain offerings and drink offerings, and a basket of bread made without yeast —
cakes made of fine flour mixed with oil, and wafers spread with oil.

¹⁶"The priest is to present them before the LORD and make the sin offering and the
burnt offering. ¹⁷He is to present the basket of unleavened bread and is to sacrifice the
ram as a fellowship offering to the LORD, together with its grain offering and drink offering.

¹⁸"Then at the entrance to the Tent of Meeting, the Nazirite must shave off the hair that
he dedicated. He is to take the hair and put it in the fire that is under the sacrifice of the
fellowship offering.

¹⁹"After the Nazirite has shaved off the hair of his dedication, the priest is to place in his
hands a boiled shoulder of the ram, and a cake and a wafer from the basket, both made
without yeast. ²⁰The priest shall then wave them before the LORD as a wave offering; they
are holy and belong to the priest, together with the breast that was waved and the thigh
that was presented. After that, the Nazirite may drink wine.

COMMENTARY

13–20 The offerings of the Nazirite at the
completion of the period of the vow (v.13) were
extensive, expensive, and expressive of the spirit
of total commitment to Yahweh during this period
of special devotion. In addition to these several
offerings (vv.14–17), there was also the presentation of the Nazirite's (shaven) hair (*nezer*) — the
sign of the vow — for burning. Burning the hair
signified the completion of the vow. That it was
burned and not kept as a trophy or memorial demonstrated that the act of the Nazirite was in devotion to the Lord.

The rites described in these verses are solemn
and the prescriptions precise. The three sacrifices
were a male lamb for the burnt offering, a ewe lamb
for the sin offering, and a ram for the fellowship
offering, each with the accompanying grain offerings and libations. These sacrifices were very dear; it
was not a trifling thing to take on oneself the vow
of a Nazirite.

The libation, or "drink offering" (*nesek*; GK
5821; v.15), is particularly interesting in the con-

text of the Nazirite vow. Since the Nazirite was
prohibited any contact whatsoever with wine and
products of the vine during the time of his vow,
one might conclude that such things are essentially
evil in themselves. However, the wine offering was
presented on the altar to the Lord along with the
clean animals and the associated grain offerings
mixed with olive oil; so such a conclusion would
be misguided. The *nesek* offering of wine poured
out on the altar of the Lord was practiced from
patriarchal times (see Ge 35:14) and became part
of the religious system commanded by the Lord
to Moses (see Ex 29:40; Lev 23:13, 18, 37; Nu 4:7;
15:5, 7; 28:7; 29:6; et al.). The conclusion respecting
the significance of the prohibition of wine and beer
to the Nazirite during the time of his vow must
take into account the use of wine in the Nazirite's
rite of vow completion as well as the notice that at
the end of the rites of purification the Nazirite was
free to drink wine again (v.20).

The priest's public presentation of the Nazirite
before the Lord at the Tent of Meeting shows that

this type of vow was not just a personal, private, and secret matter. Any public rite such as these verses describe suggests that the vow was also a matter of public knowledge. Presumably, the community could be supportive of the person during the time of his or her vow. But more important in this text than the public aspect was the personal presentation before the Lord at the Tent of Meeting (see vv.13–14, 16–17, 20). This vow, though in a public context, was an intensely personal act of relating to the Lord, properly entered only with a profound sense of one's coming into the presence of the Holy One.

(v) The summary of the Nazirite vow (6:21)

21"'This is the law of the Nazirite who vows his offering to the LORD in accordance with his separation, in addition to whatever else he can afford. He must fulfill the vow he has made, according to the law of the Nazirite.'"

COMMENTARY

21 Summary statements such as this serve not only to end a section but also to solemnize the contents of the section. This verse also indicates that the previous sacrifices and offerings are the minimal demands and that additional offerings might also be expected. The costs of the Nazirite vow were considerable and varied. In addition to numerous personal and private feelings and discomforts, a significant outlay of property was demanded as well. Again, the Nazirite vow was not a demand of God on his people; it was a provision for men and women who voluntarily desired an unusually demanding means of showing their devotion to him. This was an act of rugged discipleship!

(b) The Aaronic Benediction (6:22–27)

OVERVIEW

In the well-known words of the Aaronic Benediction, we find a broad, national complement to the restrictive words of the Nazirite vow that were so personal and demanding. These words are expansive and gracious, inclusive of the whole community. They are also a part of the purification of the camp that the book of Numbers features in these several chapters. The reader is also arrested by the form of these words. Their poetic cast not only makes them more memorable but also contributes significantly to the aesthetics of the prayer and draws one in more deeply to its meaning. The function of poetry is to intensify feeling and deepen response.

22The LORD said to Moses, 23"Tell Aaron and his sons, 'This is how you are to bless the Israelites. Say to them:

²⁴ "'"The LORD bless you
and keep you;
²⁵the LORD make his face shine upon you
and be gracious to you;
²⁶the LORD turn his face toward you
and give you peace."'

²⁷"So they will put my name on the Israelites, and I will bless them."

COMMENTARY

22–23 The words of the prayer of vv.24–26 are termed the *Aaronic Benediction*, but the words were given *to* Aaron, not developed *by* Aaron. In some ways these lovely words may be thought of as "The Lord's Prayer of the Old Testament" (cf. Mt 6:9). The priests are told here how to pray for God's blessing on the people in the same way that the disciples were instructed how to pray for God's blessing in their lives by the Savior. Perhaps the most impressive aspect of this prayer is that it is a provision for God's desire to bless his people. Blessing is his idea, his purpose. It is not something his people must beg for; it is the voluntary outreaching of his grace.

The supreme beauty of the words of this prayer (evident in translation) and the formulaic words of introduction (vv.22–23) and conclusion (v.27) give ample warrant for the concept of fixed, repeated prayers in spiritual worship. Some people suggest that only spontaneous prayer is "real" prayer; verses such as these show that such sentiment is not correct. Fixed prayers ought to interplay with spontaneous prayers in our patterns.

The pattern of the words of this prayer is exquisite; the language is poetic and emotive. There are three lines each with the divine name Yahweh ("LORD," English versions); the repetition of the divine name gives force to the expression of v.27 — "So they will put my name on the Israelites" — and is certainly fitting with the (later) Christian revelation of the three persons of the Trinity.

Each line conveys two elements of benediction, and the lines are progressively longer. In the Hebrew text the first line has three words (in the pattern 2 // 1), the second has five words (in the pattern 4 // 1), and the third has seven words (in the pattern 4 // 3). If one does not count the threefold use of the divine name, there are twelve words to the prayer, which suggest the twelve tribes of Israel. (For comments on rhythm in Hebrew poetry, refer to Note at 11:11–15.)

This prayer has a luminous sense about it. It speaks of the light of the presence of the Lord in a vivid, anthropomorphic manner; but there is a sense that the prayer itself is light-giving. This prayer prayed in faith expects God to respond by drawing near and enfolding one in his grace. In fact, the concluding words promise that he will bless his people. The Hebrew wording is emphatic: "and *I* will bless them" (v.27).

24 The first line may be rendered, "May Yahweh bless you and may he keep you." While these words are directed to the entire community, the pronouns are singular. This is characteristic of covenantal language: Yahweh blesses the whole by blessing the individuals; he blesses the individuals by blessing the whole. The invocation of God's blessing reveals that the covenantal community knew who they were: the people who were particularly blessed of the Lord because of his own choice of the patriarchs (Abraham, Isaac, and Jacob) and because of the solemn relationship he has entered into with the fathers, mothers, and their children.

"The LORD bless you and keep you" are words of reminder, words of attestation of promise. These are words whereby the community says, "Yes, Amen!" to God's promise, whereby they request from his presence the continuity of the blessing he has already begun. The buttressing words, "and keep you," further explain his blessing. God's intention for his people is for their good; he will preserve them to enjoy that good.

25 The words "make his face shine upon you" take us back to the experience of Moses on Mount Sinai. There the epiphany of the Lord appeared to Moses (see Ex 34:29–35), and he experienced God's presence in a dramatic and direct manner. (As elsewhere, I follow Claus Westermann in using the term "theophany" to describe an appearance of God, but "epiphany" to describe an experience of his grand descent.) As his glory caused Moses' face to shine, so the Lord desired to make his presence known to all his people. When Moses was on the mountain, it was in the context of terror; all the physical signs of the epiphany of God in Exodus 19–20 provoked trepidation on the part of the people. But God had come down in grace; his revelation was of mercy. Hence we have the splendidly suitable tie of the light of his face and the grace of his presence in the words: "[May] the LORD make his face shine upon you / and be gracious to you."

Again, and throughout the prayer, the pronoun "you" is in the singular in the Hebrew text; this was a prayer for the community, but its force was to be realized in the life of the individual. Only in the introductory and concluding formulas are the plurals used.

26 The climax of the prayer is: "[May] the LORD turn ['lift up'] his face toward you / and give you peace." The Hebrew word *šalôm* ("peace," NIV; GK 8934) is here seen in its most expressive fullness— not just as an absence of war, but also as the positive state of rightness and the fullness of well-being. This kind of peace comes only from the Lord. The expression "turn his face" suggests pleasure and affection. This terminology has the functional equivalent of the word "smile." Here the people are led to pray that the Lord will turn his face toward them in a gracious smile! (see Mayer I. Gruber, "The Many Faces of Hebrew 'Lift up the Face,'" *ZAW* 95, 2 [1983]: 253). We may thus translate this text: "May Yahweh smile on you, and may he grant you well-being!"

The words of this prayer are first introduced by the monocolon, "[And] the LORD said to Moses" (v.22), showing both that this is a new section in the book (see 6:1) and that it is a divine communication. The idea of invoking God's blessing, presence, and smile on his people is not a creation of the people or a development of the priests but a gracious provision by God himself. The words of the prayer are framed by an introductory formula (v.23) and a concluding formula (v.27); these framing sections highlight the words of the prayer and provide its proper setting.

Uttering the prayer was a priestly function, for the priests were God's gift to the nation to stand between himself and his people. The people might come to God through the agency of the priests, and God would speak to his people through these priests. Further, without these instructions the priests might have sought the mantic acts of their neighbors as a means of seeking the pleasure of the

Lord. God's intention was to bring his pleasure to his people; thus he presented the means whereby that might be sought and received.

27 The words of the concluding formula may be the most surprising of all, for here the Lord says that this prayer is the means of placing his name on his people. Since the name Yahweh is itself a term of blessing whereby the eternal God states his relatedness to his people, these words could not be more appropriate. The prayer was designed to help the people experience the reality of the Lord's blessing, whose delight is to bring that blessing near; his promise is that he will do that very thing.

NOTE

24 Baruch A. Levine (*Numbers 1–20: A New Translation with Introduction and Commentary* [AB 4A; New York: Doubleday, 1993], 216) reports on the discovery of two thin silver amulets in 1986 in a burial cave in the Valley of Hinnom (Keteph Hinnom) that record almost verbatim versions of the "priestly benediction" of Numbers 6:24–26. These amulets are dated between the late seventh and early sixth centuries BC. Predating the Dead Sea Scrolls (Qumran literature) by more than four hundred years, they are the earliest written texts from the Bible ever to have been discovered! See David Noel Freedman, "The Aaronic Benediction," in *No Famine in the Land* (ed. J. W. Flanagan and A. Weisbrod Robinson; Claremont, Calif.: Claremont Graduate School, 1975), 35–47; A. Yardeni, "Remarks on the Priestly Blessing on Two Ancient Amulets from Jerusalem," *VT* 41 (1991): 176–85. William Dever (*Did God Have a Wife? Archaeology and Folk Religion in Ancient Israel* [Grand Rapids: Eerdmans, 2005], 131) discusses one of the amulets and describes it as an aspect of "popular religion," possibly as something worn by a woman as a magical charm to ward off evil. But then he relents and describes the amulet as "really only an analogue for a form of the 'phylactery.'"

Walter C. Kaiser Jr. (*Mission in the Old Testament: Israel as a Light to the Nations* (Grand Rapids: Baker, 2000], 30–33) observes that the words of the Aaronic benediction are echoed in several psalms (4:6[7]; 31:16[17]; 80:3, 7, 19); he develops in particular the use of the benediction in Psalm 67.

REFLECTION

Surely this Aaronic benediction is a prayer that needs to be recovered by the believing community today. Christians may read these words and find in them not only the Lord's special covenantal relationship with Israel at Mount Sinai but also a reflection of the loving relationship God has with his people, the church, through the work of the Savior, Jesus, in whom we have experienced preeminently the smile of God. The threefold invocation of the name of the Lord is not likely to be lost on Christian readers:

> May the Lord Yahweh as Father, Son, and Spirit bless his people and keep them,
> cause them to know his presence and his grace,
> and allow them to sense his smile and his peace. Amen!

iii. The offerings at the dedication of the tabernacle (7:1–89)

OVERVIEW

In the stylized organization of the book of Numbers, the presentation of the concept of the purity of the camp moves from the prayer for the blessing of the Lord on his people to the blessings of the people that are brought to him. Chapter 7 is a text of gifts — monumental gifts — presented with great pageantry and significant pomp. Here is a festival of offerings to the Lord stretching over twelve days. The chapter stands as a monument to the pleasure of Yahweh, Israel's God, who took enjoyment in the repetition — for these were grand gifts in the good days of his early relationship with his people. These were the honeymoon days of the marital relationship of the Lord and Israel (see Jer 2:2–3). Each of the gifts was relished, each regarded as a lovely presentation by a lover in the early days of the bliss of marriage.

(a) The presentation of carts and oxen (7:1–3)

¹When Moses finished setting up the tabernacle, he anointed it and consecrated it and all its furnishings. He also anointed and consecrated the altar and all its utensils. ²Then the leaders of Israel, the heads of families who were the tribal leaders in charge of those who were counted, made offerings. ³They brought as their gifts before the LORD six covered carts and twelve oxen — an ox from each leader and a cart from every two. These they presented before the tabernacle.

COMMENTARY

1 Exodus 40:1–33 presents the prose description of the setting up of the tabernacle. That chapter ends with the report of the cloud covering and the presence of Yahweh filling the tabernacle (vv.34–35; see Note at Nu 5:3). With much repetition of language, Numbers 7 records the magnificent (and identical) gifts given to the Lord for tabernacle service by the leaders of each of the twelve tribes. It is wonderfully fitting that the record of these gifts in Numbers follows the text of the Aaronic benediction (6:24–26): in response to God's solemn promise to bless his people, they bring their blessing to him — magnificent gifts in twelve sequential days of celebrative pageantry.

The terminology of v.1 is significant. First, we observe that this is the first major section of Numbers to begin as a narrative text. Each of the other sections has begun either with the introductory monocolon of divine revelation (e.g., "And the LORD spoke to Moses"; see 1:1; 2:1; 3:11, 14, 44; 4:1; 5:1, 5, 11; 6:1, 22) or with a statement of background fact (see 3:1, "This is the account of the family of Aaron and Moses"). Chapter 7 begins with a narrative action-sequence pattern: "When Moses finished … he anointed…. Then the leaders … made offerings." Wenham, 91, has nicely summarized the relationship of the dated events of Numbers 7–9 with the events of Exodus and Leviticus. The following chart of the events of the first two months of the second year of Israel's exodus is adapted from his book:

Date (in second year)	Event	Text
Day 1, first month	Completion of tabernacle	Exodus 40:2; Numbers 7:1
	Laws for offerings begin	Leviticus 1:1
	Offerings for altar begin	Numbers 7:3
	Ordination of priests begins	Leviticus 8:1
Day 8, first month	Ordination of priests completed	Leviticus 9:1
Day 12, first month	Offerings for altar completed	Numbers 7:78
	Appointment of Levites	Numbers 8:5
Day 14, first month	Second Passover	Numbers 9:2
Day 1, second month	Census begins	Numbers 1:1
Day 14, second month	Passover for those unclean	Numbers 9:11
Day 20, second month	The cloud moves, the camp begins its trek	Numbers 10:11

The focus in the chapter is on the tabernacle (hammiškān), the "dwelling place of God" (v.1), and the altar (hammizbēaḥ), the point of approach to God's dwelling. After Moses had completed supervising the construction and erection of the sacred tent and its altar, he anointed and consecrated them for the Lord's special services. The verb "anoint" is the same term used for the anointing of special persons (see Note). The second verb used of the dedication rites is "consecrated." It was a declarative action (see Note), to be noted by those present that the tabernacle and its furnishings and the altar and its implements were no longer common items but were now marked out as special, distinct, and other. The common was now sacred; the ordinary was now set apart to the worship of God.

2–3 Then the leaders of the tribes, whom we have met already in chs. 1 and 2, came forward with their first gifts. The Hebrew word for their gifts is qorbān (GK 7933), a noun related to the verb meaning "to bring near" (qārab in the Hiphil). This type of language is particularly apt, for the leaders were "bringing near" to the symbols of God's presence their own gifts. These gifts were necessary and utilitarian.

There were six carts, each drawn by a pair of oxen, for the special use of the priests in transporting the elements of the sacred tent and its furnishings when the people would set out on their march toward Canaan. The Hebrew word for "cart" (ᶜagālâ) is modified by the noun ṣāb ("litter"), used only here and in Isaiah 66:20. This phrase has traditionally been understood to describe a covered wagon, though the precise meaning of the wording is debated. Covered wagons would certainly be appropriate for transporting the sacred items. I suspect the pairs of oxen were matched and stately, suitably chosen for their significant work.

NOTE

1 מָשַׁח (*māšaḥ*; GK 5417) has the basic meaning of "to smear, anoint" (see also discussion of this word at 3:3; 18:8). It can be used of covering a surface with paint (as in Jer 22:14) but is used especially for the anointing of a person or an object with olive oil in a ritual of consecration. When anointing was done of persons such as priests, kings, and prophets, the oil was poured on the head of the sacral person (e.g., Ex 28:41; 1Ki 1:45; 19:16). When anointing was done of objects, the oil could be poured or smeared over the surface of sacred things. Jacob anointed a sacred pillar before the Lord at Bethel (Ge 31:13), and Moses was commanded to anoint the altar of the tabernacle (Ex 29:36). The oil that was to be used in these consecrating ceremonies is described in Exodus 30:23–25. It was an extraordinary oil blended with exotic spices in exacting proportions and termed "a sacred anointing oil," the recipe for which was sacrosanct; unauthorized use or duplication of it was an affront to the holiness of God and was grounds for being cut off from the people of God (v.33).

וַיְקַדֵּשׁ (*wayqaddēš*, "and [he] consecrated") is a form of the verb קָדַשׁ (*qādaš*, "to be holy"; GK 7727). This verb in the Piel stem used here means "to make holy, set apart."

(b) The distribution of the carts and oxen (7:4–9)

> ⁴The LORD said to Moses, ⁵"Accept these from them, that they may be used in the work at the Tent of Meeting. Give them to the Levites as each man's work requires."
> ⁶So Moses took the carts and oxen and gave them to the Levites. ⁷He gave two carts and four oxen to the Gershonites, as their work required, ⁸and he gave four carts and eight oxen to the Merarites, as their work required. They were all under the direction of Ithamar son of Aaron, the priest. ⁹But Moses did not give any to the Kohathites, because they were to carry on their shoulders the holy things, for which they were responsible.

COMMENTARY

4–9 Following the command of God, Moses took these six covered carts and their respective pairs of oxen and distributed them to the three Levitical families based on their need and their particular responsibilities. Two of the carts and their four oxen he gave to the families of Gershon for their work in transporting the varied curtains of the tabernacle and the courtyard (see 4:24–28); the other four carts and their pairs of oxen went to the families of Merari for their work in transporting the frames, crossbars, posts, bases, ropes, and pegs of the tabernacle and the courtyard (see 4:29–33). Moses made these divisions of carts and oxen based on the needs that each family had for transporting the material of the tabernacle.

The Kohathites, by contrast, were not given any carts; they were to carry the holy things on their shoulders, with staves placed through the carrying loops (see 4:4–20; esp. vv.6, 8, 11–12, 14). This prohibition of the use of carts for the holiest objects was not followed by David in his first attempt to transport the ark to the city of Jerusalem, following the establishment of his kingdom (see 2Sa 6:3).

This untoward act led to the death of Uzzah, who attempted to stabilize the ark as it seemed about to tumble from the cart (v.7). The lesson was drastic, but David learned from it. He had the priests carry it the second time (v.13).

(c) The plan of the tribal offerings (7:10–11)

¹⁰When the altar was anointed, the leaders brought their offerings for its dedication and presented them before the altar. ¹¹For the LORD had said to Moses, "Each day one leader is to bring his offering for the dedication of the altar."

COMMENTARY

10–11 The Hebrew text is emphatic in v.11: "And Yahweh said to Moses, one leader for one day, one leader for one day, let them bring their offering near for the dedication of the altar" (my translation). The repetition of "one leader for one day" shows the pacing that God required. Each leader's gift was worth a day's celebration. None of the collections of gifts was to be grouped with others, none of the leaders was to be bunched with others. Each leader, with the people he represented, was to have his day in the sun—better, his *day of approach* with significant gifts to the supernal presence of Yahweh.

(d) The offerings of the twelve tribes (7:12–83)

¹²The one who brought his offering on the first day was Nahshon son of Amminadab of the tribe of Judah.
    ¹³His offering was one silver plate weighing a hundred and thirty shekels, and one silver sprinkling bowl weighing seventy shekels, both according to the sanctuary shekel, each filled with fine flour mixed with oil as a grain offering; ¹⁴one gold dish weighing ten shekels, filled with incense; ¹⁵one young bull, one ram and one male lamb a year old, for a burnt offering; ¹⁶one male goat for a sin offering; ¹⁷and two oxen, five rams, five male goats and five male lambs a year old, to be sacrificed as a fellowship offering. This was the offering of Nahshon son of Amminadab.
¹⁸On the second day Nethanel son of Zuar, the leader of Issachar, brought his offering.
    ¹⁹The offering he brought was one silver plate weighing a hundred and thirty shekels, and one silver sprinkling bowl weighing seventy shekels, both according to the

sanctuary shekel, each filled with fine flour mixed with oil as a grain offering; ²⁰one gold dish weighing ten shekels, filled with incense; ²¹one young bull, one ram and one male lamb a year old, for a burnt offering; ²²one male goat for a sin offering; ²³and two oxen, five rams, five male goats and five male lambs a year old, to be sacrificed as a fellowship offering. This was the offering of Nethanel son of Zuar.

²⁴On the third day, Eliab son of Helon, the leader of the people of Zebulun, brought his offering.

²⁵His offering was one silver plate weighing a hundred and thirty shekels, and one silver sprinkling bowl weighing seventy shekels, both according to the sanctuary shekel, each filled with fine flour mixed with oil as a grain offering; ²⁶one gold dish weighing ten shekels, filled with incense; ²⁷one young bull, one ram and one male lamb a year old, for a burnt offering; ²⁸one male goat for a sin offering; ²⁹and two oxen, five rams, five male goats and five male lambs a year old, to be sacrificed as a fellowship offering. This was the offering of Eliab son of Helon.

³⁰On the fourth day Elizur son of Shedeur, the leader of the people of Reuben, brought his offering.

³¹His offering was one silver plate weighing a hundred and thirty shekels, and one silver sprinkling bowl weighing seventy shekels, both according to the sanctuary shekel, each filled with fine flour mixed with oil as a grain offering; ³²one gold dish weighing ten shekels, filled with incense; ³³one young bull, one ram and one male lamb a year old, for a burnt offering; ³⁴one male goat for a sin offering; ³⁵and two oxen, five rams, five male goats and five male lambs a year old, to be sacrificed as a fellowship offering. This was the offering of Elizur son of Shedeur.

³⁶On the fifth day Shelumiel son of Zurishaddai, the leader of the people of Simeon, brought his offering.

³⁷His offering was one silver plate weighing a hundred and thirty shekels, and one silver sprinkling bowl weighing seventy shekels, both according to the sanctuary shekel, each filled with fine flour mixed with oil as a grain offering; ³⁸one gold dish weighing ten shekels, filled with incense; ³⁹one young bull, one ram and one male lamb a year old, for a burnt offering; ⁴⁰one male goat for a sin offering; ⁴¹and two oxen, five rams, five male goats and five male lambs a year old, to be sacrificed as a fellowship offering. This was the offering of Shelumiel son of Zurishaddai.

⁴²On the sixth day Eliasaph son of Deuel, the leader of the people of Gad, brought his offering.

⁴³His offering was one silver plate weighing a hundred and thirty shekels, and one silver sprinkling bowl weighing seventy shekels, both according to the sanctuary shekel, each filled with fine flour mixed with oil as a grain offering; ⁴⁴one gold dish weighing

ten shekels, filled with incense; [45]one young bull, one ram and one male lamb a year old, for a burnt offering; [46]one male goat for a sin offering; [47]and two oxen, five rams, five male goats and five male lambs a year old, to be sacrificed as a fellowship offering. This was the offering of Eliasaph son of Deuel.

[48]On the seventh day Elishama son of Ammihud, the leader of the people of Ephraim, brought his offering.

[49]His offering was one silver plate weighing a hundred and thirty shekels, and one silver sprinkling bowl weighing seventy shekels, both according to the sanctuary shekel, each filled with fine flour mixed with oil as a grain offering; [50]one gold dish weighing ten shekels, filled with incense; [51]one young bull, one ram and one male lamb a year old, for a burnt offering; [52]one male goat for a sin offering; [53]and two oxen, five rams, five male goats and five male lambs a year old, to be sacrificed as a fellowship offering. This was the offering of Elishama son of Ammihud.

[54]On the eighth day Gamaliel son of Pedahzur, the leader of the people of Manasseh, brought his offering.

[55]His offering was one silver plate weighing a hundred and thirty shekels, and one silver sprinkling bowl weighing seventy shekels, both according to the sanctuary shekel, each filled with fine flour mixed with oil as a grain offering; [56]one gold dish weighing ten shekels, filled with incense; [57]one young bull, one ram and one male lamb a year old, for a burnt offering; [58]one male goat for a sin offering; [59]and two oxen, five rams, five male goats and five male lambs a year old, to be sacrificed as a fellowship offering. This was the offering of Gamaliel son of Pedahzur.

[60]On the ninth day Abidan son of Gideoni, the leader of the people of Benjamin, brought his offering.

[61]His offering was one silver plate weighing a hundred and thirty shekels, and one silver sprinkling bowl weighing seventy shekels, both according to the sanctuary shekel, each filled with fine flour mixed with oil as a grain offering; [62]one gold dish weighing ten shekels, filled with incense; [63]one young bull, one ram and one male lamb a year old, for a burnt offering; [64]one male goat for a sin offering; [65]and two oxen, five rams, five male goats and five male lambs a year old, to be sacrificed as a fellowship offering. This was the offering of Abidan son of Gideoni.

[66]On the tenth day Ahiezer son of Ammishaddai, the leader of the people of Dan, brought his offering.

[67]His offering was one silver plate weighing a hundred and thirty shekels, and one silver sprinkling bowl weighing seventy shekels, both according to the sanctuary shekel, each filled with fine flour mixed with oil as a grain offering; [68]one gold dish weighing ten shekels, filled with incense; [69]one young bull, one ram and one male lamb a year

old, for a burnt offering; [70]one male goat for a sin offering; [71]and two oxen, five rams, five male goats and five male lambs a year old, to be sacrificed as a fellowship offering. This was the offering of Ahiezer son of Ammishaddai.

[72]On the eleventh day Pagiel son of Ocran, the leader of the people of Asher, brought his offering.
[73]His offering was one silver plate weighing a hundred and thirty shekels, and one silver sprinkling bowl weighing seventy shekels, both according to the sanctuary shekel, each filled with fine flour mixed with oil as a grain offering; [74]one gold dish weighing ten shekels, filled with incense; [75]one young bull, one ram and one male lamb a year old, for a burnt offering; [76]one male goat for a sin offering; [77]and two oxen, five rams, five male goats and five male lambs a year old, to be sacrificed as a fellowship offering. This was the offering of Pagiel son of Ocran.

[78]On the twelfth day Ahira son of Enan, the leader of the people of Naphtali, brought his offering.
[79]His offering was one silver plate weighing a hundred and thirty shekels, and one silver sprinkling bowl weighing seventy shekels, both according to the sanctuary shekel, each filled with fine flour mixed with oil as a grain offering; [80]one gold dish weighing ten shekels, filled with incense; [81]one young bull, one ram and one male lamb a year old, for a burnt offering; [82]one male goat for a sin offering; [83]and two oxen, five rams, five male goats and five male lambs a year old, to be sacrificed as a fellowship offering. This was the offering of Ahira son of Enan.

COMMENTARY

12−83 The leaders of the twelve tribes have already been named in 1:5−15 and 2:3−32. The order of the presentation of their great offerings to the Lord is the same as the order of march: first the triad of tribes encamped to the east of the tabernacle (Judah, Issachar, and Zebulun; 2:3−9; 7:12, 18, 24); then the triad of tribes encamped to the south (Reuben, Simeon, and Gad; 2:10−16; 7:30, 36, 42); then the triad on the west (Ephraim, Manasseh, and Benjamin; 2:18−24; 7:48, 54, 60); finally those on the north (Dan, Asher, and Naphtali; 2:25−31; 7:66, 72, 78).

The gifts of each of the twelve worthies were the same:

one silver platter weighing about 1.5 kilograms;

one silver sprinkling bowl weighing about 0.8 kilogram;

one gold ladle weighing about 110 grams;

the plate and bowl containing flour mixed with oil for a grain offering;

the ladle filled with incense;

one young bull, one ram, and one male lamb for a burnt offering;

one buck goat for a sin offering;

two oxen, five rams, five buck goats, and five male lambs for a fellowship offering.

These gifts were all to be used in the worship patterns of the temple service. The "silver plate" (v.13) may have been used in association with the bread of the Presence. The sprinkling bowls were for the blood that would be sprinkled on the altar. The golden "dish" (*kap*, lit., "palm of the hand"; v.14) may have been used for incense, as this was the way it was presented to the Lord. The shekel used to weigh the silver and gold gifts is termed the "sanctuary shekel" (v.13), as against the half-value shekel sometimes used. The MT uses this phrase with the "sprinkling bowl," which the NIV (probably correctly) implies to extend to the weight of the "dish" as well (v.13). The weight of the sanctuary shekel was established in Exodus 30:13 as "twenty gerahs" (= .403 ounce or 11.4 grams; see Gleason L. Archer Jr., "The Metrology of the Old Testament," *EBC*[1], 1:379).

Attempts to determine what something was worth in terms of our present economy are futile for at least three reasons: (1) the economy of ancient Israel was not a money-based system, as in our day; (2) the relative values of gold and silver were likely closer to each other than they are in our day; and (3) the abundance or scarcity of silver and gold at any given period is difficult to ascertain. Certainly these gifts were regarded as substantial, particularly so coming from a people so recently enslaved. They had despoiled the Egyptians (Ex 12:35–36) to enrich the worship of their God. The incense that filled the dishes was the prescribed, fragrant incense of Exodus 30:34.

Obviously the writer might more easily have said that each of the twelve leaders brought the same magnificent offerings to the Lord on his appointed day during the twelve-day celebrative period. How are we to regard his seeming *excess of repetitive detail*

throughout the long chapter? Is it not possible that in this daily listing we catch a glimpse of the magnificent pomp and ceremony attending these gifts? Do we not see the genuine spirit of worship of each of the successive tribes as their turn came to bring gifts to the Lord? And finally, do we not see the joy of the Lord in his reception of these gifts? This chapter has a stately charm, a leisurely pace, and a studied sense of magnificence as each tribe in its turn was able to make gifts to God that he received with pleasure.

This text gives warrant to the ideas of rite and ritual, of ceremony and tradition. For many Christians in free churches, ritual and ceremony are regarded with suspicion, if not with disdain. Yet ritual and ceremony are deeply imbedded in the Scriptures. This text describes events in which the people took joy and in which they believed there was the corresponding joy of the Lord. As we have noted already, the daily pacing of the gifts was the directive of the Lord; their obedience was the prompt for his joy (v.11).

Analogies of the repetition found in this chapter may be made with graduation ceremonies. Sometimes when schools are very large, degrees are granted en masse; sometimes this is done on an athletic field. No names are read, and no graduates cross the platform for a handshake and the receipt of a diploma. The class is asked to stand, all are pronounced in receipt of their degrees, and word is made that their diplomas will be in the mail. In smaller schools the situation is markedly different. Here each name is read, and each student crosses the platform; each receives a diploma and a handshake and may even hear a few personal words. This latter type of highly personalized situation is reflected in Numbers 7.

NOTE

13 Many readers of the Bible think that the term שֶׁקֶל (*šeqel*, "shekel, weight"; GK 9203) refers to coinage of silver or gold. But coinage did not develop in ancient times until the Persian period. The use of the term *shekel* in this passage to describe the actual weight of consecrated objects shows the true situation. A major work on biblical coinage is David Hendin's *Guide to Biblical Coins* (4th ed.; New York: Amphora, 2001), with values by Herbert Kreindler. Hendin's chapter 2 ("A Time before Coins," 57–69) explains varied uses of the term *shekel* and the development of the official Judean shekel-weight system in the First Temple Period. The shekel then weighed approximately 11.4 grams and was divided into 20 gerah units, with other fractions called *pim*, *nezê*, and *beka* (see Hendin, 61). Dever (*What Did the Biblical Writers Know?* 221–28) also has a helpful description (along with a graph) of the shekel-weight system.

(e) The totals of the offerings (7:84–88)

84These were the offerings of the Israelite leaders for the dedication of the altar when it was anointed: twelve silver plates, twelve silver sprinkling bowls and twelve gold dishes. 85Each silver plate weighed a hundred and thirty shekels, and each sprinkling bowl seventy shekels. Altogether, the silver dishes weighed two thousand four hundred shekels, according to the sanctuary shekel. 86The twelve gold dishes filled with incense weighed ten shekels each, according to the sanctuary shekel. Altogether, the gold dishes weighed a hundred and twenty shekels. 87The total number of animals for the burnt offering came to twelve young bulls, twelve rams and twelve male lambs a year old, together with their grain offering. Twelve male goats were used for the sin offering. 88The total number of animals for the sacrifice of the fellowship offering came to twenty-four oxen, sixty rams, sixty male goats and sixty male lambs a year old. These were the offerings for the dedication of the altar after it was anointed.

COMMENTARY

84–88 At long last the twelve-day procession of givers and gifts came to its conclusion. Each tribal leader had his moment, each tribe its opportunity, and on each day there was experienced the smile of the Lord. In characteristic Hebrew style, this paragraph gives the sums of the twelve sets of gifts, a further witness to the opulence of the offerings, the festive nature of the ritual of presentation, and the sense of celebration each tribe had in its part. The totals are given in fine mathematical detail. The addition of elements in this type of paragraph shows that numerical precision was possible in ancient Israel and that numbers may be transmitted with care. The ordinary use of numbers in this section is important, as we think of their possible rhetorical use in ch. 1, with its seemingly immense numbers of fighters for each tribe.

(f) Moses' conversation with God (7:89)

89When Moses entered the Tent of Meeting to speak with the LORD, he heard the voice speaking to him from between the two cherubim above the atonement cover on the ark of the Testimony. And he spoke with him.

COMMENTARY

89 The climax came when Moses heard the voice of the Lord speaking to him from the central shrine, amid the cherubim, and over the atonement cover. Communion was established between the Lord and his prophet; the people now had an advocate with the Lord. All the sumptuous gifts of the people through their tribal leaders had had their effect. The eternal Yahweh now spoke to Moses and through Moses to the people. Moses might also speak to God for the people. There was access to heaven within this shrine. Here was forgiveness of sin. Here was grace and here was mercy. Here was the voice of God, as promised in Exodus 25:22.

Many scholars have assumed that God is to be pictured as enthroned on the cherubim that were on the mercy seat of the ark. It seems far more

likely, however, that the cherubim and the mercy seat of the ark are symbols of the Divine Presence and that the voice of God came to Moses from amid that cluster of symbols. The description of the construction of the ark, the cover of atonement, and the cherubim is given in Exodus 37:1–9. The workmanship must have been exquisite; it was the special work of the Spirit-endowed craftsman Bezalel. But more exquisite than the cherubim of hammered gold or the atonement cover of pure gold was the invaluable voice of God. It was that voice that Moses heard (see ch. 12).

There is something of a play on words in this verse. It begins with the activities of Moses: "When Moses entered the Tent of Meeting to speak with the LORD...." The verse ends, "And he [Yahweh] spoke with him [Moses]."

iv. Setting up the lamps and the separation and age of service of the Levites (8:1–26)

OVERVIEW

Chapter 8 deals with two issues: lamps and Levites. Both the proper setting of the lamps and the distinction of the Levites from the community are further elements in the purification of the nation in preparation for the holy task God had prepared for his people. One may wonder: Is there a possible connection intended in the materials of this chapter between the proper positioning of the lamps within the tabernacle and the Levites outside in the camp?

Perhaps as the lamps were to be properly focused on the bread of the Presence, so the Levites were to have their proper stance within the community. Lamps not properly focused would give poorly diffused light; God's intent was illumination. Levites not properly positioned within the community would give a diffused picture; God's intention was that the nation should understand who the Levites were and what they presented of the nature of God.

(a) Setting up the lamps (8:1–4)

¹The LORD said to Moses, ²"Speak to Aaron and say to him, 'When you set up the seven lamps, they are to light the area in front of the lampstand.'"

³Aaron did so; he set up the lamps so that they faced forward on the lampstand, just as the LORD commanded Moses. ⁴This is how the lampstand was made: It was made of hammered gold—from its base to its blossoms. The lampstand was made exactly like the pattern the LORD had shown Moses.

COMMENTARY

1 Chapter 8 begins in the characteristic manner of the book of Numbers, with the formulaic words: "The LORD said to Moses." As noted on other occasions, these words serve a double purpose: they present a new topic and thus may be regarded as a narrator's device. But they are more than just the sign of a new topic; they are the reminder of the divine origin of the words and of the role Moses had as the intermediary between God and humans.

2 The seven lamps and the lampstand (cf. the wording of "seven golden lampstands" in Rev 1:12–13, and following) are described more fully in Exodus 25:31–40. There we find the notations of the exquisite beauty of the lampstand (see Note). It was made of hammered pure gold and consisted of a base, a shaft, and seven branches (three on each side of the central shaft), with cups shaped like almond blossoms, along with other decorative buds and blossoms. The lampstand must have been truly elegant, a stunning symbol of the God who created light as the first of his works, of the Lord who illuminates—a symbol of God, who is light.

In this chapter the new information concerns the direction of the light: it was to be cast forward from the lampstand. This chapter does not explain what might be significant in this positioning. Only when we think through the relative positioning of the other furnishings of the tabernacle are we able to see the point of the paragraph: the lamps were to be positioned so that they would light the area in front of the lampstand, that is, the area where the bread of the Presence was displayed. In this way there would always be *light* on the *bread*; the twin symbols of life would work together to speak of the life-giving mercies of the Lord, whose attention was ever on his people.

As one entered the Holy Place, the golden lampstand would be on the left side and the table of the bread of the Presence on the right side, with the altar of incense straight ahead. Beyond that altar was the veil leading into the Most Holy Place, housing the ark, with the "mercy seat" (NASB; "atonement cover," NIV) and the cherubim.

3–4 Aaron obeyed the command of God in the proper focusing of the lamps (v.3); then the text reminds us of the beauty of the design of the lampstand (v.4). The most remarkable aspect is the note that the lampstand was made in exact accordance with the pattern the Lord had given to Moses. The pattern of the lampstand was not a brilliant human artifice; its plan and design were of God (see Ex 25:40; also cf. Heb 8:5; Rev 1:12–20).

NOTES

2 מְנוֹרָה (*mᵉnôrâ*, "lampstand") is commonly Anglicized as "menorah" (see also Ex 25:31). The term for the lampstand is associated with the word נֵר (*nēr*, "lamp"), a word that is in the plural here (נֵרֹת, *nērōt*, "lamps";

see also Ex 25:37). Household lamps in the Late Bronze Age (ca. 1550–1200 BC) were terra-cotta (baked clay) bowls of about six or more inches in diameter with a depression of an inch or so to hold the olive oil, which was the fuel. A pinched area along the rim of the bowl held the wick (often made of flax). Thousands of examples of baked-clay lamps from all periods of Israel's history are available today from archaeological excavations. The typing of pottery lamps and bowls is one of the principal means used to give a relative date to a stratum of an archaeological excavation (a "dig"). The standard reference work on pottery from biblical times is Ruth Amiran's *Ancient Pottery of the Holy Land: From Its Beginnings in the Neolithic Period to the End of the Iron Age* (Jerusalem: Massada, 1969); plate 59 (189) describes lamps from the Late Bronze Age.

No examples of the grand lamps or lampstands have surfaced from the tabernacle—or from the First Temple (the temple built by Solomon). At the time of this writing, the only ancient item that has been discovered that is believed actually to have been used in the First Temple is a beautiful, pomegranate-shaped ivory censor head. It is all the more remarkable in that it has an inscription in Hebrew: *lby [yhw] h qdš khnm*, "Belonging to [Yahwe]h, holy to the priests." See André Lamaire, "Probable Head of Priestly Scepter from Solomon's Temple Surfaces," *BAR* 10/1 (January–February 1984): 24–29. The authenticity of this inscription, however, has recently been challenged.

4 מַרְאֶה (*marʾeh*, "appearance"; "pattern," NIV) is a nominal form from the verb רָאָה (*rāʾâ*, "to see"), used here in the Hiphil with the meaning "to show." This is a familiar Hebrew device in which the object is from the same root as the verb (a cognate accusative), a device that plays to the eye and the ear and brings emphasis on the object.

(b) The separation of the Levites (8:5–22)

OVERVIEW

A pattern used in Numbers is to move from the priests to the Levites (cf. 4:5–15a, priests, with 4:15b, Levites); here the brief paragraph on priestly duties is followed by a more extensive section on the Levites. Another pattern in Numbers is to interweave texts dealing with lay persons and texts dealing with sacral persons (a point noted by Victor P. Hamilton, *Handbook on the Pentateuch* [Grand Rapids: Baker, 1982], 328). Chapters 1–2 deal with laypersons, chs. 3–4 with sacral persons, the sections 5:1–6:21 with laypersons, 6:22–27 with sacral persons, 7:1–89 with laypersons; and ch. 8 with sacral persons.

Numbers 8 is a significant text on the role and nature of the Levites in ancient Israel; it is also an important reminder of the theology of redemption. The Levites belonged to the Lord in exchange for his deliverance of the firstborn sons of Israel during the tenth plague in Egypt.

(i) Their ceremonial cleansing (8:5–14)

⁵The LORD said to Moses: ⁶"Take the Levites from among the other Israelites and make them ceremonially clean. ⁷To purify them, do this: Sprinkle the water of cleansing on them;

then have them shave their whole bodies and wash their clothes, and so purify themselves. ⁸Have them take a young bull with its grain offering of fine flour mixed with oil; then you are to take a second young bull for a sin offering. ⁹Bring the Levites to the front of the Tent of Meeting and assemble the whole Israelite community. ¹⁰You are to bring the Levites before the Lord, and the Israelites are to lay their hands on them. ¹¹Aaron is to present the Levites before the Lord as a wave offering from the Israelites, so that they may be ready to do the work of the Lord.

¹²"After the Levites lay their hands on the heads of the bulls, use the one for a sin offering to the Lord and the other for a burnt offering, to make atonement for the Levites. ¹³Have the Levites stand in front of Aaron and his sons and then present them as a wave offering to the Lord. ¹⁴In this way you are to set the Levites apart from the other Israelites, and the Levites will be mine.

COMMENTARY

5–10 This section (vv.5–14) describes the cleansing of the Levites and may be compared with the account detailing the ordination of Aaron and his sons to the priesthood (Lev 8). The Levites were helpers to the priests, and the language describing their consecration is somewhat distinct from that of the priests. The priests were made holy, the Levites clean; the priests were anointed and washed, the Levites were sprinkled; the priests were given new garments, the Levites washed theirs; blood was applied to the priests, water was sprinkled over the Levites.

One of the refrains in this section is the idea that the Levites were taken from among (*mittôk*, "from the midst of") the people (see vv.6, 14, 16, 19), thus reminding us that the Levites were distinct from the other tribes. They were to have no tribal allotment; their homes would be spread throughout the other tribes, but they were drawn from the tribes to have a special service before the Lord in assisting the priests.

The verb *ṭāhar* (GK 3197) in v.6 describes ceremonial cleansing. In the Piel stem it speaks of cleansing,

making pure—of cleansing ceremonially. The verb is used, for example, in the cleansing process for the altar of incense by applying blood from a sin offering. The cleansing process of the Levites was to begin with a sprinkling of water on them rather than with a sprinkling of blood. This water is termed *mê ḥaṭṭāʾt* (lit., "water of sin"; v.7), a phrase taken to mean "water of cleansing" or "purification from sin." A similar phrase is found in 19:9, *mê niddâ* ("water of cleansing") for purification from sin. The phrase "water of sin" may also be compared with the phrase *mê hammārîm hamʾārᵃrîm* ("bitter water producing cursing") in 5:18, used in the rite of the woman suspected of adultery.

The second factor in the cleansing of the Levites was the shaving of their entire bodies (v.7). This symbolic act speaks of the fullness of their cleansing, as in the case of the ritual cleansing of one cured of a serious skin disorder (Lev 14:8; see comments on Nu 5:2). Shaving the entire body, not just the head, was in some ways a return to innocence and an initiative symbol of purity. It is well known that hair tends to be dirty; bodily hair needs to be cleansed regularly, for the follicles tend to collect and hold dirt. The ancient Egyptians were fastidious about cleanliness; they shaved their bodies regularly and wore wigs. They were also concerned with head lice, so the shaving of the head was a protection in that regard. According to Herodotus (2.37), Egyptian priests shaved their whole bodies every other day.

The cleansing of the Levites in Israel seems not to have been a repeated action but an initial rite of purification. Since Semitic men were characterized generally in the ancient world by wearing beards and by ample body hair, the shaving of these men's bodies must have been regarded as a remarkable act of devotion to God.

The third factor in cleansing the Levites was washing their garments. The verb used for washing is *kābas* (a verb meaning "to tread, walk" [GK 3891], related to the Akkadian *kabāsu*, "to tread down, wash garments by treading"). The verb pictorially represents the ancient form of washing clothing. The same verb was used to describe the cleansing that had to be done by the whole nation when Moses was about to go to the mountain to meet with the Lord (Ex 19:10, 14). On occasion *kābas* is used in parallel with *rāhaṣ* ("to wash the person"; e.g., Lev 14:8; 15:5).

Following the sprinkling with water of purification, the shaving of their bodies, and the washing of their clothes, the Levites were ready for the next step in their purification: the presentation of their offerings and sacrifices to God. They were each to bring two bulls along with the fine flour mixed with oil that constituted the grain offering. These items would then be presented by Moses before the Tent of Meeting, with the nation gathered to witness the event (vv.8–9). The people (their representatives) would then place their hands on the

Levites (v.10) as a means of identifying with them. The Levites had come from among the people; now they would stand in their place before the Divine Presence. This was a solemn act, worthy of reflection. The Levites were the substitutes for the nation; by placing hands on them, the people of the nation dramatically acknowledged this substitutionary act (see 8:16–18).

11–14 Our text makes a subtle move from the placing of the hands of the people on the Levites to the placing of the hands of the Levites on the two bulls. This is delicious—a double substitution! The Levites substituted for the people, the bulls substituted for the Levites. The bulls, with this double signification, were then made sacrifices of sin offering and burnt offering to provide atonement for the Levites. This double ritual was engaging; persons present for these actions must have had their attention riveted to the ritual, wondering at its meaning.

In v.11 Aaron is brought more directly into the picture, as he was to present the Levites as a "wave offering" before the Lord. The notion of a "wave offering" is somewhat mysterious to us. We have some concept of burning sacrifices, of pouring out libations, and of presenting grain offerings. But the "wave" offering is the most obscure. Its idea was to hold an object, usually the part of the offering that ordinarily would be the food for the priests, before the Lord, wave it back and forth, and then keep it for one's own use. Presenting an offering in this manner was unusually symbolic—as indeed was all sacrifice!

In the case of the Levites, presumably Aaron and his sons placed their hands on the Levites' shoulders and caused them to move from side to side in a symbolic way to represent the fact that they were a living sacrifice (see Ro 12:1–2)

presented before the Lord; now they belonged to the priests to assist them in their work of service in the tabernacle. In this way the Levites were separated from the rest of the community; they belonged to the Lord, and in turn they belonged to the priests.

(ii) Their position before the Lord (8:15–19)

15"After you have purified the Levites and presented them as a wave offering, they are to come to do their work at the Tent of Meeting. 16They are the Israelites who are to be given wholly to me. I have taken them as my own in place of the firstborn, the first male offspring from every Israelite woman. 17Every firstborn male in Israel, whether man or animal, is mine. When I struck down all the firstborn in Egypt, I set them apart for myself. 18And I have taken the Levites in place of all the firstborn sons in Israel. 19Of all the Israelites, I have given the Levites as gifts to Aaron and his sons to do the work at the Tent of Meeting on behalf of the Israelites and to make atonement for them so that no plague will strike the Israelites when they go near the sanctuary."

COMMENTARY

15–16 Here the Lord acknowledged the Levites as his particular possession. The Hebrew uses the Qal passive participle $n^e tunîm$ (meaning "a given one," from $n\bar{a}tan$, "to give") and doubles the word: $n^e tunîm$ $n^e tunîm$, "given, given," meaning "given wholly" (v.16). The Levites were the substitutes for the firstborn of every mother in Israel.

The story line of salvation comes through strongly here—it centers on Passover! Israel had been in Egypt. The tenth plague was imminent. Faithful people had slaughtered a lamb, roasted it, and were eating it along with bitter herbs and matzo bread. When Yahweh (see Note on v.17) was passing over the camp of the people of Israel, he looked for blood on the posts and lintel of each home. Where that blood was found, the Lord "passed over." No one inside died. All lived. But in those homes that

lacked the prescribed blood, there came blood; instead of the blood of an animal on the bracing of the door, there was blood in the bed of the oldest child; for the Lord had extracted the most vicious toll, the death of the firstborn. The firstborn children of the faithful Israelites were not killed. They lived. But for them a price needed to be paid, and that price was the Levites. The Levites were to be taken in the service of God (v.15) as a redemptive substitute for the firstborn whose lives were spared in homes displaying the sacrifical blood on post and lintel.

17 The statement "every ... man or animal" is inclusive. No similar ritual was necessary for the animals; the focus was on people.

18–19 The Levites were the people given to the Lord for his exclusive use (v.18; cf. v.14). In v.19 the

Lord gave his Levites to the priests as their aids for the work of the ministry in the tabernacle worship. The Levites had three functions: (1) they served the priests in their work at the tabernacle, generally responsible for the heavy work that priestly duties demanded (*laʿăbōd ʿet-ʿăbōdâ*, lit., "to do the work of the work"); 2) they brought redemption for the firstborn of the nation (*taḥat*, "in place of"; vv. 16, 18); and (3) they served as a protective hedge, an atonement (*ûleₑkappēr*, "and to make atonement"; v. 19), against unwarranted approaches of the holy things, "so that no plague will strike the Israelites." The Levites were a protective hedge for the community against trespass in sacred precincts of the tabernacle (see 1:53).

In this language we have portraits of both the wrath and the mercy of the Lord. His wrath would be extended against evil assaults on his holiness, but in his mercy he had a protective hedge to prevent such confrontations. Throughout these chapters there is an insistence on God's wrath and mercy and on his holiness and grace. To hold one of these excellencies out of balance with the other distorts in some manner the biblical portrait of our Father.

NOTE

17 הַכֹּתִי כָל־בְּכוֹר בְּאֶרֶץ מִצְרַיִם (*hakkōtî kol–bekôr beʾereṣ miṣrayim*, "I struck all the firstborn in the land of Egypt") sets the record straight. It is not unusual for people to speak of "the angel of death" as the instrument of God on this horrific night; in fact, I did this myself in the 1990 edition of this commentary! But it was not "the angel of death" who engaged in this awful work; *it was Yahweh himself.* The awesome fact is that *the Lord,* the Creator of all and the Redeemer of Israel, was the one who destroyed the firstborn sons in all the homes of the Egyptians. In fact, in the words of the Haggadah, the liturgy for the Passover Seder, this fact is emphasized strongly. The words of this libretto of salvation insist that it was not an angel, not a seraph, but the Lord himself in his own glory who came near to deliver his people by this awesome act of judgment on their enemies.

(iii) A summary of their separation (8:20–22)

²⁰Moses, Aaron and the whole Israelite community did with the Levites just as the LORD commanded Moses. ²¹The Levites purified themselves and washed their clothes. Then Aaron presented them as a wave offering before the LORD and made atonement for them to purify them. ²²After that, the Levites came to do their work at the Tent of Meeting under the supervision of Aaron and his sons. They did with the Levites just as the LORD commanded Moses.

COMMENTARY

20–22 This section serves two functions: it reports the completion of the act of separation as a literary device; it also reports the obedience of the people as a mark of their initial compliance to the will and work of God. Verses of complete obedience to Yahweh's commands occur regularly in the first chapters of Numbers (see 1:54; 2:34; 3:16, 51; 4:49; 5:4; 8:4, 20, 22; 9:5, 23). The implicit obedience of Moses and the people of Israel to God's commands in the areas of ritual and regimen leave us unprepared for their complaints against his loving character and their outrageous breaches of faith in the rebellions that begin in ch. 11.

(c) The age of service of the Levites (8:23–26)

²³The Lord said to Moses, ²⁴"This applies to the Levites: Men twenty-five years old or more shall come to take part in the work at the Tent of Meeting, ²⁵but at the age of fifty, they must retire from their regular service and work no longer. ²⁶They may assist their brothers in performing their duties at the Tent of Meeting, but they themselves must not do the work. This, then, is how you are to assign the responsibilities of the Levites."

COMMENTARY

23–26 At 4:3 the age for the service of the Levite is said to be from thirty to fifty. The present paragraph has the same upper limit but a new lower limit, twenty-five years. This is a controverted passage; the problem is not easily solved (see Note).

After a Levite had reached the mandatory retirement age of fifty, he was still free to assist his younger coworkers as long as he was able to do so (perhaps at the great festivals), but he was no longer to do the hard and difficult work he had done in his prime. Again, in these regulations we sense the holiness and mercy of God. His holiness demanded that his ministers had to be fully able to do the work that was required of them; to slip or err in holy things was a most grievous offense. His mercy precluded a man from doing the work that was demanded when he might be past his physical prime. There were to be no elderly, doddering Levites stumbling about in the precincts of the Holy Place, carrying poles too heavy for them or doing things they were no longer fit to do.

The last words of the chapter, "This, then, is how you are to assign the responsibilities of the Levites," serve as a fine finish for the section that begins, "Take the Levites from among the other Israelites" (v.6). This is another example of the beauty of order in the book of Numbers. Not only was the camp to be ordered and the work of the cultic personnel to be done in order, so was the written record of these descriptions to be one in superb order. Finally, the order and organization presented by this chapter further elevated the significance of the Levites. They were treated with dignity and honor, for they held a special function in the worship of God for the good of the community.

NOTE

24 We know King David reduced to twenty the age for entering Levitical service (1Ch 23:24, 27), as the circumstances of the Levites' work had greatly changed by the time of the monarchy (v.26). Yet it is difficult to imagine a change in circumstances between Numbers 4:3 and 8:24 (as Noordtzij, 81, suggests), if these texts are regarded as both from Moses and ultimately from God. Critical scholars, of course, seize on such contradictions as indicators of varied sources used in the making of the Pentateuch (Noth, 67, calls this "a later correction," and Budd, 90–92, posits a highly complex picture of late editing). Yet one would think that such an obvious "blunder" could have been smoothed over by even a rather lazy redactor.

The blatant distinction between the ages given in these two chapters (which naturally call for comparison) suggests the possibility that at the time these words were written no one saw any contradiction in these numbers. For these reasons the rabbinical harmonization of these two texts appears to be appropriate with their suggestion of a five-year period of apprenticeship. The contrary data in the texts themselves call for harmonization on the part of the reader—a demand for the careful reading of Scripture by those who are sympathetic to the integrity of the text. And this is the critical issue—*prior sympathy* with the text.

Here is a *negative* example of the concept of prior sympathy, presented by means of analogy. As I am revising the words on this page, angry reports flood the American airwaves concerning charges by some African Americans whose lives were devastated by the ravages of Hurricane Katrina in New Orleans in August 2005. These hurt, angry people testified before a committee of the American Congress, making damning, incendiary claims, that the levees of their city were deliberately destroyed by white officials as planned acts to annihilate the city's black communities. People can believe such unfounded claims of "American genocide" only if they already have the mindset that white people (powerful and evil) could (and would) perpetrate such atrocities. A person who does not have that prior mindset finds the testimony of these unfortunate individuals to be misguided rantings of pain, not reliable reports of truth.

So we revert now to a *positive* example of prior sympathy. The late Dr. John F. Walvoord, long-time president of the Dallas Theological Seminary, used to say in his classes something of the following, with regard to the issue of what to do when facing difficulties in the biblical text. "Imagine the Bible as a long-time friend," he would say, "a friend whom you have learned to trust, to appreciate, to rely on—even with your very life. Then imagine that someone reports in your hearing something truly evil about your friend. What would your first inclination be?" Walvoord would say that if one's knowledge, trust, and confidence in his or her friend were truly deep and stemmed from long-practiced experience, such a person would not immediately believe the accusation. "You would have a 'wait and see' attitude. You would want to investigate; you would not jump to a negative conclusion. You would look for a solution." So it is with a *prior sympathy* toward the biblical text.

v. The celebration of the Passover (9:1 – 14)

OVERVIEW

Numbers 9 begins with instruction and interaction—a dynamic exchange between the Lord and Moses that provides a rare glimpse into how the Lord's instruction for his people could be modified on the basis of new conditions and circumstances (cf. also Nu 27). The theological implications of this dynamic are enormous, as we will see. The particular issue addressed in Numbers 9 concerns the command of the Lord for the celebration of the Passover in the second year of Israel's redemption and the request for special treatment prompted by those who were ceremonially unclean at the time and hence excluded from participating in this sacred festival. The first Passover was celebrated in Egypt on the eve of the redemption of the nation from bondage (see Ex 12 for details). Now, a year later, the celebration was to be commemorated by the redeemed populace in the shadow of Mount Sinai.

(a) The command to keep the Passover (9:1 – 5)

> [1]The LORD spoke to Moses in the Desert of Sinai in the first month of the second year after they came out of Egypt. He said, [2]"Have the Israelites celebrate the Passover at the appointed time. [3]Celebrate it at the appointed time, at twilight on the fourteenth day of this month, in accordance with all its rules and regulations."
>
> [4]So Moses told the Israelites to celebrate the Passover, [5]and they did so in the Desert of Sinai at twilight on the fourteenth day of the first month. The Israelites did everything just as the LORD commanded Moses.

COMMENTARY

1–2 The arrangement of materials in Numbers is not strictly chronological, as we have observed from time to time. The events of this chapter actually precede the beginning of the census of 1:2 ("the first day of the second month of the second year"; 1:1). The first two months of the second year of redemption were an exceedingly busy period of activity. (See the Notes for a chronological listing of the events of chs. 1 – 10.) The long stay at the base of Mount Sinai was not a time of inactivity or indolence. It was a time of much activity in celebration of the goodness and mercy of the Lord and in preparation for what was expected to have been the soon triumphal march into the land of Canaan. The chronological discontinuity of this book suggests that the principle of arrangement is not time related (see Introduction: Unity and Organization).

The first Passover was held in Egypt in the midst of the saving works of the Lord (Ex 12); this next one is to be celebrated in the Desert of Sinai in commemoration of his works, as commanded by him (Ex 12:14: "for the generations to come"). The celebration of Passover was to become a regular commemorative act by the redeemed Hebrew community, just as celebrating the Lord's Supper is the regular commemorative act by the redeemed community in Christ.

Verses 1–2 have two discreet emphases. The first concerns the appropriate time and the proper regulations for the Passover; the second is found in the verb "to celebrate." Repeatedly in these few verses we find an interchange between the words "appropriate time" and "celebrate." In these two words are compelling complementary ideas. The first is a proper focus on the demands, obligations, and rites of worship in Hebrew Scripture. The second is the opportunity for the people to reach out for the celebrative, enjoyable, and festive nature of that worship.

Error may come in omitting either aspect. To lose sight of the regulation is to trespass in presumption. To forget the celebrative is to lose the joy and heart of worship; merely to follow the obligation is to slip into the dreary work of "religion." Any approach to God by his people ought to meld these two ideas. Only in that which is appropriate is there really room for true celebration; celebration apart from a sense of the appropriate is the bittersweet failure of pseudo-happiness.

3–4 The Hebrew term *bên haᶜarbayim*, translated "at twilight" (v.3), speaks poignantly: "between the evenings," denoting that period just between sunset and true darkness. In traditional Hebrew practice, this period is regarded as the end of one day and the beginning of the next. The official determination of the precise moment of twilight in Jewish tradition became that point where one could no longer distinguish between white and black threads when standing outside in the growing darkness.

In addition to the emphasis on the appropriate timing of the Passover, we find ourselves impressed with the necessity for complete obedience to the legislation of the celebration. It was to be celebrated according to all of its statutes and judgments. These correlative words speak in hendiadys of complete compliance to detail, a full respect for and obedience to the regulations that God had established. This emphasis on complete obedience in the minute details can lead in two directions: (1) to the obedience of faith that regarded the minute details as important and that understood that compliance to them was that which would bring the pleasure of the Lord; (2) to legalism that found itself so preoccupied with the details and regulations as to lose the primary sense of the meaning God had in the legislation in the first place. We observe with sadness that the latter direction has characterized postbiblical Judaism, even as was the case in the lives of so many Hebrew people in the NT era.

5 Verse 5 is a report of compliance—yet another example of the obedience of Israel to the demands of the Lord in these early chapters of Numbers. Reports such as this assure us that things were as they should have been. Yet these same reports ill-prepare us for the dreadful rebellion of Israel at Kadesh, described in the following chapters.

NOTES

1 The chronology of the first two months of the second year after the exodus is as follows.

1. The setting up of the tabernacle (7:1) was declared to be completed on the first day of the first month of the second year (Ex 40:2). On this day the cloud covered the tabernacle, as we will see later in this chapter (Nu 9:15–23). Then, in response to the symbol of God's presence over the completed tabernacle, also on that day the first of the offerings from the twelve leaders of the tribes

was given to the Lord (7:3–17). The presentation of the gifts from each tribe extended until the twelfth day of this month.

2. The setting apart of the Levites (8:26) presumably followed immediately after the twelve days of gifts, perhaps on the thirteenth day of the month. It seems unlikely that the setting apart of the Levites would have been on the same day as the last of the tribal gifts; to have another significant action on that day would have minimized the importance of the gifts of Ahira of Naphtali (7:78–83).

3. The second Passover was celebrated on the fourteenth day of the first month (9:5).

4. The census began on the first day of the second month (1:1–2).

5. Those who were ceremonially unclean at the time of the second Passover were permitted to celebrate it on the fourteenth day of the second month (9:11).

6. Then the cloud lifted and the march from Sinai began on the twentieth day of the second month (10:11).

2 The verb used throughout this section is the common term עָשָׂה (ʿāśâ, "to do"). It has an extraordinary range of meaning in biblical usage. The translation "celebrate" for וְיַעֲשׂוּ (weyaʿăśû) is appropriate here because of the environment of the festival that Passover suggests.

הַפֶּסַח (happesaḥ, "the Passover") has three basic usages in the MT: (1) the sacrifice of the Passover, the associated communion meal (as in Ex 12:11, 27); (2) the animal that is sacrificed, the particular lamb or goat of Passover (as in Ex 12:21); and (3) the Feast of the Passover, which is the broader use (as in 9:2).

בְּמוֹעֲדוֹ (bemôʿădô, "at the appointed time") is from the verb יָעַד (yāʿad, "to appoint"). This word is the same as that used to describe the "Tent of Meeting" (12:4), which could also be called "the tent of the appointed meeting."

(b) The ceremonially unclean (9:6–8)

> [6] But some of them could not celebrate the Passover on that day because they were ceremonially unclean on account of a dead body. So they came to Moses and Aaron that same day [7] and said to Moses, "We have become unclean because of a dead body, but why should we be kept from presenting the LORD's offering with the other Israelites at the appointed time?"
>
> [8] Moses answered them, "Wait until I find out what the LORD commands concerning you."

COMMENTARY

6–7 Crisis developed within the community because of ritual impurity on the part of some; they had come in contact with a dead body. As seen in 5:1, such contact rendered a person ritually unclean and no longer able to participate in the community until rites of purification had been completed (see v.2). Hence a person in a state of ritual impurity would not have been permitted to participate in the celebrative Feast of the Passover. The section points to two issues: (1) the desire of these people to obey God fully in his calls for worship and festivals, and (2) the formidable obstacle of participation based on ritual uncleanness.

The concept of ritual impurity is so foreign to modern thinking as to be nearly unintelligible to most readers. The idea of being "unclean" is not simply that of being physically soiled, of course, though that which was dirty might have been a physical presentment of what was "unclean." The best way for us to think of the notion of "uncleanness" is as a teaching device to remind the people of Israel of the holiness of God. The idea that any person at all might have the effrontery to dare to approach the presence of the Lord is audacious in itself. Only by God's grace might anyone come before him to worship. By developing a concept of ritual purity, an external symbol, the notion of internal purity might be presented.

In the Bible the notions of external symbols are representative of internal realities. Only the obdurate miss the point here. In Jesus' numerous confrontations with the Pharisees, the principal battle was not over the essential demands of God but centered on the tendencies the Pharisees had in focusing on external compliance without due attention to internal meaning (see, e.g., Mt 23:27–28). In the present passage, the recognition of ceremonial uncleanness on the part of some people and their consequent inability to participate in the activities of celebrative worship in the Passover speaks of their high level of compliance to the dictates of Torah and their keen desire to worship the Lord in spirit and truth (see Jn 4:24).

8 Moses responded that he would seek an answer from the Lord to redress the people's need; this answer presents an amazing dynamic in Scripture (see Notes). In this instance there were two conflicting ideals: the demand of the Lord for the community-wide celebration of Passover was confronted by ceremonial uncleanness of a part of the community. In a case of such conflict, Moses sought the intervention of the Lord—a new word from glory (see comments on 27:5, 21). That word would bring a means of maintaining the best of both ideals without compromising either.

We may also observe that Moses' response to the genuine needs of believing people is a mark of his spiritual leadership, his humility before God, and his desire to be the spokesman not only for the Lord to the people but also for the people back to the Lord. In this scenario we have not only a historical instance but also a template for how such decisions should be made. Another dramatic example of this process is found in ch. 27 regarding the problem of the estate of a father who has daughters but no sons.

NOTES

6 לְנֶפֶשׁ (l\ enepeš, "to a person, to a soul"; "on account of a dead body," NIV) employs the preposition "to" or "for" plus the noun often translated as "soul" or "person."

8 מַה־יְּצַוֶּה יהוה לָכֶם (mah-y\ eṣawweh yhwh lākem, "what Yahweh may command for you") suggests that Moses would consult the Lord through the priest by means of the Urim and Thummim; see Note at 27:21 for a development of this concept.

(c) Divine permission for a legitimate delay (9:9–13)

⁹Then the LORD said to Moses, ¹⁰"Tell the Israelites:'When any of you or your descendants are unclean because of a dead body or are away on a journey, they may still celebrate the LORD's Passover. ¹¹They are to celebrate it on the fourteenth day of the second month at twilight. They are to eat the lamb, together with unleavened bread and bitter herbs. ¹²They must not leave any of it till morning or break any of its bones. When they celebrate the Passover, they must follow all the regulations. ¹³But if a man who is ceremonially clean and not on a journey fails to celebrate the Passover, that person must be cut off from his people because he did not present the LORD's offering at the appointed time. That man will bear the consequences of his sin.

COMMENTARY

9–11 The grace of God can be seen not only in the words of his response to Moses but also in that he responded at all. We need to grasp anew the concept of the audacity of faith: by what right, excepting only God's great grace, did Moses dare to go before Yahweh, the Creator of the universe, and request a provision for exception from his demands? All God's actions and words to his people were gracious, undeserved, and unmerited. That he spoke at all, even in demands, was a mark of his condescension; that he spoke favorably in response to the request of Moses is a marvel. Throughout we have a sense of the ongoing wonder of grace.

God's gracious provision for those ritually unclean was an alternative opportunity to celebrate the Passover on a day one month later so that they would not be excluded totally from its observance. The text thus presents the reality of the distancing that uncleanness brought between a believer and his or her participation in the worship acts of the community; it also provided a merciful alternative from the Lord. Further, the answer of the Lord went even beyond the request by add-

ing the alternative of a later celebration for those who might be away on a trip in addition to those who were ritually impure.

This gracious and provident provision of the Lord is not dissimilar to some modern civil legislation. For example, the United States' tax code emphasizes strongly the notion of an "appointed time" for filing one's tax returns; yet it also includes provisions for late filing because of personal exigency or foreign travel. As in the case of the law of the Lord, these provisions do not nullify the obligation; they only delay it. There is no mercy for one who merely decides not to obey. The text gives no room for indifference (KD 3:52); God's mercy must never be trampled by the uncaring.

Even when the Passover was celebrated a month later, it was still to be done fully in order. The text emphasizes the essentials of the meal and the essentials of the ritual. In terms of the meal, there was to be the lamb (noted by the word "Passover"), the unleavened bread, and the bitter herbs. In our own day, in the traditional Passover Haggadah ("recitation"), Rabbi Gamaliel, the teacher of Saul (renamed Paul, the apostle; see Ac 22:3 [5:34–39]; also Ac 21:39; 26:4–5; Gal 1:13–14), is quoted as saying that if anyone does not eat the lamb, the unleavened bread, and the bitter herbs, he has not kept the Passover. He built his direction on this passage.

12 The strictures for the Passover include two additional items in this verse: (1) none of the feast was to be left over until morning, and (2) the bones of the sacrificial lamb were not to be broken. Eating the Passover lamb and its attendant foods was to be done entirely in one evening. This provision follows the original command for Passover in Exodus 12:10 (and 12:46, which even insists that the meal be consumed in one house, family by family, and not carried from one house to another), where Moses was commanded to have the people burn any of the meat not eaten the night before.

The concept of not leaving sacred foods over until morning also extended to the legislation respecting manna (see Ex 16:19) and the fat of the three annual sacrifices (Ex 23:18). No reasons are given for this part of the legislation, but we surmise these possibilities: (1) the meal of Passover was not to be regarded as an ordinary meal but as a great feast that was a sacred occasion between the Lord and his people; (2) hence the food of the Passover was not like ordinary food that could with impunity be used as leftovers at one's next meal; and (3) secondary to these religious reasons was (perhaps) an implied health aspect that underlies some of the legislation in Torah concerning food: there was, of course, no refrigeration in ancient times, and cooked meats that were exposed to heat and humidity would soon go bad. The Hebrew people would eat meat infrequently, in part because of the difficulties of safe food preservation.

The second emphasis in v.12 is in the words "or break any of its bones." This was also a provision of the first legislation of Passover in Exodus 12:46. When the Lord Jesus ("our Passover lamb," 1Co 5:7; see also Jn 1:29) was crucified, John writes that none of his bones was broken, in fulfillment of Scripture (Jn 19:36). The passages John points to include Numbers 9:12 (plus Ex 12:46; Ps 34:20). This concept is one of many in the Hebrew Scriptures that we may presume the first readers would not have understood to be predictive of the Messiah. It may be that there are similar surprises awaiting us with respect to the fulfillment of prophecy in his second coming.

13 Wherever there is grace, there are those who will make presumption. Those who had no reason not to celebrate the Passover and simply failed to do so were to be cut off from the community. God's gracious provision for the distressed to have an alternative time of celebration was not to be license for the careless person to ignore the Passover altogether. Such people, by their own neglect, showed that they were not part of the community and were not deserving of further union with it. The obdurate were to be "cut off," a phrase signifying either death by divine agency or perhaps banishment. In either case the judgment was severe indeed. The NT also gravely warns against the abuse or misuse of the celebration of the Lord's Table (1Co 11:28–30).

NOTES

10 אִישׁ אִישׁ (ʾîš ʾîš, "man man") is repetition for distribution, "if any man" or "any of you" (NIV; noted in Williams, *Hebrew Syntax*, sec. 15; see also 1:4; 14:34).

רְחֹקָה (rᵉḥōqâ, "away, distant") is marked on the final ה (h, הָ = āh or â) with a superior dot or point (see Note at 3:39), an early scribal mark, explained by the *Sipre* on Numbers 9: "to denote that even he who is on a short journey and is defiled must not offer with them the Passover" (Ginsburg, 319). Ginsburg's own conclusion is that this letter (indicating a feminine adjective) should be dropped, as דֶּרֶךְ (*derek*, "way, journey") is more frequently found with a masculine adjective (ibid., 323).

(d) The rights of the alien at Passover (9:14)

> [14]"'An alien living among you who wants to celebrate the LORD's Passover must do so in accordance with its rules and regulations. You must have the same regulations for the alien and the native-born.'"

COMMENTARY

14 An alien male had to be circumcised before he could participate in the Passover celebration (cf. Ex 12:48). But there was an opening for the non-Israelite who had come to faith in the God of Israel to participate fully with the Israelites in holy worship. This is the point of Yahweh's gracious promise to Abram: "and all peoples on earth / will be blessed through you" (Ge 12:3). The inclusion of the alien in covenantal legislation such as this reminds us of God's great grace and also of his determined purpose to reach out through his people to all peoples.

vi. The covering cloud (9:15–23)

> [15]On the day the tabernacle, the Tent of the Testimony, was set up, the cloud covered it. From evening till morning the cloud above the tabernacle looked like fire. [16]That is how it continued to be; the cloud covered it, and at night it looked like fire. [17]Whenever the cloud lifted from above the Tent, the Israelites set out; wherever the cloud settled, the Israelites encamped. [18]At the LORD's command the Israelites set out, and at his command they encamped. As long as the cloud stayed over the tabernacle, they remained in camp. [19]When the cloud remained over the tabernacle a long time, the Israelites obeyed the LORD's order and did not set out. [20]Sometimes the cloud was over the tabernacle only a few days; at the LORD's command they would encamp, and then at his command they would set out. [21]Sometimes the cloud stayed only from evening till morning, and when it lifted in the morning, they set out. Whether by day or by night, whenever the cloud lifted, they set out. [22]Whether the cloud stayed over the tabernacle for two days or a month or a

year, the Israelites would remain in camp and not set out; but when it lifted, they would set out. ²³At the LORD's command they encamped, and at the LORD's command they set out. They obeyed the LORD's order, in accordance with his command through Moses.

COMMENTARY

15 The cloud (*he^cānān*; GK 6727) was the dramatic symbol of the presence of the Lord hovering above the tabernacle (cf. Ex 13:21; 40:34; see Notes). That this was no ordinary cloud is attested not only by its spontaneous appearance at the completion of the setting up of the tabernacle but also by the fact that at night it had the appearance of fire. It was by means of the cloud that the Lord directed the movements of his people (see R. B. Allen, ^cānān, *TWOT*, 2:684, #1655a).

16 It must have been an extraordinary sight — this mystic cloud, this fiery heaviness, this enveloping presence. In the words "that is how it continued to be," the text suggests the permanent abiding of the cloud over the camp. The Hebrew word *tāmîd* has the sense of "continually, incessantly." The idea of the presence was so impressive that there was an implied threat if ever this presence was found missing. The cloud and fire were both reversals of the expected phenomena of the time. Both the cloud and the fire were striking, unusual, and unexpected symbols of Yahweh's protective care for his people. These were symbols one would not, could not ignore. They were awesome and eerie, unnatural and unexpected, comforting and protective. To relieve the heat of the wilderness sun, there was the symbol of a cloud by day. To reverse the cold darkness of the wilderness night, there was the symbol of a comforting fire overhead. Everything about this paragraph is wrapped in mystery, a mystic sense of the Divine Presence. The passage shimmers with awe and delight.

But this text also manifests something of regret, of loss. The vantage point of the language of the passage is to describe something that used to be true but is no longer visible. The description is not unlike that of manna in 11:7. The tense of the verbs does not suggest a present reality but a historical experience. In this paragraph in which something from the past is evoked, we sense the possibility of a later hand's adding this description to the text of Numbers. That is, Moses and his original audience were the participants in these events, the ones who observed directly the manifestation of the cloud of the presence. There would be no need for Moses to say to his contemporaries that the cloud reminded them of fire at night or that it gave the signals for encampment or for setting out on the march. All this was a vital part of their personal experience. However, if we view the second generation as the original readers of Numbers and their children as the readers to come, we may maintain the idea that Moses did write this section.

17 Two significant verbs are used to describe the presence of the cloud as the symbol of God's nearness. One is the verb meaning "to cover" (v.15; see Notes); the other is the verb meaning "to settle" (v.17; see Notes). The expression "wherever the cloud settled" uses the significant verb *šakan* (GK 8905), which gives us the basis for the idea of the "Shekinah glory" (see Note on 5:3). "Shekinah," surprisingly, is not a biblical word. It is built on the verb meaning "to dwell" [[see Note at 5:3]]. The

Hebrew text rings with the sound of *šākan* as this verb is also the basis for the term for "tabernacle," *miškān*. This phrasing symbolizes both God's nearness and his remoteness. He is present as a cloud, but he hovers above; he is near as a fire, but one cannot draw very close. He is *God*!

18 The words "at the LORD's command" are more literally, "by the mouth of Yahweh." The cloud was one of the ways in which the Lord spoke to his people. The identification of the lifting and settling of the cloud and the command of the Lord was made sure in this and the following verses. The cloud was the means God used to direct the movements and the resting times of his people Israel.

19–22 The movement of the cloud and its presence were unpredictable, without discernable pattern. This was to impress on the people the sense that it was God who was leading them, not some pattern of creation or some whim from above. The cloud might linger only a day or so, or it might linger in one spot nearly indefinitely. The wording of these verses allowed for a lengthy stay (v.19), a briefer stay (v.20), or a very short stay (v.21). Whatever the duration, the people were to move or to encamp based on the movement or settling of the cloud.

23 This verse gives a report of compliance: "They obeyed the LORD's order." The repetitious nature of this section (vv.15–23) enhances the expectation of continued obedience to the sure direction of the Lord in Israel's movements through the wilderness. The role of Moses is mentioned for balance: Moses was the Lord's agent who interpreted the movement of the cloud as signaling the movement of the people. The level of the tragedy of their subsequent disobedience is heightened by this paragraph of great obedience.

The whole section (vv.15–23) is harmonious. There are several repeated phrasings ("by the mouth of," "the cloud," "settling/lifting," and "journeying/encamping"). The perspective seems to be distant from the event. The narrator uses broad strokes of summary, suggesting the ideals of God's direction and the promptness of the people's response. There is no hint of disobedience here.

NOTES

15 וּבְיוֹם (*ûbᵉyôm*, "on the day," NIV) can be translated as "when." The Hebrew expression for "on the day" is more properly וּבַיּוֹם (*ûbayyôm*, i.e., with the definite article indicated).

כִּסָּה (*kissâ*, "covered," the Piel perfect of the verb כָּסָה, *kāsâ*) is a lovely pictorial image of the presence of Yahweh in the form of a "covering cloud" over the tabernacle (found also in Ex 40:34, paired with the verb "to settle"; see Note on v.17).

16 The versions read the word "by day" in the phrase "the cloud covered it *by day*." The Hebrew word יוֹמָם (*yômām*, "by day") is lacking in the MT, but its insertion is likely a proper emendation.

17 On יִשְׁכָּן־שָׁם הֶעָנָן (*yiškān-šām heʿānān*, "the cloud would settle there") using the Qal imperfect form of the verb שָׁכַן (*šākan*, "to settle down, abide"), see Note at 5:3.

18 עַל־פִּי יהוה (*ʿal-pî yhwh*, "according to the mouth of Yahweh," i.e., according to the command of the Lord; "the LORD's order," NIV) is a characteristic phrase of compliance to the word of God in Numbers. The expression is found seven times in vv.18–23 (twice in v.18; twice in v.20; three times in v.23). The repetition of this phrase seven times in this pericope is inescapably emphatic. The phrase is also found in 3:16, 39; 4:37, 41, 45, 49; and 10:13.

REFLECTION

The emphasis in this section is on God's grace and the people's recognition of his grace, marked by their prompt response. God's grace is apparent in his giving them direction at all, his giving it by clear signs, and his provision of Moses as the interpreter of his meaning (v.23). A passage that speaks in this manner is didactic of how his people should respond to God. The second generation should obey God this well, and future generations (down to our own day!) should take a lesson. God will be directing them also, and they (and we) must attend to his voice.

Note too an emphasis on the sovereignty of God in this text. The variation from a night's rest, to a camp of a couple of days, to a month-long rest, to a lengthy period of many years was all dependent on the work and will of God. In no case was there an explanation given by or needed from God. "Just watch the cloud," one might say, "and we will know what to do." George Bush (*Notes on Numbers* [1856; repr., Minneapolis: James & Klock, 1976], 132) writes, "In this there is evidently nothing capricious or unstable to be charged upon the people, as their movements were constantly regulated by the divine direction, and this again was undoubtedly governed by reasons of infinite wisdom, though not expressly made known."

vii. The two silver trumpets (10:1–10)

OVERVIEW

All seemed to be in readiness for the triumphal march of the people of God. They have been mustered for battle and stationed for encampment. They have been put through numerous paces of purification ritual, celebrated their deliverance from Egypt in the Feast of Passover, worshiped the Lord with sumptuous gifts, responded faithfully to his every word through his prophet Moses, and sensed the awe of his presence through cloud and fire. Two tasks remained: the fashioning of trumpets and the establishment of the appropriate tattoos they will signal. Then, let the march begin!

(a) The command to fashion two silver trumpets (10:1–7)

¹The LORD said to Moses: ²"Make two trumpets of hammered silver, and use them for calling the community together and for having the camps set out. ³When both are sounded, the whole community is to assemble before you at the entrance to the Tent of Meeting. ⁴If only one is sounded, the leaders—the heads of the clans of Israel—are to assemble before you. ⁵When a trumpet blast is sounded, the tribes camping on the east

are to set out. [6]At the sounding of a second blast, the camps on the south are to set out. The blast will be the signal for setting out. [7]To gather the assembly, blow the trumpets, but not with the same signal.

COMMENTARY

1 Ordinarily, an expectation in the wording in such a verse as this is a sequential act, one that follows one event and precedes another. However, it is possible that this introductory sentence may be intended to be read as something that God had said on an earlier occasion; its placement here between the narrative reporting the enveloping cloud (9:15–23) and that describing the beginnings of the march (10:11–35) may not be sequentially significant but it may indeed be topically appropriate. Throughout these early chapters of Numbers there is a topical presentation rather than a chronological arrangement of the material. God may have instructed Moses to have these trumpets fashioned months before the people actually set out on their triumphant march. I suspect that considerable time would have been needed for Moses (and/or his artisans; see Note) to make these trumpets of hammered silver.

2 While it is possible that the Lord's command to Moses allowed an artisan to work under his direction, the MT has the type of construction that often means the command is to be done by the person addressed. Perhaps Moses himself hammered out these trumpets. It is evident that the idea of the hammered trumpet was well known to Moses; the Lord did not need to give him directions on what one would look like or how it would function (see Note).

The Bible speaks of two types of trumpets. One is the silver trumpet, such as this chapter presents

(see also 31:6; 1Ch 13:8; 2Ch 13:12; 29:26; Ps 98:6). The other is the ram's horn trumpet, called the shofar (*šôpār*; see Jos 6:4) or the horn (*qeren*; see Jos 6:5). Both the ram's horn and the silver metal instruments are far removed from the modern trumpet, as, lacking valves, they only are capable of producing notes of certain intervals, such as fourths or fifths. But like all trumpets these instruments would amplify and channel the sound made by the rapid buzzing of pursed lips.

These two trumpets may be compared to the post horn. They were a long, straight, slender metal tube with a flared end. As in the case of the fashioned cherubim and the lampstand, the trumpet or clarion was made of hammered metal. Trumpets would be blown for order and discipline; the immense numbers of the people presented an evident need for demonstrating order and discipline among the ranks.

3–7 Two trumpets were blown for assembly of the people (v.3) and one for assembly of the leaders (v.4). Trumpets were also blown as a signal to the people to set out on a march (vv.5–6), at times of battle (v.9), and during festivals of worship (v.10). Obviously, different tattoos would be used ("but not with the same signal"; v.7); hence we may presume the development of a guild of priestly musicians was demanded (v.8). These were not casual players who would "jam" from time to time; they were professional players whose music making was as serious as the work of a soldier on the battlefield and as sacred as the tasks done by a sacrificing priest in the tabernacle courts. See comments on 21:14–15 respecting songs and warfare in ancient Israel.

NOTE

2 Language similar to עֲשֵׂה לְךָ (*caśēh lekā*, "make to you," i.e., "*you* make!") is used by God in his initial command to Abram (Ge 12:1), "*you* go!" (see also Nu 13:2; 35:11). This type of command (sometimes termed the dative of personal reference) means that it must be obeyed by the one addressed; it may not be delegated. Williams (*Hebrew Syntax*, sec. 272) terms this function of the letter *lamed* (*l*) as "reflexive, restricted to the same person as the subject of the verb." Hirsch, 151, presents a Jewish tradition that the prepositional phrase *lekā* in this text was used to exclude others from using these trumpets after the death of Moses. My suggestion is that the hammering of silver to make a trumpet would have taken a particular skill. Moses may have been commanded by God to supervise this work, to see that it was done in the best manner possible. In this way he could obey the command in the particular way communicated by the verbal form here.

Yahweh's command to Moses that he make שְׁתֵּי חֲצוֹצְרֹת (*šettê haṣôṣerōt*, "two trumpets") did not come with instructions. That is, the concept of the hammered silver trumpet was sufficiently well known for the work to be accomplished as ordered by God. This factoid is a piece of a larger whole: None of the musical instruments used by God's people under his direction was of original Hebrew design or manufacture! That is, all of the instruments used in Yahweh's holy worship and under his blessing were borrowed from neighboring peoples.

In other words, these instruments had first been used in pagan temples by pagan peoples in the worship of pagan gods. But the Lord directed his people to take these instruments and to dedicate them to his use (see Allen and Allen, 160, 275). Joachim Braun (*Music in Ancient Israel/Palestine: Archaeological, Written, and Comparative Sources* [trans. Douglas W. Stott; Grand Rapids: Eerdmans, 2002], 207–9) describes ancient biblical trumpets (including the relevance of the disputed graphic display of trumpets from the Second Temple on the Arch of Titus).

(b) The ordinance for the silver trumpets (10:8–10)

⁸"The sons of Aaron, the priests, are to blow the trumpets. This is to be a lasting ordinance for you and the generations to come. ⁹When you go into battle in your own land against an enemy who is oppressing you, sound a blast on the trumpets. Then you will be remembered by the LORD your God and rescued from your enemies. ¹⁰Also at your times of rejoicing—your appointed feasts and New Moon festivals—you are to sound the trumpets over your burnt offerings and fellowship offerings, and they will be a memorial for you before your God. I am the LORD your God."

COMMENTARY

8 The role of the sons of Aaron as the sole players of these silver trumpets in ancient Israel further signals the sacral function of this music. These instruments were not just noisemakers; they were like the lampstand and the censures, sacred implements in the worship of God.

9 In times of battle the distinctive Israelite trumpet tattoo for war would be blown so that (1) Israel would be remembered before the Lord, and (2) the people might be rescued from their enemies. In this way the blowing of the trumpet is seen to be analogous to prayer, a means of participation in activating the will of God. God's will *will* be done whether we pray or not. But by praying we become expectant of his response, and we praise him when he does respond in the manner of our prayer. The blowing of trumpets was another means for participating in the "activating" of God's will. By blowing the trumpets before the battle, Israel could confidently expect God's active presence in the battle scene. The blowing of these trumpets prepared the people for the presence of God.

10 As in the case of battle, it appears that the blowing of the trumpets was a means of knowing that the people were remembered by the Lord: "They will be a memorial for you before your God." The trumpets were blown not as an invocation of deity, as in pagan societies, but as an introit to prepare the people for an active confrontation with God. Here, then, is one of the OT's bases for the use of instrumentation in divine worship.

Trumpets in the worship of God in the tabernacle and later the temple were used similarly. The blowing of the trumpets was not a charm to summon a deity but an active response to his presence, an appeal to his will, a participation in his work. Trumpets were to be played in times of festive worship, including feasts, New Moon festivals, and ceremonies surrounding burnt offerings and fellowship offerings. They serve as a memorial of the people to God and of him to them.

This text ends with the solemn assertion, "I am the LORD [Yahweh] your God." This is a slogan that marks the importance of a text; here it also indicates the completion of a major unit of our book.

Certain biblical words evoke strong associations. Many readers of the Bible think of a trumpet blast as initiating the resurrection of the righteous dead to life imperishable (1Co 15:52). Here, at the beginning of organized religious practice in the OT, the trumpet blast has more modest but still significant associations.

2. Setting Forth the People on the Triumphal March (10:11–36)

OVERVIEW

Many commentators divide the book of Numbers into three parts, with the second major section beginning at 10:11. The approach in this commentary is to treat the book of Numbers as a biped of two unequal parts (chs. 1–25; 26–36), structured on the basis of the two census lists (chs. 1–4; 26). In this approach, suggested by Dennis T. Olson (see Introduction: Unity and Organization), 10:11 does not begin the second major unit of the book; it leads instead to the conclusion of the first part of the first major section. Thus 10:11–36 is a key to our understanding the book of Numbers.

But the function of this section is not to introduce Israel's gradual failure, as is commonly supposed. It presents Israel at last on the move, under the hand of God, faithful to his word, and on the way to victory in Canaan. This section celebrates the triumphalism of the first generation. Nothing prepares us for the shock of their rebellion as described beginning in ch. 11. The fact that their triumphant march lasts only briefly, with Israel still in the wilderness, is a great sadness.

a. The March Begins (10:11–13)

¹¹On the twentieth day of the second month of the second year, the cloud lifted from above the tabernacle of the Testimony. ¹²Then the Israelites set out from the Desert of Sinai and traveled from place to place until the cloud came to rest in the Desert of Paran. ¹³They set out, this first time, at the LORD's command through Moses.

COMMENTARY

11–13 After eleven months in the region of Mount Sinai (see Note on 9:1) the people moved out, for the first time led by the Lord in his wondrous cloud (v.11). Israel, on the move from the Desert of Sinai (v.12), was on a journey that in a few weeks could lead them to conquer the land of Canaan. This was a day not to be forgotten: the second year, the second month, the twentieth day. Generations later, one suspects, this day might have been memorialized. At last the Israelites were on their way to Canaan!

Once again we sense the spirit of Yahweh's initiation, of the peoples' compliance, of the role of the cloud of his presence, and of the work of Moses in guiding the people. Possibly the command of Moses in v.13 included blowing the trumpets (as described in vv.1–10). The journey this text describes is not detailed fully here. It is not until 12:16 that the people achieved the destination of the Desert of Paran. More specifically, they settled at Kadesh in the Desert of Zin (20:1). There are at least three stops on this initial journey: Taberah (11:3), Kibroth Hattaavah (11:35), and Hazeroth (11:35).

The Desert of Paran is a large plateau in northeastern Sinai, south of what later would be called the Negev of Judah and west of the Arabah. This area forms the southernmost portion of the Promised Land, the presumed staging area for the assault on the land itself. The principal lines of assault on the land of Canaan are from the southwest, following the Way of the Sea from Egypt, and from the northwest, following the Way of the Sea from Phoenicia. Israel's staging for attack in the Desert of Paran was a brilliant strategy. In this way they would avoid the fortified routes to the west, presumably under the control of Egypt. This unusual line of attack from the south would stun the inhabitants of the land. They would come like a sirocco blast from the wilderness, and the land would be theirs, under the hand of God.

NOTE

13 One of the ways in which significant events are highlighted in biblical narrative is by a finely crafted structure. Number 10:11–28 shows such a structure:

v.11: The time frame
vv.12–13: Introductory summary of the people setting out on their journey
vv.14–17: Setting out of the tribes in the camp of Judah (see 2:3–9)
vv.18–21: Setting out of the tribes in the camp of Reuben (see 2:10–16)
vv.22–24: Setting out of the tribes in the camp of Ephraim (see 2:18–24)
vv.25–27: Setting out of the tribes in the camp of Dan (see 2:25–31)
v.28: Concluding summary of the line of march

b. The Grand Procession of Tribes and Levites (10:14–28)

[14]The divisions of the camp of Judah went first, under their standard. Nahshon son of Amminadab was in command. [15]Nethanel son of Zuar was over the division of the tribe of Issachar, [16]and Eliab son of Helon was over the division of the tribe of Zebulun. [17]Then the tabernacle was taken down, and the Gershonites and Merarites, who carried it, set out.

[18]The divisions of the camp of Reuben went next, under their standard. Elizur son of Shedeur was in command. [19]Shelumiel son of Zurishaddai was over the division of the tribe of Simeon, [20]and Eliasaph son of Deuel was over the division of the tribe of Gad. [21]Then the Kohathites set out, carrying the holy things. The tabernacle was to be set up before they arrived.

[22]The divisions of the camp of Ephraim went next, under their standard. Elishama son of Ammihud was in command. [23]Gamaliel son of Pedahzur was over the division of the tribe of Manasseh, [24]and Abidan son of Gideoni was over the division of the tribe of Benjamin.

[25]Finally, as the rear guard for all the units, the divisions of the camp of Dan set out, under their standard. Ahiezer son of Ammishaddai was in command. [26]Pagiel son of Ocran was over the division of the tribe of Asher, [27]and Ahira son of Enan was over the division of the tribe of Naphtali. [28]This was the order of march for the Israelite divisions as they set out.

COMMENTARY

14–28 The names of the leaders of the twelve tribes are given for the fourth time in the book (see 1:5–15; 2:3–31; 7:12–83); the order for the tribes in the line of march is the same as that presented in ch. 2. The new detail is that the Gershonites and the Merarites, bearing the tabernacle, followed the triad of Judah – encampment tribes in the line of march (v.17). The Kohathites, carrying the holy things, followed the triad of Reuben – encampment tribes (v.21). Each of the four triads of tribes had a standard or banner for rallying and organization (cf. 2:3, 10, 18, 25).

It is difficult to read these words without wincing. We know what is coming, for we have already read the story. But there is nothing in these chapters to suggest that the worthies mentioned here for the fourth time would not be the leaders who would make their mark with their tribes, their armies, and their banners in the Promised Land. The stately pageantry of this section is — it turns out — the setup for a terrible fall.

c. The Request for Hobab to Join the March (10:29–32)

²⁹Now Moses said to Hobab son of Reuel the Midianite, Moses' father-in-law, "We are setting out for the place about which the LORD said, 'I will give it to you.' Come with us and we will treat you well, for the LORD has promised good things to Israel."

³⁰He answered, "No, I will not go; I am going back to my own land and my own people."

³¹But Moses said, "Please do not leave us. You know where we should camp in the desert, and you can be our eyes. ³²If you come with us, we will share with you whatever good things the LORD gives us."

COMMENTARY

29–32 Hobab was Moses' brother-in-law; he was the son of Reuel (also known as Jethro; see Ex 2:18; 3:1). Earlier, Reuel had been most helpful to Moses (see Ex 18). Now Reuel's son, with expert knowledge of the wilderness lands of the Sinai, would be a significant aid in locating water and pasturage in regions unknown to Moses.

It is significant that Moses appealed to Hobab on several lines. One was likely in terms of their relatedness through marriage, a not insignificant bond among peoples of the wilderness; another was based on the goodness of God that was promised to Israel and in which Hobab might participate; and another is the expertise of Hobab, that is, an appeal to his sense of a special ability. In this latter aspect Moses said that Hobab might become the "eyes" of the people (v.31). Moses then reinforced the benefits that would come to Hobab: he would share in the benefits the Lord was about to bestow on the nation (v.32).

At first Hobab refused, citing the need to care for his own family in his own land (Midian), following the traditional ancient Near Eastern pattern of adherence to family and place. Possibly his refusal also involved ties to his family gods, though he did not clearly say so. Moses continued to urge Hobab to join Israel. In a sense this urging was an act of evangelism. Hobab did not come easily. But subsequent biblical texts indicate that at last he did come. In his compliance he is like Ruth, who, leaving all behind, joined Naomi en route to the Promised Land with the promise of something ahead that was of more value than anything left at home. To come with Moses was not just to change Hobab's address; this act was a radical reorientation of life itself. To come with Moses was to have a new family. To come with Moses was to gain a new land. To come with Moses was to come to believe in a new God—Yahweh of Israel.

Judges 1:16 indicates that Hobab acceded to Moses' request to be "eyes" for the people in the wilderness (v.31), as his descendants received a share in the land. But he himself did not share in the land. Presumably, the sadness of Israel's impending rebellion against the Lord included Hobab in the judgment. He experienced God's goodness in the same way that the rest of the people did, in the providential care that God gave his erring people in the inhospitable wilderness of their banishment. Hobab must have been an invaluable aid to Moses. The anticipated journey of a few weeks turned out to last a lifetime.

NOTE

29 Words of familial relationships such as חֹתֵן (*hotēn*, "father-in-law") are troublesome in Hebrew. The basic idea of the root חָתַן (*hātan*; GK 3162) relates to the idea of ritual circumcision done by the prospective bride's father on the prospective groom shortly before the marriage. See Ronald B. Allen, "The 'Bloody Bridegroom' in Exodus 4:24–26," *BSac* 153 (July–September 1996): 259–69. The noun חֹתֵן (*hotēn*) came to be used of an in-law relationship, usually of the father-in-law; the precise relationship in some uses is sometimes debated. In the case of Hobab, v.29 suggests he was the brother of Zipporah, wife of Moses. He was thus the brother-in-law of Moses. Judges 4:11 complicates the issue; in some translations this verse reads that Hobab was the father-in-law of Moses. Judges 4:11 should be read in the light of Numbers 10:29, however. Upon the death of his father, Reuel (Jethro), Hobab would become the head of his household. Since he was the one who joined in the fortunes of Israel, he was regarded by later generations as the head of his household. His tie to Moses through marriage made him particularly memorable.

d. The Three-Day Procession behind the Ark of the Lord (10:33–36)

[33]So they set out from the mountain of the LORD and traveled for three days. The ark of the covenant of the LORD went before them during those three days to find them a place to rest. [34]The cloud of the LORD was over them by day when they set out from the camp. [35]Whenever the ark set out, Moses said,

"Rise up, O LORD!
    May your enemies be scattered;
    may your foes flee before you."

[36]Whenever it came to rest, he said,

"Return, O LORD,
    to the countless thousands of Israel."

COMMENTARY

33–34 The journey began with a three-day march. Eleven months earlier the people of Israel had emerged as a rag-tag group of former slaves, gathered in the wilderness in the first rush of deliverance, but unorganized and unruly. Now they were prepared for the march, the battle, and the victory. Because of the significant numbers of people in the tribes of Israel, and since this was their first organized march, it is not likely that the first journey of three days covered much territory. But it was marked by sufficient success to be regarded as a victory march in these verses.

35–36 The sense of a victory march is enhanced by the recording of what we may call the "Battle Cry of Moses" (contrast the "Lament of Moses" in 11:11–15). This little poem is potent in its living theology (see Note); it rests ultimately on the notion of cursing and blessing that goes all the way back to Yahweh's promises to Abraham (Ge 12:2–3). As the cloud of the Lord arose and as it settled for the people to rest, Moses would call out, "Rise up, O LORD!" and "Return, O LORD!" The words of v.35 are a cursing of the enemies of Yahweh and his people; the words of v.36 are a blessing on the people of his promise.

Finally, the wording of the blessing section is significant for the presentation of the idea of the rhetorical use of numbers in the census lists. The Hebrew phrase for "countless thousands" is "myriads of thousands" (v.36, see Note). The idea is akin to our conventions in the phrases "untold numbers" or "teeming millions." This deliberate hyperbole (no matter how many peoples the census lists indicate) is perhaps an example of Moses' using "power numbers" in his battle cry (see Note; see also Introduction: The Problem of Large Numbers; The Large Numbers—Toward a Solution).

Thus in these words of Moses we have a shout of victory based solidly on the faithfulness of the Lord to his covenantal promise to the patriarchs. The people were on their way to Canaan; soon Canaan would be the land of Israel, or so we might think, based on these words of exuberant confidence in God. Significantly, David used these words of Moses in the beginning of his triumphal song in Psalm 68.

NOTE

35–36 The structure of the little poem is as follows:

Introductory prose line: At the time of the departure of the ark (five words)
A call for Yahweh to rise and to scatter his enemies (bicolon—2:2:3)
Introductory monocolon: At the time of the resting of the ark (two words)
A call for Yahweh to return and to bless his people (bicolon—2:3)

The descriptions of poetic structure in this commentary include counts of accents. This structure is not based on a concept of Western meter; Semitic and Egyptian poetry do not demonstrate the metrical concepts we find in much (but not in all) Western poetry (ancient and modern). But the poetry of Israel and her neighbors was infused with rhythm, and the accentuation (with basically one "beat" per word) most likely signifies that pattern. Describing Egyptian poetry, Kitchen (*Poetry of Ancient Egypt*, 480) writes, "It would seem clear that principal words (nouns, verbs, adjectives) and certain compound clusters bore the rhythmic stresses in a line."

The second and third members of the tricolon, "may your enemies be scattered / may those who hate you flee before you," form a synonymous pair; the two units are strongly contrasting: Rise/Return, Curse/Bless.

In the MT these verses are braced with an unusual phenomenon, long debated in meaning—the use of two letters נ (*nûn*), which are inverted (called by Hebrew writers, *nûn m⁽e⁾nûzeret*). These are found only here in the MT and in seven verses in Psalm 107 (vv.21–26, 40). There is an inverted *nûn* before v.35 and another at the end of v.36.

Medieval Jewish tradition suggested that these two verses were not from Moses but from an otherwise suppressed book by Eldad and Medad (see 11:26–27). This view is explained and then critiqued by Sid Z. Leiman, "The Inverted Nuns at Numbers 10:35–36 and the Book of Eldad and Medad," *JBL* 93 (September 1974): 348–55. His view is that these two verses did not come *from* an independent book but that the two cases of the inverted letters *nûn* suggest that they *form* an independent "book." Milgrom, 375–76, presents a study on the topic: "Excursus 23: The Inverted 'Nuns.'" Compare also Ginsburg, 342, for a discussion: "These inverted letters or their equivalents are among the earliest signs by which the Sopherim designed to indicate the result of their textual criticism." Ginsburg, 343, believed the use of inverted *nûns* here indicates that these two verses are misplaced, that they belong between vv.33 and 34.

רִבְבוֹת אַלְפֵי יִשְׂרָאֵל (*rib⁽e⁾bôt ʾalpê yiśrāʾēl*, "the countless thousands of Israel") speaks rhetorically of the vast numbers of people constituting the tribes of Israel as they set off on their march on the way to Canaan. The word רְבָבָה (*ribābâ*) may signify a specific numerical term meaning "ten thousand" (see Jdg 20:10). More common, however, is its use in a phrase such as here to describe innumerable people. The words in our phrase are reversed in Genesis 24:60: לְאַלְפֵי רְבָבָה (*l⁽e⁾ʾalpê r⁽e⁾bābâ*, "for thousands of myriads"). Here are indisputable examples of the rhetorical use of numbers in Torah (see Introduction: Large Numbers—Toward a Solution).

B. The Rebellion and Judgment of a Fearful People (11:1–25:18)

OVERVIEW

We now begin an entirely new and unexpected account in the experience of the people of the first generation. They had been prepared by Moses, at the instruction of Yahweh, to be a holy people on a march of triumph bound for the Promised Land. But by the third day of the march the people faltered; the holy people became sullied with contempt for Yahweh. Chapters 11–20 present a dismal record of their acts of ingratitude and of God's consequent judgments on his ungrateful people. Yet within these chapters are innumerable instances of his continuing grace. The reader of these texts goes astray if he or she focuses solely on God's wrath or on the constant provocations to his anger by his meandering people. The more impressive feature in this text is God's continuing mercy against continuing, obdurate rebellion.

Chapters 21−25 bring the narrative to an arresting climax by coupling the motifs of rebellion and hope. The materials of these chapters do not present a complete record of Israel's experiences in the wilderness. The writing is focused, the choice of stories selective. The aspect of God's grace is presented arrestingly in the amazing narrative of Balaam, the pagan mantic who failed to destroy Israel by the power of his words but who nearly destroyed the people by the persuasion of his guile (chs. 22−25). The judgment of God at the final rebellion of the people in ch. 25 ends the record of rebellion of the first generation. The experience of the new generation begins in ch. 26.

1. A Cycle of Rebellion and Atonement and the Record of Death (11:1−20:29)

OVERVIEW

These ten chapters now balance and contrast with the ten chapters that present the record of Israel's preparation. Barely did the march begin before the rebellion was underway—a rebellion of the spirit of the people that manifested itself in a variety of ways. But always it came down to this: God's demand of complete obedience and robust faith, a devotion of the whole person, was infrequently found in his people. These chapters call to mind the observation of Gleason L. Archer Jr., who reacted against the hypothesis of "Israel's genius for religion" as an explanation for the lofty spirituality of the Bible and especially as the source of its grand monotheistic faith. Certain theologians ascribe to Israel a penchant for religion that is akin to the Greeks' love for beauty and the Romans' gift for order. Archer correctly rejoins, "It was not [a] product of the natural Hebrew 'genius for religion' (as is often asserted), for the Scripture record witnesses rather to the natural Hebrew genius for irreligion and apostasy" (SOTI-rev, 145). Such a judgment is not a slur against Jewish people, by the way; throughout the ages, many of those who have presented themselves as God's people have displayed similar traits of irreligion and apostasy. Therein lies another reason the book of Numbers is so important for readers today.

a. The Beginning of Sorrows (11:1−35)

i. A judgment of fire (11:1−3)

OVERVIEW

There is a cyclical nature to Israel's rebellions against God—obdurate people tend to repeat the sins of the past. The first rebellion of the redeemed people came on the third day of marching toward the mount of God after their miraculous crossing of the Red Sea (Ex 15:22−24). Now, three days out on their triumphal march to Canaan from Mount Sinai (cf. Nu 10:35), they fall back into their complaining behavior. The pattern of "three days" in both cases shows both similarities of actions as well as an intemperate, impatient attitude on the part of the people.

> ¹Now the people complained about their hardships in the hearing of the Lord, and when he heard them his anger was aroused. Then fire from the Lord burned among them and consumed some of the outskirts of the camp. ²When the people cried out to Moses, he prayed to the Lord and the fire died down. ³So that place was called Taberah, because fire from the Lord had burned among them.

COMMENTARY

1 Instead of "Now the people complained," the MT may also be translated, "Now the people became murmurous—an offense to Yahweh's ears." Nothing in the first ten chapters of Numbers has prepared us for this verse; rather, those chapters have emphasized repeatedly the complete obedience of Moses and the people to the dictates of Yahweh. But only three days into their march, the people revert to the disloyal complaining they expressed a year earlier, only three days past their deliverance from the waters of the Red Sea (Ex 15:22–27). In that earlier experience they had vented their subsequent complaints about manna (Ex 16) and a lack of water (17:1–7). Now the people revert to the behavior of ingratitude that marked their early experience in the wilderness. This attitude of ingratitude was seditious against the covenant and malicious against the person of God. They were actually in breach of covenant, deserving of the divine suzerain's wrath.

Moses, the narrator of Numbers, has arranged his materials so carefully that this sudden outbreak of renewed pettiness against God seems unprecedented, unexpected—unbelievable. How, we wonder, with all the preparation for a holy walk, could there come such stumbling so soon?

The response of Yahweh to this outbreak of murmuring was one of wrath. The text says that "fire from the Lord burned among them." This purging fire was limited to the outskirts of the camp—even this was a mercy of Yahweh. He might have cast his fire into the very midst of the camp and killed many more persons than suffered this terrible judgment. The judgment by "fire" is suggestive not only of judgment but also of refining, of cleansing. Perhaps a burst of fire will not only judge the offenders of God's grace but will serve as well as a symbol of cleansing for the entire camp.

At times the expression "fire from the Lord" may refer to fire ignited by the divine casting of lightning (as seems possible in 1 Kings 18:38, in the encounter of Elijah with the prophets of Baal on Mount Carmel). The imagery of Baal (Baʿal) in the nature religion of Canaan often presents him in association with lightning and storm, as the one who casts his bolt, beats the drums of the heavens, then drives the clouds across the sky as he rides in his heavenly chariot. The poets of the Bible sometimes built on this imagery but applied it to Yahweh. In this way they despoiled Baal of his titles, and they ascribed greatness to Yahweh, the true God of heaven. For example, Psalm 68, to which reference was made at 10:35, extols Yahweh as the one "who rides on the clouds" (see NIV's text and margin at Ps 68:4).

It seems altogether possible that the "fire from the LORD" in this text is judgment in the form of a bolt (or bolts) of lightning that caused terrible destructive fires among the people on the outskirts of the camp. (There are other times when it may be that the phrase refers to a flash from the fires of his altars.)

2 In the midst of his wrath, Yahweh remembered mercy. This is one of the ongoing themes of Scripture and is a truism emphasized in Numbers. The people truly deserved God's considerable wrath. But the survivors of this outburst of his anger cried out to Moses for help in their behalf before Yahweh. Moses prayed, and the fire subsequently subsided. The Hebrew verb is *šāqaʿ*, a word meaning "to sink down" and thus a particularly picturesque term for the dying out of a raging fire.

3 The place name "Taberah" comes from a Hebrew noun meaning "burning"; it is mentioned only here and in Deuteronomy 9:22. This name comes in association with the verb "had burned." Because of the raging of the fire of God in their midst, the people named that place of awful memory "Taberah" ("Burning").

NOTES

1 כְּמִתְאֹנְנִים (*kᵉmiṯʾōnᵉnîm*, "complained") is a Hithpoʿel participle from the root אנן (*ʾānan*). It may be related to an Akkadian term *anānu* (*ênênu, unnînu*), "to sigh" (see BDB, 59d). The Hebrew word is used only here and in Lamentations 3:39. The problem with the grammatical form is the כְּ (*kᵉ*) prefix. It is possible to take this prefix as the preposition כְּ (*kᵉ*, "like, as") and to translate, "they have become as those who complain." But it is more likely that the use of כְּ (*kᵉ*) here is asseverative, expressing identity (see Williams, *Hebrew Syntax*, sec. 261). The idea seems to be: "Now the people became truly murmurous, an offense to the LORD's ears."

The NIV reads רַע (*raʿ*, "evil thing, an offense") as a prepositional phrase following the participle "they complained," thus rendering it "hardships." However, the *BHS* text has a strong disjunctive accent with the participle; the term רַע (*raʿ*) goes with the following phrase. I suggest the translation: "Now the people became truly murmurous, an evil offense to the LORD's ears."

ii. A surfeit of quail (11:4–34)

OVERVIEW

We observe with sadness that the memory of the cause of the burning at Taberah seems to have been lost quickly. It was followed directly by another, even more serious attack on God's mercy in the people's rejection of manna, the bread of heaven. It is possible that there was a considerable lapse of time between the provocation of burning (vv.1–3) and the provocation of the plague of quail (vv.4–35), but the placement of these stories in abrupt linking suggests that the time lapse is negligible. It seems that this new rebellion transpired during the next stop along the march (see v.34).

There is symmetry in these narratives of rebellion in the Bible. The scream for "real food" rather than the divine provision of manna takes us back to the initial complaint about food in Exodus 16:1–3, where God initiated his wonder of manna; it also carries us forward to the last rebellion about food near the end of the generation in the wilderness (21:4–9), where the people spurned manna as detestable, only to have a purposed focus on the image of the truly detestable, the snake, be their only means of escape from God's plague.

Indeed, God's provision of food for his people (and their common actions of ingratitude for his mercy) is one of the dominant motifs of the journey of biblical faith. The biblical vista of humankind's adventure with God began in the midst of a garden teeming with all manner of food (Ge 2); the eating of one forbidden item led to expulsion from Paradise (Ge 3). The Bible ends with the portrait of a glorious day in the future in which there will be no lack of provision for the people of God, and nothing is prohibited (Rev 22:1–5). Along the way, on the journey from the paradise of Eden to the coming garden of glory, the provision of food is a mark of God's love and care for his people (cf. Ps 111:5).

Further, the provision of food is often a sign of the worship of God's wonder and grace (as in the fellowship offerings of the OT and the Lord's table of the NT). Food is more than "fuel" for the body, more than nutrients for living. The biblical view is that food is sacral; there are no "common meals." Paul attacks the ideas of some in his day who minimized food to the mechanical processes of digestion (see 1Co 8:13). There is more to eating than food and stomach. This is why we must bless God (i.e., mark him out as the source of our blessing; see Ps 103:1–2) especially at mealtimes. Eating a satisfying meal provides the believer a wonderful provocation for the praise of Yahweh, who gives good gifts (Dt 8:10). Similarly, to attack God for meagerness in food or for a lack of variety may be a cowardly act of impiety. So we learn in the story that follows.

[4]The rabble with them began to crave other food, and again the Israelites started wailing and said, "If only we had meat to eat! [5]We remember the fish we ate in Egypt at no cost — also the cucumbers, melons, leeks, onions and garlic. [6]But now we have lost our appetite; we never see anything but this manna!"

[7]The manna was like coriander seed and looked like resin. [8]The people went around gathering it, and then ground it in a handmill or crushed it in a mortar. They cooked it in a pot or made it into cakes. And it tasted like something made with olive oil. [9]When the dew settled on the camp at night, the manna also came down.

[10]Moses heard the people of every family wailing, each at the entrance to his tent. The LORD became exceedingly angry, and Moses was troubled. [11]He asked the LORD, "Why have you brought this trouble on your servant? What have I done to displease you that you put the burden of all these people on me? [12]Did I conceive all these people? Did I give them birth? Why do you tell me to carry them in my arms, as a nurse carries an infant, to the land you promised on oath to their forefathers? [13]Where can I get meat for all these people? They keep wailing to me, 'Give us meat to eat!' [14]I cannot carry all these people by myself; the burden is too heavy for me. [15]If this is how you are going to treat me, put me to death right now — if I have found favor in your eyes — and do not let me face my own ruin."

[16]The Lord said to Moses: "Bring me seventy of Israel's elders who are known to you as leaders and officials among the people. Have them come to the Tent of Meeting, that they may stand there with you. [17]I will come down and speak with you there, and I will take of the Spirit that is on you and put the Spirit on them. They will help you carry the burden of the people so that you will not have to carry it alone.

[18]"Tell the people: 'Consecrate yourselves in preparation for tomorrow, when you will eat meat. The Lord heard you when you wailed, "If only we had meat to eat! We were better off in Egypt!" Now the Lord will give you meat, and you will eat it. [19]You will not eat it for just one day, or two days, or five, ten or twenty days, [20]but for a whole month — until it comes out of your nostrils and you loathe it — because you have rejected the Lord, who is among you, and have wailed before him, saying, "Why did we ever leave Egypt?"'"

[21]But Moses said, "Here I am among six hundred thousand men on foot, and you say, 'I will give them meat to eat for a whole month!' [22]Would they have enough if flocks and herds were slaughtered for them? Would they have enough if all the fish in the sea were caught for them?"

[23]The Lord answered Moses, "Is the Lord's arm too short? You will now see whether or not what I say will come true for you."

[24]So Moses went out and told the people what the Lord had said. He brought together seventy of their elders and had them stand around the Tent. [25]Then the Lord came down in the cloud and spoke with him, and he took of the Spirit that was on him and put the Spirit on the seventy elders. When the Spirit rested on them, they prophesied, but they did not do so again.

[26]However, two men, whose names were Eldad and Medad, had remained in the camp. They were listed among the elders, but did not go out to the Tent. Yet the Spirit also rested on them, and they prophesied in the camp. [27]A young man ran and told Moses, "Eldad and Medad are prophesying in the camp."

[28]Joshua son of Nun, who had been Moses' aide since youth, spoke up and said, "Moses, my lord, stop them!"

[29]But Moses replied, "Are you jealous for my sake? I wish that all the Lord's people were prophets and that the Lord would put his Spirit on them!" [30]Then Moses and the elders of Israel returned to the camp.

[31]Now a wind went out from the Lord and drove quail in from the sea. It brought them down all around the camp to about three feet above the ground, as far as a day's walk in any direction. [32]All that day and night and all the next day the people went out and gathered quail. No one gathered less than ten homers. Then they spread them out all around the camp. [33]But while the meat was still between their teeth and before it could be consumed, the anger of the Lord burned against the people, and he struck them with a severe plague. [34]Therefore the place was named Kibroth Hattaavah, because there they buried the people who had craved other food.

COMMENTARY

4 This account appropriately begins with the "rabble," an apt term for the non-Israelite mixed group of people who followed the Hebrews from Egypt. This term points to a recurring source of complaints and trouble in the camp. Those who did not know Yahweh and his mercies too easily incited those who did know him to rebel against him. But however the murmuring began, it soon spread throughout the camp of Israel. It is likely that familiar texts on the need for separation from people who do not share biblical faith have their first instance in this account (see 1Co 6:14–18; see also prohibited mixtures in Torah at Dt 22:10–11). Not all the people termed "rabble" (or who began as "rabble") were unbelievers! That is, we may expect that many non-Hebrew people would have come to faith in God in view of their daily contact with Hebrew people who did believe (see Ex 14:30–31). Among the non-Hebrew people we may presume had come to full faith in Yahweh was the Kushite (African) wife of Moses (see 12:1 and Note there).

In any event, as in Exodus 16, the people, forgetting what God had done for them, had begun to complain concerning their diet: "in the desert they gave in to their craving; / in the wasteland they put God to the test" (Ps 106:14). We may suspect that meat was not the common fare of the slaves in Egypt. By romanticizing the past, the people tended to minimize earlier discomforts when in a new type of distress—a common human failing.

The verb "to crave" (ʾāwâ, in the Hithpael; GK 203) leads to the name of the location of the subsequent judgment, Kibroth Hattaavah, "Graves of Craving" (v.34). The verb can be used for positive and proper desires, but it is especially fitting for feelings of (improper) lusts and bodily appetites. The verb is enhanced by its cognate accusative taʾăwâ ("desire"; GK 9294), a word that may be used in a good sense (as Pss 10:17; 38:9[10]; Pr 11:23; et al.), as well as in contexts of covetousness and lust (Pss 10:3; 112:10; Pr 21:25–26). The wording used here, "they craved a craving," is emphatic in nature; the meaning is something on the order of, "they had an intense craving [for meat]."

5–6 The several types of vegetables and fruit mentioned in this verse are suggestive of the varieties of foods available in Egypt, in contrast to the diet solely of manna in the wilderness (v.6). Further, the poor in Egypt were able to supplement their diet with fish still found in many canals and waterways (see Gray, 103). They may have been exaggerating the variety and plenty of their diet in Egypt, but it is true even today that food is plentiful in Egypt because of the richness of the deposits of particles of soil amid the waters of the Nile River in its annual flooding. Every year there is not only abundant water but also a refreshing of the particulates that enrich the soil.

The contrast for Israel was sure: there were no fish or vegetables to be had in the wilderness. The focus of faith, however, is that there should have been no food at all in the wilderness. That there was anything at all to eat was solely by God's mercy. To spurn a regularly occurring, abundant, and nutritious food only because it was boring is understandably human—a pitiable mark of our tendency toward ingratitude.

7–9 The description of the manna in terms of its appearance and taste would be meaningful only to people who lived later than the time of its provision (cf. also Ex 16 for a description of manna). As in the instance of the description of the hovering cloud and fire (9:15–23), the nature and appearance of manna would have been familiar to the persons of this story. In fact, that is the point: they were sick of it!

These words could have been written by Moses in anticipation of the curiosity of later generations; but conceivably these descriptive words were added considerably later than Moses, based on the memory of the food at a time when it was no longer a part of Israel's experience. (See Introduction: Authorship and Date, for a discussion of possible post-Mosaic additions to the book.) To speak in this way of the possibility of later additions to the text of Numbers is not to imply that these additions, if that is what they are, are not accurate, are untrustworthy, or are not inspired by God. They are, in fact, an essential part of this text. Even though descriptions such as these may come from a time later than Moses, they may still be viewed as the work of the Spirit—i.e., true Scripture. In such a case the concept of inspiration—and its corollary inerrancy—extends to such bona fide additions. The issue of the "autograph" of a biblical book is far more complex in some books of Hebrew Scripture than perhaps in some NT writings.

Numerous naturalistic explanations have been given to account for the provision of manna by those who have traveled in the Sinai. Some point to a secretion of the tamarisk tree of small, yellow-white balls that have a sweet taste. Others believe this secretion is not the product of the tree but is the excreta of certain scale insects made on the leaves of these trees during June in some areas of the Sinai. But no naturally occurring substance truly fits the data of the text. Several factors suggest that manna was a unique provision from the Lord for the people of Israel in the wilderness, not just a natural substance given in greater-than-usual abundance (see Notes).

10 The people's rejection of his gracious gift of heavenly food (called "bread from heaven" in Ex 16:4) was extremely evil to Yahweh. Israel's rejection of his provision was a failure of the test of faith. God had said that the reception of the manna by the people would be a significant test of their obedience (Ex 16:4). The people had allowed themselves to think back to their lives in slavery and to regard that estate as more pleasurable than their present walk with the Lord on their way to the land of his promise. In view of the "good things" the Lord was to give them (see 10:32), the people were expected to receive each day's supply of manna as a gracious gift of a merciful God and a promise of abundance to come. When they spurned the manna, the people contemned him—they were rejecting his mercy as they reacted with disgust!

They repeated this grave evil thirty-eight years later (ch. 21). There is a sense that the rebellion of Israel in Numbers begins and ends on the subject of food and a despising of God's provision. In our own journey through life, we need to be on guard that we do not despise God's present mercies, even as we may long for our future home in heaven.

11–15 The reaction of the people to God's mercy in providing manna was greatly troubling to Moses as well. Instead of turning to the Lord to ask that he understand the substance of their complaint, Moses turned to the Lord to ask why he was given such an ungrateful people to lead. There is a human touch in all this; Moses is caught off guard, as it were—ill-prepared for the magnitude of the problem he faced in leading this sinful people.

Moses' frustration leads to what we may call "Moses' Lament" (vv.11–15), a studied contrast with the "Battle Cry of Moses" (10:35–36). There are elements in this section that remind one of the Bible's psalms of lament. The layout of the text in the standard MT is presented as prose, as in the NIV. But there is a musical, poetic feel to these words. It is possible to present this section in a poetic format and thus to sense more thoroughly, breathe more deeply, the rich passions that underlie them. Here follows my translation of "Moses' Lament":

[11]And Moses said to Yahweh:

"Why have you brought calamity to your
    servant?
  Why do I still not find grace in your eyes?
    [Why have you] placed the burden of all
    this people on me?
[12]Surely it is not I who conceived all this people?
  Did I give birth to them?
Why should you say to me,
  'Hold them to your bosom;
    Carry them as a nurse does a nursing child
      to the land you promised to their
      fathers'?
[13]Wherever may I find meat
  to give to all this people?
For they come weeping against me saying,
  'Give us meat that we may eat!'
[14]I am unable to do it alone!
  I cannot bear all this people;
    They are too heavy for me!
[15]If this is what you wish to do to me,
  then slay me quickly!
Do this, if I still have any favor in your sight!
  Only let me not see my calamity!"

Viewed in this manner, this lament has a highly poetic cast to it. It is marked by lines of tricola (three elements) and bicola (two elements) in standard parallel structures familiar from other poetry of the Bible (see Notes). Moreover, the rhetoric is poetic in nature; it expresses deep passion in hyperbolic flourishes. The lament is marked by an inclusio, the use of the same or a similar element at the beginning and end to give a sense of binding and unity.

The poem begins (v.11) with Moses' using the verbal form *hᵃrēʿōtā* (a Hiphil from the verb *rāʿaʿ*, "to treat badly") to ask God why he has brought calamity on him. It ends (v.15) with Moses' using the nominal form *bᵉrāʿātî* (the noun *rāʿâ*, "trouble,

misery," plus preposition and pronominal suffixes) to beg Yahweh not to let him see the full extent of his calamity.

Moses brought all this on himself. He would rather die than continue to be so troubled by this obdurate people. In this deeply moving lament, which I take to be an exquisite poem of great artistry, Moses serves as a mirror of the feelings of God!

The language is impassioned when we hear it from Moses. It is unbearable when we hear it from the Lord. That is where these words drive us. After all, it is Yahweh who has conceived this people. It is he who has given them birth. He is their nurse, their mother, their succor in the wilderness. He has promised them their land; he will give them their place. The people were screaming out to Moses, but ultimately they were ranting against Yahweh. When Moses rhetorically contemplated death as escape, there is the suggestion of unrelieved horror: What if the Lord were to "die" to his people? What if he were to be no more their God? The words of this poem are troubling enough when we hear them from Moses, servant of the Lord. When we realize they mirror the rage of God, in anthropopathic feelings of frustration and incredulity, then this poem is expressive of genuine mystery and wonder!

16–17 The response of Yahweh to the great distress of his prophet was twofold—mercy and curse: (1) there was mercy to Moses in that his workload was now to be shared by seventy leaders who would help him carry the burden of the people in future encounters (vv.16–17); (2) there was a curse on the people in keeping with their complaint: they asked for meat and would now become sick with it (vv.18–34).

The blessing of the provision of seventy elders must have brought an enormous sense of relief to Moses. It is dangerous, perhaps even silly, to attempt to psychoanalyze someone from antiquity. Nonetheless, the language of Moses' Lament (vv.11–15) suggests that he may have suffered from a form of depression. Moses' desire to die (v.15) was not unlike the death wish of Elijah following the ultimate failure of his revival at Mount Carmel (1Ki 19:4; see Ronald B. Allen, "Elijah the Broken Prophet," *JETS* 22 [September 1979]: 193–202). It is my suggestion that the enormous weight of these feelings of depression serve as the signal elements of understanding the troublesome words of 12:3, the celebrated announcement of the "meekness" of Moses (12:2; "very humble," NIV; see below).

The language used with reference to the Spirit in this section is of high interest. God told Moses that he would take of the Spirit that was on Moses and put that Spirit on the seventy (v.17). The idea in this strange wording is clear enough: they would share the same Holy Spirit who animated and empowered Moses.

18–20 The people's distress at the lack of variety in the daily manna led them to challenge the goodness of Yahweh. Ultimately, it would be such a challenge to his essential goodness that would lead to their own deaths in the land (chs. 13–14). At present the judgment was partial; the judgment that would come would be all-inclusive. They had screamed for meat. Now they were going to get a surfeit of meat—so much meat that it would make them physically ill. There is sardonic humor in this development, a sense of comic justice. In effect, God told them he would give them all the meat they wanted and then some! They claimed that manna was a boring diet, that they could not live without variety, without some meat to eat. Now they were going to receive a diet of constant meat—not for a day or so but for a full month. They would be so filled with meat that it would spew from their nostrils.

The principal issue was not meat, of course. Yahweh explained to Moses what the real issue was; he said of the people, "You have rejected

the LORD" (v.20). The language is emphatic and gripping: "Surely you have rejected Yahweh who is among you!" The idea is a statement of incredulity. He was near in grace, but they had turned their back on him. He was in their midst, and they wished he were not so close. He had come down, and they wished he would go away. The issue was not just failure to demonstrate proper gratitude to the Lord, who was in their midst and who was their constant source of good; it was turning from him entirely and grudgingly rejecting his many acts of mercy in their behalf. I suspect the only apt comparison for the modern reader would be to consider one who has made a Christian commitment saying to the Savior, "I wish you had not died for me! Leave me alone!" Only in these terms may we sense the enormity of impact in the language of this verse.

21–23 The response of Moses in these verses was not to the basic theological issue of the rejection of the Lord by the people. His head was still spinning from the declaration of the Lord that he would provide meat for all the people for a month. Moses reminded God (!) of the numbers involved: six hundred thousand men on foot. The numerics of the men numbered for war are consistent throughout the book of Numbers, thus presenting a strong argument, it seems, against arbitrary judgments of textual corruption. A marching force of this size suggests a total population of over two million people (or perhaps one tenth of this total; see the sections on large numbers in the Introduction). Moses' distress at providing meat for this immense number of people (and it is immense, even if the numbers are rhetorically inflated!) is nearly comical—the task is staggering, impossible. The Christian has an advantage over Moses by knowing already the corresponding works of Jesus in the Gospels of feeding immense crowds from the meagerest of provisions.

The familiar level of the dialogue between Moses and the Lord highlights the level of trust and relationship that Moses, God's servant, was able to have with his Suzerain. The special nature of Moses' relationship with God and the level of intimacy in his communication with the Lord and the Lord with him are detailed in 12:6–8. The response of God was, "Is the LORD's arm too short?" (v.23; the Hebrew idiom is, "Is the hand of Yahweh too short?" where the meaning of the word "hand" includes the full arm). The human impossibility of the task of providing meat for the immense numbers of Israelites was an occasion to demonstrate the wonder of Yahweh. Moses also needed an encouragement to his faith. His depression made him like Elijah after Carmel, a prophet in need of a fresh experience of the wonder and presence of Yahweh.

24–25 This chapter interplays several themes: the arrogant lust of the people, the impassioned distress of Moses, the plan of God to bring an answer of judgment to the people, and the purpose of the Lord to bring an answer of grace to his servant. These two verses relate to the subject of the seventy elders, introduced in vv.16–17. The coming near of the Lord in the cloud (v.25) brings us back to 9:15–23, the description of the hovering cloud and fire. But this text advances it by speaking of the cloud as coming down or, better, of the Lord as coming down by means of the cloud. Sovereignly, mysteriously, graciously, Yahweh apportioned to the seventy elders the same Spirit that was on Moses.

The emphasis is not that the Spirit was divided into smaller units but that it was the very same Spirit of God, who still empowered Moses, that now animated these men. The Christian cannot but think of Pentecost in Acts 2. In a sense what occurred here in the wilderness is a presentment ahead of time of the bestowal of the Spirit on the believers in the upper room following the resurrection of the

Lord Jesus. The taking of "some" of the Spirit from Moses suggests the release of some of the burden he bore. They would share in that work with him.

The text states that these elders prophesied for a while but that they did not continue to do so. It seems that the temporary gift of prophecy to these elders was primarily to establish their credentials as Spirit-empowered leaders rather than to make of them ongoing agents of the prophecy of the Spirit. Their principal task would not be revelatory; God still spoke through Moses. The task of the elders would be to help in the administration of the immense population, in its varied needs, especially in the context of the increasing impiety of the people.

26–30 Two of the designated elders did not meet with the others when the Spirit of God came on the group. For some reason they remained in the camp. But they also received the gift of the Spirit and began to prophesy. A young man devoted to Moses rushed to his master to inform him of this phenomenon and to beg his master to have them cease. The prophesying of Eldad and Medad in the camp where the common people would see them was perceived as an opportunity for further personal attacks on Moses. If these men had the same gift as Moses, and if they were in the midst of the people making prophetic proclamations, would they not be able to use their new gifts to bring about further sedition against God's servant?

Here the true spirit of Moses is demonstrated. Rather than being threatened by the public demonstration of the gifts of the Spirit by Eldad and Medad, Moses desired that all God's people might have the full gifts of the Spirit! This verse is a suitable introduction to the inexcusable challenge to the leadership of Moses in Numbers 12. Moses' magnanimity compares with that of Jesus in Mark 9:38–41 and Paul in Philippians 1:15–18. His expression of the desire for the Spirit of God to fall on all the people is anticipatory of the promise of God through the prophet Joel (2:28–32) and the experience of the early Christians in Acts 2:5–21.

The "young man" of v.27 so protective of the reputation of Moses was likely the same as the person named in v.28—Joshua son of Nun. How propitious it is that the first time we read of him is in association with his service to Moses as an aide from youth. Perhaps it was this very close association with Moses that emboldened Joshua, along with Caleb, to take his stand with the promise of God rather than with the fears of the people when he withstood the evil report of the majority of the tribal agents (or "spies"; chs. 13–14).

31–34 The sickening feast of the plague of quail ends this chapter of Numbers. The people had begged for meat. In a tragicomic act of miraculous provision, the Lord supplied more quail than the people could possibly eat. The Hebrew text is somewhat ambiguous in the phrasing translated, "about three feet above the ground" (lit., "about two cubits"; v.31). The NIV suggests that the quail were borne along by the wind of the Lord at the height of about three feet; the birds may have been stupefied by the supernatural wind and hence were low enough to be seized readily by the people. The Hebrew phrase has also been read by some to mean that the quail were found in stacks upwards of three feet deep. In any event, the supply of the birds was stupendous. One who

did not do very well at the gathering of birds still captured "ten homers" of birds (nearly sixty bushels; v.32).

The figures here are staggering! In some ways it reminds us of the great provision of the Lord Jesus in the feedings of the five thousand (Mt 14:13–21) and the four thousand (Mt 15:29–39). In those cases the feeding of many from God's plenty was a demonstration of God's grace; in the instance in Numbers it was a manifestation of God's wrath.

The scene must have been similar to a riot: people screaming, birds flapping their wings, everywhere the pell-mell movement of a meat-hungry people in a sea of birds. Dare we picture people ripping at the birds, eating flesh before cooking it, bestial in behavior? They must have been like a sugar-crazed boy in a child's daydream, the boy afloat a chocolate-sandwich-cookie raft in a sea of chocolate syrup and nibbling at the cookie before drowning in the dark, sweet sea.

The drama of the text is exquisite: "while the meat was still between their teeth" (v.33), the plague of the Lord struck them down. Before they could swallow, God made them choke. Thus, this place took on an odious name: Kibroth Hattaavah (v.34), "Graves of Craving." These graves marked the death camp of those who had turned against the food of the Lord's mercy. What a contrast with the ending of ch. 10! We are in a different world—and certainly not a better one.

NOTES

4 The term וְהָאסַפְסֻף (wᵉhāʾsapsup, "the rabble"), found only here in the MT, is a negative designation of the camp followers of the Hebrews at the exodus. The *aleph* is quiescent; the noun is a reduplicative type of the pattern *qetaltul*. The form ᵃsapsup is augmented from אֹסֶף (ʾāsup).

6 הַמָּן (hammān, "manna"; GK 4942) appears to be comprised of the particle *man*, meaning "what?" coupled to the definite article. The idea seems to be idiomatic: "What is it?" Thus the very name indicates the unusual nature of the bread from heaven.

The following factors support the idea that manna was indeed a special, miraculous gift from the Lord and not a naturally occurring phenomenon.

1. The very Hebrew word manna ("What [is it]?") suggests that it was something unknown by the people at the time (see Ex 16:15).
2. The description of the appearance and taste of the manna (Ex 16:31; Nu 11:7) suggests that it was not something experienced by other peoples in other times.
3. The daily abundance of the manna and its regular periodic surge and slump (double amounts on the sixth day but none on the seventh; Ex 16:22, 27) hardly suggest a natural phenomenon.
4. The fact that it was available in ample supply for the entire wilderness experience, no matter where the people were (Ex 16:35), goes against the idea of a naturally occurring substance.
5. The fact that there was a cessation of manna when the wilderness years were completed (Ex 16:35; Jos 5:12) shows the particularity of this provision.
6. The keeping of a sample of the manna in the ark for future generations (Ex 16:33–34) suggests that this was a unique food, a holy provision.

William G. Dever (*Who Were the Early Israelites?* 21) writes:

The description of the mysterious "manna" (the Hebrew name means "What is it?" Exodus 16:14–21) has been connected to the secretion of a sweet sticky substance by tamarisk shrubs in the desert, caused by two species of scale insects. Considerable quantities of the edible stuff could have been gathered; but it is seasonal, and in any case would hardly have been enough to feed several million people for even a short time. Once again, such "naturalistic" explanations beg the question of miracles and their religious significance in the Hebrew Bible. The events are the *magnolia dei*, the "mighty acts of God," or they are nothing.

11–15 In the introduction to his great work on Egyptian poetry, Kenneth A. Kitchen (*Poetry of Ancient Egypt*, xiii) describes Egyptian-Semitic poetry in this manner:

Poetry is the artistic use, and variation in use, of language in non-mundane formats, to create special effects in the minds of readers or hearers. It can be created at the will of a writer for its own sake, to satisfy nothing more than his or her inner creative urges, or else to serve some specific aim: e.g., to praise a deity (hymnody), or a leader (paean), or to express feelings on a subject, or to entertain (cf. the love-lyrics in this book).

The recognition of new poetic islands such as this "new" poem of Moses, in what was once viewed by many as a dense sea of prose, is a continuing delight. The Hebrew Scriptures abound with great poetry. See my chapter "Poetry—the Language of the Psalms" in Ronald B. Allen, *And I Will Praise Him: A Guide to Worship in the Psalms* (repr., Grand Rapids: Kregel, 1999), 41–56.

20 In לָמָה זֶּה (*lāmmâ zeh*, "Why ever?") the demonstrative pronoun *zeh* is enclitic as an undeclined word for emphasis. Compare 1 Samuel 10:11, "What in the world?" and 1 Samuel 17:28, "Why ever?" The pattern is noted in Williams, *Hebrew Syntax*, sec. 118.

25 וְלֹא יָסָפוּ (*wᵉlōʾ yāsāpû*, "and did not do so again") is from the root יָסַף (*yāsap*, "to do again, repeat"). The standard understanding is that these elders were given a temporary gift of prophecy that served to validate their ministry as the aides of Moses, but they did not continue to prophesy. The NIV margin has,

"Or *prophesied and continued to do so.*" This is derived from an alternative reading found in the Targums, presumably based on וְלֹא יָסֻפוּ (*wᵉlōʾ yāsupû*) from סוף (*sûp*, "to come to an end"), meaning, "and they did not stop." The MT's reading is surely preferable here. Incidentally, the verb סוף (*sûp*, "to come to an end") is the root for סוֹף (*sôp*, "end"), the word used in a suggested emendation of יַם־סוּף (*yam-sûp*, "Sea of Reeds") to יַם־סוֹף (*yam-sôp*, "Sea's End"), suggested at Numbers 33:10; see Note there.

26 On Eldad, see the note at 34:21.

iii. A journey note (11:35)

³⁵From Kibroth Hattaavah the people traveled to Hazeroth and stayed there.

COMMENTARY

35 Surely there was a sense that the people could not leave Kibroth Hattaavah quickly enough. "Hazeroth" (*ḥᵃṣērôt*) means "enclosures." This was a location that allowed them a temporary residence on their journey northward. But it also became the locus of yet another place of trouble, the attack on Moses by Miriam and Aaron (12:1–15).

b. The Opposition of Miriam and Aaron (12:1–16)

OVERVIEW

If the issues of ch. 11 were troubling, those of ch. 12 are nearly unbearable. The challenges to Moses in the complaints of the people at Taberah (11:1–3) and Kibroth Hattaavah (vv.4–34) drove him to such a state of depression that he asked God to take his life in the stirring poem (so I have argued above) I have called the Lament of Moses (vv.11–15). Moses was well aware that the attacks were not on him exclusively; in a sense he was but a foil for God as the people had rejected their Savior (v.20). Nonetheless, the attacks on his person had affected him deeply.

We recall that when God first spoke to Moses, the man shrank from the task (cf. Ex 4), believing that he was not capable of doing the work God wanted him to do. Likely the burlesque of dialogue from that confusing period came back to him in these days of assault. If there was any compensating factor in the attacks on Moses and the Lord described in ch. 11, it was that the people called the "rabble" (v.4) were the prime instigators. These were other escaped slaves or displaced persons who, presumably, decided for their own reasons, not for spiritual commitment, to attach themselves to the populace of Israel in her adventure in leaving Egypt. In ch. 12 the attacks against Moses came from his sister and his brother. These are the unkindest cuts of all.

i. The attack on Moses from his family (12:1-3)

¹Miriam and Aaron began to talk against Moses because of his Cushite wife, for he had married a Cushite. ²"Has the LORD spoken only through Moses?" they asked. "Hasn't he also spoken through us?" And the LORD heard this.

³(Now Moses was a very humble man, more humble than anyone else on the face of the earth.)

COMMENTARY

1 The attack against Moses in this chapter comes as a surprise. We are stunned to find that the principal provocateur in this case was Miriam, Moses' sister. We are unprepared for the opening salvo, an attack on Moses' wife; and we discover amid these questions the real issue: Why was Moses God's favorite? The story becomes a classic example of sibling rivalry—a haunting reminder of Cain's anger against Abel, so long ago (Ge 4:1-16).

The feminine singular verb that initiates the chapter (*watt*ᵉ*dabbēr*, lit., "and she spoke"; v.1; see Notes) and the placement of her name before that of Aaron both indicate that Miriam was the principal protagonist in the attack against Moses. Aaron apparently joined her at her instigation. Some modern interpreters have read the narrative of this chapter as an attack on women in general in Scripture and especially an attack on the person of Miriam. (For some contemporary readers, any presentation of moral failure or bad behavior on the part of a woman in a biblical narrative is a red flag for misogynous attitudes in OT patriarchy.) It appears to me, however, that this account does not unduly demean Miriam; rather, it presents her in a human, understandable manner. She was not judged because she was a woman; she, like any other person, was judged for her sin.

Women, like men, are capable of great acts of piety and valor; they are equally able to act in the most debased of manners. Further, although this may seem tortuous to some, Miriam's significance in the history of Israel is assured in a curious manner by the inclusion of this story in the Torah. I suspect that in the male-oriented culture of the biblical world, a question might have been given to the propriety of including in Torah a major section devoted to the misadventure of a (mere) woman. In the highly selective account of Israel's thirty-eight years in the wilderness, the story of Miriam's attack on her brother is included because of how important she really was. Finally, this is not the last we hear of Miriam. In Micah 6:4 she is celebrated along with Moses and Aaron as God's gifts to his people in his gracious actions. This prophetic verse becomes her long-overdue reappraisal.

Miriam is a grand biblical character. She preserved the life of her young brother, the helpless infant who later became the great Moses, servant of Yahweh (see Ex 1). She made it possible for Moses' (and her!) actual mother to become his nurse when he was adopted into the household of Pharaoh in Egypt. She led the singing of the first psalm we find recorded in the Scriptures, the Song of Moses (Ex 15; cf. vv.1, 20)—the praise of the people of

God celebrating their deliverance from the army of Egypt at the Red Sea. Again, it is not because Miriam was a woman that she is presented in this chapter in an unfavorable light; it is precisely because she was such a magnificent person in the history of salvation that her act of rebellion is recorded as a significant event. On a final note, it would be a strange male conspiracy that would later bring even Moses under judgment (see Nu 20). Miriam behaved badly in this chapter, yet so did Moses in a text yet to come.

The initial attack on Moses concerned his wife. It is a human phenomenon, in the context of personality clashes, for one to present a smoke screen before coming out with the real issue. The marriage of Moses to a Cushite woman is not the central issue. This was only pretext; the real issue concerned Moses' special relationship with God.

But we begin where Miriam began, with Moses' new wife. The reference to the "Cushite wife" of Moses is puzzling, to say the least. As to the word "Cush," there was a man named "Cush" who was the first son of Ham (Ge 10:6–7). Traditionally, many Bible interpreters have associated "Cush" with Ethiopia (e.g., Merrill, 228; Budd, 136; the LXX translated the Hebrew term as *Aithiopia*). Others have associated the word "Cush" with the Kassites (Akk. *kaššû*) in Mesopotamia (see Harrison, 194). Presently, however, Cush (better, Kush) is believed to speak of the Nubian people of ancient Sudan. These are black Africans who had periods of close contact with Egypt; there were even periods of Kushite dominance over the local Egyptian population (see Notes).

Some have thought that Moses' wife Zipporah was intended by the words "his Cushite wife" (see Ex 2:15–22). If so, her foreign ancestry (as a Midianite) was attacked rhetorically by exaggeration. More likely, however, the possibility is that Moses had taken a new wife. In this case the new wife could have been a second wife, if Zipporah was still alive. Or he may have married again after the death of Zipporah (which is not recorded) or following a divorce from her (which is also not recorded).

Following their traumatic disagreement concerning circumcising their second son (see Ex 4:24–26 and the Notes below), it seems possible that Moses divorced Zipporah. The language of 12:1 seems to point to a recent marriage of Moses (lit., "concerning the issue of the Cushite woman that he had married, for it was a Cushite woman whom he had married"). The repetition of the phrases suggests an emphasis as well as a sense of the appropriateness of the charge, if not a validation of the attitude that underlies it. The language suggests a basic ethnic resentment (so Milgrom, 93). In any event, the attack on the marriage of Moses was a pretext; the focus of the attack was on the prophetic gift of Moses and his special relationship with Yahweh.

2 Miriam and her brother Aaron asked, rhetorically, "Has the LORD spoken only through Moses? Has he not spoken as well through us?" Of course he had. Exodus 15:20 specifically marks Miriam as a prophet in her own right (*hannᵉbîʔâ*, the definite feminine form of the term "prophet"). Micah 6:4 speaks of Moses, Aaron, and Miriam as God's gracious provisions for Israel. God spoke through Aaron and Miriam, but his principal spokesman was Moses. The prophetic gifting of the seventy elders (11:24–30) seems to have been an immediate provocation for the attack of Miriam and Aaron on their brother.

Verse 2 ends in an ominous manner: "And the LORD heard this." The writer is well aware that the Lord "hears" everything. This special notice means that the Lord heard with an intention of acting, of intervening in behalf of his servant. The phrasing is not unlike that in Exodus 2:23–25, where four verbs are used of Yahweh's relatedness to his people: he hears, he remembers, he sees, and he knows (see Ronald B. Allen, "What Is in a Name?" in *God: What Is He Like?* [ed. William F. Kerr; Wheaton, Ill.: Tyndale, 1977], 107–27).

3 The most difficult line in the chapter, and one of the most difficult verses in the entire book, is v.3. Critical and conservative scholars have long (and, it would seem, correctly) observed that it is not likely that a truly humble person would write in such a manner about himself. Some have used this verse as a cudgel against those who believe in the Mosaic authorship of the Torah. The supposition is that this verse, and the general use of the third person (e.g., "Moses said," "Moses did"), constitute clear evidence of later authorship of the book. It is theoretically possible that Moses might have authored such a line about his abject humility by inspiration, just as it is possible that he might have recorded the account of his death and burial by prophetic insight (Dt 34). These possibilities, however, are not likely. It may be observed that our Lord spoke of himself in the words, "I am gentle and humble in heart" (Mt 11:29). But even he (who alone could legitimately speak in such a manner!) did not add, " … more than all the people on the face of the earth."

Some scholars have argued that the verse began as a marginal gloss, which, through time, slipped into the text of the book. Scribes might have added this note to the margin to help the reader understand how unfair the attack against Moses was. Later scribes, not realizing this was an explanatory gloss, may have included the verse in the text proper. Yet there is no textual evidence that this is the case; that is, we do not presently have Hebrew manuscripts or ancient versions that omit this phrase or suggest it was a later insertion.

Cleon Rogers has presented a suggestion that appears to be preferable. He states that the key term

in v.3 should be translated "miserable" rather than "meek" (see Notes). When we read the narratives in which he plays a role, we may observe that Moses was not really an exceptionally meek or humble man. He was a man given at times to rage, self-pity, questioning, and debate. He was also a man capable of true greatness. He is one of the most impressive figures in biblical history, certainly one of the most pivotal. But this verse aside, it is not likely that observers of the story line of the Torah would automatically include "meekness" among the character traits of this most significant biblical personage (see Notes).

The word "miserable," however, could hardly be more fitting to describe his situation in the context of this chapter. Moses had been under assault on every front. He found his lot so difficult, his task so unmanageable, his pressure so intense, that he called out to God saying, "It's too much!" (cf. 11:14). With the assault now coming from within his family, he passed even beyond that feeling of desperation observed in the Lament of Moses (11:11–15). At this point he was utterly speechless; he was a broken man. He was like Elijah following that prophet's great work on Mount Carmel (see 1Ki 19:3; see Notes). Verse 3, in my judgment, should be translated confidently in this manner: "Now the man Moses was exceedingly miserable, more than any man on the face of the earth!" Many have felt like this from time to time; none has felt it so deeply as Moses did at this nadir of his life. Hence there is nothing in this verse that speaks against the role of Moses as the author of Numbers. It is merely in keeping with the third-person nature of the general recitation.

An obvious objection to this point of view would be that if it were true, would not someone have suggested it as an alternative explanation before Rogers presented his case? An answer, perhaps also obvious, is that there really could be no advance in biblical understanding if there were not the possibility of "new understandings" of ancient textual conundrums. The issue is whether the viewpoint of Rogers fits the text at hand and the larger picture. In my view, his idea works wonderfully for both. See also the commentary at 16:1 for an application of the results of this line of inquiry.

NOTES

1 וַתְּדַבֵּר (*watteᵉdabbēr*, "and she spoke"), the Piel preterit verb that begins the chapter, is feminine singular, which serves to heighten our understanding of Miriam's leadership in the conspiracy against Moses. When a clause has a compound subject ("Then Miriam and Aaron spoke"), the tendency in Hebrew style is to have the verb agree in person, number, and gender with the noun that is nearer the verb. The word order of the Hebrew clause is "then-she-spoke, Miriam, and-Aaron, against-Moses." The notion of speaking "against" is captured by the בְּ (*bᵉ*) that is prefixed to the name "Moses." This is the *bēt* adversative (see Williams, *Hebrew Syntax*, sec. 242) with the verb "to speak." It has the meaning, "to speak with hostility" or "to speak against." The same use of בְּ is found, for example, in v.8; 21:5, 7; Psalms 50:20; 78:19.

הַכֻּשִׁית (*hakkušît*, "the Kushite"), the term used derisively by Miriam respecting Moses' wife, is now understood by some scholars to refer to Nubians—black African peoples of ancient Sudan, south of Egypt. In antiquity there were periods when there were extensive contacts between the Kushites (Nubians) of Sudan and the Egyptians, including periods when Kushites actually ruled Egypt. It is possible that the new wife of Moses was a (black) African woman who was one of the numbers of people who left Egypt along with the Hebrews. Some of these people formed the infamous "mixed multitude," but some could well have been people who had come to true faith in Yahweh. In a splendid treatment of the issue, Edwin M. Yamauchi concludes: "In light of the ample Egyptian evidence of the presence of many Nubians in Egypt from as early as the Old Kingdom and of intermarriage between Egyptians and Nubians, we should not doubt the possibility of Moses' marriage to a Kushite or Nubian woman" (*Africa and the Bible* [Grand Rapids: Baker, 2004], 75). For recent studies of Kush and Egypt in the ancient periods, see Derek A. Welsby and Julie R. Anderson, eds., *Sudan: Ancient Treasures* (London: The British Museum, 2004); Julie R. Anderson, ed., *Treasures from Sudan* (London: The British Museum, 2004).

Regarding the phrase "for he had married a Cushite," I have presented the idea of the strong disagreement between Zipporah and Moses concerning circumcision as the likely provocation for their separation in Ronald B. Allen, "The 'Bloody Bridegroom' in Exodus 4:24–26," *BSac* 153 (July–September 1996): 259–69. Their dispute was so severe that Zipporah disappeared from the story line in the narrative of the exodus. She was not present during the grand events in which her husband was so prominent in Egypt. Before he proceeded to the stage of his acts of divine destiny in Egypt, Moses had sent his wife back to her father Jethro in Midian, to where she took along their two sons (see Ex 18:2).

After the events of the exodus, Moses had a joyful reunion with Zipporah's father (see Ex 18:1–27), but there appears to have been no joy in Moses' meeting with his wife. We may presume that when Jethro returned to Midian (v.27), he took Zipporah with him again, but the sons remained with Moses, as they continued with their families in the heritage of Israel (see, e.g., 1Ch 23:15–16). Thus Moses seems to have married another woman, "the Kushite," concerning whom there was such consternation by Miriam. (Explanations of Zipporah as the subject of the controversy in ch. 12 fail the smell test as to why, after so many years, would the issue of the ethnicity of Zipporah be seized upon by Miriam? Further, Zipporah the Midianite [a Semite] was not a Kushite [i.e., a black African woman].)

We may review another option in relation to what I have presented here. The Kushite wife of Moses could, of course, have been a second wife; that is, she may have been a wife of Moses in addition to Zipporah. However, the usual reasons in biblical times for a (godly) man to marry a second wife (while his first wife was still living and in his home) do not seem to be present here. These reasons would be: (1) contracting a second marriage to fulfill the desire for children when the first wife was judged to be infertile, or (2) marrying out of obligation the widow of one's close relative (the so-called "levirate marriage"; see Dt 25:5–10). Since Moses already had sons by Zipporah, the first reason seems moot. The second reason, marrying a widow of a close relative, is even less likely, given the lack of explanation given in the text.

If indeed my presentation is correct, then the words of Jesus respecting divorce take on an added irony. Jesus spoke of the hardness of the human heart as being the reason Moses allowed divorce (see Mt 19:7–8). If my take is correct, then Moses *himself* may have been divorced.

A final option for a godly man to marry a second wife in biblical times was following the death of his first wife. So one may suppose that Zipporah had died and that the second wife, the Kushite, was a sequential marriage to that of Zipporah. It would seem strange, however, that a notice of Zipporah's death is not mentioned. Less strange would be the omission of a note concerning the divorce of Moses, the moral leader of the nation! If this were the case, then the fact of Moses' divorce would not be paraded, just assumed. How such a realization of Moses as a divorced leader of the nation Israel might play in current issues of divorce and Christian leadership, well ... this may be a biblical "Pandora's Box"!

2 The interrogative particle הֲ (hᵃ) is attached to the adverb רַק (raq, "only"), thus resulting in הֲרַק (hᵃraq, "only?"). This word is then followed by the adverb אַךְ (ʾak, "surely"). The two words placed together at the beginning of the clause in Hebrew make the question emphatic: "Is it *truly only* through Moses that Yahweh has spoken?"

3 Instead of the Kethiv's עָנָו (ʿānāw, "meek"), the Qere reading is עָנָיו (ʿānāyw), an indication that the last syllable is to be pronounced. Cleon Rogers ("Moses: Meek or Miserable?" *JETS* 29 [September 1986]: 257–63) presents evidence from etymology and usage that "miserable" is a possible reading for this word, and from the context that meaning is preferable in this text. The basic meaning of the root עָנָה (ʿānâ; GK 6705) is "to be bowed down" (root עָנָה III in BDB, 776a). One could be bowed down by force (i.e., be subdued), bowed down with submissiveness (i.e., be humbled), or bowed down by issues of care and trouble (i.e., be miserable or afflicted). Among the uses of ʿānāw in the Prophets and the Wisdom Literature are descriptions of the socially oppressed and the miserable (see, e.g., Am 2:7); similarly, the word can also be used to describe one who has his or her full confidence in God and thus is humble before him (see, e.g., Pr 3:34).

As we have traced the story line of Numbers beginning in 11:1, one thing after another has brought pressure on Moses so that in 11:14 he whimpers to God that he is not able to bear the load any longer. He even asks God that he might die to be relieved of the pressures that are grinding him down. With the added assault of his sister and brother on his character, it was simply too much. He was now the most miserable man on earth. As Rogers, 262–63, says, "In the complaining of the people heightened by the complaining of his own sister and brother it would be the most natural thing in the world for someone to describe himself as the most miserable person on earth." I regard Rogers' argument and conclusion to be genuine contributions to our understanding of a biblical conundrum.

On the comparison of Moses' feeling of intolerable misery and Elijah's sense of overwhelming futility (1Ki 19:3), see Ronald B. Allen, "Elijah the Broken Prophet," *JETS* 22 (September 1979): 193–202.

On the idea that it is not likely that our first thought concerning Moses would be of his humility or meekness, I suggest a comparison with a situation relating to David that is found in Psalm 40:2. The standard translations read something like, "I waited patiently on Yahweh." Yet the adverb "patiently" is not written in the text. The words are קַוֹּה קִוִּיתִי (*qauwōh qiwwîtî*, "waiting, I waited"). In many translations the adverb "patiently" is supplied "for sense." Yet when we think of the character of David as described in Samuel and Kings, "patience" is not one of the first qualities that emerges. David was sometimes marked by rash acts (see, e.g., see the story of Nabal in 1Sa 25). Further, in this very verse he speaks of "screaming" out to Yahweh by using the word שַׁוְעָתִי (*šaw'ātî*, "my scream"). This word is hardly consequent in a passage describing patience. I suggest that in this verse the infinitive construct ("waiting") is used not to describe the adverb "patiently" but to insist on the *singularity* of David's focus on Yahweh. The form is emphatic and focused: "I *waited* on Yahweh."

This case is confirmed further in the poem when David states that, against the direction of his advisors, he did not seek other gods for help (see v. 4). David may have displayed patience in some circumstances, but the point of Psalm 40 is that his focus was on Yahweh and on Yahweh alone. Here again a familiar text and common translation is subject to review and reassessment.

ii. The defense of Moses by the Lord (12:4–9)

⁴At once the LORD said to Moses, Aaron and Miriam, "Come out to the Tent of Meeting, all three of you." So the three of them came out. ⁵Then the LORD came down in a pillar of cloud; he stood at the entrance to the Tent and summoned Aaron and Miriam. When both of them stepped forward, ⁶he said, "Listen to my words:

"When a prophet of the LORD is among you,
    I reveal myself to him in visions,
I speak to him in dreams.
    ⁷But this is not true of my servant Moses;
he is faithful in all my house.
    ⁸With him I speak face to face,
clearly and not in riddles;
    he sees the form of the LORD.
Why then were you not afraid
    to speak against my servant Moses?"

⁹The anger of the LORD burned against them, and he left them.

COMMENTARY

4 The Hebrew adverb *piťōm* ("at once") expresses suddenness, an abrupt response of the Lord that is pregnant with terror (see Job 22:10; Isa 47:11; Jer 4:20). Ordinarily God is slow to anger and hesitant in judgment; he longs for repentance in place of stubbornness and desires to forgive rather than destroy. But the association of the Lord to his servant Moses is so strong that here suddenly even he bursts in to redress the wrong done to his friend. That God speaks to Moses along with Aaron and Miriam suggests that he is near and present as they berate Moses so unfairly. (Here I speak not of God's omnipresence but of his gracious personal involvement in the affairs of human beings.)

5 When the trio comes to the Tent of Meeting according to the command of the Lord, he descends to them in the cloud (as in 11:25; see above). The language here is even more dramatic: "Then the LORD came down in a pillar of cloud" (see Ex 13:21 for this expression used to describe the Lord's guidance of his people). Descriptions of the appearances of God in Hebrew Scripture are usually styled "theophanies." Here I follow a lead from Claus Westermann in suggesting that the term "epiphany" may be used, in distinction from "theophany," where Scripture presents a *dramatic descending* of God, as in Psalm 18:7–15.

The Hebrew verb *yārad* ("to come down") is often used in these contexts. In 11:25, Yahweh came down in grace; in Genesis 11:5–8, Yahweh came down in judgment. It is beyond comprehension to reflect on the wonder of the Lord's "coming down." Psalm 113 speaks of his incomparable glory, "exalted with respect to sitting" (cf. v.5). Yet it is his unfathomably condescending nature to stoop down, as it were, to see and even to come down to meet with humans. In a sense, each theophany (appearance of God) and epiphany (descent of God) is a pictorial

promise of the grand theophany, the great epiphany of the Lord Jesus Christ, and a "gentle tease" of his future dwelling in the midst of his people (see, e.g., Zep 3:16–20, esp. v.17, "the LORD your God in your midst").

There is a bad side to the good news, however, for God may come down in wrath as well as in grace. When Yahweh appeared from the midst of the cloud before the Tent of Meeting, he spoke to Aaron and Miriam. They came forward. What a dramatic moment in the history of salvation! Then he told them to listen. And then he spoke.

6–9 This oracle of Yahweh in vv.6–8 is presented in poetic format. As in the Battle Cry of Moses (10:35–36) and the Lament of Moses (11:11–15), so the Oracle of Yahweh here functions more impressively in poetry than in prose. The genius of poetry is to make much little; that is, poetry compresses the greatest significance into the fewest words. The overall effect of great poetry is the feeling or experience one receives of the impact of the words.

Below I offer my translation of this poem, with a couple of difficult text-critical decisions included (and explained in the Note):

> [6]And he said:
> "Hear my words:
>   'If there is one of your prophets
>   —I am Yahweh!
>   I may speak to him by means of vision,
>   or I may talk to him by means of a prophetic dream.
> [7]But not so with my servant Moses;
>   in all my household he is reliable.
> [8]Face to face I speak with him,
>   in personal presence and not in riddles;
>   he gazes on the semblance of Yahweh.
> Why then are you not terrified,

to speak against my servant, against Moses?'"

Some salient features of this poem may be noted. The usual wording, "if there is a prophet among you," is likely the correct meaning of the phrase. The Hebrew word as it stands (see Note) is more usually translated "your prophet." There seems to be a subtle effect in play here. All other prophets are "your prophets." Only Moses is "my" prophet.

Second, the poem stresses in an unusual manner the sovereignty of Yahweh in the way he deals with prophets and other persons. He decides how he will speak, when, to whom, and in what manner. This is why I suggest the interjection, "I am Yahweh," is so fitting. Commonly in solemn utterances the words ʾănî yhwh ("I am Yahweh/I am the LORD") will be inserted. This feature is especially common in the book of Leviticus.

Third, the poem presents in a powerful manner the distinctiveness of Moses as against all other agents of divine disclosure. The contrasts are in the areas of levels of intimacy. To other prophets God might speak in a variety of ways, with some more clearly than with others (see Heb 1:1; 1Pe 1:10–11). But with Moses, Yahweh had a one-on-one relationship. Only Moses could approach the holy mountain and gaze on the Divine Person. Only his face radiated following these sublime encounters. Others might have heard the words; only Moses "saw" God's person (see Ex 34:5–7). What we are to make of these words is somewhat uncertain, given the language of mystery in the Hebrew Bible and the denial in the NT that anyone ever saw God at any time (see Jn 1:18). At the very least, these words speak of an unprecedented level of intimacy between God and Moses.

At the most, it is possible to argue that Moses spoke with the person of Jesus (a "preincarnate appearance of Christ"). John 1:18 suggests that no one has ever seen the Father but that the role of the Son is specifically revelatory of the Father to others. The one sure thing in this text is that there was no one who was on such familiar ground with God as was Moses (see also Dt 34:10). The expression "my house" refers to the household of the nation.

The reason given for this special relationship is unexpected: Moses' faithfulness is what has set him apart from all others. It is intriguing to associate this idea with the description of Abram in Genesis 15:6. It is also ominous to contrast the faithfulness of Moses as described in this poem with the faithlessness of the people in the story to follow (chs. 13–14).

Finally, the last bicolon of the poem is chilling. In feigned incredulity God asks the potent question, "Why then are you not terrified, / to speak against my servant, against Moses?" (my translation). "Why are you not very afraid?" Clearly, the axe of God's wrath was about to fall on the block below! Verse 9 speaks of the wrath of God and of his awesome departure. Just reading the text is stunning. To have been present must have been chilling beyond comprehension.

NOTE

6 The phrasing of the words, נְבִיאֲכֶם יהוה (nebîʾăkem yhwh, "your [masculine plural] prophet, Yahweh"), is difficult; the Hebrew pronominal suffix ("your") is plural; it may not refer to Yahweh. The first word would usually be translated "your prophet." It is customary to read this word as though it were two words, נָבִיא בָכֶם (nābîʾ bākem, "a prophet among you"), as in the versions. More difficult, however, is the relationship of this word to the divine name that follows it. The term נְבִיאֲכֶם (nᵉbîʾăkem) has a major disjunctive accent (zaqeph parvum) that ordinarily would separate it from what follows; further, a noun with a pronominal suffix ("your prophet") would not form a binding unit (a construct chain) with a following word. Hence the rendering "a prophet of the LORD among you" in the NIV is one approximation of the situation.

Generally, there are three solutions presented: (1) transpose the divine name to follow the introductory verb at the beginning of verse 6 to read, "And the LORD said ...."; (2) add a preposition "to" to the divine name, as is suggested in the LXX, and leave the divine name where it is but ignore the accents, thus leaving a translation such as the NIV's; (3) presume the loss of the pronoun "I" אֲנִי (ᵃnî) before the divine name and maintain the accents as they are, thus resulting in a new colon: "I am the LORD"—the solution of the Syriac (and Targum). This last solution I find the most convincing; it is reflected in the translation I have given above. See also Note at 15:41.

iii. The punishment of Miriam (12:10–15)

> ¹⁰When the cloud lifted from above the Tent, there stood Miriam—leprous, like snow. Aaron turned toward her and saw that she had leprosy; ¹¹and he said to Moses, "Please, my lord, do not hold against us the sin we have so foolishly committed. ¹²Do not let her be like a stillborn infant coming from its mother's womb with its flesh half eaten away."
> ¹³So Moses cried out to the LORD, "O God, please heal her!"
> ¹⁴The LORD replied to Moses, "If her father had spit in her face, would she not have been in disgrace for seven days? Confine her outside the camp for seven days; after that she can be brought back." ¹⁵So Miriam was confined outside the camp for seven days, and the people did not move on till she was brought back.

COMMENTARY

10 The immediate effect of God's wrath was seen on the body of Miriam. The fact that Miriam became "leprous" but Aaron did not is a signal to the reader that our initial impression was correct: Miriam was the principal offender. Now God spoke out against her; his hand struck her. She broke out with a type of skin disease that excluded persons from participation in the activities of the community (see 5:1–4).

It has long been asserted that the term "leprous" in such contexts may be misleading for the modern reader. While today's Hansen's disease may be a subset of the biblical disease cluster, they may not be the same illness (see Note). The result of this judgment

was that Miriam, the principal offender against her brother Moses, became a pariah, an outcast, as she now suffered from the type of infectious skin disease that excluded her from the community of Israel.

11–13 The repentance of Aaron for the sin of presumption (v.11) is touching both in its intensity and in his concern for their sister. His description of the appearance of Miriam's skin (v.12) is ghastly but effective. Moses, their brother, then called out to God to heal her. His prayer is remarkable in its urgency and simplicity, as he screamed out, "O God [ʾēl], please heal her!"

14–15 The response of God was graciousness mingled with sobriety. He granted Miriam healing, but he still demanded her public shame for a period of time. Building on cultural elements of the day, the Lord referred to a public rebuke and the time of shame that rebuke would entail (v.14). It would seem that seven days' time was the briefest of periods of such shame before restoration might be accomplished. A period of seven days was a standard time for uncleanness occasioned by touching or coming into contact with a dead body (see 19:11, 14, 16).

NOTE

10 R. K. Harrison, 197 (also "Leper, Leprosy," *ISBE*[2], 3:103–6), suggests that the form of skin disease Miriam suffered from—מְצֹרַעַת (*mᵉṣōraʿat*, "leprous")—as well as that which Moses suffered as a sign (Ex 4:6)—may well have been leucoderma or psoriasis. In both texts the word כַּשָּׁלֶג (*kaššāleg*, "[white] as snow") describes the form of the skin disorder; yet chronic צָרַעַת (*ṣāraʿat*, "leprosy"; see Dt 24:8; Lev 13–14) was not noted for a white aspect.

iv. A journey note (12:16)

[16]After that, the people left Hazeroth and encamped in the Desert of Paran.

COMMENTARY

16 At last the destination of the grand march was achieved (see 10:12 and comments). The Desert of Paran was the staging area for the attack on the land of Canaan. Despite numerous terrible events that marred the dream of the triumphal march, at last the people were at their destination. Now was the time for regrouping, for reconnaissance and evaluation, for putting strategy in place, and for mounting the assault of victory over the Canaanite peoples. Yes, there had been troubled times on the journey. But glory awaited—at least it should have.

c. The Twelve Agents and the Mixed Report (13:1–33)

OVERVIEW

We appear to be at a new beginning of greatness for Israel when we enter this chapter. The vindication of Moses as the servant of Yahweh had been stunning and unforgettable. The presence of the people in the vastness of their numbers there on the plateau of Paran was undeniable. The desire of the people to enter the Land of Promise was unquestionable. The faithfulness of the Lord to his promise and his commitment to his people were sure and unalterable. Given all the experiences the people had gone through in the previous months of preparation and journey, at last—at long last—it was time for them to claim Yahweh's word, to believe in his power, to march in his name, and to enter his land.

Hence the surprise that comes in the unexpected turn of events in this and the following chapter is even more startling than the surprise we felt as we first read the narrative of the rebellion of the people in ch. 11, after the record of their compliance in chs. 1–10. Chapters 13–14 become "the road of sorrows" of the Torah. These passages are a blight on Israel and a warning to all who read the story. That which marked Moses apart from all others was his utter faithfulness to Yahweh (see again 12:7). That which now marks the nation as a whole is fear (fright) of their enemies instead of fear (reverence) of Yahweh.

i. The command of the Lord (13:1–2)

¹The LORD said to Moses, ²"Send some men to explore the land of Canaan, which I am giving to the Israelites. From each ancestral tribe send one of its leaders."

COMMENTARY

1–2 Years after these events, Moses reflected on them. As he recounted the story in his homily in Deuteronomy to the sons and daughters of those who lived the account, he filled in some details this chapter omits. Moses' words to the people were to rise, to go up, to begin the attack, and to seize the land (see Dt 1:21). But the people petitioned him first to send forth spies to discover the best routes for making their assault successful (1:22). This idea seemed reasonable to Moses; so he selected twelve men, one from each tribe, to reconnoiter (*tûr*, "to explore" [v.2], with the special meaning "to reconnoiter" in this text) the land (1:23).

But when we return to Numbers 13:1–2, we see that the command to send the men was also made by Yahweh. It is likely that Deuteronomy 1:21–23 presents the story from the point of view of the people, and that Numbers 13:1–2 presents the same account from the divine perspective. When the people requested that men be sent, Moses decided, on the basis of the will of God, to accede to their request. Both accounts meld into a whole. What we gain from putting the two accounts together, however, is the idea that sending men to scout the land was a further example of God's grace to the people.

It is customary to speak of these twelve men as "the twelve spies." Milgrom, 100, makes an interesting observation: these were not like the unnamed military spies of Joshua 2:1 who scouted out the city of Jericho before Israel's attack on that city—these individuals in Numbers 13–14 were significant tribal leaders. They should be thought of as "special agents"—but not agents sent to act clandestinely as military spies. Rather, they are agents sent by Moses in an act of faith to display the power of Yahweh that would soon become evident as the Hebrew people marched in victory over a good and plentiful land. So, while perhaps a bit awkward, I will avoid the term "spies" in this section. However, I doubt that this change of terminology will ever catch on, since the notion of the "twelve spies" is so fixed in our vocabulary, such a part of our common currency, that I may be singing in the dark here.

The specification of the type of men to be selected reminds us that, while God is not a respecter of persons with regard to the outworking of his mercy (see Dt 10:17), he does use select persons for his leadership tasks. Yet ten of the twelve men in this list turn out to be dismal failures. That they were each leaders of their tribes did not guarantee they would measure up for the leadership role God desired them to have. The term used to describe them as "leaders" is the same used for the tribal leaders in the making of the rosters of the tribes in ch. 1 (nāśîʾ; see 1:16).

NOTE

2 In שְׁלַח־לְךָ (šᵉlaḥ-lᵉkā, "send to you"), the preposition and pronominal element form the so-called dative of personal reference (also termed "the reflexive use of the preposition"), which emphasizes active participation on the part of the one who receives the command. It has the force, "*you* send!" ("send one," NIV). This is the same construction we find in God's command to Abram in Genesis 12:1: "*You* go!" See also Notes at Numbers 10:2; 35:11. On the phrase "From each … tribe," see Note on 9:10.

ii. The roster of names (13:3–16)

³So at the Lord's command Moses sent them out from the Desert of Paran. All of them were leaders of the Israelites. ⁴These are their names:

from the tribe of Reuben, Shammua son of Zaccur;
⁵from the tribe of Simeon, Shaphat son of Hori;
⁶from the tribe of Judah, Caleb son of Jephunneh;
⁷from the tribe of Issachar, Igal son of Joseph;
⁸from the tribe of Ephraim, Hoshea son of Nun;
⁹from the tribe of Benjamin, Palti son of Raphu;
¹⁰from the tribe of Zebulun, Gaddiel son of Sodi;
¹¹from the tribe of Manasseh (a tribe of Joseph), Gaddi son of Susi;
¹²from the tribe of Dan, Ammiel son of Gemalli;
¹³from the tribe of Asher, Sethur son of Michael;
¹⁴from the tribe of Naphtali, Nahbi son of Vophsi;
¹⁵from the tribe of Gad, Geuel son of Maki.

¹⁶These are the names of the men Moses sent to explore the land. (Moses gave Hoshea son of Nun the name Joshua.)

COMMENTARY

3 As in the records of chs. 1–10, the story begins with the compliance of Moses to the will of God. He did just as God had commanded in selecting one worthy individual from each tribe to represent his people on the reconnaissance mission. There is a sense in these chapters that when God speaks, Moses acts—thus our terrible shock when even he falters in ch. 20! The names listed in vv.4–15 are different from those given for the tribal leaders in chs. 1, 2, 7, and 10. Presumably the tribal leaders in the four earlier lists were older men. The task of the special agents called for men who were younger and more robust, but who were no less respected by their peers.

There is symmetry in this chapter, as we have found on other occasions. The whole impression is orderly and straightforward, thus granting a sense of importance and dignity. There is nothing casual about this text. The travel of the tribal agents begins in the Desert of Paran (v.3); it is to that wilderness they return in v.26. The text comes full circle geographically. But the men who came back were not the same as the men who left. Presumably they left in confidence, with a spirit of divine adventure; but they returned in fear, groveling before human beings and no longer trusting in God. This factor provides intertwining circles of geography and character development in the chapter.

4–15 The significance of the list of names in these verses (cf. 1:5–15) is multiple: (1) the names add a certain historical verisimilitude; (2) they provide a level of accuracy in the narrative; (3) they should have given the occasion for pride of family, clan, and tribe; (4) they become, because of the failure of the majority in this case, markers of sadness, as do the names of places of Israel's judgment (e.g., "Taberah" [11:3]; "Kibroth Hattaavah" [11:34]); and (5) they, like all lists of names in Scripture, remind

us of the significance of names to God (e.g., the Lamb's "book of life" [Rev 20:12]).

The names of the tribal leaders and their respective tribes are listed in vv.4–15. Note these observations about these names and the meanings that may be suggested for them (see Notes for suggested derivations of names).

1. While few of these names are specifically theophoric (built with a term for deity, such as the names "Gaddiel," "Ammiel," and "Geuel"), most of them are implicitly theophoric (e.g., "Sethur" and "Nahbi," both likely having the idea of being hidden [in God]).
2. Only the name of the superb leader Caleb does not seem to have a moral or theophoric meaning (see Notes).
3. Joseph is mentioned along with Manasseh (v.11) but not with Ephraim (v.8); further, these allied tribes are separated in this listing—an unusual feature in such lists.
4. The tribe of Levi is omitted, as is common in lists of the laic tribes; the omission of Levi allows for the listing of both Ephraim and Manasseh.

16 The particular significance of Joshua is noted here. We have already discovered that Joshua was an attendant of Moses from his youth and was particularly concerned about his master's reputation when it seemed threatened by the independent prophesying of Eldad and Medad (see comments on 11:27–28). Here we learn that Joshua's name was first known as Hoshea, but it was Moses who changed it to Joshua. This parenthetical statement anticipates the later prominence of Joshua. The reader is alerted to the significance of this name among those of the special agents; here is a man of great destiny. The Hebrew word Hoshea (hôšēaʿ)

means "salvation [ofYahweh]"; the new form of the name, "Joshua," (*yᵉhôšuaᶜ*) means "Yahweh saves." Both forms are precursors of the Hebrew spelling for the name of Jesus: Yeshua (*yēšuaᶜ*).

Moses' act in changing Hoshea's name to Joshua was a mark of a special relationship between the two men. This change of name, which is slight—something of a play on words—is a fatherly action on Moses' part; it is also a prophetic action. It is as though Moses has adopted his young aide and marked him for greatness. We are reminded of the way the Lord changed the name of Abram to Abraham (Ge 17). The names are related, but in this changing of name a new relationship results.

It is notable that the two agents who rendered a report that was faithful to the promise of God represented the two tribes that later would become most prominent in the land. Joshua was from the tribe of Ephraim, the tribe that would become dominant in the north; Caleb was from the tribe of Judah, the dominant tribe in the south. There is something salutary in this fact as

well—the two men who stood for faithfulness in God came from prominent tribes.

The ancestry of Caleb is particularly intriguing. Verse 6 says that he is Caleb son of Jephunneh (*ben-yᵉpunneh*). Jephunneh is called "the Kenizzite" in Numbers 32:12; Joshua 14:6, 14. In 1 Chronicles 2:18 he is called "son of Hezron" (*ben-ḥeṣrôn*). Hezron was the son of Peres, the grandson of Judah (see Ge 38:29). If we put all these data together, we may conclude that Caleb was of the tribe of Judah, the son of Jephunneh, a descendant of Hezron the son of Peres, the son of Judah. It may have been Judah's relationship with Tamar that linked the family with the Kenizzite group, a Canaanite people. It is also possible, however, that Caleb was more immediately Canaanite in his ancestry. "Jephunneh the Kenizzite" may have been a slogan of triumph, much like the phrase "Ruth the Moabitess" in the book of Ruth (Ru 1:22); here was a man from a Canaanite people group (see Ge 15:19–20) who had come to faith in Yahweh; now his son Caleb was the leader of the tribe of Judah. See Note.

NOTES

4–15 The names of the selected leaders of Israel, and their meanings, are as follows:

1. Shammua, שַׁמּוּעַ (*šammûaᶜ*, related to the verb שָׁמַע, *šāmaᶜ*, "to hear"; perhaps meaning, "Report [of God]"), leader of the tribe of Reuben;
2. Shaphat, שָׁפָט (*šāpāṭ*, from the verb שָׁפַט, *šāpaṭ*, "to judge"; perhaps meaning, "He has judged"), leader of the tribe of Simeon;
3. Caleb, כָּלֵב (*kālēb*, related to כֶּלֶב, *keleb*, "dog"; perhaps meaning, "Dog [of God]" (see Note on v.6), leader of the tribe of Judah;
4. Igal, יִגְאָל (*yigʾāl*, from the verb גָּאַל, *gāʾal*, "to redeem"; perhaps meaning, "He [God] redeems"), leader of the tribe of Issachar;
5. Hoshea, הוֹשֵׁעַ (*hôšēaᶜ*, from the verb, יָשַׁע, *yāšaᶜ*, "to save"; perhaps meaning, "Salvation"), leader of the tribe of Ephraim;
6. Palti, פַּלְטִי (*palṭî*, perhaps related to the verb פָּלַט, *pālaṭ*, "to escape"; perhaps meaning, "My escape [is God]"), leader of the tribe of Benjamin;
7. Gaddiel, גַּדִּיאֵל (*gaddîʾēl*, perhaps related to the noun גָּד, *gad*, "fortune"; perhaps meaning, "My fortune is God"), leader of the tribe of Zebulun;

8. Gaddi, גַּדִּי (*gaddî*, a name with the same meaning as that of the leader of Zebulun, "My fortune [is in God]"), leader of the tribe of Manasseh;

9. Ammiel, עַמִּיאֵל (*ʿammîʾēl*, a name combining the words עַמִּי, *ʿammî*, "my people," and אֵל, *ʾēl*, "God"; perhaps meaning, "God is my kinsman"), leader of the tribe of Dan;

10. Sethur, סְתוּר (*sᵉtûr*, a name perhaps related to the verb סָתַר, *sātar*, "to hide"; perhaps meaning, "Sheltered [by God]"), leader of the tribe of Asher;

11. Nahbi, נַחְבִּי (*naḥbî*, a name perhaps related to the verb חָבָה, *ḥābâ*, "to withdraw, hide"; perhaps meaning, "My hiding [is God]"), leader of the tribe of Naphtali;

12. Geuel, גְּאוּאֵל (*gᵉʾûʾēl*, a name perhaps relating the verbal root גָּאָה, *gāʾâ*, "to rise up [in majesty]" with the word "God"; perhaps meaning, "Majesty of God"), leader of the tribe of Gad.

As in all attempts to determine the meaning of biblical names, the suggestions here are, of necessity, tentative. The attempt to pin down the relationship of names to so-called verbal roots is a precarious adventure, in part due to the multiplicity of homonyms (words with the same spelling but unrelated in meaning) in Hebrew (which, for example, has four words spelled עָנָה, *ʿānâ*, each with a different etymology). The principal difficulty with the meaning of names, however, is usage. A noun or a verb has its meaning in the context of its use. A name, by its very nature, cannot be tied precisely to a meaning based simply on the narrative in which the name is found. The situation is even more difficult when names appear simply in lists. But in the list given above, each of the names may be regarded as a positive affirmation of faith in and service to God. It is this feature of these names that makes the list so haunting as we reflect on the actions and behavior of ten of these divinely appointed, humanly designated special agents.

The order of the tribes varies in the several listings. No reason seems to be given for these variations. Below is a comparison of the lists of chs. 1 and 13:

Numbers 1:5–16	Numbers 1:20–43	Numbers 13:4–15
(1) Reuben	(1) Reuben	(1) Reuben
(2) Simeon	(2) Simeon	(2) Simeon
(3) Judah	(3) Gad	(3) Judah
(4) Issachar	(4) Judah	(4) Issachar
(5) Zebulun	(5) Issachar	(5) Ephraim
(6) Ephraim	(6) Zebulun	(6) Benjamin
(7) Manasseh	(7) Ephraim	(7) Zebulun
(8) Benjamin	(8) Manasseh	(8) Manasseh
(9) Dan	(9) Benjamin	(9) Dan
(10) Asher	(10) Dan	(10) Asher
(11) Gad	(11) Asher	(11) Naphtali
(12) Naphtali	(12) Naphtali	(12) Gad

These variations raise questions. Why is Gad listed third in 1:24 but last in 13:15? Why is Judah third in 1:7 and 13:6 but fourth in 1:26? The birth order of the sons of Jacob is given piecemeal in Genesis, which also notes the birth of Jacob's daughter Dinah:

1. Reuben (mother: Leah; Ge 29:32)
2. Simeon (mother: Leah; Ge 29:33)
3. Levi (mother: Leah; Ge 29:34)
4. Judah (mother: Leah; Ge 29:35)
5. Dan (mother: Bilhah, maid of Rachel; Ge 30:6)
6. Naphtali (mother: Bilhah, maid of Rachel; Ge 30:8)
7. Gad (mother: Zilpah, maid of Leah; Ge 30:10)
8. Asher (mother: Zilpah, maid of Leah; Ge 30:13)
9. Issachar (mother: Leah; Ge 30:18)
10 Zebulun (mother: Leah; Ge 30:20)
11. Joseph (mother: Rachel; Ge 30:24)
12. Benjamin (mother: Rachel; Ge 35:18)
13. Dinah (mother: Leah; Ge 30:21)

Genesis 35:23–36 lists the sons in the order of their mothers. Two other significant listings of the sons of Jacob are found in the blessing of Jacob (Ge 49) and the blessing of Moses (Dt 33). In the blessing of Jacob, Zebulun and Issachar are out of birth order but are grouped with the other sons of their mother, Leah. In the blessing of Moses the tribe of Simeon is missing.

6 כָּלֵב (kāleb, "Caleb") is the name of the special agent from the tribe of Judah. Because of the usual, negative associations of the word "dog," כֶּלֶב (keleb), in ancient Hebrew culture, it appears that the scribes may have altered the pronunciation of this name when it was used of various individuals in the Bible. Gerhard F. Hasel ("Caleb," ISBE[2], 1:573) surmises that the positive associations of a dog as faithful and humble might have given rise to this name in Israel. We tend to think of these ideas as modern; but at times the ancients must have had some sense of a dog as "man's best friend." So, though slightly disguised in pronunciation, the name of this heroic companion of Joshua is a word that means "dog"—but in a positive sense. Perhaps we may think of him as "Dog of God," in an honorable sense. Milgrom, 101, points to Akkadian names such as Kalbi-Sin or Kalbi-Marduk, where a servant is the "dog [in service] of a god"—that is, an obsequious servant.

iii. The instructions of Moses (13:17–20)

[17]When Moses sent them to explore Canaan, he said, "Go up through the Negev and on into the hill country. [18]See what the land is like and whether the people who live there are strong or weak, few or many. [19]What kind of land do they live in? Is it good or bad? What kind of towns do they live in? Are they unwalled or fortified? [20]How is the soil? Is it fertile

or poor? Are there trees on it or not? Do your best to bring back some of the fruit of the land." (It was the season for the first ripe grapes.)

COMMENTARY

17–20 The instructions of Moses to the twelve special agents were comprehensive; a thorough report of the land—its produce, the peoples, and their towns—was required in the reconnaissance mission. The plan of approach was practical, showing that Moses had some sense of the lay of the land of Canaan. From their location in the northernmost boundary of the Desert of Paran, the men were to move into the Negev, the southernmost part of the land of Canaan. Then they were to ascend the hill country and journey as far as they could through the land. The journey upward was not only geographical; there is a sense in which we may see this upward journey as a symbol of assault, conquest, and victory.

The scouts were to give special attention to the people and the produce of the land, to the cities and towns, to the soil and the presence or absence of forests. Since the journey was at the time of the harvest of grapes, there is a personal note that they should bring back some of the fruit they might discover in the land. They were to show themselves courageous in taking some of the fruit (see Note)—words that would later come to haunt the nation. But the quest for a sampling of fruit is a nice touch; it had been a long time since the wilderness community had seen grapes. They had experienced a long hiatus since last enjoying wine. The principal harvesting of grapes in the land of Canaan/Israel comes in September and October, after the long, hot summer. But the first, early grapes may be harvested by mid- or late July. So the journey of the scouts would have come in the summer months.

NOTE

20 The NIV translation of וְהִתְחַזַּקְתֶּם (wᵉhithazzaqtem) as "Do your best" seems weak for this strong verb, a Hithpael perfect with the *waw* consecutive, used as a command, from the verb חָזַק, ḥāzaq, meaning "show yourselves courageous!" The act of heroism was in fact the bracing for thievery! They were told to take a sample of the fruit of the land—not to purchase from a stand but to seize from a field. Since the whole of the land was to be theirs, including cities they had not built, vineyards they had not cultivated, and trees they had not planted (Dt 6:10–11), in a sense the taking of the sample of the fruit of the land is a sampling of that which would all become theirs.

iv. A summary of the reconnaissance (13:21–25)

²¹So they went up and explored the land from the Desert of Zin as far as Rehob, toward Lebo Hamath. ²²They went up through the Negev and came to Hebron, where Ahiman,

Sheshai and Talmai, the descendants of Anak, lived. (Hebron had been built seven years before Zoan in Egypt.) ²³When they reached the Valley of Eshcol, they cut off a branch bearing a single cluster of grapes. Two of them carried it on a pole between them, along with some pomegranates and figs. ²⁴That place was called the Valley of Eshcol because of the cluster of grapes the Israelites cut off there. ²⁵At the end of forty days they returned from exploring the land.

COMMENTARY

21 The journey of the special agents began in the southernmost extremity of the land (the Desert of Zin) and took them to the northernmost point (Rehob, near Lebo Hamath; see 34:8). This journey of about 250 miles in each direction took them forty days (v.25)—possibly a rounded number indicating an approximate period of time similarly to "a month" in modern English idiom. Since a month is nearer to thirty days, forty days is regarded as more than a month, a complete cycle, a fullness of time. Nonetheless, the citing of forty days is a number suitably fitting for the sacral nature of their task.

22 Hebron was the first city the men came to in the land of Canaan. The parenthetical comment about the building of the city seven years before Zoan in Egypt may have been prompted by their amazement at the size and fortification of the city that was so closely associated with the lives of their ancestors four centuries before this time (see Ge 13:14-18; 14:13; 23:1; 25:9; 35:27-29; 50:13). In the stories of the ancestors of their people, Hebron had not been a great city but a dwelling and trading place for shepherds and herdsmen.

What is strange in the agents' interest in the city of Hebron is what they do *not* mention. This was the burial place of Abraham and Sarah, Isaac and Rebekah, Jacob and Leah! Why would they not have said, "Here we have arrived at the place where

our fathers and mothers were buried. Where they now lie, soon we shall live"?

Instead of looking to the patriarchs and the promises, the agents noticed sizes of buildings and statures of persons. Moreover, they ignored the clear timetable of God as recorded in Genesis 15. They were in the land at the time of promise. Yet they averted their glance from the tombs of the fathers, and they neglected the promise of God; they were too preoccupied with the sandal sizes of three huge men who lived in Hebron.

The other association with Hebron was the population of Anakites who lived there. Three notables from the descendants of Anak are mentioned as living at Hebron. The Anakites were men of great stature; their physical size became a rallying point for the fear of the people (see vv.32-33 and Note). In a later day of faith, Caleb was to drive these giants from their city (Jos 15:14; Jdg 1:10). Would that he had been given his chance forty years earlier!

23-25 Due to the size of the grape cluster they found, the special agents named the valley in which it was found "the valley of the cluster" (v.24; cf. NIV margin). The Valley of Eshcol is near Hebron; presumably the men cut the cluster of grapes on their return journey, but they may well have marked the location as they passed through this valley on their journey north. The very size of the grape cluster, indicated by the item describing the manner of transporting it to the camp (v.23), was a mark of the goodness of the land God was giving them. To think of clusters of grapes so large that two men would transport a cluster suspended from a pole—why, the people should have thought they had discovered Eden!

The grapes they brought back to the camp were wine grapes, of course. Hence these grapes were a symbol of the joy the land would provide for the people. The good land would provide for them the good life. As is well known, the present state of Israel uses the logo of the two men carrying an immense cluster of grapes on a pole as the symbol of the Department of Tourism. The Bible does not specify which of the men carried the grapes; the modern tourism department supplies the names freely: Caleb and Joshua!

Alas, the size of the cluster these agents brought back to the camp became a provocation of fear for the faithless. Such a large cluster of fruit was intimidating and unnerving to them. It ought to have intoxicated them with joy; instead, it inebriated them with paralyzing terror.

v. The mixed report (13:26–33)

> ²⁶They came back to Moses and Aaron and the whole Israelite community at Kadesh in the Desert of Paran. There they reported to them and to the whole assembly and showed them the fruit of the land. ²⁷They gave Moses this account: "We went into the land to which you sent us, and it does flow with milk and honey! Here is its fruit. ²⁸But the people who live there are powerful, and the cities are fortified and very large. We even saw descendants of Anak there. ²⁹The Amalekites live in the Negev; the Hittites, Jebusites and Amorites live in the hill country; and the Canaanites live near the sea and along the Jordan."
>
> ³⁰Then Caleb silenced the people before Moses and said, "We should go up and take possession of the land, for we can certainly do it."
>
> ³¹But the men who had gone up with him said, "We can't attack those people; they are stronger than we are." ³²And they spread among the Israelites a bad report about the land they had explored. They said, "The land we explored devours those living in it. All the people we saw there are of great size. ³³We saw the Nephilim there (the descendants of Anak come from the Nephilim). We seemed like grasshoppers in our own eyes, and we looked the same to them."

COMMENTARY

26–29 The first portion of the report of the special agents was truthful, if timorous. The clear goodness of the land was offset in their eyes by the many and mighty peoples who dwelt in it. They did give assent to the bounty of the land in the proverbial phrase "a land flowing with milk and honey." This phrase takes us back to Exodus 3:8 and the words of God to Moses at the beginning of his call to return to Egypt to rescue God's people from slavery and to bring them to the good land. This phrase forms a leitmotif of blessing with respect to the land. The biblical emphasis in this phrase is on productivity and abundance. As Moses heard these words from the men, his heart must have leaped within. This phrase was given by Moses again to the second generation, after the first generation lost their opportunity to enjoy the land (see Dt 11:9–12).

But immediately after praising the land for its bounty, the agents lamented its people and cities. Verse 28 begins with the limiting phrase, *'epes kî* ("except that"; "but," NIV). This reversal of mood was deadly. The size of the grape cluster now became ominous. No longer did it point to plenty but to people; no longer did it speak of joy but of fear. The cities were described as being inaccessible, impregnable. The term *bᵉṣurôt* ("fortified," NIV) is used in 2 Kings 18:13 of inaccessible cities and in Jeremiah 33:3 of inaccessible things. The cities of Canaan were said to be beyond the reach of the people of Israel. The listing of the nations that inhabited the land became a new reason for terror—the Amalekites, the Hittites, the Jebusites, the Amorites, and the Canaanites. Yet this listing of nations should have been taken as an indication of the numerous victories God was going to give to his people in fulfillment of his promise to Abraham in the covenant between the parts (see Ge 15).

30 The report of the majority must have caused the people to become frightened, as indicated by the words that speak of Caleb's silencing the people. Only Caleb and Hoshea (Joshua) returned a report that was prompted by faith in God. Caleb's words, "We can certainly do it," were not merely bravado; they were the words of one who really believed that Yahweh was giving the land to the people. These words were in the spirit of Moses, who knew that "the LORD has promised good things to Israel"

(10:29). Boldly, confidently, Caleb encouraged the people, "We are most assuredly able to do it" (see Notes).

31–33 But the evil report prevailed. Ten fearful men can outshout, and certainly outscare, two brave men. At last they stated explicitly what they had implied, "We are unable to do it" (cf. v.31). In this strong denial they did not give a negative cast to the words of faith that Caleb had just spoken; they clearly said that God was not sufficient to bring the task to completion. At this point these men were denying the power and presence of God, the promises and assurances of God, their own resources—indeed, even their own names. Those wonderful names their parents had given them—most of which names speak of the blessing of being the people of God—were being denied as they spoke their words of calumny (see Notes on the meanings of the names on 13:3–15; cf. Ge 37:2; Jer 20:10).

The Land of Promise was a good land, a gracious gift of Yahweh. By speaking evil concerning the land, the faithless agents were speaking evil of him. At this point their words became exaggerations and distortions. The Anakites (who were of large size) were now said to be Nephilim, the race of giants described briefly in the mysterious context of the cohabitation of the sons of God and the daughters of men (Ge 6:4). The use of the "Nephilim" seems to be deliberately provocative of fear, a term not unlike the concept of bogeymen and hobgoblins (see Notes). The exaggeration of the faithless led them to their final folly: "We seemed like grasshoppers in our own eyes, and we looked the same to them."

We have noted the possible use of deliberate rhetorical exaggeration or hyperbole in the numbers of the tribes of Israel—power numbers designed to bring encouragement to the nation in the confidence they would need to have in the fulfillment of the promises of God (see in the Introduction the sections on large numbers). In the report of the evil agents, we see that rhetorical exaggeration can work both ways. By describing themselves as mere grasshoppers in the sight of the fabulous Nephilim, they frightened the sandals off the people and led a nation to the grievous sin of unbelief against their caring God.

NOTES

30 The phrase כִּי־יָכוֹל נוּכַל לָהּ (*kî-yākôl nûkal lāh*, lit., "we are most assuredly able to do it!"; "we can certainly do it," NIV) begins with an asseverative *kî*, meaning "surely." Then a Qal passive infinitive absolute is joined to a Qal passive imperfect, both from the same root, יָכוֹל (*yākôl*, "to be able"). Sadly, we do not have to go far to find a contrast (v.31).

32 The report from the majority of the agents ("spies") was not just a "bad report" (NIV); it was truly evil. וַיּוֹצִיאוּ דִּבַּת (*wayyôṣîʾû dibbat*, "and they spread about an evil report"). The noun דִּבָה (*dibâ*, "whispering, defamation, evil report") is modified in 14:37 by the adjective רָעָה (*rāʿâ*, "evil"). See 14:36–37.

33 The hyperbole in the evil report came to an extreme in the reference to הַנְּפִילִים (*hannᵉpîlîm*, lit., "the fallen ones") in the "majority report." The NIV's rendering suggests that there is an editorial, explanatory comment: "the descendants of Anak come from the Nephilim." These words, presented in parentheses in the NIV, would appear to be the official teaching of Torah, the explanation of Moses. It appears to be better, however, to understand these words as an integral part of the false report of the spies; they were manipulating the evidence—putting their spin on things.

The Anakites (who were a people group of great stature in Canaan) were made even more frightful by this charge by its connecting them to the progeny of the spirit beings and human women described in the antediluvian account of Genesis 6:1–4. Milgrom, 107, correctly I believe, writes: "Now their identification as the Nephilim could have only one purpose—instill greater fear in the hearts of the people, for the gigantic stature and strength of these Anakites are now measured against a primordial and divine dimension." Their words are, in short, a complete fabrication. The real (and ancient) Nephilim all perished in the waters of the great flood.

d. The Rebellion of the People and Defeat by the Amalekites (14:1–45)

OVERVIEW

The narrative of this section of Numbers is tied directly to the events of ch. 13; indeed, these two chapters are the most tightly connected of all the narrative sections of the book. This chapter brings to climax and conclusion the story of the central rebellion of the people against Yahweh and his ser-vant Moses. The location of the rebellion is Kadesh in the Desert of Zin, in the northernmost reaches of the Desert of Paran. Poised at the base of the Land of Promise and presumably ready for their assault on the land in completion of their divine destiny, the people spurn the land, contemn their

Savior, and make plans to return to slavery in Egypt. Their acts of rebellion on this occasion are so grievous, so outrageous, that God is said bitterly to regret that he had ever reached out to them.

The Lord threatens to destroy the people utterly and to begin anew with Moses. But Moses implores God to reconsider, to extend anew his mercy, to be again their Savior. The decision of the Lord is one of mitigated judgment. Instead of killing off the rebellious nation at once, he condemns those over the age of twenty to a sentence of a listless existence in the wilderness. They are like banished peoples, landless and homeless, without a place—in a period in which having a sense of place is more important than even in our own day. Only their children—whom they claim outrageously that God desired dead—will be able to enter the land. But of the first generation none save the two righteous agents, Caleb and Joshua, will enter the land of God's promise. (Note: See comment on 13:2 for the use of "special agents" rather than "spies" for these individuals.)

The central ideas of this chapter are simply overwhelming. Here is the original "lost generation." All over the age of twenty are to mark time until they breathe their last and the sands of Sinai enwrap their remains. All is to be a waiting game. Throughout the years as parents aged, they will look at their children and live for them; for only through their children's hope of seeing the Promised Land can another day in the wilderness be livable. It is one thing to have a passive impression of the story line of Numbers. But when we really begin to think about the enormity of the sentence of the population, the sense of the text overwhelms us.

As stated in the Introduction, this passage forms the heart of the book. "God has time, and the wilderness has sand." Yahweh is not in a hurry. If his people are faithless, he will allow them to live their lives in the wilderness and be buried there. But one day a generation will rise in faith and follow his mercy and power into the Land of Promise.

i. The final rebellion of the faithless people (14:1–4)

¹That night all the people of the community raised their voices and wept aloud. ²All the Israelites grumbled against Moses and Aaron, and the whole assembly said to them, "If only we had died in Egypt! Or in this desert! ³Why is the Lord bringing us to this land only to let us fall by the sword? Our wives and children will be taken as plunder. Wouldn't it be better for us to go back to Egypt?" ⁴And they said to each other, "We should choose a leader and go back to Egypt."

COMMENTARY

1–2 The malicious report of the ten spies or special agents (see comment on 13:2; cf. 13:26–33) spread throughout the populace like a virus on a rampage. The words of Caleb and Joshua were not heard. Everywhere people heard of walled cities, strong men, giants—even the fabled Nephilim. The giant clusters of grapes were a portent of doom. If clusters of grapes were as great as these, imagine what the people would be like! No one talked about Yahweh's grace. None recited his miracles. Forgotten was God's act of stymying Egypt, then the most powerful nation of the world, by sending the parted waters of the Red Sea back to their beds to engulf the pursuing Egyptian army. The thunder of Sinai, the fire of God, his speaking and delivering and gracing his people beyond imagination—all these things were forgotten in their paroxysm of fear, which, unchecked, becomes its own fuel, a self-propelling force that expands as it expends. The words of a mid-twentieth-century American president, "The only thing we have to fear is fear itself," have their outworking in the self-consuming absorption with terror that raged through the camps of the people of Israel that night.

Verses 1–2 emphasize the pervasiveness of the fear and the outrage of the entire populace. The words are "all the people of the community" (v.1), "all the Israelites" (v.2), and "the whole assembly" (v.2). This threefold emphasis on the extent of the rebellion is important, for the judgment of God will extend to the entire community, which has been given over to wailing—a distinctively Eastern practice. This is not a scene of passive resignation, of silent ruing. We are to imagine the worst sort of rage, a picture of screaming, rending, throwing, cursing anger—an intoxication of grief.

Moses and Aaron were regarded as the principal culprits, the central targets of the anger of the nation. The people "grumbled" against Moses and Aaron (v.2), even as they grumbled against Yahweh. They became "The Grumblers of Israel"; Scripture accords them their own distinctive verbal expression (see Notes; also comments on 16:41).

As the people gave themselves over to more and more outrageous attitudes, they began to wish that they had already died. It seemed to them that it would have been preferable to have died in Egypt or even in the wilderness than to come this close to

their goal, only to discover that it was unattainable. The irrationality of their words is understandable from the perspective of weakened, sinful humanity. But from the vantage of faith, from the stance of belief in God, these words are intolerable; they are self-destructive, self-fulfilling prophecies. The people who wished to have died in the wilderness will find that is exactly what they will have to do.

3–4 The more the people wail, the more excessive are their words. The more the people cry, the more they outdo one another in protests of rage. This is the pattern of crowd psychology that leads to riots, lynchings, stormings, and rampages. Now they begin to aim their anger more directly at Yahweh himself. Moses and Aaron are the fall guys, but the Lord is the one really to blame; he delivered them from Egypt. He brought Pharaoh to his knees, cast horse and rider into the sea, led them through a barren land, and provided bread from heaven and water from a gushing rock. He had spoken, revealing grace and wonder, power and gentleness, direction and Torah. God is the one at fault! And they begin to curse him, to contemn his goodness, to reject his grace.

Forgetful of God's power against Egypt—surely a nation stronger than any petty Canaanite city-state—the people work themselves into such a frenzy of fear that they wish that God had not brought them here at all. Why had he not just left them alone? Slavery began to look good to them. The hovels in Egypt became home again. The memory of a variety of food made the memory of oppressive taskmasters less fearsome.

So it was that the frightening words of the faithless agents led to the mourning of the entire community and to their great rebellion against the Lord. They forgot all the miracles the Lord had done for them; they contemned his mercies and spurned his might. In their ingratitude they preferred death (v.2). Unfortunately, it was death they deserved and death they were to get. The most reprehensible charge against God's grace was that concerning their children (see vv.31–33). Only their children would survive. All the rest would die in the wilderness they had chosen over the Land of Promise.

NOTES

1 The syntax of the verse is somewhat abrupt and rough. The word order of the first clause literally reads: "and-they-raised all-the-congregation and-they-gave their-voices." Despite their separation, we expect that the two verbs—"they raised" and "they gave"—work together in hendiadys: "and they gave themselves over completely to wailing." This is buttressed by the last colon of the verse: "and the people wept all that night." The use of three verbs here is powerful.

2 The verb לוּן (lûn, "to murmur, grumble") is a term of special use for the wilderness community. (There is another verb לוּן that means "to lodge, spend the night.") This verb is used only in Exodus 15–17; Numbers 14; 16–17; and Joshua 9:18. In the Niphal and Hiphil forms (used interchangeably with this verb), לוּן becomes the marker of a generation of people. Instead of "the greatest generation," this was "the murmuring generation."

ii. The words of the faithful warning against rebellion (14:5–9)

> [5]Then Moses and Aaron fell facedown in front of the whole Israelite assembly gathered there. [6]Joshua son of Nun and Caleb son of Jephunneh, who were among those who had explored the land, tore their clothes [7]and said to the entire Israelite assembly, "The land we passed through and explored is exceedingly good. [8]If the LORD is pleased with us, he will lead us into that land, a land flowing with milk and honey, and will give it to us. [9]Only do not rebel against the LORD. And do not be afraid of the people of the land, because we will swallow them up. Their protection is gone, but the LORD is with us. Do not be afraid of them."

COMMENTARY

5 In the midst of this riot of rebellion, only a few voices still spoke of God's grace and remembered his power. This text mentions four such persons: Moses, Aaron, Joshua, and Caleb. These people are the only ones mentioned as not being part of the larger, rebellious community. I suspect that these four are listed because of their prominence in the central story. But I also suspect that they were not in fact the only persons in the entire community who were faithful to God. In any period of great apostasy, we—and Scripture—tend to focus on the pervasiveness of the rebellion and to minimize the numbers of those who are exceptions to the general depravity. Certainly this was the experience of Elijah at Carmel (1Ki 19:10, 14; cf. v.18).

When we consider the emphasis of Numbers 14 on faithlessness of the entire community, countered by only four individuals (these exceptions being the notables), it is reasonable to posit that here and there was a mother in Israel who did not capitulate to her husband's rage or a son in the land who raised his doubts against his parents' folly. But "all" versus "four" is used to impress on the reader the enormity of the collapse of the nation because of the malicious report of the ten faithless agents.

Be that as it may, the only voices of reason and faith we hear in the text are those of Moses, Aaron, Caleb, and Joshua. Their passion for truth in the midst of monumental error caused Moses and Aaron to fling themselves to the ground, to prostrate themselves before the enraged leaders of the people. In this posture they symbolized their awareness that the anger of the Lord was likely to burst on the people in a moment.

6–7 Joshua and Caleb tore at their clothing (v.6) in a ritual symbolic of mourning. They were mourning not the loss of parent or loved one but the loss of faith, the death of hope. Yet even as they mourned, Joshua and Caleb tried to revive the dead. They extolled the land and its virtues in extravagant language. Joshua and Caleb had been there—the land they described to be "exceedingly good" (v.7; see Notes). They reminded the people that the land still "flows with milk and honey" (see comments on 13:27).

8 Then these righteous men presented the posture of faith. It is still possible to gain the land and to enjoy its fruit. The only thing necessary is that "the LORD is pleased with us." The Hebrew verb *ḥāpēṣ* ("to be pleased with, enjoy, smile over"; GK 2911) is one of the rich verbs expressive of the relationship God desires with his people. The biblical view of God is not one picturing an angry deity smoldering with rage, nastily looking for yet another miserable wretch to zap from on high. Bib-

lical faith believes in the great grace of God, the Lord of mercy, who desires to smile on his people. (See again the words of the Aaronic Benediction [6:24–26] and commentary there.) Judgment is God's "strange work," his "unusual task" (Isa 28:21). Anger is as alien to his inner nature as it is awful to those who are its target, as those four worthies knew. If only the people would listen, repent, and believe—then the land could still be theirs and be enjoyed under the smile of heaven.

9 Two changes were required: the people needed to stop their rebellion against the Lord, and they had to cease being afraid of the people of the land. The worthy agents shouted, "Their protection is gone." The word translated "protection" is *ṣēl* (GK 7498), often rendered "shadow" or "shade." In the hot and arid regions of the Middle East, the notion of a shadow or shade is a symbol of grace and mercy, a relief from the searing heat (cf. Ps 91:1). Sometimes the wings of a mother bird form the shadow of protection for her young; in the imagery of the poets of Israel, this mother-hen language is used of the protective care of God (e.g., Ps 17:8). God has served as a protecting shadow for the peoples of the land of Canaan; now that protection is gone. Yahweh was with his people. They could swallow their foes alive!

The depth of the faith of Joshua and Caleb is seen particularly in this vivid expression of the loss of the protective shade in Canaan. There are no walls, no fortifications, no factors of size or bearing, and certainly no gods that could withstand the onslaught of God's people when they know that Yahweh is with them. Perhaps these words were based on the covenantal language of Genesis 15, which relates an incident that came to mind in this crisis. At the covenant between the parts, the Lord had assured Abram that his descendants would return to the land in the fourth generation, at the time when the sins of the Amorites had reached full measure (Ge 15:15–16).

NOTE

7 The repetition of the modifier מְאֹד מְאֹד (*m°ōd m°ōd*, "very, very"), which means "exceedingly," is used to elaborate the surpassing goodness of the land. This type of repetition is a way of presenting a heightened sense of things, a superlative.

iii. The appearance of the Lord to withstand the rebels (14:10– 12)

¹⁰But the whole assembly talked about stoning them. Then the glory of the Lᴏʀᴅ appeared at the Tent of Meeting to all the Israelites. ¹¹The Lᴏʀᴅ said to Moses, "How long will these people treat me with contempt? How long will they refuse to believe in me, in spite of all the miraculous signs I have performed among them? ¹²I will strike them down with a plague and destroy them, but I will make you into a nation greater and stronger than they."

COMMENTARY

10 Despite the impassioned language of Joshua and Caleb and the portent of the prostrate forms of Moses and Aaron, the people were deaf to mercy and blind to truth. In a grand perversion the people began to shout to one another, "Stone them!" We are reminded of similar attempts to take the life of Jesus (see, e.g., Jn 8:59). When Yeshua spoke truth to an obdurate people in his day, their response was not unlike that of their distant ancestors in the wilderness.

Certainly one of the more chilling lines in Scripture is the description of the irruption of Yahweh in the middle of verse 10. In the midst of the people's rage, which was building into a storm that might lead to the stoning of the righteous, the holy God in an awesome display of his wonder burst into their midst at the entrance of the tabernacle.

Moses and Aaron had a foreboding this would happen; likely this is the reason they were prostrate (v.5). There they lay, grieving and praying; there they lay, waiting, for God was near. The sudden theophany of Yahweh at this moment must have been staggering in its abrupt and intense display of his wonder and wrath.

11 When God appeared, he did not thunder against the people; instead he spoke to his servant Moses about their outrageous behavior. His words have the sense of incredulity: "How long will these people treat me with contempt?" The verb *nāʾaṣ* (here and in v.23; GK 5540; cf. 16:30; Ps 10:3, 13; Isa 1:4) is a strong term for utter disregard of a person. As we think of God's promise to bless those who bless Israel and to curse the individual who treats the people with less than a sense of dignity and respect (cf. Ge 12:3), we wonder what must be in store for one who holds God in contempt! This is the central issue. By refusing to believe in the power of the Lord, especially in view of all the wonders they had experienced themselves, the people of Israel are holding him in contempt by their unbelief.

12 God's anger against his people is at fever pitch. In a moment he will destroy them all. With a word they will cease to afflict him with their arrogance. By a plague the populace could be reduced to a handful. And God could begin again. Moses could be the new paterfamilias; he could be Abra-ham redivivus. God says, "I will make you into a nation." For the second time since the exodus, Yahweh speaks of starting over with Moses in order to create a people faithful to himself (see Ex 32:10).

REFLECTION

As we read these words, we are aware of several dynamics at work. One is the real anger of the Lord, expressed here anthropopathically, that is, in the feelings and frustrations that mirror our own ways of reacting to stress. By using language to describe the "feelings" of God in such palpable terms, God is brought near! Even the expressions of his wrath ultimately are manifestations of his grace!

A second dynamic in these words is their effect on Moses. God does not lead his people into temptation, but he does allow them to pass through the tempering fires of stress. He does not do this to break them but for the righteous to have the opportunity to demonstrate what they really believe. The stinging fires lap the dross, but they harden metals that matter. While we hear the words of God, we are anticipating the response of Moses.

A third dynamic in these words is their effect in the lives of those who read them after the fact. The book of Numbers, as in the case of all Scripture, has a target audience. The primary audience for this book is the second generation, the sons and daughters of these people who behaved so egregiously. The second generation was to learn a lesson that their parents did not learn: God can be provoked only so far. Finally, his wrath is kindled. "God has time, and the wilderness has sand."

A fourth dynamic in these words is their effect in the lives on the more distant readers, including us. We moderns tend to ignore passages that speak of God's wrath; we prefer more comfortable passages — texts with "possibilities." Surely the Spirit of God measures our own response to these words. The question they pose is inescapable: Do we or do we not really believe in the concept of the judgment of God? And if we do believe that finally he will bring judgment on the wicked, those who hold him in contempt, what difference does it make in the way we live?

My point is this: No one should dare to remain unmoved by these words of the expression of the wrath of God. We remember that this wrath was not against Canaanites or Hittites, not against the Egyptians or the Assyrians, but against his own people. There is a measured, almost dispassionate judgment of remote peoples who pass by the world scene. But when God is forced by his own majesty and holiness to rise up in judgment against his own people, we are made to feel what that anger means to him.

iv. The pleading of Moses on behalf of the rebellious people (14:13–19)

¹³Moses said to the Lᴏʀᴅ, "Then the Egyptians will hear about it! By your power you brought these people up from among them. ¹⁴And they will tell the inhabitants of this land about it. They have already heard that you, O Lᴏʀᴅ, are with these people and that

you, O LORD, have been seen face to face, that your cloud stays over them, and that you go before them in a pillar of cloud by day and a pillar of fire by night. ¹⁵If you put these people to death all at one time, the nations who have heard this report about you will say, ¹⁶'The LORD was not able to bring these people into the land he promised them on oath; so he slaughtered them in the desert.'

¹⁷"Now may the Lord's strength be displayed, just as you have declared: ¹⁸'The LORD is slow to anger, abounding in love and forgiving sin and rebellion. Yet he does not leave the guilty unpunished; he punishes the children for the sin of the fathers to the third and fourth generation.' ¹⁹In accordance with your great love, forgive the sin of these people, just as you have pardoned them from the time they left Egypt until now."

COMMENTARY

13–16 To the extent that the expression of the wrath of God was a test of the character of Moses, we see in his response one of his grandest moments. Not for a second does he mull the possibility of a new people of God, "the sons of Moses." Instead, zealous for the protection of the perception of the character of God among the nations (who do not know him!), Moses burst with protest, "But the Egyptians will hear!" (cf. v.13). For Moses there was something far more important than his own pride and destiny, something even more important than the people themselves—this was the reputation of God! Impassioned with zeal for the Lord (see Phinehas's similar reaction [25:11] and the comparison Moses makes in that text between his own zeal for the Lord and that of the young priest), Moses shouted, "No!"

The idea of the reputation of Yahweh among the nations may sound strange to us, but it is a vital concern of Scripture. This idea relates to the manifestation of the glory of God. It also speaks to the "pre-evangelism" of the nations. There was a marketplace of ideas about gods in the ancient world. But there was no God like Yahweh; never had a deity done for a people what Yahweh had done for

his people by signs and wonders and outstretched arm (see Dt 4:32–40).

And the nations were watching! A generation later, when Israel finally entered the land of Canaan under Joshua, the nations still remembered what they had heard of Israel's deliverance from Egypt. The sadness is that the nations at large did not fall captive to the grace of God. But individuals did do so from time to time. One of the most interesting stories concerns a pagan harlot who lived at Jericho. She heard. She remembered. She believed. And this harlot was transformed. She became a means of deliverance for the two spies from the camp of Israel. Indeed, Rahab became an honored mother in Israel and an ancestress of the Savior (see Jos 2; Ru 4:18–22 [Salmon married Rahab]; Mt 1:5; Heb 11:31; Jas 2:25)!

The response of Moses, thus, was in keeping with his character and was in deference to his desire to maintain the reputation of Yahweh. He shouted, "Then the Egyptians will hear!" (v.13). After all the demonstration of the reality of God as against the shallow, hollow, vapid nature of their supposed deities, Moses was aghast at the thought that word would get back to Egypt that God had not been able to complete the deliverance of his people. Moses knew that the enemies of God's people would charge Yahweh with an inability to complete his work of delivering them and would thus add their own contempt to that of the rebellious people of Israel. To Moses such a prospect was intolerable.

17–19 The second tack that Moses took was to affirm the splendors of the character of God, particularly his grace. He says, "Now may the Lord's strength be displayed!" (v.17). At this point Moses moved from the reputation of Yahweh to his character by presenting a composite quotation of God's own words of loyal love for and faithful discipline of his people (see Ex 20:6; 34:6–7). These ideas are basic to the Hebrew Bible in its revelation of the character of God.

Moderns who have rejected the message of the OT have often done so on the basis of its false "bad rap." They have been taught through popular culture and through misinformed religionists that the "God of the OT" is a god of wrath, whereas the God of the NT is all mercy and grace. Milgrom, xxxvii, writes: "It is to [Yahweh's] attribute of ḥesed [GK 2876] that Moses appeals in his plea that God not destroy Israel (14:18–20). Ḥesed stands for God's constancy, His fidelity to His covenant with Israel."

But Moses knew God intimately. He knew him as a consuming fire; he also knew his warm embrace. We tend to focus on the flashes of God's wrath. Moses reminds us that while the wrath is real, it is long delayed. The most remarkable feature of God's exercising of wrath is how much provocation he tolerates before he finally acts in righteous judgment. I suspect that there are occasions when we all have wished that God would "zap" this evil or reach out and destroy that evil. But the fact that he has not yet done so is a loving reminder that he may extend his patience with us as well.

NOTE

19 The phrase כְּגֹדֶל חַסְדְּךָ (kegōdel ḥasdekā, "in accordance with your great love") contains one of the most significant terms in Hebrew Scripture to describe the gracious aspect of the character of God. This word is חֶסֶד (ḥesed, "great love"; GK 2876), perhaps best translated "loyal love," as this pair of words ties together both the aspects of mercy and loyalty conveyed by the word ḥesed. In his impassioned plea that God forgive the people, Moses heightens the focus on the Lord's loyal love by using the phrase kegōdel ("according to the greatness of").

v. The judgment of the Lord against the rebels (14:20–35)

²⁰The Lord replied, "I have forgiven them, as you asked. ²¹Nevertheless, as surely as I live and as surely as the glory of the Lord fills the whole earth, ²²not one of the men who saw my glory and the miraculous signs I performed in Egypt and in the desert but who disobeyed me and tested me ten times — ²³not one of them will ever see the land I promised on oath to their forefathers. No one who has treated me with contempt will ever see it. ²⁴But because my servant Caleb has a different spirit and follows me wholeheartedly, I will

bring him into the land he went to, and his descendants will inherit it. ²⁵Since the Amalekites and Canaanites are living in the valleys, turn back tomorrow and set out toward the desert along the route to the Red Sea."

²⁶The LORD said to Moses and Aaron: ²⁷"How long will this wicked community grumble against me? I have heard the complaints of these grumbling Israelites. ²⁸So tell them, 'As surely as I live, declares the LORD, I will do to you the very things I heard you say: ²⁹In this desert your bodies will fall — every one of you twenty years old or more who was counted in the census and who has grumbled against me. ³⁰Not one of you will enter the land I swore with uplifted hand to make your home, except Caleb son of Jephunneh and Joshua son of Nun. ³¹As for your children that you said would be taken as plunder, I will bring them in to enjoy the land you have rejected. ³²But you — your bodies will fall in this desert. ³³Your children will be shepherds here for forty years, suffering for your unfaithfulness, until the last of your bodies lies in the desert. ³⁴For forty years — one year for each of the forty days you explored the land — you will suffer for your sins and know what it is like to have me against you.' ³⁵I, the LORD, have spoken, and I will surely do these things to this whole wicked community, which has banded together against me. They will meet their end in this desert; here they will die."

COMMENTARY

20–21 Finally God spoke. He was moved by the words of Moses. Think about that; it is another aspect of his grace. In response to Moses' request, "Pardon the iniquity of this people on the basis of the greatness of your loyal love" (cf. v.19), God declared that his forgiveness of them (v.20). The verb used in this sentence is *sālaḥ*, a term that basically means "to pardon." There is a sense that this verb may be seen as the antonym to the word "to requite" (*nāqâ*), the word used by Moses to describe God's righteous judgment of the wicked in v.18.

But the forgiveness in this case was not without consequences for the horrible sins of the Israelites. The people who had behaved so intolerably would not be put to death, but neither could things go back to the way they had been on the day before the rebellion. The words of God in v.21 are forceful

and direct; as surely as he lives, as surely as his glory fills the earth, there was a sentence to be paid.

22–23 The judgment is mitigated. The people are not put to death, but neither will they live as God intended. They will not be allowed to see the land (v.23), the prize of his grace for the faithful. As vv.1–2 emphasized the term "all" (see comments above), so vv.22–23 emphasize "not one." Since all the people are in rebellion, not one will escape the mitigated judgment.

Yahweh spoke of ten times when the people tested (*nāsâ*; see Notes) him. Possibly this use of the number "ten" is a rhetorical way of saying "these many times" (see Notes). Whether or not the list in the Notes is *the* list of ten (for it may be that God was not intending ten in the sense of one more than nine), the list still represents a dismal record. It is as though the people had a penchant for disobedience, a special gifting for murmuring. Yet time after time God forgave them in the midst of his judgment. And that may be the point; the story of the rejecting attitudes and evil actions of the people is not the proper center of Scripture. Instead, we ought to focus on the Lord, watch his actions and reactions, his invitations and his responses.

24 The Lord singles out Caleb, calling him "my servant" and remarking with affection on his "different spirit." It may be that Caleb was the principal spokesman in the defense of the goodness of the land and the sureness of the character of God in vv.7–9; perhaps Joshua joined in Caleb's faithful celebration of God. Caleb's ultimate vindication came forty-five years later (see Jos 14:10; see also comment on 13:22).

25 Here is a verse of sadness. The Lord reminded Moses that there were inhabitants already living in the land, Amalekites and Canaanites; hence the people needed to turn back to the wilderness. They had been brought near for the purpose of confronting these inhabitants of the land in a struggle for possession. But now they were not to fight. They had lost their opportunity; it was back to the sand, back to God's time.

26–35 These verses appear as a second take on the mitigated judgment of God on the nation. Verses 20–25 present a unity of forgiveness and judgment, concluding with a travel notice. Then v.26 seems to take us back to the point at which we were in vv.20–21. The observation of such phenomena in the Torah was part of the prompting for many scholars to argue for varied sources (the documentary approach). I confess I am no fan of the "JEDP" approach to the Torah. I find this approach atomizing, with its splitting of the text into smaller and smaller pieces with little interest in the whole of Scripture as we have it. Usually the practitioners of this method approach Scripture in a judgmental rather than reverential manner; and

rarely is the concept of the divine inspiration of Scripture taken seriously in a context that does not credit the text with basic integrity or the authority of God. Nonetheless, some of the features that documentary scholars have noticed in the text are actually there. This section presents an instance.

Verses 26–35 form a unit of address by the Lord to Moses and Aaron that overlaps in some way with the unit of vv.20–25, where God spoke directly to Moses in response to his plea for the forgiveness of the people. Explanations for this feature do not have to proceed along the classic lines of putative documentary research. One may suggest that one or the other of these two units was "original" and that the other is a later addition to the text to fill it out. But one also may observe that a peculiar feature of Hebrew stylistics is just this very thing: two accounts take on the same issue, each a self-contained unit, but the two together forming a more significant whole. Many of the "doublets" of the documentary approach may be viewed in this manner. The most obvious example is the pairing of two dissimilar (but, I believe, complementary) accounts of creation: Genesis 1 and Genesis 2.

I regard vv.26–35 as a distinct entity from vv.20–25. It is possible that these two blocks had a different history; it is possible that one was added to the book of Numbers considerably later than the other. But it is also possible that both sprang from the experience of Moses, that both were deliberately used by him consciously from the beginning. The resultant impression of these two overlapping blocks heightens the mitigated judgment of God on his errant people, just as the dissimilar, overlapping, but complementary blocks of God's response to the faithfulness of Abraham on Mount Moriah worked together for a greater whole (see Ge 22:11–14, 15–18).

The heart of the second oracle of judgment is one of comic justice. The rash words of the people who asked to die in the wilderness become in a sense the judgment of the Lord. They had brought on themselves their punishment. They had said that they would prefer to die in the wilderness (v.2) rather than to be led into the land of Canaan to die by the sword. All those who were above the age of twenty, who were counted in the census, were indeed to die in the wilderness. The only exceptions would be Joshua and Caleb (v.30).

God's sharpest rebuke of his errant people came in response to their charge that he wanted to kill their children (v.3). The attacks on his grace and the rebuffs of his mercy he will tolerate. The forgetfulness of his power and the ignoring of his acts of deliverance he will set aside. But there is one thing that God simply will not tolerate—the accusation that he had brought the people into the wilderness with the intent that

he might thereby destroy their children, so that they would die in the wilderness or be taken as plunder by victorious enemies. Hence a further element in the comic justice of this section is the notice that the children, concerning whose safety the people made such a false charge against the Lord—these children would be the only ones who actually *would* come to enjoy the land (v.31). The rest of the people's bodies would "fall in this wilderness" (v.32).

The forty days of the travels of the agents became the numerical paradigm for the suffering of the people: one year for one day—for forty years they would recount their misjudgment (v.34), and for forty years the people over the age of twenty would be dying (v.35). Thus, when the time was fulfilled, only the younger generation would enter the land.

NOTES

22 וַיְנַסּוּ (*waynassû*, "and they tested") is from the verb נָסָה (*nāsâ*; GK 5814), which means "to test, try." This verb may be used with God as the subject with the intent of testing the character of someone, as used in Genesis 22:1 when God put Abraham to the test of his life. When God is the object of this verb, the idea is usually one of trying his patience. This is its meaning here and in Exodus 17:2, 7; Deuteronomy 6:16; Psalms 78:18; 95:9; 106:14.

זֶה עֶשֶׂר פְּעָמִים (*zeh ʿeśer pᵉʿāmîm*, "this ten times"). We have seen numerous rhetorical uses of numbers in this book; the words "these ten times" may be another such use. Yet it may be valuable to attempt to count the number of instances of rebellion to see whether we can arrive at a listing of ten discrete occurrences. The ten instances of rebellion by the people against the grace of the Lord may be enumerated as follows:

1. At the Red Sea, where it seemed that Pharaoh's army would destroy them (Ex 14:10-12)
2. At Marah, where they found bitter water (Ex 15:22-24)
3. In the Desert of Sin, as they hungered (Ex 16:1-3)
4. In the Desert of Sin, as they paid no attention to Moses concerning the storing of the manna until the morning (Ex 16:19-20)
5. In the Desert of Sin, as they disregarded Moses concerning the gathering of the manna on the seventh day (Ex 16:27-30)
6. At Rephidim, as they complained for water (Ex 17:1-4)
7. At Mount Sinai, as they worshiped the golden calf, which (false) god they had pressured Aaron to make for them (Ex 32:1-35)

8. At Taberah, where they raged against the Lord (Nu 11:1–3)

9. At Kibroth Hattaavah, in the rabble's grumbling for meat (Nu 11:4–34)

10. At Kadesh in the Desert of Paran, when they refused to receive the good report of Joshua and Caleb and instead wished themselves dead (Nu 14:1–3)

25 יָם־סוּף (*yam-sûp*, "Red Sea" or "Sea of Reeds") is the phrase used to describe the body of water where the people of Israel crossed in God's great act of redemption as they were delivered from the pursuing Egyptians (see Ex 14–15). Presumably, the references in Exodus to this body of water signify an area on the west of the Sinai Peninsula (the arm of the Red Sea known as the Gulf of Suez). In the book of Numbers, however, the phrase is used to describe the body of water *east* of the Sinai Peninsula (the arm of the Red Sea known as the Gulf of Aqaba; see 21:4; 33:8, 10). It is possible that the phrase יָם־סוּף (*yam-sûp*) may be emended to יָם־סוֹף (*yam-sôp*, "Sea's End"). If this approach turns out to be correct, the phrase would refer in all cases to the same body of water, the Gulf of Aqaba, to the east of the (consequently, misnamed) Sinai Peninsula. See the discussion on this alternative viewpoint in the Note on 33:8, 10.

27 תְּלֻנּוֹת (*t⁰lunnôt*, "complaints") is a noun (singular, תְּלֻנָּה, *t⁰lunnâ*) that is related to the verb לוּן (*lûn*, "to grumble, murmur") discussed in Note on 14:2. As with the verb with which it is associated, this noun is a part of the distinctive language Torah uses to describe the Israelites in their wilderness sojourn; they were "The Grumblers."

34 The repetition, יוֹם לַשָּׁנָה יוֹם לַשָּׁנָה (*yôm laššānâ yôm laššānâ*, "a day for a year, a day for a year"), is for distribution: "one day for each year" (see Williams, *Hebrew Syntax*, sec. 15; also used in Nu 1:4; 9:10).

vi. The death of the evil agents (14:36–38)

> [36] So the men Moses had sent to explore the land, who returned and made the whole community grumble against him by spreading a bad report about it — [37] these men responsible for spreading the bad report about the land were struck down and died of a plague before the LORD. [38] Of the men who went to explore the land, only Joshua son of Nun and Caleb son of Jephunneh survived.

COMMENTARY

36–38 The people as a whole received a commuted sentence, a mitigated judgment. But not the men who were responsible for the attitudes that led to this debacle of doubt! Those responsible for spreading the bad report had to be put to death. The judgment on the ten evil agents was immediate; the generation they influenced would live out their lives in the wilderness, but their lives were forfeit. Only Joshua and Caleb were exempt from this judgment. The repeated mention of these

two men is deserved, for together they withstood a nation.

vii. Defeat by the Amalekites (14:39–45)

³⁹When Moses reported this to all the Israelites, they mourned bitterly. ⁴⁰Early the next morning they went up toward the high hill country. "We have sinned," they said. "We will go up to the place the LORD promised."

⁴¹But Moses said, "Why are you disobeying the LORD's command? This will not succeed! ⁴²Do not go up, because the LORD is not with you. You will be defeated by your enemies, ⁴³for the Amalekites and Canaanites will face you there. Because you have turned away from the LORD, he will not be with you and you will fall by the sword."

⁴⁴Nevertheless, in their presumption they went up toward the high hill country, though neither Moses nor the ark of the LORD's covenant moved from the camp. ⁴⁵Then the Amalekites and Canaanites who lived in that hill country came down and attacked them and beat them down all the way to Hormah.

COMMENTARY

39–45 Here is a classic example of too little, too late. Now too late to be in faith, the people determined to go up to the land they had earlier refused to enter. They confessed that they had sinned (v.40), but it is difficult to know what they meant by this confession since it is not elaborated. But their confession was partial at best, as their actions were rash and foolish, not measured and deliberate. Such a course of action was doomed to failure. Not only was the Lord not with them in this belated act—he was against them (v.41). In fact, he had warned them not to go this way at all but to turn back to the wilderness (v.25). Their subsequent defeat (v.45) was another judgment that the rebellious people brought on their heads. In fact, any soldiers who died in this abortive warfare only hastened their own punishment for the rebellion at Kadesh.

e. Laws on Offerings, the Sabbath, and Tassels on Garments (15:1–41)

OVERVIEW

After reading the dramatic, if depressing, story of the rebellion of Israel at Kadesh and their mitigated judgment by the Lord on the edge of the land (chs. 13–14), it is difficult for the reader to move to a priestly text on sacrifice, Sabbath, and tassels. The change of topic is too abrupt; the shift of mood is too distinct; the issue is anticlimactic. In fact, such seeming mismatching of texts has led many scholars to wring their hands over the book of Numbers (see Introduction: Unity and Organization).

Umberto Cassuto, in an paper delivered to the World Congress of Jewish Studies in Jerusalem, 1947 ("The Sequence and Arrangement of the Biblical Sections," *Biblical and Oriental Studies, Vol. I: Bible* [Jerusalem: Magnes/Hebrew University, 1973], 1–6) offered a Jewish perspective on this issue, suggesting that the principles for arrangement in the Torah, which at times seem to be so random and arbitrary to us, may have been more meaningful and tangential to the ancients. He suggests, and I paraphrase here, that instead of what we might think of as "logical" ties, there was on occasion an association of words and ideas on a nearly subliminal level that guided the ancient sages in their arrangement of material. This case seems to apply to Numbers 15, whose material on spiritual propriety follows the dramatic narrative of apostasy and rebellion in chs. 13–14.

The possible association consists in the following. Chapter 14 of Numbers leaves us with a sunken feeling. The people have responded in such a grossly inappropriate manner to the mercy of God, and had so arrogantly reacted against his servant Moses, that they had been excluded from their inheritance in the land. Only their children would inherit what should have been theirs.

Then ch. 15 begins as though nothing has happened! It begins precisely the same way that ch. 1 does ("The LORD said to Moses"). In fact, the opening, with some variation, is found repeatedly through chs. 1–10. Those chapters were meant to prepare the people for their march to Canaan and their entrance into the land. Chapter 15 is another collection of texts designed to prepare the people

for their life in the land. Hence this chapter is one of promise. Though a great deal *has* happened, and the results are overwhelming for the adult population involved, nonetheless there is a sense in which we may say that *nothing has happened*. God has pardoned his people (14:20), the second generation will enter the land (14:31), and preparations still need to be made for that period after the conquest and the achieving of "normalcy" in Canaan. All these factors evince the grace of Yahweh— overwhelming grace!

The connecting thought between chs. 14 and 15 is the wording in 15:2, "when you enter the land of your dwelling places that I am giving to you" (my translation). This verse ties to 14:31: "I will bring them in to enjoy the land you have rejected." The connection is not a rubbing of salt into the wound; rather, it is the connection of promise. Although much has happened, nothing has happened. The land still awaits the people; the people must now wait for the land.

Further, the people are to know through both of these verses that the land belongs to the Lord and that granting it to Israel will be his work. Often the question is raised, "To whom does the land of Israel belong?" The correct answer, both in antiquity and in our own day, is clear: the land is the Lord's. The Canaanites who lived in the land did not own the land. God has the right to give the land to Israel, but he may also take it back again. He holds the title; he grants the use of the land but may withhold it for his own reasons.

Not only is the "holiness code" material of ch. 15 an abrupt change from the action of the previous chapters, the inner structure of the chapter is difficult to determine as well. There are three times in the chapter where the same introductory phrasing is used (vv. 1, 17, 37), but it seems that there are six discrete sections to the chapter (counting breaks at vv. 22, 30, 32). My analysis follows these lines.

i. Teaching on special offerings (15:1–16)

¹The Lord said to Moses, ²"Speak to the Israelites and say to them:'After you enter the land I am giving you as a home ³and you present to the Lord offerings made by fire, from the herd or the flock, as an aroma pleasing to the Lord — whether burnt offerings or sacrifices, for special vows or freewill offerings or festival offerings — ⁴then the one who brings his offering shall present to the Lord a grain offering of a tenth of an ephah of fine flour mixed with a quarter of a hin of oil. ⁵With each lamb for the burnt offering or the sacrifice, prepare a quarter of a hin of wine as a drink offering.

⁶"With a ram prepare a grain offering of two-tenths of an ephah of fine flour mixed with a third of a hin of oil, ⁷and a third of a hin of wine as a drink offering. Offer it as an aroma pleasing to the Lord.

⁸"When you prepare a young bull as a burnt offering or sacrifice, for a special vow or a fellowship offering to the Lord, ⁹bring with the bull a grain offering of three-tenths of an ephah of fine flour mixed with half a hin of oil. ¹⁰Also bring half a hin of wine as a drink offering. It will be an offering made by fire, an aroma pleasing to the Lord. ¹¹Each bull or ram, each lamb or young goat, is to be prepared in this manner. ¹²Do this for each one, for as many as you prepare.

¹³"Everyone who is native-born must do these things in this way when he brings an offering made by fire as an aroma pleasing to the Lord. ¹⁴For the generations to come, whenever an alien or anyone else living among you presents an offering made by fire as an aroma pleasing to the Lord, he must do exactly as you do. ¹⁵The community is to have the same rules for you and for the alien living among you; this is a lasting ordinance for the generations to come. You and the alien shall be the same before the Lord: ¹⁶The same laws and regulations will apply both to you and to the alien living among you.'"

COMMENTARY

1–2 The conjunction of these verses with the sad ending of the narrative of Numbers 14 is dramatic. The sins of the people were manifold; they would be judged. The grace and mercy of the Lord are magnified as he points to the ultimate realization of his ancient promise to Abraham (Ge 12:7) and his continuing promise to the nation that they would indeed enter the land.

3–12 Leviticus 1–7 presents the basic standards of offerings for the community, with a focus on those sacrifices that deal with the issues of sin and guilt. The offerings in Numbers 15 are special; that is, they relate more to the desire of the Hebrew believer for spontaneous, grateful response to the wonder of knowing God. Verse 3 is broad in scope on the subject of offerings by fire (*ʾiššeh*; see Notes). Grain and wine offerings were to accompany the offerings by fire; the grain was to be mixed with oil. We may observe that the grain and wine offerings increased in amounts as the size of the sacrifical animal increased (vv.6–7; vv.8–12). These passages are the first to indicate that wine offerings, or libations, must accompany all burnt or fellowship offerings.

The provision of "fine flour" (*sōlet*; v.4) speaks of luxurious food rather than ordinary flour. This type of flour was used in fine cooking (Eze 16:13), at the table of the king (1Ki 4:22), for honored guests (Ge 18:6), and in the worship of God. Hence the attitude toward the flour was the same as toward the animals one might bring to the worship of God: only the best was good enough, for the gift was to the Lord. We suspect that the oil and wine used in these offerings were similarly selected from choice, not common, stocks.

The NIV's marginal notes aid the modern reader in gauging the ancient measurements used in these sacrifices. The tenth ephah of fine flour (vv.4–5) is about two quarts; the quarter hin of oil or wine is about one quart. The other measurements are proportional to these rough conversions. Some may wish to make some mystical meaning of these varied proportions, but my judgment is that the real issue in these proportions is not some special sense of the numbers; rather, the point of view ought to be in the recognition that God has dictated as to how these offerings were to be presented. If God demanded one-quarter hin of wine as the drink offering with the sacrifice of a lamb (v.5), then one-quarter hin of the finest wine is precisely what he should receive. If God demanded one-half hin of wine with the sacrifice of a young bull (v.10), then one-half hin of the finest wine is precisely what he should receive. Worship is about God, not us! The strength of the particulars helps one to focus on God rather than on oneself.

Verse 4 stresses the concept of approach to the Lord, with all the awe and wonder such a concept should evince. The first three words in the MT are each from the same root (*qārab*, "to make an approach"; see Notes), with each word speaking of coming near and making an approach to deity. Our modern notions of biblical worship sometimes suffer from distaste, distance, and a sense of strangeness. For us to understand the issues of this chapter, the verb meaning "to come near to God" ought to be stressed in our thinking. It is in our approach of him that we begin to think more and more of what is meant by "holy."

The system of sacrificial worship in ancient Israel was far more complex than we may have imagined. We tend to focus on those sacrifices that relate directly to the issue of sin, those that many regard to typify most clearly the death of Christ. Some of the sacrifices God demanded were presented in the context of a mournful admission of sin, a guilt-laden expression of repentance. But other sacrifices in the biblical period were presented in contexts of celebration and a joyful, heartfelt expression of one's delight in knowing Yahweh. The tone and texture of this chapter lead us to focus on the celebrative aspect of worship. Even the celebrative and spontaneous acts were done in a context of method, order, and proportion.

Another arresting element in these worship texts is the concept of "an aroma pleasing to the LORD" (vv.7, 10 [see Notes]; see also Lev 1:9). The odor of sacrifice, whether of the whole burnt offering or the burning of heavy organs and fat, would be heavy, acrid, and pungent. Further, unpleasant smells, heat, flies, stressful sounds, and disgusting sights were all part of the worship setting. The addition of flour, oil, and fine wine to the fire added an exotic element to the smells. In pagan nations the production of certain odors likely was designed to soothe an angry deity. In some cultures, we are told, odorous gifts used to be placed near the openings of volcanoes to pacify the demons beneath. But the God of Israel did not need to be soothed. The point of these phrases seems to be the bringing of pleasure to him.

Then we ask, would mere smell and smoke make God happy? To ask is to answer: Of course not! It is the person bringing the offering, not the offering itself, that brought pleasure to God (see Ps 40:6–8; Mic 6:8–10; see especially Allen and Allen, ch. 8 ["Worship in Spirit and Truth"]). In this case, the smells and the smoke, the flesh and the flour were all elements that made the offering "real" by adding substance and action to the feeling of worship. Ultimately the odor of the sacrifice of the Hebrew festivals pointed to the "fragrance" of the offering of the Savior (see Eph 5:2).

13–16 The "native-born" (hā'ezrāḥ; see Notes) and the alien were likewise to follow these same regulations. As in the case of the celebration of the Passover (see comment on 9:14), the alien who participated with the people of Israel in God's worship had the same regulations as native-born Israelites. The point about the alien was to ensure that the commonwealth of Israel would always be open to proselytes. Indeed, the charter of Israel's faith embraces "all peoples on earth" (Ge 12:3). Because

the gēr, the one who sojourned with Israel, was under the same Torah, he also was able to bring pleasure to Yahweh. If the gēr continued to please God, soon he might become a part of the community as a whole.

In Israel the concept of native and alien was not designed to enforce the distinction forever; ultimately it provided a process for assimilation. While still an alien, the proselyte must learn to worship in the same manner as the native populace; and together they needed to learn their worship from the Lord.

In summarizing this section (vv.1–16) I make the following observations: (1) the varied offerings needed to be done in order; (2) the proportion of wine, grain, and oil to the specified animal sacrifice was prescribed, with no reasons given for these ratios and with the issue seeming to be simply one of compliance; (3) the rules were the same no matter who the players were—the free citizen and the resident alien both were to follow the same statute.

NOTES

3 The word אִשֶּׁה ('iššeh, "offerings made by fire") is built on the word אֵשׁ ('ēš, "fire") and is used chiefly of sacrifices of animals; the word is also used of the מִנְחָה (minḥâ, the "offering" of grain). Grain offerings and wine offerings were also burned on the altar.

The word זֶבַח (zebaḥ, "sacrifice") is a general term for all sacrifices that culminate in the eating of feasts. The whole burnt offering עֹלָה ('ōlâ, "holocaust") was not the only type of animal sacrifice in Israel. Many sacrifices were occasions for festivity, dancing, music, and feasting—a celebration of the wonder of knowing God.

לְפַלֵּא־נֶדֶר (lᵉpallē'-neder, "to make a special offering, special vow") is a phrase from the verb פָּלָא (pālā', "to be special, extraordinary, wondrous") that is coupled to the noun נֶדֶר (neder, "vow"). The verbal root פלא (pl'; GK 7098) and its nominal complements mainly have to do with the person and works of Yahweh—usually with the attached idea of the divinely miraculous and the human response of astonishment; the verb in these cases is found principally in Niphal themes. When the verb is in the Piel form (as here), it means "to fulfill a vow." Here the words describe the presentation of an extraordinary offering (only in

15:3, 8 and Lev 22:21), motivated by a heart of gratitude to God. See also Numbers 6:2, where פָּלָא (*pālāʾ*) in the Hiphil is used in the making of an extraordinary vow; the "Torah of the Nazir."

The word נְדָבָה (*nᵉdābâ*, "freewill offering"; GK 5607) has a particular joyfulness about it. When used of human's gifts to God, it speaks of a noninstitutionalized, perhaps even spontaneous act of worship; when used with God as subject, it may describe Yahweh's gracious love for his people (Hos 14:4[5]: "I will love them freely") and his lovely gift of rain (Ps 68:9[10]: "You gave abundant showers, O God"). See J. P. Weinberg, "The word *ndb* in the Bible: A Study in Historical Semantics and Biblical Thought," in *Solving Riddles and Untying Knots: Biblical, Epigraphic, and Semitic Studies in Honor of Jonas C. Greenfield* (ed. Ziony Zevit et al.; Winona Lake, Ind.: Eisenbrauns, 1995), 371.

4 Each of the words in the phrase וְהִקְרִיב הַמַּקְרִיב קָרְבָּנוֹ (*wᵉhiqrîb hammaqrîb qorbānô*, lit., "and-he-offers the-one-who-offers his-offering"; "the one who brings his offering shall present," NIV) is related to the root קרב (*qrb*, "to make an approach, to offer [to God]"). This use of three words with the same verbal root is striking in Hebrew style.

7, 10 The idea of the phrase רֵיחַ־נִיחֹחַ (*rêah-nîhōah*, lit., "a scent of soothing"; "an aroma pleasing," NIV) is presented first in Genesis 8:21, where it describes Yahweh's approval of the offerings of Noah following the great flood; fascinatingly, the name "Noah" (נֹחַ, *nōah*) is (likely) related etymologically to the noun "soothing" (נִיחֹחַ, *nîhōah*; GK 5767); both words are related to the verbal root נוּחַ (*nûah*, "to rest"). However, the name "Noah" is also associated with the verb נָחַם (*nāham*, "to be sorry for, comfort"; see Ge 5:29). I believe this association may be an example of paronomasia in biblical names—a double entendre that makes the name even more powerful (see, e.g., the double meaning of the name "Samuel" in 1Sa 1:20). Thus the aroma of the sacrifices is said in some way to bring "rest" to God; the aroma is "soothing," "tranquillizing" (see also Nu 28:2 and Notes; Ex 29:18; Lev 1:9).

13 הָאֶזְרָח (*hāʾezrāh* "the native-born") points directly to the time of being settled in the land. At the time of the writing of the book of Numbers, there were no "native-born" Hebrews; all had been born in a foreign place. This word has led some scholars to believe this whole section comes from a later period and has been inserted into this book. This is possible, for one pericope (vv.32–36) is surely from a later time. However, it is still possible to argue that the stance of the chapter is deliberately set by Moses in a future time frame of being settled in the land (see again v.2, "after you enter the land"; cf. v.18). In this way the function of the chapter is anticipatory and encouraging to the people who were still living in the wilderness.

ii. Instructions for the cake offering (15:17–21)

¹⁷The LORD said to Moses, ¹⁸"Speak to the Israelites and say to them: 'When you enter the land to which I am taking you ¹⁹and you eat the food of the land, present a portion as an offering to the LORD. ²⁰Present a cake from the first of your ground meal and present it as an offering from the threshing floor. ²¹Throughout the generations to come you are to give this offering to the LORD from the first of your ground meal.

COMMENTARY

17–21 This small section begins with the same introductory formula as vv.1–16 (see also v.37), a notice of the source of the instruction being Yahweh's revelation to Moses. This law also looks forward to the time the Israelites will be in the land. There is a synergism of sorts in the wording, "when you enter," and, "I am taking you" (v.18). They must enter; yet God will have brought them. The attempt to enter the land on their own ended in disaster (14:44–45). God's actions in bringing the Israelites near to the land were not effective when they were unwilling to move in at his command (14:4).

Since Numbers presents two generations, we must always remember who is being addressed in each section. The "you" here may have been spoken to the community as a whole, but these verses were principally addressed to the people of the second generation, for only they would actually enter the land. The words of 14:29 are riveting in this regard: every individual who was numbered in the census (chs. 1–4) would perish in the wilderness; all those twenty years of age and older, except Joshua and Caleb, had forfeited their prospects for the land.

The first of the threshed grain was to be made into a cake and to be presented to the Lord (v.20). This concept of the firstfruits is a symbol that all blessing is from Yahweh and all produce belongs to him—a foreign notion in biblical times. When the people would be blessed to eat of the varied products of the land, this sacred offering was to be presented as a reminder that their food was not just the product of their hands or, as understood in Canaanite religion, a gift of "nature." Each meal is a gift from Yahweh; his people must have a conscious sense of being ever dependent on his largess.

This offering is made of coarse grain (*ʿarîsâ*, "ground meal"; v.20) instead of the fine grain of the previous offerings (see comment on v.4). The idea seems to be one of immediacy. Right at the time of the threshing of the grain, before beginning the process of refining for princely flour, a cake is to be made in worship of God and held high from the threshing floor. As v.4 is marked so strongly by the verb *qārab* ("to offer"), so v.20 is marked by elegance in the use of four forms of the word *rûm* ("to raise up").

The raising of the first cake of coarse grain is similar to the custom today for small businesses to frame the first dollar earned. The difference is notable as well, for the cake was raised in gratitude to the Lord—likely a less common motive in the case of framing a dollar bill. Verse 21 repeats and extends the teaching on this offering. This is a perpetual ordinance. The further removed the people became from the events of their salvation, the more likely they would forget the nature of their salvation. The first generation was not able to remember for much longer than three days (11:1–3)!

iii. Instructions about offerings for unintentional sins (15:22–29)

²²"Now if you unintentionally fail to keep any of these commands the LORD gave Moses—²³any of the LORD's commands to you through him, from the day the LORD gave them and continuing through the generations to come—²⁴and if this is done

unintentionally without the community being aware of it, then the whole community is to offer a young bull for a burnt offering as an aroma pleasing to the Lord, along with its pre-scribed grain offering and drink offering, and a male goat for a sin offering. [25]The priest is to make atonement for the whole Israelite community, and they will be forgiven, for it was not intentional and they have brought to the Lord for their wrong an offering made by fire and a sin offering. [26]The whole Israelite community and the aliens living among them will be forgiven, because all the people were involved in the unintentional wrong.

[27]"'But if just one person sins unintentionally, he must bring a year-old female goat for a sin offering. [28]The priest is to make atonement before the Lord for the one who erred by sinning unintentionally, and when atonement has been made for him, he will be forgiven. [29]One and the same law applies to everyone who sins unintentionally, whether he is a native-born Israelite or an alien.

COMMENTARY

22–29 These verses comprise a new section, but they do not have the customary introductory formula of their revelatory origin. This unit deals with the failure to comply with all the commands of the Torah and the provisions of restitution. Verse 22 could be translated, "And *when* you err," for the expectation is that by acts of omission and commis-sion there will be failures of compliance. The verb *šagâ* ("to go astray, err, swerve") focuses on sins of ignorance and inadvertence. This verb can be used even of the reeling of drunkenness (see Isa 28:7).

This section reminds us that God's attitude toward his Torah is complex: (1) he is serious about his commands—they are not trivial nor are they subject to the trifling attitudes of casual people; (2) but he is also gracious—just as human beings are not made for the Sabbath but the Sabbath for human beings (see Mk 2:27), so we may aver that human beings were not made for the Torah but the Torah for human beings. This second point sug-gests the error of the theological approach that presents *Yahweh's original intent* in Hebrew law as that of establishing an impossible standard destined

to make sinners of its people. Von Rad, 1:230, has written:

> All the commandments are simply a grand expla-nation of the command to love Yahweh and to cling to him alone (Deuteronomy vi. 4f.). And this love is Israel's return of the divine love bestowed upon her. The many imperatives in Deuteronomy are therefore appeals, sometimes implicit and sometimes explicit, for gratitude to be shown in action, and Deuteronomy regards them as easy to fulfill.

God could not justly have commanded impossi-bilities, for he knows our frame (see Ps 103:13–17; cf. 1Co 10:13). God made high demands and expected compliance, but he also provided avenues for redress when one did not comply fully. There-fore we conclude that in the Torah God speaks in grace; in the most exacting law there is mercy, and in the entire Torah the intention is to know him and to relate to him. These ideas are developed more fully in Ronald B. Allen, *Grace, Always Grace* (Grand Rapids: Kregel, forthcoming).

Hence sins may be unintentional, but they still need to be covered (see Lev 4:2). Such unintentional sins might be committed by the people as a whole (Nu 15:22–26) or by individuals (vv.27–29). In either case procedures were to be followed for restoration to a sense of God's presence and grace. As in the case of other sacrifices, the alien and the citizen fall under the same demands of compliance.

NOTE

22 אֶל־מֹשֶׁה (ʾel-mōšeh, "[which Yahweh gave] to Moses") is a phrase that compares with the wording of 15:23: בְּיַד־מֹשֶׁה (beyad-mōšeh, "[which Yahweh your God commended] by the hand [i.e., by means] of Moses ['through him,' NIV]"). These phrases, which are not isolated, suggest that it is nearly a misnomer to speak of "the law of Moses," which designation merely comprises a shorthand way of stating the full title, "the law of Yahweh given through [by the hand of] Moses." The Torah is the Lord's; he is the source of the law. It belongs to him. Moses is the means, the agent, the transmitter. See the wording of John 1:17: "the law was given through Moses"; the true giver of the Torah is Yahweh. See Ronald B. Allen, "Affirming Right-of-Way on Ancient Paths," *BSac* 153 (January–March, 1996): 3–11.

iv. Instructions about punishment for sins of defiance (15:30–31)

³⁰"But anyone who sins defiantly, whether native-born or alien, blasphemes the LORD, and that person must be cut off from his people. ³¹Because he has despised the LORD's word and broken his commands, that person must surely be cut off; his guilt remains on him.'"

COMMENTARY

30–31 Quite another case is presented by defiant sin. The Hebrew idiom is "sins with a high hand," a posture of arrogance, blasphemy, and revolt. Unlike the unintentional sinner, for whom the law makes provisions of God's mercy, one who sets his hand defiantly to despise the word of God and to blaspheme his name must be punished. The punishment is one of death, not just banishment or exile. Such a person is doomed. Walter C. Kaiser Jr. compares the "sin of the high hand" here to the NT expression of the offense of blasphemy against the Holy Spirit (Mark 3:28–19; Heb 10:26–39):

"As such it becomes an unpardonable sin, since it represents high treason and revolt against God" (*Toward Rediscovering the Old Testament* [Grand Rapids: Zondervan, 1987], 132).

This verse should not be understood to include all manner of evil actions, most of which could be forgiven. Rather, it deals with outrageous behaviors of blasphemy. But what the Torah regards as outrageous behavior may surprise us, as the illustration in the next paragraph demonstrates. Before we move to that paragraph, however, we may reflect on the application of this unit to the experience of Israel in her rebellion at Kadesh. The Israelites deserved to be cut off, utterly destroyed. The grace of God is seen in his commuting their sentence to banishment in the wilderness (see again 14:20).

NOTE

30 The phrase בְּיָד רָמָה (bᵉyād rāmâ, "with a high hand"; "defiantly," NIV) can be used positively (see 33:3 [and Note]; Ex 14:8 ["boldly"]; Dt 32:27 ["our hand has triumphed"]). But here the phrase is used of a person's acting in deliberate presumption, pride, and disdain. Moreover, the phrase is modified in v.30 with the words "blasphemes the LORD"! Hence the posture presented in this verse is one of treason; there is no provision in the Torah for escaping the results of this sin.

A postscript is demanded: David's sins respecting Bathsheba, Uriah, the army, the nation, and Yahweh (!) may certainly be described as "sins of a high hand." Yet in the wideness of God's mercy and in response to David's utter depths of personal repentance (see 2Sa 11–12; Pss 32; 51), there was forgiveness even here. David's subsequent years were marked by family tragedy, but he was forgiven—fully forgiven!

v. A man who violated the Sabbath (15:32–36)

³²While the Israelites were in the desert, a man was found gathering wood on the Sabbath day. ³³Those who found him gathering wood brought him to Moses and Aaron and the whole assembly, ³⁴and they kept him in custody, because it was not clear what should be done to him. ³⁵Then the LORD said to Moses, "The man must die. The whole assembly must stone him outside the camp." ³⁶So the assembly took him outside the camp and stoned him to death, as the LORD commanded Moses.

COMMENTARY

32–36 The introductory phrasing of this pericope suggests that this narrative was inserted into the text of Numbers at a later time, but the experience it relates derives from the time of the wilderness sojourn of Israel (as seems to be demanded by the references to Moses, Aaron, and the elders of Israel [see v.33], unless, of course, these references are regarded as elements of stereotypical formulae). It is not likely that a story beginning with the phrase, "While the Israelites were in the desert," was an original part of a narrative that has its primary setting in the desert. The phrasing is similar to the opening words of the book of Ruth, which, from the point of view of the writer and the original readers, reflect events that happened long before.

Whatever the history and origin of this story, it is something of a cause célèbre of the very thing vv.30–31 describe—and the account is based on the profound seriousness of the concept of Yahweh's Sabbath in Israel (see Nu 28:9 and Note). The breaking of the Sabbath was not akin to using one-third rather than one-quarter hin of oil or a two-year-old goat instead of a yearling. The point of the story is that Sabbath-breaking was the act of a raised fist in defiance of Yahweh—the offense strikes at the very center of Israel's responsibility before the Lord. By his action (v.32) this man was thumbing his nose at God. Incidentally, the severity of the issue in this text helps to explain, in part, the severe attitudes of the enemies of Jesus, who routinely charged him with breaking the Sabbath (see, e.g., Mk 3:2).

The brief account is presented in fine narrative style. The ones who discovered the man in violation of the Sabbath did not know quite what to do. Perhaps they were stunned by his brazenness. They presented him to Moses, Aaron, and the elders to see what must be done (v.33). The answer came from the Lord: "The man must die" (v.35, see Note). And the sentence was to be carried out by the people, outside the camp. The public participation in his execution must have sent a chilling message deeply impressed on the psyche of the nation: "For this transgression, I too might die."

The penalty for breaking the Sabbath was death (Ex 31:15; 35:2). As in the case of the willful blasphemer (Lev 24:10–16), the Sabbath-breaker was guilty of high-handed rebellion and was judged with death.

NOTE

35 The verbs מוֹת יוּמַת (*môt yûmat*, "must die") are both old Qal passive forms (not Qal and Hophal forms, respectively, as is sometimes stated) of the imperfect and the infinitive of the verb מוּת (*mût*, "to die"). The meaning is "violent death" (see 35:16; Ex 21:12; 22:19[18]; Lev 20:2; 24:16). The stoning of Stephen (Ac 7:54–60) is of a piece with the stoning of the Sabbath-breaker from the vantage point of those who participated. Saul may well have had this text in mind when he consented to Stephen's death. Only later did Saul as Paul realize that it was not blasphemy but praise of the risen Savior that led Stephen to speak as he did.

REFLECTION

By the time of the life of our Lord, Sabbath-keeping had become distorted to the point that the regulations concerning the Sabbath were regarded as more important than the genuine needs of people. Our Lord confronted the Pharisees on this issue on several occasions (e.g., Mt 12:1–14). From their point of view, the regulations in Numbers 15:32–36 gave the Pharisees their reasons to seek his death (Mt 12:14).

We may add a comment on "Christian Sabbath-keeping." The Sabbath, as the seal of Yahweh's covenant with Israel (see Ex 20:8–11; Dt 5:12–15), was a distinctly Israelite institution. We speak in something of an oxymoron if we describe Sunday, the Lord's Day, as a "Christian Sabbath." Sabbath, of course, is Saturday. If we really believe that Sunday is the "Christian Sabbath," then not only would we need to transform it to a day of rest (rather than the frenetic activities that mark most church-going families nowadays!), but we would also logically have to consider this pericope's serious applications against infraction. Sabbath-breaking in this story is a blatant revolt against God that is deserving of death.

The Sabbath was Yahweh's covenantal seal with Israel. Sunday is the historic day for Christians to worship, as it was on a glorious Sunday that the Lord Jesus was raised from death, and it was on another glorious Sunday that the church was born at Pentecost. We recognize that this issue is contentious, that great scholars in the Protestant tradition and many sincere Christian laypeople *do* think of Sunday as "our" Sabbath. But doing so requires that the term "Sabbath" be invested with new meaning, as its OT meaning can hardly apply in the fullest, original sense.

vi. Instructions for tassels on garments (15:37–41)

³⁷The Lord said to Moses, ³⁸"Speak to the Israelites and say to them: 'Throughout the generations to come you are to make tassels on the corners of your garments, with a blue cord on each tassel. ³⁹You will have these tassels to look at and so you will remember all the commands of the Lord, that you may obey them and not prostitute yourselves by going after the lusts of your own hearts and eyes. ⁴⁰Then you will remember to obey all my commands and will be consecrated to your God. ⁴¹I am the Lord your God, who brought you out of Egypt to be your God. I am the Lord your God.'"

COMMENTARY

37–40 As in many of the pericopes of this sort, the connection with the preceding is not at once clear. What has the wearing of tassels to do with the stoning of a Sabbath-breaker? Yet there is a connection of sorts. The story of the execution of the high-handed offender is designed to bring fear to all people that they, too, might be led to the breaking of the demands of the Lord in his Torah. Hence, a most practical device is given: the wearing of tassels on one's garment as a perpetual reminder of the demands of God in his Torah. Again, this reminder is a mark of grace—as is all the Torah.

The reason for wearing the tassels is given in this paragraph. As one walked along, the tassels would swirl about at the edge of one's garment. These would be excellent prods of memory for the wearer to keep faith with the Torah, to obey the commands of God. Each step of the believer was to be encircled by tassels that symbolized the restraints and freedoms of knowing Yahweh (cf. Dt 6:8–9). The tassels on the fringes of the garment were made of blue or violet color (v.38).

41 This pericope—as with the chapter—ends on a high note of the self-revelation of the Lord and his declaration of purpose for his people. The words "I am the Lord your God" (repeated) have about them the sound of a litany, a recitation of faith. The demands God made on his people came from his right of redemption. By his act of deliverance, Yahweh speaks in accordance with the demands of his character. The literary form of the chapter demonstrates an inclusio by beginning and concluding with the continuing promise of God to bring his people into the land. He was still at work in the process of completing their redemption from Egypt. The command to turn back to the wilderness (14:25) dictated a lengthy detour, not an abandonment of the journey itself.

This verse is nearly poetry. It can be displayed in this manner:

I am Yahweh your God,
the one who is bringing you from the land of Egypt
to be your God;
I am Yahweh your God!

NOTE

41 The words יהוה אֲנִי (ʾᵃnî yhwh, "I am the LORD") at the beginning and again at the end of this verse serve as the regular assertion of the self-declaration of Yahweh at points of singular emphasis of his sovereign grace in the lives of his people. Recall that it is possible that this phrase was intended to be in the beginning of the poem of the Oracle of the Lord (12:6–8; see comment and Note there). Here the language is even more expressive; the full phrasing at the beginning and the end of this verse (thus forming an inclusio) is, "I am the LORD your God." This declaration of Yahweh, coming after the people's terrible rebellion at Kadesh, should have been especially comforting.

f. The Rebellion of Korah and His Allies (16:1–50)

OVERVIEW

Earlier there had been a rebellion against the leadership of Moses led by Miriam and Aaron (see ch. 12). This chapter presents an attack on the leadership of Moses and Aaron by Korah and his allies. Korah was descended from Levi through Kohath. As a Kohathite he had high duties in the service of the Lord at the tabernacle (see 4:1–20), but he desired something higher. His passion was to assume the role of priest; he used subterfuge to further his claim by advancing the false piety of common holiness before the Lord.

Korah was joined by the Reubenites Dathan, Abiram, and On and some 250 other leaders of Israel (perhaps from several tribes), who had their own complaints and their own pretensions. Politics and strange bedfellows are not exclusively modern phenomena. Their charge was that Moses had "gone too far" in taking the role of spiritual leadership of the people; they asserted that the whole community was equally holy, hence Moses and Aaron had no special privilege with the Lord or special authority over them. To these scurrilous charges Moses retorted, "You Levites have gone too far!" (v.7), and he set up a trial by fire. The chapter is dramatic in nature and is profound in its basic teaching.

The text does not have a temporal indicator. We may presume by its placement, however, that it records an event that took place after the debacle at Kadesh. In this manner the rebellion of Miriam and Aaron (ch. 12), which came before Kadesh, serves to balance this post-Kadesh assault on the character of Moses. The story of Moses' own failure before the Lord (ch. 20) can only be understood with these stories of rebellion against his leadership by trusted people. Finally, even Moses capitulated to rage.

This narrative is one of a few instances in which the wilderness experience following the mitigated judgment of God against the people is detailed for later generations. I suggest that with few exceptions, such as this story, the reason Moses passes over most of the experiences of the people in the wilderness is that these experiences were not properly part of the *Heilsgeschichte* of the people. The movement from Egypt to Kadesh was detailed fully. The movement of the people toward Moab is also nicely developed. Intervening years are lost time, the working out of judgment, a waiting for a generation to pass from the scene. Only occasionally, when an event of great import transpires, does Moses break his "code of silence" and inform the later generation of the event.

i. The beginning of revolt (16:1–3)

> ¹Korah son of Izhar, the son of Kohath, the son of Levi, and certain Reubenites — Dathan and Abiram, sons of Eliab, and On son of Peleth — became insolent ²and rose up against Moses. With them were 250 Israelite men, well-known community leaders who had been appointed members of the council. ³They came as a group to oppose Moses and Aaron and said to them, "You have gone too far! The whole community is holy, every one of them, and the LORD is with them. Why then do you set yourselves above the LORD's assembly?"

COMMENTARY

1 This is the second account of a presumptuous, unprincipled rebellion against Moses by prominent figures who were not content to continue in subservient positions under his leadership. Given the results of that first rebellion (ch. 12), this account seems to be particularly grievous.

There may always have been some resentment of Moses among leading persons in the community. Petty, insecure people, pushing and pressing to assert their own ends, sometimes rise up against constituted leadership with questions of an unbalanced nature. On the first occasion when Moses intervened on behalf of righteousness among his people while still a young man in Egypt, he found himself rebuffed by a ruffian who challenged his right to intervene. At that time Moses was still living as a privileged scion in the household of Pharaoh, and he intervened in a fight between two Hebrews (see Ex 2:13–14). Now, long the leader of the nation, Moses still found himself under terrible attack by others who ought to have been supporters of his leadership. They may have been jealous of his privileged upbringing in the household of Pharaoh (2:1–11), resentful of his futile attempt to redress wrong in his rash behavior against the slave master, suspicious of his forty-year absence while they continued to suffer under Pharaoh (2:15–25), and doubtful of his audacious claim to have been singled out by God as his mediator for the nation (3:1–15).

It is also possible that Moses was a difficult person to function under. Since we have discovered that the classic text ascribing meekness or humility to Moses is likely a misunderstanding (see comments on 12:3), it may be time to reassess his personal character. Rebellion against persons in authority can spring from a variety of reasons. But when principled people of varied sorts rise against a leader from time to time, it is possible that there is something amiss in that person. Scripture clearly places the blame on others in this case. But Moses may unwittingly have given rise from time to time to opposition to his leadership. This possibility does not dismiss the error of the insurrections, but it may help to explain why they occurred.

The name "Korah" (*qōraḥ*; v.1) may mean "baldness" (see Note). His paternity is traced through Izhar and Kohath to Levi. As we will see, his name later became famous for the role his descendants played in the making of music in the time of David and following. The phrase "A son of B son of C" in this instance extends over four hundred years. Levi, third son of Jacob, was one of the twelve patriarchs who entered the land of Egypt over four hundred years before the time of the events of this text. Numerous intervening generations are demanded. This may explain, for example, the name "Amminadab" instead of "Izhar" between Kohath and Korah in 1 Chronicles 6:22. We might paraphrase today, "Korah was a Levite whose line may be traced through Kohath and Izhar."

Korah's cohorts in this evil plan of insurrection were the Reubenites Dathan (*dātān*, "decree, law") and Abiram (*ʾabîrām*, "the exalted One is my Father"), sons of Eliab (*ʾelîʾāb*, "God is Father"), and On (*ʾôn*, "vigor"), a man mentioned only here. The father of On is said to be Peleth (*pelet*), but this may be a substitution for the name Pallu (*pallûʾ*; see Ge 46:9; Ex 6:14; 1Ch 5:3).

2 The principals were joined by another 250 men. These were not rogues, however. They were dignified leaders and are credited with three descriptive phrases in the MT: (1) they were chiefs of the congregation (*nāśîʾ*, "one lifted up as a chief"; "community leaders," NIV; the same term used for the tribal leaders in chs. 1–2; 7; and 34, and for the spies in ch. 13); (2) they were official representatives of the assembly (*qᵉrîʾê môʿēd*, "the summoned ones of the assembly"; "appointed members of the council," NIV; an expression found in 1:16); and (3)

they were "men of name" (*ʾanšê-šēm*, that is, men of reputation; untr. in NIV).

The text thus draws considerable attention to the fact that this rebellion was not carried out by rude, impudent ruffians but by credible leaders, esteemed men of rank. Their malcontent with the privilege they had received by God's grace makes their rebellion even more tragic. They wanted more. Korah was a direct descendant of Levi from an esteemed line. The brothers Dathan and Abiram and their friend On were Reubenites. The men associated with them were constituted officials, men of name. Together this was a formidable company of nobles who brought their seditious attempt to discredit Moses.

3 Aaron was under attack as well. Perhaps Korah's real desire was not only to demean Moses but also to have himself made priest instead of Aaron. Both Moses and Aaron were (at least) in their eighties at this time. The nation was under sentence of God's judgment, and these men knew that they were a part of the doomed community. Perhaps the rebels thought that by a forced change of guard they might even reverse the fortunes of the people. The verb translated "they came as a group" suggests an organized, well-thought-out conspiracy. This was not just a momentary, casual play of a motley crew. They had not just come up to Moses and Aaron but "against" ("to oppose," NIV) them; the preposition is significant.

The conspirators' words to Moses and Aaron are compressed and impassioned; they are difficult to translate smoothly: "Much to you" (*rab-lākem*). The idea is that Moses and Aaron arrogated too much, that they had presumed on their power for self-aggrandizement. Perhaps they were charged as well with failure sufficiently to share their power with these antagonists. The charge was much the same in ch. 12, but on the present occasion Aaron was not a coconspirator; here he was also charged with the same offense.

When Korah and his cohorts said that the entire congregation was holy, they emphasized the word "all." They also insisted that the Lord was in the midst of the whole community, not just residing in the privacy of the Tent of Meeting.

Their claims bore truth, but it was distorted. The entire nation was, indeed, holy, but the claims of Korah and company ignored the gradations of holiness in the divine intent. By their words they appeared to be arguing for a democratization of the divine privilege. In fact, they merely desired a shift of power — to themselves. The pattern of leadership the Lord established in Israel was *not* an even-handed, ideal democracy. His pattern was theocratic — rule by God — mediated through a divinely sanctioned regent. The Lord was present with all the people. The leaders had more privilege than the common people, and Moses and Aaron were the most privileged and had the greatest responsibilities. A prudent response of a privileged person is gratitude to God and loyal service to his praise. Only a fool would attack the structure of God's rule based on a mistaken notion of democracy. Fools these worthies became!

NOTE

1 The name קֹרַח (qōraḥ, "Korah") is presumably derived from the verbal root קָרַח (qāraḥ, "to be bald"). However, there is another word with the same spelling that is the presumed root for the word "frost" or "ice." When the meaning of a name is not commented on in Scripture, suggestions may be precarious.

The verb וַיִּקַּח (wayyiqqaḥ, "became insolent"[?]) appears at first to be the word regularly rendered "and he took," a Qal preterit of the common verb לָקַח (lāqaḥ, "to take"). The NIV's translation, "became insolent," is suggested by comparison with an Arabic word, leading to an as yet unattested Hebrew verb יָקַח (yāqaḥ, "to become insolent, act with impudence"). I am attracted to this translation for two reasons: (1) the verb "to take" has no accusative given in the verse; rather the sentence is construed as though the verb is not a transitive word; and (2) the verb "to become impudent" is suggestively significant in this context. Other suggestions have been offered to resolve this difficulty, but the NIV's solution seems convincing.

ii. Moses' rejoinder (16:4– 7)

⁴When Moses heard this, he fell facedown. ⁵Then he said to Korah and all his followers: "In the morning the LORD will show who belongs to him and who is holy, and he will have that person come near him. The man he chooses he will cause to come near him. ⁶You, Korah, and all your followers are to do this: Take censers ⁷and tomorrow put fire and incense in them before the LORD. The man the LORD chooses will be the one who is holy. You Levites have gone too far!"

COMMENTARY

4 The response of Moses was sudden, dramatic, and decisive. He fell to his face on the ground. The baseless attack of Korah and his company is superbly demonstrated by this action. An arrogant man might have lashed out at them. A threatened man might have become defensive. Moses was neither. He fell to his face in obeisance to the Lord, whose regent he was and to whom his sole allegiance belonged. Although Aaron was also under attack, all the focus was on Moses. If he were to stumble, Aaron would stumble as well. If Aaron stumbled, Moses might still stand.

5 There is no indication of the length of time Moses lay prone to the earth. But when he rose, he spoke decisively. His words were now the Lord's words. Tomorrow would be "High Noon" in the encampment of Israel. Once and for all the role of Moses in Israel would be defined. One way or another tomorrow would tell. The verb rendered "will show" is likely a jussive; the flow may be translated: "In the morning, let Yahweh make known ['will show,' NIV] who belongs to him." This phrasing may be compared with the words of 2 Timothy 2:19: "The Lord knows those who are his" (see also Na 1:7; Jn 10:14). Moses used language of the prayer of faith, commingled with his sense of the certainty of his own position.

Further, Moses' term for the choice one of God is "the holy" (*weʾet-haqqādôš*, perhaps "the holiest"; the term "holy" with the article may be an example of the article's indicating the superlative). The Lord will bring near to himself the one who is the holiest, so determined by his own choice of that person.

The enemies had asked for a showdown. Moses would give them one, and it would be far more than they had bargained for. When Moses rose from his prone position, it was with resolution and grim determination. Finally, it had come to him that it was neither he nor his brother who were under attack; it was the Lord himself. If Moses had indeed arrogantly assumed power that was not properly his, he would have been in error and Korah would be vindicated. But Moses knew. It was his story. It was Moses who had heard the voice of the Lord from the burning bush. It was Moses who had withstood Pharaoh to his face. It was Moses who had stood on the holy mount to receive the word of God. And it was Moses who had faced a similar challenge from his own sister and brother. Now the rebels would get their chance, but it would be their ruin.

6–7 Only the initial provisions for the test are laid out at this point; more would come later. Moses told each of those involved to take a censer and fire and incense. This instruction is remarkable, since the priests alone were to hold the censers. While Korah was of the house of Levi, he was not a member of the priestly family. The others, as Reubenites, were not even remote candidates for priestly service. But Moses dared them to do as he demanded, for then the Lord would make his choice known to all in a dramatic, vivid manner. Here would be an unforgettable demonstration of the supernal power of God and of his gracious choice of his true servant. In an arresting turn of phrase using the same words (*rab-lākem*, "much to you!") the detractors had used against Moses and Aaron (v.3), Moses countered by shouting that it was they who "have gone too far" (v.7).

iii. Moses' warning to the rebels (16:8–11)

⁸Moses also said to Korah, "Now listen, you Levites! ⁹Isn't it enough for you that the God of Israel has separated you from the rest of the Israelite community and brought you near himself to do the work at the LORD's tabernacle and to stand before the community and minister to them? ¹⁰He has brought you and all your fellow Levites near himself, but now you are trying to get the priesthood too. ¹¹It is against the LORD that you and all your followers have banded together. Who is Aaron that you should grumble against him?"

COMMENTARY

8 Although the text says "Korah," Moses was addressing all the assembled insolent men. The verb "listen" is in the plural and is strengthened by the energic ending, giving special force to his charge. Since the principals along with Korah were Reubenites, it is difficult to know whether Moses' words, "you Levites," are inclusive of other Levites who were joined with Korah or were meant to include Dathan, Abiram, and On in a sarcastic manner.

9 "Isn't it enough for you" translates the Hebrew idiom (*hamᵉ῾aṭ mikkem*), "Is it a little thing from you?" In other words, Moses was saying: "In your judgment was it nothing that the Lord had marked you out as distinct from the entire community for a special work for his pleasure?" They were already in a special place in God's economy, but they were not satisfied. They desired more than ever.

There is an emphasis in these verses on God's grace being trampled shamelessly by these arrogant men. Korah was the ringleader, but all in his company were culpable. The issue was gratitude versus pride. A humble, grateful person thanks God for any task and carries it out faithfully. A prideful person such as Korah, selfishly desiring a bigger place, a larger slice of the action in God's kingdom, was in fact an enemy of God. Anytime one begins to emphasize (grandly) his or her ministry as "my ministry," such a one is in danger of standing in Korah's sandals.

10 That the conspirators were really after the priesthood became clear to Moses. It was not that Moses was in error or that Aaron was at fault. It was simply that these wicked men wanted their positions.

11 The phrase "banded together" shows the determination of Korah and his followers. This was not a rag-tag group but a congealed body who were on the make. Moses adds the trump "and Aaron!" after "against the LORD." His language is incredulous, as though to say, "What did he ever do to you that you should strike out against him?"

iv. Confrontation with Dathan and Abiram (16:12–14)

¹²Then Moses summoned Dathan and Abiram, the sons of Eliab. But they said, "We will not come! ¹³Isn't it enough that you have brought us up out of a land flowing with milk

and honey to kill us in the desert? And now you also want to lord it over us? [14]Moreover, you haven't brought us into a land flowing with milk and honey or given us an inheritance of fields and vineyards. Will you gouge out the eyes of these men? No, we will not come!"

COMMENTARY

12–14 It is difficult to believe the level of acrimony we find in Dathan and Abiram. They were not even willing to come to appear before Moses to face charges. Twice they refused absolutely (vv.12, 14). The charge of Dathan and Abiram against Moses was to sing again the old song that he had not led them into the Land of Promise. The ludicrous level of their apostasy shows in their absurd charge that Moses had in fact led the people *from* "a land flowing with milk and honey" (v.13). By some strange alchemy, in their minds the land of Egypt had changed from prison to paradise, and Moses was presented as some sort of dunce who had been leading them in the wrong direction. Moreover, they charged Moses with play-acting the role of a prince (*śārar*, in the Hithpael; "to lord it," NIV). Their contempt is simply audacious.

The behavior of Dathan and Abiram was, if possible, even more intolerable than that of Korah: (1) they refused to appear before Moses; (2) they mocked his words, throwing the language of "a little thing" ("Isn't it enough?" NIV; v.13) back on him;

(3) they abused the language of choice for Canaan to describe contemptuously the land of Egypt; (4) they accused Moses of causing their plight in the wilderness, while quite forgetting all the events of Kadesh; (5) they mocked him as a strutting prince always prancing about; (6) they blamed him that they did not yet possess the fields and vineyards of Canaan; (7) they tauntingly accused him of misusing his power by attempting to blind others to his faults; and (8) they reasserted their obstinate outrage in the disobedient refusal, "We will not come!" (v.14). Was there ever such impudence against Moses as came from these men? Later in Israel's history a poet would write a psalm chronicling the experience of Israel from her roots. This poet included the rebellion of Dathan and Abiram but failed even to mention Korah (see Ps 106:17–18).

The expression "to gouge out their eyes" (v.14) is a rhetorical exaggeration. The rebels charged Moses with blinding men to his true intentions. It is as though he wanted to gouge out their eyes so that they could not see the wicked things he was alleged to have been doing to them.

v. Judgment on his enemies (16:15–35)

[15]Then Moses became very angry and said to the LORD, "Do not accept their offering. I have not taken so much as a donkey from them, nor have I wronged any of them."

[16]Moses said to Korah, "You and all your followers are to appear before the LORD tomorrow—you and they and Aaron. [17]Each man is to take his censer and put incense in

it—250 censers in all—and present it before the Lord. You and Aaron are to present your censers also." [18]So each man took his censer, put fire and incense in it, and stood with Moses and Aaron at the entrance to the Tent of Meeting. [19]When Korah had gathered all his followers in opposition to them at the entrance to the Tent of Meeting, the glory of the Lord appeared to the entire assembly. [20]The Lord said to Moses and Aaron, [21]"Separate yourselves from this assembly so I can put an end to them at once."

[22]But Moses and Aaron fell facedown and cried out, "O God, God of the spirits of all mankind, will you be angry with the entire assembly when only one man sins?"

[23]Then the Lord said to Moses, [24]"Say to the assembly, 'Move away from the tents of Korah, Dathan and Abiram.'"

[25]Moses got up and went to Dathan and Abiram, and the elders of Israel followed him. [26]He warned the assembly, "Move back from the tents of these wicked men! Do not touch anything belonging to them, or you will be swept away because of all their sins." [27]So they moved away from the tents of Korah, Dathan and Abiram. Dathan and Abiram had come out and were standing with their wives, children and little ones at the entrances to their tents.

[28]Then Moses said, "This is how you will know that the Lord has sent me to do all these things and that it was not my idea: [29]If these men die a natural death and experience only what usually happens to men, then the Lord has not sent me. [30]But if the Lord brings about something totally new, and the earth opens its mouth and swallows them, with everything that belongs to them, and they go down alive into the grave, then you will know that these men have treated the Lord with contempt."

[31]As soon as he finished saying all this, the ground under them split apart [32]and the earth opened its mouth and swallowed them, with their households and all Korah's men and all their possessions. [33]They went down alive into the grave, with everything they owned; the earth closed over them, and they perished and were gone from the community. [34]At their cries, all the Israelites around them fled, shouting, "The earth is going to swallow us too!"

[35]And fire came out from the Lord and consumed the 250 men who were offering the incense.

COMMENTARY

15 In Moses' plea of innocence, we sense his humanity. In his pleading for mercy from the Lord for the people (v.22), we sense again his magnanimity. In his wrath Moses asked God not to turn his face with gracious favor on their offering; he proclaimed himself innocent of misuse of his office for personal gain; he proclaimed himself guiltless of any harm. He had not enriched himself by one donkey or brought harm to one person.

16 The trial was to be by fire. The test was to determine which men Yahweh would accept as his priests in the holy tabernacle. The 250 men allied with Korah came with arrogance to withstand Moses and Aaron at the entrance of the Tent of Meeting. The revelation of the glory of Yahweh was sudden, with words of impending doom for the rebellious people. The punishment was sure and with fitting irony. Those 250 men who dared to present themselves as priests before the Lord with fire in their censers were themselves put to death by fire from the Lord (v.35).

This section is similar to the command Moses gave earlier (vv.5–7), though it has more refinements. Some scholars might regard this restatement as an example of a tortured history of the text. But it is also possible to see statement and refinement such as this as a standard pattern of Hebrew style. The reader is drawn into the experience by not being told exactly what will happen.

17–18 The text emphasizes the participation of the individual by its repeated use of the term "man" (ʾîš) in vv.17–18 ("each man," NIV). There also seems to be a focus on Korah versus Aaron, rather than Korah versus Moses. It seems that with Aaron now quite old, Korah wanted his position. Even though the "job" is the service of the Lord in his holy precincts, it seems that Korah believed he would be able to wrest that service by force. Somehow he must have decided that the Lord would acquiesce to his demands!

19 But God is not one to capitulate to the base charges of wicked people! Suddenly the glory of the Lord burst into their midst. The "glory of the Lord" speaks of the weight of his presence, the semblance of his majesty. This is a way of referring to God in potent, frightful mystery.

20–21 The Lord spoke again that he had had it with the people. He was about to wipe out the nation — not just the company of evil, grasping men, but the entire congregation. Moses and Aaron understood that it was all the people, not just the foolish rebels, whom God was about to destroy.

22 Again we see the richness of the character of Moses and Aaron, who prayed to God to preserve the nation despite yet another outrageous attack. The prayer is unusual in the manner of address: "O God, God [ʾēl ʾĕlōhê] of the spirits of all mankind." Perhaps in this unusual phrasing Moses and Aaron were urging God to act in mercy since all life is ultimately dependent on him. They asked whether it was right that the whole nation be destroyed just because one man had sinned (or perhaps, "Shall just a single man sin, and the whole be destroyed?").

23–27 The Lord seems to have acceded to the reasoning of these words, for he demanded that the people move away from the tents of Korah, Dathan, and Abiram. In saying, "Yahweh acceded," the impression is not that God was recalcitrant until presented with a powerful argument. It is my view that situations such as these are opportunities that God provided for Moses to work through in his own mind issues that would ultimately bring great glory to Yahweh. (See also Ex 32:8, where Moses pleaded with Yahweh to spare the people after the debacle of the golden calf in the shadow of Mount Sinai.) The judgment of the Lord was going to be severe, but he did not wish to have it lash out on the bystanders.

It appears as if Korah himself had left the 250 priests and was standing with Dathan and Abiram to continue their opposition to Moses. The use of the term for "tent" (miškān) is unusual here, as this is the word normally used for the tabernacle of the Lord. We may wonder whether the term is not used sarcastically. It is as though the Lord has his miškān and now these false claimants to the priesthood have their miškān. It is possible that we find here a dark witticism against the enemies of God.

28–30 Moses wished to assure the people that the judgment that was coming was certainly the direct work of Yahweh and not a happenstance that might be interpreted differently. The opening of the earth to swallow the rebels was a sure and evident sign of the wrath of God and the vindication of Moses and Aaron. It was a new phenomenon (*berîʾâ*, "something totally new," NIV), something unmistakably the work of God. The earth was pictured as a ravenous monster whose jaws suddenly opened and whose gullet descended to the inner chambers of Sheol. This passage is frightful, a thing of horror. The new phenomenon was that these people would not die and then go into Sheol—they would fall into Sheol alive (v.33). This is a grisly spiritual antithesis of Enoch's being caught alive into heaven; they were to descend alive into "hell."

31–34 It happened as soon as Moses finished speaking (v.31); the earth split open and swallowed the rebels, with their households (v.32). Numbers 26:11 explains that the sons of Korah did not die. Apparently they did not join their father in his rash plan. The households of the other rebels died with them. The men and all those with them were under "the ban" (*ḥerem*; cf. the story of Achan in Jos 7). There was no mercy, no pleading, no help. The children, wives, and even toddlers died with their wicked fathers. Whole families were wiped out. This judgment was immediate, catastrophic, horrible, and complete. Yet there is something in it that is also satisfying: something of the honor of the Lord and the servants he had named, of the purity of the camp, and, in a sense, of poetic justice.

35 The 250 men were then devoured by fire (perhaps lightning); the smell of their incense would not be able to cover that of their stinking, burning flesh. After these revolts, the word would be out: those who would seek to take the positions of Moses and Aaron might find that God would have no more use for them. He might take them to

the home they had chosen when they decided not to follow him.

The horror of the story is that the punishment included women and children. No easy answer presents itself to deal with this issue in a satisfactory manner. One may speak of corporate solidarity, of the sense of family compliance, of the possibility that the children would grow to be like their fathers. Yet ultimately one has to back away from such problems and simply, humbly admit that we really do not know. But there is one thing that we do know: The God of Israel will do right!

The issue is *theodicy*. Not just the ego of Moses was at stake here, but also the vindication of God's work, his name, and his glory. Possibly Korah felt with his leadership the nation might overcome God's judgment, and he and the others might not die in the wilderness. Perhaps his original intention had been a self-deluded attempt to give the nation one more chance. Such a theory provides Korah with a sense of motivation that otherwise seems lacking.

We would expect that the line of Korah would have been obliterated in this event, along with the families of Dathan and Abiram. Yet it turns out that there are survivors of Korah's family who extended all the way to the time of David and beyond. Numbers 26:10–11 tells us that Korah was among those whom the earth swallowed but that his sons did not die with him. His descendants would later become the temple singers, responsible for the crafting of numerous psalms (see headings to Pss 42; 44–49; 84–85; 87–88; cf. Ex 6:21, 24; 1Ch 6:22–31).

In the survival of the house of Korah and their ongoing participation in the worship of God, we find both irony and mercy. The irony is self-evident. The mercy ought to be that God would allow this family to resume its former prestige—carrying the name of their infamous father—as a remarkable tribute to his grace. At the same time the memory of their father was not lost; it is cited in the NT (Jude 11) as one of the prime exemplars of rebellion and evil in the biblical record.

NOTE

30 The word בְּרִיאָה (*bᵉrîʔâ*, "a new thing," i.e., "a new phenomenon, unique creation"; "something totally new," NIV) is related to the root בָּרָא, *bārāʔ* ("to create"; GK 1343), which, I argue, has the basic idea of "to fashion anew—a divine act." See Ronald B. Allen, "The Meaning of the Hebrew Verb *Bara*ʔ," appendix in *The Majesty of Man: The Dignity of Being Human* (rev. and exp. ed.; Grand Rapids: Kregel, 2000), 181–84.

vi. The aftermath of the contest—more distress (16:36–50[17:1–15])

³⁶The Lord said to Moses, ³⁷"Tell Eleazar son of Aaron, the priest, to take the censers out of the smoldering remains and scatter the coals some distance away, for the censers are holy—³⁸the censers of the men who sinned at the cost of their lives. Hammer the censers into sheets to overlay the altar, for they were presented before the Lord and have become holy. Let them be a sign to the Israelites."

³⁹So Eleazar the priest collected the bronze censers brought by those who had been burned up, and he had them hammered out to overlay the altar, ⁴⁰as the Lord directed him through Moses. This was to remind the Israelites that no one except a descendant of Aaron should come to burn incense before the Lord, or he would become like Korah and his followers.

⁴¹The next day the whole Israelite community grumbled against Moses and Aaron. "You have killed the Lord's people," they said.

⁴²But when the assembly gathered in opposition to Moses and Aaron and turned toward the Tent of Meeting, suddenly the cloud covered it and the glory of the Lord appeared. ⁴³Then Moses and Aaron went to the front of the Tent of Meeting, ⁴⁴and the Lord said to Moses, ⁴⁵"Get away from this assembly so I can put an end to them at once." And they fell facedown.

⁴⁶Then Moses said to Aaron, "Take your censer and put incense in it, along with fire from the altar, and hurry to the assembly to make atonement for them. Wrath has come out from the Lord; the plague has started." ⁴⁷So Aaron did as Moses said, and ran into the midst of the assembly. The plague had already started among the people, but Aaron offered the incense and made atonement for them. ⁴⁸He stood between the living and the

dead, and the plague stopped. ⁴⁹But 14,700 people died from the plague, in addition to those who had died because of Korah. ⁵⁰Then Aaron returned to Moses at the entrance to the Tent of Meeting, for the plague had stopped.

COMMENTARY

36–40 [17:1–5] After the terrible conflagration that destroyed the 250 rebels who had joined with Korah and his cohorts, Moses received a new command from the Lord. He was told to have Eleazar, son of Aaron, take the censers from the midst of the smoldering remains (v.37). Perhaps the most chilling incident in the narrative is the description of the true priests taking the censers of the 250 deceased impostors from their charred remains and employing these holy instruments in hammered bronze sheets for the altar (v.38). Can you imagine the scene? True priests were picking among the bodies, charred flesh, stench, smoke, smoldering embers, and twisted parts. They were to make a count. There were 250 censers; not one was to be lost. Each one was recorded, each one cleansed, each one holy. And the fire was to be scattered yonder. It was strange fire, not worship fire. It was a fire of judgment.

Even with the death of the false priests, the holy things had to be treated as holy things. This is amazing! The men were wicked and had to be destroyed; the implements were holy and needed to be preserved! From that time on the sheet of bronze over the altar would be a memorial of the utter folly of the self-proclaimed priest of the most holy God (v.40). Their families would know. Their neighbors would remember. Every time they looked at the altar or thought of it again, they would be forced to remember the folly of their fathers.

Moreover, those who went to pick out the censers became unclean because of their contact with the bodies of their foes. Everything was a lesson in ancient Israel. All was a mix of holy and profane, of clean and unclean, of good and evil.

The censers were hammered together to form the overlay for the altar, to fit the shape and contours of the stones. This metal sheath over the stone, gleaming and resplendent, with a patina, became a thing of beauty, a decoration of loveliness. Yet it was also a reminder of horror, a stab of vengeance. As the pieces were hammered together, the identity of each individual piece was lost. The collective guilt of the troop was identified with the resultant single sheet; no one would be able to approach the altar and say of one section of the bronze sheath, "This part belonged to so-and-so."

As we think about the notion of the "holy," we recognize that things are made holy in Scripture not because people are holy, but because things are presented to Yahweh, who is holy. Since these wicked men presented their censers to the Lord, the censers were holy, despite the men's own wickedness.

A mark of Eleazar's faith is that he did precisely what Moses commanded him to do (v.39). He was thus a strong contrast to Korah and his allies (v.40). Just as the name of God is a memorial of his grace (see Ex 3:15) and as the stones in the Jordan would later make a memorial for Israel on their entry into the land (Jos 4:7), so these censers and the resultant metal plate were a memorial to God's wrath and a witness to his holiness.

God has established his personnel; he would allow none to breach their ranks. The sons of

Eliab — Dathan and Abiram — were Reubenites, not Levites (v.1); they were not of the proper tribe to serve as priests. Korah was a Levite but not a son of Aaron; hence he was not suited for the priesthood either. Each was a "strange man" (ʾîš zar, v.40 [17:5]) to seek to serve at the altars of God.

We suspect that God's desire in the memorial was not to perpetuate his wrath but to prevent further reasons to provoke it. This was a preventative symbolism. If another man were to approach the altar with his censer and if he were not of the descendants of Aaron, the sparkling light of the sun dancing on the hammered metal should sparkle in his eyes as a threat of doom.

After the smoke cleared, it was now certain that Eleazar would follow his father, Aaron the priest, not Korah. And as we conclude this section, we feel that surely things will settle down now before we come to the time to enter Canaan.

41 [17:6] With all the results of murmuring against Moses, Aaron, and the Lord, one would think that the people would have had their bellies' worth of grumbling. Nevertheless, they were at it again. On the next day following the terrible judgment of God against the apostate nobles, the would-be priests of God, we read that the entire Israelite community grumbled against Moses — again! The verb used here and in similar contexts is the Hebrew term lûn (see Note at 14:2). The people who had seen the judgment of God in such a remarkable manner still did not interpret things correctly. Again they blasted against Moses and Aaron by unfairly charging them with the death of "the LORD's people."

The attack on Moses and Aaron was audacious in its language. The pronoun "you" is emphatic; they said to them, "You are responsible! You have killed the men of Yahweh!" Oblivious to the vindication of Moses and Aaron by the Lord, the frenzied crowd, mad as rabid wolves, pressed in on them.

42-43 [17:7-8] Verse 42 speaks of the men's turning toward the Tent of Meeting. This may merely mean that they looked toward the tent. But it may also mean that the crowd was about to take over the territory, to seize the tent as their own holding.

At once, as before, the glory of the Lord was in the midst of the people — in judgment. Fear must have seized them as a bulldog grabs a pant leg. They must have been wrenched with terror, sickened with self-loathing, ashen faced, trembling, weeping. The Lord had come!

Moses and Aaron were not groveling with fear. They were where they belonged — in the presence of the Lord. Calmly, sedately they approached. Only they were permitted to do so; all others who dared draw near would become smoking brands. Moses and Aaron approached the tent and entered into the eerie darkness within the mysterious cloud, with lightning flashing and darkness enveloping — they came to God.

44-45 [17:9-10] Again, but for the intervention of Moses and Aaron (see vv.4, 22), the entire nation might have been destroyed by the Lord because of their continued rebellion (v.45). The Lord told them to depart so that he might destroy the nation; instead they fell to the ground, just as they had done in the incident with Korah and his allies (see v.4). There is a sense that v.45 is a reprise of vv.21-22, with slightly different phrasing (see Notes). Again the Lord was about to destroy the nation. Again Moses and Aaron, under unbelievable personal assault, bowed down to seek his mercy, to turn away his wrath.

In each of the dialogues of Moses and the Lord, there is a sense in which the Lord uses Moses as a foil. As the words of the Lord evoked responses in Moses, praise comes to the Lord; and the true spirit of Moses is displayed. In each instance the falseness of the attacks on Moses was exposed.

The very one the people were attacking was the one praying that they might be spared. There is something in the praying of Moses for his enemies that may be viewed as a forward directing thought (*Heilsgeschichte*) of the praying of the Savior for his enemies.

46 [17:11] Moses told Aaron to take his censer and to begin his work as an atoning priest. This chapter has turned on the account of holy censers being used by unholy men in mock piety. Now the rightful Aaron was to take his censer and do the work of the true priest to stay the plague of the Lord and to bring mercy to the people.

In the former revolt Moses stayed the anger of God by debate; only the guilty died. This time the wrath of God had already burst out in indiscriminate slaughter by means of a virulent, rapidly spreading plague, a supernatural visitation of sickness unchecked by natural protection. People who were railing against Moses and Aaron were now screaming in death throes.

Moses and Aaron might have said, "Let them die." Instead, Moses called to Aaron to act, to take a censer and do his priestly work. How precious is this text! What poetic justice! The very implement used by the enemies to force God's hand to wrath now has to be used by his true priest to force his hand to mercy.

This presents a conundrum: Is God fickle? Is man the hero? Or does God use these crises to occasion heroic acts among his servants, who then display in palpable terms his mercy and his grace?

We notice that the priest was told to take fire from the altar. He was not to use "strange fire" but fire of propriety. He used only the fire that would be efficacious. Earlier there were censers with strange fire to attack Moses and Aaron, thus provoking the wrath of God. Now there was a censer with the proper fire to protect the people against God's wrath.

Moses told his brother to "hurry" (*m^{e}hẽrâ*, used adverbially). This word communicates the rush of grace by two old men to protect the people who moments before had shouted their virulent hatred of them. Surely in the brothers' actions we find God's mercy! Their character mirrors his own. Moses knew that the plague had already begun before he had even looked. But Moses also knew that the plague might be stemmed—but they had to hurry to make that happen.

47–50 [17:12–15] So Aaron ran (v.47)! This old priest with sacral items ran to save and to heal. This old man stood in the breach between the dead and the living (v.48). This old man stopped the plague. What drama! And what loss! Thousands died needlessly. The text says that fourteen thousand seven hundred people died (v.49; see Notes), and these were in addition to those who died in the incident of Korah. All these people died needlessly, too soon, before their time—forlorn, forsaken, victims of their own folly.

But at last the plague was stemmed. Moses and Aaron met again at the entrance to the Tent of Meeting. Verse 50 is a salutary vindication of the role God had given to these two men. Despite repeated attempts by powerful persons to wrest away from them their special place in the work of God, there they stood, two old men, blessed of the Lord.

We who read this verse, weary with the wickedness of many men and women, finally come to a sense of peace. Surely now, at last, there will be no more offense. Surely now there is a new beginning for the new people, now a new generation, now a new day. Soon, surely, they will come to Canaan.

NOTES

36 [17:1] The English versions have vv.36–50 as a continuation of ch. 16. In the MT these fifteen verses form the first part of ch. 17. This means that verse numbers will present unusual problems for some readers in these two chapters.

45 [17:10] הֵרֹמּוּ (*hērōmmû*, "Remove yourselves!"; "Get away," NIV) is a rare word, the Niphal imperative masculine plural of רָמַם (*rāmam*, "to be removed"). In v.21 the verb used is הִבָּדְלוּ (*hibbād⁼lû*), a Niphal imperative masculine plural from בָּדַל (*bādal*, "to separate oneself from"). The meaning is nearly the same, but this similar story uses a more unusual word.

49 [17:14] The number of people who died (14,700) because of the arrogance of Korah and his allies is staggering. As with all reports of large numbers in this narrative, questions continue to rise as to "common numbers" or numbers used in exaggeration for effect. In thinking through some passages, all one can do is to raise the question yet another time. To "solve" the issue in one passage does not necessary lead to one's "solving" the issue in another.

g. The Budding of Aaron's Staff (17:1–13 [16–28])

OVERVIEW

The connection of this chapter with the narrative of ch. 16 is obvious; indeed, chs. 16 and 17 overlap in versification as we move from the MT to the English versions (see Note at 16:37 [17:1]). This text presents the final vindication of the Lord's confidence in his selection of Aaron as the true high priest. It is especially important as Aaron's life was reaching its end that there would be no question concerning God's choice of him and his posterity.

Aaron and his wife, Elisheba, daughter of Amminadab and sister of Nahshon, the prince of the tribe of Judah listed in 1:7, had four sons. The first two, Nadab and Abihu, had died because of arrogant acts of impiety (see Lev 10). The other two, Eleazar and Ithamar, were to become the twin lines of the divine priesthood of Israel throughout their generations. The issues of this chapter ensured that this line would continue.

i. The test for the true priest (17:1–7 [16–22])

¹The LORD said to Moses, ²"Speak to the Israelites and get twelve staffs from them, one from the leader of each of their ancestral tribes. Write the name of each man on his staff. ³On the staff of Levi write Aaron's name, for there must be one staff for the head of each ancestral tribe. ⁴Place them in the Tent of Meeting in front of the Testimony, where I meet

with you. ⁵The staff belonging to the man I choose will sprout, and I will rid myself of this constant grumbling against you by the Israelites."

⁶So Moses spoke to the Israelites, and their leaders gave him twelve staffs, one for the leader of each of their ancestral tribes, and Aaron's staff was among them. ⁷Moses placed the staffs before the LORD in the Tent of the Testimony.

COMMENTARY

1 [16] As we have often seen, this text is introduced in the standard manner, "The LORD said to Moses." We have noted before but may assert anew: If these words are just the mechanical device of a late redactor to introduce a new story he pieces into the flow of his gradually developing book, then these words really have no more significance than other stylistic devices used in other narrative sections of the Bible, devices such as, "After these things," or "Some time later" (e.g., Ge 22:1). But if the words in this introductory clause mean what they seem to mean, we have a constant punctuation throughout the book of Numbers (in over 150 instances!) that Yahweh has spoken and that he has spoken principally to Moses, and through Moses to his people.

2 [17] God's word to Moses was to collect twelve staffs, one staff from the leader of each of the tribes of Israel. Each staff was to have the name of its owner written on it so that the identification would be sure in the test that followed. This story comes on the heels of the account of the divine judgment of Korah (16:1–35) and the narrative of the symbolic use given to the censers of the rebels and its aftermath (vv.36–50). Numbers 17 is thus the third in a series of accounts vindicating the Aaronic priesthood against all opposition. The selection of the twelve staffs, one from each tribe, provided for a dramatic symbolic act that would manifest the divine choice of Aaron.

3 [18] The incidental line concerning writing the name of each staff's owner is significant in terms of the history of writing in Israel. Some scholars regard this notice as anachronistic; they believe that the use of writing would not possibly have been known by the Hebrews at this stage of their experience. Conservative scholars find this verse to be a confirmation of the idea of literacy among the Hebrew peoples from their beginnings, and certainly among those who were in leadership positions. It is difficult to believe that it was not too many years ago that radical scholars denied the Mosaic authorship of the Torah in part because they thought that even if he were a historical person, he certainly would not have known how to write!

The test for legitimacy of the Aaronic priesthood needed to be unequivocal. In addition to the staffs from each of the other tribes, the staff of the tribe of Levi had to have Aaron's name clearly written on it. The staff of Levi had to be chosen over the staffs of the other tribes; this was necessary again because of the broad community support given to the rebellion of Korah. The 250 who joined with Korah presumably represented many of the tribes. The name of Aaron on the staff of Levi would limit the choice to him and his descendants; this was necessary to ward off attacks on his leadership similar to that of Korah by others of the tribe of Levi but not of the family of Aaron.

4–5 [19–20] These several staffs were to be placed "in front of the Testimony," the "Testimony" referring to the Ten Words (Commandments) placed in the ark of the covenant (v.4). In other words, the staffs were to be brought not only to the Tent of Meeting but were actually to be brought within the Most Holy Place. I suspect the staffs would have been placed as near the ark as was practical. The symbolism is that these staffs were placed, as it were, in the "lap" of God. This must have been chilling!

Moses, who brought these staffs near, must have realized that he was performing a highly unusual act. The most immediate placement of the staffs in the presence of God is assured by these words. The intention was to rid the nation of their grumbling (*t*e*lunnôt*, from the verb *lûn*, "to murmur, grumble") concerning the validity of the priests (v.5); see the Note at 15:2. The verb *lûn* is used also in v.10: "their grumbling against me" (*t*e*lûnnōtām me*ʿ*ālay*).

6–7 [21–22] As we have come to anticipate, Moses complied with God's command without reservation. Hebrew narrative style, which is deliberately repetitive for clarity and emphasis, rehearses Moses' acts of obedience to the Lord's command (vv.6–7), thus making certain that the reader is alert to the fact that among the several staffs is the one with Aaron's name on it.

The ordeal, if one can term it that way, was to identify the "right" staff by having it sprout (v.5). Now it was patent in that ancient day, as in our own, that a sprout may arise from a living branch and even from the trunk of a tree that has been felled (see Isa 6:13). But it is clearly not possible for a wooden staff that is long dead to sprout again as though it were still part of a growing tree.

The story demands nothing short of a miracle — an intervention of the power of God in the normal order of things in such a way as to produce wonder and awe. This demonstration of the power of God and his sovereign work was to be wondrous, something for the people to remember throughout all their generations. It was the call for a major demonstration of the power of God, something truly stunning. It was also to be regarded as absolutely and finally convincing, for the act of God would be impossible for anyone else to duplicate.

NOTES

1 [16] The English versions have the story of Aaron's staff as a separate chapter (17:1–13). In the MT the first fifteen verses of ch. 17 correspond to 16:36–50, and the English section 17:1–13 appears as 17:16–28 in the MT. Despite the difficulty of finding corresponding verses presented by this arrangement, both the MT and the translations have the same number of verses.

5 [20] In the MT there is a marginal note that this verse forms the center of the book, by verse numbers.

ii. The outcome of the ordeal (17:8–13 [23–28])

⁸The next day Moses entered the Tent of the Testimony and saw that Aaron's staff, which represented the house of Levi, had not only sprouted but had budded, blossomed

and produced almonds. ⁹Then Moses brought out all the staffs from the LORD's presence to all the Israelites. They looked at them, and each man took his own staff.

¹⁰The LORD said to Moses, "Put back Aaron's staff in front of the Testimony, to be kept as a sign to the rebellious. This will put an end to their grumbling against me, so that they will not die." ¹¹Moses did just as the LORD commanded him.

¹²The Israelites said to Moses, "We will die! We are lost, we are all lost! ¹³Anyone who even comes near the tabernacle of the LORD will die. Are we all going to die?"

COMMENTARY

8 [23] On the next morning Moses entered the Most Holy Place. When he looked at Aaron's rod, he found that not only had it sprouted, it had budded! This development exemplifies God's exceeding the demands of a test so that there may be no uncertainty as to who accomplished the act or what was intended by it. (Compare Elijah's experience on Mount Carmel, where the response of God [1Ki 18:38] went considerably beyond the specific request [v.24].) One could surmise that it might be possible for a staff to have a small sprout, given the right conditions. But none would dare to say that what happened to Aaron's rod did so by chance; for not only did it sprout, "it budded, blossomed and produced almonds"—all on the next day!

Miracles in the Bible are often of this sort—natural events in unnatural conditions, timing, and placement. For almonds to grow from an almond branch is normal. It is not normal, however, for a dead pole to sprout, flower, and produce its fruit—and all in the process of a night. Almond trees are notable for their rapid production of blossoms, but this example is without parallel. This miracle is stunning!

9 [24] It must have been humbling for the men from the other tribes to take back their staffs. But only those who aspired to an office that was not theirs would feel shame. Moses' actions in having

each of the men take back his staff allowed them to give silent assent to the decision of the miracle of God and the choice of Aaron as his priest.

10–11 [25–26] Aaron's rod, however, was not returned to him. It was to be a perpetual reminder of the wonder of the night and God's choice of his priest. Hence the rod was to remain in front of the Testimony (the Ten Words/Commandments) in perpetuity (v.10). Aaron's rod would keep company with the stone tables of the law of Moses (see Ex 25:16) and the jar of manna (Ex 16:33–34), both housed in the ark of the Lord, as a reminder to rebels and malcontents as long as the ark and the Holy Place would stand. (The writer of Hebrews suggests that at some point the staff of Aaron was kept inside the ark [Heb 9:4], but it seems not to have been inside the ark at the time of the dedication of the temple [1Ki 8:9].) The presence of these reminders in the central shrine was designed by God as an act of his mercy; people who were sufficiently warned would escape dying for breach of propriety.

It is remarkable, however, that these memorials were put in a place where no one would ordinarily see them. People in later generations would be told of the reminders, but they would not be on public display. None, save the high priest, would enter the Holy Place, excepting Moses on rare occasions (such as this chapter presents). While the text focuses on the role these symbols would have in the memory of the people, the placement of these symbols in the seclusion of the shrine indicates that the one who will be ever reminded is the Lord! These holy symbols were ever before him as memorials of his special works with his people. Should anyone of a later age dare to question the unique and holy place of the Aaronic priests in the service of the Lord, this memorial of God's symbolic choice of Aaron would stand poignantly in opposition to such audacity.

It is difficult to overestimate the importance of the role of Aaron and his sons in the worship system of Israel. It is *impossible* to overestimate the role of the Priest who replaced Aaron, the Lord Jesus Christ (Heb 4:14–8:13). The extensive treatment of the priesthood of the Savior is necessary, given the divine validation of the priesthood of Aaron in Numbers 16–17.

12–13 [27–28] The larger pericope begins with insolent, bragging language of grasping people (v.1). Now it ends with the disconsolate weeping of the people (vv.12–13), all fearful of dying. At last the enormity of the arrogant sin of the people in challenging the role of Aaron hit them. Their remorse was justified; death was deserved. Any untoward approach of the holy tabernacle would result in disaster. But there are appropriate manners of approaching the Lord, as detailed in the next two chapters. The people really did not need to die as a result of trespassing against holy things.

NOTE

13 [28] In הַאִם תַּמְנוּ לִגְוֺעַ (*haʾim tamnû ligôaʿ*, "Are we all going to die?"), the common verb מוּת (*mût*, "to die") is paired with the less common גָּוַע (*gāwaʿ*, "to expire, perish"; GK 1588); the verb גָּוַע is also used in 17:12, "we will die," where it is paired with אָבַד (*ʾabad*, "to perish, be lost"). See also Numbers 20:3, 29, where the verb גָּוַע is used to describe the deaths of Miriam and Aaron.

h. The Priests and the Levites (18:1–32)

OVERVIEW

The crisis of leadership in the spiritual ministry of the people provoked by the revolt of Korah (ch. 16) leads the writer of the book of Numbers to detail anew the regulations and responsibilities that affect the true priests of God. There is reason, then, to see how the material of chs. 18–19 fits into the larger structure of the book of Numbers. It is possible that the materials in these chapters constitute later additions to the book, as they do not relate directly to the historical flow of the narrative. But they do form an essential part of its deep theol-

ogy, and these two chapters are certainly part of the book as we receive it in God's gift of canon.

The preoccupation with priestly themes has led many scholars to believe that the book of Numbers is the product largely of the putative P source. Those who reject this source-critical approach to the composition of the Pentateuch may point out that there is sufficient reason inherent within the story line of Numbers to give such a strong emphasis to priests and Levites in the Hebrew culture. The issue of rightful priests is not just a record of power struggles between competing families, stories that can be paralleled in cultures throughout time. In Israel the issue was more significant because the stakes were higher. In this case it is the worship of Yahweh, the true God, and his choice of who may be serving at his altars that are at issue.

The house of Aaron has already been convincingly validated by the miracle of the budding, blossoming, and fruit-producing staff (Nu 17). Now, as Aaron is growing older and his sons Eleazar and Ithamar are assisting him more and more in his sacred duties—tasks that will be theirs alone after Aaron's demise—it is necessary to explain more fully the manner of the priesthood. The inclusion of chs. 18–19 in the story line of the wilderness experience is not intrusive but compelling.

Nevertheless, the modern reader comes to chs. 18–19 with a sense of foreboding; what, we may wonder, is in these chapters for us? The answer to that question is fivefold:

1. The reader of Scripture needs to have general knowledge about the major institutions of the biblical period just for Scripture to make sense;
2. Our understanding of the true worship of God begins with the sense that he controls and directs true worship; who the priests are and how they function are first his concerns.

This means that worship is not a game where we may make up the rules as we play;

3. A general knowledge of the work of the priests in the Hebrew Bible gives many insights to the modern reader as to the interests of God in our own worship. Often we think of worship in terms of what we like and appreciate. This perspective misses the mark; worship is principally for God's pleasure;
4. A general knowledge of the work of priests in the time of Hebrew worship gives the Christian reader significant insights into the priestly work of the Lord Jesus Christ. The book of Hebrews has an intense priestly orientation in its presentation of the Lord Jesus Christ, priest of God in the order of Melchizedek;
5. In contrast with the highly regulated, highly structured patterns demanded of the priests of the Hebrew economy, the believer in the Lord Jesus Christ today has almost unbelievably direct access to God through the Savior. We are all priests; we can come near the presence of the Lord without an intermediary. Yet our privilege as believer-priests may only really be appreciated against the background of priests in the biblical period.

Thus it is not just for arcane, antiquarian reasons that we come to this chapter and the one following.

i. Their general duties (18:1–7)

¹The LORD said to Aaron, "You, your sons and your father's family are to bear the responsibility for offenses against the sanctuary, and you and your sons alone are to bear the responsibility for offenses against the priesthood. ²Bring your fellow Levites from your ancestral tribe to join you and assist you when you and your sons minister before the Tent of the Testimony. ³They are to be responsible to you and are to perform all the duties of the Tent, but they must not go near the furnishings of the sanctuary or the altar, or both

they and you will die. ⁴They are to join you and be responsible for the care of the Tent of Meeting — all the work at the Tent — and no one else may come near where you are.

⁵"You are to be responsible for the care of the sanctuary and the altar, so that wrath will not fall on the Israelites again. ⁶I myself have selected your fellow Levites from among the Israelites as a gift to you, dedicated to the LORD to do the work at the Tent of Meeting. ⁷But only you and your sons may serve as priests in connection with everything at the altar and inside the curtain. I am giving you the service of the priesthood as a gift. Anyone else who comes near the sanctuary must be put to death."

COMMENTARY

1–4 The Lord's choice of Aaron and his family as the true priests of holy worship presented an onerous task. The lament of the people in 17:12–13 was a genuine expression of distress; grievous sins against the holy meeting place of the Lord and his people would be judged with death. It was only in the mercy of the Lord in providing a legitimate priesthood that there could be any hope for deliverance from judgment. Modern readers are not always aware that the Lord's provision of the priesthood was an aspect of his grace. Without proper priests doing their work effectively, there would be only death among the sinning community. Psalm 99:6 points to the grace of God in providing priests for his people. The provision of the Great Priest, the Lord Jesus Christ (Heb 4:14), is in line with this work of his grace.

In Numbers, a characteristic phrase, troubling to understand, is the line, "you … are to bear the responsibility for offenses against the sanctuary." This rendering by the NIV is somewhat expansive but is a development of the meaning of the Hebrew term ᶜᵃwōn ("iniquity"; GK 6411). At times it is used to describe the iniquity that one commits or that mars one's life. But in this context ᶜᵃwōn relates to the whole sphere of sin, guilt, and responsibility for offense.

The words of the people in 17:13 were based on reality: it was a fearful thing to make an inappropriate approach to the shrine of God's dwelling. The priests, who had their work in the precincts of his dwelling, had to realize that they were there at the leave of God. But they could not forget where they were or be casual in what they were to do. To act foolishly, brazenly, and carelessly in the holy places was to invite disaster. Their priestly ministry put them in roles of awesome responsibility (see Ex 28:38).

The priests of the line of Aaron were to be assisted in their work by the people of the tribe of Levi (v.2), but the assistants were not to usurp their serving role. Were they to do so, not only would they die, so would the priests who were responsible (v.3). Aaron and his sons were the only true priests of God in the worship of Israel. The Levites were joined (see Notes) to the priests as their assistants. But the Levites were never to be regarded as "priests in training." They had a serious "career ceiling" in their vocation. The sanctity of the Holy Place was not to be underestimated.

Aside from the Levites, who had their limited functions in the worship of God in the sacred places, no other individual might come near at all (v.4). The term "stranger" (zār; "no one else," NIV), which often speaks of a foreign national, is used to describe all other people in the Holy Place. The only people who had a right to work in the shrine were the Levites under the supervision of the priests. All others were "foreigners."

5–7 The frightful obligations of the priests and Levites and their responsibilities were balanced in the sense of the importance and honor of the work they did in the presence of God (v.5). The divine vantage point is that they should regard their service of the priesthood as a gift—a gift that is priceless (v.6). The gift was to the priests; they of all people were able to approach the Holy Place

and minister before the Lord (v.7). The Lord's gift of the priesthood was also to the people; that there was a legitimate priesthood was an act of God's mercy.

The priests had a dual identity. On their shoulders rested the protection of the nation before God. The weight of that responsibility must have been enormous. But the priests were also the most privileged persons in the community, for they could draw near to God. The stranger (*hazzār*; "anyone else," NIV) would approach the holy place only under the threat of death (see also 1:51; 3:10, 38).

NOTES

2 וְיִלָּווּ עָלֶיךָ (*weyillāwû ʿāleykā*, "to join you") forms a wordplay on the word for "Levite," לֵוִי (*lēwî*). The text may be read (woodenly): "the tribe of Levi ... will 'levi' with you." The presumed root of the word "Levi" is the verb לָוָה (*lāwâ*, meaning "to be joined" [in the Niphal]).

5 מִשְׁמֶרֶת (*mišmeret*, "service, charge"; "to be responsible," NIV; GK 5466), related to the Hebrew verbal root שָׁמַר (*šāmar*, "to keep"), has the idea of charge and responsibility. The work of the priests was a sacred trust. The fulfillment of the trust provided for the peace of the nation with God.

ii. Their offerings and support (18:8–13)

> ⁸Then the LORD said to Aaron, "I myself have put you in charge of the offerings presented to me; all the holy offerings the Israelites give me I give to you and your sons as your portion and regular share. ⁹You are to have the part of the most holy offerings that is kept from the fire. From all the gifts they bring me as most holy offerings, whether grain or sin or guilt offerings, that part belongs to you and your sons. ¹⁰Eat it as something most holy; every male shall eat it. You must regard it as holy.
>
> ¹¹"This also is yours: whatever is set aside from the gifts of all the wave offerings of the Israelites. I give this to you and your sons and daughters as your regular share. Everyone in your household who is ceremonially clean may eat it.
>
> ¹²"I give you all the finest olive oil and all the finest new wine and grain they give the LORD as the firstfruits of their harvest. ¹³All the land's firstfruits that they bring to the LORD will be yours. Everyone in your household who is ceremonially clean may eat it.

COMMENTARY

8 The priests were to be supported, to earn their livelihood, in their work of the ministry of God (see Lev 6:14–7:36). Since the Levites as a whole and the priests in particular had no inheritance in the land God was going to give to the nation, it was necessary that the means for their provision be spelled out fully. They were not to have a part in the land; their share was the Lord himself (v.20). The language of this chapter is anticipatory of the settlement in the land of Canaan. Moses continued to speak about God's revelation for the new land; for in doing so he assured the fathers and mothers that, while they would not enjoy the land because of their sins, their lives had not been valueless: their children would be able to enter the land.

The language of God in v.8 is strongly expressive, with a pronounced emphasis on himself and his work in making Aaron his priest. The priesthood in Israel was not to be regarded as the result of self-aggrandizement; the priests were the choice of God himself. Here is God's gracious provision for the care and maintenance of his priests. The sacral gifts were their provisions. They could enjoy the things they received without guilt. This provision was from the hand of the Lord.

9–10 Verse 9 helps the priests to know what of the offerings belonged to them for their support. The starting point was to know that the offerings that were not put through fire would be given to the priests. In v.10 we find a helpful use of the concept of the holy. Something was regarded as holy not because of some mysterious inner quality,

but because it had been presented to the Lord for his use. He then transferred the use of some of his holy things to the priests.

Among the gifts he gave to the priests was abundant food. But the food was no longer ordinary; it was holy food that had to be regarded as such. The basic meaning of the word "holy" (*qōdeš*; GK 7731) is clearly seen here: something was *qōdeš* when it was set apart for special use in the service of God. These holy foods were specifically restricted to the males and had to be eaten only by those who were ritually clean.

11 The wave offerings were for the entire family to eat. Provision was made not only for the priests themselves (v.10) but for their families as well. Only the ceremonially unclean family members were forbidden the eating of the gifts and offerings of the people (cf. v.13). Provisions for cleansing are stated in Leviticus 22:4–8.

12–13 Since the best items of produce were to be given to the Lord, they became the special foods of the priests and their families: the best oil, the finest wine, and the choicest grains were theirs (v.12). On the basis of the provisions God intended for the priests in the OT, the NT writers argued that those who minister the Word of God in the present period should also be paid suitably for their work (see 1Co 9:3–10). The grace of God is manifest in this provision for his servants, but so are the demands of God: the priests and their families were to be in a state of ritual purity when they ate sacred foods (v.13). The foods remained sacred; they were not to be profaned by unclean persons.

NOTES

8 תְּרוּמָה (*tᵉrûmâ*, "contribution, offering") is a noun built on the verb רוּם (*rûm*, "to be high, raised"). This is something set apart for or "presented to" (NIV) the priests (see 5:9; Lev 22:12; 2Ch 31:10, 12, 14; Eze 44:30).

לְמָשְׁחָה (lᵉmoŝḥâ, "portion") is a hapax legomenon. It is related to the verb מָשַׁח (māŝaḥ, "to anoint, consecrate"; GK 5417; see at 3:3, 25; 7:1). A similar noun is מִשְׁחָה (miŝḥâ, "anointing [oil]"; 4:16). Because of its association with the verbal root meaning "to anoint, consecrate," perhaps לְמָשְׁחָה (lᵉmoŝḥâ) should be translated "consecrated portion."

11 תְּנוּפָה (tᵉnûpâ, "swinging, waving, brandishing") is from the verb נוּף (nûp, "to move to and fro, wave"). The term may be used in contexts of hostility; e.g., of God's brandishing his hand in a menacing manner (Isa 19:16). But in the context of people coming to him in holy worship, this noun is a technical term for the "wave offering." By holding up grain or produce and waving it back and forth in the air in a respectful manner, the one making the offering was marking out Yahweh as the source of his plenty; God had given life and growth to his grain. Since this food was not put to fire, it was given over to the priests for their own family use.

12 חֵלֶב יִצְהָר (ḥēleb yiŝhār, "finest oil") and חֵלֶב תִּירוֹשׁ (ḥēleb tîrôŝ, "finest wine") are constructed by using the noun חֵלֶב (ḥēleb, "fat"; GK 2693) as a descriptive term. This use goes back to the offering of Abel in Genesis 4:4, where the Hebrew word וּמֵחֶלְבֵהֶן (ûmēḥelbēhen, "and of their fat") may describe "the best of the firstborn" rather than "their fat portions." The term חֵלֶב (ḥēleb) is used in these cases as a superlative adjective; only the best is good enough for God (see also Note at vv.30–32).

REFLECTION

The concept that God gets "the best of the first" is a constant in the worship texts of the Bible. The oil and the wine mentioned in v.12 were not the dregs but the finest of the firstfruits. In giving the first and best to the Lord, believers were affirming with confidence that there will be something left for their own needs. And if not, true believers will still bless the Lord. As today, believers did not worship God just because it was a way to a full stomach. But in their worship of God, they (then, and we now) expect that the giving of the first and best to God will often result in enjoying more than ever for themselves and for their family.

Perhaps a farmer who practices giving to the Lord is more likely to be a better farmer than one who does not give to the Lord. It may be that the very act of giving makes demands on him for greater diligence in his work. But even if such a farmer does not prosper, he will continue to trust in the Lord even if no more food is to come at all. This idea is found in a marvelous text in the prophets. The prayer of Habakkuk (Hab 3) ends in a marvelous declaration of the faith of the farmer, even in times of failed crops and herds: "Yet I will rejoice in the LORD, / I will be joyful in God my Savior" (Hab 3:18).

Here is where we tend to fall down. Often we find ourselves giving out of our surplus. When there is no surplus, we are not giving to the Lord. Others find that when they give to God of the first of their best, they wind up with a surplus they had not even anticipated.

iii. The firstborn offerings and redemptions (18:14–19)

14"Everything in Israel that is devoted to the LORD is yours. ¹⁵The first offspring of every womb, both man and animal, that is offered to the LORD is yours. But you must redeem every firstborn son and every firstborn male of unclean animals. ¹⁶When they are a month old, you must redeem them at the redemption price set at five shekels of silver, according to the sanctuary shekel, which weighs twenty gerahs.

¹⁷"But you must not redeem the firstborn of an ox, a sheep or a goat; they are holy. Sprinkle their blood on the altar and burn their fat as an offering made by fire, an aroma pleasing to the LORD. ¹⁸Their meat is to be yours, just as the breast of the wave offering and the right thigh are yours. ¹⁹Whatever is set aside from the holy offerings the Israelites present to the LORD I give to you and your sons and daughters as your regular share. It is an everlasting covenant of salt before the LORD for both you and your offspring."

COMMENTARY

14–16 Anything under the ban (*ḥērem*; "devoted," NIV in v.14; GK 3051) belonged to the priests (unless, of course, such things were destroyed, as in the story of Jericho). The firstborn of every womb was to be consecrated to the Lord (Ex 13:2). Now we learn that the firstborn were a means of supporting the priests. They would receive the firstborn of animals and humans, or their redemption price (v.15).

There was to be no sacrifice of humans (!) and no sacrifice of unclean animals, which instead needed to be redeemed (i.e., their owners would pay a price to the priests). The priests were to take the redemption price in exchange for the firstborn of people. The price set for the redemption of the firstborn of women was five shekels, a considerable sum (v.16). The shekel is specified by weight (twenty gerahs — otherwise unknown; "about 2 ounces," NIV margin), a reminder of the differing standards of weights and measures in the ancient

Near East. (Note: There was no coinage until the Persian period; all silver and gold exchanges were made by weight, the meaning of the Hebrew word "shekel.")

Seemingly, the reason for paying a redemption price for the firstborn of humans and unclean animals and the sacrifice of the firstborn of clean animals was to provide a perpetual reminder that conception, birth, and life are gifts of God. Thus Exodus 22:29–30 reads, "You must give me the firstborn of your sons. Do the same with your cattle and your sheep." As we think of these rituals throughout the biblical period, we realize that they extended to the life of the Savior. Since Jesus was the firstborn of Mary, he had to be redeemed; then he became the Redeemer of all.

17–19 The firstborn of clean animals were not to be redeemed; they were holy, devoted to the Lord (v.17). They were to be sacrificed in the usual manner (see ch. 15 on offerings by fire), but the meat would belong to the priests (v.18). This was a permanent obligation, symbolized by salt (v.19) — a lasting compound. The precise idea of the covenant of salt (see 2Ch 13:5) remains somewhat obscure. We know that salt was sometimes a medium of trade in the ancient world. Perhaps an exchange of salt was a part of some covenantal ceremonies. We also know that salt was used in some of the sacrifices to the Lord (Lev 2:13; Eze 43:24) and in special incense that was used in the worship of God (Ex 30:35). Moreover, salt was a common table element; its mention here speaks of eating and, hence, of communion (see Ge 31:54; Ex 24:5–11; Ps 50:5).

iv. Aaron's special portion (18:20)

²⁰The LORD said to Aaron, "You will have no inheritance in their land, nor will you have any share among them; I am your share and your inheritance among the Israelites.

COMMENTARY

20 The basic idea of v.20 has been stated before (see ch. 3), but this verse presents the issue definitively. A mechanical layout of the verse (my translation), representing the word order (emphasis) of the MT, shows how impressive these ideas are:

And Yahweh said to Aaron:
"In their land you will not gain possession,
and a portion will not be for you in their midst;
   I am your portion
   and [I am] your possession
     in the midst of the Israelites."

This verse, marked by emphatic repetition and chiasm (see Note), gives Yahweh's special blessing on Aaron. The second-person pronouns in this verse are singular: This is a remarkable word to Aaron, which, by extension, would continue to be the portion of the true priests of Israel. While Aaron did not have a part in the land that the rest of the people would inherit, he had more — a peculiar relationship to the Lord.

Verse 20 in some way anticipates the possession of God's people in the church age. Today believers have no land promise, but they do enjoy a special relationship with the Lord. There is a sense in which we enjoy what the high priest, along with all priests and Levites in Israel, enjoyed — and more.

NOTE

20 The idea of chiasm is an inverting of the order of parallel elements; the term comes from the Greek letter *chi*, which looks something like an X. In the somewhat wooden translation I have given, there is an attempt to represent this pattern in the first two lines of the quotation. The verb תִנְחָל (*tinḥal*, "you [will not] take possession") in the first colon (accentual unit) is followed by the noun וְחֵלֶק (*wᵉḥēleq*, "and a portion") in the second; חֶלְקְךָ (*ḥelqᵉkā*, "your portion") then precedes the use of the nominal form וְנַחֲלָתְךָ (*wᵉnaḥᵃlātᵉkā*, "and your possession") in the remaining cola. This literary device helps to make the verse more memorable.

v. The tithes and the Levites (18:21–24)

21"I give to the Levites all the tithes in Israel as their inheritance in return for the work they do while serving at the Tent of Meeting. 22From now on the Israelites must not go near the Tent of Meeting, or they will bear the consequences of their sin and will die. 23It is the Levites who are to do the work at the Tent of Meeting and bear the responsibility for offenses against it. This is a lasting ordinance for the generations to come. They will receive no inheritance among the Israelites. 24Instead, I give to the Levites as their inheritance the tithes that the Israelites present as an offering to the LORD. That is why I said concerning them: 'They will have no inheritance among the Israelites.'"

COMMENTARY

21–24 Much of the previous section has already been explained in other portions of the Torah. But giving tithes to the Levites is a new development; vv.21–24 form an independent unit. This gift of God was in return for their work of ministry of service in the tabernacle precincts. These verses are marked by considerable emphasis and repetition, all designed to make the deepest impression on the people who read them.

There is a sense in which this text presents the "exchange of the Lord"—full reward for full service. Verse 21 uses forms of the word "to serve" (*ʿābad*). The term the NIV translates as "in return for" (*ḥēlep*; here and v.31 [though left untranslated in the NIV]) speaks of God's justice in rewarding them for their work. But no longer might any but Levites approach the Tent of Meeting. The precincts were now sacred, fitted only for sacral people. The wrong people approaching for even a "right" reason would die.

Verses 21–24 form a complete *tôrâ*, an authoritative instruction, dealing with the rationale for the tithes going to the Levites. The section is highly repetitive. God is in control; it is he who speaks. And in the section we notice that the Levites were cared for very well. The Levites had a double portion: they were related to the Lord in a special way, and they were provided for by him from special sources.

The Levites had a special work. Only they might perform the service of the Tent of Meeting, and only they might bear the consequences for their own guilt. They could come near and live; others who approached would die. This section does not have the ordinary introduction, "the LORD said to Moses," but it does represent itself as God's voice speaking ("I give"; v.21).

Possibly this section is a later addition to the book of Numbers, as seems to be the case with

15:32–34. Chapter 18 is a logical part of the flow of Numbers, as earlier sections were divine addresses to Aaron on priestly duties, responsibilities, and care. But this section both adds to the chapter (tithes as well as meat) and overlaps the chapter (no portion in Israel). Hence perhaps this unit was later inserted here, at what seemed to be a logical point. In any event, the approach I take is that insertions into Numbers are divinely intended, are inspired Scripture, and are authoritative.

vi. The contributions of the Levites (18:25–32)

²⁵The Lᴏʀᴅ said to Moses, ²⁶"Speak to the Levites and say to them:'When you receive from the Israelites the tithe I give you as your inheritance, you must present a tenth of that tithe as the Lᴏʀᴅ's offering. ²⁷Your offering will be reckoned to you as grain from the threshing floor or juice from the winepress. ²⁸In this way you also will present an offering to the Lᴏʀᴅ from all the tithes you receive from the Israelites. From these tithes you must give the Lᴏʀᴅ's portion to Aaron the priest. ²⁹You must present as the Lᴏʀᴅ's portion the best and holiest part of everything given to you.'

³⁰"Say to the Levites:'When you present the best part, it will be reckoned to you as the product of the threshing floor or the winepress. ³¹You and your households may eat the rest of it anywhere, for it is your wages for your work at the Tent of Meeting. ³²By presenting the best part of it you will not be guilty in this matter; then you will not defile the holy offerings of the Israelites, and you will not die.'"

COMMENTARY

25–32 Now we return to a word addressed specifically to Moses; the earlier sections were addressed to Aaron (vv.1, 8, 20), including a specific *tôrâ* for the Levites (vv.21–24). The instruction of this section, which Moses was to relate to the Levites, is impressive: those who make their living by contributions for the Lord's work were themselves to be responsible for giving to the Lord as well. There is a tendency, then and now, for persons to believe that if their lives are spent in the Lord's work, they are exempt from contributing financially to that work. This leads to a concept, lamentably more and more observed in our own day, that payment for ministry is something deserved and is something to be demanded.

The last phrase, "a tithe from the tithe" (lit. Heb.; "a tenth of that tithe," NIV) is sharp and pointed (v.26). As others give, so must the Levites give; how can they who live from the contributions of others be less giving than the community? That this was regarded as a most serious matter is seen in the promise that by keeping faith in these matters, the Levites would escape judicial death (v.32).

The offerings the Levites would render to the Lord were not themselves fresh. Their grain was not new; neither was their wine. But since they themselves were not doing the harvesting of their own lands to bring their firstfruits to the Lord, the produce of others would be regarded as their own.

For those who cannot harvest for themselves, God reckoned (*neḥšab*, Niphal perfect of *ḥāšab*, "to be reckoned"; v.27) their gifts as though they were just harvested. As in the case of the people, the Levites were to render to the Lord "the best and holiest part of everything" (v.29). Never is God pleased to receive of shoddy gifts; his demands are for the best that one has.

NOTE

30–32 חֶלְבּוֹ (*ḥelbô*, "its fat") is used to mean "the best part." This word is used twice here (vv.30, 32); compare the use of חֵלֶב (*ḥēleb*) as a superlative adjective in v.12 and Note. This small *tôrâ* repeats and amplifies the preceding section (vv.25–29) and makes its obligation of signal importance: "and you will not die."

The chapter begins with the concept that the holy persons in the worship of God served in an awesomely wondrous ministry, one that addressed a life-and-death issue. Not only might the lay person who presumed on holy things receive a sentence of death (v.22); neither should those who were in the holy service of God presume on holy things, for they too might die if they did. But the thrust of the text was not just to be a threat: "Do this and you may die." It was to be a gracious provision: "Do *this* and you will *not* die." Thus the sovereign grace of Yahweh displayed itself in ever-varied ways in the Torah.

i. The Red Heifer and the Cleansing Water (19:1–22)

OVERVIEW

Chapter 18 presented basic instruction on the role, responsibilities, duties, and privileges of the priests and Levites. Chapter 19 follows with ritual instruction for the purification of people, the laic (non-Levitical) segment of the population of Israel. Its flavor and intention are priestly in some sense, but the chapter does not concern sacral persons so much as common people. The issue is one of ritual cleansing, answering a basic question in ancient, biblical culture: How may a person be ritually "clean" before the Lord?

This also is a chapter that presents unusual problems in interpretation and understanding for the modern reader. This is a fascinating text that rewards the patient reader. The subject of the chapter reminds us of other bizarre sections in the Torah, such as the rituals of Numbers 5.

i. The statute of the red heifer (19:1–10)

¹The Lord said to Moses and Aaron: ²"This is a requirement of the law that the Lord has commanded: Tell the Israelites to bring you a red heifer without defect or blemish and that has never been under a yoke. ³Give it to Eleazar the priest; it is to be taken outside the camp and slaughtered in his presence. ⁴Then Eleazar the priest is to take some of its blood

on his finger and sprinkle it seven times toward the front of the Tent of Meeting. [5]While he watches, the heifer is to be burned — its hide, flesh, blood and offal. [6]The priest is to take some cedar wood, hyssop and scarlet wool and throw them onto the burning heifer. [7]After that, the priest must wash his clothes and bathe himself with water. He may then come into the camp, but he will be ceremonially unclean till evening. [8]The man who burns it must also wash his clothes and bathe with water, and he too will be unclean till evening.

[9]"A man who is clean shall gather up the ashes of the heifer and put them in a ceremonially clean place outside the camp. They shall be kept by the Israelite community for use in the water of cleansing; it is for purification from sin. [10]The man who gathers up the ashes of the heifer must also wash his clothes, and he too will be unclean till evening. This will be a lasting ordinance both for the Israelites and for the aliens living among them.

COMMENTARY

1–4 The material of this chapter is not congenial to modern, Western readers. Many have no understanding of or appreciation for the concept of ritual; the concept of the slaughter of a magnificent animal for the purpose of burning its flesh for ash is repugnant. For such readers the opening words of this verse should have a special importance. The ritual of the cleansing waters is presented here as a direct requirement of God. For all of its strangeness, this chapter too presents the righteous works of the Lord.

The chapter was addressed to Moses and Aaron, but Eleazar was the one who was to perform the ritual the text demands, thus suggesting that Eleazar was operating as an associate with his father and proving that the threat to his ascendancy by the rebellion of Korah and his allies (ch. 16) was now a thing of the past.

Verse 2 begins in the NIV, "This is a requirement of the law that the LORD has commanded." Likely the term "law" in this verse is a scribal confusion for the word "cow" or "heifer" (see Notes); the words in Hebrew are close in spelling. I suggest that the verse should begin thus: "This is the statute of the [red] heifer that the LORD has commanded." This,

then, would be the proper heading for the section (so Vulgate).

The words used to describe the heifer are familiar in the context of sacrificial worship. The heifer was to be perfect, without defect, and unused, i.e., one that has not been used as a draft animal with a yoke about its neck. As in all the legislation respecting the use of animals in worship, God would accept no culls. The tendency of people presented with commands to kill animals in ritual worship would be to use those occasions to rid themselves of animals that were not worth the demands of their feed and care. But the demands of the Lord are specific: only the finest animals, ones that ordinarily would be used for the improvement of the herd, are acceptable for him. This means a person had to have sufficient faith to believe that though using his finest animals for sacrifice, the other animals would still improve the herd and flock — or that it simply would not matter, because obedience was more important than anything else.

There are several unusual items in sacrificial ritual in this text. First, the color of the heifer was important. It was to be red, presumably because of the color of blood. In the standard sacrifices of Leviticus 1–9, there is no mention of the color of the animal that was to be offered; the only requirements were in configuration and perfection.

The factor that makes this pericope unique is that the animal involved was not a standard sacrificial beast. This was a cow, not a bull (contrast Lev 1:3, "a male without defect"). It was to be slaughtered (*šāḥaṭ*) outside the camp, not at the holy altar. In contrast to the blood of sacrificial animals sprinkled against the altar on all sides (see Lev 1:5), some of the blood of the heifer was to be sprinkled from the priest's finger seven times toward the front of the Tent of Meeting (v.4).

5–6 Instead of the animal sacrifice's having its hide and offal separated from the meat and fat, as was the case of the sin offering (see Lev 4:3–12), the heifer was to remain intact while it was burned (v.5). The fire of the holocaust was to be augmented with cedar, hyssop, and scarlet stuff (perhaps scarlet-colored wool). These elements were associated in the Hebrew mind with cleansing properties (see Lev 14:4). They help us to see the cleansing association the resultant ashes were to have in the Hebrew consciousness.

It is primarily the ashes of the red heifer (v.9) that were the focus of this act, for they would be used in the ritual of the waters of cleansing. It is striking that the animal was to be burned in its entirety—"hide, flesh, blood and offal" (v.5). The burning of the beast with its blood and offal is unprecedented in the OT.

The normal pattern for the sacrifice of the burnt offering is given in Leviticus 1:3–9. There are several differences there from killing the red heifer in Numbers 19. In Leviticus 1:3–9: (1) the burnt offering was to be a male; (2) the animal was to be presented at the entrance to the Tent of Meeting; (3) the priest was to place his hand on it in identification of the act of atonement; (4) the animal was to be sacrificed at the altar; (5) the blood was to be

sprinkled on the altar, not burned with the animal; (6) the animal was to be skinned and cut in pieces; (7) special attention was to be given to burning the head and the fat; (8) the various parts were to be cleansed and washed before being burned.

In nearly every respect the killing of the red heifer was distinctive: this was a female animal, taken outside the camp to be killed; the priest had to be present, but there was no identification made with it; a bit of blood was sprinkled from the priest's finger toward the tabernacle seven times; the rest of the animal was to be burned in its entirety, without draining the blood or cleansing its offal.

7–8 The priest who officiated at the burning of the heifer was ceremonially unclean for the rest of the day, as was the one who did the actual work at his command; both would be considered clean after washing their bodies and their clothes.

9–10 In a fascinating turn of events, the priest and the worker, since they were ritually unclean, were not to handle the ashes after the fire had died down (v.9). A third person, one who was ritually clean, was designated to gather the ashes and then to put them outside the camp in a place that was ceremonially clean. The ashes could not be brought into the camp, but they were holy. Only the clean could touch them, but in touching them a person became unclean (v.10). Hence the one who subsequently gathered the ashes after the burning became ritually unclean because of his contact with the dead remains. He too was unclean for the rest of the day and needed to bathe before returning to the camp.

This text gives rise to innumerable questions. We would like to have a precise signification for each of the elements. In fact, a text such as this makes for something of a field day for allegorists. But the point of the text is probably best seen in broad strokes rather than in purported symbolism we might find in the minutiae. The minutiae are there, but the overall effect lies in our recognition that the passage describes a ritual. The major meaning is in the ritual nature of the matter, not the details that comprise the ritual.

The text is like a dance: each move is specified, each step choreographed. There are elements of color and pageantry. There are also the factors of drama and death. The senses are assaulted throughout. One hears the mooing of the cow as she is led outside the camp. There is the violent stroke of the knife against the bound animal's neck, likely the severing of the carotid artery as the quickest way to kill an animal with a knife. One hears her muffled bleating as she bleeds from her death wound. There

is the priest dipping his finger in the blood and making seven flicks of the dripping finger toward the holy altar. One smells the acrid odor of the fire, with the admixture of cedar and hyssop adding their sweet-awful smells.

The conclusion of the matter is that this is a lasting statute pertaining to both the native-born and the aliens who live among them (v.10). The importance of the passage is assured by language such as this, but the meaning still escapes us. The next paragraphs illuminate the uses of the ashes of the red heifer. All we know for certain in this section is that the ashes would be used in the water of cleansing (see Notes) as a rite of purification from sin.

NOTES

2 The opening phrasing of the verse is awkward and unusual: "This is the statute of the Torah." It seems likely that the Hebrew word הַתּוֹרָה (*hattôrâ*, "the Torah" or "the law") is a scribal error for the word הַפָּרָה (*happārâ*, "the cow" or "the heifer"), in which case the verse should begin: "This is the statute of the [red] heifer." Compare the wording of 6:13: "This is the Torah for the Nazirite." The Vulgate (Latin version of the Bible) reads: "This is the regulation of the *victima* [animal offered in sacrifice]" here.

9 The term נִדָּה (*niddâ*, "impurity"; GK 5614) is a feminine noun likely related to the verb נָדַד (*nādad*, "to flee, depart"). See now Moshe Greenberg, "The Etymology of נִדָּה '(Menstrual) Impurity,'" in *Solving Riddles and Untying Knots: Biblical, Epigraphic, and Semitic Studies in Honor of Jonas C. Greenfield* (ed. Ziony Zevit et al.; Winona Lake, Ind.: Eisenbrauns, 1995), 69–77. Greenberg summarizes that the basic meaning of נָדַד (*nādad*) is "distancing"—physical (e.g., flight from) and moral (e.g., abhorrence of). The noun is used to describe ceremonial impurity in such cases as a man having sexual congress with a brother's wife (a forbidden act; Lev 20:21) and a woman's uncleanness caused by her menstruation (Lev 12:2). The phrase לְמֵי נִדָּה (*lᵉmê niddâ*, "for waters of purification") thus literally means "waters of defilement" but has the derived meaning, "waters that purify from defilement"; hence "waters of cleansing," as in the NIV. Compare the phrase in 8:7, מֵי חַטָּאת (*mê ḥaṭṭāʾt*, lit., "water of sin"; v.7), a phrase taken to mean "water of cleansing" or "purification from sin." Compare also the phrase in 5:24, מֵי הַמָּרִים הַמְאָרְרִים (*mê hammārîm hamᵉārᵉrîm*, "the bitter, curse-bringing waters"), used in the trial of the woman charged with adultery.

אִישׁ טָהוֹר ... בְּמָקוֹם טָהוֹר (*ʾîš ṭāhôr ... bᵉmāqôm ṭāhôr*, "a clean man ... in a clean place"); the doubling of the concept for "clean" is impressive here. Shimon Gibson (*The Cave of John the Baptist: The Stunning Archaeological Discovery That Has Redefined Christian History* [New York: Doubleday, 2004], 204) suggests that the expression "a clean place" in 19:9 (misstated in his book as Nu 22:9) may refer to such a place as the cave that he identifies as associated with John the Baptist but which was in use in the Iron Age as a sacred place for water rituals in the hills west of Jerusalem.

10 The *BHS* text has a space following the phrase עַד־הָעָרֶב (*‘ad-hā‘areb*, "till evening"). It is as though the scribes felt a new verse should have begun before the words, "This will be for the Israelites." There are few problems of versification in Numbers; see 26:1.

ii. Application of cleansing waters (19:11–13)

> ¹¹"Whoever touches the dead body of anyone will be unclean for seven days. ¹²He must purify himself with the water on the third day and on the seventh day; then he will be clean. But if he does not purify himself on the third and seventh days, he will not be clean. ¹³Whoever touches the dead body of anyone and fails to purify himself defiles the Lord's tabernacle. That person must be cut off from Israel. Because the water of cleansing has not been sprinkled on him, he is unclean; his uncleanness remains on him.

COMMENTARY

11–13 This paragraph reveals the nature of the phrase in v.9, "for purification from sin." It is not that the ashes would take on a magical property or that they would replace the sacrificial rites that were so important in the worship patterns of people of biblical faith. These ashes were to be used in the ritual of cleansing from impurity, particularly in cases of impurity occasioned by contact with dead bodies.

The ashes from the red heifer were kept outside the camp in a ritually pure place. Then a portion of these ashes would be mixed as needed with water to provide means for cleansing from contact with dead bodies. The period of uncleanness was to be seven days; acts of purification were to be done on both the third and the seventh days.

Anyone who refused to follow the rites of purification or who was neglectful in this area was said to defile the tabernacle. This means that willful neglect of the provision for cleansing brought not only judgment on the person but also pollution of the tabernacle itself. Willful neglect to avail oneself of the waters of purification would be a most serious matter. The idea of being in a state

of cultic uncleanness is found in many contexts: of men (Lev 5:3), of women (Lev 15:25–27), of food (Jdg 13:7–14), and of things (Eze 24:11); Zechariah 13:2 speaks of a "spirit of impurity."

Perhaps there are several ideas associated with ritual uncleanness. One has to do with being soiled. The fact that the word "unclean" is used suggests that, at the very least, this is the place to begin. A woman's menstrual flow, certain mildews and skin diseases, animals that feed on cadavers — these things in some way or other speak of something soiled. But it is difficult to go far with this notion.

Moreover, the association of a woman's menstrual flow with mildew and mold is an odious one to make; such linking leads easily to demeaning views of biological functions of women viewed as in some manner "dirty." Allen P. Ross observes, "The English word *unclean* is so freighted with negative connotations that one should try to find another translation, or else take time to explain that unclean does not necessarily mean sinful or loathsome. (This is seen most clearly when a woman who just gave birth to a child in compliance with divine will and in enjoyment of divine blessing is for a time classified as unclean)" (*Holiness to the Lord: A Guide to the Exposition of the Book of Leviticus* [Grand Rapids: Baker Academic, 2002], 244).

We report with sadness that there are some teachers with wide followings who attempt to press the laws of purity and holiness from Hebrew Scripture into the everyday life of Christians today. William "Bill" Gothard is a prime example. Not only does he commend circumcision of Christian men as a perpetual biblical rite, he also imposes the ancient laws of sexual abstinence for a certain number of days following childbirth. For a thorough, "fair and balanced" discussion of his teaching, see Don Veinot, Joy Veinot, and Ron Henzel, *A Matter of Basic Principles: Bill Gothard and the Christian Life* (Lombard, Ill.: Midwest Christian Outreach, 2002), especially ch. 4, "IBLP: Institute in Basic Legalistic Practices," 119–38.

Since the people of ancient Israel lived long before the discovery of microbiology, it would be an error to assume that it was principally concerns for infectious disease that led them to their ideas of clean and unclean. While a certain sense of cause and effect might be granted, nonetheless, we (anachronistically) read back into the text our own ideas if we determine that clean and unclean in ancient times had to do principally with health concerns. Ultimately, the ideas of clean and unclean had to do with appropriateness and inappropriateness for participation in the cultus of Israel. The ideas go all the way back to the time of Noah (see Ge 7:2) but were routinely being developed and refined through the biblical period.

Finally, the idea of clean and unclean had to do with the basic idea of holiness, which is separation and distinction. Animals were regarded as clean and unclean not because they necessarily would or would not make a person sick if they were used as food, but primarily because God desired his people to live in a world of (divine) discrimination (see esp. Lev 11:44–47). We may look back from a twenty-first-century understanding of infection and disease and remark, "How kind it was of God that some of the animals he declared to be unclean to Israel are foods that might be conveyers of disease." But the principal issue was distinction, discrimination, the marking out of that which is different from something else.

In v.13 the basic idea seems to be accidental contact with a corpse because of the death of a person in the proximity of the one affected. This could be a member of one's family in the home or a total stranger in the marketplace.

The idea of contact with the dead as causing disease might have been discovered empirically in the ancient world. But the wording of v.13 suggests contact with the body of someone who was recently dead. The risk of bacterial infection would be less in this case. The ancient idea of the uncleanness of a dead body more likely sprang from a sense of the mystery of life. Life is a force; the leaving of life from a body is a terror of the unknown. Yet it is not that the people of Israel were unacquainted with death. The incidents of famine, disease, pestilence, war, and the interminable dying in the wilderness made death something the people saw all about them. More likely the context was in some way related to sin, for death—ultimately—is the result of sin.

NOTE

13 זֹרַק (*zōraq*, "sprinkled") is to be parsed as a Qal passive perfect rather than a Pual (as in BDB, 284c). The general rule is this: If a verb is used as the passive of the simple, basic stem and there is no Piel attested, then the supposed Pual is really a passive formation of the simple (Qal) stem. The use of the Qal passive has nearly disappeared, except in the participle; the Masoretes tended to treat them as Puals. See, for example, the exquisite phrasing כִּי־יֶלֶד יֻלַּד־לָנוּ (*kî-yeled yullad-lānû*, "a child will be born for us") in Isaiah 9:6[5]; יֻלַּד (*yullad*) is a simple passive (Qal) rather than a Pual ("a child is born," NIV).

REFLECTION

The Lord is the Great Teacher. He is the one who uses teaching aids. Inadvertent contact with the body of a dead person was a time for a reminder of the ultimate: life and death, sin and forgiveness, cleanness and uncleanness.

There is an issue of responsibility here. The person who was contaminated had to initiate the action. But there is also a sense of consequences. For the community, the individual's state of uncleanness would pollute the dwelling place. This means that one person's sinful state might endanger God's continuing presence in the midst of his people. A holy God demands a holy people. The second danger

was for oneself. Such a one who refused the provision of cleansing was to be a castoff. To protect the whole, such a one was to be consigned outside the camp (cf. 1Co 5:5).

In this passage we have the ideas of corporate solidarity and individual responsibility seen together. Yahweh condescended to dwell with his people, but he was not constrained to continue to do so in the event of unrestrained contempt for the demands of his presence. See, especially, Ezekiel 8–10 for a visionary portrayal of Yahweh's gradual removal from the temple as he removed his presence from those who had rejected his glory.

iii. Specifics of uncleanness (19:14–16)

¹⁴"This is the law that applies when a person dies in a tent: Anyone who enters the tent and anyone who is in it will be unclean for seven days, ¹⁵and every open container without a lid fastened on it will be unclean.

¹⁶"Anyone out in the open who touches someone who has been killed with a sword or someone who has died a natural death, or anyone who touches a human bone or a grave, will be unclean for seven days.

COMMENTARY

14–16 That these two short paragraphs (vv.14–15 and v.16) and the preceding one overlap some is suggestive of a complex process of assimilation of these various *tôrōt* (plural of *tôrâ*, sacral instructions) into

the text of Numbers. Yet there is no real conflict between them; they meld together into a coherent whole. The resultant repetition may be used for emphasis. It may be that these two units (vv.14–15 and v.16) came as the result of specific instances of ritual defilement in which petitioners came to Moses asking what they should do in their specific circumstance. When Moses ruled, under the direction of the Spirit, then these became *tôrōt* for cleanness as well.

The point of v.16 seems to be that the cause of death was not the issue; rather, the fact of death was what rendered a corpse unclean. The person might have died in battle from a sword wound or might have expired of age in a natural death. In either case the result was an unclean corpse that made all who touched it unclean. If such is the case in v.16, then the situation in vv.14–15 seems to be the result of a question concerning a corpse that was out in the open in a tent or that might be in a container. If the container was open, the result was uncleanness

for persons who were in the room; it is as though the corpse were in the room with them. If the container was fastened, then, presumably, there was no effect on others nearby.

As we think of this text with its restrictions and limitations, we should also reflect on the opportunities it granted for relief from the bondage of uncleanness. There would be many occasions on which a person would become unclean not because of a deliberate act of contact with a dead body, but just by being in the proximity of one who died. Given the factor of uncleanness, the cleansing water became a great gift of grace. Moreover, family members were freed to minister to the bodies of their deceased loved ones, knowing that their ritual impurity could be removed (see Note).

NOTE

16 Touching a dead body was a matter of serious consequence. One would think twice before extending a casual touch, given these laws. All those who cared for the bodies of the deceased came into ritual impurity. Dealing with the dead was not to be thought of as a casual thing. Even today, Jewish people strive to complete their task for burial preparation within a day's time and under strict conditions. These factors heighten our appreciation of those who cared for the body of the Savior Jesus, helped with his burial, and planned for the full anointing and preparation of his body after the Passover and Sabbath were completed. These loving disciples were voluntarily placing themselves in a position of ritual uncleanness for seven days. Yet it was something they did without hesitation, such was their love for him.

iv. Application of the cleansing waters for uncleanness (19:17–22)

¹⁷"For the unclean person, put some ashes from the burned purification offering into a jar and pour fresh water over them. ¹⁸Then a man who is ceremonially clean is to take some hyssop, dip it in the water and sprinkle the tent and all the furnishings and the people who were there. He must also sprinkle anyone who has touched a human bone or a grave or someone who has been killed or someone who has died a natural death. ¹⁹The man who is clean is to sprinkle the unclean person on the third and seventh days, and on the seventh day he is to purify him. The person being cleansed must wash his clothes

and bathe with water, and that evening he will be clean. ²⁰But if a person who is unclean does not purify himself, he must be cut off from the community, because he has defiled the sanctuary of the LORD. The water of cleansing has not been sprinkled on him, and he is unclean. ²¹This is a lasting ordinance for them.

"The man who sprinkles the water of cleansing must also wash his clothes, and anyone who touches the water of cleansing will be unclean till evening. ²²Anything that an unclean person touches becomes unclean, and anyone who touches it becomes unclean till evening."

COMMENTARY

17–22 The ritual application of the cleansing waters for purification rites is detailed in this section. First was the preparation of the water (v.17). Ashes from the heifer were placed in a clay pot. Then fresh water was added and mixed. This is not magic but ritual. The water was still water, the ashes were still ashes. The resultant swill was ordinary in its components but holy in its designation and divine in its application. The Christian may wish to make comparisons with the "ordinariness" of the substances we use in our own rituals. There is no mystery in the baptismal waters, no magic in bread and wine. Ordinary things, however, may be used for extraordinary rites; ordinary items—not magic!—may be used by the Spirit of God to effect any result in which he takes pleasure.

We notice that hyssop, a plant long associated with cleansing in the ancient Near East (e.g., Ex 12:22) and already associated with the ashes of the heifer (v.6), was used to dip into the water and then was a means to sprinkle water on all that was unclean, both persons and things (v.18). Here the methodology of the cleansing ritual is explained. It took a ceremonially clean person to sprinkle the ceremonially unclean person or thing (v.19). Following the sprinkling the person being cleansed would then bathe and wash all of his clothes. A person's failure to avail himself of these provisions would result in his being cut off from the community, for his failure affected both him and the sanctuary (v.20).

REFLECTION

The cleansing noted in this section was twofold. One was the sprinkling with the waters of cleansing; the other was bathing and washing with ordinary water (and soap). David's prayer in Psalm 51:7 [9] takes on special significance in this regard: "Cleanse me with hyssop, and I will be clean; / wash me, and I will be whiter than snow" (cf. v.2 [4]). The parallel members speak of the two washings of the ceremony; in David's case, he requested that the entire cleansing be done by God himself!

The cleansing water of the ashes of the red heifer is specifically related to the cleansing property of the blood of Christ in the NT (Heb 9:13; notice the words, "How much more," v.14) and is a portrait of the cleansing of the believer available on confession of sin (1Jn 1:7–9). The *tôrâ* of the cow (see comment on v.2) turns out to be another of the great texts on the grace of God in the Hebrew Scriptures.

j. The Ultimate Rebellion in the Sin of Moses (20:1-13)

OVERVIEW

Numbers 20 is made up of three significant units. The first concerns the rebellion of Moses against God as he struck the rock to gain the waters of God (vv.1-13); the second concerns an arrogant rebuff by Edom to allow Israel right of passage through their territory (vv.14-21); and the third describes the sad story of the death of Aaron, priest of the Lord (vv.22-29). The death of Miriam is nearly unnoticed among these sad events. She was a prophet of Yahweh; sadly, her death merits only one line (v.1). The resultant chapter has a grim structure to it, with four (!), not just three, sad events:

1. The death of Miriam, prophetess of the Lord (v.1)

2. The rebellion of Moses, prophet of the Lord (vv.2-13)

3. The arrogant inhospitality of Edom (vv.14-21)

4. The death of Aaron, priest of the Lord (vv.22-29)

The result of these varied events, with the book-end nature of the deaths of Miriam and Aaron (comprising an inclusio), presents a central picture that is most grim indeed: Moses was now a rebel against Yahweh! Further, a petty power stymied the march of the armies of Israel. This is a chapter of unrelieved gloom. Between the death of Miriam and the death of Aaron are the stories of the waters of Meribah and the borders of Edom.

[1]In the first month the whole Israelite community arrived at the Desert of Zin, and they stayed at Kadesh. There Miriam died and was buried.

[2]Now there was no water for the community, and the people gathered in opposition to Moses and Aaron. [3]They quarreled with Moses and said, "If only we had died when our brothers fell dead before the LORD! [4]Why did you bring the LORD's community into this desert, that we and our livestock should die here? [5]Why did you bring us up out of Egypt to this terrible place? It has no grain or figs, grapevines or pomegranates. And there is no water to drink!"

[6]Moses and Aaron went from the assembly to the entrance to the Tent of Meeting and fell facedown, and the glory of the LORD appeared to them. [7]The LORD said to Moses, [8]"Take the staff, and you and your brother Aaron gather the assembly together. Speak to that rock before their eyes and it will pour out its water. You will bring water out of the rock for the community so they and their livestock can drink."

[9]So Moses took the staff from the LORD's presence, just as he commanded him. [10]He and Aaron gathered the assembly together in front of the rock and Moses said to them, "Listen, you rebels, must we bring you water out of this rock?" [11]Then Moses raised his arm and struck the rock twice with his staff. Water gushed out, and the community and their livestock drank.

¹²But the Lᴏʀᴅ said to Moses and Aaron, "Because you did not trust in me enough to honor me as holy in the sight of the Israelites, you will not bring this community into the land I give them."

¹³These were the waters of Meribah, where the Israelites quarreled with the Lᴏʀᴅ and where he showed himself holy among them.

COMMENTARY

1 In several ways this is a problematic verse. There are problems with respect to the geographical and chronological issues as well as with the obituary. The order of phrases in the MT follows along these lines: "Then the entire community of the Israelites entered the Desert of Zin, in the first month, and the people dwelled in Kadesh. And it was there that Miriam died, and there she was buried" (my translation).

Several suggestions are available to explain what seems to be a redundancy in the first words, describing the arrival of the people in the Desert of Zin (see Notes) and their dwelling at Kadesh (see 13:21, 26).

(1) This notice may be read as sequentially chronological; it would thus describe the return to Zin and Kadesh from a lengthy period of wandering about elsewhere in the Desert of Sinai.

(2) The notice may betray its origin in a different source than the earlier record from which ch. 13 was drawn; hence the writer of this section was not aware that earlier mention had been made of Zin and Kadesh (see 13:21, 26).

(3) The verb translated "they arrived," although a preterit (see Notes), may be used in a pluperfect sense: "They had arrived ... and they had dwelled." In this sense the action of the verbs is a throwback to ch. 13.

(4) Yet another solution is to understand that this phrase is a narrator's device designed to take us back

into the narrative story line by the use of recall. This is my own preference. There have been numerous sections dealing with a wide variety of topics; now it was time to remind the reader of the geographical setting of the main narrative story line. Hence it is as though the narrator were saying, "Now you will recall that the nation had moved to the Desert of Zin and had dwelled for a lengthy period at Kadesh. It was at Kadesh that Israel had rebelled against the Lord, thus losing the opportunity for the people to enter the land of Canaan for an entire generation." In this way the words "Desert of Zin" and "Kadesh" serve as an ominous cloud over the entire chapter.

We have already observed that the larger part of the peoples' sojourn in the wilderness is left without record. This may be deliberate on Moses' part. It is as though the time of sojourn was time that did not really count in the history of salvation. The *Heilsgeschichte* of the exodus traditions is one of movement and victory, not stagnation. We are left to ourselves to try to imagine what it was like for the people during this long, dreary time in the wilderness. (Recall the ongoing theme, "the wilderness has sand.")

It is often thought that the people were constantly on the move in the Desert of Sinai during the thirty-eight years of their exile. Yet the indication of Deuteronomy 1:46 is that Israel may have made Kadesh her principal base for the long sojourn in the wilderness: "And so you stayed in

Kadesh many days—all the time you spent there." Perhaps the best reconstruction of events is to presume that the people may have sent out parties on a cycle of roving travels, following the slight water sources and the sparse vegetation, supported primarily by the manna, the bread from heaven. But their circuits would bring them back to the central camp at Kadesh, the scene of their great rebellion (Nu 13–14). They had now come full circle; the Land of Promise lay before them again.

The chronological notice in v.1 is incomplete. It indicates that this was the "first month," but it does not give us the year (cf. 9:1, "the first month of the second year after they came out of Egypt"). Textual notes in *BHS* raise the question about the possible dropping of the year from this verse. A comparison of 20:22–29 and 33:38 leads us to conclude that this chapter begins in the fortieth year from the exodus (see Notes on 1:1; 9:1). The larger number of people over the age of twenty at the time of the rebellion at Kadesh (Nu 13–14) already would have died. This is the winding up of the clock of God's program of redemption. *Heilsgeschichte* (the forward movement of the history of salvation), long on hold, is about to resume. Yahweh's saving work is about to begin again. But not yet! First, there is a sad story of dying and a sadder one of rebellion.

Verse 1 notes the passing of Miriam, sister of Aaron and Moses, herself a prophet of Yahweh. It is at least of interest that her death and burial are mentioned in this record, but it is sad to see that only a clause or two are given to record these events. It seems as though after her challenge of the authority of Moses, along with her brother Aaron (ch. 12), Miriam nearly disappears from the scene. She may never have fully recovered the position of trust and privilege she had enjoyed before this rebellion.

This is not just to be explained by the anti-women stance of the Torah (see comments on ch.

12), as some writers aver. It may be a notice that even when a person has been forgiven of enormous sin, the subsequent realm of influence that person has in the work of God may be limited thereafter. In any event, when we read of her death, we grieve. It really is true: all those over the age of twenty at the time of the rebellion would die; even Miriam was buried in the sands of the wilderness instead of being given the opportunity to enter the Land of Promise. God has time, and the wilderness has sand.

Centuries later another Miriam, her namesake, would be the happy agent for the birth of the Promised One. We pronounce her name as "Mary."

2–8 In the opening words of v.2, "now there was no water," we have a sense of déjà vu. We think back forty years to the incident at Rephaidm when the people screamed to Moses to give them water to drink (Ex 17:1–3). Moses was instructed by the Lord to take the staff he had used to strike the Nile in the curse of plague (7:20) and to strike the rock at Horeb to initiate a flow of the water of blessing. Now, forty years later, at the place of Israel's worst act of rebellion, the story is being rerun. The people of the rebellious nation now desire to die with those who have already passed away in earlier judgments of the Lord (vv.3–4; see 14:22; 16:31–35). It takes an especially desperate people to wish themselves dead by God's judgments. The complaints against the bread of heaven are repeated by the sons even as earlier by their fathers.

The response of Moses and Aaron to this new assault on their persons is similar to that on earlier occasions; they go to the entrance of the Tent of Meeting and fall down in obeisance to Yahweh (v.6; see 14:5; 16:4, 22, 45). As in times past, they are prepared for an awesome display of God's presence and the scourge of his flaming judgment against a people who continually rebel against him, despite repeated acts of mercy and grace.

Then, as they anticipated, Yahweh appears (v.6). There he is in glory. There he is in wonder. In this case, however, there is no fire. There is no judgment. There is no anger. There is just a gentle word, telling Moses to take his staff and to go with Aaron to bring water from the rock for the thirsting community. The instructions of the Lord are clear: "Speak to that rock before their eyes" (v.8). We notice that the staff is not the rod of Aaron that had budded but the same staff that Moses had used to do wonders in Egypt (see Ex 17:5) and in the wilderness all these years. While he is to take his staff, the symbol of his power through the Lord, he is merely to speak to the rock, and it will give its water for the people.

9–12 This paragraph begins with words that we are accustomed to hear respecting Moses, prophet of Yahweh. He begins by doing exactly as the Lord has instructed him (v.9). He takes his staff in hand and gathers the assembly (see Note on v.2) before the rock (v.10a).

Then, at long last, Moses explodes! Is he disappointed that the Lord had not burst out against his people, as happened time after time? Moses bursts out against them — and against the rock — to his lasting regret (vv.10b–11). Suddenly the accumulated anger and frustration of forty years bears down on Moses, servant of Yahweh. The death of his sister marked the end of an era. Yet nothing had changed; the children were as rebellious as ever. He addresses the assembly in harsh words, "Listen, you rebels" (v.10). In a sense all Moses is saying is what God had said numerous times to the same people and for the same reasons. The term "rebels" (*hammōrîm*, a plural Qal active participle) that Moses uses is similar to the noun the Lord used to describe their contentious behavior in 17:10 [25]: *libnê-merî*, lit., "to [these] rebellious sons."

Moses' words — "must we bring you water out of this rock?" — express the intense level of his exasperation and pain. At this point he reaches out with

the rod of wonder and strikes the rock twice (v.11). In his rage Moses disobeys the clear instructions of the Lord to speak to the rock (v.8). While the water is released and the people and their livestock are refreshed with its blessing, the rash action of Moses brings a stern rebuke from the Lord.

The nature of Moses' offense is not clearly stated in this text. Below are elements we may bring together.

(1) In some way the action of Moses demonstrated a lack of trust in the Lord. This is part of the charge of the Lord against him (see v.12). It is not clear how Moses failed to trust God in this story. One might suppose that he did not believe a word alone would suffice to bring water from the rock, that he felt a blow against the rock was necessary. However, I believe it is more likely that he was disappointed with the failure of God this time to respond in wrath to the rebellious people as he had in the past. It is almost as though he thought it was necessary to do the work of vengeance himself; hence his harsh, condemnatory words, his sarcasm, and his blows against the rock. In this action Moses forgot a basic stipulation of the Torah concerning judgment: "Vengeance is mine, I will repay, says the LORD" (see Dt 32:35–43; Ro 12:19).

(2) In some way Moses' rash action assaulted the holiness of the Lord (v.12; see also 27:14), for Moses had not treated with sufficient deference the rock of God's presence. In some manner the rock speaks of God. This was a mysterious symbol of his person, a gracious provision of his presence. In the NT we learn that the rock actually speaks of the person of the Lord Jesus Christ; it is called "Christ" by Paul in 1 Corinthians 10:4. Hence, unwittingly, Moses in his wrath had lashed out against the physical symbol of the embodiment of God's grace. What an awful moment this is! Had Moses an opportunity to erase one sequence of events in his life, to do the sequence correctly, surely this was it! But Moses,

like us, had no erase track. All is forward play; for the rest of his life he would relive the infamy of this moment.

(3) Even the rash words of Moses were an act of rebellion against the Spirit of God. This is the conclusion of the poet in Psalm 106:32–33; he rehearses these events in song:

> By the waters of Meribah they angered the
>   LORD,
>   and trouble came to Moses because of them;
> for they rebelled against the Spirit of God,
>   and rash words came from Moses' lips.

(4) A factor we easily may miss is that Moses was not alone in his rash action and violent words; he was accompanied in word and deed by his brother, Aaron, the aged priest. We learn so from the divine words of judgment on the two of them (v.12: "the LORD said to Moses and Aaron, 'Because you [plural] did not trust in me'"). Here is an awful example of the coming full circle for both of these men. In Numbers 12 Moses was the object of the wrath and jealousy of his sister and brother; in Numbers 16 Aaron was the object of the wrath and jealousy of

Korah and his allies. Now both Moses and Aaron, who had behaved so marvelously in these past times, were rebellious against God.

The judgment of God had not flashed out against the people, but now it burst against his (usually) faithful servants: "You [plural] will not bring this community into the land" (v.12). The end result of Moses' action is sure: neither he nor Aaron will enter the Land of Promise; of their contemporaries only Joshua and Caleb will survive to enter the land. The inclusion of Aaron here demonstrates his partnership with his brother in the breach against the holiness of Yahweh.

13 Once again a name of judgment was given to a place of Israel's journey. This time the name is Meribah, a word that means "a place of strife" or "quarreling." The same name was used forty years earlier at the first occasion of bringing water from the rock (Ex 17:7; also called Massah, "testing"). Psalm 95:8 laments the rebellion at Meribah and Massah, and Psalm 114:8 celebrates both occasions of God's grace. For Meribah and Massah serve for both; they are reminders of the rebellion and symbols of the celebration of God's mercy.

NOTES

1 The spelling of the place name מִדְבַּר־צִן (*midbar-ṣin*, "Desert of Zin") is with the Hebrew *tsade* (ṣ) rather than with the *zayin* (z), as may be suggested by the English rendering. This northerly outreach of the Sinai wilderness area, just south of Judah and west of the southern shore of the Dead Sea, is mentioned in 13:21; 20:1; 27:14; 33:36; 34:3–4; Deuteronomy 32:51; Joshua 15:1, 3. Often the Desert of Zin is associated with its principal oasis, Kadesh (see 13:26; 20:1, 14, 16, 22; 27:14; 33:36–37; cf. also Dt 1:46; 32:51; Jdg 11:16–17; Ps 29:8; Eze 47:19; 48:28). Kadesh is also known by its longer name, "Kadesh Barnea" (32:8; 34:4; Dt 1:2, 19; 2:14; 9:23; Jos 10:41; 14:6–7; 15:3). For a new approach to the wilderness traditions, see now James K. Hoffmeier. *Ancient Israel in Sinai: The Evidence for the Authenticity of the Wilderness Tradition* (New York: Oxford, 2011).

The tense of the verbs וַיֵּשֶׁב ... וַיָּבֹאוּ (*wayyābōʾû ... wayyēšeb*, "[they] arrived ... and they stayed") is preterit (termed by some authorities as an imperfect with *waw* consecutive); see Williams (*Hebrew Syntax*, sec. 176) for the newer terminology. This type of verb is the workhorse of Hebrew narrative prose. It normally speaks of sequential acts: such-and-such happened, then such-and-such, then such-and-such. On occasion the preterit may take on special uses (determined by environment), such as the pluperfect ("had done"), as in Genesis 12:1: "The LORD had said to Abram."

2, 10 וַיִּקָּהֲלוּ (*wayyiqqāhᵃlû*, "[they] gathered") is a play on words on the term "community" (see v.4). The verb is the Niphal of the root קָהַל (*qāhal*, here meaning "to gather together for conflict, rebellion"; see also 16:3, 42). In v.10 the expression ... אֶת־הַקָּהָל ... וַיַּקְהִלוּ (*wayyaqhilû* ...*ʾet-haqqāhāl*, "and they gathered [Hiphil of קָהַל, *qāhal*] the assembly") speaks of the usual construction, an assembly gathered for a religious purpose.

3 The verb גָּוַע, *gāwaʿ* ("to expire, perish, die"), is found also in 17:12–13 [27–28]. It is a less common synonym of the verb מוּת (*mût*, "to die").

k. The Resistance of Edom (20:14–21)

> ¹⁴Moses sent messengers from Kadesh to the king of Edom, saying:
>
> "This is what your brother Israel says: You know about all the hardships that have come upon us. ¹⁵Our forefathers went down into Egypt, and we lived there many years. The Egyptians mistreated us and our fathers, ¹⁶but when we cried out to the LORD, he heard our cry and sent an angel and brought us out of Egypt.
>
> "Now we are here at Kadesh, a town on the edge of your territory. ¹⁷Please let us pass through your country. We will not go through any field or vineyard, or drink water from any well. We will travel along the king's highway and not turn to the right or to the left until we have passed through your territory."
>
> ¹⁸But Edom answered:
>
> "You may not pass through here; if you try, we will march out and attack you with the sword."
>
> ¹⁹The Israelites replied:
>
> "We will go along the main road, and if we or our livestock drink any of your water, we will pay for it. We only want to pass through on foot—nothing else."
>
> ²⁰Again they answered:
>
> "You may not pass through."
>
> Then Edom came out against them with a large and powerful army. ²¹Since Edom refused to let them go through their territory, Israel turned away from them.

COMMENTARY

14–17 The grief of this chapter is unrelieved. Moses' attempt to pass through the territory of the Hebrews' brother nation, Edom, on the basis of peaceful negotiation and payment for services rendered was met by an arrogant rebuff and a show of force that dissuaded Israel from taking the most direct route toward their rendezvous with destiny.

The nation was now about to begin her last trek in the wilderness; the people were now ready to begin the march that would lead them to the land. When they came to Kadesh thirty-eight years before, it seemed that their plan of attack was to march northward through the land of Canaan, conquering as they went. But the evil reports of the spies and the rebellion of the people against the Lord changed all that. This time the plan appears to be one of circumventing the south of the land, traversing southern Transjordan, then bursting into the land from the east. This means the nation planned to take the "King's Highway" (v.17), the major north-south highway in Transjordan from Arabia to Damascus. The first nation whose land they would cross to take this route was Edom, a brother nation to Israel, as the people of Edom were descended from Esau, brother of Jacob (see Ge 36:1).

Moses diplomatically sent messengers from his camp at Kadesh to the king of Edom to request passage through his land. The message is summarized in vv. 14–17, a highly interesting document from the ancient world. In this message Moses used language and appeals that were designed to bring the most favorable decision. He called Edom a brother; he rehearsed the Hebrews' experience in Egypt and in the wilderness (a section that sounds almost creedal—a confession of faith); he spoke of the deliverance of the Lord; he stated their present condition; and he asked permission to pass through the land of Edom, with a promise that they would not forage along the way or veer to one side or the other. In all the above Moses evinced humility of person and confidence of purpose. He betrayed no desire for military aggrandizement; his only request was passage through their land.

18 The response of Edom was unusually hostile. It was an unprovoked stroke of anger with rash threats of war.

19 Moses countered with an elaboration of his purpose. Again he assured Edom that he had no intention of conquest; they had no desire even to live off the land as they passed through on the major highway. If in fact there would be any need for local water for the people or their flocks, they would pay for it fully. In truth, Israel was forbidden by the Lord to take even a foothold of the land of Edom (Dt 2:4–6).

20 Once more, even more abruptly, Edom refused. And Edom backed up its haughty behavior with a show of force of their large army in the field.

21 With a sigh, Israel turned away to the east to make a broad circuit of the territory. As we read this story, we may make the following observations.

(1) Israel was likely a more numerous people than Edom, the people from whom they requested passage. If the population of Israel is indeed the 2.5 million or more that the numbers of the census of an army of six hundred thousand would indicate (if these numbers are, as many believe, "common numbers"), then Israel must have been immensely larger in population than the nation of Edom. The territory of Edom is rather arid, being sparsely populated in biblical times as well as today. If the army of Israel numbered sixty thousand instead of six hundred thousand (as we have suggested in the Introduction: The Large Numbers—Toward a Solution), then the story becomes more plausible.

It is difficult to imagine that an army raised by the people of Edom could be much of a threat to an army of over half a million, even one comprised of green troops! Yet if the army of Israel was about sixty thousand in number, the Hebrew people might have felt that even though they were a larger force than the army of Edom, they were not ready to take on the seasoned troops of Edom, particularly in their rugged terrain.

(2) We may posit two reasons that Israel preferred to turn away rather than force the issue and enter a

war they might have won. First, they were brother nations, and Israel had no claim at this time on the territorial integrity of Edom. Second, the Hebrews wanted to make their first military campaign for reasons of conquest and righteousness rather than spite and pettiness.

(3) Moses believed that the experiences of his people were well known to the other nations of the region. He said to the king of Edom through his messengers, "You know" (v.14). This issue is significant in the story of the exodus; the saving work of Yahweh was not done in a vacuum or in a hiding place. The nations round about were expected to understand something of what had happened, that it was the Lord who had brought deliverance for his people.

Nevertheless, the Hebrews turned away and began a long circuit around the nation of Edom. The rebuff and its aftermath must have been especially galling to Moses and Aaron; it was another step in their decline.

1. The Death of Aaron and the Succession of Eleazar (20:22–29)

OVERVIEW

Finally we come to the end of this grim chapter. It began with a note of the death of Miriam; it ends with the story of Aaron's death. In the midst of these sadnesses was the death of the hope of Moses to enter the land and the end of the opportunity to take the King's Highway to mid-Transjordan.

---

²²The whole Israelite community set out from Kadesh and came to Mount Hor. ²³At Mount Hor, near the border of Edom, the LORD said to Moses and Aaron, ²⁴"Aaron will be gathered to his people. He will not enter the land I give the Israelites, because both of you rebelled against my command at the waters of Meribah. ²⁵Get Aaron and his son Eleazar and take them up Mount Hor. ²⁶Remove Aaron's garments and put them on his son Eleazar, for Aaron will be gathered to his people; he will die there."

²⁷Moses did as the LORD commanded: They went up Mount Hor in the sight of the whole community. ²⁸Moses removed Aaron's garments and put them on his son Eleazar. And Aaron died there on top of the mountain. Then Moses and Eleazar came down from the mountain, ²⁹and when the whole community learned that Aaron had died, the entire house of Israel mourned for him thirty days.

COMMENTARY

22 At last the people were on the move north and east from their long stay in the wilderness near the oasis of Kadesh. They came to Mount Hor, a place that may possibly be identified with Jebel Madurah, a mountain about fifteen miles northeast of Kadesh on the northwestern border of Edom. This mountain is on the direct route from Kadesh to Moab and fits the particulars of the story in this section quite well (S. Barabas, "Mount Hor," ZPEB, 3:201).

23-24 As Israel came to the region of Mount Hor on the border of Edom (v.23), the word of the Lord came to Moses and Aaron that Aaron, the aged priest, was now about to die. The reason for his death is stated (v.24), a reminder of the sin of the two brothers at Meribah, as described earlier in this chapter. Yet the grace of God is still apparent here. The language is merciful, not vindictive. The interests of Moses and Aaron in the transfer of power were also the interests of God. Even in the death of his servant, the Lord showed his continuing grace.

25-29 Before Aaron died, he was to see that his son Eleazar became his successor. This must have been the one comfort that came to him as he knew that his days were at an end. In a dramatic symbol of this transfer of power, Moses took from his brother the garments, the insignia of his divine office, and placed them on his dutiful son Eleazar (v.28). At this point Moses did precisely as the Lord commanded (v.27); there was no more rash action on his part, no more flashes of anger.

Three men ascended the mountain; two returned. One—Aaron—died there (v.28). The presumption is that Aaron was buried there by his brother and his son. From the mount there was a sense of looking out to the land to the northwest; this was as close as Aaron would get to the Promised Land. Later, Moses would have a view of the land from another hill; like his brother, he, too, would see the land only from a distance. Both brothers are associated with mountains at their deaths. Their sister was buried near the oasis of Kadesh.

With the death of Aaron, the story of the first generation is quickly winding down. The promise of the next generation is soon to be realized.

NOTES

24 The idiom for the approach of death, "be gathered to one's people" (see also Dt 32:50), is characteristic of the OT narrators, particularly when the death is of a notable person of saving faith in Yahweh (see Ge 25:8, 17; 35:29; et al.). See also how this phrase is used of the impending death of Moses (Nu 27:13). The expression seems to be a spiritual double entendre. (1) The laying of a body in a grave is a step in returning the body to the dust from which humans have come (Ge 3:19); (2) but the expression also presents hope that the person will be gathered to his people in the realm of life beyond death. Although Aaron was about to die and would not enjoy the blessings of the Land of Promise, he would still have his part in the life to come.

Further in this passage we have another notice of the culpability of the two brothers in the rebellion at Meribah. Aaron had joined Moses in rebelling against God (v.12); the impending death of Aaron was a precursor of the death of Moses as well (see Dt 34).

25 A principal issue of this section is that the death of Aaron was not to leave in doubt the question of his successor, any more than the death of Moses was to leave in doubt the one who would succeed him (see Dt 34). While Aaron was still alive, his garments were to be placed on his son; only then did Aaron die. The mourning of the people (v.29) was not only for the death of the old priest; it was also mourning that marked the end of an era. The old generation was now nearly gone; in forty years there had been almost a complete turnover of the population over the age of twenty.

29 See Note on v.3; the verb גָּוַע, gāwaʿ ("to expire, perish, die") also occurs here.

REFLECTION

It is often alleged that the Hebrew people in OT times had no real view of the afterlife, the resurrection of the body, or heaven. This common assumption is found to be incorrect when one looks at the tombs of Hebrews from the biblical periods. As in the case of Egyptian tombs (and the tombs of neighboring peoples throughout Canaan), the tombs of Hebrews were filled with material things: bowls, jars, lamps, and implements. In fact, it is primarily the pottery from these tombs that has found its way to antiquities dealers — and ultimately to private and museum collections in centers around the globe. If Hebrew people who lived in the OT periods did not believe in the afterlife, in resurrection, in life to come, they would have been the only

people group in their neighborhood *not* to share these beliefs — and they were the only ones who had come to faith in the living God! Such a situation, prima facie, seems preposterous.

Certainly we believe in and champion the idea of progressive revelation. There is far more information concerning life to come in the books of the NT writers than may clearly be found in OT texts. But in an attempt to magnify the glory of this new revelation in the NT, there has been (perhaps inadvertently) a denigration of the hope of the future in the Hebrew Scriptures. See the words of Jesus in Matthew 22:29-33, and see my book *Grace, Always Grace* (Grand Rapids: Kregel, forthcoming) for a chapter on this issue.

2. A Climax of Rebellion and Hope and the End of Their Dying (21:1-25:18)

OVERVIEW

If Numbers 20 is a tableau of unrelieved gloom, ch. 21 begins to show some glimmers of light in the dark sea of Israel's wilderness experience. This is not to say that there would be no more trouble and no more rebellion; such is hardly the case. Indeed, this chapter and ch. 25 present notorious instances of Israel's continued acts of rebellion against Yahweh. But this chapter presents some victories — victories against hostile enemies as well as victories against the dark side of themselves. Chapter 21 also presents the setting for the enormously important set

of texts on the dramatic story of Balaam the pagan mantic, who confronted the power of Yahweh, Israel's God, in one of the most amusing, wondrous, and engaging of biblical narratives (chs. 22-24).

Numbers 21 has five discrete sections. Our commentary will proceed along those lines. Then follows Numbers 22-24, the account of Balaam and Balak, with two major movements. On the heels of this story is the dramatic, unexpected, and frightful aftermath, the seduction of Israel at Baal Peor. Altogether, then, Numbers 21-25 has eight sectional divisions.

a. The Destruction of Arad (21:1-3)

¹When the Canaanite king of Arad, who lived in the Negev, heard that Israel was coming along the road to Atharim, he attacked the Israelites and captured some of them. ²Then Israel made this vow to the LORD: "If you will deliver these people into our hands, we will

totally destroy their cities." ³The LORD listened to Israel's plea and gave the Canaanites over to them. They completely destroyed them and their towns; so the place was named Hormah.

COMMENTARY

1 The first battle of the new community against the Canaanites was provoked by the king of Arad, perhaps as he was on an incursionary raid. The result was a complete victory for the Israelites. Indeed this was a new day for Israel since their defeat by the Amalekites a generation earlier (14:41–45).

Unlike the situation with Edom in ch. 20, Arad was a Canaanite region that was a part of the people and territory under the interdict of Yahweh. Here was the first occasion for a military operation by the new generation. The text emphasizes several matters: (1) the king of Arad was a Canaanite (vv.1, 3); (2) he deliberately provoked an attack on Israel, including the taking of hostages (v.1); and (3) unlike their rebellious fathers (14:41–45), the people of Israel fought this time under the blessing and empowerment of Yahweh (v.3).

The site of biblical Arad is identified with Tell ʿArad, about twenty miles south of Hebron in the eastern Negev. While the 1962–67 Israeli excavations at Arad demonstrated a large, fortified city of the Early Bronze II period (ca. 2900–2700 BC) and complex ruins from the Iron Age, there was no evidence found of a Late or Middle Bronze city on the tell (mound of ruins). It is possible that in the time of Moses the term Arad was used for a region of the Negev rather than a city proper, or that at that time the name "Arad" had "floated" to another site nearby. (Compare the "floating" of the city of Jericho through its long history.) Y. Aharoni ("Arad," *ISBE*², 1:229) suggests this possibility and cites as a candidate Tell el-Milḥ (eight miles south of Tell ʿArad), where strong Hyksos fortifications have been found and which may be mentioned along with Tell ʿArad in the Shishak list (see Note).

2 The vow of the people of Yahweh speaks of their full dependence on him for their victory, as well as their determination to fulfill their vow by making a complete destruction of their cities. The verb translated "totally destroy" (*ḥāram* in the Hiphil; GK 3049) is the verbal form related to the word *ḥerem*, meaning "to devote to the ban." This ruthless action was determined not just by the rugged spirit of the age, but also from a sense that the people were engaging in holy war, where the extermination, not just the subjugation, of their enemies was the spiritual goal for the people in their conquest of Canaan. The cup of iniquity of the people of the land was now full (see Ge 15:16); Israel was to be the instrument of the Lord's judgment to cleanse the land of the people who had polluted it.

3 The success of the military action against the Canaanite army of the king of Arad was thorough. They named the place "Hormah" (*ḥormâ*), a noun related to the verb *ḥāram* (used in the Hiphil theme, meaning "to devote to destruction"). Since the name Hormah was used in the first (and unsuccessful) battle against the Canaanites and Amalekites of the region (14:45), it is possible that the naming of the region came as a result of this present battle and that the earlier passage uses the name (of what became a well-known place) proleptically (see the example of the city of Rameses at 33:3). In any event, the association of the victorious battle with Israel's earlier defeat is made certain by the use of this place name. The new generation faced a new day; victory ahead seemed to be assured.

NOTE

1 Shishak (or Sheshonq I) was a Libyan war chief who became the pharaoh of Egypt (ca. 945–924 BC). Following the death of Solomon, Shishak invaded Judah and captured many of its cities (see 1Ki 14:25). The record of his campaign was inscribed on a wall of the temple of Amon at Karnak (Thebes). In the lists of cities conquered are two called עֲרָד (ʿᵃrād, "Arad"): "Arad of the House of Yrhm" and "the Great Arad." See also Note at 33:2.

REFLECTION

All contemporary feelings of revulsion against the seeming "barbarism" of holy war need to be evaluated in terms of the later history of Israel. As is well attested in biblical history, except on rare occasions the people did not carry out the policy of ḥerem on the peoples of the land. The Canaanite peoples who survived became instruments of Israel's defection from the pure worship of Yahweh. Their practice of the seductive patterns of the worship of Baal became the allure for Israel as she turned from the Lord—and this subsequently became the reason for Yahweh's judgment on them. A recent work presents the views and interactions of four evangelical scholars on the issue of "holy war" and total destruction in ancient Israel. See C. S. Cowles, Eugene H. Merrill, Daniel L. Gard, and Tremper Longman III, *Show Them No Mercy: 4 Views on God and Canaanite Genocide* (ed. Stanley N. Gundry; Grand Rapids: Zondervan, 2003).

b. The Bronze Snake (21:4–9)

OVERVIEW

It is not unusual in Scripture—or in our own lives—to experience defeat following quickly on an event of victory. The narrator of Numbers places two such contrasting stories side-by-side in this chapter, perhaps to show the reader that while progress was being made toward dependence on the Lord, there was still a long way to go for these wilderness people! On the heels of the story of Israel's great victory over the Canaanites of the Negev, they fell on their own swords, again over the issue of food in the rebellion that led to the story of the bronze serpent.

⁴They traveled from Mount Hor along the route to the Red Sea, to go around Edom. But the people grew impatient on the way; ⁵they spoke against God and against Moses, and said, "Why have you brought us up out of Egypt to die in the desert? There is no bread! There is no water! And we detest this miserable food!"

⁶Then the LORD sent venomous snakes among them; they bit the people and many Israelites died. ⁷The people came to Moses and said, "We sinned when we spoke against the LORD and against you. Pray that the LORD will take the snakes away from us." So Moses prayed for the people.

⁸The LORD said to Moses, "Make a snake and put it up on a pole; anyone who is bitten can look at it and live." ⁹So Moses made a bronze snake and put it up on a pole. Then when anyone was bitten by a snake and looked at the bronze snake, he lived.

COMMENTARY

4 This passage has a geographical and logical connection to the account of the death of Aaron on Mount Hor (20:27–29) and to the rebuff of Edom in not permitting Israel to pass through its territory for any price (20:14–21). There is no real connection indicated with the little pericope of the victory over the Canaanites of Arad (vv.1–3). These accounts are separate but juxtaposed for effect.

The people had to journey on a detour because of the intransigent attitude of Edom. Each step they made south and east, rather than north and west, must have seemed unbearably tedious—such backtracking. They rejoined the road to the Red Sea (or "Sea of Reeds," but here connoting the eastern arm of the Red Sea, the Gulf of Arabah; see Note at 33:8, 10) to make a broad circuit around Edom. Finally, it got to them again. They had been so near the land of Canaan and had even tasted the sweet wine of victory. But now they were wandering again, and in their wanderings they seemed to be as far away from "real" food as ever.

With Moses' determination not to engage Edom in battle (see comment on 20:19), the people became impatient with him and with the direction Yahweh was taking them. Flushed with victory, their confidence was now in themselves. They forgot that their victory over the army of Arad was a victory granted to them by Yahweh in response

to their solemn pledge to him (vv.2–3). Now they were ready to rebel again.

5 The people began to complain and spoke against both God and Moses. They, like their fathers, asked why they had not been left in Egypt and why they should be brought to this awful place to die. They did not deny the miracle God had done for them, but they disparaged their deliverance from Egypt. Again they complained about the lack of food and water. Then they went beyond their fathers and mothers—they not only spoke of the monotony of manna, but they described it as "miserable bread" (see Notes). In their styling the "bread of heaven" (see Ps 78:23–24) as something vile and despicable, the people were actually contemning the Lord, its giver.

The venom of the people's anger led them to blaspheme Yahweh (v.4), to reject his servant Moses, and to contemn the bread of heaven. This is the most vitriolic of their several attacks on the manna (see Note on 11:6). Just as the attack of Moses on the rock was more than it appeared to be (see comment on 20:11), so the contempt of the people for the heavenly bread was more serious than one might think. The Lord Jesus speaks of the manna as a type of himself, that he is the true Bread from heaven (Jn 6:32–35, 48–51, 58). A rejection of the heavenly manna, it turned out, was tantamount to spurning the grace of God in the Savior.

6 Once more God's people had rejected him; again he brought judgment on their heads. The pattern of rebellion by the people followed by God's judgment is well established in the book of Numbers. It is possible that the basic trigger that provoked the outrageous actions and words of Moses in his rebellion against Yahweh (20:9–11) was precisely because he felt this pattern had been broken at that time. God had not burst out against the people as Moses might have expected in response to their attack on him as described in 20:2–5. So Moses raged against them, and in the process he forgot who was (and is) God and who was servant. He confused the holy with the profane. For that moment he seemed not to have believed that God would vindicate his own name (see 20:12).

But this time God acted as Moses expected. He brought a new instrument of his judgment on the people. This time it was snakes. The KJV's "fiery serpents" has led some readers to think of burning snakes—indeed, some have thought of fiery dragons! (Compare the Hebrew phrase *hannᵉḥāšîm haśśᵉrāpîm*, "the burning snakes" or, better, "the snakes that produce burning.") The "fire" was in their venom, of course; hence the NIV's "venomous snakes." The poison in these snakebites must have been particularly virulent, thus leading to horrible, agonizing deaths.

We notice something in these snakes that points to what is common in the miracles of the Bible; naturally occurring phenomena may come in unnatural ways, in exaggerated numbers, or in unusual timings. Manna, as we have argued above (see 11:5), seems to have been an exception. Manna was not naturally occurring—it was wholly divine. And the people spurned it.

The people received something from the wilderness rather than from heaven. They received a sting instead of a blessing. They found themselves dying instead of being preserved alive by "that miserable bread." There is something very human about the people in their complaints about their diet. The timing of their renewed complaint is understandable, given the fact that they were backtracking into the wide waste of the wilderness in order not to provoke Edom. But acting understandably human or not, they were again engaging in outrageous rebellion, coupled to an almost visceral hatred of God's gift to them in the "bread of angels" (Ps 78:25).

There is a pattern to complaining; it is habit forming. The tendency among people is to go beyond where one left off the last time, to become ever more egregious, ever more outspoken. Rarely does a complaining person become milder in his or her complaints. Finally, complaining becomes self-destructive.

7 Nonetheless, there was change of sorts in the people as they are described in this chapter. They continued to rebel (and they would rebel again in ch. 25), but now they asked for forgiveness. They were sinners, but they were confessing their wrong. They screamed out to Moses, "We sinned when we spoke against the Lᴏʀᴅ and against you." In this act of repentance, we witness the seeds for renewal. In their desire for forgiveness, there was hope for their future.

So Moses prayed for the people as he had prayed before (e.g., 11:2). And God answered, but in a most unusual way. In the case of the fire that flashed from heaven at the beginning of their troubles (11:1–3), the prayer of Moses eventuated in the fire's dying out. In this case the snakes did not slither away, nor did they lose their fangs; the fiery serpents continued to plague the people with their horrible bites, and the people continued to grow ill and die.

8 Instead of losing the snakes, the people had to get their fill of them, as they had been forced to stomach quail at another time (11:31–34). Meanwhile, Moses was told to make an image of a snake (see Notes)! As we think about this, we realize several levels of incongruity.

1. The description of the plague seems to be of something that was spreading quickly; yet Moses had to take the time to fashion, or direct the fashioning of, a metal image of one of the poisonous snakes. Sometimes even in a crisis one needs to move purposefully, surely.

2. Moses had transmitted to Israel God's prohibition against making images of any animal or other life form (see Ex 20:4–6) because of the dangers of idolatry that were so inherent in graphic art in the biblical period; yet now he was asked to make a graven image. This command must have been inordinately surprising, even to Moses.

3. There are few things so intensely disliked and feared the world over as snakes. Herpetologists cannot understand the revulsion in the lay opinion of snakes, and they seem to suffer umbrage at what they regard to be silly misinformation about snakes in popular culture. No matter. Most people simply do not care for snakes; we may presume (from the tenor of this text) that this is a value we share with people who lived thirty-five hundred years ago.

4. More specifically, in biblical culture it was a snake that became associated with the Evil One himself (Ge 3). Satan's first manifestation in the biblical story is as a serpent; he is later to be called the primordial serpent, the Dragon (see Rev 20:2). There is a sense in biblical thought that snakes are not only detestable in themselves—they may even be symbolic of the prince of darkness himself.

With all these factors in view, now we think again of the enormity of what Moses was asked to do, of the taboos he was asked to break. This is not unlike Peter's being told to kill and eat food he regarded as unclean (Ac 10). The people had called the bread of heaven detestable. Moses was commanded of God to make an image of something truly detestable in their culture and to hold that high on a pole as their only means of deliverance from disease. Only those who looked at the image of the snake would survive the venom that coursed through their bodies. This is an extraordinary act of cultural shock, an exceptionally daring use of potent symbols. As the people had transformed (in their own thinking) the gracious bread of heaven into detestable food, so the Lord now transformed a symbol of death into a source of life and deliverance. The rejection of God's grace brought a symbol of death. The intervention of God's grace brought a source of life.

9 Some interpreters err in their evaluation of the "salvation" that came from looking at this snake. Some contemporary theologians and Bible teachers debate on how intense one's gaze at the bronze serpent had to be for one to be "saved." Discussions rage on the meaning of the verb "to look" (*nābaṭ*, in the Hiphil; GK 5564). One party says merely a glance was needed; the other says the text demands a constant, groping stare. The one party says the glance is akin to making a commitment of faith in Christ; the other party says that the gaze is akin to making Christ the Lord of one's life.

In this arcane debate these teachers appear to have missed the point of this text. It does not speak of eternal salvation or of what a Hebrew person had to do to be saved forever before God. It certainly should not be used as a touch-point for the debate over "lordship salvation." The passage speaks plainly of physical healing from a critical disease. Health, not heaven, is the issue here. The people were redeemed already by blood and covenant and by Passover deliverance. They had come to saving faith (see Ex 14:30–31; the language is the same as in Ge 15:6). The issue remained for each of them: How long may they continue to live this life? Those over twenty were already on a death course; those under twenty had an opportunity for a long life in the land. Many would die in the wilderness of the fiery venom of these snakes, but not all had to die. God would keep many alive if they would only do as he demanded.

NOTES

4 יַם־סוּף (*yam-sûp*, "the Red Sea" or "the Sea of Reeds") is the phrase used to describe the crossing point for Israel in Yahweh's great act of delivering them, presumably at some point along the western arm of the Red Sea, the Gulf of Suez (see Ex 14–15). However, in Numbers (see also 14:25; 33:8, 10) this phrase does not refer to the western arm of the Red Sea (the "Gulf of Suez"), but to the eastern arm (the "Gulf of Aqaba"). It is possible that the phrase "Sea of Reeds" may be emended to יַם־סוֹף (*yam-sôp*, "Sea's End"). In this case the name would refer in all cases to the eastern arm of the Red Sea. See the Note at 33:8, 10 for discussion of this alternative viewpoint.

5 בַּלֶּחֶם הַקְּלֹקֵל (*ballehem haqqelōqēl*, "contemptible, worthless bread") is rendered "miserable food" in the NIV. The adjective קְלֹקֵל (*qelōqēl*; GK 7848) is a hapax legomenon. It is derived from the verb קָלַל (*qālal*, "to be slight, trifling," which verb, incidentally, gives us our stem name "Qal"). The verb can refer to something that is light, inconsequential; it may also speak of cursing someone or something in the sense of treating as of no value. This is the verb used by God in the promise to Abram at the beginning וּמְקַלֶּלְךָ (*ûmeqallelkā*, "whoever curses you"; Ge 12:3); now the people were cursing the food God had given.

8 In this verse only the word שָׂרָף (*śārāp*, "fiery [i.e., venomous] [serpent]"; GK 8597) is used; compare הַנְּחָשִׁים הַשְּׂרָפִים (*hannehāšîm haśśerāpîm*, "the venomous snakes") in v.6, and נְחַשׁ נְחֹשֶׁת (*nehaš nehōšet*, "bronze snake," a wordplay) in v.9. This word שָׂרָף (*śārāp*, "fiery") is the term used to describe the "burning" angelic beings described by Isaiah ("seraphim"; Isa 6:2). The singular term נָחָשׁ שָׂרָף (*nāhāš śārāp*) is used in Deuteronomy 8:15 of the "venomous snakes" (collective) of the wilderness. Wenham, 156–57, associates the making of a metal snake with a Midianite shrine near Timna in which a copper snake was found.

REFLECTION

What is distinctive in this essentially judgmental text is the unusual symbol of God's grace that reaches all the way to the Savior. In the earlier judgments of the book of Numbers there was regularly the demonstration of God's wrath, the prayer of Moses for help, and the repentance of the people. These acts then usually led to some lessening of the pain of the plague until the evil ebbed away. In this plague something was truly different: there was a symbol of hope that was disgusting in nature but had healing properties that were most surprising. We find an amazing sense of God's presence in the most unlikely of places, the symbol of evil—a snake.

This was not magic but the dramatic provision of Yahweh to demand personal responses from the people. Similar actions demanded of people are found elsewhere in the OT; an example is the story of leprous Naaman, who was told to dip seven times in the Jordan to be cleansed (2Ki 5:10). The healing of the afflicted people of Israel was not in the efficacy of the metal snake any more than the cleansing of Naaman was in the purging waters of the Jordan; the issue was a purposeful and deliberate response of faith in the mercy of the Lord. The improbability of a person's being able to survive a deadly snake bite simply by looking at a metal image of a snake held high on a pole is seized on by our Lord to affirm an even greater imponderability: "Just as Moses lifted up the snake in the desert, so the Son of Man must be lifted up, that everyone who believes in him may have eternal life" (Jn 3:14-15).

The reader of John 3 is impressed with the interplay of judgment and salvation themes. This creative admixture lends itself splendidly to the interplay of serpents and deliverance. By the initiative of God, the curse becomes the basis for salvation. This is a paradox that spans the testaments.

No one reading this passage can shirk the sense of foreboding that the snake conjures in many people. The snake reaches all the way back to the garden, the unwelcome and cunning intruder. (See the pun on ʿārûm, "crafty," in Genesis 3:1, compared with ʿărûmmîm ["naked"] in 2:25.) Yet it is principally to the gospel of John that this text drives us:

the contemptible bread leads to John 6:48-51, the contemptible snake to John 3:14.

In both parallels there are portraits of the Savior, Jesus. In some circles these days, it has fallen out of style to speak of biblical types. Typology has fallen on hard times. The abuse of typology in former generations, where every spiritual lesson one might derive from a text was declared to be a "type," has led to a gradual but sure reaction against typology of any kind. Yet the idea of typology is a factor of the text of Scripture, not an innovation of "creative" interpretation (see John Bright, *The Authority of the Old Testament* [Nashville: Abingdon, 1967], 79-95).

If ever there was a less expected pairing of types, this would be it. The manna was an altogether gracious gift of God, which the people turned against as it eventually turned their stomachs. The snakes were an instrument of God's judgment because of the peoples' ingratitude and rebellious spirits; yet it was a metal copy of just such a snake that became the means of their deliverance.

The bread is a picture of Jesus; as the Bread of heaven he is the proper nourisher of his people. The bronze snake is a picture of Jesus, who became sin for us as he was suspended on that awful tree. The manna had to be eaten. The snake had to be seen. The commands of Scripture are for doing. The manna was no good if left to rot. The metal snake would not avail if none looked at it. The manna and the snake are twin aspects of the grace of God.

c. The Journey toward Moab and the Song of the Well (21:10-20)

> [10]The Israelites moved on and camped at Oboth. [11]Then they set out from Oboth and camped in Iye Abarim, in the desert that faces Moab toward the sunrise. [12]From there they moved on and camped in the Zered Valley. [13]They set out from there and camped alongside the Arnon, which is in the desert extending into Amorite territory. The Arnon is the

border of Moab, between Moab and the Amorites. ¹⁴That is why the Book of the Wars of the Lord says:

" ...Waheb in Suphah and the ravines,
   the Arnon ¹⁵and the slopes of the ravines
that lead to the site of Ar
   and lie along the border of Moab."

¹⁶From there they continued on to Beer, the well where the Lord said to Moses, "Gather the people together and I will give them water."

¹⁷Then Israel sang this song:

"Spring up, O well!
   Sing about it,
¹⁸about the well that the princes dug,
   that the nobles of the people sank—
   the nobles with scepters and staffs."

Then they went from the desert to Mattanah, ¹⁹from Mattanah to Nahaliel, from Nahaliel to Bamoth, ²⁰and from Bamoth to the valley in Moab where the top of Pisgah overlooks the wasteland.

COMMENTARY

10–12 At last the people were on the march; they skirted Edom and made their way to the Arnon (v.13), the wadi that serves as the border between the region of Moab and that of the Amorites; the Arnon flows west into the midpoint of the Dead Sea. Along the way the people made encampments at Oboth (v.10), Iye Abarim (v.11), and the Zered Valley (v.12).

13–15 This portion of the itinerary includes a quotation from a fragment of a song in an ancient book called the "Book of the Wars of the Lord" (cf. the "Book of Jashar" in Jos 10:13; 2Sa 1:18), which is mentioned only here in the OT. We may presume that this book was an ancient collection of songs of war in praise of God (see comments on 10:3 for music in war); the poem fragment attests to the variety of sources used by the author of the book.

We may call this song fragment the "Song of Places." It shows how distant we are from those days and the life they represent, for the song fragment is nearly unintelligible to us today. It seems merely to be a simple listing of names of places and their relative locations. Some have attempted to emend this text rather drastically in order to produce a "spiritual song" in which the Lord plays a significant role (see Notes). Such reconstructions are intriguing and may be (partly) correct. Yet in biblical times one might well have used songs to set in the memory various places of encampment in the wilderness. Those who were training for war in the army of the Lord (if that is the intent of the title of this old fragment) might have found that their lives would depend on knowing this ancient ditty. The reason for its inclusion here seems to be based on the catchwords "Arnon" and "Moab."

While the three short poems in this chapter (vv.14–15, 17–18, 27–30) bristle with difficulties, they provide evidence of robust poetic activity in the period of Moses and the early history of the Hebrew people. These brief songs pale beside the beauty of the "Psalm of Moses" in Exodus 15. Perhaps the most significant recent book on the poetry of the ancient world is the magnum opus by Kitchen (*Poetry of Ancient Egypt*). He terms the first (rather bare) poem that he presents "A Litany of Victory" (pp. 3–6). He dates it to ca. 3000 BC and concludes: "it ranks accordingly as the oldest known written poem in the world." All the talk from nineteenth century German critics aside—there should now be no question concerning the possibility of poetry (even great poetry) being written by Moses and his contemporaries, whether dated in the fifteenth or the thirteenth centuries BC.

16–18a The "Song of Places" (vv.14–15) leads to the "Song of the Well" in vv.17–18. The quest for water had been a constant problem during the wilderness experience (see Ex 17; Nu 20). At this new promise of water from Yahweh, the people burst forth with the triumphant words of the "Song of the Well," a dramatic departure from their earlier behavior! When the people came to a likely spot, Yahweh instructed Moses to have a well dug.

The place received the happy name *bᵉʾēr* ("Beer," meaning "well" in Hebrew). Here come also happy words from the Lord: "Gather the people together and I will give them water" (v.16). How fitting it is that this is a place of song!

The NIV's rendering of the "Song of the Well" has much energy and enjoyment to it. Quite possibly this song came from the same collection as the "Song of Places," also known as the "Book of the Wars of the LORD" (see v.14). It is possible to draw a spiritual lesson from this song, particularly since the idea of salvation and wells and springs are so closely connected (see, e.g., Isa 12). But it seems more likely that this was simply a song one might have sung in conjunction with digging a well. Instead of attempting to make some spiritual lesson from this brief song, this song is probably the nearest we come in the Bible to "popular music"—better, "folk music." In this song there is a sense of the joy of knowing God even though the name of God is not mentioned. The association of princes and nobles with the digging of a well is likely a use of "power language" to ensure that the well will last a lengthy period.

18b–20 From Beer the people journeyed ever onward and finally came to the valley of Moab; there Pisgah was a fine lookout from which to spy out the land of Canaan. Only later (Dt 34:1) do we associate this peak with Moses' final moments.

NOTES

14 C. L. Christensen ("Numbers 21:14–15 and the Book of the Wars of Yahweh," *CBQ* 36 [1974]: 359–60) translates the poem as follows:

Yahweh came in a whirlwind;
    He came to the branch wadis of the Arnon;
    He marched through the wadis;
    He marched, he turned aside to the seat of Ar.
    He leaned toward the border of Moab.

This translation involves the following emendations: (1) The term וָהֵב (wāhēb; v.14) is usually translated as a place name, "Waheb," otherwise unknown. Christensen emends it to "Yahweh" (yhwh). (2) The definite direct object marker אֶת (ʾet), which precedes this word, is emended to the verb "he came" אָתָה (ʾātâ, a fairly rare verb meaning "to come"; see its use in Dt 33:2, where אָתָה is used in parallel with the more common verb בּוֹא [bôʾ], "to come, enter"), here and in the next colon. (3) The supposed place name "Suphah" סוּפָה (sûpâ) is translated as "whirlwind" (as in Ps 83:15 [16]; Hos 8:7; Am 1:14; Na 1:3; et al.). (4) The term translated "slopes" וְאֶשֶׁד (wᵉʾešed; v.15) is emended to "he marched" אָשַׁר (ʾāšar, "to advance, move forward"), as is the relative pronoun "that" אֲשֶׁר (ʾᵃšer) in the next colon.

Christensen's approach is viewed as quite attractive by Wenham, 159–60, but as indemonstrable because of the numerous conjectures involved. Any perusal of the MT of these two verses, however, shows that this little fragment has presented numerous problems to interpreters through the ages. This fragment is a text-critical minefield.

18 נְדִיבֵי הָעָם (nᵉdîbê hāʿām, "nobles of the people") is more poetic than official in function. The noun נָדִיב (nādîb, "noble") does not have a fixed, social meaning as much as an honorific significance (paralleled with words such as צַדִּיק [ṣaddîq], "righteous," as in Pr 17:26). See J. P. Weinberg, "The word ndb in the Bible: A Study in Historical Semantics and Biblical Thought," in *Solving Riddles and Untying Knots: Biblical, Epigraphic, and Semitic Studies in Honor of Jonas C. Greenfield* (ed. Ziony Zevit et al.; Winona Lake, Ind.: Eisenbrauns, 1995), 371.

d. The Defeat of Sihon of Heshbon (21:21–31)

OVERVIEW

The victories over Sihon and Og are celebrated throughout Israel's history, even to our own day in the Passover *Haggadah*. These battles formed the true beginning of victories. The defeat of Arad was a nuisance issue. Sihon and Og represented formidable opponents; their land became part of the inheritance of the tribes of Israel. There is a sense in which the area of Transjordan is somewhat touchy; we are ambivalent about these territories. They were a part of the promise, yet they were not the heart of the land. But they were the scenes of the first victories of the Hebrew people, a note of assurance from God that the greater victories were still to come (see Notes).

²¹Israel sent messengers to say to Sihon king of the Amorites:
²²"Let us pass through your country. We will not turn aside into any field or vineyard, or drink water from any well. We will travel along the king's highway until we have passed through your territory."
²³But Sihon would not let Israel pass through his territory. He mustered his entire army and marched out into the desert against Israel. When he reached Jahaz, he fought with

Israel. ²⁴Israel, however, put him to the sword and took over his land from the Arnon to the Jabbok, but only as far as the Ammonites, because their border was fortified. ²⁵Israel captured all the cities of the Amorites and occupied them, including Heshbon and all its surrounding settlements. ²⁶Heshbon was the city of Sihon king of the Amorites, who had fought against the former king of Moab and had taken from him all his land as far as the Arnon.

²⁷That is why the poets say:

"Come to Heshbon and let it be rebuilt;
    let Sihon's city be restored.
²⁸"Fire went out from Heshbon,
    a blaze from the city of Sihon.
It consumed Ar of Moab,
    the citizens of Arnon's heights.
²⁹Woe to you, O Moab!
    You are destroyed, O people of Chemosh!
He has given up his sons as fugitives
    and his daughters as captives
    to Sihon king of the Amorites.
³⁰"But we have overthrown them;
    Heshbon is destroyed all the way to Dibon.
We have demolished them as far as Nophah,
    which extends to Medeba."

³¹So Israel settled in the land of the Amorites.

COMMENTARY

21–23 The Amorites, unlike the Edomites, were not related to the Israelites. But as in the case of their approach to Edom (20:14–19), Israel first requested a right of passage. The language of the request (v.22) is similar to what Israel had used with Edom. And the response of Sihon, king of the Amorites, was the same as Edom's—a show of force to block the Hebrews' path (v.23).

24–26 When Sihon tried to meet Israel with a show of force, he suffered an overwhelming defeat (v.24). The Transjordanian land of the Amorites extended from the Arnon River at the midpoint of the Dead Sea to the Jabbok River (v.24), which flows into the Jordan River some twenty-four miles north of the Dead Sea. Among Israel's conquests were the cities of Heshbon and its dependent settlements (v.25). Heshbon had originally been a Moabite territory (see vv.25–30); Israel, however, wrested it from Sihon and the Amorite conquerors. It was this victory that cast a pale of fear into the Moabites (see 22:2–3). The syllogism was clear: Sihon had defeated Moab; Israel now defeated

Sihon; Moab was next, and their defeat seemed imminent. Thus Balak king of Moab wished to transfer the battle arena from the field of men to the realm of the gods (see comment on 22:5–7).

27–30 Numbers 21 is unusual in its inclusion of three short songs. Possibly each of the three (vv.14–15, 17–18, 27–30) was included in the "Book of the Wars of the LORD" (see v.14). This third song in ch. 21, the "Taunt Song of Heshbon," was originally an Amorite song celebrating their earlier victory over Moab (v.29); thus the phrase, "why the poets say" (v.27). Heshbon, the capital city of Sihon, had been wrested by the Amorites from an earlier Moabite king. Perhaps this king was Zippor, the father of Balak (see 22:2). A. H. van Zyl (*The Moabites* [Praetoria Oriental Series 3; Leiden: Brill, 1960], 7–10) observes that taunt songs were regularly used in warfare. If this was a song originally used against the Moabites, whom the Amorites had recently conquered, its reuse here by Israel must have been particularly galling to Moab. Indeed, it may serve as the "last nail in the coffin"—the reason for Moab's call for Balaam.

In any ancient taunt song such as this, more was at stake than the reputation of the armies or the kings who participated in the battle. Ultimately, the outcome of a war in the ancient Near East was evaluated in terms of victories and defeats of respective gods. Note, for example, the dramatic story in 1 Kings 20 of the first battle between Ben

Hadad of Aram (Syria) and Ahab of Israel. When the Israelites won this battle, the counselors of Ben Hadad instructed him on ways to improve his position for the next year's encounter (1Ki 20:23–25). Their first line of advice was to fight the next battle on a plain rather than in the hills. They were positive that the Israelites won the battle because "their gods are gods of the hills" (v.23). Presumably, if they moved the battle to a turf that Israel's "gods" did not control, the battle would be won for the Arameans (whose gods were believed to be powerful on level plains).

In the "Taunt Song of Heshbon," it was not just the people of Moab who had been defeated by Sihon in the earlier engagement; it was their god Chemosh as well (v.29). But now a new God had come on the scene. His name was Yahweh, and his power was not limited by geography at all!

Since Israel had defeated the nation that had been the victor over Moab, the Moabites knew that they would likely fare poorly in battle against Israel. The victory of Israel over this nation gave them a new song to sing in irony and triumph. Verse 30 of the Song of Heshbon must have sent Moab reeling (see Notes).

31 The concluding verse of this section is a dramatic mark of accomplishment. After forty years of sojourn in the Desert of Sinai, now, at last, the people had entered the land of the Amorites—the land that would become theirs.

NOTES

21 J. van Seters ("The Conquest of Sihon's Kingdom: A Literary Examination," *JBL* 91 [1972]: 182–97) has argued strongly against the historical validity of the account of Israel's conquest of these Transjordanian kingdoms. He maintains that the editor-redactor of Numbers 21 borrowed heavily from the (late) Deuteronomic tradition (see Dt 2:26–37; Jdg 11:19–26). His rather negative assessment is countered by John R. Bartlett in his rejoinder, "The Conquest of Sihon's Kingdom: A Literary Re-Examination," *JBL* 97 (1978): 347–51. Bartlett deals with each of van Seters' points seriatim and concludes that it is more likely that the

Deuteronomic passage is dependent on the text of Numbers, "for Deuteronomy removes the inconsistencies and clarifies the point left obscure in Numbers" (351). See also John R. Bartlett, "Sihon and Og, Kings of the Amorites," *VT* 20 (1970): 257–77, for a critical analysis of the biblical representation of these two kings and their kingdoms in the biblical traditions.

30 Critical scholars have suggested numerous settings for this song other than that presented in this chapter. Martin Noth, for example, relates the victory song of Numbers 21 to the events of 32:28–36, the story of Gad's victory in Transjordan (*The Old Testament World* [trans. Victor I. Gruhn; Philadelphia: Fortress, 1966], 75). Earlier, Bruno Baentsch (*Exodus–Leviticus–Numeri* [HAT; Göttingen: Vandenhoeck und Ruprecht, 1903], 584) held that the song referred to the defeat of Mesha, king of Moab, by Omri, king of Israel.

אֲשֶׁר (ᵃšer, "which") is one of fifteen words in the MT that the scribes questioned by adding a dot or point over a letter (*punctum extraordinarius*); in this case the dot is over the ר (r). Ginsburg, 326–28, concludes that the ancient reasons proffered for this dot are unsatisfactory; he argues that the dot was added to mark a word that was defective and concludes that the word should be read as אִישׁ (ᵓîš, "man") as the parallel for וַנַּשִּׁים (wannaššîm, "women") in the earlier, parallel colon. He gives the following reconstruction as the probably original text of this difficult verse (with the explanation that the second bicolon explains that it was the people of Heshbon who were killed rather than that cities were destroyed):

We have shot at them,
    Heshbon is destroyed even unto Dibon
The women also even unto Nopha
    And the men even unto Medeba.

31 J. van Seters ("The Terms 'Amorite' and 'Hittite' in the Old Testament," *VT* 22 [1972]: 64–81) views the term "Amorite" as an ideological and rhetorical term superimposed according to the Hebrew writer's later thought rather than reflecting the historical situation in the land. To him the term moves in the direction of representing "super-human evil." Without our accepting his critical evaluation of the historicity of the text of Numbers 21, it is possible for us to agree that van Seters points in a constructive direction when he speaks of the connotation of this term. He says (81), "One must be very skeptical about attributing any historicity to the conquest of the Amorite kingdoms of Sihon and Og in Transjordan. The accounts serve primarily as etiologies legitimizing Israel's territorial claims east of the Jordan." The "Amorites" were a symbol of evil, and Israel now rightly had come to dispossess them.

e. Israel's Defeat of Og of Bashan (21:32–22:1)

³²After Moses had sent spies to Jazer, the Israelites captured its surrounding settlements and drove out the Amorites who were there. ³³Then they turned and went up along the road toward Bashan, and Og king of Bashan and his whole army marched out to meet them in battle at Edrei.

> ³⁴The Lᴏʀᴅ said to Moses, "Do not be afraid of him, for I have handed him over to you, with his whole army and his land. Do to him what you did to Sihon king of the Amorites, who reigned in Heshbon."
> ³⁵So they struck him down, together with his sons and his whole army, leaving them no survivors. And they took possession of his land.
> ²²:¹Then the Israelites traveled to the plains of Moab and camped along the Jordan across from Jericho.

COMMENTARY

32–35 The region of this king and his people was east of the Sea of Galilee. By defeating Og, Israel became the victor over Transjordan from the region of Moab to the heights of Bashan in the vicinity of Mount Hermon. The victories over Sihon and Og were matters for singing (Pss 135:11; 136:19–20) and regular parts of the commemoration of the works of the Lord in the Passover celebration.

Significantly, this section begins with a notice that Moses sent spies to scout out the land before he began his attack on the region of Bashan (v.32). These spies must have done as they were instructed, in contrast to the rebellious tribal agents or spies of chs. 13–14. It is also notable that the battle was joined with the army of Og only after the word of the Lord had come to Moses assuring him of a divine victory (vv.33–34). This was to be the pattern of holy war, an obedient people following the sure word of their great God. The victory was complete because God's ways were followed (v.35).

22:1 This section ends in 22:1 with the statement of the journey of Israel to the plains of Moab and their subsequent encampment near the Jordan River across from the city of Jericho. They were now on the lip of the land; Canaan—God's gift—was in view. Soon the land would be theirs. But this verse also sets the stage for one of the most remarkable stories in the Bible—the dramatic encounter of Balaam, the pagan mantic, with Yahweh the God of Israel (22:2–24:25).

Thus ch. 21 of Numbers presents a remarkable shift in the fortunes of the people. They were still rebellious (and would continue to rebel—see ch. 25), but they were now on a victory march, not fearful of battle against the people of the land. At least they had learned this lesson from their parents: When God is for us, what can humans do against us? (cf. Ps 118:6). The wilderness still had sand, but the Hebrews were now moving with God—and they were moving away from that sand!

f. Balak and Balaam (22:2–41)

OVERVIEW

The misplaced verse number at the beginning of ch. 22 helps us read the story of Balak and Balaam in the context of the emerging power and nascent victories of Israel. The story of Balaam's dramatic encounter with the Lord is of a piece. It stands by itself as a remarkable unit of great writing. Even though documentary scholars believe these three chapters afford them something of a field day in putative source analysis (see Note on 22:2), none-theless the story reads as a unified whole; and it stands alone on its own merit.

i. The "call" of Balaam (22:2–20)

²Now Balak son of Zippor saw all that Israel had done to the Amorites, ³and Moab was terrified because there were so many people. Indeed, Moab was filled with dread because of the Israelites.

⁴The Moabites said to the elders of Midian, "This horde is going to lick up everything around us, as an ox licks up the grass of the field."

So Balak son of Zippor, who was king of Moab at that time, ⁵sent messengers to summon Balaam son of Beor, who was at Pethor, near the River, in his native land. Balak said:

"A people has come out of Egypt; they cover the face of the land and have settled next to me. ⁶Now come and put a curse on these people, because they are too power-ful for me. Perhaps then I will be able to defeat them and drive them out of the country. For I know that those you bless are blessed, and those you curse are cursed."

⁷The elders of Moab and Midian left, taking with them the fee for divination. When they came to Balaam, they told him what Balak had said.

⁸"Spend the night here," Balaam said to them, "and I will bring you back the answer the Lord gives me." So the Moabite princes stayed with him.

⁹God came to Balaam and asked, "Who are these men with you?"

¹⁰Balaam said to God, "Balak son of Zippor, king of Moab, sent me this message: ¹¹'A people that has come out of Egypt covers the face of the land. Now come and put a curse on them for me. Perhaps then I will be able to fight them and drive them away.'"

¹²But God said to Balaam, "Do not go with them. You must not put a curse on those people, because they are blessed."

¹³The next morning Balaam got up and said to Balak's princes, "Go back to your own country, for the Lord has refused to let me go with you."

¹⁴So the Moabite princes returned to Balak and said, "Balaam refused to come with us."

¹⁵Then Balak sent other princes, more numerous and more distinguished than the first. ¹⁶They came to Balaam and said:

"This is what Balak son of Zippor says: Do not let anything keep you from coming to me, ¹⁷because I will reward you handsomely and do whatever you say. Come and put a curse on these people for me."

¹⁸But Balaam answered them, "Even if Balak gave me his palace filled with silver and gold, I could not do anything great or small to go beyond the command of the Lord my God. ¹⁹Now stay here tonight as the others did, and I will find out what else the Lord will tell me."

> ²⁰That night God came to Balaam and said, "Since these men have come to summon you, go with them, but do only what I tell you."

COMMENTARY

2–3 The story of Balaam begins with the gut-wrenching fear of Balak, son of Zippor, king of Moab. With the vast army of Israel now encamped on the edge of his territory, he feared the worst. The text uses the verb *gûr* ("was terrified"; v.3) to describe his fear, indicated by the adverb *meʾōd* ("very") as intensified, then brought into even sharper focus by the strong term *qûṣ* ("to feel a sickening dread"; "filled with dread," NIV; GK 7762). Rabbi Hirsch, 390, explains that this verb suggests that which causes such violent emotion within that it may provoke one to vomit: "All that they had became distasteful, despicable, yea repulsive at the thought of the children of Israel" (cf. Marcus Jastrow, *A Dictionary of the Targumim, the Talmud Babli and Yerushalmi, and the Midrashic Literature* [2 vols.; New York: Pardes, 1950], 2:1339).

Balak's fear was intensified because of the victories Israel had recently won over his neighboring northern enemies (see Nu 21). A new, stronger enemy was now present—one before whom Balak and his people seemed powerless. Balak was not aware that Israel actually had no designs on the land of Moab. Yahweh was about to give Canaan to Israel, but the land of Moab was a gift of the Lord to Moab. In fact, the Lord had prohibited the Hebrews from any attack on the territorial integrity of Moab in their wars of conquest (Dt 2:9). Israel, under God's blessing, fell under divine limits. God was sovereign over all Israel's actions.

Yet there was a reason for Moab's fear: The events of the exodus and the salvation of Israel were designed by the Lord to provoke fear in all nations

(see Dt 2:25). The defeat of the Amorite kings Sihon and Og to the north of Moab (21:21–35; cf. Dt 2:26–3:11) put it in an especially difficult position. The taunt song of 21:27–30 would have been particularly galling to Moab (see above).

4 The proverbial figure of an ox licking the grass is particularly fitting for a pastoral people. Balak knew how quickly the fragile grasses of the lands of Moab could be eaten by large numbers of beasts given free range. The image of Israel as an ox is an emphatic symbol of her strength and power. The association of Moab to the Midianites in this verse is more significant than we might first think. It would be another plot developed by the Midianites in collusion with Moab that would finally bring great disaster on Israel (ch. 25, Israel's apostasy at Baal Peor).

5–7 Balak believed that there was no available military means to allow them to withstand the forces of Israel. Hence he sought to battle Israel on the level of pagan divination. He sent for a diviner with an international reputation, Balaam son of Beor (v.5)—a drastic move to use the supernatural means of the effective curse. This move was predicated on the pervasive belief in the ancient world of the power of the spoken word. The diviner with the most remarkable reputation of the day, it turns out, was Balaam.

Balaam should be understood to be the pagan counterpart to Moses the man of God. The discovery of texts attributed to Balaam at Deir ʿAlla in Jordan compares to the 1993 discovery at Tel Dan of the "Beit David" inscription, concerning which many articles have been written. Pride of place goes to the initial presentation by its discoverers. See Avraham Biran and Joseph Naveh, "An Aramaic Stele Fragment from Tel Dan," *IEJ* 43 (1993): 81–98; the same authors prepared this major report, "'David' Found at Dan: Inscription Crowns Twenty-Seven Years of Exciting Discoveries," *BAR* 20/2 (March/April, 1994): 26–39. In each case, we now have the first instance of these names (Balaam and David) found in demonstrably ancient texts outside the Bible.

The recovery of the prophetic texts of Balaam in Aramaic from the sixth century at Deir ʿAlla demonstrates how famous this man was in the ancient Near East, even centuries after his death (see Jacob Hoftijzer, "The Prophet Balaam in a 6th-Century Aramaic Inscription," *BA* 39/1 [March 1976]: 11–17). The fact that the prophetic text was written on a wall indicates that it was an important historical example of the oracles of this diviner that might be preserved for posterity. Stephen A. Kaufman observes that the texts of these inscriptions "remain enticingly obscure" and that perhaps we need the powers of a Balaam to help banish the darkness ("Review Article: The Aramaic Texts from Deir ʿAlla," *BASOR* 239 [Summer 1980]: 71–74).

Balaam, it turns out, was an internationally known prophet, a diviner expert in examining the entrails of animals and observing natural phenomena to determine the will of the gods. He was not a good prophet who went bad or a bad prophet who was trying to be good. He was altogether outside Israel's prophetic tradition, but he must have thought that the Lord God of Israel was like any other deity he could manipulate by mantic acts. But from the early part of the narrative, when he first encountered the true God in visions, and in the humorous narrative of the journey on the donkey, Balaam began to learn what for him was a strange, bizarre, even incomprehensible lesson: An encoun-

ter with the God of reality was fundamentally different from anything he had ever known.

Verse 5 presents several problems of the interpretation of words. The name "Balaam" seems to be an example of a deliberate corruption of names by the Hebrew scribes; the transparent meaning of his name, *bilʿām*, is "devourer of the people" (see Notes). The letter of Balak to Balaam indicates the intent he had: to bring a curse on a people who were under a blessing of a god. This story thus takes us into the mysterious world of blessing and cursing in the ancient Near East. It was believed that some persons were agents of the gods who could utter curses or blessings that would bind the will of the gods to these declarations. Since Israel seemed to Moab to be too formidable a force to attack on the battlefield, the decision—prompted by Balak's Midianite advisors—was to attack them on a spiritual level. If their blessing could be destroyed, they would no longer be a threat.

8–11 The language of v.8 and the conversation Balaam had with the Lord in this section have led many readers to believe that Balaam actually was a believer in Yahweh, the God of Israel. The most significant phrasing along this line comes in his words of v.18: "the LORD my God." It seems best, however, based on the subsequent narrative, to take Balaam's words as examples of braggadocio. Balaam is universally condemned in the Scripture for moral, ethical, and religious faults (see 31:8, 16; Dt 23:3–6; Jos 13:22; 24:9–10; Jdg 11:23–25; Ne 13:1–3; Mic 6:5; 2Pe 2:15–16; Jude 11; Rev 2:14).

The character of Balaam continues to be a conundrum in biblical study. From the early church fathers to the most recent interpreters, many have argued that he was a good prophet who went bad, or a bad prophet who attempted to go right. The classic study of his person by Bishop Joseph Butler ("Upon the Character of Balaam," in *The Works of the Right Reverend Father in God Joseph Butler, D.C.L., Late*

Lord Bishop of Durham [Oxford: Oxford Univ. Press, 1850], 2:80) concluded: "So ... the object we have now before us is the most astonishing in the world: a very wicked man, under a deep sense of God and religion, persisting still in his wickedness, and preferring the wages of unrighteousness, even when he had before him a lively view of death.... Good God, what inconsistency, what perplexity is here!"

Rather than see Balaam as a true believer in Yahweh who was caught up in greed, it is preferable for us to understand that he was a sorcerer, more specifically, a *bārū* ("diviner"; see Note on v.8), for whom the God of Israel was just another deity he thought he might manipulate. Samuel Daiches ("Balaam—A Babylonian *bārū*," in *Assyrische und Archaeologische Studien: H. V. Hilprecht gewidmet* [Leipzig: Hinrichs, 1909], 60–70) argued that the considerable emphasis on magical elements in these chapters is best explained by understanding Balaam as a *bārū* diviner of the Mesopotamian type (see esp. v.7, "the fees for divination"; Jos 13:22 speaks of Balaam as "the soothsayer" [*haqqôsēm*] "who practiced divination" [NIV]). Daiches finds special interest in the descriptions in 22:40–41, the preparatory sacrifice; 23:1–2, the offering of seven bulls and seven rams on seven altars; 23:2, the sacrifices brought by both the diviner and the person for whom he divines; 23:3, the expression of Balak as "the owner of the sacrifice" standing by his offering; 23:3, the difficult word *šepî*, usually translated "barren height" but possibly instead better rendered as "quietly" or "step by step," describing the manner of Balaam's mantic acts. William Albright, 231, regarded the researches of Daiches as in the main valid and impressive; they seem to point to the correct view.

The narrator of this chapter shows his strong aversion to the pagan prophet Balaam by the interchange of the name for God (Yahweh, "the LORD") in Balaam's mouth (v.8) and the term "God" as the narrator speaks of him (v.9). By this subtle interchange, the narrator demonstrates his distance from Balaam's outrageous claims. That God did speak to Balaam is not to be denied; it is just that Balaam did not yet realize that the God of Israel was not like the supposed deities of his usual machinations.

12–20 The words of v.12 reveal the nature of the crisis. Israel was under the blessing of the Lord as the heritage of the Abrahamic covenant (Ge 12:1–3). Balaam was being sought by Balak to bring Israel under a divine curse; this situation God would not allow, for Israel was "blessed." Moreover, one who would attempt to curse Israel would bring himself under God's curse (cf. Ge 12:3). The story of Balaam is thus an example of the folly of attempting to destroy the eternal blessing of the people of the Lord.

The first words of God to Balaam prohibited him from accompanying the emissaries of Balak (v.12). But when these emissaries returned to Balak, he would not accept their report of Balaam's refusal to come with them. He sent grander and nobler representatives, with greater and finer promises of gifts for this mantic to return with them (v.15). In these descriptions we discover potent images from the Eastern world. Balaam first said that nothing could change his mind (v.18). Then in a dream he was given permission to go with them (v.20).

There appears to be a contradiction between the permission God granted to Balaam in v.20 and the prohibition he had issued earlier (v.12), as well as the anger of the Lord that was displayed against Balaam on his journey (v.22). The difficulty is best seen as lying in the contrary character of Balaam rather than in some fickle flaw in the character of God. God first had forbidden him to go to Moab to curse Israel; then God allowed Balaam to go to Moab, but only as he would speak at the direction of the Lord. Balaam's real intentions, however, were known to the Lord, and hence in his severe displeasure he confronted the pagan mantic on the road.

NOTES

2 The text of Numbers 22 has been used by some critical scholars as a primary locus to test their approaches to the source analysis of the Bible. A. H. Edelkoort (*Numeri* [Tekst en Uitleg: Praktische Bijbelverklaring; Groningen: Bij J. B. Wolters' Uitgevers-Maatschappij, 1930], 170), for example, speaks of the Balaam story as the result of "three threads promiscuously twisted"; he concludes (p. 21) that the final redaction did not come before the time of Second Isaiah, after ca. 500 BC. Ladislas Martin von Pákozdy ("Theologische Redaktionsarbeit in der Bileam-Perikope [Num 22–24]," in *Von Ugarit Nach Qumran* [Berlin: Alfred Töplemann, 1958], 176) remarks on the masterful skill of the final redactor who, "forming so artfully of his ancient and written tradition, and in the spirit of the prophetic religion, was able to create such a unity out of diverse theological concepts" (all trans. of foreign sources are mine). My approach will presume a unified whole in the text as it stands. Questions of the origin of these chapters are highly interesting, but the answers appear to be unusually subjective.

5 Some critical scholars, such as Sigmund Mowinckel ("Der Ursprung der Bil'amsage," *ZAW* 48 [1930]: 237), have suggested that Balaam and Bela (Ge 36:32) were confused in the Scriptures, as they are both called "the son of Beor." However, Albright, 231, argued strongly that such an association cannot be maintained, suggesting that the original name of Balaam might have been something such as *Yabil-ʿammu* (an Amorite name from the thirteenth century BC made up of an imperfect plus a divine name), a name meaning "The [divine] uncle brings forth." The Hebrew connotation, "The devourer of the people," was an intentional change, not unlike the change of the original name of Jezebel from that which honored Baal to that which held Baal in contempt. The process in debasing her name involved the dropping of the letter בּ (*bĕt*); an original אֲבִיזֶבֶל (*ᵃbîzebel*, "My [divine] Father is Prince") became the corrupted form אִיזֶבֶל (*ʾîzebel*, "Un-exalted"; see Leah Bronner, *The Stories of Elijah and Elisha as Polemics against Baal Worship* [Leiden: Brill, 1968], 9–10); the element אִי (*ʾî*) is the Phoenician negation. See also the discussion below on the meaning of the name of Cozbi (Nu 25:14), the woman who joined Zimri in defiling the entrance to the Holy Place.

פְּתוֹרָה (*pᵉtôrâ*, "at Pethor") may be identified as a reference to the city Pitru (Pi-it-ru) of the Assyrian texts, a city located on the river Sagur, near its junction with the Euphrates (indicated by the words "the River" in this verse). Pitru is mentioned by Shalmaneser III (ca. 859–824 BC) in the annalistic report of 853 BC. L. Yaure, however ("Elymas–Nehelamite–Pethor," *JBL* 79 [1960]: 297–314), says that this term should be translated not as a place name but as a descriptive nomen agentis, "the interpreter."

בְּנֵי־עַמּוֹ (*bᵉnê-ʿammô*, "in his native land") is perhaps the most difficult of the phrases to identify in this verse. The NIV has rephrased the traditional understanding, "in the land of the sons of his people" (as in the LXX). Albright ("Some Important Recent Discoveries: Alphabetic Origins and the Idrimi Statue," *BASOR* 118 [1950]: 11–20), in an article describing an inscription on a statue of King Idrimi of Alalakh (ca. 1480–1450 BC), believed he had found the solution to this phrase as a place name. He observed that Idrimi, king of Alalakh, ruled also over three lands: Mukishkhe, Niʾ, and ʿAmau, the last being the place intended by our text—the land of ʿAmau, the region of the Sajur Valley between Aleppo and Carchemish. This translation has been accepted by the NEB, JB, and La Sainte Bible/Segond. The resultant translation of v.5 with all these data in place would be: "So he sent messengers to Balaam the son of Beor, to Pethor [Pitru], which is near the River [Euphrates] in the land of the people of ʿAmau."

These several data all suggest that Balaam was a North Syrian from the northern Euphrates Valley, near Haran of the patriarchal stories. Such accords remarkably well with the words of his opening bicola (23:7a, pers. trans.):

Balak brought me from Aram,
the king of Moab from the eastern mountains.

Further, this location for Balaam places him in the general area of Laban, called "the land of the eastern peoples" (Ge 29:1) and Paddan Aram (Ge 25:20). It is also the general area of the newer view of the possible location of Ur, the hometown of Abram and Sarai (rather than the great city of Ur near the Persian Gulf, excavated by Sir Leonard Woolley). This viewpoint has been advanced since the discovery and publication of texts from Ebla (beginning in 1976), where a northwestern Ur is indicated. (See Barry J. Beitzel, *The Moody Atlas of the Bible Lands* [Chicago: Moody Press, 1985], 82–83, map 24; see also discussion by Walter C. Kaiser Jr., *A History of Israel: From the Bronze Age through the Jewish Wars* [Nashville: Broadman & Holman, 1998], 55–57.)

On Balaam as a "liver diviner" (one who engaged in extispicy) as described in the text, see William W. Hallo, "Before Tea Leaves: Divination in Ancient Babylonia," *BAR* (March/April 2005): 32–39; a review and explanation article of a major work by Danish Assyriologist Ulla Koch-Westenholz, *Babylonian Liver Omens: The Chapters Manzazu, Padanu and Pan Takalti of the Babylonian Extispicy Series, Mainly from Aššurbanipal's Library* (Copenhagen: Carsten Niebuhr Institute of Near Eastern Studies, University of Copenhagen, Museum Tuscalam Press, 2000).

6 Three times in this verse Balak uses forms of the Hebrew verb אָרַר (*'ārar*, "to curse, bind with a curse"; GK 826). This verb is cognate to the Akkadian *'araru* A ("to curse," or in weaker contexts, "to treat with disrespect"; *CAD* I, "A" Part II, 234–36). One example of this word in an Akkadian text illustrates its foreboding connotation:

May the great gods of heaven and nether world curse him [*li-ru-ru (šu)*], his descendants, his land, his soldiers, his people, and his army with a baleful curse; may Enlil with his unalterable utterance curse him [*li-ru-ur-šu-ma*] with these curses so that they speedily affect him. [*CAD* I, "A" Part II, 235]

This example has the element of the inflexible nature of a curse once uttered. There is a sense in which the curse may be said to be "bound" on one. The Hebrew cognate אָרַר (*'ārar*) seems to be associated with effective force, too, as is certainly true when God is the actor or the subject of the verb (see Ge 3:14, "cursed [אָרוּר, *'ārûr*] are you more than all cattle"; 12:3, "I will curse [אָאֹר, *'ā'ōr*]."

Paul van Imschoot writes in *Theology of the Old Testament* (trans. Kathryn Sullivan and Fidelis Buck; Tournai: Desclee & Co., 1965), 1:189–90:

The efficacy of the word is attributed either to the formula itself—this is the case of the magic formulas of all countries and times—or to the power of him who says it; also then it may be considered as capable of constraining the gods and remains in the sphere of magic.... In Israel, without doubt, the use of magic formulas has existed at all times among the lower classes, but has been reproved by the official religion (Ex 22:17; Lev 20:6, 27; Dt 18:9–13; 1Sa 15:23; 28:3; Mic 5:11; Jer 27:9; Ez 13:18–20; Mal 3:5). The efficacy of curses and of blessings is derived from Yahweh (Pr 3:33; Sir 4:6; Ge 12:3; Nu 22:6; 23:8); the curse can be obstructed

(Nu 22:22 ff.), weakened (Pr 26:2), or changed into a blessing by Yahweh (Dt 23:6); it is ordinarily pronounced in the form of a prayer (Jer 15:15; 18:19–23; Ps 109, etc.).

U. Cassuto (*A Commentary on the Book of Genesis* [trans. Israel Abrahams; Jerusalem: Magnes Press, The Hebrew University, 1961, 1964], 2:155) also observed the ancient belief in the power of the spoken curse to effect the will of gods in the lives and destinies of the peoples:

> In the ancient East there was current the belief, based on the concept of the magic power of the spoken word, that blessings and curses, and particularly curses, once uttered, act automatically and are fulfilled of their own accord, as it were, unless another force opposes and annuls them.

But Cassuto goes on to explain, 2:156, that in the true religion of Israel such ideas are intolerable:

> The sublime religion of Israel cannot acquiesce in such a conception. In the view of Israel's Torah, it is impossible to imagine that a man's word should have the power to effect anything without God's will, for only from the Lord do evil and good issue. Human blessings are, according to the Torah, no more than wishes and prayers that God may be willing to do this or that. So, too, human imprecations, in so far as they are not iniquitous, are, in the ultimate analysis, but prayers that God may act in a given way.

8 On the meaning of *bārū*, Noordtzij, 199, says:

> The *bārū* belongs to the priestly class, and his specialty is "seeing" what will happen on the basis of phenomena that escape the common person, but are found, e.g., in the liver of a ritually slaughtered animal, or in the configuration of drops of oil on water, or in the stars, or in the shape of the clouds. Such *bārūs* were believed to be able to influence the will of the gods because of their secret knowledge and mysterious manipulations, and to force the gods to do, or not to do, a given thing.

A most freakish approach to the complex problem of the character of Balaam was taken by James Black ("A Discharge for Balaam," in *Rogues of the Bible* [New York: Harper & Brothers, 1930], 59–79). (I owe thanks to Tremper Longman III for his apt suggestion of the use of "freakish" to describe this anti-Semitic and racist point of view.) He argued that the *good* Balaam has been confused by "Jewish prejudice in the Bible" with a *wicked* man of the same name; one was a true worshiper of the Lord, and the other was a soothsayer or oracle-monger of the Midianites. With great passion, he said that it is the duty of Christian people to rediscover and then "to rehabilitate the true Balaam, to grant him a discharge from the world's calumnies." The good Balaam was a "great white soul who loved the will of God to his own worldly loss," but Jewish prejudice against seeing a Gentile believer in the Lord led them deliberately to confuse the textual witness to his character.

An unusually bizarre approach to Balaam is proffered by Mary Douglas, self-described as an "anthropologist of Scripture." She opines that the story was written in the fifth century as a veiled satire against the pompous Nehemiah! In *In the Wilderness: The Doctrine of Defilement in the Book of Numbers* (Oxford: Oxford Univ. Press, 2001), 233, she writes:

> Nehemiah is a natural butt. One of the strange things about his political history is that it is written like a private confession to God. The way he dramatizes himself, his sanctimoniousness and self-glorification, are ridiculous. He thinks he can do anything, he admits he beats people up (Ne 13:25), he makes out he knows what God

wants, but he does not. Balaam works well as a skit on Nehemiah, stupidly berating and beating the ass on which he rides. With this reading the animal has to be a female, because she stands for Israel. The people of Israel recognize the Lord better than the governor.

ii. The donkey story (22:21–41)

²¹Balaam got up in the morning, saddled his donkey and went with the princes of Moab. ²²But God was very angry when he went, and the angel of the Lord stood in the road to oppose him. Balaam was riding on his donkey, and his two servants were with him. ²³When the donkey saw the angel of the Lord standing in the road with a drawn sword in his hand, she turned off the road into a field. Balaam beat her to get her back on the road.

²⁴Then the angel of the Lord stood in a narrow path between two vineyards, with walls on both sides. ²⁵When the donkey saw the angel of the Lord, she pressed close to the wall, crushing Balaam's foot against it. So he beat her again.

²⁶Then the angel of the Lord moved on ahead and stood in a narrow place where there was no room to turn, either to the right or to the left. ²⁷When the donkey saw the angel of the Lord, she lay down under Balaam, and he was angry and beat her with his staff. ²⁸Then the Lord opened the donkey's mouth, and she said to Balaam, "What have I done to you to make you beat me these three times?"

²⁹Balaam answered the donkey, "You have made a fool of me! If I had a sword in my hand, I would kill you right now."

³⁰The donkey said to Balaam, "Am I not your own donkey, which you have always ridden, to this day? Have I been in the habit of doing this to you?"

"No," he said.

³¹Then the Lord opened Balaam's eyes, and he saw the angel of the Lord standing in the road with his sword drawn. So he bowed low and fell facedown.

³²The angel of the Lord asked him, "Why have you beaten your donkey these three times? I have come here to oppose you because your path is a reckless one before me. ³³The donkey saw me and turned away from me these three times. If she had not turned away, I would certainly have killed you by now, but I would have spared her."

³⁴Balaam said to the angel of the Lord, "I have sinned. I did not realize you were standing in the road to oppose me. Now if you are displeased, I will go back."

³⁵The angel of the Lord said to Balaam, "Go with the men, but speak only what I tell you." So Balaam went with the princes of Balak.

³⁶When Balak heard that Balaam was coming, he went out to meet him at the Moabite town on the Arnon border, at the edge of his territory. ³⁷Balak said to Balaam, "Did I not send you an urgent summons? Why didn't you come to me? Am I really not able to reward you?"

³⁸"Well, I have come to you now," Balaam replied. "But can I say just anything? I must speak only what God puts in my mouth."

³⁹Then Balaam went with Balak to Kiriath Huzoth. ⁴⁰Balak sacrificed cattle and sheep, and gave some to Balaam and the princes who were with him. ⁴¹The next morning Balak took Balaam up to Bamoth Baal, and from there he saw part of the people.

COMMENTARY

21–28 The pagan mantic, the donkey, and the angel of the Lord were brought together in this truly tragicomic scene. The internationally known seer was blind to the reality of the angel of the Lord, but his proverbially dumb beast was able to see the spiritual reality of the living God on the path. Balaam as a *bārû* prophet was a specialist in animal divination. Here his own "stupid" animal saw what he was too blind to observe.

Against the assertion of many critical scholars who state that the episode with the donkey contributes nothing to the story line, both Mowinckel ("Der Ursprung," 260) and von Pákozdy ("Theologische Redaktionsarbeit," 17–72; see Notes on 22:2–20) have noted that the episode serves the purpose of slowing the action and heightening the tension of the story. In fact, it is the "best part" of the story (so Goldberg, 106), which is one of studied ridicule. We observe the prophet Balaam as the blind seer who saw less than a dumb animal. In this graphic representation of Balaam pitted against the donkey, we also notice a more important contrast, as Goldberg avers: the contrast of Balaam and Moses. The long shadow of Moses falls across the pages of the Balaam story even though Moses is never named once. Moses spoke face to face with God (see ch. 12); Balaam did not even know that God was near—but his donkey did!

This section is the ultimate in polemics against paganism. It is well known that the ass has been depicted from the earliest times in proverbial thought and literature as a subject of stupidity and contrariness. Yet here the "stupid" ass saw the angel of the Lord and she then attempted to protect her rider from God's drawn sword. Three times the hapless Balaam beat his donkey.

Then the donkey spoke (v.28). Some have imagined too much here. The donkey did not give a prophetic oracle; she merely said what a mistreated animal might say to an abusive master if given the chance. There was no preaching from the donkey! Others have stumbled, of course, at the improbability of an animal's speaking, for such is the stuff of fairy tales. What keeps this story from the genre of legend or fairy tale is the clear fact that the animal did not speak of its own accord but as it was given the power to do so by the Lord. Only an exceedingly limited view of God would deny him the ability to open the mouth of a dumb animal; such an objection should lead one to a rereading of Job 40–41.

Noth, 179, observes that the speaking of the ass is not particularly stressed but is an integral part of the story and is attributed to a miracle on the part of the Lord, "which indicates how directly and unusually Yahweh acted in this affair of blessing or curse for Israel." The speaking of the donkey is affirmed in the NT (2Pe 2:16); it was a genuine element in the righteous acts of the Lord. It is not that this miracle is the focus of the text; on the contrary, the miracle is just an amazingly humorous way to humiliate the prophet Balaam. Before the Lord revealed himself to Balaam, he first "got his attention" in this dramatic fashion. Balaam had to learn from a donkey before he could learn from God. This episode is one of the most amusing stories in the Bible.

29–30 The high camp of the story is furthered by Balaam's words, "If I had a sword in my hand, I would kill you right now" (v.29). The ridiculous picture of the hapless Balaam looking for a sword is precious; there was a sword very near, but the object was not about to be the donkey (vv.23, 31–33). Again, the donkey said only what a donkey who was being so abused might say. We err in talking about this text as though God spoke through the donkey. Here is no oracle, no prophecy, no poem; she merely said she had been a good donkey. We also laugh as we hear Balaam talking with her, as though nothing were out of the ordinary. So heightened is his rage that he doesn't even show surprise at the voice that comes from his donkey. So who (or what) is really "dumb" here?

31–33 The wording "Then the LORD opened Balaam's eyes" follows the same structure as in v.28, "Then the LORD opened the donkey's mouth." The opening of the eyes of the pagan prophet to see the reality of the living God was the greater miracle. The animal was but a brute beast; the prophet was a man bent on trafficking with false gods.

34–35 The words of Balaam to God, "I have sinned" (v.34), might lead us to think that he was truly repentant. Only the later outcome of the story shows this conclusion to be false (see chs. 25 and 31). His appears to have been the confession of error of sorts, but it was a confession that fell short of the repentance of saving faith. Doubtless Balaam spoke with one eye on the sword that menaced from above.

The Lord told Balaam to continue on his journey but to "speak only what I tell you" (v.35). The point of the whole chapter is this: Balaam the pagan mantic would not be able to utter curses as he had planned to do. Instead, he would be the most surprised of all; he would be the most remarkable instrument of God in blessing his people, Israel. The one great gain was that Balaam was now more aware of the seriousness of the task before him; he would not be able to change the word that the Lord would give to him (see 23:12, 20, 26).

36–38 Balak's sense of urgency heightens the comic element in this story. He was so anxious to have Balaam begin his work of cursing that he went to some distance to meet him at the border of his land, and then he upbraided his visitor for the delay in his journey. Doubtless Balak was puzzled over the words with which Balaam greeted him: "I must speak only what God puts in my mouth" (v.38). My interpretation is based on the presupposition that ordinarily Balaam believed he could say pretty much what he pleased to say—if the price was right—in the belief that the will of the gods would in some manner correspond with his words; but not this time. Nevertheless, we are led by the narrative into the enemy's camp, and we learn of their consternation over the power of God in the camp of Israel.

39–41 Verses 39–41 speak of the propitiatory sacrifices that Balak and Balaam engaged in as they prepared for the mantic acts. It seems unlikely that these sacrifices were for Yahweh. The pieces given to Balaam presumably would have included the livers; for as a *bārū* diviner, Balaam was a specialist in liver divination. Numbers 24:1 reports that Balaam subsequently gave up on his acts of sorcery, as the power of the word of the Lord came on him. But at the beginning, he started his procedures as he always had. Yet never had he spoken as he was about to speak.

g. Balaam's Seven Oracles (23:1-24:25)

OVERVIEW

Chapters 23-24 of Numbers form a close unit based on the oracles of Balaam. Characteristically to elegant Semitic style, these oracles come in a set of seven. The first four oracles are lengthier, the last three brief; nonetheless, each oracle has its own independent nature within the corpus and is introduced in the same manner (23:7a, 18a; 24:3a, 15a, 20b, 21b, 23a). Considering the role that the number seven plays in the narrative of this section (see the sevens in 23:1, 14, 29) and in the Torah in general, this feature can hardly be accidental. The oracles also show a sense of progression and development. The structure shows a repetitive nature, but the repetition is not static, as the text displays a development, a growing intensity—indeed, a crescendo. My analysis follows this line of approach.

i. Balaam's first oracle (23:1-12)

(a) The setting of the oracle (23:1-6)

¹Balaam said, "Build me seven altars here, and prepare seven bulls and seven rams for me." ²Balak did as Balaam said, and the two of them offered a bull and a ram on each altar.

³Then Balaam said to Balak, "Stay here beside your offering while I go aside. Perhaps the LORD will come to meet with me. Whatever he reveals to me I will tell you." Then he went off to a barren height.

⁴God met with him, and Balaam said, "I have prepared seven altars, and on each altar I have offered a bull and a ram."

⁵The LORD put a message in Balaam's mouth and said, "Go back to Balak and give him this message."

⁶So he went back to him and found him standing beside his offering, with all the princes of Moab.

COMMENTARY

1-6 The elaborate sacrificial actions of Balaam and Balak in these verses are to be contrasted to the sacrificial texts already described in Numbers. The sacrifices here are not those of chs. 15 and 28-29. These sacrifices are pagan acts that contrast with the true worship of God. The use of the number seven is significant in this section: seven bulls and seven rams on seven altars. These sacrifices were prepared as a part of Balaam's actions as a *bārû* (see comments on 22:8). The number seven was held in high regard among Semitic peoples in general; the numerous animals would provide abundant livers and organs for the diviner from the east. Balaam was in charge; Balak was now his subordinate.

The most arresting element of the introductory section is in the words, "God met with him" (v.4), and, "the LORD put a message in Balaam's mouth" (v.5). Despite the pagan and unsavory actions of this ungodly man, the Lord deigned to meet with him and to speak through him. These actions are utterly remarkable. Our presumption in saying that God never uses an unclean vessel is not quite accurate. God may use whatever vessel he wishes; the issue concerns what happens to an unclean vessel when God has finished using it for his purposes. It appears that such vessels are tossed aside, dashed on the road.

The story is dramatic as Balaam returned to those who had sent for him (v.6). They were standing by the altar and hoping for a word from heaven that would destroy their presumed foe. They received a word from heaven, all right; but that word was far from what they expected.

NOTE

3 שְׁפִי (*šepî*, "barren height") is a word Samuel Daiches believes to be a term of pagan mantic actions (for more on this, see comment on 22:8, describing the manner of Balaam's behavior). More recently Karl Elligen defends the meaning "bare height" ("Der Sinn des hebraischen Wortes שְׁפִי," *ZAW* 83 [1971]: 317-29).

(b) The oracle: The blessing of Israel is irrevocable (23:7-10)

OVERVIEW

The theme of this first oracle centers on the notion of the blessing of Israel. This blessing was unique. It was altogether different from anything Balaam (or Balak) had ever experienced. It was an irrevocable blessing; hence, any attempt to curse Israel would be ineffective. Israel was a nation distinct from all others. Her uniqueness was to be found in her God. The oracle may be outlined in the following way.

I. Introductory formula: Balaam takes up his oracle (v.7a)
II. Exordium: Balaam states his purpose to curse Israel (v.7b)
III. Blessing
  A. Balaam is unable to curse Israel (v.8)
    1. God has not cursed Israel
    2. Balaam cannot curse Israel
  B. Balaam blesses Israel as unique among the nations (vv.9-10a)
    1. Balaam views Israel as unique among the nations
    2. Balaam regards Israel as immune from curses
  C. Balaam expresses a desire to share in Israel's blessing (v.10b)

> [7]Then Balaam uttered his oracle:
>
> "Balak brought me from Aram,
>   the king of Moab from the eastern mountains.

'Come,' he said, 'curse Jacob for me;
    come, denounce Israel.'
[8]How can I curse
    those whom God has not cursed?
How can I denounce
    those whom the LORD has not denounced?
[9]From the rocky peaks I see them,
    from the heights I view them.
I see a people who live apart
    and do not consider themselves one of the nations.
[10]Who can count the dust of Jacob
    or number the fourth part of Israel?
Let me die the death of the righteous,
    and may my end be like theirs!"

7 The Hebrew word *māšal* (GK 5442) is more usually translated as "proverb"; here the translation "oracle" is appropriate. The distinctive nature of the prophecies of Balaam is established in the use of this word; none of the prophecies of the true prophets of Israel is described by this term. There are seven poetic oracles in the set: the first four are longer, have introductory narrative bridges, and are set as exquisite poetry (23:7–10, 18–24; 24:3–9, 15–19); the last three oracles are brief, are much more difficult to understand, and follow one another in what we may call a staccato pattern (24:20, 21–22, 23–24).

The words of the exordium (v.7b) are problematic in terms of their poetic arrangement. The accents suggest an imbalanced pair of bicola with a 4:1 count, with the resultant translation:

Balak the king of Moab brought me from Aram,
    from the mountains of the east.

But a more natural alignment of the bicolon would be a more balanced pair with a 3:2 count:

From Aram Balak brought me,
    the king of Moab from the eastern mountains.

The result is a balanced line of what we may call complementary parallelism. The verb gaps the couplet, and the words of the second member explain more fully the meaning of the corresponding words of the first.

Then follow the instructions Balak gave to the erstwhile agent of curse:

Go, curse for me Jacob!
And go, execrate Israel!

These words form a balanced bicolon of 3:3 meter, with emphatic verbal forms expressing the great urgency with which Balak beseeched Balaam to come. The two verbs are *ʿārar* (the verb "to curse," as in 22:6) and *zāʿam* ("to speak against with indignation"; see Ps 7:11, "a God who expresses his wrath every day"). In the couplet, these verbs work together to give the sense of anger and indignation, to speak of execration. "Jacob" and "Israel" are regularly occurring pairs, of course; they are interchangeable words marking out the people of Yahweh's covenant. In these words there is the call, witting or not, for Yahweh to break his promise to the patriarchs.

8 Yet that which Balaam had been hired to do he was unable to do. The blessing of Israel was inviolable; Balaam had no power to attack their blessing. God forbade him to speak in a curse on his people, who were unlike the nations of the world:

How may I imprecate
  whom God has not imprecated?
How may I execrate
  whom Yahweh has not execrated?

The pattern is unusual here, with long bicola subdivided into two units: 2/3:2/3. The word *mâ* is used at the beginning of each of the two units to indicate utter impossibility. The new synonym for curse is *qābab*, a word used elsewhere in the corpus (22:11, 17; 23:8, 11, 13, 25, 27; 24:10). God is called both *ʾēl* and *yhwh* in the parallel cola.

9 In verse 9 Balaam viewed Israel as unique among the nations:

As I see him from the top of the mountains,
and as I gaze at him from the hills—
  Look! A people that dwells alone;
  it is not reckoned among the nations!

These two lines of bicola are also nicely balanced with clear parallel terms and concepts. There seems to be a protasis and an apodosis in the respective lines of the bicola. We are brought alongside Balaam, and with him we look down. With him we discover with shock: this people was not like any other; they were alone, not a part of the families of the nations. Their distinction was in their relationship with their God. As he is holy, so they are holy. The first bicolon of the verse has a 3:2 pattern; the second a 3:3 pattern (in accents). The term "look!" adds a degree of excitement and urgency.

10 Here is Balaam's wistful desire to share in Israel's blessing! He who had come to curse the people wished himself to be blessed along with them. This irony is exquisite. The expression rendered "my end" speaks of the glorious future, of life beyond the grave. That Balaam never participated in the death of the righteous is not learned until 31:8, 16.

Who may number the dust of Jacob?
Who can count the dust-cloud of Israel?
O that I might die the death of the upright!
Ah, that my latter end might be like his!

These two lines of bicola are nicely balanced (4:3 and 4:3), with the relationship between them presenting exasperation and futility. Just as Balaam could not "get their number," so he realized that he was not a part of their destiny. One almost comes to a point of feeling sorry for Balaam at this point. Further, the words concerning "getting the number" of Israel serve as a double entendre in this book. Balaam wanted to "get the number" in a mantic sense, to have a handle for control. The book has made much of "numbers" as a means of displaying God's great blessing on his people. This feature is an unexpected, though minor, confirmation of the rhetorical use of numbers within this text.

NOTES

7 As I mentioned in the comments on ch. 10, the descriptions of poetic structure in this commentary include counts of accents. This system is not based on a concept of Western meter; Semitic and Egyptian poetry do not demonstrate metrical concepts that we find in much (but not all) Western poetry (ancient and modern). But the poetry of Israel and her neighbors was infused with rhythm, and the accentuation (with basically one "beat" per word) most likely signifies that pattern. Describing Egyptian poetry, Kitchen

(*Poetry of Ancient Egypt*, 480) writes, "It would seem clear that principal words (nouns, verbs, adjectives) and certain compound clusters bore the rhythmic stresses in a line."

The principal, classic work on the accents used in the MT is William Wickes, *Two Treatises on the Accentuation of the Old Testament* (Library of Biblical Studies; ed. Harry M. Orlinsky; repr., New York: Ktav, 1970). The accents are discussed briefly in GKC (sec. 15, 57−63). See also P. Paul Joüon, *Grammaire de l'Hebreu biblique* (Rome: Pontifical Biblical Institute, 1947), sec. 15, 45; cf. 39−46.

10 Rather than emending וּמִסְפָּר (*ûmispār*, "or number"), as many have done, it seems best to regard this word as an "abbreviation" (or shorter formation) for וּמִי סָפַר (*ûmî sāpar* ("and who may count?"). This approach yields a nice balance with the first word, "who may number?" See Ginsburg, 168; G. R. Driver, "Abbreviations in the Massoretic Text," *Text* 1 (1960): 112−31.

רֹבַע (*rōbaʿ*, "the fourth part," NIV) seems to be a rather poor parallel to the word "dust" in the first colon. I accept as probable a solution proposed by a long line of scholars, namely, that the word *rbʿ* may be compared with the Akkadian *turbuʿu* ("dust cloud") and the Arabic *rabaʿun*, with the same meaning. See H. L. Ginsberg, "Lexicographical Notes. 3. *rōbaʿ*, Dust," *ZAW* 51 (1933): 309; James Barr, *Comparative Philology and the Text of the Old Testament* (Oxford: Clarendon, 1968), index; D. Miller, "Animal Names in Ugaritic," *UF*, 2:184.

(c) The aftermath (23:11−12)

> ¹¹Balak said to Balaam, "What have you done to me? I brought you to curse my enemies, but you have done nothing but bless them!"
> ¹²He answered, "Must I not speak what the LORD puts in my mouth?"

COMMENTARY

11−12 In the introductory oracle the major elements of the passage are on display. Balaam was unable to curse Israel; Israel was unique because of her blessing from the Lord. Balak is furious—and Yahweh is sovereign. The words of the consternation of Balak and those forming the response of Balaam are marvelous; we are supposed to chuckle as we witness the work of God among the enemies of his people.

ii. Balaam's second oracle (23:13−26)

(a) The setting of the oracle (23:13−17)

> ¹³Then Balak said to him, "Come with me to another place where you can see them; you will see only a part but not all of them. And from there, curse them for me." ¹⁴So he

took him to the field of Zophim on the top of Pisgah, and there he built seven altars and offered a bull and a ram on each altar.

¹⁵Balaam said to Balak, "Stay here beside your offering while I meet with him over there."

¹⁶The Lord met with Balaam and put a message in his mouth and said, "Go back to Balak and give him this message."

¹⁷So he went to him and found him standing beside his offering, with the princes of Moab. Balak asked him, "What did the Lord say?"

COMMENTARY

13–17 Trying to cover all the angles, Balak attempted to reduce the power of the people by selecting a point where their immense numbers would be obscured. Alas for Balak, the oracle that followed exceeded the first in its blessing on Israel. Again we sense the idea of numbers in this text. There was a power in numbers in the ancient world. If one were confronted only with a small percentage of the whole, Balak reasoned, the enormity of the nation would not cause the gods to bless when they were requested to curse Israel. Again sevens were used in the offerings, meant as magical charms like those used in mantic rites of idolatry, not presentations of the true worship of holy Yahweh. The note of "Pisgah" (v.14; see 21:20) causes the reader to think of Moses, even though he is not mentioned. His long shadow is everywhere present.

The result of all this frenetic activity was the same as at first. Again the Lord met Balaam and gave him a new word, to the consternation of Balak, positioned as he was in pious pretense at his pagan altar.

(b) The oracle: the source of Israel's unique blessing (23:18–24)

OVERVIEW

The theme of this oracle extends the first oracle's theme by making it more explicit. The uniqueness of Israel was found in her unique relationship to Yahweh. The oracle may be outlined as follows.

I. Introductory formula: Balaam takes up his oracle (v.18a)
II. Exordium: Balaam demands the attention of his hearer for the stunning oracle he is about to pronounce (v.18b)
III. Blessing

A. Israel's unique blessing issues from her unique God (v.19)
  1. God is unlike humans in his person
  2. God is unlike humans in his word
B. Israel's unique blessing is irrevocable in her God (v.20)
  1. Balaam is commanded to bless
  2. Balaam is powerless to curse
C. Israel's unique blessing is explained by the presence of her God (vv.21–23)

1. God permits no cursing of Israel (v.21a)
2. God is present with Israel (v.21b)
3. God is the protector of Israel (v.22)
4. God is the power effective in Israel (v.23)

D. Israel's unique blessing is to be exhibited by her power in battle (v.24)

1. As a lion she rises for the kill
2. As a lion she feasts on the slain

The introductory formula and exordium (v.18) are characterized by a full use of fixed pairs of parallel words as well as by the use of arresting figures. The person of God as the effective force in Israel permeates the passage. God is different from humans; his word is different from that of humans. God, not humankind, is the source of blessing. God is with his people and is their King. God is the Deliverer from Egypt and is the strength of his people. Because of God, his people become victorious.

---

¹⁸Then he uttered his oracle:

"Arise, Balak, and listen;
  hear me, son of Zippor.
¹⁹God is not a man, that he should lie,
  nor a son of man, that he should change his mind.
Does he speak and then not act?
  Does he promise and not fulfill?
²⁰I have received a command to bless;
  he has blessed, and I cannot change it.

²¹"No misfortune is seen in Jacob,
  no misery observed in Israel.
The Lord their God is with them;
  the shout of the King is among them.
²²God brought them out of Egypt;
  they have the strength of a wild ox.
²³There is no sorcery against Jacob,
  no divination against Israel.
It will now be said of Jacob
  and of Israel, 'See what God has done!'
²⁴The people rise like a lioness;
  they rouse themselves like a lion
that does not rest till he devours his prey
  and drinks the blood of his victims."

COMMENTARY

18 The introductory monocolon is followed by a bicolon of 3:4 meter and marked by unusual energy. The introduction reads:

And he took up his oracle and said:

"Rise up, O Balak, and hear!
Give ear to me, O son of Zippor!"

The naming of Balak in the second member as "son of Zippor" is a fine use of parallelism.

19 The words "God is not a man, that he should lie" describe both the immutability of the Lord and the integrity of his word. Balaam is himself a foil for God. Balaam is constantly shifting, prevaricating, equivocating, changing—he is himself the prime example of the distinction between God and humanity.

God is not a man, that he is able to lie,
Nor is he human, that he is able to change;
Has he said, and will he not do it?
Or has he spoken, and will he not confirm it?

Again two lines of bicolon mark this verse (4:2 and 4:3 meter), with the pairs enhancing each other. Balaam's view of gods was based on his own human failings. Now he confronts God, who is not at all like humans in their failures. This fact is the stunning reality. All others may change; God—even with all of his power—cannot change, for he cannot deny himself (cf. 1Sa 15:29; Ps 89:35–37; Heb 6:16–18). God must fulfill his promise, for he has bound his character to his Word.

20 The blessing of God is thus irrevocable:

Look! I have received [orders] to bless;
since he has blessed, I am unable to revoke it!

Verse 20 is a bicolon with 3:3 meter that advances the implication of v.19 to the present situation.

Since Yahweh is unlike fickle people, the command to bless is not subject to change.

21 That the first declaration of the kingship of the Lord in the Pentateuch was made by Balaam is a suitable improbability. It was precisely because God is the King that he was able to use Balaam for his own ends—to bless his people in a new and wonderful manner.

He does not see evil in Jacob,
nor does he regard trouble in Israel.
Yahweh his God is with him.
And the battle cry of a King is in him.

The negative wording of the first bicolon contrasts with the most positive elements in the second. The meter is 3:3 and 3:3. At first blush the wording of this verse is nearly incredible. The whole course of Israel's experience in the wilderness was one evil after another, one trouble on another. Yet it was evidently the standing of Israel that was in view here rather than her state. It is also possible that the words "evil" and "trouble" in this verse are not used to refer to moral issues but to mantic concerns. That is, God does not look on his people with "an evil eye" or a hostile glance. This interpretation may fit better with the first bicolon of v.23. When Israel was presented in the context of a hostile environment, it was the blessing of Israel that was maintained. Only within the family context was the sinfulness of the people addressed. Since Yahweh the King was in their midst, they were invincible from outside attack.

22 The wild ox (aurochs) of the ancient Near East is a traditional image of power (see also 24:8). The KJV's "unicorn" was wrong from the beginning; the Hebrew expression speaks of two horns (dual), which the NIV paraphrases as "strength."

God is bringing them out of Egypt,
he is their aurochs' horns!

This bicolon (3:3) is powerful in its imagery. The verbal form is a participle, describing ongoing action. God was still in the process of bringing his people from Egypt; he would soon complete his work by bringing them into his land. And along the way he was their strength. They were not empowered by magic but by his person, not by potion but by his presence.

23 The reason for Israel's eventual triumph is given in a new way in this verse: there is "no sorcery against Jacob." Balaam speaks here from his frightful experience. He had no means in his bag of tricks to withstand the blessing of Israel. Instead of the tricks of the sorcerer, it will be said of Israel: "See what God has done!"

For there is no divination against Jacob,
neither is there augury against Israel.
Now it must be said for Jacob,
and for Israel—"What God has done!"

These two bicola display 3:2 and 3:3 meter; the first is complementary and the second is completive. The two lines form a contrastive parallel, the first negative and the second positive (as in v.19); there is a relationship of cause and effect here. Since there is no possibility of the use of magic either for or against Israel, whatever comes of Israel will truly be regarded as the work of God. This verse forms an insider's key to the whole of Balaam's work. He

had come to use magic, but he could not "get their number" (v.10). He had come to bring a curse, but he found them blessed. He had come to bring a divination and an augury, but he found such ineffective. God was in control, and Balaam was his puppet in this spiritual Punch and Judy show.

24 As a lioness on the hunt, Israel was about to arise and devour its foes (see 24:9).

Ah! A people rises as a lioness,
and as a lion it rouses itself.
It will not lie down until it devours its prey,
and drinks the blood of the slain.

At this point the would-be victim of the curse of Balaam and Balak becomes the instrument of the destruction of its own enemies. As a lioness (the huntress), Israel was about to rouse herself and would soon bring her foes to destruction. She would not rest until the enemy was devoured, its blood lapped clean at the end of the chase. These two bicola (of 3:2 and 4:2 meter) are closely connected with contrasting verbs of rising and lying down and with their display of positive and negative contrasts. The effectiveness of the lion image was not lost on Israel. Witness the seal from Megiddo with the figure of the roaring lion, inscribed, "Belonging to Shemaᶜ, / servant of Jeroboam" (*ANEP*, item 276). The image hearkens back to the earliest patriarchal period (cf. Ge 49:9). The use of the image of the lion is a way of speaking of Israel's vocation as the warrior of God (see Mic 5:8).

NOTE

23 נַחַשׁ (*naḥaš*, "sorcery"; GK 5728) is an important term in the context of the Balaam oracles. This noun is used here and in 24:1. The verbal form is used in the Piel with the meaning, "to practice divination, observe signs." It may even have the sense of "to cast a spell" or "to utter a magical curse" (key texts include Ge

30:27; 44:5, 15; Lev 19:26; Dt 18:10; 2Ki 17:17; 21:6; 2Ch 33:6). Divination in all its forms was prohibited in Israel; here we learn that there is no divination that may be made against Israel. The other mantic word used in this verse is קֶסֶם (*qesem*, "divination, augury"; GK 7877). This is also a word that is always used in a negative cast in the viewpoint of normative Yahwistic faith. It is prohibited in Israel in Deuteronomy 18:10 (along with *naḥaš*; cf. 1Sa 15:23; Eze 13:6, 23).

(c) The aftermath (23:25–26)

> ²⁵Then Balak said to Balaam, "Neither curse them at all nor bless them at all!" ²⁶Balaam answered, "Did I not tell you I must do whatever the LORD says?"

COMMENTARY

25–26 The tragicomic nature of the story is seen in the aftermath. Balak appeared incredulous. He gasped, "What have you done to me!" in v.11. Then he said, in essence, "Stop it all together." But Balaam was unstoppable in his mission from Yahweh, Lord of Israel.

iii. Balaam's third oracle (23:27–24:14)

(a) The setting of the oracle (23:27–24:2)

> ²⁷Then Balak said to Balaam, "Come, let me take you to another place. Perhaps it will please God to let you curse them for me from there." ²⁸And Balak took Balaam to the top of Peor, overlooking the wasteland.
> ²⁹Balaam said, "Build me seven altars here, and prepare seven bulls and seven rams for me." ³⁰Balak did as Balaam had said, and offered a bull and a ram on each altar.
> ²⁴:¹Now when Balaam saw that it pleased the LORD to bless Israel, he did not resort to sorcery as at other times, but turned his face toward the desert. ²When Balaam looked out and saw Israel encamped tribe by tribe, the Spirit of God came upon him.

COMMENTARY

23:27–24:2 Once more Balak tried another tack. Perhaps a change of location might lead to a change of words (23:27). The mention of Peor (v.28) takes on a horrible association in Numbers 25; it would appear that this place was the Moabite center for the worship of the god Baal. Von Pákozdy ("Theologische Redaktionsarbeit," 174; see Note on 22:2) believes this section means that Balaam was being asked by Balak to call up his own deity (a demon), one on whom he had some hold, some handle.

Again the sevens both of altars and of animals were prepared (23:29-30), but this time there was a significant change. Balaam did not go about his normal routine of sorcery (24:1). This time, "the Spirit of God came upon him" (v.2). This unexpected language (*rûaḥ ᵉlōhîm*) is used to prepare the reader for the heightened revelation that was about to come from the bizarre messenger. The oracles build in intensity and depth of meaning.

(b) The oracle: the beauty and strength of Israel (24:3-9)

OVERVIEW

Here follows an outline of the oracle.

I. Introductory formula: Balaam takes up his oracle (v.3a)
II. Exordium: Balaam, empowered by the Holy Spirit, speaks in a new way of the source of his revelation (vv.3b-4)
III. Blessing
  A. The blessings of Israel will be demonstrated in the land (vv.5-7)
    1. Israel's dwellings will be beautiful (v.5)
    2. Israel's productivity will be bountiful (v.6)
    3. Israel's resources will be plentiful (v.7a)
    4. Israel's king and kingdom will be powerful (v.7b)
  B. The blessings of Israel are in her God (v.8)
    1. Israel's God is her deliverer (v.8a)
    2. Israel's God is her protector (v.8b)
    3. Israel's God makes her victorious (vv.8c-e)
  C. The blessings of Israel are certain (v.9)
    1. Israel is like a lion, sovereign and grand (v.9a)
    2. Israel's blessing is vouchsafed by the promise of God (v.9b)

³And [Balaam] uttered his oracle:

"The oracle of Balaam son of Beor,
    the oracle of one whose eye sees clearly,
⁴the oracle of one who hears the words of God,
    who sees a vision from the Almighty,
    who falls prostrate, and whose eyes are opened:

⁵"How beautiful are your tents, O Jacob,
    your dwelling places, O Israel!

6"Like valleys they spread out,
    like gardens beside a river,
like aloes planted by the LORD,
    like cedars beside the waters.
7Water will flow from their buckets;
    their seed will have abundant water.

"Their king will be greater than Agag;
    their kingdom will be exalted.

8"God brought them out of Egypt;
    they have the strength of a wild ox.
They devour hostile nations
    and break their bones in pieces;
    with their arrows they pierce them.
9Like a lion they crouch and lie down,
    like a lioness — who dares to rouse them?

"May those who bless you be blessed
    and those who curse you be cursed!"

COMMENTARY

3–4 The introduction to this oracle is extensive and descriptive of Balaam's experience in the presence of the Lord. Now Balaam's eyes are opened (see 22:31, where the Lord opened Balaam's eyes to see his presence). Balaam then took up his third oracle:

The utterance of Balaam son of Beor,
    even the utterance of the strong man whose
        eye[s] is [are] opened;
    the utterance of one who hears the words of
        God,
who sees the vision of Shadday —
falling down, but whose eyes are uncovered.

These words are truly remarkable. The use of the term "oracle, revelatory utterance" ($n^{e\supset}um$)

three times adds significant solemnity — and divine authority — to these words, as do the lines descriptive of his own personal experience on the road. As Saul had his experience on the road to Damascus, so Balaam had his experience on the road to Moab. In both cases there was divine revelation. In the case of Saul, the revelation was one of grace; in the case of Balaam, it was one of judgment. But both revelations included the protection of the true people of God from those who wished to do them harm.

The (now customary) introductory monocolon of this verse is followed by a bicolon (4:4) that is self-descriptive of past and present experience. A tricolon (3:4:3) follows in v.4, where the first colon repeats the word $n^{e\supset}um$ of the previous verse. These words are so expressive of something new in Balaam's experience: he has now heard God and seen the vision of him. He lay prone before him, but his eyes were now opened (in the Hebrew, the word "eye" is first singular [v.3] and then plural [v.4]) to a wonder he had never even dreamed of—the true God! The *seer now saw*, but the seer Balaam was still not a man of faith, not a familial member of the people of God (see again 23:10: "Let me").

5 Balaam spoke prophetically. He looked down on the tents in which the people were dwelling and was given a vision of their future. When he saw the orderliness of the encampments, he saw their coming grandeur.

> O how beautiful are your tents, O Jacob,
>   your encampments, O Israel.

This verse is one bicolon (3:2) celebrating the astonishment of Balaam as he gazed on the beauty of the encampments of Israel and viewed, by a divine gift of true vision, their coming glory. The words "your tents" (*ʾōhāleykā*) and "your encampments" (*miškᵉnōteykā*, from the verb *šākan*, "to dwell"; see "he saw Israel *dwelling*" [*šōkēn*; Qal active participle], v.2) provide a lovely example of synonymous parallelism. Balaam was looking at tents in the wilderness; the Spirit of God gave him a vision of future cities with homes and buildings.

6 Balaam exulted in luxuriant terms concerning the blessings that would waft upon the people of Israel in their future dwelling in their new land. The people would have a sense of Eden in the lushness of their blessing from Yahweh. These words are among the most treasured in Torah respecting the blessings of the Lord on his people.

> As palm trees that stretch themselves out,
>   as orchards beside a river,
>   as aloes planted by Yahweh,
>   as cedars by the waters.

Verse 6 has two lines of bicola with complementary parallelism throughout. The first line displays 2:3 meter, the second 3:2, thus forming an altogether satisfactory set. The meaning of the first word (translated here as "palm trees") is problematic. The word *nāḥal* appears to be the common term "wadi" (see the NIV's "like valleys"). Yet the other nouns in this verse are terms for trees. It seems that here we find a homonym of *nāḥal* that denotes a type of tree or a cluster of trees. The NEB and the JPS's Torah translation render "palm tree" by following a suggestion made already in BDB (636), which compares the Hebrew word with an Arabic term for the date palm. Further, the verb "to stretch" (*nāṭâ*) seems more suitable to the stretching of the boughs of trees than the sprawl of wadis.

7 This potent, prophetic verse speaks of luxurious productivity as well as of the majesty of the coming king of Israel.

> Water flows from his buckets,
>   and his seed is by many waters;
>   his king is higher than Agag,
>   and his kingdom is exalted.

This verse has two lines of bicola (2:3 and 3:2) in an unusual pairing of ideas: "water and seed" tied to "king and kingdom." The ideas of water and seed probably point to vital luxuriance in the future inhabitation of the land. The words may also have a double entendre: sexual fecundity and productivity (see Note).

The most problematic issue here is the reference to "Agag" (*ʾᵃgag*). Because a man named Agag was the opponent of King Saul in the tenth century BC (see 1Sa 15:7–33), the mention of this name in a text that is ostensibly from a period hundreds of years earlier has led critical commentators to take this reference to Agag as a telltale sign that this oracle, and the others like it, were written in the time of David (or later) and were then projected backward into the remote past (see, e.g., Otto Eissfeldt, "Sinai-Erzählung und Bileam-Sprache," *HUCA* 32 [1961]: 188).

But what may seem like a "slam dunk" by the critical player here may turn out to be only an "air ball." First, why would a passage that critics believe was designed to magnify David use the name of the Amalakite king whom Saul defeated? Even though Saul's behavior following the battle turned out to be seriously compromised (see the powerful condemnation of Saul by Samuel in 1 Samuel 15:22–23), nonetheless, the story presents Saul—not David—as the victor over Agag (see Note). How could a reference to the might of Agag advance David's prestige?

Second, it is possible, that the reference to Agag is based on a common, royal name among the Amalekite kings (as the names Abimelech in Philistia and Ben-Hadad in Syria). In this case the use of this name here may grow out of memories of the attack on Israel by Amalek (see Ex 17:8–13) and, more recently, when Israel first entered battle against Canaan—and lost! (see Nu 14:45).

Third, it is also possible the name "Agag" is used in a specific, predictive prophecy of a future victory of a king of Israel over a great enemy. In the words, "Their king will be greater than Agag," we may have a *heilsgeschichtliche* continuity that begins in the wilderness with the attacks of Amalek in Israel's recent past (Nu 14:45), that leads to the future victory of Saul over his nemesis, Agag (1Sa 15:32–33), and that culminates in the final victory of Israel's greatest King (Yeshua) over all her enemies (styled under the title "Agag"). This interpretation seems to fit with the prophecies that follow in the fourth oracle (see v.17). The fact that the Spirit of God fell on Balaam (v.2) gives the reverent reader a sense of expectation for just such a dramatic convergence of ideas.

8 This broad interpretation suggested for v.7 also fits with the direction of v.8. It is stunning to hear the central words of Israel's salvation ("God is bringing him out of Egypt") recited by one who was an outsider and a hostile foe (see comments on 25:1).

> God is bringing him out of Egypt,
> he is his aurochs horns!
> He will devour the nations, his enemies,
> their bones he will crush,
> and their arrows he will shatter.

That the first couplet is repetitive of the second oracle (see 23:22) helps tie the corpus together, as well as emphasize its central importance. The only change is in the pronoun "him" (here singular, but plural ["them"] in 23:22). Again the power of Israel's God is compared to that of the horns of the aurochs. A tricolon projecting a time of ultimate victory over all enemies (as in v.7's reference to Agag) follows. The imagery of victory is in the manner of a lion (as in v.9).

There is a tightly woven connection in these verses. The tricolon has the pattern 3:2:2, with complementary parallelism of the strong verbs "to devour," "to crush," and "to shatter." An Akkadian text speaks of the crushing of bones in battle: "I had his (own) sons crush these bones, the bones of PN, which they had taken to Assyria from GN" (*CAD* IV, 342; here "PN" stands for "personal name," "GN" for "geographical name"). This is a stark image of complete victory over one's enemy.

9 The theology of blessing and cursing in the Abrahamic covenant (Ge 12:2–3) is now made an explicit part of the oracle of blessing. Perhaps here Balaam was reasserting his wistful desire to be a part of Israel's blessing (see 23:10).

> He crouches, he lies down as a lion,
> and as a lion, who dares to rouse him?

All who bless you are blessed;
but all who curse you are cursed.

These two lines of bicola have 3:3 and 2:2 meter, thus giving a sense of balance and conclusion. The idea of the lion is taken from the second oracle (see 23:24). The stunning climax is in the blessing of God on all who bless Israel. This theme, of course, takes us back to the original promise of God to Abram (Ge 12:3). The irony cannot be missed. In his actions Balaam brings a curse on his own head even as he speaks words of blessing!

NOTE

7 Rembert Sorg (*Ecumenic Psalm 87* [Fifield, Wis.: King of Martyrs Priory, 1969], 36, 46–52) presents an argument that the phrasing of the first part of the verse is to semen virile; he makes similar comments on the words of our Lord in John 7:37–39: "out of his belly shall flow rivers of living water" (KJV). His point is not without problems (!), but he argues that John 7:37–39 is based on our text.

Concerning the use of the name אֲגַג (ʾagag, "Agag"), we may observe that David did defeat the armies of the Amalekites, but no particulars are given of these events, just a summary of the loot he took and what he did with what he seized from many nations (Edom, Moab, Ammon, Philistia, Amalek, and Zobah; see 2Sa 8:11–12; 1Ch 18:11). There is no mention of the name "Agag" in these verses.

(c) The aftermath (24:10–14)

> ¹⁰Then Balak's anger burned against Balaam. He struck his hands together and said to him, "I summoned you to curse my enemies, but you have blessed them these three times. ¹¹Now leave at once and go home! I said I would reward you handsomely, but the LORD has kept you from being rewarded."
>
> ¹²Balaam answered Balak, "Did I not tell the messengers you sent me, ¹³'Even if Balak gave me his palace filled with silver and gold, I could not do anything of my own accord, good or bad, to go beyond the command of the LORD—and I must say only what the LORD says'? ¹⁴Now I am going back to my people, but come, let me warn you of what this people will do to your people in days to come."

COMMENTARY

10–14 The oracles could well have ended with the great third utterance from Balaam. But there was one grander yet to come. Balak was beside himself with anger (see Note). He raged and struck his hands while ranting. He observed that at this point Balaam had given three distinct blessings on Israel (v.10). At least Balak got that much right. In his disgust with the failure of Balaam to curse Israel, Balak now dismissed him without pay—the ultimate insult in answer to his greed (2Pe 2:15).

Balaam was ready to leave; the whole situation must have been uncomfortable for him as well! But before he left, he was constrained by the Lord to speak again — this time his greatest oracle. In the phrase "in days to come," we recognize the signal in biblical literature for the distant future.

NOTE

10 Balak's anger, וַיִּחַר־אַף בָּלָק (*wayyiḥar-ʾap bālāq*, "and Balak's anger raged"), is expressed in the idiom, "his nose became red with rage"; this suggests a famous line from a popular Hollywood film; Balaam might have been the first to say to a powerful man, "The truth? You can't handle the truth!"

iv. Balaam's fourth oracle (24:15–19)

OVERVIEW

Unlike the preceding oracles, there is no set up for this fourth one, nor is there any aftermath. Of sole importance is the oracle itself; its outline follows.

I. Introductory formula: Balaam takes up his oracle (v.15a)

II. Exordium: Balaam, about to utter his most important oracle, expands the exordium of the preceding section (vv.15b–16)

III. Blessing

A. Israel has a coming deliverer (v.17)

1. The deliverer will come in the future (v.17a–b)
2. The deliverer will be like a star and a scepter (v.17c–d)
3. The deliverer will bring victory over his enemies (v.17e–f)

B. Israel has a coming dominion (vv.18–19)

1. Her enemies will be destroyed (v.18)
2. Her people will have dominion (v.19)

¹⁵Then he uttered his oracle:

"The oracle of Balaam son of Beor,
    the oracle of one whose eye sees clearly,
¹⁶the oracle of one who hears the words of God,
    who has knowledge from the Most High,
who sees a vision from the Almighty,
    who falls prostrate, and whose eyes are opened:

¹⁷"I see him, but not now;
    I behold him, but not near.
A star will come out of Jacob;

a scepter will rise out of Israel.
He will crush the foreheads of Moab,
   the skulls of all the sons of Sheth.
[18]Edom will be conquered;
   Seir, his enemy, will be conquered,
   but Israel will grow strong.
[19]A ruler will come out of Jacob
   and destroy the survivors of the city."

COMMENTARY

15–16 As in the third oracle (vv.3–4), the introduction to the fourth oracle is lengthy (vv.15–16), thus helping to prepare the reader for the startling words of the prophecy to come:

The utterance of Balaam the son of Beor,
even the utterance of the strong man whose eye
   is opened;
the utterance of one who hears the words of
   God,
who knows the knowledge of the Most High,
who sees the vision of Shadday—
   falling down, but whose eyes are uncovered.

As we compare this section with 23:3–4, we find one new colon: "who knows the knowledge of the Most High." This expansion changes the arrangement of the lines in the second verse from a tricolon to two lines of bicola (3:3 and 3:3). The addition of the new colon tends to intensify the anticipation of the blessing that follows; the repetition helps to tie these oracles together, to give us a sense of crescendo and climax.

17 Without question the most debated and the most important verse in the oracular corpus is v.17. While arguments may be presented to the contrary, the approach here is to take the prophecy of the star out of Jacob and the scepter out of Israel as ultimately a specific prophecy of the coming messianic Ruler, the Lord Yeshuaᶜ, the Messiah (see Note). Israel's future Deliverer will be like a star and a scepter in his royalty and will bring victory over the enemies of his people (see also v.19). That a prophecy of the Lord himself would be given through the improbable prophet Balaam is remarkable and reminds us of the unexpectedness of the thoughts of God (Isa 55:8).

I see him, but not now,
I behold him, but not near,
a star shall march out from Jacob,
and a scepter shall rise from Israel—
   and shall crush the temples of Moab,
   even the skulls of the sons of Sheth.

This verse presents the grand idea that Israel has a coming deliverer. This keenly debated verse has been debased by some, devalued by others, and allegorized by still others (see Note). For our part, in agreement with many in the early church and in early Judaism (see Note), we believe this text speaks of the coming of the Messiah. That this prophecy should come from one who was unworthy makes the prophecy all the more dramatic and startling.

Indeed, the notion that Balaam, of whom no part was God's, could speak of the coming of the

Messiah, who is completely God, is a fascinating aspect of the biblical doctrine of inerrancy. The truth of Scripture could never finally be dependent on the worthiness of the writer or the personal piety of the speaker, else we would have gradations in inspiration and shades in trustworthiness. I say this reverently but strongly: The words of Balaam the pagan mantic, *when he was speaking under the control of the Holy Spirit of God*, were as sure as the words of the Savior Jesus found in a red-letter edition of the NT!

Balaam was unworthy of the words that passed through his lips, even as others were unworthy of the role they played in the salvation history of the Bible. But the words were not compromised; it was the Spirit who gave him utterance (v.2). It was also the Spirit who directed the process that led to these words' being included in the Torah of God (a point I develop more fully in my essay "The Theology of the Balaam Oracles," in *Tradition and Testament: Essays in Honor of Charles Lee Feinberg* [ed. John S. Feinberg and Paul D. Feinberg; Chicago: Moody Press, 1981], 79–119).

The terms "star" and "scepter" do not demand a future, messianic interpretation. These words certainly may speak of the promise of a king such as David, Israel's greatest king in the historical period. In fact, a type of fulfillment of these words may be seen in the heroic actions of Phinehas in his smiting of the couple who offended all decency at the entrance of the Tent of Meeting (see 25:7–8). But I believe and argue that the hints in the verse point farther than to David; ultimately these words reach beyond him. The setting for the text is "in days to come" (see again v.14), an eschatological notice. The inclusion of these words in the text is for the final victory over the enemies of Israel. The section reaches to the end because it reaches all the way to the Savior.

The first bicolon has the meter 3:3 in a complementary parallelism that is unusually moving: "but not now," "but not near"—words that stress the futurity of the referent. The second line of bicola has a 3:3 meter and speaks of the marching of the star-scepter as a great victor. These nouns speak of the royalty of the Messiah.

The third bicolon in the verse has a 3:2 meter with complementary parallelism, describing the shattering of the enemies in a complete judgment. That Jeremiah 48:45 serves as an important parallel of our words helps to solve the problem of the word the NIV renders "skulls" (see Note). The other problematic word in this verse is "Sheth," a word that may refer to early inhabitants of Moab (and so a parallel word to "Moab"; see Note). The point of the verse, of course, is that the coming King will be the ultimate victor over all of his enemies (cf. Pss 2; 110; Rev 19–20).

18–19 There is a sense in which the modern reader might regard these verses as somewhat anticlimactic compared to what follows. Yet this feature is not at all unusual in biblical prophecy. One can pick almost any well-known messianic text (Isa 9:6–7; Mic 5:2) and find it to have what appear to be rather humble associations. Yet the wording of these two verses does not present something insignificant; the verses advance the idea of v.17 that the coming Deliverer will have the great victory and will provide a dominion for his people.

> And Edom will become a possession,
> and Seir, his enemies, will be a possession,
> while Israel is demonstrating power.
>> One from Jacob will have dominion,
>> and shall destroy the remnant of the city.

Verse 18 is made of one line of tricolon with a 3:4:4 meter; the first two cola are complementary, and the third is expansive of these two. Edom and Seir are correlative terms (Ge 32:3; 36:8–9; Dt 1:44; 2:4, 8, 12; et al.). The pairing of these two words may be the key to understanding the pairing of Moab and Sheth in v.17 (see Note on v.17). In the time of Moses, Edom was a nation that Israel was forbidden to attack. The future projection of the text assumes a time of Edomite enmity against Israel (cf. the book of Obadiah), for which the nation finally receives its comeuppance for refusing passage to the Hebrews (see 20:14–21). David became a victor over Edom (2Sa 8:14). But after the division of the kingdom, Edom became independent (2Ki 8:20–22) and remained an implacable foe of Israel, thus inviting the final wrath of God (Isa 63:1–6).

In the eschaton, words such as "Edom" and "Seir" stand for any enemies of the people of God and of their Messiah. That is, it is not necessary to this prophecy that these nations exist in the end times; they stand for all peoples who are in opposition to the work of Yahweh and the establishment of His Anointed (see Ps 2:1–2). Conversely, it *is* necessary for Israel to be in place in the end times in order for this prophecy (and other such texts) to be fulfilled (see Ro 9–11).

The words contrasting to the ultimate downfall of Edom at the end of v.18 are to be stressed: Israel will grow strong while her enemies languish. This promise is also the point of v.19: Jacob will provide the ruler who will destroy all survivors of the enemies of God's people.

Verse 19 forms a bicolon with 2:3 meter. There is no subject for the verb "will come out"; likely the referent is the Star-Scepter of v.17. The Star-Scepter makes Israel triumphant as he gains dominion over the enemies of God's people. Messiah in his kingdom will exercise dominion over all peoples. The theme of this oracle is sustained: Israel's ultimate blessing centers in her Deliverer from all enemies.

NOTES

17 Views on the interpretation of this "star and scepter" prophecy have ranged widely through time. Following are some significant samples of the range of opinion through time.

In early Judaism, *Targum Onqelos* commented on this verse: "When a mighty king of Jacob's house will reign, and the Messiah will be magnified." *Targum Jonathan* commented: "When there shall reign a strong king of the house of Jacob, and Messiah shall be anointed, and a strong scepter shall be from Israel." In rabbinic works this section is tied to Messiah in *y. Taʿanit* (68.4); *Debarim Rabba* (sec. 1); *Pesiqta Zutarta* (58.1). Further, in the Dead Sea Scrolls, the *Damascus Document* (CD 7.9–20) ties this verse to Amos 9:11, the raising of the fallen booth of the house of David; in the *War Scroll* (1QM 7), the star-and-scepter passage is linked to the final battle of good and evil. Indeed, the text was a particular favorite among the Qumran covenanters (see F. F. Bruce, *The Teacher of Righteousness in the Qumran Texts* [London: Tyndale, 1956], 10).

Among the church fathers who interpreted the "star" of Numbers 24:17 to be prophetic of the Lord Jesus Christ was Justin Martyr (d. 166). His *First Apology* 32 presents an amalgam of Numbers 24:17; Isaiah 11:1; and 51:5: "Isaiah, another prophet, prophesying the same things in other words, said: 'A star shall rise out of Jacob, and a flower will come forth from the root of Jesse, and upon his arm will the nations hope.' The shining star has risen and the flower has grown from the root of Jesse—this is Christ." Another is Athanasius the Great (d. 373); his *On the Incarnation of the Word* 33 includes the lines of Numbers 24:17 in a christological section.

However, the great Martin Luther was unable to see this prophecy as speaking of Christ because he regarded Balaam as unworthy of such a sublime subject (see Heinrich Bornkamm, *Luther and the Old Testament* [ed. Victor I. Gruhn; trans. Eric W. and Ruth C. Gritsch; Philadelphia: Fortress, 1969], 240, n. 72).

E. W. Hengstenberg (*The Christology of the Old Testament and a Commentary on the Messianic Predictions* [trans. Reuel Keith; abridg. Thomas Kerchever Arnold; repr., Grand Rapids: Kregel, 1970], 34–37), the great nineteenth-century defender of Christian orthodoxy, balked at this issue as well. After stating that the early Jewish scholars were unified in their understanding that this passage was predictive of the coming Messiah, he listed three reasons why he did not believe Numbers 24:17 was predictive of the Messiah Jesus: (1) Jewish traditional understanding of this passage was misguided, as this passage speaks of this-worldly expectations; (2) no NT passage explicitly cites this verse as fulfilled in Jesus the Messiah; and (3) the passage was fulfilled completely in David. Moreover, the martial imagery of the figure in the "star and scepter" prophecy is far removed from the Messiah, who will bring blessings to the peoples.

Many interpreters have allegorized the text. Some point, for example, to the star of Bethlehem in Matthew 2:1–12 as the fulfillment of the passage (see Paul L. Maier, "The Magi and the Star," *Mankind* 3 [February 1972]: 5).

The most bizarre of approaches may have been that of John Allegro, who attempted to join this verse of the star and the scepter to his theory of a pan-phallic and hallucinogenic cult in Israel (*The Sacred Mushroom and the Cross: A Study of the Nature and Origins of Christianity within the Fertility Cults of the Ancient Near East* [repr., New York: Bantam Books, 1971]).

The word וְקַרְקַר (*wᵉqarqar*, "even tear down") as it stands is a Pilpel infinitive of the rare root קָרַר (*qārar*, meaning "to tear down [a wall]"), used elsewhere only in Isaiah 22:5, where it is also in dispute. Many emend this word to וְקָדְקֹד (*wᵉqodqōd*, a word meaning "crown, head, skull"); see *BHS* marginal suggestion of Isaiah 3:17, where this word for "head" is used in parallel construction to פֵּאָה (*pēʾâ*, "temple")—the word used in our verse's פַּאֲתֵי מוֹאָב (*paʾᵃtê mōʾab*, "temples of Moab"; cf. also Jeremiah 48:45, where these two words are parallel, but the pairing is slightly rephrased).

כָּל־בְּנֵי־שֵׁת (*kol-bᵉnê-šēt*, "all the sons of Sheth") is apparently a parallel ethnic term for Moab—the Shutu people in ancient Egyptian documents (so Albright, 220, n. 89). As v.18 balances "Edom" and "Seir," so we may expect that v.17 balances "Moab" and "Sheth."

v. Balaam's fifth oracle (24:20)

20Then Balaam saw Amalek and uttered his oracle:

"Amalek was first among the nations,
  but he will come to ruin at last."

COMMENTARY

20 The remaining three oracles seem to spring almost involuntarily from the fourth oracle. They overlap the promise of the victory of Israel over all enemies; hence these oracles are "curse oracles," imprecations. It may be that these were similar to the types of oracles that Balaam intended to present against Israel; instead these harsh words lash out against the foes of the covenantal community. Herein lies the final irony: Balak and Balaam had plotted to bring Israel under a curse, but in their machinations they only assured their own doom.

> And he saw Amalek,
>> and he took up his oracle and said:
>>> "First among the nations was Amalek,
>>> but its end will be destruction."

The structure of this brief oracle is simple. There is a bicolon that serves as the introduction, then a bicolon of prophetic indictment with a 3:3 metrical pattern.

The first defeat of Israel in the wilderness was at the hand of the Amalekites, when Israel went against them foolishly without the blessing of God (see 14:44–45; compare also the story of Israel's defeat of the Amalekites in Ex 17:8–16). There will come a day of reckoning on Amalek that will be dreadful. The Amalekites were defeated by Saul (1Sa 14:48; but see 15:1–35) and David (1Sa 30:18; 2Sa 8:12). These defeats may be regarded as fulfillments of this prophecy. But there is also the possibility that the implications of this verse, as with the others in the set (see esp. Ex 17:16, which projects war with the Amalekites "from generation to generation"), extend into the days of the Messiah's final victory over all enemies (see Ps 110; Rev 19). The final victory would be couched in the names familiar in the day in which they were given. Later on these names become prototypes for the enemies of Israel in the future.

vi. Balaam's sixth oracle (24:21–22)

²¹Then he saw the Kenites and uttered his oracle:

"Your dwelling place is secure,
  your nest is set in a rock;
²²yet you Kenites will be destroyed
  when Asshur takes you captive."

COMMENTARY

21–22 The spotlight of judgment turns now from Amalek to the Kenites:

> And he saw the Kenite,
>> and he took up his oracle and said:

> "Your dwelling place is enduring,
>> and your nest is set in the cliff;
> nevertheless, the Kenite shall be consumed
>> when Asshur takes him captive."

The structure of this little oracle is somewhat similar to the preceding one. It begins with a couplet of introduction continues with a double bicola in the pattern 2:3 and 4:3.

This oracle is problematic in several respects; it is based on wordplays (the word "nest" [*qēn*; see Jer 49:16; Ob 4; Hab 2:9] is a pun (paronomasia) on the word "Kenite" [*qēnî*]) and seems to point to the distant day when the seemingly unassailable Kenites will be taken captive by Asshur (Assyria). Why the Kenites come under attack here is not explained, except that it is possible that they became associated with the Midianites, who come under the scourge of Israel (Nu 31). The mention of Assyria is also a surprise, as its ascendancy to power in the ancient Near East was centuries away from Balaam's day; yet Assyria was known as a powerful city-state even in this early period. This text may be a powerful insight into the way of the prophets — the taking of familiar things and peoples and juxtaposing them in startling ways (cf. the celebrated series of puns [paronomasia] on city names in the preaching of Micah [Mic 1:10–16]).

vii. Balaam's seventh oracle (24:23–25)

²³Then he uttered his oracle:

"Ah, who can live when God does this?
    ²⁴Ships will come from the shores of Kittim;
they will subdue Asshur and Eber,
    but they too will come to ruin."

²⁵Then Balaam got up and returned home and Balak went his own way.

COMMENTARY

23–24 Balaam now presents his last oracle, one that is more difficult than any of the others to interpret — perhaps a fact that is fitting. The relative obscurity of the words compels attention; clarity may come as the time period of the oracle is realized in the future.

And he took up his oracle and said:
"Woe! Who can live except God establish him?
    For ships will come from the direction of
        Kittim,
and they will afflict Asshur and they will afflict
    Eber,

and he also will come to destruction."

The first verse has a bicolon with 3:5 meter; the introductory words set a grim stage for the words that follow. The second verse is in the form of a tricolon with 3:3 meter; yet the text is so corrupt that it presents an assortment of opportunities for guesses as to meaning and interpretation.

The translation (above) of the second colon of verse 23 leads one to a sense of utter dependence on the Lord. This is the lesson that is taught throughout the oracles. None is able to live, except by God's establishment. All is in his grasp, "Ah!" Balaam realizes the ultimate futility of his vocation.

Verse 24, as it stands, mentions Asshur, which connects it with the preceding oracle (v.22). The reference to "ships from Kittim" presents unusual difficulties. The identification of Kittim in the early period of Israel's history seems to be Cyprus. But ultimately the word was applied to Rome, as at Qumran (see, e.g., [1QM1:9-10] "From of old Thou hast announced to us the time appointed for the mighty deed of Thy hand against the Kittim") and perhaps also (prophetically!) in Daniel (e.g., 11:30). The resulting meaning may refer to the final battle between forces of the west (the Kittim) and forces of the east (Asshur and Eber)—a battle in which both will be destroyed, presumably before a greater power than either (the Lord of glory).

The difficulties we face in interpretating this verse with precision do not obscure its general direction: one nation will rise and supplant another, only to face its own doom. In contrast there is the implied ongoing blessing on the people of Israel and their sure promise of a future Deliverer who will have the final victory (vv.17-19). Further, the difficulties in this text suggest an early date for composition of the poem (the time of Balaam), not a late date (the time of David or later).

25 With these promises of a future Deliverer ringing in their ears, the defeated collaborators, Balaam and Barak, depart.

NOTE

25 We really have no idea how the story of Balaam and his donkey or the oracles of Balaam came into the Torah. That the question was asked from antiquity is evinced by the wording of *b. Baba Batra* 14b–15a: "Moses wrote his own book and the section concerning Balaam, and Job." The inclusion of the section on Balaam and Job could only have been provoked by the question, "How did these sections come into the Bible?"

E. W. Hengstenberg (*A Dissertation of the History and Prophecies of Balaam* [trans. J. E. Ryland; Edinburgh: T&T Clark, 1848], 513) attempted to present a credible scenario for the authorship of the section by Moses. He says that when Balaam left Balak, he sought from the Israelites the payment he had been refused by Balak. In return for payment, he offered to relate the whole story to Moses. When Moses refused to give him payment, in revenge he turned to the Midianites and advanced the plan that led to the debacle of Numbers 25. Keil, 3:203, surmises that Balaam, in a (failed) attempt to save his life, communicated the events and the prophecies to whomever would have captured him after the battle with Midian (Nu 31).

Samuel Cox (*Balaam: An Exposition and a Study* [London: Kegan, Paul Trench, & Co., 1884], 14–15) suggested that Balaam suffered a judicial death (his understanding of Nu 31:8); at the trial he would have used the relating of the story and the prophecies as a part of his defense. Oswald T. Allis (*The Old Testament: Its Claims and Its Critics* [Philadelphia: Presbyterian & Reformed, 1972], 127) has suggested that the events and prophecies may have been granted to Moses by a direct revelation of the Holy Spirit.

Others posit that the story and the oracles may not have been added to the book of Numbers during the life of Moses but sometime later in Israel's history as a way of finishing the story of Israel's wilderness account. Harrison (*IOT*, 620, 630), for example, suggests the possibility that the materials may even have come from a Moabite source or through a disciple of Balaam. In point of fact, we simply do not know how these chapters became part of the book. All we know is that these chapters form an essential part of Numbers as God has had it come to the synagogue and the church. As Scripture, the words of Balaam's prophecies are as true as the gospel, of which they—astonishingly—ultimately form a part.

h. Israel's Final Rebellion with the Baal of Peor and the Death of the First Generation (25:1–18)

OVERVIEW

Many readers of Numbers have considered the events of this chapter as just another example of rebellion and judgment in the long, sorry story of Israel's intransigence in the wilderness. Norman C. Habel was one of the first to observe that these events are something more than that; this was no mere peccadillo (see his *Yahweh versus Baal: A Conflict of Religious Cultures: A Study in the Relevance of Ugaritic Materials for the Early Faith of Israel* [New York: Bookman Associates, 1964], 24–25). As Rabbi Hirsch, 426, writes, "The sword of no stranger, the curse of no stranger had the power to damage Israel. Only it itself could bring misfortune, by seceding from God and his Torah."

This chapter presents a formative encounter with Baal worship, an instance in the soon-to-be lengthy disaster that would one day engulf and destroy the nation. It is evocative of the sad images of Genesis 38, when Judah nearly became a practicing Canaanite in his separation from his brothers, his marriage to a Canaanite woman, the marriages he arranged for his sons with a Canaanite woman, and his participation in Canaanite ritual prostitution. It projects the images of the end of Israel and of Judah, which resulted in their becoming like the peoples of Canaan.

This section presents the ultimate rebellion of Israel in the wilderness. The time was at the end of the forty-year period of their wilderness experience. The place was the staging area for the conquest of the land of Canaan. The issue is that of apostasy from the Lord by participation in the debased, sexually centered Canaanite religious rites of Baal worship—that which would become the bane of Israel's experience in the land. This chapter is an end and a beginning. It marks the end of the first generation; it also points to the beginning of a whole new series of wicked acts that would finally lead to Israel's punishment (see comments on 33:50–56).

All the rebellions up to this point described in Numbers have centered in murmurings against Yahweh and against his servants Moses and Aaron. The people have provoked the anger of the Lord by grumbling about water and food and by refusing to believe that he was able to deliver on his promise to bring them into the land of Canaan. But this chapter stands out in the record of the experience of the Hebrews in their move from Sinai to Moab—it describes their involvement in the worship of another deity.

In a sense this chapter matches the grim account of Israel's involvement in the pagan rites of the worship of the golden calf at the base of Mount Sinai (Ex 32). The apostasy of Israel in flagrantly worshiping the golden calf pointed back to Egypt. The golden calf was a symbol of the Egyptian bull-god Apis, likely referred to in Jeremiah 46:15 (see *EBC*[1], 6:652). Apis was the sacred bull in Egypt, the incarnation of Osiris, a principal deity in Egypt. Exodus 32:6 reads, "So the next day the people rose early and sacrificed burnt offerings and presented fellowship offerings. Afterward they sat down to eat and drink and got up to indulge in revelry"; see 1Co 10:6–8). The verb translated "to indulge in revelry" (*lᵉṣaḥēq*, Piel infinitive construct of *ṣāḥaq* [GK 7464], meaning "to laugh" in the Qal and

forming the base for the name "Isaac") sometimes speaks of sexual involvement. It is a euphemism for "caressing" in sexual play (as in Ge 26:8). The present chapter describes Israel's engaging in sexual acts in the worship of a god of Canaan.

i. The involvement of Israel in the worship of Baal Peor (25:1–3)

¹While Israel was staying in Shittim, the men began to indulge in sexual immorality with Moabite women, ²who invited them to the sacrifices to their gods. The people ate and bowed down before these gods. ³So Israel joined in worshiping the Baal of Peor. And the LORD's anger burned against them.

COMMENTARY

1 Shittim (*haśśiṭṭîm*, "the acacias"; see 33:49, *ʾābēl haśśiṭṭîm* [Abel Shittim], "the brook of the acacias") is another name for the region of Israel's staging for the conquest of the land; Shittim lay in Transjordan, across from the ancient city of Jericho (see Jos 2:1). The story of Numbers 25 has some breaks in it; it is not until 31:8, 16 that we learn that the principal instigator of the apostasy of the people of Israel was Balaam son of Beor (see Note on 22:5). Failing to destroy Israel by the means of the mantic curse, Balaam then seduced Israel with Canaanite practices of the sexually centered worship of the god Baal.

The phrase "Moabite women" is the connecting link that ties this chapter to the preceding ones (chs. 22–24). What the fathers of Moab could not do, their daughters accomplished by bringing Israel to its knees—sexually, morally, in false worship, and in great judgment. The verb *zānâ* ("to partake in immorality"), used to describe the action of the men, is often used to describe the behavior of a loose woman, a harlot. Here the people, as a unit, *bewhored themselves* with foreign, pagan women.

Regularly in the ancient Near Eastern context, references to sexual imagery such as this suggest interconnecting circles of sexual immorality tied to sacral rites of prostitution, which were essential parts of pagan religious systems of the day.

2 The phrase "to the sacrifices of their gods" reminds us that the true worship of the Lord, which was sacrificial in nature, was easily compromised in the minds of the people, due in part to the nature of the sacrificial systems of their neighbors (see Ex 34:15; Dt 32:38; Jdg 16:23; 2Ki 10:19; Isa 57:7; Eze 20:28; Hos 4:19). Psalm 106:28 terms these pagan acts "sacrifices ... to lifeless gods" (*zibḥê mētîm*)—as against sacrifices to the living Yahweh.

There is nothing in 24:25 to prepare us for the suddenness of 25:1. This chapter is the last word on the old generation. This was the end; the new was coming. The events in this chapter are no mere petty sins on Israel's part. Israel's engagement in the sexually centered worship of Baal was not only the evil of immorality; it was also a breach of the covenant with Yahweh, a worship of the gods of the land (v.3), and a foretaste of the ruin of the people in the unfolding of their history. That this terrible evil followed so closely on the heels of the blessings the Lord pronounced through the improbable prophet Balaam is most lamentable.

The Torah is hesitant to describe these licentious actions of pagan worship in detail; it refers to these events with considerable restraint for at least two reasons. (1) The people for whom these texts were first written were well aware of the issues; only we on this side of the vast chasms of time, culture, history, and language have questions about them. (2) To dwell unduly on the licentious character of the nature religions of the neighbors of Israel could itself become a subtle enticement to draw one in rather than to repel the reader from the evil itself. Consider a modern example: Few people peruse racy magazines to read essays, despite common protestations to the contrary.

3 Verse 3 is especially telling; the crafting of the verse is powerful. The wording contrasts the actions of Israel with God's evaluation of her:

And so Israel was yoked to Baal Peor;
but Yahweh was enraged against Israel.

The verb "to be yoked" (ṣāmad; "joined," NIV) is a binding together, as oxen are yoked in a common task. In this case Israel was "yoked" to pagan peoples in the worship of their god. The verb speaks of adapting to the worship patterns of a foreign people—an abhorrent concept, such as the false yokings from which Israel was prohibited (see Dt 22:10; cf. 2Co 6:14). This passage is the first encounter of Israel with Baal, and it forms the death rattle of the first generation.

The word "Peor" describes a mountain in Moab (see 23:28) where the local manifestation of Baal was worshiped. In v.18 Peor is used alone of the god (see 31:16; Jos 22:17). Some writers see this religion as distinct from the Baal worship of Canaan; we agree with Habel (*Yahweh Versus Baal*, 25; see Overview) that the Baal worship at Peor was a part of the same broad religion as that which was found throughout Canaan.

The wrath of the Lord is *wayyiḥar-ʾap* (lit., "a reddening of his nose"), a flashing of his rage. These anthropomorphisms (better, anthropopathisms) are vivid ways to describe what is unimaginable—to be on the receiving end of the wrath of God. The point of the Torah is not to show how often God rages or how violent are his judgments. The texts regularly assert how slow he is in coming to rage (see again Ex 34:5–7). But God has his flash point; his rage has a trigger. The rage of the Lord should have been expended against Moab and Balaam because of their effrontery; but here it is directed against Israel. They have deflected his rage from others to themselves by their obdurate folly.

NOTES

1 וַיָּחֶל (*wayyāḥel*, "began") may be an example of double entendre. The root חָלַל (*ḥālal*) III means "to pollute, defile, profane," in the Niphal, Piel, and Pual stems. In the Hiphil, as here, the verb means "to begin." It is used in the same way in other odious contexts (e.g., Ge 6:1; 10:8 ["grew to be"]). In any event, the next verb, לִזְנוֹת (*liznôt*, "to play the whore") leaves nothing to the imagination. The root זָנָה (*zānâ*) has the idea of "fornication" in Genesis 38:24; Leviticus 21:9; Deuteronomy 22:21; Hosea 4:13–14; et al.—all of which refer to women who engage in illicit sexual relationships. Here the verb is used of men. They went "whoring" after the women priestesses of Canaanite Baalism. It is a deficiency of our language that we have numerous words for loose women but few suitable terms for loose men. I say this is a "deficiency," as we have no shortage of varieties of outrageous male sexual behavior in our culture.

2 The verb וַיִּשְׁתַּחֲוּוּ [emended; MT has חֲוו-] (*wayyištaḥᵃwû*, "and [they] bowed down") is now parsed as a Hishtaphel preterit of the root חָוָה, *ḥāwâ* ("to make oneself lie prostrate, bow oneself down"; GK 2556; see *HALOT*, 1:295–96) rather than a Hithpael preterit of the root שָׁחָה (*šāḥâ*, "to bow down"), as listed in BDB 1005b. The force of the stem speaks of "causing oneself to bow down"; the Hishtaphel (used in the MT only with this verb) is causative-reflexive. This is the principal Hebrew term in the Bible for acts of worship, used of the worship of Yahweh (see Ge 22:5; Pss 29:2; 95:6; cf. Eph 3:14) as well as of pagan gods (as here). It is fitting that the biblical term for worship is physical in nature, but it entails internal realities. See Ronald Allen and Gordon Borror, "The Body of the Believer in Worship," in *Worship: Rediscovering the Missing Jewel* (Portland, Ore.: Multnomah, 1982), 119–35; cf. Allen and Allen, 116–18.

ii. The judgment of the Lord on his errant people (25:4–5)

> ⁴The LORD said to Moses, "Take all the leaders of these people, kill them and expose them in broad daylight before the LORD, so that the LORD's fierce anger may turn away from Israel."
> ⁵So Moses said to Israel's judges, "Each of you must put to death those of your men who have joined in worshiping the Baal of Peor."

COMMENTARY

4–5 God's rage against his people provoked a terrible judgment: those who were the leaders of the people in this awful act of impiety were to be put to death. The gravity of the sin called not only for death but also for a special display of the corpses of the offenders (see Note) in "broad daylight" so that those who would survive would be strongly warned of the consequences. As the animals and birds had been cut in half in the covenantal ceremony at the beginnings of Israel's history (Ge 15:10), so the bodies of these rebels were to be dismembered and displayed in an awful symbol of divine judgment.

The expression "in broad daylight" (lit., "before the sun") speaks of something done openly, publicly (so 2Sa 12:12; cf. "before the eyes of the sun" in the MT of v.11). The execution of the leaders was designed to divert his anger from the populace as a whole. The expression *ḥᵃrôn ʾap-yhwh* ("fierce anger of Yahweh") is used elsewhere of the anger of the Lord (32:14; Ex 32:19, 22; Dt 13:17; Jos 7:26; 1Sa 28:18; 2Ki 23:26; 2Ch 28:11; Zep 2:2; 3:8; et al.); but this anger may be averted or turned back, once it flashes against its target.

So Moses commanded the judges of Israel to kill those persons who had attached themselves to Baal Peor. The verb *hārag* ("to kill"; v.5) is usually used to speak of ruthless violence, murder (as in Ex 5:21). Here its use to speak of the judicial taking of life by the command of God is a rare one (so Ex 32:27; Lev 20:15–16; Dt 13:10).

Chapter 25 is the nadir of the book of Numbers. The sin it relates is worse even than the sins of chs. 12–14. This account describes the great sin at the end of the road. This may be one of the most indelicate texts of Scripture, one in which Israel's judges are commanded to kill their own people who were engaged in the worship of Baal (v.5). At times we have trouble coming to grips with Scripture's commands that Israel kill her enemies. This chapter is even more difficult for us to face, for it commands Hebrews to kill fellow Hebrews.

But these rebellious persons were like a cancer in the body. If they were not excised, they would soon ruin the lot. So the call was to kill and execute, and to do it quickly. Chapter 15 told of the public execution of one person, a blasphemer. Now the whole population was in danger.

NOTE

4 The NIV's translation "kill them and expose them" is a rendering of וְהוֹקַע (wᵉhôqaʿ, "expose [them]"). From v.5 we understand that this verse calls for Moses to take the leaders of the people, execute them, and then "set them aside" or "expose them" to the Lord in broad daylight. The verb יָקַע (yāqaʿ, "to set aside, expose"; GK 3697) is used in the Qal stem to describe a bone dislocation (Ge 32:25 [26], of Jacob's thigh). Possibly here the meaning of the Hiphil is "to [kill them and then] expose them with legs and arms broken" (so KB, 398c; BDB says, "[used] of some solemn form of execution, but mng. uncertain," 429c). Second Samuel 21:6, 9 may describe the same type of "exposing" of mutilated bodies (see also the Hophal in 2Sa 21:13). The Samaritan recension reads an explanatory line: "And Yahweh said to Moses, 'Let them kill the men who have joined themselves to Baal Peor.'" This seems to be a smoothing of the Hebrew of v.4 based on the words of v.5. It is reading back a clearer idea into a verse where the text is less clear to later readers — a characteristic feature of the Samaritan text.

iii. The zeal of Phinehas (25:6–9)

⁶Then an Israelite man brought to his family a Midianite woman right before the eyes of Moses and the whole assembly of Israel while they were weeping at the entrance to the Tent of Meeting. ⁷When Phinehas son of Eleazar, the son of Aaron, the priest, saw this, he left the assembly, took a spear in his hand ⁸and followed the Israelite into the tent. He drove the spear through both of them — through the Israelite and into the woman's body. Then the plague against the Israelites was stopped; ⁹but those who died in the plague numbered 24,000.

COMMENTARY

6 The wording of verse 6 is problematic. It is possible to take the verse as the NIV has rendered it and to sense in these words that something quite — but unspecified — was happening.

But I suspect the actions described here were so very shocking that the scribes of Scripture found it to be quite repellent and that the precise nature of the offense was softened by slight euphemistic revisions in the wording through time (see Note).

Perhaps the verse is best read this way: "Then a certain Israelite man brought the Midianite woman to *the Tent [of God]* right before the eyes of Moses and the eyes of all the congregation of Israel; *and they were sporting* at the entrance of the Tent of Meeting." This translation is based on some textual considerations (represented in the emphasized phrases; see Note) and on an attempt to reconstruct what may have been the most outrageous action of apostate behavior recorded anywhere in the Torah.

The MT reads in the first italicized instance "to his brothers" (ʾel-ʾeḥāyw), a phrase the NIV smoothes out as "to his family." The LXX translates, "the man brought his brother to the Midianite woman." Yet the mention of "brother" or "family" is not nearly as shocking as the possibility that the phrase should read "to his tent" (reading ʾel-ʾohŏlô [as in Ge 31:25, "Jacob pitched ʾet-ʾohŏlô [his tent]"] instead of ʾel-ʾeḥāyw). Because of what follows, the emended text "to his tent" must refer to the Tent of the Lord; i.e., a specific tent is in view. It is most shocking that the tent may be the Tent of Meeting.

This emendation and the change of meaning are prompted by the last phrase of the verse, which the NIV renders, "while they were weeping at the entrance to the Tent of Meeting." This suggests that it was Moses and the congregation of Israel who were weeping at the entrance to the holy precincts. This is certainly possible; the outrage of the events might have driven Moses and pious persons to weep and to beg God for forgiveness.

It seems likely, however, that the subject of the verb *bōkîm*, "weeping," is not Moses and the congregation but the sinning Israelite and his Midianite partner. The focus of action in the verse is on them, not Moses. What they did was before Moses, in his presence—under his nose! And what they did was to engage in a sexual embrace in the manner of Baal worship—right at the entrance of the holy Tent of God! They were no longer copulating before an image of Baal, but—in outrageous behavior—in front of the Holy Place of Yahweh!

Thus the scribes, I suggest, have made a deliberate substitution of an opposite word, "weeping," to replace "caressing," in order to stress euphemistically the heightened enormity of this act. They were not weeping; they were laughing (*śōqēp*)—that is, they were engaged in delirious love-making (cf. Ge 26:8; Ex 32:6). Just as to say "curse God" was for the godly scribe an unthinkable thing actually to write down, so one might write "bless God" when "curse God" was intended (see 1Ki 21:10, 13; Job 1:5, 11; 2:5, 9; Ps 10:3; see Ginsburg, 366–67); here, to "cry" in the sacred precincts (as in a cry of remorse) is used to disguise the antithetical meaning, "to laugh in sexual pleasure"—while engaged as "one flesh" at the opening of the sacred tent.

The audacious action of this Israelite man and the Midianite woman is unparalleled and totally unexpected. The contempt for the holy things and the word of the Lord shown by Zimri and his Midianite lover, Cozbi (v.15), is unimaginable. This is the nadir of the first section of Numbers; here is Israel at her very worst. This provides an unhappy justification for the ways of the Lord; it also provides a theodicy of his judgment of the entire first generation.

The man was a blasphemer in the strongest sense. His sin was a deliberate provocation of the wrath of the Lord. He was flaunting and taunting holiness in an almost unbelievable crudity. The issue was so blatant, so outrageous, so unspeakable—I suggest—that the ancients had to hide the meaning somewhat in coded words. Those who read the text today find between the words that stand (which are awful enough) something that is truly an outrage against Majesty—something that is nearly unbelievable.

Many of those who saw this happening must have been so shocked that they were motionless. They must have been stunned by audacity, numbed by horror. Someone had to do something; finally, one man did act. Notice that the evil man in this verse is a Hebrew. It would have been bad enough had this been a foreign man with his foreign mate. But it was a prominent man from the congregation. This act, then, is the cause célèbre of v.1, the principal action of "playing the whore" with foreign women. This man's disregard for the sacred (*qōdeš*) is so outrageous as to shock us even today, in our jaded, secular age.

The point was that in joining the sexual frenzies of the sacrificial feasts of Baal, the man and his priestess partner were attempting to transform the worship of Yahweh into the pattern of sexual rites that were the mode of Canaan. Had this outrage not been stopped, there could never have been true worship in the Holy Place again. They were making the place of entrance into a bordello, the entrance of the meeting place of God with humankind into a trysting spot. No wonder the ancients may have been uncomfortable with this text.

The woman was a Midianite. The enemy people were Moabites. This situation alerts us to the complexities involved in the relationships of the transient peoples of the ancient Near East at this time (cf. the Ishmaelites and Midianites in Ge 37:25–36). More importantly, the Hebrew of v.6 uses the definite article to identify the woman: "the Midianitess." This suggests that she was not just one of the local sacred prostitutes but a person of prominence. I suggest that the article is used to mark her as a pivotal player. Perhaps she was the high priestess of the religion at Baal Peor. The story when read in this way explains the action of Phinehas in the next verses.

Priests were always male in Israel. Women could be priests in the pagan religions that surrounded Israel. In fact, the sexually centered religions of Canaan would have catered to women in their priestly orders, as some lists of priestly guilds in Ugarit attest. Women priests were so closely tied to the sexual outrages of Baal and Asherah worship that the very notion of a female priest conjured up images of sexual worship. Perhaps this reason helps explain why Israel had no women priests.

It was the brazenness of the acts of these two people that made them not just sinners but an abomination to the Lord. Here was a frontal assault on the true, high, and pure worship of the Lord that the priestly interests in Numbers stress repeatedly. Only an act of force equal to the nature of the affront would suffice. That powerful act came in the person of Phinehas.

7–8 When Phinehas the son of Eleazar saw what was happening right at the entrance of the tent (v.7), he reached for a "spear" (*rōmaḥ*) and drove it through the licentious couple (v.8; see 3:10 and notes for background to his actions). Everyone had observed what was happening; but Phinehas not only watched, he also acted. He came from the midst of the people as the protagonist. Possibly the implement he used was a spear that he took from a nearby soldier. It is hard to know what a priest would be doing with a spear (yet see the use of spears by pagan priests in 1Ki 18:28). It is just possible that here the Hebrew *rōmaḥ* might mean "knife," as this would be the more expected tool for a priest to possess. It would be suitably ironic for him to have used a tool he normally used to kill animals in sacrifice to the Lord as the weapon to kill this sinning couple.

Phinehas was a grandson of Aaron (Ex 6:25). His name may have been Egyptian in origin; BDB (810) suggests *Pe-nehasi* ("the negro"), speaking of dark complexion. Phinehas was like a "man of the in-between" (*'îš habbēnayim*), as Goliath had been a "champion" to the Philistines (1Sa 17:4; cf. v.23—and by extension, the same phrase could have been used for David as he represented Israel). Phinehas was like a "mighty man of valor" (*gibbôr ḥayil*; "man of standing," NIV), as Kish the father of Saul is described (1Sa 9:1). He was also a true "servant of Yahweh" (*ʿebed yhwh*), as Moses is described (Dt 34:5). Ultimately, he was typical of Christ the Victor (see Pss 2; 110; Rev 19). He was an early embodiment of the "star" and "scepter" of 24:17, the smiter of Moab. He was the hand of God extended in rage against the profanation of his joy. Phinehas is one of the great heroes of faith in Scripture; though he is quite unknown to most of us, he is never forgotten by God. His zeal was that of one who feared the Lord, who waited on his mercy (Ps 147:11), but who also acted when not to act would be to sin.

Verse 8 says that Phinehas pursued the couple into the "vaulted canopy" (*haqqubbâ*; "tent," NIV), a word used only here in the Bible. If our conceptualization of this story is correct, it is possible that the term *qubbâ* (GK 7688) refers to some canopy at the entrance of the Tent of Meeting. It would not be necessary to imagine that the couple was actually within the Most Holy Place, nor does it seem likely that they were in the man's tent, as is commonly supposed. In any event, there is a grisly pun on the word *haqqubbâ* and the word for "her belly" (*qobātâ*).

That Phinehas pierced through the two of them is forcefully stressed: (1) the knife or spear could not have been a little thing but could well have been a narrow, sharp blade; (2) there would have taken a tremendous force for him to plunge the knife or spear through both bodies; (3) the emphasis on "both" stresses that they were oblivious to Phinehas,

both caught up in their licentiousness, so that the knife would have gone through his back, pass below his sternum, and into her abdomen; and (4) with this bold act of the young priest the plague was stayed, which indicates that this couple's act was not just an outrageous instance of debauchery; rather, likely they were the instigators of the pagan rites! Contemporary radio social commentator Dr. Laura Schlessinger would likely have a lively comment to describe their actions and sudden death—perhaps something along the lines of "hoping they had a lovely orgasm." The purposeful shock in her hypothetical barb strikes at the blasé attitudes of so many people in our day who seem willing to break all bonds for momentary pleasure.

9 The number of those who died because of the flagrant actions of the people in their worship of the Baal of Peor (24,000 here; see 1Co 10:8, where the number 23,000 is given; see *EBC*[2], 11:344) exceeded even those who died in the rebellion of Korah and his allies (14,700; see 16:49). If the numbers of the two census lists (1:46; cf. 26:51) are taken at face value (i.e., as "common numbers"), then the loss of 24,000 people, while certainly significant, is not overwhelming. If the numbers of the census lists are rhetorically inflated, as I have argued (see Introduction: Large Numbers), then we must ask whether this number was also inflated. It seems possible that this number and the number of those who died in Korah's rebellion may be "common, rounded numbers." If so, the enormity of the numbers who died in this plague was truly impressive—nearly 10 percent of the total population of 250,000.

NOTE

6 אֶל־אֶחָיו (*ʾel-ʾeḥāyw*, "to his brothers") is not a felicitous phrase in this verse. The NIV translates "to his family," an attempt to smooth out an awkward idea. *BHS* lists a proposal in the apparatus to emend this term to אֶל אָהֳלוֹ (ʾel ʾohºlô, "to his tent"); this reading appears to be superior—albeit adventuresome.

Ginsburg has sections on scribal activity in this vein entitled, "The Removal of Indelicate Expressions, Anthropomorphisms, &c. from the Text" (11.8.345–47), "The Emendations of the Sopherim" (11.9.347–63), and "Impious Expressions Towards the Almighty" (11.10.363–67). I propose that this verse constitutes another instance, one that Ginsburg did not himself mark.

iv. The Lord's covenant with Phinehas (25:10–13)

¹⁰The LORD said to Moses, ¹¹"Phinehas son of Eleazar, the son of Aaron, the priest, has turned my anger away from the Israelites; for he was as zealous as I am for my honor among them, so that in my zeal I did not put an end to them. ¹²Therefore tell him I am making my covenant of peace with him. ¹³He and his descendants will have a covenant of a lasting priesthood, because he was zealous for the honor of his God and made atonement for the Israelites."

COMMENTARY

10–11 The words of the Lord to Moses concerning Phinehas (v.10) take us back to the words of the Decalogue (Ex 20:4–6). The zeal of Phinehas for the honor of Yahweh became the occasion for the Lord's covenanting with him and his descendants as God's true priests. What a contrast this son of Eleazar is with the casual wickedness of his uncles Nadab and Abihu (see comment on 3:4).

Standard criticism regards the present shape of Numbers to be the work of P, the priestly source, lately designed to elevate the priests in the life of the people and their institutions. Thus, not only are chapters such as 15 and 19 significant in their calm presentation of sacrifices, worship, duties, and tithes, but so also is this chapter, as the hero of the piece was a priest.

For the more conservative reader whose understanding does not proceed from the putative P source, the emphasis on priesthood should still be maintained. Since the hero of our story is a priest,

our estimation of the righteous priests should be enhanced. These men could be noble and brave; they were not just cultic functionaries. Then we remember that Christ is priest; he is noble and brave. The best in priests points to Christ. This is true of Aaron, Eleazar, and Phinehas. The chapter celebrates a great priest, just as it excoriates a terrible evil.

Verse 10 introduces an oracle of the Lord attached directly to the preceding, dramatic narrative. Its focus is on Phinehas, who had acted with the zeal of the Lord. There is almost a sense of pride in the way Phinehas is addressed in this text: "Phinehas son of Eleazar, the son of Aaron, the priest" (v.11). This is the language of celebration. The zeal of Phinehas stayed the rage of Yahweh; the zeal of Phinehas restrained the zeal of the Lord to annihilate the nation. Perhaps in these words we should stand beside his father, Eleazar, and sense his pride in his son.

12 The Lord instituted his covenant with the priests through Phinehas. We often speak of the Abrahamic, Mosaic, and Davidic covenants. We should also speak of Yahweh's covenant with Phinehas. He was priest by divine right, descended from the right family in an immediate line. He showed himself to be the rightful priest by his interest in divine righteousness. He was now confirmed priest by the rite of the divine covenant.

13 As in Yahweh's covenant with Abram, this covenant was God's doing; it involved the priest's

"seed," and it is lasting (ʿôlām). In the case of Abram, God first chose him; then by Abram's action of faith, the Lord confirmed his covenant with him (see Ge 12; 15; 22). In the case of Phinehas, he was already chosen by God, but in his action God's covenant with him was confirmed.

Most surprisingly, by the action of Phinehas "atonement" (wayekappēr) was made for the people, for the plague was stopped (v.9). This chapter is a pivotal section in the theology of the Torah.

NOTE

12 The phrase אֶת־בְּרִיתִי שָׁלוֹם (ʾet-bᵉrîtî šālôm, "my covenant of peace") is somewhat problematic, as we do not usually find intervening pronominal suffixes in bound constructions. We would have expected אֶת־בְּרִית שְׁלוֹמִי (ʾet-bᵉrît šᵉlômî, "the covenant of my peace") as in בְּכָל־הַר קָדְשִׁי (bᵉkol-har qodšî, "in all my holy mountain"; Isa 11:9). Some have emended the word שָׁלוֹם (šālôm, "[my covenant of] peace") to שִׁלּוּם (šillûm, "[my covenant of] requital").

v. The aftermath of the rebellion (25:14–18)

> ¹⁴The name of the Israelite who was killed with the Midianite woman was Zimri son of Salu, the leader of a Simeonite family. ¹⁵And the name of the Midianite woman who was put to death was Cozbi daughter of Zur, a tribal chief of a Midianite family.
>
> ¹⁶The LORD said to Moses, ¹⁷"Treat the Midianites as enemies and kill them, ¹⁸because they treated you as enemies when they deceived you in the affair of Peor and their sister Cozbi, the daughter of a Midianite leader, the woman who was killed when the plague came as a result of Peor."

COMMENTARY

14–18 Only after the role of Phinehas had been suitably celebrated were the names of the antagonists given. The Israelite was a prince of the house of Simeon, Zimri son of Salu (v.14). It is important that we realize this individual was

not insignificant—here was one who should have ennobled himself and his father's house. As the great pride of Eleazar must have swelled over the actions of his son that day, so there must have been extraordinary shame among the members of

Zimri's family on realizing what this promising young man had done.

Zimri had been named in praise of God. However, he is now remembered as the one who nearly destroyed his people in his flagrant, wanton attack on the pure worship of God. With his name turned on its head, he serves as a memorial to destruction. The name of his Midianite partner is given as Cozbi daughter of Zur (v.15). Her name is likely another example of names deliberately changed by Israel because of the contempt in which she was held (see comments on the name of Balaam in 22:5). "Cozbi" means "My Lie" or "Deception." She stands forever memorialized as a prime example of the deception of the allure of pagan worship. Verse 18 speaks of her as one who was also from

a noble house of her own people. Likely she was a priestess of her religion, a prototype of Jezebel, who would later be instrumental in bringing Baal and Asherah worship into the center of the life of Israel.

Because of their active participation in the seduction of the sons of Israel, the Midianites were put under the curse of God and were henceforth to be treated as enemies (v.17). They had been in league with Balak from the beginning of the confrontation (see comment on 22:4) and became the objects of a holy war of Israel to declare the glory of the name Yahweh (see ch. 31).

In the MT the words "after the plague" (see 26:1 NIV) actually form a separate verse at the end of the chapter (25:19). See Note on 26:1.

II. THE PROSPECTS FOR THE SECOND GENERATION TO ENTER THE PROMISED LAND (26:1–36:13)

OVERVIEW

Following the lead of Olson (see Introduction: Unity and Structure), I suggest that this chapter begins the second major part of the book of Numbers. The book is best seen as a bifid based on the two generations that are celebrated in the two census lists. Other approaches to the book use chronological or geographical clues to determine the relevant portions. However, the chronological notes are too few and piecemeal to be helpful, and the arrangement of some of the blocks of materials turns out not to be in chronological sequence.

Similarly, the geographical issues, which at first seem to be more helpful than the chronology for discovering the author's purpose, do not yield convincing results. Most scholars who follow the

geographical approach are able to agree on the first major division at 10:11, the beginning of the march from Sinai. But there is no consensus as to the beginning of the third movement, the march to or the sojourn in Moab. But more problematic than the issue of which verses should be included in which geographical section (and the lack of the precise indicator in the text of Numbers ought to be regarded as a problem in this approach) is that this approach slights the most prominent feature of the book — *its census lists*!

The book of Numbers is correctly named; its organization is simple. There are two grand sections: (1) the census and preparation for the march of the first generation, and its subsequent failure and judgment (chs. 1–25); (2) the census and preparation for the march of the second generation, and the hope that they will not repeat the sins of their fathers and mothers (chs. 26–36).

The unequal length of the two sections results from the nature of the case. The story is told more fully of the first generation; they were prepared, but they rebelled and did not inherit the land. The second generation is prepared, but their subsequent success or failure is left to be decided another day. As we saw at the beginning, God has time and the wilderness has sand.

The first section begins with the preparation of a holy camp and is followed by material describing the rebellion of the people, their subsequent judgment, and their return to the wilderness to wait for the dying of the rebellious people. The chapters on priesthood, purification, and the like are included in this section as encouragements to the people. Even though the one generation would never be able to participate in the blessings of the land, yet those blessings have not been forgotten by God. The new generation may be making confident preparation for their day in glory.

Then the story of Balaam comes as the new generation was about to have its opportunity. The pagan prophet is a foil for the person of Moses, and his attempted cursings of Israel are opportunities for God to renew his promises of blessings and to affirm them to the people. Thus there is in this incident tremendous assurance that despite all the sins, rebellions, and untoward actions of the people on so many occasions and in the most diverse of circumstances, the Lord not only was not finished with his people, but he was now more ready than ever to bless them and complete his promise of salvation for them. Yet immediately on the heels of God's monumental blessing of the people, they rebelled again(!) in the most egregious way possible.

Chapter 25 records Israel's bowing to the lust of Baal Peor, the last rebellion of the first generation. And the plague is their last judgment, the final judicial assault of God on wicked persons, the final purging of the people.

Then chapter 26 begins with the idea that after the plague the Lord commanded that Moses take a census of the people. The expression "after the plague" is to be regarded as the turning point from the first generation to the second, the shift from the fathers and mothers to sons and daughters. God was about to begin a new work with a new people. The younger generation would begin to have their day.

The second section of Numbers presents only the positive, preparatory side of things. It deals with the taking of the new census, a demonstration that God has kept faith with the people in a remarkable manner. Despite innumerable setbacks and plagues that touched many lives, and despite God's judgment that decreed that everyone over age twenty would have to die in the forty years spent in the wilderness, the total numbers of God's people remain nearly precisely the same. This is an enormous miracle, a great demonstration of God's power to do his will and work even in the most unlikely of places.

But the new generation will also have to face its tests. What those will be are anybody's guess, but they will not likely be easier than those suffered by their parents. The great question, looming like a heavy cloud on the horizon, is asked all along the way through these last chapters of this book: Is it possible that the new generation will finally be used of God to enter the land, to conquer the inhabitants, to displace them, and to enjoy the land that is God's great and gracious gift for them? Or will this new, second generation be like its predecessors? Will they also come to the lip of the land, send out their spies, and find that the evil report of these spies will also dissuade them? God forbid! The hope is this: May the new generation truly be *new*! May they be faithful to God in their entire house even as Moses was for most of his illustrious career. And may they enter the land with joy and delight, while praising God for giving them the opportunity that their parents had forsworn.

So the book of Numbers ends with a great, haunting question: What will the children be like? Will they be like their parents? Or will they be like Moses and Aaron, like Joshua and Caleb, like Miriam and others faithful to God? Will they believe in him, obey his commands, and take up their weapons as they march in victory song?

Incidentally, the bifid approach to the book of Numbers greatly heightens the importance of the subsequent story of the sending out of the spies from Israel's encampment in Transjordan to the city of Jericho (Jos 2). The work of those spies and their report is the accomplishment of daring men of faith. They are like Caleb and Joshua (and, notably, this time there are just two spies). The plan is on. The people will do as God demands.

A. The Preparation for the Triumphal March to the Promised Land, the Second Generation (26:1–32:42)

OVERVIEW

In view of the approach I have suggested, chs. 26–36 match and mirror the basic thrust of chs. 1–10. In each case there is the enumeration of the people in celebration of the Lord's grace to his people, their preparation for a holy march, and the anticipation that soon they will be in Canaan, and Canaan will become the land of Israel.

1. The Second Census, That of the New Generation, Who Will Enter the Land (26:1–65)

a. The Command of the Lord to Take the Census (26:1–4)

¹After the plague the LORD said to Moses and Eleazar son of Aaron, the priest, ²"Take a census of the whole Israelite community by families—all those twenty years old or more who are able to serve in the army of Israel." ³So on the plains of Moab by the Jordan across from Jericho, Moses and Eleazar the priest spoke with them and said, ⁴"Take a census of the men twenty years old or more, as the LORD commanded Moses."

These were the Israelites who came out of Egypt.

COMMENTARY

1–4a The first phrase, "after the plague," is the key for our understanding of this text. The plague of ch. 25 was not just another plague; it was the final judgment of God on the first generation and the opportunity to unleash God's blessing on the second generation, those people who have now reached their majority.

The first census of the redeemed community had been taken over thirty-eight years earlier. This was a census for conscription to the army of the people, soldiers who were drafted for the war of conquering the Land of Promise. That first generation of men over the age of twenty had died. It was now time for the new generation to be numbered and mustered for the campaign of conquest that now awaited them. The aged Moses was joined in the task this time by his nephew Eleazar. Aaron was dead (20:28). Miriam was dead (20:1). And Moses was soon to die as well.

How sad it must have been for Moses to realize what might have been! Yet there must have been enormous satisfaction to realize that it still might be—though without him. This was a bittersweet time, one of ruing the past while still anticipating the future. It was the same task: number the able-bodied men over the age of twenty to conscript them for the army of Israel. But it was a different task. The place had changed from Sinai to Moab. The personnel had changed; Moses was assisted now by Eleazar instead of his brother Aaron. More importantly, the people had changed; they were a new generation.

The passage thus presents the opportunity for a collective sigh. At last we will be at it. We will finally be on the trail again. Yet the passage also evokes a certain element of sadness. What we are now doing has already been done. What we are about to do should have been done long ago. Our parents should have entered the land, and we should have grown up there rather than here in this wilderness. The passage is also a warning. Those mustered earlier were disqualified; just being in the roll call of the Lord's army does not mean acquittal in his service.

Eleazar was not the only son who participated this day; the participants were *all* sons of fathers who had died. There is a final poignancy in the heart of Moses. The last time, he was going as the leader of the people. This time he is involved in their preparation, but he will not be with them in their campaign. This prospect must have eaten away at his inner being—it must have felt like a tourniquet of regret wrenching his heart.

4b These words actually serve as the section heading for the tribe-by-tribe list that follows. How impressive it is that the phrasing is inclusive of the departure from Egypt! This new generation is regarded as the people of the exodus. It is as though their parents had not lived, as though they had not rebelled. The new generation substitutes for the first. The story begins anew, as though the people have just left bondage in Egypt.

NOTES

1 For the first phrase of v.1 in the NIV, וַיְהִי אַחֲרֵי הַמַּגֵּפָה (*way^{e}hî $^{\,}$ah^{a}rê hammaggēpâ*, "after the plague"), is problematic in that the chapter division is misplaced in the present MT. In *BHS* these words form 25:19 (observe that there is no v.19 in the English versions), but these words do not form a complete verse. These three words end in an *athnah* accent, a major disjunctive within a verse; then 26:1 in Hebrew begins with the words "and Yahweh said." There is no *athnah* within 26:1; it clearly is the same verse begun with the words, "After the plague." This verse indicates that the old generation is gone, and the new one is now in place.

A further complication in the Hebrew here is in the inclusion of the Hebrew letter פ (*p*) as a section marker after this introductory phrase. In this case we may have an example of a chapter number's being written inadvertently in the midst of the first verse of the unit; the first part of the verse was then assigned a supernumerary for convenience of citation. (Another problem in verse division is found at 19:10 [see Note].)

2 The listing of the clans in the second census calls for special mention. These names would be important for the nation later in the land as people would wish to be able to trace with certainty their ancestry for purposes of tribal inheritance. The listing of the clans is also a dramatic mark on the part of the narrator; this is the list that will count! We may observe that not all who were part of Israel were genetically descended from Jacob through his twelve sons. From the beginning, persons of varied backgrounds joined their destinies with the people of Israel. However, to have their part in the land, they had to have a tie with a tribe and a family. Perhaps ritual adoption was the means used to include such persons in the communal rosters.

The number of the tribe of Reuben in the second listing is a slight decrease from the first. Several of the tribes (namely, Judah, Issachar, Zebulun, Manasseh, Benjamin, Dan, and Asher) increase in number in the second census compared to the first. Like Reuben, Gad suffers a slight decline, Ephraim and Naphtali a greater decline, and the tribe of Simeon takes a decisive cut.

Possibly the slight reduction of the families of Reuben (46,500 in 1:20; 2:10) was brought about by the judgment on their members during the rebellion of Korah and his Reubenite allies (see comment on 26:9). In the intervening years the family of Reuben had nearly caught up with its former numbers.

Here is a comparison of the numbers of each of the tribes from the first census to the second:

Tribe	First Census	Second Census
Reuben	*46,500*	43,730
Simeon	59,300	22,200
Gad	45,650	40,500
Judah	74,600	76,500
Issachar	54,400	64,300
Zebulun	57,400	60,500
Ephraim	40,500	32,500
Manasseh	32,200	52,700
Benjamin	35,400	45,600
Dan	62,700	64,400
Asher	41,500	53,400
Naphtali	53,400	45,400
Total	603,550	601,730

As we observed in the first census listings in ch. 1, there are several interesting factors in these various numbers. First, none of these numbers is brought down to a final digit; only two are rounded to the tens (Gad in the first census, at 45,650, and Reuben in the second, at 43,730); all the others are rounded to the hundreds. In both lists there are six tribes that number over 50,000 men and six that number fewer than 50,000. Twelve units of about 50,000 is a convenient way to reach the grand totals of about 600,000.

Tribes with More Than 50,000 Men

First Census	Second Census
Simeon: 59,300	
Judah: 74,600	Judah: 76,500
Issachar: 54,400	Issachar: 64,300
Zebulun: 57,400	Zebulun: 60,500
	Manasseh: 52,700
Dan: 62,700	Dan: 64,400
	Asher: 53,400
Naphtali: 53,400	

Tribes with Fewer Than 50,000 Men

First Census	Second Census
Reuben: 46,500	Reuben: 43,730
	Simeon: 22,200
Gad: 45,650	Gad: 40,500
Ephraim: 40,500	Ephraim: 32,500
Manasseh: 32,200	
Benjamin: 35,400	Benjamin: 45,600
Asher: 41,500	
	Naphtali: 45,400

3 עַל־יַרְדֵּן יְרֵחוֹ (ʿal-yardēn yᵉrēḥô, "by the Jordan of Jericho") seems to be an older way of speaking of the region of the Jordan River that is across from the city of Jericho (so NIV; see also v.63; 31:12; 33:48, 50; 35:1; 36:13).

b. The Enumeration of the People by Their Ancestral Tribes and Clans (26:5–50)

i. The tribe of Reuben (26:5–11)

⁵The descendants of Reuben, the firstborn son of Israel, were:
through Hanoch, the Hanochite clan;
through Pallu, the Palluite clan;
⁶through Hezron, the Hezronite clan;
through Carmi, the Carmite clan.
⁷These were the clans of Reuben; those numbered were 43,730.
⁸The son of Pallu was Eliab, ⁹and the sons of Eliab were Nemuel, Dathan and Abiram. The same Dathan and Abiram were the community officials who rebelled against Moses and Aaron and were among Korah's followers when they rebelled against the Lord. ¹⁰The earth opened its mouth and swallowed them along with Korah, whose followers died when the fire devoured the 250 men. And they served as a warning sign. ¹¹The line of Korah, however, did not die out.

COMMENTARY

5–7 Pride of place is given to Reuben, firstborn of Jacob. These chapters serve as the account of the generations of Jacob (see comment on 1:17–19). The four clans are descended from his sons Hanoch, Pallu, Hezron, and Carmi, whose names are given first in Genesis 46:9. Numbers 26 should be compared with Genesis 46:8–27. Genesis 46 is a full mustering of the fathers' houses as Israel went down to Egypt. Numbers 26 is a full mustering of the fathers' houses as they were about to reenter Canaan. From the seventy persons of Genesis 46:27 to the quarter million (or two and one-half million, if the traditional understanding of the numbers is maintained) of Numbers 26:51, there is an enormous increase. And this came despite the conditions in Egypt for four hundred years, coupled to the experience in the wilderness for another forty

years. Reuben's sons are also mentioned in Exodus 6:14 (the same listing as in Genesis 46 and Numbers 26).

8–11 The listing of the families of Reuben becomes an occasion to remind the reader of the part that certain of their number (especially Dathan and Abiram) had played in the rebellion of Korah (16:1; On is not mentioned in ch. 26). The tragic memory of the rebellion of Korah is made as well in Jude 11.

This paragraph is impressive. It is something of an intrusion into the ordered format of the tribal listings, clans, and numbers. But it is important that the reader know this list is not just business as usual. The overwhelming judgment of those who joined Korah in his ill-advised rebellion was to remain a *nēs*, "a warning sign" or "signal flag of warning," to succeeding generations (v.10). They, too, may suffer a similar fate if ever they attempted similar folly.

The wording of v.9 is dramatic: "the very Dathan and Abiram" (*hû^ɔ-dātān waⁿᵃbîrām*). Further, the verb translated "rebelled" (*nāṣâ*) against Moses and Aaron is rare and signifies a strong contest of wills. But ultimately they found they were struggling not just with man but also with God. He had used heaven (fire) and earth (the sink hole) to destroy them. Take on God and one finds he has a no-holds-barred fight. After all, "The LORD is a warrior" (Ex 15:3).

Some names of infidels and rascals are to be forgotten. They are to be treated as though they never had lived. But others have behaved so shamefully that their names are to be preserved as bywords for future generations, a warning to others not to be like them. These names are like the salten image of the unfortunate wife of Lot, a symbolic barrier to misbehavior.

Names are of interest in the biblical narrative. These men were named for God but became his enemies. As in the case of Elimelech in the book of Ruth, bearing a godly name does not necessarily mean leading a godly life. Nor is a godly name a device effective to ward off his judgment. A godly name on an ungodly person is in fact a double offense, more deserving than ever of God's judgment.

In summary, the tribe of Reuben numbered 43,730 in the second census, a decrease of 2,770 from the 46,500 of the first census (a loss of about 6 percent). There are four clans. The further history of the Reubenites is found in 1 Chronicles 5:1–10.

NOTES

7 For a discussion concerning the large numbers in this chapter and in the census lists for the first generation, see in the Introduction the sections on large numbers.

9 קָרִיא (*qārîⁿ*, singular), the Hebrew word underlying the phrase "the men appointed," is a technical term for representatives; it is used only here and in 1:16. In both cases there are problems of Kethiv-Qere spellings, but the adjectival form is passive in function and means "one called," from the common root קָרָא (*qārāⁿ*, "to call").

ii. The tribe of Simeon (26:12–14)

¹²The descendants of Simeon by their clans were:
    through Nemuel, the Nemuelite clan;
    through Jamin, the Jaminite clan;
    through Jakin, the Jakinite clan;
¹³through Zerah, the Zerahite clan;
    through Shaul, the Shaulite clan.
¹⁴These were the clans of Simeon; there were 22,200 men.

COMMENTARY

12–14 The greatest loss was among the tribe of Simeon (down to 22,200 from 59,300). The exceedingly wicked Zimri (see ch. 25) was a prince of the house of Simeon (v.14). Perhaps the larger number of the 24,000 who died in the plague of that time had been of the house of Simeon. The judgment was so recent that the tribe had not had time to recover as Reuben had (see comment on v.7).

Five clans are listed as descended from Simeon in v.12: Nemuel, Jamin, Jakin, Zerah, and Shaul. Nemuel is called Jemuel in Genesis 46:10 and Exodus 6:15. Further, Ohad of Genesis 46:10 and Exodus 6:15 is not mentioned in Numbers; perhaps he died childless or for some other reason did not establish a bona fide clan. Genesis 46:10 observes of Shaul that his mother was a Canaanite—an interesting note when compared with the story of Judah and Tamar in Genesis 38.

In summary, the tribe of Simeon numbered 22,200 in the second census, a decrease of 37,100 from the 59,300 of the first census (a decrease of about 63 percent). There are five clans. The tribe of Simeon is ranked second in both lists. In 1 Chronicles 4:24 the sons of Simeon are listed as Nemuel, Jamin, Jarib, Zerah, and Shaul; 1 Chronicles 4:24–43 develops the later history of the family of Simeon.

iii. The tribe of Gad (26:15–18)

> ¹⁵The descendants of Gad by their clans were:
>   through Zephon, the Zephonite clan;
>   through Haggi, the Haggite clan;
>   through Shuni, the Shunite clan;
> ¹⁶through Ozni, the Oznite clan;
>   through Eri, the Erite clan;
> ¹⁷through Arodi, the Arodite clan;
>   through' Areli, the Arelite clan.
> ¹⁸These were the clans of Gad; those numbered were 40,500.

COMMENTARY

15–18 Here we notice a standard, even stereotypical pattern of the tribal listings. Only in the rebellious tribe of Reuben is there a strong variation. The other lists follow a bookkeeper's tidy pattern, at least in format.

In parallel passages, there are several problems with the names of these sons of Gad. Further, when we compare the names of the sons of Gad in Genesis 46:16, we find some variations of names. Zephon of v.15 is Ziphion in Genesis 46:16 (NIV margin); Ozni of v.16 is Ezbon in Genesis 46:16. The problems with these names in parallel passages could be regarded as an embarrassment to the tenet of inspiration. Yet in a sense the very problems we find in these parallel lists of names may be strong indicators of the tradition of textual integrity. If the text were not highly regarded by the scribes as the Word of God, then blemishes such as these would have been smoothed over. Spellings would have been agreed on, divergences expunged. Surely we are not the first to read one name in Numbers 26 and another in Genesis 46, one in Numbers 26 and another in one of the chapters of 1 Chronicles.

The preservation of discordant spellings and even dissimilar names argues for, not against, integrity. At one time the names were known and were correct. When errors crept in, or when alternative names were used that resulted in some confusion, the scholars of later generations did not disturb the evidence they had. This is not to say that scribes never meddled with names; in fact they did. But the amazing thing is that they did not meddle more, especially in instances such as these. In cases of such "muddled" names, there are several alternative explanations: (1) different spellings for the same name, (2) different names for the same person, and (3) confusion of scribes and hence mistakes in the copying of the names.

In summary, the tribe of Gad numbered 40,500 in the second census, a decrease of 5,150 from the 45,650 of the first census (a decrease of about 11 percent). There are seven clans. The tribe of Gad is ranked third in both lists. The further history of the tribe of Gad is found in 1 Chronicles 5:11–17.

iv. The tribe of Judah (26:19–22)

> ¹⁹Er and Onan were sons of Judah, but they died in Canaan.
> ²⁰The descendants of Judah by their clans were:
>   through Shelah, the Shelanite clan;
>   through Perez, the Perezite clan;
>   through Zerah, the Zerahite clan.
> ²¹The descendants of Perez were:
>   through Hezron, the Hezronite clan;
>   through Hamul, the Hamulite clan.
> ²²These were the clans of Judah; those numbered were 76,500.

COMMENTARY

19–22 Compare v.19 with Genesis 46:12: "The sons of Judah: Er, Onan, Shelah, Perez and Zerah (but Er and Onan died in the land of Canaan). The sons of Perez: Hezron and Hamul." As in the case of the sons of Eliab of Reuben (vv.9–11), the sadnesses of the fathers' families are not glossed over in these lists but are to be remembered for posterity. The family of Judah was unique among the tribes of Israel in that two of the father's sons died childless in Canaan because of their perfidy before their father ever left for Egypt. Now, hundreds of years later, the sordid story of Er and Onan was alluded to, not to titillate but to warn, to cause the people to remember.

Here we are reminded that Shelah went on to marry and to father a clan. Further, the sons of Judah by his son's wife, Tamar, each fathered a clan. The firstborn twin, Perez, has two subclans—a mark of significance, since most of the grandsons are not mentioned here. It is likely that the listing of these subclans makes up for the loss of the clans that might have been founded by the two deceased older sons. Perez has the double honor; indeed, his is the line that Yahweh selected for his great king David (Ru 4:18–22) and for David's greater Son, Jesus (Mt 1:3; Lk 3:33). It is fascinating that already in Genesis 46:12 the precedence

of Perez was asserted. He alone is noted of the grandsons.

In summary, the tribe of Judah numbered 76,500 in the second census, an increase of 1,900 from the 74,600 of the first census (a gain of less than 3 percent). There are five clans (two are subclans). The tribe of Judah is ranked fourth in both lists. The further history of the tribe of Judah is found in 1 Chronicles 2:3–4:23, which includes an extensive list not only of sons but also of mothers and daughters—an unusual feature in these lists. Since it is from the tribe of Judah that the kings were traced, the unusual listing is made significant. For obvious reasons Christian readers are aware of the special care of the Spirit of God in these lists.

v. The tribe of Issachar (26:23–25)

²³The descendants of Issachar by their clans were:
through Tola, the Tolaite clan;
through Puah, the Puite clan;
²⁴through Jashub, the Jashubite clan;
through Shimron, the Shimronite clan.
²⁵These were the clans of Issachar; those numbered were 64,300.

COMMENTARY

23–25 The clans of Issachar are traced through Tola, Puah, Jashub, and Shimron. Two of these names are problematic; there is difficulty with the spelling of Puah (see Note on v.23), and the name Job (*yôb*, "Iob") is mistakenly written in the MT of Genesis 46:13 for Jashub (*yāšûb*). There is also a slight variation in spelling for the name Shimron (*šimrōn* in Numbers; *šimrôn* in Genesis). The point is that we are able to put these various data together and we may attempt to harmonize them. The scribes did

not do so, presumably based on their sense of caution against destroying the varied evidence that was before them.

In summary, the tribe of Issachar numbered 64,300 in the second census, an increase of 9,900 from the 54,400 of the first census (a gain of about 18 percent). There are four clans. The tribe of Issachar is ranked fifth in both lists. The further history of the tribe of Issachar is found in 1 Chronicles 7:1–5.

NOTE

23 The name פֻּוָה (*puwâ*, "Puah") is spelled variously in different texts and is represented differently in the versions. Many Hebrew manuscripts read the word as פֻּוָּה (*puwwâ*); the Samaritan Pentateuch, LXX, Syriac, and Vulgate read פֻּוָאה (*pûᵓâ*). Genesis 46:13 reads פֻּוָּה (*puwwâ*); 1 Chronicles 7:1 reads פֻּוָאה (*pûᵓâ*). In each case the same individual is intended, but the spelling variations suggest some confusion; perhaps these are variations in pronunciation.

Matters are a bit more difficult in the case of תוֹלָע (*tôlāᶜ*, "Tola"), who is here the founder of a clan ("the Tolite clan") in Issachar that is parallel to the clan founded by Puah ("the Puite clan"). In Judges 10:1 we read of a judge called "a man of Issachar, Tola son of Puah, the son of Dodo." Some scholars suggest that this judge was assigned to an earlier time by the P source in Genesis and Numbers (e.g., BDB, 1069a). However, it would not be at all unusual for patronymic names to be used in later generations in alternating sequences; such was common in ancient (and is so in modern) times.

vi. The tribe of Zebulun (26:26–27)

> ²⁶The descendants of Zebulun by their clans were:
> through Sered, the Seredite clan;
> through Elon, the Elonite clan;
> through Jahleel, the Jahleelite clan.
>
> ²⁷These were the clans of Zebulun; those numbered were 60,500.

COMMENTARY

26–27 Sered, Elon, and Jahleel, sons of Zebulun, founded the three clans of this tribe; the names are the same in Genesis 46:14. In summary, the tribe of Zebulun numbered 60,500 in the second census, an increase of 3,100 from the 57,400 of the first census (a gain of over 5 percent). There are three clans. The tribe of Zebulun is ranked sixth in both census lists. Unlike the other tribes, the further history of the tribe of Zebulun is not recorded in 1 Chronicles 2–8; only the name of the tribe is given in 2:1. This is a strange omission (but see on Dan, vv. 42–43).

vii. The tribe of Manasseh (26:28–34)

> ²⁸The descendants of Joseph by their clans through Manasseh and Ephraim were:
> ²⁹The descendants of Manasseh:

through Makir, the Makirite clan (Makir was the father of Gilead);
through Gilead, the Gileadite clan.
[30]These were the descendants of Gilead:
through Iezer, the Iezerite clan;
through Helek, the Helekite clan;
[31]through Asriel, the Asrielite clan;
through Shechem, the Shechemite clan;
[32]through Shemida, the Shemidaite clan;
through Hepher, the Hepherite clan.
[33](Zelophehad son of Hepher had no sons; he had only daughters, whose names were
Mahlah, Noah, Hoglah, Milcah and Tirzah.)
[34]These were the clans of Manasseh; those numbered were 52,700.

COMMENTARY

28–34 There is an inclusio of sorts grouping the tribes of Manasseh and Ephraim. Verse 28 introduces these two tribes as the descendants of Joseph; v.37 ends with a notice that these were the descendants of Joseph. In this way the reader is reminded that Joseph received the double honor of his father, Jacob, by having two sons receive equal status with his brothers among the tribes of Israel. With the removal of the tribe of Levi from the lay tribes, this "bonus" to Joseph maintained the sacral number twelve for the fathers' houses.

The order of the tribes is the same in the two census lists, with the exception of the inversion of Manasseh and Ephraim among the tribes of Joseph. One observation we may make about this inversion of order is that the tribe of Ephraim was superior in number to Manasseh in Numbers 1; the reverse is true in Numbers 26. Later in Israel's history, the tribe of Ephraim became the counterpart in the north to the importance of Judah in the south. Yet at this point the tribe of Ephraim was among the smallest (only Simeon with 22,200 was smaller than Ephraim's 32,500). This datum seems to argue against the critical theory from a number of German scholars that the lists in these chapters of Numbers were projections backward from late in Israel's history (when these lists were manufactured), based on their conceptions of the ideal state of affairs during the times of David and Solomon. Yet these numbers do not accord with any later period of Israel's history. To be blunt, if the numbers do not accord with the time of Moses in some manner, then they are simply manufactured.

There are a couple of unusual features in the roster of the clans of Manasseh. First, only one son of Manasseh is listed; his name is Makir (see Ge 50:23; Nu 27:1; 32:39–40; Dt 3:15; Jos 13:31; 17:1, 3). Joshua 17:1–2 suggests that Makir was the firstborn of Manasseh and that Abiezer (= Iezer), Helek, Asriel, Shechem, Shemida, and Hepher were other "sons." These other sons are actually descended from Gilead, son of Makir.

Thus the tribe of Manasseh is distinctive in that it did not divide into sub-clans until the fourth generation. The line of descent is Joseph – Manasseh – Makir – Gilead – six sons, including Hepher. From Hepher came Zelophehad, who had five daughters. The listing of the sons of Gilead is prominent in our text: Iezer, Helek, Asriel, Shechem, Shemida, Hepher (followed by Zelophehad).

It is the last name that presents the second unusual factor in this listing; Zelophehad, actually the grandson of Gilead, "had no sons, only daughters" (v.33). This factor became the subject matter for chapter 27 (and a followup in ch. 36).

The family of Makir is developed in 1 Chronicles 7:14–19. Of Manasseh it is said that his Aramean concubine (no name given) bore him Makir (v.14). Makir then married Maacah, from the people of Huppim and Shuppim, and they became the parents of Gilead. Gilead had six sons: Iezer (see Note on v.30), Helek, Asriel, Shechem, Shemida, and Hepher. Hepher was the father of Zelophehad.

While the descendants of Jacob had a remarkable propensity to father sons, surely there were daughters along the way! Yet Zelophehad's daughters (Mahlah, Noah, Hoglah, Milcah, and Tirzah; v.33) are nearly the only ones mentioned in this chapter (see v.46). Since the chapter records a roster of men being mustered for war, the lack of the mention of daughters elsewhere can be explained. But it is interesting to see how 1 Chronicles mentions women abundantly, especially in chs. 2 and 7. The purpose of Numbers 26 in listing men for war is granted, but hardly any other mention of women is unsettling. Who was mothering all these sons? The reason to mention Zelophehad's daughters in v.33 was to set the stage for the narrative of ch. 27. And that stage is a most dramatic one indeed.

The most significant gain among all the tribes in the wilderness period was that of Manasseh (52,700, up from 32,200). No reason is known for this dramatic increase. In summary, the tribe of Manasseh numbered 52,700 in the second census, an increase of 20,500 from the 32,200 of the first census (a stunning gain of 64 percent). There are two clans, that of Makir and that of his son Gilead; then there are six subclans of the Gileadites. The tribe of Manasseh is ranked eighth in the first list and seventh in the second, thereby changing places with its brother tribe Ephraim—perhaps because of its phenomenal increase in numbers. The further history of the tribe of Manasseh is found in 1 Chronicles 7:14–19.

NOTE

30 אִיעֶזֶר (ʾîʿezer, "Iezer"), this first-named son of Gilead, may in fact have been the son of his sister Hammoleketh but was regarded as Gilead's "son" for genealogical purposes; see 1 Chronicles 7:18, where "Iezer" seems to be intended by אֲבִיעֶזֶר, (ʾabîʿezer, "Abiezer"). The genealogies are exceedingly complex in this section.

viii. The tribe of Ephraim (26:35–37)

³⁵These were the descendants of Ephraim by their clans:
through Shuthelah, the Shuthelahite clan;
through Beker, the Bekerite clan;

through Tahan, the Tahanite clan.
³⁶These were the descendants of Shuthelah:
through Eran, the Eranite clan.
³⁷These were the clans of Ephraim; those numbered were 32,500.

These were the descendants of Joseph by their clans.

COMMENTARY

35–37 The clans of Ephraim are listed under three sons — Shuthelah, Beker, and Tahan — and one subclan, through Eran son of Shuthelah (yet Eran is not mentioned elsewhere).

In summary, the tribe of Ephraim numbered 32,500 in the second census, a drop of 8,000 from the 40,500 of the first census (a decrease of about 20 percent). There are three clans and one subclan. The tribe of Ephraim is ranked seventh in the first list and eighth in the second, thereby changing places with its brother tribe, Manasseh. Further history of the tribe of Ephraim is found in 1 Chronicles 7:20–29.

ix. The tribe of Benjamin (26:38–41)

³⁸The descendants of Benjamin by their clans were:
through Bela, the Belaite clan;
through Ashbel, the Ashbelite clan;
through Ahiram, the Ahiramite clan;
³⁹through Shupham, the Shuphamite clan;
through Hupham, the Huphamite clan.
⁴⁰The descendants of Bela through Ard and Naaman were:
through Ard, the Ardite clan;
through Naaman, the Naamite clan.
⁴¹These were the clans of Benjamin; those numbered were 45,600.

COMMENTARY

38–41 The lists of names of sons and clans in the earlier rosters have presented problems of spelling and identification from time to time when the lists in Numbers 26 are compared with similar lists in Genesis and 1 Chronicles. But in the case of the tribe of Benjamin, we come to

361

nearly insurmountable problems of correlation. It appears that the lists of the clans of Benjamin are fluid, perhaps depending on differing purposes of their sources, as well as considerable confusion in the transmission of these names. Again, the most hopeful observation one can make about the confused state of the matter is that scribes did not attempt to go through these lists to sanitize them of these astringencies.

The lists that are to be compared are from Genesis 46:21; Numbers 26:38; 1 Chronicles 7:6; and 1 Chronicles 8:1–2. Below are parallel tables of these four texts of the sons of Benjamin:

Genesis 46:21	Numbers 26:38	1 Chronicles 7:6	1 Chronicles 8:1–2
Bela	Bela	Bela	Bela
Beker		Beker	"his firstborn" (see Note)
		Jediael (only here)	
Ashbel	Ashbel		Ashbel
Gera (only here)			
Naaman	[Naaman; name of a son of Bela; v.40]		[Naaman; name of a son of Bela; v.3]
Ehi	Ahiram		Aharah
Rosh			Nohah (only here)
			Rapha (only here)
Muppim	Shephupham or Shupham [v.39]		
Huppim	Hupham [v.39]		
Ard	Ard [name of a son of Bela; v.40		

Some possible reasons for the differences follow.

1. The name "Beker" may have been misunderstood in 1 Chronicles 8:1 as the Hebrew term $b^e\underline{k}\bar{o}r\hat{o}$, "his firstborn," leading to the unusual list of ordinals in the rest of the names in that listing.

2. The name "Ahiram" in Numbers 26:38 (= Aharah of 1Ch 8:1) may be identified with Ehi of Genesis 46:21; alternatively, perhaps there is a confusion of the two names "Ahi" and "Rosh" of Genesis 46:21 in the name "Ahiram."

3. Shephupham (MT = Shupham of Sam., Pent., Vulg., Syr.) is confused perhaps with "Muppim" of Genesis 46:21.

4. "Hupham" of Numbers 26:39 may equal "Huppim" of Genesis 46:21; but he may be a descendant, not the son (see 1Ch 7:12; yet 1Ch 7:12 may list descendants who have similar names as their forebears, this issue being complex).

5. Ard in Numbers 26:40 is listed as a son of Bela, along with Naaman. Perhaps these men were not born in the period described in Genesis 46.

In summary, the tribe of Benjamin numbered 45,600 in the second census, an increase of 10,200 from the 35,400 of the first census (a gain of 29 percent). There are five clans and two subclans (but the other lists give different figures). The tribe of Benjamin is ranked ninth in both census lists. The further history of the tribe of Benjamin is found in 1 Chronicles 7:6-12; 8:1-39. This latter, extended excursus on the family of Benjamin is occasioned by interest in the line of Israel's first king, Saul (see 1Ch 8:33).

NOTE

38 In the complex listing of the sons of Benjamin, as compared with other lists, one name, בֶּכֶר (beker, "Beker"), is omitted in Numbers 26:38 but found in Genesis 46:21 and 1 Chronicles 7:6. In 1 Chronicles 8:1 the text reads בְּכֹרוֹ (bᵉkōrô, "his firstborn").

x. The tribe of Dan (26:42-43)

⁴²These were the descendants of Dan by their clans:
through Shuham, the Shuhamite clan.
These were the clans of Dan: ⁴³All of them were Shuhamite clans; and those numbered were 64,400.

COMMENTARY

42-43 The briefest of all the tribal notations is given for Dan, and only one clan is listed, Shuham. Yet surprisingly, the total population is quite large, at 64,400; only Judah (76,500) is larger. Genesis 46:23 lists one son for Dan, namely, Hushim. The relationship of the words "Shuham" and "Hushim" is unknown (but a confusion of letters is certainly possible; see Note). It is unexpected that such a large tribe would be descended from only one son.

In summary, the tribe of Dan numbered as 64,400 in the second census, an increase of 1,700 from the 62,700 of the first census (a gain of about 3 percent). There is only one clan. The tribe of Dan is ranked tenth in both census lists. Alone among the tribes, the name of Dan is not mentioned at all in the tribal genealogies of 1 Chronicles 1-8 (see also on vv.26-27, the situation with respect to Zebulun).

NOTE

42 The name of the son of Dan is שׁוּחָם (*šûḥām*, "Shuham"); in Genesis 46:23 the son of Dan is חֻשִׁים (*ḥušîm*, "Hushim"). These different names may have resulted from a transposition of the Hebrew letters שׁ (*š*) and ח (*ḥ*) in transcription.

xi. The tribe of Asher (26:44–47)

44The descendants of Asher by their clans were:

through Imnah, the Imnite clan;

through Ishvi, the Ishvite clan;

through Beriah, the Beriite clan;

45and through the descendants of Beriah:

through Heber, the Heberite clan;

through Malkiel, the Malkielite clan.

46(Asher had a daughter named Serah.)

47These were the clans of Asher; those numbered were 53,400.

COMMENTARY

44–47 In Numbers 26 one name, "Ishvah" (*yišwâ*), has dropped from the listing of the names of the sons of Asher in Genesis 46:17 and 1 Chronicles 7:30. Perhaps Ishvah did not establish a clan and so is not listed in Numbers. The other sons who are listed are Imnah, Ishvi, and Beriah, besides Heber and Malkiel, the sons of Beriah who founded subclans.

The mention of Serah, daughter of Asher (v.46), is remarkable (and she is mentioned as well in Genesis 46:17 and 1 Chronicles 7:30). The appearance of her name in these lists raises some questions: Is it possible she was the only daughter born to the twelve sons of Jacob, even as Jacob had only one daughter, Dinah? Do sons (or daughters) run in families that prominently? Or were there numerous other daughters from the many wives of these twelve sons of Jacob though only Serah is mentioned? Her name is mentioned without any note of marriage or progeny—what happened to her? These unanswered questions remind us of how little we know of women in the patriarchal stories.

Genesis 46:26 adds up the persons who went down to Egypt thus: "all those who went to Egypt with Jacob ... not counting his sons' wives—were sixty-six persons." Since these women were not descended from Jacob, out of his body, they were not named. By contrast, the mothers of Jacob's twelve sons are named prominently in Genesis 46 (and elsewhere). But note what we are not told. By the time of the account of Genesis 46, Rachel is dead. What became of Leah, Zilpah, and Bilhah? Did they go to Egypt, or were they already dead? Did Jacob outlive all four wives before he went down to Egypt?

Further, we learn of the occasional inappropriate wife—Judah's Canaanite wife and his daughter-in-law Tamar (see 1Ch 2:3)—and the exceptional, but apparently fitting, foreign wife, such as Asenath, the wife of Joseph (Ge 41:50). But we wonder where the other sons got their wives. Were they also women of the land?

We read of Zelophehad, who had only daughters, and in 1 Chronicles 2:34–35 of Sheshan, who also had only daughters. He gives one unnamed daughter in marriage to a named slave, whose son he regards as his grandson!

Again, we think of David (1Ch 3:1–9), who has six sons at Hebron from six different wives, then four sons by Bathsheba, plus nine others from wives not specified, and unnumbered sons by concubines.

But only one daughter is named: Tamar, the sister of Absalom, daughter of Maacah (2Sa 13:1). This ratio of nineteen sons to one daughter, by numerous wives, stands out! So we ask: Were there actually many more daughters? Was Tamar only mentioned because of the story of Absalom and Amnon, as Dinah may have been mentioned alone among many sisters only because of the story of Shechem and her brothers?

In summary, the tribe of Asher numbered 53,400 in the second census, an increase of 11,900 from the 41,500 of the first census (a gain of 29 percent). There are three clans, two subclans, and one daughter. The tribe of Asher is ranked eleventh in both census lists. The further history of the tribe of Asher is found in 1 Chronicles 7:30–40.

xii. The tribe of Naphtali (26:48–50)

48The descendants of Naphtali by their clans were:
    through Jahzeel, the Jahzeelite clan;
    through Guni, the Gunite clan;
49through Jezer, the Jezerite clan;
    through Shillem, the Shillemite clan.
50These were the clans of Naphtali; those numbered were 45,400.

COMMENTARY

48–50 The families of Naphtali are descended from four sons, Jahzeel, Guni, Jezer, and Shillem (all mentioned in Ge 46:24 and 1Ch 7:13).

In summary, the tribe of Naphtali numbered 45,400 in the second census, a decrease of 8,000 from the 53,400 of the first census (a drop of 15 percent). There are four clans. The tribe of Naphtali is ranked twelfth in both census lists. The names of the sons of Naphtali, but no further history of the tribe, are found in 1 Chronicles 7:13.

c. The Grand Celebrative Number, to the Praise of the Lord (26:51)

51The total number of the men of Israel was 601,730.

COMMENTARY

51 Despite all the people who had died during the years of wilderness experience, the total of the people was 601,730 — nearly the same as the total of those who were first numbered. This remarkable fact is to be regarded as the signal blessing of the Lord, in fulfillment of his many promises to give numerical strength to the people descended from Abraham through Jacob (see Ge 12:2). The loss of 1,820 persons, from 603,550 mentioned in 1:46 in the first census, is a drop of only 0.3 percent — a negligible sum!

This grand total and its integers are in accord with the general pattern of the numbers of the book. The numbers show a wonderful consistency, despite the shifting totals among the various tribes (see Note). It is utterly remarkable that the total number has remained nearly unchanged even though the people have lived under the most try-ing conditions for a period of thirty-eight years. There had been the deaths of all those who were over the age of twenty at the time of the rebellion at Kadesh, and there had been numerous judgments of God that came on the people because of that rebellion and others. Then there was the harsh reality of living out life in the Desert of Sinai. Given all these factors, the birth rate was not just equal but prolific. God's faithfulness to his people is grandly celebrated with this triumphant chapter of census!

The point of this number is principally the praise of the Lord. The number may have been inflated rhetorically; but if so, it is *a celebrative inflation*, glorying in God and anticipating the time when Israel, the people of God, will be in number like the stars of the heavens and as countless as the grains of sand on the seashore.

NOTE

51 For the large totals of the tribes and the grand total for the full complement of able-bodied men over the age of twenty, see the Introduction, the sections on the large numbers; also see the comment and Note on 1:46. The numbers in the second list are consistently large, as are those in the first census. Any conclusion drawn about the one must affect the other. Again in this chapter we find numerous problems in the textual transmission of names but none concerning the transmission of these large numbers. If one wishes to argue for problems of textual transmission as the source of the large numbers, the errors would have had to come at such an early period that there was no record left of the errors — a most unlikely situation. Again, the numbers are added as real integers; 1,000 is 1 more than 999. Further, the math is correct; the sum of the twelve tribal rosters adds up to the total: 601,730.

d. The Allotment of the Land on the Basis of the Names of the Families of Israel (26:52–56)

[52]The LORD said to Moses, [53]"The land is to be allotted to them as an inheritance based on the number of names. [54]To a larger group give a larger inheritance, and to a smaller

group a smaller one; each is to receive its inheritance according to the number of those listed. ⁵⁵Be sure that the land is distributed by lot. What each group inherits will be according to the names for its ancestral tribe. ⁵⁶Each inheritance is to be distributed by lot among the larger and smaller groups."

COMMENTARY

52–56 This pericope is an impressive addition to the census record as compared to 1:44–46 and following. In the first census the emphasis was fully on preparation for warfare ("all ... who are able to serve in the army," 1:3; and "who were able to serve in Israel's army," 1:45). The second census begins in the same manner ("who are able to serve in the army of Israel," 26:2), but it ends differently. The second census relates not only to military service in the conquest of the land but also to inheritance rights once the land was made theirs. This pericope of promise was designed to compel the people to lives of faithfulness.

The listing of names was not only the means for demonstrating God's faithfulness to his people; it was also a basis for an equitable distribution of the land they were about to enter. Larger tribes would receive larger shares, but the decisions of place would be made by lot (v.56). Until the end, Moses was still in charge of these matters—more bittersweet experiences that marked his last days. The distribution of the land was to be based on the dual principles of fairness and lot (with the understanding that the fall of the lot lay in the hands of the Lord). The land was God's gift to his people; hence their shares in it were their inheritance from him.

e. The Families and Numbers of the Levites, the Holy Tribe of Israel (26:57–62)

⁵⁷These were the Levites who were counted by their clans:
through Gershon, the Gershonite clan;
through Kohath, the Kohathite clan;
through Merari, the Merarite clan.
⁵⁸These also were Levite clans:
the Libnite clan,
the Hebronite clan,
the Mahlite clan,
the Mushite clan,
the Korahite clan.
(Kohath was the forefather of Amram; ⁵⁹the name of Amram's wife was Jochebed, a descendant of Levi, who was born to the Levites in Egypt. To Amram she bore Aaron, Moses and their sister Miriam. ⁶⁰Aaron was the father of Nadab and Abihu, Eleazar

and Ithamar. ⁶¹But Nadab and Abihu died when they made an offering before the LORD with unauthorized fire.)

⁶²All the male Levites a month old or more numbered 23,000. They were not counted along with the other Israelites because they received no inheritance among them.

COMMENTARY

57–58a This pericope corresponds to the separate counting of the Levites in the first census (see 1:47–53; 3:1–39; see also Ex 6:16–25). The Levites are grouped in three clans (Gershon, Kohath, and Merari) with five subclans in this text: Libni (of Gershon; see 3:18; Ex 6:18), Hebron (of Kohath; see 3:19; Ex 6:18), Mahli and Mushi (of Merari; see 3:20; Ex 6:19), and Korah (a descendant of Kohath through Izhar; see Ex 6:21). A comparison of the line of Levi in Exodus 6 shows that not all the sons of Gershon, Kohath, and Merari founded families that were reckoned among the Levites.

58b–61 The parenthetical pericope on Kohath, Amram, and Jochebed is a reminder of earlier sections of the Torah (3:1–10; Ex 6:20), likely inserted here to assert anew the lineage of Aaron and to remind the priests of the debacle of Nadab and Abihu. The record of Amram and Jochebed is compressed, as is generally recognized. Kohath must have lived perhaps 350 years before Moses, as he was born before Jacob went down to Egypt (see Ge 46:11). Further, there is a family of Amramites that numbered several hundred at the time of Moses (see Nu 3:27). Most probably Amram and Jochebed are celebrated ancestors of Aaron, Miriam, and Moses rather than their immediate parents (see W. H. Gispen, *Exodus* [Bible Student's Commentary; trans. Ed van der Maas; Grand Rapids: Zondervan, 1982], 77, n. 10); for Nadab and Abihu, see comments on

3:4 and Leviticus 10:1–3. From the direction of these verses, it is clear that the listing of the families of Levi is focused on the need to document the family line of Miriam, Aaron, and Moses one more time.

A question remains, however. If Amram and Jochebed are not the immediate parents of Miriam, Aaron, and Moses, why are they mentioned so prominently? Perhaps the issue concerns something of a scandal about their marriage. Exodus 6:20 says that Amram married his aunt. Such a breech of taboo would not soon be forgotten. So scandalized was Israel that the names of these remote persons are preserved, though the immediate parents' names are forgotten. On Amram see also 1 Chronicles 6:1–3; contrast Exodus 2:1, which speaks of the parents of Moses without giving their names. Even in the birth narratives of some of its most illustrious heroes, the Torah does not seem to answer the types of basic questions the modern reader has.

62 The number of male Levites over the age of one month increased from 22,000 in the first census (3:39) to 23,000 in the second (26:62), an increase of 1,000 (about 5 percent). The pericope ends with the restated reason for the separate numbering of the Levites: They were not part of the army, nor would they be inheritors of the land; they were a tribe holy to the Lord. But they were a part of the nation, and their families had to be listed along with the names of the other family names in Israel.

f. A Recapitulation of the Point of the Census: This Is the New Generation (26:63–65)

> ⁶³These are the ones counted by Moses and Eleazar the priest when they counted the Israelites on the plains of Moab by the Jordan across from Jericho. ⁶⁴Not one of them was among those counted by Moses and Aaron the priest when they counted the Israelites in the Desert of Sinai. ⁶⁵For the LORD had told those Israelites they would surely die in the desert, and not one of them was left except Caleb son of Jephunneh and Joshua son of Nun.

COMMENTARY

63–65 This chapter has a fine style to it, despite the seemingly mundane issues it presents. The second census was, of course, of enormous importance to Israel and a central aspect of the Lord's dealings with her. The style is not ornate or given to literary flourish; yet in the simplicity of its format, in the sense of order and control, its strong salvific message is proclaimed—Yahweh had a people ready to enter his land!

Verses 63–65 serve as the fitting conclusion to the section begun in vv.1–4a. There are numerous ties between the two: (1) the mention of Moses and Eleazar the priest; (2) the location on the plains of Moab; and (3) the words "after the plague" in v.1, which tie to the notice in v.64 that, except for Caleb and Joshua, not one of the original group of rebels was still alive. The text emphasizes the expression "not one of them" (vv.64–65). This phrase, of

course, speaks of the sure righteousness of the Lord. But the survival of Caleb and Joshua reminds us of the grace of Yahweh, who keeps his promise to save, even as he remembers his oath to punish.

In truth it is all of grace, as Moses elaborates in his homily in Deuteronomy. In Deuteronomy 1:31 he speaks of the Lord's carrying the people in the wilderness as a father carries a son; in 2:7 he speaks of God's presence with them throughout the forty years so that they lacked nothing; and in 4:32–40 he speaks of the actions of the Lord in these years as unparalleled in all human history.

The name "Eleazar" is significant in its linking with Moses in v.63. The next verse reminds us of the first census, in which Aaron joined Moses in making the tabulation. Of the first generation none—except Caleb and Joshua—would enter the land (v.65). Even old Moses was excluded.

2. The Inheritance of Women on Entering the Land (27:1–11)

> ¹The daughters of Zelophehad son of Hepher, the son of Gilead, the son of Makir, the son of Manasseh, belonged to the clans of Manasseh son of Joseph. The names of the daughters were Mahlah, Noah, Hoglah, Milcah and Tirzah. They approached ²the entrance

to the Tent of Meeting and stood before Moses, Eleazar the priest, the leaders and the whole assembly, and said, [3]"Our father died in the desert. He was not among Korah's followers, who banded together against the LORD, but he died for his own sin and left no sons. [4]Why should our father's name disappear from his clan because he had no son? Give us property among our father's relatives."

[5]So Moses brought their case before the LORD [6]and the LORD said to him, [7]"What Zelophehad's daughters are saying is right. You must certainly give them property as an inheritance among their father's relatives and turn their father's inheritance over to them.

[8]"Say to the Israelites, 'If a man dies and leaves no son, turn his inheritance over to his daughter. [9]If he has no daughter, give his inheritance to his brothers. [10]If he has no brothers, give his inheritance to his father's brothers. [11]If his father had no brothers, give his inheritance to the nearest relative in his clan, that he may possess it. This is to be a legal requirement for the Israelites, as the LORD commanded Moses.'"

COMMENTARY

1–4 The substance of this chapter has a distinctly modern ring to it. Here is a story impinging on the rights of women in early Israel. The issue in the chapter is the question brought to Moses by five daughters of a man who had no sons. As such, this is a significant chapter in the sociology of early Israel. It is also an important contribution to the biblical theology of the book of Numbers. While we tend to focus on the fact that it was women who were presenting a claim to Moses, the substance of their claim did not center in gender but only sprang from it. The issue centered in the concept of the land and one's share in it as the geographical and spiritual destiny of the redeemed community of Israel.

The five women were daughters of Zelophehad, whose genealogy is traced back to Manasseh (v.1, a reprise of 26:33). In a sense this chapter is an extension of the genealogies of ch. 26, thus showing how complications may have had to be worked out when the people would come to inherit their share in the land of Canaan. The principal concern

of Mahlah, Noah, Hoglah, Milcah, and Tirzah was the securing of the inheritance and the preservation of their father's name in the land (v.4). Their action in approaching Moses, Eleazar, and the leaders of the nation was unprecedented, a great act of courage, conviction, and faith. It is not to be missed that the actual names of these women are given; so often in biblical narratives the names of women are lacking, even when they have a significant role to play (e.g., the wife of Noah, the wife of Lot, etc.).

The women's act of coming near (*qārab*, "to make an approach") to Moses is detailed rather graphically (v.2). They stood before Moses, before Eleazar the priest, and before the leaders and the entire congregation at the entrance of the Tent of Meeting (v.3). This march to the central shrine by these women must have been incredible to those who were watching. In ancient Israel, this act was akin to the refusal of Rosa Parks, an African-American woman, to give up her bus seat in Montgomery, Alabama, a half-century ago! With the exception of Miriam, sister of Moses and Aaron, we do not read of righteous women coming to such sacral precincts in these ancient narratives (but recall the horrible actions of Cozbi in ch. 25).

When the women made their claim to Moses, they specified that their father, Zelophehad, had not died because of an act of participation in the rebellion of Korah (see Nu 16); his death was the more common fate of all members of the entire doomed first generation (v.3). In this explanation, the daughters showed their understanding of the reality of God's judgment combined with a sense of his mercy. It appears from this verse that the rebels associated with Korah not only lost their lives in the judgment of God on them, but also their survivors may have lost their inheritance. Here is a particular death notice from among the huge statistic of 26:64. There is something touching in this notice.

But these women did not excuse their father either. These pious women demonstrated sound understanding of the nature of the wilderness experience and a just claim for their family. Further, they were women of faith. The people were not yet in the land, but these women knew that they would enter it soon. Their claim to Moses was anticipatory of the Lord's coming deliverance of the people from the awful wilderness to the Land of Promise.

So the women came with a suit asking for a decision from the Lord that their father's name not disappear from among the clans of his family. The tie of name to land in the expectation of Israel is demonstrated clearly here (v.4). One's meaning in the community was considered to be dependent on the survival of the family name in the distribution of land in the time of conquest.

5 A mark of the leadership of Moses is seen in v.5, where he heard the women's complaint and then took their case before Yahweh. In the MT of this verse, the term "their case" is written with an oversized, darkened letter "n" (nun—the so-called majuscule nun), indicating the suffixed pronoun

"their" (feminine plural). It seems that the scribe used this unusual letter to bring special attention to the fact that this appeal came from women.

6–11 This section is not only instructive in terms of the issues it presents; these verses also give an indication how case law might have operated in Israel. The general laws would be promulgated. Then legitimate exceptions or special considerations would come to the elders and perhaps be brought to Moses himself. He then would await a decision from the Lord. The language is specific in this regard; Moses did not decide by himself but waited for a decision from the Lord. Then after the decision for the specific case was rendered (see v.7), an application for other situations was also able to be rendered (see vv.8–11).

In cases such as this, Moses would have consulted Yahweh by means of the Urim and Thummim. Much speculation has centered on these words (see comments on vv.18–21 and Notes).

In this case Yahweh gave a favorable decision to these women. In fact, the response of the Lord went beyond their request. In v.4 they requested *ʾaḥuzzâ* ("landed property"). The response of the Lord was for *ʾaḥuzzat naḥᵃlâ* ("a hereditary possession of landed property"; v.7). The point seems to be that not only would these women receive their property; they could transfer it to their heirs as well. Thus they shared with the sons of other fathers who were deceased. It is as though their father had had sons!

Throughout this section there is a balanced presentation of the grace of God to hear and to review the case as well as a firmness with which the command is worded. The decision is clear, prompt, and exact. This special case would then be used as a legal precedent for other cases like it. An extension was made of those kinds of applications considered binding. The first decision respected the five women; the eventuating law affected all Israel (v.11).

The first in line for inheritance of one's father was the father's son(s). If the father had no son, then his daughter would inherit in his stead. If there was no daughter either, then the inheritance would pass to nearest relatives: brothers, uncles, or other kin. The intent in each case was to keep the inheritance as close as possible to the deceased man's family line. His name and his possession in the land were inseparable.

This decision becomes a *ḥuqqat mišpāṭ* (v.11), a statutory legal decision or "requirement" (v.11); compare "their case" of v.5. Moreover, the section closes by saying that the decision was mediated through Moses but originated from Yahweh.

Numbers 36 provides an appendix to this account. This deals with the complicating factor of the case of women who were now inheritors of the land and who might marry outside their families and thus muddle the subsequent inheritance claims of Israel.

NOTES

1 The story of the daughters of Zelophehad is discussed in several critical articles. Snaith argues that the law really only served as a justification for the settlement of the half-tribe of Manasseh to the west of the Jordan; he regards this law as fiction and as "bad" law (N. H. Snaith, "The Daughters of Zelophehad," *VT* 16 [1966]: 124–27). But Weingreen points out how this section speaks of a new process of lawmaking in Israel, "a rule of law" (J. Weingreen, "The Case of the Daughters of Zelophehad," *VT* 16 [1966]: 518–22).

7 It seems that the feminine suffixes are used so infrequently in Scripture that (copyist) errors are found from time to time. Here is a mix of forms: לָהֶן ... אֲבִיהֶם ... לָהֶם (*lāhem* ...ᵃᵃ*bîhem* ... *lāhen*, "[to] them [masculine plural] ... their [masculine plural] father ... to them [feminine plural]"). It is also possible that a strict standard was not in place in these early times; similar factors are found in the book of Ruth (Ruth 1:8). Numerous MT MSS normalize these spelling errors to the feminine gender.

8 תְּדַבֵּר (*tᵉdabbēr*, "say") is an example of the instructional use of the imperfect.

3. The Successor to Moses (27:12–23)

[12]Then the LORD said to Moses, "Go up this mountain in the Abarim range and see the land I have given the Israelites. [13]After you have seen it, you too will be gathered to your people, as your brother Aaron was, [14]for when the community rebelled at the waters in the Desert of Zin, both of you disobeyed my command to honor me as holy before their eyes." (These were the waters of Meribah Kadesh, in the Desert of Zin.)

[15]Moses said to the LORD, [16]"May the LORD, the God of the spirits of all mankind, appoint a man over this community [17]to go out and come in before them, one who will lead them out and bring them in, so the LORD's people will not be like sheep without a shepherd."

[18]So the LORD said to Moses, "Take Joshua son of Nun, a man in whom is the spirit, and lay your hand on him. [19]Have him stand before Eleazar the priest and the entire assembly and commission him in their presence. [20]Give him some of your authority so the whole

Israelite community will obey him. [21]He is to stand before Eleazar the priest, who will obtain decisions for him by inquiring of the Urim before the Lord. At his command he and the entire community of the Israelites will go out, and at his command they will come in."

[22]Moses did as the Lord commanded him. He took Joshua and had him stand before Eleazar the priest and the whole assembly. [23]Then he laid his hands on him and commissioned him, as the Lord instructed through Moses.

COMMENTARY

12–14 The conjunction of the story of the daughters of Zelophehad with their request for an inheritance in the land (vv.1–11) and the Lord's words to Moses about his own lack of participation in the land (vv.12–14) is touching indeed. Provisions were made for the exceptions and irregularities of the inheritance laws, but there was no provision made for Moses, the (usually) faithful servant of the Lord. His sin at the waters of Meribah at Kadesh (20:1–13) was always before him. Aaron had already died; Moses was soon to die. He would be allowed a glimpse of the land from a distant mountain, but not even he would be allowed a footfall in the land itself.

There is some sense in which we are not sure how to react to the provision of Yahweh for Moses to gaze at the land from a distance. This was a provision of mercy, for at least he was able to see the land. Nevertheless, this must have been a bittersweet experience. It may have been too hard for Moses even to look, knowing that the land would never be his own. Deuteronomy 3:23–25 describes the pleading of Moses with the Lord for an opportunity to walk through the land. But the Lord would not listen; Moses was not allowed even to speak of the issue further (v.26). The mountain from which Moses was to see the land is not specified here; Deuteronomy 3:27 and 34:1 describe it as Mount Nebo and the top of Pisgah (see Note on Dt 34:1).

The sin of Moses is tied to Aaron in this text, as in Numbers 20; hence both had to die before the people could enter the land. The ominous name "Meribah" is used again in this passage (v.14) to remind us of the rebellion of the leader of the people against the Lord (see comment on 20:13). The punishment of Moses seems to be a significant element of the *Heilsgeschichte* of Numbers. Balaam was an utter reprobate and was entirely deserving of God's judgment; yet God's judgment came as well even on Moses because of his rebellion. As in 20:12, the principal error of Moses and Aaron was in failing to regard Yahweh as holy. (See Dt 32:48–51 for a close parallel to this paragraph.)

The solemnity of this passage is remarkable. In a context of mercy to the daughters of Zelophehad (vv.1–11) that displays the righteousness ($s^e d\bar{a}q\hat{a}$) of Yahweh, here we sense something of his holiness ($q\bar{o}de\check{s}$). The assault on the holiness of God by Moses and Aaron was disastrous. The fact of Aaron's death adds a level of certainty to Moses' own soon demise.

15–17 Moses then requested, in the light of his own impending death, that the Lord appoint a successor for him, even as he clearly indicated a successor for Aaron the priest (see 20:22–29). Without such a certain leader, the people would be like shepherdless sheep in wandering each his own way across the wastelands. In this request to God, Moses used an unusual form of address: "Yahweh God of the spirits of all flesh" (v.16, lit. tr.; "the LORD, the God of the spirits of all mankind," NIV; a similar expression is used by Moses in 16:22). This expressive title of Yahweh speaks of his ultimate sovereignty over all peoples. If God is sovereign over all, then surely God will wish to show his sovereignty over his people in their evident need for a shepherd to follow Moses.

Thus we see that Moses' reaction to this reassertion of his restriction from enjoying the land was to bless the Lord and to offer a prayer for his successor. Here is the Moses of old! Gone is his terrible moment of anger. He had the good of the community at heart. He did not grieve at his own loss but desired a successor so that at last the people would be able to enjoy the end of their salvation. In this sense his life would not have been for naught. Note that Moses did not select his own heir. This post was neither hereditary nor one that was his to dispose — only Yahweh could provide a successor to Moses. Since the Lord knows all persons, he would be the judge of the inner qualities demanded for the task.

The successor to Moses was not chosen because of a blood relationship to Moses; he was not a king. Nor was he chosen by a popular election, for Moses had not been elected by the people — a fact of which they had constantly reminded him (cf. 14:4, where the people wanted to select a leader other than Moses)! The successor was to be appointed directly by God. The Lord was (and is) King; Moses was only an agent. The successor was not to be a figurehead or a symbol, but a leader who would stand before his people and lead them in the direction they should go. He is pictured as a shepherd, one needed by the flock. Moses' concern was that his flock not be left without a shepherd.

18–21 The response of the Lord was to take Joshua son of Nun and to consecrate him as the true successor of Moses. As Moses and Aaron needed to determine the true successor of Aaron

before his death (20:22–29), so the true successor of Moses needed to be established. Joshua and Caleb were the two heroes in the darkest day of Israel's apostasy (Nu 13–14). It was fitting that the Lord selected one of these two. Further, Joshua had been an aide of Moses from his early youth (11:28), a fact that made him especially well suited to follow his master's steps.

The wording of v.18 is expressive of Moses' own part in the selection process. He would be the one to single out Joshua; the Hebrew wording for Yahweh's command is one that demands personal participation ("you yourself take" — an imperative followed by a dative of personal reference). If another person had taken this step, some of the people might think it was an act against the leadership of Moses. Since he himself was the one to reach out to Joshua, there could only be the sense that this act was deliberate on his part.

The arresting phrase in v.18 concerning Joshua is that he was "a man in whom is the spirit." The term "spirit" can refer to his own leadership capacity, as would be suggested by the NIV's lowercased reading; perhaps "the spirit [of leadership]" is intended. But it is also possible, as the NIV margin has it, to read the word "Spirit" as a distinct reference to the Holy Spirit. This latter possibility seems to be more likely. The Hebrew term *rûaḥ* ("spirit") is indefinite by spelling but may be regarded as inherently definite when used as a reference to deity. It is possible that this phrase means that Joshua was Spirit-endowed as the leader of the people (see Dt 34:9: "Joshua son of Nun was filled with the [S]pirit of wisdom"); such phrasing is hauntingly suggestive of NT language concerning the work of the Spirit of God (see Ac 6:5).

The procedure for succession was to include the laying on of hands, a visual representation of the transfer of power while Moses was still alive (cf. the laying on of hands in the NT, Ac 6:6). This action was intended to forestall any doubts as to the legitimacy of the transfer of power among the people. This investiture of power (see Dt 34:9, "because Moses had laid his hands on him") was to be done under the most solemn and public of circumstances. It was done before Eleazar and the whole congregation (v.19). Moreover, the transfer was to be put into operation on a gradual basis but was to begin immediately. Some of Moses' authority was to be given to Joshua that the people might begin to obey him (v.20). After forty years, the transition from the leadership of Moses to any successor would be difficult. The change would be made smoother by a gradual shift of power while Moses was still alive.

Joshua was to stand before Eleazar while Moses was alive so that there would be no priestly objections either. Joshua would go before the priest for consultation and for the decision of the Urim before Yahweh (v.21). Joshua was to begin leading the movement of the congregation as well.

The mention of the Urim in v.21 is significant, as it helps to explain the procedures Moses used in making inquiry of Yahweh and the manner in which his successor was to continue this practice. There has been a great deal of speculation on the nature of the Urim and Thummim (see Lev 8:8; Ezr 2:63; Ne 7:65), sometimes referred to (as here) simply as the Urim (see Ex 28:30; Dt 33:8; Isa 28:6). Some have thought these were two special stones that were kept by the high priest within a fold of his ephod in his priestly garment.

These stones might have been cast on the ground before the Lord, as in the case of Chinese stones called *poe* in Taoism even today. In that case, round stones (or ivory pieces) have a flat side and a curved side. When they are cast before an idol in a temple with a question for the god to answer, they may land both on the flat side (with the answer from the god believed to be "yes"), both on the rounded side so they are rocking (with the answer from the god believed to be "no"), or one on the flat side and the other on the rounded side (with the answer from the god believed to be ambiguous, or even mocking of the questioner).

More recently, however, a view has been presented that seems superior. The Hebrew words "Urim and Thummim," a hendiadys of two supercharged words ("lights" and "purities"), speak of a *dazzling light* (see Note). Together they would indicate a shimmering brilliance that would be a divine sign. When Moses went before Yahweh with a question, it is possible that he would speak to the high priest. The priest would pray to Yahweh; then, when he received a divine answer, he would turn to Moses with the stones of his ephod shining in dazzling light. This light would be the symbol of a divine response. When the priest spoke, it would be the word of God, a divine revelation. And the function of the dazzling light from the stones on the ephod would validate the message. This dazzling light would be the visual sign of Yahweh's revelation.

22-23 These verses conclude the pericope on the transfer of power by reporting Moses' complete obedience to the Lord in the matter of Joshua. Moses followed God's command to the letter. Each time we read of Moses' complete obedience to the Lord in Numbers, we wistfully glance back to ch. 20 and wish that he had stayed in character at that time as well.

NOTES

13 וְנֶאֱסַפְתָּ אֶל־עַמֶּיךָ גַּם־אָתָּה (wene'esap̄tā 'el-'ammeykā gam-'attâ, "and you will be gathered to your people—even you!"); see the development of this phrase respecting Aaron in 20:26 (Note) and respecting

Moses in 31:2 (Note). Here the arresting element is the added phrase גַּם־אָתָּה (gam-ʾattâ). It is difficult enough to face the facts of the early, judicial deaths and burials of Miriam (20:1) and Aaron (20:22–29); it is nearly inconceivable to think that this grim event would also happen to Moses. In each case, the deaths and burials in the wilderness of these notables, these divinely gifted people (see Mic 6:4), were because of their sins against Yahweh. This judgment was true even for Moses—גַּם־אָתָּה (gam-ʾattâ), "even you!"

17 אֲשֶׁר־יֵצֵא לִפְנֵיהֶם וַאֲשֶׁר יָבֹא לִפְנֵיהֶם (ʾašer-yēṣēʾ lipnêhem waʾašer yābōʾ lipnêhem, "who will lead them out and bring them in") exhibits a play on the words "to go out" and "to come in," as the next phrases use Hiphil forms of these same words, יוֹצִיאֵם (yôṣîʾēm, "to lead them out") and יְבִיאֵם (yebîʾēm, "to bring them in"). The idea of these phrasings is to mirror the activities of Moses, who was a faithful leader.

20 The term מֵהוֹדְךָ (mēhôdekā, "of your authority") is from הוֹד (hôd; GK 2086), which may mean "weight, power, splendor, authority." Here the prefixed portative מִן (min) suggests the idea, "some of your authority." It is not clear in this text whether the idea, "some of," was limited and immediate or lasting. That is, it could be that while Moses was alive, "some of" his authority would be given to his assistant so that there would be a gradual shift in leadership, not unlike a coregency of son and father as king. It is also possible that this phrase is used to indicate that no matter how important Joshua became and how significant his role, he was never to be thought of as on the same level with Moses. Joshua was the true successor of Moses but never his equal (see Dt 34:10–12). There was to come another who would be greater than Moses, but his name is not "Joshua"; his name is *Yeshua* ("Jesus"; see Heb 3:1–6).

21 The pattern of divine revelation to Moses through the high priest involved in some way the mysterious words, הָאוּרִים וְאֶת־הַתֻּמִּים (hāʾûrîm weʾet-hattummîm, "the Urim and the Thummim"). The words have to do with light. הָאוּרִים (hāʾûrîm) is a plural intensive of the word אוּר (ʾûr, "light"; GK 242), along with the definite article. הַתֻּמִּים (hattummîm), similarly, is a plural intensive of the word תֹּם (tōm, "completeness, integrity"; GK 9448), along with the definite article. The combination of an intensive word for light followed by an intensive word for completeness makes a hendiadys (one concept through two words), meaning something like "purest of brilliant light, most dazzling light." The definite article on each of the nouns makes it specific: "the purest, most dazzling of light."

What a powerful phrase for a symbol of God's self-revelation! Josephus (*Ant.* 3.8.9) thought the words referred to an action of the stones on the priest's ephod; they would shine, thus giving a decision from the Lord. But this view and similar ones limit the response of God by the Urim and Thummim to "yes" or "no" concepts, a binary oracle that was a sort of "sacred lot" (see suggestions in BDB, 22a). It is the advantage of the view of Douglas Dale Bookman ("The Urim and Thummim in Relation to the Old Testament Theocracy" [Ph.D. diss., Dallas Theological Seminary, 2001]) that when the high priest would speak an oracle from Yahweh, the stones on his ephod would burst into dazzling light, thus giving an inescapable sense of the divine revelation that would be revealed orally through the priest in response to the question from Moses or Joshua and their successors. Bookman observes that the use of הָאוּרִים (hāʾûrîm) alone in this passage (also in 1Sa 28:6) suggests that light is the principal idea; the term הַתֻּמִּים (hattummîm) is descriptive of the perfection of the light (p. 110). Also see Cornelis Van Dam, *The Urim and the Thummim: A Means of Revelation in Ancient Israel* (Winona Lake, Ind.: Eisenbrauns, 1997).

23 The Samaritan Pentateuch adds the words, "and said to him," to the end of this verse and then interpolates a lengthy section from Deuteronomy 3:21–22. This item is in keeping with the Samaritan

Pentateuch's penchant for adding explanatory glosses from other sections of the Torah. See Bruce K. Waltke, "The Samaritan Pentateuch and the Text of the Old Testament," in *New Perspectives on the Old Testament* (ed. J. Barton Payne; Waco, Tex.: Word, 1970), 212–39.

4. Commands for the Second Generation on Regular Offerings, Festival Offerings, and Vows (28:1–30:16)

OVERVIEW

Numbers 28–30 is a section on varied laws that interrupts the narrative flow of this section of the book, much like chs. 5–10 and ch. 15 break the narrative flow of the first sections of the book. The intrusion of laws on holiness, worship, and vows in the narrative serves to remind the readers that they are engaging not only a story of dramatic power but also an account that is profoundly religious in nature. This is not just a story to entertain but also an account that serves to present the highest demands of purity, worship, and obedience on God's people. As the first generation had been given numerous laws on worship and behavior in preparation for its entry into the Land of Promise (chs. 5–10), so now the second generation, which is the heir of all, received its own new *tōrōt* ("laws, instructions") on offerings and vows. They will be God's people in his land; in everything they do they are to reflect his character by obeying his word.

The offerings in chs. 28–29 should be contrasted with the offerings of ch. 15 (see 29:39). These are offerings demanded by the Lord and expected by him on a regular basis. Numbers 15 presented supplementary offerings that would be prompted by grateful people who would respond out of joyful hearts to the Lord. Both the required offerings and the supplementary gifts were governed by stipulations and regulations, and both needed to be pre-

sented with attitudes of wonder and response to the Lord. Perhaps the reason for the insertion of these passages at this time was to indicate a sense of continuity in the impending transition from the leadership of Moses to that of Joshua (27:12–23). This change of leadership does not indicate a change in the worship patterns of Israel; these must continue. The modern reader likely has only a vague awareness of the role of sacrifice in the worship patterns of the OT. These extended chapters attest to the all-pervasiveness of sacrifice in the life of the people as well as the enormity of the work of the priests on their behalf.

Chapters 28–29 follow a clear order and progression. They do not give all new material; much has been given in earlier sections of the Torah. But the repetition and restatement of these sacrificial gifts to the Lord serves to remind the people who were about to enter the land that it was not an ordinary land they were about to enter, nor were they an ordinary people. The land was God's Promised Land, and they were his covenantal people. Everything they were to become was extraordinary, for they were the people of God. Everything they were to do was special, for they were in league with him. So offerings pile on offerings, sometimes overlapping in what seems to us today to be a bewildering, benumbing collage. But these offerings were the perpetual reminders of who the people were, who their God was, and the enormity of their need to respond to him in overwhelming gratitude. For what people has ever received the blessings of deity that this people enjoyed? And what god is there who is like their God?

a. Regular Offerings (28:1-15)

OVERVIEW

The first part of ch. 28 gives lengthy descriptions of the offerings to be made to the Lord each day (vv. 1–8), each Sabbath (vv. 9–10), and each new month (vv. 11–15).

i. The daily offerings (28:1–8)

¹The LORD said to Moses, ²"Give this command to the Israelites and say to them: 'See that you present to me at the appointed time the food for my offerings made by fire, as an aroma pleasing to me.' ³Say to them: 'This is the offering made by fire that you are to present to the LORD: two lambs a year old without defect, as a regular burnt offering each day. ⁴Prepare one lamb in the morning and the other at twilight, ⁵together with a grain offering of a tenth of an ephah of fine flour mixed with a quarter of a hin of oil from pressed olives. ⁶This is the regular burnt offering instituted at Mount Sinai as a pleasing aroma, an offering made to the LORD by fire. ⁷The accompanying drink offering is to be a quarter of a hin of fermented drink with each lamb. Pour out the drink offering to the LORD at the sanctuary. ⁸Prepare the second lamb at twilight, along with the same kind of grain offering and drink offering that you prepare in the morning. This is an offering made by fire, an aroma pleasing to the LORD.

COMMENTARY

1–8 This paragraph reiterates the laws of sacrificial worship in the daily offerings in their order (see Ex 29:38–41; Lev 1–7). The most significant issue for the modern reader, I suspect, is not in the details in each of these sacrifices so much as in the wording of these commandments. The personal involvement of Yahweh, the emphasis on his speaking, and the direction of worship to him—these issues are paramount. The original text of v. 2 has some diffi-

culties, but great stress is presented on the pronouns "me" and "my." Here is my translation of vv. 2–3a, one that presents this emphasis:

Then Yahweh spoke to Moses saying:
   "Command the Israelites, and say to them,
      'You must be careful to present to me my offering,
      my food of my offerings by fire, my soothing

aroma, at the appointed time for each.'
'And you will say to them,
'This is the offering by fire that you shall present to Yahweh.'"

The repeated use of personal pronouns in God's words in this verse contrast strongly with his words from a later time, one when he distanced himself from these very types of sacrifices presented by a people whose hearts were far from God. At that later time, the sacrifices were "yours," not "mine" (see Isa 1:10–15).

When we look at the daily offerings, the following factors are emphasized:

1. *The concept of the "appointed time" (v.2).* Sacrifices were part of the rhythm of worship. The ordering of the sacrifices was a fixed element in the ritual of the people. Each day began and ended in sacrifice; each Sabbath had its special sacrifices, as did each new month. All time was marked by sacrifice.

2. *The concept of the "acceptable gift."* Just as there was a time, so there was a specified offering that was to be presented (see Lev 22:17–33). Not just any animal or any amount of flour, oil, and wine could be used; all was according to pattern. The flour was as important as the animal; the wine was as significant as the oil. The sacrifices would not be appropriate if any element was not acceptable or if any element was not in the correct proportion. Again, we may err if we try to determine spiritual significance in each of the varied proportions; the issue is one of obedience to the revealed will of God.

3. *The concept of a "pleasing aroma to the LORD" (vv.2, 6–7).* There is a sense in which these sacrifices brought pleasure to the Lord. Yet as we reflect on them, we realize that it was not the sacrifice that brought him pleasure—

God is not a ghoul! God did not take some heavenly perverse pleasure in the blood of animals and the bleating of lambs! The offerers who obeyed him in these demands were the ones who pleased him! This is the clear teaching of Psalm 40:6–8 and Micah 8:6–8. The acrid odor of the burning flesh and attendant grain, oil, and wine were the physical symbols of the spiritual reality; obedient people brought pleasure to the Lord.

4. *The concept of a living sacrifice (Ro 12:1–2).* This concept is not a distinctly NT teaching. It is the clearer statement of that which had always been the major issue in sacrifice from the time of Abel until the atonement of *Yeshua* (see the words of Ps 40:6–8 quoted in Heb 10:5–7). God looked first on the one who brought the sacrifice (notice the word order in Ge 4:4–5), then he looked on the sacrifice that person brought. But when all was as it should be—person and sacrifice—then there was a "pleasing aroma" that ascended to the Lord. I have written elsewhere on these issues (see Allen and Allen, esp. ch. 6 ["Worship as Response to God"]).

5. *The sense of the enormity of it all.* Wenham, 197, expanding on an article by Anson Rainey ("The Order of Sacrifices in Old Testament Ritual Texts," *Bib* 51 [1970]: 485–98), calculates that the yearly sacrifices at a minimum would include the following: 113 bulls, 32 rams, 1,086 lambs, more than a ton of flour, and a thousand bottles of oil and wine. These numbers suggest that Israel would have to become an exceedingly prosperous nation in which agriculture would be especially blessed of the Lord. Thus in these required sacrifices there was considerable promise: God would bless his people in such a manner as to allow them to do all that he demanded.

NOTES

2 רֵיחַ נִיחֹחִי (*rēaḥ nîḥōḥî*, lit., "an aroma of [i.e., producing] my soothing"; "an aroma pleasing to me," NIV); this phrase speaks of the satisfaction Yahweh takes in sacrifices that are made according to his stipulations and are carried out by people who worship him truly. As in 15:10, the phrase has a certain irony to it, as the actual odors of burning sacrifices (even with admixtures of oil, spices, and wine) would not be pleasant.

7 Usually the drink offering is specified to be יַיִן (*yayin*), "wine"; here it is שֵׁכָר (*šēkār*; GK 8911), "beer." Wine is the naturally fermented product of grapes and fruit; beer is the naturally fermented drink of grains. The traditional translation, "strong drink" (KJV), and the more recent rendering, "fermented drink" (NIV), for the word שֵׁכָר (*šēkār*) might lead one to think that the alcoholic content of this beverage (beer) was more than that of wine, but such is not the case. Often the associations of this word are unsavory; they depict drunkenness and untoward behavior (e.g., Pr 20:1; Isa 5:11; 28:7; Mic 2:11). But the word is also used as a parallel to wine and was a common drink of the people (Dt 29:6), a part of the sacred festal meals of Israel (Dt 14:26), and commended for the weak and weary (Pr 31:6). Because of the abundant growth of grape vines in Israel (viticulture) in ancient and modern times, wine was (and is) plentiful. Beer was the more common drink in Assyria and Babylon. Decisions for or against abstinence by Christians are best made from other considerations than from the meaning and usage of the several words for wine and beer in the Bible.

REFLECTION

Careful attention to the wording particularly in v.2 should correct the notion common among Christians in our day that the OT is filled with "the laws of Moses" concerning sacrifice and that it was the purpose of Jesus to set us free from such bondage to ritual. The underlying assumption is that Moses brought trouble and then Jesus delivered us from the trouble Moses brought on the Jewish people. But our understanding of these laws should be conditioned by the wording of the text. These were not the laws of Moses but the *tôrôt* ("laws, instructions") of Yahweh. In fact, to speak of "the law of Moses" is something of a misnomer—at best, it is a shorthand expression. The law is the law of God, as this wording makes abundantly clear.

Second, we should focus on the regularity of these sacrifices. They form part of the rhythm of

life of the redeemed community. Each morning there was sacrifice. Each evening there was sacrifice. On the Sabbath there were special sacrifices, and there were also sacrifices on the first of each month. These sacrifices would overlap and intertwine—no matter; they were to be so much a part of the life of the people that one would find it impossible to think of the worship of God apart from sacrifice.

The Hebrew Scriptures are clear that any sacrifice—even sacrifice to the Lord—made apart from obedience was valueless; indeed, sacrifice apart from obedience is an affront to God. It remains true that "to obey is better than sacrifice" (see 1Sa 15:22). Indeed, there are significant texts in Scripture that call sacrifice into question when one is apart from God's will (see Isa 1:10–18) or when one has lost a sense of purpose in sacrifice (see Ps 40:6–8; Mic

6:6–8). But these various passages were not intended by the Spirit of God to destroy sacrificial worship in Israel. The texts have a common intent, namely, to keep those engaging in sacrificial worship to be thinking rightly about their service to the Lord.

When modern readers of Numbers think scripturally, this overwhelming emphasis on sacrificial worship has a common intent: to cause each reader to think of the enormity of the offense of our sin against the holiness of God, thus driving the repentant sinner to the foot of the cross. All God's ordained sacrifices in the Hebrew Scriptures — whether of the morning or evening, of the Sabbath,

or of the New Moon — had their ultimate meaning in the death the Savior died. Apart from the Savior's death, these sacrifices were just the killing of animals and the burning of their flesh with attendant ceremonies. After the Lord's death, sacrifices such as these became redundant — indeed, offensive — for they would suggest that something was needed in addition to the Savior's death. But before his death, these sacrifices were the means God lovingly gave his people to help them face the enormity of their sin, the reality of their need for his grace, and — in some mysterious way — to point them to the coming cross of the Savior, Jesus.

ii. The Sabbath offerings (28:9–10)

> [9] "On the Sabbath day, make an offering of two lambs a year old without defect, together with its drink offering and a grain offering of two-tenths of an ephah of fine flour mixed with oil. [10] This is the burnt offering for every Sabbath, in addition to the regular burnt offering and its drink offering.

COMMENTARY

9–10 The Sabbath (see Note) offerings were additional to the daily offerings. The special offerings made on this day marked it as "holy." Its status as such does not mean that the Sabbath was to be the "day of worship," as is sometimes supposed. It was to be a day of rest — except for the priests, who had additional service to perform before the Lord. Each day was a day of the worship of God; hence the daily offerings.

The passages concerning the Sabbath festivals of ancient Israel are brought into focus for the Christian reader in Hebrews 4, where we learn that the Savior Jesus embodies our Sabbath rest (Heb 4:1–5). Other significant references in the NT to the Sabbath include Matthew 12:1–14; 28:1; Luke 4:16; John 5:9; Acts 13:42; and Colossians 2:16.

NOTE

9 וּבְיוֹם הַשַּׁבָּת (ûbᵉyôm haššabbāt, "on the Sabbath day") is a phrase that occurs in Numbers only here (vv.9–10) and in 15:32–36 (see comments and Note). The word "Sabbath" is merely a transliteration of the Hebrew word (as indicated in the script and transcription above). The transliteration of biblical terms is both serviceable and troublesome. It is serviceable in that specific terms in biblical records (such as "baptism") take on a life of their own when they are transliterated into a receiving language; it is troublesome, however, in that the principal idea inherent in the biblical term may eventually be lost. Few people who have even a modest knowledge of the content of the Bible are aware that the inherent meaning of the word "Sabbath" is rest, for the word is related to the verb שָׁבַת (šābat, "to cease, desist, rest"; GK 8701).

This basic concept was given in the story of the manna: "This is what the LORD commanded: 'Tomorrow is to be a day of rest [שַׁבָּתוֹן, šabbātôn], a holy Sabbath to the LORD [שַׁבַּת־קֹדֶשׁ לַיהוה, šabbat-qōdeš la-yhwh]. So bake what you want to bake and boil what you want to boil. Save whatever is left and keep it until morning'" (Ex 16:23). The fourth commandment in Exodus 20:8–11 ties Israel's "day of rest" to the Lord's rest on the seventh day of Genesis 2:2–3; the fourth commandment when restated in Deuteronomy 5:12–15 connects Israel's "rest" to Yahweh's work in delivering his people from slavery in Egypt. The Sabbath was to be for Israel both a day "to rejoice in God's creation … and for Israel to remember that God is an emancipator, a liberator" (see Victor P. Hamilton, "שָׁבַת (šābat)," *TWOT*, 2:902–3).

iii. The monthly offerings (28:11–15)

11"'On the first of every month, present to the LORD a burnt offering of two young bulls, one ram and seven male lambs a year old, all without defect. 12With each bull there is to be a grain offering of three-tenths of an ephah of fine flour mixed with oil; with the ram, a grain offering of two-tenths of an ephah of fine flour mixed with oil; 13and with each lamb, a grain offering of a tenth of an ephah of fine flour mixed with oil. This is for a burnt offering, a pleasing aroma, an offering made to the LORD by fire. 14With each bull there is to be a drink offering of half a hin of wine; with the ram, a third of a hin; and with each lamb, a quarter of a hin. This is the monthly burnt offering to be made at each new moon during the year. 15Besides the regular burnt offering with its drink offering, one male goat is to be presented to the LORD as a sin offering.

COMMENTARY

11–15 The sacrifices at the beginning of the month were of great proportion. These occasions were times for celebration and the blowing of trumpets in worship (see 10:10). Whereas two lambs were specified for the daily offerings (and two more on each Sabbath), the animals for the New Moon burnt sacrifices included two bulls, one ram, and seven lambs. Each animal sacrifice was accompanied with flour, oil, and wine; in addition, a goat also was to be offered as a sin offering.

The NIV translates the beginning of v.11 as "on the first of every month." This rendering communicates the intent, but the Hebrew phrasing is, "in the first of your months." As the land is Yahweh's gift to his people, so time is his gift to enjoy the land. Each month is a marker of his blessing, a time for special rejoicing. Later in Israel's history, the New Moon festivals may have become opportunities for excess, for licentious behavior. In the Prophets there are times when God says to his erring people, "Your New Moon festivals and your appointed feasts my soul hates" (Isa 1:14). There is always a latent danger in the most festive of occasions for people to be forgetful of God's intention for us to respond to his wonder. Compare contemporary celebrations of once-Christian holidays (e.g., Christmas) in many Western cultures; often during these times few celebrants appear to give serious thought to God. Holy-days have become merely holidays.

b. Festival Offerings (28:16–29:40)

OVERVIEW

Passages demanding regular offerings are followed by the Lord's demands for offerings to be made during the great festivals: Passover (vv.16–25), the Feast of Weeks (vv.26–31), Feast of Trumpets (29:1–6), Day of Atonement (vv.7–11), and Feast of Tabernacles (vv.12–38). All these sections conclude by connecting these sacrifices and those of ch. 15 (see 29:39) and by stating that Moses instructed the people just as he had been commanded by Yahweh (29:40). As in the earlier section, these paragraphs display a sense of order, propriety, and measure.

i. The Passover (28:16–25)

[16]"'On the fourteenth day of the first month the LORD's Passover is to be held. [17]On the fifteenth day of this month there is to be a festival; for seven days eat bread made without yeast. [18]On the first day hold a sacred assembly and do no regular work. [19]Present to the LORD an offering made by fire, a burnt offering of two young bulls, one ram and seven male lambs a year old, all without defect. [20]With each bull prepare a grain offering of three-tenths of an ephah of fine flour mixed with oil; with the ram, two-tenths; [21]and with each of the seven lambs, one-tenth. [22]Include one male goat as a sin offering to make atonement for you. [23]Prepare these in addition to the regular morning burnt offering. [24]In this way prepare the food for the offering made by fire every day for seven days as an aroma pleasing to the LORD; it is to be prepared in addition to the regular burnt offering and its drink offering. [25]On the seventh day hold a sacred assembly and do no regular work.

<h1 style="text-align:center">COMMENTARY</h1>

16–25 This passage instructs the priests as to the proper preparation for the Passover in the first month of the year. Passover is the spring feast at which the nation celebrates the marvel of redemption from Egypt, the great work of God in freeing the people to worship him and to enjoy him in the land that he was giving them (see comments on 9:1–14). The focus of these passages in Numbers is on the work of the priests; the participation of the families of Israel is not the concern of these texts. Documentary-critical scholars, therefore, have regularly styled these sections as "P" for the putative "Priestly" source.

The Torah has already spoken on the subject of Passover (see Ex 12:14–20; Lev 23:4–8; also Dt 16:1–8). The Feast of Passover is also associated with the Feast of Unleavened Bread (v.17; see Ex 12:15; Lev 23:4–8). This paragraph is studded with the number seven (and its multiple of fourteen). The Feast of Passover was to be a time during which the people were not to do any work. It was akin to a week of Sabbaths in this regard. It is from such a concept that the idea of "holy days" originates; the modern "holiday" lies far afield from the original concept. On several occasions the NT speaks of the Passover celebration and its fulfillment in Christ (Mt 26:17; Mk 14:12–16; Jn 2:13; 11:55; 1Co 5:7; Heb 11:28).

ii. The Feast of Weeks (28:26–31)

26"'On the day of firstfruits, when you present to the LORD an offering of new grain during the Feast of Weeks, hold a sacred assembly and do no regular work. 27Present a burnt offering of two young bulls, one ram and seven male lambs a year old as an aroma pleasing to the LORD. 28With each bull there is to be a grain offering of three-tenths of an ephah of fine flour mixed with oil; with the ram, two-tenths; 29and with each of the seven lambs, one-tenth. 30Include one male goat to make atonement for you. 31Prepare these together with their drink offerings, in addition to the regular burnt offering and its grain offering. Be sure the animals are without defect.

<h1 style="text-align:center">COMMENTARY</h1>

26–31 The Feast of Firstfruits is also called the "Feast of Weeks" (see Ex 23:16; 34:22). This festival came fifty days after the Feast of Unleavened Bread (see Lev 23:9–22); from this number the Greek term "Pentecost" (meaning "fifty") was used in the NT period (Ac 2:1). For other texts on the Feast of Weeks, see Leviticus 23:15–22 and Deuteronomy 16:9–12. In the NT the association of Pentecost and the beginning of the church is of signal importance (see Ac 2:1–4; 20:16; 1Co 16:8).

Each of these feasts is associated in some way with the agricultural year, thus leading some scholars to assume that there was a gradual development from a purely agricultural festival, to a quasi-agricultural-cum-spiritual festival, to a purely spiritual festival. It is preferable to assume that the Lord graciously used the agricultural year, with its natural rhythm, to stimulate his people to the worship of his name. Thus the association of the agricultural calendar and the spiritual worship were framed together from the beginning by the Lord through his servant Moses.

These texts contain a couple of emphases we should not miss. First, the special offerings of these feasts were to be made in addition to the regular daily sacrifices (v.31); so on the days on which the people were to do no regular labor (v.26), the priests were unusually busy. Second, the animals had to be without any defect, as indicated by the final note at v.31. For the Christian reader, the reminders of this standard point irresistibly to the person of Christ, the one perfect sacrifice for the sins of humankind who "offered himself unblemished to God" (Heb 9:14).

iii. The Feast of Trumpets (29:1−6)

> ¹"'On the first day of the seventh month hold a sacred assembly and do no regular work. It is a day for you to sound the trumpets. ²As an aroma pleasing to the LORD, prepare a burnt offering of one young bull, one ram and seven male lambs a year old, all without defect. ³With the bull prepare a grain offering of three-tenths of an ephah of fine flour mixed with oil; with the ram, two-tenths; ⁴and with each of the seven lambs, one-tenth. ⁵Include one male goat as a sin offering to make atonement for you. ⁶These are in addition to the monthly and daily burnt offerings with their grain offerings and drink offerings as specified. They are offerings made to the LORD by fire—a pleasing aroma.

COMMENTARY

1−6 This feast came at the beginning of the seventh month, an exceedingly busy month for faithful people who worshiped the Lord by keeping the holy festivals (see Lev 23:23−25); later in Jewish tradition this feast became the time of the New Year (Rosh Hashanah). The blowing of the trumpet on this feast day, yôm tĕrûʿâ ("a day of blowing [trumpets]"), was the blowing of the shofar (šōpār), the ram's horn, rather than the silver trumpet of Numbers 10.

The contribution of this text in Numbers is to detail for the priests the sacrifices that must be made on this holy day. The sacrifices fall into a certain pattern. On the first day of the seventh month there was to be the sacrifice of one bull, one ram, and seven male lambs, each along with the requisite grain and libation offerings. The goat for the sin offering accompanied these celebrative whole burnt offerings, and the daily offerings were also to be made. The language is somewhat repetitive in these sections, thus emphasizing the soothing aroma of the sacrifices and the fact that the male animals offered must be without defect.

iv. The Day of Atonement (29:7–11)

> [7]"'On the tenth day of this seventh month hold a sacred assembly. You must deny yourselves and do no work. [8]Present as an aroma pleasing to the LORD a burnt offering of one young bull, one ram and seven male lambs a year old, all without defect. [9]With the bull prepare a grain offering of three-tenths of an ephah of fine flour mixed with oil; with the ram, two-tenths; [10]and with each of the seven lambs, one-tenth. [11]Include one male goat as a sin offering, in addition to the sin offering for atonement and the regular burnt offering with its grain offering, and their drink offerings.

COMMENTARY

7–11 The Feast of Trumpets leads into the Day of Atonement, or Yom Kippur, on the tenth day of the seventh month. The name of the day of assembly is not given in vv. 7–11, but we pick up this name from the parallel texts in Leviticus. Yom Kippur (properly, *yôm hakkippurîm*, "the day of atonings") was a time of confession, contrition, and celebration (see Lev 16; 23:26–32). This was the most solemn of Israel's holy days. It was a time of fasting rather than of feasting, of solemnity rather than rejoicing. The NIV reads, "You must deny yourselves" (v.7; *wᵉʿinnîtem*, from *ʿānâ* in the Piel); the implication of this verb is that one was to deny oneself by means of fasting (see Lev 16:29, 31; 23:27, 32; Ps 35:13; Isa 58:3, 5).

Even today the Day of Atonement is regarded by traditional Jewish people as the holiest day of the year. Men still fast during this day, and they lie prostrate for a time in their synagogues in a posture of repentance for the sins of the people. In the NT, Yom Kippur is fulfilled in the death of the Savior, who made full atonement for us (see Ro 3:24–26; Heb 9:7; 10:3, 19–22).

v. The Feast of Tabernacles (29:12–38)

> [12]"'On the fifteenth day of the seventh month, hold a sacred assembly and do no regular work. Celebrate a festival to the LORD for seven days. [13]Present an offering made by fire as an aroma pleasing to the LORD, a burnt offering of thirteen young bulls, two rams and fourteen male lambs a year old, all without defect. [14]With each of the thirteen bulls prepare a grain offering of three-tenths of an ephah of fine flour mixed with oil; with each of the two rams, two-tenths; [15]and with each of the fourteen lambs, one-tenth. [16]Include one male goat as a sin offering, in addition to the regular burnt offering with its grain offering and drink offering.
> [17]"'On the second day prepare twelve young bulls, two rams and fourteen male lambs a year old, all without defect. [18]With the bulls, rams and lambs, prepare their grain offerings and drink offerings according to the number specified. [19]Include one male goat as a

sin offering, in addition to the regular burnt offering with its grain offering, and their drink offerings.

²⁰"'On the third day prepare eleven bulls, two rams and fourteen male lambs a year old, all without defect. ²¹With the bulls, rams and lambs, prepare their grain offerings and drink offerings according to the number specified. ²²Include one male goat as a sin offering, in addition to the regular burnt offering with its grain offering and drink offering.

²³"'On the fourth day prepare ten bulls, two rams and fourteen male lambs a year old, all without defect. ²⁴With the bulls, rams and lambs, prepare their grain offerings and drink offerings according to the number specified. ²⁵Include one male goat as a sin offering, in addition to the regular burnt offering with its grain offering and drink offering.

²⁶"'On the fifth day prepare nine bulls, two rams and fourteen male lambs a year old, all without defect. ²⁷With the bulls, rams and lambs, prepare their grain offerings and drink offerings according to the number specified. ²⁸Include one male goat as a sin offering, in addition to the regular burnt offering with its grain offering and drink offering.

²⁹"'On the sixth day prepare eight bulls, two rams and fourteen male lambs a year old, all without defect. ³⁰With the bulls, rams and lambs, prepare their grain offerings and drink offerings according to the number specified. ³¹Include one male goat as a sin offering, in addition to the regular burnt offering with its grain offering and drink offering.

³²"'On the seventh day prepare seven bulls, two rams and fourteen male lambs a year old, all without defect. ³³With the bulls, rams and lambs, prepare their grain offerings and drink offerings according to the number specified. ³⁴Include one male goat as a sin offering, in addition to the regular burnt offering with its grain offering and drink offering.

³⁵"'On the eighth day hold an assembly and do no regular work. ³⁶Present an offering made by fire as an aroma pleasing to the LORD, a burnt offering of one bull, one ram and seven male lambs a year old, all without defect. ³⁷With the bull, the ram and the lambs, prepare their grain offerings and drink offerings according to the number specified. ³⁸Include one male goat as a sin offering, in addition to the regular burnt offering with its grain offering and drink offering.

COMMENTARY

12–38 The seventh month began with the Feast of Trumpets on the first day and moved to the Day of Atonement on the tenth day. Then the Feast of Tabernacles began on the fifteenth day and lasted for seven more days (see Lev 23:33–44). Each day of the Feast of Tabernacles (or Booths) had its own order for sacrifice; the small paragraphs in the rest of this chapter note each of these orders of procedure. The somewhat repetitive nature of these paragraphs adds to the solemnity and pageantry of this text, much like the repeated sections in Numbers 7. These texts are not just explanatory; they are themselves a ritual celebration. To read these texts is to enter into a world of rhythm and ritual, where the patterns have a satisfying nature to them.

This Feast of Booths (*ḥag hassukkôt*; Lev 23:34) made the greatest demands on the numbers of animals to be sacrificed. On each of the first seven days, there were two rams and fourteen male lambs sacrificed, along with their requisite grain and libation offerings. In addition, there were thirteen bulls sacrificed on the first day, twelve on the second, and one less on each of the days leading to the seventh day, on which seven bulls were sacrificed—a total of seventy bulls for the seven days. On the eighth day there were the following: one bull, one ram, and seven male lambs sacrificed along with requisite grain and libation offerings. In each of the days of this festival there was also a male goat offered as a sin offering, along with the normal daily offerings. This was an exceedingly busy time of sacrificing to the Lord (see also Ex 23:16; 34:22; Dt 16:13-15; Zec 14:16-19). In the NT the Feast of Booths is mentioned in John 7:2, 37. It was on the last, the most significant day of the feast, that Jesus stood in the temple in Jerusalem and invited the spiritually thirsty to come to him (Jn 7:37-38).

NOTE

15 The doubling phrase עִשָּׂרוֹן וְעִשָּׂרוֹן (*wᵉʿiśśārôn ʿiśśārôn*, "a tenth, a tenth") was observed by the scribes as suspicious, so they marked the first word with a superior dot or point (*puncta extraordinarius*); its occurrence here marks one of fifteen times in the MT that such superior points are used (see Nu 3:39; see also Ginsburg, 329). The word "a tenth" occurs in 29:4 and is doubled in 29:10 (as here). I suggest these doublings of the word "tenth" are for distribution (see Williams, *Hebrew Syntax*, sec. 15), "one tenth for each"; cf. 3:47, "five, five," meaning "five for each."

vi. Summary (29:39-40)

> ³⁹"'In addition to what you vow and your freewill offerings, prepare these for the Lord at your appointed feasts: your burnt offerings, grain offerings, drink offerings and fellowship offerings.'"
> ⁴⁰Moses told the Israelites all that the Lord commanded him.

COMMENTARY

39-40 The recapitulation of each of these festivals was a necessary part of the transfer of power from Moses to Joshua. The new community would soon be in the Land of Promise, wherein these festivals would take on their full meaning in the life of the people. It would be in the good land that they would be able to bring all these sacrifices to the Lord because of his bountiful provision. The restatement of these various offerings is a mark of faith and trust in the Lord that at last he will complete his promise to bring his people into the land that is his gift for them.

Verse 39 explains that these sacrifices elaborated in Numbers 28–29, with special attention to the priestly participation in the worship of God, are in addition to any voluntary offerings one might bring (see ch. 15), as well as any vow one might make to the Lord (see ch. 30). Thus we understand that there was to be a regular pattern of sacrifice without regard to the special offerings one might bring because of a heart overflowing with joy to God or because of a desire to make a special need known to him.

NOTES

39 Below is a tabulation of the varied offerings mentioned in these two chapters. There are several observations we may make. All the animals that were to be sacrificed were to be young males and without blemish. The grain offerings were always mixed with oil, in regular proportion to the animal sacrificed: with a bull one presented three tenths of an ephah (אֵיפָה, ʾêpâ) of grain, with a ram two-tenths, and with a male lamb one tenth of an ephah of flour. The amount of oil is not always noted, but the proportions used with the daily and monthly offerings might serve as a guide. The libation is not always mentioned. It is not certain that libations accompanied every one of these offerings. Note that the daily and—where appropriate—the monthly offerings were to be made in addition to the special offerings.

Daily Offerings

- Two male lambs (one in the morning; one in the evening)
- Each lamb accompanied by a grain offering of one tenth of an ephah (about two quarts) of fine flour mixed with one-quarter hin (הִין, hîn [about one quart]) of oil
- Each lamb also accompanied by one-quarter hin of beer (שֵׁכָר, šēkār, "fermented drink," NIV) as a libation

Sabbath Offerings

- Two male lambs
- Grain offering of two tenths of an ephah (about four quarts) of fine flour mixed with oil (unspecified amount)
- A libation (unspecified amount)

Monthly Offerings

- Two bulls, one ram, seven male lambs
- With each bull: A grain offering of three tenths of an ephah (about six quarts) of fine flour, mixed with oil libation of one-half hin (about two quarts) of wine
- With the ram: A grain offering of two tenths of an ephah (about four quarts) of fine flour, mixed with oil, plus a libation of one-third hin (about two quarts) of wine
- With each lamb: A grain offering of one tenth of an ephah (about two quarts) of fine flour, mixed with oil libation of one-quarter hin (about one quart) of wine

- One male goat as a sin offering
- Regular daily offerings and libations

Passover

- Two bulls, one ram, seven male lambs
- With each animal, grain offerings of the same proportions specified for the monthly offerings, each mixed with oil (no mention of an accompanying libations)
- One male goat as a sin offering
- Regular daily offerings and libations
- Emphasis on unleavened bread for seven days

Feast of Weeks

- Two bulls, one ram, seven male lambs
- With each animal, grain offerings of the same proportions specified for the monthly offerings, each mixed with oil, plus accompanying libations
- One male goat as a sin offering
- Regular daily offerings

Feast of Trumpets

- One bull, one ram, seven male lambs
- With each animal, grain offerings of standard proportions (no mention of accompanying libations)
- One male goat as a sin offering
- Daily and monthly offerings, with attendant grain and libation offerings

The Day of Atonement

- One bull, one ram, seven male lambs
- With each animal, the same proportion of grain offerings as with the others (no mention of accompanying libations)
- One male goat as a sin offering
- Regular daily offerings

The Feast of Tabernacles

On the first day of the feast, the fifteenth day of the seventh month

- Thirteen bulls, two rams, fourteen male lambs, plus the same proportion of grain offerings as with the others
- One male goat as a sin offering
- Regular daily offerings

On the second day of the feast

- Twelve bulls, two rams, fourteen male lambs
- With each animal, grain offerings and libations, as before
- One male goat as a sin offering
- Regular daily offerings

On each successive day from day three to day seven

- One less bull, plus the two rams and the fourteen male lambs
- With each animal, all the attendant sacrifices

On the eighth day

- One bull, one ram, seven male lambs
- With each animal, grain offerings and libations, as before
- One male goat as a sin offering
- Regular daily offerings

40 [30:1] That this verse is given as 30:1 in the MT means that each verse in ch. 30 will be one number lower when the English text is compared to the Hebrew text. The placement of this verse as the end of ch. 29 is correct; it is the completion of a section, not the beginning of a new unit.

REFLECTION

Sacrifice was a continual process in the courts of the Lord, a theme picked up by the writer to the Hebrews, who speaks of "the same sacrifices repeated endlessly year after year" (Heb 10:1). This writer then points to the sacrifice of our Savior Jesus, which was singular and non-repeatable (v.10) and in whom the priestly sacrifice was fulfilled; in him all meaning has been realized. He now sits "at the right hand of God" (v.12). No one reading these sections in Numbers would ever imagine a godly priest as sitting down; the work was never done. But in Jesus' sacrifice, all the work was complete (v.10). Sacrifices of animals, offerings of grain, and libations of wine—all were fulfilled in Christ's work, to the praise of the Father.

c. Vows (30:1–16)

OVERVIEW

The third part of the legislative "intrusion" of chs. 28–30 deals with the issue of vows. Again, there must have been some purpose for inserting this material in the book of Numbers at this point. I suggest that these chapters are placed here as guarantors of hope: the very fact that plans were being made for the sacrifices and vows that would be performed in the land are sure indicators that Yahweh was going to complete his work for his people. All one needed to do was to prepare for the coming battles. The hope for the people of the second generation was victory under Yahweh's gracious hand.

Significantly, the problematic issue in this section (ch. 30) has to do with vows that were made by women. In the male-oriented culture of biblical times, numerous complications could arise when a woman made a religious vow. Was she a free agent? Might her vow needlessly entangle her father or husband? Nevertheless, we should not miss the fact that women did make vows, a

fact that shows they really did participate in some manner as responsible individuals in the worship patterns of Israel.

That the vows of women were considered problematic reminds us of the cultural astringencies of the day. This chapter—as well as ch. 27 on the daughters of Zelophehad—points to some elements of change in the rights and responsibilities of women, even though its message did not effect many changes in its own day. These chapters speak of a gradual shifting from patriarchy to a more egalitarian relationship between women and men. The actual change was gradual in biblical times, but the process of transformation was underway.

i. The issue of vows to the Lord (30:1–2)

¹Moses said to the heads of the tribes of Israel: "This is what the Lord commands: ²When a man makes a vow to the Lord or takes an oath to obligate himself by a pledge, he must not break his word but must do everything he said.

COMMENTARY

1–2 [2–3] Each verse in this chapter is one number higher in the Hebrew text; Numbers 30:1 in the MT is (correctly) presented in standard English versions as the last verse (v.40) of ch. 29.

This chapter is a significant OT text on the subject of the vow (see Dt 23:21–23). The principal issue is that a vow was not to be made rashly (see Ecc 5:1–7), for a vow to the Lord must be kept. The chapter begins with the words, "When a man makes a vow to the LORD" (v.2). The Hebrew word ʾiš ("man") does not always indicate "male" exclusively. (See, e.g., Ps 1:1, where the use of Hebrew ʾiš does

not necessarily indicate "a man" and not "a woman.") Note how in the following verses of this chapter the ones making the vows are not men but women.

The rest of the chapter develops some of the problems that would eventuate when women began making vows to the Lord in a society that was male oriented. These ideas suggest the beginning of a movement to bring more personal freedom to women, but there were also numerous brakes applied here and there. This chapter is one of several that indicate that a change was in the works, even though significant change was to be slow in coming.

ii. The vows of a woman who lives with her father (30:3–5)

³"When a young woman still living in her father's house makes a vow to the LORD or obligates herself by a pledge ⁴and her father hears about her vow or pledge but says nothing to her, then all her vows and every pledge by which she obligated herself will stand. ⁵But if her father forbids her when he hears about it, none of her vows or the pledges by which she obligated herself will stand; the LORD will release her because her father has forbidden her.

COMMENTARY

3–5 [4–6] The vow of an unmarried woman who was still under her father's protection might be nullified by her father. We may presume that this law and the following one were designed for the protection of women, who in ancient Near Eastern society were subject to strong societal pressures, some of which would have left them defenseless. That is, this text provided not simply the right of denial of a vow to the Lord by a woman's male protector (her father), and his right to nullify her con-

tractual agreements with another party; the text also protected her from the abuse of others. And it also protected her father, who might be the one who would have to come up with whatever the vow entailed if his daughter were remiss in fulfilling it. Again, the very fact that women were making vows in ancient times is a step of great significance. But, as with every step of progress, there were attendant problems as well.

NOTE

3–4 [4–5] The phrasing וֶאֱסָרָה אֲשֶׁר אָסְרָה עַל-נַפְשָׁהּ (we³sārāh ³ăšer ³āsᵉrâ ᶜal-napšāh, "the pledge by which she obligates herself") in verse 4 [5] is used to amplify and to make more specific the usual term for making a vow, כִּי-תִדֹּר נֶדֶר (kî-tiddōr neder, v.3 [4], "surely she had made a vow"; "makes a vow," NIV). In both cases the verbs are used with their cognate accusatives. The verb אָסַר (³āsar) basically means "to bind" or "to tie"; hence, in the context of making a vow, the idea is "to tie oneself to do something." The full phrase from v.3 could be translated rather woodenly: "and her binding, by which she has bound her own being." This language is most serious indeed!

וְאִשָּׁה ... בִּנְעֻרֶיהָ (wᵉ³iššâ ... binᶜureyhā, "a woman ... in her youth"; "young woman," NIV) is the manner in which this text speaks of the young, unmarried woman (see also v.16 [17]). The term binᶜureyhā is an example of a plural noun used as an abstraction ("youth"), plus the feminine pronominal suffix. In both cases the phrase is further defined in terms of her living in her father's house.

iii. The vows of a (newly) married woman (30:6–8)

> ⁶"If she marries after she makes a vow or after her lips utter a rash promise by which she obligates herself ⁷and her husband hears about it but says nothing to her, then her vows or the pledges by which she obligated herself will stand. ⁸But if her husband forbids her when he hears about it, he nullifies the vow that obligates her or the rash promise by which she obligates herself, and the LORD will release her.

COMMENTARY

6–8 [7–9] The vow of a married woman might be nullified by her husband. A comparison of this section with vv. 10–15 suggests that these verses relate to young couples who had recently married, insofar as a woman may have taken on a vow prior to her marriage that could easily place heavy obligations and restrictions on her husband. Again, we may presume that in this law there was something protective for the woman (an escape clause) as well as for the husband. The woman in this case is treated like a minor child, lacking independent authority to enter into a vow or an obligation in her own right. She was either subject to her father or to her husband.

In addition to the protective element, v. 6 would also work for her if she were pressured into making a vow that was not at all in her best interest to keep. This provision freed her from unnecessary complications to her life. In both the case of the married woman and the woman who lived with her father, the vows might be released by another person, but only if that person acted immediately on the information he had.

iv. The vows of a widow or a divorced woman (30:9)

> ⁹"Any vow or obligation taken by a widow or divorced woman will be binding on her.

COMMENTARY

9 [10] A widowed or divorced woman was her own agent in the taking of vows. She was no longer under the household of her father or husband. This verse contributes significantly to our understanding of the ramifications of divorce in ancient Israel.

Some people claim that divorce in biblical times was only a certain legal fiction, that the woman was always considered the wife of the husband who had dismissed her. (See Dt 24:1–4 for the basic text on divorce in the OT.) Yet this verse clearly indicates that a divorced woman (*gᵉrûšâ* [v. 10], the Qal feminine passive participle of *gāraš*, "to be driven out"; see also Lev 21:7, 14; 22:13; Eze 44:22) had the same legal status as a widow (*ʾalmānâ*). She became an independent agent. Like the widow, her former husband was in a sense "dead" to her. Since she had been married, she was no longer under the protection of her father (unless she sought to regain that status). So, strangely, this woman along with the widow was able to negotiate contracts, take vows, make promises — to function, in some respects, like any man in society.

This is not to say that she could do anything; certainly some restrictions were placed on her just by virtue of her gender and her status as one who was divorced (see Lev 21:7 again). Even though she was among the freest of women, she was also the one most apt to be bound by vows.

v. The vows of a married woman (30:10–15)

¹⁰"If a woman living with her husband makes a vow or obligates herself by a pledge under oath ¹¹and her husband hears about it but says nothing to her and does not forbid her, then all her vows or the pledges by which she obligated herself will stand. ¹²But if her husband nullifies them when he hears about them, then none of the vows or pledges that came from her lips will stand. Her husband has nullified them, and the LORD will release her. ¹³Her husband may confirm or nullify any vow she makes or any sworn pledge to deny herself. ¹⁴But if her husband says nothing to her about it from day to day, then he confirms all her vows or the pledges binding on her. He confirms them by saying nothing to her when he hears about them. ¹⁵If, however, he nullifies them some time after he hears about them, then he is responsible for her guilt."

COMMENTARY

10–15 [11–16] This paragraph illustrates the complications that would come in the taking of vows within the woman-man relationship. In contrast to vv.6–8, which deal with young couples in the early stages of their marriage, vv.10–15 deal more with those who had been married for a longer period of time. One gains the impression that these several complications may have arisen in much the same way as the case of the daughters of Zelophehad (27:1–11). That is, one case after another presented itself; the resulting chapter is the final codification.

We may well presume that in the centuries leading to NT times, legal decisions on the subject of vows became even more complex. The instruction of the Lord Jesus to avoid the complications of these oaths (Mt 5:33–37) is liberating. After a while, serious language about holy things was being used in the most trivializing manner possible. So for his disciples Jesus forswore oaths and vows altogether. He urged them to let their words speak for themselves, apart from the calling of heaven and earth to witness. Actually, this teaching is great grace on his part.

vi. A summary statement (30:16)

¹⁶These are the regulations the LORD gave Moses concerning relationships between a man and his wife, and between a father and his young daughter still living in his house.

COMMENTARY

16 [17] From this summary, it is evident that this chapter has to do specifically with the making of vows by women, not the making of vows in general. This chapter is much like ch. 27. It deals with exceptions for women to general rules for men in a patriarchal age. Like ch. 27, it deals rather sympathetically with women and presents some glimmer of light in terms of their growing partnership with men in praising God and their living their lives here on earth as God's gift to them would suggest. But we also recognize that the door to full participation is only cracked briefly in this chapter. That it is cracked at all is the most hopeful sign.

5. The Reprisal against Midian, Moses' Last Campaign (31:1–54)

OVERVIEW

Chapter 31 picks up the story line of ch. 25, the account of the debauchery of Israel at Baal Peor. The delay of relating this battle report adds punch to the content. We remember that Yahweh placed Midian under interdict because of its part in inciting the failure of Israel in that ignoble event. Yahweh had said to Moses, "Treat the Midianites as enemies and kill them" (25:17). This chapter tells the story of the holy war of Israel, the vendetta of Yahweh, against these enemies of God and his people.

That such an idea as "holy war" is distasteful to many believers today is granted, particularly in the aftermath of the events of 9/11, the terrorist attacks against the United States in 2001. Muslim terrorists proclaim their jihads against the infidels of the West, and we all shudder. But the reader of Scripture can only come to a sense of the meaning of this text if he or she abandons for a moment the ethical and moral crises of our day and attempts to read the Bible within the standards of the day in which the text stood. This is not to present an idea of moral relativism or to censor the morality of the Bible. It is merely to observe that conditions in the robust and rugged world of the ancient Near East differ from those we are used to or are comfortable with in our own living.

On their own grounds, the frightful events of this chapter are moral and are from God. The most important issue in approaching texts such as this is not to concentrate on the suffering and pain the chapter describes but to reflect on the holiness of the Lord that it celebrates. In the midst of terrible wrath, God remembers mercy—the story of this chapter, as we will see. A recent work that presents the views and interactions of four evangelical scholars on the issue of "holy war" in ancient Israel is *Show Them No Mercy: 4 Views on God and Canaanite Genocide*, by C. S. Cowles, Eugene H. Merrill, Daniel L. Gard, and Tremper Longman III (ed. Stanley N. Gundry; Grand Rapids: Zondervan, 2003).

a. The Report of the Battle (31:1–24)

i. The instructions for the battle (31:1–6)

> [1] The LORD said to Moses, [2] "Take vengeance on the Midianites for the Israelites. After that, you will be gathered to your people."
>
> [3] So Moses said to the people, "Arm some of your men to go to war against the Midianites and to carry out the LORD's vengeance on them. [4] Send into battle a thousand men from each of the tribes of Israel." [5] So twelve thousand men armed for battle, a thousand from each tribe, were supplied from the clans of Israel. [6] Moses sent them into battle, a thousand from each tribe, along with Phinehas son of Eleazar, the priest, who took with him articles from the sanctuary and the trumpets for signaling.

COMMENTARY

1–2 This war is Moses' last one before God brings his life to an end. On the expression, "to be gathered to your people" (v.2), see Note on 20:24. Moses did not get to lead the war of conquest in Canaan; that would be for his successor. But at least he was to lead a punitive war against the foes who nearly had destroyed his people, seemingly on the eve of their greatest triumph. This war was to be a war of vengeance against Midian, a holy war of the people of God.

The war is announced by the Lord, not Moses. Moses did not regard this war as motivated by petty jealousy. It was "the LORD's vengeance" (v.3) because of the wickedness of the Midianites, who caused the seduction of the Israelites in the pagan worship system of Baal of Peor (25:16–18). Yahweh's strong words came specifically to Moses: "avenge an avenging" ($n^e\bar{q}\bar{o}m$ $niqmat$; v.2). The cognate accu-

sative is a means of emphasis in Hebrew style. See also Deuteronomy 32:43, a text speaking of God's avenging the blood of his servants, and Nahum 1:2, of vengeance against Nineveh. We may also notice the phrase, "avenge the breaking of the covenant" (Lev 26:25).

3–4 On hearing the commandment of the Lord, Moses turned to the people and called for a strike force, an elite corps of soldiers who would carry out the punitive war. This was a limited, contained, special task calling for a limited army of special forces. One thousand men were to come from each of the tribes of Israel. The entire nation has been jeopardized, so all the tribes were to share in vengeance. If the figures of the census of 26:51 are "common numbers" (see the discussion on large numbers in the Introduction), then twelve thousand of the six hundred thousand men make a very small proportional force (one fiftieth of the whole). If twelve thousand are taken from a smaller army of approximately sixty thousand men, then a force of twelve thousand would be relatively small but still significant (one fifth of the whole). In any case, reduced force is a part for the whole, a representative army for the whole nation.

5–6 Verse 5 is somewhat celebrative in nature, as is so much of the historical narrative of this book. The "thousand of the thousands" is a nice tie of words, having an almost mystical ring to it. The holy war was a vendetta of God that called for special uses of numbers and men.

In biblical thought a blood relative may take vengeance on the killer of the slain (see ch. 35). There is a sense that the Lord is the kinsman of his people, who issues a command for his own holy vendetta. The war is one of divine reprisal for the near destruction of his people by the Midianites. The mention of Phinehas in v.6 is especially noteworthy. It was his zeal for the honor of the Lord that led him to spear Zimri and Cozbi in their licentious act at the entrance to the Tent of Meeting (25:15, 18). Now his leadership in the sacral aspects of the battle demonstrates that this was truly holy war. To the site of the battle he took along "articles from the sanctuary and the [priestly] trumpets for signaling" (see 10:9).

The "articles from the sanctuary" do not appear to include the holy ark of the covenant (despite the desire of some scholars to connect this phrasing to the story of the ark in warfare in Jos 6:6 and 1Sa 4); surely the ark would have been mentioned if it were used in this battle. More likely the priest took small implements from the worship of God in the tent; the focus is on the trumpets. Whatever implements he took with him, the belief was sure: Yahweh was with his people in the sacred place, so he was with his people as they went to war.

The trumpet in this text is the "sacred clarion" ($h^a\bar{s}\bar{o}\bar{s}^e r\hat{a}$) from 10:8 (see also 2Ch 13:12). This was a long, straight metal tube with a flowing bell; it is distinguished from the shofar ($\bar{s}\bar{o}p\bar{a}r$), the ram's horn of ancient Israel. The verbal root hsr (GK 2955) is denominative and means "to sound a clarion" (see 2Ch 5:13, Piel; 1Ch 15:24, Hiphil). The blowing of the sacred clarion was an act of celebrative worship. While the concept is alien to us today, even the warfare that Israel was to engage in was regarded as a sacral act—in some way an act of the worship of God (see Ps 149:6, the praise of God linked to the wielding of a sword). "Onward *Hebrew* Soldiers" was more than a metaphor for Israel; it was a descriptive reality of army life.

NOTE

2 The words נְקֹם נִקְמַת ($n^e q\bar{o}m$ $niqmat$, "take vengeance") form a powerful imperative. Not only are these words reported to be the command of Yahweh directly to Moses, which he then was to bring to the people of Israel, but also the two forms of the same verb (the root נָקַם [$n\bar{a}qam$], "to avenge") make the expression emphatic.

A second striking factor in this verse is the phrasing used to describe the forthcoming death of Moses, אַחַר תֵּאָסֵף אֶל־עַמֶּיךָ (ʾahar tēʾāsēp ʾel-ʿammeykā, "After that, you will be gathered to your people"; cf. the use of this phrase respecting the impending death of Aaron in 20:26; see also its use respecting Moses in 27:13). A first impulse might be to shrug at these words and simply to dismiss them as a common rhetorical device, a euphemism for death. But several issues are in play in the use of this phrase in this particular case:

1. Others die of illness, infirmity, or injury, or simply from the cumulative effects of aging in a postfall world. Moses' death, however, was not to be from any common cause; his death was to be at the express agency of God (see also Dt 32:50; cf. 34:5). Moreover, at the time of his death Moses was in superb health and physical vigor (see Dt 34:7).

2. The expression "to be gathered to one's people" might have been a gentle phrase in Hebrew culture to describe death and its aftermath. When a person's body was placed in a family vault, after the process of decay that person's bones might be taken by relatives and placed farther back in a burial cave amid the bones of those in the family who had died earlier. In this way one might say that one was "gathered to one's people" through the intermingling of their bones.

3. But the description of the burial of Moses is unique in biblical literature: "He [Yahweh] buried him in Moab, in the valley opposite Beth Peor, but to this day [i.e., the day of the writing of this text] no one knows where his grave is" (Dt 34:6). Moses was *not* "gathered to his people" in the customary understanding of that phrase. His bones remained alone, in a burial site about which we know no more today than was known by faithful people in Israel in the fifteenth (or later) century BC.

4. For this reason, and against the common (Sadducean? see 5, below) viewpoints of scholars today, I suggest that this phrase should be considered as a part of the inquiry into and study of the hope of life after death and the resurrection of the body in the text of the Hebrew Scriptures. The only manner in which Moses could be "gathered to his people" was to experience life after death, along with those who also shared such blessed hope. Thus I propose that this phrase should be used to consider life, not death—the ongoing person, not the rotting of flesh and the resultant cache of bones.

5. As Jesus told the unbelieving Sadducees of his day, God "is not the God of the dead but of the living" (Mt 22:32). In fact, in that same verse Jesus argued this very point from the words Yahweh had spoken to Moses at the beginning of Moses' ministry: "I am the God of Abraham, the God of Isaac, and the God of Jacob" (Ex 3:6). Abraham, Isaac, and Jacob were alive with God when Yahweh called Moses to serve him. Now, after all the events in his life with God, Moses was "gathered to his people"—in heaven!

ii. The report of the victory (31:7–12)

> [7]They fought against Midian, as the LORD commanded Moses, and killed every man. [8]Among their victims were Evi, Rekem, Zur, Hur and Reba—the five kings of Midian. They also killed Balaam son of Beor with the sword. [9]The Israelites captured the Midianite women and children and took all the Midianite herds, flocks and goods as plunder. [10]They burned all the towns where the Midianites had settled, as well as all their camps. [11]They took all the plunder and spoils, including the people and animals, [12]and brought the captives, spoils and plunder to Moses and Eleazar the priest and the Israelite assembly at their camp on the plains of Moab, by the Jordan across from Jericho.

COMMENTARY

7 The narrator stresses the fact that this battle was the Lord's; it was not merely the result of human pique. The narrator does not say much at all about the battle, but he is concerned to detail the aftermath of the victory of Israel. Our modern difficulty in comprehending the concept of holy war and its annihilation of a populace is understandable but somewhat shortsighted. Yahweh was about to bring Israel into the land of Canaan to engage in a war of conquest and extermination of all the peoples in that land (see Dt 20:1–16) because of their gross wickedness and the threat they represented to the integrity of the worship of Israel—in fact, to Israel's very survival in the land. The cup of the Amorites was now full (see Ge 15:16). Further, the judgment of the Lord on the peoples of Canaan is a paradigm of final judgment, a teaching of both Old and New Testaments and all orthodox creeds.

So it is that v.7 reports that Israel obeyed the word of the Lord through his servant Moses. They fought as they were taught, an act of faithfulness, courage, and obedient trust. The report that they "killed every man" does not necessarily mean that they killed every individual without exception, but that there was complete defeat with a focus on the males of the enemy army who were slain. Some of the enemies must have fled. The emphasis in this report is that the Hebrews killed only the men, thus allowing for the report of v.9 respecting women and children.

8 Verse 8 lists the notables the Israelites killed and then impaled (see Notes). The list of the Midianite kings (Evi, Rekem, Zur, Hur, and Reba) is like a list of trophies. These five chieftains are memorialized forever as enemies of the Lord who were impotent before his armies. Their wounds and their impaling poles point to ghastly deaths and grisly display. There is here a vindictiveness of the sacred, a display of triumph—a celebration of God, who has given glorious victory.

Among the names are two surprises. One is Zur (*ṣûr*), whom we remember as the father of Cozbi (see 25:15), the Midianite woman who was stabbed to death with Zimri by Phinehas. The supposition we had in ch. 25 that she was a significant person is now confirmed. Cozbi was like an early Jezebel. She was a priestess-princess of paganism. As in the case of Jezebel, so also Cozbi's name has been defiled in Israel (Cozbi means "Deception"). We have a name to use for her if we wish to recall her at all, but it is a name of infamy.

The other surprise, of course, is the mention of Balaam. The Hebrew wording is striking: "And Balaam son of Beor they also killed by the sword." Until now, following the text, we would have had no idea he would appear in the narrative of Scripture again. The story of ch. 25 lacks the name of the principal instigator in the seduction of the men of Israel to the orgiastic worship of Baal. But here he is found among the dead of the princes of Midian; what trouble Balaam failed to accomplish by the use of mantic arts he was able to achieve by the evil direction he gave to the Midianites (v.16; see chs. 22–24).

Balaam's name, amid the recital of the names of the Midianite kings, suggests that he was their advisor, their spiritual guru. Always after a shekel, Balaam had a new gig. It must have seemed ironic to him to have his pay and to know that Israel was in trouble. But the irony came full circle; he was now dead. There is considerable discussion as to the manner of his death, indicated in this verse. Some feel he may have died in war; others believe that he was executed, that he died a judicial death. It is possible that the second case is true and that after he was run through with a sword, he was also impaled with the princes he had so misdirected.

9-12 While the men of Midian were killed by the victorious Hebrew soldiers, the women and children were spared by the troops as plunder (v.9). Moses commanded that only the virgin women (who were thus innocent of the indecencies at Peor) could be spared; the guilty women and the boys (who might endanger the inheritance rights of Israelite men) were to be put to death (vv.15-17). We may make some observations about this shocking situation:

1. Jericho is the first city of Cisjordan (the near side of Jordan) that Israel would win by warfare. In the case of Jericho, all the inhabitants and all of their possessions were placed under the ban (ḥerem); all was to be devoted to the Lord. In the case of Midian, this was a punitive strike; Midian was not the firstfruits of the land. There were, therefore, many items of booty and plunder (including surviving people) to be distributed among the men of the army, as well as among the people who had remained in camp. The burning of the cities was a mark that they were not to be inhabited by the Hebrews; burning them would greatly impede their being reinhabited by enemies.

2. The sparing the lives of the women and children was likely considered by the soldiers of Israel to be an act of mercy. They could have killed them or abandoned them to their own devices. By sparing them, the soldiers must have thought themselves magnanimous.

3. There is a sense of poetic justice in that the Midianites had conspired to destroy Israel through licentious behavior of their priestess-cult functionaries. Now their young women and daughters were about to be added to the families of Israel in what seems to be a proper despoiling of the enemies.

4. At the same time we see here, and often, how in the ancient Near East (and in the Bible, which grew out of that world) that women and children were regarded as property to be listed with cows, trinkets, and assorted booty. The sad truth is that the times were rarely merciful to women as persons.

Throughout the war, Phinehas was intensively involved as a priest-warrior. There was a sense in which his father, Eleazar, was still the high priest who functioned in the camp at the altars of the Lord. But Phinehas was more like a field priest who functioned with the armies of Israel to remind them that the Lord was in their midst, fighting for them.

This section is marked by an orderliness that is characteristic of so much of the book of Numbers and that stands in studied contrast to the horrors the verses recount. Verse 8 gives a list of the kings, v.9 a list of the booty, v.10 an accounting of the burnings, and v.12 a list of possessions. There is also a redundancy of verbs describing the taking of captives ("the Israelites captured ... plundered ... burned ... took ... brought").

Verse 12 is particularly triumphant in tone, with a formal pageantry to its cadences. The victorious Hebrews proved that they could do it. They were unlike their parents, who could not win wars against their enemies; with only a fraction of the entire army they had been able to win a great victory. So they come to Moses, to Eleazar, and to the people who had remained behind in camp. This scene is not unlike the later Roman victory processionals after a distant campaign by a great general. This display shows forth God's accomplishments to the entire community.

There is an episodic nature to this book. In some ways it is like the memoirs of Moses in the wilderness, as evidenced in the way this story ties up three loose ends: the matters of Cozbi's father, Balaam, and the meaning of the events at Baal Peor. The tone so far in this story is one of victory march. The people must have been thinking, "We are faithful, and so is the Lord."

NOTES

8 In the phrase הָרְגוּ עַל־חַלְלֵיהֶם (*hārᵉgû ʿal-ḥallêhem*, "they killed ... with the sword"), the meaning of the word *ḥallêhem* (GK 2728) remains debated. The basic meaning of the verb חָלָל (*ḥālāl*) means "to profane"; in certain contexts it means "to pierce, wound." Here it seems preferable to think of the word's nominal form as denoting "impaling stakes," used in the ancient Near East for brutal, grisly displays of vanquished foes as potent symbols of their destruction. The body of a man would be thrust down on a sharpened stake that would pierce through his rectum to enter his abdomen. There was a double shame to this action; the awful display of the corpse would also preclude its decent burial.

11 בָּאָדָם וּבַבְּהֵמָה (*baʾadām ûbabbᵉhēmâ*, "the people and animals") aptly illustrates how the Hebrew term *ʾadām* ("man") may be used from time to time in the Bible to speak generally of persons, rather than specifically of males. Here the word is used specifically of women and children; all the adult males had been slain in the battle and the subsequent judgment.

12 The phrasing אֶל־עַרְבֹת מוֹאָב אֲשֶׁר עַל־יַרְדֵּן יְרֵחוֹ (*ʾel-ʿarbōt môʾab ᵃšer ʿal-yardēn yᵉrēḥô*, "on the plains of Moab, by the Jordan across from Jericho") presents a perspective of Transjordan from Cisjordan; perhaps this reflects the work of a post-Mosaic redactor. The expression "across from Jericho" has the sense of "over there." Similarly, the association of the Jordan River with the city of Jericho is also the perspective that later people would have found helpful in visualizing the site in their minds. The perspective of geography in the Bible regularly centers on the land of Israel, even when the people are not there. Everything else is designed to give us a sense of "out there"—a regular metaphor for distance from God's dwelling.

iii. The destruction of the women and boys (31:13–18)

¹³Moses, Eleazar the priest and all the leaders of the community went to meet them outside the camp. ¹⁴Moses was angry with the officers of the army—the commanders of thousands and commanders of hundreds—who returned from the battle.

¹⁵"Have you allowed all the women to live?" he asked them. ¹⁶"They were the ones who followed Balaam's advice and were the means of turning the Israelites away from the Lord in what happened at Peor, so that a plague struck the Lord's people. ¹⁷Now kill all the boys. And kill every woman who has slept with a man, ¹⁸but save for yourselves every girl who has never slept with a man.

COMMENTARY

13–18 We may be shocked when we find the people are facing anger from Moses instead of approval. The meeting outside the camp is an omen; something is unclean. The Bible says that Moses was furious against the officers of the armies. He does not come to bless them in their victory but to vent his rage at the victories. Even in victory the people can grossly err.

Moses asks almost incredulously, "Have you allowed all the women to live?" (v.15). The text has led us down a line that leads to deliberate surprise. We find ourselves as startled by these words, even as some of the soldiers might have been. But then Moses explains: These were the very women whom Balaam had used to cause the seduction of the people of Israel and to provoke the terrible plague that had broken out among the Hebrew congregation (v.16). So boys and women were to be killed; there was to be no mercy, no exception (v.17). The lives of young girls (demonstrable virgins) only would be spared; for only they had not contaminated themselves with the debauchery of Midian and Moab in Baal worship (v.18). The suggestion is that the participation of Midianite women in the debased orgiastic worship of Baal described in ch. 25 was extensive, not selective. Who would know which of these women was innocent of participation in these rituals? The presumption is that each one was guilty in some manner.

Verse 17 is rather powerful in its formation. It is framed with a chiasm using the imperative verb "kill." The following format shows the word order, the pungency, of the original:

And now, kill every male among the children;
> and every woman who knows a man,
a male sexually, kill!

The brutality demanded by this verse is nearly unimaginable — the killing of boys and babies. One has to ask, what separates this action from the Egyptians' killing of Hebrew male babies in Exodus 1? Since most women were married young in biblical times, most women would have had to be killed as well. Here is the sort of text that troubles us deeply. It is one thing to kill a man. It is one thing to kill a woman in battle. It is one thing even to kill children in a frenzy of hatred. But this verse demands the calm, selective, purposeful executing of women and children after the battle was over.

Verse 18 only increases our sense of unrest in this text. Those girls who were to be kept alive would have had to be rather young. Though the lives of these little girls were to be preserved, their mothers would have to be killed. For more on this and its relationship to morality in the OT, see the Reflection.

NOTE

17 The phrase יֹדַעַת אִישׁ לְמִשְׁכַּב זָכָר (yōdaʿat ʾîš lᵉmiškab zākār, "to know a man, lying with a male"; "who has slept with a man," NIV) is noteworthy. The word מִשְׁכַּב (miškab; GK 5435) is a noun that means "place of lying, couch, act of lying (down)." Here it is used idiomatically as an adverb to define further the intention of the line. To the first phrase, "who had not known a man," this word adds the idea "lying with a male." The two phrases together are a definitive statement of virginity. It has been observed that no single word in biblical Hebrew unequivocally means "virgin." A qualifying phrase is needed to make the idea clear. In discussing a Ugaritic term, Cyrus Gordon writes, "There is no word in the Near Eastern languages that by itself means *virgo intacta*" (*UT*, #540). The use of the noun *miškab* as an adverb indicating sexual behavior is seen also in Judges 21:11–12 and in Leviticus 18:22; 20:13 (of man-to-man relations, i.e., sodomy).

REFLECTION

Such stories as Numbers 31 are bound to raise questions about morality in the OT. Ultimately, these questions are darts directed against the person of God. One cannot debate the "morality" of the OT apart from the "morality" of God, who is represented in these passages. And once one begins to ask, "Is God moral?" the very question damns the speaker. For who is humankind to instruct the Lord (see Job 40:1–2)? This is not to say that these passages do not cause us to shriek with inner tension—for they do! But our shout had best not be an arrogant attack on Majesty. Ultimately, people of faith affirm—in the midst of the most negative environment: "The God of Israel will do right."

The only way to understand such a ghastly command is to realize what was at stake in the story of Baal Peor (ch. 25), the incident that gave rise to the holy war in the first place. This story is not just another account of sin and rebellion in the wilderness. Indeed, if the story of Baal Peor was not an unusual and remarkable account, then the punishment meted out in ch. 31 was not in keeping with the crime.

Numbers 25 is unique. It records an altogether new type of sin and rebellion—one that bears within itself the threat of the doom of the nation as a whole. Since we have read the rest of the story,

we know that the evil described in ch. 25 was the very type of evil that finally destroyed the Israelite kingdoms in the land. While it is difficult to make such a statement, the commanded destruction of the women and boys was actually an act of God's mercy—for Israel. There is a sense of perspective here that is so difficult to grasp, yet which permeates the Word of God: Divine judgment is sure for the nations who are a threat to the existence of God's people or who have rejected his grace.

And that truth remains in our own "sophisticated" day. Modern nations, and the ungodly among all peoples, are at risk. They are aware of risks from the possibility of nuclear disaster, from the threat of war, from the tweaks of nature, and from the freaks of chance. But nations today are also at risk from the judgment of God—whether or not they acknowledge so. One day that judgment will come. At that time there will be no weeping over women and boys who died in ancient Midian three and a half millennia ago; at that time the judgment of God will transcend anything ever written in the harshest OT Scripture. And God will still be merciful and holy, who will maintain glory and honor in the midst of havoc and ruin. The God of Israel will still do right.

iv. The purification of the soldiers (31:19–20)

19"All of you who have killed anyone or touched anyone who was killed must stay outside the camp seven days. On the third and seventh days you must purify yourselves and your captives. ²⁰Purify every garment as well as everything made of leather, goat hair or wood."

COMMENTARY

19–20 The "seven days" of v.19 help us to sense the full weight of what the laws of cleanness pertained to, as this was holy war (see 19:11–13). Both people (31:19–20) and things (31:21–24) had to be cleansed. The rites of purification from contact with a dead body would demand the waters of cleansing from the ashes of the red heifer (see 19:12).

There is an emphatic pronoun at the beginning of this verse: "And you!" Here all who had been involved in the killing of others are addressed, even though those who were killed were the enemies of God and his people. The death of any person makes unclean the one who comes in contact with the corpse, even when the killing was commanded by God. Thus even in a text of judgment, there are still the lessons of ritual cleansing for the people of God.

NOTE

19 תִּתְחַטְּאוּ (tithatt°û, "purify yourselves") is a Hithpael imperative from the root ḥāṭāʾ ("to purify oneself from uncleanness"), a verb used of the Levite in 8:21. Those who had had any contact with the dead were impure (see 19:12) and needed to undergo the rite of purification.

v. The purifying of the goods (31:21–24)

²¹Then Eleazar the priest said to the soldiers who had gone into battle, "This is the requirement of the law that the LORD gave Moses: ²²Gold, silver, bronze, iron, tin, lead ²³and anything else that can withstand fire must be put through the fire, and then it will be clean. But it must also be purified with the water of cleansing. And whatever cannot withstand fire must be put through that water. ²⁴On the seventh day wash your clothes and you will be clean. Then you may come into the camp."

COMMENTARY

21–24 Purification extends to things as well as to people. Things that were ritually impure would contaminate people who were otherwise clean. Hence it is another mark of the grace of God to provide a means for the purification of goods as well. Metal objects had to be purified by having them pass through fire and then the waters of cleansing. Some of these metal objects that were so cleansed became gifts to the Lord (see v.50). Those items that could not withstand fire had to be cleansed in the water alone. Possibly Paul's description of the *bēma* judgment of the work of believers (1Co 3:10–15) is patterned in part after this passage. In the case of the cleansing of these soldiers, they had to wait until the seventh day, then wash their clothes before they could enter the camp. This pattern of seven days of exclusion from the camp because of uncleanness is well established in Israel (see the story of Miriam in ch. 12).

b. The Division of the Spoils (31:25–54)

OVERVIEW

Another aspect of holy war was the just distribution of the spoils of war, both among those who fought in the battle as well as among those who stayed with the community, with appropriate shares to be given to the Lord, whose battle it was (v.28). This section describes rather elaborately that process of division. As in so many such sections in Numbers, this rather prosaic text reads with a certain grandeur—for it, too, is celebrative. These texts were meant to be read aloud as a declaration of the work of God in the lives of his people. Much like the antiphonal responses in Psalm 136, the patterns of remembrance of the works of the Lord in the deliverance of his people were designed to be recited in a variety of ways.

i. The share for the soldiers (31:25–41)

²⁵The Lord said to Moses, ²⁶"You and Eleazar the priest and the family heads of the community are to count all the people and animals that were captured. ²⁷Divide the spoils between the soldiers who took part in the battle and the rest of the community. ²⁸From the soldiers who fought in the battle, set apart as tribute for the Lord one out of every five hundred, whether persons, cattle, donkeys, sheep or goats. ²⁹Take this tribute from their half share and give it to Eleazar the priest as the Lord's part. ³⁰From the Israelites' half, select one out of every fifty, whether persons, cattle, donkeys, sheep, goats or other animals. Give them to the Levites, who are responsible for the care of the Lord's tabernacle."
³¹So Moses and Eleazar the priest did as the Lord commanded Moses.
³²The plunder remaining from the spoils that the soldiers took was 675,000 sheep, ³³72,000 cattle, ³⁴61,000 donkeys ³⁵and 32,000 women who had never slept with a man.
³⁶The half share of those who fought in the battle was:
337,500 sheep, ³⁷of which the tribute for the Lord was 675;
³⁸36,000 cattle, of which the tribute for the Lord was 72;
³⁹30,500 donkeys, of which the tribute for the Lord was 61;

[40]16,000 people, of which the tribute for the LORD was 32.

[41]Moses gave the tribute to Eleazar the priest as the LORD's part, as the LORD commanded Moses.

25–41 The book of Numbers delights in lists, in the numbering of persons and things. Here in this section of the chapter is the command of the Lord to Moses to total up the spoils of the battle, both human and beast. The term "people" (*bā'adām*, "among [the] men") in this section relates only to the little girls who were spared from the ban (*ḥerem*); the animals included sheep, cattle, donkeys, and goats. Eleazar and heads of fathers' houses were to aid Moses in taking this inventory. The task must have been enormous, given the numbers involved. The purpose of making this sum seems to be twofold: (1) it is a celebrative declaration of the work of God in their behalf; (2) it is a means to assure the equitable distribution of the spoils of war. Dividing such spoils was a proverbial symbol for exquisite joy in the ancient world (e.g., Isa 9:3, where the celebration of spoils is paired with that of the bringing in of a harvest).

The division of the spoils was to be made in two sections, one for those who had fought in the war and the other for the rest of the congregation. The two halves were equal, but their distribution was deliberately unequal—there were far fewer soldiers than those who remained in the camp. Yet it was the soldiers who had risked their lives, so theirs was the larger personal share. The term used for soldiers in v.27 is indicative of the type of man who had been called to serve in the elite corps. They are described as *tōp̄e'śê hammilḥāmâ*, "those who are skilled for battle" (cf. Jer 2:8, "those who deal with the law").

Before the men of war could enjoy their allotment of the spoils, there first had to be a tax set apart for the Lord. The ratio in this case was one to five hundred. Again, the soldiers who had risked their lives received larger personal shares (as they were a smaller collective unit than the vast numbers of the congregation), and their share to the Lord was also smaller than the share that was demanded of the people. The proportion to be given to the Lord is termed a "tax" or a "tribute" (*mekes*, from the verb *kāsas*, "to compute," v.28; see Ex 12:4). This tribute was given to Eleazar the priest as a sacred offering (*te rûmâ*) to the Lord (v.29).

From the half of the booty that was to be distributed to the members of the congregation, one unit of each fifty was to be given as a tribute to the Lord for the special use of the Levites in return for their sacral service at the tabernacle. Thus the people's tax in this booty was ten times that of the soldiers' share—one fiftieth compared to one five-hundredth.

The instructions the Lord gave to Moses (vv.25–30) are followed by a report of accomplishment (v.31). In this verse we find again the familiar words of obedience. Each time we read these words of compliance on the part of Moses, we groan within at the thought of the one time that Moses did not do as God had commanded him (ch. 20).

The list of the plunder as a whole is given in vv.32–35. The numbers were enormous; the victory was staggering. This was just the beginning; on the other side of the Jordan lay the rest of the land of God's promise. The people should have been thinking, "If we received this much booty in a punitive war, just think what will be our portion when we are on the campaign of conquest!"

The table reads:

- 675,000 sheep (presumably including goats)
- 72,000 cattle
- 61,000 donkeys
- 32,000 young (virgin) women

The half share follows with correct, simple arithmetic:

- 337,500 sheep (including goats)
- 36,000 cattle
- 30,500 donkeys
- 16,000 young (virgin) women

The Lord's tax (to be given to Eleazar; ratio of one unit of five hundred):

- 675 sheep
- 72 cattle
- 61 donkeys
- 32 young (virgin) women

Again, the section concludes with a summary statement of complete obedience on the part of Moses with regard to the presentation of the tax as a sacred contribution to the Lord; he gave these items to Eleazar the priest (v.41).

We may make a few observations about these numbers:

1. They are immense numbers, indicative of a great victory with enormous booty.
2. Though the numbers of the animals and women are rounded off to the thousands, the proportion of one to five hundred gets quite exacting; the supposition is that these numbers may well be "common numbers" rather than inflated sums.
3. The supposition, so often heard, that numbers are not copied well in the Bible is not buttressed in these sections of Numbers. It seems that in this book, at least, the copying of numbers (in the awkward manner of words rather than symbols) was done carefully. Perhaps the necessity for the sums and totals to work out correctly was a check against carelessness by later scribes.

As to the use to which the women would be put in the service of the priests, we can only guess. It is possible that they were given menial tasks to do in the service of the Lord, as many commentators suggest (see Ex 38:8). In these women there is something redemptive in the whole dismal record of the defeat of Midian. Though most of their countrymen had been slain, including their parents and brothers, the surviving young girls would eventually become part of the redeemed community. Eventually these few girls became mothers in Israel.

ii. The share for the people (31:42–47)

⁴²The half belonging to the Israelites, which Moses set apart from that of the fighting men — ⁴³the community's half — was 337,500 sheep, ⁴⁴36,000 cattle, ⁴⁵30,500 donkeys ⁴⁶and 16,000 people. ⁴⁷From the Israelites' half, Moses selected one out of every fifty persons and animals, as the LORD commanded him, and gave them to the Levites, who were responsible for the care of the LORD's tabernacle.

42–47 The statistics of the half share for the people follow in much the same procedure as the previous section for the soldiers. The numbers of the half are the same but are listed in a celebrative manner. In this case the tax, which would become a sacred tribute to the Lord, was proportionally higher: one unit of fifty (rather than one unit of five hundred).

This proportion would result in the following:

- 6,750 sheep
- 720 cattle
- 610 donkeys
- 320 young (virgin) women

Again, Moses followed faithfully in the distribution of the Lord's share. In this case it was given to the Levites.

iii. The extra share for the Lord (31:48–54)

⁴⁸Then the officers who were over the units of the army — the commanders of thousands and commanders of hundreds — went to Moses ⁴⁹and said to him, "Your servants have counted the soldiers under our command, and not one is missing. ⁵⁰So we have brought as an offering to the Lord the gold articles each of us acquired — armlets, bracelets, signet rings, earrings and necklaces — to make atonement for ourselves before the Lord."

⁵¹Moses and Eleazar the priest accepted from them the gold — all the crafted articles. ⁵²All the gold from the commanders of thousands and commanders of hundreds that Moses and Eleazar presented as a gift to the Lord weighed 16,750 shekels. ⁵³Each soldier had taken plunder for himself. ⁵⁴Moses and Eleazar the priest accepted the gold from the commanders of thousands and commanders of hundreds and brought it into the Tent of Meeting as a memorial for the Israelites before the Lord.

COMMENTARY

48–54 For a chapter that begins with such a grim story, there is a perfectly lovely ending. This is the account of a spontaneous extra gift to the Lord by the officers' corps. Beyond the tax they were required to give of the animals and persons that had been distributed to them in the sharing of the booty of the war, there were innumerable objects the soldiers had taken for their own use as they looted the camps (v.53). Now the captains of thousands and of hundreds approached Moses (v.48) and made a mag-

nanimous offering of numerous beautiful objects of gold — armlets, bracelets, signet rings, earrings, and other ornaments (v.50). This gift, they assured Moses, was in gratitude for a most remarkable fact: not one soldier of the elite Hebrew corps had died in the war (v.49)! The only explanation for this outcome was the presence of the Lord among his people in his holy sanctuary (cf. the comment of Goldberg, 134, "Gott ist im Israel gegenwartig im Heiligtum"; "God is present in Israel in his sanctuary").

That no Israelite soldiers were lost was a miracle. But it was a miracle that compelled response on the part of God's people. As Walther Eichrodt (*Theology of the Old Testament* [trans. J. A. Baker; Philadelphia: Westminster, 1967], 163) points out, the important issue for the belief in miracles in Scripture lies not so much in the material facts of the miracles but in what they present of the person and work of God. The real importance of the miraculous for faith is in "its evidential character," particularly "a clear impression of God's care or retribution within it."

Of course, the people made a special gift to the Lord. He had made a special gift of life to them. The gift by the officers' corps is reminiscent of the extravagant gifts of the people from the despoiling of the Egyptians (Ex 35). This is a mark of the gratitude of the new generation. Moses and Eleazar the priest took from them the gold items, all of fashioned work (v.51). When they weighed them, they found the cumulative weight to be 16,750 shekels (about 420 pounds; v.52)! This gift is enormous—and it came from grateful men to an all-protective God.

Moses and Eleazar brought the gold into the Tent of Meeting, where it became a "memorial" (*zikkārôn*) of the victory the Lord had won (v.54). We suspect, though without specificity from the text, that the gold would have been melted down and reworked into a suitably fashioned symbol—an extravagant offering to the Lord.

The most interesting phrase in this entire section concerns the motivation of the chiefs. It was "to make atonement for ourselves before the Lord" (v.50). Thus the making of atonement was not prompted by sin or guilt but by overwhelming gratitude. They knew, as all officers know, that every battle is a calculated risk in which some soldiers will die. A good officer seeks to minimize his losses as he maximizes his gain. In this case the gain was overwhelming—complete victory. The losses were nil—not one Hebrew soldier died. The making of atonement, then, was an offering of expiation in gratitude to God for the gift he made of the lives of those who could have died. This is a payment, if you will, in return for what they might have lost.

REFLECTION

We have no reason to believe that the protection of the lives of every soldier in the wars of Israel ever happened again. This must have been a singular event in the history of Israel. If so, it is suitably predictive of the army of Christ in his final victory over all wickedness (Rev 19). No doubt in that final

battle there will be no casualties among his forces. So here is a battle at the beginning of the wars of Israel that in one particular aspect points forward to the final battle of Savior Jesus. Gratitude to him will be in the measure of the gratitude of these officers back then.

6. The Settlement of the Transjordan Tribes (32:1–42)

OVERVIEW

There is a sense of direction and symmetry to the book of Numbers that is satisfying to the patient reader. Within the book, as we have seen, there are passages of dramatic encounters, miracu-

lous acts, robust theology, and even comedic drama. There are also texts, such as the present chapter, that bear none of these characteristics. Yet the chapter is significant because it deals with the ways the will of God was manifest through the tribes of Israel as the new generation was taking its place in the world God had given to them. This chapter presents the account of the first of the tribes to settle in the land of their choice. In the case of two and one-half tribes, Transjordan was the inheritance of choice. For them—Reuben, Gad, and half of the tribe of Manasseh—the victories over Sihon and Og (ch. 21) and the punitive victory over Midian (ch. 31) signaled victory aplenty. It was time at last to make a home.

This chapter is most significant in what it presents of the life and character of Moses. Here we find another block to add to our view of his complex humanity—he flashes here in rage, it seems, before he knows fully what is being asked. But his rage is based on a lifetime of disappointment, a generation of waste, and the ever-present wilderness.

a. The Request of Reuben and Gad to Settle in Transjordan (32:1–19)

OVERVIEW

The chapter begins, as several chapters do, with the approach of petitioners to Moses. They come to him not because he is king but because he is the regent of the Lord who mediated the divine word in the league of tribes. As in the case of the daughters of Zelophehad in ch. 27, and as in the instance of the relatives of these women in ch. 36, so the leaders of the tribes of Reuben and Gad make their approach to Moses for the settlement of their landed claim. The abundance of fertile grazing land in Transjordan prompted the leaders of these two tribes to request of Moses and Eleazar that they might settle there, not across (west of) the Jordan River.

There are several approaches we may take in evaluating the request of these tribal leaders. It is customary among Christian commentators to regard their actions as sinful, an acceptance of lesser things rather than having faith to cling on for the best. But it is possible to see in the actions of the men of Gad and Reuben nothing untoward at all, only a pragmatic decision that led to a remarkable negotiation with the Lord and his servant Moses.

Transjordan, too, was a gift of God won by conquest. When we think of Canaan, we are prone to think of Cisjordan; Canaan proper is described this way in ch. 34. Yet the full inheritance of God's people extended to the regions of Transjordan as well. But it was, in a sense, the fringe of the garment. It was not the heart and soul of the land. To settle on the fringe was a mixed blessing. The people who lived in Transjordan were able to do so by conscious choice.

But because they were somewhat removed from the center of the life of the land, they were the most prone to be influenced by outsiders. And clearly they were the most open for territorial expansion by their neighbors. Territorial living has both its advantages and its disadvantages. Ultimately, their request and the Lord's decision through Moses expanded the territory of Israel. If we put the best construction on things, we may see this chapter as a rash adventure in faith rather than a record of rebellion.

As these tribal leaders evaluated the lands they had won from the people of Sihon and Og, they found themselves particularly attracted to these areas. The region and its habitations (Ataroth, Dibon, Jazer, Nimrah, Heshbon, Elealeh, Seban, Nebo, and Beon—cities and regions that are relatively well located) looked especially promising to these chiefs. Extensive excavations and surface surveys were conducted in these areas of Transjordan in the 1970s and 1980s. The consensus is that these regions did not support a high population density in the period of the exodus and conquest (however this period may be dated); yet the biblical evidence from this chapter accords well with the archaeological evidence. This was an ideal place for the running of large flocks and herds.

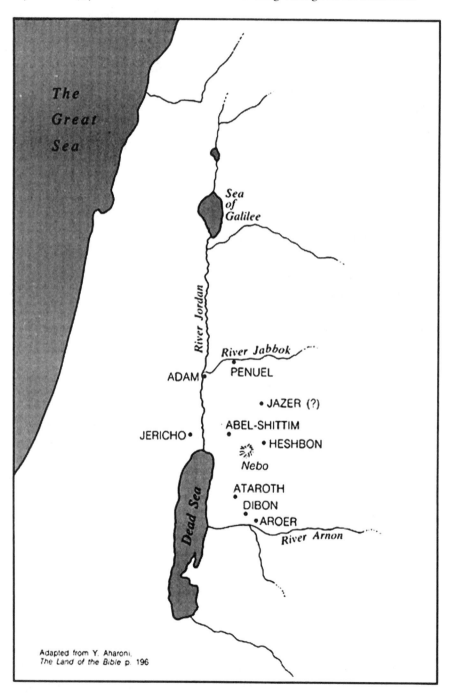

Adapted from Y. Aharoni.
The Land of the Bible p. 196

i. The original request (32:1-5)

> ¹The Reubenites and Gadites, who had very large herds and flocks, saw that the lands of Jazer and Gilead were suitable for livestock. ²So they came to Moses and Eleazar the priest and to the leaders of the community, and said, ³"Ataroth, Dibon, Jazer, Nimrah, Heshbon, Elealeh, Sebam, Nebo and Beon — ⁴the land the LORD subdued before the people of Israel — are suitable for livestock, and your servants have livestock. ⁵If we have found favor in your eyes," they said, "let this land be given to your servants as our possession. Do not make us cross the Jordan."

COMMENTARY

1 Verse 1 is characteristic of well-formed prosodic structure by exhibiting a chiasm based on the word "herds" or "livestock" (*miqneh*). Here is an attempt to render the order of the words of the verse and its emphasis:

Now the livestock was great of the people of
  Reuben,
        and of the people of Gad, it was exceedingly numerous;
            and they saw the land of Jazer
            and the land of Gilead,
and they provided a region ideal for livestock.

2–5 There is a subtle shift in the wording of v.2 from that of v.1. In v.1 Reuben precedes Gad; in v.2 this order is reversed. Perhaps this is a gentle way to suggest that both tribes had an equal stake in the affair. Only later (see v.33) do we find that some clans of Manasseh were involved as well. The listing of sites within the land they desired (see v.3) adds verisimilitude to their request; specificity of this sort helps the story to be more believable. But these nobles of Gad and Reuben do more than add place names; they put the issue of the land in the realm of divine gift in v.4:

The land that Yahweh smote
    before the congregation of Israel;
it is a land for livestock,
    and your servants have livestock.

The repetition of the word "livestock" (*miqneh*) is for emphasis; their herds must have been exceptionally large. The conquest of the Midianite livestock would have further expanded the holdings of these tribes as well as the others. But their language suggests that their holdings in livestock were out of proportion to the other tribes. They needed the room that Transjordan seemed to provide. But it is not just the matter of livestock that animates these particular tribes; it is also the fact that God in his power has provided the land as a gift for his people. The battles of victory over the peoples of Transjordan were the battles of Yahweh. His people were his agents, but the outcome was his.

As we read these verses, we might wonder what the motivation of the two tribes really was. We may wonder how they knew that the region of Transjordan was more suitable for their needs than a share in Cisjordan would be. We may wonder whether they were selfish, grasping for land ahead of the other tribes. It is also possible that the people of Reuben, at least, were still operating under a mistaken notion of their right of primogeniture by desiring that the first share of the land be given to them as descendants of the firstborn of Israel's tribal fathers.

Based on their subsequent words in this chapter, however, we may conclude that none of these issues was paramount. The text breathes a certain naïve transparency, a simplicity and candor that does not seem to admit complex reasoning. We may observe, simply, that these were two tribes with unusually large holdings of herds and flocks, and they believed that Transjordan was quite suitable for their needs. So the two tribes requested of Moses that the land of Transjordan be given to them as their singular possession on the basis of any grace that they had found in his sight as his servants (v.5). All seems respectful and deferential in tone and manner.

The possibility existed, however, that these polite words were covering a rebellious spirit. It was not just that they felt at home and should be allowed to settle in the place of their choice; these two tribes might have been abandoning their place in the league as a whole by saying something like, "We have ours; good luck with yours!" At least Moses read their words this way.

NOTES

1 יַעְזֵר (ya'zēr, "Jazer") is a place name of a region of Transjordan often associated with Heshbon (vv.1, 3, 35; 21:32; Jos 13:25; 21:39 [37]; 2Sa 24:5) and with vineyards (Isa 16:8–9 = Jer 48:32).

5 The tendency is to view verbs such as יֻתַּן (yuttan, "be given") as Pual imperfects. It is better, however, to parse this verb as a Qal passive jussive: "let [this land] be given [to your servants]."

ii. The angry response of Moses (32:6–15)

⁶Moses said to the Gadites and Reubenites, "Shall your countrymen go to war while you sit here? ⁷Why do you discourage the Israelites from going over into the land the LORD has given them? ⁸This is what your fathers did when I sent them from Kadesh Barnea to look over the land. ⁹After they went up to the Valley of Eshcol and viewed the land, they discouraged the Israelites from entering the land the LORD had given them. ¹⁰The LORD's anger was aroused that day and he swore this oath: ¹¹'Because they have not followed me wholeheartedly, not one of the men twenty years old or more who came up out of Egypt will see the land I promised on oath to Abraham, Isaac and Jacob — ¹²not one except Caleb son of Jephunneh the Kenizzite and Joshua son of Nun, for they followed the LORD wholeheartedly.' ¹³The LORD's anger burned against Israel and he made them wander in the desert forty years, until the whole generation of those who had done evil in his sight was gone.

¹⁴"And here you are, a brood of sinners, standing in the place of your fathers and making the LORD even more angry with Israel. ¹⁵If you turn away from following him, he will again leave all this people in the desert, and you will be the cause of their destruction."

COMMENTARY

6–7 The response of Moses reveals his flash point. He raged against the two tribes that they had become no better than their fathers, for neither had they been willing to go to the land to fight the battle of conquest. We may wonder at the reason for Moses' anger; it seems to be complex in nature. He may have suspected that the real reason for the request of these tribes was that they really did not want to participate in the war of conquest. This suspicion could not have come by their words alone, which seem respectful and reasonable, but by other information he may have had.

Additionally or alternatively, Moses may have reacted the way he did not because of their words but because of the torment within him that must have welled up constantly, uncontrollably. Moses could not enter the land; could it be possible that these two tribes who *could* enter the land chose not to do so? The words of the tribal spokesmen may have rubbed the wound of his own limitation with stinging salt.

Moses' words may have been provoked by his anger, but they became the opportunity to review the basic theology of the wilderness period. He was able to contrast the first and second generations, to warn the second on the basis of the experience of the first. In this case our approach to the book of Numbers is vindicated by his homily: The old generation is dead; the new generation must act differently from their ancestors.

In any event, Moses charged these tribal leaders with posing an intolerable situation. By granting them the right to settle outside Canaan proper, not only would these tribes be lost from the battle plans, but their absence would be a means of hindering the other tribes from crossing the Jordan as well. "Think of it," Moses seemed to be saying. "Could we have come this far after so long and still never enter the land?" For him, then, their question seemed not only selfish but also seditious. The entire nation might become discouraged (v.7), thus perhaps leading to an ominous replay of the failure of their parents—and this possibility forms the thesis of Numbers. Will the sons behave like their parents, or will they believe and inherit?

8 Here Moses rages, "This is what your fathers did." Moses' fear was that the failure of these two tribes to stay with the whole community in the war of conquest of Canaan would be the beginnings of a general revolt among the people against entering the land. It would be the failure of Kadesh (chs. 13–14) all over again.

In fact, this chapter has numerous word associations with chs. 13–14. In addition to the reporting of the story of those chapters in vv.6–15, several terms cause the reader to juxtapose the chapters. Among the most prominent are the following: (1) the verb "cross over" (ʿābar)—cf. 32:21 ("go over"), 27, 29–30, with 13:32 (untr. NIV); 14:7 ("passed through"), 41 ("disobeying"); (2) the term "children" (ṭap)—cf. 32:16–17, 24, 26, with 14:3, 31; (3) the phrase, "the inhabitants of this land" (yōšbê hāʾareṣ)—cf. 32:17 with 14:14. Wenham (213, n. 1) lists other words as well, but those mentioned above seem the more convincing.

9–13 All these happenings afford Moses the opportunity to preach a brief homily (certainly shortened considerably in this chapter from what he might really have said) on the history of the national experience in the wilderness. Moses presents an example of a biblical use of history for the instruction of the people of God. He speaks with specificity, passion, and historical insight with a contemporary feel—the tying of the experience of the past into the present of his audience. In some ways this section may be thought of as a model of biblical exhortation. The section is also a splendid review of the core of the historical narrative in Numbers. The materials center particularly on the debacle of chs. 13–14, the rebellion of the first generation at Kadesh Barnea, which led to the divine sentence that they spend the rest of their lives in the wilderness.

The underlying theology is based on the notion that the land is the gift of Yahweh. How would it be possible for the Israelites to spurn his gift? Even though their ancestors had despised the gift, is it really possible that such an act of cowardice and ingratitude might be committed again? In asking these questions, Moses is developing the central message of this book. The new generation has a new opportunity to be different from their parents. They could be the people who will succeed. They do not have to repeat the failure of their parents.

But what if they are to fail? This possibility is the hidden horror in Numbers. What if the new generation is no better than their fathers and mothers? Will God then give a third generation an opportunity? Will God keep waiting until he finally has a people who will act on his word? Or is it possible that God could be spurned one time too many, and the Land of Promise will revert to its present, wicked inhabitants? These emotionally charged questions may be looming in the forefront of Moses' mind as he preaches this homily.

The sermon is more than homily. It is also litany. The words of vv.10–12 are a confession of sorts—not the confession of faith that begins with "I believe," but a litany of life beginning with, "This we have experienced." The book of Numbers not only describes worship; it *is* a book of worship. Remembering failure is also a part of worship. (See Ps 95:6–11 for a splendid example.) Worship is not just responding to grace; it is also remembering past disaster—and learning to avoid it in the present.

With the words of v.11 we are in the heart of covenant—a covenant that was promised but rebuffed. Yet the promise is still present. God's oath to the patriarchs—to Abraham, Isaac, and Jacob—is present in eternity. Jesus' words to the Sadducees recorded in Matthew 22 are to the point here: "But about the resurrection from the dead—have you not read what God said to you, 'I am the God of Abraham, the God of Isaac, and the God of Jacob'? He is not the God of the dead but of the living" (22:31–32). This is not just a past oath. Since he lives, so does the promise. The only question will be in the generation that stands before him now: Will they be the ones, or must he wait for others? These words are liturgical in form; they are meant to be recited and remembered. The reference to twenty years and older speaks of the generational change represented by these emissaries from Reuben and Gad.

The promise to Caleb and Joshua is also part of the litany (v.12). This section is like the preaching of the apostles in the early NT. There is a pattern, a *kerygma* of grace and wrath. The NT preaching of the evangelists begins in grace but moves to wrath. The OT preaching of the prophets often begins in wrath but moves to grace. In both approaches there is a pattern of historical citation and present adjuration. There is no truly biblical preaching that does not ultimately tie history to the current message; neither the evangelist nor the prophet would draw his message merely from his existential situation.

14–15 Moses' words in vv.14–15 are unusually harsh. In the phrase "brood of sinners" (v.14) he is prescient of the preaching of Jesus (e.g., Mt 12:34; cf. 3:7). There is moral culpability in the action of disunity that may bring divine ruination on the entire community. Moses' words are as expressive of his deep, personal feelings as are Paul's words in texts such as 2 Corinthians 1–3. This moment is intensely personal for the great prophet of God.

Rightly or wrongly, he has been provoked to give vent to his deepest feelings. But those feelings are based on his experience—and the deep feelings of God that he experienced as none other in his day.

NOTES

11 The LXX adds an explanatory phrase after the words "twenty years old or more" that serves to explain it more fully: "who know [the difference between] good and evil." This phrase suggests that the age of twenty was possibly regarded as an age of adult accountability (not unlike our consideration of twenty-one as the age of maturity).

13 וַיְנִעֵם (*wayᵉniʿēm*, "and he made them wander"; GK 5675) is an unusual use of the verb *nuaʿ*, a word meaning "to quiver, wave, tremble" (GK 5675; see 2Ki 19:21 = Isa 37:22; Pss 22:7 [8]; 109:25; Da 10:10). Here, in 2 Samuel 15:20, and in Psalm 59:11 the verb has the idea "to cause to wander." The connotation likely ties something of the latent meaning of this verb to this more unusual usage. The time in the wilderness was wandering, not as an aimless and pleasurable jaunt but as a journey that is like a quivering, trembling walk.

14 לִסְפּוֹת (*lispôt*, "to increase") is a Qal infinitive construct of the root *sāpâ* ("to snatch away"). But the intent seems related to the root *yāsap* ("to add to"); hence the verb should be read as לָסֶפֶת (*lāsepet*).

The prepositional phrase at the end of the verse, אֶל־יִשְׂרָאֵל (*ʾel-yiśrāʾēl*), is also unusual. This phrase would normally be translated "to Israel," but the expected meaning is "against" or "with Israel" (as though the preposition were misspelled for ʿal). However, the preposition ʾel may sometimes have the idea of "against."

iii. The assurances of Reuben and Gad (32:16–19)

¹⁶Then they came up to him and said, "We would like to build pens here for our livestock and cities for our women and children. ¹⁷But we are ready to arm ourselves and go ahead of the Israelites until we have brought them to their place. Meanwhile our women and children will live in fortified cities, for protection from the inhabitants of the land. ¹⁸We will not return to our homes until every Israelite has received his inheritance. ¹⁹We will not receive any inheritance with them on the other side of the Jordan, because our inheritance has come to us on the east side of the Jordan."

COMMENTARY

16–19 The response from the men addressed so angrily seems to be something like, "You have us all wrong. We are sincere in our desire to find the pleasure of the Lord. We will gladly go with the people into Canaan; only let us prepare temporary pens for our sheep and places to live for our children and our wives. Then we will come; and to them we will return." They say these and similar things (see Note on v.17) in an attempt to assure Moses that they do not wish to shirk their part in conquering the land. They will join their brothers in battle but wish to leave their families and livestock behind in the portion of their choosing. Their promises are sound; they have met the demands implicit within the charge of Moses.

Many commentators believe that the chiefs of Gad and Reuben were acting disingenuously here, that they were covering their original intention with hastily drawn plans to accede to Moses' desires. It appears to me, however, that it is possible the intentions of these men were honorable from the beginning. The reaction of Moses to them may have been based on *his own fears* of rebellion (and he had been given ample opportunity in the previous forty years to develop such a jaundiced view!) rather than a truly rebellious spirit in these men.

If this more positive view is correct, then both the implicit and explicit comparisons we might draw between this chapter and chs. 13–14 are invalid. In the former generation there was a rebellion that did spell ruin for the nation. But in this generation there is not rebellion, only petition; there is not a lack of faith, only an alternative plan. As long as both parties are clear as to the governing intention, then the story of the second generation will wind up differently from the account of the first. Nonetheless, the goal still needed to be upheld: God has time and the wilderness has sand!

NOTE

17 The term חֻשִׁים (*ḥušîm*, "ready") is problematic. It may be parsed as a Qal masculine plural passive participle from *ḥûš* ("to make haste, be ready"). There are numerous alternative words suggested for this difficult term. *BHS* suggests [*ḥᵉmiššîm*, "fifty,"] as in [Joshua 1:14; 4:12; Judges 7:11]. Some think this verb should be repointed as an active verb, *ḥušîm*, rather than the passive, for a more likely spelling. [Others emend to [*ḥᵃmušîm*] (as in Ex 13:18), a plural adjective meaning "in battle array" (see Jos 1:14; 4:12; Jdg 7:11).] I prefer this emendation to *ḥᵃmušîm*.

b. The Decision of Moses for Their Settlement (32:20–30)

²⁰Then Moses said to them, "If you will do this—if you will arm yourselves before the LORD for battle, ²¹and if all of you will go armed over the Jordan before the LORD until he has driven his enemies out before him—²²then when the land is subdued before the LORD, you may return and be free from your obligation to the LORD and to Israel. And this land will be your possession before the LORD.

²³"But if you fail to do this, you will be sinning against the LORD; and you may be sure that your sin will find you out. ²⁴Build cities for your women and children, and pens for your flocks, but do what you have promised."

²⁵The Gadites and Reubenites said to Moses, "We your servants will do as our lord commands. ²⁶Our children and wives, our flocks and herds will remain here in the cities of

Gilead. ²⁷But your servants, every man armed for battle, will cross over to fight before the LORD, just as our lord says."

²⁸Then Moses gave orders about them to Eleazar the priest and Joshua son of Nun and to the family heads of the Israelite tribes. ²⁹He said to them, "If the Gadites and Reubenites, every man armed for battle, cross over the Jordan with you before the LORD, then when the land is subdued before you, give them the land of Gilead as their possession. ³⁰But if they do not cross over with you armed, they must accept their possession with you in Canaan."

COMMENTARY

20–30 Moses was not easily calmed. He spoke to the people as, in a sense, a father to an errant but repentant child. He gave them words of comfort and also words of strong warning: "Your sin will find you out" (v.23). The language is striking: it is not just that their sin would be discovered but that their sin would be an active agent in discovering them. This is not unlike the picture of sin as lying at the door of Cain's life (Ge 4:7). Moses' words of v.20 are especially vivid: "If you are willing to do this thing, then prepare yourselves before Yahweh for war" (my translation).

Moses' adjuration also reminded the people of Gad and Reuben that it was not just their participation he desired but also their commitment to the affirmation of faith. They needed to prepare for battle, but they also needed to know that the Lord was going to be the one to win the battle (v.21). The actions were the Lord's; the people were partners with him in his holy war. Verse 22 also strongly emphasizes the role of Yahweh in the taking of the land. It will be subdued "before the LORD"; they

will be innocent from "obligation to the LORD and to Israel[!]"; and the land will be their possession "before the LORD."

The bargain was struck, but not without strong warnings of the seriousness of the matter if the people failed to live up to their word. In the permission Moses granted to them, we sense the negotiation that was possible in Israel, even from the hand of the Lord. The story of Abraham's and the Lord's bartering over the fate of Sodom (Ge 18:16–33) comes to mind as an example. In a sense the bargain with Moses was a bargain with God. Like the daughters of Zelophehad (ch. 27), these men had come to Moses in order to come to the Lord. When they agreed with Moses, they said, "Your servants will do just as my lord commands" (v.25). They were also saying that they would do as the Lord commanded. The specifying elements — children, wives, livestock, and cattle — were a part of the bargain. The language was like that of a contract; agreement was full and complete.

NOTE

24 The term צֹנֶה (ṣōneʾ) has an unusual spelling of the more common צֹאן (ṣōʾn); it is used only in Psalm 8:7 [8] and here—לְצֹנַאֲכֶם (leṣōnaʾakem, "your flocks").

c. The Public Declaration of the Agreement (32:31–32)

> ³¹The Gadites and Reubenites answered, "Your servants will do what the LORD has said. ³²We will cross over before the LORD into Canaan armed, but the property we inherit will be on this side of the Jordan."

COMMENTARY

31–32 These two verses serve as a public declaration of the decision to which the men of Gad and Reuben had come before the presence of Moses. Now it is made formal and binding before the congregation.

d. The Territories of Reuben and Gad (32:33–42)

OVERVIEW

It appears that after the principle of the settlement of Transjordan was established with the tribes of Reuben and Gad, a portion of the tribe of Manasseh joined with them in their agreement to settle east of the Jordan River and then to participate in the battle for Canaan. It is possible that the chapter has been compiled from two different records and that according to one of the traditions the men of Manasseh were present in the beginning of the bargaining. But since the text as we have it mentions Manasseh only at this late point in the negotiation, it may more likely be that the leaders of Manasseh were hesitant to approach Moses and that they only came forward with their own participation in the plan after the deal was made.

> ³³Then Moses gave to the Gadites, the Reubenites and the half-tribe of Manasseh son of Joseph the kingdom of Sihon king of the Amorites and the kingdom of Og king of Bashan — the whole land with its cities and the territory around them.
> ³⁴The Gadites built up Dibon, Ataroth, Aroer, ³⁵Atroth Shophan, Jazer, Jogbehah, ³⁶Beth Nimrah and Beth Haran as fortified cities, and built pens for their flocks. ³⁷And the Reubenites rebuilt Heshbon, Elealeh and Kiriathaim, ³⁸as well as Nebo and Baal Meon (these names were changed) and Sibmah. They gave names to the cities they rebuilt.
> ³⁹The descendants of Makir son of Manasseh went to Gilead, captured it and drove out the Amorites who were there. ⁴⁰So Moses gave Gilead to the Makirites, the descendants of Manasseh, and they settled there. ⁴¹Jair, a descendant of Manasseh, captured their settle-

ments and called them Havvoth Jair. ⁴²And Nobah captured Kenath and its surrounding settlements and called it Nobah after himself.

COMMENTARY

33 So the chapter that began with such hostility on the part of Moses ends with happy portents. The territory of Transjordan became part of the new homeland for some of the tribes of Israel. As the representative of God on earth, Moses bestowed the territory of Transjordan on Gad, Reuben, and some of the families of Manasseh.

34–38 Verses 34–38 are the happy record of the rebuilding and settling of the people of the Lord in that portion of the land he had given to them. The section includes as well notices about continuing conquests, which mark the Lord's continuing pleasure. The listing of towns and cities adds to this text a sense of verisimilitude and a note of celebration. The citation of these habitations by name (e.g., Dibon, Ataroth, Aroer, Atroth Shophan, Jazer, and the like) is important not just for cartography but also for theology. This land now really belonged to Israel. The cities that had been destroyed were now being rebuilt, and in some cases they were being renamed (v.38) to show new relationships and to evince the new reality. The old gods were no longer

in control; this was now the land of the people of Yahweh.

39–42 This pericope may well be a later addition to this chapter. It features the exploits of the family of Makir, of which the celebrated daughters of Zelophehad were a part (see chs. 27; 36), and their conquest of Gilead, along with the heroic exploits of Jair and Nobah. This is a further expansion of the people in Transjordan. Their territorial aggression was a part of the plan of God in further dispossessing the Amorites from the region. The taking of cities and renaming them after heroic persons is a part of the celebrative nature of the chapter, a projection of what lies ahead on the other side of the Jordan for the people of God.

The settlement of Transjordan was a considerably more complex issue than this chapter presents; this text relates only a few instances in the process. The point of the chapter is not to give a complete record or to present a full mapping of the territory; rather, the chapter speaks of territorial expansion and gifting by God.

B. A Review of the First Generation's Journey, and Words of Warning and Encouragement to the Second Generation (33:1–56)

OVERVIEW

Numbers 33 is a somewhat curious piece in the book. Principally, it is a list of places (an onomasticon), similar to how some chapters in this book have been lists of numbers and names. It is the one chapter in which we read that Moses was

commanded by the Lord to write an account of his experience in the wilderness (v.2)—a notice that certain critical scholars find to be the most potent argument *against* Moses' having written the book!

For example, Gray, xxix–xxx, writes, "In one passage only (33:2) does the book lay any claim to the authority of Moses for its statements; that passage is closely related to others (P) which are clearly of far later origin than the age of Moses, and consequently the Mosaic authorship even of this particular passage cannot be seriously considered." Noth, 243, says, "Yet the sentence contained in verse 2a, which follows awkwardly on verse 1, and has occasioned a brief summary of verse 1 in verse 2b, is certainly an addition to what is already a very late passage." (Further discussion on the subject of the Mosaic authorship of Numbers is found in the Introduction: Authorship and Date.)

Yet Gray, Noth, and others notwithstanding, Moses certainly wrote this travel itinerary; Scripture explicitly states so. Gray's rejection of the statement is based on an appeal to prior late-dating of the so-called Priestly document. His claim is simply nothing more than an example of special pleading. Gray argues that Moses cannot have been the author since the book does not assert his authorship; concerning the one verse of the book that does claim Mosaic authorship of a particular section, Gray dismisses its claim for other reasons. Using this approach, one can deny just about anything.

Greenstone, 337, tells a rabbinic story that points out a reason for the inclusion of this itinerary in the book of Numbers:

A king took his son who was ill to a distant place to be cured. On his return, with the son entirely cured, the king points out to him various places they had passed through and recalls certain occurrences that happened there. [In a similar manner this] list was written by Moses at the command of God as a record for future generations (Num. R. 23:3; Tan., Masseè 2).

Wenham (see pp. 216–30 for his extended discussion) has an elaborate schematization of the place names in six columns of seven entries each (by adding the beginning at Rameses and the ending on the plains of Moab to achieve a total of forty-two places). He finds some interesting correlations between several of these cycles, based in part on significant uses of certain numbers in the Bible (one, three, four, seven, and twelve).

R. Dennis Cole ("The Challenge of Faith's Final Step: Israel's Journey toward Victory in Numbers 33," in Howard and Grisanti, eds., *Giving the Sense*, 359) presents a strong case that this chapter should be considered as Israel's victory march:

Hence, the didactic intent of Numbers 33 is to challenge each generation of God's people toward living faithfully according to that which he has revealed in his Word. His abiding presence and power are available in fullness to those who accept the challenge with vision and hope.

This view fits nicely into our motif: "God has time, and the wilderness has sand" (see Introduction).

1. The Stages of the Journey in the Wilderness (33:1–49)

a. Introduction (33:1–2)

¹Here are the stages in the journey of the Israelites when they came out of Egypt by divisions under the leadership of Moses and Aaron. ²At the LORD's command Moses recorded the stages in their journey. This is their journey by stages:

COMMENTARY

1–2 The listing of the numerous "stages" (*maṣṣāʿîm*—significantly, forty in number between Rameses in Egypt and the plains of Moab) in Israel's wilderness experience appears at first to be a rather straightforward list that might easily be charted on a map. The chapter presents numerous difficulties, however, once one actually looks at the map. William G. Dever (*Who Were the Early Israelites?* 19) writes, "Dozens of sites are listed matter-of-factly here and there in the overall account, as though the reader of a later day knew of their existence. But the fact is that only a few sites in the entire biblical text have ever been persuasively identified." Most of the sites were wilderness encampments, not cities with lasting archaeological evidence.

Many of the place names in the list (e.g., most of the place names in vv.19–29) are not recorded elsewhere in Exodus and Numbers. Moreover, some of the places names mentioned elsewhere in Numbers are lacking here (e.g., Taberah [11:3; see also 21:19]). Some of the places names mentioned in this list are found in a recapitulation in Deuteronomy, though with slightly different spellings and in an irregular order (cf. vv.30–34 with Dt 10:6–7); but even these place names are otherwise unknown. Wenham, 220, is correct in describing these data as being among the most intractable that biblical scholars face.

We may observe the following factors:

1. The recording of the list was stated as having been done by the hand of Moses at the command of the Lord (v.2).
2. The listing thus should be taken seriously as an accurate reprise of the stages of the journey, despite our difficulty in locating many of the sites today.
3. The numerical factor of forty sites between Rameses and the plains of Moab suggests some stylizing of the list, which may help to account for the inclusion or exclusion of some sites.
4. As in the case of genealogies in the Torah, not all the factors of significance in antiquity may be apparent to the modern reader.
5. Ultimately, the record is a recital of faith in the Lord's blessing over his people for the extended period of their wilderness experience. Although certainly not without geographical importance, the list of the stages of Israel's experience in the wilderness is fundamentally a religious document, a spiritual geographical litany of the Lord's deliverance of his people. Harrison, 403–4, writes:

> The locations were thus not so much areas on a map as memorials to God's power and humanity's weakness, as stages on a journey through life that were as much spiritual as physical, and above all else as a constant reminder of the justice and mercy of the Lord of the covenant, who had bound a self-willed, nomadic people to Himself in His great love for them.

Despite the many places that are mentioned in these verses, they do not really record a travel story. One of the most durable literary formats is the travel narrative, found in both ancient and modern writings. An Egyptian example is called "The Journey of Wen-Amon to Phoenicia," a travel narrative from the Twenty-First Dynasty (eleventh century BC; see *ANET*, 25–29). In a travel narrative, the journey is the setting for the story, for character development, and for plot conflict and resolution. But Numbers 33 has none of these elements. It is merely an itinerary, the barest listing of place names. Even when great events are associated with places, they are only rarely noted in this chapter. The book of Numbers as a whole is a travel narrative; this chapter is simply a routing list (an onomasticon).

NOTE

2 The noun מַסַּע (*massaʿ*, "stage") is derived from the verb נָסַע (*nāsaʿ*, "to set out, journey"). It records the stopping places of the Hebrews in the wilderness, but it presents them not so much as their sites of dwelling (as though they were there to stay) as it does as staging points for the continuation of their journey. This word thrusts us forward in a recital of a journey that moves toward completion. Cole, 518, makes an interesting comparison between the onomasticon (list of names) in this chapter to those of the victorious campaigns of Egyptian monarchs, including Thutmose III, Seti I, Rameses II, and Shishak (Sheshonq); records are included in *ANET*, 234–58. On Shishak (Sheshonq), see Note at 21:1.

b. The Point of Departure (33:3–4)

³The Israelites set out from Rameses on the fifteenth day of the first month, the day after the Passover. They marched out boldly in full view of all the Egyptians, ⁴who were burying all their firstborn, whom the LORD had struck down among them; for the LORD had brought judgment on their gods.

COMMENTARY

3–4 Only at the beginning of the journey and at one point along the way (Mount Hor; vv.37–39) does the listing of places give way to narrative. These verses both note the specific time of the Israelites' departure from Egypt and describe its manner (see Ex 12:37). They left disdainfully (see Ps 114:1–2) without watching the burial details of the many grieving Egyptian families whose firstborn had been slain by the hand of the Lord; as they did so, they were relishing the victory that Yahweh had won over the gods of the land (v.4). This section is a triumphant taunt, though even the mention of the dead adds a gentle note of sadness.

The city of Rameses (v.3) has traditionally been identified with Tanis (San el-Hajar [San el-Hagar]; cf. Ge 47:11; Ex 1:11). However, evidence now points to a location near Qantir-Khataana–Tell Daba as the correct site (see *The New International*

Dictionary of Biblical Archaeology [ed. E. M. Blaiklock and R. K. Harrison; Grand Rapids: Zondervan, 1983], 384, 435). Tell Daba (also spelled Tell el-Dabʾa) is a bit more than twelve miles south of Tanis. The area of the ancient city is truly immense — six miles long and two miles wide (see the description by Kitchen, *Reliability*, 255).

The name "Rameses" is derived most likely from the great Pharaoh Rameses II, who is dated centuries later than the story of Joseph (Ge 47:11) and, many believe, later than the Hebrews' time in Egypt (Ex 1:11). This chronology means that we have an example here of a historical updating of an ancient place name to a more current, recognizable name for later generations (see Notes; see also the use of "Hormah" and comments at Nu 21:3).

The stages of the journey of Israel may be viewed in a variety of ways. The simplest way is to see the stages as grouped in two sections, with an emphasis on the stop at Mount Hor, where Aaron the priest died; only at this point does the onomasticon breaks into narrative (vv.37–39).

NOTES

3 Many scholars have used the mention of רַעְמְסֵס (*raʿmᵉsēs*, "Rameses") to argue that since this city was named for Pharaoh Rameses II (ca. 1290–1213 BC), he must have been the pharaoh of the exodus, and the exodus was therefore in the thirteenth century BC (see, e.g., *OTS*–1996, 59–60). William H. Shea ("The Date of the Exodus," in Howard and Grisanti, eds., *Giving the Sense*, 248) observes that Joseph reports that when the family of Jacob came into Egypt, they settled in "the district of Rameses" (Ge 47:11). But no chronology would place the *entrance* of the Hebrew family into Egypt during the reign of this pharaoh.

In other words, in Genesis 47:11 we have a certain updating of a place name to help the readers understand. The same phenomenon may also be the case in Numbers 33:3—a later updating of a place name for a new generation of readers. That is, Pharaoh Rameses II may have lived considerably later than both Israel's entrance into and leaving of Egypt, despite the mention of a place name likely tied to his fame and reign. A most passionate argument for the thirteenth-century dating of the exodus is given by Kitchen, *Reliability*, especially 307–10.

In contrast to its negative use in 15:30, the expression בְּיָד רָמָה (*bᵉyād rāmâ*, "with a high hand") is used here in a positive sense as a figure of triumph (note the NIV's "boldly"). With hands held high, the Israelites left on their journey in a deliberate and conscious sense of the presence of the grander, higher hand of Yahweh held over them in blessing.

3–4 Cole, 520–27, following a suggestion of Wenham, 217–19, observes that the departure and encampment sites may have been organized into six groups, or stages, of seven sites; the seventh stage is then implied in the concluding paragraph (33:50–56)—the last stage will be the conquest of Canaan. Cole gives extensive charts to display this pattern. Timothy R. Ashley (*The Book of Numbers* [NICOT; Grand Rapids: Eerdmans, 1990], 623–24) is more skeptical of Wenham's approach and calls it too speculative.

c. The Stages of the Journey from Rameses to Mount Hor (33:5–37)

⁵The Israelites left Rameses and camped at Succoth.

⁶They left Succoth and camped at Etham, on the edge of the desert.

⁷They left Etham, turned back to Pi Hahiroth, to the east of Baal Zephon, and camped near Migdol.

⁸They left Pi Hahiroth and passed through the sea into the desert, and when they had traveled for three days in the Desert of Etham, they camped at Marah.

⁹They left Marah and went to Elim, where there were twelve springs and seventy palm trees, and they camped there.

¹⁰They left Elim and camped by the Red Sea.

¹¹They left the Red Sea and camped in the Desert of Sin.

¹²They left the Desert of Sin and camped at Dophkah.

¹³They left Dophkah and camped at Alush.

¹⁴They left Alush and camped at Rephidim, where there was no water for the people to drink.

¹⁵They left Rephidim and camped in the Desert of Sinai.

¹⁶They left the Desert of Sinai and camped at Kibroth Hattaavah.

¹⁷They left Kibroth Hattaavah and camped at Hazeroth.

¹⁸They left Hazeroth and camped at Rithmah.

¹⁹They left Rithmah and camped at Rimmon Perez.

²⁰They left Rimmon Perez and camped at Libnah.

²¹They left Libnah and camped at Rissah.

²²They left Rissah and camped at Kehelathah.

²³They left Kehelathah and camped at Mount Shepher.

²⁴They left Mount Shepher and camped at Haradah.

²⁵They left Haradah and camped at Makheloth.

²⁶They left Makheloth and camped at Tahath.

²⁷They left Tahath and camped at Terah.

²⁸They left Terah and camped at Mithcah.

²⁹They left Mithcah and camped at Hashmonah.

³⁰They left Hashmonah and camped at Moseroth.

³¹They left Moseroth and camped at Bene Jaakan.

³²They left Bene Jaakan and camped at Hor Haggidgad.

³³They left Hor Haggidgad and camped at Jotbathah.

³⁴They left Jotbathah and camped at Abronah.

³⁵They left Abronah and camped at Ezion Geber.

³⁶They left Ezion Geber and camped at Kadesh, in the Desert of Zin.

³⁷They left Kadesh and camped at Mount Hor, on the border of Edom.

COMMENTARY

5–37 Succoth, Etham, and Pi Hahiroth (vv.5–7) were in Egypt. On traditional maps, the other sites are all located in the Sinai Peninsula. Below is a list of their staging areas in the order they are given; their English names; their verse numbers; a transcription of their Hebrew names (helpful in precision of names); their suggested English meanings (many of which are provisional in nature); and further comments about identification, significance, or parallel Scriptures. (Additionally, there exists the possibility —so far unverified by scientific research—that sites 4–40 are not in the Sinai Peninsula at all, but instead in Saudi Arabia! See further on this speculation in the Note on 33:8, 10.) The following identifications are given with the assumption of the traditional route of the journey that followed first the west side of the peninsula in a southerly direction, then arrived at the traditional site of Mount Sinai, and then moved northerly along the eastern side of the peninsula.

(1) Succoth (*sukkōt*, "Booths"; v.5)—see Exodus 13:20; Succoth is likely identified with modern Tell el-Maskhutah in the Wadi Tumeilat, about forty miles southeast of Tanis/Rameses.

(2) Wilderness of Etham (*ʾetām*, meaning unknown; v.6)—see Exodus 13:20; site of the first mention of the pillar of cloud and pillar of fire.

(3) Pi Hahiroth (*pî haḥîrōt*, "Mouth of Burning"; v.7)—see Exodus 14:2, 9; the Hebrews' encampment was near Pi Hahiroth, between Migdol (*migdōl*, "Tower") and the sea, to the east of Baal Zephon (*baʿal ṣᵉpôn*, "Baʿal of the North"). It was from this encampment that they made their miraculous escape across the divinely dried seabed of the Red Sea (or Sea of Reeds; see Notes; Ex 14:2) in the great exodus (v.8). Alternatively (see Note on 33:8, 10), it is possible that the crossing of the Red Sea was near the lower eastern tip of the peninsula and that it proceeded to what is now Saudi Arabia, and then the march continued to Jebel al-Lawz, an alternative site for Mount Sinai.

(4) Marah (*mārâ*, "Bitter Spring"; v.8)—see Exodus 15:23; site of the bitter waters cleansed by the Lord through his servant Moses.

(5) Elim (*ʾêlim*, "Place of Trees," "Terebinths"; v.9)—see Exodus 15:27; curiously, this site is the only place that is described in this list.

(6) Red Sea (*yam-sûp*, perhaps "Sea of Reeds"; v.10)—not mentioned in Exodus as a place of encampment, but mentioned in reference to a southwestwardly move before turning eastward to the south-central Sinai. See the Note on 33:8, 10.

(7) Desert of Sin (*midbar-sîn*, meaning for *sîn* unknown; v.11)—see Exodus 16:1; the arrival of the people of Israel here was on the fifteenth day of the second month; the location seems to be in the south-central Sinai Peninsula.

(8) Dophkah (*dopqâ*, "Beaten"; v.12)—not mentioned in Exodus; location unknown.

(9) Alush (*ʾalûš*, meaning unknown; v.13)—not mentioned in Exodus; location unknown.

(10) Rephidim (*rᵉpîdim*, "Spreading"; v.14)—see Exodus 17:1; curiously there is a note on the significance of this site ("no water") when other sites are mentioned without any notice.

(11) Desert of Sinai (*midbar sînay*, the meaning of *sînay* unknown; v.15)—see Exodus 19:2; traditionally believed to be the central, southern section of the Sinai Peninsula. (This well-known peninsula is given its name precisely because of the traditional location of Mount Sinai here; see Notes.) Here Israel lingered for about eleven months. That the giving of the Torah is not mentioned in this passage is especially surprising. The departure from Sinai is recorded in Numbers 10:11-36.

(12) Kibroth Hattaavah (*qibrōt hattaʾᵃwâ*, "Graves of Desire"; v.16)—see Numbers 11:34; all that is known about the site is that it lay a three-day journey's distance from Sinai.

(13) Hazeroth (*hᵃṣērōt*, "Settlements"; v.17)—see Numbers 11:35; 12:16; Deuteronomy 1:1; location unknown.

(14) Rithmah (*ritmâ*, "Binding"; v.18)—not mentioned elsewhere (as with each of the next eleven sites).

(15) Rimmon Perez (*rimmōn pāreṣ*, "Pomegranate Breach"; v.19)—not mentioned elsewhere.

(16) Libnah (*libnâ*, "White"; v.20)—not to be confused with the Libnah of Joshua 10:29; the Libnah in Numbers is not mentioned elsewhere.

(17) Rissah (*rissâ*, meaning unknown; v.21)—not mentioned elsewhere.

(18) Kehelathah (q^ehēlātâ, "Assembly"; v.22) — not mentioned elsewhere.

(19) Mount Shepher (har-šāper, "Mount of Beauty"; v.23) — not mentioned elsewhere.

(20) Haradah (h^arādâ, "Frightening"; v.24) — not mentioned elsewhere.

(21) Makheloth (maqhēlōt, "Place of Assembly"; v.25) — not mentioned elsewhere.

(22) Tahath (tāḥat, "Lower"; v.26) — not mentioned elsewhere.

(23) Terah (tāraḥ, meaning unknown; v.27) — not mentioned elsewhere.

(24) Mithcah (mitqâ, "Sweetness"[?]; v.28) — not mentioned elsewhere.

(25) Hashmonah (ḥašmōnâ, meaning unknown; v.29) — not mentioned elsewhere. The non-mention elsewhere of twelve staging places in a row (nos. 14 to 25) means that these sites are otherwise completely unknown to us. Given this fact, little ground is lost (pun intended) by giving attention to the alternative view respecting the crossing of the Red Sea and the alternative location for Mount Sinai (see Note on 33:8, 10).

(26) Moseroth (mōserôt, "Bands"; v.30) — another form of "Moserah" (môserâ), mentioned in Deuteronomy 10:6 as the place where Aaron died; but see on v.37.

(27) Bene Jaakan (b^enê-ya^c aqan, "Sons of Ya'aqan"; v.31) — a place in Edom mentioned in Genesis 36:27 and 1 Chronicles 1:42 as "Akan" (^c aqan). In Deuteronomy 10:6 this site is called b^e'ērōt b^enê-ya^c aqan ("The Wells of the Sons of Ya'aqan"; "the wells of the Jaakanites," NIV), but the order of the sites in Deuteronomy 10:6 is the reverse of that in Numbers 33:30–31. The somewhat extemporaneous nature of Deuteronomy sometimes has events in a less regular order than in the (presumably) more orderly patterns of Numbers.

(28) Hor Haggidgad (ḥōr haggidgad, "The Hollow of Gidgad"; v.32) — called Gudgodah (gudgōdâ) in Deuteronomy 10:7.

(29) Jotbathah (yoṭbātâ, "Pleasantness"; v.33) — mentioned in Deuteronomy 10:7 as a land with streams of water. So we have four otherwise unknown places (staging areas 26–29) that are mentioned in Deuteronomy 10:6–7 with slightly different spellings and some irregularity in order. Again, there is little to be lost in considering the alternatives for the location of the crossing of the Red Sea and the new idea for the location of Mount Sinai, mentioned in the Note on 33:8, 10.

(30) Abronah (^c abrōnâ, "Regions Beyond"; v.34) — not mentioned elsewhere.

(31) Ezion Geber (^c esyôn gāber, "Mighty Trees"[?]; v.35) — see Deuteronomy 2:8; 1 Kings 9:26; the well-known oasis near Elath on the Gulf of Aqaba. If the alternative view is considered (see Note at 33:8, 10), then this stage would be a movement north along the *eastern* side of the Red Sea (the region of Midian), rather than a movement north along its *western* side (the Sinai Peninsula).

(32) Kadesh (qādēš, "Sanctuary"; v.36) — see Numbers 13:21; 20:1; 27:14; 34:3; Deuteronomy 32:51; Joshua 15:1 (see also Dt 1:46; Nu 27:14); the well-known 'Ain Qedeis oasis, also known as Kadesh Barnea, in the Desert of Zin. At this point the alternative route (see Note at 33:8, 10) and that of the traditional view now come together. It is over seventy miles from Ezion Geber to Kadesh; numerous intermediate stops would be indicated. It was here that the revolt against Yahweh took place as the people listened to the evil majority report of the spies (Nu 13–14). God's judgment of a forty-year period of wilderness waiting was given at Kadesh. It is possible that much of the thirty-eight years of Israel's experience in the wilderness was

spent with Kadesh as the central location. But if the alternative view is considered (see again the Note at 33:8, 10), it would also be possible that Moses led the people back to the region of Midian, where he was so familiar with the territory from *his* forty-year sojourn among the family group of Jethro. But

at some point they would have returned to Kadesh; here also Miriam died (see 20:1).

(33) Mount Hor (*hōr hāhār,* "Hor the mountain"; v.37) — perhaps identified with Jebel Nebi Harum, about fifty miles south of the Dead Sea, southwest of Petra.

NOTES

8, 10 The full designation for םַיַּה (*hayyām,* "the sea") is ףוּס־םַי (*yam-sûp*), traditionally translated "the Red Sea" (Vul. following LXX) but in recent decades, as in the NIV's margin, "the Sea of Reeds" (ףוּס [*sûp*] meaning "reeds") — a translation already suggested in BDB, 693a [1909]); see the recent discussion by Kitchen, *Reliability,* 261–63. The term "the Red Sea" as the location of Yahweh's victory over the armies of Pharaoh (Ex 14–15) has been commonly understood to refer to a site on the northwestern branch of the Red Sea, the area of the Gulf of Suez today. The more recent translation, "the Sea of Reeds," has been thought by many to speak of an inland lake area (perhaps near, or including, "the Bitter Lakes" region). A suggestion is that in antiquity this area may have been marked by many reeds (see BDB, 693b). But in its uses in the book of Numbers (14:25; 21:4; 33:10, 11; also in Ex 23:31; Dt 1:40), ףוּס־םַי (*yam-sûp*) speaks of the Gulf of Aqaba (the northeastern branch of the Red Sea), not the western branch (the Gulf of Suez) at all. The phrase is not unambiguous.

A more recent, speculative proposal for the location of the miraculous crossing of the Red Sea suggests the southern end of the Sinai Peninsula, across the Gulf of Aqaba, to modern Saudi Arabia (ancient Midian, as virtually all Bible maps show). The proposal includes evidence of a partly submerged "land bridge" that nearly traverses the distance across the gulf from the Sinai Peninsula to the land of Midian (modern Arabia). Passageway for modern ships has to be dredged, as the wind-borne wilderness sands, pushed by currents and tides, keep this "land bridge" largely in place. This idea is also linked to a proposal for an alternative site of Mount Sinai in Arabia (see Gal 4:25), at Jebel al-Lawz. At present, the speculation remains fascinating, but it cannot be validated one way or the other; the political situation in the Middle East precludes a scientific inquiry in Saudi Arabia to identify the location of the place so closely associated with the Hebrew Moses!

Here is one more element in the idea: If this new proposal gains more currency, it is possible that the phrase ףוּס־םַי (*yam-sûp,* "Sea of Reeds") may be emended to ףוֹס־םַי (*yam-sôp,* "sea's end"; see Note at 11:25). That is, we may describe the tip of a peninsula as "land's end." Was it possible that *yam-sôp* ("sea's end") was another way of saying the same thing? If so, the issue of "reeds" becomes moot. Is it possible that later in Hebrew history, when the people were so far removed from these places, the pronunciation shifted slightly — a shift that has caused such confusion in our own day? Award-winning author Howard Blum has written a best-selling narrative that describes the story of two adventurers (Bob Cornuke and Larry Williams) who have been central to this story. Blum's book is titled, *The Gold of Exodus: The Discovery of the True Mount Sinai* (New York: Pocket, 1999). Cornuke has written his story with a similar title: *In Search of the Mountain of God: The Discovery of the Real Mt. Sinai* (Nashville: Broadman & Holman, 2000).

R. Dennis Cole, in his essay "The Challenge of Faith's Final Step" (in Howard and Grisanti, eds., *Giving the Sense*, 352, n. 17) demurs rather strongly from this idea. He notes that the area of Midian is not so fixed on the eastern shore of the Gulf of Aqaba as this view maintains, and that Paul's reference to Arabia in Galatians 1:17 is not a precise geographical term. Kitchen (*Reliability*, 274) is also strongly critical of shifting the location of either the crossing of the Sea of Reeds or the site of Mount Sinai: "As the Midianites could readily penetrate the Sinai Peninsula ... there are no compelling grounds to move 'Mount Sinai' into Midian proper or anywhere else in northwest Arabia either." Beitzel is likewise critical of this point of view. He believes that each of the arguments for the Saudi Arabia location for Mount Sinai may be answered and that none is decisive for rejecting the traditional viewpoint (see Barry J. Beitzel, ed., *The Moody Atlas of the Bible* [rev. ed.; Chicago: Moody Press, 2009], 109–10). See also Hoffmeier, *Ancient Israel in Sinai*, for a strong dissent of the new proposal.

15 סִינַי (*sînay*, "Sinai"), the mountain of God (also known as הַר חֹרֵב (*har ḥōrēb*, Mount Horeb; see 1Ki 19:8), is the most significant mountain locale in the Bible aside from Mount Zion and Jerusalem. However, the location of the mountain is as "iffy" as its pronunciation! Many people pronounce the word with three syllables rather than two. The letters "ai" (Heb. *ay*) form a diphthong in Hebrew. As with the name of the prophet Haggai, the word "Sinai" has two syllables. Sinai is the most elusive mountain in biblical geography to identify with precision. Not only is the site of the revelation of the Lord to Moses of importance on its own merits; but also, most of the other sites of the wilderness wanderings and the route that connects them are dependent on where one identifies Sinai. And, as LaSor, Hubbard, and Bush observe, "Direct evidence for the location of Sinai and the Israelite presence there may never be forthcoming. That presence was, historically speaking, ephemeral" (*OTS*–1996, 61).

The oldest tradition centers on Jebel Musa ("the Mountain of Moses"), a mountain of about 8,500 feet in the central-southern Sinai Peninsula (and it is that identification, of course, that has given the peninsula its name). But this tradition goes back only to the fourth century of our era. The broad plain at the base of Jebel Musa seems to serve as an admirable site for the encampment of the thousands of Israel. H. G. Andersen ("Mount Sinai," *ZPEB*, 5:447–50) presents a defense of this traditional site. Another suggestion, particularly of some nineteenth-century writers, is Jebel Serbal, a mountain of about 6,700 feet in the central Sinai Peninsula. Yet another is Jebel Sin Bisher, a mountain of about 1,900 feet located about thirty miles southeast of Suez. This last suggestion, enthusiastically endorsed by Cole ("The Challenge of Israel's Faith," in Howard and Grisanti, eds., *Giving the Sense*, 352), is that of M. Harel (*Masei Sinai* [Tel Aviv: Am Oved, 1968]; "The Route of the Exodus of the Israelites from Egypt" [Ph.D. diss., New York University, 1964]) and is cautiously accepted by Wenham, 220–27, his discussion being a fine summary of the difficulties one faces concerning this issue. See also the discussion by W. C. Kaiser Jr., *A History of Israel: From the Bronze Age through the Jewish Wars* (Nashville: Broadman & Holman, 1998), 113–14.

d. The Events at Mount Hor (33:38–40)

38At the Lord's command Aaron the priest went up Mount Hor, where he died on the first day of the fifth month of the fortieth year after the Israelites came out of Egypt. **39**Aaron was a hundred and twenty-three years old when he died on Mount Hor.

⁴⁰The Canaanite king of Arad, who lived in the Negev of Canaan, heard that the Israelites were coming.

COMMENTARY

38–40 Unexpectedly, it is the staging area of Mount Hor that is singled out for special mention in this chapter. The area became the setting for a memorial notice to Aaron, the high priest and the brother of Moses and Miriam, who died here at the hoary age of 123. Not only is his age given, but so also is the date: the first day of the fifth month of the fortieth year. This date is the second one in the list; the first date was that of their leaving Rameses on the fifteenth day of the first month of the first year (v.3). This information reveals that the journeying from Tanis/Rameses to Mount Hor completed the forty years of wilderness wanderings.

The death of Aaron marked a pivotal date in the history of Israel. The death of the high priest was regarded as having an atoning effect (see ch. 35).

Aaron was three years older than Moses (see Ex 7:7; cf. Dt 1:3; 34:5–7). His death came at a great age—a mark of Yahweh's blessing on his life. By the mercy of the Lord, his time was extended to the very last year of Israel's wilderness experience; his own sin (Nu 20) kept him from living into the time of—and participating in—the conquest of the land.

The second notice given with respect to Israel's time at the staging area of Mount Hor is a word concerning the king of Arad (v.40). Even the king who dwelled in the Negev of the land of Canaan knew of the coming of the people of Israel; the reference is to the story of 21:1–3, the first of Israel's victories on the military field—promise for a new generation's being different from their ancestors.

e. The Stages of the Journey from Mount Hor to the Mountains of Abarim (33:41–47)

⁴¹They left Mount Hor and camped at Zalmonah.

⁴²They left Zalmonah and camped at Punon.

⁴³They left Punon and camped at Oboth.

⁴⁴They left Oboth and camped at Iye Abarim, on the border of Moab.

⁴⁵They left Iyim and camped at Dibon Gad.

⁴⁶They left Dibon Gad and camped at Almon Diblathaim.

⁴⁷They left Almon Diblathaim and camped in the mountains of Abarim, near Nebo.

COMMENTARY

41–47 The listing of place names continues:

(34) Zalmonah (ṣalmōnâ, "Resemblance"; v.41) — not mentioned elsewhere; there is an es-Salmaneh about twenty-five miles south of the Dead Sea.

(35) Punon (pûnōn, meaning unknown; v.42) — perhaps the same as the Edomite site pînōn in Genesis 36:41; 1 Chronicles 1:52; located between Petra and Zoar, famous for its mines.

(36) Oboth (ʾōbōt, "Water Skins"; v.43) — see Numbers 21:10–11 for the story of the stay at Oboth; probably the eastern outskirts of Idumea, not far from Moab. The route from Punon to Oboth is not as simple as this list might indicate. Eugene H. Merrill, 254, suggests that the people probably went southward from Punon to Ezion Geber, then eastward and northward around Edom along the wilderness road of Moab (cf. 21:4; Dt 2:8).

(37) Iye Abarim (ʿîyê hāʿăbārîm [v.44]; short form ʿîyîm [v.45], meaning unknown; hāʿăbārîm means

"Beyond" [for location, see number 40 below]; v.47) — see Numbers 21:11; a location on the border of Moab.

(38) Dibon Gad (dîbōn gād, "Built Up by Gad"; v.45) — see Numbers 21:30; 32:3a; city in Moab north of the Arnon (Dhiban); also mentioned in the Mesha Inscription.

(39) Almon Diblathaim (ʿalmōn diblātāyim, meaning unknown, but perhaps "Hidden Figs" [dᵉbēlâ means "a lump of figs"]; v.46) — mentioned in Jeremiah 48:22; a site north of Dibon Gad but of unknown location.

(40) The mountains of Abarim (hārê hāʿăbārîm, "The Mountains Beyond"; v.47) — see Numbers 27:12; the fortieth station, a mountainous region of northwestern Moab just northeast of the Dead Sea. Pisgah and Nebo are two ridges in this mountainous region.

f. The Encampment in Moab as the Staging Area for the Assault on the Land of Canaan (33:48–49)

48They left the mountains of Abarim and camped on the plains of Moab by the Jordan across from Jericho. **49**There on the plains of Moab they camped along the Jordan from Beth Jeshimoth to Abel Shittim.

COMMENTARY

48–49 At last, after a period of forty years, the people are situated on the plains of Moab across from the city of Jericho — the firstfruits of the land. Now only the Jordan River separates them from their goal, the Promised Land. The encampments of the thousands of Israel stretched from Beth Jeshimoth (bêt hayšimōt, "Place of Desolation"; see Jos 12:3; 13:20) to Abel Shittim (ʾābēl haššiṭṭîm, "Field/

Brook of Acacias"; see Nu 25:1, where it is called Shittim; cf. Mic 6:5), in the lowlands of Moab. The distance from these two sites, north to south, was over five miles — a suitable spread for the thousands of the tribes of Israel.

Now we may make some concluding observations about this listing of the massāʿîm ("staging areas"; see 33:1) of Israel in the wilderness.

1. That there are forty places may be signifi-cant as a mnemonic device: as the people dwelled in the wilderness for forty years, so there are forty sites of their journeys.

2. Most of the "places" were temporary abodes; we should not be surprised that they are not easily located on modern maps. They are not made-up places, just encampments in the wilderness.

3. The principal story line was omitted from this listing; here only the names of the places are important. There is an assumption that the reader would know the basic associations as the places were listed.

4. The intrusion made by the account of the death of Aaron (vv. 38–40) is remarkable. This travel account is something of an obitu-ary for Moses, as he was about to die. But in the midst of it he memorializes his brother.

5. The fact that many of the names are not sites that can be located or that are found in other passages is an indication that this is an ancient text. The notice that the Lord commanded Moses to write it (v. 2) is more credible because of our uncertainty over locations.

6. Most significantly, the document speaks not of rebellion but only of continuity. Were one only to read this list of staging places, the reader would likely conclude that Israel marched faithfully from one place to another in an orderly progression from Egypt to Moab. This point is that the new generation has become the replacement for the old. *It is as though there had never been a first generation.* The people who arrive at Moab are regarded as the people who left Egypt. The plan and purpose of God will be realized, despite the loss (and disappearance!) of an entire generation. But the new genera-tion should still take into account the facts that God has time and the wilderness has sand!

2. Words of Warning and Encouragement to the Second Generation (33:50–56)

⁵⁰On the plains of Moab by the Jordan across from Jericho the LORD said to Moses, ⁵¹"Speak to the Israelites and say to them:'When you cross the Jordan into Canaan, ⁵²drive out all the inhabitants of the land before you. Destroy all their carved images and their cast idols, and demolish all their high places. ⁵³Take possession of the land and settle in it, for I have given you the land to possess. ⁵⁴Distribute the land by lot, according to your clans. To a larger group give a larger inheritance, and to a smaller group a smaller one. Whatever falls to them by lot will be theirs. Distribute it according to your ancestral tribes.

⁵⁵"But if you do not drive out the inhabitants of the land, those you allow to remain will become barbs in your eyes and thorns in your sides. They will give you trouble in the land where you will live. ⁵⁶And then I will do to you what I plan to do to them.'"

COMMENTARY

50–54 It is on the basis of triumphalism that the final pericope of this chapter has its meaning. The instructions of the Lord to the new generation come at the climax of the record of their triumphal march. They were now at their last *massaʿ*, their last staging area. Before them lies the land, behind them an exceedingly long and tortuous journey. Now is the time for their obedience so that their salvation will be made sure in the new land.

The commands of the Lord to the people are expressed in several significant verbs in v.52: (1) they are to "dispossess" (Hiphil of *yāraš*) the present inhabitants, (2) "destroy" (Piel of *ʾābad*) their idolatrous symbols, (3) "destroy" (Piel of *ʾābad*) all of their molten images, and (4) "shatter" (Hiphil of *šāmad*) their high places. Verse 53 repeats the verb "to dispossess" and then speaks of living in the land as God's divine grant to the people. The land is his to give; he chooses to give the gift to his people.

The manner of the distribution of the land will be by lot, with the assurance that the lot will not be by chance but by the disposition of the Lord. In this way the people will be able to "take possession" (Hithpael of *nāḥal*, "to possess oneself of something") of the land as a lasting inheritance. As in 35:8, consideration will be given for the size of the clans of Israel (v.54); there will be no claim of inequity or "influence-peddling," to use a modern term. Possession will come by God's will expressed through the fairness of divine lots.

55–56 The positive admonitions of vv.50–54 are followed by a strong warning. If the people do not succeed in their divine commission to dispossess the pagan inhabitants, they will experience two consequences: (1) the native peoples who remain will be perpetual trouble to the Israelites' enjoyment of the land, and (2) the Lord will bring on Israel the dispossession he demanded that they themselves accomplish.

The description of trouble is, of course, sadly prophetic. The remaining Canaanites were to be barbs in the eye and pricks in the side (images Joshua uses in his farewell address; see Jos 23:13). These expressions describe constant annoyance (at the least) to terrible pain (at the most)—constant harassment. The most chilling words, however, are not the troubles that might come from peoples but that which may come from the Lord (v.56):

> And it will happen,
> > just as I intend to do to them,
> > > I will do to you.

This verse encapsulates the theology of the land *in nuce*. It is God's land. He will give and will take it back as he wills.

These words, coming at the end of the travel itinerary, are most threatening indeed. For the present—that is, the time of the writing of Numbers—the outcome is uncertain. But the prospects are good. The second generation has fully replaced their erring fathers and mothers. The land lies before them as they wait in the final staging area. There is the Jordan. Over yonder is Jericho, the firstfruits of the land. And with them is the eternal Yahweh!

NOTE

52 מַשְׂכִּיֹתָם (*maśkiyōtām*, "their carved images") is from the word מַשְׂכִּית (*māśkît*), which means "showpiece, something to be displayed." Here it is used of carved figures, idolatrous symbols of the pagan religious practices of the Canaanite peoples. These images include sexual symbols of the fertility deities that were so pervasive in that region (see Lev 26:1; Eze 8:12).

The second term, מַסֵּכֹתָם (*massēkōtām*, "their cast idols"), is also found in Exodus 32:4, 8; 34:17; Leviticus 19:4; Deuteronomy 9:16.

The third term, בָּמֹתָם (*bāmōtām*, "their high places"), refers to hilltops (or artificial mounds) that were used in worshiping the nature gods of the ancient Near East. The licentious system of sexually centered worship was particularly exhibitionist in nature. Baal and Asherah were regarded as voyeuristic deities whose own libidos would be raised by viewing orgiastic rites or sacrificial acts. The raised platform was an enhancement "to let the gods" see more clearly. As is well known from the reading of the historical books, Israel adapted the use of בָּמוֹת (*bāmôt*, "high places") for their own local patterns of the worship of Yahweh (or for syncretistic systems of worship of Yahweh and Baal). As the most enduring of paganisms even into Israel's later history, the *bāmôt* were the banes of godly kings who fought desperately to destroy these "high places." On the warfare of the righteous against the cult of Baal in ancient Israel, see Leah Bronner, *The Stories of Elijah and Elisha as Polemics against Baal Worship* (Leiden: Brill, 1968).

C. An Anticipation of the Promised Land (34:1–36:13)

OVERVIEW

These last three chapters of Numbers round out the book. They have about them the sense of appendages. Chapter 33, with its itinerary, final blessing, and warning (vv.50–56), admirably serves as the climax of the book. The prospects for conquest and the warning of failure are just what the new generation needs to be the people God wants them to be.

Although these last three chapters are somewhat anticlimactic, they also play a role in furthering the general driving force presented to the new generation. This message is: The land is before you for

your habitation; do not behave as your fathers and mothers did, but instead move on in faith to take the land he offers. You are responsible for the decisions you are about to make. And recall that God has time and the wilderness has sand. If you behave as your parents did, God has time to wait for your children or your children's children to behave courageously and to respond in faithful action; and the wilderness has no shortage of sand to accommodate your remains. (On this summary theme of Numbers, see the Introduction.)

1. A Preview of the Land (34:1–26)

a. The Boundaries (34:1–12)

i. Introduction (34:1–2)

¹The LORD said to Moses, ²"Command the Israelites and say to them: 'When you enter Canaan, the land that will be allotted to you as an inheritance will have these boundaries:

COMMENTARY

1–2 The listing of the four boundaries in this section of Numbers is given not only for informational purposes but also to display again the dimensions of God's great gift to his people in the Land of Promise. The initial covenant specified the land in terms of the peoples who lived there (see Ge 15:18–21). This chapter presents the land in terms of an outline of its borders. The language is covenantal in nature; the description is that of a contract. Those who were in the final staging area in the plains of Moab would have their sensibilities greatly encouraged by the dimensions and directions of the land so described.

Some critical scholars tend to dismiss this chapter as an unauthentic piece from the vantage of anticipating the land; rather, they suggest this section is a later, backward projection based on some experience in the land itself. Noth, 248, for example, judges the situation this way: "In short, this whole section presupposes, on the one hand, the Pentateuchal narrative at an already late stage, and on the other, the deuteronomistic historical work, and is, therefore, part of the editorial unification of these two literary complexes."

Yet it is possible to argue that the spies who scouted out the land in chs. 13–14 brought with them sufficient information for Moses to be able to construct this general outline of the land. The manner of the description of the borders certainly accords with what we know of Egyptian concepts of Canaan in the period of the exodus. Presumably, Moses would have kept the records of the spies. Further, both Caleb and Joshua may have assisted Moses in the construction of this outline of the land. We may further presume that had things gone differently in the events described in chs. 13–14 and had the majority report been one of confident expectation and courage, just such a report as this chapter presents may have been given thirty-eight years earlier. But at last, for the new generation, the report is given—as God's promise.

Moreover, the text itself presents the outlines to have come directly from the Lord to Moses (vv.1–2). Based on the information Moses had before him from the report of the spies and with the assistance of Caleb and Joshua at hand, the direction of the words of the Lord to Moses would have been understandable and clear.

The presentation of the boundaries follows an orderly format. This is the way of the book of Numbers. Even when we have difficulty in making identifications of geographical sites (not a surprising matter, given the nature of the case), we may still be impressed with the order and format of these texts. They were designed to be read aloud. In Numbers even geography is a matter of worship, a litany of promise. This chapter is a celebration of God's gifting. It is a liturgy of geography. It presents a deed of trust, a legal document from God to his people. Prophetically, it points to realization in Joshua 15. The repetition of the phrase "the land of Canaan" (Heb.) in v.2 has something triumphant about it. These chapters were designed to build confidence in the people and also to provoke their continuing worship of the Lord.

NOTE

2 In the phrase אֲשֶׁר תִּפֹּל לָכֶם (ʾašer tippōl lākem, lit., "which will fall to you"), the use of the verb נָפַל (nāpal, "to fall") adds a colorful touch; reference is made to the distribution of the land by lot, but that lot will be the outworking of the will of the Lord (see the same wording in Jdg 18:1; Ps 16:6; Eze 47:14). The NIV ("that will be allotted to you") is a more sedate rendering of this phrase.

ii. The southern boundary (34:3–5)

³"Your southern side will include some of the Desert of Zin along the border of Edom. On the east, your southern boundary will start from the end of the Salt Sea, ⁴cross south of Scorpion Pass, continue on to Zin and go south of Kadesh Barnea. Then it will go to Hazar Addar and over to Azmon, ⁵where it will turn, join the Wadi of Egypt and end at the Sea.

COMMENTARY

3–5 The southern boundary does not run on a straight east-west line; it forms a rough, broad angle with the southernmost point south of Kadesh. Similarly, the northern boundary forms a rough, broad angle with the northernmost curve extending through Lebo Hamath (v.8) and then reaching into northeastern Syria (v.9) before turning south and west in a swoop to the Sea of Galilee. The resultant picture of the land is somewhat ideal, jewel-like. The western and eastern boundaries are formed principally by the waterways; but the north and south are peaked outward, giving a dynamic shape to the outline of the land. However, the land is a real entity, not just an ideal in someone's mind. Hence the exotic place names that form the outline of the borders are of signal importance.

The line of the border begins with the south, that which was more familiar to the people from their wilderness environment. There is a sense that movement is from the known to the unknown. The southern border would include part of the Desert of Zin near Edom, with the Dead Sea (*yām-hammelaḥ*, "The Salt Sea") as the easternmost extension. The line moves southwest just south of "Scorpion Pass," traverses Zin, and extends to the

south of Kadesh Barnea. Then the border moves westward and northward passing through Azmon to the Wadi of Egypt (the Wadi el-ʿArish) on the Mediterranean.

Scorpion Pass (*maʿᵃlēh ʿaqrabbîm*; v.4) is mentioned in Joshua 15:3 and Judges 1:36 and remains today a well-known feature of the wilderness. The inclusion of Kadesh Barnea, the site of Israel's long sojourn in the wilderness (see comment on 33:36), is arresting. There was a sense in which during all those years they lived in the region of Kadesh, they were living on the fringe of the land. Certainly by their occupation of that region for a generation, it was fitting that it was to become a hereditary feature of the Land of Promise. The Wadi of Egypt (Wadi el-ʿArish) is a well-known geographical feature that separates Canaan proper from Egypt as it empties into the Great Sea. This wadi was part of the original promise (see Ge 15:18: "from the river of Egypt"). One should not confuse it with the great Nile River.

So with Edom on the east and the Great Sea (the Mediterranean) on the west, and with Kadesh Barnea as the southernmost extension of the border, the general sense of the line is fairly clear.

NOTES

3 The language used in this chapter—e.g., פְּאַת־נֶגֶב (peʾat-negeb, "southern side")—to describe the four sides of the land by their boundaries is similar to that used in Exodus 27 to describe the sides of the tabernacle and in Ezekiel 47 to describe the new (prophetic) borders of the land (see vv. 13–20).

4 Cole, 536, describes the "Scorpion Pass," מַעֲלֵה עַקְרַבִּים (maˤaleh ˤaqrabbîm) as "a winding road from the Nahal Zin basin into the Negeb south of Mampsis, that continued to be known by that name through the Roman period." At some points the Roman road of the same name may be seen today from the modern road.

iii. The western boundary (34:6)

6"Your western boundary will be the coast of the Great Sea. This will be your boundary on the west.

COMMENTARY

6 The Great Sea is the Mediterranean and its coastlands. Certainly there was no misunderstanding of the western boundary. The Great Sea was feared by the peoples of Canaan; it was viewed as a malevolent, powerful, unpredictable force. It was deified by the Canaanites as Yammu (the Sea God) and was believed to be the home of Lotan (Heb. Leviathan), the fearsome sea monster deity.

iv. The northern boundary (34:7–9)

7"For your northern boundary, run a line from the Great Sea to Mount Hor **8**and from Mount Hor to Lebo Hamath. Then the boundary will go to Zedad, **9**continue to Ziphron and end at Hazar Enan. This will be your boundary on the north.

COMMENTARY

7–9 The northern boundary may be something of a bloated, mirror image of the southern. It does not form a straight line from west to east but moves northeastward to Lebo Hamath, where it turns, either dropping sharply to the eastern area north of the Sea of Galilee (so Greenstone, 384; see also Walter C. Kaiser Jr., "The Promised Land: A Biblical Historical View," *BSac* 138 [October–December 1981]: esp. 304), or, more likely, moving even more northerly as it reaches to the sites of Zedad,

Ziphron, and Hazar Enan (towns that Wenham, 231–33, suggests are considerably north and east of Damascus in Syria). The Mount Hor of v.7 cannot be confused with the Mount Hor in the south where Aaron died (see 33:37); the mountain here is in the region of Lebanon, perhaps Jebel ʿAlekar.

These two constructions of the northern boundary are dissimilar. That which presents Lebo Hamath as the northernmost point (forming a "cap" to the land) is more in line with the historical reality, where Lebo Hamath is presented as the remote north of the land (see Jos 13:5; 1Ki 8:65 = 2Ch 7:8; 2Ki 14:25; 1Ch 13:5; Am 6:14). The view that the northern boundary includes much of northeastern Syria seems not to correspond to biblical events but may present the biblical ideal that was never fully realized (see Ge 15:18: "from the river of Egypt, to the great river, the Euphrates"). Had Israel continued to expand under glorious kings such as David and Solomon, then perhaps the completion of the amalgamation of the northern territories as a part of Canaan would have been realized. Certainly the incongruity of this ideal northern boundary with the historical facts of occupation during Israel's history would have been known by people at the time. Finally, the northern border is an eschatological promise.

NOTES

7–8, 10 תְּתָאוּ (tᵉtāʾû, "mark out"; vv.7–8), which the NIV translates as "run a line," is problematic. The word in the text in these two verses appears to be a Piel imperfect from the root תָּאָה (tāʾâ), but BDB (1060d) lists it as dubious; similarly, BDB finds dubious וְהִתְאַוִּיתֶם (wᵉhiṯʾawwîtem), a supposed Hithpael of אָוָה (ʾāwâ, "to mark, describe with a mark"; BDB 16c [a hapax legomenon]) in v.10. The suggested emendation for both verbs in these three verses is to connect them to the root תָּאַר (tāʾar), which in the Piel is a denominative verb that may mean "to draw, trace an outline." There is a noun תֹּאַר (tōʾar) meaning "outline, form." See, for example, the use of this noun in the phrase, "lovely in form" (יְפַת תֹּאַר, yᵉpat tōʾar), describing Rachel in Genesis 29:17. This emendation of difficult words seems to be an appropriate decision. Thus the verb in vv.7–8 may be emended to תְּתָאֲרוּ (tᵉtāʾărû, a Piel imperfect second masculine plural of תָּאַר [tāʾar], "to trace out a line"). Similarly, the verb in v.10 should be emended to וְתֵאַרְתֶּם (wᵉtēʾartem, a Piel perfect second masculine plural of tāʾar with waw consecutive, meaning "and trace out a line").

8 In לְבֹא חֲמָת (lᵉbōʾ hᵃmāt, "Lebo Hamath"), the term "Lebo" may also be translated "to the entrance of." The phrase seems to be used as a geographical limit (Jdg 3:3, NIV margin).

v. The eastern boundary (34:10–12a)

10"'For your eastern boundary, run a line from Hazar Enan to Shepham. **11**The boundary will go down from Shepham to Riblah on the east side of Ain and continue along the slopes east of the Sea of Kinnereth. **12**Then the boundary will go down along the Jordan and end at the Salt Sea.

COMMENTARY

10–12a The line from the northernmost point that traverses to the south finally to join the southern tip of the eastern side of the Sea of Galilee is the most precarious to attempt to draw. Perhaps a grand curve is intended that includes the sweep of much of southeastern Syria. The sites of Shepham and Riblah are unknown today. The Sea of Kinnereth (*yām kinneret*, another name for the Sea of Galilee) and the Jordan River form the traditional eastern border for the southern part of the line.

NOTES

10 See Note on 34:7–8, 10.

12 The Jordan River meanders in a valley from the southern point of the Sea of Galilee (600 feet below sea level) to the northern point of the Dead Sea (now nearly 1,400 feet below sea level—the lowest point on the earth!), a distance of about 75 miles. Today, that twisting, serpentine journey nearly doubles the distance to about 150 miles. The valley of the Jordan is a part of the massive Syrian-African rift, extending all the way to Uganda and Kenya in East Africa.

vi. Summary (34:12b)

12b"'This will be your land, with its boundaries on every side.'"

COMMENTARY

12b "This will be your land, with its boundaries on every side." These words convey grand gifting; the role of Yahweh as the Giver of the land cannot be stressed too greatly. At no time in Israel's history did Israel ever realize the full extent of the land as these verses present it (but cf. Jos 23:14). But the ideal was always there. One day, many Christians believe, the rule of David's greater son, the Lord Jesus, will fulfill each of these promises to overflowing. At that time the boundaries of ancient promise will form living markers for the heartland of his reign; yet ultimately, there is no line that may be drawn to show the full extent of his rule.

b. The Inheritance in Transjordan (34:13–15)

¹³Moses commanded the Israelites: "Assign this land by lot as an inheritance. The LORD has ordered that it be given to the nine and a half tribes, ¹⁴because the families of the

tribe of Reuben, the tribe of Gad and the half-tribe of Manasseh have received their inheritance. ¹⁵These two and a half tribes have received their inheritance on the east side of the Jordan of Jericho, toward the sunrise."

COMMENTARY

13–15 The new realities that the settlement of Reuben, Gad, and the half-tribe of Manasseh in Transjordan brought about (see ch. 32) demanded that this section be added. Since the Jordan River is the traditional eastern boundary of the land of Canaan, these tribes are outside the boundaries in a strict sense. Yet it is possible to see them as deliberately extending the borders of the Land of Promise. Again in these verses we find the obedience of Moses to the word of God as he allots the land of Canaan proper to the nine and one-half tribes.

c. The Personnel of the Inheritance (34:16–29)

¹⁶The Lord said to Moses, ¹⁷"These are the names of the men who are to assign the land for you as an inheritance: Eleazar the priest and Joshua son of Nun. ¹⁸And appoint one leader from each tribe to help assign the land. ¹⁹These are their names:

Caleb son of Jephunneh,
    from the tribe of Judah;
²⁰Shemuel son of Ammihud,
    from the tribe of Simeon;
²¹Elidad son of Kislon,
    from the tribe of Benjamin;
²²Bukki son of Jogli,
    the leader from the tribe of Dan;
²³Hanniel son of Ephod,
    the leader from the tribe of Manasseh son of Joseph;
²⁴Kemuel son of Shiphtan,
    the leader from the tribe of Ephraim son of Joseph;
²⁵Elizaphan son of Parnach,
    the leader from the tribe of Zebulun;
²⁶Paltiel son of Azzan,
    the leader from the tribe of Issachar;
²⁷Ahihud son of Shelomi,
    the leader from the tribe of Asher;

²⁸Pedahel son of Ammihud,
    the leader from the tribe of Naphtali."
²⁹These are the men the LORD commanded to assign the inheritance to the Israelites in
the land of Canaan.

COMMENTARY

16–29 The list of the new tribal leaders recalls the list of the leaders of the first generation (1:5–16). This time the promise will be realized; these new leaders will assist Eleazar and Joshua in actually allotting that land.

Below is a list of the leaders' names, along with suggested meanings for the transliterated Hebrew terms. The meanings of these names are somewhat speculative; Hebrew has so many homonyms in its verbal (triliteral) root structure that one is often unsure which presumed root is correctly identified with the name in question. Many of these names are theophoric; that is, they are constructed with a form of the divine name (here, largely a form of "El" [Heb. *ʾēl*, "God") as a statement of the faith of the parents in Yahweh when they lovingly assigned these names to their children.

(1) Caleb (*kālēb*, "Dog"; see 13:6) son of Jepunneh (*yᵉpunneh*, meaning unknown; perhaps, "He Makes Clear," if related to the Piel of the verb *pānâ*, "to turn, make clear"), was the leader of tribe of Judah (v.19). He is a figure well known to us by this time (see chs. 13–14).

(2) Shemuel (*šᵉmûʾēl*, "His Name Is God") son of Ammihud (*ʿammîhûd*, "My Kinsman Is Majesty") was the leader of the tribe of Simeon (v.20).

(3) Elidad (*ʾᵉlîdād*, "My God Loves") son of Kislon (*kislôn*, "Confidence") was the leader of the tribe of Benjamin (v.21). It does not seem possible that this is the same person as the prophet Eldad (*ʾeldād*, "God Loves") of 11:26; presumably

that Eldad (whose father's name is not given) was already deceased, unless he was very young when the Spirit fell on him in that unusual event.

(4) Bukki (*buqqî*, "Proven"[?]) son of Jogli (*yoglî*, "Led Away") was the leader of the tribe of Dan (v.22).

(5) Hanniel (*ḥannîʾēl*, "Grace of God") son of Ephod (*ʾēpōd*, "Ephod," as in the vestment of the priest) was the leader of the tribe of Manasseh, from the families of Joseph (v.23).

(6) Kemuel (*qᵉmûʾēl*, "God Establishes") son of Shiphtan (*šipṭan*, "Judgment") was the leader of the tribe of Ephraim (v.24).

(7) Elizaphan (*ᵉlîṣāpān*, "My God Protects") son of Parnach (*parnāk*, meaning unknown) was the leader of the tribe of Zebulun (v.25).

(8) Paltiel (*palṭîʾēl*, "My Deliverance is God") son of Azzan (*ʿazzān*, "Mighty") was the leader of the tribe of Issachar (v.26).

(9) Ahihud (*ᵃḥîhûd*, "My Brother is Majesty") son of Shelomi (*šᵉlōmî*, "My Peace") was the leader of the tribe of Asher (v.27).

(10) Pedahel (*pᵉdahʾēl*, "God Ransoms") son of Ammihud (the same name as the father of Shemuel; v.20) was the leader of the tribe of Naphtali (v.28).

The chapter ends with the report of accomplishment: "These are the men" (v.29). These are the names of the second generation; the leaders of the earlier lists were now dead. But with the outlines of the land now in mind and with new leaders of the tribes now in place, certainly soon the new generation will begin its long-anticipated conquest of the land under the hand of God. Cole, 541, writes: "The basic challenge lay before them: Be faithful to the Lord's commands and he will bring abundant blessing. But if they rebelled as the previous generation in the wilderness did, they would likewise not inherit the land." It remains true: God has time and the wilderness has sand.

NOTE

24 The NIV's text adds "son of Joseph" to the words "from the tribe of Ephraim" to allow the patterning of the previous verse to be understood. Further, the MT begins adding the word "leader" (*nāśîʾ*) to each of the names in v. 22; it is possible that each verse should have this word included but that it was dropped from vv. 19–21.

2. Levitical Cities and Cities of Refuge (35:1–34)

OVERVIEW

The materials of this chapter serve as a further appendage to the major story line of Numbers; the climax of the theology of the book comes in 33:50–56. Yet there is a sense of logic to this chapter, especially as it follows the account of the divine dimensions of the Land of Promise in ch. 34. There is a pattern in the book of Numbers that deals first with the laic tribes and their concerns and then moves to the holy tribe of the Levites and their concerns. This was true in the census enumerations and in various other sections throughout the book.

Chapter 34 presents the ideal dimensions of the whole land of Canaan, including the acknowledgment of God's sanctioning the settlement of the two and one-half tribes in Transjordan. Now it was necessary for Moses to speak more clearly on the prospects for the settlement of the Levites. They were not to have a landed tribal holding as the other tribes, but they certainly needed places to live. The solution came in the concept of cities spread throughout the entire land, in and among the other tribes. In this way the Levites could serve as a "holy leaven" that would permeate the laic tribes with their presence as special representatives of the work of God in their midst. Among the people they would serve as holy guides to the truth and work of God (see Ge 49:7; Lev 10:11; Dt 31:9–13; 33:10).

We should not be surprised that critical scholars do not regard this chapter as an authentic piece from the time of Moses. Because of its thematic connection with Joshua 20–21, where the distribution of the cities of refuge and other Levitical cities is enacted, some scholars regard Numbers 35 as dependent on Joshua 20–21 rather than anticipatory of it (see, e.g., Noth, 253; see commentary on Joshua 21). Other passages that deal with the distribution of land among the families of the Levites include Leviticus 25:32, 34; Joshua 14:4; 1 Chronicles 13:2; 2 Chronicles 11:14; 31:15, 19. Later texts reflecting on these issues include Ezra 2:70; Nehemiah 7:73; 11:3, 20, 36. A prophetic perspective of future Levitical landed arrangements is given in Ezekiel 48:8–14.

Despite the fact that the distribution of land for the Levites is such a major theme in Scripture, critical scholars doubt whether there was any enactment at all of this arrangement in the history of the nation. Noth, 253–54, for example, concludes:

> These considerations are perhaps, however, superfluous, since the whole passage is purely theoretical, as is clear from the prescriptions for the schematic measuring out of the pasture lands. According to these, the "city" with its "wall" must have been only a point without extension (v.5). The idea of cities of residence for the Levites must, in itself, go back to Deuteronomic-Deuteronomistic ideology (so, too, surely the original form in Joshua 21); the present elaboration is a very late product.

In response to Noth, we may grant the concept that the provisions of this chapter were indeed an ideal, just as the outlines of the boundaries of the land were an ideal (see Nu 33) never fully realized in the historical period. Nonetheless, there were boundaries that corresponded at least in part to the ideal of the boundaries in Numbers; similarly, in the historical experience of the people there were provisions made for the dwellings of the Levites and for the cities of refuge that correspond at least in part to the ideal of this chapter, as Joshua 20–21 details.

a. The Levitical Cities (35:1–5)

¹On the plains of Moab by the Jordan across from Jericho, the Lord said to Moses, ²"Command the Israelites to give the Levites towns to live in from the inheritance the Israelites will possess. And give them pasturelands around the towns. ³Then they will have towns to live in and pasturelands for their cattle, flocks and all their other livestock.

⁴"The pasturelands around the towns that you give the Levites will extend out fifteen hundred feet from the town wall. ⁵Outside the town, measure three thousand feet on the east side, three thousand on the south side, three thousand on the west and three thousand on the north, with the town in the center. They will have this area as pastureland for the towns.

COMMENTARY

1–3 Since the Levites will not receive a landed tribal allotment (1:47–53), they will need towns in which to live and raise their families and places to care for their livestock. The Levites are to be spread among the other tribes throughout the land, not placed in an isolated encampment. Joshua 21 presents the partial fulfillment of this command.

This chapter begins in the same pattern as ch. 34, with a command from Yahweh to Moses respecting the provisions the people need to have in mind as they contemplate the land of Canaan. The notation of their present location across from Jericho (v.1) adds pungency to the account. In their final staging area for their assault on the land, the people must have a perspective of how the land is to be apportioned. Some of the cities and territory will be given to the Levites. But these shares make up only a small portion of the whole; Greenstone, 352, estimates that the total holdings of the Levites envisioned here are a little over fifteen square miles—a small proportion of the nearly six thousand square miles of the land of Canaan.

The Levites are to be given cities along with adjacent open areas for pasture and farming activities. The term the NIV translates as "pasturelands" (*migraš*, from the verb *gāraš*, "to drive out") includes open land for agriculture as well as for herds and flocks (see Jos 14:4; 21:2). These cities will be for their habitation, and the surrounding area will be for their use. It is not clear that these cities will be inhabited exclusively by Levites, but this plan seems to be the aim of the text—a notice that suggests the arrangement is rather idealistic.

However, we do know of priest towns in later Scripture. Anathoth is the most celebrated of such towns (Jos 21:18; 1Ki 2:26; Jer 1:1; 32:7–8), Bethel (Jdg 20:18; 1Sa 10:3; 2Ki 17:28), Nob (1Sa 21:1; 22:19), and Shiloh (1Sa 1:3) also come to mind. Greenstone, 352, concludes: "The exact distribution of the towns and the measurements of the open land as given here may not have been carried out, but there is no reason to doubt the fact that certain definite localities were set aside by each tribe for the priests and the Levites, where they might find homes for their families."

4–5 The description of the allotment of land in each of these cities is not clear as we compare v.4 with v.5. Verse 4 speaks of a distance of one thousand cubits (the NIV converting this figure to "fifteen hundred feet") from the town wall round about for the open land; v.5 speaks of a measurement of two thousand cubits (NIV's "three thousand feet") on each side of the city for the open

land. These apposite dimensions have caused commentators to exercise remarkable mathematical creativity. We may observe that the juxtapositioning of these verses suggests that for the ancients there must have been a workable solution to what seems to us to be a considerable problem. If these two verses were separated by a large block of material, one might argue that they are possibly contradictory and that it was carelessness on the part of scribes or redactors not to see how they do not meld together. Since they are adjacent, they must work—or the work of the writer (or redactor) was most careless indeed! The situation is not unlike the comparison of Proverbs 26:4 and 26:5, verses that seem to be mutually exclusive but may be seen to speak in a complementary and comprehensive manner.

The simplest explanation for these two verses in Numbers is given by Wenham, 234. The city is regarded as a point encompassed by a square that is two thousand cubits to a side. From the central point of the city, each direction would be one thousand cubits. That this solution suggests a very small city is not really a difficulty; most of the towns and settlements of the land of Canaan were small—often just a matter of a few acres. Again, the small size of the settlements of Canaan fits better with the reduced numbers of Israel that we have suggested in terms of the census listings. If a city were to become larger, then correspondingly larger dimensions could have been added. The issue in the verses was not mathematics but simply an adequate provision for the landed needs of the people who would live in the cities. One might imagine that, were this provision of open lands not made, a grudging tribe might allow some Levitical families to live within a settlement but not give them any space (except at great cost) for their flocks, herds, and farming needs. A city apart from arable land and sufficient pasturelands was no great gift.

NOTE

4–5 Milgrom, 502–4 ("Excursus 74—The Levitical Town: An Exercise in Realistic Planning"), presents a more complex—but perhaps more workable—idea. He suggests that the length of the city walls (the city's being viewed as a square for simplicity) would be factored in as "X" (for the east-west axis) and "Y" (for the north-south axis). The resultant pasturage would actually be two thousand cubits plus X by two thousand cubits plus Y. In this way the relative size of the city would be taken into account in the measurements for pasturage (see also Cole, 546).

b. The Cities of Refuge (35:6–33)

i. The basic concept of the cities of refuge (35:6–8)

⁶"Six of the towns you give the Levites will be cities of refuge, to which a person who has killed someone may flee. In addition, give them forty-two other towns. ⁷In all you must give the Levites forty-eight towns, together with their pasturelands. ⁸The towns you give the Levites from the land the Israelites possess are to be given in proportion to the inheritance of each tribe: Take many towns from a tribe that has many, but few from one that has few."

COMMENTARY

6–8 Six Levitical cities were to be stationed strategically in the land—three in Transjordan and three in Cisjordan (Canaan proper)—as cities of refuge, or asylum, where a person guilty of unintentional manslaughter might escape blood revenge. Joshua 20 describes the sites that were eventually chosen.

The situation here arose, of course, from conditions of an age in which family members were expected to seek retribution for harm against one of their number. Here the term "refuge" or "asylum" (*hammiqlāṭ*; v.6) conveys safety for a manslayer from the avenger of blood out to kill him retributively. The term for "manslayer" is *hārōṣēaḥ* (GK 8357) a word that can point to premeditated murder (see Ex 20:13 = Dt 5:17, the commandment against murder; 1Ki 21:19; Jer 7:9; Hos 4:2; cf. Dt 22:26). It may also be used of one who has taken human life without premeditation, or inadvertently, as here (Dt 4:42; 19:3–4, 6; Jos 20–21). Further, the same verb may be used to describe the act of the blood-avenger (vv.27, 30).

These six cities of asylum were to be chosen in addition to forty-two cities for the Levites, thus giving a total of forty-eight cities (v.7). Further, the ideal was that the selection of the cities would be based on the relative size of the holdings of the various tribes and their relative populations (v.8). Though the prescription is ideal in nature, the general application is still clear. The cities that were later selected as the cities of asylum include Bezer, Ramoth-Gilead, and Golan in Transjordan, and Hebron, Shechem, and Kedesh in Cisjordan (see Dt 4:43; Jos 20:7–8; 21:13, 21, 27, 32, 36, 38).

ii. Further details on the cities of refuge (35:9–15)

⁹Then the LORD said to Moses: ¹⁰"Speak to the Israelites and say to them:'When you cross the Jordan into Canaan, ¹¹select some towns to be your cities of refuge, to which a person who has killed someone accidentally may flee. ¹²They will be places of refuge from the avenger, so that a person accused of murder may not die before he stands trial before the assembly. ¹³These six towns you give will be your cities of refuge. ¹⁴Give three on this side of the Jordan and three in Canaan as cities of refuge. ¹⁵These six towns will be a place of refuge for Israelites, aliens and any other people living among them, so that anyone who has killed another accidentally can flee there.

COMMENTARY

9–15 Verse 9 is worded as a new oracle from Yahweh. It may be that the chapter is made of varied materials that were worked into a unified whole; it is also possible that the revelation of the Torah on the cities of asylum came in stages, not unlike the pattern we find elsewhere in Scripture (cf. the two oracles to Abraham following his obedience in the binding of Isaac; Ge 22:11–12, 15–18).

Through Moses, the Lord commanded the people who were about to enter the land personally to select special cities of asylum for manslayers seeking safety from blood-avengers. Verse 11 specifies the provision of these cities as being for accidental (*bišḡāḡâ*; see GK 8705) killers, those whose actions are opposite to purposeful sins of the "high hand" (15:30). Other references to inadvertent sins are found in 15:25; Leviticus 4:2, 22; and Joshua 20:3, 9.

The avenger of blood was a relative of the slain person who would take it on himself to protect the family rights by avenging his relatives of the loss suffered by the family. In fact, the term *gōʾēl* (GK 1457), often translated "redeemer," has this basic idea. The *gōʾēl* was principally the "protector of family rights" (definition of Don Glenn, formerly of Dallas Seminary; see Lev 25:48; Ru 3:13). A redeemer is one who redeems the loss sustained by the family. This can be by payment of a price or by taking a life. In the latter case, one is an "avenger of blood" (*gōʾēl haddām*; vv.19, 21). But in his rage against the loss of a family member, the *gōʾēl haddām* might rashly kill the offender before he knew the circumstances of the death. If the killing was not premeditated or was accidental, the slaying of the offending party would add wrong to wrong.

Basically, the provision of the cities of asylum was another instance of the mercy of Yahweh in supplying the needs of his people living in their particular world setting. Note that this text does not *demand* that a relative act as a blood avenger; it simply *assumes* that in that culture, taking such action was precisely what would be done. As a result, given the ethos of the times, the provision of the cities of asylum was merciful and righteous.

There seems to be no significance to the number of the cities (six), but there is certainly significance to their placement. There would be three cities on each side of the Jordan River, thus providing accessibility from all parts of the land. Also, the inclusion of three cities of asylum in Trans-jordan served further to legitimize the holdings of the two and one-half tribes in the expanded territories.

Verse 15 explains that there will be equal access to these cities by all persons in the land — free citizens as well as sojourners or even temporary aliens. This provision is another aspect of God's grace, who provides one law for all persons who come under the purview of the Torah of his grace.

NOTE

11 The verb וְהִקְרִיתֶם (wᵉhiqrîtem, "select") is a Hiphil perfect with *waw* consecutive of the root *qārâ*. In the Qal stem this verb means "to encounter, meet." In this formation the verb has the idea "to make a suitable selection, make one's choice in." Moreover, the command came through Moses in a direct manner: "You [plural] are personally to select." The construction includes what is sometimes called the dative of personal reference, in which the action-command verb (the perfect with the *waw* consecutive here functioning as an imperative) is followed by a preposition with a pronominal suffix לָכֶם (lākem, "to you"; both the verb and the pronoun are plural). For more on this construction, see Note on 10:2.

iii. Basic stipulations concerning the taking of life and the cities of refuge (35:16–21)

> ¹⁶"'If a man strikes someone with an iron object so that he dies, he is a murderer; the murderer shall be put to death. ¹⁷Or if anyone has a stone in his hand that could kill, and he strikes someone so that he dies, he is a murderer; the murderer shall be put to death. ¹⁸Or if anyone has a wooden object in his hand that could kill, and he hits someone so that he dies, he is a murderer; the murderer shall be put to death. ¹⁹The avenger of blood shall put the murderer to death; when he meets him, he shall put him to death. ²⁰If anyone with malice aforethought shoves another or throws something at him intentionally so that he dies ²¹or if in hostility he hits him with his fist so that he dies, that person shall be put to death; he is a murderer. The avenger of blood shall put the murderer to death when he meets him.

COMMENTARY

16–21 These verses present various descriptions of the taking of life that would indicate willful murder. The intent is all practical, as is the listing of stipulated foods for the household in Leviticus 11. Rather than having to keep in mind a vastly complicated system of classifying animals, for example, a cook in ancient Israel had only to know whether an animal ruminated and whether it had cloven hooves. If so, the meat was acceptable for the table; if not, the meat was to be excluded.

Similarly—but in contrast to the inordinately complicated system of modern jurisprudence concerning criminal homicide law—the provisions of this section are clear and straightforward. They are based on the notions of evident intent. The manner of a person's death may suggest willful intent or accidental demise. If a person were killed with a lethal instrument, the means of death seemed purposeful and guilt of the killer was presumed. Lethal instruments might be iron implements (v.16), (heavy) stones (v.17), or wooden implements (v.18).

Further, if the person died by a physical blow delivered in hatred or in the context of an ambush (v.20), the killer was viewed as guilty and would have to die. For such a one was a murderer, not just an inadvertent manslayer. Modern gradations of murder by degree and extending to manslaughter continue some of these ideas.

NOTE

20 יֶהְדָּפֶנּוּ (*yehdāpennû*, "shoves") may be used to describe a mere push or rejection (2Ki 4:27; Pr 10:3). The word is used of the Lord's intended actions in driving the enemies of Israel from Canaan (Dt 6:19; 9:4). Here the idea is a "shove" that results in a fatality—perhaps, for example, if the one who is pushed falls against a rock. Again, intentionality is the point. One might shove another person playfully and the result might be death, or one might shove someone out of violent hatred with the intention of killing him.

iv. Cases to be decided concerning the taking of life and the cities of refuge (35:22–32)

22"'But if without hostility someone suddenly shoves another or throws something at him unintentionally 23or, without seeing him, drops a stone on him that could kill him, and he dies, then since he was not his enemy and he did not intend to harm him, 24the assembly must judge between him and the avenger of blood according to these regulations. 25The assembly must protect the one accused of murder from the avenger of blood and send him back to the city of refuge to which he fled. He must stay there until the death of the high priest, who was anointed with the holy oil.

26"'But if the accused ever goes outside the limits of the city of refuge to which he has fled 27and the avenger of blood finds him outside the city, the avenger of blood may kill the accused without being guilty of murder. 28The accused must stay in his city of refuge until the death of the high priest; only after the death of the high priest may he return to his own property.

29"'These are to be legal requirements for you throughout the generations to come, wherever you live.

30"'Anyone who kills a person is to be put to death as a murderer only on the testimony of witnesses. But no one is to be put to death on the testimony of only one witness.

³¹"'Do not accept a ransom for the life of a murderer, who deserves to die. He must surely be put to death.
³²"'Do not accept a ransom for anyone who has fled to a city of refuge and so allow him to go back and live on his own land before the death of the high priest.

COMMENTARY

22–32 The cities of refuge were to be established for the person who had committed an act of involuntary manslaughter. But such cases are not always simple to determine, then or now. The killing of an individual by a lethal weapon brings a presumption of guilt on the slayer. Yet it is possible that this death was still inadvertent. In cases of doubt, judgments would have to be made by the people (v.24), presumably by their town elders (the term "assembly" can refer to the whole nation or to any group within the nation). The text is not specific, but apparently the judgment was made in the city in which the death occurred. If the council decided that the death was premeditated and deserving of death, the guilty party was delivered over to the blood avenger. But if the council decided the slayer was innocent of premeditated malice, the slayer had to go to the city of asylum for protection from the avenger. He would be protected only so long as he remained within that city (v.26); if the slayer left it for any reason, the avenger was allowed to kill him without any personal consequence (ʾên lô dām, "there is no blood guilt"; "without being guilty of murder," NIV; v.27).

Most interestingly, permanent protection was guaranteed only if the refuge seeker remained in the city of asylum until the death of the high priest (vv.25, 28). There was an atoning significance for the entire populace when the high priest (notice the phrasing: "who was anointed with holy oil") died. If the high priest died during the period of the slayer's exile in the city of asylum, he was not only free to leave the city, but he could also resume his normal life again, including his stake in his ancestral land. Historical sources tell us that in the case of the death of a pharaoh in ancient Egypt, capital crimes were forgiven. The notice of the death of the pharaoh of the Hebrews' oppression in Egypt (Ex 2:23) was the political opportunity God provided for Moses to return to Egypt without fear of reprisal for his crime of murder some forty years earlier.

As we think about the application of the high priest's death to the freedom of the manslayer, we realize that the sin of killing, no matter how unintended, is serious. It cannot be passed over or left free of serious consequence. For an exile in a city of asylum, life was characterized by discontinuity and estrangement—but it was life. If the high priest should die while the slayer was in, he was free to leave without being subject again to the avenger of blood. This picture portrays redemption—the remission of sin. The sins do matter—they do affect one's life; but they may be forgiven, and a person may be set free (see also Jos 20:6).

A further provision of mercy in these cases was the requirement of witnesses to confirm guilt (v.30). This provision was made to avoid the possibility of an innocent party's being accused and sentenced to death on insufficient evidence. A minimum of two witnesses was required to forestall malicious false testimony from one isolated voice. As we know, even the provision of multiple witnesses does not automatically preclude collusion; recall the shocking perversion of Israel's judicial system by the foreign priestess Jezebel in the incident of Naboth (1Ki 21; note also the false witnesses at the trial of Jesus before the Sanhedrin [Mk 14:55–64]).

The stipulations concerning ransom payments are also designed as extensions of mercy (vv.31–32). Conceivably, a wealthy person might take the route of paying ransom as a means of getting out of a sticky situation, while the poor person, who could not afford a ransom payment, would be at the mercy of the avenger or be forced to live for years in a city of asylum. Hence the alternative for the guilty party to pay a ransom did not figure in cases involving murder or manslaughter — deliberate or accidental killing. Exodus 21:29–30 presents an exception, namely, the case of a man's ox lethally goring a neighbor.

REFLECTION

Christians reading these words about the salvific effect of the high priest's death find their thoughts turning to the book of Hebrews, with its presentation of Christ as our High Priest (Heb 5–10). His death as high priest is the antitype for the atoning deaths of Israel's high priests in antiquity. There can be no salvific merit in the death of a high priest in isolation; only when the death of that high priest is seen in a *heilsgeschichtliche* continuity with the death of Christ — as an arrow pointing forward to the death of the one who really mattered for the salvation of the community — can we understand this provision. Hence, even though many modern writers shy away from typological relationships between the Old and New Testaments, this connection is one we should not miss.

v. The divine perspective on murder and the land (35:33–34)

33"Do not pollute the land where you are. Bloodshed pollutes the land, and atonement cannot be made for the land on which blood has been shed, except by the blood of the one who shed it. 34Do not defile the land where you live and where I dwell, for I, the LORD, dwell among the Israelites.'"

COMMENTARY

33–34 The underlying theology of this text is most significant: the shedding of human blood pollutes the land. The crime of murder is not only an offense against the sanctity of life; it is in fact a pollutant to the Lord's sacred land. It is like the blood of innocent Abel screaming out to the Lord (Ge 4:10). Only the blood of Christ will be able to speak a better word (Heb 12:24).

The point of the present passage is not merely that there be cities for the Levites to inhabit or that there be cities of asylum in which the inadvertent manslayer can find refuge. All the theology of the chapter culminates in the last words of v.34: "For I am Yahweh who dwells in the midst of the people of Israel" (my translation). This statement encapsulates the central issue. If God is to reside among his people, the land may not be polluted. With all the attention we (rightly) give to issues of ecology and pollution in our own day, there is an act of pollution that far transcends the trashing of rivers, the killing of lakes, the denuding of forests, and the spilling of oil to mar even the seas; the transcendent pollution is the abuse of persons. The worst abuse of all is to cause wrongful death. God will not draw near to a land polluted with wrongly shed human blood.

3. A Review of the Inheritance of Women (36:1–13)

OVERVIEW

Each of the last three chapters of the book of Numbers is an appendage to the book; its theological climax comes directly in the last pericope of ch. 33. It is there that the will of the Lord for his people is stated in definitive form as they are about to enter the land. Of the last three chapters, this one is the most transparently additional, as it presents an interesting further development of the account of Zelophehad's daughters (see 27:1–11). Since the Lord had instructed Moses that women who had no brothers might inherit their father's land, new questions arose: What would happen to the family lands if these daughters were to marry men from other tribes? Would not the original intent of the first provision be frustrated? Such questions led to the decision that marriage was to be kept within one's own tribe so that the family allotments would not "pass from tribe to tribe" (v.9).

Even though we may regard this chapter as somewhat anticlimactic, this observation is not to deny that the chapter is instructive. It shows a continuing pattern of the development of Torah in Israel. As the Lord spoke to Moses in general terms, specific cases arose that did not seem to fit the general framework of the revelation. In such instances, Moses presented the needs of the people to the Lord; then he received new instructions that not only addressed the immediate needs but also served as a further basis for application in Israel. (This system of case law and the establishing of precedent ["casuistic" law] shaped one of the two major types of Torah, the other type [termed "apodictic"] being that of nonnegotiable stipulations.)

The fact that these chapters are appendages does not preclude their having been written by Moses. In fact, Moses is still the principal human player in these chapters. The present account has three divisions followed by a summary statement (v.13).

a. Concerns of the Gileadites for the Daughters of Zelophehad (36:1–4)

[1]The family heads of the clan of Gilead son of Makir, the son of Manasseh, who were from the clans of the descendants of Joseph, came and spoke before Moses and the leaders, the

heads of the Israelite families. ²They said, "When the Lᴏʀᴅ commanded my lord to give the land as an inheritance to the Israelites by lot, he ordered you to give the inheritance of our brother Zelophehad to his daughters. ³Now suppose they marry men from other Israelite tribes; then their inheritance will be taken from our ancestral inheritance and added to that of the tribe they marry into. And so part of the inheritance allotted to us will be taken away. ⁴When the Year of Jubilee for the Israelites comes, their inheritance will be added to that of the tribe into which they marry, and their property will be taken from the tribal inheritance of our forefathers."

COMMENTARY

1–4 The grandiloquent pageantry of the setting demonstrates the importance of the issue. The family of the daughters of Zelophehad brought to Moses their petition. They did not dispute the former decision of the Lord that the brotherless daughters might inherit land to carry on their father's heritage. But the family worried about the problems that would eventuate if these daughters should marry outside their clan and tribe. Upon marrying, their husband(s) would gain title to their land — part and parcel of the ancient patriarchal system. This would result in transfer of that land to a different tribe and threaten the very basis of the concept of tribal inheritance.

At issue was not a complaint or a grievance against women per se so much as a concern for the continuity of the lines of inheritance within the tribes. At the Year of Jubilee (*hayyôbēl*, "the cornet"; see Lev 25:12, 29–55; 27:17–25), when problems concerning lines of inheritance were to be resolved, this issue would remain unresolvable unless further instruction was obtained from the Lord through Moses.

So the perspective is not antiwoman but concern for the integrity of the landed distribution. At the same time, from the vantage of women's right to participate equally in the community, this chapter in some manner diminishes the slight advance that was made in ch. 27. By this observation, I mean that women were still not considered independent entities within the community; their definition, their sense of their part in the community, continued to be connected to their husbands (and fathers and sons).

Nonetheless, this sequence of events (chs. 27–31) is a significant entry in the history of women's issues. It takes two steps forward and one step back; but there is some forward movement — a countercultural thrust that has the blessing of God.

NOTE

3 The two forms of the verb גָּרַע (*gāraʿ*) — וְנִגְרְעָה (*wᵉnigrᵉʿâ*, "will be taken") and יִגָּרַע (*yiggāraʿ*, "will be taken away") — speak of something that abates or is withdrawn. The point is that this is the verb used in 27:4 on the part of the daughters in their initial complaint. The tie between these chapters (inclusio) is made compelling by the use of this same word.

b. The Law for the Marriages of the Women Who Inherit Familial Land (36:5–9)

⁵Then at the LORD's command Moses gave this order to the Israelites:"What the tribe of the descendants of Joseph is saying is right. ⁶This is what the LORD commands for Zelophehad's daughters:They may marry anyone they please as long as they marry within the tribal clan of their father. ⁷No inheritance in Israel is to pass from tribe to tribe, for every Israelite shall keep the tribal land inherited from his forefathers. ⁸Every daughter who inherits land in any Israelite tribe must marry someone in her father's tribal clan, so that every Israelite will possess the inheritance of his fathers. ⁹No inheritance may pass from tribe to tribe, for each Israelite tribe is to keep the land it inherits."

COMMENTARY

5–9 Again, in great grace, the word of Yahweh came through Moses to present a decision. In this case, as in the case of the daughters of Zelophehad, the petitioners were correct in their observations — and the issue was decided in their favor. The women were permitted to marry whomever they chose — a surprising turn, as we usually think of women as being chosen in biblical times! Perhaps the fact that they inherited land made them active rather than passive agents in marriage. But they had to choose husbands from within their own clans. The issue was not their personal happiness but the solidarity of the larger family unit. As a man is to cleave to his wife (Ge 2:24), so a person in Israel was to cleave to the family inheritance. The destiny of the family in Israel was tied to the land.

The instance of these women becomes a law that is applicable in other, similar cases (v.8). The basic issue was to keep the inheritance of a family in the clan and the tribe of the fathers. Verse 9 summarizes the earlier elements and so reinforces them.

c. The Compliance of the Daughters of Zelophehad (36:10–12)

¹⁰So Zelophehad's daughters did as the LORD commanded Moses. ¹¹Zelophehad's daughters — Mahlah, Tirzah, Hoglah, Milcah and Noah — married their cousins on their father's side. ¹²They married within the clans of the descendants of Manasseh son of Joseph, and their inheritance remained in their father's clan and tribe.

COMMENTARY

10–12 In a book (and in a culture) in which names of women are given only rarely, the names of these women are repeated: Mahlah, Tirzah, Hoglah, Milcah, and Noah (see again 27:1–11). They were married within their families, to paternal "cousins" (*dodehen*, "[sons of] their uncles"; v.11). In this manner the inheritance of their father remained within the clan.

The book of Numbers, which so often presents the rebellion of God's people against his grace and in defiance of his will, ends here on a happy note. These noble women, who were concerned for their father's name and their own place in the land, obeyed the Lord. This concluding section of Num-

bers ties in nicely with the epilogue of Proverbs. Its acrostic portrayal of the wise woman (Pr 31:10–31) exemplifies wisdom in action—through the life of a woman. Significantly in Numbers, a book so marred by disobedience, there is a final statement of obedience; and it is in the lives of these noble daughters of Zelophehad. Likely, we would never have heard of this man had he fathered sons instead of these daughters!

d. A Summary Statement of the Law of the Lord (36:13)

¹³These are the commands and regulations the LORD gave through Moses to the Israelites on the plains of Moab by the Jordan across from Jericho.

COMMENTARY

13 The book of Numbers is far more than a record of commands and regulations. The true climax of the book comes in 33:50–56. Yet in this chapter there is a salutary feeling of theoretical issues being put to practical work. There is hope in the actions of the daughters of Zelophehad that

they will be representative of the nation: this generation will do well.

There is an unstated supplement to the book. We follow the lead of Olson (see Introduction), who suggests a heading such as:

[D. The Prospects for the Second Generation Are for Good, but the Warning from the Experience of the First Generation Must Not Be Forgotten]

Chapter 36 presents the idea of Psalm 78:8: Let this people not be like their fathers and mothers, but let them obey the Lord and enjoy the good land! As stated in the Introduction, God has time and the wilderness has sand. If the second generation *were* to be like the first, then they, too, would be buried in the copious sands. And Yahweh in great mercy would use his time in his manner to await a generation that would obey him.

Yet based on the story of the daughters of Zelophehad, the provisional outlook appears to be good indeed! Harrison, 428, has it right: "The promises of God to Abraham (Ge 17:8), so long in the fulfilling, are now on the point of becoming reality as the Israelite warriors stand opposite Jericho, poised and waiting to cross the Jordan under Joshua's leadership in order to occupy their heritage."

DEUTERONOMY

MICHAEL A. GRISANTI

Introduction

1. TITLE

The book's Hebrew title, *ʾēlleh haddᵉbārîm* ("these are the words of"), conforms to the practice of taking the title from the first word or two of an OT book. The English title, "Deuteronomy," derives from the Septuagint (LXX), *deuteronomos* (and the Latin Vulgate *Deuteronomium*), "second law" or "repeated law." This idea draws on Deuteronomy 17:18, where the king is instructed to make a "copy of this law" (*mišnēh hattôrâ hazzōʾt*). This title is somewhat inappropriate because the book of Deuteronomy is not a mere replica of Exodus (or Exodus–Leviticus), nor is it a second or distinct law. Although it shares several features and themes with other pentateuchal books, i.e., restating the Mosaic law, it also serves as an exposition of the original law (1:5–7). In addition, the book of Deuteronomy is not primarily a legal document. It constitutes sermonic exposition rather than legislation. The legal material is incorporated into the exposition.

2. AUTHORSHIP AND DATE

Before the Enlightenment period (18–19 centuries AD), the consensus view of Christian and Jewish scholars was that Moses authored the book of Deuteronomy (and the Pentateuch). Although several scholars questioned Mosaic authorship prior to the nineteenth century,[1] William de Wette laid the cornerstone for Pentateuchal literary criticism by proposing that Deuteronomy had been composed as a "pious fraud" during the reign of Josiah.[2] Wellhausen's synthesis of de Wette's proposal (as part of the documentary hypothesis) made his explanation a "linchpin" of OT studies. Most scholars have since rejected the notion

---

1. Cf. the survey by R. K. Harrison, *Introduction to the Old Testament* (Grand Rapids: Eerdmans, 1969), 3–11.
2. D. L. Christensen, *Deuteronomy 1:1–21:9* (WBC 6A; Nashville: Nelson, 2001), lxviii.

that the book of Deuteronomy is a *purely* fictional work (i.e., "pious fraud").[3] But they did not return to accepting Moses as the author. The biblical claim of Mosaic authorship was viewed as "fiction." Various writers have suggested that the book derived from Levitical circles,[4] the prophetic guild,[5] the realm of the Jewish court,[6] or wisdom traditions.[7]

In 1943, M. Noth introduced a new paradigm for explaining the composition of Deuteronomy.[8] Noth proposed that Deuteronomy through Kings was the work of a single exilic historian (the Deuteronomist). This writer appropriated Deuteronomy 4:44–30:20 (composed in the seventh century) and composed the Deuteronomistic History (Samuel–Kings). More recently, R. N. Whybray has proposed that the book reached its final form in the sixth century by one author who drew on a variety of sources.[9]

The alleged connection between the book of Deuteronomy and the Josianic reforms in 621 BC appears to be flawed on several grounds. In the first place, Deuteronomy appears to be the basis for earlier reforms, by Jehoshaphat (1Ki 22:42–49, ca. 873–849 BC), Amaziah (2Ki 14:6, ca. 800–783 BC), and Hezekiah (2Ki 18:3–8, ca. 700 BC). Second, the book also *presupposes* the existence of earlier canonical legislation in several instances (e.g., sacrificial ritual, tithes, the Ten Commandments). Third, Josiah's reform reflects some laws not found in Deuteronomy (e.g., laws concerning sacrifice to Molech). Finally, the centralization of worship at Jerusalem is not a primary or fundamental concern in Deuteronomy (as had been conceived by the critics). Although it does address the issue of the proper kind of place to worship Yahweh (Dt 12), the book never explicitly mentions high places, a temple, or Jerusalem.

Several scholars have proposed that a substantial portion of Deuteronomy was composed by Moses (including the words of Moses and Yahweh). A later narrator added about fifty-two verses as part of inspired Scripture[10] (see Note on 10:5, 10). Robert Polzin also made this proposal but did not regard the rest of the book to be Mosaic.[11]

Although the last position deserves consideration, one must be careful not to minimize the biblical evidence for Mosaic authorship of Deuteronomy. The book opens with the statement "These are the words which Moses spoke to all Israel" (1:1), attributing the immediately following passage and, by implication, the entire book to Moses (cf. 1:5; 31:9, 24, 26). Other OT books attribute this book to Moses as well

---

3. S. R. Driver, *A Critical and Exegetical Commentary on Deuteronomy* (ICC; New York: Charles Scribner's Sons, 1895), lvi–lxii.

4. G. von Rad, *Deuteronomy* (OTL; Philadelphia: Westminster, 1966), 23–26.

5. E. W. Nicholson, *Deuteronomy and Tradition* (Oxford: Basil Blackwell, 1967), 122–24.

6. N. Lohfink, "Deuteronomy" (IDBSup; ed. K. Crim; Nashville, Abingdon, 1976), 229–30.

7. M. Weinfeld, *Deuteronomy 1–11* (AB; New York: Doubleday, 1991), 44–53.

8. M. Noth; cf. the English translation of part of his original German work: *The Deuteronomistic History* (JSOTSup 15; Sheffield: JSOT, 1981).

9. R. N. Whybray, as noted by G. J. Wenham, "Pondering the Pentateuch: The Search for a New Paradigm," in *The Face of Old Testament Studies* (ed. David Baker and Bill Arnold; Grand Rapids: Baker, 1999), 133; cf. R. N. Whybray, *The Making of the Pentateuch: A Methodological Study* (JSOTSup 53; Sheffield: JSOT, 1987), 240–42.

10. See R. Dillard and T. Longman, III, *An Introduction to the Old Testament* (Grand Rapids: Zondervan, 1994), 100; D. I. Block, "Recovering the Voice of Moses: The Genesis of Deuteronomy," *JETS* 44 (2001): 392.

11. R. Polzin, *Moses and the Deuteronomist: A Literary Study of the Deuteronomistic History* (New York: Seabury, 1980), 25–36.

(Jos 1:7; 8:31–32; 23:6; 2Ki 14:6; Ne 8:1; 13:1; 2Ch 25:4; 35:12; et al.). The NT also refers to the laws that Moses commanded Israel to obey (Mt 8:4; 19:7–8; 22:24; Mk 1:44; 7:10; 10:3–4; Lk 5:14; Jn 8:5; Ac 6:14), the "Law of Moses" (Lk 2:22; 24:44; Jn 7:23; Ac 13:39; 15:5; 28:23; 1Co 9:9; Heb 10:28), and the book of Moses (Mk 12:26).

The literary form of Deuteronomy (see below) may also contribute to one's conclusions concerning the date of the book's composition. Although the book of Deuteronomy is substantially from Moses, a small portion of it was added by prophetic figures after the time of Moses. At the very least, the epilogue (ch. 34) was added sometime after Moses' death. There are also some possible geographical and historical updates added after Moses finished his writing (2:10–11, 20–23; 3:9, 11, 13b–14; 10:6–9).[12]

3. HISTORICAL BACKGROUND

The date of the primary composition of Deuteronomy as proposed above draws on several other interpretive decisions. First, having accepted Moses as the author, the date of Israel's Exodus from Egypt provides a chronological benchmark for dating Deuteronomy. Although not delineated here,[13] one can assign the date of 967/966 BC for the fourth year of Solomon's reign. First Kings 6:1 affirms that Solomon began building the temple in Jerusalem in his fourth year as king, an event that was 480 years after Israel's exodus from Egypt. Consequently, the exodus took place in around 1447/46 BC.[14]

Second, the book itself claims to have originated in the "plains of Moab" at the end of the wilderness wanderings and on the eve of Israel's conquest of Canaan (Dt 34:1–8).

Third, a number of passages assign forty years to Israel's trek from Egypt to the brink of the Promised Land. In fact, the celebration at Gilgal (after Israel crosses the Jordan River) occurs precisely forty years after Israel's first celebration of the Passover (Jos 5:6). In the light of those facts, Moses completed the book of Deuteronomy (in near final form) in 1407/06, shortly prior to Israel's crossing the Jordan River.

4. OCCASION AND PURPOSE

Various factors constitute the human setting and delineate the relevance of the book of Deuteronomy (to the original audience in particular). The following are some of the "needs" met by Moses' writing of this book: Israel's identity as God's chosen people, the transition in national leadership, and the preservation of God's revelation for Israel.

First, with regard to Israel's divine calling, the book of Genesis introduces a reader to the patriarchal roots of the nation and the covenant Yahweh established with the descendants of Abraham (Ge 12:1–3: promising a people, land, and blessing). The book of Exodus depicts Israel's transition from a people to a

---

12. Cf. M. A. Grisanti, "Inspiration, Inerrancy, and the Old Testament Cannon: The Place of Textual Updating in an Inerrant View of Scripture," *JETS* 44 (2001): 577–98.

13. Cf. E. H. Merrill, "Palestinian Archaeology and the Date of the Conquest: Do Tells Tell Tales?" *GTJ* 3 (Spring 1982): 107–21; B. K. Waltke, "Palestinian Artifactual Evidence Supporting the Early Date of the Exodus," *BSac* 129 (January–March 1972): 33–47.

14. See W. Shea, "The Date of the Exodus," in *Giving the Sense: Understanding and Using Old Testament Historical Texts* (ed. D. Howard and M. A. Grisanti; Grand Rapids: Kregel, 2003), 236–55; I. Provan, V. Long, and T. Longman III, *A Biblical History of Israel* (Louisville: Westminster John Knox, 2003), 129–32, 140.

nation, a nation to whom God gave his law. Their sincere obedience to that law was central to fulfilling their God-given calling to represent his character before the pagan nations of the world (Ex 19:4–6). After describing how the nation could have access to and live before a holy God (Leviticus), the book of Numbers details Israel's journey toward the Land of Promise. Their rebellion at Kadesh Barnea occasioned divine judgment, i.e., wandering in the wilderness for almost forty years.

The book of Deuteronomy then depicts God's people camped on the plains of Moab, across the Jordan Rift Valley from the Promised Land. Facing the significant challenge of expelling the Canaanites from their land, the Israelites needed this reminder of their God-given identity. Moses reiterates the covenant established at Sinai by applying it directly to this new generation. The Canaanites before them were a vile and idolatrous people. Once the Israelites crossed the Jordan River, they would not only face a military challenge but also encounter temptations to compromise their conduct as God's chosen people. The book of Deuteronomy reminds Israel of who they are and where they originated and delineates what God intends for them in the coming years.

Second, Moses' role in the original forging of the covenant at Sinai had been so significant that, for many Israelites, Moses and the covenant must have seemed inseparable. With the approaching time for Israel's entrance of Canaan came the time for Moses' death. Although God was the true leader of the covenantal people, Moses had been the divinely appointed covenantal mediator. The children of Israel would soon have to face life without Moses and switch their full allegiance to Joshua, God's new covenantal mediator. The book of Deuteronomy prepares God's people for this change. It helps to demonstrate the continuity between Moses' and Joshua's leadership.

Third, Merrill argues that it was urgent for Moses to commit this material to writing because this book "would serve as the corpus of law and practice for the covenant community from that day forward. For Moses to hand on to Joshua the mediatorship of the covenant necessitated the transmission of the covenant text itself."[15] According to Deuteronomy 17, each king was to commission a new copy of Deuteronomy. No doubt this measure would ensure that a good copy was always available for God's people. The project was also intended to be part of the transition of covenantal leadership. For the sake of the entire nation of Israel, the entire book of Deuteronomy was to be read in its entirety before all those gathered at the Feast of Tabernacles every seven years (31:9–13, 24–26).

5. LITERARY FORM

Although the book of Deuteronomy involves three lengthy speeches by Moses (chs. 1–4; 5–28; and 29–30), several scholars have observed that it also closely follows the structure of ancient Near Eastern vassal treaties. The book contains five elements common in Hittite suzerain-vassal treaties:

(1) Preamble (1:1–5). This section delineates the setting and occasion of the covenant: Who are the parties of the covenant and what is its function?

(2) Historical Prologue (1:6–4:49). A ruler's right to have dominion over his vassals is often based on their past relationship. This historical review reminds the vassals of the suzerain's accomplishments on their behalf (hence his right to rule them) and certifies his promise to protect them in the future.

---

15. E. H. Merrill, *Deuteronomy* (NAC; Nashville: Broadman & Holman, 1994), 27.

(3) Stipulations (5:1–26:15). In Deuteronomy, Moses first presents "general" stipulations (5:1–11:32), which outline the broad principles that should guide the relationship between the suzerain and his vassals. (These principles focus on the kingship of the suzerain and the proper response of the vassals—total allegiance.) Moses goes on to detail the "specific" stipulations (12:1–26:15), which expand the general principles in the form of clear and specific statements of the King's expectations (casuistic laws).

(4) Blessings and Curses (27:1–29:1 [28:69]). This section states the rewards and sanctions of a treaty. Vassals who are loyal to the treaty's expectations will enjoy the favor of the suzerain, while those who are disloyal and disobedient will experience the king's wrath and judgment.

(5) Witnesses (30:19; 31:19; 32:1–43). Proper protocol required that a treaty be drawn up before and certified by appropriate witnesses. In pagan treaties, the gods served as witnesses. However, in Deuteronomy the hills and mountains and the heavens and earth function as the witnesses of this covenant between Yahweh and Israel.

By means of suzerain-vassal treaties, a conquering nation would impose conditions on a smaller state and promise its people protection.[16] Various scholars have compared the structure of Deuteronomy to early Hittite treaties (second millennium BC), various law codes (e.g., laws of Hammurabi, ca. 1750 BC), and late Assyrian treaties (first millennium BC). K. Kitchen points to several aspects of close correspondence between Deuteronomy and second millennium treaties and law collections.[17] This similarity in structure supports a second millennium date for the composition of the book.

Why are there differences between Deuteronomy and these ancient Near Eastern treaties if Deuteronomy is modeled after them? In the first place, Deuteronomy was not given simply to serve as a treaty document, but a sermon patterned after a treaty. The treaty form is modified for homiletic reasons. Moses' use of the treaty form serves to strengthen the significance of Israel's responsibilities to God and to assure them of God's faithfulness to Israel. Second, chs. 31–34 (which are not attested in ancient Near Eastern treaties) are not fundamental to customary treaty structure but are essential to Moses' argument.

6. SUMMARY

After delineating the setting for this recitation of Yahweh's covenant with Israel (1:1–5), Moses overviews Yahweh's dealings with his chosen people from the time of Israel's encampment at Sinai until their encampment on the plains of Moab (chs. 1–3). This historical summary demonstrates that Yahweh is their provider, protector, and redeemer. In the light of those realities, God's people must not worship any other gods or attempt to make an image of Yahweh (ch. 4).

Moses reminds his people of Yahweh's expectations of them in chs. 5–26. Building on chs. 1–4, Yahweh has the right to demand total loyalty from Israel because he has redeemed them. Moses presents those demands in two sections. Chapters 5–11 present Yahweh's broad expectation of absolute allegiance. Chapters 12–26 remind the Israelites of Yahweh's specific legislative demands. These expectations reach a

---

16. For more information, see D. J. McCarthy, *Treaty and Covenant: A Study in the Form in the Ancient Oriental Documents and in the Old Testament* (2nd ed.; Rome: Biblical Institute, 1978), 51–85.

17. K. Kitchen, *On the Reliability of the Old Testament* (Grand Rapids: Eerdmans, 2003), 284–88; cf. G. J. Wenham, "The Date of Deuteronomy: Linch-pin of Old Testament Criticism: Part One," *Them* 10/3 (1985): 19.

crescendo at the end of ch. 26, where Moses reminds Israel of their divine calling to represent his character before the surrounding pagan nations (26:16–19). Yahweh's demand for heartfelt loyalty is not something optional for his servant-nation. He promises to bless his nation if they are characterized by obedience and to curse them if they choose to rebel against him (27:1–29:1[28:69]).

In the face of that sober expectation, Israel must renew their wholehearted commitment to their covenantal relationship with Yahweh (29:2[1]–30:20). A casual, ritualistic attempt to conform to God's demands is incompatible with a genuine relationship with Yahweh. Moses ends Deuteronomy by dealing with issues related to the transfer of national leadership to Joshua as well as giving final challenges to the nation (chs. 31–34).

The covenantal structure of Deuteronomy contributes to the overall message of the book as well as to its date of composition. A covenant between people and/or nations assumes the existence of a relationship. What Yahweh asks of his chosen people is not arbitrary or unreasonable. He demands absolute loyalty of a people whom he has redeemed from long-term subservience and to whom he has shown his compassion and absolute power. His demands for wholehearted obedience arise from an intimate relationship between him and his beloved nation. Also, the covenantal structure indicates the sobriety of his demands. To rebel against his expectations was much more than breaking some rules. For Israel, disobedience was tantamount to treachery. It represented the violation of an established and deep relationship.

7. CANONICITY AND TEXT

Deuteronomy is the fifth book of the Pentateuch, a term derived from the Greek *pentateuchos*, "five scrolls" (indicating that they were regarded as a discrete collection of books). Although the term "law" (*tôrâ*) can refer to individual regulations, the Pentateuch, or the entire OT, it can also designate the book of Deuteronomy (Jos 1:7; 1Ki 2:3). From intertestamental times until the present day, the place of Deuteronomy in the OT canon has been uncontested. This book is the second-most quoted book in the NT (ca. fifty times; only Psalms is quoted more frequently)[18] and is the book from which Jesus quoted most frequently. Quotations from Deuteronomy also figure prominently in various Qumran documents.[19]

The Hebrew text of Deuteronomy has been preserved in "excellent condition, generally free from expansions and serious problems."[20] The most significant textual difficulties occur in the two poetic chapters (chs. 32 and 33). The Qumran manuscripts and fragments of Deuteronomy demonstrate the remarkable accuracy with which the text of Deuteronomy was transcribed over the centuries. Portions of Deuteronomy were found in seven of the Qumran caves as well as three nearby locations (Masada, Murabaʿat, and Naḥal Ḥever).[21] The majority of the differences between the standard Hebrew text and the Qumran texts are minor in nature (orthography or grammar). In one case (32:43) the Qumran text is longer than the MT.

---

18. See K. Aland et al., *The Greek New Testament* (4th rev. ed.; Stuttgart: United Bible Societies, 1993), 887–88.

19. See a chart of these occurrences in P. Craigie, *The Book of Deuteronomy* (NICOT; Grand Rapids: Eerdmans, 1976), 84–86.

20. P. Kyle McCarter, *Textual Criticism: Recovering the Text of the Hebrew Bible* (Philadelphia: Fortress, 1986), 88.

21. Cf. F. G. Martínez, "Les Manuscrits du Désert de Juda et le Deutéronome," in *Studies in Deuteronomy* (ed. F. G. Martínez et al.; Leiden: Brill, 1994), 64–65.

8. THEOLOGICAL VALUES

As the book of Romans does for the NT, Deuteronomy provides an important theological foundation for the OT. It graphically delineates the character of God and various fundamental aspects of his relationship with his chosen nation. The book provides the theological foundation on which later biblical writers base their teaching. Later Israelite historians evaluate the direction of the chosen nation from a Deuteronomic perspective and with Deuteronomic phraseology. The prophets call the people of Yahweh to repentance and threaten horrific judgment in terms of the blessings and curses delineated in chs. 27 and 28.

Yahweh

Yahweh is the only God for Israel (4:35; 32:39) and is the Lord of the covenant (6:4). He reveals himself to his covenantal nation by means of his acts, theophany, and direct revelation (his words). He has been, is, and will be their Redeemer (1:30–31; 6:21–23; 26:6–9), Warrior (2:21–22, 30–31; 7:1–2, 20–24), and Judge (7:13–16; 11:14–15; 30:3–9). He is "gracious (5:10; 7:9, 12), loving (1:31; 7:7–8, 13), righteous or just (4:8; 10:17–18), merciful (4:31; 13:17), powerful (4:34, 37; 6:21–22), holy (5:11), glorious (5:24–26), faithful or loyal (7:9, 12), and upright (32:4). But he is also an angry God (1:37; 3:26; 9:18–20), one zealous for his own honor (4:24; 13:2–10; 29:20)."[22]

Covenant

The covenant serves as the bond between Yahweh and his people. The source of the covenant rests in Yahweh alone and represents his steadfast love for his servant-nation. He has committed himself to them in this unique relationship, not because of their uprightness or strength but because of his elective choice (7:7–8). The covenant is grounded in the past, gives meaning to the present, and promises hope for the future.[23] The provision of the covenant at Sinai was not merely a historical event but inaugurated a continuing relationship between Yahweh and Israel.[24]

Israel's Task

Israel's God-given task is to model his character before the other nations of the earth (26:16–19; cf. Ex 19:4–6). Although they live among the "nations" (*gôyim*), they are a "people" (*ʿam*) of Yahweh (27:9). As his people, they are the ones whom Yahweh redeemed, to whom he gave the land of promise as an inheritance, and through whom he intended to affect the world (9:26, 29; 21:8; 26:15; 32:9, 36, 43).

---

22. Merrill, *Deuteronomy*, 50.
23. G. H. Hall, *Deuteronomy* (Joplin, Mo.: College, 2000), 27.
24. Craigie, *Deuteronomy*, 37.

The Land

The land is a fundamental theme throughout Deuteronomy. God had promised the land to Israel's ancestors (Ge 12:7) and pledged to bring them into that land because of that divine commitment (4:37–38; 9:4–6). It is a land of abundant blessings (6:3; 8:7–10; 11:9; 26:9, 15; 27:3; 31:20). A key part of God's promise to his people is long tenure in that land (4:40; 5:16, 33; 6:2; 11:9; 22:7; 25:15; 32:47), where life will "go well" for them (4:40; 6:3, 18; 12:25, 28; 22:7). If Israel chooses rebellion, Yahweh will evict his people from this land of promise (4:26; 28:32, 63–66).

9. BIBLIOGRAPHY

Aharoni, Yohanan. *Land of the Bible: A Historical Geography*. Rev. ed. Philadelphia: Westminster, 1979.

Barker, Paul A. *The Triumph of Grace in Deuteronomy: Faithless Israel, Faithful Yahweh in Deuteronomy*. Waynesboro, Ga.: Paternoster, 2004.

———. "The Theology of Deuteronomy 27." *Tyndale Bulletin* 49 (1998): 277–303.

Beckwith, R. *The Old Testament Canon of the New Testament Church*. Grand Rapids: Eerdmans, 1985.

Biddle, Mark E. *Deuteronomy*. Smyth & Helwys Commentary. Macon, Ga.: Smyth & Helwys, 2003.

Block, Daniel I. "How Many Is God? An Investigation into the Meaning of Deuteronomy 6:4–5." *Journal of the Evangelical Theological Society* 47 (2004): 193–212.

Braulik, Georg. *Deuteronomium 1–16, 17*. Würzburg: Echter, 1986.

———. *Deuteronomium 16, 18–34, 12*. Würzburg: Echter, 1992.

———. "The Sequence of the Laws in Deuteronomy 12–26 and in the Decalogue." Pages 313–35 in *A Song of Power and the Power of Song: Essays on the Book of Deuteronomy*. Edited by Duane L. Christensen. Winona Lake, Ind.: Eisenbrauns, 1993.

Cairns, Ian. *Word and Presence: A Commentary on Deuteronomy*. International Theological Commentary. Grand Rapids: Eerdmans, 1992.

Christensen, Duane L. *Deuteronomy 1:1–21:9*. Word Biblical Commentary 6A. Nashville: Nelson, 2001.

———. *Deuteronomy 21:10–34:12*. Word Biblical Commentary 6B. Nashville: Nelson, 2002.

Craigie, P. *The Book of Deuteronomy*. New International Commentary on the Old Testament. Grand Rapids: Eerdmans, 1976.

De Vaux, Roland. *Ancient Israel*. 2 vols. New York: McGraw-Hill, 1965.

Driver, S. R. *A Critical and Exegetical Commentary on Deuteronomy*. International Critical Commentary. 3rd ed. Edinburgh: T&T Clark, 1901.

Grisanti, Michael A. "1 Kings." Pages 227–97 in vol. 2 of *The Bible Knowledge Word Study*. Edited by Eugene H. Merrill. Colorado Springs, Colo.: Cook, 2004.

———. "2 Kings." Pages 298–327 in vol. 2 of *The Bible Knowledge Word Study*. Edited by Eugene H. Merrill. Colorado Springs, Colo.: Cook, 2004.

———. "1 Samuel." Pages 123–72 in vol. 2 of *The Bible Knowledge Word Study*. Edited by Eugene H. Merrill. Colorado Springs, Colo.: Cook, 2004.

———. "2 Samuel." Pages 173–227 in vol. 2 of *The Bible Knowledge Word Study*. Edited by Eugene H. Merrill. Colorado Springs, Colo.: Cook, 2004.

———. "Inspiration, Inerrancy, and the Old Testament Canon: The Place of Textual Updating in an Inerrant View of Scripture." *Journal of the Evangelical Theological Society* 44 (2001): 577–98.

Hall, Gary H. *Deuteronomy*. Joplin, Mo.: College, 2000.

Harman, Allan. *Deuteronomy: The Commands of a Covenant God*. Ross-shire, Great Britain: Christian Focus, 2001.

Hartley, John E. *Leviticus*. Word Biblical Commentary 4. Dallas: Word, 1992.

Kalland, Earl. "Deuteronomy." Pages 3–235 in vol. 3 of *The Expositor's Bible Commentary*, first edition. Edited by Frank E. Gaebelein. Grand Rapids: Zondervan, 1992.

Kaufman, S. "The Structure of the Deuteronomic Law." *Maarav* 1–2 (1978–79): 105–58.

Keel, Othmar. *The Symbolism of the Biblical World: Ancient Near Eastern Iconography and the Book of Psalms*. Translated by Timothy J. Hallett. Winona Lake, Ind.: Eisenbrauns, 1997.

Keil, C. F. *The Fifth Book of Moses (Deuteronomy)*. In vol. 3 of Commentary on the Old Testament. Repr., Grand Rapids: Eerdmans, 1981.

Kline, Meredith G. *The Structure of Biblical Authority*. Rev. ed. Grand Rapids, Mich.: Eerdmans, 1975.

———. *Treaty of the Great King—The Covenant Structure of Deuteronomy: Studies and Commentary*. Grand Rapids: Eerdmans, 1963.

Lenchak, Timothy A. *"Choose Life!": A Rhetorical-Critical Investigation of Deuteronomy 28, 69–30, 20*. Analecta biblica 129. Rome: Pontifical Biblical Institute, 1993.

Lohfink, Norbert. *Das Hauptgebot: Eine Untersuchung literarischer Einleitungs-fragen zu Dtn 5–11*. Analecta biblica 20. Rome: Pontifical Biblical Institute, 1963.

Mayes, A. D. H. *Deuteronomy*. New Century Bible Commentary. Greenwood, S.C.: Attic, 1987.

McCarthy, Dennis J. "Notes on the Love of God in Deuteronomy and the Father-Son Relationship between Yahweh and Israel." *Catholic Biblical Quarterly* 27 (1965): 144–47.

———. *Treaty and Covenant: A Study in the Form in the Ancient Oriental Documents and in the Old Testament*. 2nd ed. Rome: Pontifical Biblical Institute, 1978.

McConville, J. G. *Deuteronomy*. Apollos Old Testament Commentary. Downers Grove, Ill.: InterVarsity Press, 2002.

Merrill, Eugene H. *Deuteronomy*. New American Commentary. Nashville: Broadman & Holman, 1994.

———. "Deuteronomy." Pages 441–522 in vol. 1 of *The Bible Knowledge Word Study*. Edited by Eugene H. Merrill. Colorado Springs, Colo.: Cook, 2004.

Milgrom, Jacob. *Leviticus 1–16*. Anchor Bible. New York: Doubleday, 1991.

———. *Leviticus 17–22*. Anchor Bible. New York: Doubleday, 2000.

Millar, J. G. *Now Choose Life! Theology and Ethics in Deuteronomy*. Grand Rapids: Eerdmans, 1998.

Miller, Patrick D. *Deuteronomy*. Interpretation. Louisville, Ky.: John Knox, 1990.

Moran, W. L., ed. and trans. *The Amarna Letters*. Baltimore: Johns Hopkins University Press, 1992.

Nelson, Richard. *Deuteronomy*. Old Testament Library. Louisville, Ky.: Westminster John Knox, 2002.

Ortlund, R. *Whoredom: God's Unfaithful Wife in Biblical Theology*. Grand Rapids: Eerdmans, 1996.

Phillips, Anthony. *Ancient Israel's Criminal Law: A New Approach to the Decalogue*. Oxford: Basil Blackwell, 1970.

———. *Deuteronomy*. Cambridge Bible Commentary. Cambridge: Cambridge University Press, 1973.

Ridderbos, J. *Deuteronomy*. Bible Student's Commentary. Translated by Ed M. van der Maas. Grand Rapids: Zondervan, 1984.

Taylor, Richard A. "1 Chronicles." Pages 329–77 in vol. 2 of *The Bible Knowledge Word Study*. Edited by Eugene H. Merrill. Colorado Springs, Colo.: Cook, 2004.

Thompson, J. *Deuteronomy*. Downers Grove, Ill.: InterVarsity Press, 1974.

Tigay, Jeffrey. *Deuteronomy*. JPS Torah Commentary. Philadelphia: Jewish Publication Society, 1996.

———. "Some Archaeological Notes on Deuteronomy." Pages 373–80 in *Pomegranates and Golden Bells: Studies in Biblical, Jewish, and Near Eastern Ritual, Law, and Literature in Honor of Jacob Milgrom*. Edited by D. Wright, D. Freedman, and A. Hurvitz. Winona Lake, Ind.: Eisenbrauns, 1995.

Vogt, Peter T. "Religious Concepts in the Theology of Deuteronomy: A Re-appraisal of Deuteronomic Theology and the Significance of Torah." Ph.D. diss., University of Gloucestershire, 2003.

Von Rad, Gerhard. *Deuteronomy*. Old Testament Library. Philadelphia: Westminster, 1966.

Walton, J. H., and M. B. Matthews. *Genesis–Deuteronomy*. IVP Bible Background Commentary. Downers Grove, Ill.: InterVarsity Press, 1997.

Weinfeld, Moshe. *Deuteronomy 1–11*. Anchor Bible. New York: Doubleday, 1991.

———. *Deuteronomy and the Deuteronomic School*. Winona Lake, Ind.: Eisenbrauns, 1992.

Wenham, G. J. *Genesis 1–15*. Word Biblical Commentary 1. Dallas: Word, 1987.

———. *Leviticus*. New International Commentary on the Old Testament. Grand Rapids: Eerdmans, 1979.

Wright, Christopher. *Deuteronomy*. New International Biblical Commentary. Peabody, Mass.: Hendrickson, 1996.

———. *God's People in God's Land: Family, Land, and Property in the Old Testament*. Grand Rapids: Eerdmans, 1990.

10. OUTLINE

Text and Exposition

I. GENERAL INTRODUCTION (PREAMBLE) (1:1–5)

OVERVIEW

Following the pattern of a bilateral covenantal treaty document (suzerain-vassal treaty; see Introduction), the book of Deuteronomy begins with a preamble. This introductory section provides the backdrop for the book of Deuteronomy, the parties involved, and other relevant information (elements commonly found in treaty documents). It provides the geographical and historical setting for Moses' covenantal message.

---

¹These are the words Moses spoke to all Israel in the desert east of the Jordan—that is, in the Arabah—opposite Suph, between Paran and Tophel, Laban, Hazeroth and Dizahab. ²(It takes eleven days to go from Horeb to Kadesh Barnea by the Mount Seir road.) ³In the fortieth year, on the first day of the eleventh month, Moses proclaimed to the Israelites all that the LORD had commanded him concerning them. ⁴This was after he had defeated Sihon king of the Amorites, who reigned in Heshbon, and at Edrei had defeated Og king of Bashan, who reigned in Ashtaroth. ⁵East of the Jordan in the territory of Moab, Moses began to expound this law, saying:

COMMENTARY

1 Almost forty years after the law was given at Sinai, Moses provides an exposition of that law to the surviving second-generation Israelites encamped at the edge of the Promised Land. As the covenantal mediator, Moses speaks "the words" (that God commanded him; v.3) to Israel. Although Moses indeed communicates through words, the term here signifies the covenantal text and its demands in a broad sense (cf. 1:18; 4:2; 6:6; 11:18; 30:14). Moses addresses these speeches to "all Israel," or rather representatives of the nation instead of the entire nation. Beyond this address, the material was intended for all Israel, in Moses' time and later, and would be accessible to all after it was committed to written form.

Moses provides three relatively clear geographical and topographical reference points, then six that are less clear. The "desert" (or wilderness) is a broad term for the opposite of urban and semiurban territory. It refers to actual desert as well as transitional semiarid land that is suitable for pasturage (Diamond, *NIDOTTE*, 4:520). The area on the eastern side of the Jordan River was a high plateau (ca. 3,500 ft above sea level) and served better

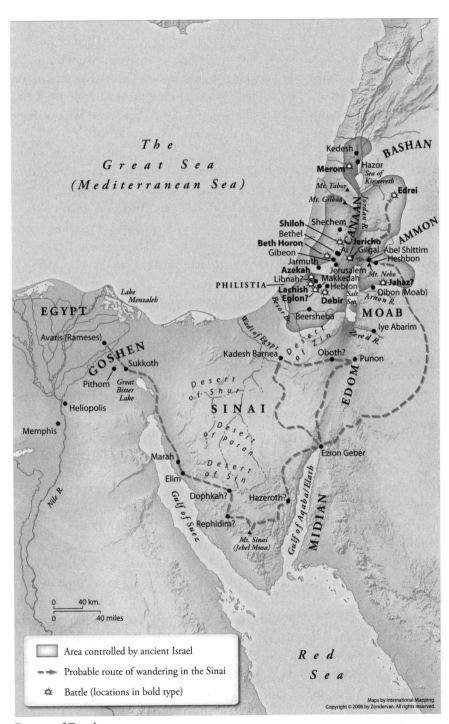

Route of Exodus

as pastureland than for raising crops. While the "Arabah" could signify a less than abundant region around a given city (Ge 21:14; 37:22), here it refers to a specific geographical region that follows a fault line in the earth that extends north–south through this region. The biblical writers call the depression or valley that extends along this fault line the "Arabah."

The phrase "opposite Suph" probably describes the part of the Arabah Moses had in view. Although some scholars regard Suph as a city in the area of Edom or Moab (Craigie, 90; Mayes, 114), the designation probably refers to the part of the Arabah that is near the Gulf of Elath, the eastern branch of the Red Sea (both are called *yam sûp*, "Red Sea"—Ex 10:19; 15:4, 22; "Gulf of Elath"—Nu 21:4; Dt 1:40; 2:1). Of the remaining five sites (see Tigay, *Deuteronomy*, xlv, 417–22, for a helpful overview of geographical references and a map), only Paran and Hazeroth can be identified with any confidence. "Paran" refers to much of the Sinai Peninsula and the southern region of the Negev (Nu 10:12; 12:16; 13:26), while "Hazeroth" has been identified with sites in southern or northeastern Sinai (Tigay, *Deuteronomy*, xlv, 419). Although a number of scholars locate these places on the route Israel took between Sinai and Kadesh Barnea (Kalland, 20; Merrill, *Deuteronomy*, 63), others identify them as places in the area around the Israelite encampment on the plains of Moab (Craigie, 90–91; Ridderbos, 52). The reference to Israel's journey from Sinai to Kadesh Barnea in the next verse favors the former alternative.

2 The Israelites took eleven days to journey from Sinai to Kadesh Barnea (ca. 140 miles apart). This time frame indicates the ruggedness of the terrain and serves as a clear contrast to the almost forty years of wilderness wandering occasioned

by their rebellion at Kadesh (see comments on 1:26–40). "Mount Seir" serves as a broad reference for the region of Seir or Edom (Aharoni, 40). "Horeb" is an alternative term for "Sinai" favored by the book of Deuteronomy, in which "Horeb" occurs nine times (1:2, 6, 19; 4:10, 15; 5:2; 9:8; 18:16; 29:1), compared with a single instance of "Sinai" (33:2).

3 Moses begins addressing the Israelites slightly less than forty years (thirty-nine years, nine months, sixteen days) after they departed from Egypt (first year, first month, and fifteenth day — the day after their first Passover celebration; Ex 12:18), ca. 1406 BC (see Introduction). Since the Israelite crossing of the Jordan River (Jos 4:19 — forty-first year, first month, tenth day) represented the beginning of the conquest of Canaan, the transition from Moses to Joshua (with Moses preaching the content of Deuteronomy, his death, burial, and the transferral of leadership to Joshua) occurred within about one and one-third months of Moses' addressing the Israelites with this material.

4 In addition to this calendric information, Moses begins this address after the Israelite conquest of two Amorite kings, Sihon and Og (3:8; 4:47; cf. Nu 21; see comments on 2:26–3:11).

5 The chiastic structure of these verses (see Craigie, 92, n. 17; Tigay, *Deuteronomy*, 3, for different elements of this chiasm) gives emphasis to the geographical, chronological, and theological backdrop for Deuteronomy. In addition to the geographical and chronological features already discussed (see above), these verses prepare the way for the following context. They introduce two pivotal themes: the disastrous effects of not trusting God and the overwhelming victory provided by God to those who trust him.

A These are the words Moses spoke

  B In the desert east of the Jordan

    C Kadesh Barnea—a place of judgment because of Israel's rejection of God's intervention

      D The time of Moses' address: fortieth year, on the first day of the eleventh month

    C' Sihon and Og—victory because of Israel's reliance on God's intervention

  B' East of the Jordan in the territory of Moab

A' Moses began to expound this law, saying:

"This law," along with "the words" (1:1), refers in a broad sense to the covenantal document as a whole (see Notes on 4:44) and represents all that the Lord commanded (1:3). The "law" served as the foundation for Israel's covenantal relationship with Yahweh. In his addresses to the Israelites, Moses provides an exposition of "this law." Although the verb *bʾr* can mean to write or inscribe something clearly (27:8; Hab 2:2), here it signifies Moses' explanation or elucidation of the Law (*HALOT*, 106; cf. Satterthwaite, *NIDOTTE*, 1:578).

It is essential for any reader of Deuteronomy to understand that this book represents an exposition of the law, which God had already given at Sinai, and not a second giving of the law. It does not serve as a simple repetition of the law, nor does it constitute a contradiction of those divine standards. Moses provides an exposition of God's law as a means of preparing God's children for the daunting task that lay before them.

NOTES

1, 5 The expression הַדְּבָרִים (*haddᵉbārîm*, "the words") and related ones can also refer to individual stipulations (12:28; 15:15; 24:18, 22) as well as to the Decalogue as a whole (4:10, 13, 36; 5:5, 22; 9:10; 10:2, 4).

The expression בְּעֵבֶר הַיַּרְדֵּן (*bᵉʿēber hayyardēn*, "on the other side of the Jordan") can refer to the territory to the east (1:1, 5; 3:8; 4:41, 46–47; Jos 1:14–15; etc.) or to the west (Dt 3:20, 25; 11:30; Jos 9:1; etc.) of the Jordan River. Many have argued that the expression requires that the writer be located on the opposite side of the river. Consequently, this phrase would serve as an example of a post-Mosaic expression. Although this argument is plausible, the usage of this expression by the same author (e.g., Jos 1:14–15; 9:1) suggests that it is simply a regional reference whose precise connotation the immediate context makes clear. The phrase is a technical geographical expression for the area near the Jordan River that does not make explicit the location of the speaker/writer (cf. B. Gemser, "*Bᵉʿēber Hajjardēn*: In Jordan's Borderland," *VT* 2 [1952]: 355).

II. HISTORICAL RETROSPECT (1:6–4:49)

OVERVIEW

Moses reviews the manner in which the Lord brought Israel safely through the wilderness wanderings (the consequence of their faithless rebellion at Kadesh Barnea) and assisted them in the conquest of Heshbon and Bashan, and he exhorts the nation once again to obey the Lord and worship him alone.

This historical overview has two parts. In the section's first three chapters, Moses summarizes Israel's experiences from the time of lengthy encampment at Mount Sinai to the time depicted by the book of Deuteronomy. In ch. 4, building on that presentation of God's expectations of his chosen people and the many examples of his intervention in their behalf, Moses exhorts God's people to obey God's demands sincerely and wholeheartedly, i.e., to render total allegiance to their covenantal Lord.

These chapters provide a backward and a forward look (which both had implications for Moses' day). In conjunction with Deuteronomy's structure (paralleling a covenantal treaty document), Moses provides this brief overview as a way of reviewing the history of the relationship between the divine suzerain (Yahweh) and his national vassal (Israel). As was the custom in ancient Near Eastern treaties, the preamble and the historical review demonstrated the past relationship of the suzerain and his vassal to prepare the nation for the stipulation section, in which the suzerain makes demands of the vassal. This part of the treaty document clearly demonstrates that the suzerain has the right to make these demands of them and can expect their unquestioned obedience. This historical prologue

also gives credence to God's ability to bring to pass all that he has promised.

This historical section also lays emphasis on Yahweh's faithfulness. Moses makes it clear that history is the sphere in which God works out the fulfillment of his promises. His provision of victory over Israel's enemies (1:28; 2:24–25; 30) and his care for his covenantal nation during their wilderness wanderings (1:31; 2:6–7) serve as part of his fulfillment of his oath to their ancestors that he would bring Israel into this landed inheritance (1:8, 21, 35).

In his delineation of Israel's experiences since the time of their encampment at Sinai, Moses frankly examines Israel's repeated acts of faithlessness and the dire consequences their conduct occasioned. Israel's refusal to trust in God's promise to deliver the land of Canaan into their hands (regardless of its powerful defenses) indicated the capriciousness of the human heart. In spite of all that Yahweh had done up to the time of Israel's rebellion at Kadesh Barnea, his people rebelled against him and declared that God hated them (1:26–27). Because of their treacherous conduct, Israel experienced the full force of God's anger (1:34, 37; 2:14–15; 3:26; 4:21, 24–25) and faced divine rejection of sorts. God withdrew his presence (1:42) and closed his ears to their cries (1:45; 3:26).

Finally, these chapters also have a forward look. Moses is not simply filling space with encyclopedic information; rather, he intends that this overview of Israel's experience since their encampment at Sinai will have clear implications for their future attitudes and conduct. Remembering and not forgetting (see comments and Note on 4:9–10) does not simply represent the presence or absence of cognitive activity but signifies life-transforming remembrances of God's character and activity. Moses provides this overview to prepare God's servant-nation for the great challenge ahead of them. They will be able to conquer the land of Canaan and live in accordance with God's expectations only if they live in the light of God's awesome power and majesty. God's promise and past faithfulness provide the grounds to trust him in the present and future (1:32), and God's swift and harsh response to rebellion serves as a warning against rebellion and unbelief in the days to come.

A. Yahweh's Past Dealings with Israel (from Horeb to the Jordan River) (1:6–3:29)

OVERVIEW

Moses demonstrates that the Lord was consistently faithful to his chosen people from the time of their encampment at Sinai onward (when he gave them their national foundation—his law). He did so in spite of their abhorrent rebellion at Kadesh Barnea and in the face of the threat of enemy nations. The historical scope of these chapters extends from Israel's encampment at Sinai to their gathering on the plains of Moab. The ratification of the covenant at Sinai served as the beginning of Israel's existence as a nation. Throughout these chapters Moses depicts Yahweh as the One orchestrating every historical event.

1. Events at Horeb (1:6–18)

OVERVIEW

After commanding Israel to break camp and leave Sinai for the Promised Land and to assist Moses in effective leadership, the Lord exhorted Moses to appoint several respected men from each tribe to function as his subordinates.

a. Yahweh Exhorts Israel to Advance toward Canaan (1:6–8)

[6]The LORD our God said to us at Horeb, "You have stayed long enough at this mountain. [7]Break camp and advance into the hill country of the Amorites; go to all the neighboring peoples in the Arabah, in the mountains, in the western foothills, in the Negev and along the coast, to the land of the Canaanites and to Lebanon, as far as the great river, the Euphrates. [8]See, I have given you this land. Go in and take possession of the land that the LORD swore he would give to your fathers — to Abraham, Isaac and Jacob — and to their descendants after them."

COMMENTARY

6 Moses begins this historical overview with Israel's encampment at Sinai/Horeb. The initial giving of the law at Sinai provides the theological backdrop for Moses' call for covenantal renewal in Deuteronomy. After God's children spent about a year camped at the base of Mount Sinai, God exhorted them to continue their journey toward the land of promise.

7 As part of his command that the Israelites break camp and travel toward Canaan, the Lord provided an overview of the principal geographical divisions of that region (see Aharoni, 41–42, for a summary of those terms). The land described covers an area that exceeds even the boundaries of Israel during the glorious days of David and Solomon. The "hill country of the Amorites" and the "land of the Canaanites" respectively refer to the central hill country and the coastal area (cf. Nu 13:29), inhabited by the two people groups customarily referenced in these geographical descriptions. "Canaanites" serves as an umbrella term for the diverse peoples who inhabited the land of Canaan.

After Yahweh named "the hill country of the Amorites," he referred to the various groups of people who inhabited the land in general. In that regard, God methodically cited four divisions of Canaan: the Arabah (primarily the Jordan Rift Valley), Shephelah (the transitional region between the hill country of Judah and the coastal region to the west), Negev (the arid region in southern Palestine), and coast (possibly referring to the coastline farther to the north, in the area of Phoenicia, since he seems to refer to the Canaanite coast with the phrase "land of the Canaanites"). The region of Lebanon and the Euphrates River serve as the far northern boundaries for the land of promise. This territorial overview approximates the promise given to Abraham in Genesis 15:18: "from the river

of Egypt to the great river, the river Euphrates" (cf. Ex 23:31; Dt 11:24).

8 As the foundation for his command that Israel depart from Sinai and travel toward the Land of Promise, the Lord reaffirmed his promise, originally made to Abraham, Isaac, and Jacob, that he would indeed enable them to take possession of the land of Canaan.

Moses presents both sides of the conquest endeavor: God's part and Israel's part. God "set before" Israel this land of promise. The unique combination of the verb "to give" (*ntn*) and the preposition "before" (*lipnê*) highlights God's action of placing the land of promise before the nation of Israel (see Note). Yahweh first promised this land to Abraham (as a pledge) in Genesis 12:7. His reaffirmation of this promise to Abraham (Ge 15:18) and Jacob (28:13–15) regarded this promise as a reality ("I have given/I gave"). In his reaffirmation to Jacob (Ge 35:12), the Lord affirmed that the land he *gave* to Abraham and Isaac he *will give* to Jacob and his descendants. The Lord promised this land to Abraham and his descendants by oath (1:8—"the land that the LORD swore he would give").

In Moses' day, God is placing the land of promise at the disposal of the Israelites, the anticipated descendants of Abraham, Isaac, and Jacob. In conjunction with the interjection "See," Yahweh is declaring: "I hereby give/place ..." (Weinfeld, *Deuteronomy 1–11*, 134).

God required that Israel "take possession" of this land of promise. Although this verb can signify a peaceful occupation of land (cf. Pss 25:13; 37:9), in covenantal contexts it highlights taking possession of a land by dispossessing the former inhabitants (Dt 4:14, 26; 6:1; 7:1; 8:1; 11:8 et al.). Just as God directed other nations to "possess" certain lands (2:12, 21–22),

God demands that Israel take possession of what he has allotted to them. Although taking possession of a land relates to Israel's inheriting the land, the verb *nḥl* more precisely highlights that nuance (1:38; 3:28). God's servant-nation was not merely taking land that belonged to another nation but was receiving "the land as gift from its divine owner, coming into their own rightful claim as vassals who work the royal estate of the Lord their God (cf. 1:39; 3:20; 10:11; Josh 1:15; 21:43)" (Merrill, *Deuteronomy*, 68).

NOTE

8 The juxtaposition of נָתַתִּי לִפְנֵיכֶם (*nātattî lipnêkem*, "I have set … before you")—the verb נתן (*ntn*) and the preposition לִפְנֵי—occurs twenty-eight times in the OT. In all but three occurrences God serves as the subject of the action. (In three instances Abraham [Ge 18:8], Elisha [2Ki 4:44], or Jeremiah [Jer 35:5] sets food before someone present.) In the political and military realm, God sets Sihon before Israel (Dt 2:31), threatens to give Jewish exiles to a conquering nation (1Ki 8:46 = 2Ch 6:36; Jer 15:9), and promises to give nations to the disposal of Cyrus (Isa 41:2). As the covenantal Lord, he is the dispenser of land (Dt 1:8; Ne 9:35), his law (Dt 4:8; 11:32; 1Ki 9:6 = 2Ch 7:19; Jer 9:13 [12]; 26:4; 44:10; Da 9:10), blessings and curses (Dt 11:26; 30:1, 15, 19; Jer 21:8), general provision for Israel (Eze 16:19), and the right to bring judgment against his chosen nation (Eze 23:24). In the ceremonial realm, he appoints Levites to their position (1Ch 16:4) and sets a certain stone before Joshua the high priest (Zec 3:9). The expression seems to emphasize what God makes available and accessible.

Regarding the phrase אֲשֶׁר נִשְׁבַּע יְהוָה (*ʾ ašer nišbaʿ yhwh*, "that Yahweh swore"), and unlike in contemporary vernacular usage, "swearing" in the OT had nothing to do with foul language but communicated a person's assurance that he will keep his promise or that a certain course of events will take place. God swore "by himself" or "by his name" to emphasize the surety of something's happening (Jer 22:5; 44:26; 49:13). The promised event was as sure as God's character was absolutely reliable. The expression "that [Yahweh or a personal pronoun referring to him] swore" occurs twenty-nine times in Deuteronomy. It refers to the Promised Land in twenty instances (1:8, 35; 6:10, 18, 23; 7:13; 8:1; 10:11; 11:9, 21; 19:8; 26:3, 15; 28:11; 30:20; 31:7, 20–21, 23; 34:4; cf. Ex 33:1; Nu 14:23; 32:11; Jer 11:5). It also emphasizes God's promise of the covenant (Dt 4:31; 7:8, 12; 8:18; 9:5), judgment (2:14), compassion (13:17 [18]), and his unique relationship with Israel (28:9; 29:13). This statement serves as a reminder to Israel that he remains committed to his promise to his chosen people. God's covenantal nation can rely on him to do exactly as he promised or swore.

b. Yahweh Commands Moses to Appoint Qualified Leaders (1:9–18)

OVERVIEW

Because of the increasing burden of Moses' position of leadership, the Lord commanded him to appoint several qualified men (selected by their respective tribes) to judicial offices. In this section Moses recognizes the need for new leadership (vv.9–12), chooses those leaders (vv.13–15), and gives them a charge (vv. 16–18). Although some scholars view this section as a digression (because 1:8 flows into 1:19 seamlessly), it does prepare the reader (and Moses' audience) for the reality before them. The breadth of the land into which they are about to enter (the wilderness initially and the land of Canaan in Deuteronomy) and the growing population of Israel (a fulfillment of Yahweh's promise to them) provide the occasion for this appointment of leaders to serve as Moses' assistants. It will also pave the way for a smoother transition once Moses passes off the scene. Finally, Yahweh's ultimate supremacy receives recognition once again (1:17, "judgment belongs to God"). Moses and these newly appointed leaders serve in submission to Yahweh's authority.

---

⁹At that time I said to you, "You are too heavy a burden for me to carry alone. ¹⁰The LORD your God has increased your numbers so that today you are as many as the stars in the sky. ¹¹May the LORD, the God of your fathers, increase you a thousand times and bless you as he has promised! ¹²But how can I bear your problems and your burdens and your disputes all by myself?

¹³Choose some wise, understanding and respected men from each of your tribes, and I will set them over you." ¹⁴You answered me, "What you propose to do is good." ¹⁵So I took the leading men of your tribes, wise and respected men, and appointed them to have authority over you — as commanders of thousands, of hundreds, of fifties and of tens and as tribal officials.

¹⁶And I charged your judges at that time: Hear the disputes between your brothers and judge fairly, whether the case is between brother Israelites or between one of them and an alien. ¹⁷Do not show partiality in judging; hear both small and great alike. Do not be afraid of any man, for judgment belongs to God. Bring me any case too hard for you, and I will hear it. ¹⁸And at that time I told you everything you were to do.

COMMENTARY

9–10 Moses reminds Israel that during their tenure at Mount Horeb he faced the challenge of providing efficient leadership for the numerically growing Israelites (cf. Ex 18:13–27; Nu 11:11–17). The fact that Israel had become too heavy a burden for Moses was not a problem about which Moses was complaining, but a reality that demonstrated Yahweh's faithfulness to his promises (cf. Ge 15:5; 17:2; Dt 10:22; 26:5).

11–12 The growing population of Israel has not discouraged Moses; on the contrary, he prays that God will cause them to multiply even more. In vv. 10–11 he uses hyperbolic language ("as many as the stars in the sky," "increase you a thousand times") to highlight his confidence that Yahweh not only has been faithful to his promise to Abraham but will continue to do so (cf. Ge 22:17; 26:4; Ex 32:13; Dt 28:62). This language provides a clear connection between Israel's present situation and Yahweh's original commitment in the Abrahamic covenant.

Moses describes the overwhelming legislative and judicial load he faced with three terms: problems, burdens, and disputes. The noun translated "problems" only occurs in one other passage (Isa 1:14), where it designates the burdensome nature of Israel's false worship. The term for their "disputes" (*rîb*) occurs in Exodus 17:7 to describe Israel's complaining, but here the word concerns their legal disputes (vv.16–18). Moses was well aware of the weight of leadership, having experienced their murmuring, complaining, and arguing.

13–14 Moses requested that the Israelites choose from their midst men who were qualified to function as potential rulers to serve under Moses' direction. Even though the parallel account in Exodus 18:21, 24 mentions that Moses selected the appointees, this passage demonstrates that his choices were based on the recommendation of the people. The people recognize the value of Moses' proposal.

Moses states three qualifications for these potential leaders: wisdom, understanding, and respectedness. Some interpreters unnecessarily contrast these qualifications with those found in Exodus 18:21 ("men who fear God, trustworthy men who hate dishonest gain"). The previously stated, more virtue-oriented requirements are assumed in the qualifications stated here and are taken up in the following verses (1:16–17). Intelligence or understanding was foundational to being able to adjudicate disputes. The skill involved in taking knowledge and helpfully applying it to concrete situations is wisdom (cf. others who utilized discernment and discretion in their governance — Joseph (Ge 41:33, 39); David (2Sa 14:20); and

Solomon (1Ki 2:9; 3:12; 5:12); cf. Merrill, "Deuteronomy," 442). Since these two qualifications are not theoretical, their presence assumes some life experience. These appointees must also have a good reputation ("known"); they had to be recognized by the community and be people in whom others had confidence. These leaders had to have passed the test of close scrutiny and enjoy respect by their peers.

15 Moses took those men who fit the required qualifications and gave them authority over various groups of people (descending in size). These leaders functioned in a civil and military capacity. The "tribal officials" assisted the "commanders" by communicating and implementing the decisions they made (McConville, 66).

16–18 Moses gave these leaders clear instructions to guide them in rendering judgments. Regardless of whether they faced a dispute between fellow Israelites or between an Israelite and an alien (a non-Israelite who lived among the Israelites), they were to resolve the dispute fairly (v.16). They were also to render their judicial decisions without partiality (lit., "do not regard faces"; cf. Dt 16:19; Pr 24:23; 28:21). The reputation or social standing of the people bringing disputes to the leaders was to play no role in the decision they made, nor was it to affect the cases they allowed to come before them (v.17a). Since justice is God's domain, these leaders were not to allow fear of any person to affect their judicial decisions (v.17b). As the perfectly just God, the Lord would protect his representatives as well as hold them accountable for their conduct. Since God provides the ultimate standard of justice, adjudicating these cases was more than a legal process — the task represented a process that had theological significance. These judges were to send to Moses any case that exceeded their legal expertise or ability (v.17c).

NOTES

9, 18 The expression בָּעֵת הַהִוא (*bāʿēt hahiwʾ*, "at that time") opens and closes this section, thus forming an inclusio (cf. 1:16; 2:34; 3:4, 8, 12, 18, 21, 23; 4:14; 9:20; 10:1, 8). Throughout chs. 1–11 this phrase usually introduces a digression, material that does not advance the narrative but serves an important purpose.

10 The word הַיּוֹם (*hayyôm*, "today") occurs over ninety times in Deuteronomy and serves as a rhetorical device to signify the idea of contemporaneity (S. DeVries, *Yesterday, Today and Tomorrow* [Grand Rapids: Eerdmans, 1975], 45–47). In a number of instances this use of "today" serves to epitomize the past, present, and future (ibid., 253–55). In this sense, the present is intentionally and firmly linked with the past day and has significant implications for the future (based on the decision Israel makes; ibid., 275).

13 "Wise" (חָכָם, *ḥākām*; GK 2682) and "understanding" (נָבוֹן, *nābôn*; GK 1067) occur as synonyms and might represent a hendiadys meaning "very wise" (Merrill, *Deuteronomy*, 69). The words occur as synonyms in a number of passages (Ge 41:33, 39; 1Ki 3:12; Job 28:28; Pr 1:5; 4:5, 7; 9:10; 16:16, 21; 17:28; 18:15; Isa 5:21; Jer 4:22).

15 The term רָאשִׁים (*rāʾšîm*, "heads") occurs once in 1:13 and twice in 1:15: (lit.) "I will appoint them as your *heads* … I took the *heads* of your tribes … set them as *heads* over you." Since 1:15 deals with Moses' making these men leaders or "heads" among the Israelites, some people have struggled with the first occurrence of the term in v.15. A solution is to regard the first occurrence of the term as proleptic, i.e., used by Moses in view of their imminent appointment to that task.

Moses appoints these leaders to function as "commanders" (שַׂר, *śar*; GK 8569) and "officials" (שׁוֹטֵר, *šōṭēr*; GK 8853). These terms commonly signify military leaders, but the surrounding context deals primarily with judicial officials. These men likely functioned in a military and a civil/judicial capacity. The term שַׂר (*śar*) originally designated a chieftan or clan leader, but it can also refer to a military leader (Ge 21:22; Jdg 4:7; 7:25; 8:3; 1Sa 18:30; 1Ki 15:20; Baker/Nel, *NIDOTTE*, 3:1295). The word occurs in a broad sense for an "official" in 1 Kings 4:2. Although this noun refers to Assyrian leaders as kings (Isa 10:8), it more frequently refers to various kinds of advisers or underlings (Ge 12:15; 1Ch 22:17; Est 1:18; Jer 24:1).

The second term, שׁוֹטֵר (*šōṭēr*), is difficult to translate more precisely than "officials." It refers to Egyptian overseers (Ex 5:6, 10, 14–19), subofficials of the seventy elders of Israel (Nu 11:16), who at times were involved in military affairs (Dt 20:5–9; Jos 1:10; 3:2). This noun appears to derive from the Akkadian verb *šṭr*, "to write" (Tigay, *Deuteronomy*, 12). If such is in fact the case, these officials may have provided to the judges assistance with "secretarial" work (cf. Dt 16:18; as in Egypt [Weinfeld, *Deuteronomy 1–11*, 138]).

16 A גֵּר (*gēr*; GK 1731), or "alien," belonged to a class of people who traveled with Israel from Egypt to the Promised Land but who did not receive a landed inheritance. Without the blessing of a landed allotment and family connections, aliens (like orphans and widows) were vulnerable to exploitation and oppression (Ex 22:21; Lev 19:33–34; 23:22; Dt 24:17, 19; 27:19; Wright, *Deuteronomy*, 28; cf. Wright, *God's People*, 58–64, 99–103).

2. Events at Kadesh Barnea (1:19–46)

OVERVIEW

After arriving in Kadesh Barnea (1:19), Moses commissioned twelve spies to survey the Promised Land, but ten of them brought back a discouraging report, which caused the children of Israel to reject the Lord's promise of a victorious conquest. Consequently, God's punishment on these rebels was that no adult from that generation (except Joshua and Caleb) would enter the land. Their rebellious attempt to enter Canaan on their own strength was thwarted by the Amorites.

a. Israel Arrives at Kadesh Barnea and Sends Out the Spies (1:19–25)

¹⁹Then, as the LORD our God commanded us, we set out from Horeb and went toward the hill country of the Amorites through all that vast and dreadful desert that you have seen, and so we reached Kadesh Barnea. ²⁰Then I said to you, "You have reached the hill country of the Amorites, which the LORD our God is giving us. ²¹See, the LORD your God has given you the land. Go up and take possession of it as the LORD, the God of your fathers, told you. Do not be afraid; do not be discouraged."

²²Then all of you came to me and said, "Let us send men ahead to spy out the land for us and bring back a report about the route we are to take and the towns we will come to."

²³The idea seemed good to me; so I selected twelve of you, one man from each tribe. ²⁴They left and went up into the hill country, and came to the Valley of Eshcol and explored it. ²⁵Taking with them some of the fruit of the land, they brought it down to us and reported, "It is a good land that the LORD our God is giving us."

COMMENTARY

19 In accordance with the Lord's command (cf. comments on 1:8), the Israelites departed from the area around Horeb and set out for the "hill country of the Amorites" (cf. comments on 1:7). Kadesh Barnea, an eleven-day journey from Horeb (see comments on 1:2), was a stopping-off point on their way north to the Promised Land (at the southern perimeter of Canaan). On this journey Israel passed through the "vast and dreadful wilderness" (cf. 8:15; Nu 11:1–12:16). This dry and dusty journey should have heightened Israel's anticipation of the land awaiting them. God's provision of sustenance throughout this journey should have served to deepen their ability to take God at his word (cf. 1:31).

20-21 Moses told the Israelites that the Lord "is giving" (or "about to give"; 1:20) and "has given" (1:21) them the land of the Amorites. The present reality of the land's being given by the Lord to Israel is based on God's perspective (in the light of Yahweh's covenantal promise of the land, Ge 13:14-17) that this gift is an accomplished fact. Only Israel's actual occupation of that Land of Promise awaited fulfillment. In that light, Moses commanded the Israelites to enact this theological reality by taking possession of this divine stewardship. Reference to "the LORD, the God of your fathers" cements the link between the commanded conquest of the land of Canaan and God's past promises to Abraham, Isaac, and Jacob (Ge 12:1; 13:14-17; 15:18-21; 17:8; 26:3-4; 48:3). Moses exhorted God's people to be courageous ("do not be afraid, do not be discouraged") in light of the fact that Yahweh himself had promised this land to them.

In v.21 the narrative shifts from the plural to the singular (cf. 1:31), and then in v.22 it shifts back to the plural. This transition between plural and singular forms (with no clear textual rationale) has occasioned various explanations. Christensen (*Deuteronomy 1:1-21:9*, ci) relates this "number" switch (*Numeruswechsel*) to the suggestion that Deuteronomy (or some of it) was composed for a musical reading. (He regards the switches as structural markers; see ibid., xcix-c, for a bibliography on this debate.) Lohfink (239-60, esp. 246-51) suggested that the singular sections are paraenetic (preaching) in character while the verses with plural forms are primarily historical in orientation. Switching back and forth would stimulate the attention of the audience.

Others have argued that this change in number indicates the literary development of the book of Deuteronomy (the result of a compilation of various sources; e.g., H. Cazelles, "Passages in the Singular within Discourse in the Plural of Dt. 1-4," *CBQ*

29 [1967]: 207-19), but most find this explanation unacceptable and unnecessary (cf. Driver, 21). This kind of switching from plural to singular and back also occurs in various ancient Near Eastern treaties (K. Kitchen, "Ancient Orient, 'Deuteronism,' and the Old Testament," in *New Perspectives on the Old Testament* [ed. J. B. Payne; Waco, Tex.: Word, 1970], 4-5). It appears best to regard these changes from plural to singular and back to plural as intentional changes by the author to emphasize the individual's responsibility in the midst of a passage that addresses a larger group (cf. Driver, 21). McConville, 57, suggests these switches are common features of "Deuteronomic discourse."

22 The people encouraged Moses to enlist several men to spy out the land before them so that they could better plan their route through that region and see the size and disposition of enemy forces they would face there. Although the Numbers account (Nu 13:1-2) affirms that Moses received this command from Yahweh, several scholars have proposed that the people first suggested it, and after receiving the Lord's approval Moses put the plan into action (cf. Merrill, *Deuteronomy*, 73; Craigie, 101).

23-25 Moses selected one leader from each tribe of Israel to investigate the land to their north (cf. Nu 13:3-16). They explored several regions of the land of Canaan (see 13:17-25 for a more detailed summary), but Moses here focuses on their discovery of abundant fruit in the "valley of Eschol" (a fertile valley apparently near Hebron, an area still known for vineyards). The fruit these spies brought back to the Israelite encampment provided clear and tangible evidence that the land God had promised to them and was "giving them" was a "good land," i.e., a land flowing "with milk and honey" (Nu 13:27; see comments and Note on Dt 6:3). The return to a present tense verb form highlights the fact that this divine reality was not yet a practical one.

NOTE

21 The exhortation אַל־תִּירָא וְאַל־תֵּחָת (ʾal-tîrāʾ wᵉʾal-tēḥāt, "do not fear and do not be discouraged") occurs repeatedly in the OT as a word of encouragement from Yahweh to his people or to one of his servants in the face of an overwhelming dilemma (Dt 31:8; Jos 8:1; Isa 51:7; Jer 23:4; 30:10; 46:27; Eze 2:6; 3:9; 2Ch 20:15, 17) or from a ruler to his military forces (Jos 10:25; 2Ch 32:7) or a regal descendant (1Ch 22:13; 28:20). Although the first verb (ירא, yrʾ; GK 3707) often connotes the reverential awe humans should have for Yahweh (positive), it also occurs negatively concerning a fear that focuses on human weakness and inability in the face of seemingly insurmountable obstacles (Taylor, "1 Chronicles," 368). The second verb (חתת, ḥtt; GK 3169) means "to be shattered" or "be filled with terror" (*HALOT*, 365). It refers to a sense of dismay over challenges that appear to exceed one's ability to cope. Because of Yahweh's choice of and promises to his chosen people, such fear is unnecessary.

b. Israel's Rebellion against the Lord (1:26–33)

²⁶But you were unwilling to go up; you rebelled against the command of the LORD your God. ²⁷You grumbled in your tents and said, "The LORD hates us; so he brought us out of Egypt to deliver us into the hands of the Amorites to destroy us. ²⁸Where can we go? Our brothers have made us lose heart. They say, 'The people are stronger and taller than we are; the cities are large, with walls up to the sky. We even saw the Anakites there.'"

²⁹Then I said to you, "Do not be terrified; do not be afraid of them. ³⁰The LORD your God, who is going before you, will fight for you, as he did for you in Egypt, before your very eyes, ³¹and in the desert. There you saw how the LORD your God carried you, as a father carries his son, all the way you went until you reached this place."

³²In spite of this, you did not trust in the LORD your God, ³³who went ahead of you on your journey, in fire by night and in a cloud by day, to search out places for you to camp and to show you the way you should go.

COMMENTARY

26–28 In spite of God's command that Israel should conquer Canaan, God's promise of the land (Ge 12:1), and the recent evidence of the land's abundance (Dt 1:25), Israel was unwilling to proceed. This refusal to move forward toward Canaan represented nothing less than covenantal treachery, an abhorrent offense against their loving cov-

enantal Lord. The parallel account in Numbers 13 (vv.25–29) provides a fuller rendition of the spies' account, which focuses on the powerful inhabitants and their fortified cities. Regardless of the military likelihood of an Israelite victory over Canaan, Israel's refusal to believe that their faithful covenantal Lord would and could give them a sweeping victory over the Canaanites signifies a practical denial of the many acts of deliverance carried out by Yahweh in their behalf already.

While grumbling about the unfairness of this task Yahweh had set before them (the conquest of Canaan), the Israelites (the frequent recipients of God's redemptive intervention) accused God of hating them (1:27)! They claimed the Lord had brought them to this barren wilderness to exterminate them at the hands of the Amorites. The Israelites' use of this term, "hate" has clear covenantal overtones (cf. Merrill, *Deuteronomy*, 75–76). Throughout Deuteronomy Moses insisted that Yahweh acted in their behalf because he loved them (4:37; 7:8). In the Ten Commandments, those who love Yahweh are those who are wholeheartedly committed to living in conformity with God's covenantal expectations, and those who hate Yahweh want nothing to do with that covenantal relationship (Ex 20:5–6; see Note on Dt 5:9). Rather than "giving" them the Land of Promise, they believed that the Lord intended to "give" them over to the Amorites. Instead of heeding Moses' exhortation that they not fear or be discouraged (1:21), the people became frightened by the report of ten of the spies Moses had commissioned—frightened to the point that they preferred to rebel against Yahweh's authority.

29–31 Moses once again exhorted the Israelites to put away their fear (v.29). The basis for his exhortation is the fact that Yahweh is their beloved God, who would go before them and fight on their behalf against their enemies (cf. 20:3–4; 31:6; Jos 1:9). This was not just their battle, it was also and

primarily Yahweh's. He had sent Israel on this mission and had ordained the land of Canaan as the future dwelling place of his servant-nation (Ge 12:1; 13:14–17). Besides the fact that his divine power stood behind them, Yahweh had already given them clear demonstrations of his willingness to fight on their behalf, both in Egypt (through the ten plagues [Ex 7:4–5; 12:29; 13:3, 14–15]) and during their wilderness wanderings (through the crossing of the Red Sea and the battle against the Amalekites [Ex 14:4, 13–14; 15:1–18; 17:8–16; Nu 10:35]).

Moses likens Yahweh's care for Israel to a father's compassionate treatment of his son (1:31; cf. 8:5; 14:1; Jer 3:4; Hos 11:1–4). Not only does this familial language signify the intimacy of a father-son relationship, but it also highlights the covenantal relationship that existed between Yahweh and Israel. In various ancient Near Eastern treaties, the one who established a covenant would be the "father" and the recipient would be the "son" (McCarthy, "Notes on the Love of God," 144–47).

32–33 In spite of repeated demonstrations of God's faithfulness to his promises, Israel refused to believe that Yahweh was able and willing to orchestrate a victory over Israel's foes in Canaan (1:32). Since their departure from Egypt, the Lord had provided infallible guidance through a barren wilderness, where the wrong turn meant certain death. He had gone before them to guide them and locate ideal places for them to set up camp (1:33). Israel's refusal to believe God was not prudence in the face of an unwise venture but rebellion. Israel's belligerence exhausted his patience and occasioned severe divine judgment.

NOTES

26 Although the root of the verb וַתַּמְרוּ (*wattamrû*, "and you rebelled"; root מרה, *mrh*) can refer to rebellion in a noncovenantal context (e.g., a rebellious son [21:18, 20]), in all but three passages it refers to Israel's tragic rebellion against their gracious Lord. Its occurrences address Israel's treacherous conduct following

Yahweh's deliverance of them from Egypt (Ps 107:11; Isa 63:10) or at the time of their moral decline leading to exile (Isa 1:20; Jer 4:17; 5:23; La 1:18, 20; 3:42; Eze 5:6). The juxtaposition of this verb with the expression "command of Yahweh" (פִּי יהוה, *pî yhwh*) occurs ten times (Nu 20:24; 27:14; Dt 1:26, 43; 9:23; Jos 1:18; 1Sa 12:14–15; 1Ki 13:21, 26) and signifies rebellion against specific instructions or commands of their covenantal Lord. This rebellion is especially reprehensible because of its theological backdrop, a covenantal relationship with Yahweh (Carpenter/Grisanti, *NIDOTTE*, 2:1101).

28 The statement אַחֵינוּ הֵמַסּוּ אֶת־לְבָבֵנוּ (*ʾaḥênû hēmassû ʾet-lᵉbābēnû*, "Our brothers have made us lose heart") can be rendered literally, "our brothers have made our hearts melt." This expression occurs frequently in war contexts, especially concerning "holy war" (Dt 20:8; Jos 2:11; 5:1; 7:5; 2Sa 17:10; Isa 13:7; 19:1; Eze 21:7[12]; Na 2:10[11]).

The "Anakites" (בְּנֵי עֲנָקִים, *bᵉnê ʿanāqîm*), called the "Nephilim" in Numbers 13:32–33, belonged to a race of giants known as the Rephaim (cf. Dt 2:10–11, 21). Og of Bashan, an Anakite, had an iron bedstead that was over thirteen feet long (3:11). The Rephaites/Anakites were also found in Philistia (esp. Gath; Nu 13:22; Jos 11:21–22; 1Sa 17:4–7; 2Sa 21:16, 20).

c. The Lord's Judgment on Israel (1:34–40)

> [34] When the LORD heard what you said, he was angry and solemnly swore: [35] "Not a man of this evil generation shall see the good land I swore to give your forefathers, [36] except Caleb son of Jephunneh. He will see it, and I will give him and his descendants the land he set his feet on, because he followed the LORD wholeheartedly."
>
> [37] Because of you the LORD became angry with me also and said, "You shall not enter it, either. [38] But your assistant, Joshua son of Nun, will enter it. Encourage him, because he will lead Israel to inherit it. [39] And the little ones that you said would be taken captive, your children who do not yet know good from bad — they will enter the land. I will give it to them and they will take possession of it. [40] But as for you, turn around and set out toward the desert along the route to the Red Sea."

COMMENTARY

34–36 Israel's refusal to obey Yahweh's command to march against Canaan and their unwillingness to believe God's promise of victory caused him to respond in anger. Since Moses had already delineated the penalties for covenantal treachery (Lev 26:14–39), Yahweh made a solemn promise ("swore"; see Note on 1:8) that those who refused to believe he was able to give them a victory over the Canaanites would never see the land he promised them. The same land that Yahweh had sworn to give to Israel (Ge 50:24; Ex 33:1; Nu 14:16; Dt 1:8) would be denied from those adult Israelites who rebelled against Yahweh's directive to enter the land.

This declaration did not represent a final revocation of that promise but instead the exclusion of the present generation from ever enjoying its benefits. Except for Caleb (and Joshua; see below), all men over twenty years of age in that generation would perish before Israel entered the Promised Land (cf. Nu 14:22–23, 29, 31). The announcement implied that adult women and young people and children under twenty were spared from this fate. Because of Caleb's wholehearted obedience, Yahweh promised that he would inherit the land on which he had walked as an Israelite spy (cf. Jos 15:13–19).

37 Moses declared to the Israelites camped on the plains of Moab (lit.), "*Even with me* the LORD was angry on your account and said, 'Even you will not enter there.'" Not only did Yahweh exclude the generation of rebels from the Land of Promise, Yahweh also prohibited Moses from entering that land. He shared their fate. He mentions that this fate of his was "because of you." Is Moses shifting the blame off himself? He mentions the issue at least four times in his own words (1:37; 3:26–27; 4:21; 31:2) and twice more in the book (32:48–52; 34:1–4). Eventually, the Lord told him to stop bringing up the issue (3:26).

To what event does Moses refer as that occasioning his fate of not entering the land? Because of the contextual proximity of Moses' statement here with the discussion of Israel's rebellion at Kadesh Barnea, several scholars regard that rebellion as the correct backdrop for Moses' affirmation (Christensen, *Deuteronomy 1:1–21:9*, 32; Craigie, 105; Driver, 26–27; Thompson, 88; Tigay, *Deuteronomy*, 19; Weinfeld, *Deuternomy 1–11*, 150). Most proponents of this interpretation describe Moses as himself being innocent. But as leader of Israel he had to share in their punishment for this national rebellion. Regardless, however, Moses' exclusion from the land was not a divine punishment, nor did it indicate any divine displeasure with Moses (e.g., Cairns, 37–38). Some have even suggested that Moses suffers "vicariously" for Israel's sin (Mayes, 147; cf. von Rad, 45). Others associate Moses' declaration with Israel's rebellion against Yahweh at Meribah (Nu 20:1–5; Hall, 99; Keil, 289; McConville, 71; Wright, *Deuteronomy*, 41–42).

Although Moses' statement that Yahweh had been angry with him and was excluding him from the Land of Promise as well occurs as part of his overview of Israel's rebellion at Kadesh Barnea, there is no need to require that event to serve as the backdrop for his exclusion from Canaan. Because of the reference to Caleb and Joshua (before and after this verse), reference to Moses' exclusion from the Land of Promise represents an obvious logical corollary (McConville, 71). Moses does not appear to be as chronologically concerned as he is interested in overviewing these historical events thematically.

In summary, how can one resolve the tension between Moses' statement here (1:36; cf. 3:26; 4:21) and the statement at the end of Deuteronomy (32:51) that connects his exclusion from the land to his striking the rock at Meribah (cf. Nu 20:11–12)? As many have pointed out, Israel's rebellion at Meribah occurred over three decades after their rebellion at Kadesh Barnea. Briefly put, Israel's rebellion at Meribah and Moses' sinful striking of the rock never would have happened if Israel had entered the Promised Land when Yahweh told them to do so (Raymond Brown, *The Message of Deuteronomy* [Downers Grove, Ill.: InterVarsity Press, 1993], 43). Sadly, sin always reproduces itself. One act of rebellion quickly leads to another.

Note too that Moses' comments do not place on Israel's shoulders the entire blame for his exclusion from the land of Canaan; rather, his words demonstrate the seriousness and far-reaching implications of sin. This message is one that the Israelites camped in the plain of Moab need to take to heart. The ultimate point here is that Moses wants his fellow Israelites to recognize the full extent of the guilt and sin of the previous generation so that his present audience can avoid doing the same thing.

38–40 Moses mentions Joshua as the other survivor from the rebellious generation who will enter the Promised Land because Moses' own exclusion from that land occasioned the need for a replacement to lead the nation in the coming years. God will enable Joshua to make the divine promise of a land for Israel (a divine inheritance) a reality. Yahweh exhorts Moses to "encourage" Joshua in light of the challenge before him, i.e., to strengthen or equip him for the task ahead (cf. 3:28; 31:7).

Moses goes on to point out the irony of Israel's rebellion that his present audience will clearly understand (1:39). The generation of Israelites who rebelled against God out of a desire to protect themselves and their children from what they thought was certain death have been survived by those very children. They, rather than their parents, will inherit the land sworn to their parents by Yahweh. These children were not morally responsible when their parents chose to rebel against Yahweh. They did not know "good from bad" (cf. Isa 7:15–16; 8:4; Jnh 4:11). This phrase does not signify innocence but a lack of ability to discern morally. The prophets denounced those who knew better and who called "evil good and good evil" (Isa 5:20; cf. Mic 3:2; Am 5:14). The Lord told the Israelites who rebelled at Kadesh Barnea to turn around and head back the way they came. Yahweh closed the door of opportunity for them to enter Canaan.

NOTES

34 As examplified by וַיִּקְצֹף (*wayyiqṣōp*, "and he was angry"), Deuteronomy contains a number of references to God's anger (twenty-six times, various Hebrew words). The verb that occurs here (קָצַף, *qṣp*; GK 7911) occurs in the OT with both a human and a divine subject. God's anger, however, is not occasioned by human frailties or by pride, nor is it uncontrolled. It is anger occasioned by Israel's consistent pattern of rebellion and unbelief. This verb also occurs to describe God's angry response to Israel's decision to build the golden calf while Moses was on Mount Sinai receiving the law from God (Dt 9:7, 19). This anger does not arise from a divine character defect but is a divine response to human treachery and sinfulness (cf. Merrill, "Deuteronomy," 446; Sauer, *TLOT*, 3:1157–58).

36 In observing מִלֵּא אַחֲרֵי יהוה (*mille*ʾ *aḥărê yhwh*, "he followed the Lord wholeheartedly"), Moses writes that Caleb (lit.) "completely filled [himself] with Yahweh." This statement is applied to Caleb in four other passages (Nu 14:24; Jos 14:8–9, 14) and refers to both Caleb and Joshua once (Nu 32:12). Those who rebelled against God's directive to conquer Canaan are described as those who "have not" followed the Lord wholeheartedly (32:11). In Joshua 14 Caleb's own testimony that he wholeheartedly followed the Lord contrasts his evaluative statement that the testimony of the ten other spies caused the heart of the Israelites to melt (Jos 14:8). Concerning Solomon's reign, after the statement "Solomon did evil in the eyes of the Lord," the biblical historian also writes that "he did not follow the Lord completely" (1Ki 11:6). In light of the contrasting statements that accompany this expression in certain contexts, this statement as applied to Caleb depicts him as a man who was totally submitted to God's expectations and commands, regardless of their difficulty (cf. Snijders, *TDOT*, 8:300–301).

37 A different verb for anger, אָנַף (ʾnp [GK 647]; cf. קָצַף [qṣp] in 1:34) occurs with regard to God's response to Moses: הִתְאַנַּף יְהוָה (hiṯʾannap yhwh, "the LORD became angry"). This verb, wherever it occurs, has only Yahweh as its subject. It is a near synonym of qṣp, for both verbs occur to describe God's reaction to Israel's making of the golden calf (see אָנַף [ʾnp] in 9:8, 20; קָצַף [qṣp] in 9:7–8, 19, 22). The verb ʾnp also occurs in 4:21 with regard to Moses' exclusion from entering the Promise Land. This verb describes God's anger in light of the anticipated rebellion of Israel (1Ki 8:46), Solomon's apostasy (1Ki 11:9), and Israel's penchant for covenantal treachery (2Ki 17:18).

The term בִּגְלַל (biḡlal, "because of you") occurs only ten times in the OT and can mean "because of" or "on account of" (Merrill, *Deuteronomy*, 82). In one sense the term can denote direct causation, or it can highlight a less direct "occasion" of something's happening. For example, Joseph was not the primary cause for God's blessing of Potiphar's household, but he did provide the occasion for that blessing (Ge 39:5; cf. Jacob and Laban—Ge 30:27, 30). Especially when the word is used to refer to Israel's sin, there is a more direct connection between the cause and the result (1Ki 14:16; Jer 11:17; 15:4). Moses is not absolving himself of responsibility by saying that the rebellious Israelites occasioned his own sin.

38 Regarding יַנְחִלֶנָּה אֶת־יִשְׂרָאֵל (yanḥilennâ ʾeṯ-yiśrāʾēl, "he will enable Israel to inherit the land"), Israel's promised possession of the land of Canaan represents much more than a territorial acquisition. The Land of Promise was an "inheritance" provided for the nation of Israel by God. The verb "to inherit" (נחל, nḥl; GK 5706) signifies the permanent allocation of land within the tribal and family structure of Israel. It can also refer to the "metaphorical" reality of Israel's serving as Yahweh' inheritance (Dt 32:8–9; 2Sa 21:3) or even Yahweh's functioning as Israel's inheritance (Ps 119:57; Jer 10:16; 51:19; La 3:24; C. Wright, *NIDOTTE*, 3:77). On the national level, the land was portrayed as the inheritance of Israel as a whole. It was given to Israel by virtue of their covenantal relationship with Yahweh, and their continued enjoyment of that land was effected by their wholehearted allegiance to their God (4:40; 24:4).

The verb nḥl occurs eight times in Deuteronomy and in all but one instance (19:14) refers to someone's causing another to receive his inheritance. Yahweh (12:10; 19:3) and Joshua (1:38; 3:28; 31:7—as God's instrument) will cause Israel to receive his divine allotment of land. A father can provide an inheritance for his children (21:16), and Yahweh will provide an inheritance for all the nations of the earth (32:8). The noun derived from this verb (נַחֲלָה, naḥălâ) occurs twenty-five times in Deuteronomy, ten of which are part of the clause, "the land the LORD your God is giving you as your inheritance" (4:21, 38; 15:4; 19:10; 20:16; 21:23; 24:4; 25:19; 26:1; 29:8). Israel is called the people of Yahweh's inheritance (4:20; cf. 9:26, 29; 32:9). The land of Canaan is not just property for Israel to possess but is a stewardship given to them by their gracious God as a marvelous benefit. Various Mosaic regulations guard their permanent enjoyment of that inheritance. In the end, however, a given generation's enjoyment of that inheritance is integrally connected to the nation's covenantal conformity (or lack of it; cf. the covenantal curses in ch. 28).

40 The verb "to set out" (נסע, nsʿ, root form of וּסְעוּ, ûseʿû, "and set out") occurs frequently in the Pentateuch to describe the movement of people, i.e., they break camp and set off on a journey. The two verbs "turn" (פנה, pnh) and "set out" (נסע, nsʿ) occur together four times (Nu 14:25 = Dt 1:40; 1:7; 2:1). God's command that Israel turn in a different direction (away from the Promised Land) stands in painful contrast with his command that they leave their encampment at the base of Mount Horeb and travel toward the Promised Land (1:7). Their day of opportunity and fulfillment of divine promises became a day of judgment and divine wrath.

d. Israel's Unsuccessful Attempt to Invade Canaan (1:41–46)

⁴¹Then you replied, "We have sinned against the LORD. We will go up and fight, as the LORD our God commanded us." So every one of you put on his weapons, thinking it easy to go up into the hill country.

⁴²But the LORD said to me, "Tell them, 'Do not go up and fight, because I will not be with you. You will be defeated by your enemies.'"

⁴³So I told you, but you would not listen. You rebelled against the LORD's command and in your arrogance you marched up into the hill country. ⁴⁴The Amorites who lived in those hills came out against you; they chased you like a swarm of bees and beat you down from Seir all the way to Hormah. ⁴⁵You came back and wept before the LORD, but he paid no attention to your weeping and turned a deaf ear to you. ⁴⁶And so you stayed in Kadesh many days—all the time you spent there.

COMMENTARY

41–42 God's message of judgment shocked the Israelites into "confessing" their sin. Faced with no hope of ever seeing the long-awaited Promised Land, the Israelites decided they would fight against the Canaanites, just as Yahweh had commanded them. Through Moses, the Lord declared to them that fighting against the Canaanites was no longer an act of obedience to him since he had withdrawn the promise of his presence. Obedience after the fact does not change the judgment God had determined for his covenantal nation; without God, the Israelites had no hope of defeating the Canaanite forces.

The promise of God's presence is a key element throughout the OT. Statements that refer to his presence as being with someone at times appear to serve as a recognition of God's blessings in their life (Ge 26:28; Dt 2:7; 1Sa 16:18; 2Ki 18:7; 1Ch 22:18;

2Ch 1:1; 15:9), a reference to the provision or lack of provision of military enablement (Nu 14:43; Dt 20:1, 4; Jdg 1:22; Zec 10:5; 2Ch 15:2), or the evidence of divine enablement (Jdg 2:18; 6:12–13; 2Sa 7:3; 1Ki 1:37; 1Ch 22:11, 16).

The Israelites after Moses' death longed that God would be with Joshua as he had been with Moses (Jos 1:17; cf. Solomon's prayer in 1Ki 8:57). Even pagans such as Balaam (Nu 23:21) and Cyrus (2Ch 36:23) recognized the importance of God's presence with his people. The phrase found here, "I will not be with you" (lit., "there will not be me in your midst"), is similar to the Lord's statement in Numbers 14:42 ("the LORD is not with you"; lit., "there is no Yahweh among you"). It occurs again toward the end of Deuteronomy when the Lord tells Moses of his impending death. The Lord predicts that Israel will commit covenantal treachery and affirms that he will hide his face from his servant-nation and will bring disaster on them. In the wake of this punishment, God's people will ask, "Have not these disasters come upon us because our God is not with us?" (31:17).

43 Israel gave no heed to Moses' warning and marched toward the region of Canaan. By deciding to press forward with their plans to attack Canaan anyway, the Israelites presumed on the grace of God. They had rebelled against Yahweh and now were counting on his forgiveness. They assumed that Yahweh would bless them and provide them the promised victory even though he had clearly told them otherwise. Their actions in the face of God's explicit statement represented the epitome of presumption and arrogance. Just as their refusal to march in battle against Canaan after hearing the report of the spies signified treacherous rebellion against their covenantal Lord (1:26), their refusal to heed his warning and their decision to march against Canaan after God's announcement of judgment also demonstrated their rebellious spirit. (The same wording occurs in both places.)

44–46 The Amorite forces attacked the Israelite army in the southern part of their territory. They, like enraged bees pursuing a trespasser, put the Israelite men to flight (cf. Ps 118:12; Isa 7:18–19). In the wake of this convincing and painful defeat, the Israelites returned in sorrow to their encampment at Kadesh Barnea. Although they wept "before the LORD" (at the tabernacle), Yahweh paid no attention to their sorrow. Just as he had promised, he was not "with them." Just as the people refused to listen to the words of Yahweh and Moses up to this point, Yahweh did not listen to their weeping. The people finally realized that Yahweh had meant what he said. They spent "many days" in the region around Kadesh Barnea (1:46) and in the hill country of Seir to the south (2:1). A comparison of various chronological notations in Numbers and in the subsequent narrative here suggests that they remained in this region over thirty-eight years until God's judgment on this rebellious generation was fulfilled (2:14).

When Israel had departed from Horeb, there has been genuine hope and anticipation. They were approaching a day of fulfillment. However, because of their rebellion God's chosen nation was right back where it started in 1:19, namely, as a people without a land. In God's eyes, the Israelites had become nothing more than Canaanites.

NOTES

41 The verb וַתָּהִינוּ (wattāhînû, "thinking it easy," from הון, hwn) might be better rendered "dared" or "prepared themselves." The verb occurs only here in the OT. If this verb is compared with a similar root in Arabic ("to slight, treat with disdain"), it may mean to act recklessly, a meaning that would thus highlight the Israelites' swift transition from panic to heedless overconfidence (Tigay, *Deuteronomy*, 348, n. 118). But it might simply render the idea of the word unit in Numbers 14:40 (הִנֶּנּוּ, hinnennû) that could be rendered "Here we are" (NASB, NKJV, NRSV) or "Now we are ready" (NLT, TEV; Weinfeld, *Deuternomy 1–11*, 151).

43 The statement וַתָּזִדוּ וַתַּעֲלוּ (wattāzidû wattaʿalû, "in your arrogance you marched up") represents two verbs (a verbal hendiadys): "you acted presumptuously and you marched up." The first verb (זיד, zyd) occurs ten times in the OT and depicts people or nations that presume to have authority that is not legitimately theirs (Smith, *NIDOTTE*, 1:1094). God brought judgment on Babylon because she defied him in thinking she could accomplish anything significant without God's blessing (Jer 50:29). A person who kills another human being with full knowledge of the legal consequences acts in arrogance (Ex 21:14). False prophets, who claimed to speak a word given to them by Yahweh when he had not, in fact, spoken to them, evidenced arrogance that received the death penalty (18:20–22). Israel's conduct after God warned them against attacking the Canaanites demonstrated that they assumed God would still come to their aid. The Numbers account clarifies the intensity of their presumption. They marched against Canaan without Moses or the ark of the covenant (Nu 14:44).

44 The reference here to הָאֱמֹרִי (*hā᾽emōrî*), "the Amorites," has caused some to question the relationship of this account to the Numbers 14 passage, which mentions the Amalekites and Canaanites (Nu 14:43). But as has already been seen in 1:7, throughout Deuteronomy Moses uses the term "Amorites" as a broad general description for the inhabitants of Canaan (cf. Merrill, *Deuteronomy*, 87; Weinfeld, *Deuternomy 1–11*, 132–33; Tigay, *Deuteronomy*, 14).

3. Israel's Passage through Edom, Moab, and Ammon without Fighting (2:1–25)

OVERVIEW

Toward the end of Israel's wilderness wanderings the Lord commanded the children of Israel to begin their journey to the Promised Land, thus causing them to leave the region surrounding Kadesh Barnea and to pass near the territory held by the Edomites, Moabites, and Ammonites. Although the ensuing narrative (2:1–3:11) shares the basic details of the parallel account in Numbers 20–24, the present narrative demonstrates greater interest in theology than in the details of geography and chronology.

With regard to the Edomites, Moabites, and Ammonites, Yahweh prohibited Israel from taking any land from these peoples (2:1–25). Yahweh is the owner of the entire "estate" of the world. He allocates his properties to those he desires. God was orchestrating all these events for the Israelites. At this point in time in biblical history, the blood relationship of these three peoples with Israel protected them from the destruction that God promised to bring on the Amorites, Bashanites, and Canaanites. These "Amorites" had no such relationship with God's people and faced a quite different fate.

Israel's victories over Sihon and Og figure more prominently here (2:26–3:11) than in Numbers (21:21–35) because Sihon and Og (and their peoples) represent the firstfruits of the dispossession of the inhabitants of the entire region around Canaan. Those victories served as a paradigm of holy war in which God's covenantal nation utterly would destroy his enemies (cf. 2:34; McConville, 81).

a. Events in the Hill Country of Seir (2:1–8)

OVERVIEW

After Israel wandered in the Kadesh Barnea region (and south of it) for many years, the Lord commanded his children to pass around the hill country of Mount Seir and then pass north toward the Promised Land without disturbing the Edomites or their possessions in any way.

¹Then we turned back and set out toward the desert along the route to the Red Sea, as the Lord had directed me. For a long time we made our way around the hill country of Seir.

²Then the Lord said to me, ³"You have made your way around this hill country long enough; now turn north. ⁴Give the people these orders: 'You are about to pass through the territory of your brothers the descendants of Esau, who live in Seir. They will be afraid of you, but be very careful. ⁵Do not provoke them to war, for I will not give you any of their land, not even enough to put your foot on. I have given Esau the hill country of Seir as his own. ⁶You are to pay them in silver for the food you eat and the water you drink.'"

⁷The Lord your God has blessed you in all the work of your hands. He has watched over your journey through this vast desert. These forty years the Lord your God has been with you, and you have not lacked anything.

⁸So we went on past our brothers the descendants of Esau, who live in Seir. We turned from the Arabah road, which comes up from Elath and Ezion Geber, and traveled along the desert road of Moab.

COMMENTARY

1 The Israelites obeyed God's command (1:40) to begin their journey away from the land of Canaan and in the direction of the Red Sea (after their abortive attempt to evade its consequence in 1:41–46 [McConville, 82]). The language describing Israel's travels ("we turned back and set out") fulfilled God command in 1:40 but provided a painful contrast with similar wording in 1:19 (where God commanded his people to begin the "final" phase of their trek to the Promised Land). The "hill country of Seir" refers to the mountain range of Edom located south of the Dead Sea and extended down the eastern flank of the Arabah (Craigie, 107; see comments on 1:1).

2–6 God then told the Israelites that they had wandered in the wilderness long enough. It was time to begin their trek toward the Land of Promise (once again). The command to "turn north" may imply that God's people were located near the southern extremity of Edomite territory when this command came to them, or it simply serves as a summary statement of their travels given more detail in Numbers. God instructed Moses to lead the Israelites around the Edomites without disrupting them. The Edomites were the descendants of Esau, the brother of Jacob (Nu 20:14). In the light of that fact, God commanded that the Israelites leave the Edomites alone. Hostility between Israel and Edom had not yet developed. More specifically, Yahweh demanded that Israel not provoke them to war, nor take any of their land (as it is God's allotment for them), and they were to pay them for any food and water they consumed.

Although the narrative mentions Israel was about to "pass through" Edomite territory, the Numbers account makes clear that the Edomites prohibited Israel from taking the customary route through their region (the King's Highway) and required that they skirt the borders of Edom (Nu 20:14–21). As predicted in Exodus 15:14–16, the Edomites (among others) had heard of Yahweh's great deeds in Israel's behalf and feared the Israelites as a result. This fear explains the Edomites' refusal of safe passage through the midst of their territory and the need for Israel to be extra careful in their relations with the Edomites during their time in the area.

The Lord used three statements (2:5) to emphasize Edom's inviolable claim to the land (at this time). God had not "given" Israel any of their land (cf. 1:8, 20–21, 25, 35–36, 39; 2:12, 29), which was Edom's "possession" (cf. Dt 3:20; Jos 1:15; 12:6–7). Israel could not take even as much as would be necessary for a footprint! Since the Lord had not allot-ted the land of Edom to Israel, God's people were to avoid any conduct that could provoke conflict. He is sovereign over his entire creation and over all peoples, and he allocates the territories of the earth as he deems fit.

Up to this point the Israelites had been exclusively dependent on Yahweh for all their material needs. Even though God's provision of manna continued until their first celebration of the Passover in the land of Canaan (Jos 5:10–12; cf. Ex 16:35), the Israelites were also able to purchase food and water as they passed around Edomite areas.

7 Yahweh's blessing on Israel precluded any need for them to take resources from Edom. Even during their experience of almost forty years of divine judgment, Yahweh blessed them (cf. 7:13; 14:29; 15:10, 18; 16:15; 24:19; 30:9), watched over them (cf. Pss 1:6; 37:18; Ne 1:7–8; Jer 29:11; Hos 13:5), and made sure that they lacked nothing. Even though the Lord had told them that he would not be with them in any effort to conquer the Canaanites after his word of judgment (1:42; see comments there), he was with them throughout their wilderness wanderings.

8 That the Israelites bypassed the region of Edom by means of a "round-about" route probably meant they traveled on the Transjordanian plateau, near the transition between habitable land and the Arabian desert.

NOTES

1 The expression יָמִ֥ים רַבִּ֖ים (*yāmîm rabbîm*, "many days") occurs in both 1:46 and 2:1. Although some scholars suggest that the reference in 1:46 highlights Israel's relatively short stay at Kadesh Barnea during and shortly after their rebellion there (Tigay, *Deuteronomy*, 22; Ridderbos, 64–65), it is more likely that both occurrences of the expression refer to the time of Israel's wandering in the general wilderness region around Kadesh Barnea and the hill country of Seir (2:1). According to Numbers 20:1, it appears that the Israelites returned to Kadesh Barnea at least once during their almost four decades of wandering.

The directional statement דֶּרֶךְ יַם־סוּף (*derek yam-sûp*, "route to the Red Sea") refers to the same Red Sea Israel crossed when they came out of Egypt. However, the Red Sea encompasses the region that separates the continent of Africa from the Saudi Arabian peninsula as well as the smaller gulfs that sit between the African continent and the Sinai peninsula (the Gulf of Suez), and the Sinai peninsula and the Saudi Arabian peninsula (the Gulf of Aqaba).

3 Scholars have long debated how to harmonize the accounts found in Numbers and here in Deuteronomy. Although some despair of finding that harmony (Driver, 31–33; Tigay, *Deuteronomy*, 425–29; Weinfeld, *Deuteronomy 1–11*, 165–67), various helpful suggestions have been made (e.g., Hall, 65–67; Wright, *Deuteronomy*, 35). Although space does not allow their retelling here, one point is essential: The itinerary information in Deuteronomy is intentionally sketchy and arranged more thematically. Consequently, differences between the two accounts should not be overemphasized.

4 Moses refers to the inhabitants of the region of Seir as בְּנֵי־עֵשָׂו (*b[e]nê-'ēśāw*), the "descendants of Esau," rather than Edomites (Nu 20:14–21), in order to highlight the kinship between Israel and Edom (cf. Ge 36).

5 The term מִדְרָךְ (*midrak*, "a foot's breadth"; *HALOT*, 550) is a *hapax legomenon* derived from the verb דרך (*drk*). In 1:36 God promised Caleb the land on which his feet had walked (Nu 14:24; Jos 14:6–15). According to Yahweh, any place Israel "walked" belonged to the nation as though she had subdued and conquered it (Merrill, "Deuteronomy," 446); thus Moses emphasized the warning to be careful in Seir — territory that was off-limits to Israel.

b. Events in the Territory of Moab (2:9–15)

OVERVIEW

As the children of Israel approached the boundary of Moab, the Lord forbade them to attack and plunder the territory of Moab since he had allocated this land to the Moabites (2:9–12). Moses also points out that Israel's crossing over the Zered Valley represented the official end of God's punishment of Israel for their rebellion at Kadesh Barnea (2:13–15).

> ⁹Then the LORD said to me, "Do not harass the Moabites or provoke them to war, for I will not give you any part of their land. I have given Ar to the descendants of Lot as a possession."
>
> ¹⁰(The Emites used to live there — a people strong and numerous, and as tall as the Anakites. ¹¹Like the Anakites, they too were considered Rephaites, but the Moabites called them Emites. ¹²Horites used to live in Seir, but the descendants of Esau drove them out. They destroyed the Horites from before them and settled in their place, just as Israel did in the land the LORD gave them as their possession.)

¹³And the LORD said, "Now get up and cross the Zered Valley." So we crossed the valley. ¹⁴Thirty-eight years passed from the time we left Kadesh Barnea until we crossed the Zered Valley. By then, that entire generation of fighting men had perished from the camp, as the LORD had sworn to them. ¹⁵The LORD's hand was against them until he had completely eliminated them from the camp.

COMMENTARY

9 As with Edom, since the Lord had "given" as a "possession" (see comments at 2:5) the region of Moab (located east of the Dead Sea) to the descendants of Lot (Ge 19:30–38), the Israelites were to pass through the area without taking any territory. Even though these peoples (Moabites and Ammonites) came into existence through immoral circumstances, God saw fit to guard their possession of land (for now). "Ar" was a city in Moab and served (by synecdoche, a figure of speech where a part stands for the whole) as a reference to the region of Moab.

10–12 This "parenthetical note," the first of several (cf. 2:20–23; 3:9, 11, 13), points out that both the Moabites and the Edomites had gained their territory by dispossessing peoples who earlier inhabited this region of Transjordan (cf. Ge 14:5–6), just as Israel would do to Sihon and Og. The Edomites, Moabites, and Ammonites had supplanted these earlier peoples, just as Israel would supplant the people inhabiting the land of Canaan (Tigay, *Deuteronomy*, 26). If nothing else, these verses demonstrate that the phenomenon of land's changing hands by means of military conquest is part of God's sovereign plan. In fact, in 2:21–22 God receives the credit for giving land to the Ammonites and Edomites.

Besides the fact that Yahweh uses the theological language of "inheritance" to describe the Edomites',

Moabites', and Ammonites' claim to land (see comments at 2:5), these parenthetical notes provide several significant insights into God's role with regard to the world at large (see Wright, *Deuteronomy*, 36–37). First of all, Yahweh is not only the suzerain of Israel but also exercises multinational sovereignty. Facilitated by the God to whom the whole earth belongs (Ex 9:14, 16, 29), Israel's conquest of these Transjordanian kingdoms (2:26–3:11) was not the first time Yahweh was behind transitions in rulership. Later in Israel's history, his use of Assyria, Babylon, and Persia as tools of judgment and preservation evidences God's sovereignty over all nations (cf. Dt 32:8; Jer 18:1–10; 27:1–7).

Second, Israel's covenantal relationship with Yahweh, and not only her possession of some land, distinguished Israel from all other nations of the world. This reality does not diminish the significance of Yahweh's allocating the Land of Promise to Israel or its role in yet future events; rather, it places the primary focus where it needs to be, namely, on Israel's relationship with Yahweh as the key to her distinct identity and destiny.

Finally, since this land was part of Israel's relationship with Yahweh and since his promised victory over Israel's enemies would result from that relationship, Israel must live in genuine conformity with that relationship. If they commit covenantal treachery, God can and will evict them from this divine allotment of land, just as he evicted Sihon, Og, and various Canaanite peoples before them (Lev 18:24–28; 20:22–24; Dt 28:36–37, 58–68).

What should one conclude from the statement at the end of v.12, "just as Israel did in the land the LORD gave them as their possession"? One of three interpretations is normally offered. In the first place, the clause refers to the Transjordan region that was conquered prior to the time of writing of the book of Deuteronomy (cf. 2:24–3:11). Consequently, Moses wrote these verses. Moses is probably seeking to bolster the faith of the Israelites as they approach the land of Canaan for the second time (Hall, 73; Kalland, 32; Merrill, *Deuteronomy*, 94). Merrill suggests that Moses could have written this material as an encouragement to his immediate audience, the Israelites who faced the specter of invading the land of Canaan, by employing a "perfect of confidence" (Merrill, *Deuteronomy*, 94; *IBHS*, 489–90, §30.5.1e).

Second, it could refer to the land of Canaan itself, not yet conquered at the time depicted in Deuteronomy 2. Consequently, someone added this material sometime after Moses as minor editorial addition that is part of the inspired text of Scripture (Craigie, 24, n. 17, 111; R. K. Harrison, *Introduction to the Old Testament* [Grand Rapids: Eerdmans, 1969], 637–40; McConville, 39–40, 84; Ridderbos, 68–69; Thompson, 49–53, 92; Wright, *Deuteronomy*, 7–8).

Finally, some agree with the second alternative (describing the land of Canaan itself, not yet conquered) but contend that this reality evidences a *final composition* of the entire book of Deuteronomy much later than the time of Moses (Mayes, 42–43, 137; Tigay, *Deuteronomy*, xxiv–xxvi, 26; von Rad, 42–43; Weinfeld, *Deuteronomy 1–11*,

13–14, 163). Scholars who prefer the second or third option customarily appeal to the following two arguments (at least). First, Moses normally uses the second person ("you") in his addresses to the Israelites, while in these "notes" the third person predominates. Second, the most likely meaning for the phrase "the land the LORD gave them" would be the land of Canaan and not the region of Transjordan.

Even if those arguments are valid, there is no need to assume that the book of Deuteronomy did not reach a final stage of composition until the seventh century BC or later. On the one hand, I do not have a problem with a prophetic figure's making minor additions to Deuteronomy after the death of Moses (e.g., ch. 34, the narrative of Moses' death and burial; cf. Grisanti, "Inspiration, Inerrancy," 577–98; Merrill, *Deuteronomy*, 94; Ridderbos, 84; Thompson, 49–53). If such were the case, these verses were added by an authorized individual under the direction of the Holy Spirit. Even if such is not the case, however, there is no need to conclude that the final composition of the book (involving major reworking) did not happen until the seventh century BC.

13–15 The crossing of the Wadi Zered by the children of Israel marked the end of the former generation, who had rebelled against the Lord at Kadesh and were condemned to die in the wilderness. This wadi represented the southernmost boundary of Moab. (The northernmost boundary was the Wadi Arnon.) In general, these verses signify that the era of desert sojourning was over, that God's oath of judgment had reached total fulfillment (cf. 1:35), and that impending victories in Transjordan and Canaan will be due to God's intervention, not Israel's military prowess.

NOTES

11 The designation רְפָאִים (*rᵉpāʾîm*, "Rephaim") appears to have been a generic name or epithet for a race of giants who lived in the region of Transjordan (Ge 15:20; Jos 17:15). Their descendants appear in Philistia during David's reign (2Sa 21:16–22). The Moabites called them the "Emim" and the Ammonites called them the "Zamzummim." These "local" names may have been more descriptive than ethnic designators. "Emim" might mean "fearsome ones" (because they occasioned fear) and "Zamzummim" might mean "buzz-buzzers" in imitation of their speech (Tigay, *Deuteronomy*, 27, 29).

12 הַחֹרִים (*haḥōrîm*), "the Horites," might refer to the Hurrians, a non-Semitic people who lived in various places in Mesopotamia, Syria, and Palestine (Craigie, 111; Tigay, *Deuteronomy*, 27; Weinfeld, *Deuteronomy 1–11*, 162–63).

c. Events in the Territory of Ammon (2:16–25)

¹⁶Now when the last of these fighting men among the people had died, ¹⁷the LORD said to me, ¹⁸"Today you are to pass by the region of Moab at Ar. ¹⁹When you come to the Ammonites, do not harass them or provoke them to war, for I will not give you possession of any land belonging to the Ammonites. I have given it as a possession to the descendants of Lot."

²⁰(That too was considered a land of the Rephaites, who used to live there; but the Ammonites called them Zamzummites. ²¹They were a people strong and numerous, and as tall as the Anakites. The LORD destroyed them from before the Ammonites, who drove them out and settled in their place. ²²The LORD had done the same for the descendants of Esau, who lived in Seir, when he destroyed the Horites from before them. They drove them out and have lived in their place to this day. ²³And as for the Avvites who lived in villages as far as Gaza, the Caphtorites coming out from Caphtor destroyed them and settled in their place.)

²⁴"Set out now and cross the Arnon Gorge. See, I have given into your hand Sihon the Amorite, king of Heshbon, and his country. Begin to take possession of it and engage him in battle. ²⁵This very day I will begin to put the terror and fear of you on all the nations under heaven. They will hear reports of you and will tremble and be in anguish because of you."

COMMENTARY

16–19 As with Edom and Moab, the Lord commanded the Israelites to pass through Ammon without provoking its inhabitants to war since he gave this territory to the Ammonites (see comments at 2:5). They were located parallel with the area held by the Amorites of Heshbon (as far as its north–south location), but to its east, i.e., farther inland from Sihon's Amorite territory. After explaining some of the prehistory of this region, Yahweh exhorted the Israelites to enter into conflict with Sihon, the Amorite king. Even before the battle had begun the Lord had delivered Sihon into Israel's hand (2:24–25).

20–23 As with the Moabites and Edomites (2:10–12), the Ammonites and the Caphtorites had gained their territory by dispossessing peoples who had earlier inhabited this region.

24–25 Yahweh's exhortation that Israel "set out" and cross the Arnon River represented a great blessing to all Israelites aware of their history. After they were encamped at Horeb for almost one year, the Lord commanded Israel to "set out" for the Promise Land (1:7, 19). Unfortunately, in the wake of their faithlessness and rebellion at Kadesh Barnea, the Lord demanded that his people "set out" for the "way of the Red Sea," away from Canaan (1:40; 2:1). In 2:24 Yahweh commanded them to do what every Israelite should have longed to do — enter the Land of Promise and see God provide

them his promised victory. Once the Israelites crossed the Arnon River, they entered the region controlled by the Amorites (and part of the Promised Land). The Lord commissioned the Israelites to engage the Amorites in battle, who served King Sihon of Heshbon, and promised to bring fear to the enemies' hearts and to give victory to Israel.

Yahweh's exhortation that Israel should begin "taking possession" of Sihon's land draws on theological language of inheritance (see comments at 2:5). It is encouraging to notice the pairing together of a divine command with a divine promise. God does not ask that his people do what they cannot do or promise to them what he cannot give. He commanded them to engage their first significant military opponent in battle and promised that the outcome of that conflict had already been determined — by God himself. The Lord employed a tool against the Amorites that had been at work in their midst since Israel's crossing of the Red Sea. News of Yahweh's powerful intervention in Israel's behalf had preceded Israel's arrival in this area by almost four decades (Ex 15:14–18).

NOTES

20 Like the Moabites, the Rephaites had once occupied Ammon. The Moabites had called this people group the "Emim" (2:11), but the Ammonites called them the "Zamzummim" (cf. Ge 14:5; see Note on 2:11).

23 Although scholars debate the exact origin of the Philistines, it appears that Caphtor, an island or coastland in the area of the Aegean Sea, was the point of origin for the Philistines (Ge 10:14; 1Ch 1:12; Am 9:7; Jer 47:4). Because of the language of Zephaniah 2:5, some contend that Crete and the surrounding islands was that place (Roland de Vaux, *Early History of Israel* [Philadelphia: Westminster, 1978], 504–7; cf. Tigay, *Deuteronomy*, 30; *ABD*, 5:327, 329; Trude Dothan and Moshe Dothan, *People of the Sea: The Search for the Philistines* [New York: Macmillan, 1992], 8–11, 34–35).

24 The expression נתן בְּיָד (*ntn b*ᵉ*yād*; here נָתַתִּי בְיָדְךָ, *nātattî b*ᵉ*yād*ᵉ*kā*, "I have given into your hand") occurs over 130 times in the OT. It can mean simply to place something in someone's hand (Ge 27:17;

Dt 24:1, 3) or to place something in the care of another (Ge 9:2; 30:35). More importantly, this expression occurs in military and legal settings to signify the delivery or abandonment of a person(s) or matter into the power of another (Grisanti, *NIDOTTE*, 3:210). B. Albrektson (*History and the Gods* [Lund: Gleerup, 1967], 38–39) has pointed out that in ancient Near Eastern literature, a king would use the expression "the gods delivered it into my hand" to express his belief that a given course of events was directed by the gods and that his victory over his enemies was a divine gift.

An alternative form of this expression is "give [object] … before" נתן ... לִפְנֵי [*ntn* … *lipnê*]; see Note on 7:2). The Israelites incorrectly thought that Yahweh had brought them into the wilderness to deliver them over to the Amorites (1:27). Joshua wondered whether God was going to destroy them or deliver them from the Canaanites (Jos 7:7). This statement occurs in several instances as part of Yahweh's promise to his servant-nation (Ex 23:31; Dt 7:24; Jos 8:1) and also as a description of what Yahweh actually accomplished for Israel's benefit (Jos 2:24; 6:2; 11:8; 21:44; 24:8, 11). The possibility of Yahweh's delivering Israel into the hands of their enemies was part of the covenantal curses God would bring on his chosen people if they violated their covenantal relationship with him (Lev 26:25). In the present passage Yahweh promised that he had already determined Sihon's fate, namely, he had delivered the Amorites into the hand of the Israelites (cf. 2:30; 3:3).

25 עַל־פְּנֵי הָעַמִּים תַּחַת כָּל־הַשָּׁמָיִם (*ʿal-pᵉnê hāʿammîm taḥat kol-haššāmāyim*, "all the nations under heaven") is a hyperbolic statement; it emphasizes that Israel has no need to fear since their God is the ultimate sovereign of the world. Any nation that Israel encountered would not be able to resist their advance (cf. 11:25; 28:10; Ex 23:27–29; Jos 2:8–11), and all other nations who heard this report would tremble in fear.

4. Israel's Conquest of the Transjordanian Kingdoms (2:26–3:11)

OVERVIEW

After passing through Edom, Ammon, and Moab peacefully, God enabled the children of Israel to defeat two Amorite kings (cf. 3:8), Sihon and Og, and then gave this newly won territory in Transjordan to the tribes of Reuben, Gad, and half the tribe of Manasseh as their tribal inheritance. The Amorites first appear in third-millennium Mesopotamian texts, where they are referred to as *Martu / Amurru*, or "westerners" (*ISBE²*, 1:113). This reference serves as a geographical indicator of their origins, probably the region of Syria.

In addition to signifying a direction, the term could also connote a region or a people. In its various OT occurrences, the word "Amorite" can broadly refer to people living in Canaan (Ge 15:16; 36:2–3; Jos 24:15; Jdg 1:34–35; Eze 16:3), more specifically to the hill country located in the central part of Canaan or those living there (Nu 13:29; Dt 1:7, 19–20), or to non-Israelites who lived on the eastern side of the Jordan River (Nu 21:26; Dt 4:46; Jos 13:10, 21). Although Numbers 13:29 identifies the Canaanites as those who inhabited the valleys and the Amorites as the dwellers of the hill country, there also appears to be some overlapping of these two designations. Liverani ("The Amorites," in *Peoples of Old Testament Times* [ed. D. Wiseman; Oxford: Clarendon, 1973], 125–26) and Stiebing ("When Was the Age of the Patriarchs? — Of Amorites, Canaanites, and Archaeol-

ogy," *BAR* 1/2 [June 1975]: 21) suggest that the terms "Canaanites" and "Amorites" were ethnically and culturally identical but geographically distinct. These two Amorite kings, Sihon and Og, ruled over the entire region of Transjordan, from the Wadi Arnon in the south to Mount Hermon in the north (Dt 4:48–49; Jos 12:1).

a. Israel's Conquest of Sihon, King of Heshbon (2:26–37)

OVERVIEW

Moses sent messengers to Sihon, king of Heshbon, requesting safe and unhindered passage through his territory but was firmly refused (because Yahweh hardened Sihon's heart). In the battle between Israel and Sihon, the Israelites destroyed Sihon's entire army and completely subjugated all of his territory (but not the territory of the Ammonites).

²⁶From the desert of Kedemoth I sent messengers to Sihon king of Heshbon offering peace and saying, ²⁷"Let us pass through your country. We will stay on the main road; we will not turn aside to the right or to the left. ²⁸Sell us food to eat and water to drink for their price in silver. Only let us pass through on foot — ²⁹as the descendants of Esau, who live in Seir, and the Moabites, who live in Ar, did for us — until we cross the Jordan into the land the LORD our God is giving us." ³⁰But Sihon king of Heshbon refused to let us pass through. For the LORD your God had made his spirit stubborn and his heart obstinate in order to give him into your hands, as he has now done.

³¹The LORD said to me, "See, I have begun to deliver Sihon and his country over to you. Now begin to conquer and possess his land."

³²When Sihon and all his army came out to meet us in battle at Jahaz, ³³the LORD our God delivered him over to us and we struck him down, together with his sons and his whole army. ³⁴At that time we took all his towns and completely destroyed them — men, women and children. We left no survivors. ³⁵But the livestock and the plunder from the towns we had captured we carried off for ourselves. ³⁶From Aroer on the rim of the Arnon Gorge, and from the town in the gorge, even as far as Gilead, not one town was too strong for us. The LORD our God gave us all of them. ³⁷But in accordance with the command of the LORD our God, you did not encroach on any of the land of the Ammonites, neither the land along the course of the Jabbok nor that around the towns in the hills.

COMMENTARY

26–29 After the Israelites crossed the Arnon River, they set up camp in the wilderness of Kedemoth (about eight miles north of the Arnon [Aharoni, 202–3]). From there Moses sent a message to Sihon asking that he allow the Israelites to pass through his territory unmolested, as the Edomites and Moabites had done. They would stay on the main route and purchase (rather than steal) any supplies they needed along the way. Although there is no evidence that the Israelites were able to trade with the Edomites or Moabites (cf. 23:4), they did pass through those regions without provoking any military conflict. As part of his message to Sihon, Moses manifested his confidence with God's ultimate plan for Israel. He asked for free passage until they arrived at the boundary of Sihon's neighbor (Canaan), whose land the Lord "is giving" to Israel (2:29).

30 Sihon, however, refused to grant Moses' request. Whether or not from a sense of arrogance or military supremacy (Sihon having taken his territory from the Moabites in the recent past; cf. Nu 21:26–30), Sihon refused primarily because God hardened his heart. The terms "spirit" and "heart" are virtually synonyms in this verse. In brief, God "fossilized" Sihon's inner being (cf. God's dealings with the Egyptian pharaoh [Ex 4:7–10; 7:3; 9:34–35; 10:27] and the division of Israel after Solomon [1Ki 12:15]).

Throughout this passage, notice the interplay of *divine sovereignty* and *human responsibility*. Sihon is responsible and culpable (vv.30a, 32), and Yahweh was accomplishing his agenda (vv.24a, 25a, 30b, 31a, 33a, 36b). Whenever we attempt to consider the complexity of the interrelationship of divine responsibility and human responsibility, we must be careful not to abuse one facet of that equation out

of a desire to give enough credence to the other. As Craigie, 116, points out: "Man is free and responsible in action, but the actions of all men are set within the sphere of history, and God was the Lord of history." The natural comparison between God's hardening Sihon's heart and his hardening Pharaoh's heart also demonstrates that the upcoming conquest of the land of Canaan continues the history of deliverance that began back in Egypt. Now as then, no human power can prevent the ultimate accomplishment of God's plan (McConville, 87).

At the end of v.30 Moses added, "as he has now done" (lit., "as it is today"). Moses wants to remind his current audience (camped just across the Jordan River from the land of the Canaanites and the great challege they represented) that their God does exactly what he says. Moses is saying, "Yahweh did this … so that this would happen … and it did!" The Israelites who were preparing to begin their conquest of Canaan could take courage in the light of God's past intervention in their behalf.

31 The Lord promised to Israel total victory ("*I have begun to deliver Sihon and his country over to you*") and exhorted his chosen people to trust him to bring that victory to pass ("Now [you] begin to conquer and possess his land"). God had set everything in place. Now Israel had to believe God had given the victory and engage Sihon and his army on the battlefield.

32–35 Exactly what God promised would happen in fact came to pass! Because God had orchestrated the demise of Sihon, Israel was able to achieve total victory over Sihon and his people. In accordance with the parameters of holy war (cf. 20:10–18), the Israelites "completely destroyed" Sihon and his people (cf. Achan in Jos 7 and the Amalekites in 1Sa

15). Although they left no human survivors, the Israelites recovered the flocks, herds, and valuables left behind by the Amorites who lived in this region.

36–37 The geographical extent of Israel's victory encompassed Sihon's territory but not that of the Ammonites. This region extended from the Arnon Gorge in the south as far as Sihon's boundary with Og (Gilead) in the north, i.e., the Jabbok River (Nu 21:24; ca. fifty-five miles). The Dead Sea and the Jordan River served as the western boundaries, and the territory of Ammon provided the eastern limits to Israel's recently conquered land (an east–west span of ca. twenty-five miles). In accordance with God's demand, the Israelites did not encroach on the territory of the Ammonites (blood relatives through Abraham's nephew Lot; 2:19 [cf. Ge 19:30–38]).

NOTES

31 Just as God "gave" (נתן, *ntn*) the land to Israel (cf. 1:8, 20–21, 25, 35–36, 39; 2:12) and could give (deliver) enemies into the hands of Israel (see Notes on 2:24 and 7:2), God "gave" (הַחִלֹּתִי תֵּת לְפָנֶיךָ, *hah̠illōtî tēt lᵉpāneykā*, "I have already begun to give ... to you") Sihon as a conquered foe to Israel.

34 The verb חרם (*h̠rm*; GK 3049), "to completely destroy" (root of וַנַּחֲרֵם, *wannah̠ᵃrēm*, "and we completely destroyed them") highlights the devoting of condemned people or things to Yahweh (and destruction). The OT uses two verbs for devoted things: חָרַם (*h̠ērem*; positive—something dedicated to Yahweh) and קָדוֹשׁ (*qādôš*; negative—something separate from what is sinful or common). The noun *h̠ērem* and the verb חָרַם can refer to something that is forbidden (13:18; Jos 6:18). In the context of holy war (as in 1Sa 15), the verb highlights a religious act that dedicates the enemies (and sometimes even the booty) to God (Brekelmans, *TLOT*, 2:475). Those people and/or things are banned from human use and consigned for destruction.

The exact "look" of חָרַם (*h̠ērem*) varied to some degree. In conjunction with Israel's conquest of Jericho, it involved the destruction of the entire population and the burning of anything valuable in the condemned city (Jos 6:17–19). With regard to Sihon and the Amorites, the inhabitants were wiped out, but the Israelites were able to take livestock and other spoils. The devoted things could be totally destroyed, turned over to the priests (Nu 18:14), or given to the sanctuary/tabernacle (Jos 6:24). Throughout the Israelite conquest of Canaan, חָרַם most regularly referred to the extermination of the inhabitants of a given city. Chapter 6 will make clear that even though the human population is "completely destroyed," the practice of חָרַם did not require widespread destruction. The Israelites plan on living in the cities and homes left empty and will eat from the vineyards and orchards left untended. The key principle was that Yahweh was to be Israel's only sovereign! Anything that stood in the way of his sovereignty was to be removed. For a helpful treatment of the concept of חָרַם, see *Show Them No Mercy: 4 Views on God and Canaanite Genocide* (ed. S. Gundry et al.; Grand Rapids: Zondervan, 2003), especially the essays by E. H. Merrill (61–94) and T. Longman III (161–87).

36 Although the NIV's translation of לֹא הָיְתָה קִרְיָה אֲשֶׁר שָׂגְבָה מִמֶּנּוּ (*lōʾ hāyᵉtâ qiryâ ᵃšer śāgᵉbâ mimmennû*, "not one town was too strong for us") is accurate and valid, it obscures a play on words that points back to the faithless report of ten of the spies Moses had sent out from Kadesh Barnea. These spies had bemoaned the fact that "the cities are large, with walls *up to the sky*" (1:28). According the NASB, Moses wrote here "there was no city that was *too high* for us." Israel's victory over Sihon and the Amorites provided the assurance that Israel could also conquer the walled cities of Canaan. As with Sihon, the ultimate end of that battle had been established by Yahweh as well.

b. Israel's Conquest of Og, King of Bashan (3:1–11)

¹Next we turned and went up along the road toward Bashan, and Og king of Bashan with his whole army marched out to meet us in battle at Edrei. ²The LORD said to me, "Do not be afraid of him, for I have handed him over to you with his whole army and his land. Do to him what you did to Sihon king of the Amorites, who reigned in Heshbon."

³So the LORD our God also gave into our hands Og king of Bashan and all his army. We struck them down, leaving no survivors. ⁴At that time we took all his cities. There was not one of the sixty cities that we did not take from them—the whole region of Argob, Og's kingdom in Bashan. ⁵All these cities were fortified with high walls and with gates and bars, and there were also a great many unwalled villages. ⁶We completely destroyed them, as we had done with Sihon king of Heshbon, destroying every city—men, women and children. ⁷But all the livestock and the plunder from their cities we carried off for ourselves.

⁸So at that time we took from these two kings of the Amorites the territory east of the Jordan, from the Arnon Gorge as far as Mount Hermon. ⁹(Hermon is called Sirion by the Sidonians; the Amorites call it Senir.) ¹⁰We took all the towns on the plateau, and all Gilead, and all Bashan as far as Salecah and Edrei, towns of Og's kingdom in Bashan. ¹¹(Only Og king of Bashan was left of the remnant of the Rephaites. His bed was made of iron and was more than thirteen feet long and six feet wide. It is still in Rabbah of the Ammonites.)

COMMENTARY

1–2 Israel's conquest of the kingdoms that controlled the territory in Transjordan continued in their victory over Og of Bashan. As the region ruled by Og, Bashan involved the territory to the north and east of the Jordan River. According to the prophet Amos, this region was famous for its fertility and rich pastureland (cf. 32:14; Am 4:1). In a more abbreviated narrative (though it could have contained some of the features that were part of Israel's conquest of Sihon), Israel marched farther north and engaged Og's army in battle at Edrei (a city almost as far north as the Sea of Galilee on the Yarmuk River). As an Amorite king, Og and his people were subject to the same fate as Sihon and the Amorites under his control, i.e., total destruction. As with Sihon, God determined the outcome

of the battle but required that Israel trust his promise and conquer the Bashanites.

3–7 The Lord enabled the children of Israel to defeat Og and his forces. They "completely destroyed" the entire Amorite population and took possession of all of his cities (sixty fortified cities as well as a number of unwalled villages). Since this endeavor was "holy war," God's involvement guaranteed Israel's success. Although that fact was abundantly evident in Israel's victories over Sihon and Og, the same reality existed during the conquest of Canaan proper. God determined the final outcome but required that his people take that reality to heart and engage their (and God's) enemy in battle.

Israel's failure to evict the Canaanites during the conquest of Canaan does not reflect God's inability but humans' unwillingness. After the defeat of Og and his people, the Israelites were able to keep for themselves the cattle and spoils left behind. Although the exact location and extent of Argob are never specified, it apparently was a subregion of Bashan.

8–10 The victory over Sihon and Og gave Israel control over the territory in Transjordan that extended from the Arnon River as far as Mount Hermon (also called Sirion or Senir by the Sidonians and Amorites, respectively, and spanning a distance of ca. 140 miles). The Israelites

captured and were able to inhabit all the cities in this region.

11 This verse states that Og's immense bed (thirteen feet long and six feet wide) "is still in Rabbah of the Ammonites." Ridderbos, 75–76, identifies this statement as a post-Mosaic gloss, perhaps from the time of David when Rabbah was the capital city of Amman, a place where antiquities such as Og's bed would likely be stored for display (cf. Merrill, *Deuteronomy*, 106; see comments on 2:10–12). Recording the location of Og's bed would have made little sense coming from Moses, one of Og's contemporaries.

NOTES

2 On אַל־תִּירָא (ʾal-tîrāʾ, "Don't be afraid), see Notes on 1:21.

3 On וַיִּתֵּן ... בְּיָדֵנוּ (wayyittēn ... bᵉyādēnû, "So he gave ... into our hands"), see Notes on 2:24.

11 Some contend that the word translated "bed" (עַרְשׂוֹ, ʿarśô, "his bed") would be better rendered "sarcophagus" or "coffin" (as his final "resting place"; Craigie, 120; Weinfeld, *Deuteronomy 1–11*, 184–85). Regardless of the translation, the item was large (ca. thirteen and a half feet by six feet). However, A. Millard makes a good case for regarding Og's "iron bed" as just that—a wooden bed frame decorated with or covered with iron ("King Og's Iron Bed—Fact or Fancy?" *BRev* 6 [1990]: 16–21, 44). Since iron did not come into common use until the first millennium BC (four hundred years after the events described by Moses) and because of the bed's immense size, it garnered attention as a "museum piece."

5. The Distribution of the Land in Transjordan (3:12–20)

OVERVIEW

Moses recalls once again the allotment of the newly conquered land to the Reubenites, Gadites, and half the Manassites, as well as

his challenge to these specific tribes to participate in the conquest of the land of Canaan proper.

a. The Division of the Transjordanian Land (3:12–17)

> **12**Of the land that we took over at that time, I gave the Reubenites and the Gadites the territory north of Aroer by the Arnon Gorge, including half the hill country of Gilead, together with its towns. **13**The rest of Gilead and also all of Bashan, the kingdom of Og,

I gave to the half tribe of Manasseh. (The whole region of Argob in Bashan used to be known as a land of the Rephaites. [14]Jair, a descendant of Manasseh, took the whole region of Argob as far as the border of the Geshurites and the Maacathites; it was named after him, so that to this day Bashan is called Havvoth Jair.) [15]And I gave Gilead to Makir. [16]But to the Reubenites and the Gadites I gave the territory extending from Gilead down to the Arnon Gorge (the middle of the gorge being the border) and out to the Jabbok River, which is the border of the Ammonites. [17]Its western border was the Jordan in the Arabah, from Kinnereth to the Sea of the Arabah (the Salt Sea), below the slopes of Pisgah.

COMMENTARY

12–13 In the parallel account in Numbers (32:1–5), tribal representatives from Reuben and Gad approached Moses to request that they be allowed to possess and occupy the territory just conquered on the eastern side of the Jordan River. In general, Reuben and Gad share the southern half while the half-tribe of Manasseh receives the northern part of Gilead and Bashan.

14–15 Moses gives more detailed information about the territory he assigned to the part of the tribe of Manasseh that would dwell in this region. Since Jair, a descendant of Manasseh, played a key role in capturing the cities of Bashan (Nu 32:41; 1Ch 2:22–23), Moses assigned this region to his family or clan. He renamed that area "Havvoth Jair," or "the settlements of Jair." Consequently, "to this day" the area formerly known as Bashan was called "Havvoth Jair." Most scholars estimate that God's children were encamped at the brink of the Promised Land for about three months. It had been a

little over seven months since they had begun their final approach to this land.

The events that occurred during that brief time span may have proceeded as follows: the peaceful passing through Edom, Moab, and Ammon; the conquest of Transjordanian peoples (Sihon and Og); the beginning of settling into a landed inheritance by the tribes of Reuben, Gad, and the half-tribe of Manasseh, while the rest of the tribes set up camp across the Jordan River from Jericho; Moses' composition of the book of Deuteronomy and presentation of it to the people; Moses' death; the mourning of God's people for Moses; and the preparation of God's people for entrance into Canaan. The key question is, Would the passage of three months' time from the conquest of Transjordan to the time of the writing of Deuteronomy provide enough time for it to be said that a certain part of Transjordan was called "Havvoth Jair until this day"?

Chronological Setting for Moses' Speeches			
	Year	Month	Day
Israel begins wilderness wanderings (Nu 13–14): approx.	2	3	20
Israel ends wilderness wanderings and begins conquest of Transjordan (38 years—Dt 2:14)	40	3	20
Elapsed time:	38	–	–

	Year	Month	Day
Israel ends wilderness wanderings and begins the conquest of Tranjordan (38 years—Dt 2:14)	40	3	20
Moses' last words (Dt 1)	40	11	1
Elapsed time:		7	9

	Year	Month	Day
Moses' last words (Dt 1)	40	11	1
Israel's crosses the Jordan (Jos 4:19)	41	1	10
Elapsed time:		1	9

16–17 Families from the tribes of Gad and Reuben settled from Gilead to the Arnon and as far east as the Jabbok River (where it makes a sharp turn to the north). The Dead Sea and the Jordan River formed the tribes' western border.

b. All Twelve Tribes Must Participate in the Conquest of Canaan (3:18–20)

[18]I commanded you at that time: "The Lord your God has given you this land to take possession of it. But all your able-bodied men, armed for battle, must cross over ahead of your brother Israelites. [19]However, your wives, your children and your livestock (I know you have much livestock) may stay in the towns I have given you, [20]until the Lord gives rest to your brothers as he has to you, and they too have taken over the land that the Lord your God is giving them, across the Jordan. After that, each of you may go back to the possession I have given you."

COMMENTARY

18–20 The fact that God sanctioned Israel's possession of this land serves as a key theme in these verses (Jos 22:1–9). They had not gained this land through their own merit or military prowess. It was a bequest to them from God. Notice the repetition of the verb "to give": "The Lord your God has given you this land ... the towns I have given you, until the Lord gives rest ... the land that the Lord your God is giving them ... the possession I have given you." They are also told to "take possession" of the land of Canaan and, after that is finished for all the tribes, they can return to their "possession." (See comments at 1:8 and 1:20–21 and Notes on 1:38 for further discussion of inheritance terminology.)

Another important point Moses makes in this section is that God holds these tribes (Reuben, Gad, and half-Manasseh) responsible to assist the other tribes in conquering the rest of the land of Canaan (3:20). Although their wives and children can remain behind to take care of their affairs in their newly possessed territory (3:19), the fighting men of these tribes must join their brethren for the conquest of Canaan proper. At the heart of this section is the reality that God seeks to maintain the solidarity and unity of the children of Israel. They need to conquer the entire region of Canaan and enjoy their new possession as one people.

This was an essential emphasis since the topographical barrier represented by the Jordan River could become an obstacle to national unity. Unfortunately, later on in Israelite history the tribes on the eastern side of the Jordan River became less interested in the affairs on the other side of the Jordan. In Judges 5, when Deborah and Barak led Israel against the Canaanites from Hazor, the tribes from Transjordan offered no assistance.

NOTE

14 Different forms of the expression "until this day" (here עַד הַיּוֹם הַזֶּה, *ʿad hayyôm hazzeh*, "to this very day") occur in the OT. The formulaic phrase "until this day" occurs eighty-four times in the OT (cf. Brevard Childs, "A Study of the Formula, 'Until This Day,'" *JBL* 82 [1963]: 280). It occurs twelve times in the Pentateuch (Ge 26:33; 32:32 [33]; 47:26; 48:15; Ex 10:6; Nu 22:30; Dt 2:22; 3:14; 10:8; 11:4; 29:3; 34:6). The phrase כַּיּוֹם הַזֶּה (*kayyôm hazzeh*, "as it is today") occurs twenty-four times in the OT and seven times in the Pentateuch (Ge 50:20; Dt 2:30; 4:20, 38; 8:18; 10:15; 29:28). The expression כְּהַיּוֹם הַזֶּה (*kᵉhayyôm hazzeh*, "as is the case today") only occurs six times in the OT and twice in the Pentateuch (Ge 39:11; Dt 6:24). This general expression often directs the attention of the audience to an event whose impact is still obvious. For example, Moses could remind the children of Israel that Egypt was still in shambles at the time of the Israelite conquest of Canaan (Dt 11:4; cf. 4:20; 29:4). Moses constantly reminded the Israelites that they had witnessed or were witnessing the things of which he spoke (1:19; 2:30; 11:1–19).

In addition to this usage of the phrase "until this day," which does not carry any chronological or compositional implications, eight occurrences may represent a post-Mosaic editorial note (Ge 26:33; 32:32 [33]; 47:26; Dt 2:22; 3:14; 10:8; 29:28; 34:6). The following section briefly considers the three most promising examples. Deuteronomy 34:6, part of a post-Mosaic section, affirms that the location of Moses' grave is unknown "to this." Deuteronomy 29:28 [27] occurs in the midst of the proposed answer to the question by the surrounding nations concerning God's future judgment of his chosen nation. Consequently, the expression "as it is this day" in reference to Israel's experience of exile could simply be part of that proposed answer with no implication of a post-Mosaic date of composition, or it could have been inserted by a later writer for special emphasis to the exilic or postexilic community. (Craigie, 360, and Merrill, *Deuteronomy*, 385, regard both alternatives as worthy of consideration.) Finally, the statement that Bashan was called Havvoth Jair "to this day" in honor of Jair, the son of Manasseh who was influential in the conquest of that region (3:14), would make little sense in the time of Moses when that region was first taken over by Israel. This phrase suggests the passage of some time. According to the chronology of this period before the conquest of Canaan, Moses arrived at the plains of Moab approximately three months before Joshua led the children of Israel across the Jordan River. In that brief time frame, Moses wrote the bulk of the book of Deuteronomy, he died, Israel mourned for him for thirty days, and preparations were made for the conquest. This scenario hardly leaves time for Jair to become memorialized "until this day" as the great conqueror of Bashan. Thus, I suggest that a divinely authorized representative inserted this parenthetical note for the sake of later readers (see comments at 2:10–12; cf. Ridderbos, 22, 68–69, 77; Grisanti, "Inspiration, Inerrancy," 585–86).

6. Preparations for the Israelite Invasion of the Land of Canaan (3:21–29)

OVERVIEW

In accordance with God's command, Moses exhorted Joshua to lead the children of Israel courageously in the light of all that God already had done for Israel in their victories over Sihon and Og. Then Moses requested the Lord to permit him to enter the Promised Land; he was refused, but God gave him permission to view the land from the top of Pisgah.

a. Joshua Needs to Look Forward with the Past in Mind (3:21–22)

²¹At that time I commanded Joshua: "You have seen with your own eyes all that the LORD your God has done to these two kings. The LORD will do the same to all the kingdoms over there where you are going. ²²Do not be afraid of them; the LORD your God himself will fight for you."

COMMENTARY

21–22 What Joshua had seen with his own eyes, God will continue to do on the other side of the Jordan River. According to Wright (*Deuteronomy*, 40): "If God could defeat two kings, He could defeat many more. Yahweh was a God who was not coincidentally lucky, but consistently victorious." Joshua need not fear, for God has promised to fight for him (and Israel) just as he had done against Sihon and Og. This theme is repeated in 31:1–8 and in Joshua 1:1–9.

b. Moses Needs to Rejoice in the Future in Spite of the Past (3:23–29)

OVERVIEW

Moses fervently requested the Lord's permission to enter the Promised Land but will only be allowed to view the land from the top of Pisgah.

God commanded Moses to invest his final energies in preparing Joshua for his leadership of the nation of Israel.

[23] At that time I pleaded with the LORD: [24] "O Sovereign LORD, you have begun to show to your servant your greatness and your strong hand. For what god is there in heaven or on earth who can do the deeds and mighty works you do? [25] Let me go over and see the good land beyond the Jordan — that fine hill country and Lebanon."

[26] But because of you the LORD was angry with me and would not listen to me. "That is enough," the LORD said. "Do not speak to me anymore about this matter. [27] Go up to the top of Pisgah and look west and north and south and east. Look at the land with your own eyes, since you are not going to cross this Jordan. [28] But commission Joshua, and encourage and strengthen him, for he will lead this people across and will cause them to inherit the land that you will see." [29] So we stayed in the valley near Beth Peor.

COMMENTARY

23–25 Although Moses was the great lawgiver and the ruler of Israel, he addresses his God as the "Sovereign LORD" and regards himself as his "servant." Moses realized that he had only begun to comprehend his great God's majesty because God had only begun to manifest himself to Moses and his people. The phrase "your greatness and your strong hand" refers to Yahweh's awe-inspiring character and his impressive interventions in Israel's behalf.

Moses breaks out in praise of his incomparable God because there were no gods like him. His question, "For what god is there in heaven or on earth ...," is a rhetorical question asked for emphasis. Moses was addressing the "marketplace of ideas" that existed in his day. He was referring to the conception of pagans (and certain Israelites) for the sake of argument. He was not granting the existence of other powerful gods and concluding that Yahweh is the winner out of many; rather, he was emphasizing that Yahweh is unique and unparalleled, the one and only true God (cf. 4:32–29). Moses pleaded (3:23) for God to allow him to witness personally the fulfillment of God's promise to provide Israel with a land (Ge 12:1; 13:14–17; 15:18–21; 17:8; 26:3–4; 48:3–4).

26–27 Moses once again points out to the Israelites that "because of/on account of you" Yahweh was angry with him and would not allow Moses to enter the Promised Land (see comments at 1:37). Moses is not affirming that he was blameless and punished despite his innocence; rather, Israel's rebellious conduct at Meribah (Nu 20) may have occasioned Moses' sin, but their behavior did not excuse his departure from God's clear instructions about striking the rock. Although Moses was affected by Israel's rebellious heart, he himself had sinned against Yahweh (Nu 20:12; Dt 32:51). Whether Israel provoked him or not, God held Moses accountable for his own sin.

Moses mentions this reality (which was painful for him at that time, when he was so near the Land of Promise) because he wants the Israelites to comprehend the far-reaching implications of sin. Their sin of grumbling occasioned (not caused) his sin, and his sin served as the grounds for his exclusion from Canaan. God demanded that Moses not request again that God might change his mind about this punishment. Instead, he exhorted Moses to go to the top of Mount Pisgah and view the land from that vantage point.

28–29 Since there was no possibility that Moses would lead Israel across the Jordan River into the land of Canaan, Yahweh directed Moses to prepare Joshua for that task (31:23; Jos 1:7, 9; cf. Nu 27:18–23). Israel waited at Beth Peor (exact location unknown) until God would command them to commence their long-anticipated entrance into the Promised Land.

At the end of this historical overview, everything is in place for the conquest of Canaan. Moses has commissioned Joshua, the people are located at Beth Peor (about one day's journey from the Promised Land), and Moses has stirred up the people's remembrance of their failures and God's rich blessing on them. Now Israel needs to look ahead, taking to heart God's surpassing character and abundant intervention in their behalf.

NOTES

23 The verb "to plead" (חנן, ḥnn [GK 2858], root of וָאֶתְחַנַּן, wāʾethannan, "and I pleaded with [the LORD]") means to "implore favor" from someone (*HALOT*, 335). When used with God as the object of the plea the word suggests seeking God's favor or compassion in a pointed, specific way (Merrill, *Deuteronomy*, 111; cf. Ps 30:8–10 [9–11]).

24 Although a number of translations render the divine title אֲדֹנָי יְהוִה (ʾᵃdōnāy yhwh, "O Sovereign LORD") as "LORD God" (ESV, NASB, NCV, NKJV, NRSV), the NIV (cf. NET, NLT, TEV) has rendered it more appropriately "Sovereign LORD." Both of these divine titles can be rendered "Lord" (hence, lit., "Lord, LORD"). The Masoretes, who added the vowel points to the consonantal text, normally pointed the second title (the divine title often translated with all capital letters—"LORD") to direct the reader's attention to a different divine title for "Lord" (יְהוָה [yhwh] → אֲדֹנָי [ʾᵃdōnāy]), to make sure that everyone avoided "profaning" the revered name, "Yahweh." However, when this compound title occurred as it does here, with two somewhat repetitive titles, the Masoretes provided vowel marks that directed the reader's attention to the divine title "God" (יְהוִה [yhwh] → אֱלֹהִים [ʾᵉlōhîm]).

If one sets aside this Jewish convention, the meaning of these two titles is redundant and emphatic and best rendered in a way that highlights God's sovereignty: "Sovereign Lord." Moses uses this title to emphasize God's sovereign control over history. Since the title "Yahweh" highlights God's capacity as the covenant-maker and covenant-keeper, this title also introduces a strong personal nuance. In historical literature this title almost always occurs in fervent prayers (Ge 15:2; Dt 9:26; Jos 7:7; Jdg 6:22; 16:28; 2Sa 7:18; 1Ki 8:53; not 1Ki 2:26, where it modifies the ark of the covenant). In the prophetic books, this title often serves to introduce the speaker of a prophetic message: "this is what the Sovereign Lord says" (Isa 7:7; 28:16; 30:15; 49:22; Am 1:8; 3:11).

B. Moses Exhorts God's People to Obey God's Law (4:1–40)

OVERVIEW

Although the next section of Deuteronomy that "formally" corresponds to the structure of suzerain-vassal treaties common in the middle of the second millennium begins in 5:1 (see comments on covenantal structure in Introduction and 1:1), ch. 4 plays a key role in Moses' message for the nation of Israel.

Based on the Lord's repeated demonstration of faithfulness toward the children of Israel (1:6–3:29), Moses exhorts them to be obedient and

prohibits them from practicing idolatry (4:1–40). Moses here moves from relating Israel's itinerary to pointed preaching (paraenesis) to the next generation of Israelites. Having traced the highlights of their experience over the past forty years, he now draws conclusions from that experience and urges a course of action that will affect both the present and the future. Finally, this chapter paves the way for the presentation of Yahweh's expectations of his servant-nation in chs. 5–11.

1. Observe God's Commands: The Extent and Result (4:1–8)

¹Hear now, O Israel, the decrees and laws I am about to teach you. Follow them so that you may live and may go in and take possession of the land that the Lord, the God of your fathers, is giving you. ²Do not add to what I command you and do not subtract from it, but keep the commands of the Lord your God that I give you.

³You saw with your own eyes what the Lord did at Baal Peor. The Lord your God destroyed from among you everyone who followed the Baal of Peor, ⁴but all of you who held fast to the Lord your God are still alive today.

⁵See, I have taught you decrees and laws as the Lord my God commanded me, so that you may follow them in the land you are entering to take possession of it. ⁶Observe them

carefully, for this will show your wisdom and understanding to the nations, who will hear about all these decrees and say, "Surely this great nation is a wise and understanding people." ⁷What other nation is so great as to have their gods near them the way the LORD our God is near us whenever we pray to him? ⁸And what other nation is so great as to have such righteous decrees and laws as this body of laws I am setting before you today?

COMMENTARY

1–2 Moses commands Israel to obey God's law so that they will enjoy the Lord's blessings and the surrounding pagan nations will recognize Israel's wisdom and understanding. The first two words in the Hebrew text, "and now," remind the reader that this exhortation does not come in a vacuum but is based on the historical remembrance of chs. 1–3. The exhortation "Hear, O Israel" (4:1; 5:1; 6:3–4; 9:1; 20:3; et al.) functions to call Israel to attention. The verb "to hear" (*šmʿ*; GK 9048) occurs almost one hundred times in Deuteronomy. It does not simply make reference to sound waves affecting the ear, but to focusing one's entire being on the Lord and what he says.

Moses exhorts God's people to give attention to Yahweh's "decrees and laws." These terms are pervasive in covenantal literature and denote the stipulations of the covenant. The Israelites are to give attention to Moses' teaching with the immediate goal of obedience (4:1 — "follow them"). God gave the law to Israel through Moses to provide parameters for Israel's conduct, not to function as a museum piece. The ultimate goal of their "hearing" and obedience is tenure in the land of promise.

The juxtaposition of living in obedience to the law and enjoy long tenure in the land has confused many readers of Deuteronomy. God, as the great sovereign of the universe, promises to give Israel the land but declares that the people's long-term enjoy-

ment of it is dependent on their response of committed loyalty and obedience (Lev 18:5; Dt 4:1; 5:33; 8:1; 16:20; 30:19; Wright, *Deuteronomy*, 46). According to the law of Moses, life for Israel meant life in the Promised Land. The duty of obedience and the gift of the land are interdependent. On the one hand, living in that land should serve to motivate God's people to obey their great God (cf. 7:6–11). On the other hand, tenure in the land is clearly linked with obeying the Mosaic law (30:15–20). Their disobedience might bring about their eviction from that land.

In the ultimate sense, whether or not Israel remained in the Land of Promise was determined by fidelity to the covenant made between them and God. The key observation to make from this interdependence is that "life" in the truest sense was only to be enjoyed when an Israelite lived in conformity with God's expectations. Living in the land God gave them provided Israel with an international platform to demonstrate his character to the surrounding nations.

As with other ancient Near Eastern treaties, Moses provides a nontampering clause for this covenantal document (4:2), thus highlighting the canonical status of Torah. Even though a suzerain-vassal treaty (after which Deuteronomy is modeled) can be called a bilateral agreement, it was the sovereign alone who could set the terms of the covenant. The vassal's responsibility was to accept the covenantal stipulations as given and to make every effort to keep them. Although various scholars regard this commandment as a divine one with regard to the canonical writings of both Old and New Testaments, in the immediate context the divine mandate in Deuteronomy 4:2 (cf. 12:32 [13:1]) relates to the God's law, which Moses is about to present to the children of Israel.

This injunction primarily refers to the essence of the law rather than the letter of the law (Craigie, 130; cf. Beckwith, 134). For example, the wording of the law in Deuteronomy 5 differs at several points from its wording in Exodus 20; nevertheless, the essence of the law is clear and the same in both chapters. The meaning or sense of these laws and not their exact wording is at stake. The covenant-treaty stipulations Moses gave to Israel lacks nothing. He prohibits anything that will adulterate, contradict, or render ineffective these divine requirements (Kalland, 42).

The placement of the almost identical injunctions in 4:2 and 12:32 [13:1] affirms the covenantal context of this warning. The mandate in 4:2 introduces a section of verses that exhort Israel to obey all God's commands. Deuteronomy 12:32 concludes the general stipulation section, in which Moses calls Israel to worship their God in total and absolute allegiance. Only what the Lord has spoken, but *all* that he has spoken, is incumbent on them. These warnings are against willful tampering with or distorting of the message of God's servant. In addition, they emphasize the fact that God's Word is sufficient or complete.

This reality occasions at least three observations. First, it highlights the unity of the law of Moses. It cannot be divided up into three sections: ceremonial, civil, and moral. Second, this nontampering clause is not referring to the presence or absence of certain words in a given biblical verse

that become apparent when one compares various modern translations. Finally, it exalts God's position as the sole maker or establisher of the covenant with Israel. The covenant is not a community project. Yahweh himself demands their total and undiluted loyalty.

3-4 As a motivation for Israel to obey, Moses reminds God's children of the Lord's curse on those who strayed from God's ways and his blessing on those who faithfully adhered to his ways at Baal Peor. The call to "see" suggests that there is a lesson for this new generation of Israelites to learn. If Israel's rebellion at Kadesh Barnea represented Israel's lowest point in their relationship with Yahweh, their rebellion at Baal Peor was the freshest in their memory (Nu 25; cf. Ps 106:28; Hos 9:10). There the Moabite women seduced many Israelite men and led them into idolatry. God struck down many Israelites through a plague because they had "followed after" another god. He demanded that they "hold fast" to him. Those who did so were still alive to hear this message by Moses. God offered his people life in the Land of Promise and demanded loyal allegiance if they were to continue to enjoy abundant blessings there. Rebellion occasioned the forfeiture of those blessings.

5-8 Although Moses was the great lawgiver, he is presently teaching and explaining ("I am teaching" instead of "I have taught") the laws God gave to Israel through him. As he affirmed in 4:1, the immediate objective of his teaching is obedience ("you may follow them"). In this case, however, the ultimate objective relates to the nations around them (not to Canaan). Israel's faithful observation of God's lofty expectations will uniquely affect those nations (cf. Ex 19:1-6). They will recognize Israel's "greatness" (mentioned three times) by seeing Israel as a wise and understanding people, having a God who is near, and having righteous laws. Respect for Israel implies respect for Yahweh, the one from whom Israel has received these laws.

According to Moses, the essence of wisdom and understanding is heartfelt conformity to God's will (Merrill, *Deuteronomy*, 116). The pagan nations, who all placed great value on wisdom, will recognize a wisdom more pure than they have ever seen in their own teachings or national life. The fact that Yahweh has given Israel a tangible set of regulations and in the light of his consistent efforts to cultivate (and demand) an intimate rela-

tionship with his servant-nation will astound the nations. Unlike their accustomed relationships with remote and inaccessible gods, Israel's loving relationship with Yahweh will amaze the nations. Finally, even though many law codes claim to be wise and righteous (e.g., the Code of Hammurabi 1:30–31; 4:9–10; 47:1–8, 9–58 [*COS*, 2:336–37, 351]), Yahweh's laws exceed everything these nations have ever heard. As these nations marvel at Israel's greatness, they will also marvel at Israel's great God.

NOTES

1, 40 These verses form an inclusio that encompasses the entire section, thus drawing attention to the section's key theme: wholeheartedly obeying Yahweh's commands.

1 The two nouns חֻקִּים (*ḥuqqîm*; GK 2976) and מִשְׁפָּטִים (*mišpāṭîm*; GK 5477) occur as a pair fourteen times in the book (4:1, 5, 8, 14, 45; 5:1, 31; 6:1, 20; 7:11; 11:32; 12:1; 26:16–17). They represent technical terms that signify the specific terms of the covenant, i.e., the specific laws incumbent on the parties of the covenant that are based on an underlying principle (the "commandment"; cf. 6:1). When this pair occurs with other words for law (עֵדֹת, *ʿēdōt* [4:45]; מִצְוָה, *miṣwâ* [5:31; 7:11]), those two words refer to individual commands. In other passages, especially points of transition (5:1; 11:32; 12:1; 26:18), they stand for the whole body of law as propounded in Deuteronomy 5–26 (McConville, 103). חֻקִּים (*ḥuqqîm*, derived from חקק, *ḥqq*) signifies a law that has been inscribed permanently (Enns, *NIDOTTE*, 2:231), and מִשְׁפָּטִים (*mišpāṭîm*) implies a judicial decision or an authoritative precedent. Although these terms have some distinct shades of meaning, they are often used interchangeably.

2 Prohibitions such as וְלֹא תִגְרְעוּ ... לֹא תֹסִפוּ (*lōʾ tōsipû ... weʾlōʾ tigreʿû*, "you will not add ... you will not subtract") are attested throughout ancient Near Eastern law and covenantal texts. For example, an Assyrian treaty states: "(You swear that) you will not alter (it) [the covenantal text], you will not consign (it) to the fire nor throw (it) into the water, nor [bury (it)] in the earth nor destroy it by any cunning device, nor make [(it) disappear], nor sweep it away. If you do, may Ashur, king of the gods who decrees the fates, decree for you evil and not good" (D. J. Wiseman, *The Vassal-Treaties of Esarhaddon* [London: British School of Archaeology, 1958] 60; cf. the epilogue of the Lipit-Ishtar lawcode, *COS*, 2:413; Kline, *Treaty of the Great King*, 43).

A nontampering clause like this is found in several ancient Near Eastern documents. In a unilateral arrangement of this type, the sovereign alone sets its terms. Since this revealed covenant is sacred (as part of the canonical Scriptures), "no one has the authority to alter it in any way, or even to supplement it, unless he shares the prophetic gift of its original author, Moses" (Beckwith, 134). This statement warns against supplementation (only what Yahweh prescribes is normative) and against deletion (or reduction; all that Yahweh prescribes is normative).

The basic idea of the verb לִשְׁמֹר (lišmōr, "by keeping"; GK 9068) is to pay careful attention to something (Schoville, *NIDOTTE*, 4:182). It can refer to maintaining (Ex 22:6; 1Sa 19:11; 28:2) or guarding something (Ge 3:24; 2Ki 11:5–7; 12:9; 22:4, 14; 23:4; 25:18). By keeping an oath one demonstrates careful adherence to verbal commitments (1Ki 2:43). The most frequently found meaning of this verb relates to persons diligently carrying out their moral and/or spiritual responsibilities. God expects his people to keep his way (Ge 18:19; Ex 20:6; Lev 18:26; Dt 26:16; Eze 11:20) and to give diligent attention to his decrees and commandments (Lev 22:31; Dt 4:40; 6:2; 26:17). This verb occurs repeatedly with the verb הלך (hlk; GK 2143; often translated "follow, walk [after]") with reference to obeying (or not obeying) God's commands (Lev 18:4; Dt 8:6; 28:9; Jdg 2:22; 1Ki 2:4; 3:14; 2Ki 10:31; 23:3; Ps 78:10; Mic 6:16). The "keeping" that Yahweh demands of Israel is not just a theoretical issue but must manifest itself in practical living. This verb also describes the careful attention Yahweh gives to his covenantal commitment to Israel (Dt 7:8–9, 12).

3 To "walk after" other gods (cf. 6:14; 8:19; 11:28; 13:2 [3]; 28:14) was a political idiom in the ancient Near East for giving allegiance to a ruler, hence to defect from the Lord here (Tigay, *Deuteronomy*, 44); so the expression אֲשֶׁר הָלַךְ אַחֲרֵי (ʾašer hālak ʾaḥᵃrê, "who followed") implies a wholehearted commitment of life and purpose (cf. Jdg 2:19; Ru 3:10; 1Ki 11:10; 21:26; Merrill, *NIDOTTE*, 1:1035).

4 To "hold fast" (דבק, dbq; GK 1816), as in the phrase וְאַתֶּם הַדְּבֵקִים (wᵉʾattem haddᵉbēqîm, "but you who held fast"), refers to covenantal commitment or undeviating loyalty (cf. 10:20; 11:22; 13:4 [5]; 30:20; Brooke, *NIDOTTE*, 1:911).

2. The Dangers and Consequences of Idolatry (4:9–31)

OVERVIEW

In light of the theophany at Mount Horeb, Moses prohibits Israel to practice any form of idolatry and promises that any such conduct will be severely punished.

a. A Reminder of God's Revelation at Mount Sinai (4:9–14)

OVERVIEW

Moses warns the children of Israel to be careful lest they stray from God's expectations of them. He reminds them that the Lord's intangible appearance before them was intended to cause them to fear him and to communicate that same reverence to their children.

⁹Only be careful, and watch yourselves closely so that you do not forget the things your eyes have seen or let them slip from your heart as long as you live. Teach them to your children and to their children after them. ¹⁰Remember the day you stood before the LORD your God at Horeb, when he said to me, "Assemble the people before me to hear my words so that they may learn to revere me as long as they live in the land and may teach them to their children." ¹¹You came near and stood at the foot of the mountain while it blazed with fire to the very heavens, with black clouds and deep darkness. ¹²Then the LORD spoke to you out of the fire. You heard the sound of words but saw no form; there was only a voice. ¹³He declared to you his covenant, the Ten Commandments, which he commanded you to follow and then wrote them on two stone tablets. ¹⁴And the LORD directed me at that time to teach you the decrees and laws you are to follow in the land that you are crossing the Jordan to possess.

COMMENTARY

9 In this call to remembrance, Moses uses multiple terms to emphasize the great significance of Israel's responsibility to maintain a living and dynamic relationship with Yahweh (which would naturally affect the next generation). He affirms that Israel must first and foremost give all diligence that they "do not forget" what they witnessed at Sinai/Horeb and since that time. This "forgetting" does not simply signify loss of memory but actually failing to live in the light of God's repeated intervention in their behalf, i.e., living as though those great and awesome events never took place. Instead of forgetting those realities, Moses exhorts the Israelite parents to devote themselves to making God's character and activity part of the fabric of their children's (and grandchildren's) lives. Life-transforming modeling before and training of one's descendants provides the only sure prevention for apostasy (cf. Jdg 2:10; Hos 4:6).

10–14 Moses reminds the Israelites of Yahweh's revelation of himself and his law to Israel when they were encamped at the base of Horeb/Sinai. Yahweh gave them his law so that the Israelites would know how to revere him properly (see Note on 6:13; cf. 10:12–13) and that they would be able to pass on those truths to the next generations. The Ten Commandments (lit., "ten words"; cf. 10:4; Ex 34:28) represent the heart or epitome of the Mosaic law. The fire, black clouds, and deep darkness bring together the concepts of self-disclosure and self-obscurity, i.e., immanence and transcendence. Although God revealed himself to Israel at Sinai in an unparalleled fashion, he did not reveal himself in any form that his people could visualize. God gave Moses the task of teaching the Israelites his expectations so that they would be able to live in conformity with those expectations from that day forward, but especially after they took possession of the Promised Land.

NOTES

10 "Remember" (זכר, *zkr*; 5:15; 7:18; 8:2, 18; 9:7; 16:3, 12; 24:18, 22) and do not "forget" (שׁכח, *škḥ*; 4:9; 9:7; 25:19; 26:13; 32:18) are common imperatives in Deuteronomy. ("Remember" is only implied in 4:10.) The verb "forget" serves as the antonym of the verb "remember." It can refer to something's or someone's slipping from memory (24:19; Ps 31:12). But when it is used of God's people with reference to their relationship with Yahweh, it refers to practical behavior rather than the act of a mere memory lapse. Moses connects the idea of forgetting God with tangible obedience or disobedience (Dt 4:23; 6:12–13; 8:11, 19; 9:7; 26:13). Deuteronomy 4:31 states that Yahweh himself does not forget his covenant with Israel. Yahweh's not "forgetting the covenant" did not simply represent the absence of cognitive activity (i.e., amnesia) on God's behalf with regard to the Abrahamic covenant! Instead, not forgetting this covenant meant that God will be faithful to its provisions. This covenant will affect his conduct in Israel's behalf.

Likewise, the verb "to remember" can refer to simple reflection or recollection, primarily on something in the past (e.g., Nu 11:5). But more often than not, remembering generates some impact on the person involved (Job 21:6; Ecc 5:20). In Deuteronomy remembering often induces present action, i.e., it provides a positive constraint for God's children. Out of its fifteen occurrences, ten instances refer to remembering some aspect of Israel's experience in and exodus from Egypt. For Israel to remember (and not forget) places the focus of their attention on God. Since God is living and is always present, the past can affect the present. Reflecting on the past will enable individual Israelites to believe that Yahweh can be counted on to remain true to his character. The same God who demonstrated his power in specific events "there and then" is prepared to do the same "here and now." Remembering God does not merely signify recreating or revisiting some historical aspect; rather, it demonstrates the contemporary validity of his promises. Remembering God gives evidence to his always continuing faithfulness.

The statement עָמַדְתָּ לִפְנֵי יְהוָה (*'āmadtā lipnê yhwh*, "you stood before the LORD") does not primarily refer to location but means "to have an audience with" someone. It is often used with royal overtones, e.g., standing before the suzerain (e.g., before Pharaoh; Ge 41:46; 47:7; Ex 9:10).

13 Various commentators have suggested that the Ten Commandments were divided between אֲבָנִים שְׁנֵי לֻחֹת (*šᵉnê luḥôt ᵃᵃbānîm*), "the two stone tablets." It seems more accurate, however, to regard these two tablets as two copies of the Ten Commandments rather than one tablet for the first four commandments (addressing humans' relationship with God) and the other tablet for the final six commandments (addressing relationships between humans). It was common in ancient Near Eastern treaties for the suzerain and the vassal each to receive a copy of the covenantal agreement, which they deposited in their temples. With Israel, both copies of the Ten Commandments were deposited in ark of the covenant housed in the Most Holy Place (Ex 25:16, 21; 40:20; Dt 10:2). The tabernacle/temple was Israel's sanctuary as well as the residence for the *shekinah* glory of Yahweh (Kline, *The Structure of Biblical Authority*, 113–26).

b. The Intangible Nature of Israel's God (4:15–24)

OVERVIEW

The Lord appeared to the children of Israel apart from any tangible form, and the Israelites are not to worship any tangible form lest they experience the divine wrath of their jealous God.

---

[15]You saw no form of any kind the day the LORD spoke to you at Horeb out of the fire. Therefore watch yourselves very carefully, [16]so that you do not become corrupt and make for yourselves an idol, an image of any shape, whether formed like a man or a woman, [17]or like any animal on earth or any bird that flies in the air, [18]or like any creature that moves along the ground or any fish in the waters below. [19]And when you look up to the sky and see the sun, the moon and the stars — all the heavenly array — do not be enticed into bowing down to them and worshiping things the LORD your God has apportioned to all the nations under heaven. [20]But as for you, the LORD took you and brought you out of the iron-smelting furnace, out of Egypt, to be the people of his inheritance, as you now are.

[21]The LORD was angry with me because of you, and he solemnly swore that I would not cross the Jordan and enter the good land the LORD your God is giving you as your inheritance. [22]I will die in this land; I will not cross the Jordan; but you are about to cross over and take possession of that good land. [23]Be careful not to forget the covenant of the LORD your God that he made with you; do not make for yourselves an idol in the form of anything the LORD your God has forbidden. [24]For the LORD your God is a consuming fire, a jealous God.

COMMENTARY

15–18 In their observation of the theophany at Horeb, the Israelites did not see Yahweh in any tangible form. Since all pagan nations objectified their gods in some tangible form, Moses warns God's chosen people against following that practice. He is obviously drawing on the first two of the Ten Commandments. To make and worship idols will horribly corrupt or ruin the purpose for which God made Israel. He commissions Israel to demonstrate his character to the nations around them (Ex 19:5–6), but making and worshiping images will divert the attention of the worshipers and the nations around them away from their great God.

Moses commands Israel not to depict their God in any fashion because doing so will reduce the omnipotent God to the level of pagan imagination (Merrill, *Deuteronomy*, 122). He employs four relatively synonymous terms that are part of idolatry: idol, image, shape, form. Most idolatrous religions do not technically regard the image or pattern as the god itself, rather, as a representation of the god. But in almost every case the image or pattern takes on divine qualities in the minds of its worshipers. In other words, the idol replaces the god it supposedly represents. Israel must not replace God with any human creation. The other danger of idolatry is that the worshiper ends up repudiating the true God.

Moses frames his description of the potential idolatry of Israel after the pattern of creation texts. In Genesis 1 God clearly delineated proper spheres of sovereignty: God over humankind over all creation. Yahweh created every celestial body and all animal life, and he commissioned humankind to have dominion over that creation. Idolatry overturns and rearranges these spheres of sovereignty (cf. Ge 1:14–27; Dt 4:16–19 and the reversal of the creation order). As Merrill (*Deuteronomy*, 122) points out, "humankind worships the creation rather than rules over it and repudiates the sovereignty of God rather than submitting to it." These prohibitions against animal worship and celestial worship have special relevance for the Israelites. The pagan world around them was wholly given over to this kind of worship (Craigie, 135–37, and footnotes; Christensen, *Deuteronomy 1:1–21:9*, 86–87).

19 What does Moses mean when he says, "do not be enticed into bowing down to them and worshiping things the LORD your God has apportioned to all the nations under heaven"? Some have suggested that Yahweh either sanctions or allows the worship of heavenly bodies by pagan nations (Craigie, 137; Driver, 70; Weinfeld, *Deuteronomy 1–11*, 206). Ridderbos, 87, writes that "idolatry ... occurs in accordance with His plan and providential governance." This view flies in the face of Romans 1:24–25 and seems totally out of harmony with the biblical presentation of God's demand for exclusive worship. It is unlikely that Yahweh would assign the lower parts of his creation to be objects of worship for the highest part of his creation (humankind).

Finally, this passage may simply affirm that these celestial bodies were given to all humankind for the physical benefit of the entire earth, not that they were proper objects of worship (cf. Ge 1:14–18). The implied contrast is between the heavenly creation, which was given to all humanity, and Yahweh himself, who was the portion of Israel (McConville, 108; Merrill, *Deuteronomy*, 123–24; Kalland, 45; Wright, *Deuteronomy*, 52). This verse does not demonstrate divine toleration of the worship of false gods; rather, it prepares the way for the stark contrast between Israel's favored position (4:20) and the status of the pagan nations (Mayes, 154).

20 Yahweh had delivered Israel from the blasting furnace of Egyptian affliction in order to make them a nation of his own. He made it possible for them to be a people of his inheritance, his special possession. As Israel's Redeemer, Yahweh has every right to demand absolute allegiance from Israel, and Israel has every obligation to render comprehensive allegiance to him.

21–22 The fact that Israel is Yahweh's special possession (inheritance) leads to the need for that special people to have a land of its own. Not only is the land Israel's inheritance, but Israel is Yahweh's inheritance. Moses mentions once again his exclusion from the landed inheritance as a reminder to God's people that they too can fail to enjoy this inheritance if they commit covenantal treachery (McConville, 109).

23–24 Moses warns his fellow Israelites against violating this covenant by means of idolatry and thereby risking the experience of Yahweh's all-consuming wrath. Moses regards idolatry as treachery for the Israelites because it constitutes "forgetting" the covenant. The God who is a consuming fire has forbidden this! The God who delivered Israel from Egypt (4:20), the fiery furnace, will bring his wrath against that same people if they violate his covenant with them (4:24). As the jealous God, he will not tolerate the worship of other gods by his special people, Israel. He demands unqualified allegiance.

NOTES

15 The exhortation וְנִשְׁמַרְתֶּם מְאֹד לְנַפְשֹׁתֵיכֶם (wᵉnišmartem mᵉʾōd lᵉnapšōtêkem, "watch yourselves very carefully"; lit., "give great care to your souls") occurs three times in the OT (2:4; 4:15; Jos 23:11). In Deuteronomy 2 Yahweh warns Israel against taking any land from the Edomites because he had allotted to them that land. In Joshua 23 Joshua exhorts the Israelites: "So be very careful to love the LORD your God." In the present passage Moses warns God's children to be very careful to avoid any connection with idolatry (4:16–19). The same verbal form of the root שָׁמַר (šmr; GK 9068) occurs eleven other times in Deuteronomy. In nine of those passages the particle "lest" (פֶּן, pen) follows the verb and provides the conduct being warned against: forgetting (4:9, 23; 6:12; 8:11), being seduced by idolatry (11:16; 12:30), failing to treat fellow Israelites with equity (15:9), offering sacrifices anywhere (at unacceptable locations; 12:13), or forsaking a Levite (12:19).

16 To "become corrupt" (שָׁחַת, šḥt [GK 8845], in the phrase, פֶּן־תַּשְׁחִתוּן, pen-tašḥitûn, "so that you do not become corrupt") describes the ruining or destruction of any number of things (morals [Ge 6:11–12; Dt 32:5; Eze 20:44]; a spring [Pr 25:26]; a covenant [Mal 2:8]; Van Dam, *NIDOTTE*, 4:92). This verb includes both the ideas of corruption and destruction. Genesis 6 depicts the world as corrupt (vv.11–12), and that corruption leads to destruction (v.17). In the present passage "corruption" (Dt 4:16, 25) represents a danger Israel faces, but Yahweh promises never to corrupt or destroy his covenant with Israel (v.31). This section and the next (vv.15–16, 25) begin with the danger of corruption. Idolatry represents intolerable corruption because it confuses the Creator with the creature (cf. Ro 1:25, 28).

24 The juxtaposition of the terms "fire" (אֵשׁ, ʾēš) and "jealous" (קַנָּא, qannāʾ) is interesting in the light of Deuteronomy 6:15, where the Lord is seen as a jealous God whose anger bursts into a destructive fire (cf. Lev 10:2; Nu 16:35). For God to be "jealous" means that his holiness and uniqueness cannot tolerate pretended or imaginary rivals. It is not petty envy but a divine response to an act of insubordination that must be severely judged (Peels, *NIDOTTE*, 3:937–40; cf. NET footnote).

c. The Potential Punishment for Covenantal Treachery (Idolatry) (4:25–31)

> ²⁵After you have had children and grandchildren and have lived in the land a long time — if you then become corrupt and make any kind of idol, doing evil in the eyes of the LORD your God and provoking him to anger, ²⁶I call heaven and earth as witnesses against you this day that you will quickly perish from the land that you are crossing the Jordan to possess. You will not live there long but will certainly be destroyed. ²⁷The LORD will scatter you among the peoples, and only a few of you will survive among the nations to which the LORD will drive you. ²⁸There you will worship man-made gods of wood and stone, which cannot see or hear or eat or smell. ²⁹But if from there you seek the LORD your God, you will find him if you look for him with all your heart and with all your soul. ³⁰When you are in distress and all

these things have happened to you, then in later days you will return to the Lord your God and obey him. ³¹For the Lord your God is a merciful God; he will not abandon or destroy you or forget the covenant with your forefathers, which he confirmed to them by oath.

COMMENTARY

25–28 Moses' overview of God's past dealings with Israel (chs. 1–3) and his exhortation for the generation camped at the brink of the Promised Land (ch. 4) leads to his concern for future generations. If future generations of Israelites violate this divine prohibition of idolatry, the curses of the covenant will become operative, i.e., Israel will be scattered among the nations (cf. chs. 27–32). By calling heaven and earth as witnesses, Moses emphasizes the intensity of his concern. Moses warns them that they will experience divorce from the land if they rebel against Yahweh. As part of his relationship with Israel, Yahweh has given the land of Canaan to Israel as their inheritance. He also regards Israel as his inheritance and demands that they live in accordance with that relationship. Moses wants Israel to understand that if covenantal faithfulness is missing, Israel has no claim to the land. There is no divinely granted right to the land they are entering without covenantal faithfulness. If they violate their relationship with Yahweh, their relationship with or enjoyment of the land will be interrupted as well.

He also promises that they will experience the shortening of life (long life's being an honor and blessing), dispersion among the nations, and destruction among the nations (become few in number), and they will be allowed to practice devotion to futile idolatry. Contrary to the pagan assumption that the gods ate the sacrifices offered to them, saw their devotees' processions, and smelled the incense, idols were in fact man-made, formed from inanimate substances, and insensitive to their surroundings, let alone their worshipers. Under divine judgment, the Israelites will have to do what they have freely chosen to do—serve other gods!

According to Moses, if Israel, knowing a God who has carried them (Ex 19:4; Dt 1:31; Isa 46:3–4), wants to serve gods that they will have to carry for themselves, they have some hard lessons to learn. In 4:16–19, Moses shows how idolatry reverses the divine order of creation. In a similar fashion, the judgment God promises for rebellion represents the reversal of the Abrahamic covenant. According to the Abrahamic covenant, God promised to provide a great land and a great people. However, God promises he will evict his people from the land and drastically reduce their population if they practice idolatry in rebellion against him.

29–31 Moses does not just have bad news for Israel. Even in the midst of divine judgment of great severity God provides the potential of covenantal restoration. He first establishes the precondition: genuine seeking after Yahweh (4:29–30). From their place of dispersion ("from there"), Yahweh will hear the repentant cry of his people. Unlike the pagan gods, who are territorial, Yahweh is not limited to his land. He can respond to his people wherever they might be. For Israel to seek after God wholeheartedly (see Note on 6:5) will obviously entail the abandonment of idolatry.

One of the features of a covenantal relationship with Yahweh is that "a rebel may return." The basis for any hope of restoration resides in God himself. Because Yahweh is characterized by compassion, he longs to spare his people from unnecessary sorrow and judgment. Even in the midst of judging his covenantal people, Yahweh will not forget his covenantal commitments to them. The fact that he has sworn (see Note on 1:8) to be their God guarantees his perpetual love for them and willingness to restore them. Some might think that the statements about God in 4:24 (God is a consuming fire and a jealous God) and 4:31 (above) are mutually exclusive or contradictory. Consider Wright's (*Deuteronomy*, 53) helpful comments about these verses:

The fire of Yahweh as *a jealous God* is the fire of an exclusive commitment to this people that demands an exclusive commitment in return. It is, in short, the fire of redeeming love that had brought them out of the fires of bondage (v.20) and would therefore tolerate no rival. The apparent contradiction between verse 24 and verse 31 is in reality a vital consistency. For mercy functions precisely in the context of judgment. It was the fire of God's mercy and covenantal faithfulness to this people. In rebellion and idolatry they would find the God of verse 24. In return and obedience they would find the God of verse 31. This is the same unchanged God, responding to a tragically changeable people.

NOTES

26 The word pair "heavens and earth" (in אֵת־הַשָּׁמַיִם וְאֶת־הָאָרֶץ, *ʾet-haššāmayim weʾet-hāʾāreṣ*, "the heavens and the earth") occurs repeatedly in the OT and can designate something that is fixed and reliable (11:21; Jer 33:25), refer to creation (2Ki 19:15 = Isa 37:16; 51:13, 16; 65:17; 66:1; Jer 32:17; Zec 12:1), or serve as a merism (referring to totality—Dt 4:39; 10:14; Jos 2:11; 1Ki 8:23; Isa 55:9; 66:1; Hag 2:21). Here Moses calls the heavens and earth as witnesses of Yahweh's demand for unqualified allegiance (not corrupted by any semblance of idolatry; cf. Dt 30:19; 31:28; 32:1; Ps 50:4–6; Isa 1:2; 49:13).

In a similar fashion, in various ancient Near Eastern treaties heaven and earth (along with gods and other parts of nature) are called as witnesses to the agreement (cf. McCarthy, *Treaty and Covenant*, 34, n. 11, 192–93). In ancient Near Eastern treaties the witnesses were generally deified and were instruments of punishment to those who violated the agreement. Because they are enduring and reliable witnesses, the heavens and earth can serve as sources of testimony against later generations of Israelites who break covenant. They too will be instruments of divine judgment against God's covenantal nation (Dt 11:17; 28:23–26, 38–40). However, unlike ancient Near Eastern treaty witnesses who possess great authority as deities, the heavens and earth are subject to Yahweh's ultimate authority and carry out his bidding.

31 The adjective רַחוּם (*raḥûm* [GK 8157], in אֵל רַחוּם, *ʾēl raḥûm*, "a merciful God") is related to the word for a woman's womb (רֶחֶם, *reḥem*; Ex 13:2, 12, 15; Nu 3:12; Eze 20:26). The verbal form related to this noun can signify a mother (Isa 49:15) or a father (Ps 103:13) who has mercy on a loved one as well as showing mercy to an enemy (1Ki 8:50; Isa 13:18; Jer 6:23; 21:7; 42:12). The usage of *raḥûm* to denote the emotion of mercy is similar to the metaphorical usage of another anatomical organ (the heart) for the seat or center of a person's emotions, intellect, and will. The fact that a mother has strong feelings for her child, the product of her womb, provides a clear illustration for this feeling of compassion.

It is important to note that this term for compassion not only describes the feelings a mother has for her children. In a number of instances it refers to the love of a father. The psalmist compares the "love" (רחם, *rḥm*) a father has for his children to the compassion (רחם, *rḥm*) the Lord feels for those who fear him (Ps 103:13; cf. Hos 1:6; 2:3, 6, 25). This noun and verb signify more than an emotionally rooted fatherly concern; it also denotes a compassion occasioned by the intentional acknowledgment of a relational foundation. This recognition of "paternity" triggers the acceptance of caring for the "child's" security and protection (Stoebe, *TLOT*, 3:1226). The OT always uses the nominal and verbal forms to describe the compassion felt by the "superior" figure toward the "inferior" party, never the reverse.

Along with the feeling of compassion based on an intimate relationship, the verbal and nominal forms at times emphasize the idea of sparing the person loved from some horrible fate. To show compassion in those instances concretely manifests itself in protecting that person (or nation) from extinction. In the first place, the Lord's "compassion" for Israel served to protect God's chosen people from total extinction or permanent banishment. Second, this "showing mercy" was rooted in God's ongoing covenantal relationship with his servant-nation. In summary, this noun and verb connote an intimate compassion, a love that goes beyond what is expected, a relationally grounded concern or mercy that gladly forgives sin and replaces judgment with favor. This demonstration of mercy goes far beyond what one could expect. Even though this compassion represents the outgrowth of a committed relationship, the recipient of the mercy has no automatic claim to it.

3. Observe God's Commands: The Motivation (4:32–40)

OVERVIEW

In this last section Moses returns to the need for Israel to obey God's commands wholeheartedly (cf. 4:1–8). In these verses, however, Moses focuses on the motivation for that obedience: who God is and what he has done in behalf of Israel. He recalls for Israel the distinctiveness of their God (in character and activity; 4:32–34), reminds them why God took care of them as he had (4:36–38), and gives them a final exhortation (4:39–40).

> ³²Ask now about the former days, long before your time, from the day God created man on the earth; ask from one end of the heavens to the other. Has anything so great as this ever happened, or has anything like it ever been heard of? ³³Has any other people heard the voice of God [a] speaking out of fire, as you have, and lived? ³⁴Has any god ever tried to take for himself one nation out of another nation, by testings, by miraculous signs and wonders, by war, by a mighty hand and an outstretched arm, or by great and awesome deeds, like all the things the LORD your God did for you in Egypt before your very eyes?

³⁵You were shown these things so that you might know that the L<small>ORD</small> is God; besides him there is no other. ³⁶From heaven he made you hear his voice to discipline you. On earth he showed you his great fire, and you heard his words from out of the fire. ³⁷Because he loved your forefathers and chose their descendants after them, he brought you out of Egypt by his Presence and his great strength, ³⁸to drive out before you nations greater and stronger than you and to bring you into their land to give it to you for your inheritance, as it is today.

³⁹Acknowledge and take to heart this day that the L<small>ORD</small> is God in heaven above and on the earth below. There is no other. ⁴⁰Keep his decrees and commands, which I am giving you today, so that it may go well with you and your children after you and that you may live long in the land the L<small>ORD</small> your God gives you for all time.

COMMENTARY

32–34 In order to challenge Israel's appreciation for and understanding of her God, Moses asks four specific rhetorical questions concerning the Lord's activity in their behalf. In general, Moses poses the question, "Has Israel's experience ever been duplicated?" He challenges them to review all past history and include all God's creation to see whether anything like "this" has happened before. Notice that Moses is not just saying that nothing *greater* has happened before, but that nothing *like it at all* has happened before! The "this" that is unparalleled in the present context refers to God's making a nation for himself, a nation that he has commissioned to lift up his name before the other nations of the world.

Moses goes on to ask two rhetorical questions that develop this thought (rather than introducing something new). When he asks, "Has any people ever heard the voice of God and survived like this before?" he is not asking, "Has anyone heard the voice of God and died as a result?" Rather, he is emphasizing that no other nation had ever received

direct revelation from its God (cf. Ps 147:19–20). He then asks whether another "god" had ever taken a people from the powerful grasp of another people and made them his own, as Yahweh had done. Although the mythology of other nations may include claims of divine intervention, none of these epic tales can compare to God's deliverance of a disorganized, dispirited, militarily inexperienced horde of slaves from the dominion of one of the mightiest powers on earth at that time (Merrill, *Deuteronomy*, 131). What Yahweh did in and through the events of the exodus and the Sinai revelation was unprecedented and unparalleled.

35–38 Moses points out that the Lord acted in Israel's behalf so that they could know by experience that the Lord is indeed God, the only true God. The powerful point of 4:32–34 is not simply that God is one, a belief in monotheism (as important as that might be). Rather, Moses proclaims that Yahweh, the God of Israel, is the exclusive, one-and-only true God. Moses then circles back to remind God's covenantal nation of their God's greatness and what he has done in their behalf. He revealed his expectations to them (4:36), chose them as his own people (4:37a), and delivered them from bondage in Egypt (4:37b–38).

39–40 Based on all the marvelous things the Lord has done for them already, God's children are exhorted to acknowledge his utter uniqueness and obey his commands with the result that this generation and all future generations will experience God's abundant blessings. Moses challenges his fellow Israelites to "take to heart" or internalize the fact that Yahweh is the universal sovereign ("in heaven above and on the earth below") and the only sovereign ("there is no other"). In the light of that theological reality, they should gladly obey his commands. Moses affirms that Israel's genuine obedience to God's commands will occasion long tenure in the land (and continued enjoyment of covenantal blessings).

As seen in 4:1 (see comments there), Moses is not simply holding before Israel the hope of long tenure in the Promised Land as a bribe or incentive. Granted, Israel's obedience or disobedience to God's covenantal expectations did affect whether they would remain in the Land of Promise. Nevertheless, Yahweh intended that Canaan would serve as a platform for his people to demonstrate his greatness to the surrounding world. God offered them the opportunity to live lives that exalt his greatness before the world around them for the undetermined future.

NOTE

37 The juxtaposition of these verbs "to love" (אהב, *ʾhb*) and "to choose" (בחר, *bḥr*), as in the phrase אָהַב ... וַיִּבְחַר (*ʾāhab ... wayyibḥar*, "he loved ... and chose"), occurs in several passages to highlight the concept of Yahweh's elective choice. In this passage and Deuteronomy 10:15 they occur in this order ("love," then "choose"). In at least four other passages these terms occur in the reverse order, but with the same notion (7:7–8; Pss 47:4 [5]; 78:68; Isa 41:8). In a word, to choose is to love and to love is to choose.

William Moran ("The Ancient Near Eastern Background of the Love of God in Deuteronomy," *CBQ* 25 [1963]: 78–79) has capably pointed out that as early as the eighteenth century ancient Near Eastern treaties used the term "love" (a different word in Akkadian, but a parallel term) to describe the loyalty and friendship that joined independent kings, a sovereign and his vassal, or a king and his subject. On the human side, the vassal or subject was expected to demonstrate loyalty (wholehearted obedience) to his suzerain or supreme ruler. However, God's love for Israel is in view in the present context. God's love represented an act of covenantal initiation (Dt 10:15; 23:5; Isa 43:4; 48:14; Jer 31:3; Hos 11:1; Mal 1:2; Merrill, "Deuteronomy," 459). The second verb, "to choose," highlights God's initiative in making Israel his servant-nation, an outgrowth of his love. J. B. Payne wrote: "God was the God of love because he was the God of the covenant; the establishment of the covenant and the giving of the Law had been the supreme expression of his love" (*Theology of the Older Testament* [Grand Rapids: Zondervan, 1962], 162).

C. Internal Matters, Recapitulation, and Transition (4:41–49)

1. The Cities of Refuge (4:41–43)

[41]Then Moses set aside three cities east of the Jordan, [42]to which anyone who had killed a person could flee if he had unintentionally killed his neighbor without malice aforethought. He could flee into one of these cities and save his life. [43]The cities were these: Bezer in the desert plateau, for the Reubenites; Ramoth in Gilead, for the Gadites; and Golan in Bashan, for the Manassites.

COMMENTARY

41–43 In order to ensure long life and to protect innocent people, Moses provides information concerning the purpose for and identity of the cities of refuge (cf. 19:2–13; cf. Nu 35:6–34; Jos 20:1–9). He sets aside three cities that will provide refuge for any person who commits unintentional murder. These cities are located on the eastern side of the Jordan River, the territory recently taken from Sihon and Og. Although the exact location of Bezer and Golan is uncertain, Ramoth was located in the eastern part of the territory given to Gad (modern Tell Ramith).

Moses addresses this issue here (an interlude of sorts) because these cities are likely chosen for this function at this time (while Israel is camped in the plains of Moab). The conquest of Transjordan has been accomplished, and there is no need to delay the fulfillment of the divine requirement for these locations (cf. Nu 35).

2. Recapitulation and Preparation (4:44–49)

OVERVIEW

Scholars have long debated whether these verses represent a conclusion to chs. 1–4 or an introduction to chs. 5–11 (or to ch. 26). Numerous scholars view them as a preface to the presentation of the Ten Commandments and the general stipulations (Yahweh's demand for total allegiance), especially in the light of 4:44–45 (Craigie, 146–47; Hall, 110–11; Ridderbos, 96–97; Thompson, 111; Tigay, *Deuteronomy*, 58–59; Weinfeld, *Deuteronomy 1–11*, 234–36; Wright, *Deuteronomy*, 61). Others contend on rhetorical and content grounds that these verses provide a fitting conclusion to chs. 1–4 (Christensen, *Deuteronomy 1:1–21:9*, 98–103; Harman, 68–70; Merrill, *Deuteronomy*, 135–38; McConville, 101–2, 114; cf. J. Lundbom, "The Inclusio and Other Framing Devices in Deuteronomy," *VT* 46 [1996]: 302–4). This passage, as other sections in narrative literature, looks backward and forward—

hence the divided opinion about its proper placement in the flow of argument. The content and wording of 4:44–49 is similar to 1:1–5. Fundamentally, these verses are not forward-looking but backward-looking, focusing more on historical and itinerary issues (which characterize chs. 1–4). Chapters 1–4 provide a prologue or introduction to chs. 5–11, not just to 4:44–49.

Moses asserts that the laws he is about to present have been given to the children of Israel encamped on the brink of the Jordan River. They have been given in the wake of God's impressive intervention in their behalf and in preparation for their conquest of the long-anticipated Land of Promise.

---

⁴⁴This is the law Moses set before the Israelites. ⁴⁵These are the stipulations, decrees and laws Moses gave them when they came out of Egypt ⁴⁶and were in the valley near Beth Peor east of the Jordan, in the land of Sihon king of the Amorites, who reigned in Heshbon and was defeated by Moses and the Israelites as they came out of Egypt. ⁴⁷They took possession of his land and the land of Og king of Bashan, the two Amorite kings east of the Jordan. ⁴⁸This land extended from Aroer on the rim of the Arnon Gorge to Mount Siyon (that is, Hermon), ⁴⁹and included all the Arabah east of the Jordan, as far as the Sea of the Arabah, below the slopes of Pisgah.

COMMENTARY

44–46 What Moses sets before Israel as they are camped on the plain of Moab is not a new covenant but instead represents the renewing of an old covenant (established at Sinai). Specifically, "the law" to which he refers encompasses chs. 5–26. More broadly, it refers to all the legislation Moses has delivered to Israel since their time at Sinai. Moses reminds his fellow Israelites of the immediate historical context, namely, their coming out of Egypt and their conquest of the land formerly occupied by the Amorites (under Sihon [2:26–37] and Og [3:1–11]). God's intervention in their behalf in both events (and repeatedly during the years between them) positions Yahweh as the one with the prerogative to demand their unqualified loyalty to his covenantal expectations.

47–49 Moses reviews the land Israel now occupies: all the Transjordanian region (except the land controlled by nations with a blood-relationship with Israel—the Edomites, Moabites, and Ammonites), all allocated to them by Yahweh.

NOTES

44 The term "the law" (הַתּוֹרָה, hattôrâ; 4:44; cf. 30:10) or "this law" (הַתּוֹרָה הַזֹּאת, hattôrâ hazzōʾt; 1:5; 4:8; 17:18–19; 27:3, 8, 26; 28:58, 61; 29:20, 28; 31:11–12, 24, 26; 32:46) normally refers to the entire corpus of Mosaic law.

45 On הָעֵדֹת וְהַחֻקִּים וְהַמִּשְׁפָּטִים (hāʿēdōt wᵉhahuqqîm wᵉhammišpāṭîm, "stipulations, decrees and laws"), see Note on 4:1.

48 The topographical reference שִׂיאֹן (śîʾōn, "Mount Siyon") should be rendered "Mount Sirion" (cf. 3:9), which is another name for Mount Hermon. The reading of the Hebrew text represents a variant of the original (cf. Craigie, 147, for an explanation of this problem).

III. EXPOSITION OF THE COVENANTAL STIPULATIONS (5:1-26:19)

A. General Stipulations of the Covenant (5:1-11:32)

OVERVIEW

Through Moses, the Lord reveals several general stipulations for Israel to follow; they can be summarized as an exhortation to love and obey the Lord wholeheartedly. Building on the historical overview of chs. 1-3 and Moses' sermon in ch. 4, these chapters constitute a broad exhortation to covenantal loyalty and obedience. With broad strokes, Moses depicts the kind of character and conduct Yahweh expects from his covenantal nation.

1. The Ten Commandments (5:1-6:3)

OVERVIEW

Moses reminds the Israelites of the relationship they enjoy with the Lord; it revolves around the Ten Commandments given at Horeb. He exhorts them to live faithfully in accordance with all that God expects of them (both the commandments God has already given and the ones he is about to give through Moses).

The covenant the Lord made with Israel at Horeb has clear relevance for the Israelites camped on the plains of Moab. It is not simply an agreement into which their forefathers have entered that has no ongoing significance.

a. The Historical Background for and Relevance of these Commandments (5:1-5)

> ¹Moses summoned all Israel and said: Hear, O Israel, the decrees and laws I declare in your hearing today. Learn them and be sure to follow them. ²The LORD our God made a

covenant with us at Horeb. ³It was not with our fathers that the LORD made this covenant, but with us, with all of us who are alive here today. ⁴The LORD spoke to you face to face out of the fire on the mountain. ⁵(At that time I stood between the LORD and you to declare to you the word of the LORD, because you were afraid of the fire and did not go up the mountain.) And he said:

COMMENTARY

1 Moses summons the Israelites (or their tribal representatives) to a covenantal assembly and calls for them to give careful attention ("hear"; see comments below) to Yahweh's expectations (cf. 4:1; 6:4; 9:1; 20:3; 27:9; Pr 1:8; 4:10; 23:19). The nouns "decrees" and "laws" can refer to the specific terms of the covenant (see comments and Note on 4:1), but in the present passage (a key transition point) they refer to the whole body of law delineated in the following chapters (chs. 5–26; McConville, 103). Although these terms would encompass what Moses had said (as Yahweh's prophetic spokesman) at Horeb, they more properly focus on Moses' teaching for the generation camped on the plains of Moab. The clear implication of a proper hearing of God's covenantal demands is that all Israel will "learn" and "be sure to follow them."

2–3 By means of overstatement, Moses makes clear that his presentation of God's expectations to Israel does not represent something unrelated to the events at Horeb, but is a renewal of the existing covenantal relationship between Yahweh and Israel. Further, Moses emphasizes that this covenant into which Israel entered at Horeb is just as much for the present generation as it had been for their forefathers.

Moses' statement that Yahweh made a covenant "with us" and "*not* with our forefathers" provides an initial shock to the reader and listener. He adds five more phrases to heighten his emphasis: "with us," "with all of us," "who are alive," "here," and "today."

God had established this covenant with the nation of Israel, and that covenant had implications for all Israelites for generations to come. The covenant was never simply a past event, because Yahweh (as the living covenantal Lord) is the suzerain of every succeeding Israelite generation (Wright, *Deuteronomy*, 62).

The mention of "Horeb" in v.2 indicates that Moses is referring to the generation of Israelites who agreed to God's covenantal demands there forty years earlier (rather than to the patriarchs). Although in the OT this term "fathers" often refers to the patriarchs (Abraham, Isaac, and Jacob; cf. 1:8; 6:3), Moses compares and contrasts the generation of Israelites living right before the conquest of Canaan with those who stood at the base of Mount Sinai four decades earlier (29:14). That Moses does so supports the contention that the covenant established at Sinai and renewed in Deuteronomy is distinct from the Abrahamic covenant both in form and function.

The covenant Yahweh made with Abraham represents an irrevocable and unilateral grant that promised Abraham's descendants land, seed, and blessing (Ge 12:1–3). The "Israelite" (often called Mosaic) covenant follows the pattern of a suzerain-vassal arrangement between Yahweh and Israel wherein the Lord (the suzerain) promised to care for Israel's welfare and destiny and Israel (the vassal) pledged their total allegiance to him. This latter covenant regulated Israel's life as the chosen people "within the framework of the Abrahamic covenant"

(Merrill, *Deuteronomy*, 141). Even though Israel's existence was never in ultimate question (based on the Abrahamic covenant), their enjoyment of covenantal blessings and their ability to function as a servant-nation (Ex 19:4–6) depended on their wholehearted obedience to the demands of the covenant made at Horeb.

4–5 After dealing with the continuity of the covenant, Moses speaks about the immediacy of Yahweh's dealing with Israel by means of the covenant. In view of 4:12, 15, "face to face" in 5:4 does not literally mean that Yahweh appeared before the Israelites but instead seems to emphasize the directness of Yahweh's revelation of himself to his servant-nation. Israel is the only nation ever to have witnessed God's revelation of himself (Ex 19:16–19; Dt 4:32–33). Even though Yahweh spoke to Moses "face to face" (Ex 33:11), Moses was not allowed to see his "face" (Ex 33:20). In addition to drawing attention to the unique immediacy of Yahweh's relationship with Israel, Moses points to his role as covenantal mediator. Yahweh utilizes Moses as his revelatory spokesman to present the covenantal stipulations to the chosen nation.

NOTE

1 The command for Israel to "hear" (שְׁמַע) (*š^ema^c*, "Listen!") calls Israel to give careful attention to God's message through Moses. As the only singular verb in this passage, it serves as an interjection. It commonly serves to introduce a didactic address (Weinfeld, *Deuteronomy 1–11*, 199).

The two verbs שְׁמַרְתֶּם לַעֲשֹׂתָם (*š^emartem la^{ca}śōtām*, "be careful to keep them") occur in immediate or close juxtaposition to each other in forty OT passages; twenty-five of those OT occurrences are in Deuteronomy and signify "carefully obey." The verbs can occur together as two infinitive constructs (Dt 15:5; 28:1, 13, 15; 32:46), two finite verbs (4:6; 7:12; 16:12; 23:24; 26:16; 29:9 [8]), or a finite verb and an infinitive construct (as here; 5:1, 32; 6:3, 25; 8:1; 11:32; 12:1; 13:1; 17:10; 19:9; 24:8 [2x]; 28:58; 31:12). They represent a verbal hendiadys of sorts (where two verbs carry one primary significance that draws on both verbs). Moses uses this combination of verbs to call the Israelites to invest themselves wholeheartedly in living according to the covenantal stipulations.

b. The Ten Commandments (5:6–21)

OVERVIEW

Moses reviews the Ten Commandments and the context of their being given. The first four commandments address the vertical dimensions of the covenant (5:7–15), while the last six commandments give attention to its horizontal dimensions (5:16–21). In addition to these two dimensions (cf. Mt 22:34–40), these commandments present a scale of values that reflects God's design for human life: God, society, family, life, sex, and property. Sadly, modern society constantly inverts this scale of values (Wright, *Deuteronomy*, 66).

As was common when certain covenants were renewed because of changing times and circumstances (Harman, 71; Merrill, *Deuteronomy*, 141), Moses makes some modifications to the Ten Commandments (see below). As the covenantal spokesman and mediator, Moses presents to Israel once again God's clear demands of them, but his audience will soon experience many changes in their life's experience. Leaving an itinerant existence in the wilderness, they will soon occupy a land that will be theirs and face circumstances and challenges that are somewhat different from those encountered over the past forty years.

The Ten Commandments, distinct from most of the rest of the law, entail terse, divine demands, called "apodictic" law. Apodictic law normally begins with the second person ("you shall/shall not"), involves statements of principle or general commands without qualifications, and leaves unstated any consequences of nonobservance. Most of Mosaic law is "casuistic" or "case law." This latter legal form normally begins with "if" or "when" and is usually in the third person. A specific situation receives attention, and the law often contains long explanatory comments or qualifications. It normally identifies the consequences of nonobservance.

i. The preamble (5:6)

⁶"I am the LORD your God, who brought you out of Egypt, out of the land of slavery."

COMMENTARY

6 Paralleling the suzerain-vassal treaty form evident in the book of Deuteronomy as a whole (in which 1:6–4:43 provides the historical prologue), this verse delineates Yahweh's conduct toward Israel as the basis for Israel's obeying the stipulations of the covenant. God does not deliver his covenantal demands to Israel in a vacuum but in the context of an intimate relationship, clearly evidenced by his character and activity in Israel's behalf. He addresses Israel through Moses as "the LORD your God" (cf. Lev 26:11–12), the God who has pledged to care for their welfare and destiny.

As the faithful, covenant-keeping, and absolutely sovereign God, Yahweh has tangibly demonstrated his character by means of his activity in history. In an absolutely unparalleled fashion, he delivered Israel, a subject people, from the domination of Egypt, a powerful empire (4:32, 34). He redeemed them out of slavery in Egypt in order to establish them in a land he promised to them, so that they will be able to demonstrate his character to the surrounding world (cf. Ex 19:5–6). This divine deliverance from bondage should serve as a clear indication that Yahweh is not bringing on Israel another (different but just as miserable) form of bondage by giving to them these commandments and the various laws to follow.

ii. The First Commandment: Give exclusive allegiance to Yahweh (5:7)

⁷"You shall have no other gods before me."

COMMENTARY

7 This line states literally, "There will not be for you other gods before my face." In biblical Hebrew, "there will be/not be ... for you" signified either possession or relationship. In Leviticus 26:12 Yahweh affirms (lit.), "I will be for you, as God." Yahweh demands that Israel have a relationship with him alone. For them, there are to be no other gods. Although this verse does not provide concrete grounds for the idea that Moses was a henotheist (regarding Yahweh as the supreme God but recognizing the existence of other, lesser gods), its primary function is not to establish philosophical monotheism or to deny the validity of polytheism in theory. This verse clearly denies the legitimacy of polytheism for Israel. Its fundamental thrust is not Yahweh's sole deity as much as it is Yahweh's sole sovereignty over Israel. It serves to emphasize and protect Yahweh's exclusive covenantal sovereignty over Israel and his legitimate demand for their exclusive covenantal loyalty (Wright, *Deuteronomy*, 68).

Yahweh prohibits Israel from establishing a relationship with any alleged "god" "before" him or "in his presence" (cf. Merrill, *Deuteronomy*, 146; Weinfeld, *Deuteronomy 1–11*, 276–77). This prepositional phrase has both locational and relational significance. In the first place, as their suzerain lord and worthy object of their worship, no other god should receive worship in his holy structure (the tabernacle and later the temple). Beyond that, as the omnipresent God, he prohibits the worship of any other "god" by his chosen people in any location. Second, any worship rendered to another "god" represents relational treachery. This commandment does not primarily concern philosophical orthodoxy but demands absolute covenantal loyalty.

iii. The Second Commandment: Allow Yahweh alone to define his image (5:8–10)

> 8"You shall not make for yourself an idol in the form of anything in heaven above or on the earth beneath or in the waters below. 9You shall not bow down to them or worship them; for I, the LORD your God, am a jealous God, punishing the children for the sin of the fathers to the third and fourth generation of those who hate me, 10but showing love to a thousand generations of those who love me and keep my commandments."

COMMENTARY

8 Yahweh also prohibits his chosen people from fashioning images to worship. On the one hand, forming images of pagan gods was clearly unacceptable and was deemed an act of covenantal treachery. Since the first commandment prohibited Israel from worshiping anyone but Yahweh, this command states that they may not fashion any images of those forbidden gods. Doubtless, the present commandment adds emphasis to that prohibition.

Nevertheless, it primarily deals with the shaping of idols in an attempt to present a visual image of Yahweh. In greater detail than Exodus 20, the Lord specifies every part of his creation as an insufficient image to depict accurately his character. It was abundantly clear throughout the ancient Near East and even in Israelite history (e.g., bronze serpent, bulls made by King Jeroboam I) that an image or idol made to represent some kind of deity became the object of worship itself. In 4:12, 15, Moses emphasized that Yahweh had not revealed himself to his people in visible form. There is no physical image sufficient to capture the glories of a great, powerful, and majestic God. Also, a visible representation of God is not only insufficient to serve as an accurate representation, it would also horribly limit or confine God's greatness and transcendence. An image would depict the living God as a lifeless God, the speaking God as a gagged God, and the incomparable God as a comparable (or limited) God.

9–10 Yahweh prohibits the worship of any image, even one made to facilitate an Israelite's worship of him. His chosen people are not to bow down to them or to offer their allegiance to them. The basis for this prohibition is the fact that Yahweh is a jealous God, firmly committed to protect and defend an exclusive relationship with his covenantal people. Since he has exclusively committed himself to Israel, he demands that they render to him exclusive loyalty. Unlike the petty jealousy and anger that characterizes human relationships, God has the right to a monopoly on our love and will act to protect that special relationship (as in a husband-wife relationship).

God promises to "punish" the iniquity of those who "hate" (see Notes) him even to the third or fourth generation. Does Moses here refer to "cross-generational retribution," the idea that later generations will be held responsible for the sins their ancestors committed? Not only do later prophets

emphasize that God does not punish innocent people (Jer 31:29–30; Eze 18:1–20), but Moses himself writes that "fathers shall not be put to death for their children, nor children put to death for their fathers; each is to die for his own sin" (Dt 24:16). In general, four generations marks the common span of human life (Ge 50:23; Job 42:16; 2Ki 10:30; 15:12). By using this expression the Pentateuch is not seeking to be precise but is rather speaking of the third or fourth generation (x or x + 1, a pattern common in biblical language; cf. Am 1–2).

While God holds none of us *responsible* for the sins committed by someone else (guilt), we can experience *consequences* that result from someone else's sinful choices. Because extended Israelite families often included three and often four generations, "the effects of one generation's failure in covenant loyalty … would detrimentally affect the succeeding ones" (Wright, *Deuteronomy*, 72). In addition to providing an idolatrous example, those who "hate" Yahweh will not instruct their children in proper covenantal loyalty.

In contrast to this horrific fate, Yahweh promises "covenant faithfulness" (*ḥesed*; GK 2876) as long as a thousand generations for those who love (see Notes) Yahweh. This term has several possible translations: loyal love, lovingkindness, covenantal faithfulness, mercy, love, steadfast love, kindness. In general, when used of Yahweh it signifies the steadfast love of God toward his people in the context of a covenantal relationship (cf. 7:9). Mention of "thousands" of generations signifies a *long time*. A thousand generations was a very, very long time, almost as good as "for ever." God's punishment lasts for generations, just as his grace endures for generations. God speaks of punishment in terms of *living memory* and of covenantal love in terms of *an unimaginable long-distance future* (see Wright, *Deuteronomy*, 72).

NOTES

8 A פֶּסֶל (*pesel*; GK 7181), "idol," refers to an object made of wood (Dt 27:15; 1Ki 21:7), stone (Lev 26:1), or metal (Jdg 17:3–4; Isa 40:19; 44:10; Jer 10:14) that depicts things, animals, or people. This noun includes reference to an image of Yahweh that an Israelite might be tempted to form in order to facilitate Israel's worship of their god rather than exclusively addressing the making of idols of pagan gods. The similarity of the first and second commandments (dealing with worship) caused Augustine, Catholic, and Lutheran tradition incorrectly to regard the first two commandments as one. This choice forced them to divide the tenth commandment into two commands in order to maintain ten of them.

9 As in the phrase לֹא־תִשְׁתַּחֲוֶה לָהֶם וְלֹא תָעָבְדֵם (*lōʾ-tištaḥʷaweh lāhem welōʾ tāʿobdēm*, "you shall not bow down to them or worship them"), the verbs חוה (*ḥwh*; GK 2556) and עבד (*ʿbd*; GK 6268) occur in close juxtaposition thirty-four times in the OT (seven times in Deuteronomy: 4:19; 8:19; 11:16; 17:3; 29:26 [25]; 30:17), fourteen of those in this order. The first verb generally means "to bow down" and always refers to an attitude or action directed toward an authority figure, whether human or divine. This act of self-abasement could be performed before relatives or strangers (Ge 33:3; 48:12; 18:2), superiors (Nu 22:31; Ru 2:10), or even before royalty (2Sa 14:4, 22; 15:5; 16:4). It often occurs in the context of divine worship (110 times out of its 170 occurrences in the OT). It can be used of the true worship of God as well as the worship of false gods.

The second verb can signify work (Ge 2:5; 4:2, 12; Ex 20:9; Dt 28:39; 2Sa 9:10), service rendered as a servant (Ex 21:2, 6; Lev 25:39–46; Dt 15:12), political loyalty (Ge 27:29; 1Ki 9:21; 12:4, 7; 2Ki 18:7; 25:24), or service rendered to false gods (Dt 4:28) or the true God (Ex 4:23; Dt 6:13; Grisanti, "1 Kings," 236, 257). In all but two instances where these two verbs occur together (Ge 27:29; Ps 72:11), this verbal pair delineates covenantal treachery, i.e., the worship of false gods in place of worshiping Yahweh.

Rather than introducing distinct ideas, the two verbs most likely serve as a broad reference to any kind of worship of submission (Tigay, *Deuteronomy*, 65). Since serving God entails a recognition of his lordship and supremacy, to "serve" other gods meant much more than practicing a certain kind of worship. It represents acknowledging another god as lord, i.e., choosing the lordship of another god (Westermann, *TLOT*, 2:829). Israel was redeemed from bondage or service in Egypt in order to serve Yahweh. To serve other gods, then, is to reverse the exodus and go back under bondage, thus betraying the grace and favor of Yahweh (Merrill, *Deuteronomy*, 147–48).

Although the verb "to hate" (שׂנא, *śnʾ* [GK 8533], root of לְשֹׂנְאָי, *leśōneʾāy*, "of those who hate me") can literally signify the emotion of hatred, in this context the term probably has the basic idea of *rejection*. This verb and the next (אהב, *ʾhb*, "love") are often used in describing familial relationships and, in a derived sense, political relationships (Tigay, *Deuteronomy*, 66). The following examples highlight this aspect of rejection: a husband or father may disfavor one of his wives or children (Ge 29:31, 33; Dt 21:15); members of a group may reject one of their number (Ge 26:27; 37:4–8); enemies are often described as "haters" (Pss 25:19; 139:21–22).

When used in the realm of spiritual or religious relationships, the verb "to hate" does not likely mean that a polytheistic Israelite would hate or even reject (in a final sense) the Lord. They might worship him along with a host of other gods or even ignore him. However, since the Lord demands exclusive fidelity, the worship of other gods alongside of him is viewed as tantamount to rejecting him. According to Merrill (*Deuteronomy*, 75), the verb and cognate noun frequently are technical terms to describe covenantal rejection, i.e., nonelection (cf. Dt 1:27).

10 As with the term "hate," the verb אהב (*ʾhb*, "love") can refer to the emotional concept to "love." In light of the manner in which "hate" is used in this passage, "love" connotes election to covenantal fellowship. In covenantal contexts it appears to mean "to choose." Tigay (*Deuteronomy*, 67) points out that in political contexts this verb includes friendship and loyalty, including loyalty of allies and of a vassal toward his suzerain, i.e., to act loyally. The prophet Hosea especially develops the idea of love to express Yahweh's covenantal choice of Israel (Hos 3:1; 11:1; cf. Mal 1:2−3). In a covenantal context, love is demonstrated by keeping Yahweh's commandments. It is inseparable from action.

Like the numerical adjectives "third" and "fourth" in 5:9, the adjective "thousand" (לַאֲלָפִים, *laʾᵃlāpîm*, "to a thousand generations") does not modify a noun in the passage. For a number of reasons, most scholars insert the word "generation" with "third" and "fourth" in v.9. Commentators and Bible translations are mixed on what they do with the numerical adjective in v.10. Some translate it "thousands," referring to the vast number of people in view (ESV, NASB, NET, NKJV). Others insert the word "generations" as in v.9 (see comment above; NIV, NLT, NRSV; NCV has "lifetimes").

iv. The Third Commandment: Honor and respect Yahweh (5:11)

¹¹"You shall not misuse the name of the LORD your God, for the LORD will not hold anyone guiltless who misuses his name."

COMMENTARY

11 The Lord prohibits his children from making use of his name for ends that stand opposed to God's purposes. God's name is often regarded as an extension of or even a substitute for God himself (cf. 12:5, 11, 21; 14:23−24; 16:2, 6, 11; 26:2; Pss 25:11; 79:9; 145:1−2; cf. Merrill, *Deuteronomy*, 149; Ross, *NIDOTTE*, 4:150). Several scholars have argued that the clause "to lift the name of" primarily concerns the issue of swearing or making oaths (Hamilton, *NIDOTTE*, 3:162; Tigay, *Deuteronomy*, 67; Weinfeld, *Deuteronomy 1−11*, 278−79, 300−301; Kalland, 54). More likely, this clause

refers more broadly to speaking the name of the Lord (Stolz, *TDOT*, 10:38; idem, *TLOT*, 2:771).

"Taking up" the name of Yahweh can be an idiom for worship (Ps 16:4) or can describe how God's adversaries misuse his name (139:20). Making use of God's name for deceptive purposes (see Note) encompasses both the manner and the purpose for which someone uses God's name. To invoke God's name in support of a statement or deed that in reality does not have God's authority behind it is to use his name for deceptive purposes (Biddle, 110). By so doing one creates the impression that God stands behind what is affirmed or done, when such is far from the truth (C. Houtman, *Exodus* [Leuven: Peeters, 2000], 3:36). In these circumstances, truth is violated and fellow citizens are misled and harmed.

Further, with regard to a people that is to be characterized by internal harmony, such a betrayal of trust threatens to unravel the moral fiber holding that society together. Perjury, false oaths, and even false prophecy are condemned by this command. As those who bear God's name ("the people of God"), to live as "Canaanites" is to bear his name deceptively.

Yahweh also promises that he will not acquit anyone (i.e., find them innocent or exempt them from punishment; *HALOT*, 720) who uses his name in this prohibited fashion. This characteristic of God receives mention at least seventeen times in the OT (e.g., Ex 34:7; Nu 14:18; Job 9:28; Jer 30:11; 46:28; Na 1:3). This negative statement is a common way of affirming that God will punish all who use his name inappropriately.

NOTE

11 God's "name" (שֵׁם, *šēm* [GK 9005], in שֵׁם יהוה אֱלֹהֶיךָ, *šēm-yhwh ʾelōheykā*, "the name of Yahweh your God") signifies more than a mere title—it highlights God's character. In the Semitic world, a name often signified something about a person's character. In Exodus 34:5–7, the Lord's declaration of his name to Moses is followed by a recitation of his marvelous attributes. The special names listed in Isaiah 9:6 represent more than titles to pronounce by connoting his nature. When prophets were sent in the name of Yahweh, they carried his personal authority as if present with them (Dt 18:20; Ross, *NIDOTTE*, 4:148, 150). A prophetic curse carried God's authority (2Ki 2:24). The Lord swore by his "great name" (Jer 44:26) and will one day sanctify his "great name" (Eze 36:23). The psalmist exhorted all nations to praise his "great name" (Ps 99:3).

In the wake of Israel's defeat at Ai, Joshua asked God how a Canaanite extermination of Israel would affect his "great name" or reputation (Jos 7:9). God's reputation is wrapped up in Israel's existence; consequently, he will not destroy his reputation and deny his character by permanently forsaking his chosen people (2Ki 14:27). Something done "for the sake of his name" is done to uphold God's great fame and reputation (1Ki 8:41).

In a few passages the noun שָׁוְא (*šāwʾ* [GK 8736]; cf. here לַשָּׁוְא, *laššāwʾ*, "for worthless purposes") can refer to something that is empty or futile without any connotation of deceit (Jer 2:30; 4:30; 6:29; 46:11; Mal 3:14). In some places, the word clearly implies deceit or falsehood, even if it carries the idea of something worthless or unrestrained (Eze 13:6, 9, 23; 21:34; Pss 24:4; 119:37; La 2:14; cf. *HALOT*, 1426). In most passages, however, the concept of deceit or falsehood is primary (Ex 23:1; Ps 144:8, 11; Pr 30:8; Isa 1:13; 59:4; Jer 18:15).

This noun also appears in the ninth commandment (Dt 5:20). Whether the primary idea in that instance is "empty" or "without substance" is immaterial in the end. One who is accused on invalid or worthless evidence is accused falsely (Merrill, *Deuteronomy*, 155). Note that in the Exodus 20 account, the noun שָׁוְא (*šāwʾ*) occurs in the third commandment (v.7), and a closely related term, שֶׁקֶר (*šeqer*), occurs in the ninth commandment (v.16). There appears to be no basic difference between these nouns.

v. The Fourth Commandment: Celebrate Yahweh's accomplishments (5:12–15)

¹²"Observe the Sabbath day by keeping it holy, as the LORD your God has commanded you. ¹³Six days you shall labor and do all your work, ¹⁴but the seventh day is a Sabbath to the LORD your God. On it you shall not do any work, neither you, nor your son or daughter, nor your manservant or maidservant, nor your ox, your donkey or any of your animals, nor the alien within your gates, so that your manservant and maidservant may rest, as you do. ¹⁵Remember that you were slaves in Egypt and that the LORD your God brought you out of there with a mighty hand and an outstretched arm. Therefore the LORD your God has commanded you to observe the Sabbath day."

COMMENTARY

12–14 This is one of two commandments that are expressed positively (the other is the command to honor parents). God demands that his chosen people observe or celebrate this special day. The noun "Sabbath" derives from the verb *šbt*, which means "to cease or desist" (*HALOT*, 1407; cf. Ex 23:12; Lev 23:32). Consequently, the Sabbath was a day of ceasing and/or resting from work. While the first six days of the week are given to labor, the seventh day must be set aside as a special day.

The second verb, "to make it holy," expresses the purpose of remembering or observing the Sabbath (contra NIV and D. Christensen, *Deuteronomy 1:1–21:9*, 117, 119, whose translation of the second verb "by keeping" suggests the first verb is primary and the second describes the manner in which one should "remember"; cf. P. Enns, *Exodus* [NIVAC; Grand Rapids: Zondervan, 2000], 418; NET, NKJV, NASB). "Making it holy" is the purpose for or result of observing this special day. This verb does not signify here the idea of moral purity but describes a day set apart for a special or particular purpose (Naudé, *NIDOTTE*, 3:885). Unlike an ordinary day of work, the Sabbath is to be set aside for a special function: to celebrate God's activity in behalf of his people.

This Sabbath is a day "to the LORD your God." The deeds and person of Yahweh are to serve as the grounds for and focus of this holy day. Since this day belongs to Yahweh, Israel is to utilize the time for the Lord's purposes rather than their own (Isa 58:13; Tigay, *Deuteronomy*, 68). The statement "as the LORD your God has commanded you" (also found with the fifth commandment [5:16] but not found in Exodus 20:8 or 12) looks back to the original statement of the Ten Commandments and is part of the sermonic or hortatory style of Deuteronomy. Israel's disobedience of this command during the years since the first giving of the law may also have occasioned this statement.

All people (both free and enslaved) and all animals normally used for work are to enjoy this Sabbath rest. No person or animal is supposed to work on this special day. The Deuteronomic version of this command provides more specifics than the parallel passage in Exodus 20:10. After referring to "your male slave, your female slave,"

Exodus refers only to "your animals" before referencing foreigners. The Deuteronomy passage adds, "your ox and your donkey and any of...." It appears that Deuteronomy 5:14 simply provides a fuller explanation of who and what is covered by this commandment.

15 Moses goes on to describe the theological rationale for this command. According to Deuteronomy, Israel's keeping of the Sabbath constitutes a celebration of God's mighty deliverance of them from their oppressive bondage in Egypt. The phrases "a mighty hand" (3:24; 4:34; 6:21; 7:8, 19; 9:26; 11:2; 26:8; 34:12) and "an outstretched arm" (4:34; 7:19; 9:29; 11:2; 26:8) occur repeatedly throughout the OT (twenty-six times and fifteen times, respectively) as references to God's powerful intervention in Israel's affairs. To rest, i.e., abstain from labor for one day, serves as a powerful reminder of God's deliverance of them from perpetual slavery, thus making the final clause of v.14 especially significant. The Israelites, redeemed from slavery at the exodus, must be sure the slaves and servants in their society also enjoy the rest of the Sabbath.

This focus on the exodus event rather than God's creation of the universe (Ex 20:11) provides one of the major differences between the articulation of this commandment in Deuteronomy and in Exodus. Exodus focuses on God's cessation of creative activity as the theological backdrop for this command. Deuteronomy looks to God's redemption of Israel from bondage as slaves in Egypt for this command's theological foundation. The covenantal "renewal" context of Deuteronomy may lend itself to an emphasis on redemption and Yahweh's intervention in Israel's behalf.

This shift does not remove all significance from creation as a legitimate rationale for Sabbath-keeping in the OT period; the fact that Yahweh rested on the seventh day provides the pattern for the Sabbath day, sabbatical year, and Year of Jubilee. Rather, as God's people prepare for the conquest of Canaan, the exodus provides them with a historically "nearer" rationale for keeping the Sabbath. Yahweh, as their Redeemer, deserves their obedience in this area, and Israel's redemption from slavery demonstrates that this "rest" is to be society-wide, including all slaves.

The Sabbath day is not simply intended as a day of inactivity, but also as a day of celebration. God's people are to take this opportunity to celebrate God's purposes demonstrated in his creative and redemptive work.

NOTE

12 The verb שָׁמוֹר (šāmôr, "observe"; GK 9068) occurs in this passage, in contrast with זכר (zkr) in the parallel passage in Exodus (20:8). Both verbs can refer to keeping a commandment or doing something (*HALOT*, 270, 1582). They occur together in Psalm 103:18 as parallel verbs. Although there is not much difference in these verbs as they occur here and in Exodus 20, שמר (šmr) perhaps focuses on the observance of the commandment and זכר (zkr) gives attention to its theological foundation (cf. Dt 5:15; Weinfeld, *Deuteronomy 1– 11*, 303). As a common word of exhortation, שמר (šmr) presupposes the existing form of the Decalogue and shows that the present passage is a deliberate re-presentation of it (McConville, 121).

REFLECTION

Of the Ten Commandments, this command is the only one that Christ or the apostles never restate in the NT. Jesus sought to correct the legalistic understanding of the Sabbath in his day (Mt 12:1–13; Jn 7:21–24). Paul pointed out that observing special days was an individual choice in a post-cross setting (Ro 14:5–9; Col 2:16). Since the seven-day week was established at the time of creation and the Lord rested on the seventh day, the principle of a day of "rest" still has relevance. The NT church's gathering together on the first day of the week looks back to Christ's final provision of redemption and his resurrection. However, it is inappropriate to view church worship on Sunday as the Christian's Sabbath. In addition to looking back to Christ's provision of redemption, the gathering of the church on the first day of the week looks ahead to God's provision of ultimate rest to believers (in present salvation and future glory [Heb 4:1–11]; cf. Hall, 121).

vi. The Fifth Commandment: Respect Your Parents (5:16)

¹⁶"Honor your father and your mother, as the LORD your God has commanded you, so that you may live long and that it may go well with you in the land the LORD your God is giving you."

COMMENTARY

16 As with all these commandments, this exhortation for the Israelites to respect their parents addresses adults in the first place (and would have included children). Although many regard it as the first of six commandments that deal with horizontal relationships (with the first four focusing on one's relationship with God), this commandment deals with both perspectives. Its linkage with the command to keep the Sabbath (Lev 19:3) suggests that both deal with the important issue of giving proper honor to key authority figures: God (fourth commandment) and parents (fifth commandment).

The requirement for God's people to honor their parents demands careful attention because the family unit stands at the core of the covenantal community. Although the apostle Paul focuses on the importance of this command for children (Eph 6:2), in this setting Moses gives this exhortation to parents. Proper relationships between children and parents (of all ages) serve as part of the structure and fabric of Israel's covenantal relationship with God (Wright, *Deuteronomy*, 77). Whatever threatens the family unit eventually threatens the wider basis of the covenantal relationship.

What is the theological significance of "honoring" one's parents? The verb "to honor" (*kbd*; GK 3877) signifies the idea of weighing down someone or something with honor or respect. It is derived from a term that refers to something that is heavy, just as the verb for "to dishonor" (*qll*) derives from a term that means something light or insignificant (E. Merrill, "Deuteronomy," 462; cf. 1Sa 2:30; 2Sa 6:22; Isa 23:9; Hos 4:7; Hab 2:16; Pr 3:35). Cursing one's parents is the clear opposite of honoring them (Ex 21:17; Lev 20:9; cf. Dt 27:16; Eze 22:7; Pr 20:20; 30:11). To honor one's parents means to declare to someone or to effectively convey to something the quality of honor (Merrill, *Deuteronomy*, 153). It represents more than an attitude by requiring that God's people demonstrate their respect for parents in tangible, empirical ways. Treating parents with honor involves reverence or respect and care (Tigay, *Deuteronomy*, 69–70; Weinfeld, *Deuteronomy 1–11*, 311).

The second half of 5:16 clarifies the significance of this command by affirming that obedience to it will occasion long and enjoyable tenure in the Promised Land. This promise and hope for long life in the land occurs repeatedly in Deuteronomy as a standard promise for those who keep covenant (4:40; 7:12–16; 12:25; 22:7; 25:15; 28:1–14; cf. Lev 26:3–13). The idea of "prolonging the days" is typical of Deuteronomy and occurs elsewhere in the OT (Isa 53:10; Pr 28:16; Ecc 8:13) and in certain Phoenician and Aramaic inscriptions. However, the combination of "long life" with "faring/going well with you (*yṭb*)" is distinct to Deuteronomy (4:40; 5:29; 6:2–3, 24; 22:7). Some have suggested this promise indicates that those who provide proper care for their parents will themselves enjoy long life and receive proper care themselves (Weinfeld, *Deuteronomy 1–11*, 312; Hall, 121), while others regard it as essential to the economic viability of the nation (Wright, *Deuteronomy*, 78).

This promise of long and enjoyable tenure in the Promised Land should be understood against the backdrop of God's ultimate intentions for his chosen nation. The Mosaic law makes it absolutely clear that Israel's continued presence in the land is directly related to their conformity with God's covenantal expectations (30:15–20). Disobedience or covenantal treachery will occasion Israel's eviction from that land (28:21–44, 63–68). Even though obedience to the covenant is an essential part of Israel's continued possession of their divine landed inheritance, is enjoying this landed inheritance an ultimate value? According to Exodus 19:4–6, God intended to use Israel as a servant-nation among the pagan nations of the world. He intended to lift up his name before those nations through his chosen people. Although continued presence in the land of his promise is indeed a great blessing, it is preliminary to a more ultimate value. Continued presence in the land gives God's chosen people the continued honor, privilege, and opportunity to manifest God's character to the surrounding world.

vii. The Sixth Commandment: Guard life (5:17)

17"You shall not murder."

COMMENTARY

17 The verb "to murder" (*rṣḥ*; GK 8357) can refer to unintentional murder (Nu 35:11, 22, 23; Dt 4:42; 19:3–4, 6; Jos 20:3–6) or to premeditated killing (murder or homicide; Nu 35:16–21; 1Ki 21:19; Job 24:14; Ps 94:6; Isa 1:21; Jer 7:9; Hos 4:2). Mosaic law indicates that the person who kills someone, but not as the consequence of "malice aforethought" or as the result of premeditation ("manslaughter"), can avoid the legal penalty for murder by fleeing to a city of refuge (Ex 21:12–14; Nu 35:6–31; Dt 4:41–43; 19:3–6; Jos 20–21). Apparently, based on the idea of capital punishment, relatives of a victim of manslaughter were allowed to kill the one who killed their loved one. Since the OT regarded manslaughter differently from premeditated murder, protection was offered to the manslayer. A person could flee to one of these cities, where a judgment would be made as to the kind of murder that had taken place. If it was deemed manslaughter, the priest would "atone" for the guilty person's deed.

Outside manslaughter, "to murder" generally denotes illegal behavior against the Israelite community that was always directed against an individual (*HALOT*, 1283). If intentional murder had taken place, the guilty person would be sent out of the city of refuge to face the punishment for his crime. These cities of refuge were evenly distributed throughout the land of Israel. Three cities were located on the eastern side of the Jordan River and three on the western side.

Based on the larger context of the OT, in this passage "to murder" (*rṣḥ*) does not refer to all killing. The central idea involves the taking of life outside divinely established parameters (cf. W. Zimmerli, *Old Testament Theology in Outline* [trans. D. Green; Atlanta: John Knox, 1978], 135). Human life carried a special value in God's sight. To take a life outside the divinely delineated parameters demanded some form of restitution. In the OT it could involve a penalty passed down by the Israelite court system or through carrying out blood vengeance (Domeris, *NIDOTTE* 3:1189). Against that backdrop, at least three categories of killing are not condemned in the OT: killing as a representative of the government (e.g., as a soldier, police officer, etc.; Dt 20:13, 16–17), killing as capital punishment (Ge 9:6; Dt 13:5, 9), and unintentional killing (for which the cities of refuge offer the "killer" protection from relatives of the victim, see above).

Genesis 9:6 provides the theological grounds for this commandment. The fact that humans are created in God's image confers supreme value on human life (Tigay, *Deuteronomy*, 71). As von Rad, 128, writes: "The establishment of the divine sovereign right over human life is expressed apodictically and unconditionally ... not for man's sake because of some law of humanity, or 'reverence for life,' but because man is God's possession and was created in God's image."

viii. The Seventh Commandment: Protect the purity of marriage (5:18)

¹⁸"You shall not commit adultery."

COMMENTARY

18 This commandment specifically addresses the sin of adultery. Other passages condemn fornication (Nu 25:1), prostitution (Dt 23:17–18), infidelity (Dt 22:22), and homosexuality (Lev 18:22; Jdg 19:22). This verb (*n'p*; GK 5537) occurs thirty-one times in the OT (in twenty-seven passages). Two-thirds of them refer to physical adultery (e.g., Lev 20:10; Pr 6:32; Jer 7:9; Hos 4:13–14), while the rest signify spiritual adultery—treachery in one's relationship with God (Jer 3:8–9; 5:7; Eze 23:37, 45). Adultery refers to the sexual liaison between a man and a married woman (Lev 18:20; 20:10; Eze 16:32; Hos 4:13) or a man and a betrothed girl (Dt 22:23–27). Note that the *man* involved in such a union makes himself an "adulterer" (Lev 20:10) regardless of his own marital status, which goes unmentioned in the texts.

Why is adultery regarded as such a serious offense? In the first place, marriage, grounded in a divine ordinance (Ge 2:24), is a covenantal arrangement that requires faithfulness and love. It mirrors God's covenant with his people. Marriage is a unique human relationship that most closely parallels our relationship with God. It is the only human relationship that demands exclusive fidelity. In Song of Songs 8:6–7 the woman wants the man to place her like a seal on his arm. That seal is like a stamp with a form of personal identification; it acts like a signature, marking identity and ownership (T. Longman III, "Adultery: Betrayed Commitments," *Decision* 41:7–8 [July–August 2000]: 33).

Second, physical adultery serves as a sad example of treachery in one's relationship with God. The sin of adultery uniquely strikes at the heart of a committed relationship. It represents horrific treachery. As such it paves the way for an understanding of the treachery of idolatry, spiritual adultery. Later passages speak of whoredom—playing the role of a prostitute with regard to one's relationship with God. Worshiping other gods represents our abandonment of our Redeemer in favor of another god who has no covenantal claim or legitimacy (Hos 4:1–9; Jer 3:9–13; Merrill, *Deuteronomy*, 154). Finally, adultery, like all sin, represents a violation of holiness.

ix. The Eighth Commandment: Do not steal (5:19)

¹⁹"You shall not steal."

COMMENTARY

19 Several scholars (rabbinic: *b. Nez.* 86a; Biddle, 113; Craigie, 161–62) argue that this verse deals with the specific issue of kidnapping (cf. Dt 24:7)—someone's forcibly taking and selling a person for personal profit or gain (e.g., the sale of Joseph by his brothers; see Weinfeld [*Deuteronomy 1–11*, 314–15] for a fairly thorough critique of this suggestion). Since violating all the other commandments occasions the death penalty and no manner of property theft carried the death penalty, these scholars contend that kidnapping, as a capital offense, must be the intended offense addressed here.

Although this observation about the other nine commandments is valid, there is no need to limit it to kidnapping; it prohibits all forms of theft, i.e., all forms of unjust gain at the expense of others, including kidnapping (Ex 21:16) but also extending to the theft of animals (22:1, 12) and other material possessions (22:7). Merrill (*Deuteronomy*, 155) points out a progression in commandments six through eight: theft of life (sixth), theft of the purity and sanctity of the marriage relationship (seventh), theft of goods and possessions (eighth).

Throughout the OT, Yahweh (as the sovereign ruler of Israel) is the ultimate owner of everything (Ps 24:1). His allotments to his people were not temporary. God was the owner of all, but he entrusted his gifts to human beings, and the use of property had to be respected. As a matter of fact, there were various laws in the Pentateuch that provided for a family's continuing possession of their divinely granted allotment of land. There were certain times (sabbatical years and the years of Jubilee) when loans were forgiven and land reverted back to its original owner (Ex 21:1–3; Lev 25:23–34; Dt 15:1–11). What God gave belonged to the recipient and what God gave was enough. At a fundamental level, theft manifests dissatisfaction with what God has provided. The person who steals tries to gain more than God has given to him by taking it from others.

x. The Ninth Commandment: Do not destroy an honest reputation (5:20)

20"You shall not give false testimony against your neighbor."

COMMENTARY

20 This commandment prohibits Israelites from giving false testimony (see Note on v.11 for comments on the noun *šāwʾ*, "false") against someone else and against a member of the covenantal community in particular. The verb "to give, offer" used here occurs at least fifteen times in the OT with the idea "to witness against" (Beck, *NIDOTTE*, 3:448; cf. *HALOT*, 852; cf. Dt 19:16, 18). Given the covenantal context of this section, it probably anticipates some kind of a legal case between two members of the covenantal community (cf. 19:15–21). The fundamental principle appears to be faithfulness in the context of covenantal relationships. This prohibition would cover any form of general, false accusations as well as false testimony in a legal or court setting. The placement of this command between the prohibition against theft and coveting may relate to the fact that false accusation is one way of depriving a fellow member of the covenantal community of what belongs to him (cf. Lev 19:11; see Note).

According to other passages, false testimony occasions severe penalties. The false accuser will himself receive the penalty that would have been levied against the innocent defendant, however severe that may be (Dt 19:15–21: *lex talionis*, "show no pity: life for life, eye for eye, tooth for tooth, hand for hand, foot for foot" [v.21]). To help prevent false witnessing, the Mosaic law required at least two or three witnesses giving corroborating testimony. One need only look at various historical and prophetic passages to see the horrific impact of false testimony in the life of the nation of Israel (1Ki 21; Isa 5:20–23; Jer 5:1–3, 26–28; 7:9; Hos 4:1–3; Am 5:7–15).

Yahweh abhors the giving of false testimony to the detriment of an innocent person for at least three reasons. First, as the God of truth (Isa 65:16; Ps 119:142, 151) who hates a "lying tongue" (Pr 6:17, 19), he demands that his chosen people speak the truth. Second, at various junctures of the Mosaic law the Lord establishes guidelines that are intended to ensure the practice of justice and equity among God's people. Consequently, giving false testimony represents a direct violation of God's required justice. Finally, in all human relationships false testimony represents a betrayal of trust; it strikes at the heart of any society, especially one that God intends will demonstrate his character to the surrounding nations.

NOTE

20 The noun רֵעַ (*rēaʿ*, "neighbor") general refers to a fellow Israelite (Lev 19:18; Dt 15:2), though it can also refer to a pagan (Ex 11:2). The covenantal context here suggests that its primary referent is those individuals who are part of Israelite society. Thus, this emphasis does not allow for false testimony in cases that involve non-Israelites. In any setting where evidence is being gathered in order for the arrival at a just and accurate verdict, giving a false witness is prohibited regardless of the ethnicity of the "neighbor."

xi. The Tenth Commandment: Do not covet (5:21)

²¹ "You shall not covet your neighbor's wife. You shall not set your desire on your neighbor's house or land, his manservant or maidservant, his ox or donkey, or anything that belongs to your neighbor."

COMMENTARY

21 Unlike the Exodus passage that prohibits coveting a neighbor's house and then refers to the neighbor's wife (listed with servants, animals, and miscellaneous belongings), the present passage prohibits in a stand-alone statement the coveting of a neighbor's wife and then addresses everything else (house, land [not listed in Exodus], servants, animals, and miscellaneous belongings). The change in location of "wife" does not imply that before this time a man's wife was regarded as property (like slaves, animals, and possessions). It does, however, preclude any misunderstanding of the proper treatment of women (cf. Dt 15:12–18; 22:28–29).

Unlike all the other commandments, the tenth one places more direct emphasis on the inner disposition than on the outward act. This commandment serves as a powerful summary of the previous commandments as well as a clear indication of the nature of God's expectations of his chosen people. In the first place, the violation of this command represents the first step leading to the transgression of any of the preceding commands (J. Durham, *Exodus* [WBC; Waco, Tex.: Word, 1987], 298–99). Second, notice how this command shifts the point of indictment from vile actions and words to hidden thoughts and cravings.

Even in the time of Moses, a wicked internal attitude was an abomination. Even if other nations found external conformity to their laws acceptable, God demands obedience of the heart and mind. Merrill (*Deuteronomy*, 157) points out: "At the same time it is the least overtly violent and injurious, it is the commandment most at the root of covenant disobedience in that it logically precedes the rest." Wright (*Deuteronomy*, 85) adds that the inclusion of coveting in the Ten Commandments shows that covenantal loyalty in Israel goes far deeper than external conformity to statute law. This commandment anticipates Christ's rebuke of covetous greed during his ministry (Mt 19:16–22; Lk 12:13–21; cf. Eph 5:5; Col 3:5; Jas 4:1–2).

NOTE

21 Two verbs, חמד (*ḥmd*; GK 2773) and אוה (*ʾwh*; GK 203), occur in the two clauses of 5:21 (וְלֹא תִתְאַוֶּה ... לֹא תַחְמֹד, *lōʾ taḥmōd ... wᵉlōʾ titʾawweh*, "you must not desire ... nor must you crave"), while חמד (*ḥmd*) occurs twice in Exodus 20:17. Weinfeld (*Deuteronomy 1–11*, 316–18) suggests that the first verb means "to plan to appropriate" and the second means to "crave." William Moran ("The Conclusion of the Decalogue (Ex 20, 17 = Dt 5, 21)," *CBQ* 29 [1967]: 543–54) contends that the first verb refers to a desire stimulated by sight, while the second verb denotes a desire arising from an inner need. Since the first verb can have sexual overtones (cf. SS 2:3) and refers to the neighbor's wife, Moses may have used a different verb for the other potential objects of coveting for the sake of clarity.

c. The Mediatorial Role of Moses (5:22–6:3)

OVERVIEW

Moses describes his mediatorial role at the time of the giving of the law at Mount Horeb (which he carried out at their request because of their fear of the Lord; cf. Ex 19:18–21) and points out the Lord's commendation of their spirit of reverence. After rehearsing that stupendous revelation of Yahweh to his covenantal nation (vv.22–27), Moses gives attention to the response Yahweh demanded of his chosen people — wholehearted obedience (vv.28–33).

i. The rehearsal of the theophany (5:22–27)

²²These are the commandments the LORD proclaimed in a loud voice to your whole assembly there on the mountain from out of the fire, the cloud and the deep darkness; and he added nothing more. Then he wrote them on two stone tablets and gave them to me.

²³When you heard the voice out of the darkness, while the mountain was ablaze with fire, all the leading men of your tribes and your elders came to me. ²⁴And you said, "The LORD our God has shown us his glory and his majesty, and we have heard his voice from the fire. Today we have seen that a man can live even if God speaks with him. ²⁵But now, why should we die? This great fire will consume us, and we will die if we hear the voice of the LORD our God any longer. ²⁶For what mortal man has ever heard the voice of the living God speaking out of fire, as we have, and survived? ²⁷Go near and listen to all that the LORD our God says. Then tell us whatever the LORD our God tells you. We will listen and obey."

COMMENTARY

22 Moses graphically describes the divine transcription of the terms of the covenant. Notice some of the features of the Ten Commandments highlighted by this verse: their divine source, their authority over all Israel, their majesty, their completeness and finality, and their fixed and permanent nature (Wright, *Deuteronomy*, 90). Yahweh "speaks" these commandments ("words") directly to the gathered assembly of the covenantal nation, thus emphasizing the fact that the entire nation is involved in the reception of the Decalogue. The fact that Yahweh adds nothing more to these commandments and inscribes them on stone tablets (cf. Dt 4:13) highlights the sacredness of this divine declaration. The Ten Commandments represent the central core of Yahweh's expectations of his people.

23–27 God's people were amazed at the dramatic revelation of God's presence and by the sound of his voice (vv.24, 26; cf. 4:33) and, consequently, feared for their lives (cf. Ex 20:18–21). After Moses received from Yahweh the Ten Commandments, which the Israelites had heard Yahweh announce aloud, their leaders approached Moses and proposed that he serve as their intermediary (Dt 5:27a). They granted the reality that human beings could survive God's verbal revelation of himself (v.24), but they would rather not expose themselves to the potential danger of continued encounters with Yahweh. The fact that they (and Moses) received direct revelation from their God was unparalleled in the ancient Near East (v.26). Unlike unresponsive wooden and stone idols, their God is a living being. These leaders then committed themselves and their brothers to listen to Yahweh's other requirements and to live according to those demands (v.27).

NOTES

22 הַדְּבָרִים הָאֵלֶּה (haddᵉbārîm hāᵓēlleh), "these words," serves as the standard reference to the Ten Commandments (Ex 20:1; 24:3; Dt 4:13; 9:10; 10:2, 4). Their position at the front of this verse emphasizes the central role they play in what God demands from his covenantal nation.

26 The reference to בָּשָׂר (bāśār), "all flesh" or "all mankind," highlights humans' frailty and mortality before this living and powerful God.

ii. The preparations for the covenantal stipulations (5:28–31)

²⁸The LORD heard you when you spoke to me and the LORD said to me, "I have heard what this people said to you. Everything they said was good. ²⁹Oh, that their hearts would be inclined to fear me and keep all my commands always, so that it might go well with them and their children forever!

³⁰"Go, tell them to return to their tents. ³¹But you stay here with me so that I may give you all the commands, decrees and laws you are to teach them to follow in the land I am giving them to possess."

COMMENTARY

28–31 God commended the elders of Israel for their reverent and humble response (v.28). Apparently, however, God was not convinced that this attitude was true of every Israelite, nor that it would characterize the nation for all time (v.29; cf. Jer 32:39–40). He was too aware of their past (as well as their future). He longed that his covenantal nation would wholeheartedly revere him and obey his commands (*miṣwōt*—generic for the law as a whole; see Note on 6:1). The consequence of this kind of attitude and conduct would be long-term blessing for God's people (a common theme in Deuteronomy [5:16, 29; 6:18; 12:25, 28; 22:7]).

In this light, Yahweh spoke to Israel through his covenantal mediator, Moses (vv.30–31). God commanded the elders of Israel to return to their tents and told Moses to stay and receive the stipulations of this covenant. Yahweh's invitation publicly confirmed Moses' role as mediator between Yahweh and his covenantal nation. Yahweh promised to reveal through Moses all the "commands, decrees and laws" (see comments on 6:1) that he expected Moses to teach to the Israelites. The Lord once again makes a clear connection between expected obedience by Israel and their continued enjoyment of the landed inheritance, given to them by their covenantal Lord.

NOTES

29 The collocation מִי־יִתֵּן (*mî-yittēn*, "if only") occurs twenty-five times in the OT and serves to introduce a wish (e.g., Dt 28:67; Jdg 9:29; Isa 27:4; Jer 8:23; 9:1; Grisanti, *NIDOTTE*, 3:209). The construction is most abundant in Job (eleven occurrences: 6:8; 11:5; 13:5; 14:4, 13; 19:23 [2x]; 23:3; 29:2; 31:31, 35) and is followed either by a nominal form (noun, participle, infinitive), pronominal suffix, or finite verb.

The fear (לְיִרְאָה, *lᵉyirʾâ*, "to fear") Yahweh desires from his people manifests itself in reverence and genuine worship, unlike the sentiment alluded to when the people "feared" a continued encounter with Yahweh (v.25; see Note on 6:13).

iii. The rationale for this covenant/law (5:32–6:3)

³²So be careful to do what the LORD your God has commanded you; do not turn aside to the right or to the left. ³³Walk in all the way that the LORD your God has commanded you, so that you may live and prosper and prolong your days in the land that you will possess.

⁶:¹These are the commands, decrees and laws the LORD your God directed me to teach you to observe in the land that you are crossing the Jordan to possess, ²so that you, your children and their children after them may fear the LORD your God as long as you live by keeping all his decrees and commands that I give you, and so that you may enjoy long life. ³Hear, O Israel, and be careful to obey so that it may go well with you and that you may increase greatly in a land flowing with milk and honey, just as the LORD, the God of your fathers, promised you.

COMMENTARY

32–33 The narrative, i.e., the recollection by Moses of this stupendous historical event, ends with 5:31, and Moses' exhortation begins with 5:32. Moses makes it clear that he is not talking about the words or commandments of Moses but the words of Almighty God. God's covenantal people are not to "turn aside to the right or to the left" (a common expression in Deuteronomy and other historical books—Dt 17:11, 20; 28:14; Jos 1:7; 23:6; 2Ki 22:2) from those divine expectations. Instead, the Israelites are to live ("walk"; see comment on 10:12–13) in accordance with those requirements and, consequently, enjoy long tenure in the Promised Land.

6:1–3 In preparation for his exposition of God's law, Moses proclaims to Israel the rationale for it: that they might fear the Lord so that the covenantal blessings (long and abundant tenure in the Promised Land) will come on them. Scholars do not agree on the structural role of 6:1–3, i.e., whether it belongs with 5:32–33 or introduces a new section. There are insightful arguments for both options (with

5:32–33: Christensen, *Deuteronomy 1:1–21:9*, 132–33; Lohfink, 67–68; Thompson, 120; Weinfeld, *Deuteronomy 1–11*, 327; Wright, *Deuteronomy*, 92–93; beginning a new section: Craigie, 167–68; G. H. Hall, "Rhetorical Criticism, Chiasm, and Theme in Deuteronomy," *Stone-Campbell Journal* 1 [1998]: 92–94; Merrill, *Deuteronomy*, 160–61; Tigay, *Deuteronomy*, 74). There is no doubt that these verses look backward and forward.

However, on structural grounds they appear to fit best with the preceding verses. Verse 1 refers to "the commandment [see Note], the decrees and laws," as does 5:31. This repetition "recaptures" Moses' primary point after the "digression" of 5:32–33. The flow of these verses appears to be: God gave this command (v.31) … So you be careful to do it (vv.32–33) … And this is it (6:1–3; Wright, *Deuteronomy*, 93). The MT reading/paragraph divisions (*perashoth*) do not indicate a break until 6:4. Lohfink, 67, points out the chiastic arrangement of verbal pairs, which favors viewing 5:22–6:3 as a structural unit:

A hear ... do (5:27);
  B fear ... keep (5:29);
    C teach ... do (5:31);
      D keep ... do ... turn aside ... walk
        (5:32−33);
    C' learn ... do (6:1);
  B' fear ... keep (6:2);
A' hear ... keep ... do (6:3).

It is clear that in some sense these verses serve as a preamble to this section of general stipulations and clearly demonstrate that the laws and rules that Moses is about to relate to Israel are identical to the ones given at Mount Sinai. Also, from a geographical point of view, ch. 6 introduces a transition from the theophany at Sinai to Israel's encampment at Moab. Regardless, by connecting 6:1−3 with 5:22−33, Moses demonstrates the coherence of the giving of the law at Sinai and his re-presentation of that law on the plains of Moab.

As in 5:29, Moses links God's demand that Israel fear him with their fulfillment of his expectations. Since he, their covenantal Lord, has given these requirements to them, they, as his covenantal people, should devote their entire lives to submission to his demands.

After exhorting God's people to live in wholehearted accordance with God's covenantal demands, which action will trigger their longevity (6:1−2), Moses repeats that formula (obedience occasions abundant blessings; 6:3). This reality exactly corresponds to what Yahweh promised to his people for several generations. Yahweh is a God who brings to pass all that he promises. Moses also likens the Promised Land to "a land flowing with milk and honey." Yahweh, the living God, is giving to his covenantal nation a land that he will abundantly furnish. This expression occurs eighteen times in the OT (thirteen times in the Pentateuch, including five times in Deuteronomy [6:3; 11:9; 26:9, 15; 27:3]). In all but one instance (Nu 16:13) it refers to the land of Canaan and depicts it as a land of abundance and fertility. The clause may be somewhat hyperbolic, but it is also possible that present-day Israel is not as fertile as that land was in the time of Moses.

NOTES

33 The expressions "that it may go well with you" (לְמַעַן תִּחְיוּן וְטוֹב לָכֶם, *lᵉmaᶜan tiḥyûn wᵉṭôb lākem*) and "that you may prolong your days" (וְהַאֲרַכְתֶּם יָמִים, *wᵉhaᵃraktem yāmîm*) occur repeatedly throughout Deuteronomy. In Deuteronomy, with regard to the nation's potential fate the former clause occurs with the verb יטב (*yṭb*) nine times (4:40; 5:16, 29; 6:3, 18; 8:16; 12:25, 28; 22:7) and with the verb טוב (*ṭôb*) three times (5:33; 6:24; 19:13). The promise of "lengthened" (ארך, *ʾrk*) days occurs as a positive benefit for the nation in seven passages (4:40; 5:16; 6:2; 11:9; 22:7; 25:15; 32:47) and as something they will not receive because of their disobedience in two passages (4:26; 30:18). These statements occur together four times (4:40; 5:16; 6:2−3; 22:7).

One cannot question that God promises to his chosen nation longevity in the Promised Land and enjoyable life in the wake of covenantal conformity. Is that the ultimate end Yahweh has in mind for his people? In the light of Exodus 19:4−6 and Deuteronomy 26:16−19, where Yahweh commissions his chosen people to represent his character before the surrounding world, these materialistic blessings appear to be immediate objectives rather than ultimate goals. God gave Israel the land of Canaan as a stewardship to provide them with a platform from which they could serve as a witness-nation before the world. Long tenure in the land would give Israel the continued opportunity to carry out their God-given role of demonstrating to the pagan world the awesome and incomparable character of their covenantal Lord.

6:1 The triad הַמִּצְוָה הַחֻקִּים וְהַמִּשְׁפָּטִים (hammiṣwâ haḥuqqîm wᵉhammišpāṭîm, "the commandment, the statutes and judgments") possesses unusual technical and theological significance. In Deuteronomy, "commandment" (מִצְוָה, miṣwâ) occurs forty-three times, "statutes" (חֻקִּים, ḥuqqîm) twenty-one times, and "judgments" (מִשְׁפָּטִים, mišpāṭîm) thirty-seven times. In thirteen of the forty-three instances of "commandment," the word occurs in the singular with the prefixed article. In all but two of those thirteen occurrences "commandment" is followed by the expression, "which I commanded/am giving you" (6:1, 25; 7:11; 8:1; 11:8, 22; 15:5; 19:9; 27:1; 30:11; 31:5). In 5:31 "commandment" is followed by the expression, "which you shall teach," and in 17:20 it serves as the benchmark for covenantal conduct.

In Deuteronomy the triad of terms appears in four passages: 5:31; 6:1; 7:11; 26:17. In the first three occurrences (5:31; 6:1; 7:11) it occurs in the order found here in 6:1; in the last occurrence (26:17), the term for "commandments" is in the plural form and the order is "his statutes, and his commandments, and his judgments." Most scholars argue that the phrase, "this is the commandment" (6:1), summarizes all that is commanded as a unit (the legal corpus; Tigay, *Deuteronomy*, 74) or denotes the same principle underlying the entire law (Christensen, *Deuteronomy 1:1–21:9*, 135; Craigie, 166; Ridderbos, 112). Weinfeld (*Deuteronomy 1–11*, 326) suggests that "the commandment" (הַמִּצְוָה, hammiṣwâ; GK 5184) refers to the basic demand for loyalty (to which chs. 5–11 are devoted). "The commandment" consequently deals with the demand for love of God, following his ways, serving him, and holding fast to him. It may correspond to the basic stipulation of allegiance demanded by the treaties or loyalty oaths of the ancient Near East. (Compare Jer 32:11, where "the commandment and the statutes" may refer to "the basic stipulation and the specified terms of the deed.")

The two words "statutes" and "judgments" occur as a pair fourteen times in Deuteronomy (4:1, 5, 8, 14, 45; 5:1, 31; 6:1, 20; 7:11; 11:32; 12:1; 26:16–17). They represent technical terms that signify the specific requirements of the covenant, i.e., the specific laws based on the underlying principle. Tigay (*Deuteronomy*, 43) points out that in traditional Jewish exegesis, "statutes" (חֻקִּים, ḥuqqîm; GK 2976) and "judgments" (מִשְׁפָּטִים, mišpāṭîm; GK 5477) are understood as referring to two broad categories of commandments. Jewish interpreters consider the מִשְׁפָּטִים (mišpāṭîm) to be those laws whose purpose is evident and which people would have instituted even if God never commanded them (basic ethics; e.g., prohibitions of murder and theft). The חֻקִּים (ḥuqqîm) are commandments for which the reason is not obvious, such as the dietary regulations; they must be obeyed as expressions of divine sovereignty. Although this interpretation is interesting, it appears best to see these two terms as general references to the specific stipulations of the Mosaic covenant.

3 P. Stern ("The Origin and Significance of 'The Land Flowing with Milk and Honey,'" *VT* 42 [1992]: 554–57) compares the descriptive statement אֶרֶץ זָבַת חָלָב וּדְבָשׁ (ʾereṣ zābat ḥālāb ûdᵉbāš, "a land flowing with milk and honey") to the Ugaritic account of Baal's death (*KTU*, 1.6.III; *COS*, 1:271) and suggests that, in addition to connoting the idea of fertility, it represents a polemical critique of the alleged efforts of Baal to bring fertility to the land. The living God, Yahweh, will do what the dead god, Baal, cannot do. The juxtaposition of milk, the product of human labor, and honey, the product of nature, represents the fullness of blessings associated with the Promised Land (Merrill, *Deuteronomy*, 161). The Egyptian Sinuhe's account of his travels in Syria-Palestine (ca. 2000–1900 BC) describes the abundant fertility of this region and mentions its plentiful honey and milk (*COS*, 1:79).

2. Moses Exhorts Israel to Manifest Tangibly Their Love for Yahweh (6:4–25)

OVERVIEW

Moses exhorts the Israelites to manifest their love for the Lord (who alone is God) by both obeying all that Moses has been (and is) teaching them and by passing on those same truths to their children.

a. Yahweh's Uniqueness and Humanity's Obligation to Love Him (6:4–9)

OVERVIEW

In this passage Moses summarizes the significance of the law with its two most fundamental and important truths: the Lord's uniqueness and humanity's obligation to love him. He goes on to challenge them to make these truths central in every part of their lives and pass them on to their children.

i. The focus and essence of allegiance (6:4–5)

⁴Hear, O Israel: The LORD our God, the LORD is one. ⁵Love the LORD your God with all your heart and with all your soul and with all your strength.

COMMENTARY

4–5 Verse 4, known by Jews as the *Shema*, is "as close as early Judaism came to the formulation of a creed" (Block, 195). The call for Israel to "hear," a common form of address in Deuteronomy (5:1; 6:3; 9:1; 20:3; 27:9), draws attention to the rest of the Hebrew line, which focuses on God himself as the object of Israel's allegiance. Scholars have often debated whether v.4 teaches the singularity (one as opposed to many) or unity (internal consistency) of Yahweh or his uniqueness (incomparability) or exclusivity (the only one for Israel). A key interpretive problem is the unparalleled nature of this line in Hebrew. After the summons, "Hear, O Israel," four Hebrew words occur without any verbs. Although verbless clauses occur throughout the Hebrew Bible, the construction found here has no counterpart.

Space precludes giving attention to many of these details, but certain key affirmations deserve mention. Regardless of where one places a form of the verb "to be," at least three truths arise from the divine names used in these verses. (1) This God is Yahweh, the faithful, covenant-making, and covenant-keeping God. He is God, the sovereign Creator. (2) He is also "our God," the God who entered into an intimate and special covenantal relationship with his nation, Israel. (3) Although the OT makes it clear that Israel's God is singular, in stark contrast to the pagan gods, another idea seems prominent in this context (cf. 4:35, 39; 5:7) and in this verse. One of the realities that sets Israel apart from the world is the exclusive relationship they have with this remarkable God. He is Yahweh alone! Not only is he incomparable, but he is the only God for the Israelites and they are the people on whom he has set his love. Yahweh and only Yahweh is to be the object of Israel's wholehearted and undivided loyalty. A potential translation of v.4 is, "Hear, O Israel: Yahweh is our God, Yahweh alone!"

In v.5 Moses develops the essence of covenantal allegiance, i.e., loyalty or obedience. He demands that Israel "love" Yahweh with their entire being. In covenantal settings, "love" connotes a commitment that "seeks the well-being and the pleasure of one's covenant partner, often without regard for oneself" (Block, 201). Love described the loyalty rendered by a vassal on behalf of his suzerain (Els, *NIDOTTE*, 1:278, 287–88). Moses correlates this duty to "love" Yahweh with the demand that God's

covenantal nation fear him (10:12), walk in his ways (10:12; 11:22; 19:9; 30:16), serve him (10:12; 11:13), keep his commands (10:13; 11:22; 19:9; 30:16), hold fast to him (11:22; 30:20), and listen to or obey his voice (11:13; 30:20).

The second part of v.5 delineates the extent or intensity of the love God demands his people to have for him: "with all your heart and with all your soul and with all your strength." Moses does not mention these three nouns primarily as attributes of human personality but to demonstrate the far-reaching nature of this demanded commitment. The heart often signifies the seat of a person's intellect, emotion, and will (4:29; 10:12; 11:13; 26:16). The soul designates one's entire being or person (Ps 103:1). The word translated "strength" or "might" usually signifies the adverbial idea of "very" or "much" and only here and one other place (2Ki 23:25) connotes "might."

Moses piles up relatively synonymous terms to emphasize the totality of this allegiance. The task of expressing this love for Yahweh (in loyalty) encompasses one's entire person. These three phrases do not express three precise modes of expressing love or refer to three distinct spheres of life. They combine together to serve as an intense affirmation of absolute commitment. In summary, vv.4 and 5 make a statement about God as well as demanding absolute commitment to God.

REFLECTION

Jesus taught that the truths contained in these two verses constitute the foremost or central demand of the OT law (Mt 22:37–38; Mk 12:29–30; Lk 10:27). Minor differences between the gospel quotations and Deuteronomy include Matthew's replacing "might" with "mind," while

Mark and Luke include both (with "mind" and "strength" in different order). Regardless, the NT writers do not subtract anything from the meaning of the passage in Deuteronomy. As with Moses, Christ sought to emphasize the life-invasive extent of this commitment to allegiance.

ii. The internal and generational impact of allegiance (6:6–9)

⁶These commandments that I give you today are to be upon your hearts. ⁷Impress them on your children. Talk about them when you sit at home and when you walk along the road, when you lie down and when you get up. ⁸Tie them as symbols on your hands and bind them on your foreheads. ⁹Write them on the doorframes of your houses and on your gates.

COMMENTARY

6 Building on God's incomparable identity and his demand for absolute loyalty from Israel, Moses addresses how to live out this divine expectation. How will a recognition of Yahweh's exclusive relationship with Israel and Israel's total allegiance manifest itself? Those who live in the light of these realities will have transformed lives and invest themselves in passing on those life-changing beliefs to the next generation. They will not be content with leading lives for God's glory but will earnestly desire to help give to their children a life-changing awareness of their great and mighty God.

Moses delineates the inward perspective (v.6) and the generational perspective (vv.7–9) that characterizes a life transformed by undivided allegiance to the incomparable God. God's people are to internalize God's expectations of them. The "words" that Yahweh commands them to appropriate do not refer only to the Ten Commandments but also to the sum total of what he expects of them. Those words should be "upon your hearts"—perpetually kept in mind.

Moses here affirms that a clear understanding of God's character that results in a sincere commitment to one's relationship with God (loving God wholeheartedly) should strike at the very heart of one's being (4:9; 10:16; 11:18; Pr 3:1; 4:4; 6:21; Jer

4:4). In other words, understanding who God is (6:4) should lead to absolute loyalty (6:5), which leads to internal transformation (6:6). It is essential to notice that God did not command external conformity to his requirements, nor did he expect this wholehearted obedience just from the religious "elite."

7–9 God's covenantal demands should also have a powerful impact on future Israelite generations. God requires that his people diligently teach these truths to their children. Moses demands that God's people teach God's expectations to their children and grandchildren repeatedly, in all life's settings. After commanding them to do so (v.7a), Moses delineates the means for doing so (vv.7b–9). They should take opportunities to speak of these marvelous truths in every part of life. These pairs of expressions—"sit ... walk," "lie down ... get up"—are called merisms. These opposite terms refer not just to the actions they specify but also to everything between them (cf. our expression "A to Z"; cf. Pr 6:21–22). They signify totality. By using these two phrases, Moses highlights the fact that God's people are to teach their children about God and his expectations of them in all contexts of life. They are to permeate every realm of a believer's life. God's truth was and is to be the topic for ordinary conversation in ordinary homes in ordinary life from breakfast to bedtime, whether we are busy or not. Moveover, there needs to be deliberate teaching as well as repetitive instruction.

In addition to teaching God's expectations in every part of life (v.7b), God's people must make God's requirements an obvious part of their own entire lives (vv.8–9). Moses exhorts the Israelites to tie and bind "them" on their hands and foreheads (v.8). In the context, "them" must refer to God's expectations of his covenantal people. What are these bound expectations to symbolize? A person with God's expectations bound on hands and head (actions and attitudes) represents a member of God's people who lives life under the authority of God's expectations.

Moses also tells the Israelites to write God's covenantal demands on the "doorframes" and "gates," i.e., the entrances to their homes and cities (v.9) — the two primary points of access in their lives. They will pass through their "doorposts" (*mᵉzûzōt*—see Note) whenever they enter or leave their homes. In the ancient world, the gate of a city was the center of public activity. Buying and selling took place near the gate. Judicial decisions were rendered in the area of the city gate. "Writing" God's expecta-

tions on the gates of the city ensures the widest visibility. Binding God's expectations on their wrists or foreheads and writing them on the doorposts of their homes and the gates of their cities pictures something that will perpetually remind God's people of his love for them and what he expects of them.

Does Moses expect God's people to enact this command literally? Most likely he is speaking figuratively. In Exodus 13:9 and 16 the word for "signs" is figurative, and Proverbs 3:3 and 6:21 refer to figurative "binding." Although Moses may not have envisioned a literal practice, biblical readers must be careful not to miss the point of his exhortation. What is the point of doing what Moses says? He wants the Israelites to be sure that God's Word is preeminent in their lives! Wright (*Deuteronomy*, 100) forcefully writes:

> Christian readers of 6:8–9 may be tempted to dismiss the Jewish use of *tefillin* (phylacteries) and *mezuzot* ... as unnecessary literalism. However, the question is whether we are any more serious or successful in flavoring the whole of life with conscious attention to the law of God as a personal, familial, and social strategy for living out our commitment to loving God totally.

NOTES

4 The meaning of the word אֶחָד (ʾeḥād; GK 285), "one," has occasioned most of the scholarly discussion on this verse. The most common meaning for this term is "one" (*HALOT*, 30), and numerous scholars advocate that meaning in the present verse. They correctly point out that the adverb לְבַדּוֹ (lᵉbaddô) more properly signifies the idea of "alone." However, since the *Shema* consists of a nominal or verbless clause, an adverb would be inappropriate (Weinfeld, *Deuteronomy 1–11*, 338). Finally, several OT passages make use of אֶחָד (ʾeḥād) with the idea of "alone" or "only" (Jos 22:20; 2Sa 7:23 [= 1Ch 17:21]; 1Ch 29:1; Job 23:13; 31:15; SS 6:9; Eze 7:5; Zec 14:9). See Block, 195–201, for a fuller overview of the lexicographical and syntactical issues in this verse.

5 The triad in בְּכָל־לְבָבְךָ וּבְכָל־נַפְשְׁךָ וּבְכָל־מְאֹדֶךָ (*bᵉkol-lᵉbābᵉkā ûbᵉkol-napšᵉkā ûbᵉkol mᵉʾōdekā*, "with all your heart and with all your soul and with all your might") occurs only here in Deuteronomy (and only one other time in the OT: 2Ki 23:25). "Heart" and "soul" occur as a pair signifying totality ("all your heart and all your soul") in eight other passages in Deuteronomy. The verb they adverbially modify varies: "search" (דרשׁ, *drš*; 4:29), "love" (אהב, *ʾhb*; 13:4; 30:6), "serve" (עבד, *ʿbd*; 10:12; 11:13), "be careful to do" (עשׂה, *ʿśh*, + שׁמר, *šmr*; 26:16), "obey" (שׁמע, *šmʿ*; 30:2), and "turn" (שׁוב, *šûb*; 30:10). The distribution of this "totality statement" suggests that, even though each verb may signify a unique facet of Yahweh's expectations of Israel, the verbs should not be viewed as conveying entirely different concepts. Also, when it comes to covenant, Yahweh expects nothing less than his people's wholehearted commitment.

7 The verb שׁנן (*šnn* [II], in וְשִׁנַּנְתָּם, *wᵉšinnantām*, "and you must teach them") generally means to repeat or recount something (*HALOT*, 1606–7). This may be the only occurrence of the verb in the OT. There is a homonymic root (שׁנן, *šnn* [I]) that means "to sharpen" or "to pierce" (Jenson, *NIDOTTE*, 4:195). A cognate root in Ugaritic (J. Gibson, ed., *Canaanite Myths and Legends* [Edinburgh: T&T Clark, 1978], 99, 160) and Akkadian (*AHw*, 3:1165b–66a) means "to do twice, a second time" or "to repeat." The form *wᵉšinnantām* can only mean "to sharpen, pierce, or inscribe" if it is related to *šnn* I. Rather than signifying the idea of engraving, it seems best to view this word as connoting repetitive teaching. The fact that a parallel passage (11:19) uses the verb למד (*lmd*), "to teach," instead of *šnn* also suggests this meaning. The following merisms (in vv. 7b–9) also point to repetitive teaching.

8 In modern Judaism, Jews use something called "phylacteries" (cf. Mt 23:5: φυλακτήρια, *phylaktēria*) to obey the command regarding לְטֹטָפֹת (*lᵉṭōṭāpōt*, "as frontlets" [also called *tefillin* by the Jews]). A phylactery is a small box that contains several verses from the Pentateuch (usually some or all of Ex 13:1–10, 11–16; Dt 6:4–9; 11:13–21). This box is in a leather pouch that has leather straps (called טֹטָפֹת, *ṭōṭāpōt*) on both sides (Tigay, *Deuteronomy*, 441). The leather straps are wrapped around the wrist or forehead so that the box containing the Scriptures rests on the middle of the forehead or wrist. It was the hypocritical wearing of these items that occasioned Jesus' scathing rebuke of the Jews (Mt 23:5).

9 The term מְזוּזֹת (*mᵉzûzōt*, "doorframes") literally means "doorposts" and occurs in seventeen passages for the side posts of a city gate, door of a building, or window. By the Second Temple period many Jews were taking this command literally and eventually transferred the significance of a מְזוּזָה (*mᵉzûzâ*) from the doorpost itself to the passages affixed to the doorpost. In Jewish tradition, the mezuzah consists of a glass or metal receptacle that contains a piece of parchment on which certain words from Deuteronomy (6:4–9 and 11:13–21) are written, traditionally in twenty-two lines (L. Rabinowitz, "Mezuzah," *EncJud*, 11:1475). The parchment is rolled up and inserted in the receptacle so that the word שַׁדַּי (*šadday*), written on the back of the parchment, is visible through a small aperture. One of the caves at Qumran yielded a mezuzah parchment that contained the Hebrew text of Deuteronomy 10:12–11:21 (DJD 3 [1962], 158–61). Customarily, a mezuzah is fixed to the outer right hand doorpost at the entrance to every dwelling room of a house.

b. Yahweh Demands That Israel Worship and Obey Him Exclusively (6:10–19)

OVERVIEW

Looking to the near future (after Israel conquers Canaan) and in the light of all the Lord has done for Israel, Moses exhorts the nation not to forget the Lord, but instead to manifest their fear of him by obeying his commands.

[10]When the LORD your God brings you into the land he swore to your fathers, to Abraham, Isaac and Jacob, to give you — a land with large, flourishing cities you did not build, [11]houses filled with all kinds of good things you did not provide, wells you did not dig, and vineyards and olive groves you did not plant — then when you eat and are satisfied, [12]be careful that you do not forget the LORD, who brought you out of Egypt, out of the land of slavery.

[13]Fear the LORD your God, serve him only and take your oaths in his name. [14]Do not follow other gods, the gods of the peoples around you; [15]for the LORD your God, who is among you, is a jealous God and his anger will burn against you, and he will destroy you from the face of the land. [16]Do not test the LORD your God as you did at Massah. [17]Be sure to keep the commands of the LORD your God and the stipulations and decrees he has given you. [18]Do what is right and good in the LORD's sight, so that it may go well with you and you may go in and take over the good land that the LORD promised on oath to your forefathers, [19]thrusting out all your enemies before you, as the LORD said.

COMMENTARY

10–12 When the Lord finally fulfills his pledge to bring Israel into the Promised Land and when they dwell securely there, they must be careful to worship Yahweh exclusively and not to become apathetic or to forget (see Note on 4:9–10) the Lord who redeemed them from slavery in Egypt. Moses envisions a time after Yahweh has established Israel in the land of Canaan. The conquest he describes will be generally nondestructive of buildings, cisterns, orchards, and vineyards. Although the Israelites are to exterminate the Canaanite inhabitants and their idolatrous altars and worship appara-

tus, God intends that Israel will be able to benefit from the material culture in place at the time of the conquest (cf. 19:1; Jos 24:13; cf. E. H. Merrill, "Palestinian Archaeology and the Date of the Conquest: Do Tells Tell Tales?" *GTJ* 3 [Spring 1982]: 107–21; B. Waltke, "Palestinian Artifactual Evidence Supporting the Early Date of the Exodus," *BSac* 129 [January–March 1972]: 33–47).

In the wake of the completed conquest of Canaan, Moses gives Israel a stern warning not to forget Yahweh, their Redeemer (6:12). The two titles Moses uses highlight the very reason God's covenantal people should not forget him (i.e., live as though he does not exist). Their God is Yahweh, the ever-faithful, covenant-keeping God, and their Redeemer, the one who had just extricated them from bondage in Egypt and made them his chosen nation. There is absolutely no justification for God's people then (and now) to conduct their lives like practical atheists.

13–15 Moses wraps up this section by demanding that the Israelites worship God exclusively. In vv.13–14 he gives the injunctions and then sets forth the basis for these demands in v.15. He first tells them what they must do: fear Yahweh, serve only him (see Note on 5:9), and swear by his name. In other words, the only way for them to function as God's servant-nation (cf. Ex 19:5–6; Dt 26:16–19) is to maintain a fervent commitment to their covenantal relationship with Yahweh. Yahweh has delivered them from the house of slaves (v.12) and now demands that they serve him instead (v.13).

Swearing by Yahweh's name (see Note on 5:11) is an expression of loyalty to him and recognition of him as the supreme authority. A true worshiper of Yahweh is one who swore by his name (Ps 63:11; Isa 48:1; Jer 4:2; 5:2; 12:16). To swear by other gods will represent a betrayal of his authority (Jos 23:7; Jer 12:16). The corollary of serving Yahweh exclusively and wholeheartedly is the absolute refusal to worship any pagan gods (v.14). To "follow after" a ruler or a god implies wholehearted commitment of one's entire life (see Note on 4:3).

The fact that Yahweh is a jealous God (*'ēl qannā'*) provides the primary reason that Israel must worship Yahweh alone and reject any idea of worshiping other gods (v.15). In 5:9, God's characterization of himself as *'ēl qannā'* serves as the theological grounds for his fierce judgment on those who choose to worship prohibited images of him in spite of his covenantal stipulation forbidding any such conduct.

As a jealous God, he judges and punishes any and all covenantal violations. God does not tolerate one of his chosen people giving to another the honor due him alone (cf. Isa 42:8; 48:11).

The *qannā'* (GK 7862) word group, when used of God, reflects the relationship between Yahweh and Israel that the prophets described metaphorically as a marital bond in which Yahweh is compared to a husband and Israel is likened to his wife. As Tigay (*Deuteronomy*, 65) points out, "This metaphor befits the exclusiveness of the relationship: Israel must restrict her fidelity to one God, just as a wife owes exclusive fidelity to her husband; worship of other gods is thus as repugnant as adultery (Ex 34:15–16; Eze 16), and God's reaction to such an offense, like that of an aggrieved husband, is jealousy." According to Ortlund, 30, n. 16, "God's morally perfect jealousy arises out of his joint longings both to vindicate his own glory and to enjoy true love with his people." Especially when used of God, *qannā'* has no associations with self-centered pettiness, fear of losing property, envy, or selfish jealousy.

That exclusivity is also seen in the political realm. The jealousy (*qin'â*; GK 7863) of Yahweh can be directed against external threats to the covenant or the covenantal nation (invading armies, false prophets, etc.). This jealous God, Yahweh, will remove ("destroy") Israel from the Promised Land if they continue to worship false gods.

16–19 Moses warns Israel against questioning Yahweh's ability to keep his promise to them. Rather than concerning themselves with his capacity to do what he said, the Israelites need to commit themselves to unreserved submission to his requirements. Their ability to enjoy continued existence in the Promised Land is at stake. Moses begins by alluding to Israel's "rebellion" at Massah (this place name deriving from the verb *nsh*, "to test"; GK 5814), where they questioned whether God was really in their midst (as he had promised to be) and demanded that he demonstrate his presence to them (cf. Ex 17:7; Ps 95:8–9). "Testing" of this kind involves a question about the capacity of the one being tested (McConville, 144). Instead of demanding something of God, Moses exhorts God's people to live in the light of the covenantal stipulations as a whole ("commands," "stipulations," and "decrees"; v.17).

Jesus quoted from this passage when Satan suggested that he cast himself from the pinnacle of the temple (Mt 4:7; Lk 4:12). Jesus did not question God's ability to rescue him, but he knew that "such an act would trivialize the power of God and his care for those he loves" (Merrill, *Deuteronomy*, 172). If the Israelites devote themselves to those practices God defines as right and good, he will make things "go well" for them (see comments on 5:16 and Note on 5:33), bring them into the Promised Land, and give them longevity there (vv.18–19).

What is the connection between the conduct of God's covenantal people, the fulfillment of God's promise to give them the land, and their continued enjoyment of it? Could Israel's disobedience prevent God's promise from becoming a reality? The ultimate fulfillment of God's promises to the patriarchs was beyond question (Ge 13:14–17; 15:18; 17:8) because Israel's receipt of the Land of Promise was integrally connected to God's character. What was "conditional" was which generation would enjoy the fulfillment of that promise (cf. the Kadesh Barnea generation that died in the wilderness; Nu 13–14) and how many generations would continue to benefit from that divine provision. The presence of conditions did not affect whether or not God would fulfill his promises, but their presence did affect when and to whom those promises would be fulfilled (cf. Jer 31:31–37; 32:36–40; Eze 36:22–31; 37:1–14). As Moses said in v.18, this is a reality that Yahweh has "promised on oath to your forefathers."

In vv.16–19 Moses demonstrates that Yahweh is fully capable of bringing to pass his promise that Israel will inherit the land of Canaan. The issue is whether Israel will enjoy long tenure in that land as the result of wholeheartedly embracing Yahweh's demands.

NOTES

13 The word order of the three clauses in this verse focuses primary attention on Yahweh. In all three cases, the object (normally last) comes first: It is Yahweh your God you must fear, him you must serve, and by his name you must swear (cf. 10:20).

The verb in אֶת־יְהוָה אֱלֹהֶיךָ תִּירָא (*ʾet-yhwh ʾělōheykā tîrāʾ*, "you must revere the LORD your God")— namely, יָרֵא (*yrʾ*; GK 3707)—occurs 435 times in the OT and can signify one of three nuances: terror, respect, or worship (Van Pelt/Kaiser, *NIDOTTE*, 2:527–28). Terror can be occasioned by various circumstances of life (Ge 19:30; Jdg 6:27), the absolute authority of a king (Da 1:10), and the threat of war (Ex 14:10; Dt 2:4; 2Ki 10:4), to name a few possibilities. Most of the occurrences of the phrase "fear the LORD," however, depict Yahweh as an object of worship (cf. Dt 6:2, 24; 8:6; 10:12; 17:19; 31:12–13; Jos 4:24; 24:14).

The verb *yrʾ* occurs thirty-seven times in Deuteronomy; in sixteen instances it refers to "horizontal" fear, so to speak—terror caused by people or circumstances (1:19, 21, 29; 2:4; 3:2, 22; 5:5; 7:18, 21; 8:15; 20:1, 3; 28:10; 31:6, 8). In three passages it describes something about God or something God did (10:17,

21; 28:58). The rest of the occurrences refer to the need for God's people to fear their covenantal Lord (e.g., 4:10; 13:11; 14:23; 21:21; 28:58). The fact that *yrʾ* occurs along with the verb "to serve" (עבד, *ʿbd*) highlights its relevance to God-honoring worship (6:13; 10:12, 20; 13:4). In 6:14, not following other gods serves as a counterpart to fearing Yahweh.

This kind of fear or worship is also characterized by obedience to his decrees and commands (Ps 119:63). Fearing God and obeying his commands will manifest itself in appropriate moral conduct (Ge 42:18; Ex 1:17, 21; Lev 25:17). To live (or rule) in accordance with the fear of the Lord is the same thing as living in accordance with God's decrees and commands. The verb *yrʾ* occurs in close juxtaposition with the verbs for "keeping" (שמר, *šmr*; 5:29; 6:2; 8:6; 13:5), "doing" (עשׂה, *ʿśh*; 6:24; 17:19; 31:12), and "walking" (הלך, *hlk*; 8:6; 10:12; 13:5; 17:19) in accordance with God's commands. God's redemptive acts in behalf of his people provide clear motivation for fearing him (1Sa 12:24; Ex 14:31). This verb also occurs in connection with swearing by his name (שבע בשם, *šbʿ bešem*; 6:13; 10:20), cleaving to him (דבק, *dbq*; 10:20; see Note on 4:4), loving him (אהב, *ʾhb*; 10:12), not acting presumptuously (זיד, *zyd*; 17:13), and not committing evil (עשׂה רע, *ʿśh rʿ*; 19:20).

15 The adjective קנא (*qannaʾ*, "jealous"; GK 7862) occurs six times in the OT (Ex 20:5; 34:14 [2x]; Dt 4:24; 5:9; 6:15). It is only used of God, and in each instance it occurs in the context of the divine prohibition against worshiping other gods or images of God. Various forms of the verbal root קנא (*qnʾ*) occur about eighty-five times in the OT. In the positive sense it can mean to advocate zealously for the benefit of someone else, and in a negative sense it can signify bearing a grudge or resenting. The cause of this jealousy is normally the infringement of someone's rights or injury to the subject's honor, whether real or imagined (Peels, *NIDOTTE*, 3:938–99). M. Greenberg (*Ezekiel 1–20* [AB; New York: Doubleday, 1983], 115) suggests that it represents "the resentful rage of one whose prerogatives have been usurped by, or given to, another." The adjective in question and most of the nominal forms (קנאה, *qinʾâ*) occur in biblical texts that relate to the issue (or threat) of idolatry practiced by the Israelites. According to Peels (*NIDOTTE*, 3:938), "Inside the covenant circle God demands of his people a completely exclusive worship (cf. 6:4). His love for Israel totally excludes any other gods."

G. Sauer (*TLOT*, 3:1146) points out that ancient Near Eastern literature refers to the gods' envy of one another but never depicts a god's zeal in relationship to his worshiper. The reason for this phenomenon is the fact that in the context of a fundamentally polytheistic viewpoint, the worship of one god is not regarded as a threat to the worship of another god. However, this free alternating between gods as objects of one's worship is unthinkable in the biblical (and covenantal) context. The one and only God, Yahweh, who chose Israel to serve as his special possession, will tolerate no rivals. He jealously guards his own uniqueness and demands Israel's undivided worship, loyalty, and allegiance.

16 Generally, the verb נסה, *nsh* (GK 5814), in the phrase לא תנסו, *lōʾ tenassû* ("do not put to the test") either captures the idea of trying to do something (Job 4:2; Dt 4:34) or denotes the act of testing people or items in order to determine something about them. At Massah and in other settings, humans attempted to test Yahweh either by forgetting his works in their behalf and subsequently calling into question his covenantal faithfulness (Nu 14:22; Ps 106:14), or by directly violating his commands (Ps 78:41, 56). Psalm 78 pictures both these aspects. The wandering Israelites tested God by demanding food (v.18) and repeatedly rebelling (v.41). Unfortunately, those who entered Canaan did no better by refusing to keep God's commands (v.56). According to Brensinger (*NIDOTTE* 3:111–12), "to question Yahweh's covenantal faithfulness is to entice him to prove himself again and again. To violate his commands is to test the boundaries and doubt his authority."

c. Yahweh Demands That Israel Remember Past Divine Activity in Their Behalf (6:20–25)

[20]In the future, when your son asks you, "What is the meaning of the stipulations, decrees and laws the LORD our God has commanded you?" [21]tell him: "We were slaves of Pharaoh in Egypt, but the LORD brought us out of Egypt with a mighty hand. [22]Before our eyes the LORD sent miraculous signs and wonders — great and terrible — upon Egypt and Pharaoh and his whole household. [23]But he brought us out from there to bring us in and give us the land that he promised on oath to our forefathers. [24]The LORD commanded us to obey all these decrees and to fear the LORD our God, so that we might always prosper and be kept alive, as is the case today. [25]And if we are careful to obey all this law before the LORD our God, as he has commanded us, that will be our righteousness."

COMMENTARY

20–25 Looking to the more distant future, Moses challenges the present generation to be sure they explain the rationale for the God-given laws to the next generation (cf. 6:7), with the result that they too will obey the Lord's commands and thereby manifest their fear of and love for him.

Moses looks forward to a day when a son, having been instructed in the requirements Yahweh had set before his people, will ask a probing question (v.20). Literally rendered, the Hebrew text reads: "What are the stipulations, decrees, and laws...?" This son could be asking, "What is the real significance of these requirements?" or "Why do we keep these rules?" The question does not appear to be asked in rebellion or skepticism, but out of genuine interest.

Moses instructs the hypothetical father to begin by providing a theological foundation for that answer. God's deliverance of his chosen people, the descendants of Abraham, from bondage in Egypt constitutes the heart of the answer. Through stupendous miracles and awesome demonstrations of his power over his creation, Yahweh brought Egypt to its knees and began the process of fulfilling his promise to provide a landed inheritance for his covenantal people. He brought them out of Egypt and across the Red Sea (a paradigmatic miracle throughout the OT), and he brought them to their encampment on the plains of Moab at the brink of the Promised Land by virtue of the pledge he had made to the patriarchs. In the light of all he had done on Israel's behalf—choosing them as a people, delivering them from Egypt, and giving them this divine inheritance—he had the right to demand their undivided loyalty. The requirements that they "obey" and "fear" Yahweh summarize the demands of his covenant with Israel. Prosperity and life have been, are, and will be occasioned by Israel's obedience to their suzerain's demands.

To that theme, mentioned both earlier and later in Deuteronomy, Moses adds that obedience to God's law "will be our righteousness" (v.25). Similarly to 5:7, which reads literally, "there will not be to you other gods" (= "you will have no other gods"), this clause reads, "righteousness will be to us," i.e., "we will have righteousness." It is unlikely that this

"righteousness" carries a forensic sense, i.e., being "in the right" legally. Wright (*Deuteronomy*, 106) provides this expanded translation: "we shall have, experience, enjoy the blessing of, everything being right—in our family, in our society, and in our relationship with God." God deserves nothing less than Israel's wholehearted submission, and obedience to his requirements has occasioned this "righteousness." As a result, an Israelite father can help his son understand the divine rationale for the covenantal requirements that so thoroughly affect their lives.

3. The Blessings and Requirements Occasioned by Yahweh's Choice of Israel (7:1–26)

OVERVIEW

Scholars have suggested variously that the focus of ch. 7 (1) warns against making an alliance with the Canaanites (Weinfeld, *Deuteronomy 1–11*, 357, 77), (2) exhorts holy and obedient conduct (Christensen, *Deuteronomy 1:1–21:9*, 152, 159), (3) centers on some aspect of the extermination of the Canaanites, i.e., holy war (Craigie, 177; Merrill, *Deuteronomy*, 176; Thompson, 127; Tigay, *Deuteronomy*, 84), or (4) highlights God's faithfulness to his promises (Hall, 149). Although ch. 7 relates to all those issues, the following thematic statement more completely summarizes the heart of the chapter. God's choice of Israel as his special nation (and his continued faithfulness to them) must always be central to their identity. As a result, God demands the extermination of the Canaanites. God's choice

of Israel should be a treasured reality, and Israel's identity must be guarded against corruption.

Scholars have also debated the structure of this chapter (see Hall, 97, for a brief overview of alternatives), but the following outline follows the traditional Masoretic division and conforms to certain key grammatical features. Scholars are fairly unified in thinking that 7:17–26 constitutes a paragraph. (The particle *kî* introduces v.17.) At the very least, a macro-syntactical marker (*wᵉhāyâ*) begins a new section at v.12, and it is likely that a negative particle begins a section at v.7. The following outline (modified from that suggested by Hall) lays out the chapter in chiastic fashion. Israel's covenantal relationship with Yahweh (central elements) provides the rationale for the demanded extermination of the Canaanites (outside elements):

A Destroy the Canaanites from the land (vv.1–6);

  B God has chosen Israel, therefore obey (vv.7–11);

  B' Obey, and God will provide covenantal blessings (vv.12–16);

A' God will destroy the Canaanites from before you (vv.17–26).

a. Destroy the Canaanites from the Land (7:1–6)

OVERVIEW

After dispossessing the various peoples of Canaan, the children of Israel are to avoid any friendly relationships with them; instead, the Israel- ites are to destroy them and their idolatrous objects of worship utterly, for Yahweh has made Israel his special possession.

¹When the Lord your God brings you into the land you are entering to possess and drives out before you many nations — the Hittites, Girgashites, Amorites, Canaanites, Perizzites, Hivites and Jebusites, seven nations larger and stronger than you — ²and when the Lord your God has delivered them over to you and you have defeated them, then you must destroy them totally. Make no treaty with them, and show them no mercy. ³Do not intermarry with them. Do not give your daughters to their sons or take their daughters for your sons, ⁴for they will turn your sons away from following me to serve other gods, and the Lord's anger will burn against you and will quickly destroy you. ⁵This is what you are to do to them: Break down their altars, smash their sacred stones, cut down their Asherah poles and burn their idols in the fire. ⁶For you are a people holy to the Lord your God. The Lord your God has chosen you out of all the peoples on the face of the earth to be his people, his treasured possession.

COMMENTARY

1–2a These verses detail the time frame in which the events of the following verses take place. The defeat of the Canaanites is not questioned in any way but is an assumed reality. Moses shifts from focusing on the conquest to the occupation of Canaan. The implications of the first commandment (no other gods) serve as the foundation for Moses' exhortation.

Moses mentions seven nations that then occupied the land of Canaan and that God commanded Israel to dislodge. Various listings of nations occur twenty-seven times in the OT, with the number of nations mentioned ranging from two to twelve. Six nations are mentioned in eleven passages (Ex 3:8, 17; 23:23; 34:11; Dt 20:17; Jos 9:1; 11:3; 12:8; Jdg 3:5; Ne 9:8 [omitting Girgashites]), while only seven occur in two passages outside the present context (Jos 3:10; 24:11). It is likely that "seven" reflects the idea of completeness or totality (Merrill, *Deuteronomy*, 177).

The center of the Hittite empire (1800–1200 BC) was located in Asia Minor. It is unclear whether the Hittites mentioned here are directly related to that empire or migrated there much earlier and share a common ancestor (Heth; cf. H. Hoffner, "Hittites," in *Peoples of the Old Testament World* [ed. A. Hoerth, G. Mattingly, and E. Yamauchi; Grand Rapids: Baker, 1994], 152–53). Although the Amorites and the Canaanites originated from different places (the Amorites being originally from the upper Euphrates region and having migrated to Canaan in the late third millennium, and the Canaanites being the descendants of Ham and indigenous to Canaan), it appears that the Amorites generally occupied the hill country, while the Canaanites inhabited the coastal and lowland areas (cf. Dt 1:7; K. Schoville, "Canaanites and Amorites," in ibid., 165–67, 180–81; see comments on 2:26–3:11).

Most scholars identify the Hivites with the Hurrians or Horites (cf. Ge 14:6; 36:20–22, 29, 30; Nu 13:5; Dt 2:12, 22). They lived in various parts of Canaan (Ge 34:2; Jos 9:7; 11:19) and Lebanon (Jos 11:3; Jdg 3:3). The Jebusites were descendants of Ham (through Canaan; Ge 10:16) and occupied the hill country of Canaan (Nu 13:29; Jos 11:3). Named after them was the city of Jebus, which remained in their hands until David conquered it (and renamed it Jerusalem). Little is known about the Girgashites (Ge 10:16; Jos 3:10; 24:11; 1Ch 1:14; *ABD*, 2:1028) or the Perizzites (Ge 13:7; 34:30; Jos 3:10; 7:1; Jdg 1:4–5; *ABD*, 5:231; for a helpful overview of these peoples, see E. Hostetter, *Nations Mightier and More Numerous* [Richland Hills, Tex.: Bibal Press, 1995], 51–83).

These seven nations are called "larger and stronger" than Israel. Although on grammatical grounds this statement could be true of these Canaanite peoples individually or collectively, it is most likely that *as a group* they outnumber the Israelites. Consequently, there is little hope that Israel can successfully conquer this region on their own. Moses finishes delineating the time frame by adding, "when the LORD your God has delivered them over to you and you have defeated them"; this phrase emphasizes Israel's desperate need for Yahweh's enablement for the task ahead of them.

2b–5 Once Yahweh enables Israel to defeat the peoples of Canaan (7:2a), he makes of them various requirements, which fall into political, social, and religious categories (Wright, *Deuteronomy*, 110–11). Politically, the Israelites must exterminate them and refuse to enter into any covenants with them (7:2b). The Israelites have been bound to an exclusive relationship with Yahweh because of their "covenant" with him. Even though this covenant is primarily religious in orientation, it is also a political reality. This covenant sets them apart as a distinct nation.

In addition, if the Israelites were to pursue a treaty (which would include a peace agreement) with the nations of Canaan, they would be disobeying God's demand to exterminate them. It would also represent a human attempt to facilitate taking control of Canaan and a lack of trust that God will bring it to pass. Socially, the Israelites are forbidden to allow their sons or daughters to intermarry with Canaanite men and women (7:3); such marital alliances would result from making treaties with these peoples. Marriages between Israelites would strengthen the fabric of God's people; marriages made with non-Israelites would weaken that fabric (McConville, 153). Israel's history is replete with examples of idolatry that followed Israelite intermarriage with pagan peoples (cf. Solomon [1Ki 11:3] and Ahab [1Ki 16:30–33]). Though "mixed" marriages were not prohibited across the board (Nu 12:1; Dt 21:10–14), intermarriage would generally lead to idolatry, which would in turn occasion the wrath of Yahweh.

Religiously, the Israelites must destroy any kind of religious equipment involved in Canaanite worship (cf. 12:3). Altars, also used in Israelite worship, would have been used to offer food, drink, or incense to Baal. They could have been made out of dirt or stones. Sacred stones refer to cut or uncut stones that pagan worshipers used to mark out an area as belonging to the pagan deity. Asherah poles involved live trees or wooden poles that symbolized the fertility-goddess, Asherah (cf. Ex 34:13; Dt 16:21–22; Jdg 6:25. 28), and idols were images to facilitate pagan worship. All these must be broken, smashed, cut down, and burned.

6 Israel's identity as God's covenantal nation provides the primary basis or rationale for the preceding requirements. Moses highlights three facets of that unique status (cf. Ex 19:5–6). In the first place, they are (and are to be) "holy" to Yahweh, i.e., have a distinctive witness in the midst of pagan nations. It is important to notice that this holiness did not simply place limitations on Israel's relationships with other people groups and religions. Israel's holy

calling served as the foundation for many of the laws delineated in Deuteronomy 12–26. Yahweh intends that their separation from what is sinful and profane and their absolute consecration to Yahweh will have far-reaching implications.

Second, their unique status is not deserved but the result of Yahweh's choice of them (cf. 7:7–8; 4:37; 10:15; 14:2). God has chosen them to be his own people "out of" the midst of all the world's nations so that they will be distinct "from" all those nations.

Finally, by choosing Israel (see comments on 10:14–16) Yahweh has made them his "treasured possession" (*sᵉgullâ*), i.e., "a people particularly for him" (McConville, 155; cf. 1Pe 2:9).

NOTES

2a In the phrase וּנְתָנָם לְפָנֶיךָ (*ûnᵉtānām lᵉpāneykā*, "when he gives them over ... to you"), the combination of the verb "to give" (נתן, *ntn*) with the preposition "before" (לִפְנֵי, *lipnê*), yielding "to give ... before," occurs seventeen times in Deuteronomy to highlight what God bestows on people: statutes and ordinances (11:32), blessing/life and curse/death (11:26; 30:1, 15, 19), the law (4:8), the land of promise (1:8, 21; 2:36), victory/defeat (28:7, 25), and vanquished enemies for Israel (2:31, 33; 7:2, 23; 23:14; 31:5). It serves as a counterpart to נתן בְּיָד (*ntn bᵉyād*), "to give into the hand of" (see Note on 2:24).

2b The occurrence of the verb חרם (*ḥrm* [GK 3049], in הַחֲרֵם תַּחֲרִים, *haḥᵃrēm taḥᵃrîm*, "you must annihilate"), in the present context in particular, has occasioned some scholarly debate. If the verb means to totally annihilate a people (see Note on 2:34), why does Moses command Israel not to enter into political arrangements with, intermarry, or worship the gods of the Canaanites, the very people they are to exterminate? Does חרם mean something different from "devote to destruction"? Weinfeld (*Deuteronomy 1–11*, 365, 382–84) resolves the tension by regarding the requirement of extermination as a later ideal (from Deuteronomistic sources) that was never actually implemented. Others redefine the verb (based on J. Lilley, "Understanding the Ḥerem," *TynBul* 44 [1993]: 169–77, esp. 176–77) as "renounce for any personal benefit" (Hall, 152–53; Wright, *Deuteronomy*, 109, 120) and suggest that Moses is prohibiting the Israelites from taking any gain or profit from the conquered peoples.

However, it appears best to maintain the idea of "total destruction" as central to the meaning of חרם (cf. Naudé, *NIDOTTE*, 2:276–77; Giesen, *TDOT*, 5:199–203; McConville, 87–88). Subsequent verses in ch. 7 support that interpretation: "You must destroy all the peoples the LORD your God gives over to you" (7:16); "until even the survivors who hide from you have perished" (7:20); "you will not be allowed to eliminate them all at once" (7:22); "until they are destroyed" (7:23); "you will wipe out their names from under heaven" (7:24); "you will destroy them" (7:24). The failure of God's people to carry out this requirement will have long-term consequences (Jdg 1:21–34; 1Ki 9:20–21).

But why issue these other prohibitions if total extermination is in view? The forbidding of covenants with Canaanites, intermarriage, and worship of false gods provides the divine rationale for this sobering demand to exterminate these peoples (McConville, 153). Because those practices will be so enticing and so far-reaching in the corruption they occasion for God's people, God requires them to "devote [the Canaanites] to destruction."

The verb כרת (*krt* [GK 4162], in the phrase לֹא־תִכְרֹת לָהֶם בְּרִית, *lōʾ-tikrōt lāhem bᵉrît*, "Make no treaty with them") can mean to cut or cut down something, such as trees (1Ki 5:6[20]; 2Ki 19:23) or pagan idols (1Ki 15:13; 2Ki 18:4; 23:14). In several passages it means to excommunicate, eliminate, or destroy. Its most significant theological use is in conjunction with the noun "covenant." To "cut" a covenant means to make, establish, or enter into a covenantal relationship with someone (Dt 4:23; 5:2–3; 9:9; 29:1, 14, 25 [28:69; 29:13, 24]; 31:16). It refers to renewing one's commitment to the covenant as well (2Ki 23:3). This verb probably came to be used for establishing a covenant because the slaughtering of animals was a part of the covenantal ritual (cf. Ge 15:9–11, 17; Jer 34:18–19; cf. Weinfeld, *TDOT*, 2:259; Hasel, *TDOT*, 7:349–52).

6 The קדשׁ (*qdš*) word family signifies that which belongs to the realm of the sacred and is, consequently, distinct from the common or profane (Naudé, *NIDOTTE*, 3:878–79). Just as devoting something to destruction (חרם, *ḥrm*; see comments on 7:2b) is part of "holy war," certain items and people are to be consecrated to Yahweh. The nation is to have a distinctive witness and impact on the world

The noun סְגֻלָּה (*sᵉgullâ*; GK 6035), "treasured possession," also occurs in five other passages to describe Israel's privileged status (Ex 19:5; Dt 14:2; 26:18; Ps 135:4; Mal 3:17) and Yahweh's affection for his chosen people. Elsewhere it refers to a king's private fortune (1Ch 29:3; Ecc 2:8). In an Akkadian text a king is depicted as the special possession (*sikiltum*) of a god, and in a Ugaritic letter a Hittite king (the suzerain) reminds a Ugaritic king (the vassal) that he is the Hittite king's servant and *sglt* (Weinfeld, *Deuteronomy 1–11*, 368). In language reminiscent of Exodus 19:4–6 (where Moses lays before the covenantal nation God's primary expectations of them, so that they are a "banner nation" before the nations of the world), Moses explains the theological foundation for this demand to exterminate the Canaanites and all of their religious utensils. Because of their identity (chosen, holy people, treasured possession), Israel must avoid idolatry and clearly manifest their God-given identity to all surrounding nations (cf. Dt 14:2; 26:18; Ps 135:4; Mal 3:17; Tit 2:14; 1Pe 2:9).

b. God Has Chosen Israel, Therefore Obey (7:7–11)

[7]The Lord did not set his affection on you and choose you because you were more numerous than other peoples, for you were the fewest of all peoples. [8]But it was because the Lord loved you and kept the oath he swore to your forefathers that he brought you

out with a mighty hand and redeemed you from the land of slavery, from the power of Pharaoh king of Egypt. ⁹Know therefore that the Lord your God is God; he is the faithful God, keeping his covenant of love to a thousand generations of those who love him and keep his commands. ¹⁰But

> those who hate him he will repay to their face by destruction;
>   he will not be slow to repay to their face those who hate him.

¹¹Therefore, take care to follow the commands, decrees and laws I give you today.

COMMENTARY

7–8 Moses here pursues one of the deep mysteries of the entire Bible, i.e., the unexplained, self-motivated love of God for humanity at large and Israel in particular. He uses three pairs of verbal phrases to make his point: "[He] did not set his affection on you and choose you … [he] did love you [see Note on 4:37] and kept the oath he swore … that he brought you out and redeemed you." The first and second pairs of verbs are generally synonymous, and the last set of verbs delineate the consequence of God's action or choice. Yahweh's desire for and choice of Israel had nothing at all to do with their population. His relationship with them was totally unrelated to their (nonexistent!) numerical strength (and consequent reputation).

The next pair of verbs does not provide an outside reason for God's choice. Moses' simply saying that the Lord loved Israel leaves the reader with only one alternative: God's choice to set his love on Israel was based in God alone. (For a brief discussion of "love," see Note on 4:37.) The oath (see Note on 1:8) he made to (or covenant he established with) the patriarchs was also grounded in his character alone. Although God makes certain demands on Abraham's descendants if they are to enjoy the fulfillment of the covenantal pro-

visions, the ultimate fulfillment of that covenant was never in question. Its fulfillment was as sure as God's character was reliable (cf. Ge 15:9–20). Yahweh's decision to love Israel and his fixed commitment to his oath provided the theological foundation for his delivering them from bondage in Egypt.

Moses uses other repeated ideas to drive his point home: "you … your forefathers" (relevant to this new generation), "brought you out … redeemed you" (God himself extricated them), "from the land of slavery … from the power of Pharaoh" (not just from a difficult situation but also in the face of overwhelming human odds).

9–11 What does Yahweh expect from his redeemed people in light of the undeserved and miraculous demonstration of his great power in their behalf? He wants them to have a life-transforming knowledge of their covenantal Lord (7:9–10) and devote their entire beings to living in accordance with his demands (7:11). Moses wants Israel to know "the Lord your God," a title that occurs abundantly (over 230 times) in Deuteronomy and highlights the covenantal relationship that exists between them and Yahweh. This covenantal Lord is "the God," i.e., the one and only God. Also, he is a God who is characterized by a fixed commitment to his promises. He is trustworthy and reliable. He demonstrates this dependability in the way he deals with his covenantal citizens.

His subjects fall into two categories: those who love him and those who hate him (see comments and Note on 5:10, where these two categories appear in reverse order). Yahweh unfailingly delivers on his covenantal commitments for the unimaginable future with reference to those who wholeheartedly and loyally embrace this covenantal relationship (those who love him). The ones who genuinely submit to his covenantal demands are they who obey those requirements. The ones who reject this covenantal relationship and its demand for unswerving loyalty will experience a different fate. Moses uses a chiastic structure (evident in the Hebrew; cf. McConville, 158) to focus on the fact that God will destroy these covenantal rebels, and none will escape (7:10):

A Repay
  B Those who hate him
    C Destroy
    C' Do Not Delay
  B' Those who hate him
A' Repay

The "compensation" envisioned here is full repayment in kind. Unlike 5:9–10, which considered the generational implications of covenantal treachery, the present passage focuses on the personal consequences for those Israelites who reject a heartfelt relationship with their covenantal Lord. Moses concludes this section by exhorting the Israelites to invest themselves in obeying Yahweh (7:11). They must carefully obey (see Note on 5:1) the stipulations of the covenant Yahweh established with them at Sinai and reaffirmed at Moab.

NOTES

7 The verb/preposition collocation חָשַׁק בְּ (ḥšq bᵉ, "to set affection on"), present in the phrase חָשַׁק יְהוָה בָּכֶם (ḥāšaq yhwh bākem, "that Yahweh set his love on you"), occurs eleven times in the OT. In three instances it refers to metal strips used to bind things together in the tabernacle (Ex 27:17; 38:17, 28). It also describes the longing a man could have for a woman (Ge 34:8; Dt 21:11). It signified the structures Solomon "desired" to build in Jerusalem (1Ki 9:19 = 2Ch 8:6). The psalmist used it to describe a believer who passionately cleaves to Yahweh (Ps 91:14). In the present passage and 10:15 the verb describes God's desire for his covenantal people. When used of relationships, the verb does not emphasize the emotional side but presupposes "a reasoned and unconditioned decision" (Wallis, *TDOT*, 5:263).

9 The verb יָדַע (ydʿ, "to know"; here וְיָדַעְתָּ, wᵉyādaʿtā, "Know therefore") is part of an important theological triad (know, remember, forget—see Note on 4:10 for the last two). It occurs eleven times as part of an exhortation to God's covenantal people (4:9, 35, 39; 7:9; 8:5; 9:3, 6; 11:2; 29:3, 6, 16; 31:13). This verb has a fairly wide variety of meanings in the OT. It can refer to something as basic as sensory perception or awareness (Ex 3:7; Jer 12:3) and can signify the idea of discernment or careful consideration (cf. Pr 18:15). It can even carry the idea of sexual intimacy (Ge 4:1). In general, for one to "know" something means for that person to live in light of the various truths and events around him or her (e.g., 4:39: "take to heart").

Normally, ydʿ does not signify cognitive exercise alone. As a matter of fact, this verb shows up repeatedly in the context of God's relationship with his children. God knows his people, they are supposed to know God (4:35, 39), and they are required to pass on this life-transforming understanding of God (4:9; 31:13).

It is instructive to take a glance at those who, according to the Bible, do not know the Lord (Ex 5:2; 1Sa 2:12; Hos 5:4). In each case, the life of the person(s) who did not know God was not influenced by God's character. In Deuteronomy in particular, Yahweh exhorts his people to "know" him and his activities in their behalf because genuine knowledge of God is always life-changing.

Scholars have offered various translations for the two nouns in the phrase שֹׁמֵר הַבְּרִית וְהַחֶסֶד (*šōmēr habbᵉrît wᵉhaḥesed*, "keeping covenant and steadfast love"): "keeps covenant and displays steadfast love" (Thompson, 131); "maintaining covenant and faithful love" (Craigie, 180; Hall, 156; McConville, 158); and "keeps his covenant faithfully (Tigay, *Deuteronomy*, 88). Weinfeld (*Deuteronomy 1–11*, 370–71) and Merrill (*Deuteronomy*, 181) regard these two nouns as a hendiadys, with the two terms expressing a complete idea. Weinfeld translates the expression "gracious covenant" and Merrill renders it "loyalty to covenant." Although "covenant" and "steadfast love" are important concepts in the OT and occur frequently on their own, the construction in this passage supports regarding them as a hendiadys. An almost identical construction occurs in 7:12 with the same meaning.

c. Obey, and God Will Provide Covenantal Blessings (7:12–16)

OVERVIEW

As suggested above, four pericopes make up ch. 7. The first and last section focus on God's demand for the extermination of the Canaanites. The central sections focus on Israel's standing with God, his expectation of them, and his commitment to glorifying himself through them. In the preceding verses (7:7–11), Moses has exhorted God's covenantal nation to obey Yahweh wholeheartedly in the light of all he has done in their behalf. In the present passage, Moses moves on to deal with the covenantal implications of genuine obedience—covenantal blessings.

[12]If you pay attention to these laws and are careful to follow them, then the LORD your God will keep his covenant of love with you, as he swore to your forefathers. [13]He will love you and bless you and increase your numbers. He will bless the fruit of your womb, the crops of your land — your grain, new wine and oil — the calves of your herds and the lambs of your flocks in the land that he swore to your forefathers to give you. [14]You will be blessed more than any other people; none of your men or women will be childless, nor any of your livestock without young. [15]The LORD will keep you free from every disease. He will not inflict on you the horrible diseases you knew in Egypt, but he will inflict them on all who hate you. [16]You must destroy all the peoples the LORD your God gives over to you. Do not look on them with pity and do not serve their gods, for that will be a snare to you.

COMMENTARY

12 The first line of this pericope summarizes the preceding section. If Israel gives diligent attention to obey the covenantal stipulations ("are careful to follow"—see Note on 5:1), God will be faithful to the covenant he established with his covenantal nation. Once again, what God promises does not depend on Israel's strength or merit. Rather, it resides in the character of their God, the one who has chosen to initiate this relationship with them.

13–15 These three verses carry significant covenantal overtones. Although "love" is more frequently associated with the duty of Israelites (covenantal citizens), it does describe Yahweh's choice to make Israel his own (4:37; 10:5; 23:5) and his tender care of them (10:18–19). The verbs "bless" (*brk*) and "multiply" (*rbh*) occur as a word pair (Ge 22:17; 26:24; 28:3; Dt 7:13; Isa 51:2) to emphasize God's intent to pour out abundant blessings on his covenantal people. He promises to make them numerous and to provide for them abundantly. God's promise to multiply their population (Ge 17:2, 20; 48:4; Ex 32:13; Lev 26:9; Dt 1:10) contrasts with the way he found them, small and insignificant (cf. 7:7–8).

This blessing will manifest itself in large families, productive fields, and growing herds and flocks. The triad "grain, new wine and oil" occurs six times in Deuteronomy (7:13; 11:14; 12:17; 14:13; 18:4; 28:51; twelve times in the rest of the OT) and the doublet "grain and new wine" occurs once (33:28; eight times in the rest of the OT). These agricultural products represent the chief food products of Israel and designate a fruitful land (Weinfeld, *Deuteronomy 1–11*, 373). All these blessings accord with his covenantal commitment or oath (see Note on 1:8). He will also deliver his people from the many sicknesses they had witnessed in Egypt. Indeed, he will inflict such sicknesses on their enemies.

This positive message of abundant, divine blessing on Israel also represents a veiled rebuke against Baalism (and anyone tempted to worship that false god). What Yahweh promises to Israel here are the very things the Canaanite gods were supposed to provide for their worshipers. Yahweh, the only living God, is the one to whom the Israelites must look rather than any dead, pagan gods.

16 Making a transition to the next paragraph, Moses reminds the Israelites of their God-given task, the extermination of the Canaanites. Moses warns them against the natural sympathy (see Note on 13:8 [9]) they will feel for these pagans and presses them to carry out God's bidding. If they spare the Canaanites and then worship their pagan gods, it may lead to Israel's own ruin.

NOTE

13 The idea of divine blessing (וּבֵרַכְךָ, *ûbērakkā*, "and he will bless you") plays a central role in Yahweh's covenant with Israel. The verb *brk* occurs 327 times in the OT and thirty-nine times in Deuteronomy (esp. chs. 28–33). In the context of a covenantal relationship, nothing was more important than securing the blessing of God in one's life or nation. The Bible and ancient Near Eastern literature give evidence of multitudes of people who sought a blessing from their God or gods. As Brown (*NIDOTTE*, 1:758) points out:

How crucial it was, then, for the people of Israel to secure the blessing of the all-powerful god, the only creator, the ruler of the ends of the earth, their true lord and rightful king, whose blessing no one could reverse and whose curse no one could lift. And where there was a covenantal (or family) blessing passed on through the generations, there was nothing more urgent than being properly positioned so as to receive (or inherit) that blessing (cf. 1Ki 2:45). A blessed life was the ideal; a life without God's blessing (a fortiori, a life under God's curse; cf. Jer 20:14) was the ultimate nightmare (cf. Ps 129:8; Jer 17:5–6; Mic 2:9).

Wenham (*Genesis 1–15*, 24) aptly wrote: "Where modern man talks of success, Old Testament man talked of blessing."

d. God Will Destroy the Canaanites From Before You (7:17–26)

OVERVIEW

In case the Israelites become discouraged from carrying out their task because of the strength of the Canaanites, Moses exhorts them to focus on the Lord's greatness instead. The Lord will deliver their enemies into their hands, after which the children of Israel are to destroy utterly all the Canaanite idols. Verses 17–19 look back at the ways Yahweh had already demonstrated his great power, and vv.20–24 look forward to his enabling Israel for the task God has set before his people, the extermination of the Canaanites. Moses concludes his exhortation by warning the Israelites about the danger of worshiping false gods (vv.25–26).

[17]You may say to yourselves, "These nations are stronger than we are. How can we drive them out?" [18]But do not be afraid of them; remember well what the LORD your God did to Pharaoh and to all Egypt. [19]You saw with your own eyes the great trials, the miraculous signs and wonders, the mighty hand and outstretched arm, with which the LORD your God brought you out. The LORD your God will do the same to all the peoples you now fear. [20]Moreover, the LORD your God will send the hornet among them until even the survivors who hide from you have perished. [21]Do not be terrified by them, for the LORD your God, who is among you, is a great and awesome God. [22]The LORD your God will drive out those nations before you, little by little. You will not be allowed to eliminate them all at once, or the wild animals will multiply around you. [23]But the LORD your God will deliver them over to you, throwing them into great confusion until they are destroyed. [24]He will give their kings into your hand, and you will wipe out their names from under heaven. No one will be able to stand up against you; you will destroy them. [25]The images of their gods you are to burn in the fire. Do not covet the silver and gold on them, and do not take it for yourselves, or you will be ensnared by it, for it is detestable to the LORD your God. [26]Do not bring a detestable thing into your house or you, like it, will be set apart for destruction. Utterly abhor and detest it, for it is set apart for destruction.

COMMENTARY

17–19 Moses turns Israel's attention to past events in which the Lord intervened spectacularly to carry out his purposes. If the Israelites feel inadequate for the task before them, afraid of the greater strength and larger numbers of the Canaanite people, Moses directs their attention to God, the one who will enable them to carry out the assigned task. He commands them not to fear (see Note on 6:13) the Canaanites but instead to remember Yahweh's activity in their behalf, in particular his deliverance of them from Egypt. Throughout Deuteronomy, remembering God does not merely signify recreating or revisiting some historical aspect. It demonstrates the contemporary validity of his promises. Remembering God gives evidence to his always-continuing faithfulness (see Note on 4:10). Just as Yahweh miraculously and stupendously delivered the Israelites from bondage in Egypt, he will deliver the Canaanites (the people the Israelites fear) into the hands of his covenantal nation.

The word pair "miraculous signs and wonders" (*hāʾōtōt wᵉhammōpᵉtîm*) occurs twelve times in the OT to refer to Yahweh's unparalleled deliverance of Israel from Egypt (Ex 7:3; Dt 4:34; 7:19; 26:8; 29:2; 34:11; Ne 9:10; Pss 105:27; 135:9; Jer 32:20–21). On the paired anthropomorphic expression "a mighty hand and an outstretched arm," see comment on 5:15. Because Yahweh is with them, they have nothing to fear!

20–24 Building on his pattern of faithfulness to his covenantal nation, Yahweh, the great God, guarantees that he will deliver the Canaanites into Israel's hands. Just as God chased the Israelites back to Kadesh Barnea ("like a swarm of bees") when they failed to trust him (Dt 1:44), God promises to drive any surviving Canaanites into the hands of Israel. Yahweh commands them not to be terrified by the more numerous Canaanites and points to

himself as the enabler of that lack of terror. They are not to be afraid (*ʿrṣ*) because Yahweh himself is a terrifying God ("awesome," derived from *yrʾ*, "to fear"). Unlike the dead Canaanite gods, Yahweh is a living God, who promises his presence in the midst of his covenantal people.

The *shekinah* cloud serves as a visible reminder of that reality. God's presence occurs repeatedly as the grounds for God's people to find encouragement (Ex 33:3, 5; Dt 1:42; 7:21; 23:14 [15]; Jos 3:10; Ps 46:5 [6]; Jer 14:9; Hos 11:9; Zep 3:17) as well as to motivate them to avoid covenantal treachery (Dt 6:15; 31:17). The settlement of all the land will not be immediate. God will enable the Israelites to conquer the land they occupy, lest wild animals overrun their territory (see comment on 9:3).

In 7:23–24 Moses delineates the combined divine and human involvement in the conquest of Canaan. Yahweh will deliver the Canaanites to the Israelites and give their kings into Israelite hands. Israel will destroy the Canaanites and wipe out their names. The potential before an obedient Israel is that, because of God's enablement, the Canaanites will be unable to avoid total defeat. Israel's eventual inability to conquer the Canaanites completely does not reflect on Israel's God but on the nation's unwillingness to take God at his word.

25–26 Moses here returns to a theme found earlier in the chapter, a theme that served as part of the rationale for God's demand that Israel exterminate the Canaanites. Lest the Israelites also be destroyed, they are prohibited from taking for personal use anything of value from the Canaanite images; the Israelites must destroy everything connected with idolatrous Canaanite worship. Even though the gold and silver utilized to make pagan images still carry significant value, their association with false worship make them totally unsuitable for use by

God's people, a holy people. Since God has devoted all instruments of idolatry to destruction (*ḥrm*; see Note on 7:2b), God's people risk ensnarement by that same fate if they keep for themselves anything associated with idolatry. Anything associated with false worship is detestable to Yahweh and is to be absolutely loathed and detested (emphatic structure in Hebrew) by God's people.

NOTES

20 Scholars have debated the correct rendering of הַצִּרְעָה (*haṣṣirʿâ*, "the hornet"). All three passages that have this word (Ex 23:28; Dt 7:20; Jos 24:12) refer to God's act of driving out the peoples in Canaan before Israel. It could serve as a literal reference to a hornet's nest, wasp's nest, hornet, or wasp (so LXX, σφηκιά, *sphēkia*, "wasp's nest"; cf. σφηξ, *sphēx*, "wasp"; *HALOT*, 1056–57; Craigie, 182; Driver, 104; Tigay, *Deuteronomy*, 90; Weinfeld, *Deuteronomy 1–11*, 375). Some regard it as a figurative reference to the dread or fear that will come on Israel's enemies when they hear of what Yahweh did to Egypt (with no reference to hornets—McConville, 149, 161; cf. several references in *HALOT* entry). In Exodus 23:28 it serves as a parallel term for "my terror" (v.27). In that case, the report psychologically incapacitated them much as a wasp's or hornet's sting does (Jos 2:10–11; Carpenter/Grisanti, *NIDOTTE*, 3:847).

The strongest evidence favors translating the term as "hornets," but that answer does not settle whether actual hornets are in view or whether the terror and panic occasioned by a ferocious swarm of insects are intended. Weinfeld (*Deuteronomy 1–11*, 375) concludes that the hornets serve as metaphors for invading armies. Craigie, 182, suggests that the Canaanites will find no hiding place from the victorious pursuit of God's people. At the very least, the hornet designates some instrument God will use to facilitate Israel's conquest of the Canaanites.

21 The verb ערץ (*ʿrṣ*, "to be terrified," in לֹא תַעֲרֹץ, *lōʾ taʿᵃrōṣ*, "you must not tremble") occurs fifteen times in the OT. In Deuteronomy and Joshua it occurs in a prohibition, "Do not be terrified" (Dt 1:29; 7:21; 20:3; 31:6; Jos 1:9). In each case the prohibition is directed either to Israel or to one of Israel's leaders (Moses or Joshua). A motive or purpose clause follows each prohibition to delineate the ground for such a prohibition: e.g., "for the LORD your God goes with you; he will never leave you nor forsake you" (Dt 31:6); "for the LORD your God is the one who goes with you to fight for you against your enemies to give you victory" (20:4). Each instance focuses on the idea of Yahweh's actual presence in the face of a great task or the enemy's threat as the motivation for not fearing (Van Pelt/Kaiser, *NIDOTTE*, 3:543–44).

24 In the OT, the survival of one's name was highly valued. God instituted levirate marriage to guarantee that each Israelite family would have an heir (25:6). God's commitment to preserving his chosen people prevented him from blotting out Israel's name, i.e., wiping them out totally (2Ki 14:27). To have one's name blotted out (וְהַאֲבַדְתָּ אֶת־שְׁמָם, *wᵉhaʾᵃbadtā ʾet-šᵉmām*, "you will wipe out their names") is the same thing as dying (Ps 41:5 [6]) or having no descendants (Ps 109:13). God threatened to blot out Israel's name in the wake of the incident with the golden calf (Dt 9:14). Most of the above examples use the verb מחה (*mḥh*) for "blot out." The verb אבד (*ʾbd*) occurs in three passages to indicate the blotting out of one's name: Deuteronomy 7:14; 12:3; Ps 41:5 [6]. Paralleling Deuteronomy 7:25–26 (the destruction of all idolatrous utensils), Moses commands the Israelites to "wipe out their name" from the place where the pagan gods are worshiped (12:3). For examples of this concept in ancient Near Eastern curses, see Weinfeld (*Deuteronomy and the Deuteronomic School*, 107).

25–26 Fundamentally, תּוֹעֵבָה (*tôʿēbâ*, "something detestable" [GK 9359], which occurs sixteen times in Deuteronomy [twice here—once in the phrase תּוֹעֲבַת יְהוָה אֱלֹהֶיךָ הוּא, *tôʿabat yhwh ʾelōheykā hûʾ*, "it is detestable to Yahweh your God"]) denotes the persons, things, or practices that offend one's ritual or moral order, while the verb תעב (*tʿb*, "to detest," which occurs twice here and twice in 23:7) delineates the loathing of that offensive person, thing, or practice. Throughout the OT, the noun refers to three categories of things that are offensive to Yahweh: pagan worship practices, deceit and insubordination, and superficial worship of Yahweh.

In Deuteronomy, the following practices are regarded as "something destestable": idolatry (7:25–26), child sacrifice (12:31), unclean food (14:3), sacrifice of blemished animals (17:1), child sacrifice/occult (18:9–12), gender confusion (22:5), temple prostitution (23:18), remarriage after divorce in a certain situation (24:4), and inequitable measures (25:16). In the light of Yahweh's covenant with his people, he has a number of expectations for Israel stemming from his desire that they demonstrate his character to the surrounding nations. Those divine expectations entail the avoidance and loathing of certain prohibited items and practices, which, having been demarcated by Yahweh himself, are incompatible with his character and therefore must be rejected and abhorred by any worshiper of Yahweh.

All these abominations constitute a threat to the harmony and existence of Israel, Yahweh's covenantal community. The fundamental issue appears to be Yahweh's desire to preserve the purity of his chosen people so as to enable them clearly to mirror his character to the surrounding pagan nations. More particularly, the phrase תּוֹעֵבָה יְהוָה (*tôʿēbâ yhwh*) occurs in only two books of the OT: Deuteronomy (eight times) and Proverbs (eleven times). In Deuteronomy it is always connected with a demand for exclusive devotion to the worship of Yahweh, while in Proverbs it primarily concerns moral deviation and interpersonal relationships without reference to an explicit covenantal background (W. McKane, *Proverbs: A New Approach* [OTL; Philadelphia: Westminster, 1970], 301).

4. The Need for Israel to Depend Totally on Yahweh (8:1–20)

a. Yahweh's Loving Care for His Covenantal People Should Occasion Wholehearted Obedience (8:1–6)

OVERVIEW

Looking back at God's faithfulness to Israel as they wandered in the wilderness and looking forward to the good land God is giving them, Moses exhorts the Israelites to avoid a spirit of independence and self-sufficiency and instead to remember the Lord by keeping his commandments, lest he cause them to perish. Moses uses two "double themes" to strengthen his challenge for Israel to live in the light of their covenantal relationship with Yahweh: remember/forget and wilderness/Promised Land (Craigie, 184).

¹Be careful to follow every command I am giving you today, so that you may live and increase and may enter and possess the land that the LORD promised on oath to your forefathers. ²Remember how the LORD your God led you all the way in the desert these forty years, to humble you and to test you in order to know what was in your heart, whether or not you would keep his commands. ³He humbled you, causing you to hunger and then feeding you with manna, which neither you nor your fathers had known, to teach you that man does not live on bread alone but on every word that comes from the mouth of the LORD. ⁴Your clothes did not wear out and your feet did not swell during these forty years. ⁵Know then in your heart that as a man disciplines his son, so the LORD your God disciplines you.

⁶Observe the commands of the LORD your God, walking in his ways and revering him.

COMMENTARY

1 This verse serves as an introduction to the entire chapter by calling Israel to covenantal conformity that will occasion tremendous blessings, all in accordance with Yahweh's promise to his covenantal people. Moses exhorts them to "carefully follow" (see Note on 5:1) "every command." He does not have in mind a particular requirement Yahweh had given to his people; rather, in several passages this singular noun ("command") refers to the basic demand for loyalty (to which chs. 5–11 are devoted; see Note on 6:1). The Israelites' genuine obedience will enable them to live, multiply in number, and enter and possess the land Yahweh had sworn to give to them (see Note on 1:8). The verb "to live" serves as the first element in a triad or a doublet in six passages in Deuteronomy. The other elements commonly cited are "go in and take possession," "go well," "multiply," "inherit/take possession," or "lengthen days" (4:1; 5:33; 6:24; 8:1; 16:20; 30:16). What God desires for his covenantal people is abundant life in the Promised Land, where they will live long and multiply in number.

2–4 Moses urges the Israelites to remember (see comments and Note on 4:10) the Lord's repeated faithfulness to them during their wilderness wanderings and consequently to be motivated to obey all that the Lord demands of them. Moses directs their attention to Yahweh's flawless guidance of and provision for them during their nearly forty years of wandering in the wilderness—divine acts meant to humble them.

Verse 2b can be rendered, "that he might humble you, by testing you to know what was in your heart." God applied pressure to Israel during the wilderness wanderings as a way to discern the disposition of their heart. Were they committed to covenantal obedience or covenantal treachery? By letting them feel hunger and then providing them with manna, he sought to teach his people an important lesson: As indispensable as bread is to life, God's demands and expectations are even less dispensable. The bread that came from God (i.e., life-giving manna) dwarfs in comparison to what God himself has to say to his people. When Christ quotes this part of the verse (Mt 4:4; Lk 4:4), he contrasts physical food with spiritual food, an application that is not as prominent in the present context. Finally, Moses reminds the Israelites that God arrested normal wear and tear to their clothing and sandals as well as their bodies (even in that period of covenantal judgment!).

5–6 Moses concludes this section with two commands. First, the Israelites must be fully aware of or know (see Note on 7:9) that God's dealings with them are like that of a father disciplining his child (cf. Pr 3:11–12; 19:18; 29:17). His actions toward them may involve admonition and punishment, but they are motivated by love. Second, and in concert with multiple other statements like it, Moses exhorts Israel to live in accordance with (i.e., keep) Yahweh's demands. They can manifest that internal conformity by "walking" in those ways and by "revering" their covenantal Lord (see Note on 6:13).

NOTE

2 The basic idea of the verb עָנָה (ʿnh [GK 6700], in the phrase לְמַעַן עַנֹּתְךָ (lemaʿan ʿannōteka, "that he might humble you"), is, in the Piel, to apply force on someone so that their state or existence becomes worse. This verb describes the "affliction" Israel experienced at the hands of the Egyptians (26:6). In the Davidic covenant Yahweh promised David that evildoers would no longer be able to "afflict" God's people (2Sa 7:10). With Delilah's help, the Philistines were able to "subdue" Samson (Jdg 16:5–6, 19). This verb can also connote physical or sexual violation, i.e., rape. When the men of God sought to "know" the visiting Levite, they were given access to his concubine. Throughout the night they humiliated or violated her, causing her death (Jdg 19:24; 20:5). The Mosaic law uses this verb to address situations in which rape took place away from the community (Dt 22:24, 29). The OT at times describes God himself as one who can humble people. In the present passage, Yahweh "humbled" the Israelites by having them wander in the wilderness in absolute dependence on his provision of food and drink (8:2, 13, 16).

The thread that runs through all these occurrences is conduct that humiliates or lowers the existence of the object of the action. The humiliation done by people to other people is always demeaning. The humiliation done by God to his people is either part of his judgment on sin or a tool of refinement.

When God tests (נסה, nsh; GK 5814) people, as remembered here in the word לְנַסֹּתְךָ (lenassōteka, "to test you"), he has certain objectives or goals to accomplish: "to measure obedience (Ex 15:25; 16:4; Dt 8:2; Jdg 2:22), instill fear (Ex 20:20), prevent sinning (Ex 20:20), discern what is in the heart (Dt 13:3[4]; 2Ch 32:31), and ensure future prosperity (Dt 8:16). At issue here is Yahweh's desire both to evaluate specific aspects of his people's character as well as to influence and shape them" (Brensinger, *NIDOTTE*, 3:112). Contrast this purpose with the Israelites' attempt to test God (see comments and Note on 6:16).

b. Yahweh's Generous Gift of an Abundant Land Should Occasion Wholehearted Praise (8:7–10)

⁷For the LORD your God is bringing you into a good land — a land with streams and pools of water, with springs flowing in the valleys and hills; ⁸a land with wheat and barley, vines and fig trees, pomegranates, olive oil and honey; ⁹a land where bread will not be

scarce and you will lack nothing; a land where the rocks are iron and you can dig copper out of the hills.

¹⁰When you have eaten and are satisfied, praise the LORD your God for the good land he has given you.

COMMENTARY

7–9 Moses' description of the land stands in stark contrast with what Israel had seen and experienced in the wilderness. It is a good land (1:25, 35; 3:25; 4:21–22; 6:18) that has abundant resources: water (streams, pools, and springs), agricultural produce, and mineral deposits. This land has everything the Israelites will need to enjoy life under God's direction.

10 God's provision of a marvelous land of abundance should occasion nothing less than robust praise! Humans cannot provide God with blessings as he does for his children, but they can bless God by pronouncing to all around them the superlative character of their God.

NOTE

10 Of the thirty-nine times the verb ברך (*brk*, root of וּבֵרַכְתָּ, *ûbēraktā*, "and then bless") appears in Deuteronomy, it only occurs once to describe humans' blessing of God. God blesses human beings by speaking well of them, and by so doing God imparts "blessing" (good things) to them. Humans bless God by speaking well of him, i.e., attributing "blessing" (good qualities) to him. In this fashion, God is "blessed," i.e., praised and declared praiseworthy. As M. Brown (*NIDOTTE*, 1:764) summarizes, "God blesses people by conferring good on them; we bless God by praising the good in him." See Note on 7:13 for a consideration of God's blessing his people.

c. Yahweh's Gracious Provision of Flawless Guidance and Material Prosperity Should Occasion
Wholehearted Obedience (8:11–18)

OVERVIEW

Looking to Israel's near future, Moses warns the people against feeling proud and self-sufficient as a result of the prosperity and abundance they will experience in the Promised Land.

¹¹Be careful that you do not forget the LORD your God, failing to observe his commands, his laws and his decrees that I am giving you this day. ¹²Otherwise, when you eat and are

satisfied, when you build fine houses and settle down, ¹³and when your herds and flocks grow large and your silver and gold increase and all you have is multiplied, ¹⁴then your heart will become proud and you will forget the LORD your God, who brought you out of Egypt, out of the land of slavery. ¹⁵He led you through the vast and dreadful desert, that thirsty and waterless land, with its venomous snakes and scorpions. He brought you water out of hard rock. ¹⁶He gave you manna to eat in the desert, something your fathers had never known, to humble and to test you so that in the end it might go well with you. ¹⁷You may say to yourself, "My power and the strength of my hands have produced this wealth for me." ¹⁸But remember the LORD your God, for it is he who gives you the ability to produce wealth, and so confirms his covenant, which he swore to your forefathers, as it is today.

COMMENTARY

11 In the light of God's abundant provision for his people, Israel's heart should be full of gratitude. So Moses warns them to beware of "forgetting" their covenantal Lord (see Note on 4:10). He delineates the reason why this forgetting is so reprehensible. It manifests itself in failing genuinely to obey God's covenantal demands. The terms "commands," "laws," and "decrees" serve as near synonyms to refer to God's detailed expectations of his servant-nation (cf. chs. 12–26; see Note on 6:1).

12–16 Moses delineates the setting in which this "forgetting" might take place. When the Israelites enjoy the benefits of the conquest of Canaan (= covenantal blessing)—that is, they have plenty to eat and are settled in comfortable residences, their herds and flocks are becoming more numerous, and they have abundant material wealth—the potential exists to become proud and forget their covenantal Lord, the One who has made their abundance possible. In the midst of their experience of overflowing covenantal blessings, they might become arrogant ("lift up their hearts," 17:20; Eze 31:10; Da 11:12; Hos 13:6) and forget God (see Note on 4:10).

So Moses goes on to delineate why such pride and forgetfulness are so abhorrent. The God they are forgetting is the same one who brought them out of Egypt (and their bondage there; 8:14), flawlessly led them through the barren wilderness, made water come out of rock (8:15), and fed them with manna (8:16). And he did all this to test them (see Note on 8:2) for their own benefit (so that it might "go well" for them; see Note on 5:33). All along Yahweh has had their best interests in mind. It is this kind of God whom Israel might forget. A person who "forgets" God and his deeds has closed his or her eyes to the many marvelous things God did in behalf of his people. Such a person conducts a life completely untouched by who God is and what he does.

17–18 Even though the Israelites might attempt to take credit for their abundance and prosperity, Moses challenges them to maintain a proper (and theologically correct) perspective. They must remember (see Note on 4:10) that Yahweh (and not they) is the one who continually gives them the ability to generate their wealth. This provision of God for them is just one more indication of Yahweh's fixed commitment to his covenantal relationship with Israel. As always, he perfectly conducts himself as their God, whether or not they live as though they are his people.

That truth stood when he established his particular covenant at Sinai and remains true at the time of Moses' call to covenantal renewal ("as it is today").

NOTE

12 The verbal pair אכל (*ʾkl*, "to eat"; GK 430) and שׂבע (*śbʿ*, "to satisfy"; GK 8425), in the phrase פֶּן־תֹּאכַל וְשָׂבָעְתָּ (*pen-tōʾkal weśābāʿtā*, "when you eat to your satisfaction"), serves as a verbal hendiadys, in which two verbs joined by a conjunction describe one event. In this instance, the first verb retains its full verbal sense, while the second functions adverbially: "they ate and were filled" = "they ate until they were full" (NET footnote for Ne 9:25). This pair of verbs occurs thirteen times to describe some aspect of covenantal favor and blessing (Dt 6:11; 8:10, 12; 11:15; 14:29; 26:12; 31:20; Ru 2:14; 2Ch 31:10; Pss 22:26 [27]; 78:29; Joel 2:26). To eat and not be satisfied is an evidence of covenantal curse (Lev 26:26; Isa 9:20; Hos 4:10; Mic 6:14). On a coming day when Yahweh judges his covenantal people, he declares that the sword will eat and be satisfied (Jer 46:10)!

d. Israel's Failure to Live in the Light of All Yahweh Has Done For Them Will Occasion Their Destruction (8:19–20)

> ¹⁹If you ever forget the LORD your God and follow other gods and worship and bow down to them, I testify against you today that you will surely be destroyed. ²⁰Like the nations the LORD destroyed before you, so you will be destroyed for not obeying the LORD your God.

COMMENTARY

19–20 Moses gives Israel a stern warning. If Israel chooses to forget the Lord and instead worships pagan gods, Yahweh will destroy them just as he intends to judge the Canaanite nations. If the Israelites want to live like Canaanites, God will treat them like Canaanites. Just as the destruction of the

Canaanites was theologically or morally justified, the same would be true of God's judgment of his own covenantal nation. The "forgetting" of God and worshiping of idols are symptoms or manifestations of the fundamental problem: not obeying, or disregarding, their covenantal Lord.

NOTE

19 Although the verbal root אבד (*ʾbd* [GK 6], in אָבֹד תֹּאבֵדוּן, *ʾābōd tōʾbēdûn*, "you will surely be destroyed") can mean "to become lost" (22:3) or "to go astray" (1Sa 9:3, 20), it more frequently signifies "to perish" (Nu 17:12) or "to destroy" (Dt 11:4; *HALOT*, 2–3). In most of its OT occurrences Yahweh is the direct or indirect agent of destruction. Whoever experiences this devastation is regarded as God's enemy (*TLOT*, 1:14). In Deuteronomy it describes the destruction Yahweh accomplished against Egypt (11:4) and refers to the future extermination of the Canaanites (7:20, 24; 8:20; 9:3). He also commands his covenantal nation to destroy all idolatrous high places (12:2–3). It is interesting to note that the verb describes the potential destruction of Israel (as a consequence of covenantal treachery) more frequently than all the other uses of this verb in Deuteronomy (4:26; 7:10; 8:19–20; 11:17; 28:20, 22, 51, 63; 30:18). The emphatic structure (cognate infinitive absolute and finite verb) stresses the surety of God's destruction of his chosen people if they choose to commit covenantal treachery.

5. Moses Warns Israel against Self-righteousness and Rebellion (9:1–10:11)

OVERVIEW

Moses warns Israel to avoid the feeling of self-righteousness and the practice of rebellion that might arise from their imminent dispossession of the Canaanite nations. In spite of the fact that they (Israel) have repeatedly acted corruptly (instead of righteously), the Lord will enable them to defeat the Canaanite nations for two basic reasons: to judge the wickedness of those peoples and to be faithful to the covenant he made with their ancestors. As Merrill (*Deuteronomy*, 189) points out, the importance of this passage lies primarily "in its emphasis on the gracious initiative of the Lord in bringing his people to the present hour despite their contrariness. No matter their sin in the past, up to and including their unbridled idolatry, Israel was the nation of promise and election, and the Lord would guarantee their ultimate salvation and sovereignty."

a. God's Provision of Victory over the Canaanites Is Totally Unrelated to Israel's "Righteousness" (9:1–6)

OVERVIEW

Moses exhorts the children of Israel to realize that their future conquest of Canaan is not in any way the fruit of their righteousness but is the result of the Lord's holiness (which demands that he judge sin) and faithfulness (to his covenant made with their ancestors).

¹Hear, O Israel. You are now about to cross the Jordan to go in and dispossess nations greater and stronger than you, with large cities that have walls up to the sky. ²The people are strong and tall — Anakites! You know about them and have heard it said: "Who can stand up against the Anakites?" ³But be assured today that the LORD your God is the one who goes across ahead of you like a devouring fire. He will destroy them; he will subdue them before you. And you will drive them out and annihilate them quickly, as the LORD has promised you.

⁴After the LORD your God has driven them out before you, do not say to yourself, "The LORD has brought me here to take possession of this land because of my righteousness." No, it is on account of the wickedness of these nations that the LORD is going to drive them out before you. ⁵It is not because of your righteousness or your integrity that you are going in to take possession of their land; but on account of the wickedness of these nations, the LORD your God will drive them out before you, to accomplish what he swore to your fathers, to Abraham, Isaac and Jacob. ⁶Understand, then, that it is not because of your righteousness that the LORD your God is giving you this good land to possess, for you are a stiff-necked people.

COMMENTARY

1–2 In the face of strong and powerful enemies in Canaan, Moses assures Israel that Yahweh will go before them and fight in their behalf, just as he promised. As in several other passages, this paragraph begins with the exhortation "Hear" — a call that gives this section a sense of urgency and importance (cf. 4:1; 5:1; 6:4). Moses depicts the crossing of the Jordan and the dispossession of Canaan as something in their immediate future.

Their foes, however, present a daunting challenge for Israel. They are greater and stronger and their cities have "walls up to the sky." This last statement is clearly hyperbolic, heightening the sense of the impossibility of what they are about to do (cf. Merrill, *Deuteronomy*, 189). The Anakites (9:2) were both strong and tall (Nu 13:33; Dt 2:10, 21; 9:2). They descended from a certain Anak, whose own ancestor Arba founded the city of Kiriath Arba, i.e., Hebron (Jos 21:11). The question "Who can stand up against the Anakites?" apparently was a proverbial saying concerning the giants who lived in this region. (For other proverbial sayings, such as "Who can withstand his icy blast?" [Ps 147:17], see Job 38:41; Ps 89:49; Pr 30:4.)

3 Since Yahweh has promised to go before Israel in this conquest, the people can rest assured of victory. As Merrill (*Deuteronomy*, 190) points out: "But what is insurmountable to humankind is of no consequence to God, the one who like a 'devouring fire' (cf. 4:24) leads the battle" (cf. 1:30; 3:22). Moses affirms that God himself will destroy and subdue the enemy. In the light of that promise, Israel must do their part: "quickly" drive out the Canaanites and exterminate them (in accordance with the divine promise).

4 Moses carefully points out that Israel's imminent possession of the Promised Land will not be accomplished because of their righteousness but rather because of the wickedness of the Canaanites and because of the oath Yahweh made with their ancestors. Moses makes the point clear to God's chosen nation: All that they are and everything they are able to accomplish is due to the mercy and grace of Yahweh. None of these things is based on their merit or worth. In light of the decision to extend Moses' quotation of the Israelite sentiment to the end of 9:4 (in contrast to the NIV; see Note below), it appears that God's people thought: our victory = our righteousness + their wickedness. In this context, both "righteousness" (*ṣᵉdāqâ*) and "wickedness" (*rišᶜâ*) are legal terms referring to Israel's "innocence" and the nations' "guilt." They correctly understand the moral condition of the Canaanites but horribly overestimate their own situation.

5–6 In no uncertain terms, Moses rejects their argumentation. It is "not because of your righteousness [*ṣᵉdāqâ*; GK 7407] or your intergrity [*yōšer*; GK 3841; lit., 'uprightness of your heart']." What is the point of these two terms that relate to righteousness? The first word, though generally synonymous with the second, signifies the idea of conformity to an objective standard. The second term focuses more on an inner, moral quality. Neither, however, provides grounds for appealing to the Lord's favor. He acts as he does on the basis of his grace and promises (see NET footnote on 9:4). In contrast to the Israelites' idea, Yahweh's equation was: Our victory = God's promise to Abraham, Isaac, and Jacob + their wickedness (Wright, *Deuteronomy*, 131).

Moses does not deny that the Canaanite nations are indeed guilty. However, the guilt of the Canaanites does not justify the conclusion by Israel that they themselves are totally innocent. As McConville, 182, points out, "it is not for legal reasons that Yahweh's decision has been made, but only because of his ancient oath to Abraham, Isaac, and Jacob." The fact of the matter is that God's covenantal nation was characterized by rebellion, i.e., they were a "stiff-necked people" (9:6).

NOTES

3 The presence of a redundant subjectival pronoun (הוּא, *hûʾ*) in this verse stresses the actor rather than the action, thus emphasizing that Yahweh and only Yahweh will accomplish Israel's victory in the land of Canaan. The meaning "quickly" (מַהֵר, *mahēr*) is somewhat unclear when compared with 7:22, where Moses affirms that the Israelites will not be able to conquer the Canaanites "all at once." Weinfeld (*Deuteronomy 1–11*, 406) suggests that this term means "easily" in 9:3 rather than "quickly" (cf. Ecc 4:12, "a cord of three strands is not quickly broken"). It --might be better to retain the normal meaning and regard it as a word of encouragement to give the Israelites an assurance of success (Wright, *Deuteronomy*, 142). The same adverb in 7:4 pronounces certainty and completeness of Yahweh's judgment on Israelites who practice idolatry.

4 Where does Moses' quotation of Israel's sentiment end? The NIV (and other translations) end the quotation after "because of my righteousness." They insert "No" at that point (without basis in Hebrew) in an attempt to highlight the contrastive response of Moses. What Israel declares is the incorrect notion that God brought Israel into the land of promise because of their righteousness. It would be better to regard the entire verse as part of the incorrect perception of the Israelites. This approach also avoids unnecessary redundancy between the end of v.4 and v.5: "Do not think to yourself after the LORD your God has run them out before you, 'Because of my own righteousness the LORD has enabled me to possess this land, and because of the wickedness of these nations he is dispossessing them from before *me*.'"

There is one problem with this understanding of v.4. Various scholars who accept this suggestion wrestle with a textual "problem" at the end of the verse. The Hebrew text has the second person pronoun at the end of the verse, but some translations have changed it to read "me," concluding that the second masculine singular suffix on the preposition "before" was perhaps originally the conjunction/particle כִּי (*kî*), which would have then introduced the next verse. This textual emendation may be unnecessary. As McConville, 182, suggests, the "you" at the end of 9:4 refers to Moses as the leader of God's people. This understanding of v.4 avoids the abruptness of the NIV's reading and its repetition with part of 9:5. Moreover, it allows v.5 to provide a response to both points of Israel's thinking. The nation is correct in one facet but horribly wrong about the other facet.

6 The construction עַם־קְשֵׁה־עֹרֶף (*ʿam-qĕšēh-ʿōrep*, "stiff-necked people"—three nouns in construct) occurs six times in the OT (Ex 32:9; 33:3, 5; 34:9; Dt 9:6, 13; cf. 31:27). The verbal form (קָשָׁה, *qšh*; GK 7996) occurs in numerous passages to describe the obstinacy of someone's heart. The nominal phrase here depicts an animal that is trained to pull or carry a load but is not submissive to the reign or yoke. It refuses to give in to its master. According to Weinfeld (*Deuteronomy 1–11*, 407), "Stiff-necked is the opposite of 'turn the ear (*hth ʾzn*)' by bending the neck in order to listen (cf. Jer 17:23)." Israel was characterized by a refusal to listen to their covenantal Lord.

b. Israel's Rebellion and Yahweh's Forgiveness (9:7–10:11)

OVERVIEW

Instead of "going after" the Canaanites and pointing out various examples of their abhorrent wickedness, the Lord focuses on the rebellion that has characterized the Israelites all too frequently. This entire section seeks to dispatch any delusions Israel might have about their own righteousness or worth. Although it was true that the Canaanites were far more wicked than the Israelites in many ways, for Moses to have dwelt on the wickedness of the Canaanites could have fed the fire of Israel's pride. Instead, Moses seeks to banish any notion of a superiority complex from the Israelites' minds. They are deserving of divine judgment, and only God's grace has spared them.

i. Israel's brush with extinction because of rebellion (9:7–24)

OVERVIEW

Verses 7 and 24 (and possibly 9:7–8 and 9:22–24) form an "inclusio" for this passage, which emphasizes Israel's perpetual rebellion against Yah- weh. Both verses refer to Israel's rebellion and the perpetual nature of that treachery. Also, notice that midway through 9:7, after the expression "from the day that you left Egypt," the style changes from singular to plural address, a style that continues until Moses finishes describing Israel's rebellion against Yahweh in 9:24. A transition takes place from exhortation (9:1–6) to history (9:7–24). In 9:8–21 Moses reviews Israel's rebellion at Horeb, when they erected the golden calf. He goes on to cite instances of Israelite rebellion at four other locations (9:22–23).

A reading of Exodus 32 and followed by Deuteronomy 9:8–10:11, with careful comparison of each passage's chronological delineation of events, reveals that the passage in Deuteronomy does not always closely track with the presentation of this account in Exodus (when Moses went up and down the mountain, when he fasted and prayed, and when

God made various responses). Various critical scholars account for these chronological divergences by saying that the editor of the book confused some of his sources and/or by referring to this section's complex redactional history.

These attempts at "solving" any chronological variations are unnecessary and incorrect. The passage in Deuteronomy represents a recollection of the events recorded in Exodus 32 with a view toward highlighting the significant theological points of that account. It is not a chronologically driven account but a theologically driven one. In Deuteronomy 9, the focus is on Israel's sin and the nearly calamitous results of this covenantal breach, not on Yahweh's forgiveness and the renewal of the ruptured covenant (Merrill, *Deuteronomy*, 192).

---

[7]Remember this and never forget how you provoked the LORD your God to anger in the desert. From the day you left Egypt until you arrived here, you have been rebellious against the LORD. [8]At Horeb you aroused the LORD's wrath so that he was angry enough to destroy you. [9]When I went up on the mountain to receive the tablets of stone, the tablets of the covenant that the LORD had made with you, I stayed on the mountain forty days and forty nights; I ate no bread and drank no water. [10]The LORD gave me two stone tablets inscribed by the finger of God. On them were all the commandments the LORD proclaimed to you on the mountain out of the fire, on the day of the assembly.

[11]At the end of the forty days and forty nights, the LORD gave me the two stone tablets, the tablets of the covenant. [12]Then the LORD told me, "Go down from here at once, because your people whom you brought out of Egypt have become corrupt. They have turned away quickly from what I commanded them and have made a cast idol for themselves."

[13]And the LORD said to me, "I have seen this people, and they are a stiff-necked people indeed! [14]Let me alone, so that I may destroy them and blot out their name from under heaven. And I will make you into a nation stronger and more numerous than they."

[15]So I turned and went down from the mountain while it was ablaze with fire. And the two tablets of the covenant were in my hands. [16]When I looked, I saw that you had sinned against the LORD your God; you had made for yourselves an idol cast in the shape of a calf. You had turned aside quickly from the way that the LORD had commanded you. [17]So I took the two tablets and threw them out of my hands, breaking them to pieces before your eyes.

¹⁸Then once again I fell prostrate before the LORD for forty days and forty nights; I ate no bread and drank no water, because of all the sin you had committed, doing what was evil in the LORD's sight and so provoking him to anger. ¹⁹I feared the anger and wrath of the LORD, for he was angry enough with you to destroy you. But again the LORD listened to me. ²⁰And the LORD was angry enough with Aaron to destroy him, but at that time I prayed for Aaron too. ²¹Also I took that sinful thing of yours, the calf you had made, and burned it in the fire. Then I crushed it and ground it to powder as fine as dust and threw the dust into a stream that flowed down the mountain.

²²You also made the LORD angry at Taberah, at Massah and at Kibroth Hattaavah.

²³And when the LORD sent you out from Kadesh Barnea, he said, "Go up and take possession of the land I have given you." But you rebelled against the command of the LORD your God. You did not trust him or obey him. ²⁴You have been rebellious against the LORD ever since I have known you.

COMMENTARY

7 Moses labors to impress firmly on the children of Israel their perpetual tendency toward rebellion. By juxtaposing the commands "remember … and never forget" (see Note on 4:10), Moses makes a fervent plea that Israel will live in the light of what they have seen and know to be true. As Craigie, 194, points out: "If the people were ever foolish enough to claim that the gift of the land was a result of their righteousness, then they would be suffering from a severe case of religious amnesia. They are called, therefore, to remember the long history of their stubbornness and provocation of God, which had extended from the time of the Exodus from Egypt up till the present moment on the plains of Moab (v.7b)." Sadly, Israel's future propensity to choose rebellion over obedience was based on their history, something Moses refers to repeatedly (4:9–14; 6:10–15; 8:1–4, 11–16; cf. Ps 106:32–33; Merrill, *Deuteronomy*, 192).

8–14 Moses reminds the Israelites that their rebellion occurred at the same time that Moses was receiving the law from Yahweh himself. Notice how Israel's rebellion at Horeb is doubly significant. First,

while the Israelites were waiting for Moses to come down from Mount Horeb/Sinai with the tablets containing the essence of their covenantal relationship with Yahweh, they rebelled against their God! No sooner had the covenant between Yahweh and Israel been made than the Israelites violated its most basic demand: worship Yahweh alone and worship no images (even of Yahweh). As Wright (*Deuteronomy*, 135) observes: "The covenant had not been based on, and certainly could not be sustained by, Israel's own righteousness, so any grounds for future boasting were cut off from under them." Second, Yahweh was angry enough to destroy the Israelites, but he chose not to. Yahweh told Moses that his people had already sinned against the Lord by forming an idol.

Moses went up on Mount Horeb to receive the stone tablets that epitomized the covenantal relationship between Yahweh and Israel (probably the Ten Commandments). During his entire stay on Horeb (forty days and nights), Moses did not eat or drink (9:9; cf. 8:3; Mt 4:2). God himself inscribed the text onto these stones. Nowhere else in Scripture is God said to have written anything. As Merrill (*Deuteronomy*, 193) notes, "The personal attention to the Ten Commandments underscores their fundamental importance to the entire covenant revelation."

When Yahweh commanded Moses to descend the mountain to confront the Israelites for their treachery, he referred to the Israelites as "your people whom you brought out of Egypt" (9:12–13). He does not refer to them as "my people"! In fact, Yahweh threatened utterly to destroy the Israelites and to start over with Moses alone (9:12–14). In 7:23–24 he had promised to destroy (*šmd*) the Canaanites and wipe out (*ʾbd*) their names (cf. 9:3; 12:3). In the wake of the rebellion involving the golden calf, he threatened to destroy (*šmd*) Israel and blot out (*mḥh*) their name as well (9:14). By affirming this potential of extermination and blotting out of their name, God suggested an abandonment of the Abrahamic and Mosaic covenants, i.e., the termination of his relationship with his chosen people (an aspect of covenantal curse; 29:19–20 [18–19]).

15–19 After seeing their wicked conduct, Moses broke the tablets of the covenant, thus symbolizing the nullification of the covenant. Then he prayed for Yahweh to spare this undeserving people. Unlike in the Exodus account, where Moses' intercession in behalf of the children of Israel immediately followed this sober pronouncement of Yahweh (and perhaps for dramatic effect), here Moses delineates his reaction to Israel's treachery before he refers to his pleading for the sake of God's chosen nation.

As soon as Moses witnessed the Israelite conduct, he declared that they had "sinned" and "turned aside" from God's way by constructing this golden calf. The making of this image could have been a lapse into idolatry, an attempt to make a physical representation of Yahweh, or an attempt to make

an object symbolizing the footstool of God (cf. Craigie, 195). In any case, it represented a violation of the first or second commandment (cf. 5:7–10). As a symbol or emblem of the broken covenant, Moses intentionally threw the two stone tablets to the ground, thus causing them to shatter (9:17). Craigie (195) writes:

> Moses' act was not simply a spontaneous reaction of anger, in which he shattered the tablets because they just happened to be in his hands; rather, the evil act of the Israelites had violated the covenant God had just granted to them. Thus Moses' act of smashing the covenantal tablets symbolized in a very forceful way the potential meaning of the Israelites' act in constructing the calf. At the very time that God had given the people the tablets of the covenant through Moses, the people broke the conditions of the covenant and potentially rendered it null and void.

Weinfeld (*Deuteronomy 1–11*, 410) observes that breaking a tablet in ancient Near Eastern legal and covenantal traditions signified invalidating a document.

After breaking the two stone tablets, Moses, burdened by God's stated intention to exterminate the Israelites, fasted for forty days and nights (9:18–19). He was terrified by Yahweh's "anger and wrath" (or "intense anger," a nominal hendiadys that emphasizes the intensity of Yahweh's anger).

20–21 Moses prayed for Aaron's deliverance (since Aaron made the calf) and completely destroyed the evidence of Israel's treacherous behavior. The statement, "and I took that sinful thing of yours," literally reads, "and I took your sin." In this metonymy of effect for cause, the effect (sin) stands for the cause (the molten image). What Moses did with the golden calf (grinding it to fine dust) served as an object lesson of what God's people were to do with all pagan images (cf. 7:25).

22–24 Moses also cites instances of Israelite rebellion at four other sites—Taberah (Nu 11:1–3; the second instance), Massah (Ex 17:1–7; the first instance), Kibroth Hattaavah (Nu 11:31–33; the third instance), and Kadesh Barnea (Nu 13–14; Dt 1:19–46; the fourth instance)—and highlights Israel's penchant to rebel against Yahweh. Although these place names are slighly out of chronological order, for rhetorical effect Moses may have listed the sites from the least serious breach of loyalty to the most severe one (Kalland, 82).

To emphasize the depth of Israel's treachery, Moses piles up terms that refer to Israel's disobedi-ent conduct: provoke (*qṣp*; 9:22), rebel (*mrh*; 9:23), did not believe (*ʾmn*; 9:23), did not obey (*šmʿ*; 9:23), and rebel (*mrh*; 9:24). What is obvious at this point in the narrative? Yahweh's gift of the land could never be regarded as a reward for Israel's righteousness! As it began, this pericope (9:7–24) ends with this sad note concerning Israel's constant rebellion. From the first day Moses knew the children of Israel, he had witnessed their perpetual rebellion against Yahweh, their covenantal Lord. As Craigie, 197, points out: "But for God's grace in the past, they would not even be standing in the plains of Moab, renewing their covenant with God."

NOTES

7 The expression עַד ... לְמִן־הַיּוֹם (*lᵉmin-hayyôm ... ʿad*, "since the day ... until") occurs seven times in the OT (Ex 9:18; Dt 9:7; Jdg 19:30; 2Sa 7:6; 19:24 [25]; Jer 7:25; 32:31) to provide temporal parameters for a certain event or practice (*HALOT*, 599, #10b).

8 In this verse the preposition לְ (*lᵉ*), in לְהַשְׁמִיד אֶתְכֶם ... וַיִּתְאַנַּף (*wayyiṯʾannap ... lᵉhašmîd ʾeṯkem*, "angry ... enough to destroy you"), indicates the degree of Yahweh's anger (R. Williams, *Hebrew Syntax: An Outline* [2nd ed.; Toronto: Univ. of Toronto Press, 1992], 50, §275; cf. Dt 9:20; 2Sa 13:2).

9 The number אַרְבָּעִים (*ʾarbāʿîm*, "forty") occurs frequently in the OT, commonly in the expressions "forty days and forty nights" and "forty years." The former expresssion occurs ten times in the OT: with regard to the Noahic flood (twice; Ge 7:4, 12); concerning Moses' time on the top of Mount Sinai (seven times; Ex 24:18; 34:28; Dt 9:9, 11, 18, 25; 10:10); and regarding Elijah's trip from the area around Mount Carmel to Horeb (once; 1Ki 19:8). The expression "forty days" occurs eight times: for Noah's flood (twice; Ge 7:17; 8:6); to describe Egyptian embalming practices (once; Ge 50:3); for the duration of the Israelite spies' mission (twice; Nu 13:25; 14:34); for the number of days Goliath challenged the Israelite army (once; 1Sa 17:16); for the duration of Ezekiel's lying on his right side (once; Eze 4:6); and as part of Jonah's message of judgment to Nineveh (once; Jnh 3:4).

"Forty years" occurs thirty-two times to describe a certain time span: age at the time of an important event (four times; Ge 25:20; 26:34; Jos 14:7; 2Sa 2:10); the duration of the wilderness wanderings (thirteen times; Ex 16:35; Nu 14:33–34; 32:13; Dt 2:7; 8:2, 4; 29:4; Jos 5:6; Am 2:10; 5:25; Ps 95:10; Ne 9:21); the duration of judgeship or rest of land (four times; Jdg 3:11; 5:31; 8:28; 1Sa 4:18); the time of Philistine oppression (one time; Jdg 13:1); the reign of a king (seven times; 2Sa 5:4; 1Ki 2:11 = 1Ch 29:27; 1Ki 11:42 = 2Ch 9:30; 2Ki 12:1 = 2Ch 24:1); a time of judgment and devastation on Gentile nations (three times; Eze 29:11–13).

How are we to regard the number "forty" in the OT? Is it a clear historical reference or is it symbolic? According to R. K. Harrison (*Numbers* [WEC; Chicago; Moody Press, 1990], 217 [commenting on Nu 14:33–34]):

> The forty-year sentence was also an appropriate symbol of rejection. The number is commonly held to characterize a generation and is thus a round number (cf. Ps 95:10).
>
> This symbolism should not necessarily be regarded as a reliable guide, however. If a generation was reckoned from a person's birth to that of his firstborn, it need only have involved a period of some twenty years. But if it was calculated from a person's birth to his death, it could involve sixty years or even more. The number forty can also be understood literally in some instances, as R. L. Harris has pointed out in connection with the occurrence of the forty-year figure mentioned on the Moabite Stone.

B. Birch (*ISBE*, 3:558) explains the use of "forty" as a rounded number:

> The most frequently used round number in the Bible is forty ... which has the sense of a relatively long period of time and more specifically is the traditional number of years in a generation.... A sense of completeness or maturity is attached to the number (perhaps because it is the product of four times ten). A man was considered to reach full adulthood at forty (Jos 14:7; 2Sa 2:10; Ac 7:23).... The abundant occurrences of the number forty indicate that it was used as a rounded rather than an exact figure.

In most contexts there is no need to conclude that the number "forty" meant anything other than "forty." Although "forty" may have served as a rounded number in certain instances, in those cases it was a historically reliable rounded number. The number of days, years, or months it represented is best regarded as "forty." It is not a symbolic number that does not convey a clear idea of time.

10 The שְׁנֵי לוּחֹת הָאֲבָנִים אֶת (*ʾet-šᵉnê lûḥōt hāˀᵃbānîm*), "two stone tablets," probably represented two *copies* of the Ten Commandments rather than certain commandments on one tablet and the rest on the other tablet (Craigie, 134; cf. Kline, *Treaty of the Great King*, 13–26; idem, *The Structure of Biblical Authority*, 113–30). In ancient Near Eastern suzerain/vassal treaties, each partner to the treaty received a copy of the agreement. In the context of the Mosaic covenant, both parties had a copy of this information, and they were to be stored in a safe place, i.e., the ark of the covenant.

According to the NET's footnote for the expression בְּאֶצְבַּע אֱלֹהִים (*bᵉˀeṣbaʿ ˀᵉlōhîm*, "by the [very] finger of God"): "This is a double figure of speech (1) in which God is ascribed human features (anthropomorphism) and (2) in which a part stands for the whole (synecdoche). That is, God, as Spirit, has no literal finger nor, if he had, would he write with his finger. Rather, the sense is that God himself—not Moses in any way—was responsible for the composition of the Ten Commandments (cf. Exod 31:18; 32:16; 34:1)."

12 The noun מַסֵּכָה (*massēkâ*, "cast image") occurs twenty-eight times in the OT; seventeen times it occurs alone as a generic reference to a "cast image" and seven times it is preceded by a term for "image." In four passages it is preceded by the term "calf" (עֵגֶל, *ʿēgel*; Ex 32:4, 8; Dt 9:16; Ps 106:19). In the present passage, the term occurs by itself in v.12 and with "calf" in v.16. The NET suggests that the absence of the term "calf" in v.12 might indicate Moses' contempt for it. However, its inclusion in v.16 makes that case unlikely. The term by itself and its coupling with "calf" are interchangeable. The juxtaposition of מַסֵּכָה (*massēkâ*) and עֵגֶל (*ʿēgel*) provides a clear allusion to the incident with the golden calf recorded in Exodus 32.

23 The word translated "command" in פִּי יְהוָה (*pî yhwh*, "the command of Yahweh") is literally the word for "mouth" (פֶּה, *pî*). In this instance, mouth = command as a metonymy of cause for effect. This expression occurs elsewhere in the OT. In Deuteronomy (1:26, 43; 9:23) it refers to Israel's rebellion at Kadesh Barnea. In 1 Samuel 12:14–15 it occurs twice with reference to Yahweh's warning Israel and her king not to rebel against him. It occurs twice with reference to a prophet who does not carry out all Yahweh's instructions (1Ki 13:21, 26).

ii. Yahweh forgives Israel and provides a second revelation of the Ten Commandments (9:25–10:11)

OVERVIEW

In the face of national extinction, Moses interceded in behalf of Israel, and the Lord responded with clemency and graciously provided a second revelation of the Ten Commandments.

²⁵I lay prostrate before the LORD those forty days and forty nights because the LORD had said he would destroy you. ²⁶I prayed to the LORD and said, "O Sovereign LORD, do not destroy your people, your own inheritance that you redeemed by your great power and brought out of Egypt with a mighty hand. ²⁷Remember your servants Abraham, Isaac and Jacob. Overlook the stubbornness of this people, their wickedness and their sin. ²⁸Otherwise, the country from which you brought us will say, 'Because the LORD was not able to take them into the land he had promised them, and because he hated them, he brought them out to put them to death in the desert.' ²⁹But they are your people, your inheritance that you brought out by your great power and your outstretched arm."

¹⁰:¹At that time the LORD said to me, "Chisel out two stone tablets like the first ones and come up to me on the mountain. Also make a wooden chest. ²I will write on the tablets the words that were on the first tablets, which you broke. Then you are to put them in the chest."

³So I made the ark out of acacia wood and chiseled out two stone tablets like the first ones, and I went up on the mountain with the two tablets in my hands. ⁴The LORD wrote on these tablets what he had written before, the Ten Commandments he had proclaimed to you on the mountain, out of the fire, on the day of the assembly. And the LORD gave them to me. ⁵Then I came back down the mountain and put the tablets in the ark I had made, as the LORD commanded me, and they are there now.

⁶(The Israelites traveled from the wells of the Jaakanites to Moserah. There Aaron died and was buried, and Eleazar his son succeeded him as priest. ⁷From there they traveled to Gudgodah and on to Jotbathah, a land with streams of water. ⁸At that time the LORD set apart the tribe of Levi to carry the ark of the covenant of the LORD, to stand before the LORD

to minister and to pronounce blessings in his name, as they still do today. ⁹That is why the Levites have no share or inheritance among their brothers; the LORD is their inheritance, as the LORD your God told them.)

¹⁰Now I had stayed on the mountain forty days and nights, as I did the first time, and the LORD listened to me at this time also. It was not his will to destroy you. ¹¹"Go," the LORD said to me, "and lead the people on their way, so that they may enter and possess the land that I swore to their fathers to give them."

COMMENTARY

25–29 In the wake of God's threatened judgment, Moses begged the Lord to spare Israel from their well-deserved judgment for the sake of his prestige before the nations of the world. On his second trip up Mount Horeb, Moses once again interceded in Israel's behalf for forty days and forty nights (9:25). He fell down to the ground to pray for Israel's sparing. (The verb "to fall" occurs twice, at the beginning and end of the clause, probably to emphasize Moses' humility before Yahweh.) His request that Israel be spared was based on Yahweh's prior promise to the patriarchs (9:27) as well as his prestige before the nations of the world (9:28–29). The divine title "O Sovereign LORD" is only used to introduce prayers and "may indicate the relationship between Moses and God on which the petition was based, namely the recognition of God's Lordship and sovereign power" (Craigie, 197; cf. 3:24).

When Moses prayed "do not destroy" (9:26), he was not demanding something of God but was pleading in Israel's behalf. The two nouns in "your people and your inheritance" are probably a hendiadys for "your very own people." Moses used this emphatic construction to counter Yahweh's disassociation of himself from Israel (9:12). They were the people with whom he had established his enduring covenant. Notice the relational and theological basis of Moses' entreaty for Israel's continued existence (vv.26b–29): "your own [very] inheritance" (9:26), "that you redeemed" (9:26), "that you ... brought out of Egypt" (9:26), "remember" the ancestors (9:27), consider what the nations will say and think (9:28), "your people, your inheritance" (9:29), "that you brought out" (9:29). Moses piles up these terms to emphasize the covenantal foundation of this unique relationship Israel had with Yahweh. From a different perspective, Moses does not underestimate the depth of Israel's sin ("stubbornness," "wickedness," "sin"; 9:27).

In summary, Moses raises three important issues in his response to Yahweh. (1) Yahweh had entered into a covenantal relationship with this people (through the Mosaic covenant). (2) The status of Israel before Yahweh was founded on Yahweh's oath to their ancestors (in the Abrahamic covenant). (3) Finally, Yahweh's glory before the nations was at stake. According to Craigie, 198:

> Thus the recollection of the prayer in Moses' address served to bring a sobering influence on his audience; in the past, there had been moments when the whole future of the people of Israel had been in the balance. In the present, therefore, the people were to remember the past mercies of God and to commit themselves wholeheartedly in allegiance to their Lord.

10:1-5 At the command of Yahweh, Moses hewed out two stone tablets, on which Yahweh would again write the Ten Commandments, and he deposited them in the prescribed wooden chest, where they were safely stored for centuries. As Wright (*Deuteronomy*, 143) points out:

> The point of Deut. 10:1-5 is not to give a detailed physical description of the ark or to explain every aspect of its religious significance, but rather, in the context of ch. 9, to see its construction for the purpose of storing the *new* tablets of the Law as tangible proof of the forgiveness of the people and the renewal of the covenant by God's grace.

Unlike with the first set of tablets, which apparently were provided by God himself, Yahweh instructed Moses himself to hew these tablets out from rock. After God wrote his stipulations on these tablets, Moses was to place them in a sacred place, the ark of the covenant. In 10:3 and 5 Moses said he made the ark, but it was actually Bezalel who made it (Ex 37:1-9). Moses, however, commanded that the work be done and was ultimately responsible for its completion. This new set of tablets was more than simply a replacement copy of what was broken. As Craigie, 200, points out: "The shattering of the first tablets symbolized the breaking of the covenant relationship because of Israel's sin in making the calf. The second writing of the Law and the gift of the tablets is indicative of the graciousness of God and the response of God to the intercession of Moses."

6-7 Moses reviews Israel's travels after their time at Kadesh Barnea and relates Aaron's death near Mount Hor and the succession of Eleazar (Aaron's son) to the high priesthood. Although there is a slight difference between this listing of sites and that found in Numbers 33:30-33, that difference need not be attributed to variant traditions of Israel's itinerary during the wilderness wanderings. Instead, since Israel probably passed through this region repeatedly during their almost four decades of wanderings, they likely visited these sites in different sequences. Most of these sites cannot be identified with any certainty. The death of Aaron (10:6) took place almost forty years after the incident with the golden calf (Nu 33:37-39); reference to his death here might signify that although he was spared from death at the time of the incident involving the golden calf, he did not altogether escape punishment for his role in Israel's idolatry (Tigay, *Deuteronomy*, 105).

8-9 Moses describes how Aaron's tribe, the Levites, had been set apart to perform priestly duties: carrying the ark of the covenant, ministering in the sanctuary, and pronouncing God's blessings on the people. Although vv. 6-9 may appear somewhat parenthetical, these verses serve at least three important contextual purposes (drawn from Wright, *Deuteronomy*, 141). (1) The note about Israel's itinerary implicitly demonstrates that Moses' intercession for Israel was successful. (2) The reference to Aaron's death and Eleazar's succession to the high priesthood indicates that Moses' intercession for Aaron was also successful. Not only did Aaron not die at that time, but also his family remained heirs of the priesthood. (3) Finally, by summarizing the duties of the Levites, Moses makes clear that all God's gifts mediated through the Levites remain intact. The Levites, as members of the priestly tribe, lacked a tribal allotment like those of the other tribes. Instead, they had the use of forty-eight towns set apart for them by God (Nu 35:1-8; Jos 21:1-42). According to Moses, Yahweh himself is the inheritance of the Levites (10:9). In other words, the Levites would live "by participating in that which was given directly to the Lord. Though they would not have the physical security derived from their own personal property, they had the high honor of directly serving the Lord on behalf of their fellow Israelites" (Craigie, 201).

10–11 The Lord listened to Moses during his second visit to the top of Mount Horeb and chose not to destroy the Israelites. Verse 10 affirms that "it was not his will to destroy you"; that is, "Yahweh did not want to exterminate you." What is Yahweh unwilling to do? This verb (*'bh*) appears with Yahweh as the subject in six passages. The normal construction is the negative adverb "not" (*lō'*) + finite verb + Yahweh + infinitive. Three passages affirm that Yahweh refuses to destroy the covenantal nation in spite of their (or their leaders') treachery (Dt 10:10; 2Ki 8:19 = 2Ch 21:7). Twice the text states that Yahweh is unwilling to pardon or forgive the Israelite guilty of covenantal treachery (Dt 29:20 [19]; 2Ki 24:4). Once Yahweh refuses to listen to Balaam, the false prophet (Dt 23:6).

Something that God is unwilling to do is something he *chooses* not to do.

In the present context, Moses did not convince Yahweh to spare the Israelites against his will. God's threat of extermination and his decision to spare his covenantal people were part of his determined will. In v.11 Yahweh exhorts Moses to return to the business of leading his chosen nation toward the land of promise. As Wright (*Deuteronomy*, 141) points out:

> The whole section ends, as it began in 9:1, with the onward movement of the people into the land of promise. In the light of all that has come between the beginning and the end of this section, this should be a chastened people about to move into the land; a people with every confidence in their God, but with no illusions about themselves.

NOTES

26 The pointing of the "tetragrammaton" here יְהֹוִה (*yhwh*, "GOD") is not the customary one (יְהוָה, *yhwh*), for this divine title is preceded by the word to which the normal pattern points the reader's attention (אֲדֹנָי, *'ădōnāy*). The translation that follows the Jewish tradition would be "LORD God" (cf. NASB, NET, NKJV, NRSV). A few translations have "O Sovereign LORD" (NIV, NLT). Since the pointing of the tetragrammaton here is a Jewish convention and the Hebrew text does have two titles that carry the idea of "lord," the translation "Sovereign LORD" is preferable.

The verb פָּדָה (*pdh*, "to redeem" [GK 7009], in אֲשֶׁר פָּדִיתָ, *'ăšer pādîtā*, "that you redeemed") occurs fifty-three times in the OT and has a narrow meaning in cultic/sacrificial contexts and a broader significance in the rest of the OT. Compared to a near synonym (גָּאַל, *g'l*), the verb פָּדָה (*pdh*) gives more emphasis to the *act* of redeeming than to the object of the redeeming. According to the Mosaic law, all firstborn (animals and people) belong exclusively to Yahweh (Ex 13:1–2; 34:19). The Lord permitted Israel to redeem firstborn donkeys and sons (by paying a certain amount or offering an animal sacrifice; Ex 13:13; 34:20; Nu 18:15–16). The tribe of Levi was set aside for exclusive service of Yahweh. All firstborn of sheep, cows, and goats were unredeemable and dedicated for sacrifice to Yahweh.

More broadly, this verb (פָּדָה, *pdh*) signifies the redemption or deliverance of either an individual or a nation. God's redemption of Israel from bondage in Egypt serves as a classic example of divine redemption (Ex 4:22; Dt 15:15; 21:8; 24:18) and something on which various biblical writers looked back with fondness (2Sa 7:23; Pss 78:42; 111:9; Mic 6:4). God's future deliverance of Israel is patterned after that historical deliverance (Isa 35:10; 51:11). The verb פָּדָה (*pdh*) also describes the redemption or deliverance of an individual. An Israelite could redeem a slave girl for the purpose of marriage (Lev 19:20). The psalmists often speak of God's deliverance of a person from some threatening danger (Pss 26:11; 31:5 [6]; 34:22 [23]; 44:26 [27]; 71:23) or human oppression (Pss 55:18 [19]; 69:18 [19]).

The prepositional phrase בְּגָדְלְךָ (*beǧodlekā*, "by your great power/greatness") either highlights an instrumental notion, "by your great power/greatness" (NIV, NASB), or carries an adverbial nuance, "that you have powerfully redeemed" (NET). Four out of the five times that the noun גֹּדֶל (*gōdel*) occurs, it does so with a pronominal suffix (Dt 9:26; Eze 31:2, 7, 18) and maintains its nominal translation ("greatness"), thus suggesting that the instrumental notion fits best here.

27 To "remember" (זְכֹר, *zekōr*; see Note on 4:10) the patriarchs means remembering the oath made to them (namely, to make their descendants numerous and to give them the Promised Land; Ge 12:1–3; Ex 32:13).

10:2 Regarding וְשַׂמְתָּם בָּאָרוֹן (*weśamtām bāʾārôn*, "you will place them in the ark"), Tigay (*Deuteronomy*, 104, 362, n. 37) points out:

> Documents were sometimes stored in chests or other types of containers in the ancient world, protecting them from damage or loss. In the case of a contractual document this would help protect the evidence of the agreement. Placing a document in a sanctuary enhanced its safety and brought the agreement under the sponsorship of the deity. For this reason the texts of treaties were deposited in temples, sometimes 'at the feet' of a deity [cf. Kline, *Treaty of the Great King*, 19–20; COS 2:106; Pritchard, *ANET*, 205].

3 A question arises concerning the statement וָאַעַשׂ אֲרוֹן (*wāʾaʿaś ʾarôn*, "I made the ark"). In the Exodus account (37:1–9), the ark of the covenant was not constructed until after Moses descended Mount Sinai for the second time. The present context suggests that the ark was completed before he ascended the mountain for the second time and that Moses deposited the tablets in the ark immediately after arriving at the bottom. Is Driver, 118, correct when he says that these differences cannot be reconciled? Some scholars (and several rabbinic sources [Tigay, *Deuteronomy*, 362, n. 40]) have suggested that Moses built a temporary ark or box (referred to here) before the permanent one was made (Ex 25:10–22; 40:20).

A number of evangelical commentators suggest that one of the passages is out of chronological order. The narrative in Exodus demonstrates that the command to make the ark was given before the sin involving the golden calf (Ex 25:10–22) and that the ark was made as part of the building of the tabernacle, while the tablets were not placed in the ark until the dedication of the tabernacle (40:20). Merrill (*Deuteronomy*, 198; cf. Keil, 340) suggests that the incident with the golden calf occurred sometime before the tabernacle and all of its related furnishings were completed. After the rebellion involving the golden calf, the ark was constructed. The juxtaposition of the rebellion and Moses' reascent of Mount Sinai helps to connect clearly Moses' return to Mount Sinai with the events that occasioned the need for that return. Regardless, one need not expect exact chronological agreement of the narratives in Exodus and Deuteronomy.

עֲצֵי שִׁטִּים (*ʿaṣê šiṭṭîm*, "shittim wood") is wood from the acacia, a flat-topped tree that is the most common tree in the Sinai region. It thrives in the wadis of the Sinai and the Arabah (F. Hepper, *Baker Encyclopedia of Bible Plants* [Grand Rapids: Baker, 1992], 56–57, 63–64; Jacob and Jacob, *ABD*, 2:804).

5, 10 Because of the change from first person in 10:5 and 10 to third person in 10:6–9, various scholars contend that this section of verses (10:6–9) was added by a later editor (e.g., Tigay, *Deuteronomy*, 105).

Others have suggested that Deuteronomy contains three "voices":Yahweh, Moses, and a narrator (Robert Polzin, *Moses and the Deuteronomist: A Literary Study of the Deuteronomistic History* [New York: Seabury, 1980], 25–36; R. Dillard and T. Longman III, *An Introduction to the Old Testament* [Grand Rapids: Zondervan, 1994], 100; D. I. Block, "Recovering The Voice of Moses: The Genesis of Deuteronomy," *JETS* 44 [2001]: 392). They have suggested that this passage (along with about fifty-two other verses) comes from the hand of the narrator. Evangelical proponents of this alternative view the narrative's work as part of the inspired text of Scripture. However, as Craigie (200, n. 6) and others (G. Manley, *The Book of the Law: Studies in the Date of Deuteronomy* [London: Tyndale, 1957], 157; H. Segal, *The Pentateuch: Its Composition and Its Authorship and Other Biblical Studies* [Jerusalem: Magnes, 1967], 95) point out, Moses may have simply excerpted it from a travel itinerary similar to that found in Numbers 33.

6. Yahweh Deserves and Demands Israel's Undivided Loyalty (10:12–11:32)

OVERVIEW

The Lord required one thing of Israel: wholehearted commitment to him and obedience to his covenantal demands because of his character and activity in their behalf and in order that they might be able to possess the land he promised them. In 10:12–11:25 he describes that loyalty and then concludes the general stipulation section by delineating the consequences of Israel's conduct: blessing for obedience and curse for disobedience (11:26–32).

Like Moses' sermon in ch. 4, 10:12–11:32 serves as a summary of the preceding chapters (1–3 and 5:1–10:11, respectively) and marks a shift from historical survey (chs. 1–3 and 9:7–10:11, respectively). Both passages begin with the call to attention, "And now, Israel" (*weʿattâ yiśrāʾēl*; the only two times this phrase occurs in Deuteronomy). Both sections call Israel to obey God's covenantal requirements and focus on God's character and conduct. (See Weinfeld, *Deuteronomy 1–11*, 453–55, for other points of comparison.)

a. The Lord Requires Total Commitment from His Vassals (10:12–11:25)

i. Yahweh demands (and deserves) Israel's undivided loyalty (10:12–22)

OVERVIEW

Yahweh makes it absolutely clear that all the detailed requirements God has Moses present to the covenantal people have a driving purpose. Yahweh

requires one thing of his chosen people: to live in wholehearted and undiluted allegiance to him. As Wright (*Deuteronomy*, 144) points out:

These verses begin the buildup toward the climax of the opening exhortation of the book in chapter 11. Deuteronomy 10:12–22 is unquestionably one of the richest texts in the Hebrew Bible, exalted and poetic in its language, comprehensive and challenging in its message. It purposely tries to "boil down" the whole theological and ethical content of the book into memorable phraseology, packed and pregnant, rich and resonant of all the surrounding preaching. Indeed, there are not many dimensions of "Old Testament theology," that are not directly expressed or indirectly echoed in this mini-symphony of faith and life.

Merrill (*Deuteronomy*, 201) adds:

As has been noted repeatedly, covenant relationship between the Lord and Israel had to be expressed in both a vertical and horizontal dimension. To love God is to love one's neighbor, and to serve God necessitates societal obligation. The point is made here again, in perhaps its strongest statement in the entire book of Deuteronomy, for the litany of covenant failure since Sinai as just elaborated in 9:6–10:11 calls for a fresh appeal by Moses that the sins of the past not be repeated.

The present passage (10:12–22) appears to have an envelope structure, with vv. 12–13 and 20–22 serving as the boundary elements of the pericope (cf. Merrill, *Deuteronomy*, 201). Both sections of verses emphasize the "what" and the "why": Obey Yahweh wholeheartedly because of who he is and what he does. This envelope structure surrounds a central section (10:14–19) in which Moses grounds his exhortation for God's people on the high and lofty character and conduct of Yahweh. Because of this reality, they need to live in genuine submission to his expectations and demands (10:16) and live out his character before others, especially before those of whom it would be easy to take advantage (10:19).

---

¹²And now, O Israel, what does the Lord your God ask of you but to fear the Lord your God, to walk in all his ways, to love him, to serve the Lord your God with all your heart and with all your soul, ¹³and to observe the Lord's commands and decrees that I am giving you today for your own good?

¹⁴To the Lord your God belong the heavens, even the highest heavens, the earth and everything in it. ¹⁵Yet the Lord set his affection on your forefathers and loved them, and he chose you, their descendants, above all the nations, as it is today. ¹⁶Circumcise your hearts, therefore, and do not be stiff-necked any longer. ¹⁷For the Lord your God is God of gods and Lord of lords, the great God, mighty and awesome, who shows no partiality and accepts no bribes. ¹⁸He defends the cause of the fatherless and the widow, and loves the alien, giving him food and clothing. ¹⁹And you are to love those who are aliens, for you yourselves were aliens in Egypt. ²⁰Fear the Lord your God and serve him. Hold fast to him and take your oaths in his name. ²¹He is your praise; he is your God, who performed for you those great and awesome wonders you saw with your own eyes. ²²Your forefathers who went down into Egypt were seventy in all, and now the Lord your God has made you as numerous as the stars in the sky.

COMMENTARY

12–13 The first words of this section, "and now, O Israel," look back at the preceding section. Based on the mercy and grace of God as demonstrated in his forgiving them in the wake of their horrific treachery (the incident involving the golden calf; 9:1–10:11), Moses exhorts God's covenantal nation to live in accordance with his demands. God's character should have clear implications for Israel's conduct.

Moses then asks a probing and far-reaching question: "What does the LORD ask of you but [except] ... " (cf. Mic 6:8). Moses wants Israel to understand that Yahweh's claim on them is not "complicated and esoteric but fundamentally simple" (Wright, *Deuteronomy*, 144), i.e., straightforward (not necessarily easy). Concerning the five verbs that follow, Wright (ibid., 145) suggests that this sentence "is like a five-note musical chord. Each note has its own distinct tone, but taken all together they sound forth in a harmony that expresses the whole content of Deuteronomy and the Torah." Some scholars try to categorize these five verbs. For example, Hall, 197, divides them into verbs of action ("walk," "serve," "observe") and attitude ("fear," "love"). Others try to demonstrate logical order in the verbs. Merrill (*Deuteronomy*, 203) contends that fear gives rise to walking and that love serves as the basis for serving and observing.

The present writer is not convinced that either approach is necessary. These five verbs demonstrate the multifaceted expectation of God. They thoroughly show that God expects much more than external obedience to a disparate collection of laws. God demands the kind of obedience that affects every part of a person's being.

1. "To fear" can connote terror, but in the context of one's relationship with God it signifies reverential awe (cf. 5:29; 6:2, 13, 24; 10:20; 31:12–13). It describes the attitude of someone standing before the King of kings and Lord of lords and the disposition that would motivate that person to worship and obey the Lord (cf. Ro 3:18; 2Co 5:11; 7:1; 1Pe 2:17).

2. The idea of traveling or walking serves as a common metaphor for "adherence to principles and pathways of obedience" (Merrill, *Deuteronomy*, 202; cf. 5:33; 8:6; 11:22; 19:9; 26:17; 28:9; 30:16; 1Co 7:17; 2Co 5:7; Gal 5:16, 25; 6:16; Eph 2:10; 4:1; 5:2, 8; Col 1:10; 2:6; 1Th 2:12; 1Jn 1:7; 2Jn 4, 6; 3Jn 3, 4).

3. When used of God, "love" represents more than an emotive term. It serves as a synonym for election. God's choices reflect and express his love. God's love "must find its response and counterpart in the commitment of the chosen one to love (i.e., choose) God in return" (Merrill, *Deuteronomy*, 202). Throughout Deuteronomy, love is manifested in deeds or loyalty to the covenant (cf. 5:10; 6:5; 7:9, 13; 11:1, 13, 22; 13:3; 19:9; 30:6, 16, 20; cf. 1Co 8:3; 2Th 3:5; 1Jn 2:5; 3:17; 4:9, 20, 21; Jude 21).

4. Since Yahweh is Israel's Redeemer, Israel is obligated to render service to her God lovingly, without reservation, and with total devotion (see Note on 6:5; cf. 6:13; 7:4; 10:20; 11:13; 13:4; cf. Mt 4:10; Lk 4:8; Ro 1:9; 12:11; 14:18; Col 3:24; 1Th 1:9; 2Ti 1:3).

5. God demands that his people observe or live in accordance with his expectations (cf. 4:6; 6:1; 7:11; 8:6, 11; 11:1, 8, 13, 22; 12:14; 26:16; 28:45; 1Jn 2:3–4; 3:22; 5:3).

The source of these commands does not consist in Moses but in Yahweh himself, and he gave them to Israel "for your own good." Throughout the Mosaic covenant, Yahweh offers Israel the potential for enjoying covenantal blessings: secure possession of the land, long life, abundant enjoyment of life, the chance to serve as a witness before the pagan nations, etc. (cf. 4:1, 5–8; 5:29, 33; 6:24; 30:15–20; see Note on 5:33).

14–16 Because of who God is and the many ways in which he has demonstrated his love for his people, the children of Israel should be compelled to keep all of his commandments and willingly submit to his intentions for them. Both of the subsections (vv. 14–16 and 17–19) serve as repetitive triplets, thus founding the exhortation squarely on God himself. In both units, Moses points to Yahweh's superlative character (vv. 14, 17), unique conduct (vv. 15, 18), and covenantal demands (vv. 16, 19). In the first subsection, Moses affirms that because the great God of the universe has set his love on them, Israel should gladly submit to his directives and not rebel against him (vv. 14–16).

Moses begins by considering Yahweh's marvelous (superlative) character (10:14). To Israel's covenantal Lord belongs the entire universe. The parallel repetition of heavens and earth, "the heavens [A], the highest heavens [B] ... the earth [A] and everything in it [B]," signifies that the totality of heaven and the totality of earth are under God's ownership! Wright (*Deuteronomy*, 146) points out: "This verse, with wonderful rhythmic cadence, affirms the universal exaltation and cosmic ownership of Yahweh (cf. 1 Kings 8:27; Pss 24:1; 47:7–9; 68:34; 95:4–5; 115:16; 148:4–5; Jer. 10:10–13). There is absolutely nothing in creation ... that does not belong to him." This affirmation would seem to leave little room in Moses' thinking for henotheism, i.e., the idea that Moses recognized that other gods existed with certain limited domains of creation under their control. It is Yahweh and Yahweh alone who exercises sovereignty over the universe.

One of the realities that sets Yahweh apart is his decision to love/choose the descendants of Abraham to be his nation. The fact that he "loved them" (the patriarchs) and "chose you" (Moses and the Israelites) highlights his role as the covenant-maker and covenant-keeper. The juxtaposition of the verbs "to love" (*'hb*) and "to choose" (*bḥr*) occurs in several passages to highlight the concept of Yahweh's elective choice. In this passage and in 4:37 (see Note there), they occur in this order ("love," then "choose"). In at least four other passages these terms occur in the reverse order, but with the same notion (Dt 7:7–8; Pss 47:4 [5]; 78:68; Isa 41:8). In a word, to choose is to love and to love is to choose. There is a clear continuity between God's oath to Abraham, Isaac, and Jacob and what God is declaring to God's people through Moses in this setting. One of the astounding aspects of this divine choice is that Yahweh chose Israel out of or above all the nations of the world (cf. Ex 19:4–6).

In the light of God's character and conduct, Moses commands the Israelites to do two things: circumcise their hearts (cf. Dt 30:6; Jer 4:4; 9:26) and stop being stiff-necked (see Note on 9:6; 10:16). The reference to a circumcised heart in this context is grounded in the practice of circumcising every Israelite boy eight days after birth (Ge 17:9–14). Physical circumcision, the token of the Abrahamic covenant, represented entrance into the covenantal community of Israel. Israelite history after Abraham makes it absolutely clear that physical circumcision made no necessary impact on a person's spiritual condition.

Why use the imagery of circumcision to make Moses' point? Some interpreters emphasize the hygenic issue, i.e., physical circumcision prevented disease-causing organisms from collecting on the male sexual organ and thereby prevented the spread of that disease through sexual contact. Along that line, spiritual circumcision signifies the cleansing of the heart from sin's deadly disease (J. MacArthur, ed., *MacArthur Study Bible* [Nashville: Word, 1997], 1067). Although purity or holiness would characterize the life of the Israelite who had a circumcised heart, I believe that spiritual circumcision has a different point of primary significance. Physical circumcision constituted an outward sign of covenantal allegiance and conformity. Consequently, circumcision of the heart would signify the internal commitment to covenantal allegiance and conformity. Rather than resisting his will, God wanted his children to submit gladly to it.

17–19 Because Israel's supreme God himself deeply cares about the needy among Israel, the Israelites themselves must also live out that same compassion for the alien, orphan, and widow. Once again, Moses gives attention to Yahweh's unparalleled character (10:17). The title "the LORD your God" highlights his role as Israel's covenantal Lord as well as all-powerful Creator. This God is the unparalleled God. There is no god like him.

Moses then utilizes three descriptive terms to delineate one aspect of Yahweh's uniqueness: "the great God, mighty and awesome" (cf. 3:24; 4:35, 39). Clearly, he is the all-powerful God. All three terms occur together twice (10:17; Ne 9:32). Two of them, "great God, the awesome one," occurs three times (Dt 7:21; Da 9:4; Ne 1:5), and "great God, the mighty one" occurs once (Jer 32:18). These occurrences suggest that this collection of terms serves as a common way of describing Yahweh. Three of the passages in which these terms occur have the modifying phrase, "who keeps covenant and steadfast love" (Da 9:4; Ne 1:5; 9:32).

Israel's God also "accepts no bribes." Throughout the OT, taking bribes is condemned because it corrupts one's judgment. Besides the present verse, in which Moses presents God as one who takes no bribes (Dt 10:17), taking a bribe is prohibited (Ex 23:8; Dt 16:19), the one who takes bribes is cursed (Dt 27:25), taking bribes is a mark of covenantal treachery (1Sa 8:3; Eze 22:12), and refusing to take bribes is a mark of covenantal conformity (Ps 15:5). The pairing of showing partiality and taking bribes occurs here and in Deuteronomy 16:19.

In this subsection, Yahweh's unique conduct relates to the fact that he "defends the cause of the fatherless and the widow, and loves the alien" (10:18; cf. Ps 146:9; Eze 22:7). Yahweh "executes justice" for the orphan and widow, members of Israel who were easily (and regularly) treated unjustly. He "loves" the alien (see Note on 1:16) as though he were a member of the covenantal community.

Moses demands that the Israelites conduct themselves toward the weaker members of their society just as God does, with justice and love (10:19). In this verse, the "alien" is the only one of these three terms that receives explicit mention, although it likely serves as a pointer to all three terms. It is probably cited because the Hebrews had been "aliens" during their tenure in Egypt. One can make at least two observations from this usage of these three terms. First, God's concern for the alien, orphan, and widow serves as the foundation for his demand that Israel take care of these people. Second, throughout the prophets in particular, Israel's treatment of these people often serves as a barometer or indicator of their covenantal conformity or lack of it.

20–22 Moses repeats his exhortation to God's chosen people. They should genuinely serve and fear God as the one who has repeatedly manifested his great power in their behalf. He begins by affirming God's demand of them (v.20) and concludes by focusing on his character and identity (vv.21–22). He returns to his emphasis at the beginning of this section. God's servant-nation must fear, serve, cleave to, and swear by Yahweh.

Moses ends the passage where he should, with the focus on Israel's God. As Merrill (*Deuteronomy,*

205) points out: "The justification for this uncompromising allegiance was both the person and the works of God.... A God so faithful to his promise and with sufficient resources to bring it to pass was surely worthy of his people's wholehearted commitment to the covenant he had graciously made with them." Moses affirms that God is "your praise," i.e., (by metonymy) the object of their praise. By referring to Yahweh as "your God," he reminds Israel of the heart of the Mosaic covenant. One could summarize that covenant with these words: "I will be your God and you will be my people." Yahweh is also Israel's wonderworker. He has performed an abundance of marvelous works in behalf of his chosen nation. Finally, he is their multiplier. He has taken Jacob's convoy of seventy people who descended into Egypt and made them into a numerous people—a nation—in fulfillment of his promise to make them "as numerous as the stars in the sky" (Ge 15:5; 22:17).

NOTES

14 Although left untranslated most of the time, the particle הֵן (*hēn*, "behold") does serve to focus the reader's attention on the utterance that follows (C. van der Merwe, J. Naudé, and J. Kroeze, *A Biblical Hebrew Reference Grammar* [Sheffield: Sheffield Academic Press, 1999], 330).

Since biblical (and modern) Hebrew lack a verb for "have" or "belong to," the language has no explicit way to express possession; therefore, Hebrew normally shows possession by prefixing a *lamed* (as a preposition) to the person or possessor and then stating the item possessed, as in לַיהוָה אֱלֹהֶיךָ (*layhwh ʾelōheykā*), roughly rendered, "to Yahweh your God is/belongs...."

The expression הַשָּׁמַיִם וּשְׁמֵי הַשָּׁמַיִם (*haššamayim ûšemê haššamayim*, "the heavens, indeed/even the highest heavens") is rendered literally, "the heavens and the heavens of the heavens." Waltke and O'Connor (*IBHS*, 267, §14.5b) describe this construction as a "comparative superlative" (two instances of the same noun that occur in a construct relationship in which the second noun is determined). With this kind of superlative, "some person or object is judged to surpass all others in its class with respect to some quality" (ibid.). As Merrill (*Deuteronomy*, 203) points out, this phrase does not suggest "some cosmological scheme in which there are levels of heavenly realm, but it is merely a Hebrew construction indicating totality."

15 The particle רַק (*raq*) can introduce a limitation or a contrast to what has preceded, i.e., "yet" (Van der Merwe et al., *Biblical Hebrew Reference Grammar*, 317). If such is the case here, Moses is highlighting the "shocking" fact that the God to whom the universe belongs has chosen Israel, clearly unworthy of such an honor (Hall, 199; McConville, 195; Wright, *Deuteronomy*, 146). It also occurs as an emphatic adverb, "only" (*HALOT*, 1286; T. Muraoka, *Emphatic Words and Structures in Biblical Hebrew* [Jerusalem: Magnes, 1985], 131). Weinfeld (*Deuteronomy 1–11*, 436) translates it with both words: "yet only." Even if it carries the emphatic notion of "only," it demonstrates a clear contrast with the preceding truth—Yahweh's universal sovereignty.

16 How is the perfect verb וּמַלְתֶּם (*ûmaltem*, "you circumcise") to be translated? Is the construction the normal perfect + *waw* consecutive (after a nonperfective verb)? No, for perfect and preterite verbs occur in the preceding line. Waltke and O'Connor (*IBHS*, 532−33, §32.2.3d) point out: "In some contexts, especially legal literature, relative *wqtl* with a consecutive notion takes on a subordinate volitional force." According to the theology of Deuteronomy, Israel should offer to God future obedience on the basis of his past gracious acts toward them, and here as elsewhere *waw* + perfect (v.16) represents the entreaty form, and perfect + preterite + *waw* consecutive (v.15) signifies past acts (cf. Dt 29:2, 4, 8; 30:19). As with v.16, the initial verb of v.19 represents the logical consequence of the divine reality in v.18: Because Yahweh loves the sojourner, so should you love the sojourner (see *IBHS*, 535–36, §32.2.5a).

17 Both pairs of terms in the phrase אֱלֹהֵי הָאֱלֹהִים וַאֲדֹנֵי הָאֲדֹנִים (*ᵉlōhê hāᵉlōhîm waᵃdōnê hāᵃdōnîm*, "God of gods and Lord of lords") have a construct noun followed by a genitive noun in the plural. Waltke and O'Connor (*IBHS*, 154, §9.5.3j; cf. GKC, 431, §133i) call this construction a "superlative genitive," and they call the two plural nouns (the second element of each pair) an "honorific plural" (*IBHS*, 122–23, §7.4.3b).

Although the expression יִשָּׂא פָנִים (*yiśśāᵓ pānîm*, lit., "lift the face") can simply mean to meet someone (2Sa 2:22) or refer to prominent persons ("ones lifted up with respect to the face"—2Ki 5:1; Isa 3:3; 9:15 [14]; Job 22:8), in at least seven instances it refers to showing partiality, once in reference to God (here in Dt 10:17 in the negative: "who shows no partiality") and the rest with regard to people (Ge 32:20 [21]; Lev 19:15; Dt 28:50; Job 32:21; Pr 18:5; Mal 2:9). Such conduct is prohibited by God (Lev 19:15) and abhorred by godly individuals (Job 32:21; Pr 18:5).

18 The three terms יָתוֹם וְאַלְמָנָה ... גֵּר (*yātôm wᵉᵓalmānâ ... gēr*, "the fatherless and the widow ... alien") occur together fourteen times in the OT (ten times in Deuteronomy; "fatherless" and "widow" occur together as a pair once, in Isa 9:17 [16], without "alien"). God is their defender (Dt 10:18; Ps 146:9), and the triad serves as part of a Mosaic exhortation for Israel to provide for these needy people, either by leaving gleanings (Dt 24:19–21) or through the Levitical tithe (14:29; 26:12–13); twice the text invites these less fortunate people to join with the rest of Israel in festival celebrations (16:11, 14); and once a curse is pronounced on those who deprive the needy of justice (27:19). The triad occurs three times as part of a prophetic exhortation or indictment in which Israel's treatment of these three groups of people is in view (Jer 7:6; 22:3; Eze 22:7), and in eleven passages as a reference to those in Israelite society who are at the fringe of existence and need special care. In three passages the term "alien" is governed by one verb and the other two terms ("orphan/fatherless" and "widow") by another verb.

ii. God's deliverance of Israel from Egypt should motivate Israel to be loyal to him (11:1–7)

OVERVIEW

Having provided a broad understanding of God's character and conduct (Dt 10:12–22), Moses focuses on God's miraculous deliverance of his covenantal nation from bondage in Egypt. In the light of that divine rescue, God's people should long to obey him wholeheartedly.

¹Love the LORD your God and keep his requirements, his decrees, his laws and his commands always. ²Remember today that your children were not the ones who saw and

experienced the discipline of the LORD your God: his majesty, his mighty hand, his out-stretched arm; [3]the signs he performed and the things he did in the heart of Egypt, both to Pharaoh king of Egypt and to his whole country; [4]what he did to the Egyptian army, to its horses and chariots, how he overwhelmed them with the waters of the Red Sea as they were pursuing you, and how the LORD brought lasting ruin on them. [5]It was not your children who saw what he did for you in the desert until you arrived at this place, [6]and what he did to Dathan and Abiram, sons of Eliab the Reubenite, when the earth opened its mouth right in the middle of all Israel and swallowed them up with their households, their tents and every living thing that belonged to them. [7]But it was your own eyes that saw all these great things the LORD has done.

COMMENTARY

1 Moses begins ch. 11 with two "covenantal" verbs: "love" (*ʾhb*; see Note on 5:9) and "keep" (*šmr*; see Note on 4:2). The Israelites are to live as loyal subjects to Yahweh and conform their lives to his expectations. The four terms referring to Yahweh's requirements point to the multifaceted nature of Israel's obedience. To love Yahweh is to obey him in every way possible (Merrill, *Deuteronomy*, 206).

2–7 Moses exhorts God's chosen people to "know" (*ydʿ*) Yahweh's "discipline" of them. They must not only maintain a memory of a historical event but also to allow this knowledge to transform their lives (see Note on 7:9). Unlike their children (both survivors of the wilderness wanderings as well as future generations), who have not witnessed Yahweh's miraculous deeds performed in Israel's behalf, Israelite adults, whose choices had

far-reaching implications, must keep in mind his "discipline" or teaching of them.

As in 5:3, Moses seeks to focus on the immediacy of Israel's experience and the urgent responsibility for them to obey their covenantal Lord (McConville, 202). He begins broadly by referring to Yahweh's greatness and his "mighty hand [and] outstretched arm" (v.2; see comment on 7:17–19). Then he points to three concrete examples (two positive and one negative). He reminds them of the way God crushed Egypt's power and released them from the slavery and land of Egypt by performing one of the most stupendous miracles recorded in the OT (11:3–4). God remained with them during their travels in the wilderness (11:5) and provided them with flawless guidance. He also judged two rebellious Israelites, Dathan and Abiram, for their treachery (11:6).

NOTES

1 Certain verses seem to serve "double duty." This verse provides an apt conclusion to ch. 10 as well as a needed introduction to ch. 11. Since ch. 11 seems abrupt without this verse, it is included with the outline point for ch. 11.

2 Does the clause בְנֵיכֶם־אֶת לֹא (*lōʾ ʾet-bᵉnêkem*), "it was not your children," serve as a brief parenthetical statement or play a primary role in vv.2–6? One's conclusion clearly affects the translation of these verses and the emphasis of the passage but does not change the primary significance of the unit: Pay attention to what God has done. Several translations (NASB, NCV, NET, NIV, NKJV, NLT) emphasize that it was "not your children" who "saw and experienced" all the activities detailed in vv.2–6. Two of the translations (NIV, NLT) insert verbs at various spots to continue this emphasis. Verse 7 then affirms that it was "you" who saw these things. This translation of these verses highlights what the "children" did not see or perceive (cf. Ridderbos, 144).

At least two translations (ESV, NRSV) regard the clause in question to be a brief parenthetical statement (Craigie, 202, 208; McConville, 193, 195). For example, the NRSV has: "Remember today that it was not your children (who have not known or seen the discipline of the LORD your God), but it is you who must acknowledge...." The emphasis of the passage rests on Moses' command that the adults and leaders of the present generation live in the light of all that God has done for them. The latter option best deals with the Masoretic accentuation in v.2 (Weinfeld, *Deuteronomy 1–11*, 442) and provides the best emphasis in the paragraph.

The noun מוּסָר (*mûsār*, "discipline"; GK 4592) is derived from the verb יסר (*ysr*), which occurs in four passages in Deuteronomy and signifies either instruction (4:36) or loving, parental punishment (8:5; 21:18; 22:18). The noun occurs only this one time in Deuteronomy. It places the emphasis not on Israel's punishment but on what they learned as they observed Yahweh's deeds. Fundamentally, the noun concerns teaching or learning by exhortation and example and is often accompanied by warnings and the application of punishment for failure to adhere to the instruction (Merrill, *NIDOTTE*, 2:480–81). In the present passage, the people had already experienced the negative aspects of this "discipline" in the past and are now exhorted to benefit from what they have learned.

iii. Israel's enjoyment of the Promised Land is connected to their covenantal obedience (11:8–25)

⁸Observe therefore all the commands I am giving you today, so that you may have the strength to go in and take over the land that you are crossing the Jordan to possess, ⁹and so that you may live long in the land that the LORD swore to your forefathers to give to them and their descendants, a land flowing with milk and honey. ¹⁰The land you are entering to take over is not like the land of Egypt, from which you have come, where you planted your seed and irrigated it by foot as in a vegetable garden. ¹¹But the land you are crossing the Jordan to take possession of is a land of mountains and valleys that drinks rain from heaven. ¹²It is a land the LORD your God cares for; the eyes of the LORD your God are continually on it from the beginning of the year to its end.

¹³So if you faithfully obey the commands I am giving you today — to love the LORD your God and to serve him with all your heart and with all your soul — ¹⁴then I will send rain on your land in its season, both autumn and spring rains, so that you may gather in your grain, new wine and oil. ¹⁵I will provide grass in the fields for your cattle, and you will eat and be satisfied.

¹⁶Be careful, or you will be enticed to turn away and worship other gods and bow down to them. ¹⁷Then the LORD's anger will burn against you, and he will shut the heavens so that it will not rain and the ground will yield no produce, and you will soon perish from the good land the LORD is giving you. ¹⁸Fix these words of mine in your hearts and minds; tie them as symbols on your hands and bind them on your foreheads. ¹⁹Teach them to your children, talking about them when you sit at home and when you walk along the road, when you lie down and when you get up. ²⁰Write them on the doorframes of your houses and on your gates, ²¹so that your days and the days of your children may be many in the land that the LORD swore to give your forefathers, as many as the days that the heavens are above the earth.

²²If you carefully observe all these commands I am giving you to follow — to love the LORD your God, to walk in all his ways and to hold fast to him — ²³then the LORD will drive out all these nations before you, and you will dispossess nations larger and stronger than you. ²⁴Every place where you set your foot will be yours: Your territory will extend from the desert to Lebanon, and from the Euphrates River to the western sea. ²⁵No man will be able to stand against you. The LORD your God, as he promised you, will put the terror and fear of you on the whole land, wherever you go.

COMMENTARY

8–9 Moses repeats his exhortation for the Israelites to accept Yahweh's requirement of their total loyalty (singular form of "command"; see Note on 6:1) but gives more attention to its "consequences." If they wholeheartedly conform to God's expectations, they will be able to conquer and possess the Promised Land and enjoy long tenure there. This is the land of abundance that Yahweh promised by oath to the patriarchs (see Note on 1:8; comment on 6:3).

10–12 Moses compares the land of Egypt with the land of Canaan. In Egypt the Nile River flooded annually, watering the land running alongside the river and depositing fertile soil there. During the other parts of the year, most Egyptians depended on an intricate system of manmade canals to water

their fields. Egypt received relatively little rain. In the Promised Land, God's chosen people will have to rely exclusively on their God, who causes the rain to fall. But they need not worry, for Yahweh deeply cares for this land. His eyes are only on those things of great importance (see Note on 11:12). The theme of the land is a key part of the theology of Deuteronomy and has a central role in the Abrahamic covenant as well (Ge 12:1, 7; 13:15; 15:7, 16, 18; 17:8; 26:3).

13–17 In a land of potential abundance, Israel will be tempted to take the fullness of the land for granted. They must realize that their enjoyment of abundance is not just the coincidence of an agricultural cycle. Verses 13–15 follow an "if … then" construction. The condition Moses sets before Israel is God's demand for wholehearted obedience (see Note on 6:5) to the covenant, and he does so using three "covenantal" verbs: "obey," "love," and "serve." If they live in accordance with God's demands, he will cause the land to be productive in every sense by means of the autumn and spring rains. He will cause the land to produce grain, new wine, and oil (chief products of agriculture in this region), as well as abundant grass for their cattle. They will be able to eat to their satisfaction (see Note on 8:12). For a brief consideration of this consistent connection between Israel's conduct and their experience of material blessings, see comments on 4:1.

Since Yahweh demands absolute loyalty of his covenantal nation, he prohibits Israel from worshiping any other gods (Dt 11:16–17; cf. 4:15–19; 6:14). The Canaanite gods might seem enticing to the Israelites because they were allegedly responsible for rain and the fertility of the land (Baal/Hadad; *ABD*, 1:546–49). However, if the Israelites fail to recognize that Yahweh alone brings rain and fertility to the land, and if they worship other gods to accomplish that end, they will learn a painful lesson. God will cause the rain to stop and prevent the fields from producing. Because of their rebellion, rather than enjoying a long tenure in the land they will not survive.

18–21 These verses strongly resemble 6:6–9, though in a slightly different order here (see comments there). As part of the concluding material for the general stipulations section (chs. 5–11), this challenge returns to the exhortation given in ch. 6 (right after the delineation of the Ten Commandments). Yahweh demands that his covenantal nation "flavor" their entire lives with his covenantal demands. Before Moses begins his recitation of the details of Yahweh's covenantal requirements (chs. 12–26), he reminds them that God's expectations need to influence them internally and externally, in every realm of their existence.

22–25 Moses returns to a theme developed in the beginning of this section (11:8–9): Israel's genuine obedience to Yahweh's demands will ensure a successful conquest of the Promised Land. As in other places, he "piles up" covenantal verbs: "carefully observe" (*šmr*), "love" (*ʾhb*), "walk" (*hlk*), "hold fast" (*dbq*; see comments on 10:12–13). If they live in this fashion, they will conquer nations larger and stronger than themselves and will be able to take possession of all the land God has promised to them. Moses gives the boundaries of this Promised Land in general terms: the desert to the south, Lebanon to the north, the Euphrates River to the east, and the Mediterranean Sea to the west.

NOTES

10 Scholars have offered various interpretations of the phrase וְהִשְׁקִיתָ בְרַגְלְךָ (*wᵉhišqîtā bᵉraglᵉkā*, "irrigated it by foot") and its role in the passage (in addition to the one offered above). Merrill (*Deuteronomy*, 208) regards this clause as a reference to the foot-operated water wheel, the *shadû*. Although "by foot" may in part refer to the *shadû*, the phrase probably more broadly refers to various activities involved with the Egyptian irrigation system, e.g., opening and closing sluice gates, breaking down ridges of dirt, etc. (Craigie, 210, n. 20; Tigay, *Deuteronomy*, 112). Others suggest that here Moses makes a sarcastic contrast between the desirability of the Land of Promise and the land of Egypt. Understanding "foot" as a euphemism for the genitals, they see Moses as contrasting the Egyptian practice of irrigating with impure water (i.e., urine), whereas God provides Canaan with pure rainwater (Walton and Matthews, 233). Some suggest he contrasts the small fields in Egypt (small enough to be watered with urine) with the spacious lands of Canaan (G. Nicol, "Watering Egypt (Deuteronomy xi 10–11) Again," *VT* 38 [1988]: 347–48).

12 The expression עֵינֵי יְהֹוָה (ʿênê yhwh, "eyes of the LORD") occurs about one hundred times in the OT; ninety-four times it is part of a prepositional phrase, "in the eyes of the LORD," referring to God's presence or knowledge. In seven passages this expression (or "his eyes," referring to Yahweh) describes God's eyes as looking at something. "His eyes" carefully watch the whole earth (2Ch 16:9), are on those who fear him (Ps 33:18) and are toward the righteous (Ps 34:15[16]), are in every place and watch over knowledge (Pr 15:3; 22:12), and range over the whole earth (Zec 4:10). In each case, God's eyes are on something of great value to him.

14 Referred to in the phrase יוֹרֶה וּמַלְקוֹשׁ (yôreh ûmalqôš, "autumn and spring rains"; also called the "former and latter rains"), the autumn rain falls in October and November (thus preparing the soil for plowing and sowing), and the spring rain falls in April and early May (thus facilitating the final maturation of the grain). It is not just the provision but also the timing of these rains that was (and is) essential. The absence or presence of rain at the wrong part of the growing season could be disastrous (cf. Tigay, *Deuteronomy*, 113–14).

24 While the verb דרך (drk, in the phrase אֲשֶׁר תִּדְרֹךְ כַּף־רַגְלְכֶם, ²⁴ʾšer tidrōk kap-raglᵉkem, "where you set your foot") can signify the literal idea of "treading" or "marching" (Ps 91:13; Isa 59:8), it can also speak figuratively of conquest (Merrill, *NIDOTTE*, 1:992). Caleb received land on which he had walked in faith (Dt 1:36; cf. Jos 14:9). The word may refer to a legal procedure resulting in legal title to the land (Hall, 212).

b. Israel's Obedience or Treachery Has Far-Reaching Implications (11:26–32)

OVERVIEW

In addition to serving as a conclusion for chs. 5–11 (the general stipulations), these verses form a chiastic framework with the subsequent chapters (a revision of Craigie, 212):

11:26–28: the blessing and curse in the *present* renewal of the covenant (at Moab)
    11:29–32: the blessing and curse in the *future* renewal of the covenant (on Ebal and Gerizim)
        12:1–26:19: specific covenantal stipulations
    27:1–26: the blessing and curse in the *future* renewal of the covenant (on Ebal and Gerizim)
28:1–29:1: the blessing and curse in the *present* renewal of the covenant (at Moab)

²⁶See, I am setting before you today a blessing and a curse — ²⁷the blessing if you obey the commands of the LORD your God that I am giving you today; ²⁸the curse if you disobey the commands of the LORD your God and turn from the way that I command you today by following other gods, which you have not known. ²⁹When the LORD your God has brought you into the land you are entering to possess, you are to proclaim on Mount Gerizim the blessings, and on Mount Ebal the curses. ³⁰As you know, these mountains are across the Jordan, west of the road, toward the setting sun, near the great trees of Moreh, in the territory of those Canaanites living in the Arabah in the vicinity of Gilgal. ³¹You are about to cross the Jordan to enter and take possession of the land the LORD your God is giving you. When you have taken it over and are living there, ³²be sure that you obey all the decrees and laws I am setting before you today.

COMMENTARY

26–28 For the first time in Deuteronomy (cf. 27:9–28:68), Moses utilizes the technical terms of the covenant, "blessing" and "curse." Ancient Near Eastern treaties generally included a section promising blessings and threatening curses contingent on the faithfulness of the vassals to their covenantal commitments. Yahweh "sets before" or "gives" these promises and threats to Israel. Throughout Deuteronomy, Yahweh affirms that he has or is giving to Israel the land he has promised.

Many of the blessings delineated in ch. 28 concern that land. The curses involve God's making the land unproductive and even evicting the Israelites from it. Consequently, it is apparent that God's gift of the land to his chosen people is not without conditions. From God's perspective, the gift of the land to Israel is an accomplished fact. He *will* bring them into the land of Canaan. Whether Israel continues to possess that land, however, is the issue in question. For their obedience (*šmᶜ*) he will bless them, but for their disobedience (*lōʾ šmᶜ*) he will bring curses on them. Specifically, the worship of other

gods is central to covenantal treachery. Whether or not the Israelites conduct themselves as loyal citizens under Yahweh's rule will have far-reaching implications.

29–30 After arriving in the Promised Land, the Israelites are to rededicate themselves to submission to this covenantal agreement by proclaiming these blessings and curses while standing on Mounts Ebal and Gerizim. The Israelites had pledged mutual fidelity to the Sinaitic covenant and to Yahweh at Horeb (Ex 24:3–8); now Moses demands that God's people renew their commitment to this covenantal relationship with Yahweh in a tangible fashion (cf. Jos 8:30–35). The city of Shechem, rich in patriarchal history (Ge 12:6–7; 33:19–20; cf. Jn 4:6), sits at the base of the two mountains mentioned. Although the specific significance of the geographical features has been debated, Moses' reference to these two mountains is without question.

31–32 Knowing the manifold challenges that await them, Moses encourages the Israelites one more time to take this exhortation seriously and dedicate themselves to obeying the Lord and his commandments. Just as God expects of Israel before the conquest of Canaan, he demands that they "be careful to obey" (see Note on 5:1) his covenantal requirements once they receive this gracious inheritance of land.

NOTE

28 The verb "to know" (ידע, *ydʿ*, in the phrase אֲשֶׁר לֹא־יְדַעְתֶּם, *ʾăšer lōʾ-yᵉdaʿtem*, "which you have not known") occurs almost fifty times in Deuteronomy. It frequently occurs, along with "remember" and "do not forget" (see Note on 4:10), to delineate God's desire for an intimate relationship with Israel. He wants them to know him in a way that transforms their lives. In the present context Moses refers to pagan gods as those whom the Israelites have not known. This reference does not mean that by this time God's people had never heard of these pagan deities. Indeed, when they passed through Moab, they encountered the enticing nature of false gods from this region. Moses' point is rather that these pagan gods have never tangibly intervened in Israel's behalf. Israel had not had any genuine relationship with them.

B. Specific Stipulations of the Covenant (12:1–26:15)

OVERVIEW

Having already dealt with the general stipulations (a call to absolute loyalty, chs. 5–11), Moses delineates Yahweh's specific requirements of his covenantal people (in accordance with various ancient Near Eastern treaties). While some (e.g., Kaufman, 110) have suggested that chs. 5–11 provide an exposition of the first two commandments, various scholars have suggested that the specific stipulations elaborate all ten commandments (Kaufman, 105–58; J. Walton, "Deuteronomy: An Exposition of the Spirit of the Law," *GTJ* 8 [1987]: 213–35).

Kaufman first suggested a *literary* correlation between the Decalogue and the Deuteronomic laws. However, Walton takes the connection a step further; he contends that the Deuteronomic stipulations (laws) exemplify the "spirit" of each of the Ten Commandments, with the result that one does not have to wait until Jeremiah or Christ to recognize that the Ten Commandments are to be understood as broader in scope than the "letter of the law." Rather, as Walton, 214, suggests, "the commandments serve as doors into the discussion of a transcendent morality which they are fully understood to require. In other words, the Ten Commandments, even as early as Moses, were understood to oblige the individual to a lifestyle of moral conduct both with regard to God and to man." Although it seems clear that this section of Deuteronomy (and the specific legislation in Exodus and Leviticus) explicates the Ten Commandments, scholars do not agree concerning the arrangement of the verses under those broad headings (cf. Hall, 31–32, who outlines this section in accordance with the Decalogue).

1. The Place and Kind of Worship Yahweh Accepts (12:1–16:17)

a. Being God's People Demands that Israel Be Totally Distinct in Their Object, Place, and Manner of Worship (12:1–13:18 [19])

i. Worship at the place and in the Way Yahweh prescribes (12:1–32)

OVERVIEW

Chapters 5–11 have focused on Yahweh's demand for Israel's absolute loyalty. It is significant that the first requirement Yahweh gives to his covenantal nation in the present section (after the introductory statement in v.1) is to destroy any vestige of Canaanite religion. False worship is totally incompatible with conducting oneself in exclusive allegiance to Yahweh (Vogt, 207). A key way for the Israelites to demonstrate their loyalty to Yahweh is to worship him properly. The outline found below (revised from Vogt, 182; cf. Christensen, *Deuteronomy 1:1–21:9*, 234–35) could be presented in a chiastic fashion to highlight its internal coherence as well as its central focus:

A Introductory Statement: "These are the laws you shall observe" (12:1)

   B No God but Yahweh: Destroy idolatrous centers of worship (12:2–4)

      C Demonstrate loyalty to Yahweh alone in all aspects of worship (12:5–28)

   B' No God but Yahweh: Do not imitate idolatrous worship (12:29–31)

A' Closing statement: "Observe all that is commanded" (12:32 [13:1])

This entire section (12:1–13:18 [19]) affirms that Israel must not worship Yahweh in the same manner that the nations worshiped their gods. They must worship in the manner he dictates and at the places he chooses.

(a) Introductory statement (12:1)

¹These are the decrees and laws you must be careful to follow in the land that the LORD, the God of your fathers, has given you to possess — as long as you live in the land.

COMMENTARY

1 As in 5:1 and 29:1, this heading introduces a new major section of the book, by which Moses exhorts God's covenantal nation to obey wholeheartedly Yahweh's covenantal stipulations. The intended "context" for this obedience is the Promised Land, given to them by their covenantal Lord as an inheritance. Their continued enjoyment of this landed gift and their covenantal obedience are interrelated.

(b) No God but Yahweh: Destroy idolatrous centers of worship (12:2–4)

²Destroy completely all the places on the high mountains and on the hills and under every spreading tree where the nations you are dispossessing worship their gods. ³Break down their altars, smash their sacred stones and burn their Asherah poles in the fire; cut down the idols of their gods and wipe out their names from those places. ⁴You must not worship the LORD your God in their way.

COMMENTARY

2–4 Moses commands the Israelites to destroy utterly the centers of Canaanite worship scattered throughout the land of Canaan once they gain possession of it. These places (called "high places" in a number of other historical books, e.g., 1Sa 9:12–14, 19) were located on various hills and mountains. The vast number of worship centers, suggested by "under every spreading tree," highlights the "indiscriminateness" of Canaanite worship (McConville, 218), in clear contrast with Yahweh's requirement of a specific place to worship him (Dt 12:5–12).

In addition to destroying all the religious instruments connected with pagan worship (see comment on 7:5), the Israelites are to "wipe out" the "names" of the pagan idols worshiped at these locations (see Note on 7:24) and all remembrances of pagan worship practices there (see comments on 7:5). Verse 4 literally reads, "you shall not do so to Yahweh your God." The Israelites' worship of Yahweh should be distinct from the way in which the Canaanites worshiped their lifeless gods. As Miller (131) writes:

> Negating one group of names and establishing another name in effect calls for a new order, a transformation: a shift from an order where there are multiple claims for human allegiance ... and where human design determines the place and nature of worship. This order is to give way to another, wherein divine control is placed over human worship and one name replaces all other names.

(c) Demonstrate loyalty to Yahweh alone in every aspect of worship (12:5–28)

OVERVIEW

Although these verses deal with diverse issues related to the worship of Yahweh, they share a common focus: the need for the Israelites to manifest their absolute loyalty to Yahweh through every aspect of their worship of him.

⁵But you are to seek the place the LORD your God will choose from among all your tribes to put his Name there for his dwelling. To that place you must go; ⁶there bring your burnt offerings and sacrifices, your tithes and special gifts, what you have vowed to give and your freewill offerings, and the firstborn of your herds and flocks. ⁷There, in the presence of the LORD your God, you and your families shall eat and shall rejoice in everything you have put your hand to, because the LORD your God has blessed you.

⁸You are not to do as we do here today, everyone as he sees fit, ⁹since you have not yet reached the resting place and the inheritance the LORD your God is giving you. ¹⁰But you will cross the Jordan and settle in the land the LORD your God is giving you as an inheritance, and he will give you rest from all your enemies around you so that you will live in safety. ¹¹Then to the place the LORD your God will choose as a dwelling for his Name—there you are to bring everything I command you: your burnt offerings and sacrifices, your tithes and special gifts, and all the choice possessions you have vowed to the LORD. ¹²And there rejoice before the LORD your God, you, your sons and daughters, your menservants and maidservants, and the Levites from your towns, who have no allotment or inheritance of their own. ¹³Be careful not to sacrifice your burnt offerings anywhere you please. ¹⁴Offer them only at the place the LORD will choose in one of your tribes, and there observe everything I command you.

¹⁵Nevertheless, you may slaughter your animals in any of your towns and eat as much of the meat as you want, as if it were gazelle or deer, according to the blessing the LORD your God gives you. Both the ceremonially unclean and the clean may eat it. ¹⁶But you must not eat the blood; pour it out on the ground like water. ¹⁷You must not eat in your own towns the tithe of your grain and new wine and oil, or the firstborn of your herds and flocks, or whatever you have vowed to give, or your freewill offerings or special gifts. ¹⁸Instead, you are to eat them in the presence of the LORD your God at the place the LORD your God will choose—you, your sons and daughters, your menservants and maidservants, and the Levites from your towns—and you are to rejoice before the LORD your God in everything you put your hand to. ¹⁹Be careful not to neglect the Levites as long as you live in your land.

²⁰When the LORD your God has enlarged your territory as he promised you, and you crave meat and say, "I would like some meat," then you may eat as much of it as you want. ²¹If the place where the LORD your God chooses to put his Name is too far away from you, you may slaughter animals from the herds and flocks the LORD has given you, as I have commanded you, and in your own towns you may eat as much of them as you want. ²²Eat them as you would gazelle or deer. Both the ceremonially unclean and the clean may eat. ²³But be sure you do not eat the blood, because the blood is the life, and you must not eat the life with the meat. ²⁴You must not eat the blood; pour it out on the ground like

water. ²⁵Do not eat it, so that it may go well with you and your children after you, because you will be doing what is right in the eyes of the LORD.

²⁶But take your consecrated things and whatever you have vowed to give, and go to the place the LORD will choose. ²⁷Present your burnt offerings on the altar of the LORD your God, both the meat and the blood. The blood of your sacrifices must be poured beside the altar of the LORD your God, but you may eat the meat. ²⁸Be careful to obey all these regulations I am giving you, so that it may always go well with you and your children after you, because you will be doing what is good and right in the eyes of the LORD your God.

COMMENTARY

5–7 Verse 5 introduces an abrupt contrast to the false worship of the Canaanites. In addition to the shift in perspective indicated grammatically (the compound particle, *kî ʾim*, indicates a restriction or contrast, especially after a negative clause, as in 12:4; *IBHS*, 671, §39.3.5d), key wordplays heighten the contrast that should exist between the worship of Canaanite gods and that of Yahweh. The Israelites are to destroy the "places" of Canaanite altars but worship only at the "place" God chooses. They are to wipe out the "names" of the Canaanite gods from those places but worship at the place where God causes his "Name" to dwell.

Moses does not place the emphasis on the number or location of the proper place of worship but on the *kind* of place, namely, one that Yahweh chooses (especially in contrast with Canaanite practices of worship; Miller, 131). Until God has given Israel rest from all their enemies (12:10–11, presaging the time of David), the Israelites can follow the pattern established in Exodus 20:24 (namely, allowing God's people to offer their sacrifices at more than one place).

But what kind of place must that location be? Just as God chose Israel (Dt 4:37; 7:6–7; 10:15;

14:2) and their priests (18:5; 21:5), he alone will chose the place in which he will receive worship (12:5, 11, 14, 18, 21, 26; 14:23–25; 16:2, 6–7; 17:8, 10, et al.). Yahweh will "cause his Name to dwell" (see Note on 12:11) in that place of his choosing. Establishing Yahweh's "name" at the acceptable place of worship demonstrates that he has the ability to mark out a place for himself in the light of his sovereignty over and ownership of the Promised Land (Vogt, 183; cf. Wright, *Deuteronomy*, 159).

In the light of 12:5 and 14, does ch. 12 mandate one altar at one place for all time, or only Yahweh-ordained locations (see Note on 12:5, 14 for a summary of the views)? Exodus 20:24 affirms that the Israelites were to erect an earthen altar "wherever I cause my name to be honored/remembered." The essential element in a location for sacrifice is a place where Yahweh reveals himself or brings himself glory by intervening in behalf of the Israelites. Also, it is clear from subsequent biblical narratives that sacrifices were occasionally offered (without divine condemnation) at locations other than the primary location for the given period of time (Jos 8:30–35; Jdg 2:5; 6:26; 13:16–23; 20:26–27; 21:4; 1Sa 6:14–15; 7:9–10, 17; 10:8; 11:15; 2Sa

6:13; 24:22, 24–25; 1Ki 3:4 [cf. 2Ch 1:3–6]; 1Ki 18:30–38).

The general picture in ch. 12 as it relates to proper worship of Yahweh is one of anticipation. The Lord desires that sacrifices offered to him take place only at a location among the tribes of Israel where he "places his Name." At all times in Israel's history as a nation (i.e., after Sinai), the Israelites could offer sacrifices only at locations marked out by Yahweh (and not associated with any pagan forms of worship). Once Solomon erected the temple of Yahweh, the restriction was narrowed: the Israelites were not to offer Levitical sacrifices at any location other than that temple.

Verses 6–7 and 11–12 (cf. vv. 17–19) call on Israel to bring their offerings (of various kinds) to Yahweh, to eat those portions of the offering not burned by fire, and to rejoice together as families and fellow members of the nation. Moses demands that the Israelites bring their offerings and sacrifices to the place God chooses. These sacrificial terms do not constitute an exhaustive delineation of their sacrificial responsibilities but broadly refer to whatever one needed to present to Yahweh in a sacrificial setting (see Note on 12:6).

Moses also wants the Israelites to worship and rejoice together as citizens of God's covenantal nation. In numerous OT passages, rejoicing and worship occur together (Feast of Tabernacles—16:14; Ne 8:17; Passover and Feast of Unleavened Bread—2Ch 30:21, 23, 25–26; Ezr 6:22; First-fruits—Dt 26:11; Feast of Purim—Est 8:16–17; 9:17–19, 22; fasting—Zec 8:19; and all worship activities—Nu 10:10; cf. Est 9:17–18; see Grisanti, *NIDOTTE*, 3:1252). The very fact that God's people will be able to offer these sacrifices and rejoice together represents a fulfillment of God's pledge to bring them into the land he has promised and to provide for them abundantly ("blessed"; Dt

12:7). The Israelites are to celebrate in this way at the approved location "in the presence of the LORD" (12:7). The land is his, and everything they do is before him (cf. 12:18, 25, 28).

8–12 From the time of their departure from Sinai until Yahweh settles them in the Promised Land, there will be a certain ad hoc quality to their worship. Although some compare the phrase "everyone as he sees fit" to a similar statement in Judges (17:6; 21:25—during a time of moral anarchy), it is unlikely that this clause signifies total anarchy in Israel's worship practices. In the light of their unsettled existence, however, this period in Israel's history was characterized by more freedom in the details of worship. This passage envisions a time when the nation will experience a relative degree of peace and will be able to bring more order and consistency to their worship of Yahweh (12:10). Once that happens, the Lord will require that his people bring their offerings and sacrifices to the place where he causes his name to dwell. The worship and rejoicing commanded by Moses here (see Note on 16:11) must include their own families, their servants, and the Levites (who will not receive a landed tribal inheritance; 12:12).

13–14 Reemphasizing his exhortation earlier in the chapter, Moses reminds the Israelites that they must not conduct their worship as the Canaanites did by worshiping wherever they please. God's covenantal nation must offer their sacrifices at one kind of a place: a place that Yahweh chooses.

15–28 With some repetition, 12:15–19 and 12:20–25 address an issue occasioned by Israel's future settled existence in the Promised Land. After they settle in their tribal inheritances at various distances from the central sanctuary (the tabernacle and eventually the temple), how should they to deal with slaughtering animals for meat if they live a significant distance away? According to Leviticus 17:1–6, oxen, lambs, and goats killed for consumption could be eaten only after certain sacrificial rituals (with those animals) took place at the tabernacle. The intention of this requirement was to prevent the people from making idolatrous sacrifices away from the Israelite encampment (Lev 17:7). Regardless, wild animals caught by hunting could be killed and consumed without this limitation (as long as their blood was properly drained—17:13; cf. 1:2), since they were nonsacrificial animals.

In a post-conquest setting, Moses allows the Israelites who live some distance from the central sanctuary to slaughter and eat "sacrificial" animals as though they were not "sacrificial" animals ("as if it were [i.e., as you would] gazelle or deer"; 12:15, 22). Further, the ceremonial purity of the person who desires to eat the meat is inconsequential (12:16, 22).

However, anyone presenting tithes, firstborn animals, vow offerings, freewill offerings, or special gifts (see Note on 12:6), i.e., sacrifices from which they would receive a share for personal consumption, must do so at the central sanctuary (12:17–18, 26). This requirement ensures that God's people will periodically worship and rejoice together at the central sanctuary. Whenever this unifying event takes place, the entire family, their servants, and the Levites are to participate in the celebration (12:18–19). A key regulation placed on God's people, whether they slaughter an animal away from or at the central sanctuary, is that they pour the blood of the slain animal on the ground (12:16, 23–25; cf. 12:27) because "the blood is the life" (12:23).

Some scholars refer to the slaughter of animals away from the central sanctuary as "profane" or "secular" slaughter; but it might be better to view this allowance as "nonsacrificial" slaughter (Vogt, 209). Yahweh desires that even in this act his people recognize that their presence in the land and their enjoyment of its abundance is a consequence of his faithfulness to them. By obeying God in each of these areas, they are demonstrating their loyalty to him. To consume the blood in violation of this requirement is viewed as covenantal treachery (12:25). Moses exhorts Israel diligently to obey "all these regulations" (12:28). The fact that their continued prosperity in the land is at stake reveals that their obedience is not profane in orientation but covenantal.

NOTES

5 The translation "you are to seek" (תִּדְרְשׁוּ, *tidrešû*; GK 2011) the place God chooses does not do justice to the combination of the verb "to seek" with the preposition "to" (אֶל, *'el*). Although the verb *drš* can mean "to seek" or "to inquire" (Denninger, *NIDOTTE*, 1:993), when used with this preposition it signifies "turning to" or "choosing" God (Job 5:8; Isa 8:19b), idols (Isa 19:3), or false religious intermediaries (Dt 18:11; Isa 8:19a). In the present verse, "seek" does not mean that the people should find the identity of this place, but that they "should decide to resort to Yahweh's place of worship, as a deliberate choice of him and rejection of the other nation's gods" (McConville, 219).

5, 14 A fundamental interpretive crux in ch. 12 concerns the issue of "centralization"; that is, does this chapter establish something brand new by mandating worship at only one place (הַמָּקוֹם, *hammāqôm*, "the place")? Scholars have proposed three major views (with some variety).

(1) This chapter may require God's people to have *one altar at Jerusalem*. Proponents of this view connect the message of ch. 12 to centralization of worship in Josiah's day (since they date the composition of Deuteronomy to that general period). During the reign of the kings preceding Josiah, pagan altars had multiplied throughout Israel's territory. This chapter demands that an Israelite offer sacrifices only at the approved sanctuary in Jerusalem. Critical scholars generally hold some version of this position (e.g., Driver, 140–45; Weinfeld, *Deuteronomy 1–11*, 76–77). Without any connection at all to the critical assumptions of the preceding view, some evangelicals affirm that ch. 12 looks forward to the establishment of a central sanctuary after Israel enjoys "rest" in the land—something that did not take place until the reign of Solomon (T. Longman III, *Immanuel in Our Place* [Phillipsburg, N.J.: Presbyterian & Reformed, 2001], 39–45). Prior to that time, multiple altars were permissible.

(2) Ch. 12 may look forward to the establishment of a single sanctuary at Jerusalem, but until then it mandates that sacrifices to Yahweh be offered at the one and only approved location in existence at a given time (*only one altar at a time*). As the tabernacle was relocated from place to place, the new erection site for the tabernacle became that one site for acceptable sacrifices to Yahweh (e.g., Craigie, 217; McConville, 220; Ridderbos, 153–55; Thompson, 166–67; Vogt, 185–86).

(3) Along with an emphasis on a central sanctuary (whose location varied until Solomon built the temple in Jerusalem), this chapter could envision *only those locations that are undeniably devoted to worship of Yahweh* (J. Neihaus, "The Central Sanctuary: Where and When?" *TynBul* 43 [1992]: 5–20; G. Wenham, "Deuteronomy and the Central Sanctuary," *TynBul* 22 [1971]: 109–16). Wenham points out a key distinction between the idea of a *central* sanctuary and a *sole* sanctuary. This passage does envision a general norm of one primary location for sacrifice at any given time. However, its prime concern is not to mandate a single centralized location without exception, but to prohibit syncretism. The real thrust of ch. 12 is not so much to centralize worship as it is to eliminate idolatry and guard against syncretism. In other words, these verses focus on the character or nature of the altar's location rather than on the number of permissible altar locations (e.g., Averbeck, *NIDOTTE*, 2:893–96; Merrill, *Deuteronomy*, 223–24). The historical books provide numerous examples of acceptable offerings made at locations other than the central sanctuary (see passages cited at 12:5–7). Most of the altars and sacrifices identified as apart from the central sanctuary were generally for special purposes and not in violation of Deuteronomy 12:5 (Niehaus, "The Central Sanctuary," 15).

6 The sacrificial terms in this verse are only some of those delineated in Leviticus 1–7. "Burnt offerings" (עוֹלָה, ʿōlâ) and "sacrifices" (זֶבַח, zebaḥ), both of which words occur in the phrase עֹלֹתֵיכֶם וְזִבְחֵיכֶם (ʿōlōtêkem wᵉzibḥêkem, "your burnt offerings and sacrifices"), often appear together as a broad reference to the OT sacrificial system (Averbeck, *NIDOTTE*, 1:1070). In a burnt offering, the entire animal was consumed by fire on the altar, but in a "sacrifice" only the fat was burned. (The priest and worshiper [and family] were allowed to eat the rest of the animal [cf. Lev 1–7].)

"Vows" (נֶדֶר, nēder) involved offerings given as part of a vow made earlier, and "special gifts" (תְּרוּמָה, tᵉrûmâ; lit., "offering of your hand") represented a voluntary expression of devotion or gratitude (cf. Lev 7:14, 32; 22:12). "Tithes" (מַעֲשֵׂר, maʿᵃśēr) refers to an offering of 10 percent of a worshiper's agricultural abundance (Dt 14:22–29), while "freewill offerings" (נְדָבָה, nᵉdābâ) involved additional gifts

(12:6, 17). "Firstborn" (בְּכֹר, *bᵉkōr*) refers to firstborn male oxen or sheep, which were sacrificed to God (15:19–23; cf. Nu 18:15–18). As Merrill (*Deuteronomy*, 223) points out, the tithe "should be viewed as tribute paid to the sovereign by his grateful and dependent servant" (cf. Lev 27:30–32; Nu 18:26, 28; Dt 14:23–25, 28).

11 The idiom לְשַׁכֵּן שְׁמוֹ שָׁם (*lᵉšakkēn šᵉmô šām*, "to make his name dwell") occurs seven times in the OT (Dt 12:11; 14:23; 16:2, 6, 11; 26:2; Ne 1:9). S. Richter ("The Deuteronomistic History and the Place of the Name" [Ph.D. diss., Harvard University, 2001], 243; cf. Vogt, 201) has observed that a cognate form of this construction was employed in ancient Near Eastern parallel texts to demonstrate the inscribing of someone's name on a victory stele or foundation stone. The purpose of this inscription was to demonstrate ownership, "victory," or even "to become famous by heroic deeds." Richter, 256, goes on to conclude that this phrase is especially appropriate in ch. 12 because "it emphasizes *yhwh*'s role as conquering king by communicating hegemony in the context of kingship, allegiance in the context of sovereignty, and fame due to battles won ... [it] serves as a shorthand reference to the historical prologue of Israel's covenant with her God which served as the theological catalyst for the proper cultic behavior."

(d) No God but Yahweh: Do not imitate worship of false gods (12:29–31)

²⁹The LORD your God will cut off before you the nations you are about to invade and dispossess. But when you have driven them out and settled in their land, ³⁰and after they have been destroyed before you, be careful not to be ensnared by inquiring about their gods, saying, "How do these nations serve their gods? We will do the same." ³¹You must not worship the LORD your God in their way, because in worshiping their gods, they do all kinds of detestable things the LORD hates. They even burn their sons and daughters in the fire as sacrifices to their gods.

COMMENTARY

29–31 After reminding the Israelites of Yahweh's part in conquering of Canaan (namely, that he will "cut off" the nations), Moses again looks to a future day when the Israelites will have driven out the Canaanites, destroyed them, and settled in the land (12:29b–30a). At that time, they must be careful not to become enticed by the Canaanite ways of worshiping their gods. In direct contrast to 12:4, where Moses commands, "you must not [do thus]," the hypothetical future Israelites affirm, "we will do [thus]" (12:30).

Rather than giving careful consideration to pagan worship practices, Moses prohibits God's covenantal subjects from worshiping Yahweh in accordance with Canaanite practices. These pagan practices are an "abomination" (*tôʿēbâ*) to Yahweh, something he despises or hates (see Note on 7:25–26). The depravity of their abhorrent worship practices finds its epitome in their custom of sacrificing their children to a pagan god (12:31; see Note).

NOTE

31 The practice of sacrificing one's children to a pagan god (described here as יִשְׂרְפוּ בָאֵשׁ, *yiśrᵉpû bāʾēš*, "they burn with fire") is attested in various ancient Near Eastern cultures, especially in Phoenicia (G. Heider, *The Cult of Molek: A Reassessment* [JSOTSup 43; Sheffield: Sheffield Academic Press, 1985], 174–94, 196–203; cf. *ABD*, 4:895–97). The fact that the OT harshly condemns this practice indicates that at different times the Israelites committed this awful treachery (Lev 18:21; Jer 7:31; 19:4–6; 32:35; Eze 23:37; Ps 106:37–38; cf. Wright, *God's People*, 231–35). Biblical historians indict Ahaz (2Ki 16:3 [= 2Ch 28:3]), Manasseh (21:6), and the northern kingdom (17:17–18) for performing this act. Apparently, the Moabites appropriated the practice of child sacrifice from the Canaanites (J. Day, *Molech: A God of Human Sacrifice in the Old Testament*, University of Cambridge Oriental Publications 41 [Cambridge: Cambridge Univ. Press, 1989], 31). Although not all scholars agree (e.g., Tigay, *Deuteronomy*, 464–65), both the present passage as well as those that speak of causing a child to "pass through" the fire refer to child sacrifice (Heider, *The Cult of Molek*, 258–73; Day, *Molech*, 67–68). The other way to understand the latter expression is "make pass over to a deity by means of a fire," i.e., as an act of dedication.

(e) Closing statement (12:32 [13:1])

> ³²See that you do all I command you; do not add to it or take away from it.

COMMENTARY

32 [13:1] Moses ends this section where he began, by exhorting the Israelites genuinely to obey all that God demands of them. Since God's covenantal stipulations are both of paramount importance and sufficient, Israel must not alter them in any way. What God expects of his covenantal people is not open to debate or up for negotiation (see Note on 4:2).

ii. Purge all idolatrous practices (and practitioners) from your midst (13:1–18 [2–19])

> ¹If a prophet, or one who foretells by dreams, appears among you and announces to you a miraculous sign or wonder, ²and if the sign or wonder of which he has spoken

takes place, and he says, "Let us follow other gods" (gods you have not known) "and let us worship them," ³you must not listen to the words of that prophet or dreamer. The LORD your God is testing you to find out whether you love him with all your heart and with all your soul. ⁴It is the LORD your God you must follow, and him you must revere. Keep his commands and obey him; serve him and hold fast to him. ⁵That prophet or dreamer must be put to death, because he preached rebellion against the LORD your God, who brought you out of Egypt and redeemed you from the land of slavery; he has tried to turn you from the way the LORD your God commanded you to follow. You must purge the evil from among you.

⁶If your very own brother, or your son or daughter, or the wife you love, or your closest friend secretly entices you, saying, "Let us go and worship other gods" (gods that neither you nor your fathers have known, ⁷gods of the peoples around you, whether near or far, from one end of the land to the other), ⁸do not yield to him or listen to him. Show him no pity. Do not spare him or shield him. ⁹You must certainly put him to death. Your hand must be the first in putting him to death, and then the hands of all the people. ¹⁰Stone him to death, because he tried to turn you away from the LORD your God, who brought you out of Egypt, out of the land of slavery. ¹¹Then all Israel will hear and be afraid, and no one among you will do such an evil thing again.

¹²If you hear it said about one of the towns the LORD your God is giving you to live in ¹³that wicked men have arisen among you and have led the people of their town astray, saying, "Let us go and worship other gods" (gods you have not known), ¹⁴then you must inquire, probe and investigate it thoroughly. And if it is true and it has been proved that this detestable thing has been done among you, ¹⁵you must certainly put to the sword all who live in that town. Destroy it completely, both its people and its livestock. ¹⁶Gather all the plunder of the town into the middle of the public square and completely burn the town and all its plunder as a whole burnt offering to the LORD your God. It is to remain a ruin forever, never to be rebuilt. ¹⁷None of those condemned things shall be found in your hands, so that the LORD will turn from his fierce anger; he will show you mercy, have compassion on you, and increase your numbers, as he promised on oath to your forefathers, ¹⁸because you obey the LORD your God, keeping all his commands that I am giving you today and doing what is right in his eyes.

COMMENTARY

1–5 [2–6] Moses warns the Israelites about the dangerous threat posed by false prophets. (The next two units subsequently refer to idolatrous family members [13:6–11] and rebellious groups [13:12–18].) Each group in view here encourages God's people to practice idolatry, which constitutes the danger. The importance of Yahweh's demand for absolute loyalty (ch. 12) is apparent in the face of competition for that loyalty.

A prophet was a divine spokesman (cf. Ex 4:15–16; 7:1), and the OT provides examples of God's revealing something to a prophetic figure by means of dreams (Ge 37:1–10; Nu 12:6). Even if the prophet in question is able to perform some miraculous deed and thereby authenticate (theoretically) his prophetic function (cf. Ex 4:8, 21; 7:3; 11:9–10; Dt 4:34; 6:22; 7:19; 26:8), if he exhorts the Israelites to worship pagan gods, the Israelites must refuse to do so. They must heed (smᶜ; 13:4) God rather than give ear (smᶜ; 13:3) to the message of the false prophet.

This set of circumstances represents a divine test (see Note on 8:2) to discern the status of Israel's heart, i.e., whether they love God wholeheartedly (live in absolute loyalty; see comments and Note on 6:5). Instead of following after pagan gods (hlk + ʾaḥᵃrê; 13:2), they should follow (hlk + ʾaḥᵃrê; 13:4) and revere Yahweh, keep his commands, obey and serve him, and hold fast to him (the longest collection of "covenantal" verbs in Deuteronomy). Because this (hypothetical) false prophet has preached rebellion and sought to turn the Israelites aside from Yahweh's way, he must be killed, thereby purging the evil from the covenantal nation. Such conduct was so abhorrent because it represented a rejection of the God who brought Israel out of and redeemed them from Egypt (cf. 7:8). The ultimate test that trumps all other prophetic tests is whether the prophet incites the covenantal people to rebel against their covenantal Lord.

6–11 [7–12] Moses turns from false prophets to family members as a potential source for treachery. A blood relative (brother, son, daughter), a beloved wife, or a dear friend—in fact, anyone who encourages an Israelite to worship any god, from any place, other than Yahweh (in direct opposition to the second commandment, see 5:7)—must be swiftly executed (see comment on 24:16). Especially in the light of Israel's social structure based on the extended family, one relative had significant potential to influence other relatives for evil or for good. But loyalty to God supersedes personal relationships (cf. Lk 14:26).

Moses warns God's people against two possible responses: paying attention to the enticements, or feeling sorry for the enticers and trying to protect them because of the fate they face (13:8). Instead, the one who hears a corrupt message must take the lead in putting the covenantal rebel to death by stoning. Along with other members of the community, this covenantally faithful relative must swiftly bring the divinely mandated punishment to bear on the corrupt loved one or friend to prevent that corruption from spreading to others. Such obedience will cause others to think twice about heeding enticements to treachery by their relatives.

12–18 [13–19] The third potential case for religious seduction concerns a nearby village that is considering engaging in idolatry (the widest of the three examples in scale). The fact that this city was Yahweh's gift (13:12) to the Israelites makes this corruption even more detestable. Once a report is received that a town has turned to idolatry, a thorough investigation must be conducted to discern the accuracy of the report. If it proves true (nākôn) that the nearby town had embraced this detestable practice (tôᶜēbâ; see Note on 7:25–26), the faithful Israelites in that region were to exterminate *all* the inhabitants of that rebellious community. As they were commanded to do with the Canaanites, they were to devote everything (all livestock and property) in that town to destruction (ḥrm; see Note on 7:2b). If an Israelite town embraced Canaanite conduct, they were to suffer the divinely ordained fate of the Canaanites.

The destruction of the city represented a "whole offering" totally devoted to Yahweh, the covenantal Lord they had rejected. That destroyed town was never to be rebuilt. Such total obedience would occasion two sets of consequences. First, God would withdraw his promised expres-sion of wrath against his nation. Second, he would grant them the mercy (*rḥm*; see Note on 4:31) and increased numbers (see comments on 7:13–15) he promised to their ancestors, the patriarchs. By being vigilant against the seduction of idolatry, God's chosen people would be keeping his commands and doing what was covenantally right (13:18).

NOTES

1 [2] Both nouns in the phrase אוֹת אוֹ מוֹפֵת (*ʾōt ʾô môpēt*, "[miraculous] sign or wonder") refer to a supernatural act done to authenticate that the one performing it was a divine representative (Merrill, *Deuteronomy*, 231). Throughout Israel's history signs and wonders were performed either to impart truth (Ex 7:5, 17; Dt 4:34; 6:22; 7:19; 11:3; et al.) or to help the people witnessing these deeds to believe that Yahweh alone is God (4:35; Kruger, *NIDOTTE*, 1:332).

4 [5] Moses uses various "covenantal" verbs to refer to the multifaceted nature of Yahweh's expectations of his covenantal people. Notice the following collections of such terms:

6:13:	fear, serve, take oaths in his name
8:6:	observe, walk, revere
10:12–13:	fear, walk, love, serve, observe
10:19–20:	fear, serve, hold fast, take oaths in his name
11:1:	love, keep
11:13:	obey/hear, love, serve
11:22:	carefully observe, love, walk, hold fast
13:4–5:	follow, revere, keep, obey/hear, serve, hold fast
13:18:	obey/hear, keep, do what is right
19:9:	carefully follow, love, walk
30:16:	obey/hear, love, walk, keep
30:20:	love, obey/listen, hold fast

5 [6] In Deuteronomy, the verb בָּעַר (*bʿr*, "to burn"), used in the phrase וּבִעַרְתָּ הָרָע מִקִּרְבֶּךָ (*ûbiʿartā hārāʿ miqqirbekā*, "you must purge the evil in your midst"), occurs in six passages (nine times) with רַע (*raʿ*, "evil") as its object. It always occurs in passages that require the death penalty and delineates the far-reaching impact of that penalty on the rest of Israel. By exterminating the guilty party, they "burn out" or remove the evil (and evil influence) from the midst of the covenantal nation as a sobering deterrent for others. The crimes whose evil must be purged from Israel include idolatry (13:5), holding priests in contempt (17:7, 12), malicious witness (19:18–19), unsolved murder (21:9), rebellion by a son (21:20–21), sexual immorality (22:21, 22, 24), and kidnapping (24:7). The authorities at a city of refuge are to hand over one who has committed premeditated murder to the relatives of his victim in order to purge "innocent blood" from the land (19:11–13).

8 [9] The two verbs in the phrase לֹא־תָחוֹס ... וְלֹא־תַחְמֹל (lōʾ-tāḥôs ... weʾlōʾ-taḥmōl, "show him no pity. Do not spare him") occur as a pair once in Deuteronomy (here) and seven times in other OT passages (Jer 21:7; Eze 5:11; 7:4, 9; 8:18; 9:5, 10). In every case outside Deuteronomy, Yahweh affirms that he will have no compassion on the nation of Israel in the light of their covenantal treachery. The verb חוס (ḥws; GK 2571) occurs eighteen times in the OT most often to depict God (Eze 5:11; 7:4, 9; 8:18; 9:10; 24:14) or his instrument of judgment (Jer 21:7) as having no compassion on his rebellious nation. According to Deuteronomy, the Israelites are not to have compassion for the Canaanites (7:16), a committer of premeditated murder (19:13), a false witness (19:21), or a woman who intervenes in a fight and crushes the testicles of her husband's opponent (25:12). Every occurrence of the word in Deuteronomy has "your eyes" as the subject, thus highlighting the fact that what one sees can sometimes trigger the emotion of pity or compassion. In Ezekiel 20:17 the "eye" serves as the subject of חוס (ḥws) to describe the feeling of compassion. The point of this command is that Yahweh did not want the Israelites to allow human emotion to prevent them from carrying out the penalty he had mandated. An "emotional" verdict constituted a corruption of divine justice (Butterworth, *NIDOTTE*, 2:51). The second verb, חמל (ḥml, "spare"; GK 2798), signifies holding back from an action that might be expected (Butterworth, *NIDOTTE*, 2:74). Yahweh allows for no hesitation in carrying out the required punishment.

11 [12] The verbal pair יִשְׁמְעוּ וְיִרָאוּן (yišmeʿû weʾyirāʾûn, "hear and fear") occurs four times in Deuteronomy to describe the far-reaching impact of such execution on the rest of Israel (cf. 17:13; 19:20; 21:21). It occurs twice in 31:12–13 to describe positive results. Israelites are to be gathered together for a national assembly so that they can hear and learn to fear Yahweh.

13 [14] Although scholars debate the etymology of the term "worthlessness" (בְּלִיַּעַל, beʾlîyaʿal; GK 1175), its usage in the OT is clear. It refers to a person who has become so corrupt and wicked that he is a detriment to society (Wegner, *NIDOTTE*, 1:662). This person is characterized by rebellion against authority and social order. Although the noun does occur alone (2Sa 23:6; Job 34:18; Pr 19:28), it normally belongs to a nominal phrase and is joined by "sons of," "daughters of," or "men of." Proverbs 6:12 parallels the phrase "worthless person" with the phrase "wicked man" (NASB), thereby equating the two. The conduct of a "worthless man" strikes at the moral fabric of any society. This descriptive phrase can refer to a person who is good for nothing in general, such as Nabal (1Sa 25:17, 25) or some of David's men who did not want to share the spoils of battle with their exhausted compatriots (30:22).

Those who are willing to give false witness for whatever reason are regarded as men of worthlessness (1Ki 21:10, 13; cf. Pr 19:28). At times their worthless activity involves sexual deviation (Jdg 19:22; 20:13). However, with regard to the sons of Eli, not only did they rape women in the tabernacle area, but they also "had no regard for Yahweh" (1Sa 2:12). Worthless men sometimes attempted to undermine Israel's monarchy (1Sa 10:27; 2Sa 16:7; 20:1; 2Ch 13:7). Such people can plot evil and have destructive speech (like a scorching fire; Pr 16:27). The worthless man seeks to convince people to worship false gods instead of the only true God (Dt 13:13). A "son of worthlessness" violates basic social order, undermines the monarchy, mocks moral standards, and cares nothing about genuine worship of Yahweh (Grisanti, "1 Samuel," 125).

b. Daily Implications of Bearing Yahweh's Name (14:1–21)

OVERVIEW

This pericope begins and ends with a focus on Israel's identity as God's "children" (14:1), a people "holy to the Lord" (14:2, 21). This repeated emphasis forms an inclusio (the repetition of a theme or an explicit statement "enveloping" the passage) that highlights the theme of the entire section, namely, the impact of a holy identity on daily life. The practices delineated in the ensuing verses are not holy themselves but were ordained by Yahweh to mark out Israel more clearly from the pagan nations around them.

In addition to this, these mirroring statements (concerning Israel's identity) at the beginning and end of the passage may suggest an answer for the placement of the practices addressed in 14:1–2 and 21b. Reference to mourning practices and cooking a kid in its mother's milk appears to be out of place in juxtaposition to regulations dealing with clean and unclean food. They may both represent pagan practices that the Israelites were to avoid to maintain their distinctiveness.

i. Mourning practices (14:1–2)

¹You are the children of the Lord your God. Do not cut yourselves or shave the front of your heads for the dead, ² for you are a people holy to the Lord your God. Out of all the peoples on the face of the earth, the Lord has chosen you to be his treasured possession.

COMMENTARY

1–2 In emphatic grammatical fashion (with the nouns "children/sons" and "holy people" beginning both clauses), Moses gives attention to Israel's identity as God's covenantal nation. As their father, Yahweh had cared for them (1:31) and disciplined them (8:5). Verse 1 emphasizes the duty of Israel to obey their Father's will (the other side of the parent-child relationship). The next verse emphasizes the depth of that special covenantal relationship in a nearly exact quotation of 7:6 (see comments and Notes there).

Because of their identity, God's chosen people need to manifest their distinctiveness by avoiding all pagan mourning practices. They are prohibited from self-mutilation (Jer 16:6; 41:5; 47:5; cf. Lev 19:27–28) and shaving the front part of their heads (see Note). The prophets of Baal repeatedly cut themselves as a means of inciting Baal to action (1Ki 18:28; cf. Zec 13:4–6). For examples of this pagan conduct in Ugarit, see the comments of Craigie, 229–30, and T. Lewis (*Cults of the Dead in Ancient Israel and Ugarit* [HSM 39; Atlanta, Ga.:

Scholars, 1989], 100–101). God demanded that Israel not cloud their identity as his special possession by accepting practices that had clear pagan connotations.

NOTE

1 The prohibition וְלֹא־תָשִׂימוּ קָרְחָה בֵּין עֵינֵיכֶם (wᵉlōʾ-tāśîmû qorḥâ bên ʿênêkem, "or shave the front of your heads"), i.e., of making one's forehead bald (lit., "do not place baldness between your eyes") echoes a similar requirement made of the priests (Lev 21:5). The fact that such shaving was done "for the dead" (14:1b) indicates that such conduct was part of some pagan practice (the precise significance of which is unclear). Shaving the head or pulling hair out was apparently associated with mourning (Isa 15:2; Jer 47:5). The fact that other passages mention the practice indicates that the Israelites did not always heed this prohibition (Isa 3:24; Jer 16:6; 48:37; Eze 7:18; 27:31; Mic 1:16).

The fact that Yahweh calls for baldness (Isa 22:12) and threatens to make Israel bald (Am 8:10) introduces a unique twist to the question. Why does God call for something he condemns? On the one hand, it could be that Yahweh simply uses the vocabulary of mourning without necessarily approving a pagan practice. On the other hand, one might need to distinguish between intentional actions as part of a pagan practice and impetuous actions by a grieving person without association with godless customs (Milgrom, *Leviticus 17–22*, 1802).

ii. The distinction between clean and unclean food (14:3–21)

³Do not eat any detestable thing. ⁴These are the animals you may eat: the ox, the sheep, the goat, ⁵the deer, the gazelle, the roe deer, the wild goat, the ibex, the antelope and the mountain sheep. ⁶You may eat any animal that has a split hoof divided in two and that chews the cud. ⁷However, of those that chew the cud or that have a split hoof completely divided you may not eat the camel, the rabbit or the coney. Although they chew the cud, they do not have a split hoof; they are ceremonially unclean for you. ⁸The pig is also unclean; although it has a split hoof, it does not chew the cud. You are not to eat their meat or touch their carcasses.

⁹Of all the creatures living in the water, you may eat any that has fins and scales. ¹⁰But anything that does not have fins and scales you may not eat; for you it is unclean.

¹¹You may eat any clean bird. ¹²But these you may not eat: the eagle, the vulture, the black vulture, ¹³the red kite, the black kite, any kind of falcon, ¹⁴any kind of raven, ¹⁵the horned owl, the screech owl, the gull, any kind of hawk, ¹⁶the little owl, the great owl, the white owl, ¹⁷the desert owl, the osprey, the cormorant, ¹⁸the stork, any kind of heron, the

hoopoe and the bat. [19] All flying insects that swarm are unclean to you; do not eat them. [20] But any winged creature that is clean you may eat. [21] Do not eat anything you find already dead. You may give it to an alien living in any of your towns, and he may eat it, or you may sell it to a foreigner. But you are a people holy to the LORD your God. Do not cook a young goat in its mother's milk.

COMMENTARY

3 Since the Israelites have been chosen to be Yahweh's holy people, Moses asserts that they are not to eat unclean birds, animals, or fish and calls them "detestable" (see Note on 7:25–26).

4–20 Moses employs the same categories found in Leviticus 11:1–23, in accordance with the animals' primary habitats — land (vv.4–8), water (vv.9–10), and air (vv.11–20; cf. the creation account in Ge 1:20–25). A number of the creatures referred to in these verses are difficult to identify exactly. For some helpful suggestions, see Milgrom (*Leviticus 1–16,* 645–67) and Driver, 159–63.

Scholars have long debated the rationale or underlying principles that gave rise to the animals designated as clean and unclean. (For a helpful overview of these alternatives, see J. Moskala, who discusses fourteen views in "Categorization and Evaluation of Different Kinds of Interpretation of the Laws of Clean and Unclean Animals in Leviticus 11," *BR* 46 [2001]: 5–41; J. Sprinkle, who cites seven views in "The Rationale of the Laws of Clean and Unclean in the Old Testament," *JETS* 43 [2000]: 645–54; Wenham, *Leviticus,* 166–71.) The various alternatives can be grouped under five headings: arbitrary, cultic, hygienic, sacrificial, and symbolic.

(1) *Arbitrary.* Some scholars have proposed that one cannot find a rationale that explains all the animals in the unclean realm, so that the distinc-

tion between clean and unclean animals is relatively arbitrary. Just as Yahweh's choice of Israel is without final explanation (Dt 7:7–8), so his choice of clean and unclean animals cannot be fully fathomed (cf. Merrill, *Deuteronomy,* 236, n. 39). Even though other ancient Near Eastern nations may have regarded various animals as unclean, what Yahweh asked of his covenantal nation was unique.

(2) *Cultic.* Others scholars have connected these distinctions to pagan cultic practices (e.g., M. Noth, *The Laws in the Pentateuch and Other Studies* [Edinburgh: Oliver & Boyd, 1966], 56–60). A key problem with this view is that Israel used most of the same animals for sacrifices as her pagan neighbors did (G. Wenham, "The Theology of Unclean Food," *EvQ* 53 [1981]: 7).

(3) *Hygienic.* Yet another a popular rationale suggests that the dietary laws promote good health (R. L. Harris, "Leviticus," in EBC[1], 2:528–30; R. K. Harrison, *Leviticus* [TOTC; Downers Grove, Ill.: InterVarsity Press, 1980], 124–26). But God's withdrawal of these dietary limitations in the NT (Ac 10:9–16) does not give the sense that he is thereby encouraging his children to eat unhealthy food. Certain health benefits may have been a by-product or result of these dietary regulations, but they do not seem to provide the rationale for them.

(4) *Sacrificial.* W. Houston has proposed that since only certain animals were fit to be offered

as sacrifices to Yahweh, faithful Israelites were to restrict their diet to those animals (*Purity and Monotheism: Clean and Unclean Animals in Biblical Law* [JSOTSup 140; Sheffield: JSOT, 1993]; cf. E. Firmage, "The Biblical Dietary Laws and the Concept of Holiness," in *Studies in the Pentateuch* [ed. J. Emerton; Leiden: Brill, 1990], 177–208).

(5) *Symbolic.* Finally, various symbolic explanations have been offered over the years (see Wenham, "Theology of Unclean Food," 8–9, and Hartley, 143, for some of the suggested symbolic explanations). Mary Douglas (*Purity and Danger* [London: Routledge and Kegan Paul, 1966], 41–57; idem, "The Abominations of Leviticus," in *Anthropological Approaches to the Old Testament* [ed. B. Lang; Philadelphia: Fortress, 1985], 100–16) has proposed a symbolic understanding based on anthropological studies that several scholars have found commendable (W. Bellinger, *Leviticus* [NIBC; Peabody, Mass.: Hendrickson, 2001], 9–10, 72; P. Budd, *Leviticus* [NCBC; Grand Rapids: Eerdmans, 1996], 159–60; Hartley, 144–46; Wenham, *Leviticus,* 23–25, 168–71; Wright, *Deuteronomy*, 185–86). She suggests that holiness involves more than separation from evil but also includes the positive concepts of wholeness and integrity. Any anomaly in that wholeness causes uncleanness. The animal world can be divided into three realms: those that fly in the air, those that walk on the land, and those that swim in the sea (cf. Ge 1:20–30). Any animals that do not conform to the customary features of each division are regarded as unclean (e.g., insects that fly like birds but have four legs like land animals, fish without fins and scales, the regular means of locomotion).

Although Douglas's proposal deserves attention, like others it fails to answer certain questions. For example, why must the hoofs of a land animal be split for it to be considered pure? J. Moskala has sought to connect the distinctions between

clean and unclean to the creation ideal of life. Unclean animals are linked to death for various reasons, including their carnivorous diets, use in war, and hygienic dangers (*The Laws of Clean and Unclean Animals of Leviticus 11* [Berrien Springs, Mich.: Adventist Theological Society, 2000], 315–48; cf. idem, "Dietary Laws in Leviticus 11 and Creation," in *Creation, Life, and Hope: Essays in Honor of Jacques B. Doukhan* [ed. J. Moskala; Berrien Springs, Mich.: Andrews Univ. Press, 2000], 17–28).

Milgrom (*Leviticus 1–16*, 722) has developed the concept of holiness as the rationale for these regulations and made the following comparison: All animals, clean animals (fewer), and sacrificial animals (fewest), correspond to humankind, the nation of Israel, and Israel's priests, respectively. The dietary system delineated in Leviticus 11 and Deuteronomy 14 would teach the Israelites reverence for life by "(1) reducing his choice of flesh to a few animals; (2) limiting the slaughter of even these few permitted animals to the most humane way ... and (3) prohibiting the ingestion of blood ... as acknowledgement that bringing death to living things is a concession of God's grace and not a privilege of man's whim" (735).

Only land animals that both chewed the cud and had cloven hooves were acceptable for the Israelites to eat (Dt 14:4–8). An animal that possessed only one of these features was to be regarded as unclean. Even touching the carcass of an unclean animal was prohibited. Marine creatures had to possess both fins and scales to be fit for consumption by an Israelite (14:9–10). This requirement left available a limited variety of fishes. The category of birds presents the most complicated section of unclean animals (14:11–18). These verses list twenty-one species or subspecies, some of which are difficult to identify. By way of observation, most of the unclean birds are carnivores that consume other dead animals. This list concludes with the insect world (14:19–20) and declares off-limits all insects that swarm. Without providing any specifics, this passage affirms that Israelites could eat any clean insect or bird. Leviticus 11:20–23 provides more information by dividing the entymological world into those insects that walk on all fours (forbidden) and those that have jointed legs for hopping (permitted).

In Acts 10:9–16 (cf. 11:4–10), Peter's vision of various unclean animals and God's encouragement of him to eat any of those animals indicates that maintaining the unclean/clean distinction was not required of believers after Christ's death. The animals Peter saw were no longer unclean. The Lord had made clean (pure) what had been unclean (Ac 10:15; 11:9). This significant shift is related to the transition from a focus on the nation of Israel to the church, where there is "neither Jew nor Greek, slave nor free, male nor female, for you are all one in Christ Jesus" (Gal 3:28).

21 Regardless of an animal's status as clean or unclean, the Israelites could not eat the meat of any animal they found already dead. They were allowed to give it to one of the "aliens" (non-Israelites who lived in the midst of them) or sell it to a foreigner. As this paragraph began, so does it conclude, namely, by prohibiting the Israelites from appropriating any pagan practices, including cooking a young goat in its mother's milk.

NOTES

21b The difficult statement לֹא־תְבַשֵּׁל גְּדִי בַּחֲלֵב אִמּוֹ (lōʾ-tᵉbaššēl gᵉdî baḥᵃlēb ʾimmô, "Do not cook a young goat in its mother's milk"; cf. Ex 23:19; 34:26) has occasioned scholarly debate for centuries. Some scholars (Craigie, 232–33; McConville, 251; Merrill, *Deuteronomy*, 239; Wright, *Deuteronomy*, 186) regard it as an allusion to a Canaanite fertility rite (based on a fragmentary Ugaritic text). The Ugaritic evidence cited in favor of this view is debatable (Ratner and Zuckerman, "'A Kid in Milk'? New Photographs of *KTU* 1.23, Line 14," *HUCA* 57 [1986]: 46–52). Regardless of whether or not this Ugaritic text provides a backdrop for the practice addressed in 14:21, the inclusio (see above) that bounds this passage favors the idea that a pagan custom is in view.

Other scholars regard the issue as ethical or humanitarian. To cook a young goat in its mother's milk would be cruel and savage (cf. Lev 22:28; Dt 22:6–7; U. Cassuto, *A Commentary on the Book of Exodus* (Jerusalem: Magnes, 1967), 305; Haran, "Seething A Kid in Its Mother's Milk," *JJS* 30 [1979]: 29–30; Tigay, *Deuteronomy*, 140; cf. Sasson, "Should Cheeseburgers Be Kosher?" *BR* 19 [December 2003]: 50, for a variation of this view).

A final interpretation focuses on the symbolism of the act. It seems improper to use lifegiving milk as a cause of death (Knauf, "Zur Herkunft und Sozialgeschichte Israels: 'Das Böckchen in der Milch seiner Mutter,'" *Bib* 69 [1988]: 153–54; Ridderbos, 176). Although I prefer the first alternative, one's conclusion must be tentative. All three references to this condemned practice occur in contexts devoted to rituals, festivals, and offerings (Ex 23:19; 34:26; Dt 14:21b). In the light of that contextual emphasis, the boiling of a young goat in its mother's milk was likely rooted in pagan festival practices. For some reason, it had become especially abhorrent to Yahweh and represented the epitome of evil (Merrill, *Deuteronomy*, 239).

c. Tribute for Yahweh, the Covenantal Lord (14:22–16:17)

OVERVIEW

Moses now delineates stipulations that concern periodic obligations and institutions: tithing (14:22–29), sabbatical years (15:1–18), firstlings (15:19–23), and the three annual pilgrim festivals (16:1–17). In line with suzerain–vassal relationships in the ancient Near East in which the vassal regularly rendered tribute to the suzerain, Israel is to demonstrate their submission to their covenantal Lord by providing tribute. This tribute will not "purchase" anything for them but instead represents their gratitude for the benefits provided to them by the Sovereign.

i. Tithes (14:22–29)

²²Be sure to set aside a tenth of all that your fields produce each year. ²³Eat the tithe of your grain, new wine and oil, and the firstborn of your herds and flocks in the presence of the LORD your God at the place he will choose as a dwelling for his Name, so that you may learn to revere the LORD your God always. ²⁴But if that place is too distant and you have been blessed by the LORD your God and cannot carry your tithe (because the place where the LORD will choose to put his Name is so far away), ²⁵then exchange your tithe for silver, and take the silver with you and go to the place the LORD your God will choose. ²⁶Use the silver to buy whatever you like: cattle, sheep, wine or other fermented drink, or anything you wish. Then you and your household shall eat there in the presence of the LORD your God and rejoice. ²⁷And do not neglect the Levites living in your towns, for they have no allotment or inheritance of their own.

²⁸At the end of every three years, bring all the tithes of that year's produce and store it in your towns, ²⁹so that the Levites (who have no allotment or inheritance of their own) and the aliens, the fatherless and the widows who live in your towns may come and eat and be satisfied, and so that the LORD your God may bless you in all the work of your hands.

COMMENTARY

22–23 Building on other tithing passages (Ge 14:20; 28:22; Lev 27:30–32; Nu 18:21–28), Moses commands the children of Israel to set aside one-tenth of their produce (grain, new wine, and oil) and the firstborn of their herds and flocks each year and devote them to the Lord. As families, they will eat from that "tithe" in the central sanctuary ("at the place he will choose"; see comments on

12:5–7). The pedagogical purpose for this practice is to teach God's chosen people to fear him always (cf. 4:10; 17:19). Their prosperity will not result from their irrigation or advanced agricultural techniques but is due to Yahweh's fixed commitment to his covenantal promises (Craigie, 233). This abundance will not be caused by Canaan's fertility god but by the one and only God of the world, Israel's marvelous God.

24–27 Those who live too far from the central sanctuary (and thus face logistical challenges in bringing their livestock and tithe a long distance) have the opportunity to exchange their property for silver and bring the silver (the most common metal of exchange) to the central sanctuary. At that location they can purchase what they want to give to Yahweh as their tithe. The worshiper and his family as well as the priests and Levites at the sanctuary will eat part of what they have brought (or purchased). Their enjoying this banquet "in the presence of the LORD" implies that this act of tithing is indeed part of their worship of their faithful God. One can assume that they will not consume all that the many Israelite families have brought with them (ten percent of an Israelite's "production"). Even as they bring their tithes to the central sanctuary and celebrate God's abundant provision for them through this banquet, the Israelites must consider the needs of the Levites who serve Yahweh in their communities away from the central sanctuary.

28–29 In order to help care for these Levites, Yahweh mandates that every third year the Isra-

elites direct their tithe to the Levites in their local community as well as for the benefit of the alien, fatherless, and widows (the triennial tithe). This loving care for the needy in their midst manifests a genuine commitment to enacting God's desire for justice and equity among the members of his servant-nation. God promises to bless sincere conformity to his covenantal expectations.

Rabbinic writings refer to three kinds of tithes (Tigay, *Deuteronomy*, 141–42; Averbeck, *NIDOTTE*, 2:1052–53): a "first" tithe given to the Levites (Nu 18:1–28); a second tithe, part of which was eaten by the Israelites who offered their tithe to Yahweh (Lev 27:30–31; Dt 14:22–27); and a third tithe (for the poor) every third year (Dt 14:28–29). Other scholars contend that there were two distinct tithes, with the second tithe being an additional tithe sent to local Levites every third year (14:28–29; Merrill, *Deuteronomy*, 241). A number of scholars identify only one tithe. In that case, the triennial tithe was sent to the local communities *rather than* to the central sanctuary (Averbeck, *NIDOTTE*, 2:1047; G. McConville, *Law and Theology in Deuteronomy* [Sheffield: JSOT, 1984], 68–78; Ridderbos, 180; Thompson, 184). Although one must remain tentative in light of the limited evidence, the second option appears to be the most likely. The central sanctuary (and the priests and Levites serving there) would always have the same needs. It seems unlikely that they could have functioned without the tithe for a year. Also, the tithe referred to in 26:12–15 suggests a distinct tithe.

NOTES

26 The permission to bring money for purchasing one's animals and tithed items at the central sanctuary (וְנָתַתָּה הַכֶּסֶף, *weⁿātattâ hakkesep*, "use the silver to buy") provides the backdrop for Jesus' encounter with the moneychangers in the temple during his ministry (Mt 21:12–13; cf. Jn 2:13–16). Although God ordained this feature, the abuse of it by greedy profiteers occasioned Jesus' ousting them from the temple area.

29 Five passages in Deuteronomy affirm this truth that the Levites אֵין־לוֹ חֵלֶק וְנַחֲלָה עִמָּךְ (*ʾên-lô ḥēleq wᵉnaḥᵃlâ ʿimmāk*), "have no allotment or inheritance of their own" (10:9; 12:12; 14:27, 29; 18:1). Five other times they are listed with the aliens, fatherless, and widow (14:29; 16:11, 14; 26:12–13) or just the alien (26:11). All four categories of people are also said to be "in your towns" (12:12, 18; 14:27, 29; 16:11, 14; 26:12), which emphasizes their established presence in Israelite communities. The Levites and these other people at the fringe of Israelite society are absolutely dependent on their covenantal Lord and the justice and equity of his people for their continued existence.

ii. Sabbatical year—measures to protect the poor (15:1–18)

¹At the end of every seven years you must cancel debts. ²This is how it is to be done: Every creditor shall cancel the loan he has made to his fellow Israelite. He shall not require payment from his fellow Israelite or brother, because the LORD's time for canceling debts has been proclaimed. ³You may require payment from a foreigner, but you must cancel any debt your brother owes you. ⁴However, there should be no poor among you, for in the land the LORD your God is giving you to possess as your inheritance, he will richly bless you, ⁵if only you fully obey the LORD your God and are careful to follow all these commands I am giving you today. ⁶For the LORD your God will bless you as he has promised, and you will lend to many nations but will borrow from none. You will rule over many nations but none will rule over you.

⁷If there is a poor man among your brothers in any of the towns of the land that the LORD your God is giving you, do not be hardhearted or tightfisted toward your poor brother. ⁸Rather be openhanded and freely lend him whatever he needs. ⁹Be careful not to harbor this wicked thought: "The seventh year, the year for canceling debts, is near," so that you do not show ill will toward your needy brother and give him nothing. He may then appeal to the LORD against you, and you will be found guilty of sin. ¹⁰Give generously to him and do so without a grudging heart; then because of this the LORD your God will bless you in all your work and in everything you put your hand to. ¹¹There will always be poor people in the land. Therefore I command you to be openhanded toward your brothers and toward the poor and needy in your land.

¹²If a fellow Hebrew, a man or a woman, sells himself to you and serves you six years, in the seventh year you must let him go free. ¹³And when you release him, do not send him away empty-handed. ¹⁴Supply him liberally from your flock, your threshing floor and your winepress. Give to him as the LORD your God has blessed you. ¹⁵Remember that you were slaves in Egypt and the LORD your God redeemed you. That is why I give you this command today.

¹⁶But if your servant says to you, "I do not want to leave you," because he loves you and your family and is well off with you, ¹⁷then take an awl and push it through his ear lobe

into the door, and he will become your servant for life. Do the same for your maidservant. [18]Do not consider it a hardship to set your servant free, because his service to you these six years has been worth twice as much as that of a hired hand. And the LORD your God will bless you in everything you do.

COMMENTARY

1–6 At the end of every seven years (the sabbatical year), Yahweh requires his covenantal people to cancel all loans made with fellow Israelites. They are to forgive the loan totally at that point, regardless of the personal loss to themselves (Ex 23:10–11; Lev 25:2–4). However, they may continue receiving payments for their loans to foreigners.

Verses 4–6 provide the theological rationale for this divine mandate. In the land God is giving them as their divine inheritance (see Note on 1:38), the Lord will pour out his abundant covenantal blessings on them, and there should therefore be no poor Israelites. The key for that to be a reality (as it is throughout Deuteronomy) is that God's people "fully obey" and "diligently follow" (for this combination of verbs, see Note on 5:1) all of his requirements. If they genuinely obey Yahweh, they will experience his blessing.

The two areas specified in this passage are financial abundance (they will lend to many and not need to borrow from any) and sovereignty over the nations (cf. Dt 28:12–13). Chapter 28 specifies that disobedience will occasion covenantal curses, including financial disaster (they will not lend but will have to borrow; 28:44) and rule by other nations (28:25, 43, 49–52).

7–11 Knowing that this mandate might cause some Israelites to refuse making loans to needy fellow Israelites as the sabbatical year approaches, Moses demands that they do not allow this divine requirement to limit their lending practices. Rather than being hardhearted or tightfisted, they should be openhanded and lend willingly (15:8). A refusal to lend in that setting represents "wicked thought," "ill will," and "sin" (15:9). Because Yahweh is the one who provides them with all they possess, they need not worry. That the verb "to bless" (*brk*; GK 1385) occurs six times in this brief section (vv. 4 [2x], 6, 10, 14, 18; see Note on 7:13) clearly emphasizes God's role in their ability to even offer a loan.

12–18 Since poverty can lead to slavery or servanthood, this section provides an appropriate sequel to the forgiveness of loans (15:1–11; cf. Ex 21:2–11). Being unable to provide for oneself (or experiencing some other financial distress) could lead a person voluntarily to become a slave (an "indentured" servant) to obtain basic needs or to pay off a debt (cf. Lev 25:39–55; Ne 5:4–5). The length of time for this kind of slavery was six years. The master must release the slave in the seventh year (not necessarily the same as the sabbatical year) and in addition send the freed slave away with enough supplies to start a new life.

The master must "supply him liberally" (see second Note on 15:4) from every category of his resources (flock, threshing floor, and winepress) for at least two reasons. Because all the master has is a direct blessing from Yahweh, he will simply be sharing what God has given him. Also, since the Israelites were slaves in Egypt and experienced a unique provision of their needs from the Egyptians (pagans non-Israelites; Ex 12:35–36) they left behind, the

Israelites should be more than willing to treat their fellow Israelites with abundant generosity.

In certain instances, because of the insurmountable challenges of life before them if released or because of their love for ther master, slaves could commit themselves to lifelong servitude. In Exodus 21:5, the slave may have been married and had children during his term of servitude and did not want to leave them behind. The owner would formalize that decision by piercing the slave's ear lobe with an awl. Perhaps the ear was chosen because it is associated with hearing and hearing with obedience (Ridderbos, 184).

There is no good reason for the master to oppose the mandate to set a servant free, for all that the master has constitutes a blessing provided by Yahweh, and Yahweh will continue to provide for

his needs. Indeed, the master benefited from the work of this servant, worth "twice as much" as a hired hand (see text note) — he labored for six years without pay and was available around the clock, while a hired hand only worked certain hours, and for wages.

Throughout the OT, Israel's treatment of the poor, fatherless, and widows served as a barometer of the nation's conformity to Yahweh's covenantal expectations. Treating these needy people with compassion, justice, and equity was a fundamental part of being able to lift up God's name before the surrounding nations. The health of the covenantal nation was often measured by the quality of their care for these needy people, not by its accumulation of wealth (Hall, 257; Wright, *Deuteronomy*, 195).

NOTES

1 What is remitted or released in ch. 15? A key issue involves the question: Does the noun שְׁמִטָּה (*šᵉmiṭṭâ*, "remission" [GK 9024], with "of debt" being implied from the context) refer back to the same kind of practice as it does in Exodus 23:10–11 (cf. Lev 25:1–7)? In Exodus 23, when the land is "released" it is allowed to lie fallow for the year. Consequently, various scholars conclude that payment for a loan would be suspended for the sabbatical year, though the loan was not forgiven (Craigie, 236; Driver, 174–75; Keil, 3:369; McConville, 259–60; Ridderbos, 180–81). Others focus on the "pledges" that a lender would have taken possession of as collateral. According to that interpretation, the lender returns the "pledge" to the debtor, giving him access to whatever economic benefit might be produced for the sabbatical year (or until the next payment is due; Wright, *Deuteronomy*, 188; cf. Christopher Wright, "What Happened Every Seven Years in Israel? Old Testament Sabbatical Institutions for Land, Debt and Slaves," *EvQ* 56 (1984): 129–38, esp. 136–37; Wakely, *NIDOTTE*, 4:157–58). Nelson, 194–95, agrees that a release of the pledge is in view, but for him that is tantamount to making the debt uncollectible, i.e., an indirect way of canceling the debt.

A number of scholars affirm that the passage requires a lender to forgive the entire loan (Braulik, *Deuteronomium 1–16, 17*, 111; Cairns, 147; Christensen, *Deuteronomy 1:1–21:9*, 312; Hall, 250; J. M. Hamilton, *Social Justice and Deuteronomy: The Case of Deuteronomy 15* (SBLDS 136; Atlanta: Scholars, 1992), 16–18; Mayes, 247–48; Merrill, *Deuteronomy*, 243–44; Thompson, 186–87; Tigay, *Deuteronomy*, 144–45). Kaufman suggests that Deuteronomy 15 addresses a slightly different scenario than that envisioned in Exodus 23 (Stephen Kaufman, "A Reconstruction of Social Welfare Systems of Ancient Israel," in *In the Shelter of Elyon* [ed. W. B. Barrick and J. R. Spencer; JSOTSup 31; Sheffield: JSOT, 1984], 282). The fact that 15:2 reads "this is the nature of the remission" suggests that something new is introduced. If Exodus 23 was in view, there would be no need for an explanation. Although forgiving the remaining part of a loan would be more economically difficult for the lender, that seems to be the precise point of 15:7–11. Finally, the release of the Hebrew slaves in 15:12–18 was not temporary, for the sabbatical year only, but permanent. The economic "pain" of that practice was to have no impact on the Israelite masters' obedience.

4 The noun אֶבְיוֹן (ʾebyôn, "poor"; GK 36) occurs seven times in Deuteronomy (sixty-one times in the OT), six of which are in ch. 15 (4, 7 [2x], 9, 11 [2x]; cf. 24:14). One of six terms for the poor or oppressed, this noun signifies people who are virtually destitute—the day laborers of the ancient world, who were totally dependent on others for their daily survival (Domeris, *NIDOTTE*, 1:228). In legal and prophetic texts, this term signifies those who are exploited (Ex 23:6, 11; Jer 2:34; 5:28; Am 2:6; 4:1; 5:12). Throughout the Psalms, Yahweh is the deliverer of the ʾebyôn (Pss 9:18 [19]; 35:10; 40:17 [18]; 69:33 [34]; 70:5 [6]; 72:4, 12–13). A tension exists between the statement "there should be no poor among you" (15:4) and "there will always be poor people in the land" (15:11). Verse 5 points out that obedience to Yahweh's requirements will prevent the existence of poverty. Conversely, covenantal treachery leads to poverty in Israel. If the Israelites consistently lived out the dictates of 15:1–18, there indeed *would* be no poor among them.

The juxtaposition of an infinitive absolute and a finite verb of the same verbal root in the phrase בָּרֵךְ יְבָרֶכְךָ (bārēk yᵉbārekkā, "he will richly bless you") places increased emphasis on the verbal action (*IBHS*, 585–88, §§35.3.1a–i). Verse 4 ends with the declaration that Yahweh will surely or greatly bless Israel. The same construction occurs five other times in the passage to describe what Yahweh expects of his covenantal people. They must "fully obey" (15:5) Yahweh's instructions, "be openhanded" and "willingly" or "freely lend" (15:8), "give generously" (15:10), and "supply him liberally" (15:14). In accordance with the abundance of Yahweh's blessing, the Israelites are to obey their covenantal Lord and carry out his demands regarding the poor and needy.

11 The adjective עָנִי (ʿānî, "poor"; GK 6714) occurs four times in Deuteronomy (15:11; 24:12, 14–15; eighty times in the OT) and describes people who have no land of their own and, consequently, need economic protection (Domeris, *NIDOTTE*, 1:228). The word refers to someone who has been afflicted by some necessity or circumstance and stresses the difficulty and ongoing nature of the affliction. It never refers to deserved poverty and is always linked to those who have been exploited and wrongfully impoverished (Job 24:4; Ps 37:14; Isa 32:7; Dumbrell, *NIDOTTE*, 3:454–55). As with אֶבְיוֹן (ʾebyôn; 15:4), Yahweh is the defender of the ʿānî (10:17–18); his prophets exhorted Israel to treat these poor people justly (Isa 10:2; 58:7).

12 Some scholars regard הָעִבְרִי (hāʿibrî, "your brother, a Hebrew man"; NIV, "a fellow Hebrew") not as an ethic designator but as a socioeconomic term referring to a class of people who existed at the fringe of Israelite society (similar to the ʿapîru of the Amarna letters; Wright, *Deuteronomy*, 192). The ʿapîru were social outsiders who either harassed the people in power or sold their services to them. Proponents of this parallel suggest that, in general, non-Israelite outsiders used the term hāʿibrî to refer to Israelites (cf. Ge 14:13; 39:14, 17; 41:12; Ex 1:15–16, 19; 2:6–7, 11, 13; 1Sa 4:6; Jon 1:9). Although Thompson, 190, grants this interpretation as a possibility, he considers that Leviticus 25:39–55 might indicate that in view here is an Israelite who has chosen to become a slave (to repay a debt); and the parallel term, "your brother," may suggest an Israelite rather than a non-Israelite (Mayes, 250–51). Further, it is unlikely that Moses would address a set of laws to a marginal people who were not even Israelites. Perhaps this term was used "to remind Israel that when they were 'Hebrews,' that is, when they were in Egypt, they were slaves. Now that they are free they must not keep their fellow Israelites in economic bondage" (NET note).

18 The NRSV and certain scholars (e.g., Braulik, *Deuteronomium 1–16, 17*, 115; Craigie, 239; Mayes, 252–53) translate the noun מִשְׁנֶה (*mišneh*) as "equivalent to" rather than "twice as much as," based on the a supposed parallel term in texts from Alalaḫ. J. M. Lindenberger ("How Much for a Hebrew Slave? The Meaning of *Mišneh* in Deuteronomy 15:18," *JBL* 110 [1991]: 479–82, esp. 481–82) has demonstrated the unlikelihood of this Akkadian term's serving as the backdrop for the Hebrew word here.

iii. Firstborn animals (15:19–23)

¹⁹Set apart for the LORD your God every firstborn male of your herds and flocks. Do not put the firstborn of your oxen to work, and do not shear the firstborn of your sheep. ²⁰Each year you and your family are to eat them in the presence of the LORD your God at the place he will choose. ²¹If an animal has a defect, is lame or blind, or has any serious flaw, you must not sacrifice it to the LORD your God. ²²You are to eat it in your own towns. Both the ceremonially unclean and the clean may eat it, as if it were gazelle or deer. ²³But you must not eat the blood; pour it out on the ground like water.

COMMENTARY

19–23 The sabbatical year involved some kind of "release" for land and debt; the seventh year was a time for slaves to be freed; and the present paragraph delineates the "release" of firstborn animals from customary work or economic productivity by dedicating them as sacrifices to Yahweh. The Israelites were to set apart or consecrate (see Note on 7:6) every firstborn male oxen or sheep for use by Yahweh. This practice recalls the tenth plague Yahweh sent against the Egyptians (in which most of the Egyptian firstborn died and God spared the Israelite firstborn; Ex 11:1–9; 12:29–30) and Yahweh's subsequent demand that the Israelites dedicate all firstborn sons to him (Ex 13:11–16).

Just as offering the firstfruits demonstrated God's ownership of and blessing on the land (Lev 25:2; Dt 8:10–18), the sacrifice of these firstborn animals represents the recognition of God's ownership of and blessing on the herdsmen (Hall, 259). Each year (most likely at one of the three pilgrimage feasts [see below]—perhaps the Feast of Tabernacles; Ex 22:29–30), Israelite families are to bring their firstborn animals to the central sanctuary and participate in the sacrificial meal (cf. 14:23). If they have a firstborn animal with a serious defect or blemish, they may not sacrifice it to Yahweh. Since that animal is exempt from work and economic productivity, however, they are permitted to eat it at a local communal meal (which had requirements for ritual purity). As with any consumption of meat, they must not consume any of the animal's blood but instead let it drain onto the ground (see comments on 12:15–16).

iv. Three pilgrimage feasts (16:1–17)

OVERVIEW

Along with giving tithes, celebrating the sabbatical year, and consecrating their firstborn animals to Yahweh, these three feasts—Passover (and Unleavened Bread), Feast of Weeks, and Feast of Tabernacles—represent part of the homage due Yahweh (cf. Ex 23:14–18; 34:18–26; Lev 23). They form part of the "sacred rhythm" of Israel's life (Braulik, "The Sequence of the Laws," 321). The first two feasts frame the spring grain harvest, while the Feast of Tabernacles occurs in the fall, when the new grain and wine are stored away for the winter (Tigay, *Deuteronomy*, 152). All three commemorate God's deliverance of his people through the exodus from Egypt and express gratitude for the harvest.

For these three feasts, all Israelite men are to make the pilgrimage to the central sanctuary "to appear before the Great King" (Merrill, *Deuteronomy*, 250). This "national" gathering of Israelites from all parts of the land of promise will remind them of their national identity as God's covenantal people.

Jewish Calendar and Key Feasts

# of the month, religious calendar	# of the month, civil calendar	Hebrew name	Modern calendar equivalent	Feast(s)
1	7	Nisan (14–21)	March–April	Passover/Unleavened Bread
2	8	Iyyar	April–May	
3	9	Sivan (6)	May–June	Pentecost ("Weeks")
4	10	Tammuz	June–July	
5	11	Ab	July–August	
6	12	Elul	August–September	
7	1	Tishri (10)	September–October	Day of Atonement
		(15–21)		Tabernacles
8	2	Marchesvan	October–November	
9	3	Kislev	November–December	
10	4	Tebeth	December–January	
11	5	Shebat	January–February	
12	6	Adar (13–14)	February–March	Purim

(a) Passover (16:1–8)

¹Observe the month of Abib and celebrate the Passover of the LORD your God, because in the month of Abib he brought you out of Egypt by night. ²Sacrifice as the Passover to the LORD your God an animal from your flock or herd at the place the LORD will choose as a dwelling for his Name. ³Do not eat it with bread made with yeast, but for seven days eat unleavened bread, the bread of affliction, because you left Egypt in haste — so that all the days of your life you may remember the time of your departure from Egypt. ⁴Let no yeast be found in your possession in all your land for seven days. Do not let any of the meat you sacrifice on the evening of the first day remain until morning. ⁵You must not sacrifice the Passover in any town the LORD your God gives you ⁶except in the place he will choose as a dwelling for his Name. There you must sacrifice the Passover in the evening, when the sun goes down, on the anniversary of your departure from Egypt. ⁷Roast it and eat it at the place the LORD your God will choose. Then in the morning return to your tents. ⁸For six days eat unleavened bread and on the seventh day hold an assembly to the LORD your God and do no work.

COMMENTARY

1–2 The Passover feast is to be observed in the month of Abib (also called Nisan, lasting from about mid-March to mid-April; cf. Ex 12:1–16; Lev 23:4–8; Nu 28:16–25 for more detailed description of this feast). The celebration will commemorate Yahweh's deliverance of Israel from Egypt and his establishing them as his covenantal nation. Although the original celebration of this feast involved the sacrifice of a lamb (Ex 12:6–7), an ox or a lamb can serve as a Passover sacrifice. The animal is to be slain at the place where God will cause his name to dwell (16:2; cf. 16:6, 11; see Note on 12:11). Although the Passover began as a family event, once Israel becomes established in the Promised Land God's people (as families) must celebrate it together as a nation (2Ch 35:4, 12).

3–4 The Israelites are to eat unleavened bread during the week following the Passover to remind them of their hasty departure from Egypt. (Unleav-

ened bread could be made quickly; cf. Ex 12:11, 39.) In addition to refraining from any use of leaven for seven days, the Israelites are to consume all the meat of the sacrificed animal before the following morning (probably to prevent decay; Ex 12:10; 23:18; 34:25; Nu 9:12). The unleavened "bread of affliction" will cause them to recall their hardships in Egypt and the pharaoh's vain opposition to Yahweh's demands.

The fundamental reason for the Israelites to celebrate the Passover and the Feast of Unleavened Bread is so that they will remember (see comments and Note on 4:10) Yahweh's stupendous deliverance of them from bondage in Egypt. This historical reality should have a life-transforming impact on their present and future existence. Each new generation, made up of Hebrews who did not witness this great event, should through the commemorative event bring to life that national deliverance and gladly accept the privileges and obligations that accompany a treasured covenantal relationship with Yahweh.

5–8 On the anniversary of their departure from Egypt (Nisan/Abib 14), God's people are to gather at the central sanctuary to commemorate that great day of deliverance. After slaying the sacrificial animal at dusk, Israelite families are to consume the meat and unleavened bread into the night and early morning. Once the meat has been totally eaten, the Israelites can return to their tents, the temporary dwellings of the thousands of Israelites who have traveled from their homes to gather at the central sanctuary for this important feast. At the end of the Feast of Unleavened Bread, the Israelites are to refrain from working (as on the Sabbath).

NOTE

7 The original command establishing the Passover feast mandated that the Israelites bake, not boil (בָּשַׁל, *bšl*, root of וּבִשַּׁלְתָּ, *ûbiššaltā*, "and boil [it]"), the meat of the Passover lamb (Ex 12:3–9). Although this verb can clearly connote boiling something, it can signify the broad idea of cooking (Nu 11:8) or baking (2Sa 13:8). Several passages mention the liquid in which the meat is to be cooked or some kind of pot or vessel when boiling is in view (Ex 23:19; Lev 6:28 [21]; Dt 14:21; 2Ki 4:38; Eze 24:3–5). Second Chronicles 35:13 affirms that King Josiah's Passover offering was "cooked" (*bšl*) in fire. By comparison, the Akkadian cognate verb refers to several kinds of cooking (Tigay, *Deuteronomy*, 155; contra Biddle, 263; Levinson, *Deuteronomy and the Hermeneutics of Legal Innovation* [New York/Oxford: Oxford Univ. Press, 1997], 73).

In various passages the expression וְהָלַכְתָּ לְאֹהָלֶיךָ (*weḥālaktā leʾōhāleykā*, "return to your tents") serves as a stock phrase for returning home (1Ki 8:66; 12:16; cf. 2Sa 20:1). Driver, 194, proposed that it originated from a time when Israel was wandering in the wilderness, long before the time he sees Deuteronomy as being composed (seventh century BC). Ridderbos, 189, suggests that the expression represents divine permission to return home for those who came to the central sanctuary just for the Passover feast. In the present context, however, the phrase refers to the Israelites' returning to their temporary housing set up in the vicinity of the central sanctuary (Mayes, 259; Merrill, *Deuteronomy*, 253; Hall, 265).

(b) Feast of Weeks (16:9–12)

⁹Count off seven weeks from the time you begin to put the sickle to the standing grain. ¹⁰Then celebrate the Feast of Weeks to the LORD your God by giving a freewill offering in proportion to the blessings the LORD your God has given you. ¹¹And rejoice before the LORD your God at the place he will choose as a dwelling for his Name — you, your sons and daughters, your menservants and maidservants, the Levites in your towns, and the aliens, the fatherless and the widows living among you. ¹²Remember that you were slaves in Egypt, and follow carefully these decrees.

COMMENTARY

9–12 Seven weeks after the grain harvest began, the children of Israel are to celebrate the Feast of Weeks (cf. Ex 23:16; 34:22; Lev 23:15–20; Nu 28:26–31) as an expression of their thankfulness for the Lord's provision of abundant material blessings. A freewill offering and a communal meal constitute the focus of this celebration. In accordance with Yahweh's blessing of their labors, God's people are to bring an offering to the central sanctuary. God does not demand that they give "out of" their blessings but "according to" the degree of his blessing. Those who have had great harvests will bring more than those who had a difficult year.

This giving is not to be done with grudging resignation but accompanied by great rejoicing. Part of what they bring to the central sanctuary is to provide a banquet for the Israelite families and their servants, as well as all those who do not own land from which to gain blessing—Levites, aliens, the fatherless, and widows (see comments and Note on 14:29). Yahweh's abundant blessings on their crops, herds, and flocks, as well as his gracious deliverance of them from slavery in Egypt, should motivate them to participate gladly in this celebration of his provision for them. Since they had been slaves in Egypt, God's people should welcome all needy people to join them in this celebratory banquet. What God asks of his people—whether the OT Hebrews or the NT church—should be done in grateful and obedient response in the light of his prior blessing of them (Wright, *Deuteronomy*, 199).

NOTES

10 "Weeks" (שָׁבֻעוֹת, *šābu'ôt*) in the title of this feast derives from the fact that it was observed exactly seven weeks after the beginning of the grain harvest (Ex 34:22). This feast is also known as the "Feast of the Harvest" (Ex 23:16) and "the day of the firstfruits" of the grain harvest (Ex 34:22; Nu 28:26). The Feast of Weeks always began fifty days after the conclusion of the Feast of Unleavened Bread (Lev 23:15–16), thus giving rise to the NT's name for this festival, "Pentecost" (πεντηκοστή, *pentēkostē*, "fiftieth").

11 Moses mandates tangible expressions of joy (וְשָׂמַחְתָּ לִפְנֵי יְהוָה אֱלֹהֶיךָ, *weśāmaḥtā lipnê yhwh 'elōheykā*, "and rejoice [from שׂמח, *śmḥ*] before the LORD your God") as part of the Israelites' celebration of feast days, offering sacrifices and tithes, or other national gatherings. The expression "before Yahweh" (לִפְנֵי יְהוָה, *lipnê yhwh*) at the very least connotes Yahweh's presence at these celebrations and may signify his participation as a covenantal partner with Israel (D. Sheriffs, "The Phrases *ina IGI DN* and *lip^eney yhwh* in Treaty and Covenant Contexts," *JNSL* 7 [1979]: 61–65). This expression occurs in seven verses in connection with the celebration of the Feast of Tabernacles (Lev 23:40), Feast of Weeks (Dt 16:11), fellowship offerings (27:7), tithing (14:26), and national convocations. (For its connection with covenantal reaffirmation and renewal, see 12:7, 12, 18.)

This idea is implied in other exhortations to and demonstrations of joyfulness in the celebration of religious feasts (Feast of Tabernacles—Dt 16:14; Ne 8:17; Passover and Feast of Unleavened Bread—2Ch 30:21, 23, 25–26; Ezr 6:22; Firstfruits—Dt 26:11; Feast of Purim—Est 8:16–17; 9:17–19, 22), fasting (Zec 8:19), all worship activities (Nu 10:10), and coronation ceremonies (1Sa 11:15). In a few contexts, the feast day is called "the day of your rejoicing" (יוֹם שִׂמְחַתְכֶם‎, *yôm śimḥatkem*; Nu 10:10; cf. Est 9:17–19, 22; Grisanti, *NIDOTTE*, 3:1252).

(c) Feast of Tabernacles (16:13–15)

¹³Celebrate the Feast of Tabernacles for seven days after you have gathered the produce of your threshing floor and your winepress. ¹⁴Be joyful at your Feast — you, your sons and daughters, your menservants and maidservants, and the Levites, the aliens, the fatherless and the widows who live in your towns. ¹⁵For seven days celebrate the Feast to the LORD your God at the place the LORD will choose. For the LORD your God will bless you in all your harvest and in all the work of your hands, and your joy will be complete.

COMMENTARY

13–15 After they have completed the fall harvest (grain, grapes, olives, dates, and figs), the children of Israel are to celebrate the Feast of Tabernacles (i.e., "booths" or "huts") as an expression of their gratitude for God's blessings in all of their harvests. This feast is also called the Feast of Ingathering (Ex 23:16; 34:22). In genuine gratitude for God's abundant provision on them in all realms of life and economy, all Israelites (those with and without land) are to celebrate Yahweh's goodness at a seven-day communal banquet at the central sanctuary. Not only is this celebration an expression of the Israelites' gratitude for Yahweh's provision but also an expression of their confidence in his promise to continue providing for them.

(d) Summary of the pilgrimage feasts (16:16–17)

¹⁶Three times a year all your men must appear before the LORD your God at the place he will choose: at the Feast of Unleavened Bread, the Feast of Weeks and the Feast of Tabernacles. No man should appear before the LORD empty-handed: ¹⁷Each of you must bring a gift in proportion to the way the LORD your God has blessed you.

COMMENTARY

16–17 This long section (14:22–16:17) began with the giving of tithes (14:22–29), and it ends with a summary of Israel's "festal" responsibilities. The varied duties described in these verses represent "tribute" that Israel has the privilege of offering to her covenantal Lord. By obeying these divine mandates, God's covenantal people both manifest and pledge their continuing loyalty to Yahweh, their Redeemer.

God demands that for all three of these pilgrimage feasts, all Israelite men must travel to the central sanctuary to celebrate his stupendous deliverance of and abundant provision for Israel. In the light of those factual realities, no one should come to these great gatherings without a gift proportionate to Yahweh's blessing of them.

2. Kingdom Officials (16:18–18:22)

OVERVIEW

Moses delineates the qualifications for and expectations of various officials (judge, king, priest, and prophet) in the theocratic state. He also delineates various areas on which the judicial process is to have an impact in order to maintain legitimate national leadership and ensure that judicial righteousness will be exercised over the nation.

a. Judges and Judicial Procedures (16:18–17:13)

i. The appointment of judges (16:18–20)

[18]Appoint judges and officials for each of your tribes in every town the LORD your God is giving you, and they shall judge the people fairly. [19]Do not pervert justice or show partiality. Do not accept a bribe, for a bribe blinds the eyes of the wise and twists the words of the righteous. [20]Follow justice and justice alone, so that you may live and possess the land the LORD your God is giving you.

COMMENTARY

18–20 Moses was the first mediatorial and judicial figure to provide guidance for Israel. After Sinai, because of the overwhelming burden of adjudicating cases, Moses selected wise men to assist him with this task (Ex 18:13–26; Dt 1:14–17). He appointed them as "commanders" and "officials" (*šōṭerîm*; see Note on 1:15). In the present section he appoints "judges" and "officials" (*šōṭerîm*). Since the people will soon be established in the Promised Land, these judges will have a more established role in the nation and be present in each Israelite community ("in your gates"). Moses gives them five mandates.

1. Israelite judges must render their decisions in accordance with God's standards of justice ("judge with a judgment of righteousness," i.e., fairly; cf. 1:16).

2. They must not twist judgment. The notion of perverting or twisting judgment occurs eight times in the OT. To pervert justice is to deprive a person of the justice due that person (La 3:35). This expression occurs in juxtaposition to partiality (Pr 18:5) and bribery (Dt 16:19; 1Sa 8:3; Pr 17:23) and normally affects the poor, the alien, and the fatherless (Ex 23:6; Dt 24:17; 27;19).

3. They may not show partiality. Just as Moses did with the judges he appointed soon after Sinai, so here he exhorts these judges not to show favor based on a person's status or wealth. The phrase used is literally "recognize the face" (cf. Dt 1:17; Job 34:19; Pr 24:23; 28:21), a phrase much like "lifting the face" (10:17 [see Note]; 28:50); it is antithetical to genuine justice.

4. Moses demands that judges refuse all bribes (cf. Ps 15:5; Pr 17:23; Isa 1:23; 5:23; Eze 22:12). Taking a bribe violates Israel's function as a banner nation given the responsibility of representing God's character before the world (Ex 19:4–6). As the God who does not take bribes (10:17; see comments there), these judges must not corrupt the world's understanding of Yahweh's character. As a matter of fact, among the blessings and curses to be pronounced from Ebal and Gerizim (11:29–30) is a curse on anyone "who accepts a bribe to kill an innocent person" (27:25)! In the present verse, bribery is abhorrent because it has destructive implications: it blinds the eyes of the wise and distorts or renders ineffective the words of the righteous (Ex 23:8). In other words, it chokes justice rather than achieving it!

5. Finally, the solitary purpose of these judges must be the pursuit of justice above all else. As is true throughout Deuteronomy, genuine obedience to covenantal requirements results in long life in the land that Yahweh will deliver into their hands.

NOTES

18 The two nouns מִשְׁפַּט־צֶדֶק (mišpāṭ-ṣedeq, "fairly") can be literally rendered "[with] a judgment of righteousness." As McConville, 287, points out, the first word refers to the individual case or a just decision, while the second noun denotes the more abstract quality on which the decision is based.

19 The verb סלף (slp, root of וִיסַלֵּף, wîsallēp, "and it distorts") occurs seven times in the OT. When applied to people this verb can describe something that is brought to ruin (Pr 19:3; 21:12). It can signify "overthrowing" something or someone established on a certain course. God himself will overthrow those who think they are well-established but do not honor him (Job 12:19; Pr 22:12). Even the wickedness of sinners will overthrow them, i.e., their treachery is ultimately self-destructive (Pr 13:6).

20 Most occurrences of the verb רדף (rdp, root of תִּרְדֹּף, tirdōp, "you must pursue"; GK 8103) involve military terminology of some kind. In those contexts it denotes the active pursuit of one or more persons, with hostile intent (Ge 14:14–15; Dt 1:44; 11:4; Frevel, TDOT, 13:343). The goal of this pursuit is always to catch and exterminate the enemies (cf. pursuit of a murderer by relatives; Dt 19:6). The word occurs repeatedly in the cursing section of Leviticus 26 (vv.7, 8 [2x], 17, 36 [2x], 37) and Deuteronomy 28 (vv.22, 45; cf. 30:7; 32:30). All occurrences of *rdp* without a personal object have "ethical" overtones. People can pursue evil (Pr 11:19), fantasies and emptiness (Pr 12:11; 28:19), gifts (= bribes; Isa 1:23), or strong drinks (Isa 5:11). But they can also pursue goodness (Ps 38:20 [21]), peace (Ps 34:14 [15]) or righteousness (Pr 15:9; 21:21; Isa 51:1 [= seeking Yahweh]), as in the present passage. This verb does not envision a casual or inconsistent pursuit. Here the repetition צֶדֶק צֶדֶק (*ṣedeq ṣedeq*, "only justice alone"), the only time it occurs, highlights the exclusivity of the pursuit exhorted.

ii. Guidance for judges (16:21–17:13)

OVERVIEW

Although several scholars question the originality of 16:21–17:1 because of their "awkward" flow (see Merrill [*Deuteronomy*, 258] for a brief overview), Kaufman, 134, helpfully explains a possible reason for this arrangement of verses. After instructions concerning the appointment of judges (16:18–20), 16:21–17:1 lays down some fundamental requirements, and 17:2–13 serves as "case law" showing how to deal with offense in that area (cf. Wright, *Deuteronomy*, 205).

²¹Do not set up any wooden Asherah pole beside the altar you build to the LORD your God, ²²and do not erect a sacred stone, for these the LORD your God hates.

¹⁷:¹Do not sacrifice to the LORD your God an ox or a sheep that has any defect or flaw in it, for that would be detestable to him.

²If a man or woman living among you in one of the towns the LORD gives you is found doing evil in the eyes of the LORD your God in violation of his covenant, ³and contrary to my command has worshiped other gods, bowing down to them or to the sun or the moon or the stars of the sky, ⁴and this has been brought to your attention, then you must investigate it thoroughly. If it is true and it has been proved that this detestable thing has been done in Israel, ⁵take the man or woman who has done this evil deed to your city gate and stone that person to death. ⁶On the testimony of two or three witnesses a man shall be put to death, but no one shall be put to death on the testimony of only one witness. ⁷The hands of the witnesses must be the first in putting him to death, and then the hands of all the people. You must purge the evil from among you.

⁸If cases come before your courts that are too difficult for you to judge — whether bloodshed, lawsuits or assaults — take them to the place the LORD your God will choose. ⁹Go to the priests, who are Levites, and to the judge who is in office at that time. Inquire

of them and they will give you the verdict. [10]You must act according to the decisions they give you at the place the LORD will choose. Be careful to do everything they direct you to do. [11]Act according to the law they teach you and the decisions they give you. Do not turn aside from what they tell you, to the right or to the left. [12]The man who shows contempt for the judge or for the priest who stands ministering there to the LORD your God must be put to death. You must purge the evil from Israel. [13]All the people will hear and be afraid, and will not be contemptuous again.

COMMENTARY

21–22 As Moses has affirmed already (7:25–26; cf. 12:3, 31; 13:15), God's chosen people were not to set up any religious instruments that were part of Canaanite worship (Asherah poles and sacred stones; see comments on Dt 7:5). To erect these abhorrent things (which were supposed to be totally destroyed) will bring great offense to their suzerain because he "hates" these. As seen in 5:9 (see Note), this verb is a technical covenantal word that does not primarily refer to an emotion but instead illustrates the absolute incompatibility of syncretism (the combining of religions) and Yahweh worship. Yahweh "could enter into no relationship with, make no accommodation to" (Wright, *Deuteronomy*, 205) these pagan religious utensils (or the gods they represent).

The two commands in 16:21–22 primarily deal with Yahweh's claim on Israel's exclusive loyalty. The next command repeats Yahweh's requirement of unblemished animals for use in sacrifices to him. Taken together, these three commands seem to affirm one key point: Israel's wholehearted adherence to Yahweh is the sum total of the Mosaic law (McConville, 288). Who God is and how he is to be worshiped are at stake (Thompson, 201).

17:1 No animal with any kind of serious defect or flaw is fit for use in sacrificial worship. Yahweh regards negligence in this area as an abomination (see Note on 7:25–26). Defective sacrifices serve as evidence of carelessness and a lack of gratitude on Israel's part (Dt 15:21; Lev 22:17–25; Mal 1:6–14).

2–7 Moses describes a hypothetical situation in which an Israelite man or woman is caught worshiping other gods (or celestial bodies). To "bow down" (*ḥwh*) and "worship" (*ʿbd*) false gods represented acknowledging another god as lord, i.e., choosing the lordship of another god (Westermann, *TLOT*, 2:829; see Note on 5:9). Multiple negative phrases highlight the abhorrent aspect of this sin: "evil," "in violation of his covenant" (17:2), "contrary to my command" (17:3), and "destestable thing" (17:4).

Upon hearing a report of such apostasy, the Israelite leaders in the vicinity must conduct a thorough examination to determine the accuracy of the charge. There must be at least two witnesses to this covenantal treachery for the Israelite leaders to bring the mandated punishment to fruition: death by stoning (17:5; see comment on 24:16). Because the crime is a capital offense, the witnesses must initiate the penalty, with others from the community joining in. The participation of the entire community emphasizes the far-reaching impact of the offense and the response. If the witnesses have given false testimony, they have exposed themselves to blood revenge by the victim's relatives (cf. 19:15–21). By carrying out this punishment the community is able to "purge the evil" from their midst (see Note on 13:5).

8–13 The local judges and officials must relegate to the central tribunal, made up of priests and a chief judge, cases that are too difficult for them to adjudicate. This body will issue a binding decision, and all who fail to abide by it will face the death penalty. It is possible that the priests would give special attention to cases with ceremonial implications, while the judges would focus on civil and criminal issues. The fundamental point is that whatever ver-dict is rendered by this central tribunal, its decision is totally nonnegotiable.

Verses 10–11 contain four repetitive statements that emphasize this fact ("act ... be careful to do [see Note on 5:1] ... do ... do not turn aside"). Anyone who refuses to carry out this verdict, thereby acting arrogantly, must be stoned to death. To refuse a directive of one of God's representatives is to stand in opposition to Yahweh. The death of that person will serve as a deterrent against any similar presumption.

NOTES

17:2 In general, the verb עבר (ʿbr) denotes movement from one place to another. The specific form of the verb in the phrase לַעֲבֹר בְּרִיתוֹ (laʿăbōr bᵉrîtô, "in violation of his covenant," lit., "to cross over [the stipulations of] the covenant") depicts causing that movement to take place. It is used to describe God's causing wind to blow on the earth after the flood (Ge 8:1); the verb occurs ten times in the OT with the noun "covenant" (בְּרִית, bᵉrît; Dt 17:2; Jos 7:11, 15; Jos 23:16; Jdg 2:20; 2Ki 18:12; Isa 33:8; Jer 34:18; Hos 6:7; 8:1) and refers to the violation of Israel's covenantal relationship with Yahweh (Dt 26:13; cf. Grisanti, "2 Kings," 317).

12 The noun בְּזָדוֹן (bᵉzādôn, "with contempt"; GK 2295) occurs eleven times in the OT and twice in Deuteronomy, here and with reference to a presumptuous false prophet (18:22). Derived from the verb זיד (zyd), "to act presumptuously" or "be arrogant," it describes people who think more of themselves than they should (Pr 11:2; Jer 49:16; 50:31–32; Ob 3). To claim God's grace apart from a life of righteousness is the height of presumption (Eze 7:10). In the present passage it describes direct defiance against Yahweh and his representatives (priests and judges). In ch. 18 the verb depicts the arrogance of a false prophet who deceptively claims to represent the living God.

b. Kings (17:14–20)

OVERVIEW

Regulations concerning kingship do not occur elsewhere in the Pentateuch. In this section Moses does not mandate a monarchy but permits a king under Yahweh's ultimate sovereignty. The potential of a king's ruling over Israel is not intrinsically bad. Just as judges will help adjudicate legal cases under God's sovereignty, a king must rule with derived authority. The placement of these requirements for a potential king after instructions concerning judges (16:21–17:13) finds rationale in the probability that a judge will precede a king by several centuries and can function in Israel with or without a king.

¹⁴When you enter the land the LORD your God is giving you and have taken possession of it and settled in it, and you say, "Let us set a king over us like all the nations around us," ¹⁵be sure to appoint over you the king the LORD your God chooses. He must be from among your own brothers. Do not place a foreigner over you, one who is not a brother Israelite. ¹⁶The king, moreover, must not acquire great numbers of horses for himself or make the people return to Egypt to get more of them, for the LORD has told you, "You are not to go back that way again." ¹⁷He must not take many wives, or his heart will be led astray. He must not accumulate large amounts of silver and gold.

¹⁸When he takes the throne of his kingdom, he is to write for himself on a scroll a copy of this law, taken from that of the priests, who are Levites. ¹⁹It is to be with him, and he is to read it all the days of his life so that he may learn to revere the LORD his God and follow carefully all the words of this law and these decrees ²⁰and not consider himself better than his brothers and turn from the law to the right or to the left. Then he and his descendants will reign a long time over his kingdom in Israel.

COMMENTARY

14–17 Moses anticipates Israel's thought process once they become settled in the land of promise. Seeing the rulership of kings over surrounding nations, the Israelites might one day desire a king to rule over them. Moses provides two key requirements and three limitations if they ever decide to appoint a king. First of all, he must be a man chosen by Yahweh. Just as the nation/people, the place of worship, and the priestly tribe had been chosen by Yahweh, so Israel's king must be divinely chosen. Rather than being "like all the other nations" (cf. 1Sa 8:5, 20), the distinctive nation of Israel is to have a king who is, in his qualifications and the manner of his ruling, also distinctive. Moreover, he must be an ethnic Israelite (probably because a non-Israelite ruler might be more likely to introduce idolatry into the land). This requirement does not mean that non-Hebrews are "second-class" citizens in Israel. Numerous passages make it clear that the Israelites are to treat "aliens" with tender compassion (see Notes on 1:16 and 10:17).

Three provisions aimed at curbing three kinds of excess common among monarchs appear in 17:16–17: excessive accumulation of horses, wives, and wealth. A king might be tempted to increase his number of horses so he could have a larger number of chariots and, consequently, field a more powerful army (cf. 1Sa 8:11–12). Absalom and Adonijah, two of David's sons, signaled their desire to take the Israelite throne for themselves by acquiring horses and chariots (2Sa 15:1; 1Ki 1:5). The psalmist pits trusting horses and chariots against trusting in God (Ps 20:7 [8]). Marriages of a king to princesses from other peoples regularly took place as a means of ratifying treaties between two countries (e.g., 1Ki 3:1). After Solomon took multiple wives, these women turned his heart aside from exclusive Yahweh worship (1Ki 11:1–4). The warning against increasing wealth may represent a limitation on the taxes a king might try to levy. In all three instances, to multiply the prohibited items could give a king the mistaken notion that he is self-sufficient and has no pressing need for Yahweh.

Moses does not deal with the question of the legitimacy of a king over Israel; rather, he concerns himself with the qualifications for any king that might one day rule over Israel. In summary, like the people of Yahweh, God expects the king to live in wholehearted conformity to the covenant he has established with the nation.

18–20 Yahweh makes one primary requirement of any king to rule over God's chosen people: Pay careful attention to his covenantal demands. Apparently, the Levites kept an official "copy of this law" in the central sanctuary. Moses mandates that as soon as a new king takes the throne of Israel, he must commission the making of a fresh copy of this covenantal text. Once the copy is made, the king must not live as though it does not exist. Rather, it must be with him, and he must read it "all the days of his life."

In other words, the king must "always" compare his reign to the demands of Yahweh—not every moment of every day, just as Yahweh does not demand that parents do nothing else but train their children (Dt 6:6–9). Rather, the parent-child relationship is to be characterized by consistent training in every arena and setting of life. Similarly, the king is regularly to read this law, and for an important reason: that he might revere his covenantal Lord! If he genuinely fears Yahweh, he will consistently live in accordance with God's covenantal demands. He will realize that he, just like his fellow Israelites, is not above God's law. As Yahweh does with them, Yahweh prohibits the king from departing from his laws and decrees. Even the highest human ruler of Israel is a subject of the great God of Israel. If he puts these regal demands into practice, he and his descendants will rule over Israel for a long time.

NOTES

14 The idea of Yahweh's "bringing" Israel (6:10; 7:1; 8:7; 9:28; 11:29; 26:9; 30:5; 31:20, 21) or Israel's "coming into/entering" (17:14; 18:9; 26:1, 3; both with the verb בוא, *bw*ʾ) the Promised Land occurs repeatedly in Deuteronomy (here נֹתֵן לָךְ ... כִּי־תָבֹא אֶל־הָאָרֶץ, *kî-tābōʾ ʾel-hāʾāreṣ ... nōtēn lāk*, "when you enter the land ... [he] is giving you"). In most of these instances, the idea points chronologically to a time (namely, the completion of conquest and being established in the land) when God's chosen nation must put into practice one of Yahweh's covenantal stipulations. The "formula of land-gift" (McConville, 293), "the land that ... [Yahweh] is giving," occurs twenty-nine times in Deuteronomy (4:1; 5:31; 11:31; 12:1; 15:4, 7; 16:20; 19:2, 10, 14; et al.). This expression reaffirms Yahweh's role in giving this land. That divine function gives him the wherewithal to make certain requirements of his covenantal nation.

The reference in this passage to "a king" (מֶלֶךְ, *melek*) has caused several scholars to conclude that Deuteronomy was composed in a later time, when a king was ruling over Israel. Since the passage focuses on several specific issues (multiplying horses, wives, silver and gold), some scholars, assuming a post-Mosaic composition for the passage, posit Solomon's activities as the likely catalyst for this legislation. Such a catalyst is unnecessary, however, since the Pentateuch foresaw kingship as early as the times of Abraham (Ge 17:6, 16). Also, Moses would have been aware of kingship from his time in the court of Pharaoh's daughter.

18 In ancient Near Eastern suzerain-vassal treaties, a duplicate copy of the treaty was provided for the vassal king, and it was to be read in public periodically (Thompson, 206). When a different king came to the throne, copying this version of the treaty would represent the new king's submission to the terms of the treaty (as reflected in the phrase וְכָתַב לוֹ, *weḵāṯaḇ lô*, "and he will write for himself"). For an Israelite king, making a new copy of the law would tangibly indicate his recognition that he rules the nation with derived authority. Yahweh is the ultimate king. The king would most likely commission royal scribes to make this copy rather than writing it out himself. In a similar literary fashion, Moses said he made the ark, but it was actually Bezalel who made it (10:3, 5; cf. Ex 37:1–9); Moses commissioned the work to be done.

The LXX translates the phrase אֶת־מִשְׁנֵה הַתּוֹרָה הַזֹּאת (*'eṯ-mišnēh hattôrâ hazzō'ṯ*, "a copy of this law") with τὸ δευτερονόμιον τοῦτο (*to deuteronomion touto*), "this second law," the basis for the modern name for the book of Deuteronomy. This title incorrectly suggests that Deuteronomy represents a second giving of the law. In reality, "a copy of this law" provides a more accurate translation of this phrase. The book of Deuteronomy gives in sermonic format a re-presentation of the Mosaic law given at Sinai, not a different, second law (see Introduction). In this phrase, the term "law" (תּוֹרָה, *tôrâ*) probably means only the book of Deuteronomy and not the whole Pentateuch. "This law" could refer to the legislation concerning a king (17:14–20), the specific stipulation section of the book (chs. 12–26), the entire book of Deuteronomy, or the book of the covenant (cf. Ex 24:7). Since this expression repeatedly occurs in Deuteronomy to refer to the entire book (1:5; 4:44; 27:3, 8, 26; 29:21, 29 [20, 28]; 30:10; et al.), that is likely its referent here.

19 The requirement that an Israelite read the book of the law כָּל־יְמֵי חַיָּיו (*kol-yemê ḥayyāyw*, "all the days of his life") is not an impossible or merely ideal demand. The term refers broadly to the life in view, not every moment of that life. There is no doubt that this practice is to be for the king a consistent or regular practice, not one occupying every moment of every day, which thereby leaves him no time for any other regal matters. The Israelites are not to let Yahweh's demands depart from their hearts (4:9) and must keep his commands (6:2) "all the days of" their lives. King David is said to have done what was right in the eyes of Yahweh "all the days of his life" (1Ki 15:5), yet not in the matter with Uriah the Hittite. Other references indicate that this phrase indicates an overall consistent life pattern but not perpetual activity without exception (cf. Ge 3:17; Jos 4:14; 1Sa 7:15 et al.).

c. Priests and Levites (18:1–8)

OVERVIEW

The tribe of Levi, and more specifically the line of Aaron (the priests), constitute the next category of theocratic officials concerning which Moses provides regulations. The general point of this passage is that every member of the tribe of Levi has a right to share in the "proceeds" of the offerings made at the altar. Verses 1–2 refer to all Levites, vv.3–5 concern Levitical priests, and vv.6–8 return to the broad category of Levites (in a specific circumstance).

¹The priests, who are Levites — indeed the whole tribe of Levi — are to have no allotment or inheritance with Israel. They shall live on the offerings made to the LORD by fire, for that is their inheritance. ²They shall have no inheritance among their brothers; the LORD is their inheritance, as he promised them.

³This is the share due the priests from the people who sacrifice a bull or a sheep: the shoulder, the jowls and the inner parts. ⁴You are to give them the firstfruits of your grain, new wine and oil, and the first wool from the shearing of your sheep, ⁵for the LORD your God has chosen them and their descendants out of all your tribes to stand and minister in the LORD's name always.

⁶If a Levite moves from one of your towns anywhere in Israel where he is living, and comes in all earnestness to the place the LORD will choose, ⁷he may minister in the name of the LORD his God like all his fellow Levites who serve there in the presence of the LORD. ⁸He is to share equally in their benefits, even though he has received money from the sale of family possessions.

COMMENTARY

1–2 Since the Levites will not receive a landed inheritance (see Note on 14:29), they must rely on Yahweh alone, for he is their inheritance (cf. 10:9; Nu 18:20). In accordance with sacrificial legislation, select parts of animals and agricultural produce brought to the temple as an offering (see Note) will be given to the priests and Levites who minister to the Israelites on behalf of Yahweh. Within the allotments of other Israelite tribes, God will set aside certain cities as Levitical cities (Nu 35; Jos 20–21) and apparently, in some situations, allow for private holdings by Levites (18:8; Jer 32:6–15). Their lack of a land allotment allows them to focus more fully on their God-given ministry.

3–5 Moses specifies the parts of Israelite offerings to be dedicated to the priests (and their fellow Levites; cf. Ex 29:26–28; Lev 7:31–34; Nu

18:11–12, 18; Dt 14:27–29). The shoulders, the two cheeks ("jowls"), and the stomach of a sacrificed animal; the grain, wine, and oil (a standard triad highlighting Yahweh's abundant blessing; 7:13; 11:14; 12:17; 14:23; cf. Ne 10:40; 13:12; Jer 31:12; Hag 1:11) from the firstfruits; and the first wool sheared from sheep belong to members of the priestly tribe. Their distinctive position among their fellow Israelites derives from the fact that Yahweh has chosen them for this role (cf. Nu 3:11–13; 8:12–26; cf. Yahweh's choice of Israel "out of all the peoples" [7:6]). As a tribe, they serve and minister in Yahweh's interest.

6–8 The Levites will be scattered throughout the land of Israel, where they will teach God's people the law and facilitate their worship. If a Levite assigned to some outlying community in the

Promised Land (Nu 35:1–8) desires to come to the central sanctuary and minister there, he may do so (by this permissive rather than mandated legisla-tion) and thereby become an equal participant in the Levitical income.

NOTES

1 The first two nouns in the phrase כֹּהֲנִים הַלְוִיִּם כָּל־שֵׁבֶט לֵוִי (kōhᵃnîm halᵉwîyim kol-šēbeṭ lēwî, "The priests, who are Levites—indeed the whole tribe of Levi") occur together five times in Deuteronomy (17:9, 18; 18:1; 24:8; 27:9), but not in the rest of the Pentateuch, and could be rendered "Levitical priests." The debated issue is how that first expression relates to "the whole tribe of Levi." Some believe that the second expression, as an appositional phrase, is to be equated with the first expression (Driver, 214; J. A. Emerton, "Priests and Levites in Deuteronomy," *VT* 12 [1962]: 133–34; McConville, *Law and Theology in Deuteronomy* [Sheffield: JSOT, 1984], 142–49; ESV, NASB, NKJV, NRSV). From this, several proponents of this translation (not McConville) conclude that Deuteronomy introduced a change concerning the priesthood; now any Levite could be a priest.

Other scholars view the second expression as an explanatory apposition (R. Abba, "Priests and Levites in Deuteronomy," *VT* 27 (1977): 257–67, esp. 262–63; R. K. Duke, "The Portion of the Levite: Another Reading of Deuteronomy 18:6–8," *JBL* 106 [1987]: 193–201, esp. 197–98; ASV, NET, NIV, NLT); they insert "and" or "indeed" between the two expressions and believe Moses addresses an issue that directly relates to the Levitical priests as well as to the entire tribe of Levi (cf. also 27:9–14; 31:9, 25).

Wright (*Deuteronomy*, 220) takes all three expressions to refer to different groups, each wider than the former: priests of the Aaronic line, Levites who serve in some way at the sanctuary, and Levites who have no responsibilities at the sanctuary (cf. Emerton, 133–34). The common juxtaposition of the first two terms makes his view less likely. Regardless, the point of this passage is not to introduce a pivotal piece of legislation but to emphasize the means of provision for this important segment of Israelite society.

אִשֵּׁי יְהוָה (ʾiššê yhwh, "offerings made by fire," lit., "fires of Yahweh") is a technical expression (אִשֶּׁה, ʾiššeh) that occurs frequently in Exodus (four times), Leviticus (forty-two times), and Numbers (sixteen times), and in Leviticus for the burnt offering (Lev 1:9), meal offering (2:3), peace offering (3:3), and guilt offering (7:5). Except in the case of the burnt offering, specified portions of all these offerings were allotted to the priests (Lev 2:3; 7:6–10; Nu 18:9–10). In Deuteronomy the expression occurs only here.

7 Some of those who contend that this passage introduces a change in the pentateuchal requirements for priests suggest that "ministering in the name of Yahweh" and "serving/standing before Yahweh" (here הָעֹמְדִים ... שֵׁרֵת, šērēt ... hāʿōmᵉdîm, "he may minister ... who are serving") are clearly priestly duties (Driver, 121–23; Mayes, 206, 278). The verb "to serve" (with or without an object) occurs repeatedly to describe the function of nonpriestly Levites (Nu 1:50; 3:6, 31; 4:9; 16:9; 1Ch 15:2; 16:37; 2Ch 23:6; 29:11; Ezr 8:17; cf. Duke, "The Portion of the Levite," 199). The idea of standing before Yahweh does frequently apply to the priests but also encompasses the Levites' service (Dt 10:8; 2Ch 29:4–5, 11; Eze 44:15).

d. Prophets (18:9–22)

i. Pagan attempts to know or affect the future (18:9–14)

OVERVIEW

Before delineating the prophetic office, Moses warns the Israelites against imitating Canaanite counterfeit religious practice. God's gift of the land of Canaan and his dispossession of the Canaanites from that land begin and end this section. The land Yahweh is giving to them as an inheritance is a land in which God's covenantal people are to conduct themselves as loyal citizens of Yahweh's kingdom.

[9]When you enter the land the LORD your God is giving you, do not learn to imitate the detestable ways of the nations there. [10]Let no one be found among you who sacrifices his son or daughter in the fire, who practices divination or sorcery, interprets omens, engages in witchcraft, [11]or casts spells, or who is a medium or spiritist or who consults the dead. [12]Anyone who does these things is detestable to the LORD, and because of these detestable practices the LORD your God will drive out those nations before you. [13]You must be blameless before the LORD your God. [14]The nations you will dispossess listen to those who practice sorcery or divination. But as for you, the LORD your God has not permitted you to do so.

COMMENTARY

9–11 Israel's conquest of Canaan will bring them into direct contact with a religious system that is the diametric opposite of what Yahweh intends for his servant-nation. The Israelites must take great care that they do not learn to imitate Canaanite pagan practices, which Yahweh views as detestable (see Note on 7:25–26). Learning about Yahweh and wholeheartedly obeying him (4:1; 5:1) is incompatible with their learning these pagan practices and submitting to these pagan gods.

Most ancient cultures manifested a keen need to receive some kind of direction from their god and created various practices to facilitate that endeavor (Ex 7:11; Eze 21:21–22 [26–27]; Da 2:2). Their sacrifices were intended to prod their gods into certain courses of action. The practice of child sacrifice, though not a divinatory rite (an attempt to determine future events), represented an attempt to convince a god to do something in particular in light of the total dedication of the worshiper (evidenced in the willingness to sacrifice his or her own flesh and blood; see Note on 12:31). For example, the king of Moab, losing ground in a battle with Israel, offered his son (and heir) in an attempt to convince his god to give him the victory (2Ki 3:26–27). This abhorrent practice, along with various forms of divination and occult, "must never be found among" God's chosen people.

Divination or sorcery was practiced by the Philistines (Isa 2:6) and the Judean king Manasseh (2Ki 21:6) and condemned by God (Lev 19:26; Isa 57:3; Jer 27:9). Manasseh also utilized the practice of interpreting omens (2Ki 17:17; 21:6), condemned as well by God (Lev 19:26; Mic 5:12 [11]). Witchcraft and casting spells involved trying to change the direction of human affairs. The last three (mediums, spiritists, and consulting the dead; cf. 1Sa 28:3–14; Isa 8:19) represented attempts to communicate with the dead as a way of predicting or determining future events. See Merrill (*Deuteronomy*, 271–72) and Tigay (*Deuteronomy*, 173–74) for suggestions on more precise understandings of these difficult and rarely used terms.

12–14 These "detestable" practices represent an important part of Yahweh's rationale for demanding the extermination of the Canaanite peoples.

Consequently, all who engage in these "detestable" activities have become "detestable" to Yahweh themselves. In light of the horrific practices Yahweh regards as detestable (see Note on 7:25–26), a more powerful warning is difficult to imagine. Moses demands that the Israelites conduct blameless lives so as not to become detestable to their God.

Moses returns to where he began by reminding the Israelites of the fundamental issue before them. An exclusive relationship with Yahweh leaves no room for these failed human attempts at discerning or determining future affairs. Yahweh is going to use his chosen people to evict the Canaanites (who engaged in these detestable practices) from the land they have been occupying. God's covenantal nation can trust Yahweh himself as worthy of their absolute trust with regard to any future events. The structure of the Hebrew line emphasizes the contrast between what the Canaanites are doing and what Yahweh expects of his chosen people ("these nations … [listened], but you, not thus, did Yahweh your God give to you").

NOTE

13 The adjective תָּמִים (*tāmîm*, "blameless"; GK 9459) occurs frequently to describe offerings that perfectly match the priestly requirements, i.e., they are whole, perfect, or blameless (Ex 12:5; Lev 9:2; 22:21; Nu 6:14; 28:19). It can also depict the serenity of a relationship between God and the righteous that is complete or without blemish (Ge 6:9; 17:1; Dt 18:13; Jos 24:14). It describes a genuine and loyal relationship between persons (Jdg 9:16; Am 5:10). To be blameless signifies a person is upright before Yahweh (Ps 101:2; Grisanti, "2 Samuel," 222–23).

ii. Yahweh's provision of prophets (18:15–22)

¹⁵The LORD your God will raise up for you a prophet like me from among your own brothers. You must listen to him. ¹⁶For this is what you asked of the LORD your God at Horeb on the day of the assembly when you said, "Let us not hear the voice of the LORD our God nor see this great fire anymore, or we will die."

¹⁷The LORD said to me: "What they say is good. ¹⁸I will raise up for them a prophet like you from among their brothers; I will put my words in his mouth, and he will tell them everything I command him. ¹⁹If anyone does not listen to my words that the prophet speaks in my name, I myself will call him to account. ²⁰But a prophet who presumes to speak in my name anything I have not commanded him to say, or a prophet who speaks in the name of other gods, must be put to death."

²¹You may say to yourselves, "How can we know when a message has not been spoken by the LORD?" ²²If what a prophet proclaims in the name of the LORD does not take place or come true, that is a message the LORD has not spoken. That prophet has spoken presumptuously. Do not be afraid of him.

COMMENTARY

15 In light of the fact that Israel is about to enter a land filled with abominable practices, Moses clarifies for Israel the means of discerning a true messenger of God, i.e., a true prophet. The Lord will provide a succession of prophets from among the Israelites as well as for their benefit. The true prophet will function as Yahweh's mouthpiece, just as Moses has done. Moses, that model prophet, exhorts his fellow Israelites to pay close attention to the message of any true prophet. Other people in Israel's history before Moses had been given that title (Ge 20:7; Nu 11:29; 12:6–8), but the office of a prophet seems to crystallize in Moses' ministry as God's prophet.

16–19 When the Israelites were gathered at the base of Mount Horeb (Sinai), they feared a face-to-face encounter with Yahweh and begged Moses to function as their intermediary (5:23–27). God's revelation of his covenantal expectations to his people through his prophet Moses, a divinely certified individual, provided the paradigm for God's instituting the prophetic office. Wright (*Deuteronomy*, 217–18) points out four key elements of this important position.

1. True prophecy will be a matter of divine initiative (18:15, 18). Yahweh does not allow

for self-appointed or self-perpetuating people. Just as God will raise them up, so will he speak through them.

2. A true prophet will follow God's model, Moses, as a mediator and example of God's will (18:18a).

3. A true prophet will speak God's message (18:18b). That is why a prophet can say and write, "this is what the LORD says" (cf. Isa 6:9–10; Jer 1:9; 5:14; Eze 2:9–3:4).

4. Finally, a true prophet carried Yahweh's authority, speaking in God's "name" (18:19). The very character of God stands behind the prophetic message (and messenger). To reject the message of a true prophet represents a rejection of God himself.

20–22 The Israelites need to know that some who claim to be prophets of God will be deceivers (cf. 1Ki 22:11–28; Jer 28). A false prophet is someone who speaks words not authorized by God himself or speaks on behalf of a god other than Yahweh (cf. 13:1–11). Falsely claiming divine authority represents the epitome of presumption and arrogance (*zyd* in 18:20; see Note on 17:12). The Israelites must put to death such a pretender (cf. 17:12).

While it would be a simple matter to recognize the treachery of an alleged prophet of God who encourages them to worship other gods, discerning the authenticity of a prophet's message represents a greater challenge. A prophet whose proclamation does not come to pass is not a prophet whom God has sent. Yahweh requires truth, i.e., the correspondence between the prophetic word and the realities of history (Miller, 153; cf. 1Sa 3:19–20; 10:2–9; 1Ki 17:1–7; 21:23; 2Ki 9:32–36). Whenever a prophet makes a prediction (his ministry involved both preaching and predicting), the failure of that prediction to come to pass provides an clear verdict about the prophet's lack of divine authority.

While the fulfillment of a prediction *by itself* does not *prove* the authenticity of a prophet (13:1–3 [2–4]), failed prophecy serves as an unmistakable indication of his treachery. Do the Israelites, then, have to wait for years (until a prophetic procla-mation comes to pass) before knowing whether a given prophet has been sent by God? For example, what about Jeremiah, some of whose prophecies did not find fulfillment for decades? No, a prophet "like Moses" will have credibility with God's chosen people, who will accept his messages as divinely authorized unless one of his declarations fails to take place. The coherence of a prophet's message with the rest of Scripture will be a primary test to apply to authenticating any biblical prophet. The Israelites need not fear a prophet operating under his own authority.

By combining the input of chs. 13 and 18, a true prophet's declarations will be confirmed by history, will be consistent with the rest of Yahweh's instructions, and will maintain a demand for exclusive worship of Yahweh (Miller, 154; cf. C. H. Bullock, *An Introduction to the Old Testament Prophetic Books* [Chicago: Moody Press, 1986], 26–27).

NOTE

15 The "prophet" alluded to in the phrase יָקִים לְךָ יְהוָה אֱלֹהֶיךָ (*yāqîm lekā yhwh ʾelōheykā,* "Yahweh your God will raise up for you …") has a collective sense, i.e., it refers to prophetism as an institution. However, late Jewish writings (especially Qumran documents; see Craigie, 263, for specific citations) and various NT passages indicate the presence of an expectation of "an incomparable eschatological prophet who would be either a messianic figure or the announcer of the Messiah (cf. Jn 1:21, 25; Ac 3:22; 7:37" (E. H. Merrill, "Deuteronomy, NT Faith, and the Christian Life," in *Integrity of Heart, Skillfulness of Hands* [ed. Charles H. Dyer and Roy B. Zuck; Grand Rapids: Baker, 1994], 28). In particular, Peter's linking of Jesus with Deuteronomy 18 depicts Jesus as the fulfillment of the OT prophetic witness and the greatest of all prophets (Ac 3:12–26).

3. Laws Delineating the True Administration of Justice (19:1–22:8)

OVERVIEW

Various commentators associate this section with the sixth commandment (prohibition of murder; see Braulik, "The Sequence of Laws," 322 [omitting 22:1–8]; idem, *Deuteronomium 16, 18–34,*

12, 139–40; Hall, 297–98; Harman, 188–89). Several verses evidence that broad association, but a *close* connection between this section and the sixth commandment seems untenable. Issues such as boundary stones (19:14), female prisoners of war (21:10–14), and the right of the firstborn (21:15–17) seem only loosely related to that commandment. Also, any outline of this section is somewhat tentative because of the loose structure of chs. 19–25.

a. Cities of Refuge (19:1–13)

¹When the Lord your God has destroyed the nations whose land he is giving you, and when you have driven them out and settled in their towns and houses, ²then set aside for yourselves three cities centrally located in the land the Lord your God is giving you to possess. ³Build roads to them and divide into three parts the land the Lord your God is giving you as an inheritance, so that anyone who kills a man may flee there.

⁴This is the rule concerning the man who kills another and flees there to save his life — one who kills his neighbor unintentionally, without malice aforethought. ⁵For instance, a man may go into the forest with his neighbor to cut wood, and as he swings his ax to fell a tree, the head may fly off and hit his neighbor and kill him. That man may flee to one of these cities and save his life. ⁶Otherwise, the avenger of blood might pursue him in a rage, overtake him if the distance is too great, and kill him even though he is not deserving of death, since he did it to his neighbor without malice aforethought. ⁷This is why I command you to set aside for yourselves three cities.

⁸If the Lord your God enlarges your territory, as he promised on oath to your forefathers, and gives you the whole land he promised them, ⁹because you carefully follow all these laws I command you today — to love the Lord your God and to walk always in his ways — then you are to set aside three more cities. ¹⁰Do this so that innocent blood will not be shed in your land, which the Lord your God is giving you as your inheritance, and so that you will not be guilty of bloodshed.

¹¹But if a man hates his neighbor and lies in wait for him, assaults and kills him, and then flees to one of these cities, ¹²the elders of his town shall send for him, bring him back from the city, and hand him over to the avenger of blood to die. ¹³Show him no pity. You must purge from Israel the guilt of shedding innocent blood, so that it may go well with you.

COMMENTARY

1–3 As he has done in several preceding passages (12:20, 29; 13:12 [13]; 15:7; 17:2, 14; 18:9), Moses envisions a future day when Yahweh will establish his covenantal people in the Promised Land.

After God destroys the nations (divine role) and the Israelites drive them out and settle in their towns (human role), God's people are to set aside three cities to serve as cities of refuge (cf. Nu 35:6–34). Joshua later designated these cities as Kedesh in Galilee (northern region), Shechem in Ephraim (central region), and Hebron in Judah (southern region; Jos 20:7–9), thereby providing a city of refuge for each "third" of the land. Moses had already set aside three cities in Transjordan (Bezer, Ramoth, and Golan) to serve this purpose (4:41–43). The people are to make sure that these cities are accessible to all Israelites in case a murder takes place. A murderer, further defined in the next verses, can flee to one of these cities for refuge (to escape a "blood avenger"; 19:6, 12).

This entire passage lays great emphasis on God's role in providing this land for his chosen nation. It is a land that he "is giving you" (19:1), "is giving you to possess" (19:2), "is giving you as an inheritance" (19:3, 10; see Note on 1:38), "enlarges your territory" with (19:8), and "promised on oath to your forefathers" (19:8; see Note on 1:8)—a promise he fulfills as he "gives you the whole land he promised them" (19:8).

4–7 This legislation does not allow all murderers to flee (successfully) to a city of refuge—only those who have committed murder unintentionally (lit., "without knowledge" [*biblî-daʿat*, "premeditation"] and not driven by hatred [*śnʾ*], i.e., the legal category of manslaughter). Moses gives one example of this kind of murder: while a person is chopping wood near another person, the axehead slips off the handle and strikes and kills the other person. Since there has been no premeditation, that "murderer" has the opportunity to flee to the closest city of refuge for the protection it offers.

The reason he must flee for his life is that a victim's near relative, the "avenger of blood," was permitted by Mosaic law to kill the murderer (Nu 35:22–23). This blood avenger must not, however, act rashly and take the life of the "murderer" in the heat of anger (19:6; see Note below). The guilt of a "murderer" must be established before any execution takes place (probably by elders of the city nearest the crime scene).

8–10 Verses 1–3 delineate the legislation concerning these cities of refuge; vv.4–7 present a scenario to explain the function of these cities; and vv.11–13 deal with the fate of a person guilty of premeditated murder. The present verses deal with a more hypothetical issue, namely, Israel's need to set aside three additional cities of refuge if the nation reaches her most expansive boundaries (so that all Israelites will have easy access to such cities). Although the nation of Israel held sway over most of the divinely promised territory during the period of the united monarchy, that territory was never fully integrated as part of Israel (Craigie, 267, n. 14).

The condition envisioned in v.8 never took place (e.g., Dt 11:22–25). This passage connects the divine provision of additional land with Israel's covenantal obedience—"to love the LORD your God and to walk always in all his ways" (19:9; see Note on 4:37 and comments on 10:12–13). The NIV's rendering of v.9, "you carefully follow all these laws I command you," might be better rendered, "then you are careful to observe all this commandment" (cf. NET). The "whole commandment" (*kol-hammiṣwâ hazzōʾt*) refers here to the entire covenantal agreement of the book of Deuteronomy as encapsulated in the *Shema* (6:4–5; NET note; see Note on 6:1).

Verse 10 not only provides the rationale for setting aside these three additional cities, but it also refers to the legislation in 19:1–7. The Israelites are to make these refuge cities available to avoid the shedding of innocent blood (see comment on 19:13).

11–13 Unlike the scenario delineated in 19:4–7, these verses address the issue of a person who is driven by hatred (*śnʾ*) and plans and carries out a murder. If that person flees to a city of refuge, the elders of the town near the scene of the crime must go to that city and bring him back to their community, where they will render a verdict. They will allow the "blood avenger" to execute this murderer. The Israelites are prohibited from showing this murderer any pity (see Note on 13:8 [9]).

By putting him to death, they are purging from their land the guilt of shedding innocent blood (cf. Dt 21:8–9; see Note on 13:5). Only shedding the blood of the one who shed someone else's "innocent" blood can provide atonement for the land (cf. Nu 35:33–34). Israel's enjoyment of God's covenantal blessings is directly related to their obedience concerning the shedding of innocent blood ("so that it may go well with you"; see comments on 5:16).

NOTES

3 The difficult Hebrew construction תָּכִין לְךָ הַדֶּרֶךְ (*tākîn leka hadderek*, "build roads to them") can signify building or preparing roads (NASB, NET, NKJV, NIV; Hall, 299) or measuring the distance of roads (ESV, NRSV). The meaning of "measure out" for this verb (כון, *kwn*) might also occur at Exodus 16:5, where the Israelites are told to "prepare" or "measure out" a double portion on the Sabbath. Although both meanings highlight the need to provide easy access to these cities, the latter option appears preferable (cf. Dion, "Deuteronomy 19:3: Prepare the Way, or Estimate the Distance?" *Église et théologie* 25 (1994): 333–41; A. R. Hulst, *Old Testament Translation Problems* (Leiden: Brill, 1960), 15; Christensen, *Deuteronomy 1:1–21:9*, 422; Craigie, 265; McConville, 307; Nelson, 238; Tigay, *Deuteronomy*, 180). Since this verse emphasizes the equitable distribution of these cities throughout the land and v.6 refers to the danger of great distance, the idea of carefully measuring the distance between the cities seems to fit the context best.

The verb רצח (*rṣḥ*, here in the form רֹצֵחַ, *rōṣēaḥ*) occurs in the sixth commandment, which prohibits "murder" (Dt 5:17). Although the verb can refer to killing or murdering regardless of the circumstances (*HALOT*, 1283; Domeris, *NIDOTTE*, 3:1188–89), a comparison of that commandment with other parameters established by Yahweh (e.g., holy war, capital punishment, the present legislation concerning cities of refuge) suggests this verb in the sixth commandment refers to taking someone's life outside those divinely established parameters.

6, 12 Although the familial connection between the victim and the blood avenger is not explicitly mentioned, the verbal root "to redeem" (גאל, *gʾl*; in the light of its usage for a relative in Ru 2:20) and the reference to "in a rage" (lit., "when his heart burns" כִּי־יֵחַם לְבָבוֹ, *kî-yēḥam lebābô*; 19:6) suggests that a relative enraged by the death of one of his kin is in view in the term גֹּאֵל הַדָּם (*gōʾēl haddām*, "avenger of blood"; Nelson, 241). The actions of Gideon (Jdg 8:18–21) and Joab (2Sa 3:26–30) may also support this idea. Phillips (*Ancient Israel's Criminal Law*, 102–6) has suggested that this expression refers instead to a representative commissioned by the elders of the city near the scene of the crime. As Craigie, 266–67, suggests, a correct understanding might involve aspects of both alternatives.

The warning against acting out of anger suggests that the "blood avenger" must not act rashly and may imply that he must bring the "murderer" back to the city near the location of the crime for adjudication.

If they find the "murderer" guilty, the "blood avenger" will be allowed to carry out the death penalty. The "redemption" in view may carry the idea of restoring the wholeness that was disturbed by a premeditated murder (Ringgren, *TDOT*, 2:352; Hubbard, *NIDOTTE*, 1:791; Tigay, *Deuteronomy*, 181).

10, 13 The most common use of "blood" in the OT denotes the shedding of blood through violence, often resulting in death (2Ki 21:16; 24:4; Isa 1:15; 4:4; Jer 2:34; Hos 4:2; Trebilco, *NIDOTTE*, 1:963). The Hebrew phrase דָּם נָקִי (*dām nāqî*, "innocent blood") refers to the blood of a person who is "blameless" (*HALOT*, 720) because either he is not guilty of premeditated murder (19:10) or was the innocent victim of premeditated murder (19:13). The juxtaposition of this adjective and noun occurs twenty-one times in the OT as a fixed expression referring to guiltless people who are threatened with murder (Dt 27:25; 1Sa 19:5) or those who have been killed (Dt 19:13; 2Ki 21:16; Jnh 1:14). It signifies innocent people who, from a judicial point of view, were "powerless, guiltless, and blameless" (Olivier, *NIDOTTE*, 3:153). The shedding of innocent blood played a central role in numerous prophetic indictments (Ps 106:38; Jer 2:34; 7:6; 19:4; 22:3) and was an act that characterized Israel in some of her darkest days (2Ki 21 [during the reign of Manasseh]; Hall, 301, n. 15).

b. Boundary Stones (19:14)

14Do not move your neighbor's boundary stone set up by your predecessors in the inheritance you receive in the land the LORD your God is giving you to possess.

COMMENTARY

14 Although this legislation may seem out of place, it relates to the preceding passage through the repetition of certain key words: "borders" (*gᵉbûl*; 19:3, 8), "inheritance" (*naḥᵃlâ*; 19:10), and the verb "to inherit" (*nḥl*; 19:3). The legislation concerning cities of refuge recalls 3:12–17 and 4:41–43, passages that deal with boundary issues and cities of refuge in the region of Transjordan and pave the way for this legislation concerning boundary markers (Wright, *God's People*, 128–31).

Not only is Yahweh giving Israel the land as their inheritance (see Note on 1:38), but the land is also allocated to the tribes, clans, and individual families. The continued possession of one's land is a primary means to a family's economic security. A person might move someone's boundary for personal advantage, i.e., to gain more land. The fact that the curses of ch. 27 include a reference to this kind of conduct highlights its treacherous nature (27:17). Both wisdom writers (Job 24:2–4; Pr 15:25; 22:28; 23:10–11) and the prophets (Isa 5:8; Hos 5:10; Mic 2:2–4) refer to land grabbing as part of their warning or rebuke. To take land from a fellow Israelite represents theft (prohibited in the eighth commandment; 5:19) and covetous lack of contentment with God's allotment (prohibited in tenth commandment; 5:21).

c. False Witnesses (19:15–21)

¹⁵One witness is not enough to convict a man accused of any crime or offense he may have committed. A matter must be established by the testimony of two or three witnesses. ¹⁶If a malicious witness takes the stand to accuse a man of a crime, ¹⁷the two men involved in the dispute must stand in the presence of the LORD before the priests and the judges who are in office at the time. ¹⁸The judges must make a thorough investigation, and if the witness proves to be a liar, giving false testimony against his brother, ¹⁹then do to him as he intended to do to his brother. You must purge the evil from among you. ²⁰The rest of the people will hear of this and be afraid, and never again will such an evil thing be done among you. ²¹Show no pity: life for life, eye for eye, tooth for tooth, hand for hand, foot for foot.

COMMENTARY

15 One witness is not sufficient to convict a person accused of any crime (Nu 35:30 and Dt 17:6 deal with witnesses in capital offenses in particular). At least two or three witnesses must testify before an appointed judge before the rendering of any verdict. But ungodly people can still thwart the intent of this legislation (1Ki 21:10, 13), which is to ensure that genuine justice takes place.

16–19 If there is only one witness and that witness wants to prosecute the case, the judges and priests appointed to adjudicate it will thoroughly examine (cf. 13:14; 17:4, 9) the testimony of the "witness" as much as the accused person. Since the witness and the accused must appear at the central sanctuary before those divinely appointed to this judicial role, both plaintiffs (see Note) are standing, as it were, in Yahweh's presence. If examination of the testimony demonstrates it is false (*šeqer*; cf. 5:20 and comments there), the adjucators must punish the witness with the same penalty the accused

would have borne. The "equitable" punishment of this malicious witness is necessary for God's covenantal nation to "purge the evil" from their midst (see Note on 13:5).

20–21 It is essential that adjudicating judges and priests obeyed this legislation for the sake of the rest of the covenantal nation. The appropriate punishment of malicious witnesses will have a deterrent effect that prevents the widespread bearing of false testimony (see Note on 13:11). Rather than succumb to feelings of compassion for the witness caught up in a web of destructive lies, the adjucators must show him or her no pity whatsoever (see Note on 13:8 [9]). Instead, their judgment must accord with the principle of *lex talionis* (cf. Ex 21:23–25; Lev 24:19–20).

This often misunderstood principle does not legitimize vengeance in kind but provides appropriate limits or parameters for penalties. The punishment must be commensurate with the crime, thus preventing both leniency and excess. When Jesus addressed this issue in the Sermon on the Mount (Mt 5:38–42), he did not criticize the principle of *lex talionis* in general; rather, he affirmed that a strict

equivalence between the "crime" and the "punishment" was appropriate in legal settings but never intended to be a guide for offenses in interpersonal relationships.

NOTE

16 The noun חָמָס (*ḥāmās*, in the term עֵד־חָמָס, ʿ*ēd-ḥāmās*, "a malicious witness") occurs sixty times in the OT and can signify affliction on the international level, i.e., a stronger nation's abusing of a weaker nation (Jer 51:46; Hab 1:9; 2:8, 17). It can also connote affliction within the nation, i.e., injustices perpetrated against fellow Israelites by an individual or a group of individuals (Isa 59:6; 60:18; Jer 6:7; Eze 7:23; Am 3:10; Mic 6:12; Swart/Van Dam, *NIDOTTE*, 2:177). Often it refers to affliction brought on the poor and needy. In the present passage, it concerns legal testimony motivated by a desire to bring affliction on the accused for personal gain (cf. Ex 23:1; Ps 58:2 [3]). In light of the scrutiny placed on the "witness" and because of the seriousness of the accusation (a capital crime), both the accused and the "witness" are viewed as plaintiffs (Haag, *TDOT*, 4:484).

d. Rules for Warfare (20:1–20)

¹When you go to war against your enemies and see horses and chariots and an army greater than yours, do not be afraid of them, because the LORD your God, who brought you up out of Egypt, will be with you. ²When you are about to go into battle, the priest shall come forward and address the army. ³He shall say: "Hear, O Israel, today you are going into battle against your enemies. Do not be fainthearted or afraid; do not be terrified or give way to panic before them. ⁴For the LORD your God is the one who goes with you to fight for you against your enemies to give you victory."

⁵The officers shall say to the army: "Has anyone built a new house and not dedicated it? Let him go home, or he may die in battle and someone else may dedicate it. ⁶Has anyone planted a vineyard and not begun to enjoy it? Let him go home, or he may die in battle and someone else enjoy it. ⁷Has anyone become pledged to a woman and not married her? Let him go home, or he may die in battle and someone else marry her." ⁸Then the officers shall add, "Is any man afraid or fainthearted? Let him go home so that his brothers will not become disheartened too." ⁹When the officers have finished speaking to the army, they shall appoint commanders over it.

¹⁰When you march up to attack a city, make its people an offer of peace. ¹¹If they accept and open their gates, all the people in it shall be subject to forced labor and shall work for you. ¹²If they refuse to make peace and they engage you in battle, lay siege to that

city. [13]When the LORD your God delivers it into your hand, put to the sword all the men in it. [14]As for the women, the children, the livestock and everything else in the city, you may take these as plunder for yourselves. And you may use the plunder the LORD your God gives you from your enemies. [15]This is how you are to treat all the cities that are at a distance from you and do not belong to the nations nearby.

[16]However, in the cities of the nations the LORD your God is giving you as an inheritance, do not leave alive anything that breathes. [17]Completely destroy them — the Hittites, Amorites, Canaanites, Perizzites, Hivites and Jebusites — as the LORD your God has commanded you. [18]Otherwise, they will teach you to follow all the detestable things they do in worshiping their gods, and you will sin against the LORD your God.

[19]When you lay siege to a city for a long time, fighting against it to capture it, do not destroy its trees by putting an ax to them, because you can eat their fruit. Do not cut them down. Are the trees of the field people, that you should besiege them? [20]However, you may cut down trees that you know are not fruit trees and use them to build siege works until the city at war with you falls.

COMMENTARY

1-4 Moses introduces some broad principles (rather than detailed instructions) to govern Israel's conduct whenever the nation engages another people in warfare. The hypothetical future situation that Moses delineates involves Israel's facing an army not only larger than their own but also having numerous horses and chariots. There is no need for God's chosen people to fear this more numerous and better equipped army because Yahweh, the one who has stupendously delivered them from Egypt, will be with them (see comments on 1:42).

To prepare his people for any (future) battle, the Lord requires a priest to exhort them before they engage the enemy. Moses calls for their attention with the command to "hear" (directing their attention to his recurrent call for obedience to and faith in Yahweh [6:4; cf. 4:1; 5:1]). Then, piling up four related verbs ("fainthearted ... afraid ... terrified ... give way to panic"), he emphasizes that Israel has nothing to fear. Yahweh himself serves as the ground or basis for this lack of fear. He will be with them, will fight for them, and will give them victory (20:4).

5-9 The appointed officials (see Note on 1:15) must announce to the fighting men four circumstances that exempt them from battle (thus reducing an already outnumbered Israelite army!). The first three rest on humanitarian grounds, while the last one will help maintain better morale among those who remain. Various scholars liken these exemptions to "futility curses" (cf. Dt 28:30; Pritchard, *ANET*, 48 [lines 50-53], 143-44 [lines 96-103, 184-91]; McConville, 319; Nelson, 250). Such curses generally express an underlying fear that something that is begun but not finished might have ongoing destructive results.

A more likely understanding is to recognize the integral connection between the possession and enjoyment of the land of promise and war. Since the enjoyment of God's provision of land is such a central theme throughout Deuteronomy, it would be tragic for Israelites to be killed without having the chance to experience the very gifts and blessings for which the war is being fought (Wright, *Deuteronomy*, 229)! A man should be able to move into and occupy a house he has built (see Note below), to enjoy the fruits of the vineyard he has planted and cultivated, and to begin married life into which he has entered with his wife (20:5–6). Moses' reference to these same issues in his delineation of potential covenantal curses (28:30) emphasizes the trauma experienced by the one who misses out on these unique privileges. People who have no just claim to his house, his wife, and his vineyard will possess or enjoy them if he dies in battle. The last exemption benefits the army rather than the people released through it. A terrified soldier can devastate the morale of fellow soldiers (cf. Jdg 7:3).

10–15 These verses delineate Israel's military policy with regard to nations of non-Canaanite peoples ("at a distance" from them; v.15). When they come against the city of an enemy, they must not offer a diplomatic proposal of peace but present a nonnegotiable demand of absolute surrender, i.e., a vassal treaty (Nelson, 251; cf. Jos 9:15; 11:19; Jdg 21:13; 2Ki 18:31). If the inhabitants of the enemy city agree to these terms and open their gates, the Israelites will subject them to forced labor (20:11). However, if they refuse the terms, the Israelites will lay siege to the city. Once they conquer it they must kill all the men (thus diminishing its future threat to Israel), but spare the women (cf. 21:10–14), children, livestock, and anything of value. This plunder will become theirs to enjoy.

16–18 In accordance with instructions Moses has already given God's chosen people, they must treat the Canaanite peoples differently from those "distant" nations. Since their land and the people themselves are part of God's inheritance (see Note on 1:38) for Israel, the Israelites must destroy the Canaanite inhabitants completely, leaving no survivors (*ḥrm*; see Note on 7:2b). The phrase "anything that breathes" here refers only to the human population. As with the distant nations, they are allowed to keep the livestock as part of their booty (2:34–35; 3:4–7; Jos 10:40; 11:11). Moses provides a representative listing of the nations; he omits the Girgashites, mentioned in the list of 7:1–2a (see comments there).

This note fully accords with Yahweh's requirements (cf. Ex 23:23, 32–33; Dt 7:1–2). The rationale for this demand is spiritual, not military strategy: If the Israelites do not exterminate the Canaanites with their vile religious practices, the Israelites will be seduced by these abhorrent forms of worship, regarded by Yahweh as detestable (*tôʿēbâ*; see Note on 7:25–26). For Israel to assimilate Canaanite worship practices represents sin against Yahweh himself, their covenantal Lord.

19–20 For the immediate benefit of the Israelite army and the long-term benefit of the besieged people, the Israelites are to chop down only non-fruit-bearing trees for the construction of siege equipment. The spared fruit trees will give the Israelite soldiers an available source for food during their siege of the enemy city and provide necessary economic benefits for the ongoing life of anyone who lives in that city.

NOTES

1 Although there is evidence of chariots (רֶכֶב [*rekeb*]) as far back as the late fourth millennium BC (in southern Mesopotamia), it was not until the early to mid-second millennium that the chariot underwent significant development and found more widespread use as an effective tool of warfare. The chariot provided an army with a mobile platform from which to fire volleys of arrows, particularly effective in softening up enemy infantry. In close quarters, javelins or short, light spears could wreak havoc against an army on foot (Littauer/Crouwel, *ABD*, 1:889−90; cf. Y. Yadin, *The Art of Warfare in Biblical Lands* (New York: McGraw-Hill, 1963), 1:4−5, 86−90).

The prohibition לֹא תִירָא (*lōʾ tîrāʾ*), "do not fear" (without an explicit object) occurs eight times in the OT (three times outside Deuteronomy; Job 11:15; Isa 8:12; 54:14). In every case in which the expression occurs in Deuteronomy, it is grounded in the fact that Yahweh will fight for his people (1:29; 3:22) or is with them (31:8), or it is related to his devastation of Egypt (1:29; 7:18; 20:1).

A similar construction occurs in 20:3−4 (אַל־תִּירְאוּ ... כִּי, *ʾal-tîreʾû ... kî*, "do not fear ... because"). This encouragement formula occurs seventy-five times in the OT and appears in four kinds of scenarios. Although it is used as a bland word of encouragement in everyday life (Ge 35:17; 43:23; 50:19; Ru 3:11), it occurs frequently to encourage God's people in the context of holy war (four times in Deuteronomy). As with the other construction, this prohibition of fear is grounded in God's previous activity (he set the Promised Land before them [1:21]; he had already delivered Sihon into their hands [3:2]), the fact that he was with them (20:4; 31:6), and his promise to fight for them (20:4).

5 Although scholars are divided on whether the verb חנך (*ḥnk*, root of חֲנָכוֹ, *ḥᵃnākô*) should be translated "to dedicate" (Merrill, *Deuteronomy*, 284; Ridderbos, 214; Thompson, 220) or to "initiate" or "begin using" (Christensen, *Deuteronomy 1:1−21:9*, 438; Craigie, 273, n. 12; Dommershausen, *TDOT*, 5:19−21; McConville, 319; Nelson, 244; Reif, "Dedicated to חנך," *VT* 22 (1972): 495−99; Tigay, *Deuteronomy*, 187), most translations render it "to dedicate." Those favoring this translation commonly point to the usage of the verb with regard to the dedication of Solomon's temple (1Ki 8:62−64 = 2Ch 7:5−7) or to the derived noun (חֲנֻכָּה, *ḥᵃnukkâ*), associated with the consecration of the great temple altar (2Ch 7:9) as well as the postexilic wall of Jerusalem (Ne 12:27). In Maccabean times the festival of Hanukkah, the name of which is based on this verb, was introduced to celebrate the rededication of the temple following its desecration by Antiochus IV Epiphanes (1Mc 4:36−61; 2Mc 10:1−8; Dommershausen, *TDOT*, 5:21). According to this view, what is being done is a sacred ceremony to Yahweh (Merrill, *Deuteronomy*, 284).

Those who favor "to begin using" point out that there is no evidence for a ritual of dedication for a home in Israel (only for public structures) and that the "dedication" usages could just as easily signify "beginning to use" the thing in question (cf. M. Cogan, *1 Kings* [AB; New York: Doubleday, 2000], 289).

10 To וְקָרָאתָ אֵלֶיהָ לְשָׁלוֹם (*wᵉqārāʾtā ʾēleyhā lᵉšālôm*), "make ... an offer of peace," represents nothing less than terms for absolute surrender. The Israelites will promise to spare the city if its inhabitants agreed to submit to their dominion. In both an Akkadian letter from Mari and an Egyptian inscription, cognate words for the Hebrew שָׁלוֹם (šālôm) depict submission or surrender (Tigay, *Deuteronomy*, 188–89, 380, n. 27; D. Wiseman, "'Is It Peace?'—Covenant and Diplomacy," *VT* 32 (1982): 320–21; cf. ARM, 2, 42:8; Pritchard, *ANET*, 378).

11 The noun לָמַס (*lāmas*, "to forced labor") refers to a contingent of conscripted laborers working for the state on agricultural or construction projects (*HALOT*, 603–4; cf. 2Sa 12:31; 1Ki 9:15, 20–22).

19 If left as is, the statement הָאָדָם עֵץ הַשָּׂדֶה (*hāʾādām ʿēṣ haśśādeh*, lit., "men are the trees of the field") seems quite confusing. It could mean that men live on the trees of the field, i.e., as the trees go, so man goes (because he needs them for food). Nelson, 245, suggests that it could mean that "the life-giving products of the trees are the equivalent of the enemy humans they would otherwise be sustaining: 'for the tree of the field is [worth] a human life.'" Several scholars, following various ancient versions (LXX, Syriac), repoint the article to make it an interrogative particle: הֶאָדָם (*heʾādām*; Christensen, *Deuteronomy 1:1–21:9*, 444, 448; Craigie, 277, n. 20; McConville, 316; Mayes, 296). This change makes the clause a rhetorical question: "Are the trees of the field human beings ...?" either meaning that the trees are not human and hence unable to protect themselves, or that since they are not human they do not need to be killed indiscriminately. Tigay (*Deuteronomy*, 380, n. 38) suggests that no repointing is necessary since in some passages the interrogative appears with this very form (Ge 17:17; and before an *aleph* in Nu 16:22).

e. Issues of Life and Death (21:1–23)

OVERVIEW

Although the contents of this chapter are diverse, the passage has several features that contribute to its cohesiveness. It begins and ends with a focus on the Promised Land as Yahweh's gift to his chosen people (21:1, 23), deals with the need to purge the land of sin (21:9, 21), and juxtaposes issues of death and life.

i. Atonement for unsolved murder (21:1–9)

[1]If a man is found slain, lying in a field in the land the LORD your God is giving you to possess, and it is not known who killed him, [2]your elders and judges shall go out and measure the distance from the body to the neighboring towns. [3]Then the elders of the town nearest the body shall take a heifer that has never been worked and has never worn a yoke [4]and lead her down to a valley that has not been plowed or planted and where there is a flowing stream. There in the valley they are to break the heifer's neck. [5]The priests, the sons of Levi, shall step forward, for the LORD your God has chosen them to minister and to pronounce blessings in the name of the LORD and to decide all cases of dispute and assault. [6]Then all the elders of the town nearest the body shall wash their hands over the

heifer whose neck was broken in the valley, ⁷and they shall declare: "Our hands did not shed this blood, nor did our eyes see it done. ⁸Accept this atonement for your people Israel, whom you have redeemed, O Lord, and do not hold your people guilty of the blood of an innocent man." And the bloodshed will be atoned for. ⁹So you will purge from yourselves the guilt of shedding innocent blood, since you have done what is right in the eyes of the Lord.

COMMENTARY

1–4 Moses delineates a scenario in which an unknown person has killed a fellow Israelite and someone else happens to discover the corpse. Since this crime has occurred on Israel's land, bestowed on them by Yahweh, it is an offense against him as well as the victim. Israel's land is where God "lives" (Nu 35:34). If this scenario takes place, elders and judges (probably from the central sanctuary; Craigie, 279; Tigay, *Deuteronomy*, 191) will determine which community lies nearest to the scene of the crime. Elders from that city are to bring a young cow (that has not been used for work) to a nearby valley. That valley has to be undisturbed by agricultural activity and have a stream flowing through it (perhaps to show the symbolic removal of guilt). This unused heifer and valley have not been contaminated by human activity. In that valley the elders are to break the neck of the young cow (apparently a death not involving shedding the cow's blood [as a sacrifice], contra David P. Wright, "Deuteronomy 21:1–9 as a Rite of Elimination," *CBQ* 49 [1987]: 387–403, esp. 394).

People have understood this requirement in various ways (Wright, "Deuteronomy 21:1–9 as a Rite of Elimination," 388–93, provides a helpful overview of interpretive possibilities). Two options appear most likely. Some have suggested it is a symbolic, judicial execution (Thompson, 227). That is, the cow serves as a symbolic substitute for the unknown murder. Hence the killing of this cow is not viewed as a sacrifice but as an execution. However, this option does not seem to explain the obscure location for the mandated action (thus depriving it of public impact). Others view the action as a rite of expiation or elimination (Hall, 315; Merrill, *Deuteronomy*, 288; Tigay, *Deuteronomy*, 472–74; Wright, *Deuteronomy*, 232–33). In this view, the death of the cow represents a reenactment of the murder as the grounds for eliminating guilt from the land (for ancient Near Eastern parallels, see Tigay, *Deuteronomy*, 539, n. 1; D. P. Wright, "Rite of Elimination," 401–3).

The elders of the nearby community are responsible to deal with this offense by virtue of the concept of corporate responsibility. There is a sense in which Yahweh holds the entire nation responsible for certain sins—an approach reflected in other ancient Near Eastern law codes (Code of Hammurabi, §§23–24 [*COS*, 2:338]; Hittite Laws, §IV [late version of §6], [*COS*, 2:107]).

5 The priests, God's chosen representatives, must be present at this ceremony even though their precise involvement is not clear. The verse summarizes their role in the life of Israel: to minister, pronounce blessings in Yahweh's name, and adjudicate certain legal cases.

6–9 After the priests have presented themselves, the elders will symbolically affirm their innocence with regard to the unsolved murder case by washing their hands over the dead cow (cf. Pss 26:6; 73:13; cf. Mt 27:24). By doing so they will affirm their noninvolvement in and total lack of knowledge concerning the tragic event (for their sake as well as for their community's). They will ask Yahweh to accept their profession of innocence as his redeemed people (see Note on 9:26) and "to atone for" this bloodshed. God requires this action of them in order to purge (see Note on 13:5) the guilt of shedding innocent blood (see Note on 19:10, 13) on the land over which the Lord is sovereign. Reference to "your people Israel ... your people" (21:8) as those who need this divine atonement demonstrates that the nation as a whole, not just the nearby community, needs to rectify their relationship with Yahweh.

NOTES

1 The expression כִּי־יִמָּצֵא (*kî-yimmāṣēʾ*, "if ... is found") occurs four times in Deuteronomy (17:2; 21:1; 22:22; 24:7) and implies discovery by the community. It does not describe a situation in which a person is caught "redhanded." Rather than emphasizing the fearfulness of the crime itself, it stresses its seriousness because it was done before Israel's covenantal Lord (C. Carmichael, *The Laws of Deuteronomy* [Ithaca, N.Y.: Cornell Univ. Press, 1974], 45–46). Since the issue stands unresolved before Yahweh, it is something offensive that the Israelites must remove from Yahweh's presence (McConville, 327).

The adjective חָלָל (*ḥalāl*, "slain") accompanied by the participle נֹפֵל (*nōpēl*) can refer to people who have died in battle (1Sa 31:1; Eze 32:20). In this passage it refers to a homicide victim (Nu 19:16; 23:24; Jer 51:52; Eze 26:15; 30:24; 31:17–18; cf. Dommershausen, *TDOT*, 4:419).

8 Scholars have offered three basic meanings for the important OT verb כַּפֵּר (*kappēr*, "Accept this atonement"; GK 4105): (1) "to cover" (BDB, 497; Jenni, *Das Hebräische Piʿel* [Zürich: EVZ, 1968], 241); (2) "to ransom" (W. Eichrodt, *Theology of the Old Testament* [trans. J. A. Baker; Philadelphia: Westminster, 1961–67], 2:444–47; B. Levine, *In the Presence of the Lord: A Study of Cult and Some Cultic Terms in Ancient Israel* [Leiden: Brill, 1974], 67–77 [proposing a distinct verb, כפר II (*kpr* II)]; Harris, *TWOT*, 1:453); and (3) "to wipe away" (Averbeck, *NIDOTTE*, 2:696–98; J. Hartley, 63–66; B. Levine, *Leviticus* [JPS Torah Commentary; Philadelphia: Jewish Publication Society, 1989], 23–24 [כפר I (*kpr* I)]; Milgrom, *Leviticus 1–16*, 1079–80). Without going into detail, the third option appears to provide the best understanding of this verb. It always carries a resultative nuance, i.e., it does not describe an ongoing process but emphasizes a result to be achieved (Maass, *TLOT*, 2:626).

This passage is one of the few places that has God as the subject of this verb (cf. Dt 32:43; 2Ch 30:18; Pss 65:3 [4]; 78:38; 79:9; Jer 18:23; Eze 16:63, each of which passages concerns a situation in which the lives of the persons involved are forfeit because of some legal, moral, or religious guilt). The desired act of atonement by God relates to "an exceptionally critical situation in which not simply some aspect of human life but its very existence is at stake" (Lang, *TDOT*, 7:300). The atonement envisioned here is not part of the sacrificial system but concerns the correction of a horrible injustice. The death of the cow clears the land and the people of Israel from their corporate guilt.

ii. Female prisoners of war (21:10–14)

> ¹⁰When you go to war against your enemies and the LORD your God delivers them into your hands and you take captives, ¹¹if you notice among the captives a beautiful woman and are attracted to her, you may take her as your wife. ¹²Bring her into your home and have her shave her head, trim her nails ¹³and put aside the clothes she was wearing when captured. After she has lived in your house and mourned her father and mother for a full month, then you may go to her and be her husband and she shall be your wife. ¹⁴If you are not pleased with her, let her go wherever she wishes. You must not sell her or treat her as a slave, since you have dishonored her.

COMMENTARY

10–14 Envisioning a similar circumstance to that depicted in 20:1 (when Israel engages a people in battle and God gives his people victory), this legislation provides guidance for the man who notices among the captives an attractive woman whom he desires to marry. The fact that Israel takes captives in this scenario demonstrates that the battle has been against non-Canaanite peoples (see 20:13–15 and comments there). Hence these instructions do not contradict those given in 7:3 (contra Mayes, 303).

In the scenario depicted, the Israelite man is permitted to take this woman as his wife, but with certain requirements.

1. He must house her in his home and have the woman shave her hair, trim her nails, and wear new clothing (rather than the garb of prisoners). Although in part perhaps relating to her mourning her parents (see below), the primary significance of these requirements consists in her need to make a clearcut transition to life as an Israelite.

2. She must be given the chance to mourn her parents for one month (whether they have died in the conflict or simply because she will likely never see them again).

3. The marriage is not to be consummated until the month of mourning is over. During that period the Israelite man might reconsider his decision.

4. Finally, if he finds her displeasing for any reason, he has to release her from the relationship with no consequences (e.g., he cannot make her his slave [ʿmr] or sell her as a slave to someone else [mkr]; see Note on v.14). After all, he has "dishonored" or "humiliated" (ʿnh) this woman by rejecting one with whom he has (likely) had sexual relations. The verb ʿnh occurs in several OT passages to refer to rape (Ge 34:2; 2Sa 13:12, 14, 22, 32; Jdg 19:24; see Note on 8:2). Whether or not the Israelite man decides to send the foreign woman away before or after

their marriage is consummated, he must not treat her as a slave but as a free citizen.

Although this passage raises legitimate concerns about the potential religious or spiritual influences this foreign wife might have on her husband (cf. 7:3–4), it focuses on a different issue, namely, the humane treatment of a captive woman. Regardless of whether or not the passage envisions an "official" divorce (*šlḥ*, "to send away," can have that connotation; Dt 22:19, 29; 24:1–3; Jer 3:1; Mal 2:16), it does not give divine approval for divorce. Numerous OT and NT passages present divorce in a negative light or prohibit it altogether (Lev 21:7, 14; Dt 22:19, 29; Mal 2:16; Mt 5:31–32; 19:3–9; 1Co 7:10–16). In this legislation, as with Deuteronomy 24:1–4 (see comments there), God addresses a real-life situation without mandating or even recommending divorce.

NOTE

14 The verb עמר (*ʿmr*, in the phrase לֹא־תִתְעַמֵּר, *lōʾ-titʿammēr*, "do not treat her as a slave"; GK 6683) occurs only twice in the OT (here and 24:7). In both passages it is juxtaposed with the verb מכר (*mkr*), "to sell." The Targums (Aramaic paraphrases of the OT) render this verb "treat as merchandise" or "engage in trade with" (Tigay, *Deuteronomy*, 382, n. 35). Alt compared עמר to a cognate noun in Ugaritic texts that designated a group of people liable for military service (A. Alt, "Zu *Hitʿammēr*," *VT* 2 [1952]: 153–57). If Alt is correct, the verb signifies the actions of a person who claims unlimited power over the disposal of others (Mayes, 304). Along this line, Nelson, 254 (cf. *HALOT*, 849) suggests a translation of "exercise one's power of commercial disposal."

Given the agricultural backdrop for another form of this verb ("to gather grain"; Ps 129:7b), M. David suggested the translation "treat as merchandise" ("*Hitʿāmēr* [Dt XXI 14; XXIV 7]," *VT* 1 [1951]: 219–21). Swart and Cornelius (*NIDOTTE*, 3:441) posit that the verb "intends to express an oppressive deed that has devastating physical and psychological impact on the afflicted person. The latter is mistreated, forced to submit to the will of a stronger party, reduced to servile existence, and his or her whole person degraded." Brin (*Studies in Biblical Law: From the Hebrew Bible to the Dead Sea Scrolls* [JSOTSup 176; ed. D. J. A. Clines and P. R. Davies; Sheffield: JSOT, 1994], 28, n. 17) points out that the two verbs (מכר, *mkr*, "to sell," and עמר, *ʿmr*, "to treat as a commodity") are not redundant—the second verb describes the "non-humanitarian relationship expressed in the sale of the captive woman."

iii. The right of the firstborn (21:15–17)

[15]If a man has two wives, and he loves one but not the other, and both bear him sons but the firstborn is the son of the wife he does not love, [16]when he wills his property to his sons, he must not give the rights of the firstborn to the son of the wife he loves in preference to his actual firstborn, the son of the wife he does not love. [17]He must acknowledge the son of his unloved wife as the firstborn by giving him a double share of all he has. That son is the first sign of his father's strength. The right of the firstborn belongs to him.

COMMENTARY

15–17 If an Israelite man who has two wives, one of which he loves more than the other (cf. Jacob and his wives, Ge 29:21–30:24), he is prohibited from preferring the son(s) of his most-loved wife when deciding matters of inheritance. He is not permitted to "give the rights of the firstborn" (i.e., transfer the benefits of the firstborn) to the son of the beloved wife merely by his declaration of that intent ("to treat as firstborn" [factitive Piel]; *HALOT*, 130). The eldest son, regardless of the intensity of his father's love for his mother, is to receive two-thirds of his father's inheritance (see Note).

The Mosaic law made this requirement because the firstborn son was the "sign of his father's strength." His birth demonstrated his father's ability to perpetuate the family name (Ge 49:3; Pss 78:51; 105:36). The key issue addressed by this passage is that a husband's attitude toward his wife must not influence his legal responsibilities to her or her children (Merrill, *Deuteronomy*, 292).

NOTES

15 Not only does the OT fail to condemn polygamy (the practice of taking more than one wife), but in this passage it actually assumes the practice (שְׁתֵּי נָשִׁים, *šᵉtê nāšîm*, "two wives") in ancient Israel. Is the OT condoning polygamy? In the light of Genesis 2:23–24 (which depicts a monogamous relationship as the creation model), any form of polygamy was a departure from the original institution of marriage. Even though the practice of polygamy was tolerated during the time of the OT, it represented a violation of God's instituted order (the biblical ideal). Also notice that despite this toleration in OT times Mosaic legislation sought to prevent worse evils and abuses from occurring, and the absence of stiff civil or religious penalties for polygamy does not imply its legitimacy. Even if polygamy was "allowed" in certain OT scenarios, this allowance does not imply that polygamy was desirable or recommended. The absence of any word of censure or condemnation does not necessarily indicate the condoning of a given practice. The teaching and practice of the NT resoundingly supports monogamous marriage.

The most controversial problem is this: How does one fit the biblical ideal of monogamy with any "allowance" of polygamy in the life of an OT believer? In that regard, notice this chronological progression. Before the law of Moses, instances of polygamy are cited without positive or negative comments. In each case, however, the chaos and tension that results from polygamy suggest that it was not a wise choice by the men involved. At the time of the law of Moses, the Mosaic legislation either deals with a practice that was already in place or mandates a marriage in certain cases that *may* involve polygamy (e.g., Dt 25:5–10). Finally, at the time of the NT, monogamous marriage relationships are clearly reaffirmed.

In spite of the clear biblical ideal for marriage (permanent and monogamous), two concessions to fallen humanity (with regard to marriage) appear to manifest themselves in the Bible. First, the phenomenon of divorce deviated from the biblical ideal of the permanence of marriage. With regard to divorce, Jesus affirms that the permitting of divorce arose on account of the hardness of the human heart (Mt 19:8). Both Moses and Jesus placed regulations on divorce to avoid a number of excesses and abuses. Divorce never was, never is, and never will be an expression of the divine intent for marriage. The biblical regulations placed on divorce by Moses and Jesus were not to make divorce easy or to elevate it to an accepted practice. On the contrary, these regulations were intended to prevent wanton, illegitimate, and repeated divorce and remarriage.

Second, the phenonemon of polygamy represented a compromise of God's ideal that marriage be monogamous. From the OT, it is readily apparent that polygamy became part of the fabric of Israelite society early in the patriarchal period. The Mosaic regulations placed on polygamous marriages served to prevent a number of potential abuses that customarily occurred in polygamous relationships (Ex 21:7–11; Dt 21:15–18, 25:5–10).

17 The Hebrew expression פִּי שְׁנַיִם (*pî šᵉnayim*, "the double portion," lit., "a mouth/measure of two"), based on an Akkadian fraction for two-thirds (*šinipû/āt*, which also involves the two ideas "two" and "mouth"), should be consistently rendered "two-thirds" (Barry J. Beitzel, "The Right of the Firstborn [*Pî Šᵉnayim*] in the Old Testament [Deut. 21:15–17]," in *A Tribute to Gleason Archer* [ed. Walter C. Kaiser Jr. and Ronald F. Youngblood; Chicago: Moody Press, 1986], 182; cf. 2Ki 2:9; Zec 13:8). This practice is implied in Isaac's blessing of Jacob (Ge 25:31–34) and Jacob's blessing of Ephraim (Ge 48:8–22). Consequently, the firstborn son is to inherit the majority and not just a plurality of his father's estate (Beitzel, 183; contra Tsevat, *TDOT*, 2:125–26).

iv. Punishment of rebellious sons (21:18–21)

> **18**If a man has a stubborn and rebellious son who does not obey his father and mother and will not listen to them when they discipline him, **19**his father and mother shall take hold of him and bring him to the elders at the gate of his town. **20**They shall say to the elders, "This son of ours is stubborn and rebellious. He will not obey us. He is a profligate and a drunkard." **21**Then all the men of his town shall stone him to death. You must purge the evil from among you. All Israel will hear of it and be afraid.

COMMENTARY

18–21 These verses describe a situation that any parent would find horrifying: a child who refuses to obey and does not heed any disciplinary measures. In the setting of the covenantal nation, the parents of that rebellious son must present him to their town's elders so they can adjudicate the situation. Judicial and economic decisions customarily took place in the area of the town gate (Ge 23:10, 18; Dt 16:18; 17:5; 22:15, 24; Pr 24:7; Jer 20:2). This case of a rebellious son represents more than a family matter because the family unit is an essential part of the fabric of the covenantal nation (see comments on 5:16).

After presenting their son to the elders, the parents describe his rebellious conduct and add that he is leading a dissolute lifestyle. The harshness of the mandated penalty (much harsher than the general practice in the contemorary ancient Near East [cf. David Marcus, "Juvenile Delinquency in the Bible and the Ancient Near East," *JANESCU* 13 (1981): 33–44]) relates to the fact that rejection of parental authority is tantamount to violating the covenant in Israel (McConville, 331). Also, the son's unswerving commitment to rebellion mirrored Israel's tendency to rebel against Yahweh, for which disobedience he eventually "extinguishes" them as a nation (E. Bellefontaine, "Deuteronomy 21:18–21: Reviewing the Case of the Rebellious Son," *JSOT* 13 [1979]: 24–26). Whether or not the parents pursue the mandated legal process, juvenile rebellion incurs a divine curse (27:16).

Once the town elders have heard the case and rendered their guilty verdict, all the men of the town will participate in carrying out the death penalty (by stoning). Not only will this execution have a powerful impact on all the fathers who have to participate in it (thus motivating them to be diligent in placing the stamp of God's character on the lives of their sons), but it should also have a deterrent effect on the young men and women viewing and hearing of the fate of this rebellious son. Although disobedient conduct begins in the household, it affects the whole community and indeed the entire nation. Yahweh demands that the Israelites carry out this severe penalty in order to "purge the evil" from the nation (see Note on 13:5).

NOTES

18, 20 Both adjectives in the phrase בֵּן סוֹרֵר וּמוֹרֶה (*bēn sôrēr ûmôreh*, "a stubborn and rebellious son") connote the idea of rebellion. They occur as a word pair twice in this passage as well as in Psalm 78:8 and Jeremiah 5:23. The psalmist bemoans the fact that the Israelites' ancestors were characterized by rebellion, and Jeremiah indicts the Israelites of his day for their stubbornness and departure from God's covenantal expectations.

The verb סרר (*srr*; GK 6253), which occurs first in the phrase, may signify a rebellious attitude more than some specific action (Patterson, *TWOT*, 2:635); elsewhere the word appears by itself to describe the rebellious attitude of the nation (Ne 9:29; Hos 4:16; cf. Carpenter/Grisanti, *NIDOTTE*, 3:299). The second verb (מרה, *mrh*; GK 5286) occurs more frequently in the OT, in general to describe persons in some kind of subordinate position rebelling before another to whom they owe obedience. The act of rebellion is a conscious, intentional, consummate decision to disobey or rebel (Carpenter/Grisanti, *NIDOTTE*, 2:1100). As a pair, these verbs present a "paradigm of the incorrigible youth" (W. McKane, *Proverbs, A New Approach* [OTL; Philadelphia: Westminster, 1970], 388) or a "cliché for self-indulgence and lack of constructive activity" (Merrill, *Deuteronomy*, 294–95). For a helpful overview of "juvenile delinquency" in the Bible and the ancient Near East, see Marcus, "Juvenile Delinquency," 31–52.

20 The verb זלל (*zll*, in the phrase זוֹלֵל וְסֹבֵא, *zôlēl weṣōbēʾ*, "a profligate and a drunkard"; GK 2361) occurs eight times in the OT and means to be despised or to regard something lightly. Four instances (in the Qal) condemn gluttony, the squandering of food for lack of appreciation of its value. This passage and Proverbs 23:20–21 link together drunkards and gluttons. This kind of behavior is reprehensible and brings poverty (Pr 23:21), heaps disgrace on one's father (28:7), and, as a practice of the rebellious son, receives the death penalty (Dt 21:20; Grisanti, *NIDOTTE*, 1:1109). The second verb, סבא (*sbʾ*; GK 6010), describes those who characteristically drink too much beer (Isa 56:12) or wine (Pr 23:20). This pair of descriptive terms and the one in 21:18, 20 might have served as stock epithets for rebellion and the dissolute lifestyle that often follows (R. Whybray, *Proverbs* [NCBC; Grand Rapids: Eerdmans, 1994], 338). The OT soundly condemns the laziness that accompanied this sort of lifestyle (Pr 10:4; 12:27; 26:15; Ecc 10:18).

v. Proper treatment of executed criminals (21:22–23)

²²If a man guilty of a capital offense is put to death and his body is hung on a tree, ²³you must not leave his body on the tree overnight. Be sure to bury him that same day, because anyone who is hung on a tree is under God's curse. You must not desecrate the land the LORD your God is giving you as an inheritance.

COMMENTARY

22–23 While 21:1–9 deal with protecting the land from cursedness through contact with the corpse of a murder victim (whose killer was unknown), the present passage concerns the corpse of an executed criminal. The hanging of his body on a tree is not the reason for the curse but an expression of his cursed status. The Israelites probably hung his body on a tree (or wooden post) for the deterrent effect the sight would have on other would-be criminals. The law presented here limits the time that the body can be left to hang—the daylight hours that remain after the execution. To be hung on a tree is tantamount to being under God's curse, and to leave the corpse hanging there overnight is to desecrate the land that Yahweh has bestowed on his chosen nation and to invite God's curse to fall on the entire land.

NOTES

22 As indicated in the phrase וְתָלִיתָ אֹתוֹ עַל־עֵץ (*wᵉtālîtā ʾōtô ʿal-ʿēṣ,* "and his body is hung on a tree"), the Israelites (Fitzmyer, "Crucifixion in Ancient Palestine, Qumran Literature, and the New Testament," *CBQ* 40 [1978]: 493–513), as well as some of their ancient Near Eastern neighbors, practiced the hanging of bodies in a public place (e.g., Epic of Gilgamesh, 12:151–52 [Pritchard, *ANET*, 99]; Code of Hammurabi, §153 [*COS*, 2:345]; Middle Assyrian Laws, §53 [*COS*, 2:359]; Sennacherib's siege of Jerusalem [*COS*, 2:303]; Pritchard, *ANEP*, §362, 368, 373). The Israelites did so either as a means of execution (Jos 8:29; Est 2:23; 5:14; 7:10; 8:7) or as a public display after the criminal died (cf. Ge 40:19, 22; Jos 10:26–27; 2Sa 4:12; 21:12). Crucifixion continued this practice of public exposure and combined the execution with humiliation. The Jews removed Jesus' body before nightfall in conformity with the stipulation found here (see Mt 27:57–58).

23 The expression קִלְלַת אֱלֹהִים (*qillat ʾᵉlōhîm,* "under God's curse") literally reads, "a curse of God." Scholars have debated whether this genitival construction should be regarded as an objective genitive ("a curse to God") or a subjective genitive ("cursed by God"). Fox renders the phrase "an insult to God" (Everett Fox, *The Five Books of Moses* [New York: Schocken, 1995], 945), and Phillips (*Ancient Israel's Criminal Law*, 25, 41–42) offers "a repudiation of God" (cf. The Message). Most translations and scholars correctly translate it as a subjective genitive (supported by the LXX and Gal 3:13). Yahweh commands the Israelites to hang a criminal's body on a tree as an expression of that person's accursed state, i.e., to provide tangible evidence that this criminal is the object of curse. Being accursed is not the result of hanging on a tree but instead the cause for it. Paul (Gal 3:13–14) makes use of this passage to affirm that Christ hung "upon the tree" to bear the curse of the violated covenant and to turn away God's wrath from his people by delivering them from the curse of the law (A. Caneday, "Redeemed from the Curse of the Law: The Use of Deut. 21:22–23 in Gal. 3:13," *TJ* 10 [1989]: 208).

f. Acts of Justice and Equity (22:1–8)

> [1]If you see your brother's ox or sheep straying, do not ignore it but be sure to take it back to him. [2]If the brother does not live near you or if you do not know who he is, take it home with you and keep it until he comes looking for it. Then give it back to him. [3]Do the same if you find your brother's donkey or his cloak or anything he loses. Do not ignore it.
>
> [4]If you see your brother's donkey or his ox fallen on the road, do not ignore it. Help him get it to its feet.
>
> [5]A woman must not wear men's clothing, nor a man wear women's clothing, for the LORD your God detests anyone who does this.
>
> [6]If you come across a bird's nest beside the road, either in a tree or on the ground, and the mother is sitting on the young or on the eggs, do not take the mother with the young. [7]You may take the young, but be sure to let the mother go, so that it may go well with you and you may have a long life.
>
> [8]When you build a new house, make a parapet around your roof so that you may not bring the guilt of bloodshed on your house if someone falls from the roof.

1–4 In contrast to the natural human tendency toward noninvolvement in matters that do not directly relate to one's life, Moses exhorts God's people to take the initiative in assisting their fellow Israelites in various basic realms of life. If an Israelite finds one of his brother's oxen or sheep astray from its pasture (cf. Ex 23:4), he must take the time and energy to return it to his brother's home. If the owner lives at a distance or is unknown, he must take care of the lost animal until the owner comes to claim the animal.

This policy applies to whatever a fellow Israelite might lose. This particular stipulation is not warning God's people against theft but is requiring that they go out of their way to restore any found property to its rightful owner. Also, if they come across a beast of burden that has collapsed on the road (surely weighed down by a heavy load and accompanied by its owner), any passing Israelite must help with getting the animal back on its feet and its way. In both scenarios, an Israelite must not succumb to the temptation to ignore the problem because it concerns someone else. All members of the covenantal nation must show genuine interest in the welfare and success of their fellow Israelites.

5 Although some interpreters apply this verse to fashions or styles of dressing, it more likely refers to some kind of deviant sexual conduct, i.e., transvestism and/or homosexuality. The word for men's "clothing" ($k^e l\hat{\imath}$) can refer to weapons (1:41) or utensils (23:24) as well as clothes (1Sa 21:6), while the term used in connection with women ($\acute{s}iml\hat{a}$) more clearly signifies a garment of some kind. W. H. Römer ("Randbemerkungen zur Travestie von Dt 22,5," in *Travels in the World of the Old Testament* [ed. M. van Voss, P. Houwink ten Cate, and N. van Uchelen; Assen: Van Gorcum, 1974], 19–22; cf. Braulik, *Deuteronomium 16, 18–34, 12*, 161–62) has gathered various examples from Mesopotamian sources of transvestism, the confusion of the sexes, or emasculation that are related to the worship of the goddess Ishtar. Even though the text does not specify the particular background of this covenantal requirement, the fact that Yahweh regards the behavior as detestable (see Note on 7:25–26) suggests that it is related to false worship or horrible perversion.

6–7 An Israelite who finds a bird's nest that has fallen from its resting place must not take the mother bird for personal consumption, not necessarily out of humanitarian concerns (as some argue) but as a means of protecting a long-term source of food (cf. 20:19–20). The released mother bird can produce other eggs, care for those chicks, and thus in the future provide potential food for Israelites.

The statement "so that it may go well with you and you may have a long life" (22:7) is cited several times as a consequence of wholehearted obedience to the Mosaic law (4:40; 5:33; 6:2; 11:9; et al.; see comments on 4:1). It also occurs as the anticipated consequence of just three specific covenantal requirements: honoring one's parents (5:16), using just weights (25:15), and the protection of birds in the present context. Although the thread that ties these three elements together is not altogether clear, the stipulation does demonstrate that some covenantal demands that at first glance might not seem far-reaching in fact have great importance.

8 Houses in the ancient Near East generally had flat roofs and were regularly used for various purposes: drying and storing produce, sleeping, relaxation, and entertaining guests (Jos 2:6; 1Sa 9:25; 2Sa 11:2; 16:22; Isa 22:1; Jer 19:13; Tigay, *Deuteronomy*, 201). The owner of a house whose roof does not have a parapet, i.e., a retaining wall, must build one. If the owner fails to do so, he is legally culpable for the (even accidental) injury or death of anyone who falls off that roof (as in other cases of accidental death; cf. Ex 21:33–34; Dt 19:1–13).

NOTES

1 The noun אָחִיךָ (*'āḥîkā*, "your brother"), which occurs forty-eight times in Deuteronomy, can describe foreigners (2:4, 8; 23:7) and blood relationships (Dt 25:5–7, 9; 32:50) but most often refers to fellow members of the covenantal nation (as in the present passage). All the laws concerning filial relations in Deuteronomy urge compassion and concern. A brother could be a poor person (15:1–11) or someone whose property is jeopardized (22:1–4; Hamilton, *NIDOTTE*, 1:348). Every Israelite, whether a king, prophet, servant, or priest, should regard fellow Israelites as members of Yahweh's covenantal nation.

1, 4 The root of the word וְהִתְעַלַּמְתָּ (wᵉhitᶜallamtā, "and ignore")—namely, עלם (ᶜlm)—can refer to something hidden or concealed (1Ki 10:3; 2Ch 9:2), unintentional sin overlooked by others (Lev 4:13; 5:2–3), or deliberate sin (Nu 5:13; Ps 90:8). However, in contexts of covenantal requirements it signifies "to ignore" something important (Hill, *NIDOTTE*, 3:426).

2 The phrase אֶל־תּוֹךְ בֵּיתֶךָ (ʾel-tôk bêtekā, "home with you") could be rendered literally "inside your house" (cf. 21:12; 1Ki 6:27), though most translations render it similarly to the NIV's rendering. Tigay ("Some Archaeological Notes," 374–75, fig. 1) points out that in multistoried houses, especially in villages, the ground floor served as a stable for livestock. The Israelites are to treat stray animals every bit as well as their own.

4. Various Laws of Distinctiveness/Purity (22:9–23:18)

OVERVIEW

If one thinks of purity only in terms of moral separation, they will miss the point of several of the laws discussed below. The biblical concept of purity or holiness has two primary aspects: separation from sin (negative aspect) and consecration to a dedicated usage (positive aspect). So the idea of holiness does concern "separation" from or the careful avoidance of sin, but also deals with something that is dedicated for special purposes. At least two things are true about something dedicated for consecrated purposes. On the one hand, it is taken out of common or ordinary circulation; it is not used for everyday needs. On the other hand, it has been taken out of ordinary usage in order to dedicate it for special purposes. That is how a building, a table, bread, or a day could be holy. It stands distinct from normal or everyday things and is dedicated for some lofty purpose.

a. Miscellaneous Examples of Distinctiveness (22:9–12)

⁹Do not plant two kinds of seed in your vineyard; if you do, not only the crops you plant but also the fruit of the vineyard will be defiled. ¹⁰Do not plow with an ox and a donkey yoked together. ¹¹Do not wear clothes of wool and linen woven together. ¹²Make tassels on the four corners of the cloak you wear.

COMMENTARY

9–11 Although the rationale for these laws (cf. Lev 19:19) may be unclear to the modern reader (and is often debated by scholars; see Milgrom [*Leviticus 17–22*, 1656–64] for a helpful comparison of Dt 22:9–11 and Lev 19:19 and an overview of primary interpretive options), they may have symbolic value as "badges" of Israel's distinctiveness from the nations (as with clean/unclean food requirements [14:1–21]; Wright, *Deuteronomy*, 242). An interpretive option of preliminary appeal suggests that these requirements mirror divinely established points of distinction in the animal and plant world (Wenham, *Leviticus*, 269–70; C. Houtman, "Another Look at Forbidden Mixtures," *VT* 34 [1984]: 227–28).

What might seem trivial to a modern reader fits perfectly with God's pattern for his creation. At creation God separated light from darkness, waters of the sky from waters on the earth, and waters on the earth from dry ground (Ge 1:3–9). God's chosen nation must be careful to maintain the distinction between those things that God has made distinct. Whether concerning the issue of whom to marry (with marriage of Israelites to non-Israelites prohibited; Dt 7:3–6) or how to plant crops (with the planting together of different kinds of seeds prohibited), the Israelites must keep separate what God has made separate. Breaking down divinely established distinctions constitutes callous disregard for Israel's unique relationship with Yahweh and their distinctiveness from the surrounding nations.

The first example (regarding seeds) is the only one with stated consequences for disobedience. If an Israelite chooses to disregard this requirement, his entire crop (even from the grape vineyard in which he did plant only one kind of seed) is "defiled" and consequently unavailable for his consumption.

12 Numbers 15:37–41 provides a fuller delineation of this command. In that passage Moses instructs God's chosen people to attach these tassels (lit., "twisted threads") to the four corners of the outer garment they wore during the day and covered themselves with at night. The requirement ensures that whenever the Israelites see the tassels, at any time of the day or night, they will "remember all the commands of the LORD, that you may obey them and not prostitute yourselves by going after the lusts of your own hearts and eyes. Then you will remember to obey all my commands and will be consecrated to your God" (Nu 15:39–40). Even the clothing the Israelites wear must serve as a reminder of God's promises, their identity as his people, and his demand for their absolute loyalty.

b. Purity in Sexual Conduct (22:13–30 [22:13–23:1])

[13]If a man takes a wife and, after lying with her, dislikes her [14]and slanders her and gives her a bad name, saying, "I married this woman, but when I approached her, I did not find proof of her virginity," [15]then the girl's father and mother shall bring proof that she was a virgin to the town elders at the gate. [16]The girl's father will say to the elders, "I gave my daughter in marriage to this man, but he dislikes her. [17]Now he has slandered her and said, 'I did not find your daughter to be a virgin.' But here is the proof of my daughter's virginity." Then her parents shall display the cloth before the elders of the town, [18]and the elders shall take the man and punish him. [19]They shall fine him a hundred shekels of silver and give them to the girl's father, because this man has given an Israelite virgin a bad name. She shall continue to be his wife; he must not divorce her as long as he lives.

²⁰If, however, the charge is true and no proof of the girl's virginity can be found, ²¹she shall be brought to the door of her father's house and there the men of her town shall stone her to death. She has done a disgraceful thing in Israel by being promiscuous while still in her father's house. You must purge the evil from among you.

²²If a man is found sleeping with another man's wife, both the man who slept with her and the woman must die. You must purge the evil from Israel.

²³If a man happens to meet in a town a virgin pledged to be married and he sleeps with her, ²⁴you shall take both of them to the gate of that town and stone them to death — the girl because she was in a town and did not scream for help, and the man because he violated another man's wife. You must purge the evil from among you.

²⁵But if out in the country a man happens to meet a girl pledged to be married and rapes her, only the man who has done this shall die. ²⁶Do nothing to the girl; she has committed no sin deserving death. This case is like that of someone who attacks and murders his neighbor, ²⁷for the man found the girl out in the country, and though the betrothed girl screamed, there was no one to rescue her.

²⁸If a man happens to meet a virgin who is not pledged to be married and rapes her and they are discovered, ²⁹he shall pay the girl's father fifty shekels of silver. He must marry the girl, for he has violated her. He can never divorce her as long as he lives.

³⁰A man is not to marry his father's wife; he must not dishonor his father's bed.

COMMENTARY

13–21 This legislation addresses a situation in which a man who has recently consummated his marriage to an Israelite woman accuses her of not being a virgin at the time of their marriage. Something not specified in the context has occasioned that belief ("I did not find proof of her virginity"; see Note). In the first part of this scenario, the reader learns that the husband "dislikes" or "hates" his wife. Although this term (*śnʾ*) can connote the emotion of hatred, it better signifies "rejection" in this passage (see 21:15–17; cf. Ge 29:31, 33 [Leah]; see Note on 5:9). By making this accusation, he gives her a bad name or defames her reputation.

In the Semitic world, a name (*šēm*) often signified something about a person's character (see Note on 5:11). Since the accusation reflects on the parents as well, they have the opportunity to bring before the town elders evidence of their daughter's virginity at the time of the marriage — some garment or sheet (*HALOT*, 1337–38). If the evidence proves credible, the elders will punish the husband who has falsely accused his wife. This would seem to be some kind of corporeal punishment, such as flogging (Branson, *TDOT*, 6:130; in this case, the false accuser does not receive the punishment the accused would have received [19:15–21]). The husband must also pay to his wife's father one hundred shekels (twice the amount required of the man who rapes an unbetrothed woman [cf. 22:29]).

The final aspect of the penalty levied against the husband is that he can never divorce this wife. Although this prohibition may seem less than desirable for the woman, in fact it protects her—a defamed and maritally undesirable divorcée—from deprivation in a culture characterized by women's economic dependence on men (Wright, *Deuteronomy*, 243).

Verses 20–21 present a different version of the above scenario, one in which there is no evidence to confirm the virginity of the wife at the time of her marriage. In that case, the men of the city (cf. 21:21) must stone her to death at the entrance to her father's home. The location of the execution emphasizes the shame resting on the family. Whether or not the father was aware of her immorality, as the head of his home he was responsible for his children's behavior. What she did was disgraceful and reflected poorly on her parents as well as on the entire nation ("a disgraceful thing in Israel"; see Note). Apparently, she is killed, not only for the immorality but also for the deceit of misrepresenting herself as a virgin.

The key point is not her sexual condition, i.e., that only virgins could become married in Israel; rather, she has concealed her immorality, which is an act of treachery (like any lie). By stoning her, God's people are able to purge the evil from their midst (cf. 22:22, 24, see Note on 13:5).

22 Adultery entails a sexual relationship between two persons, one or both of whom are married to someone else (cf. Lev 20:10; see comments on 5:18). If a person witnesses a man and woman committing adultery (the verbal phrase "to lie down with" generally indicates consensual sex), God's people must execute both adulterers. (The manner of execution is not specified in the context.)

23–27 Because betrothal in Israel required sexual fidelity by both parties, the law treats sexual immorality in the same way that it does adultery.

Israelites from the town where the sin has taken place must stone both partners at the city gate. The phrase "he sleeps/lies down with her" and her failure to cry out for help indicate the woman's complicity. The man is executed for "violating" this young woman (cf. 22:29; see comments on 21:14), who was pledged to another man.

But if a man rapes a betrothed young woman away from the town, where no one could hear her cries or intervene, the town elders will hold only him responsible. Unlike the "in-town" scenario, in which the man "finds" and "lies down" with the young woman, the man here "finds," "seizes" (*ḥzq*), and "lies down" with her, implying force.

28–29 If a man rapes a woman who is not betrothed (and hence does not violate marriage or betrothal commitments), he must pay to the woman's father fifty shekels of silver, marry her, and never divorce her. The fact that he "seizes" her (a somewhat weaker verb than *ḥzq*, but still showing coercion) and the remark in 22:29 that he "has violated" her suggest that the sexual encounter was not consensual.

The primary question raised in this passage is its relationship to Exodus 22:16–17 [15–16], which deals with a man who has "seduced" and had sexual relations with an unbetrothed woman. There the man must pay the bridal gift (*mōhar*) to her father and marry her. The father, however, has the option of refusing the marriage (but still receiving the bridal gift). Various scholars have suggested that the father may do the same in the present scenario (McConville, 342; Merrill, *Deuteronomy*, 306). But since Deuteronomy 22 does not repeat the clause allowing the refusal of the marriage and since the passage does prohibit the man from ever divorcing the woman, the option of refusal does not appear to be available to the father in the present context.

30 [23:1] Mosaic law did not permit an Israelite man to marry his biological mother (Lev 18:7) or his father's wife (the man's stepmother; Lev 18:8); these prohibitions assume the divorce or death of the man's father. This passage in Deuteronomy concerns the latter potential relationship (cf. 27:20, where such conduct is included in the covenantal curses). As Merrill (*Deuteronomy*, 306) points out: "For a man to have sexual intercourse with a woman who had enjoyed such intimacy with his own father was tantamount to having exposed his father's nakedness."

NOTES

14 In the light of v.17, בְּתוּלִים (*bᵉtûlîm*, "evidence of virginity") could refer to blood-stained sheets indicative of the first instance of intercourse (Tsevat, *TDOT*, 2:342; Craigie, 292; McConville, 339; Merrill, *Deuteronomy*, 302–3; Nelson, 264; Tigay, *Deuteronomy*, 204–5; C. Pressler, *The View of Women Found in the Deuteronomic Family Laws* [BZAW 216; Berlin: de Gruyter, 1993], 24–29). The preservation of this bloodied sheet may have been part of the wedding ritual. G. J. Wenham ("Bᵉtûlāh, 'A Girl of Marriageable Age,'" *VT* 22 [1972]: 330–36; cf. Hall, 336; Mayes, 310; Thompson, 236; Wright, *God's People*, 214–15) suggests that this "evidence" (a garment stained by blood) points to the fact that she was menstruating and not pregnant before they married.

Although there is not enough evidence to make a dogmatic conclusion, the traditional (former) alternative is preferable. The evidence of a similar custom in various ancient Near Eastern cultures (though not attested in OT literature for Israel; Tigay, *Deuteronomy*, 384, n. 47; Braulik, *Deuteronomium 16, 18–34, 12*, 165) and the difficulty of certifying or dating a stained garment for the purposes of this legal case slightly favor that position. It is more likely that parents might keep the blood-stained sheets from the wedding night as part of a ritual than keeping sheets stained by their daughter's menstrual blood sometime before the wedding. One does wonder why a husband would make this kind of an accusation if he knew that the parents had such evidence.

21 The noun נְבָלָה (*nᵉbālâ*; GK 5576) occurs eighteen times in the OT and only here in Deuteronomy (נְבָלָה בְּיִשְׂרָאֵל, *nᵉbālâ bᵉyiśrā'ēl*, "a disgraceful thing in Israel"). Although it can signify mental deficiency, it frequently refers to one who acts foolishly in a moral or religious sense by breaking social orders or behaving treacherously toward God (Pan, *NIDOTTE*, 3:11). Anthony Phillips ("NEBALAH—A Term for Serious Disorderly and Unruly Conduct," *VT* 25 [1975]: 241) asserts that "נְבָלָה is a general expression for serious, disorderly and unruly action resulting in the break-up of an existing relationship whether between tribes, within the family, in a business arrangement, in marriage or with God."

Nᵉbālâ occurs in three other passages in the phrase "a disgraceful thing in Israel" (Achan's sin [Jos 7:15]; the abusive rape of the Gibeonite's concubine [Jdg 20:6; cf. 19:23–24 for background]; committing adultery with the wife of a neighbor [Jer 29:23]), and it applies as well to Shechem's rape of Dinah (Ge 34:7) and Amnon's rape of Tamar (2Sa 13:12), for a total of six passages in which the word refers to a disgraceful act. To commit a treacherous act such as this is not only an offense against the victim but also an affront against the covenantal nation.

The related verb נבל (*nbl*) occurs once in Deuteronomy (32:15) when Moses rebukes Israel for their abhorrent treatment of Yahweh: (lit.) "he treated the Rock who saved him with contempt." The verb signifies breach of relationship with Yahweh or treachery against the accepted social order (Mic 7:6). Moses accuses God's people of apostasy for abandoning Yahweh at the time of their prosperity (given to them by God!).

30 [23:1] The clause וְלֹא יְגַלֶּה כְּנַף אָבִיו (wᵉlōʾ yᵉgalleh kᵉnap ʾābîw, "he must not dishonor his father's bed") reads literally, "he must not uncover his father's skirt." This form of the verb (Piel) occurs chiefly to refer to prohibited sexual activity. It appears about forty times (twenty-four times in Lev 18 and 20) concerning uncovering a person's private parts or concerning that which covers a person (e.g., skirt, veil, etc.). The most frequent object of this verb is עֶרְוָה (ʿerwâ), "nakedness" or "shame" (nineteen occurrences). In those instances it refers either to committing fornication (Lev 18:6–19; 20:11, 17–21; Eze 16:36–37; 23:10) or rape (Eze 23:10, 29). Along with "uncover the skirt" here, other OT passages refer to uncovering the bed (Isa 57:8), lewdness (Hos 2:10 [12]), the robe and legs (Isa 47:2), and skirts (Jer 13:22; Na 3:5).

c. Purity in Public Worship (23:1–8 [2–9])

OVERVIEW

The verses in this section delineate who may "enter" the assembly of Yahweh. Although the noun "assembly" occurs eleven times in Deuteronomy (referring to the gathering at Sinai [5:22; 9:10; 10:4; 18:16]; at Horeb [31:30]; six times in ch. 23), the expression "the assembly of the LORD" occurs only in this chapter (23:2–3 [2x], 4 [2x], 9). This passage looks forward to the day after the conquest of Canaan when "the assembly of the LORD" will be able to gather together to worship their covenantal Lord.

Eligibility to "enter" this assembly indicated that a person was a full citizen of the covenantal nation and was physically whole. The "assembly" was not coextensive with the "nation" of Israel, for the nation, as a political unit, included individuals who were not ethnic Israelites. In other OT passages, this assembly conducts war (Jdg 21:5, 8), crowns a king (1Ki 12:3), adjudicates legal cases (Jer 26:17), worships Yahweh (1Ch 29:20; Joel 2:16), and will participate in the eschatological allocation of land (Mic 2:5). The following verses exclude three categories of people from participation in the assembly of Yahweh for at least some period of time. Keep in mind that this exclusion does not represent eviction from the nation of Israel but ineligibility to participate in certain formal gatherings and at certain places of national worship.

¹No one who has been emasculated by crushing or cutting may enter the assembly of the LORD.

²No one born of a forbidden marriage nor any of his descendants may enter the assembly of the LORD, even down to the tenth generation.

³No Ammonite or Moabite or any of his descendants may enter the assembly of the LORD, even down to the tenth generation. ⁴For they did not come to meet you with bread

and water on your way when you came out of Egypt, and they hired Balaam son of Beor from Pethor in Aram Naharaim to pronounce a curse on you. [5]However, the LORD your God would not listen to Balaam but turned the curse into a blessing for you, because the LORD your God loves you. [6]Do not seek a treaty of friendship with them as long as you live.

[7]Do not abhor an Edomite, for he is your brother. Do not abhor an Egyptian, because you lived as an alien in his country. [8]The third generation of children born to them may enter the assembly of the LORD.

COMMENTARY

1 [2] A man who had been emasculated (by crushing or surgery) is barred from entering Yahweh's assembly. It is not clear whether this prohibition applies to men who have become emasculated involuntarily (e.g., from a genetic problem, as the result of an accident, or as an act perpetrated by someone else [cf. 25:12 and comments]). Eunuchs (castrated men) were not allowed to be priests because they were blemished, or not whole (Lev 21:17–20). The text does not specify why emasculated men are barred from Yahweh's assembly, but several scholars point to the practice of various ancient Near Eastern peoples that made castration part of pagan worship (cf. 14:1; Craigie, 297, n. 6; Tigay, *Deuteronomy*, 210).

2 [3] The phrase "one born of a forbidden marriage" renders the noun *mamzēr* (which occurs only here and in Zec 9:6). It could refer to children born of incestuous relationships (cf. 22:29), those born to cultic prostitutes (cf. 23:17–18), or the offspring of a marriage between an Israelite and a foreigner (cf. 7:3). A person in this category can never (meant by the figure of speech, "even down to the tenth generation") enter Yahweh's assembly (see next category).

3–6 [4–7] The Ammonites and Moabites are also permanently barred from participation in this assembly. In addition to the fact that the number

ten often stands for "countless times" (Ge 31:7; Nu 14:22; Job 19:3; Ne 4:6), the expression "forever" at the end of 23:3 [4] (in Hebrew) suggests the endlessness of this ban. The first cause of this exclusion is best applied to both the Ammonites and Moabites, while the second one applies only to the Moabites (the first clause being plural and the second one singular).

In contrast to customary ancient Near Eastern hospitality, the Ammonites offered no common courtesies to the Israelites when they passed through that region. Even worse, the Moabites hired Balaam to curse God's people (cf. Nu 22:5–6), though their efforts were unsuccessful (Nu 23:5–12, 26; 24:13). Not only were the Ammonites and Moabites excluded from participation in Yahweh's assembly, but the Israelites were also prohibited from entering into any political or economic relationships with them.

7–8 [8–9] The Edomites and the Egyptians are to be excluded from the assembly of Yahweh for a time, but the Israelites must not "abhor" these two people groups. The Edomites were their kinfolk (the descendants of Esau, brother of Jacob [the father of Israel]; Ge 36:1–19), and the Egyptians had "hosted" (focusing on the Hebrews' preslavery days) God's people for a number of centuries. Although the noun *tôʿēbâ* occurs frequently in Deuteronomy (seventeen times, to denote the persons, things, or practices that offend one's ritual or moral order [see Note on 7:25–26]), the verb *t‘b* occurs only four times in the book (in two passages: 7:26 and 23:8), where it denotes the loathing of an offensive person, thing, or practice. An abominable or repugnant nature is determined by a person's character, values, or culture. God prohibits his covenantal nation from treating the Edomites and Egyptians as loathesome, and the three-generation time frame provides sufficient time for people of these ancestries to demonstrate their enthusiastic desire to function as part of the Israelite community.

NOTE

6 [7] לֹא־תִדְרֹשׁ שְׁלֹמָם וְטֹבָתָם (*lōʾ-tidrōš šᵉlōmām wᵉṭōbātām*, "Do not seek a treaty of friendship," lit., "do not seek peace and friendship"). Cognate forms of the two nouns שָׁלוֹם (*šālôm*; cf. Akkadian *sulummû*) and טוֹבָה (*ṭôbâ*; cf. Akkadian *ṭūbtu*) were used to describe friendly international relations. Wiseman ("'Is It Peace?'—Covenant and Diplomacy," *VT* 32 [1982]: 313) points out that the Akkadian phrase *sulummû u ṭūbtu* denotes a state of nonhostility and was used of equal parties whether or not they had established a covenant with each other (cf. D. Hillers, "Notes on Some Treaty Terminology," *BASOR* 176 [1964]: 46–47; W. Moran, "Notes on the Treaty Terminology of the Sefire Stelas," *JNES* 22 [1963]: 173–76).

d. Purity in the Military Camp (Holy War) (23:9–14 [10–15])

> ⁹When you are encamped against your enemies, keep away from everything impure. ¹⁰If one of your men is unclean because of a nocturnal emission, he is to go outside the camp and stay there. ¹¹But as evening approaches he is to wash himself, and at sunset he may return to the camp.
>
> ¹²Designate a place outside the camp where you can go to relieve yourself. ¹³As part of your equipment have something to dig with, and when you relieve yourself, dig a hole and cover up your excrement. ¹⁴For the LORD your God moves about in your camp to protect you and to deliver your enemies to you. Your camp must be holy, so that he will not see among you anything indecent and turn away from you.

COMMENTARY

9–11 [10–12] Moses delineates stipulations to ensure the ceremonial purity of Israel's military camp. The military camp is subject to more detailed requirements of ritual purity than the encampment of the general population of the nation (because the soldiers are conducting "holy war"). After providing a general principle, Moses deals with two areas of personal hygiene, or ceremonial purity (seminal emission and a bowel movement). For the first issue, an "accidental" occurrence that creates ritual impurity, there is a prescribed process for cleansing. If the emission (see Note on vv.9–10) "happens" during the night, the man must leave the camp the next morning, wash himself with water, and return to the camp after sunset.

12–13 [13–14] The Israelites are to designate a site outside the camp proper to serve as a latrine. Anyone who has a bowel movement is responsible to dig a small hole and bury the excrement. In addition to the obvious hygienic benefits of doing so, the divine requirement maintains the ritual purity of the camp.

14 [15] Moses gives the rationale for this legislation: Since the Lord is in their midst, "anything indecent" could turn the Lord and his promise of victory away from Israel's military camp. Ritual impurity is incompatible with God's holy presence. He "moves about" the Israelite encampment as its commander. As the God who will go before them and fight for them, he travels with them every-

where they go as his army (with or without the ritual implements).

Even though God's presence is often associated with the ark of the covenant, it is unnecessary to conclude that the ark will travel along with the fighting men of Israel to every battleground. There is no evidence in later biblical passages that the ark was transported with the army when it conducted military campaigns. This use of the verb "to walk" (Hithpael of *hlk*) equates Yahweh's walking among and with Israel with the exercise of his sovereignty (Ge 3:8; Job 22:14; Merrill, *NIDOTTE*, 1:1034). Wherever God "walks," God has absolute dominion.

The potentially impure activities envisioned in the above verses are not intrinsically sinful or impure. However, since the nation is soon to embark on holy war against Canaan, they need to take great care to maintain their ritual purity lest they offend their covenantal Lord, who will go before them and fight on their behalf.

NOTES

9–10 [10–11] The Hebrew noun מִקְרֶה (*miqreh*) generally means "something that happens," i.e., an event unplanned and unexpected, but not random. Another noun, derived from the same verb (קָרֶה, *qāreh*), might signify a nocturnal emission. Because of the daghesh forte in the ק (*q*) here, this latter noun is more likely the one that occurs in v.10 in the phrase מִקְרֵה־לָיְלָה (*miqqᵉrēh-layᵉlâ*, "a nocturnal emission," lit., "an event/happening of the night"), containing the only occurrence of this word in the OT. A potentially parallel passage seems to refer euphemistically to a seminal discharge (Lev 15:16–18; cf. 22:4 [note the requirement of ritual bathing]). However, the word found in the present passage does not occur there. This term could refer more broadly to any unintentional activity that occasions ritual impurity (e.g., urination in the camp; cf. 23:12–13 [Craigie, 299]).

Like its "parent" verb (רעע, *rᶜᶜ*), the adjective רַע (*raᶜ*; GK 8273), in the expression דָּבָר רָע (*dābār rāᶜ*, "anything impure"), can carry a wide range of meanings. In general it describes an unacceptable action or state of being of a person. It can serve as a general term for evil (1Ki 3:9) or refer to something that is of poor quality (e.g., bad water; 2Ki 2:19) or is harmful (2Ki 4:41). In Deuteronomy 17:1 it refers to a defect that makes an animal totally unacceptable for ritual purposes. The present context demonstrates that *rāᶜ* signifies ritual impurity and not moral impurity. It is "evil" in the sense that it disbars one from certain religious activities.

12 [13] Although the noun יָד (*yād*, "a place") most frequently means "hand," it can also refer to a monument or memorial (1Sa 15:12; 2Sa 18:18), a "signpost" (Eze 21:19 [24]), or a place, i.e., a portion of a field in which a given shepherd grazes his sheep (Jer 6:3; cf. Nu 2:17). Consequently, this noun could refer to a signpost directing soldiers to the proper area or to the demarcated place itself.

14 [15] Literally, the expression עֶרְוַת דָּבָר (*ʿerwat dābār*, "anything indecent") means "nakedness of a thing." Though the term עֶרְוָה (*ʿerwâ*) usually has to do only with indecent exposure of the genitals, it can also include behavior that involves the genitals, such as adultery (cf. Lev 18:6–18; 20:11, 17, 20–21; Eze 22:10; 23:29; Hos 2:10). This noun occurs fifty-five times in the OT, primarily in Leviticus (thirty-two times) and only twice in Deuteronomy (here and in 24:1 [see comments]). Apart from Leviticus, where it stands for sexual intercourse, it is used of nakedness, genitals, the shame associated with their exposure, or related figurative meanings (Seevers, *NIDOTTE*, 3:528).

In the present passage this expression refers to the "night happening" and human excrement, which occasions ritual impurity, shames the military encampment, and consequently offends God. In light of the context of its other occurrence (in 24:1, concerning divorce and remarriage), this expression may refer to some gross sexual impropriety.

e. Purity concerning Escaped Slaves (the Disadvantaged) (23:15–16 [16–17])

> **15**If a slave has taken refuge with you, do not hand him over to his master. **16**Let him live among you wherever he likes and in whatever town he chooses. Do not oppress him.

COMMENTARY

15–16 [16–17] If a non-Israelite slave takes refuge with the Israelites, they are not to extradite that slave to his or her owner. For several reasons this law appears to refer to slaves who escaped from their owners in other nations (contra D. Patrick, *Old Testament Law* [Atlanta: John Knox, 1985], 133; Weinfeld, *Deuteronomy and the Deuteronomic School*, 272, n. 5; Wright, *Deuteronomy*, 249). The "you" with whom the slave finds refuge in the context is the nation of Israel, and it would not make sense for a fleeing Israelite slave to find refuge within Israel. Whereas an Israelite would be expected to live in his tribal region, a foreigner could be given permission to live anywhere in the land. Also, the prohibition of oppression occurs in other contexts with reference to "resident aliens," i.e., non-Israelites who choose to live in the midst of Israel.

This "nonextradition" policy is important for at least two reasons. First, it went against the general practice of other ancient Near Eastern peoples. Various ancient Near Eastern treaties include several clauses that deal with this very issue (Code of Hammurabi, §§15–20 [*COS*, 2:338]; Sefire Treaty, 3:4–7, 19–20 [*COS*, 2:216–17]; cf. Pritchard, *ANET*, 200–201, 203–4, 531 [§5], 532 [§2]) and place great importance on returning fugitives to the places from which they took flight. Second, for Israel to return foreign slaves would imply the existence of treaty relationships with pagan nations, thus undermining Israel's total commitment to

Yahweh (Craigie, 301). The prohibition against returning foreign slaves constitutes part of Israel's distinctive witness before foreign nations. After all, Yahweh delivered his covenantal nation from slavery in Egypt and never returned them to their Egyptian overlord.

The Israelites are to allow fugitive slaves to settle in a place of their choosing in Israel. The NIV's reading "in whatever town he chooses" could be rendered "in the place which he will choose in one of your towns." The wording of this statement echoes one found throughout Deuteronomy with reference to the central sanctuary. The land of God's

promise and a place to worship chosen by Yahweh provide the theological foundation for this exhortation that the Israelites show compassion to these slaves.

Neither are the Israelites to "oppress" fugitive slaves. This verb occurs several times in the OT with regard to the way Israelites should relate to each other (Lev 25:14, 17), the way they should deal with "anyone" (Eze 18:7, 16), and, in particular, the manner in which they should deal with those at the fringe of Israelite society (the poor, orphans, widows, and aliens; Ex 22:21; Lev 19:33; Jer 22:3; Eze 18:12; 22:7, 29).

f. Purity concerning Cultic Personnel (23:17–18 [18–19])

¹⁷No Israelite man or woman is to become a shrine prostitute. ¹⁸You must not bring the earnings of a female prostitute or of a male prostitute into the house of the LORD your God to pay any vow, because the LORD your God detests them both.

COMMENTARY

17–18 [18–19] This brief passage brings to a close a series of laws dealing with Israel's purity or distinctiveness (22:9–23:18). Israelite men and women are prohibited from becoming cultic prostitutes (common practice in Canaanite idolatry). Further, no funds generated by cultic prostitution have any place whatsoever in the worship of

Yahweh. Yahweh regards both male and female prostitution as detestable (see Note on 7:25–26). Sadly, the nation of Israel adopted this practice at different times until a godly king arose to the throne and removed them from places of worship scattered throughout the land (1Ki 14:24; 15:12; Hos 4:14).

NOTES

17 [18] The nouns קָדֵשׁ and קְדֵשָׁה (*qādēš* and *qᵉdēšâ*, "sacred male prostitute" and "sacred female prostitute") both derive from the Hebrew verb meaning "to be holy or consecrated" (קדשׁ, *qdš*) and are associated with a customary word for prostitute in v.18 (see Note there) and with sexual activity in other

OT passages (cf. Ge 38:21–22; 1Ki 14:24; 15:12; 22:46; 2Ki 23:7; Hos 4:14). The individuals designated by these names were dedicated to temple duty (at pagan worship sites). These cultic prostitutes would engage in various immoral activities with pagan worshipers (for pay that funded the pagan temple) in an effort to stimulate the pagan gods to bring fertility to the worshipers' land, herds, flocks, and families.

This practice seems to have occurred in different parts of the ancient Near East (though the evidence is sketchy; cf. E. Yamauchi, "Cultic Prostitution: A Case Study in Cultural Diffusion," in *Occident and Orient: Essays Presented to Cyrus H. Gordon on the Occasion of his Sixty-Fifth Birthday* [ed. Harry A. Hoffner Jr.; AOAT; Neukirchen-Vluyn: Neukirchener, 1973], 213–22). More recently, several scholars have questioned or denied the identification of these terms with sacred prostitution (Goodfriend, *ABD*, 5:507–8; van der Toorn, *ABD*, 5:509–12; Ringgren, *TDOT*, 12:523–27, 542–43; Tigay, *Deuteronomy*, 480–81; Westenholz, "Tamar, Q*edēšā*, Qadištu, and Sacred Prostitution in Mesopotamia," *HTR* 82 [1989]: 245–65, esp. 248–49). They suggest that these terms envision individuals involved with pagan worship (priests or priestesses), but without any sexual connotation. While it should be recognized that ancient Near Eastern evidence is not abundant, the biblical evidence seems to make that association clear.

18 [19] The noun זוֹנָה (*zônâ*) refers to a noncultic female prostitute, and כֶּלֶב (*keleb*) is the colloquial term for a noncultic male prostitute. The second designation, *keleb*, disparagingly refers to this kind of person as a "dog" (lit. trans.).

5. Laws of Interpersonal Relationships (23:19 [20]–25:19)

a. Respect for the Needs and Possessions of Fellow Israelites (23:19 [20]–24:7)

i. Laws on lending (23:19–20[20–21])

[19]Do not charge your brother interest, whether on money or food or anything else that may earn interest. [20]You may charge a foreigner interest, but not a brother Israelite, so that the LORD your God may bless you in everything you put your hand to in the land you are entering to possess.

COMMENTARY

19–20 [20–21] This is the third passage in the Pentateuch that addresses the issue of charging interest on loans (cf. Ex 22:25; Lev 25:36–37). Although the other passages focus on the poor and needy (the most likely to suffer from interest-bearing loans), this passage encompasses all Israelites in the prohibition against charging interest (an intent that probably underlies all three passages). Exodus and Leviticus mention loans only of money and food, but here any substance is included. Generally in this nonindustrial, agrarian society, the only reason people would seek a loan consisted in their facing some kind of difficulty. This law prevents unscrupulous Israelites from exploiting a struggling person in the face of a stiff challenge. The prohibition against charging interest is unparalleled in the ancient Near East, where interest rates could vary between 20 percent and 50 percent (McConville, 352; Tigay, *Deuteronomy*, 217).

The Israelites are permitted, however, to charge interest on loans made to foreigners for reasons including the likelihood that an Israelite would have to pay interest on a loan from a foreigner. More importantly, a foreigner seeking a loan was likely a kind of businessman seeking a profit, not a person facing a dire tragedy. Maintaining a difference

between lending practices involving foreigners and fellow Israelites constitutes a tangible way for God's people to demonstrate their distinctiveness by carefully treating each other with unparalleled justice and equity. Note that the prohibition against charging interest to a fellow Israelite assumes that an Israelite lender would be willing to make a loan even though it might not benefit him financially. Since Yahweh is the source of blessing for his people (see Note on 7:13), financial profit is not to be the ruling standard for the way they treat their Israelite kinsfolk.

ii. Laws on making vows (23:21–23 [22–24])

²¹If you make a vow to the LORD your God, do not be slow to pay it, for the LORD your God will certainly demand it of you and you will be guilty of sin. ²²But if you refrain from making a vow, you will not be guilty. ²³Whatever your lips utter you must be sure to do, because you made your vow freely to the LORD your God with your own mouth.

COMMENTARY

21–23 [22–24] A vow entailed a promise made to God and often involved offering a sacrifice at the central sanctuary (Lev 7:16–17; Ps 22:25 [26]). A vow could involve goods, property (as here), or pledges of service (Ge 28:20; 31:13; Nu 6:2, 5, 21; 1Sa 1:11) and was an integral part of worship at the central sanctuary (though not always a sacrifice; Nu 15:8; 29:39; Dt 12:6, 17). The psalmists repeatedly speak of fulfilling the vows they have made to Yahweh (Pss 56:12–13; 61:5, 8; 66:13–15; 116:12–14). A vow, by its very nature, was voluntary (Dt 23:22), but once a person made a vow he or she was obligated to fulfill the promise (and with some haste). Rash promises were (and are) to be avoided (Jdg 11; Pr 20:25; Ecc 5:4–6), for failure to keep one's vow reflects poorly on one's honesty and integrity and

incurs the guilt of sin. It is better not to make the vow in the first place.

The importance of doing precisely what one has promised is modeled and demanded by Israel's covenantal Lord. The word he has spoken to his covenantal nation is totally reliable and sure to find fulfillment. His character is at stake where his promises are concerned. He has not made promises or vows just to stimulate a certain kind of conduct (i.e., offer a bribe). He has made them because he is totally committed to doing (and is able to do) exactly what he has said. For his covenantal people to make vows and not keep them would be to provide their fellow Israelites and the pagan nations around a corrupt picture of the character of the God whom they serve and whose name they bear.

iii. Law on finding provisions for travels (23:24–25 [25–26])

²⁴If you enter your neighbor's vineyard, you may eat all the grapes you want, but do not put any in your basket. ²⁵If you enter your neighbor's grainfield, you may pick kernels with your hands, but you must not put a sickle to his standing grain.

COMMENTARY

24–25 [25–26] If an Israelite passes through a fellow Israelite's vineyard or field (whether on a long journey or taking a shortcut), this law allows him to eat some of the grapes or grain produced by that vineyard or field as he passes through. He may eat until his hunger is satisfied. In ancient days, travelers had no means to prevent perishable food from spoiling during their journey. This requirement seeks to create an atmosphere of compassion between fellow members of Yahweh's people (cf. Mt 12:1–8; Mk 2:23–28; Lk 6:1–5), for after all, Yahweh is the one responsible for the abundance of any given field. This permission does not, however, include taking some of a fellow Israelite's harvest for personal advantage. The property and its produce belong to the owner of the land, and those passing through his property must respect his ownership.

iv. Law concerning remarriage (24:1–4)

¹If a man marries a woman who becomes displeasing to him because he finds something indecent about her, and he writes her a certificate of divorce, gives it to her and sends her from his house, ²and if after she leaves his house she becomes the wife of another man, ³and her second husband dislikes her and writes her a certificate of divorce, gives it to her and sends her from his house, or if he dies, ⁴then her first husband, who divorced her, is not allowed to marry her again after she has been defiled. That would be detestable in the eyes of the LORD. Do not bring sin upon the land the LORD your God is giving you as an inheritance.

COMMENTARY

1–4 Moses' presentation of the Deuteronomic law (chs. 12–26) turns next to matters of divorce and remarriage (Dt 21:10–14; 22:13–19, 28–29; Ezr 9–10; Isa 50:1; Jer 3:1–8; Mal 2:10–16), a topic much at home in the larger context of respect for property and personal rights. The specific issue here concerns a man who, having married, becomes displeased with his wife (lit., "she finds no favor in his sight") because "he finds something indecent about her" (v.1). His divorcing her (in most cases) necessitates her remarrying (for economic security, since ancient Israelite women lacked means to support themselves). If her second husband also divorces her (because he "dislikes" her) or if he dies, the first husband may not remarry her, for she has become ritually "defiled" by her second marriage. Though her first husband occasioned this defilement by initially divorcing her, his remarrying his now ritually defiled ex-wife would be "detestable" to the Lord (v.4).

What is the basic idea of the word "indecent" or "offensive"? Although the noun by itself can signify nakedness, a unique expression occurs here and in one other place (*'erwat dābār*; see Note on 23:14 for a fuller treatment). There it refers to issues that make ritually impure the Israelite military camp or soldiers in it. More specifically, the expression points back to two matters: a "night happening" (seminal emission?) and human excrement, in need of proper disposal.

What is it that the husband would have "found" in his wife to occasion his seeking a bill of divorce? Although several writers suggest that "something indecent" refers to adultery, the Pentateuch presents several reasons why that interpretation is unlikely. The most important of these reasons is that the Mosaic law prescribed death for both adulterous partners (Lev 20:10; Dt 22:22; cf. J. Murray, *Divorce* [Phillipsburg, N.J.: Presbyterian & Reformed, 1961], 10–11, where he offers five other reasons for the Pentateuch's ruling out adultery). If this expression does not refer to adultery, what does it signify? It is clear (see above) that in the light of OT usage and the other use of this precise phrase it refers to something that is shameful. It seems to refer to some impropriety of behavior that the husband finds worthy of censure or condemnation.

In other words, it appears to be a fairly broad term. It probably refers to some kind of serious and shameful conduct of indecent exposure that is something less than illicit sexual intercourse (R. Davidson, "Divorce and Remarriage in the Old Testament," *Journal of the Adventist Theological Society* 10 [1999]: 7; cf. R. Gane, "Old Testament Principles Relating to Divorce and Remarriage," *Journal of the Adventist Theological Society* 12 [2001]: 42–49).

What is the law or legislation introduced by this passage? The way a person views the structure of the passage can influence his or her interpretation. In OT legal material (as it occurs in ancient Near Eastern law codes), the legislation is commonly arranged in an "if … then" format (called "case law" or "casuistic law"). This kind of law often has three parts: protasis (description of condition[s]), apodosis (the actual legislation), and a motive clause (explaining the fundamental rationale for the law). Some early English translations located the protasis or conditional circumstance in the first half of v.1, with the apodosis or the potential result in 24:1b–4 (cf. KJV, ASV). In this case, the provision of a bill of divorce played an integral role in the legislation proper. Most modern English translations regard 24:1–3 as the protasis, with the legislation proper found in 24:4 (cf. ESV, NASB, NET, NIV, NKJV, NLT, NRSV). In this instance, the required conduct focuses on the husband's nonpermission to remarry his ex-wife after she has been married to another man (the scenario depicted in vv.1–3).

In other words, the divorce is not the focus of the law but the circumstance in which God gives his requirement through Moses. This law deals with a specific case and does not provide a general rule governing all possible instances of divorce and remarriage. These verses do not establish divorce either as a right or as a requirement; they do not encourage Israelite husbands to put away their wives because of "uncleanness" but merely recognize that contemporary practice. This passage focuses on one issue: A woman who was divorced because of "uncleanness" and married to a second man may not return to her first husband after divorce from or the death of her second husband. Moses is regulating a current practice in Israel—a practice Yahweh regards as "detestable" (see Note on 7:25–26) and one that all Israelites must avoid, lest they bring sin upon the land God has graciously given to them as an inheritance.

In other words, Moses is not in any sense saying that in the scenario addressed, divorce is required, legitimated, sanctioned, or even encouraged (Murray, *Divorce*, 14). In fact, the legislation hinders the husband from divorcing his wife rashly, since a divorce will likely occasion her ritual defilement, which will, in turn, make it religiously illegal to take her back (cf. the preceding warning against making vows to God rashly; 23:21–23).

NOTES

1 When Jesus alluded to this text, it seems clear that he had adultery or sexual infidelity in mind by his use of the Greek term πορνεία (*porneia*) as the only justification for divorce (Mt 5:31–32; 19:7–9). Moses' regulation, which merely acknowledges the current practice of divorce for reasons of עֶרְוַת דָּבָר (*ʿerwat dābār*, "something indecent"), provides the occasion or backdrop for Christ's teaching; but Christ does not state that he is perpetuating Moses' teaching.

A. Warren ("Did Moses Permit Divorce?: Modal *wᵉqāṭal* as Key to New Testament Readings of Deuteronomy 24:1–4," *TynBul* 49 [1998]: 42–50) has suggested a slight revision of the consensus understanding of the structure of these verses. He contends that the statement וְכָתַב (*wᵉkātab*, "and he may write"), which I regard as part of the protasis or conditions, is a brief apodosis ("and he must write") followed by the full apodosis in 24:4. According to his view, the passage *mandates* the husband to write a bill of divorce.

1, 3 Obtaining a סֵפֶר כְּרִיתֻת (*sēper kᵉrîtut*, "certificate of divorce," lit., "a writing of cutting off") was essential for the woman to protect her status in the eyes of other Israelites. This document "certified" the divorce, allowed her to remarry, and spared her from accusations (and the penalty) of adultery. Generally in the ancient Near East, a husband could reclaim an abandoned wife until she had a certificate of divorce from him (D. Brewer, "Deuteronomy 24:1–4 and the Origin of the Jewish Divorce Certificate," *JJS* 49 [1998]: 237).

4 The verb הֻטַּמָּאָה (*huṭṭammāʾâ*, "she has been defiled") takes a rare form, the Hothpael, that has a passive reflexive significance and could be rendered in several ways: (1) "she has been declared defiled" (McConville, 358; Warren, 43; J. Walton, "The Place of the *hutqaṭṭēl* within the D-Stem Group and Its Implications in Deuteronomy 24:4," *HS* 32 [1991]: 12—"she has been made to declare herself unclean"); (2) "she has been made to defile herself" (Davidson, "Divorce and Remarriage in the Old Testament," 12); or (3) "she has been defiled" (Craigie, 305; Hall, 359). The latter translation seems least likely in light of the verbal form used here. Those who prefer this translation regard the second marriage as a nontechnical kind of adultery that would get worse if she remarried her husband.

Both of the first two alternatives place the responsibility of the defilement on the husband's shoulders. According to the second view, the husband's decision to divorce his wife has caused her to marry again and be in a quasi-adulterous relationship (Davidson, ibid., 13). The first view does not regard the second marriage as adulterous in any sense. The first husband's decision to divorce his wife brought shame on her and, consequently, defiled her with respect to any relationship with her first husband. Proponents of this translation vary on the precise cause of that defilement. This verb makes it clear that the husband's decision does occasion her defilement. See J. Laney, "Deuteronomy 24:1–4 and the Issue of Divorce," *BSac* 149 (1992): 9–13, for various interpretations offered for the purpose of this legislation.

v. An Exemption from military service (24:5)

⁵If a man has recently married, he must not be sent to war or have any other duty laid on him. For one year he is to be free to stay at home and bring happiness to the wife he has married.

COMMENTARY

5 An Israelite man who is newly married is exempt from all kinds of military service (or other compulsory service) for one full year. During that time, the husband will "bring happiness" to his new wife, and the new couple will have time to lay a good foundation for their life together and, possibly, to have a child before he is liable to assume compulsory military service. This law complements the exemptions granted in 20:5–8 but focuses on the married man (rather than the betrothed man) and gives a specific time period for the exemption. The former passage focused on the man's opportunity to enjoy his wife, while this passage concerns itself with the joy he can bring to his loving wife. If he were to remain in military service and die before enjoying life with his wife (and possibly fathering a child), it would be comparable to his being stolen from his loved ones.

vi. Law concerning millstones (24:6)

⁶Do not take a pair of millstones — not even the upper one — as security for a debt, because that would be taking a man's livelihood as security.

COMMENTARY

6 It was common practice in the ancient Near East for a lender to receive something as collateral when providing a loan to someone (contra Tigay [*Deuteronomy*, 223–24], who sees it as a lien against the item of property). As stated above, in biblical times most people who took a loan did so only because they faced difficult circumstances and were needy. Such people would have little of value to offer to the lender. This law, while not denying the legitimate stake of the lender in the loan's repayment, prohibits the lender from taking collateral that was central to the borrower's ability to make a living.

A millstone consisted of two pieces of rock, the top one resting on the lower one, and was used to grind grain to flour for bread. The bottom stone ("nether stone") could weigh ten to twenty pounds, and the upper stone ("rider stone") would weigh much less (about five pounds; van der Toorn, *ABD*, 4:831; cf. Tigay, "Some Archaeological Notes," 374–76). Though taking both stones would be difficult, taking the upper stone would be relatively easy. But by taking just the upper stone, a person could render a millstone worthless and thus "take the life" (i.e., the livelihood) of the debtor.

vii. Law concerning kidnapping (24:7)

⁷If a man is caught kidnapping one of his brother Israelites and treats him as a slave or sells him, the kidnapper must die. You must purge the evil from among you.

COMMENTARY

7 This law addresses the theft of a fellow member of the covenantal nation. Anyone who does so and treats the kidnapped person as a piece of property (ʿmr), including selling (mkr; see Note on 21:14) the victim, must be treated as a criminal and executed. By carrying out this punishment God's people will purge evil from the land God has given them as a stewardship (see Note on 13:5).

b. Respect for the Dignity of Others (24:8–25:4)

i. Law concerning leprosy (24:8–9)

⁸In cases of leprous diseases be very careful to do exactly as the priests, who are Levites, instruct you. You must follow carefully what I have commanded them. ⁹Remember what the LORD your God did to Miriam along the way after you came out of Egypt.

COMMENTARY

8–9 Leprosy in the OT is likely not the leprosy spoken about in modern times (also known as Hansen's disease). "Leprosy" is commonly used to translate the noun ṣāraʿat, which in fact refers to various kinds of skin diseases (cf. Lev 13–14; Wright and Jones, *ABD*, 4:277). This law demands that the Israelites pay close attention to the instruction of the priests as they treat their "leprosy" (Lev 13:1–14). The rebellious example of Miriam (who resisted Moses' leadership; Nu 12:10–15) serves as their motivation and is an event they must remember (with life-changing impact; see Note on 4:10). Just as it was important for Miriam to submit to Moses' leadership, even concerning an issue of skin diseases, God's people must pay attention to the leaders God has appointed.

ii. Laws concerning pledges (24:10–13)

¹⁰When you make a loan of any kind to your neighbor, do not go into his house to get what he is offering as a pledge. ¹¹Stay outside and let the man to whom you are making the loan bring the pledge out to you. ¹²If the man is poor, do not go to sleep with his pledge in your possession. ¹³Return his cloak to him by sunset so that he may sleep in it. Then he will thank you, and it will be regarded as a righteous act in the sight of the LORD your God.

COMMENTARY

10–13 This legislation focuses on a key issue in the realm of loans and collateral (Ex 22:25–26; Lev 25:35–37; Dt 23:19–20; 24:6), i.e., the dignity of the person who needs a loan. First, a lender is to honor the privacy of the borrower. His property is still his property, and he is worthy of respect. The lender should allow the debtor to bring the pledge out to him rather than himself dig through the man's possessions in search of something he might find adequate. Also, if the indebted man is poor, he might offer his outer cloak as a pledge or collateral for the loan. Since that cloak is also his covering when he sleeps, the lender must return it to him by sunset. Not only would the poor man thank him for the compassionate treatment, but also Yahweh will regard such conduct as "righteous," i.e., as conforming or measuring up to his covenantal expectations.

NOTE

13 The word family of צדק (*ṣdq*), which includes צְדָקָה (*ṣᵉdāqâ*, "a righteous act"; GK 7407), can signify what one is, does, or declares others to be. Whenever words from this family refer to behavior (whether human or divine), they clearly imply conduct that is measured in accordance with some standard, whether or not that standard is ever explicitly spelled out. (It could be natural law, the Mosaic law, or even the character of God, depending on the context.) As sinners, people have a natural tendency to seek what is best for them regardless of what is just or right. In a world full of sinners (whether redeemed or not), it is imperative for a ruler and his subjects to practice what is just and right (Grisanti, "2 Samuel," 195–96).

iii. Laws concerning proper wages (24:14–15)

¹⁴Do not take advantage of a hired man who is poor and needy, whether he is a brother Israelite or an alien living in one of your towns. ¹⁵Pay him his wages each day before sunset, because he is poor and is counting on it. Otherwise he may cry to the LORD against you, and you will be guilty of sin.

COMMENTARY

14–15 This legislation considers a hired man (*śākîr*; cf. de Vaux, 1:76) who is "poor and needy." These two terms occur as a pair seventeen times in the OT and twice in Deuteronomy (15:11; 24:14; see Notes on 15:4, 11). They refer to people who have no property, are destitute, and are experiencing some kind of affliction. God's people must be sure that they do not exploit these needy people, whether they are fellow Israelites or foreigners. Just as the lender should return the cloak to a debtor by sunset, Israelite employers must pay their laborers by that same time, for the men have no other resources to provide for their families. If employers fail to obey Yahweh in this matter, Yahweh will hear the pleading of these poor workers and find the selfish Israelites guilty of sin (rather than crediting them with righteous conduct; cf. 24:13).

The OT prophets frequently refer to the oppression of the poor and needy, orphans and widows, and aliens (all of whom existed at the fringe of Israel's society) as the classic indication of a life of covenantal treachery. An Israelite could live in general conformity to a number of covenantal stipulations and appear submissive to Yahweh. However, God is always interested in the condition of his people's heart (10:12; Mic 6:8). The compassion or affliction that God's people heap on the poor in their midst serves as a clear indicator of their loyalty to their covenantal Lord or their commitment to covenantal rebellion.

NOTE

14 The verbal command לֹא־תַעֲשֹׁק (*lōʾ-taʿăšōq*, "do not take advantage of") prohibits abuses of power or authority, i.e., burdening or taking advantage of those who belong to a lower social stratum than the perpetrator of the exploitation. The widow, the orphan, the sojourner, and the poor—people lacking adequate defense of their rights—were the most likely to experience oppression. The primary purpose of oppression is personal gain for the perpetrator. Whether by using false scales (Hos 12:7 [8]), withholding wages (Jer 22:13), or accepting bribes (Eze 22:12, 29), the oppressor seeks personal advantage by exploiting a weaker person (Grisanti, "1 Samuel," 143).

iv. Law concerning individual responsibility (24:16)

¹⁶Fathers shall not be put to death for their children, nor children put to death for their fathers; each is to die for his own sin.

COMMENTARY

16 In the midst of Deuteronomy's consistent emphasis on Israel's destiny as a nation, the reader must not overlook the book's emphasis on the individual. Yes, Yahweh does set before his covenantal people two fates: covenantal blessing or covenantal curse (cf. chs. 27–28). Those blessings or curses will be experienced by individuals but triggered by the conduct of the nation (an aggregate of individuals; see comments at ch. 28). Yahweh, however, does not hold innocent individuals responsible for another individual's sin. A father's treachery can have far-reaching effects on ensuing generations (cf. 5:9–10; Ex 20:5–6), and people can experience the consequences of sin without having committed the sin that occasioned those consequences. Recognizing the integrity of the individual, Moses promises that fathers will not be punished for their children's rebellion, nor will children be punished for the disobedience of their father. Yahweh holds individuals responsible for their own sin.

NOTE

16 The verbal form לֹא־יוּמְתוּ (*lōʾ-yûmᵉtû*, "shall not be put to death"; Hophal of מוּת, *mût*, "put to death") generally refers to judicial execution (rather than divine punishment) for some act of covenantal treachery (Tigay, *Deuteronomy*, 227). This form of the verb "to die" occurs forty-five times in the OT (twenty-eight times in the Pentateuch, and six times in Deuteronomy [13:5, concerning a false prophet; 17:6, concerning false witnesses [2x]; and three times in the present passage). There are various examples in the Code of Hammurabi (§§116, 209–10, 230 [*COS*, 2:343, 348–49]) and the Middle Assyrian Laws (§§50, 55 [*COS*, 2:359]) of children being executed or severely fined for the crime of their parent.

v. Justice for the poor (24:17–22)

¹⁷Do not deprive the alien or the fatherless of justice, or take the cloak of the widow as a pledge. ¹⁸Remember that you were slaves in Egypt and the LORD your God redeemed you from there. That is why I command you to do this.

> ¹⁹When you are harvesting in your field and you overlook a sheaf, do not go back to get it. Leave it for the alien, the fatherless and the widow, so that the LORD your God may bless you in all the work of your hands. ²⁰When you beat the olives from your trees, do not go over the branches a second time. Leave what remains for the alien, the fatherless and the widow. ²¹When you harvest the grapes in your vineyard, do not go over the vines again. Leave what remains for the alien, the fatherless and the widow. ²²Remember that you were slaves in Egypt. That is why I command you to do this.

COMMENTARY

17–18 Moses gives three pointed commands that will affect the Israelites' treatment of aliens, orphans, and widows (see Note on 10:17). First, God's people must not deprive such individuals of the justice God intends for them to have. (Depriving them would have been a perversion of justice; see comments on 16:19.) Many of the covenantal stipulations found in the first and second presentation of the Mosaic covenant spell out God's expectation that his covenantal people treat each other with justice and equity.

Second and specifically, no lender should take as a pledge (collateral; cf. 24:12–13) the cloak of a widow, her covering at night. And why should the Israelites heed this exhortation? They themselves had been slaves in Egypt and experienced life at the fringe (or bottom) of Egyptian society. Since God himself redeemed them (see Note on 9:26)

from that horrific existence (which they did not deserve), he is in a position to demand that they take proper care of the poor and needy in their communities. Notice how their remembrance of God's intervention in their affairs is not simply to involve a recitation of facts but must serve as the motivation for their obedience. Throughout Deuteronomy, remembering and not forgetting are to be life-transforming activities (see Note on 4:10).

19–22 Finally, when they harvest their fields, olive orchards, and vineyards (epitomizing agricultural efforts throughout the land of Israel), they must leave behind (intentionally and gladly) part of the harvest for poor Israelites (gleaners; Lev 19:9–10; cf. Ru 2:2–19). Grain, oil, and wine, the commodities produced by fields, orchards, and vineyards, function in the same summarizing way in Deuteronomy (see comments on 7:13–15).

NOTE

19–21 The combination of the verb "to be" (היה, *hyh*) with the preposition "to" (לְ, *le*), in the phrase לַגֵּר לַיָּתוֹם וְלָאַלְמָנָה יִהְיֶה (*laggēr layyātôm welā'almānâ yihyeh*, "it belongs to the alien, the fatherless, and the widow"), indicates possession or ownership. The crops left behind are viewed as the possessions of the needy in Israel.

vi. Proper limits for punishment (25:1–3)

¹When men have a dispute, they are to take it to court and the judges will decide the case, acquitting the innocent and condemning the guilty. ²If the guilty man deserves to be beaten, the judge shall make him lie down and have him flogged in his presence with the number of lashes his crime deserves, ³but he must not give him more than forty lashes. If he is flogged more than that, your brother will be degraded in your eyes.

COMMENTARY

1–3 This legislation assumes a scenario in which at least two men have a dispute that they have brought before the appointed judges. The judges will find one of them guilty and one of them innocent. If the guilty man deserves punishment (lit., "is a son of flogging," a Hebrew idiom to describe his fate), the judge will prescribe a penalty of a certain number of lashes "that his crime deserves" (*kᵉdê rišᵉʿātô*, lit., "according to the sufficiency of his wickedness"). The punishment must fit the crime. Forty lashes are not the required penalty but the maximum penalty. To beat a man excessively would be to treat him like an animal, thus "degrading" him. This law does not focus on preventing this person's death but preserving his dignity. As with other Deuteronomic laws (e.g., regarding forgiveness of debt and release of slaves), this law envisions the restoration of an offending member of the covenantal community to a dignified place among his people (McConville, 368).

NOTES

1 Regarding the phrase וְהִרְשִׁיעוּ ... וְהִצְדִּיקוּ (*wᵉhiṣdîqû ... wᵉhiršîʿû*, "acquitting ... condemning"), the verb רשׁע (*ršʿ*; GK 8399) always includes the idea of wickedness, evil intent, and injustice against God or persons. Its most appropriate antonym is צדק (*ṣdq*), "to act, do righteously." רשׁע (*ršʿ*) signifies negative behavior—evil thoughts, words, and deeds that are not only contrary to God's character but also hostile to the surrounding community. When it occurs in the Hiphil verbal form as here, it can connote either wicked conduct or the pronouncement of guilt. In the latter sense (as in 25:1), it signifies condemning the guilty judicially (Carpenter/Grisanti, *NIDOTTE*, 3:1201).

In a similar sense, the next verb (from צדק, *ṣdq*; GK 7405) denotes acquitting the innocent. (See Note on 24:13 for a noun derived from this verb.) It describes behavior that conforms to a certain standard and can describe someone who "acts rightly" or "is right." In the latter sense, a person is judged or declared to be righteous (Ex 23:7–8; Pr 17:15; Reimer, *NIDOTTE*, 3:746, 750).

3 The limit of lashes to אַרְבָּעִים (*ʾarbāʿîm*, "forty") provides the backdrop for the later Jewish practice of administering only thirty-nine lashes to allow a margin of error in case the flogger lost count.

The base form of the verb *qll* (root of וְנִקְלָה, *wᵉniqlâ*, "he will be degraded") means "to be light/slight" (Keller, *TLOT*, 3:1142). In its present form, the verb means to declare or make someone light, i.e., despicable, insignificant, or meaningless (ibid., 3:1142). This verb is the most common one used to denote mocking and reviling speech in which the speaker who feels uncertain or weak elevates himself by degrading the other person. The OT prohibits despising persons worthy of respect, such as parents (Ex 21:17; Lev 20:9; Pr 30:11) and political leaders (Ex 22:28; 2Sa 19:22; Ecc 10:20; Grisanti, "1 Samuel," 153–54). It is the antonym of the verb "to honor" (כבד, *kbd*), used in 5:16 for honoring (i.e., regarding as heavy) one's parents (cf. 27:16).

vii. Respect for animals (25:4)

⁴Do not muzzle an ox while it is treading out the grain.

COMMENTARY

4 Just as Yahweh desires that his covenantal nation practice justice and equity in all of their relationships with each other as well as with foreigners from surrounding nations, God wants his people to manifest compassion toward animals that help provide them with life-giving food. In ancient times, after the grain was harvested from the field the workers lay the grain stalks on a threshing floor of rock or packed earth. Sometimes they would have oxen walk over the grain stalks while pulling a wooden sledge with sharp objects on its bottom. This action would chew up the grain stalks and release the grain from the stalk (thereby leaving straw, chaff, and grain). To benefit from the labor of the oxen and yet refuse the animal any food while it is working demonstrates a lack of compassion. God's people should provide proper care for the animals that are integral to God's provision for the Israelites' own sustenance.

The apostle Paul used this passage twice (1Co 9:9–14; 1Ti 5:17–18) to show that those who minister the Word of God to his people are also worthy of proper care. Paul does not allegorize or spiritualize this OT law. Just as God requires the fair treatment of a working animal, so do working human beings deserve fair consideration, including people who have given their lives to ministry. Paul uses a clear principle from this passage without diminishing the meaning of this legislation in the time of Moses. He points out that a God who cares about the daily provision for an ox would care no less about the material needs of someone who is serving him (Wright, *Deuteronomy*, 265).

c. Respect for the Sanctity of Others (25:5–16)

i. Levirate marriage (25:5–10)

⁵If brothers are living together and one of them dies without a son, his widow must not marry outside the family. Her husband's brother shall take her and marry her and fulfill the duty of a brother-in-law to her. ⁶The first son she bears shall carry on the name of the dead brother so that his name will not be blotted out from Israel.

⁷However, if a man does not want to marry his brother's wife, she shall go to the elders at the town gate and say, "My husband's brother refuses to carry on his brother's name in Israel. He will not fulfill the duty of a brother-in-law to me." ⁸Then the elders of his town shall summon him and talk to him. If he persists in saying, "I do not want to marry her," ⁹his brother's widow shall go up to him in the presence of the elders, take off one of his sandals, spit in his face and say, "This is what is done to the man who will not build up his brother's family line." ¹⁰That man's line shall be known in Israel as The Family of the Unsandaled.

COMMENTARY

5–6 The law delineates that Yahweh intends both to allot certain parts of the land of promise to each of the tribes of Israel (and clans and families in each tribe) and to make sure all the land remain "connected" to the families to whom it was given originally. Other laws in Exodus through Numbers address different aspects of that question. According to this passage, a deceased man's brother should take his brother's widow as his wife and raise a family to perpetuate his brother's name and to keep inherited land in the family (a practice called levirate marriage; *levir* is the Latin word for "brother-in-

law"). A deceased man's lack of an heir will cause his name to be "blotted out"—a tragedy often connected with divine judgment (Ex 17:14; Dt 25:19; Ps 9:5; see Note on 7:24).

7–10 If the surviving brother refuses to carry out this duty, he risks social ostracism. The widow can present his refusal to the town elders, who will verify that he stands by the decision. If he does so, the widow, with the town elders watching, will take off one of her brother-in-law's sandals and spit in his face as an act of derision.

NOTES

5 It is important to notice that levirate marriage appears to contravene the legislation found elsewhere that prohibited marriage to the wife of one's brother (cf. Lev 18:16; 20:21). The practice of doing so

(וּלְקָחָהּ לוֹ לְאִשָּׁה, *ûleqāḥāh lô leʾiššâ*, "marry her," lit., "take her for himself for a wife") is not to be a commonplace occurrence. A deceased man's lack of an heir provides the occasion for a levirate marriage. Here is the point of contact with the issue of polygamy (see Note on 21:15). On the one hand, at least one of the OT examples of levirate marriage apparently involves a brother or relative who was unmarried (Ge 38:8–10; Ru 4:1–12 does not make this issue clear). However, the legislation that deals with levirate marriage does not address the issue of polygamy; it does not specify that only an unmarried brother could perform this duty. If that silence leaves the door open for a married brother to perform the levirate duty with regard to his brother's widow, his doing so might result in a polygamous relationship.

Furthermore, the "duty of the brother-in-law" would seem to involve more than sleeping with his brother's widow until she conceives. The text says that he should "take her for himself as a wife." On the one hand, the inheritance of his deceased brother would be divided among the child or children of his brother's widow (now his wife). On the other hand, the text implies that she remains his wife. In addition, the reference to the "firstborn son" (v.6) would imply that other children would be born from this union. The purpose of this legislation is not simply to provide an heir for the deceased brother (the heir's *legal* father), but also to ensure the welfare of his (otherwise economically destitute) widow; for the heir fathered by the deceased man's brother and born to the man's widow would not be able to care for the landed inheritance for many years. That task was left to the brother (the heir's biological father) in the interim.

There is a group of three words in Hebrew that share a common meaning and etymology: a masculine noun, "brother-in-law" (יָבָם, *yebāmāh*), a feminine noun, "sister-in-law" (יְבִמְתּוֹ, *yebbimtô*), and a verb, "to perform the levirate duty of a brother-in-law" (יבם, *ybm*, root of וְיִבְּמָהּ, *weyibbemāh*, "fulfill the duty of a brother-in-law to her"). Both nominal forms are much more specific than our English "brother-in-law" or "sister-in-law." The masculine noun refers to the brother of the man who died without a male heir and is related by marriage to the surviving widow. The feminine noun refers to the deceased brother's widow (who in this case is related by marriage to a surviving brother). The verb is used to delineate the act of "brother-in-lawing"—a specific responsibility in cases in which a man's deceased brother has no male heir.

9 Scholars have offered numerous suggestions concerning the symbolic significance of the removal of the brother-in-law's sandal (נַעֲלוֹ, *naʿalô*, "one of his sandals"; cf. P. Kruger, "The Removal of the Sandal in Deuteronomy XXV 9: 'A Rite of Passage,'" *VT* 46 [1996]: 535–38, for some of the primary alternatives). The first of the two most likely alternatives is that the removal of the sandal has a meaning distinct from the "spitting."

Various scholars posit that the removal of a sandal signifies the forfeiture of some right or authority (cf. Pss 60:8 [10]; 108:9 [10], where putting a sandal over something indicates ownership; *HALOT*, 705). It may indicate that the brother-in-law has no right to conjugal relations with the widow (McConville, 370) or may emphasize her right to freedom, i.e., full control of her destiny (Hamilton, *ABD*, 4:567). The man has shirked his responsibility to his brother (Craigie, 315; Driver, 283; Tigay, *Deuteronomy*, 233). Kruger ("The Removal of the Sandal," 536) suggests that the removal of the sandal represents a sort of bill of divorce providing protection of the widow by freeing her from any obligations to her dead husband's family. While this view may be true, it seems to understand this custom in the light of Ruth 4:7, which refers to the sandal as a symbol of the legal transfer of property. However, there Ruth does not remove the sandal from the "redeemer," so the symbolism of the sandal might be different.

The other primary interpretation views both the sandal's removal and the spitting as acts of derision (Hall, 376–77). Since no property changes hands and the following statements emphasize the despicable nature of the man's choice, it may be that no legal notion is in mind. Hoffner ("Some Contributions of Hittitology to Old Testament Study," *TynBul* 20 [1969]: 44) has pointed out a Hittite parallel in which the removal of a sandal "constitutes a public stigmatization." Several scholars suggest that the sandal imagery and the spitting may carry sexual overtones (and they link this law with the next one; C. Carmichael, "A Ceremonial Crux: Removing a Man's Sandal as a Female Gesture of Contempt," *JBL* 96 [1977]: 329–32; L. Eslinger, "More Drafting Techniques in Deuteronomic Law," *VT* 34 [1984]: 222–25; Wright, *Deuteronomy*, 269). One wonders whether the hearers and readers of this law would have recognized this symbolism as a sexual euphemism.

ii. Stopping a fight (the wrong way) (25:11–12)

[11]If two men are fighting and the wife of one of them comes to rescue her husband from his assailant, and she reaches out and seizes him by his private parts, [12]you shall cut off her hand. Show her no pity.

COMMENTARY

11–12 Whereas the preceding law dealt with the way to guarantee that a woman could bear a child to be the heir of her dead husband, this law concerns a man who loses his ability to father a child (cf. Kaufman, 143). The envisioned situation involves two men fighting and the wife of one of the fighters intervenes in her husband's behalf (cf. Ex 21:22–25, with a different outcome) by seizing the genitalia of her husband's opponent. The penalty for this act is the removal of her hand. This law appears to be a somewhat broad application of the principle of *lex talionis*. Since she, as a woman, did not have the same anatomy as a man (hence no exactly corresponding penalty), the removal of her hand (which had seized the man's private parts) serves as the appropriate penalty (Craigie, 316; Phillips, *Ancient Israel's Criminal Law*, 94–95).

Although the text does not make the point explicitly, it appears that such intervention injures the man's ability to father children, hence the severity of the penalty (Tigay, *Deuteronomy*, 485). Although this is the only OT law that mandates "mutilation," that penalty has various ancient Near Eastern parallels (Code of Hammurabi, §§116, 195, 210, 230 [*COS*, 2:343, 348–49]; Middle Assyrian Laws, A §§8, 50, 55 [*COS*, 2:354, 359]). Although one might be tempted to feel sorry for the woman because she intervened in her husband's behalf, the law requires that the Israelites show her no pity (see Note on 13:8 [9]).

NOTE

12 As with the preceding law, several scholars have suggested that "her hand" (כַּפָּהּ, *kappāh*) refers to the woman's sexual genitalia, thus making the punishment commensurate to her action (L. Eslinger, "The Case of an Immodest Lady Wrestler in Deuteronomy XXV 11–12," *VT* 31 [1981]: 269–81; idem, "More Drafting Techniques in Deuteronomic Laws," *VT* 34 [1984]: 225; Wright, *Deuteronomy*, 269).

iii. Honest weights and measures (25:13–16)

¹³Do not have two differing weights in your bag — one heavy, one light. ¹⁴Do not have two differing measures in your house — one large, one small. ¹⁵You must have accurate and honest weights and measures, so that you may live long in the land the Lᴏʀᴅ your God is giving you. ¹⁶For the Lᴏʀᴅ your God detests anyone who does these things, anyone who deals dishonestly.

COMMENTARY

13–16 Using false weights occurred regularly throughout the biblical world. The book of Leviticus addresses the same issue (Lev 19:35–37; cf. Eze 45:10), and biblical prophets indict those who are resorting to incorrect weights and measures (Hos 12:7; Am 8:5; Mic 6:10–12; cf. Pr 11:1; 16:11; 20:10, 23). In biblical times there was no apparent standard for weights and measures. (See de Vaux, 1:195–209, for a helpful overview of various kinds of weights and measures utilized in biblical times.) Regardless of the precise measuring tool in use at a given place, the professed unit of measurement and the actual unit of measurement are to be identical. A person should receive the exact amount he expects and pay only what he has agreed to. (Money was also weighed out.)

Ancient merchants used weights ("stones") and measures (baskets or jars for liquids or grains) when buying and selling goods; they could use these tools to their own financial advantage. When buying, they could use a heavier stone or a larger container measure in order to receive more than the fair amount. When selling, they could use a lighter stone or smaller container so that the customer received less than expected for the price paid. God's people only need one set of weights and measures — a set that is precise and full.

In addition to the fact that using false weights represented deception (a practice condemned by various biblical passages), it was primarily done to take advantage of those who had nowhere else to turn: the poor and needy, the fatherless and widows, and aliens. Yahweh consistently condemns mistreating people at the fringe of Israelite society; he regards such conduct as detestable (see Note on 7:25–26). Moreover, to use accurate and honest weights is part of a life of covenantal conformity and will bring to the honest merchant longevity in the Promised Land (see comments on 5:16).

NOTES

15 The verb שָׁלַם (*šlm*; GK 8966), reflected in the phrase שְׁלֵמָה וָצֶדֶק (*šelēmâ wāṣedeq*, "accurate and honest"), has three primary areas of meaning: to make peace (1Ki 22:44 [45]), to repay or compensate (Ex 21:33–22:14; 2Ki 4:7 [paying debts]; 9:26 [divine vengeance]), and to bring something to completion or fulfillment (Dt 20:12; Jos 10:1, 4; 2Sa 10:19; 1Ki 7:51; 9:25 [temple construction]; Grisanti, "1 Kings," 250). Some occurrences of the related adjective שָׁלֵם (*šālēm*) carry the idea of completeness. Stones used for altars and the temple were "complete" or unhewn (Dt 27:6; Jos 8:31; 1Ki 6:7). Similarly, correct weights would be complete, i.e., all that was intended, or "accurate." They are also to be "honest" (from the noun צֶדֶק, *ṣedeq*). As with the verb and other derivative forms (see Note on 24:13), these weights and measures must conform to a standard. God's people must not depart from or pervert that standard.

16 The noun עָוֶל (*ʿāwel*, "dishonesty" [here translated adverbially as "dishonestly"]; GK 6404) commonly occurs in contrast with nouns such as "righteousness," "justice," "truth," "instruction," and "good." Rather than referring to a specific deed, this noun connotes a broad, negative assessment of a person's behavior and actions (Schreiner, *TDOT*, 10:524). It often carries the meaning of "perversity" and "inequity." The perversion of a legal decision by bribery (Eze 18:8) is called "injustice" (Lev 19:15; cf. related words in Isa 61:8; Zep 3:5). In this passage and others, unfair business or trade practices are also regarded as a perversion or injustice (Lev 19:35; Eze 28:18; Baker, *NIDOTTE*, 3:342).

d. Dealing with the Amalekites (25:17–19)

> ¹⁷Remember what the Amalekites did to you along the way when you came out of Egypt. ¹⁸When you were weary and worn out, they met you on your journey and cut off all who were lagging behind; they had no fear of God. ¹⁹When the LORD your God gives you rest from all the enemies around you in the land he is giving you to possess as an inheritance, you shall blot out the memory of Amalek from under heaven. Do not forget!

COMMENTARY

17–19 The Amalekites were a nomadic or semi-nomadic people, the descendants of Esau, and one of Israel's traditional enemies (Jdg 3:13; 6:3–5, 33; 7:12; 10:12; 1Sa 15; 28:18; 30:18; 2Sa 1:1; 8:12). The OT provides the only written evidence about this relatively obscure people. No extrabiblical sources refer to them by name (see Mattingly, *ABD*, 1:169). In their wanderings, they inhabited the desert areas of the Sinai peninsula, the Negev, and the Arabah. The Israelites defeated them in battle near Rephidim (Ex 17:8–15) and were defeated by them when they tried to enter the land of Canaan after Yahweh's pronouncement of judgment (Nu 14:44–45).

This passage ignores the details of the battle at Rephidim and focuses on the Amalekites' attack of those least capable of defending themselves, those who were weary, worn out, and lagging behind. Clearly this group would have involved the elderly, the sick, and the weak, who were unable to keep up with the main group. To attack these vulnerable people evidenced the Amalekites' lack of any fear of God. Rather than referring to Yahweh's expectation that his covenantal people revere him, this "fear-of-God" deficit with reference to the Amalekites demonstrated that they did not fear divine punishment for their barbaric cruelty. They lacked even the most basic principles of morality. Because of this cowardice, Yahweh reserves for them total extermination.

As a result, once the Israelites become established in the Promised Land, God requires that they "blot out the memory of Amalek from under heaven" (see Note on 7:24; cf. Ex 17:14). These verses are framed by the Deuteronomic expression "remember ... do not forget" (see Note on 4:10). This exhortation to remember (and not forget) past events or realities always had some resultant conduct in view. The remembrance was to motivate (and enable) the Israelites to put into practice some aspect of what Yahweh expected of them. In this instance, the extermination of the Amalekites represents "unfinished business" for Israel, a backward-looking perspective. It provides a transition to 26:1-15, which looks forward to Israel's living out their God-given identity as the people of Yahweh once they are established in the land he has sworn to give them.

6. Ceremonial Fulfillment of the Law (26:1-15)

OVERVIEW

Just as ch. 12 began this section (chs. 12-26) with instructions concerning Israel's worship of Yahweh, ch. 26 ends the section with a similar emphasis (cf. 12:5-7; 26:1-2). Set against the backdrop of Israel's conquest of Canaan (by means of Yahweh's enablement), the offering of firstfruits (26:1-11) and the tithe offering (26:12-15) serve as clear examples of the attitudes of gratitude and obedience Yahweh expects from every member of the covenantal nation (Miller, 178) and represent the vertical and horizontal dimensions of Israel's existence as such.

The offering of firstfruits tangibly demonstrates Israel's gratitude for and recognition of God's provision of abundance in the Promised Land. The offering of tithes serves as Yahweh's appointed means to care for the priests and Levites as well as the poor of the nation. Also, these offerings represent the *homage* Israel must pay to Yahweh in recognition of his sovereignty over them (Merrill, *Deuteronomy*, 331).

a. Firstfruits (26:1-11)

¹When you have entered the land the LORD your God is giving you as an inheritance and have taken possession of it and settled in it, ²take some of the firstfruits of all that

you produce from the soil of the land the LORD your God is giving you and put them in a basket. Then go to the place the LORD your God will choose as a dwelling for his Name ³and say to the priest in office at the time, "I declare today to the LORD your God that I have come to the land the LORD swore to our forefathers to give us." ⁴The priest shall take the basket from your hands and set it down in front of the altar of the LORD your God. ⁵Then you shall declare before the LORD your God: "My father was a wandering Aramean, and he went down into Egypt with a few people and lived there and became a great nation, powerful and numerous. ⁶But the Egyptians mistreated us and made us suffer, putting us to hard labor. ⁷Then we cried out to the LORD, the God of our fathers, and the LORD heard our voice and saw our misery, toil and oppression. ⁸So the LORD brought us out of Egypt with a mighty hand and an outstretched arm, with great terror and with miraculous signs and wonders. ⁹He brought us to this place and gave us this land, a land flowing with milk and honey; ¹⁰and now I bring the firstfruits of the soil that you, O LORD, have given me." Place the basket before the LORD your God and bow down before him. ¹¹And you and the Levites and the aliens among you shall rejoice in all the good things the LORD your God has given to you and your household.

COMMENTARY

1–4 Israel's conquest of and settlement in the land of Canaan serves as the chronological point (cf. 17:14; 18:9; 27:3) after which God's people must celebrate Yahweh's provision for them through offerings. Verse 1 draws on themes found in preceding chapters that focus on Yahweh's gracious gift of the land (the verb "to give" [*ntn*] occurs six times in this passage concerning the land; 26:1–3, 9–11) as a stewardship to his covenantal people. Israel's entrance into the land was commanded (1:8; 4:1), performed by God himself (4:38; 8:7; 9:28; 31:21), and presented as an outcome of covenantal obedience (6:18; 8:1; 10:11; 11:8, 31), and it will be brought to completion in the near future (26:3). This land represents a divine inheritance (see Note on 1:38) of which they are to take possession (see comments on 1:8) and in which they are to settle.

After that day comes, each Israelite family must bring some of the "firstfruits" of their agricultural abundance in a basket to the priest at the central sanctuary, i.e., the place where God has caused his name to dwell (see Note on 12:11). It is important to notice that this ability to bring firstfruits represented the inauguration of Israel's life in the Promised Land. No longer an enslaved or wandering people after they settle in their God-given inheritance, the Israelites will enjoy Yahweh's provision of agricultural abundance and must offer the first part of that harvest to their faithful, covenantal Lord.

The worshiper begins by making the first of two affirmations (both of which focus on Israel's history): I stand here today in fulfillment of what Yahweh has sworn to us (see Note on 1:8). The statement recognizes God's promise to Israel's ancestors and his bringing that oath to reality. He is indeed the ever-faithful God. The priest will take the basket and set it before the altar.

5-11 The worshiper's second affirmation provides a more detailed review of Israel's past experience. Israel's "father," Jacob (renamed "Israel" in Ge 32:28), moved his entire (extended) family to Egypt and settled there, where "he lived as an alien" (*gwr*; in contrast with the worshiper who has settled in Canaan). Although they were originally few in number ("seventy souls"; Dt 10:22; cf. Ge 46:27), Yahweh has multiplied their population in the intervening years in fulfillment of his promise to the patriarchs (Ge 15:5; 22:17; see comments at 10:22). They had been an inconsequential people but have become a powerful and numerous nation.

Because of the affliction they experienced in Egypt, they cried out to Yahweh, who attentively heard their plea. As he had done consistently (Ps 34:17 [18]), Yahweh intervened in their behalf and delivered them from Egypt through Moses' leadership. The fact that Yahweh "brought out" Israel from the land of Egypt serves as a fundamental theme in the book of Deuteronomy (a theme surfacing twenty-one times; 1:27; 4:20, 37; 5:6, 15; 6:12, 21, 23; et al.). Yahweh is the kind of God who honors his word to his people by hearing their cry and coming to their aid (cf. Ex 2:23-25).

The three nouns for affliction emphasize the burdensome nature of Israel's suffering in Egypt.

Yahweh delivered his people "with a mighty hand and an outstretched arm" (cf. 4:34; 11:2; see comment on 5:15 and 7:17-19). The word pair "signs and wonders" occurs in five other passages in Deuteronomy to describe Yahweh's miraculous intervention (4:34; 6:22; 7:19; 29:2; 34:11; paralleled with *môrā*ʾ, "terror," in 4:34 and 34:12; see comments on 7:17-19). Not only did Yahweh deliver his people from Egyptian bondage, but (from the perspective envisioned in ch. 26) he also brought his covenantal nation to and settled them in this land "flowing with milk and honey," i.e., having the fullness of blessings associated with the Promised Land (cf. v.15; see comments and Note on 6:3).

Because of the many things Yahweh did in Israel's behalf, the worshiper will be able to stand before the priest at the central sanctuary to offer the firstfruits in recognition that they have come from Yahweh himself. The offerer will set the basket before the altar and worship (see Note on 5:9) his marvelous covenantal Lord. Because the Levites and aliens (non-Israelites living among God's people; see Note on 1:16) lack an allotment in the land (12:12; 14:27, 29; see Note on 14:29), they will join with the worshiper in rejoicing (see Note on 16:11) in God's abundant provision (for all three groups through various means).

NOTES

5 Most view the patriarch Jacob as the individual to whom the phrase אֲרַמִּי אֹבֵד (ᵃᵃ*rammî ʾōbēd*, "wandering Aramean") refers. The designation "Aramean" probably derives from Jacob's extended stay in that region (twenty years; Ge 31:41-42). Scholars have offered three primary alternatives for the verbal form אבד (ʾ*bd*) in this expression. Several scholars point to ancient Near Eastern parallels in offering "wandering" as the best translation for the verb in question (Otzen, *TDOT*, 1:20; McConville, 376; A. Millard, "A Wandering Aramean," *JNES* 39 [1980]: 155; Nelson, 304; Tigay, *Deuteronomy*, 240). According to this meaning, Jacob went from being a man without roots to fathering a nation that became established in its divinely promised and granted inheritance.

Craigie (321, n. 4), however, posits that this verb is best rendered "ailing" and points to the fact that Jacob was already quite old when he moved his family to Egypt. Alternatively, Janzen ("The 'Wandering

Aramean' Reconsidered," *VT* 44 [1994]: 373–75; cf. Hall, 388–89) suggests the translation "starving" and highlights the fact that a famine in the land of Canaan occasioned his moving his entire family to Egypt. He also suggests that this meaning provides a nice contrast of Israel's enjoyment of abundance in the land of God's promise with the barrenness of the wilderness through which they had recently traveled.

Although the meaning of this verb here is not entirely clear, the contextual emphasis on the homelessness of Jacob in contrast with Israel's settled existence in the time envisioned by ch. 26 favors the first interpretive alternative. This translation may be supported by references to lost or "strayed" property (Dt 22:3; 1Sa 9:3, 20). The prophet Jeremiah (Jer 50:6) describes Israel as a lost or straying sheep. Ezekiel indicts the watchmen/shepherds of Israel for failing to bring in the lost or straying sheep of Israel (Eze 34:16; cf. Ps 119:176).

A fourth alternative, offered more recently, seems quite unlikely: "an Aramean [i.e., Laban] sought to destroy my father [i.e., Jacob]" (S. Norin, "Ein Aramäer, dem Umkommen Nahe—ein Kerntext der Forschung und Tradition," *SJOT* 8 [1994]: 101–4; R. Steiner, "The 'Aramean' of Deuteronomy 26:5: *Peshat and Derash*," in *Tehillah le-Moshe: Biblical and Judaic Studies in Honor of Moshe Greenberg* [ed. M. Cogan, B. Eichler, and J. Tigay; Winona Lake, Ind.: Eisenbrauns, 1997], 136–38). It implies a reading that is not attested in any MSS and does not match the contextual contrast between impermanence and permanence.

The three adjectives in the phrase לְגוֹי גָּדוֹל עָצוּם וָרָב (*lᵉgôy gādôl ʿāṣûm wārāb*, "a great nation, powerful and numerous") occur several times to describe the might of non-Israelite peoples (2:10, 21; 7:1, 17). Yahweh promised Israel that he would make them into a nation that was greater (רַב, *rāb*) and mightier (עָצוּם, *ʿāṣûm*) than the Canaanites (9:14).

7 The noun עֳנִי (*ʿŏnî*, occurring thirty-six times in the OT; here the first word in the phrase עָנְיֵנוּ ... עֲמָלֵנוּ ... לַחֲצֵנוּ, *ʿonyēnû ... ʿᵃmālēnû ... laḥᵃṣēnû*, "our misery, toil and oppression") describes the condition of pain, suffering, and anguish of the person who experiences affliction. This noun can refer to significant suffering by the nation, as in their sojourn in Egypt (Ex 3:7, 17; Dt 26:7; Ne 9:9) or the Babylonian exile (La 1:3, 9; 3:1; Isa 48:10). It can also signify the suffering of an individual (Ge 31:42; Ps 88:9 [10]). It can depict actual physical suffering (Job 30:16, 27; 36:8) or mental anguish (1Sa 1:11; Wegner, *NIDOTTE*, 3:451).

The other two nouns occur only here in Deuteronomy. Based on the verb from which the second one is derived (עמל, *ʿml*, "to work"), the noun עָמָל (*ʿāmāl*) highlights the idea of burdensome and laborious toil, with which Israel was well acquainted in Egypt (Ecc 4:8; 5:16[15]). The third noun emphasizes the pressure and weight of affliction (cf. Ex 3:9; Pss 42:9 [10]; 43:2, where it is paired with *ʿŏnî*).

10 Whereas in 26:4 the worshiper is to hand the basket to the priest, who will place it before the altar, by the word וְהִנַּחְתּוֹ (*wᵉhinnaḥtô*, "then you must set it down") this verse affirms that the worshiper will place the basket before Yahweh. Some scholars regard this difference as evidence of layers of redactional activity (i.e., one statement was added later without giving careful attention to the other statement; Mayes, 335). Several scholars view v.10 as a summarizing statement based on the preceding description of the priest's placing the basket before Yahweh (on behalf of the worshiper; Kalland, 157; Ridderbos, 244). Christensen (*Deuteronomy 21:10–34:12*, 638) delineates a chiastic structure to which he appeals in asserting that v.10a parallels vv.3–4 and describes the same procedure. Others believe that the basket is twice placed before the altar as part of the liturgy (Craigie, 320; Merrill, *Deuteronomy*, 333; Nelson, 307; Wright, *Deuteronomy*, 274).

The NJPS resolves the tension by translating the verb in v.10 as "leave it," so that, unlike in other firstfruits celebrations, the worshiper leaves the offering with the priest and does not participate in a communal meal. That the basket is placed on the altar twice seems the most likely interpretation.

b. Tithes (26:12-15)

¹²When you have finished setting aside a tenth of all your produce in the third year, the year of the tithe, you shall give it to the Levite, the alien, the fatherless and the widow, so that they may eat in your towns and be satisfied. ¹³Then say to the LORD your God: "I have removed from my house the sacred portion and have given it to the Levite, the alien, the fatherless and the widow, according to all you commanded. I have not turned aside from your commands nor have I forgotten any of them. ¹⁴I have not eaten any of the sacred portion while I was in mourning, nor have I removed any of it while I was unclean, nor have I offered any of it to the dead. I have obeyed the LORD my God; I have done everything you commanded me. ¹⁵Look down from heaven, your holy dwelling place, and bless your people Israel and the land you have given us as you promised on oath to our forefathers, a land flowing with milk and honey."

COMMENTARY

12 This ceremony concerns the setting aside of the triennial tithe (i.e., tithe of the third year) for the benefit of various categories of needy people in Israel. Whereas the preceding section concerned the vertical dimension of Israel's relationship with Yahweh, these verses address the horizontal dimension of Yahweh's expectations of his covenantal nation. Scholars have debated whether this triennial tithe referred to the normal tithe that would be diverted for these needy people every third year, was a second tithe required every third year, or was a third tithe (see comments on 14:28-29).

Regardless of the correct answer, the triennial tithe taken up here is to be dedicated for the consumption of those who, for various reasons, have little ability to provide for their own material needs. Rather than the tithe's being sent to the central sanctuary, it is to be given to needy recipients in the region. The Levites, unlike the other tribes, lack a landed allotment. Consequently, their ability to generate food for themselves is limited. Aliens, orphans, and widows were socially powerless people who often faced severe economic hardship and for whom God's people are to show abundant compassion (see comments on 10:17-19 and Note on 14:29).

13-14 As with the offering of the firstfruits (26:1-11), the setting aside of the tithe is to be accompanied by an affirmation from the worshiper, who first testifies to his own obedience and then asks Yahweh to continue blessing him. His testimony involves a positive and a negative statement, both of which are followed by a "global" affirmation of obedience.

The giver begins by declaring that he has, in fact, "removed" this tithe from his home and turned it over to the needy people for whom it was intended. This form of the verb (Piel of *bᶜr*) occurs thirteen times in Deuteronomy, eleven of which are part of the statement "purge the evil from ..." (see Note on 13:5). Clearly, it indicates a rigorous separation (McConville, 381) to emphasize that the worshiper has kept absolutely none of the tithe for personal consumption. In his "global" affirmation, he declares that he has not turned aside from nor forgotten (two common verbs for covenantal treachery; see Note on 4:10 and 17:2) Yahweh's expectations in this area of his life. The worshiper then states what he has not done with the "sacred offering."

All three statements affirm the ritual purity of the offered tithe (hence its acceptability for the recipients). The worshiper affirms that he has not touched the tithe when he was unclean, whether as the result of coming into contact with a corpse (Lev 22:4) or other reasons, or from some affiliation with pagan practices.

15 The worshiper ends his declaration with a prayer. He asks Yahweh to observe his obedience from his heavenly (set apart) residence (see Note) and to bless his covenantal people. God's blessings on Israel are not something they *deserve* in the light of their obedience in this area; their covenantal Lord has simply determined to bless them. The worshiper is asking Yahweh to continue blessing them. These blessings (being in the land God promises and enjoying abundance of agriculture and livestock) are a fulfillment of the oath Yahweh made to the patriarchs.

NOTES

13 Because the phrase לִפְנֵי יְהוָה (*lipnê yhwh*, "to the LORD") often refers to something done at the temple, some scholars conclude that the tithe is presented to the Lord at the central sanctuary (12:7, 12, 18; cf. Cairns, 144, 223; Driver, 290; Mayes, 336). However, the common phrase "the place where the LORD will choose to establish his Name" is absent. Also, ch. 14 refers to this tithe as given at the local community rather than the central sanctuary. Some scholars contend that the tithe was not taken to the central sanctuary, but the affirmation had to be uttered there on one of a worshiper's later trips to that holy place (Ridderbos, 245; Thompson, 257). Nevertheless, this phrase references Yahweh's presence in all Israel and, in particular, at the worshiper's home or where the needy people partake of the tithe (Ge 27:7; cf. Craigie, 322–23; Hall, 391; Tigay, *Deuteronomy*, 243).

Because this offering was הַקֹּדֶשׁ (*haqqōdeš*, "the sacred portion"), Yahweh owns it exclusively (Lev 5:15–16; 19:24; 27:28). The holiness of this tithe demonstrates that giving to the needy is no less sacred an act than giving a tithe at the central sanctuary. This noun occurs two other times in Deuteronomy. In 12:26 it refers to offerings in general, and in v.15 of this chapter it designates Yahweh's heavenly dwelling place. As applied to the tithe, this term highlights the consecrated nature of the portion set aside.

14 Scholars are not agreed on whether the noun represented in בְאֹנִי (*bᵉʾōnî*, "in mourning") is derived from the verb "to mourn" (אנה, *ʾnh*, "mourning"), or from the conjectured verb "to be strong" (און, *ʾwn*, "vigor/strength") with the meaning of "power" or "strength." Craigie, 323 (cf. Georg Fohrer, "Twofold Aspects of Hebrew Words," in *Words and Meaning* [ed. P. Ackroyd and B. Lindars; Cambridge: Cambridge Univ. Press, 1968], 98; Christensen, *Deuteronomy 21:10–34:12*, 642), opts for the latter alternative and translates the expression "trusting in my own strength," referring to something produced by his own cleverness or skill. In light of the contextual emphasis on uncleanness, the first option is preferable. Although some writers connect these mourning rites with pagan rituals (Merrill, *Deuteronomy*, 336; Thompson, 257), this statement seems to refer to uncleanness caused by touching a corpse (T. Lewis, *Cults of the Dead in Ancient Israel and Ugarit* [HSM 39; Atlanta: Scholars, 1989], 103; McConville, 381; Nelson, 310; Tigay, *Deuteronomy*, 243–44).

There are two common interpretations of the phrase לְמֵת (*lᵉmēt*, "to the dead"). Some (e.g., Lewis) argue that it refers to placing food and other items at a relative's grave, some kind of offering or pagan rite for dead relatives (for their spirits in Sheol; cf. Ps 106:28; Driver, 292; Nelson, 305; Tigay, *Deuteronomy*, 244, 482), or a meal furnished in a house of mourning (Jer 16:5–9; Hos 9:4). Other interpreters suggest that the reference is to offerings presented to either Baal (Craigie, 323; Merrill, *Deuteronomy*, 336), Molech (McConville, 381), or Mot, i.e., "the Dead One." In that case, the food offerings were meant to sustain the pagan god (who was consigned to the Netherworld) until it could revive and resume its earthly role (Merrill, *Deuteronomy*, 336). Regardless of the exact reference, however, all such offerings are unacceptable to Yahweh.

C. Mutual Commitments of Covenantal Renewal (26:16–19)

OVERVIEW

Forming a conclusion to Moses' articulation of the various covenantal stipulations (5:1–26:15, and more specifically, 12:1–26:15 [cf. the wording of 12:1 and 26:16]), the Lord commands the children of Israel carefully to obey the stated laws and rules in the light of their reciprocal affirmation to live in accordance with the covenantal agreement (26:16). In this ratification of the covenant, Israel declares their allegiance to the Lord (26:17), and God declares his faithfulness to his promises (26:18–19). Both affirmations are to serve as a motivation for Israel's obedience to the covenantal stipulations.

> [16]The Lord your God commands you this day to follow these decrees and laws; carefully observe them with all your heart and with all your soul. [17]You have declared this day that the Lord is your God and that you will walk in his ways, that you will keep his decrees, commands and laws, and that you will obey him. [18]And the Lord has declared this day that you are his people, his treasured possession as he promised, and that you are to keep all his commands. [19]He has declared that he will set you in praise, fame and honor high above all the nations he has made and that you will be a people holy to the Lord your God, as he promised.

COMMENTARY

16 Every member of God's covenantal nation must wholeheartedly live in accordance with all the covenantal requirements ("decrees and laws"; see Note on 4:1) stated in the preceding chapters, "with all your heart and with all your soul" (see Note on 6:5).

17 By embracing this covenantal relationship with Yahweh, the nation of Israel affirms a reality and an intention. The reality is that Yahweh is their God. This fact of relationship is not an obligation that Yahweh accepts but a commitment that he makes. The "central covenant reality" (Wright, *Deuteronomy*, 272) is that Yahweh perfectly fulfills his role as the God of his people by caring for their welfare, protecting them, and guaranteeing their future destiny. The other side of that "covenantal formula" is that Israel is his people. Their promises to "walk," "keep," and "obey" (see Note on 13:4 and comments on 10:12–13) are the means by which they can demonstrate their identity as the people of Yahweh to the surrounding nations.

18–19 In accordance with his earlier declarations, the Lord affirms that Israel is his specially chosen nation and that he will one day set them in a grand position over all the nations of the world. The terms "his people," "treasured possession" (*sᵉgullâ*, see Note on 7:6), and "a people holy [see Note on 7:6] to the LORD your God" highlight their role as God's elect nation, by means of whose distinctive witness he intends to influence the surrounding nations. This potential for Yahweh's covenantal people to influence the world around them is central to what God promised them in Exodus 19:5–6.

God's promise here is also conditioned by Israel's full and wholehearted obedience to his covenantal requirements ("you are to keep all his commands"). Just as God affirmed in Exodus 19, Israel's voluntary obedience to the covenant (its conditional "if" clause) was the prerequisite for their ability to function as Yahweh's banner nation (the covenantal "then" consequence). Yahweh's intent is to establish them in a renowned position before the nations ("in praise, fame and honor") for his ultimate glory. The first two terms of this triad occur as a pair in Zephaniah 3:19–20, which looks forward to the future day when Yahweh will judge the oppressors of his people, regather his chosen ones, and give them honor and praise.

All three terms occur in Jeremiah 13:11 and 33:9 in a slightly different order ("fame ... praise ... honor"). In Jeremiah 13 Yahweh affirms that he commissioned Israel "to be my people for my renown and praise and honor" and then indicts his covenantal nation for rejecting this role. In ch. 33, which is similar to the present passage, Yahweh looks forward to the day when the city of Jerusalem will bring him "renown, joy, praise and honor before all nations on earth." Bringing glory to Yahweh before every inhabitant of the world is the ultimate goal of Yahweh's relationship with his covenantal people.

NOTES

16–19 The expression הַיּוֹם (*hayyôm*, "this day") occurs three times in these verses to return the hearer's attention to the time of Israel's encampment on the plains of Moab (since the preceding verses looked to a future day). The text of Deuteronomy never refers to a dialogue or a ceremony like that described here. It could be that there was a covenant-renewal ceremony not recorded in the book, or that Yahweh did not require a formal covenant-renewal ceremony. Regardless, Yahweh's covenantal relationship with his chosen nation is not something to be relegated to the past or future; rather, the covenant is always to be a *present* concern for the Israelites.

17–18 These verses contain the only two OT occurrences of the Hiphil form of the verb אמר (*ʾmr*, here in the clause הֶאֱמַרְתָּ ... הֶאֱמִירְךָ, *heʾĕmartā ... heʾĕmîrᵉkā*, "you have declared ... the LORD has declared ...

you"). This form of the verb signifies an official, binding statement (Wagner, *TDOT*, 1:329): "to proclaim or vow to do something" (*DCH*, 1:325). McConville, 382, in a rendering that spells out the mutual commitment of Yahweh and Israel, translates the clause as follows: "You have today confirmed the declaration of the Lord ... and the Lord has today confirmed your declaration." These two verbs highlight the commitments made by both parties and emphasize the solemnity of this covenantal renewal. Nelson, 304 (cf. 305), offers the less helpful translation, "you have caused Yahweh to agree ... and Yahweh has caused you to agree" (cf. NRSV's "you have obtained the LORD's agreement" and the helpful footnote of Tigay [*Deuteronomy*, 393, n. 47] critiquing this translation).

REFLECTION

The divinely intended impact of covenantal requirements. What should an understanding of these stipulations produce among God's chosen people? For an Israelite to keep these stipulations, this passage:

1. Provides an awareness of what is abominable to Yahweh (see Note on 7:25–26). When people do abominable things, they become an abomination themselves and face the treatment reserved for those items or actions (7:25).

2. Emphasizes the need for the purgation of evil from the community (see Note on 13:5). In each passage that demands purging (except 19:19), the death penalty is prescribed. Death by stoning allows the people to carry out the penalty without defiling their hands.

3. Highlights Israel's status as Yahweh's chosen people (14:1–2, 21; 26:19).

4. Stresses concern for the purity of the land (21:23; 24:4; cf. Lev 18:25–28; 20:22). Sadly, around the time of the exile (before and afterward) the prophets refer to the defiled condition of the land (Jer 2:7; 16:18; Eze 36:18).

5. Evokes the memory of their experience in Egypt (15:14–15; 16:3, 12; 24:9, 18, 22; 25:17).

6. Draws attention to the means for their enjoyment of the covenantal blessings (14:29; 15:4, 10, 18; 16:15; 23:20; 24:19; 26:15).

IV. COVENANTAL BLESSINGS AND CURSES (27:1–29:1 [28:69])

OVERVIEW

These chapters possess a clear link with the preceding section (chs. 12–26). In addition to serving their own purpose (to present covenantal blessings and curses), chs. 27–28 form a chiastic framework with the preceding chapters (cf. Craigie, 212; Lohfink, 233–34; McConville, 387):

11:26–28: The blessings and curses in the *present* renewal of the covenant (at Moab)

11:29–32: The blessings and curses in the *future* renewal of the covenant (on Ebal and Gerizim)

12:1–26:19: Specific covenantal stipulations

27:1–26: The blessings and curses in the *future* renewal of the covenant (on Ebal and Gerizim)

28:1–29:1: The blessings and curses in the *present* renewal of the covenant (at Moab)

This connectedness has caused several commentators to include chs. 27–28 with chs. 12–26 (Biddle, Craigie, Hall, Kalland, Tigay). However, the obvious linkage between these sections does not require one to ignore their distinctiveness (e.g., 11:26–32 in above framework).

In this section, Moses exhorts the children of Israel to renew their covenant with the Lord (ch. 27) and declares in clear terms the blessings and curses (covenantal sanctions) that will be occasioned by their obedience or disobedience (respectively) to the covenantal stipulations (as is common in various ancient Near Eastern treaties; ch. 28).

A. The Call for Covenantal Renewal (27:1–26)

OVERVIEW

Moses exhorts the children of Israel to renew their covenant with the Lord, commands that they provide for the preservation of the covenantal stipulations, and charges that they symbolically place themselves under the suzerainty of the stipulations of the covenant with the Lord by means of a ceremony on Mounts Ebal and Gerizim. The nation is to "act out" this covenant-renewal ceremony shortly after they entered the land God has promised them.

1. Instructions for the Covenant-Renewal Ceremony (27:1–13)

OVERVIEW

Moses commands the children of Israel to record the laws spoken by Moses as part of the ceremony of this covenantal renewal and to erect an altar on Mount Ebal, where they are to make various offerings and pronounce the covenantal curses on Israelites who will practice various kinds of covenantal treachery.

¹Moses and the elders of Israel commanded the people: "Keep all these commands that I give you today. ²When you have crossed the Jordan into the land the LORD your God

is giving you, set up some large stones and coat them with plaster. ³Write on them all the words of this law when you have crossed over to enter the land the LORD your God is giving you, a land flowing with milk and honey, just as the LORD, the God of your fathers, promised you. ⁴And when you have crossed the Jordan, set up these stones on Mount Ebal, as I command you today, and coat them with plaster. ⁵Build there an altar to the LORD your God, an altar of stones. Do not use any iron tool upon them. ⁶Build the altar of the LORD your God with fieldstones and offer burnt offerings on it to the LORD your God. ⁷Sacrifice fellowship offerings there, eating them and rejoicing in the presence of the LORD your God. ⁸And you shall write very clearly all the words of this law on these stones you have set up."

⁹Then Moses and the priests, who are Levites, said to all Israel, "Be silent, O Israel, and listen! You have now become the people of the LORD your God. ¹⁰Obey the LORD your God and follow his commands and decrees that I give you today."

¹¹On the same day Moses commanded the people:

¹²When you have crossed the Jordan, these tribes shall stand on Mount Gerizim to bless the people: Simeon, Levi, Judah, Issachar, Joseph and Benjamin. ¹³And these tribes shall stand on Mount Ebal to pronounce curses: Reuben, Gad, Asher, Zebulun, Dan and Naphtali.

COMMENTARY

1 For the first time in Deuteronomy, the elders of Israel are associated with Moses as God's spokesmen to the chosen nation. Since Yahweh will not allow Moses to enter the Promised Land, the elders (and Joshua) will assume the responsibility of leading the nation.

2–4, 8 After crossing the Jordan River into the land of "milk and honey" promised to them by Yahweh (see comments and Note on 6:3), the children of Israel are to plaster several large stones, clearly inscribe on them "all the words of this law," and place those stones on Mount Ebal. Unlike an inscription carved into a rock surface (with a very durable result), God's people were to "write on" these stones. This task involves covering the stone(s) with plaster and then either writing on them with some sort of ink or inscribe the plaster (a practice more common in Egypt than in Mesopotamia;

Tigay, *Deuteronomy*, 248). Although this writing will not last as long as an inscription carved in rock, it will provide the Israelites access to Yahweh's expectations of them and serve as a silent witness (cf. Jos 24:27; McCarthy, *Treaty and Covenant*, 196) of Israel's need to live in accordance with those expectations in the soon-to-be-conquered land. They will also serve as a witness *against* the nation when they disobey Yahweh's covenantal demands.

It seems striking that these stones are to be placed on Mount Ebal (not Mount Gerizim) and that the sacrifices detailed below are to be offered there, for Mount Ebal is the mountain of cursing (27:13), while Mount Gerizim is the mountain of blessing (27:12). Six of the Israelite tribes are to announce the threatened curses while standing on Mount Ebal. This location for the stones probably emphasizes, first, the need for Israel to recognize that failure to keep the covenant means that Israel must accept the resultant curses (McConville, 389). Second, the stones' deposit on Mount Ebal may symbolize the expectation that Israel will indeed disobey Yahweh's demands and experience covenantal cursing (Barker, "The Theology of Deuteronomy 27," 288). If Israel seeks to obey the law without a faith relationship with Yahweh, they are doomed to fail.

5–7 At the same site (Mount Ebal) the children of Israel are to set up an altar of unhewn stones (cf. Ex 20:25) on which they will make burnt offerings and peace offerings to express their dependence on and thankfulness for Yahweh. Scholars have debated the reason for Yahweh's prohibition of using hewn stones, i.e., stones carved into specific shapes with metal blades or chisels. It could be that carving stones with metal blades had some connection with Canaanite religion (Craigie, 329, n. 7) or that doing so could indicate dependence on non-Hebrews (for the tools; Craigie, 329; Hall, 401). The Philistines, for example, provided the necessary expertise and equipment for iron-working in later periods (1Sa 13:19–23).

Instead of focusing on the use of an iron tool as the defiling element, however, the reader should focus on the fact that only unhewn rather than hewn stones can be used for this altar. It does appear that the Canaanites, whose religious practices were proscribed for Israel, made their altars of hewn stones (though they also made some altars with unhewn stones; Brevard Childs, *The Book of Exodus* [OTL; Philadelphia: Westminster, 1974], 466; J. Philip Hyatt, *Commentary on Exodus* [NCBC; Grand Rapids: Eerdmans, 1980], 226). But beyond that presumably forbidden parallel, the prohibition of hewn stones probably signifies the idea that all human effort (devoted to shaping or "improving" the altar's stones) is unacceptable as a means of approaching God (J. M. Sprinkle, *"The Book of the*

Covenant": A Literary Approach [JSOTSup 174; Sheffield: Sheffield Academic, 1994], 48).

Yahweh requires the Israelites to offer burnt offerings and fellowship (peace) offerings, both of which were presented at the conclusion of the covenant at Sinai (Ex 24:5), as often happened in conjunction with important occasions (Ex 32:6; Jos 22:27; Jdg 20:26; 1Sa 10:8; 2Sa 6:17–18; 24:25; 1Ki 3:17; cf. Hall, 401; Tigay, *Deuteronomy*, 250). The entire animal was offered in the burnt offering, but only the fat and entrails of the animal were burned on the altar in the fellowship offering. The remainder of the animal was eaten by the worshiper and his family. Some scholars regard the burnt offerings as vertically oriented (i.e., expressing human worship of God) and the fellowship offerings as horizontally oriented (i.e., occasioning or restoring human-to-human relationships; Hall, 401; Wright, *Deuteronomy*, 276). Although the fellowship offerings did involve a joyful celebration with other Israelites, it seems that their primary significance was peace between Yahweh and his chosen people, i.e., that the Israelites are in a state of well-being before their covenantal Lord (Averbeck, *NIDOTTE*, 4:136–37, 1000–1001; Barker, "Theology of Deuteronomy 27," 296).

Various critical scholars (e.g., Mayes, 342) suggest that a conflict exists between this command to offer sacrifices in the area of Shechem and the law in ch. 12 concerning the location of the altar (at a place where Yahweh will choose to establish his name [assumed to be Jerusalem]; see comments at ch. 12). However, these scholars misunderstand the real aim of the law concerning an altar and the function of the sacrifices in ch. 27. Here the law seeks to establish Yahweh's exclusive sovereignty over Israel's worship and deals with Israel's regular practice of worship. Also, the nation has not yet entered into the "rest" Yahweh has promised to give them (Dt 12:9–10). The sacrifices envisioned in ch.

27 represent a unique, rather than an ongoing, event (McConville, 389).

In fact, Shechem is the place of Yahweh's choice for this important celebration of covenantal renewal. There are at least four potential reasons for the choice of Mounts Ebal and Gerzim as the site for this covenant-renewal ceremony: The valley between these two mountains provides a natural amphitheater (the acoustical factor); Shechem was an important site throughout biblical history (Ge 12:6–7; Jos 24:32; the historical factor); Shechem was centrally located among the tribal allotments (the geographical factor); and mountains and hills were often appealed to as witnesses in covenantal contexts (the covenantal factor).

9–10 To motivate Israel to obey the commands of the Lord, Moses, the priests, and the Levites point out that in this renewal of the covenant the Israelites have renewed their status as God's chosen people. Moses demands their undivided attention by exhorting his fellow Israelites, "Hear" (see comments on 4:1–2). After referring to their renewed status as Yahweh's elect nation, he exhorts them to obey their covenantal Lord wholeheartedly. ("Obey" and "follow" are two of several "covenantal verbs" that occur throughout Deuteronomy [see Note on 13:4].) It is essential to notice that the obedience Yahweh demands of his people is the consequence of their relationship with Yahweh and not its cause (Barker, "Theology of Deuteronomy 27," 300; Cairns, 234; Thompson, 264).

11–13 After crossing the Jordan River, the children of Israel are to gather in the region of Mounts Ebal and Gerizim for a ceremony to demonstrate the sovereignty of God's law over the soon-to-be-conquered Promised Land. Moses instructs the children of Israel to divide into two groups when they gather near Shechem to renew the covenant with Yahweh, one to agree with (by saying "amen") the blessings and the other with the curses. In this covenant-renewal ceremony, six specified tribes will stand on Mount Gerizim to affirm the blessings that will result from obedience to the law, while the other six tribes will stand on Mount Ebal to affirm the curses that will result from disobedience to that same law.

The tribes who echo the blessings (Simeon, Levi, Judah, Issachar, Joseph, and Benjamin) have their tribal allotments in the heart of the land and descend from Rachel and Leah (Jacob's "legitimate wives" [Driver, 298]). Those echoing the curses (Reuben, Gad, Asher, Zebulun, Dan, and Naphtali) have their tribal allotments at the fringe of the land; four of these tribes descend from Jacob's handmaidens, Bilhah and Zilpah, while the other two are Leah's oldest and youngest sons (Reuben, who lost his birthright, and Zebulun). In analyzing these tribal groupings, some scholars emphasize the maternal relationship of the tribes (Driver, 298; Mayes, 344; Ridderbos, 251). Other interpreters emphasize the geographical proximity of the landed allotments in each group, with the tribes assigned to Mount Ebal receiving territory in the north and east of the Promised Land, while the tribes assigned to Mount Gerizim settling in the south and west (Cairns, 235; Merrill, *Deuteronomy*, 345, n. 15). Insufficient contextual evidence makes a final conclusion elusive.

NOTES

2 Several scholars suggest that 27:2 and 27:4 contradict each other because the Israelites will not be able to perform this covenantal celebration בַּיּוֹם אֲשֶׁר תַּעַבְרוּ (*bayyôm ʾăšer taʿabrû*, "on the day you cross over"), i.e., on the day they arrive in the Promised Land (Driver, 295; Mayes, 340–41; Nelson, 316; Tigay,

Deuteronomy, 486–87). A celebration at Gilgal is the only location that would have worked immediately after entering the land. These scholars regard the reference to Ebal as a later addition. Although the combination of the noun "day" with the particle אֲשֶׁר (*ʾăšer*) can refer to a specific day (Jdg 4:14; Est 9:1; Jer 20:14), it can also signify more broadly an important time or an event in salvation history (Nu 15:23; Dt 9:7; 1Sa 29:8; 2Sa 7:11; 1Ki 8:16; 2Ki 21:15; Ps 78:42; Jer 7:25; Eze 39:8; Mal 3:17; 4:3; Jenni, *TLOT*, 2:529–30). Also, prefixing the preposition *bᵉ* ("on") to the noun "day" generally "weakens" its meaning (Sæbø, *TDOT*, 6:15).

Finally, the biblical record of Israel's compliance with this command (Jos 8:30–35) places the event after the defeat of Jericho and Ai. A. Hill ("The Ebal Ceremony as Hebrew Land Grant," *JETS* 31 [1988]: 401–2; cf. Wright, *Deuteronomy*, 278–79) offers a different resolution. He compares ch. 27 to a land-grant treaty rather than a vassal treaty. Consequently, ch. 27 primarily concerns Israel's possession of the Promised Land rather than functioning as a covenant-renewal document (ibid., 403). Hill identifies a celebration at Gilgal and one at Shechem as ceremonies within a ceremony and compares them to Joshua 4–5 and 8 (ibid., 404–5). Deuteronomy 27, however, does not seem to envision a twofold implementation of this ceremony.

3 Scholars have suggested that the phrase כָּל־דִּבְרֵי הַתּוֹרָה הַזֹּאת (*kol-dibrê hattôrâ hazzōt*, "all the words of this law") refers to all of Deuteronomy (Braulik, *Deuteronomium 16, 18–34*, 12, 203; Christensen, *Deuteronomy 21:10–34:12*, 655; Ridderbos, 248); the entire legal section of the book (chs. 5–26; Driver, 296; McConville, 388) or some large section of it (Hall, 398; Tigay, *Deuteronomy*, 248); salient parts of the law reiterated in Deuteronomy (Kalland, 160); the Ten Commandments (Merrill, *Deuteronomy*, 342); or the law of covenant from Exodus 19–24 (Craigie, 328). Size and space is not really an issue. Two stela the size of that on which the laws of Hammurabi's code were written could easily contain more than Deuteronomy (Tigay, *Deuteronomy*, 248).

4 In this verse's בְּהַר עֵיבָל (*bᵉhar ʿêbāl*, "on Mount Ebal") the Samaritan Pentateuch reads "Gerizim," not "Ebal." After the Jews who returned from Babylonian exile rejected the Samaritans, the latter claimed that Mount Gerizim was the divinely approved place for worship. Although some regard "Gerizim" as the original reading (changed by later Jews as a polemic against the Samaritans, who claimed Gerizim as their holy mountain; E. Würthwein, *The Text of the Old Testament* [2nd ed.; trans. E. F. Rhodes; Grand Rapids: Eerdmans, 1995], 46, n. 4; Cairns, 231–32; Mayes, 341; Phillips, *Deuteronomy*, 179), "Ebal" seems to be the best reading (E. Tov, *Textual Criticism of the Hebrew Bible* [2nd ed.; Minneapolis: Augsburg Fortress, 2001], 94, 266, n. 37; R. Bratcher and H. Hatton, *A Handbook on Deuteronomy* [New York: United Bible Societies, 2000], 433–34; Tigay, *Deuteronomy*, 394, n. 12). If later Jews replaced "Ebal" with "Gerizim" here, it seems odd that they would not also have made "Gerizim" the place from which the curses were pronounced (27:12–13).

8 The verb בָּאַר (*bāʾar*, "expound, [write] clearly, make plain"; GK 930) occurs only three times in the OT. In Deuteronomy 1:5, it affirms that Moses was elucidating or expounding God's law. In the present passage and Habakkuk 2:2, it connotes writing something clearly to produce a full impact on the readers. By writing with painstaking clarity "all the words of this law," the leader of the Israelites will make God's expectations of his people easily accessible to them and emphasize their accountability to that law. In light of the two occurrences of this expression in Deuteronomy (1:5; 27:8), some have argued that the intervening chapters (chs. 1–26) are referenced by "all the words of this law" (Barker, "Theology of Deuteronomy 27," 286; see Note on 27:3).

9 As demonstrated in the phrase נִהְיֵיתָ לְעָם (*nihyêtā lecām*, "you have now become the people"), the juxtaposition of the verb "to be" plus the preposition "to" (הָיָה + לְ, *hyh* + *le*) commonly means to be in a relationship with someone and is used to express the establishing of family relationships, especially marriage (Tigay, *Deuteronomy*, 64; Weinfeld, *Deuteronomy and the Deuteronomic School*, 80–81, 327; cf. Ex 2:10; Dt 24:2; 2Sa 7:14; Eze 16:8 et al.). In Genesis 17:7–8, Yahweh first promised that he would be his chosen people's God. From Leviticus onward, the formula "I will be your/their God … you will be my/his people" occurs thirteen times (Lev 26:12; Jer 7:23; 11:4; 24:7; 30:22; 31:1, 33; 32:38; Eze 11:20; 14:11; 36:28; 37:23, 27), thus affirming the unique relationship enjoyed by Israel and their God (Grisanti, *NIDOTTE*, 1:1024).

The Niphal form of the verb normally carries a passive or reflexive nuance, but here it signifies a causative meaning, i.e., "you were caused to become" (cf. 1Ki 1:27; 12:24 = 2Ch 11:4; *HALOT*, 244). Deuteronomy has made it abundantly clear that Israel already possesses the lofty status of God's chosen people (4:20; 7:6–7; 9:26–29; 10:15; 14:2; 21:8; 26:17–18; 29:13). In this renewal of the covenant, God's chosen nation renews their status as his people (Craigie, 329). The Israelites must repeatedly actualize their awareness of the historical fact of Yahweh's election (divine initiative; Hall, 403).

2. The Pronouncements of Covenantal Curses (27:14–26)

¹⁴The Levites shall recite to all the people of Israel in a loud voice:
¹⁵"Cursed is the man who carves an image or casts an idol — a thing detestable to the LORD, the work of the craftsman's hands — and sets it up in secret."

Then all the people shall say, "Amen!"
¹⁶"Cursed is the man who dishonors his father or his mother."

Then all the people shall say, "Amen!"
¹⁷"Cursed is the man who moves his neighbor's boundary stone."

Then all the people shall say, "Amen!"
¹⁸"Cursed is the man who leads the blind astray on the road."

Then all the people shall say, "Amen!"
¹⁹"Cursed is the man who withholds justice from the alien, the fatherless or the widow."

Then all the people shall say, "Amen!"
²⁰"Cursed is the man who sleeps with his father's wife, for he dishonors his father's bed."

Then all the people shall say, "Amen!"
²¹"Cursed is the man who has sexual relations with any animal."

Then all the people shall say, "Amen!"
²²"Cursed is the man who sleeps with his sister, the daughter of his father or the daughter of his mother."

Then all the people shall say, "Amen!"

> ²³"Cursed is the man who sleeps with his mother-in-law."
>
> Then all the people shall say, "Amen!"
>
> ²⁴"Cursed is the man who kills his neighbor secretly."
>
> Then all the people shall say, "Amen!"
>
> ²⁵"Cursed is the man who accepts a bribe to kill an innocent person."
>
> Then all the people shall say, "Amen!"
>
> ²⁶"Cursed is the man who does not uphold the words of this law by carrying them out."
>
> Then all the people shall say, "Amen!"

COMMENTARY

14 Certain appointed Levites (probably those who customarily cared for the ark of the covenant) are to stand in the valley between Mounts Ebal and Gerizim and declaratively list the kinds of people who will be cursed. After the pronouncement of each curse, all the tribes are to shout "Amen."

At first glance, it appears that this section is redundant when compared with the curses found in ch. 28. However, there are some clear differences. The present section (27:15–26) affirms that the violation of specific covenantal stipulations will trigger covenantal curses. Unlike the upcoming section of curses (28:15–68), ch. 27 does not specify what the curses are for any violations. It delineates certain representative covenantal violations of God's law, and God's children affirm their recognition of the curses by shouting out "Amen" (a verbal exclamation point). Chapter 28, by contrast, carefully delineates the nature of the curses the nation will experience for covenantal violations. The curses in the present section follow a set formula: (1) passive participle ("A cursed one is"); (2) individual address ("the man"); (3) objective statement of the offense ("who does …"); (4) national recognition ("Amen").

15 Anyone who makes an idol (carved from wood) or a molten image (cast in metal) in violation

of the first (if the idol/image depicted a god other than Yahweh) and second commandments (if it represented an attempt to provide a visual representation of Yahweh; Ex 20:3–6; Dt 5:7–10) and sets it up secretly for the purpose of worship is cursed. Yahweh regards any such act as detestable (see Note on 7:25–26). Various OT prophets also condemn this activity (Isa 40:19–20; 41:7; 44:9–20; 45:16; Jer 10:3, 9; Hos 8:6; 13:2). Manmade idols/images have no place as objects of worship by God's chosen people.

Only this curse and the one found in 27:24 have the phrase "in secret"; these curses expose the fact that idolatry and murder that escape the attention of the authorities and go unpunished nevertheless do not escape God's attention. Anyone who does those things, whether or not discovered and/or punished by humans, is, as it were, in a divine "curse zone" (Keller, *TLOT*, 1:180). Since each of the condemned practices in the twelve curse statements has been prohibited elsewhere, several scholars suggest that this "secrecy" motif runs through all the curses (E. Bellefontaine, "The Curses of Deuteronomy 27: Their Relationship to the Prohibitives," in *No Famine in the Land* [ed. James W. Flanagan and A. W. Robinson; Claremont, Calif.: Institute for Antiquity and Christianity, 1975], 58–59; Craigie, 331; Driver,

299–300; Keil, 434; Wright, *Deuteronomy*, 277; contra Cairns, 237). By uttering these curses, the nation affirms their desire that all violations, known or unknown, be punished. Also, since all sin is against Yahweh, he will ultimately bring the necessary justice (McConville, 392).

16 The second curse is pronounced on anyone who dishonors (*qlh* [GK 7829], an antonym of *kbd*, "honor"; see comments at 5:16) his parents (cf. Ex 20:12; 21:17; Dt 5:16). God gave parents the role of teaching their children, so parents are to be honored as God's covenantal representatives. To dishonor one's parents is to disrespect the authority of God.

17–19 These next three curses relate especially to the needy among Israel (the poor, the blind, aliens, orphans, and widows). The first of these three curses concerns property rights. The only reason for intentionally moving of a boundary stone would be to steal a section of a neighbor's property (condemned in 19:14). Since Yahweh himself has allotted land to each tribe, clan, and family, any stealing of a neighbor's land constitutes arrogant rebellion and lack of contentedness (Lev 25:23). Babylonian boundary stones (*kudurru*-stones) were inscribed with curses directed against anyone who dared to move them or alter their inscription (to change the stated owner; Tigay, *Deuteronomy*, 255; *COS* 1:117). The disadvantaged in Israel were especially susceptible to this abuse because they lacked the means to defend themselves or pursue the issue legally.

The second of these three curses condemns those who seek to exploit the blind. Although the expression "leads the blind astray on the road" can be taken literally, it seems more likely to refer to any treatment of a blind person for personal gain that exploits his lack of sight (which state absolves him of accountability for straying). Leviticus 19:14 proscribes taking advantage of the deaf and the blind by pronouncing a mocking curse before one who

cannot hear or putting a stumbling block in front of someone who cannot see. The word pair "deaf and blind" occurs in various ancient Near Eastern sources to denote complete incapacity (Milgrom, *Leviticus 17–22*, 1640).

The final curse in this trio condemns the perversion of justice, commonly directed against aliens, orphans, and widows (cf. 16:19; 24:17). Lacking ethnic belonging, a father, or a husband, respectively, these needy people served as tempting targets for unscrupulous Israelites who seek their own gain at whatever cost to others. Not only is any such conduct heartless, it also represents treachery against God's intentions for his covenantal nation, the relationships between whose members God desires to be characterized by equity and justice (e.g, Mic 6:8). Yahweh presents himself as the protector of the disadvantaged (Dt 10:18).

20–23 This quartet of curses concerns various kinds of sexual offenses (cf. Ex 22:19; Lev 18:6–23; 20:10–21). The nonmention of adultery does not lessen the detestable nature of that offense; but these curses focus on less easily detected sexual offenses. Fellow Israelites would think nothing of a man's keeping regular company with his stepmother (called "his father's wife," not his mother), sister, mother-in-law, or animals (whereas his spending time in the company of another man's wife would be highly noticed). And family members aware of his aberrant sexual behavior might be tempted to hide it to spare the entire family from great shame.

Because marriage makes a husband and wife to be "one flesh" (Ge 2:24), to engage in sexual intercourse with the wife of one's father brings great shame on the father, as though his nakedness were exposed (cf. Ge 9:21–23; see comments at 22:30).

Because God created humankind as distinct from the animal world (Ge 1:24–25, 26–27), and having sexual relations with an animal would seem to equate animals with humans (cf. Ge 1:28), a curse is pronounced on anyone who practices bestiality. The Canaanite and Hittite practice of bestiality in certain cultic settings may also serve as the backdrop for the pronouncement of this curse (Hittite laws 187–88, 199–200a [*COS*, 2:118–19]; the Ba‘lu Myth [*COS*, 1:267]; Epic of Gilgamesh, in Pritchard, *ANET*, 84; cf. Hoffner, "Some Contributions of Hittitology to Old Testament Study," *Tyn Bul* 20 [1969]: 41–42).

Incest—that is, in this case sexual relations with a sister or half-sister—is also unacceptable (cf. Lev 18:9; 20:17). Proper conduct between family members who would be living in close proximity to each other was essential to stability within the covenantal nation. The final curse dealing with sexual offenses is pronounced on anyone who (at any time) enters into a sexual relationship with his wife's mother.

24–25 Paralleling the pronouncements in 27:17–19, murdering an unwary neighbor or committing murder for hire places the guilty party in a divine "curse zone." The text explicitly addresses the case of a first murder that takes place in secret, while the second murder would only benefit the murderer if he lived to enjoy the payment received for committing it. In the light of other legislation, premeditated murder rather than manslaughter is in view (Ex 21:12–14; Lev 24:17). Although the first scenario depicts the actual occurrence of murder, the second scenario condemns even the acceptance of a bribe to commit that crime, whether or not the murder takes place. The giving and acceptance of bribes always leads to a corruption of justice (E. Bellefontaine, "The Curses of Deuteronomy 27," 56; see comments on 10:17–19).

26 This final curse concerns the law as a whole rather than focusing on a single issue. In an all-inclusive manner, a curse is pronounced on anyone who does not wholeheartedly obey God's law in

every area of life. Even though one can imagine a person's avoiding the eleven offenses cited in the previous verses, no one can perfectly and always avoid committing this offense. This last pronouncement of curse encompasses all covenantal violations not mentioned in the preceding list.

Why does this section only contain curses but no blessings? Some have suggested that the corresponding blessings were omitted at some point (Thompson, 265). Others have suggested that 27:11–14 anticipates the blessing section of ch. 28 (I. Lewy, "The Puzzle of Deuteronomy XXVII: Blessings Announced, but Curses Noted," *VT* 12 [1962]: 209) or refers to ch. 28 as a whole (P. Buis, "Deutéronome XXVII 15–26: malédictions ou exigenses de l'alliance," *VT* 17 [1967]: 478–79). Several scholars compare the twelve curses in ch. 27 to the Ten Commandments (Cairns, 236; Mayes, 346, 348; Merrill, *Deuteronomy*, 347; Tigay, *Deuteronomy*, 253–54; in this regard, von Rad, 167, refers to 27:15–26 as the Dodecalogue).

However, this focus on the curses to the exclusion of blessings appears to be an integral part of Moses' theological agenda. Moses understands that the nation, on its own, will fail to live up to Yahweh's expectations and experience the pain of covenantal cursing (Barker, "Theology of Deuteronomy 27," 284; cf. Keil, 432). Chapter 27 expects Israel to fail and disobey (Barker, ibid., 280). In spite of this "pessimism," the ceremony of covenantal renewal "acknowledges a future for Israel, not premised on Israel's ability but rather on Yahweh's faithfulness" (ibid., 294; cf. 302). Alongside this "pessimism," the erection of the altar and offering of sacrifices points to Yahweh's role in his relationship with Israel. On their own the people of the chosen nation are totally incapable of honoring their covenantal Lord. However, they can obey Yahweh as a consequence of a genuine relationship with him (ibid., 302–3).

NOTES

15–26 Forms of the verb אָרוּר (*'ārûr*, "cursed") occur sixty-eight times in the OT (forty-one times with the same verbal form as that found here), and nineteen of those occurrences are concentrated in Deuteronomy 27:15–26 (thirteen times) and 28:16–19 (six times). When used in the form here (Qal passive participle), it functions as a formulaic pronouncement that the person or category of persons is "destined for divinely imposed misfortune" (Tigay, *Deuteronomy*, 254). The verbs "to curse" (אֲרָר, *'rr*) and "to bless" (בָּרַךְ, *brk*) occur in contrast to each other in several passages (Ge 9:25–26; 12:3; 27:29; Nu 22:6, 12; 24:9; Dt 28:3–6, 16–19; Jdg 5:23–24; Jer 17:5–8; 20:14). Spoken by another person, "cursing" could signify some kind of disapproval, but when spoken by Yahweh it represents a powerful declaration of divine judgment (Hall, 406, n. 36). Covenantal cursing promises devastation, and covenantal blessing offers success and favor (see Note on 28:3).

The word אָמֵן (*'āmēn*, "Amen") always occurs in the OT as a response to what someone else has said. It has the basic idea of "let it be so" or "may it come true" (Moberly, *NIDOTTE*, 1:428). When uttered in response to a pronounced curse (as here), it expresses more than a wish: those who pronounce the "Amen" acknowledge the fate as their own if they practice the specified offense (Wildberger, *TLOT*, 1:146). The speakers of the "Amen" are also committing themselves to abhor and avoid the practices to which the curse is attached.

B. Covenantal Blessings and Curses (28:1–68)

OVERVIEW

Moses, having completed his look forward to the anticipated celebration of covenantal renewal at Shechem after the nation enters the land, returns his attention to the covenant he is presenting to the Israelites encamped on the plains of Moab (cf. 28:1, "this day"). He delineates the blessings and the curses (covenantal sanctions occasioned by the people's obedience or disobedience) as part of the covenantal relationship between the Lord and Israel (cf. Lev 26).

This section constitutes an important part of the covenant-renewal function of the book of Deuteronomy. Although no covenantal blessings occur in a number of ancient Near Eastern treaty documents (blessings being found in late second millennium treaties and then disappearing again in first millennium treaties; see K. Kitchen, *On the Reliability of the Old Testament* [Grand Rapids: Eerdmans, 2003],

284–88), Yahweh begins with the covenantal blessings, in part as motivation for Israel to obey him. Unfortunately, the children of Israel all too often forgot about the implications of their conduct. The prophets, seeking to drive God's people back to covenantal conformity, often appeal to these curses as the grounds for Israel's experience of divine judgment.

Unlike the covenantal curses of ch. 27, which record a series of covenantal violations without specifying curses or judgments, the following material includes both the condition for blessing or cursing (protasis) and the nature of the resulting blessing or cursing (apodosis). Although ch. 27 delineates many examples of reprehensible behavior, ch. 28 emphasizes only one issue: absolute and total loyalty and obedience to Yahweh.

1. Covenantal Blessings (28:1–14)

[1]If you fully obey the LORD your God and carefully follow all his commands I give you today, the LORD your God will set you high above all the nations on earth. [2]All these blessings will come upon you and accompany you if you obey the LORD your God:

[3]You will be blessed in the city and blessed in the country.

[4]The fruit of your womb will be blessed, and the crops of your land and the young of your livestock—the calves of your herds and the lambs of your flocks.

[5]Your basket and your kneading trough will be blessed.

[6]You will be blessed when you come in and blessed when you go out.

[7]The LORD will grant that the enemies who rise up against you will be defeated before you. They will come at you from one direction but flee from you in seven.

[8]The LORD will send a blessing on your barns and on everything you put your hand to. The LORD your God will bless you in the land he is giving you.

[9]The LORD will establish you as his holy people, as he promised you on oath, if you keep the commands of the LORD your God and walk in his ways. [10]Then all the peoples on earth will see that you are called by the name of the LORD, and they will fear you. [11]The LORD will grant you abundant prosperity—in the fruit of your womb, the young of your livestock and the crops of your ground—in the land he swore to your forefathers to give you.

[12]The LORD will open the heavens, the storehouse of his bounty, to send rain on your land in season and to bless all the work of your hands. You will lend to many nations but will borrow from none. [13]The LORD will make you the head, not the tail. If you pay attention to the commands of the LORD your God that I give you this day and carefully follow them, you will always be at the top, never at the bottom. [14]Do not turn aside from any of the commands I give you today, to the right or to the left, following other gods and serving them.

COMMENTARY

1–2 Moses here articulates the blessings Yahweh promises that the children of Israel will experience if they faithfully obey his commandments and do not worship any other gods. Because of the covenantal relationship between Israel and the Lord, he expects certain kinds of conduct from his chosen people and promises to bless them abundantly before the entire world for their obedience. Two emphatic verbal constructions highlight the nature of this obedience. First, the combination of two verbs from the same root (*šmʿ*, "to hear/obey"; GK 9048) carries the idea of full or total obedience. Second, the juxtaposition of the verbs "keep" and "do" demonstrates that Yahweh demands diligent or careful obedience of his covenantal nation (see Note on 5:1). The phrase "all his commands" refers, as it does throughout the book, to the totality of Yahweh's covenantal expectations for his chosen nation. The contents of this "covenantal treaty document" are nonnegotiable (see comments on 4:2).

Verses 1–2 contain two conditional statements, presented chiastically (condition [v.1a], result [v.1b], result [v.2a], condition [v.2b]). Verse 1 affirms that total and wholehearted obedience will occasion the nation of Israel's international prominence. The statement that Yahweh "will set you high above all the nations" occurs only twice in the OT—here and in 26:19 (see comments there). In both places, the conformity of Israel to Yahweh's covenantal demands is integrally linked to their ability to affect the world (cf. Dt 4:5–8). Israel's covenantal responsibilities are *set in an international context*, i.e., for all the world to see (cf. 28:10). Israel's response to God's expectations and their experience of covenantal blessing or cursing will be noticed internationally.

When will this blessing and/or cursing find ultimate fulfillment? Merrill (*Deuteronomy*, 35) writes: "Ultimately, however, the promise must find fulfillment in an eschatological setting in which Israel (or Zion) would enjoy unrivaled preeminence among the nations as the object of God's gracious favor (cf. Num 24:7; Ps 89:28; Isa 2:2)." Verse 2 first affirms the result—Israel's experience of covenantal blessings—before it presents the condition of obedience.

3–6 After delineating the importance and implications of genuine obedience (vv.1–2), Moses provides a brief statement of the blessings (vv.3–6; see vv.15–19 for the curses) and then provides a short exposition of those blessings (vv.7–14; see vv.20–68 for the curses). In six brief and rhythmic statements, Moses declares that the one who faithfully observes the Lord's commandments will be abundantly blessed in every area of his or her life. The blessings cited in these verses provide a picture of comprehensive blessing in every realm of life.

The first and third statements of blessing refer to two "polar" features or realms in which the blessing will operate (e.g., "city" and "country"). This literary device of using bipolar forms is called

"merism"; the merisms used here are meant to encompass every aspect of life. Simply put, a merism expresses totality in abbreviated form. The significant point in a merism is not the individual elements themselves but what they amount to together, as a unit (W. G. E. Watson, *Classical Hebrew Poetry: A Guide to Its Techniques* [2nd ed., corrected; Sheffield: Sheffield Academic, 1995], 321). The six occurrences of the verb "to bless" in these verses fall into three pairs (in an ABA' pattern). The first and last pairs (vv.3, 6) each use three Hebrew words and refer to the completeness or comprehensive nature and extent of this blessing, while the middle pair (vv.4–5) involves many more words and highlights the abundance of fertility and food. Some have suggested that the six blessings (vv.3–6) and six curses (vv.15–19) correspond to the twelve tribes of Israel.

In every location (totality of space) Yahweh promises to pour out his blessings on Israel (v.3). As a predominantly agrarian society, they depend on fertility for their survival, not to mention abundance. Yahweh promises to provide them with large families, abundant crops, and growing herds and flocks (v.4). The vessels used to collect and work with the produce from the fields will be full (v.5). Finally, they will experience God's blessing in the entire range of their efforts (v.6).

This promise of abundant blessings from the hand of Yahweh in all areas of life is relevant to the challenge Israel has before them. The Canaanite gods, Baal and Asherah/Astarte, were gods of fertility. Part of the seductive appeal of Baalism was the practice of "sacred/ritual sex" in an effort to induce these gods to provide the desired fertility. Against this backdrop, the presentation of Yahweh as the exclusive source of fertility is fundamental for Israel's life as God's covenantal nation (7:14–15).

7–13 In a more elaborate fashion, as part of his exposition of these covenantal blessings Moses describes the way in which the Lord will bless his vassals by giving them military victories, material abundance, an impressive reputation, and international prominence if they will only obey his commandments. Notice the chiastic structure:

A Foreign Relations: Yahweh will provide total security (28:7);

  B Domestic Affairs: Yahweh will provide prosperity in barns and land (28:8);

    C Covenantal Relationship: Yahweh will establish Israel as his holy people (28:9-10);

  B' Domestic Affairs: Yahweh will provide prosperity in barns and land (28:11-12);

A' Foreign Relations: Yahweh will provide total security (28:13-14).

Israel's enemies will come against them as an organized army with a concentrated battle front but will flee from them in scattered groups (in seven directions; v.7). "Seven" can signify a large number, carrying the idea of completeness or fullness (Tigay, *Deuteronomy*, 259; cf. 1Sa 2:5; Pr 24:16; Isa 4:1; 11:15). Rather than being the subjected nation ("the tail"), Yahweh's chosen people will be the victorious nation ("the head") at God's doing; further, Yahweh will give them a place of international prominence among the many nations of the world (v.13). Interwoven with this focus on Israel's supremacy is Moses' reminder to the covenantal people that they must, on the positive side, follow God's requirements wholeheartedly and, on the negative side, avoid any semblance of idolatry (and therefore any violation of the covenantal relationship [5:8-9]; see comments on 5:32-33).

As promised in the preceding section (vv.3-6), Yahweh will bless all that Israel has and all that they do. Their storage facilities will be full, and their efforts will be productive (v.8). The expression "in the land he is giving you" serves as a reminder to the Israelites that Yahweh is the one giving to them

the land as well as these blessings. All this potential blessing stems from their covenantal relationship with Yahweh. Also, the Promised Land itself is the realm in which covenantal blessing will occur. As the rest of the blessings and all the curses will make clear, the enjoyment of or eviction from the land plays a central role in what Israel can expect and what Yahweh intends to do.

In vv.11-12 Moses describes what Yahweh will do, how he will do it, and what the implications of those blessings will be. Yahweh promises to bless his people with abundant prosperity in the fundamental areas of their lives: family, livestock, and crops, once again, in the land he has promised them. He will facilitate this abundance by pouring out on the earth rain that comes from "his abundant treasure house," i.e., the heavens. Also, he will send this rain at the right time, in season; for heavy rains at the wrong time and lack of rain during key growth periods can devastate a crop.

Yahweh will also bless all of their labors. To bless their labors means to make them successful or prosperous (see Notes). In 28:8 the "storehouse" is something Yahweh fills as part of blessing his covenantal nation and in 28:12 is something he empties (the heavens) in order to bless his chosen people (see Notes). The far-reaching result of this divine blessing is economic supremacy (material surplus), i.e., God's chosen nation will lend to the nations rather than borrow from them.

In addition to serving as a genuine promise from Yahweh, this promise to bless Israel with abundant fertility provides a stark contrast with the "theology" of the Canaanites in the land they are soon to conquer. According to Canaanite mythology, Baal, as god of fertility, had a window placed in the roof of his home so he could pour out rain on the earth (Craigie, 337; *KTU* 1.1.VII, *COS*, 1:262-63). But there are two fundamental differences between Baal and Yahweh that Israel must understand. In the first place, while the Canaanites regarded Baal as the god of fertility, Yahweh is the absolute sovereign over the entire universe, including the realm of fertility. Second, the Canaanites had to stimulate Baal into action by their ritual sexual relations. In contrast, Yahweh will bestow his blessings on Israel out of grace and mercy. Israel's obedience does not make them deserve Yahweh's blessings but enables them to appropriate those blessings (Wright, *Deuteronomy*, 281).

In the central section of this exposition of the covenantal blessings Moses focuses on the rationale for Yahweh's blessing his covenantal nation (vv.9–10). He delineates what Yahweh will do, what he expects of Israel, and what the potential impact of covenantal obedience will be. First, Yahweh promises to "establish" Israel as his holy people, in accordance with his covenantal oath (28:9a; see Note on 1:8). He has already made them his people, but here he promises to fix or establish them in a place of international impact as a witness-nation before the world. Yahweh intends that their distinctiveness as his holy people will draw the attention of the surrounding nations to his greatness.

Second, in order for the chosen nation to bring Yahweh great glory and so to accomplish their God-given function, they must live in heartfelt conformity to his covenantal expectations (keep his commands and walk in his ways; 28:9b). Their obedience does not help them earn this place of international impact; rather, their conformity to Yahweh's demands makes them able to have a powerful impact on the surrounding nations. It is only as they wholeheartedly conform their lives to God's requirements that they will provide the vivid demonstration of Yahweh's awe-inspiring character that will have a powerful impact on the world. Covenantal obedience does not merit God-glorifying prominence but enables it to happen.

Third, the idea of impact on the world constitutes the "big idea" of Yahweh's covenantal relationship with Israel (cf. 7:6; 26:19). The nations will recognize Yahweh's selection of Israel as his special people and will "fear." Although the verbal root of this word can connote reverence and awe (which could be part of the idea here; see Note on 5:29), here it also indicates that the nations will be afraid of Israel and their God when they witness his uncontested power.

NOTES

1–69 The title יְהוָה אֱלֹהֶיךָ (*yhwh ʾelōhêkā*, "the LORD/Yahweh your God") occurs almost 320 times in Deuteronomy, and the title "the LORD/Yahweh" occurs by itself another 230 times. In this chapter alone the compound title occurs 13 times, and "Yahweh" occurs by itself 28 times. Broadly speaking, the title "Yahweh" standing by itself focuses on his capacity as the maker and keeper of the covenant. The compound title highlights his connection with Israel as the one who promises to be their protector and to take care of their destiny. In the light of all that Yahweh has done, is doing, and will do in behalf of his servant-nation, he deserves nothing less than Israel's absolute loyalty.

The juxtaposition of the infinitive absolute before the finite verb in the phrase שָׁמוֹעַ תִּשְׁמַע (*šāmôaʿ tišmaʿ*, "you fully obey"), both forms using the same verbal root, emphasizes the verbal action of that root as completed "fully," "certainly," or "surely" (*IBHS*, 584–86). For a similar construction, see Note on 8:19.

2 As evidenced in the phrase וּבָאוּ עָלֶיךָ ... וְהִשִּׂיגֻךָ (*ûbāʾû ʿāleykā ... weḥiśśîgukā*, "will come upon you ... and overtake you"), throughout ch. 28 the blessings and curses are almost personified by the verbs used of them:

"come" (בוֹא, *bwʾ*; vv.2, 15, 45), "overtake" (נָשַׂג, *nśg*; vv.2, 15, 45), and "pursue" (רָדַף, *rdp*; v.45). Yahweh commands or ordains (v.15), sends (v.20) these realities, and strikes (v.22) Israel with them. Similar wording is found in Psalm 23:6, where God's goodness and mercy pursue (רָדַף, *rdp*; GK 8103) or "hound" the believer.

3–6 The verb בָּרַךְ (*brk*, "to bless") occurs 327 times in the OT, in 63 passages as a passive participle (as here, in בָּרוּךְ אַתָּה, *bārûk ʾattâ*, "you will be blessed") and part of a formulaic pronouncement of blessing (with 38 of the 63 passages referring to God and 25 to people). *Brk* signifies the state of possessing blessing (Keller and Wehmeier, *TLOT*, 1:268). In the OT, nothing was more important than securing God's blessing for oneself or the nation. A blessed life was an ideal to aim for. For an Israelite, divine blessing was the key to genuine success (Wenham, *Genesis 1–15*, 24), and a life without God's blessing was the ultimate nightmare (Ps 129:8; Jer 17:5–6; Mic 2:9; M. Brown, *NIDOTTE*, 1:758; see Note on 7:13).

8 The noun בַּאֲסָמֶיךָ (*baʾăsāmeykā*, "on your barns") only occurs twice in the OT—here and in Proverbs 3:10—and signifies a storehouse or barn. Barns filled with harvested crops clearly evidence Yahweh's faithfulness to the covenant.

10 The NIV's "called by the name of the LORD" does not do justice to the statement, שֵׁם יְהוָה נִקְרָא עָלֶיךָ (*šēm yhwh niqrāʾ ʿāleykā*, "the name of Yahweh has been pronounced over you"). To pronounce one's name over something is to declare one's ownership and intention to protect that person or thing (Nelson, 330). The expression carries the idea of a mark of identification (Merrill, *Deuteronomy*, 354). As a nation marked out as Yahweh's possession, Israel can totally rely on Yahweh as their protector. The surrounding nations have a legitimate cause for fear if they attack this "chosen" people. A Canaanite vassal appealed to the Egyptian pharaoh: "As the king has placed his name in Jerusalem forever; he cannot abandon it—the land of Jerusalem" (EA 287; Moran, 328). His placing his name over Jerusalem obligated him to protect that region.

11 Although the verb יָתַר (*ytr*; GK 3855) can signify simply leaving something behind (Ex 16:19–20; Lev 22:30; Nu 33:55; 2Sa 17:12), in the present passage and 30:9 it carries the more causative notion of "cause to abound" (thus here, וְהוֹתִרְךָ ... לְטוֹבָה, *wᵉhôtirᵉkā ... lᵉṭôbâ*, "will grant you abundant prosperity"; Kronholm, *TDOT*, 6:486).

12 Based on the verb אָצַר (*ʾṣr*), which means "to store up, accumulate, amass" (e.g., 2Ki 20:17 = Isa 39:6; Hamilton, *NIDOTTE*, 1:487), the noun (found here in אוֹצָרוֹ הַטּוֹב, *ʾôṣārô haṭṭôb*, "his abundant treasure house") can mean the treasure itself (Isa 30:6) or a place to store it (Jos 6:19, 24; treasury or storehouse). It can refer to storehouses at Yahweh's temple in Jerusalem (1 Kgs 7:51) or to the heavens as a repository for blessing (Dt 28:12) or judgment (Job 38:22). To those who live in wholehearted covenantal conformity and manifest it by giving their tithe faithfully, Yahweh promises to "throw open the floodgates of heaven and pour out so much blessing that you will not have room enough for it" (Mal 3:10).

REFLECTION

Do these blessings and curses represent promises for individuals to claim or promises that were national in scope? One of the interpretive challenges one faces in dealing with these blessings and curses concerns their relevance to believers then and now. Was the divine provision of blessings and curses triggered by individual conduct and experienced by specific individuals in the covenantal nation? Does God still act in this way today?

In the first place, both OT and NT teach the general principle that God blesses the righteous and judges the wicked (cf. Gal 6:7–8).

Second, it is important to understand that people can never "earn" divine blessings. God provides his children (those who have a faith relationship with him) with an abundance of eternal and infinite blessings through salvation. He never (in OT or NT times) asks people to do something *in order to* be blessed. The pattern has always been, "you have been richly blessed, therefore, obey me wholeheartedly."

Finally, it is essential for any student of the Bible to recognize that the blessings and curses of Deuteronomy 28 are part of a covenant made between Yahweh and the nation of Israel. Although individuals make up that nation, the blessings and curses envisioned in this chapter are not something selectively invoked by Yahweh. As the nation of Israel is characterized by covenantal obedience, God will pour out covenantal blessings on them. However, as that same nation is characterized by covenantal treachery, he will bring covenantal curses on them.

This chapter relates to the conduct of the nation as a whole as well as their corporate experience of these blessings or curses. Consequently, this chapter does not justify individuals' expecting or demanding God to act in a certain way toward them personally because of their "righteous" conduct. Conversely, a person's experience of "cursing" does not necessarily represent divine judgment for sin.

2. Covenantal Curses (28:15–68)

OVERVIEW

If God's children refuse to obey the Lord's commands faithfully, he will bring a great number of curses on them for their failure to maintain their part of the covenantal agreement. Numerous scholars have sought to identify the various sources that were brought together in the process through which these curses reached their present form. They cite the repetition of key concepts and the lack of a clear organizational outline as part of the evidence that this section is not a cohesive whole written by one individual.

However, a number of scholars, conservative and liberal, argue that the repetitious and "disorganized" format of the following verses matches the general ancient Near Eastern pattern for covenantal curse sections. For example, McCarthy (*Treaty and Covenant*, 176) writes concerning the genre of the blessing-curse list: "its object was fullness, not symmetry or logical unity. The more the better, and the more mouth-filling the curses the more satisfying they were." He goes on to point out that, as in Deuteronomy 28, this ancient Near Eastern genre is characterized by an "imbalance of blessings and curses, repeated introductions and conclusions, repetitions, and changes in style.... [Dt 28] has been put together so as to accent the danger of infidelity by means of standard rhetorical devices: key words (repetitions!), expansion, climactic order, inclusion, ironic reversal" (ibid.). There is a mixing of curses that affect home and family as well as those that affect the nation, thus moving toward a more national perspective (McConville, 404). As with the blessings, Moses begins by giving a brief statement of the curses (vv.15–19) followed by a more lengthy exposition of those painful potentialities (vv.20–68).

a. A Basic Statement of the Covenantal Curses (28:15-19)

¹⁵However, if you do not obey the LORD your God and do not carefully follow all his commands and decrees I am giving you today, all these curses will come upon you and overtake you:

¹⁶You will be cursed in the city and cursed in the country.

¹⁷Your basket and your kneading trough will be cursed.

¹⁸The fruit of your womb will be cursed, and the crops of your land, and the calves of your herds and the lambs of your flocks.

¹⁹You will be cursed when you come in and cursed when you go out.

COMMENTARY

15 Moses clearly defines the people on whom the curses will fall, namely, those who do not obey the stipulations of the covenant. This verse is a near replica of 28:1, except for the last clause. Instead of Israel's being set high above all the nations of the earth, "all these curses shall come upon you and overtake you" (same verbs as 28:2) The presence of this curse language, also found in various ancient Near Eastern treaties, emphasizes the seriousness of infidelity in Israel's relationship with Yahweh. It is interesting to notice the parallels between the curse topics addressed in Deuteronomy and those in other ancient Near Eastern treaty documents (McCarthy, *Treaty and Covenant*, 173-74):

Subject	Dt 28	Code of Hammurabi	Matiʾilu	Sefire	Esarhaddon vassal treaties
Breadmaking utensils	17				444
Drought	23-24	xxvii, 68ff.	IV, 13-14		528-31
Defeat	25	xxvii, 20-21, 90			454
Plague, Illness	27, etc.	xviii, 55	IV, 5		419-20
Blindness	28				423-24
Spoilation	29				430
Slavery	32			I.A, 41	428; 588-90
Exile	36, etc.	xvii, 22-23, 74	IV, 6	I.A, 42	
Locusts	38		V, 6	I.A, 27	443
Ruin of city	52		V, 6	I.A, 32	599
Cannibalism	53 ff.		IV, 10		448; 549-50; 568-72

16–19 In six brief and rhythmic statements (modeled after the blessings in 28:3–6), Moses declares that the one who refuses to observe faithfully the Lord's commands will be terribly cursed in every area of his life (curses 3 and 4 appear in reverse order in comparison with the blessings). For the content of the curses, see the comments on 28:3–6, and replace the idea of blessing with curse. Although various authors have suggested that the reversal of the third and fourth curses (and the omission of "the young of your livestock" [28:4], which the LXX also lacks) is the result of a long editorial process (e.g., Mayes, 348–51), the author could have changed the order for rhetorical variety (Merrill, *Deuteronomy*, 357). Nelson, 330, suggests that this reversal provides "a rhetorical boost in intensity" by providing a clearer transition from material things (28:16–17) to living creatures (28:18).

b. An Exposition of the Covenantal Curses (28:20–68)

OVERVIEW

In more elaborate fashion, Moses describes the way in which the Lord will curse his vassals by bringing various kinds of judgment into their lives as a form of punishment for their flagrant violation of the covenantal relationship between them and him. As noted, there are many parallels between the following Deuteronomic curses and curses found in ancient Near Eastern treaty documents (especially Neo-Assyrian treaty texts such as Esarhaddon's vassal treaties). Some conclude that the Deuteronomic material is totally dependent on the Assyrian models and consequently must have been composed in the monarchic period (e.g., Weinfeld, *Deuteronomy and the Deuteronomic School*, 116–29).

There are, however, several differences between the two materials. Craigie, 339–40, offers six responses to Weinfeld's contention that the close similarity between this Deuteronomic curse section and Esarhaddon's vassal treaties (first millennium); his responses (three of which will receive mention here) demonstrate that these similarities do not establish a first millennium date for this section of Deuteronomy. First, there are enough differences between ch. 28 and late Assyrian treaties to preclude direct *borrowing* but allow for *adaptation*. Second, several curses in 28:26–35 also have parallels in older second millennium treaties. Finally, several curse elements in 28:26–35 have their only parallels in the older treaties. Moses probably made use of certain covenantal curse terminology common in his day to express the potential covenantal judgment. It is likely that there existed a common collection of covenantal curse statements that appear with slight variations throughout ancient Near Eastern treaties.

i. Disease and drought (28:20–24)

²⁰The Lᴏʀᴅ will send on you curses, confusion and rebuke in everything you put your hand to, until you are destroyed and come to sudden ruin because of the evil you have done in forsaking him. ²¹The Lᴏʀᴅ will plague you with diseases until he has destroyed

you from the land you are entering to possess. ²²The LORD will strike you with wasting disease, with fever and inflammation, with scorching heat and drought, with blight and mildew, which will plague you until you perish. ²³The sky over your head will be bronze, the ground beneath you iron. ²⁴The LORD will turn the rain of your country into dust and powder; it will come down from the skies until you are destroyed.

COMMENTARY

20–21 Yahweh's pledge to use the chaos of disease and drought to judge his chosen but disobedient vassals almost to the point of extinction counters the blessings of vv.8–12. The triad of terms, "curses, confusion and rebuke," reinforces each other. The first noun derives from the verb "to curse" (ʾrr), found in 28:16–19. This cursing will bring about total "confusion" (mᵉhûmâ). This word refers to confusion that can be caused by war, social disorder, and pestilence (Tigay, *Deuteronomy*, 262). In 7:23, God threatened to strike the Canaanites with confusion. The third noun (migʿeret) occurs only here in the OT. Scholars have suggested that it refers to Yahweh's fierce anger (Craigie, 342) or frustration (Tigay, *Deuteronomy*, 262).

Not one area of Israel's efforts will be spared from experiencing these agonies. He will cause pestilences to "cling" to them, i.e., be impossible for the Israelites to shake, until their demise. The occasion for these curses is Israel's covenantal treachery or "forsaking him." The expression "the evil you have done" (lit., "the evil of your deeds") occurs eleven times in the OT, and nine of those instances signify Israel's rebellion against their covenant with Yahweh (Isa 1:16; Jer 4:4; 21:12; 23:2, 22; 25:5; 26:3; 44:22; Hos 9:15; cf. Ps 28:4).

22–24 Moses then lists seven afflictions, signifying the comprehensive nature of these curses (as "seven" is commonly the number for completion). The first three are clearly human diseases (con-

sumption, fever, and inflammation). The last three describe climatic or agricultural conditions. The fourth term, which means "feverish heat," could refer to either category (an illness [Craigie, 343] or severe heat [NIV; Merrill, *Deuteronomy*, 359]). All seven terms can be associated with heat. The diseases will plague them personally or their crops "until you perish."

"Drought" (see Note) refers to the absence of rain, and "scorching heat" (ḥarḥur) may connote the hot wind (sirocco) that blows in the desert. The last two terms, "blight and mildew," occur as a word pair in four other passages (1 Kgs 8:37; 2Ch 6:28; Am 4:9; Hag 2:17) to refer to some kind of disease that leads to crop failure. Craigie, 342, suggests the latter term may signify a kind of mildew that kills the plant by extracting its moisture and that leaves a white powdery substance on the leaves.

The fact that many of the above maladies relate to heat leads to a vivid depiction of drought (vv.23–24; cf. Lev 26:19, where iron and bronze are reversed). The bronze heavens will not allow any moisture to leak out, and the earth will be too hard to receive it (or the farmer's seed). Instead of sufficient rain (a covenantal blessing; 28:12), winds will kick up the waterless soil into duststorms and the desert wind will bring in sandstorms (G. Smith, *The Historical Geography of the Holy Land* [New York: Harper and Row, 1966], 65). Compare this reference to the bronze heaven and iron earth to a section from the vassal treaties of Esarahaddon:

> May all the gods who are named in this treaty tablet reduce your soil in size to be as narrow as a brick, turn your soil into *iron*, so that no one may cut a furrow in it. Just as rain does not fall from a *copper* sky, so may there come neither rain nor dew upon your fields and meadows, but let it rain burning coals in your land instead of dew. (lines 526–33, §§63–64, in Pritchard, *ANET*, 539)

The obvious point is that the farmer will not be able to break up earth, which will not be able to receive the farmer's seed, and the heavens will not provide any rain.

NOTES

20 The statement עַד הִשָּׁמֶדְךָ (ʿad hiššāmedkā, "until you are destroyed") occurs six times in ch. 28 (vv. 20, 24, 45, 48, 51, 61) like repeated hammer blows or "a tolling death knell" (Kalland, 176). The experience of covenantal cursing will bring Israel to the brink of extinction; and this function of covenantal cursing provides a sad contrast to what God intends for his chosen nation. God promised that he would enable the Israelites to "wipe out their [enemies'] names from under heaven … you will destroy them" (Dt 7:23–24, which contains the other two occurrences of this construction in the book). The fact that Yahweh did not exterminate Israel when he evicted them from Promised Land (covenantal curse) later in their history indicates that this verb (and "perish") is somewhat hyperbolic. The strength of the language, however, prevents one from minimizing the extent of this threat.

The expression וְעַד־אֲבָדְךָ (wᵉʿad-ʾᵃbodkā, "until you come … to ruin") parallels the one treated in the preceding note. The first time it occurs in Deuteronomy it refers to Yahweh's pursuing every surviving Canaanite until they all perish (7:20). The expression occurs three times in ch. 28, twice in the same verse as the expression "until you are destroyed" (28:20, 51; cf. 28:22). In 28:51 it describes the non-Israelite attacker who pursues his enemy until he causes him to perish. The fate that Yahweh had reserved for the Canaanites will come upon his covenantal nation if they persist in rebellion.

22 The fourth word of these seven terms for calamities— חֶרֶב (ḥereb)—means "sword" as it appears in the Hebrew text. In light of the context, most scholars (cf. Latin Vulgate) agree that this noun should be repointed to חֹרֶב (ḥōreb), meaning "heat."

ii. Defeat and deportation (28:25–37)

OVERVIEW

As in the preceding section, the curses flow forth without any introduction by means of a protasis giving the grounds or reason for them. These verses look back to 28:15. They spell out the opposite conditions of 28:7. The basic thesis of this section is that God's rebellious nation will *not* enjoy covenantal blessings! While the preceding section concerned disasters in the domestic realm, the following section gives attention to the calamities caused by invading armies. One of the interesting features of this section is the pairing of a pronouncement of curse with a statement that emphasizes the Israelites' total inability to escape the weight of the curse. Indeed, there is no rest for the wicked! Consider the summary of the "bad news" found below:

28:26	Your carcass will be food for the birds ... and beasts	no one to startle (them)
28:27	The LORD will afflict you with boils ... tumors ... sores and the itch	you cannot be cured
28:29	You will be oppressed and robbed	no one to rescue you
28:30	You will build a house	you will not live in it
	You will plant a vineyard	and you will not begin (to use) it
28:31	Your ox will be slaughtered before your eyes	you will eat none of it
	Your donkey will be forcibly taken from you	[it] will not be returned
	Your sheep will be given to your enemies	no one will rescue them
28:32	Your sons and daughters will be given to another nation	[you will be] powerless to lift a hand
28:35	The Lord will afflict you ... with painful boils	that cannot be cured.

Five statements in this section make it clear that Yahweh is orchestrating these events. He causes their defeat (28:25, 35), afflicts them with boils (28:27), afflicts them with madness and blindness (28:28), and drives them to an unknown nation (28:36).

25The LORD will cause you to be defeated before your enemies. You will come at them from one direction but flee from them in seven, and you will become a thing of horror to all the kingdoms on earth. 26Your carcasses will be food for all the birds of the air and the beasts of the earth, and there will be no one to frighten them away. 27The LORD will afflict you with the boils of Egypt and with tumors, festering sores and the itch, from which you cannot be cured. 28The LORD will afflict you with madness, blindness and confusion of mind. 29At midday you will grope about like a blind man in the dark. You will be unsuccessful in everything you do; day after day you will be oppressed and robbed, with no one to rescue you.

30You will be pledged to be married to a woman, but another will take her and ravish her. You will build a house, but you will not live in it. You will plant a vineyard, but you will not even begin to enjoy its fruit. 31Your ox will be slaughtered before your eyes, but you will eat none of it. Your donkey will be forcibly taken from you and will not be returned. Your sheep will be given to your enemies, and no one will rescue them. 32Your sons and daughters will be given to another nation, and you will wear out your eyes watching for them day after day, powerless to lift a hand. [33]A people that you do not know will eat what your land and labor produce, and you will have nothing but cruel oppression all your days. [34]The sights you see will drive you mad. [35]The LORD will afflict your knees and legs with painful boils that cannot be cured, spreading from the soles of your feet to the top of your head.

[36]The LORD will drive you and the king you set over you to a nation unknown to you or your fathers. There you will worship other gods, gods of wood and stone. [37]You will become a thing of horror and an object of scorn and ridicule to all the nations where the LORD will drive you.

COMMENTARY

25–26 Yahweh, who has repeatedly promised to give his chosen nation victory over their enemies (cf. 6:19; 12:10; 20:4; 21:10), promises his nation defeat (cf. 28:31, 48, 49, 52, 55, 57). Unlike the absolute victory Yahweh promised in v.7, where the enemy flees in total disarray, Israel will approach their enemy as a unified force but flee away in seven groups (i.e., totally shattered). Rather than causing Israel's enemies to fear them and their great God, the nation's defeat and flight will horrify all witnesses (cf. Jer 15:4; 24:9; 29:18; 34:17). Israel will become a land filled with corpses, a banquet for various scavengers (birds and beasts; cf. Jer 7:33; 16:4; 19:7). One cannot escape the irony here: Israel, a nation Yahweh intends to feed from the land he has promised them, will become the food supply for a multitude of carnivorous beasts (Merrill, *Deuteronomy*, 360).

27 Depicting a reversal of the exodus, Yahweh promises that Israel will experience some of the agony of "ten plague-like" judgments paralleling those that Egypt faced. In the same way that the exodus event epitomized Yahweh's power and his intention to redeem his chosen people, it will also serve as a paradigm of overwhelming judgment (Merrill, *Deuteronomy*, 361; cf. Dt 28:60–61; Hos 8:13; 9:3). Israel will experience various painful and uncomfortable eruptions of the flesh involving boils (cf. Ex 9:9–11), tumors (perhaps hemorrhoids; cf.

1Sa 5:6, 9, 12; 6:4–5), sores (cf. Lev 21:20; 22:22), and the itch (the Hebrew word for which occurs only here in the OT). Tigay (*Deuteronomy*, 263–64) and Driver, 309–10, offer helpful explanations of each of these afflictions. Israel has no hope for any cure from these painful conditions of the skin.

28–29 As in Esarhaddon's vassal treaties, the covenantal curses move from skin disease to blindness (lines 419–24, §§39–40, in Pritchard, *ANET*, 538). Yahweh will also afflict his rebellious people with madness, blindness, and mental confusion (lit., "bewilderment of heart"; all three terms occur in Zec 12:4 to describe horses and their riders struck by panic when in battle). Since two of the three terms are psychological in nature, it could be that the blindness is metaphorical (i.e., the inability to think clearly or make intelligent judgments; Merrill, *Deuteronomy*, 361; cf. Ps 146:8; Isa 29:18; 35:5; 42:7, 16; 43:8; 56:10). In such a disoriented state, they will be unsuccessful in their own efforts and will be easy prey for robbers and exploiters. Once again, no one will rescue them from this predicament.

30–34 These curses will have a destructive impact on their family and property as well. They are known as "futility curses" because they frustrate the proper enjoyment of something (McConville, 406). All that a given Israelite has done for his or his family's benefit will be taken and enjoyed by a non-

Israelite (thus undoing the blessings of 28:4, 8, 11). The curses of 28:30 depict a breakdown of Deuteronomic protections (Dt 20:5–7; 24:5). These laws were meant to ensure that a man could enjoy the wife he married and the house he built. In other passages the prophets describe similar indignities as threats against God's covenantal nation (Jer 6:12; 8:10; Am 5:11; Mic 6:15; Zep 1:13; Hag 1:6).

Non-Israelites will take away their ox, donkey, sheep, children, and crops, and the Israelites will not receive them back. In the ancient Near East, stealing someone's ox or donkey was a proverbial example of oppression (Tigay, *Deuteronomy*, 265; Nu 16:15; 1Sa 12:3; cf. Pritchard, *ANET*, 280). The Israelites will know nothing but oppression, and the experience of their traumatic losses will drive many of them to insanity.

35 Moses returns to the threat of horrible skin conditions. Painful sores will appear on their knees and legs and spread to cover their entire bodies (reminiscent of Job's experience; Job 2:7–8; 7:3–5; 17:7; 19:17, 20; 30:17).

36–37 For the first time in the curse section, Moses refers to the threat of conquest by a foreign power and deportation to some unknown land, away from those things and places they know and love. Yahweh will "drive" them there, i.e., forcibly evict them and send them far from the land Yahweh promised to give to them. There they will be able to worship and serve the worthless gods that triggered these covenantal curses (cf. 4:28). Rather than Israel's being a prominent nation respected by the surrounding nations (cf. 26:18–19; 28:1–2, 13), Yahweh will cause Israel to become an occasion of horror (Jer 18:16; 49:17), a proverb (a classic example of extreme misfortune), and an object of ridicule (1 Ki 9:7 = 2Ch 7:20; Jer 24:9).

What is the significance of this reference to deportation and the mention of a king (28:36)? Since the monarchy did not arise in Israel until several centuries after Moses, was this verse added later in Israel's history (cf. Mayes, 350–51; von Rad, 25–28)? Since the book of Genesis is the first to refer to the institution of the monarchy (Ge 17:6, 16; 35:11; 36:31; 49:10; cf. Dt 17:14–20), and since siege, cannibalism, and exile—features mentioned elsewhere in ch. 28—were common experiences in the ancient world (cf. Lev 26:27–45; Tigay, *Deuteronomy*, 491), there is no need to date this verse "late" because of its referring to a "king."

NOTES

25 Some connect שִׁבְעָה (*šibʿâ*, "seven") to the seven curses mentioned in 28:20–24, but the number more likely refers to the extent (complete or total) of the scattering of Israel (as it did in 28:7).

30 The verb יִשְׁגָּלֶנָּה (*yišgālennâ*, "he will rape her") occurs only four times in the OT, and outside the present passage it never describes legitimate sexual relations (always "ravish" or "violate") and does occur in prophetic threats against Israel (Isa 13:16; Jer 3:2; Zec 14:2). The *Qere* marginal reading has the verb שכב (*škb*, "to lie down with"), a more conventional term for sexual relations (and a reading supported by the Syriac, Targum, and Vulgate). The Masoretes may have suggested using it since the verb שגל (*šgl*) was too vulgar for public reading in the synagogue (Tigay, *Deuteronomy*, 265). However, there is no need to avoid the distasteful verb and minimize the offense in view.

32 The OT uses a particular idiom to express an ability to do something (Ge 31:29; Ne 5:5; Pr 3:27; Mic 2:1): "it is in my power ..." (יֶשׁ־לְאֵל יָדִי, *yeš-leʾēl yādî*). The expression וְאֵין לְאֵל יָדֶךָ (*weʾên leʾēl yāʿdekā*, "you will be powerless to do anything about it" [NET]) in this verse represents the negative form of that idiom. What does the phrase found here mean? Scholars have debated the precise meaning of the term אֵל (ʾēl) in this phrase. Medieval Hebraists assumed that אֵל (ʾēl) came from the verb אִיל (ʾyl), which means "to have power" (cf. Tigay, *Deuteronomy*, 265): e.g., "so-and-so's hand has/has no power." Others regard אֵל (ʾēl) as a noun for "God" (see Tigay, *Deuteronomy*, 396, n. 54): e.g., "God/god has/does not have [control of] so-and-so's hand" (i.e., enables or does not enable so-and-so to do something). This interpretation has grammatical problems and is contrary to the MT's punctuation (Tigay, *Deuteronomy*, 396, n. 54). According to Wakely (*NIDOTTE*, 1:398–99), this noun signifies power or strength. The point is that these parents will helplessly watch their children be taken away because they do not have the power to intervene.

iii. Agricultural deprivation and political subjugation (28:38–44)

³⁸You will sow much seed in the field but you will harvest little, because locusts will devour it. ³⁹You will plant vineyards and cultivate them but you will not drink the wine or gather the grapes, because worms will eat them. ⁴⁰You will have olive trees throughout your country but you will not use the oil, because the olives will drop off. ⁴¹You will have sons and daughters but you will not keep them, because they will go into captivity. ⁴²Swarms of locusts will take over all your trees and the crops of your land.

⁴³The alien who lives among you will rise above you higher and higher, but you will sink lower and lower. ⁴⁴He will lend to you, but you will not lend to him. He will be the head, but you will be the tail.

COMMENTARY

38–42 These verses continue the "futility curses" of 28:32–34. The three staple crops of Israel (Dt 7:13)—grain, wine, and oil—commonly served as clear indicators of God's blessing on his servant-nation (Lev 26:20; Dt 6:11; 8:8; Isa 5:10; Jer 12:13; Mic 6:15). Along with various kinds of crops, one's children were also a key part of covenantal blessings (Dt 28:3b–5). Verses 38–41 present a painful contrast between a significant expenditure of labor and having nothing to show for it. Notice the repeated pattern:

Sow much seed	harvest little	harvest consumed by locusts
Plant and cultivate vineyards	no wine to drink	grapes consumed by worms
Have numerous olive trees	no oil to use	olives drop off prematurely
Have sons and daughters	no enjoyment of their company	children go into captivity

Also, the envelope structure of this passage strengthens its emphasis:

A destruction by locusts (v.38)

   B you will not enjoy what belonged to you (vv.39–41)

A' destruction by locusts (v.42)

Another part of the ironic impact of this section is the fact that these "locusts" in 28:42 will "take over" (*yrš*) all of Israel's crops and trees. This verb occurs repeatedly in Deuteronomy to signify Israel's "taking possession" of the land of Canaan or "dispossessing" the Canaanites from their land. As part of the covenantal curses, these locusts (or destructive insects) will take possession of the land God promised to Israel.

43–44 Whereas 28:1, 12–13, 36–37 compare Israel to other nations outside the land of promise, these verses contrast Israel with aliens who live in their midst. (Aliens were normally part of the lowest level of Israelite society [10:19; 24:17–21].) Merrill (*Deuteronomy*, 364; cf. Ridderbos, 259) contends that this contrast heightens "the sense of humiliation and chagrin Israel would experience in the coming day of judgment." This curse turns one of the covenantal blessings on its head (28:12b–13a). The crop failure envisioned in vv.38–42 leads to an economic collapse so significant that the poor aliens will be among Israel's creditors.

NOTE

38 This passage mentions the "locust" twice but uses two different words and may have two different kinds of insects in mind. The first term, הָאַרְבֶּה (*hāʾarbeh*), is the most common word for locusts in the OT. Yahweh sent locusts against Egypt as part of the eighth plague, causing great damage to Egypt's crops. A large swarm of locusts could consume enough food in one day to feed 1.5 million people (Tigay, *Deuteronomy*, 266). The second term, הַצְּלָצַל (*haṣṣelāṣal*; 28:42), is an onomatopoeic word (a word that, when pronounced, sounds like what it signifies) referring to some kind of buzzing or whirring insect. Although several scholars believe this word also refers to a locust, the referent could be another kind of insect (e.g., a cricket; see Tigay, *Deuteronomy*, 267, for some suggestions). Notice the following translational alternatives: "buzzing insects" (NAB), "the cricket" (NASB), "the cicada" (NRSV), "swarms of insects" (NLT), and "whirring locusts" (NET).

iv. Military siege (28:45–57)

⁴⁵All these curses will come upon you. They will pursue you and overtake you until you are destroyed, because you did not obey the LORD your God and observe the commands and decrees he gave you. ⁴⁶They will be a sign and a wonder to you and your descendants forever. ⁴⁷Because you did not serve the LORD your God joyfully and gladly in the time of

prosperity, [48]therefore in hunger and thirst, in nakedness and dire poverty, you will serve the enemies the LORD sends against you. He will put an iron yoke on your neck until he has destroyed you.

[49]The LORD will bring a nation against you from far away, from the ends of the earth, like an eagle swooping down, a nation whose language you will not understand, [50]a fierce-looking nation without respect for the old or pity for the young. [51]They will devour the young of your livestock and the crops of your land until you are destroyed. They will leave you no grain, new wine or oil, nor any calves of your herds or lambs of your flocks until you are ruined. [52]They will lay siege to all the cities throughout your land until the high forti-fied walls in which you trust fall down. They will besiege all the cities throughout the land the LORD your God is giving you.

[53]Because of the suffering that your enemy will inflict on you during the siege, you will eat the fruit of the womb, the flesh of the sons and daughters the LORD your God has given you. [54]Even the most gentle and sensitive man among you will have no compassion on his own brother or the wife he loves or his surviving children, [55]and he will not give to one of them any of the flesh of his children that he is eating. It will be all he has left because of the suffering your enemy will inflict on you during the siege of all your cities. [56]The most gentle and sensitive woman among you — so sensitive and gentle that she would not venture to touch the ground with the sole of her foot — will begrudge the husband she loves and her own son or daughter [57]the afterbirth from her womb and the children she bears. For she intends to eat them secretly during the siege and in the distress that your enemy will inflict on you in your cities.

COMMENTARY

45–48 With these verses it is as though Moses has reached a plateau in his presentation of cov-enantal curses. He has made it abundantly clear that the experience of covenantal curses will be hor-rific and agonizing. He provides here a summary in the heart of the long presentation of curses. Moses pauses to provide the theological rationale for these terrible curses once again, namely, to punish Israel for her disobedience of the agreed-upon covenantal stipulations (their covenantal treachery; vv.45–47) and to serve as a warning to all future generations. He also summarizes the impact of the curses: hun-ger, thirst, nakedness, and poverty. The following section (vv.49–57) then describes the gruesome details of a military siege, a destiny that Yahweh will allow his chosen people to experience at the hands of a pagan nation because of Israel's refusal whole-heartedly to obey Yahweh's covenantal demands.

Verses 45–48 also introduce a new perspec-tive. It no longer seems as though covenantal curs-ing is a mere possibility — now that fate appears to be a foregone conclusion (Nelson, 332). The defeat envisioned by these verses is total. The pagan enemy pursues the Israelites until their attacker has destroyed them (vv.45, 48, 51, 61; see Note on 28:20), caused them to perish (v.51; see Note on

28:20), and knocked down their walls of fortification (v.52). Using language similar to that found earlier in the chapter (28:2, 15), Moses declares that these curses will pursue Israel like a relentless predator. The two verbs *rdp* and *nśg* occur together to describe the tireless pursuit that ends with the capture of the prey (Ex 15:9; Dt 19:6; 1Sa 30:8; Ps 7:5 [6]). The cause for Israel's experience of covenantal curses is without question: They have refused to obey Yahweh's voice (contrary to his central expectation of them in Ex 19:5–6) and have not kept his commandments and statutes (umbrella terms for Yahweh's covenantal demands).

The curses Yahweh will send on his people will serve as "a sign and a wonder" to those who experience those curses and to all their descendants (v.46). In Israel's exodus experience, the ten plagues had served as exciting signs and wonders. What a reversal in Israel's fate this experience of judgment represents! The pair "signs and wonders" commonly signifies anything that testifies to Yahweh's presence and power (Dt 4:34; 7:19; 26:8; 29:3 [2]; Jer 32:21). As Merrill (*Deuteronomy*, 364) writes: "The inevitable calamities that befall the disobedient nation would be indelibly engraved in their memories and forever after would witness to the truth that the Lord and his covenant will cannot be flaunted."

Israel's covenantal treachery will occasion a military siege and all the agony that accompanies such an experience (28:47–48). Once again notice the sad progression from Israel's conduct to their fate. Because Israel "did not serve" Yahweh, they "will serve" pagan nations. This fate represents a reversal of the exodus, i.e., a return to bondage. Although somewhat hyperbolic (since other passages in Deuteronomy refer to a restoration to Yahweh), the language of 28:48 provides no indication of any respite or hope for survival.

There is also a clear contrast between v.47 and v.48. On the one hand, in the midst of Yahweh's

abundant provision for his covenantal people on repeated occasions, his vassal nation did not serve their suzerain with gladness and joy. (God is never interested in grudging obedience.) On the other hand, in the light of that neglect God will permit them to serve pagan nations without those blessings, in hunger, thirst, nakedness, and poverty. That "service" to the pagan nations will be like an "iron yoke." It is a servitude that will weigh them down and from which they cannot release themselves. One wonders why God's people, then and now, cannot understand that it is only eternal values that have ultimate worth. As the late missionary Jim Elliot said so powerfully, "He is no fool who gives what he cannot keep to gain what he cannot lose."

49–52 Moses demonstrates how the nation of Israel, which had been offered great glory by the Lord, will experience the horrors and destruction of a military siege. The central concept throughout this inventory of covenantal curses (vv.49–57) is "the catastrophe of serving one's enemies rather than Yahweh" (Nelson, 332). This section describes the enemy Yahweh will send against his people, while the next section (vv.53–57) delineates the horrific conduct of God's people in the midst of a siege. Whereas vv.20–46 focus on internal disintegration, vv.49–57 delineate the external threat to Israel. This delineation of military conquest at the hands of a foreign power represents the total reversal of all that God has done for Israel: no land, no cities, no possessions, no crops, no herds or flocks, no loved ones.

Yahweh will raise up against his chosen people a fierce enemy who will epitomize covenantal curse. They will come from afar and speak a language foreign to Israel's ears (cf. 2Ki 18:26–28 = Isa 36:11–13). The comparison of this attacking nation to an eagle's swooping down signifies the suddenness, speed, and power of the attack (Tigay, *Deuteronomy*, 269). As Habakkuk (Hab 1:8) wrote about the Babylonian army: "Their horses are swifter than leopards, fiercer than wolves at dusk. Their cavalry gallops headlong, their horsemen come from afar. They fly like a vulture swooping to devour" (cf. Job 9:26; Jer 48:40; 49:22). The attackers will be ruthless, even merciless to noncombatants (cf. Isa 13:18; 47:6; La 4:16; 5:12–13).

The attacking army will devastate the heart of Israel's economy. They will consume all of their calves, lambs, and crops (cf. three staple crops [grain, wine, and oil] in 28:38–40). Because the enemy consumes Israel's material resources, the Israelites will be unable to feed themselves. In laying siege to all of their cities the enemy will be able to overcome any fortifications in which the Israelites have mistakenly placed their confidence.

This last indictment ("walls in which you trust," v.52) is Israel's fundamental problem. Yahweh repeatedly demanded that his covenantal nation trust him. He demonstrated his stupendous power and willingness to intervene in their behalf on numerous occasions. Nevertheless, on too many occasions in the face of an insuperable challenge (humanly speaking), the chosen nation either turned back (cf. Nu 13–14; Dt 1:28) or resorted to other sources of strength (political alliances, idolatry, etc.). Their refusal to trust in their covenantal Lord led to their rebellion and idolatry and, eventually, to their experience of covenantal curse.

53–57 As the result of this siege, God's people will depart from any semblance of justice, equity, and compassion. Because of the severity of the siege placed on the cities of Israel, even the most gentle and sensitive person will abandon all restraint and loyalty and turn to gruesome cannibalism. A pampered husband, who would normally treat his loved ones with kindness and love, will be unfriendly toward those closest to him and share with them only grudgingly. The reference to "his surviving children" adds to the pain of this anticipated reality. In 28:11 the same verb refers to Yahweh's promise to provide his covenantal nation with an abundance of children, livestock, and crops. Here, these children are those who have not died yet and "remain" (*ytr*). His "beloved" wife will treat others in the same way and will seek to keep for her own consumption a newborn child and the afterbirth that her body expels.

NOTES

48 The "yoke" (here עֹל בַּרְזֶל, *'ol barzel*, "an iron yoke") is a common metaphor in ancient Near Eastern literature employed to signify submission to the rule of gods and kings. It can refer, in a positive sense, to loyal service to a legitimate ruler (Jer 27:11–12; 28:14; Tigay, *Deuteronomy*, 269). Ancient Near Eastern rulers commonly boasted of placing the yoke of overlordship on those they subjugated (Pritchard, *ANET*, 297, 314; Moran, 310, 339 [EA 257, 296]). Throughout the OT, a "yoke" refers to political domination and oppression (Ge 27:40; Lev 26:13; 1Ki 12:4, 9–11, 14; Isa 9:4 [3]; 10:27; Jer 2:20; 27:8, 11–12; et al.; Biddle, 420).

Jeremiah fashioned a wooden yoke and wore it on his neck in the temple precincts to symbolize the Babylonian domination of Judah that he had been predicting (Jer 28:5–9). Hananiah, a false prophet, broke that wooden yoke and declared that Babylon's domination over Judah would be brief (Jer 28:10–11). Jeremiah returned to the temple with an iron yoke around his neck to demonstrate visibly the durability of Babylon's subjugation of Judah (Jer 28:13–14).

52 Walls played a key role in the overall fortification system of ancient cities (2Sa 5:6; 1Ki 4:13; 2Ki 25:4; Isa 22:11; 25:12). In parallel to the reference here, חֹמֹתֶיךָ הַגְּבֹהוֹת וְהַבְּצֻרוֹת אֲשֶׁר אַתָּה בֹּטֵחַ בָּהֵן (ḥōmōteykā haggᵉbōhôt wᵉhabbᵉṣurôt ʾᵃšer ʾattâ bōṭēaḥ bāhēn, "the high fortified walls in which you trust"), the OT prophets regularly condemn trusting in human resources instead of Yahweh — resources such as chariots (Isa 31:11; Hos 10:13), fortified cities (Jer 5:17), false gods (Jer 13:25), foreign powers (Jer 46:25), and personal wealth (Jer 48:7; 49:4). Confidence in military strength, carefully laid fortifications, or other resources implies that trust in Yahweh alone is insufficient.

Israel should have clearly understood that human fortifications have no ultimate significance. When they defeated Og of Bashan, Yahweh had enabled them to conquer and take possession of a number of walled cities (Dt 3:5). The fortified or impregnable (בָּצוּר, bāṣûr; 1:28) cities that had terrified them when they heard the report of ten of the twelve spies (Nu 13:28; Dt 1:28) did not stand in the way as they conquered the region of Transjordan (Dt 3:5), nor would such fortifications prevent them from conquering Canaan (Dt 9:1).

53 The expression פְּרִי־בִטְנְךָ (pᵉrî-biṭnᵉkā, "the fruit of your womb") occurs eleven times in the OT, and six of those instances are found in Deuteronomy. As Israel prepared to conquer Canaan, Yahweh promised to bless his covenantal nation with children (7:13). "Fruit of the womb" is also a central part of covenantal blessing (28:4, 11), and the denial of it is a covenantal curse (28:18, 53). When Yahweh restores his chosen people to the land of his promise after they experience covenantal curse and repent of their rebellion, he promises to bless "the fruit of the womb" once again (30:9). The disgusting consumption of "the fruit of the womb" is especially offensive in light of the central role children played in Yahweh's covenantal blessings. This same painful prediction appears several times in the vassal treaties of Esarhaddon (lines 440–52, 547–62, 568–69, §§47, 69–72, 75 [Pritchard, *ANET*, 538–40]).

53, 55, 57 The clause בְּמָצוֹר וּבְמָצוֹק אֲשֶׁר־יָצִיק לְךָ אֹיְבֶךָ (bᵉmāṣôr ûbᵉmāṣôq ʾᵃšer-yāṣîq lᵉkā ʾōyᵉbekā, "the stressful siege in which your enemies will constrict you") gathers together two nouns and a verb that share a number of sounds or letters; the alliteration would catch a listener's or reader's attention. These nouns and verb also share the notion of stress and pressure (cf. Lamberty-Zielinski, *TDOT*, 12:303, 305; Thiel, *TDOT*, 12:308). The two nouns can serve as a hendiadys with one emphatic translation: "desperate straits." The following verb, "to constrict, inflict" adds weight to that emphasis. The juxtaposition of these three terms (in three verses in this section) serves to depict the choking, stifling nature of the covenantal curses envisioned for Israel in the event of their persistent covenantal rebellion.

54 The adjective רַךְ (rak; GK 8205) occurs sixteen times in the OT and three times in Deuteronomy (20:8; 28:54 [הָאִישׁ הָרַךְ בְּךָ וְהֶעָנֹג מְאֹד (hāʾîš hārak bᵉkā wᵉheʿānōg mᵉʾōd), "the most gentle and sensitive man"], 56). A good-quality calf that is slaughtered for special guests is called "tender" (Ge 18:7). The adjective describes children who are young and need protection (Ge 33:13; cf. Pr 4:3); when used with the noun heart (לֵב, lēb; Dt 20:3; 1Ch 29:1; 2Ch 13:7; Job 23:16), it describes someone who is inexperienced or weak. The adjective עָנֹג (ʿānōg) carries the idea of "delicate" (Kronholm, *TDOT*, 11:213) or "pampered, molly-coddled" (*HALOT*, 851). Outside Deuteronomy 28, it occurs one other time (with רַךְ, rak; Isa 47:1).

The woman mentioned in 28:56 is so "gentle" (רַכָּה, rakâ) that she does not even consider allowing her bare feet to touch the ground directly (probably indicating that she is accustomed to being carried around on a litter or a carriage). Although some scholars understand this description in positive terms, indicating a gentle and sensitive heart (as in loyalty, faithfulness, and devotion; cf. Carew, *NIDOTTE*, 3:445), in light of the additional description of the woman it seems to refer to someone who is pampered or indulged (Tigay, *Deuteronomy*, 270). Even a person who avoids menial or filthy tasks will consume her own children and refuse to share the cannabilized flesh.

The combination of the verb רעע (r^c) and the noun "eyes," as in the phrase תֵּרַע עֵינוֹ (*tēra^c ^cênô*, "will look with evil"), occurs fifteen times in the OT. It generally refers to something that displeases someone else (Ge 21:12; 48:17; 1Sa 8:6; 18:8; 1Ch 21:7; Pr 24:18; Isa 59:15). It can also refer to feelings of hostility (Dt 15:9). In the present passage, close relatives, who would normally be treated with kindness and compassion, will be regarded as hostile competitors for the human flesh that is available for consumption.

v. Reversal of covenantal love (28:58–68)

OVERVIEW

This final section of covenantal curses demonstrates that through them Yahweh will reverse the manifestations of his covenantal love for his people. Their refusal to revere him serves as the theological occasion for the curses (28:58). Because of their rebellion, he will decimate his chosen people through disease (28:59–63a) and divorce them from their land (28:63b–68). The covenantal curses will undo much of what Yahweh has done in Israel's behalf up to that time; the use of expressions from the Abrahamic covenant intensifies the significance of this reversal. Notice also the contrast made between Israel's experience (or promise) of divine blessings at the end of their sojourn in Egypt and Israel's promised experience of these covenantal curses (Craigie, 351–52).

	Redemption in Egypt	**Cursed by Covenantal Treachery**
28:60–61	Diseases on Israel's enemies	Diseases on Israel
28:62–63	Multiplied in numbers	Decimated in numbers
28:64a	Anticipation of the Promised Land	Eviction from the Promised Land
28:64b	Fullness of life found in serving Yahweh	Emptiness of life seen in worshiping false gods
28:65–67	Nations will fear Israel	Israel will be overwhelmed by fear
28:66	Long life in the Promised Land	Unsure of life in exile
28:68	Freed from slavery in Egypt	Returned to bondage in Egypt

One must not fail to recognize that the strength of Yahweh's negative response is directly proportional to his positive commitment to the covenant.

⁵⁸If you do not carefully follow all the words of this law, which are written in this book, and do not revere this glorious and awesome name — the LORD your God — ⁵⁹the LORD will send fearful plagues on you and your descendants, harsh and prolonged disasters, and severe and lingering illnesses. ⁶⁰He will bring upon you all the diseases of Egypt that you dreaded, and they will cling to you. ⁶¹The LORD will also bring on you every kind of sickness and disaster not recorded in this Book of the Law, until you are destroyed. ⁶²You who were as numerous as the stars in the sky will be left but few in number, because you did not obey the LORD your God. ⁶³Just as it pleased the LORD to make you prosper and increase in number, so it will please him to ruin and destroy you. You will be uprooted from the land you are entering to possess.

⁶⁴Then the LORD will scatter you among all nations, from one end of the earth to the other. There you will worship other gods — gods of wood and stone, which neither you nor your fathers have known. ⁶⁵Among those nations you will find no repose, no resting place for the sole of your foot. There the LORD will give you an anxious mind, eyes weary with longing, and a despairing heart. ⁶⁶You will live in constant suspense, filled with dread both night and day, never sure of your life. ⁶⁷In the morning you will say, "If only it were evening!" and in the evening, "If only it were morning!" — because of the terror that will fill your hearts and the sights that your eyes will see. ⁶⁸The LORD will send you back in ships to Egypt on a journey I said you should never make again. There you will offer yourselves for sale to your enemies as male and female slaves, but no one will buy you.

COMMENTARY

58 Like many of the other sections of curses, these verses fall into a protasis−apodosis pattern. Verse 58 serves as the protasis or condition, and vv.59−68 provide the apodosis or conclusion/result. The fundamental cause for this divine judgment does involve Israel's conduct (not following "all the words of this law," i.e., all the covenantal demands of Deuteronomy), but it also encompasses their attitude of heart — an adamant refusal to revere God's lofty character.

The verb "to fear" (*yr*) can signify terror, respect, or worship (see Note on 6:13). The fact that in several passages it occurs along with the verb "to serve" (*ʿbd*) highlights its relevance to God-honoring worship (6:13; 10:12, 20; 13:4). Not following other gods serves as a counterpart to fearing Yahweh (Dt 6:14) as well as obeying his decrees and commands (Ps 119:63). Fearing God and obeying his commands will manifest itself in appropriate moral conduct (Ge 42:18; Ex 1:17, 21; Lev 25:17). To live in accordance with the fear of the Lord is the same as living in accordance with God's decrees and commands. Israel's refusal to revere Yahweh manifests itself in their penchant to worship other gods and in their rebellion against his covenantal requirements. His glorious and awesome "name" refers to his lofty character (see Note on 5:11).

59–63a Yahweh will send afflictions and diseases that are "harsh and prolonged" and "severe and lingering." The second adjective in both pairs is the same and highlights the abiding or enduring nature of these curses. Verses 60–61 describe those diseases in further detail (cf. 28:21–22, 35). Some will be like those diseases Yahweh sent against Egypt (e.g., murrain [Ex 9:1–7], boils [Ex 9:8–12]) while others will be those unmentioned in Deuteronomy. These diseases will be inescapable ("will cling to you"), comprehensive in extent ("every kind of sickness and disaster"), and punitive ("until you are destroyed").

This overabundance of terrible diseases will result in a vastly reduced population of Israelites (28:62–63a). Even though Yahweh promised his people to be as numerous as the stars in the sky (cf. Ge 15:5; 22:17; 26:4; Ex 32:13; Dt 1:10; 7:7; 10:22), Israel will become only few in number. Just as it served God's purposes to multiply their population and give them prosperity, so will he accomplish his intentions for his servant-nation by ruining (*ʾbd*) and destroying (*šmd*) them (see Notes on 28:20)!

63b–68 Yahweh will also evict (*nšḥ*, lit., "forcibly remove from" or "tear out") his covenantal nation from the Promised Land as part of the covenantal curses (cf. 28:36–37; Lev 26:33). Imagine what this aspect of the covenantal curse represents for Israel. From the time of Abraham on, generations of Israelites longed for the day when God's promise of a land for this special people would be fulfilled. Their departure from Egypt after Yahweh's great demonstration of power through the ten plagues surely heightened the excitement of the Israelites. Forty years later, after the trip through the Sinai peninsula, a year spent in the barren regions around Mount Sinai, and over thirty-eight years consumed in wilderness wandering, Israel's entrance into Canaan was surely a glorious experience. To be in that land

was to be in the place where an Israelite could experience the abundance of God's covenantal blessings. This threat of eviction from the land strikes at the foundation of God's promise to his chosen nation.

Yahweh will scatter them among numerous nations ("from one end of the earth to the other"), where the Israelites will have the chance to worship numerous false gods (many of which they had never heard of before; 28:64). Not only will Israel's existence in exile be characterized by the absence of rest and comfort (28:65a), but they will also experience emotional upheaval (28:65b). The reference to three anatomical and psychological terms—"mind," "eyes," and "heart"—emphasizes the internal and far-reaching nature of this distress (28:65). Their lives will be so consumed by instability that they will have absolutely no confidence of another day or night of life. They will find each segment of a day so unbearable that they will long for the next (Tigay, *Deuteronomy*, 273).

As a final step of covenantal reversal, Yahweh will send his chosen people back to Egypt, where they came into existence as a nation (28:68). Scholars have offered various suggestions to explain the significance of this return to Egypt on ships. A return to Egypt and the enslavement from which they had just been redeemed serves as a summary statement of covenantal curses that undo Yahweh's activity in Israel's behalf.

Why will they return to Egypt on ships? On the one hand, their departure from Egypt, wandering in the wilderness, and approach to the Promised Land were entirely due to Yahweh's miraculous intervention in their behalf (Merrill, *Deuteronomy*, 372; P. Head, "The Curse of Covenant Reversal: Deuteronomy 28:58–68 and Israel's Exile," *Churchman* 111 [1997]: 225). Their expatriation from that land, however, will be the work of men, who return the Israelites to a slave market in which they will have no redeeming value whatsoever.

NOTES

58 As in the phrase אִם־לֹא תִשְׁמֹר לַעֲשׂוֹת ... לְיִרְאָה (ʾim-lōʾ tišmōr laʿăśôt ... lᵉyirʾâ, "If you refuse to obey ... and refuse to fear"), the juxtaposition of the first two verbs (שׁמר, šmr, and עשׂה, ʿśh) occurs repeatedly in Deuteronomy (see Note on 5:1) as part of Moses' call for Israel to invest themselves wholeheartedly (lit., "be careful to do") in living according to the covenantal stipulations. The introductory particles "if not" and the first verb also govern the infinitive in the second half of this verse—"to fear" (ירא, yrʾ). Yahweh faults his covenantal nation for failing to invest themselves with all diligence in obeying his requirements and fearing or revering him (see Note on 6:13).

59 The verb פלא (plʾ; GK 7098), in the phrase וְהִפְלָא יְהוָה אֶת־מַכֹּתְךָ (wᵉhiplāʾ yhwh ʾet-makkōtᵉkā, "then the LORD will increase your punishments" [NET]), generally means "to do something wonderful" (*HALOT*, 928). It often refers to an event or activity that, when compared to the normal or expected, appears extraordinary, impossible, and even wonderful (Albertz, *TLOT*, 2:982). The form of this verb (Hiphil) refers to someone's making a "special" vow (Lev 27:2; Nu 6:2), the marvelous temple (2Ch 2:8), Yahweh's stupendous help (2Ch 26:15), and something that is almost too great to describe (Jdg 13:19; Ps 31:21 [22]; Isa 28:29; Joel 2:26). Yahweh affirms that he will do something incomprehensible for or to his hypocritical people (Isa 29:14). The passage does not clarify whether he is referring to future judgment or restoration. The verb can carry a negative nuance as it does in 28:59. Yahweh will do something unparalleled and indescribable by sending these "smitings" against his covenantal nation.

C. Narrative Interlude (29:1 [28:69])

¹These are the terms of the covenant the LORD commanded Moses to make with the Israelites in Moab, in addition to the covenant he had made with them at Horeb.

COMMENTARY

1 [28:69] Although all scholars recognize the transitional nature of this verse, there is debate as to whether the verse concludes the preceding section or introduces the following material (see text note). As Merrill (*Deuteronomy*, 373) points out, the division of the Hebrew text favors the former, and the placement of the chapter division in most English translations supports the latter. Merrill also suggests that this verse forms part of an inclusio (bracketing the book up to this point) with the preamble section of the book (1:1–5), since both passages begin with the words "these are the words ... which Moses," locate the setting in Moab, and make reference to Horeb and the earlier covenant. Consequently, this verse may bring a close to the covenantal text proper.

What does Moses mean when he writes that his sermons to Israel on the plains of Moab are "besides" or "in addition to" (millᵉbad habbᵉrît) "the covenant he had made with them at Horeb"?

Does the comment refer to a separate or distinct "Palestinian covenant," or does it look back to the Mosaic covenant originally established at Mount Sinai/Horeb?

In order to understand the relationship of Moses' presentation of the covenant at Moab to the covenant established at Mount Sinai, McConville, 401, directs readers' attention to 5:2–3. In that passage, the Horeb/Sinaitic covenant was presented as having been made with the present (Moab encamped) generation (no chronological distinction). The point of blurring those temporal horizons is to demonstrate that Moses' teaching of the commandments is a "new embodiment" of the Horeb/Sinaitic covenant. The present passage affirms that the covenant presented in Moab does not replace the Horeb/Sinaitic covenant but exists alongside it. McConville, 401–2, concludes that "the latter does not invalidate the earlier. Rather, the two co-exist. This is part of the tendency of Deuteronomy to telescope a succession of covenants into an ever renewed challenge to faithfulness. 29:1 [28:69] refers back to what has preceded it, as does the same phrase in 29:9 [8]." McConville, 409, later adds that the covenant at Moab represents

the renewal of the covenant at Horeb mediated by Moses' preaching of the laws in Deuteronomy. The relationship of the Moab covenant to the Horeb covenant is not one of clean distinction, but rather a new realization. Moses' preaching is, on the one hand, the teaching of the terms of Horeb (5:27; 6:1), but on the other constitutes the covenant entered into "today" in Moab (cf. 26:16–19). (Cf. R. E. Clements, "Deuteronomy," in *New Interpreter's Bible* [ed. L. Keck et al.; Nashville: Abingdon, 1998], 511; Keil, 446; Millar, *Now Choose Life* [Grand Rapids: Eerdmans, 1998], 92)

Consequently, one needs to recognize the different emphases in Deuteronomy concerning the relationship of what Moses presents to the covenantal nation camped at Moab and the covenant presented at Sinai. On the one hand, the covenant presented at Sinai was made with the Israelites camped at Moab, whether they were in attendance at that time or not (5:2–3). On the other hand, the need for this new generation of Israelites to recommit themselves to this covenantal relationship with Yahweh gives Moses' preaching at Moab its own identity as well. It is not a brand new covenant but represents a renewal of the covenant first given at Sinai.

NOTE

1 [28:69] The following commentators conclude that this verse serves as a subscript to 27:1–28:68 in particular and perhaps the entire book up to this point: R. E. Clements (*The Book of Deuteronomy: A Preacher's Commentary* [London: Epworth, 2001], 127; Craigie, 353; Driver, 319; Hall, 429–30; McConville, 409; Merrill (*Deuteronomy*, 372–73), Tigay (*Deuteronomy*, 274); and H. van Rooy ("Deuteronomy 28,69—Superscript or Subscript?" *JNSL* 14 [1988]: 219–21). A number of scholars place this verse as an introduction to the following section (29:2–30:20): Biddle, 435–37; Cairns, 253–54; Harman, 245; Kalland, 178–79; Keil, 446–47; Lenchak, 173–74; Mayes, 358–60; J. G. McConville and J. G. Millar (*Time and Place in Deuteronomy* [JSOTSup 179; Sheffield: Sheffield Academic, 1994], 77–78); Miller, 200–202; Nelson, 338–39; Phillips (*Deuteronomy*, 193–94); Ridderbos, 263; Thompson, 278–79; von Rad, 178–79; and Wright (*Deuteronomy*, 284).

This litany of proponents demonstrates that there is no clear unanimity about the place of 29:1 in the structure of Deuteronomy. The first argument for interpreting the verse as a subscript is the structure suggested by the Hebrew text. More importantly, the phrase "the terms of the covenant" (הַבְּרִית אֵלֶּה דִבְרֵי, ʾēlleh dibrê habbᵉrît) clearly points back to the context of chs. 27−28. The next section (chs. 29−30) does not delineate "the terms of the covenant." But one of the strongest arguments for regarding this verse as a superscript to the next section consists of the phrase "these are ... which." In almost every case in Deuteronomy, this phrase points forward (1:1; 4:45; 6:1; 12:1; 14:4, 12; 15:2; 19:4; 33:1). That observation aside, the same phrase can provide a summary of a paragraph or a large section (Ex 19:6; Lev 27:34; Nu 36:13).

Traditionally, dispensationalists have affirmed that ch. 29 presents the Palestinian covenant (R. Showers, *There Really Is a Difference: A Comparison of Covenant and Dispensational Theology* [Bellmawr, N.J.: Friends of Israel Gospel Ministry, Inc., 1990], 77−83; C. Ryrie, *The Basis of the Premillennial Faith* [Neptune, N.J.: Loizeaux Brothers, 1953], 58−59). This distinct "covenant" (הַבְּרִית, habbᵉrît) presents God's promises to his people that will be realized when he restores them to the Promised Land. This interpretation seems unlikely. Of the five other occurrences of "the covenant" in this section, three clearly have the Mosaic covenant in view (29:9, 21, 25), and the others might be referring to it (29:12, 14).

For the expression מִלְּבַד (millᵉbad, "in addition to"), various translations suggest "besides" (ESV, NASB, NKJV) or "in addition to" (NCV, NET, NIV, NLT, NRSV). This construction also appears in Genesis 26:1; Numbers 6:21; 16:49 [17:14]; Deuteronomy 4:35; and Daniel 11:4. In each instance it clearly means "besides" or "in addition to," setting the item referenced alongside something else.

V. THE GROUNDS AND NEED FOR COVENANTAL RENEWAL (29:2 [1]−30:20)

OVERVIEW

Moses begins this section by reminding the children of Israel of Yahweh's faithfulness to them in bringing them from Egypt to the plains of Moab, as well as of the covenantal relationship into which they are entering with the Lord—a relationship that promises cursing for disobedience and blessing for obedience. In the light of those realities, Moses challenges Israel to renew this covenant and choose life and blessing rather than death and cursing.

Merrill (*Deuteronomy*, 375) points out that chs. 29 and 30 serve at least four purposes in the larger context of Deuteronomy. They (1) provide a summation of God's past dealings with Israel; (2) restate the present occasion of covenantal offer and acceptance; (3) address the options of covenantal disobedience and obedience respectively; and (4) exhort the assembled throng to covenantal commitment.

A. Reminder of Yahweh's Faithfulness and Call to Covenantal Renewal (29:2–29 [1–28])

1. Historical Review (29:2–9 [1–8])

OVERVIEW

In ch. 29 Moses reminds the Israelites of God's abundant faithfulness to them as demonstrated in the exodus from Egypt and his care for them throughout their pilgrimage to Canaan (29:2–8). He also challenges them to renew their commitment to Yahweh (29:9–16) lest they become objects of his destructive wrath (29:16–28). This call to covenantal renewal, like several exhortation sections in the book, begins with a historical overview (29:2–8). In that regard, Craigie, 356, points out that in these verses Moses develops themes presented earlier in the book (with 29:2–3, cf. 1:30;

5:1; 7:17–19; 11:2–3; with 29:5–6, cf. 8:2–3; and with 29:7–8, cf. 2:32–36; 4:34; 11:3–7).

The entire nation has seen and experienced Yahweh's might and miraculous power, by means of which he delivered his people from Egyptian bondage and brought them through the barren wilderness (29:2–3). During that lengthy wandering in the wilderness, Yahweh supernaturally provided for their physical needs (29:5–6). After arriving in the region of Transjordan, he delivered Heshbon and Bashan into their hands (29:7–8).

---

²Moses summoned all the Israelites and said to them:

Your eyes have seen all that the LORD did in Egypt to Pharaoh, to all his officials and to all his land. ³With your own eyes you saw those great trials, those miraculous signs and great wonders. ⁴But to this day the LORD has not given you a mind that understands or eyes that see or ears that hear. ⁵During the forty years that I led you through the desert, your clothes did not wear out, nor did the sandals on your feet. ⁶You ate no bread and drank no wine or other fermented drink. I did this so that you might know that I am the LORD your God.

⁷When you reached this place, Sihon king of Heshbon and Og king of Bashan came out to fight against us, but we defeated them. ⁸We took their land and gave it as an inheritance to the Reubenites, the Gadites and the half-tribe of Manasseh.

⁹Carefully follow the terms of this covenant, so that you may prosper in everything you do.

COMMENTARY

2–3 [1–2] As is typical in Deuteronomy, covenantal exhortation is preceded here by a reflection on Yahweh's acts of deliverance in bringing the Israelites out of Egypt (McConville, 414). Moses'

reference to what Israel had seen Yahweh do in their behalf in Egypt (29:1–2) echoes Moses' words when Israel was encamped at the base of Mount Sinai, where he explained to them the divine rationale for the law (Ex 19:4: "You yourselves have seen what I did to Egypt, and how I carried you on eagles' wings and brought you to myself"). This historical summary serves as a motivation for action (cf. 1:30–32; 11:2–7).

God's intent was for Israel to witness his powerful deeds when he delivered them from Egypt and to trust him to guide them throughout the wilderness and give them victory against the Canaanites (Hall, 432). Deuteronomy 1 depicted Israel's earlier failure to trust Yahweh even though he had performed great miracles before their eyes. Although the terms "miraculous signs and great wonders" in 29:3 draw readers' attention to the ten plagues and Yahweh's deliverance of Israel from Egypt, the pair may serve more broadly to refer to Israel's pilgrimage from the time of their departure from Egypt to their present encampment at Moab (Barker, *The Triumph of Grace*, 117–18).

The repetition of the verb "to see" and the repeated reference to "eyes" emphasizes that God's people had personally witnessed what Yahweh had done in their behalf. For this new generation, some of whom had not themselves witnessed those events in Egypt or at the Red Sea, Moses makes it clear that this indictment for failing to trust Yahweh was not simply based on hearsay evidence from some previous generation. God had continued to intervene miraculously in Israel's affairs even after their rebellion at Kadesh Barnea. And they continued to lack the spiritual perception that they should have had.

4 [3] The rebuke presented by this verse is powerful for several reasons. While the verb "to see" in 29:2–3 refers to those acts of divine intervention that Israel saw with their own "eyes," the reference in v.4 to eyes that do not see presents an abrupt contrast. Also, historical remembrances of Yahweh's activity in their behalf immediately precede and follow 29:4 (29:2–3, 5–8). This triad of heart, eyes, and ears occurs in only one other place with

a similar significance — Isaiah 6:10, where Yahweh tells the prophet Isaiah that the Israelites will not generally be responsive to his message. The repeated mention of these three organs emphasizes Israel's ability to understand God's dealings with the nation.

The "heart," in addition to signifying the physical organ, often connotes "the seat of understanding and knowledge" (Ridderbos, 264) or the "organ of understanding" (Driver, 321). Deuteronomy also makes clear exactly what God's people are supposed to know. In 29:6 Moses affirms that Israel's wanderings in the wilderness took place "so that you might know [*yd^c*] that I am the LORD your God!" (cf. 4:35, 39; 7:9). These passages and others affirm that God expected his chosen people "to understand and acknowledge that the one they know as the Lord, who has acted powerfully, redemptively, and providentially in their history, is God and God alone" (Miller, 205). However, according to Deuteronomy 29:4 God did not give them "a mind that understands."

The "eyes" and "ears," in addition to being organs for physical sight and hearing, refer to "the capacity of moral and spiritual perception (Is. 6:10; 32:3)" (Driver, 321). The expression "before your eyes" (*l^e^{c}êneykā*) occurs eleven times in Deuteronomy, seven of which occurrences refer to important covenantal acts performed before God's chosen people, i.e., "before the eyes" of all Israel: Yahweh's deliverance of Israel from Egypt (1:30; 4:34; 6:22), Moses' breaking the tablets (9:17), Moses' exhortation that Joshua be courageous (31:7), the miraculous deeds performed by Moses (34:12), and Israel's future experience of covenantal curses (28:31). The combination of the verb "to see" and the noun "eyes" refers to Yahweh's defeat of Sihon and Og (3:21), his judgment on the Israelite rebels at Baal Peor (4:3), his deliverance of Israel from Egypt (4:9; 7:19; 11:7; 29:2), and the future experience of covenantal curse (28:32, 34, 67).

Throughout Deuteronomy, these references to eyes and seeing consistently highlight acts of divine deliverance and providential care. Weinfeld (*Deuteronomy and the Deuteronomic School*, 173) writes that the purpose of this repeated emphasis on "seeing" and "eyes" serves "to implant in his listeners the feeling that they themselves have experienced the awe-inspiring events of the Exodus." There is no doubt that this seeing is not an end in itself, but rather a means to an end. In the present passage, Moses makes use of sight to heighten the contrast between what Israel saw physically and what they perceived (or did not perceive) spiritually. Although the Israelites saw the many miraculous activities of Yahweh in their behalf (29:2), they did not really "see" what God was doing because Yahweh had not given them eyes to see (29:4; cf. Jer 5:21; see Reflection, below). "Heart" and "eyes" occur five times in Deuteronomy (4:9; 11:18; 15:9; 28:65, 67) as parallel terms (without "ears") referring to the internalization of what is seen, taught, or heard.

Although the "ear" is not referred to often in Deuteronomy (5:1; 15:17; 31:11, 28, 30; 32:44 — in all but 15:17 for physical hearing), the command "to hear" occurs abundantly in the book (ninety times, most frequently in chs. 4–5, 28, and 30). Moses repeatedly exhorts God's chosen people to listen to and heed the voice of God, i.e., his instruction and teaching embodied in all the commandments, statutes, and ordinances that constituted the Mosaic law (Miller, 205). When followed by the noun "voice" (with a prefixed preposition b^e), to "hear" means to obey (nineteen times [4:30; 8:20; 9:23; 28:1–2, 15, 45, 62; 30:2, 8, 10, 20; et al.]). It means "to do what Yahweh says and wants" (Schult, *TLOT*, 3:1379). Also, when this verb occurs in covenantal contexts within a relationship of sovereignty

and submission, to hear Yahweh means to obey him (ibid.). The addition of "ears" to make up the triad of "heart," "eyes," and "ears" seems to add emphasis to Yahweh's statement. God had not given his chosen people "ears to hear."

This inability to perceive has lasted "to this day" (v.4), an expression that generally extends whatever is described in the context to the day of the reader or listener (and beyond). By using this phrase, Moses makes his audience aware that this problem of spiritual perception is not just an issue that plagued the previous generation, who died in the wilderness. It continues to be a problem of national significance for those camped on the plains of Moab. Sadly, the events of the exodus and the wanderings in the wilderness have not caused Israel to reach a full understanding of Yahweh's ultimate purposes for them.

5–6 [4–5] During their lengthy wanderings, instead of providing for their physical needs via normal means, the Lord sustained them through his gracious provision. By limiting Israel's sources of food to manna, Yahweh drove his children to utter dependence on him. What God does, gives evidence of who he is (cf. Ex 6:7; 7:5, 17; 8:10, 22; 9:14; 10:2; 14:4; Eze 6:7, 10, 13–14; et al.).

7–8 [6–7] Upon reaching the region of Transjordan, the Lord gave into Israel's hands the entire territory of Heshbon and Bashan to serve as part of Israel's tribal inheritance (see comments on 2:26–3:11).

9 [8] In the light of God's repeated faithfulness to his children, the Israelites should obey his commands so that they might enjoy the covenantal blessings of the Lord. The exhortation to wholehearted obedience of Yahweh's covenantal demands is again predicated on his abundant acts of faithfulness in behalf of his covenantal nation.

NOTES

4 [3] Regarding לֵב לָדַעַת (*lēb lādaʿat*, "a heart to know"), the noun *lēb* (or *lēbāb*) occurs fifty-one times in the book of Deuteronomy, and it occurs in general proximity with the verb "to know" in five other passages (4:39; 8:2, 5; 13:4; 18:21). Verse 4 especially resonates with Deuteronomy 8:2–5, which deals with Israel's capacity to keep the covenant with Yahweh. In that passage Moses writes that Yahweh tested Israel (by means of their wanderings in the wilderness) to discern (יד״ע, *ydʿ*) what was "in their heart" (לְבָב, *lēbāb*; 8:2). He then exhorts them to "know [יד״ע, *ydʿ*] in your heart [לְבָב, *lēbāb*]" that Yahweh disciplines Israel as a father would discipline his son (8:5). This inability to perceive also reminds the reader of 9:4–6, in which Moses indicts Israel for a disposition to covenantal treachery. Similarly, Yahweh wanted his chosen people to know (יד״ע, *ydʿ*) his purpose for wiping out the Canaanites (9:4–6). See Barker (*The Triumph of Grace*, 119) for several other words shared by Deuteronomy 8:2–5 and 29:1–3.

The phrase עַד הַיּוֹם הַזֶּה (*ʿad hayyôm hazzeh*, "until this day") occurs five other times in Deuteronomy (2:22; 3:14 [see Note]; 10:8; 11:4; 34:6). In none of these cases is there any indication that the situation relating to "until this day" is about to change or is in the process of changing (Barker, *The Triumph of Grace*, 118–19). Although in a few instances (3:14; 29:28; 34:6) this expression seems to point to a time later than Moses', it aptly fits Moses' day in most of its occurrences in Deuteronomy.

9 [8] Since the verb represented in וּשְׁמַרְתֶּם (*ûšᵉmartem*, "therefore, keep") follows several *wayyiqtol* (narrative) forms, the translation "and you kept" may at first seem preferable. However, Waltke and O'Connor (*IBHS*, 532–33, §32.2.3d) point out that in certain contexts, especially in legal literature, a perfect verb with a prefixed waw (here called a *wᵉqatal*) following one or more *wayyiqtol* forms "takes on a subordinate volitional force." According to the theology of Deuteronomy, Israel should show future obedience to God on the basis of his past gracious acts in their behalf. Here, as elsewhere, the verb in question (*wᵉqatal*) represents the entreaty form, and the preceding verbs (*wayyiqtol*) signify the past acts on which that entreaty is based.

REFLECTION

Was Israel able to do what Yahweh demanded of them?

The nation of Israel's penchant for rebellion and their imperceptiveness of Yahweh's dealings are not unheard of. In Moses' first speech he clearly demonstrated that seeing is not the same as believing. Their witness of God's stupendous deliverance of them from Egypt did not prevent God's people from outright rebellion at Kadesh Barnea (1:19–46). What God had done "there and then" seemed to have no impact on his covenantal people "here and now." In addition, the problem Israel faced did not involve a lack of clarity concerning God's expectations. Even in this passage, Yahweh says that he had delivered and cared for them "so that you might know [*ydʿ*] that I am the LORD your God" (29:6; cf. 4:35; 7:9; 9:3). Yahweh desired that his chosen people know (in a way that transformed their lives) that "the Lord, who has acted powerfully, redemptively, and providentially in their history, is God and God alone" (Miller, 205).

Although the entire book of Deuteronomy makes it abundantly clear that Israel was, for the most part, a rebellious nation, the central point of 29:3–4 is the fact that God gives or does not give his people the ability to understand what he has done, is doing, and will do for them as his covenantal nation. According to v.4, the Israelites still lack "the moral understanding that can produce right action" (McConville, 415). If this verse means that only God can give the perception necessary to understand the ultimate significance of historical realities and that God had not given Israel this perceptive ability, how could God have held the rebellious generation of Israelites responsible for its faithlessness?

First, Deuteronomy 29–30 have a national focus. In these chapters, as in the rest of the book, Moses always has the nation of Israel in mind as his audience. Yahweh's expectation of the nation and the fate or destiny of the nation are always in view. The Mosaic covenant (better called the Israelite covenant) was made with the entire nation (Ex 19:7–8). Moses opens ch. 29 with a call for "all Israel" to listen to his message. Since the Mosaic covenant was established between Yahweh and the nation of Israel, the exhortations and instruction throughout Deuteronomy always have the nation in mind (though not to the exclusion of individual Israelites).

Second, one must consider the nature of the Mosaic covenant. Although Yahweh established this covenant with the entire nation of Israel, not all the Israelites who made up that nation were believers. After the original establishment of this covenant, each new generation of Israelites automatically became participants in it by virtue of their physical birth and external circumcision (R. Showers, *The New Nature* [Neptune, N.J.: Loizeaux Brothers, 1986], 33). Because the majority of Israelites were unregenerate, "they were enslaved by their con-

firmed, sinful dispositions of enmity against God" (ibid., 33).

Consequently, not only did they fail to live in accordance with Yahweh's covenantal expectations, but as well they were absolutely unable to do so (Ro 8:7). Only when Yahweh wrote his law on their heart (i.e., "radical surgery") would Israel be able to avoid rebellion and live in genuine submission to his demands. The promise of the new covenant later in Jeremiah refers to that very phenomenon (Jer 31:31–34). Although Judah's sin is written on the heart of God's chosen nation in general, God's law will be written on the heart of every Israelite in that new-covenant setting.

In this regard, it is essential to notice a key difference between the nature of the Mosaic covenant and the new covenant. Since the Mosaic covenant included believing and unbelieving Israelites, participating in that covenant did not necessarily include an internal conformity to Yahweh's requirements. God's law was not written on the heart of an Israelite as a necessary or automatic part of participating in the Mosaic covenant. Israel's perpetual hardheartedness (Ps 95:8; Eze 3:7; Zec 7:12), stiffened neck (Dt 9:6, 13; 10:16; 31:27; 2Ki 17:14; Jer 7:26; 17:23; 19:15), and stubbornness (Ne 9:29; Isa 30:1; 65:2; Jer 6:28; Hos 4:16; 9:15; Zec 7:11) make this reality abundantly clear.

Although the Mosaic covenant was external in nature, it would be incorrect to conclude that it had nothing to do with an Israelite's internal disposition. After giving the Ten Commandments to Moses, Yahweh declares: "Oh, that their hearts would be inclined to fear me and keep all my commands always, so that it might go well with them and their children forever!" (Dt 5:29; cf. 1Sa 16:7; Ps 40:8 [9]; Pr 3:1; 4:23). It would not be until the inauguration of the new covenant that *every* participant in this covenantal relationship would have an internal spiritual reality. Consequently, as Wright (*Deuteronomy,*

286) points out, "the persistent and wholly culpable failure of Israel to make the right response to God and to live accordingly was indeed because the gift was not yet *fully* given" (emphasis mine).

Third, the OT both assumes and presents an internal spiritual reality for God's people. In Deuteronomy 10:12–13, when Moses summarized Yahweh's expectations of his covenantal nation, he affirmed that God wanted his chosen people "to fear the LORD your God, to walk in all his ways, to love him, to serve the LORD your God with all your heart and with all your soul, and to observe the LORD's commands and decrees." His description of God's expectations of Israel clearly does not ignore practical obedience to specific laws, but it does place the focus on Yahweh's expectation of obedience from the heart.

As well, the "loyalty language" of Deuteronomy (some of which is seen in 10:12–13) provides abundant evidence that Yahweh's demands of his covenantal nation were primarily internal in their emphasis. Moses uses various "covenantal" verbs to refer to the multifaceted nature of Yahweh's expec-

tations of his covenantal people. Notice the following collections of these terms.

6:13	fear, serve, take oaths in his name
8:6	observe, walk, revere
10:12–13	fear, walk, love, serve, observe
10:19–20	fear, serve, hold fast, take oaths in his name
11:1	love, keep
11:13	obey/hear, love, serve
11:22	carefully observe, love, walk, hold fast
13:3–5	love, follow, revere, keep, obey/hear, serve, hold fast
13:18	obey/hear, keep, do what is right
19:9	follow, love, walk
30:20	love, obey/listen, hold fast

Finally, the suggestion that OT believers were unable to live in accordance with the covenantal stipulations established by Yahweh in a way that honored and pleased him flies in the face of another passage in Deuteronomy, namely, 30:11–14 (see comments there).

2. The Significance and Scope of This Covenantal Renewal (29:10–15 [9–14])

OVERVIEW

Tigay (*Deuteronomy*, 277) suggests that the verses in this section are organized in a chiastic pattern with the covenantal formula, its focal point, at the center:

A You [present generation] stand ... this day before the LORD your God (vv. 10–11)
    B to enter the covenant ... which the LORD ... is concluding ... with its sanctions (v. 12)
        C that he may establish you as his people and be your God (v. 13)
    B' I am concluding this covenant ... with its sanctions (v. 14)
A' Those standing here ... this day before the LORD our God and [future generations] (v. 14)

The entire reason for Israel's existence as a covenantal nation and for their gathering to renew their commitment to this covenant is Yahweh's position as their covenantal Lord, who remains fixed in his commitment to his covenantal people.

> ¹⁰All of you are standing today in the presence of the LORD your God — your leaders and chief men, your elders and officials, and all the other men of Israel, ¹¹together with your children and your wives, and the aliens living in your camps who chop your wood and carry your water. ¹²You are standing here in order to enter into a covenant with the LORD your God, a covenant the LORD is making with you this day and sealing with an oath, ¹³to confirm you this day as his people, that he may be your God as he promised you and as he swore to your fathers, Abraham, Isaac and Jacob. ¹⁴I am making this covenant, with its oath, not only with you ¹⁵who are standing here with us today in the presence of the LORD our God but also with those who are not here today.

COMMENTARY

10–11 [9–10] Moses describes the comprehensive nature of this covenantal renewal. This listing of diverse individuals demonstrates that the entire believing community, without reference to social, economic, gender, or age differences, has been invited to enter into a covenantal relationship with Yahweh.

12–13 [11–12] The primary function of this gathering of the Israelites is to renew the covenant the Lord originally made with Israel at Sinai, with the result that they may serve him as his people and he will be their God (along with all the obligations that accompany those relationships). Merrill (*Deuteronomy*, 379) points out:

It is important to remember that this was not so much a ceremony of covenant making as it was one of covenant affirmation or renewal. The original covenant had been made at Horeb, so what was in view here was the Lord's offer of the same covenant (albeit, with necessary amendments) to the next generation of Israelites. Arrangements agreed to by their parents were not sufficient for them. They also had to go on record as committing themselves to the Lord and his theocratic program.

14–15 [13–14] This covenant and its obligations concern not only the Israelites gathered in that day, but all future generations as well. In ch. 5, Moses had emphasized the relevance of the Sinaitic covenant to the Israelites camped at Moab, many of whom were born after the one-year stay at Mount Horeb (see comments there). In this passage Moses looks forward instead of backward. He stresses the continuity of this covenant from the present audience to all future generations.

NOTES

10 [9] In several passages the verb represented in אַתֶּם נִצָּבִים (ʾattem niṣṣābîm, "you stand") has a religious connotation for people assembling together (1) to select a king (1Sa 10:19), (2) to make (Dt 29:10) or renew (Jos 24:1) a covenant, or (3) to formally discharge someone from office (1Sa 12:7, 16; Reindl, *TDOT*, 9:528). It implies some kind of formal arrangement (Craigie, 356, n. 4). A less formal verb for "stand" occurs in v.15 and serves to frame the passage (and the chiastic structure; see above).

The phrase רָאשֵׁיכֶם שִׁבְטֵיכֶם (rāʾšêkem šibṭêkem, "your heads, your tribes") presents a vexing textual problem. As it stands, "your heads, your tribes" presents an unclear meaning (though preserved in many English translations [NASB, NCV, NIV, NKJV, NLT, NRSV]). The simplest solution is to leave it as is (even though its meaning is unclear). Some interpreters give the second word a unique meaning (e.g., "leaders" instead of "tribes"). Others emend the second word to "judges" (שֹׁפְטֵיכֶם, šōpᵉṭêkem, which looks somewhat similar; e.g., Driver, 322; Merrill, *Deuteronomy*, 378; TEV). One could emend the first word to read "heads of" (regarding the suffix "your" as added by dittography from the second word), resulting in "the heads/chiefs of your tribes." Finally, the two words as they stand could be a rare variant of the construct relationship and mean "the heads/chiefs of your tribes" (A. Sperber, *A Historical Grammar of Biblical Hebrew* [Leiden: Brill, 1966], 610 [citing Ge 9:5; 37:27; Dt 18:15; 23:25; and this passage as examples]. The last option seems the best, since there is some grammatical evidence for it and since it provides a clearer meaning for the two words. Also, the MT's reading is the more difficult reading and probably should be retained.

12, 14 [11, 13] The noun אָלָה (ʾālâ ["curse" or "oath"; *HALOT*, 51], in the construction וּבְאָלָתוֹ, ûbᵉʾālātô, "with its sanctions") occurs six times in Deuteronomy, five of which are in ch. 29 (see also vv.20–21). In three of those instances it is juxtaposed with "covenant" (בְּרִית, bᵉrît): "enter into a covenant … sealing with an oath" (v. 12), "the covenant, with its oath" (v.14), and "all the curses of the covenant" (v.21). Several English translations regard the term as having a positive sense: "into the sworn covenant" (ESV), "and a promise" (NCV), "and sealing with an oath" (NIV), and "sworn by an oath" (NRSV). Interestingly, these translations switch to "curse" in vv.19–21 (NASB, NCV) or vv.20–21 (ESV, NIV, NRSV).

The translation "oath" does not communicate the term's central idea, namely, "curse" (H. Brichto, *The Problem of "Curse" in the Hebrew Bible* [Philadelphia: Society of Biblical Literature and Exegesis, 1963], 25–31, esp. 28–31). The Tanak renders the expression "with its sanctions." Merrill (*Deuteronomy*, 379) suggests that "covenant" and "oath" comprise a hendiadys expressing the covenantal relationship as a whole, while Craigie, 357, suggests that these two terms highlight both the renewal of the relationship as well as the legacy into which Israel will enter. It seems more appropriate to render it as the Tanak does or as a hendiadys, "a covenant enforced by sanctions" (cf. Tigay, *Deuteronomy*, 278). R. Gordon (*NIDOTTE*, 1:403–4) points out that אָלָה (ʾālâ) "is properly a curse by which a person is bound to an obligation that is most often contractual in nature." The following verses (vv.20–21) delineate the curses that would befall the person who committed covenantal treachery.

13 [12] The Hiphil form of the verb קוּם (*qûm*), in הָקִים־אֹתְךָ (*hāqîm-ʾōtᵉkā*, "to affirm/confirm you"), occurs regularly to speak of establishing and/or ratifying an already existing agreement (such as a covenant; cf. Ge 6:18; 9:9, 11; 17:19, 21; Ex 6:4; Dt 8:18; 9:5; Merrill, *Deuteronomy*, 379–80; cf. W. J. Dumbrell, *Covenant and Creation* [Nashville: Nelson, 1984], 25–26; Martens, *NIDOTTE*, 3:903–4).

15 [14] In the phrase אֲשֶׁר יֶשְׁנוֹ פֹּה עִמָּנוּ עֹמֵד הַיּוֹם (*ʾᵃšer yešnô pōh ʿimmānû ʿōmēd hayyôm*, "who are standing here with us today"), Moses piles up terms to emphasize that he is addressing the generation of Israelites who are camped in Moab, on the brink of entering the Promised Land. The four terms could be rendered literally, "he is, here, with us ... today." The last three terms also occur in 5:3 (though substituting a different preposition for "with") in a similar "overstatement." Moses goes on to say that this covenantal renewal is also made "with those who are not here today," literally, "he is not, here, with us, today." The only difference is that the first line has the particle of existence (יֵשׁ, *yēš*), whereas the second line has the particle of nonexistence (אֵין, *ʾayin*).

3. The Results of Covenantal Treachery (29:16–28 [15–27])

OVERVIEW

Moses describes the painful consequences, for the individual and for the nation, of failing to obey the covenantal stipulations. His warning here suggests that God's chosen people had been tempted by idolatry and had defected from Yahweh in the past. That reality adds weight to Moses' concern that Israel might do the same in the future. Moses looks to the future from the perspective of his time (29:16–21) and then looks back hypothetically from some future day (29:22–28).

a. From Moses' Present Perspective, Looking to the Future (29:16–21 [15–20])

¹⁶You yourselves know how we lived in Egypt and how we passed through the countries on the way here. ¹⁷You saw among them their detestable images and idols of wood and stone, of silver and gold. ¹⁸Make sure there is no man or woman, clan or tribe among you today whose heart turns away from the LORD our God to go and worship the gods of those nations; make sure there is no root among you that produces such bitter poison.

¹⁹When such a person hears the words of this oath, he invokes a blessing on himself and therefore thinks, "I will be safe, even though I persist in going my own way." This will bring disaster on the watered land as well as the dry. ²⁰The LORD will never be willing to forgive him; his wrath and zeal will burn against that man. All the curses written in this book will fall upon him, and the LORD will blot out his name from under heaven. ²¹The LORD will single him out from all the tribes of Israel for disaster, according to all the curses of the covenant written in this Book of the Law.

COMMENTARY

16–18 [15–17] Moses warns individual Israelites against thinking that since the nation was involved in this covenantal relationship with Yahweh, their own conduct is not essential to the fate of the nation. He reminds them of the various forms and instruments of idolatry they had seen on their pilgrimage from Egypt to Moab. He uses unique descriptive terms to highlight their vile and detestable nature. Drawing on Deuteronomy 13 and 17:2–7 (cf. 21:9, 21; 22:21), he prohibits any Israelite from worshiping any god other than Israel's incomparable God.

The series "man or woman, clan or tribe" begins with the individual because God holds each one accountable. He is not looking just for "group" obedience. He ends with corporate terms because entire cities and tribes could devote themselves to some horrible form of covenantal treachery (as with, e.g., the tribe of Benjamin [Jdg 19–21]). To worship other gods was tantamount to turning one's heart "away from the LORD our God" (29:18; cf. 30:17; 31:18; Lev 19:4). An individual's choosing to worship false gods affects many others besides him or her. A covenantal rebel is like a single root that produces abundant poisonous fruit (Driver, 325). Bitterness often signifies the devastating affects of idolatry (Pr 5:4; Jer 9:15 [14]; 23:15; La 3:15, 19; Am 5:7; 6:12).

19–21 [18–20] Any Israelite who worships other gods and hopes to escape divine judgment by some deceptive means can expect to experience the full force of covenantal curse. Moses depicts an individual Israelite who, upon hearing the covenantal curses and the judgment they pronounce on idolatry, thinks he can escape that curse and still worship false gods. The clause at the end of this verse can be rendered literally, "thus destroying the watered with the parched." The expression appears to be a proverbial observation employing a figure of speech called a merism, which suggests totality by referring to two polar elements. This clause affirms that the Israelite who violates the letter and even the spirit of the covenant will harm not only himself but also everything he touches—"the watered and the parched" (NET note). Although the sin might appear hidden and committed by only one person, it will affect the entire nation.

To highlight the severity of the divine judgment this person will experience, Moses makes five powerful statements: Yahweh will never be willing to forgive him, his zealous wrath will burn against him, all the covenantal curses will fall on him, Yahweh will blot out his name (see Note on 7:24), and the Lord will single him out for disaster or calamity. In this covenantal relationship between Israel and Yahweh, there are no secret sins in the ultimate sense.

NOTES

17 [16] In the phrase אֶת־שִׁקּוּצֵיהֶם וְאֵת גִּלֻּלֵיהֶם (ʾet-šiqqûṣêhem weʾēt gillûlêhem, "their detestable images … and their idols"), the terms for idols emphasize their offensive nature. The term שִׁקּוּץ (šiqqûṣ, occurring twenty-eight times in the OT) focuses almost exclusively on certain aspects of idolatrous worship. It is used as an exact or near synonym of תּוֹעֵבָה (tôʿēbâ, "abomination"; cf. 2Ki 23:13; Jer 16:18; Eze 5:11; 7:20; 11:18, 21). Whether or not the Israelites loathe the שִׁקּוּצֵיהֶם (šiqqûṣêhem), i.e., forbidden pagan practices, clearly demonstrates their spiritual condition and serves as an indication of their coming fate. The prophet Hosea

(Hos 9:10) describes how Israel changed from being a beloved nation to a שִׁקּוּץ (*šiqqûṣ*), a detestable nation. The term generally signifies anything Yahweh regards as detestable (Grisanti, *NIDOTTE*, 4:244–45). The other noun, גִּלֻּלֵיהֶם (*gillûlêhem*), may come from the root גֵּל (*gēl*), "dung," and consequently carry the unsavory appellation of these idols as "dung things" (Preuss, *TDOT*, 3:2). These two terms occur together in Ezekiel 20:30–31.

20 [19] The phrase אַף־יְהוָה וְקִנְאָתוֹ (*ʾap-yhwh wᵉqinʾātô*, "his intense anger" [NET]) could be translated literally, "the anger of Yahweh and his zeal." However, the two nouns in the phrase form a nominal hendiadys, i.e., a figure in which the second noun functions as an adjective modifying the first (NET note).

b. From a Distant Future Perspective, Looking Back (29:22–28 [21–27])

OVERVIEW

In a hypothetical scenario in which the nation of Israel has disobeyed the stipulations of the covenant and has been judged appropriately, later generations of Israelites as well as the nations of the world will be amazed at the destruction that has fallen on Israel. They will learn that the cause of all this sorrow was Israel's violation of their covenant with the Lord by worshiping other gods.

---

²²Your children who follow you in later generations and foreigners who come from distant lands will see the calamities that have fallen on the land and the diseases with which the Lord has afflicted it. ²³The whole land will be a burning waste of salt and sulfur—nothing planted, nothing sprouting, no vegetation growing on it. It will be like the destruction of Sodom and Gomorrah, Admah and Zeboiim, which the Lord overthrew in fierce anger. ²⁴All the nations will ask: "Why has the Lord done this to this land? Why this fierce, burning anger?"

²⁵And the answer will be: "It is because this people abandoned the covenant of the Lord, the God of their fathers, the covenant he made with them when he brought them out of Egypt. ²⁶They went off and worshiped other gods and bowed down to them, gods they did not know, gods he had not given them. ²⁷Therefore the Lord's anger burned against this land, so that he brought on it all the curses written in this book. ²⁸In furious anger and in great wrath the Lord uprooted them from their land and thrust them into another land, as it is now."

COMMENTARY

22–24 [21–23] Because of Israel's future covenantal treachery, Yahweh will bring such severe judgment against Israel that future Israelites and pagans will ask in bewilderment, "Why did Yahweh do this to his servant-nation?" They will see the carnage left behind by "calamities" (28:59, 61) and "disease" (cf. 28:21, 60, using different Hebrew words). Likening the land of Israel to the devastation caused by Yahweh's destruction of Sodom and Gomorrah, the land will be characterized as "brimstone, salt, and burning debris" (NET).

Sodom and Gomorrah often serve in the OT as a paradigm for God's destructive judgment (Isa 1:9; 13:19; Jer 49:18; 50:40; Am 4:11; Zep 2:9; Admah and Zeboiim were located near Sodom and Gomorrah, probably near the southern end of the Dead Sea). Three distinct statements emphatically affirm that the land will be totally denuded of vegetation ("nothing planted, nothing sprouting, no vegetation growing on it"). The land "flowing with milk and honey" (see comments and Note on 6:3) will be divested of any evidence of fertility and abundance—a reversal of Yahweh's provision of the Promised Land. The sentiment of horror and amazement expressed by these future onlookers is attested elsewhere in the OT experience of horror

(1 Ki 9:6–9; Jer 19:8; 22:8–9; 49:17; 50:13; Eze 27:35–36).

25–28 [24–27] The answer to the question "Why?" (v.24) is given without equivocation: Israel's covenantal treachery constitutes the primary grounds for this horrible judgment. Idolatry—an act of absolute disloyalty—was the paradigmatic sin in the context of Israel's relationship with Yahweh. Even though the incomparable God, the only God of the universe, chose to establish a covenantal relationship with the nation of Israel, his chosen people abandoned that unique relationship and pursued gods they had not known by experience, i.e., gods that had done nothing to demonstrate the compelling need to offer them worship.

Because of that rebellion, Yahweh (according to the depicted scenario) brought upon his covenantal people the curses delineated in chs. 27–28. Using two verbs of violence, he "uprooted" them from their land and "thrust" them into a foreign land, away from the place of covenantal blessing—all this for the opportunity to worship gods that are lifeless and powerless!

NOTES

22 [21] The phrase הַדּוֹר הָאַחֲרוֹן (haddôr hāʾaḥᵃrôn, "the generation to come") could refer to a distant future generation (Tigay, *Deuteronomy*, 281) or to "the next generation" (McConville, 412, 418). Sometimes the expression refers to a generation close enough that one can still have contact with it (Pss 48:13 [14]; 78:4, 6; 102:18 [19]; cf. Tigay, *Deuteronomy*, 281). Although this expression can refer to the next generation, it seems here to have a more distant and ambiguous perspective, i.e., some future generation.

24 [23] The wrath of Yahweh (הָאַף הַגָּדוֹל הַזֶּה; hāʾap haggādôl hazzeh, "this great anger") receives more attention in this passage than anywhere else in Deuteronomy. Here the noun אַף (ʾap) occurs five times (29:20, 23–24, 27–28) out of its twelve occurrences in the book. Other nouns that occur once include "jealousy" (קִנְאָה, qinʾâ; 29:20), "heated anger" (חֳרִי, ḥŏrî; 29:24), "rage" (קֶצֶף, qeṣep; 29:28), and "wrath" (חֵמָה, ḥēmâ; 29: 28). Verbs commonly associated with the expression of anger—"burn" (חמה, ḥmh; 29:27) and "smoke" (עשׁן, ʿšn; 29:20)—occur once each.

25 [24] The verbal root עזב (ʿzb, in the phrase עָזְבוּ אֶת־בְּרִית, ʿāzᵉbû ʾet-bᵉrît, "they abandoned the covenant") occurs over two hundred times in the OT and has God, the nation of Israel, and individual men and women as its subject. In various passages God speaks of having abandoned (Jer 12:7) or says that he will abandon (Dt 31:17) the nation of Israel, an individual king (2Ch 32:31), or a psalmist (Ps 71:11). In several instances the verb is negated: "God will not forsake his people" (Ge 28:15; Dt 31:6, 8). The psalmists often prayed, "Do not forsake me" (Pss 38:21 [22]; 71:9, 18; 119:8). God's covenantal nation (or citizens of that nation) at times abandoned Yahweh (Jdg 2:12–13; 2Ki 21:22), his covenant (Jer 22:9), the law (2Ch 12:1), or his statutes (1 Kgs 18:18). Less frequently, people left or abandoned other people (Ru 2:11; 2Ch 28:14). Sometimes people left something behind (Ge 39:13; 50:8) or left a city (1Ch 10:7; Alden, *NIDOTTE*, 3:364). Over half of the occurrences of this verb signify breaking the covenant Yahweh made with Israel (Dt 28:20; 29:25; 31:16; Jer 2:13, 17, 19; 22:9; Da 11:30; Grisanti, "1 Samuel," 138).

28 [27] Was the phrase כַּיּוֹם הַזֶּה (*kayyôm hazzeh*, "as it is today") written by Moses (cf. Hall, 440), or is it a post-Mosaic addition (cf. Cairns, 261; Mayes, 367) to emphasize the relevance of this answer to his day? This phrase occurs in the midst of the proposed answer to the question by the surrounding nations concerning God's future judgment of his chosen nation. Consequently, the expression "as it is this day" in reference to Israel's experience of exile could simply be part of that proposed answer, with no implication of a post-Mosaic date of composition, or could have been inserted by a later writer for special emphasis to the exilic or postexilic community. Craigie, 360, and Merrill (*Deuteronomy*, 385) regard both alternatives as worthy of consideration. But in light of the "hypothetical future" perspective of these verses, there is no compelling need to see this section as post-Mosaic.

REFLECTION

Do chs. 28 and 29 represent prophetic predictions, and if so, what kind of fulfillment should the reader look for? Although these chapters are clearly forward-looking, it would be incorrect to regard them as predictive prophecy in the strictest sense of the term. They present the threat of covenantal curse and, in this last section in particular (29:22–28), a hypothetical future scenario. Will Israel's experience of covenantal curse entail every single disease or calamity listed in ch. 28? Will the land of promise be absolutely denuded of vegetation?

Israel's experience of covenantal curse in the Assyrian and Babylonian exiles certainly did not bring about those disastrous effects to the degree envisioned in these passages. It seems that this last section of ch. 29 presents what might happen to Israel, not a prophecy of something that would happen inevitably. Israel's obedient or disobedient conduct would determine exactly what fate or destiny the nation received from God's hand. The threat of devastation was not sure and certain. It was possible, but not inevitable (Craigie, 360–61). It appears best to recognize that Moses makes use of stock covenantal terminology to communicate graphically the horrific nature and impact of covenantal curse in chs. 28 and 29.

4. Live Faithfully in the Light of God's Revelation (29:29[28])

²⁹The secret things belong to the Lᴏʀᴅ our God, but the things revealed belong to us and to our children forever, that we may follow all the words of this law.

COMMENTARY

29 [28] Knowing that the people's tendency would be to speculate concerning the future, which is only known and controlled by the Lord, Moses exhorts the children of Israel to live faithfully in the light of what has been revealed to them, namely, God's law and his promise of blessing for obedience or cursing for disobedience. Many individuals use this verse as a "catch-all" category for some verse, theological issue, or divine activity they do not understand. What are the "secret things" and the "revealed things" and how do they relate to the immediate context? Do they primarily look backward or forward?

Tigay (*Deuteronomy*, 283) relates this passage to concealed and overt sins. Concealed sins are known to God, and he will punish them. God requires that his followers punish the overt sins, however. Especially in light of the contextual treatment of an individual who tries to practice idolatry in secret, Tigay contends that God will not hold the nation collectively responsible for sins committed by individuals in secret. God will, however, punish those individuals; he will hold the nation responsible only if they fail to effect punishment for sins of whose commission they are aware.

Merrill (*Deuteronomy*, 385) and Craigie, 360–61, suggest that this verse has a backward-looking or narrow perspective. In light of the threat of devastation given in the preceding verses and the

conundrum it would occasion in the minds of God's chosen people (wrestling with the concepts of the continuation of Israel and their apparent termination), this verse directs their attention toward what they know to be true. Even though God's plans for his covenantal nation ("the secret things") may elude the comprehension of his children, he has given them something sure and certain ("the revealed things")—"the words of this law." To go beyond God's revelation and speculate about future events is not humankind's prerogative but God's.

Ridderbos, 268, and Wright (*Deuteronomy*, 293) conclude that this verse has a forward-looking or broad outlook. The "secret things" refer to the future that God alone knows, i.e., anything that has not been revealed. The expression "revealed things" connotes God's known law, which can be obeyed.

Primarily, this passage affirms that God has made it clear what he expects from his children. Their responsibility is not to wonder about the future but to live in accordance with his expectations. Yahweh is fully capable of taking care of those issues beyond human comprehension and control. What he expects of his children is that they live in the light of the knowledge he has graciously given to them. Having said that, and secondarily, since the human mind is bound by its finitude, it will never be possible to know all things.

B. The Potential for Restoration after Repentance (30:1–10)

OVERVIEW

In order to emphasize the need for Israel to obey the Lord in the present, Moses looks forward to a future day in which, after having experienced the covenantal curses for their disobedience, the

children of Israel will return to the Lord, will be brought back to the Promised Land, and will enjoy the abundant blessings of a proper relationship with the Lord.

Scholars have offered various outlines for this passage and identified different verses as the climax or center of the section (generally v.6, vv.6–8, or v.8; cf. Wright, *Deuteronomy*, 289; Barker, *The Triumph of Grace*, 141–44; McConville, 424, respectively). The pattern of an imperfect verb followed by a chain of perfect verbs begins in vv.1, 4, and 8, thus suggesting that the passage is best divided into three sections: vv.1–3, 4–7, and 8–10. The presence of the conditional particle in v.1 (*kî*) and v.4 (*ʾim*) confirms this outline. (Although v.8 does not begin with a conditional particle, it presents a condition, something Israel must do.)

Also, the clear contrast between what Yahweh will do (vv.4b–7) and what Israel must do (v.8), coupled with the presence of the emphatic pronoun "you," suggests that a break occurs between vv.7 and 8. As Lenchak, 199, proposes, the first and third sections (vv.1–3 and vv.8–10) deal with conversion and obedience, while the middle section (vv.4–7) gives attention to the blessings Yahweh will bestow on his repentant people. Also, in light of the themes they share, vv.1–2 and 10 serve as an inclusio (an envelope structure) that emphasizes the theme of the entire section: Israel's wholehearted return to Yahweh.

[1] When all these blessings and curses I have set before you come upon you and you take them to heart wherever the LORD your God disperses you among the nations, [2] and when you and your children return to the LORD your God and obey him with all your heart and with all your soul according to everything I command you today, [3] then the LORD your God will restore your fortunes and have compassion on you and gather you again from all the nations where he scattered you. [4] Even if you have been banished to the most distant land under the heavens, from there the LORD your God will gather you and bring you back. [5] He will bring you to the land that belonged to your fathers, and you will take possession of it. He will make you more prosperous and numerous than your fathers. [6] The LORD your God will circumcise your hearts and the hearts of your descendants, so that you may love him with all your heart and with all your soul, and live. [7] The LORD your God will put all these curses on your enemies who hate and persecute you. [8] You will again obey the LORD and follow all his commands I am giving you today. [9] Then the LORD your God will make you most prosperous in all the work of your hands and in the fruit of your womb, the young of your livestock and the crops of your land. The LORD will again delight in you and make you prosperous, just as he delighted in your fathers, [10] if you obey the LORD your God and keep his commands and decrees that are written in this Book of the Law and turn to the LORD your God with all your heart and with all your soul.

COMMENTARY

1–3 Moses describes a time when the children of Israel will experience the consequences of disobeying the covenantal stipulations. In their affliction

they will call to mind the terms of the covenant and be restored to the land and its abundance (30:1). In the midst of their exile, the Israelites will realize that their own rebellion against the Lord is to blame, and they will genuinely return to the Lord ("with all your heart and with all your soul" [30:2]; cf. v.10; see Note on 6:5).

The particle (*kî*) that introduces this passage might be presenting an assumption or a time frame ("when") rather than a condition ("if"). Moses is not being skeptical by saying "if" but presenting the clear truth. Yahweh will only restore his people when they repent and turn back to him. As Wright (*Deuteronomy*, 289) points out, "After the dire curses of chapter 28 and the compressed warnings of 29:22–28, this section comes like an oxygen mask to revive hope.... God will not be defeated by Israel's response or bound and imprisoned by the past. For beyond past, present, and even future failure, stands the great covenant faithfulness of Yahweh."

Although that hope is indeed sure, the ultimate restoration of God's servant-nation is predicated on their returning to a genuine faith relationship with him (v.2). Here again we encounter the interesting interplay between divine sovereignty and human responsibility. God expects his chosen people to return to him. Nevertheless, various OT texts speak of God's bringing about a spirit of repentance and obedience among them (cf. Lev 26:40–45; Jer 30:3, 18–22; 31:23–24, 31–34; Eze 34:11–16; 36:22–36).

In response to their repentance (the condition/protasis), Yahweh will gather his chosen people from their various locations of exile and install them in the Promised Land (the conclusion/apodosis). This action will involve Yahweh's turning from his judgment on them and having compassion (see Note on 4:31) on his repentant nation. Even great distance will not hinder the accomplishment of God's plans.

Israel's repentance does not obligate Yahweh to act, but he chooses to restore his people to a place of favor. He will turn from sending judgment on them to showing favor to them and to gathering them to the land he promised them.

4–7 In the midst of sections that focus on conversion and obedience (vv.1–3, 8–10), these verses delineate the blessings Yahweh will bestow on his repentant people. Regardless of their location of exile, the Lord will regather them (v.4) to the land of his promise and will bless them even more abundantly than their ancestors (v.5). Once the Lord reinstates them in the land, he will reconstitute Israel and give them the ability to obey him and to enjoy his continued blessings. By an act of God alone, these returned Israelites and their descendants will be given the ability to love the Lord ("circumcise your hearts") and consequently experience the abundant blessings of the covenant (v.6). In addition to this great blessing, he will transfer the curses endured by the children of Israel to the nations that brought about Israel's exile (v.7).

8–10 After making it clear that Yahweh alone can remake Israel's heart (McConville, 428), Moses returns to Yahweh's expectations of his covenantal people. For Israel to enjoy the promised blessings of the covenant, they must repent, obey Yahweh, and wholeheartedly live in accordance with his covenantal demands. If they act like covenantal citizens, he will treat them as such by delighting in them and making them prosperous. This message, however, is not just for some distant generation of Israelites. The emphatic pronoun that begins v.8 (*wĕʾattâ*, "but as for you") applies the need for covenantal renewal to Moses' own audience as well.

NOTES

3 The verb שׁוּב (*šûb*; GK 8740) occurs seven times in this passage (vv.1, 2, 3 [2x], 8, 9, 10). The related noun שְׁבוּת (*šĕbût*, "restoration"; GK 8654) occurs in this verse as well (וְשָׁב ... אֶת־שְׁבוּתְךָ, *wĕšāb ... ʾet- šĕbûtĕkā*, "restore your fortunes"; see comments below). This passage employs this word family repeatedly to emphasize dramatically the "inversion of the course of history and restoration of the happy past" (A. Rofé, "The Covenant in the Land of Moab (Dt 28,69–30,20)," in *Das Deuteronomium: Entstehung, Gestalt, und Botschaft* [ed. N. Lohfink; Leuven: Leuven Univ. Press, 1985], 311). Although scholars have argued over the etymology of the noun שְׁבוּת (šᵉbût), it seems best to treat the phrase as a whole (the verb with the noun). On literary grounds the phrase seems to mean "restore to an earlier state of well-being" (J. Bracke, "*šûb šᵉbût*: A Reappraisal," *ZAW* 97 [1985]: 244), i.e., "God's reversal of his judgment" (233). When Israel returns to Yahweh, he will reverse the curses threatened in Deuteronomy 28.

Although most translations combine the two verbs וְשָׁב וְקִבֶּצְךָ (wᵉšāb wᵉqibbeṣkā) as "he will gather you again" (ESV, NASB, NIV, NKJV, NLT, NRSV), in light of the repeated use of the verb שׁוּב (šûb) for some kind of reversal it seems best to translate them distinctly: "he will turn and gather" (cf. McConville, 422; W. Holladay, *The Root Šûb in the Old Testament with Particular Reference to Its Usage in Covenantal Contexts* [Leiden: Brill, 1958], 68–69). A similar construction occurs in v.8, where Israel will turn and obey Yahweh (cf. 30:9).

6 The verb מוּל (mûl, in the phrase וּמָל ... אֶת־לְבָבְךָ, ûmāl ... ʾet-lᵉbābᵉkā, "and he will circumcise ... your heart"), occurs thirty-two times in the OT and means "to circumcise" (thirteen times, Qal stem) or "to circumcise oneself" or "to be circumcised" (nineteen times, Niphal stem). The object of this verb can be the person himself (Ge 17:10, 12–13, 26–27; 21:4; 34:15, 22, 24; Ex 12:44, 48; Jos 5:2–5, 7), "the flesh of the foreskin" (בְּשַׂר עָרְלָה, bᵉśar ʿorlâ; Ge 17:11, 14, 23–25; Lev 12:3), the "foreskin" (עָרְלָה, ʿorlâ; Jer 9:25 [24]), "the flesh of the heart" (עָרְלַת לְבָב, ʿorlat lēbāb; Dt 10:16; Jer 4:4), or "the heart" (לְבָב, lēbāb; Dt 30:6). In all but three passages (Dt 10:16; 30:6; Jer 4:4) the verb describes the physical act of circumcision.

Scholars have offered three categories of meaning for spiritual circumcision: removal of something (Christensen, *Deuteronomy 21:10–34:12*, 739; Nelson, 137; Ridderbos, 142; cf. 270; Tigay, *Deuteronomy*, 108; NET) or cleansing (NET note on 10:16; Phillips, 1973: 76), sensitivity to God (Cairns, 111; Driver, 125; Thompson, 149), and internal conformity to God's expectations (Craigie, 205; Fabry, *TDOT*, 7:433; Merrill, *Deuteronomy*, 388; McConville, 200; Wright, *Deuteronomy*, 151). Just as external conformity demonstrated internal conformity to the demands of the Abrahamic covenant, spiritual circumcision manifests internal conformity to Yahweh's requirements.

REFLECTION

How do 10:16 and 30:6 harmonize?

How should one explain the "tension" between Yahweh's demand that Israel circumcise their hearts (10:16) and his own promise to circumcise their hearts (30:6)? The fact that Israel's "story" is one in which the nation perpetually fails to live in accordance with God's covenantal expectations (cf. 1:26–46; 9–10) contributes to this question. The

OT teaches that Israel rebels against God for a large segment of her history. As a whole, Israel remains unregenerate until the last part of redemptive history (Jer 31:31–34; Eze 36:22–28; 37:14).

In contrast to the command in 10:16, Deuteronomy 30:6 "speaks of circumcision of the heart as something that would be done by Yahweh in order to restore Israel" (Nelson, 137). How does this promise of a future reality relate to God's demand that Israelites in Moses' day circumcise their hearts? There is no doubt that 30:1–10 envisions a future day when God will restore his people and enable them to worship him. On the one hand, is circumcision of heart an entirely future reality? If so, what does this situation say about Israel's spiritual existence or capacity in Moses' day and in the centuries after that time (and the command for Israelites to circumcise their hearts in 10:16)? On the other hand, if this promised circumcision is not entirely or exclusively future, how can one explain the future orientation of this promise?

In addition to the comments made in the Reflection on 29:2–9 (which are also relevant here), one other important observation must be offered: 29:22–28 and 30:1–10 are not "primarily prophetic" (Craigie, 364). Rather, Moses makes use of past experience and the notion of the *potential future* to drive home Israel's need to obey Yahweh in the present. By referring to the nation's experience of

covenantal curse and later restoration, Moses is not "predicting" those events. If so, he would be telling the Israelites that they are doomed and do not have a chance. He shows them, in graphic detail, what covenantal curse will look like, but he moves on to demonstrate that Yahweh holds the final answer. He will restore them if they will repent in their exiled state.

Consequently, this "prediction" of Yahweh's circumcising their hearts should not be regarded as something he will do in some distant future day that he will not have done until then. No, for Moses' point is that in this set of conjecture or potential future events, God's internal work is a prerequisite for Israel to be able genuinely to love Yahweh. In the same way that God will provide *the only means* for restoration and genuine obedience in the wake of covenantal judgment, God's intervention in the hearts of Israelites of Moses' day represents *the only way* for those Israelites to carry out God's expectations of them as well.

C. The Appeal for Covenantal Obedience (30:11–20)

1. The Accessibility of the Covenant (30:11–14)

[11]Now what I am commanding you today is not too difficult for you or beyond your reach. [12]It is not up in heaven, so that you have to ask, "Who will ascend into heaven to get it and proclaim it to us so we may obey it?" [13]Nor is it beyond the sea, so that you have to ask, "Who will cross the sea to get it and proclaim it to us so we may obey it?" [14]No, the word is very near you; it is in your mouth and in your heart so you may obey it.

COMMENTARY

11–14 Unlike 30:1–10 (which was forward-looking, though with clear relevance for Moses' audience), 30:11–20 returns to a focus on those alive in Moses' day (as well as later generations; contra Barker, *The Triumph of Grace*, 182–87; Millar, 94). Moses affirms that the law of the covenant is not incomprehensible or inaccessible, nor does it require a specially qualified interpreter; rather, it was given in such a way that each person can know God's expectations and obey them.

The two negative statements in v.11 are illustrated by vv.12 and 13 ("not too difficult" = "not ... in heaven"; "beyond your reach" = "nor ... beyond the sea"). Verse 14 concludes the section by making a positive affirmation. In addition to addressing the accessibility question, this passage also serves as a polemic against other religions. In concert with his repeated warnings against idolatry, Moses polemically compares the way Yahweh reveals his demands to his chosen people (clearly) with the way pagan gods reveal their will to their worshipers (ambiguously).

By saying that Yahweh's demands of Israel are "not too difficult," Moses could be referring to one's ability to understand them (Christensen, *Deuteronomy 21:10–34:12*, 742–43; Hall, 447; McConville, 429; Merrill, *Deuteronomy*, 391; Nelson, 349; Ridderbos, 271; Tigay, *Deuteronomy*, 286) or to fulfill them (Craigie, 364; Wright, *Deuteronomy*, 290). Although the end of the section refers to obedience, this statement affirms that what Yahweh has set before his people is not beyond their comprehension (cf. Dt 17:8). There is no need to send an envoy to heaven, a feat deemed impossible in biblical (Pr 30:4) and ancient Near Eastern literature (cf. Tigay, *Deuteronomy*, 286), or to some distant location on earth, to receive an explanation of Yahweh's covenantal demands. The covenantal commandment is not so lofty and high that only a specially qualified person has access to it. It is not beyond Israel's capacity. Their obedience does not require that someone first receive a special revelation to explain Yahweh's demands.

Moses concludes this section by affirming that God has clearly revealed what he wants his chosen people to know (v.14—the converse of vv.11–13). Rather than being difficult and far off, it is very near. Yahweh's expectations of his chosen nation are accessible and knowable. Some commentators have suggested that this reference to "mouth" and

"heart" signifies the recitation and memorization of the covenantal requirements (cf. 6:4–9; Ridderbos, 271; Tigay, *Deuteronomy*, 286–87). Although the comparison to ch. 6 is appropriate, this statement has broader significance. God expects his people to speak about his commandments with each other, to train their children in the light of them, and to maintain these requirements in their hearts. Truths that they can internalize and pass on to others are divine demands that are understandable and doable ("so that you may obey it"; 30:14).

The apostle Paul referred to this passage to emphasize the accessibility of the gospel (Ro 10:6–8). Through the incarnation, God made salvation and righteousness readily available. As Moo writes: "One does not have to ascend into heaven or plumb the depths of the sea to discover it. All one needs to do to attain righteousness is to respond in faith to the gospel as it is preached" (D. Moo, *Romans* [NIVAC; Grand Rapids: Zondervan, 2000], 332). Because Christ and the gospel are accessible, people have no excuse for missing the message of salvation.

Although most scholars conclude that this section concerns Israel's ability to live in accordance with the Mosaic law, they do not agree on when Israel will have that ability. In light of the proximity of this pericope to the preceding, future-looking verses (30:1–10), some interpreters have suggested that Israel will not enjoy that ability until Yahweh circumcises their hearts in the eschaton (McConville, 429; idem, *Grace in the End: A Study in Deuteronomic Theology* [Grand Rapids: Zondervan, 1993], 137–38; Barker, *The Triumph of Grace*, 187–98; Dennis Olson, "How Does Deuteronomy Do Theology?" in *A God So Near: Essays on Old Testament Theology in Honor of Patrick D. Miller* [ed. B. Strawn and N. Bowen; Winona Lake, Ind.: Eisenbrauns, 2003], 209–10). This interpretation seems to ignore numerous OT passages that speak of godly Israelites who were able genuinely to obey Yahweh (see Reflection on 29:2–9).

NOTES

11, 14 The noun מִצְוָה (*miṣwâ*), "commandment" (v.11), occurs repeatedly in Deuteronomy to denote the entire covenantal text, i.e., Yahweh's expectations of the chosen nation (cf. 4:2; 5:29; 7:9; 8:2, 6; 11:8, 13, 22, 27; 26:13, 18; 28:1, 9, 13; 30:8; et al.). In light of the context, הַדָּבָר (*haddābār*), "the word" (v.14), serves as synonym for "this commandment" (הַמִּצְוָה הַזֹּאת, *hammiṣwâ hazzōt*).

11 The verb פלא (*plʾ* [GK 7098], in the phrase לֹא־נִפְלֵאת הִוא מִמְּךָ, *lōʾ-niplēʾt hiwʾ mimmᵉkā*, "it is not too difficult for you"), can refer to something that is wonderful or difficult. People regard something as "wonderful" because it exceeds their expectations or because they consider it impossible in a specific situation (Albertz, *TLOT*, 2:984). This meaning of the verb ("to be wonderful") highlights a person's response to something unique. The idea of "difficult" emphasizes a person's inability to attain to or grasp a given concept or event. In a judicial setting it can refer to a case that is "too difficult" to judge (Dt 17:8). In Proverbs 30:18 it characterizes certain aspects of life that are beyond the sage's understanding.

2. The Significance of One's Acceptance or Rejection of the Covenant (30:15–20)

OVERVIEW

With clarity and urgency the first and third sections of this pericope (vv.15–16, 19–20) present Israel with the choice they are facing (obedience or treachery), with a focus on the potential blessings. The middle section (vv.17–18) spells out the negative side, the curses that God will send against his people if they rebel against him.

---

¹⁵See, I set before you today life and prosperity, death and destruction. ¹⁶For I command you today to love the LORD your God, to walk in his ways, and to keep his commands, decrees and laws; then you will live and increase, and the LORD your God will bless you in the land you are entering to possess.

¹⁷But if your heart turns away and you are not obedient, and if you are drawn away to bow down to other gods and worship them, ¹⁸I declare to you this day that you will certainly be destroyed. You will not live long in the land you are crossing the Jordan to enter and possess.

¹⁹This day I call heaven and earth as witnesses against you that I have set before you life and death, blessings and curses. Now choose life, so that you and your children may live ²⁰and that you may love the LORD your God, listen to his voice, and hold fast to him. For the LORD is your life, and he will give you many years in the land he swore to give to your fathers, Abraham, Isaac and Jacob.

COMMENTARY

15–16 After setting the choices before the children of Israel, Moses exhorts them to manifest their love for the Lord by walking in accordance with his commandments so that they can enjoy his abundant blessings. In stark clarity, Moses presents Israel with the choices before them: life and prosperity or death and destruction. At issue is whether or not they heed the exhortation in v.16 (cf. v.20). The use of "command" and "today" highlights the urgency in Moses' appeal to the Israelites. This is not a decision to be delayed!

Using stock expressions for genuine covenantal conformity ("love," "walk," "keep"; see Note at 13:4 and Reflection on 29:2–9), Moses demands that his fellow Israelites wholeheartedly submit to Yahweh's authority. If they do, they will receive the blessings of that covenantal relationship: life, multiplication of numbers, and blessing (see Note on 7:13). This blessing is centered in the Promised Land, a land they will soon possess (from the perspective of Moses).

17–18 Those individuals who decide to disobey God and worship other gods will perish and will forfeit abundant life in the Promised Land. Covenantal treachery will occasion the exact opposite of the marvelous blessings Yahweh wants to bestow on his people. Moses piles up terms for disobedience: "heart turns away," "not obedient," "drawn away," "bow down to other gods" (cf. 4:19; 13:5, 10, 13; see Note at 5:9). In no uncertain terms, Moses declares that Yahweh will destroy (see Note

at 8:20 for this emphatic construction) his covenantal nation if they rebel in this way. Rather than receiving life, they will not live long in the land (cf. 4:26).

19–20 For a final time, Moses solemnly exhorts God's children to choose life (for themselves and for their descendants) and all the other blessings that accompany a proper relationship with the God of their ancestors. To emphasize the importance of this demand, Moses for the third time uses the expression "today" (cf. 30:15, 18). He presents heaven and earth as enduring witnesses to this call to covenantal conformity (see Note on 4:26). Appeals to creation as part of a rebuke for covenantal disobedience also occur in other OT passages (Isa 1:2; Mic 1:2; 6:1 [mountains and hills]).

Israel's choice to obey or disobey Yahweh will have far-reaching implications: life or death, blessings or curses (cf. ch. 28). Choosing life (for them and their descendants) is equated with wholehearted commitment to a genuine covenantal relationship with Yahweh. Verse 20 delineates that commitment by employing stock "covenantal" verbs: "love," "listen," "hold fast" (see Note at 13:4). Moses concludes this section by affirming that Yahweh, Israel's covenantal Lord, will give them long tenure in the land if they live as loyal citizens. Just prior to that statement he declares a powerful reality: "For the LORD is your life." True life is only to be found in God, i.e., in an intimate relationship with him.

NOTE

18 The expression לֹא־תַאֲרִיכֻן יָמִים (lōʾ-taʾărîkun yāmîm, "you will not live long") occurs in nine other passages in Deuteronomy to describe one aspect of covenantal blessings (4:40; 5:16, 33; 6:2; 11:9; 17:20; 22:7; 25:15; 32:47). It is always connected with some area of covenantal obedience. In addition to the

Promised Land itself, long tenure in that land is a treasured blessing for God's covenantal nation. To not live long in that land represents the undoing of the covenant. See comments on 4:40 for more on the significance of this expression.

VI. THE CONTINUITY OF THE COVENANT FROM MOSES TO JOSHUA (31:1–34:12)

OVERVIEW

Moses provides for the continuity of the covenant during the change in national leadership from himself to Joshua by appointing and commissioning Joshua and arranging for the deposition of the law (chs. 31–32). Moses then composes a song celebrating Yahweh's role in their existence as a covenantal people, a song that will serve a central role in their continuing life as his servant-nation (ch. 33). Chapter 34 describes Moses' final view of the land, his death, and the transition to Joshua's direction of the nation.

These chapters parallel chs. 1–3 in various ways. A sermon (ch. 4) follows the historical narrative of chs. 1–3 and provides a transition to the heart of the book of Deuteronomy (chs. 5–28, patterned after a treaty document). In reverse order, chs. 29–30 serve as a sermon (call to covenantal renewal) that leads into the concluding historical narrative (chs. 31–34).

A. Moses' Final Arrangements (31:1–29)

OVERVIEW

In preparation for Israel's entrance into the Promised Land subsequent to his death, Moses appoints Joshua (before all Israel) as the next national leader. He arranges for the reading of his addresses, given on the plains of Moab, every seven years and for the deposition of the law. The Lord commissions him to write a final poem that will serve as a witness against Israel when they forsake him.

1. The Succession by Joshua (31:1–8)

¹Then Moses went out and spoke these words to all Israel: ²"I am now a hundred and twenty years old and I am no longer able to lead you. The Lord has said to me, 'You shall not cross the Jordan.' ³The Lord your God himself will cross over ahead of you. He will destroy these nations before you, and you will take possession of their land. Joshua also

will cross over ahead of you, as the LORD said. ⁴And the LORD will do to them what he did to Sihon and Og, the kings of the Amorites, whom he destroyed along with their land. ⁵The LORD will deliver them to you, and you must do to them all that I have commanded you. ⁶Be strong and courageous. Do not be afraid or terrified because of them, for the LORD your God goes with you; he will never leave you nor forsake you."

⁷Then Moses summoned Joshua and said to him in the presence of all Israel, "Be strong and courageous, for you must go with this people into the land that the LORD swore to their forefathers to give them, and you must divide it among them as their inheritance. ⁸The LORD himself goes before you and will be with you; he will never leave you nor forsake you. Do not be afraid; do not be discouraged."

COMMENTARY

1–2 Moses' inability to lead God's people occasions this transfer of leadership responsibility to Joshua. His advanced age may have limited his effectiveness as the nation's leader, especially in light of the challenges ahead of them. More significantly, however, is Yahweh's refusal to allow Moses to cross the Jordan River and enter the Promised Land (cf. 3:23–29).

3–6 Moses' capacity for leadership of the nation may have diminished, but Yahweh remains their ultimate leader (cf. 1:30; 3:18–21; 7:1–2, 17–24; 9:3–4; 20:1–4). As is affirmed previously in Deuteronomy, Yahweh is the commander-in-chief who will lead their army, destroy the Canaanites, and deliver the land to his chosen people. Although Joshua may be stepping into Moses' shoes, his role is still a subordinate one. Yahweh's role, not Joshua's, is decisive (Tigay, *Deuteronomy*, 290). The primacy of Yahweh's leadership is seen in the chiastic pattern: Yahweh crosses (v.3a), Joshua crosses (v.3b), Joshua goes (v.7), Yahweh marches (v.8).

Moses refers to Israel's God-given victories over Sihon and Og (2:26–3:11) as a paradigm of God's promised intervention in behalf of Israel in their conquest of the Canaanites. In the light of what Yahweh will do, Moses exhorts the Israelites to be strong and courageous and not to fear their enemies. What God did in their past he will also do in their near future. Since the accomplishment of this daunting task rests on Yahweh alone, Israel has no need to fear. They can rest assured that he will not fail them or abandon them (cf. 31:8; Jos 1:5; 1Ch 28:20).

7–8 What is true for God's people is also true for their divinely appointed leader. Joshua can be courageous (v.7) and without fear (v.8) because Yahweh will be with and guide his chosen leader just as he will be with and guide his chosen nation. The presence of a redundant pronoun "he" in vv.3 and 8 emphasizes God's role in leading the nation and their leader. Throughout the OT, whenever Yahweh promises his presence, he offers his limitless assistance and protection (Ge 21:22; 26:3, 28; 28:15, 20; 39:2–3; Ex 3:12; Jos 1:5, 9; Jdg 6:12–13; Isa 8:10; Jer 1:8, 19; cf. Tigay, *Deuteronomy*, 290).

NOTES

1 For the MT's reading וַיֵּלֶךְ (*wayyēlek*; "Then Moses went out"), the LXX reflects and a fragment of a Qumran scroll has וַיְכַל (*waykal*, "and he finished"), involving a reversal of the last two consonants. Several scholars favor this variant as an indication that Moses is bringing his comments in chs. 29–30 to a close (Mayes, 372–73; Nelson, 353; Tigay, *Deuteronomy*, 289). The difficulty of the MT's reading favors its genuineness. Although the verb seems somewhat out of place, Christensen (*Deuteronomy 1:1–21:9*, cvii–cviii) has pointed to the use of similar verbs at key structural points in the book.

2 The expression לֹא־אוּכַל עוֹד לָצֵאת וְלָבוֹא (*lōʾ-ʾûkal ʿôd lāṣēʾt wᵉlābôʾ*, "no longer able to lead you") reads literally, "I am not able to go out and come in." It refers to all human activity (cf. Nu 27:17) and may comprise technical terminology applied to a military or royal leader (Jos 14:11; 1Sa 18:13–16; 1Ki 3:7).

6 The pair of verbs represented in the phrase חִזְקוּ וְאִמְצוּ (*ḥizᵉqû wᵉʾimᵉṣû*, "be strong and courageous") occurs nine times in Deuteronomy (3:28; 31:6–7, 23) and Joshua (1:6–7, 9, 18; 10:25), all of which verses focus on the transition of leadership from Moses to Joshua. The pair occurs eight more times in the rest of the OT, with four of them relating to the Davidic monarchy (1Ch 22:13; 28:20; 2Ch 11:17; 32:7). Some interpreters call the exhortation a formula of encouragement.

The first verb, "be strong," can refer to physical strength (Jdg 7:11; 2Sa 2:7; 16:21) or to the strength necessary to recover from a physical illness (Isa 39:1). Groups of people can be strong (Dt 11:8; Jos 17:13; Jdg 1:28), and a spoken word that is effective is regarded as something strong (2Sa 24:4; 1Ch 21:4). This verb is used often for courageous confidence in the face of some danger that threatens success. When the imperative form appears (as here), "individuals are urged to display the tenacity and resolve necessary to accomplish a worthy goal" (Taylor, 367).

The second verb, "be courageous," describes inner strength that displays fortitude, commitment, and perseverance even in the face of potentially overpowering circumstances (Taylor, 367). Seven of the above occurrences are accompanied by the command not to fear (using the verbs יָרֵא [*yrʾ*], עָרַץ [*ʿrṣ*], and חָתַת [*ḥtt*]; Dt 31:6, 7–8; Jos 1:9; 10:25; 1Ch 22:13; 28:20; 2Ch 32:7; see Note at 1:21).

2. Moses Arranges for the Regular Reading of the Law (31:9–13)

⁹So Moses wrote down this law and gave it to the priests, the sons of Levi, who carried the ark of the covenant of the LORD, and to all the elders of Israel. ¹⁰Then Moses commanded them: "At the end of every seven years, in the year for canceling debts, during the Feast of Tabernacles, ¹¹when all Israel comes to appear before the LORD your God at the place he will choose, you shall read this law before them in their hearing. ¹²Assemble the people — men, women and children, and the aliens living in your towns — so they can listen and learn to fear the LORD your God and follow carefully all the words of this law.

¹³Their children, who do not know this law, must hear it and learn to fear the Lord your God as long as you live in the land you are crossing the Jordan to possess."

COMMENTARY

9 This transition of leadership also has implications for other Israelite leaders — the priests and elders. After completing his writing of the law, Moses makes the priests (cf. 10:8; 18:1) and elders (cf. 27:1; 31:28) the custodians of that law. Although "this law" can broadly refer to Mosaic writings, in Deuteronomy it customarily refers to the book itself or some section of the book (cf. 1:5; 4:8; 17:18–19; 27:3, 8, 26) — perhaps, as suggested by various scholars, chs. 12–26 (Merrill, *Deuteronomy*, 398) or chs. 1–30 (Craigie, 370). Written law codes were common in the ancient Near East and served to manifest a ruler's commitment to maintaining justice (Walton and Matthews, 265).

As a written document, the Mosaic law will be preserved for the benefit of future generations. It makes the law more permanent and less susceptible to revision. Throughout Israel's history it was primarily Israel's kings and priests who had direct access to this law. Yahweh commissions the priests and Levites to teach the law of Moses to their fellow Israelites. Although many copies of this written law were not produced, its existence was essential as a covenantal witness to the nation (cf. 31:26).

10–13 Moses commands these leaders to make certain that this law is read every seven years at the time of the Feast of Tabernacles (at "the place he will choose"). That feast was one of three celebrations that all Israelite males were required to attend (Dt 16:13–15). Reference to women and children may suggest that entire families were expected to attend this feast during the sabbatical year. After all, women shared the responsibility for raising their children, and the children represented the next generation responsible for continuing this covenantal relationship. Yahweh also required that the "aliens" who lived in Israel participate in this important assembly.

More than all the other required feasts, the Feast of Tabernacles will remind all Israelites that Yahweh delivered them from bondage in Egypt and chose them to be his servant-nation (Lev 25:43). As a celebration of an abundant harvest, the Feast of Tabernacles involves great joy and thanksgiving. Since this reading of the Mosaic law to the nation will occur during the same year in which all debts are cancelled ("the year of release"), it contains vivid memories of historical redemption and the joyous celebration of Yahweh's abundant provision. Various Hittite treaties also included stipulations mandating their periodic public reading (Weinfeld, *Deuteronomy and the Deuteronomic School*, 64–65; Pritchard, *ANET*, 205).

This special gathering "was to provide a forum for a regular and formal renewal of the covenant before the Lord" (Merrill, *Deuteronomy*, 399). Listening to God's revelation in any setting represents something of great value in itself. However, the reading of the Law is intended to have a direct and powerful impact on the lives of God's people. They are to learn what it means to fear Yahweh (see Note on 6:13) and to be motivated to arrange their lives in conformity with ("carefully obey"; see Note on 5:1) his demands. Although Yahweh clearly wants the conduct (external) of his people to manifest practically their reception of his expectations, a life of external conformity without internal reality (fear of Yahweh) is unacceptable to Yahweh. Israel's obedience to this requirement of reading the Mosaic law to the nation every seven years is part of Yahweh's plan to keep reminding his chosen nation of the blessings and responsibilities of their intimate covenantal relationship.

As Tigay (*Deuteronomy*, 498) points out, this writing and reading of the law of Moses signified various truths about that law. The Israelites clearly regarded it as sacred and canonical, i.e., inspired and authoritative. Further, God did not reserve this law for the religious or political elite, but for all of his people. He wanted every Israelite to be aware of and understand his expectations of them. The Bible records only two occasions on which Israel carried out this requirement (2Ki 23:1–3; Ne 8:13–9:38).

3. Final Instructions for Moses and Joshua (31:14–23)

[14]The LORD said to Moses, "Now the day of your death is near. Call Joshua and present yourselves at the Tent of Meeting, where I will commission him." So Moses and Joshua came and presented themselves at the Tent of Meeting.

[15]Then the LORD appeared at the Tent in a pillar of cloud, and the cloud stood over the entrance to the Tent. [16]And the LORD said to Moses: "You are going to rest with your fathers, and these people will soon prostitute themselves to the foreign gods of the land they are entering. They will forsake me and break the covenant I made with them. [17]On that day I will become angry with them and forsake them; I will hide my face from them, and they will be destroyed. Many disasters and difficulties will come upon them, and on that day they will ask, 'Have not these disasters come upon us because our God is not with us?' [18]And I will certainly hide my face on that day because of all their wickedness in turning to other gods.

[19]"Now write down for yourselves this song and teach it to the Israelites and have them sing it, so that it may be a witness for me against them. [20]When I have brought them into the land flowing with milk and honey, the land I promised on oath to their forefathers, and when they eat their fill and thrive, they will turn to other gods and worship them, rejecting me and breaking my covenant. [21]And when many disasters and difficulties come upon them, this song will testify against them, because it will not be forgotten by their descendants. I know what they are disposed to do, even before I bring them into the land I promised them on oath." [22]So Moses wrote down this song that day and taught it to the Israelites.

[23]The LORD gave this command to Joshua son of Nun: "Be strong and courageous, for you will bring the Israelites into the land I promised them on oath, and I myself will be with you."

COMMENTARY

14–15 Because Moses will soon die, God commands him to bring his faithful servant Joshua to the Tent of Meeting outside the Israelite encampment. As the Lord had done with Moses, Yahweh himself commissions Joshua to carry out the staggering task of leading God's chosen nation. Yahweh's appearance to Joshua removes any doubt (for Joshua and the watching Israelites) that God has chosen him to take over the reins of leadership. The pillar of cloud (by day) and fire (by night) manifests Yahweh's presence to his people (Ex 13:21–22; 14:19–24; 19:19; 34:5; Nu 11:25). It serves both to reveal Yahweh to his people (as a visible reminder of his presence) and to conceal (only in intangible form; Hall, 460).

16–18 After reminding Moses again of his impending death, Yahweh describes the apostasy of Israel that will follow in a rebellion that will occasion severe judgment. God's servant-nation will prostitute themselves, forsake (see Note on 29:25) Yahweh, and break their covenant with him. Their treachery will trigger Yahweh's anger, and he will forsake his people and hide his face from them until they are destroyed. He will send calamities and affliction against them. This trauma will cause Israel to ask whether Yahweh is still with them. If God's being with them signified the provision of his assistance and protection (see comments on 31:7–8), his absence will signify the withholding of divine enablement and protection for the agonies of life in a sinful world.

The Lord employs powerful language in describing his response to Israel's sin. One might think that he is affirming a permanent disruption of his relationship with his chosen people. However, one must understand these statements in concert with other OT passages. In Isaiah 54:8 he declares: "'In a surge of anger I hid my face from you for a moment, but with everlasting kindness I will have compassion on you,' says the LORD your Redeemer." In Ezekiel 39:29 he says, "I will no longer hide my face from them, for I will pour out my Spirit on the house of Israel, declares the sovereign LORD."

19–22 Yahweh commands Moses to compose (probably through Joshua, as signified by the plural verb) the following "song" to serve as a witness against his covenantal nation. As they sing it, the words will remind the Israelites of their commitment to a loyal relationship with Yahweh.

Verses 20–21 set God's grace and Israel's sin side-by-side. After he has brought to fulfillment all that he has promised ("milk and honey" [see comments and Note on 6:3] "I promised them on oath" [see Note on 1:8]) and his chosen people are enjoying their abundant covenantal blessings, they will commit treachery by breaking their covenantal vows (in turning to other gods, worshiping them, rejecting Yahweh, and thus breaking their covenant with him). However, when the promised covenantal curses fall on Israel, the words of this song will ring in their ears. To their dismay, their descendants (who will experience the agony of the covenantal curses) will not be able to forget its words (in contrast to their constant tendency to forget their God; see Note on 4:10). Even before all these eventualities take place, the Lord knows the sinful tendencies of his chosen people.

23 Just as Moses commissioned Joshua, the Lord himself exhorts Joshua to be courageous in the light of his promise to install the chosen people in the land he has promised them (cf. Jos 1:6–7), just as he had sworn to their ancestors. God's promise of his continued presence will serve as the ultimate foundation for Joshua's hope.

NOTES

14 The expression בְּאֹהֶל מוֹעֵד (*bᵉʾōhel môʿēd*, "at the tent of meeting") occurs 145 times in the OT and in most passages refers to the tabernacle and later the temple (cf. Ex 25–40). This designation draws on the fact that it served as the meeting place of Moses and Yahweh (and indirectly between Yahweh and the Israelites). The visible presence of God rested in the Most Holy Place. The tabernacle, in use in Moses' day, was located at the center of Israel's encampment during the journey to the Promised Land.

Although various scholars do not distinguish this "tent" from the tabernacle (Kalland, 196; Thompson, 293; Walton and Matthews, 266), several clues (in the present passage and elsewhere) suggest their distinctness. The tent was located outside the encampment (Ex 33:7–11; Nu 11:16; 12:4), was frequented by Moses and other leaders who sought counsel from Yahweh (Ex 33:7–11; cf. 18:7–16; Nu 11:16, 24, 26; 12:4), and appears to have existed before the building of the tabernacle (Ex 33:7–11). Yahweh's presence stood at or over the door of this tent (Ex 33:9–10; Nu 12:5; Dt 31:15), and Joshua stayed in this tent most of the time (Ex 33:11; cf. Merrill, *Deuteronomy*, 401; Koch, *TDOT* 1:124–25).

16 The expression הִנְּךָ שֹׁכֵב עִם־אֲבֹתֶיךָ (*hinnᵉkā šōkēb ʿim-ʾᵃbōteykā*, "you are going to rest with your fathers") serves as a common OT idiom for death. It could depict the spirit of the dead person's joining relatives in Sheol or refer to the ancient practice of burying bodies in a family tomb (Hall, 460, n. 21).

Moses repeatedly warned Israel against worshiping other gods (7:1–6; 12:1–3, 13; 28:20). However, the idea of spiritual prostitution—foreseen here in the phrase וְזָנָה אַחֲרֵי אֱלֹהֵי נֵכָר (*wᵉzānâ ʾaḥᵃrê ʾᵉlōhê nēkar*), "they will prostitute themselves with [lit., 'after'] foreign gods"—evokes a much stronger warning. Although the verb *znh* occurs only here in Deuteronomy, it appears often in the prophets (cf. Jer 3:6–12; Eze 16:26, 28; 23:5, 7; Hos 4:12; 5:4). Notice that the preposition "after," rather than "with," follows the verb (a construction modeled after the expression "walk after other gods"; see Note on 4:3). To "play the harlot after" other gods means "to cultivate a relationship with them, to render unto them one's obedience and devotion, to walk in their ways and pursue their ideals" (Ortlund, 32; cf. Lev 17:7; 20:5–6; Nu 15:39; Jdg 2:17; 8:27, 33).

The Samaritan Pentateuch, LXX, and Targums read the plural "they" for this singular pronoun in the phrase אֲשֶׁר הוּא בָא־שָׁמָּה (*ʾᵃšer hûʾ bāʾ-šammâ*, "into which they are going"). Third person singular forms occur in the Hebrew text twice more in this verse, three times in v.17, once in v.18, five times in v.20, and four times in v.21. Although there is no need to change the singular to a plural in the Hebrew text, each singular form can be translated as a plural for stylistic purposes. Throughout Deuteronomy, singular forms function to emphasize the individual in the midst of the nation.

16, 20 Although the verb in the phrase וְהֵפֵר אֶת־בְּרִיתִי (*wᵉhēpēr ʾet-bᵉrîtî*, "and break my covenant") occurs only twice in Deuteronomy (31:16, 20), it presents a graphic picture of the implications of Israel's treacherous conduct. In twenty-one other OT passages it appears with the noun "covenant" (cf. Lev 26:15–20; Isa 24:5–6; Jer 11:10–11; 31:32; Eze 16:59; 44:7). The verb means to remove or withdraw (whether intentionally or not) one's support for or validation of an agreement (Williams, *NIDOTTE*, 3:696). Its juxtaposition with the verb "to forsake" (עזב, *ʿzb*) demonstrates that forsaking Yahweh is one way to break the covenant (cf. 29:25 and Note; 1Ki 19:10, 14; Pr 2:17; Jer 22:9). In other passages, Moses refers to Israel's "forgetting" (4:23) and "transgressing" (17:2; cf. Jos 7:11, 15; 2Ki 18:12; Jer 34:18; Hos 6:7; 8:1) the covenant.

17, 21 The noun רָעָה (rāʿâ; GK 8288) and its synonym רַע (raʿ) can signify a wide range of meanings, as suggested by the generalizing expression הָרָעוֹת הָאֵלֶּה (hārāʿôt haʾelleh, "these difficulties"). Both of these nouns describe the action or the state of being of people who are not acceptable, and both can serve as general terms for evil (1Ki 3:9) or refer to something that is of poor quality (e.g., bad water; 2Ki 2:19) or harmful (2Ki 4:41). The nouns refer not only to a person's deeds but also to the results or consequences of those actions (i.e., direct punishment or the experience of calamity; Baker, *NIDOTTE*, 3:1155). The Bible depicts those who mistreat God's chosen people as doing evil (1Ki 20:7; Est 8:3; Na 3:19). Certain kings of Israel (1Ki 13:33; 16:7) and the nation itself (2Ki 17:11, 13; 21:9, 15; Isa 3:9; Jer 6:7; 11:17; Eze 16:57; Hos 7:2) are also said to have committed evil deeds. As a result of those actions, God punished the evildoers by sending calamity into their lives (1Ki 22:8, 18). God brought disaster and harm on Israel's enemies (Isa 47:11; Jer 2:3; 48:2, 16; 49:37) as well as on his chosen people (1Ki 9:9; 14:10; 21:21, 29 [2x]; 22:23; 2Ki 6:33; 21:12; 22:16, 20), sometimes through foreign powers (2Ki 8:12).

18 The hiding of one's face can refer to looking away from someone (Ex 3:6) and to hiding oneself or someone else (1Sa 26:1; 1Ki 17:3; 2Ki 11:2). Here God affirms, וְאָנֹכִי הַסְתֵּר אַסְתִּיר פָּנַי (wᵉʾānōkî hastēr ʾastîr pānay), "and I myself will surely hide my face" (cf. Dt 32:20; Isa 54:8; Jer 33:5; Eze 39:23–24); other passages refer to the fact that God has hidden his face from individuals or his people (Pss 13:1 [2]; 30:7 [8]; 88:14 [15]; Isa 8:17; 59:2; 64:7; Mic 3:4). The position of the infinitive absolute before the finite verb, both using the same verbal root, emphasizes the verbal action of that root with the idea "fully," "certainly," or "surely" (*IBHS*, 584–86; for a similar construction, see Note on 8:19). The above-cited passages and others depict a causal connection between the people's sin and God's absence. Because Israel has turned away from Yahweh, he will turn away from them in an action that will also involve removing his protection of them (Eze 39:23–24). Biddle, 462, suggests that from a theological perspective (both for individuals and the nation), "God's absence — not God's punitive acts — represents the extreme of human pain and despair."

19 The noun עֵד (ʿēd, "witness"; GK 6332) occurs fourteen times in Deuteronomy and generally refers to a legal witness to the truth or factuality of a charge (5:20; 17:6–7; 19:15–18). The related verb עוד (ʿwd) occurs five times in the book, with all occurrences having a theological nuance: God's testifying of truth (32:46), or his doing so against his people in the light of their rebellion (4:26; 8:19; 30:19; 31:28). In the present passage, both the scroll (= "Book of the Law"; 31:26) and the song of Moses (31:19, 21) are to serve as witnesses testifying of the clarity of Yahweh's covenantal demands and, hence, against treacherous Israel for rebelling. According to 31:26, Israel's copy of the covenant served as a "documentary witness" (Kline, *The Structure of Biblical Authority*, 123). Kline adds that it was a "witness to and against Israel, reminding of obligations sworn to and rebuking for obligations violated, declaring the hope of covenant beatitude and pronouncing the doom of the covenant curses" (ibid., 124).

20 The verb וְנִאֲצוּנִי (wᵉniʾᵃṣûnî, "and will reject me"; GK 5540) occurs in conjunction with Israel's breaking covenant with Yahweh. In its basic form the verb means to reject or disdain something or someone. In the Piel form as here, it connotes declaring someone or something to be contemptible.

It refers to an attitude rather than conduct and signifies neglecting Yahweh in favor of other gods (cf. 32:19). It may be that Israel will not overtly reject him so much as ignore him. Although one might expect this kind of treatment of God by pagans (Ps 10:3, 13), Israel will be guilty of it as well (cf. Nu 14:11; Isa 1:4). As Merrill ("Deuteronomy," 514; cf. idem, *NIDOTTE*, 3:5−6) points out, "to belittle or despise the Lord is in itself an act of insubordination [so] as to render his covenant with Israel null and void."

21 The clause יָדַעְתִּי אֶת־יִצְרוֹ אֲשֶׁר הוּא עֹשֶׂה (*yādaʿtî ʾet-yiṣrô ʾăšer hûʾ ʿōśeh*, "I know what they are disposed to do") could be rendered literally, "I know his tendency that he is doing." The noun יֵצֶר (*yēṣer*; GK 3671) connotes the pattern, disposition, or inclination of a person's thoughts, i.e., those things that impact his or her conduct (Hartley, *NIDOTTE*, 2:506). In later Jewish literature and the Qumran scrolls, the word signifies the human disposition toward wrong (ibid.) or someone's "inexorable impulse, something beyond one's control" (Merrill, *Deuteronomy*, 403, n. 15; cf. Otzen, *TDOT*, 6:265).

4. The Deposition of the Law as a Witness against the Nation (31:24−29)

²⁴After Moses finished writing in a book the words of this law from beginning to end, ²⁵he gave this command to the Levites who carried the ark of the covenant of the LORD: ²⁶"Take this Book of the Law and place it beside the ark of the covenant of the LORD your God. There it will remain as a witness against you. ²⁷For I know how rebellious and stiff-necked you are. If you have been rebellious against the LORD while I am still alive and with you, how much more will you rebel after I die! ²⁸Assemble before me all the elders of your tribes and all your officials, so that I can speak these words in their hearing and call heaven and earth to testify against them. ²⁹For I know that after my death you are sure to become utterly corrupt and to turn from the way I have commanded you. In days to come, disaster will fall upon you because you will do evil in the sight of the LORD and provoke him to anger by what your hands have made."

COMMENTARY

24−26 Moses returns to a subject introduced in 31:9, namely, the preservation of the written legal document (see comments on 31:9). The Levitical priests are to store it beside the ark of the covenant (probably in a jar), where it will be safe as well as accessible to the priests. These instructions complete, rather than compete with, those found earlier. As with the song of Moses (31:19, 21), this legal document will serve as a witness (see Note on 31:19) to Yahweh's demands of his people and serve as clear evidence when his people rebel against him. It contains the terms of the covenant that Israel has gladly accepted.

27−29 Moses is well aware of Israel's penchant for rebellion. By drawing on expressions employed earlier in the book, he piles up terms to emphasize the darkness of the Israelites' hearts ("rebel" [1:26, 43; 9:7, 23–24], "stiff-necked" [9:6, 13; 10:16], "corrupt" [4:16, 25; 9:12; 32:5; see Note on 4:16], "turn away" [11:28; 28:14], "do evil" [4:25; 9:18; 17:2], and "provoke to anger" [4:25; 9:18; 32:16, 21]). Moses also knows that the intensity of Israel's rebellion will only increase after his death. Consequently, he calls for Israel's leaders to gather before him so that he can give them another weighty exhortation. He wants to make sure they understand that their choices and conduct will have far-reaching implications.

By calling heaven and earth as witnesses against Israel (see Note on 4:26), Moses sets before the nation's leaders the options of covenantal acceptance or repudiation (cf. 30:19; Merrill, *Deuteronomy*, 404). Covenantal treachery will face nothing less than disaster! Moses does not intend that the negative flavor of this exhortation will make the Israelites give up on the idea of obedience; rather, it serves to confront them with the predilections of a nation not totally comprised of believers in Yahweh. In the light of what Yahweh has revealed to his people through Moses, they are without excuse.

NOTES

24–25 Books as we moderns know them were not invented until after the time of the writing of the NT. Here the word סֵפֶר (*sēper*, "a book") simply refers to some kind of document, whether written on papyrus, parchment, or some other substance (e.g., stone, plaster, pottery, clay). A parchment scroll is likely in view (cf. Jer 32:11–16).

27 Since the emphatic personal pronoun appears in the phrase אָנֹכִי יָדַעְתִּי (*ʾānōkî yādaʿtî*, "I know"), it can be rendered, "I in particular know well" or "no one knows better than I," in the light of Moses' firsthand knowledge of Yahweh's historical dealings with his recalcitrant people (Tigay, *Deuteronomy*, 297).

29 In the phrase הַשְׁחֵת תַּשְׁחִתוּן (*hašḥēt tašḥitûn*, "you are sure to become utterly corrupt"), the position of the infinitive absolute before the finite verb, with both using the same verbal root, emphasizes the verbal action of that root with the idea "fully," "certainly," or "surely" (*IBHS*, 584–86). For a similar construction, see Note on 31:18.

B. The Song of Moses (31:30–32:52)

OVERVIEW

The poetic genre and the varied contents of this song challenge any interpreter who attempts to explain its meaning. Critical scholars have often suggested that the song was not composed until

much later in Israel's history. The genre of this lengthy poem approximates that of a covenantal lawsuit (cf. G. Ernest Wright, "The Lawsuit of God: A Form-Critical Study of Deuteronomy 32," in

Israel's Prophetic Heritage [ed. B. Anderson and W. Harrelson; New York: Harper & Brothers, 1962], 26–67; cf. Isa 1; Jer 2:4–13; Mic 6:1–8). In this "covenantal courtroom," Yahweh is without guilt and Israel is warned about and presented with the consequences for their guilt.

1. Introduction (31:30)

³⁰And Moses recited the words of this song from beginning to end in the hearing of the whole assembly of Israel:

COMMENTARY

30 These words form the prosaic introduction to Moses' poem, the entirety of which he recites before the whole assembly of Israel. This poem serves as the climax of the book and provides a theological summary that clearly distinguishes covenantal rebels from genuine believers in Yahweh. It celebrates the glory of Yahweh, Sovereign of Israel (E. H. Merrill, "A Theology of the Pentateuch," in *A Biblical Theology of the Old Testament* [ed. Roy B. Zuck; Chicago: Moody Press, 1991], 86).

In addition to the heavens and the earth (Dt 30:19; 31:28) and the book of the law (31:26), Yahweh gives this song to Israel through Moses as a witness to them. These witnesses are given to remind Yahweh and Israel of their mutual commitments. This song recites Yahweh's many gracious acts in their behalf, as well as his demand for absolute loyalty. Any long-term departure from genuine obedience will invite the experience of covenantal cursing.

2. Call of Witnesses (32:1–3)

¹Listen, O heavens, and I will speak;
    hear, O earth, the words of my mouth.
²Let my teaching fall like rain
    and my words descend like dew,
like showers on new grass,
    like abundant rain on tender plants.

³I will proclaim the name of the LORD.
    Oh, praise the greatness of our God!

COMMENTARY

1–3 As he has done elsewhere, Moses calls the heavens and earth as witnesses to this "legal proceeding" (cf. 4:26; 30:19; 31:28; Jer 2:12; see Note on 4:26). They serve as silent, objective onlookers observing the justice of the charges made against Israel and the fairness of Israel's punishment (Tigay, *Deuteronomy,* 299). Moses' instructive words are to have a powerful impact on his hearers, his fellow Israelites.

Moses uses four similes to describe the life-giving and growth-inducing results of Moses'

teaching. Both rain (Dt 11:14; 28:12; Job 5:10; Ps 72:6) and dew (Dt 33:13, 28; Ps 133:3; Pr 19:12; Isa 26:19; Hos 14:5 [6]) are part of God's beneficent provision for his vassal nation. Moses declares that he will proclaim Yahweh's name and affirm his greatness. To proclaim his "name" means much more than pronouncing a title (see comments and Note on 5:11); in this song Moses will declare his character and recount his many deeds.

NOTES

2 כִּשְׂעִירִם (*kiśʿîrim,* "like showers") occurs only here in the OT. Various Ugaritic texts (e.g., *KTU* 1.19.I:44–45; *COS,* 1:351) employ this word as part of a triple parallel expression: "dew [*ṭl*] ... rain [*rbb*] ... and fountain [*šrʿ*]."

3 The noun גֹּדֶל (*gōdel,* "greatness") occurs thirteen times in the OT, five of which are in Deuteronomy (3:24; 5:24; 9:26; 11:2; 32:3). In each of these passages (and Nu 14:19) it emphasizes the greatness of God demonstrated by delivering his chosen nation from slavery in Egypt (cf. Pss 79:11; 150:2). When it is used with reference to humankind, it connotes arrogance (Isa 9:9 [8]; 10:12; Eze 31:2, 7, 18). God's greatness is a trait that sets him apart from all the gods worshiped by other peoples. He is totally transcendent.

3. Yahweh's Graciousness and Israel's Ingratitude (32:4–6)

⁴He is the Rock, his works are perfect,
   and all his ways are just.
A faithful God who does no wrong,
   upright and just is he.

⁵They have acted corruptly toward him;
   to their shame they are no longer his children,
   but a warped and crooked generation.
⁶Is this the way you repay the LORD,
   O foolish and unwise people?
Is he not your Father, your Creator,
   who made you and formed you?

COMMENTARY

4–6 This section introduces Yahweh's case against Israel by contrasting his perfection with their guilt. Moses likens Yahweh to a rock, totally immovable. Then, using four statements and five nouns or adjectives, he describes God's perfections. God is perfect, i.e., totally reliable and without flaw (see Note on 18:13). His ways are just, and he is absolutely dependable. Unlike sinful humanity, he is not at all characterized by perversity or inquity (see Note on 25:16). The last two terms highlight the fact that his character and conduct perfectly conform with standards of perfection.

Unlike Yahweh, his covenantal people have "acted corruptly" (see Note on 4:16) or committed apostasy (cf. 9:12; 31:29). Their failure to conduct themselves as his children constitutes their mark of "shame" (an antonym of "perfect" in v.4). Yahweh is perfect (*tāmîm*) and just (*ṣaddîq*), but his people are twisted (*ʿiqqēš*) and crooked (cf. Pr 8:8, where *ʿiqqēš* contrasts with *ṣedeq*, and Pr 11:20, where it contrasts with *tāmîm* [cf. 19:1; 28:6]).

Moses then asks incredulously, "Is this how you treat your marvelous and wonderful God?" Using terms characteristic of wisdom literature, Moses likens their rebellion to folly. This rebellious response is so shocking because the God they have rebelled against is the very God who has brought them into existence. By forming them as a nation, he has brought them into the special status of being the "son" of Yahweh (Hos 11:1).

NOTES

4 The noun צוּר (*ṣûr*) can refer to literal mountains or rocky formations (Nu 23:9; Job 24:8; 28:10; Jer 21:13). In this passage, הַצּוּר (*haṣṣûr*, "the Rock") serves as a divine epithet. Particularly in poetic passages, an unshakeable rock provides a stereotypical image for God's help (Pss 18:46 [47]; 62:2 [3]; 89:26 [27]; 95:1), the protection he provides (Isa 17:10; Pss 28:1; 31:2 [3]; 62:7 [8]; 71:3), the refuge he offers (Pss 18:2, 31 [3, 32]; 94:22; 144:1), his redemptive activity (Pss 19:14 [15]; 78:35), and his steadfast faithfulness (Pss 73:26; 92:15 [16]; Isa 26:4; Van der Woude, *TLOT*, 2:1070; Grisanti, "2 Samuel," 219). The word also appears in vv.15, 18, and 30 of this song.

The verb שׁפט (*špṭ*) describes a range of actions that concern restoring or preserving order in society. The goal of this activity is to guarantee justice and involves adjudicating legal disputes, punishing those found guilty of crimes, and ruling in general. "Just" and "justice" (מִשְׁפָּט, *mišpāṭ*; GK 5477) describe and denote the act of carrying out שׁפט (*špṭ*). Being more than legal terms, these words connote conduct characterized by justice (Grisanti, "2 Samuel," 196).

Derived from the verb אמן (*ʾmn*), "to be firm, trustworthy" (*HALOT*, 63), the noun אֱמוּנָה (*ʾemûnâ*, here translated adjectivally as "faithful"; GK 575) carries the idea of dependability. Something or someone who is dependable is able to support the weight of trust.

The word family of צדק (*ṣdq*) can signify what one is, does, or declares others to be. Whenever referring to behavior (human or divine), words from this stem, such as צַדִּיק (*ṣaddîq*, "upright"; GK 7404) here, clearly imply conduct measured in accordance with some standard. It was imperative for a ruler and his subjects to practice what is just and right. After presenting Yahweh as the one who practices these things (loyal love, justice, and righteousness) and delights in them (Jer 9:24 [23]), the prophet Jeremiah challenged the Davidic king and all of his officials to rule as Yahweh rules (Jer 22:3, 15; cf. Eze 45:9). Not only does Yahweh rule in this way, but the coming Davidic ruler (Messiah/Branch) will also do what is just and right (Jer 23:5; 33:15). The prophet Isaiah used these two nouns with other verbs to emphasize that the Messiah will indeed reign justly and righteously (Isa 9:7 [6]; Grisanti, "1 Kings," 278–79).

The verb ישׁר (*yšr*) and its related adjective (יָשָׁר, *yāšār*, "just") signify what is legally and ethically right, i.e., in accordance with Yahweh's revealed truth (Isa 45:19; Olivier, *NIDOTTE*, 2:565). They refer to conduct that is "straight" or "upright"—to actions that conform to God's moral and ethical demands.

5 The terse expression לֹא בָּנָיו (*lōʾ bānāyw*, "not his sons") matches others found elsewhere in the song: "non-wise" (v.6), "no-gods" (vv.17, 21), and "no-people" (v.21; cf. Isa 1:2–4; Hos 1:6, 9).

Although the noun מוּמָם (*mûmām*, "their blemish"; GK 4583) can refer to a physical blemish (Lev 21:21, 23; Nu 19:2; Dt 15:21; 17:1), it can also signify a moral blemish (Job 11:15; Pr 9:7). Scholars have suggested some creative renderings of the line incorporating this word (cf. Craigie, 377, n. 15; Tigay, *Deuteronomy*, 301), but the line can be understood as it stands. Nelson, 363, offers this translation: "his nonchildren have dealt corruptly with him as their blemish."

6 The verb קָנָה (*qnh*) occurs eighty-four times in the OT and in most cases means "to acquire, buy." Based on six passages (Ge 4:1; 14:19, 22; Dt 32:6; Ps 139:13; Pr 8:22), several scholars have suggested another meaning for this verb: "to beget, bear" (Lipinski, *TDOT*, 13:60–61) or "to create" (as adopted by the NIV in the rendering of קָנֶךָ, *qāneka*, as "your Creator"; Cornelius/Van Leeuwen, *NIDOTTE*, 3:941). Whether or not this alternative indicates a distinct Hebrew verb (*qnh* II), the primary meaning "to acquire" does not seem to satisfy the contextual demands of most of the above six passages.

Here the verbs that follow *qāneka*—namely, "he made you and formed you"—support its underlying idea as creation (or "begetting"). Since this verb and not בָּרָא (*brʾ*) is used, creation out of nothing is not the primary point. Yahweh brought Israel into existence as a nation, his vassal. On the one hand, the reference to God as Israel's "Father" might highlight his expression of love, concern, and patience toward his chosen people (Ex 4:22; Dt 1:31; Ps 103:13; Hall, 470). On the other hand, it could also have covenantal overtones (Dt 1:31). In various ancient Near Eastern treaties the one who establishes a covenant would be the "father" and the recipient would be the "son" (McCarthy, "Notes on the Love of God," 144–47).

4. Overview of Yahweh's Care for His Covenantal Nation (32:7–14)

⁷Remember the days of old;
    consider the generations long past.
Ask your father and he will tell you,
    your elders, and they will explain to you.
⁸When the Most High gave the nations their inheritance,
    when he divided all mankind,

he set up boundaries for the peoples
  according to the number of the sons of Israel.
⁹For the LORD's portion is his people,
  Jacob his allotted inheritance.

¹⁰In a desert land he found him,
  in a barren and howling waste.
He shielded him and cared for him;
  he guarded him as the apple of his eye,
¹¹like an eagle that stirs up its nest
  and hovers over its young,
that spreads its wings to catch them
  and carries them on its pinions.
¹²The LORD alone led him;
  no foreign god was with him.

¹³He made him ride on the heights of the land
  and fed him with the fruit of the fields.
He nourished him with honey from the rock,
  and with oil from the flinty crag,
¹⁴with curds and milk from herd and flock
  and with fattened lambs and goats,
with choice rams of Bashan
  and the finest kernels of wheat.
You drank the foaming blood of the grape.

COMMENTARY

7–9 The preceding section has laid the foundation for the covenantal lawsuit brought by Yahweh against his chosen people. Even though he is perfectly blameless, his covenantal nation is unfaithful and rebellious. In the present section Moses provides proof that supports this charge. Yahweh is undoubtedly Israel's generous benefactor. In parallel poetic lines (two sets of parallel constructions), Moses exhorts his fellow Israelites to consider Yahweh's past dealings with them and the nations around them. The verbs "to remember" (see Note on 4:10) and "to consider/understand" are part of a bookwide emphasis in life-transforming remembrance (seen also in the numerous exhortations, "do not forget …").

The "prosecutor" is not accessing secret, hidden information helpful to his case but instead is appealing to knowledge of which every Israelite should have been well aware. Moses directs his audience's attention to the distant past, even before Yahweh brought the nation of Israel into existence. The expressions "days of old" and "long past" include God's dealings with his people for the last forty years but also extend even further back in time. When the Lord set up boundaries for all the nations and allocated to them spreads of land as part of his plan for the world, Israel was at the center of his efforts. He sets his election of Israel as an essential part of his plans for the entire world.

Yahweh's abundant provision of blessings to Israel began when he chose them as his own after dividing humanity into nations (vv.9–14). "His people" (= "Jacob") are Yahweh's "allotment" (= "portion of his inheritance"; v.9). The repetition of parallel terms emphasizes Israel's role as that nation of people who are the inheritance of Yahweh and will receive the land of Canaan as their own, God-given inheritance (see Note on 1:38 for discussion of *naḥᵃlâ*). Not only is Yahweh giving this land to Israel as their special possession, but he is also claiming the nation itself as his special possession. Such a privileged position out of all the nations of the world (Ex 19:5; Dt 7:6; 14:2, 21) should surely motivate his chosen people to conduct themselves as loyal citizens.

10–14 Moses employs a number of vivid metaphors to describe Yahweh's abundant care and consistent compassion for his chosen people. Although the nation's experience in the wilderness occurred in the preceding four decades, the wilderness to which Moses refers here predates that period by centuries. It refers to the time when Yahweh transformed them from a loose collection of ethnically related individuals into a nation designed to demonstrate his character to the surrounding nations.

In a wilderness a person faces the serious threat of starvation, thirst, and exposure. In a situation from which there was no human deliverance (bondage in Egypt), Yahweh provided care for Abraham's descendants. He surrounded and shielded his people (*sbb*), gave careful attention to them (*byn*), and guarded (*nṣr*) them, just as a person

ducks or covers his or her eye with a hand if something comes near to it (v.10).

The Lord also cared for his servant-nation like a (hovering) eagle protects its young (v.11). Also, this carrying of Israel as on eagle's wings pictures Yahweh's loving care for Israel during their journey from Egypt toward the land he promised them (H. Peels, "On the Wings of the Eagle (Dtn 32,11) — An Old Misunderstanding," *ZAW* 106 [1994]: 302). Yahweh alone, and no pagan god, was responsible for their deliverance from Egypt, successful transit through the wilderness, and arrival at the plains of Moab, just across the Jordan River from the Promised Land (v.12). It was this truth that made Israel's penchant for idolatry so reprehensible. Yahweh, who had repeatedly and miraculously intervened in their affairs, deserved their loyalty. These foreign (and false) gods, however, have done absolutely nothing to deserve their worship. They have absolutely no claim on God's chosen nation (cf. Dt 5:6–7).

Not only did Yahweh protect and guide his chosen people, but he also abundantly provided for them (vv.13–14). The clause "he made him ride on the heights of the land" highlights Yahweh's absolute sovereignty over the land and his ability to lead his people wherever they needed to go (cf. Isa 58:14; Job 9:8; Am 4:13; Hab 3:19). He enabled them to eat the produce of the fields and to "suck," like an infant nursing at his mother's breast, all that they needed and more: honey and olive oil, curds and milk, lambs, goats, and rams, and wheat. They were able to drink their fill of wine. Moses piles up these terms to highlight Yahweh's superabundant provision for his vassal nation. The phrases "from the rock" and "from the flinty crag" demonstrate that Yahweh will even provide for his children from places where one would not expect abundance.

NOTES

8 In the light of its etymology and the occurrence of similar names in other ancient Near Eastern literature, the divine title עֶלְיוֹן (ʿelyôn; GK 6610) means "the most high" or the "exalted one" (Zobel, *TDOT*, 11:121, 130–33). This title focuses on Yahweh as the supreme ruler over his creation. As the "most high" God, he is omnipotent (La 3:38), rules over the entire creation, and is incomparable (Ps 83:18 [19]) and immovable (Ps 21:7 [8]). He provides protection and shelter for Israel (Pss 9:2 [3]; 91:1, 9) and for her king (Ps 21:7 [8]; Grisanti, "2 Samuel," 221). This title seems to be used in contexts emphasizing the more universal aspects of God's plan.

Instead of the MT's reading בְּנֵי יִשְׂרָאֵל (bᵉnê yiśrāʾēl, "the sons of Israel"; cf. NASB, NCV, NET, NIV, NKJV, Tanak), a Qumran scroll fragment, the LXX (and Symmachus), and some Old Latin texts have or suggest the Hebrew reading בְּנֵי אֵל (bᵉnê ʾēl/ʾēlîm/ʾelōhîm, "sons of God" = "angels"; cf. NLT, NRSV). Several scholars accept the MT as it stands (Driver, 355–56; Hall, 472; Kalland, 203; Merrill, *Deuteronomy*, 413; Ridderbos, 284). According to their view, Yahweh allocated the boundaries of the nations so as to reserve among them a home for his chosen nation that was adequate to support its numbers (Driver, 355). In other words, land was set aside for each nation based on Israel's population (Merrill, *Deuteronomy*, 413; perhaps a reference to a correspondence between the number of nations mentioned in Ge 10 [seventy] and the descendants of Jacob who moved to Egypt in Ge 46:27 and Dt 10:22 [seventy]).

A number of other scholars, however, regard the above-noted variant as part of the original text (D. I. Block, *The Gods of the Nations: Studies in Ancient Near Eastern National Theology* [2nd ed.; Grand Rapids: Baker, 2000], 29–32; Christensen, *Deuteronomy 21:10–34:12*, 791, 796; Craigie, 378–79; M. Heiser, "Deuteronomy 32:8 and the Sons of God," *BSac* 158 [2001]: 52–74; McConville, 448; Nelson, 367; Thompson, 299; Tigay, *Deuteronomy*, 302–3, 513–15; Wright, *Deuteronomy*, 306–7). According to this view (generally), the heavenly court (or divine council) involved Yahweh and a certain number of angelic beings ("sons of God"). Yahweh divided humankind into a number of nations that corresponded to the number of members of the heavenly court and designated each of them as guardian over a given nation. Israel, however, was cared for directly by Yahweh (Block, *Gods of the Nation*, 32).

In light of the MSS evidence and the fact that the variant represents the more difficult reading, the variant ("the sons of God") appears to be the preferred reading. Accepting this variant, however, does not require one to regard this verse as providing a biblical legitimization of pagan religions (as Miller, 229, suggests). One should be careful about concluding too much from this statement. As Skehan points out, this verse serves as "a poetic representation of theological truth" ("The Structure of the Song of Moses," *CBQ* 13 [1951]: 155). See Note on a similar issue in 32:43.

10 The Hebrew idiom כְּאִישׁוֹן עֵינוֹ (kᵉʾîšôn ʿênô, "like the apple of his eye") can be translated literally, "like the little man (the noun אִישׁוֹן, ʾîšôn, being a diminutive of the noun אִישׁ, ʾîš, "man") of his eyes." The idiom seems to be similar to the Arabic idiom "the little man in the eye" (ʾinsan ʾal-ʿayin), referring to one's reflection in the pupil of another person (Tigay, *Deuteronomy*, 403, n. 63). The pupil is a sensitive and important part of the eye, something to be guarded jealously. David later prays to God, "keep me as the apple of your eye" (Ps 17:8), a request for divine protection.

11 The noun כְּנֶשֶׁר (kᵉnešer, "like an eagle") occurs twenty-six times in the OT. In those contexts that refer to feeding on carrion (Pr 30:17), baldness of a scavenging bird's head or neck (Mic 1:16), or nesting on cliffs (Job 39:27–28; Jer 49:16), the word probably refers to a vulture (G. Cansdale, *All the Animals of the Bible Lands* [Grand Rapids: Zondervan, 1970], 142; Kronholm, *TDOT*, 10:79). When also considering v.10, scholars debate the issue of where the comparison to the eagle ends and where Moses resumes referring to Yahweh.

Although many commentators believe that יָעִיר קִנּוֹ (yāʿîr qinnô, "he stirs up his nest") refers to an aspect of an eagle's treatment of its young, others deny that an eagle disturbs its eaglets by chasing them out of the nest to force them to fly, though catching their young on adult wings if needed (Cansdale, 143; A. Parmelee, *All the Birds of the Bible* [New Canaan, Conn.: Keats, 1959], 99; Peels, "On the Wings of the Eagle (Dtn 32,11)," 300; contra Driver, 356). Another point of debate relates to the meaning of the verb עוּר or עִיר (ʿwr or ʿyr). According to Peels (ibid., 301–2; cf. *HALOT*, 820), this verb is עִיר (ʿyr) and means "to protect or keep" (cf. Job 8:6). If so, it refers to an eagle's protection of its young by hovering over the nest rather than stirring them from the nest. Whether it means "to rouse" or "to protect" is not clear.

Several English translations regard the entire verse as an extended comparison to an eagle's treatment of its young (ESV, NCV, NIV, NKJV, NRSV), while others see a transition from the simile to a direct reference to Yahweh's conduct at the phrase יִפְרֹשׂ כְּנָפָיו (yiprōś kᵉnāpāyw), "he spreads out his wings" (NASB, NET, NLT). Drawing on the image of an eagle (v.11a), Moses develops the metaphor in the superlative. Just as an eagle hovers over its young to protect them, so Yahweh watches over his people. However, what the eagle cannot do, Yahweh does. He takes his covenantal nation and carries them on his back (cf. Ex 19:4; Dt 1:31; Isa 46:3; Hos 11:3). In other words, the second half of this verse does not depict an eagle's flight training; rather, it depicts Yahweh's special providential care for his servant-nation (Peels, "On the Wings of the Eagle [Dtn 32,11]," 302). As Keel, 190–92, points out, the imagery of God's spreading his wings over his people to protect them is common in the OT (Pss 17:8; 36:7 [8]; 57:1 [2]; 61:4 [5]; 63:7 [8]; 91:4; cf. Isa 31:5) and occurs more broadly in ancient Near Eastern literature (especially of Egypt, Palestine, and Syria).

13 The phrase וְשֶׁמֶן מֵחַלְמִישׁ צוּר (wᵉšemen mēḥalmîš ṣûr, "and oil from the flinty crag") probably refers to the fact that olive trees are able to grow in such inhospitable places as dirt-filled cracks in rocky regions that get little water.

5. Yahweh's Indictment against His People (32:15–18)

15Jeshurun grew fat and kicked;
   filled with food, he became heavy and sleek.
He abandoned the God who made him
   and rejected the Rock his Savior.
16They made him jealous with their foreign gods
   and angered him with their detestable idols.
17They sacrificed to demons, which are not God—

> gods they had not known,
> gods that recently appeared,
> gods your fathers did not fear.
> [18]You deserted the Rock, who fathered you;
> you forgot the God who gave you birth.

COMMENTARY

15–18 In spite of enjoying Yahweh's abundant provision, the Israelites abandoned their Father and Maker in order to worship pagan gods that were powerless. These verses present three sad contrasts. First, Israel responded to Yahweh's abundant provision by rejecting his authority and treating him with contempt (*nbl*; v.15; see Note on 22:21). Unlike most animals, which are docile when fed, Israel kicked at Yahweh, their Maker and Protector, and resisted his directives.

Second, even though Yahweh had chosen and flawlessly guided his people to the brink of the Promised Land, Israel often turned to pagan ("strange"; cf. *HALOT*, 279), do-nothing gods (vv.16–17)—behavior prohibited by Yahweh and regarded as vile (*tôʿēbâ*; see Note on 7:25–26). The incomprehensible part consisted in the fact that there was nothing about these "gods" to compel Israel to worship them. Israel had not experienced any blessings through their activity, and Israel's forefathers knew nothing about them. This horrific treatment of Yahweh provoked his jealousy (see comments on 5:9 and 6:15). As Ortlund, 30, n. 16, points out, "God's morally perfect jealousy arises out of his joint longings both to vindicate his own glory and to enjoy true love with his people."

Finally, they deserted and forgot (see Note 4:10) the God who brought them into existence (v.18).

NOTES

15 The name יְשֻׁרוּן (*yᵉšurûn*, "Jeshurun") occurs only three other times in the OT (Dt 33:5, 26; Isa 44:2). This title derives from the verb יָשַׁר (*yšr*), "to be upright." In the present passage it depicts Israel "in an ideal situation, with its 'uprightness' due more to God's help than his own efforts" (Mulder, *TDOT*, 6:475). It is a term of affection that often parallels "Jacob."

The verb וַיִּשְׁמַן (*wayyišman*, "but he grew fat") alludes back to the "oil" or "fat" (שֶׁמֶן, *šemen*) that Yahweh had extracted for Israel from the "flinty rock" (v.13). The verb and its related noun normally highlight abundance. The verb occurs twice in this verse to emphasize Israel's "fatness." In its other three occurrences in the OT (Isa 6:10; Jer 5:28; Ne 9:25), this abundance or "fatness" is always associated with some form of covenantal treachery. The problem with this generous, divine provision is not with the abundance itself but with Israel's attitude of heart following Yahweh's provision. Without justification, it appears that Israel takes credit for the things Yahweh has generously provided and disregards him.

In addition to the ordinary meaning of leaving something behind (1Sa 10:2; 17:20, 28) or letting land lie fallow ("leaving" the land; Ex 23:11), the verb וַיִּטֹּשׁ (*wayyiṭṭōš*, "and he abandoned"; GK 5759) means "to forsake" or "to reject" in half of its forty occurrences. It occurs frequently concerning God's rejection of his chosen people (Jdg 6:13; 1Sa 12:22; 2Ki 21:14; Pss 27:9; 94:14; Isa 2:6; Jer 7:29; 23:33, 39) and also relates to Israel's rejection of their covenantal Lord (Dt 32:15; Jer 15:6), not through "leaving" Yahweh but by disregarding him, by giving him no consideration. Since abandoning something involves a deliberate act, the one who abandons bears responsibility for doing so. Consequently, Israel's abandonment of Yahweh represents treachery. Although this verb never occurs in juxtaposition with the noun covenant, it clearly presupposes a covenantal relationship that is violated (Grisanti, "1 Kings," 273).

17 The term לַשֵּׁדִים (laśśēdîm, "to demons") only occurs here and in Psalm 106:37. In both settings the demons are objects of Israel's worship and sacrifices. According to Y. Kaufmann (*The Religion of Israel* [Chicago: Univ. of Chicago Press, 1960], 65, n. 1), "they are insubstantial shades, 'no-gods,' with neither divine nor demonic function." Tigay (*Deuteronomy*, 403, n. 92) refers to an Assyrian inscription in which Ashurbanipal (the king) says that he captured the gods or idols of the Elamites and treated them as mere ghosts, i.e., powerless beings. Not only does Israel worship pagan gods rather than the one-and-only, all-powerful God, but they worship entities that are also absolutely powerless!

18 The verbal root of מְחֹלְלֶךָ (mᵉḥōlᵉlekā, "who gave you birth") normally refers to a mother's writhing in pain as she delivers a child (Job 39:1; Isa 26:17–18; 45:10; 51:2; Jer 4:19; Mic 4:10). Here the verb graphically depicts Yahweh's intense involvement in forming Israel as a nation.

6. Yahweh's Determination to Judge Israel (32:19–25)

> ¹⁹The LORD saw this and rejected them
>   because he was angered by his sons and daughters.
> ²⁰"I will hide my face from them," he said,
>   "and see what their end will be;
> for they are a perverse generation,
>   children who are unfaithful.
> ²¹They made me jealous by what is no god
>   and angered me with their worthless idols.
> I will make them envious by those who are not a people;
>   I will make them angry by a nation that has no understanding.
> ²²For a fire has been kindled by my wrath,
>   one that burns to the realm of death below.
> It will devour the earth and its harvests
>   and set afire the foundations of the mountains.
>
> ²³"I will heap calamities upon them
>   and spend my arrows against them.
> ²⁴I will send wasting famine against them,
>   consuming pestilence and deadly plague;

I will send against them the fangs of wild beasts,
  the venom of vipers that glide in the dust.
²⁵In the street the sword will make them childless;
  in their homes terror will reign.
Young men and young women will perish,
  infants and gray-haired men.

COMMENTARY

19–20 Yahweh will witness Israel's rebellion and, in response to their rejection of him (31:19–20; see Note), will reject his covenantal nation. The rare occurrence of reference to both "sons and daughters" demonstrates the comprehensive extent of this treachery. Yahweh will withdraw his blessing ("hide his face"; see Note on 31:18) and watch the tragic outcome. He affirms that his chosen nation is perverse and disloyal (in stark contrast to their God, who is faithful; v.4 [see Note there]).

21–25 Verse 21 clearly demonstrates the appropriateness of Yahweh's promised judgment on Israel. The nation that has provoked his jealousy (*qn'*) by "non-gods" and angered (*k's*) him with "worthless idols" will be made jealous (*qn'*) by a "non-people" and made angry (*k's*) by a nonunderstanding nation. Although these elements seem to mirror each other, there are key differences between them. The anger and jealousy elicited in Yahweh *trigger* judgment but for Israel *represent* the judgment they experience. The "non-gods" that Israel pursues are just that, nonexistent gods; however, the "non-people" who conquers Israel will not be a phantom or just an idea. Yahweh will employ a nation that does not share the chosen status of Israel to bring his judgment on them.

Moses uses similar-sounding words to demonstrate the poetic justice of the judgment Yahweh will send against his people. In response to Israel's decision to worship "worthless things" (*hebel*), God

will send against his people a nation characterized by foolishness (*nābāl*). The folly of this nation probably involves their insensitivity to spiritual things, i.e., they are spiritual dullards.

Moses continues in the first person his description of Yahweh's judgment of his chosen people and uses the graphic language of covenantal cursing. The fire (metaphorical for judgment) reaches the lowest depths, consumes the earth and all of its produce, and even scorches the foundations of the mountains. This hyperbolic language may seem to imply total destruction, but it vividly depicts destruction that is far-reaching in its impact. He will heap numerous calamities (see Note on 31:17, 20) on Israel. Each affliction specified in v.24 is modified by an intensifier: "*wasting* famine against them, *consuming* pestilence and *deadly* plague." He refers to the fangs and venom of the creatures that will attack God's chosen people. These calamities will afflict young as well as old, women as well as and men.

Moses refers to future divine judgment in this section but does not provide enough detail for one to identify the attacking nation(s). Paul later makes use of this "non-people" nomenclature for a different reason. Whereas the "non-people" in the present context are God's tool of judgment on his chosen nation, the Gentile "not a people" Paul speaks of will be used by God to drive his chosen people Israel back to himself (Ro 9:24–26).

NOTES

20 The noun תַּהְפֻּכֹת (*tahpukōt*, "perversity"; GK 9337), derived from the verb "to overturn" (הפך, *hpk*), describes Israel's overturning of God's requirements. The ancient Near Eastern cognates for the verb signify betraying or reneging on an oath, treaty, or agreement (Tigay, *Deuteronomy*, 404, n. 104).

21 The nominal root of בְּהַבְלֵיהֶם (*bᵉhablêhem*, "with their worthless idols") can refer to breath or vapor (Job 7:16; Pr 21:6; Isa 57:3) or metaphorically to something vain (2Ki 17:15; Ecc 6:4, 11; Jer 10:15). Included in the OT's dubbing as הֶבֶל (*hebel*; GK 2039) are: human activity (Ecc 1:2, 14), wasted effort (Isa 49:4), empty comfort (Zec 10:2), humankind (Ps 39:5, 11 [6, 12]; 62:9 [10]), and life itself (Ps 78:33). As Merrill ("Deuteronomy," 517–18) points out,

> only God can transform the nothingness of life into purpose and value. The present text equates vanities with "not God".... The existence and presence of God provide significance of life to those who know him. Those who disavow him, however, and chase after idols (no gods, v.17) embrace vanity and therefore live empty and unfulfilling lives.

22 In the OT שְׁאוֹל (*šᵉʾôl*, "death, grave") does not generally refer to the fires of hell but to the realm of the dead (cf. Pss 9:17 [18]; 16:10; 139:8; Isa 14:9, 15; Am 9:2; cf. P. Johnston, *Shades of Sheol: Death and Afterlife in the Old Testament* [Downers Grove, Ill.: InterVarsity Press, 2002], 71–81). The parallel expression "the foundations of the mountains" suggests that עַד־שְׁאוֹל תַּחְתִּית (*ʿad-šᵉʾôl taḥtît*, "to the lowest Sheol") signifies the innermost parts of the earth—as low as one can go.

7. Yahweh's Reconsideration of Judging His Chosen People (32:26–35)

²⁶I said I would scatter them
 and blot out their memory from mankind,
²⁷but I dreaded the taunt of the enemy,
 lest the adversary misunderstand
and say, 'Our hand has triumphed;
 the LORD has not done all this.'"

²⁸They are a nation without sense,
 there is no discernment in them.
²⁹If only they were wise and would understand this
 and discern what their end will be!
³⁰How could one man chase a thousand,
 or two put ten thousand to flight,
unless their Rock had sold them,
 unless the LORD had given them up?

> [31]For their rock is not like our Rock,
>   as even our enemies concede.
> [32]Their vine comes from the vine of Sodom
>   and from the fields of Gomorrah.
> Their grapes are filled with poison,
>   and their clusters with bitterness.
> [33]Their wine is the venom of serpents,
>   the deadly poison of cobras.
>
> [34]"Have I not kept this in reserve
>   and sealed it in my vaults?
> [35]It is mine to avenge; I will repay.
>   In due time their foot will slip;
> their day of disaster is near
>   and their doom rushes upon them."

COMMENTARY

26–27 At this point the song begins a transition from Yahweh's judgment on his servant-nation to his judgment of the arrogant nations that carry out his intentions. Yahweh first mentions the comprehensive extent of his intended judgment of Israel. It will blot out any remembrance of them to all humankind (see Note on 7:24 for a similar concept but with different wording). Israel's covenantal treachery justifies their extermination.

However, Yahweh is concerned that the pagan nations might see the extermination of Israel as their victory rather than Yahweh's judgment (a clear part of his plan). They will regard Israel's destruction as evidence of the defeat of Yahweh's plan for the world. This delineation of Yahweh's deliberation does not evidence God's going through a process in his own understanding and thinking; rather, he lays out the process *for the readers* so they can understand the rationale driving his conduct.

28–29 Scholars debate whether the subject of these verses is Israel (Craigie, 386; Kalland, 210;

Merrill, *Deuteronomy*, 421; Thompson, 301–2) or the pagan nations (Hall, 478; Ridderbos, 291; Tigay, *Deuteronomy*, 310; Wright, *Deuteronomy*, 302; McConville, 457, and Nelson, 375–76, waffle on the issue). This interpretive debate draws on the fact that both Israel and the nations are characterized by lack of wisdom and inability to recognize Yahweh's key role in the events of history. Proponents of both options identify a shift from Israel to the nations either at v.28 or at v.31. Recognizing the relevance of this description to God's servant-nation, since the passage begins and ends with the nations as the subject, it would appear that these verses are directed to the pagan nations as well. Their inability to recognize Yahweh's role in their victory over the rebellious Israelites displays their lack of discernment.

30–33 How could they have gained an overwhelming victory against the "odds" except for Yahweh's (the Rock; see Note on 32:4) intervention in their behalf? The pagan nations have no such defender. This disparity between the attackers and Israel does not point to any specific historical conflict, nor does it necessarily connote a great disparity between their military forces. Unless Yahweh delivers his chosen people into the hands of an enemy nation, no nation will have victory over Israel. In numerous instances Yahweh gave his people an astounding victory over much larger armies. The side that Yahweh backs is always victorious.

The "vine" of these pagan nations seems to refer metaphorically to their pagan gods, who find their root in Sodom and Gomorrah—OT paradigms for perversion and wickedness (cf. Ge 18:20; 19:4–28; Isa 1:10; 3:9; Jer 23:14; La 4:6; Eze 16:44–52; Mt 10:15; 11:23–24). The grapes and wine produced from the fruit of these vines is bitter and poisonous, even comparable to the poisonous venom of a cobra (Jer 25:15–16; Eze 23:31–34). The worship of these pagan gods is not only displeasing but ultimately induces certain death. Both Israel and the pagan nations must recognize the death-inducing rather than life-producing consequences of worshiping false gods if they are to survive, i.e., avoid the devastating fate experienced by Sodom and Gomorrah.

34–35 Yahweh resumes speaking (as vv.31–33 reflect the words of the Moses) and presents the demise of the wicked as a certainty. The "this" Yahweh has stored in his vaults refers to his intent to bring judgment on the pagan nations, who are devoted to their false gods. This judgment will take place at the time and in the manner that Yahweh determines. Because these nations have overstepped their bounds as agents of divine wrath, Yahweh alone will punish them (cf. Isa 10:5–19, 24–27; Jer 25:12–14).

NOTES

27 The verb אָגוּר (ʾāgûr, "but I dreaded") occurs only ten times in the OT with this meaning. Unlike other verbs for "fear," this verb does not signify the visceral reaction of terror as much as the dread of some anticipated threat or danger (Dt 1:17; 18:22; 1Sa 18:15; Job 19:29). Yahweh's reputation is so important to him and to Israel that he will not damage it by allowing the pagan nations to attribute failure to him. He will save his people—not just for their sakes, but also for the sake of his own name (1Sa 12:22; 2Ki 19:34; 20:6; Ps 25:11; Isa 37:35; 43:25; Jer 14:7). The expression יָדֵינוּ רָמָה (yādênû rāmâ, "our hand is high") appears to be a metaphor that indicates military arrogance (Craigie, 385).

32 The connection between the reference to גַּפְנָם (gapnām), "their vine," and the pagan gods may be that of a metonymy in which the effect is put for the cause. In this case vines, grapes, and wine represented the gods (often gods of fertility) that made their production possible (Merrill, *Deuteronomy*, 422).

34 The second verb in this verse, in the question הֲלֹא־הוּא ... חָתֻם (hªlōʾ-hûʾ ... ḥātum, "Is it not sealed up?"), refers to an ancient Near Eastern practice of closing royal storerooms by placing clay over the door-latch and then imprinting the royal seal in the clay (Tigay, "Some Archaeological Notes," 378–80). This verse affirms that Yahweh has securely stored the announced punishment until he determines to bring that judgment to pass.

35 Biblical vengeance relates to lawfulness, justice, and salvation (Peels, *NIDOTTE*, 3:154), whose ultimate source, in most instances, is God (as exemplified here in the statement לִי נָקָם, lî nāqām, "vengeance is mine"); humans (if involved at all) are a secondary source (Eze 25:14). God, being holy, cannot allow sinful rebellion to remain unpunished. Divine vengeance entails God's setting the record straight. His perfect justice and righteousness serve as both the occasion and guide for vengeance. Divine vengeance takes place on an international level (Isa 47:3; Jer 46:10; Na 1:2), in a covenantal setting (Nu 31:2; Lev 26:15; Ps 79:10; Jer 5:9, 29; 9:9[8]), and in behalf of individuals (Pss 58:11; 79:10; 94:1; 149:7; Grisanti, "2 Kings," 2:306).

As exemplified in the phrase תָמוּט רַגְלָם (*tāmûṭ raglām*, "their foot will slip"), the slipping of one's foot is a regular biblical idiom for the experience of misfortune (Pss 38:16 [17]; 66:9; 94:18; 121:3; cf. Ps 73:2).

8. Israel and Yahweh Are Vindicated (32:36–43)

> 36The LORD will judge his people
>   and have compassion on his servants
> when he sees their strength is gone
>   and no one is left, slave or free.
> 37He will say: "Now where are their gods,
>   the rock they took refuge in,
> 38the gods who ate the fat of their sacrifices
>   and drank the wine of their drink offerings?
> Let them rise up to help you!
>   Let them give you shelter!
>
> 39"See now that I myself am he!
>   There is no god besides me.
> I put to death and I bring to life,
>   I have wounded and I will heal,
>   and no one can deliver out of my hand.
> 40I lift my hand to heaven and declare:
>   As surely as I live forever,
> 41when I sharpen my flashing sword
>   and my hand grasps it in judgment,
> I will take vengeance on my adversaries
>   and repay those who hate me.
> 42I will make my arrows drunk with blood,
>   while my sword devours flesh:
> the blood of the slain and the captives,
>   the heads of the enemy leaders."

> [43]Rejoice, O nations, with his people,
>   for he will avenge the blood of his servants;
> he will take vengeance on his enemies
>   and make atonement for his land and people.

COMMENTARY

36–38 The judgment to which Moses refers does not connote divine punishment but Yahweh's vindication of his covenantal nation (cf. Ge 30:6; Pss 54:1 [3]; 135:14; Pr 31:9). He will "right a wrong" and relent from the promised punishment ("have compassion"). He will extend this to "his servants" and "his people," thus reminding the Israelites singing this song that they are in an intimate relationship with Yahweh, their covenantal Lord. Only when they have exhausted all resources and are forced to recognize their total inability to face their predicament alone will Yahweh come to their aid. He will, appropriately, point out the foolishness of their preference for false gods. With some sarcasm, Yahweh refers to the "rock" that can provide no protection and the idols that consume their sacrifices and drink offerings but provide absolutely nothing for their worshipers. He knows that his exhortation for these "do-nothing" gods to come to Israel's aid will generate nothing but silence since they do not even exist.

39–43 The goal of Yahweh's dealings with Israel, especially his judgment of them for their rebellion, is to elicit the nation's realizing that he is the only true God, who possesses all power and will judge every one of his enemies in an act that will affect the entire world. In stark contrast to the pagan gods that the Israelites found so alluring, Yahweh is unique—"I am he," declares the Lord. He makes the same affirmation in the book of Isaiah, where he announces that he has no rival among

the pagan gods (Isa 41:4; 43:10, 13; 48:12). In the context (here and in Isaiah), Yahweh is stating that he alone, unlike the non-gods, controls the events of history. The affirmation of Yahweh's uniqueness and exclusivity ("there is no other") is echoed in several other OT passages (Dt 4:35, 39; 1Ki 8:60; Isa 45:5–6, 14, 18, 21–22; 46:9; Joel 2:27). He alone wields absolute sovereignty over life and death and has the ability to cause and heal wounds, which only God can do perfectly.

Yahweh buttresses the irrevocability of his ensuing statements by using oath language: "I lift my hand to heaven" and "as surely as I live forever" (v.40; see Notes). In vv.41–42 Yahweh describes his judgment of Israel's enemies in graphic, militaristic terms. His sword and arrows cause much bloodshed. As a matter of fact, his arrows become "drunk" with blood and his sword "devours" flesh—images that emphasize the devastation caused by divine judgment. This punishment represents divine vengeance (cf. 32:43; see Note on 32:35) and makes complete (*šlm*; cf. 7:10) or repays those pagans who hate Yahweh (i.e., have no covenantal relationship with him; see Note on 5:9).

This stanza concludes with a call for the nations to rejoice, along with Israel, because of Yahweh's role in history. This joy does not involve reveling in the carnage left behind by divine judgment but instead entails celebrating Yahweh's resolution of numerous moral and ethical inequities (Merrill, *Deuteronomy*, 425). Although God's people had the responsibility of offering a sacrifice for the atonement of the land

(21:8 [see Note]), Yahweh will make atonement for both the land and his people—a declaration anticipating the redeeming (and atoning) death of Jesus Christ.

NOTES

36 Scholars have offered various interpretations of the difficult phrase עָצוּר וְעָזוּב (*ʿāṣûr wᵉʿāzûb*), "slave or free" (cf. *HALOT*, 871; M. Cogan and H. Tadmor, *II Kings* [New York: Doubleday, 1988], 107). It occurs here and in four passages in Kings (1Ki 14:10; 21:21; 2Ki 9:8; 14:26), all four of which predict total annihilation. Cogan and Tadmor, 107, based on the present passage's reference to a lack of strength, suggest the phrase signifies incapable or incapacitated individuals. If so, even the sick and feeble will be unable to escape whatever the surrounding context delineates. At the very least, it is a phrase that highlights totality in some fashion.

40 J. Lust ("For I Lift up My Hand to Heaven and Swear: Dt 32:40," in *Studies in Deuteronomy* [ed. F. Martínez et al.; Leiden: Brill, 1994], 155–64) has suggested that the statement אֶשָּׂא אֶל־שָׁמַיִם יָדִי (*ʾeśśāʾ ʾel-šāmayim yādî*, "I lift my hand to heaven") signifies Yahweh's intention to intervene in behalf of his people. But the immediate context and the statement's use in several other passages (Eze 20:5–6, 15, 23, 28, 42; 36:7; et al.) to indicate something Yahweh swears he will do favor the traditional interpretation.

The oath formula חַי אָנֹכִי לְעֹלָם (*ḥay ʾānōkî lᵉʿōlām*, "as I live forever") occurs twenty-two times in the OT (with the pronoun אָנֹכִי, *ʾānōkî*, here but אֲנִי, *ʾᵃnî*, everywhere else), sixteen of which are in Ezekiel. The phrase represents a modification of a more common oath formula, "as the Lord lives" (which appears forty times in the OT). These formulas fall into two general categories. In several passages, the latter formula emphasizes that Yahweh indeed lives, in direct contrast to the dead gods (e.g., Baal) that Israel was worshiping (1Ki 17:1; 18:10, 15; Jer 4:2; 5:2; Hos 4:15; et al.). In these instances the phrase could be translated: "so truly Yahweh lives."

Several other instances of this latter formula and all the occurrences of the former formula appear in the context of personal relationships, often when a person's life is threatened. In those instances the formula offers security in the face of danger or strengthens the intentionality of the vow (e.g., Nu 14:21; Isa 49:18; Jer 22:24; Eze 5:11; 20:3, 31, 33 et al.; J. Wozniak, "Bedeutung und Belege der Schwurformel *ḥaj* Jahwe," *BZ* 28 [1984]: 248–49). Yahweh swears by his own life that what he has promised will take place (Grisanti, "1 Kings," 236–37).

43 This verse has a number of textual "problems." While the MT for this verse only has four poetic lines, the Qumran text (4QDeut^q) has six lines and the LXX eight lines. Consult the following works for a helpful summary and treatment of the issues: A. van der Kooij, "The Ending of the Song of Moses," in *Studies in Deuteronomy* (ed. F. G. Martínez et al.; Leiden: Brill, 1994), 93–100; Nelson, 379–80; Tigay, *Deuteronomy*, 516–18. This note discusses only one of the questions, namely, whether or not the MT is missing a line found in both the Qumran document and the LXX—"Bow to him, all sons of God" (based on the Heb. והשתחוו לו כל אלהים, *whštḥww lw kl ʾlhym*)—in the light of the line's similarity with a textual variant in 32:8. The external evidence for this variant reading is strong (as both the Qumran fragments and the LXX agree). This line was probably omitted because of concerns that it taught incorrect angelology or polytheism. The quotation of this passage in Hebrews 1:6 suggests that this line belongs in the original version of the MT. Just as this song gives attention to the heavenly/cosmic and earthly/historical dimensions of Yahweh's activity, this verse includes the "sons of God" and the "nation" in this call to praise (עַמּוֹ גּוֹיִם, *gôyim ʿammô*, "O nations, with his people").

9. Epilogue (32:44–52)

⁴⁴Moses came with Joshua son of Nun and spoke all the words of this song in the hearing of the people. ⁴⁵When Moses finished reciting all these words to all Israel, ⁴⁶he said to them, "Take to heart all the words I have solemnly declared to you this day, so that you may command your children to obey carefully all the words of this law. ⁴⁷They are not just idle words for you — they are your life. By them you will live long in the land you are crossing the Jordan to possess."

⁴⁸On that same day the LORD told Moses, ⁴⁹"Go up into the Abarim Range to Mount Nebo in Moab, across from Jericho, and view Canaan, the land I am giving the Israelites as their own possession. ⁵⁰There on the mountain that you have climbed you will die and be gathered to your people, just as your brother Aaron died on Mount Hor and was gathered to his people. ⁵¹This is because both of you broke faith with me in the presence of the Israelites at the waters of Meribah Kadesh in the Desert of Zin and because you did not uphold my holiness among the Israelites. ⁵²Therefore, you will see the land only from a distance; you will not enter the land I am giving to the people of Israel."

COMMENTARY

44–47 Looking back on the message of this song in particular and the law in general, Moses charges the nation of Israel to live in accordance with the Lord's expectations. Not only must they wholeheartedly obey Yahweh's demands, but they must also pass on to each successive generation that passion for genuine conformity of heart to his law. Only then will they and their descendants enjoy long tenure in the Promised Land.

Their submission to this exhortation is of vital importance because God himself is testifying about them, and his demands represent nothing less than

life itself (cf. 4:1; 30:20). These words are not empty or inconsequential (*rēq*). Full and satisfying life directly depends on Israel's willing submission to Yahweh's expectations. The involvement of Joshua in this appearance before the nation paves the way for his imminent assumption of leadership.

48–52 After Moses has finished reciting the preceding song, the Lord tells him to ascend Mount Nebo (cf. Nu 27:12–14; see Note on "Pisgah" at 34:1) to view the land of Canaan. The Lord will not allow Moses to enter the land because of the offense he committed during Israel's wanderings in the wilderness (cf. Nu 20:10–13; Dt 1:37; 3:23–28). Sometime shortly after seeing the Promised Land, Moses will die.

The text specifies two reasons for this painful reality. In the first place, Moses "broke faith" with Yahweh. This verb signifies a breach of a relationship of trust between persons or with God (Wakely, *NIDOTTE*, 2:1020). The covenantal mediator's conduct at Meribah represented dis-

loyalty. That whole episode was regarded as an act of rebellion throughout Israelite history (Nu 20:24; cf. 27:14; 1Sa 12:15). Second, Moses failed to "uphold holiness." His actions at Meribah did not demonstrate a proper recognition of Yahweh's absolute sovereignty and uniqueness. In spite of this offense, Yahweh will allow Moses the privilege of viewing the long-anticipated land before he dies.

NOTE

44 הוֹשֵׁעַ (*hôšēaʿ*), "Hoshea," appears in the MT for Joshua (יְהוֹשֻׁעַ, *yehôšuaʿ*) in this verse. That name was a common alternative for Joshua (Nu 13:8, 16). The difference in the meanings of these two names is slight but significant: "Hoshea" means "he saves," whereas the more specific "Joshua" means "the LORD saves."

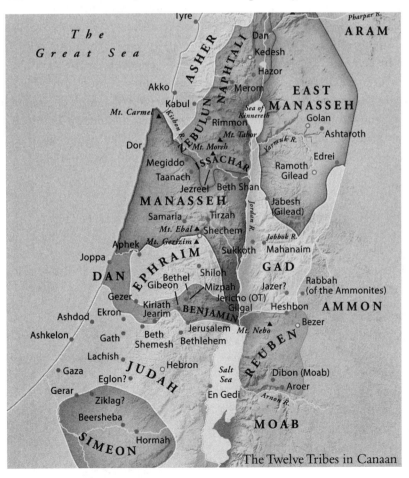

The Twelve Tribes in Canaan

C. The Blessing of Moses on the Israelite Tribes (33:1–29)

OVERVIEW

As with ch. 32, this chapter is poetic in form, and as with Jacob in Genesis 49, Moses pronounces blessings on the Israelite tribes. Although the pronouncements in Genesis 49 are clearly predictive, the blessings in the present chapter represent Moses' desire for God's people (his "prayerful intercession"; Merrill, *Deuteronomy*, 432). As Driver, 388–89, suggests, the aim is "to rally the nation anew around the banner of the Mosaic institutions" and to give God's people a fresh reminder of the blessing of being the people of Yahweh.

It is also important to notice that the chapter does not delineate Israel's responsibility to the exclusion of Yahweh's role. As a matter of fact, the idea of blessing in ch. 33, according to Barker ("The Theology of Deuteronomy 27," 293), "is not bound to the law but ultimately derives from Yahweh's grace. Thus Deuteronomy 33 ... is an expression of optimism, with confidence placed not in

Israel's possibility of covenantal obedience, but in Yahweh's grace." J. Heck ("A History of Interpretation of Genesis 49 and Deuteronomy 33," *BSac* 147 [1990]: 23) suggests that Deuteronomy 33 and Genesis 49 have various shared features in order to connect Israel's "present" circumstances with Yahweh's promise of a land to Jacob. Moses legitimately appears as a leader of Israel akin to Jacob, one of the patriarchs. God has kept his promise, so Israel needs to obey him genuinely.

After a brief introduction (v.1) and historical review (vv.2–5), Moses pronounces blessings on the tribes (vv.6–25) and ends with a general praise of and blessing for the nation (vv.26–29). Only eleven tribes find mention in ch. 33. (Joseph is counted as one, and Simeon is omitted). The numbering of the tribes in Numbers 1:5–15 and 26:5–51 omits Levi but divides Joseph into Manasseh and Ephraim (thus retaining twelve tribes).

1. Introduction and Historical Review (33:1–5)

¹This is the blessing that Moses the man of God pronounced on the Israelites before his death. ²He said:

"The LORD came from Sinai
　and dawned over them from Seir;
　he shone forth from Mount Paran.
He came with myriads of holy ones
　from the south, from his mountain slopes.
³Surely it is you who love the people;
　all the holy ones are in your hand.
At your feet they all bow down,

> and from you receive instruction,
>
> ⁴the law that Moses gave us,
>
>   the possession of the assembly of Jacob.
>
> ⁵He was king over Jeshurun
>
>   when the leaders of the people assembled,
>
>   along with the tribes of Israel.

COMMENTARY

1–2a In anticipation of his death, Moses gathers the Israelite tribes (who bear the names of Jacob's sons) much as Jacob did according to Genesis 49. As their theocratic leader, Moses delineates these forward-looking blessings. He is called "the man of God," a term normally reserved for biblical prophets.

2b–5 Moses describes Yahweh's appearance to Israel at Sinai in graphic terms. He is their conquering hero and covenantal Lord, who came to them at Sinai and brought them to the Promised Land (cf. Jdg 5:4–5; Ps 68:7–8, 17–18 [8–9, 18–19]; Hab 3:3–7). He mentions Sinai (for the only time in Deuteronomy), Seir, and Paran as parallel terms for places along Israel's trek to Canaan. The fact that he "dawned over" and "shone forth" refers to his impressive revelation of himself (theophany) at Sinai. He led a host of Israelites from the south (Kadesh Barnea) toward the land of Canaan.

Yahweh loves his chosen people (evidenced in his election of and care for them), and they should respond in submission by gladly accepting his instruction (v.3), mediated to them through Moses (v.4). Their reception of this special provision from Yahweh is part of what has made them his special possession in the world (Ex 19:5–6; Dt 7:6). A fundamental element of Israel's relationship with Yahweh is to recognize and submit to his kingship. He is sovereign over them, i.e., over Jeshurun (see Note on 32:15). As their king he can lay before them his requirements, demand their submission, and provide the blessings (or curses) he promised them.

Wright (*Deuteronomy*, 309–10) helpfully summarizes three key themes in these verses: Yahweh's transcendent power (clearly demonstrated at Sinai), the reciprocal nature of this covenantal relationship (Yahweh's love and Israel's obedience or loyalty), and Yahweh's kingship, which rested on three basic premises: his deliverance of Israel from Egypt (Ex 15:18), his provision of the law at Sinai, and the victory over Canaan he is about to give to Israel (see also Craigie, 394).

NOTES

2 Regarding the phrase הוֹפִיעַ ... זָרַח (*zāraḥ ... hôpîaʿ*, "he rose up ... he shone forth"), the first verb (זרח, *zrḥ*) usually describes the rising of the sun (Ge 32:31; Ex 22:3; Jdg 9:33; 2Ki 3:22; Ps 104:22) or the shining of the stars (Nu 24:17). Here it refers to Yahweh's revelation of himself in his theophanic glory when he gave the law to Israel at Sinai (Ex 19:16; 24:17). The second verb (יפע, *ypʿ*) represents the natural consequence of rising up. Once a bearer of light rises, its light radiates to others (Merrill, "Deuteronomy," 519). Yahweh has displayed his glory to Israel, both through theophany and by means of the revealed law.

Verses 2 and 3 in this section have various textual problems; we will discuss only two of the issues here (cf. Nelson, 380, 383–84, for an overview). First, the second word in the phrase וְאָתָה מֵרִבְבֹת קֹדֶשׁ (weʾātâ mēribbōt qōdeš, "and he came with multitudes from Kadesh") can mean "myriads/many" (most commentators) or constitute a place name (Christensen, *Deuteronomy 21:10–34:12*, 832, 836; Tigay, *Deuteronomy*, 320). The former is more likely. The third term (קֹדֶשׁ, qōdeš) can refer to Kadesh Barnea (McConville, 465; Merrill, *Deuteronomy*, 435) or to holy ones (= "angels"; Craigie, 392; Nelson, 380). Although angels fit into Yahweh's plans, the abundance of place names in the context favors the first option.

Second, the line מִימִינוֹ אֵשְׁדָּת לָמוֹ (mîmînô ʾēšdāt lāmô, "from the south, mighty ones with him") bears several points of debate. The primary change evidenced in the translation provided above is at variance with the NIV ("from the south, from his mountain slopes") and involves a slight emendation following the LXX (אשרו אלים, ʾšrw ʾlym, "with him mighty ones"; cf. McConville, 465; Merrill, *Deuteronomy*, 435).

3 Although several MSS and versions emend the noun עַמִּים (ʿammîm) to a singular, the next line probably defines what "peoples" mean. The "holy ones" in the context refer to the Israelites. Accordingly, one should recognize that this reference constitutes the only use of the plural of עַם (ʿam), i.e., "peoples," for Israel in the OT.

2. The Blessings on the Tribes (33:6–25)

OVERVIEW

The pronouncement of blessings on the Israelite tribes is not only one of Moses' last acts but also looks forward to the victory Yahweh will give Israel in the Promised Land. The order in which the blessings are pronounced departs from that found in Genesis 49. It appears roughly to follow their divinely intended geographic distribution of the land, from south to north.

a. Reuben (33:6)

> [6]"Let Reuben live and not die,
>   but let his men be few."

COMMENTARY

6 As Jacob's eldest son (Ge 29:32), Reuben is the first to receive a blessing (as in most tribal lists). This blessing is brief and negative. Reuben lost the blessing because of an affair with his father's concubine (Ge 35:22). Although this tribe was not especially small in the censuses of Numbers 1 and 26, it will struggle to survive in Israel's ensuing history (cf. 2Ki 10:32–33).

NOTE

6 Scholars and English translations are divided on whether the line מְתָיו מִסְפָּר (*mᵉtāyw mispār*, "let his men be few") envisions for Reuben great numbers (Christensen, *Deuteronomy 21:10–34:12*, 848; Hall, 489; Merrill, *Deuteronomy*, 436; NASB, NET, NIV, NKJV) or small numbers (Craigie, 394; Driver, 394–95; McConville, 466; Nelson, 389; Thompson, 309; Tigay, *Deuteronomy*, 322–23; Wright, *Deuteronomy*, 314; ESV, NCV, NLT, NRSV). Interpreters suggesting that this verse affirms that Reuben will become numerous regard the negative adverb in the first poetic line as also governing the second line (i.e., translated, "may his numbers not be few"). However, in most cases in which the negative adverb serves "double duty," it holds the principal place in the first of two clauses (Driver, 395). Here it seems to hold a subordinate place. The Hebrew reads literally, "may his men be a number," probably echoing the expression "men of number," which means "men of small number" (Ge 34:30; McConville, 466).

b. Judah (33:7)

⁷And this he said about Judah:

"Hear, O LORD, the cry of Judah;
  bring him to his people.
With his own hands he defends his cause.
  Oh, be his help against his foes!"

COMMENTARY

7 This blessing on Judah is much shorter than the one found in Genesis 49:8–12 and has no messianic overtones. It does not deny those overtones but assumes that the Israelites are already aware of them. This blessing by Moses has clear military overtones. After all, Judah was to march at the head of the Israelite army whenever they entered the field of battle (Nu 2:9). The prayer to bring Judah to his people may be a prayer that the tribe will survive all battles and return to their loved ones at home. Judah will be personally involved in all battles ("with his own hands"), but their victory hinges on receiving Yahweh's help.

c. Levi (33:8–11)

⁸About Levi he said:

"Your Thummim and Urim belong
    to the man you favored.
You tested him at Massah;
    you contended with him at the waters of Meribah.
⁹He said of his father and mother,
    'I have no regard for them.'
He did not recognize his brothers
    or acknowledge his own children,
but he watched over your word
    and guarded your covenant.
¹⁰He teaches your precepts to Jacob
    and your law to Israel.
He offers incense before you
    and whole burnt offerings on your altar.
¹¹Bless all his skills, O LORD,
    and be pleased with the work of his hands.
Smite the loins of those who rise up against him;
    strike his foes till they rise no more."

COMMENTARY

8–11 Unlike the negative "blessing" found in Genesis 49 (appropriate in the light of Levi's sin in Ge 34:1–29), Moses' words focus on the role of the descendants of Levi as priests and teachers of the law. As a tribe, they had been set apart by Yahweh. Their fulfillment of this role is integral to their duties as members of the covenantal nation and thus has clear covenantal overtones. In some fashion, the Israelites tested the Levites at Massah and Meribah. It may be that their testing of Yahweh and Moses represented a testing of the Levites as well, since both Moses and the Levites were Yahweh's spokesmen (Craigie, 396).

Verse 9 appears to allude to Israel's rebellion in fashioning the golden calf (Ex 32:26–29). In the wake of that rebellion, Yahweh directed the Levites to execute those who were committed to rebelling against him, regardless of their blood relatedness. By obeying Yahweh, they were guarding the covenantal relationship between the nation and their God. The Levites' assigned tasks involved teaching the Torah to God's people, offering incense, and presenting other types of offerings (v.10).

Moses' blessing on Levi ends with a prayer that Yahweh will bless or enhance Levi's efforts (v.11). Even this tribe, dedicated to leading Israel's worship, needs Yahweh's assistance if they are going to be effective in carrying out their God-given role. Like all the other tribes, the Levites will enter battle with the rest of the army of Israel and need God's protection against the nation's foes. This request is not for for military prowess but for protection against attackers.

NOTE

8 The phrase תֻּמֶּיךָ וְאוּרֶיךָ (tummeykā wᵉʾûreykā, "your Thummim and your Urim") reverses the normal order of "Urim and Thummim," denoting sacred stones used by Israel's leaders to ascertain from Yahweh "yes" or "no" answers to specific requests for guidance. The high priest (a member of the tribe of Levi) carried the stones in a pouch of his priestly breastplate (Ex 28:30; Lev 8:8; for more information, see Van Dam, *NIDOTTE*, 1:329–30; idem, *ISBE*², 4:957–59). As Merrill (*Deuteronomy*, 438) points out, by synecdoche (a figure by which a more comprehensive term is used for a less comprehensive one, or vice versa) Moses mentions the Urim and Thummim as representative of the entire office and function of the priesthood.

The adjective in the phrase לְאִישׁ חֲסִידֶךָ (lᵉʾîš ḥᵃsîdekā, "to the man you favored") has two primary meanings. It can refer to someone who is kind in his treatment of others (2Sa 22:26; Ps 18:26), but more frequently it signifies a godly person whose conduct evidences a desire to be faithful to Yahweh. The word is especially common in the Psalms, where it identifies a faithful remnant of people loyal to Yahweh and seeking to serve him (Pss 16:10; 30:4 [5]; 32:6; 37:28; 50:5 et al.; R. A. Taylor, "2 Chronicles," *The Bible Knowledge Word Study* [ed. E. H. Merrill; Colorado Springs, Colo.: Cook, 2004], 2:395). In the present context it refers to the Levites, who are set apart by Yahweh for devoted service to him.

d. Benjamin (33:12)

¹²About Benjamin he said:

"Let the beloved of the LORD rest secure in him,
    for he shields him all day long,
    and the one the LORD loves rests between his shoulders."

COMMENTARY

12 Unlike the blessing in Genesis 49, which depicts Benjamin as a ravenous wolf, Moses pronounces a tender blessing on Benjamin—one reminiscent of Benjamin's close relationship with his father, Jacob (Ge 42:4, 38; 44:18–34). The term "beloved" refers to someone who enjoys a special relationship with Yahweh or with another person (2Sa 12:25; Ps 127:2; Isa 5:1; Jer 11:15). Benjamin can rest securely in Yahweh, who shields him from all threats.

The anthropomorphism of resting between Yahweh's shoulders speaks of tender compassion and unshakeable security (Merrill, *Deuteronomy*, 440). In the light of a Ugaritic parallel, it may refer to being held close to the breast or bosom of Yahweh (F. Cross and D. Freedman, *Studies in Ancient Yahwistic Poetry* [Grand Rapids: Eerdmans, 1997], 77, n. 40; cf. Jn 13:23).

NOTE

12 One's interpretation of the phrase בֵּין כְּתֵיפָיו (*bên kᵉtêpāyw*, "between his shoulders") hinges on whether God is taken as the subject or the object of the "resting." If God is "resting," the "shoulders" could refer to the hills or mountains around the sanctuary where his presence dwells (Bethel or Jerusalem; Tigay, *Deuteronomy*, 326; McConville, 463, 467; ESV, NLT), or to his weapons as the warrior God (Craigie, 396–97). The verb "to dwell" (שׁכן, *škn*) occurs twice, apparently in a chiastic pattern (ABB'A') in the MT: "will dwell securely ... between his shoulders he will dwell." The chiasm may support the interpretation that Benjamin is the subject of both verbs; thus he rests on Yahweh's bosom—a mark of intimacy (Hall, 491; Merrill, *Deuteronomy*, 440; Nelson, 390; NET, NASB, NIV, NKJV, NRSV).

e. Joseph (33:13–17)

¹³About Joseph he said:

"May the LORD bless his land
   with the precious dew from heaven above
   and with the deep waters that lie below;
¹⁴with the best the sun brings forth
   and the finest the moon can yield;
¹⁵with the choicest gifts of the ancient mountains
   and the fruitfulness of the everlasting hills;
¹⁶with the best gifts of the earth and its fullness
   and the favor of him who dwelt in the burning bush.

Let all these rest on the head of Joseph,
　　on the brow of the prince among his brothers.
¹⁷In majesty he is like a firstborn bull;
　　his horns are the horns of a wild ox.
With them he will gore the nations,
　　even those at the ends of the earth.
Such are the ten thousands of Ephraim;
　　such are the thousands of Manasseh."

COMMENTARY

13–16 This blessing on Joseph (the second longest in ch. 33) applies by extension to the tribes of Ephraim and Manasseh. Moses desires that Yahweh will abundantly bless the land occupied by "Joseph" (vv.13–16) and enable him to have the strength to defeat Israel's enemies (v.17). These tribes received the largest amount of land compared to the other tribes, and much of their land was fertile. Here Moses presents four pairs of statements with parallel items:

v.13—"precious dew" and "deep waters";
　　"from heaven above" and "that lie below"
v.14—"best" and "finest"; "the sun brings
　　forth" and "the moon can yield"
v.15—"choicest gifts" and "fruitfulness";
　　"of the ancient mountains" and "of the
　　ever lasting hills"
v.16—"best gifts" and "favor of him"; "the
　　earth and its fullness" and "him who
　　dwelt in the burning bush."

Strengthening the obvious theme of abundance, the term for "bounty" (*meged*; "precious dew" [v.13], "best" and "finest" [v.14], "choicest gifts" [v.15], and "best gifts" [v.16]) occurs five times in vv.13–16. The parallelism of the places or topographical features emphasizes the comprehensive nature of these blessings. All parts of creation, under the control of Yahweh, will produce abundantly for Joseph's descendants. In light of the relatively arid climate, rain, dew, and springs are of the utmost importance. The sun (with the moon as a parallel) is essential to a productive harvest. The hills and mountains are valuable not only as sources for needed minerals but also for their slopes, on which are planted vineyards and olive trees.

The last of these parallel lines points to the ultimate source of all these blessings: the One who dwells in the burning bush, i.e., Yahweh (Ex 3:2–4). The request that these blessings rest on Joseph's head (v.16b) alludes to the prominence Joseph's descendants will have over his brothers (fulfilling Ge 37:5–11).

17 The tribes of Joseph are likened to a powerful bull that gores the enemies around it. "Horns" are common metaphors for strength (Nu 23:22; Job 39:9–12; Ps 22:21 [22]). Although Manasseh was the older brother, Ephraim received the primary blessing (Ge 48:12–14) and is listed first here. For the purposes of emphasis, Moses reverses the normal order of "thousands ... ten thousand" (cf. Dt 32:30; 1Sa 18:7; 21:12; 29:5).

f. Zebulun and Issachar (33:18–19)

> [18]About Zebulun he said:
>
> "Rejoice, Zebulun, in your going out,
>   and you, Issachar, in your tents.
> [19]They will summon peoples to the mountain
>   and there offer sacrifices of righteousness;
> they will feast on the abundance of the seas,
>   on the treasures hidden in the sand."

COMMENTARY

18–19 Moses pronounces a corporate blessing on Zebulun and Issachar, who also appear side-by-side in Jacob's last words (Ge 49:13–15) and are paired in the Song of Deborah (Jdg 5:14–15). This blessing is to affect every aspect of their lives. The statements "going out" and "in your tents" appear to comprise a merism (polar elements that signify totality, e.g., "top to bottom"; see comments on Dt 6:7–9; Nelson, 391). They will summon fellow Israelites to offer proper or acceptable (*ṣedeq*) sac-

rifices, probably at a shrine on Mount Tabor (Jos 19:12, 22; Jdg 4:6, 12). Although the prophet Hosea (Hos 5:1) later condemns this shrine, it was a legitimate place for sacrifice before the temple was built.

Although neither of these tribes appears to inherit territory directly touching the Mediterranean Sea, their proximity to the Sea of Galilee and the Esdraelon Valley will give them access to the sea and products taken from it (e.g., seafood, shells, etc.).

g. Gad (33:20–21)

> [20]About Gad he said:
>
> "Blessed is he who enlarges Gad's domain!
>   Gad lives there like a lion,
>   tearing at arm or head.
> [21]He chose the best land for himself;
>   the leader's portion was kept for him.
> When the heads of the people assembled,
>   he carried out the LORD's righteous will,
>   and his judgments concerning Israel."

COMMENTARY

20–21 Gad was one of three tribes who received their inheritance (or part of it) on the eastern side of the Jordan River. Gad's territory occupied the central part of Transjordan with Reuben to the south and Manasseh to the north. Yahweh is to be blessed because he has seen fit to enlarge Gad in population and territory (although some take the reference as signifying anyone who helps Gad become larger; cf. McConville, 472; Tigay, *Deuteronomy*, 331).

The reference to Gad as a lion (cf. Ge 49:9; Nu 23:24; 24:9; 1Ch 12:8) may look forward to their

pivotal role in the conquest of Canaan (Jos 22:1–8) and look back to their involvement in the conquest of Transjordan. The "best land" could refer to the fertility of the land allotted to Gad or to the fact that they received part of the land first conquered by the nation. The "leader's portion" may refer to land so superb as to be fit for a ruler (Nelson, 391). Eventually, Gad occupied the land originally given to Reuben. Later, after the Moabite king (Mesha) freed himself from Israelite dominion, he referred to Transjordan as "Gad" (Moabite Stone, line 10; *COS*, 2:137)

NOTE

21 The verb מְחֹקֵק (*mᵉḥōqēq*) derives from חקק (*ḥqq*), to "inscribe" (*HALOT*, 347). Although it normally refers to writing laws and decrees, it could connote a leader responsible for that important task (cf. Jdg 5:14; Isa 33:22; Ringgren, *TDOT*, 5:141). The phrase חֶלְקַת מְחֹקֵק (*ḥelqat mᵉḥōqēq*, "the leader's portion"), could be translated, "the portion of the inscriber of laws."

h. Dan (33:22)

> ²²About Dan he said:
>
> "Dan is a lion's cub,
>   springing out of Bashan."

COMMENTARY

22 As with the last words of Jacob (Ge 49:16–17, where Dan is said to be a serpent; see Note), Moses' blessing is brief and includes animal metaphors. Here Moses likens Dan to a lion cub that leaps forth out of Bashan. Dan's original tribal inheritance, after the conquest of Canaan,

was in the Shephelah region (central Israel). Eventually, after being unable to evict the Canaanites, the tribe relocated to the far northern region of Israel and conquered a community named "Laish." The comparison of Dan to a lion may have been related to that conquest (prophetically), since

"Laish" (לַיִשׁ, *layiš*) is another Hebrew term for "lion." The reference to Bashan might draw on the fact that lions were known to be found there (Nelson, 392).

NOTE

22 Because of the cryptic nature of מִן־הַבָּשָׁן (*min-habbāšān*, "from Bashan") in this verse, several scholars have suggested that "Bashan" is a cognate form for the Ugaritic noun *btn*, "viper" (Craigie, 401; *HALOT*, 165). If this suggestion is true, it may allude to Genesis 49:17, where Dan is described as a serpent.

i. Naphtali (33:23)

²³About Naphtali he said:

"Naphtali is abounding with the favor of the LORD
    and is full of his blessing;
    he will inherit southward to the lake."

COMMENTARY

23 Naphtali receives one of the most positive blessings in this chapter; the tribe is satiated with Yahweh's "favor" and full of his "blessing." Naphtali will spread to the south and west from its territorial core. One of the blessings enjoyed by this tribe was that the Messiah spent much of his ministry in their territory and in neighboring Zebulun (Isa 9:1–2 [8:23–9:1]; Mt 4:12–17). Naphtali and Asher, the last two tribes to receive a word of blessing, were descendants of the last two sons of Jacob by the concubines Bilhah and Zilpah, respectively (cf. Ge 30:7–8, 12–13).

NOTE

23 Although the noun יָם (*yām*, "to the lake") does mean "sea," it can refer to the direction "west" (*HALOT*, 414). It is unclear whether it refers to the Sea of Galilee redundantly or to their territory toward the west.

j. Asher (33:24–25)

24About Asher he said:

"Most blessed of sons is Asher;
   let him be favored by his brothers,
   and let him bathe his feet in oil.
25The bolts of your gates will be iron and bronze,
   and your strength will equal your days.

COMMENTARY

24–25 This pronouncement of "blessing" (brk) on Asher is likely related to the meaning of "Asher" as "happy, blessed." Not only is this tribe blessed above all others, but it is also regarded highly by its brother tribes. The hyperbolic metaphor of bathing one's foot in oil suggests abundant prosperity. Even though olive groves were abundant in the territory of Asher, it seems that here the oil, which often symbolizes blessing in the OT (Dt 32:13; Job

29:5–6, 11), provides a metaphor of prosperity in general.

The iron and bronze bolts refer to bolts that held a city gate in place as an essential component to the city's defense. The basic idea of this line may be: "May your land be as secure as if it were locked with bolts of iron or bronze" (Tigay, *Deuteronomy*, 333). As long as the tribe lives, they will enjoy Yahweh's protection.

---

3. Conclusion (33:26–29)

26"There is no one like the God of Jeshurun,
   who rides on the heavens to help you
   and on the clouds in his majesty.
27The eternal God is your refuge,
   and underneath are the everlasting arms.
He will drive out your enemy before you,
   saying, 'Destroy him!'
28So Israel will live in safety alone;

> Jacob's spring is secure
> in a land of grain and new wine,
>   where the heavens drop dew.
> ²⁹Blessed are you, O Israel!
>   Who is like you,
>   a people saved by the LORD?
> He is your shield and helper
>   and your glorious sword.
> Your enemies will cower before you,
>   and you will trample down their high places."

COMMENTARY

26 This final stanza continues the theme found in vv.1–5, i.e., the favor that Yahweh, the unique God, has shown to his beloved nation, Jeshurun (see Note on 32:15). Unlike earthbound, pagan, so-called gods, Yahweh rides on the clouds, thus evidencing his mastery over the elements of nature (2Sa 22:11 = Ps 18:10 [11]; 68:4, 33 [5, 34]; 104:3; Isa 19:1). As Moses has affirmed repeatedly in Deuteronomy, so here he affirms that Yahweh is without comparison (3:24; 4:32–39; 32:39; 33:29). As their all-powerful God, Yahweh comes to Israel's aid when needed. Since he is the God who wields absolute control over creation, he is able to make his promises of abundance found in the preceding verses come to pass.

27–28 Although the imagery in v.26 may have directed the attention of Moses' audience to certain pagan gods, Moses reminds them of Yahweh's eternality (cf. Ps 74:12; Isa 51:9; Hab 1:12). For his chosen people he is a refuge who will protect them against their enemies. His eternally supporting arms hold up his chosen people. In addition to carrying the common nuance of deliverance (Dt 4:34; 5:15; 7:19; 26:8; cf. Ex 6:6; 15:16), the arms of Yahweh highlight his care of and support for Israel.

In addition to instigating the defeat of Israel's enemies, the Lord demands that Israel act in dependence on his promise of victory. Because of Yahweh's intervention in their behalf, Israel will live in safety, free from the threat of attacking armies (v.28). The "fountain" or spring of Jacob does not refer to springs of water in the land but is a synonym for Israel (the parallel term) and their descendants. The guaranteed presence of grain, new wine, and dew represents the epitome of the "good life" in the Promised Land (cf. Dt 7:13; 11:10–12; 33:13–16; Ge 27:28).

29 Moses brings his conclusion to a climax by exulting over Israel's blessed position. Because of their special relationship with Yahweh, demonstrated by his deliverance of them from Egypt (and other calamities), they are unique among all the nations of the world. The question "Who is like you?" is normally addressed to God (Ex 15:11; Pss 35:10; 71:19; 89:8 [9]) to emphasize his incomparability.

Another demonstration of the unparalleled relationship between Israel and Yahweh is God's consistent care for them. He is their shield, helper, and sword. Those metaphors describe not only what

Yahweh does for his chosen people but also his very character (Ps 115:9–11). Israel's enemies will be enemies of Yahweh, who will cower before this God-enabled nation.

NOTES

26 The imagery of God as one רֹכֵב שָׁמַיִם (rōkēb šāmayim), "who rides on the heavens" through the clouds, draws on imagery from various ancient Near Eastern texts (COS, 1:248–49, 251–52, 258, 261, 266). Canaanite literature, for example, depicts Baal-Hadad (the storm god) riding on the clouds as his chariot. In Babylonian and Canaanite literature, riding on clouds or the wind represents the god's military prowess (see examples cited above). By applying this imagery to Yahweh, Moses affirms that not only is Yahweh in absolute control of history, but he also has total sovereignty over nature — a power that would have been important to Israel in light of the relative lack of rain in the land of Canaan (Cairns, 302). Although the pagan gods claimed to ride the clouds to carry out their rule over various elements of the world, their efforts are ultimately vain. Yahweh alone has total sovereignty over all creation and history.

27 The noun מְעֹנָה ($m^{e c}\bar{o}n\hat{a}$, "a dwelling place") occurs nine times in the OT and frequently refers to the den or hiding place of a wild animal (Job 37:8; 38:40; Ps 104:22). Derived from this usage, the noun can occur in connection with human and divine dwelling. Stressing the remoteness and inaccessibility mentioned above, the word can occasionally mean "refuge," in which humans take shelter from their enemies (Dt 33:27; Pss 71:3; 91:9; Jer 21:13). God is the refuge that protects those who fear him from enemies and distress (Dt 33:27; Pss 71:3; 91:9; Wilson, *NIDOTTE*, 2:1016).

29 With reference to what the world might call "lucky" or "fortunate," the Scriptures use אַשְׁרֵי (ʾašrê, "blessed"; GK 897) to describe genuine happiness "with a decided emphasis on a life in right relationship with God" (M. Brown, *NIDOTTE*, 1:50). This term occurs only here in Deuteronomy. The more common term for "blessed" is the passive participle בָּרוּךְ (bārûk; Dt 28:3–6).

With reference to the phrase בָּמוֹתֵימוֹ תִדְרֹךְ (bāmôtêmô tidrōk, "on their back you will trample"), although the noun בָּמָה (bāmâ) normally refers to a "high place" used for pagan worship, the word can also mean "back," whether the back of a person, the back of a cloud (Isa 14:14), or the back of a hill, i.e., a ridge (Dt 32:13; 2Sa 1:19, 25; Schunck, *TDOT*, 2:140; *HALOT*, 136). Placing one's foot on the neck or back of a conquered foe was a biblical (Jos 10:24) and ancient Near Eastern gesture of triumph (Keel, 253–55). The verb דָּרַךְ (drk) occurs frequently to signify the exercise of sovereignty over one's enemies by humankind (Dt 1:36; 11:24–25; Jos 1:3; 14:9; Mic 5:5 [4]) or by God (Am 4:13; Mic 1:3; Hab 3:15).

D. The Death of Moses (34:1–12)

OVERVIEW

Sometime after the completion of the conquest and the allocation of the tribal inheritances, an anonymous prophetic figure records the death of Moses and the beginning of Joshua's era of leadership (at least vv.5–12, though some argue that here Moses writes prophetically). These verses provide a final sequel to 32:48–52, in which Yahweh exhorted Moses to climb Mount Nebo and view the land of Canaan.

¹Then Moses climbed Mount Nebo from the plains of Moab to the top of Pisgah, across from Jericho. There the Lᴏʀᴅ showed him the whole land — from Gilead to Dan, ²all of Naphtali, the territory of Ephraim and Manasseh, all the land of Judah as far as the western sea, ³the Negev and the whole region from the Valley of Jericho, the City of Palms, as far as Zoar. ⁴Then the Lᴏʀᴅ said to him, "This is the land I promised on oath to Abraham, Isaac and Jacob when I said, 'I will give it to your descendants.' I have let you see it with your eyes, but you will not cross over into it."

⁵And Moses the servant of the Lᴏʀᴅ died there in Moab, as the Lᴏʀᴅ had said. ⁶He buried him in Moab, in the valley opposite Beth Peor, but to this day no one knows where his grave is. ⁷Moses was a hundred and twenty years old when he died, yet his eyes were not weak nor his strength gone. ⁸The Israelites grieved for Moses in the plains of Moab thirty days, until the time of weeping and mourning was over.

⁹Now Joshua son of Nun was filled with the spirit of wisdom because Moses had laid his hands on him. So the Israelites listened to him and did what the Lᴏʀᴅ had commanded Moses.

¹⁰Since then, no prophet has risen in Israel like Moses, whom the Lᴏʀᴅ knew face to face, ¹¹who did all those miraculous signs and wonders the Lᴏʀᴅ sent him to do in Egypt — to Pharaoh and to all his officials and to his whole land. ¹²For no one has ever shown the mighty power or performed the awesome deeds that Moses did in the sight of all Israel.

COMMENTARY

1–4 Yahweh introduced himself to Moses on a mountain (Ex 3), gave his law to Moses on the same mountain (Ex 19–20), and now brings an end to his physical life on another mountain. From the top of Mount Pisgah, Yahweh shows Moses "the whole land" (v.2). The text describes the panorama (semicircle) before Moses in a counterclockwise direction, starting at the north, proceeding westward, and continuing southward (including the compass points between).

None of these locations would have been visible to the unaided human eye from Pisgah. It could be that what Moses "saw" was representative (Hall, 498), or perhaps it was a "divinely assisted visualization granted to Moses" (Nelson, 396). Since Dan did not become a northern location until the days

of the judges, the matter of when one dates the composition of this chapter affects the decision as to whether the place name "Dan" was written prophetically, was a replacement for "Laish" by a later author (Ridderbos, 315), or was simply part of the original chapter, in which case the chapter would have been written (by an unnamed prophetic figure) sometime after that tribe moved to the north (cf. Grisanti, "Inspiration, Inerrancy," 583–84, 597).

After showing to Moses the land of Canaan, God reminds him of the theological significance of this day. It brings to fulfillment an oath he made to Moses' ancestors (Ge 12:1, 7; 13:15; 18:18; 28:13; Dt 1:8, 21, 25; cf. Ex 33:1). The Lord reminds Moses one last time that he will not be allowed to cross over the Jordan River into the land itself (thus providing the reason for that prohibition elsewhere; Dt 1:37; 3:23–29; 31:2, 14, 16, 27–29).

5–9 The record of Moses' death refers to him as a "servant of the LORD." Although this term connotes a subservient position, the title represented a great honor. While various individuals who ministered on God's behalf received this title (Jos 24:29; Jdg 2:8; 2Sa 3:18; 1Ki 11:13 et al.), Moses is referred to as "servant" most frequently (Dt 3:24; Jos 1:1–2, 7, 13, 15; 8:31, 33; 9:24; et al.). He epitomized what a servant of the Lord should be.

The statement "he buried him" could imply that Yahweh himself buried Moses. Others have suggested that the verb should be plural, "they buried him" (as in the LXX and Samaritan Pentateuch; McConville, 475, 477) or translated as an indefinite plural, "he was buried" (Ridderbos, 316). Regardless, the location of his burial place was kept secret. The people were unable to venerate Moses or take his corpse across the Jordan River into the land.

Moses' death was in accordance with Yahweh's intentions for him, but not the result of health problems. He still was physically vigorous. Having strong or weak eyes constituted an ancient Near Eastern idiom to describe a person's physical condition (cf. Ge 27:1; 1Sa 4:15; 1Ki 14:4; Pritchard, *ANET*, 412, 561, 661). As the Israelites had done for Moses' brother Aaron (Nu 20:29), so they mourn Moses' death for thirty days.

9 Yahweh provides Joshua, Moses' successor, with a spirit of wisdom to enable him to lead this nation in accordance with the Lord's expectations.

All God's leaders of Israel need this wisdom to carry out their God-given role effectively (cf. 1Ki 4:29; 5:12; 2Ch 1:10–12; Isa 11:1–5). Years earlier, when Moses laid hands on Joshua (Nu 27:15–23), his actions symbolized the transferral of covenantal authority to Joshua, even though Joshua would not exercise that authority for a long time. The Israelites now pay attention to Joshua's guidance because he is their God-certified leader.

10–12 The book of Deuteronomy concludes with an affirmation of Moses' uniqueness. Since the time of his death (whenever this chapter was composed), no prophet came on the scene who compared with Moses. This statement does not mean that no true or powerful prophets had arisen since Moses' death; rather, no prophet since the time of Moses had enjoyed the intimacy with Yahweh that Moses experienced ("face to face"; cf. Nu 12:8).

Also, even though God would do great things through other prophets, God had not seen fit to use any other true prophet to accomplish as many stupendous signs and wonders as Moses had performed (cf. Ex 7:3; Dt 4:34; 6:22; 7:19 [see comments there]; 26:8; 29:3; Ne 9:10; Ps 78:43; 105:27). Yahweh had brought great glory to himself before the entire Egyptian population (and Pharaoh in particular) through his servant Moses. Not only had these great deeds affected the Egyptians, they also demonstrated to God's chosen people with perfect clarity that Yahweh is a God who performs all that he has promised and is able to bring to pass whatever he chooses.

NOTES

1 The place name "Pisgah" occurs eight times in the OT (רֹאשׁ הַפִּסְגָּה, *rōʾš happisgâ*, "the top of Pisgah" [Nu 21:20; 23:14; Dt 3:27; 34:1]; "the slopes of Pisgah" [Dt 3:17; 4:49; Jos 12:3; 13:20]). Pisgah is part of the Abarim range (32:49), a high plateau region located east of the Jordan River (and Dead Sea). According to G. Mattingly (*ABD*, 5:373), most scholars identify Mount Nebo and Mount Pisgah as the two peaks on

Jebel Shayhan, with Pisgah located ca. 1.5 miles west-northwest of Nebo, beyond a small saddle. Though this widely accepted location of Pisgah is slightly lower than Nebo (Jebel en-Nebu), Pisgah would afford Moses a magnificent view of the Jordan Rift Valley and points beyond.

Some scholars have suggested that this viewing of the land (וַיַּרְאֵהוּ יהוה אֶת־כָּל־הָאָרֶץ, *wayyarʾēhû yhwh ʾet-kol-hāʾāreṣ*, "there the LORD showed him the whole land") represents a legal transfer of land from Yahweh to Moses (and Israel; D. Daube, *Studies in Biblical Law* [New York: Macmillan, 1947], 25–39; Cairns, 303–4; Hall, 498). In several ancient law codes, the two parties would view the property in question before transferring ownership. In Genesis 13 Yahweh invited Abraham to view the land, and here he does the same with Moses. The difference between that legal reality and the present context is that Yahweh still owns the land. He has given it to his covenantal nation as a stewardship. If this expression has legal implications, it simply serves to emphasize the significance of Israel's upcoming conquest of the Promised Land.

9 Various OT passages refer to the Holy Spirit's coming upon an individual (cf. in this passage Joshua's being filled with רוּחַ חָכְמָה, *rûaḥ ḥokmâ*, "the spirit of wisdom"). The people who received this anointing were theocratic figures of a sort; they carried out some function in the theocracy. This anointing involved leaders (e.g., Moses [Nu 11:17]; Israelite elders [Nu 11:17, 25]; Joshua [Nu 27:18–23; Dt 34:9]; judges [Jdg 3:10; 6:34; 11:29]; Saul [1Sa 10:6; 11:6]; David [1Sa 16:13; Ps 51:11 (13)]; Solomon [1Ki 4:29]); Levites (2Ch 20:14), prophets (Nu 11:26; 2Ch 15:1); and tabernacle and temple craftsmen (Ex 28:3; 31:3, 8). Hence this ministry of the Holy Spirit can be called "theocratic anointing." It appears to have involved Yahweh's provision of enablement so that a theocratic figure could carry out a God-given task. The anointing does not appear to have any relationship to a person's spirituality.

JOSHUA

HÉLÈNE M. DALLAIRE

Introduction

1. CONTENT OF THE BOOK

The book of Joshua presents a dramatic exposition of the conquest and settlement of the Israelites in the land of Canaan promised to them centuries earlier. During the patriarchal period, God promised to Abraham that through his seed all the nations of the earth would be blessed, and that he would give to Abraham's descendants a land where they would live in covenant relationship with him (Ge 12:7; 13:14–17; 15:7; 17:4–8; Ex 33:1). This divine promise was reaffirmed through Abraham's descendants, Isaac (Ge 26:1–5) and Jacob (28:10–17; 35:9–13), and saw initial fulfillment under Joshua's leadership.

The book does not provide a complete and exhaustive record of all major events that occurred under Joshua's leadership. Rather, it provides a description of the main events (e.g., the crossing of the Jordan, the spies in Jericho, the conquest of cities, the treatment of inhabitants, land distribution, the covenant renewal) that undergird the following key theological themes: (1) the initial fulfillment of God's promise of land to the children of Israel, (2) the establishment of a national identity for Israel, and (3) God's active participation in the conquest of the land.

The content of Joshua is both thrilling and disturbing. It is thrilling in that it reveals the mighty acts of God on behalf of his people, and it serves as a compelling testimony of God's faithfulness to Israel. It is disturbing in that it records a series of violent and bloody military encounters that are directly related to the fulfillment of God's promises to his people. It touches a raw nerve in most readers and raises crucial theological, ethical, and moral questions. For some, its presentation of brutal scenes of genocide, seeming discrimination against indigenous people, and the colonization of an inhabited land can hardly be reconciled with the God of love who is revealed throughout Scripture. The concept of God as a Divine Warrior who fights for one nation at the expense of another is uncomfortable for most readers. For this reason, many "simply ignore it, thus letting the book languish in a kind of scriptural ghetto from which its voice is seldom heard."[1]

On a more positive note, the book of Joshua provides the necessary bridge between the nomadic life of the Israelites and their establishment as a nation. Only in a "homeland' could the social, political, and religious systems of Israel flourish.

2. JOSHUA—THE MAN

Joshua, son of Nun, of the tribe of Ephraim and thus a descendent of Joseph, is the principal character in the book. His name means "Yahweh is salvation" or "Yahweh has saved" (*yᵉhôšûᶜa*). It appears in an abbreviated form as Hoshea in Nu 13:8, 16 and Dt 32:44 (*hôšēᶜa*). Joshua's name was expanded by Moses from Hoshea to Joshua when the spies were sent from the desert of Paran to explore the land of Canaan and to find out if its inhabitants were strong or weak, if the land was good or bad, if the cities were fortified or unwalled, if the soil was fertile or poor, and if the trees were abundant or few (Nu 13:16, 20). The LXX renders Joshua's name both in the short and long form: *Ausē* and *Iēsous* respectively. The meaning of Joshua's name is appropriate for a book that focuses primarily on the deliverance of God's people. It carries the same etymology as that of the name Yeshua (Jesus), whose purpose for coming to earth was the "salvation" of mankind.

In the introduction of the book, the leadership is transferred from Moses to Joshua (cf. Nu 27:18–23), who had up to this point been identified as "the servant," "the aide," or "the minister" of Moses since his youth (*mᵉšārēt mōšeh*, Nu 11:28; Jos 1:1). At the end of his life and in later texts, Joshua is honored by a new lofty designation previously used exclusively to honor Moses—"the servant of the LORD" (*ᶜebed yhwh*, Dt 34:5; Jos 1:1, 15; 8:31, 33; 11:12; 12:6; 13:8; 14:7; 18:7; 22:2, 4). In Jos 24:39, Joshua is no longer called "the servant of Moses"; he is given the honorable designation of "the servant of the LORD" (cf. also Jdg 2:8).

Scripture tells us that God had chosen Joshua to succeed Moses before he became the chief leader of Israel. Joshua is first identified as a valiant and fearless military man whose exploits brought defeat to the Amalekites (Ex 17:8–15). So significant was this event that Moses was instructed by Yahweh to record it as a remembrance for Joshua (Ex 17:13–14). This introduction of Joshua as a conqueror confirms him as a brilliant military leader, as the perfect prospect to lead the conquest of Canaan, and as an exceptional future leader of God's people. His skills as a military man are noticed on Mount Sinai when he identifies the noise coming from the Israelite encampment as the "sound of war" (Ex 32:17), referring to the commotion that surrounded the worship of the golden calf.

Joshua's prominent and unique position is confirmed soon after his appearance on the scene. Scripture tells us that Joshua was the only individual who accompanied Moses to the top of Mount Sinai, where he spent forty days and forty nights in the glorious presence of Yahweh (Ex 24:12–18). Although the text is unclear as to the exact location of Joshua during Moses' face-to-face encounter with God, we know that Joshua was lingering somewhere on Mount Sinai above the Israelite encampment and below the clouded

---

1. Jerome F. D. Creach, *Joshua* (Interpretation; Louisville, Ky.: Westminster John Knox, 2003), 3.

place where Moses met with God. On Mount Sinai, God gave Moses the Torah—the rules and regulations that would serve as the primary authority for the cultic, social, moral, and political life of the Israelites both during their desert wanderings and during their existence in the Promised Land.

Following the Sinai experience, Moses sent Joshua to explore the land of Canaan for a period of forty days along with a representative from each tribe (Nu 13:1–16). His positive report contradicted that of the other spies (except for Caleb) and nearly cost him his life (14:6–10). In his opinion, the land was exceedingly good (14:7), it flowed with milk and honey (14:8), and its inhabitants were not to be feared (14:9). The Israelites, by contrast, had been convinced by ten of the spies that the land was unconquerable, that it swarmed with the presence of strong giants (the Nephilim), and that numerous large and fortified cities peppered the land (13:25–33). The skepticism and cowardice of the ten spies earned them death in the desert. As for Joshua and Caleb, God rewarded them for their bravery and courage and granted them the privilege of entering Canaan with the next generation of Israelites (14:26–30, 36–38).

Joshua's faithfulness earned him the greatest and the most challenging reward. God chose him to become Moses' successor and to lead the Israelites into the Promised Land (Dt 1:38; 3:28). Shortly before his death, God instructed Moses to lay hands on Joshua, to present him before Eleazar the priest, and to commission him as Israel's next leader (Nu 27:12–23; Dt 31:14). During this commissioning, the Spirit of the Lord filled Joshua with wisdom, and consequently, the Israelites recognized him as their leader and obeyed his instructions as they had previously done with Moses (Dt 34:9). Although chosen, confirmed, and anointed by God for this new task, Joshua's life as the official leader of God's people would not be easy. God and Moses repeatedly exhort Joshua to "be strong and courageous" (Dt 31:7, 23; Jos 1:6, 7, 9, 18), and to remember that God would accompany him and strengthen him as a leader all the days of his life, just as God had done with Moses (Jos 1:5).

Joshua dies at the ripe old age of 110 (Jos 24:29; Jdg 2:8) after having successfully led the Israelites into the land of Canaan, distributed the land to the eleven tribes, allotted portions to the Levites, and renewed the covenant between God and his people at Shechem (Jos 24:1–28).

Centuries after his death, Joshua is remembered when Hiel of Bethel rebuilt the city of Jericho, laying its foundation and setting up its gates at the cost of his two sons, Abiram and Segub (1Ki 16:34). After the conquest of Jericho, Joshua had declared in Joshua 6:26:

Cursed before the LORD is the man who undertakes to rebuild this city, Jericho.

> At the cost of his firstborn son
>   will he lay its foundation;
> at the cost of his youngest
>   will he set up its gates.

3. AUTHORSHIP AND COMPOSITION

The book of Joshua appears as the sixth book of the Hebrew Bible, immediately following the Pentateuch. It makes no specific claim regarding its authorship. Most scholars agree that the book is comprised of a collection of texts from various authors who provided materials that reflect different foci (e.g., etiologies, chronologies, historical narrative) and were composed over an extended period of time. The canonical version—with its interwoven narratives, formulaic religious ceremonies, battle records, and boundary/town lists—reflects a compilation of sources rather than a single piece of literature written by a single author.

The book of Joshua is the first of the so-called Historical Books (Jos, Jdg, 1–2Sa, 1–2Ki); in the Hebrew Bible it belongs to a subsection known as the Former Prophets. To the subsection designated as the Latter Prophets belong the books of Isaiah, Jeremiah, Ezekiel, and the twelve Minor Prophets. In Jewish and Christian scholarship, the prevailing view on the place of the book of Joshua in the canon points toward the first of the historical books. This choice is based on the link that exists between the acquisition of the land in Joshua and the Israelites' new life in that land as described chronologically in Judges through 2 Kings.

Most scholars agree that Joshua is not the author of the book that carries his name. As is common, especially in the Old Testament canon, the personal names that appear in the titles of books do not always reflect the name(s) of the author(s). Rather, they often identify the protagonist or the principal character around whom the story revolves (e.g., 1 & 2 Samuel, Ruth, Jonah). The accounts are primarily described in the third person by a narrator who may or may not have been a participant in the events. The narrators offer their perspective of the accounts, using skillful literary strategies that create tension, build suspense, and entice the reader (e.g., hyperbole, wordplays, repetition, alliteration, assonance).

Ancient Jewish tradition claims that Joshua was the author of the entire book,[2] a view no longer popular in modern scholarship. The narratives of Joshua could have been written by an eyewitness or by an individual who first received them through oral transmission and subsequently recorded them in written form. Scholars agree that a specific date for the composition of the book is elusive. The recurring expression "to this day" points to the recording of some events at a time later than that of the events themselves (4:9; 5:9; 7:26; 8:28–29; 9:27; 10:27; 13:13; 14:14; 15:63; 16:10).

Although Joshua is not recognized as the author, the book mentions two accounts where he is said to have recorded incidents. In the first account (8:32), Joshua writes the law of Moses on tablets of stone in the presence of the Israelites after having built an altar to God on Mount Ebal to celebrate the recent conquest of Ai. In the second account (24:26), Joshua records the events that surround the renewal of the covenant at Shechem in "the Book of the Law of God." As for the rest of Joshua, narratives and lists were no doubt provided by a collection of writers whose traditions are reflected in their personal contributions.

According to Gerhard von Rad, Joshua belongs to a corpus of literature that underwent deliberate editing over an extended period of time, along with the Pentateuch, the story of David's accession to the throne, and the late historical work of the Chronicler.[3] In his view, such redacted works demonstrate "how Israel from time to time went back afresh to write her history. These great literary works often took a century to mature to their final form or to be framed ingeniously with others by editors."[4] In Trent Butler's words, "Israelite theologians were continually at work under the leadership of God seeking to interpret

---

2. See *b. Baba Bathra* 14b. M. H. Woudstra notes that Rashi and Kimchi attributed the writing of the book to Joshua, while Avravanel advocates for a Samuel authorship. See M. H. Woudstra, *The Book of Joshua* (NICOT; Grand Rapids: Eerdmans, 1981), 5; D. M. Howard Jr., *Joshua* (NAC 5; Nashville: Broadman & Holman, 2002), 29.

3. Gerhard von Rad, *God at Work in Israel* (trans. John. H. Marks; Nashville: Abingdon, 1974), 12.

4. Ibid.

the holy traditions for the people of God....The inspired canonical writer understood and interpreted the sacred traditions transmitted to him by the community of faith."[5]

A prevailing scholarly view regarding the composition of Joshua is that of a Deuteronomistic History, first presented by Martin Noth and subsequently adopted by much of the scholarly community.[6] Noth proposed a literary complex that stretches from Deuteronomy (at least the narratives at the beginning and end of the book) through 2 Kings, a corpus composed during the exilic period by one author whose personal editing of earlier historical sources reflects the theology of Deuteronomy and Jeremiah. According to this view, the literary unit is interconnected by the unyielding monotheistic tone of the books, and it was composed to provide a historical-theological explanation of the fall of the northern (722 BC) and southern (586 BC) kingdoms. This hypothesis also seeks to explain the direct linguistic, literary, and thematic correlations that exist between the books of Joshua and Deuteronomy: the repeated formula "be strong and courageous" (Dt 31:7, 23//Jos 1:5, 7, 9, 18), the dispossession of people groups from Canaan (Dt 7:1//Jos 3:10), the renewal of covenant (Dt 29//Jos 24), the inheritance of Levites (Dt 10:9//Jos 18:7), and the treatment of the "devoted things' (ḥērem, Dt 13:16//Jos 10:39). The cohesive phrase "to this day" appears throughout the two books (Dt 2:22; 3:14; 10:8; 11:4; 29:3; 34:6//Jos 4:9; 5:9; 6:25; 7:26; 8:28–29; 9:27; 10:27; 13:13; 15:63; 16:10; 23:9; etc.).[7]

According to Noth, the narrative portions of Joshua (Jos 1–12, 22–24) could belong to a Hexateuch, but the text of Joshua 13–21 certainly represents a compilation of documents that belongs to the Deuteronomistic stage and not to a pre-Deuteronomistic literary unit.[8] This view had been challenged by scholars who advocate an earlier date of composition based on the following arguments: (1) the theological strands that unite the so-called Deuteronomistic History are not simply characteristic of seventh-century themes, as proposed by Noth and his followers, but they appear in the ancient Near Eastern literature of the first and second millennia BC;[9] (2) the historical narratives from Joshua 1 to 12 reflect the realities of conquest accounts of the first and second millennia BC (e.g., Akkadian from Mari, Egyptian, Neo-Assyrian);[10]

5. T. C. Butler, *Joshua* (WBC 7; Waco, TX: Word, 1983), xxi. Butler lists the following editorial passages in Joshua: 1:1–18; 2:9b–11; 3:7, 10; 4:10, 12, 14, 24; 5:1, 5–6; 6:21, 26; 7:7–9, 11, 15; 8:18, 26, 29, 30–35; 9:9b–10, 24aB, 27bB; 10:25, 40; 11:3, 11–12, 14b–15, 20b–23; 12:1–13; 13:1–14, 32–33; 14:1–5, 14–15; 15:13–15; 17:3–6; 18:1, 7; 19:51; 20:8–9; 21:1–3, 43–45; 22:1–6; 23:1–16; 24:1, 11aB, 12b–13, 24, 31–32.

6. M. Noth, *Überlieferungsgeschichte Studien* (Tübingen: Max Niemeyer, 1957), 1–110. Translated and reprinted as *The Deuteronomistic History* (2nd ed.; JSOTSup 15, Sheffield: Sheffield Academic, 2002); A. G. Auld, *Joshua, Moses and the Land: Tetrateuch-Pentateuch-Hexateuch in a Generation Since 1938* (Greenwood, S.C.: Attic Press, 1980), 1–51; Creach, *Joshua*, 5; L. D. Hawk, *Joshua* (Berit Olam; Collegeville, Minn.: Liturgical, 2000), xxiv–xxviii.

7. B. Childs, "A Study of the Formula '"Until this Day,'" *JBL* 82 (1963): 279–92; R. D. Nelson, *Joshua: A Commentary* (OTL 9; Louisville, Ky.: Westminster John Knox, 1997), 10.

8. Noth, *The Deuteronomistic History*, 61–68.

9. Woudstra, *Joshua*, 7–18.

10. K. L. Younger Jr., *Ancient Conquest Accounts: A Study in Ancient Near Eastern and Biblical History Writing* (JSOTSup 98; Sheffield: Sheffield Academic, 1990), 197–237; J. K. Hoffmeier, "The Structure of Joshua 1–11 and the Annals of Thutmose III," in *Faith, Tradition, History: Old Testament Historiography in Its Near Eastern Context* (ed. A. R. Millard, J. K. Hoffmeier, and D. W. Baker; Winona Lake, Ind.: Eisenbrauns, 1994), 165–79; J. Van Seters, "Joshua's Campaign of Canaan and Near Eastern Historiography," *Scandinavian Journal of the Old Testament* 2 (1990): 1–12; M. Weinfeld,

(3) the anti-Canaanite polemic points to an early date, especially since the Canaanites do not appear in historical literature after 1 Kings 9:20–21.[11]

Tradition has for a long time preserved a penta-designation for the first five books of the Hebrew Bible (Genesis to Deuteronomy). After the rise of the literary-critical method, a six-book literary unit was proposed — the *Hexateuch*. The apparent similarities that exist between Joshua and Deuteronomy — their overlapping themes, corresponding language, logical sequence of events, evidence of sources (J, E, D, P), and the seamless continuity of leadership transferred from Moses to Joshua — have led some scholars (e.g., Wellhausen, von Rad) to lump Joshua with the Pentateuch, thus creating a Hexateuch.[12] Furthermore, advocates of this view claim that clear connections between Numbers and Joshua (e.g., repetition of Shittim in Nu 25:1; 33:49, and Jos 2:1; 3:1) prove the existence of a literary unit that includes both books. In addition, they point to (1) the "settlement tradition" of the Yahwist, (2) the Deuteronomic link between the Sinai event and the exodus-conquest complex, and (3) the covenant renewal at Shechem in Deuteronomy 27 and Joshua 24.

Today, this Hexateuch hypothesis has been mostly abandoned or a number of reasons: (1) no copy of the Hebrew Scriptures connects the book of Joshua with the Pentateuch; (2) Joshua begins with a large narrative section (chs. 1–12), which shows limited connection with the Pentateuch; (3) the Hexateuch theory is hypothetical; and (4) the book of Joshua has never been included in "the books of Moses' in Jewish and Christian tradition.

Scholarly studies of Joshua have proposed dates of composition ranging from before the end of the second millennium BC to the Hellenistic period, but internal and external evidence for exact dating is wanting. While the recurring formula "to this day" seems to distance the composition of the book from the time of the events, a comparison of themes in Joshua and West Semitic literature of the second millennium BC, focusing primarily on the Hittite and Hurrian evidence, supports early dating (Late Bronze Age-Iron I, late second millennium BC) for the composition of the book.[13] Hess highlights the following points that indicate a second millennium BC composition:[14]

- From the group of seven foreign nations mentioned in Jos 3:10 (Canaanites, Hittites, Hivites, Perizzites, Girgashites, Amorites, Jebusites; see also 9:1; 11:3; 12:8), three are clearly identified in second millennium BC texts — Hivites (Gibeonites), Perizzites (*pi-ri-iz-zi* from fourteenth century BC Mitanni), and Girgashites (mentioned in Ugaritic and Egyptian sources).[15]

The Promise of the Land: The Inheritance of the Land of Canaan by the Israelites (The Taubman Lectures in Jewish Studies; Berkeley: Univ. of California Press, 1993), 142–43.

11. R. S. Hess, *Joshua: An Introduction and Commentary* (TOTC; Downers Grove, Ill.: InterVarsity Press, 1996), 34.

12. See Gerhard von Rad, *The Problem of the Hexateuch and Other Essays* (trans. E. W. Trueman Dicken; New York: McGraw-Hill, 1966); Hartmut N. Rösel, "The Book of Joshua and the Existence of a Hexateuch," in *Homeland and Exile: Biblical and Ancient Near Eastern Studies in Honour of Bustenay Oded* (eds. G. Galil, M. Geller, and A. Millard; VTSup 130 (Leiden: Brill, 2009), 559–70; Auld, *Joshua, Moses and the Land*.

13. R. S. Hess, "West Semitic Texts and the Book of Joshua," *BBR* 7 (1997), 64; Hess, *Joshua*, 31–35, 56–60.

14. Ibid.

15. Ibid., 68.

- Divine intervention in the fall of the walls of Jericho finds a parallel in a second millennium BC Hittite text. The goddess Shaushga causes the fortifications of a city to collapse.[16]
- The description of the borders of the land promised to Israel in Jos 1:4 corresponds to a second millennium BC Egyptian depiction of Canaan.[17]
- Ugaritic and Hittite treaty documents from the second millennium BC include boundary descriptions similar to those found in Jos 13–21.[18] These boundary descriptions include (1) an introduction and conclusion; (2) brief narrative notes; and (3) comparable duplicate descriptions of boundaries with similar linguistic features.[19]
- Texts from Ugarit and Alalakh include second millennium BC town lists similar to those in Jos 13–21.[20]
- The list of towns mentioned in the southern campaign (10:28–42) uses the repetition of a peculiar formula—"king of" and "one." This formula resembles a list of Canaanite towns mentioned in Egyptian texts of the second millennium BC.[21]
- The presence of West Semitic names identified with second millennium BC sources connects the book of Joshua with an early date.[22]
- The town of Hazor, prominent during Joshua's day, is identified with the Late Bronze Age (second millennium BC).[23]
- The covenant renewal ceremony of Jos 24 reflects the structure of a Hittite vassal treaty unique to the second millennium BC.[24]

In addition to the evidence highlighted by Hess, the formula "to this day" mentioned throughout Joshua does not necessary imply an extended period between the time of the events and the writing of the account. For example, after the destruction of Jericho, Rahab and her family were allowed to dwell in Israel "to this day," indicating that she was still alive at the time of the recording of the narrative (Jos 6:25). If so, the Jericho conquest narrative could very well have been composed during the thirteenth or twelfth century BC.

The LXX translation of Joshua reveals a shorter version than that of the Masoretic Text (MT). The Qumran fragments of Joshua correspond to the MT with few variants, but the fragmentary nature of the text prevents us from reaching definite conclusions as to the sources available to the scribes. The New Testament occasionally points to the events and characters of this book. Joshua is remembered for having led the Israelites into the Promised Land (Acts 7:45) and bringing the tabernacle with him (7:45).

---

16. Ibid.
17. Ibid.
18. Ibid., 69.
19. Ibid., 70.
20. Ibid., 71.
21. Ibid., 72.
22. Ibid., 73. Richard S. Hess, "Non-Israelite Personal Names in the Book of Joshua," *CBQ* 58 (1996): 205–14.
23. Hess, *West Semitic Texts*, 74.
24. Ibid.

The fall of Jericho is featured as a major historical event (Heb 11:30). Rahab is highlighted in a list of those who exerted great faith, and she was considered righteous because she hid the spies and saved their lives (Heb 11:31; Jas 2:25). The conquest of the land and the overthrow of the seven Canaanite nations are remembered by the author(s) of Acts (13:19). God's people are exhorted to abstain from the love of money, for God said: "I will never leave you nor forsake you" (Jos 1:5b; cf. Heb 13:5b).

4. LITERARY FORM

The book of Joshua begins with the transition of power from Moses to Joshua (1:1–6) and ends with the latter's death and burial (24:29–31). It is presented as the complete story of a leader whose public life focuses primarily on one objective — to facilitate the transition of the Israelites from a wandering state to an established people in the land promised to them.

The book is divided into three main sections: the conquest of the land (chs. 1–12), the division of the land (chs. 13–21), and the settling of the Israelites in their new land (chs. 22–24). Each section is further divided in subunits:[25] (1) The conquest (chs. 1–12) includes four main subplots: the conquest of Jericho (5:13–6:27), the conquest of Ai (7:1–8:29), the conquest of southern cities (10:1–43), and the defeat of the kings of the north (11:1–12:24). Literary devices link smaller sections. References to "three days" appear primarily in chapters 1–3 (1:11; 2:16, 22; 3:2). The list of seven foreign nations is mentioned in several chapters (2:13; 9:1; 12:8). The repetition of "be strong and of good courage" appears in chapters 1 and 10 (1:6, 7, 9, 18; 10:25).

(2) The descriptions of tribal boundaries and town lists (13–21) are joined together with brief narrative summaries and transitional statements. The formula "(X) could not dislodge (Y)" appears in 15:63 (cf. Jdg 1:21) and 16:10 (see also 13:13; 17:12–13). Summary statements such as "these were the boundaries that maked out the inheritance of the clans of (X)" appear after allotments for Benjamin (18:20), Simeon (19:8), Zebulun (19:16), Issachar (19:23), Asher (19:31), Naphtali (19:39), and Dan (19:48).

(3) The conclusion of the book includes the conflict between the eastern and western tribes (ch. 22) and Joshua's final instructions to Israel (chs. 23–24). A detailed structure of the book appears in the outline below.

5. HISTORICAL BACKGROUND AND THE DATING OF THE BOOK[26]

a. Historical Background

The events of the book of Joshua take place during the second half of the second millennium BC (Late Bronze and Early Iron Age) and span approximately thirty years. The book itself does not specify

---

25. Based on a comparison of the literary features of Joshua and those of the Keret epic, some scholars have proposed that chs. 1–8 of Joshua form a specific unit that reflects the Ugaritic text. See Marieke den Braber and Jan-Wim Wesselius, "The Unity of Joshua 1–8, its Relation to the Story of King Keret, and the Literary Background to the Exodus and Conquest Stories," *SJOT* 22.2 (2008): 253–74.

26. For summaries of the historical background of the book, see Robert G. Boling and G. Ernest Wright, *Joshua* (AB 6; New Haven, Conn.: Yale Univ. Press, 1982), 80–88; Howard, *Joshua*, 31–50; Pekka M.A. Pitäknen, *Joshua* (Apollos OT Commentary 6; Downers Grove, Ill.: InterVarsity Press, 2010), 32–64; Robert L. Hubbard Jr., *Joshua* (NIVAC; Grand Rapids: Zondervan, 2009), 27–30; Woudstra, *Joshua*, 18–26.

precise dating, nor does it give a clear chronology linked to dates of known historical events. Scholars have attempted to interpret archaeological data for the purpose of dating the book, but this data fails to answer all the questions and thus specific dating remains inconclusive.

During the second millennium BC, Egypt dominated Syria-Palestine. Egyptian outposts had been strategically positioned throughout the coastal areas, the lowlands, and the hill country (e.g., Gaza, Megiddo, Byblos, Beth-Shean, Dor). The Amarna letters—fourteenth-century BC correspondence between rulers of Canaan and their Egyptian overlords—provide snapshots of Egyptian-Canaanite relationships, with the rulers of Canaanite city-states functioning as vassals under Egyptian economic and military domination.

Some of the Amarna letters speak of a pastoral group of people named the *hapiru/apiru* that migrated to western areas of the Fertile Crescent during the Late Bronze Age. These *hapiru/apiru* are identified in the literature as agriculturalists, mercenaries, raiders, merchants, and slaves. Because of the etymological connection between the words *hapiru/apiru* and *Hebrews*, scholars have attempted to identify the *hapiru/apiru* people with the Hebrews (*ʿibrîm*) of the biblical text. Scholars have been unsuccessful in proving this link because their description as "outlaws" and "disenfranchised" people conflicts with the description of the Hebrews recorded in Joshua and in the rest of Scripture.[27]

Around 1200 BC, major changes swept through the entire region. The once prominent Hittite empire disintegrated, major urban centers were destroyed (e.g., Ugarit, Emar), and large populations migrated to other areas of the Levant. The arrival of the Sea Peoples mentioned in Egyptian sources changed the ethnic landscape, and the whole region of Canaan experienced a shift in economic and material culture.

As to dating the events of this book, over the years scholars have proposed two main paradigms. These two models are based on biblical chronologies, extrabiblical textual evidence, archaeological records, and sociohistorical trends in the Levant during biblical times. These two models are also closely connected with the primary scholarly views on the dating of the exodus. In general, evangelical scholars favor an *early* date while critical scholars advocate for a *late* date, but this view is currently being revisted in evangelical scholarship.[28] These two major views are still being debated in scholarly circles, but one important point of agreement exists among scholars: the Israelites were in the land of Canaan by the end of the thirteenth century BC.[29]

b. Dating the Exodus and the Conquest of Canaan

The dating of the events in Joshua is directly related to the dating of the exodus from Egypt. Since Joshua does not provide explicit internal evidence for that dating, scholars have turned to other data in

27. Jean Bottéro, *Le Problème des Habiru à la 4ᵉ rencontre assyriologique internationale* (Cahiers de la Société asiatique 12; Paris: 1954), 160–61; idem, "Entre nomades et sédentaires: Les Habiru," *Dialogues d'histoire ancienne* 6 (1980): 201–13. According to Bottéro, Benno Landsberger was the first to propose the designation of "fugitives" or "refugees" to the term "Habiru." See N. P. Lemche, "Habiru, Hapiru," *ABD*, 3:6–10.

28. For discussion, see Ralph K. Hawkins, "Propositions for Evangelical Acceptance of a Late-Date Exodus-Conquest: Biblical Data and the Royal Scarabs From Mt. Ebal," *JETS* 50 (March 2007): 31–46.

29. For a summary of the main views, see the following: J. M. Golden, *Ancient Canaan and Israel: An Introduction* (New York: Oxford Univ. Press, 2004; repr., 2009), 266–70; Howard, *Joshua*, 31–32; Pitkänen, *Joshua*, 51–64; Hubbard, *Joshua*, 27–42; Woudstra, *Joshua*, 18–26.

order to support their views. Those who advocate for an early date for the Exodus focus primarily on textual evidence while those who promote a late date highlight mainly archaeological data.

Early Exodus/Early Conquest.[30] A proposed early date for the Exodus is c. 1446 BC with a conquest date of c. 1406 BC. Proponents of this dating present the following arguments:

1. According to 1 Kings 6:1, the fourth year of Solomon's reign is "480 years" after the exodus. Since the fourth year of Solomon's reign is commonly accepted as being around 966 BC, this would date the exodus at around 1446 BC, with the conquest of Canaan taking place forty years later.

2. The cumulative number of years for the rule of the judges seems to support an early date. In addition, the Judges 11:26 reference to 300 years of occupation of Israel in the land of Canaan between the time God had driven out the Amorites from before Israel and the time of Jephthah seems to point to an early date for the conquest.

3. The Amarna letters[31] written by Abdi-Hepa of Jerusalem around 1375 BC (EA 286–290) mention a group of people named *apiru*, a nomadic people who are thought to have invaded the land of Canaan during the fourteenth century BC. Basing their argument on the etymological correspondence between this word and the word "Hebrew," some scholars identify these *apiru* with Israelites of the Bible. This view has been discredited by many scholars who explain the term as "a catchall word for a diverse group living on the margins of ancient society."[32] The *apiru* have been identified as migrants, refugees, fugitives, brigands, and landless peasants whose presence is attested in the Fertile Crescent throughout much of the second millennium BC.[33] It is possible that a connection between the *apiru* of the Amarna texts and the Hebrews of the Bible existed, but it is unlikely that the term *apiru* equates to *Hebrews.*

---

30. For discussion by proponents of an early date, see the following: B. G. Wood, "The Rise and Fall of the 13th-Century Exodus-Conquest Theory," *JETS* 48 (2005): 489; idem, "The Biblical Date for the Exodus Is 1446 BC: A Response to James Hoffmeier," *JETS* 50 (2007): 249–58; Howard, *Joshua*, 31–35; J. J. Bimson and D. Livingston, "Saving the Biblical Chronology," *BAR* 13.5 (1987): 40–53, 66–68; E. H. Merrill, *Kingdom of Priests: A History of Old Testament Israel* (Grand Rapids: Baker, 1987), 66–67; idem, "Palestinian Archaeology and the Date of the Conquest: Do Tells Tell Tales?" *GTJ* 3 (1982): 107–21; W. H. Shea, "Exodus, Date of the," *ISBE*, 2:230–38; and B. K. Waltke, "Palestinian Artifactual Evidence Supporting the Early Date of the Exodus," *BSac* 129 (January 1972): 33–47. In their study of an Egyptian fragmentary name ring on a topographical pedestal relief preserved in the Berlin Museum, P. van der Veen, C. Theis, and M. Görg suggest that "Israel" is mentioned on a pre-Israel Stele of Merneptah as a place name in Canaan during the Nineteenth Dynasty (P. van der Veen, C. Theis, and M. Görg, "Israel in Canaan [Long] Before Pharaoh Merneptah? A Fresh Look at Berlin Statue Pedestal Relief 21687," *Journal of Ancient Egyptian Interconnections* 2.4 [2010]: 15–25). This interpretation of the text is accepted by Bryant Wood ("The Rise and Fall" and "The Biblical Date") and rejected by James Hoffmeier (James K. Hoffmeier, "What Is the Biblical Date for the Exodus? A Response to Bryant Wood," *JETS* 50.2 [2007]: 225–47).

31. Dated to 1400–1350 BC, the Amarna letters comprise political correspondence between rulers of Canaan and Mesopotamia, whose territories were under Egyptian control and Egyptian administration.

32. Hubbard, *Joshua*, 28.

33. Iain Provan, V. Philips Long, and Tremper Longman III, *A Biblical History of Israel* (Louisville, Ky.: Westminster John Knox, 2003), 170–71. The term ʿ*apiru* appears in Hittite archives from Boghazköy (Ḫattušaš), Lemche, "Habiru, Hapiru," *ABD*, 3:7.

4. The Merneptah Stele, dated to the thirteenth century BC, mentions the presence of a group of people called *Israel* who were settled in Canaan during Merneptah's rule (1213–1203 BC). This view assumes that Israel was already established as a people in the land of Canaan.

Late Exodus/Late Conquest.[34] A proposed late date for the exodus is c. 1260 BC. This author adopts a late date for the conquest of Canaan for the reasons listed below. Scholars who advocate for a late exodus and consequently a late conquest present the following claims:

1. According to Exodus 1:11, the Israelites built the store cities of Rameses and Pithom while they were in Egypt. The city of Rameses is thought to have been named after Rameses II, the Egyptian pharaoh who ruled during the thirteenth century BC (c. 1279–1213 BC).[35]
2. Proponents of a late date understand 1 Kings 6:1 as representing a symbolic number for twelve generations of forty years, between the time of the exodus and the time of Solomon, not a literal 480 years as interpreted by proponents of an early conquest.[36]
3. Based on interpretation of archaeological data, some conclude that Transjordan and Cisjordan were not highly populated until approximately 1300 BC, and that the dramatic population increase in Canaan around 1200 BC is attributed to the entrance of a new people in the land.[37] Furthermore, the emergence of "pillared-rim storage jars, the four-roomed or pillared house, the plastered pits for retaining water, and the creation of terraces"[38] and the sudden multiplication of towns in the highlands of Canaan during this period corroborate a late settlement (Late Bronze Age). The absence of cultic figurines and the non-porcine diet of the inhabitants of the land support the presence of a culture whose religious life did not permit images of the deity and a daily life that included restrictive dietary laws.

---

34. The original proponents of *late* dating for the exodus and conquest include William Foxwell Albright and his disciples (John Bright, *A History of Israel* [3rd ed.; Philadelphia: Westminster, 1981]). See also K. A. Kitchen, "The Exodus," *ABD*, 2:700–708; Hoffmeier, "What Is the Biblical Date for the Exodus?" 225–47; Hess, *Joshua*, 139–43. For a brief summary of this position, see W. G. Dever, *Who Were the Early Israelites and Where Did They Come From?* (Grand Rapids: Eerdmans, 2003), 41–49.

35. Provan et al., *A Biblical History of Israel*, 131.

36. A generation may have been closer to twenty-five years than forty years. See ibid., 131; Kitchen, "The Exodus," *ABD*, 2:702.

37. Early generations of archaeologists supported a late date based on their identification of burnt layers at various sites dated to the thirteenth century BC, concluding that these sites were destroyed during Joshua's campaigns in the land of Canaan. See W. F. Albright, "Ceramics and Chronology in the Near East," in *So Live the Works of Men: Seventieth Anniversary Volume Honoring Edgar Lee Hewett* (eds. D. B. Brand and F. E. Harvey; Albuquerque: Univ. of New Mexico Press, 1939), 49–63; G. E. Wright, *The Bible and the Ancient Near East: Essays in Honor of William Foxwell Albright* (Winona Lake, Ind.: Eisenbrauns, 1961); Y. Yadin, "The Transition from a Semi-Nomadic to a Sedentary Society in the 12th Century B.C.E.," in *Symposia Celebrating the Seventy-Fifth Anniversary of the Founding of the American Schools of Oriental Research (1900–1975)* (ed. F. M. Cross; Cambridge, Mass.: American Schools of Oriental Research, 1979), 57–68.

38. Richard S. Hess, "Joshua," in *Zondervan Illustrated Bible Backgrounds Commentary: Old Testament* (ed. John H. Walton; Grand Rapids: Zondervan, 2009), 2:7.

4. According to advocates of a late date, the data provided by the Merneptah Stele (thirteenth century BC) presents a recent take-over of the Canaanite towns of Ashkelon, Gezer, and Yenoam, and the beginning of the settlement of a people called Israel in Canaan during Merneptah's reign (1213–1203 BC).

Neither of the two major positions on the dating of the exodus and conquest is convincing beyond reasonable doubt. Scholars all agree that additional data is still needed in order to authenticate either of these working hypotheses. This author agrees that absolute dating is impossible due to the lack of direct evidence, but after reviewing the arguments for both positions, she remains a proponent of a late exodus and conquest for the following reasons:

1. The 480 years mentioned in 1 Kings 6:1 can be interpreted figuratively rather than literally. Numbers that appear in the biblical text are often symbolic representations of groups of people, items, times periods, etc. (e.g., "three days," "forty days," "seven").
2. The cumulative number of years for the period of the judges is 300. A literal interpretation of this number precludes an overlap of years for the rule of each judge.
3. Most scholars agree that the *hapiru/apiru* mentioned in the EA texts of the fourteenth and thirteenth centuries BC are not the Hebrews who left Egypt.
4. The Merneptah Stele does not confirm that Israel had been in the land of Canaan for a substantial period of time. It is possible that Israel had arrived in Canaan shortly before the writing of the inscription.

c. Conquest and Settlement Models[39]

Scholars remain divided on the origin of Israel; thus the reading of Joshua continues to provide a colorful landscape of scholarly interpretations. Several major theories on that topic have appeared over the years

Military conquest model (exogenous—W. F. Albright, Y. Yadin).[40] This model takes into account the biblical evidence that highlights a military conquest of the land of Canaan. Scholars who support this view point to archaeological data that reveal a thirteenth-century destruction of several cities in Canaan (e.g., Bethel, Debir, Eglon, Hazor, Lachish). Scholars who challenge this view raise several objections. (1) The book of Joshua mentions only two cities that suffered total destruction during the conquest; thus, evidence of a major military conquest is barely evident. (2) This book does not note who destroyed the two Canaanite cities; they could have been destroyed by other invaders. (3) Joshua mentions that only three cities were

---

39. For a brief discussion of the major views on the conquest of Canaan, see the following: Hubbard, *Joshua*, 35–40; Provan et al., *A Biblical History of Israel*, 138–49; Pekka Pitkänen, "Ethnicity, Assimilation and the Israelite Settlement," *TynBul* 55.2 (2004): 161–82; K. L. Younger Jr., "Early Israel in Recent Biblical Scholarship," in *The Face of Old Testament Studies* (ed. D. W. Baker and B. T. Arnold; Grand Rapids: Baker, 1999), 178–200.
40. W. F. Albright, "The Israelite Conquest of Canaan in the Light of Archaeology," *BASOR* 74 (1939): 11–23; Y. Yadin, "Is the Biblical Account of the Israelite Conquest of Canaan Historically Reliable?" *BAR* 8.2 (March/April 1982): 16–23.

burned (Jericho, Ai, and Hazor—6:24, 8:28, 11:13). A military campaign such as the one described in Joshua may have included more burnt cities.

Peaceful infiltration model (exogenous—A. Alt and M. Noth).[41] At the beginning of the twentieth century, Albrecht Alt and Martin Noth suggested that the Israelites were nomads or seminomads who infiltrated Canaan over a long period of time and settled in the sparsely populated regions of the land, primarily in the hill country. This view is incongruent with the information provided by the book of Joshua and denies the historical reliability of the biblical text. In addition, it dismisses the archaeological evidence that reveals a sudden increase in population in Canaan during the thirteenth century BC.

Peasant revolt model (exogenous/endogenous—G. Mendenhall and N. Gottwald).[42] The major arguments in favor of this theory point toward the formation of an alliance between the rural inhabitants of the land and a new group of people of low social status, resulting in an uprising of the lower class against the oppression of the upper class nobility. This view has been linked to a Marxist ideology "as the revolutionary attempt of a proletariat peasantry to overthrow their feudal overlords."[43]

Collapse model (endogenous—W. Dever).[44] At the end of the Middle Bronze age and the beginning of the Late Bronze Age, the inhabitants of Canaan lived under Egyptian dominance (see Amarna letters from Syro-Phoenicia). Around the end of the fourteenth century, the socio-cultural landscape of Canaan experienced an overall population decline, the abandonment of towns, and the economic weakening of the middle class.[45] The increased tax burden of the Egyptians and the disrupted trade network resulted in major economic decline in the region. The arrival of the Sea Peoples further contributed to the instability of the area. According to Dever, during this period, rural farmers from the lowlands of Canaan, "urban dropouts" who sought to escape the pressures of city life, *apiru* (rebels and brigands) from the countryside, refugees who fled social disasters, and local nomads moved to the highlands.

For Dever, this heterogeneous group with no specific ethnic identity and located primarily in the highlands formed "the *ancestors*—the authentic and direct progenitors—of those who later became the biblical Israelites."[46] They developed new methods of farming, built four-room houses (a new style), dug cisterns, built silos and storage pits, and so on. These developments evident during the period of the monarchy show ethnic continuity from the end of the second millennium into the first half of the first millennium—the monarchic period. This view completely discards the idea of an exodus out of Egypt during the second millennium and distances the events from the biblical text.

---

41. A. Alt, "The Settlement of the Israelites in Canaan," in *Essays on Old Testament History and Religion* (trans. R. A. Wilson; Sheffield: JSOT, 1989), 135–69; M. Noth, *The History of Israel* (2nd ed.; London: A & C Black, 1960), 53–84.

42. G. E. Mendenhall, "The Hebrew Conquest of Palestine," *BA* 25 (1962): 66–87; N. K. Gottwald, *The Tribes of Yahweh: A Sociology of the Religion of Liberated Israel, 1250–1050 B.C.E.* (Maryknoll, N.Y.: Orbis, 1979).

43. Hubbard, *Joshua*, 36.

44. Dever, *Who Were the Early Israelites?* 194.

45. J. M. Golden, *Ancient Canaan and Israel: New Perspectives* (New York: Oxford Univ. Press, 2009), 58–60.

46. Dever, *Who Were the Early Israelites?* 194.

Cyclic model (endogenous—I. Finkelstein, Coote and Withelam).[47] Along with some of the afore-mentioned theories, this model denies any possibility of an Israelite conquest; it argues that the Israelites had settled in the highlands of Canaan during one of the cycles of settlement of the third and second millennia, interrupting their nomadic lifestyle and establishing permanent roots in Canaan. These cycles of immigration were separated by periods of decline and reflected the socioeconomic changes that occurred during these centuries. Coote and Whitelam advocate that the emergence of Israel and the later formation of the Davidic kingdom were not isolated incidents. Rather, they were part of a complex cycle of growth, stagnation, and depletion in the ancient world. In their view, climate change, the collapse of trade structures, the ravage of territory by foreign powers, and the movement of masses triggered these cycles.[48]

Mixed multitude model (endogenous—A. Killebrew, J. M. Miller and J. H. Hayes, P. Pitkänen).[49] In her recent publication on biblical ethnicity, Killebrew proposes an endogenous model in which a mixed multitude of peoples, slaves, nomads, and others formed a distinct entity through a process called "ethnogenesis."[50] This group of largely indigenous peoples inhabited the land of Canaan and formed a loosely organized society that populated the region.[51]

Miller and Hayes describe the conditions in Palestine at the end of the Late Bronze Age and the beginning of the Early Iron Age as:

> a "melting pot," composed of diverse elements living under various "ad hoc" political and religious circumstances. It is our impression, correspondingly, that the early clans and tribes that formed the basis of the later kingdoms of Israel and Judah derived from diverse backgrounds and origins. They too, at least to a certain degree, represented a "melting pot."[52]

In their understanding, this melting pot would have been comprised of inhabitants of Palestine of old Semitic stock who already lived in the land, some who settled in the land gradually, some *Habiru*, escaped slaves from Egypt, some Sea Peoples, and migrating Arameans who settled in the area temporarily.

No conquest—minimalist approach (P. R. Davies and W. Lemke).[53] Scholars who join the minimalists reject the idea of a conquest and exclude any biblical evidence from their theory, advocating that the biblical text was composed too late—during the postexilic/Persian period—to provide information about the origin of Israel, and that it is "legendary, too theologically tainted, [and] too dependent on unreliable

---

47. I. Finkelstein, "State Formation in Israel and Judah: A Contrast in Context, a Contrast in Trajectory," *Near Eastern Archaeology* 62 (1999): 35–52; idem, "The Great Transformation: The Conquest of the Highlands Frontiers and the Rise of the Territorial States," in *The Archaeology of the Holy Land* (3rd ed.; ed. T. E. Levy; New York: Facts on File, 2003), 349–67; R. B. Coote and K. W. Whitelam, *The Emergence of Early Israel in Historical Perspective* (Sheffield: Almond, 1987).

48. Coote and Whitelam, *The Emergence of Early Israel*, 117–66.

49. A. Killebrew, *Biblical Peoples and Ethnicity* (Atlanta: Society of Biblical Literature, 2005), 184–85; J. M. Miller and J. H. Hayes, *A History of Ancient Israel and Judah* (Philadelphia: Westminster Press, 1986); P. Pitkänen, "Ethnicity," 161–82.

50. Killebrew, *Biblical Peoples and Ethnicity*, 149.

51. Ibid.

52. Miller and Hayes, *A History of Ancient Israel and Judah*, 78–79.

53. P. R. Davies, *In Search of Ancient Israel* (Sheffield: JSOT, 1992); W. Lemke, *The Israelites in History and Tradition* (Louisville, Ky.: Westminster John Knox, 1998).

oral tradition ... to contribute to any discussion of history."[54] Most biblical scholars reject this view as too extreme, too exclusive, and unsustainable.

Biblical and archaeological approach (R. L. Hubbard Jr.). Recently, Hubbard proposed a model that allows for literary (biblical and extrabiblical) and archaeological features to provide a partial description of the conquest of the land and to play a partial role in the reconstruction of Israel's history. Hubbard's view presents a worthy solution for combining the strengths of various scholarly positions in order to provide a better understanding of the message and context of Joshua. The following features are noteworthy: (1) the literary qualities of the text (e.g., hyperbolic language, lists, repetition, treaty formulae); (2) the archaeological evidence discovered during the last two centuries (e.g., wall at Jericho, burnt layer at Hazor, sudden increase of towns in Canaan); (3) intertextual data in the biblical text (e.g., OT and NT references to events of the book); and (4) extrabiblical documented evidence (e.g., town lists, military campaigns, conquest accounts). In our view, the sum of these features points to a conquest partially recorded toward the end of the second millennium BC, with necessary editing completed during the monarchical period. In addition, this method removes the need to "pit biblical texts against each other (e.g., Jos 10 versus Jos 13 or Jdg 1)."[55] Only when consideration is given to all these components can the message of Joshua be understood, and only then can the seemingly contradictory accounts of the conquest be treated with fairness.

6. THE PEOPLE OF THE LAND

During their journey to the Promised Land, the Israelites faced numerous groups of people (mostly hostile) who had heard of the extraordinary miracles God had performed on their behalf (e.g., Jos 2:10–11; 5:1—parting of the Red Sea, defeat of Amorite kings). The fear of the God of Abraham, Isaac, and Jacob had fallen on the inhabitants of Canaan and on the people of the surrounding region. Their hearts melted and their courage failed (2:11; 5:1; 7:5); yet they were determined to stand their ground and to remain in the land they had occupied and called home. While most of the people resisted Israel in military conflicts, others (such as the Gibeonites) chose to deceive the newcomers with trickery (Jos 9). The following alphabetical list identifies the people groups Israel encountered during her journey to and into the Promised Land.

Amorites[56] (Nu 13:29; 21:13–35; 32:33–39; Dt 7:1; 20:17; Jos 2:10; 3:10; 5:1; 7:7; 9:1, 10; 10:6, 12; 11:3; 12:2, 8; 13:4, 10, 21; 24:8, 11, 15, 18). In the Table of Nations, the Amorites are listed as sons of Canaan of the line of Ham, a non-Semitic line (Ge 10:16). They appear in the biblical text as one of the seven major people groups that inhabited Canaan before Israel entered the land. Akkadian sources refer to the *amurru* as an ethnic group of people who lived west of Mesopotamia and whose language was an independent branch of NW Semitic (identified primarily by its verbal system with prefix- and suffix-conjugations analogous to

---

54. Hubbard, *Joshua*, 38.

55. Ibid., 39.

56. G. E. Mendenhall, "Amorites," *ABD*, 1:199–202; K. N. Schoville, "Canaanites and Amorites," in *Peoples of the Old Testament World* (eds. A. J. Hoerth, G. L. Mattingly, and E. M. Yamauchi; Grand Rapids: Baker, 1994), 157–82; J. A. Dearman, "Amorites," *NIDB* (eds. K. Doob Sakenfeld et al.; Nashville: Abingdon, 2006), CD-ROM; H. B. Huffmon, *Amorite Personal Names in the Mari Texts: A Structural and Lexical Study* (Baltimore, Md.: Johns Hopkins Univ. Press, 1965).

other NW Semitic languages).[57] As mentioned in texts from Alalakh, in Amarna letters, and in Hittite literature during the Late Bronze Age, the Amorites had established a kingdom in the upper Orontes Valley.[58] They also inhabited parts of Canaan and Transjordan.

Anakites[59] (Dt 1:28; 2:10, 11, 21; 9:2; Jos 11:21, 22; 14:12, 15; 15:14; Jdg 1:20). The Anakites are first mentioned in Deuteronomy. Their name originates from the noun *anak* meaning "neck" or "necklace," a corollary of "giants" (long-necked).[60] Anak was the son of Arba (Jos 15:13), who founded the town of Kiriath-Arba/Hebron (Jos 21:11). The Anakites are described as strong and tall, a people to be feared (Dt 2:10, 21; 9:2). They inhabited the hill country of Judah and the area of Hebron. When Caleb settled in Hebron, he attacked the Anakites, and those who survived fled Israelite territory and relocated in Gaza, Gath, and Ashdod (Jos 11:22).

Avvites[61] (Dt 2:23; Jos 13:3). The Avvites inhabited the southern part of Canaan when Israel entered the land. They were southern neighbors to the Philistine cities, probably occupying the area between Egypt and Gaza. The LXX identifies them with the Hivites. The Avvites were deported to Samaria by the Assyrians during the eighth century BC and worshiped the gods of Assyria at the shrines they built to their deities (2Ki 17:27–34).

Canaanites[62] (Ex 3:8, 17; Num 13:29; Jos 9:1–2; Jdg 1:1–10). In the Table of Nations, the Canaanites are listed as descendants of the line of Ham, a non-Semitic line (Ge 10:6). The "land of Canaan" and "Canaanites" are mentioned in eighteenth-century texts from Mari, in fourteenth-century texts from Alalakh, on an Egyptian stele of Amenhotep II of the fifteenth century, and on the "Israel stele" of Merneptah in the thirteenth century.[63] The Canaanites occupied the land of Canaan long before the patriarchs traveled the area (Ge 13:7). They lived in the valleys (Nu 14:25; Dt 11:30) and in the hill country (Nu 14:40–45). God promised to drive out the Canaanites before Israel (Dt 7:1; Jos 3:10) and commanded the Israelites to completely destroy them (Dt 20:17); yet they remained in the land even after Israel settled in Canaan (Jos 13:1–4; 16:10; 17:12).

Gebalites[64] (Jos 13:5). The Gebalites appear only once in the Hebrew Bible. The men of Gebal (a port city on the Mediterranean, also called Byblos) participated in the building of Solomon's temple in Jerusalem (1Ki 5:18). They are identified as "shipwrights" in Ezekiel 27:9. Byblos was a major trade city known for its production of paper from Egyptian papyrus. It is mentioned in many ancient Near Eastern texts such

57. Mendenhall, "Amorites," 199.

58. Ibid., 201.

59. G. L. Mattingly, "Anak," *ABD*, 1:222; L. M. Wolfe, "Anak, Anakim, Anakites," *NIDB* (2006), CD-ROM.

60. Mattingly, "Anak," 222.

61. S. E. McGarry, "Avvim," *ABD*, 1:531–32; "Avvim, Avvites," *NIDB* (2007, CD-ROM).

62. See Y. Aharoni, *The Land of the Bible: A Historical Geography* (2nd ed.; trans. A. F Rainey; Philadelphia: Westminster, 1979), 61–63; W. F. Albright, "The Role of the Canaanites in the History of Civilization," in *The Bible and the ANE* (ed. G. E. Wright; repr., Winona Lake, Ind.: Eisenbrauns, 1979), 328–62; P. C. Schmitz, "Canaan (Place)," *ABD*, 1:829–31; K. N. Schoville, "Canaanites and Amorites," in *Peoples of the Old Testament World* (eds. A. J. Hoerth, G. L. Mattingly, and E. M. Yamauchi; Grand Rapids: Baker, 1994), 157–82; J. A. Dearman, "Canaan, Canaanites," *NIDB* (2006), CD-ROM.

63. Schoville, "Canaanites and Amorites," 158.

64. R. L. Roth, "Gebal," *ABD*, 2:922–23; S. Frolov, "Gebal, Gebalites," *NIDB* (2007, CD-ROM).

as the Egyptian (execration texts), Assyrian (campaign reports), and Akkadian (Amarna texts). The area of Byblos was not conquered under Joshua's leadership (Jos 13:5).

Geshurites[65] (Dt 3:14; Jos 13:2; 1Sa 27:8). The Geshurites lived in an area not conquered under Joshua's leadership. Some scholars have placed them at the base of the Golan Heights, east of the Sea of Galilee (Dt 3:14; Jos 12:5; 13:11, 13), while others have located them in an area between Philistia and Sinai (Jos 13:1−4; 1Sa 7:8−11).

Gibeonites[66] (Jos 9; 10:6; 2Sa 21). The Gibeonites were descendants of the Amorites, a non-Semitic people (2Sa 21:2). They inhabited the town of Gibeon in Benjamin, located in the hill country approximately five miles northwest of Jerusalem. The Gibeonites (a subgroup of Hivites, Jos 9:7) would have been annihilated by Israel during the conquest were it not for their ability to deceive Joshua through trickery. After hearing of the destruction of Jericho and Ai by the Israelites, the inhabitants of Gibeon went to Joshua at Gilgal and fooled him into thinking they were strangers from a distant country who had come to request a treaty with the Israelites because of the fame of their God. Duped by these con-artists, Joshua made a treaty with the Gibeonites, a deed strictly forbidden by Yahweh (Dt 7:1−2). After discovering the trick of the Gibeonites, Joshua decided to let them live and to make them woodcutters and water carriers for the Israelites and for the Solomonic temple. During the united monarchy, Saul attempted to annihilate the inhabitants of Gibeon, thereby breaking the treaty established earlier between them and Joshua and inviting severe consequences on Saul's family — the execution of seven of his descendants (2Sa 21). After the exile, ninety-five Gibeonites returned to Judah from Babylon (Ne 7:25).

Gileadites[67] (Nu 26:29; 32:40; Jos 17:1; Jdg 12:4, 5). Gilead was the son of Makir and grandson of Manasseh. His descendants lived east of the Jordan between the Yarmuk River and the Dead Sea in an area suitable for keeping livestock (Nu 32:1). In the Bible, the term "Gilead" often designates an area inhabited by several people groups (Amorite kings, Dt 4:47−49; Reuben and Gad settle in Gilead, Nu 32:1, 25−27). Moses gave the area of Gilead to the descendants of Manasseh (Nu 32:30). The daughters of Zelophehad, who received an inheritance of land in Transjordan, were Gileadites (Nu 27:1, granddaughters of Gilead). The King's Highway went through Gilead, making it a strategic commercial area for the whole region. Ramoth in Gilead served as a city of refuge for individuals accused of manslaughter (Jos 21:38).

Girgashites[68] (Ge 15:18−21; Dt 7:1; Jos 3:10; 24:11). In the Table of Nations, the Girgashites are listed as sons of Canaan of the line of Ham, a non-Semitic line (Ge 10:16). The Girgashites are included in the list of the seven nations God promised to drive out before the Israelites. Ancient Near Eastern texts include names that are linked to this designation (e.g., Ugaritic "son of Grgs" in *UT* 3:381, no. 619; Hittite "Karkisa"; Egyptian "*krkr*").[69]

65. G. J. Petter, "Geshurites," *ABD*, 2:996−97; K. A. Wilson, "Geshur, Geshurites," *NIDB* (2007, CD-ROM).

66. P. M. Arnold, "Gibeon," *ABD* 2:1010−13; Kah-Jim Jeffrey Kuan, "Gibeon, Gibeonites," *NIDB* (2007), CD-ROM.

67. M. P. Graham, "Gilead (Person)," *ABD*, 2:1019−21; M. Ottosson, "Gilead (Place)," *ABD*, 2:1020−22; S. L. Klouda, "Gilead, Gileadites," *NIDB* (2007), CD-ROM.

68. D. W. Baker, "Girgashite," *ABD*, 2:1028; M. G. Vanzant, "Girgashite," *NIDB* (2007), CD-ROM.

69. Baker, "Girgashite," 1028.

Hittites[70] (Ex 3:8; Num 13:29; Dt 7:1; 20:17; Jos 3:10; 9:1; 11:3; 12:8; 24:11; Jdg 1:26; 3:5). In the Table of Nations, the Hittites are listed as sons of Canaan of the line of Ham, a non-Semitic line (Ge 10:15; 1Ch 1:13). They are sometimes referred to as "the sons of Heth" ($b^e n \hat{e} \; h\bar{e}t$—Ge 23:3, 5, 10, 16, 18, 20; 25:10; 49:32) and "the daughters of Heth" ($b^e n\hat{o}t \; h\bar{e}t$—27:46). In the standard list of the seven major people groups of Canaan, the Hittites are normally listed in first or second place (Ex 3:8, 17; 13:5; 23:23; Dt 7:1; 20:17; Jos 3:10; 9:1; 11:3; 12:8). They were present in Canaan before the patriarchal period. Abraham purchased a cave in the field of Machpelah from a Hittite to bury his wife Sarah (Ge 23:19–20). Abraham, Isaac, Rebekah, Jacob, and Leah were later buried in this cave (49:30–32; 50:13). During the second millennium BC, the Hittites are found in the hill country, in the Negev, and in the coastal region; they are never completely eradicated from Canaan. During the period of the judges, the Israelites began to intermarry with them and regrettably adopted some of their religious practices (Jdg 3:5–6).

Hivites[71] (Ex 3:8, 17; 13:5; 23:23; Dt 7:1; 20:17; Jos 3:10; 9:1, 7; 11:3, 19; 12:8; 24:11; Jdg 3:3, 5; 2Sa 24:7). In the Table of Nations, the Hivites are listed as sons of Canaan of the line of Ham, a non-Semitic line (Ge 10:17). Speiser associates the Hivites with the Hurrians, who had the oversight of cities in Canaan during the fourteenth century BC.[72] In Joshua 9:7, the MT reads "Hivite" while the LXX reads "Horite." According to Deuteronomy 20:17, the Israelites were strictly forbidden to have contact with them; they were to treat them as *ḥērem* ("devoted to Yahweh") and to destroy them completely along with the Hittites, Amorites, Canaanites, Perizzites, and Jebusites. Israel violated this rule when they made a peace treaty with the Hivites at Gibeon (9:7; 11:19). Israelite women were given in marriage to Hivite men, who led them to worship their gods (Jdg 3:5–6). Consequently, the anger of Yahweh burned against the Israelites, and they were defeated in battle by the king of Aram Naharaim (Jdg 3:5–8).

Jebusites[73] (Num 13:29; Dt 7:1; 20:17; Jos 3:10; 9:1; 11:3; 12:8; 15:63; 24:11; Jdg 1:21; 3:5; 19:11; 2Sa 5:6, 8; Ne 9:8). In the Table of Nations, the Jebusites are listed as sons of Canaan of the line of Ham, a non-Semitic line (Ge 10:16; Jdg 19:11). The pre-Israelite name for Jerusalem is "Urusalim" in the Amarna texts and documents from Ebla, and "Jebus" in the biblical text (Jos 15:63; 18:28; Jdg 19:10–11; 2Sa 5:6; 1Ch 11:4). According to the biblical text, Jebusites lived in and beyond Jerusalem and occupied land up to the southern border of Benjamin. Long before the Israelites entered Canaan, God promised that he would drive the Jebusites out of the Promised Land (Dt 7:1), and he commanded Israel to destroy them completely (20:17). In reality, their recurring presence in the land reveals that this was never fulfilled. During the united monarchy, David captured Jerusalem from the Jebusites and made it his capital (2Sa 5:6–7; 1Ch 11:4–9).

70. A. Kempinsky, "Hittites in the Bible," *BAR* 5 (September–October 1979): 21–45; G. McMahon, "Hittites in the OT," *ABD*, 3:231–33; H. A. Hoffner Jr., "Hittites" in *Peoples of the Old Testament World* (eds. A. J. Hoerth, G. L. Mattingly, and E. M. Yamauchi; Grand Rapids: Baker, 1994), 127–56; B. J. Collins, "Hittites," *NIDB* (2007), CD-ROM.

71. E. A. Speiser, "Hurrians," *IDB*, 2:665. See also H. A. Hoffner, "Hittites and Hurrians," in *Peoples of Old Testament Times* (ed. D. J. Wiseman; Oxford: Clarendon, 1973), 225; Hess, "West Semitic Texts," 67; D. W. Baker, "Hivites" *ABD*, 3:234; R. de Vaux, "Les Hurrites de l'histoire et les Horites de la Bible," *RB* 74 (1967): 497–503; O. Margalith, "The Hivites," *ZAW* 100 (1988): 60–70.

72. Speiser, "Hurrians," 665.

73. Boling and Wright, *Joshua*, 167; S. A. Reed, "Jebus," *ABD*, 3:652–53; J. Kah-Jin Kuan, "Jebus, Jebusites," *NIDB* (2008), CD-ROM.

Kenizzites[74] (Ge 15:19; Nu 32:12; Jos 14:6, 14). Caleb is listed as the son of Jephunneh the Kenizzite, a possible descendant of Kenaz, a grandson of Esau (Ge 36:11). The grandsons of Esau settled in Seir (Edom), south/southeast of the Dead Sea. The plural Kenizzites appears only once in the Hebrew Bible — in the Abrahamic covenant account (Ge 15:19).

Makirites (Nu 32:40; Jos 17:1). The Makirites are descendants of the tribe of Manasseh. They were known to be great soldiers and settled in the area of Gilead in Transjordan.

Perizzites[75] (Ge 15:20; Ex 3:8, 17; 23:23; Dt 7:1; 20:17; Jos 3:10; 9:1; 11:3; 12:8; 17:15; 24:11; Jdg 1:4, 5; 3:5). The Perizzites inhabited Canaan before the time of the patriarchs. They are first mentioned in the account where Abram and Lot's herdsmen quarrel during their journey from the Negev to Bethel (Ge 13:7). The Perizzites are mentioned in the list of seven nations encountered by Israel during their conquest of Canaan. Where the list is reduced to only two names, the Canaanites and the Perizzites are mentioned and may represent combinations of various people groups (Ge 13:7; 34:30; Jdg 1:4, 5). Some have suggested that the Canaanites refer to Semitic people while the Perizzites represent non-Semitic people.[76] Speiser suggests that the etymology of "Perizzite" may come from Hurrian.[77]

Philistines[78] (Ge 10:14; 26; Ex 23:31; Jos 13:2; Jdg 3:3; 13:1; Ps 56:1; Isa 2:6). The Philistines are listed as descendants of Cush of the line of Ham, a non-Semitic people. Their origin is still unknown but scholars point to the arrival of the Philistines in Canaan partly via Anatolia and partly via Caphtor (Jer 47:4−5; Am 9:7). The Philistines ("Peleshet") were Sea Peoples who aspired to dwell in Egypt; opposition from Egyptian naval forces sent them toward Canaan. They settled in the Philistine Pentapolis — Ashdod, Ashkelon, Gaza, Ekron, and Gath. Ashdod, Ashkelon, and Gaza were port cities on the Mediterranean (the "Sea of the Philistines," Ex 23:31) while Ekron and Gath were located inland.

Israel failed to drive out the Philistines from Canaan and consequently fought against them for centuries, at times suffering defeat (1Sa 4:1−10) and at other times obtaining victory (7:1−14). Judges (Samson, Shamgar), kings (Saul, David), and prophets (Samuel) encountered the Philistines in battle throughout Canaan. The Philistines erected shrines to Dagon in Gaza (Jdg 16:21−23) and Ashdod (1Sa 5:1−8), and a temple to Ashtoreth was built at Beth Shan. During the first millennium BC, the Philistine Pentapolis was invaded by the Assyrians (under Tiglath-pileser III, Sargon, Sennacherib, Esarhaddon, Assurbanipal), the Egyptians (under Psammetichus, Neco II, Neco I), the Babylonians (under Nebuchadnezzar), the Persians (under Cyrus), and the Greeks (under Alexander the Great).[79] Philistines were deported by Nebuchadnezzar to the region of Nippur, where they settled in locales named Gaza, Ashkelon, and Bit Arsa.[80]

---

74. J. K. Kuntz, "Kenaz," *ABD*, 4:17; R. K. Hawkins, "Kenaz, Kenizzite," *NIDB* (2008), CD-ROM.

75. S. A. Reed, "Perizzite," *ABD*, 5:231; "Perizzites," *NIDB* (2009), CD-ROM; N. Na'aman, "Canaanites and Perizzites," *BN* 13 (1988): 42−47.

76. Reed, "Perizzite," 231.

77. E. A. Speiser, "Hurrians," *IDB*, 2:665.

78. See "Philistines, Philistia," *NBD*, 988−91; H. J. Katzenstein, "Philistines," *ABD*, 5:326−28; T. J. Schneider, "Philistines," *NIDB* (2009), CD-ROM.

79. Katzenstein, "Philistines," 328.

80. Ibid.

Rephaites (Rephaim)[81] **(**Ge 14:5; 15:20; Dt 2:11, 20; 3:11, 13; Jos 12:4; 13:12; 17:15; 1Ch 20:4). The Rephaites (called Emites by the Moabites, Dt 2:11, and Zamzummites by the Ammonites, Dt 2:20) are compared with the Anakites, who were a strong and giantlike people. Og, king of Bashan, was a Rephaite, whose iron bed measured thirteen feet long and six feet wide (Dt 3:11). Some scholars have proposed that the Rephaites were not a group of people as distinct as the other people groups who lived in Canaan and Transjordan, but rather that they were a remnant of an ancient warrior tribe of giants.[82]

Sidonians[83] (Dt 3:9; Jos 13:4, 6; Jdg 3:3; 10:12; 18:7; 1Ki 5:6; 11:1−33; 16:31; 2Ki 23:13; 1Ch 22:4; Eze 32:30). The Sidonians inhabited the prominent coastal city of Sidon on the Mediterranean, located approximately twenty-five miles north of Tyre. The Phoenician city of Sidon is mentioned in texts from Ugarit (*KTU* 1.14.IV.35, 39), in Hittite incantations (*ANET*, 352), in the Amarna letters (EA 75, 85, 92, 101, 114, 118, 144, 146 [reconstructed], 147, 148, 149, 151, 152 [reconstructed], 154, 155, and 162), and in Egyptian documents (Papyrus Anastasi I). The Assyrians (under Tiglath-pileser I, Sennacherib, Esarhaddon) invaded it, as did the Babylonians (under Nebuchadnezzar) and the Persians (under Cyrus).[84]

With a natural harbor and an offshore reef, the city of Sidon was strategic for commerce and trade. Among the many artifacts uncovered at Sidon, King Eshmunazar and King Tabnit of Sidon provided the scholarly world with 3000-year-old Phoenician inscriptions on their personal sarcophagi. Famous for their glass making and bronze artifacts, Sidonians were also known for their mastery in shipbuilding.[85] According to the book of Joshua, Sidon was given as an inheritance to Israel but was not conquered during the days of Joshua (Jos 13:1−6).

7. THEOLOGY

a. The Land

The theological significance of "the land' in Joshua is directly linked to the national and ethnic identity of Israel and to the fulfillment of God's promise to Abraham, Isaac, Jacob, and Moses. The word for "land" (ʾereṣ) occurs over 2,400 times in the Hebrew Bible. The patriarchs, former prophets, latter prophets, kings, priests, and even some foreign nations believed and acknowledged that the land was a gift from Yahweh to Israel. This land is Israel's divine legacy, the place God has chosen for his people and the instrument of God's blessings to his children. Without a divine promise of land, the book of Joshua is incomprehensible.

The Bible speaks of two types of land, the earthly and the heavenly. Vis-à-vis the earthly, the narratives of the Old and New Testaments emerge (for the most part) in the physical land of Canaan (i.e., Jerusalem, Shechem, Hebron, Bethlehem, Nazareth, Galilee). From the beginning of the patriarchal narratives to the end of the New Testament, the land is a primary component of Israel's history. First came the *promise* of land to Abram (Ge 12:7; 15:7, 18; 24:6−7) that was *renewed* to Isaac (Ge 26:2−3) and Jacob (Ge 35:11−12), and reiterated to Joseph (Ge 48:3−4). The promise was followed by the *journey* to this very land with Moses

---

81. M. S. Smith, "Rephaim," *ABD*, 5:674−76; E. T. Mullen Jr., "Rephaim," *NIDB* (2008), CD-ROM.

82. Smith, "Rephaim," *ABD*, 5:676.

83. P. C. Schmitz, "Sidon (Place)," *ABD*, 6:17−18; D. Doumet-Serhal, "Sidon," *NIDB* (2009), CD-ROM.

84. Schmitz, "Sidon (Place)," *ABD*, 6:18.

85. Doumet-Serhal, "Sidon," *NIDB* (2009), CD-ROM.

and the children of Israel. Finally, with Joshua as leader came the *procurement* of the land. Exile from the land never assumed the permanent loss of the land. On the contrary, the *return* from exile always meant a return to *that* land—no other location is ever mentioned as a homeland for Israel, neither in ancient times nor in modern times. The lenses of biblical history are permanently fixed on that land, and the events of eschatology center on that land.

Scripture is consistent when revealing Yahweh's will for the land. God never intended for his people Israel to be without a homeland. From the beginning of Israel's history, the plan was disclosed. To Abraham, God promised a growing family and a place where this family would thrive and flourish (Ge 12:1–3). The place was chosen by God and given to Abraham and his offspring as an inheritance forever (Ge 13:15; Ex 32:13; Jos 14:9). The patriarchs (Abraham, Isaac, and Jacob) settled in Canaan—the Promised Land. Living elsewhere always meant living in a foreign land (Gen 15:13//Acts 7:6; Ex 2:22; 3:18; Ps 137:4). The purpose of the exodus was to free Israel from slavery in Egypt and to bring her to the land promised to her centuries earlier (Ex 3:8, 17; 6:8; 13:5; 20:12; 23:23). The journey in the wilderness always pointed toward the land (Num 14:7–9; 15:1–2; 26:52–55; Dt 11:10–15), and the rest of Israel's history takes place primarily in the land.

Yahweh's gift of land to Israel never precluded the blessings declared to Abraham for the sons of Ishmael. In Genesis 17:20, God said of Ishmael: "I will surely bless him; I will make him fruitful and will greatly increase his numbers. He will be the father of twelve rulers, and I will make him into a great nation." Regarding Hagar's son, God said to Abraham: "I will make the son of the maidservant into a nation also, because he is your offspring" (21:13). In God's plan, Ishmael and his descendants were never destined to be outcasts, oppressed, and reduced to a minor people group. In fact, we can say that God has fulfilled his promise as there are currently approximately 58,000,000 sons of Ishmael in the Middle East and dispersed in the rest of the world. Throughout history, God provided huge territories for Ishmael's sons, from Egypt to Syria to Iraq to Saudi Arabia, and most of the land in between. The small land of Israel, by contrast, has been reserved for the sons of Isaac, according to the biblical promise confirmed to the patriarchs, to Moses, to David, and to many other biblical characters.

In Yahweh's promise of land to Abraham, he swore to give it as an inheritance to his people Israel. The terms employed to speak of the promise of land to Israel—"to swear" (*nišbaʿ*), "to give" (*lātēt*), "the land" (*ʾereṣ*), "inheritance" (*naḥªlā*), "Israel," and "forever" (*ʿôlām*)—leaves little room for misinterpretation of the divine promise. Throughout Scripture, where Yahweh *swears* to accomplish a task, it is always performed absolutely, without ever relenting (e.g., Ge 22:16; Dt 1:8; 2:16; 4:21; 6:10, 18; 7:8; 8:1; 9:5; 11:9, 21; 19:8; 26:3; 28:9, 11; 30:20; 31:7; 34:4; Jos 5:6 [2x]; Jud 2:15; 2Sa 3:9; Pss 110:4; 132:11; Isa 13:24; 62:8; Jer 22:5; 44:26; 49:13; 51:13; Am 4:2; 6:8; 8:7).

As for "the land' (*ʾereṣ*), it is included in the major biblical covenants with Israel (e.g., Abrahamic, Ge 15; 17; Mosaic, Ex 20:12; 23:31–33; Davidic, 2Sa 7). The term used to express *forever* (*ʿôlām*) can signify (1) a limited duration of time (e.g., during a life span, Pr 10:25; 1Sa 20:15); (2) an indefinite period of time (past or future); and (3) an unceasing period of time or from now to perpetuity (e.g., Ge 9:12, 16; 17:7, 13; Pss 78:69; 104:5). Regarding the use of *forever* or *everlasting* (*ʿôlām*) in contexts of covenant, Anthony Tomasino writes that *ʿôlām* "means that they were made with no anticipated end point."[86]

---

86. Anthony Tomasino, "עוֹלָם," *NIDOTTE*, 3:349.

In biblical times, the land is identified as a divine inheritance (*naḥᵃlâ*). Today as in ancient times (Nu 27:8–11), an inheritance bequeathed from one generation to the next cannot be taken away after it is given. The new "owner" is responsible to care for the acquired possession until he/she grants it to another. Once bequeathed, the gift cannot be retrieved, even if it is mishandled by the new owner. The promise of the land for the descendants of Abraham did not change after the coming of the Messiah. The land is and will forever remain a gift to the chosen people. Jesus never denied the permanent significance of the land for his people. His ministry took place in Judah and Samaria. His respect for the sacredness of Jerusalem, and the temple is highly significant (Lk 19:41–47).

Gary Burge maintains that Jesus' silence about the Jewish hope for a homeland indicates that "Israel's national ambitions tied to reclaiming the land live on the margin of Jesus' thinking."[87] Although this may be true, an argument from silence can neither negate nor deny that the land was *promised to*, *given to*, and *received by* Israel centuries earlier as an inheritance *forever*. Jesus' love for the nations, the poor, the landless, and the foreigner opens a door for the inclusion of all in his *spiritual* kingdom, but it never replaces the promise of an *earthly* estate for the chosen people—a place from which they can reach the world with the gospel.

Scholars are divided in their hermeneutical discussion of the land. The views are polarized and the issues are complex.[88] For one people, the land is home; for the other, the land signifies homelessness. The cry of the dispossessed accuses the possessor who has finally come home. There is no simple solution to the issues

---

87. G. M. Burge, *Jesus and the Land: The New Testament Challenge to "Holy Land" Theology* (Grand Rapids: Baker, 2010), 28.

88. In 1992, Palestinian Christian Samir Munayer founded the organization *Musalaha* (meaning "reconciliation") for Arab/Palestinian and Jewish believers who live in "the land" today and who seek to address difficult social, political, and religious matters through a biblical paradigm—the love of Jesus Christ (www.musalaha.org [accessed June 10, 2011]). The Executive Board of the organization is comprised equally of Palestinian Christian leaders, Messianic Jewish leaders, and church leaders. One of the major issues addressed by the organization is the "theology of the land." A collection of Palestinian, Messianic, and Christian theological perspectives on "the promised land" has been published by Musalaha in *The Bible and the Land: An Encounter—Different Views: Christian Arab Palestinian, Israeli Messianic Jews, Western Christian* (ed. L. Loden, P. Walker, and M. Wood; Jerusalem: Musalaha, 2000). In his recent book *Once an Arafat Man: The True Story of How a PLO Sniper Found a New Life* (Cambridge: Tyndale, 2009), Taas Saada highlights that what matters most for believers in *Yeshua/Yasooa* is not one's stance on the land, but the souls of men. He says: "When I speak to groups of messianic Jews, I often say, 'A soul is worth more than land. To bring a single Palestinian soul to Jesus is more important than hanging onto acreage.' When I address Arab Christians, I make the same point in reverse. 'So far, most Jews are not finding their true Messiah. For us to bring them in that direction is worth far more in God's eyes than proving our point about the land'" (p. 226). Additional sources on the topic of the land include P. Church et al., eds, *The Gospel and the Land of Promise: Christian Approaches to the Land of the Bible* (Eugene, OR: Pickwick, 2011); Jean-Paul Rempp, *Israël: peuple, foi et territoire* (Charols, France: Excelsis, 2010); G. M. Burge, *Jesus and the Land*; idem, *Whose Land? Whose Promise? What Christians Are Not Being Told about Israel and the Palestinians* (Cleveland: Pilgrim, 2003); W. Brueggemann, *The Land: Place as Gift, Promise, and Challenge in Biblical Faith* (rev. ed.; Minneapolis: Augsburg Fortress, 2002); C. Chapman, *Whose Promised Land?* (rev. ed.; Tring, UK: Lion, 1989); W. C. Kaiser Jr., "The Promised Land, A Biblical-Historical View," *BSac* 138 (1981): 302–12; D. Miller, "Messianic Judaism and the Theology of the Land," *Mishkan* 26 (1997): 31; B. F. Skjott, "Messianic Believers and the Land of Israel—a Survey," *Mishkan* 26 (1997): 75; C. Urbach, "The Land of Israel in Scripture," *Mishkan* 26 (1997): 21–30; P. W. L. Walker, ed., *Jerusalem Past and Present in the Purposes of God* (Croydon, UK: Deo Gloria, 1994); L. A. Hoffman, ed., *The Land of Israel: Jewish Perspectives* (Notre Dame, Ind.: Univ. of Notre Dame Press, 1986); S. J. Munayer and L. Loden, eds., *The Land Cries Out: Theology of the Land in the Israeli-Palestinian Context* (Eugene, OR: Cascade, 2012).

associated with the land, neither from a theological perspective nor from a political standpoint. According to Brueggemann:

> The Church is immobilized by phony polarizations, as though the issue was liberal/conservative, revolutionary/reactionary, when in fact the real radicalness is the agenda of land that undercuts all other postures. We have yet to face how odd and discomforting is the biblical affirmation that God wills land for his people and he will take it from others for the sake of the poor.[89]

In the Abrahamic, Mosaic, and Davidic covenants, physical land was promised to Israel and given as "a gift not to be presumed upon ... [but] as an arena for justice and freedom."[90] Brueggemann adds, "It is recognized that life in the land must be lived in conformity with the creator's intention."[91] Misappropriation and misuse of the land by Israel were always costly and brought about severe consequences. Religious corruption, syncretism, and breach of the covenant were punished with the loss of the land in 586 BC to live in exile for an extended period of time (Jer 17:4).

The divine promise of land to Israel is unique. No other nation has been promised such a gift. As Brueggemann and Burge point out, the promise was not given in a void, but rather it was given in the context of a covenant relationship between God and his people. Living in the Promised Land required justice, righteousness, and holiness from Israel; her sins against Yahweh resulted in the temporary loss of land. Where the Old Testament declares the uprooting of Israel from the land because of her disobedience to the covenant (e.g., Dt 28:15, 63), the text also provides hope for territorial restoration for God's people (e.g., Jer 31:16–17; Ezra; Nehemiah; Haggai). Once her sins were atoned for, Israel returned home to the very place she had been given centuries earlier. Never in biblical history was the divine promise revoked.

Although Yahweh is the ultimate "owner" of the land, he chose Israel to be its caretaker (Lev 25:23), and for this reason, the land could never be bequeathed to non-Israelites. Today, Israel is responsible to care for the same land, to bless all its inhabitants — including the aliens and the sons of Ishmael in her midst — and to serve Yahweh wholeheartedly. Unfortunately, the realities on the ground do not reflect the biblical mandate. Today, the State of Israel is primarily secular, her social responsibilities are wanting towards the alien and foreigner, her devotion to Yahweh is contemptible, and consequently, her rights to the land are disputed fiercely and incessantly. But with the rise of the Messianic movement throughout the world, and especially in Israel, there is great hope that Israel will one day be who she was called to be and that her light will shine before men, that they may see her good works and glorify God who is in heaven (Mt 5:16). There is hope that, in the future, the Word will again go forth into the world from Zion, the Word of the Lord from Jerusalem (Isa 2:3), as it was in the first century with Paul and the other apostles of Christ.

In modern Jewish thought as well as in ancient Judaism, "one cannot divide the Jewish people into two parts, the 'enlandised' and the 'disenlandised.' Those in the land look outward. Those outside look toward the land."[92] Land is intertwined with the identity of all Jews; the two are inseparable.

---

89. Brueggemann, *The Land*, 206.
90. Ibid., 204.
91. Ibid., xix.
92. Brueggemann, *The Land*, 202–3.

Brueggemann speaks of an "urgent and difficult connection of *God, land,* and *Torah,* a convergence that is inescapable."[93] In his words, "the Jewish community—in all its long, tortuous history—has never forgotten that its roots and its hopes are in a storied earth, and that is the central driving force of its uncompromising ethical faith."[94]

Burge dismisses the promise of a homeland for modern Jews. He spiritualizes elements of the land and interprets them as literary metaphors for spiritual formation (e.g., desert = testing place; tumultuous Sea of Galilee = a place without control; mountains = place of refuge; Jordan River = boundary between dry place and Promised Land).[95] Such an appropriation of Scripture issues from replacement theology in which the church is thought to have completely replaced Israel. This interpretation ignores the divine promise of land to Israel, the revival and growth of the modern Messianic movement, and the past-present-future mission of the Jewish people in the world.

The following question has been asked by modern biblical scholars: "Who owns the land today?"[96] As mentioned above, the situation is difficult and complex on many levels—primarily on the sociopolitical and religious levels. Hubbard advocates that progressive revelation from the Old Testament to the New Testament has redefined the promise of land to Israel and has removed it from God's paradigm for his people Israel.[97] Yet nowhere in the New Testament is this implicitly or explicitly stated by the authors of Scripture. If progressive revelation requires replacement by the New Testament of all that is explicitly stated in the Old Testament, then what are Christians to do with the eschatological prophecies of the Old Testament not reiterated in the New Testament? Are these not to be understood as yet-to-be-fulfilled historical events? The silence of the New Testament on matters related to the Old Testament does not preclude their fulfillment in a postbiblical timeframe.

Burge alleges that the support of the Western evangelical movement for Israel as a homeland for the Jews is primarily based on the following:

- a sense of guilt for the horrors perpetrated against Jews over the centuries, especially during the Holocaust
- the kinship felt by the evangelical world toward the Jews because of the Jewish background of Jesus, the Jewish traditions observed in the church, the fact that the canon of Scripture is 80 percent of Hebrew origin, and Paul's rejection by the Jews of his day because of his newfound faith
- the miraculous survival of God's chosen people after suffering multiple exiles, after experiencing assimilation into other nations, and after witnessing the resurrection of its primary language (Hebrew)
- the need to be on the "right side" before the eschatological event of the last days[98]

---

93. Ibid., xxiii.
94. Ibid., 203.
95. Burge, *Jesus and the Land,* 33.
96. Hubbard, *Joshua,* 48.
97. Ibid., 49.
98. Burge, *Whose Land? Whose Promise?* 9–12.

The assumption that Western evangelical support for Israel as a homeland for the Jewish people is based primarily on guilt, kinship, and need is subjective and dismissive of the opinions of many trustworthy evangelical scholars.[99]

b. Warfare and the "Devoted Things" (h̄erem)[100]

The most controversial theological issue that emerges from Joshua is the notion that a loving God would ordain and participate in the annihilation and massacre of large groups of people (men, women, and children). This concept (h̄erem) seems contrary to the high value Scripture places on human life. Scholars have reached various conclusions concerning this dilemma. Calvin argued "that the Canaanites were rightly the

---

99. Scholars (such as Burge) who dismiss the state of Israel as a homeland for modern Jews often highlight the plight of the Palestinians (including Palestinian Christians) and the injustices committed by Israelis. Palestinians have indeed suffered from persecution, oppression, and injustice. Many have been displaced, lost homes and possessions, and suffered profoundly. Their suffering is unjust and undeserved. But Jews have also suffered deeply at the hands of their oppressors. What then should the evangelical response be toward those—both Palestinians and Jews—who are oppressed and persecuted, and who continue to hope for a place called home? The biblical response is to love both of them, to seek their reconciliation through prayer and bridge building, to honor those who have been dishonored, and to bring hope to them with the gospel of the Lord Jesus Christ (Yeshua the Messiah). In Marvin Wilson's words, "A biblical view can't be anti-Arab and pro-Israel, or anti-Israel and pro-Arab. God's heart is where justice is" (K. Sidey, "For the Love of Zion," *Christianity Today* [March 9, 1992], 50). Many modern evangelical scholars stand with the Jewish people in support of Israel as a homeland for the Jews. In 1989, the World Evangelical Fellowship, supported by the Lausanne Committee for World Evangelization, held a Consultation on The Christian Gospel and the Jewish People at Willowbank, Bermuda. After several days of intense discussion and much prayer, the international committee (from USA, Kenya, France, Norway, Philippines, England, India and Canada), led by Chairman Vernon Grounds, redacted and signed the Willowbank Declaration in which affirmations are made regarding Jewish evangelism, anti-Semitism, observance of Jewish traditions by Messianic Jews, and the land of Israel. In Article V.27, the committee declares the following: "We affirm that the Jewish quest for a homeland with secure borders and a just peace has our support. We deny that any biblical link between the Jewish people and the land of Israel justifies actions that contradict biblical ethics and constitute oppression of people-groups or individuals" (www.lcje.net/willowbank.html [accessed September 19, 2011]). Strongly committed to Israel as a homeland for the Jewish people, the committee acknowledges that with ownership of land come ethical and social responsibilities towards all of its inhabitants.

100. On the topic of warfare in the Bible see T. Longman III and D. G. Reid, *God Is a Warrior* (Studies in Old Testament Biblical Theology 1; eds. W. A. vanGemeren and T. Longman III; Grand Rapids: Zondervan, 1995); P. C. Craigie, *The Problem of War in the Old Testament* (Grand Rapids: Eerdmans, 1978); R. S. Hess and E. A. Martens, *War in the Bible and Terrorism in the Twenty-First Century* (Winona Lake, Ind.: Eisenbrauns, 2008); L. L. Rowlett, *Joshua and the Rhetoric of Violence: A New Historicist Analysis* (JSOTSup 226; Sheffield: Sheffield Academic, 1996); P. D. Miller Jr., *The Divine Warrior in Early Israel* (2nd ed.; Atlanta: SBL, 2006); K. Latvus, *God, Anger and Ideology: The Anger of God in Joshua and Judges in Relation to Deuteronomy and the Priestly Writings* (JSOTSup 279; Sheffield: Sheffield Academic, 1998); K. L. Younger Jr., *Ancient Conquest Accounts*; S. Niditch, *War in the Hebrew Bible: A Study in the Ethics of Violence* (New York: Oxford Univ. Press, 1993). On the term h̄erem, see William L. Lyons, *A History of Scholarship on the Biblical Word Herem: The Contributions of Walter C. Kaiser Jr., Peter C. Craigie, and Tremper Longman III* (New York: Edwin Mellen, 2010); Philip D. Stern, *The Biblical Herem: A Window on Israel's Religious Experience* (Brown Judaic Studies 211; Atlanta: Scholars, 1991); Frédéric Gangloff, "Joshua 6: Holy War or Extermination by Divine Command (Herem)?" *TR* 25/1 (2004): 3–23.

object of God's wrath because they were so depraved."[101] Some scholars deny the historical nature of the book of Joshua, thereby dismissing the idea of conquest and "holy war."[102] Others see the need for holy war as a means to restore the moral order of the universe.[103]

The subject of warfare and violence in the Bible has received considerable attention in the scholarly world, with renewed interest demonstrated after the terrorist attack on the World Trade Center and the Pentagon on September 11, 2001.[104] Following this tragedy, some scholars have brought accusations against the three monotheistic religions (Judaism, Christianity, and Islam) and charged them with advocating violence through their "*them* and *us*" paradigms.[105] Evangelical scholars have joined their voices in defense of Christianity and have shown how religious belief based on the pure message of the Bible does not condone violence but advocates for peace. The Old and the New Testaments reveal God's overwhelming love for humanity. How can we then reconcile God's love for humanity with the concept of genocide in the book of Joshua? How can God command, condone, and participate in the destruction of entire populations of Canaanites, Hittites, Hivites, Perizzites, Girgashites, Amorites, and Jebusites?

As mentioned above, in Joshua (as in ancient Near Eastern literature), warfare is theological. Warfare involves God, and therefore the conquest of the land of Canaan is religious in nature and not simply militaristic. It is Yahweh's war and not solely that of humankind. That God is a warrior is a theme woven through many biblical books. In Exodus, God fights on behalf of his people to destroy the Egyptians, who are preventing them from marching toward their divine destiny (Ex 15:1–18). In 2 Samuel, God strikes the Philistines on behalf of David and brings him military victory (2Sa 5:22–25). The author of Psalm 68 praises God for scattering Israel's enemies and blowing them away like smoke (Ps 68:1–2). The book of Joshua introduces no new theological concept. It simply depicts God fighting on behalf of his people (Jos 3:10; 5:13–15; 9:9–10; 23:3).

In order for a reader to understand the concept of holy war, he or she must read the biblical text in its ancient Near Eastern context. Ancient Near Eastern literature reveals that the concept of conquering "devoted things" for a deity was practiced by foreign nations outside of the borders of Canaan. During the eighteenth century BC, a military commander who led the troops against Mari declared the spoils of war to be "things

---

101. Creach, *Joshua*, 41.

102. Ibid., 42.

103. Stern, *The Biblical Herem: A Window on Israel's Religious Experience*.

104. J. J. Collins, *Does the Bible Justify Violence?* (Minneapolis: Augsburg Fortress, 2004); W. Brueggemann, *Divine Presence Amid Violence: Contextualizing the Book of Joshua* (Eugene, Ore.: Cascade, 2009); E. A. Seibert, *Disturbing Divine Behavior: Troubling Old Testament Images of God* (Minneapolis: Fortress, 2009); P. D. Miller Jr., *The Divine Warrior in Early Israel*; S. N. Gundry, ed., *Show Them No Mercy: 4 Views on God and Canaanite Genocide* (Grand Rapids: Zondervan, 2003); Hess and Martens, eds., *War in the Bible and Terrorism in the Twenty-First Century*. See also Longman and Reid, *God Is a Warrior*; Craigie, *The Problem of War in the Old Testament*; Younger, *Ancient Conquest Accounts*; Niditch, *War in the Hebrew Bible*.

105. R. Schwartz, *The Curse of Cain: The Violent Legacy of Monotheism* (Chicago: Univ. of Chicago Press, 1997). Schwartz argues that all monotheistic religions (Judaism, Islam and Christianity) advocate violence. Miroslav Volf challenges her view in "Christianity and Violence" in *War in the Bible and Terrorism in the Twenty-First Century*, 1–17, and in "Jehovah on Trial," *Christianity Today* (April 27, 1998), 32–35. Volf points to the Trinitarian monotheism of Christianity as the perfect paradigm for harmony and love (*perichoretic* model) in which each person of the Trinity gives perfectly, receives perfectly, imposes nothing on the other, and "is characterized by mutually uncoerced and welcomed generosity" (9).

devoted to the god(s)."[106] During the ninth century BC, the Moabite ruler King Mesha destroyed the inhabitants of Ataroth and Nebo, including women and children, as a sacrifice to his god Chemosh.[107] In Assyria, diviners and astrologers consulted with the god Ashur in order to obtain approval for military operations. In cases of defeat, the religious leaders who had consulted with the god(s) paid dearly, often with their lives.[108]

In Joshua, warring against the inhabitants of Canaan was a sacred act (*ḥerem*) first described in Deuteronomy 20:16–18.[109] It involved exterminating the enemy population that inhabited a region and obtaining its plunder for divine use. This religious act was intended to destroy the evil that prevailed and to enable the manifestation of the holiness of God in the midst of his people. It required ritual purity on the part of the Israelites. The *ḥerem* often weds warfare with holiness. In Leviticus 27:28, the *ḥerem* comprises people, animals, and objects that are devoted to the Lord and are considered most holy to the Lord.

In Deuteronomy and Joshua, God promises to destroy the Hittites, Amorites, Canaanites, Perizzites, Hivites, Girgashites, and Jebusites—seven nations stronger than Israel—and commands Joshua and his men to exterminate all the inhabitants of Canaan (Dt 7:1–2; 20:17; Jos 3:10; 24:11). His command to exterminate the inhabitants seems harsh, especially from a loving and gracious God, but the purpose for the cleansing of the land was for the establishment of a holy people in a place where Yahweh's name would be glorified.

Israel engaged in warfare and conquest long before she entered Canaan. Years earlier in the Negev, the Israelites were attacked by the Canaanite king of Arad, whose army took captive some of the Israelites (Nu 21:1–3). In response to this act of warfare, the Israelites vowed to Yahweh that if he would deliver the captives out of the hands of the enemies, they would completely destroy (21:2, *ḥāramtî*) the cities of the Canaanites who had captured them. God answered their prayer, and consequently the Israelites completely destroyed them (*wayyaḥᵃrēm*) and named the place Hormah (*ḥormā*) to commemorate the victory.

The most recent study on the concept of *ḥerem* appears in Lyons' *A History of Modern Scholarship on the Biblical Word Herem*. Lyons studies the interpretation of three evangelical scholars who have wrestled with the text and contributed significantly to the scholarship on this topic: Walter C. Kaiser Jr., Peter C. Craigie, and Tremper Longman III. The complimentary views of Kaiser, Craigie, and Longman provide a good representation of the evangelical positions on biblical warfare and the *ḥerem*.

In *Hard Sayings of the Old Testament*, Walter C. Kaiser Jr. concludes that the concept of *ḥerem* cannot be separated from the omniscience, justice, and righteousness of God.[110] In his opinion, the rejection of natural revelation by the Canaanites reflected a rejection of God and consequently invited the judgment of God, who had patiently observed their moral decline and had not previously acted against them.[111] The biblical text specifies that the Canaanites were wicked and could have easily contaminated Israel with their wickedness (e.g., bestiality, sodomy, idol worship, syncretism). For this reason, God chose

---

106. A. Malamat, *Mari and the Early Israelite Experience* (The Schweich Lectures of the British Academy 1984; Oxford: Oxford Univ. Press, 1989), 70–79.

107. *ANET*, 360.

108. Younger, *Ancient Conquest Accounts*, 260.

109. M. Weinfeld notes it as "the law of *Herem*" in his *Deuteronomy 1–11: A New Translation with Introduction and Commentary* (AB 5; New York: Doubleday, 1991), 172.

110. Ibid., 63.

111. Ibid., 60; W. C. Kaiser Jr., *Hard Sayings of the Old Testament* (Downers Grove, Ill.: InterVarsity Press, 1988), 206.

to drive them out from before the Israelites who were entering Canaan—the Promised Land. Kaiser indicates that today, anyone who attempts to justify war with the biblical *ḥērem* would surely be brought before a war tribunal and charged with crimes against humanity.[112] The biblical *ḥērem* is always connected to the divine promise of land and cannot be applied today since the land was officially given to Israel in Joshua's day.

In *The Problem of War in the Old Testament*, Peter C. Craigie notes that the prevalence of war in the Hebrew Bible is indeed disturbing and depressing for most Christians, but since it is a common and recurrent theme in the historical writings of the biblical world, its presence in the Bible should not be surprising.[113] The Bible identifies God as a warrior in numerous passages (e.g., Ex 15:21; Jdg 5:31; Pss 24:8; 35:1–3) fighting for (and against, Jer 21:4–6) his people. Historically, Christians have tended to spiritualize the message of the Old Testament and have ignored or rejected any seemingly offensive material, including the difficult portions of Joshua. For this reason, the church is mostly illiterate on the history, content, and theology of the Old Testament. The need to reconcile the God of love and the difficult texts of the Old Testament is now urgent. Failure to do so will continue to propagate an erroneous view of God's love, mercy, grace, and true *šālôm* ("wholeness, completeness").

Craigie distinguishes "holy war" from "Yahweh war." He states that there is nothing holy about war even when it is orchestrated by Yahweh. Craigie focuses on the broader context of military activities rather than on the term *ḥērem*. He identifies two categories for the war passages: (1) battles with foreign enemies outside of the Promised Land, and (2) battles with inhabitants of the land of Canaan. Craigie points to the Deuteronomic law (Dt 20:10–15) that allowed Israel to make peace agreements with cities outside of the Promised Land. Outside of the land, if the inhabitants agreed to make a treaty with Israel, they became vassals; if they refused, males were killed and everything else was taken as plunder.[114]

But when a battle occurred in Canaan, the situation was different. Israel was forbidden to make peace treaties with the inhabitants of the land. Israel was instructed to *completely destroy* all the inhabitants of the land and to leave no one alive, including men, women, and children lest they teach Israel to worship other gods and sin against Yahweh (Dt 20:16–18). Craigie gives two reasons for the complete annihilation of the inhabitants of Canaan: (1) Israel served as the hand of God in judgment against the Canaanites (cf. Kaiser's view), and (2) the presence of Canaanites in the midst of Israel provided an opportunity for syncretism, an evil forbidden by Yahweh.[115] According to Craigie, the *ḥērem* was indispensable in order for Israel to become established as a holy nation to the Lord in the Promised Land.

In *God Is a Warrior*, Tremper Longman III identifies five main motifs of divine warfare that are central to the biblical story: (1) God fights for Israel; (2) God fights against Israel; (3) hope for the future; (4) Jesus Christ, the divine warrior; and (5) the coming day of Christ.[116] Only the first theme will be discussed here.

---

112. Lyons, *A History of Modern Scholarship*, 66.

113. Ibid., 96–97; Craigie, *The Problem of War*, 10.

114. Peter C. Craigie, *The Book of Deuteronomy* (NICOT; Grand Rapids: Eerdmans, 1976), 57; Lyons, *A History of Modern Scholarship*, 113.

115. Craigie, *Deuteronomy*, 276; Lyons, *A History of Modern Scholarship*, 114.

116. Longman and Reid, *God Is a Warrior*, 17.

Longman notes that holy war is never initiated by Israel. It is introduced by God, who qualifies the process and watches over its execution. Where Israel initiates warfare without explicitly seeking God, it is never called *ḥērem* and more often than not, it ends in defeat (e.g., Ai, Jos 7). Contrary to expectation, holy war (*ḥērem*) appears in the Hebrew Bible as an act of worship that required spiritual preparation (Jos 3:5) and at times required the offering of a sacrifice. Before engaging in battle, both the warriors and the camp of Israel were required to go through a form of ritual cleansing (Dt 23:9–14). Compromise in this area could jeopardize military success and bring about severe consequences.

During the battle, Israel was to rely on Yahweh. Her lack of military arsenal was an advantage as it allowed the warring men to move about freely, and it afforded God an opportunity to show himself strong on behalf of his people (e.g., Jdg 7, Gideon; 1Sa 17:45–47, David and Goliath). Success in battle brought corporate praise to Yahweh, who time and again delivered the enemy into Israel's hands (e.g., Ex 15; Jdg 5).

Echoing the voice of many scholars, Longman maintains that the *ḥērem* was not unique to Israel but that it must be understood in the cultural context of the ancient Near East (e.g., Moab offers "devoted things' to Chemosh; see examples above). For Longman, the *ḥērem* is "a temporal judgment against a wicked nation, in essence becoming a minipreview of the horrors that await the unbeliever in phase five."[117] In accord with Kaiser, Longman denies the place of *ḥērem* or holy war in the church today. God has never permitted the church to use physical violence in order to establish his kingdom on earth. According to Scripture, "our struggle is not against flesh and blood, but against the rulers, against the authorities, against the powers of this dark world and against the spiritual forces of evil in the heavenly realms" (Eph 6:12). The warfare of the church is to be conducted in the spirit realm and not in the physical realm.

During the conquest of Jericho, the Israelites were instructed to abstain from taking any of the "devoted things" from the city (Jos 6:18) lest they be destroyed themselves (Dt 7:26). Joshua commanded his men to destroy every living thing (human and animal) and to place the articles of silver, gold, bronze, and iron ("the devoted things") into the treasury of the Lord's house (Jos 6:19, 24). By contrast, during the conquest of Ai, the Israelites were given permission to take plunder for themselves, including objects and livestock (8:2). The disparity between the treatment of the "devoted things" at Jericho and Ai has raised questions in the minds of scholars. Some have proposed that the divine permission to keep the occasional plundered items from a city could be attributed to God's care and providence for his people. The Owner of all property is ultimately God himself, who has the authority to determine how his belongings are to be used and distributed on the earth (see Ps 24:1–2). Scripture never glorifies the *ḥērem* of Joshua, nor does it advocate for violent conquest of land for future times.

Conquest of the Promised Land through *ḥērem* did not guarantee permanent settlement in the land. As long as the Israelites obeyed God and walked uprightly in covenant relationship with him, God allowed them to live in the land; when the Israelites became unfaithful to God, they too could be driven out of the land — as evidenced by the Babylonian exile (Dt 28:49–68).

---

117. Lyons, *A History of Modern Scholarship*, 152, quoted in T. Longman III, "Should I Go to War?" in *Streams from Scripture II* (Philadelphia: Westminster Media, 1993; cassette SS205).

c. Yahweh as Divine Warrior

Divine intervention in warfare is a theme foreign to the church today; it was not so in biblical times. Throughout Scripture, God devised strategies, led attacks, joined in battle, fought against flesh-and-blood, and gave Israel victory over her enemies. As mentioned above, the warfare of Israel was treated as a sacred act that often required spiritual preparation (Nu 21:2; Dt 23:9–14 [cf. Lev 15:16–18]; Jos 3:5). Warfare was performed under the leadership of Yahweh.

Scripture reveals God as warrior in the Torah (e.g., Ex 14:14; Dt 1:30; 3:22; 20:4; 21:10), in the Prophets (e.g., Jos 10:11; 1Sa 17:47; Zec 14:3), and in wisdom literature (e.g., Ne 4:20; Ps 24:8). Throughout Israelite history, God fought both *for* and *against* Israel—*for her* in times of warfare (e.g., Dt 1:30; 3:22; 7:22–24;) and *against her* in times of disobedience and judgment (e.g., Isa 7:17–20; 10:5–6; Jer 21:4–7; 32:27–35). Shortly after crossing the "Sea of Reeds," the Israelites acclaimed Yahweh as a warrior God and burst forth with singing:

[1]"I will sing to the LORD,
    for he is highly exalted.
The horse and its rider
    he has hurled into the sea.
[2]The LORD is my strength and my song;
    he has become my salvation.
He is my God, and I will praise him,
    my father's God, and I will exalt him.
[3]*The LORD is a warrior,*
    the LORD is his name.
[4]Pharaoh's chariots and his army
    he has hurled into the sea.
The best of Pharaoh's officers
    are drowned in the Red Sea.
[5]The deep waters have covered them;
    they sank to the depths like a stone.
[6]*"Your right hand, O LORD,*
    was majestic in power.
Your right hand, O LORD,
    shattered the enemy.
[7]In the greatness of your majesty
    you threw down those who opposed you.
You unleashed your burning anger;
    it consumed them like stubble.
[8]By the blast of your nostrils
    the waters piled up.
The surging waters stood firm like a wall;
    the deep waters congealed in the heart of the sea.

9"The enemy boasted,
   'I will pursue, I will overtake them.
I will divide the spoils;
   I will gorge myself on them.
I will draw my sword
   and my hand will destroy them.'
10*But you blew with your breath,*
   and the sea covered them.
They sank like lead
   in the mighty waters.
11"Who among the gods is like you, O LORD?
   Who is like you—
      majestic in holiness,
      awesome in glory,
      working wonders?
12You stretched out your right hand
   and the earth swallowed them. (Ex 15:1–12, emphasis added)

The ark—the primary symbol of Yahweh's presence—plays a prominent role in Joshua, especially in the battle at Jericho (Jos 6), in which the priests carrying the ark march thirteen times around the city before the walls collapsed (cf. 2Sa 11:11). Taking the ark to the battlefield was a must. Without the presence of God—the ark—there could be no victory. As long as Israel was walking in obedience to the covenant, the ark brought victory. Whenever Israel broke the covenant, the ark was impotent. When the enemies of Israel captured the ark, the consequences were devastating. Israel lost fighting men (Jos 7:3–5) and was defeated in battle (e.g., 1Sa 4), and leaders perished (e.g., 1Sa 4:18).

In the book of Joshua, God fought *for* Israel. Joshua and the Israelites could proceed confidently knowing that Yahweh would be with them wherever they went (Jos 1:9). On several occasions, God exhorted Israel with the following words: "Do not be terrified; do not be discouraged," affirming that the battle was his (Jos 1:9; cf. Dt 20:3–4). He had promised to drive out the inhabitants of the land (e.g., Ex 23:29–30; 34:11; Dt 7:22; 11:23; Jos 3:10) and to give the enemies into her hands (Dt 7:23–24; Jos 8:7).

Such a display of divine power was well received by Israel, but sometimes, it was taken for granted. For example, in chapter 7, Joshua and his men proceeded to take the city of Ai without consulting Yahweh. Consequently, they lost thirty-six fighting men and returned to the camp defeated. Had Joshua taken time to seek the face of the Commander of the army, he would have discovered that there was sin in the camp and that Yahweh would not fight for Israel until the sin was removed. This error by the leader was not soon repeated!

d. Covenant and Obedience

The presence of the ark with Israel was a constant reminder of the covenant Yahweh established with his people. After Israel entered Canaan, Joshua led the Israelites in the renewal of the covenant at Mount

Ebal and Mount Gerizim. Joshua built an altar to Yahweh on Mount Ebal—built according to the dictates of the Mosaic covenant (Jos 8:30–31)—and offered sacrifices. Later, he copied on a white-washed stone the law of Moses (cf. Dt 17:18–19) while the people stood at the edge of the mountains, facing the ark of the covenant. Joshua read to the entire community of Israel—men, women, children, and aliens—all the words "written in the Book of the Law of Moses" (Jos 8:31).

In the second ceremony (Jos 24), Joshua assembled Israel at Shechem and recounted the history of his people, from the patriarchs to the current day, highlighting the mighty deeds of the Lord and underlining Israel's responsibility toward him. The Israelites renewed their commitment to serve Yahweh only and to forsake all other gods. Joshua recorded the events in the Book of the Law of God. "He took a large stone and set it there under the oak near the holy place of the LORD" (24:26). The stone was to serve as a testimony against Israel should she break the covenant and live a life of compromise.

Covenant is closely related to obedience. During each covenant renewal ceremony, Israel heard the words of the law of Moses (8:34–35; 24:25–27); she was reminded of the blessings and the curses—blessings for obedience and curses for disobedience. With Israel now in her homeland, she was responsible to live a life of holiness (Ex 31:13; Lev 19:2; Dt 7:6; 14:2, 21; 26:19), to abstain from all things that made her unclean (Lev 15:31; Nu 19:13, 20), and to be distinct from all the other nations of the world (Ex 19:5). In the presence of Joshua at Shechem, the Israelites declared their complete devotion to Yahweh and proclaimed, "We too will serve the LORD, because he is our God" (24:18); "we will serve the LORD" (24:21); "we will serve the LORD our God and obey him" (24:24).

8. BIBLIOGRAPHY

Boling, Robert G., and G. Ernest Wright. *Joshua*. Anchor Bible 6. New Haven, Conn.: Yale University Press, 1982.

Butler, Trent C. *Joshua*. Word Biblical Commentary 7. Edited by D. A. Hubbard, G. W. Barker, and J. D. W. Watts. Nashville: Nelson, 1983.

Dallaire, Hélène. "The Syntax of Volitives in Northwest Semitic Prose." PhD diss., Hebrew Union College, 2002.

Hess, Richard S. *Joshua: An Introduction and Commentary*. Tyndale Old Testament Commentaries. Downers Grove, Ill.: InterVarsity Press, 1996.

———. "The Book of Joshua as Land Grant." *Biblica* 83 (2002): 493–506.

Howard, David M. Jr. *Joshua*. The New American Commentary 5. Nashville: Broadman & Holman, 2002.

Hubbard, Robert L. Jr. *Joshua*. The NIV Application Commentary. Grand Rapids: Zondervan, 2009.

Junkkaala, Eero Kalevi. *Three Conquests of Canaan: A Comparative Study of Two Egyptian Military Campaigns and Joshua 10–12 in the Light of Recent Archaeological Evidence*. Åbo, Finland: Åbo Akademi University Press, 2006. Pdf version at https://oa.doria.fi/handle/10024/4162.

Kitchen, K. A. *On the Reliability of the Old Testament*. Grand Rapids: Eerdmans, 2003.

Nelson, Richard D. *Joshua*. The Old Testament Library. Louisville, Ky.: Westminster John Knox, 1997.

Pitkänen, Pekka M. A. *Joshua*. Apollos Old Testament Commentary 6. Downers Grove, Ill.: InterVarsity Press, 2010.

Waltke, B. K., and M. O'Connor. *An Introduction to Biblical Hebrew Syntax*. Winona Lake, Ind.: Eisenbrauns, 1990.

Watson, W. G. E. *Classical Hebrew Poetry*. JSOT Supplement 26. Sheffield: Sheffield Academic, 1995.

Woudstra, Marten H. *The Book of Joshua*. New International Commentary on the Old Testament. Grand Rapids: Eerdmans, 1981.

Younger, K. Lawson Jr. *Ancient Conquest Accounts: A Study in Ancient Near Eastern and Biblical History Writing*. JSOT Supplement 98. Sheffield: Sheffield Academic, 1990.

9. OUTLINE

I. Conquest of the Land (1:1–12:24)
  A. Joshua—A New Leader for Israel (1:1–9)
  B. Preparing for the Conquest (1:10–2:24)
    1. Joshua Organizes the People (1:10–15)
    2. Joshua's Leadership Confirmed (1:16–18)
    3. Rahab and the Spies (2:1–24)
      a. The Spies Enter Jericho (2:1–7)
      b. The Spies Covenant with Rahab (2:8–21)
        i. Rahab pleads for mercy (2:8–14)
        ii. The spies promise mercy on Rahab and her family (2:15–21)
      c. The Spies' Report to Joshua (2:22–24)
  C. Moving to Canaan and Initial Conquest (3:1–8:35)
    1. Crossing the Jordan (3:1–4:24)
      a. Joshua's Instructions at the Jordan (3:1–13)
      b. Crossing the Jordan on Dry Ground (3:14–17)
      c. The Stone Memorial (4:1–9)
      d. The Crossing of the Ark of the Covenant (4:10–24)
    2. Renewal of the Covenant and Passover Celebration (5:1–12)
    3. Conquest of Jericho (5:13–6:27)
      a. Joshua and the Messenger (5:13–15)
      b. The Fall of Jericho (6:1–21)
      c. Rahab's Rescue (6:22–27)
    4. Achan and the "Devoted Things" (7:1–26)
      a. Achan's Sin and Israel's Defeat at Ai (7:1–5)
      b. Joshua's Intercession and the "Devoted Things" (7:6–15)
      c. Achan Punished for His Sin (7:16–26)
    5. Conquest of Ai (8:1–29)
      a. The Ambush (8:1–17)
      b. The Attack (8:18–23)
      c. The Victory (8:24–29)
    6. Renewal of the Covenant at Mount Ebal (8:30–35)
  D. Conquering the Land (9:1–12:24)
    1. A Treaty with the Gibeonites (9:1–27)
      a. The Gibeonite Deception and the Peace Treaty (9:1–15)
      b. The Deception Is Discovered (9:16–21)
      c. The Gibeonites Are Cursed for Their Deception (9:22–27)
    2. The Amorite Kings against Gibeon (10:1–15)
      a. The Amorite Kings against Gibeon (10:1–5)

Text and Exposition

I. CONQUEST OF THE LAND (1:1—12:24)

OVERVIEW

The first twelve chapters of this book highlight the conquest/subjugation of the land of Canaan under Joshua's leadership. The accounts preserved in the narrative are well-crafted summaries of battles — defeats and victories — that took place during Israel's initial penetration into the Promised Land. Conquest narratives are not unique to biblical Israel. Ancient Near Eastern texts provide numerous accounts of military campaigns led by prominent kings who sought to expand their territories and include neighboring lands (e.g., annals of Egyptian, Hittite, Assyrian, and Babylonian kings). The surrounding nations would have interpreted Israel's conquest of Canaan as a natural step toward establishing a people in a new region or expanding a people's territory.

The first part of Joshua points to the following two major events: the crossing of the Jordan (1:1–5:12) and the conquest of Canaan (5:13–12:24). The events recorded in 1:1–11:15 seem to have occurred over a relatively short period of time, conceivably over the course of a few months, but statements in chapter 11 contradict this notion. The narrator points out that "Joshua waged war against all these kings for a long time" (11:18) and that after the conquest, "the land had rest from war" (11:23; cf. 14:15). This information echoes what Yahweh clearly declared in Exodus 23:29–30, "I will not drive them out in a single year, because

the land would become desolate and the wild animals too numerous for you. Little by little I will drive them out before you, until you have increased enough to take possession of the land."

Several events described in Joshua 1–12 reflect events that appear in a similar chronological order in Exodus. For example:

- removal of the leader's sandals while standing on holy ground — Ex 3:5//Jos 5:15
- Passover celebration by the community — Ex 12//Jos 5:10–12
- destruction of enemies and taking of plunder — Ex 12:35–36; 14:23–28//Jos 6:24
- presence among Israelites of aliens whose lives have been preserved — Ex 12:43–49//Jos 6:22–25
- circumcision — Ex 12:43–49//Jos 5:2–8
- crossing a body of water on dry ground — Ex 13:17–14:31//Jos 3
- trouble in the camp — Ex 16–17//Jos 7
- leader is rebuked — Ex 18:17–27 (Jethro rebukes Moses)//Jos 7:6–15 (Yahweh rebukes Joshua)
- the consecration of Israelites the day before Yahweh's manifestation — Ex 19:10–15//Jos 7:13
- giving/renewal of the covenant — Ex 20//Jos 8:30–35

A. Joshua—A New Leader for Israel (1:1–9)

OVERVIEW

Joshua 1 includes three discourses, one by each of the three main characters— *God, Joshua,* and *Israel.* First, *God* addresses Joshua and infuses him with the drive to lead boldly and to manage courageously the huge undertaking of conquering the land (vv.1–9). Second, *Joshua* commands the Reubenites, Gadites, and half-tribe of Manasseh to assist their brothers in the conquest of Canaan (vv.12–15). Joshua's words are direct and his message unambiguous. Third, the *fighting men's* response to Joshua confirms their loyalty to their new leader and their determination to execute fearlessly the task at hand. Based on these three "speeches," everyone is ready for the difficult task ahead.

The beginning of the narrative reflects on the events at Mount Nebo—the death of Moses—and points forward to the imminent conquest of and settlement in the land. The introduction echoes the language of Deuteronomy and reminds the reader that the theological foundation for the conquest of the land has been laid by Moses.

Following Moses' death, Joshua escorts Israel into a new era. He assumes his leadership role and leads Israel into the land given to her as an inheritance centuries earlier (Abram [Ge 12:7; 13:14–18; 15:7, 18–21]; Isaac [Ge 26:1–5]; Jacob [Ge 35:9–15]; Joseph [Ge 50:24]; and Moses [Ex 2:23–24; 3:8; 6:6–8; 13:15]). Before any movement of people can take place, God confirms Joshua as the new leader and commissions him to prepare the people to cross the Jordan River (1:2, 6–9). After a series of commands to "be strong and courageous" (1:6, 7, 9), Joshua orders the people to prepare for the long-awaited move into Canaan (1:10–11).

¹After the death of Moses the servant of the LORD, the LORD said to Joshua son of Nun, Moses' aide: ²"Moses my servant is dead. Now then, you and all these people, get ready to cross the Jordan River into the land I am about to give to them—to the Israelites. ³I will give you every place where you set your foot, as I promised Moses. ⁴Your territory will extend from the desert to Lebanon, and from the great river, the Euphrates—all the Hittite country—to the Great Sea on the west. ⁵No one will be able to stand up against you all the days of your life. As I was with Moses, so I will be with you; I will never leave you nor forsake you.

⁶"Be strong and courageous, because you will lead these people to inherit the land I swore to their forefathers to give them. ⁷Be strong and very courageous. Be careful to obey all the law my servant Moses gave you; do not turn from it to the right or to the left, that you may be successful wherever you go. ⁸Do not let this Book of the Law depart from your mouth; meditate on it day and night, so that you may be careful to do everything written in it. Then you will be prosperous and successful. ⁹Have I not commanded you? Be strong and courageous. Do not be terrified; do not be discouraged, for the LORD your God will be with you wherever you go."

COMMENTARY

1 The book's opening formula provides both the link between the two great leaders — Moses and Joshua — and the official transition between their leadership. Moses had been the hero of the story for decades, and now Joshua's turn had come to assume the headship over Israel. Joshua had followed Moses closely since his youth (Ex 33:11; Nu 11:28) and had assisted him during numerous major events (e.g., Mount Sinai, the golden calf, spying Canaan). He had observed Moses closely and taken every opportunity to be mentored by him both in glorious and in challenging times.

Joshua was a faithful and devoted servant of Yahweh. One day, after a face-to-face encounter between Yahweh and Moses at the tent of meeting, Joshua failed to return to the camp with Moses. Instead, he remained still at the entrance of the tent, unable to pry himself away from the awesomeness of the place where Yahweh had just manifested his presence (Ex 33:7–11). The reader is left to wonder what thoughts raced through Joshua's mind as he stood there, hypnotized by what he had just witnessed in that holy place.

On another occasion, while serving Moses in the wilderness, Joshua learned of two men — Eldad and Medad — who were prophesying in the name of Yahweh. Responding in a manner typical of an unseasoned leader, Joshua reported the unusual incident to Moses and called on him to stop them from prophesying. Moses rebuked Joshua saying, "Are you jealous for my sake? I wish that all of the Lord's people were prophets and that the Lord would put his Spirit on them!" (Nu 11:29). The account is similar to that found in Mark 9:38–39, where the apostle John tells Jesus that he saw a man driving out demons in Jesus' name and requested that he stop doing so. Jesus replied, "Do not stop him. No one who does

a miracle in my name can in the next moment say anything bad about me, for whoever is not against us is for us."

2 The hardships that would accompany the leadership position were not unknown to Joshua. He had observed the people's rebellion at the base of Sinai (Ex 32:1–6), the jealousy of the elders against their leader (Nu 12:1–2), the deep personal struggles Moses had experienced since Egypt (Nu 11:10–15), and the stubbornness of the people in the desert (Nu 14:1–4). Nonetheless, Joshua showed no sign of hesitation or wavering in accepting his new task. He received his call with courage and determination, but would the Israelites accept him as their new leader? The answer is clear. As the end of the first chapter points out, the Israelites make a pledge of obedience to Joshua; they promise to follow his instructions wholeheartedly and to go wherever he commands them to go (1:16–17).

The death of a leader often requires a period of mourning, but in the case of Moses and Joshua the transfer of leadership is seamless, interrupted only by a thirty-day period of bereavement for the Israelites (Dt 34:8). Soon after Moses' death, God turns to Joshua and gives him directives for the next step of the journey. The tone of his instructions is both militaristic and sacred. The command to proceed is unambiguous and the direction in which the people are to march is clear — westward, across the Jordan.

For forty years, the Israelites had been led by Moses in all aspects of life — religious, social, judicial, political, and military. With Moses' death, one would expect an interruption in the flow of events, but in this case, the transfer of leadership is anticipated, having been previously announced and sanctioned by Moses himself. In the presence of all

Israel, Moses had pronounced words of exhortation to Joshua to "be strong and courageous," for Yahweh was surely going to be with him as he had been with Moses (Dt 31:7–8; Jos 1:9). Shortly before crossing the Jordan, Joshua was anointed with the spirit of wisdom as Moses laid hands on him before the entire assembly (Nu 27:22–23; Dt 34:9).

As a proven military leader (Ex 17:9, 13) and a faithful servant of God, Joshua picks up where Moses left off. He is ready to be at the helm and to lead where God directs. Joshua had witnessed the divinely orchestrated crossing at the Red Sea forty years earlier under Moses. He had full confidence in the God who had sustained his people for centuries, who had performed miracles in their midst, and who had promised long ago to give a homeland to his people.

The intermediary, Moses, who once stood between Joshua and Yahweh, is no longer present; consequently, the door is open for direct communication between Yahweh and his new appointee.

3 The expression "I will give you every place where you set your foot" echoes the very words pronounced earlier by Moses to the Israelites (Dt 11:24). In order for the Israelites to see the fulfillment of the divine promise, their feet will have to tread the land. No benefit will come to them without their active participation. The gift had already been given; the time had now come for the recipients—the Israelites—to possess it.

4 The territory described here in a crisscross pattern covers an area much larger than the territory conquered and settled by the Israelites at any time in history, unless the phrase "all the land of the Hittites" refers only to the northern areas of Canaan where Hittites lived during this period (for discussion on the Hittites, see Introduction). Before its demise around 1200 BC, the entire Hittite empire covered a vast area (ancient Anatolia [modern Turkey]). In Joshua, the territory to be conquered is bordered in the *south* by the desert, in the *north* by Lebanon, in the *east* by the Euphrates or "the great river," and in the *west* by the Mediterranean or "the Great Sea" (lit., "the Great Sea where the sun sets"). This description can be interpreted as the literal expanse of the territory promised by God, or it can be interpreted as a hyperbolic note intended to point toward Israel's upcoming challenges.

The land given to Israel is described in several biblical passages with varying boundary markers and a different order of cardinal points (e.g., north, south). For example:

- Genesis 15:18 mentions only two borders— *southwest* (river of Egypt) and *northeast* (Euphrates)
- Deuteronomy 1:7 presents a different order than Joshua 1:4—*south* (Negev), *west* (along the coast), *north* (Lebanon), *east* (Euphrates)
- Deuteronomy 11:24 is almost identical to Joshua 1:4—*south* (desert), *north* (Lebanon), *east* (Euphrates), *west* (Western Sea)
- Joshua 1:4 reflects Deuteronomy 11:24 except for the designation of the western border— *south* (desert), *north* (Lebanon), *east* (Euphrates), *west* (Great Sea)
- Numbers 34:3–12 presents the most detailed list of boundaries—*south* (Desert of Zin along border of Edom, v.3), *east* (end of Salt Sea, south of Scorpion pass, onto Zin, south to Kadesh Barnea, to Hazar Addan, Azmon, Wadi of Egypt, and end at the Sea, vv.3–5; Hazar Enan, Shepham, Riblah, Ain, eastern slopes of Kinnereth, along Jordan to Salt Sea [vv.10–12]), *west* (coast of Great Sea, v.6), *north* (Great Sea to Mount Hor, Lebo Hamath, Zedad, Ziphron, end at Hazar Enan, vv.7–9)

The area to be conquered was extensive. Undeterred by the task at hand, Joshua sets his face like a flint toward the goal and remains focused on the divine promises: "I will give you every place where you set your foot" (Dt 11:24; Jos 1:3); "no one will be able to stand up against you" (Dt 7:24; 11:25; Jos 1:5); and "I will never leave you nor forsake you" (Dt 31:6, 8; Jos 1:5). Joshua reflects courage and bravery throughout his leadership, and when the vast territory to be conquered is described to him, he neither flinches nor recoils. Joshua is familiar with certain areas since he previously scouted the southern part of Canaan, but he may have been less familiar with the northern and eastern boundaries.

5–7 Under Moses' leadership, Joshua had experienced God's faithfulness and omnipotence in times of seemingly insurmountable obstacles. Therefore, words of reassurance, such as "as I was with Moses, so I will be with you," become significant. The formula "be strong and (very) courageous" is repeated three times in the divine discourse (vv.6, 7, 9). The

hendiadys highlights the ultimate strength and bravery required from Joshua for the task set before him. The phrase is echoed later by the Reubenites, the Gadites, and the half-tribe of Manasseh, who pledge their complete support to Joshua as they prepare to cross the Jordan River and help their brothers conquer the Promised Land (1:18).

The combination of the pronouncements "be strong and courageous," "do not be terrified" (v.9), and "I will never leave you nor forsake you" (v.5) always appears in contexts where the challenges faced by an individual or a community are humanly impossible and the task at hand is risky and momentous (e.g., the conquest of the land— Dt 31:7, 23; Jos 1:6, 7, 9, 18; the building of Solomon's temple—1Ch 22:13; 28:20; the protection of Jerusalem from the Assyrian invasion—2Ch 32:7). In each case, the formulae are uttered by superiors to inferiors (except for Jos 1:18):

Phrases	God	Moses	Joshua	David	Hezekiah
"Be strong and courageous"	**To Joshua:** Dt 31:23; Jos 1:6, 7, 9	**To Joshua:** Dt 3:28; 31:7 **to Israelites:** Dt 31:6	**To Israelites:** Jos 10:25 **to Joshua by Israelites:** Jos 1:18	**To Solomon:** 1Ch 22:13, 28:20 **Psalms:** Ps 27:14; 31:25	**To his men:** 2Ch 32:7
"Do not be afraid or terrified"	**To Joshua:** Jos 8:1 **to Jehosaphat & Israelites:** 2Ch 20:15, 17 **to Israelites:** Jer 30:10; 46:27 **to Ezekiel:** Eze 2:6	**To Israelites:** Dt 1:21; 31:6	**To Israelites:** Jos 1:9; 10:25	**To Solomon:** 1Ch 22:13; 28:20	**To his men:** 2Ch 32:7

| "I will never leave you nor forsake you" | **To Joshua:** Jos 1:5 (Heb 13:5) | **To Israelites:** Dt 31:8 **to Joshua:** Dt 31:8 | | **To Solomon:** 1Ch 28:20; Ps 37:8 (**Solomon to Israelites:** 1Ki 8:57) | |
| "Do not turn to the right or to the left [of the Torah]" | **To Joshua:** Jos 1:7 | **To Israelites:** Dt 5:32; 17:11, 20; 28:14 | **To Israelites:** Jos 23:6 | | |

8–9 According to Deuteronomy, a godly leader must conform to the following behaviors: (1) meditate on the law day and night (Dt 17:19; Jos 1:8); (2) keep the law in one's mouth (to be read aloud before the people—Dt 17:19, 31:11, 12; Jos 1:8); and (3) abstain from turning from the law to the right or to the left (Dt 17:20; Jos 1:7). In other words, the Book of the Law was to remain the unchanging foundation on which any leader should guide the community (cf. Ps 1:2). The instructions given to Joshua here correspond to the Mosaic paradigm of leadership. The success of Joshua's undertaking is conditional upon his scrupulous obedience to the law. He must be resolute and steadfast in the pursuit of his divine assignment.

One who studies the history of Israel soon notices that when a leader disobeys the commands given by God, the whole community suffers. Therefore, the instructions given to Joshua—to meditate on the Torah and not turn to the right or to the left—cannot be overestimated. The future of the nation depends on the leader's faithful adherence to God's commands. God instructs Joshua to meditate on the Book of the Law, and the results of active meditation are success and prosperity. In Western culture, Christians often mistakenly interpret "success" and "prosperity" for financial wealth and the acquisition of material possessions. True biblical success and prosperity are demonstrated through wisdom, knowledge, insight, understanding, morality, holiness, obedience, harmony, righteousness, and grace.

God's charge to Joshua concludes by restating the words of exhortation: "Be strong and courageous. Do not be terrified; do not be discouraged, for the LORD your God will be with you wherever you go" (v.9).

NOTES

1 The introductory phrase "after the death of [name]" (וַיְהִי אַחֲרֵי מוֹת מֹשֶׁה, *wayyᵉhî ʾaḥᵃrê môt mōšeh*) appears at the beginning of several books of the Bible, where the end of a leader's life is linked to the beginning of another's reign (e.g., Jdg 1:1—"after the death of Joshua"; 2Sa 1:1—"after the death of Saul"; 2Ki 1:1—"after the death of Ahab"). The expression "the servant of the Lord" (עֶבֶד יהוה, *ʿebed yhwh*) appears fourteen times with regard to Moses in Joshua. Only after his death is Joshua called "the servant of the LORD" (Jos 24:29), a title previously only used for Moses (e.g., Dt 34:5; Jos 1:1, 13, 15; 8:31, 33; 11:12; 12:6 [2x]; 13:8; 14:7; 18:7; 22:2, 4, 5).

2 The two verbs that form the expression "get ready to cross" (קוּם עֲבֹר, *qûm ʿăbor*) are a hendiadys. A hendiadys uses two separate words, often joined by a conjunction, to express one complex concept (Watson, 324–25). When followed by a verb of motion, the verb "to arise" (קוּם, *qûm*) often takes an inceptive meaning, indicating the beginning of the motion—thus "get ready to...."

3 The use of the perfect of the verb "to give" *ntn* (נְתַתִּיו, *nᵉtatîw*, "I have [already] given it") points back to the promise of land made to Abram centuries earlier (Ge 15:7).

4 The phrase "all the Hittite country" is omitted from the LXX, thus reflecting the variant of Dt 11:4, where "all the Hittite country" is also absent.

5–9 Pairs of synonyms fill these verses: "As I was with Moses, so I will be with you" (v.5); "I will never leave you nor forsake you" (v.5); "be strong and courageous" (v.6, 9); "be strong and very courageous" (v.7); "to the right or to the left" (v.7); "day and night" (v.8); "prosperous and successful" (v.8); "do not be terrified, do not be discouraged" (v.9). In biblical literature, the use of pairs or doublets is intentional and serves to intensify, emphasize, and ensure that the message is heard clearly. The verb that indicates "to stand up" (v.5, יִתְיַצֵּב; *yityaṣṣēb*) implies "taking a solid stance," "taking a firm stance," "taking one's position," and not simply standing in one place, as indicated by the common verb "to stand" (עמד, *ʿmd*). The author highlights the idea that no opposition will succeed in taking a firm stand against Israel.

6 The verb "to inherit, dispossess" (נחל, *nḥl*) and the noun "inheritance, possession" (נַחֲלָה, *naḥᵃlā*) are key terms in Joshua. The use of the Hiphil here indicates that Joshua will take charge in leading Israel to dispossess the land and acquire her inheritance.

8 Joshua is instructed to "meditate" (וְהָגִיתָ, *wᵉhāgîtā*) on the Book of the Law with his mouth and not simply with his mind. The Hebrew verb used here (הגה, *hgh*) includes participation in an activity that is done "aloud" and not silently (e.g., muttering, groaning, uttering), involving the heart, mind, and mouth (M. V. Van Pelt & W. C. Kaiser Jr., "הגה," *NIDOTTE*, 1:1008–9). The word is translated elsewhere in the NIV as "moaning [like a dove]" (Isa 38:14), "growling [like a lion]" (Isa 31:4), "mourning" (Isa 16:7), "speaking [with the tongue]" (Ps 35:28), and "plotting" (Ps 2:1).

B. Preparing for the Conquest (1:10–2:24)

1. Joshua Organizes the People (1:10–15)

OVERVIEW

After listening to God's charge, Joshua turns his attention toward the leaders of Israel and issues his first directives. To the officers, he gives instructions to prepare the Israelites—men, women, and children—for the upcoming journey in which they will cross the Jordan and take possession of the land. To the fighting men of the tribes of Reuben, Gad, and the half-tribe of Manasseh, Joshua issues the command to assist the rest of the Israelite tribes in their conquest of the land west of the Jordan. By the tone of Joshua's message, there is a sense that entering the land of Canaan is equally as significant as the exodus from Egypt. The Israelites who had left behind four hundred years of history are now ready to begin a new and long area of permanent settlement in their own homeland.

---

¹⁰So Joshua ordered the officers of the people: ¹¹"Go through the camp and tell the people, 'Get your supplies ready. Three days from now you will cross the Jordan here to go in and take possession of the land the LORD your God is giving you for your own.'"

¹²But to the Reubenites, the Gadites and the half-tribe of Manasseh, Joshua said, ¹³"Remember the command that Moses the servant of the LORD gave you: 'The LORD your God is giving you rest and has granted you this land.' ¹⁴Your wives, your children and your livestock may stay in the land that Moses gave you east of the Jordan, but all your fighting men, fully armed, must cross over ahead of your brothers. You are to help your brothers ¹⁵until the LORD gives them rest, as he has done for you, and until they too have taken possession of the land that the LORD your God is giving them. After that, you may go back and occupy your own land, which Moses the servant of the LORD gave you east of the Jordan toward the sunrise."

COMMENTARY

10–11 The "officers of the people" (šōṭᵉrê hāʿām) summoned by Joshua are most likely administrative officials who assisted leaders in carrying out their duties. Their responsibilities include standing before God as witnesses in covenant ceremonies (Dt 29:10; Jos 8:33; 23:2; 24:1) and delivering judgments in legal cases (Dt 16:18). These officers have received the Spirit of the Lord for specific tasks (Nu 11:16–17; Dt 1:15–16), and in this case, they are called upon to command the people to prepare for the journey ahead.

The "supplies" (ṣêdā) carried by the Israelites during their journey across the Jordan often refers elsewhere to food brought along during an excursion (e.g., Ge 27:3; 42:25; Jdg 7:8; 1Sa 22:10). The command to prepare food over a period of three days contrasts the hastiness with which the previous generation of Israelites left Egypt forty years earlier. Before crossing the Red Sea, the Israelites were instructed to be prepared to leave Egypt quickly and without prepared food (ṣêdā, Ex 12:10, 33–39). The crossing of the Jordan, by contrast, requires less haste, leaving sufficient time to prepare food supplies for the expedition. The text makes no mention of bringing weapons of war or other arsenals for the conquest, only food for the crossing.

Joshua declares to the Israelites that in "three days" they will cross the Jordan. The number "three" can hardly be interpreted literally since the total number of days after which the Israelites cross into Canaan turns out to be at least six to seven days. As per the events of chapters 2 and 3, there are at least two periods of "three days" between the officers' orders to prepare for the journey and the actual crossing. In chapter 2, Joshua sends spies to explore the region of Jericho. After their encounter with Rahab, the spies remain in the hill country for "three days" before returning to the Israelite encampment on the east side of the Jordan (2:21–23). If the events of chapter 3 are to be interpreted sequentially with those of chapter 2, an additional three to four days occurs before the crossing actually takes place (3:1–5). Thus, there is a total of six to seven days between the original officers' message and the time of the crossing. The phrase "in three days" appears numerous times in Scripture with a symbolic meaning (see Ge 1:13; 40:12–23; Est 5:1; Hos 6:2; Jnh 1:17; Mt 26:61; Jn 2:20; Rev 11:9, 11). A similar use of "three days" appears in a Hittite text where warriors are instructed to follow their enemies for a period of "three days" before returning to the king with an account of the victory or defeat (Hess, *Joshua*, 20–21).

The purpose for the journey toward Canaan is clear. The Israelites are about to inherit (*lārešet*) the land and to dispossess it of its inhabitants. The fulfillment of a promise made to the patriarchs centuries earlier is approaching its culmination, and a life of vulnerability among foreign nations is nearing its end.

12–15 The Israelites are expected to protect one another and fight together for the good of the community. For this reason, the Reubenites, Gadites, and half-tribe of Manasseh are instructed to participate in the conquest of Canaan before settling permanently in their own territory on the east side of the Jordan.

The command to "remember" (*zākôr*) points to the instructions given earlier by Moses to the fighting men of the eastern tribes. Moses had charged them to help their brothers acquire their territorial inheritance on the west side of the Jordan (Dt 3:18–20). He had ordered them to march into Canaan in front of the western tribes, probably in formations of fifty across (*ḥᵃmušîm*). They were to support the western tribes in their military activities until Canaan was completely subjugated and until God gave them rest within their new territorial borders. In the meantime, their wives, children, and animals were instructed to remain on the east side of the Jordan and begin their new lives in their assigned territories.

NOTES

10 The verb "to order" (צוה, *ṣwh*) is one of several key words in Joshua. It appears seven times in this chapter (1:7, 9, 11, 13, 16, 18) and over twenty times in the book. Other important key words in Joshua include "to cross" or "crossing" (עבר, *ᶜbr*,) occurring six times in this chapter (1:2, 11 [2x], 14 [2x], 15) and over eighty times in Joshua. The verb "to give" (נתן, *ntn*) is repeated eight times in this chapter (1:2, 3, 6, 11, 13, 14, 15 [2x]) and appears over eighty times in the book, commonly referring to the gift of land.

11 The expression "to take possession" (לָרֶשֶׁת, *lārešet*) is theologically significant in Joshua as it is primarily connected to the conquest of the land by driving out and dispossessing the inhabitants of the land. Scholars are undecided as to the origin of this word, especially whether it originates from a violent military practice or from a common secular usage related to acquiring possessions. Deuteronomy gives it a moral association, emphasizing that the conquest is an act of divine judgment on the wickedness of the Canaanites (C. J. H. Wright, "ירשׁ," *NIDOTTE*, 2:547–48).

13 "Remember!" (זָכוֹר, *zākôr*). When an infinitive absolute expresses a command, it indicates a strong command from someone of higher social status to someone of lower social status (Dallaire, 184).

14 "Fully armed" (חֲמֻשִׁים, *ḥᵃmušîm*). Wherever the text uses this term, the Israelites are in a distinct battle formation, in groups of fifty, facing enemy combatants (Ex 13:18; Jos 4:12; Jdg 7:11). The Hebrew term is based on the number "five" (חָמֵשׁ, *ḥāmēš*).

2. Joshua's Leadership Confirmed (1:16–18)

> ¹⁶Then they answered Joshua, "Whatever you have commanded us we will do, and wherever you send us we will go. ¹⁷Just as we fully obeyed Moses, so we will obey you. Only may the LORD your God be with you as he was with Moses. ¹⁸Whoever rebels against your word and does not obey your words, whatever you may command them, will be put to death. Only be strong and courageous!"

COMMENTARY

16–18 The Reubenites, Gadites, and half-tribe of Manasseh affirm Joshua's leadership and respond with readiness and determination: "Whatever you have commanded us, we will do, and wherever you send us, we will go." Their commitment is complete and their response exemplary. But whoever refuses to obey the orders will suffer a most severe penalty—the rebellious individual will be put to death (v.18). The sentence will ensure that no rebellious behavior deserving of capital punishment will persist in the community.

The three statements pronounced by the men of the eastern tribes are absolute—"we will do" (*naʿᵃśeh*), "we will go" (*nēlēk*), and "we will obey" (*nišmaʿ*). Their declarations indicate total commitment to the charge, complete loyalty to the leader, and a determination to accomplish the task without turning back. Their verbal commitment concludes with words of exhortation for their new leader: "May the LORD your God be with you as he was with Moses.... Be strong and courageous!" (vv.17–18).

NOTES

17–18 The thrice repetition of the root "obey" (שׁמע, *šmʿ*) in two subsequent verses is significant. Such a concentration of occurences highlights the theme of the passage—that Israel is committed to obey Joshua as they had obeyed Moses. In an oral culture, repetition enables the audience to hear more deeply the message of the speaker (Watson, 278).

REFLECTION

The central theme of Joshua is unmistakable from the beginning. The time had finally come for Israel to take possession of her inheritance and to establish herself as a nation. Acquisition of the land required obedience, faithfulness, commitment, and determination. Israel was to live holy before the Lord in her new home and become a blessing to world. The task at hand for Israel was complex and challenging. For this reason, God required complete devotion to him and wholehearted loyalty to Joshua. With the acquisition of land came stewardship responsibilities.

Such are also the requirements for those who are called to serve the church as apostles, prophets, pastors, teachers, and evangelists. The commitment to the call must be total, without reservation; they must trust that God will be there every step of the way as he was with Moses. As with Israel, the church must learn to wait for God's timing to move forward, lest she walk in her own strength and proceed in the wrong direction.

Changes in leadership are not always as seamless as the transition of power between Moses and Joshua. In the church, such changes often create periods of uncertainty and tension. Searching for a new leader may take a prolonged period of time. And for the new leader, the risk of facing a stiff-necked people with high expectations can create apprehension. When God confirms and commissions someone to a new position of leadership, he also calls a congregation to join the leader—to support, encourage, and walk with him/her. So it was with God's people here. They are called to obey the commands of Joshua and to serve him in the divine mission.

The theme of land is woven throughout the fabric of Scripture (Ge 15:18; Lev 25:2; Nu 33:53; Dt 1:8; Jos 2:9, 14, 24; 5:6; 8:1; 9:24; 18:3; 22:4; 23:13, 15, 16; 24:13; see the Introduction). She was called to "love the LORD your God with all your heart and with all your soul and with all your strength" (Dt 6:5) and to bless all the nations of the world (Ge 12:3). God fulfills his plan in his own time, according to his purposes and for his glory.

3. Rahab and the Spies (2:1–24)

OVERVIEW

Acquainted with spying new territory (cf. Nu 13–14), Joshua sends two secret agents to Jericho to scout out the area in and around Jericho (2:1). The spies encounter a prostitute named Rahab, who hides them from the king's messengers (2:2–6). After making a promise to save her and her family (2:14), they return to Joshua at Shittim with a good report (2:24).

The structure of the chapter is an inclusio—the spies leave Shittim at the beginning (v.1) and return to Shittim at the end (vv.23–24). Within this inclusio, the chapter includes three important dialogues—between Rahab and the king's messengers (vv.2–7), between Rahab and the two spies (vv.8–13), and between the spies and Rahab

(vv. 14–21). Each discourse creates tension and advances the plot toward the realization of the primary theme of the book—the conquest of Canaan.

In her first speech, Rahab gives a swift and clever response to the king's messengers. She acknowledges the arrival of the spies in the city and promptly deflects the attention of the pursuers eastward, pointing to the road that goes to the Jordan River. In her second speech, Rahab addresses the spies with an urgent message, filled with emotion, intensity, and supplication. She discloses historical facts that contribute to the long-standing fear of the inhabitants of Jericho toward the Israelites. According to her, it is well-known that God has given them land (2:9). As a result, with dread and anxiety the inhabitants of Canaan await the arrival of this privileged group of invaders. In the third dialogue, the spies negotiate an agreement with Rahab and promise to save her and her family from the impending attack on the city. They present their stipulations and give Rahab instructions for the liberation of her family.

The number of participants mentioned in this chapter is significant (e.g., spies, king of Jericho, king's messenger, pursuers, and Rahab's parents and siblings); yet only Joshua and Rahab are mentioned by name. Given that their pronouncements will exclusively determine the outcome of the events, it is justifiable that the spotlight focuses on them.

The spy and hospitality motifs are not unique to this account. In Genesis 19, Lot hosts two angels who have come to announce that Yahweh is about to destroy Sodom (Ge 19:14). Lot cooks a meal for the messengers and prepares a room for them to spend the night. The next morning, Lot and his family—his wife and two daughters—hurry out of Sodom with the angels of the Lord. As they flee, the city is completely destroyed by burning sulfur raining down from heaven (Ge 19:23–24). In Judges 1, spies from the tribe of Joseph agree to spare the life of a man from Bethel who assists them in infiltrating the city. After entering Bethel, the spies put the city to the sword and spare the lives of the man and his family (Jdg 1:22–25).

In both of these cases, as in the Rahab narrative, messengers are sent with a warning of impending judgment (spies, angels), an inhabitant and his/her family are delivered from destruction (Rahab, Lot, man from Bethel), Yahweh is involved in the battle (Jos 2:8, 11, 14; cf. Ge 19:14; Jdg 1:22), and a city is completely destroyed (Jericho—Jos 6; Sodom—Ge 19:24; Bethel—Jdg 1:25).

The spy story of Joshua 2 displays similarities with the spy narrative of Numbers 13–14, in which Moses sent twelve spies (including Caleb and Joshua) into southern Canaan to assess the conditions of the land (13:17–20). Here in Joshua 2, the spies journey to and around Jericho for three days before bringing a glowing report back to Joshua. In Numbers 13, the expedition lasted forty days. In Joshua 2, the report is positive while in Numbers 13, the report was mostly negative (except for Joshua's and Caleb's testimony). In Joshua 2, the spies return to their leader empty-handed while the spies in Numbers 13 returned with plump and delicious fruit from the land. With this in mind, there is no reason for Joshua to disbelieve the report of the two spies when they return from Jericho, especially since their message reflects what Caleb and Joshua had reported to Moses forty years earlier—that the land could be conquered and inhabited by Israel.

a. The Spies Enter Jericho (2:1–7)

¹Then Joshua son of Nun secretly sent two spies from Shittim. "Go, look over the land," he said, "especially Jericho." So they went and entered the house of a prostitute named Rahab and stayed there.

²The king of Jericho was told, "Look! Some of the Israelites have come here tonight to spy out the land." ³So the king of Jericho sent this message to Rahab: "Bring out the men who came to you and entered your house, because they have come to spy out the whole land."

⁴But the woman had taken the two men and hidden them. She said, "Yes, the men came to me, but I did not know where they had come from. ⁵At dusk, when it was time to close the city gate, the men left. I don't know which way they went. Go after them quickly. You may catch up with them." ⁶(But she had taken them up to the roof and hidden them under the stalks of flax she had laid out on the roof.) ⁷So the men set out in pursuit of the spies on the road that leads to the fords of the Jordan, and as soon as the pursuers had gone out, the gate was shut.

COMMENTARY

1 The Israelites had reached Shittim, a town on the eastern shore of the Jordan, before the death of Moses (Nu 25:1). The name of the place means "acacia tree." It is possible that the name of the site where the Israelites encamped implies a concentration of vegetation in that location—an oasis of acacia trees. As seen in chapter 1, Joshua is proactive in his mission to conquer Canaan. As expected from a competent military leader, Joshua's strategy incorporates a preliminary examination of the area to be conquered. He sends two spies to Jericho to accomplish the task. Acting wisely, Joshua refrains from moving in haste and waits for the spies' report before taking the next step.

Joshua understands the value of spying and scouting out territory. Decades earlier, Moses had sent him along with eleven other men to examine Canaan's population, strength, agricultural conditions, and habitability (Nu 13:17–25). Joshua had learned that twelve spies were much too numerous to bring back an accurate and helpful report. He had learned that only two spies could do the job well (as he and Caleb had done); consequently, he sees fit to send only two men to scout out the area of Jericho.

This military practice did not originate with the Israelites. Mari texts from the eighteenth century BC speak of sending spies to Suhum as a prelude to the attack on the town (R. H. Hess, "Joshua," in *Zondervan Illustrated Bible Backgrounds Commentary* [ed. J. H. Walton; Grand Rapids: Zondervan, 2009], 2:17). Centuries later, at the battle of Qadesh (1275 BC), a Hittite king used spies as decoys in order to provoke the Egyptian pharaoh into battle (Kitchen, 167).

Knowing full well that if the word of the scouting mission becomes public, members of the community might want to join in the clandestine operation, so Joshua sends the two men "secretly." The Hebrew word for "secretly" (*ḥereš*) can be applied to the context in at least three ways. The first way involves the *secret* sending of spies, a method used by Joshua to avoid making the operation public. Though this may be an accurate interpretation of the passage, it is clear from the text that the king finds out about the *secret* mission very quickly! According to the second way, the *secrecy* could refer to the spies themselves — *secret spies* — whose identity remains concealed to the reader. A third way highlights the *secret* words that Joshua said to the spies, "Go, look over the land." Although these words are not concealed from the reader, they are probably kept secret from the rest of the community.

The spies are sent out to explore the area of Jericho — more specifically, to find out the feasibility of conquering the city first and then the rest of the land. Jericho was strategic in the conquest of Canaan. The city controlled the major pass between east and west, and it was strategically located to provide a place of rest and respite for travelers. Conquering Jericho was a must! Joshua could not have proceeded further into Canaan without controlling this area.

Rahab is introduced as a female prostitute (*zônā*), a term used in Scripture for one who provides sexual services either for personal pleasure or as a profession (cf. Ge 38). Rahab was possibly an "innkeeper" or a "madam" who took care of the home and managed the business for other prostitutes who offered services in her house. Had it become known that she was hiding the two spies, Rahab could have suffered severe consequences for lying to the king. In ancient Near Eastern texts (e.g., Laws of Hammurabi), if an innkeeper learned about villains who plotted evil while at the inn and did not report it to the king, the innkeeper could be put to death (M. Weinfeld, *The Promise of the Land: The Inheritance of the Land of Canaan by*

Israelites [Berkeley: Univ. of California Press, 1993], 142–43; M. T. Roth, *Law Collections from Mesopotamia and Asia Minor* [SBLWAW 6; Atlanta: Scholars, 1995], 101).

Some scholars have suggested that the weaving of suggestive language in the story is simply a playful literary device intended to entice the reader. The name *Rahab* is a non-Israelite name. It comes from a Semitic root whose verb form denotes "opening oneself wide" and the noun means "open public square" (R. S. Hess, "Getting Personal: What Names in the Bible Teach Us," *BRev* 13/6 [December 1997], 34–35).

2 The king of Jericho finds out about the coming of the spies, but the text is silent on the identity of the one(s) who divulges the clandestine mission to him. The king was likely the leader of a city-state, with limited influence over the surrounding areas. There is no evidence that he controlled areas beyond Jericho. Whoever informed the king considered it important and worthy of disclosure and possibly knew about the reputation of the dreaded Israelites. Knowledge of the arrival of the spies was sufficient to prompt the messenger to run to the king and inform him of the threat that had reached Jericho. According to the courier, the spies had come to Jericho with a specific purpose in mind — to investigate and scout out the land.

3 The king reacts at once with direct orders to expose those who have entered Rahab's house deviously. The verb "to enter, come" (*bôʾ*) appears three times in this verse. It highlights the fact that the king knows of the spies coming to the city and entering Rahab's dwelling. Nothing is said about the king's relationship with Rahab. It could be assumed that the king is personally familiar with the services she provides and may have even benefited from her professional skills. As for the spies, it is doubtful that they were involved sexually with anyone in the house. There is no hint of immoral behavior in the chapter, nor is there any evidence that Rahab made any sexual advances toward them during their brief stay.

4–5 Subject to the king's orders, Rahab finds herself in need of devising a quick scheme, one that will satisfy the ruler and keep her safe from harm. Rahab is a smooth operator who thinks quickly on her feet! She hides the men on the roof of her house under a pile of flax and returns to the messengers with a clever description of the recent events. Most houses in Jericho had flat roofs that allowed for the storage of grain, furniture, and other items. During the summer months, residents often used the roof as living space.

In the doorway of her house, Rahab reacts with confidence. She admits to the king's messengers that, indeed, the spies did come to her house. But Rahab lies to them about the present whereabouts of the spies and sends them running out of the city toward the Jordan River. Since it was well-known that the Israelites were encamped at Shittim, on the eastern side of the Jordan, it seemed logical for the messengers to believe Rahab's story and to trust that the spies are fleeing eastward, back to their base camp.

6–7 Once she sees that the messengers are in hot pursuit outside of the city gates, Rahab climbs to the roof of her house and engages in conversation with the well-hidden spies. In this area, flax was known to grow up to three or four feet high, so it would have been possible for the spies to hide under a pile without being detected. It is known from the Gezer Calendar (900 BC) that flax was harvested before barley, probably in February or March. Flax was used for the production of oil and for the production of fibers from which linen was made. Once flax was harvested, it was soaked, dried, and bleached on the roof of a house, and later crushed, beaten, and spun.

The spies exhibit great faith in the goodness of humanity as they place their lives in the hands of a prostitute whom they do not know. The possibility of treason by this questionable woman puts the spies at risk of being discovered by one of her confidantes at any moment. Almost to the surprise of the reader, the New Testament announces that Rahab was justified through her faith (Heb 11:31), a faith evidenced by her efforts to spare the lives of the spies and to save the members of her family.

It is ironic that the officers of the king, who should have been safe inside the city, are locked *outside* of the city gates, while the spies, who should have been outside, are locked up *inside* the walled city.

NOTES

1 The word for "prostitute" (זוֹנָה, *zônā*, also meaning "fornicator") refers to the idolatry of the Israelites in prophetic books. This term identifies a common prostitute while a different Hebrew word (קְדֵשָׁה, *qᵉdēšâ*) is used for the temple or sacral prostitute. The word used here in Joshua 2 is also used metaphorically for people and cities that have made alliances with foreign nations and worshiped foreign gods. In God's eyes, such compromises are equated to prostitution. It is possible in the context of this narrative that Rahab was an innkeeper whose house allowed the drinking of alcohol and catered to visitors or merchants who came from other regions. The expression "and [they] stayed there" (וַיִּשְׁכְּבוּ, *wayyiškᵉbû*, "they lay down") has no sexual connotation, as some have suggested, since the spies went to sleep on the open roof and were visited later by Rahab, who made no apparent advances toward them.

2 The use of the passive stem, Niphal, for the expression "it was said" (וַיֵּאָמֵר) (*wayyēʾāmēr*) allows for the subject who did the actual reporting to the king to remain faceless. The particle הִנֵּה (*hinnēh*) + the perfect verb בָּאוּ (*bāʾû*) indicates that the spies "had just arrived," implying that their secret presence was revealed almost instantly.

4, 6 Hebrew uses several words to indicate "hiding, concealing" (e.g., טמן [*ṭmn*], צפן [*ṣpn*], חבא [*ḥbʾ*], כחד [*kḥd*], סתר [*str*], עלם [*ʿlm*]). This portion of the narrative uses two different Hebrew words for "to hide," צפן (*ṣpn*, v.4) and טמן (*ṭmn*, v.6). In verse 4, the verb "to hide," צפן (*ṣpn*), emphasizes hiding someone or something in order to protect it; in verse 6, the verb טמן (*ṭmn*) indicates that something is buried so as to be out of sight (A. E. Hill, "צפן," *NIDOTTE*, 3:839–40; "טמן," *NIDOTTE*, 2:377). Rahab buries the spies on the roof of her house with two purposes in mind: (1) to hide them from sight, and (2) to protect their lives.

5 The author uses adverbs to intensify the drama of the story: "secretly" (חֶרֶשׁ, *ḥereš*, v.1) and "quickly" (מָהֵר, *mahēr*).

b. The Spies' Covenant with Rahab (2:8–21)

OVERVIEW

As is often the case in the Bible, the least likely character becomes the hero of the narrative (e.g., Joseph, Moses, Esther, Mordecai). This literary feature is called the *reversal motif*. The story of Rahab and the spies exemplifies this motif. Rahab, whose occupation should have kept her in the margins of society, unable to contribute to the deliverance of her people, becomes the hero of the story. In spite of her distasteful profession, she succeeds in becoming the liberator of her entire family.

Rahab quickly reveals her exceptional knowledge of history. She is an intelligent woman who listens well to the conversations of her guests and who makes a point to retain critical information. As a businesswoman who understands strategic planning, she devises a plan to be revealed only to the two spies. None of her family members knows of her strategy and of her negotiations with her unusual guests.

i. Rahab pleads for mercy (2:8–14)

⁸Before the spies lay down for the night, she went up on the roof ⁹and said to them, "I know that the LORD has given this land to you and that a great fear of you has fallen on us, so that all who live in this country are melting in fear because of you. ¹⁰We have heard how the LORD dried up the water of the Red Sea for you when you came out of Egypt, and what you did to Sihon and Og, the two kings of the Amorites east of the Jordan, whom you completely destroyed. ¹¹When we heard of it, our hearts melted and everyone's

courage failed because of you, for the LORD your God is God in heaven above and on the earth below. ¹²Now then, please swear to me by the LORD that you will show kindness to my family, because I have shown kindness to you. Give me a sure sign ¹³that you will spare the lives of my father and mother, my brothers and sisters, and all who belong to them, and that you will save us from death."

¹⁴"Our lives for your lives!" the men assured her. "If you don't tell what we are doing, we will treat you kindly and faithfully when the LORD gives us the land."

COMMENTARY

8–9 Before settling in for the night, the spies receive a visit from Rahab, who discloses at once that the inhabitants of the region are gripped with fear. Their hearts are melting at the thought of being massacred by the threatening assailants. The people of Jericho know they are no match for Israel, and even less for their God—Yahweh. Before presenting her request, Rahab discloses her knowledge of Israel's history and identifies several miraculous deeds done by Yahweh on behalf of his people. Rahab is a good negotiator. In her profession, she has learned to deal shrewdly with clients and to manipulate her way into their good favor. Her discourse with the spies is compelling as she highlights what she knows of history and what the inhabitants of the city have heard about Israel and her God.

Surprisingly, Rahab reveals significant theological knowledge as she discloses her familiarity with Yahweh and his deeds. One wonders how she would have had knowledge of Yahweh's promise of land to Abraham, Isaac, Jacob, and Moses. Had previous guests in her home mentioned that Yahweh had given the land to the Israelites? Had they made reference to the Abrahamic and Mosaic covenants in which Yahweh promised land to his people? The reader is left wondering how and when Rahab acquired this crucial information.

10–11 The whole city is keenly aware of the miraculous events that took place years earlier in the Israelite community. The inhabitants of Jericho had heard that God dried up the waters of the Red Sea (*yam sûp*) when he delivered his people out of the slavery of Egypt. The defeat of the Amorite kings—Sihon and Og—was etched in their memory, and understandably, they were very afraid. Their hearts melted with despair at the prospect that their fate might be identical to that of the Amorite kings.

For the first time in Joshua, the verb "to possess" (*ḥrm*) appears in reference to the defeat of the Amorite kings, indicating that their destruction was divinely ordained (see discussion on "Warfare and the Ban (*ḥērem*)" in the Introduction). It is possible that Rahab would have understood the full meaning of the word (*ḥērem*) with its theological ramifications and its impending effects on the people of Jericho. She probably recognized that without the divine promise of land, there would be no threat of annihilation; and since the arrival of the spies in Jericho indicated that the subjugation of Canaan was at hand, she knew that the only means of survival was to join the people of God.

If only the God of the Israelites were not fighting for his people, maybe the inhabitants of Jericho would have a chance. But since Yahweh—the God of heaven and earth—was orchestrating the events, there was no chance of survival without an alliance with the enemy. The God of Israel is the supreme divine authority against whom no one can stand.

12 Rahab demands an oath, a promise of protection and a confirmation that the spies will spare her and her family from the impending destruction. In a patriarchal culture where the father or eldest male led major negotiations, it is somewhat surprising that a woman such as Rahab is at the helm, negotiating audaciously with those who could destroy her and her family. Her language is demanding yet polite. She orders the spies politely and emphatically (with the particle of politeness *nāʾ*, "please") to swear to her in the name of Yahweh that they will extend mercy to her and her family. Her forceful language reveals a woman who is in control, and yet who is well aware of her dependence on the gracious response of her guests. She demands a sign, a guarantee of rescue by the spies.

13 Rahab nobly pleads for her own deliverance and for that of her extended family. One is left to wonder what would have happened had she interceded on behalf of all the inhabitants of the city. Would God have spared all of them? With her knowledge of Israelite history, it is possible that she

had heard about Abraham's intercession for the city of Sodom years earlier, when God was willing to spare the city for fifty, forty-five, forty, thirty, twenty, and even ten righteous people (Ge 18:20–33). The destruction of Sodom and Gomorrah may very well have been a popular legend in the area during the time of Joshua.

14 The spies' response to Rahab's request is unequivocal and convincing. With sharp life-or-death language, they vow to lay down their lives in order to rescue Rahab and her family on the condition that she conceal their identity and their mission from the inhabitants of the city. Tension builds as both parties find themselves in a vulnerable position, expecting freedom at the hand of another. The spies acknowledge the vulnerability of their lives in the hands of Rahab while Rahab acknowledges her dependence on the integrity of the spies and on their willingness to fulfill their promise to her and her family. As seen above (v.1), secrecy is crucial to the success of the mission. The spies were sent by Joshua *secretly*. Rahab keeps the presence of the spies in her home a *secret*, and the life-or-death agreement between Rahab and the spies must be kept in *secrecy*.

NOTES

10 The root for "to possess" (חרם, *ḥrm*) appears here for the first time in Joshua. The noun "devoted things" (*ḥērem*) from the same root appears numerous times (for additional information on this word, see Introduction, "Warfare and the Ban [*ḥērem*]").

11 "In heaven above and on earth below" (בַּשָּׁמַיִם מִמַּעַל וְעַל הָאָרֶץ מִתָּחַת, *baššāmayim mimmaʿal-weʿal hāʾāreṣ mittāḥat*). This expression functions as a hendiadys, a combination of two words or phrases of the same grammatical form, used to indicate more than the sum of the two elements (see Note on 1:2). In this case, the two phrases signify "the whole universe."

12 "Please swear" (הִשָּׁבְעוּ נָא, *hiššābʿû-nāʾ*). Long imperatives with the particle *nāʾ* typically appear in the language of absolute politeness, primarily when someone of lower social status addresses someone of higher social status (Dallaire, 77). Rahab subordinates herself to the spies by requesting from them with extremely politeness—almost begging—for mercy for her and her family.

14 The narrator uses language of life and death, "our lives for your lives" (נַפְשֵׁנוּ תַחְתֵּיכֶם לָמוּת, *napšēnû taḥtēkem lāmût*), indicating that the commitment is serious and even absolute. The spies utter strong language, implying that an oath binds them to their commitment to save Rahab and her family. The plural verb for "tell" (תַּגִּידוּ, *taggîdû*) may indicate that the spies are speaking with Rahab and members of her family. Several Hebrew manuscripts, the LXX, and the Vulgate adopt the singular form (cf. v.20). The word pair "kindly and faithfully" (חֶסֶד וֶאֱמֶת, *ḥesed weʾemet*) highlights an extremely good situation, more than the sum of the two words. The spies' answer pleases Rahab, who ends the conversation quickly and released them through the window. For a discussion of the word "kindly" (חֶסֶד, *ḥesed*), see K. D. Sakenfeld, *The Meaning of Hesed in the Hebrew Bible* (HSM 17; Missoula, Mont.: Scholars, 1978).

ii. The spies promise mercy on Rahab and her family (2:15–21)

¹⁵So she let them down by a rope through the window, for the house she lived in was part of the city wall. ¹⁶Now she had said to them, "Go to the hills so the pursuers will not find you. Hide yourselves there three days until they return, and then go on your way."

¹⁷The men said to her, "This oath you made us swear will not be binding on us ¹⁸unless, when we enter the land, you have tied this scarlet cord in the window through which you let us down, and unless you have brought your father and mother, your brothers and all your family into your house. ¹⁹If anyone goes outside your house into the street, his blood will be on his own head; we will not be responsible. As for anyone who is in the house with you, his blood will be on our head if a hand is laid on him. ²⁰But if you tell what we are doing, we will be released from the oath you made us swear."

²¹"Agreed," she replied. "Let it be as you say." So she sent them away and they departed. And she tied the scarlet cord in the window.

COMMENTARY

15 Archaeological discoveries have shown that casemate walls (empty or rubble-filled double walls) built around a city could serve to encase domestic residences. Rahab's house was seemingly built in a casemate wall and was therefore accessible from inside and outside the city. Some point out that the use of casemate walls appears only around the tenth century BC, making Rahab's house an unlikely candidate for a residence in the city wall. But since Jericho was inhabited during the second millennium BC, it is possible that Rahab's residence was one of many houses that formed the perimeter of Jericho.

The window of Rahab's residence was probably not high, but too high for someone to climb out or jump out without injury. In this case, the lowering of the spies by a rope would have been necessary to prevent personal injury, and it could have taken place in a matter of minutes. In the 1930s, John Garstang's team of archaeologists uncovered an ancient mud brick wall at Jericho that, according to archaeologist Kathleen Kenyon, may have existed long before the Israelites' entrance into Canaan (Boling and Wright, 148). Other known walled cities of Canaan are Lachish, Megiddo, Hazor, and Jerusalem.

The location of Rahab's house was practical for those who needed a place to stay for the night and for those who desired her services. Close to the main gate and visible from inside and outside of the city, Rahab's residence was strategically located and allowed for maximum exposure for her business. It is, therefore, not surprising that the spies enter her residence to seek refuge for the night. Soon after their arrival, they are rushed to the roof and hidden under a bundle of flax.

It is possible that after their initial conversation with Rahab on the roof, they are taken to a room on the second floor since the text indicates they were let down by a rope through a window. This account reminds the Christian reader of the method used by Jesus' followers when they let down their handicapped friend into the living room of a house in Capernaum through a man-made hole in the roof (Mk 2:1-5). In both cases, the individuals let down to the ground depended on the strength of the ropes and on the power of those who held them.

16 Before the spies exit the house, Rahab instructs them to run to the hills and to hide there for a period of three days in order to allow their pursuers to lose sight of them (for discussion on the meaning of "three days," see comments on 1:11). The logical place for the spies to hide is west of the city, in the hills somewhere between Jericho and Jerusalem. In their pursuit, the messengers of the king would no doubt conclude that the spies have been running eastward, toward the Jordan River and Shittim, where the Israelites are encamped. But with Rahab's ruse, the spies are safely tucked into one of the wadis (dry river bed) west of the city.

The text does not tell us if Rahab ever sent other individuals to the mountains after they had conducted business in her house. This could have been a method she used frequently with her clients. She may have spared other lives through this means of escape. The presence of a strong rope close to an open window seems to indicate that the idea was not a novel one!

17-20 Just before leaving, the spies realize that their oath to rescue Rahab and her family was not included in the original mission. It consisted of a compromise between the instructions of Joshua and the passionate petition of a foreign woman. Joshua had originally commissioned them to spy out the land, not to negotiate special arrangements with individuals in the city! Furthermore, the Mosaic law forbade making any covenant with Canaanites (Dt 7:1-3). While at Rahab's mercy, the spies opted for survival rather than obedience. Now that they have declared an oath to her, they will have to fulfill it, unless they can come up quickly with an alternative plan.

Sharp-witted as they are, the spies blame Rahab for pressuring them into this agreement (*hišbaʿtānû*, "this oath you made us swear"). Attempting to undo the arrangement they have just made, the spies declare their innocence three times (through the repetition of the Hebrew word *nᵉqiyyîm*, "innocent," vv.17b, 19a, 20b) and reframe their commitment to Rahab, adding three conditions to the original oath. Compromising any of the stipulations will free the spies from their oath, but also, it will guarantee deathly consequences for Rahab and her family.

(1) Rahab is required to tie a scarlet string (*tiqwat ḥûṭ šānî*) to the window. The Hebrew phrase used for "scarlet string" is significant. In Hebrew, the word *tiqwā* refers either to a "cord" (only in Jos 1:18, 21) or to "hope, expectation" (e.g., Ru 1:12; Job 5:16; Ps 71:5). The word *ḥûṭ*—translated *cord*,

thread, or *string*—appears in a variety of contexts (e.g., Ge 14:23; 1Ki 7:15; Ecc 4:12). The "scarlet thread" (*ḥûṭ šānî*) appears in only two biblical passages—Joshua 2:18 and Song of Songs 4:3, in which a lover describes the appearance of the lips of his beloved ("Your lips are like a scarlet ribbon"). In both passages, a sensuous woman is highlighted. This use of *ḥûṭ šānî* may well indicate that Rahab is more than an innkeeper. She may have been involved in sexual activity with the men who frequented her residence.

(2) In verses 18–19, the spies refer to the blood-guilt formula typically connected to legal discourse (cf. 2Sa 1:16; 1Ki 2:32, 33, 37). Whoever is in Rahab's house at the time of the invasion, his/her blood (life) will be the responsibility of the spies; but whoever has gone out of Rahab's house, his/her blood (life) will be his/her own responsibility. With the blood-guilt formula comes the declaration of innocence (*nāqî*) also common in legal declarations. If the oath is compromised in any way by Rahab or any member of her family, the spies will be declared innocent (*nāqî*) and not held responsible for the loss of life.

(3) In verse 20, Rahab is required to keep the plan in the deepest of secrecy lest the spies are relieved of their oath and destruction comes to her or her family.

The sequence of events in verses 15–21 is unclear. It seems logical that the conversation between Rahab and the spies took place while they were still inside the house rather than after they rapelled down through the window (v.15). It seems almost inconceivable that the spies and Rahab would have discussed the three stipulations in the hearing of everyone, risking the public disclosure of the plan to anyone living near Rahab's house, especially since the spies insisted on confidentiality and absolute secrecy.

21 Wishing to ensure the safety of her family, Rahab quickly accepts the stipulations of the spies. Immediately after their departure, she ties the scarlet cord (*tiqwâ*) to the window in a location that can be seen from a distance. That will serve as a sign to the Israelites who will pass by her house seven times before entering the city. It will also serve as a sign of hope (*tiqwâ*) for Rahab and her family, who anxiously anticipate deliverance.

Scholars have offered several interpretations for the scarlet thread. Some have interpreted it symbolically, pointing back to the Passover night in Egypt when God instructed Moses to put blood on the doorpost in order to spare the inhabitants of the house from certain death (Ex 12:7). Others point to the future messianic fulfillment, when the blood of Christ is shed for the redemption of all mankind. This type of symbolism must be handled with caution since nothing in the text of Joshua mentions the events of the Passover night. A christological interpretation obviously comes much later and represents prophetic insights that could not have been intended by the original author of Joshua. Nonetheless, an allegorical interpretation of Joshua 2 is not impossible in retrospect.

NOTES

18 The use of הִנֵּה (*hinnēh*) with a participle indicates that something "*is about to happen*," adding to the sense of urgency in the context. The expression expresses vivid immediacy (Waltke and O'Connor, §40.2.1b).

19 In oaths, the particle אִם (*'im*, "if") is translated as a negative "not" (D. J. A. Clines, ed. *The Dictionary of Classical Hebrew* [Sheffield: Sheffield Academic, 1993], 1:304).

c. The Spies' Report to Joshua (2:22–24)

²²When they left, they went into the hills and stayed there three days, until the pursuers had searched all along the road and returned without finding them. ²³Then the two men started back. They went down out of the hills, forded the river and came to Joshua son of Nun and told him everything that had happened to them. ²⁴They said to Joshua, "The LORD has surely given the whole land into our hands; all the people are melting in fear because of us."

COMMENTARY

22 Without delay, the spies obey Rahab's instructions and hide in the hills for three days, just enough time for the pursuers to abandon their search and return to Jericho. Had the spies attempted to run back to Shittim upon leaving the city, they would surely have been apprehended and the mission would have been aborted. But thanks to Rahab's clever strategy, the spies are safe from harm, and the pursuit by the king's messengers is abandoned. The spies are young men who could have been enticed by Rahab's erotic schemes, but fortunately, they remain faithful to their duty and accomplish their mission without falling to temptation.

23–24 After hiding for three days, the spies leave their secret location and journey eastward toward the Jordan River. They return to the camp where Joshua is eagerly awaiting their return. The mission is accomplished, and their report to Joshua includes details of "everything that had happened to them." The report is both positive and puzzling. On the positive side, the spies report to Joshua that the "whole land" has been given into their hands and that "all the people are melting in fear" before the presence of the Israelites. These two statements echo Rahab's earlier proclamation to the spies (vv. 9, 11).

On the puzzling side, however, how can the spies mention the "whole land" and "all the people" when their expedition has only included Jericho and its surroundings? What about the dangers that loomed in the rest of the land? Were all the inhabitants of Canaan as fearful as those who lived in Jericho? The integrity of the spies is in question as they seem to embellish their report to Joshua with details that cannot be confirmed by textual evidence. One wonders if the details of the agreement made between Rahab and the spies are shared with Joshua upon their return. If so, the reader is left to speculate on Joshua's response to the news.

REFLECTION

How amazing that the most unlikely character in Jericho, a prostitute, becomes the liberator of a large group of people. Socially this is a problem. Her occupation, which should have prevented her from appearing at center stage, is overlooked and her social status casts no shadow on the narrative. Rahab's lies and deception are never condemned or condoned by the author.

In the end, God's grace prevails, and the divine paradigm reveals inclusion and hope for the outcast who is often persecuted and considered worthless. In Matthew 21:31–32, Jesus reveals that among the outcasts of Israel, the prostitute who turns to God will inherit the kingdom of heaven. In God's plan, Rahab will become the great-great-great-great grandmother of King David and an ancestor mentioned in the genealogy of Jesus (Mt 1:5–16). In Hebrews 11:31, Rahab is lauded for her strong faith as demonstrated through her hospitality for the spies. The author of James (Jas 2:25) acclaims

her behavior toward the king's messengers, whom she redirected away from Joshua's men.

The content of this chapter raises a number of questions related to the purpose and rationale of the Rahab narrative in the larger context of Joshua. According to some, Joshua 2 is simply a spy story that reveals a known ancient Near Eastern method of conquest, in which undercover agents are sent ahead of an army in order to scout out the territory to be conquered. Other scholars view Joshua 2 as an etiology intended to explain why Rahab's descendents remain in the land after the conquest (6:25). Still others have interpreted the chapter as a story of hospitality in which foreigners live under someone's roof for a short period of time during a journey between two locations. As I understand this passage, the mention of Rahab in several New Testament passages, in contexts where other well-known historical figures are listed by name, highlights her actual existence in the history of Israel (Mt 1:5; Heb 11:31; Jas 2:25).

C. Moving to Canaan and Initial Conquest (3:1–8:35)

OVERVIEW

In Joshua 3–8, the narrator describes the events that occur between the departure from Shittim on the eastern side of the Jordan and Israel's first encounter with a coalition of rulers in Canaan. Before crossing the Jordan (3:3–4), the Israelites prepare for the journey, and the priests who carry the ark of the covenant move into place at the edge of the river (3:1–10). During the crossing, the priests lead the procession (3:14–17), followed by the men from the eastern tribes (4:12), with Joshua and the Israelites

at the rear. The priests standing in the middle of the Jordan (3:17) exit behind the last of the Israelites (4:15–17) and reach the western shore before the waters of the Jordan begin to flow again (4:18).

After the entire community of Israel has crossed the Jordan, Joshua and the tribal representatives build two memorial stone structures, one in the river and another at Gilgal (4:4–9, 19–24). The stone memorials are to serve for future generations as testimonies of God's miraculous deeds during the crossing of the Jordan. Two major events occur between the erection of the memorials and the conquest of the first city: Joshua circumcises the men who were born in the desert (5:1–9), and Israel celebrates the Passover at Gilgal (5:10–11). Two days later, the manna stops, and the Israelites begin feasting on the produce of the land (5:11–12). The theophany near Jericho confirms to the Israelites that the land on which they are standing has indeed been given to them by Yahweh—it is holy ground (5:13–15).

With Israel finally in Canaan, the time has come to possess the land and to dispossess its inhabitants. Chapter 6 describes the conquest of the first city— Jericho—where Rahab and her family are living. This event is followed by the first attack against the city of Ai. Unfortunately, this attempt fails because of Achan's sin, who took from the ḥērem and hid it for future personal use. The last chapter of this unit describes the complete destruction of Ai (8:1–29) and the renewal of the covenant at Mount Ebal (8:30–35).

1. Crossing the Jordan (3:1–4:24)

OVERVIEW

Chapters 3 and 4 describe the events that surround the symbolic and miraculous crossing of the Jordan. This narrative includes a series of discourses between Yahweh, Joshua, the priests, the officers, and the Israelites. Of all the characters in the account, the only silent actors are the Israelites. The unfolding of the narrative of these two chapters is complex and contains nonsequential events and apparent inconsistencies.

Some of the details here seem to be repeated unnecessarily, and the chronology of events is unclear. For example, (1) the time lapse between the priests' initial departure from Shittim with the ark of the covenant and their actual entrance into the waters of the Jordan is blurred; (2) there is mention of events taking place "today," "tomorrow," and "in three days"; (3) the priests are instructed both to stand at the edge *and* in the middle of the Jordan (3:8, 13, 15, 17); (4) memorial stones are set up in the middle of the Jordan (4:9) *and* on the western shore of the river (4:3–5, 8); (5) there is inconsistency in the nomenclature for the ark of

the covenant ("ark of the covenant of the Lord" [3:3, 11, 17; 4:7, 16]; "ark" [3:4, 15; 4:10]; "ark of the covenant" [3:6, 8; 4:9]; "ark of the Lord" [3:13; 4:5, 11]; "ark of the Testimony" [4:16]; (6) the ark of the covenant and the priests, who should have reached the western shore in 4:11, are still in the water in 4:16; and (7) twice, Yahweh instructs Joshua to summon a representative from each of the twelve tribes (3:21; 4:2).

Literary critics regard the text either as a merging of two or more accounts, or as one original account with complex editing. Hess, however, views the chapters as a multilayered literary unit in which the "groups are acting simultaneously. Like a film in which the camera switches back and forth between the various scenes of action, the narrative moves back and forth between these three groups [priests, twelve tribal representatives, Israelites]" (Hess, *Joshua*, 103).

The repeated mention of the ark of the covenant is significant. It highlights the presence of Yahweh in the midst of his people during this miraculous event and serves as a constant reminder of the covenant he established with his people at Mount Horeb. It was common in the ancient world to carry on a journey an object that represented the god(s) of the community. Cultic objects were normally preserved in a shrine or temple, but during long journeys or in times of battle, the god was carried along by the priests in a chest (Pitkännen, 144–46). Whenever the god was in the midst of the camp, people were assured of victory and protection from the enemy; but whenever the idol was captured by an adversary, defeat and chaos normally ensued.

The ark of the covenant was sacred. It could not be touched by the common individual without consequences (e.g., 1Sa 6:19–20; 2Sa 6:6–7). In the Jordan crossing, Joshua instructs Israel to keep a safe distance from the priests carrying the ark and forbids them to go near it (3:4). The reason given here for the distance between the ark and the community is simply for the sake of orientation. But elsewhere in Scripture, the distance between people and the ark indicates respect and honor.

As mentioned in the Overview to 1:1–12:24, chapters 3–4 convey a substantial number of details linked to the exodus out of Egypt. For example, (1) Yahweh orchestrates a major move for his people;

(2) individuals are instructed to keep a distance from the manifested presence of God; (3) a major body of water is removed; (4) Yahweh leads the way; (5) the community enters foreign territory; (6) the leader receives the allegiance of the tribes through a verbal oath; (7) a covenant is established/renewed; and (9) Yahweh promises to be with the leader during the entire mission.

The reader who peruses through the events of Joshua 3–4 experiences a sense of confusion and disarray in the community. Simultaneously, leaders give and receive instructions, priests walk down the hill cautiously while holding on to the ark, Israelites pack up their weighty belongings and place them on beasts of burden, the overflowing Jordan rushes southward with a deafening sound, priests move westward while tribal leaders gather before Joshua at Shittim, women chase after their young ones, children scurry about with intense laughter or piercing screams, and a great multitude marches forward in formation stomping on a dry river bed. Anyone who has been in this area can easily imagine the vast dust cloud that would have arisen from the ground as people dragged their sandals on the dusty and rocky terrain from Shittim to the shore of the Jordan River.

a. Joshua's Instructions at the Jordan (3:1–13)

[1]Early in the morning Joshua and all the Israelites set out from Shittim and went to the Jordan, where they camped before crossing over. [2]After three days the officers went throughout the camp, [3]giving orders to the people: "When you see the ark of the covenant of the Lord your God, and the priests, who are Levites, carrying it, you are to move out from your positions and follow it. [4]Then you will know which way to go, since you have never been this way before. But keep a distance of about a thousand yards between you and the ark; do not go near it."

⁵Joshua told the people, "Consecrate yourselves, for tomorrow the LORD will do amazing things among you."

⁶Joshua said to the priests, "Take up the ark of the covenant and pass on ahead of the people." So they took it up and went ahead of them.

⁷And the LORD said to Joshua, "Today I will begin to exalt you in the eyes of all Israel, so they may know that I am with you as I was with Moses. ⁸Tell the priests who carry the ark of the covenant: 'When you reach the edge of the Jordan's waters, go and stand in the river.'"

⁹Joshua said to the Israelites, "Come here and listen to the words of the LORD your God. ¹⁰This is how you will know that the living God is among you and that he will certainly drive out before you the Canaanites, Hittites, Hivites, Perizzites, Girgashites, Amorites and Jebusites. ¹¹See, the ark of the covenant of the Lord of all the earth will go into the Jordan ahead of you. ¹²Now then, choose twelve men from the tribes of Israel, one from each tribe. ¹³And as soon as the priests who carry the ark of the LORD — the Lord of all the earth — set foot in the Jordan, its waters flowing downstream will be cut off and stand up in a heap."

COMMENTARY

1 The Israelites had been in Shittim in the plains of Moab since the events of Numbers 22 and 25, when Israel defeated kings Sihon and Og—kings of the Amorites. Assuming that Abel Shittim is the same location as Shittim, scholars have proposed Tell el-Kefrein and Tell el-Hammam as possible modern sites for this ancient city. Archaeologists have unearthed remains from Iron I and II in these two areas (J. C. Slayton, "Shittim," *ABD*, 5:1222).

The time has now come for Israel to complete her forty-year excursion in the desert and to enter the land promised centuries earlier. The journey from Shittim to the edge of the Jordan is approximately seven miles. The excursion in the hot rugged desert of the Jordan valley would have been challenging for men, women, children, and animals, but with Canaan in sight and the promise of a better life in a homeland, the prize merited the effort.

2–4 After completing the seven-mile walk from Shittim and spending three days on the eastern shore of the Jordan, the officers instruct the Israelites to prepare for the crossing. This scene points to a well-organized system of leadership, involving a distribution of tasks according to rank. Acting on the previous instructions from Joshua (1:10), the officers direct the people to pay close attention to the movement of the Levites who carried the ark of the covenant and to follow them attentively with a space of a thousand yards (about a half mile) between them and the ark.

Without remaining at a distance and keeping their eyes on the ark of the covenant and the priests, the Israelites could have attempted to enter the land at the wrong entry point and could have suffered greatly in a geographical area with unbearable heat and scarce drinking water. Although it is difficult to imagine that the Israelites would have lost sight of each other in this narrow stretch of land, it is possible that they could have lost sight of the Levites. Keeping the ark in sight ensured their safety. The warning given by the officers and the mention that they had "never been this way before" indicate that the possibility of getting lost or losing sight of the leaders was real.

The ark of the covenant is mentioned here for the first time in Joshua. It is central to the Jordan crossing in the same manner as the cloud by day and the pillar of fire by night were necessary in the desert. The ark signifies a divine witness in the midst of the people (Dt 31:24–26), the constant presence of Yahweh in times of transition (Nu 14:40–45), and a divine compass for physical direction (Nu 10:31–33). To follow the ark was to follow the Lord himself, and losing sight of its presence was to lose sight of the divine manifestation.

The instructions to keep a safe distance of at least a thousand yards between the people and the ark echo directives given earlier to Moses at the burning bush (Ex 3:5) and to the Israelites at Mount Sinai (19:12). In the Exodus accounts, there is a sense that respect for God requires that humans keep a healthy distance from his manifested presence. Some scholars have linked the thousand yards mentioned in Joshua to the distance between the town wall and the pasture land given to the Levites in Numbers 35:5 (Hess, *Joshua*, 100, n.1).

When the ark was built, God gave Aaron specific instructions as to how to approach it. Disobedience to these instructions was a matter of life or death. God forbade Aaron to approach the ark whenever he wished, lest he die (Lev 16:2). He could approach it in the Most Holy Place only once a year, on the tenth day of the seventh month, to offer sacrifices for himself, for his family, and for the entire Israelite community (16:3–11). Only after the sacrifices were offered could Aaron enter the Most Holy Place and stand before the ark. During the Davidic monarchy, Uzzah, one of the sons of Abinadab, touched the ark as it was traveling from Baalah of Judah to the City of David on the back of oxen and paid with his life (2Sa 6:6–7).

5 Joshua tells the people to "consecrate yourselves" (*hitqaddāšû*) before crossing the Jordan. This command reiterates the directives Yahweh gave to Israel at Mount Horeb three days before Moses received the law. In Exodus 19:22, God commanded the people, including the priests, to "sanctify themselves'" (*hitqaddešû*) before witnessing his mighty deeds. In Joshua, the reason given for the sanctification is for the consecration of the community before witnessing the miracle of the crossing—"for tomorrow, the LORD will do amazing things [*niplāʾôt*] among you" (Jos 3:5). Throughout Scripture, personal sanctification is associated with theophanies (Nu 11:18; Jos 7:13; 1Sa 16:5; 1Ch 15:12; 2Ch 29:5; 35:6).

6–13 Joshua commands the priests to take the ark and to pass ahead of the people in preparation for the long-awaited crossing of the Jordan.

Once again, the time for the official exaltation of Joshua as the new leader of the community has come (cf. 1:1–2). It is at this juncture that the transfer of power from Moses to Joshua receives divine endorsement and that Joshua's leadership begins to crystallize. Moses is no more, so God confirms Joshua as the new leader of *all* Israel. God says, "I will begin to exalt you," which indicates that further exaltation will take place in the future. The purpose for the promotion is revealed: "so they may know that I am with you as I was with Moses" (cf. 1:5, 17). This purpose is fulfilled in the next chapter (4:14).

Following the confirmation of Joshua's leadership, God gives Joshua directives for the priests. He is to say to them: "When you reach the edge of the Jordan's waters, go and stand in the river."

The priests are not instructed to go to the middle of the river, but rather, they are told to stand at the edge of the Jordan with their feet ankle-deep in the water and the ark of the covenant on their shoulders.

Before the crossing, Joshua addresses the people with a three-part message. (1) He invites them to listen to the words of the Lord (v.9). In a nonliterate society where oral tradition is the norm, it is crucial that divine instructions be transmitted with clarity and precision. Therefore, when Joshua summons the people and tells them to come and to "listen to the words of the LORD your God," it is vital that they give their full attention to the message. This call highlights the importance of listening to God's instructions before embarking on a journey, especially one as significant as this one. The word of God is worthy of attention since it includes the blueprint and the directives for every aspect of the journey.

(2) Joshua reminds the people that it was God's plan to "drive out" (dispossess) the Canaanite, Hittites, Hivites, Perizzites, Girgashites, Amorites, and Jebusites (Ex 23:23; Dt 7:1). A similar list of peoples appears throughout the Pentateuch and throughout Joshua (e.g., Ge 15:19–21; Ex 3:8, 17; 23:23; 33:2; 34:11; Dt 20:17; Jos 9:1). The dispossessing of the land is a fulfillment of God's promise (e.g., Nu 14:24; 32:21; 33:52–53, 55; Dt 4:38; 7:17; 9:3–5). The inhabitants whom the Lord promises to drive out are well-known from anicent Near Eastern literature (see Introduction—"The People of the Land").

(3) Joshua describes briefly the Jordan crossing. The ark of the covenant, a symbol of God's presence, is the first element to enter the Jordan ahead of the people; this indicates that God is at the forefront of the expedition, leading the way into Canaan. Joshua then instructs the people to choose twelve men, one from each tribe, for an unspecified task. The reason for this selection is revealed only later, after the crossing has been completed, unless the two groups of tribal representatives include different individuals for different assignments (4:1–3).

The Israelites must journey forward in faith, trusting that God will lead the way and manifest himself on their behalf. Since their supreme leader is proclaimed as "the Lord of all the earth," there is no reason for them to doubt that Yahweh has the power and ability to grant them success in their mission. This honorific title confirms that Yahweh is not simply a local deity whose power is anemic and limited; rather, it indicates that in the mind of ancient Israelites, their God is sovereign, omniscient, and omnipotent.

NOTES

1 The name "Jordan" (יַרְדֵּן *yardēn*) comes from the root *yrd*, "to go down." East of Jericho, the Jordan River is more than one thousand feet below sea level. Whether one comes from Moab or from Canaan, one must "go down" in order to reach the Jordan River. The river flows from north to south and ends in the Dead Sea. The key word "to cross over" (עבר, *ʿbr*) is repeated twenty-two times in chapters 3 and 4. This repetition highlights the significant transition of the Israelites from their preconquest state to their new beginning in Canaan.

3 "When you see" (כִּרְאוֹתְכֶם, *kirʾôtᵉkem*; see also vv.8, 13, 15). A temporal clause introduced with the preposition *kᵉ* and an infinitive construct (followed by subject of the infinitive) indicates urgency. Most modern translations render the temporal phrase as "when you see," losing the sense of urgency. A preferred translation of the phrase is, therefore, "*As soon as* you see the ark of the covenant, you are to move ..." and not simply "When you see the ark of the covenant." The phrase "the ark of the covenant of the LORD your God" (אֲרוֹן בְּרִית־יְהוָה אֱלֹהֵיכֶם, *ᵃrôn bᵉrît-yhwh ᵉlōhêkem*) occurs only once in the book of Joshua (the only other occurrence in the Hebrew Bible is in Dt 31:26). In Jos 3:11, the phrase is extended to include "the ark of the covenant of the Lord of all the earth." This phrase is unique to this passage. The ark is mentioned numerous times in Joshua under a variety of names (e.g., 3:3, 6, 11, 13, 14, 15, 17; 4:5, 7, 9, 10, 11, 16, 18; see Butler, 45).

5 "Amazing things" (נִפְלָאוֹת, *niplāᵓôt*) is translated in other passages as "miracles" (Jos 5:9), "great things" (Job 37:5), "[great] wonders" (Job 37:14; Ps 136:4; Mic 7:15), "wonderful things" (Job 42:3; Ps 119:18), "marvelous deeds" (Ps 72:18), "awesome deeds" (Ps 106:22). Such "amazing things" are impossible in the natural realm. These acts that characterize Yahweh's deliverance and the outcome of such deeds typically prompt joy and praise. The same word appears in Exodus 3:20 in reference to the divine miracles about to take place in Egypt and lead Israel to freedom from bondage (the plagues). See R. Albertz, "פלא," *TLOT*, 2:981–86.

10 The expression "the living God" (אֵל חַי, *ᵓēl ḥay*) occurs in this form only four times in the Hebrew Bible (Jos 3:10; Pss 42:3; 84:3; Hos 2:1). In other passages, the phrase "the living God" appears as אֱלֹהִים חַיִּים (*ᵉlōhîm ḥayyîm*, Dt 4:4; 5:26; 1Sa 17:26, 36; Jer 10:10; 23:36) or אֱלֹהִים חַי (*ᵉlōhîm ḥay*, 1Ki 19:4, 26; Isa 37:4, 17). This designation confirms to Israel that the God who is in their midst is not like the gods of the foreign nations, whose mouths cannot speak, whose eyes cannot see, whose ears cannot hear, and whose noses cannot smell (Ps 115:5–7). Their God is alive and dwells in their midst; he speaks, sees, hears, and smells.

b. Crossing the Jordan on Dry Ground (3:14–17)

[14]So when the people broke camp to cross the Jordan, the priests carrying the ark of the covenant went ahead of them. [15]Now the Jordan is at flood stage all during harvest. Yet as soon as the priests who carried the ark reached the Jordan and their feet touched the water's edge, [16]the water from upstream stopped flowing. It piled up in a heap a great distance away, at a town called Adam in the vicinity of Zarethan, while the water flowing down to the Sea of the Arabah (the Salt Sea) was completely cut off. So the people crossed over opposite Jericho. [17]The priests who carried the ark of the covenant of the LORD stood firm on dry ground in the middle of the Jordan, while all Israel passed by until the whole nation had completed the crossing on dry ground.

COMMENTARY

14 The picture engendered by the phrase "the people broke camp" is one of intensive labor as men, women, children, the elderly, and the animals prepare to cross the river. The reader can visualize the folding of heavy tents, the loading of beasts of burden, the gathering of excited children, the assembling of animals, and the clash of intense personalities, with the loud voices of people who are both excited and stressed by the circumstances.

15–17 The statement that "the Jordan is at flood stage all during harvest" is crucial in order for a miracle to take place. During the dry season, it may have been possible to cross the Jordan on foot, but during harvest time, the fast-flowing river was at its highest (today more than ten feet deep) and at its widest (today more than a hundred feet wide) (H. O. Thompson, "Jordan River," *ABD*, 3:956). In these conditions, it would be impossible for anyone to cross the river on foot. The crossing could not have taken place except through divine intervention.

At the very moment that the priests enter the Jordan, the waters stop flowing and the dry ground appears. The Jordan dries up at Adam, approximately eighteen miles north of Jericho. Adam was located just south of the Jabbok River, a river that flowed into the Jordan and caused it to rise during harvest time. Only after the waters recede do the priests proceed forward to the middle of the river, carrying the ark and watching as the Israelites cross on dry ground (v.15). The miraculous event becomes a testimony of the power of God for future generations.

The "ark (of the covenant)" is mentioned nine times in this chapter (vv.3, 4, 6, 8, 11, 13, 14, 15, 17). This repetition suggests that the focus of the crossing is not meant to be on the event but on God's presence in the midst of his people during an expedition that will change their lives forever. The placements of the ark during the crossing indicated that Yahweh is before, in the midst of, and after the Israelites during this event. The text does not reveal how long it takes for the entire community to cross from the eastern to the western shore. But it is unthinkable that such a multitude could complete the crossing in a short period of time.

NOTES

16 By mentioning that the waters of the Jordan "were flowing down" (הַיֹּרְדִים, *hayyōreʿdîm*), the author contrasts the root *yrd* (ירד, "to go down") with the root *ʿmd* (עמד, "to stand still"). The waters that normally "flowed down" now "stood still," an event fully orchestrated by Yahweh. The state of the Jordan that allowed for the crossing of the river reminds the reader of the events at the Red Sea in Exodus 15:8 (cf. Ps 78:13).

c. The Stone Memorial (4:1–9)

¹When the whole nation had finished crossing the Jordan, the LORD said to Joshua, ²"Choose twelve men from among the people, one from each tribe, ³and tell them to take up twelve stones from the middle of the Jordan from right where the priests stood and to carry them over with you and put them down at the place where you stay tonight."

⁴So Joshua called together the twelve men he had appointed from the Israelites, one from each tribe, ⁵and said to them, "Go over before the ark of the LORD your God into the middle of the Jordan. Each of you is to take up a stone on his shoulder, according to the number of the tribes of the Israelites, ⁶to serve as a sign among you. In the future, when your children ask you, 'What do these stones mean?' ⁷tell them that the flow of the Jordan was cut off before the ark of the covenant of the LORD. When it crossed the Jordan, the waters of the Jordan were cut off. These stones are to be a memorial to the people of Israel forever."

⁸So the Israelites did as Joshua commanded them. They took twelve stones from the middle of the Jordan, according to the number of the tribes of the Israelites, as the LORD had told Joshua; and they carried them over with them to their camp, where they put them down. ⁹Joshua set up the twelve stones that had been in the middle of the Jordan at the spot where the priests who carried the ark of the covenant had stood. And they are there to this day.

COMMENTARY

1–3 As soon as the Israelites have completed their journey on dry ground, from the eastern shore to the western shore of the Jordan, God tells Joshua to instruct the twelve tribal representatives (cf. 3:12) to take large stones from the Jordan in order to build an altar to Yahweh at the location where they will set up camp on their first night. Each man is to take one stone (presumably) from the very spot where the priests who carried the ark stood during the crossing. Since the river bed is still dry and the priests are still standing in the middle of the Jordan, the task can be accomplished relatively quickly and without difficulty.

The chronology of events in these verses is ambiguous. It is not clear if the twelve tribal representatives are the same individuals chosen by Joshua in chapter 3. The language in both passages (3:12 and 4:2) is almost identical—"choose twelve men from among the tribes of Israel [4:2: from among the people], one from each tribe." It is possible that the double set of instructions refers to the same event, but it is also possible that two groups of men were chosen for two different tasks—one undisclosed (3:12) and one disclosed (4:2).

A second ambiguous point that puts the sequence of the events into question is whether Joshua commanded the twelve men to walk back to the middle of the Jordan after having reached the shore, in order to gather stones for the memorial. One can easily imagine that the men picked up large stones during their initial crossing and carried them to the western shore.

As pointed out by Howard (133), the phenomenon found in this passage may conform to a literary pattern of "anticipation/confirmation" or "command/fulfillment" rather than to a description of the sequence of events. Hubbard (157) refutes this view and points to the theological difficulty of having God "confirm" and "fulfill" the command of Joshua in the same breath. He suggests that the text "may in fact also serve a thematic purpose — to enhance the portrait of Joshua as leader and close divine confidante."

4–6a There is no doubt that the stones collected by the twelve men were large since they are instructed to carry them on their shoulders rather than in their hands. In anticipation of the questions asked by curious future generations, Joshua explains the purpose for the collection of stones (vv.6–7, 21–24): to serve as a visible sign for the community that the Jordan had dried up before Israel exclusively through divine intervention. The stone structure erected at Gilgal is not an altar for sacrifice; rather, it will serve as a perpetual memorial of the crossing for the people of Israel, both for the current generation and for generations to come (v.7).

The Hebrew Bible provides numerous accounts where stone structures are erected in memory of significant events (e.g., Ge 28:18–22: theophany at Bethel [Jacob]; 31:45–47: covenant between Laban and Jacob; Ex 24:4: Moses' receipt of the law; Jos 7:26: destruction of the ḥērem [Achan]; 24:26–27: renewal of covenant at Shechem; 1Sa 7:12: Israel's victory over the Philistines). The gathering of the twelve stones symbolizes the unity of the entire nation of Israel, even though two and one-half tribes — Reuben, Gad, and the half-tribe of Manasseh — remain in Transjordan, the territory Moses assigned to them earlier (Nu 34:13–15).

6b–7 The miracle of the crossing is not to be celebrated only by the generation who experiences

it, but it must be remembered by future generations forever. During the first Passover, the Lord said to Moses: "In days to come, when your son asks you, 'What does this mean?' say to him, 'With a mighty hand the Lord brought us out of Egypt, out of the land of slavery'" (Ex. 13:14; cf. 12:26). Before Moses died, he said to the Israelites: "In the future, when your son asks you, 'What is the meaning of the stipulations, decrees and laws the Lord our God has commanded you?' tell him, 'We were slaves of Pharaoh in Egypt, but the Lord brought us out of Egypt with a mighty hand'" (Dt 6:20–21). Oral transmission of historical information and miraculous events was a norm in the life of Israel. The Israelites were to teach the mighty deeds of God to their children and to their children's children (Dt 6:6–9) so that they might celebrate the miraculous events and glorify God who had performed mighty deeds on their behalf. It is, therefore, important for Joshua to command the Israelites to teach future generations the details of the miraculous crossing of the Jordan.

8–9 The men take the stones from the middle of the Jordan and bring them to the location where Israel encamps the first night. The text refers to two piles of stones — one in the middle of the Jordan and another at the location where the Israelites set up camp (see NIV text note). Is there one pile or two piles of stones? Is there one pile in the river and another one on land? Howard suggests two possible scenarios (Howard, 136):

1. Joshua built a stone structure in the middle of the Jordan during the crossing. This structure was concealed by the waters of the Jordan during the harvest season and visible during the dry season.
2. Joshua may have initially set up twelve stones in the middle of the Jordan, the place where the priests stood with the ark of the

covenant. During the crossing, the tribal representatives picked up these stones and brought them to the western shore of the Jordan, to the camp where Israel spent the first night.

If the first scenario is accurate, the final comment "and they are there to this day" indicates that a stone structure built by Joshua was still at the bottom of the Jordan when the text was written. It is unthinkable that a stone structure in the middle of the gushing Jordan would have remained in place for long. They would, no doubt, have been carried down the river toward the Dead Sea. If the second scenario is accurate, the pile of stones was erected where Israel encamped the first night after the crossing, a location known to the writer of the story but one that cannot be identified by modern archaeologists. In this part of the world, stones were used to build houses, fences, roads, memorials, and other structures. The original pile of stones set up in the camp by Joshua has certainly been reused many times since.

In our interpretation of the events, the text refers to one set of stones handled first by Joshua and then by the twelve men. Initially, Joshua set up the stones in the middle of the Jordan at the place where the priests were standing (v.9); subsequently, the twelve picked them up from that place (v.8) and carried them to the western shore of the river.

NOTES

2 The expression "one [man] from each tribe" (אִישׁ־אֶחָד אִישׁ־אֶחָד, *ʾîš ʾeḥād ʾîš ʾeḥād*) uses the repetition of the same Hebrew phrase for "one man" (אִישׁ אֶחָד, *ʾîš ʾeḥād*)—"one man one man" (see also v.4). A similar expression also appears in 22:14 with "one [leader] for each of ..." (נָשִׂיא אֶחָד נָשִׂיא אֶחָד *nāśîʾ ʾeḥād nāśîʾ ʾeḥād*).

4 The number "twelve" (שְׁנֵים הֶעָשָׂר, *šᵉnêm heʿāśār*) is written this way (with definite article) only here and 1Ki 19:19. The phrase is normally written שְׁנֵים־עָשָׂר (*šᵉnêm-ʿāśār*; Ge 17:20; Nu 1:44; 17:17; Dt 1:23; 2Ch 4:4; Est 2:12; Jer 52:20). The unusual spelling may reflect on the dialect of the author or redactor of the text.

6 "Sign" (אוֹת, *ʾôt*). Biblical signs include objects (e.g., blood, Ex 12:13; stones, Jos 4:5–6), supernatural phenomena (e.g., appearances, Jdg 6:17), natural phenomena (e.g., rainbow, Ge 9:12; plagues, Ex 8:23; storm, drought), acts (e.g., circumcision, Ge 17:11), days (e.g., Sabbath, Ex 31:17), and so on. The purpose of a sign was to help the audience to recognize, learn from, and remember the credibility of a significant event (F. J. Helfmeyer, "אוֹת," *TDOT*, 1:167–88) .

7 The theme for "remembering" (NIV "memorial," זִכָּרוֹן, *zikkārôn*) the Lord and his mighty deeds is common throughout Scripture. Israel is commanded to "remember" numerous times in the Pentateuch (e.g., Ex 13:3; 20:8; 32:13; Nu 15:39–40; Dt 5:15; 7:18; 8:2, 18; 9:7, 27; 15:15; 24:9; 25:17; 32:7). This command is sometimes complemented with the command: "do not forget" (אַל תִּשְׁכַּח [*ʾal tiškaḥ*], Dt 9:7; cf. Pr 3:1; 4:5).

9 "Joshua set up the twelve stones" (וּשְׁתֵּים עֶשְׂרֵה אֲבָנִים הֵקִים יְהוֹשֻׁעַ, *ûšᵉtêm ʿeśrēh ʾᵃbānîm hēqîm yᵉhôšûaʿ*). The syntax of this verse points to two sets of stones (the following scholars advocate for two sets of stones [one in the Jordan and one set up as a memorial in the camp]: see Hubbard, 158; Woudstra, 92; Butler, 49; R. Polzin, *Moses and the Deuteronomist* [New York: Seabury, 1980], 95, 114; see also LXX and Vulgate: "the twelve other stones"). The introductory disjunctive clause and the use of the perfect (pluperfect) in verse 9 seem to indicate that Joshua had already set up stones before the twelve men picked them up and carried them to the edge of the river. Based on the syntax of the sentence, the following translation is possible: "As for the twelve stones, Joshua had erected them." This interpretation requires that the final comment "and they are there to this day" be read as follows: "and they are there [on dry land] to this day."

d. The Crossing of the Ark of the Covenant (4:10–24)

[10]Now the priests who carried the ark remained standing in the middle of the Jordan until everything the LORD had commanded Joshua was done by the people, just as Moses had directed Joshua. The people hurried over, [11]and as soon as all of them had crossed, the ark of the LORD and the priests came to the other side while the people watched. [12]The men of Reuben, Gad and the half-tribe of Manasseh crossed over, armed, in front of the Israelites, as Moses had directed them. [13]About forty thousand armed for battle crossed over before the LORD to the plains of Jericho for war.

[14]That day the LORD exalted Joshua in the sight of all Israel; and they revered him all the days of his life, just as they had revered Moses.

[15]Then the LORD said to Joshua, [16]"Command the priests carrying the ark of the Testimony to come up out of the Jordan."

[17]So Joshua commanded the priests, "Come up out of the Jordan."

[18]And the priests came up out of the river carrying the ark of the covenant of the LORD. No sooner had they set their feet on the dry ground than the waters of the Jordan returned to their place and ran at flood stage as before.

[19]On the tenth day of the first month the people went up from the Jordan and camped at Gilgal on the eastern border of Jericho. [20]And Joshua set up at Gilgal the twelve stones they had taken out of the Jordan. [21]He said to the Israelites, "In the future when your descendants ask their fathers, 'What do these stones mean?' [22]tell them, 'Israel crossed the Jordan on dry ground.' [23]For the LORD your God dried up the Jordan before you until you had crossed over. The LORD your God did to the Jordan just what he had done to the Red Sea when he dried it up before us until we had crossed over. [24]He did this so that all the peoples of the earth might know that the hand of the LORD is powerful and so that you might always fear the LORD your God."

COMMENTARY

10–11 The priests carrying the ark of the covenant remain standing in the middle of the Jordan until everyone has crossed over. The crossing takes place relatively quickly and without interruption (cf. Ex 12:33). As the eyes of the Israelites had been on the Levites before the crossing, so they are also on them afterwards. Standing on the western shore of the Jordan, the people watch the end of the procession until everyone—including the priests—have crossed.

12–13 Approximately forty thousand fighting men of Reuben, Gad, and the half-tribe of Manasseh have crossed the Jordan in battle formation ahead of the Israelites. This number has been challenged by scholars based on the interpretations of the events in Judges 5:8 and 2 Samuel 10:18 (1Ch 19:18), where a battalion of approximately forty thousand men refers to a relatively large group of people but not to a literal group of forty thousand individuals (Hubbard, 159). Large numbers are often used in hyperbolic language. They may also represent a literary tradition of historiography used by Israel during this period.

As per Moses' instructions, these "forty thousand' fighting men are to assist in the conquest of Canaan and to remain with their brothers until the whole land is dispossessed of its inhabitants (Nu 32:16–42).

14 As noted in 3:7, Yahweh exalts Joshua in the eyes of all the people. Joshua is quickly becoming the new Moses. The Israelites had been grateful for Moses' leadership during their deliverance out of Egypt and the crossing of the Red Sea. Now, recognizing that Joshua has brought them safely across the Jordan, the people do not hesitate to "revere him" ("fear him, be in awe of him") as their new leader. As Moses had been God's instrument in Egypt and in the desert, Joshua is God's instrument

in the crossing of the Jordan and in the events that follow.

The verse seems somewhat out of place since what follows tells us that the crossing has not yet been completed. The priests are still standing in the middle of the Jordan. One would expect to find the Israelites revering Joshua only once everyone was safe and sound on the western shore.

15–18 Once Israel has reached the land of Canaan, Joshua instructs the priests carrying "the ark of the Testimony" to come out of the Jordan (cf. v.11). As they set foot on the western shore, a surge of water comes rushing down from Adam, and the waters of the Jordan begin to flow again until they reach flood stage. What an amazing sight that must have been!

19–20 The date of the event—the tenth day of the first month—points to springtime, when the Jabbok River pours a plentiful amount of water into the Jordan River, causing it to swell its banks and flow at high speed toward the Dead Sea. The date of the Jordan crossing corresponds to the date of the first Passover in Egypt (Ex 12:1–3), an event celebrated four days after Israel has entered Canaan (Jos 5:10–12). Once at Gilgal, Joshua erects the required stone memorial using the rocks carried on the shoulders of the twelve men. The exact location of Gilgal is still uncertain, but most scholars agree that it was located somewhere between Jericho and the Jordan.

21–24 Although the question to be anticipated by future generations is identical in 4:6 and 21— "What do these stones mean?"—the answer given by Joshua differs in each case. In the earlier passage (4:6–7), the answer highlights the "cutting off" (*krt*) of the waters of the Jordan and the presence of the ark of the covenant during the crossing. In the later passage (4:21–24), the answer emphasizes the "dry ground/drying up" (*ybš*) of the Jordan, the active participation of Yahweh, and the rationale behind the miraculous event. Moreover, the similarities between the crossing of the Jordan and the crossing of the Red Sea are mentioned in this passage (4:21–24) while they are excluded from the earlier passage (4:6–7). As the crossing of the Red Sea had marked the end of a lengthy period in Egypt, so the crossing of the Jordan marks the end of a difficult and long journey in the desert. The time has come for a new adventure with Yahweh at the helm and Israel in tow!

NOTES

14 The Israelites "revered" Joshua (וַיִּרְאוּ, *wayyirʾû*), meaning that they feared, respected, and honored him as their new leader. Now that Yahweh has confirmed his authority, the Israelites commit themselves to remain loyal and faithful to Joshua as they had been loyal and faithful to Moses. The verb "to fear" is often combined with other expressions such as "to love" (Dt 10:12), "to cleave to" (10:20), "to serve" (6:13; 10:12, 20; 17:19; 31:12), "to walk in his ways" (8:6), "to follow" (13:5[4]), "to hearken to his voice" (13:4[5]), and "to do his commands" (6:24) (see H. F. Fuhs, "ירא," *TDOT*, 6:290–315).

19 Most scholars agree that the name "Gilgal" derives from the root *gll* (גלל, "to roll") or from the word *gl* (גל, "heap, wave") (see E. S. Kalland, "גלל," *TWOT*, 1:162–65; G. Münderlein, "גלל," *TDOT*, 3:20–23). Joshua 5:9 connects the root *gll* with the name of town of Gilgal: "Then the LORD said to Joshua, 'Today I have rolled away [*gll*] the reproach of Egypt from you.' So the place has been called Gilgal [*glgl*] to this day."

21 In verse 6, the question is introduced with the particle *kî* (כִּי) while in verse 21, the same question is introduced with the particle *ʾăšer* (אֲשֶׁר). Both particles carry the secondary function of temporal marker. The use of *kî* (כִּי) in temporal clauses appears in situations that are *contemporary* to those of the main clause while the particle *ʾăšer* (אֲשֶׁר) is more common in temporal clauses that express a *preceding* situation (Waltke and O'Connor, §38.7.a).

22–23 The root for "to [be] dry" or "dry land" (יבש, *ybš*) appears three times in verses 22 and 23. The repetition is intentional. It highlights the fact that only God could provide dry land on which Israel would cross to the other side, at a time of the year when the Jordan was at its highest.

REFLECTION

The miracle at the Jordan highlights important theological points. First, the story confirms that God is faithful to his promises and true to his word. The Israelites had waited for a long time before reaching their homeland. The journey had been turbulent and at times gruesome, but God reassured them that he would never leave them nor forsake them. In the same manner, the Christian journey requires patience and the constant assurance that God is present with us in good times as well as in difficult times.

Second, God is omnipotent and omniscient. He is the God "of all the earth" (3:13; Isa 54:5). Natural elements are under his control and the earth moves at his command. The waters stop at his word, the river beds dry up underfoot, the peoples of the earth fear him, and his plans unfold in the least favorable conditions. As we witness the events of the crossing, we find comfort in knowing that no enemy and no physical obstacle can thwart the plans God has for his people. His timing is perfect and his instructions absolute. His power is manifested on the earth "so that all people may fear him."

Finally, the command to "remember" the mighty deeds of the Lord appears throughout Scripture. Moses commands Israel to "remember that you were slaves in Egypt and the LORD your God redeemed you" (Dt 15:15); "remember well what the LORD your God did to Pharaoh and to all Egypt" (7:18); "remember how the LORD your God led you all the way in the desert these forty years" (8:2). One generation was responsible to remember the events and to inform the next generation of all the miracles God has done for his people. Joshua perpetuates this tradition and instructs Israel to explain to future generations the miracle at the Jordan River. In the same manner, Christians must never forget the mighty works of the Lord and the miracles God has performed on their behalf. They are responsible to teach them from one generation to the next, until the end of time.

2. Renewal of the Covenant and Passover Celebration (5:1–12)

OVERVIEW

Once the news of the crossing of the Jordan reaches the inhabitants of the surrounding area, fear strikes them. The kings of the Amorites and Canaanites tremble at the prospect of having to face this great nation whose God is "God in heaven above and on the earth below" (2:11). One can imagine these rulers planning their response to Israel and working on their military strategy, should the invaders approach their territory (cf. Ps 2:1–2). The tension mounts as conflict is now inevitable. And for Israel, there is no turning back. The waters of the Jordan River have returned to flood stage, and retreat is impossible and out of the question.

Three major events take place in chapter 5: (1) the circumcision of males born in the wilderness (vv.2–9); (2) the celebration of the Passover (vv.10–12); and (3) the theophany near Jericho (vv.13–15). (1) Before the land can be dispossessed of its inhabitants, God requires that Joshua circumcise all Israelite males born in the desert. This sacred act reestablishes the covenantal relationship between God and his people before the land is conquered. There are three occurrences of circumcision in the Torah (Ge 17; 34; Ex 4:24–26). (a) Circumcision had been ordained as a sign of the covenant during the days of Abraham (Ge 17). (b) After Hamor's son Shechem sexually violated Jacob's daughter Dinah, Dinah's brothers deceitfully agreed to intermarriage with the house of Hamor if all the males underwent circumcision (Ge 34). Hamor and the men of the city agreed to the proposal and every male was circumcised. Three days later while the men were still in great pain, Simeon and Levi took swords and killed every male in the city. (c) In Exodus 4, Moses' wife Zipporah circumcises her son while they are on their journey to Egypt, where Moses will negotiate before Pharaoh the release of the Israelites. The text is ambiguous and does not explain why God was angry with Moses (4:24) and why Zipporah performed the circumcision (4:25–26).

(2) As seen above, the date of the crossing of the Jordan corresponds to the date of the first Passover in Egypt (preparation on the tenth day of the first month, Ex 12:3; Jos 4:19; celebration on the fourteenth day of the first month, Ex 12:18; Jos 5:10). The description of the celebration in Exodus is not repeated in Joshua, and the reader is simply told that the Israelites celebrate the Passover at Gilgal and begin to eat the produce of the land thereafter.

(3) While standing near Jericho, Joshua encounters the commander of the army of the Lord, whose hand holds a drawn sword. Overwhelmed at the presence of the divine messenger, Joshua falls facedown to the ground. The messenger repeats a command uttered by God to Moses at the burning bush, "Take off your sandals, for the place where you are standing is holy" (v.15). This encounter is similar to the one at Peniel, when Jacob encountered the man of God (Ge 32:22–32), and to the encounter between Moses and God at the burning bush (Ex 3:1–4:17). This event will be discussed in the next section.

¹Now when all the Amorite kings west of the Jordan and all the Canaanite kings along the coast heard how the Lord had dried up the Jordan before the Israelites until we had crossed over, their hearts melted and they no longer had the courage to face the Israelites.

²At that time the Lord said to Joshua, "Make flint knives and circumcise the Israelites again." ³So Joshua made flint knives and circumcised the Israelites at Gibeath Haaraloth.

⁴Now this is why he did so: All those who came out of Egypt—all the men of military age—died in the desert on the way after leaving Egypt. ⁵All the people that came out had been circumcised, but all the people born in the desert during the journey from Egypt had not. ⁶The Israelites had moved about in the desert forty years until all the men who were of military age when they left Egypt had died, since they had not obeyed the Lord. For the Lord had sworn to them that they would not see the land that he had solemnly promised their fathers to give us, a land flowing with milk and honey. ⁷So he raised up their sons in their place, and these were the ones Joshua circumcised. They were still uncircumcised because they had not been circumcised on the way. ⁸And after the whole nation had been circumcised, they remained where they were in camp until they were healed.

⁹Then the Lord said to Joshua, "Today I have rolled away the reproach of Egypt from you." So the place has been called Gilgal to this day.

¹⁰On the evening of the fourteenth day of the month, while camped at Gilgal on the plains of Jericho, the Israelites celebrated the Passover. ¹¹The day after the Passover, that very day, they ate some of the produce of the land: unleavened bread and roasted grain. ¹²The manna stopped the day after they ate this food from the land; there was no longer any manna for the Israelites, but that year they ate of the produce of Canaan.

COMMENTARY

1 As soon as the Amorite and Canaanite kings learn about the miraculous crossing of the Jordan by the Israelites, their hearts melt with fear. Rahab had told the spies before the crossing that the people of the region were terrified of the Israelites because of the fame of their God (2:9, 11). They had heard that Yahweh had given the land of Canaan to Israel (2:9). They had learned about the miracle of the exodus and the crossing at the Red Sea, as well as about the death of the two Amorite kings — Sihon and Og (2:9–10). The Amorite and Canaanite kings inhabited the entire southern region of Canaan, from the western shore of the Jordan to the hill country and as far west as the coast of the Mediterannean Sea.

2–3 In obedience to God's command, Joshua makes flint knives and circumcises the Israelite males at Gibeath Haaraloth (location unknown). As is often the case, the name of the town is related to the events that take place in that location. Gibeath Haaraloth means "the hill of the foreskins," so anyone who approached the city remembered that the Israelite males had been circumcised there immediately after the crossing of the Jordan. In Exodus, circumcision was required for all males — Israelites and aliens — before the celebration of Passover.

Flint was readily available in Canaan at that time. Flint knives were used in the ancient Near East for ritual and nonritual purposes (Hess, *Joshua*, 119). In Israel, the ritual of circumcision served as an outward sign of the covenant between God and his people (Ge 17; Acts 7:8), yet it never confirmed a person's right relationship with God (1Co 7:18–19; Gal 5:6; 6:15; Php 3:3–9). Both the Old and New Testaments place greater value on circumcision of the heart than on circumcision of the flesh (Dt 10:16; 30:6; Jer 4:4; Rom 2:25–29).

4–5 A historical note explains why the Israelites had to be circumcised immediately after the crossing of the Jordan. Although the previous generation of Israelite males had been circumcised — the generation that had left Egypt under the leadership of Moses — none of them was permitted to enter Canaan. As for the generation born in the desert, none of them had been circumcised. The circumcised people had died, and the uncircumcised were alive. This reversal of the paradigm is ironic since in Scripture, the "circumcised" are normally favored over the "uncircumcised." Some have proposed that the rebellious nature of Israel caused her to consciously reject circumcision during her journey through the desert. Others have suggested that the desert may not have been a safe place to perform the surgery since the dust and grime created unsanitary conditions. There is no textual evidence to support either view.

It is somewhat puzzling that God would require the Israelite fighting men to become physically vulnerable through circumcision at a time when kings were plotting against them, especially since the healing process took place over several days (Ge 34:24–25). Since the rulers of the land were gripped with fear and unprepared for an offensive assault, there was most likely sufficient time to recover from the surgical procedure before a military confrontation could occur.

6–8 Disobedience to God in the desert proved costly. A journey of forty challenging years concluded with the death of the disobedient rather than with the reward of a land flowing with milk and honey (Ex 3:8, 17). Soon after the Israelites left Egypt, God gave them an opportunity to enter Canaan from the south, but the people chose to believe the evil report of the ten spies rather than the positive account of Joshua and Caleb (Nu 13–14).

Consequently, God determined that only Caleb and Joshua would enter the land and that the rest of the men would die in the desert. God raised up another generation of men to replace those who died. It was imperative that this new generation of men be circumcised in order to establish their own identity as the people of God.

9 Israel now found herself in Gilgal, a site that is yet to be identified by archaeologists. As with Gibeath Haaraloth, the name Gilgal (*gll*) reveals a wordplay with the root *gll* (see Note on 4:19). God rolled back (*gll*) "the reproach of Egypt" from Israel here. This reproach may refer to the shame of living as homeless slaves in Egypt for four hundred years, oppressed by foreign rulers who refused to acknowledge the living God—Yahweh. It was important for Israel to begin a new life in a new land without the guilt and shame of previous generations. Therefore, Yahweh removed the burden from her and commemorated the event by naming the place Gilgal.

10 As mentioned above, the entry into Canaan corresponds to the time of the Passover—the fourteenth day of the month (see 4:19; Ex 12:2, 6, 18). Along with circumcision, Passover had been neglected by the previous generation. Both circumcision and Passover are reinstated immediately after the entry into Canaan. A new beginning required a new commitment to Yahweh's ordinances.

11–12 For forty years, the Israelites had been sustained by manna provided daily by the hand of God. The day had finally come for them to graduate from this strict and dull diet to a regimen that included unleavened bread, roasted grain, and fresh produce from the land—probably the first harvest of the season. This changed eating habit signified that Israel would now have access to seasonal harvests to create scrumptious and delectable recipes. The nomadic lifestyle of the desert was finally being substituted with a sedentary one in a land flowing with milk and honey.

NOTES

1 "When all the kings of the Amorites ... heard" (וַיְהִי כִשְׁמֹעַ כָּל־מַלְכֵי הָאֱמֹרִי, *wayyᵉhî kišmōaᶜ kol malkê hāᵉmōrî*). The use of the preposition *kᵉ*- ("in, with") with infinitive construct in temporal clause indicates urgency. This temporal expression (וַיְהִי כִשְׁמֹעַ, *wayyᵉhî kišmōaᶜ*) appears again at the beginning of chapters 9, 10, and 11 and serves as a transitional phrase between major events of the three chapters. In all of these cases (5:1; 9:1; 10:1; 11:1), the urgency should be translated with "as soon as he/they heard" rather than "when he/they heard ..." (see Waltke and O'Connor, §32.2.b). "*We* had crossed over" (עָבְרֵנוּ) (ᶜōbᵉrānû). Several Hebrew manuscripts adopt the *Qere* עָבְרָם (ᶜobrām), which changes the meaning to "*they* had crossed over."

2 "Circumcise" (מֹל, *mōl*). The Hebrew word not only refers to the physical act of circumcising, but it also appears as a metaphor, in contexts where circumcision refers to the heart (Dt 10:16; 30:6; Jer 4:4).

6 "The land flowing with milk and honey" (אֶרֶץ זָבַת חָלָב וּדְבָשׁ, *ᵉreṣ zābat ḥālāb ûdᵉbāš*, in Ex 3:8, 17; 13:5; 33:3; Lev 20:24; Nu 13:27; 14:8, 16:13, 14; Dt 6:3; Jer 11:5; 32:22; etc.) is described in Deuteronomy 11:11–12 as "a land of mountains and valleys that drinks rain from heaven. It is a land the LORD your God cares for; the eyes of the LORD your God are continually on it from the beginning of the year to its end." Ezekiel 20:6 and 15 describe it as "the most beautiful of all lands."

3. Conquest of Jericho (5:13–6:27)

a. Joshua and the Messenger (5:13–15)

> ¹³Now when Joshua was near Jericho, he looked up and saw a man standing in front of him with a drawn sword in his hand. Joshua went up to him and asked, "Are you for us or for our enemies?"
>
> ¹⁴"Neither," he replied, "but as commander of the army of the LORD I have now come." Then Joshua fell facedown to the ground in reverence, and asked him, "What message does my Lord have for his servant?"
>
> ¹⁵The commander of the LORD's army replied, "Take off your sandals, for the place where you are standing is holy." And Joshua did so.

COMMENTARY

13–14 After celebrating the Passover, Joshua wanders from Gilgal toward the city of Jericho. Suddenly, as he looks up, he sees a man with a drawn sword in his hand standing in front of him. Joshua inquires into his reason for being in the immediate vicinity of Jericho. *Was this man friend, or foe, or something else?* he thinks. The man quickly reveals that he is the "commander of the army of the LORD."

Surprise encounters with supernatural beings who hold drawn swords in their hands and bring messages from God occur in other biblical passages. In Numbers 22, the donkey on which Balaam of Pethor is traveling sees "the angel of the LORD standing in the road, with a drawn sword in his hand" (Nu 22:23). The donkey's immediate reaction is to turn off the road into the field. For this, Balaam beats it. The donkey sees the angel of the Lord a second time and a third time; finally, the animal lays down under Balaam and refuses to move. For this, Balaam beats his donkey two more times with his staff. Finally, Yahweh opens the eyes of Balaam and he sees "the angel of the LORD standing in the road with his sword drawn" (Nu 22:31).

In a later incident, while standing at the threshing floor of Araunah the Jebusite, David looks up and sees "the angel of the LORD standing between heaven and earth, with a drawn sword in his hand" (1Ch 21:16).

In each case, the individual falls down to the ground and receives instructions from the Lord. The response of biblical characters who encounter a messenger of the Lord is not unusual. The cultural gesture of falling down to the ground at the feet of a superior is well known from ancient Near Eastern texts (e.g., Ru 2:10; 2Sa 9:6; Amarna texts, Egyptian art, Assyrian reliefs). For example, several Amarna letters from Rib-Haddi to the king of Egypt (fourteenth century BC) include the following greeting: "I fall at the feet of my lord, my sun, seven times and seven times" (EA 74, 75, 76, 79, 81, etc.).

15 The instructions given to Joshua by the commander of the Lord's army echo the words spoken to Moses by the Lord at the burning bush (Ex 3:5). Both messengers instruct Moses and Joshua to take off their sandals, for the ground on which they stood is holy. When the two leaders remove their sandals, their feet feel the scorching heat of the sand—Moses in the desert of Midian and Joshua in the Jordan Valley. This burning feeling may have symbolized the harshness of the journey they are facing. In both cases, the journey is just beginning. For Moses, it would be forty difficult years in the desert, and for Joshua, it would be a season of warfare in Canaan. "Holy ground" always indicates that Yahweh is present, and that a major event is about to unfold. In this case, Israel is about to conquer Canaan, and Jericho is on the verge of being destroyed.

b. The fall of Jericho (6:1–21)

OVERVIEW

The conquest of the first town, Jericho, follows the crossing of the Jordan (3:1–4:18), the building of the memorial structure (4:8–9), the circumcision of the Israelite males (5:2–9), and the celebration of Passover (5:10–12). Joshua 6 describes the process through which Jericho is conquered. A city wall protected the inhabitants from intruders and foreign armies. The remains of a wall of Jericho with a defensive tower can be seen to this day. This structure dates to the Neolithic period (6800 BC) (A. Mazar, *Archaeology of the Land of the Bible* [ABR; New York: Doubleday, 1990], 331).

Yahweh commands Joshua, the priests, and the fighting men to march around the city. They must do so once each day for six days, and seven times on the seventh day (6:3–9). During the daily procession, the priests blow the shofar while the rest of the men remain silent (6:10). On the seventh day, the plot reaches its climax. The entire convoy circles Jericho seven times (6:15). On the seventh time, the priests blast their shofars, Joshua gives the charge to "Shout!" and the walls of the city collapse before Joshua and his men (6:16–20). The militia enters Jericho, gathers the articles of silver, gold, bronze, and iron for the treasury of the Lord, and destroys every living thing in the city, including men, women, children, cattle, sheep, and donkeys (6:21).

Rahab and her relatives are the only ones delivered from the wrath that befalls the city. By faith, Rahab had negotiated a rescue plan for herself and her entire family (Jos 2; Heb 11:31; Jas 2:25). Once she and her kinfolk are removed from harm's way, the city and everything in it is burned (6:22–25). The chapter ends with a curse pronounced by Joshua over anyone who dares to rebuild the foundations of the city and to set up its gates (6:26).

In this chapter, the reader encounters the difficult concept of "holy war" or "things devoted to Yahweh" (ḥērem) (see discussion in the Introduction—"Warfare and the Devoted Things [ḥērem]"). The concept is connected to the wholesale extermination of people—men, women, children—and animals through military conquest. This kind of genocide is not unique to Israel. As noted in the Introduction, a text from Mari from the eighteenth century BC indicates the spoils of war being placed under a ban (Heb. ḥērem; Akk. asakkum; see Hess, *Joshua*, 43). Similar ideology appears in Egyptian literature from the twelfth century BC and in Moabite and Assyrian texts of the ninth century BC (Hess, *Joshua*, 43).

Through Moses, God had instructed the Israelites to destroy completely (*ḥērem*) all the inhabitants of Canaan — the Hittites, Girgashites, Amorites, Canaanites, Perizzites, Hivites and Jebusites — upon entering the land (Dt 7:1–2). No compromise was allowed. Israel must annihilate the inhabitants of Canaan. As for the inhabitants of cities outside of the Promised Land, Deuteronomy 20 allowed Israel to make an offer of peace to the people of such a city (20:10). If the people consented to negotiate a peace treaty and opened the gates of the city to Israel, its inhabitants were to be conscripted into forced labor (20:11). But if the people refused to surrender peacefully, the Israelites were to attack the city, kill the men, and take everything else — women, children, livestock — as plunder. God permitted Israelite men to take foreign wives from these conquered cities (20:10–14), while Israelites were not to marry foreign women from Canaan, the land of their inheritance (20:16–17). The purpose of the complete destruction (*ḥērem*) in Canaan was to prevent the inhabitants of those cities from teaching Israel to worship foreign gods and, consequently, to sin against Yanweh (20:18).

In summary, Deuteronomy provides one scenario for the treatment of inhabitants of towns in the Promised Land — complete annihilation (*ḥērem*) — and another scenario for the treatment of cities outside of the Promised Land, where peace treaties were permitted. In Jericho, all living things are to be put to death, except for Rahab and her family. Their lives are spared, and thereafter they are allowed to live among the Israelites.

[1]Now Jericho was tightly shut up because of the Israelites. No one went out and no one came in.

[2]Then the LORD said to Joshua, "See, I have delivered Jericho into your hands, along with its king and its fighting men. [3]March around the city once with all the armed men. Do this for six days. [4]Have seven priests carry trumpets of rams' horns in front of the ark. On the seventh day, march around the city seven times, with the priests blowing the trumpets. [5]When you hear them sound a long blast on the trumpets, have all the people give a loud shout; then the wall of the city will collapse and the people will go up, every man straight in."

[6]So Joshua son of Nun called the priests and said to them, "Take up the ark of the covenant of the LORD and have seven priests carry trumpets in front of it." [7]And he ordered the people, "Advance ! March around the city, with the armed guard going ahead of the ark of the LORD."

[8]When Joshua had spoken to the people, the seven priests carrying the seven trumpets before the LORD went forward, blowing their trumpets, and the ark of the LORD's covenant followed them. [9]The armed guard marched ahead of the priests who blew the trumpets, and the rear guard followed the ark. All this time the trumpets were sounding. [10]But Joshua had commanded the people, "Do not give a war cry, do not raise your voices, do not say a word until the day I tell you to shout. Then shout!" [11]So he had the ark of the LORD carried around the city, circling it once. Then the people returned to camp and spent the night there.

¹²Joshua got up early the next morning and the priests took up the ark of the LORD. ¹³The seven priests carrying the seven trumpets went forward, marching before the ark of the LORD and blowing the trumpets. The armed men went ahead of them and the rear guard followed the ark of the LORD, while the trumpets kept sounding. ¹⁴So on the second day they marched around the city once and returned to the camp. They did this for six days.

¹⁵On the seventh day, they got up at daybreak and marched around the city seven times in the same manner, except that on that day they circled the city seven times. ¹⁶The seventh time around, when the priests sounded the trumpet blast, Joshua commanded the people, "Shout! For the LORD has given you the city! ¹⁷The city and all that is in it are to be devoted to the LORD. Only Rahab the prostitute and all who are with her in her house shall be spared, because she hid the spies we sent. ¹⁸But keep away from the devoted things, so that you will not bring about your own destruction by taking any of them. Otherwise you will make the camp of Israel liable to destruction and bring trouble on it. ¹⁹All the silver and gold and the articles of bronze and iron are sacred to the LORD and must go into his treasury."

²⁰When the trumpets sounded, the people shouted, and at the sound of the trumpet, when the people gave a loud shout, the wall collapsed; so every man charged straight in, and they took the city. ²¹They devoted the city to the LORD and destroyed with the sword every living thing in it—men and women, young and old, cattle, sheep and donkeys.

COMMENTARY

1 The mention that Jericho is "tightly shut up" is understandable since the fearful inhabitants of the city have anticipated the arrival of the Israelites. With the recent visit of the spies, the people of Jericho suspect an imminent attack and set in place special measures of security in order to protect the city and its inhabitants. In reality, Jericho is now under siege. As a rule, walled cities opened their gates every day to allow the inhabitants to plow the surrounding fields, to permit foreign merchants to come in for business purposes, and to enable travelers to enter the city. Gates were closed at night for protection against intruders and during the day when the city was under siege or under attack. Walled cities mentioned in biblical texts include Jerusalem (2Ki 18; 25:1–4; Jer 39:4) and Jericho (Jos 6), as well as unnamed cities (Lev 25:29–30; 1Ki 4:13). Archaeologists have also identified walls and gates at other sites, such as Megiddo, Hazor, and Dan.

2 The city of Jericho is the first gift of land given by Yahweh to Israel. The process that follows can be viewed as a ceremonial ritual rather than a military maneuver, especially since the conclusion of the operation is already predetermined by Yahweh. The passage expresses clearly that the upcoming victory is from the Lord and is not attributed to the skill and prowess of the Israelites.

3–7 Joshua receives instructions for the pre-conquest proceedings. The organized procession—

Joshua, his armed men, the seven priests with seven rams' horns, the priests who carry the ark of the covenant, and the rearguard—is to set out marching around Jericho once a day for six days. On the seventh day, the delegates are to walk around the city seven times, with the seven priests blowing the seven shofars. On the seventh time around the city, the priests are to sound a loud blast and the people are to join in with a loud shout. The walls of the city will then collapse before them and provide the opening necessary for them to take over the city. This ritual does not reflect a typical military strategy; rather, it is a divine technique intended to confound the inhabitants of the city.

The number seven is repeated thirteen times in the chapter and is significant throughout the Hebrew Bible, denoting completion. It is often used in reference to periods of seven days (e.g., creation narrative [Ge 1]; Passover [Ex 12–13]; Feast of Tabernacles [Lev 23:34; Eze 6:22]; Moses on Mount Sinai [Ex 24:16]). The number seven is also used for bulls (Nu 23:2), cows (Ge 41:2, 3, 4), rams (1Ch 15:26), lambs (Ge 21:28–30), days (Ge 7:4, 10), months (1Sa 6:1), years (Ge 41:26, 27, 29, 30, 34, 36, 47, 48, 53, 54), altars (Nu 23:1, 4, 14, 29), braids of hair (Jdg 16:13, 19), sons (Ru 4:15; Acts 19:14), daughters (Ex 2:16), times (Lev 4:6, 17), hundreds (Jdg 20:15), thousands (1Ki 19:18), steps (Eze 40:22, 26), lamps (Ex 25:37; Rev 4:5), and so on. In this chapter, there are *seven* days before the conquest of the city, *seven* priests who carry *seven* rams' horns, and a march of *seven* times around the city on the *seventh* day. On a literary note, the verb "to surround" (*sbb*) appears *seven* times in the chapter.

The presence of the ark of the covenant is significant as it represents the presence of Yahweh in the midst of the procession. The ark encircling the city signifies that Yahweh himself is encircling the city. Never before has Israel conquered a walled city. The men do not have the equipment necessary to build battering ramps, dig tunnels, puncture holes through the wall, or climb over it. Only God can bring victory.

8–14 Verses 8–11 describe the activities of the first day of the march. Joshua leads the procession, followed by the armed guards, the priests who blow the trumpets, the ark of the covenant, and finally, the rearguard. The rest of the Israelites remain in the camp nearby and watch the events unfolding from a distance. The sound of the trumpets is heard during the entire march. Nothing else is said. The same activities take place every day for six days (vv.12–14). One is left to wonder what went through the minds of the inhabitants of the city as they watched this daily disturbance. Were they arming for battle, shoring up their residences, hiding their families and valuables in safe places, or plotting a surprise attack on the Israelite camp? Although no word is heard from Jericho, one can easily imagine the increasing tension in a city where demoralized and confused defenders have no control over their ominous circumstances.

15–16 On the seventh day, the Israelites rise up early in the morning, having a full day of military activities ahead of them. The men circle the city seven times while the priests blow the shofars during the entire march. The biblical text does not reveal the distance between the wall of the city and the Israelites encircling it. Evidently, Jericho must be quite small in circumference in order for this task—going around the city seven times—to be completed in one day. The seventh time around the city, Joshua commands the people: "Shout! For the LORD has given you the city!" The shouts of the men join the deafening sound of the shofars, and the walls collapse, allowing the men to charge straight in and plunder the city (v.20).

17–19 Joshua commands the Israelites to destroy all living beings—humans and animals—and to preserve inanimate objects. He orders the men to stay away from the "devoted things" (ḥērem) lest they become "devoted things" themselves and bring about their own destruction (for discussion on "devoted things," see Introduction, "Warfare and the 'Devoted Things' [ḥērem]"). The preservation of inanimate things and the destruction of living beings created in God's image seems paradoxical since Scripture places much more value on human life than on physical things. God determines how things that belong to him, the "devoted things" (in this case, silver, gold, articles of bronze, and iron) are to be treated. In ancient times, the plunder of cities often served to resupply an army with provisions and equipment for the rest of the journey. Therefore, what seems to be inconsistent in taking from the "devoted things" (plunder) of Ai and not of Jericho points to the practicality of carrying just enough for the journey in time of war.

As per the narrator, ḥērem is instituted at Jericho to prevent the Israelites from being contaminated by the belongings of the Canaanites. The consequences for disobeying the orders related to the "ban" were serious, not only for the individual who committed the offense but also for the family of the sinner and for the whole camp of Israel. As we will see in the next chapter, Achan mishandled the "devoted things," and as a result, he and his family were stoned and burned to ashes. After the conquest of Jericho, the "devoted things" were to go into the treasury of the Lord, out of reach of the members of the Israelite community.

20–21 Once the walls of Jericho have collapsed, the Israelites charge into the city and destroy every living being in it. The collapse of the walls of Jericho finds a parallel in a Hittite text of the second millennium BC, in which the goddess Shaushga of Shamuha caused the fortifications of a city to fall down (Hess, *Joshua*, 28; M. Liverani, *Prestige and Interest: International Relations in the Near East ca. 1600–1100 BC* [History of the Ancient Near East/Studies 1; Padova: Sargon, 1990], 155). Scholars have also pointed to parallels between the conquest of Jericho and the Ugaritic stories of King Keret at Udum (Marieke den Braber and Jan-Wim Wesselius, "The Unity of Joshua 1–8, Its Relation to the Story of King Keret, and the Literary Background to the Exodus and Conquest Stories," *SJOT* 22.2 [2008]: 253–74; D. E. Fleming, "The Seven-Day Siege of Jericho in Holy War," in *Ki Baruch Hu: Ancient Near Eastern, Biblical, and Judaic Studies in Honor of Baruch A. Levine* [eds. R. Chazan, W. W. Hallo, and L.H. Schiffman; Winona Lake, Ind.: Eisenbrauns, 1999], 211–28).

NOTES

1 "Tightly shut" (סֹגֶרֶת וּמְסֻגֶּרֶת, *sōgeret ûmᵉsuggeret*). The reduplication of a root often occurs in idiomatic expressions (e.g., Ge 37:6, 9; 41:15; Jdg 7:13; Dan 2:3) and for emphasis in verbal clauses where an infinitive absolute appears before a conjugated verb of the same root (e.g., Ge 2:16; Ex 3:7; 15:1; Lev 20:2, 9, 10, 11, 12). In this passage, the repetition of the root *sgr* emphasizes that the inhabitants of Jericho allowed "no one" to enter or to go out of the city because of the looming threat by the Israelites.

3 "March around the city" (וְסַבֹּתֶם אֶת־הָעִיר, *wᵉsabbōtem ʾet hāʿîr*). The verb סבב (*sbb*, "to surround, go around") is repeated "seven" times in the chapter. This can hardly be coincidental since the number "seven" is highlighted throughout the chapter. A synonym for the verb *sbb* appears in the same chapter (נקף, *nqp*, "to surround"). Both verbs appear in contexts of hostile or military conflicts (e.g., סבב [sbb]—Ge 19:22; Jdg 19:22; נקף [nqp]—2Ki 6:14), in laments (e.g., סבב [sbb]—Pss 17:11; 88:18; נקף [nqp]—Ps 17:9; 22:17), and in sacred processions (e.g., סבב [sbb]—Pss 26:6; 32:7; 48:13; נקף [nqp]—Ps 48:13). Jericho was only a small settlement during this period; thus, surrounding the site did not take much time.

4. The sound of seven trumpets (שׁוֹפָרוֹת, šôpārôt, "rams' horns") would have resounded in the Jordan Valley and confused the inhabitants of Jericho. The sound of multitudes of trumpets was to be heard on the fiftieth year, the year of jubilee (Lev 25:8–11). The blowing of the rams' horns around Jericho may have symbolized a kind of jubilee for Israel.

5 "Have all the people give a loud shout" (יָרִיעוּ כָל־הָעָם תְּרוּעָה גְדוֹלָה, yārî'û kōl-hā'ām tᵉrû'ā gᵉdôlā). In warfare, a loud shout functioned as a tactic of intimidation and a sign of victory. Scripture also refers to a loud shout as a call to battle in war (e.g., Jer 20:16; Am 1:14; 2:2) and a shout of joy (1Sa 4:5–6; Ps 98:6; Zep 3:14).

18 "But [as for *you*,] keep away from the devoted things" (וְרַק־אַתֶּם שִׁמְרוּ מִן־הַחֵרֶם, wᵉraq-ʾattem šimrû min-hahērem). The text reveals forceful language with the use of disjunctive syntax (וְרַק, wᵉraq) and an independent pronoun 2mp "you" ('attem) that precedes the imperative (שִׁמְרוּ, šimrû). The root ḥrm that designates "devoted things" appears five times in two verses (vv. 17–18). For "so that you will not bring about your own destruction," פֶּן־תַּחֲרִימוּ, pen taḥᵃrîmû) the LXX suggests an emendation to "so that you will not covet" (פֶּן־תַּחְמְדוּ, pen taḥmᵉdû) (cf. 7:21).

20 "The people went up toward the city" (וַיַּעַל הָעָם הָעִירָה, wayya'al hā'ām hā'îrā). The men *went up* into the city, implying that they were in a valley or that they had to climb over the crumpled walls in order to get into the city. Otherwise, one would expect the verbs "to come, enter" (בוא, bwʾ), "to go" (הלך, hlk) or "to reach" (נגע, ng').

c. Rahab's Rescue (6:22–27)

²²Joshua said to the two men who had spied out the land, "Go into the prostitute's house and bring her out and all who belong to her, in accordance with your oath to her." ²³So the young men who had done the spying went in and brought out Rahab, her father and mother and brothers and all who belonged to her. They brought out her entire family and put them in a place outside the camp of Israel.

²⁴Then they burned the whole city and everything in it, but they put the silver and gold and the articles of bronze and iron into the treasury of the LORD's house. ²⁵But Joshua spared Rahab the prostitute, with her family and all who belonged to her, because she hid the men Joshua had sent as spies to Jericho — and she lives among the Israelites to this day.

²⁶At that time Joshua pronounced this solemn oath: "Cursed before the LORD is the man who undertakes to rebuild this city, Jericho:

"At the cost of his firstborn son
   will he lay its foundations;
at the cost of his youngest
   will he set up its gates."

²⁷So the LORD was with Joshua, and his fame spread throughout the land.

COMMENTARY

22–23 No one but Rahab and her family are spared the wrath that befalls Jericho. Joshua commands the spies, with whom Rahab had negotiated the rescue, to fulfill their oath to her and to bring her and her kinfolk out of Jericho to safety. The spies know the exact location of her house, and for unspecified reasons, the wall where her house is located did not collapse with the rest of the city walls. No mention is made here of the scarlet thread tied to the window. At first, Rahab and her family are not invited to join the Israelite community but are placed outside the camp, quarantined from the community of Israel. At a later, unspecified time, she and her relatives join the Israelite community and live among them presumably until their death (v.25).

24–25 Once Rahab and her family are rescued, the metal objects are taken for "the treasury of the LORD's house"—the tabernacle—and the city is burned completely. The comment "she lives among the Israelites to this day" may indicate that the account was written while she was still alive.

26 Joshua pronounces a curse over anyone who rebuilds Jericho, with a penalty of the death of the firstborn son for laying its foundation and the slaying of the youngest son for setting up its gates. This curse is fulfilled five centuries later. During the reign of Ahab (8th century BC), Hiel of

Bethel lays the foundations of Jericho at the cost of his firstborn and sets up its gates at the cost of his youngest son (1Ki 16:34).

Although the narrative indicates that the city was destroyed and burned to the ground under Joshua's leadership, there is biblical evidence that Jericho (i.e., "the City of Palms") remained habitable during the time of the Judges (Jdg 3:13–14) and during the period of the united monarchy (2Sa 10:5). It is possible that the comment "they burned the whole city and everything in it" (v.24) is hyperbolic, not intended to represent historical reality. It is also possible that since Jericho was a *ḥērem*—a city devoted to destruction—it was destined to be in ruins, in a poor habitable condition, until Yahweh allowed its rebuilding. The ruin may have served as a memorial of God's judgment on the sins of the Canaanites.

Ancient Near Eastern literature provides numerous examples of curses pronounced on people who modify features of physical structures (e.g., buildings, sarcophagi, monuments). For example, the Azitawadda Phoenician inscription from Karatepe (near modern Adana, Turkey) concludes with a curse similar to that pronounced by Joshua:

> If there be a king among kings and a prince among princes or a man who is (just) called a man who shall wipe out the name of Azitawadda from this gate and put down his

own name, even if he has good intentions toward this city but removes this gate which was made by Azitawadda and makes for the (new) gate a (new) *frame* and puts his name upon it, whether he removes this gate with good intentions or out of hatred and evil, let Ba'l-shamem and El-the-Creator-of-the-Earth and the Eternal-Sun and the whole Group of the Children of the Gods (*El*) wipe out that ruler and that king and that man who is (just) called a man. (*ANET*, 654).

The Phoenician inscription of Kilamuwa, discovered in northwest Syria at the beginning of the twentieth century includes a similar curse:

He who smashes this inscription, may his head be smashed by Ba'l-Samad who belongs to Gabbar, and may his head be smashed by Ba'l-Hamman who belongs to *Bmh*, and by Rakabel, the Lord of the dynasty! (*ANET*, 655).

The Phoenician funerary inscriptions of Ahiram and Eshmunazar offer similar threats for anyone who should open their sarcophagi (*ANET*, 661–62).

27 Once again, Joshua's leadership is confirmed (cf. 1:1–9; 2:9–11; 4:14; 5:1–3). Not only is he revered by all Israel but, as indicated in the texts, "his fame spread throughout the land." This climactic conclusion to the conquest of Jericho loses its energy in the events of the next chapter.

NOTES

26 "Cursed ... is the man who undertakes to rebuild this city" (אָרוּר הָאִישׁ ... יָקוּם וּבָנָה אֶת הָעִיר, *ʾārûr hāʾîš ... yāqûm ûbānā ʾet hāʿîr*). The language echoes Phoenician curses placed on anyone who opens the coffin of a royal or defaces the name of a ruler after his death (e.g., Eshmunazar, http://en.wikipedia.org/wiki/Eshmunazar; and Kilamuwa, http://en.wikipedia.org/wiki/Kilamuwa_Stela, accessed on October 9, 2011).

4. Achan and the "Devoted Things" (7:1–26)

OVERVIEW

In this chapter, Joshua faces the harsh reality that leading a sinful and rebellious people comes at a cost. With the campaign against Jericho completed, Joshua sets his eyes on the next town—Ai (Beth Aven). Because of the absence of archaeological evidence, the existence of Ai has been questioned. Of those who adhere to its historical existence, some locate it at et-Tell (Arabic for "the ruin heap"), approximately five miles east of Bethel. Others point to the site of Khirbet al-Maqatir located one mile east of et-Tell (Hess, *Joshua*, 157–59; Howard, 178–80). According to Bryant Wood,

The location of Joshua's Ai has been a matter of mystery and controversy since the beginnings of archaeological research in Palestine. Most archaeologists locate Joshua's Ai at et-Tell, 6 miles east of our site. At et-Tell there is no indication of occupation at the time of Joshua.... This has led scholars to doubt the historicity of the account of the capture of

Ai, and the Conquest in general.... Topography, fortifications, and pottery finds all suggest that Kh. el-Maqatir is a strong candidate for the Ai of Joshua 7–8. This is an enormously important apologetic project that is critical in defending the historical reliability of the Bible in this age of rampant skepticism. ("The Search for Joshua's Ai: The Excavations at Khirbet el-Maqatir 2012—Is the Bible in error about the city of Ai, recorded in Joshua 7–8"; www.biblearchaeology.org/outreach/ [site visited February 23, 2011])

Without first consulting Yahweh, Joshua sends men to spy the town of Ai. According to their report, this campaign should present no problem since the city is small, with only "a few men in it" (v.3). Following the spies' advice, Joshua sends three thousand men — or three contingents of men — instead of a large delegation, but these are quickly overtaken by the "few men" of Ai. Thirty six Israelites are killed and the rest are thrown into disarray and return to the camp defeated.

Unlike the battle devised and led by Yahweh at Jericho, the conquest of Ai is initiated and led by Joshua. At this point, he is unaware of the disobedience of Achan and unprepared for the devastating consequences when the troops are engaged. Distraught at the loss of men and the overthrow of the battalion, Joshua tears his clothes, falls face down on the ground before the ark of the Lord, and remains there prostrate until evening. Similar rituals of mourning and penitence are known from other biblical passages (e.g., 2Sa 12:15–16 [David]; Job 1:20 [Job]; Joel 1:8–14 [priests]). Joshua cries out to God with a petition that is reminiscent of the Israelites' complaint to Moses when, after leaving Egypt, they bemoaned the harsh realities of living in a barren and parched land (Ex 14:11–12; 16:2–8). "Why?"; "If only ..."; "What then will you do...?"

These are but a few of the concerns Joshua expresses in his attempt to receive a divine explanation for the defeat at Ai. God's answer is swift and to the point: "Stop it! Get up! Israel sinned. Disobedience requires punishment. Find the guilty party! Kill him and his family!" After a parade of tribes, clans, families, and individuals, Achan confesses his sin and discloses the location of the "devoted things" (ḥērem). Along with his family, Achan is stoned and burned to ashes, a treatment strictly reserved for the "devoted things."

Not only had Achan taken of the things devoted for destruction, but he had become a "devoted thing" (ḥērem) himself, like Jericho, through disobedience to Yahweh's instructions. In the account at Jericho, Israel had been warned to "keep away from the devoted things [ḥērem], so that you will not bring about your own destruction [ḥērem] by taking any of them [ḥērem]. *Otherwise you will make the camp of Israel liable to destruction* [ḥērem].... All the silver and gold and the articles of bronze and iron are sacred to the LORD and must go into his treasury" (6:18–19, emphasis added). The message was clear: do not touch the ḥērem lest you become a ḥērem and suffer destruction.

The Achan narrative is a reversal of the Rahab account. Rahab, the ultimate outsider and Canaanite outcast, should have been obliterated along with the inhabitants of Jericho, but she and her relatives are spared and allowed to live among the Israelites. In contrast, Achan receives the consequences reserved for the Canaanites—death for himself and for his family—because he is contaminated by the "devoted things" (ḥērem) he stole and has become a "devoted thing" destined for destruction.

The account at Ai reveals a number of similarities with the earlier aborted invasion of Kadesh Barnea (Dt 1:9–3:11). In both accounts, we find: (1) the sending of spies (Dt 1:22–26; Jos 7:2–3); (2) the interruption of the campaign because of sin in the camp (Dt 1:26–36; Jos 7:11–12); (3) Yahweh's angry reaction (Dt 1:37; Jos 7:1); (4) Yahweh's refusal to accompany his unrepentant people in battle (Dt 1:41–42; Jos 7:12); (5) Israel's defeat and outcries to Yahweh (Dt 1:43–46; Jos 7:5–9); (6) melting hearts (Dt 1:28; Jos 7:5); and (7) guilty parties who confess their sin (Dt 1:41; Jos 7:20).

a. Achan's Sin and Israel's Defeat at Ai (7:1–5)

¹But the Israelites acted unfaithfully in regard to the devoted things; Achan son of Carmi, the son of Zimri, the son of Zerah, of the tribe of Judah, took some of them. So the Lord's anger burned against Israel.

²Now Joshua sent men from Jericho to Ai, which is near Beth Aven to the east of Bethel, and told them, "Go up and spy out the region." So the men went up and spied out Ai.

³When they returned to Joshua, they said, "Not all the people will have to go up against Ai. Send two or three thousand men to take it and do not weary all the people, for only a few men are there." ⁴So about three thousand men went up; but they were routed by the men of Ai, ⁵who killed about thirty-six of them. They chased the Israelites from the city gate as far as the stone quarries and struck them down on the slopes. At this the hearts of the people melted and became like water.

COMMENTARY

1 No sooner have the triumphant celebrations at Jericho ended than a dark cloud descends on the narrative. Achan has disobeyed by taking secretly from the "devoted things" at Jericho. His behavior arouses Yahweh's wrath against *all* Israel. One individual sins, but the entire community is accused of having "acted unfaithfully." Consequently, the entire nation finds itself in a vulnerable position before its enemies.

2–3 Unaware of the offense of Achan, Joshua initiates the next campaign without Yahweh's consent and dispatches a reconnaissance team to spy out the town of Ai, east of Bethel. Their report is positive, and no problem is anticipated since "only a few men are there." Full of confidence, the spies recommend sending only a small contingent of fighting men.

4–5 Joshua sends approximately three thousand fighters — or three bands of men — to Ai instead of a full delegation of soldiers. To their surprise, the "few men" of Ai overcome them, killing thirty-six Israelites and clobbering the rest of the men as they flee for their lives. Defeated by this commanding defense, the wounded fighters return to the camp and face Joshua, who is befuddled by the devastating results of the campaign. Surprised by the defeat, the hearts of the Israelites melt "like water," just as those of their enemies had done before their attack on Jericho (2:11; 5:1).

NOTES

1 "The Israelites acted unfaithfully" (וַיִּמְעֲלוּ בְנֵי־יִשְׂרָאֵל מַעַל, *wayyim'alû b*e*nê yiśrā'ēl ma'al*). The verb describes an act that is counter to one's duty, a "slanderous, calumnious, deceitful" act performed against God, in this case, the misappropriation of the "devoted things" (H. Ringgren, "מעל," *TDOT*, 8:460–63). The verb points to a serious breach of trust between Israel and Yahweh. The repetition of the root reflects a common Semitic linguistic phenomenon where the root appears both in verbal and nominal forms to express one thought or action (e.g., חָלַמְתִּי חֲלוֹם [*ḥālamtî ḥālôm*, "I dreamed a dream"], Ge 37:6, 9; 41:15; Jdg 7:13; Dan 2:3; הֶעֱבַרְתָּ הַעֲבִיר [*hē'ebartā ha'abîr*, "you made us cross the crossing"], Jos 7:7). Achan appears as "Achar" (Αχαρ) in the LXX—a play on words with the "valley of Achor/valley of trouble," where Achan and his family are killed and burned because of the "trouble" caused by Achan/Achor (vv.25–26).

4 In the expression "about three thousand men" (כִּשְׁלֹשֶׁת אֲלָפִים אִישׁ, *kišlōšet 'alāpîm 'îš*), the Hebrew word for "thousands" (אֲלָפִים, *'alāpîm*) does not always represent a literal thousand. The word is "understood either as a precise or round number. But it can also describe a social grouping that is smaller than the tribe but larger than the 'father's house' (*bêt 'ab*). It thus appears to be broadly equivalent to the extended family (*mišpāḥā*)" (P. P. Jenson, "אֶלֶף (*'elep* II)" *NIDOTTE*, 1:416–18). For further discussion on the word "thousand" and other large numbers, see Woudstra, 137; Howard, 189, n. 76; Butler, 84.

b. Joshua's Intercession and the "Devoted Things" (7:6–15)

⁶Then Joshua tore his clothes and fell facedown to the ground before the ark of the Lord, remaining there till evening. The elders of Israel did the same, and sprinkled dust on their heads. ⁷And Joshua said, "Ah, Sovereign Lord, why did you ever bring this people across the Jordan to deliver us into the hands of the Amorites to destroy us? If only we had been content to stay on the other side of the Jordan! ⁸O Lord, what can I say, now that Israel has been routed by its enemies? ⁹The Canaanites and the other people of the country will hear about this and they will surround us and wipe out our name from the earth. What then will you do for your own great name?"

¹⁰The Lord said to Joshua, "Stand up! What are you doing down on your face? ¹¹Israel has sinned; they have violated my covenant, which I commanded them to keep. They have taken some of the devoted things; they have stolen, they have lied, they have put them with their own possessions. ¹²That is why the Israelites cannot stand against their enemies; they turn their backs and run because they have been made liable to destruction. I will not be with you anymore unless you destroy whatever among you is devoted to destruction.

> ¹³"Go, consecrate the people. Tell them, 'Consecrate yourselves in preparation for tomorrow; for this is what the LORD, the God of Israel, says: That which is devoted is among you, O Israel. You cannot stand against your enemies until you remove it.
>
> ¹⁴"'In the morning, present yourselves tribe by tribe. The tribe that the LORD takes shall come forward clan by clan; the clan that the LORD takes shall come forward family by family; and the family that the LORD takes shall come forward man by man. ¹⁵He who is caught with the devoted things shall be destroyed by fire, along with all that belongs to him. He has violated the covenant of the LORD and has done a disgraceful thing in Israel!'"

COMMENTARY

6 Joshua's role quickly changes from leader to intercessor. He tears his clothing and throws himself to the ground before the ark of the covenant, remaining prostrate until evening. The elders join him, sprinkling dust on their heads as a sign of mourning. These gestures are normally associated with sorrow over death or grief over devastating circumstances (Ge 37:33–34; Job 2:11–13; La 2:10–11).

7–9 Joshua's response is reminiscent of the reaction of Moses and the Israelites at Kadesh Barnea, after the spies had returned from Canaan with a negative report (Nu 14:1–5). Echoing the complaint of the Israelites in the desert, Joshua questions Yahweh's plan and expresses regret for crossing the Jordan (Nu 14:1–5; 20:2–6; 21:4–5). Joshua desperately addresses Yahweh with three questions: "Why did *you* ever bring this people across the Jordan ...?"; "What can I say now ...?"; "What then will *you* do for your own great name?" (emphasis added). Imitating Moses the intercessor, Joshua falls face down on the ground in despair over the tragic situation and laments to Yahweh regarding his plight as the leader of a vanquished people (Nu 11:1–2; 21:7). Joshua blames Yahweh for leading them across the Jordan and for giving them into the hands of the Amorites. Afraid of a Canaanite offensive, Joshua dramatizes before Yahweh the threat that Israel will become the laughingstock of the surrounding nations and that Yahweh's great name will be wiped out from the earth and thus he will lose his good reputation. At this point, Joshua is still unaware of the reason for the defeat.

10–12 Unimpressed by Joshua's display of emotions, Yahweh snaps swiftly with a firm statement, "Get up! What are you doing down on your face?" He follows up with a list of accusations against Israel. God's people have sinned *and even* (w^egam) violated the covenant *and even* (w^egam) taken of the devoted things *and even* (w^egam) stolen *and even* (w^egam) deceived and *and even* (w^egam) hid the devoted objects. The reason for the defeat at Ai is clear. There is sin in the camp. The guilty party has transgressed the covenant of the Lord and has brought disgrace on all Israel (v.15). Yahweh will not stand with Israel in battle when Israel *has become* the very thing it stole—a "devoted thing" destined for destruction.

Israel had witnessed a few years earlier Yahweh's abandonment of his people in the desert. Because of rebellion and disobedience, an entire generation perished and was prevented from receiving the promise of a homeland (Nu 14:26–35). Was this generation going to be rejected also? The threat is ominous. It could only be rescinded if the devoted things — including those who had become "devoted things" — were destroyed from the midst of the community.

13–15 Now comes the task of exposing the culprit and removing the "devoted things" from the camp. The first phase of the operation demands the consecration of Israel. The second phase requires that Israel present herself before Yahweh, first by tribe, then by clan, then by family, and finally by individual. Once identified, the guilty one — the contaminant — and all that belongs to him are to be destroyed by fire and removed from the community. Only then can the conquest of the land continue successfully. No detail is given as to the specific dynamics involved in the selection process, but one thing is known from the repeated use of the verb *lqd*. The snatching of the tribe, clan, family, and individual by Yahweh resembles more a swift capture (*lqd*) — the term used for the capture of a city — than a relaxed selection process.

NOTES

7 "Ah, Sovereign Lord" (אֲהָהּ אֲדֹנָי יְהוִה, *ʾăhāh ʾădōnāy yhwh*). The author uses language of petition common in prophetic literature, normally used by an individual who addresses God or his messenger (Jer 1:6; 4:10; 14:13; 32:17; Ez 4:14; 9:8; 11:13; 21:5) (E. Jenni, *TLOT*, 1:54–55).

8 The phrase "O Lord" (בִּי אֲדֹנָי, *bî ʾădōnāy*) reflects language of petition typically used by an inferior in addressing a superior (Ge 43:20; 44:18; Ex 4:10, 13; Nu 12:11; Jdg 6:13, 15; 1Sa 1:26; 1Ki 3:17, 26). The phrase is omitted from LXX.

"Israel has been routed by its enemies" (הָפַךְ יִשְׂרָאֵל עֹרֶף לִפְנֵי אֹיְבָיו, *hāpak yiśrāʾēl ʿōrep lipnê ʾōyᵉbāyw*) can be translated literally, "Israel has turned her back before her enemies." Turning one's back and running away from an enemy shows weakness and vulnerability. The root *hpk* appears in numerous idiomatic expressions such as "changing direction" (with "hand," 1Ki 22:34), "conversion" (with "heart," Ex 14:5), "perversions" (e.g., Dt 32:20), etc. (K. Seybold, "הפך," *TDOT*, 3:423–27).

10 The command "Stand up!" (קֻם לָךְ, *qum lāk*) is a hendiadys (see Note on 1:2).

11 The Hebrew text uses five occurrences of the marker of emphasis *wᵉgam* ("and even," וְגַם). The word *gam* ("even") functions primarily as an emphatic particle that signals the "climax in an exposition" (Waltke and O'Connor, §39.3.4d). The NIV does not account for these literary markers in the translation; consequently, it misses the forceful and climactic nature of the verses.

13 "Go, consecrate!" (קֻם קַדֵּשׁ, *qum qaddēš*). As mentioned in the Note for 1:2, the verb "to arise" (קוּם, *qûm*) often takes an inceptive meaning, pointing to the beginning of an event; thus, "*get busy* consecrating the people."

c. Achan Punished for His Sin (7:16–26)

¹⁶Early the next morning Joshua had Israel come forward by tribes, and Judah was taken. ¹⁷The clans of Judah came forward, and he took the Zerahites. He had the clan of the Zerahites come forward by families, and Zimri was taken. ¹⁸Joshua had his family come forward man by man, and Achan son of Carmi, the son of Zimri, the son of Zerah, of the tribe of Judah, was taken.

¹⁹Then Joshua said to Achan, "My son, give glory to the LORD, the God of Israel, and give him the praise. Tell me what you have done; do not hide it from me."

²⁰Achan replied, "It is true! I have sinned against the LORD, the God of Israel. This is what I have done: ²¹When I saw in the plunder a beautiful robe from Babylonia, two hundred shekels of silver and a wedge of gold weighing fifty shekels, I coveted them and took them. They are hidden in the ground inside my tent, with the silver underneath."

²²So Joshua sent messengers, and they ran to the tent, and there it was, hidden in his tent, with the silver underneath. ²³They took the things from the tent, brought them to Joshua and all the Israelites and spread them out before the LORD.

²⁴Then Joshua, together with all Israel, took Achan son of Zerah, the silver, the robe, the gold wedge, his sons and daughters, his cattle, donkeys and sheep, his tent and all that he had, to the Valley of Achor. ²⁵Joshua said, "Why have you brought this trouble on us? The LORD will bring trouble on you today."

Then all Israel stoned him, and after they had stoned the rest, they burned them. ²⁶Over Achan they heaped up a large pile of rocks, which remains to this day. Then the LORD turned from his fierce anger. Therefore that place has been called the Valley of Achor ever since.

COMMENTARY

16–18 With a heightened sense of anxiety looming over those who assemble before Yahweh, those left unselected breathe a sigh of relief. Of the tribe of Judah, the Zerahites are chosen. Of the clan of Zerah, the family of Zimri is taken; finally, Achan son of Carmi is identified and is left standing alone—vulnerable, shaking, and humiliated before Yahweh, Joshua, and the whole community. The guilty one has been publicly singled out.

19 Joshua calls Achan "my son," an expression used by a superior to address a subordinate (1Sa 3:16; 4:16; 24:16). With a tone of brokenness and compassion in his voice (nā᾽, "please"), Joshua calls for a confession. He says to Achan, "Give glory to the LORD.... Tell me what you have done. Do not hide it from me." Only Joshua knows that the guilty and his family will be burned with fire. His heart must have been racing and aching intensely at the thought that Yahweh's wrath will be poured out on this man and his family. At this point, Achan is still unaware of the grave consequences that await him.

20–21 Confronted with the severity of his offense, Achan confesses and discloses the location of the "devoted things." One can only speculate that, had Achan not been caught, he may not have confessed and Israel may have continued to be defeated in battle. Achan's silence during the procession of tribes, clans, families, and individuals points to his hope of avoiding detection and to his continued desire to keep the looted objects.

The objects of temptation include fine textiles from Babylon, silver, and gold. Such items appear in ancient Near Eastern inventory lists of the fourteenth and thirteenth centuries BC at Emar, Ugarit, and Alalakh (Hess, *Joshua*, 152). The verb "to covet" appears in the tenth commandment of the Decalogue—"You shall not covet.... You shall not set your desire on ..." (Ex 20:17; Dt 5:21). Like Eve in the garden, Achan fell for what he *saw* because it looked *good*, an offense that called for the death penalty in both cases.

22–23 The stolen items are found exactly where Achan has hidden them—in the ground inside his tent, with the silver underneath. The messengers spread them out at the feet of Joshua, the Israelites, and Yahweh. What belonged to Yahweh is finally returned to its rightful place. One can only imagine the quivering body of Achan, standing there horrified at the impending verdict.

Achan's deception was clearly premeditated. He has chosen a safe location for the stolen plunder—so he thought—and executed his plan in secret. God saw Achan's scheming heart; he watched him hide what belonged to him. Achan could not conceal his sin forever.

24–26 The gavel falls and the verdict is read: death by stoning and fire. Joshua gathers Achan (LXX, "Achor"), his sons, his daughters, his oxen, his donkeys, his sheep, his tent, and all his belongings, along with the devoted things before all Israel. Before the execution, Joshua addresses Achan:"Why have you brought this trouble on us? [ʿakartānû]. The LORD will bring trouble on you [yaʿkᵒrᵉkā] this day." All Israel participates in the execution of the sentence. Every hint of devoted thing is destroyed by fire, along with those who brought trouble to Israel. The wordplay emphasizes the *trouble* (ʿkr) brought on the nation by a *troublemaker* (ʿkr) who receives mortal *trouble* (ʿkr) as a punishment for his crime. Stoning and burning had been used earlier to destroy Jericho, leaving only piles of rubble in the place of judgment. Once restored to its pre-Achan state of innocence, Israel can proceed forward with the conquest of the land.

NOTES

19 "My son, I implore you" (בְּנִי שִׂים־נָא, *bᵉnî śîm-nāʾ*). Joshua addresses the offender in a surprisingly polite fashion, considering the offense he has committed and the impending consequences to be inflicted on Achan and his family. The precative particle *nāʾ* (נָא) typically softens the tone of a discourse (Dallaire, 77).

21 The items taken by Achan reflect a second millennium list of precious items. In biblical literature, the term *šinʿār* (שִׁנְעָר) refers to Babylon (e.g., Ge 10:10; 11:2; 14:1, 9; Dan 1:2; Zec 5:11). In cuneiform texts, the term is found only during the second millennium. The expression "a wedge [tongue] of gold weighing fifty shekels" finds a parallel in second millennium ancient Near Eastern literature. An Amarna letter from King Tushratta of Mitanni to Pharaoh Amenhotep IV includes a list of gifts that mentions "a wedge ['tongue'] of gold weighing one thousand shekels" (EA 27 ln. 61, EA 29 lns 34 and 39; see Hess, *Joshua*, 152, n.1).

21 "I coveted [desired, craved] them" (וָאֶחְמְדֵם, wāʾehmᵉdēm). The verb "to covet" (חמד, ḥmd) indicates that an individual finds something or someone "desirable or precious on account of its form or splendor.... This act begins with the visual impression made by the desired object or person" (G. Wallis, "חמד," *TDOT*, 4:453–54). The act of coveting is offensive to Yahweh and strictly prohibited by Mosaic law (Ex 20:17; Dt 5:21).

24–26 "Trouble" (עָכוֹר, ʿākôr). This word (verb and noun) is repeated several times in these verses. In 1Ch 2:7, Achan's name is Achor, "who brought trouble on Israel by violating the ban on taking devoted things." Both Achor and Yahweh appear as subjects of the verb "to trouble"; both bring "trouble" on the community. Achor *troubles* the community by committing sin and disrupting its progress; Yahweh *troubles* the community by dealing with the sin and restoring the community.

REFLECTION

First, had Joshua consulted God before attempting to conquer Ai, the thirty-six men killed in battle may have lived long and fruitful lives. An unfortunate and pointless tragedy resulted in devastated families, young widows, and children without fathers. Yahweh witnessed silently the unfolding of the disaster, waiting patiently for Joshua to turn to him for guidance. It never happened. Joshua's eyes remained on the horizon, looking toward the next target—Ai.

Astounded by the defeat and the loss of men, Joshua staggers to the ark, falls on the ground, and finally lifts his eyes to the one who could have prevented the catastrophe—Yahweh. O how costly it is when God's people forget to consult God for important decisions, when they walk in their own strength, and when they become self-sufficient. The psalmist said it well, "With your help I can advance against a troop; with my God I can scale a wall" (Ps 18:29[30]), and "some trust in chariots and some in horses, but we trust in the name of the LORD our God (Ps 20:7[8]). The battles of life cannot be fought without God. He is our counselor (Ps 73:24; Isa 9:6), our warrior (Ex 14:14; 15:3), and our guide forever (Pss 31:3[4]; 48:14[15]; Isa 58:11; Jn 16:13).

Second, crime never pays. It pollutes both the perpetrator and the community. Our sins rarely remain private and harmless. They impact our hearts, our minds, and our behavior, and consequently, they affect our relationships—with God and with people. In the case of Achan, sin in the tent of one meant sin in the tent of all. Thus, Yahweh rose up in anger against the whole community, not just against the perpetrator. Human tendency is to lie about sin, to cover it, and to hope no one ever finds out. Divine tendency, by contrast, is to call to repentance, reveal sin, and restore the repentant. Achan had lied to himself (and maybe to others) and plotted evil in his heart, hoping that no one would find out what he had done. The psalmist speaks of the consequences of such behavior:

¹An oracle is within my heart
concerning the sinfulness of the wicked:
There is no fear of God
before his eyes.
²For in his own eyes he flatters himself
too much to detect or hate his sin.
³The words of his mouth are wicked and deceitful;
he has ceased to be wise and to do good.
⁴Even on his bed he plots evil;

he commits himself to a sinful course
and does not reject what is wrong....
¹²See how the evildoers lie fallen —
thrown down, not able to rise! (Ps 36:1b–4,
12[1b–5, 13])

Achan showed ignorance of an important truth, namely, that "the secret things belong to the LORD" (Dt 29:29). The prophet Jeremiah testifies, "Can anyone hide in secret places so that I cannot see him?... Do I not fill heaven and earth?" (Jer 23:24). As stated by the author of Hebrews, "nothing in all creation is hidden from God's sight. Everything is uncovered and laid bare before the eyes of him to whom we give account" (Heb 4:13). Achan's sinful behavior causes the annihilation of his entire family. This sad event certainly brought grief and sorrow to colleagues and comrades and created confusion in children who did not understand the loss of their friends.

5. Conquest of Ai (8:1–29)

a. The Ambush (8:1–17)

¹Then the LORD said to Joshua, "Do not be afraid; do not be discouraged. Take the whole army with you, and go up and attack Ai. For I have delivered into your hands the king of Ai, his people, his city and his land. ²You shall do to Ai and its king as you did to Jericho and its king, except that you may carry off their plunder and livestock for yourselves. Set an ambush behind the city."

³So Joshua and the whole army moved out to attack Ai. He chose thirty thousand of his best fighting men and sent them out at night ⁴with these orders: "Listen carefully. You are to set an ambush behind the city. Don't go very far from it. All of you be on the alert. ⁵I and all those with me will advance on the city, and when the men come out against us, as they did before, we will flee from them. ⁶They will pursue us until we have lured them away from the city, for they will say, 'They are running away from us as they did before.' So when we flee from them, ⁷you are to rise up from ambush and take the city. The LORD your God will give it into your hand. ⁸When you have taken the city, set it on fire. Do what the LORD has commanded. See to it; you have my orders."

⁹Then Joshua sent them off, and they went to the place of ambush and lay in wait between Bethel and Ai, to the west of Ai — but Joshua spent that night with the people.

¹⁰Early the next morning Joshua mustered his men, and he and the leaders of Israel marched before them to Ai. ¹¹The entire force that was with him marched up and approached the city and arrived in front of it. They set up camp north of Ai, with the valley between them and the city. ¹²Joshua had taken about five thousand men and set them in ambush between Bethel and Ai, to the west of the city. ¹³They had the soldiers take up their positions — all those in the camp to the north of the city and the ambush to the west of it. That night Joshua went into the valley.

¹⁴When the king of Ai saw this, he and all the men of the city hurried out early in the morning to meet Israel in battle at a certain place overlooking the Arabah. But he did not know that an ambush had been set against him behind the city. ¹⁵Joshua and all Israel let themselves be driven back before them, and they fled toward the desert. ¹⁶All the men of Ai were called to pursue them, and they pursued Joshua and were lured away from the city. ¹⁷Not a man remained in Ai or Bethel who did not go after Israel. They left the city open and went in pursuit of Israel.

COMMENTARY

1–2 Immediatly after the execution of Achan and his family, Yahweh takes charge of the situation. He instructs Joshua to prepare for the military offensive against Ai. There is no time for grief or sorrow over the recent loss of life. The *ḥērem* has been purged from the midst of the community; consequently, Israel is free to continue her journey with confidence. Yahweh instructs Joshua, "Do not be afraid; do not be discouraged," for the time has come to reorganize and continue the mission.

Contrary to the spies' counsel in the previous chapter (7:3), Yahweh tells Joshua to take "the whole army" with him. During the first attempt at Ai, the spies had recommended sending only three to five thousand men for the battle (or three to five units) because the men of Ai "were few" (7:3). According to Yahweh's directive, all warriors are summoned to enlist for the battle. The prebattle decree, "I have delivered into your hands [the king of Ai]" (8:1), appears throughout Scripture, especially in contexts where Israel conquers new territory (Dt 3:3; 20:13; 21:10; Jos 2:24; 6:2; Jdg 1:2; 2:14; 13:1; 20:28; 2Ki 3:18). The decree guarantees victory, but only if Israel obeys Yahweh's instructions.

Surprisingly, Yahweh allows Israel to carry off the plunder and the livestock from Ai. In Jericho, everything — human, animal, object, structure — was destroyed by fire (except for the consecrated articles of silver, gold, bronze, and iron, which were placed into the treasury of the Lord's house [6:24]). The treatment of booty is determined by Yahweh, and the rationale for his decision is not always stated in the text. The practice of taking plunder was not a novel idea for Israel. Before entering Canaan, Israel had burned cities and taken plunder from towns controlled by Sihon king of Heshbon and Og king of Bashan (Dt 2:34–35; 3:6–7).

3–8 Joshua instructs thirty thousand men (or thirty units) to prepare a surprise attack on the city and to set up an ambush between Bethel and Ai. The use of ambush in military warfare is not unique to Israel. It appears in several ancient Near Eastern texts (e.g., Egyptian Papyrus Anastasi I; Annals of Ashurnasirpal; see Hess, *Joshua*, 160). It is unlikely that *thirty thousand* men chosen by Joshua would have tried to hide west of the city since the city was probably small in circumference. Such a large number of fighting men would have been easily noticed by the people of Ai. The number

910

of fighting men seems inordinately exaggerated since the inhabitants of Ai numbered only twelve thousand, including the men, women and children (v.25). With Hess, we estimate that the five thousand men (or five military units) mentioned in verse 12 probably form the ambush while the thirty thousand (or thirty military units) join Joshua in the camp for the night (Hess, *Joshua*, 162).

Joshua's plan of luring the people of Ai away from the town gives the men in the ambush the opportunity to attack the city from behind and to set it on fire quickly. The strategy devised by Joshua—under Yahweh's leadership—is similar to that found in Judges 20:29–38, where the Israelites set up an ambush against Gibeah (20:29–30), entice the men away from the city, provoke them to engage in battle (20:31–36), and finally, burn the city behind them (20:37–38). At Ai, the response is predictable. Joshua anticipates that the men of Ai will replicate the defensive strategy used during the first attack. They will undoubtedly pursue Israel down the slope and leave the gates of the city unprotected, vulnerable to the attack of intruders. Before the men leave to set up the ambush, Joshua instructs them to "listen carefully," to "be on the alert" and to "see to it" that the plan is successfully implemented. This time, there is no room for error!

9 The five thousand men (or five military units) hide between Bethel and Ai, west of Ai, while Joshua and his men return to the camp to spend the night with the rest of the Israelites. The men who set up the ambush spend the night in the vicinity where Abram had built an altar to Yahweh centuries earlier (Ge 12:8). This is probably the region that Abram's father, Terah, had wished to make his home (11:31). Terah left Ur of the Chaldees, with Canaan in mind, long before Abram received

his call (12:1–3). Terah never saw the fulfillment of his dream. He took his family as far as Haran and settled there until his death. Perhaps this brief historical note (11:31) indicates that the region of Canaan was chosen by God as the place where his people would dwell long before Yahweh promised to give it to them (Ex 3:8; Lev 20:24; Dt 6:3).

10–13 Early in the morning, Joshua leads the march and sets up camp across the valley from Ai. The men take their positions—the ambush west of Ai and the rest of the men north of the city—and await the command of their leader. The events are reminiscent of the early morning marches of Joshua and the priests around Jericho on the first and seventh days of the siege of the city (6:12). The events outside of Ai unfold in a similar orderly fashion under the instructions of their military leader.

14 As soon as the king of Ai sees Joshua and his army, he and his men hurry (*way^{e}mah^{a}rû*) out of the city and run to meet Israel in battle, eastward, in the direction of the Arabah—the Jordan Valley. Unaware that men lie in wait on the west side of the city, the king and his men exit the city confidently, expecting to defeat the army of Israel as easily as they had done during the first attack.

15–17 Joshua and his men lure away the men of Ai and Bethel, "eastward into the desert" (*derek hammidbār*) in the direction of the Jordan. Completely fooled by the ruse of the Israelites, the king of Ai and his men abandon the city, leaving it vulnerable to an attack from the west. It is not surprising that the men of Bethel join in the offensive against Israel because Bethel was probably the next town to be victimized by the new intruders. It is also possible that Ai was a small outpost for the larger city of Bethel, and consequently, Bethel valued Ai's military strength during conflicts.

NOTES

1 The expression "Do not be afraid; do not be discouraged" (אַל־תִּירָא וְאַל־תֵּחָת, ʾal-tîrāʾ weʾal-tēḥāt) appear also in 10:8 and 11:6. For the verb יר׳ (yrʾ, "to fear"), see H. F. Fuhs, *TDOT*, "יר׳," 6:304−5; for the verb חתת (ḥtt, "to be discouraged") see F. Maass, *TDOT*, "חתת," 5:280−81. For the combination of these two verbs, see Dt 1:21; 31:8; 1Sa 17:11; 1Ch 22:13; 28:20; 2Ch 20:15, 17; 32:7; Jer 23:4; 26:47. Other similar doublets include "be strong and courageous" (חֲזַק וֶאֱמָץ, hªzaq weʾeªmāṣ) in 1:6, 7, 9, 18; 10:25.

b. The Attack (8:18−23)

> ¹⁸Then the Lord said to Joshua, "Hold out toward Ai the javelin that is in your hand, for into your hand I will deliver the city." So Joshua held out his javelin toward Ai. ¹⁹As soon as he did this, the men in the ambush rose quickly from their position and rushed forward. They entered the city and captured it and quickly set it on fire.
>
> ²⁰The men of Ai looked back and saw the smoke of the city rising against the sky, but they had no chance to escape in any direction, for the Israelites who had been fleeing toward the desert had turned back against their pursuers. ²¹For when Joshua and all Israel saw that the ambush had taken the city and that smoke was going up from the city, they turned around and attacked the men of Ai. ²²The men of the ambush also came out of the city against them, so that they were caught in the middle, with Israelites on both sides. Israel cut them down, leaving them neither survivors nor fugitives. ²³But they took the king of Ai alive and brought him to Joshua.

COMMENTARY

18−23 So far, no mention has been made of the weapon (*kîdôn*, "javelin") held by Joshua (cf. Ex 14:16, *maṭṭeh*, "staff" of Moses). Yahweh instructs Joshua to raise the weapon that is "in your hand," for "into your hand" Yahweh is going to deliver the city. The repetition of the idiom is certainly intentional. The javelin in Joshua's hand is not the instrument of victory; rather, it is Yahweh's hand that brings the victory. As soon as Joshua turns toward Ai and raises his weapon, the men set to ambush the city come out of hiding, swarm the city, capture it, and quickly set it on fire. The language of the text highlights a fast-moving sequence of events: "the men of the city hurried out [*wayeªmahªrû*]" (14); "they fled [*wayyānusû*]" (v.15); "they pursued [*wayyirdepû*]" (vv.16; cf. 17); "the men ... rose quickly [*qām meḥērā*]" (v.19); "[they] rushed [*wayyārûṣû*]" (v.19); "they entered" [*wayyābôʾû*] (v.19); "they captured it" [*wayyilkedûhā*] (v.19); "[they] quickly [*wayeªmahªrû*] set it on fire" (v.19).

Unprepared for such a scenario, the king of Ai and his men are stunned and trapped, uncomfortably squeezed between Joshua's men on the east and the ambush that is now approaching from the west. Surrounded by Israel's forces, the Aiites scramble and stagger in shock, unable to defend themselves. The Israelites annihilate the men of Ai and Bethel and capture the king of Ai alive. The hearts of the men of Ai must have melted in fear and sorrow (cf. 2:9–11; 5:1; 7:5) as they watched their city burn and imagined their wives and children attacked mercilessly, put to the sword, and burned alive. What was meant to be a simple victory for them turns into a terrible tragedy.

In Judges 20, the Israelites use a similar tactic to defeat the Benjaminites at Gibeah. While some of the Israelites ambush Gibeah, others lure the Benjaminites outside of the city. As the men of Gibeah pursue the Israelites, the men in the ambush make a sudden dash into Gibeah, kill everyone with swords, and set the city on fire. When the Benjaminites see the smoke rising from the city, they cease chasing the Israelites, who turn toward them and try to entrap them. The Benjaminites flee "eastward into the desert" (*derek hammidbār*, 20:42, 45, 47; cf. Jos 8:15) and are defeated.

NOTES

18 "Javelin" (כִּידוֹן, *kîdôn*). This weapon, understood by some as "a short curved sword," is the same type of instruments found strapped on Goliath's back when he encountered David (1Sa 17:6, 45). This word occurs only eight times in the Hebrew Bible. Other Hebrew words for "sword," "javelin," "spear," and "lance" include *laḥaṭ* (לַחַט), *ḥereb* (חֶרֶב), *rōmaḥ* (רֹמַח) and *ḥᵃnît* (חֲנִית) (see G. Molin, "What is a *Kidon?*" *JSS* 1 [1956]: 334–37; also *HALOT*, "כִּידוֹן," 472).

c. The Victory (8:24–29)

> ²⁴When Israel had finished killing all the men of Ai in the fields and in the desert where they had chased them, and when every one of them had been put to the sword, all the Israelites returned to Ai and killed those who were in it. ²⁵Twelve thousand men and women fell that day — all the people of Ai. ²⁶For Joshua did not draw back the hand that held out his javelin until he had destroyed all who lived in Ai. ²⁷But Israel did carry off for themselves the livestock and plunder of this city, as the LORD had instructed Joshua.
>
> ²⁸So Joshua burned Ai and made it a permanent heap of ruins, a desolate place to this day. ²⁹He hung the king of Ai on a tree and left him there until evening. At sunset, Joshua ordered them to take his body from the tree and throw it down at the entrance of the city gate. And they raised a large pile of rocks over it, which remains to this day.

COMMENTARY

24–25 The entire population of Ai—twelve thousand—is annihilated. Israel kills all who are both inside and outside the city—men, women, and children. As noted earlier, the Israelites carry off the plunder and livestock from Ai for their own use and enjoyment (8:2).

26–27 Reminiscent of Moses' upraised arms during the battle against the Amalekites (Ex 17:10–13), Joshua keeps his arm outstretched during the entire conquest of Ai. During the battle against the Amalekites, Moses kept his arms raised high, holding "the staff of God" in his hand until the enemy was overcome. When his arms grew tired, his aides brought a stone on which Moses sat. They then held his arms up—one aide on each side of him—until the Amalekites were defeated at sunset (Ex 17:8–16). In a similar manner, Joshua holds the javelin (*kîdôn*) up in the air from the beginning to the end of the battle, until Ai and its inhabitants are completely destroyed—treated as devoted things (*ḥērem*). The "staff of God" (*maṭṭeh haᵉlōhîm*) and the "javelin" (*kîdôn*) were not instruments of warfare. Rather, they were symbols of the presence of God in the midst of the battles.

28–29 Ai and its king receive the same treatment as Jericho and its king—total annihilation. The king of Ai, who was taken alive, is hung on a tree and left there to die. At sunset, Joshua orders his men to take down the body (cf. Dt 21:22–23) and to throw it down at the gate of the city, where a large pile of rocks is placed over it (cf. 7:26). The heap of stones serves as a memorial of the victory at Ai "to this day."

Ancient Near Eastern methods of warfare often included hanging bodies in public places—near gates and walls of cities (e.g., Jos 10:26; 2Sa 31:11–12; Est 7:10; Assyrian relief of Lachish). This cruel treatment served to intimidate the adversary. The Assyrian king Sennacherib hung the bodies of the governors of Ekron on poles around the city (Annals of Sennacherib, Third Campaign, Col. III.8–10; Younger, 223). Egyptian pharaohs also practiced this method of warfare. In one of his military campaign annals, Merneptah states: "They [the Lybians] are cast to the ground by hundred-thousands and ten-thousands, the remainder being impaled [put to the stake] on the South of Memphis" (*KRI* IV, 34/13–14; Younger, 317, n.88).

6. Renewal of the Covenant at Mt. Ebal (8:30–35)

OVERVIEW

After a strategic military advance on Ai and the conquest of the city, the Israelites renew the covenant at Mount Ebal. Joshua reads all the words of the covenant and formally reminds the people of the blessings and the curse of the Mosaic covenant, exactly as they were recorded in "the Book of the Law" (8:34–35). In the manuscript tradition, this pericope appears in different locations. In the Joshua text from Qumran, this incident appears at the beginning of chapter 5, between the statements regarding the terrified Amorite kings (5:1) and the ritual of circumcision (5:2–9). In the LXX, verses 30–35 appear after 9:2. This portion has been called the "floating pericope" (Nelson, 116);

consequently, some scholars have viewed it as a fictional addition inserted into the text of Joshua much later. Nonetheless, the theme of this "floating pericope" blends in perfectly with the overarching topics of covenant, obedience, and commitment to Yahweh.

---

³⁰Then Joshua built on Mount Ebal an altar to the Lord, the God of Israel, ³¹as Moses the servant of the Lord had commanded the Israelites. He built it according to what is written in the Book of the Law of Moses—an altar of uncut stones, on which no iron tool had been used. On it they offered to the Lord burnt offerings and sacrificed fellowship offerings. ³²There, in the presence of the Israelites, Joshua copied on stones the law of Moses, which he had written. ³³All Israel, aliens and citizens alike, with their elders, officials and judges, were standing on both sides of the ark of the covenant of the Lord, facing those who carried it—the priests, who were Levites. Half of the people stood in front of Mount Gerizim and half of them in front of Mount Ebal, as Moses the servant of the Lord had formerly commanded when he gave instructions to bless the people of Israel.

³⁴Afterward, Joshua read all the words of the law—the blessings and the curses—just as it is written in the Book of the Law. ³⁵There was not a word of all that Moses had commanded that Joshua did not read to the whole assembly of Israel, including the women and children, and the aliens who lived among them.

COMMENTARY

30–31 While in Transjordan, Moses had given specific instructions to Israel regarding the dedication ceremony that was to follow their entry into Canaan. Under the leadership of Joshua, the Israelites were instructed to (1) set the tribes of Simeon, Levi, Judah, Issachar, Joseph, and Benjamin on Mount Gerizim in order to proclaim the blessings of the covenant (Dt 11:29; 27:12); (2) set the tribes of Reuben, Gad, Asher, Zebulun, Dan, and Naphtali on Mount Ebal to proclaim the curses (11:29; 27:13); (3) set up large plastered stones on Mount Ebal (27:2, 4); (4) write the law on these stones (27:3, 8); (5) build a stone altar to Yahweh (27:5–6); (6) offer burnt offerings and fellowship offerings on the altar (27:6–7); and (7) have the Levites recite in a loud voice the curses of the covenant (27:14–26). After the conquest of Ai,

Joshua and the people follow these instructions precisely. The ceremony signifies a renewal of Israel's commitment to obey and serve Yahweh, and him only, in the land of Canaan.

The location of the celebration, the town of Shechem between Mount Gerizim and Mount Ebal, is famous for several historical events: (1) Abraham was in the area of Shechem when he received the promise of the land (Ge 12:6–7); (2) Jacob bought a parcel of land from a resident of the area and built an altar there to "El, the God of Israel" (33:18–20); and (3) Jacob buried the foreign gods that were in his possession under the oak tree at Shechem (35:1–4). Shechem is later designated by Joshua as a city of refuge (Jos 20:7) and a Levitical city assigned to the Kohathites (21:21).

32 Joshua writes the law of Moses on white-washed stones (cf. Dt 27:2–8). The method used to prepare these stone tablets is not the same as that used for Sumerian, Akkadian, Ugaritic, and Hittite cuneiform tablets. Cuneiform tablets are never whitewashed. They are made of clay and are inscribed with a pointed stick or reed. Cuneiform texts written on stone are inscribed with a sharp-pointed metal stylus (see C. B. F. Walker, "Cunei-form," in *Reading the Past: Ancient Writing from Cuneiform to the Alphabet* [London: British Museum Press, 1990], 15–74; E. Chiera, *They Wrote on Clay: The Babylonian Tablets Speak Today* [Chicago: Univ. of Chicago Press, 1966]).

Inscribing God's law on a stone covered with a white, plasterlike substance was used for the Aramaic text of Balaam found on the walls of Tell Deir ʿAlla in the Jordan Valley. This text is written in red and black ink on a section of a wall covered with white plaster (Jo Ann Hackett, "Balaam," *ABD*, 1:569–72); a portion of the text is preserved in the Amman museum. The technique of whitewashing stone before inscribing a text was also used in Egypt (P. C. Craigie, *The Book of Deuteronomy* [NICOT; Grand Rapids: Eerdmans, 1976], 328).

33–35 In biblical terms, "all Israel" includes both Israelites and the resident aliens (*gērîm*) who lived permanently among them. Men, women, children, and aliens stand on the fringes of Mount Ebal and Mount Gerizim, and they listen to Joshua reading of the Book of the Law—both blessings and curses. Rahab and her relatives certainly participate in the celebration. The cultic life of Israel was intended to be inclusive of non-Israelites (*gērîm*).

The inclusion of aliens who had joined the Israelite community to worship the God of Abraham, Isaac, and Jacob is anticipated in a covenant renewal ceremony. After leaving Egypt, Yahweh had commanded Israel, "Do not mistreat an alien or oppress him, for you were aliens in Egypt" (Ex 22:21; cf. 23:9; Lev 19:34; Dt 10:19). Along with the poor, the foreigners (*gērîm*) who dwelt with Israel were to receive food rations by being permitted to glean from the edge of the fields and reap from the harvest of Israel (Lev 19:10; 23:22). The aliens were also invited to participate in the festivals, such as the Passover (Ex 12:48–49), the Feast of Tabernacles (Dt 16:13–15), the Sabbath (Ex 20:10; Dt 5:13–14), and the Feast of Weeks (Dt 16:10–12). Cities of refuge welcomed aliens who had committed accidental manslaughter (Nu 35:15). At the end of every third year, the aliens, the fatherless, the widows, and the Levites benefited from the tithe of that year (Dt 14:28–29; 26:11–12). They were invited to eat until they were satisfied. The inclusion of foreigners in the life and worship of Israel fulfills the missiological agenda proclaimed by Yahweh to Abram (Ge 12:1–3).

At Mount Ebal, Joshua reads the entire law of Moses before the whole community—young and old, men and women, Israelite and foreigner, official and commoner, child and adult. Special emphasis is placed on the blessings for obedience and curses for disobedience. The law of Moses covered all aspects of life—cultic, civil, social, and personal. Israel was now ready to occupy the land, to transition from the nomadic to the sedentary life, and to serve Yahweh in the Promised Land.

D. Conquering the Land (9:1–12:24)

OVERVIEW

Chapters 9–12 reveal the complexities of conquering a land inhabited by people whose leaders do not fear intruders. Whereas Israel's early victories involved individual cities, she is now confronted by deceivers—the Gibeonites—and by coalitions of rulers who band together for the sole purpose of defeating her in battle.

Yahweh's fame is known throughout the land; therefore, the Gibeonites devise a plan to circumvent the subjugation of their land by the Israelites. Some scholars have proposed that the pact established between Joshua and the people of Gibeon was a vassal treaty. According to Blenkinsopp, "the Gibeonites as servants corresponded to vassals and Israel to an overlord" (J. Blenkinsopp, *Gibeon and Israel: The Role of Gibeon and the Gibeonites in the Political and Religious History of Early Israel* [Cambridge: Cambridge Univ. Press, 1972]; Pitkänen, 209). This interpretation supports the view that the purpose of the military offensive by the kings of the south—led by the king of Jerusalem—was to revoke the treaty and to cancel the alliance. The reference to details of the Gibeonite deception in 2 Samuel 21 confirms the historical reliability of the account in Joshua 9. The kings from the southern regions of Canaan refuse to bow to the threat engendered by the presence of Israel in the land. They band together, plot against Israel, and come against her with full military force (ch. 10). Doomed to failure from the beginning, their efforts are thwarted by Joshua and his men.

Following the victory over southern cities, Joshua and his men turn northward, only to be confronted by the kings of the north (ch. 11).

Undeterred by this new complication and encouraged by Yahweh's exhortation, "Do not be afraid of them" (11:6), Joshua attacks the armies of the north at the Waters of Merom and defeats them until no survivor remains. Finally, Joshua and his men conquer a good portion of the southern and northern territories promised to Israel centuries earlier. The time has come to settle in the land.

The formula "when X heard that ..." (*wayᵉhî kišmōaʿ*) links chapters 9, 10, and 11 (see Note on 5:1). This formula appears in Assyrian military conquest accounts. For example, on the prism of Assurbanipal, we read: "Tarharqa, the king of Egypt and Nubia, in Memphis *heard of the coming of my expeditionary force ...*" ([Rassam] 1.78–80 in Younger, 200). In another Assyrian conquest account, we read: "4,000 Kasku (and) Urumu ... *heard of my coming* to the land of Subartu" (M. Streck, *Assurbanipal*, 1.56–60 [first campaign] in Younger, 200).

Chapter 12 provides a list of all the southern and northern kings defeated by Israel. The gradual inflation of the military opposition against Israel since her entrance into Canaan is noticeable. In Jericho (ch. 6), there are no fighting men. At Ai (ch. 8), the men of Bethel and Ai join forces only to be defeated by Israel. In the military confrontation with the kings of the south (ch. 10), six cities (five kings) are represented—Jerusalem, Hebron, Jarmuth, Lachish, Debir, and Gibeon. In the north (ch. 11), the coalition has grown to include the kings of Hazor, Madon, Shimron, Acshaph, the mountain cities, the Jordan valley, the western foothills, Naphoth Dor, the land of the Canaanites, Amorites, Hittites, Perizzites, Jebusites, and the Hivites below Hermon:

"They came out with all their troops and a large number of horses and chariots—a huge army, as numerous as the sand on the seashore" (11:4). This gradual inflation of Israel's enemies represents either hyperbolic language intended to create tension in the narrative or historical reality.

1. A Treaty with the Gibeonites (9:1–27)

OVERVIEW

Israel's triumph over Ai and her festive disposition at Shechem is short-lived. Her strong leadership and divine call do not preclude her susceptibility to succumb to deception. The events of chapter 9 reveal the vulnerability of God's people, charged with taking the land and destroying its inhabitants. Already at Jericho, Rahab and her family were allowed to negotiate their redemption. Now it is the Gibeonites' turn to strategize deliverance from annihilation.

Afraid that the treatment of Jericho and Ai might be a precursor for the fate of their own cities, the kings west of the Jordan join forces and plan a military offensive against Israel. The Gibeonites, a local people on the ḥērem hit list, resort to a different approach. They contrive a fraudulent plan and successfully trick Joshua and his men into making a peace treaty with them, ratified by an oath in the name of the Lord (9:15).

Deuteronomy 20 provides the background for this pericope. Before the Israelites entered the land, Moses had made pronouncements regarding the treatment of foreign cities. With cities outside of the boundaries of the land, Israel could establish a peace treaty and subject its inhabitants to forced labor (20:10–11). Such was not the case for cities within the borders of the land. Israel was forbidden to make peace agreements with them. Rather, Moses instructed Israel to annihilate completely the inhabitants of these cities to prevent the integration of abhorrent religious practices into their worship of Yahweh (Dt 20:15, 18). The Joshua narrative does not refer explicitly to Deuteronomy 20; yet the Gibeonites seem to be familiar with the permissive ordinance given to Israel. In their address to Joshua, they stress that they are "from a very distant country" (Jos 9:9), echoing the words of Moses to Israel, to establish peace treaties only with cities "that are at a distance from you and do not belong to the nations nearby" (Dt 20:15).

After three days, the Israelites discover the deception, but since the treaty had been sworn by an oath in the name of the God of Israel, Joshua is unable to harm them. Instead, Joshua curses them and makes them into slaves—woodcutters and water carriers—for Israel for the rest of their lives (9:23, 26–27).

Some scholars have rejected the historical interpretation of the account and treated it as etiological. Its purpose would be to explain the origin for the Gibeonites' service at the altar of Yahweh in Gilgal (Pitkänen, 201). According to others, the account contains both a historical tradition and the deceit motif, in order to justify the events of 2 Samuel 21, in which a famine afflicts Israel as a result of Saul's killing of Gibeonites (Pitkänen, 201).

a. The Gibeonite Deception and the Peace Treaty (9:1–15)

[1]Now when all the kings west of the Jordan heard about these things — those in the hill country, in the western foothills, and along the entire coast of the Great Sea as far as Lebanon (the kings of the Hittites, Amorites, Canaanites, Perizzites, Hivites and Jebusites) — [2]they came together to make war against Joshua and Israel.

[3]However, when the people of Gibeon heard what Joshua had done to Jericho and Ai, [4]they resorted to a ruse: They went as a delegation whose donkeys were loaded with worn-out sacks and old wineskins, cracked and mended. [5]The men put worn and patched sandals on their feet and wore old clothes. All the bread of their food supply was dry and moldy. [6]Then they went to Joshua in the camp at Gilgal and said to him and the men of Israel, "We have come from a distant country; make a treaty with us."

[7]The men of Israel said to the Hivites, "But perhaps you live near us. How then can we make a treaty with you?"

[8]"We are your servants," they said to Joshua.

But Joshua asked, "Who are you and where do you come from?"

[9]They answered: "Your servants have come from a very distant country because of the fame of the LORD your God. For we have heard reports of him: all that he did in Egypt, [10]and all that he did to the two kings of the Amorites east of the Jordan — Sihon king of Heshbon, and Og king of Bashan, who reigned in Ashtaroth. [11]And our elders and all those living in our country said to us, 'Take provisions for your journey; go and meet them and say to them, "We are your servants; make a treaty with us."' [12]This bread of ours was warm when we packed it at home on the day we left to come to you. But now see how dry and moldy it is. [13]And these wineskins that we filled were new, but see how cracked they are. And our clothes and sandals are worn out by the very long journey."

[14]The men of Israel sampled their provisions but did not inquire of the LORD. [15]Then Joshua made a treaty of peace with them to let them live, and the leaders of the assembly ratified it by oath.

COMMENTARY

1–2 Determined to stop the invasion of the intruders, the kings of the region — Mediterranean coastal region, Shephelah (western foothills), hill country, as far north as Lebanon — join forces against Joshua and Israel. Unlike in previous accounts, where the hearts of the people melted with fear (2:11; 5:1; 7:5), the kings of the Hittites, Amorites, Canaanites, Perizzites, Hivites, and Jebusites (cf. 3:10) promptly organize a coalition and plan for war against Israel. This merging of forces is noted several more times in this section of Joshua (see 10:3, 5; 11:1–3). Each attempt is unsuccessful.

3–6 Determined to avoid annihilation, the people of Gibeon devise a ruse. They send a small delegation of men wearing tattered garments and patched sandals, and carrying dried-up wineskins and crumbling bread, to meet Joshua in the camp at Gilgal. The plan is to deceive Joshua into making a peace treaty with them. Such a ploy reminds the reader of the ambush and military craftiness of Israel during the conquest of Ai. In the same way they had deceived the people of Ai, they will soon be swindled by the Gibeonites.

The Gibeonite visitors pretend to come from a distant country. Most scholars identify the town of Gibeon with the site of el-Jib, located approximately eight miles northwest of Jerusalem (Hess, *Joshua*, 177). A strategic location at a major crossroads in the hill country, it guarded the roads that went from the coastal region through the Aijalon Valley via Beth Horon and Kiriath Jearim, as well as the north-south road that controlled international commerce. This proposition is supported by the archaeological evidence found at the site; several Iron Age jar handles contain the Hebrew word for *Gibeon*. Others point to a site located approximately four miles west of Bethel, based on the list of Palestinian towns provided by Eusebius (in *Onomasticon*; see Woudstra, 154).

The location of Gilgal, where the Israelites encamped after the covenant renewal, is still a matter of debate. Several sites have been proposed, including the locality where Israel first encamped immediately after the Jordan crossings, and possibly a site in the vicinity of Mount Gerizim and Mount Ebal. If the Gilgal mentioned here is indeed the same city as the one mentioned in chapter 4, Israel would have retreated approximately twenty-five miles southeast and traveled down into the Jordan Valley after renewing the covenant at Shechem. This is unlikely since the towns that remained to be conquered were northward and southward in the hill country and westward toward the Mediterranean Sea. There was no reason for Israel to return

to a site east of Jericho before engaging in battle with the inhabitants of the hill country.

The language for "make a treaty" (v.7) is the official language used when a covenant is "cut" between the following: (1) God and his people (Ex 34:10, 27; Dt 5:2–3); (2) rulers (1Ki 20:34: Ahab and Ben-Hadad); (3) individuals (1Sa 18:3: David and Jonathan); and (4) people groups (1Sa 11:1–2: Ammonites and Israelites). Before entering Canaan, the Israelites had been forbidden to cut a covenant with the inhabitants of the land "lest they become a snare among" them (Ex 34:12–15).

7 The Gibeonites are identified by Israel as Hivites—a Canaanite group to be destroyed completely (Ex 34:11; Dt 20:17; Jos 3:10) or a people whose origin is from the Hittite empire in Anatolia. The latter is possible since in verse 11, the Gibeonites refer to their leaders as "elders" and not as "kings." Ancient Near Eastern literature reveals an Anatolian system in which the Hittite kings and their representatives interacted with the "local governments" of towns, cities, and regions, in which the governing bodies were led by elders (O. R. Gurney, *The Hittites* [2nd ed.; New York: Penguin: 1966], 68, 72, 92–93; Hess, *Joshua*, 179; see also J. Berman, "CTH 133 and the Hittite Provenance of Deuteronomy 13," *JBL* 130 [2011]: 25–44). In 2 Samuel 21, the Gibeonites are identified as survivors of the Amorites (2Sa 21:2).

Joshua makes a treaty with the Gibeonites. The Hebrew text reveals the standard covenant making formula "to cut a covenant" (*k-r-t bᵉrît*), whose origin appears to be related to the ancient ritual of "cutting" one or more sacrificial animals. This practice is well-known from ancient Near Eastern literature (e.g., in treaties between Naram-Sin and the Lamites, between Lagash and Umma, between Abba-AN and Yarim-Lim of Alalakh; G. F. Hasel, *TDOT*, "כרת," 7:336–52). In the context of covenants, the act of "cutting" ratifies the agreement.

Once Joshua has identified the men as Hivites, the Israelites challenge their identity and origin. Fully aware that the law of Moses forbade making a peace treaty with Canaanites (Ex 34:12; Dt 20:10–18), the Israelites are reluctant to give in quickly to the foreigners' request. Suspicious of the provenance of the strangers, Joshua raises the question of establishing a covenant with a people who conceivably live nearby.

8 With a quick retort, the Gibeonites identify themselves as servants seeking to become vassals of Israel, a status that would provide them with protection from the attack of any enemy. Suspecting trickery, Joshua replies sternly and questions both their identity and their place of origin (cf. Jnh 1:8). But without first seeking the Lord, how could Joshua and Israel know if the Gibeonites were telling the truth? Had they not learned from their military defeat at Ai, in which Joshua had not consulted Yahweh before the first attempt to conquer the city?

9–13 The men of Gibeon reply astutely and with a lengthy explanation, having probably rehearsed the possible scenarios among themselves before approaching Joshua. Striking at Joshua's heart strings, they first refer to the great fame of Yahweh and mention his mighty deeds on behalf of Israel in Egypt and Transjordan. The comment of the men regarding Yahweh's fame mirrors that of Rahab in Jericho, in which she attributes the fame of Israel to Yahweh's exploits on behalf of his people in Egypt and in Transjordan (2:9–11). Following the Gibeonites' moving introduction comes the pretense related to their true identity. With sincere and convincing woes regarding their worn-out clothing and spoiled provisions, the men of Gibeon persuade Joshua successfully to form an alliance with them.

14 This verse can be interpreted in several ways: (1) The Israelites examine some of the Gibeonites' provisions and determine that their story is true, without seeking Yahweh's opinion on the matter; (2) the Gibeonites partake of their own stale bread in order to substantiate their words while the Israelites watch the feast; or (3) the Israelites partake of the moldy bread in a covenantal ritual that involves sharing food. The Hebrew text is unclear. The two plural verbs ("[they] sampled" and "[they] did not inquire") may or may not have the same subject. The text simply states that "the men" sampled and/but they did not inquire of the Lord. These men were either the Gibeonites or the Israelites. The syntax provides no solution for this dilemma.

Most translations adopt the first of the three possible interpretations. If indeed Israel partook of the bread, her biggest mistake is not to taste the food but to make the critical decision of forming an alliance with the men of Gibeon without first consulting Yahweh. This was a serious offense. The fact that Israel was deceived by the Gibeonites is secondary.

15 In the end, Joshua extends "a treaty of peace" (*šālôm*) to the men of Gibeon and ratifies it, allowing them and their people to live as vassals in the land. The Gibeonites no doubt breathe a sigh of relief once the treaty is ratified, and they may have even laughed at Israel, who fell for the deception. Joshua had been duped!

The treaty includes the stipulation that Israel will allow the Gibeonites to live in their midst. A few centuries later, a famine in the land is attributed to Saul's breach of Joshua's treaty—he violated its terms and killed Gibeonites (2Sa 21:1–14). Consequently, Saul's descendants are executed at Gibeah of Saul as retribution for the suffering of the Gibeonites during the famine. Mephibosheth, the grandson of Saul, is spared because of the oath established earlier between David and Saul's son Jonathan (2Sa 21:7).

NOTES

1 The LXX reads "Horites" for the MT "Hivites" (also v.7; cf. Isa 17:9). This variant may be a misreading by the scribes of the *reš* and *waw* in the early Hebrew script (D. W. Baker, "Hivites," *ABD*, 3:234). Studies on the Gibeonite treaty include F. C. Fensham, "The Treaty between Israel and the Gibeonites," *BA* 27 (1964): 96–100; J. M. Grintz, "The Treaty of Joshua with the Gibeonites," *JAOS* 86 (1966): 113–26.

2 "[They came] together" (פֶּה אֶחָד, *peh ʾeḥād* = lit., "one mouth"). Parts of the body are common in idiomatic expressions (e.g., "Yahweh burned with anger" [וַיִּחַר אַף יהוה, *wayyiḥar ʾap yhwh* = lit., "the nose of Yahweh burned"]; "with a mighty hand Yahweh brought us out" [בְּחֹזֶק יָד הוֹצִי אָנוּ יהוה, *beḥozeq yād hôṣîʾānû yhwh* = lit. "with the strength of a hand, Yahweh brought us out"].

6–7 "The men of Israel" (אִישׁ יִשְׂרָאֵל, *ʾîš yiśrāʾēl*). The phrase (lit., "a man of Israel") appears in the singular. In this context, it functions as a collective, thus representing "the men of Israel." See also Jdg 7:23; 9:55; 1Sa 13:6; 14:22; 17:2, 19–25; 2Sa 23:9. This collective use of a singular noun is common with other Hebrew words, such as, "Israel/Israelites" (יִשְׂרָאֵל, *yiśrāʾēl*), "fruit" (פְּרִי, *peri*), "birds" (עוֹף, *ʿôp*), "livestock" (בְּהֵמָה, *behēmâ*), "children" (טַף, *ṭap*), etc.

b. The Deception Is Discovered (9:16–21)

> [16]Three days after they made the treaty with the Gibeonites, the Israelites heard that they were neighbors, living near them. [17]So the Israelites set out and on the third day came to their cities: Gibeon, Kephirah, Beeroth and Kiriath Jearim. [18]But the Israelites did not attack them, because the leaders of the assembly had sworn an oath to them by the LORD, the God of Israel.
>
> The whole assembly grumbled against the leaders, [19]but all the leaders answered, "We have given them our oath by the LORD, the God of Israel, and we cannot touch them now. [20]This is what we will do to them: We will let them live, so that wrath will not fall on us for breaking the oath we swore to them." [21]They continued, "Let them live, but let them be woodcutters and water carriers for the entire community." So the leaders' promise to them was kept.

COMMENTARY

16–18a Shortly after the treaty is ratified, Israel learns that the Gibeonites live nearby and are much more numerous than originally thought, with inhabitants in Gibeon, Kephirah (Khirbet el-Kefireh, five miles west-south-west of Gibeon), Beeroth (possibly Khirbet Raddana), and Kiriath Jearim (Tell el-Azhar, eight miles northwest of Jerusalem). Joshua and his men have been fooled! The Gibeonites have tricked them! And because of the oath sworn in the name of the Lord—the

God of Israel—the Israelites are unable to attack Gibeonite cities.

The expressions translated "three days after" and "on the third day" may or may not represent an exact period of time between the oath and the disclosure of the Gibeonites' deception. As discussed earlier (see Notes on 1:11), the phrase "three days" appears throughout Scripture, often to represent relatively short period of times of three or more days, even up to one week. It is, therefore, possible that the Israelites discovered the deception of the Gibeonites a week after the treaty was ratified—not a literal three days later.

18b–21 Humiliated by the deception, the community of Israel "grumble against" the leadership for having to endure the permanent presence of the deceivers in their midst. According to the community leaders, the oath cannot be broken since it was ratified by the Lord, the God of Israel. The only solution is to make the Gibeonites slaves—woodcutters and water carriers for the entire community. These tasks are normally associated with the aliens living among them (Dt 29:11[10]). One of the largest ancient cisterns in the hill country has been discovered at Gibeon (Hess, *Joshua*, 183). This cistern probably served as the source of water from which the Gibeonites brought water to the camp of Israel.

The Hebrew verb for "grumble" (Niphal of *lûn*) appears primarily in narratives related to the desert wanderings (Ex 15:24; 16:7; Nu 14:2, 36; 16:11; 17:6). The shift of leadership seems somewhat strange at this point. Thus far, Joshua is the one who led the oath ceremony with the Gibeonites, but during the grumbling, Joshua is silent. Instead, "all the leaders" respond to the communal complaint. If Joshua was not included in "all the leaders," then he only reappears to issue the judgment on the Gibeonites and for the curse ritual (v.23).

NOTES

18–21 "The leaders" (הַנְּשִׂיאִים, *hannᵉśîʾîm*) is repeated five times in these four verses. The Hebrew word *nāśîʾ* ("leader") is linked to the verbal root *nśʾ* ("to lift up, elevate, raise, exalt"). The noun *nāśîʾ* is to be understood as one who has been raised up or exalted above others. One who is a *nᵉśîʾ nᵉśîʾîm* ("a leader of leaders," Nu 3:32) fulfills a position superior to that of the *nāśîʾ*. In Israel, a *nāśîʾ* could be over a family (Nu 1:4), a tribe (Nu 17:2), a kingdom (1Ki 11:34), and so on. See H. Niehr, "נָשִׂיא," *TDOT*, 10:44–53.

23 The "woodcutters and water carriers" (*ḥōṭᵉbê ʿēṣîm wᵉśōʾăbê-mayim*) fulfilled menial tasks and were considered as one of the lowest ranks in Israelite society. They are mentioned at the end of a list of social classes in Deuteronomy 29:10–11, after the leaders and chief men, elders and officials, and all other Israelites (including children and women).

c. The Gibeonites Are Cursed for Their Deception (9:22–27)

22Then Joshua summoned the Gibeonites and said, "Why did you deceive us by saying, 'We live a long way from you,' while actually you live near us? **23**You are now under a curse: You will never cease to serve as woodcutters and water carriers for the house of my God."

²⁴They answered Joshua, "Your servants were clearly told how the L<small>ORD</small> your God had commanded his servant Moses to give you the whole land and to wipe out all its inhabitants from before you. So we feared for our lives because of you, and that is why we did this. ²⁵We are now in your hands. Do to us whatever seems good and right to you."

²⁶So Joshua saved them from the Israelites, and they did not kill them. ²⁷That day he made the Gibeonites woodcutters and water carriers for the community and for the altar of the L<small>ORD</small> at the place the L<small>ORD</small> would choose. And that is what they are to this day.

COMMENTARY

22–23 Joshua interrogates the Gibeonites, who have lied to him, and pronounces a curse over them. They are condemned to serve perpetually as woodcutters and water carriers for Israel. The Hebrew word for "curse" (*ʾārar*) appears only twice in Joshua—here and in 6:26, after the conquest of Jericho, when Joshua cursed anyone who would attempt to rebuild the city, reestablish its foundation, and hang its gates.

24–25 Like Rahab, the men of Gibeon acknowledge their fear of Yahweh, having heard of his mighty deeds and of his command to wipe out all the inhabitants of the land. The Gibeonites faced only two choices: (1) suffer annihilation or (2) become vassals of the newcomers. They decided to try the latter—thus the response of the Gibeonites, "We are now in your hands. Do to us whatever seems good and right to you."

26–27 Joshua becomes the deliverer of the Gibeonites. He prevents the angry and grumbling Israelites from killing them. The Gibeonites are condemned to the menial service of cutting wood and drawing water for the entire community of Israel and for the rituals at the sanctuary. Ironically, they had sought military protection from Israel, not slavery!

REFLECTION

During her long history, Israel was joined by a mixed multitude that chose—either out of conviction or out of fear—to join the community and submit to its tenets (Ex 12:38; 23:9; Lev 18:26; Nu 35:15). Such is the body of Christ with the grafting in of the Gentiles (Ro 11:17–19), the welcoming of all nations (Mt 28:19), and the universality of God's love. God is willing to bless and protect all those who join the community of faith—either out of conviction or out of fear—through the Messiah of Israel. Long before Joshua's day, Yahweh promised to multiply Abraham's seed and to bless all the nations of the world (Ge 12:1–3; Gal 3:8). The call of Abraham was not for the sake of one nation only, but for the sake of all humanity.

Moreover, although Israel had a strong military leader, the events of chapter 9 show serious weakness in Israel's leadership. For the second time, Joshua fails to seek Yahweh before making critical decision. In this case, Joshua forgets to consult Yahweh before answering the important question: "Should we or should we not make a treaty?" Failure to seek

Yahweh before the attack on Ai had proven costly. Men had lost their lives and Israel was humiliated. Unfortunately, Joshua forgot his bout with depression and his emotional outburst before Yahweh after the defeat at Ai—another costly mistake.

In the Pentateuch, Yahweh warns Israel repeatedly to refrain from making special agreements with the Canaanites, but Israel does not listen; as a result, she suffers recurring consequences. Joshua lacked judgment and ensured the protection of Israel's neighbor without first seeking Yahweh. God's ideal is that we "make plans by seeking advice; if you wage war, obtain guidance" (Pr 20:18). As Christians, we are at war—not with flesh and blood but with principalities, powers, and the rulers of the darkness of this world (Eph 6:12). To win the

war, we must seek guidance from the Lord through worship and prayer (6:13–19). Only he can reveal the best plan of attack.

Wisdom says, "A man lacking in judgment strikes hands in pledge and puts up security for his neighbor" (Pr 17:18; cf. 22:26). Joshua put up security for the Gibeonites, and for this, the Israelites suffered. Today, Christians are warned of similar dangers. The apostle Paul states: "Do not be yoked together with unbelievers. For what do righteousness and wickedness have in common? Or what fellowship can light have with darkness?" (2Co 6:14). God sends his people into the world, not to be equally yoked with the world but to be witnesses of his love, his compassion, and his plan of redemption through the Messiah, Jesus Christ.

2. The Amorite Kings against Gibeon (10:1–15)

OVERVIEW

Alarmed by the events at Gibeon, Adoni-Zedek, the king of Jerusalem, invites the kings of surrounding areas—Hebron, Jarmuth, Lachish, Debir, Eglon—to join forces with him against the city of Gibeon (10:3–4). Seemingly without hesitation, the kings and their armies join Adoni-Zedek and his men. They take position against Gibeon and attack the city. The Gibeonites entreat Joshua to fulfill his oath and to come to their rescue.

Promised victory by the Lord, Joshua fearlessly approaches Gibeon, where the kings' armies have launched an offensive. Taken by surprise, the kings' troops fall into confusion and scurry in all directions, attempting to save their own lives. Most are killed by the sword at Gibeon while others are killed by large hailstones that fall on them as

they are fleeing on the road to Azekah (10:11). In commemoration of this great victory, Joshua orders the sun to stand still over Gibeon. The sun pauses over the city for a full day, a phenomenon that has never occurred since in history (10:12–14). This puzzling passage has generated a number of interpretations, including:

- a song that appeals for the granting of a favorable omen. This practice is known from Babylonian sources (Baruch Halpern, "Settlement of Canaan," *ABD*, 5:1136).
- a prayer for the dawn to delay and the clouds hold still in order to prevent Israel from suffering the scorching heat of the day during the battle (J. S. Holladay Jr., "The Day(s) The Moon Stood Still," *JBL* 87 [1968]: 166).

- a petition for the sun to withold its power to dissipate the early morning mist in order to enable the surprise attack (Holladay, "The Day(s) The Moon," 166).
- a poem celebrating the culmination of a great victory. The first stich is a prayer/incantation that the sun and moon stand in opposition, and the second and third stichoi report an affirmative outcome to the prayer. This interpretation takes into consideration ancient Near Eastern practices of astronomy and astrology in incantations to astral deities (Holladay, "The Day(s) The Moon," 173–74).
- a solar eclipse that occurred and confounded the Canaanites (L. D. Hawk, *Joshua* [Berit Olam; Collegeville, Minn.: Liturgical, 2000], 153).
- literal interpretation of the event—an unexplainable miracle, concluding in the extension of the day during which Joshua could complete the long and complex battle against the Canaanites.

Following this unusual natural wonder, Joshua continues the campaign, kills the five Amorite kings, and hangs their bodies on trees (10:22–26). By the end of the chapter, Israel has subdued "the whole region, including the hill country, the Negev, the western foothills and the mountain slopes, together with all their kings…. Joshua subdued them from Kadesh Barnea to Gaza and from the whole region of Goshen to Gibeon. All these kings and their lands Joshua conquered in one campaign" (10:40–42).

The description of military maneuvers in Joshua reflect ancient Near Eastern annalistic accounts of military campaigns in which the author first elaborates on the conquest of a few towns—in this case, Jericho and Ai—and concludes with a staccato summary of the conquest of numerous additional cities (e.g., the campaign records of Tuthmoses III of Egypt [Junkkaala, 95–101], Shishak [ibid., 173–75], the Hittite king Murshili II [Kitchen, 170]; see also the third campaign of Sennacherib for a summary of cities taken in Judah and Samaria [*ANET*, 288]). In Joshua 10, we encounter one such detailed list of conquered cities (see Junkkaala, 227–302).

Elements of the names of Amorite kings (chs. 10–11) appear "in personal names of the fourteenth century Amarna letters in the names of town leaders from elsewhere in Palestine and Syria" (e.g., *a-du-na* and *rabu-tsi-id-qi* [Adoni-Zedek, Jos 10:1]; Hess, *Joshua*, 29). Other names appear in the Egyptian Execration texts dated to the first half of the second millennium BC (*Anak*), and some include Late Bronze Age Hurrian or Anatolian elements (*Hoham* and *Piram*) (Hess, *Joshua*, 29–30; idem, "Joshua," in *Zondervan Illustrated Bible Backgrounds Commentary* [Grand Rapids: Zondervan, 2009], 2:44).

Striking parallels appear in chapters 10 and 11: (1) both chapters begin with a coalition of kings who join forces against Israel (10:3–5//11:1–5); (2) the coalition is instigated by one ruler (10:3//11:1); (3) Yahweh reassures Joshua with "do not be afraid" (10:8//11:6); and (4) Joshua and his men subdue the towns of the entire region (10:40//11:12, 16–17, 21–23).

a. The Amorite Kings against Gibeon (10:1–5)

¹Now Adoni-Zedek king of Jerusalem heard that Joshua had taken Ai and totally destroyed it, doing to Ai and its king as he had done to Jericho and its king, and that the people of Gibeon had made a treaty of peace with Israel and were living near them. ²He and his people were very much alarmed at this, because Gibeon was an important city, like one of the royal cities; it was larger than Ai, and all its men were good fighters. ³So Adoni-Zedek king of Jerusalem appealed to Hoham king of Hebron, Piram king of Jarmuth, Japhia king of Lachish and Debir king of Eglon. ⁴"Come up and help me attack Gibeon," he said, "because it has made peace with Joshua and the Israelites."

⁵Then the five kings of the Amorites — the kings of Jerusalem, Hebron, Jarmuth, Lachish and Eglon — joined forces. They moved up with all their troops and took up positions against Gibeon and attacked it.

COMMENTARY

1 Aware of the defeat of Jericho and Ai and the treatment of its kings, Adoni-Zedek of Jerusalem frantically organizes a united offensive against the Gibeonites, who had formed an alliance with Israel. "Jerusalem" is mentioned here for the first time in the Bible. It appears in the Amarna tablets of the fourteenth century BC as *"Urusalim"* (see Woudstra, 169). During Joshua's days, the population of Jerusalem was mixed and included at least Amorites and Hittites (Eze 16:3). Jericho and Ai were cities devoted to the ban (*ḥērem*), and consequently, they and all their inhabitants were destroyed. Suspecting that Jerusalem was also on the list of such cities, Adoni-Zedek cannot afford to take a chance. His life and that of his subjects are on the line.

2 Gibeon's alliance with Israel has become a major problem for the inhabitants of the region. Gibeon was a prominent city located only a few miles north of Jerusalem at a major crossroads between the coastal plain, the lowlands, the hill country, and the Judean wilderness. According to Adoni-Zedek, Gibeon was an important city-state, like a royal city, with "good fighters" (*gibbōrîm*) trained for combat. Gibeon's alliance with Israel becomes such a threat to the people of the region that the king of Jerusalem recruits the assistance of the armies of five additional cities in order to stop Joshua and his men. The alliance of Gibeon with Israel has created a void in the security of the region because the mighty fighters, who would have defended the whole area, have now become vassals and slaves of Israel. As a result, the Benjamite plateau is now for the most part under the control of Israel — the invader.

3–4 Adoni-Zedek sends a message to the kings of four strategically located towns south of Jerusalem — Hebron, Yarmuth, Lachish, and Eglon — and urges them to join forces with him against Gibeon. Hebron (also known as Kiriath Arba in 20:7; cf. Ge 23:2; 35:27) has been identified with Tell er-Rumeiden (ca. twenty miles south of Jerusalem). Lachish has been identified with Tel ed-Duweir (ca. twenty-five miles southwest of Jerusalem), Debir with Khirbet Rabud (southwest of Hebron), Jarmuth with Tell Yarmut/Khirbet Yarmuk (ca. sixteen miles west of Jerusalem), and Eglon with Tel el-Hesi (ca. thirty-two miles southwest of Jerusalem) (see Hess, *Joshua*, 189; Woudstra, 170). Beth Horon may represent a Canaanite sanctuary where the god Horon, mentioned in the Execration texts and in Ugaritic material, was worshiped (Butler, 115).

The four cities are located south and southwest of Jerusalem and form a line across the southern part of the Judean hills and the Shephelah. Jerusalem is the closest site to Gibeon; consequently, it is the most vulnerable of the five cities in the alliance. Adoni-Zedek's call for help is similar to those found in Amarna texts — fourteenth to twelfth century BC — in which Canaanite vassal rulers request help from Egypt for reinforcement against the attacks of foreigners (Hess, *Joshua*, 190).

The message of the king is direct and strong: "Come up and assist me in attacking Gibeon!" (pers. trans.). The author uses the root *šlm* ("peace") when describing the alliance made between Gibeon and Israel, indicating that the Gibeonites "have made peace" with Israel and have consequently become enemies of the Canaanites.

5 The narrative reveals an immediate and positive response from the Amorite kings, who quickly summon their troops, take up position against Gibeon, and attack the city. Before making an alliance with Israel, the Gibeonites had revealed to Joshua their awareness of the fate of two other Amorite kings from Transjordan — Sihon, king of Heshbon, and Og, king of Bashan. These kings were defeated by the Israelites after they refused to allow them to pass through their territories before entering the Promised Land (9:10; Nu 21:21–35). News of this devastating blow on Sihon and Og had reached Canaan and had prompted the Gibeonites to devise their survival plan, which eventually saved their lives. The Amorite kings who have not sought an alliance with Israel now expect the same fate as Sihon and Og — death.

NOTES

1 The name "Adoni-Zedeq" (אֲדֹנִי־צֶדֶק, *ʾᵃdōnî-ṣedeq*) is Semitic in origin and is a construct of "lord" and "righteousness" (or the Canaanite god "Tsaduq/Tsedeq"), thus meaning "lord of righteousness" or "righteous lord." The LXX reads "Adoni-Bezeq" of the town of Bezeq as found in Judges 1:5–7.

4 "Come up!" (עֲלוּ, *ᶜᵃlû*). The verb *ᶜlh* ("to go up") is logical when going to or gathering in Jerusalem since the city is located at one of the highest points in the land, on Mount Zion. The other towns mentioned in the coalition (Hebron, Jarmuth, Lachish, Eglon) are at lower elevations.

5 The repetition of lists of names, objects, cities, and so on, is common in Semitic languages (e.g., "Canaanites, Hittites, Amorites, Perizzites, Hivites and Jebusites," Ex 3:8, 17; 13:5; 23:23; "the sound of the horn, flute, zither, lyre, harp, pipes and all kinds of music," Da 3:5, 7, 10, 15; "men and women, children and infants, cattle and sheep, camels and donkeys," 1Sa 15:3; 22:19).

b. Joshua Rescues the Gibeonites (10:6–11)

⁶The Gibeonites then sent word to Joshua in the camp at Gilgal: "Do not abandon your servants. Come up to us quickly and save us! Help us, because all the Amorite kings from the hill country have joined forces against us."

⁷So Joshua marched up from Gilgal with his entire army, including all the best fighting men. ⁸The LORD said to Joshua, "Do not be afraid of them; I have given them into your hand. Not one of them will be able to withstand you."

⁹After an all-night march from Gilgal, Joshua took them by surprise. ¹⁰The LORD threw them into confusion before Israel, who defeated them in a great victory at Gibeon. Israel pursued them along the road going up to Beth Horon and cut them down all the way to Azekah and Makkedah. ¹¹As they fled before Israel on the road down from Beth Horon to Azekah, the LORD hurled large hailstones down on them from the sky, and more of them died from the hailstones than were killed by the swords of the Israelites.

COMMENTARY

6 Defenseless before the coalition of Amorite kings, the Gibeonites appeal to Joshua for immediate reinforcement. In the same way as the king of Jerusalem pleads for assistance from the other Amorite kings, the Gibeonites plead for assistance from Israel (v.4). Their plea is articulated with language of urgency: "Do not abandon your servants. Come up to us quickly and save us! Help us …" (a significant sequence of four imperative verbs). Although the alliance between Israel and Gibeon simply stated that Joshua would "let them live" (9:15), the text seems to indicate that the expectations from the vassal city-state are much higher. In their view, the covenant with Israel includes protection against the attacks of enemies. The alliance confirmed by Joshua is now put to the test. How will Israel respond?

The Gibeonites' statement that "all the kings of the Amorites … have joined forces against us" indicates either (1) a hyperbole on the part of the Gibeonites to strengthen their case; (2) a recognition that the cities mentioned here were the major

southern centers at that time; or (3) an awareness that only Amorites inhabited the southern region (Hess, *Joshua*, 192). The first of these is the most likely, that the Gibeonites are using exaggeration in order to serve their own purposes rather than opting for a view that limits the number of Amorite settlements in the southern area of Canaan.

7–8 Without delay, Joshua and his men climb the ascent from Gilgal to Gibeon at night to ward off the Amorite kings and the armies of the southern cities. Once again, Yahweh encourages Joshua with words that are familiar throughout the conquest narrative, "Do not be afraid of them" (Dt 31:6, 8; Jos 8:1; 10:8; 11:6), confirming to Joshua that Yahweh has already given his enemies into his hands. From this point forward, the roles are reversed. Yahweh becomes the military leader who determines the strategies, creates confusion in the enemy camp, attacks the Amorite warriors, and gives the victory to Israel. Joshua yields the military leadership to Yahweh.

9–10 The early morning arrival of Joshua and his men at Gibeon traps the Amorite armies and finds them unprepared to fight against Yahweh's stratagems. Thrown into complete panic (*hmm*) by Yahweh, the Amorites suffer a great defeat at Gibeon. The survivors are pursued all the way to Beth Horon, Azekah, and Makkedah and are killed either by the sword or by Yahweh's hailstones.

Beth Horon is located on a major route between Gibeon and the coastal plain. Azekah is located near Jarmuth, making it possible for the Amorite armies to have taken refuge there during the battle. Makkedah is identified with Khirbet el-Qom in the Shephelah, which is known for an eighth-century Hebrew tomb inscription and graffiti that includes the text "*Yahweh … and his Asherah*," hinting, according to some scholars, that the syncretism of Judah eventually included Asherah as a consort of Yahweh (A. Lemaire, "Les inscriptions de Khirbet el Qôm et l'Ashérah de Yhwh," *RB* 84 [1977]: 595–608; J. M. Hadley, "The Khirbet el-Qom Inscription," *VT* 37 [1987]: 50–62; M. Dykstra, "I Have Blessed You by YHWH of Samaria and His Asherah: Texts with Religious Elements from the Soil Archive of Ancient Israel" in *Only One God? Monotheism in Ancient Israel and the Veneration of the Goddess Asherah* [ed. B. Becking et al.; London: Sheffield Academic, 2001], 30–35; for similar inscription, see "Kuntillet Ajrud," *ABD*, 4:103–9).

An all-night military march—approximately eighteen miles in this case—is not unique to the Bible. A similar event is recorded in the *Comprehensive Annals* of the Hittite king Murshili II: "But when night fell, I turned about and advanced against Pitaggatalli. I marched the whole night through, and daybreak found me on the outskirts of Sapidduwa. And as soon as the sun rose I advanced to battle against him" (Hess, *Joshua*, 46; Younger, 207). In both texts—Joshua and Murshili II—the leader and his army leave their camp at night, march during the night, and attack the city in the morning.

11 The battle continues beyond Gibeon westward, on the road up to Beth Horon, then down to Azekah and Makkedah. From the sky, Yahweh casts large stones on the Amorite kings and their armies. So large are the stones that more perished from Yahweh's projectiles than from the weapons of Israel. The meteorological event is interpreted as an answer to Joshua's prayer. The occurrence of hailstones in warfare is not unique to the biblical narrative. An Assyrian text from the eighth century BC speaks of natural elements—including hailstones—annihilating enemies of Sargon: "Adad, the violent, the son of Anu, the valiant, uttered his loud cry against them; and with the flood cloud and hailstones, he totally annihilated the remainder" (Younger, 210). In Joshua, the victory over the Amorite kings is attributed to Yahweh, whose weapons are more efficient than the man-made weapons of Israel. In the Assyrian text, divine intervention contributes to the victory.

NOTES

10–11 The author employs a merism ("on the ascent to Beth-Horon" [מַעֲלֵה בֵית־חוֹרֹן, *maʿalēh bêt-ḥôrōn*] and "on the descent of Beth-Horon" [מוֹרַד בֵּית־חוֹרֹן, *môrad bêt-ḥôrōn*]) in order to indicate that the Amorites who had survived the battle at Gibeon were *completely* destroyed on the road to Beth Horon. A merism is a figure of speech that contrasts two extremes in order to express a totality (Watson, 321–24).

10 "Yahweh confused them" (וַיְהֻמֵּם יְהוָה, *way*ᵉ*hummēm yhwh*). Although this seems contrary to his nature, God is sometimes the initiator of confusion (*hmm*) (e.g., Ex 14:24; 23:27; Dt 2:15; Jdg 4:15; 1Sa 7:10). In such cases, Yahweh is evoking panic and terror on the enemies of Israel in order to defeat them and to bring victory to his people (H. P. Müller, "המם," *TDOT*, 3:419–22).

c. The Sun Stands Still over Gibeon (10:12–15)

¹²On the day the LORD gave the Amorites over to Israel, Joshua said to the LORD in the presence of Israel:

"O sun, stand still over Gibeon,
    O moon, over the Valley of Aijalon."
¹³So the sun stood still,
    and the moon stopped,
    till the nation avenged itself on its enemies,

as it is written in the Book of Jashar.
The sun stopped in the middle of the sky and delayed going down about a full day.
¹⁴There has never been a day like it before or since, a day when the LORD listened to a man.
Surely the LORD was fighting for Israel!
¹⁵Then Joshua returned with all Israel to the camp at Gilgal.

COMMENTARY

12–14 The text quickly changes from prose to poetry with an address from Joshua to Yahweh. However, Joshua does not speak directly to Yahweh; rather, he addresses the sun and moon, commanding them to stand still over Gibeon in the east and over the Valley of Aijalon in the west. According to the text, the extraordinary phenomenon is intended to assist Israel in its defeat of the Amorite kings, possibly by giving Israel a longer day to pursue her enemies and to complete the military task under a moonlit sky.

No sooner does Joshua utter the request than we learn of the unmitigated response of the celestial bodies—the sun stands still and the moon stops moving until the campaign is over and the nation has avenged itself on its enemies. According to the narrative, the event is recorded in "the Book of Jashar," a source mentioned only here and in 2 Samuel 1:18, where David laments over the loss of Saul and Jonathan (2Sa 1:19–27). The Hebrew word for *Jashar* (*yāšār*) means "straight, honest, just, righteous, upright." It is possible that the Book of Jashar included the story of righteous heroes who modeled honest lives for Israel (D. L. Christensen, "Book of Jashar," *ABD*, 3:646–57).

Joshua's address to the sun and moon is astounding since Israel was monotheistic and worshiped only Yahweh. Scholars remain divided as to the interpretation of the account (see Overview on 10:1–15). Some deem it a miraculous historical event (our view), when the earth would have stopped rotating, while others adopt alternative secular interpretations, such as: (1) a natural phenomenon—a solar eclipse that would certainly have scared the enemy; (2) a request for a favorable omen from the heavens, as found in Ancient Near Eastern astrological texts; (3) a syncretistic address from Joshua to astronomical deities, since both the sun and moon are mentioned in the Hebrew Bible in the context of idolatry (Dt 4:19; 2Ki 23:5); (4) a prayer to prevent the sun from dissipating the early morning mist; (5) a polemic against the Sun and Moon gods; and (6) a figurative mention of the sun and moon describing the battle in hyperbolic poetic form (see Howard, 239–49; Younger, 212).

The narrative exposes a role reversal between Yahweh and Joshua. Yahweh obeys human commands ("the LORD listened [*šmʿ*] to a man") while Joshua gives commands to the two chief astronomical bodies—the sun and moon. Just as the sun and moon listen to the voice of Joshua, so does Yahweh "obey" (*šmʿ bᵉ-*) the voice of a man.

15 This verse seems to have been inserted as a literary marker in order to complete the first scene after the battle against the Amorite kings. It is unlikely that Joshua and his men actually return to Gilgal at this point since the events that follow in this chapter take place around Makkedah, in the Shephelah. Only after the battle against the Amorite kings does Joshua return to Gilgal "with all Israel"; this hints that no Israelite life was lost during the battle.

NOTES

12 Younger (211) understands "then he spoke" (אָז יְדַבֵּר, *ʾāz yᵉdabbēr* [preterite]) as a flashback that connects and contrasts the violence of the storm of hailstones with the stillness of the sun and moon.

13 As a rule, the Hebrew word *gôy* used here for Israel (גּוֹי, "nation") refers to a community of people linked by three major components: race, government, and territory (R. E. Clemens, "גּוֹי," *TDOT*, 2:426–33). The identity of the "nation" of Israel as a *gôy* originates with Abraham, when God promises him to make his descendants into a great "nation" (Ge 12:2). Israel as a *gôy* in Joshua points to the (partial) fulfillment of the promise made to Abraham.

3. The Amorite Kings Are Executed (10:16–28)

OVERVIEW

Fearing for their lives, the Amorite kings who had joined forces against Israel and attacked Gibeon hide in a cave at Makkedah. Their secret hideout is made known to Joshua, who detains them, executes them, hangs them on trees in the sight of everyone, and throws them back into the cave. What was a sure victory in the minds of the Amorite kings ends in complete defeat. Energized by his recent victory, Joshua and his men move forward to conquer the southern cities.

¹⁶Now the five kings had fled and hidden in the cave at Makkedah. ¹⁷When Joshua was told that the five kings had been found hiding in the cave at Makkedah, ¹⁸he said, "Roll large rocks up to the mouth of the cave, and post some men there to guard it. ¹⁹But don't stop! Pursue your enemies, attack them from the rear and don't let them reach their cities, for the LORD your God has given them into your hand."

²⁰So Joshua and the Israelites destroyed them completely—almost to a man—but the few who were left reached their fortified cities. ²¹The whole army then returned safely to Joshua in the camp at Makkedah, and no one uttered a word against the Israelites.

²²Joshua said, "Open the mouth of the cave and bring those five kings out to me." ²³So they brought the five kings out of the cave—the kings of Jerusalem, Hebron, Jarmuth, Lachish and Eglon. ²⁴When they had brought these kings to Joshua, he summoned all the men of Israel and said to the army commanders who had come with him, "Come here and put your feet on the necks of these kings." So they came forward and placed their feet on their necks.

²⁵Joshua said to them, "Do not be afraid; do not be discouraged. Be strong and courageous. This is what the LORD will do to all the enemies you are going to fight." ²⁶Then Joshua struck and killed the kings and hung them on five trees, and they were left hanging on the trees until evening.

²⁷At sunset Joshua gave the order and they took them down from the trees and threw them into the cave where they had been hiding. At the mouth of the cave they placed large rocks, which are there to this day.

²⁸That day Joshua took Makkedah. He put the city and its king to the sword and totally destroyed everyone in it. He left no survivors. And he did to the king of Makkedah as he had done to the king of Jericho.

COMMENTARY

16–19 What was intended as a place of refuge for the Amorite kings becomes a place of incarceration. Joshua's men discover the cave in which the kings have sought shelter and imprison them in their own refuge. Charged by Joshua, they roll large rocks at the mouth of the cave. The boulders remind the reader of the recent storm of hailstones sent by Yahweh on Israel's enemies. The same Hebrew expression ("large stones," ʾăbānîm gᵉdōlôt) appears in both accounts. Blocking the entrance of the cave with stones proves to be a good military

tactic. It prevents Joshua from having to leave a large contingent of men to guard the kings' hiding place. Then Joshua tells his men: "Don't stop! Pursue your enemies, attack them from the rear" (v.19). The command "Don't stop!" (ʾal taʿᵃmōdû) stands in direct contrast with the command to the moon to "stand still" (dôm).

Ancient Near Eastern conquest accounts include narrations of open-field battles where "the king, kings, and/or people flee and take refuge in some place (whether high mountain, mountain cave, or across the sea). In some instances, the kings are captured; in others they are not" (Younger, 221). Younger provides numerous examples: (1) King Rusa of Urartu fled before Sargon and hid in the recesses of a mountain (W. Mayer, *MDOG* 115 [1983]: 82–83, lines 150–151); (2) King Ummanaldaši of Elam fled to the mountains after hearing that Assurbanipal's army had entered his city (Prism A [Rassam] Col. V. 11–14); (3) in a speech to Thutmoses III, Amun-Re states that his enemies hid in holes (Poetical Stela: *Urk.* 4.610.7–9); and (4) in a text of Ramses II at Karnak, we read that the enemies of the pharaoh hid in caves like jackals with the fear of the pharaoh in their hearts (G. A. Gaballa, *JEA* 55 [1969]: 82–88. Fig. no. 5; for additional details on each text, see Younger, 221–22).

The expression "the LORD your God has given them into your hand" appears throughout Scripture, both in offensive and defensive military contexts. In most cases, God gives the victory to Israel (e.g., Og, king of Bashan [Dt 3:3]; Canaanite cities [20:12]; Israel's enemies [21:10]; Jericho [Jos 2:24]; Ai [8:7]; Amorite kings and armies [10:19]; Libnah [10:30]; kings of the north [11:8]; all Israel's enemies [21:44] Cushan-Rishathaim, king of Aram [Jdg 3:10]; Sisera [4:14]; the Midianites [7:15]; the Ammonites [11:32]; the Philistines [1Sa 14:12; 2Sa 5:19]). In certain cases, the pattern is reversed and God gives Israel into the hands of her enemies (e.g., the Midianites [Jdg 6:1]; the Philistines [13:1; 1Sa 28:19]; the Babylonians [Eze 23:28]).

20–21 The hyperbolic language of verse 20 ("Joshua and the Israelites destroyed them completely") would be better translated: "as soon as [they] ... had completely overcome them with an exceedingly great blow until they had finished";

this emphasizes the magnitude of Israel's victory. While only a few Amorites survived the campaign, "the whole army then returned safely to Joshua in the camp at Makkedah." The victory brought such fear on the people of the region that no one dared utter a word against the Israelites.

22–24 Emboldened by the success of the military campaign, Joshua orders his men to open the mouth of the cave where the Amorite kings were incarcerated and to bring them out before all the people. Joshua commands his chief military men to put their feet on the necks of the humiliated kings. Putting the enemy under one's foot appears in ancient Near Eastern and Egyptian texts and reliefs, and it denotes the subjugation of an enemy. In the Annals of Tukulti-Ninurta I, one finds the description of the Assyrian king's treatment of the captured Babylonian ruler Kaštiliah IV—"his royal neck I trod with my foot, like a footstool" (Boling and Wright, 286). In Psalm 110:1, the psalmist portrays such an act as one of supreme authority, saying, "the LORD says to my Lord: "Sit at my right hand until I make your enemies a footstool for your feet.'"

The hiding–exposure motif appears in numerous pericopes in Joshua. (1) The spies sent to Jericho are hidden on the roof of Rahab's residence and then released through the window (2:4–15). (2) The spies hide for three days in the hills of the Jordan valley until the coast is clear for them to be out in the open and return to the camp (2:22–23). (3) Achan's hidden plunder—a beautiful robe from Babylonia, two hundred shekels of silver, and a wedge of gold weighing fifty shekels (7:21)—is found and laid out before the Lord. (4) Now in chapter 10, the Amorite kings who are first hidden in the cave are discovered and displayed in humiliation before their conquerors.

25 Joshua's commands "do not be afraid; do not be discouraged" and "be strong and courageous" echo declarations made earlier by Moses to Joshua (Dt 3:28; 31:6–7, 23; Jos 1:7, 9, 18; see also 1Ch 22:13; 28:20; 2Ch 32:7) and by Yahweh to Joshua (Jos 1:6, 7, 9, 18).

26–27 Following the public humiliation of the Amorite kings, Joshua decides to kill and hang the rulers on trees outside the city of Makkedah, for all to see, until evening. It is possible that the "trees" were "poles" on which the bodies were impaled, as seen in the Lachish relief. In an ironic twist, Joshua orders that their bodies be removed from the poles and thrown into the cave where they had hidden earlier. According to Mosaic law, anyone who was hung on a tree was to be taken down before sunset in order to prevent the land from being defiled

(Dt 21:22–23; see Jos 8:29). Once the deceased kings are thrown back into the cave, piles of stones are placed at the mouth of the cave as a memorial to the victory against Israel's enemies.

28 The city of Makkedah is conquered as a *ḥērem*—a city devoted to Yahweh where everything is to be completely destroyed. The treatment administered to the king of Makkedah reflects that previously inflicted on the king of Jericho (6:20–21, 24; 8:2). We presume that the king of Jericho was hung on a tree based on information given in chapter 8. In 8:2, Yahweh instructed Joshua to do to the king of Ai what he did to the king of Jericho, and in 8:29 we are told that the king of Ai was hung on a tree. We can, therefore, conclude that the king of Makkedah was also hung on trees or poles outside of the city.

4. Conquest of Southern Cities (10:29–43)

OVERVIEW

The conquest of the southern cities is highly formulaic, hyperbolic, and redundant in its language. This section describes briefly the conquest of eight named cities (Makkedah, Libnah, Lachish [and king of Gezer], Eglon, Hebron, Debir, Kadesh Barnea, and Gaza) and concludes with a summary statement (vv.40–42). The following formulaic elements delineate the narrative: (1) Joshua and all Israel move from one town to another (vv.29, 31, 34, 36, 38); (2) Joshua and his men take position and attack the city (vv.29, 31, 34, 36); (3) the Lord hands over the city into the hands of Israel (vv.30, 32); (4) everyone in the city is put to the sword (vv.28, 30, 32, 35, 37, 39); (5) the text points to treatment

of a previous conquered city (vv.30, 32, 35, 37, 39); and (6) the Israelites leave no survivors in the city (vv.28, 30, 33, 35, 37, 39, 40).

The summary statement reveals Yahweh's role in the conquest. Without divine intervention, Joshua and his men could not have succeeded in this extraordinary military undertaking. It is "because the LORD, the God of Israel, fought for Israel" that the mission was accomplished in one campaign (v.42). Once the southern region is secure under Israelite control, Joshua and his men return to the camp at Gilgal, the locale from which they had been summoned to protect Gibeon (vv.6–7).

²⁹Then Joshua and all Israel with him moved on from Makkedah to Libnah and attacked it. ³⁰The LORD also gave that city and its king into Israel's hand. The city and everyone in it Joshua put to the sword. He left no survivors there. And he did to its king as he had done to the king of Jericho.

³¹Then Joshua and all Israel with him moved on from Libnah to Lachish; he took up positions against it and attacked it. ³²The LORD handed Lachish over to Israel, and Joshua took it on the second day. The city and everyone in it he put to the sword, just as he had done to Libnah. ³³Meanwhile, Horam king of Gezer had come up to help Lachish, but Joshua defeated him and his army — until no survivors were left.

³⁴Then Joshua and all Israel with him moved on from Lachish to Eglon; they took up positions against it and attacked it. ³⁵They captured it that same day and put it to the sword and totally destroyed everyone in it, just as they had done to Lachish.

³⁶Then Joshua and all Israel with him went up from Eglon to Hebron and attacked it. ³⁷They took the city and put it to the sword, together with its king, its villages and everyone in it. They left no survivors. Just as at Eglon, they totally destroyed it and everyone in it.

³⁸Then Joshua and all Israel with him turned around and attacked Debir. ³⁹They took the city, its king and its villages, and put them to the sword. Everyone in it they totally destroyed. They left no survivors. They did to Debir and its king as they had done to Libnah and its king and to Hebron.

⁴⁰So Joshua subdued the whole region, including the hill country, the Negev, the western foothills and the mountain slopes, together with all their kings. He left no survivors. He totally destroyed all who breathed, just as the LORD, the God of Israel, had commanded. ⁴¹Joshua subdued them from Kadesh Barnea to Gaza and from the whole region of Goshen to Gibeon. ⁴²All these kings and their lands Joshua conquered in one campaign, because the LORD, the God of Israel, fought for Israel.

⁴³Then Joshua returned with all Israel to the camp at Gilgal.

COMMENTARY

29–30 Libnah is a Levitical city in the Judah/ Simeon list (21:13). Archaeologists have suggested Tell es-Safi, Tell Judeideh, and Tell Bornat as possible sites for biblical Libnah (J. L. Peterson, "Libnah," *ABD*, 4:322–23). The three sites stood between the coast and the Shephelah, and they protected one of the main routes that linked the valley and the mountains.

31–32 Lachish — Tell ed-Duweir — is well-known from the Assyrian relief found in Sennacherib's palace in Nineveh. During his third campaign into Canaan, Sennacherib conquered a number of Judean and coastal towns, including Ashkelon, Ashdod, Ekron, Gaza, and Lachish. A portion of Sennacherib's relief is preserved in the British Museum in London. Lachish is mentioned in a fifteenth-century BC Egyptian document (the Hermitage papyrus) and in the Amarna letters of the fourteenth and thirteenth centuries BC (e.g., EA

328, 329) (Pitkänen, 223). Japhia, the Amorite king of Lachish, was killed by Joshua and hung outside Makkedah during the southern campaign (10:3, 22–26). The death of the leader may have weakened the political infrastructure of Lachish and left it vulnerable to the attack of an enemy.

33 King Horam of Gezer and his troops joined forces with the men of Lachish against Israel. The king and his men are quickly defeated and no survivors are left standing. Gezer is located at the base of the Judean hills and is identified with Tell Jezer. The site guards a major road that connects the Via Maris and Jerusalem (W. G. Dever, "Gezer," *ABD*, 2:998–1003).

34–35 Eglon has yet to be located by archaeologists. This town is mentioned nowhere else in the Bible, but its king, Debir, is mentioned with the Amorite kings who joined Adoni-Zedek of Jerusalem against the attack on Israel (10:3). Debir was killed by Joshua and hung on a tree in the vicinity of Makkedah. The city of Eglon is conquered as a *ḥērem*—a city devoted to Yahweh.

36–37 Hebron, a Canaanite city, dates back to Early Bronze Age I (EB I) and is located on the crest of the Judean hills. The ancient site has been identified as Jebel er-Rumeidah at the junction of two routes—one coming from the Shephelah in the west and another on the main north-south ridge route linking Jerusalem and Beersheba. The city of Hebron is conquered by Joshua as a *ḥērem*— a city devoted to Yahweh (P. W. Ferris Jr., "Hebron [Place]," *ABD*, 3:107–8).

38–39 Debir identifies both a Canaanite king and a city (10:3). The town of Debir—also called Kiriath Sepher (Jos 15:15–16) and Kiriath Sanna (15:49)—was located in the most southern part of the hill country of Judah. The city of Debir is conquered by Joshua as a *ḥērem*—a city devoted to Yahweh.

40–43 The entire region, including the hill country, the Negev, the western foothills, and the mountain slopes, is conquered by Joshua as a *ḥērem*—a region devoted to Yahweh. The language of this section is highly hyperbolic: "Joshua subdued the *whole* [*kol*] region ... together with *all* [*kol*] their kings.... He *totally* destroyed *all* [*kol*] who breathed ... the *whole* [*kol*] region of Goshen.... *All* [*kol*] these kings and their lands Joshua conquered in one campaign" (emphasis added). Following the conquest, Joshua and his men return to Gilgal. The repetition of the identical statement in verses 15 and 43 is highly dubious. Joshua and his men could not have accomplished all the events of that day twice. There was not sufficient time for Joshua and his men to return to Gilgal between the killing of the Amorite kings and the subduing of Makkedah, Libnah, Lachish, Eglon, Hebron, and the region from Kadesh Barnea to Gaza. The LXX omits verse 15, leaving only one return to the camp at Gilgal after the conquest of the southern region (v.43).

NOTES

29–43 For additional information on Canaanite cities, see J. N. Tubb, *Canaanites (People of the Past)* (Oklahoma City: Univ. of Oklahoma Press, 1999); S. N. Gundry, ed., *Show Them No Mercy: 4 Views on God and Canaanite Genocide* (Grand Rapids: Zondervan, 2003); F. M. Cross, *Canaanite Myth and Hebrew Epic: Essays in the History of the Religion of Israel* (Cambridge, MA: Harvard Univ. Press, 1997); E. Stern, ed. *The New Encyclopedia of Archaeological Excavations in the Holy Land* (Jerusalem: Carta, 1993); E. M. Meyers, ed. *Oxford Encyclopedia of Archaeology in the Near East* (Oxford: Oxford Univ. Press, 1997).

5. Conquest of Northern Cities (11:1–23)

a. The Northern Kings against Israel (11:1–5)

OVERVIEW

Since its entry into Canaan, Israel has seen a substantial increase in opposition to its presence in the land. At Jericho (ch. 6), no army was present during the destruction and conquest of the town. In the second battle for Ai (ch. 8), the opposition increased as the men of Ai and Bethel joined forces against Israel, only to be defeated through an ambush. At Gibeon (ch. 10), Joshua is not only battling against a band of fighting men but against the Amorite kings and the armies of five southern cities.

Now when Jabin the king of Hazor in the north hears of the great defeat of the Amorite cities in the south, he forms a coalition with the kings of Madon, Shimron, Acshaph, and rulers of northern cities (of cities in the Arabah, in the western foothills, and in Naphoth-Dor [ch. 11]). He also calls on Canaanite, Amorite, Hittite, Perizzite, Jebusite, and Hivite rulers and their troops to join his coalition against Israel at the Waters of Merom. The opposition against Israel has swelled significantly since she entered into Canaan; nevertheless, through divine intervention, Israel subdues its enemies and conquers the land promised to her centuries earlier.

The chapter is replete with hyperbolic language. The repetition of *all, every, entirely, completely, totally, large numbers of, everyone,* and other such expressions is significant. These terms contribute to the tension of the story and add to the tone of urgency in the narrative. Essentially, this chapter ends the initial description of Israel's military conquest of the land.

¹When Jabin king of Hazor heard of this, he sent word to Jobab king of Madon, to the kings of Shimron and Acshaph, ²and to the northern kings who were in the mountains, in the Arabah south of Kinnereth, in the western foothills and in Naphoth Dor on the west; ³to the Canaanites in the east and west; to the Amorites, Hittites, Perizzites and Jebusites in the hill country; and to the Hivites below Hermon in the region of Mizpah. ⁴They came out with all their troops and a large number of horses and chariots — a huge army, as numerous as the sand on the seashore. ⁵All these kings joined forces and made camp together at the Waters of Merom, to fight against Israel.

COMMENTARY

1–3 Troubled at the swift advance of the Israelites, King Jabin of Hazor summons the rulers of the surrounding regions and assembles the largest army gathered in Canaan until now. With a population of approximately thirty thousand inhabitants, Hazor was a significant urban center at the end of the Late Bronze Age situated ten miles north of the Sea of Galilee on a major road that ran from northern Canaan down to Egypt. Hazor is identified with Khirbet Waqqâf (Tell el-Qedaḥ) southwest of Lake Huleh. According to archaeological evidence, the city was destroyed around the end of the thirteenth century BC, a time frame that corresponds well with a late date of the conquest of the land by the Israelites. Hazor is resettled during the Iron Age but is less important than during the previous centuries.

The name of King Jabin also appears in the story of Barak and Deborah (Jdg 4). Scholars are divided as to the relationship between the Jabin of Joshua 11 and Jabin of Judges 4. Those who opt for one King Jabin propose that the battle mentioned in Judges 4 is the same as that fought by Joshua and his men in Joshua 11. For others, Joshua 11 and Judges 4 describe two separate military conflicts. King Jabin summons King Jobab of Madon, a site identified by some with the "Horns of Hattin" (Tell Qarnei Hittin) five miles west of Tiberias (P. Benjamin, "Madon," *ABD*, 4:463).

The kings of Shimron and Achsaph are not identified by name. Shimron has been linked with Khirbet Sammuniyeh, located in the Jezreel Valley five miles west of Nazareth (C. F. Mariottini, "Shimron," *ABD*, 5:1218). Achsaph has been identified with several possible sites: Tell Keisan, a site destroyed around 1200 BC; Tell Berweh in the foothills; and Tell Harbaj (M. W. Prausnitz, "Achzib," *ABD*, 1:57; J.-B. Humbert, "Keisan, Tell," *ABD*, 4:14–16; Junkkaala, 293–94, 118–20). It is mentioned in several Egyptian second millennium documents (e.g., Papyrus Anastasi 1, the Execration texts and the Amarna letters [366:23; 267:1]). The locations of Shimron and Achsaph reveal the large area under the rulership of the king of Hazor.

The other military men summoned by King Jabin are not mentioned by name, only by location. These include the kings of the Arabah, south of the Kinnereth (Kinnereth refers to the Sea of Galilee and the Arabah is identified with the Jordan Valley, south of the Sea of Galilee); the kings of the lowland (the Shephelah); the king of Naphoth Dor on the west (Naphoth Dor is identified with Khirbet el-Burj on the Mediterranean coast, a locale mentioned in thirteenth-century BC Egyptian literature [e.g., Ramses II inscription, story of Wenamun]; see P. Benjamin, "Naphoth-Dor," *ABD*, 4:1020–21); the kings of the Canaanites in the east and west; the kings of the Amorites, Hittites, Perizzites, and Jebusites in the hill country, and the Hivites at the base of Hermon in Mizpah (Hermon probably refers to Mount Hermon in modern Syria).

4–5 With hyperbolic language, the author describes the military might gathered against Israel: "They came out with all their troops and a large number of horses and chariots—a huge army, as numerous as the sand on the seashore." The author makes a clear contrast between the large size of the enemy forces and the small number of Israelites who take part in the conquest of the land under Joshua's leadership. Canaanite states relied on horses and chariots for military victory. By contrast, the Israelites did not multiply horses (Dt 17:16) nor did they trust in chariots (Ps 20:8). Rather, they traveled on foot, used basic weapons for warfare, and depended primarily on Yahweh's help for victory in battle. As seen in the Exodus from Egypt, chariots and horses were no match for Yahweh. Regardless of its strong military advantage, Pharaoh's army was defeated in a fell swoop and swallowed up by the Red Sea.

The location of the Waters of Merom is unclear, but some have proposed Lake Semechonitis, west-northwest of modern Safed (D. C. Liik, "Merom, Waters of," *ABD*, 4:705; Junkkaala, 165–67).

The hyperbole "as numerous as the sand on the seashore" appears in several passages with reference to people, supplies, and wisdom. For example:

• God promises to bless Abraham and make his descendants so numerous that they will be "as the sand on the seashore" (Ge 22:17).

- Jacob fears his encounter with Esau and reminds God of his promise to "make his descendants like the sand of the seashore" (32:12).
- Joseph stores such a huge quantity of grain ("like the sand of the seashore") that it is impossible to keep count (41:49).
- Gideon and his three hundred men face the Midianites, the Amalekites, and a multitude of people from the east who had settled in the valley with their camels that were as countless "as the sand of the seashore" (Jdg 7:12).
- The Philistine soldiers who set up camp against Israel are "as numerous as the sand on the seashore" (1Sa 13:5).
- Hushai instructs Absalom to gather a band of men from Dan to Beersheba "as numerous as the sand on the seashore" to come against David and his men (2Sa 17:11).
- The people of Judah and Israel grow to be "as numerous as the sand on the seashore" during Solomon's reign (the mention of "Judah and Israel" is curious since during Solomon's reign, the kingdom was not yet divided [1Ki 4:20]).
- Solomon's wisdom, insight, and breadth of understanding was so great that it is described as "measureless as the sand on the seashore" (1Ki 4:29).

(For additional examples, see Isa 10:22; 48:19; Jer 33:22; Hos 1:10; Heb 11:12 (Israel); Job 29:18; Ps 78:27; Rev 20:8.)

NOTES

1 "When Jabin heard" (וַיְהִי כִּשְׁמֹעַ יָבִין, *way*[e]*hî kišmōa*[c] *yābîn*). The use of *k*[e]- + infinitive construct introducing a temporal clause indicates urgency ("as soon as Jabin heard"). The city of Madon appears as Maron in ancient Greek. Hess suggests that the site of Madon may be the same as that of Merom (Hess, *Joshua*, 208). Shimron appears as Symoōn (Συμοων) and Achsaph appears as Aziph (Αζιφ) in LXX.

4 The repetition of keywords contribute to the hyperbolic tone of the narrative include *rāb* (רָב, "great, large"), *rōb* (רֹב, "great, large,") and *rāb m*[e]*ʾōd* (רַב מְאֹד, "huge, very large"). The cumulation of the terms implies that the armies of Israel's enemies are exceedingly large in number and powerful in strength. Consequently, Israel's victory in battle against such a legion is theologically symbolic—Yahweh gives Israel the victory.

b. Joshua Defeats the Northern Kings (11:6-15)

> [6]The LORD said to Joshua, "Do not be afraid of them, because by this time tomorrow I will hand all of them over to Israel, slain. You are to hamstring their horses and burn their chariots."
> [7]So Joshua and his whole army came against them suddenly at the Waters of Merom and attacked them, [8]and the LORD gave them into the hand of Israel. They defeated them and pursued them all the way to Greater Sidon, to Misrephoth Maim, and to the Valley

of Mizpah on the east, until no survivors were left. ⁹Joshua did to them as the LORD had directed: He hamstrung their horses and burned their chariots.

¹⁰At that time Joshua turned back and captured Hazor and put its king to the sword. (Hazor had been the head of all these kingdoms.) ¹¹Everyone in it they put to the sword. They totally destroyed them, not sparing anything that breathed, and he burned up Hazor itself.

¹²Joshua took all these royal cities and their kings and put them to the sword. He totally destroyed them, as Moses the servant of the LORD had commanded. ¹³Yet Israel did not burn any of the cities built on their mounds — except Hazor, which Joshua burned. ¹⁴The Israelites carried off for themselves all the plunder and livestock of these cities, but all the people they put to the sword until they completely destroyed them, not sparing anyone that breathed. ¹⁵As the LORD commanded his servant Moses, so Moses commanded Joshua, and Joshua did it; he left nothing undone of all that the LORD commanded Moses.

COMMENTARY

6–9 Maintaining the hyperbolic language of the previous section, the story proceeds with the conquest narrative. Joshua and his relatively small band of men face an enormous military force and, in what seems to be an impossible situation, Yahweh gives a swift and comprehensive victory to Israel. Within twenty-four hours, Joshua and his small band of men surprise the huge enemy army gathered at the Waters of Merom and overcome it instantly. They hamstring their horses (render them inoperable) and burn their chariots with fire — ancient methods of warfare that disable an enemy permanently. As in previous battles, Yahweh gives the enemies of Israel into her hands (see 10:28–43), and the enemy scatters in all directions — northward toward Sidon (coastal region north of the Litani River), westward toward the sea to Misrephoth Maim (probably at the northern plain of Acco), and eastward into the Valley of Mizpeh (probably a valley in the Lebanon mountains). Once again, the victory is complete and no enemy is left standing.

The expression "be not afraid because of them" reminds the reader of Yahweh's words of encouragement to Moses (Nu 21:34; Dt 3:2), Moses' words to Israel (Dt 1:21; 20:1), and Yahweh's words to Joshua before the defeat of Ai (8:1) and the dismantling of the southern coalition (10:8).

10–11 Since Jabin the king of Hazor (Tell el-Qedah) had initiated this military endeavor, Joshua turns his attention to his city and captures it, destroying its king with the sword and killing all its inhabitants (cf. 10:28, 30, 32, 35, 37). The pattern of events is similar to that of the southern campaign (cf. 10:28–39): Joshua captures the city, puts its king to the sword, and spares no one. The only addition at Hazor is the burning of the city. Unlike most of the cities conquered so far, Hazor is burnt to the ground, the third city in Canaan to be set ablaze by Joshua (the other two cities are Jericho [6:24] and Ai [8:8, 19]) (archaeologist Yigael Yadin identified a burnt layer in stratum 13). The fate of Hazor is defined as a *ḥērem* — a town devoted to destruction for Yahweh. The repetition of terms such as "destroyed" (*yayyakkû*) and "sword" (*ḥereb*) in this chapter reinforces the idea of the complete destruction of the enemy (cf. 10:28, 30, 32, 25, 27, 29).

The destruction of Hazor is significant, especially since archaeologists have identified it as a large Bronze Age urban center whose king ruled the entire region. Hazor is mentioned in Egyptian literature (e.g., Amarna letters 148 and 364), texts from Mari (A. Malamat, *Mari and the Early Israelite Experience* [Oxford: Oxford Univ. Press, 1989], 56–68), and records from Pella, Tyra, and Hazor itself. Omen, legal, lexical, administrative, and epistolary texts written in cuneiform have been found at the tell (for bibliography, see Hess, *Joshua*, 213, n.1). Verses 1 and 10–11 form a literary *inclusio* as the battle begins at Hazor and ends at Hazor.

12 As Joshua and his men did to the cities of the south, so also they do to the northern cities, putting their kings to the sword and killing their inhabitants. As per Moses' instructions (cf. 1:7, 13; 4:10, 12; 8:30–33; 11:15; 20:2, 8; 22:2), Hazor is completely destroyed (*ḥērem*).

13–14 Of all the northern cities conquered, only Hazor is burnt. The other towns that sit on top of tells (mounds) are left standing. Unlike at the battle of Jericho, the Israelites are permitted to plunder Hazor and take the livestock for themselves.

15 The events end with a confirmation that all was ordained by God. The instructions to conquer the entire region had originally come from Yahweh through Moses to Joshua, who left nothing undone of what had been commanded. Since the military conflict was conducted under divine mandate, one could only anticipate victory for Israel. Although not explicitly stated, Yahweh acts as the military commander of the entire campaign. Under his leadership, victory is guaranteed. Israelite history shows that when Israel takes military matters into her own hands, the battle is often lost; but when Yahweh ordains the maneuvers, victory is guaranteed.

NOTE

13 "[All] of the cities built on their mounds" (כָּל־הֶעָרִים הָעֹמְדוֹת עַל־תִּלָּם), *kol-heʿārîm hāʿōmdôt ʿal-tillām*). A "tel" or "mound" is a man-made mound on which a town is built. The word is sometimes translated as "ruin" or "heap of ruins" (Dt 13:16; Jos 8:28). Materials found in "tells" provide information for interpreting the social, familial, political, cultural, and cultic life of the inhabitants of the town (J. C. H. Laughlin, "Tel, Tell," *NIDB*, 5:486).

c. The Conquest of Northern Cities (11:16–23)

> [16]So Joshua took this entire land: the hill country, all the Negev, the whole region of Goshen, the western foothills, the Arabah and the mountains of Israel with their foothills, [17]from Mount Halak, which rises toward Seir, to Baal Gad in the Valley of Lebanon below Mount Hermon. He captured all their kings and struck them down, putting them to death. [18]Joshua waged war against all these kings for a long time. [19]Except for the Hivites living in Gibeon, not one city made a treaty of peace with the Israelites, who took them all in

battle. ²⁰For it was the LORD himself who hardened their hearts to wage war against Israel, so that he might destroy them totally, exterminating them without mercy, as the LORD had commanded Moses.

²¹At that time Joshua went and destroyed the Anakites from the hill country: from Hebron, Debir and Anab, from all the hill country of Judah, and from all the hill country of Israel. Joshua totally destroyed them and their towns. ²²No Anakites were left in Israelite territory; only in Gaza, Gath and Ashdod did any survive. ²³So Joshua took the entire land, just as the LORD had directed Moses, and he gave it as an inheritance to Israel according to their tribal divisions.

Then the land had rest from war.

COMMENTARY

16–18 Although the summary of events indicates that the entire land (from south to north) is conquered by Joshua in what seems to be quick and easy military confrontations, the author soon reveals that the campaign was not as swift and painless as described in this chapter. The warfare took place over an extended period of time (v.18), so that additional battles occurred besides those mentioned thus far.

The exact length of time it took to subdue the land is not specified. A survey of the area conquered includes "the entire land," meaning the hill country (south and central regions), the Negev (south), the region of Goshen (Transjordan), the western foothills (Shephelah), the Arabah (the Jordan Valley), from Mount Halak (southeast of Beersheba) toward Seir (Edom) to Baal Gad (in the Valley of Lebanon), south of Mount Hermon. Noticeably absent from the summary of the conquest is the coastal region (Philistine area) and the Galilee. In Joshua 13, these two regions are identified as "unconquered territory."

19 Thanks to a special (and deceitful) peace treaty made between Joshua and the Hivites (9:3–27), the inhabitants of Gibeon are the only ones who are protected from the *ḥērem*; consequently, they suffer no loss during the conquest.

20 Could the Canaanites also have made a peace agreement with Israel and lived? Not according to Deuteronomy 20:10–15. Such a peace treaty was forbidden. The Canaanites had no chance of survival. Their fate was sealed. The text reveals that Yahweh had hardened their hearts and had incited them to wage war against Israel "so that he may destroy them totally, exterminating them without mercy." This statement can be troubling to us today, but, as proposed by some scholars, Yahweh's "hardening of the hearts" of the Canaanites was not simply an act of manipulation; rather, it may have been intended to establish Yahweh's superiority over human powers, especially the enemies of Israel. As mentioned above, the Canaanites had to be driven out of the land lest they teach the Israelites to worship their gods.

Some have suggested that the Canaanites would have opposed Israel regardless, even without Yahweh's intervention. The "hardening of the hearts" of the Canaanites points back to the "hardening of the heart" of Pharaoh, whose blind self-confidence contributed to his refusal to let Israel go (Ex 7–14).

Pharaoh's fate was inevitable. He was an enemy of God's people and had to be treated as such. As mentioned earlier, a number of features in the conquest narrative reflects details of the Exodus account (e.g., parting of waters, hardening of the hearts of enemies, Yahweh as divine warrior). The rebellion of Pharaoh and the Canaanites against God's plan brought them the same fate—destruction. In contrast, the obedience of God's people in Egypt and Canaan brought them the same conclusion—victory over their enemies.

21–22 The Anakites (sons of Anak associated with the Nephilim [Nu 13:33] and also with the Rephaim [Dt 2:11]) are described in Deuteronomy as "strong and tall" (1:28; 2:10–11, 21); yet these features do not deter Joshua from attacking them, destroying their towns, and annihilating them completely (*ḥērem*), except for Gaza, Gath, and Ashdod (three of the five Philistine cities). Victory over the Anakites foretold decades earlier (Dt 9:1–5) is a fitting conclusion to the conquest of the land. It communicates the fulfillment of the divine promise given through Moses that "the LORD your God ... will destroy them; he will subdue them before you. And you will drive them out and annihilate them quickly" (9:2–3).

For Hebron and Debir, see comments on 10:3–5. Hebron (Kiriath Arba) and its surroundings are eventually given to Caleb as an inheritance (15:13–14). And Debir (Kiriath Sepher) is conquered by the nephew of Caleb, Othniel, who is subsequently given in marriage to Caleb's daughter (15:15–19). Anab (P. Benjamin, "Anab," *ABD*, 1:219) is identified with Khirbet ʿAnâb located

approximately fourteen miles from Hebron. Gaza (H. J. Katzenstein, "Gaza (Pre-Hellenistic)," *ABD*, 2:912–15; *NEAEHL*, 464–67) is identified with Tell Harube. Gath (J. D. Seger, "Gath," *ABD*, 2:908–09) is identified with Tell es-Safi, where Late Bronze Age and Early Iron Age remains have been found. Ashdod (M. Dothan, "Ashdod," *ABD*, 1:477–82; *NEAEHL*, 98–102) has been excavated and reveals remains from the Late Bronze Age and Early Iron Age, with the evidence of an burnt layer. The mention of "the hill country of Judah" and "the hill country of Israel" serves as a hyperbole to point to the comprehensiveness of the conquest.

23 The entire land is conquered over an extended period of time. The tribal division described in chapters 13–21 is mentioned in summary here, a clue that this portion of the text was written after the division of the land was completed. The mention that "the land had rest from war" (cf. 14:15) indicates that this verse was written much later than the events described in the chapter, after "the land" had experienced a significant period of renewal and rest. A similar expression appears in an Akkadian text from Alalakh (AT 456.30) while the governor of the land (Zitraddu) revolts against a ruler (Yarimlim), engages in warfare with his men, defeats them, and eventually returns to Aleppo in peace (Hess, "The Book of Joshua as Land Grant," 501). A concluding statement after Joshua's defeat of the southern and the northern kings is a fitting conclusion to the conquest narrative and provides a natural segue for the next section of the book—the division of the land.

NOTES

18 The NIV reads: "Joshua waged war against all these kings for a long time" (יָמִים רַבִּים עָשָׂה יְהוֹשֻׁעַ אֶת־כָּל־הַמְּלָכִים הָאֵלֶּה מִלְחָמָה, *yāmîm rabbîm ʿāśā yᵉhôšuaʿ ʾet-kol-hammᵉlākîm hāʾēlleh milḥāmā*). In the Hebrew, the main clause is fronted by the temporal phrase "for a long time." The place of this temporal phrase emphasizes that the conquest took an extended period of time (possibly "*over a very long period of time,* Joshua waged war against all these kings").

6. List of Defeated Kings (12:1–24)

OVERVIEW

Chapter 12 provides a summary of the conquest by Moses on the eastern side of the Jordan (12:1–6), a summary of the land conquered by Joshua west of the Jordan, and a list of kings defeated in battle in Canaan (12:9–24). What Moses did in Transjordan, Joshua did in Cisjordan. The land conquered east of the Jordan is described with the formula "from X to Y," mapping out the territory conquered by the children of Israel as it appears in Numbers 21:21–35 and Deuteronomy 2:24–3:11. The list of defeated kings includes the names of towns/regions conquered by Joshua on the west side of the Jordan rather than the names of the rulers who governed them. After each king, the number "one" is repeated. This number may indicate that only "one" king ruled over the city at the time of the conquest.

The list of kings includes nine cities not mentioned in the conquest narrative (*southern*—Geder, Hormah, Arad, Adullam; *northern*—Bethel, Tappuah, Hepher, Aphek, Lasharon). The addition of these names may indicate that there were more towns and cities conquered in Canaan than what could be described in detail in the narrative. Lists of defeated kings and conquered towns/regions are not unique to the biblical narrative; they appear in ancient Near Eastern reports of military campaigns (e.g., lists from Thutmoses III in the Temple at Karnak, Sennacherib's third campaign in Canaan). Rulers were known for recording their military conquests as a sign of personal greatness and honor, often using the expression "I captured, destroyed [name of city]." In contrast to the boastful ancient Near Eastern campaign reports, the language of Joshua 12 does not attribute the victory to the leader but to the Israelites as a people.

Verses 6–7 confirm the connection between the two outstanding leaders. Together with the Israelites, Moses and Joshua "conquer" (*nkh*) the land of their enemies and set the stage for the distribution of land to Israel. The conclusion of Moses' long and fruitful ministry is the beginning of Joshua's successful leadership.

a. Kings East of the Jordan Defeated by Moses (12:1–6)

¹These are the kings of the land whom the Israelites had defeated and whose territory they took over east of the Jordan, from the Arnon Gorge to Mount Hermon, including all the eastern side of the Arabah:

²Sihon king of the Amorites, who reigned in Heshbon.

He ruled from Aroer on the rim of the Arnon Gorge — from the middle of the gorge — to the Jabbok River, which is the border of the Ammonites. This included half of Gilead. ³He also ruled over the eastern Arabah from the Sea of Kinnereth to the Sea of the Arabah (the Salt Sea), to Beth Jeshimoth, and then southward below the slopes of Pisgah.

⁴And the territory of Og king of Bashan, one of the last of the Rephaites, who reigned in Ashtaroth and Edrei.

⁵He ruled over Mount Hermon, Salecah, all of Bashan to the border of the people of Geshur and Maacah, and half of Gilead to the border of Sihon king of Heshbon.

⁶Moses, the servant of the Lord, and the Israelites conquered them. And Moses the servant of the Lord gave their land to the Reubenites, the Gadites and the half-tribe of Manasseh to be their possession.

COMMENTARY

1 The chapter begins with a summary of the territory conquered in Transjordan under Moses' leadership. The two kings who ruled over the vast area are mentioned by name — Sihon, king of the Amorites, and Og, king of Bashan. This differs from the list of defeated leaders in Cisjordan, where the kings are identified by the names of towns/regions rather than by personal names. The Arnon Gorge, identified as modern Wadi el-Mujib, marks the southern border of Sihon's territory and the northern border of Moab. The Arnon River flows into the Jordan from the eastern side. Mount Hermon (altitude 9,232 ft.) marks the northern border of the territory conquered by Israel under Moses' leadership before the crossing of the Jordan. The area conquered under Moses' leadership is approximately 130 miles, south to north.

2–3 The first king defeated in Transjordan is Sihon, king of the Amorites, who reigned in Heshbon and whose defeat is described in Numbers 21:21–31 and Deuteronomy 2:24–37. His territory extended from Aroer to the Jabbok River, on the eastern Arabah from the Sea of Kinnereth to the Dead Sea, from Beth Jeshimoth and southward to Pisgah. Transjordan is primarily a plateau that rises approximately seven thousand feet above the Jordan Valley and the Dead Sea.

Heshbon is identified with Tell Hesban, located approximately fourteen miles southwest of modern Amman and fifteen miles east of the area where the Jordan River flows into the Dead Sea. An earlier site also identified as Heshbon is linked to Tell Jalul or Tell el-Umeiri, sites occupied during the Late Bronze Age and Early Iron Age. Aroer

(G. L. Mattingly, "Aroer," *ABD*, 1:199) is identified with modern Khirbet ʿAraʿir and located on the rim of the Arnon Gorge. Aroer was occupied during the Late Bronze Age and Early Iron Age.

The Jabbok River is identified with modern Wadi ez-Zerqa, a river that carves its way through the mountains of Gilead to empty out into the Jordan River approximately halfway between the Sea of Galilee and the Dead Sea. The Jabbok River marked the southern border of Ammonite territory. The Eastern Arabah is the area east of the Jordan River, from the Sea of Galilee in the north to the Dead Sea in the south. The Sea of Kinnereth is the Sea of Galilee, and the Sea of the Arabah is the Dead Sea (also called the Salt Sea).

Beth Jeshimoth is identified with modern Tell el-ʿAzeimeh, located on the northeastern corner of the Dead Sea. The slopes of Pisgah are at the western edge of the Moabite plateau and located on the east side of the Dead Sea.

4–5 The next king defeated in Transjordan is Og, king of Bashan, who ruled over Ashtaroth and Edrei, Mount Hermon, Salecah, Geshur, and Maacah. His defeat is described in Numbers 21:33–35 and Deuteronomy 3:1–10. Og is noted as "one of the last of the Rephaites." The Rephaites (see Introduction) may be associated with the Rapi'u mentioned in Late Bronze Age Ugaritic texts (primarily RS 24.252; see B. Margulis, "A Ugaritic

Psalm [RS 24.252]," *JBL* 89 [1970]: 292–304; R. M. Good, "On RS 24.252," *UF* 23 [1991]: 155–60).

Located east-northeast of the Sea of Galilee, Ashtaroth is identified with Tell ʿAshtarah. It is mentioned in Egyptian texts of the second millennium (e.g., Amarna letters) (see B. MacDonald, *East of the Jordan: Territories and Sites of the Hebrew Scriptures* [ASOR Books 6; Boston: American Schools of Oriental Research, 2000], 152–53). The name of the area may be linked to the worship of Ashtoreth (Astarte, Ishtar), a Canaanite goddess. Edrei is identified with modern Derʿa. Both Ashtaroth and Edrei are located in eastern Bashan on different tributaries of the Jarmuk River.

Salecah has been identified as modern Salkhad and is located in the extreme eastern area of Bashan, southeast of Ashtaroth. The people of Geshur and Maacah are Arameans who lived east of the Sea of Galilee. Geshur is located northeast of the Sea of Galilee. Maacah was in the same area, with Geshur to the south and Mount Hermon to the north. The Geshurites and Maacahites were not driven out of the area but continued to live in areas inhabited by Israelites (13:13).

6 This pericope ends with a summary statement attributing the conquest of this land east of the Jordan to Moses, who distributed it to the Reubenites, the Gadites, and the half-tribe of Manasseh.

NOTES

5 The Rephaites are also mentioned in Ge 14:5; 15:20; Dt 2:11, 20; 3:11, 13; Jos 13:12; 17:15; 1Ch 20:4; Job 26:5; Ps 88:11; Pr 2:18; 9:18; 21:16; Isa 14:9; 26:14; 26:19. In some cases, they refer to a people group in Transjordan (e.g., 1Ch 20:4) or Cisjordan (e.g., Jos 13:12). In other cases, the term refers to the dead (e.g., Job 26:5; Ps 88:11; Pr 2:18) or the place of the dead (e.g., Isa 26:19).

b. Kings West of the Jordan Defeated by Joshua (12:7–24)

⁷These are the kings of the land that Joshua and the Israelites conquered on the west side of the Jordan, from Baal Gad in the Valley of Lebanon to Mount Halak, which rises toward Seir (their lands Joshua gave as an inheritance to the tribes of Israel according to their tribal divisions — ⁸the hill country, the western foothills, the Arabah, the mountain slopes, the desert and the Negev — the lands of the Hittites, Amorites, Canaanites, Perizzites, Hivites and Jebusites):

⁹the king of Jericho	one
the king of Ai (near Bethel)	one
¹⁰the king of Jerusalem	one
the king of Hebron	one
¹¹the king of Jarmuth	one
the king of Lachish	one
¹²the king of Eglon	one
the king of Gezer	one
¹³the king of Debir	one
the king of Geder	one
¹⁴the king of Hormah	one
the king of Arad	one
¹⁵the king of Libnah	one
the king of Adullam	one
¹⁶the king of Makkedah	one
the king of Bethel	one
¹⁷the king of Tappuah	one
the king of Hepher	one
¹⁸the king of Aphek	one
the king of Lasharon	one
¹⁹the king of Madon	one
the king of Hazor	one
²⁰the king of Shimron Meron	one
the king of Acshaph	one
²¹the king of Taanach	one

the king of Megiddo	one
[22] the king of Kedesh	one
the king of Jokneam in Carmel	one
[23] the king of Dor (in Naphoth Dor)	one
the king of Goyim in Gilgal	one
[24] the king of Tirzah	one

thirty-one kings in all.

COMMENTARY

7–8 Verses 7–8 correspond to verses 1 and 6, noting identical elements: (1) the names of the leaders, (2) the conquest of the areas by the Israelites, (3) the formula "from X to Y," (4) a description of the land conquered, and (5) the distribution of land by the leader to the tribes of Israel.

9–24 The following section lists towns/regions conquered by Joshua roughly in the order in which the conquest occurred, with the addition of a few sites (e.g., Adullam, Taanach, Megiddo). For an explanation of the grid number, see Carl G. Rasmussen, *Zondervan Atlas of the Bible* (rev. ed.; Grand Rapids: Zondervan, 2010), 273.

Town	Modern name (Arab/Israeli; see NEAEHL)	Primary Scripture references	Tribal allocation	Notes (grid #)
Jericho	Tell es-Sultan	Jos 2; 6; 1Ki 16:34; Mt 20:29–34; Heb 11:30	Benjamin	Border city between Ephraim & Benjamin "City of Palms" #192142
Ai near Bethel	Et-Tell?	Ge 12:8; 13:3; Jos 7–8; Ezr 2:28; Neh 7:32	Benjamin	2nd Ai in Transjordan? (Jer 49:3) #174147
Jerusalem	El-Quds/ Jerusalem	Jos 10; 12:10; 15:63; Jdg 1:6–8, 21; 19; 2Sa 5:5–7, 13; 9:13; 11; 15; 1Ki 8:1; 10; 11; 2Ki 21:7; 25:8–9; Ezr 1; 6; 7; Jer 24:1–2; Mic 3:12; Mt 11:15–17; Rev 3:12	Judah	Southern coalition #172131

Hebron	Tell er-Rumeideh (el-Khalil)	Ge 13:18; 23:2, 19; Jos 10; 11:21; 12:10; 14:13–15; 15:13–14; 20:1–7; 2Sa 2:1–5, 11; 5:5; 1Ki 2:10–11	Judah	Southern coalition city of refuge Levitical city— Kohathites "Kiriath-Arba" Given to Caleb King David's 1st capital city #160103
Jarmuth	Khirbet el-Yarmuk/Yarmut	Jos 10:3, 5, 23; 12:11; 15:35; 21:29; Neh 11:29	Judah	Southern coalition Levitical city— Gershonites #147124
Lachish	Tell ed-Duweir/ Tell Lachish	Jos 10; 12:11; 15:39; 2Ki 14:18–19; 18:14–17 (Isa 36:2); 19:8 (Isa 37:9); Neh 11:30; Jer 34:6–7; Mic 1:13	Judah	Southern coalition Captured by Nebuchadnezzar & Sennacherib #135108
Eglon	Tell ʿAiṭûn/ Tell ʿEton	Jos 10; 12:12; 15:39	Judah	Southern coalition #143099
Gezer	Tell Jezer (Abu Shusheh)/Tell Gezer	Jos 10:33; 12:12; 16:3, 10; 21:21; Jdg 1:29; 2Sa 5:25; 1Ki 9:15–17	Ephraim	Levitical city— Kohathites #142140
Debir	Khirbet Rabûd	Jos 11:21; 12:13; 15:7, 15, 49; 21:15; Jdg 1:11	Judah	Levitical city— Kohathites "Kiriath Sepher" "Kiriath Sannah" #151093
Geder	Khirbet Jedûr?	Jos 12:13	Judah? Simeon?	?
Hormah	Khirbet el-Meshâsh/Tell Masos or Tell es-Sebeta	Num 21:3; Jos 12:14; 15:30; Jdg 1:17	Judah/ Simeon	"Zephath" #146069

Arad— LBA, IA I and IA II	East of Beersheba: *Tell el-Milh* (Tell Malhata) and south of Hebron: *Tell Arad*	Num 21:1; Jos 12:14; Jdg 1:16	Judah	*#152069* (Tell el-Milh) *#162076* (Tell Arad)
Libnah	Tell Bornât Tell Burna? Tell el-Beida/ Khirbet Lavnin?	Jos 10; 12:15; 15:42; 21:13; 2Ki 8:22; 19:8 (Isa 37:8); Jer 52:1	Judah	Levitical city— Kohathites *#145116*
Adullam	Tell esh-Sheikh Madhkûr/Khirbet ʿAdullam	Ge 38:1–5; Jos 12:15; 15:35; 1Sa 22:1; 2Sa 23:13; Neh 11:30; Mic 1:13–16	Judah	Fortified by Rehoboam *#150117*
Makkedah	Khirbet el-Qôm	Jos 10; 12:16; 15:41	Judah	*#146104*
Bethel	Beitîn	Ge 12:8; 13:3; 35; Jos 7:2; 8:9, 12, 17; 12:9; 16:1–2; Jdg 4:4–5; 20; 21; 1Sa 7:15–17; 1Ki 12:26–33; 13; 2Ki 2:1–3; 23; Jer 48:13; Hos 10:15; Am 3:14; 5:4–6; 7:10–17	Benjamin	Jeroboam built worship center & golden calf "Luz" *#172148*
Tappuah	Sheikh Abū Zarad	Jos 12:17; 15:34; 16:8; 17:8	Judah (Jos 15:34) Ephraim (Jos 16:8; 17:8)	*#172168* (Ephraim) #? (Judah)
(Gath) Hepher	Tell el-Mumâar? Tell el-Ifshar? (Hepher) Khirbet ez-Zurra/Tell Gat Hepher (Gath Hepher)	Jos 12:17; 19:13; 1 Ki 4:10; 2Ki 14:23–25	Zebulun	Home of prophet Jonah *#141197* (Hepher) *#180238* (Gath Hepher)
Aphek	Tell Kurdaneh/ Tell Afeq	Jos 12:18; 13:1–4; 19:30; Jdg 1:31; 1Sa 4:1–2; 2Ki 13:14–20	Asher	*#160250*
Lasharon	Sharon Plain	Jos 12:18	?	LXX "Aphek of Sharon"

Madon	Qarn Hattin/ Tell Qarnei Hittin? (Merom)	Jos 11:1; 12:19	? in Galilee	Northern coalition #193245 (Merom)
Hazor	Tell el-Qedah/ Tell Hazor	Jos 11; 12:19; 19:36–37; Jdg 4:1–2; 1 Ki 9:15; 2 Ki 15:29; Jer 29:38–43	Naphtali	Northern coalition Major international route #203269
Shimron Meron	Khirbet Sammuniya/ Tell Shimron	Jos 12:20	Zebulun	Northern coalition LXX reads "Shimron" and "Meron" #?
Acshaph	Khirbet el-Harbaj?/ Tell Regev?	Jos 11:1; 12:20; 19:25	Asher	Northern coalition #158240
Taanach	Tell Ti'innik/ Tell Ta'anakh	Jos 12:21; 21:25; Jdg 1:27; 1Ki 4:7–12	Manasseh	Levitical city— Kohathites #171214
Megiddo	Tell el-Mutesellim/ Tell Megiddo	Jos 12:21; 17:11; Jdg 1:27; 1Ki 4:7–12; 9:15; 2Ki 9:27–28; 23:29–30	Manasseh	Major city Ahaziah and Josiah died there #167221
Kedesh	Khirbet Qedish/ Tell Qedesh	Jos 12:22; 20:1–7	Naphtali	Upper Galilee city of refuge Levitical city— Gershonites #199279 Another Kedesh in Judah (Jos 15:23)
Jokneam in Carmel	Tell Qeimûn/ Tell Yoqneam	Jos 12:22; 19:11; 21:34	Zebulun	Levitical city— Merarites #160230
Dor in Naphoth-Dor	Khirbet el-Burj/ Tell Dor	Jos 11:1–3; 12:23; Jdg 1:27; 1Ki 4:7–19	Manasseh	Northern coalition Levitical city— Gershonites

				Port city; also inhabited by Ephraim (1Chr 7:29) #142224
Goyim in Gilgal	Galilee?	Jos 12:23		LXX "Galilee" "Geliloth" (Jos 18:17)
Tirzah	Tell el-Farah north	Jos 12:24; 1Ki 14:1–18; 16; SS 6:1–4	Manasseh/ Ephraim	#182188

II. DIVIDING THE LAND (13:1–21:45)

OVERVIEW

The second section of Joshua (chs. 13–21) differs substantially from the first (chs. 1–12). The description of battles, confrontations with enemies, and military maneuvers has ended. In chapters 13–19, boundary markers and lists of towns permeate the text. In chapter 20, we find a list of six cities of refuge, where individuals who have committed involuntary manslaughter may flee for protection against the avenger of blood. In chapter 21, Levitical cities and their surrounding pastoral lands are apportioned to the Levites who did not receive an allotment among the tribes (13:14, 33; 18:7). The descendants of Aaron (Kohathites) receive thirteen towns from Judah, Simeon, and Benjamin, and the rest of the Kohathites receive ten towns from Ephraim, Dan, and the half-tribe of Manasseh (west of the Jordan). The Gershonites settle in thirteen towns given to them by the tribes of Issachar, Asher, Naphtali, and the half-tribe of Manasseh in Bashan. Finally, the descendants of Merari receive twelve towns from Reuben, Gad, and Zebulun. Emphasis on exclusive areas for Levites reveals the author's special interest in the cultic life of Israel. The list of Levitical cities indicates that Israel was willing to return to Yahweh a portion of the divine gift of land she had received—a sort of exchange of gifts between the giver and the recipient.

The Israelites who subjugated the towns and cities of Canaan are now ready to occupy the land. Just as Yahweh led the conquest in chapters 1–12, now he oversees the allotment of land for each tribe. The first list of towns and boundaries describes the areas given by Moses to the tribes in Transjordan—Reuben, Gad, and the half-tribe of Manasseh (ch. 13). The description of the allotments to the other nine and a half tribes west of the Jordan (chs. 14–19) is meshed together with brief narrative portions. Some of the narrative statements are formulaic. For example, after the description of certain tribal allotments, the reader discovers that the Israelites could not dislodge the Canaanites from their assigned territory (e.g., 13:13; 15:63; 16:10; 17:12). This formula points toward future trouble in the camp because Yahweh had commanded Israel to drive out *all* the Canaanites from the land, lest these people teach Israel's descendants to serve foreign gods (Dt 7:1–4).

A second formulaic statement reveals the absence of a territorial inheritance for the tribe of Levi (13:14, 33; 14:3, 4; 18:7). The Levites receive, from the other tribes, towns with the surrounding pasturelands for their flocks and herds. Their inheritance also comes through the sacrificial system (13:14; 18:7) and directly through Yahweh (13:33). The nonformulaic narratives include the giving of land to Caleb (14:6–15a; 15:13–19), the fulfillment of the promise of land to the daughters of Zelophehad son of Hepher (17:3–6), the request for more land by the tribe of Joseph (17:14–18), and the survey of the undivided land for the last seven tribes (18:1–10).

The distribution of land to the tribes of Israel is defined in terms of boundaries and town lists. Similar town lists appear in accounts of Assyrian and Egyptian military conquests (e.g., topographical list of Tutmose III, third campaign of Sennacherib, Onomasticon of Amenope). Scholars have compared the structure of these chapters with that of "land grants" common in ancient Near Eastern literature (e.g., Hittite, Ugaritic, Akkadian) (Hess, "The Book of Joshua as a Land Grant," 493–506; includes discussion on Alalakh AT 456). The following questions regarding the order of tribal allotments have been raised by scholars, though no consensus has been reached: (1) Does the pericope that describes the division of the land reflect historical conditions, utopian ideas, or Davidic ideological restorations? (2) Does the land promised to the patriarchs (Ge 15:18) correspond to the territory outlined in Joshua? If not, how does one handle the discrepancy? (3) Does the "Dan to Beersheba" territory include Transjordan?

The land conquered by Joshua in Cisjordan together with the unconquered territory mentioned in Joshua 13:1–5 represent the area of Israelite territory described after the expansion during David's reign (2Sa 24:5–7) and Solomon's twelve districts (1Ki 4:7–19). However, the apportionment of the land in Joshua differs substantially from that found in the eschatological vision of Ezekiel 47–48, in which each tribe will have an equal portion and the aliens receive an inheritance among the tribes (47:21–23).

Here is a summary of tribal allotment in Joshua 13–19:

- *Transjordan*: (1) summary of Transjordanian area conquered under Moses (13:8–13); (2) Reuben (boundaries and towns, 13:15–23); (3) Gad (boundaries and towns, 13:24–28); (4) half-tribe of Manasseh (boundaries, 13:29–31)
- *Cisjordan*: (1) Caleb's inheritance (Hebron, 14:1–15); (2) Judah (boundaries and towns, 1–12, 20–63); (3) Ephraim (boundaries, 16:5–9); (4) half-tribe of Manasseh (boundaries, 17:1–11)
- *By lot at Shiloh*: (1) first lot to Benjamin (boundaries and towns, 18:12–19, 21b–28a); (2) second lot to Simeon (towns taken from Judah, 19:1–9); (3) third lot to Zebulun (boundaries and towns, 19:10–16); (4) fourth lot to Issachar (towns, 19:17–23); (5) fifth lot to Asher (boundaries and towns, 19:24–31); (6) sixth lot to Naphtali (boundaries and towns, 19:39); (7) seventh lot to Dan (towns, 19:40–48); (8) land for Joshua (19:49–51)

A. Unconquered Land (13:1−7)

OVERVIEW

The previous chapter has provided an account of an ostensibly complete conquest report in Transjordan under Moses and in Cisjordan under Joshua. However, the introduction to chapter 13 reveals that even after an extended period of time in the land, Israel has not taken over Canaan completely; a large area still remains unconquered. The unoccupied territory includes the area of the Philistines with its five major cities — Gaza, Ashdod, Ashkelon, Gath, and Ekron — in the southwestern region of Canaan, the coastal district of Phoenicia, and the northern territory from Lebanon to the eastern region of Mount Hermon. In his old age, Joshua has not fully accomplished his mission. Consequently, Yahweh nudges him and reminds him of the task at hand.

A similar account appears in chapter 18 — this time at Joshua's initiative and without Yahweh's prodding. In this case, seven tribes have not yet received their inheritance. Therefore, Joshua sends men to survey the land before he distributes the rest of the inheritance. It is somewhat puzzling, after what seems to be a complete subjugation of the land, that Israel has waited so long to divide it and to settle in it. Why did the tribes west of the Jordan not receive their allotments soon after entering Canaan? Was there a purpose for the waiting period? The text does not answer these important questions.

> [1]When Joshua was old and well advanced in years, the LORD said to him, "You are very old, and there are still very large areas of land to be taken over.
> [2]"This is the land that remains: all the regions of the Philistines and Geshurites: [3]from the Shihor River on the east of Egypt to the territory of Ekron on the north, all of it counted as Canaanite (the territory of the five Philistine rulers in Gaza, Ashdod, Ashkelon, Gath and Ekron — that of the Avvites); [4]from the south, all the land of the Canaanites, from Arah of the Sidonians as far as Aphek, the region of the Amorites, [5]the area of the Gebalites; and all Lebanon to the east, from Baal Gad below Mount Hermon to Lebo Hamath.
> [6]"As for all the inhabitants of the mountain regions from Lebanon to Misrephoth Maim, that is, all the Sidonians, I myself will drive them out before the Israelites. Be sure to allocate this land to Israel for an inheritance, as I have instructed you, [7]and divide it as an inheritance among the nine tribes and half of the tribe of Manasseh."

COMMENTARY

1 The mention of Joshua's age — he "was old and well advanced in years" — serves as a transitional comment between the conquest of Canaan and the division of the land. Joshua's service, first as Moses' loyal aide since his youth (Nu 11:28) and then as his anointed successor (Nu 27:18–23), had now lasted over four decades. After the exodus, Joshua fought the Amalekites (Ex 17:8–16), journeyed for forty years in the desert, and lived in Canaan for an extended period of time. He could easily have been in his mid-eighties by this time, about the same age as Caleb (14:10), who had served alongside him since the exodus out of Egypt.

The mention of Joshua's old age (*zāqēn bā' bayyāmîm*) highlights the fact that a lengthy period of time elapsed between the conquest and the distribution of the land west of the Jordan. Joshua personally mentions his old age later, before the renewal of the covenant at Shechem and shortly before his death (23:1–2). The expression used in this case is exclusively reserved for prominent leaders who have served Yahweh for extended periods of time. Note how the same phrase identified Abraham and Sarah as "advanced in years" (*zᵉqēnîm bā'îm bayyāmîm*, Ge 18:11). Shortly thereafter, Abraham alone was described as being "old' (*zāqēn bā' bayyāmîm*, 24:1). It is possible that the use of the idiom in Joshua attempts "to connect Joshua to Abraham, perhaps to convey the notion that Joshua has taken the land promised to the patriarch" (J. Bembry, *Yahweh's Coming of Age* [Winona Lake, Ind.: Eisenbrauns, 2011], 29).

The idiomatic expression *zāqēn bā' bayyāmîm* also later identifies King David as being "old and well advanced in years" (1Ki 1:1). His old age and frail body — probably impotent — prevent him from being comfortably warm. David's servants bring a beautiful young virgin — Abishag, a Shunammite — to lie beside him. She takes care of him (probably until his death) but has no sexual relations with him (1Ki 1:2–4). In Samuel, four individuals are listed as "old" (*zāqēn*): Eli (1Sa 2:22; 4:18), Samuel (8:1; 12:2), Jesse (17:12), and Barzillai (2Sa 19:33). Eli and Barzillai were "very old" (*zāqēn mᵉ'ōd*) at the respective ages of ninety-eight (1Sa 4:15) and eighty (2Sa 19:32). Samuel's long and fruitful life is described in detail in 1 and 2 Samuel. As for Jesse, the father of eight sons (1Sa 17:12), little is known except for his relationship with David.

2–5 The land that remains to be conquered includes the land of the Philistines with its five major cities in Canaanite territory. Gaza, Ashdod, and Ashkelon are on the Mediterranean coast, while Gath and Ekron are located inland in the Shephelah (foothills). The Philistines were not Canaanites (see Introduction, "The People of the Land"). They came from Caphtor (Crete) during the migration of the Sea Peoples in the twelfth century BC. They settled on the southern coastal area of Canaan, on the major trade route between Syria and Egypt. The mention of Philistines in Genesis 21:32–34; 26:1, 8, 14–15 and Exodus 13:17; 15:14; and 23:31 is anachronistic. Their mention in the patriarchal narratives points to the redaction or editing of the Genesis and Exodus passages after the thirteenth century BC, after the arrival of the Philistines on the eastern coast of the Mediterranean Sea (C. Westermann, *Genesis 12–36: A Commentary* [trans. J. J. Scullion; Minneapolis, Minn.: Augsburg, 1985], 349).

Since the entire area that belonged to the Canaanites was given to Israel (Ge 12:7; Ex 3:8–9; Nu 33:53; 34:1–12), the land of the Philistines was destined to be conquered (for information on the

Geshurites, Avvites, Canaanites, Amorites, Gebalites, and Sidonians, see Introduction, "The People of the Land"). The following chart provides a description of the land that remains, with the modern name of each site (Arabic and Israeli names), Scripture references, location of sites, tribal allocations, and grid numbers (for information on the charts in chs. 13–19, see C. R. Rasmussen, *Zondervan Atlas of the Bible* [Grand Rapids: Zondervan: 2010]; B. J. Beitzer, *The New Moody Atlas of the Bible* [Chicago: Moody Press, 2009]; J. D. Currid and D. P. Barrett, *ESV Bible Atlas* [Wheaton, Ill.: Crossway, 2010]; A. F. Rainey and R. S. Notley, *The Sacred Bridge* [Jerusalem: Carta, 2006]).

Town / Region — Modern name (Arabic / Israeli)	Location — Tribal allocation — Grid #
Shihor River — ("black river") Jos 13:3; 1Ch 13:5; Isa 23:3; Jer 2:18	Northeast Egypt NE portion of the Pelusaic branch of the Nile in the E delta of Egypt or the frontier canal in the far E delta
Gaza — Ghazzeh / Azza Jos 13:3; 15:47; Jdg 16:1; Am 1:6; Acts 8:26	3.5 mi. inland from the Mediterranean Sea Judah (15:47); *#099101*
Ashdod — Esdud / Tel Ashdod Jos 11:22; Ne 13:23; Zec 9:6; Acts 8:40	3 mi. inland from the Mediterranean Sea Judah (15:46, 47); *#117129*
Ashkelon — Asqalan / Ashqelon Jdg 14:19; Jer 47:5; Zep 2:7	On the Mediterranean Sea Judah (Jdg 1:18)l *#107118*
Gath — Tel es-Safi / Tel Zafit Jos 13:3; 1Sa 17:4; Ps 56:0; Mic 1:10	25 mi. SSE of Joppa; *#135123*
Ekron Kh. el-Muqennaᶜ / Tell Miqne Jos 13:3; 2Ki 1:6; Zep 2:4; Zec 9:5	South of the Sorek River; 20 mi. SE of Joppa Judah (15:11) and Dan (19:43); *#136131*
Arah — Unknown Jos 13:4	In Sidonian territory
Aphek — Afqa; Afeq Jos 13:4; Ju 1:31; 1Ki 20:30	23 miles north of Beirut Asher (Jos 19:30); *#231382*
Area of Gebalites (Gebal = Byblos) — Jebeil Jos 13:5; 1Ki 5:18; Eze 27:9	18 mi. NNE of Beirut; on the Med coast; *#210391*
Lebanon Dt 1:7; Jos 13:5; 2Ch 25:18; SS 4:15; Hos 14:5–7	The area of modern Lebanon, excluding the narrow coastal plain (= Phoenicia), but possibly including a portion of W Syria
Baal Gad — Unknown Jos 11:17; 12:7; 13:5	In Valley of Lebanon at W foot of Mt. Hermon

Lebo Hamath—Lebweh Nu 13:21; Jos 13:5; Jdg 3:3	In Lebanese Beqa, 45 mi. N of Damascus; #277397
Misrephoth Maim—Kh. el-Mushrefeh? Jos 11:8; 13:6	N of Galilee in the vicinity of Sidon; possibly in the area of Litani River (Lebanon)

6–7 Yahweh himself promises to drive out the inhabitants of the unconquered areas (southern and northern) and to ready them for occupation by Israel. This theocentric approach to land conquest and ownership places Yahweh as its owner and ultimate caretaker. Israel is primarily accountable to God for its maintenance and usage.

NOTES

1 "You are very old" (אַתָּה זָקַנְתָּה בָּאתָ בַיָּמִים, ʾattā zāqantā bāʾtā bayyāmîm). In order to preserve the vigor of the expression, the sentence could be translated more accurately as: "As for *you*, *you* have become old, *you* have now come of age." Focus is placed on the second person singular—in this case, Joshua. A stative verb in the perfect (here zāqantā, זָקַנְתָּ) is often translated in the present tense. Such verbs emphasize a durative or continuative state (Waltke and O'Connor, §30.2.3a). In this passage, the verb for "to be taken over" (לְרִשְׁתָּהּ, lᵉrištâh) indicates that the land had not yet been taken fully, or that it had been taken but was not yet occupied by the Israelites (see Howard, 300–302; N. Lohfink, "ירשׁ yaraš," *TDOT*, 6:368–96; C. J. H. Wright, "ירשׁ," *NIDOTTE*, 2:547–49).

B. Land Allotment East of the Jordan (13:8–33)

OVERVIEW

The rest of chapter 13 describes the area east of the Jordan, given by Moses to the tribes of Reuben, Gad, and the half-tribe of Manasseh. The land was divided among them before Israel entered Canaan, but no description of this territory has previously been given. It is significant at this point to indicate that the tribes settling east of the Jordan (two and a half tribes) were united with the tribes that settled on the west side of the Jordan (nine and a half tribes). The twelve tribes were one unit; this can never be ignored. The mention of Moses, "the servant of the LORD," is also significant as it reminds the Israelites that Moses participated actively in the acquisition of Israel's homeland and in the assignment of the territory before he died (cf. 12:6). For the first time, the reader learns that "the Israelites did not drive out the people" from various areas (13:13; cf. 15:63; 16:10; 17:12). This distressing report suggests that trouble is brewing on the horizon.

1. Introduction (13:8–14)

⁸The other half of Manasseh, the Reubenites and the Gadites had received the inheritance that Moses had given them east of the Jordan, as he, the servant of the LORD, had assigned it to them.

⁹It extended from Aroer on the rim of the Arnon Gorge, and from the town in the middle of the gorge, and included the whole plateau of Medeba as far as Dibon, ¹⁰and all the towns of Sihon king of the Amorites, who ruled in Heshbon, out to the border of the Ammonites. ¹¹It also included Gilead, the territory of the people of Geshur and Maacah, all of Mount Hermon and all Bashan as far as Salecah — ¹²that is, the whole kingdom of Og in Bashan, who had reigned in Ashtaroth and Edrei and had survived as one of the last of the Rephaites. Moses had defeated them and taken over their land. ¹³But the Israelites did not drive out the people of Geshur and Maacah, so they continue to live among the Israelites to this day.

¹⁴But to the tribe of Levi he gave no inheritance, since the offerings made by fire to the LORD, the God of Israel, are their inheritance, as he promised them.

COMMENTARY

8–12 The first tribes to receive their inheritance are those that settled in Transjordan. Moses distributed the land to Reuben, Gad, and the half-tribe of Manasseh (see Nu 32:33–42; Dt 3:8–17). Before providing a list of towns for each of the eastern tribes, the author presents a general survey of the area. Most of the locations listed in this section (vv.9–13) appear in the tribal lists of the eastern tribes (vv.15–31).

Eastern tribes Borders/Towns *(13:9–13)*	*Comments and Grid #*
13:9—**Aroer** (Reuben)	• see Reuben (13:16)
13:9—**Arnon Gorge** (Reuben) Nu 21:13–14, 24–26; Dt 2:24; 3:12–16; Jdg 11:12–22; 2Ki 2:32–33	• southern border of Reuben; northern border of Moab
13:9—**Medeba** (Reuben)	• see Reuben (13:16)
13:10—**Dibon** (Reuben)	• see Reuben (13:17)
13:11—**Geshur** (Manasseh) 2Sa 3:3; 13:37, 38; 1Ch 2:23; 3:2	• David married the daughter of Talmai the king of Geshur, and she bore to him Absalom • Absalom fled to Geshur after executing Amnon

	• Geshur and Aram capture the Israelite territory of Havvoth Jair • 1.5 mi. N of the Sea of Galilee • et-Tell, *#209257*
13:11—**Maacah** (Manasseh) Jos 12:5; 2Sa 10:6, 8; 1Ch 19:7	• a small Aramean (Syrian) kingdom in N Israel • its inhabitants were not driven out and they were initially one of David's adversaries but became his vassal • NE portion of the Huleh Valley and the NW slopes of the Golan Heights
13:11—**Mount Hermon** Dt 3:8; Jos 12:1; 1Ch 5:23; Ps 133:3	• high mountain in NE Israel that marked the N most limit of Joshua's conquests • snow covered much of the year; tributaries of the Jordan River originate at its base • also called Senir, Sirion, and Baal Hermon • 27 mi. WSW of Damascus; 9,232 feet high • Jebel esh-Sheikh/Jebel eth-Thalj
13:11—**Bashan** (Manasseh) Nu 32:33; 1Ch 6:62; Ne 9:22; Isa 33:9; Am 4:1	• area E and NE of the Sea of Galilee, bounded by the Rift Valley on the W, Mount Hermon on the N, Mount Bashan on the E, and Gilead on the S
13:11—**Salecah** (Manasseh) Dt 3:10; Jos 12:5; 1Ch 5:11	• on E edge of Bashan; had been controlled by Og • allotted to Manasseh but settled by Gadites • in Jordan, ca. 62 mi. ESE of S end of Sea of Galilee and 8 mi. S of Jebel Druze • Salkhad, *#311212*
13:12—**Ashtaroth** (Manasseh) • Levitical city Dt 1:4; Jos 9:10; 1Ch 6:71	• capital city of Og, king of Bashan before captured by Israel • in Transjordan, 22 mi. E of Sea of Galilee • Tell Ashtarah, *#243244*
13:12—**Edrei** (Manasseh) Nu 21:33; Dt 3:1, 10	• town in Bashan; the residence of Og, king of Bashan, who was defeated by the Israelites • 60 mi. S of Damascus • Dera, *#253224*
20:8—**Golan** (Manasseh) • city of refuge and Levitical city Dt 4:43; Jos 21:27; 1Ch 6:71	• Transjordanian city • 18 mi. E of Sea of Galilee. In NT times there was a district known as Gaulanitis • Sahm el-Jolan, *#238243*

13 The Israelites do not dispossess (*weˀlōˀ hôrîšû*) all the inhabitants of Geshur and Maacah, even though both areas had already been conquered (12:5). The Geshurites continue to live in the area at least until the time of the united monarchy (2Sa 13:37–38; 14:23, 32; 15:8).

14 The Levites receive no territorial inheritance — neither on the eastern nor on the western side of the Jordan River. Their inheritance is Yahweh himself and the tithes from Israel in return for their service at the tabernacle (Jos 13:14, 33; 18:7). This directive was given to Aaron earlier in the desert years (Nu 18:20–24). Israel was not always consistent in providing tithes for the Levites. During the Persian period, after the exiles returned to Jerusalem, Nehemiah rebuked the Israelites for not bringing the portions assigned to the Levites (Neh 13:10–14). Consequently, in order to survive, the priests had gone back to their own fields to harvest the produce of their own land.

NOTE

8 "The Reubenites and the Gadites" (הָרְאוּבֵנִי וְהַגָּדִי, *horeˀûbēnî weˀhaggādî*). The MT does not include "the other half of Manasseh" by name, but most English versions include it (e.g., NIV, NASB, NJPSV, NRSV, NLT).

2. Land Allotment for Reuben (13:15–23)

[15]This is what Moses had given to the tribe of Reuben, clan by clan: [16]The territory from Aroer on the rim of the Arnon Gorge, and from the town in the middle of the gorge, and the whole plateau past Medeba [17]to Heshbon and all its towns on the plateau, including Dibon, Bamoth Baal, Beth Baal Meon, [18]Jahaz, Kedemoth, Mephaath, [19]Kiriathaim, Sibmah, Zereth Shahar on the hill in the valley, [20]Beth Peor, the slopes of Pisgah, and Beth Jeshimoth [21] — all the towns on the plateau and the entire realm of Sihon king of the Amorites, who ruled at Heshbon. Moses had defeated him and the Midianite chiefs, Evi, Rekem, Zur, Hur and Reba — princes allied with Sihon — who lived in that country. [22]In addition to those slain in battle, the Israelites had put to the sword Balaam son of Beor, who practiced divination. [23]The boundary of the Reubenites was the bank of the Jordan. These towns and their villages were the inheritance of the Reubenites, clan by clan.

COMMENTARY

15–20 The territorial inheritance to the tribe of Reuben is mentioned first.

Tribe of Reuben Borders/Towns (13:15–23)	Comments and Grid #
13:16—Aroer Dt 2:36; Jos 12:2; Ju 11:26; 2Ki 10:33; Jer 48:19	• S limit of Sihon's kingdom • allotted to Reuben but built by sons of Gad • located near Arnon Gorge • here Joab began a census for David • ca. 14 mi. E of Dead Sea on N bank of Arnon • Arair, *#228097*
13:16—Medeba Nu 21:30; 1Ch 19:7; Isa 15:2	• a Moabite town captured from Sihon • Joab laid siege to the town and captured it • in Jordan, 20 mi. S of Amman, 12.5 mi E of Dead Sea • Madeba, *#225124*
13:17—Heshbon • Levitical city Nu 21:25–34; Dt 2:24; Ju 11:26; SS 7:4; Isa 15:4; 16:8, 9; Jer 48:45	• capital city of Sihon, king of the Amorites, conquered by Israel • allotted to Reuben but became Gadite • later recovered by Moab • possibly Hesban, 12 mi. SW of Amman, may preserve the name, but the OT site may have been at nearby Jabul, where the archaeological profile fits the historical data better in some periods, *#226134*
13:17—Dibon Nu 21:30; 32:3, 34; Isa 15:2; Jer 48:18, 22	• one of the chief cities of Moab, captured by Israel • allotted to Reuben but built by Gad • later reclaimed by Moab; mentioned in the Moabite stone and in prophetic oracles • 13 mi. E of Dead Sea and 3.5 mi. N of Arnon Gorge • Dhiban, *#224101*
13:17—Bamoth Baal Nu 22:41	• allotted to Reuben but claimed by Moabites • site NE of Dead Sea to which Balak took Balaam to curse Israel
13:17—Beth Baal Meon Nu 32:38; 1Ch 5:8; Eze 25:9; Jer 48:23	• settled by Reubenites but at times under Moabite rule • also called Baal Meon, Beth Meon, and possibly Beon • 23 mi. SW of Amman; 10 mi. E of Dead Sea • *#219120*

13:18 — Jahaz • Levitical city Nu 21:23; Jos 21:36; Ju 11:20; Isa 15:4	• captured from Sihon, king of Amorites • mentioned in prophetic oracles as town of Moab • possibly E of Dead Sea, 11 mi. SE of Medeba • possibly Kh. el-Medeiyineh, *#236110*
13:18 — Kedemoth • Levitical city — Dt 2:26; Jos 21:37; 1Ch 6:79	• possibly 20 mi. E of Dead Sea, N of Arnon River • possibly Aleiyan, *#233104*
13:18 — Mephaath • Levitical city Jos 21:37; 1Ch 6:79; Jer 48:21	• possibly 7 mi. S of Amman in Jordan • possibly Tel Jawah, *#239140*
13:19 — Kiriathaim Nu 32:37; Jer 48:1, 23; Eze 25:9	• mentioned in prophetic oracles against Moab • possibly 9 mi. E of Dead Sea • possibly Qaryat el-Mekhaiyet, *#220128*
13:19 — Sibmah Nu 32:38; Isa 16:8, 9; Jer 48:32	• from domain of Sihon • passed into Moabite hands • famous for its vineyards
13:19 — Zereth Shahar	• possibly on E shore of Dead Sea • possibly ez-Zarat, *#203111*
13:20 — Beth Peor Dt 3:29; 4:46; 34:6	• in or near the plains of Moab where Israel camped • setting for giving of laws of Deuteronomy • where Moses was buried • possibly 18 mi. WSW of Amman • possibly Kh. esh-Sheikh Jayil, *#215133*
13:20 — Pisgah Nu 21:20; 23:14; Dt 3:17, 27; 4:49; 34:1; Jos 12:3	• hilltop to which Balaam was taken to curse Israel • place from which Moses surveyed Canaan prior to his death • had been ruled by Sihon, king of Amorites • probably near Mount Nebo, ca. 9 mi. E of N end of Dead Sea
13:20 — Beth Jeshimoth Nu 33:49; Jos 12:3; Eze 25:9	• last camping place for Israel before crossing the Jordan River into Canaan (on plains of Moab) • on extremity of Sihon the Amorite's territory • later a town of Moab • possibly 22 mi. WSW of Amman • possibly Tel el-Azeimeh, *#208132*
20:8 — Bezer • city of refuge and Levitical city — Dt 4:43; Jos 21:36; 1Ch 6:78	• E of the Jordan River • possibly 11 mi. S of Amman • possibly Umm el-Amad, *#235132*

21-22 Following the list of towns given to the tribe of Reuben, we learn that Moses had defeated Sihon, king of the Amorites, and the Midianite chiefs Evi, Rekem, Zur, Hur, and Reba, who lived in that region. In addition, Balaam the diviner, summoned by Balak to curse Israel, died by the sword of the Israelites.

23 The western border of the Reubenite territory is the Jordan River.

3. Land Allotment for Gad (13:24-28)

[24] This is what Moses had given to the tribe of Gad, clan by clan:

[25] The territory of Jazer, all the towns of Gilead and half the Ammonite country as far as Aroer, near Rabbah; [26] and from Heshbon to Ramath Mizpah and Betonim, and from Mahanaim to the territory of Debir; [27] and in the valley, Beth Haram, Beth Nimrah, Succoth and Zaphon with the rest of the realm of Sihon king of Heshbon (the east side of the Jordan, the territory up to the end of the Sea of Kinnereth). [28] These towns and their villages were the inheritance of the Gadites, clan by clan.

COMMENTARY

24-28 The territorial inheritance to the tribe of Gad is mentioned second.

Tribe of Gad Borders/Towns (13:25-28)	Comments and Grid #
13:25 — **Jazer** • Levitical city Nu 21:32; 32:1; Jos 21:39; 2Sa 24:5; 1Ch 6:81; 26:31; Isa 16:8, 9; Jer 48:32	• Transjordanian town of Sihon captured by Israelites • David stationed soldiers there. • Joab passed through area while taking a census • later taken over by Moabites • possibly 6 mi. W of Amman • possibly Kh. es-Sar, *#228150*
13:25 — **Gilead**	• geographical term referring to the mountainous region E of the Jordan, S of the Yarmuk, and N of an E-W line drawn at the N end of the Dead Sea and stretching to the edge of the desert on the E
13:25 — **Aroer** Nu 32:34; Dt 2:36; 3:12; Ju 11:26; 2Sa 24:5; 2Ki 10:33; Jer 48:19	• S limit of Sihon's kingdom • allotted to tribe of Reuben (Jos 12:2) but repaired/ built by sons of Gad

	• located near Arnon Gorge • here Joab began census for David • ca. 14 mi. E of Dead Sea on N bank of Arnon • Arair, *#228097*
13:25 — Rabbah Dt 3:11; 2Sa 11:1; 12:26, 27, 29; 17:27; 1Ch 20:1; Jer 49:2, 3; Eze 21:20; 25:5; Am 1:14	• major Transjordanian town where Og's gigantic bed was kept • excluded from tribal allotments; later Joab and David captured it for Israel and its king assisted David when he fled from Absalom • capital of Ammonites mentioned in prophetic oracles • in NT times it was called Philadelphia • now capital of Jordan, 24 mi. E of Jordan River • Amman, *#238151*
13:26 — Heshbon • Levitical city Nu 21:25 – 34; Dt 2:24; Ju 11:26; SS 7:4; Isa 15:4; 16:8, 9; Jer 48:45	• capital city of Sihon, king of the Ammorites, conquered by Israel • allotted to Reuben but inhabited by Gadites • later recovered by Moab and mentioned as Moabite in prophetic oracles • Hesban, 12 mi. SW of Amman, may preserve the name, but the OT site may have been at nearby Jalul where the archaeological profile fits the historical data better in some periods • Hesban, *#226134*
13:26 — Ramath Mizpah	• possibly NW of Amman • possibly Kh. Jelad, *#223169*
13:26 — Betonim	• 16 mi. NE of Jericho in Transjordan • Kh. Batneh, *#217154*
13:26 — Mahanaim • Levitical city Ge 32:2; Jos 21:38; 2Sa 2:8, 12, 29; 17:24, 27; 19:32; 1Ki 2:8; 4:14; 1Ch 6:80	• place where Jacob met angel of God on return to Canaan • on border between Gad and Manasseh • where Abner set up Saul's son, Ish-bosheth, as king • David fled there when Absalom revolted • Solomonic district center • possibly edh-Dhahab el-Gharbi, *#214177*, 7 mi. E of Jordan River, N of Jabbok

	• or possibly Tel er-Reheil, *#228177*, 15.5 mi. E of Jordan River, N of Jabbok
13:26 — **Debir**	• in Gilead; in Jordan Valley, 10 mi. S of Sea of Galilee • if Lo Debar then Umm ed-Dabar, *#207219*
13:27 — **Beth Haram**	• in Transjordan; 18 mi. WSW of Amman • Tell Iktanu, *#214136*
13:27 — **Beth Nimrah** Nu 32:36	• in Transjordan, 18 mi. E of Amman • Tel el-Bleibil, *#210146*
13:27 — **Succoth** Ge 33:17; Ju 8:14–16; 1Ki 7:46; 2Ch 4:17; Ps 60:6	• where Jacob camped after encountering angel of the Lord • Gideon punished its leaders after they refused to help him against the Midianites • Solomon cast bronze vessels for the Temple in the area • 22 mi. SSE of Beth Shan, E of Jordan near Jabbok • Tel Deir ʿAlla, *#208178*
13:27 — **Zaphon** Jdg 12:1; Ps 48:2	• where Ephraimites met with Jephthah • possibly Tel es-Saidiyeh, 17 mi. SSE of Beth Shan, just E of Jordan River; *#204186*
20:8 — **Ramoth** • city of refuge and Levitical city Dt 4:43; 1Ki 4:13; 22:3, 4; 2Ki 8:28, 29; 1Ch 6:80; 2Ch 22:5, 6	• also called Ramoth in Gilead • headquarters for Ben-Geber in a Solomonic district • there Ahab and Jehoshaphat fought against the Arameans, as did Joram; there Jehu was anointed king • 36 mi. N of Amman in Jordan • Tel Ramith, *#244210*

4. Land Allotment for the Half-Tribe of Manasseh (13:29–31)

[29]This is what Moses had given to the half-tribe of Manasseh, that is, to half the family of the descendants of Manasseh, clan by clan:

[30]The territory extending from Mahanaim and including all of Bashan, the entire realm of Og king of Bashan — all the settlements of Jair in Bashan, sixty towns, [31]half of Gilead, and Ashtaroth and Edrei (the royal cities of Og in Bashan). This was for the descendants of Makir son of Manasseh — for half of the sons of Makir, clan by clan.

COMMENTARY

29-31 The territorial inheritance to the eastern half-tribe of Manasseh is mentioned third.

Half-tribe of Manasseh (eastern)— Borders and Towns (13:30-31)	Comments and Grid #
13:30—Mahanaim Ge 32:2; Jos 21:38; 2Sa 2:8, 12, 29; 17:24, 27; 19:32; 1Ki 2:8; 4:14; 1Ch 6:80	• place where Jacob met angel of God on return to Canaan • on border between Gad and Manasseh • Abner set up Saul's son, Ish-bosheth, as king • David fled there during Absalom's revolt
13:30—Bashan Nu 32:33; 1Ch 6:62; Ne 9:22; Isa 33:9; Am 4:1	• area E and NE of the Sea of Galilee, bounded by the Rift Valley on the W, Mt. Hermon on the N, Mt. Bashan on the E, and Gilead on the S
13:30—Jair Dt 3:14; Ju 10:4; 1Ki 4:13; 1Ch 2:23	• in N Gilead; had been part of the kingdom of Og; settled by a descendant of Manasseh named Jair, a judge • in Solomonic district • captured by Geshur and Aram • probably the region of N Gilead between Jabal 'Ajlun and the Yarmuk River
13:31—Ashtaroth • Levitical city Dt 1:4; Jos 9:10; 1Ch 6:71	• capital of Og the king of Bashan before captured by Israel • in Transjordan, 22 mi. E of Sea of Galilee • Tell Ashtarah, *#243244*
13:31—Edrei Nu 21:33; Dt 3:1, 10	• in Bashan; residence of Og, king of Bashan, who was defeated by the Israelites • 60 mi. S of Damascus • Dera, *#253224*
21:27—Golan • Levitical city and city of refuge—Dt 4:43; Jos 21:27; 1Ch 6:71	• Transjordanian city • 18 mi. E of Sea of Galilee; in NT times, known as Gaulanitis • Sahm el-Jolan, *#238243*
21:27—Additional Levitical cities	• Beth Eshtarah

5. Summary (13:32–33)

> ³²This is the inheritance Moses had given when he was in the plains of Moab across the Jordan east of Jericho. ³³But to the tribe of Levi, Moses had given no inheritance; the LORD, the God of Israel, is their inheritance, as he promised them.

COMMENTARY

32 Here ends the summary of the territory allotted under Moses' leadership to two and a half tribes on the eastern side of the Jordan. The final statement reiterates Moses' involvement in the distribution of land to Israel (vv.8, 12, 15, 24, 29).

33 This verse echoes 13:14 and provides further theological information, specifying that Yahweh himself is the inheritance of the landless Levites.

C. Land Allotment West of the Jordan (14:1–19:51)

OVERVIEW

The following chapters alternate between personal narratives and geographical descriptions. The personal narratives introduce characters who demand, through convincing discourses, portions of land or bodies of water as part of their inheritance. First come the men of Judah with Caleb, who states his case before Joshua and requests his inheritance as promised to him at Kadesh Barnea (14:6b–12). In response, Joshua gives him Hebron (14:13–14).

Second is Caleb's daughter Achsah, who requests a spring of water to irrigate her land in the Negev (15:19). Without hesitation, Caleb gives her the upper and lower springs (15:19).

Third, Zelophehad's daughters remind Joshua and the elders of Israel to give them an inheritance among their brothers, as promised years earlier by Yahweh through Moses (17:3–4; cf. Nu 27:1–8).

Joshua gives them a portion of land from the share of the eastern half-tribe of Manasseh (17:4).

Finally, the tribe of Joseph demands a greater territory for their growing community (17:14–18). Joshua gives them forested hills in the land of the Perizzites and the Rephaites and challenges them to clear it for their personal use (17:15–18).

The introduction to chapter 14 highlights three important points: (1) the land in Transjordan was divided among two and a half tribes (Reuben, Gad, and the half-tribe of Manasseh) by Moses; (2) the territory west of the Jordan was divided through a lot system; and (3) the Levites received no share of land but instead, specific towns with their surrounding pasturelands for themselves and their flocks. The remainder of chapter 14 is dedicated to Caleb's request for land and Joshua's response.

Chapter 15 provides the longest account of tribal allotments. It describes the boundaries and towns given to the tribe of Judah. Alternating between narrative and descriptions of boundaries, chapters 16–19 provide a meticulous description of the distribution of the rest of the land west of the Jordan to the nine and a half tribes of Israel.

1. Introduction (14:1–5)

¹Now these are the areas the Israelites received as an inheritance in the land of Canaan, which Eleazar the priest, Joshua son of Nun and the heads of the tribal clans of Israel allotted to them. ²Their inheritances were assigned by lot to the nine-and-a-half tribes, as the LORD had commanded through Moses. ³Moses had granted the two-and-a-half tribes their inheritance east of the Jordan but had not granted the Levites an inheritance among the rest, ⁴for the sons of Joseph had become two tribes — Manasseh and Ephraim. The Levites received no share of the land but only towns to live in, with pasturelands for their flocks and herds. ⁵So the Israelites divided the land, just as the LORD had commanded Moses.

COMMENTARY

1 The division of the land west of the Jordan differs in several ways from that of Transjordan. First, Eleazar the priest, who has not been identified as a major active participant in the distribution of land in Transjordan, is mentioned as a leader in the allotment of land to the western tribes (cf. Nu 34:17). The reader first encounters Eleazar before the exodus (Ex 6:24–25) and then during the desert wanderings, where he is appointed to tend to sacrifices (Lev 10); he receives the mantle of his father Aaron (Nu 20:23–29), takes a census of Israel (26:1–4), and participates in the commissioning of Joshua (27:22–23).

Second, the inheritance of the western tribes is determined by casting lots (v.2), unlike the method of land distribution in Transjordan. Lots were probably small engraved stones that were placed in a container and cast to the ground. Their configuration determined outcomes. Through the lot system, the land could be divided among the tribes without partiality, removing any possible accusation of impropriety (J. Lindblom, "Lot-Casting in the OT," *VT* 12 [1962]: 164–78; A. M. Kitz, "The Hebrew Terminology of Lot Casting and Its Ancient Near Eastern Context" *CBQ* 62 [2000]: 207–14; idem, "Undivided Inheritance and Lot Casting in the Book of Joshua," *JBL* 119 [2000]: 601–18).

2–4 The casting of lots for dividing the inheritance is first mentioned in Numbers, where Yahweh commands Moses to distribute the land through this system (Nu 26:52–56; 33:54; 34:13–14). The technique is also known in Scripture as a cultic ritual used by the high priest on the Day of Atonement (e.g., Lev 16:8–10). On that day, the high priest cast lots in order to determine which goat would become a sin offering and which goat was to be sent alive into the desert as a scapegoat. The phrase "as the LORD commanded" recurs throughout the book (Jos 4:10; 7:11; 8:27, 31, 33, 35; 10:40; 11:12, 15, 20; 13:6) and highlights Israel's need to depend on God for direction and instruction.

In order to preserve the scheme of twelve tribes, Joseph's sons Ephraim and Manasseh assume the status of tribes and receive a land allotment, while the sons of Levi receive towns with their surrounding pasturelands for their inheritance. The Levites receive no territorial inheritance; God is their inheritance (13:14, 33). The comment about the Levites seems to be redundantly inserted into a brief report regarding the distribution of land to the eastern tribes; the end of the previous chapter has provided the same information (13:33). The biblical text reveals two systems for naming the twelve tribes of Israel. The first system includes Joseph and Levi (Ge 49:1–27; 29:31–30:24; Ge 35:23–26; 46:8:25; Ex 1:2–4; Dt 27:12–13; 1Ch 2:1–2; Eze 48:31–35), while the second system omits Levi and divides Joseph into the tribes of Ephraim and Manasseh (Ge 48; Nu 1:5:15, 20–43; 2:3–31; 7:12–83; 10:14–28; 26:5–51).

5 Once more we read that the land in Transjordan was divided, "just as the LORD had commanded Moses." This is another seemingly redundant statement since the same information appears in 13:32.

NOTES

1–3 The root *nḥl* (נחל), "to inherit, inheritance," appears five times in these first three verses (v.1, נָחֲלוּ, *nāḥᵃlû*, "[they] received as an inheritance"; v.1, נִחֲלוּ, *niḥᵃlû*, "[the heads] ... allotted to them"; v.2, נַחֲלָתָם, *naḥᵃlātām*, "their inheritances"; v.3, נַחֲלַת, *naḥᵃlat*, "[their] inheritance"; v.3, נַחֲלָה, *naḥᵃlā*, "an inheritance"). A cluster of terms from the same root, appearing together within a few verses typically points to a significant theme or matter. In this case, the author highlights the "inheritance" received by Israel.

2. Hebron Given to Caleb (14:6–15)

⁶Now the men of Judah approached Joshua at Gilgal, and Caleb son of Jephunneh the Kenizzite said to him, "You know what the LORD said to Moses the man of God at Kadesh Barnea about you and me. ⁷I was forty years old when Moses the servant of the LORD sent me from Kadesh Barnea to explore the land. And I brought him back a report according to my convictions, ⁸but my brothers who went up with me made the hearts of the people melt with fear. I, however, followed the LORD my God wholeheartedly. ⁹So on that day Moses swore to me, 'The land on which your feet have walked will be your inheritance and that of your children forever, because you have followed the LORD my God wholeheartedly.'

¹⁰"Now then, just as the LORD promised, he has kept me alive for forty-five years since the time he said this to Moses, while Israel moved about in the desert. So here I am today, eighty-five years old! ¹¹I am still as strong today as the day Moses sent me out; I'm just as

vigorous to go out to battle now as I was then. ¹²Now give me this hill country that the LORD promised me that day. You yourself heard then that the Anakites were there and their cities were large and fortified, but, the LORD helping me, I will drive them out just as he said."

¹³Then Joshua blessed Caleb son of Jephunneh and gave him Hebron as his inheritance. ¹⁴So Hebron has belonged to Caleb son of Jephunneh the Kenizzite ever since, because he followed the LORD, the God of Israel, wholeheartedly. ¹⁵(Hebron used to be called Kiriath Arba after Arba, who was the greatest man among the Anakites.)

Then the land had rest from war.

COMMENTARY

6–9 As noted above, the account of the land distributed in Cisjordan appears in the form of a "land grant" similar to those in cuneiform texts of the ancient Near East (Hittite, Ugaritic, and Akkadian; see Overview of 13:1–21:45). Caleb's request for his inheritance introduces the section on the allotment of land to the tribe of Judah. At eighty-five years of age (v.10), Caleb still has a tremendous memory. For forty-five years, he had been thinking about the portion of property he would one day receive in Canaan. Eager to acquire his inheritance, Caleb approaches Joshua at Gilgal, where he and his men are encamped after the military victory in northern Canaan. Gilgal, a major center of activities, appears primarily in the first half of Joshua (4:19, 20; 5:9, 10; 9:6; 10:6, 7, 9, 15, 43; 12:23; 14:6; 15:7).

Caleb had become familiar with his territorial inheritance when he explored the area forty-five years earlier. While he was in the desert, Yahweh promised to "give him and his descendants the land he set his feet on, because he followed the LORD wholeheartedly" (Dt 1:36). His dream is now coming true! The reader can easily imagine Caleb walking proudly in the southern region of Judah,

looking with excitement for places familiar from his first expedition in the land. What an exciting moment! He can now claim the area for himself and his descendants.

Caleb had been deeply touched by Moses' pledge to him in the desert, which came in response to his report about the spies' expedition in southern Canaan. Caleb recalls exactly where he was when Moses uttered this promise—in Kadesh Barnea (Dt 1:19). A major site of Israelite activity, Kadesh Barnea appears numerous times in the wilderness narrative (Nu 13:26; 20:1, 14, 16, 22; 27:14; 32:8; 33:36, 37; 34:4; Dt 1:2, 19, 46; 2:14; 9:23; 32:51). In his request for land, Caleb recounts the details of the events in the desert exactly as they had occurred (Dt 1:18–38). Caleb reminisces about his colleagues' troubling report to Moses, a report so disturbing that it made the hearts of the Israelites melt in fear (Jos 14:8).

With a compelling speech peppered with hyperbolic expressions of self-confidence, Caleb reminds Joshua that Yahweh had *promised* to give him land in Canaan (Dt 1:35–36). The speech abounds with glaring linguistic and literary markers for emphasis. For example:

- In verses 6, 8 and 12, an independent pronoun appears before the finite verb, emphasizing the subject of the verb.
- In verse 6, the emphatic structure (ʿal ʾōdôt, "precisely because of [me, you]") appears twice.
- The first person singular pronouns "I," "my," "me," "myself" appear nineteen times in the speech (vv.6, 7 [4x], 8 [5x], 10 [2x], 11 [4x], 12 [3x]).
- The text repeats that Yahweh was a witness to the promise made to Caleb at Kadesh Barnea (vv.6, 9, 10 [2x], 12 [3x]).
- The text also emphasizes that Moses, the man of God, swore (wayyiššābaʿ) to fulfill God's promise (vv.6, 7, 9, 10, 11).
- Caleb's proclaims (lit.), "Here I am today, eighty-five years old," a statement that has been uttered elsewhere only by Moses (v.10; cf. Dt 31:2).
- The repetition of the word lēb/lebab ("heart") contrasts Caleb's "honest heart" (v.7) with the "melting hearts' of the people (v.8).
- The Piel verb millēʾtî ("I wholeheartedly fulfilled") is preceded by the first person independent pronoun, confirming Caleb's unquestionable obedience to Yahweh's instructions (v.8; cf. Dt 1:36).
- The repetition of "[on] that day" (bayyôm hahûʾ) points to Caleb's clear recollection of the events that had occurred forty-five years earlier (vv.9, 11, 12[2x]).
- The use of ʾim lōʾ ("surely") stresses that the land on which Caleb had earlier trodden would surely be his (v.9).
- The use of ʿad ʿôlām ("forever") indicating that the land would be a gift from Yahweh forever (v.9).
- The passage repeats the particle of emphasis (ʿattā /weʿattā, "now/and now") (v.10 [2x], 11, 12).

In this context, Caleb exemplifies on a small scale what Israel is experiencing on a larger scale: Caleb and Israel both await the gift of land promised to them decades earlier. Caleb receives a town while Israel receives an expanse of land.

10 Caleb here makes a contrast between the disobedient Israelites, whom Yahweh killed in the desert, and himself, whom Yahweh "kept alive" (heḥᵉyeâ) for forty-five years, because of his obedience and faithfulness to him (Nu 14:28–30).

11 In his old age, Caleb is still "strong" (ḥāzāq— the same word is used in the commands to Joshua "be strong, do not be afraid") and "vigorous" (kōaḥ, 2x). According to him, he has not aged a day. He is still as strong as he was forty-five years earlier, with sufficient stamina to defeat the Anakites in their walled and fortified cities! Had Caleb discovered a secret fountain of youth? He certainly seems to think so. It is important for Caleb to acknowledge his strength before mentioning that the Anakites are still in the land. He sees himself powerful enough to overcome them with "the LORD helping me" (v.12, almost an afterthought!) and to drive them out of the area.

12 The climax of Caleb's request finally bursts forth with the following words, "Give me this hill country [mountain] that the LORD promised me that day." Caleb's petition nears the height of arrogance with its back-to-back repetition of "that the LORD promised me that day" (ᵃšer dibber yhwh bayyôm hahûʾ) and "just as [the LORD] said" (kaᵃšer dibber yhwh).

13 After patiently listening to the splendid address of his personal assistant, Joshua politely blesses him and gives him Hebron (one city!) as an inheritance (naḥᵃlā) instead of the whole mountain Caleb had originally requested. Was this a ploy used by Joshua to make Caleb humble? Maybe. In his speech, Caleb had listed all the reasons why he should receive the hill country—at least the mountain where Gilgal was located. Since the text contains no response from Caleb, one cannot be certain whether Caleb is pleased or disappointed with the limited territory assigned to him.

14–15 The narrative closes with a brief historical note concerning Kiriath Arba (Hebron), named after Arba, one of the greatest Anakites in the land. The meaning of the name is literally "city of four," which suggests that Hebron and neighboring Anakite settlements formed a geographical unit. Hebron would eventually become the city where David was anointed king and his first capital, where he ruled for seven and a half years before moving the throne to Jerusalem (2Sa 5:1–5). The chapter concludes with the same literary marker that ends chapter 11, "then the land had rest from war" (cf. 11:23).

REFLECTION

A promise is not easily forgotten! Caleb remembers vividly the events at Kadesh Barnea and the promise Yahweh made to him decades earlier. Prominent leaders — Moses and Joshua, whom Caleb admired so much — had sworn to give him a gift. Caleb trusted them; he knew in his heart that he could depend on their words. He had seen them fulfill their promises in the past, and there was no reason for him to doubt their commitment to him. Has someone made a pledge to you and failed to fulfill it? Or did they keep their promise and fulfill it at the perfect time? Have you ever broken a promise to someone — a spouse, a child, a friend — who trusted your words? Words are not easily forgotten. People remember them years later. It is never too late to fulfill your vows to others.

Caleb was deeply moved by Moses' approval of him when he returned from southern Canaan with a good report. Moses' words had marked Caleb profoundly, and he would never forget the affirmation he received. Can you think of personal moments in your life when someone whom you genuinely admire expressed appreciation for a job well done? How rewarding it is to be affirmed and encouraged by the people you admire and respect. Do you have a habit of affirming those around you who are faithful, trustworthy, and committed to their tasks? May we become like Moses and Joshua, who fulfilled their promises, encouraged those around them, and remained steadfast until the job was done.

3. Tribal Land Allotment (15:1–19:48)

a. Land Allotment for Judah (15:1–63)

i. Borders of Judah (15:1–12)

¹The allotment for the tribe of Judah, clan by clan, extended down to the territory of Edom, to the Desert of Zin in the extreme south.
²Their southern boundary started from the bay at the southern end of the Salt Sea, ³crossed south of Scorpion Pass, continued on to Zin and went over to the south of Kadesh Barnea. Then it ran past Hezron up to Addar and curved around to

Karka. ⁴It then passed along to Azmon and joined the Wadi of Egypt, ending at the sea. This is their southern boundary.

⁵The eastern boundary is the Salt Sea as far as the mouth of the Jordan.

The northern boundary started from the bay of the sea at the mouth of the Jordan, ⁶went up to Beth Hoglah and continued north of Beth Arabah to the Stone of Bohan son of Reuben. ⁷The boundary then went up to Debir from the Valley of Achor and turned north to Gilgal, which faces the Pass of Adummim south of the gorge. It continued along to the waters of En Shemesh and came out at En Rogel. ⁸Then it ran up the Valley of Ben Hinnom along the southern slope of the Jebusite city (that is, Jerusalem). From there it climbed to the top of the hill west of the Hinnom Valley at the northern end of the Valley of Rephaim. ⁹From the hilltop the boundary headed toward the spring of the waters of Nephtoah, came out at the towns of Mount Ephron and went down toward Baalah (that is, Kiriath Jearim). ¹⁰Then it curved westward from Baalah to Mount Seir, ran along the northern slope of Mount Jearim (that is, Kesalon), continued down to Beth Shemesh and crossed to Timnah. ¹¹It went to the northern slope of Ekron, turned toward Shikkeron, passed along to Mount Baalah and reached Jabneel. The boundary ended at the sea.

¹²The western boundary is the coastline of the Great Sea.

These are the boundaries around the people of Judah by their clans.

COMMENTARY

1–12 The description of Judah's territorial inheritance includes the most comprehensive and detailed list of boundaries and towns. In fact, the list of boundaries—southern, eastern, northern, and western—introduces the chapter. The territory of Judah extends from the Desert of Zin, in the extreme southern part of Canaan, along the Dead Sea on the east, to the mouth of the Jordan River; it then turns westward up the Judean hills, passing north of Jerusalem, and continuing west to the Great Sea (Mediterranean Sea). The southern and eastern borders parallel those listed in Numbers 34:3–5 for the boundaries of Israel.

Tribe of Judah Borders and Towns (15:1–12)	Comments and Grid # on most common sites
Southern Boundary 15:2–4 Salt Sea, Scorpion Pass, **Desert of Zin**, **Kadesh Barnea**, Hezron, Addar, Karka, Azmon, Wadi of Egypt	• Desert of Zin Moses sent spies into Canaan from there (Nu 13:21) formed the SSE boundary of the land of Canaan (Nu 34:3, 4) and Judah uncertain location; located W of Rift, SW of Dead Sea, NW of Elath/Aqaba

	• Kadesh Barnea in or beside the Desert of Zin (Nu 20:1; Dt 32:51) mentioned with Abraham (Ge 14:7; 16:14; 20:1) men who spied Canaan returned Kadesh (Nu 13:26) where Moses' sister, Miriam, died (Nu 20:1) Israel encampment (Dt 1:46) about 50 mi. SW of Beersheba Ain el-Qudeirat, #096006
Eastern Boundary 15:5a Salt Sea	• Salt Sea common biblical name for the "Dead Sea" (Ge 14:3; Nu 34:3, 12; Dt 3:17; Jos 3:16; 12:3; 15:2, 5; 18:19) also called the Sea of the Arabah and the Eastern Sea
Northern Boundary 15:5b–11 Beth Hoglah, Beth Arabah, Stone of Bohan, Debir, Valley of Achor, Gilgal, Pass of Adummim, **En Shemesh**, En Rogel, Valley of Ben Hinnom, Jerusalem, Valley of Rephaim, Nephtoah, Mount Ephron, **Kiriath Jearim**, **Mount Seir**, Kesalon, Beth Shemesh, Timnah, Ekron, Shikkeron, Mount Baalah, Jabneel	• En (Beth) Shemesh in N Shephelah; N boundary of Judah, allotted to Dan (Jos 19:38), who was unable to occupy it (Ju 1:33) a Levitical city (Jos 21:16; 1Ch 6:59) Judean outpost on border with the Philistines; ark of covenant returned there (1Sa 6) in Solomon's second administrative district; fortified by Rehoboam (2Ki 14:8–14) 16 mi. W of Jerusalem Tel er-Rumeileh/Tell Bet Shemesh, #147128 • Kiriath Jearim town in the old Hivite league with which Israel made a treaty (Jos 9:17) N border of Judah and SW boundary of Benjamin (Jos 18:14, 15) Danites camped there (Ju 18:12) ark of God stored there (1Sa 6:21; 7:1, 2) David brought the ark from there to Jerusalem (1Ch 13:5, 6) Jeremiah mentions a prophet from the town (Jer 26:20) Israelites return there after Babylonian exile (Ezr 2:25; Ne 7:29) also called "Kiriath Baal" (Jos 15:60; 18:14), "Baalah of Judah" (Jos 15:9, 10; 2Sa 6:2; 1Ch 13:6), "Kiriath" (Jos 18:28), "Jaar" (Ps 132:6), and "Baalath" (2Ch 8:6; 1Ki 9:18) 8.5 mi. W of Jerusalem Deir el-Azar/Tell Qiryat Yearim, #159135 • Mount Seir N boundary of Judah location uncertain—possibly ridge W of Kiriath Jearim and N of Kesalon, ca. 11 mi. W of Jerusalem
Western Boundary 15:12	• Great Sea used 13 times in the NIV for the Mediterranean Sea

ii. Caleb's Daughter Receives Land (15:13–19)

¹³In accordance with the LORD's command to him, Joshua gave to Caleb son of Jephunneh a portion in Judah — Kiriath Arba, that is, Hebron. (Arba was the forefather of Anak.) ¹⁴From Hebron Caleb drove out the three Anakites — Sheshai, Ahiman and Talmai — descendants of Anak. ¹⁵From there he marched against the people living in Debir (formerly called Kiriath Sepher). ¹⁶And Caleb said, "I will give my daughter Acsah in marriage to the man who attacks and captures Kiriath Sepher." ¹⁷Othniel son of Kenaz, Caleb's brother, took it; so Caleb gave his daughter Acsah to him in marriage.

¹⁸One day when she came to Othniel, she urged him to ask her father for a field. When she got off her donkey, Caleb asked her, "What can I do for you?"

¹⁹She replied, "Do me a special favor. Since you have given me land in the Negev, give me also springs of water." So Caleb gave her the upper and lower springs.

COMMENTARY

13 This brief interlude recaps the events of 14:13–15, in which Caleb receives Hebron as his land grant (cf. Jdg 1:9–15).

14 Ready to settle in his own land, Caleb dispossesses the dreaded and colossal Anakites (Sheshai, Ahiman, and Talmai) from their land and settles his family in the area bequeathed to him by Joshua (cf. Jdg 1:14). Terrified by their reputation and by their sheer size, Israel had previously avoided the Anakites in southern Canaan. The spies had described them as giants in whose eyes the Israelites appeared like mere grasshoppers (Nu 13:31–33). Undeterred by their stature and frightful demeanor, Caleb proceeds to expunge them from his newly acquired land.

15 Debir, a city previously conquered by Joshua (10:36–39), was originally called Kiriath Sefer ("book city" or "scribal city"). Its original name may indicate that at one time, the city was a repository for official records. The phenomenon of secondary names for towns is not unique to Debir (Jdg 1:11). Other such towns include Hebron

(Kiriath Arba, Ge 23:2; 35:27; Jdg 1:10), Bethel (Luz, Ge 28:19; 35:6; Jos 16:2; 18:13; Jdg 1:23), Dan (Laish, Jdg 18:29), and Jerusalem (Jebus, Jdg 19:10; 1Ch 11:4; Salem, Ge 14:18). A dual name for a town may indicate that the inhabitants were a mixed group or that the town had been conquered at some point and given a new name (Hess, *Joshua*, 244–45). Individuals also have dual names (e.g., Abram-Abraham [Ge 17:5], Sarai-Sarah [Ge 17:15], Jacob-Israel [Ge 32:28]). The same biblical name is sometimes given to geographical locations and to individuals (e.g., Ziph [Jos 15:24; 1Ch 2:42], Shema [Jos 15:26; 1Ch 2:44], Naamah [Jos 15:41; 1Ki 14:31], Zanoah [Jos 15:34; 1Ch 4:18]).

16–17 In addition to serving as a matchmaker for his daughter Achsah, Caleb grooms mighty men under him and rewards them for courage and heroism. He promises to give his daughter in marriage to the valiant one who attacks and captures Kiriath Sepher (Debir). Othniel, Caleb's nephew, overcomes the inhabitants of the city and receives the prize (cf. Jdg 1:12–13).

18–19 In ancient times, donkeys and camels were favorite modes of transportation. They carried people (*donkey*—Ex 4:20; Nu 22:21–33; Jdg 19:26–28; 1Sa 25:20–23; 2Sa 19:25–26; Zec 9:9; *camel*—Ge 24:61–64; 31:17; 1Sa 30:17) and supplies (*donkey*—Ge 42:25–26; 1Sa 16:20; Isa 30:6; *camel*—Ge 37:25; 1Ki 10:2; Isa 30:6). In most cases where these animals were used for transporting people, the text indicates a significant distance traveled during the trip. For example, after a long journey from Aram-Naharaim to Beer Lahai Roi in the Negev, Rebekah saw Isaac her soon-to-be-husband. She descended from her camel (lit., "fell off her camel" [*wattippōl mēʿal haggāmāl*], Ge 24:64) and covered her face with a veil before meeting Isaac.

In Numbers 22, Balaam was summoned by Balak, king of Moab, to curse Israel. Balaam traveled from his hometown to northern Moab, on the border of the Arnon River (22:36). Balaam's mode of transportation was a donkey, which, on seeing the angel of the Lord, turned off the road into a field, crushed Balaam's foot against a rock wall, and sat on the road refusing to move forward (22:21–34).

Oblivious to the presence of the angel, Balaam beat his donkey three times (22:32).

It is possible that in the case of Achsah, the period of time that elapsed between the request to her husband, Othniel (15:18a), and the visit to her father (15:18b) was significant. The text is silent on the response of Othniel, but what is clear is that he did not go to Caleb; Ashcah made the journey. Her use of a donkey for the trip indicates that her property in the Negev was not next to her father's property, but was at a significant distance from Hebron.

After her marriage to Othniel, Achsah asks her father to give her water sources to irrigate the land bequeathed to her in the Negev. Since Caleb had already given her the land, there was reason to expect him to grant her request. Without hesitation, Caleb gives Achsah the upper and lower springs. This biblical account is one of several in which women request special resources from leaders for their own survival and that of their families. See also Joshua 17:3–6 for the account of Zelophehad's daughters, who approach Joshua, Eleazar the priest, and the elders of Israel with a request for land among their father's brothers (17:3–6).

NOTES

13 "[Joshua] gave to Caleb son of Jephunneh a portion" (וּלְכָלֵב בֶּן־יְפֻנֶּה נָתַן חֵלֶק, *ûlĕkālēb ben-yᵉpunneh nātan ḥēleq*). In this text, the use of disjunctive syntax (fronted *waw* + nonverb) indicates a shift of scene and provides a flashback to the events of the previous chapter (14:6–15).

14 It is possible that Sheshai, Ahiman, and Talmai represented family clans rather than individuals (cf. Nu 13:22; Woudstra, 240). The etymology and meaning of their names are uncertain.

19 "Do me a special favor" (תְּנָה־לִּי בְרָכָה, *tᵉnā-lî bᵉrākā*; lit., "[Please] grant me a blessing"). More often than not, a long imperative expresses a polite request uttered by someone of lower social status to someone of higher social status (e.g., Ge 43:8; Nu 10:35; Jos 14:12; 1Sa 8:6; Ps 86:16) (see Dallaire, 61–77).

iii. Towns of Judah (15:20–63)

²⁰This is the inheritance of the tribe of Judah, clan by clan:

²¹The southernmost towns of the tribe of Judah in the Negev toward the boundary of Edom were:

Kabzeel, Eder, Jagur, ²²Kinah, Dimonah, Adadah, ²³Kedesh, Hazor, Ithnan, ²⁴Ziph, Telem, Bealoth, ²⁵Hazor Hadattah, Kerioth Hezron (that is, Hazor), ²⁶Amam, Shema, Moladah, ²⁷Hazar Gaddah, Heshmon, Beth Pelet, ²⁸Hazar Shual, Beersheba, Biziothiah, ²⁹Baalah, Iim, Ezem, ³⁰Eltolad, Kesil, Hormah, ³¹Ziklag, Madmannah, Sansannah, ³²Lebaoth, Shilhim, Ain and Rimmon — a total of twenty-nine towns and their villages.

³³In the western foothills:

Eshtaol, Zorah, Ashnah, ³⁴Zanoah, En Gannim, Tappuah, Enam, ³⁵Jarmuth, Adullam, Socoh, Azekah, ³⁶Shaaraim, Adithaim and Gederah (or Gederothaim) — fourteen towns and their villages.

³⁷Zenan, Hadashah, Migdal Gad, ³⁸Dilean, Mizpah, Joktheel, ³⁹Lachish, Bozkath, Eglon, ⁴⁰Cabbon, Lahmas, Kitlish, ⁴¹Gederoth, Beth Dagon, Naamah and Makkedah — sixteen towns and their villages.

⁴²Libnah5, Ether, Ashan, ⁴³Iphtah, Ashnah, Nezib, ⁴⁴Keilah, Aczib and Mareshah — nine towns and their villages.

⁴⁵Ekron, with its surrounding settlements and villages; ⁴⁶west of Ekron, all that were in the vicinity of Ashdod, together with their villages; ⁴⁷Ashdod, its surrounding settlements and villages; and Gaza, its settlements and villages, as far as the Wadi of Egypt and the coastline of the Great Sea.

⁴⁸In the hill country:

Shamir, Jattir, Socoh, ⁴⁹Dannah, Kiriath Sannah (that is, Debir), ⁵⁰Anab, Eshtemoh, Anim, ⁵¹Goshen, Holon and Giloh — eleven towns and their villages.

⁵²Arab, Dumah, Eshan, ⁵³Janim, Beth Tappuah, Aphekah, ⁵⁴Humtah, Kiriath Arba (that is, Hebron) and Zior — nine towns and their villages.

⁵⁵Maon, Carmel, Ziph, Juttah, ⁵⁶Jezreel, Jokdeam, Zanoah, ⁵⁷Kain, Gibeah and Timnah — ten towns and their villages.

⁵⁸Halhul, Beth Zur, Gedor, ⁵⁹Maarath, Beth Anoth and Eltekon — six towns and their villages.

⁶⁰Kiriath Baal (that is, Kiriath Jearim) and Rabbah — two towns and their villages.

⁶¹In the desert:

Beth Arabah, Middin, Secacah, ⁶²Nibshan, the City of Salt and En Gedi — six towns and their villages.

⁶³Judah could not dislodge the Jebusites, who were living in Jerusalem; to this day the Jebusites live there with the people of Judah.

COMMENTARY

20–62 The first part of the territorial inheritance of Judah is described in a list of boundaries. The second part appears in a list of cities organized from the southernmost towns, to the western foothills, to the hill country, and concluding with towns in the desert.

Tribe of Judah *Borders and Towns (15:20–62)*	*Comments and Grid # on most common sites*
In Negev 15:21–32 Kabzeel, Eder, Jagur, Kinah, Dimonah, Adadah, **Kedesh**, Hazor, Ithnan, Ziph, Telem, Bealoth, Hazor Hadattah, Kerioth Hezron, Amam, Shema, Moladah, Hazar Gaddah, Heshmon, Beth Pelet, Hazar Shual, **Beersheba**, Biziothiah, Baalah, Iim, Ezem, Eltolad, Kesil, **Hormah**, Ziklag, Madmannah, Sansannah, Lebaoth, Shilhim, Ain, Rimmon	• Kedesh town in Negev district of Judah (Jos 15:23) unknown location; some believe it to be identical to Kadesh Barnea but not likely • Beersheba capital of the Negev, mentioned 34 times in the OT associated with the patriarchs—Abraham, Isaac, and Jacob allotted to both Judah and Simeon (Jos 15:28; 19:2) mentioned as the S boundary of Israel in the phrase (from Dan to Beersheba) mentioned in Joab's census (2Sa 24:7) and Elijah's flight from Jezebel (1Ki 19:3) evidently, a shrine or temple was there (Am 5:5; 8:14) Jews lived there in the postexilic period (Ne 11:27) 25 mi. SW of Hebron Tel es-Seba/Tell Beer Sheva, *#134072* • Hormah village in Negev allotted to Judah (Jos 15:30) and then to Simeon (Jos 19:4) There, Israel had first been defeated by the Canaanites (Nu 14:45) but later they captured and destroyed the town, which formerly had been called Zephath (Nu 21:3; Jos 12:14; Ju 1:17) Later, David sent booty to its inhabitants (1Sa 30:30) Uncertain location—possibly Kh. el-Meshash/Tell Masos (*#146069*), 8 mi. ESE of Beersheba, or Tel Khuweilifeh/Tell Halif (*#137087*), 9.5 mi. NNE of Beersheba
In Western foothills 15:33–47 Eshtaol, Zorah, Ashnah, Zanoah, En Gannim, Tappuah, Enam, Jarmuth,	• Adullam in the Shephelah; conquered by Joshua (Jos 12:15); allotted to Judah (Jos 15:35) residents intermarried Judahites (Ge 38:1) David fled to a cave there (1Sa 22:1; 2Sa 23:13; 1Ch 11:15) fortified by Rehoboam (2Ch 11:7) Micah laments over

Adullam, Socoh, **Azekah**, Shaaraim, Adithaim and Gederah (or Gederothaim), Zenan, Hadashah, Migdal Gad, Dilean, Mizpah, Joktheel, **Lachish**, Bozkath, Eglon, Cabbon, Lahmas, Kitlish, Gederoth, Beth Dagon, Naamah and **Makkedah**, **Libnah**, Ether, Ashan, Iphtah, Ashnah, Nezib, Keilah, Aczib and Mareshah, **Ekron**, with its surrounding settlements and villages; west of Ekron, all that were in the vicinity of **Ashdod**, together with their villages; Ashdod, its surrounding settlements and villages; and **Gaza**, its settlements and villages, as far as the Wadi of Egypt and the coastline of the Great Sea

Adullam before Assyrian invasion (Mic 1:15) reinhabited after the Babylonian exile (Ne 11:30) 16.5 mi. WSW of Bethlehem in Shephelah Kh. esh-Sheikh Madhkur/H. Adullam, *#150117*

- Azekah allotted to Judah; in the Shephelah (Jos 15:35) Joshua pursued Amorite coalition in its direction (Jos 10:10, 11) David fought Goliath there (1Sa 17:1) between Judah and coastal plain, Rehoboam fortified it (2Ch 11:9); Nebuchadnezzar attacked it (Jer 34:7; Lachish Letter 4) reoccupied after Babylonian exile (Ne 11:30) 15 mi. NW of Hebron Kh. Tel Zakariyeh/ Tell Azeqa, *#144123*
- Lachish in Judean Shephelah (Jos 15:39); king was defeated by Joshua (Jos 10; 12:11) fortified by Rehoboam (2Ch 11:9) Amaziah assassinated there (2Ki 14:19; 2Ch 25:27) Sennacherib and Nebuchadnezzar captured town (2Ki 18:14, 17; 19:8; 2Ch 32:9; Isa 36:2; Mic 1:13; Jer 34:7) Babylonian exiles returned there (Neh 11:30) frequent in extrabiblical documents 29 mi. WSW from Jerusalem Tel ed-Duweir/Tell Lachish, *#135108*
- Makkedah five Amorite kings hid cave at Makkedah; captured by Joshua (Jos 10) Shephelah town conquered by Joshua (Jos 12:16); allotted to Judah (Jos 15:41) 8.5 mi. W of Hebron Kh. el-Kum, *#146104*
- Libnah Shephelah town conquered by Joshua (Jos 10; 12:15); allotted to Judah (15:42) Levitical city (Jos 21:13; 1Ch 6:57) revolted against Judean rule during reign of Jehoram (2Ki 8:22; 2Ch 21:10) Sennacherib besieged the village (2Ki 19:8; Isa 37:8) mother of Zedekiah was from there (2Ki 23:31; 24:18; Jer 52:1) Disputed location; possibly Kh. Tel el-Beida/H. Lavnin (*#145116*), 20 mi. SW of Jerusalem, 8 mi. NE of Lachish or Tell Bornat/Burna, *#138115*
- Ekron in coastal plain; N border of Judah and S border of Dan (Jos 15:11, 46; 19:43) Judah had difficulty controlling it (LXX of Ju 1:18) important Philistine

	center (Jos 13:3) prominent in capture of the ark (1Sa 5 & 6) and David and Goliath (1Sa 17:52)20 mi. SE of Joppa Kh. el-Muqanna/Tell Miqne, *#136131* • Ashdod in Philistine plain 22 mi. S of Joppa, 10 mi. N of Ashkelon 21 times in OT as well as Acts 8:40 (Azotus) usually under Egyptian, Philistine, Assyrian, etc., influence 3 mi. inland from the Mediterranean Sea Esdud/Tell Ashdod, *#117129* • Gaza in SW Israel on border between Canaan and desert of N Sinai Philistines settled there (Jos 13:3; Ju 1:18; 1Sa 6:17) mentioned 22 times in OT and once in NT (Acts 8:26) usually under non-Israelite control: the Egyptian military base for expeditions N; Assyrian, Babylonian, etc. military base for invasions of Egypt3.5 mi. inland from the Mediterranean in SW Israel Ghazzeh/Azza, *#099101*
In Hill Country 15:48−60 Shamir, Jattir, Socoh, Dannah, **Kiriath Sannah** (that is, **Debir**), Anab, Eshtemoh, Anim, Goshen, Holon Giloh, Arab, Dumah, Eshan, Janim, Beth Tappuah, Aphekah, Humtah, **Kiriath Arba** (that is, **Hebron**) and Zior, Maon, Carmel, Ziph, Juttah, Jezreel, Jokdeam, Zanoah, Kain, Gibeah and Timnah, Halhul, Beth Zur, Gedor, Maarath, Beth Anoth and Eltekon, **Kiriath Baal** (that is, **Kiriath Jearim**) and Rabbah	• Kiriath Sannah/Debir Canaanite city also known as "Kiriath Sepher" (Jos 15:15, 49) conquered by Israelites (Jos 10; 11:21; 12:13) and by Othniel (Jos 15:15; Ju 1:11); allotted to Judah (Jos 15:49) Levitical city (Jos 21:15; 1Ch 6:58) 8.5 mi. SSW of Hebron Kh. Rabud, *#151093* • Kiriath Arba/Hebron town in hill country of Judah; 64 times in OT Abraham pitched a tent; built altar (Ge 13:18); purchased cave of Machpelah where wives of patriarchs were buried (Ge 23:19) Israelite spies surveyed Hebron (Nu 13:22) captured by Joshua; given to Caleb (Jos 14:6:15) Levitical city (Jos 21:11, 13); city of refuge (Jos 20:7) David ruled from Hebron 7½ years before moving capital to Jerusalem (2Sa passim) Absalom began his revolt there (2Sa 15); Rehoboam refortified the city (2Ch 11:10) 20 mi. SSW of Jerusalem El-Khalil—Jebel er-Rumeideh/Hebron, *#160103* • Kiriath Baal/Kiriath Jearim (see chart "Tribe of Judah—Northern Boundaries," 15:5b−11)
In desert 15:61−62	• En Gedi allotted to tribe of Judah; on the W shore of the Dead Sea (Eze 47:10) borders Judean Desert

| Beth Arabah, Middin, Secacah, Nibshan, the City of Salt and **En Gedi** | • David flees there from Saul (1Sa 23:29; 24:1) also called Hazazon Tamar (2Ch 20:2) oasis famous for its vineyards (SS 1:14) 25 mi. SE from Jerusalem Tal Jurn/ Tell Goren, *#187097* |
| 21:11–16—additional Levitical cities | • Judah and Simeon—Libnah, Jattir, Eshtemoa, Holon, Debir, Ain, Juttah, Beth Shemesh |

63 Of all the towns in the territory of Judah, Jerusalem is mentioned as a city from which the Jebusites could not be dislodged. Similar statements appear in the list of towns for the tribes of Ephraim and Manasseh. We are told that the Ephraimites did not dislodge the Canaanites living in Gezer (16:10). The Manassites were unable to inhabit some of their cities because the Canaanites were determined to remain there (17:12–13).

NOTES

36 "Shaaraim" (שַׁעֲרַיִם, *ša^{ca}rayim*, meaning "two gates"). In 2008, archaeologists dug the Khirbet Qeiyafa site in the Shephelah, near the Elah Valley, and discovered two gates—one facing west and one facing east toward Jerusalem. The following year, a Semitic inscription written on a large pottery fragment was found inside the fortified city, near one of the two gates. Scholars dated the inscription to the time of the united monarchy. The text is written in a dialect of Hebrew, in Proto-Canaanite script, with ink, and contains five rows with ten letters in each row. Based on the evidence, scholars have concluded that the site of Khirbet Qeiyafa is biblical Shaaraim, a location that had not previously been identified (see Jos 15:36; 1Sa 17:52; 1Chr 4:31–32) (Y. Garfinkel and S. Ganor, "Khirbet Qeiyafa: Sha'arayim," *JHS* 8 [2008], 2–10; http:// qeiyafa.huji.ac.il/ [accessed February 9, 2011]).

b. Land Allotment for the Sons of Joseph (16:1–17:18)

OVERVIEW

The two sons of Joseph, Ephraim and Manasseh, each receive a portion of land in the central hill country, north of Benjamin and south of Asher and Issachar. Both tribal allotments are bordered on the east by the Jordan River. The western border of Manasseh's allotment is the Great Sea (Mediterranean Sea), while the western border of Ephraim is the territory of the Danites. The biblical text presents the tribe of Joseph both as a single unit—the people of Joseph (Jos 16:1–3; 17:14–18; 18:5, 11;

Jdg 1:22, 35; 2Sa 19:20)—and as two separate tribes (Jos 16:4; 17:9–10; 1Ch 9:3).

The introduction of chapter 16 describes briefly the boundaries of the joined territories of Ephraim and Manasseh (vv.1–4). This section is followed by a list of geographical markers that identify the land of Ephraim (vv.5–9). A brief genealogy of Manasseh introduces chapter 17; then follows an account of the land distribution to the daughters of Zelophehad (vv.3–6). The description of (western) Manassite territory (vv.7–11) ends with a meeting of the people of Joseph—Ephraim and Manasseh—who question Joshua for giving them "only one allotment and one portion for an inheritance" (17:14). In their opinion, they are much too numerous to settle in this small area. Joshua answers wisely and tells them to clear the forested area of the Perizzites and Rephaites. If they do so, they will have enough room for their entire tribes and even for future growth.

i. Land for Sons of Joseph (16:1–4)

¹The allotment for Joseph began at the Jordan of Jericho, east of the waters of Jericho, and went up from there through the desert into the hill country of Bethel. ²It went on from Bethel (that is, Luz), crossed over to the territory of the Arkites in Ataroth, ³descended westward to the territory of the Japhletites as far as the region of Lower Beth Horon and on to Gezer, ending at the sea. ⁴So Manasseh and Ephraim, the descendants of Joseph, received their inheritance.

COMMENTARY

1–3 The sons of Joseph receive their allotments through a "lot" (*gôrāl*) system. The eastern boundary begins at the Jordan River, east of the "waters of Jericho"—the spring Ain es-Sultan that watered the oasis of Jericho (T. A. Holland and E. Netzer, "Jericho," *ABD*, 3:724). It then runs westward up the hill toward Bethel, crosses over to the territory of the Arkites, continues on to Lower Beth Horon and Gezer, and ends at the Great Sea. The distance between Gezer and the sea is approximately fifteen miles. The Arkites are descendants of Canaan (Ge 10:17). Hushai, who lived during the united monarchy, is identified as an Arkite (2Sa 15:32; 16:16; 17:5, 14).

4 The unified tribe of Joseph—Ephraim and Manasseh—now has its allotment. The following section separates the two tribes and describes their respective areas.

NOTES

1 The "allotment" (וַיֵּצֵא הַגּוֹרָל, *wayyēṣēʾ haggôrāl*; lit., "the lot went out"). "Lots" were small stones or pieces of wood that were shaken in a small vessel and cast onto the ground (*yrh*, e.g., Jos 18:6; *npl*, e.g., 1Chr 24:21; 25:8; 26:13; Ne 10:34; *šlḥ*, Jos 18:8, 10; *yrd*, Joel 3:3; *yṣʾ*, Jos 16:1). Lot casting was done for secular (e.g., Pr 18:18; Na 3:10; Ne 10:35[34]; Est 3:7) and religious (e.g., Lev 16:8; Jos 18:6, 8, 10) purposes. In Joshua, the lot is cast to determine the boundaries of tribal allotments (see W. Dommershausen, "גּוֹרָל," *TDOT*, 2:450−56).

ii. Land for Ephraim (16:5−10)

> [5]This was the territory of Ephraim, clan by clan:
> The boundary of their inheritance went from Ataroth Addar in the east to Upper Beth Horon [6]and continued to the sea. From Micmethath on the north it curved eastward to Taanath Shiloh, passing by it to Janoah on the east. [7]Then it went down from Janoah to Ataroth and Naarah, touched Jericho and came out at the Jordan. [8]From Tappuah the border went west to the Kanah Ravine and ended at the sea. This was the inheritance of the tribe of the Ephraimites, clan by clan. [9]It also included all the towns and their villages that were set aside for the Ephraimites within the inheritance of the Manassites.
> [10]They did not dislodge the Canaanites living in Gezer; to this day the Canaanites live among the people of Ephraim but are required to do forced labor.

COMMENTARY

5−9 The first tribe of Joseph to receive its inheritance is Ephraim.

Tribe of Ephraim Borders/Towns (16:5−8)	Comments and Grid #
16:5 — **Ataroth Addar** Jos 18:13	• on border of Benjamin and Ephraim • possibly Kh. Raddana, *#169146*
16:5 — **Upper Beth Horon** • Levitical city Jos 10:10,11; 1Ch 6:68; 2Ch 8:5	• on a ridge guarding hill country from the coastal plain • Joshua pursued fleeing Amorites there (Jos 10:10−11) • near Benjamin-Ephraim border; in Ephraim • Solomon rebuilds it to protect western approach to Jerusalem

	• 12 mi. NW of Jerusalem • Beit Ur el-Foqa, *#160143*
16:6 — Micmethath Jos 17:7	• on boundary between Ephraim and Manasseh • possibly 2.5 mi. SSW of Shechem • possibly Kh. Makhneh el-Foqa, *#175176*
16:6 — Taanath Shiloh	• on NE border of Ephraim • 4.5 mi. SE of Shechem • Kh. Tana el-Foqa, *#185175*
16:6 — Janoah 2Ki 15:29	• on NE boundary of Ephraim • captured by Tiglath-Pileser, Assyrian king (2Ki 15:29) • 6 mi. SE of Shechem • Kh. Yanun, *#184173*
16:7 — Ataroth Nu 32:3, 34; Jos 18:13	• in NE Ephraim on border with Manasseh
16:7 — Naarah 1Ch 7:28	• on SE border of Ephraim between Ataroth and Jericho • also called Naaran (1Ch 7:28) • 1.8 mi. NW of Jericho • Tel el-Jisr, *#190144*

16:7 — Jericho
Nu 34:15; Jos 2; 6; 2Ki 2; Ezr 2:34;
Ne 3:2; 7:36; Jer 52:8
	• W of Jordan River; border between Ephraim and Benjamin
	• spies sent there (Jos 2); conquered by Israel (Jos 6)
	• there, Ehud killed Eglon; mentioned in Elijah and Elisha
	  narratives
	• after Babylonian exile, Jews resettled there
	• 6 mi. W of Jordan River and 10 mi. NNW of Dead Sea
	  alongside a powerful spring that waters the oasis
	• Tel es-Sultan, *#192142*

16:8 — Tappuah Jos 12:17; 15:34, 53; 16:8; 17:8; 1Ch 2:43	• on border between Ephraim and Manasseh • allotted to Ephraim, but the land around it to Manasseh • 8 mi. SW of Shechem • Sheikh Abu Zarad, *#172168*
16:8 — Kanah Ravine Jos 16:8; 17:9	• boundary for Ephraim and Manasseh • Wadi Qana flows W out of hill country of Ephraim and Manasseh; joins Nahal Yarkon W of Aphek

20:7 — Shechem
• city of refuge and Levitical city
  Ge 12:6; 37:12; Ju 9; 1Ch 6:67;
  Hos 6:9
	• important non-Israelite city; prominent in stories of Abraham,
	  Jacob, and Abimelech
	• Israelite tribal and religious center during the days of Joshua
	• on the boundary between Manasseh and Ephraim

	• first capital of the N kingdom; replaced by Tirzah and then Samaria • 30 mi. N of Jerusalem, on E side of Nablus • Tel Balatah, #176179
21:21–22	• Additional Levitical cities of Ephraim — Gezer, Kizbaim

9 Ephraim's territory also includes towns in Manasseh's inheritance. This description blurs the boundaries for the descendants of Joseph and anticipates the question asked by the people of Joseph: "Why have you given us only one allotment and one portion for an inheritance?" In chapter 17, we find another blurring of borders. The towns of Beth Shan, Ibleam, Dor, Endor, Taanach, and Megiddo are shared by Issachar, Asher, and Manasseh (17:11).

The Ephraimites succeed in taking over their assigned territory except for Gezer, from which they are unable to dislodge the Canaanites, who are allowed to remain as forced labor. During the Middle Bronze Age, Gezer was an important walled city in the Shephelah, located approximately twenty miles west of Jerusalem. The town had a large defensive tower that was over fifty-two feet wide (www.

bibleplaces.com/gezer.htm [accessed on October 10, 2011]). During the united monarchy, Gezer was captured by the Egyptians and set on fire, and its Canaanite inhabitants were decimated. The pharaoh of Egypt gave the city to his daughter when she married King Solomon. Among his building projects, Solomon rebuilt the cities of Gezer, Hazor, and Megiddo (1Ki 9:15–17).

Towns in the Shephelah were typically larger than those in the hill country, which fact may have impacted the Ephraimites' ability to subdue the town completely. This incomplete conquest reflects a similar situation in Judah, where the Jebusites continue to dwell in Jerusalem (15:63). This inability to subdue the entire land is problematic according to Deuteronomy 7:1–7; failure to eradicate the inhabitants from the land — including the Canaanites and the Jebusites — is displeasing to Yahweh.

iii. Land for Manasseh (17:1–13)

¹This was the allotment for the tribe of Manasseh as Joseph's firstborn, that is, for Makir, Manasseh's firstborn. Makir was the ancestor of the Gileadites, who had received Gilead and Bashan because the Makirites were great soldiers. ²So this allotment was for the rest of the people of Manasseh — the clans of Abiezer, Helek, Asriel, Shechem, Hepher and Shemida. These are the other male descendants of Manasseh son of Joseph by their clans.

³Now Zelophehad son of Hepher, the son of Gilead, the son of Makir, the son of Manasseh, had no sons but only daughters, whose names were Mahlah, Noah, Hoglah,

Milcah and Tirzah. ⁴They went to Eleazar the priest, Joshua son of Nun, and the leaders and said, "The LORD commanded Moses to give us an inheritance among our brothers." So Joshua gave them an inheritance along with the brothers of their father, according to the LORD's command. ⁵Manasseh's share consisted of ten tracts of land besides Gilead and Bashan east of the Jordan, ⁶because the daughters of the tribe of Manasseh received an inheritance among the sons. The land of Gilead belonged to the rest of the descendants of Manasseh.

⁷The territory of Manasseh extended from Asher to Micmethath east of Shechem. The boundary ran southward from there to include the people living at En Tappuah. ⁸(Manasseh had the land of Tappuah, but Tappuah itself, on the boundary of Manasseh, belonged to the Ephraimites.) ⁹Then the boundary continued south to the Kanah Ravine. There were towns belonging to Ephraim lying among the towns of Manasseh, but the boundary of Manasseh was the northern side of the ravine and ended at the sea. ¹⁰On the south the land belonged to Ephraim, on the north to Manasseh. The territory of Manasseh reached the sea and bordered Asher on the north and Issachar on the east.

¹¹Within Issachar and Asher, Manasseh also had Beth Shan, Ibleam and the people of Dor, Endor, Taanach and Megiddo, together with their surrounding settlements (the third in the list is Naphoth).

¹²Yet the Manassites were not able to occupy these towns, for the Canaanites were determined to live in that region. ¹³However, when the Israelites grew stronger, they subjected the Canaanites to forced labor but did not drive them out completely.

COMMENTARY

1 The introduction to chapter 17 revisits Transjordan. The narrative highlights the descendants of Makir, the Gileadites, who are great men of war and inhabitants of the land of Gilead and Bashan. The names Makir and Gilead serve to identify both people (Nu 26:1, 29–30; 36:1; Jdg 5:17) and geographical locations (Ge 31:21; Nu 32:29, 39; Dt 2:36; 3:12; 34:1; 2Sa 24:6). The focus on Transjordan provides the background for the narrative about Zelophehad's daughters' request for a portion of land among Manasseh (eastern tribe) (vv.3–6). This pericope has the main characteristics of a "land grant," in which (1) an individual petitions a leader

for land, (2) Moses had already promised land to the petitioner, and (3) the request is granted.

2 The territory outside of Gilead and Bashan belongs to the other male descendants of Manasseh. This gender pronouncement is set in contrast with the following request for land made by females.

3 A great-great-grandson of Manasseh, Zelophehad, had five daughters—Mahlah, Noah, Hoglah, Milcah, and Tirzah—but no sons. With no male heir, Zelophehad's family risked losing its inheritance.

4–6 Aware of their predicament, Zelophehad's daughters approach the leaders of Israel—Joshua,

Eleazar the priest, and the heads of the tribal clan—who are responsible for distributing the conquered territory (14:1; 19:51; 21:1; Nu 32:28; 34:17–17). They remind the leaders that Moses had promised to give them an inheritance among their father's brothers (Nu 27:1–11). The promise made by Moses belongs in a legislative context, and it appears here in a "promise/fulfillment" structure (e.g., Dt 1:8, 21; 3:18–20; 4:1; 6:10–12; 8:1; 11:31; 19:8; 26:1–3). According to Numbers, land was first bequeathed to sons; but if none were present, the land was given to daughters, then to brothers, then to the deceased individual's brother; finally, if none of these existed, the land was given to the next of kin in the dead person's clan (Nu 27:8–11).

Legally, the daughters of Zelophehad were entitled to their father's inheritance since they had no brothers. Without hesitation, Joshua grants them territory in one of Manasseh's tracts of land beside Gilead and Bashan, east of the Jordan. The narrative notes that "because the daughters of the tribe of Manasseh received an inheritance among the sons," the land remained in the hands of Manasseh's descendants permanently. According to Numbers 27 and 36, Zehophelad's daughters marry their Manassite cousins, obeying Moses' instructions and thereby ensuring that their inheritance remains in the family (Nu 27:8–11; 36:6–13). The story of Zelophehad's daughters portrays Israel as a reasonably well-integrated people among whom women had a (mitigated) voice and played a role in society. This evidence decentralizes the privileged male paradigm, as it reveals Yahweh as one who provides for all his children indiscriminately.

This brief return to Transjordan is mentioned here for several reasons: (1) to meet the legal interests of Zelophehad's daughters; (2) to confirm that the inheritance is distributed according to Moses' directives; (3) to link the distribution of land in Transjordan to that in Cisjordan.

7–11 At this point, the digression into Transjordan ends and the reader returns to Cisjordan, to the territory given to the western half-tribe of Manasseh. The southern boundaries overlap slightly with Ephraim, whose towns lie among those of Manasseh. The northern boundaries of Manasseh overlap with those of Issachar and Asher.

Half-tribe of Manasseh—Borders and Towns (17:7–11)	Comments and Grid #
17:7—**Micmethath**	• see Tribe of Ephraim—16:6
17:7—**Shechem** • a Levitical city • city of refuge	• see Tribe of Ephraim—16:5–8
17:7—**En Tappuah**	• see Tribe of Ephraim—16:8
17:9—**Kanah Ravine**	• see Tribe of Ephraim—16:8
17:11—**Beth Shan** Jos 17:16; Ju 1:27; 1Sa 31:10, 12; 2Sa 21:12; 1Ki 4:12	• major Canaanite city in or near Issachar • Manasseh not able to drive out inhabitants (Jdg 1:27)

	• bodies of Saul and Jonathan were hung on wall (2Sa 21:12) • located in the 5th Solomonic district • in Hellenistic period called Scythopolis and Nysa • 15 mi. SSW of Sea of Galilee • Tel el-Husn/Tell Bet Shean, #197212
17:11—Ibleam • Levitical city Ju 1:27; 2Ki 9:27; 1Ch 6:70	• Manassites did not drive out Canaanites • Jehu killed Ahaziah nearby (2Ki 9:27) • probably "Bileam" (1Ch 6:70) • 12 mi. SE of Megiddo • Kh. Belameh, #177205
17:11—Dor Jos 11:12; 12:23; Ju 1:27; 1Ki 4:11; 1Ch 7:29	• port city; king defeated by Joshua; allotted to Manasseh but possessed by Ephraim • Canaanites not driven out (Jdg 1:27) • area around Dor called "Naphoth Dor" (Jos 11:2) • often under non-Israelite control • 15 mi. S of Haifa, 8 mi. N of Caesarea • Kh. el-Burj/Tell Dor, #142224
17:11—Endor 1Sa 28:7; Ps 83:10	• assigned to Manasseh, but in Issachar • there, Saul consulted a medium (1Sa 28:7) • 2.5 mi. due S of Mt. Tabor • Kh. Safsafeh/H. Zafzafot, #187227
17:11—Taanach • Levitical city Jos 12:21; Ju 1:27; 5:19; 1Ki 4:12	• town conquered by Israelites • "beside" or "on the border of" rather than "within" Issachar (Jos 17:11) • Canaanites lived there • in 5th Solomonic administrative district • 4 mi. SE of Megiddo • Tel Tinnik, #171214
17:11—Megiddo Jos 12:21; Ju 1:27; 1Ki 4:12; 9:15; 2Ki 9:27; 23:29, 30; 1Ch 7:29; 2Ch 35:22; Zec 12:11	• major Canaanite city captured by Joshua • Manassites not able to take possession of it • under Israelite control during the reign of David; fortified district capital of Solomon • Ahaziah and Josiah died at Megiddo (2Ki 9:27; 23:29–30)

	• mentioned in an oracle of Zechariah (12:11) • SW edge of Jezreel Valley, guarding important pass through Carmel Range • Tel el-Mutesellim/Tell Megiddo, *#167221*
17:11—**Naphoth**	• Naphoth Dor—forested region around coastal city of Dor; a king fought against Joshua (Jos 11:2; 12:23); 4th Solomonic district (1Ki 4:11)
21:23-24—additional Levitical cities	• Gath Rimmon (also with Dan)

12-13 As mentioned above, the Canaanite threat does not cease with the conquest of the area. In fact, the Canaanites have no intention of leaving their homeland. They are deeply entrenched in the region, profiting greatly from the resources of the land and inhabiting an area deemed militarily strategic. The failure of Israel to eradicate the Canaanites is significant as it sets the stage for later syncretism and for relentless conflicts between the two groups.

This is the third mention of Israel's inability to drive out all the inhabitants of the land (see also 15:63, the Jebusites; 16:10, the Gezerites). But only here do we read about the determination of the Canaanites to remain in their land. As noted by D. M. Howard, the Israelites "had the power to remove the Canaanites from the land and so to be God's instruments of judgment to remove wickedness, but they chose to tolerate wickedness and to use for their own purposes that which God had devoted to destruction. And so they sowed the seeds of their own destruction" (Howard, 354).

iv. Complaint of the Sons of Joseph (17:14-18)

¹⁴The people of Joseph said to Joshua, "Why have you given us only one allotment and one portion for an inheritance? We are a numerous people and the LORD has blessed us abundantly."

¹⁵"If you are so numerous," Joshua answered, "and if the hill country of Ephraim is too small for you, go up into the forest and clear land for yourselves there in the land of the Perizzites and Rephaites."

¹⁶The people of Joseph replied, "The hill country is not enough for us, and all the Canaanites who live in the plain have iron chariots, both those in Beth Shan and its settlements and those in the Valley of Jezreel."

¹⁷But Joshua said to the house of Joseph—to Ephraim and Manasseh—"You are numerous and very powerful. You will have not only one allotment ¹⁸but the forested hill country as well. Clear it, and its farthest limits will be yours; though the Canaanites have iron chariots and though they are strong, you can drive them out."

COMMENTARY

14 Disappointed with the size of their allotment, the people of Joseph—Ephraim and Manasseh—approach Joshua and complain that their inheritance is insufficient. Thus far, those who approached Joshua with special requests all received a positive answer. In the previous requests for land, Caleb and the daughters of Zelophehad had appealed to an earlier promise of Yahweh; but in the case of the people of Joseph, there was no such divine pledge. The Ephraimites and Manassites ironically describe themselves as "a numerous people," abundantly blessed by Yahweh; yet, when the time comes to defeat the Canaanites, they see themselves as too weak to overcome their foes!

15 In a first attempt to satisfy the demand for more land, Joshua bluntly suggests that the Ephraimites and Manassites clear the forest occupied by the Perizzites and Rephaites and spread out in that area. This solution is less than pleasing to their ears. The Rephaites (Zamzummites in Dt 2:20) were known as fearsome giants similar to the Anakites (e.g., Dt 2:20–21), who lived in Bashan east of the Jordan (Dt 2:11, 20; 3:11–13; Jos 12:4; 13:12). The Perizzites had lived in the area since before the time of the patriarchs, and they certainly had no desire to

be uprooted (e.g., Ge 13:7; 15:20; 34:30). Despite Yahweh's promise to drive them out from the land (e.g., Ex 33:2; 34:11; Dt 7:1–2; 20:17; Jos 3:10), they remained there through Israel's return from exile (Ezr 9:1).

16 Still dissatisfied at the limited space for their large tribe, the people of Joseph express grave concern at the presence, in the surrounding areas, of Canaanites, who had iron chariots at their disposal. The Israelites were primarily on foot, so the thought of facing warriors on wheels was particularly alarming to them. Chariots reinforced with iron were used in warfare, especially in valleys, where the terrain was suitable for this type of military equipment (R. Drews, "The 'Chariots of Iron' of Joshua and Judges," *JSOT* 45 [1989]: 15–23).

17–18 Unyielding to the demands of the people of Joseph, Joshua repeats his original response. In a hortatory tone, he reassures them that they are well able to subdue the Canaanites and to settle safely in the area. His reply to the people of Joseph is a clear, "Go for it! You can do it! Clear the forest and settle there! There is no other solution!"

NOTES

15 The phrase *har-ʾeprayim* (הַר־אֶפְרָיִם) is rendered "Mount Ephraim" in the KJV; "the hill country of Ephraim" in the ESV, NAS, NIV, NRS, RSV, and TNK; "the hills of Ephraim" in CJB; "the mountains of Ephraim" in NKJV; and "the highlands of Ephraim" in NJB. Common in biblical Hebrew (ca. 550x), the word *har* can refer to an individual mountain (e.g., 1Ki 18:19–20) or to a mountain range (e.g., Ps 78:54). This author agrees with translators who adopt the idea of a mountainous area rather than a single mountain. Since Joshua instructs the people of Joseph (Ephraim and the half-tribe of Manasseh) to "go up into the forest and clear land for yourselves ... the land of the Perizzites and Rephaites," so as to accommodate the "numerous people" whom God blessed abundantly (probably with sheep, cattle, donkeys, camels), the expanse of the area to be cleared needed to be substantial—more than just one mountain top (see S. Talmon, "הר," *TDOT*, 3:427–47).

The root of the verb to "clear" (וּבֵרֵאתָ, *ûbē rē'tā*) the forested area may not be the same root as that found in Genesis 1:1 (ברא, *br'*, "to create"). BDB (135) considers only one root to cover both meaning, in the Qal for Genesis 1:1 ("to create") and in the Piel for Joshua 17:15 ("to cut, clear"); see also K. H. Bernhardt, "ברא," *TDOT*, 2:245). *HALOT* (146–47) proposes two different roots ברא I ("to create") and ברא II ("to divide, cut"). Since the etymology of the root is unknown and the root does not appear in other Semitic languages, both views are possible.

16 "Beth-Shan and its settlements" (בְּבֵית־שְׁאָן וּבְנוֹתֶיהָ, *b⁰bêt-š⁰'ān ûb⁰nôteyhā*). The word for "settlements" is personified with the Hebrew word for "daughter" (בַּת, *bat*). The "daughters of Judah" are the "towns of Judah" (Ps 97:8), and the "daughter(s) of Zion" refer to Jerusalem (Isa 1:8) or to the towns around Jerusalem (SS 3:10–11; cf. Eze 16:53, 57). The same expression is used for cities outside of Israel's territory and for nations (e.g., "daughter of Tyre" = Tyre, Ps 45:13[12]); "daughter of Babylon" = city of Babylon, Ps 137:8; "daughter of Tarshish" = Tarshish, Isa 23:10) (see H. Haag, "בַּת," *TDOT*, 2:332–38).

c. Survey of the Rest of the Land (18:1–10)

¹The whole assembly of the Israelites gathered at Shiloh and set up the Tent of Meeting there. The country was brought under their control, ²but there were still seven Israelite tribes who had not yet received their inheritance.

³So Joshua said to the Israelites: "How long will you wait before you begin to take possession of the land that the LORD, the God of your fathers, has given you? ⁴Appoint three men from each tribe. I will send them out to make a survey of the land and to write a description of it, according to the inheritance of each. Then they will return to me. ⁵You are to divide the land into seven parts. Judah is to remain in its territory on the south and the house of Joseph in its territory on the north. ⁶After you have written descriptions of the seven parts of the land, bring them here to me and I will cast lots for you in the presence of the LORD our God. ⁷The Levites, however, do not get a portion among you, because the priestly service of the LORD is their inheritance. And Gad, Reuben and the half-tribe of Manasseh have already received their inheritance on the east side of the Jordan. Moses the servant of the LORD gave it to them."

⁸As the men started on their way to map out the land, Joshua instructed them, "Go and make a survey of the land and write a description of it. Then return to me, and I will cast lots for you here at Shiloh in the presence of the LORD." ⁹So the men left and went through the land. They wrote its description on a scroll, town by town, in seven parts, and returned to Joshua in the camp at Shiloh. ¹⁰Joshua then cast lots for them in Shiloh in the presence of the LORD, and there he distributed the land to the Israelites according to their tribal divisions.

COMMENTARY

1–2 The scene changes from the encampment at Gilgal to Shiloh, a location theologically significant for the cultic life of Israel until the time of Eli the priest/prophet (1Sa 1:4). Shiloh is located at the center of the tribal allotment west of the Jordan; therefore its location was favored for the setting up of the Tent of Meeting. Identified with modern Khirbet Seilun, the site reveals Middle Bronze Age and Late Bronze Age occupation. The Tent of Meeting appears before the distribution of the land to the seven remaining tribes and again after the allotment is completed, forming a literary inclusio (Jos 19:51). The Tent of Meeting at Shiloh highlights the importance of the cultic life of Israel and its establishment as a formal institution in the new conquered land. At this point, the land is under Israelite "control," but seven tribes are still without assigned territory.

3 Joshua reprimands Israel impatiently, "How long will you wait before you begin to take possession of the land?" His accusatory tone seems to imply that the Israelites have become idle in their effort to inhabit the land. According to Joshua, there is still much work to be done; there is no time for apathy. Undeniably, conquest must be followed by occupation,

Joshua's question to Israel echoes a query made by Jacob to his sons. During a time of famine in Canaan, Jacob turned to his sons and said: "Why do you just keep looking at each other? ... I heard that there is grain in Egypt. Go down there and buy some for us" (Ge 42:1–2). Akin to Joshua's frustration with Israel, Jacob projects a tone of impatience and implies that his sons were complacent in the face of potential peril.

4–5 Three representatives from each tribe are appointed for a special survey mission, but the text is unclear as to how many map makers Joshua sends out. If the representatives are sent out from only the seven tribes that had not yet received their inheritance, there are twenty-one surveyors. If the tribal representatives include all twelve tribes (since they were all assembled at Shiloh), there are thirty-six surveyors; and if the landless tribe of Levi is excluded, there are thirty-three surveyors. The map makers are to survey the land, divide it into seven parts, write a description of their findings, and report to Joshua. Then the land will be assigned by lot to the seven remaining tribes. The details of the mission are repeated three times in the passage, twice in the form of instructions (vv.4–6, 8b) and once as a report of the survey work (vv.9–10). This repetition highlights the importance of the event.

6 The map makers are to write descriptions of the seven parts and bring the report to Joshua. Subsequently, Joshua will assign the seven portions through casting lots. Throughout Scripture, only crucial information is recorded in written form. For example, Yahweh instructed Moses to write on a scroll Joshua's defeat of the Amalekites (Ex 17:13–14); Moses wrote the words of the law on chiseled stone tablets (34:1); Moses wrote down a song and taught it to the Israelites (Dt 31:19–22); the prophet Jeremiah dictated the words of the Lord to Baruch, who wrote them on a scroll (Jer 35:1–4); Yahweh instructed the prophet Habakkuk to write down his revelation on tablets (Hab 2:2).

7 Every tribe that has received an inheritance is mentioned in this pericope—Judah (v. 5), house of Joseph (v.5), tribe of Levi (v.7), Gad, Reuben, and the half-tribe of Manasseh (v.7). Upon the return of the surveyors, Joshua will cast lots for the seven remaining tribes.

8–9 The repetitive information again reveals the importance of the situation. What was commanded by Joshua in verses 4–6 is accomplished here. The information written on the scroll is surely the description of the seven allotments in 18:11–19:48.

10 The casting of lots at Shiloh "in the presence of the LORD" highlights Yahweh's approval of the process and his endorsement of the choice of localities for each of the remaining tribes.

d. Land Allotment for Benjamin (18:11–28)

> ¹¹The lot came up for the tribe of Benjamin, clan by clan. Their allotted territory lay between the tribes of Judah and Joseph:
>
> ¹²On the north side their boundary began at the Jordan, passed the northern slope of Jericho and headed west into the hill country, coming out at the desert of Beth Aven. ¹³From there it crossed to the south slope of Luz (that is, Bethel) and went down to Ataroth Addar on the hill south of Lower Beth Horon.
>
> ¹⁴From the hill facing Beth Horon on the south the boundary turned south along the western side and came out at Kiriath Baal (that is, Kiriath Jearim), a town of the people of Judah. This was the western side.
>
> ¹⁵The southern side began at the outskirts of Kiriath Jearim on the west, and the boundary came out at the spring of the waters of Nephtoah. ¹⁶The boundary went down to the foot of the hill facing the Valley of Ben Hinnom, north of the Valley of Rephaim. It continued down the Hinnom Valley along the southern slope of the Jebusite city and so to En Rogel. ¹⁷It then curved north, went to En Shemesh, continued to Geliloth, which faces the Pass of Adummim, and ran down to the Stone of Bohan son of Reuben. ¹⁸It continued to the northern slope of Beth Arabah and on down into the Arabah. ¹⁹It then went to the northern slope of Beth Hoglah and came out at the northern bay of the Salt Sea, at the mouth of the Jordan in the south. This was the southern boundary.
>
> ²⁰The Jordan formed the boundary on the eastern side.
>
> These were the boundaries that marked out the inheritance of the clans of Benjamin on all sides.
>
> ²¹The tribe of Benjamin, clan by clan, had the following cities:
>
> Jericho, Beth Hoglah, Emek Keziz, ²²Beth Arabah, Zemaraim, Bethel, ²³Avvim, Parah, Ophrah, ²⁴Kephar Ammoni, Ophni and Geba — twelve towns and their villages.
>
> ²⁵Gibeon, Ramah, Beeroth, ²⁶Mizpah, Kephirah, Mozah, ²⁷Rekem, Irpeel, Taralah, ²⁸Zelah, Haeleph, the Jebusite city (that is, Jerusalem), Gibeah and Kiriath — fourteen towns and their villages.
>
> This was the inheritance of Benjamin for its clans.

COMMENTARY

11–28 This is most detailed list of geographical markers regarding the allotment for Benjamin. This tribe receives the east-west strip of land north of Judah and south of Ephraim.

Tribe of Benjamin— Borders/Towns (18:11–20)	Comments and Grid #
Boundaries for Benjamin	
18:12—Beth Aven Jos 7:2; 1Sa 13:5; 14:23; Hos 4:15; 5:8; 10:5	• on N boundary of Benjamin, W of Jericho, E of Luz, near Ai • site noted for illicit worship (Hos 4:15; 5:8; Am 1:5) • possibly Tel Maryam, 7 mi. NE of Jerusalem, *#175141*
18:13—Luz/Bethel Ge 28:19; 35:6; 48:3; Ju 1:23; 1Ki 12:29, 32, 33; Am 4:4; Ezr 2:28; Ne 7:32	• Canaanite town where Jacob met with God; renamed it Bethel • on boundary between Ephraim and Benjamin • captured by house of Joseph; Jeroboam built worship center and placed a golden calf; resettled after Babylonian exile • 12 mi. N of Jerusalem; Beitin, *#172148*
18:13—Ataroth Addar Jos 16:5	• on border of Benjamin and Ephraim • possibly Kh. Raddana, *#169146*
18:13—Lower Beth Horon • Levitical city Jos 16:3, 5	• built up by Solomon (1Ki 9:17; 2Ch 8:5) • 12 mi. NW of Jerusalem • Beit Ur et-Tahta, *#158144*
18:14—Kiriath Baal/Kiriath Jearim	• see Tribe of Judah—northern boundaries (15:5b–11)
18:15—Waters of Nephtoah Jos 15:9	• site on the border between Judah and Benjamin • 3 mi. NW of Jerusalem; Lifta/Me-Neftoah, *#168133*
18:16—Valley of Ben Hinnom 2Ki 23:10; 2Ch 28:3; 33:6; Jer 7:31	• valley W and S of OT Jerusalem; joins Kidron S of Jerusalem • formed part of border between Judah and Benjamin • idolatrous worship took place there (2Ki 23:10; Jer 7:31)
18:16—Valley of Rephaim 2Sa 5:18, 22; 23:13; Isa 17:5	• WSW of Jerusalem; border between Judah and Benjamin • Philistines camped there as they attempt to invade Judah • relatively flat; breadbasket of Jerusalem
18:16—En Rogel 2Sa 17:17; 1Ki 1:9	• spring S of Jerusalem between Benjamin and Judah • David's spies hid here (2Sa 17:16–17); where Adonijah's coronation takes place (1Ki 1:9) • less than a mile S of Jerusalem in Kidron Valley; Bir Ayyub, *#172130*

18:17—**En Shemesh** Jos 15:7	• spring on boundary between Benjamin and Judah, between Jericho and Jerusalem; 2 mi. E of Jerusalem • Ain Hod/"Spring of the Apostles," *#175131*
18:17—**Geliloth** Jos 22:10–11	• point SE boundary of Benjamin near Pass of Adummim • eastern tribes build large altar there (Jos 22:10–11) • possibly same as Gilgal in Jos 15:7
18:17—**Pass of Adummim** Jos 15:7	• on N boundary of Judah and S boundary of Benjamin • Eusebia places it between Jericho and Jerusalem, possibly "modern" Talaat ed-Damm ("ascent of blood"), 8 mi. ENE of Jerusalem, *#184136*
18:17—**Stone of Bohan** Jos 15:6	• marker on NE border of Judah, SE Benjamin • in Jericho region; closer to Dead Sea
18:18—**Beth Arabah** Jos 15:6	• boundary between Judah and Benjamin; assigned to both • possibly 4 mi. SE of Jericho • possibly Ain el-Gharabah, *#197139*
18:19—**Beth Hoglah** Jos 15:6	• town SE of Jericho on border of Judah and Benjamin but allotted to Benjamin • possibly Deir Hajlah, 3.5 mi. SE of Jericho; possibly *#197136*
Towns for Benjamin (not mentioned above)	
18:21—**Jericho**	• see tribe of Ephraim—16:7
18:21—**Emek Keziz**	• in eastern portion of territory
18:22—**Zemaraim** 2Ch 13:4	• mountain associated with this town figures in war between Abijah and Jeroboam I (2Ch 13:4) • possibly Ras et-Tahuneh, 9 mi. N of Jerusalem; *#170146*
18:23—**Avvim**	• probably near Bethel
18:23—**Parah**	• 4.7 mi. NE of Jerusalem; Kh. Abu Musarrah, *#177137*
18:23—**Ophrah** 1Sa 13:17	• Philistine raiding party advanced (1Sa 13:17) • 13 mi. NNE of Jerusalem; Et-Taiyibeh, *#178151*
18:24—**Kephar Ammoni**	• possibly N of Jerusalem, on E side of watershed
18:24—**Ophni**	• unknown location; possibly on Benjamin plateau, E of watershed

18:24—**Geba**
• Levitical city
  1Ki 15:22; 2Ki 23:8; 1Ch 6:60;
  Ezr 2:26; Isa 10:29
	• in area disputed by Judah and Israel; near N border of Judah after fall of northern kingdom; along the N approach to Jerusalem
	• Jews resettled after Babylonian exile
	• 6 mi. NNE of Jerusalem; Jeba, *#175140*

18:25 — **Gibeon**
• Levitical city
  Jos 10:4; 2Sa 3:30; 5:25;
  1Ch 9:35–39; Ne 3:7; Jer 28:1;
  41:12, 16
	• major hill country town
	• Gibeonite tricked Joshua into making treaty (Jos 10); probably Saul's hometown; Joab fought Abner here (2Sa 2); David drove the Philistines from area (2Sa 5:25); Jeremiah cursed a prophet from Gibeon (Jer 28:1); Jonathan fought with Ishmael here; men from town helped rebuild walls of Jerusalem after exile (Ne 3:7)
	• 6 mi. NW of Jerusalem; El-Jib, #167139

18:25 — **Ramah** Jdg 4:5; 19:13; 1Sa 1:1, 19; 7:15–17; 1Ki 15:17–22; Ne 7:30; 11:33; Isa 10:29; Jer 40:1; Hos 5:8	• north of Gibeah; also called Ramathaim; along traditional N invasion route towards Jerusalem • Deborah judged Israel there (Jdg 4); home of Samuel; frequently in stories of Saul and David; Baashah, king of Israel, fortified it (1Ki 15:17); Asa removed fortifications (1Ki 15:22); Jeremiah released by Babylonians there (Jer 40:1); after Babylonian exile, Jews settled there • 5 mi. N of Jerusalem; Er-Ram, #172140
18:25 — **Beeroth** Jos 9:17; 2Sa 4:2, 3; 23:37; Ezr 2:25; Ne 7:29	• a Gibeonite city that made a treaty with Joshua (Jos 9:17) • inhabitants flee to Gittaim and murder Ishbosheth (2Sa 4) • Jews resettled here after the exile • Kh. el-Burj (#167137), 4.5 mi. NW of Jerusalem and/or el-Bira 8 mi. N of Jerusalem
18:26 — **Mizpah** Ju 20–21; 1Sa 7; 10:17; 1Ki 15:22; 2Ki 25:23; Ne 3:7; Jer 40–41	• Israelites gather here; prepare for war against Benjamin because atrocities committed against Levite's concubine; important cult center during days of Samuel; fortified by Asa, Judean king; administrative center of Gedaliah, governor appointed by Babylonians over defeated Judah; men from Mizpah help rebuild Jerusalem after exile (Neh 3:7) • 7.5 mi. NNW of Jerusalem; Tel en-Nasbeh, #170143
18:26 — **Kephirah** Jos 9:17; Ezr 2:25; Ne 7:29	• a Gibeonite city that made a treaty with Joshua (Jos 9:17) • later resettled by Jews after Babylonian exile • 8.5 mi. WNW of Jerusalem; Kh. el-Kefireh, #160137
18:26 — **Mozah**	• 5 mi. WNW of Jerusalem; Qalunyah/ Mevasseret Ziyyon, #165134
18:27 — **Rekem**	• unknown location; probably W of watershed
18:27 — **Irpeel**	• unknown location; probably in area N of Jerusalem

18:27 — **Taralah**	• unknown location; probably in W Benjamin plateau, NW of Jerusalem
18:28 — **Zelah** 2Sa 21:14	• David buried bones of Saul and Jonathan there (2Sa 21:14) • unknown location; in W Benjamin plateau, NNW of Jerusalem
18:28 — **Haeleph** (Jerusalem)	• unknown location; probably W of watershed
18:28 — **Gibeah** Jdg 19–20; 1Sa 13:2, 15; 14:16; Hos 9:9	• wicked men of Gibeah abuse Levite's concubine; city is destroyed as punishment (Jdg 19) • 3 mi. N of Jerusalem (site later called "Gibeah of Saul"); Tel el-Ful, *#172136* • two or three hundred years later, Jonathan launches attack on Philistines from "Gibeah of Benjamin," located 3 mi. NE of the old site; Jeba, *#175140*
18:28 — **Kiriath** Jos 9:17; 1Sa 6:21; 1Ch 13:5; Ezr 2:25; Jer 26:20	• on N border of Judah, SW border of Benjamin, allotted to Judah • also called Baal of Judah; possibly Kiriath, Jaar, Baalath • 8.5 mi. W of Jerusalem; Deir el-Azar/ Tell Qiryat Yearim, *#159135*
21:17–18 — Additional Levitical cities	• Anathoth, Almon

e. Land Allotment for Simeon (19:1–9)

[1]The second lot came out for the tribe of Simeon, clan by clan. Their inheritance lay within the territory of Judah. [2]It included:

Beersheba (or Sheba), Moladah, [3]Hazar Shual, Balah, Ezem, [4]Eltolad, Bethul, Hormah, [5]Ziklag, Beth Marcaboth, Hazar Susah, [6]Beth Lebaoth and Sharuhen — thirteen towns and their villages;

[7]Ain, Rimmon, Ether and Ashan — four towns and their villages — [8]and all the villages around these towns as far as Baalath Beer (Ramah in the Negev).

This was the inheritance of the tribe of the Simeonites, clan by clan. [9]The inheritance of the Simeonites was taken from the share of Judah, because Judah's portion was more than they needed. So the Simeonites received their inheritance within the territory of Judah.

COMMENTARY

1–9 The second lot came out for the tribe of Simeon, but the boundaries of the allotment are not listed. The area is identified with the names of towns only. Simeonite cities are included within the borders of Judah and are located at the southern end of the Judahite territory. The stated reason for the overlap is that "Judah's portion was more than they needed" (v.9). It is also possible that the Simeonites did not receive a separate territory because their ancestor had violently killed the freshly circumcised Shechemites (Ge 34:13–30) and carried away their wealth, women, children, and animals. Jacob had prophesied at the end of his life that the violence of Simeon would cause them to be scattered among the tribes (49:5–7; see Boling and Wright, 439–40; A. L. Harstad, *Joshua* [Concordia Commentary; Saint Louis: Concordia, 2004], 597; Howard, 366; Woudstra, 280).

Tribe of Simeon — Borders and Towns (19:2–8a)	Comments and Grid #
19:2—**Beersheba** Ge 21:14; Jos 15:28; 2Sa 24:7; 1Ki 19:3; 1Ch 4:28; Ne 11:27; Am 5:5	• allotted to both Judah and Simeon; S boundary of Israel; 25 mi. SW of Hebron; • associated with the patriarchs (Abraham, Isaac, and Jacob); capital of the Negev; mentioned in Joab's census and story of Elijah's flight from Jezebel; a shrine or temple was there; Jews lived there in postexilic period • Tel es-Seba/Tell Beer Sheva, *#134072*
19:2—**Moladah** Jos 15:26; 1Ch 4:28; Ne 11:26	• in Negev; allotted to Judah and Simeon • Jews lived there after the Babylonian exile • location unknown — possibly Kh. el-Waten/H. Yittan, *#142074*, 5 mi. E of Beersheba
19:3—**Hazar Shual** Jos 15:28; 1Ch 4:28; Ne 11:27	• in Negev; allotted to Judah and Simeon • Jews settled there after the exile • location unknown
19:3—**Balah**	• in Negev; location unknown
19:3—**Ezem** Jos 15:29; 1Ch 4:29	• in Negev; allotted to Judah and Simeon • location unknown
19:4—**Eltolad** Jos 15:30	• allotted to the tribe of Simeon within allotment of Judah • location unknown; in the Negev
19:4—**Bethul**	• in Negev; probably also "Bethel" to which David sent plunder (1Sa 30:27) • parallel Judean list (Jos 15:30) has "Kesil"; unknown location

19:4—**Hormah** Nu 14:45; 21:3; Jos 12:14;15:30; Ju 1:17; 1Sa 30:30	• in Negev; allotted to Judah and Simeon • Israelites were defeated by Canaanites; later, Israelites capture and destroy town, formerly called Zephath; David sent booty to its inhabitants • possibly Kh. el-Meshash/Tell Masos, *#146069*, 8 mi. ESE of Beer Sheba, or Tel Khuweilifeh/Tell Halif, *#137087*, 9.5 mi. NNE of Beersheba
19:5—**Ziklag** Jos 15:31; 1Sa 27:6; 2Sa 1:1; 4:10; Ne 11:28	• town allotted to Judah and Simeon • after fleeing from Saul to Achish, David was settled here • Jews settled there in postexilic period • possibly Tel esh-Shariah/Tell Sera, *#119088*, 15 mi. ESE of Gaza
19:5—**Beth Marcaboth** 1Ch 4:31	• village in Negev allotted to Simeon • may be Madmannah; preceded by Ziklag in Negev list of Judah (Jos 15:31) • if not, then location unknown; in S Judah
19:5—**Hazar Susah**	• Negev village allotted to Simeon; name means "corral of the mare" • probably identical to Hazar Susim, "corral of the horses" (1Ch 4:31) • location unknown—possibly stables or military stations
19:6—**Beth Lebaoth**	• in Negev; possibly same as Lebaoth (Jos 15:32) and Beth Biri (1Ch 4:31) • location unknown—in S Israel/Judah
19:6—**Sharuhen**	• in W Negev; also called Shilhim (Jos 15:32) • probably T. el-Ajjul, *#093097*, 4 mi. SW of Gaza, or possibly Tel el-Farah (S), *#100076*
19:7—**Ain** • Levitical city—Nu 34:11; Jos 15:32; 21:16; 1Ch 4:32	• assigned to Judah and Simeon; probably in W Negev • location uncertain—probably a compound town name: Ain Rimmon
19:7—**Rimmon** Jos 15:32; 1Ch 4:32; Zec 14:10	• town in Negev allotted to Judah and Simeon; Zechariah also seems to place it in S Judah • location uncertain—possibly Tel Khuweilifeh/Tell Halif; *#137087*, 9.5 mi. NNE of Beersheba
19:7—**Ether** Jos 15:42	• Judean town in the Shephelah; later assigned to the tribe of Simeon • 4 mi. NE of Lachish; Kh. el-Ater/Tell Eter, *#138112*

19:7 — **Ashan**	• village allotted to Judah in Shephelah district; later given to

• Levitical city
Jos 15:42; 1Sa 30:30; 1Ch 4:32
	Simeon
	• David and men roamed there
	• location uncertain — possibly Tell Beit Mirsim, *#141096*,
	  12.5 mi. SW of Hebron (two Ashan's: Judahite in Shephelah;
	  Simeonite in Negev)

19:8 — **Baalath Beer/Ramah**	• in Negev; also called "Ramah in the Negev" • possibly Bir Rekhme/Beer Yeroham, *#138043*

f. Land Allotment for Zebulun (19:10–16)

¹⁰The third lot came up for Zebulun, clan by clan:
The boundary of their inheritance went as far as Sarid. ¹¹Going west it ran to Maralah, touched Dabbesheth, and extended to the ravine near Jokneam. ¹²It turned east from Sarid toward the sunrise to the territory of Kisloth Tabor and went on to Daberath and up to Japhia. ¹³Then it continued eastward to Gath Hepher and Eth Kazin; it came out at Rimmon and turned toward Neah. ¹⁴There the boundary went around on the north to Hannathon and ended at the Valley of Iphtah El. ¹⁵Included were Kattath, Nahalal, Shimron, Idalah and Bethlehem. There were twelve towns and their villages.
¹⁶These towns and their villages were the inheritance of Zebulun, clan by clan.

COMMENTARY

10–16 The third lot came up for Zebulun. The tribal allotment includes the towns and their villages that appear in the boundary list.

Tribe of Zebulun — Borders and Towns (19:10–15)	Comments and Grid #
19:10 — **Sarid**	• on S boundary of Zebulun from which the boundary ran W (19:10) and E (19:12); 6 mi. NE of Megiddo on N edge of Jezreel Valley; Tel Shadud, *#172229*

19:11 — **Maralah**	• on W border of Zebulun; possibly Tel el-Ghaltah/Tell Reala, *#166232*, on NW edge of Jezreel Valley, 7 mi. NNW of Megiddo, or possibly Tel Thorah/Tell Shor, *#166228*, 5 mi. NNW of Megiddo
19:11 — **Dabbesheth**	• in description of the S border of Zebulun; between Sarid and Jokneam • 6 mi. NW of Megiddo; Tel esh-Shammam/Tell Shem, *#164230*
19:11 — **Jokneam** • Levitical city Jos 12:22; 21:34; 1Ch 6:77	• Canaanite town conquered by Israel; border of Zebulun extended to ravine nearby; 7 mi. NW of Megiddo on S edge of Jezreel Valley at foot of Mt. Carmel; Tel Qeimun/Tell Yoqneam, *#160230*
19:12 — **Kisloth Tabor**	• alternate name for Kisloth; in boundary description of Zebulun; perhaps the same as Kesulloth (town allotted to Issachar)
19:12 — **Daberath** • Levitical city Jos 21:28; 1Ch 6:72	• on border of Zebulun; in Issachar; possibly the same as Rabbith (Jos 19:20); 5 mi. E of Nazareth at the NW foot of Mt. Tabor; Daburiyeh, *#185233*
19:12 — **Japhia**	• on S border of Zebulun; possibly Yafa, *#176232*, but archaeological data do not correspond with historical record
19:13 — **Gath Hepher** 2Ki 14:25	• on the E border of Zebulun in Lower Galilee; 3 mi. NE of Nazareth • home of prophet Jonah; Kh. ez-Zurra/Tell Gat Hefer, *#180238*
19:13 — **Eth Kazin**	• on NE boundary of Zebulun between Gath Hepher and Rimmon; possibly Kefr Kenna, *#182239*, 4 mi. NE of Nazareth
19:13 — **Rimmon** • Levitical city 1Ch 6:77	• on NE border of Zebulun; Dimnah (Jos 21:35); Rimmono (1Ch 6:77) • Rummaneh/H. Rimona (*#179243*), or possibly nearby H. Romah at *#177243*, 6 mi. NNE of Nazareth
19:13 — **Neah**	• on N border of Zebulun between Rimmon and Hannathon; possibly Tel el-Wawiyat, *#178244*
19:14 — **Hannathon**	• on NW boundary of Zebulun; 14 mi. SE of Acco; Tel el-Bedeiwiyeh/Tell Hannaton, *#174243*
19:14 — **Valley of Iphtah El** — Jos 19:27	• valley on boundary between Zebulun and Asher; possibly Wadi el-Malik
19:15 — **Kattath** 1Ch 6:77 — **Kartah** • Levitical city — Jos 21:34	• possibly the same as "Kitron" of Ju 1:30; location unknown • location unknown
19:15 — **Nahalal** • Levitical city — Jos 21:35	• called Nahalol (Ju 1:30), where Canaanites lived • location unknown; in or just N of Jezreel Valley
19:15 — **Shimron** Jos 11:1	• Canaanite town whose king fought against Israel; allotted to Zebulun • possibly "Simeon" in 2Ch 34:6 refers to this place; 9 mi. NNE of Megiddo; Kh. Sammuniyeh/Tell Shimron, *#170234*

19:15—**Idalah**	• possibly Kh. el-Huwarah, *#167236*, 6.5 mi. W of Nazareth
19:15—**Bethlehem** Jdg 12:8, 10	• town from which the minor judge Izban came; 7 mi. WNW of Nazareth; Beit Lahm/Bet Lehem Hagelilit, *#168238*
21:34–35—Additional Levitical cities	• Dimnah

NOTES

11 "Jokneam" (יָקְנְעָם, *yoqnᵉ ā m*) is identified as a Levitical city in Joshua 21:34. In the Zebulun list of Levitical cities from 1 Chronicles 6:77[62], Jokneam is omitted from the MT and from most English translations, while it is listed in the NIV.

13 The town of "Rimmon" appears as *rimmôn* (רִמּוֹן) in Joshua 19:13 and as *rimmônô* (רִמּוֹנוֹ) in 1 Chronicles 6:77[62].

15 "Kattath" (קַטָּת, *qaṭṭāt,*) and "Kartah" (קַרְתָּה, *qartā*). "Kattath" appears in Joshua 19:15. The same city appears as "Kartah" in Joshua 21:34. In 1 Chronicles 6:77[62], the MT and many English translations omit "Kattath" and "Kartah" while the NIV preserves "Kartah."

g. Land Allotment for Issachar (19:17–23)

¹⁷The fourth lot came out for Issachar, clan by clan. ¹⁸Their territory included:
Jezreel, Kesulloth, Shunem, ¹⁹Hapharaim, Shion, Anaharath, ²⁰Rabbith, Kishion, Ebez, ²¹Remeth, En Gannim, En Haddah and Beth Pazzez. ²²The boundary touched Tabor, Shahazumah and Beth Shemesh, and ended at the Jordan. There were sixteen towns and their villages.
²³These towns and their villages were the inheritance of the tribe of Issachar, clan by clan.

COMMENTARY

17–23 The fourth lot came out for Issachar. Their territorial allotment comprised sixteen towns and extended eastward to the Jordan River. Its western and southern borders met the northern border of Manasseh; its northern border touched Zebulun and Naphtali. The towns of Issachar were located primarily in the Jezreel Valley and in Lower Eastern Galilee.

Tribe of Issachar— Borders and Towns (19:17–22)	Comments and Grid #
19:18—**Jezreel** 1Sa 29:1–11; 2Sa 2:9; 1Ki 4:12; 18:45; 21:1; 2Ki 9–10; Hos 1:4	• Saul's troops camped near it in battle with Philistines and later his son, Ish-Bosheth, ruled over area; included in the 5th Solomonic district; Ahab had a secondary palace; Naboth's vineyard here; site of Jehu's coup in which Joram and Jezebel were killed • 11 mi. WNW of Beth Shan and 8.5 mi. ESE of Megiddo; Zerin/Tell Yizreel, #181218
19:18—**Kesulloth**	• probably same as Kisloth Tabor mentioned in boundary description of Zebulun (Jos 19:12); 2 mi. SE of Nazareth; Iksal, #180232
19:18—**Shunem** 1Sa 28:4; 1Ki 1, 2; 2Ki 4:8	• Philistines camped in preparation for battle with Saul; Abishag was from there; woman of Shunem assisted Elisha • 9 mi. E of Megiddo, at S foot of Mt. Moreh; Solem, #181223
19:19—**Hapharaim**	• 6.5 mi. ENE of Megiddo; Affuleh, #177223
19:19—**Shion**	• possibly Kh. Mugheir, #183232, 4 mi. SE of Nazareth
19:19—**Anaharath**	• possibly Tel el-Mukharkhash/Tell Rekhesh, #194228, 8 mi. SW of S tip of Sea of Galilee
19:20—**Rabbith** 19:20—**Kishion** • Levitical city—Jos 21:28	• possibly a variant of Daberath, a Levitical town in Issachar (Jos 21:28; 1Ch 6:72) • parallel for Jos 21:28; in 1Ch 6:72 is "Kedesh" • 6.5 mi. SE of Nazareth near foot of S slope of Mt. Tabor
19:20—**Ebez**	• possibly the unnamed site at grid #197227, 9 mi. N of Beth Shan
19:21—**Remeth**	• 9 mi. SSW of Sea of Galilee; probably the same as Ramoth (1Ch 6:73) and Jarmuth (Jos 21:29); En Hayadid/Tell Remet, #199221
19:21—**En Gannim** • Levitical city—Jos 15:34; 21:29; 1Ch 6:72	• 5 mi. SW of the Sea of Galilee; Kh. ed-Dir, #200229
19:21—**En Haddah**	• 6 mi. WSW of the Sea of Galilee; el-Hadatheh, #195231
19:21—**Beth Pazzez**	• possibly Sheikh Mazghith (#199221), 5.5 mi. N of Beth Shan
19:22—**Tabor** (Mount) Ju 4:6, 12, 14; 8:18; Ps 89:12; Jer 46:18	• on NW boundary of Issachar; 4.5 mi. ESE of Nazareth • only mentioned in story of Deborah and Barak (Ju 4:6, 12, 14); nearby Zebah and Zalmunna kill Gideon's brothers; mentioned in poetic and prophetic literature • Jebel et-Tur/Har Tavor, #186232

19:22 — **Shahazumah**	• on N border of Issachar; probably between Mt. Tabor and Jordan River
19:22 — **Beth Shemesh**	• in E Lower Galilee on boundary of Issachar; possibly Kh. Sheikh esh-Shamsawi/H. Shemesh, #*199232*, but more probably Tel el-Abeidiyeh, #*202232*, 2 mi. S of Sea of Galilee near Jordan River
21:28–29 — Additional Levitical cities	• Daberah (also mentioned in Zebulun), Jarmuth

h. Land Allotment for Asher (19:24–31)

[24]The fifth lot came out for the tribe of Asher, clan by clan. [25]Their territory included: Helkath, Hali, Beten, Acshaph, [26]Allammelech, Amad and Mishal. On the west the boundary touched Carmel and Shihor Libnath. [27]It then turned east toward Beth Dagon, touched Zebulun and the Valley of Iphtah El, and went north to Beth Emek and Neiel, passing Cabul on the left. [28]It went to Abdon, Rehob, Hammon and Kanah, as far as Greater Sidon. [29]The boundary then turned back toward Ramah and went to the fortified city of Tyre, turned toward Hosah and came out at the sea in the region of Aczib, [30]Ummah, Aphek and Rehob. There were twenty-two towns and their villages. [31]These towns and their villages were the inheritance of the tribe of Asher, clan by clan.

COMMENTARY

24–31 The fifth lot came out for Asher. The long and narrow allotment for Asher included twenty-two towns (v.30b; yet twenty-three are listed). Its western boundary was the Great Sea, from Carmel to Greater Sidon. On the east, Asher touched the border of Naphtali and Zebulun, and to the south, western Manasseh.

Tribe of Asher — Borders and Towns (19:25–30)	Comments and Grid #
19:25 — **Helkath** • Levitical city — Jos 21:31	• on boundary of Asher; parallel for Jos 21:31; in 1Ch 6:75 "Hukok" • possibly Tel el-Qassis/Tell Qashish, #*160232*, at the NW exit of the Jezreel Valley, 17 mi. S of Acco
19:25 — **Hali**	• 11 mi. SSE of Acco; Kh. Ras Ali/Tell Hali, #*164241*

19:25 — **Beten**	• possibly Kh. Ibtin/H. Ivtan (#*160241*), in N coastal plain of Israel, 11 mi. SSE of Acco
19:25 — **Acshaph** Jos 11:1; 12:20	• its king participated in battle of Merom against Joshua; mentioned in extrabiblical documents • possibly Kh. el-Harbaj/Tell Regev, #*158240*, 12 mi. S of Acco
19:26 — **Allammelech**	• location unknown
19:26 — **Amad**	• location unknown
19:26 — **Mishal** • Levitical city — Jos 21:30	• called "Mashal" in 1Ch 6:74; possibly Tel Kisah/Tell Kison, #*164253*, 5 mi. SE of Acco
19:26 — **Carmel** 1Ki 18; 2 Ki 2:25; 4:25; SS 7:5; Isa 35:2; Am 1:2	• Carmel range interrupts coastal plain in N Israel; stretches ca. 30 mi. from Mediterranean, SE. NE and W slopes of triangular-shaped range are quite steep; formed S border of tribe of Asher • site of great contest between Elijah and the prophets of Baal; Elisha frequented the region; symbol of beauty and fruitfulness; its withering became a symbol of destruction and desolation
19:26 — **Shihor Libnath**	• point on S boundary of Asher in the Mt. Carmel area • possibly Libnath is Tel Abu Huwam, #*152245*, 9 mi. SSW of Acco in modern Haifa
19:27 — **Beth Dagon**	• boundary town of Asher in N Israel; location unknown
19:27 — **Valley of Iphtah El** — Jos 19:14	• on the boundary between Zebulun and Asher; possibly Wadi el-Malik
19:27 — **Beth Emek**	• on boundary of Asher; 5 mi. NE of Acco; Tel Mimas/Tell Bet Ha-Emeq, #*164263*
19:27 — **Neiel**	• 8.5 ESE of Acco; Kh. Yanin/H. Yaanin, #*171255*
19:27 — **Cabul** 1Ki 9:13	• near/in Plain of Acco; allotted to Asher; also name of a district, "Land of Cabul," in same area; given by Solomon to Hiram, king of Tyre; 8 mi. ESE of Acco; Kh. Rosh Zayith, #*171253*
19:28 — **Abdon** • Levitical city — Jos 21:30; 1Ch 6:74	• along N coast of Israel; Kh. Abdeh/Tell Avdon, #*165272*
19:28 — **Rehob** (northern Asher)	• on N (NE?) border of Asher; possibly Tel el-Balat (#*177280*), 12 mi. SE of Tyre in Lebanon
19:28 — **Hammon** 1Ch 6:76	• in Lebanon, 14.5 mi. NNE of Acco; Umm el-Awamid, #*164281*
19:28 — **Kanah**	• 7.5 mi. SE of Tyre in Lebanon; Qana, #*178290*

19:28 — **Greater Sidon** Jos 11:8; 2Sa 24:6; Mt 15:21; Mk 7:31; Ac 27:3	• main city of Phoenicia on the NW border of Israelite settlement; frequently mentioned in connection with Tyre; Jesus visited the region and mentioned it in cursing Korazin and Bethsaida; Paul's ship stopped there at the beginning of his journey to Rome • 24 mi. SSW of Beirut on Lebanese coast; Saida, *#184329*
19:29 — **Ramah**	• on N border of Asher in vicinity of Tyre and Sidon; location unknown
19:29 — **Tyre** 2Sa 5:11; 1Ki 9:11; Isa 23:1; Eze 26-28; Am 1:9	• Phoenician city on island until Alexander connected it to the mainland by a causeway (332 BC); famous for maritime activities and trade; located on the border of Asher; probably never controlled by Israel; Hiram, its king, assisted David and Solomon in building projects, as well as in maritime activities; mentioned frequently in prophetic literature • in Lebanon, 46 mi. SSW of Beirut, 12 mi. N of Israeli/Lebanese border; Es-Sur, *#168297*
19:29 — **Hosah**	• on N border of Asher; possibly Tel Rashidiyeh, *#170293*, in Lebanon, 3 mi. SSE of Tyre near Mediterranean coast
19:29 — **Aczib** Jdg 1:31	• Asherites did not drive out its inhabitants • 10 mi. N of Accol Ez-Zib/Tel Akhziv, *#159272*
19:30 — **Ummah**	• in Plain of Acco region; some LXX manuscripts suggest Acco
19:30 — **Aphek** Jdg 1:31	• they did not drive out inhabitants • 7 mi. SSE of Acco; Tell Kurdaneh/T. Afeq, *#160250*
19:30 — **Rehob** (southern Asher) • Levitical city — Jos 21:31; Ju 1:31; 1Ch 6:75	• Asherites did not drive out the Canaanites • possibly Tel el-Bir el-Gharbi/Tell Bira, *#166256*, 5 mi. ESE of Acco

i. Land Allotment for Naphtali (19:32-39)

[32]The sixth lot came out for Naphtali, clan by clan:

[33]Their boundary went from Heleph and the large tree in Zaanannim, passing Adami Nekeb and Jabneel to Lakkum and ending at the Jordan. [34]The boundary ran west through Aznoth Tabor and came out at Hukkok. It touched Zebulun on the south, Asher on the west and the Jordan on the east. [35]The fortified cities were Ziddim, Zer, Hammath, Rakkath, Kinnereth, [36]Adamah, Ramah, Hazor, [37]Kedesh, Edrei, En Hazor, [38]Iron, Migdal El, Horem, Beth Anath and Beth Shemesh. There were nineteen towns and their villages. [39]These towns and their villages were the inheritance of the tribe of Naphtali, clan by clan.

COMMENTARY

32–39 The sixth lot came out for Naphtali, which received nineteen towns and their villages in a richly forested land in Galilee. Its eastern borders reached the allotment of Manasseh (east of the Jordan) and the Sea of Galilee. In the south, Asher's territory touched the northern border of Zebulun. The western border of Naphtali was adjacent to the territory of Asher.

Tribe of Naphtali— Borders and Towns (19:33–38)	Comments and Grid #
19:33 — **Heleph**	• at SW corner of boundary of Naphtali; possibly Kh. Irbadeh/H. Arpad, *#189236*, 3 mi. NE of Mt. Tabor
19:33 — **Zaanannim** Jdg 4:11	• along S border of Naphtali; site where Heber the Kenite camped near Kedesh; possibly Sjajarat el-Kalb/Hurshat Yaala, *#200232*, 3 mi. SW of S tip of Sea of Galilee
19:33 — **Adami Nekeb**	• on S tribal boundary of Naphtali; 6 mi. SW of Tiberias; Kh. et-Tell (ed-Damiyeh)/Tell Adami, *#193239*
19:33 — **Jabneel**	• on S border of Naphtali; same name as a town in Judah (15:11); 3.5 mi. W of S end of Sea of Galilee; Tel en-Naam/Tell Yinam, *#198235*
19:33 — **Lakkum**	• on S boundary of Naphtali; possibly Kh. el-Mansurah/Kh. Kush, *#202233*, 1.7 mi. SW of Sea of Galilee
19:34 — **Aznoth Tabor**	• on SW border of Naphtali; possibly Tell Aznot Tavor, #186237, 3 mi. N of Mt. Tabor
19:34 — **Hukkok**	• on W border of Naphtali; possibly Kh. el-Jemeijmeh/H. Gamon, *#175252*, 12 mi. ESE of Acco
19:35 — **Ziddim**	• probably W of Sea of Galilee
19:35 — **Zer**	• probably to the S or W of Hammath
19:35 — **Hammath**	• on W shore of Sea of Galilee; Hammam Tabariyeh/Hame Teveriya, *#201241*
19:35 — **Rakkath**	• between Hammath and Kinnereth, on W shore of the Sea of Galilee; 2.5 mi. NW of Tiberias; Kh. el-Quneitireh/Tell Raqqat, *#199245*
19:35 — **Kinnereth** 1Ki 15:20	• on NW shore of Sea of Galilee called "Gennesaret" in NT; Ben-Hadad conquered the town, or the area; Kh. Ureime/Tell Kinrot, *#200252*
19:36 — **Adamah**	• fortified cities of Naphtali; possibly Qarn Hattin/H. Qarne Hittim, *#193245*, 5 mi. W of Tiberias

19:36 — **Ramah**	• on boundary between Lower and Upper Galilee; 19 mi. E of Acco; same name as a town in Asher (v.29); Kh. Zeitun er-Rameh, *#187259*
19:36 — **Hazor** Jos 11:1, 10, 11, 13; 12:19; Ju 4:2, 17; 1Sa 12:9; 1Ki 9:15; 2Ki 15:29	• large Canaanite city conquered by Joshua; allotted to Naphtali; had been head of the kingdoms in the area; its forces fought against Deborah and Barak; lying along the international route through the country; Solomon fortified the city; conquered by Tiglath-Pileser III • 9.5 mi. N of Sea of Galilee; Tel el-Qedah/Tell Hazor, *#203269*

19:37 — **Kedesh**
(Upper Galilee)
• city of refuge and
  Levitical city — Jos
  12:22; 20:7; 21:32; 2Ki
  15:29; 1Ch 6:76
	• conquered by Israel; allotted to Naphtali
	• captured by Tiglath-Pileser III; later called Cadasa
	• 17 mi. NNW of Sea of Galilee in Upper Galilee
	• same name as a town in Judah (15:23); Tel Qades/Tell Qedesh, *#199279*

19:37 — **Edrei**	• probably in Upper Galilee; same name as a town in Transjordan (13:12)
19:37 — **En Hazor**	• probably in Upper Galilee
19:38 — **Iron**	• in Upper Galilee; 22 mi. NE of Acco; Yarun, *#189276*
19:38 — **Migdal El**	• probably in Upper Galilee
19:38 — **Horem**	• in Upper Galilee
19:38 — **Beth Anath** Jdg 1:33	• inhabitants became forced laborers for Naphtali • possibly Safed el-Battikh (Lebanon), *#190289*, 15 mi. SE of Tyre in Upper Galilee
19:38 — **Beth Shemesh** Jdg 1:33	• in Upper Galilee; Canaanites continued to live in town; served as laborers for Naphtali; same name as a town in Judah (15:10) and Issachar (v.22) • 17 mi. NE of Acco; Kh. Tel er-Ruweisi/Tell Rosh, *#181271*
21:32 — Additional Levitical cities	• Hammoth Dor, Kartan

NOTE

34 The NIV's "and the Jordan on the east" (וּבִיהוּדָה הַיַּרְדֵּן מִזְרַח הַשָּׁמֶשׁ, *ûbîhûdā hayyardēn mizraḥ haššāmeš*; also NJB) is translated "and Judah on the east at the Jordan" (ESV, NRSV, TNK), "and to Judah at the Jordan toward the east" (NASB), and "and ended at Judah by the Jordan toward the sunrise" (NKJV). The text is problematic in that the territory of Naphtali did not touch the "(Judah at) the Jordan on the east," as stated in the Hebrew text. The land of Naphtali was located on the west and northwest of the Sea of Galilee. The tribes of Issachar, Manasseh, and Ephraim stood between the territory of Naphtali and the allotment of Judah. The reference to Judah is curious and seemingly out of place, unless the common eastern border—the Jordan—enabled the two tribes to reach each other by means of the river (G. Bush, *Joshua and Judges* [Minneapolis: Klock & Klock, 1981, repr.], 179).

j. Land Allotment for Dan (19:40–48)

[40]The seventh lot came out for the tribe of Dan, clan by clan. [41]The territory of their inheritance included:

Zorah, Eshtaol, Ir Shemesh, [42]Shaalabbin, A.ijalon, Ithlah, [43]Elon, Timnah, Ekron, [44]Eltekeh, Gibbethon, Baalath, [45]Jehud, Bene Berak, Gath Rimmon, [46]Me Jarkon and Rakkon, with the area facing Joppa.

[47](But the Danites had difficulty taking possession of their territory, so they went up and attacked Leshem, took it, put it to the sword and occupied it. They settled in Leshem and named it Dan after their forefather.)

[48]These towns and their villages were the inheritance of the tribe of Dan, clan by clan.

COMMENTARY

40–48 The seventh and last lot was for the tribe of Dan, whose territory is described by a list of towns. Abutted by the Mediterranean on the west, it is bordered by Manasseh on the north, Ephraim and Benjamin on the east, and Judah in the south. The Danites were unable to settle in their land because of the fierce opposition of the Philistines (Ekron) and the Canaanites who lived in the area (cf. Jdg 1:34). The tribe eventually traveled to northern Galilee, attacked the town of Leshem, later renamed Dan, and settled there.

Tribe of Dan (19:41–46)	Comments and Grid #
19:41 — **Zorah** Ju 13:25; 16:31; 18:2, 8, 11; 2Ch 11:10; Ne 11:29	• in N Shephelah allotted to Judah and to Dan; Danites migrated from the area to Laish in the N • Manoah, Samson's father and a Danite from Zorah; Samson was active in area and was buried nearby; Rehoboam fortified the town; Jews settled there in the postexilic period • 15 mi. W of Jerusalem; Sarah/Tell Zora, #148131
19:41 — **Eshtaol** Jos 15:33; Ju 13:25; 16:31; 18:2, 8, 11	• in N Shephelah first allotted to Judah, then to Dan; some Danites moved N from the area; Samson's family was from the area • 14 mi. W of Jerusalem; Ishwa/Eshtaol, #1511132

19:41 — **Ir Shemesh** Jos 21:16; Ju 1:35; 1Sa 6; 2Ki 14:8–14; 2Ch 25:21	• probably an alternate form of Beth Shemesh, a town in N Shephelah on N boundary of Judah allotted to Dan, who was unable to occupy it; served as a Judean outpost on their border with the Philistines • ark of the covenant was returned there; in Solomon's 2nd administrative district; fortified by Rehoboam; disputed over by both Israel and the Philistines • 16 mi. W of Jerusalem; Tel er-Rumeileh/Tell Bet Shemesh, *#147128*
19:42 — **Shaalabbin**	• probably a variant of Shaalbim (1Ki 4:9), a Danite district 19 mi. SE of Joppa, Selbit/Tell Shaalevim (#148141) • Solomon later placed Ben-Deker in charge of this district (1Ki 4:9)

19:42 — **Aijalon**
• Levitical city
  Jos 21:24; Ju 1:35; 1Sa
  14:31; 1Ch 6:69; 8:13;
  2Ch 11:10; 28:18
	• Danites failed to take it; inhabited by Ephraimites and Benjamites
	• fortified by Rehoboam; occupied by Philistines during reign of Ahaz
	• 13 mi. NW of Jerusalem in N Shephelah; Yalo, *#152138*

19:42 — **Ithlah**	• location unknown
19:43 — **Elon**	• in coastal plain, E of Joppa; in Solomon's 2nd administrative district (1Ki 4:9 = Elon Beth-hanan)
19:43 — **Timnah** Ju 14; 2Ch 28:18	• on NW border of Judah; allotted to Dan • occupied by Philistines in Samson's day; passed into and out of Philistine and Israelite hands; conquered by Sennacherib in 701 BC • 21 mi. SE of Joppa; Tel el-Batashi/Tell Batash, *#141131*
19:43 — **Ekron**	• see tribe of Judah — borders and towns — 15:46
19:44 — **Eltekeh** • Levitical city — Jos 21:23	• possibly Tel esh-Shallaf/Tell Shalaf, *#128144*, 11 mi. SSE of Joppa
19:44 — **Gibbethon** • Levitical city — Jos 21:23; 1Ki 15:27; 16:15	• Philistine village in N Philistia assigned to Dan; 15 mi. SE of Joppa, 3mi. W of Gezer • Baashah murdered Nadab; Omri was proclaimed king of Israel
19:44 — **Baalath**	• possibly el-Mughar (*#129138*); possibly referred to in 1Ch 4:33 (N boundary of Simeonites in Shephelah) and in 2Ch 8:6 and 1Ki 9:18 (fortified by Solomon); latter two references could be to Kiriath Jearim
19:45 — **Jehud**	• 8.5 mi. E of Joppa in coastal plain; El-Yehudiyeh/Yehud, *#139159*
19:45 — **Bene Berak**	• attacked by Sennacherib; 4.5 mi. ESE of Joppa; Kheiriyeh/Bene-beraq, *#133160*

19:45 — **Gath Rimmon** Jos 21:24; 1Ch 6:69	• later occupied by Ephraim; usually identified with Tel Jerisheh/Tell Gerisa, *#132166*, located in modern Tel Aviv, 4.5 mi. NE of Joppa; archaeological data is problematic
19:46 — **Me Jarkon**	• means "the waters of the Jarkon"; maybe Nahr el-Auja/N. Yarkon, which begins near Aphek and flows into Mediterranean Sea in N Tel Aviv or possibly to W. el-Auja/N. Aijalon
19:46 — **Rakkon**	• if a town, then in vicinity of Joppa
19:46 — **Joppa** 2Ch 2:16; Ezr 3:7; Jnh 1:3; Acts 9–11	• Mediterranean seaport allotted to Dan • intermittently served as a Judean port; logs for two temples were shipped there from Lebanon; in non-Israelite hands throughout much of the OT period; from there, Jonah set sail; there, Peter had his vision and receive messengers from Cornelius; mentioned frequently in extrabiblical literature; just S of modern Tel Aviv; Yafa/Yafo, *#126162*

4. Land Allotment for Joshua (19:49–51)

[49]When they had finished dividing the land into its allotted portions, the Israelites gave Joshua son of Nun an inheritance among them, [50]as the LORD had commanded. They gave him the town he asked for — Timnath Serah in the hill country of Ephraim. And he built up the town and settled there.

[51]These are the territories that Eleazar the priest, Joshua son of Nun and the heads of the tribal clans of Israel assigned by lot at Shiloh in the presence of the LORD at the entrance to the Tent of Meeting. And so they finished dividing the land.

COMMENTARY

49 The mention of land given to Joshua marks the conclusion of the distribution of land in Cisjordan and forms an inclusio with the Caleb account at the beginning of this section (chs. 14–19). Joshua and Caleb have now been rewarded for their faithfulness to Yahweh.

50 Joshua receives Timnath Serah (Timnath Heres, Jdg 2:9) in the hill country of Ephraim, where he was later buried. Joshua receives his inheritance in the presence of Eleazar the priest and the tribal leaders at the sanctuary in Shiloh and not by lot. Joshua's courteous and humble spirit prompts him to wait until everyone else has received an inheritance before requesting his own. This approach to leadership is the antithesis of abuse of power and exhibits a model that should be imitated by Christian leaders. While establishing roots in Timnath Serah, Joshua completes renovations to the town and stays there with his family, accessible to all Israel while living in security, until his death.

51 The chapter's concluding statement confirms four main points: (1) the land was completely distributed to the seven remaining tribes; (2) the leaders (Joshua, Eleazar the priest, and the tribal leaders) were actively involved in the distribution; (3) the territories were assigned by lot; and (4) the decisions were made in the presence of the Lord, at the entrance of the Tent of Meeting in Shiloh. The conclusion also confirms that all Israel partakes of the blessings of God.

D. Special Land Provisions (20:1-21:42)

OVERVIEW

Following the distribution of land to the twelve tribes, Joshua sets apart forty-eight cities for the Levites (ch. 21; cf. Nu 35:2-8), from which six are designated as cities of refuge for individuals who commit manslaughter (ch. 20; cf. Nu 35:6, 9-15, 22-29; Dt 4:41-42; 19:1-14). A "law of asylum" for accidental killers first appeared in the Mosaic law (Ex 21:12-14). It was instituted to protect an accidental killer from the retribution of an avenger of blood (*gō'ēl haddām*, Nu 35:16-34). If accepted by the leaders of a city of refuge, a killer who fled there was given a fair trial, received shelter, and remained there until the death of the high priest, after which time he was free to return home (Nu 35:25, 28). No such protection was granted for premeditated murder — a capital offense punishable by death (Ex 21:12, 14).

The forty-eight cities set apart for the Levites came from the portions allocated to the twelve tribes (Jos 21:1-3; Nu 35:1-8). The allotment for the Levites was divided according to the three descendants of Aaron. The Kohathites received twenty-three cities — ten for the priests and thirteen for the rest of the clan. The Gershonites received thirteen towns and the Merarites twelve towns.

1. Cities of Refuge (20:1-9)

¹Then the LORD said to Joshua: ²"Tell the Israelites to designate the cities of refuge, as I instructed you through Moses, ³so that anyone who kills a person accidentally and unintentionally may flee there and find protection from the avenger of blood.

⁴"When he flees to one of these cities, he is to stand in the entrance of the city gate and state his case before the elders of that city. Then they are to admit him into their city and give him a place to live with them. ⁵If the avenger of blood pursues him, they must not surrender the one accused, because he killed his neighbor unintentionally and without malice aforethought. ⁶He is to stay in that city until he has stood trial before the assembly and until the death of the high priest who is serving at that time. Then he may go back to his own home in the town from which he fled."

⁷So they set apart Kedesh in Galilee in the hill country of Naphtali, Shechem in the hill country of Ephraim, and Kiriath Arba (that is, Hebron) in the hill country of Judah. ⁸On the east side of the Jordan of Jericho they designated Bezer in the desert on the plateau in the tribe of Reuben, Ramoth in Gilead in the tribe of Gad, and Golan in Bashan in the tribe of Manasseh. ⁹Any of the Israelites or any alien living among them who killed someone accidentally could flee to these designated cities and not be killed by the avenger of blood prior to standing trial before the assembly.

COMMENTARY

1–3 Yahweh commands Joshua to designate cities of refuge for manslayers. These cities are to be centrally located (Dt 19:2), and the Israelites are to build roads to them for easy access (19:4). In the Mosaic law (Ex 21:12–14), accidental killing was distinguished from premeditated murder. After accidentally taking a life, someone—Israelite or alien (Nu 35:6, 9–34)—could flee to a city of refuge. If someone who killed accidentally fled to a city of refuge, the avenger of blood could not kill, unless the manslayer ventured outside of the city gates before the death of the high priest (Nu 35:26–27). The purpose for cities of refuge was to prevent further innocent blood from being shed in the land.

4–6 Before entering the city, a manslayer was required to stand at the gates and state his case in the presence of the elders. If presumed innocent, the inhabitants of the city would give him a place to live. The approval of the elders indicated that the leaders and the inhabitants of the city (1) believed the account of the killer, (2) trusted him sufficiently to permit him to live in their midst, and (3) were willing to protect him from the avenger of blood. To remove his guilt and gain the freedom to return home, a manslayer was required to remain in a city

of refuge until the death of whoever was high priest at the time of the killing.

Some have suggested that since the high priest represented the sacrificial system, his death meant atonement for the sin of the manslayer (Howard, 386; Woudstra, 301; M. Greenberg, "The Biblical Conception of Asylum," *JBL* 78 [1959]: 125–32). Avengers of blood in pursuit of manslayers undoubtedly tried to enter cities of refuge in search of people whom they wished to kill. It was necessary, therefore, to guard the city gates securely from such dangerous intruders.

7–8 Cities of refuge were located on both sides of the Jordan River—three on each side. They were centrally located for easy and quick access by those in need. West of the Jordan (from north to south), Naphtali set apart Kedesh in Upper Galilee; Ephraim set apart Shechem in the hill country; and Judah set apart Kiriath Arba (Hebron) in the highlands of Judah, approximately fifteen miles south of Jerusalem. East of the Jordan (from south to north), Reuben set apart Bezer on the desert area of the plateau, Gad designated Ramoth in Gilead, and Manasseh dedicated Bolan in Bashan. Each city of refuge could be reached by manslayers on foot in a matter of hours.

City of refuge	Location	For information, see the following charts:
Kedesh	Upper Galilee	Tribe of Naphtali—19:37
Shechem	Hill country	Tribe of Ephraim—20:7
Kiriath Arba	Judean hills	Tribe of Judah—in hill country—15:13
Bezer	On desert plateau	Tribe of Reuben—21:8
Ramoth	Gilead	Tribe of Gad—20:8
Golan	Bashan	Half-tribe of Manasseh (eastern)—21:27

9 Foreigners (*gērîm*) who lived among the Israelites were afforded the same protection as Israelites. They could seek refuge in the designated cities and could expect a fair trial before the assembly.

NOTES

3 "Anyone who kills a person accidentally and unintentionally" (רוֹצֵחַ מַכֵּה־נֶפֶשׁ בִּשְׁגָגָה בִּבְלִי־דָעַת, *rôṣēaḥ makkēh-nepeš bisgāgā biblî-dāʿat*; cf. Nu 35:11). In Exodus 21:13, the accidental killer is identified literally as "one who does not lie in wait" or "one who does not hunt [for someone to kill]" (אֲשֶׁר לֹא צָדָה, *ʾašer lōʾ ṣādā*). The intentional killer is identified as "a man [who] schemes and kills another man deliberately," (יָזִד אִישׁ עַל־רֵעֵהוּ לְהָרְגוֹ, *yāzid ʾîš ʿal-rēʿēhû lᵉhorgô*, Ex 21:14), and one who pushes his neighbor "with malice" (בְּשִׂנְאָה) (*bᵉśinʾā*; lit., "with hatred," Nu 35:20) or "in hostility" (בְּאֵיבָה, *bᵉʾêbā*, Nu 35:21). This man is forbidden to seek protection in a city of refuge for he has committed premeditated murder. The murderer is condemned to death at the hands of the avenger of blood (Nu 35:21).

2. Levitical Cities (21:1–42)

OVERVIEW

The only Israelites who have yet to receive land are the Levites. Chapter 21 provides a summary of the territory given to them, according to the "land grant" process discussed above (see comments on 17:1). The introduction to the chapter discloses the number of towns the tribes are required to give to each clan of Levites (vv.3–8)—for a total of forty-eight cities, including the six cities of refuge.

The only city of refuge not mentioned in this chapter is Bezer, a Reubenite city (cf. 20:8). An almost identical list of Levitical cities appears in 1 Chronicles 6:54–58[39–66]. These cities are to be apportioned by lot to the three sons of Levi—Kohath, Gershon, and Merari (Ge 46:11).

Some scholars view the list of cities in Joshua as a scribal imitation and a "rhetorical strategy ... so effective that it has induced many scholars to accept the historical existence of this artificial system" (Nelson, 236–37). Others argue for the historical nature of the list and support their view with the Iron Age II archaeological evidence uncovered from many of the Levitical cities (J. Peterson, *A Topographical Surface Survey of the Levitical "Cities" of Joshua and 1 Chronicles 6* [Chicago Institute of Advanced Theological Studies; Evanston, Ill.: Seabury-Western, 1977], cited in Hess, *Joshua*, 281, n. 2).

After the introductory summary comes a description of the land allotment to the Levites. The following tribes distribute towns and pasturelands to the Kohathites: Judah and Simeon (vv.9–16), Benjamin (vv.17–19), Ephraim (vv.20–22), Dan (vv.23–24), the half-tribe of Manasseh (western) (v.25). Second, the Gershonites receive towns and pasturelands from the half-tribe of Manasseh (eastern) (v.27), Issachar (vv.28–29), Asher (vv.30–31), and Naphtali (v.32). Finally, Zebulun (vv.34b–35), Reuben (vv.36–37), and Gad (vv.38–39) give towns and pasturelands to the Merarites. The chapter closes with a statement confirming that all Israel has received land (v.43), that each tribe settles in its own territory (v.43) and that all of Yahweh's good promises have been fulfilled (v.45).

The discrepancies between the list in Joshua 21 and the tribal inheritance lists can, for the most part, be explained. First, Shechem (v.21) appears here as an Ephraimite city, yet also as a border town in western Manasseh (17:2). Since the people of Joseph — Ephraim and Manasseh — were often treated as a single tribe and their territories were adjacent, we see no inconsistency. Second, Gath Rimmon (v.24) is given by the Danites (cf. 19:45) and also by the Manassites (v.25). It is possible that the scribe meant to write "Ibleam" in verse 25 (cf. Jos 17:11; Jdg 1:27), since this is what appears in the Old Greek text. Third, Daberah appears here from Issachar and in the boundary list of Zebulun (19:12). Since these tribes also shared borders, we see no problem. Fourth, Jarmuth is given by Issachar (v.29). A city named Jarmuth also appears on Judah's list (15:35), but is almost certainly a separate place with the same name. Such is also the case with En Gannim, a town listed in Issachar (v.29; 19:21) and in Judah (15:34).

a. Towns for the Levites (21:1–8)

¹Now the family heads of the Levites approached Eleazar the priest, Joshua son of Nun, and the heads of the other tribal families of Israel ²at Shiloh in Canaan and said to them, "The LORD commanded through Moses that you give us towns to live in, with pasturelands for our livestock." ³So, as the LORD had commanded, the Israelites gave the Levites the following towns and pasturelands out of their own inheritance:

⁴The first lot came out for the Kohathites, clan by clan. The Levites who were descendants of Aaron the priest were allotted thirteen towns from the tribes of Judah, Simeon and Benjamin. ⁵The rest of Kohath's descendants were allotted ten towns from the clans of the tribes of Ephraim, Dan and half of Manasseh.

⁶The descendants of Gershon were allotted thirteen towns from the clans of the tribes of Issachar, Asher, Naphtali and the half-tribe of Manasseh in Bashan.

⁷The descendants of Merari, clan by clan, received twelve towns from the tribes of Reuben, Gad and Zebulun.
⁸So the Israelites allotted to the Levites these towns and their pasturelands, as the LORD had commanded through Moses.

COMMENTARY

1–3 The tribe of Levi includes three clans: Kohath (Ex 6:18–25a; Nu 3:19; 1Ch 6:2–15, 22–28; 23:12–20), Gershon (Ex 6:17; Nu 3:18; 1Ch 6:17; 23:12–20), and Merari (Ex 6:19a; Nu 3:20a; 1Ch 6:19a; 23:21–23). In previous chapters, we read that no territory was given to the tribe of Levi (13:14, 33; 14:3; 18:7). Rather, their inheritance was "the offerings made by fire to the LORD" (13:14), "the LORD, the God of Israel" (13:33), and "the priestly service of the LORD" (18:7). But, as promised by Yahweh through Moses, each tribe is to give towns with their surrounding pasturelands to the clans of the Levites.

The family heads of the Levites appear before Eleazar, Joshua, and the tribal leaders in order to request their respective inheritance or "land grant." The petitioners meet the criteria that identify a "land grant." First, they approach the leadership; second, they remind the leaders of a divine promise made through Moses; third, portions of land are granted to the petitioners through a "lot" system in the presence of the Lord at Shiloh.

4–7 The Kohathites are mentioned first. They receive a portion larger than that of the other clans, with a total of twenty-three towns: thirteen towns from the tribes of Judah, Simeon, and Benjamin for the descendants of Aaron, and ten towns from the tribes of Ephraim, Dan, and the western half-tribe of Manasseh. Second, the descendants of Gershon receive thirteen towns with their surrounding pasturelands from the tribes of Issachar, Asher, Naphtali, and the eastern half-tribe of Manasseh. Finally, the descendants of Merari receive twelve towns with their pasturelands from the tribes of Reuben, Gad, and Zebulun.

8 As Yahweh commanded through Moses, all Israelites have a home in the Promised Land, where men, women, and children can settle and live before him.

b. Towns for the Kohathites (21:9–26)

i. Towns for the Sons of Aaron, Kohathites (21:9–19)

⁹From the tribes of Judah and Simeon they allotted the following towns by name ¹⁰(these towns were assigned to the descendants of Aaron who were from the Kohathite clans of the Levites, because the first lot fell to them):
¹¹They gave them Kiriath Arba (that is, Hebron), with its surrounding pastureland, in the hill country of Judah. (Arba was the forefather of Anak.) ¹²But the fields and villages around the city they had given to Caleb son of Jephunneh as his possession.

¹³So to the descendants of Aaron the priest they gave Hebron (a city of refuge for one accused of murder), Libnah, ¹⁴Jattir, Eshtemoa, ¹⁵Holon, Debir, ¹⁶Ain, Juttah and Beth Shemesh, together with their pasturelands — nine towns from these two tribes.

¹⁷And from the tribe of Benjamin they gave them Gibeon, Geba, ¹⁸Anathoth and Almon, together with their pasturelands — four towns.

¹⁹All the towns for the priests, the descendants of Aaron, were thirteen, together with their pasturelands.

COMMENTARY

9–26 The tribes of Judah, Simeon, and Benjamin give thirteen towns to the sons of Aaron (Kohathites) (for information on Levitical cities, see the chart for Judah in ch. 15, the chart for Simeon in ch. 19, and the chart for Benjamin in ch. 18).

Judan and Simeon (vv.9–16)	Kiriath Arba (Hebron), Libnah, Jattir, Eshtemoa, Holon, Debir, Ain, Juttah, Beth Shemesh
Benjamin (vv.17–19)	Gibeon, Geba, Anathoth, Almon

ii. Towns for the Rest of the Kohathites (21:20–26)

²⁰The rest of the Kohathite clans of the Levites were allotted towns from the tribe of Ephraim:

²¹In the hill country of Ephraim they were given Shechem (a city of refuge for one accused of murder) and Gezer, ²²Kibzaim and Beth Horon, together with their pasturelands — four towns.

²³Also from the tribe of Dan they received Eltekeh, Gibbethon, ²⁴Aijalon and Gath Rimmon, together with their pasturelands — four towns.

²⁵From half the tribe of Manasseh they received Taanach and Gath Rimmon, together with their pasturelands — two towns.

²⁶All these ten towns and their pasturelands were given to the rest of the Kohathite clans.

COMMENTARY

20–26 The tribes of Ephraim, Dan, and the half-tribe of Manasseh (western) give ten towns to the rest of the Kohathites (for information on Levitical cities, see the chart for Ephraim in ch. 16, the chart for Dan in ch. 19, and the chart for the half-tribe of Manasseh [western] in ch. 16).

Ephraim (vv.20–22)	Shechem (city of refuge), Gezer, Kibzaim, Beth Horon
Dan (vv.23–24)	Eltekeh, Gibbethon, Aijalon, Gath Rimmon
Half-tribe of Manasseh (western) (v.25)	Taanach, Gath Rimmon (probably Ibleam)

c. Towns for the Gershonites (21:27–33)

²⁷The Levite clans of the Gershonites were given:
from the half-tribe of Manasseh, Golan in Bashan (a city of refuge for one accused of murder) and Be Eshtarah, together with their pasturelands — two towns;
²⁸from the tribe of Issachar,
Kishion, Daberath, ²⁹Jarmuth and En Gannim, together with their pasturelands — four towns;
³⁰from the tribe of Asher,
Mishal, Abdon, ³¹Helkath and Rehob, together with their pasturelands — four towns;
³²from the tribe of Naphtali,
Kedesh in Galilee (a city of refuge for one accused of murder), Hammoth Dor and Kartan, together with their pasturelands — three towns.
³³All the towns of the Gershonite clans were thirteen, together with their pasturelands.

COMMENTARY

27–33 The half-tribe of Manasseh (eastern) and the tribes of Issachar, Asher, and Naphtali give thirteen towns to the Gershonites (for information on Levitical cities, see the chart for the half-tribe of Manasseh [eastern] in ch. 13, the chart for Issachar in ch. 19, the chart for Asher in ch. 19, and the chart for Naphtali in ch. 19).

Half-tribe of Manasseh (eastern)	Golan (city of refuge), Be Eshtarah
Issachar	Kishion, Daberath, Jarmuth, En Gannim
Asher	Mishal, Abdon, Helkath, Rehob
Naphtali	Kedesh (city of refuge), Hammoth Dor, Kartan

d. Towns for the Merarites (21:34–40)

³⁴The Merarite clans (the rest of the Levites) were given:

from the tribe of Zebulun, Jokneam, Kartah, ³⁵Dimnah and Nahalal, together with their pasturelands — four towns;

³⁶from the tribe of Reuben,

Bezer, Jahaz, ³⁷Kedemoth and Mephaath, together with their pasturelands — four towns;

³⁸from the tribe of Gad,

Ramoth in Gilead (a city of refuge for one accused of murder), Mahanaim, ³⁹Heshbon and Jazer, together with their pasturelands — four towns in all.

⁴⁰All the towns allotted to the Merarite clans, who were the rest of the Levites, were twelve.

COMMENTARY

34–40 The tribes of Zebulun, Reuben, and Gad give twelve towns to the Merarites (for information on Levitical cities, see the chart for Zebulun in ch. 19, the chart for Reuben in ch. 13, and the chart for Gad in ch. 19).

Zebulun	Jokneam, Kartah, Dimnah, Nahalal
Reuben	Bezer, Jahaz, Kedemoth, Mephaath
Gad	Ramoth (city of refuge), Mahanaim, Heshbon, Jazer

e. Summary of Levitical Cities (21:41–42)

⁴¹The towns of the Levites in the territory held by the Israelites were forty-eight in all, together with their pasturelands. ⁴²Each of these towns had pasturelands surrounding it; this was true for all these towns.

COMMENTARY

41–42 In total, the Levites receive forty-eight towns together with their pasturelands. The division of the land is now complete.

E. Peace in the Land (21:43–45)

⁴³So the LORD gave Israel all the land he had sworn to give their forefathers, and they took possession of it and settled there. ⁴⁴The LORD gave them rest on every side, just as he had sworn to their forefathers. Not one of their enemies withstood them; the LORD handed all their enemies over to them. ⁴⁵Not one of all the LORD's good promises to the house of Israel failed; every one was fulfilled.

COMMENTARY

43–45 As seen earlier, hyperbolic summaries are not unusual (11:16–23). The conclusion to chapter 21 provides an overstated synopsis of the events related to the conquest: (1) *all* the land is in Israel's possession; (2) *all* her enemies have been given into her hands; and (3) *all* of Yahweh's promises have been fulfilled. Israel has gloriously received what was promised to her forefathers centuries earlier (Ge 12:1–3; 15:18–21; 22:17–18; 24:7; 26:3; 50:24; Nu 11:12; 14:16, 23; Dt 1:8, 35; 6:10). The Lord *gave rest* to his people from their enemies round about (e.g., Dt 12:9–10; Jos 1:13, 15; 22:4; 23:1). Not one word from *all* of Yahweh's good promises have failed.

But in reality, much work remained to be done, since the Canaanites could not be dislodged from the land (e.g., 13:1–7; 15:63; 16:10; 17:12–13). So, why do we find a discrepancy between the final summary and historical reality? Perhaps the author wishes to contrast Yahweh's faithfulness in accomplishing *all* he had promised and the unfaithfulness of Israel in failing to accomplish the *entire* mission.

REFLECTION

The prominent place given to the description of each tribe's inheritance highlights the theological significance of the material. Yahweh had covenanted with Abraham and Moses to provide a homeland for his people; the promise is now fulfilled. Israel is home! Nomadic life has ended and sedentary life is beginning. Priests can fulfill their obligations in permanent cultic sites; judges can perform their duties in stable locations; society can establish roots and prepare the ground for the next generation. But, as Israel quickly discovers, the blessings of land ownership come with challenges. The enemy is never far away, and the temptation to create alliances for the sake of temporary peace is often appealing. Israel is exhorted to serve Yahweh with all her heart, mind, and strength in the land

God has given her. In this land, she must be a testimony to all the nations of the world. Her responsibility is great!

In many ways, the Christian journey reflects that of Israel. God has provided a temporary home for his people here on earth. The journey is both challenging and rewarding. Life is filled with ups and downs, twists and turns, peaks and valleys, defeats and victories. There are times of celebration and times of mourning. And the enemy is never far away. Temptation to compromise integrity, faithfulness, justice, and righteousness faces Christians on a daily basis. Our responsibility is great! God has called us to be faithful witnesses of his love and mercy to a lost world, until we reach our permanent homeland in heaven.

F. Preparing for Life in Canaan (22:1–24:33)

OVERVIEW

In chapters 22–24, Joshua gives three farewell addresses: first, to the men of the eastern tribes who are to return home after the conquest of Canaan (22:2–5); second, to the elders, leaders, judges, and officials of Israel who will be responsible to guide the people according to the law of Moses (ch. 23); and third, to all Israel at Shechem, during a covenant renewal ceremony (ch. 24). In the first speech, Joshua addresses the Reubenites, the Gadites, and the half-tribe of Manasseh, and he praises them for helping their brothers carry out their mission in Canaan, as previously ordered by Moses (vv.1–3). Joshua urges the Transjordanians to keep the commands of the Lord, to follow the law of Moses, to love Yahweh with all their heart and soul, to walk in his ways, and to serve him faithfully on the east

side of the Jordan (v.5). Joshua sends them with his blessings and with great material wealth (vv.6–8).

When the men of the eastern tribes reach Geliloth on the edge of the Jordan, they build an imposing altar. The structure is to serve as a testimony that they, with their western brothers, will offer burnt offerings, sacrifices, and fellowship offerings to Yahweh—not there, but at his sanctuary in Shiloh (vv.10, 26–28). The structure quickly becomes controversial as the western tribes misinterpret the significance of the memorial and accuse the Reubenites, Gadites, and the half-tribe of Manasseh of rebellion against Yahweh (vv.11–20). After reassuring the western tribes of their noble intentions, the eastern tribes give the altar the following name: "A Witness Between Us that the Lord is God" (v.34).

In his second speech, Joshua announces his impending death and reminds the elders of Yahweh's mighty deeds for Israel during the conquest of the land (23:1–5). He urges the leaders to be strong, to obey the law of Moses faithfully, to worship Yahweh only, and to abstain from intermarrying with the Canaanites, lest they become a snare to Israel (vv.6–13).

In his final speech, Joshua reviews the major historical events that have brought Israel to a land they did not plow, to cities they did not build, and to vineyards and olive groves they did not plant (24:2–13). He urges them to serve Yahweh faithfully all the days of their lives. The people respond three times with a resounding, "We will serve the LORD" (vv.18, 21, 24). Before his death, Joshua renews the covenant with Israel at Shechem, in a format similar to that of Hittite treaties — with introduction, historical prologue, stipulations, deposit in the temple, public reading, witnesses, and curses for disobedience and blessings for obedience (Hess, *Joshua*, 299). After his oral exchanges with Israel, Joshua records the event in the Book of the Law of God and sets up a memorial stone near "the holy place of the LORD" (vv.25–26, 29). Finally, Joshua dies at the age of 110 (v.29). After his burial at Timnath Serah, Joseph's bones are buried at Shechem (v.32). Finally, Eleazar the priest dies and is buried at Gibeah (v.33).

1. The Eastern Tribes Return Home (22:1–9)

OVERVIEW

Joshua is pleased with the accomplishments of the Reubenites, Gadites, and half-tribe of Manasseh, who obeyed Moses' instructions faithfully by aiding their brothers in carrying out Yahweh's assignment and remaining with them until Joshua releases them to return home. The mission is only fully accomplished when the eastern tribes return to Transjordan. They leave Shiloh with a warning to remain faithful to Yahweh, a special blessing from their leader, and great riches to be shared with their people in Transjordan.

[1]Then Joshua summoned the Reubenites, the Gadites and the half-tribe of Manasseh [2]and said to them, "You have done all that Moses the servant of the LORD commanded, and you have obeyed me in everything I commanded. [3]For a long time now — to this very day — you have not deserted your brothers but have carried out the mission the LORD your God gave you. [4]Now that the LORD your God has given your brothers rest as he promised, return to your homes in the land that Moses the servant of the LORD gave you on the other side of the Jordan. [5]But be very careful to keep the commandment and the law that Moses the servant of the LORD gave you: to love the LORD your God, to walk in all his ways, to obey his commands, to hold fast to him and to serve him with all your heart and all your soul."

[6]Then Joshua blessed them and sent them away, and they went to their homes. [7](To the half-tribe of Manasseh Moses had given land in Bashan, and to the other half of the tribe Joshua gave land on the west side of the Jordan with their brothers.) When Joshua sent

them home, he blessed them, [8]saying, "Return to your homes with your great wealth — with large herds of livestock, with silver, gold, bronze and iron, and a great quantity of clothing — and divide with your brothers the plunder from your enemies."

[9]So the Reubenites, the Gadites and the half-tribe of Manasseh left the Israelites at Shiloh in Canaan to return to Gilead, their own land, which they had acquired in accordance with the command of the LORD through Moses.

COMMENTARY

1–3 With the same language as 1:13, Joshua praises the Reubenites, Gadites, and half-tribe of Manasseh for their fervent obedience, saying, "You have done all that Moses the servant of the LORD commanded." East of the Jordan, Moses had commanded them to assist their brothers in conquering Canaan (Nu 32:16–32; Dt 3:18). The eastern tribes did not abandon their brothers; rather, they stayed with them until the end, "for a long time now — to this very day."

4 Yahweh has given rest to the western tribes, as he had promised (Dt 3:18–20; 25:19; Jos 1:13, 15). The eastern tribes, knowing that all Israel is at rest, are now ready to return home and build pens for their livestock and cities for their women and children (Nu 32:16).

5 This verse echoes exhortations previously given to Israel to love the Lord, to walk in his ways, to keep his commandments, and to serve him with all their heart and mind (Dt 4:29; 6:5; 11:1, 13; 19:9;

30:16, 20). This behavior will serve as a testimony of their covenant relationship with Yahweh to the nations of the world.

6–8 Joshua blesses the men with an abundance of livestock, silver, gold, bronze, iron, and clothing to be distributed among the members of the tribes east of the Jordan, and he sends them away. It is possible that the sons of Aaron recite the Aaronic blessing over the men of the eastern tribes, especially since Aaron and his sons had been instructed to do so over Israel years earlier (Nu 6:24–26). The blessing is certainly fitting for the occasion. The send-off is interrupted by a parenthetical note regarding the division of land for the tribe of Manasseh — Moses gave land in Bashan and Joshua gave land west of the Jordan (v.7).

9 The men return to their assigned territory in Transjordan. They travel eastward from Shiloh toward Gilead, where their wives and children are waiting.

NOTES

1 "Then [Joshua] summoned" (אָז יִקְרָא, ʾāz yiqrāʾ). ʾāz + a preterite indicates past tense ("at that time") and highlights "consequence" rather than "sequence" (Waltke and O'Connor, §31.1.1d, §31.6.3; see Howard, 238, n. 191, 192; I. Rabinowitz, "ʾāz Followed by Imperfect Verb-Form in Preterite Contexts:

A Redactional Device in Biblical Hebrew," *VT* 34 [1984]: 53–62). In this passage, sometime after the warfare was over ("at that time"), Joshua is free to send the eastern tribes home.

4 "Now" (וְעַתָּה, *wᵉᶜattā*). The disjunctive marker *wᵉᶜattā* appears twice in the verse. Waltke and O'Connor (§38.1e) identify this marker as one of several "macrosyntactic signs [that serve] as introductory and transitional signals in dialogue." In our text, the marker indicates the end of a major event—Canaan has been conquered—and the beginning of another—the eastern tribes can settle in their assigned territories.

2. The Jordan Altar Controversy (22:10–34)

OVERVIEW

The departure of the Reubenites, Gadites, and half-tribe of Manasseh is not without incident. As soon as they reach Geliloth near the Jordan, they build a memorial so large that it is visible from a great distance. The memorial will serve as a reminder to future generations that the eastern tribes worship Yahweh and offer sacrifices at his sanctuary.

This stone monument is completely misunderstood by the Israelites west of the Jordan, whose anger arises quickly. They accuse the Reubenites, Gadites, and half-tribe of Manasseh of building an altar in rebellion against Yahweh, and they threaten to wage war against them. Phinehas, son of Eleazar the priest, and ten tribal chiefs travel to Transjordan to confront the men of the eastern tribes. The exchange is heated and animated but beneficial. The eastern tribes clarify their original intent in building the memorial, and peace is maintained. From a literary standpoint, this chapter highlights the unity of the twelve tribes. The reiteration of the "whole assembly of the LORD" (v.16), "the whole community of Israel" (vv.18, 20), "each of the tribes of Israel" (v.14) and "the Israelites" (vv.30–32) emphasizes the sense of community.

a. The Crisis (22:10–14)

> ¹⁰When they came to Geliloth near the Jordan in the land of Canaan, the Reubenites, the Gadites and the half-tribe of Manasseh built an imposing altar there by the Jordan. ¹¹And when the Israelites heard that they had built the altar on the border of Canaan at Geliloth near the Jordan on the Israelite side, ¹²the whole assembly of Israel gathered at Shiloh to go to war against them.
>
> ¹³So the Israelites sent Phinehas son of Eleazar, the priest, to the land of Gilead—to Reuben, Gad and the half-tribe of Manasseh. ¹⁴With him they sent ten of the chief men, one for each of the tribes of Israel, each the head of a family division among the Israelite clans.

COMMENTARY

10–12 When the men reach Geliloth, near the western shore of the Jordan, they build "an imposing altar" (*mizbēaḥ gādôl lemarʾeh*, cf. Ex 3:3) by the river—one that can be seen from both sides of the Jordan. This structure causes alarm at Shiloh. The Cisjordanians take offense at this seemingly distasteful act and gather an assembly in order to decide the best course of action to take against their brothers. They decide to go to war against them (though not a *ḥērem*, "holy war"; see Introduction, "Theology, Warfare, and the Devoted Things (*ḥērem*]"). Altars built on territorial boundaries also appear in 1 Kings 12, where Jeroboam I makes two golden calves and sets up altars at the northern and southern borders of Israel—Dan in the north and

Bethel in the south (vv.31–33). From that point forward, evil kings of Israel and Judah are accused of identifying with the "sins of Jeroboam."

13–14 The Israelites send Phinehas, son of Eleazar the priest, and a delegation of ten tribal representatives to Gilead to address the matter of the altar. Phinehas was known as a courageous defender of the faith, who killed individuals involved in the worship of Baal at Baal Peor (Nu 25). He and the tribal leaders are unafraid and ready for battle. With a priest to oversee such an expedition, we can assume its purpose is religious in nature. Since the unity of Israelite worship appears threatened by the altar, it is fitting to send a priest to lead the delegation.

NOTES

10 Agreeing with the LXX, some scholars have proposed that Geliloth is a site located west of the Jordan, connected to Gilgal, where Israel first camped after crossing the Jordan—the location where Joshua had set up a stone memorial (Butler, 240). Others propose a site east of the Jordan based on the Hebrew text of verse 11, *ʾel-ʿēber benê yiśrāʾēl* (אֶל־עֵבֶר בְּנֵי יִשְׂרָאֵל, lit., "across from the Israelites"), in sight of the western tribes (see discussion in M. H. Woudstra, 321 n. 6). In 13:2, the term *gelîlôt* means "regions," "districts," or "boundaries." Since the text mentions "near the Jordan, in the land of Canaan," it seems more logical that the Reubenites, Gadites, and half-tribe of Manasseh build the altar on the west side of the Jordan, but the text is not specific as to the exact location.

b. The Confrontation (22:15–20)

¹⁵When they went to Gilead—to Reuben, Gad and the half-tribe of Manasseh—they said to them: ¹⁶"The whole assembly of the LORD says:'How could you break faith with the God of Israel like this? How could you turn away from the LORD and build yourselves an altar in rebellion against him now? ¹⁷Was not the sin of Peor enough for us? Up to this very day we have not cleansed ourselves from that sin, even though a plague fell on the community of the LORD! ¹⁸And are you now turning away from the LORD?

"'If you rebel against the LORD today, tomorrow he will be angry with the whole community of Israel. ¹⁹If the land you possess is defiled, come over to the LORD's land, where the LORD's tabernacle stands, and share the land with us. But do not rebel against the LORD or against us by building an altar for yourselves, other than the altar of the LORD our God. ²⁰When Achan son of Zerah acted unfaithfully regarding the devoted things, did not wrath come upon the whole community of Israel? He was not the only one who died for his sin.'"

COMMENTARY

15–18a The men of Reuben, Gad, and the half-tribe of Manasseh cross over to the eastern shore and gather in Gilead. The exact location of the encounter of the leaders is not specified, and the reason why the two and a half tribes find themselves together in Gilead is unclear. One anticipates that each tribe would have made its way home — Reuben to the south, Gad to the center of the country, and the half tribe of Manasseh to the north.

Phinehas and the tribal representatives approach the leaders of the eastern tribes in Gilead with a provocative tone and ask three questions: (1) "How could you break faith with the God of Israel like this?" (v.16). This question assumes that the eastern tribes have acted unfaithfully (*mᶜl*) toward Yahweh and broken faith arrogantly.

(2) "How could you turn away (*šûb*, 22:8, 9, 16, 18, 23, 29, 32 [2x]) from the LORD and build yourselves an altar in rebellion against him now?" (v.16). With the second question, the western leaders presume that the building of an altar is a gesture of rebellion, an offense deserving of severe punishment (cf. 1Sa 15:23).

(3) "Was not the sin of Peor enough for us?" (v.17). The third question refers to the events at Shittim, in which Israel engaged in sexual immorality with the women of Moab and worshiped

the Baal of Peor (Nu 25:1–5). The behavior of Israel angered Yahweh, who sent a plague to the Israelite camp and ordered Moses to kill all the men who had taken part in the worship of Baal. Phinehas remembered the incident clearly. Following the orgy, an Israelite by the name of Zimri brought a Midianite woman named Cozbi into his tent in the sight of all Israel. Undeterred by Israel's cries at the Tent of Meeting, Zimri engaged in sexual intercourse with Cozbi in his family tent. Angered by the arrogance of Cozbi, Phinehas grabbed a spear, entered the tent, and drove the spear through the bodies of the man and woman, united in sexual transgression. Only then did the plague stop, after 24,000 Israelites had perished. According to Phinehas, the consequences of this sin were still being felt "to this very day." The concluding statement summarizes the misunderstanding: "And you, you are now turning away from the LORD!!" (v.18a; the NIV translates as a question).

18b–19 The stern and panic-stricken reaction of Phinehas is explained in verse 18b. According to him the safety of all Israel is at stake. Rebellion from one part of the community results in consequences for the entire community. According to Phinehas, the building of an altar outside of a designated area (e.g., Shiloh) indicates rebellion against Yahweh and causes defilement of the land. Phinehas proposes a solution: come back to the western side of the Jordan and live where the land is undefiled, where the tabernacle of the Lord has been erected. But do not rebel against God.

20 Phinehas reminds his audience of Achan's unfaithfulness with the devoted things at Ai and the wrath poured on him and his entire family. Many innocent lives were lost because of his sin. One man's sin can cause Yahweh's wrath to fall on an entire community.

NOTES

16–31 "Break faith" (מעל, *mʿl*, "to act faithlessly, be unfaithful") appears in various forms seven times in the chapter (vv. 16 [2x], 20 [2x], 22, 31 [2x]; cf. 7:1), as does "to turn away" (מרד, *mrd*, "to be rebellious, rebellion") (vv. 16, 18, 19 [2x], 22, 29). The combination of these two roots sharpens the tone of the accusation and intensifies the dynamics of the discourse. The tension is heightened with the repetition of "this (very) day, now" (היום, *hayyôm*; vv. 3, 16 [2x], 17, 18 [2x], 22, 29, 31).

17–19 The author contrasts the words "to be clean, pure" (טהר, *ṭhr*, v. 17) and "to be defiled, impure" (טמא, *ṭmʾ*, v. 19). The most frequent use of these words is in cultic contexts. In Leviticus, the priests were given the assignment to distinguish what was "clean" and what was "unclean" (10:10), a job they often failed to accomplish (Eze 22:26). The use of these two cultic terms in this passage emphasizes the gravity of being unclean as well as the severe consequences possible for acting unfaithfully and for being unclean (cf. Jos 7:1; 22:16; H. Ringren, "טהר," *TDOT*, 5:287–96; H. Ringren and G. André, "טמא," *TDOT*, 5:330–42).

c. The Response (22:21–29)

²¹Then Reuben, Gad and the half-tribe of Manasseh replied to the heads of the clans of Israel: ²²"The Mighty One, God, the Lord! The Mighty One, God, the Lord! He knows! And let Israel know! If this has been in rebellion or disobedience to the Lord, do not spare us this day. ²³If we have built our own altar to turn away from the Lord and to offer burnt offerings and grain offerings, or to sacrifice fellowship offerings on it, may the Lord himself call us to account.

²⁴"No! We did it for fear that some day your descendants might say to ours, 'What do you have to do with the Lord, the God of Israel? ²⁵The Lord has made the Jordan a boundary between us and you — you Reubenites and Gadites! You have no share in the Lord.' So your descendants might cause ours to stop fearing the Lord.

²⁶"That is why we said, 'Let us get ready and build an altar — but not for burnt offerings or sacrifices.' ²⁷On the contrary, it is to be a witness between us and you and the generations that follow, that we will worship the Lord at his sanctuary with our burnt offerings, sacrifices

and fellowship offerings. Then in the future your descendants will not be able to say to ours, 'You have no share in the LORD.'

²⁸"And we said, 'If they ever say this to us, or to our descendants, we will answer: Look at the replica of the LORD's altar, which our fathers built, not for burnt offerings and sacrifices, but as a witness between us and you.'

²⁹"Far be it from us to rebel against the LORD and turn away from him today by building an altar for burnt offerings, grain offerings and sacrifices, other than the altar of the LORD our God that stands before his tabernacle."

COMMENTARY

21–22 The Reubenites, Gadites, and Manassites are appalled at Phinehas's accusations. They react fiercely with an extremely emphatic exclamation, invoking Yahweh before whom they consider themselves blameless. As is seen in the chart below, the superlative nature of the exclamation is not easy to translate from Hebrew to English. Some modern versions have reduced the number of designations for Yahweh in their translation.

MT	ʾēl ʾĕlōhîm yhwh ʾēl ʾĕlōhîm yhwh hûʾ yōdēaʿ weyiśrāʾēl hûʾ yēdāʿ
NIV, ESV	The Mighty One, God, the LORD! The Mighty One, God, the LORD! He knows! And let Israel know!
CJB	The Mighty One, God, is ADONAI! He knows, and Israel will know.
NKJV, NRSV	The LORD God of gods, the LORD God of gods, He knows and let Israel itself know.
NAB	The LORD the God of gods, knows and Israel shall know.
NJB	The God of Gods, Yahweh, the God of gods, Yahweh well knows, and let Israel know it too.
TNK	God, the LORD God! God, the LORD God! He knows, and Israel too shall know!

23 The leaders of the eastern tribes become transparent before the western leaders and before Yahweh. Never had they intended to offer sacrifices to Yahweh on the altar. The sacrifices mentioned here are the first three found in Leviticus (1:3; 2:1; 3:1).

24–27 The answer is clearly "No!" The Transjordanians did not set up an altar as a place for offerings, but rather as a memorial to celebrate and guarantee the unity of the tribes for generations to come. If one day descendants of the Cisjordanians consider the Jordan River as the border of Israel's inheritance and exclude anyone east of the Jordan, "let Israel know" that the altar is a symbol of unity between the twelve tribes. The altar is intended to serve as "a witness" (ʿēd) between the tribes. The Hebrew word for "witness" is often used in legal contexts, implying that the eastern tribes are legally bound by their oath to worship Yahweh with their brothers in Cisjordan.

28 The purpose of the altar is repeated for emphasis — the altar is a "replica" (*tabnît*) and not the actual altar for offerings.

29 Israel was familiar with the consequences of rebellion. In the desert, the previous generation of Israelites had revolted against God and his servant Moses (Nu 21:5) by wishing to return to Egypt. As a consequence, multitudes of Israelites perished before they could enter the land of Canaan (Nu 14:1–35).

NOTES

22 The Hebrew marker *wᵉʾim* (וְאִם, "and even") appears five times in verses 22–24. The quick repetition of this disjunctive marker intensifies the dynamics in the discourse. The Reubenites, Gadites, and the half-tribe of Manasseh explode with an escalating discharge of defenses, declaring that "Yahweh and Israel indeed know *if* she has acted in rebellion, *and even* with unfaithfulness against the Lord.... *and if* she offered a burnt offering ... *and if* she sacrificed fellowship offerings...." To the accusations of Joshua, the men of the eastern tribes voice every possible scenario that could have brought guilt on them, knowing full well that they are innocent.

d. The Resolution (22:30–34)

³⁰When Phinehas the priest and the leaders of the community — the heads of the clans of the Israelites — heard what Reuben, Gad and Manasseh had to say, they were pleased. ³¹And Phinehas son of Eleazar, the priest, said to Reuben, Gad and Manasseh, "Today we know that the LORD is with us, because you have not acted unfaithfully toward the LORD in this matter. Now you have rescued the Israelites from the LORD's hand."

³²Then Phinehas son of Eleazar, the priest, and the leaders returned to Canaan from their meeting with the Reubenites and Gadites in Gilead and reported to the Israelites. ³³They were glad to hear the report and praised God. And they talked no more about going to war against them to devastate the country where the Reubenites and the Gadites lived.

³⁴And the Reubenites and the Gadites gave the altar this name: A Witness Between Us that the LORD is God.

COMMENTARY

30–33 Phinehas son of Eliazar, the priest, and the leaders (repeated 3x) are pleased with the reply of the Reubenites, Gadites, and half-tribe of Manasseh. What began as a tense accusation turns into a sigh of relief! The indictment of "acting unfaithfully" (*mâ hammâ'al hazzeh ᵃšer mᵉᶜaltem*) in verse 16 is reversed here with "you have not acted unfaithfully toward the Lord" (*lō' mᵉᶜaltem … hammâ'al hazzeh,* v.31).

32–34 Phinehas and the tribal leaders return to Shiloh with a good report. The Israelites praise Yahweh and abandon their thought of war against the eastern tribes. The Reubenites and Gadites declare their faithfulness to Yahweh by naming the altar: "A Witness Between Us that the LORD is God."

REFLECTION

Actions can often be misunderstood, and miscommunication often creates chaos. Such was the case with Israel when the deeds of the eastern tribes were misinterpreted by the western tribes, who quickly concluded that war with their brothers was necessary. There is no evidence that the Israelites at Shiloh ever consulted with Yahweh before deciding on their course of action. Had they prayed, sought divine counsel, and waited for a brief moment, they would surely have discovered the truth of the matter. Consequently, the confrontation in Gilead would have been avoided.

Without clear communication between individuals, the innocent actions of one are often considered inappropriate by another. In hindsight, more communication between parties is often the key to avoiding confrontations and misunderstandings. Had the men of the eastern tribes shared their plan with Joshua before forging ahead with their brilliant idea, the confrontation could have been avoided. But it is possible that their spontaneous spirits led them to build the stone structure without even considering the possibility of negative consequences. As Christians, how quickly we are to diagnose problems and to propose solutions for what we think are crises, before ever taking the time to consult God, who is omniscient and has the solution to every problem of life.

3. Joshua's Farewell Speech (23:1–16)

OVERVIEW

At the end of his life, Joshua convenes two assemblies. The first includes the elders, leaders, judges, and officials of Israel (ch. 23). He acknowledges in their presence that his life is coming to a close, and he exhorts them to remain faithful to the Yahweh. This final farewell by Joshua is typical of Deuteronomistic history (e.g., 1Sa 12; 1Ki 2:1–9; 1Ki 8:1–2, 12–53), in which leaders (1) reflect on the mighty deeds of God, (2) urge the Israelites to remain faithful to the Lord (22:5; Dt 6:5; 10:20; 30:16, 20), (3) advise Israel to refrain from turning to the right or to the left (1:7; Dt 17:20; 28:14), and (4) prohibit the people from worshiping foreign gods. Farewell addresses also appear before the deaths of Jacob (Ge 48–49), Joseph (Ge 50), Moses (Dt), and David (1Ki 2:1–9).

The structure of this chapter includes an introduction (v.1) and Joshua's farewell speech (vv.2–16). The speech is interwoven with highlights of Yahweh's participation in the conquest of the land (vv.3–5, 9–10, 14), exhortations to remain strong and obedient to the law of Moses (vv.6–8, 11), and admonitions against disobedience (vv.12–13, 15–16). The exhortations to be obedient follow a pattern of *positive–negative–positive*.

Positive	Negative	Positive
"Be very strong; be careful to obey" (v.6)	"Do not associate with these nations … do not invoke … [do] not serve them or bow down to them" (v.7)	"Hold fast to the LORD" (v.8)

The chapter concludes with a reality check: Yahweh gave you the land and Yahweh can take it away (vv.15–16).

a. Blessings of Obedience (23:1–11)

¹After a long time had passed and the LORD had given Israel rest from all their enemies around them, Joshua, by then old and well advanced in years, ²summoned all Israel—their elders, leaders, judges and officials—and said to them: "I am old and well advanced in years. ³You yourselves have seen everything the LORD your God has done to all these nations for your sake; it was the LORD your God who fought for you. ⁴Remember how I have allotted as an inheritance for your tribes all the land of the nations that remain—the nations I conquered—between the Jordan and the Great Sea in the west. ⁵The LORD your God himself will drive them out of your way. He will push them out before you, and you will take possession of their land, as the LORD your God promised you.

⁶"Be very strong; be careful to obey all that is written in the Book of the Law of Moses, without turning aside to the right or to the left. ⁷Do not associate with these nations that remain among you; do not invoke the names of their gods or swear by them. You must not serve them or bow down to them. ⁸But you are to hold fast to the LORD your God, as you have until now.

⁹"The LORD has driven out before you great and powerful nations; to this day no one has been able to withstand you. ¹⁰One of you routs a thousand, because the LORD your God fights for you, just as he promised. ¹¹So be very careful to love the LORD your God.

COMMENTARY

1 By now Joshua is almost 110 years old (cf. 24:29). The reader learns about Joshua's old age in 13:1, in 24:29, and here; the repetition of the identical sentence in 13:1 and 23:1 — "Joshua was old and well advanced in years" — serves as a literary inclusio for chapters 13 through 23. The same statement is mentioned with regards to two other prominent leaders — Abraham and David (see comments on 13:1).

2 The elderly state of Joshua is repeated in the introduction of his farewell speech. Aware that his time of departure is at hand, Joshua summons all the leaders of Israel and urges them to lead Israel according to the law of Moses. While some scholars envision the entire community of Israel gathered before Joshua, others see only the leaders standing in his presence. The latter scenario seems more likely for logistical reasons. It would have been practically impossible to have all the Israelites from every region of the land come before the leader, presumably in his home town of Timnath Serah or at Shiloh.

Farewell speeches — different from patriarchal blessings — are intended to instruct disciples on the steps to follow in order to avoid deviating from Yahweh's plan. Included in farewell speeches are some or all of the following elements: (1) mention of the leader's old age; (2) mention of significant historical events; (3) exhortations to follow God; and (4) a response by the audience. These serve to validate the authority of the leader and to confirm the successor (e.g., Dt 31:7–8; 1Ki 2:2–4).

3 Joshua's statement is emphatic (*weʾattem reʾîtem*, "you yourselves have seen"). With this declaration, Joshua places the burden on Israel for continuing to serve Yahweh faithfully, since their success in acquiring the land is due solely to his

work and not to their own human efforts. The mention of God's great and mighty deeds serves to deepen Israel's identity as the people of God. "These nations" have failed to thwart the plans of Yahweh for Israel.

4 The expression "Look!" (NIV "Remember") is a wordplay with "you have seen" (v.3). Joshua addresses only the leaders of the western tribes in his statement regarding Israel's inheritance — between the Jordan and the Great Sea — seemingly ignoring the leaders of the eastern tribes. His focus is on the occupation of Canaan by Israel.

5 Joshua indicates that Yahweh *will* fulfill his plan in its entirety. This seems to contradict earlier hyperbolic statements that the *entire* land was conquered and the *all* the enemies of Israel had been defeated (cf. 11:10–23; 21:43–44). In reality, much work remained to be done. Joshua declares that "the LORD your God, he himself will drive out" (*yhwh ʾelōhêkem hûʾ yehdāpēm*) the nations that remain, as they pose a serious threat to Israel.

6 The charge to "be strong" appears also in 1:6, 7, 9, 18 (cf. Dt 31:6, 7, 23). This exhortation is crucial for the future of Israel. Joshua has witnessed on several occasions the vulnerability and failings of the Israelites. Thus far, his resolve has kept them proceeding forward, but what would transpire after his death without his steadfastness and tenacity to remain faithful to Yahweh? The "Book of the Law (of Moses)" ("the Book of the Covenant," Ex 24:7) contains the standard for Israel's behavior in the land. From this book, Israel is admonished to refrain from "turning aside to the right or to the left."

7–8 The author uses five negative commands to emphasize the dangers of associating with Canaanites: "Do not associate ... do not invoke ... [do not]

swear … [do] not serve …[do not] bow down." The command "do not associate" uses a Hebrew word (*bw*ʾ, "to enter") that is sometimes applied in contexts of sexual intercourse and procreation (Ge 16:4; 30:4; 38:18; Eze 23:44; Jos 23:12). In this case, the term implies spiritual intercourse that leads to syncretism. Worshiping foreign gods was forbidden by the Law of Moses (Ex 20:2–5; Dt 5:6–9).

The Canaanite gods who were the most likely to compete with the worship of Yahweh included El, his consort Athirat, the goddesses Ashtarte and Anat, the gods Yam and Baal, whose epithet appears in several place names in and around Canaan (e.g., Baal Peor, Baal Zaphon, Baal Shamen, Baal Gad, Baal Meon, Kiriath Baal, Baal Perazim, Baal Hazor, Baal Hermon). One of the major texts from Ugarit—just north of Canaan—is entitled "The Baal Cycle" (fourteenth century BC). Considered among other things to be a storm god, Baal was appealing to people who lived in an agricultural setting. Some of the religious rites performed for foreign gods included sexual relations with cult prostitutes (e.g., Dt 23:17–18; Hos 4:12–14). This act of sexual intercourse symbolically "encouraged the god(s) to inseminate the land with abundant fertility" (Hubbard, 525).

Since Israel now lived a sedentary, agricultural lifestyle, the temptation to compromise in order to enhance the fertility of the land was appealing. As is seen throughout history, Israel succumbed to the temptation numerous times and consequently received repeated severe punishment. Sexual offenses are judged harshly in the Hebrew Bible. For example, the rape of Dinah by Shechem the Hivite is condemned and punished by death at the hands of Simeon and Levi, who call the incident "a disgraceful thing … [something] that should not be done" (Ge 34:7). (For additional examples of

sexual offenses, see Judah and Tamar, Ge 38; David and Bathsheba, 2Sa 11; Amnon and Tamar, 2Sa 13).

Joshua exhorts Israel to hold fast to Yahweh and to maintain an exclusive relationship with him. The verb "to hold fast" (*dbq*) indicates intimacy, closeness, loyal embrace, and propinquity in relationship. In Modern Hebrew, the verb means "to glue together." God is deserving of fidelity and devotion from his people. According to the text, this type of intimacy with Yahweh can be maintained by Israel since she has "done it until this day."

9 To Yahweh only belongs the glory for driving out the great and powerful nations from before Israel (cf. Ex 23:28–31; 33:2; 34:11, 24; Lev 18:24; 20:23; Nu 32:21; 33:52, 55; Dt 4:38; 7:1, 22; 9:3–5; 11:23; 12:29; 18:12; 19:1; 33:27). Since God had initiated the conquest and participated in its fulfillment, how could Israel now attempt to become self-sufficient? Joshua's message is clear: "There is no victory without Yahweh's intervention."

10 The comparison of "one" to "one thousand" may indicate (1) that the number of Israelites was quite small in comparison to the rest of the inhabitants of the land, and/or (2) that with Yahweh, victory is guaranteed without reliance on human effort.

11 The command "to love the LORD your God" echoes several Deuteronomistic passages (e.g., Dt 6:5; 11:1, 13, 22; 30:16, 20; 1Ki 3:3). Loving Yahweh is an appropriate response from a people whom he protected from harm in battle and for whom he defeated all enemies. Ancient Near Eastern treaties provide examples in which "love" is compelled by the superior in a treaty relationship and discussed as important among equals (K. D. Sakenfeld, "Love," *ABD*, 4:376). Love undergirds faithfulness in covenants, whether religious (e.g., marriage) or secular (e.g., political).

b. Curses of Disobedience (23:12–16)

[12]"But if you turn away and ally yourselves with the survivors of these nations that remain among you and if you intermarry with them and associate with them, [13]then you may be sure that the LORD your God will no longer drive out these nations before you. Instead, they will become snares and traps for you, whips on your backs and thorns in your eyes, until you perish from this good land, which the LORD your God has given you.

[14]"Now I am about to go the way of all the earth. You know with all your heart and soul that not one of all the good promises the LORD your God gave you has failed. Every promise has been fulfilled; not one has failed. [15]But just as every good promise of the LORD your God has come true, so the LORD will bring on you all the evil he has threatened, until he has destroyed you from this good land he has given you. [16]If you violate the covenant of the LORD your God, which he commanded you, and go and serve other gods and bow down to them, the LORD's anger will burn against you, and you will quickly perish from the good land he has given you."

COMMENTARY

12 Intermarriage between Israelites and Canaanites never produced favorable results. As seen in the account at Peor, Yahweh condemned sexual intercourse with foreign women and punished it severely. Since family ties were of utmost importance in Israel, marrying outside the clan, the tribe, or the nation jeopardized Israel's unique identity. Her identity was connected to her ethnic origin and racial purity. Intermarriage allowed for compromise with people who practiced a non-Yahwistic religion. Joshua forbids alliances (*dbq*, "to ally") with foreign nations. As mentioned above (v.8), the verb *dbq* indicates loyal embrace, intimacy, and closeness in relationship.

13 Yahweh has limits in his willingness to advocate for Israel. As long as Israel obeys the law of Moses, Yahweh will fight for her; but if she chooses disobedience, Yahweh will withhold his protection (cf. Dt 28:15, 25–26). The consequences of disobedience are enslavement by foreign nations, who would act as cruel whips and thorns in the eyes, and finally result in destruction and the loss of land.

14–15 Once again, Joshua declares his imminent death to the listening community. He will be silenced by death, but he hopes that his voice will still be heard in the hearts of the Israelites. Yahweh has been faithful and will continue to be faithful to Israel. Joshua will depart, but Yahweh will not!

16 Joshua repeats his concern: "If you violate the covenant of the LORD your God ... and serve other gods ...the LORD's anger will burn against you." Compromise and unfaithfulness will not go unpunished. They will provoke God to anger and jealousy; consequently, great disasters will come on Israel.

4. Renewal of the Covenant at Shechem (24:1–27)

OVERVIEW

At Shechem Joshua addresses Israel for the last time (cf. 8:30–5); the entire community is present to participate in the ceremony. The content of this chapter is comparable to that of ancient Near Eastern treaties, especially to second millennium BC Hittite treaties. The outline of Joshua 24 follows closely the typical outline of such treaties:

1. *Introduction* (v.2b)
2. *Historical Prologue* (vv.2c–13)
   a. The Patriarchs (vv.2–4)
   b. The Exodus (vv.5–7)
   c. The Victory in Transjordan (vv.8–10)
   d. The Conquest (vv.11–14)
3. *Stipulations* (vv.14–24)
4. *Reading of Document and Deposit in the Holy Place of the Lord* (vv.25–26)
5. *Witnesses* (vv.26–27)
6. *Curses and Blessings* (vv.19–20)

This chapter reflects on every book of the Torah (Pentateuch) and on the events of the book of Joshua. The historical comments about Terah and the patriarchs are from Genesis (vv.2–4). The mention of Moses and Aaron, especially in relationship to deliverance from Egypt, reflects on the events of Exodus (vv.5–7). The mention of the holiness of Yahweh in verse 19 echoes Leviticus. The retelling of the journey in the desert, highlighting conflict with the Amorites and encounters with Balak and Balaam, reminds the reader of Numbers (vv.8–10). The stipulations of the covenant, together with blessings for obedience and curses for disobedience, recall Deuteronomy (vv.19–20). Finally, the crossing of the Jordan, conquest of Jericho, and battles against the Canaanites point to the book of Joshua (vv.11–13). The picture is complete. What Yahweh promised to the patriarchs has now been fulfilled. The time has come for an earnest recommitment by Israel to the covenant relationship with Yahweh.

a. Introduction and Historical Prologue (24:1–13)

¹Then Joshua assembled all the tribes of Israel at Shechem. He summoned the elders, leaders, judges and officials of Israel, and they presented themselves before God.

²Joshua said to all the people, "This is what the LORD, the God of Israel, says: 'Long ago your forefathers, including Terah the father of Abraham and Nahor, lived beyond the River and worshiped other gods. ³But I took your father Abraham from the land beyond the River and led him throughout Canaan and gave him many descendants. I gave him Isaac, ⁴and to Isaac I gave Jacob and Esau. I assigned the hill country of Seir to Esau, but Jacob and his sons went down to Egypt.

⁵"'Then I sent Moses and Aaron, and I afflicted the Egyptians by what I did there, and I brought you out. ⁶When I brought your fathers out of Egypt, you came to the sea, and the

Egyptians pursued them with chariots and horsemen as far as the Red Sea. ⁷But they cried to the LORD for help, and he put darkness between you and the Egyptians; he brought the sea over them and covered them. You saw with your own eyes what I did to the Egyptians. Then you lived in the desert for a long time.

⁸"I brought you to the land of the Amorites who lived east of the Jordan. They fought against you, but I gave them into your hands. I destroyed them from before you, and you took possession of their land. ⁹When Balak son of Zippor, the king of Moab, prepared to fight against Israel, he sent for Balaam son of Beor to put a curse on you. ¹⁰But I would not listen to Balaam, so he blessed you again and again, and I delivered you out of his hand.

¹¹"Then you crossed the Jordan and came to Jericho. The citizens of Jericho fought against you, as did also the Amorites, Perizzites, Canaanites, Hittites, Girgashites, Hivites and Jebusites, but I gave them into your hands. ¹²I sent the hornet ahead of you, which drove them out before you — also the two Amorite kings. You did not do it with your own sword and bow. ¹³So I gave you a land on which you did not toil and cities you did not build; and you live in them and eat from vineyards and olive groves that you did not plant.'

COMMENTARY

1 Joshua summons the leaders listed in the previous chapter — elders, leaders, judges, and officials (23:2) — to an assembly at Shechem. They "present themselves" (*wayyityaṣṣ^ebû*) before God. The same verb appears in Exodus 19, when the Israelites prepared to meet God, shortly before Moses received the law on Mount Sinai. The verb appears also in Deuteronomy 31:14, when Moses commissioned Joshua in Transjordan.

2–4 *Historical prologue: the patriarchs.* "Long ago," Terah, an idol worshiper from Mesopotamia, and his three sons (only Abram and Nahor are mentioned here) left Ur of the Chaldees and traveled toward Canaan. Terah's desire was to settle there (Ge 11:31), but once he and his family had reached the great city of Haran on the Euphrates River, Terah decided to remain there until his death. Subsequently, God called Abram to move his family to Canaan. Obedient to the call, Abram traveled to the land where God established a covenant with him.

The patriarchs settled in Canaan, in Seir (Edom), and in Egypt.

5–7 *Historical prologue: the exodus.* After 430 years in Egypt, the Israelites cried out to the Lord, who then raised Moses and Aaron up to deliver them from slavery in Egypt. God afflicted the Egyptians, destroyed their chariots and horses in the sea, and brought Israel out on dry ground (Ex 12:31–39) to a desert region, where they lived for the next forty years.

Johsua then shifts the perspective from the history of ancestors to the history of the present generation. For the first time, the discourse uses "you" (v.5b), implying that those who are standing in the presence of Joshua at Shechem crossed the Red Sea with their parents. Yahweh reminds Israel of the great miracle they witnessed when they were very young. He states: "You saw with your own eyes what I did to the Egyptians. Then you lived in the desert for a long time" (v.7). God worked on the behalf of Israel long ago, during the days of the patriarchs, and he is still working mightily in their midst as they stand in Shechem.

8–10 *Historical prologue: victory in Transjordan.* Before crossing the Jordan, the Israelites encountered several foes who tried to prevent them from settling in the areas of Transjordan and Canaan. Again, God performed miracles for this generation of Israelites. He gave the Amorites (probably referring to Og and Sihon) into their hands and thwarted the plans of Balak, who summoned Balaam to pronounce a curse on Israel (cf. Nu 21–24).

11–13 *Historical prologue: the conquest.* Finally, Israel entered the Promised Land. Following the conquest of Jericho, the Israelites subdued the Amorites, Perizzites, Canaanites, Hittites, Girgashites, Hivites and Jebusites, as Yahweh gave them into their hands.

Scholars have offered three interpretations regarding the identity of "the hornet" in verse 12.

(1) Most likely it represents the terror that Israel's enemies experienced when they encountered Israel's God. This description corresponds to the reaction of the enemies in Exodus 15:14–16, the description of the events in Exodus 23:27–30 and Joshua 2:11, 24; 5:1; 6:27. (2) The hornet represents Egypt by metonymy; a bee or hornet was a pharonic symbol. This is improbable since Egypt did not pose a threat to the Canaanites at that time. (3) It refers to insects used in warfare. Although there is evidence that insects have been used in conflicts (e.g., plagues of Egypt, locusts in Joel), there was no threat from insects at any time in the conquest narrative. The conclusion to the historical prologue highlights the fact that Yahweh has given Israel a land on which they did not toil, cities they did not build, and vineyards and olive groves they did not plant. God has been generous with his gifts to Israel. But with gifts come responsibilities.

NOTES

1–13 Twenty verbs with Yahweh as the subject appear in chapter 24. "I took" (וָאֶקַּח, *wāʾeqqaḥ*, v.3), "I led" (וָאוֹלֵךְ, *wāʾôlēk*, v.3), "I gave (him many descendants)" (וָאַרְבֶּה, *wāʾarbeh*, v.3), "I gave" (וָאֶתֵּן, *wāʾetten*, v.3, 4 [2x], 8, 11, 13), "I sent" (וָאֶשְׁלַח, *wāʾešlaḥ*, v.5, 12), "I afflicted" (וָאֶגֹּף, *wāʾeggōp*, v.5), "I did" (עָשִׂיתִי, *ʿāśîtî*, v.5, 7), "I brought [you] out" (הוֹצֵאתִי, *hôṣēʾtî*, v.5), "I brought [your fathers] out" (וָאֹצִיא, *wāʾôṣîʾ*, v.6), "I brought [you]" (וָאָבִיא, *wāʾābîʾ*, v.8), "I destroyed them" (וָאַשְׁמִידֵם, *wāʾšmîdēm*, v.8), "I would not listen," (וְלֹא אָבִיתִי, *wᵉlōʾ ʾābîtî*, v.10), and "I delivered [you]," (וָאַצִּל, *wāʾaṣṣil*, v.10). This historical survey cements the relationship between Yahweh and his people with credal language in a treatise format and should provoke the Israelites to godly behavior in their new homeland.

b. Joshua's Charge to the People (24:14–24)

> ¹⁴"Now fear the LORD and serve him with all faithfulness. Throw away the gods your forefathers worshiped beyond the River and in Egypt, and serve the LORD. ¹⁵But if serving the LORD seems undesirable to you, then choose for yourselves this day whom you will serve, whether the gods your forefathers served beyond the River, or the gods of the

Amorites, in whose land you are living. But as for me and my household, we will serve the LORD."

¹⁶Then the people answered, "Far be it from us to forsake the LORD to serve other gods! ¹⁷It was the LORD our God himself who brought us and our fathers up out of Egypt, from that land of slavery, and performed those great signs before our eyes. He protected us on our entire journey and among all the nations through which we traveled. ¹⁸And the LORD drove out before us all the nations, including the Amorites, who lived in the land. We too will serve the LORD, because he is our God."

¹⁹Joshua said to the people, "You are not able to serve the LORD. He is a holy God; he is a jealous God. He will not forgive your rebellion and your sins. ²⁰If you forsake the LORD and serve foreign gods, he will turn and bring disaster on you and make an end of you, after he has been good to you."

²¹But the people said to Joshua, "No! We will serve the LORD."

²²Then Joshua said, "You are witnesses against yourselves that you have chosen to serve the LORD."

"Yes, we are witnesses," they replied.

²³"Now then," said Joshua, "throw away the foreign gods that are among you and yield your hearts to the LORD, the God of Israel."

²⁴And the people said to Joshua, "We will serve the LORD our God and obey him."

COMMENTARY

14–24 From this point on, Joshua addresses the Israelites and exhorts them passionately to remain faithful to Yahweh. The root (*ʿbd*, "to serve") appears fifteen times in this section of the chapter (vv.14 [3x], 15 [4x], 16, 17, 18, 19, 20, 21, 22, 24).

14–15 Joshua instructs them to "serve him with all faithfulness [with integrity and truth] ... serve the LORD ... [and] choose ... whom they will serve" (vv.14–15). The choices are few—Israel will either *serve* Yahweh or the gods of the nations. Joshua links his discourse with the first portion of the *historical prologue*. He commands the Israelites to throw away the gods of their forefathers (Terah and Abraham) as well as the gods of the Egyptians. There is no direct textual evidence that Israel brought Mesopotamian and Egyptian gods with

them. The "gods of their forefathers" may foreshadow the "gods of the Canaanites" Israel will soon encounter in the land.

16–18 The Israelites remember the mighty deeds of Yahweh, when he delivered them from Egypt. They recall his protection in the desert during the entire journey, and they acknowledge his mighty power that drove out the inhabitants of the land from before them. And finally, they declare loudly and confidently: "Far be it from us to forsake the LORD to serve other gods! [v.16] ...We too will serve the LORD [v.18] ...We will serve the LORD [v.21] ...We will serve the LORD our God and obey him" (v.24).

19–20 The quick and seemingly artificial response of the Israelites startles Joshua. His hortatory tone changes to one of accusation as he shamelessly retorts: "You are not able to serve the LORD. He is a holy God; he is a jealous God. He will not forgive your rebellion and your sins" (v.19). The statement echoes Leviticus 19:2, "Be holy because I, the LORD your God, am holy." Mention of Yahweh's holiness (*qdš*) appears here for the second time in the book of Joshua; the other references are in 5:15, where the commander of the Lord's army commands Joshua to take off his shoes because he is standing on "holy" ground, and in 24:26, where Joshua places the large memorial stone near the "holy place of the LORD."

The statement regarding Yahweh's jealousy points to the Decalogue. The second commandment states (Ex 20:5-6), "I, the LORD your God, am a jealous God, punishing the children for the sin of the fathers to the third and fourth generation of those who hate me but showing love to a thousand generations of those who love me and keep my commandments." God wants his children's undivided attention and will not allow them to compromise in their relationship with him. If they turn to other gods, Yahweh will surely bring disaster on them. God will not share his glory with another.

21-24 The discourse between Joshua and Israel ends after the people reaffirm, twice more, their resolve to serve Yahweh. Joshua holds the people accountable for their commitment and makes them a witness against themselves. If they break their oath to Yahweh, that is, their pledge to serve him only, they will reap severe consequences. As mentioned above, witnesses were present when an ancient Near Eastern treaty was established. In this case, the witnesses are Yahweh and his people. Whoever breaks the agreement is held responsible by the other party.

c. Sealing and Recording of the Covenant (24:25-27)

²⁵On that day Joshua made a covenant for the people, and there at Shechem he drew up for them decrees and laws. ²⁶And Joshua recorded these things in the Book of the Law of God. Then he took a large stone and set it up there under the oak near the holy place of the LORD.

²⁷"See!" he said to all the people. "This stone will be a witness against us. It has heard all the words the LORD has said to us. It will be a witness against you if you are untrue to your God."

COMMENTARY

25-27 "On that day Joshua made [cut] a covenant for the people" at Shechem. Joshua records the events in the Book of the Law of the Lord before setting up a large memorial stone under a tree, near the holy place of the Lord. The structure is the last of several memorials erected by Israel during the conquest of the land. Joshua seals the covenant between Yahweh and his people, and he fulfills the "reading of the law and deposit of the document" (#4) and the involvement of the "witnesses" (#5) of the treaty (see Overview of 24:1-27).

5. Deaths and Burials (24:28–33)

a. Death and Burial of Joshua (24:28–31)

²⁸Then Joshua sent the people away, each to his own inheritance. ²⁹After these things, Joshua son of Nun, the servant of the LORD, died at the age of a hundred and ten. ³⁰And they buried him in the land of his inheritance, at Timnath Serah in the hill country of Ephraim, north of Mount Gaash.

³¹Israel served the LORD throughout the lifetime of Joshua and of the elders who outlived him and who had experienced everything the LORD had done for Israel.

COMMENTARY

28 After the ceremony at Shechem, Joshua sends the people to their respective tribal allotments. Here ends the mission given to Moses and Joshua, and here begins a new chapter in the life of Israel.

29–30 For the first time, Joshua is called "the servant of the LORD." Until now, only Moses had carried this epithet (Dt 34:5; Jos 1:1, 13, 15; 8:31, 33; 11:12; 12:6; 13:8; 14:7; 18:7; 22:2, 3, 5). Joshua's faithfulness and dedication to the mission of Yahweh has won him the honor. Joshua dies at age 110 and is buried at Timnath Serah, in the land of his inheritance, in the city he had chosen as a dwelling place.

31 Israel remained faithful to Yahweh during the days of Joshua and at least during the next generation who outlived him. They had promised Joshua to continue to "serve" (ᶜbd) Yahweh and him only. The book ends with the open-ended question of whether Israel will indeed continue to serve Yahweh in the land of her inheritance.

b. Burial of Joseph's Bones (24:32)

³²And Joseph's bones, which the Israelites had brought up from Egypt, were buried at Shechem in the tract of land that Jacob bought for a hundred pieces of silver from the sons of Hamor, the father of Shechem. This became the inheritance of Joseph's descendants.

COMMENTARY

32 Years earlier, Joseph had asked his brothers to swear that they would bring his bones to the Promised Land (Ge 50:25–26). The promise is fulfilled here when those bones are buried at Shechem, in the tract of land Jacob had purchased for his family during the time of the patriarchs.

c. Death and Burial of Eleazer, Son of Aaron (24:33)

³³And Eleazar son of Aaron died and was buried at Gibeah, which had been allotted to his son Phinehas in the hill country of Ephraim.

COMMENTARY

33 Finally, Eleazar the high priest, who had helped with the distribution of the tribal allotments, dies and is buried at Gibeah, in the hill country of Ephraim. In the end, both the living and the dead are where they should be — in the Promised Land.

REFLECTION

The mission of God for Israel was demanding and grueling, but also inspiring and rewarding. Yahweh called his people to a special place, reserved only for them. The leaders — Moses and Joshua — remained faithful during the conquest. The people of Israel could now continue their tradition of faithfulness as their journey progressed in the land Yahweh had given into their hands. In the same manner, the Christian life is a journey that is both challenging and rewarding. There are battles to be won and enemies to be defeated. There are also moments made precious by the awareness that Yahweh is forever present and at work in the life of the believer. As the narrative reveals so clearly, "God's faithfulness to his people shines brightly" throughout the entire book of Joshua (Howard, 445).

JUDGES

MARK J. BODA

Introduction[1]

1. JUDGES AND ITS CANONICAL FORMS

Names

The name of the book of Judges in English Bibles is taken from Jerome's Latin translation (Vulgate): *Liber Iudicum* ("Book of Judges"), a title that echoes the name used in the Greek (Κριταί, "Judges") and Hebrew (שֹׁפְטִים, *šōpṭîm*, "Judges") textual and interpretive traditions. Like the book of Kings, this title is based on designations used to describe some of the key characters in the core of the book. (On the designation "judge," see further below.)

Canons

The book of Judges appears in the same location in both modern Jewish and Christian Bibles, that is, after the book of Joshua. These two modern biblical orders reflect the orders of two ancient traditions, the modern Jewish order based on the ancient Jewish Hebrew order and the modern Christian order based on

---

1. I began my study of the book of Judges in Hebrew twenty years ago in my introductory Hebrew course at Westminster Theological Seminary with the late J. Alan Groves, to whom I dedicate this commentary. Al fostered in us a passion for this language and its literature and in me a desire to pass this on to my students. I am thankful to those students (a more sensitive "third generation" than that found in Judges) who have journeyed with me through these chapters in my own Hebrew courses, with special thanks to B. Baxter, M. Conway, and S. Smith for reading over the manuscript, J. Barker and C. Lortie for research work, D. Beldman and S. Locke for shared research, as well as to J. Bowick, A. Brown, E. Filyer, N. Evans, A. Groen, J. Hussain, H. Kim, J. Sanders, R. Van Middelkoop, and T. Yeo for insightful translations and interaction.

an ancient Jewish Greek order.[2] In the Jewish Hebrew order, Judges appears within the canonical division called the "Prophets" (*Nebi'im*) and is identified in Jewish tradition as among the Former Prophets (along with Joshua, Samuel, and Kings) in distinction from the Latter Prophets, which comprise Isaiah, Jeremiah, Ezekiel, and the Book of the Twelve (minor prophets). In modern Christian Bibles, Judges appears in a division often referred to as the "Historical Books," among which are found not only Ruth (between Judges and Samuel), but also Chronicles, Ezra, Nehemiah, and Esther, books that in modern Jewish Bibles appear among the "Writings" (*Ketubim*).[3]

Judges is a Hebrew "prophetic" book in which one can discern the voice of God in the dual modes of warning and promise. While the accent is clearly on the mode of warning, there are ideal moments in which Israel and its leaders follow Yahweh and experience his presence and aid. In addition, the negative portrayals highlight the need for another approach to leadership, one that will have its own faults but that will also introduce a royal hope, which will capture the imagination of later generations.

As a "historical" book, Judges traces a key phase in the drama of Scripture,[4] that redemptive story shared by all who possess this book within their canon and which will find its ultimate fulfillment for Christians in the coming of Jesus and the establishment of a community that includes both Jew and Gentile. As an earlier phase of our redemptive story, it plays an ethical role (see further below).

Manuscripts

Judges has been preserved in ancient manuscripts written in many languages, key among which are Hebrew, Greek, Aramaic/Syriac, and Latin.[5] Of these the most important are extant Hebrew witnesses, which range from those of the medieval Masoretic tradition (with the major codices originating around the tenth century AD) to witnesses discovered at Qumran (1QJudg: 6:20–22; 8:1[?]; 9:1–3; 9:4–6; 9:28–31; 9:40–43; 9:48–49; 4QJudg[a]: Jdg 6:2–6, 11–13; and other smaller fragments; 4QJudg[b]: 19:5–7; 21:12–25; XJudg[c]:

---

2. See Mark Boda, *A Severe Mercy: Sin and Its Remedy in the Old Testament* (Winona Lake, Ind.: Eisenbrauns, 2009), 7–10.

3. J. Clinton McCann, *Judges* (Interpretation; Louisville, Ky.: Westminster John Knox, 2002), 12–16.

4. Craig G. Bartholomew and Michael W. Goheen, *The Drama of Scripture: Finding Our Place in the Biblical Story* (Grand Rapids: Baker, 2004).

5. Cf. Julio C. Trebolle Barrera, "Édition préliminaire de 4QJudges[b]: Contribution des manuscrits qumrâniens des Juges à l'étude textuelle et littéraire du livre," *RevQ* 15 (1991): 79–100; idem, "Light from 4QJudg[a] and 4QKgs on the Text of Judges and Kings," in *The Dead Sea Scrolls: Forty Years of Research* (ed. Devorah Dimant and Uriel Rappaport; Studies on the Texts of the Desert of Judah 10; Leiden: Brill, 1992), 315–24; idem, "The Text-critical Value of the Old Latin and Antiochean Greek Texts in the Books of Judges and Joshua," in *Interpreting Translation: Studies on the LXX and Ezekiel in Honour of Johan Lust* (ed. F. G. Martínez et al. (BETL 192; Leuven: Leuven Univ. Press, 2005), 401–13; idem, "Textual Affiliation of the Old Latin Marginal Readings in the Books of Judges and Kings," in *Biblische Theologie und gesellschaftlicher Wandel: Für Norbert Lohfink* (ed. Georg Braulik, Walter Gross, and Sean E. McEvenue; Freiburg: Herder, 1993), 315–24; idem, "Textual Variants in 4QJudg[a] and the Textual and Editorial History of the Book of Judges (1)," *RevQ* 14 (1989): 229–45; Robert O'Connell, *The Rhetoric of the Book of Judges* (VTSup 63; Leiden: Brill, 1996), 369–84; Natalio Fernández Marcos, "The Genuine Text of Judges," in *Sôfer mahîr: Essays in Honour of Adrian Schenker* (ed. Yohanan Goldman, Arie van der Kooij, and Richard D. Weis; VTSup 110; Leiden: Brill, 2006), 33–45 ; Susan Niditch, *Judges: A Commentary* (OTL; Louisville, Ky.: Westminster John Knox, 2008), 21–25; with thanks to S. Locke.

4:5–6) and dating to the turn of the common era. 4QJudg[b] displays more affinity with the MT, while 4QJudg[a] with the Old Greek.

Earlier reflection on the Old Greek witnesses to Judges identified two major Greek textual traditions, one closely associated with the great Codex Alexandrinus and two groups of manuscripts associated with Origen and Lucian, and the other associated with Codex Vaticanus. Recent scholarship has nuanced this considerably, identifying the "Lucianic" manuscripts as representing the original Old Greek translation (second-first century BC) and the others representing later revisions.[6] In general, the Greek tradition "mainly represents a form of text very close to MT," though there are a few places of divergence that must be considered.[7]

The Aramaic *Targum Jonathan* of Judges (fourth–fifth centuries AD) represents "a literal translation of a text that is very close to [the Masoretic Text] with occasional glosses and Midrashic expansions (cf. Jdg 5, Deborah's song and 11:39, Jephthah's daughter)."[8] The Syriac Peshitta (fifth century AD, if not earlier) at times preserves only a few significant variants for determining the original text of the book of Judges (2:7; 14:4; 15:20; 18:29).[9] The Old Latin (esp. the Lyons Manuscript of the fifth–sixth century) has proved extremely helpful for the reconstruction of the Old Greek.[10] Jerome's later Vulgate (AD 383–405) often provides insights into the early Hebrew manuscript tradition; however, Jerome's translation of Judges "abounds in free renderings."[11] Overall, these many witnesses do not point to significantly diverse textual traditions for the book of Judges.[12]

2. HISTORICAL CONTEXTS

When speaking about history and biblical books, it is important to distinguish carefully between the historical context of the early writers and readers of the book (compositional historical context) and the historical context of the original actors and events in the book (referential historical context).

---

6. Walter Ray Bodine, *The Greek Text of Judges: Recensional Developments* (HSM 23; Atlanta: Scholars, 1980), 134–36, 185–86; Trebolle Barrera, "Textual Affiliation of the Old Latin Marginal Readings"; idem, "The Text-critical Value of the Old Latin"; Karen H. Jobes and Moisés Silva, *Invitation to the Septuagint* (Grand Rapids: Baker, 2000), 45–46; Natalio Fernández Marcos, *The Septuagint in Context: Introduction to the Greek Version of the Bible* (Boston: Brill Academic, 2001), 94–95; Jennifer M. Dines and Michael A. Knibb, *The Septuagint* (London/New York: T&T Clark, 2004), 16; Philip E. Satterthwaite, *A New English Translation of the Septuagint and the Other Greek Translations Traditionally Included under that Title* (ed. Albert Pietersma and Benjamin G. Wright; Oxford: Oxford Univ. Press, 2007), 195–97.

7. Satterthwaite, "Judges," 196–97.

8. Fernández Marcos, "The Genuine Text of Judges," 36; cf. O'Connell, *The Rhetoric of Judges*, 373.

9. See Fernández Marcos, "The Genuine Text of Judges," 37; cf. P. B. Dirksen, *The Transmission of the Text in the Peshitta Manuscripts of the Book of Judges* (Leiden: Brill, 1972).

10. Trebolle Barrera, "Textual Affiliation of the Old Latin Marginal Readings"; "The Text-critical Value of the Old Latin."

11. Fernández Marcos, "The Genuine Text of Judges," 39.

12. O'Connell, *The Rhetoric of Judges*, 384.

Compositional Historical Context

While early Jewish tradition identified Samuel as the author of Judges (*b. B. Bat.* 14b), the book as it stands is anonymous. Discerning the historical context for the composition of the texts found in Judges is partly based on one's view of the boundaries and development of the literature.[13] Early critical scholarship, influenced by Wellhausen's documentary hypothesis, traced the development of the book from an original form (J/E) that was later revised by a late preexilic Deuteronomic editor and again by a postexilic priestly editor (e.g., Moore, Cooke, Burney, Simpson). This approach was largely supplanted after 1943 by Noth's theory that the books of Deuteronomy–2 Kings comprised a single exilic work. Revisions to Noth's theory by later German (e.g., Richter, Smend, Dietrich, Veijola, Becker) and American (e.g., Cross, McKenzie, Friedman, Peckham) scholars pointed to multiple Deuteronomic editions throughout the Babylonian and Persian periods. If Judges is part of this larger literary complex, the historical context for reading the texts in Judges must be discerned from evidence found within this entire literary complex, which ends with the exilic experience of Judah in the sixth century BC.

Recent works on the book of Judges have argued for the rhetorical integrity of the book of Judges as a literary complex (e.g., Webb, Klein, Amit, O'Connell, Wong), opening the way for proposals of an earlier dating for the book in its present form, with, for example, O'Connell[14] pointing to the conditions depicted in 2 Samuel 1–4 and Amit[15] to the period of Hezekiah's reign. Most of these studies, however, admit that the book was constructed from preexistent materials and contributes to a larger Deuteronomic corpus or tradition.

A careful look at the book of Judges reveals a narrator who is at some temporal distance from the events in the book. This distance is indicated in references to former names of locations (1:11, 23; 19:10) and phrases such as "until this day" (*ʿad hayyôm hazzeh*; 1:21, 26; 6:24; 10:4, 30; 15:19; 18:12), "on that day" (*bayyôm hahûʾ*; 5:1), and "in those days" (*bayyāmîm hāhēm*; 17:6; 18:1; 19:1; 20:28; 21:25), which appear in what are often considered various layers of the book. While most of these passages do not provide precise information on the *amount* of temporal distance between the narrator and the events, a few texts do. Judges 1:21 refers to Jebusites living with the Benjamites in Jerusalem "to this day." While this reference may indicate the period prior to the Judahite capture of Jerusalem from the Jebusites by David (2Sa 5:6–7), it must be remembered that 2 Samuel 24:18–25 describes the presence of Araunah the Jebusite in Jerusalem well after this capture. The reference to the lack of a king in Israel in the refrains of Judges 17:6; 18:1; 19:1; 21:25 suggests compositional activity in the period of the monarchy. Contrasts between the tribes of Benjamin and Judah and between the towns of Gibeah and Bethlehem in Judges 1 and 19–21 suggest a period after the rise of David, when tensions arose between the competing royal houses of Saul and David (such as in the period of the civil war of 2Sa 1–4).

---

13. Cf. Gale A. Yee, "Introduction: Why Judges?" in *Judges and Method* (Minneapolis: Fortress, 1995), 5–14; O'Connell, *The Rhetoric of Judges*, 345–68; Gregory T. K. Wong, *Compositional Strategy of the Book of Judges: An Inductive, Rhetorical Study* (VTSup 111; Leiden/Boston: Brill, 2006), 1–23; Paul S. Evans, *The Invasion of Sennacherib in the Book of Kings: A Source-Critical and Rhetorical Study of 2 Kings 18–19* (VTSup 125; Leiden/Boston: Brill, 2009), 19–27.

14. O'Connell, *The Rhetoric of Judges*, 305–42.

15. Yairah Amit, *The Book of Judges: The Art of Editing* (Biblical Interpretation Series 38; Leiden/Boston, 1999), 367, 374–75.

The most explicit reference to a time period appears in 18:30–31, with its notation of the "time of the captivity of the land" (v.30) and "the time the house of God was in Shiloh" (v.31). The focus of the preceding material in chs. 17–18 is on events foundational to an illicit cult center in the far north of Israel at Dan. The book of Kings links a cult center at Dan (and Bethel) to the schismatic northern kingdom established by Jeroboam (1Ki 12:25–33), whose sin of idolatry at these cult centers is explicitly linked to the exile of the northern kingdom (2Ki 17:21–23; cf. 1Ki 14:15–16). This has suggested to many that the reference to the "captivity of the land" in Judges 18:30, along with the consistently negative portrayal of northern figures and parallels between Micah and Jeroboam in chs. 17–18, points to the captivity of the northern kingdom in the late eighth century BC (2Ki 15:29–30; 17:1–6).[16]

But the parallel temporal reference in Judges 18:31 to "the time the house of God was in Shiloh" has suggested to others that an earlier captivity may be in view. This captivity may be one associated with the defeat of Israel under Eli, the loss of the northern Cisjordan, including Shiloh, to the Philistines, and the capture of the ark, which precipitated the transition in leadership from Eli to Samuel (1Sa 4; cf. Ps 78:60; Jer 7:12, 14; 26:6);[17] or with the defeat of Israel under Saul and the loss of the northern Cisjordan to the Philistines, which precipitated the transition in leadership from Saul to David (see 1Sa 31–2Sa 5).[18] This evidence has suggested to some that the book as an independent entity may have originated as early as the initial phase of David's rule,[19] a conclusion that would explain the positive view of kingship that dominates parts of the book.

But evidence of an anti-northern polemic throughout Judges 1–16 and links to Jeroboam's illegitimate royal rule and cult in chs. 9 and 17–18 cannot be ignored and suggest to some that an original focus on tension between the royal houses of Saul and David[20] is now viewed through the vantage point of tension between the royal houses of the north and south in the wake of the fall of the northern kingdom. Even in the case of those who hold to an earlier date, it must be admitted that the book of Judges plays a key function in the literary complex now stretching from Joshua to 2 Kings, which describes the rise of the monarchy and its ultimate failure. Thus, any original message in the wake of the Saulide-Davidic civil war ultimately took on new significance in the aftermath of the exile of Israel and Judah

---

16. Cf. Daniel I. Block, *Judges, Ruth* (NAC 6; Nashville: Broadman & Holman, 1999), 483; Nadav Na'aman, "The Danite Campaign Northward (Judges XVII–XVIII) and the Migration of the Phocaeans to Massalia (Strabo IV 1,4)," *VT* 55 (2005): 47–60; Victor H. Matthews, *Judges and Ruth* (NCBC; Cambridge: Cambridge Univ. Press, 2004), 170; Niditch, *Judges*, 184.

17. J. Gordon McConville, *Grace in the End: A Study of Deuteronomic Theology* (Studies in Old Testament Biblical Theology; Grand Rapids: Zondervan, 1993), 110.

18. O'Connell, *The Rhetoric of Judges*, 305–42.

19. See ibid., 306–7; with thanks to Brian Peterson and his unpublished paper "The Authorship of Judges Considered."

20. See A. E. Cundall, "Judges—An Apology for the Monarchy?" *ExpTim* 81 (1969–70): 178–81; Sam Dragga, "In the Shadow of the Judges: The Failure of Saul," *JSOT* 38 (1987): 39–46; Marc Z. Brettler, "The Book of Judges: Literature as Politics," *JBL* 108 (1989): 395–418; O'Connell, *The Rhetoric of Judges*; Tammi J. Schneider, *Judges* (Berit Olam; Collegeville, Minn.: Liturgical, 2000), with thanks to Peterson, "Authorship."

either within a larger Deuteronomic work comprised of distinct literary units[21] or the broader canonical context of the Former Prophets.[22]

Referential Historical Context

It is not possible in the introduction to this commentary to review in detail the history of debate over the referential historical context for the events presented in the book of Judges.[23] Among many scholars there remains general agreement that the monarchy arose in Israel around 1000 BC, thus placing the events in the book of Judges in the period prior to this date. There has been vigorous debate, however, over the dating of the period before the events in Judges, that is, the exodus from Egypt and entrance into Canaan.[24] The two dominant chronological theories place the exodus and entrance in the fifteenth and thirteenth centuries BC.

In addition to this chronological diversity, there is also variety in the explanation of the way Israel originated in the land, ranging from exogenous models that posit a violent conquest of or peaceful infiltration into the land, to endogenous models that posit a peasant revolt against the elite in the land or a sociological shift (either through collapse or natural shift) in the main Canaanite population.[25] Other streams of research have largely abandoned any attempt to reconstruct early Israel under the conclusion that it is based on myth. It will be obvious that the approach taken in this commentary resonates with that articulated in recent days by Provan, Long, and Longman in their *Biblical History of Israel*. This approach considers the biblical account as a legitimate source alongside the material record for reconstructing the history of Israel. What is found in the books of Joshua and Judges are not contradictory accounts but rather a "picture of a reasonably successful initial conquest of the land—the invading Israelites gaining the upper hand—followed by increasingly unsuccessful attempts to control and occupy the 'conquered' territories."[26] While

---

21. Robert Polzin, *Moses and the Deuteronomist* (Literary Study of the Deuteronomic History 1; New York: Seabury, 1980); Barry G. Webb, *The Book of the Judges: An Integrated Reading* (JSOTSup 46. Sheffield: JSOT, 1987), 211; McCann, *Judges*, 8–12; Wong, *Strategy*, 255; Peterson, "Authorship."

22. O'Connell, *The Rhetoric of Judges*, 307; Block, *Judges, Ruth*, 49.

23. For such a detailed review, see the vigorous debate across the continuum often called Minimalist-Maximalist among such key figures as, for example, Niels Peter Lemche, Philip Davies, Israel Finkelstein, John J. Collins, J. Maxwell Miller/John H. Hayes, Iain Provan/V. Philips Long/Tremper Longman III.

24. Richard Hess, "Early Israel in Canaan: A Survey of Recent Evidence and Interpretations," *PEQ* 125 (1993): 125–42; K. Lawson Younger, "Early Israel in Recent Biblical Scholarship," in *The Face of Old Testament Studies: A Survey of Contemporary Approaches* (ed. David W. Baker and Bill T. Arnold; Grand Rapids: Baker, 1999), 176–206; Ian Provan, V. Philips Long, and Tremper Longman III, *A Biblical History of Israel* (Louisville, Ky.: Westminster John Knox, 2003); David M. Howard and Michael A. Grisanti, *Giving the Sense: Understanding and Using Old Testament Historical Texts* (Grand Rapids: Kregel, 2003); S. A. Meier, "History of Israel 1: Settlement Period," in *Dictionary of the Old Testament: Historical Books* (ed. Bill T. Arnold and H. G. M. Williamson; Downers Grove, Ill.: InterVarsity Press, 2005), 425–34.

25. Cf. Naomi Steinberg, "Social Scientific Criticism: Judges 9 and Issues of Kinship," in *Judges and Method* (ed. Gale A. Yee; Minneapolis: Fortress, 1995), 45–64.

26. Provan, Long, and Longman, *Biblical History*, 189.

the first sections of Joshua and Judges point to an initial subjugation of certain key areas, both books attest to failure in complete occupation of the land.

As for the precise chronological setting of the events in Judges, one can say that they clearly occurred prior to the rise of the monarchy (1000 BC) in Israel and most likely prior to the activities of Eli and Samuel rehearsed in the initial chapters of 1 Samuel. Debatable, however, are the precise dates of the events in the book in this pre-1000 BC period. The earliest event described in the book of Judges appears to be the dismissal of the tribes by Joshua after the conquest of the land (2:6). Dating this event, however, is dependent on the resolution of the dates of the exodus from Egypt and entrance into the Promised Land, which (as noted above) have been placed in either the fifteenth or thirteenth centuries BC, a resolution that does not appear to be achievable based on the present biblical, inscriptional, and material data.

Complicating the issue further is the ambiguity over whether the presentation of the period between Joshua and Eli as described in the book of Judges follows a strictly chronological order. Surely chronology is not of utmost concern at the outset of the book, with its double introduction—the first (1:1–2:5) beginning with the death of Joshua (1:1) and the second (2:6–3:6) before the death of Joshua (2:6). Evidence that the book is not organized strictly chronologically can be culled from a closer look at the generational schema used at various points in the book. In Judges 2:6 the narrator identifies two generations: that of Joshua and the elders (2:7) and "another generation" (2:10), which sets in motion the narratives that follow in ch. 3. The closing chapters of the book of Judges (chs. 17–21) also point to multiple generations (18:30; 20:28), beginning with the generation prior to Joshua (Moses/Aaron), moving to the generation of Joshua (Gershom/Eleazar), and ending with a third generation contemporary with that "another generation" (Jonathan/Phinehas). These groupings suggest that the "young Levite" of chs. 17–18 is to be identified with the generation that immediately followed Joshua's death. As we return to the beginning of the book, Judges 1:1 links the events of ch. 1 also with those of the generation that immediately followed the death of Joshua. These events are joined to the "elders" who outlived Joshua (2:7), especially in light of the mention of Caleb's exploits in 1:10–15, 20. They may also relate, however, to the initial phase of the "another generation" of 2:10.

What this initial evidence reveals, however, is that the events described in chs. 17–21 are linked by the narrator to the same generation that set in motion the stories that follow ch. 2.[27] Othniel, for instance, appears to be from this third generation, since he is identified (most likely) as the nephew of Caleb (Joshua's generation), whose daughter he married. The stories that follow Othniel through chs. 3–16 provide a record of years of oppression under enemies and rest from enemies that clearly move beyond the "another" generation of 2:10, which arose immediately after Joshua's generation.

While the flow of the narrative throughout much of chs. 3–16 may suggest chronological succession, in some cases succession is at best implicit (3:11–12; 5:31b–6:1; 10:5–6; 12:15–13), and in one case the activity of the judge appears to overlap that of the earlier and later judges (3:30–4:1; 5:6). This last piece of evidence is important since it reveals that some of these stories may reflect simultaneous realities in different tribal allotments. Furthermore, the lack of strict chronological order is also suggested by a comparison of

---

27. Amit, *The Book of Judges: Editing*, 311–12; Erik Eynikel, "Judges 19–21, An 'Appendix': Rape, Murder, War and Abduction," *Communio Viatorum* 47 (2005): 101–15.

the story of Samson in chs. 13–16 with that of Micah in chs. 17–18—the former depicting the Danites still in their original southern tribal allotment and the latter reflecting the period when the Danites abandoned their allotment and moved to the far north. If chs. 17–18 reflect the generation immediately after Joshua's death (Jonathan, son of Gershom, son of Moses), then the story of Samson must be even earlier than this, thus identifying Samson as a contemporary of Othniel.[28]

This evidence helps make sense of the anomaly of at least one of the numerical figures associated with this period in Israel's history. Jephthah's speech in 11:26 identifies a period of 300 years since the conquest of Canaan by Israel. If one adds up the years cited to that point in the book of Judges (Othniel to Jephthah), the result is 319 years, a sum that does not even include the period preceding Othniel's judgeship. This evidence confirms that the narrator is aware of some overlap between the judgeships described in the book.[29]

3. SOCIOLOGICAL DYNAMICS

Tribal Confederacy

The biblical portrait of Israel is one that displays clear developments in the sociology of the nation.[30] Consistent throughout the biblical account is the smallest sociological unit, the *bêt-ʾab* ("house of the father"), headed by a patriarchal figure and consisting of three to four generations of the figure's sons and their families.[31] The stories of Abraham, Isaac, and Jacob are focused on this particular sociological unit only.

Beginning with the book of Exodus, however, Israel is depicted as having grown to the size of a nation, one bound together by tribal identity. The depiction of this phase reveals tribes consisting of clans, which are units comprised of related houses of fathers (see Jos 7:15–18). This tribal confederacy dominates the accounts from Exodus to Joshua as the people are depicted as leaving Egypt and entering Canaan. These tribes are joined by a common cause around central leadership and religious site. It is instructive that in its

---

28. Yairah Amit, *The Book of Judges* (Biblical Encyclopaedia Library 6; Jerusalem: Chaim Rosenberg School of Jewish Studies, 1992), 311.

29. See further David L. Washburn, "The Chronology of Judges: Another Look," *BSac* 147 (1990): 414–25; David Faiman, "Chronology in the Book of Judges," *JBQ* 21 (1993): 31–40.

30. See John Bright, *A History of Israel* (4th ed.; Louisville, Ky.: Westminster John Knox, 2000); James Maxwell Miller and John Haralson Hayes, *A History of Ancient Israel and Judah* (2nd ed.; Louisville, Ky.: Westminster John Knox, 2006), 84–114, on tribal confederacy, though on its history of criticism see A. G. Auld, "Amphictyony, Question of," in *Dictionary of the Old Testament: Historical Books* (ed. Bill T. Arnold and H. G. M. Williamson; Downers Grove, Ill.: InterVarsity Press, 2005), 26–32; on Israel and sociology see C. J. H. Wright, "Family," *ABD*, 2:761–67; N. Gottwald, "Sociology (Ancient Israel)," *ABD*, 6:79–89; K. Lawson Younger, *Judges and Ruth* (NIVAC; Grand Rapids: Zondervan, 2002), 25–29; C. E. Carter, "Socio-Scientific Approaches," in *Dictionary of the Old Testament: Historical Books* (ed. Bill T. Arnold and H. G. M. Williamson; Downers Grove, Ill.: InterVarsity Press, 2005), 905–21; Steinberg, "Social Scientific Criticism," 51–52.

31. S. Bendor, *The Social Structure of Ancient Israel: The Institution of the Family (Beit ʾAb) from the Settlement to the End of the Monarchy* (Jerusalem Biblical Studies 7; Jerusalem: Simor, 1996); J. David Schloen, *The House of the Father as Fact and Symbol: Patrimonialism in Ugarit and the Ancient Near East* (Studies in the Archaeology and History of the Levant 2; Winona Lake, Ind.: Eisenbrauns, 2001).

early phase this central leadership is dominated by figures from the priestly-Levitical clan (Moses, Aaron). At its core, then, this tribal unity was religious in character. Fissures within this confederacy are already evident in the distinctions between Cisjordanian and Transjordanian tribes (see esp. Jos 22) and between the various tribes and even factions of tribes throughout the book of Judges.[32]

Foreshadowed by events in the lives of Gideon and Abimelech, the beginning of the book of Samuel depicts the sociological transition from tribal confederacy to dynastic monarchy. After the initial phase of monarchy fails miserably under Saul, identities forged during the phase of tribal confederacy reemerge as the northern tribes follow the house of Saul and the southern tribes follow the house of David. Under David and especially his son Solomon, however, the shift to monarchy will reach its zenith. David makes Jerusalem, with its central position and neutral identity, his capital, while Solomon reorganizes the land into royal districts, which disrupt the original tribal geographic allotments.

Interestingly, however, after Solomon's death the older tribal identities reemerge (or, better, come to the surface), dividing the nation into what appears to be its natural northern and southern sociological identities, with the northern tribes following Jeroboam and the southern tribes following Solomon's son Rehoboam. The later history of the northern and southern monarchies reveals incremental accommodation to the emerging imperial sociological realities: first under the Assyrians, then the Egyptians and Babylonians.[33] The final stages for both kingdoms involved first vassal-kingdom status and finally incorporation as a province into the empire. With the demise of the kingdoms a sociological entity called *bêt-ʾabôt* ("house of the fathers"), resembling the original clan structures, emerges as the dominant sociological structure. Southern and northern tension (Ezr 4) and rapprochement (Chronicles; Zec 9–14) can be discerned in the early Persian period.

This sociological review of the portrayal of Israel in the biblical account is important for understanding the book of Judges, since the book refers to a historical context that is premonarchical, looks to the monarchy as a preferred system of governance, and yet is aware of postmonarchical realities. It is also aware of tensions between northern and southern royal claims. In contrast to the book of Joshua, the book of Judges shifts the focus from tribes to local families and clans.[34] It is this emphasis on the family that will drive most of the plots and provide insight into success and failure.[35] The shift to families and clans parallels a consistent lack of tribal cooperation, which had been centered on religion. At times clans and tribes operate together, but only in an ad hoc fashion.

---

32. A. D. H. Mayes, *Israel in the Period of the Judges* (SBT: Second Series 29. Naperville, Ill.: Allenson, 1974).

33. Mark J. Boda, "Walking in the Light of Yahweh: Zion and the Empires in the Book of Isaiah," in *Empire in the New Testament* (ed. Stanley E. Porter and Cynthia Long Westfall; McMaster New Testament Studies; Grand Rapids: Eerdmans, 2010), 54–89.

34. See Corrine L. Patton, "From Heroic Individual to Nameless Victim: Women in the Social World of the Judges," in *Biblical and Humane: A Festschrift for John F. Priest* (ed. Linda Bennett Elder, David L. Barr, and Elizabeth Struthers Malbon; Scholars Press Homage Series 20; Atlanta: Scholars, 1996), 33–46; Matthews, *Judges and Ruth*, 11–15.

35. Michael J. Smith, "The Failure of the Family in Judges, Part 1: Jephthah," *BSac* 162 (2005): 279–98; idem, "The Failure of the Family in Judges, Part 2, Samson," *BSac* 162 (2005): 424–36.

Judges

It is in such a context that one would expect the kind of leadership described at the core of the book of Judges, that is, by the "judge" and "deliverer" figures depicted in chs. 3–16. Earlier sociological distinctions between major and minor judges are no longer sustainable.[36] These various figures arise as charismatic chieftains who lead ad hoc militia from a variety of tribal units and territories within Israel. These individuals, used by Yahweh to rescue Israel, are described using one or two Hebrew roots, the first usually associated with saving or rescuing (*yšʿ*: 2:16, 18; 3:9, 15, 31; 6:14, 15; 8:22; 10:1, cf. 6:36–37; 7:2, 7; 10:12–14; 13:5) and the second with dispensing justice (*špṭ*: 2:16–19; 3:10; 4:4; 10:2–3; 12:7–9, 11, 13–14; 15:20; 16:31). In some instances these terms are used together, such as in 3:9, where Yahweh raises up the deliverer (*môšîaʿ*) Othniel to deliver (*yšʿ*, Hiphil) Israel, and who, after the Spirit of Yahweh comes upon him (3:10), then "judges" (*špṭ*) Israel by going on a military mission ("when he went out to war … ").

The term "judge" is rarely associated with the dispensing of justice, being attached only to Deborah in Judges and Samuel in 1 Samuel 7:15–17 (cf. 12:11). But in view here may be something more akin to "decision maker," a role made possible by the endowment of the divine Spirit and at times even prophetic access or ability.[37] Extrabiblical texts (Mari, Ebla, Ugarit, Phoenicia, Punic) do attest to the use of terms cognate with the Hebrew "to judge" to describe provincial governors serving under a king, whose duties included dispensing justice, maintaining order, collecting taxes, and providing information and hospitality.[38] It is possible that as chief military leader, the "savior" was responsible for dispensing justice, much as the king was during the monarchical period.

4. LITERARY SHAPE

Analysis of the book of Judges has consistently highlighted the double introduction to the book, the first beginning with the death of Joshua (1:1–2:5) and the second with the final moments of Joshua's life (2:6–3:6). A close look at these two introductions does suggest that on a thematic level the first one (1:1–2:5) relates more closely to the concluding chapters of the book (chs. 17–21) and the second one (2:6–3:6) to the inner core of stories about the judges/deliverers (3:7–16:31). The cyclical pattern found in this inner core separates six major judges from six minor judges and Abimelech, thus suggesting the use of a variety of source materials.[39]

These kinds of observations, while possibly granting insight into the development of the book (see above), may also provide foundational insights into the rhetorical shape of the book in its present form. Recent rhetorical work (esp. Webb, Klein, Amit, O'Connell, Wong) has revealed that the first introduction foreshadows developments not only in the final chapters of the book (chs. 17–21), but also in the central

---

36. Richard D. Nelson, "Ideology, Geography, and the List of Minor Judges," *JSOT* 31 (2007): 347–64.
37. Niditch, *Judges*, 2–3; cf. Klaas Spronk, "Deborah, a Prophetess: The Meaning and Background of Judges 4:4–5," in *Elusive Prophet: The Prophet as a Historical Person, Literary Character and Anonymous Artist* (ed. Johannes C. De Moor; Leiden: Brill, 2001), 236; and see the Ugaritic text KTU 1.124.
38. See *NBD*, 627; Nelson, "Ideology," 348.
39. See, however, Pauline Deryn Guest, "Can Judges Survive without Sources? Challenging the Consensus," *JSOT* 78 (1998): 43–61; cf. Nelson, "Ideology."

core of the book (2:6–16:31).[40] This first introduction also plays a role in transitioning the reader from the book of Joshua by drawing on proleptic material from that book.[41]

In the light of these observations, it is important to note that Judges in its present form, which is the dominant object of the present study, is structured into three basic parts. The first is the introduction to the book as a whole, an introduction that focuses on tribal identity rather than charismatic leadership (1:1–2:5). The second is the complex of stories of the judges/deliverers that constitute the inner core of the book (3:7–16:31), which is introduced by the material in 2:6–3:6. This complex of stories is arranged into thirteen sections. Six of these sections constitute elongated accounts of major judge-deliverer figures structured according to a cyclical narrative pattern (Othniel: 3:7–11; Ehud: 3:12–30; Deborah–Barak: 4:1–5:31; Gideon: 6:1–8:32; Jepthah: 10:6–12:7; Samson: 13:1–16:31). These six longer accounts are matched by six short accounts, which do not employ the cyclical pattern but do appear in groups of increasing size: first one judge (Shamgar: 3:31), then two (Tola: 10:1–2; Jair: 10:3–5), and finally three (Ibzan: 12:8–10; Elon: 12:11–12; Abdon: 12:13–15) judges. Lastly, one account presents the anomalous royal figure of Abimelech (8:33–9:57), whose story mimics the cyclical pattern established in the accounts of the judge-deliverers.

The book ends with an epilogue (chs. 17–21) arranged into two distinct yet interconnected subsections (chs. 17–18 and 19–21), which bring closure to the book as a whole. The social context of these final stories, with their focus on tribe rather than on charismatic figure, echoes that of the first introduction of the book. But in this case the challenges faced by Israel are no longer from the nations who possessed (1:1–2:5) or surrounded (2:6–16:31) Canaan, but from their own compatriots who act like these nations. The book closes, therefore, not with a return to its opening state, but with a digression to a worse state, even as the narrator looks for a new type of leader who will guide the nation into purity of worship (see further below).

One can discern rhetorical movement as the book unfolds. There appears to be a general geographic movement from south to north, both in the first introduction of the prologue in 1:1–31 and in the overall flow of the accounts of the judge-deliverers in the central core accounts of 3:7–16:31. More important, however, are signs of regression throughout the book. Both prologues trace a progressive decline. The first traces this decline in the decreasing ability of first the southern and then especially the northern tribes to occupy their tribal territories allotted in the book of Joshua (ch. 1), ending with a judgment on the nation that leaves the Canaanite nations in possession of the land (2:1–5). The second prologue traces this decline through a cyclical pattern that becomes increasingly worse (2:6–19), ending again with a judgment on the nation accomplished by God's leaving Canaanite nations behind (2:20–3:6).

While the central core of the book of Judges (3:7–16:31) is dominated by the repeated cyclical pattern established in the second introduction of 2:6–19, it is important to notice that this cyclical pattern follows a downward spiral as the situation worsens, the people become less active in seeking Yahweh, and the

40. See Webb, *Judges*, 118–19; Wong, *Strategy*, 27–46, 143–90.

41. Polzin, *Moses and the Deuteronomist*, 146–48; K. Lawson Younger, "The Configuring of Judicial Preliminaries: Judges 1:1–2:5 and Its Dependence on the Book of Joshua," *JSOT* 68 (1995): 75–92; Wong, *Strategy*, 47–77.

behavior of the judge-deliverer becomes increasingly erratic,[42] especially from Gideon on.[43] Exum notes "the increasingly problematic character of the human protagonists, and ... the increasingly ambiguous role of the deity,"[44] while Wong[45] sees this progressive deterioration in five areas: (1) the judges' decreasing faith in Yahweh; (2) the increasing prominence of the judges' self-interest as motivation behind their actions; (3) decreasing participation of the tribes in successive military campaigns; (4) the judges' increasing harshness in dealing with internal dissent; (5) Yahweh's increasing frustration with his people as the cyclical pattern breaks down. Ultimately, leadership is eliminated from the account after Samson's demise, thus highlighting the ultimate failure of the charismatic judge-deliverer phase of Israel's history and prompting the need for the monarchy in an Israel that has assimilated to the Canaanites (chs. 17–21).

5. RHETORICAL PURPOSE

In recent years there have been two major contenders for the dominant theme of the book of Judges, the first being kingship (esp. Amit, Brettler, Patton, O'Connell, Schneider, Sweeney, Auld, Midden, Matthews) and the second, assimilation (esp. Guest, Block, Wong), a phenomenon borne out in my analysis of the literary structure of the book above. One needs to question, however, whether it is necessary to choose between these two themes.

Clearly, assimilation is articulated in the first introduction to the book (1:1–2:5) as the tribes progressively fail in their attempts to conquer their tribal territories. The stories of the judges rehearsed in the core of the book reveal that the people and ultimately the leaders of Israel are sucked into the religious and social vortex of the Canaanites, ultimately compromising their covenantal relationship with Yahweh and one another. The refrains in chs. 17–21 note that "everyone did as he saw fit," a phrase drawn from Deuteronomy 12:8, which addresses the issue of assimilation to Canaanite religious practices. The behavior of Micah, the Danites, the Benjamites, and all Israel throughout chs. 17–21 is indistinguishable from that of the Canaanites who were in the land.

While the theme of assimilation is undeniably important to the book of Judges, so also is the theme of leadership (see further detail in the Excursus "Royal Polemic in Judges," at 1:20). This theme is apparent from the outset of the book, especially when comparing it to the beginning of the book of Joshua.[46] Joshua 1 reveals a clear transition plan for leadership in Israel, one in which the mantle was transferred from Moses to Joshua. This same concern for transition in leadership reappears at the beginning of Judges, which again notes the death of the leader (Joshua) and then depicts an inquiry of Yahweh that explicitly asks about leadership in the new era. Past study has typically highlighted not only the dominant role played by the judge-deliverers in this book, but also the progressive decline in their success and character, ending

---

42. Cf. Don M. Hudson, "Living in a Land of Epithets: Anonymity in Judges 19–21," *JSOT* 62 (1994): 50–51.

43. Pauline Deryn Guest, "Dangerous Liaisons in the Book of Judges." *SJOT* 11 (1997): 254; P. J. van Midden, "A Hidden Message? Judges as Forward to the Books of Kings, in *Unless Some One Guide Me ... : Festschrift for Karel A. Deurloo* (ed. J. W. Dyk; Amsterdamse cahiers voor exegese van de Bijbel en zijn tradities 2; Maastricht: Shaker, 2001), 78–79.

44. Cheryl Exum, "The Centre Cannot Hold: Thematic and Textual Instabilities in Judges," *CBQ* 52 (1990): 410–29.

45. Wong, *Strategy*, 156–85.

46. Cf. Schneider, *Judges*, 2; Matthews, *Judges and Ruth*, 38; and also Polzin, *Moses and the Deuteronomist*, 152, who speaks of "Joshua's failure."

with their disappearance after the successively worse disappointments of Barak, Gideon, Jephthah, and especially Samson.

Scholars have highlighted both pro- and antimonarchical streams within Judges. The former (promonarchical) is usually linked to those places in the book that glorify the actions of the entire tribe of Judah or individuals within it, often in contrast to those of other tribes to the north, or that allude to places or actions associated with David or Saul. The latter (antimonarchical) stream is usually linked to the presentation of Canaanite kingship at various points in the book and especially to the Abimelech traditions at the center of the book. Serious questions have been asked about the legitimacy of the evidence for each of these monarchical streams. Some have questioned the promonarchical approach by noting that Davidic connections are not always positive, such as the Judahite failure in 1:19, the Judahite capitulation to the Philistines in ch. 15, the Bethlehemite Levite's apostasy in chs. 17–18, the Bethlehemite concubine's marital unfaithfulness in ch. 19, and the Judahite failure in the initial battle against Benjamin in ch. 20.[47] Others have questioned the antimonarchical approach by highlighting idealization of Judahite efforts (Judahite conquest, Othniel) and noting that Jotham's fable suggests that Gideon's refusal of kingship actually opened the way for the rise of the murderous Abimelech.[48]

It appears that one cannot completely eliminate the tension between these two approaches to the issue of leadership in the book of Judges. Buber explained this tension diachronically, linking the antimonarchical stream to an earlier stage in the development of the book.[49] Interestingly, similar tension has been discerned in the book of Samuel, an observation that has also prompted a diachronic solution to this tension; that is, there was a development in the Deuteronomic tradition.[50] But its presence in an adjacent book in which scholars have discerned Deuteronomic themes may also indicate that this tension may be a feature typical of the Deuteronomic historiographic tradition in general. The book of Deuteronomy does envision a role for the royal house within Israel's leadership after the death of Moses.[51] The way this vision is expressed in Deuteronomy 17:14–20 suggests that human kingship will arise due to human rather than divine mandate ("Let us set a king over us like all the nations around us," 17:14). Yahweh, however, clearly provides legislation for dealing with this political arrangement—legislation that demands covenantal obedience from the royal house.

In the same way the book of Judges sends a mixed message about kingship. On the one side it makes clear in Gideon's refusal (8:22–27) that Yahweh is to be king in Israel. But the depiction of the failure of both Abimelech's reign as well as the leadership of the judges and the resulting anarchic tribal conditions is designed to lead the reader to the realization that royal rule is necessary in Israel. This rule, however, is carefully circumscribed. While Yahweh remains king, a royal figure is needed who will ensure that people do not simply do as they see fit; that is, the king must be someone who will ensure that Israel worships Yahweh alone at the central shrine (see commentary on 17:6). Allusions in the book suggest that this

47. See, e.g., Block, *Judges, Ruth*, 485.

48. See, e.g., Amit, *The Book of Judges: Editing*, 96, 113.

49. Martin Buber, *Kingdom of God* (3rd ed.; London: Allen and Unwin, 1967).

50. Though see Gerald Eddie, *Kingship according to the Deuteronomistic History* (SBLDS 87; Atlanta: Scholars, 1986), 18–38.

51. See A. D. H. Mayes, "Deuteronomistic Royal Ideology in Judges 17–21," *BI* 9 (2001): 255–57.

kingship is linked to the tribe of Judah rather than to Saulide Benjamin or the northern tribes. But kingship is no carte blanche offered to the Davidides, in whose closet there are many skeletons and whose potential for failure is subtly admitted in Judges. This admission reminds the reader that kingship is no panacea for leadership in Israel, even as it affirms the rise of royal Judahite rule through the Davidic dynasty.

The dual refrain of chs. 17–21 ("in those days Israel had no king" and "everyone did as he saw fit") brings together the two dominant themes highlighted in past scholarship. The first phrase points to kingship, with all its promise and peril, while the second to assimilation, the protection from which was to be the primary responsibility of the royal house through maintenance of the central shrine in Jerusalem. In this way Judges sets up the book of Samuel, where two models of kingship will be depicted: the first kingship according to Israel's desire and the second kingship according to Yahweh's desire.[52]

6. THEOLOGICAL POTENTIAL

With its dual themes of assimilation and leadership, the book of Judges has great potential for the church today as both a redemptive-historical and redemptive-ethical document.[53] First, the book traces the story of the church's founding community, a story that began with Abraham, flowed through Moses and David, and reached its climax in Jesus the Christ and his community, who have received the promises (Heb 11:39–40) and on whom the fulfillment of the ages has come (1Co 10:11). Judges identifies, therefore, the conditions that prompted the royal messianic hope, that one on whom the Spirit would come and through whom God would rule the nation and nations perfectly and powerfully (Ps 2). In this way the book of Judges functions with the rest of the OT as a testimony "to make you wise for salvation through faith in Christ Jesus" (2Ti 3:15).

Second, the book also plays a role in shaping our lives as Christians, for as 2 Timothy 3:16 says, all Scripture "is useful for teaching, rebuking, correcting and training in righteousness, so that the [person] of God may be thoroughly equipped for every good work." Judges provides sometimes positive examples to emulate (Heb 11:32), but more often negative examples to avoid (1Co 10:6–11). In the stories of this book the church is instructed on issues related to godly leadership, human faithfulness, divine testing, pure worship, and proper revelation.

7. BIBLIOGRAPHY

Alonso Schökel, Luis, and Daniel Legters. "Narrative Art in Joshua–Judges–Samuel–Kings." Pages 255–78 in *Israel's Past in Present Research: Essays on Ancient Israelite Historiography*. Edited by V. Philips Long. Sources for Biblical and Theological Study 7. Winona Lake, Ind.: Eisenbrauns, 1999.

Amit, Yairah. *The Book of Judges: The Art of Editing*. Biblical Interpretation Series 38. Leiden/Boston: Brill, 1999.

———. "Hidden Polemic in the Conquest of Dan: Judges 17–18." *Vetus Testamentum* 40 (1990): 4–20.

Bach, Alice. "Rereading the Body Politic: Women and Violence in Judges 21." *Biblical Interpretation* 6 (1998): 1–19.

Bal, Mieke. *Death and Dissymmetry: The Politics of Coherence in the Book of Judges*. Chicago Studies in the History of Judaism. Chicago: University of Chicago Press, 1988.

---

52. Dragga, "In the Shadow of the Judges," 39–46.

53. Mark Boda, *Haggai/Zechariah* (NIVAC; Grand Rapids: Zondervan, 2004), 63–65; see also idem, *After God's Own Heart: The Gospel according to David* (Phillipsburg, N.J.: Presbyterian and Reformed, 2007).

Barré, Michael L. "The Meaning of *pršdn* in Judges 3:22." *Vetus Testamentum* 41 (1991): 1–11.

Bendor, S. *The Social Structure of Ancient Israel: The Institution of the Family (Beit ʾAb) from the Settlement to the End of the Monarchy.* Jerusalem Biblical Studies 7. Jerusalem: Simor, 1996.

Block, Daniel I. *Judges, Ruth.* New American Commentary 6. Nashville: Broadman & Holman, 1999.

Bluedorn, Wolfgang. *Yahweh versus Baalism: A Theological Reading of the Gideon–Abimelech Narrative.* Journal for the Study of the Old Testament Supplement Series 329. Sheffield: Sheffield Academic, 2001.

Boda, Mark J. *1–2 Chronicles.* Cornerstone Biblical Commentary 5a. Carol Stream, Ill.: Tyndale, 2010.

———. *After God's Own Heart: The Gospel According to David.* Phillipsburg, N.J.: Presbyterian and Reformed, 2007.

———. *Haggai/Zechariah.* NIV Application Commentary. Grand Rapids: Zondervan, 2004.

———. "Recycling Heaven's Words: Receiving and Retrieving Divine Revelation in the Historiography of Judges." In *Prophets and Prophecy in Ancient Israelite Historiography.* Edited by Mark J. Boda and Lissa Wray Berl. Winona Lake, Ind.: Eisenbrauns, forthcoming.

———. *A Severe Mercy: Sin and Its Remedy in the Old Testament.* Winona Lake, Ind.: Eisenbrauns, 2009.

Bohmbach, Karla G. "Conventions/Contraventions: The Meanings of Public and Private for the Judges 19 Concubine." *Journal for the Study of the Old Testament* 83 (1999): 83–98.

Boling, Robert G. *Judges.* Anchor Bible 6a. Garden City, N.Y.: Doubleday, 1975.

Bowman, Richard G. "Narrative Criticism of Judges: Human Purpose in Conflict with Divine Presence." Pages 17–44 in *Judges and Method.* Edited by Gale A. Yee. Minneapolis: Fortress, 1995.

Brenner, Athalya. "A Triangle and a Rhombus in Narrative Structure: A Proposed Integrative Reading of Judges 4 and 5." *Vetus Testamentum* 40 (1990): 129–38.

Brettler, Marc Z. *The Book of Judges.* Old Testament Readings; London/New York: Routledge, 2002.

———. "The Book of Judges: Literature as Politics." *Journal of Biblical Literature* 108 (1989): 395–418.

Brooks, Simcha Shalom. "Was There a Concubine at Gibeah?" *Bulletin of the Anglo-Israel Archaeological Society* 15 (1996): 31–40.

Chisholm, Robert B. "The Role of Women in the Rhetorical Strategy of the Book of Judges." Pages 34–49 in *Integrity of Heart, Skillfulness of Hands: Biblical and Leadership Studies in Honor of Donald K. Campbell.* Edited by Charles H. Dyer and Roy B. Zuck. Grand Rapids: Baker, 1994.

Craigie, Peter C. "Reconsideration of Shamgar Ben Anath (Judg 3:31 and 5:6)." *Journal of Biblical Literature* 91 (1972): 239–40.

Crenshaw, James L. *Samson: A Secret Betrayed, A Vow Ignored.* Atlanta: John Knox, 1978.

Dumbrell, William J. "'In those days there was no king in Israel, every man did what was right in his own eyes': The Purpose of the Book of Judges Reconsidered." *Journal for the Study of the Old Testament* 25 (1983): 23–33.

Emmrich, Martin. "The Symbolism of the Lion and the Bees: Another Ironic Twist in the Samson Cycle." *Journal of the Evangelical Theological Society* 44 (2001): 67–74.

Exum, J. Cheryl. "Aspects of Symmetry and Balance in the Samson Saga." *Journal for the Study of the Old Testament* 19 (1981): 3–29.

———. "The Centre Cannot Hold: Thematic and Textual Instabilities in Judges." *Catholic Biblical Quarterly* 52 (1990): 410–29.

———. "Feminist Criticism: Whose Interests are Being Served?" Pages 65–90 in *Judges and Method.* Edited by Gale A. Yee. Minneapolis: Fortress, 1995.

———. *Fragmented Women: Feminist (Sub)versions of Biblical Narratives.* Sheffield/Philadelphia: JSOT/Trinity International, 1993.

Exum, J. Cheryl, and J. William Whedbee. "Isaac, Samson, and Saul: Reflections on the Comic and Tragic Visions." Pages 272–308 in *Beyond Form Criticism: Essays in Old Testament Literary Criticism.* Edited by Paul R. House. Sources for Biblical and Theological Study Old Testament 2. Winona Lake, Ind: Eisenbrauns, 1992.

Eynikel, Erik. "Judges 19–21, An 'Appendix': Rape, Murder, War and Abduction." *Communio Viatorum* 47 (2005): 101–15.

Fensham, Frank Charles. "Literary Observations on Historical Narratives in Sections of Judges." Pages 77–87 in *Storia e tradizioni di Israele: scrittin in honore di J Alberto Soggin.* Edited by Daniele Garrone and Felice Israel. Brescia: Paideia, 1991.

Galpaz-Feller, Pnina. "'Let My Soul Die with the Philistines' (Judges 16:30)." *Journal for the Study of the Old Testament* 30 (2006): 315–25.

———. *Samson the Hero and the Man: The Story of Samson (Judges 13–16)*. Bern/New York: P. Lang, 2006.

Gray, John. "Israel in the Song of Deborah." Pages 421–55 in *Ascribe to the Lord: Biblical and Other Studies in Memory of Peter C. Craigie*. Edited by Lyle M. Eslinger and J. Glen Taylor. Sheffield: JSOT, 1988.

———. *Joshua, Judges, Ruth*. New Century Bible Commentary. Grand Rapids: Eerdmans, 1986.

Guest, Pauline Deryn. "Dangerous Liaisons in the Book of Judges." *Scandinavian Journal of the Old Testament* 11 (1997): 241–69.

Handy, Lowell K. "Uneasy Laughter: Ehud and Eglon as Ethnic Humor." *Scandinavian Journal of the Old Testament* 6 (1992): 233–46.

Hobbs, T. Raymond. "Hospitality in the First Testament and the 'Teleological Fallacy.'" *Journal for the Study of the Old Testament* 95 (2001): 3–30.

Hudson, Don Michael. "Living in a Land of Epithets: Anonymity in Judges 19–21." *Journal for the Study of the Old Testament* 62 (1994): 49–66.

Ishida, Tomoo. "The Structure and Historical Implications of the Lists of Pre-Israelite Nations." *Biblica* 60 (1979): 461–90.

Janzen, David. "Why the Deuteronomist Told About the Sacrifice of Jephthah's Daughter." *Journal for the Study of the Old Testament* 29 (2005): 339–57.

Jones-Warsaw, Koala. "Toward a Womanist Hermeneutic." *Journal of the Interdenominational Theological Center* 22 (1994): 18–35.

Kaminsky, Joel S. *Corporate Responsibility in the Hebrew Bible*. Journal for the Study of the Old Testament Supplement Series 196. Sheffield: Sheffield Academic, 1995.

Kim, Jichan. *The Structure of the Samson Cycle*. Kampen: Kok Pharos, 1993.

Kirkpatrick, Shane. "Questions of Honor in the Book of Judges." *Koinonia* 10 (1998): 19–40.

Klein, Lillian R. "Structure, Irony and Meaning in the Book of Judges." Pages 83–90 in *Proceedings of the 10th World Congress of Jewish Studies, Division A. Jerusalem*. Jerusalem: Magnes, 1990.

———. *The Triumph of Irony in the Book of Judges*. Bible and Literature Series 14. Decatur, Ga.: Almond, 1988.

Kooij, Arie van der. "On Male and Female Views in Judges 4 and 5." Pages 135–52 in *On Reading Prophetic Texts: Gender-specific and Related Studies in Memory of Fokkelien van Dijk-Hemmes*. Edited by Bob Becking and Meindert Dijkstra. BIS 18. Leiden: Brill, 1996.

Lasine, S. "Guest and Host in Judges 19: Lot's Hospitality in an Inverted World." *Journal for the Study of the Old Testament* 29 (1984): 37–59.

Latvus, Kari. *Anger and Ideology: The Anger of God in Joshua and Judges in Relation to Deuteronomy and the Priestly Writings*. Journal for the Study of the Old Testament Supplement Series 279. Sheffield: Sheffield Academic, 1998.

Lindars, Barnabas. *Judges 1–5: A New Translation and Commentary*. Edinburgh: T&T Clark, 1995.

Malamat, A. "The Danite Migration and the Pan-Israelite Exodus-Conquest: A Biblical Narrative Pattern." *Biblica* 51 (1970): 1–16.

Matthews, Victor H. "Freedom and Entrapment in the Samson Narrative: A Literary Analysis." *Perspectives in Religious Studies* 16 (1989): 245–57.

———. "Hospitality and Hostility in Genesis 19 and Judges 19." *Biblical Theology Bulletin* 22 (1992): 3–11.

———. *Judges and Ruth*. New Cambridge Bible Commentary. Cambridge: Cambridge University Press, 2004.

McCann, J. Clinton. *Judges*. Interpretation. Louisville, Ky.: Westminster/John Knox, 2002.

Mehlman, Israel. "Jephthah." *Jewish Bible Quarterly* 23 (1995): 73–78.

Miller, Geoffrey P. "Verbal Feud in the Hebrew Bible." *Journal of Near Eastern Studies* 55 (1996): 105–17.

Mobley, Gregory. *Samson and the Liminal Hero in the Ancient Near East*. Library of Hebrew Bible/Old Testament Studies 453. New York: T&T Clark, 2006.

Mueller, E. Aydeet. *The Micah Story: A Morality Tale in the Book of Judges*. Studies in Biblical Literature 34. New York: Peter Lang, 2001.

Naʾaman, Nadav. "The Danite Campaign Northward (Judges XVII–XVIII) and the Migration of the Phocaeans to Massalia (Strabo IV 1,4)." *Vetus Testamentum* 55 (2005): 47–60.

Nelson, Richard D. "Ideology, Geography, and the List of Minor Judges." *Journal for the Study of the Old Testament* 31 (2007): 347–64.

Niditch, Susan. *Judges: A Commentary.* Old Testament Library. Louisville, Ky.: Westminster John Knox, 2008.

———. *The Symbolic Vision in Biblical Tradition.* Chico, Calif.: Scholars, 1983.

Noth, Martin. *Überlieferungsgeschichtliche Studien.* Halle: Max Niemeyer, 1943.

O'Connell, Robert H. *The Rhetoric of the Book of Judges.* Vetus Testamentum Supplements 63. Leiden: Brill, 1996.

Ogden, Graham S. "Poetry, Prose, and Their Relationship: Some Reflections Based on Judges 4 and 5." Pages 111–30 in *Discourse Perspectives on Hebrew Poetry in the Scriptures.* Edited by Ernst R. Wendland. United Bible Societies Monograph Series 7. New York: United Bible Societies, 1994.

Patton, Corrine L. "From Heroic Individual to Nameless Victim: Women in the Social World of the Judges." Pages 33–46 in *Biblical and Humane: A Festschrift for John F. Priest.* Edited by Linda Bennett Elder, David L. Barr, and Elizabeth Struthers Malbon. Scholars Press Homage Series 20. Atlanta: Scholars, 1996.

Perdue, Leo G., ed. *Families in Ancient Israel.* The Family, Religion, and Culture. Louisville, Ky.: Westminster John Knox, 1997.

Peterson, Brian. "Judges: A Polemic for Davidic Kingship?—An Inductive Approach." Unpublished paper.

Polzin, Robert. *Moses and the Deuteronomist.* A Literary Study of the Deuteronomic History 1. New York: Seabury, 1980.

Pressler, Carolyn. *Joshua, Judges, and Ruth.* Westminster Bible Companion. Louisville, Ky.: Westminster John Knox, 2002.

Provan, Iain, V. Philips Long, and Tremper Longman III. *A Biblical History of Israel.* Louisville, Ky.: Westminster John Knox, 2003.

Revell, E. J. "The Battle with Benjamin (Judges XX 29–48) and Hebrew Narrative Techniques." *Vetus Testamentum* 35 (1985): 417–33.

Römer, Thomas C. "Why Would the Deuteronomists Tell about the Sacrifice of Jephthah's Daughter?" *Journal for the Study of the Old Testament* 77 (1998): 27–38.

Satterthwaite, Philip E. "Narrative Artistry in the Composition of Judges XX 29ff." *Vetus Testamentum* 42 (1992): 80–89.

———. "'No King in Israel': Narrative Criticism and Judges 17–21." *Tyndale Bulletin* 44 (1993): 75–88.

Schloen, J. David. "Caravans, Kenites, and *Casus belli*: Enmity and Alliance in the Song of Deborah." *Catholic Biblical Quarterly* 55 (1993): 18–38.

Schneider, Tammi J. *Judges.* Berit Olam. Collegeville, Minn: Liturgical, 2000.

Sjöberg, Mikael. *Wrestling with Textual Violence: The Jephthah Narrative in Antiquity and Modernity.* The Bible in the Modern World 4. Sheffield: Sheffield Phoenix, 2006.

Soggin, J. Alberto. *Judges: A Commentary.* Old Testament Library. Philadelphia: Westminster, 1981.

Spronk, Klaas. "Deborah, a Prophetess: The Meaning and Background of Judges 4:4–5." Pages 232–42 in *Elusive Prophet: The Prophet as a Historical Person, Literary Character and Anonymous Artist.* Edited by Johannes C. De Moor. Leiden: Brill, 2001.

———. "A Story to Weep About: Some Remarks on Judges 2:1–5 and Its Context." Pages 87–94 in *Unless Some One Guide Me … : Festschrift for Karel A. Deurloo.* Edited by J. W. Dyk. Amsterdamse cahiers voor exegese van de Bijbel en zijn tradities 2. Maastricht: Shaker, 2001.

Steinberg, Naomi. "Social Scientific Criticism: Judges 9 and Issues of Kinship." Pages 45–64 in *Judges and Method.* Edited by Gale A. Yee. Minneapolis: Fortress, 1995.

Stone, Kenneth Alan. "Gender and Homosexuality in Judges 19: Subject-Honor, Object-Shame?" *Journal for the Study of the Old Testament* 67 (1995): 87–107.

Sweeney, Marvin A. "Davidic Polemics in the Book of Judges." *Vetus Testamentum* 47 (1997): 517–29.

Szpek, Heidi M. "Achsah's Story: A Metaphor for Societal Transition." *Andrews University Seminary Studies* 40 (2002): 245–56.

Talmon, S. "The Presentation of Synchroneity and Simultaneity in Biblical Narrative." *Scripta Hierosolymitana* 27 (1978): 9–26.

Tanner, J. Paul. "The Gideon Narrative as the Focal Point of Judges." *Bibliotheca Sacra* 149 (1992): 146–61.

Tatu, Silviu. "Jotham's Fable and the Crux Interpretum in Judges IX." *Vetus Testamentum* 56 (2006): 105–24.

Webb, Barry G. *The Book of the Judges: An Integrated Reading.* Journal for the Study of the Old Testament Supplement Series 46. Sheffield: JSOT, 1987.

Weinfeld, Moshe. "Judges 1.1–2.5: The Conquest under the Leadership of the House of Judah." Pages 388–400 in *Understanding Poets and Prophets: Essays in Honour of George Wishart Anderson.* Edited by George W. Anderson and A. Graeme Auld. Journal for the Study of the Old Testament Supplement Series 152. Sheffield: JSOT, 1993.

Wong, Gregory T. K. *Compositional Strategy of the Book of Judges: An Inductive, Rhetorical Study.* Vetus Testamentum Supplements 111. Leiden/Boston: Brill, 2006.

———. "Ehud and Joab: Separated at Birth?" *Vetus Testamentum* 56 (2006): 399–412.

Yadin, Azzan. "Samson's *ḥîdâ*." *Vetus Testamentum* 52 (2002): 407–26.

Younger, K. Lawson. "The Configuring of Judicial Preliminaries: Judges 1:1–2:5 and Its Dependence on the Book of Joshua." *Journal for the Study of the Old Testament* 68 (1995): 75–92.

———. "Judges 1 in its Near Eastern Literary Context." Pages 207–27 in *Faith, Tradition, and History: Old Testament Historiography in Its Near Eastern Context.* Edited by A. R. Millard, James Karl Hoffmeier, and David W. Baker. Winona Lake, Ind.: Eisenbrauns, 1994.

8. OUTLINE

    a. The Levite, His Concubine, Their Journeys to Bethlehem, and Hospitality of the Concubine's Father (19:1b–10a)

    b. The Levite, His Concubine, and Their Journey to Gibeah (19:10b–15)

    c. An Old Man from Ephraim Takes In the Levite and Concubine (19:16–21)

    d. The Evil of the Men of Gibeah (19:22–26)

    e. The Levite Takes His Dead Concubine Home and Alerts the Rest of Israel of the Evil Act of Gibeah (19:27–30)

3. Israel's Punishment of Gibeah and Benjamin (20:1–48)

    a. The Gathering of Israel at Mizpah to Investigate the Matter (20:1–11)

    b. Israel's Proposal to Benjamin Rebuffed (20:12–13)

    c. Israel and Benjamin Muster Their Troops (20:14–17)

    d. Civil War: First Battle (20:18–21)

    e. Civil War: Second Battle (20:22–25)

    f. Civil War: Third Battle (20:26–48)

4. Wives for the Benjamites (21:1–24)

    a. Introductory Inquiry (21:1–5)

    b. Providing Wives from Jabesh-Gilead for Four Hundred Benjamites (21:6–14)

    c. Providing Wives from Shiloh for the Remaining Two Hundred Benjamites (21:15–23a)

    d. Conclusion (21:23b–24)

5. Refrain (21:25)

Text and Exposition

I. THE TRIBES OF ISRAEL—PART ONE (1:1–2:5)

OVERVIEW

Judges 1:1–2:5 represents the first of two introductions at the outset of the book of Judges. While the second introduction (2:6–3:6) orients the reader to the cyclical accounts of the judge-deliverer figures, which constitute the core of the book (3:7–16:31), this first introduction transitions the reader from the book of Joshua (Polzin, 146–48) by drawing on proleptic material from that book (Younger, "Configuring"; Wong, *Strategy*, 47–77) and prepares the reader for both the central core of 2:6–16:31 and the grand finale of the book in chs. 17–21 (see Webb, 118–19; Schneider, 1; Wong, *Strategy*, 27–46, 143–90). Both this introduction (1:1–2:5) and the central core (2:6–16:31) move geographically from south to north and progressively from success to failure.

In both this introduction (1:1–2:5) and the conclusion to the book (chs. 17–21), tribal identity is emphasized. Not surprisingly, the two tribes whose behavior is attacked in chs. 17–21—Benjamin and Dan—are the two identified as the greatest failures in the south and north in the anticonquest of 1:1–31. One particular tribe, Judah, is identified as the one that will lead the other tribes in battle (Amit, *Judges*, 146–47). One finds in both 1:1–2:5 and chs. 17–21 the same question in the nation's inquiry of Yahweh regarding battle:

> The Israelites asked [*šʾl*] the Lord, "Who [*mî*] will be the first [*battᵉḥillâ*] to go up [*ʿlh*] and fight [*lḥm*, Niphal] for us [*lānû*] against the Canaanites?" (1:1)

> The Israelites went up to Bethel and inquired [*šʾl*] of God. They said, "Who [*mî*] of us [*lānû*] shall go

[*ʿlh*] first [*battᵉḥillâ*] to fight [*milḥāmâ*] against the Benjamites?" (20:18a)

And the answer in both cases is Judah.

> The Lord answered [*ʾmr*], "Judah is to go; I have given the land into their hands." (1:2)

> The Lord replied [*ʾmr*], "Judah shall go first." (20:18b)

By highlighting the tribe of Judah, this first introduction prepares the way for the fundamental concern of the book of Judges as a whole, that is, the ultimate failure of the generation that followed Joshua and the leadership of their judges. The problem lies with the people's doing what is right in their own eyes because of the lack of royal leadership in the land. The proposed solution to the problem of the Canaanites and the temptation of their false worship is subtly linked to a royal hope. Certainly the second introduction and its related section will introduce an early solution to Israel's dilemma, but the progressive failure of people and leadership during the generations after Joshua will only highlight the need for divinely anointed and appointed royal leadership.

While the account in ch. 1 does echo the style of royal military annals in the ancient Near East (Younger, "Judges 1 in its Near Eastern Literary Context"; cf. idem, *Ancient Conquest Accounts: A Study in Ancient Near Eastern and Biblical History Writing* [JSOTSup 98; Sheffield: Sheffield Academic, 1990], 198), one should not overlook two interlinked trajectories in Judges 1, the first in terms of geography as the description moves from south to north and the second in terms of conquest as the description moves from initial Judahite success to increasing northern failure to possess the land (Amit, *Judges*, 150–51; Wong, *Strategy*, 150; cf. Younger, "Judges 1 in its Near Eastern Literary Context"; idem, "Configuring"). This arrangement is strikingly similar to the geographic progress of the central section of the book (2:6–16:31), revealing the role of this chapter in preparing the way for that part of the book as well (Dumbrell, 25; Brettler, *Judges*, 110; Wong, *Strategy*, 154) by subtly indicting the northern tribes for the lack of conquest.

The structure of 1:1–2:5 (note use of the verb ʿlh, "go up," at the key junctures 1:4, 22; 2:1; cf. Webb, 103; O'Connell, 12, n. 2; McCann, 28) suggests that Judah, Simeon, and Benjamin constitute the southern tribes and that the Joseph tribes (Manasseh, Ephraim), Zebulun, Asher, Naphtali, and Dan constitute the northern tribes, called Israel in v.28. Judges 1:3–21 displays the structure of successful conquest by the dominant tribe (Judah, vv.3–19a), with whom Yahweh presences himself (v.19a). This success is followed, however, by ultimate failure by that dominant tribe (v.19b) and complete failure by another tribe (Benjamin, v.21; cf. Webb, 92).

With v.22 the account shifts to the successful conquest by the dominant northern tribes (Joseph), with whom Yahweh presences himself, followed by the ultimate failure of those dominant tribes (vv.27–29) and complete failure by the other tribes (vv.30–36). One should not miss how ch. 1 gives "the impression of a process by which the people are gradually swept up into a situation of coexistence with the inhabitants of the land" (Amit, *Judges*, 151). This process, which will restrict Israel largely to the central highlands, not only "explains much of the nation's subsequent history," but it also "fits the archaeological record" (Matthews, *Judges and Ruth*, 46). This first introduction concludes with the indictment by the "angel of the LORD" for Israel's failure to complete the conquest (2:1–5).

A. Inquiring of Yahweh (1:1–3)

> ¹After the death of Joshua, the Israelites asked the LORD, "Who will be the first to go up and fight for us against the Canaanites?"
> ²The LORD answered, "Judah is to go; I have given the land into their hands."
> ³Then the men of Judah said to the Simeonites their brothers, "Come up with us into the territory allotted to us, to fight against the Canaanites. We in turn will go with you into yours." So the Simeonites went with them.

COMMENTARY

1–2 The chapter begins by noting the death of the great leader of the people in conquering the land. This opening statement suggests that a leadership crisis lies at the heart of this book, especially when read in the light of Joshua 1, where, after the death of the great leader (Moses), a new leader was already in place (Joshua; cf. Schneider, 2; Matthews, *Judges and Ruth*, 28).

While passages such as Joshua 21:43–45 emphasize the successes in the conquest and the fulfillment of God's promises to Israel, passages such as Joshua 13 (see v.1) suggest that the conquest was far from complete by the end of Joshua's life. It is interesting how these two perspectives are intertwined in Joshua 23:1–5, which claims that Yahweh "had given Israel rest from all their enemies around them" when Joshua was "old and well advanced in years" (v.1), even as Joshua admits that there are remaining nations (v.4) that "the LORD your God himself will drive ... out of your way. He will push them out before you, and you will take possession of their land, as the LORD your God promised you" (v.5).

The narrator merely informs the reader that the Israelites made inquiry (*š'l*) of Yahweh without specifying through what means, whether priest (Urim and Thummim, cf. Nu 27:21) or prophet (inquiry of Yahweh, cf. Jer 47:1–7; Schneider, 4). The tribes are searching for direction for their first military campaign after the death of Joshua. With the loss of their military leader, it appears they are looking for leadership; however, this leadership is linked not to an individual, but rather to an entire tribe — that of Judah. This tribe will be the answer to Israel's inquiry again at the end of the book of Judges in their battle against Gibeah and Benjamin (Jdg 20:18; cf. Wong, *Strategy*, 32–35). There, however, Judah will suffer defeat, typical of those times, but that also serves as a reminder of Judah's vulnerability.

3 What is interesting is that Judah does not immediately respond to the divine instruction. Instead, Judah invites Simeon to join in on the expedition, pledging support for Simeon's future campaign (see the background for natural affinity of these two full brothers in Ge 29:33, 35; cf. Block, 88). Judah does follow through on his promise to Simeon (see v.17); however, Judah's deal with Simeon suggests compromise on Judah's part (see Klein, *The Triumph of Irony*, 23; Matthews, *Judges and Ruth*, 38). Additionally, it presages the ultimate fate of Simeon, spelling disaster for Simeon as a tribe. Over time Simeon, both the tribe and its territory, would be amalgamated into the tribe of Judah, a reality presaged in the absence of Simeon's name in the lists of tribes in Deuteronomy 33 and Judges 5 and the relatively small size of Simeon compared to the other tribes in Numbers 26. This development is also presaged by the prophecy of Simeon's distribution (along with Levi) among the rest of the tribes in Genesis 49:5–7 (cf. Block, 88). The statement in Joshua 19:1 that Simeon's "inheritance lay within the territory of Judah" also reflects an awareness of its ultimate amalgamation into Judah.

NOTES

1 לְהִלָּחֶם ... יַעֲלֶה (*yaʿaleh ... lᵉhillāḥem*, "go up and fight"). The combination here of "go up" (עלה, *ʿlh*) and "fight" (לחם, *lḥm*) is one typical of military maneuvers in the OT (Dt 1:41–42; Jos 10:5, 36; 19:47; Jdg 12:3; 1Ki 12:24; 20:1; 2Ki 3:21; 12:18; 16:5; 2Ch 11:4; 35:20; Isa 7:1).

הַכְּנַעֲנִי (*hakkᵉnaʿanî*, "Canaanites"). Reference to Canaan/Canaanites can be found in ancient texts in the latter half of the second millennium BC (from Mari: *ANET*, 557; Ugarit: KTU 4.96.7; Tell el-Amarna:

EA 36.15; 148.46; 109.46; 131.61; 137.76; Egypt: *ANET*, 246, 378; cf. *ABD*, 1:829). While the meaning of the term "Canaan" remains obscure, biblical descriptions of its boundaries (Nu 34; Eze 47–48) line up with ancient descriptions (Niditch, *Judges*, 38).

2 נָתַתִּי (*nātattî*, "I have given"). This verb could be translated in English in the present: "I am giving," reflecting the performative use of the perfect ("a performative action is an action that occurs by means of speaking" [*BHRG* 19.2]).

3 עֲלֵה ... וְנִלָּחֲמָה (*ʿᵃlēh* ... *wᵉnillāhᵃmâ*, "Come up ... to fight"). The combination of an imperative followed by *waw* plus cohortative identifies the second verb as the purpose of the first (*BHRG*, 21.5).

B. Southern Tribes: Judah with Simeon, Benjamin (1:4–21)

OVERVIEW

That Judah constitutes the future hope of the nation is clear not only from the divine answer to their inquiry in vv.1–2, but also in the fact that Judah dominates the account both in quantity (length of account) and quality (success of exploits). The narrator is careful to mention Judah's successful capture of Jerusalem and defeat of various territories in the hill country, Negev, and lowlands as well as the fact that Yahweh was with Judah (v.19a). Simeon also experiences success because Judah accompanies that tribe in battle (v.17). The only indication of failure in the Judah account is found near its close with the notation of their lack of success in driving out the inhabitants of the valley (v.19b). Although leader of the nation, Judah is reminded it is not invincible. The account of Judah is followed immediately by the complete failure of Benjamin to drive out the Jebusites from Jerusalem (v.21), a city easily defeated by Judah in v.8. This notation initiates the negative portrayal of Benjamin in the book of Judges, a portrayal directed at the royal house of Saul. This negative evaluation will reach its zenith in chs. 19–21.

1. Judah's Victory at Bezek (1:4–7)

OVERVIEW

Here the narrator follows a narrative pattern that recurs throughout the Former Prophets (1Sa 4:10; 4:17; 13:1; 2Sa 2:17; 18:6–7). This pattern briefly describes the battle, its outcome, and its casualties (v.4), followed by an account of the death of person(s) of importance on the defeated side (vv.5–7; cf. Webb, 85).

> **4**When Judah attacked, the LORD gave the Canaanites and Perizzites into their hands and they struck down ten thousand men at Bezek. **5**It was there that they found Adoni-

Bezek and fought against him, putting to rout the Canaanites and Perizzites. ⁶Adoni-Bezek fled, but they chased him and caught him, and cut off his thumbs and big toes.

⁷Then Adoni-Bezek said, "Seventy kings with their thumbs and big toes cut off have picked up scraps under my table. Now God has paid me back for what I did to them." They brought him to Jerusalem, and he died there.

COMMENTARY

4a Whereas in 1:1–3 the term "Canaanites" seems to be a general term for all the inhabitants of the land promised to Abraham, in v.4 it is accompanied by a second term, "Perizzites," which suggests that it refers to a particular group within the land. Possibly "Canaanites" refers to the dominant people group (see Note on 1:1).

The term "Perizzites" occurs regularly in various lists of the pre-Israelite inhabitants of the Promised Land (e.g., Ge 15:20; 34:20; Ex 3:8; 33:2; Jos 3:10; 7:1; 12:8; Jdg 3:5; 1Ki 9:20; Ezr 9:1; Ne 9:8). On two other occasions in the OT outside of Judges 1:4–5 (Ge 13:7; 34:30), "Canaanites" and "Perizzites" appear in a two-name list of the inhabitants of the land. It is possible that "Perizzite" is derived from the term *pᵉrizzî* ("rural country"), so that the term "Canaanites" indicates those in fortified urban space, while "Perizzites," those in the rural areas (unwalled villages, farms). But it may be that the distinction is along ethnic lines and that, in the light of Genesis 15:19–21; Joshua 11:3; 17:15, they were located in the territory between Judah and Ephraim (see *ABD*, 5:231, and Ishida).

4b–5 The precise location of Bezek remains unknown, though according to 1 Samuel 11:8 Saul counts his troops at Bezek after mustering them using a dismembered yoke of oxen—a fact that associates Saulide kingship with this city defeated by Judahites

(Schneider, 6; similarly Gibeah and Jabesh-Gilead in chs. 19–21). Here is the first sign of a polemic that pits Judah-David against Benjamin-Saul. Verse 4 appears to be a summary of the entire battle, with v.5 then introducing the key character, "Adoni-Bezek," which may be a name or, more likely, a position: "lord of Bezek." He should not be confused with Adoni-Zedek, the king of Jerusalem in Joshua 10 (contra Weinfeld, 391).

6–7 Adoni-Bezek is clearly leading this combined force of Canaanites and Perizzites and, once defeated, flees for his life (v.6a). The Judahites who capture him brutally cut off his thumbs and big toes, an action that is interpreted by the voice of Adoni-Bezek himself as retribution for his regular violent treatment of his defeated foes (v.7). His wounds prove fatal according to v.7b, but not before he is paraded before the inhabitants of Jerusalem—a form of psychological warfare used throughout the ancient Near East (cf. Boling, 55). The violence connected to Adoni-Bezek serves as an appropriate "thematic prelude to the book as a whole" with its gory depictions of violence (R. Alter, *The World of Biblical Literature* [London: Basic, 1992], 97), but also with its negative depiction of Canaanite kingship (Webb, 119) as well as Abimelech's royal pretensions (see comment on 9:6; cf. Wong, *Strategy*, 204–6). Thus a certain kind of kingship is disqualified as a leadership model in Israel.

NOTES

5 אֲדֹנִי בֶזֶק (*ʾadōnî bezeq*, "Adoni-Bezek"). The MT of Joshua 10 calls the king of Jerusalem who orga-nized a coalition against Gibeon after its treaty with Israel אֲדֹנִי־צֶדֶק (*ʾadōnî-ṣedeq*), while the LXX calls him Αδωνιβεζεκ (*Adōnibezek*). The latter is most likely a scribal accommodation to this story in Judges 1.

6 בְּהֹנוֹת יָדָיו וְרַגְלָיו (*bᵉhōnôt yādāyw wᵉraglāyw*, "his thumbs and big toes"). The Hebrew reads here "thumbs/big toes of his hands and his feet." Hebrew uses the same word to describe the opposable digit on the hand and foot.

2. Judah's Victory at Jerusalem (1:8)

> ⁸The men of Judah attacked Jerusalem also and took it. They put the city to the sword and set it on fire.

COMMENTARY

8 In a short note with little detail (v.8), the narrator relates Judah's military success at Jerusalem, where they not only take the city but also practice *ḥerem* (putting the city to the sword; see Jos 6) and set it on fire. Interestingly, in Joshua 10 after Israel's successful battle against a coalition that included Jerusalem, Jerusalem is the one city of the coalition for which no attack and destruction are recorded (Schneider, 8). Furthermore, Joshua 15:63 explicitly relates the failure of Judah to conquer Jerusalem. This failure is clearly rectified in Judges 1:8.

Jerusalem lay at the boundary between the allotted tribal territories of Judah (Jos 15:8) and Benjamin (18:28). While Judah has great success against Jerusalem here in v.8, at the end of this narrative section on the southern tribes (v.21) Benjamin will prove unable to dislodge the Jebusites in Jerusalem (see further below; cf. Weinfeld, 392).

3. Judah's Battles against the Canaanites in the Hill Country, Negev, and Lowland (1:9–20)

> ⁹After that, the men of Judah went down to fight against the Canaanites living in the hill country, the Negev and the western foothills. ¹⁰They advanced against the Canaanites living in Hebron (formerly called Kiriath Arba) and defeated Sheshai, Ahiman and Talmai.
> ¹¹From there they advanced against the people living in Debir (formerly called Kiriath Sepher). ¹²And Caleb said, "I will give my daughter Acsah in marriage to the man who attacks and captures Kiriath Sepher." ¹³Othniel son of Kenaz, Caleb's younger brother, took it; so Caleb gave his daughter Acsah to him in marriage.

¹⁴One day when she came to Othniel, she urged him to ask her father for a field. When she got off her donkey, Caleb asked her, "What can I do for you?"

¹⁵She replied, "Do me a special favor. Since you have given me land in the Negev, give me also springs of water." Then Caleb gave her the upper and lower springs.

¹⁶The descendants of Moses' father-in-law, the Kenite, went up from the City of Palms with the men of Judah to live among the people of the Desert of Judah in the Negev near Arad.

¹⁷Then the men of Judah went with the Simeonites their brothers and attacked the Canaanites living in Zephath, and they totally destroyed the city. Therefore it was called Hormah. ¹⁸The men of Judah also took Gaza, Ashkelon and Ekron — each city with its territory.

¹⁹The LORD was with the men of Judah. They took possession of the hill country, but they were unable to drive the people from the plains, because they had iron chariots. ²⁰As Moses had promised, Hebron was given to Caleb, who drove from it the three sons of Anak.

COMMENTARY

9 After the initial phase at Bezek and Jerusalem, the narrator now moves to the remainder of Judah's exploits, providing here an overview of the rest of the account of Judah by dividing the account into three phases: the hill country (vv. 10–15, Hebron, Debir), the Negev (vv. 16–17, Arad, Zephath/Hormah), and the western foothills (v. 18, Gaza, Ashkelon, Ekron).

10 The first of Judah's successes in the "hill country" was at Hebron. The book of Joshua depicts Joshua and all Israel as fighting against Hebron (and Debir) and its Anakim inhabitants and practicing *herem* (Jos 10:36–37; 11:21–22). The account of the defeat of Hebron and Debir found here in Judges 1:10–15, 20 is drawn from the book of Joshua as well (Jos 15:13–19; cf. 14:13–15; see Weinfeld, 393–94; Szpek, 246–47, for contrasts between the two narratives and their respective contexts). In Judges, however, these events are explicitly linked to the period after the death of Joshua. Although it

is clear in Judges 1 (see vv. 12, 20) that Caleb was responsible for these battles in the "hill country," these accounts are depicted as victories for Caleb's tribe, Judah (cf. Jdg 1:10–11 with Jos 15:14–15; notice how Jdg 1:10, 20 splits up the information provided in Jos 15:14).

Hebron was located about eighteen miles due west of the midpoint of the Dead Sea. It lay about nineteen miles south-southeast of Jerusalem along the Judean mountain ridge and twenty-three miles northeast of Beersheba (*ABD*, 3:107), thus at about the halfway point between Jerusalem (far north of Judah) and Beersheba (far south of Judah). Hebron's former name, Kiriath Arba, is mentioned as a place where the patriarchs and matriarchs of Israel had lived. In Genesis, Hebron is close to the Cave of Machpelah, where Sarah was buried (Ge 23:2) and where Isaac died (35:27). According to Joshua 14:15 and 15:13 Kiriath Arba was named after one of the Anakim named "Arba." The Anakim are linked to the Nephilim in Numbers 13:32–33 as the reason why Israel did not take the land. It is therefore not surprising that Caleb, whose claim to fame in Israel is linked with his exhortation to Israel to trust Yahweh for the conquest of the land, would be given Hebron as his inheritance in the land. Sheshai, Ahiman, and Talmai were the three descendants (clans?) of Anak (see Jdg 1:20; cf. Jos 15:13–14).

11–15 The second phase of Judah's campaign in the hill country, this time against the town of Debir, is an account connected in Joshua 15:15–19 to Caleb's fight against the Anakim. The book of Joshua also includes other stories of Joshua and all Israel fighting against Debir and practicing *ḥerem* (Jos 10:38–39; 11:21). This account in Judges, however, is explicitly placed after the death of Joshua. Debir's previous name was Kiriath Sepher, which possibly meant "scribe/book town" or "town of the treaty-stele" (*ABD*, 2:112; 4:85; cf. Jos 15:49, where scribal error has resulted in the name Kiriath Sannah). Debir lay eleven miles southwest of Hebron and is identified usually with modern Tell Beit Mirsim (cf. Jos 10:36–39; 12:13; *HBD*, 214).

Judges 1:12 finally brings to light what is clear in Joshua 15, namely, that Caleb is the driving force behind these Judahite attacks in the hill country. Caleb, who with his fellow spy Joshua had encouraged Israel to conquer the land of Canaan from the south (Nu 13–14), is identified as the son of Jephunneh the Kenizzite (Nu 13:6; 14:6; 32:12; Jos 14:6). The Kenizzites appear to have been a clan that at some point was incorporated into the tribe of Judah either from the Canaanites (Ge 15:19) or Edomites (36:11, 15, 42).

Caleb's offer of the prize of his daughter for the warrior whose troop could conquer Debir foreshadows the role that women will play in the bracket surrounding this book (1:1–2:5; chs. 17–21) — one in which women are used to both satisfy the lusts of men and incite them to war. (On the evidence of customs related to marriage and inheritance in this section, see Szpek, 247–48. For the bride price as fulfillment of a task by the groom, see Genesis 29. For the dowry as territory, see 1 Kings 9:16 and the Ugaritic myth Nikkal and the Moon.) Caleb's offer also allows the narrator to introduce the first and ideal major character of the inner core of the book of Judges, that is, the judge Othniel (cf. Jdg 3:9), who is identified here as the nephew of Caleb and, because of his valiant capture of Debir, Caleb's son-in-law. (On ambiguity in the description of the relationship between Caleb and Othniel, see *ABD*, 1:56–57.)

After consummating the marriage (see note below), Othniel's bride Acsah persuades (see note below) her new husband to request land within Caleb's territory. Disappointed by the quality of the land, which is identified as "the Negev" (see Note below), Acsah takes matters into her own hands, possibly even leaving her husband and returning to her father (Schneider, 14–15). In a dramatic narrative that draws considerable attention (Bowman, 23), she demands and receives the valuable blessing of springs of water to sustain human, animal, and plant life. In this she foreshadows the active, positive role played by women in the core of the book, evident in the characters of Deborah and Jael in Judges 4–5. (For the narrative role of the Acsah-Othniel episode in the book as a whole, see Webb, 87, 119; Klein, "Structure, Irony and Meaning," 87; Chisholm, 35–37.) Acsah also contrasts another Israelite daughter, whose father's (Jephthah's) decision will result in death and infertility (11:34–40; Chisholm, 37; Sjöberg, 62), and another Judahite daughter (the unnamed concubine), whose lifeless body will be placed on a donkey (ch. 19; Schneider, 14).

16–17 The reference to the Negev in v.15 functions as a subtle segue to what follows here, which, according to the overview in 1:9, describes the activity of the Judahites in the Negev region (see above). As with the previous description of activity in the hill country, it is a foreign clan that had been incorporated into Judah that initiates the action. This time the group is the Kenites, whose ancestor was the father-in-law of Moses (Nu 10:29–32; Jdg 4:11). This group travels from what is called "the City of Palms," elsewhere in Judges and the OT identified as Jericho (Jdg 3:13; cf. Dt 34:3; 2Ch 28:15), but which here may refer to Tamar on the southern border of the land of Israel (see *AEHL*, "Tamar, Tamara"; cf. Block, 98). The Kenites join the Judahites living in the wilderness of Judah (Negev) south of Arad.

Judah and Simeon together defeat the town of Zephath, renaming it "Hormah." Arad was located in the northeastern section of the Beersheba Valley, twenty-one miles south-southwest of Hebron (*ABD*, 1:331) and twenty miles east-northeast of Beersheba (*AEHL*, "Arad"), while Zephath/Hormah was most likely nearby. Zephath is possibly associated with Tell el-Meshash, eight miles southeast of Beersheba (*AEHL*, "Hormah"). Arad is mentioned in a list of cities conquered by Pharaoh Sheshonq (ca. 920 BC; *AEHL*, "Arad").

In the wilderness tradition Hormah is the site of a failed expedition at one place (Nu 14:45; Dt 1:44), while in another (Nu 21:1–3), after being defeated by Arad, Israel was given victory by Yahweh and utterly destroyed (*ḥrm*) Hormah. In the conquest tradition both Arad and Hormah had been defeated by Joshua (Jos 12:14); and interestingly, the latter is allotted to both Judah (15:30) and Simeon (19:4). This dual allotting may explain why Judah and Simeon are linked with the defeat of Hormah in 1:17, the only report in Judges 1 of the two tribes collaborating as expected in Judges 1:3.

18 The overview in v.9 identified "the western foothills" as the final region to be conquered, and with v.18 the account now shifts to this area. The Hebrew *šᵉpēlâ* (transliterated directly into English as Shephelah) means "lowland," indicative of the perspective of the Judahites who lived in the hill country (as opposed to the Philistines, from whose perspective on the flat, coastal plain the *šᵉpēlâ* would be foothills). This region, which comprised a series of east-west valleys (Aijalon, Sorek, Elah, Zephathah, Lachish) connecting the southern Mediterranean coastal plain with the central mountain ridge of Judah, extended from Carmel in the north to Beersheba in the south (seventy miles; *BEB*, 2:194). On its western edge lay the five cities of the coastal plain associated with the Philistines, who controlled this region. Here only three of them are mentioned (Gaza, Ashkelon, Ekron), with two left out (Ashdod and Gath, though see Note below).

19 This verse functions as an overview, thus forming a literary bracket with v.9. The beginning of the verse emphasizes the cause of Judah's success, which is attributed to the presence of Yahweh with that tribe. What is described as "the LORD was with them" in the double introduction to the book (1:19, 22; 2:18) is described in the account of the judges in 3:6–16:31 by reference to the "Spirit of the LORD" (see comment on 3:10; Bowman, 34–36). Judahite success is limited, however, as the narrator introduces the first sign of failure ("unable to drive out")—one attributed to the superior technology of some Canaanites (see Jos 17:16, 18; Jdg 4:3, 13; 1Sa 13:5; 2Sa 1:6).

Block, 99, defends the text against those who treat the reference to iron here as anachronistic (contra Robert Drews, "The 'Chariots of Iron' of Joshua and Judges," *JSOT* 45 [1989]: 15–23; Paula M. McNutt, *The Forging of Israel: Iron Technology, Symbolism, and Tradition in Ancient Society* [Social World of Biblical Antiquity; Sheffield: Sheffield Academic, 1990], 224–25; Lindars, 45–46). The lack of the presence of Yahweh with Judah against these valley dwellers is never explained, but it is the "beginning of a much more mixed picture of Israel's military exploits in the remainder of the chapter" (Webb, 90). This episode is a sobering reminder that Judah is not invincible.

In contrast to v.9, v.19 offers a different division of the regions by speaking in terms of topography (hill/valley) rather than in terms of area (central/south/west). The description is probably most closely related to the final stage of Judahite activity in v.18. While three of the traditional cities of the coastal plain were defeated, two were not.

20 Although earlier in the account of Judah Caleb's role is subsumed into that of Judah as a tribe (see vv.10–11 above), here the narrator makes explicit that Hebron was given to Caleb and that he drove out the three sons of Anak (cf. Jos 15:13–14). These sons, most likely clans, were already listed in v.10 as Sheshai, Ahiman, and Talmai. After the admission of Judah's military failure at the end of v.19, this description of the Judahite Caleb's success restores the positive portrayal of Judah.

NOTES

10 בְּחֶבְרוֹן (bᵉḥebrôn, "in Hebron"). The LXX has an extra phrase following this phrase: καὶ ἐξῆλθεν Χεβρων ἐξ ἐναντίας (kai exēlthen chebrōn ex enantias, "and Hebron came out in opposition" [NETS, 201]). Its absence from the Old Latin suggests it was not part of the original Old Greek, which was probably identical to the MT. This addition most likely "preserves a variant doublet" (O'Connell, 438).

14 בְּבוֹאָהּ (bᵉbôʾâh, "when she came"). The verb בוא (bwʾ; GK 995) is used at times to refer to the sexual act or the prelude to the sexual act (Jdg 15:1; cf. Ge 6:4; 16:2; 30:3; 38:8–9; 39:14; Dt 22:13; 2Sa 12:24; 16:21; 20:3; Eze 23:44; Pr 6:29). While normally it is the male who is the subject of this action, with the female introduced by a preposition (אֶל, ʾel, or עַל, ʿal), Genesis 19:34 and 2 Samuel 11:4 provide parallel cases in which females are the subjects of the verb, and in the former case there is no explicit object related to this verb as is the case in Judges 1:14. See further discussion by Lillian R. Klein, "Achsah: What Price This Prize?" in *A Feminist Companion to Judges* (ed. Athalya Brenner; Feminist Companion to the Bible 4. Sheffield: JSOT, 1993), 24, and Schneider, 12, though not the latter's conclusion, which identifies Othniel as the subject and Acsah as the object—a situation in which one would expect the preposition.

וַתְּסִיתֵהוּ (wattᵉsîtēhû, "she urged him"). The LXX has καὶ ἐπέσεισεν αὐτήν (kai epeseisen autēn, "and he nagged her"; cf. Vulgate), suggesting an original reading: וַיְסִיתֶהָ (waysîtehâ). This reading probably arose because in the story Acsah speaks, not Othniel; but the MT is the more likely original. There may be sexual connotations here, especially in light of the meaning of בוא (bwʾ, see above; Schneider, 13–14; cf. 1Ki 21:25; 2Ch 18:21).

וַתִּצְנַח מֵעַל הַחֲמוֹר (wattiṣnaḥ mēʿal haḥᵃmôr, "When she got off her donkey"). The LXX reads: καὶ ἐγόγγυζεν ἐπάνω τοῦ ὑποζυγίου καὶ ἔκραξεν ἀπὸ τοῦ ὑποζυγίου εἰς γῆν νότου ἐκδέδοσαί με (kai egongyzen epanō tou hypozygiou kai ekraxen apo tou hypozygiou eis gēn notou ekdedosai me, "And she grumbled upon her draft animal and cried out from where she was on her draft animal, 'You have given me away into the land of the south'" [NETS, 201]). This translation has raised questions about the meaning of the Hebrew verb צנח (ṣnḥ), which appears only here, in the parallel passage in Joshua 15:18, and in Judges 4:21. In the latter reference it appears to describe downward movement as well. Suggestions have ranged from "clapping the hands" (Soggin, 22) to "breaking wind" (G. R. Driver, "Problems in Judges Newly Discussed," *Annual of the Leeds University Oriental Society* 4 [1964]: 6–25), none of which are likely. The LXX appears to be an attempt to explain why Caleb would respond to her before she had spoken. But the very act of her approach to him and possibly her temporary abandonment of her husband (see Note above) could have prompted his question.

15 הַנֶּגֶב (*hannegeb*, "Negev"). This designation, which means "the South" in Hebrew, is often used for the desert region south of Beersheba (see vv. 16–17 below), but it appears to also include "the southern and southwestern foothills of Hebron" (*AEHL*, "Negev, Negeb"; cf. Szpek, 250–51).

וַיִּתֶּן־לָהּ כָּלֵב (*wayyitten-lāh kālēb*, "Then Caleb gave her"). The LXX adds: κατὰ τὴν καρδίαν αὐτῆς (*kata tēn kardian autēs*, "according to her desire" [*NETS*, 201] = Hebrew כְּלִבָּהּ, *kᵉlibbāh*), a phrase that was probably lost due to haplography.

18 וַיִּלְכֹּד (*wayyilkôd*, "took"). The LXX reads here καὶ οὐκ ἐκληρονόμησεν (*kai ouk eklēronomēsen*, "and did not acquire"). This reading appears to be an attempt to bring this verse in line with the assertion in v. 19 that Judah was unable to drive out the people from the plains. The LXX also adds to the end of this verse καὶ τὴν Ἀζωτον καὶ τὰ περισπόρια αὐτῆς (*kai tēn Azōton kai ta perisporia autēs*, "Azotus and its surrounding lands"). "Azotus" is the Greek name for Ashdod. This phrase is probably an addition for completeness and was not original to the book.

Royal Polemic in Judges

The opening scene of the book of Judges clearly establishes Judah as tribal leader in Israel, identified in their inquiry as the tribe who was to lead the nation into battle (1:2), an identification that will reappear at the end of the book in the inquiry preceding the battle against Benjamin (20:18, see below). This first case (1:2) is predominantly positive as Judah goes on to possess nearly all its tribal territory, clearly overshadowing all other tribes in the quantity and quality of their exploits (1:1–20).

But Judah's account is not spotless, as seen in Judah's request for help from Simeon (an agreement that will spell disaster for Simeon as a tribe) and then in the passing reference to Judah's one failure in 1:19. Judah's positive exploits in 1:1–20 are initially drawn from those of Caleb, whose victories are attached to the larger tribal identity of Judah. It is interesting that both Caleb (whose successes are largely attributed to Judah in ch. 1) and Othniel are identified as a Kenizzites, that is, a foreign clan grafted into the tribe of Judah. While Judah is identified as leader of the nation, it is ironic that its own leadership arises from outside its ethnic line, although admittedly the one responsible for ch. 1 has played down Caleb's role. It is probably not accidental that Caleb's power base was Hebron (1:10), the site of David's initial capital during the civil war with the Saulides (see 2Sa 2:1–4). Through this account it appears that there is a subtle attachment of Calebite victories to the tribe of Judah, a shift that paves the way for Davidic connections.

The failure of Benjamin (Saul's tribe) to conquer Jerusalem (1:21) stands as a key failure in the southern regions in ch. 1, especially as it reverses an earlier success by Judah (1:8). In the account of northern tribal exploits that follows, the narrator does include the positive account of the Joseph tribes' conquest of Bethel (1:22–26), but after this point (1:27–36) all northern tribes (including Ephraim and Manasseh) are seen as failing, and such failures prompt the judgment of Yahweh in 2:1–5.

In the depiction of Judah's success at the outset of the book, the narrator introduces the character of Othniel, son-in-law to that great Judahite military hero Caleb. In the core section of the book this same Judahite Othniel reappears as the first judge, in whose shadow the rest of the judges will appear and each be found wanting, beginning with the crafty Ehud from Benjamin drawing on Ephraimite military resources and followed by a succession of northern judges, and ending with the utter failure of the Danite Samson, who ushers in the anarchic conditions of chs. 17–21.

While ch. 1 identifies Benjamin along with Simeon within the southern political environment led by Judah, the unlikely (left-handed) Benjamite judge Ehud leads a contingent of Ephraimites against the Moabites. This collusion between Benjamin and Ephraim foreshadows the northern support for the house of Saul in the civil war that followed Saul's death (1Sa 1–4). Ehud initiates a series of major accounts of leaders from the northern tribes (Barak, Gideon, Jephthah, Samson) that progressively spiral downward in terms of the response of the people and the character and effectiveness of the leader.

This allusion to Ephraim, however, is one of many connections between Ephraim and leadership of the tribes in the book of Judges. After the death of the Ephraimite Joshua (Nu 13:8; Jdg 1:1), no other leader's lineage is explicitly linked to this dominant northern tribe, although Deborah is linked to the hill country of Ephraim (4:5), the Issacharite Tola rules in Ephraimite territory (10:1), and Abdon the judge is buried there (12:15). After the accounts of Ehud and Deborah, where Ephraim is led by figures from other tribes, Ephraim is consistently excluded from military campaigns and takes offense, often threatening violence (Gideon, 8:1–2; Jephthah, 12:1–6). These connections suggest that Ephraim's leadership role in the nation is a theme that is being developed in the background of the accounts of the judges. With the death of the Ephraimite Joshua, the story of Judges traces the shift to the leadership of the Judahite David. Interestingly, in the bracket that surrounds the book as a whole and in which the issue of leadership of the nation comes to the fore (1:1–2:5; chs. 17–21), Ephraim is depicted as unable to drive out the Canaanites (1:29) and as the location from which the two tragic plots begin (17:1; 19:1).

Recent work on the various accounts of the judges has highlighted connections between the depictions of the judges and the figure of Saul. This connection is especially prominent in the later depictions of Gideon, Jephthah, and Samson — those judges in which one can discern an acceleration of the failure of the judge-deliverer model of leadership (see Sam Dragga, "In the Shadow of the Judges: The Failure of Saul," JSOT 38 [1987]: 39–46a; Exum and Whedbee; O'Connell; Schneider; Emmrich, with special thanks to Peterson, who also argues that positive elements in Samson are related to David). Links between the Benjamite Ehud and negatively evaluated assassinations committed by Joab in 2 Samuel 3 and 20 (Wong, "Ehud and Joab") cast a shadow across this judge, who serves in the wake of the ideal figure of the Judahite Othniel.

This evidence suggests, then, not only a northern versus southern polemic in these depictions, but also a Saul versus David polemic.

There is no question that the account of Gideon emphasizes the kingship of Yahweh as he refuses the crown. Furthermore, the negative outcomes of Gideon's implicit and Abimelech's explicit assumption of royal prerogatives highlights the dangers of kingship. What is unclear, however, is whether this attack is against human royal rule per se or against human royal rule as envisioned by the Israelites in Judges 8. Favoring the latter are two pieces of evidence. First, the people approach Gideon to make him king in the wake of Gideon's military victory — a popular movement that may have been fostered by Gideon himself when he requested that the battle shout refer to victory for both Yahweh and Gideon (7:18, 20). Surely Yahweh is concerned about this very development at the outset of the military campaign when he culls the troops lest Israel think they have won the victory by their own power (7:2). This move is important because Yahweh is to be their king, a role that is tied to the one who accomplished military victory for the nation (Ex 15; Boda, *After God's Own Heart*, 6–15, 51–60). The people's royal invitation is thus based on military values that were qualities of Yahweh's royal rule.

Second, Jotham's fable in ch. 9 suggests that because more honorable individuals had refused the kingship, the nation was vulnerable to the royal rule of a dishonorable individual. In this context the former would be Gideon and the latter Abimelech.

If the Abimelech narrative is contrasting two types of royal rule, to what types does it refer? On the one side, there appears to be a contrast here between northern and southern royal models. The connection between Shechem and kingship, so important to Abimelech's kingship, brings to mind a later encounter between legitimate and illegiti-

mate royal figures in Israel's history (Schneider, 135–36). Shechem is the location where Davidic rule (Rehoboam) is rejected by the northern tribes (1 Kgs 12:1–19), where Jeroboam's rule is embraced (12:20), and from where Jeroboam rules over the northern tribes (12:25). These events create the conditions for Jeroboam to establish his twin illegitimate cult centers in Bethel and Dan (12:26–33). This contrast between royal houses suggests the similar contrast introduced by Jotham in his fable.

On the other side, however, several elements in the description of Abimelech suggest links to the later figure of Saul (Schneider, 148; Wong, *Strategy*, 210; Peterson, the latter including Ishbosheth). Both men seek to murder rivals (cf. Jdg 9:5 with 1Sa 18:11, etc.), both are plagued by injurious spirits from God (cf. Jdg 9:23 with 1Sa 16:14–16; 18:10; 19:9), and both ask armor bearers to kill them to avoid humiliation (cf. Jdg 9:54 with 1Sa 31:4).

What this evidence suggests is that while kingship belongs to Yahweh alone, there may be room for an honorable royal figure, or at least a necessity of such a figure to preserve the nation from royal rule like the surrounding nations. This kind of royal rule is linked to Saul and the northern kings. Such illegitimate foreign royal rule constantly arises in regular stories about foreign rulers throughout Judges 1–16, and these figures fill out further the picture of dishonorable kingship. But such is one model of kingship.

After the account of Gideon the progressive decline of the major accounts accelerates, moving from Abimelech to Jephthah to Samson and revealing the growing exhaustion with the judge-deliverer model. Interspersed between these major accounts, however, one finds a series of five short accounts whose elements are reminiscent of later royal annalistic accounts. "They judged

Israel outside royal structures, built alliances based on kinship, and achieved a stable and orderly sequence of leadership without royal primogeniture or dynastic succession....They 'judged Israel', but did not 'reign as king'" (Nelson, 363). These five judges thus provide an ideal model for judgeship, especially in their stability, success, and continuity—elements sorely lacking from the major accounts in chs. 9–16. But the major accounts surrounding them cast a dark shadow over these minor accounts, which do not reappear after the account of Samson, thus revealing the necessity of another (royal) way forward.

It is in the midst of the anarchy following the demise of the leadership model of the judge-deliverers in Judges 3–16 that there emerges again an explicit focus on kingship in the book through the royal refrains found in 17:6; 18:1; 19:1; and 21:25 ("In those days Israel had no king"). Linked to these refrains at the beginning and end (17:6; 21:25) is the reminder that "everyone did as he saw fit," a phrase plucked from Deuteronomy 12:8, which stipulated that when Israel entered the land they were to worship only at the divinely chosen central place of worship. The kingship envisioned in chs. 17–21 is one that would support such centralization and so unite the nation around its God in worship, rather than unite the nation around human military leadership. It is not clear whether human kingship was the express desire of Yahweh or the permissible will of Yahweh due to the hardness of Israel's heart (cf. Mt 19:8), though the latter is suggested by Deuteronomy 17:14–15 and God's response in 1 Samuel 8 and 11. In the end, however, royal leadership must recognize Yahweh's supreme kingship and their own role as promoter of central and exclusive worship of Yahweh and faith in Yahweh their warrior-king.

The identity of this human royal leadership is not clearly articulated in this section. An anti-northern (anti-Jeroboam) polemic can be discerned in chs. 17–18 (see Block, 483; Na'aman) and an anti-Benjamin (anti-Saul) polemic in chs. 19–21 (Brettler, "The Book of Judges"; Amit, *Judges*, 84–91; idem, *Hidden Polemics in Biblical Narrative* [BIS 25; Leiden/Boston: Brill, 2000], 178–88), the same two polemics evident in the account of Abimelech. Less emphatic is the identification of Davidic southern leadership in these chapters. As in the opening chapter Judah is identified by Yahweh as the tribe who is to lead (20:18). But victory is not assured in the divine response nor is it experienced in the ensuing skirmish. While this defeat does not disqualify Judah as tribal leader, it is a painful reminder of the abhorrent condition of the people at this time and also of the fact that the divine choice for leadership does not assure success. Such leadership must follow appropriate protocols for discerning God's will.

In the section explicitly nuanced by the royal theme (chs. 17–21, see refrains), one finds several references to Bethlehem, the hometown of the Davidic clan of Judah. The Levite of chs. 17–18 originates from Bethlehem and so also the Levite's concubine of chs. 19–21. On the one hand, these two characters can be viewed as victims of northern and Benjamite corruption—the Levite of chs. 17–18 being corrupted by Ephraimite and Danite influences once having left the safe environs of Bethlehem, and the concubine of chs. 19–21 being raped by the Benjamite inhabitants of Gibeah (hometown of Saul). Furthermore, the contrast between the Bethlehemite father-in-law and the Gibeahite sons of Belial in ch. 19 brings honor to Bethlehem.

On the other hand, the illicit behavior of the Levite of chs. 17–18 does cast some aspersion onto the town and tribal territory from which he came, and the concubine of chs. 19–21 is depicted as being unfaithful to her husband at the outset of ch. 19. Surely the juxtaposition of Judahite Bethlehem with Ephraim/Dan (chs. 17–18) invokes the context of political and religious tensions between northern and southern kingdoms, and the juxtaposition of Judahite Bethlehem with Benjamite Gibeah (chs. 19–21) invokes the context of the political tensions between the royal houses of Saul and David. While characterization and outcome do cast a dark shadow over northern and Saulide royal figures and kingdoms, characters connected to the Davidic clan do not emerge spotless.

These two polemics—Saulide versus Davidic kingship and northern versus southern kingdoms—have often been viewed as reflecting differing agendas and even historical periods. One way to explain these dual strategies in the book has been through diachronic argumentation, that is, an early Saul-David polemic has been taken up and reshaped through a later north-south polemic after the schism and probably in relation to Josiah's renewal. But it is not necessary to create such a strong disjunction between these two polemics. The depiction of the reign of the house

of Saul in the books of Samuel reveals a north-south distinction, especially in the civil war that followed Saul's death. This depiction expresses a tradition that the first royal figure (one attacked by the south as reflecting a desire of Israel to be like other nations) was one supported by the northern tribes who follow his successor Ishbosheth in the civil war. It is not then surprising that when the Davidic house falters after the death of Solomon, it is the northern tribes (the same group that had supported Ishbosheth) that follow Jeroboam. Saul thus lays the foundation for kingship in the north and may have been used to legitimate northern leadership, who could claim historical priority over the Davidic house.

What we find in the book of Judges, then, is a theological and historical treatise that explains the shift from Ephraimite to Judahite leadership and from nondynastic to dynastic leadership. Judahite Davidic dynastic leadership is favored over Benjamite Saulide and northern royal leadership. But the presentation provides enough ambiguity in the depiction of the Judahite Davidic solution to prepare the reader for the ultimate demise of even this royal solution.

4. Benjamin's Defeat at Jerusalem (1:21)

²¹The Benjamites, however, failed to dislodge the Jebusites, who were living in Jerusalem; to this day the Jebusites live there with the Benjamites.

COMMENTARY

21 Earlier in the account of the southern tribes (v.8), Judah was credited with victory over Jerusalem. This crediting stands in contrast to the depiction of the failure of Judah described in Joshua 15:63, a failure that is linked here to Benjamin after the death of Joshua. Verse 21 suggests that Jerusalem was reinhabited by another ethnic group, called the Jebusites, after the Judahite defeat in v.8. The Jebusites are identified as one of the Canaanite people groups who had possessed the land prior to Israel's arrival (see Ge 15:21; Ex 3:8; 33:2; Nu 13:29; Jos 11:3). In Joshua 15:8 and 18:28, Jerusalem is called "the Jebusite city."

The final phrase in the Hebrew, "to this day," emphasizes a situation enduring until the time of the one responsible for this chapter (see Introduction). It may be that this phrase highlights the time of the compiler of this chapter, since David is depicted in 2 Samuel 5 as extracting the Jebusites from Jerusalem. But Jebusites remained in Jerusalem even after David's conquest (see 2Sa 24:16). The purpose of this phrase may be to highlight for the readers the enduring ramifications of this Benjamite failure, but also to foreshadow events to come in Judges 19–21 (see Hudson, 52; Wong, *Strategy*, 29–31), which will cast a shadow not only on Benjamin, but also on the royal house of Saul (Schneider, 20).

NOTE

21 Weinfeld, 396–97, notes that it is "difficult to determine if this verse constitutes the conclusion of the preceding section about Judah's achievements or if it is attached to the following list of failures of the house of Joseph to drive out the people of the land in the second half of the chapter." He does admit that if the latter is the case, vv.22–26 would interrupt the report of failure of the northern tribes. That Benjamin is not part of the northern account is confirmed by the fact that the Hebrew verb *ʿlh* ("go up"), which structures 1:1–2:5, does not appear until v.22 (see introduction to 1:1–2:5 above).

C. Northern Tribes (1:22–36)

OVERVIEW

The account of the northern tribes of Israel begins on a positive note with success of the "house of Joseph" (Ephraim, Manasseh) in their victory at Bethel because of Yahweh's presence with them (vv.22–26). Reference to the success of the "house of Joseph" concludes the account of the northern tribes in v.35b, but between these two is a long list of failures as the northern tribes struggle to take possession of their allotted territory: Manasseh (v.27), Ephraim (v.29), Zebulun (v.30), Asher (vv.31–32), Naphtali (v.33), and Dan (v.34). These accounts of failure grow increasingly worse as the chapter progresses, beginning with Canaanites living among the tribes (vv.29–30), then the tribes living among the Canaanites (vv.31–33), and then the Canaanites forcing one tribe into the hill country (v.34). At the beginning and end of the list of failures (vv.28, 35), the narrator reminds the reader of the success of the Joseph tribes over the Canaanites, but highlights their decision to exploit them as forced labor rather than drive them out of the land as commanded (Dt 20:17–18)—a failure that will be highlighted in 2:1–5.

1. Joseph's Victory at Bethel (1:22–26)

²²Now the house of Joseph attacked Bethel, and the LORD was with them. ²³When they sent men to spy out Bethel (formerly called Luz), ²⁴the spies saw a man coming out of the city and they said to him, "Show us how to get into the city and we will see that you are treated well." ²⁵So he showed them, and they put the city to the sword but spared the man and his whole family. ²⁶He then went to the land of the Hittites, where he built a city and called it Luz, which is its name to this day.

COMMENTARY

22–26 As the leading tribe in the north, the house of Joseph (Ephraim, Manasseh) is mentioned first. Since Manasseh and Ephraim will be mentioned separately in vv.27 and 29, the focus is here on the combined efforts of both tribes (see Jos 17:17; contra Block, 102), a description that echoes the initial account of the southern tribes (1:3–19), which also begins with a successful tribal duo (Judah-Simeon; Niditch, *Judges*, 37). The Joseph tribes rally against Bethel, a key town that lay on the border of Ephraim (Jos 16:1–4), most likely situated at modern-day Beitin, about eleven miles north of Jerusalem (*AEHL*, "Beth-El"; see comment on 20:18). The narrator emphasizes this success first by noting that as with Judah (v.19), Yahweh was with Joseph (v.22; see comment on 1:19), and second, by providing details of the defeat of the city, including dialogue between spies and a man leaving the city.

The military strategy employed here bears a striking resemblance to the earlier successful attack on Jericho in Joshua 2 and 6 (see Webb, 96–97; Wong, *Strategy*, 51–55; Schneider, 21), even down to the preservation of one of the citizens who agrees to act as collaborator (cf. Jos 6:25). But the fact that this collaborator does not join the community of Israel, as Rahab did (Jos 2:12; 6:22–25), but instead is allowed to escape and build his own city, implies a different quality for this collaboration. The difference between the fate of the survivor of Judah's attack on Bezek (see above) and the survivor of Joseph's attack on Bethel, highlights the superiority of Judah (cf. Webb, 94–95; O'Connell, 67).

NOTES

24 מְבוֹא הָעִיר (*mᵉbôʾ hāʿîr*, "the entrance to the city"). This phrase probably refers to a secret entrance to the city rather than to the main gates.

26 אֶרֶץ הַחִתִּים (*ʾereṣ haḥittîm*, "the land of the Hittites"). While the heart of the Hittite empire (Hattusha) lay in Asia Minor (1650–1200 BC), its Neo-Hittite successor states endured into the seventh century BC, well after the demise of the more northern empire in the region of southern Syria/Aram (*ABD*, 3:232).

In Assyrian texts [southern Syria, the region immediately north of Israel,] became known as Hatti Land (Hittite Land), and it is in this region that the escapee from Bethel refounded his city (Matthews, *Judges and Ruth*, 46).

2. Northern Tribes' Defeats (1:27–36)

OVERVIEW

The negative tone of the rest of the account of the northern tribes is set by the monotonous repetition of two phrases (Matthews, *Judges and Ruth*, 46): X (name of tribe) "did not drive out" (*lōʾ hôrîš*; vv.27, 29–31; cf. v.19) and Y (Canaanites, Amorites) "lived" (*yāšab*) among them (vv.29–30, 32–33; cf. v.21).

> ²⁷But Manasseh did not drive out the people of Beth Shan or Taanach or Dor or Ibleam or Megiddo and their surrounding settlements, for the Canaanites were determined to live in that land. ²⁸When Israel became strong, they pressed the Canaanites into forced labor but never drove them out completely. ²⁹Nor did Ephraim drive out the Canaanites living in Gezer, but the Canaanites continued to live there among them. ³⁰Neither did Zebulun drive out the Canaanites living in Kitron or Nahalol, who remained among them; but they did subject them to forced labor. ³¹Nor did Asher drive out those living in Acco or Sidon or Ahlab or Aczib or Helbah or Aphek or Rehob, ³²and because of this the people of Asher lived among the Canaanite inhabitants of the land. ³³Neither did Naphtali drive out those living in Beth Shemesh or Beth Anath; but the Naphtalites too lived among the Canaanite inhabitants of the land, and those living in Beth Shemesh and Beth Anath became forced laborers for them. ³⁴The Amorites confined the Danites to the hill country, not allowing them to come down into the plain. ³⁵And the Amorites were determined also to hold out in Mount Heres, Aijalon and Shaalbim, but when the power of the house of Joseph increased, they too were pressed into forced labor. ³⁶The boundary of the Amorites was from Scorpion Pass to Sela and beyond.

COMMENTARY

27–29 In contrast to the success experienced at Bethel (vv.22–26), the Joseph tribes of Manasseh (v.27) and Ephraim (v.29) are unable to take possession of their territory, with Manasseh failing at Beth Shan, Taanach, Dor, Ibleam, and Megiddo and Ephraim at Gezer. At the center of this second Joseph account here, the narrator reminds the reader that although the Canaanites remained in the land, they were put to forced labor. The designation "Israel" suggests that the experience of the Joseph tribes was typical of the northern tribes. The information in these verses echoes the accounts in Joshua 17:11–13 (cf. Jdg 1:27–28) and Joshua 16:10 (cf. Jdg 1:29). The kings of Taanach, Megiddo, and Dor are listed as defeated by Joshua in Joshua 12:21, 23 and the king of Gezer in 10:33; 12:12. The book of Joshua, however, makes clear that Gezer's defeat was not total (Jos 16:10), a fact reflected here in Judges 1.

Megiddo, Ibleam, and Taanach all lay in the north-central Samarian hill country near the Jezreel Valley, while Beth Shan was situated in the far eastern Jezreel Valley, where it joins the Jordan Valley, and Dor in the far west along the Mediterranean Sea. Gezer lay in the foothills on the southwestern border of Ephraim (Jos 16:3), at a key ancient crossroad "where the trunk road leading to Jerusalem and sites in the hills branches off from the *Via Maris* [Way of the Sea] at the approach of the Valley of Aijalon" (*ABD*, 2:998).

30–33 After relating the paradigmatic failure of the Joseph tribes, the narrator then catalogues the failures of other northern tribes: Zebulun (v.30), Asher (vv.31–32), and Naphtali (v.33). The towns that resisted Zebulun included Kitron and Nahalol, cited as Kattath and Nahalal in Joshua 19:15, the latter designated a Levitical city of Zebulun in Joshua 21:35. The precise location of these towns is uncertain, but they most likely were situated in the Jezreel Valley (*ABD*, 4:93, 995). Asher's defeats are connected with towns along the coast north of Carmel. Sidon, Achzib, Aphik (Aphek), and Rehob are all mentioned in the allotment of Asher in Joshua 19:24–31. (Possibly, the Ummah of Joshua 19:30 is a scribal error of Acco; for Ahlab and Helbah see the Notes below.)

Naphtali's Beth Shemesh and Beth Anath are both mentioned in the allotment of this tribe in Joshua 19:38, an allotment situated to the west of the Sea of Galilee. This Beth Shemesh is not to be confused with its southern counterpart in the Shephelah (Jos 19:41; 21:16; cf. 1Sa 6:9–15). The reference to "Anath," violent consort of Baal in

the Canaanite pantheon, and possibly also "Shemesh" (meaning "sun"), are reminders of the dangers posed by this Canaanite remnant (see 2:1–5 below).

34–36 The failures of the northern tribes reach a climax with the struggle of Dan against the Amorites, a designation used to describe one of the nations in Canaan (Ge 15:19–21; Jos 7:7) associated with the Jebusites in Genesis 10:16. Here the term appears to be more general (cf. Jos 10:6; Niditch, *Judges*, 44), referring to highland people groups in Canaan who opposed the tribe of Dan in the southwest before the Danite migration to the far north (see Jdg 17–18). The language used here (hill country, the valley) echoes that which described Judah's struggle with the inhabitants of the valley in 1:19, which also appeared near the end of the description of the southern tribes. Aijalon and Shaalbim (variant, Shaalabbin) are placed within Dan's territory in Joshua 19:42. (Aijalon is most likely the Aialuna in the fourteenth century BC El-Amarna letters [cf. *AEHL*, "Aijalon"].)

Bringing closure to this section on the northern tribes (1:35) is an echo of the earlier statement about the power of the Joseph tribes in 1:28, a description of the ability of the Joseph tribes to gain hegemony over the former inhabitants. Rather than removing them from the land, the Joseph tribes used them as forced labor (for this practice as a Canaanite one, see Schneider, 21). This description is followed immediately in 1:36 with a description of the border of the Amorites, a striking reminder to the reader of Israel's failure in its struggle against the Canaanites introduced at the beginning of the chapter (Schneider, 22). This is what Webb, 101, called a "final sardonic comment" on a chapter that, according to Guest, 244, functions as "a programmatic anticipation for the book as a whole," that is, the "early physical co-existence with surrounding peoples leads to the possibilities of assimilation through all levels of existence—political, socio-economic and religious."

NOTES

27 בְּנוֹתֶיהָ (*bᵉnôteyhā*, "their surrounding settlements"). This term is normally used to indicate "daughters," but when used in reference to a city it refers to the surrounding unwalled settlements.

31 וְאֶת־אַחְלָב וְאֶת־אַכְזִיב וְאֶת־חֶלְבָּה (*wᵉʾet-ʾaḥlāb wᵉʾet-ʾakzîb wᵉʾet-ḥelbâ*, "or Ahlab or Aczib or Helbah"). Joshua 19:29 מֵחֶבֶל אַכְזִיבָה (*mēḥebel ʾakzîbâ*, "by the region of Aczib") may have originally read "from Ahlab to Aczib." Possibly "Helbah" is a third variant of the same name (*ABD*, 5:661)

D. Judgment (2:1–5)

OVERVIEW

The conclusion of the first introduction to the book of Judges makes clear the disappointment of Yahweh with Israelite exploits in the land. Pressler, 134, correctly calls 2:1–5 the "theological key" to the introduction in 1:1–2:5. Complementarity between this passage and elements in the cyclical accounts of 2:6–16:31 (O'Connell, 71–72)

highlights its role of introducing the book as a whole. Here is the first of three direct confrontations between Yahweh and Israel (cf. 6:7–10; 10:10–16) in the book (Webb, 102), this one making explicit the evaluation that has been implicit in the description of the progressive decline of ch. 1 (McCann, 30).

¹The angel of the LORD went up from Gilgal to Bokim and said, "I brought you up out of Egypt and led you into the land that I swore to give to your forefathers. I said, 'I will never break my covenant with you, ²and you shall not make a covenant with the people of this land, but you shall break down their altars.' Yet you have disobeyed me. Why have you done this? ³Now therefore I tell you that I will not drive them out before you; they will be thorns in your sides and their gods will be a snare to you."

⁴When the angel of the LORD had spoken these things to all the Israelites, the people wept aloud, ⁵and they called that place Bokim. There they offered sacrifices to the LORD.

COMMENTARY

1–3 These progressive failures to eradicate the Canaanite presence in the land prompt the concluding indictment by the "messenger/angel of the LORD" in 2:1–3. Gilgal was the base of military operations for Israel after entering the land (Jos

4:19–20; 6:11, 14; 10:6–7, 9, 15, 43). The fact that worship and allotment of territory occurred at this site (5:9–10; 14:6) secured its function as a cultic center throughout Israel's history (Am 4:4; 5:5; Hos 4:15; 9:15; 12:11; cf. Block, 111). The location of

Bokim, the name of which is derived from this event (see v.5), is unclear, though some suggest it was Bethel (see Webb, 105; Amit, "Hidden Polemic," 19; *Judges*, 353; O'Connell, 242; Wong, *Strategy*, 40–42).

This speech of the angel (see Notes) highlights the necessary reciprocity of covenantal relationship with Yahweh (see Ge 17), depicting first Yahweh's faithful acts of salvation (Jdg 2:1) and then rehearsing the necessary response to this gracious initiative (2:2). This indictment makes it clear that the tribes' inability to remove the Canaanites from the land signifies the establishment with them of a covenantal relationship that rivals the covenant they have made with Yahweh. The reason for this correlation is made clear in Deuteronomy 12, where the dispossessing of the Canaanite nations is directly related to the eradication of their false worship. By leaving these nations in the land, the people are implicitly opening themselves up to the worship of their gods. Thus, as Pressler, 127, has noted, this situation is not a matter of "could not" but rather of "would not," an expression of covenantal infidelity that results now in Yahweh's making permanent the condition they have allowed; that is, he will leave these nations in the land in order to ensnare the people.

4–5 The people's response to this judgment is one of deep regret (2:4–5), though it falls short of an expression of repentance (contra Spronk). Spronk ("Weep," 93) connects the people's response here to cultic weeping in Ugaritic texts, which connection, if sustained, may indicate that 2:1–5 is foreshadowing the idolatrous character of Israel throughout the book (cf. Soggin, 30–31). This weeping appears to have no effect on Yahweh. The language used to describe this response will reappear at the end of the book in 21:1–5 as Israel inquires of Yahweh for a solution to the dilemma of Benjamin's demise (see Wong, *Strategy*, 40–42). There again Yahweh does not respond to his people.

NOTES

1 מַלְאַדְ־יְהוָה (*maPak- yhwh*, "the angel of the LORD"). The term מַלְאָדְ (*maPak*; GK 4855) may refer to a heavenly being (Ge 48:16; Ex 23:20; 33:2; Hos 12:5) or a prophetic figure (Hag 1:13; Isa 44:26; 2Ch 36:15; Ecc 5:5; Mal 1:1; 3:1). The use of this phrase throughout chs. 6 and 13 to refer to a heavenly being suggests that here it is also a heavenly being. See further Webb, 239, n. 81.

אַעֲלֶה (*Pacaleh*, "I brought ... up"). The imperfect form here is odd. *BHRG*, 149, calls this one of its "problem cases," but it may be simply an example of the preterite (*IBHS*, 496–98). The LXXᵃ has here Κύριος κύριος ἀνεβίβασεν (*Kyrios kyrios anebibasen*, "the Lord, Lord brought up"), and the LXXᵇ, Τάδε λέγει κύριος ἀνεβίβασα (*Tade legei kyrios Anebibasa*, "thus says the Lord, I brought up"). The LXXᵃ's construction Κύριος κύριος usually reflects the Hebrew formulation אֲדֹנָי יְהוָה (*Padônāy yhwh*, see Dt 3:24; 9:26; Jdg 6:22), while LXXᵇ's Τάδε λέγει κύριος reflects כֹּה אָמַר יְהוָה (*kōh Pāmar yhwh*; see Hag 1:2). In both key LXX witnesses there is evidence of the presence originally of the name of God. Boling, 62, affirms the LXXᵃ and considers the MT a "fragment of the tradition behind LXXᴮ." The LXXᵇ is the text that explains the developments of all three witnesses and is most likely the original.

אֶל־הַבֹּכִים (*ʾel-habbôkîm*, "to Bokim"). The LXX has here ἐπὶ τὸν Κλαυθμῶνα καὶ ἐπὶ Βαιθηλ καὶ ἐπὶ τὸν οἶκον Ισραηλ (*epi ton Klauthmōna kai epi Baithēl kai epi ton oikon Israēl*, "to Weeping and to Baithel and to the house of Israel" [*NETS*]). These additional phrases appear to be glosses to clarify this location, at which Israel also weeps in Judges 20–21 (cf. Ge 35:8; for the association between Bethel and weeping, see Spronk, "Weep," 91–92).

2 מַה־זֹּאת (*mah-zōʾt*, "what is this"). Demonstrative pronouns combined with interrogative pronouns sometimes express surprise or amazement of a speaker (*BHRG* 259; cf. *IBHS* 312; contra Joüon, 532). See Spronk ("Weep," 90) for the striking similarity between the phrase here (מַה־זֹּאת עֲשִׂיתֶם, *mah-zōʾt ʿăśîtem*) directed at Israel and the one directed at Eve in Genesis 3:13 (מַה־זֹּאת עָשִׂית, *mah-zōʾt ʿāśît*) in the garden of Eden.

3 לְצִדִּים (*lᵉṣiddîm*, "thorns"). This is often read as an abbreviated version of the phrase וְלִצְנִינִם בְּצִדֵּיכֶם (*wᵉliṣnînim bᵉṣiddêkem*, "and thorns in your sides") in Numbers 33:55. The LXX has here εἰς συνοχάς (*eis synochas*, "for causes of oppression" [*NETS*, 203]), which assumes a Hebrew Vorlage that reads, לְצרִים (*lṣrym*). One suggestion is to see this word as a noun cognate with the Hebrew root צוּד (*ṣwd*), which means "to hunt" (Ge 27:3, 5, 33; Lev 17:13) and which would mean here "traps" (cf. מָצוֹד, *māṣôd* = "snare/net," Job 19:6; Ecc 7:26; מְצוּדָה, *mᵉṣûdâ* = "hunting net," Eze 12:13; 17:20; *HALOT*, 622; *IBHS*, 401; cf. Block, 116).

REFLECTION

In this introduction Yahweh identifies Judah as the new leadership tribe of Israel and so sets in motion a process that will result in David's rule and ultimately that of his descendant Jesus the Messiah. Key to any successes described in this chapter is the presence of Yahweh with the tribes of Judah and Joseph, but the failures of all tribes—and especially Ephraim, Benjamin, and Dan here—lays the foundation for later tragedies, especially those in chs. 17–21.

Furthermore, these failures prompt Yahweh's judgment of testing. Such testing is a reality in all ages of redemptive history (1Co 10:1–13) and has the potential to make us stronger. Although the people respond to this judgment with deep weeping, there is no sign of practical repentance or of any change in Yahweh's course of action. Ultimately, Israel will need a messiah to rescue them from the religious and social influences of the nations they failed to dispossess. The book as a whole points to a figure from Judah.

II. THE JUDGE-DELIVERERS OF ISRAEL (2:6–16:31)

OVERVIEW

At the core of the book of Judges is a series of accounts of judge-deliverers (3:7–16:31), begin-

ning with an introductory reflection that lays the foundation both structurally and thematically for these accounts (2:6–3:6). This inner core of the book traces the exploits of twelve judge-deliverers, employing the cyclical pattern introduced in the introductory 2:6–3:6 for six of these figures and a shorter notation style for six others (see further on 10:1–5; 12:8–15).

One can discern two interrelated trajectories throughout these accounts. The first is geographical moving through tribal units associated with the south (Judah's Othniel) to the north (Dan's

Samson; Dumbrell, 25). Related is the second trajectory of decline, in various ways including intensified severity of oppression, frustration of Yahweh with his people, disobedience of the people, and lack of character of their leaders (see below and Introduction). Near the center of this core section lies an intrusive thirteenth account, which mimics the cyclical pattern — that of the presumptuous royal figure Abimelech, whose reign will showcase an inappropriate royal model for Israel.

A. Introduction (2:6–3:6)

OVERVIEW

This section functions as a second introduction to the book of Judges, possibly originally standing at the beginning of an independent collection containing many of the narratives of the major judge-deliverers now found in Judges 3–16 (see Introduction). While the introduction to the present form of the book as a whole in 1:1–2:5 emphasized tribal identity and suggested a leadership role for the tribe of Judah centered at Jerusalem (1:1–2, 8), this second introduction to the judge-deliverer section ignores tribal identity and sets the tone both rhetorically and theologically for the presentation of the major judge-deliverers in several ways. (For its ideological power as "an invisible reading strategy," see David Penchansky, "Up for Grabs: A Tentative Proposal for Doing Ideological Criticism," *Semeia* 59 [1992]: 38.)

First, this section reveals that the basic narrative cycle that structures the stories of the major judge-deliverers to follow is established in the generation immediately after the death of the conquest generation.

Second, by highlighting the people's apostasy after the death of key leaders (Joshua, v.8; elders,

v.10; judges, v.19), the foundation is being laid for a new model of leadership succession that will span generations (i.e., monarchy; see chs. 17–21).

Third, by describing a progressive development in the corruption of subsequent generations (2:19), the introduction prepares the reader for the progressive downward spiral observed in the accounts of the major judges in chs. 3–16 (cf. Eze 16:47; 23:11; see J. P. U. Lilley, "A Literary Appreciation of the Book of Judges," *TynBul* 18 [1967]: 97–99; Exum, "The Centre Cannot Hold"; Guest, 254; P. J. van Midden, "A Hidden Message? Judges as Forward to the Books of Kings," in *Unless Some One Guide Me ... : Festschrift for Karel A. Deurloo* [ed. J. W. Dyk; Amsterdamse cahiers voor exegese van de Bijbel en zijn tradities 2; Maastricht: Shaker, 2001], 78–79; Wong, *Strategy*, 156–85; see Introduction). As Schneider, 32, has so aptly described it: "the cycle does not repeat itself at the same level but repeats in a descending order, with each cycle and generation beginning from a lower level of obedience to the deity than the previous period."

Fourth, it explains that the enduring presence of nations within the Promised Land was not due to the unfaithfulness of Yahweh in keeping his promise to Abraham but rather to the infidelity of Israel to their covenant with Yahweh, displayed especially in their pursuit of the deities of Canaan.

1. The Generation of Joshua (2:6–10a)

OVERVIEW

After 1:1–2:5 recounts the securing of the tribal territorial allotments after the death of Joshua (1:1), 2:6 returns the narrative to an earlier point in the story, that is, prior to the death of Joshua. For the one responsible for this introduction, the story must begin with the generation of Joshua in order to highlight its faithfulness in contrast to the unfaithfulness of the next generation. In this description there is no sense of any struggle to take the land. The conquest has been accomplished by Joshua and his generation, and now they simply each go to their inheritance and possess the land—the goal in the book of Joshua (Jos 1:1–9).

The initial section of this introduction is nearly identical to the account in Joshua 24:28–32, the final pericope in that book. In Joshua it is followed by the depiction of the reburial of Joseph's bones at Shechem and Aaron's bones at Gibeah in Ephraim. In Judges this initial section is placed immediately after a recitation of the failures of the house of Joseph (comprised of Ephraim and Manasseh) in contrast to the success of Judah — further evidence of a pro-Judah slant (Schneider, 29; Sweeney, 526; Matthews, *Judges and Ruth*, 49). It is interesting that while Moses had provided for leadership after his death (Jos 1), Joshua had not (Jdg 1); this omission is possibly a subtle critique of this Ephraimite leader of the conquest (Schneider, 2). While the tribe of Levi dominates the exodus and wilderness phases (Moses) and the tribe of Ephraim the conquest phase (Joshua), the period of the Judges represents the beginning of a transition to the tribe of Judah (David), which reaches its fullness only after the failure of the tribe of Benjamin (Saul) in 1 Samuel.

[6]After Joshua had dismissed the Israelites, they went to take possession of the land, each to his own inheritance. [7]The people served the LORD throughout the lifetime of Joshua and of the elders who outlived him and who had seen all the great things the LORD had done for Israel.

[8]Joshua son of Nun, the servant of the LORD, died at the age of a hundred and ten. [9]And they buried him in the land of his inheritance, at Timnath Heres in the hill country of Ephraim, north of Mount Gaash.

[10]After that whole generation had been gathered to their fathers …

COMMENTARY

6–7 The book of Joshua began with the exhortation to Joshua to follow the law, with the assurance that he would have success in his goal of conquering the land. The same pattern is found here since the possession of the inheritance is now linked to a generation that served Yahweh. Here the verb serve (ʿbd) speaks not only of submissive obedience to Yahweh but also of pure worship of Yahweh. It will soon be contrasted with the service of Canaanite deities by the next generation (2:11).

7 The focus shifts here from Joshua to "the people," thus revealing the impact of his leadership on their patterns. This verse also highlights the powerful role played even by "the elders who outlived" Joshua. In this verse, then, the focus is clearly on what Joshua and these elders shared in common: "who had seen all the great things the LORD had done for Israel." This generation was faithful because they followed leaders who had experienced Yahweh's miraculous deeds in the conquest of Canaan.

8–10a As 2:6–7 recounted the leadership of Joshua and then the elders, so 2:8–10a recounts their deaths in the same order. Joshua's age of 110 is a sign of Yahweh's blessing as is his burial in his "inheritance," a portion of land that the people had given to Joshua in Joshua 19:49–50 and which preserved his name in Israel (cf. Ru 4:10). Although the land was located within Ephraim (the tribe to which Joshua belonged [see Nu 13:8]), the text suggests that it had special status apart from the tribe, similar to his fellow faithful spy Caleb's inheritance of Hebron within Judah (also David's royal city of Jerusalem). Joshua's inheritance is often linked to Khirbet Tibnah on the southern slopes of Ephraim (*ABD*, 6:558).

NOTES

9 בְּתִמְנַת־חֶרֶס (bᵉtimnat-ḥeres, "at Timnath-Heres"). In the parallel text in Joshua 24:30 and the promise in Joshua 19:50 it is called תִּמְנַת־סֶרַח (timnat-seraḥ). Some (e.g., *ABD*, 6:557) suggest that the term Timnath-Heres was original since it means "portion of the sun," possibly originally relating to a cultic center that was deemed inappropriate by the editors of Joshua. The difference is more likely due to a scribal accident since the same three letters are present in both readings for the second part of the compound name. Only the first and third letters are switched. Which one was original is difficult to determine.

10a נֶאֶסְפוּ אֶל־אֲבוֹתָיו (neʾespû ʾel-ᵃbôtāyw, "gathered to their fathers"). The phrase is also found in 2 Kings 22:20//2 Chronicles 34:28, parallel to "gathered to your grave." The similar phrase "gathered to my people" in Genesis 49:29 is parallel to "bury me with my fathers." The elliptical "gathered" in Numbers 20:26 (cf. Isa 57:1) is parallel to "die." The more common phrase is "gathered to one's people" (Ge 25:8, 17; 35:29; 49:29, 33; Nu 20:24, 26; 27:13; 31:2; Dt 32:50; 2Ki 22:20//2Ch 34:28). This expression is probably a fixed idiom for death in Hebrew, arising from the practice of burying the bones of the deceased at the family gravesite, a practice important even as early as Abraham (Ge 23; 25:7–11).

2. The Next Generations (2:10b–23)

a. The Next Generation: Apostasy, Judgment, Distress, Salvation (2:10b–16)

...another generation grew up, who knew neither the LORD nor what he had done for Israel. [11]Then the Israelites did evil in the eyes of the LORD and served the Baals. [12]They forsook the LORD, the God of their fathers, who had brought them out of Egypt. They followed and worshiped various gods of the peoples around them. They provoked the LORD to anger [13]because they forsook him and served Baal and the Ashtoreths. [14]In his anger against Israel the LORD handed them over to raiders who plundered them. He sold them to their enemies all around, whom they were no longer able to resist. [15]Whenever Israel went out to fight, the hand of the LORD was against them to defeat them, just as he had sworn to them. They were in great distress.

[16]Then the LORD raised up judges, who saved them out of the hands of these raiders.

COMMENTARY

10b With 2:10b the narrator transitions to a new generation. This generation is defined from the outset in negative terms, thus creating a clear contrast to Joshua's generation: they "knew neither the LORD nor what he had done for Israel." The reference to knowing Yahweh (*yd‘*; GK 3359) builds off of the promise Yahweh gave to Moses in Exodus 6:1–8. To know Yahweh refers to the covenantal relationship between Yahweh and his people, as Exodus 6:7–8 declares: "I will take you as my own people, and I will be your God. Then you will know that I am the LORD your God, who brought you out from under the yoke of the Egyptians. And I will bring you to the land I swore with uplifted hand to give to Abraham, to Isaac and to Jacob. I will give it to you as a possession."

What Yahweh had done for that earlier generation was to bring them out of Egypt and into the land with what Yahweh describes in Exodus 6:6 as

"an outstretched arm and ... mighty acts of judgment." Those who had not experienced Yahweh as the miracle-working covenantal God were those who in Judges 2:11–13 turn to the gods of the Canaanite nations.

11–12 These verses identify a basic pattern that will shape the narratives of the major judges (see Amit, *Judges*, 37; Wong, *Strategy*, 181). This pattern begins with a statement about Israel's apostasy (Israel did evil in the eyes of Yahweh: 3:7, 12; 4:1; 6:1; 10:6; 13:1; cf. Dt 4:25; 9:18; 17:2; 22:19; Boling, 74), which is described here as worshiping other gods (Baals). The pattern then moves on to Yahweh's anger, which results in the disciplining of Israel in the form of defeat by a foreign enemy. This disciplining results in a state of distress for the people that sometimes (but not here [contra Soggin, 39] and not always) entails a cry for help (a cry *is* recorded in 3:9, 15; 6:6; 10:10). When such cries are noted, the content of this cry is not explicitly described as penitential, although this is the case for 10:10–16 and the understanding of 1 Samuel 12:9–11. God looks with compassion on the people's distress and raises up a judge to save them from their predicament.

13 Deities mentioned in this section are "Baal" ("the Baals" [*habbeʿālîm*] in v.11) and "the Ashtaroth" (*haʿaštārôt*; alternatively, "the Ashtoreths"), references to a Canaanite god and goddess known respectively as Baal (see 2:13) and Astarte. Our knowledge of these two deities is largely drawn from texts discovered at the ancient site of Ugarit (Ras-Shamra; see further Mark S. Smith, *The Early History of God: Yahweh and the Other Deities in Ancient Israel* [San Francisco: Harper & Row, 1990]; John Day, *Yahweh and the Gods and Goddesses of Canaan* [JSOTSup 265; Sheffield: Sheffield Academic, 2000]). Baal was considered the son of the otherwise unknown god Dagon, possibly suggesting that the Baal tradition was a foreign import into Canaan.

In the Ugaritic texts Baal's primary consort is named as Anath, with Astarte playing a subsidiary role. In the OT the plural Ashtaroth is also mentioned alongside Baals in Judges 10:6; 1 Samuel 7:4; 12:10. The goddess Asherah, who is mentioned in conjunction with Baal (e.g., Jdg 6:25), is paired with the high god El in the Ugaritic texts. Baal is said to reside on Mount Zaphon, the highest mountain in the range north of Canaan. This mountain is mentioned as the dwelling place of the gods in Isaiah 14:13 and is a model for the depiction of Zion in Psalm 48:2.

Baal and Astarte are two deities often depicted as challenging the Israelites' exclusive worship of Yahweh. Baal was the storm god, thus essential for fertility in the land. Astarte was the goddess of war, thus key for success in battle. These two deities were essential for survival for a people dependent on the vicissitudes of ancient agricultural production and

political instability. The temptation to worship these Canaanite gods would persist beyond the book of Judges into the monarchical age (1Sa 2:10; 1Ki 11:5, 33; 18; 2Ki 23:4).

There is some question over why the OT refers to Baal and Astarte using the plural ("Baals" in Jdg 2:11; 3:7; "Ashtaroth" in Jdg 2:13; 1Sa 7:4), or other names ("Baal-Berith" in Jdg 8:33; 9:4; "Baal-Zebub" in 2Ki 1:2–3, 6, 16), or in association with various locales (Baal Gad in Jos 11:17; Baal Hermon in Jdg 3:3; Baal Hamon in SS 8:11; Baal Hazor in 2Sa 13:23; Ashteroth Karnaim in Ge 14:5), even though the Ugaritic texts suggest that Baal was a cosmic deity. It may be that these references to Baal identify local manifestations of the one cosmic deity. Judges 2:11, 13 may use the dominant male and female deities in the plural to signify all gods and goddesses of the Canaanite peoples (*ABD*, 1:547), a trend that Moshe Weinfeld (*Deuteronomy and the Deuteronomic School* [Oxford: Clarendon, 1972]) and Soggin, 39, trace throughout Deuteronomic historiography.

14 This idolatry incites Yahweh's anger against Israel and results in his "giving them ... and selling them into the hand" of "raiders ... their enemies." The term for "raiders" here (*šāsâ*, "plunderers who plundered them") does not make clear whether these were organized army units raised by an established political entity or random bands of thieves (see Jdg 2:16; 1Sa 23:1; 2Ki 17:20; Isa 17:14; Jer 30:16; 50:11). Instead, the focus is on the devastating effect on Israel. The language of "giving/selling them into the hand of" will appear regularly throughout Judges ("selling" [*mākar*] in 3:8; 4:2, 9; 10:7; cf. 1Sa 12:9; Eze 30:12; Joel 4:8; "giving" [*nātan*] in 2:23; 6:1; 7:16; 11:21; 13:1; 15:12, 18; ubiquitous elsewhere in the OT, especially Deuteronomic texts such as Deuteronomy, Joshua, Samuel, Kings, and Jeremiah).

15 Judges 2:15a does not progress the action but instead fills in details on how and why Yahweh handed his people over to their enemies. While 2:14 speaks of Yahweh as giving/selling them over to their enemies, 2:15a speaks of Yahweh's active involvement as his "hand" was against them to defeat them. Judges 2:15b returns to the action by evaluating the effect of this defeat on Israel: "they were in great distress."

It is at this point (2:16), after signaling the despondent condition of the people, that Yahweh is roused to redemptive action. It is important to notice that the narrative makes no mention of a cry of the people, only their distressed condition. Here in the key introduction to the Judges section—an introduction that establishes the key pattern for redemption throughout the section—Yahweh acts out of compassion for the distress of his people even when they do not cry out to him.

16 His salvation comes in the form of raising up "judges" (*šōpᵉṭîm*) who "saved" (*yšᶜ*; GK 3828) them. It does appear odd that individuals named "judges" would be involved in great military exploits against oppressive enemies (see Introduction). A close look at the various figures who are called "judges" in the ensuing narratives, however, reveals that only Deborah actually judges the people (Jdg 4:4–5) by

settling disputes among them and her role in this may be more prophetic in nature (see comments on 4:4–5, 6–7 and Note on 4:5). Samuel appears to fulfill this role within Israel as well in 1 Samuel 7 (see esp. v.6), but within the book of Judges no other individual dispenses justice.

It would not be odd, however, for the military leader to play a role in dispensing justice, much as kings did in a later era. It may be that the justice these judges administer is directed toward abusive enemies who oppress God's people. This direction is suggested in the speech of Jephthah in 11:27, when he declares to the king of Ammon: "Let the LORD, the Judge, decide the dispute this day between the Israelites and the Ammonites."

Nevertheless, it is interesting that the description in 2:17–19 highlights a role for these "judges" off the battlefield, a role demanding that the people listen and neither worship idols nor turn away from Yahweh's commands. This role was similar to the role of the prophet, especially as articulated in the book of Jeremiah. (Notice how Deborah is called a prophetess in Judges 4.) This role involved holding up the standard of the Torah before the people and calling them to obey the commandments clearly laid out in the Torah. The role may have involved dispensing justice in particular cases, as we see with Deborah and Samuel, but it was certainly not restricted to this activity.

NOTES

13 וּלְעַשְׁתָּרוֹת (*wᵉlāᶜaštārôt*, "and the Ashtaroth"). Here rendered in the plural ("Ashtaroth"), the vocalization of the singular "Ashtoreth" follows the pattern of the Hebrew word בֹּשֶׁת (*bōšet*, "shame"), a term used in the OT at several points in place of the name Baal to bring disrepute to this rival god (cf. Esh-Baal in 1Ch 8:33 with Ish-Bosheth in 2Sa 2:10, 12).

15 וַיֵּצֶר לָהֶם מְאֹד (*wayyēṣer lāhem mᵉᵓōd*, "so that they were severely distressed"). The Hebrew construction here is impersonal: "and it was greatly distressful for them" (cf. 1Sa 30:6; Job 20:22).

b. Continuing Generations (2:17–19)

OVERVIEW

These three verses do not continue the linear development of the plot; rather, they present a repeated pattern of salvation-apostasy-punishment-salvation. It is this pattern that will be presented regularly throughout the narrative of Judges to follow.

¹⁷Yet they would not listen to their judges but prostituted themselves to other gods and worshiped them. Unlike their fathers, they quickly turned from the way in which their fathers had walked, the way of obedience to the LORD's commands. ¹⁸Whenever the LORD raised up a judge for them, he was with the judge and saved them out of the hands of their enemies as long as the judge lived; for the LORD had compassion on them as they groaned under those who oppressed and afflicted them. ¹⁹But when the judge died, the people returned to ways even more corrupt than those of their fathers, following other gods and serving and worshiping them. They refused to give up their evil practices and stubborn ways.

COMMENTARY

17–18 The rebellion is described in strong language that illustrates the people's covenantal infidelity of idolatry with language used for the covenantal infidelity of adultery ("prostituted themselves"). This language appears elsewhere in Judges only in 8:27, 33 and is foreshadowed by Deuteronomy 31:16. The image, though, is common in prophetic literature (see especially Jer 3; Eze 16; 23; Hosea). Interestingly, it is illegitimate marriage to foreigners in 3:6 that will lead Israel into further idolatry, and as the book progresses several key characters will be associated with prostitution (Jdg 11:1; 16:1; 19:2; Schneider, 32), a subtle reminder of the downward spiral evident in the book as a whole.

Interestingly, the people are rebellious at two points in the cycle. It appears that the people's rebellion occurs both during the judges' lifetimes (v.17) and after their deaths (v.19), thus suggesting to some (e.g., Gray, *Joshua, Judges, Ruth*, 201) that at least v.17 is a later addition. But since this section traces a repeated pattern of misbehavior, there is no need to conclude that the repetition represents two levels of editing, but rather merely two cycles of disobedience. That this section describes a repeated pattern for at least two generations is evident in the contrast between the behavior of the "fathers" in v.17 ("the way in which their fathers had walked, the way of obedience to the LORD's commands") and the "fathers" in v.19 ("ways even more corrupt than those of their fathers").

The language used in v.18 of the Lord's being with the judge is reminiscent of that associated with Judah (1:19) and Joseph (1:22). In the account of the judges in 3:6–16:31 this presence will be described as the presence of the "Spirit of the LORD" (see comments on 3:10), although see the Lord's being "with" and the presence of the "Spirit of the LORD" in the account of Gideon (cf. 6:13, 16; Bowman, 34–36).

19 Just as after the death of Joshua and his generation in the earlier part of this chapter, so here after the death of the judges, the people turn away from Yahweh. An alarming feature, however, can be discerned in v.19. The younger generation's apostasy is even deeper than the previous generation's. This comment foreshadows the eventual downward spiral that is developed as the book of Judges progresses and reveals the need for sustained leadership in Israel (see Wong, *Strategy*, 156–85).

c. God's Judgment: Nations Left to Test (2:20–23)

> ^{20}Therefore the LORD was very angry with Israel and said, "Because this nation has violated the covenant that I laid down for their forefathers and has not listened to me, ^{21}I will no longer drive out before them any of the nations Joshua left when he died. ^{22}I will use them to test Israel and see whether they will keep the way of the LORD and walk in it as their forefathers did." ^{23}The LORD had allowed those nations to remain; he did not drive them out at once by giving them into the hands of Joshua.

COMMENTARY

20 Verse 20 brings an end to the repeated pattern by noting that at a certain point Yahweh's wrath moves him to announce serious consequences for Israel (vv.20b–22). Emphasis is placed on the people's violation of "covenant" (*berît*; GK 1382), the key term for the structured relationship that Yahweh made with his people at Sinai (Ex 19–23, 34; Dt 5–6) based on the earlier covenant he had made with Abraham (Ge 15; 17).

21 Here we learn that the Lord will now leave nations in the Promised Land as a way of test-

ing Israel's faithfulness to the way of Yahweh. And here is the only time in this introduction to the judge-deliverer section of the book that a direct speech is cited, thus bringing great focus onto the section. This speech is important because it lays the blame for the enduring presence of the nations in the land promised to Abraham not on Yahweh, but rather on the enduring wickedness of Israel in the early phase of their life in the land.

22–23 Although clearly a judgment against the people (v. 20, "Because this nation has violated the covenant that I laid down for their forefathers and has not listened to me..."), Yahweh's refusal to remove the remaining nations has the potential of playing a positive role for Israel. It provides potential disciplinary resources for Yahweh to ensure the obedience of the people (v.22).

3. Textual Bridge: The Test of Remaining Nations and Failing the Test (3:1–6)

OVERVIEW

With 2:23 the narrative action comes to an end. Judges 3:1–6, however, functions as a "textual bridge"; that is, it serves as an addendum to the introduction in 2:6–23 and as an introduction to the account of the first judge in 3:7 (Sch-neider, 36). By providing a list of the nations left behind by Yahweh, this passage provides evidence of the validity of the divine word announced in 2:20–22.

---

¹These are the nations the Lord left to test all those Israelites who had not experienced any of the wars in Canaan ²(he did this only to teach warfare to the descendants of the Israelites who had not had previous battle experience): ³the five rulers of the Philistines, all the Canaanites, the Sidonians, and the Hivites living in the Lebanon mountains from Mount Baal Hermon to Lebo Hamath. ⁴They were left to test the Israelites to see whether they would obey the Lord's commands, which he had given their forefathers through Moses.

⁵The Israelites lived among the Canaanites, Hittites, Amorites, Perizzites, Hivites and Jebusites. ⁶They took their daughters in marriage and gave their own daughters to their sons, and served their gods.

COMMENTARY

1–2, 4 The lists are accompanied by statements that the role of the nations left behind by Yahweh (vv.3, 5) was to "test" (*nsh*; GK 5814) Israel (vv.1, 4). God has tested his people in the past. In Genesis 22:1 God tested Abraham's fidelity to him by demanding that he sacrifice his son Isaac. In Exodus 16:4 he tested Israel's obedi-ence through the daily portion of manna and in Deuteronomy 8:2 through the experience of the wilderness. The goal of such testing is explicitly stated as discerning whether or not the person would obey.

The use of the term "only" (*raq*) in v.2 suggests that this section is comprised of two originally separate lists, one that saw the reason for the test of the enduring presence of the nations in the land as related to military preparedness (3:1–3), and another that identified the reason (as ch. 2) as related to Israel's religious fidelity (3:4–6). While the former has closer affinities with the first introduction in ch. 1, the latter has closer affinities with the second introduction in 2:6–3:6 and will be the focus of the book of Judges (Niditch, *Judges*, 55).

3, 5 The lists in 3:3 and 5 are slightly different, the first being more specific in character and the second echoing the traditional list of Canaanites found throughout the OT (see, e.g., Ex 3:8, 17; cf. Ex 13:5; 33:2; Jos 3:10; 11:3; also Ex 34:11; 23:23;

Dt 7:1; 20:17; Jos 9:1; 12:8; 24:11; see Ishida). The second list in 3:5 largely fills out the reference to "all the Canaanites" in 3:3 but also repeats the reference to Hivites. These names of people groups play an important ideological and symbolic role throughout the OT and especially in this introductory text to Judges (Guest, 245–47).

6 The list, however, also prepares the way for the account of the first judge in 3:7. With 3:6 the introduction comes to an end with the sobering news that the Israelites utterly failed Yahweh's test by intermarrying with the Canaanites and serving their gods. This closing description sets up the first account of a specific judge, Othniel, that follows.

REFLECTION

This second introduction to Judges, which orients the reader to the accounts of the judge-deliverers, establishes basic theological principles that shape the relationship between God and his people. The cyclical pattern has both a positive and negative effect, on the one side offering hope rooted in the grace of Yahweh, who responds to the cry of his people and raises up leadership to rescue them, but on the other side accentuating the inevitability of Israel's disobedience, expressed through the image of adulterous covenantal infidelity. This infidelity becomes reality within one generation of the great leader Joshua and the exploits of the conquest, which thus highlights the fragile character of the covenantal relationship between Yahweh and his people. Infidelity is linked to a lack of "knowing," here defined as experiencing Yahweh and his miraculous ways. Without this experience the people soon fall away.

The cyclical pattern found in Judges will be leveraged by later generations to justify the righteousness of Yahweh's discipline of the nation as well as the penitential cries of the people (Ne 9). While the anger of God expresses Yahweh's character of justice, at the same time this justice is disciplinary, revealing his gracious desire to free his people from sin's bondage. This passage thus highlights the stark choice between serving Yahweh and serving the deities of Canaan and reveals a link between these deities and their related nations. It is intermarriage with these nations that leads to worship of their deities, and it is worship of their deities that leads to subjection to the nations that worship these deities. As with 2:1–5, so 3:1–6 reveals Yahweh's intention to test the community — a testing they will sorely fail in the accounts that follow and so introduce the royal hope in the closing chapters of the book.

B. Othniel (3:7–11)

OVERVIEW

Following the general introduction to the stories of the judges in Judges 2:6–3:6, which ends with a list of the nations left to test Israel's obedience to Yahweh (3:1–6), the narrator presents the first of six major accounts of judges in the book. The employment of the vocabulary and structure of the introductory 2:11–19 here in the Othniel account (Latvus, 43–44), reveal this Judahite judge's role as "concretization of the exposition" (Amit, *Judges*, 161) and "the embodiment of an institution" (Webb, 127) by which all who follow will be evaluated and found wanting (Brettler, "The Book of Judges," 405–6; Exum, "The Centre Cannot Hold," 411; Chisholm, 37). Othniel's account is "unique among the deliverer accounts in that his is the only portrayal that lacks negative aspects" (O'Connell, 83; cf. Webb, 127; Guest, 261).

---

[7]The Israelites did evil in the eyes of the Lord; they forgot the Lord their God and served the Baals and the Asherahs. [8]The anger of the Lord burned against Israel so that he sold them into the hands of Cushan-Rishathaim king of Aram Naharaim, to whom the Israelites were subject for eight years. [9]But when they cried out to the Lord, he raised up for them a deliverer, Othniel son of Kenaz, Caleb's younger brother, who saved them. [10]The Spirit of the Lord came upon him, so that he became Israel's judge and went to war. The Lord gave Cushan-Rishathaim king of Aram into the hands of Othniel, who overpowered him. [11]So the land had peace for forty years, until Othniel son of Kenaz died.

COMMENTARY

7 The narrative pattern associated with the major accounts of judges (see Amit, *Judges*, 37; O'Connell, 26, n. 18) typically begins with the notation that "the Israelites did evil in the eyes of the Lord" (2:11; 3:7, 12; 4:1; 6:1; 10:6; 13:1). The introduction to the cycles of judges (2:6–3:6) has made clear that the disobedience of Israel was religious in character, as the people abandoned Yahweh and worshiped instead the gods and goddesses of the peoples around them in Canaan (e.g., 2:11–13: Baal, Ashtoreths; cf. 2:17, 19). In 3:6 this false worship is directly related to their intermarriage with the Canaanite population.

It is not therefore surprising that the account of Othniel begins by stating that the people have "forgotten" (*škḥ*; GK 8894), a term that indicates a covenantal rejection of Yahweh (contrasting "remember"), and they are serving (*ʿbd* [2:13; 3:7; 10:6]; cf. 6:25–27) "Baals" and "Asherahs." Whereas 2:13 referred to Astarte, Baal's subsidiary consort in certain Ugaritic texts (see comment on 2:13), 3:7 refers to Asherah, a goddess associated with Baal in 6:25 but usually paired with the high god El in the Ugaritic texts. The use of the plural forms here probably relates to the various local manifestations of these deities (see comment on 2:13).

8 In the narrative pattern God responds to such disobedience with discipline. Here, as in 2:14, 20 and 10:7, Yahweh's anger burns against Israel, the practical demonstration of this anger being seen in the fact that he "sold" (*mkr*) them into the hands (or power) of an enemy (cf. 4:2; 10:7). At times this demonstration will be described as "giving" (*ntn*) them into the hands (or power) of an enemy (cf. 2:14, 22; 6:1; 13:1). The enemy is identified as Cushan-Rishathaim, the king of Aram Naharaim.

Various Aramean kingdoms arose to the north of Israelite territory, the most famous of which was Aram-Damascus. Aram Naharaim, or Aram of the two rivers, was an Aramean kingdom in upper Mesopotamia identified with Abraham's family (Ge 24:10; cf. 11:31–32). The name Cushan suggests a relationship between this king and the Kassite people, who ruled Mesopotamia in the second millennium BC (see *ABD*, 1:1219). "Rishathaim" means "the twice wicked" (cf. *HALOT*, 467), descriptive of the intensity of his eight-year oppression of Israel, but also possibly satiric in intent, reminding Israel of the folly of royal leadership models used by other nations (O'Connell, 83; see 1Sa 8; 12).

9 Such divine disciplining in the narrative sequence in Judges leads to Israel's cry to Yahweh for help (*z'q* [3:15; 4:3; 6:6–7; 10:10]). While no specific details are given as to the content of this cry (the only time any detail is given is in 10:10, 15–16), it is clear that the cry involved admission of culpability, a recognition of deserved punishment, a request for help, and a penitential response. When

the narrative sequence in Judges is described by Samuel in 1 Samuel 12:9–11, the cry is cited and includes an admission of sin, a request for deliverance, and a pledge of obedience. In the larger context of Judges and the Former Prophets, this cry is described as penitential in character (see further Boda, *Severe Mercy*).

Yahweh responds to this cry by raising up (*qwm*, Hiphil) a deliverer (cf. 2:16, 19; 3:12), identified here as Othniel, son of Kenaz and nephew (or at least relative) of Caleb. (On the ambiguity of the relationship between Caleb and Othniel, see *ABD*, 1:56–57.) This is the same Othniel who, according to Judges 1:11–15 (cf. Jos 15:15–19), was given Caleb's daughter as a wife for having successfully captured Kiriath Sepher. With Othniel linked to Kiriath Sepher (Debir) and Caleb to Hebron, it appears that this story is related to oppressive circumstances in southern Judah. As Judah was the tribe designated to advance first against the Canaanites in 1:2 (cf. 20:18), so also here the Judahite Othniel is the first of the judges to rescue Israel from Canaanite oppression (Schneider, 39).

10 The final statement in v.9 ("who saved them") is a summary of the victory described in v.10. Othniel's success is directly linked to the empowerment of "the Spirit of the LORD," which enabled him to "judge" (*špt*) Israel. This term is usually associated in Hebrew with the dispensing of justice, as displayed in the role played by Deborah in 4:4–5 and by Samuel in 1 Samuel 7:15–17. This term is connected with other figures throughout Judges (2:16–19; 4:4; 10:2–3; 11:27; 12:7–14; 15:20; 16:31), but no details are given as to their precise function (see Introduction). Here in the case of Othniel the reference to "judging" is immediately followed by the statement "and went to war," suggesting that part of the role of the judge was to lead the people into battle. Possibly, as the king functioned as the highest "judge" in the land, so also these leaders raised up by Yahweh filled this role in Israel's early period.

Othniel's victory is linked not to human ingenuity or power, but rather to its divine origin, not only in the provision of Yahweh's Spirit, but also in the statement that it was Yahweh who gave the enemy into the "hands" (power) of Othniel. Just as Yahweh sold Israel into the power of their enemy, so he now gives their enemy into the hands of their deliverer. The Spirit of Yahweh plays a key role in enabling these judge-deliverers to fulfill their divine commission (6:34; 11:29; 14:19; 15:14; cf. 1Sa 11:6; 16:13–14).

11 The account ends with statements typical of the narratives in Judges by highlighting the rest or peace enjoyed in the land (cf. 3:30; 4:31; 8:28) and noting the death of the judge (cf. 2:19; 4:1; 8:33; 12:7).

NOTES

8 וַיִּמְכְּרֵם (*wayyimkerēm*, "so that he sold them"). This economic term "expresses the passage of property by the free decision of the owner or the legitimate possessor" (Soggin, 45).

כּוּשַׁן רִשְׁעָתַיִם (*kûšan rišʿātayim*, "Cushan-Rishathaim"). This name possibly means "Cushan of Double Wickedness." For this meaning and possible historical figures, see Block, 153.

REFLECTION

As ideal judge-deliverer, Othniel foreshadows the coming Judahite David and through him Jesus the Messiah. The importance of the Spirit of Yahweh to Othniel's success lays the foundation not only for the rest of the judges, but also for David (1Sa 16:13) and ultimately Jesus (Mt 3:16) and through Jesus his new community of faith (Ac 1–2). Though for the Christian the enemy is not identified as "flesh and blood" (2Co 10; Eph 6), this nonidentification does not mean that human agents are irrelevant or that such agents are unrelated to God's permissive will. Here God's use of "wicked agents" for his disciplinary purposes is clear; however, such agents are dealt with justly by Yahweh's anointed deliverer. Reference to the rest enjoyed by the land (3:11) is a foreshadowing of God's salvific purpose accomplished through Jesus the Messiah (Heb 4).

C. Ehud (3:12–30)

¹²Once again the Israelites did evil in the eyes of the LORD, and because they did this evil the LORD gave Eglon king of Moab power over Israel. ¹³Getting the Ammonites and

Amalekites to join him, Eglon came and attacked Israel, and they took possession of the City of Palms. [14]The Israelites were subject to Eglon king of Moab for eighteen years.

[15]Again the Israelites cried out to the LORD, and he gave them a deliverer — Ehud, a left-handed man, the son of Gera the Benjamite. The Israelites sent him with tribute to Eglon king of Moab. [16]Now Ehud had made a double-edged sword about a foot and a half long, which he strapped to his right thigh under his clothing. [17]He presented the tribute to Eglon king of Moab, who was a very fat man. [18]After Ehud had presented the tribute, he sent on their way the men who had carried it. [19]At the idols near Gilgal he himself turned back and said, "I have a secret message for you, O king."

The king said, "Quiet!" And all his attendants left him.

[20]Ehud then approached him while he was sitting alone in the upper room of his summer palace and said, "I have a message from God for you." As the king rose from his seat, [21]Ehud reached with his left hand, drew the sword from his right thigh and plunged it into the king's belly. [22]Even the handle sank in after the blade, which came out his back. Ehud did not pull the sword out, and the fat closed in over it. [23]Then Ehud went out to the porch; he shut the doors of the upper room behind him and locked them.

[24]After he had gone, the servants came and found the doors of the upper room locked. They said, "He must be relieving himself in the inner room of the house." [25]They waited to the point of embarrassment, but when he did not open the doors of the room, they took a key and unlocked them. There they saw their lord fallen to the floor, dead.

[26]While they waited, Ehud got away. He passed by the idols and escaped to Seirah. [27]When he arrived there, he blew a trumpet in the hill country of Ephraim, and the Israelites went down with him from the hills, with him leading them.

[28]"Follow me," he ordered, "for the LORD has given Moab, your enemy, into your hands." So they followed him down and, taking possession of the fords of the Jordan that led to Moab, they allowed no one to cross over. [29]At that time they struck down about ten thousand Moabites, all vigorous and strong; not a man escaped. [30]That day Moab was made subject to Israel, and the land had peace for eighty years.

COMMENTARY

12–14 As with the account of Othniel (and the other major judges), the account of Ehud begins with the revelation that the Israelites did evil in the eyes of Yahweh. Unlike the account of Othniel, the precise nature of this "evil" is not identified, even though the introduction in 2:6–3:6 and the first example of Othniel in 3:7–11 suggest its nature was the worship of other gods (cf. 3:19, 26; 5:8; 6:8–10, 25–32; 10:6–16). Yahweh responds with judgment in the form of foreign domination of Israel by the

Moabite king Eglon. Traditionally, Moab constituted a narrow strip of arable land on the Transjordanian plateau bounded by the Dead Sea on the west, the Arabian Desert on the east, the Arnon River on the south, and the Zered River on the north.

While v.12b identifies the divine subject of the disciplinary action, v.13 shifts to the human subject (see Amit, *Judges*, 178) by providing details on Eglon's military strategy for subjugating Israel. His strategy involved motivating forces from other Transjordanian peoples: the Ammonites and Amalekites. The traditional territory of Ammon lay directly north of Moab on the Transjordanian plateau between the Jabbok River in the north and the Arnon River in the south. Amalekites are connected with the Edomites in the OT since Amalek was the grandson of Esau (father of the Edomites) and ruled as a chief in the land of Edom (Ge 36:11–12, 15–16), which lay to the south of Moab. The Amalekites, however, are often depicted as nomadic (Jdg 6:5; 7:12), which may explain why they are related to territories as diverse as Ephraim (Jdg 12:15) and Philistia (1Sa 30:1–2), and why they were often in the Sinai wilderness territory south of Judah (Ge 25:18; 1Sa 15:7).

Eglon thus gathers a force comprised of peoples associated with the Transjordanian plateau, and they cross the Jordan most likely just north of the Dead Sea. Eglon and company conquer Jericho, the City of Palms, so named by locals and chosen by Eglon because it possessed springs that would support plants, animals, and people (for debate over this site, see Amit, *Judges*, 177, n. 11). Cursed by Joshua (Jos 6:26), the city was to be left as rubble for an enduring sign of God's victory in Israel's behalf. Eglon's victory over Israel and possession of Israel's original beachhead in the land stands as an ironic tragedy, a sign that the conquest was being reversed (see Jos 1:2–8). Then for eighteen long years Israel experienced this divine discipline at the hand of the Moabites (v.14).

15–17 As in the other major judge sections in this book, the plot turns on the Israelites' cry (*zᶜq*) to Yahweh. Here, as in 3:9; 4:3; and 6:6–7, the content of this cry is not provided; but in Judges 10:9–16 as well as 1 Samuel 12:9–11 this cry is described as penitential, the latter showing that in the larger context of the Former Prophets (Joshua–2 Kings), Israel's rescue was based on Yahweh's grace prompted by Israel's repentance.

Yahweh's response is to raise up a deliverer (*môšîaᶜ*), this time identified as a Benjamite named Ehud son of Gera. The fact that a Benjamite judge immediately follows the first and normative Judahite judge (Othniel) continues the comparison already suggested in the opening account of the book (1:2–21) between Judah and Benjamin, underlying which is probably a David (Judah) versus Saul (Benjamin) polemic. Connections between Ehud and negative figures in the books of Samuel suggest a negative evaluation. Another Benjamite "son of Gera" named Shimei, who was a member of Saul's clan, insulted David during the rebellion led by Absalom (2Sa 16:5; 19:19–24; Schneider, 48). Most important, the later assassinations by Joab in 2 Samuel 3:27 and 20:8–10, which are evaluated negatively by the narrator of Samuel–Kings (2Sa 3:28–29; 1Ki 2:5–6), share many points of connection with the Ehud story, thus casting a shadow over this earlier account (Wong, "Ehud and Joab").

The narrator tells the reader that Ehud was "a man restricted in his right hand" (*ʾîš ʾiṭṭēr yad-yᵉmînô*). This phrase could mean he was handicapped in his right hand (as argued by John Goldingay, "Motherhood, Machismo, and the Purpose of Yahweh in Judges 4–5," *Anvil* 12 [1995]: 22; Wong, *Strategy*, 114–17), but in the light of Judges 20:16, which highlights an entire division of soldiers in Benjamin who were "restricted in the right hand," more likely means that he was left-handed (see O'Connell, 87, n. 45).

In the Hebrew text the word "Benjamin," which means "son of the right hand," and the phrase "restricted in his right hand" appear in succession, as the narrator plays humorously with this character's tribe and physical condition (Klein, *The Triumph of Irony*, 37; Handy, 236; Miller, 112, 114). These satirical jabs may be related to the larger royal theme in the book, especially in the light of Saul's emergence from the same tribe as Ehud (see Introduction), but the focus on the oddity of left-handedness is part of a regular motif in the accounts of the judge-deliverers, who are depicted as "liminal or marginal, in some cultural sense" (esp. Jepthah, Deborah, Samson; cf. Niditch, *Judges*, 57).

Ehud's opportunity to bring deliverance for Israel comes at the regular presentation of "tribute" (*minḥâ*) to Eglon at Jericho. This word denotes gifts that express "respect, thanksgiving, homage, friendship, dependence" (*HALOT*, 601). Such a gift may be offered by one person to another in the hope of restoring the relationship and calming anger (Ge 32:21). The term is also used regularly to denote a gift between royals of equal status to secure an alliance (2 Kgs 20:12; Isa 39:1) or, as here, between a smaller kingdom and an overlord to whom it is subservient (2Sa 8:2, 6; 1Ki 5:1; 10:25; 2Ki 17:3–4; Pss 45:13; 72:10; Hos 10:6; 2Ch 17:11; 26:8). It is interesting that the same term is used to denote sacrifices to Yahweh (see Jdg 13:19, 23), thus probably suggesting that such sacrifices represent recognition of Yahweh as overlord.

But one should not miss the fact that 3:18 describes Ehud as "presenting" (*qrb*, Hiphil) this "tribute" (*minḥâ*). This combination is only found elsewhere in the OT in reference to grain offerings presented to Yahweh (Lev 2:1, 4, 8, 11, 13–14; 6:7, 13–14; 7:9; 9:17; 23:16, 18, 37; Nu 5:25; 7:19; 15:4, 9; 28:26). Psalm 72:10 does use the Hiphil of *qrb* to refer to presenting tribute, but there this verb is connected to a different noun: *ʾeškâr* ("tribute"). The precise contents of the tribute are not identified, though it took at least two people to transport it to Jericho (v.18). This ambiguity is probably intentional since it will accentuate the sacrificial character of the death of Eglon (O'Connell, 94–96; see further below).

Before Ehud proceeds to Jericho, however, he makes a short, double-edged sword, which he straps in a hidden place under his clothing (v.16). Its construction (double-edged) and size (eighteen inches) make possible Ehud's violent and deceptive act (see Notes below). Placing the sword on his right side makes it possible for this left-handed Benjamite to draw his sword at the appropriate time and to fool Ehud's guards, who would not expect a left-handed soldier.

His plan finds early success as he is allowed to present the tribute to Eglon in v.17. While the narrator has already provided an observation on Ehud's physical condition (restricted in his right hand), so now in v.17 the narrator describes Eglon as a "very fat man," again possibly a pun on his name, comprised of the word "calf" (*ʿēgel*) with a diminutive ending, thus meaning "little calf" (see *HALOT*, 785). This fat king was representative of the Moabites as a whole, who according to 3:29 shared with him this quality (Handy, 235; see Note on 3:29). His obesity "symbolizes both his greed and his vulnerability to Ehud's swift blade" (Webb, 129).

Verses 15–17 serve to set up the key encounter in vv.18–22 between the "son of the right hand" who is "restricted in his right hand" and the "little calf" who is "very fat." The satire directed at Eglon throughout this account (Handy; O'Connell, 84) is another reminder of the folly of the foreign models of kingship that Israel will one day desire (cf. 1Sa 8, 12; see comments on Jdg 1:6–7; 3:8; and Introduction).

18–19 The temporal clause at the outset of v.18 signals to the reader the end of the previous scene, in which the tribute was presented, and the beginning of the core section of the story, which depicts the encounter between Ehud and Eglon. After leaving Jericho and beginning his journey home, Ehud gets as far as "the idols near Gilgal" before dismissing his attendants and returning alone to Eglon at Jericho. The precise location of Gilgal is unknown, though according to Joshua 4:19 it was on the eastern edge of Jericho. Gilgal was the place where the new wilderness generation was circumcised, the first Passover in the Promised Land was celebrated, and the manna ceased (Jos 5:1–12), and it was the location from which the conquest was launched (Jos 6).

The mention of idols in vv.18 and 26 in connection with Gilgal either points to Israel's disobedience, which has resulted in the present predicament, or to Eglon's reintroduction of pagan practices into the once-conquered land to demarcate his newly conquered territory (Gray, 1986: 263–64; Boling, 86; Handy, 237). While it is possible that the term "idols" here should be translated "stone quarries" (cf. 1Ki 5:32; Ex 34:1, 4; Dt 10:1, 3), the subsequent reference to "a divine message" (Jdg 3:20) suggests that Ehud's trip via the idols is part of his ruse to gain access to the king by claiming to have heard from Eglon's "gods" (Matthews, *Judges and Ruth*, 61; on translation see Note below). Eglon's interest is piqued and his demand for quiet (see Note) results in a clearing of his court. By the end of v.19 the attendants of the story's protagonist (Ehud) and antagonist (Eglon) have left the two main characters alone for the climactic scene in vv.20–22.

20–23 This climactic scene begins with Ehud's entrance (*bwʾ*) into the court in v.20, an action that contrasts the exit of Eglon's attendants in v.19 (*yṣʾ*). In his description of Ehud entering the court, the narrator stresses that Eglon is sitting alone. His precise location is called "the upper room," a word also used for the upper chamber that was afforded Elijah by the widow of Zarephath (1Ki 17:19, 23) and Elisha by the couple from Shunem (2Ki 4:10–11). That in Judges 3:24 Eglon's attendants think he may be relieving himself in this upper room suggests this area contained a chamber pot.

In v.20 the word for this chamber is modified by the term *mᵉqērâ* ("cool," though see Note), a sense repeated in the speech of the attendants in v.24 when they refer to it as a cool chamber by using a different word for the room from the one in v.20. Being in a higher position, this room would have taken advantage of any wind blowing through the area. As Ehud approaches the king he announces that he has a message from God/the gods (see Notes). The appearance of a message or messenger from the diety is a regular feature of the major judge accounts from this point on (see Boda, "Recycling Heaven's Words"); cf. 4:4–6; 6:7–10, 11–24; ch. 13; note also 9:7–22). This announcement prompts the obese king to rise from his seat—a term that when connected to a king refers to his throne, but which in the light of the servants' statement in v.24 may be a pun on another seat on which he regularly sat.

Ehud's divine message, however, is not from a pagan god, nor is it even in the form of words. Rather it is from Yahweh in the form of a sword, which Ehud draws with his left hand from its hiding place on his right thigh and then plunges into the king's stomach (see comments on 4:21). The sword penetrates the king's body so far that Ehud loses sight of the handle in the folds of the king's fat, where he leaves his lethal weapon.

The NIV assumes that the sword comes out the king's back, but the term used here (*parˢᵉdōnâ*) is more likely a reference to the contents of his stomach or colon that are released when the sword penetrates the king's body (Barré; another option, suggested by O'Connell [1996: 93, n. 54], is that this term refers to the "anus," with the final Hebrew letter *heh* as locative; thus, "and it [i.e., 'fecal matter'] went out the anus"). This view is based on a connection to the term *pereš*, which appears in descriptions of sacrifice in Exodus 29:14; Leviticus 4:11; 8:17; 16:27; Numbers 19:5; and Malachi 2:3. If this connection can be sustained, here it would constitute another allusion to priestly sacrificial ritual (see Amit, *Judges*, 183–85).

Earlier in the story Ehud is sent to "offer" a "tribute" (also used for grain offering) to Eglon, the very fat man whose name means "small calf." Ehud's real mission is to gut this small calf by removing his internal contents as a priest would in preparing an animal for sacrifice. As often in the sacrificial system a grain offering is offered alongside an animal offering, but here that animal offering is the king of Moab (see also Marc Z. Brettler, "Never the Twain Shall Meet?: The Ehud Story as History and Literature," *HUCA* 62 [1991]): 294–95; idem, *Judges*, 30–32).

While the content of Eglon's body (*parše dōnâ*) exits (*yṣ'*), so also does his killer Ehud (*yṣ'*)—through "the porch" (see Note). As he leaves he is sure to lock the doors of the upper, cool room behind him to slow down any who might impede his return to rally his compatriots.

24–26 As Ehud exits "stage right" ("after he had gone"), Eglon's servants arrive "stage left" at the doors of the upper room (see Alonso Schökel and Legters, 267, for the literary technique of simultaneity, here producing "a burlesque effect at the expense of the obese king"; cf. 4:16–17). Here the narrator slows the action down considerably by voicing the servants' conversation outside the room in order to explain why they do not immediately unlock the door. They are concerned not to break in on their lord when he is relieving himself, described using a euphemism that in the

Hebrew reads, "he must be covering his feet," probably describing the position of one's garment while relieving oneself (so also 1Sa 24:4). Their suggestion that he is relieving himself is most likely a literary play related to the gory release of excrement in the previous scene (R. Alter, *The Art of Biblical Narrative* [New York: Basic, 1981], 39; Barré, 5–10; O'Connell, 92; McCann, 45).

When the sense (scents?) of something amiss overcomes the fear of embarrassment, these Moabite servants finally unlock the door, only to find their lord dead on the floor. Verse 26 makes clear what the narrator only suggests: Ehud is escaping to Seirah in the hill country of Ephraim (v.27) while Eglon's servants tarry outside the locked door. Once again the narrator notes those idols at Gilgal (see v.19), a reminder of either the cause of their evil or the effect of God's discipline.

27–29 Verse 27 begins the final phase of the story as Ehud now calls together his troops using a trumpet (*šôpār*). This instrument was often employed in military contexts especially as a signal before and during a battle (Jos 6:4–20; Jdg 6:34; 7:8, 16–22; 1Sa 13:3; 2Sa 2:28; 18:16; 20:1, 22; Job 39:24–25; Jer 42:14; 51:27; Hos 5:8; Am 2:2), but here it is used to rally the troops for war. Though the precise location of Seirah is unknown at present, it was most likely positioned in the southeastern region of the Ephraimite territory close to the Jordan River Valley.

Besides the trumpet blast, the narrator provides Ehud's words to the gathered troops. These words accentuate the role of Yahweh in any victory as Ehud cries: " ... for the LORD has given Moab, your enemy, into your hands" (v.28). It is clear from vv.28b–29 that the death of Eglon strikes great fear in the Moabites posted at Jericho, causing them to retreat to their home territory in Moab via the "fords of the Jordan." Ehud's troops have stationed themselves at a place in the

Jordan where they can cross the river easily to kill Eglon's men. The narrator emphasizes the quantitative (ten thousand) and qualitative ("vigorous and strong") character of this miraculous victory caused by Yahweh.

Here is the first of three instances in Judges where the fords of the Jordan are captured in relation to an Ephraimite military operation (cf. 7:24–8:3; 12:1–6). In those that follow there will be "a lessening degree of cooperation between Ephraim and the other tribes" (O'Connell, 88, n. 46). This situation is linked by David Jobling ("Structural Criticism: The Text's World of Mean-

ing," in *Judges and Method* [ed. Gale A. Yee; Minneapolis: Fortress, 1995], 110–15) to the geographical position of the judge's tribe, which progresses from west of the Jordan (Ehud of Benjamin) to west/east of the Jordan (Gideon of Manasseh), to east of the Jordan (Jephthah of Gilead).

30 Not only is Israel freed from Moab's hegemony on that day, but also Moab is made subject to Israel. The closing note echoes those of other accounts of judges as "the land had peace." While Yahweh's discipline lasted for eighteen long years, Yahweh's blessing endures for eighty, subtly contrasting God's discipline and grace.

NOTES

15 בֶּן־הַיְמִינִי (*ben-hayᵉmînî*, "the Benjamite"). This form of the word "Benjamite" is found elsewhere (2Sa 16:11; 19:17; 1Ki 2:8), unlike בֶּן־יְמִינִי (*ben-yᵉmînî*), which occurs in 1 Samuel 9:21; Psalm 7:1; and 1 Chronicles 27:12ᴷ. In this case the narrator "seems to have preferred this distinction because it creates a basis for repetition of the word *yamin* in a new construction, *yad yemino* (his right hand)" (Amit, *Judges*, 179).

16 חֶרֶב וְלָהּ שְׁנֵי פֵיוֹת (*ḥereb wᵉlāh šᵉnê pēyôt*, "a double-edge sword"). The Hebrew text reads "a sword, and it had two edges." Such a sword would enable a quick and clean stab into the king's belly (see Lindars, 142; Amit, *Judges*, 182). The Hebrew פֶּה (*peh*, "edges") is also used to refer to the "mouth," a delightful play off Ehud's promise of a "message from God" in 3:20 (Edwin M. Good, *Irony in the Old Testament* [2nd ed.; Bible and Literature Series 3; Sheffield: Almond, 1981], 33–34; O'Connell, 85; Wong, *Strategy*, 121–22).

19 הַפְּסִילִים (*happᵉsîlîm*, "the idols"). The precise meaning of this word has been a point of much discussion, which has provided the following suggestions: (1) "quarries," (2) "boundary stones," (3) "sculptured stones," and (4) "idols" (O'Connell, 90, n. 50). O'Connell wisely concludes that its meaning in its final position in Judges must be "idols" (cf. Dt 4:16–18, 23, 25; 7:25; 12:3). The description of Ehud as "turning back" (שׁוּב, *šwb*, 3:19) and "passing by" (עבר, *ᶜbr*) the idols may be suggestive of repentance from the "evil" described in 3:12 (Polzin, 160).

אֶת־הַגִּלְגָּל (*ʾet-haggilgāl*, "near Gilgal"). Here the preposition *ʾet* is used in a spatial sense as "near" (Bill T. Arnold and John H. Choi, *A Guide to Biblical Hebrew Syntax* [Cambridge: Cambridge Univ. Press, 2003], 102; *IBHS* 11.2.4.a; cf. Jdg 4:11).

דְּבַר־סֵתֶר (*dᵉbar-sēter*, "a secret message"). This phrase is ambiguous since the first word can mean "word" or "thing." The reader knows of a secret thing hidden beneath Ehud's clothes, while the king expects a hidden divine message. Both meanings will be proven correct (see Block, 164).

הָס (*hās*, "Quiet!"). This interjection appears elsewhere in the OT at Nehemiah 8:11; Amos 6:10; 8:3; Habakkuk 2:20; Zephaniah 1:7; and Zechariah 2:17. It is uncertain whether Eglon is speaking to Ehud (prohibiting him from speaking the message until the attendants have left) or to the attendants (demanding silence in the court by clearing it).

וַיֵּצְאוּ מֵעָלָיו כָּל־הָעֹמְדִים עָלָיו (*wayyēṣᵉʾû mēʿālāyw kol-hāʿōmᵉdîm ʿālāyw,* "And all his attendants left him"). See W. H. Rose, *Zemah and Zerubbabel: Messianic Expectations in the Early Postexilic Period* (JSOTSup 304; Sheffield: Sheffield Academic, 2000), 177–207, for the use of עמד (*ʿmd*) with על (*ʿl*) to refer to attendants in a heavenly royal court (1Ki 22:19//2Ch 18:18; cf. עמד [*ʿmd*] with ממעל [*mmʿl*] in Isa 6:1–2).

20 דְּבַר־אֱלֹהִים לִי אֵלֶיךָ (*dᵉbar-ʾᵉlōhîm lî ʾēleykā,* "I have a message from God for you"). It may be that the striking similarity of the message spoken by Ehud in v.20 to that found in v.19 signals synchroneity and simultaneity (Revell, 426; cf. Talmon). But the slight differences between the two messages suggest that the one was the initial statement in public and the second a repetition in private.

בַּעֲלִיַּת הַמְּקֵרָה (*baʿᵃlîyyat hammᵉqērâ,* "the upper room of his summer palace"). The first term is used of an upper room in 2 Samuel 19:1; 1 Kings 17:19, 23; and 2 Kings 4:10–11; 23:12. But it is possible the second term is a euphemistic reference to a royal toilet (see Tom A. Jull, "MQRH in Judges 3," *JSOT* 23 [1998]: 63–75; a play on קָרֶה [*qāreh*] in Dt 23:10–15), or to "the beams" (Ne 2:8; 3:3, 6; 2Ch 34:11) over which the room was found (cf. Ps 104:3) or upon which the room was built (Baruch Halpern, *The First Historians: The Hebrew Bible and History* [San Francisco: Harper & Row, 1988], 45–46).

23 הַמִּסְדְּרוֹנָה (*hammisdᵉrônâ,* "the porch"). This term is unique to this passage in the OT and thus difficult to define. A possibly related term in Hebrew is שְׂדֵרָה (*sᵉdērâ*), which denotes a row or rank of soldiers (2Ki 11:8, 15; 2Ch 23:14) or a row of cedar beams (1Ki 6:9). The fact that Ehud is able to lock the doors of the upper chamber as he leaves suggests that this word may refer to a porch or window off the upper, cool chamber, to a colonnade, or possibly to the shaft of the toilet (for the latter see Matthews, *Judges and Ruth,* 60). Ehud certainly did not leave via the normal exit or he would have been caught by the servants.

26 אֶת־הַפְּסִילִים (*ʾet-happᵉsîlîm,* "by the idols"). See Note on v.19.

29 כַּעֲשֶׂרֶת (*kaʿᵃśeret,* "about ten"). The preposition כְּ (*kᵉ*) is used here as a marker of approximation (see *IBHS,* 11.2.9.e).

כָּל־שָׁמֵן (*kol-šāmēn,* "all vigorous"). This term is related to richness of food (Ge 49:20; Isa 30:23) and fertility of land (Nu 13:20; Ne 9:35; Eze 34:14; 1Ch 4:40), but also of plenteous nourishment of humans (Ne 9:25) and animals (1Sa 15:9; Eze 34:16). In this way it plays off the earlier description of Eglon (בָּרִיא, *bārîʾ*) in Judges 3:17 (Matthews, *Judges and Ruth,* 61, n. 55), which highlights this episode as "a victory of the thin over the fat" (Amit, *Judges,* 197).

REFLECTION

The account of Ehud is a stark reminder that the ideal conditions under God's anointed (Othniel) do not secure enduring results in future generations. In this story the original beachhead in the land (Jericho) has been taken by Eglon—a reminder to God's people that salvation for past generations does not secure salvation for the present. The natural bent of humanity is to forget Yahweh and pursue other interests, which compete with our spiritual affections. With Ehud the subtle downward spiral begins in the accounts of the judges, and so in one way he is a foreshadowing of the kind of leadership that will be rejected in the OT, one that depends on human ingenuity and deception. Nevertheless, Ehud is a sign of Yahweh's enduring compassion for Israel in that Yahweh here chooses an unlikely individual (symbolized by Ehud's left-handedness), whose courageous faith should inspire us to faithfulness.

D. Shamgar (3:31)

³¹ After Ehud came Shamgar son of Anath, who struck down six hundred Philistines with an oxgoad. He too saved Israel.

COMMENTARY

31 Between the accounts of Ehud and Deborah/Barak, the narrator has placed the short account of Shamgar, son of Anath. The fact that this account does not follow the pattern of the major judges that surround it, and that the account of Deborah and Barak begins in 4:1 with a citation of Ehud's death, suggest that it has been drawn from another source and inserted into a narrative that ran originally from 3:30 to 4:1. That Shamgar is mentioned in 5:6 gives the author and reader a clue as to Shamgar's chronological position.

While the story of Othniel took place in the south of Canaan (southern Judah) and the story of Ehud took place in east-central Canaan (eastern Benjamin and Ephraim), the story of Shamgar takes place in southwestern Canaan (western Judah), near Philistia and its five city-states (Gaza, Ekron, Gath, Ashkelon, and Ashdod) positioned along the coastal plain and highway. If Semitic in origin, Shamgar's name may be related to the Hebrew root *mgr*, meaning to "cast down" (A. van Selms, "Judge Shamgar," *VT* 14 [1964]: 299–301; see Ps 89:45)—a relationship confirmed by his role in overthrowing Philistine hegemony over Israel. But some have suggested Hurrian roots for this name since it appears in texts from Nuzi (*ABD*, 5:1155; Craigie, 240; Soggin, 58, n. 1).

Shamgar is an unlikely hero, with his lineage traced to one named after the Canaanite goddess Anath, who appears in the Ugaritic Baal epic as a violent warrior goddess and ally of Baal and in the Tale of Aqhat as a goddess seeking weapons of war (Craigie, 238–39). That Anath's name appears elsewhere in the OT in town names (Jos 19:38; Jdg 1:33) reflects the influence of Canaanite religion within the region. Some, using texts from Mari, have traced "Anath" back to the seminomadic Haneans, who functioned as mercenaries (*ABD*, 5:1155–56), thus perhaps indicating that Shamgar is a mercenary (cf. Craigie).

Because of Shamgar's weapon, however, S. D. Snyman ("Shamgar ben Anath: A Farming Warrior or a Farmer at War?" *VT* 55 [2005]: 125–29) considers this judge a farmer at war. This weapon was an "oxgoad," a stick with a nail on its end used to prod animals (cf. Sir 38:25) and with which Shamgar killed six hundred Philistines. "Hundred" (*mēʾâ*) here may refer to a military unit that was a subunit of the larger unit called a "thousand" (*'elep*). Though it most likely originally meant a literal one hundred, it came to refer to a military unit as did the Roman category "centurion." As with the Othniel and Ehud accounts, reference is made to saving Israel. But this reference probably means victory for a smaller region of Israel—in this case, the southwestern area.

While Ehud's deceptive ways seem a step down from the heroic Othniel's, Shamgar's dubious origins and the lack of details surrounding him clearly

signal to the reader that the narrator is depicting a downward trend in the story of Israel. This trend will only accelerate in the accounts that follow, an acceleration accentuated by striking links between Shamgar and Samson (in Hebrew pronounced Shimshōn), who both contest the Philistines, act alone, and use an unlikely weapon (Webb, 165). In contrast, Shamgar the Canaanite proselyte confronts the Philistines and successfully delivers Israel, while Samson the wayward Nazirite constantly courts Philistine women and fails to deliver Israel.

REFLECTION

The appearance of Shamgar is both positive and negative. On the one hand, he is a reminder that Yahweh uses the most unlikely characters, even a foreigner with a shady past ("son of Anat").

However, he represents a loss of nerve among the Israelites both in the fact that he is not Israelite, and also in the fact that he acts alone and without Israelite support.

E. Deborah and Barak (4:1–5:31)

OVERVIEW

The account of Deborah and Barak is arranged according to the structure used for the six major accounts found in the book of Judges (Othniel, Ehud, Deborah-Barak, Gideon, Jephthah, and Samson): Israel's apostasy (4:1a), Yahweh's discipline through a foreign enemy (4:2), Israel's cry (4:3), Yahweh's deliverance through a judge-deliverer (4:4–24), and Israel's peace (5:31b). The citation of the death of the previous judge Ehud (see comment on 3:31) does not appear at the end of the account of that judge, as normally happens in the book of Judges (cf. 3:11; 8:33; 12:7), but rather as a comment after the beginning of the account of Deborah and Barak in 4:1. This aberration may be

evidence of the work of an editor responsible for inserting the accounts of the six minor judges into an extant account of the six major judges. It also may indicate either that even before Ehud's death, the Israelites have fallen back into sin, and/or that Shamgar (3:31) began to function prior to Ehud's death and continued even into the time of Deborah (cf. Jdg 5:6; see Introduction).

The poem of Deborah and Barak is followed by the typical closing statement of the judge-deliverer cycles in 5:31b and thus is considered part of the basic account. There has been much debate over the historical relationship between the poem and narrative (see review by Block,

176), but this debate highlights modern insensitivity to the expression of different genres and the unique literary and theological purposes of each recounting. Brenner, 129–38, has noted the triangulation that occurs in both narrative and poetic versions of this story. In the narrative this triangulation is arranged in pairs (Deborah/Barak, Jabin/Sisera, God/Jael), with the first character initiating the action and the second implementing it. In the poem this triangulation falls along gender lines with a female triangulation of Deborah, Sisera's mother, and Jael (see further Kooij), and a male triangulation of Barak, Sisera, and God. The creative interplay of prosaic and poetic presentations of the same events (see Ogden) is strikingly similar to the presentations of the exodus in Exodus 14–15 (see O'Connell, 134–36; McCann, 59), thus heightening the theological importance of this event in the book of Judges.

1. The Story of Deborah and Barak (4:1–24)

a. Israel's Disobedience, Oppression, and Cry (4:1–3)

[1]After Ehud died, the Israelites once again did evil in the eyes of the LORD. [2]So the LORD sold them into the hands of Jabin, a king of Canaan, who reigned in Hazor. The commander of his army was Sisera, who lived in Harosheth Haggoyim. [3]Because he had nine hundred iron chariots and had cruelly oppressed the Israelites for twenty years, they cried to the LORD for help.

COMMENTARY

1–3 As is true of all the other major accounts in the book of Judges, it is Israel's sin that introduces the account and creates the basic narrative tension in the plot. The precise sin is not spelled out in this narrative (see Notes on 5:8). Elsewhere in Judges, when Israel's sin is described, it is always identified as the worship of foreign gods (2:6–3:6; 3:7–11; 6:8–10, 25–32; 10:6–16; cf. 3:19, 26).

Yahweh's response to Israel's disobedience is to "sell" (*mkr*) them into the hand (or power) of an enemy, a description identical to the one used in the accounts of Othniel (3:8) and Jephthah (10:7) and similar to the one (*ntn*, "gave into the hands of") used in the general introduction in 2:14, 22 and in the accounts of Gideon (6:1) and Samson (13:1). As is typical, this opening section ends by noting the period of oppression by the enemy (here twenty years; cf. 3:8, 14; 4:3; 6:1; 10:8; 13:1) followed by a description of Israel's desperate cry for help (*ṣʿq*; cf. 3:9, 15; 6:6–7; 10:10). As elsewhere in the accounts of the major judges, the content of this cry is not provided (3:9, 15; 6:6–7), though when it is provided in

Judges 10:10, 15–16 (cf. 1Sa 12:9–11), this cry is clearly penitential. First Samuel 12:9–11 makes explicit reference to the account of Deborah and Barak by mentioning Sisera in 12:9 and possibly Barak in 12:11. (The MT of 1 Samuel 12:11 has "Bedan," but some LXX and Syriac manuscripts have Barak.)

In Judges 4 the enemy is a Canaanite king named Jabin, who reigned in Hazor. The political structure of Canaan was dominated by independent city-states, and this chapter identifies one of these rulers in the far north (see, e.g., the El-Amarna letters in *COS*, 2:236–39; cf. McCann, 55; Niditch, *Judges*, 64). While the stories of the first three judges have taken place in the southeast (Othniel), central-east (Ehud), and southwest (Shamgar), the story of Deborah and Barak shifts the focus north to Hazor, a fortified city in Galilee that lay at a key crossroad of trade routes in northern Canaan. Its strategic position explains why Solomon fortified it during his reign (1Ki 9:15), why the Assyrians destroyed it when conquering Israel (2Ki 15:29), and why the king of this city led a Canaanite coalition against the conquering Israelites in Joshua 11:1–14 (cf. Provan, Long, and Longman, 178–81).

The fact that the king of Hazor whom Joshua faced in Joshua 11 was also named Jabin confirms the lack of enduring Israelite success in the conquest of the north (Naphtali; cf. Jdg 1:33) and suggests that the city was ruled by a dynasty that regained control of their city after the conquest. The description of Hazor's defeat in Joshua 11, however, highlights the severity of the Israelites' treatment of this leading city in the north. Although *ḥerem* (complete destruction) was practiced on Hazor (Jos 11:10–11) and the city burned, it appears that a remnant of its inhabitants survived and returned in due time. The Mari texts (eighteenth century BC) and El-Amarna Letters (fourteenth century BC) refer to the city-state of Hazor, which confirms its status as a stable political entity throughout the second millennium BC (*ABD*, 3:595; Block, 188, nn. 157, 158; Provan, Long, and Longman, 179–80).

While Jabin is the king of Hazor, the commander of his army is Sisera, who hailed from Harosheth-Haggoyim. The precise location of his hometown is unknown, but its name means "forested area [*ḥōreš* (2Ch 27:4; Isa 17:9; Eze 31:3)] of the nations/Gentiles," not an odd appellation for the northern regions (though see Note below). In the time of Isaiah the regions of Galilee associated with the tribes of Zebulun and Naphtali were also associated with the nations/Gentiles (Isa 9:1[8:23]). It is interesting that the Song of Deborah and Barak in Judges 5 (vv. 19–20) and the retrospect of their battle in 1 Samuel 12:9 highlight the role of Sisera while ignoring Jabin, thus showing that although Sisera served Jabin, the focus of the story is placed on Sisera. While this focus has been treated as evidence of the amalgamation of divergent traditions, Brenner has shown how it is part of a larger literary motif in the story (see above).

Sisera's success is linked to his superior military technology exemplified by his nine hundred iron chariots. The number "hundred" here may indicate the name of a military unit rather than a literal number, although it may also be an example of "epic exaggeration" (Block, 190; cf. Jacob Milgrom, *Numbers* [JPS Torah Commentary; Philadelphia: Jewish Publication Society, 1990], 336–39). The Israelites are no match for an army with chariotry, as was already evident in Judah's failure in 1:19.

NOTE

2 יוֹשֵׁב (*yōšēb*), "lived," may also be translated as "ruled" (as in "sat [on a throne]").

בַּחֲרֹשֶׁת הַגּוֹיִם (*baḥ*ᵃ*rōšet haggôyim*, "in Harosheth Haggoyim"). Block, 190, links this name to an Akkadian cognate *erištu*, meaning "cultivated land," which has been repointed negatively with the vowels of "shame" (*bōšet*; cf. 1Ch 8:33–34; 9:39–40; cf. 2Sa 2:8–19; 4:4; 9:6–13, where "Eshbaal" and "Merib-Baal" are changed to "Ishbosheth" and "Mephibosheth" to bring disrepute to the name "Baal"). But there is no reason to set aside the traditional reading.

b. Raising Up a Savior (4:4–10)

> ⁴Deborah, a prophetess, the wife of Lappidoth, was leading Israel at that time. ⁵She held court under the Palm of Deborah between Ramah and Bethel in the hill country of Ephraim, and the Israelites came to her to have their disputes decided. ⁶She sent for Barak son of Abinoam from Kedesh in Naphtali and said to him, "The Lᴏʀᴅ, the God of Israel, commands you: 'Go, take with you ten thousand men of Naphtali and Zebulun and lead the way to Mount Tabor. ⁷I will lure Sisera, the commander of Jabin's army, with his chariots and his troops to the Kishon River and give him into your hands.'"
> ⁸Barak said to her, "If you go with me, I will go; but if you don't go with me, I won't go."
> ⁹"Very well," Deborah said, "I will go with you. But because of the way you are going about this, the honor will not be yours, for the Lᴏʀᴅ will hand Sisera over to a woman." So Deborah went with Barak to Kedesh, ¹⁰where he summoned Zebulun and Naphtali. Ten thousand men followed him, and Deborah also went with him.

COMMENTARY

4–5 In the accounts of the major judges to this point in the book, the narrator introduces the individual whom Yahweh raises up to save Israel from its enemy immediately following the description of the cry of the people (3:9, 15). In the accounts of the major judges after this point in the book, the narrator depicts a messenger or message from God who/which confronts the people and/or calls the judge-deliverer (6:7–24; 10:10–16; cf. 13:2–23).

There is ambiguity in the presentation of Deborah, who is said to have been a judge for the people but also shares in the role of God's messenger as prophet. (On this ambiguity see Amit [*Judges*, 204–6], though Block, 191–200, may go too far in denying her judge-deliverer status.) In the light of the presentation of Barak, it is likely that her association with both roles is to be linked to Barak's failure. Deborah's and Barak's relationship to the battle is part of a larger literary motif in the story in which a figure initiates action but another completes it (Brenner).

Individuals used by Yahweh to rescue Israel are described with one or two Hebrew words. The first word is associated with saving or rescuing (*yš*: 2:16, 18; 3:9, 15, 31; 6:14–15; 8:22; 10:1, cf. 6:36–37; 7:2, 7; 10:12–14; 13:5), and the second with dispensing justice (*špṭ*: 2:16–19; 3:10; 4:4; 10:2–3; 12:7–9, 11, 13–14; 15:20; 16:31). At times these terms are used together. For instance, in Judges 3:9 Yahweh raises up the deliverer (*môšîaʿ*) Othniel to deliver (*yš*, Hiphil) Israel, but when the Spirit of Yahweh comes upon him in 3:10 the narrator declares that he "judged" (*špṭ*) Israel, a statement that is followed immediately by a description of his military exploits ("when he went out to war … "). It is possible that as chief military leader the "savior" was responsible for dispensing justice, much as the king functioned during the monarchical period.

It is in the account of Deborah that the narrator offers evidence that these judge-deliverers were actually involved in dispensing justice (though see Note). Deborah is identified here not only as a judge but also as a woman, prophetess, and wife (see Notes). These pieces of characterization are important for the ancient reader, who would have found Deborah's role odd within her particular ancient social context. She is first identified as prophetess, a description that explains why she has been given the role of handling disputes among the people of Israel. Her special spiritual gifting has qualified her to shatter the social mores of her community and settle disputes among and between the families. (For the relationship between prophecy and justice, see Spronk ["Deborah," 236–38] and Niditch [*Judges*, 2–3], though here there is no need to see ancestral cultic practice.) As prophetess Deborah joins other women throughout Israel's history who functioned as God's spokespersons (Miriam in Ex 15:20; Huldah in 2Ki 22:14; Noadiah in Ne 6:14; see Block, 192).

Second, Deborah is carefully identified as the wife of a man named Lappidoth. As male figures are often identified by their fathers ("son of …") to reveal their place within an ancient patriarchal

system, so this female figure is identified by her husband to reveal her place within this same system (so also Huldah in 2Ki 22:14).

Deborah's justice was dispensed within Ephraimite territory under a palm tree between Ramah—the hometown of Samuel, which lay in Benjamin (about seven kilometers north of Jerusalem)—and Bethel, a city in Ephraim (about eight kilometers north of Ramah). There she was at a safe distance from the hegemony of Jabin in the far north. As with the story of Ehud (3:12–30), the solution to Israel's problem came from Benjamin-Ephraim. The kinds of disputes were probably related to disagreements between families and clans that needed a higher authority for adjudication, in this case one that had access to Yahweh through prophecy.

6–7 In v.6 Deborah sends for Barak, identified as son of Abinoam and traced to the town of Kedesh in Naphtali. Kedesh was conquered by Joshua (Jos 12:22) and became one of the Levitical cities (Jos 20:7; 21:32) located in the tribal territory of Naphtali (Jos 19:37). Some identify it with a location in upper Galilee, about six miles north of Hazor in a location key for control of the fertile northern Huleh region (*ABD*, 4:11). But Judges 4 suggests that Kedesh was in southern Naphtali near or in the Jezreel Valley. This location makes sense of its position in the conquest list in Joshua 12:22, in which Kedesh is mentioned after the conquest of Taanach and Megiddo in verse 21 and before Jokneam in Carmel in verse 22b—all locations overlooking the Jezreel Valley. Since Jabin's power base is identified with Hazor, it is not surprising that a far northern Naphtalite is chosen to do battle against him.

Deborah's words to Barak constitute a prophetic revelation from Yahweh; the appearance of a prophetic messenger figure at this juncture in the cycle is an element found in most of the other major judges cycles (see Boda, "Recycling Heaven's Words"; cf. 3:19–20, 6:7–10, 11–24; 10:11–14; ch. 13; also note

9:7–22). She commissions Barak to take ten "thousand" soldiers from the northern tribes of Naphtali and Zebulun to fight Jabin's army, led by Sisera (on vv.4–10 as call narrative, see Block, 191–94). Most likely the term "thousand" (ʾlp) here refers to a large unit within a militia rather than to a literal thousand troops. Deborah tells Barak to go to Mount Tabor, which lay at the intersection of the tribal territories of Zebulun, Issachar, and Naphtali. This mountain controlled access into the Jezreel Valley from the northeast along that great ancient highway, the Way of the Sea, which linked Mesopotamia with Egypt. This route was the economic lifeblood of Hazor and the route on which troops would arrive from Jabin (cf. Jos 19:22; 1Sa 10:3; Jer 46:18; Ps 89:12; *ABD*, 6:305).

The place of battle is identified as the River Kishon, which ran just north of the Mount Carmel range and drained the Jezreel Valley into the Mediterranean Sea. Yahweh declares through Deborah that he will lure Jabin's army to this location, which would have appeared to Sisera as ideal terrain for his chariotry, thus granting him the clear military advantage over the Israelites. Yahweh assures Barak, however, that Jabin's army will be delivered into his hands.

8–9a Barak does not have the confidence to embark on this mission alone. He stipulates to Deborah that he will go only if she will accompany him. She agrees to go but makes it clear that her accompaniment will strip him of a conquering general's honor, which will go instead to a woman. Her response reveals that this deflection of honor is not the divine norm and links it to Barak's lack of faith (Wong, *Strategy*, 158; contra Niditch, *Judges*, 65). Through this dramatic narrative, Deborah seems to suggest that her role was prophetic and legal, while he was to function as the military "savior" of Israel (see Wong, *Strategy*, 242–43).

Deborah's words hint that she will be the woman into whose hands Sisera will be sold, a phrase that indicates the reversal of Israel's punishment in 4:2. In the story that follows, Deborah's presence with the army and instructions to Barak identify her as the ultimate leader of the forces that defeat the army of Sisera. But this story also reveals that Sisera himself will be killed not by Barak, nor even by Deborah, but by the woman Jael, wife of Heber and Jabin's ally (4:21–22). Barak is stripped even of the glory of killing the opposing general.

9b–10 Deborah accompanies Barak to Kedesh, where the military leader gathers together a force drawn from the local tribes of Zebulun and Naphtali. These ten divisions accompany Barak and Deborah to Mount Tabor, on the top of which was a large plateau (measuring one thousand by four hundred meters) ideal for a military camp (*ABD*, 6:304).

NOTES

4 אִשָּׁה נְבִיאָה אֵשֶׁת לַפִּידוֹת (ʾiššâ nᵉbîʾâ ʾēšet lappîdôt, "a prophetess, the wife of Lappidoth"). The first two words in the Hebrew text should be translated in apposition: "a woman, a prophetess, the wife of Lappidoth" (see Block, 192, n. 181), highlighting the narrator's intention to stress her gender.

5 יוֹשֶׁבֶת (yôšebet, "held court"). See comment on 4:2 related to Sisera. For the idea of sitting to judge, see Exodus 18:13–14; Psalms 9:5; 61:8; Isaiah 28:6; Joel 4:12.

לַמִּשְׁפָּט (lammišpāṭ, "to have their disputes decided"). For the use of this term to describe adjudication of legal cases see Numbers 35:12. But Block, 197, does not see this word as denoting the normal dispensing of justice, but rather "a specific response of justice for a specific cry" (cf. 1Ki 3:16–20; 20:39–40; 2Ki 6:26), that is, the cry of Israel in response to foreign oppression. Also possible is the suggestion of Spronk ("Deborah," 236), who links this term to the reception of a divine oracle (cf. Jdg 13:12 and the Ugaritic text KTU 1.124).

6 הֲלֹא צִוָּה יְהוָה אֱלֹהֵי־יִשְׂרָאֵל ($h^a l\bar{o}$ $siww\hat{a}$ $yhwh$ $^{x}l\bar{o}h\hat{e}$-$yi\acute{s}r\bar{a}^{\flat}\bar{e}l$ "The LORD, the God of Israel, commands you"). The Hebrew text phrases this in question format—"Has not the LORD, the God of Israel commanded you?"—which functions emphatically when introducing an exhortation—"Indeed, the LORD, the God of Israel commands you" (see *IBHS*, 40.3.b; *BHRG*, 43.2; GKC 150.e). There is no reason then to posit that Barak had disobeyed an earlier divine commission.

9 אֶפֶס כִּי ($^{\flat}epes$ $k\hat{i}$, "nevertheless"). This phrase qualifies a preceding positive statement with an exception to it (cf. Nu 13:28; Dt 15:4; Am 9:8); see Joüon, 173.a.

10 וַיַּעַל בְּרַגְלָיו ($wayya^c al$ $b^e ragl\bar{a}yw$, "followed him"). This verb could refer to those who follow or accompany another (Ex 11:8; Jdg 8:5; 1Ki 20:10; Dt 11:6; 2Ki 3:9) or simply to those who go on foot (see 4:15, 17; cf. Nu 20:19; Dt 2:28; Ps 66:6).

c. The Battle (4:11–16)

> [11]Now Heber the Kenite had left the other Kenites, the descendants of Hobab, Moses' brother-in-law, and pitched his tent by the great tree in Zaanannim near Kedesh.
> [12]When they told Sisera that Barak son of Abinoam had gone up to Mount Tabor, [13]Sisera gathered together his nine hundred iron chariots and all the men with him, from Harosheth Haggoyim to the Kishon River.
> [14]Then Deborah said to Barak, "Go! This is the day the LORD has given Sisera into your hands. Has not the LORD gone ahead of you?" So Barak went down Mount Tabor, followed by ten thousand men. [15]At Barak's advance, the LORD routed Sisera and all his chariots and army by the sword, and Sisera abandoned his chariot and fled on foot. [16]But Barak pursued the chariots and army as far as Harosheth Haggoyim. All the troops of Sisera fell by the sword; not a man was left.

COMMENTARY

11 Before describing the movements of Jabin's army in response to the advance of the Israelite army, the narrator provides "an anticipatory element that causes the reader to expect to be told of the fuller significance of the comment at some later stage" and so "draws the reader into the story" (Ogden, 115). The narrator introduces the actions of a certain Heber the Kenite. The Kenites were mentioned in 1:16 as part of the account of the tribe of Judah. There the movements of this group, related to Israel through Moses' father-in-law Hobab (cf. Nu 10:29; see Note below), are traced from "the City of Palms" to the wilderness region (Negev) in southern Judah just south of Arad.

According to 4:11, one from this group left the Kenite clan, signifying a break in their social order and identifying this breakaway clan as an enemy of Israel. That Heber was an ally of Israel's enemy Jabin is made explicit in v.17, even though vv.18–21 make clear that there remained some sympathy for Israel among certain members of the household (Jael). This clan was led by Heber, who had established his new home ("pitched his tent") at the location known as "the oak of Zaanannim," which lay on the southern border of Naphtali (Jos 19:33). Large trees were important landmarks in the ancient world, not only marking places where water was available for human civilization, but also signifying sacred sites (see Jdg 4:5; 9:37; cf. Ge 12:6; 13:18; 14:13; Dt 11:30). This location was near Kedesh, Barak's hometown and the place where Barak was raising his army. Judges 5:24–25 reveals that the members of this clan were tent dwellers with dairy herds, an important aspect of this story (see vv.17–21 below).

12–13 Being so close to Kedesh, members of this Kenite clan informed Sisera of Barak's military movements. Concerned that Israel was threatening the key highway through Jabin's land, Sisera calls up (Heb. *zʿq*, "cry") his nine units ("hundreds") of iron chariots to travel from their quarters at Harosheth Haggoyim to the Kishon River. The source of the Kishon was in the northern Samarian hills near the site of Megiddo (cf. Jdg 5:19), from where it flowed through the Jezreel Valley and emptied into the Mediterranean Sea just north of Mount Carmel.

14–16 Whereas the Kenites tip off Sisera, it is Deborah the prophetess who tips off Barak — by calling him to engage Sisera in battle. Her message emphasizes the divine dimension of this potential victory. It is Yahweh who has given Sisera into his hands by going out before the Israelite army. As Barak leads his ten large units ("thousands") of Israelites from their advantageous position atop Mount Tabor, Yahweh's role is described at the outset of the battle narrative (v.15a) as "confusing" (*hmm*) Sisera and his forces "before the sword," that is, the military advance of Israel. Seeing the defeat of his forces, Sisera flees on foot (v.15b) as the Israelite army led by Barak pursues the rump of Sisera's divisions (chariots and soldiers) back to their home base in Harosheth Haggoyim and kills them all (v.16).

NOTES

11 אֶת־קֶדֶשׁ (*ʾet-qedeš*, "near Kedesh"). See Note on 3:19.

נִפְרָד מִקַּיִן (*niprād miqqayin*, "had left the other Kenites"). This phrase is better translated, "had separated himself from the other Kenites." In Genesis 13:9 the same phrase "suggests a deliberate act of severance" (Block, 202, n. 238; cf. Pr 19:4). In both Genesis 13 and Judges 4 this separation results from tension between related clans.

חֹתֵן מֹשֶׁה (*ḥōtēn mōšeh*, "Moses' brother-in-law"). The term חֹתֵן (*ḥōtēn*) is usually to be read "father-in-law," but there has been confusion here due to the claim in Numbers 10:29 that Reuel, Hobab's father, was Moses' father-in-law. In Exodus 2–4 Reuel is also called "Jethro" (cf. 2:18 with 3:1; 4:18; cf. 18:1–12). The evidence of Numbers 10:29 suggests, then, that Hobab was actually Moses' brother-in-law. Considering the fact that the same letters vocalized differently (חָתָן, ḥātān) mean "son-in-law" (Ge 19:14; Jdg 15:6; 19:5; 1Sa 18:18; 22:14; 2Ki 8:27; Ne 6:18; 13:28; cf. חֹתֶנֶת, ḥōtenet = "mother-in-law," Dt 27:23), this designation may refer to a son-in-law or in-law in general.

13 הָעָם (hāʿām, "the men"). This word is used at times for people who bear arms, that is, an army (Nu 20:20; 31:32; Jos 8:1, 3, 11; 10:7; 11:7; 1Sa 11:11; 1Ki 20:10).

14 הֲלֹא יְהוָה יָצָא לְפָנֶיךָ (hᵃlōʾ yhwh yāṣāʾ lᵉpāneykā, "Has not the Lord gone ahead of you?"). See Note on 4:6 above.

15 הַמֶּרְכָּבָה (hammerkābâ, "his chariot"). See Joüon, 137.f (2) (cf. 143.e), for the role of the article as possessive pronoun (cf. Block, 204, n. 258).

d. The Aftermath (4:17–24)

> ¹⁷Sisera, however, fled on foot to the tent of Jael, the wife of Heber the Kenite, because there were friendly relations between Jabin king of Hazor and the clan of Heber the Kenite.
>
> ¹⁸Jael went out to meet Sisera and said to him, "Come, my lord, come right in. Don't be afraid." So he entered her tent, and she put a covering over him.
>
> ¹⁹"I'm thirsty," he said. "Please give me some water." She opened a skin of milk, gave him a drink, and covered him up.
>
> ²⁰"Stand in the doorway of the tent," he told her. "If someone comes by and asks you, 'Is anyone here?' say 'No.'"
>
> ²¹But Jael, Heber's wife, picked up a tent peg and a hammer and went quietly to him while he lay fast asleep, exhausted. She drove the peg through his temple into the ground, and he died.
>
> ²²Barak came by in pursuit of Sisera, and Jael went out to meet him. "Come," she said, "I will show you the man you're looking for." So he went in with her, and there lay Sisera with the tent peg through his temple—dead.
>
> ²³On that day God subdued Jabin, the Canaanite king, before the Israelites. ²⁴And the hand of the Israelites grew stronger and stronger against Jabin, the Canaanite king, until they destroyed him.

COMMENTARY

17–22 While Barak and his forces pursue Sisera's army back to Harosheth Haggoyim, as already noted in v.15b, Sisera flees the battle scene on foot. (See Alonso Schökel and Legters, 267, for the literary technique of simultaneity, here "to transpose the action from the wide scene of battle to the narrow space of a Bedouin tent" [cf. 3:24–26].) The description of Barak's pursuit in 4:16, 22 serves to contrast Barak's actions "first with those of Sisera, then with those of Jael achieving what Barak had hoped to achieve" (O'Connell, 127).

Verse 17 identifies the destination of his flight, which is the settlement of Heber the Kenite, his ally (see Note), who had informed him of Barak's military maneuvers in the first place (v. 11). Here Sisera thinks he will find safety and is hidden in a place that would be off limits to any Israelite warriors searching for the military leader—the tent of Heber's wife, Jael (for a woman's/wife's tent see Ge 18:6; 24:67; 31:33; cf. Schneider, 78).

On the surface, Jael seems to be expressing Near Eastern hospitality by approaching Sisera, inviting him into her tent, responding to his need for water by giving him milk, and covering him up (see V. H. Matthews, and D. C. Benjamin, "Jael: Host or Judge?" *TBT* 30 [1992]: 291–96). But Sisera violates the social code throughout this passage, which thus justifies in the minds of ancient readers Jael's murder of her rude "guest" (V. H. Matthews, "Hospitality and Hostility in Judges 4," *BTB* 21 [1991]: 13–21; idem, *Judges and Ruth*, 68–73). As with the character of Deborah earlier in the account, so here too the woman is the active character and the man the passive one (Kooij).

The narrator's provision of dramatic narrative at this point allows the reader to experience the exchange between Jael and Sisera within the secrecy of the tent. This exchange is dripping with sexual innuendo and yet leads to slaughter (Niditch, *Judges*, 66–67). Sisera, feeling secure in Jael's tent and physically drained from fighting the battle and digesting the milk, is soon fast asleep. Jael then performs the deed that appears to be planned from the outset, using a hammer to drive a tent peg through his temple and kill this enemy of Israel. In her act Jael echoes the deceptive act of Ehud (cf. 3:21), who also took/reached (*lqḥ*) a weapon in hand (*yd*) and drove/plunged (*tqʿ*) it into the

enemy (Webb, 136; Brenner, 132; Chisholm, 39; O'Connell, 121).

According to O'Connell, 118–19, the military character of Jael's actions is already foreshadowed in the wording of 4:18: "Jael went out to meet Sisera," which portrays her "going out in military fashion." In her actions she performs a deed in place of Barak as promised. The reminder that Jael is Heber's wife just prior to the description of her violent deed accentuates the irony of Sisera's death in the secure perimeter of his ally (see Note on 4:17).

When Barak finally arrives in pursuit of Sisera, Jael invites him into her tent to see the dreadful scene. Barak's discovery echoes that of Eglon's attendants in 3:24–25 (Webb, 136), thus demoting Barak to the status of foolish servant. This scene brings to fulfillment Deborah's prophetic warning to Barak in 4:9, that because Barak did not trust Yahweh to engage battle on his own without Deborah, Yahweh would "hand Sisera over to a woman." Though one might think Deborah would be that woman, it is the unlikely foreigner Jael who fulfills this prophecy; this echoes a motif evidenced elsewhere even in Canaanite literature (see the Ugaritic Tale of Aqhat, *COS*, 1.103; *CTA* 19.205–21, where Paghat, Aqhat's sister, assumes the male role and avenges his murder; cf. Baruch Margalit, "Observations on the Jael-Sisera Story [Judges 4–5]," in *Pomegranates and Golden Bells: Studies in Biblical, Jewish, and Near Eastern Ritual, Law, and Literature in Honor of Jacob Milgrom* [ed. David P. Wright, David Noel Freedman, and Avi Hurvitz; Winona Lake, Ind.: Eisenbrauns, 1995], 629–41; McCann, 65).

23–24 While the victory over Sisera is clearly significant, signaling the beginning of God's overthrow of Jabin king of Hazor, according to the narrator it is merely part of a larger complex of battles through which the Israelites grow progressively stronger until they defeat him.

NOTES

17 שָׁלוֹם (*šālôm*, "friendly relations"). Although this word may simply refer to a lack of war between enemies (see 1Sa 7:14) or to a settlement negotiated with a victorious army, the fact that the Kenites had informed Sisera of Barak's movements suggests that here *šālôm* refers to a peace treaty established between two peoples (cf. Jos 9:15). See further Soggin, 66, who points to use of the Akkadian cognate (*salīmum*) in Mari texts for a positive relationship or alliance. Interestingly, the name Heber can mean "ally" (McCann, 52)—ironic in this story since he and his wife (Jael) end up allied to opposing sides in the war.

20 עֲמֹד (*ʿᵃmôd*, "stand"). This imperatival form is masculine singular but is addressed to the woman Jael. The form may be a scribal error but most likely the word should be pointed as an infinitive absolute that here functions as an imperative (Joüon, 123.u). See Schneider, 80, for the suggestion that this apparent error is purposeful, transferring to Jael the prerogatives of a male victorious over his enemy (here Sisera).

21 בַּלְאַט (*ballāʿṭ*, "quietly"). This term, spelled also בַּלָּט (*ballāṭ*), is used elsewhere to describe an action done surreptitiously (1Sa 18:22; 24:5; Ru 3:7; *HALOT*, 527).

24 הָלוֹך וְקָשָׁה (*hālôk wᵉqāšâ*, "grew stronger and stronger"). See Joüon, 123.s, for the infinitive absolute of הלך (*hlk*) followed by *waw* plus an adjective to express continuity (1Sa 14:19; 2Sa 15:12; 18:25). The adjective here (קָשֶׁה, *qāšeh*) means "hard, difficult," and thus refers to a progressive harshness or severity to Israel's power against Jabin.

2. The Song of Deborah and Barak (5:1–31a)

OVERVIEW

The song of Deborah and Barak is often considered one of the oldest pieces in the OT (on this debate contrast H.-D. Neef, "Der Stil des Deboraliedes [Ri 5]," *Zeitschrift für Althebraistik* 8 [1995]: 275–93, who argues for pre-1000 BC; Bernd J. Diebner, "Wann sang Deborah ihr Lied? Überlegungen zu zwei der ältesten Texte des TNK [Ri 4 und 5]," *Amsterdamse cahiers voor exegese en bijbelse theologie* 14 [1995]: 106–30, who argues for the Hasmonean period, 140–37 BC]; see also Gray, *Joshua, Judges, Ruth*, 261; Schloen, 18–38). The song progressively unfolds a poetic account of the battle between Israel and Sisera already encountered in Judges 4 (5:4–8, 11b, 13–21a, 22, 25–30). The dominance of Debo-

rah and the concluding focus on the two women related to Sisera's death are evidence of the female perspective of Judges 5 in contrast to Judges 4 (Kooij; Niditch, *Judges*, 76).

While in this poetic version many details are missing from the earlier prose account, new elements in the story are added (see esp. 5:4–5, 28–30). At regular intervals this account is creatively intertwined with a series of exhortations, spoken by both singer and congregation, that exhort and express the praise of Yahweh, call the defeated foe to listen and reflect, and declare curse and blessing on various participants in the story (5:2–3, 9–11a, 12, 21b, 23–24, 31; see similar intertwining in other ancient Near Eastern texts by Alexander Globe, "Literary Structure and Unity of the Song of Deborah," *JBL* 93 [1974]: 499; contra J. Blenkinsopp, "Ballad Style and Psalm Style in the Song of Deborah: A Discussion," *Bib* 42 [1961]: 61–76).

In this way Judges 5 is not only a song praising Yahweh, but also (as heroic poetry) one that blesses and curses human characters present or absent in this deliverance (C. L. Echols, "The Eclipse of God in the Song of Deborah [Judges 5]:

The Role of Yhwh in the Light of Heroic Poetry," *TynBul* 56 [2005]: 149–52). For the social context suggested by this poem see Patton, 38–40, who concludes: "The overall impression left by the text is of a very simple society, with few mechanisms for waging war, coordinating intertribal activity, or even approaching God." On the historical and economic context reflected in this song, see Schloen, 18–38.

a. Narrative Introduction (5:1)

¹On that day Deborah and Barak son of Abinoam sang this song:

COMMENTARY

1 After providing the bulk of the story of Deborah and Barak, the narrator inserts a poetic rehearsal of the story linked to Deborah and Barak. In doing so the narrator follows the pattern established in Exodus, where the victory at the Red Sea/Sea of Reeds is first depicted in prose narrative form (ch. 14) before being rehearsed in poetic praise form (ch. 15) to underline the important victory (see Kooij, 163–64).

By placing Deborah first (and forming the main verb in relation to her [see Note]), Barak is once again identified as the passive character and Deborah as the active one. In the poem itself it is Deborah who speaks in the first person (5:3, 7, 9) and is either addressed (5:12) or listed (5:15) first. The folly of Barak's timidity is evident in this poetic rendition and gives another example of the ineptitude of northern leadership (see Introduction).

NOTE

1 וַתָּשַׁר (*wattāšar*, "sang"). The main verb is cast in the third person feminine singular, matching the first member (Deborah) of the plural subject ("Deborah and Barak"); cf. GKC, 146.g.

b. Exhortation: Bless the Lord and Sing (5:2–3)

2"When the princes in Israel take the lead,
    when the people willingly offer themselves—
    praise the LORD!
3"Hear this, you kings! Listen, you rulers!
    I will sing to the LORD, I will sing;
    I will make music to the LORD, the God of Israel.

COMMENTARY

2–3 A double refrain appears at two points in the poem (vv. 2–3, 9–11a; see Mark A. Vincent, "The Song of Deborah: A Structural and Literary Consideration," *JSOT* 91 [2000]: 69). The first component in this refrain (vv. 2, 9) praises Yahweh with reference to those Israelites who volunteered for this battle, thus preparing the way for the glorification of the tribes that gathered, as well as the questioning and cursing of those who did not respond to the call to war later in the poem (vv. 13–18). The second component (vv. 3, 10–11a) addresses a third party and either expresses the singer's desire to sing praise or issues a call to sing praise to Yahweh. These two refrains highlight the two subjects of this praise song: the divine and the human warriors who responded to Israel's predicament. The "kings" and "rulers" in view here are probably the conquered Canaanite foes (see v. 19).

NOTE

2 בִּפְרֹעַ פְּרָעוֹת (*biprōaʿ peraʿ ôt*, "When the princes ... take the lead"). The verbal root in Qal of the infinitive construct is consistently associated with leaving something unattended (e.g., Eze 24:14), sometimes in relation to letting one's hair hang loosely (esp. when used with רֹאשׁ [*rʾš*]; Lev 10:6; 13:45; 21:10; Nu 5:18; *HALOT*, 970). The LXX[a] has Ἐν τῷ ἄρξασθαι ἀρχηγούς (*En tō arxasthai archēgous*, "When chiefs take the lead" [*NETS*, 207]), while the LXX[b] has Ἀπεκαλύφθη ἀποκάλυμμα (*Apekalyphthē apokalymma*, "An unveiling was unveiled" [*NETS*, 207]). Although Peter Craigie ("Note on Judges 5:2," *VT* 18 [1968]: 397–99) suggested that in view here was "the gathering up" of hair, which preceded battle (based especially on a description in the Epic of Tikultu Ninurta [line 40], but lacking clear philological evidence), his conclusion was that it is based on a root preserved in Arabic cognates that denote "exclusive/complete dedication." This basis would render "When men wholly dedicated themselves," with the feminine plural form (פְּרָעוֹת, *pᵉrāʿôt*) representing an intensive plural emphasizing the element of exclusive dedication (cf. Gray, 1988: 423; Block, 220).

While this rendering brings the line into closer association with the second line concerning the people's volunteering, it is not necessary in Hebrew poetry (cf. James Barr, *Comparative Philology and the Text of the Old Testament* [Oxford: Clarendon, 1968], 277–82), and the lack of Hebrew evidence makes it less attractive. The reading of the LXX[b] probably reflects a creative rendering of what is found in the MT (since ἀποκαλύπτω [*apokalyptō*] means "to uncover"). The reading of the LXX[a] has suggested to some that there is a secondary meaning or a homonym related to leading/leadership (cf. Dt 32:42; Arabic *faraʾa*; Block, 220). Furthermore, when the root נדב (*ndb*, Hithpael) in reference to the people reappears in the second line of Judges 5:9, the first line speaks of "those who decree" (חָקַק, *ḥāqaq*), that is, leaders (cf. Isa 10:1).

It is interesting that Deuteronomy 32:42 uses the noun here in a context of war as well. There it is used with the noun רֹאשׁ (*rōʾš*, head), which some have interpreted as speaking of "chiefs"; but in light of the use of רֹאשׁ (*rōʾš*) with פרע (*prʿ*) in Leviticus 10:6; 13:45; 21:10; Numbers 5:18, here רֹאשׁ (*rōʾš*) may refer to hair, as it does in those places, and thus may be a reference to letting one's hair grow out during times of war. Boling favored the first gloss ("leaving something unattended"), translating here "have regained liberty" (cf. Pr 29:18; Soggin, 84). The rendering of the LXX[a] may be correct, in the light of the appearance of the root *prʿ* in Ugaritic texts to refer to "prince" (*HALOT*, 970) or as a play on the Egyptian royal title "Pharaoh" (פַּרְעֹה, *parʿōh*).

עַם (*ʿam*, "people"). This word is used at times for people who bear arms, that is, an army (Nu 20:20; 31:32; Jos 8:1, 3, 11; 10:7; 11:7; 1Sa 11:11; 1Ki 20:10).

c. Account: Advance of Divine Warrior Yahweh (5:4–5)

> [4]"O Lᴏʀᴅ, when you went out from Seir,
>   when you marched from the land of Edom,
>   the earth shook, the heavens poured,
>   the clouds poured down water.
> [5]The mountains quaked before the Lᴏʀᴅ, the One of Sinai,
>   before the Lᴏʀᴅ, the God of Israel.

COMMENTARY

4–5 The account in ch. 5 begins with a heavenly perspective, tracing at the outset, and so giving precedence to, Yahweh's activity as the Divine Warrior. This emphasis can already be discerned in the fact that even when the singers praise the human warriors in the first refrain (vv.2a, 2b, 9a, 9b), they conclude with the declaration, "praise [bless] the LORD" (vv.2c, 9c). This declaration sets the tone for the account of the battle in vv.19–22, which will show that it is action of the heavenly armies and bodies that determines the outcome rather than the strength of the human armies.

As is typical of such depictions, the march of the Divine Warrior is marked by convulsions in creation, especially those related to violent earthquakes and rainstorms, the noise of which was symbolic of divine action. Not coincidentally, in the Canaanite context it was Baal who rode the clouds and controlled the rain. According to this song, Yahweh plays this role (cf. Dt 33:26–29; Pss 68:33–34 [34–35]; 104:3, 13; Block, 223). The poem links Yahweh's appearing to ancient mountain ranges,

here identified with the regions of Edom (for Seir, cf. Ge 33:14; 36:8–9) and Sinai. Such an association is also evident in Yahweh's appearing as Divine Warrior in Deuteronomy 33:2, where he is accompanied by "myriads of holy ones" and is identified as the God "who rides on the heavens … on the clouds in his majesty" (33:26) in order to drive out Israel's enemy (33:27) and "trample down their high places" (33:29).

Here in Judges 5 Yahweh's appearance is linked more directly to Seir/Edom, yet he is also identified with Sinai. This tracks the route along which Yahweh first appeared to Israel as a nation as they moved from Egypt to the Promised Land, where he then functioned as their Divine Warrior in order to conquer the land.

NOTE

5 זֶה סִינַי (*zeh sînay*, "the One of Sinai"). The NIV treats *zeh* as a determinative use of the demonstrative (*IBHS*, 19.5.c–d; Joüon, 143.i; cf. Ex 32:1), referring here to Yahweh as the God who appeared on Sinai in Exodus through Numbers (O'Connell, 462). The MT accents the phrase differently, however—"Mountains flowed from before YHWH; This Sinai, from before YHWH God of Israel"—thus treating זֶה סִינַי (*zeh sînay*) as a specification of the more general term הָרִים (*hārîm*) in the first line. The LXX affirms the MT. But the MT's accentuation of the parallel Psalm 68:9 [8] suggests that זֶה סִינַי (*zeh sînay*) is an appellative of Yahweh, as the NIV translates here in Judges 5:5.

d. Account: Predicament of Israel (5:6–8)

⁶"In the days of Shamgar son of Anath,
    in the days of Jael, the roads were abandoned;
    travelers took to winding paths.
⁷Village life in Israel ceased,
    ceased until I, Deborah, arose,
    arose a mother in Israel.
⁸When they chose new gods,
    war came to the city gates,

and not a shield or spear was seen
among forty thousand in Israel.

COMMENTARY

6-8 In Judges 5 the presentation begins with the predicament of Israel (vv.6-8) and traces the story to the time of Shamgar (see 3:31). The fact that Ehud's death is noted at the beginning of the account of Deborah/Barak in 4:1 suggests that Shamgar's activity coincided with that of Deborah, which thus makes sense of the close association between Shamgar and Jael in 5:6. It is interesting that these individuals are chosen to set the context for the predicament. These two are unlikely saviors for Israel, both being foreigners who act in Israel's behalf. Israel's desperation in this period creates space for the rise of Deborah.

Descriptions of impediments to transportation (v.6), stifling of rural activity (v.7a; see Note), and lack of military equipment (v.8b) are symbolic of the depth of oppression perpetrated by Jabin and Sisera

at that time (see 4:2-3). Transportation in the ancient world was primarily for economic purposes, and evidence here suggests that these Canaanites "had stifled caravan traffic through the plain of Jezreel," most likely through "extortion of exorbitant tolls" (Schloen, 20). Here the abandonment of the more convenient major roadways in favor of the more difficult twisting paths creates a crisis. The villagers have refrained from dealing with the crisis (see Notes).

It is in this context that Deborah arises, identifying herself as "a mother in Israel" and thus suggesting her "life-giving" maternal care for this defenseless people (Exum, "Feminist Criticism," 72; see below on Jael). The reference to choosing "new ones" (see Notes) in v.8 follows from the rise of Deborah, and not mentioning Barak by name plays down his role (Block, 1999).

NOTES

7 פְּרָזוֹן (pᵉrāzôn, "village life"). This term only appears here in the OT (5:7, 11), but is strikingly similar to פְּרָזוֹת (pᵉrāzôt), which refers to "open country" in contrast to walled cities (cf. Eze 38:11; Est 9:19; Zec 2:8), thus possibly referring to village life or villagers. Another suggestion is that it is related to a Semitic root meaning "guidance" and, by extension, "leader/leadership" or "warrior" (see Arabic faraza; HALOT, 965). The LXX^a has φραζων (phrazōn, "a spokesman" [NETS, 207]) and the LXX^b has δυνατοί (dynatoi, "mighty ones" [NETS, 207]), possibly reflecting this other Semitic root.

חָדְלוּ (ḥodlû, "ceased"). Here the NIV understands this verb as indicating that village economic life has come to an end, but the verb can also have the meaning "to cease doing, to refrain from doing" (HALOT, 292), which would mean that the villagers refrained from dealing with the crisis until Deborah arose (Schloen, 24).

8 יִבְחַר אֱלֹהִים חֲדָשִׁים (yibḥar ᵉlōhîm hᵃdāšîm, "When they chose new gods"). This phrase is ambiguous in Hebrew and could be translated as "He [Israel?] chooses new gods" (as the NIV) or "God chooses new ones [leaders?]" (as Block, 227). The LXX has "they chose new gods" (*NETS*, 207). While the NIV's translation is possible and is thus a reference to Israel's disobedience depicted at the outset of Judges 4, the use of the singular verb here suggests it is God who is doing the choosing rather than the people.

אָז לֶחֶם שְׁעָרִים (*ʾāz lāḥem šeʿārîm*, "when … war came to the city gates"). It has been suggested that שְׁעָרִים לֶחֶם (*lāḥem šeʿārîm*, "war [came to] the city gates") should be repointed as לְחֶם שְׁעָרִים (*lāḥem šeʿārîm*, NEB: "they consorted with demons"; cf. Dt 32:17; Kevin J. Cathcart, "The 'Demons' in Judges 5:8a," *BZ* 21 [1977]: 111–12), which would bolster the NIV's translation of the first line; or that the words should be redivided as לחמש ערים (*lḥmš ʿrym*, "for five cities"; cf. Peter Craigie, "Some Further Notes on the Song of Deborah," *VT* 22 [1972]: 349–53), which may lie behind the LXX[b] ("then the cities of the rulers fought"); or that consonants should have been added to render אזלו חמשי ערים (*ʾzlw ḥmšy ʿrym*, "the armed men of the cities came forth"; Barnabas Lindars, "Deborah's Song: Women in the Old Testament," *BJRL* 65 [1983]: 168, n. 22; O'Connell, 463). This final suggestion has no versional support.

The noun לֶחֶם (*lāḥem*, "war") only occurs here. Although there is a verbal cognate that means "to fight/do battle," one would expect instead מִלְחָמָה (*milḥāmâ*). The LXX[a] reads here "barley bread," which is the more common gloss for a nominal with these letters. Little certainty is possible from these diverse witnesses, but the reference to the implements of war in the following lines suggests that war is in view rather than barley bread.

e. Exhortation: Bless the Lord and Sing (5:9–11a)

⁹My heart is with Israel's princes,
    with the willing volunteers among the people.
    Praise the LORD!

¹⁰"You who ride on white donkeys,
    sitting on your saddle blankets,
    and you who walk along the road,
consider ¹¹the voice of the singers at the watering places.
    They recite the righteous acts of the LORD,
    the righteous acts of his warriors in Israel.

COMMENTARY

9–11a Echoing the style and vocabulary of 5:2–3, the song breaks off from the account for a moment to call the audience to praise Yahweh on account of the actions of the leaders and warriors and the victory ("righteous deeds") that has been won by Yahweh. Also addressed are those riding on white donkeys, sitting on cloth, and traveling on the road—possibly a reference to the same royal figures addressed in the earlier refrain who, to this point, had exclusive access to the roadways (see v.6

above), or possibly to those figures whose trade had been encumbered by the Canaanite taxation (Schloen, 25). It is probably not coincidental that donkeys were associated with royal figures in the OT (see Ge 49:11; Zec 9:9; cf. Boda, *Haggai/Zechariah*, 416–17). This audience is called to reflect (see Note) on the righteous deeds of Yahweh being recited by the peasantry watering their flocks.

NOTES

9 בָּעָם (*bāʿām*, "among the people"). See Note on 5:2.

לְחוֹקְקֵי (*leḥôqeqê*, "with ... princes"). See Note on 5:14.

10 שִׂיחוּ (*sîḥû*, "consider"). This word is used to describe either "loud, enthusiastic, emotionally laden speech" (whether praise [Pss 105:2; 145:5; 1Ch 16:9]; lament [Pss 55:18; 77:4, 7; Job 7:11]; taunting [Ps 69:13]; or teaching [Pr 6:22]) or "meditation with thanks and praise" (Pss 77:13; 119:15, 23, 27, 48, 78, 148; cf. Job 12:8). The earlier refrain in Judges 5:3 called the audience to "hear ... listen," suggesting that what is in view here is "meditation with thanks and praise." But it is possible that in the first refrain the poet calls the audience to "hear and listen" and here now to "speak."

11a מִקּוֹל מְחַצְצִים (*miqqôl mehaṣṣîm*, "the voice of singers"). The second word is the Piel participle of the root חצץ (*ḥṣṣ*), the Qal of which is related to "dividing into groups" (Pr 30:27), which in the present context—one that speaks of watering places—may refer to those who divide the flocks or distribute the water for the purposes of drinking (Soggin, 87; Block, 229). Interestingly, the use of the Pual of this root in Job 21:21 refers to something's being at an end and so may indicate that the Piel participle here may refer to the remnant left over from the battle. A final suggestion is that since the word for arrow in Hebrew is חֵץ (*ḥēṣ*) and the present song is about military action, it may be that this word refers to archers (BDB, 346). All of these suggestions are tentative at best.

צִדְקוֹת יְהוָה צִדְקֹת פִּרְזֹנוֹ (*ṣidqôt yhwh ṣidqôt pirzōnô*, "the righteous acts of the LORD, the righteous acts of his warriors"). The word צְדָקָה (*ṣedāqâ*; GK 7407) can refer to "saving deeds" and thus to the victory that has been won (cf. Pss 71:5, 16; 98:2). Clearly the first construct pair (צִדְקוֹת יְהוָה, *ṣidqôt yhwh*) describes saving deeds accomplished by Yahweh. The second construct pair (צִדְקֹת פִּרְזֹנוֹ, *ṣidqôt pirzōnô*) is less clear. It may refer to Yahweh's saving deeds for his peasantry/warriors (see Note on 5:7) or to the saving deeds of the peasantry/warriors themselves that parallel the deeds of Yahweh. The latter seems appropriate in light of the focus of the refrain in vv. 2 and 9, which, after depicting the deeds of the leaders and warriors, calls for praise of Yahweh.

f. Account: Cry of the People, Mustering the Army (5:11b)

"Then the people of the LORD
went down to the city gates.

COMMENTARY

11b Before the account broke away to the refrain of vv.9–11a, the poet had been depicting a weaponless army facing war at the city gates. As the poetic account resumes for a brief moment in v.11b, the army (see Note) has gone down to meet the enemy at the city gates.

NOTE

11b אָז יָרְדוּ (ʾāz yārᵉdû, "Then ... went down"). This comment signals the resumption of the main account. See Note below on 5:13.

עַם־יְהוָה (ʿam-yhwh, "the people of the LORD"). See Note on 5:2.

g. Exhortation: Call to Deborah and Barak (5:12)

> ¹²'Wake up, wake up, Deborah!
>   Wake up, wake up, break out in song!
> Arise, O Barak!
>   Take captive your captives, O son of Abinoam.'

COMMENTARY

12 The account is interrupted for a brief moment again as Deborah and Barak are now exhorted by another voice, possibly now of those whom Deborah (the "I" of the song who speaks also on behalf of Barak; cf. v.1) has been exhorting to praise throughout the song (vv.2, 9). They call Deborah to awake and declare a song, and Barak to lead away the defeated captives. This exhortation assumes the successful completion of the battle, the context in which this victory song was sung.

h. Account: The Troops Assemble (5:13–18)

> ¹³"Then the men who were left
>   came down to the nobles;

the people of the LORD
    came to me with the mighty.
¹⁴Some came from Ephraim, whose roots were in Amalek;
    Benjamin was with the people who followed you.
From Makir captains came down,
    from Zebulun those who bear a commander's staff.
¹⁵The princes of Issachar were with Deborah;
    yes, Issachar was with Barak,
    rushing after him into the valley.
In the districts of Reuben
    there was much searching of heart.
¹⁶Why did you stay among the campfires
    to hear the whistling for the flocks?
In the districts of Reuben
    there was much searching of heart.
¹⁷Gilead stayed beyond the Jordan.
    And Dan, why did he linger by the ships?
Asher remained on the coast
    and stayed in his coves.
¹⁸The people of Zebulun risked their very lives;
    so did Naphtali on the heights of the field.

COMMENTARY

13 The account resumes again here in identical fashion to the earlier resumption in 5:11b (see Notes below). Here people are depicted as a remnant fleeing from defeat in battle (e.g., Nu 21:35; 24:19; Dt 2:34; 3:3; Jos 10:20, 28, 30, 33, 37, 39–40; 11:8). They rally to the nobles (cf. Jer 14:3; Ps 16:3; Ne 3:5; 10:30; 2Ch 23:20; Na 2:6; 3:18) as an army of mighty warriors.

14–18 These warriors originate from many tribes and clans, including Ephraim, Benjamin, Makir, Zebulun, Issachar, and Naphtali (vv.14–15a, 18). The fact that they are all northern tribes accords well with a threat from a Canaanite king

in the northern region of Israel. In the midst of this account of the assembling of troops the poet contrasts those tribes and clans who refused to join the coalition—that is, Reuben, Gilead, Dan, and Asher.

The names of Makir and Gilead stand out in this list of names since they are not among the usual names in tribal lists. According to Joshua 17:1–3 the Transjordanian regions of Gilead and Bashan were given to Manasseh's firstborn son, Makir, who was the father of Gilead (cf. Nu 27:1; 1Ch 7:14–19; cf. Boda, 2009, on 1Ch 7:14–19). It may be that these two clans are representative of the tribe of Manasseh, which is missing from this list of northern tribes, and the mention of both clans reflects a division among the Transjordanian Manassehites.

While the link between Makir and Manasseh is most likely, it may be that the reference to Gilead refers to the missing tribe of Gad, which settled in southern Gilead just north of Reuben, mentioned in the previous verse. According to Numbers 32:39–40; Deuteronomy 3:15–16; and Joshua 13:8–32, the land of Gilead was apportioned to both the half tribe of Manasseh and to Gad. Missing from the list, then, are only Judah and Simeon, thus suggesting this battle was a northern affair (though see Johannes C. de Moor, "The Twelve Tribes in the Song of Deborah," *VT* 43 [1993]: 483–94, who sees references to Judah and Levi in 5:13).

Throughout the book of Judges Ephraim is presented as the leader of the northern tribes, established by its actions in 1:22–26 and by expectations voiced in 8:1–3; 12:1–6 (see comments on 8:1–3). But although Ephraim is mentioned first, it is surprising that insignificant Makir and Zebulun are associated with leadership (see Note) and that Issachar is the tribe most closely associated with the leadership of Deborah and Barak. Here, as else-

where in Judges, Joshua's Ephraimite tribe is denigrated (see Introduction).

The poet emphasizes Reuben's failure by placing its mention at the center of the overall poem (Ogden, 119) and surrounding the mocking question of v.16 (see Notes) with a refrain that points to the indecision of Reuben. Gilead, Dan, and Asher are mentioned next, all in relation to bodies of water, with Gilead across the Jordan, Dan on the southern Mediterranean coastline, and Asher on the northern Mediterranean coastline. This poem reflects the period prior to Dan's migration to the far north (cf. Jdg 17–18). All of these tribes were further removed from the threat of Jabin and Sisera but also were more economically integrated with their Canaanite neighbors (see L. E. Stager, "Archaeology, Ecology and Social History: Background Themes to the Song of Deborah," in *Congress Volume: Jerusalem 1986* (ed. J. A. Emerton; VTSup 40; Leiden: Brill, 1988], 221), and so remained home. To accentuate the contrast between those who participated and those who ignored the call, the poet ends the section with a focus on the courageous risk of Zebulun and Naphtali in the battle itself. This focus foreshadows the next phase in the account, which begins in the following verse.

NOTES

12 וּשֲׁבֵה שֶׁבְיְךָ (*ûšᵃbēh šeby^ekā*, "take away your captives"). This collocation is used elsewhere in the OT in Numbers 21:1; Deuteronomy 21:10; Psalm 68:19; and 2 Chronicles 28:5, 8, 11, 17 to refer to a conquering army/leader leading away captives.

13 אָז יְרַד (*ʾāz y^erad*, "Then ... came down"). See Note on 5:11b. Notice how the Hebrew is similar in 5:11b, 13.

עַם יְהוָה (*ʿam yhwh*, "the people of the LORD"). See Note on 5:2. The Masoretes place the *atnaḥ* on עַם (*ʿam*), which results in the translation, "The LORD came to me with the mighty," possibly a reference to his heavenly army, or to an Israelite force led by Yahweh. This placement, however, leaves the term עַם (*ʿam*) in an awkward position in the first half of the verse. The LXXᵃ reads here πότε ἐμεγαλύνθη ἡ ἰσχὺς αὐτοῦ; κύριε, ταπείνωσόν μοι τοὺς ἰσχυροτέρους μου (*pote emeyalynthē hē ischys autou? kyrie, tapeinōson moi tous ischyroterous mou*, "When was his strength increased? Lord, humble for me those who are stronger than me" [*NETS*, 208]), while the LXX[b] reads τότε κατέβη κατάλειμμα τοῖς ἰσχυροῖς, λαὸς κυρίου κατέβη αὐτῷ ἐν τοῖς κραταιοῖς (*tote katebē kataleimma tois ischyrois, laos kyriou katebē autō en tois krataiois*, "Then a remnant went down for the strong ones; the people of the Lord went down for him among the powerful" [*NETS*, 208]). It is wisest to follow the MT's wording but to place the *atnaḥ* before עַם (*ʿam*).

בַּגִּבּוֹרִים (*baggibbôrîm*, "with the mighty"). As in 5:23 below, the preposition *b*ᵉ here could indicate accompaniment ("along with") or be adversative ("against"), but more likely it indicates identity; that is, it "marks the capacity in which an actor behaves" (*IBHS*, 11.2.5.e.; cf. Ex 6:3; Ps 118:7). Thus "the people of Yahweh went down to me as warriors/mighty ones."

14 מִנִּי אֶפְרַיִם שָׁרְשָׁם בַּעֲמָלֵק אַחֲרֶיךָ בִנְיָמִין בַּעֲמָמֶיךָ (*minnî ʾeprayim šoršām baʿᵃmālēq ʾaḥᵃreykā binyāmîn baʿᵃmāmeykā*, "Some came from Ephraim, whose roots were in Amalek; Benjamin was with the people who followed you"). The LXX[a] reads λαὸς Εφραιμ ἐτιμωρήσατο αὐτοὺς ἐν κοιλάδι ἀδελφοῦ σου Βενιαμιν ἐν λαοῖς σου (*laos Ephraim etimōrēsato autous en koiladi adelphou sou Beniamin en laois sou*, "People of Ephraim wreaked vengeance on them in your brother Benjamin's valley, among your peoples" [*NETS*, 208]). Clearly the LXX is reading בעמק (*bᵉmq*, "in the valley") instead of בַּעֲמָלֵק (*baʿᵃmālēq*). Furthermore, the verb τιμωρέω (*timōreō*) translates the Hebrew verb שכל (*škl*, Piel) in Ezekiel 5:17; 14:15, thus suggesting that שָׁרְשָׁם (*šoršām*) may have been שכלם (*šklm*) in the LXX Vorlage. The reference to Amalek makes little sense in this context, while in the light of the following verse the reference to "valley" does.

מְחֹקְקִים...מֹשְׁכִים בְּשֵׁבֶט סֹפֵר (*mᵉḥōqqîm ... mōšᵉkîm bᵉšēbet sōpēr*, "captains ... those who bear a commander's staff"). The first term is the Poel participle of חקק (*ḥqq*, "to order, decide"), used as a participle to refer to a commander or ruler in Genesis 49:10; Numbers 21:18; Psalm 60:9//108:9; and Deuteronomy 33:21. Interestingly, the Qal participle of this same root is used in Judges 5:9 to refer to leadership as well. The term "staff" is the scepter of a ruler/leader, as in Genesis 49:10; Isaiah 9:3; 14:5; Ezekiel 19:11; and Amos 1:5, 8. Noticeable here is that these same terms are used of Judah in Genesis 49:10. The use of סֹפֵר, usually translated "scribe," may reflect the leader's role of mustering and recording troops, or may reflect another semantic root (e.g., Akkadian *sapāru*, which means "to rule"; see Block, 232).

15 חִקְקֵי־לֵב (*ḥiqqê-lēb*, "searching of heart"). The refrain in 5:16 reads חִקְרֵי־לֵב (*ḥiqrê-lēb*, "searching of heart"), but here the MT reads "prescriptions of heart." Most likely this reading represents a scribal error in 5:15, which should read the same as 5:16.

16 הַמִּשְׁפְּתָיִם (*hammišpᵉtayim*, "the campfires"). This translation (see BDB, 1046) is most likely based on the similarity of this word to the verb שׁפת (*špt*, "set [on a fire]"; 2Ki 4:38; Eze 24:3) and the noun אַשְׁפֹּת (*ʾašpōt*, "ash heap, refuse heap, dunghill"; 1Sa 2:8//Ps 113:7; Job 2:8; La 4:5). The word appears elsewhere only in Genesis 49:14 (but see שְׁפַתָּיִם [*šᵉpattayim*] in Eze 40:43; Ps 68:14). *HALOT*, 652, however, glosses: "two saddlebaskets of a pack-mule," which is suggested by the connection to donkeys in Genesis 49:14 and other Semitic cognates (Ugar. *mtpdm*; Arab. *matafid*). Certainty on the meaning of this word eludes us.

17 לְחוֹף יַמִּים (*lᵉḥôp yammîm*, "on the coast"). This designation always refers to the Mediterranean coast (cf. Ge 49:13; Dt 1:7; Jos 9:1; Jer 47:7; Eze 25:16; Block, 233).

i. Account: The Battle (5:19–21a)

> **19**"Kings came, they fought;
> the kings of Canaan fought
> at Taanach by the waters of Megiddo,
> but they carried off no silver, no plunder.
> **20**From the heavens the stars fought,
> from their courses they fought against Sisera.
> **21**The river Kishon swept them away,
> the age-old river, the river Kishon.

COMMENTARY

19–21a What follows here is a poetic account of the battle described in 4:13–16. While ch. 4 focused mostly on the exploits of Sisera, commander of the Canaanite king Jabin, who reigned from Hazor (4:2), without losing sight of Sisera the poem in ch. 5 reminds the reader of the royal forces behind Sisera. Their defeat is indicated by their lack of silver and plunder, foreshadowing the hope of Sisera's mother at the end of the poem (vv. 28–30). The narrative in ch. 4 spoke only of a battle at the Kishon River, but the poem identifies the location as Taanach by the waters of Megiddo. Taanach was an ancient Canaanite royal town usually associated with Tell Ti'innik, which is situated in the foothills on the southern edge of the Jezreel Valley overlooking the seasonal swamps caused by poor drainage of the Kishon (*ABD*, 6:288). Megiddo is located five miles northwest along the same edge of the foothills.

The fact that the narrative describes Sisera as fleeing from his chariot on foot (4:15) and that the poem emphasizes the key role played by the Kishon River (v. 21) suggest the Canaanite chariots were incapacitated by the swampy terrain. References to the river as the "age-old river" and to stars fighting from heaven against Sisera highlight the role not of Barak and his cadre of warriors, but rather of the Divine Warrior, Yahweh, whose march from Seir/Edom/Sinai in 5:4–5 had caused similar manipulation of the cosmos. The image of stars fighting may be based on a meteorite shower or shooting stars (cf. J. F. A. Sawyer, "Joshua 10:12–14 and the Solar Eclipse of 30 September 1131 B.C.," *PEQ* 104 [1972]: 139–46; H. A. J. Kruger, "Sun and Moon Grinding to a Halt: Exegetical Remarks on Joshua 10:9–14 and Related Texts in Judges," *Hervormde teologiese studies* 55 [1999]: 1089) and is one that does appear elsewhere in ancient Near Eastern literature (see Block, 237; Matthews, *Judges and Ruth*, 77, who cite the Gebel Barkal stela of Thutmose III of Egypt as noting a star's defeat of the enemy).

j. Exhortation: Calling My Soul (5:21b)

March on, my soul; be strong!

COMMENTARY

21b For a moment there is a break in the account as the singer calls on her soul to march on in strength. In Deuteronomy 33:29 and Micah 1:3 Yahweh is depicted as marching to victory; in Micah 5:4–5 [5–6] it is the Assyrian who marches. Here the march is connected to the singer, whose victory is assured by Yahweh.

NOTE

21 תִּדְרְכִי (tidrᵉkî, "march on"). This form is the nonperfective of injunction (*IBHS*, 31.5.b; cf. Ps 51:9).

k. Account: The Horses (5:22)

²²Then thundered the horses' hoofs —
galloping, galloping go his mighty steeds.

COMMENTARY

22 Returning to the account but briefly, the poet describes the thundering of horses' hoofs. Whose "mighty steeds" are in view here is uncertain, whether those from the chariots of Sisera's army, freed from their burdens now mired in the swamps of the Kishon, or Yahweh's divine army. The Hebrew verb used for the "beating" of Sisera's horses' hoofs (*hlm*) foreshadows Jael's fatal blow (*hlm*) in 5:26 (Ogden, 116; O'Connell, 122, n. 132).

NOTE

22 אָז (ʾāz, "Then"). See Note on 5:11b. This word signals the resumption of the account.

מִדַּהֲרוֹת דַּהֲרוֹת (middahᵃrôt dahᵃrôt, "galloping, galloping"). The words used here function as onomatopoeia by sounding out the noise of horses galloping. Repetition creates intensity (GKC, 123.e;). Here the preposition מִן (min) designates instrumentality (see *BHRG*, 289).

l. Exhortation: Curse on Meroz, Who Did Not Help (5:23)

> ²³'Curse Meroz,' said the angel of the LORD.
>   'Curse its people bitterly,
>   because they did not come to help the LORD,
>   to help the LORD against the mighty.'

COMMENTARY

23 With the account of the battle complete, the poem returns to its earlier focus on those who did not respond to the muster of Deborah and Barak (see 5:16–17). Meroz is most likely a town, but it is never mentioned elsewhere in the OT. While 5:16–17 merely questions and describes those who did not participate in the battle with Deborah and Barak, Meroz is here cursed by the "angel of the LORD" (see Note on 2:1) for not joining Yahweh in the battle. This curse serves an important function at this point in the poem by standing in stark contrast to the blessing about to be pronounced on Jael in the following verse.

NOTE

23 בַּגִּבּוֹרִים (*baggibbôrîm*, "against the mighty"). See Note on 5:13.

m. Exhortation: Blessing on Jael (5:24)

> ²⁴"Most blessed of women be Jael,
>   the wife of Heber the Kenite,
>   most blessed of tent-dwelling women.

COMMENTARY

24 The curse against Meroz in 5:23 is twinned with a blessing on Jael in 5:24, possibly a continuation of the speech of the angel of the Lord in v.23. Meroz, representative of those in Israel who did not join the coalition to defend their compatriots in 5:13–18, contrasts this foreign woman, who is blessed for her courageous act described in 5:25–27. These two exhortations in 5:23–24 function as a segue to the final installments of the account, which will seal forever Deborah's prophecy in 4:9 that any human honor due for this victory will go to a woman.

n. Account: Death of Sisera (5:25–27)

²⁵He asked for water, and she gave him milk;
   in a bowl fit for nobles she brought him curdled milk.
²⁶Her hand reached for the tent peg,
   her right hand for the workman's hammer.
She struck Sisera, she crushed his head,
   she shattered and pierced his temple.
²⁷At her feet he sank,
   he fell; there he lay.
At her feet he sank, he fell;
   where he sank, there he fell—dead.

COMMENTARY

25–27 The account concludes by focusing on the death of Sisera; it juxtaposes the perspectives of two women who would have played an important role at the time of his death—his killer, Jael (vv. 24–27), and his mother (vv. 28–30; cf. Kooij). Jael plays an important role in the narrative of Judges 4 (see vv. 17–22), where she delivers the fatal blow to Sisera (see above on v. 22), commander of Jabin's army. There she invites the desperate Sisera, fresh from his defeat, into her tent, and when he asks for water she gives him milk (on maternal connotation here, see Exum, "Feminist Criticism," 72; on sexual connotations, see Brenner; Susan Niditch, "Eroticism and Death in the Tale of Sisera," in *Gender and Difference in Ancient Israel* [ed. Peggy Lynne Day; Minneapolis: Fortress, 1989], 43–57; idem, *Judges*, 81–82; Exum, "Feminist Criticism," 73; Patton, 38–39).

Jael promises to conceal his presence from anyone who asks, and when he finally falls asleep, she violently kills him by driving a tent peg through his temple. These same details are incorporated into the poem in ch. 5, now with greater flourish that draws the reader into the violent scene. The poet describes in detail the rich constitution of the milk and the elegance of the container in which it was served; both contrast with what follows—the crushing of Sisera's head, the shattering and piercing of his temple, and what appears to be a slow-motion death scene as his body reacts to the violent blow to his head. The repetition of words in 5:27 "not only provides emphasis, it also slows down the pace of the story, so that at its climax we move into slow motion; the poet wants the reader actually to visualize the enemy gradually falling to the ground under the rain of blows from Jael's hammer" (Ogden, 119).

o. Account: Mother of Sisera (5:28–30)

> ²⁸"Through the window peered Sisera's mother;
>   behind the lattice she cried out,
> 'Why is his chariot so long in coming?
>   Why is the clatter of his chariots delayed?'
> ²⁹The wisest of her ladies answer her;
>   indeed, she keeps saying to herself,
> ³⁰'Are they not finding and dividing the spoils:
>   a girl or two for each man,
> colorful garments as plunder for Sisera,
>   colorful garments embroidered,
> highly embroidered garments for my neck—
>   all this as plunder?'

COMMENTARY

28–30 Immediately after experiencing the violent death of the unsuspecting Sisera within Jael's humble tent (v.27), the reader is transported by the poet to the palace of Sisera's mother, from where she peers through the window (see Note) awaiting his arrival from the battle (v.28). The poet voices her nervous questions as she ponders the delay of both his chariot and that of his contingent. She is a woman of means served by handmaidens, but her wealth and status are based on the success of her son in battles such as the one from which he has not yet returned.

The question in v.30, voiced by her handmaidens but on her mind as well, represents a possible favorable answer to her original questions. He is delayed by the quantity and quality of the plunder (on which see Schloen, 30, as typical of caravan trade through this region), among which will be valuable items that will make up for all the worry caused by the present delay. The readers are left with this question ringing in their ears, a question for which they know the answer since they have just witnessed in all its gory detail the brutal death of this woman's only hope in that ancient world. This final character is the third "maternal" character (after Deborah and Jael, see above) identified in this poem. This feminine trio accentuates the comedy and tragedy of this account, highlighting women's role as either good or bad mother (Exum, "Feminist Criticism," 71–74).

NOTES

28 בְּעַד הַחַלּוֹן נִשְׁקְפָה ... בְּעַד הָאֶשְׁנָב (bᵉʿad haḥallôn nišqᵉpâ ... bᵉʿad hāʾešnāb, "Through the window peered ... behind the lattice"). See the use of the first phrase in 2 Samuel 6:16//1 Chronicles 15:29; Proverbs 7:6 (cf. the Hiphil in Ge 26:8; 2Ki 9:30), and the second in Proverbs 7:6, where it is paired with חַלּוֹן (ḥallôn; Block, 242). These passages all describe royal urban contexts. This image thus accentuates the contrast between Jael and Sisera's mother (O'Connell, 123).

30 רַחַם רַחֲמָתַיִם (raḥam raḥᵃmātayim, "a girl or two"). This term, used here in the singular and dual, usually refers to a woman's womb; here it is a crude reference to the sexual abuse of the women captured as spoil (Mieke Bal, *Murder and Difference: Gender, Genre, and Scholarship on Sisera's Death* [Indiana Studies in Biblical Literature; Bloomington, Ind.: Indiana Univ. Press, 1988], 134). This text is "dripping with sarcasm" in the contrast between Sisera's supposed rape and "his violent demise at the feet of a courageous woman" (Chisholm, 38–39).

p. Exhortation: Concluding Curse and Blessing (5:31a)

> ³¹"So may all your enemies perish, O LORD!
> But may they who love you be like the sun
> when it rises in its strength."

COMMENTARY

31a In keeping with the earlier rhythm of curse and blessing established in 5:23–24, the poem concludes with a curse on all enemies of Yahweh but a blessing on those who love him. Such love is identified in Deuteronomy as the normative covenantal response to Yahweh's grace and mercy expressed toward Israel (Dt 6:5; cf. 5:10; 6:5; 7:9; 10:12; 11:1, 13, 22; 13:4; 19:9; 30:6, 16, 20). In Deuteronomy 6:3–5 it is placed alongside obeying and in 10:12 alongside fearing, walking, serving, and observing. This concluding curse and blessing express the belief that Israel's success and the Canaanites' failure were directly related to their relationship to Yahweh.

NOTE

31a וְאֹהֲבָיו (wᵉʾōhᵃbāyw, "they who love you"). The MT and LXX (οἱ ἀγαπῶντες αὐτόν, hoi agapōntes auton) read here, "they who love him." The NIV's translation is based on a couple of medieval Hebrew manuscripts, the Syriac Peshitta, and the Vulgate, whose readings are inferior to the MT's and LXX's in this instance.

3. The Story of Deborah and Barak: Narrative Conclusion (5:31b)

Then the land had peace forty years.

COMMENTARY

31b That the song in Judges 5 functions within the larger narrative account of Deborah and Barak is clear from 5:31b, where the narrative peace, which commonly brings closure to the accounts of the major judges (cf. 3:11, 30; 8:28), is inserted just before the account of Gideon, which begins in ch. 6.

REFLECTION

With the Deborah-Barak narrative Yahweh not only acts in behalf of Israel but also speaks to them, here through the prophetic figure Deborah. By going into battle in response to Deborah's commission, Barak does display some measure of faith (Heb 11:32), but at the same time the passage accentuates his lack of faith, which leads to his dishonoring through the actions of the unlikely foreigner Jael, who delivers the fatal blow to the enemy's general. So also Yahweh acts more directly in this account than in any other by marching as Divine Warrior to defeat Israel's enemy.

But God's action does not discount entirely the efforts of those tribes who braved the fray, nor does it lessen the indictment against those who did not support their compatriots. This passage, then, highlights the inadequacy of the present leadership model and creates expectation for a better future. This future model will celebrate Yahweh's Divine-Warrior role as he works wonders on behalf of Israel.

F. Gideon (6:1–8:32)

OVERVIEW

The account of Gideon follows the basic structure of the six major accounts throughout the book of Judges (Othniel, Ehud, Deborah/Barak, Gideon, Jephthah, Samson): Israel's apostasy (6:1a), Yahweh's discipline through a foreign enemy (6:1b–5), Israel's cry (6:6–10), Yahweh's deliverance through a judge-deliverer (6:11–8:27), Israel's peace (8:28), and death of the judge-deliverer (8:29–32). While the overall structure is typical, the detailed account of 6:11–8:27 within this larger complex follows its own unique plot. One can discern a difference within the Gideon account between the narratives of chs. 6–7 and those of ch. 8, especially in terms of the characterization of God (who is active, then absent) and Gideon (who is fearfully timid, then courageously vengeful [Amit, *Judges*, 238; Block, 287; cf. McCann, 63]).

Such contrasts in the account suggest that Gideon represents a major juncture or "pivot point" in the accounts of the judge-deliverers (Tanner, 146, 152–53). Further evidence for this shift can be seen in the new elements introduced (detailed description of oppression, divine rebuke of Israel's cry, apostasy reported before the death of the judge-deliverer, civil strife within Israel [O'Connell, 170]), and the way Gideon's leadership prepares for the disastrous reign of Abimelech in ch. 9 (Tanner).

1. Israel's Apostasy and Yahweh's Discipline (6:1–6)

[1]Again the Israelites did evil in the eyes of the LORD, and for seven years he gave them into the hands of the Midianites. [2]Because the power of Midian was so oppressive, the Israelites prepared shelters for themselves in mountain clefts, caves and strongholds. [3]Whenever the Israelites planted their crops, the Midianites, Amalekites and other eastern peoples invaded the country. [4]They camped on the land and ruined the crops all the way to Gaza and did not spare a living thing for Israel, neither sheep nor cattle nor donkeys. [5]They came up with their livestock and their tents like swarms of locusts. It was impossible to count the men and their camels; they invaded the land to ravage it. [6]Midian so impoverished the Israelites that they cried out to the LORD for help.

COMMENTARY

1 As is typical in the major accounts in Judges, the story begins with Israel doing evil in Yahweh's sight (6:1a; cf. 2:11; 3:7, 12; 4:1; 10:6; 13:1). The precise character of this evil is not provided here, but the prophetic message in 6:8–10 and Gideon's destruction of sacred items associated with the god Baal and goddess Asherah (6:25–32) reveal that this evil is related to the worship of other gods. Elsewhere in Judges, when Israel's evil is explicitly described, it is always related to false worship (see 2:6–3:6; 3:7–11; 5:8; 10:6–16; cf. 3:19, 26).

Israel's sin prompts discipline from Yahweh, which creates the fundamental tension in the plot that will be resolved. This discipline is informed by the covenantal curses found in the Torah (Lev 26; Dt 28; see esp. Lev 26:25, and note connections between Jdg 6:2 and Lev 26:17, 25; Jdg 6:3 and Lev 26:16; Dt 28:30, 33, 38; and Jdg 6:4 and Lev 26:4, 20; cf. Block, 251). That discipline is expressed through Israel's being given into the "hands" or power of Midian for a seven-year period. This statement in 6:1b is a summary statement that is then described in detail in 6:2–5 before a second summary statement in 6:6a, which describes Israel's response.

The roots of this enemy, Midian, are linked to Israel in Genesis 25:2, which identifies Midian as the offspring of the relationship between Abraham and Keturah, the wife he took after Sarah's death (Ge 25:1–2). According to Genesis 25:1–6 Midian was sent away to "the land of the east," where his descendants are associated with Sihon, king of the Amorites (Nu 31:8), and are ultimately subjugated by the Edomites; these events suggest a settlement in the southern region of Transjordan (Ge 36:35; 1Ki 11:18). While the reference to camels in some accounts related to the Midianites has suggested to some that this people group was nomadic, biblical references to a federation of five monarchical city-states (Nu 31:8; Jos 13:21) and archaeological evidence from southern Transjordan east of the Gulf of Aqaba suggest a settled society (*ABD*, 4:815–17).

Midianite characters figure in the later exodus and wilderness stories (Ex 2:15–4:31; 18:1–27; Nu 10:29–32; 25, 31). That the stories in Exodus are positive but those in Numbers are negative reveals growing hostility between Israel and Midian. This latter tone is evident in the conquest (Jos 13:21) and here in the story of Gideon. The expeditions described in Judges 6:3–5 reveal that the Midianites' land was not adequate for feeding its population, so that they resorted to "tax-collecting expeditions" (*ABD*, 4:816).

2 So great is the Midianite oppression that Israel moves out of their vulnerable unwalled settlements into hiding places in the hill country and wilderness, including shelters, caves, and strongholds. This strategy is strikingly similar to the one adopted by Israel when they faced the greater power of Philistia in 1 Samuel 13:6 and by David when he was on the run from Saul (1Sa 23:14, 19; 24:1).

3 Although the Midianites are clearly the leaders and instigators of this oppression of Israel, they are accompanied by "Amalekites and other eastern peoples." The Amalekites are closely associated with the Edomites (see comment on 3:12–14). The "sons of the east" (lit. trans.) are mentioned in Genesis 29:1 as possessing a land through which Jacob traveled on his way to Haran. Ezekiel 25:4, 10 mentions this people group in relation to Moab and Ammon (as a threat); Isaiah 11:14 in relation to Edom, Moab, and

Ammon; and Jeremiah 49:28 in relation to Kedar (a nomadic people from the eastern desert). The use of this phrase "sons of the east" in Judges 8:10 suggests that it may be a more general term to refer to Midianites, Amalekites, and their neighbors. This coalition makes sense in light of the close proximity of all these people groups in the Transjordanian plateau and desert east of the Jordan River.

4 The oppression of these invaders appears to be limited to military expeditions that occurred after Israel had planted its crops (v.3) and after those crops had grown to maturity (vv.4, 11; see Note). The invaders' interest appears to be related not only to pillaging the harvest of these crops, but also to using the standing crops to graze their own livestock while they consumed the livestock of Israel. The reference to Gaza, one of the five Philistine city-states (which lay on the key "way of the sea" [Isa 9:1] or "way of the Philistines" [Ex 13:17] that facilitated traffic between Egypt and Asia), reveals that this oppression extended to the Mediterranean Sea and thus included the valleys of the Shephelah.

5–6 References to tents and camels and association with Amalekites do suggest that though the Midianites were a settled people group, they adopted nomadic patterns in order to supplement the resources of their own land. The comparison to "swarms of locusts" continues the allusion to the covenantal curses found in the Torah (cf. Dt 28:38; see above v.1; cf. Bluedorn, 67) and is a powerful image of the effect of this pillaging army, which stripped Israel's fields and storage facilities clean of its harvest both by military might and the grazing of their livestock. This comparison to "swarms of locusts" is also part of the narrator's agenda to accentuate the size of the group, also highlighted by the notation that the men and camels were "impossible to count." In contrast to the gargantuan size of Midian, Israel "became little before Midian" ("Midian so impoverished Israel," NIV).

NOTES

3–5 Webb, 145, notes the "sequence of iterative verb-forms in verses 3–5" as capturing "stylistically the wave after wave of pillage and destruction."

4 יְבוּל הָאָרֶץ ($y^e b\hat{u}l\ h\bar{a}^{\,}\bar{a}re\d{s}$, "the crops"). This phrase could be translated more woodenly as "the produce of the land," which refers to the harvest (see Lev 26:4, 20; Dt 11:17; 32:22; Eze 34:27; Hag 1:10; Zec 8:12; Pss 67:7; 85:13) and thus fits the fact that Gideon is threshing his grain in Judges 6:11.

2. Israel's Cry and Yahweh's Word (6:7–10)

> ⁷When the Israelites cried to the LORD because of Midian, ⁸he sent them a prophet, who said, "This is what the LORD, the God of Israel, says: I brought you up out of Egypt, out of the land of slavery. ⁹I snatched you from the power of Egypt and from the hand of all your oppressors. I drove them from before you and gave you their land. ¹⁰I said to you, 'I am the LORD your God; do not worship the gods of the Amorites, in whose land you live.' But you have not listened to me."

COMMENTARY

7 As is typical of the major accounts in Judges, divine discipline through a foreign enemy prompts a cry ($z^c q$) from Israel to Yahweh for help (vv.6b–7; cf. 3:9, 15; 4:3; 10:10). The content of this cry is not provided—a trend typical of most of the other accounts in Judges. In the one case where details are given (10:10, 15–16), the cry entails a penitential response by the people to God. Samuel's speech in 1 Samuel 12:9–11, which refers to Gideon as Jerub-Baal (cf. Jdg 6:32), reveals that the cry in Judges 6:6b–7 was penitential.

8–10 The cry of the people prompts Yahweh to send a prophetic voice (which takes the form of a classic prophetic judgment speech [Block,

255–56]). The divine word has broken into narrative at three earlier points in the book of Judges. In 2:1–3 the "angel/messenger of the LORD" confronts Israel at Bokim with their failure to eliminate the Canaanites and their shrines. In 2:20–23 God's voice breaks into the Judges cycle directly, announcing judgment on Israel for violating the covenant by worshiping other gods. In 4:6–7, 14 God delivers his word through the prophetess Deborah, calling Barak to battle (Webb, 145). The appearance of a prophet/messenger/message of God at this juncture in the cycle of a major judge is common to nearly all the accounts (see Boda, "Recycling Heaven's Words"; cf. 3:19–20; 4:4–6; 10:11–14; ch. 13; also 9:7–22).

In terms of content the unnamed prophet here is closest to the angel/messenger/prophet figures of ch. 2 (Bluedorn, 66–67; cf. Dt 29:21–27). But in terms of placement in plot and description of the character, one cannot miss the striking similarity between Yahweh's response to Israel's cry through "a woman, a prophetess" (*'šh nby'h*, Deborah) in 4:4 and his response through "a man, a prophet" (*'yš nby'*) here in 6:8 (cf. Block, 254; Schneider, 102; Bluedorn, 62).

This unnamed prophet begins with the traditional prophetic introduction: "This is what the LORD, the God of Israel says"—a phrase that identifies the speaker as merely a messenger for another authoritative figure. The speech proper first rehearses the foundational redemptive story of Israel ("I brought you up out of Egypt … gave you their land"), the foundational covenantal name of Yahweh ("I am the LORD your God"), and the foundational covenantal demand on Israel ("do not worship the gods of the Amorites, in whose land you live"), before accusing the people of failure: "you have not listened to [obeyed] me."

This prophetic attack is thus based firmly on the grace of Yahweh expressed through the exo-dus and conquest and sealed in the covenantal agreement into which Yahweh and Israel entered at Sinai. The use of the same word—"God" for Yahweh and "gods" for the foreign deities—reveals the stark choice before Israel (Bluedorn, 270). The term "oppressors" (*lḥṣ*) in v.9 is used throughout Judges (Jdg 1:34; 2:18; 4:3; 6:9; 10:12) and refers to the inhabitants of the land, who were driven out in Joshua but continued to plague Israel throughout Judges.

Uncertain, however, is the function of this prophetic speech, since it does not call for any response on the part of the people and is followed by Yahweh's providing a judge-deliverer to rescue Israel, with no mention of any response from the people. (For this reason some have suggested it should be excised, as seems to be the case in 4QJudg[a] [see Note below].) The prophetic speech appears merely to highlight the grace of Yahweh and the culpability of Israel. The rehearsal of this theological foundation may play a didactic role by reminding the people of their need to follow the covenant established by the grace of Yahweh.

NOTE

7–10 4QJudg[a] does not include vv.7–10. While this lack may reflect an earlier phase in the redactional development of the book of Judges (A. Graeme Auld, "Gideon: Hacking at the Heart of the Old Testament," *VT* 39 [1989]: 257–67; Julio C. Trebolle Barrera, "Textual Variants in 4QJudg[a] and the Textual and Editorial History of the Book of Judges (1)," *RevQ* 14 [1989]: 229–45; Emanuel Tov, *Textual Criticism of the Hebrew Bible* [2nd rev. ed.; Minneapolis/Assen: Fortress/Royal Van Gorcum, 2001], 135–36, 344–45; Eugene C. Ulrich, *The Dead Sea Scrolls and the Origins of the Bible* [Studies in the Dead Sea Scrolls and Related Literature; Grand Rapids/Leiden: Eerdmans/Brill, 1999], 105–6), more likely it is simply the result of a scribal error (see esp. O'Connell, 147, n. 178; cf. Fernández Marcos [see n. 5 in the Introduction], with thanks to S. Locke).

3. Yahweh's Deliverance through Gideon (6:11–8:27)

a. The Commissioning of Gideon (6:11–24)

[11]The angel of the LORD came and sat down under the oak in Ophrah that belonged to Joash the Abiezrite, where his son Gideon was threshing wheat in a winepress to keep it from the Midianites. [12]When the angel of the LORD appeared to Gideon, he said, "The LORD is with you, mighty warrior."

[13]"But sir," Gideon replied, "if the LORD is with us, why has all this happened to us? Where are all his wonders that our fathers told us about when they said, 'Did not the LORD bring us up out of Egypt?' But now the LORD has abandoned us and put us into the hand of Midian."

[14]The LORD turned to him and said, "Go in the strength you have and save Israel out of Midian's hand. Am I not sending you?"

[15]"But Lord,'" Gideon asked, "how can I save Israel? My clan is the weakest in Manasseh, and I am the least in my family."

[16]The LORD answered, "I will be with you, and you will strike down all the Midianites together."

[17]Gideon replied, "If now I have found favor in your eyes, give me a sign that it is really you talking to me. [18]Please do not go away until I come back and bring my offering and set it before you."

And the LORD said, "I will wait until you return."

[19]Gideon went in, prepared a young goat, and from an ephah of flour he made bread without yeast. Putting the meat in a basket and its broth in a pot, he brought them out and offered them to him under the oak.

[20]The angel of God said to him, "Take the meat and the unleavened bread, place them on this rock, and pour out the broth." And Gideon did so. [21]With the tip of the staff that was in his hand, the angel of the LORD touched the meat and the unleavened bread. Fire flared from the rock, consuming the meat and the bread. And the angel of the LORD disappeared. [22]When Gideon realized that it was the angel of the LORD, he exclaimed, "Ah, Sovereign LORD! I have seen the angel of the LORD face to face!"

[23]But the LORD said to him, "Peace! Do not be afraid. You are not going to die."

[24]So Gideon built an altar to the LORD there and called it The LORD is Peace. To this day it stands in Ophrah of the Abiezrites.

COMMENTARY

11 After Israel's cry for help, the major judge-deliverer accounts introduce the character Yahweh will use to deliver them from their enemy (see 2:15–16; 3:9, 15; 4:3–4; 10:10–11:1). In this case "Gideon" is the one raised up for this task. While the accounts of Othniel (3:9) and Ehud (3:15) speak only generally about Yahweh's "raising up a deliverer" for Israel, the account of Gideon provides details on the process by which Yahweh commissions this deliverer. In this case it is an "angel/messenger of the LORD" who arrives and sits under the "oak in Ophrah," which lay on the land owned by Gideon's father, Joash. See Note below for the close connection between the "angel/messenger" and the "prophet" in vv.8–10.

One should not miss the striking similarity to the account of Deborah and Barak in which Deborah the prophetess is first pictured under a tree before commissioning Barak to engage in battle (Bluedorn, 70–71). In contrast to the Deborah-Barak account, however, this tree marks a center of Canaanite worship. The fact that in 6:12 this figure "appears" (*yr*, Niphal—a verb commonly used for the appearance of Yahweh or an angel [as in Ge 26:24], but not always [as in Ge 46:29]), then vanishes from his sight (Jdg 6:21) and elicits Gideon's fearful response in 6:22, suggests that this figure is heavenly rather than human.

The oak in Ophrah, which appears to have served as a sacred site, here associated with the Canaanite cult, is odd in light of the Yahwistic name attributed to Gideon's father (Joash, "Yahweh is strong"). Judges 6:25 states explicitly that

Gideon's family played some role at this sacred site, which consisted of an altar to Baal, an image of Asherah, and a temple fortress (cf. *ABD*, 2:1013; Block, 257, 267). Israel's embrace of Asherah is evident throughout their material record, no more poignantly than in the drawing and inscriptions found at Kuntillet ʿAjrud, which refer to "Yahweh ... and his Asherah" (Matthews, *Judges and Ruth*, 80; cf. John A. Emerton, "'Yahweh and His Asherah': The Goddess or Her Symbol?" *VT* 49 [1999]: 315–37). Further evidence of Gideon's connection to priestly rites is seen when Gideon takes his reward from military victory. At that time he makes an "ephod" and places it in Ophrah, where it will lead Israel into false worship (8:27).

At this sacred site Gideon is busy threshing his wheat—a task that usually involved running heavy implements over the harvested stalks (Isa 28:27; 41:15), throwing the material into the air on exposed heights to take advantage of passing winds to blow away the chaff (Isa 30:24; Jer 15:7), and sifting the grain (Am 9:9; *TBD*, 21). In order to remain safely hidden from the Midianites, Gideon is forced to perform this task in a less-than-ideal fashion within a winepress, a depressed (and therefore less detectable, but also windless) area where grapes were trodden by foot (cf. Isa 5:2; 63:1–6; Jer 48:33; La 1:15).

Gideon's father, Joash, is identified as an Abiezrite, a clan within the tribe of Manasseh (Jos 17:1–2; cf. Nu 26:30; 1Ch 7:18). This clan was usually associated with Gilead, which lay east of the Jordan River. But according to Judges 6:11, 34; 8:2,

Joash's land lay west of the Jordan, since the events take place at a location in the Jezreel Valley, possibly near present-day Afuleh. This location lay exposed in the center of the Jezreel Valley (6:33–35; cf. *ABD*, 2:1013; *AEHL*, "Ophrah"). Interestingly, in Judges 12:4 the Ephraimites call the Gileadites "renegades from Ephraim and Manasseh," suggesting that some Gileadites lived in Cisjordan. The connection with Gilead is suggested by the reference in 7:3 to "Mount Gilead," which appears to be another name for the Mount Gilboa range, that is, the hills where some of the Gileadite clan from the tribe of Manasseh lived.

12–16 The appearance of this angelic figure introduces the key dialogue that constitutes the commission of Gideon to his task of rescuing Israel from Midianite oppression. There is a subtle shift in this commission from the heavenly angel/messenger of Yahweh speaking at the outset (6:12) to Yahweh himself speaking (6:14, 16, 18). This may be attributed to the fact that an angel/messenger speaks in the name of the one who sent him, that the angel/messenger is an intermediary vehicle through which Yahweh appears and speaks to Gideon, or that the angel/messenger is a theophany of Yahweh himself. Gideon is "the only judge to whom God speaks directly," the first of many divine assurances given to a Gideon who "displays more doubt" than any other character in the book (Exum, "The Centre Cannot Hold," 416).

This commission is strikingly similar to that of Moses, who also was called by Yahweh to rescue Israel from bondage to a foreign nation (Webb, 148–49; Alonso Schökel and Legters, 271; Bluedorn, 75; cf. N. Habel, "The Form and Significance of the Call Narratives," *ZAW* 77 [1965]: 316–20). That commission, also associated with prophetic figures in the OT (though see Abram in Ge 15; cf. Niditch, *Judges*, 90–91), is often divided into the following phases:

- a divine confrontation (Ex 3:1–4a; Isa 6:1–2; Jer 1:4; Eze 1:1–28)
- an introductory word that suggests the commission of the prophet (3:4b–9; Isa 6:3–7; Jer 1:5a; Eze 1:28–2:2)
- a commission that uses the imperatives "go" (*hlk*) and "send" (*šlh*; Ex 3:10; Isa 6:8–10; Jer 1:5b; Eze 2:3–5; 3:4–5)
- an objection, often in question format, from the one being commissioned (Ex 3:11; Isa 6:5, 11a; Jer 1:6; Eze 2:6, 8)
- a reassuring word from God, often saying "I will be with you" and/or "do not fear" (Ex 3:12a; Isa 6:6–7, 13; Jer 1:7–8; Eze 2:6–7)

These same components can be discerned in Judges 6:11–16. First, there is a divine confrontation as the angel of the Lord appears to Gideon (Jdg 6:11–12a).

Second, the introductory word (6:12b) suggests Gideon's commission as the angel calls him "mighty warrior," ironic in light of his cowardly activity in the winepress but prophetic in light of his future destiny.

Third, Gideon receives a clear commission using the imperatives "go" and "send" (6:14). The first imperative is a reminder of the need for Gideon to respond to Yahweh's call and is qualified by a phrase typical of the judge-deliverers in the book of Judges: "deliver Israel from the hand of...." This going and delivering is to be done "in the strength you have," possibly a reference to God's presence noted in the introductory word. The second imperative is a reminder that Gideon goes not on his own initiative but at the behest of Yahweh.

Fourth, Gideon's commission is bracketed by two objections (6:13, 15), which are directly related to Yahweh's introductory word in 6:12 ("The Lord is with you, mighty warrior"). By contrasting the present predicament of Israel with Yahweh's past miraculous care of an Israel oppressed in Egypt, Gideon questions Yahweh's statement that he is with Israel (6:13). This allusion to the exodus bolsters further connections between Moses and Gideon, all of which prompt the reader to compare and contrast these two figures. While both will deliver Israel from bondage, Gideon will ultimately receive the glory (cf. Ex 14:30–31; Jdg 8:22–27) and lead the nation into idolatry (Bluedorn, 77). By highlighting the low social status of his own clan and family within Manasseh, Gideon questions Yahweh's claim that he is "mighty warrior" (6:15).

Finally, while Yahweh could have repeated the prophetic word delivered in 6:7–10 to explain why Gideon's Israel is in such a sad state of affairs, he instead repeats his opening claims in 6:16, assuring Gideon of the divine presence ("I will be with you") and of Gideon's military commission ("you will strike down all the Midianites together"). Gideon's response to this divine word, however, is the first in a series of responses and actions that characterize him as lacking in faith, which thus shows further deterioration in the presentation of the Judges (see Overview to 2:6–16:31; cf. Barak in 4:8–9a and Jephthah in 11:30–31; Samson in 15:18; Wong, *Strategy*, 158–65).

17–19 Gideon ends this phase of the commissioning by asking his heavenly visitor for a "sign" (*ʾôt*; GK 253), a miraculous confirmation that this message has indeed come from Yahweh (cf. Dt 13:1–3; Isa 7:10–14). He seems to assume that such a sign is only possible if he offers a gift (*mnḥh*) to the messenger. The terminology "to set before" (*nwḥ*, Hiphil + *lipnê*) Yahweh is used for items placed before Yahweh's presence in the tabernacle (Ex 16:33–34; Lev 16:23; Nu 17:19, 22; 1Sa 10:25; cf. 1Ki 8:9) and, in Deuteronomy 26:4, 10, to agricultural produce offered to God at harvest time. While the word "offering" (*mnḥh*) here is one closely associated with the grain offering in priestly literature, the verb is

usually "present" (*qrb*, Hiphil), as opposed to "bring" (*yṣʾ*, Hiphil), which is used in 6:18.

Gideon's offering consists of a young goat, unleavened bread, and a pot of broth, all of which he brings out to his heavenly visitor. An entire goat and an ephah (twenty-two liters) of flour are valuable gifts, especially in a time of economic scarcity (Block, 262). This act is both one of ancient hospitality, feeding and honoring the guest who has come, and one of sacrifice to God (cf. Amit, *Judges*, 255, n. 44; see comments on Jdg 13). The fact that "the oak" is identified as the place where Gideon offers this food suggests the sacred character of this meal.

20–21 With v.20 the identity of the heavenly visitor shifts back to "the angel/messenger of the LORD," who instructs Gideon to place the items (meat, bread, broth) on a rock. The heavenly visitor then touches the items with his staff, and fire comes forth from the rock and burns up the items. Gideon has asked for a sign in connection with his gift, and the heavenly being provides this miracle through an act reminiscent of sacrificial rites in which the gifts are transferred into the heavenly realm through the smoke that arises from a burnt offering. Once the fire has consumed the offering, the heavenly being departs.

22–23 Gideon, interpreting this miracle as confirmation from Yahweh ("Sovereign LORD"), accepts the miracle as the sign he was looking for, and concludes that he has had a face-to-face encounter with a heavenly being ("angel of the LORD"). The term "Ah" (representing *ʾhâ*), sometimes translated as "alas," reflects a desperate and emotional cry (cf. Jos 7:7; Jdg 11:35; 2Ki 6:5, 15; Jer 1:6; 4:10; 14:13; Eze 4:14; 9:8; 11:13; 21:5; Joel 1:15). Yahweh interprets Gideon's response as a concern for his life, a response that later in Judges will be voiced explicitly by Samson's parents (13:22) and elsewhere in the OT expresses that to see Yahweh "face to face" is to risk death (Ge

32:30; Eze 20:35), though not so for Moses (Ex 33:11; Nu 12:8; Dt 34:10) and Israel (Nu 14:14; Dt 5:4). The phrase is used to refer to a personal encounter with another (2Ki 14:8; 2Ch 25:17; Jer 32:4; 34:3). Yahweh comforts Gideon with the word "peace," assuring him there is no need to fear, for he will not die.

24 To commemorate this personal encounter with Yahweh Gideon builds an altar on that rock, naming it after Yahweh's comforting word: "The LORD Is Peace." Such a response is reminiscent of the actions of Abraham in Genesis 12:6–7, where, after Yahweh appeared to him at the great tree of Moreh at Shechem, Abraham built an altar for Yahweh (cf. Ge 13:4; Niditch, *Judges*, 90–91). Abraham also built an altar under the oaks of Mamre at Hebron (Ge 13:18). Jacob was instructed to build an altar at Bethel, where God appeared to him (Ge 35:1–8; cf. 28:10–22). The fact that this site now becomes an altar confirms that the offering was indeed a sacrifice to God. The narrator notes that this altar is still standing in his own day—a reminder to the readers not merely of the authenticity of this event, but more so of the enduring relevance of Yahweh's peace for their present day (Bluedorn, 88).

NOTE

11 The waw-relative with prefix conjugation at the beginning of this verse picks up the narrative backbone left off in 6:8 ("he sent ... who said ...") and forges the two figures of vv.8–10 (prophet) and vv. 11–24 (messenger/angel) together.

16 כְּאִישׁ אֶחָד (kᵉʾîš ʾeḥād, "together"). The Hebrew here could be translated more woodenly "as one man," identical to Numbers 14:15, which refers to simultaneous destruction of an entire group.

b. Gideon Destroys the Altar of Baal and Asherah (6:25–32)

> ²⁵That same night the LORD said to him, "Take the second bull from your father's herd, the one seven years old. Tear down your father's altar to Baal and cut down the Asherah pole beside it. ²⁶Then build a proper kind of altar to the LORD your God on the top of this height. Using the wood of the Asherah pole that you cut down, offer the second bull as a burnt offering."
>
> ²⁷So Gideon took ten of his servants and did as the LORD told him. But because he was afraid of his family and the men of the town, he did it at night rather than in the daytime.
>
> ²⁸In the morning when the men of the town got up, there was Baal's altar, demolished, with the Asherah pole beside it cut down and the second bull sacrificed on the newly built altar!
>
> ²⁹They asked each other, "Who did this?"
> When they carefully investigated, they were told, "Gideon son of Joash did it."

³⁰The men of the town demanded of Joash, "Bring out your son. He must die, because he has broken down Baal's altar and cut down the Asherah pole beside it."

³¹But Joash replied to the hostile crowd around him, "Are you going to plead Baal's cause? Are you trying to save him? Whoever fights for him shall be put to death by morning! If Baal really is a god, he can defend himself when someone breaks down his altar."

³²So that day they called Gideon "Jerub-Baal," saying, "Let Baal contend with him," because he broke down Baal's altar.

COMMENTARY

25–27 Gideon is no sooner commissioned by Yahweh than he is called to action. Before Gideon can save Israel from the hand of the Midianites, he must first set things right within his own family unit, referred to as "the house of his father" ("his family," v.27). This social grouping is not the modern "nuclear family," but rather that family unit of multiple generations (three to four), which included all the sons (and their families) of a patriarchal figure and who all shared the family land and lived in connected quarters (see Introduction).

Gideon is instructed to tear down the altar of Baal using a prized bull from his father's herd (see Notes), cut down the image of Asherah, reconstruct an altar to Yahweh, and use the wood from the Asherah image to offer the prized bull as a whole burnt offering. The age of the bull ("seven years old") has no precedent in priestly legislation and is probably symbolic of the length of the oppression that is about to end (Dominic Rudman, "The Second Bull in Judges 6:25–28," *JNSL* 26 [2000]: 97–103; Bluedorn, 95). Gideon takes ten of his servants to accomplish this daring act, but he does so under the cloak of darkness for fear of his family's response—a fear the narrator does not hide, and in the process characterizes Gideon as a fearful individual. Throughout this narrative Gideon is consis-

tently portrayed as tentative and lacking courage, a characteristic he shares with that earlier figure, Barak (Schneider, 108). Yahweh accommodates this characteristic, however, by providing Gideon with the signs he needs.

28–32 Gideon's fears are justified, for with the morning light comes the violent response of his extended clan, who call for his death—ironic in light of the penalty in the Torah for those who worship idols (Dt 13). His father, Joash, who is responsible for his son in this patriarchal society, saves Gideon's life, reminding the people that if Baal was truly God he should have been able to defend his own altar. Gideon's survival after tearing down this altar is proof for Joash that Baal is not really a god, and any who would endanger Gideon's life will themselves be put to death by Joash.

That day Joash renames his son Jerub-Baal, which may have begun as a curse against Gideon ("Let Baal contend with him" [see Notes]) but, when nothing happens to Gideon, only serves to bolster Gideon's reputation among the people by emphasizing Baal's impotence. Before providing deliverance for Israel, Yahweh had expressed his concern over Israel's worship of other gods through the prophetic message of 6:7–10, which lay behind his disciplining of the nation.

By commissioning Gideon, Yahweh accomplishes two things. First, he shows his concern for the eradication of false worship by calling an individual within a clan that had fostered the worship of the Canaanite gods. Second, he raises up an individual who will lead Israel against their enemies. Gideon's preparation for the role of judge-deliverer entails a cleansing of the inappropriate worship practices of his own family, with whom he was inextricably linked. This principle of intra- and intergenerational identity is evident throughout the OT and is an important part of its vision for spiritual renewal (see Lev 26:39–40; Ezr 9; Ne 1; 9; Da 9; cf. Boda, *Severe Mercy*, 518–19). It is members of his own clan (the Abiezerites) who constitute the nucleus of the army he will soon raise from among the northern tribes (see v.34).

NOTES

25 אֶת־פַּר־הַשּׁוֹר אֲשֶׁר לְאָבִיךָ וּפַר הַשֵּׁנִי שֶׁבַע שָׁנִים (*ʾet-par-haššôr ʾăšer lᵉʾābîkā ûpar haššēnî šebaʿ šānîm*, "the second bull from your father's herd, the one seven years old"). This description is comprised of two phrases that at first sight suggest two bulls were involved: "your father's bull and a second bull seven years old" (NASB). But the verses that follow (vv.26, 28) only mention one bull, called the "second" bull. Most likely the second phrase in 6:25 is explicative, offering further description of the bull mentioned in the first phrase (see Bluedorn, 90–96). It may be that the word הַשֵּׁנִי (*haššēnî*, "second") represents a scribal error for דָּשֵׁן (*dāšēn*, "fat") or a root שׁנה (*šnh*, "shining of fat") as suggested by the LXXᵃ (τὸν σιτευτόν, *ton siteuton*, "the fatted one"; cf. Bluedorn, 93). It may also reflect the root שׁנה (*šnh*, "aged") attested in Hebrew, or a root שׁני (*šny*, "to be full-grown") attested in Arabic. In these latter cases it would refer to a full-grown bull ready for sacrifice. But compare Rudman, who sees in the reference to the "second bull" most likely an explanatory gloss based on Leviticus 4:21; Numbers 8:8, where a second bull was an expiatory sacrifice.

26 בַּמַּעֲרָכָה (*bammaʿărākâ*, "a proper kind of"). Here the Hebrew text reads "in/by row" (see Ex 39:37 for a row of lamps and 1Sa 4:2, 12, 16; 17:20–22, 48 for a row of soldiers in battle). This reference must be to rows of stones.

מָעוֹז (*māʿôz*, "height"). This term is used elsewhere of a mountain stronghold as a place of refuge, here as a place of safety from Gideon's enemies (cf. Isa 17:10; 23:14; 25:4; 27:5).

הַפָּר הַשֵּׁנִי (*happār haššēnî*, "second bull"). See Note on v.25.

28 נֻתַּץ מִזְבַּח (*nuttaṣ mizbaḥ*, "demolished altar"). This terminology is reminiscent of Yahweh's command in the Torah to destroy Canaanite altars (Ex 34:13; Dt 7:5; 12:3), repeated in Judges 2:2 (cf. Bluedorn, 98). Although Gideon's name is changed to Jerub-Baal (see Note below), in the light of this action his original name foreshadows his action against the pagan cults in his father's house. This name is derived from a root meaning "hacker" or "hewer," a synonym of the word used for cutting down the Asherah pole in vv.25–27 (Block, 257).

32 יְרֻבַּעַל (*yᵉrubbaʿal*, "Jerub-Baal"). The meaning of this name has been hotly debated, being linked to various roots, including ירהᴵ (*yrh*, "to lay a foundation," thus here "foundation of Baal" [cf. Job 38:6]), רבה/רבבᴵ (*rbh/rbb*, "to be/become numerous/large/great," thus here "Baal is great"), ריב (*ryb*, "to strive/quarrel," thus here "let Baal contend"). The immediate context clearly suggests the third root's meaning is in view (see further Bluedorn, 101–4). If taken as a jussive (as above), it is an invitation for Baal to act on his own behalf; the sad irony is that ultimately idolatry wins the day (see 8:27, 33; ch. 9; cf. Block, 270).

c. Gideon Defeats the Armies of Midian, Amalekites, and Sons of the East (6:33–8:21)

i. Midianites, Amalekites, and sons of the East invade the Jezreel Valley (6:33)

³³Now all the Midianites, Amalekites and other eastern peoples joined forces and crossed over the Jordan and camped in the Valley of Jezreel.

COMMENTARY

33 Here the narrator reminds the reader of the situation outside Ophrah that had prompted Gideon to thresh his wheat in a winepress. The Midianites and their allies ("Amalekites and other eastern peoples"; cf. 6:3) had invaded Canaan from the east ("over the Jordan") and were encamped in the Jezreel Valley, where they could pillage crops. (For the importance of this valley for military control of Canaan, see Matthews [*Judges and Ruth*, 88, n. 138], as confirmed by the express strategy of Pharaoh Thutmose III in *COS*, 2.2A:7–13.)

The Jezreel Valley where they camped was a broad valley that, along with the Plain of Acco (to the west) and the valley of Beth Shean (to the east), formed a valley region extending from the Mediterranean Sea to the Jordan River. This topographical depression cut northern Israel into two geographic regions: the lower hills of Ephraim, which lay south of the Jezreel Valley, and the higher hills of Galilee, which lay north of it. The name of the valley means "God sows" or "May God make fruitful," indicative of its potential to produce crops because of its fertile soil and plenteous water supply (*ABD*, 3:850). This name is ironic since Yahweh had raised up a foreign enemy to consume the harvest he had given. The numbers provided in 8:10 suggest there were 135,000 men or 135 large military units in this army.

ii. Gideon gathers troops of Israel (6:34–35)

³⁴Then the Spirit of the Lord came upon Gideon, and he blew a trumpet, summoning the Abiezrites to follow him. ³⁵He sent messengers throughout Manasseh, calling them to arms, and also into Asher, Zebulun and Naphtali, so that they too went up to meet them.

COMMENTARY

34–35 Having introduced the enemy in v.33, the narrator then presents Gideon's actions to free Israel from Midianite oppression. The indication of Yahweh's presence with and empowerment of Gideon is linked to the "Spirit of the LORD," who "clothed" (*lbš*) Gideon (see Note), a phrase reminiscent of the experience of Othniel (3:10) and Jephthah (11:29), upon whom the Spirit came (*hyh ʿl*, 3:10; 11:29), and that of Samson, upon whom the Spirit came violently (*ṣlḥ ʿl*, 14:6, 19; 15:14). The Spirit's presence with leaders set apart by Yahweh is also seen in the presentation of the first two

kings in Israel: Saul (1Sa 10:6, 10; 11:6; though see 18:10) and David (16:13). This is the "strength" to which Yahweh referred in Judges 6:14, strength that will enable Gideon to deliver Israel from the power of Midian.

Like Ehud in 3:27, Gideon summons his own clan members (Abiezerites) to war by blowing the trumpet (*šôpār*). He also uses messengers who summon not only his own tribe, Manasseh, but also members of the other northern tribes bordering the Jezreel Valley to the north: from west to east, Asher, Zebulun, and Naphtali.

NOTE

34 וְרוּחַ יְהוָה לָבְשָׁה (*wᵉrûaḥ yhwh lobšâ*, "and the Spirit of the LORD came upon"). Here the Hebrew reads better as "clothed." See Block, 272, citing Nahum M. Waldman ("The Imagery of Clothing, Covering, and Overpowering," *JANESCU* 19 [1989]: 161–70), who shows how this imagery is attested elsewhere in the ancient Near East to depict a person inundated by divine or demonic forces.

iii. Gideon asks for a sign that God will deliver (6:36–40)

³⁶Gideon said to God, "If you will save Israel by my hand as you have promised — ³⁷look, I will place a wool fleece on the threshing floor. If there is dew only on the fleece and all the ground is dry, then I will know that you will save Israel by my hand, as you said." ³⁸And that is what happened. Gideon rose early the next day; he squeezed the fleece and wrung out the dew — a bowlful of water.

³⁹Then Gideon said to God, "Do not be angry with me. Let me make just one more request. Allow me one more test with the fleece. This time make the fleece dry and the ground covered with dew." ⁴⁰That night God did so. Only the fleece was dry; all the ground was covered with dew.

COMMENTARY

36–38 While one expects at this point to find the account of the battle, it is postponed until 7:15 by a series of episodes that focus on signs given to Gideon to bolster his faith (6:36–40; 7:2–7; 7:9–14; Bluedorn, 107–8). In the first instance Gideon asks God for a sign, a request reminiscent of his commission, at the end of which he asked for a sign to confirm the divine source of this commission. The sign involves a fleece of wool that he will place on the threshing floor, possibly that same winepress where the angel of Yahweh first found him in 6:11. His request is that the fleece be sprinkled with dew while the surrounding ground remains dry.

Why Gideon asks for this particular sign is unclear, since it is precisely what one would expect to occur naturally. For this reason the narrator merely says: "And that is what happened" (v.38; cf. v.40; see Bluedorn, 121–23, who suggests that it prepares the way for the second real test).

39–40 With the first "sign" accomplished, Gideon now asks for a truly miraculous sign, one in which God will supernaturally reverse the conditions so that the fleece remains dry but the surrounding ground has dew (Bluedorn, 122). The contrast with the former request for a sign is apparent from the narrator's description: "That night God did so" (v.40).

It is clear from the way Gideon introduces this second request in 6:39 ("Do not be angry with me. Let me make just one more request"), that Gideon knows he is testing God's patience. It is true that Abraham uses similar expressions throughout his much longer debate with Yahweh over the fate of the righteous in Sodom and Gomorrah (Ge 18:23–32), and in Gideon's case God fulfills his request without any expression of anger. But the reference to "testing" God brings to mind the rehearsal of Israel's rebellion at Massah in Deuteronomy 6:16 (Bluedorn, 123).

iv. Gideon told to cull his troops (7:1–8a)

¹Early in the morning, Jerub-Baal (that is, Gideon) and all his men camped at the spring of Harod. The camp of Midian was north of them in the valley near the hill of Moreh. ²The LORD said to Gideon, "You have too many men for me to deliver Midian into their hands. In order that Israel may not boast against me that her own strength has saved her, ³announce now to the people, 'Anyone who trembles with fear may turn back and leave Mount Gilead.'" So twenty-two thousand men left, while ten thousand remained.

⁴But the LORD said to Gideon, "There are still too many men. Take them down to the water, and I will sift them for you there. If I say, 'This one shall go with you,' he shall go; but if I say, 'This one shall not go with you,' he shall not go."

⁵So Gideon took the men down to the water. There the LORD told him, "Separate those who lap the water with their tongues like a dog from those who kneel down to drink."

⁶Three hundred men lapped with their hands to their mouths. All the rest got down on their knees to drink.

⁷The LORD said to Gideon, "With the three hundred men that lapped I will save you and give the Midianites into your hands. Let all the other men go, each to his own place." ⁸So Gideon sent the rest of the Israelites to their tents but kept the three hundred, who took over the provisions and trumpets of the others.

COMMENTARY

1 In response to these signs from Yahweh, Gideon moves his army into a position that challenges his enemy. The battle, however, will not be described until 7:15. Before this description there are two digressions in the story, each initiated by Yahweh and each dealing with opposite concerns related to the human participants in Israel's victory. The first is linked to Israel's potential arrogance when Yahweh causes the victory over Midian (7:2–8a), while the second is linked to Gideon's potential fear in the face of the battle against Midian (7:8b–15).

The Harod River, flowing to the east toward the Jordan River, drained the Jezreel and Beth Shean valleys. The hill of Moreh, an inactive volcano that lay in the center of the Jezreel Valley, sat on the northern side of the basin created by the Harod River; Mount Gilboa lay on its southern side. The Midianites are positioned with their backs to the hill of Moreh, and Gideon's forces with their backs to Mount Gilboa, partly up the hill according to v.8b. Gideon's position is understandable since Mount Gilboa represents the edge of the Jezreel Valley and the beginning of the hill country to its south, where the Israelites could hide safely from their enemies. There his men find a freshwater spring to sustain them as they prepare for battle (cf. 1Sa 29:1).

2–3 While in 6:36–40 Gideon tests God, in 7:1–8 God tests Gideon. The original size of Gideon's force can be derived by adding the two figures at the end of v.3, that is, thirty-two thousand soldiers, a number that may refer to thirty-two large military units. This large number is culled by Yahweh to ensure that the people do not trust in their own strength but rather in Yahweh's power to rescue them. As Gideon looked for miraculous signs from Yahweh, Yahweh will only bring salvation through miraculous means.

The first criterion for culling troops is informed by the command in Deuteronomy 20:8 that those who are afraid and fainthearted should go home lest this fear spread to other troops. The slight change from "afraid or fainthearted" (*hayyārēʾ wᵉrak hallēbāb*) in Deuteronomy 20:8 to "afraid or trembling" (*yārēʾ wᵉḥārēd*) in Judges 7:3 is probably related to a play on the name of the river, "Harod," which shares the same root as "trembling." According to this criterion, twenty-two thousand (or twenty-two large units) were sent home, leaving only ten thousand (or ten large units). The irony of "fear" as a criterion for eliminating these troops is that this quality is consistent within the leader himself (cf. 6:27; 7:10; Tanner, 159). A further irony is that the elimination of this fear is what opens the way for an even darker dimension of Gideon's character (see comments on 8:4–9).

4–8a The second criterion for culling the troops is based on the drinking habits of the remaining men, a test that is supposedly carried out at the spring of Harod. Only three hundred men lap water out of a cupped hand, while the rest kneel down to drink directly from the water as a dog would do (see Notes below). While no reason is given for this test in the text, Josephus is probably correct when he notes that it revealed three hundred cowards (*Ant.* 5.6.3), for the test "exposed three hundred men of whom one may say that, as against the first group of fearful ones, they were even afraid to display their fear, and were only exposed by the test of water" (Amit, *Judges*, 259).

Ironically, it is these three hundred who are chosen to accompany Gideon while the remaining soldiers are sent, "each to his own place" (v.7), that is, "each to his tent" ("to their tents," v.8) — phrases used to refer to the return of people to their homes, often after an unsuccessful military engagement (Jdg 9:55; 19:28; 20:8; 1Sa 4:10; 13:2; 2Sa 18:17; 20:1, 22; 2Ki 14:12; contra Block, 277; Schneider, 112). It may be that members of this group, waiting until the next day to begin the journey home, constitute those who will be called out in v.23 ("Israelites from Naphtali, Asher, and all Manasseh") once the Midianite coalition has taken flight. Before returning to the camp, these soldiers hand their provisions and trumpets over to those who remain. Note that no weapons are mentioned in this transfer. Not only is Israel outnumbered, but it also has no weaponry save trumpets, which foreshadows the means for victory.

NOTES

3 הַר הַגִּלְעָד (*har haggilʿād*, "Mount Gilead"). "Mount Gilead" is an odd appellation since the setting of this story according to 7:1 is clearly in the Jezreel Valley. Possibly "Gilead" is a scribal error for "Gilboa." But while Gilead is usually associated with Manasseh's tribal lands east of the Jordan, according to Numbers 26:30 and Joshua 17:1–2 (cf. 1Ch 7:18) Manassehite clans (including Gideon's Abiezrite clan) that settled on lands west of the Jordan River were also descended from Gilead (cf. Jdg 12:4, where Gileadites are linked to Manasseh and Ephraim). See comments on 6:11.

4 וְאֶצְרְפֶנּוּ (*uᵉʾeṣrᵉpennû*, "I will sift them"). צרף (*ṣrp*) is used in the OT elsewhere to refer to refining metals through smelting (2Sa 22:31; Zec 13:9; Pss 12:7; 17:3; 26:2; 66:10; 105:19; 119:140; Pr 30:5; Da 11:35); here the verb is better rendered, "I will refine them."

5 כֹּל אֲשֶׁר־יָלֹק בִּלְשׁוֹנוֹ מִן־הַמַּיִם כַּאֲשֶׁר יָלֹק הַכֶּלֶב תַּצִּיג אוֹתוֹ לְבָד וְכֹל אֲשֶׁר־יִכְרַע עַל־בִּרְכָּיו לִשְׁתּוֹת (*kōl ʾᵃšer-yālōq bilšōnô min-hammayim kaʾᵃšer yālōq hakkeleb taṣṣîg ʾōtô lᵉbād uᵉkōl ʾᵃšer-yikraʿ ʿal-birkāyw lištôt*, "Separate those who lap the water with their tongues like a dog from those who kneel down to drink"). The NIV's translation of 7:5 (following the LXXᵃ, Syriac, and Vulgate) results in a contradiction between the instructions in 7:5, in which Yahweh commands a separation between those who lap water directly from the pool like a dog and those who kneel down to drink, and the report in 7:6, in which three hundred lap water from their hands and the others kneel down to drink. It is best to understand that 7:5 focuses only on the group to be eliminated. The final *waw*-phrase in v.5 is epexegetical, that is, a further description of the group described in the first phrase of v.5: "Separate those who lap the water with their tongues like a dog, that is, those who kneel down to drink" (cf. Block, 276; contra Bluedorn, 118, n. 193, who sees the contradiction as a narrative technique).

8 צֵדָה (ṣēdâ, "provisions"). This term refers elsewhere to food taken on a journey (cf. Ge 42:25; 45:21; Ex 12:39; Jos 1:11; 9:11; Jdg 20:10; 1Sa 22:10; Ps 78:25).

וּבִשְׁלֹשׁ־מֵאוֹת הָאִישׁ הֶחֱזִיק (ûbišlōš-mēʾôt hāʾîš heḥᵉzîq, "but kept the three hundred"). חזק (ḥzq) in the Hiphil with the preposition בְּ (bᵉ) refers to detaining one against one's will in 19:4 (cf. Ex 9:2; Dt 22:25; Jdg 19:25; 1Sa 15:27; 2Sa 13:11; [with לְ (lᵉ)] 2Sa 15:5). This usage suggests this smaller group wants to leave with those disqualified by the test but are forced by Gideon to remain.

v. Gideon given sign that God will deliver (7:8b–14)

> Now the camp of Midian lay below him in the valley. [9]During that night the LORD said to Gideon, "Get up, go down against the camp, because I am going to give it into your hands. [10]If you are afraid to attack, go down to the camp with your servant Purah [11]and listen to what they are saying. Afterward, you will be encouraged to attack the camp." So he and Purah his servant went down to the outposts of the camp. [12]The Midianites, the Amalekites and all the other eastern peoples had settled in the valley, thick as locusts. Their camels could no more be counted than the sand on the seashore.
>
> [13]Gideon arrived just as a man was telling a friend his dream. "I had a dream," he was saying. "A round loaf of barley bread came tumbling into the Midianite camp. It struck the tent with such force that the tent overturned and collapsed."
>
> [14]His friend responded, "This can be nothing other than the sword of Gideon son of Joash, the Israelite. God has given the Midianites and the whole camp into his hands."

COMMENTARY

8b–11 Having stripped his reluctant leader of all of the human resources necessary to challenge this imposing enemy across the valley, Yahweh now commands Gideon to initiate the battle, promising him that he has given the enemy into his hands. Knowing Gideon's pattern in past dialogues, Yahweh does not even wait for a request for a miraculous confirmation but instead offers one immediately. Gideon is instructed to take his servant Purah, sneak over to the edge of the enemy's camp, and listen to the words of those in the camp.

12 Before relating Gideon's experience at the enemy's camp, the narrator quickly reminds the reader of the massive size of the foe, thus heightening the tension in the plot. (For precise numbers comprising this force, see 8:10.) In this way the narrator is providing an insight into Gideon's own experience. The closer he gets to the enemy and the moment of encounter, the bigger the enemy becomes.

13–14 At the edge of the camp Gideon hears a man relating a recent dream and his friend's interpretation of that dream (cf. Ge 37:9). Dreams are the preferred media of revelation when the source is non-Israelite (cf. Ge 20:3, 6; 31:24; chs. 40–41; Da 2:1–3; see Block, 279), but they are also a mode used to communicate revelation to Israel, especially the prophets (e.g., Ge 31:11; Nu 12:6; 1Kgs 3:5, 15; for more on dreams and visions, see Niditch, *Symbolic Vision*, 1–19).

The image in this vision is of a common round loaf of barley, possibly symbolic of Israel's agricul-tural produce upon which their enemy was feed-ing. The images used in connection with the action of the bread (tumbling) and its effect on the tent ("overturned and collapsed") use Hebrew verbal roots associated with the defeat of an enemy. This dream is interpreted as predicting success for Gideon and defeat for the Midianites.

NOTES

8b וּמַחֲנֵה מִדְיָן הָיָה לוֹ מִתַּחַת בָּעֵמֶק (*ûmaḥ*ᵃ*nēh midyān hāyâ lô mittaḥat bāʿēmeq*, "Now the camp of Midian lay below him in the valley"). Revell, 426, notes the repetition here of 7:1 as a narrative technique in order to resume the chain of events initiated at the earlier point (cf. Talmon).

10 וּפֻרָה נַעַרְךָ (*ûpurâ naʿarkâ*, "your servant Purah"). The Hebrew term is "boy," that is, his personal servant. In Judges 9:54 and 1 Samuel 14:1 such a boy serves as an armor bearer. In Genesis 22:3; Numbers 22:22; Judges 19:11; 2 Samuel 13:17; 19:18; and Job 1:15 such a boy is a general servant.

11 קְצֵה הַחֲמֻשִׁים (*qᵉṣēh haḥ*ᵃ*mûšîm*, "outposts"). The Hebrew reads here more woodenly, "extremities of those grouped in fifties," that is, the edge of those in battle formation (cf. Ex 13:18; Jos 1:14; 4:12).

12 לָרֹב (*lārōb*, untranslated in NIV). The twofold use of this phrase ("as numerous," NASB) matches the twofold description of Gideon's army in 7:2, 4 as רָב (*rāb*), which necessitated its reduction (Bluedorn, 132).

13 מִתְהַפֵּךְ ... וַיַּהַפְכֵהוּ ... וְנָפַל (*mithappēk ... wayyahap*ᵉ*kēhû ... w*ᵉ*nāpal*, "tumbling ... overturned ... collapsed"). For "tumbling" and "overturned," both of which come from the root הפך (*hpk*), see Genesis 19:21, 25, 29; Deuteronomy 29:22; 2 Samuel 10:3; 1 Chronicles 19:3; Jeremiah 20:16; Lamentations 4:6; Jonah 3:4; and Haggai 2:22. The same stem for tumbling is also associated with the sword in Genesis 3:24. For collapsed (נפל, *npl*), see Judges 9:40; 1 Samuel 4:10; 17:52; 31:12; 2 Samuel 1:12; Isaiah 3:8; 21:9; and Ezekiel 35:8.

vi. Gideon and his troops perform their ruse against the enemy (7:15–22)

¹⁵When Gideon heard the dream and its interpretation, he worshiped God. He returned to the camp of Israel and called out, "Get up! The LORD has given the Midianite camp into your hands." ¹⁶Dividing the three hundred men into three companies, he placed trumpets and empty jars in the hands of all of them, with torches inside.

¹⁷"Watch me," he told them. "Follow my lead. When I get to the edge of the camp, do exactly as I do. ¹⁸When I and all who are with me blow our trumpets, then from all around the camp blow yours and shout, 'For the LORD and for Gideon.'"

¹⁹Gideon and the hundred men with him reached the edge of the camp at the beginning of the middle watch, just after they had changed the guard. They blew their trumpets and broke the jars that were in their hands. ²⁰The three companies blew the trumpets and smashed the jars. Grasping the torches in their left hands and holding in their right hands the trumpets they were to blow, they shouted, "A sword for the LORD and for Gideon!" ²¹While each man held his position around the camp, all the Midianites ran, crying out as they fled.

²²When the three hundred trumpets sounded, the LORD caused the men throughout the camp to turn on each other with their swords. The army fled to Beth Shittah toward Zererah as far as the border of Abel Meholah near Tabbath.

COMMENTARY

15 This dream has the desired effect on Gideon. He worships God and then returns to the Israelite camp to rouse his men and announce Yahweh's victory over the Midianites, echoing the same words Yahweh had revealed to him in 7:9.

16–18 Gideon then takes the soldiers who remain and divides the three hundred (or units) among three chiefs (see Notes below), giving each of the soldiers trumpets and empty jars with torches in them. The narrator cites Gideon's precise instructions to his men that they are to proceed to the edge of the camp, and on a trumpet signal from his group they are to blow their trumpets and shout, "For the LORD and for Gideon." The inclusion of "for Gideon" in this shout seems to suggest the emergence of Gideon's self-interest in the narrative, something warned about in 7:2 and displayed in the people's offer of kingship to him and his later royal pretensions (see 8:22–32; Wong, *Strategy*, 165; cf. Bluedorn, 139; McCann, 67). Interestingly, by holding these items in their two hands they would have had no ability to hold weapons (Amit, *Judges*, 51)—further proof that this victory is to be Yahweh's, not theirs (see 7:2).

19–22 The direct narrative that follows adds some extra elements to those provided by Gideon in his speech. First, the shout is lengthened to "A sword for the LORD and for Gideon," ironic in light of the fact that these soldiers will not even raise a sword but rely instead on the swords of the confused Midianites. Second, between the trumpet blast and the battle cry they are to smash the jars in their hands, thus suddenly revealing the torches hidden within them. The actions performed by these three hundred men would normally have been performed by one individual within each unit of men to signal the unit to engage in battle. Interestingly, three hundred is nearly 1 percent of the original Israelite force of 32,000 (or 32 large units, or 320 small units) that had assembled for battle. It appears that Gideon's ruse is designed to make the Midianites believe that each combination of trumpet/torch/shout represents one unit of soldiers at close range poised to slaughter the unprepared Midianites.

This ruse would create an incredible surprise at the beginning of the middle watch of the night, a time when many in the camp would be fast asleep, the retiring guards would be worn out from their watch, and the new guards still groggy—ideal conditions for creating considerable confusion in the camp. According to 7:19 Gideon has one hundred (or one unit of) men with him, who are distinct from the three other units that had been created according to 7:16. Whether this group with Gideon is his own band of Abiezerites and thus not included in the original three hundred (or three units) is uncertain. It appears that Gideon had this odd military strategy in mind from the beginning, since 7:8 already noted that the soldiers who left the army gave "trumpets" to those who remained, with no mention of any weaponry.

Gideon's strategy works splendidly. As the Israelite band remain in their positions surrounding the camp, the surprised and confused Midianites and their mercenaries turn their swords against one another, an act that is linked directly to Yahweh's doing (v.22; cf. 2Ki 7:6–7; 2Ch 20:17–23). Those who survive this confused slaughter retreat to the east toward and across the Jordan River. The various sites mentioned in the description of their path in 7:22 have not been securely identified, though Abel Meholah was part of Solomon's fifth district (1Ki 4:12) and the birthplace of the prophet Elijah (1Ki 19:16).

NOTES

15 שִׁבְרוֹ (šibrô, "its interpretation"). The term שֶׁבֶר (šeber), dominantly referring to a breaking—here in the context of a dream—is understood as "cracking it open" (*HALOT*, 1405), thus "its interpretation."

16 רָאשִׁים (rāʾšîm, "companies"). The Hebrew word here is better translated as "heads, chiefs," indicating that the three hundred or three units were divided among and led by three "chiefs." Dividing an army into three units is a practice also followed by Abimelech (Jdg 9:34, 37, 43), Saul (1Sa 11:11; 13:17–18), David (2Sa 18:2), and the Chaldeans (Job 1:17).

19 רֹאשׁ הָאַשְׁמֹרֶת הַתִּיכוֹנָה (rōʾš hāʾašmōret hattîkônâ, "at the beginning of the middle watch"). This notation suggests that the night was divided into three phases (possibly 8:00 p.m.–midnight; midnight–4:00 a.m.; and 4:00–8:00 a.m.) and identifies the time as most likely midnight (cf. Pss 63:7; 90:4; 119:148; La 2:19). See Exodus 24:24 and 1 Samuel 11:11 for the third or morning watch (Block, 282).

vii. Gideon summons men of Israel to finish the battle (7:23–25)

²³Israelites from Naphtali, Asher and all Manasseh were called out, and they pursued the Midianites. ²⁴Gideon sent messengers throughout the hill country of Ephraim, saying, "Come down against the Midianites and seize the waters of the Jordan ahead of them as far as Beth Barah."

So all the men of Ephraim were called out and they took the waters of the Jordan as far as Beth Barah. ²⁵They also captured two of the Midianite leaders, Oreb and Zeeb. They killed Oreb at the rock of Oreb, and Zeeb at the winepress of Zeeb. They pursued the Midianites and brought the heads of Oreb and Zeeb to Gideon, who was by the Jordan.

COMMENTARY

23 With the Midianites in retreat, the rest of the ten large military units ("thousands") who had been sent home are called into action to pursue the fleeing Midianites. This call for reinforcements does not necessarily constitute a lack of faith on Gideon's part, since Israel's role in mop-up operations after a decisive divine victory is typical in the OT (see 1Sa 17; contra Block, 283; Klein, *The Triumph of Irony*, 57–58).

24–25 At the same time, Gideon sends messengers south to request that the Ephraimites cut off the retreating Midianites as they try to cross the Jordan further south as far as Beth Barah (of unknown location), whose name may have originated from *bêt-ʿabārâ* ("house of the ford"). The Ephraimites not only respond to this request but also are able to capture and execute two of the Midianite leaders, Oreb and Zeeb, whose severed heads they bring to Gideon. The names of these two leaders reflect their violent character. "Oreb" means "raven," an unclean bird that feeds on carrion (Lev 11:15; Dt 14:14), while "Zeeb" means "wolf," an image associated with violence and linked to war in Genesis 49:27 (cf. Eze 22:27; Jer 5:6; Zep 3:3).

Here is the second of three instances in Judges where the fords of Jordan are captured in relation to an Ephraimite military operation (cf. 3:27–29; 12:1–6). In these three accounts there is a progressive decline in cooperation by Ephraim (see comments on 3:27–29), which undermines its claim to leadership.

NOTE

25 שָׂרֵי מִדְיָן (*śārê midyān*, "Midianite leaders"). Oreb and Zeeb were probably commanders of large units who served under the two kings Zebah and Zalmunna described in 8:5.

viii. Gideon calms the anger of Ephraim over not being involved in his initial battle (8:1–3)

¹Now the Ephraimites asked Gideon, "Why have you treated us like this? Why didn't you call us when you went to fight Midian?" And they criticized him sharply.
²But he answered them, "What have I accomplished compared to you? Aren't the gleanings of Ephraim's grapes better than the full grape harvest of Abiezer? ³God gave Oreb and Zeeb, the Midianite leaders, into your hands. What was I able to do compared to you?" At this, their resentment against him subsided.

COMMENTARY

1 While rising to Gideon's challenge, the Ephraimites are not pleased that they had been excluded from his earlier military strategy, a displeasure with economic (lack of plunder) as well as social (honor-shame) motivations (Matthews, *Judges and Ruth*, 94; see below). Gideon was from Manasseh, one of the two tribes of Joseph in the north, the other being the tribe of Ephraim. While Gideon's appeal to the tribes of Asher, Zebulun, and Naphtali made sense because of their common territorial claim to the Jezreel Valley, the Ephraimites may have expected to be called in the light of their common lineage, a pattern established in 1:22–26.

This allusion to Ephraim is one of many connections between Ephraim and leadership of the tribes in the book of Judges. After the death of Joshua, an Ephraimite (Nu 13:8), no other leader's lineage is explicitly linked to the tribe of Ephraim, though Deborah the prophetess-judge lived in the hill country of Ephraim (4:5), the Issacharite Tola ruled in Ephraimite territory (10:1), and Abdon the judge was buried there (12:15). While the Benjamite Ehud gathers his forces from Ephraimite territory (3:27), judges who do not involve the Ephraimites in their military campaigns (Gideon, Jephthah) risk offending this dominant tribe (8:1–2; 12:1–6).

These many connections suggest that Ephraim's leadership role in the nation is a theme being developed in the background of the accounts of the judges (see Introduction). Interestingly, in the bracket that surrounds the book as a whole and in which the issue of leadership of the nation comes to the fore (1:1–2:5; chs. 17–21), Ephraim is depicted as unable to drive out the Canaanites (1:29) and as the location from which the two tragic plots begin (17:1; 19:1).

2–3 This conflict between Gideon and Ephraim is best understood through the lens of ancient honor-shame values (Kirkpatrick, 28–32), here following a basic pattern of action-claim, perception, and response. Thus Gideon's victory (action-claim) is interpreted as a challenge to Ephraim's leadership (perception), and so is counter-challenged by Ephraim (response). This response becomes a new action-claim, which is then interpreted by Gideon (perception), who wisely responds by emphasizing his social inferiority (response).

Gideon shows his social and political acumen by diffusing the crisis (contrast Jephthah in 12:1–6, though note Josiah Derby, "Gideon and the Ephraimites," *JBQ* 30 [2002]: 118–20, who shows how Gideon slyly makes what is essentially a putdown appear to be a compliment). The metaphor he uses is drawn from the harvesting of grapes, contrasting the gleanings (those grapes left over after the harvesters have completed their work) with the full harvest. Gideon claims that even the gleanings of Ephraim's harvest are better than the full harvest of his own clan (Abiezer, see 6:11). In the same way, Ephraim's late exploits in the battle outshine anything he has accomplished because they have captured the two Midianite leaders (the choicest grapes!).

Gideon's flattery successfully calms the angry Ephraimites. This interaction reveals Ephraim's claim to leadership among the northern tribes (which will reemerge in 12:1–6), and once again threatens the unity of the tribes. Both Gideon and the Ephraimites show little concern for Yahweh's role in the battle.

NOTES

1 וַיָּרִיבוּן (*wayᵉrîbûn*, "they criticized"). The term here is one used for bringing a lawsuit against another, intensified by the adverbial phrase בְּחָזְקָה (*bᵉḥozqâ*) "with strength/force/violence."

2 עֹלֵלוֹת ... מִבְצִיר (*ᶜōlᵉlōt ... mibṣîr*, "gleanings of ... grapes ... than the full grape harvest"). עֹלֵלוֹת (*ᶜōlᵉlōt*) are "bunches of grapes or olives left behind by the pickers for the use of the poor, because they were inferior or unripe," while בָּצִיר (*bᵉṣîr*) is "the entire collected grape crop" (Derby, 119).

ix. Leaders of Succoth and Penuel refuse to feed Gideon and his troops, and Gideon promises to return and punish them (8:4–9)

⁴Gideon and his three hundred men, exhausted yet keeping up the pursuit, came to the Jordan and crossed it. ⁵He said to the men of Succoth, "Give my troops some bread; they are worn out, and I am still pursuing Zebah and Zalmunna, the kings of Midian."

⁶But the officials of Succoth said, "Do you already have the hands of Zebah and Zalmunna in your possession? Why should we give bread to your troops?"

⁷Then Gideon replied, "Just for that, when the Lᴏʀᴅ has given Zebah and Zalmunna into my hand, I will tear your flesh with desert thorns and briers."

⁸From there he went up to Peniel and made the same request of them, but they answered as the men of Succoth had. ⁹So he said to the men of Peniel, "When I return in triumph, I will tear down this tower."

COMMENTARY

4–9 While Ephraim has executed two of the Midianite leaders (Oreb and Zeeb) of lower rank, two higher-ranking kings remain on the run (Zebah and Zalmunna), and Gideon is intent on capturing them (and so in the end shame Ephraim; see above). To continue the pursuit he needs food for his troops and so asks for supplies from the leaders of two cities, Succoth and Penuel (Peniel; see Notes), the second being most likely the site of Jacob's wrestling with God along the Jabbok River in Transjordan (Ge 32:24–32). Fearful of reprisal from the much stronger Midianite force, these leaders refuse to help, and both receive Gideon's warning that he will return one day to repay them for their lack of hospitality.

One can discern a clear shift in the character of Gideon from the previous scenes, in which he was somewhat tentative and fearful (Webb, 151; McCann, 68). Following his victory he now responds with threats against those who will not assist him. Here is the beginning of a trend of self-interest and revenge among the later judges (see comments on 8:13–17).

NOTES

6 הֲכַף זֶבַח וְצַלְמֻנָּע עַתָּה בְּיָדֶךָ (*haᵏkap zebaḥ weṣalmunnā ᶜattâ beyādekâ*, "the hands of Zebah and Zalmunna"). Possibly here "hands" (used also for "palms" in Hebrew; see Note on 8:15) is used for "power" but more likely represents the ancient practice of retaining body parts as evidence of victims killed (cf. Jdg 1:6; 7:25; 1Sa 17:51, 57; 18:25).

8–9 פְּנוּאֵל (*peⁿûᵓēl*, "Peniel"). The Hebrew text reads here "Penuel" (cf. vv.9, 17; 1Ki 12:25), which means "face of God." Peniel is the name used in Genesis 32:31, while Penuel appears in Genesis 32:32.

x. Gideon pursues and defeats the Midianite kings Zebah and Zalmunna (8:10–12)

[10]Now Zebah and Zalmunna were in Karkor with a force of about fifteen thousand men, all that were left of the armies of the eastern peoples; a hundred and twenty thousand swordsmen had fallen. [11]Gideon went up by the route of the nomads east of Nobah and Jogbehah and fell upon the unsuspecting army. [12]Zebah and Zalmunna, the two kings of Midian, fled, but he pursued them and captured them, routing their entire army.

COMMENTARY

10–12 The two Midianite kings had retreated to the town of Karkor with their decimated force now comprising only fifteen large units ("thousands") of men. Judges 8:11 traces Gideon's route, showing how he travels east through Nobah and Jogbehah, towns associated with the Israelite conquest of the former territories of Sihon and Og in Transjordan. Nobah is associated with the tribe of Manasseh (Nu 32:40–42) and Jogbehah with the tribe of Gad (Nu 32:35). Most likely this route fools the remaining Midianite forces into believing the Israelites have stopped their pursuit, thus leaving the Midianites vulnerable to the devastating attack described in 8:12. No description is given of the way in which Gideon defeats this much larger force, and no reference is made to any involvement by Yahweh. Nevertheless, the army is routed and the two kings are captured. This victory is attributed to Gideon alone.

NOTE

10 וּמַחֲנֵיהֶם ... מַחֲנֶה (*ûmaḥᵃnêhem ... maḥᵃnēh*, "and their armies ... army"). Here (cf. 8:12) the term used is one designating a group that is journeying, that is, an "encampment/camp." It may be small or large, for military or nonmilitary purposes (Ge 32:9; Nu 5:3).

xi. Gideon returns to punish Succoth and Penuel (8:13–17)

¹³Gideon son of Joash then returned from the battle by the Pass of Heres. ¹⁴He caught a young man of Succoth and questioned him, and the young man wrote down for him the names of the seventy-seven officials of Succoth, the elders of the town. ¹⁵Then Gideon came and said to the men of Succoth, "Here are Zebah and Zalmunna, about whom you taunted me by saying, 'Do you already have the hands of Zebah and Zalmunna in your possession? Why should we give bread to your exhausted men?'" ¹⁶He took the elders of the town and taught the men of Succoth a lesson by punishing them with desert thorns and briers. ¹⁷He also pulled down the tower of Peniel and killed the men of the town.

COMMENTARY

13–17 Gideon does not forget his warning to the leaders of Succoth and Penuel as given in 8:4–9. Catching a young court official from Succoth, he is able to get the names of the elders of the town. Bringing with him the two captured Midianite kings, Gideon repeats the earlier words of these leaders of Succoth to them ("Do you already have the hands of Zebah and Zalmunna in your possession? Why should we give bread to your exhausted men?") before punishing them in the way he had promised.

The once timid Gideon has now become a violent tyrant and instigates, for the first time in Judges, military action against fellow Israelites — a motif that will only grow worse as the book progresses (cf. 12:1–6; 20:1–48; cf. Webb, 158). Additionally, while the earlier judges acted on behalf of Yahweh and his people, beginning with Gideon and continuing in Jephthah and Samson, the judges' actions will be based on self-interest displayed through vengeance (Schneider, xv; Wong, *Strategy*, 174–76).

NOTES

15 הֲכַף (*haᵏkap*, "the hands"). The Hebrew text here is more specific, "the hollow, the flat of the hand" (*HALOT*, 491). For the practice of severing body parts as trophies of military victory see 1:6–7 (cf. 1Sa 18:27).

16 וַיֹּדַע (*wayyōdaᶜ*, "taught … a lesson"). This probably should be read in the light of the LXXᵃ's καταξαίνω (*kataxainō*; LXXᵇ ἀλοάω, *aloaō*), כוש (*kwš*) "to thresh," here to tear to pieces with thorns, possibly through whipping.

17 פְּנוּאֵל (*pᵉnûᵓēl*, "Peniel"). See Note on 8:8–9.

xii. Gideon kills the Midianite kings Zebah and Zalmunna (8:18–21)

¹⁸Then he asked Zebah and Zalmunna, "What kind of men did you kill at Tabor?"

"Men like you," they answered, "each one with the bearing of a prince."

¹⁹Gideon replied, "Those were my brothers, the sons of my own mother. As surely as the LORD lives, if you had spared their lives, I would not kill you." ²⁰Turning to Jether, his oldest son, he said, "Kill them!" But Jether did not draw his sword, because he was only a boy and was afraid.

²¹Zebah and Zalmunna said, "Come, do it yourself. 'As is the man, so is his strength.'" So Gideon stepped forward and killed them, and took the ornaments off their camels' necks.

COMMENTARY

18–21 Gideon completes the routing of the Midianites by executing the two captured kings, Zebah and Zalmunna. He links this execution to their treatment of his own brothers in a battle that took place at Mount Tabor, a hill in the Jezreel Valley in the vicinity of the Midianites' original encampment. Gideon first commands his eldest son, Jether, to kill the two Midianite kings. When his youthful fear disables Jether, Zebah and Zalmunna challenge Gideon to do the deed himself—for them a more honorable way to die (see Niditch, *Symbolic Vision*, 105, for this challenge as evidence of the "heroic ethos of war").

Gideon is only too willing to fulfill their request. Jether is used by the narrator not only to help the reader recognize the clear contrast between the Gideon of ch. 7 and the Gideon of ch. 8 (Block, 295), but also to prepare for Jether's younger half-brother Abimelech, who will gladly kill his own royal kin, and Jether's younger full brother Jotham, who will courageously declare God's judgment (Schneider, 126, 137). The retributive practices of Gideon, showcased already in his violent treatment of Succoth and Penuel, is now directed toward the two Midianite kings. Interestingly, it is these Midianite kings who first broach the subject of kingship, flattering Gideon by likening him and his brothers to royalty (v.18; cf. Guest, 258; see Note). Ultimately, Israel will be tempted to establish kingship like that represented by Zebah and Zalmunna (1Sa 8:5; see Introduction).

NOTE

18 בְּנֵי הַמֶּלֶךְ (*bᵉnê hammelek*, "a prince"). The Hebrew reads more woodenly "sons of the king," making explicit reference to kingship.

d. Gideon Refuses Kingship but Requests Part of the Spoil, Which He Makes into an Ephod
(8:22–27)

[22]The Israelites said to Gideon, "Rule over us — you, your son and your grandson — because you have saved us out of the hand of Midian."

[23]But Gideon told them, "I will not rule over you, nor will my son rule over you. The LORD will rule over you." [24]And he said, "I do have one request, that each of you give me an earring from your share of the plunder." (It was the custom of the Ishmaelites to wear gold earrings.)

[25]They answered, "We'll be glad to give them." So they spread out a garment, and each man threw a ring from his plunder onto it. [26]The weight of the gold rings he asked for came to seventeen hundred shekels, not counting the ornaments, the pendants and the purple garments worn by the kings of Midian or the chains that were on their camels' necks. [27]Gideon made the gold into an ephod, which he placed in Ophrah, his town. All Israel prostituted themselves by worshiping it there, and it became a snare to Gideon and his family.

COMMENTARY

22–23 Identifying Gideon as the one who has saved Israel from their enemy Midian, the people ask him to establish a dynasty ("you, your son and your grandson") over them. Gideon refuses, explicitly stating that neither he nor his son will rule over them — a narrative foreshadowing of the following chapter, when his son Abimelech will assume kingship at Shechem. Gideon voices a concern that will reemerge in 1 Samuel (Amit, *Judges*, 96–97; cf. 1Sa 8:20; 9:16; 10:18–19; 12:9–12), namely, the concern that Israel's request for kingship was a direct challenge to Yahweh's kingship over Israel (see Introduction).

The one who was king in the ancient world was the one who led the nation successfully in battle. The people had linked the victory over the Midianites with Gideon rather than with Yahweh,

who had raised him up. Gideon, however, is not innocent in this matter since he did include his name in the battle cry of 7:18 (Wong, *Strategy*, 165–68).

24–27 While refusing the throne, Gideon does make a request of the people that they give him a portion of their spoil from the victory: one golden earring each. The gold from these earrings and the pendants and chains from the camels' necks are used by Gideon to create a golden ephod, which he places in his hometown of Ophrah. An ephod is a priestly vestment, appropriate for an individual whose father had once sponsored the Baal and Asherah cult at the sacred oak of Ophrah.

It may be that Gideon's original intention in creating this ephod is positive, representing a sacral offering of a portion of the plunder to Yahweh (see other ancient Near Eastern evidence in Matthews, *Judges and Ruth*, 97) and/or an act designed to facilitate proper inquiry of Yahweh (Webb, 152–53; Amit, *Judges*, 98). In the end, however, this golden ephod will lead Israel as well as Gideon and his family back into idolatry (by becoming "a snare"; cf. Jdg 2:3). This regression is ironic in light of the fact that Gideon's first act was to destroy idolatrous objects in 6:25–32 at the same Ophrah (Webb, 147, 153; Block, 250; Matthews, *Judges and Ruth*, 98). This event foreshadows the illicit ephod created by Micah in Judges 17–18 (see Wong, *Strategy*, 83–89), both events associated with the northern tribes.

4. Notation of Length of Peace and End of Gideon's Life (8:28–32)

[28]Thus Midian was subdued before the Israelites and did not raise its head again. During Gideon's lifetime, the land enjoyed peace forty years.

[29]Jerub-Baal son of Joash went back home to live. [30]He had seventy sons of his own, for he had many wives. [31]His concubine, who lived in Shechem, also bore him a son, whom he named Abimelech. [32]Gideon son of Joash died at a good old age and was buried in the tomb of his father Joash in Ophrah of the Abiezrites.

COMMENTARY

28–32 As do many of the major accounts in Judges, the narrative here closes with a notation on the final state of the enemy followed by a statement of the length of time the land enjoyed peace (3:11, 30; 5:31; 12:7; 16:20, 31). What follows is often notice of a death (2:19; 3:11; 4:1; 12:7) and sometimes a burial (12:7; 16:31), as one finds in 8:32. In the case of Gideon, however, the narrator includes a short description of his return to his home, the birth of seventy sons to his many wives, and the birth of a son named Abimelech to his concubine at Shechem (on her status see comments on 9:1).

This extra information has two effects on the reader. First, it casts doubt on the authenticity of Gideon's rejection of kingship (Webb, 154; Guest, 258; Wong, *Strategy*, 168–69), since the account suggests that Gideon acts like a royal figure in amassing a large fortune (v.26), building a harem (v.30) and a large family (v.30), and even naming his son "Abimelech" (meaning "my father is king"; cf. Dt 17:17). Abimelech's references to the rule of Gideon's children in 9:1–2 states explicitly what the narrator has communicated only implicitly in 8:28–32.

Second, this extra information prepares the reader for the narrative to follow in ch. 9 by introducing the main characters who will dominate the account. The story of Abimelech is inextricably linked with that of Gideon (Webb, 125; O'Connell, 139; Bluedorn, 265; Matthews, *Judges and Ruth*, 100), even if it has its own structural integrity (see comments on 8:33–35).

NOTE

29 וַיֵּשֶׁב בְּבֵיתוֹ (*wayyēšeb beʾbêtô*, "went back home"). This phrase probably signals Gideon's retirement to private life, though ironically in the light of its description as "far more like that of a ruler than of a private citizen" (Webb, 154).

REFLECTION

Gideon continues the presentation of unlikely characters raised up by Yahweh to save his people. This unbelieving figure does in the end respond in faith to Yahweh's call (Heb 11:32). Here Yahweh provides various forms of revelation to his leader by graciously responding to Gideon's fear. Throughout the account victory is linked to human weakness and lack of potential — here, whether Gideon or his small contingent of soldiers. Key to the victory, therefore, is God's presence and strength, spoken in word through the declaration "mighty warrior" and experienced in deed by the clothing of Gideon with God's Spirit.

It is interesting that God targets what appears to be a family who were leaders in the idolatrous rebellion that set in motion divine discipline, and it is instructive that this would-be leader must take a stand in his own family first — a family that initially threatened his life but ultimately formed the core of his army. The end of Gideon's life, however, highlights the frailty of human leadership. Although clearly affirming Yahweh's kingship verbally, there are signs even as he is about to enter battle that he is competing with Yahweh for the glory of victory.

In the end the contradiction between his word and his deed opens the way for the great tragedy in the next generation of his family, not only in taking on royal prerogatives for himself, but also in creating a cultic item that will reverse his initial stand against idolatry. Gideon's failure then creates an expectation for a greater model of leadership, one identified with the tribe of Judah in chs. 17 – 21.

G. Abimelech (8:33 – 9:57)

OVERVIEW

Judges 8:33 is thematically similar to the opening of the other major accounts of judges in the book by tracing the sin of Israel after the death of the previous judge, but it does not use the same vocabulary (see Exum, "The Centre Cannot Hold," 420, who notes similarity to 2:17). This evidence, along with the fact that the following account describes the tragedy of the failed kingship of Abimelech, sets this account apart from the major accounts of judges and can be read as an extension of the Gideon account. (On this ambiguity in 8:33 – 35, see Fensham, 81, who identifies it either "as part of the narrative of the Abimelech history or as a transitional description between the narrative of Gideon and Abimelech" [cf. Boling, 169–70, for the first, and Gray, *Joshua, Judges, Ruth*, 315, for the second].)

Yet in terms of the overall structure of the major accounts, it is possible to see in the Abimelech account the basic rhythms of cyclical accounts, with Israel's apostasy traced in 8:33–35, divine discipline in 9:1–6, followed by the rescue of 9:22–57. While Amit (*Judges*, 40–43, 99) sees the minor accounts of Judges at the beginning of ch. 10 as the missing element of the divinely commissioned judge-deliverer, these figures do not deal with the enemy identified in the divine discipline of 9:1–6 (Abimelech and the Shechemites). If any human plays this role in the story of Abimelech, it is the nameless woman of 9:52–53, though it appears that God intervenes directly in this case (see 9:23–24, 56–57). While one does not find the element of Israel's cry, the prophetic element that often follows such a cry (4:4–7; 6:7–10) may be discerned in Jotham's declaration of 9:7–21 (see Boda, "Recycling Heaven's Words").

Abimelech shares characteristics with both Saul and Jeroboam, which suggests that he is introduced into the book to highlight illegitimate kingship rather than to disqualify royal leadership in principle. That Jotham's fable brings to mind not only Shechem's anointing of Abimelech as king but also Gideon's refusal of kingship, suggests that when good leaders refuse the royal throne, they leave the nation vulnerable to inappropriate royal leadership.

1. Israel's Apostasy from Yahweh and Mistreatment of Gideon's Family after His Death (8:33–35)

> [33]No sooner had Gideon died than the Israelites again prostituted themselves to the Baals. They set up Baal-Berith as their god and [34]did not remember the LORD their God, who had rescued them from the hands of all their enemies on every side. [35]They also failed to show kindness to the family of Jerub-Baal (that is, Gideon) for all the good things he had done for them.

COMMENTARY

33–35 While Gideon led the people into idolatry through the golden ephod at Ophrah, after his death the people practice even worse activity by returning to the worship of Baal that typified their practice at the outset of the account of Gideon. Forgetting all that Yahweh did for them, they worship a god named Baal-Berith in 8:33; 9:4 and El-Berith in 9:46, meaning "Baal ('lord') of the Covenant" and "God of the Cove- nant," respectively — names that suggest they have transferred the covenant made with Yahweh to the Canaanite pantheon of Baal and El. (See esp. Bluedorn, who sees Baalistic idolatry as the key theme of the Gideon-Abimelech account, and T. J. Lewis ["The Identity and Function of El/Baal Berith," *JBL* 115 (1996): 401–23], who identifies this god as El, the lord [*ba'al*] of the covenant, the patron deity of Shechem.) The center of this cult was a temple fortress in Shechem (9:4, 46). Not only are the Israelites unfaithful to Yahweh after the death of their judge-deliverer, they are also unfaithful to Gideon by mistreating his family. This mistreatment is the focus of the narrator's attention in ch. 9.

2. Abimelech's Conspiracy and Ascension to the Throne (9:1–6)

[1]Abimelech son of Jerub-Baal went to his mother's brothers in Shechem and said to them and to all his mother's clan, [2]"Ask all the citizens of Shechem, 'Which is better for you: to have all seventy of Jerub-Baal's sons rule over you, or just one man?' Remember, I am your flesh and blood."

[3]When the brothers repeated all this to the citizens of Shechem, they were inclined to follow Abimelech, for they said, "He is our brother." [4]They gave him seventy shekels of silver from the temple of Baal-Berith, and Abimelech used it to hire reckless adventurers, who became his followers. [5]He went to his father's home in Ophrah and on one stone murdered his seventy brothers, the sons of Jerub-Baal. But Jotham, the youngest son of Jerub-Baal, escaped by hiding. [6]Then all the citizens of Shechem and Beth Millo gathered beside the great tree at the pillar in Shechem to crown Abimelech king.

COMMENTARY

1 Like Gideon's Abiezerite clan, the Shechemite clan was also descended from the line of Makir through Gilead within the tribe of Manasseh (Nu 26:29–35; cf. Jos 17:2), so it is not surprising that he would have relations with these families. The town that bore the clan's name was located twenty-five miles south of the Jezreel Valley and forty miles north of Jerusalem in the pass between Mount Ebal and Mount Gerizim. Shechem was a key site at the schism of the Davidic kingdom, hosting the coronation of Solomon's son Rehoboam (1Ki 12:1) and, after the northern tribes revolted against Rehoboam, becoming Jeroboam's first capital of his northern kingdom, Israel.

As noted in 8:31, Gideon had a concubine who continued to live with her family in Shechem. Bal,

176–77, citing also the example of the concubine in Judges 19, has argued that the term *pîlegeš* ("concubine"; GK 7108) refers to a wife who remained within her father's family, while Amit (*Judges*, 100, n. 74), citing Samson's Timnite woman, considers this a "'female friend' marriage in which the woman remains in her father's house," or a political marriage to ensure the loyalty of the aristocracy of Shechem. Bal's view has been criticized by Patton, 36, especially in light of the fact that the concubine's abandonment of the Levite's household in Judges 19 is considered abnormal and is soon rectified by the Levite (cf. Exum, *Fragmented Women*, 177; Stone, 90, n. 5; 2Sa 16:20–22).

Most likely Amit's second view is true of the relationship between Gideon and this concubine from

Shechem, but primarily a concubine was a secondary wife taken by rich males in the ancient world to ensure plenteous offspring. After Sarah's death, Abraham took another wife, Keturah (Ge 25:1), who is later called a concubine (25:6). Bilhah, Rachel's servant who was given to Jacob to bear more children (30:4), is also called a concubine (35:22). The relationship between a male and his concubine was socially binding and could not be violated by another male (35:22; 49:4; 2Sa 3:7; 1Ki 2:13−25). There are some differences in the presentation of the inheritance rights of the male offspring of the concubine. In some texts they do not inherit (Ge 21:10; 25:5−6; Jdg 11:1−2), in others they receive some gifts (Ge 25:5−6), and in still others they are treated as full sons (Ge 35:23−26). The Code of Hammurabi (§§170−71) reveals that to what extent inheritance rights apply is dependent on legal recognition of the son by the father (HBD, 422).

In 8:31 the one son Gideon's single concubine "bore him" is clearly distinguished from the seventy sons "of his own," that is, "who came out of his loins" (yōṣʾê yᵉrēkô) in 8:30 through his many wives. Jotham will refer to Abimelech's mother as a "maidservant" (ʾāmâ, 9:18), but this term may only be one of derision used for rhetorical effect (though see the Levite's description of the concubine in 19:19). Abimelech's lower status as the son of Gideon's concubine leads to his departure from Ophrah and arrival at Shechem to use his matrilineal links to gain advantage over his seventy brothers (Steinberg, 50−51, 58).

Judges 9 refers to his immediate relatives ("his mother's brothers") as well as to his mother's more distant relatives who constitute the leaders of Shechem, a group that ruled over the Shechemite clan just as the seventy sons of Gideon ruled over the tribe of Manasseh. This group (baʿᵃlê šᵉkem, "leaders of Shechem") appears regularly throughout Judges 9 (vv.2−3, 6−7, 18, 20, 23−24, 26, 39). The name Abimelech ("my father is king"), as well as the narrator's explicit reference to him as "the son of Jerub-Baal," highlights the royal function of this family. At the same time there are key differences between the father (Gideon, at least in the earlier phase of his life), who rejected kingship, smashed the altar of Baal, used spoils of war for an ephod to Yahweh, and selected his military by God's direction to avenge the blood of his brothers, and the son (Abimelech), who sought kingship, took silver from the house of Baal/El-Berith to kill his brothers, and hired worthless men to kill his own brothers (Amit, Judges, 104).

2−3 Abimelech's plan is to use his mother's immediate family to influence the leaders of the clan as a whole. He dictates an argument ("Ask all the citizens of Shechem … ") to them, which is based on quantity and quality; that is, it is better to have only one ruler you can count on since he is your close relation than seventy rulers who will favor other clans because they are your more distant relations. Reference to the rule of seventy reveals that although Gideon had functioned as a monarch in his lifetime, he had left behind an oligarchy in which seventy would rule. Abimelech's maternal family members repeat Abimelech's proposal to the leaders of the clan, who accept this argument ("he is our brother"). Ironically, it is precisely this "attempt to undermine the legitimate ancient Israelite societal norm of patrilineal kinship" that leads to Abimelech's demise (Steinberg, 57).

4−5 The Shechemites provide Abimelech with seventy shekels of silver from their temple dedicated to the god Baal-Berith (see 8:35) in order to hire mercenaries (for evidence of this temple, see Provan, Long, and Longman, 185). It is not surprising that the payment comes from the temple since in the ancient world the temple served as a key treasury for society (see ABD, 6:371, 375). The fact that the money comes from a temple dedicated to a god that has led Israel astray (8:33−35) accentuates the evil of Abimelech's action and the culpability of the Shechemites in what follows. This action is strikingly similar to the use of stolen money to create an idol for another illegitimate northern shrine in ch. 17 (Dan). The number of shekels matched the number of brothers Abimelech killed at his father Gideon's house in Ophrah; only the youngest son, Jotham, escape.

6 With all Gideon's offspring supposedly dead, Abimelech and the leaders of Shechem assemble at "the great tree" (cf. 6:11), most likely a sacred site at Shechem, for the coronation of Abimelech. While Gideon had not used the precise terminology of kingship in 8:23 (*mšl*) and Abimelech had restricted his language to that of Gideon in 9:2, the narrator makes explicit that Abimelech has demanded and accepted a royal office (*mlk*; 9:6). Wong (*Strategy*,

204–6) wisely highlights links between the stories of Adoni-Bezek (ch. 1) and Abimelech here as indicative of the negative portrayal of human kingship in Judges (seventy related victims, equal retribution, proximity of Bezek and Shechem)—what he calls "this Canaanisation of Abimelech, and the fact that he may have even out-Canaanised the Canaanites."

The crowning at Shechem of an illegitimate ruler related to an illegitimate shrine among the northern tribes after the rejection of another royal line links this story with that of Jeroboam in 1 Kings 12 (Schneider, 135–36). Jeroboam's revolt against the Davidic line would result in illegitimate shrines at Dan and Bethel, which are identified as the cause of the exile in 1 and 2 Kings.

NOTES

1 בֶּן־יְרֻבַּעַל (*ben-yᵉrubbaᶜal*, "son of Jerub-Baal"). While the account of Gideon is dominated by the name Gideon, the account of Abimelech is dominated by the name Jerub-Baal (see 9:5, 16, 24, 28, 58; cf. Amit, *Judges*, 102). This constant emphasis on the connection between Gideon and Baal reminds the reader of the Canaanite context and tone of this story.

2 כִּי־עַצְמֵכֶם וּבְשַׂרְכֶם אָנִי (*kî-ᶜaṣmēkem ûbᵉśarkem ʾānî*, "I am your flesh and blood"). This statement of family solidarity echoes the intimacy of the marriage relationship in Genesis 2:23 (cf. 29:14).

4 אֲנָשִׁים רֵיקִים וּפֹחֲזִים (*ʾᵃnāšîm rêqîm ûpōḥᵃzîm*, "reckless adventurers"). This expression is better translated "worthless and reckless fellows," or "debased and wanton men" (see Note on 11:3).

6 בֵּית מִלּוֹא (*bêt millôʾ*, "Beth Millo"). These words possibly refer to the "tower" mentioned in 9:46, most likely a stronghold area at the highest point in the city (cf. 9:20). The term *millôʾ* means "filling" and is used of a particular area in Jerusalem (2Sa 5:8; 1Ki 9:15, 24; 11:26; 1Ch 11:8; 32:5), always in reference to the fortifications of the city. Compare 2 Kings 12:20 [21] for the precise term "Beth Millo," most likely referring to a structure within the Millo.

3. Jotham's Speech on Mount Gerizim (9:7–21)

> **7**When Jotham was told about this, he climbed up on the top of Mount Gerizim and shouted to them, "Listen to me, citizens of Shechem, so that God may listen to you. **8**One

day the trees went out to anoint a king for themselves. They said to the olive tree, 'Be our king.'

⁹"But the olive tree answered, 'Should I give up my oil, by which both gods and men are honored, to hold sway over the trees?'

¹⁰"Next, the trees said to the fig tree, 'Come and be our king.'

¹¹"But the fig tree replied, 'Should I give up my fruit, so good and sweet, to hold sway over the trees?'

¹²"Then the trees said to the vine, 'Come and be our king.'

¹³"But the vine answered, 'Should I give up my wine, which cheers both gods and men, to hold sway over the trees?'

¹⁴"Finally all the trees said to the thornbush, 'Come and be our king.'

¹⁵"The thornbush said to the trees, 'If you really want to anoint me king over you, come and take refuge in my shade; but if not, then let fire come out of the thornbush and consume the cedars of Lebanon!'

¹⁶"Now if you have acted honorably and in good faith when you made Abimelech king, and if you have been fair to Jerub-Baal and his family, and if you have treated him as he deserves — ¹⁷and to think that my father fought for you, risked his life to rescue you from the hand of Midian ¹⁸(but today you have revolted against my father's family, murdered his seventy sons on a single stone, and made Abimelech, the son of his slave girl, king over the citizens of Shechem because he is your brother) — ¹⁹if then you have acted honorably and in good faith toward Jerub-Baal and his family today, may Abimelech be your joy, and may you be his, too! ²⁰But if you have not, let fire come out from Abimelech and consume you, citizens of Shechem and Beth Millo, and let fire come out from you, citizens of Shechem and Beth Millo, and consume Abimelech!"

²¹Then Jotham fled, escaping to Beer, and he lived there because he was afraid of his brother Abimelech.

COMMENTARY

7 The one brother who escaped the murderous clutches of Abimelech receives word of his coronation and, from a safe position on Mount Gerizim, proclaims a message of judgment to the people of Shechem. Shechem was located halfway between Jerusalem and the Jezreel Valley, at the heart of the hill country controlled by the Joseph tribes and near the border between Manasseh and Ephraim. It lay in a valley with Mount Ebal to the north and Mount Gerizim to the south, the location where Israel first renewed the covenant after the initial conquest of the land (Jos 8:30–35), as commanded by Moses (Dt 27–28; cf. Dt 11:29, 30). Interestingly, it was from Mount Gerizim that blessings were to be proclaimed by six tribes and from Mount Ebal that curses were to be proclaimed by the six other tribes. Mount Gerizim is now the source not of a blessing but of a curse upon Shechem from the survivor of Abimelech's bloody coup.

Jotham begins his speech with the phrase, "Listen to me ... so that God may listen to you." While it is possible that this call is an invitation for them to seek God penitentially, most likely it is a way of gaining attention by posing as a prophet who has special access to the heavenly realms.

8–15 Jotham's speech begins with a fable, that is, "a short narrative in poetry or prose that teaches a moral lesson and involves creatures, plants, and/or inanimate objects speaking or behaving like human characters" (Block, 316; for ancient Near Eastern connections, see Tatu, 108–10). The fable is about a group of "trees" (*ʿēṣîm*), a broader term that can include plants (e.g., vines), in search of a ruler whom they may anoint. The relationship between anointing and kingship is well established in the OT (see Notes).

Three plants are initially asked—the olive tree, fig tree, and vine—but all three reject the invitation by saying they were designed to bear fruit (oil, figs, wine) rather than to "hold sway." It appears that these plants know what their functions are and thus reject kingship. Whether this response means that kingship is a worthless pursuit is uncertain, though it is possible that ruling may be a function appropriate for the "cedars of Lebanon" mentioned in v.15. The olive tree, fig tree, and vine provided the three main staples for the Israelites in the hill country and thus were considered the most precious. The same phrase, "gods and humans" (*ʾĕlōhîm waʾᵃnāšîm*), is used in the response of the olive tree and vine, thus suggesting a view of the heavenly court more akin to the Canaanite pantheon than to Israelite orthodoxy—not surprising in light of the conditions of the time in the wake of Gideon's activities.

After being disappointed by the three honorable plants, the desperate plants turn to the thorn tree (NIV's "thornbush"; see Note). Unlike the earlier plants, the thorn tree, while questioning the sincerity of the invitation, not only readily accepts the invitation, promising refuge for the other plants but also demanding their submission; moreover, he threatens fiery destruction of even the greatest of all plants, the cedars of Lebanon. These cedar trees, which grew in the mountainous region to the north of Israel's traditional lands, were well known throughout the ancient world. Many a Mesopotamian emperor sent for these logs to be used in their large building projects, a practice reflected in Solomon's construction of the temple (see 1Ki 5). The thorn tree's promise of refuge is sincere (see Note), but its threat against the cedars is ridiculous, revealing the foolish desperation of the other trees and the lack of sincerity of the thorn tree.

16–20 Jotham then applies this fable to the present situation (cf. 9:57). He sets up two scenarios, one of blessing (vv.16–19) and the other of curse (v.20). If the people have acted appropriately in the recent events, then he blesses them—"may Abimelech be your joy and may you be his, too!" (v.19); but if they have not, then he declares a curse, which echoes the final scenario of his fable, with fire coming forth from both the Shechemites and Abimelech to destroy one another. The long, tortuous flow of the first scenario of blessing extinguishes any hope that this speech was intended to bless rather than curse.

The application of Jotham's fable to the situation of Abimelech has been much debated. What is often missed is that the fable seems to have in view not only the immediate context of the Abimelech story, but also the earlier story of Gideon's refusal of the throne in 8:22–28, an event that echoes the refusal of the first three trees in Jotham's fable (see Amit, *Judges*, 106–11). This context suggests that while Gideon's refusal was appropriate in the light of the Israelite desire to install a royal figure for militaristic reasons, his refusal left the nation vulnerable to the abusive royal rule of Abimelech. Appropriate human kingship that recognizes Yahweh's authority may have a role, if only to deter royal courts fashioned after the surrounding nations (see further Introduction).

21 After such a negative message to a group bent on his destruction, Jotham escapes to Beer, a disputed location tentatively identified with El-Bireh,

which was near Ophrah, Jotham's hometown (*ABD*, 1:640). This town lay far enough north to escape capture by Abimelech. Since Beer means "well" in Hebrew, it may also indicate some nondescript well in which he hid (Block, 320), and thus be eerily reminiscent of the first scene in the account of his father, Gideon.

NOTES

8 לִמְשֹׁחַ עֲלֵיהֶם מֶלֶךְ (*limšōaḥ ʿalêhem melek*, "to anoint a king for themselves"). On the relationship between kingship and anointing, for מָשַׁח (*māšaḥ*) see 1 Samuel 9:16; 10:1; 15:1, 17; 16:3, 12–13; 2 Samuel 2:4, 7; 3:39; 5:3, 17; 12:7; 19:11; 1 Kings 1:34, 39, 45; 5:15; 19:15–16; 2 Kings 9:3, 6, 12; 11:12; 23:30; 1 Chronicles 14:8; 2 Chronicles 22:7; 23:11; 29:22; Psalms 45:7 [8]; 89:20 [21]; for מָשִׁיחַ (*māšîaḥ*) see 1 Samuel 2:10, 35; 12:3, 5; 16:6; 24:7 [2x], 11; 26:9, 11, 16, 23; 2 Samuel 1:14, 16; 19:22; 23:1; Psalms 2:2; 18:51(= 2Sa 22:51); 20:7; 28:8; 84:10; 89:39, 52; 132:10 (= 2Ch 6:42), 17; Isaiah 45:1; Lamentations 4:20; Daniel 9:25–26. Compare M. J. Boda, "Figuring the Future: The Prophets and the Messiah," in *Messiah* (ed. Stanley E. Porter; McMaster New Testament Studies; Grand Rapids: Eerdmans, 2007), 35–74.

14 הָאָטָד (*hāʾāṭād*, "the thornbush"). Tatu identifies this shrub as most likely the thorn tree *Ziziphus spina-Christi*, a tree that reaches ten meters (31 ft.) in height and possesses spinous stipules. While a food resource in the wilderness (with fruit), it would not be the choice of those with access to more domesticated plants such as the fig tree, olive tree, and vine. The thornbush's offer of waving over the trees and letting trees take refuge in its shade is thus not ironic (as, e.g., Fensham, 79), but rather a sincere offer even if it is clear that a thorn tree was not as valuable to the divine and human worlds as were the olive tree, fig tree, and vine.

19 וְאִם־בֶּאֱמֶת וּבְתָמִים עֲשִׂיתֶם עִם־יְרֻבַּעַל וְעִם־בֵּיתוֹ הַיּוֹם הַזֶּה (*wᵉʾim-beʾᵉmet ûbᵉtāmîm ʿaśîtem ʿim-yᵉrubbaʿal wᵉʿim-bêtô hayyôm hazzeh*, "if then you have acted honorably and in good faith toward Jerub-Baal and his family today"). Revell, 426, notes how this repetition of 9:16 is "an example of return from a digression in an argument."

4. War between Abimelech and Shechem (9:22–49)

²²After Abimelech had governed Israel three years, ²³God sent an evil spirit between Abimelech and the citizens of Shechem, who acted treacherously against Abimelech. ²⁴God did this in order that the crime against Jerub-Baal's seventy sons, the shedding of their blood, might be avenged on their brother Abimelech and on the citizens of Shechem, who had helped him murder his brothers. ²⁵In opposition to him these citizens

of Shechem set men on the hilltops to ambush and rob everyone who passed by, and this was reported to Abimelech.

²⁶Now Gaal son of Ebed moved with his brothers into Shechem, and its citizens put their confidence in him. ²⁷After they had gone out into the fields and gathered the grapes and trodden them, they held a festival in the temple of their god. While they were eating and drinking, they cursed Abimelech. ²⁸Then Gaal son of Ebed said, "Who is Abimelech, and who is Shechem, that we should be subject to him? Isn't he Jerub-Baal's son, and isn't Zebul his deputy? Serve the men of Hamor, Shechem's father! Why should we serve Abimelech? ²⁹If only this people were under my command! Then I would get rid of him. I would say to Abimelech, 'Call out your whole army!'"

³⁰When Zebul the governor of the city heard what Gaal son of Ebed said, he was very angry. ³¹Under cover he sent messengers to Abimelech, saying, "Gaal son of Ebed and his brothers have come to Shechem and are stirring up the city against you. ³²Now then, during the night you and your men should come and lie in wait in the fields. ³³In the morning at sunrise, advance against the city. When Gaal and his men come out against you, do whatever your hand finds to do."

³⁴So Abimelech and all his troops set out by night and took up concealed positions near Shechem in four companies. ³⁵Now Gaal son of Ebed had gone out and was standing at the entrance to the city gate just as Abimelech and his soldiers came out from their hiding place.

³⁶When Gaal saw them, he said to Zebul, "Look, people are coming down from the tops of the mountains!"

Zebul replied, "You mistake the shadows of the mountains for men."

³⁷But Gaal spoke up again: "Look, people are coming down from the center of the land, and a company is coming from the direction of the soothsayers' tree."

³⁸Then Zebul said to him, "Where is your big talk now, you who said, 'Who is Abimelech that we should be subject to him?' Aren't these the men you ridiculed? Go out and fight them!"

³⁹So Gaal led out the citizens of Shechem and fought Abimelech. ⁴⁰Abimelech chased him, and many fell wounded in the flight — all the way to the entrance to the gate. ⁴¹Abimelech stayed in Arumah, and Zebul drove Gaal and his brothers out of Shechem.

⁴²The next day the people of Shechem went out to the fields, and this was reported to Abimelech. ⁴³So he took his men, divided them into three companies and set an ambush in the fields. When he saw the people coming out of the city, he rose to attack them. ⁴⁴Abimelech and the companies with him rushed forward to a position at the entrance to the city gate. Then two companies rushed upon those in the fields and struck them down. ⁴⁵All that day Abimelech pressed his attack against the city until he had captured it and killed its people. Then he destroyed the city and scattered salt over it.

⁴⁶On hearing this, the citizens in the tower of Shechem went into the stronghold of the temple of El-Berith. ⁴⁷When Abimelech heard that they had assembled there, ⁴⁸he and all his men went up Mount Zalmon. He took an ax and cut off some branches, which he lifted to his shoulders. He ordered the men with him, "Quick! Do what you have seen me do!" ⁴⁹So all the men cut branches and followed Abimelech. They piled them against the stronghold and set it on fire over the people inside. So all the people in the tower of Shechem, about a thousand men and women, also died.

COMMENTARY

22–25 The arrangement between Abimelech and Shechem lasted for but three years, a period that stands in stark contrast to the much longer tenures of the judges in this book (3:11, 30; 8:28; 10:2–3; 12:7, 9, 11, 14; 15:20; 16:31). Verse 22 suggests that this rule was "over Israel." While it is possible that this comment does refer to all the Israelite tribes, it is more likely that Abimelech ruled over the more limited region surrounding Shechem, which was, indeed, "Israel." In this way Abimelech's rule was a foreshadowing of the reign of kings over the entire nation.

Jotham's speech, however, creates an expectation in the reader for a disintegration in the relationship between Abimelech and the Shechemites. The narrator traces this relational disintegration to a divinely sent "evil spirit" or, better, "injurious spirit," linking Abimelech to that later king of Israel's choosing, Saul (cf. 1Sa 16:14–23; 18:10–12; 19:9; Wong, *Strategy*, 210). In view here is not an immoral heavenly agent, but rather a heavenly agent of Yahweh who seeds discord between king and subjects (cf. 1Ki 22:19–23). In contrast to the divine Spirit, which elsewhere in Judges empowers saviors to rescue God's people from oppression (Jdg 3:10; 6:34; 11:29; 14:6, 19; 15:14), this spirit is sent as divine judgment on

Abimelech and the leaders of Shechem for shedding the innocent blood of Gideon's seventy sons (Webb, 158–59).

The agent of judgment prompts the leaders of Shechem ("citizens of Shechem") to "act treacherously" (v.23), a term used for deceitful breaking of a previous agreement (Ex 21:8; Jer 3:20; 5:11; 12:6; La 1:2; Hos 5:7; 6:7; Mal 2:10, 14–15) and described in v.25 as setting ambushes to rob those who passed by. Since commerce would have been controlled by the king, this breach would have stripped Abimelech of his economic resources and constituted a direct affront to his rule.

26–29 According to 9:41 Abimelech did not reside in the city of Shechem but rather in the nearby town of Arumah, a move that may explain his failure to control Shechem (Steinberg, 56). Abimelech had left Zebul as his deputy over Shechem. A certain Gaal son of Ebed moved into Shechem with his brothers and was able to win over the Shechemites by claiming purer Shechemite blood than that possessed by Abimelech, whose mother was a Shechemite but whose father was an Abiezerite (8:31–32; 9:1–3). Gaal's name is related to the Hebrew root that denotes "abhorring, loathing," hardly an honorable name in the ancient world.

In his speech, Gaal mentions his ancestor Hamor, the Hivite ruler of Shechem (Ge 33:19; 34:2), and uses logic strikingly similar to that originally employed by Abimelech to entice the Shechemites to follow him rather than his brothers (Jdg 9:1–3). The festal celebration described in v.27 serves to highlight Gaal's popularity among the people, as well as the enduring pagan character of the Shechemites.

30–33 Realizing Gaal's political victory in the city, Abimelech's deputy Zebul warns his superior, who is dwelling in Arumah (9:41), and counsels him to move quickly against Gaal by taking up positions in the fields under cover of darkness. This strategy suggests that the situation in Shechem has become unbearable for Zebul, who appears to have feigned support of Gaal (see vv.36–37). It also reflects wise military advice by allowing Abimelech to attack at sunrise, leaving Gaal no time to prepare for battle.

34–41 The first phase of the battle between Abimelech and the Shechemites takes place just outside the walls of the city. Abimelech follows his deputy Zebul's advice, dividing his troops into four companies (see comments on 7:16–19). In the morning Zebul takes Gaal on a stroll to the entrance of the city gate precisely at the moment when Abimelech and his forces emerge from their hiding place. At first Zebul plays with Gaal, teasing him that he is merely seeing things. But when Gaal will not be fooled, Zebul turns against him and challenges him to follow through on his boasting by engaging Abimelech in battle.

This appeal to Gaal's honor is key since it forces the proud Shechemite to advance rashly into battle rather than retreat within the city and make adequate preparations. Gaal is soundly defeated by Abimelech, and his retreating forces are killed as they flee back into the city. Zebul is able to gain control of the city

again and force Gaal and his brothers out, while for now Abimelech returns to his home base at Arumah.

42–45 The defeat and ouster of Gaal, however, does not bring an end to Abimelech's maneuvers. He is well aware that Gaal is but a symptom of a deeper problem. The leaders of Shechem have been acting treacherously toward him (vv.23, 25), so Abimelech is intent on punishing them for this infidelity. Again the setting is the fields outside Shechem, and again Abimelech sets an ambush for the people. This time his forces are divided into three groups. Once the common people have left the city and entered the fields, possibly to engage in agricultural activity, Abimelech's companies cut off their escape route by securing the city gate, while two companies attack those in the field. The victory is decisive as the city is captured, its people are killed, and its structures are destroyed. The scattering of salt appears to be "a ritual act invoking an irrevocable curse on the site" (cf. Dt 29:23; Ps 107:34; Jer 17:6; Zep 2:9; see Block, 330).

46–49 As is typical in a siege of an ancient Near Eastern city, the commoners are the first to face defeat, while the elite are able to find safety within a stronghold at the center of the city, here attached to or synonymous with the temple of their pagan god El-Berith. With his enemy trapped in this tower, Abimelech chooses to kill them by setting fire to what appears to be the inner chamber or possibly a subterranean room ($s^e r \hat{\imath} ah$) within the tower structure. Possibly the fire is set on the roof of this room since the text refers to a fire "over the people inside" (v.49).

The wood for this fire is gathered from Mount Zalmon, a name related to the Hebrew root slm, meaning "dark" or "darkness," possibly descriptive of either Mount Ebal or Mount Gerizim, which cast shadows on Shechem (though see Ps 68:14, which refers to this mountain in the region of Bashan, further north and west). The number who die in the tower is set at about one thousand men and women. Jotham's reference to fire going out from the thorn tree and consuming the cedars of Lebanon has indeed come to pass.

NOTES

29 וַיֹּאמֶר לַאֲבִימֶלֶךְ רַבֶּה צְבָאֲךָ וָצֵאָה (wayyōʾmer laʾăbîmelek rabbeh ṣeḇāʾăkā wāṣēʾâ, "And he said to Abimelech, 'Increase your army and come out'" [NASB, following the MT]; "I would say to Abimelech, 'Call out your whole army!'" [NIV, following LXX witnesses: LXXᵃ's καὶ ἐρῶ τῷ Αβιμελεχ Πλήθυνον τὴν δύναμίν σου καὶ ἔξελθε (kai erō tō Abimelech Plēthynon tēn dynamin sou kai exelthe), "And I will say to Abimelech, 'Increase your strength and come out,'" and LXXᵇ's καὶ ἐρῶ πρὸς αὐτόν (kai erō pros auton), "And I will say to him"]), which render the beginning phrase in the first person, thus making for a continuation of the speech in 9:28–29a. Following the MT necessitates that Gaal here sends a message to Abimelech.

31 בְּתָרְמָה (beṯārmâ, "under cover"). The Hebrew word here is often used for "treachery," but it may be a scribal error for בָּארוּמָה (bāʾrûmâ), "in Arumah" (see v.41), Abimelech's dwelling place (so *BHS*, *HALOT*).

34 אַרְבָּעָה רָאשִׁים (ʾarbāʿâ rāʾšîm, "four companies"). See Note and comments on 7:16.

37 טַבּוּר הָאָרֶץ (ṭabbûr hāʾāreṣ, "the center of the land"). The first term here is used for "navel" in later Hebrew and Aramaic, and some have linked this reference to Mount Gerizim as the navel/center of the land of Israel. But there is no precedent for doing so in biblical Hebrew; the expression probably merely refers to "elevated ground" (Block, 328).

אֵלוֹן מְעוֹנְנִים (ʾēlôn meʿônenîm, "the soothsayers' tree"). This tree must have been a key sacred landmark outside the city, thus developing further the motif of sacred trees that have played both positive and negative roles within Judges. This is a reminder of the kind of pagan activity that gave rise to the divine disciplining of Israel.

40 הַשָּׁעַר (haššāʿar, "the gate"). Evidence from Qumran, the LXX, and the Vulgate suggests that the MT has left out the word העיר (hʿyr, "the city"), which originally followed הַשָּׁעַר (haššāʿar), due to haplography.

5. Abimelech's Death in Battle against Thebez (9:50–55)

⁵⁰Next Abimelech went to Thebez and besieged it and captured it. ⁵¹Inside the city, however, was a strong tower, to which all the men and women — all the people of the city — fled. They locked themselves in and climbed up on the tower roof. ⁵²Abimelech went to the tower and stormed it. But as he approached the entrance to the tower to set it on fire, ⁵³a woman dropped an upper millstone on his head and cracked his skull.

⁵⁴Hurriedly he called to his armor-bearer, "Draw your sword and kill me, so that they can't say, 'A woman killed him.'" So his servant ran him through, and he died. ⁵⁵When the Israelites saw that Abimelech was dead, they went home.

COMMENTARY

50–55 It would not only be the Shechemites who would be overtaken by Jotham's prophetic fable, but also Abimelech, both men dying in proximity to a city tower (see 2Sa 11:21). Having besieged and captured the city of Thebez, Abimelech must once again attack an inner stronghold, choosing again to use fire as his weapon. This time, however, he meets his demise as a woman drops a millstone on his head, thereby crushing his skull. A millstone was used for grinding grain and consisted of two parts, a larger one (18 to 30 inches) with a concave shape on the bottom (Job 41:24), and a smaller one (6 to 15 inches) called the "riding stone" (upper millstone) in a convex shape on the top (Dt 24:6; 2Sa 11:21; *BEB*, 2:1459).

The task of grinding was a normal sign of life and was performed by servants (Ex 11:5) or women (Isa 47:2). While it is then appropriate that a woman would drop this stone on Abimelech's head, as v.54 makes clear in this ancient patriarchal context, this reference is intended to shame Abimelech. Thus the narrator develops further a motif first introduced in the account of Deborah and Barak in Judges 4–5, where a woman delivers Israel "by a fatal blow to the head with an unconventional weapon," the difference in this case being that the oppressor is a fellow Israelite (cf. 5:26 and 9:23; Chisholm, 40; cf. O'Connell, 162).

This defeat scatters the Israelite army, which had followed Abimelech. In the account of Abimelech this nameless woman is the only human who approximates the role played elsewhere by the judge-deliverers. Here there is a great emphasis placed on God's direct intervention (see 9:23–24, 56–57), but as in the account of Deborah-Barak, a female minor character plays a significant role in the defeat of the enemy (4:17–22; 5:24–27). Abimelech's death at the hand of his armor bearer is strikingly similar to Saul's death, thus suggesting a link between the two characters (see below).

NOTE

53 אִשָּׁה אַחַת (ʾiššâ ʾaḥat, "a woman"). The use of אֶחָד (ʾeḥād) here is akin to other instances in the OT where it marks an unnamed individual ("a certain woman," so NASB; cf. A–C 33; 1Sa 1:1; 1Ki 20:13). But it also may be used for emphasis (A–C 34), here playing off Abimelech's argument that as "one man" he would be better than his seventy half-brothers (for the motif of "one" in Jdg 9, see vv.5, 18; see also J. Gerald Janzen, "A Certain Woman in the Rhetoric of Judges 9," *JSOT* 38 (1987): 33–37, with thanks to S. Locke).

6. Conclusion (9:56–57)

> ⁵⁶Thus God repaid the wickedness that Abimelech had done to his father by murdering his seventy brothers. ⁵⁷God also made the men of Shechem pay for all their wickedness. The curse of Jotham son of Jerub-Baal came on them.

COMMENTARY

56–57 The narrator closes the account of Abimelech with an evaluative note, reminding the reader, as he did in 9:23–24, that the events of 9:25–55 were divine retribution for the wickedness of both Abimelech and the men of Shechem and a fulfillment of the curse uttered by Jotham in 9:20. Israel's first experience with monarchy ends in disaster. Kingship as exemplified by Abimelech at Shechem is clearly inappropriate for Israel. That Abimelech's reign is suggestive of the later reign of Saul is argued by Wong (*Strategy*, 210), who notes

how both resort to murder to eliminate rivals (Jdg 9:5; 1Sa 18:11, 17, 21; 19:1, 10, 15; 20:31, 33; 23:15; 24:12), both are sent negative spirits as discipline from God (Jdg 9:23; 1Sa 16:14–16; 18:10; 19:9), and both ask their armor bearers to kill them to avoid humiliation (Jdg 9:54; 1Sa 31:4; cf. Schneider, 148). Abimelech's reign is also suggestive of Jeroboam's inappropriate northern rule, especially in his revolt against the reigning family, his association with an inappropriate northern cultic center, and his coronation at Shechem.

REFLECTION

Abimelech provides a model for leadership in Israel that is to be avoided at all costs. Here leadership is gained by violence and supported by money from an illegitimate shrine, and instead of the Spirit of the Lord, an injurious spirit is sent to create dissension between the leader and his people. Again God raises up an unlikely hero, the unnamed woman

of Thebez, who delivers Israel here not from a foreign enemy, but from their own leader, Abimelech. Links to Saul and Jeroboam reveal the role of the account of Abimelech to point to a different model for leadership, a model identified in the larger context of the book as that of the Judahite David, who will establish a royal model that is after God's heart.

H. Tola and Jair (10:1–5)

OVERVIEW

Just as between the major accounts of Ehud and Deborah-Barak the narrator included the short account of Shamgar, so also between the major accounts of Abimelech and Jephthah the narrator includes two further short accounts. While Shamgar is only said to have "saved Israel" (3:31), both of these men "judged" ("led") Israel. While one may be tempted to treat the account of Tola as the final

stage of the Abimelech cycle (Amit, *Judges*, 40–43), this position cannot be sustained, for the enemy of the previous cycle (Abimelech) is not defeated by Tola (see Overview to 8:33–9:57).

Three more short accounts will appear in 12:8–15 (Ibzan, Elon, Abdon); these five short accounts in chs. 10–12 are most likely drawn from an independent source (see review of evidence in Nelson, 349–51).

Elements typical of this source include: an introductory phrase ("after him X judged/arose to deliver"), identification (by genealogy, gentilic, and/or city), further information (offspring, towns, marriage practices), tenure (he judged Israel X years), death/burial (X died and X was buried in Y; Nelson, 352).

These five short accounts are placed between three longer narratives (Abimelech, Jephthah, and Samson) that accelerate the progressive decline after the account of Gideon. While most recent scholarship has deemphasized differences between the judges treated in the major and minor accounts (Alan J. Hauser, "Minor Judges: A Re-evaluation," *JBL* 94 [1975]: 190–200; E. T. Mullen, "The 'Minor Judges': Some Literary and Historical Considerations," *CBQ* 44 [1982]: 185–201), it is important not to miss distinctions in their presentation. Elements within the shorter accounts in chs. 10 and 12 are suggestive of later royal annalistic accounts (Nelson), providing especially the features of stability, success, and continuity that are lacking from the major accounts of the judges. In this way, in the wake of the debacle of Abimelech they provide ideal judge-deliverer models (Michael J. Smith, "The Failure of the Family in Judges, Part 1: Jephthah," *BSac* 162 [2005]: 288). But the major accounts they frame overshadow them and ultimately necessitate another way forward.

1. Tola (10:1–2)

¹After the time of Abimelech a man of Issachar, Tola son of Puah, the son of Dodo, rose to save Israel. He lived in Shamir, in the hill country of Ephraim. ²He led Israel twenty-three years; then he died, and was buried in Shamir.

COMMENTARY

1–2 Tola ("worm") is carefully described by his lineage, which identifies him as the son of Puah the son of Dodo within the northern tribe of Issachar. Tola's ancestral namesake was one of Issachar's four sons (Ge 46:13; Nu 26:23; 1Ch 7:1–2). This tribe's traditional territory lay on the eastern side of the Jezreel Valley immediately south of the Sea of Galilee (Jos 19:17–23), but the judge Tola is linked to the town of Shamir located in the hill country of Ephraim (cf. a Shamir in the hill country of Judah in Jos 15:48). While it may be tempting to see this Shamir as "Samaria" (as LXXᵃ), the later capital of the northern kingdom for the Omride dynasty (1Ki 16:24), that identification is unlikely because of spelling differences. The connection of this Issacharite leader to Ephraim continues the development of the satirical theme of the leadership of Ephraim within the nation (see comments on Jdg 8:1).

Tola's activities are described as both "saving" and "judging" Israel, similarly to earlier leaders in the book. But as is typical of the minor accounts of leaders in Judges, no reference is made to Yahweh's raising up this leader or to his endowment with the Spirit (3:31; 10:1–5; 12:8–15). After the brief, only three-year reign of Abimelech, Tola's twenty-three-year stint suggests greater stability and presents the model of the judges as superior to Abimelech's form of monarchy. The citation of length of reign, death, and place of burial is typical at the conclusion to the minor accounts of judges in 10:1–5 and 12:8–15.

NOTE

1 יֹשֵׁב (*yōšēb*, "he lived"). This verb could also be translated "he ruled" (see Block, 338).

2. Jair (10:3–5)

> ³He was followed by Jair of Gilead, who led Israel twenty-two years. ⁴He had thirty sons, who rode thirty donkeys. They controlled thirty towns in Gilead, which to this day are called Havvoth Jair. ⁵When Jair died, he was buried in Kamon.

COMMENTARY

3–5 Tola's account is followed immediately by that of Jair, who is linked to the clan of Gilead within the tribe of Manasseh. Other passages in the OT reveal that a region east of the Jordan was controlled by Manasseh's son Jair (Nu 32:41; Dt 3:14; Jos 13:30; 1Ki 4:13; 1Ch 2:23), who named the towns in the region Havvoth Jair, that is, "tent settlements of Jair." The judge Jair of Judges 10:3–5 is a later descendant, whose thirty sons possessed thirty towns among the Havvoth Jair.

These sons were distinguished by riding on thirty donkeys, possibly an indication of royal pretension (cf. 5:10; T. R. Hobbs, "The Language of Warfare in Zechariah 9–14," in *After the Exile: Essays in Honour of Rex Mason* [ed. J. Barton and D. J. Reimer; Macon, Ga.: Mercer Univ. Press, 1996], 124–25; Howard Eilberg-Schwartz, *The Savage in Judaism: An Anthropology of Israelite Religion and* *Ancient Judaism* [Bloomington, Ind.: Indiana Univ. Press, 1990], 127–28), but also of wealth (Nelson, 355) and military prowess (cf. Y. Yadin, *The Art of Warfare in Biblical Lands in the Light of Archaeological Study* [New York: McGraw-Hill, 1963], 2:287, who notes that donkeys were "more suited than horses to battle in hill country"; see 2Sa 13:29; 18:9). This suggestion of monarchical status, as well as reference to a large group of offspring and Gileadite stock, may reflect the narrator's design to link Jair with the earlier Gideon. Jair does not "save" Israel but rather merely "judges," which suggests that the peace in Israel established by Tola endured under Jair. Jephthah, the next judge, will also hail from the clan of Gilead (see 11:1), but the conditions that precede his rise are radically different from those sustained by Jair. Jair was buried in Kamon, a site whose provenance is unknown.

NOTE

4 וּשְׁלֹשִׁים עֲיָרִים לָהֶם (ûš^elōšîm ^cayārîm lāhem). The Hebrew text (MT) has here "and they had thirty donkeys," while the NIV rightly follows evidence from the LXX, which reads πόλεις (poleis), "cities." The difference between "donkeys" (עירים) and "cities" (ערים) is only one consonant, and that consonant (yod) is one of the matres lectionis, which may not have been present in the earliest manuscripts of the text.

REFLECTION

The five shorter accounts of judges in 10:1–5 and 12:8–15 provide pictures of idealistic leadership that points forward to a form of kingship shy of dynastic rule. These characters provide the stability, success, and continuity, which will allow them to enjoy life in the Promised Land. In this they foreshadow the kinds of qualities that will be fully realized in David.

I. Jephthah (10:6–12:7)

OVERVIEW

The account of Jephthah is the fifth of the six major accounts of judge-deliverers that dominate the core of the book of Judges (2:6–16:31). The basic structure of these accounts is first encountered in the introduction to this core, found in 2:6–3:6, and the account of Jephthah is the "most replete" with these elements and attendant vocabulary (O'Connell, 178; Latvus, 43; Sjöberg, 30). The structure comprises the following elements: Israel's sin, Yahweh's discipline, Israel's cry, Yahweh's deliverance through a deliverer, Israel's rest, and deliverer's death.

While the first three elements (in introductory notice) and the final two elements (in concluding notice) use a common range of vocabulary, the fourth element (Yahweh's deliverance through a deliverer) is dominated by a unique plot, with some vocabulary and motifs common to other accounts. At times, however, the divine word breaks into this "cycle," following Yahweh's discipline/Israel's cry and before Yahweh's deliverance (cf. 3:19–20; 4:4–6, 6:7–10, 11–24; 9:7–22; cf. Boda, "Recycling Heaven's Words"). The account of Jephthah gives another example of the prophetic word's breaking into the account (10:10–16). But unlike Gideon or Barak before him and like Samson after him, Jephthah "receives no visitation from God or prophetic word"—further evidence of the downward spiral of the accounts (Webb, 65). On the scenic structure (followed below) of the account, see Block, 342.

1. Introductory Notice (10:6–16)

⁶Again the Israelites did evil in the eyes of the Lord. They served the Baals and the Ashtoreths, and the gods of Aram, the gods of Sidon, the gods of Moab, the gods of the Ammonites and the gods of the Philistines. And because the Israelites forsook the Lord and no longer served him, ⁷he became angry with them. He sold them into the hands of the Philistines and the Ammonites, ⁸who that year shattered and crushed them. For eighteen years they oppressed all the Israelites on the east side of the Jordan in Gilead, the land of the Amorites. ⁹The Ammonites also crossed the Jordan to fight against Judah, Benjamin and the house of Ephraim; and Israel was in great distress. ¹⁰Then the Israelites cried out to the Lord, "We have sinned against you, forsaking our God and serving the Baals."

¹¹The Lord replied, "When the Egyptians, the Amorites, the Ammonites, the Philistines, ¹²the Sidonians, the Amalekites and the Maonites oppressed you and you cried to me for help, did I not save you from their hands? ¹³But you have forsaken me and served other gods, so I will no longer save you. ¹⁴Go and cry out to the gods you have chosen. Let them save you when you are in trouble!"

¹⁵But the Israelites said to the Lord, "We have sinned. Do with us whatever you think best, but please rescue us now." ¹⁶Then they got rid of the foreign gods among them and served the Lord. And he could bear Israel's misery no longer.

COMMENTARY

6–9 The account begins in typical fashion with the Israelites committing evil in the eyes of Yahweh. The precise character of this evil is not always delineated in the introductory notices found throughout Judges, but when further details are offered it is always related to the worship of other gods (2:6–3:6; 3:7–11; 5:8; 6:1, 8–10, 25–32; cf. 3:19, 26), as here. That list of foreign gods in 10:6 is the longest in this book and implies that Israel's apostasy is progressively worsening. According to Block, 343, this represents "the nadir of Israel's degradation." Now their affections are attached not only to the gods of the Canaanites (Baals, Ashtoreths), but also to those of the surrounding peoples (Aram, Sidon, Moab, Ammon, Philistia).

Although some have questioned the authenticity of these references to surrounding nations (e.g., Niditch, *Judges*, 122–23), recent archaeological work in Transjordan has revealed early activity in this region (cf. T. E. Levy et al., "Reassessing the Chronology of Biblical Edom: New Excavations and ¹⁴C Dates from Khirbat en Nahas (Jordan)," *Antiquity* 78 [2004]: 863–76). On the Baals and Ashtoreths see comments on 2:13. The narrator describes Israel as serving (ʿbd) these gods rather than serving (ʿbd) Yahweh, an action that constitutes forsaking or abandoning (ʿzb) their covenantal relationship with Yahweh.

This breach incites the anger of Yahweh (cf. 2:14, 20; 3:8) and, as is typical in the accounts of the judges, Yahweh "sells them into the hands of" their enemy (3:8; 4:2; cf. "give them into the hands of" in 2:14; 6:1; 13:1) for a set period (3:8, 14; 4:3; 6:1; 13:1). In ch. 10 the enemy is identified as the Philistines and the Ammonites—the former a people group located on the Mediterranean coastal plain on the western side of southern Israel and the latter a people group located on the Transjordanian plateau and eastern desert on the eastern side of central Israel. Philistia would become the key enemy for the tribe of Judah, while Ammon would be the key enemy of the Joseph tribes, especially Manasseh.

Although the Philistines are mentioned in v.7, the account focuses on the Ammonite oppression on the eastern side of the Jordan in the Manassehite territory of Gilead—oppression that soon affected the tribes of Judah, Benjamin, and Ephraim on the western side of the Jordan. Possibly the Philistines allied themselves with the Ammonites once the latter had moved across the Jordan, thus forcing the Israelite tribes to defend two fronts. The note about the Philistines foreshadows the account of Samson in chs. 13–16.

With four of the key tribes under foreign oppression, the narrator rightly notes that Israel was in "great distress" (cf. 2:15). It is interesting that after Israel abandons Yahweh by serving foreign gods (v.6), Yahweh sells the people into the hands of the final two foreign nations (Philistia, Ammon [v.7]) whose gods conclude the list of deities in v.6. There appears to be a link between these actions. Serving foreign gods instead of Israel's God will mean subjugation by foreign nations rather than autonomy under Yahweh's care.

10–16 As in other major accounts, such distress brought on by divine disciplining prompts Israel to cry (zʿq) to Yahweh (3:9, 15; 4:3; 6:6–7). Unlike the other depictions of Israel's cry, however, 10:10, 15–16 provides the content of the cry (cf. 1Sa 12:9–11). Here Israel admits its sin against Yahweh twice ("we have sinned"; 10:10, 15), and this confession is followed by practical repentance as they throw away their foreign gods and serve Yahweh (10:16).

After the first penitential cry Yahweh scolds the people, revealing that although he is certainly capable of saving them in the present as he has in the past (vv.11–12), because they have forsaken him by serving other gods they are no longer his responsibility but that of the gods they have chosen (vv.13–14). Reference to Yahweh's rescue of Israel from various people groups matches the various accounts in the book of Judges: the Egyptians (2:1, 12; 6:8–9, 13), Amorites (1:34–36; 3:5; 6:10), Ammonites (3:13), Philistines (3:3, 31; cf. chs. 13–16), Amalekites (3:13; 5:14; 6:3, 33; 7:12), and Midianites (chs. 6–8; cf. 9:17; see Note below). The mention of the Sidonians, however, is odd since no attack by the Phoenicians is mentioned in Judges.

It is instructive that the long list of nations in v.12 is the same length as the list of foreign gods in v.6, echoing again the principle that serving foreign gods opens Israel to control by those gods' respective foreign nations. Yahweh's instruction for Israel to cry out to their adopted gods is sarcastic, since these gods will not deliver them from control by their own people.

Yahweh's rejection of the people's first penitential cry, however, does not deter this desperate people, who again admit their sin, declare Yahweh's right to do as he pleases, and cry for him to rescue them. Their second cry in v.15 is backed up by a practical response of putting away their foreign gods and serving Yahweh alone. This second penitential response prompts a gracious response from Yahweh, who "could bear Israel's misery no longer" (v.16, see Note). The next phase in the story depicts the conditions that give rise to Jephthah, whose arrival represents the outworking of this gracious response (Sjöberg, 63).

NOTES

9 וַתֵּצֶר לְיִשְׂרָאֵל מְאֹד (*watteṣer leyiśrāʾēl meʾōd*, "and Israel was in great distress"). See Note on 2:15.

12 וּמָעוֹן (*ûmāʿôn*, "and the Maonites"). The reference to Maonites here is most likely a scribal mistake for Midianite (וּמִדְיָן, *ûmidyān*), as reflected in the Septuagint (καὶ Μαδιαμ, *kai Madiam*).

16 וַתִּקְצַר נַפְשׁוֹ בַּעֲמַל יִשְׂרָאֵל (*wattiqṣar napšô baʿᵃmal yiśrāʾēl*, "And he could bear Israel's misery no longer"). There has been considerable controversy over this final phrase in v.16. The first part of it (נַפְשׁוֹ וַתִּקְצַר, *wattiqṣar napšô*) consists of a collocation that refers to either becoming impatient or frustrated (Nu 21:4; Zec 11:8; cf. Jdg 16:16; Job 21:4), with the preposition *be* introducing that which is responsible for this impatience/frustration. The word עָמָל (*ʿāmāl*; GK 6662) in the second part of this phrase can mean "trouble" (e.g., Ge 41:51) or "difficult labor" (e.g., Ecc 1:3), but it can also have an ethical force, referring to mischief (e.g., Ps 140:10). This connotation has led some to see here not a reference to Yahweh's gracious response to Israel's cry and suffering, but rather his rejection (see Webb, 45–48; O'Connell, 186–87; Block, 348; Janzen, 347).

But the use of עָמָל (*ʿāmāl*) in the description of the cry of Israel in Deuteronomy 26:7, where Yahweh graciously responds to Israel, suggests that here we see an instance of Yahweh's gracious internal misery over the people's suffering (see Robert D. Haak, "A Study and New Interpretation of *qsr npš*," *JBL* 101 [1982]: 161–67; Terence E. Fretheim, *The Suffering of God: An Old Testament Perspective* [OBT 14; Philadelphia: Fortress, 1984], 129; McCann, 78–79). See further Boda (*Severe Mercy*, 140).

2. Jephthah and the War with Ammon (10:17–11:33)

a. Ammon Invades Gilead (10:17–18)

> [17]When the Ammonites were called to arms and camped in Gilead, the Israelites assembled and camped at Mizpah. [18]The leaders of the people of Gilead said to each other, "Whoever will launch the attack against the Ammonites will be the head of all those living in Gilead."

COMMENTARY

17–18 Verse 16 creates the expectation that Yahweh will now act on behalf of Israel, and throughout Judges it is at these points that the narrator introduces the judge-deliverers whom Yahweh will use to bring deliverance (2:16, 18; 3:9, 12; 4:4; 6:12, 14). Before introducing the judge-deliverer Jephthah, however, the narrator sets the context by describing the invasion of Gilead by the Ammonites, which prompts the army of Gilead to assemble at Mizpah.

This Mizpah is not the more famous town located in Benjamin (see Jdg 20; 1Sa 7), but rather the town by the same name in Transjordanian Gilead (Ge 31:43–55; Jos 13:26). It appears from v.18 that the leaders of Gilead lack a military leader to guide them into battle and so offer the leadership of the region to whomever is willing to lead them into battle. The statement in v.18, "whoever will launch the attack against the Ammonites," is strikingly similar (esp. in the Hebrew text) to the questions asked in 1:1 and 20:18:

1:1	*mî yaᶜăleh-lānû ʾel-hakkᵉnaᶜănî battᵉḥillâ lᵉhillāḥem bô*	"Who will be the first to go up and fight for us against the Canaanites?"
10:18	*mî hāʾîš ᵃšer yāḥēl lᵉhillāḥēm bibnê ᶜammôn*	"Whoever will launch the attack against the Ammonites ..."
20:18	*mî yaᶜăleh-lānû battᵉḥillâ lammilḥāmâ ᶜim-bᵉnê binyāmin*	"Who of us shall go first to fight against the Benjamites?"

The contrast, however, is obvious: "the Israelites seek their own counsel, not God's" (Matthews, *Judges and Ruth*, 116). While the answer in 1:1 and 20:18 is Judah, the answer in 10:18 is provided in the following verse as Jephthah the Gileadite.

NOTE

17 צָעַק (*ṣāᶜaq*, "called to arms"; GK 7590). This military term is used for gathering a military force together (see 7:23–24; 12:1) and synonymous with the similar-sounding word זעק (*zᵉq*; 4:10, 13; 6:34–35; 12:2; cf. 18:22–23). It is interesting that these two terms are also both used to describe Israel's cry to Yahweh in their distress (זעק [*zᵉq*] in 3:9, 15; 6:6–7; 10:10; cf. 10:14; צעק [*ṣᵉq*] in 4:3; 10:12). Here the cry for help from Yahweh is closely associated with the call to arms by Ammon.

b. Introducing Jephthah (11:1–3)

¹Jephthah the Gileadite was a mighty warrior. His father was Gilead; his mother was a prostitute. ²Gilead's wife also bore him sons, and when they were grown up, they drove Jephthah away. "You are not going to get any inheritance in our family," they said, "because

you are the son of another woman." ³So Jephthah fled from his brothers and settled in the land of Tob, where a group of adventurers gathered around him and followed him.

COMMENTARY

1–3 These three verses provide background information for the character who will ultimately answer the call of the leaders of Gilead in 10:18 (see Notes below). This character, Jephthah the Gileadite, is identified as a "mighty warrior" (*gibbôr ḥayil*). His origins, however, are dubious, since he was the illegitimate offspring of a tryst between a man named Gilead and a prostitute. Gilead's legitimate sons eventually drive Jephthah away. Jephthah's birth and resultant status within and treatment by his family reminds the reader of the earlier tragic figure of Abimelech (Amit, *Judges*, 87) and serves "to begin the process of disappointment," which "will grow stronger" in the ensuing stories in chs. 12–16.

The narrator uses dramatic narrative in 11:2 to accentuate how they deny Jephthah any inheritance, thus violating the Torah (Dt 21:15–17; cf. Lev 25:25–28; Nu 27:1–11; ch. 36), but possibly not broader ancient practices (see David Marcus, "The Legal Dispute between Jephthah and the Elders," *HAR* 12 [1990]: 105–14; Hannelis Schulte, "Beobachtungen zum Begriff der *Zônâ* im Alten Testament," *ZAW* 104 [1992]: 255–62; Mehlman, 74; Matthews, *Judges and Ruth*, 117). This rejection by Jephthah's half brothers forced him to flee for his own safety (e.g., Ge 16:6, 8; 35:1, 7; Ex 2:15) and adopt the life of an outcast who leads a group of young outlaws (see Note) in the land of Tob (cf. 2Sa 10:6, 8).

The social conditions reflected in the account of Jephthah "accord well with the social matrix of pre-monarchic Israel," especially with decisions based primarily in the family unit with some collaboration with higher levels of clan and tribe (cf. Patton, 40–43). Some of these elements bear striking resemblances to the accounts of Gideon and Abimelech (see further O'Connell, 202–3; Block, 342–43), the former also being called a "mighty warrior (*gibbôr heḥāyil*, 6:12) and the latter also rejected by the heirs of his father because of his illegitimacy (8:31; 9:1–6). Interestingly, the "elders of Gilead" (cf. "leaders of Gilead" in 10:18) are equated with the legitimate sons of the man Gilead (introduced in 11:2), who were the half brothers of Jephthah. The Gilead of this story seems to share a similar role to that of his namesake—Gilead the grandson of Manasseh (Nu 26:29; 36:1), the founder of the clan. It is possible that the reference to Gilead here is a reference to an anonymous Gileadite.

NOTES

1 וְיִפְתָּח (*wᵉyiptāḥ*, "Jephthah"). Here the Hebrew construction *waw* + non-verb signals the section of offline comment in 11:1–3 (see Webb, 50). This narrative technique is similar to the introduction of Heber the Kenite in 4:11 (Schneider, 165).

וְהוּא בֶּן־אִשָּׁה זוֹנָה וַיּוֹלֶד גִּלְעָד אֶת־יִפְתָּח (wᵉhûᵓ ben-ᵓiššâ zônâ wayyôled gilᶜād ᵓet-yiptāḥ, "His father was Gilead; his mother was a prostitute"). The Hebrew text has the reverse order, accentuating at the outset that he was the son of a woman, a prostitute, before mentioning Gilead. On the social meaning of זוֹנָה (zônâ; GK 2390) see Schneider, 162–63, who notes that the term could refer to a "professional prostitute," but also to a woman who "had sex outside traditional Israelite marriage."

2 בֶּן־אִשָּׁה אַחֶרֶת (ben-ᵓiššâ ᵓaḥeret, "the son of another woman"). This phrase emphasizes the difference between Jephthah and his half brothers, parallel with but more general than the earlier descriptor זוֹנָה בֶּן־אִשָּׁה (ben-ᵓiššâ zônâ, "a son of a woman, a prostitute") in 11:1 (cf. Mehlman, 74). This designation does not confer on his mother the status of "additional wife" (Sjöberg, 54).

3 וַיֵּשֶׁב (wayyēšeb, "and settled"). The Hebrew here could be "he ruled," as in "sat [on a throne]."

אֲנָשִׁים רֵיקִים (ᵃnāšîm rêqîm, "a group of adventurers"). This phrase could be translated "worthless fellows" (NASB) or "debased fellows" (Sjöberg, 56–57). Michal's use of this term when describing her husband's inappropriate and possibly lewd behavior in 2 Samuel 6:20 suggests possibly the latter, that is, someone empty or lacking dignity. The same phrase is used of the band hired by Abimelech to murder his brothers in 9:4, another similarity between these two characters in this book.

c. Elders of Gilead Invite Jephthah to Lead against the Ammonites (11:4–11)

⁴Some time later, when the Ammonites made war on Israel, ⁵the elders of Gilead went to get Jephthah from the land of Tob. ⁶"Come," they said, "be our commander, so we can fight the Ammonites."

⁷Jephthah said to them, "Didn't you hate me and drive me from my father's house? Why do you come to me now, when you're in trouble?"

⁸The elders of Gilead said to him, "Nevertheless, we are turning to you now; come with us to fight the Ammonites, and you will be our head over all who live in Gilead."

⁹Jephthah answered, "Suppose you take me back to fight the Ammonites and the LORD gives them to me — will I really be your head?"

¹⁰The elders of Gilead replied, "The LORD is our witness; we will certainly do as you say."

¹¹So Jephthah went with the elders of Gilead, and the people made him head and commander over them. And he repeated all his words before the LORD in Mizpah.

COMMENTARY

4–11 With vv. 4–5 the narrator returns to the story introduced in 10:17–18, explaining to the reader that the elders (leaders) of Gilead not only announce a general proposal (10:18), but when the Ammonites move to engage them in the battle, they finally take the initiative to travel to the land of Tob and invite their half brother, Jephthah, to lead them in battle.

The narrator includes an elongated dramatic narrative to present the interaction between the elders and Jephthah. At first the elders invite Jephthah only to be their leader (*qāṣîn*, 11:6) in battle. But when little progress is made, they are forced to repeat the proposal of 10:18 (Webb, 52), promising Jephthah the leadership (*rōʾš*; see Note) of the clan. This promise is articulated first as a proposal (11:8) and second as an oath (11:10), which is sealed with a "more solemn, ceremonial ratification of the terms" (Webb, 53) once Jephthah joins the Gileadite army at Mizpah (11:11).

This progression in the elders' proposal is caused by Jephthah's careful negotiation. First, he reminds them of their past maltreatment of him and ridicules their present predicament (v.7). Second, he questions the integrity of their offer by asking whether they will indeed give him the headship once he has defeated the Ammonites (v.9). Finally, Jephthah carefully repeats the terms of the agreement in the religious ceremony at Mizpah, which explicitly mentions his role as leader (*qāṣîn*; GK 7903) in battle and chief (*rōʾš*; GK 8031) over the clan (v.11; see Note).

The account reveals already Jephthah's penchant for negotiation and vow making, features that will reappear in his subsequent dealings with the Ammonites (11:12–28) and with Yahweh (11:29–40; Amit, *Judges*, 87). The careful negotiation of Jephthah represents further deterioration in the accounts of the judges in terms of self-interest, initiated by Gideon in 7:16–18 and reappearing in the dominance of personal vengeance in the account of Samson (Wong, *Strategy*, 171–73; cf. Webb, 54; Schneider, xv; Bluedorn, 277). Such a negotiator is a perfect match for a generation whose negotiation with Yahweh is showcased in 10:10–16 (Polzin, 178; Webb, 53–54; Sjöberg, 29).

NOTES

4 וַיְהִי מִיָּמִים וַיִּלָּחֲמוּ (*wayᵉhî mîyāmîm wayyillāḥᵃmû*, "Some time later, when [they] made war"). This circumstantial clause returns the narrative to the story line interrupted at 11:1 to introduce Jephthah (see Webb, 51).

8 עַתָּה שַׁבְנוּ אֵלֶיךָ (*ʿattâ šabnû ʾeleykā*, "we are turning to you now"). Since Jephthah is the one who is returning to them, this comment must mean that the elders are changing their mind and attitude toward Jephthah, a change of convenience out of desperation that is strikingly similar to the Israelites' return in 10:10–14 (Webb, 53).

11 לְרֹאשׁ וּלְקָצִין (*lᵉrōʾš ûlᵉqāṣîn*, "head [GK 8031] and commander [GK 7903]"). The appointment of Jephthah reveals that these two terms/positions point to different functions, the first political and the second military. At issue here also are most likely inheritance rights, reinstatement of which would be necessary for the position of "head," but not for "commander" (Timothy M. Willis, "The Nature of Jephthah's Authority," *CBQ* 59 [1997]: 34–36).

d. Jephthah Negotiates with the Ammonite King (11:12–28)

¹²Then Jephthah sent messengers to the Ammonite king with the question: "What do you have against us that you have attacked our country?"

¹³The king of the Ammonites answered Jephthah's messengers, "When Israel came up out of Egypt, they took away my land from the Arnon to the Jabbok, all the way to the Jordan. Now give it back peaceably."

¹⁴Jephthah sent back messengers to the Ammonite king, ¹⁵saying:

"This is what Jephthah says: Israel did not take the land of Moab or the land of the Ammonites. ¹⁶But when they came up out of Egypt, Israel went through the desert to the Red Sea and on to Kadesh. ¹⁷Then Israel sent messengers to the king of Edom, saying, 'Give us permission to go through your country,' but the king of Edom would not listen. They sent also to the king of Moab, and he refused. So Israel stayed at Kadesh.

¹⁸"Next they traveled through the desert, skirted the lands of Edom and Moab, passed along the eastern side of the country of Moab, and camped on the other side of the Arnon. They did not enter the territory of Moab, for the Arnon was its border.

¹⁹"Then Israel sent messengers to Sihon king of the Amorites, who ruled in Heshbon, and said to him, 'Let us pass through your country to our own place.' ²⁰Sihon, however, did not trust Israel to pass through his territory. He mustered all his men and encamped at Jahaz and fought with Israel.

²¹"Then the Lord, the God of Israel, gave Sihon and all his men into Israel's hands, and they defeated them. Israel took over all the land of the Amorites who lived in that country, ²²capturing all of it from the Arnon to the Jabbok and from the desert to the Jordan.

²³"Now since the Lord, the God of Israel, has driven the Amorites out before his people Israel, what right have you to take it over? ²⁴Will you not take what your god Chemosh gives you? Likewise, whatever the Lord our God has given us, we will possess. ²⁵Are you better than Balak son of Zippor, king of Moab? Did he ever quarrel with Israel or fight with them? ²⁶For three hundred years Israel occupied Heshbon, Aroer, the surrounding settlements and all the towns along the Arnon. Why didn't you retake them during that time? ²⁷I have not wronged you, but you are doing me wrong by waging war against me. Let the Lord, the Judge, decide the dispute this day between the Israelites and the Ammonites."

²⁸The king of Ammon, however, paid no attention to the message Jephthah sent him.

COMMENTARY

12–22 Jephthah's negotiating skills with the elders of Gilead foreshadow the more extensive negotiation he conducts with the nameless Ammonite king and for which the narrator provides an even longer dramatic narrative, slowing down the forward momentum of the story and increasing the tension (Webb,

60). This dialogue is mediated through Israelite messengers, who played a key role in ancient warfare, not only for relaying messages between opposing forces (Nu 20:14; Dt 2:26; Eze 30:9), but also in maintaining communication lines between allies (Isa 18:2; Jer 27:3; Eze 17:15; 23:16) and within an army or nation (Jdg 6:35; 1Sa 23:27; 2Sa 11:19).

Jephthah begins by asking why the king has invaded his country, and the king points to Israel's expropriation of the Ammonite Transjordanian territory at the time of the conquest (see Jos 13). Moving from north to south along the Transjordanian plateau, the Yarmuk River flowed into the Jordan River just south of the Sea of Galilee, the Jabbok River flowed into the Jordan approximately halfway between the Sea of Galilee and the Dead Sea, and the Arnon River flowed into the Dead Sea at its midpoint. The region of Gilead fell between the Yarmuk and Jabbok rivers, but the king of Ammon, expressing concern over the territory between the Jabbok and Arnon rivers, demands that it be returned to him.

That Jephthah's lengthy response reverses the Ammonite king's argument shows that Israel is not the aggressor against Ammon as he contends, but rather Ammon is the aggressor against Israel (see v.27). Since the dispute is rooted in events just before the conquest of Canaan, Jephthah begins by refuting the Ammonite king's rendition of the conquest. (The Moabite Stone, written by the later king Mesha of Moab, highlights the tradition of an early conquest of the Transjordanian region by Israelite tribes [see *ANET*, 320; *COS*, 2:137–38]).

According to Jephthah, Israel did not take land from Moab, Ammon, or Edom; instead they carefully bypassed the lands of Moab and Edom when these nations refused Israel permission to pass through their land (see Webb, 57, for links to Nu 20, 21; Dt 1–3). Territory conquered in Transjor-

dan between the Arnon and Jabbok rivers was the only territory that belonged to the Amorite king Sihon, who ruled from Heshbon. Jephthah's claim is supported by Deuteronomy 2:5, 9, 19, where Yahweh commands Israel not to harass or provoke the Edomites, Moabites, or Ammonites since their land was given by Yahweh to their ancestors (Esau and Lot). Numbers 21:24 notes that Israel attacked Sihon and took possession of his land "from the Arnon to the Jabbok, but only as far as the Ammonites." Deuteronomy 2:36–37 reveals that in the battle against Sihon, Israel took possession of his land from "Aroer on the rim of the Arnon Gorge, and from the town in the gorge, even as far as Gilead" but "did not encroach on any of the land of the Ammonites."

Even Sihon was offered peaceful treatment, since all Israel wanted was safe passage through his land. But when Sihon assembled his army for war, Israel soundly defeated him and so occupied his land. By retelling the story, Jephthah refutes not only the king's claim that Israel was the aggressor in Transjordan when they came out of Egypt, but also his assumption that Ammon had prior claim to the land that was conquered.

23–26 The second part of Jephthah's speech argues that Israel has every right to retain possession of this territory since it was given to them by their God, Yahweh (11:23–24). In the same way the Ammonites would take what their god had given them, so also Israel was justified in taking that which Yahweh had given them. The speech concludes with the final argument that neither the king at the time of the conquest (Balak of Moab [Nu 22–24]) nor Ammon throughout the past three centuries had ever contested Israel's claim to the territory between the Arnon and the Jabbok (11:25–26).

The link between Ammon and Chemosh in Jephthah's speech seems odd at first sight, since Chemosh was the chief god of the Moabites, and Molech/Milcom was the chief god of the Ammonites (see

Moabite Stone, *ANET*, 320; *COS*, 2:137–38; cf. Nu 21:29; 1Ki 11:5, 7, 33). But it is clear from Jephthah's speech that he considers this king as representative of both Ammon and Moab (see Jdg 11:15, 25, 27), probably related to an earlier expansion of Ammon into Moab (see 3:13, 29; cf. Webb, 56). What has been considered by previous scholars as an error by Jephthah or a conflation of traditions (Niditch, *Judges*, 132) is actually one of Jephthah's key rhetorical points, for it justifies Israel's possession of the disputed territory by allusion to Ammon's expansion (O'Connell, 197–98; but note Sjöberg, 59, who sees here a possible "deliberate provocation").

27–28 Jephthah's conclusion is therefore that Israel has not wronged Ammon, but rather Ammon has wronged Israel by assembling for war (11:27). It is Yahweh, the God who has given land to both Israel and Ammon (see 2:19), who will judge between the nations (Webb, 59). This reference to Yahweh as "judge" may explain why the judge-deliverers in this book are regularly called "judges," since they bring the judgment of Yahweh on Israel's oppressors (see comments on 2:16, and see Introduction). Not surprisingly, the king of Ammon does not find Jephthah's argument convincing, and this makes battle inevitable (11:28).

NOTES

16 יַם־סוּף (*yam-sûp*, "Red Sea"). The Hebrew text reads "Sea of Reeds" to describe the body of water at which the miracle of the exodus occurred (see Ex 10:19; 15:4, 22; etc.). English translations follow the LXX's rendering: θαλάσσης ἐρυθρᾶς (*thalassēs erythras*, "Red Sea").

20 וְלֹא־הֶאֱמִין סִיחוֹן (*wᵉlōʾ-heʾᵉmîn sîḥôn*, "Sihon, however, did not trust"). There may be a textual problem here, especially in the light of the LXXᵃ, which has καὶ οὐκ ἠθέλησεν Σηων διελθεῖν (*kai ouk ēthelēsen Sēōn dielthein*, "And Seon did not want ... to cross"). *BHS* suggests וְלֹא־אָבָה וַיְמָאֵן סִיחוֹן תֵּת (*wᵉlōʾ-ʾābâ waymāʾēn sîḥôn tēt*, "but he was not willing and Sihon refused to give").

e. Jephthah Defeats Ammon in War (11:29–33)

²⁹Then the Spirit of the LORD came upon Jephthah. He crossed Gilead and Manasseh, passed through Mizpah of Gilead, and from there he advanced against the Ammonites. ³⁰And Jephthah made a vow to the LORD: "If you give the Ammonites into my hands, ³¹whatever comes out of the door of my house to meet me when I return in triumph from the Ammonites will be the LORD's, and I will sacrifice it as a burnt offering."

³²Then Jephthah went over to fight the Ammonites, and the LORD gave them into his hands. ³³He devastated twenty towns from Aroer to the vicinity of Minnith, as far as Abel Keramim. Thus Israel subdued Ammon.

COMMENTARY

29–33 Although suggested by the structure of the passage (see comments on 10:17–18), there has been no explicit claim to this point that Jephthah is Yahweh's choice to rescue Israel from Ammonite oppression (Exum, "The Centre Cannot Hold," 422). The narrator has depicted how the Gileadites invited Jephthah to lead them and their taking an oath in Yahweh's name to assure Jephthah of their sincerity; but the narrator has not described any involvement by Yahweh. Verse 29, however, makes clear that Jephthah is the divine choice as the narrator describes the Spirit of Yahweh's coming upon Jephthah (see Webb, 60) in vocabulary identical to that used in connection with Othniel's endowment (*hyh*, 3:10) and similar to that used for other judges (*lbš*, 6:34; *ṣlḥ*, 14:6, 19; 15:14). Empowerment by the Spirit in Judges is always related to an endowment of physical strength to defeat a foe, so once the Spirit comes upon Jephthah, he begins his military march against the Ammonites, passing through Gilead, Manasseh, and Mizpah.

Before engaging in battle he vows that if Yahweh gives him victory, he will offer as a burnt offering to Yahweh whatever comes out of the door of his house to meet him upon his return (for such vows see esp. Nu 21:2; cf. Ge 28:20–22; 1Sa 1:11; 2Sa 15:7–8; cf. Block, 366; Niditch, *Judges*, 133; but contrast Pamela Tamarkin Reis, "Spoiled Child: A Fresh Look at Jephthah's Daughter," *Prooftexts* 17 [1997]: 279–98). This vow does emphasize that it is Yahweh who gives the victory to Israel. But it also reveals the folly, if not the moral defect, in Jephthah, who according to Webb, 64, "now slips a bribe under the table" to Yahweh and in doing so takes a great risk. (For a connection to the child sacrifice of the Moabite king Mesha in his battle against Israel, see 2 Kings

3:26–27; Moabite Stone in *ANET*, 320; *COS*, 2:137–38.)

The structure of homes in ancient Israel does show that they had room for stables, thus making it possible that an animal could come out of Jephthah's home. But sacrificial animals (cows/bulls, sheep) do not usually greet their masters, so it is also possible he knew that a human would emerge from the home, especially since the timing was his return from battle, when family members would be concerned about his well-being (see Jdg 5:28–30). Also possible is that this vow is an act of vengeance against his brothers, assuming Jephthah is the head of a larger clan unit and hopes that one of his brothers' wives or children will emerge first (Patton, 42).

In any case, a burnt offering expressed one's entire devotion to God, with the sacrifice representing the being of the offerer transferred symbolically through the smoke to the heavenly dwelling of the deity (see Samuel E. Balentine, *Leviticus* [Interpretation; Louisville, Ky.: Westminster John Knox, 2002], 19). The problem here is that the sacrificial victim is inappropriate, and this event will signal a key turning point in the story of Jephthah as it is followed by the brutal civil war of 12:1–6. Thus as Janzen, 341, has argued: "if Israel worships foreign gods or worships YHWH in the manners in which the Canaanites worshiped their gods, the nation will also act in the evil ways in which foreigners act."

There are striking similarities between Jephthah's sacrifice and that of Abraham in Genesis 22 (Römer; John L. Thompson, "Preaching Texts of Terror in the Book of Judges: How Does the History of Interpretation Help?" *CTJ* 37 [2002]: 53). Both plan to offer a whole burnt offering (ʿwlh, Ge 22:2; Jdg 11:31) of their *only* child (yḥyd/yḥydh, Ge 22:2; Jdg 11:34), call the child "my son/daughter" (Ge 22:7; Jdg 11:35), and refer to seeing the ultimate victim (Ge 22:13; Jdg 11:35). In stark contrast, however, is the outcome of these stories as Abraham is given a substitutionary animal and promised countless descendants (Ge 22:13, 17–18), while Jephthah sacrifices his daughter, and with her all hope of descendants

(Jdg 11:39). Jephthah's tragedy is accentuated by the continuity and discontinuity with the story of Abraham.

Yahweh does indeed give the enemy into the hands (or power) of Jephthah (cf. 3:10, 28; 4:14; 7:2, 9). Jephthah's forces devastate twenty towns in the areas of Minnith and Abel Keramim, the identity of which are uncertain.

NOTES

32 The repetition of the end of v.29 at this point signals the return to the narrative line that had been abandoned in vv.30–31 to describe Jephthah's vow (Revell, 426–27).

וַיַּעֲבֹר (wayyaʿăbōr, "went over"). For עבר (ʿbr) followed by אֶל (ʾel) as a collocation indicating invasion see 12:3; 1 Samuel 14:1, 6, 8; 27:2 (cf. 1Ch 21:9). See also Note on Judges 12:1.

3. Jephthah's Vow Fulfilled (11:34–40)

³⁴When Jephthah returned to his home in Mizpah, who should come out to meet him but his daughter, dancing to the sound of tambourines! She was an only child. Except for her he had neither son nor daughter. ³⁵When he saw her, he tore his clothes and cried, "Oh! My daughter! You have made me miserable and wretched, because I have made a vow to the LORD that I cannot break."

³⁶"My father," she replied, "you have given your word to the LORD. Do to me just as you promised, now that the LORD has avenged you of your enemies, the Ammonites. ³⁷But grant me this one request," she said. "Give me two months to roam the hills and weep with my friends, because I will never marry."

³⁸"You may go," he said. And he let her go for two months. She and the girls went into the hills and wept because she would never marry. ³⁹After the two months, she returned to her father and he did to her as he had vowed. And she was a virgin.

From this comes the Israelite custom ⁴⁰that each year the young women of Israel go out for four days to commemorate the daughter of Jephthah the Gileadite.

COMMENTARY

34–38 Having made his foolish vow on the verge of battle, Jephthah is devastated when his daughter is the one who is first to depart from the house upon his return. It is not surprising that she is dancing to tambourines, a response similar to that of the women of Israel led by Miriam after Yahweh's victory in the exodus (Ex 15:20–21). His despondency is accentuated by the fact that she is an only child. Jephthah was introduced to the reader as one who was disinherited by his family: "The tragic irony of the text lies in the fact that his vow leads him to sacrifice the only heir to the inheritance he has worked so shrewdly to regain, his daughter.... Jephthah has effectively disinherited himself" (Patton, 41). The focus on her virginity in vv.37–39 is related to this failure (caused by the folly of Jephthah) to bear an heir for the family (cf. Exum, "The Centre Cannot Hold," 420–22).

Having made this vow Jephthah feels compelled to fulfill it. By providing dramatic narrative at this point in the story, the narrator allows us to hear the despondency of a father over the dilemma he has brought upon himself. Interestingly, he blames the daughter for this dilemma ("you have made me miserable and wretched") rather than himself for making such a foolish vow (McCann, 84; Thompson, 53–54). But the daughter accepts her fate as necessary for the deliverance of Israel from Ammon, only negotiating (an inherited trait! [Matthews, *Judges and Ruth*, 127]) with her father the privilege of spending two months roaming and weeping among the hills with her friends as she mourns the fact that she will never marry (see Note). Jephthah grants permission and then "he did to her as he had vowed," that is, he sacrifices her as a burnt offering.

This connects and yet contrasts the vow of a later father (King Saul) concerning his son (Jonathan), which demanded death (1Sa 14:24), yet did not result in it because of the intervention of popular opinion (1Sa 14:45; Sjöberg, 62). Furthermore, one cannot help but contrast the father-daughter relationship here with that of the ideal Caleb and Acsah at the outset of the book of Judges, another case that depicts the vow of a father and negotiation of a daughter (1:11–15; Sjöberg, 62, 67). With this tragic account there is a clear shift in the portrayal of women in the book, from heroines taking an active role (Acsah, Deborah, Jael, woman of Thebez) to becoming passive victims (chs. 10–21, though not Manoah's wife in ch. 13; McCann, 86).

39–40 These verses link this event to a yearly practice among the young women of Israel, possibly a "veiled reference to some cult in the hills" (Israel Mehlman, "Jephthah's Daughter" *JBQ* 25 [1997]: 37; cf. Hos 4:13–14; Eze 8:14) indicative of the spiritual regression of this phase in the accounts of the judge-deliverers (Janzen, 351).

NOTES

35–36 פָּצִיתָה אֶת־פִּיךָ ... וְאָנֹכִי פָּצִיתִי־פִי (*wᵉʾānōkî pāṣîtî-pî ... pāṣîtâ ʾet-pîkâ*, "I have made a vow to the Lord ... you have given your word to the Lord"). These phrases could be translated more woodenly as "I have opened my mouth … you have opened your mouth." The expressions may play on Jephthah's name, which means "he has opened," using the similarly sounding synonyms פצה (*psh*) and פתה (*pth*) (Block, 351) here to accentuate the disaster caused by Jephthah's foolish open mouth.

37 בְּתוּלָי (*betûlay*, "because I will never marry"). The Hebrew phrase here is "concerning my virginity," identifying Jephthah's daughter as a pubescent woman "about to be transferred from the power of her father to that of her husband" (Sjöberg, 65; cf. Bal, 46–52; Exum, "Feminist Criticism," 76; Schneider, 179–80).

4. Jephthah and Ephraim (12:1–6)

¹The men of Ephraim called out their forces, crossed over to Zaphon and said to Jephthah, "Why did you go to fight the Ammonites without calling us to go with you? We're going to burn down your house over your head."

²Jephthah answered, "I and my people were engaged in a great struggle with the Ammonites, and although I called, you didn't save me out of their hands. ³When I saw that you wouldn't help, I took my life in my hands and crossed over to fight the Ammonites, and the LORD gave me the victory over them. Now why have you come up today to fight me?"

⁴Jephthah then called together the men of Gilead and fought against Ephraim. The Gileadites struck them down because the Ephraimites had said, "You Gileadites are renegades from Ephraim and Manasseh." ⁵The Gileadites captured the fords of the Jordan leading to Ephraim, and whenever a survivor of Ephraim said, "Let me cross over," the men of Gilead asked him, "Are you an Ephraimite?" If he replied, "No," ⁶they said, "All right, say 'Shibboleth.'" If he said, "Sibboleth," because he could not pronounce the word correctly, they seized him and killed him at the fords of the Jordan. Forty-two thousand Ephraimites were killed at that time.

COMMENTARY

1–3 The encounter between Jephthah and Ephraim in 12:1–6 most likely occurs prior to Jephthah's return home and sacrifice of his daughter in 11:34–40. This chronology does not, however, suggest a later inclusion of the vow episode into the Jephthah account (contra Römer), but rather constitutes a deliberate technique by the narrator to highlight "the parallel between foreign sacrifice and foreign morality"—the latter evident in Ephraim's

aggression (typical of foreigners) depicted in 12:1–6 (Janzen, 354).

In a scene reminiscent of the encounter between Gideon and the Ephraimites in 8:1–3, Jephthah faces the hostility of the tribe of Ephraim for not involving them in the battle against Ammon. Here, as there, economic (loss of plunder) and social (honor-shame) values lie behind the tension (see esp. the discussion in 8:1–3; cf. Kirkpatrick, 25–27). Once again a successful

Gileadite warrior offends the tribe of Ephraim for entering battle without their involvement.

The Ephraimites' threat in v.1 ("We're going to burn down your house over your head") and slur in v.4 ("You Gileadites are renegades from Ephraim and Manasseh") suggests there is little room for negotiation between the two parties. The latter slur echoes a consistent theme in the Jephthah account; what was true of Jephthah within Gilead (uncertain ancestry) is also true of Gilead within the Joseph tribes, Manasseh and Ephraim (Sjöberg, 55). But true to form Jephthah tries to reason with the Ephraimites, though unlike Gideon in 8:1–3 he is unsuccessful. (Amit [*Judges*, 88–89] sees this episode as developing "the antagonistic analogy between Jephthah and Gideon.")

As in his previous two verbal exchanges (with the elders of Gilead and the king of Ammon), Jephthah begins by challenging his audience. He contradicts the Ephraimites' accusation by claiming he had called for their help but they had not come to his aid. As a result he was forced to take his life into his own hands and mobilize against the Ammonites, and Yahweh rewarded his efforts with victory. Since they failed to act, thus forcing Jephthah to fight, and since Yahweh gave him the victory, there was no justification for their hostility.

4–6 As in his encounter with the Ammonite king, Jephthah's Ephraimite foes are not dissuaded from their course of action, and they pursue the same ends as the just-defeated Ammonites. In the ensuing battle, especially provoked by the Ephraimite slur, which questioned the Gileadites' legitimacy within the Joseph tribes (Ephraim and Manasseh), the Gileadites are victorious. As is typical of these ancient skirmishes, the mop-up operation is as important as the battle itself (see 3:26–29; 4:15–16; 7:22–8:12; cf. 1Sa 17:51–53).

Since the Ephraimites had crossed the Jordan River to attack Jephthah in Gileadite Transjordan, their retreat necessitates that they cross back over to the western side of the river. The Gileadites cunningly take control of the part of the Jordan River where a crossing is possible and there are able to slaughter the remaining Ephraimites. (See comments on 3:27–29 and 7:24–25 for the motif of Ephraimites and the fords of the Jordan. This motif reaches its lowest point here and undermines Ephraim's claim to leadership.)

Since the Gileadites are related to the Ephraimites, they use a linguistic test to distinguish friends from foes. In order to cross at the ford, the person needs to pronounce the Hebrew word for "flowing stream" correctly. It appears that the physical isolation of the Joseph tribal clans on the eastern side of the Jordan from those on western side had produced slight differences in dialect, one of which related to the pronunciation of sibilants (s-sounds; see Notes below). In this aspect Ephraim is again depicted as a foreign entity, a status that turns this "civil war" into a "foreign war." Segments of Israel are thus depicted as foreigners, a foreshadowing of the "civil war" of Judges 20.

The linguistic test proves successful as the Gileadites are able to eliminate forty-two thousand or forty-two large military units. This number probably relates to the numbers killed in the battle and its aftermath. This incident contrasts Jephthah with the earlier Ehud (3:29): whereas Ehud struck down a foreign oppressor, Jephthah kills his own people (Amit, *Judges*, 89).

NOTES

1 וַיִּצָּעֵק ... וַיַּעֲבֹר (*wayyiṣṣāʿēq ... wayyaʿᵃbōr*, "called out their forces ... crossed over"). This language is indicative of military maneuvers. For עבר (ʿbr, followed by the locative *heh*) as invasion see 2 Kings 8:21 and Note on 11:32. For צעק (ṣʿq) see Note on 10:17.

3 וָאֶעְבְּרָה (*wā'e'bᵉrâ*, "crossed over"). For עבר (*'br*) followed by אֶל (*'el*) as a collocation indicating invasion, see Note on 11:32.

6 שִׁבֹּלֶת ... סִבֹּלֶת (*šibbōlet ... sibbōlet*, "Shibboleth ... Sibboleth"). Though Hebrew manuscripts use different consonants (*shin* versus *samek*) to represent the difference in sound, at issue here is most likely not "divergent development of sibilants in Gileadite and Ephraimite dialects of Hebrew," but rather "differentiation in the pronunciation of the same sibilant in these regions" (Block, 384). David Marcus ("Ridiculing the Ephraimites: The Shibboleth Incident [Judg 12:6]," *Maarav* 8 [1992]: 95–105) argues that this incident is merely satire designed to ridicule "the Ephraimites who are portrayed as incompetent nincompoops who cannot even repeat a test-word" (cf. Matthews, *Judges and Ruth*, 129–30, who embraces both views), while Janzen, 353, wisely recognizes the way Ephraim is depicted as a foreign (Ammonite) enemy.

5. Concluding Notice (12:7)

> ⁷Jephthah led Israel six years. Then Jephthah the Gileadite died, and was buried in a town in Gilead.

COMMENTARY

7 As with other leadership figures in Judges, the account of Jephthah ends with a concluding notice that records the length of his tenure as judge (six years). While the formula "the land had peace for X years" is used to conclude the accounts of Othniel, Ehud, Deborah-Barak, and Gideon (3:11, 30; 5:31; 8:28), the formula found at the end of Jephthah's account, "X led [i.e,, judged] Israel X years," is also used to conclude the accounts of Tola, Jair, Ibzan, Elon, Abdon, and Samson (10:2–3; 12:9, 11, 14; 15:20; 16:31; cf. Abimelech in 9:22). The lack of peace thus highlights the downward spiral of the accounts of Judges.

Jephthah's record of tenure is followed by a notice of his death and burial in a town in Gilead.

While the death of the judge is often recorded in the first half of the book of Judges (2:19; 3:11; 4:1; cf. 10:1), it is only in the second half of the book that a report on the place of burial is provided (8:32; 10:2, 5; 12:10, 12, 15; 16:31), echoing the report of the death of Joshua in Judges 2:8–9. The significance of these differences is unclear, possibly pointing to reliance on different sources, but also suggesting that the account of Gideon represents a rhetorical transition in the book. Burial notices are important to accounts of royal figures in 1–2 Kings (cf. 1Ki 11:43; 14:31; 15:8, 24; 16:6, 28; 22:37, 50; 2Ki 8:24; 9:28; 10:35; 12:21; 13:9, 13; 14:16, 20; 15:7, 38; 16:20; 21:18, 26; 23:30). Possibly here is a subtle preparation for kingship.

REFLECTION

The Jephthah account confirms the principle seen elsewhere that when Israel serves foreign deities, Yahweh sells his people into service to the foreign powers who worship these deities (10:6-7). Here is also the only account that explicitly cites the cry of the people to Yahweh, and this cry is penitential. It is clear, however, that a penitential cry is not sufficient. Yahweh scolds the people for their past patterns of disobedience. This divine upbraiding suggests that the divine response of grace is not an abstract impersonal principle, but rather a personal covenantal response rooted in the mystery of God's character of justice and mercy. God's response leads to an even more desperate penitential cry of the people paralleled by repentance in deed.

Finally, Yahweh responds because of his deep consternation over their suffering. Here God uses a leader not only with suspect origins who ascends to power under dubious circumstances through his negotiating skills, but also a leader who participates in a pagan practice (child sacrifice) and participates in the massacre of fellow northern tribesmen. The text makes clear that Jephthah experienced the empowerment of the Spirit of Yahweh and led Israel by faith against foreign armies (cf. Heb 11:32), but his questionable origins and actions reveal the necessity of a faithful royal form of leadership.

J. Ibzan, Elon, Abdon (12:8-15)

OVERVIEW

The account of Jephthah is preceded by two short accounts of the judges Tola and Jair (10:1-5) and followed by three more short accounts of the judges Ibzan, Elon, and Abdon. The abundant progeny of these five judges contrast with the lack of heirs produced by Jephthah (Block, 337; McCann, 76, 91). With Abdon the number of short accounts of judge-deliverers comes to six, and with Samson in chs. 13-16 the number of long accounts will be six as well, resulting in twelve judges total, the same as the number of the tribes of Israel. The five short accounts in chs. 10 and 12 most likely have been drawn from an independent source that used certain typical elements (see Overview to 10:1-5). These accounts provide an ideal model for judgeship that is ultimately overshadowed by the dominantly negative major accounts of Jephthah and Samson.

Bluedorn, 278, has argued that the burial locations of these three judges (Bethlehem and Aijalon in the wasteland, Abdon in the hills of Amalek) imply "Israel's increasing dominance by foreign nations." It is noteworthy that the last notation of "rest" for the land occurred at the end of Gideon's reign, another indication of the downward spiral of the accounts of the judges (8:28; cf. 12:7; 15:20; 16:31).

1. Ibzan of Bethlehem (12:8–10)

⁸After him, Ibzan of Bethlehem led Israel. ⁹He had thirty sons and thirty daughters. He gave his daughters away in marriage to those outside his clan, and for his sons he brought in thirty young women as wives from outside his clan. Ibzan led Israel seven years. ¹⁰Then Ibzan died, and was buried in Bethlehem.

COMMENTARY

8–10 Since the initial accounts of Othniel, Ehud, and Shamgar, the focus of the accounts of the judges has been on the tribes in the north and northwest, with special attention on the Joseph tribes. Although it is possible that the Bethlehem in view in 12:8–10 is the one found in Zebulun (see Jos 19:15–16), it is more likely that Ibzan arose from Bethlehem in the southern tribal allotment of Judah.

Few details are offered about this individual except that he had extensive progeny: thirty sons and thirty daughters. This number is reminiscent of Jair's thirty sons, who rode on thirty donkeys. As was the social custom in ancient Israel, a fam-ily's daughters left their "father's house" to join their husband's "father's house" and in the process established a blood bond between the two families. Ibzan's children gave to him an extensive network of relationships in the southern region (Nelson, 355).

Ibzan ruled for seven years and was buried in Bethlehem. The fact that this judge from the tribe of Judah arose from Bethlehem is not coincidental and foreshadows future royal leadership from this insignificant town just over five miles south of Jerusalem. Bethlehem will appear regularly in the final section of Judges (17:7–9; 19:1–2, 18).

2. Elon the Zebulunite (12:11–12)

¹¹After him, Elon the Zebulunite led Israel ten years. ¹²Then Elon died, and was buried in Aijalon in the land of Zebulun.

COMMENTARY

11–12 The next judge mentioned, Elon ("little ram"), arose from the tribe of Zebulun and served for ten years before being buried at Aijalon in the tribal territory of Zebulun. While there was an Aijalon in the original Danite allotment in southern Israel (Jos 19:42; 21:24; Jdg 1:34–36; 1Sa 14:31;

1Ch 6:69; 8:13), which was ultimately taken over by Ephraim (Jdg 1:35) and Benjamin (1Ch 8:13), there is no other mention of an Aijalon in Zebulun in the OT. No details are offered about the tenure of Elon.

3. Abdon Son of Hillel (12:13–15)

> [13]After him, Abdon son of Hillel, from Pirathon, led Israel. [14]He had forty sons and thirty grandsons, who rode on seventy donkeys. He led Israel eight years. [15]Then Abdon son of Hillel died, and was buried at Pirathon in Ephraim, in the hill country of the Amalekites.

COMMENTARY

13–15 The last minor judge, Abdon ("little servant") son of Hillel ("he praised"), was probably from the tribe of Ephraim since that is where he lived (Pirathon, six miles southwest of Shechem; *ABD*, 1:8) and was buried. He judged for eight years, and the only information provided about his tenure besides the fact that he judged Israel is the enumeration of his progeny. While Jair had thirty sons who rode thirty donkeys (Jdg 10:3–5) and Ibzan had thirty sons and thirty daughters (12:8–10), Abdon trumped them both with forty sons and thirty grandsons who rode seventy donkeys. This large number of progeny suggests an extensive harem, not unlike ancient royal houses (see comments on 10:3–5 for the royal and military significance of donkeys). The closing reference to the territory of Ephraim as "the hill country of the Amalekites" is a reminder of the incompleteness of the conquest.

For a reflection on these final three short accounts, see the Reflection at the end of 10:1–5.

K. Samson (13:1–16:31)

OVERVIEW

While earlier scholars (esp. Noth; Wolfgang Richter, *Traditionsgeschichtliche Untersuchungen zum Richterbuch* [BBB 18; Bonn: Hanstein, 1963]) treated the Samson account as a late addition to the book of Judges, recent work has highlighted its integral connection to the rest of the book and even considered it the book's climax (Barry G. Webb, "A Serious Reading of the Samson Story (Judges 13–16)," *RTR* 54 [1995]: 112; for history of research see Kim, xi–114).

The chronological location of the Samson cycle within the period between Joshua and Samuel is unclear. The story appears to occur prior to the Danites' sojourn north in Judges 17–18, an event that is linked to the generation immediately after Joshua (see Introduction). This situation suggests that the account is one of the earliest (chronologically) in the book (contra Block, 394, who sees the Samson account as dealing with the Philistine problem introduced in 10:7). Testifying to the integrity of this account are the many parallels that have been highlighted between the three major sections (ch. 13; 14:1–16:3; 16:4–31; cf. Kim, 425).

In Samson the narrator finds the greatest of all tragedies among the judges who led Israel, as shown in his use of brilliant rhetoric to highlight the "discrepancy between Samson's epithet (a Nazirite) and his dramatic characterization (a rebel against his vocation)" (Kim, 433). This miracle baby, set apart as holy for God's service, from the beginning of his adult life places himself in vulnerable and compromising circumstances and so endangers the success made possible by the empowerment of the Spirit of Yahweh. In Samson the reader meets a judge no better, and probably worse, than sinful Israel (Webb, 158).

That Yahweh uses Samson is nothing but a sign of his gracious commitment to Israel as his chosen people. Unlike with previous judge-deliverers, who stood at the head of armies and represented tribes, Samson's acts are always "personal involvements and private vendettas" (Amit, *Judges*, 275; cf. O'Connell, 228). He is at times presented in ways that resonate with the motif of the ancient Near Eastern "wild man," a figure torn between the world of nature and domesticated urban space (Gregory Mobley, "The Wild Man in the Bible and the Ancient Near East," *JBL* 116 [1997]: 217–33; idem, *Samson*, 16–25).

In the end, Samson is unable to remove the enemy from the land and so "completes the disappointment with the leadership of the judges and prepares the ground for the concluding description of anarchy [chs. 17–21] during the period of the judges" (Amit, *Judges*, 92, see also 307; cf. McCann, 93). The links noted between Samson and Saul (cf. Jdg 14:6, 19; 15:14 with 1Sa 10:6, 10; 11:6; Jdg 16:25 with 1Sa 31:4, 9–10; 16:30 with 1Sa 31:4; O'Connell, 295–96; Emmrich, 68; Galpaz-Feller, "My Soul," 322; Peterson) further the anti-Saulide motif throughout this book.

1. Introductory Notice (13:1)

¹Again the Israelites did evil in the eyes of the LORD, so the LORD delivered them into the hands of the Philistines for forty years.

COMMENTARY

1 Chapter 13 inaugurates the episode of the final judge-deliverer, Samson. Although the account of Samson is second only to Gideon's in terms of length, its introductory notice is the shortest of all the major accounts. As usual, it begins with the description of Israel's doing evil in the eyes of Yahweh but offers no details on the precise character of this evil, which Judges often links to the worship of foreign gods (2:6–3:6; 3:7–11; 5:8; 6:1, 8–10, 25–32; cf. 3:19, 26). As a result Yahweh delivers Israel into the "hands" (power) of the Philistines, a phrase that appears in 2:14 and 6:1 and is similar to the phrase "sold them into the hands of" in 3:8; 4:2; and 10:7.

Earlier in Judges the Philistines had bothered Israel (3:31; 10:7), and they became a key enemy as Israel moved toward monarchy (1Sa 4–5, 7, 13–14, 17, 31; 2Sa 5; cf. 1Sa 9:15). This people group controlled the key international highway that ran to the west of the Judean highlands, that is, the Way of the Sea, which connected Africa with Asia and Europe.

The Philistines' origins were most likely in the islands and coastlands of the Aegean Sea (*ABD*, 5:327). Defeat at the hands of the Egyptians in the early twelfth century BC led to forced settlement along the Canaanite southern coastal plain, where they continued developing the five key cities of Gaza, Ashkelon, Ashdod, Ekron, and Gath, and where they ultimately formed an independent confederation of city-states free from Egyptian control. Their cultural remains clearly set them apart from Israel as well as the rest of Canaan (see Niditch, *Judges*, 144–45). As is typical in Judges, a set period of divine discipline through a foreign oppressor is noted—here forty years (see 3:8, 14; 4:3; 6:1; 10:8).

What is missing from this introductory notice, however, is any description of Israel's cry to Yahweh for help (3:9, 15; 4:3; 6:6–7; 10:10, 12). While Fensham, 82, argues that this lack shows the difficulty the final author had in incorporating the Samson narrative into his overall schema, it is better to see this absence as indicative of the downward spiral of the book as a whole (Schneider, xv; McCann, 94). While the Jephthah account provided the most intricate description of Israel's cry, the Samson account does not even mention it.

Amit (*Judges*, 297) sees the incompleteness of the introductory notice in ch. 13 as setting the tone for this account of a "partial deliverer," "serving as a brake to the wheel of cyclicity: no longer a complete delivery, nor a deliverer who shall assure quiet to the people." Wong (*Strategy*, 184) sees this episode as representing the final stage in the progressive deterioration depicted in the stories of the judges, as the cry of Israel disappears and the land lacks the expected rest. The people "show little sign of even *wanting* to be rescued" (Webb, 163), as showcased especially in Judah's cowering surrender of Samson into the hands of the Philistines (15:11–13; Block, 395).

2. Birth, Childhood, and Endowment of Samson (13:2–24)

OVERVIEW

Earlier in the book of Judges the major accounts of the judge-deliverers include an explicit reference to Yahweh's raising up (*qwm*, Hiphil) an individual (2:16, 18; 3:9, 12); that is, the accounts of Deborah-Barak, Gideon, and Jephthah each describe a figure who relates a divine word (Deborah in 4:4a, an unnamed prophet in 6:8–10, or Yahweh in 10:10–14), followed by the narrative about the judge-deliverer (4:4b–24; 6:11–8:32; 10:17–12:6).

The account of Samson follows the style of the latter stories, though it begins not with the judge-deliverer character himself (Samson) but rather with his parents.

In this way the Samson account incorporates another story form (type scene) well attested in the OT—the birth narrative, which often precedes the rise of a hero (Ge 18:9–15; 25:19–26; 30:1–24; 1Sa 1:1–20; cf. Lk 1:5–25; 57–80;

Block, 395; Niditch, *Judges*, 142). This particular birth narrative, however, will produce a tragic anti-hero, especially noticeable in the contrast between Samson and Samuel (Chisholm, 47) — a contrast that also serves to enhance the literary transition from Judges to Samuel and the political transition from judge-deliverer to king (Schneider, 197).

a. Introduction of Samson's Parents: Crisis in Seed (13:2)

²A certain man of Zorah, named Manoah, from the clan of the Danites, had a wife who was sterile and remained childless.

COMMENTARY

2 As is common in the OT, the husband is introduced first; this order is indicative of the patriarchal family system. He is identified with the town of Zorah, which lay in the Sorek Valley — one of five key valleys that cut through the Shephelah (see comment on 1:18), the transitional territory between the hill country, where the Judeans settled, and the Mediterranean coastal plain controlled by the five Philistine city-states. It is in another one of these valleys (the Elah) that the great battle between David and the Philistine Goliath would take place.

Manoah, whose name means "rest," lived in an era when Israel did not experience the rest that they had once been promised and had attained (cf. Jos 1:13, 15; 21:44; 22:4; 23:1). He was from the tribe of Dan, which was allotted territory in the southwest of Canaan that included the town of Zorah (Jos 19:41; cf. 19:40–48), a location mentioned in the El-Amarna letters as one of the towns experiencing attack from external forces (EA 273; *ABD*, 6:1168). The Danite struggle with the Philistines, already seen in Judges 1:34–35, ultimately prompts the Danites to abandon their allotted territory and move to the far north of Canaan (see ch. 18). After Dan's exit, Zorah became part of Judahite territory (Jos 15:33; cf. 1Ch 2:54–55).

Verse 2, then, introduces Manoah's wife, who is not only nameless in the text but also barren, a plight shared by a number of key female figures in the OT (Ge 11:30; 25:21; 29:31; 1Sa 1:2; 2:5). In the ancient world this condition was devastating and at times interpreted as a curse from God (Galpaz-Feller, *Samson*, 9; see 1Sa 1:5–6); the remedy for this was direct divine intervention. In ancient societies, in which people had short life spans and high susceptibility to fatal sickness, the continuation and preservation of the family line were dominating concerns — thus Yahweh's promise to give Abraham a multitude of descendants (Ge 17).

A woman's identity was therefore closely tied to childbearing. Without her bearing children, the continuation of the family line came under threat. In OT stories the barrenness of a woman clearly signals the greatest threat to the family, clan, and tribal units, but it also always introduces a narrative in which Yahweh will work a miracle by providing a special child who will play a significant role within the nation (Ge 21:1–4; 30:22–24; 1Sa 1:20; cf. Ru 4:13–22).

The namelessness of Samson's mother may be designed to link her with the heavenly being who soon appears and also remains nameless (cf. Adele Reinhartz, "Samson's Mother: An Unnamed Protagonist," *JSOT* 55 [1992]: 29), but possibly also introduces the key motif of women in the Samson account (so R. Alter, "Samson without Folklore," in *Text and Tradition* [ed. S. Niditch; Atlanta: Scholars, 1990], 51; cf. McCann, 96). But her barrenness and the lack of any reference to the sexual act by which Samson was conceived set her apart from all the other women in Samson's life (Matthews, *Judges and Ruth*, 140).

NOTE

2 מִשְׁפַּחַת (*mišpahat*, "clan"). One way of describing the sociological structure of Israel (see Introduction) is seen in Joshua 7:14 (from smallest to largest group): family (*byt*), clan (*mšphh*), tribe (*šbt*). These terms, however, are flexible, and here in Judges 13:2 what is usually considered a tribe within Israel is called a "clan" (though Block, 397, sees the narrator as marginalizing Manoah; see similarly 17:7, where Judah is also called a *mišpāhâ*).

b. Promise from the Angel of the Lord to Samson's Mother (13:3–5)

> ³The angel of the LORD appeared to her and said, "You are sterile and childless, but you are going to conceive and have a son. ⁴Now see to it that you drink no wine or other fermented drink and that you do not eat anything unclean, ⁵because you will conceive and give birth to a son. No razor may be used on his head, because the boy is to be a Nazirite, set apart to God from birth, and he will begin the deliverance of Israel from the hands of the Philistines."

COMMENTARY

3–5 As in the story of Gideon, the angel of the Lord plays an important role in the raising up of the judge-deliverer (Webb, 164; Amit, *Judges*, 289–90; Matthews, *Judges and Ruth*, 142). There the angel appeared to Gideon, while here he appears to Samson's parents. In both accounts the initial speech of the heavenly messenger suggests the destiny of the judge-deliverer (cf. 6:12; 13:5), the encounter ends with the presentation of a burnt and grain offering (cf. 6:19–21; 13:15–20), and it results in the human participants fearing for their lives (cf. 6:22–21; 13:21–23).

The angelic figure appears to Samson's mother and uses two words ("sterile" and "childless") to name her condition before promising a miraculous reversal, again using two, though contrasting, terms ("conceive," "have a child"). This focus on barrenness and fertility suggests the themes of death and life—themes that will reappear in the two cries of Samson to Yahweh, the first for life (15:18–19) and the second for death (16:31; Webb, 167). The angel not only appears to the woman to announce this miracle, but also to instruct her on how to carry and raise this child. The child is to be a Nazirite, set apart from the womb (see Note)—a status that demanded careful attention to practices related to eating, drinking, and caring for one's hair. Hannah's vow to Yahweh in 1 Samuel 1:11 shows another case in which a barren woman's child is dedicated to Yahweh under Nazirite rites.

Legal stipulations related to Nazirites are provided in Numbers 6:1–21. "Nazirite" was the term used for an Israelite man or woman who had made an explicit vow of consecration to Yahweh (6:2, 8) for a set period of time (6:8, 13). During this period he or she was to abstain from fermented drink (wine, alcohol, vinegar) or anything associated with grapes (6:3–4), from cutting his or her hair (6:5), and from approaching a dead body, even if it was a family member (6:6–7). The vow was concluded by rituals that took place at the sanctuary, rituals that included the presentation of a series of sacrifices (burnt, sin, peace, grain, and drink offerings; 6:13–17), the shaving of the head and burning of the hair (6:18), and finally the performance of a wave offering (6:19–20). The final stipulation (no contact with a family member's dead body) was similar to that required of the high priest (Lev 21), as is the identification of the Nazirite as "holy to the LORD" (see Ex 28:36).

These stipulations suggest that the Nazirite vow provided the Israelite laity an opportunity for consecration to Yahweh (Galpaz-Feller, *Samson*, 44; for later examples of the Nazirite practice, see 1 Macc 3:49–51; Ac 18:18; 21:23–24; see Am 2:11–12 for the vow's possible connection to prophecy; Niditch, *Judges*, 143). While priestly consecration was an enduring condition limited to a particular clan within Israel, Nazirite consecration was a condition limited in time but available to all Israelites. It is uncertain what would prompt the taking of such a vow, though the reference to a vow suggests that it may be a response of thanksgiving to Yahweh for his intervention in a person's life (Lev 7:16–17; Pss 22:25; 50:14; 56:12; 61:5, 8; 66:13; 76:11; 116:14, 18; cf. Ge 28:20; 31:13; Jdg 11:30; Jnh 2:9).

While the Nazirite rituals in the Torah point to a vow limited in time, interestingly the only two times the Nazirite rituals are described in OT narratives involve someone's being dedicated to God's service for life (Jdg 13; 1Sa 1; Galpaz-Feller, *Samson*, 46–50). Both examples note Yahweh's opening the womb of a barren woman. While the case of Hannah in 1 Samuel 1 does involve a vow (1:11), as she promises to dedicate her miracle child to Yahweh's service, no such vow is recorded on the lips of Samson's mother in Judges 13. The close relationship between the Nazirite vow and priestly consecration makes sense in the case of Hannah's Samuel, who was born to Ephraimite parents (1Sa 1:1–2) and yet served in a priestly capacity. Why the Nazirite ritual was used for Samson is unclear.

Although not identical to the legal ordinances found in Numbers 6, the stipulations commanded by the angel echo the three basic prohibitions, relating to drinking fermented liquids, contact with ritually unclean things, and cutting the hair (see Amit, *Judges*, 276–77). In the case of Samson these stipulations are in force from his conception (see Note) until his death, the latter an allusion to his ultimate fate (cf. 16:30; Webb, 166).

The angel makes clear that this child is not primarily being given to save Manoah's line from extinction, but rather to "begin the deliverance of Israel from the hands of the Philistines." While this purpose echoes earlier statements related to judge-deliverers in this book (2:16, 18; 3:9, 15; 6:14, 36), the addition of the verb "begin" suggests that his mission will be limited and incomplete (Amit, *Judges*, 90). Interestingly, Yahweh is providing salvation for his people even though they have not requested it.

NOTES

5 הִנָּךְ הָרָה (*hinnāk hārâ*, "you will conceive"). The use of the participle here most likely points to imminent future action (A–C 81; cf. Block, 401; contra Klein, *The Triumph of Irony*, 111, who sees here a description of an already existing state ["you are pregnant"]).

מִן־הַבָּטֶן (*min-habbāṭen*, "from birth"). Here the Hebrew text reads "from the belly/womb." As the narrative shows, the setting apart is from the point of conception, since Samson's mother is prohibited from drinking fermented liquids or eating unclean foods while carrying the child.

c. Samson's Mother Tells Her Husband, Who Prays for Further Guidance (13:6–8)

⁶Then the woman went to her husband and told him, "A man of God came to me. He looked like an angel of God, very awesome. I didn't ask him where he came from, and he didn't tell me his name. ⁷But he said to me, 'You will conceive and give birth to a son. Now then, drink no wine or other fermented drink and do not eat anything unclean, because the boy will be a Nazirite of God from birth until the day of his death.'"

⁸Then Manoah prayed to the LORD: "O Lord, I beg you, let the man of God you sent to us come again to teach us how to bring up the boy who is to be born."

COMMENTARY

6–7 The angel appears only to Samson's mother, who promptly reports this encounter to her husband. She describes the speaker as "a man of God," a term associated with Moses (Dt 33:1) and prophetic figures in general (e.g., 1Sa 2:27; 9:6–10; 12:22), whose appearance is "very awesome" (*nôrā' mᵉʾōd*), like that of an "angel of God." As in previous accounts (4:6–7, 14; 6:8–10; 10:11–14, cf. 2:1–3, 20–23), a divine word and/or messenger associated with such a word breaks into the account (see Boda, "Recycling Heaven's Words"). By mentioning her failure to ask this figure about his place of origin and name, this speech foreshadows the later inquiry of Manoah in the passage (13:17–18). Another foreshadowing can be discerned in the addition of an element not provided in the angel's speech cited in vv.3–5, that is, that Samson will be a Nazirite until the day of his death (v.7; cf. 16:26–31). Even before his life begins, the tragedy of his death is placed in clear view (Galpaz-Feller, *Samson*, 13).

8 This report from Manoah's wife prompts him to pray to Yahweh, asking that he send the "man of God" once again to teach them how to raise the boy. This request simultaneously reveals a spiritual sensitivity in Samson's parents and reminds the reader of the lack of instruction in Torah among the people.

d. Reappearance of the Angel of God and Dialogue with Manoah (13:9–18)

⁹God heard Manoah, and the angel of God came again to the woman while she was out in the field; but her husband Manoah was not with her. ¹⁰The woman hurried to tell her husband, "He's here! The man who appeared to me the other day!"

¹¹Manoah got up and followed his wife. When he came to the man, he said, "Are you the one who talked to my wife?"

"I am," he said.

¹²So Manoah asked him, "When your words are fulfilled, what is to be the rule for the boy's life and work?"

¹³The angel of the LORD answered, "Your wife must do all that I have told her. ¹⁴She must not eat anything that comes from the grapevine, nor drink any wine or other fermented drink nor eat anything unclean. She must do everything I have commanded her."

¹⁵Manoah said to the angel of the LORD, "We would like you to stay until we prepare a young goat for you."

¹⁶The angel of the LORD replied, "Even though you detain me, I will not eat any of your food. But if you prepare a burnt offering, offer it to the LORD." (Manoah did not realize that it was the angel of the LORD.)

¹⁷Then Manoah inquired of the angel of the LORD, "What is your name, so that we may honor you when your word comes true?"

¹⁸He replied, "Why do you ask my name? It is beyond understanding.'"

COMMENTARY

9–14 Manoah's prayer is soon answered, but once again the heavenly figure does not approach Manoah but rather his wife, who is working in the field alone. This time Samson's mother fetches her husband, who then follows his wife to the man. After identifying the individual as the one who appeared earlier, Manoah asks him to outline once again the regulations required of the expected child. The angel's abridged version brings to three the number of times the stipulations have been articulated, thus emphasizing its intricate detail. Samson will eventually disregard each of the stipulations.

15–18 Manoah's invitation to the angel to stay for a meal may be understood as a typical act of ancient hospitality, "a rite of passage in which the status of stranger is transformed into that of an intimate guest" (Galpaz-Feller, *Samson*, 14, n. 8). While reminiscent of Gideon's care for the angel of the Lord (6:17–23), comparison can also be made with the account of Abraham's care for the three heavenly guests in Genesis 18:1–10 (see Galpaz-Feller, *Samson*, 16). Interestingly, while the meal prepared by Abraham and Sarah is eaten by the heavenly beings, Manoah's is not. Rather, Manoah is encouraged to prepare a burnt offering for Yahweh.

The dialogue ends with Manoah asking the man's name so that they might honor him after the fulfillment of the prophecy. The visitor refuses to give his name since it is "beyond understanding" (*peliʾy*; cf. Ps 139:6). This refusal is reminiscent of the guarded revelation of the angelic figure in Jacob's encounter of Genesis 32:30, as well as of Yahweh throughout the book of Exodus (see Ex 3:13–15; 4:13–15; 6:3; 33:12–34:7; Amit, *Judges*, 292, 302).

NOTE

12 מַה־יִּהְיֶה מִשְׁפַּט־הַנַּעַר וּמַעֲשֵׂהוּ (*mah-yihyeh mišpaṭ-hannaʿar ûmaʿăśēhû*, "what is to be the rule for the boy's life and work?"). Here the term מִשְׁפָּט (*mišpaṭ*; GK 5477), more commonly translated as "decision, judgment" in a legal sense, may signify a divine decision/word/oracle from a messenger of God (see Note on 4:5; cf. Spronk, "Deborah," 236, and the Ugaritic text KTU 1.124). In this case וּמַעֲשֵׂהוּ (*ûmaʿăśēhû*) is epexegetical: "what is the decision concerning the boy, that is, his life's work?"

e. Manoah's Sacrifice and Concern for Life (13:19–23)

¹⁹Then Manoah took a young goat, together with the grain offering, and sacrificed it on a rock to the Lord. And the Lord did an amazing thing while Manoah and his wife watched: ²⁰As the flame blazed up from the altar toward heaven, the angel of the Lord ascended in the flame. Seeing this, Manoah and his wife fell with their faces to the ground. ²¹When the angel of the Lord did not show himself again to Manoah and his wife, Manoah realized that it was the angel of the Lord.

²²"We are doomed to die!" he said to his wife. "We have seen God!"

²³But his wife answered, "If the Lord had meant to kill us, he would not have accepted a burnt offering and grain offering from our hands, nor shown us all these things or now told us this."

COMMENTARY

19–20a Like Gideon (see Niditch, *Judges*, 146), Manoah takes burnt and grain offerings and sacrifices them on a rock (v.19), that is, a rudimentary altar (v.20a). The narrator tells the reader that Yahweh performs a miraculous wonder (see Note) before Samson's parents. Such a sign was important as confirmation of the veracity of a divine message (cf. Dt 13:1–3), as is apparent in the case of Gideon (6:17–19). As the flame and, most likely, the attendant smoke rises toward heaven, the "man of God," identified now as the "angel of the LORD," ascends in the fire.

20b–23 The response of Samson's parents is strikingly similar to that of Gideon in 6:22 as they fear their lives are in jeopardy now that they have seen God (see comment on 6:22). While Gideon is comforted by Yahweh himself, it is Samson's mother who calms the frightened Manoah by pointing to Yahweh's acceptance of their offering and revelation of his promises. Once again this unnamed woman displays greater sensitivity than her husband to heavenly realities (cf. 1Sa 1:12–18; Block, 397). O'Connell, 218, interprets this woman as a foil for Manoah, while Niditch (*Judges*, 145) highlights the contrast of "an insecure, unknowing man with a calm and wise woman" (cf. Galpaz-Feller, *Samson*, 17).

NOTE

19 מַפְלִא (*mapliʾ*, "an amazing thing"; GK 7098). In Isaiah 29:14 this term appears parallel to פֶּלֶא (*peleʾ*), a term used throughout the OT for miracles (Ex 15:11; Pss 77:15; 78:12; 88:11).

f. Birth and Growth of Samson (13:24–25)

²⁴The woman gave birth to a boy and named him Samson. He grew and the LORD blessed him, ²⁵and the Spirit of the LORD began to stir him while he was in Mahaneh Dan, between Zorah and Eshtaol.

COMMENTARY

24–25 As the man of God/angel of Yahweh promised, the woman does give birth to a child, and she names him Samson, which means "little sun" (*HALOT*, 1593). The child not only survives childhood ("grew up"), but also is blessed by Yahweh. While here this blessing (*brk*, Piel) is certainly positive, it is ironic that Samson will meet his demise on the knee (*berek*) of Delilah in 16:19–20 (Kim, 430–31). The narrator tells the reader that when Samson was grown, "the Spirit of the LORD began to stir him," thus identifying Samson as the new judge-deliverer but using vocabulary with a darker tone than other instances in the book (see Note; cf. 14:6, 19; 15:14; cf. 3:10; 6:34; 11:29).

Samson's home territory was within Mahaneh Dan, or "the camp of Dan," and extended from Zorah to Eshtaol (see comment on 13:2; cf. Jos 19:41; Jdg 18:11–12). The reappearance of these locations in the story of Micah in chs. 17–18 (see 18:1–2) highlights the way that the tragedy of Samson foreshadows the disastrous events in chs. 17–21.

NOTE

25 לְפַעֲמוֹ (*leṗaʿamô*, "to stir him"). While here is the only OT occurrence of this verb in the Qal stem, it appears in the Niphal in Genesis 41:8; Psalm 77:5; Daniel 2:3, and in the Hithpael in Daniel 2:1, to refer to a troubling disturbance within one's spirit. In this way it has the most negative tone of all the references to the Spirit's work in Judges (Mobley, 67–69).

3. Samson's Marriage to the Philistine Woman from Timnah (14:1–20)

a. Samson's Attraction to the Timnite Woman (14:1–4)

¹Samson went down to Timnah and saw there a young Philistine woman. ²When he returned, he said to his father and mother, "I have seen a Philistine woman in Timnah; now get her for me as my wife."

³His father and mother replied, "Isn't there an acceptable woman among your relatives or among all our people? Must you go to the uncircumcised Philistines to get a wife?"

But Samson said to his father, "Get her for me. She's the right one for me." ⁴(His parents did not know that this was from the LORD, who was seeking an occasion to confront the Philistines; for at that time they were ruling over Israel.)

COMMENTARY

1–3 The next story in the Samson cycle is the first to describe his exploits as a grown man. The story begins with Samson visiting the town of Timnah, which lay in the Sorek Valley (see comment on 13:2) on the northern frontier of Judah (Jos 15:7) and which was at one time associated with the tribe of Dan (Jos 19:43). During the period of the judges, however, Timnah was under Philistine control, evidence for which has been uncovered at Tel Batash (*AEHL*, "Batash [Tel] [Timnah]").

This episode introduces a key motif in the account of Samson: "Samson thrives in the wild and begins to falter once he enters Philistine society" (Mobley, 37). In civilized Timnah he is smitten by a Philistine girl, a related motif in which these foreign females seek to civilize the undomesticated Samson (Mobley, 85–108). Here, as often in the ancient world and regularly in the book of Judges, women "serve as commodities of exchange, the mediating doorways linking or separating groups of men" (Niditch, *Judges*, 154). These women will bring Samson into contact with the Philistine enemy for good or ill (Amit, *Judges*, 280–88).

Samson's attraction leads him to initiate ancient betrothal rituals ("get her for me as a wife"; cf. Ge 24). According to these rituals parents were the ones required to negotiate the betrothal (see esp. Galpaz-Feller, *Samson*, 77–92), but before agreeing to do so Samson's parents express their concern over his choice by rightfully asking why he has not chosen a wife from among his own people and referring to his choice with disdain ("the uncircumcised Philistines"). Samson ignores his parents' caution; he repeats his demand ("get her for me") and bases it on the fact that "she is right in my eyes" ("she's the right one for me"), a phrase strikingly similar to that key comment by the narrator in 17:6 and 21:25 (see comments there; cf. Wong, *Strategy*, 96–103), which condemns Israel for their lack of adherence to God's stipulations.

Here Samson is clearly violating the Torah's prohibition of intermarriage with the Canaanites (Ex 34:16; Dt 7:3), something flagged at the outset of Judges (3:5–6) as a problem that would lead Israel into idolatry (3:7). Though the Spirit is stirring within him, Samson is insensitive to Yahweh and his ways. With Samson, the deterioration of the leadership of the judges in terms of their self-interest peaks (see comments on Jdg 7:16–18; 11:4–11; Wong, *Strategy*, 174–76). Webb, 170–71, notes key distinctions between ideal Othniel in 3:7–11 and Samson in terms of their contrasting relationships with women, leadership of the military, and success in deliverance (see also David W. Gooding, "The Composition of the Book of Judges," *ErIsr* 16 [1982]: 73). While the earliest judge-deliverers acted on behalf of Yahweh and his people, Samson (and Gideon and Jephthah before him) "fight merely for personal revenge" (Schneider, xv; cf. Amit, *Judges*, 275).

4 It may seem odd to the reader that immediately following the description of the stirring of the Spirit in 13:25, the narrator relates the story of Samson's attraction to a Philistine woman in ch. 14. Samson's parents voice the concern of the reader, but interestingly the narrator counters such a response with the revelation that Samson's attraction was "of the Lord" (*kî mēyhwh*, v.4; cf. Jos 11:20), since Yahweh was seeking an opportunity to free Israel from Philistine hegemony (Amit, *Judges*, 281).

It is interesting that a similar description (*kî mēʿet yhwh*) is used in Joshua 11:20 to refer to Yahweh's hardening the hearts of the Canaanites in order to accomplish his purpose to give Israel the land. This similarity suggests that here Yahweh is using the sinful tendencies of Samson to accomplish his purpose of freeing Israel. He "manages to achieve his purpose not in spite of, but by means of, Samson's resistance" (O'Connell, 226; on the theological dilemma inherent in this verse, see Chisholm, 42, n. 20; Crenshaw, 78–83; Klein, *The Triumph of Irony*, 116–17; McCann, 102). This is hardly the ideal method for leadership raised up by Yahweh, but it is indicative of the downward spiral evidenced in the book of Judges.

NOTES

2 קְחוּ־אוֹתָהּ לִּי לְאִשָּׁה (*qᵉḥû-ʾôtâh lî lᵉʾiššâ*, "get her for me as my wife"). For לקח (*lqḥ*) as a technical term for taking a bride (cf. 1Sa 25:39–40; 2Sa 11:4; Ge 12:15; Est 2:8), often (as here) through the agency of the groom's father (Ge 34:4; 38:6; Ex 34:16; Dt 7:3), and for ancient Near Eastern evidence of this practice, see Galpaz-Feller (*Samson*, 77–79). The reciprocal term for the bride's parents' consent is נתן (*ntn*, "give"; cf. Ge 29:19, 29; 34:8–9; Ex 2:21; Jos 15:16).

3 מִפְּלִשְׁתִּים הָעֲרֵלִים (*mippelištîm hāʿărēlîm*, "uncircumcised Philistines"). Block, 424, notes how the phrase "uncircumcised X" is restricted to the Philistines in the OT (Jdg 15:18; 1Sa 14:6; 17:26, 36; 31:4 [1Ch 10:4]; 2Sa 1:20).

b. Samson, the Lion, and Honey (14:5–9)

> ⁵Samson went down to Timnah together with his father and mother. As they approached the vineyards of Timnah, suddenly a young lion came roaring toward him. ⁶The Spirit of the LORD came upon him in power so that he tore the lion apart with his bare hands as he might have torn a young goat. But he told neither his father nor his mother what he had done. ⁷Then he went down and talked with the woman, and he liked her.
>
> ⁸Some time later, when he went back to marry her, he turned aside to look at the lion's carcass. In it was a swarm of bees and some honey, ⁹which he scooped out with his hands and ate as he went along. When he rejoined his parents, he gave them some, and they too ate it. But he did not tell them that he had taken the honey from the lion's carcass.

COMMENTARY

5–9 The next scene of the story portrays Samson returning to Timnah with his parents to negotiate the betrothal (for biblical and ancient Near Eastern evidence, see Galpaz-Feller, *Samson*, 77–92). This time he moves beyond merely "seeing" the Philistine woman (14:1–2) and talks with her (14:7). By talking with her directly Samson appears to break the social convention of patriarchal negotiation, most likely an indication of his parents' "quiet opposition" to the relationship (Galpaz-Feller, *Samson*, 91). The narrator rephrases Samson's earlier evaluation ("she is right in my eyes," 14:3; see above), when he says (lit.) "she was right in the eyes of Samson" ("she looked good to Samson"), again reminiscent of the coming evaluation of Israel in chs. 17–21 (see comments on

14:1–3). Later Samson will return (14:8a) and, together with his father, put on a wedding feast (14:10).

Throughout the story line of the betrothal rituals in vv.5–9, the narrator has creatively interwoven another story line. In its first phase Samson is attacked by a young lion as he passes through the vineyards of Timnah on that initial journey with his parents (vv.5–6). This spatial setting of vineyards is a clue to the purpose of this story line in revealing that Samson foolishly endangers his Nazirite vows from the outset of the story (Webb, 113–14; McCann, 99). Nevertheless, in the face of danger the Lord's Spirit comes upon him and empowers him to tear the powerful beast to pieces with his bare hands. This event foreshadows Samson's later encounter with the Philistines not only in his use of it for the later riddle, but especially in the vocabulary and motifs shared between 14:3–6 and 15:14–19 (Emmrich, 71), the two passages that frame the first major phase of Samson's adult life (chs. 14–15).

In the accounts of Othniel, Gideon, and Jephthah, the sign of God's empowering presence with the judge-deliverer has been the coming of the Spirit, described using either the verb *hyh* (3:10; 11:29) or *lbš* (6:34). In the Samson account the verb is *ṣlḥ* (GK 7502; 14:6, 19; 15:14), a term also used in relation to the royal Spirit's entry into Saul (1Sa 10:6, 10; 11:6) and David (1Sa 16:13), as well as the injurious spirit's entry into Saul after his rejection (1Sa 18:10; see 1Sa 16:14–15, where the verb used is *bʿt*, used to denote something terrifying or frightening; cf. 2Sa 22:5//Ps 18:5; Job 3:5; 7:14; 9:34; 13:11, 21; 15:24; 18:11; 33:7; Isa 21:4). This term is used in Amos 5:6 to describe the fire of God breaking forth and consuming something. In the case of the Spirit's empowerment, this verb indicates that the Spirit forcefully enters the person, expressing "a rapid and sudden event rather than a static situation" (Amit, *Judges*, 279; Mobley, 69–70), the effects of which may be demonstrative as seen in most of the passages listed above. The use of terms unique in the book of Judges to describe Samson's experience with the Spirit, along with the darker and more violent character of these terms, sets the tone for the account of Samson—one that will combine both good and evil, suggesting at times Saul and at other times David. (For connections between Samson and Saul/David, see Exum and Whedbee; Peterson.)

For some reason, although accompanying him to Timnah, Samson's parents do not observe this feat. Possibly they hide while he struggles with the young lion, and he refrains from telling them (v.6) that he has killed the animal. Withholding infor-mation from his parents appears later in this story line and is probably related to the fact that they have been commissioned to protect his Nazirite status, which would be compromised by contact with the dead lion. This deception is the beginning of a trickster/deception motif that runs throughout the Samson account (Matthews, "Freedom and Entrapment," 245–57).

As the story line continues in vv.8–9, Samson compromises his Nazirite status even further, not only by approaching the dead carcass of the lion he has killed but also by scooping honey from the beehive subsequently built within the carcass. He is now not just touching something severely unclean (a dead carcass) but also eating food that has come in contact with such uncleanness (for uncleanness laws related to corpses, see Lev 11:24–25, 39). (One can discern within rabbinic literature a distinction between unclean [*ṭmʾ*], very unclean [*ʾb htwmʾh* = "father of impurity," for major impurity], most unclean [*ʾb ʾbwt htwmʾh* = "father of fathers of impurity," for contact with corpse; cf. Philip P. Jenson, *Graded Holiness: A Key to the Priestly Conception of the World* [JSOTSup 106; Sheffield: JSOT, 1992], 45; Boda, *Severe Mercy*, 50–52. For passing uncleanness between items, see Boda, *Haggai/Zechariah*, 143–46.)

Again Samson hides the source of the honey from his parents, who have been commissioned to protect his Nazirite status. While this episode depicts for the first time Samson's divine endowment for a great physical feat and does set up the riddle he will tell at the betrothal ceremony in vv.10–18, it also reveals the deliberate folly of Samson in compromising the first two of the three prohibitions listed by the angel of the Lord in 13:4–5 and legislated in Numbers 6 (see Note on 14:10). This folly sets up an expectation that Samson is on his way to compromising the third prohibition (against cutting his hair), which is emphasized most heavily by the angel in 13:5.

NOTE

7 וַיְדַבֵּר (*way*ᵉ*dabbēr*, "talked"). This phrase most likely refers to "pre-nuptial negotiations and not simply to a conversation" (Galpaz-Feller, *Samson*, 91).

c. Samson, the Wedding Feast, and a Riddle (14:10–18)

¹⁰Now his father went down to see the woman. And Samson made a feast there, as was customary for bridegrooms. ¹¹When he appeared, he was given thirty companions.

¹²"Let me tell you a riddle," Samson said to them. "If you can give me the answer within the seven days of the feast, I will give you thirty linen garments and thirty sets of clothes. ¹³If you can't tell me the answer, you must give me thirty linen garments and thirty sets of clothes."

"Tell us your riddle," they said. "Let's hear it."

¹⁴He replied,

"Out of the eater, something to eat;
    out of the strong, something sweet."

For three days they could not give the answer.

¹⁵On the fourth day, they said to Samson's wife, "Coax your husband into explaining the riddle for us, or we will burn you and your father's household to death. Did you invite us here to rob us?"

¹⁶Then Samson's wife threw herself on him, sobbing, "You hate me! You don't really love me. You've given my people a riddle, but you haven't told me the answer."

"I haven't even explained it to my father or mother," he replied, "so why should I explain it to you?" ¹⁷She cried the whole seven days of the feast. So on the seventh day he finally told her, because she continued to press him. She in turn explained the riddle to her people.

¹⁸Before sunset on the seventh day the men of the town said to him,

"What is sweeter than honey?
    What is stronger than a lion?"

Samson said to them,

"If you had not plowed with my heifer,
    you would not have solved my riddle."

COMMENTARY

10–14 Samson's father completes the negotiations with the woman's family in v.10, and the agreement is sealed with a feast (see below), hosted by Samson according to the custom of that time (on ancient wedding customs, see Galpaz-Feller, *Samson*, 93–116). According to vv.12 and 17–18 this custom involved a seven-day betrothal period. The Israelite custom in Genesis 29:23–27 also speaks of a seven-day betrothal feast, at the beginning of which came the sexual union (v.23). This union, however, was not the consummation of the betrothal since it required the full seven-day period (vv.27–28; see Schneider, 209; see comments on 14:19–20). It is possible that the custom described here in vv.10–14 is Philistine, in which case consummation was left until the end of the feast (Yadin, 417).

According to vv.10–14 another aspect of this custom entailed thirty young men joining Samson as his "companions" (*mērēaʿ* GK 5335), a term used elsewhere for a close friend akin to a brother (Ge 26:26; Pr 19:7; 2Sa 3:8; Job 6:14). That this group is called "the men of the town" in 14:18 reveals they are from the bride's clan and are standing in as his "groomsmen" (in modern terms) for the betrothal ritual (though possibly also as a security detail to keep control of Samson; see Note on 14:11; Block, 434).

At the feast Samson challenges his "companions" with a riddle (on the function of ancient riddles, see Galpaz-Feller, *Samson*, 109–16), which serves not only to create an opportunity for his first act of delivering Israel from the Philistines, but at the same time makes light of his earlier acts that compromised his Nazirite status. By basing his riddle on a story (14:5–9) whose vocabulary and motifs foreshadow the ultimate deadly encounter between Samson and the Philistines (15:15–19), Samson "in effect foretold the Philistines what would happen to them" (Emmrich, 73; see comments on 14:5–9). The riddle may also tragically foreshadow his demise by revealing that "sweetness/honey" (i.e., love/sex) will conquer "strength" (i.e., Samson: Crenshaw, 99–120; Philip Nel, "The Riddle of Samson [Judg 14,14.18]," *Bib* 66 [1985]: 534–45; Block, 435; for honey as symbol of fertility, see Niditch, *Judges*, 156).

Samson promises that if his "companions" can solve the riddle during the feast, he will give to them valuable items of clothing (see Note on v.12). While all thirty will receive one set of clothing each if they can solve the riddle, if they fail, Samson is to receive thirty sets for himself alone. Their request to hear the riddle signals their willingness to participate.

15–18 It may seem at first that the Philistines have little chance of solving this riddle since it describes something that no one but Samson has experienced. Some have suggested that the riddle is unsolvable (Galpaz-Feller, *Samson*, 111) or contains allusions to fertility and sexuality (see above), which may have at least given the "companions" some initial hope (see Nel; Claudia V. Camp and Carole R. Fontaine, "The Words of the Wise and their Riddles," in *Text and Tradition* [ed. Susan Niditch; Atlanta: Scholars, 1990], 127–51). While these latter nuances are likely in play, they are probably meant to mislead the Philistines, even though they contribute to the meaning on the narratival level by highlighting once again Samson's vulnerability. Kim, 252, summarizes the best argument when he writes: "The correct answer to his riddle should have been *ʾărî mēʾărî* (honey from a lion) because in early Hebrew *ʾărî* could mean both 'honey' and 'lion.' It is likely that the Philistines contemplated this solution but rejected it because of its absurdity."

On the fourth day they threaten Samson's wife and her family with a fiery death if she does not pry the answer to the riddle out of Samson; this forces the woman to plead through tears with her bridegroom. After days of imploring she gets the answer from Samson on the final day of the feast and relays the information to her violent clan members, who are able to answer Samson before the sun goes down.

The original riddle was given in poetic form, so their answer is given in poetic form as a coun-ter riddle, possibly to tease Samson or to con-ceal their source (Kim, 427). Samson will not be mocked, however, and responds in kind with more poetry, revealing that he knows the source of their information.

This experience with the woman from Timnah introduces a consistent motif seen throughout the account of Samson. Most of the motifs used here in vv.15–17 will reappear in the climactic Deli-lah account in 16:5–18, the latter leading to Sam-son's demise (Exum, "Aspects of Symmetry," 3–29; Mobley, 88). His relationship with women will prove fatal, yet Yahweh will use this attraction to bring Israel into conflict with their overlords.

NOTES

10, 12, 17 מִשְׁתֶּה (misteh, "feast"). This term denotes a banquet with wine (1Sa 25:36–37; cf. Ge 21:8; 26:30; Est 1:3, 5, 9) — an obvious problem for one designated as a Nazirite.

11 כִּרְאוֹתָם (kir'ōtām, "when he appeared"; "when they saw," NASB). Possibly this word should be translated not as an infinitive construct of רָאה (r'h) but of יָרֵא (yr') and rendered "when they feared him," identifying the reason for the "thirty companions" (Boling, 231).

12 שְׁלֹשִׁים סְדִינִים וּשְׁלֹשִׁים חֲלִפֹת בְּגָדִים (šᵉlōšîm sᵉdînîm ûšᵉlōšîm ḥᵃlipōt bᵉgādîm," thirty linen garments and thirty sets of clothes"). סָדִין (sādîn) probably refers to linen undergarments (cf. Isa 3:23; Pr 31:24), while חֲלִפֹת בְּגָדִים (ḥᵃlipōt bᵉgādîm) signifies changes of clothing beyond the undergarments (Ge 45:22; 2Ki 5:2, 22–23).

15 בַּיּוֹם הַשְּׁבִיעִי (bayyôm haššᵉbî'î, "on the seventh day"). The NIV follows the ancient versions in its reading (see the LXX's ἐν τῇ ἡμέρᾳ τῇ τετάρτῃ [en tē hēmera tē tetartē, "on the fourth day"; cf. Syriac, Old Latin). The Targum and Vulgate follow the MT, however, in reading "seventh" (see note on 14:17).

17 וַתֵּבְךְּ עָלָיו שִׁבְעַת הַיָּמִים (wattēbk 'ālāyw šib'at hayyāmîm, "She cried the whole seven days of the feast"). The Hebrew text reads, "she wept before/against him," making explicit the object of her cry-ing. Since according to v.15 it was only on the fourth (or seventh, if following the MT) day that the woman was approached by her clan members, the phrase "the seven days of the feast" ("whole" not being represented in the Hebrew text) must refer to the remainder of the seven days (Block, 434). This phrase repeats vocabulary from v.16, thus signaling a return "to the main line of thought after any digression" (Revell, 426).

d. Samson Pays His Debts and Abandons His Bride (14:19–20)

> ¹⁹Then the Spirit of the LORD came upon him in power. He went down to Ashkelon, struck down thirty of their men, stripped them of their belongings and gave their clothes to those who had explained the riddle. Burning with anger, he went up to his father's house. ²⁰And Samson's wife was given to the friend who had attended him at his wedding.

COMMENTARY

19–20 In the wake of the betrothal feast Samson once again experiences that forceful entry of the Spirit of the Lord that he first experienced when the young lion lunged at him in the vineyards of Timnah (14:6; cf. 15:14). The Spirit empowers him to go down to one of the five key Philistine cities on the coastal plain (Ashkelon), kill thirty Philistine men, and then bring back their clothes to fulfill his promise to the thirty "companions." Filled with rage, however, he does not retrieve his bride but returns without her to the house of his father (see Note).

His return leaves unfulfilled the essential final step in the betrothal process (see Ge 24; also comments on 14:10–14); therefore Samson's wife is given to one of the Philistine companions who were part of the betrothal ritual, possibly the very one who was charged with guarding the couple's bridal chamber according to ancient Philistine custom (Yadin, 418).

NOTE

19 חֲלִיצוֹתָם (ḥªlîṣôtām, "their belongings"). This word refers to plunder taken from a slain warrior; it need not refer to weaponry (contra Block, 436). Here it signifies instead the changes of clothes (הַחֲלִיפוֹת, haḥªlîpôt—notice the rhyming technique) that constituted payment for the lost contest.

בֵּית אָבִיהוּ (bêt ʾābîhû, "his father's house"). This sociological term designates the smallest family unit in Israel (see Note on 13:2; Introduction; *ABD*, 2:762).

4. Samson's Exploits against the Philistines (15:1–19)

OVERVIEW

The events of ch. 14 reveal a progression in Samson's exploits, beginning with his killing of the young lion and moving to slaying the thirty men of Ashkelon, both actions explicitly linked to the empowerment of the Spirit of Yahweh (14:6, 19). These actions in ch. 14 are restricted to the local level, beginning with Samson's involvement with the small town of Timnah and his quick foray into the city of Ashkelon to obtain the payment for his lost riddle contest. His actions, however, soon have a much greater impact and will draw Judah into military conflict with the Philistines. Once again the Spirit of Yahweh empowers him, this time in a military conflict (15:14).

a. Samson Returns for His Bride (15:1-2)

> [1]Later on, at the time of wheat harvest, Samson took a young goat and went to visit his wife. He said, "I'm going to my wife's room." But her father would not let him go in.
> [2]"I was so sure you thoroughly hated her," he said, "that I gave her to your friend. Isn't her younger sister more attractive? Take her instead."

COMMENTARY

1–2 The initial verses of ch. 15 provide a narrative segue between Samson's actions on the local level and those on the national level. As already noted at the end of ch. 14, when Samson does not complete the betrothal ritual by taking his bride into the house of his father, the bride's father gives her away to one of the thirty Philistine "companions" who accompanied Samson at the betrothal feast. The setting of the story is now placed during the wheat harvest—important information for Samson's vengeful act in vv.3–5, but also "a time ripe with conjugal possibilities" (Niditch, *Judges*, 158).

Samson, with dinner in hand ("a young goat"), arrives in Timnah to "visit" his bride in her room, possibly expressing his desire to recommence the betrothal process, which had been frustrated by his anger at the conclusion of the feast (see comments on 14:10–14, 19–20). There is ambiguity in the language used here: "go into her in the inner chamber," which may have sexual innuendo or mean lit-

erally to have sexual intercourse (Mobley, 40). The young goat may be a gift related to the betrothal or consummation ritual, or possibly an expression of remorse for not having completed the betrothal ritual before.

The woman's father, however, restricts him, explaining to him that he has given her away to one of Samson's "companions" from the betrothal ritual. But he would be happy to give the next daughter in line to Samson and even suggests that her beauty exceeds the older sister's (cf. Ge 29:14–30; 1Sa 18:17–29). While ancient Near Eastern legal codes allow for the discontinuation of a betrothal process (with penalty), they typically forbid the subsequent giving of the bride to a "friend" of the groom (Galpaz-Feller, *Samson*, 124; see, e.g., Hammurabi §161). Special laws cover cases in which a man deserts his wife (e.g., Hammurabi §136), and possibly it is such conventions that justified the action by the bride's father.

NOTE

2 שָׂנֹא שְׂנֵאתָהּ (*śānōʾ śᵉnēʾtāh*, "you thoroughly hated her"). This comment may mean that Samson's actions were interpreted as legally breaking off the relationship (Block, 439; see Dt 22:13–16; cf. 24:3; 21:15). In the later Elephantine documents, "hatred money" and "judgment of hatred" are technical terms related to divorce trials (Galpaz-Feller, *Samson*, 125).

b. Samson's Revenge (15:3–5)

³Samson said to them, "This time I have a right to get even with the Philistines; I will really harm them." ⁴So he went out and caught three hundred foxes and tied them tail to tail in pairs. He then fastened a torch to every pair of tails, ⁵lit the torches and let the foxes loose in the standing grain of the Philistines. He burned up the shocks and standing grain, together with the vineyards and olive groves.

COMMENTARY

3–5 The loss of his bride prompts Samson to utter a threat against "them," a reference to the Philistines as a whole. He takes three hundred foxes and binds their tails together in pairs with a torch between each pair of tails. The frightened and confused foxes run haphazardly throughout the ripe grain, starting a blaze that spreads even to the vineyards and olive groves, which robs the Philistines of the sources of their three basic foodstuffs.

c. The Philistines' Revenge (15:6)

⁶When the Philistines asked, "Who did this?" they were told, "Samson, the Timnite's son-in-law, because his wife was given to his friend."
So the Philistines went up and burned her and her father to death.

COMMENTARY

6 Samson's act of vengeance is the first step in a conflict that soon spins out of control. The Philistines burn to death Samson's bride and her father, fulfilling the same threat first uttered by the "companions" of Samson in 14:15 (i.e., the Philistine "men of the town" [14:18]) and returning Samson's vengeance with vengeance. The irony is that Samson's bride tried to avoid this fate by prying the answer to the riddle from Samson, but in the end this action sealed her destiny (see Block, 433).

d. Samson's Revenge and Flight (15:7–8)

⁷Samson said to them, "Since you've acted like this, I won't stop until I get my revenge on you." ⁸He attacked them viciously and slaughtered many of them. Then he went down and stayed in a cave in the rock of Etam.

COMMENTARY

7–8 The Philistines' murder of Samson's bride only stokes Samson's anger, and he attacks and slaughters many of them. He retreats to safety in a cave at the Rock of Etam. While there are two towns called Etam in the OT, one in northern Judah (2Ch 11:6; cf. 1Ch 4:3) and the other in the region occupied by Simeon (1Ch 4:32), the Rock of Etam in view here is most likely on the northern side of the Sorek Valley (*ABD*, 2:644).

e. The Philistines Assemble for War (15:9–10)

⁹The Philistines went up and camped in Judah, spreading out near Lehi. ¹⁰The men of Judah asked, "Why have you come to fight us?"

"We have come to take Samson prisoner," they answered, "to do to him as he did to us."

COMMENTARY

9–10 The Rock of Etam apparently was near the unknown location called "Lehi," which means "jawbone" (Eze 29:4; 38:4; Job 40:26; Hos 11:4; Isa 30:28) or "cheek" (1Ki 22:24; 2Ch 18:23; Job 16:10; Ps 3:8; SS 5:13; Isa 50:6; La 3:30; Mic 4:14). The origin of this name may be related to this very event (see 15:17), but on a narrative level foreshadows the weapon Samson will use to defeat the Philistines. The terms "went up" and "camped" in v.9 reveal that Samson's actions have provoked a fullscale military response from the Philistines (see Note), not just against Samson but against the entire tribe of Judah.

Knowing they have done nothing to provoke this aggression, the leaders of the tribe of Judah approach the Philistine leaders and discover that the focus of their aggression is limited to Samson and that they would be satisfied to leave the region with him bound as a prisoner.

NOTE

9 וַיַּעֲלוּ פְלִשְׁתִּים וַיַּחֲנוּ בִּיהוּדָה (*wayyaᶜᵃlû pᵉlištîm wayyaḥᵃnû bîhûdâ*, "The Philistines went up and camped in Judah"). The combination of עלה (ᶜlh) and חנה (ḥnh) signals military maneuvers (cf. Jos 4:19; 8:11; 10:5; Jdg 18:12; 1Sa 11:1; 13:5). In the phrase וַיַּחֲנוּ בִּיהוּדָה (*wayyaḥᵃnû bîhûdâ*, "camped in Judah"), most likely the preposition bᵉ here is adversative ("encamped against Judah") and takes the place of the normal preposition following חנה (ḥnh), which is על (ᶜl, adversative; see Jos 10:31, 34; Jdg 6:4; 1Sa 11:1; 2Sa 12:28; 2Ch 32:1).

f. Judahites Negotiate with Samson (15:11–13)

> ¹¹Then three thousand men from Judah went down to the cave in the rock of Etam and said to Samson, "Don't you realize that the Philistines are rulers over us? What have you done to us?"
>
> He answered, "I merely did to them what they did to me."
>
> ¹²They said to him, "We've come to tie you up and hand you over to the Philistines." Samson said, "Swear to me that you won't kill me yourselves."
>
> ¹³"Agreed," they answered. "We will only tie you up and hand you over to them. We will not kill you." So they bound him with two new ropes and led him up from the rock.

COMMENTARY

11–13 The leaders of Judah, cowering before the more powerful Philistines, are quite willing to sacrifice this Danite for the sake of peace with their overlords. This willingness reveals the demoralization of the people at this late stage in the downward spiral of the book of Judges (McCann, 105). The depiction also reminds the reader that Judah is not always glorious (see also 1:19). Thus three thousand or three large units of Judahites approach Samson's hideout to confront him. He is willing to be bound as the Philistines have requested but asks that the Judahites not kill him when he is bound. References here to "new ropes" and their inability to control Samson (v.14) foreshadow Samson's tragic episode with Delilah (16:9–12; Niditch, *Judges*, 159).

NOTE

12 פֶּן־תִּפְגְּעוּן בִּי אַתֶּם (*pen-tipgᵉʿûn bî ʾattem*, "that you won't kill me yourselves"). The LXX[a] (Lucianic and OL) has prior to this: μὴ ἀποκτεῖναί με ὑμεῖς καὶ παράδοτέ με αὐτοῖς (*mē apokteinai me hymeis kai paradote me autois*), which retroverts to פן תמיתוני ותתנוני להם (*pn tmytwny wttnwny lhm*, "that you will not kill me even though you give me to them"; Kim, 160). This *parablepsis* was most likely caused by *homoioarkton* as the scribe's eye moved from the first פֶן (*pn*) to the second פֶן (*pn*).

g. Samson Defeats the Philistine Army (15:14–17)

> [14]As he approached Lehi, the Philistines came toward him shouting. The Spirit of the LORD came upon him in power. The ropes on his arms became like charred flax, and the bindings dropped from his hands. [15]Finding a fresh jawbone of a donkey, he grabbed it and struck down a thousand men.
>
> [16]Then Samson said,
>
> "With a donkey's jawbone
>   I have made donkeys of them.
> With a donkey's jawbone
>   I have killed a thousand men."
>
> [17]When he finished speaking, he threw away the jawbone; and the place was called Ramath Lehi.

COMMENTARY

14–17 The Judahites are true to their word (v.13) and bring him safely to the Philistines, encamped at Lehi. But as Samson hears the battle cry of the Philistines (see Note), the Spirit of the Lord comes forcefully upon him (see 14:6, 19) so that he is able to tear his bonds to pieces as though they were merely burnt flax. The fact that the Philistines raise a battle cry suggests that they may have been using this incident as a ruse to inflict a military defeat on Judah. Empowered by the Spirit, Samson singlehandedly defeats a thousand men (or a large military unit) using only the jawbone of a donkey he found on the ground in an act reminiscent of Shamgar's earlier act (3:31; Webb, 165).

As seen at prior points in the account of Samson, poetry is used to make the event memorable. The poem plays off the Hebrew word for donkey, which shares the same letters with the root used for "heap"—possibly a double entendre pointing to the heaps of bodies as well as the shame of the defeated Philistines. Through this poem he cel-ebrates his killing of the thousand (or troop). In the end he throws away the jawbone from which the place, Ramath Lehi, gained its name (see below).

NOTES

14 הֵרִיעוּ (*hērî'û*, "shouting"). This term is used for raising a battle cry in Joshua 6:5, 10, 16, 20; 1 Samuel 17:20, 52; 2 Chronicles 13:12, 15; Isaiah 42:13; Jeremiah 50:15; Hosea 5:8; and Joel 2:1.

17 רָמַת לֶחִי (*rāmat leḥî*, "Ramath Lehi"). This name means "hill of a jawbone." Notice the paronomasia between רָמַת (*rāmat*, "Ramath") and the word חֲמֹרָתָיִם (*ḥᵃmōrātāyim*, "donkeys/heaps") in 15:16 (Kim, 428).

h. Samson's Cry to God (15:18–19)

> **18**Because he was very thirsty, he cried out to the LORD, "You have given your servant this great victory. Must I now die of thirst and fall into the hands of the uncircumcised?" **19**Then God opened up the hollow place in Lehi, and water came out of it. When Samson drank, his strength returned and he revived. So the spring was called En Hakkore, and it is still there in Lehi.

COMMENTARY

18–19 The physical exertion of battle leaves Samson dying of thirst, and he cries out to Yahweh for help. God miraculously opens up a spring, from which the strong man drinks and so "his spirit returned," a collocation that probably refers to regaining his physical strength while at the same time alluding to his possession of Yahweh's Spirit. As with the earlier miracle in battle, this divine wonder is commemorated in the name of the spring, En Hakkore, which means "spring of the one who called."

This cry links Samson with his ancestors in the wilderness (cf. Ex 17:1–7 with Nu 20), thus identifying him with the same community that ultimately rebelled (Dennis T. Olson, "The Book of Judges," *The New Interpreter's Bible* [ed. Leander E. Keck; Nashville: Abingdon, 1998], 2:851); but Samson's cry for help also foreshadows his final cry in 16:28, when he asks God to strengthen him one more time in order to bring vengeance on the Philistines (Amit, *Judges*, 279). This first cry is for life; the second will be for death (Webb,

167). Note that Samson is defined by physicality, whether that is in personal desires (sexual fulfillment, eating honey, drinking water) or his great feats (killing a young lion, thirty men of Ashkelon, many Philistines from Timnah, and a thousand/troop of Philistines).

NOTE

19 בַּלֶּחִי ... וַיְּחִי (*wayyeḥî* ...*ballehî*, "and he revived ...in Lehi"). Kim, 428, notes the paronomasia between these two words in the Hebrew text.

5. First Concluding Notice (15:20)

²⁰Samson led Israel for twenty years in the days of the Philistines.

COMMENTARY

20 Verse 20 echoes the concluding notices found regularly throughout the second half of Judges (10:2—Tola; 10:3—Jair; 12:7—Jephthah; 12:9—Ibzan; 12:11—Elon; 12:14—Abdon). This verse, however, does not conclude the account of Samson, which will end with the second concluding notice in 16:31. Though this verse may have marked the end of an earlier edition of the account of Samson (Fensham, 82–83; cf. Boling, 240, 252), its purpose in the final form of the book is to note the climax of the account. In the speech of Judges 13:5 the angel of Yahweh identified Samson as a "savior" or "deliverer" of Israel, words derived from a Hebrew root (*yšʿ*) associated with many figures throughout Judges (2:16, 18; 3:9, 15, 31; 6:14–15, 36–37; 7:2, 7; 8:22; 10:1, 12–13; cf. 10:14; 12:2–3). In the present verse Samson is identified as one who "judged" Israel, the other root (*špṭ*) often associated with judge-deliverers throughout the book (Jdg 2:16–19; 3:10; 4:4; 10:2–3; 11:27; 12:7–9, 11, 13–14; cf. 16:31).

6. Samson and the Harlot in Gaza (16:1–3)

¹One day Samson went to Gaza, where he saw a prostitute. He went in to spend the night with her. ²The people of Gaza were told, "Samson is here!" So they surrounded the

place and lay in wait for him all night at the city gate. They made no move during the night, saying, "At dawn we'll kill him."

³But Samson lay there only until the middle of the night. Then he got up and took hold of the doors of the city gate, together with the two posts, and tore them loose, bar and all. He lifted them to his shoulders and carried them to the top of the hill that faces Hebron.

COMMENTARY

1 While the previous episode took place on traditional Israelite land, this one is set within Philistine territory — in particular, in Gaza, one of the five main fortified cities of the Philistines. Samson had ventured into another of these cities (Ashkelon) to obtain the clothing he needed to pay off the men of Timnah (14:19), but no mention of his lodging in the city is made in that earlier episode. Fresh from his devastating victory over the Philistines at Lehi, Samson enters into the heart of the largest of the Philistine fortified cities, where a prostitute catches his eye, so he hires her for the night (for ancient evidence on prostitution see Galpaz-Feller, *Samson*, 133–48). As in the earlier episode in Timnah (14:1–2), so here Samson's sexual passions lead him into a place of danger. In contrast to the earlier episode, however, Samson has now moved beyond the cultural mores of betrothal and merely hires a woman to fulfill his sexual needs.

2–3 Knowing about his physical might, the people of Gaza devise a plan to capture him in the morning when Samson, still groggy from the deep sleep that follows his sexual activity, will be vulnerable. The narrator provides the short, pithy statements of the people of the city, accentuating the tension of the moment and their thirst for his blood.

Samson, however, beats them to the punch by arising in the middle of the night, tearing off the city gate and the posts that hold it, and carrying them off to the top of a hill facing due east, that is, toward Hebron, which lay twenty-five miles from Gaza. The removal of the protective "gate" to Judahite territory is symbolic of Samson's power over the Philistines and possibly also a challenge to Judah to resist (Matthews, "Freedom and Entrapment," 253). Furthermore, this episode reveals the Philistine inability to stop this Danite strongman. It is obvious that he can come and go as he pleases. At the same time it also accentuates the continued moral decline of this judge-deliverer, whose sexual passions leave him vulnerable to plots on his life. The Philistines will ultimately capitalize on his sexual vulnerabilities to bring an end to his life.

7. Samson and Delilah (16:4–21a)

a. Samson Falls in Love with Delilah (16:4)

⁴Some time later, he fell in love with a woman in the Valley of Sorek whose name was Delilah.

COMMENTARY

4 As with the previous three episodes in the account of Samson (14:1–20; 15:1–20; 16:1–3), so also this final episode begins with Samson's passionate attraction to a woman. While in the previous passages the woman's name is not provided, in this climactic and fatal episode her name is given as Delilah (Galpaz-Feller, *Samson*, 165), a name that has been related (1) to a Semitic root for "hang" (possibly "dangling curls"); (2) to a Semitic root for amorous/coquettish gesture (BDB; possibly, "flirtatious"; cf. *HALOT*, 222); and (3) even to the Hebrew term for "night" (*lay^elâ*), suggesting her dark role (Galpaz-Feller, *Samson*, 167). All these meanings presage her role in this story.

Delilah lived in Samson's home region in the Valley of Sorek, that Danite region between Judah and Philistia (see comments on 13:2). She is most likely a Philistine woman, given her close connections with the Philistine rulers (though see comments on 17:2), but because the text says these rulers must "go up" (*ʿlh*) to meet her (16:5), she probably does not live in one of their five cities (Mobley, 90). She is unique among women in the book in that initially she is not defined socially by any male figure (Matthews, *Judges and Ruth*, 159). The nature of the relationship between Samson and Delilah is not made clear in this episode as it was in the episodes concerning his earlier relationships, in which first Samson followed the social rituals of betrothal and marriage (chs. 14–15) and then bypassed them to hire the services of a prostitute (16:1–3). The only thing the narrator tells the reader is that Samson "loved" her—information that heightens the emotional attachment of this relationship above the previous two in the account of Samson (Matthews, *Judges and Ruth*, 158; Niditch, *Judges*, 168).

The verb "love" (*ʾhb*, GK 170) is often associated with opposite-sex relationships to describe not only the love expressed between spouses (Ge 24:67; Dt 21:15; 1Sa 18:20; Hos 3:1), but also the love expressed between the unmarried, including those anticipating marriage (1Sa 18:20), those with carnal lust (1Sa 13:1, 4, 15), and those in extramarital relationships (Isa 57:8; Jer 2:25; Eze 16:37). It may be that Samson had married Delilah, but the narrator's silence on this issue casts this relationship in a negative light.

b. The Philistines Bribe Delilah to Find Out the Secret of Samson's Strength (16:5)

5The rulers of the Philistines went to her and said, "See if you can lure him into showing you the secret of his great strength and how we can overpower him so we may tie him up and subdue him. Each one of us will give you eleven hundred shekels of silver."

COMMENTARY

5 While Samson's relationship with the woman from Timnah took some time to involve the higher levels of Philistine leadership, after the events at Lehi his encounters with the harlot in Gaza and with Delilah draw the immediate attention of the Philistines. The Philistine rulers have discovered his "Achilles heel" and intend to capitalize on it. These rulers are five in number (see note below), each a governor over one of the key Philistine city-states situated on the Mediterranean coastal plain to the west of the southern Israelite tribal territories.

Similarly to the way the men of Timnah used Samson's bride to pry out of Samson the answer to the wedding riddle in ch. 14, the rulers of the Philistines now use Delilah to pry out of Samson the answer to a much greater riddle, namely, the secret of his strength. The similarities between these two accounts are obvious, as seen especially in the use of identical vocabulary: "entice, lure" (*pth*; cf. 14:15 with 16:5), "press, nag" (*ṣwq*, Hiphil; cf. 14:17 with 16:16), "love" (*ʾhb*; cf. 14:17 with 16:16); and "he told her" (*wayyagged-lāh*; cf. 14:17 with 16:17). In contrast, however, while the men of Timnah used negative coercion, threatening to burn the woman and her family with fire (14:15), the rulers of the Philistines use positive coercion, offering a reward of 1,100 silver pieces from each of them—thus, 5,500 silver pieces in total. Additionally, while the secret in ch. 14 was intended as a game at a social gathering, the secret in ch. 16 will determine the fate of Samson and his nation.

NOTES

5 סַרְנֵי פְלִשְׁתִּים (*sarnê pᵉlištîm*, "the rulers of the Philistines"). The term סֶרֶן (*seren*; GK 6249) is only used in the OT for the leaders of the five Philistine city-states, namely, Ashdod, Gaza, Ashkelon, Gath, and Ekron, which controlled the Canaanite coastal plain (cf. Jos 13:3; Jdg 3:3; 5:8, 11; 6:4, 12, 16–18; 7:7; 29:2, 6–7; 1Chr 12:19–20). The etymology of the term is debated, though it may have originated from the Hittite word for "judge" (see *ABD*, 5:327).

לְעַנֹּותֹו (*lᵉʿannōtô*, "and subdue him"). See Note on 19:24 for the possible sexual connotation of this term, here possibly a reference to the emasculation of Samson (Galpaz-Feller, *Samson*, 168–69).

c. Attempts One through Three (16:6–14)

> ⁶So Delilah said to Samson, "Tell me the secret of your great strength and how you can be tied up and subdued."
>
> ⁷Samson answered her, "If anyone ties me with seven fresh thongs that have not been dried, I'll become as weak as any other man."
>
> ⁸Then the rulers of the Philistines brought her seven fresh thongs that had not been dried, and she tied him with them. ⁹With men hidden in the room, she called to him, "Samson, the Philistines are upon you!" But he snapped the thongs as easily as a piece of string snaps when it comes close to a flame. So the secret of his strength was not discovered.
>
> ¹⁰Then Delilah said to Samson, "You have made a fool of me; you lied to me. Come now, tell me how you can be tied."

> ¹¹He said, "If anyone ties me securely with new ropes that have never been used, I'll become as weak as any other man."
>
> ¹²So Delilah took new ropes and tied him with them. Then, with men hidden in the room, she called to him, "Samson, the Philistines are upon you!" But he snapped the ropes off his arms as if they were threads.
>
> ¹³Delilah then said to Samson, "Until now, you have been making a fool of me and lying to me. Tell me how you can be tied."
>
> He replied, "If you weave the seven braids of my head into the fabric on the loom and tighten it with the pin, I'll become as weak as any other man." So while he was sleeping, Delilah took the seven braids of his head, wove them into the fabric ¹⁴and tightened it with the pin.
>
> Again she called to him, "Samson, the Philistines are upon you!" He awoke from his sleep and pulled up the pin and the loom, with the fabric.

COMMENTARY

6–14 The narrator characterizes Delilah as showing no signs of resistance to the Philistine proposal. Instead of recording Delilah's answer to the Philistine rulers, the narrator moves immediately to depict Delilah's asking Samson to tell her the secret of his strength. Here motifs foreshadowed already in 14:15–17 reappear, but this time they spell doom for the foolish Samson (Exum, "Aspects of Symmetry," 3–29; Mobley, 88).

These verses contain Delilah's first three unsuccessful attempts, each following the same template: (1) Delilah asks Samson to tell her the secret of his strength (vv.6, 10, 13a); (2) Samson suggests a method to immobilize him (vv.7, 11, 13b); (3) Delilah applies the method and then cries out "the Philistines are upon you, Samson" (vv.8–9a, 12a, 14a); but (4) Samson easily frees himself (vv.9b, 12b, 14b). There are slight variations among these attempts. In the first attempt the Philistine rulers are involved in the preparation of the binding method, while in the other two Delilah prepares it alone. In the first and second attempts the narrator makes reference to men lying in wait, while in the third such a reference is missing, though it is assumed by Delilah's cry.

Each of the attempts involves a different method for overcoming Samson's power. For the first Samson suggests "fresh thongs" ($y^e t\bar{a}r\hat{i}m$ $lah\hat{i}m$), the latter a term also used to describe the string of a bow (Ps 11:2; Job 30:11). These thongs are "fresh" and so would tighten as they dried.

In the second attempt Samson suggests "new ropes" ($^{c}ab\bar{o}t\hat{i}m$ $h^a d\bar{a}\check{s}\hat{i}m$), the same method used by the Judahites when they delivered Samson to the Philistines in Judges 15:13–14. This term refers to ropes used for rigging that was strong enough for pulling a cart with cattle (Isa 5:18; Hos 11:4; cf. Job 39:10), for binding a sacrifice to an altar (Ps 118:27), and for bonds that could securely control a human being (Pss 2:3; 118:27; Eze 3:25; 4:8). These ropes were "new" and so not worn from use.

In the third attempt Samson suggests weaving the locks of his hair together. Samson's long hair is woven into seven braids, making it manageable, especially for physical activity. The number seven here is suggestive of the perfection of his hair as the source of his power. The braided hair was to be woven into fabric on a handloom (see 16:14). This suggestion reveals that Samson's resistance is breaking down as he comes dangerously close to revealing the true source of his strength. The description of Delilah's actions in vv.13–14 has her "tight-ening" the woven braids "with the pin" (*wattitqaʿ bayyāted*) while Samson sleeps (following the LXX; see Notes). This same phrase appears in Judges 4:21 (*wattitqaʿ ʾet-hayyāted*) to describe Jael driving the peg through Sisera's temple while he slept. Once again a great warrior entrusts himself into the hands of a cunning woman, but in "an ironic twist," for now it is Israel's hero rather than enemy who is in danger (Schneider, 227).

NOTES

7–9 יְתָרִים לַחִים (*yᵉtārîm laḥîm*, "fresh thongs"). The first term ("thongs") is used for bowstrings (Ps 11:2; Job 30:11) and possibly tent cords (Job 4:21). Such thongs were possibly made from the tendons of a slaughtered animal (*HALOT*, 452). The second term ("fresh") is used of fresh grapes in Numbers 6:3 and green wood in Ezekiel 17:24; 21:3.

9 בַּהֲרִיחוֹ אֵשׁ (*bahᵃrîḥô ʾēš*, "when it comes close to a flame"). The Hebrew here could be translated more woodenly as "when it smells [i.e., senses] the fire."

13–14 אִם־תַּאַרְגִי אֶת־שֶׁבַע מַחְלְפוֹת רֹאשִׁי עִם־הַמַּסָּכֶת ... וַתִּתְקַע בַּיָּתֵד (*ʾim-taʾargî ʾet-šebaʿ maḥlᵉpôt rōʾšî ʿim-hammassāket ... wattitqaʿ bayyāted*, "If you weave the seven braids of my head into the fabric on the loom ... and tightened it with the pin"). The MT does not contain the material after the word "the fabric on the loom" to the end of v.13. The words "' ... and tighten it with the pin, I'll become as weak as any other man.' So while he was sleeping, Delilah took the seven braids of his head, wove them into the fabric" are based on the LXX's Lucianic and Old Latin recensions, which echo the other episodes in vv.7, 11, 17. The LXXᵃ reads at the end of v.13 and beginning of v.14: καὶ ἐγκρούσῃς ἐν τῷ πασσάλῳ εἰς τὸν τοῖχον, καὶ ἔσομαι ἀσθενὴς ὡς εἷς τῶν ἀνθρώπων. καὶ ἐκοίμισεν αὐτὸν Δαλιλα καὶ ἐδιάσατο τοὺς ἑπτὰ βοστρύχους τῆς κεφαλῆς αὐτοῦ μετὰ τῆς ἐκτάσεως (*kai enkrousēs en tō passalō eis ton toichon, kai esomai asthenēs hōs heis tōn anthrōpōn. kai ekoimisen auton Dalila kai ediasato tous hepta bostrychous tēs kephalēs autou meta tēs ektaseōs*) which, if based on a Hebrew Vorlage, would retrovert as: v.13: אֶת־שֶׁבַע מַחְלְפוֹת רֹאשׁוֹ עִם־הַמַּסֶּכֶת and v.14 וְתָקַפְתְּ בַּיָּתֵד אֶל־הַקִּיר וְחָלִיתִי וְהָיִיתִי כְּאַחַד הָאָדָם וַתְּישֵׁנֵהוּ וַתַּאֲרִיג ([v.13] *wᵉtāqap bᵉyāted ʾel-haqqîr wᵉḥālîtî wᵉhāyîtî kᵉʾaḥad hāʾādām* [and v.14] *wattᵉyaššᵉnēhû wattaʾᵃrîg ʾet-šebaʿ maḥlᵉpôt rōšô ʿim-hammasseket* [BHS]). This reading is most likely due to a scribal error (haplography), with the copyist's eye moving from וְתָקַעַת בַּיָּתֵד (*wᵉtāqapat bᵉyāted*, v.13) to וַתִּתְקַע בַּיָּתֵד (*wattitqaʿ bayyāted*, v.14; cf. Kim, 161–63; for the view that here is part of a different narrative tradition, see Niditch, *Judges*, 165).

d. Final Attempt (16:15–21a)

[15]Then she said to him,"How can you say,'I love you,' when you won't confide in me? This is the third time you have made a fool of me and haven't told me the secret of your great strength." [16]With such nagging she prodded him day after day until he was tired to death.

[17]So he told her everything."No razor has ever been used on my head," he said, "because I have been a Nazirite set apart to God since birth. If my head were shaved, my strength would leave me, and I would become as weak as any other man."

[18]When Delilah saw that he had told her everything, she sent word to the rulers of the Philistines ,"Come back once more; he has told me everything." So the rulers of the Philistines returned with the silver in their hands. [19]Having put him to sleep on her lap, she called a man to shave off the seven braids of his hair, and so began to subdue him. And his strength left him.

[20]Then she called,"Samson, the Philistines are upon you!"

He awoke from his sleep and thought,"I'll go out as before and shake myself free." But he did not know that the LORD had left him.

[21]Then the Philistines seized him, gouged out his eyes and took him down to Gaza.

COMMENTARY

15–21a While the fourth attempt does contain the same elements of the first three, it is considerably longer. Delilah now does not merely accuse Samson of making a fool of and lying to her (vv.10, 13), but also questions his love for her (v.15). As happened in the earlier story of Samson and his bride from Timnah (14:16–17), this shift in argument, together with an increase in the intensity of the inquiry, ultimately breaks down Samson's will. He links his strength to his Nazirite status (v.17; see comments on ch. 13). With his long hair Samson is "holy to Yahweh," set apart for divine service, but without his hair that holy service will come to a close and with it the Spirit's physical empowerment (Webb, 170). Though known for his wise "riddles," Samson is depicted as the ultimate fool, unable to recognize that he is being led like a lamb to the slaughter, and even after revealing his secret, he continues his dangerous liaison with Delilah.

Delilah arranges with the Philistine rulers the exchange of her Samson for their silver, then hires a barber to remove the seven braids once Samson has fallen asleep on her lap (cf. Jdg 4:21; Matthews, *Judges and Ruth*, 163). Delilah's abuse of Samson (v.19) is followed by her shout that the Philistines are upon him (v.20), just as the loss of his strength (v.19) coincides with the departure of Yahweh from him (v. 20). The consequences of this loss and departure are devastating for Samson since the Philistines maim him for life by blinding him.

The loss of sight is the tragic climax of a motif that develops throughout the account, in particular by the employment of the root *r²h* in scenes that compromise Samson (14:1–3, 8; 16:5, 18; cf. Jdg 13:6, 10, 19–20, 22; Galpaz-Feller, *Samson*, 207–17). It is ironic that Samson's greatest act of deliverance will occur when he is finally blind. The Philistines

transport him to one of the five key Philistine cities (Gaza) and then bind him in the only kind of chains that will be sure to hold the former strong man—bronze. In this tragic episode the reader is presented with a striking contrast to the earlier episode in Judges 4–5. There "Israel's ally Jael lured a *foreign* general to his death; now the Philistine Delilah had lured the greatest of *Israel's* warriors to his demise. Samson was now in the role of Sisera and Delilah in the role of Jael" (Chisholm, 43, italics his).

NOTES

19 עַל־בִּרְכֶּיהָ (*'al-birkeyhā*, "on her lap"). The Hebrew reads here "on her knees," alluding possibly to a maternal scene following childbirth (Ge 30:3; 2Ki 4:20; cf. Ge 50:23; Mobley, 91–92) and suggesting that Samson the superhuman is reborn as a mere mortal (as he claimed vv. 7, 11, 13, 17), as well as severing his link to his own mother by losing the last sign of his Nazarite vow. See also Kim, 430–31, who notes the ironic connection between God's blessing (בָרַךְ [*brk*], Piel) in 13:24 and Samson's demise on Delilah's knee (בֶּרֶךְ, *berek*) here.

וַתָּחֶל לְעַנּוֹתוֹ (*wattāhel l²c'annôtô*, "and so began to subdue him"). The verb ענה (*'nh*; GK 6700) is used for Egyptian abuse of Israel (Ge 15:13; Ex 1:11–12; Dt 26:6), Sarah's abuse of Hagar (Ge 16:6), and spousal abuse (Ge 31:50). Here Delilah turns on her former lover and his strength leaves him. The LXX[a] reads here καὶ ἤρξατο ταπεινοῦσθαι (*kai ērxato tapeinousthai*), and the LXX[b] reads καὶ ἤρξατο ταπεινῶσαι: *ērxato tapeinōsai*, both meaning "and he began to weaken," thus making Samson the subject rather than Delilah.

8. Samson's Triumph through Death in Gaza (16:21b–30)

Binding him with bronze shackles, they set him to grinding in the prison. [22]But the hair on his head began to grow again after it had been shaved.

[23]Now the rulers of the Philistines assembled to offer a great sacrifice to Dagon their god and to celebrate, saying, "Our god has delivered Samson, our enemy, into our hands."

[24]When the people saw him, they praised their god, saying,

"Our god has delivered our enemy
    into our hands,
the one who laid waste our land
    and multiplied our slain."

²⁵While they were in high spirits, they shouted, "Bring out Samson to entertain us." So they called Samson out of the prison, and he performed for them.

When they stood him among the pillars, ²⁶Samson said to the servant who held his hand, "Put me where I can feel the pillars that support the temple, so that I may lean against them." ²⁷Now the temple was crowded with men and women; all the rulers of the Philistines were there, and on the roof were about three thousand men and women watching Samson perform. ²⁸Then Samson prayed to the LORD, "O Sovereign LORD, remember me. O God, please strengthen me just once more, and let me with one blow get revenge on the Philistines for my two eyes." ²⁹Then Samson reached toward the two central pillars on which the temple stood. Bracing himself against them, his right hand on the one and his left hand on the other, ³⁰Samson said, "Let me die with the Philistines!" Then he pushed with all his might, and down came the temple on the rulers and all the people in it. Thus he killed many more when he died than while he lived.

COMMENTARY

21b–22 The narrator's note that Samson is put to work as a "grinder," one who will turns the heavy millstones to grind grain (Nu 11:8; Isa 47:2; La 5:13; see comments on Jdg 9:50–55), introduces the final episode of the account of Samson. By blinding and forcing him to grind grain, the Philistines are following ancient patterns for the treatment of male prisoners, especially as grinding grain was considered the work of women (Michael J. Smith, "The Failure of the Family in Judges. Part 2, Samson," *BSac* 162 [2005]: 434). To this information the narrator adds that in time Samson's hair begins to grow again, an observation that sets the stage for the climactic episode of Samson's life, in which he will inflict through his death more damage on the Philistines than at any other point in his career.

23–24 With the great champion of Israel safely in prison, the rulers and people of the Philistines throw a grand celebration with accompanying sac-rifice in honor of their god Dagon, whom they credit with the defeat of Samson—a blasphemy in the light of the fact that it is Yahweh who is responsible for that defeat (Webb, 165–66). Dagon was a popular deity in Mesopotamia (*ABD*, 2:2), whose spread to Canaan is evidenced in names that appear in the El-Amarna letters (fourteenth century BC) and in texts that appear in Ugarit, where Dagon is identified as the father of the god Baal.

Dagon is consistently associated with the Philistines elsewhere in the OT (1Sa 5:1–7; 1Ch 10:10). Although they were not originally from Canaan, they appear to have easily assimilated to the gods of their adopted land. They built temples for Dagon in Gaza (Jdg 16:21–23) and Ashdod (1Sa 5:2–3), and to Dagon and Astarte in Beth Shean (1Ch 10:10–12; 1Sa 31:10; *ABD*, 5:327). This celebration takes place in the temple of Dagon and most likely combines sacrifice to their god with celebratory feasting with one another.

25–27 The people's merriment leads them to take a risk and call for the former mighty man to "entertain" or "provide amusement for" them by appearing before the crowd, maimed and chained. The temple is filled with the elite of the Philistines, while three thousand others look on from the roof, putting considerable strain on the structure of the building. Samson is placed between the pillars that hold up the structure and asks the young servant charged with his care to guide his hands to the pillars.

28–30 While the Philistines "called" (*qrʾ*) for Samson to amuse them (16:25, 2x), Samson "calls" (*qrʾ*) for Yahweh to come to his aid. The same verb was used in 15:18–19 (cf. Amit, *Judges*, 279) to introduce Samson's only other prayer in the account in which he asked for and received a miraculous provision of water, which made "his spirit return"—that is, he regained his strength,

which was animated by the Spirit of Yahweh. Similarly, in 16:28 Samson calls for Yahweh to send another miracle that will strengthen him and grant him vengeance for the Philistines' blinding him. Yahweh answers this prayer by enabling Samson to dislodge the two central pillars of the temple and bring the entire structure down on the Philistines and their rulers.

This final act in death, alluded to even before his birth (13:3–5), inflicts more damage on the Philistines than all of Samson's mighty deeds during his life. In this respect Samson is unique among characters in the OT who take their own lives (Abimelech, Saul, Ahithophel, Zimri): Samson does so "as an act of heroism, sacrifice, and redemption" (Galpaz-Feller, "My Soul," 325) and thus provides a sliver of light in the midst of all the darkness that concludes his life.

NOTE

21 בְּבֵית הָאֲסוּרִים (*bᵉbêt hāᵃsûrîm*, "the prison"). This expression reads in wooden Hebrew: "the house of the prisoners."

9. Second Concluding Notice: The Burial of Samson (16:31)

³¹Then his brothers and his father's whole family went down to get him. They brought him back and buried him between Zorah and Eshtaol in the tomb of Manoah his father. He had led Israel twenty years.

COMMENTARY

31 With Samson's death recorded in v.30, the narrator concludes the account with the second of two notices (see 15:20), this one explaining how the members of his family honor Samson

with a decent burial in the family tomb, which lay "between Zorah and Eshtaol," that region where the Spirit first began to stir within Samson so many years before (13:24–25). The reappearance of these locations in the story of Micah in chs. 17–18 (see 18:1–2) highlights the way the tragedy of Samson foreshadows the disastrous events in chs. 17–21.

The account ends by noting that Samson had led ("judged") Israel for twenty years.

REFLECTION

The account of Samson highlights a community that has lost all faith. By failing even to cry out for help and by handing over their judge-deliverer to the enemy, the community reveals their acceptance of the status quo of divine discipline and the reign of his agents of wrath. The spiritual insensitivity of this era is typified first by Manoah, who finds Yahweh's messenger suspect. So also his son Samson, the judge-deliverer himself, is one who receives Yahweh's Spirit violently, acts by personal vendetta, enters foolishly into dangerous zones, and is depicted largely as a powerful human who pursues his physical lusts (honey, sex, water). In this way he foreshadows the Spirit-endowed model of human kingship displayed by Saul and yet rejected in the end by Yahweh. It is possible for a leader to be empowered by the Spirit, even exercising in faith (cf. Heb 11:32), and yet operate in a fleshly way.

The failure of Samson opens the way for the rise of Davidic royal rule within Israel, a rule that foreshadows that of his scion, Jesus the Messiah. Theologically challenging is the way Yahweh uses this tragic figure's inappropriate patterns for his advantage. In no way does this action by Yahweh absolve Samson of his guilt, but it does remind the reader that God will use even one's failures for his greater glory, even if in the end these failures are destructive. Samson's personal trait of trickster ultimately rebounds to himself through the wiles of Delilah. In the end he is unable to see the approaching entrapment even though it echoes earlier patterns in his life.

III. THE TRIBES OF ISRAEL—PART TWO (17:1–21:25)

OVERVIEW

The demise of Samson signals the end of the depiction of the judge-deliverers, which has dominated the core of the book of Judges (2:6–16:31) ever since what is often considered the second introduction (2:6–3:6). This core section has traced the progressive decline in the nation and its leaders, ending with the nadir of the account of Samson in chs. 13–16.

Chapters 17–21 return to an emphasis on tribal identity, which was typical of the first introduction to the book (1:1–2:5). There tribal identity emerged in a description of conquest wars against the Canaanites in the land. Now in chs. 17–21, tribal identity reemerges not only in a description of a war of conquest against unsuspecting Canaanites in the far north, but more commonly in descriptions of civil war among Israelite tribes.

Similar inquiries are made of Yahweh in both 1:1-2:5 and chs. 17-21, asking for the identity of the tribe that would lead the nation in battle (1:1-2; 20:18). The leader in both cases is identified as Judah. The foe in each case is different, however: at first, the Canaanites (1:1), and in the end, the Benjamites (20:18). So also the results differ: success (ch. 1), and defeat (ch. 20), the latter resonating with the degenerate state to which Israel had fallen in chs. 17-21.

This emphasis on the tribe of Judah as leader, coupled with the two downward trajectories (i.e., the demise of the judge-deliverers in the core section and the shift from hopeful conquest of the land to hopeless civil strife in the outer sections of 1:1-2:5; chs. 17-21), helps to explain the repeated refrain that dominates chs. 17-21. This refrain appears in a symmetrical pattern (Robert H. O'Connell, *Concentricity and Continuity: The Literary Structure of Isaiah* [JSOTSup 188; Sheffield: Sheffield Academic, 1994], 265):

- In those days Israel had no king; everyone did as he saw fit. (17:6)
- In those days Israel had no king. (18:1)
- In those days Israel had no king. (19:1)
- In those days Israel had no king; everyone did as he saw fit. (21:25)

The story of the judge-deliverers in 2:6-16:31 has revealed the inadequacies of this leadership model. Israel always returned to its idolatrous ways and at times was even encouraged to do so by its leaders. The book of Judges subtly looks to a royal model that would arise from the tribe of Judah, one that would counter the propensity for everyone to do what was right in their own eyes. (On the various opinions of what figure is in view, whether divine king, human king, or human judge,

see Wong [2005; *Strategy*, 191-223]; see further the Introduction.)

The second part of the full refrain ("everyone did as he saw fit"), which appears only in 17:6 and 21:25, is found elsewhere in the OT only in Deuteronomy 12:8. The passage in Deuteronomy reveals that the phrase is focused primarily on the centralization of worship in Israel at one single shrine once Israel had entered the land (O'Connell, 235). It is this centralization that would be enforced ultimately by the Davidic house in Jerusalem (celebrated in Ps 122; see Boda, *After God's Own Heart*, 89-94). Such centralization would be threatened by the failure of Israel to defeat the Canaanites (see 1:1-2:5) and by the actions of Israel in setting up rival shrines throughout the land (see chs. 17-18; see the long list of connections between Jdg 17-18 and Dt 12 in O'Connell, 239-40; Matthews, *Judges and Ruth*, 172).

Judges 1:1-2:5 and 17:1-21:25 thus form a bracket around the central core of the accounts of the judge-deliverers in 2:6-16:31 and suggest a leadership model that had the potential to counter the struggles experienced during the tenure of the judge-deliverers. The question of kingship was broached and seemingly rejected through the depiction of Gideon and Abimelech in chs. 6-9; however, it appears that what was rejected was not royal leadership per se, but the kind of royal rule envisioned by Israel, a trend that resonates with 1 Samuel (see Escursus, "Royal Polemic in Judges").

In light of the link between the events in chs. 17-21 and figures who appear to be grandsons of Moses (18:30) and Aaron (20:27-28), these chapters seem to be chronologically connected to the period immediately after the death of Joshua (Amit, *Judges*, 311). Similarly, the account of Samson is not the latest material in the phase of the judge-deliverers, since it is placed prior to the Danite shift to their northern environs in ch. 18. Thus chs. 13–21 are also events that occurred historically prior to many of the judge-deliverer stories in chs. 3–12 (see Introduction).

A. Micah and the Danites (17:1–18:31)

OVERVIEW

The close relationship between 1:1–2:5 and chs. 17–21 does not, however, preclude a connection between chs. 17–21 and the preceding material in 2:6–16:31 (see Bowman; Wong, *Strategy*, 69–141). In particular, one cannot miss the close association between ch. 17 and the Samson cycle in chs. 13–16 (Sweeney). Both episodes involve Danites (cf. 13:2; 18:1), make specific reference to Zorah and Eshtaol (cf. 13:25; 18:11–12), identify Mahaneh Dan as a gathering point (cf. 13:25; 18:12), mention eleven hundred shekels of silver (cf. 16:5; 17:1; cf. O'Connell, 240), and feature ritually separated individuals who violate their regulations (Wong, *Strategy*, 89–96).

Judges 17–18 is also related to the story that follows in chs 19–21, with each story concerning Levites connected with both the hill country of Ephraim and Bethlehem in Judah (cf. 17:7–8 with 19:1) and concerning a remnant of a defeated tribe set at six hundred men (cf. 18:11 with 20:47). For an extensive list of connections between Judges 17–18 and 19–21, see Satterthwaite, "No King in

Israel"; O'Connell, 264–65; Sweeney; and Block, 474–75; see further Overview to chs. 19–21.

While the early history of scholarship sought to distance chs. 17–18 from the Deuteronomic tradition (see esp. Noth, 52–53, 59–60) by seeing the bracket around the book as a later addition, recent scholarship has highlighted the way the theology of Deuteronomy and the Deuteronomic History inform these chapters. This informing is evident not only in the refrains punctuating the accounts (17:6; 18:1; 19:1; 21:25) that play off Deuteronomy 12:8, but also in connections to various laws in Deuteronomy (see Mueller, 126; Na'aman, 52).

The story unfolds in three episodes: Micah's theft and shrine (17:1–5), Micah's appointment of a Levite (17:7–13), and the Danites' conquest and shrine (18:1b–31; Amit, "Hidden Polemic," 5). These three episodes are divided by two refrains reminding the reader that the key theme of this section is the role of the monarchy to centralize worship (see comment on 17:6; cf. Boda, *After God's Own Heart*, 87–99).

1. Micah's Theft and Shrine (17:1–5)

¹Now a man named Micah from the hill country of Ephraim ²said to his mother, "The eleven hundred shekels of silver that were taken from you and about which I heard you

utter a curse — I have that silver with me; I took it."

Then his mother said, "The LORD bless you, my son!"

³When he returned the eleven hundred shekels of silver to his mother, she said, "I solemnly consecrate my silver to the LORD for my son to make a carved image and a cast idol. I will give it back to you."

⁴So he returned the silver to his mother, and she took two hundred shekels of silver and gave them to a silversmith, who made them into the image and the idol. And they were put in Micah's house.

⁵Now this man Micah had a shrine, and he made an ephod and some idols and installed one of his sons as his priest.

COMMENTARY

1 The main character of the story is identified at the outset as Micah, whose name contains the name of Israel's God, Yahweh ("Micah" in its long form ending with -*yehu*, and in its short form ending in -*ah*). The name means "Who is like Yahweh?" — a question that praises the incomparability of Yahweh and represents a direct challenge to the other deities that have competed with Yahweh for the people's affections throughout the book (see similarly Ex 15:11; Ps 89:6; Isa 40:12–31; cf. 1Ki 8:23; 2Ch 6:14). This name is ironic in the light of the creation of an idol in this passage, thus suggesting that Micah and his family were likening this idol to Yahweh (Matthews, *Judges and Ruth*, 169; cf. E. T. Mullen, *Narrative History and Ethnic Boundaries: The Deuteronomistic Historian and the Creation of Israelite National Identity* [Semeia; Atlanta: Scholars, 1993], 166). Thereby the story reveals that worship of Yahweh must be conducted through appropriate means at the appropriate place, a major priority in the book of Deuteronomy (Dt 12).

Micah is identified as an Ephraimite at the head of a *bêt-ʾab* ("house of the father"), the smallest family unit in Israel, which included three to four generations of males descended from a patriarch along with their wives, children, servants, and priestly personnel (see Perdue; cf. Bendor; see Introduction). It appears that Micah's father has died, and as the eldest son, he has assumed the role of leader of his household (*bêt-ʾab*), a responsibility that includes caring for his mother and providing for the religious needs of the family (see Job 1 and 42). The hill country of Ephraim was the territory directly north of Judah and Benjamin. As evident in the stories of Gideon and Jephthah, the Ephraimite tribe dominated the northern tribes.

2 The story begins with Micah's confession to his mother that he has stolen from her eleven hundred silver pieces — eerily reminiscent of the amount promised by the Philistine lords to Delilah in 16:5 and thus providing another link between these two stories and possibly between these two events (if the mother was Delilah, a possibility entertained by Schneider, 231–32; McCann, 120; Matthews [*Judges and Ruth*, 171]; and Galpaz-Feller [*Samson*, 169]). It appears that the confession is prompted by fear of the curse she had uttered in his presence, possibly like the one recorded of Saul in 1 Samuel 14:24: "Cursed be any man who eats food before evening comes, before I have avenged myself on my enemies!" His admission prompts his mother to request that her curse be transformed into a blessing from Yahweh, as she declares, "The LORD bless you, my son!"

3–4 The returned money is immediately consecrated (*qdš*, Hiphil) to Yahweh by Micah's mother. The phrase translated here as "I solemnly consecrate" (*haqdēš hiqdaštî*) can also be translated as "I fully consecrate" (see Note and NASB). If the latter is the case, her decision to give only two hundred shekels of silver to the silversmith suggests that she does not follow through on her pledge (Webb, 183; cf. the strikingly similar behavior of Ananias and Sapphira in Ac 5). If the former is the case, she dedicates over eighteen percent of the returned amount to Yahweh.

This consecration of the money involves commissioning her son to have a silversmith make a carved image and cast idol. (There is some confusion in vv.3–4, for whereas in v.3 it is the son who is to make the idol, in v.4 Micah's mother gives the money to a silversmith directly.) The first term (*pesel*) is related to wooden or stone carvings depicting something in creation, such as humans or animals (Ex 20:4//Dt 5:8; Dt 4:16). The second term (*massēkâ*) indicates a metal cast image, such as the golden calf in Exodus 32:4, 8 (cf. Dt 9:16; Ne 9:18). The combination of both is found elsewhere in Deuteronomy 27:15; Judges 18:14; and Nahum 1:14.

As with Samson's mother in ch. 13, the story of Micah's mother foreshadows the role of another key mother at the outset of 1 Samuel—Hannah. Both the mother in ch. 17 and Hannah make a vow, but while the mother's vow here leads to idolatry that rivals the worship of Yahweh at Shiloh, Hannah's vow in 1 Samuel 1 leads to a revival of worship at Shiloh (see Chisholm, 48).

5 The idol, made from the stolen money as only a partial fulfillment of an abhorrent vow made to Yahweh by a woman who first cursed and then blessed the culprit, is then placed in Micah's house. The narrator reveals through the offline comment in v.5 that this idol is placed within his shrine, that is, "a house of God" (*bêt ʾelōhîm*). This comment is possibly an allusion to the later idolatrous Bethel ("house of God"; see Baruch Halpern, "Levitic Participation in the Reform Cult of Jeroboam I," *JBL* 95 [1976]: 31–42; Amit, "Hidden Polemic"), which together with Dan (the ultimate destination of these idols in this story; see 8:30–31) would become twin rival shrines to Jerusalem's centrally mandated sanctuary. The idol that is made joins other religious paraphernalia, including an ephod (see Jdg 8:27) and household idols (*terāpîm*; GK 9572). This latter term possibly refers to images used for ancestral worship (see Notes below). Micah consecrates one of his sons to wear this ephod and serve in the shrine.

NOTES

1 מִיכָיְהוּ (*mîkāyehû*, "Micah"). This designation is the longer form of the name (also found in v.4), while throughout the rest of the story the shorter form of the name (מִיכָה, *mîkâ*) is used (17:5, 8–10, 12 [2x]–13; 18:2–4, 13, 15, 18, 22–23, 26–27, 31). Block, 478, suggests the change in name has a narrative function of "reflecting the narrator's awareness of the incongruities in the story." Mueller, 53, argues that it "marks a distancing of the protagonist from YHWH.... The author subtracts YHWH, the name of the Deity, from Micah's name at the point in the story when he becomes actively involved in idolatrous worship."

2–3 אֶלֶף־וּמֵאָה הַכֶּסֶף (ʾelep-ûmēʾâ hakkesep, "eleven hundred shekels of silver"). The Hebrew here only speaks of "eleven hundred of silver." Judges 17:4 also only speaks of "two hundred of silver." The precise unit is not provided.

2 בָּרוּךְ בְּנִי לַיהוה (bārûk bᵉnî layhwh, "The LORD bless you, my son!"). The Hebrew is expressed in the passive, "blessed be my son by Yahweh." See the formula ברוך + X + ל (l + X + brwk) in Genesis 14:19; 1 Samuel 15:13; 23:21; 2 Samuel 2:5; Ruth 2:20; 3:10; Psalm 115:15 (see Block, 479).

3 הַקְדֵּשׁ הִקְדַּשְׁתִּי (haqdēš hiqdaštî, "I solemnly consecrate"). This construction—finite verb preceded by the infinitive absolute of the same root—may indicate a qualitative intensification of the action (solemnly) or quantitative (fully).

פֶּסֶל וּמַסֵּכָה (pesel ûmassēkâ, "carved image and a cast idol"; cf. 17:4, "the image and the idol"). Many have considered this construction a "hendiadys for a wooden image with an overlay of metal" (*HALOT*, 949; cf. G. W. Ahlström, *Aspects of Syncretism in Israelite Religion* [trans. Eric J. Sharpe; Horae Soederblomianae 5; Lund: Gleerup, 1963], 25–26; Malamat, 12; Boling, 256; Soggin, 265), a view that seems to be supported by the singular verb וַיְהִי (wayᵉhî) at the end of v.4 ("And they were put in Micah's house," better, "And it was put in Micah's house"). But 18:17–18 clearly distinguishes between these two items, and 18:20, 30–31 refer to the first item alone (cf. Klein, *The Triumph of Irony*, 150; Mueller, 59).

וְעַתָּה אֲשִׁיבֶנּוּ לָךְ (wᵉʿattâ ʾăšîbennû lāk, "I will give it back to you"). לָךְ (lāk) has a second feminine singular suffix and so must refer to the mother, with the "I" here being the voice of Micah, whose action is then described by the narrator at the beginning of the following verse. If the pointing is incorrect, the phrase could be a continuation of the mother's speech and refer to the mother's giving the "lost" silver to Yahweh. For a review of attempts to rearrange this text to an earlier point in the narrative, see Mueller, 54–55, who attributes the awkwardness in flow to narrative intention: "Mother and son pass the silver back and forth between them because they are too frightened to hold it in their hands for more than one moment at a time."

5 וַיְמַלֵּא אֶת־יַד (wayᵉmallēʾ ʾet-yad, "and installed"). This collocation, "and he filled the hand," is used for the ordination of priests in Exodus 28:41; 29:9, 29, 33, 35; Leviticus 8:33; 16:32; 21:10; Numbers 3:3 (Amit, *Judges*, 327, n. 22). It also appears in 1 Kings 13:33 to describe Jeroboam's installation of priests at his high places (cf. Jdg 18:30–31). The story of Micah's idols explains the origins of one of these high places. This phrase may function here as "tongue in cheek" in light of the fact that the Danites will ultimately "fill the hand" of the Levite with more than Micah can provide (Webb, 184–85).

תְּרָפִים (tᵉrāpîm, "some idols"; GK 9572). Van der Toorn argues that while broader ancient Near Eastern evidence suggests that the term tᵉrāpîm refers to either household gods or ancestral worship, an analysis of the OT reveals that it is a reference to images of dead ancestors (cf. Dt 18:11 with 2Ki 23:24, in which "dead" and תְּרָפִים, tᵉrāpîm, stand in the same place; cf. Karel van der Toorn, "The Nature of the Biblical *Teraphim* in the Light of the Cuneiform Evidence," *CBQ* 52 [1990]: 203–22; so also Carol L. Meyers and Eric M. Meyers, *Zechariah 9–14: A New Translation with Introduction and Commentary* [AB 25C; New York: Doubleday, 1993], 184–87; Boda, *Haggai/Zechariah*, 138). A key element in Canaanite worship was the consulting and veneration of ancestors (cf. Boda, "Ideal Sonship in Ugarit," *UF* 25 [1994]: 9–24).

2. Refrain (17:6)

⁶In those days Israel had no king; everyone did as he saw fit.

COMMENTARY

6 The narrator's note in v.6 provides a theological evaluation of the events described through 17:1–5, while "casting a negative light on the events to come" (Amit, "Hidden Polemic," 5). The presence of a shrine complete with priest and gods within an individual household is evidence of the Canaanization of Israel. The phrase used in the second half of v.6 ("everyone did as he saw fit") is one that appears in Deuteronomy 12:8 (see Overview to 17:1–18:31; also Andrew D. H. Mayes, "Deuteronomistic Royal Ideology in Judges 17–21," *BibInt* 9 [2001]: 255) to describe the practice of Israel in the wilderness that was akin to that of the Canaanites, who worshiped their gods "on the high mountains and on the hills and under every spreading tree" (Dt 12:2). According to Deuteronomy 12, Israel was instead to worship at the one place designated by Yahweh within the land.

This lack of adherence to a single shrine is linked to a second lack in Judges 17:6: "In those days Israel had no king." It was Israel's Davidic monarchy that would centralize worship at Jerusalem (see Boda, *After God's Own Heart*, 87–99). The story of Micah, however, is far from this ideal. So spiritually ignorant is this family that they not only create their own shrine and install their own family member as a priest, but also they dedicate stolen money to Yahweh and make it into an idolatrous image.

3. Micah and the Levite (17:7–13)

⁷A young Levite from Bethlehem in Judah, who had been living within the clan of Judah, ⁸left that town in search of some other place to stay. On his way he came to Micah's house in the hill country of Ephraim.

⁹Micah asked him, "Where are you from?"

"I'm a Levite from Bethlehem in Judah," he said, "and I'm looking for a place to stay."

¹⁰Then Micah said to him, "Live with me and be my father and priest, and I'll give you ten shekels of silver a year, your clothes and your food." ¹¹So the Levite agreed to live with him, and the young man was to him like one of his sons. ¹²Then Micah installed the Levite, and the young man became his priest and lived in his house. ¹³And Micah said, "Now I know that the LORD will be good to me, since this Levite has become my priest."

COMMENTARY

7–8 Verse 7 signals the beginning of a new scene in the chapter and with it a new character is introduced, at first only described as a young man (*na'ar*) from Bethlehem of Judah, from the clan of Judah. Here Judah is described as a "clan" (*mišpāḥâ*) rather than a "tribe" (*maṭṭeh*), a trend seen earlier in the description of Dan in 13:2 (cf. 18:2, 11; see Note on 13:2). This young man, however, is not actually from the clan of Judah, but rather is a Levite who is a temporary alien resident (*gwr*) in the Judahite tribal territory.

The tribe of Levi had a special relationship with Yahweh as it was chosen to facilitate the worship of God at the tabernacle. This tribe was considered the "firstfruits" of Israel, set apart for Yahweh (Nu 3:11–13), and did not have its own territorial inheritance (Nu 18:20) other than forty-eight towns spread throughout the other tribal allotments (Jos 21:1–42), among which were six towns of refuge (Jos 20). Though in one sense without defined tribal territory, the Levites had a status that approached "temporary alien residency," even if there were small Levitical "islands" in each tribe. Bethlehem, however, was not one of the Levitical towns in Judahite territory, so the presence of the Levite in Bethlehem was indeed a "temporary alien residency."

The fact that this Levite is not in an appropriate Levitical territory raises questions about his legitimacy. For some unexplained reason his sojourn in Bethlehem came to an end, so he left "to live as dependent alien wherever he found work." In this comment Block, 486, sees "a parody of Moses' instructions regarding Levites in Deuteronomy 18:6–9," a passage in which Moses offers guidance to Levites who leave their place of sojourn to serve at the central sanctuary. It is clear in Judges 17–18 that this Levite's sojourn will violate this principle and lead to the establishment of one of the major rival shrines to Yahweh's central sanctuary in Shiloh.

Of note is the Levite's answer to Micah in 17:9: "I am going to stay wherever I may find a place" (NASB). He went into the hill country of Ephraim, arriving at the household of Micah with the hope of carrying out his profession (see Note). The description of the Levite in vv. 7–8 is a further illustration of the narrator's commentary in 17:6 on the lack of a stable and centralized system of worship in Israel. The layman Micah was free to create his own shrine with inappropriate methods of worship, and the priestly Levite was free to wander the land and facilitate worship wherever he could find a willing patron.

9–10 The narrator now draws attention to the encounter between the two parties by providing a dramatic narrative. After inquiring after the Levite's background and discovering the answer that the Levite is looking for any place to sojourn temporarily (*gwr*), Micah invites the young and desperate Levite to settle down (*yšb*) with him. Micah offers him both significant status ("father and priest") and living allowance ("ten shekels of silver, your clothes and your food").

By calling him "father" Micah is giving the young priest authority over his household (cf. Michael K. Wilson, "'As You Like It': The Danites (Judges 17–18)," *RTR* 54 [1995]: 82; see Note below), a role in which Micah himself is serving, and by calling him "priest" he is offering him control over his shrine, a role in which his son serves. It is ironic that the "young Levite" (v. 7) is now elevated by Micah to the status of "father." The term for "food" here (*miḥyâ*) refers to that which sustains/preserves life and was used earlier in 6:4 to refer to the harvest. The Levite's basic needs of clothing and food will be cared for; in addition, he will receive a handsome wage of ten shekels of silver.

11–13 The Levite gladly takes up the offer of Micah, who installs him in the place of his own son as priest. This Levite is not merely an employee, but rather is treated as the son Micah has deposed. The description of Micah's special treatment of this Levite accentuates the depth of betrayal when the Levite abandons Micah in favor of the Danites in ch. 18.

This second major scene ends with the dramatic narrative of v.13 as Micah declares clearly his purpose for installing the Levite. Micah now expects Yahweh's blessing since he has acquired a proper priestly figure to officiate at his shrine, but his hopes will soon be dashed, since "from now on nothing will go right for him" (Webb, 184). Micah's shrine is a sanctuary of his own making, one that defies the explicit instructions in the Torah. While Micah is clearly seeking the blessing of Yahweh, his chosen means undermine any claim to God's favor.

NOTES

7 וְהוּא לֵוִי וְהוּא גָּר־שָׁם (wehûʾ lēwî wehûʾ gār-šām, "A young Levite … who had been living"; the Hebrew reads woodenly, "now he was a Levite, he was dwelling as dependent alien there"). The final two phrases of this verse in Hebrew identify the young man as a Levite who had alien status in Judahite territory.

8 לַעֲשׂוֹת דַּרְכּוֹ (laʿᵃśôt darkô, "on his way"). This phrase is probably better translated as "to carry on his profession," since דֶּרֶךְ (derek) can refer to one's enterprise/business or manner/custom/behavior (see *HALOT*, 232).

10 וֶהְיֵה־לִי לְאָב (wehyēh-lî leʾāb, "and be my father"). See how "father" is used to express honor in 2 Kings 6:21; 8:9. The same term will be used by the Danites in Judges 18:19.

לַיָּמִים (layyāmîm, "a year"). The Hebrew reads woodenly, "for the days." "Days" is used for "yearly" or "annual" at several other places in the OT (Ex 13:10; Jdg 11:40; 1Sa 1:3; 2:19; cf. 1Sa 1:21; 20:6).

12 וַיְמַלֵּא … אֶת־יַד (wayᵉmalleʾ … ʾet-yad, "installed"). See the Note on 17:5.

4. Refrain (18:1a)

> **1**In those days Israel had no king.

COMMENTARY

1a Before proceeding to the third scene in this story, the narrator interjects the phrase, "In those days Israel had no king," an abridgment (cf. 19:1) of the full refrain, which appears in 17:6 and 21:25. This phrase comes at key narrative intervals in chs. 17–21 and reminds the reader that the conditions and events being described should be understood as the result of the failure of the judge-deliverers and lack of royal leadership in Israel.

The use of this phrase in 17:6 was closely related to the sponsorship of a local shrine with idols. In 18:1a it may refer to the military protection that could be expected under a monarch but which was not available to the frustrated Danites. The focus of the early monarchy (Saul, David) was on defeating the Philistines, who oppressed the tribe of Dan. But it is also possible that the refrain has been cited in 18:1a to remind the reader once again of the crisis in religious fidelity, either as a statement reflecting on Micah's installation of the Levite in 17:7–13, or introducing the Danites' religious treachery in ch. 18.

5. The Danites' Conquest and Shrine (18:1b–31)

a. The Danites Set Out on a Reconnaissance Mission (18:1b–2a)

And in those days the tribe of the Danites was seeking a place of their own where they might settle, because they had not yet come into an inheritance among the tribes of Israel. ²So the Danites sent five warriors from Zorah and Eshtaol to spy out the land and explore it. These men represented all their clans. They told them, "Go, explore the land."

COMMENTARY

1b–2a According to Joshua 19:40–48, the Danites' inheritance was in the region to the west of Judah (19:41–46), and it is in this region that the Danite Samson is depicted in constant struggle against the Philistines (Jdg 13–16). According to Judges 1:34 the "Amorites" (there a general term describing the Philistines) were able to confine the Danites to the hill country and rob them of their inheritance. According to Joshua 19:47 and here in Judges 18, the Danites finally gave up hope of controlling their allotment and so traveled to the far north to territory that lay beyond the tribal lands of other Israelite tribes.

According to v.2 the Danites send out a reconnaissance team of five warriors from Samson's home territory, Zorah and Eshtaol (13:25), with each warrior representing a clan within the Danite tribe. Numbers 13 (cf. Dt 1) provides an account of a similar composition of a reconnaissance team, there consisting of one from each tribe within Israel. Malamat, O'Connell, 235–38, and Block, 491, all note the similarities between the conquest narratives in Numbers 12:16–14:45; Deuteronomy 1:19–46; and Judges 18:1–31, though Block is careful to call this convergence "an example of analogical narrative rather than echo narrative," the distinction apparently being related to the absence (analogical) or presence (echo) of verbal links. Even more important is the observation of Uwe F. W. Bauer ("Judges 18 as an Anti-Spy Story in the Context of an Anti-Conquest Story: The Creative Usage of Literary Genres," *JSOT* 88 [2000]: 37–47) that what we find here is actually an "anti-spy story" that highlights the "anti-conquest" represented by the Danites' actions (Uwe

Becker, *Richterzeit und Königtum: Redaktionsge-schichtliche Studien zum Richterbuch* [BZAW 192; Berlin: de Gruyter, 1990], 253–54; O'Connell, 235–37; contrast Malamat). For links and contrast to Joshua's sending out spies in Joshua 2, see Wong (*Strategy*, 55–57).

NOTE

2 לְרַגֵּל אֶת־הָאָרֶץ (*lᵉraggēl ᵓet-hāᵓāreṣ*, "to spy out the land"). The verb רגל (*rgl*), in the Piel, is used in Numbers 21:32; Deuteronomy 1:24; Joshua 2:1; 6:22–25; 7:2; 1 Samuel 26:4; and 2 Samuel 10:3; 15:10 to refer to the activity of those sent to assess the potential of a military operation by close observation of the target. The second term, וּלְחָקְרָה (*ûlᵉḥoqrâh*, "and explore it"), is a more general term that does appear in conjunction with spying in 2 Samuel 10:3.

b. The Danites Lodge at Micah's House and Inquire at Micah's Shrine (18:2b–6)

> The men entered the hill country of Ephraim and came to the house of Micah, where they spent the night. ³When they were near Micah's house, they recognized the voice of the young Levite; so they turned in there and asked him, "Who brought you here? What are you doing in this place? Why are you here?"
>
> ⁴He told them what Micah had done for him, and said, "He has hired me and I am his priest."
>
> ⁵Then they said to him, "Please inquire of God to learn whether our journey will be successful."
>
> ⁶The priest answered them, "Go in peace. Your journey has the LORD's approval."

COMMENTARY

2b–4 The five warriors from Dan head north on their mission, a route that takes them into the tribal territory of Ephraim, where they happen upon Micah's house and turn aside for the night. During their short stay with Micah they "recognized the voice" (*hikkîrû ᵓet-qôl*) of Micah's priestly officiant at his shrine. This phrase suggests that the Levite's accent was associated with a region other than the hill country of Ephraim and was most likely akin to the accent of members of the tribe of Judah among

whom the Levite had served in Bethlehem and with whom the southern Danites would have had some familiarity (Niditch, *Judges*, 182). Notice the close association between Dan and Judah in Judges 15, where, when Samson causes problems with the Philistines, they encamp against Judah.

The narrator uses dramatic narrative to depict the interchange between the Danite spies and the Levite. The warriors pummel the Levite with a series of questions in order to discern how he ended up in Ephraim. The narrator focuses the reader's attention on the fact that the Levite had been hired and had attained the status of priest, thus preparing the way for the more lucrative opportunity that will be offered by the tribe of Dan.

5-6 Happening upon this fully functioning shrine, the warriors take the opportunity to ask the priest to make an inquiry to God for them in order to discover whether their mission will be successful. To inquire (*šāʾal*) of God about a military expedition is a regular occurrence throughout Israel's history (Jdg 1:1; 20:18, 23, 27; 1Sa 10:22; 14:37; 22:10, 13, 15; 23:2, 4; 28:6; 30:8; 2Sa 2:1; 5:19, 23). Though the answer appears to be favorable, the fact that it contains some ambiguity (see Note below) and comes so quickly after the request without any details on how the will of God was discerned by this priest raises some questions as to its validity (see Schneider, 237; Mueller, 68; Boda, "Recycling Heaven's Words"). In the Torah it is the mysterious Urim and Thummim, objects related to the breastplate of the high priest (Ex 28:30), that were the priestly means for making inquiry of Yahweh (Nu 27:21; cf. 1Sa 28:6; Ezr 2:63; Ne 7:65).

NOTES

4 כָּזֹה וְכָזֶה עָשָׂה לִי מִיכָה (*kāzōh wᵉkāzeh ʿāśâ lî mîkâ*, "He told them what Micah had done for him"). The MT reads this clause as part of the Levite's speech: "according to this [feminine] and according to this [masculine] Micah has done for me." Though relating it as first person speech, the opening phrase "according to this and according to this" appears to be a summarizing statement (see NASB's "thus and so has Micah done to me"). In this way it is a melding of reported and summarized speech.

6 נֹכַח יְהוָה (*nōkaḥ yhwh*, "the LORD's approval"). The Hebrew reads "in front of Yahweh." The term here, however, is ambiguous and could refer to something agreeable or disagreeable to God (Polzin, 198; Exum, "The Centre Cannot Hold," 427; Gale A. Yee, "Ideological Criticism: Judges 17-21 and the Dismembered Body," in her *Judges and Method* [Minneapolis: Fortress, 1995], 159; Mueller).

c. The Danites Investigate Laish and Report Back to Dan (18:7-10)

⁷So the five men left and came to Laish, where they saw that the people were living in safety, like the Sidonians, unsuspecting and secure. And since their land lacked nothing, they were prosperous. Also, they lived a long way from the Sidonians and had no relationship with anyone else.

⁸When they returned to Zorah and Eshtaol, their brothers asked them, "How did you find things?"

⁹They answered, "Come on, let's attack them! We have seen that the land is very good. Aren't you going to do something? Don't hesitate to go there and take it over. ¹⁰When you get there, you will find an unsuspecting people and a spacious land that God has put into your hands, a land that lacks nothing whatever."

COMMENTARY

7 Having been blessed by the Levite at Micah's shrine in the hill country of Ephraim, the five warriors proceed to the town of Laish (called Leshem in Joshua 19:47), which lay on the far northern boundary of Israelite territory (see further Provan, Long, and Longman, 181–83). This town, situated at the base of Mount Hermon next to one of the headwaters of the Jordan River basin, is mentioned in Egyptian texts of the eighteenth century BC (*ABD*, 2:12; cf. *ANET*, 242, 329). The Danite warriors' reconnaissance reveals at least two features about the inhabitants of this city: their existence was both secluded and secure. (A third feature is clearly that of prosperity [18:10], though it is not clear from the Hebrew in 18:7 [see Notes].)

Both features are described in relation to the Sidonians, those Phoenician inhabitants along the Mediterranean coast to the northwest of Israel. The people of Laish enjoyed the seclusion and security not only in the same way as the Sidonians did, but also because they were at a safe distance from the Sidonians. These two features of Laish make it an ideal place for the Danites, not only because this tribe is hoping to put significant distance between themselves and their enemies (contrast their present close proximity to the powerful Philistines), but also because this tribe could expect easy victory over an unallied and secluded people group.

8–10 Having assessed the situation, the five spies return south to report to their Danite clans at Zorah and Eshtaol. The narrator uses dramatic narrative for this report as the spies seek to convince their clan members of the opportunity that lies at hand. The focus of the report is on the fact that the people are unsuspecting and that the land is spacious and lacking nothing. Furthermore, they claim that God has put this town and surrounding area into their hands, possibly an allusion to the priestly oracle provided by Micah's Levite. That this outcome is not Yahweh's intention is clear from his earlier revelation through Joshua, which had identified their land in the south. The Danite movement north is due to unfaithfulness in taking their inheritance.

NOTE

7 וְאֵין־מַכְלִים דָּבָר בָּאָרֶץ יוֹרֵשׁ עֶצֶר (*weʾên-maklîm dābār bāʾāreṣ yôrēš ʿeṣer*, "And since their land lacked nothing, they were prosperous"). The Hebrew reads here, "and there were no ones who harm/shame anything in the land, (that is) a possessor of oppression." For clarification see 18:10, where one finds בָּאָרֶץ מָקוֹם אֲשֶׁר אֵין־שָׁם מַחְסוֹר כָּל־דָּבָר אֲשֶׁר (*māqôm ʾašer ʾên-šām maḥsôr kol-dābār ʾašer bāʾāreṣ*, "a land that lacks nothing whatever"), which reads in Hebrew, "a place which there is not there a lack of any thing which is in the land."

עִם־אָדָם (*ʿim-ʾādām*, "with anyone else"). The Hebrew reads, "with humanity." The LXX[a] reads, μετὰ Συρίας (*meta Syrias*, "with Syria," reflecting an underlying Hebrew Vorlage with ארם [*ʾrm*] instead of אדם [*ʾdm*]), yet the LXX[b] reads, πρὸς ἄνθρωπον (*pros anthrōpon*, reflecting אדם [*ʾdm*]). The original reading was probably אָדָם (*ʾādām*), since in 18:28 where this description is repeated, the MT has עִם־אָדָם (*ʿim-ʾādām*), and both the LXX[a] and LXX[b] read, μετὰ ἀνθρώπου *meta anthrōpou*.

d. The Danites Set Out for War (18:11–12)

¹¹Then six hundred men from the clan of the Danites, armed for battle, set out from Zorah and Eshtaol. ¹²On their way they set up camp near Kiriath Jearim in Judah. This is why the place west of Kiriath Jearim is called Mahaneh Dan to this day.

COMMENTARY

11–12 The five warriors are able to convince six hundred (or six small units of) men from among the Danite clans in Zorah and Eshtaol to set out for the new territory. According to 18:21 this force is accompanied by their families and possessions, thus revealing their intention to migrate to new territory. That the fate of the rest of the Danite families is never provided suggests these families constitute the remnant after the failure of this tribe to establish tribal territory in the south.

The rallying point is Mahaneh Dan, a site that according to 13:25 was situated between Eshtaol and Zorah and the location at which the Spirit began to stir within Samson. Here in 18:11 the site is associated with Kiriath Jearim, which lay on the boundary between Judah (Jos 15:9) and Benjamin (18:14, 28). It is possible that the references to Mahaneh Dan in 13:25 and 18:11 are different locations,

reflecting Danite nomadic patterns. But the use of the same term in both passages creates a tragic link between the earlier attempt in 13:25 by Yahweh to free the Danites from oppression and the present admission of defeat in 18:11 by the Danites (see *ABD*, 4:473).

The author's voice breaks into the second half of v.12 with the observation that this story explains the origins of the name of a location near Kiriath Jearim known to his present readers ("to this day"). This phrase reveals that the implied readers of this section of Judges were those familiar with this region of the country but at some remove from the events being related. While an earlier generation of scholars saw such statements as this one as explaining the origins of the story (an etiology), they may reflect subtle attempts by the author to bolster the story's authenticity.

e. The Danites Come to Micah's House and Steal Micah's Shrine (18:13–21)

¹³From there they went on to the hill country of Ephraim and came to Micah's house. ¹⁴Then the five men who had spied out the land of Laish said to their brothers, "Do you know that one of these houses has an ephod, other household gods, a carved image and a cast idol? Now you know what to do." ¹⁵So they turned in there and went to the house of the young Levite at Micah's place and greeted him. ¹⁶The six hundred Danites, armed for battle, stood at the entrance to the gate. ¹⁷The five men who had spied out the land went

inside and took the carved image, the ephod, the other household gods and the cast idol while the priest and the six hundred armed men stood at the entrance to the gate.

[18]When these men went into Micah's house and took the carved image, the ephod, the other household gods and the cast idol, the priest said to them, "What are you doing?"

[19]They answered him, "Be quiet! Don't say a word. Come with us, and be our father and priest. Isn't it better that you serve a tribe and clan in Israel as priest rather than just one man's household?" [20]Then the priest was glad. He took the ephod, the other household gods and the carved image and went along with the people. [21]Putting their little children, their livestock and their possessions in front of them, they turned away and left.

COMMENTARY

13–14 The journey of the Danite force once again takes them into the hill country of Ephraim and past the house of Micah (v.13). The five spies alerted their comrades to the presence of a holy shrine and associated religious paraphernalia, that is, the ephod, household gods, carved image, and cast idol (v.14; cf. 17:4–5). It is soon clear that they intend to entice the tribe to steal the contents of the shrine, ironic in light of the fact that the idols were made from stolen silver in the first place (17:1–5). In the short run these religious paraphernalia would prove helpful for securing divine help for their approaching battle, but in the long run for ensuring blessing for their tribe in their new territory.

15–21 According to 18:15 they approach the young Levite directly without any consultation with Micah. The narrator is careful to mention the intimidating presence of the six small units ("six hundred") of armed warriors standing outside the gate as the five spies greet the Levite and steal the items (18:16–17). While the Levite expresses initial concern over their brazen act (18:18), he is happily silenced by the lucrative offer of the men that he serve as priest of an entire tribe and clan (Dan) rather than an insignificant household (Micah).

It is interesting that while 18:18 describes the five spies as taking the contents of the shrine, 18:20 links the same action to the young Levite. These traditions do not compete, but rather narratively signal the young Levite's willing participation with the Danites in the theft. It is not surprising that this Levite, who had been lured by Micah's offer of ten shekels of silver, clothes, and food and the status of priest and son (17:10–13), would be enticed by the lucrative offer of the Danites. The Danites leave with their newly acquired priest and shrine and carefully put their children, livestock, and possessions in front of them, thus indicating their fear of reprisal from forces loyal to Micah.

NOTES

14 וְעַתָּה דְּעוּ מַה־תַּעֲשׂוּ (weʿattâ deʿû mah-taʿaśû, "Now you know what to do"). The verb יָדַע (ydʿ; GK 3359) can also mean to consider or reflect on something and often occurs with the imperative mood as here (e.g., Dt 4:39; 2Sa 24:13; 1Ki 20:7, 22; cf. Dt 8:5). Better is the translation, "Consider what you might do."

15 וַיִּשְׁאֲלוּ־לוֹ לְשָׁלוֹם (wayyišªlû-lô lᵉšālôm, "and greeted him"). The MT reads here, "and they asked concerning his well-being" (Block, 505), a standard expression of greeting (1Sa 10:4; 17:22; 25:5; 30:21; 2Sa 8:10; Jer 15:5; 1Ch 18:10; cf. 1Sa 17:56; Jer 18:13; 30:6), contrasted with the farewell: "go with reference to well-being" (הלך ל, hlk l: Ex 4:18; Jdg 18:6; 1Sa 1:17; 20:42; 2Ki 5:19; cf. הלך ב, hlk b: Ge 26:31; 1Sa 29:7; 2Sa 3:21−23; 15:9; cf. Block, 505).

f. Micah Pursues the Danites (18:22−26)

> ²²When they had gone some distance from Micah's house, the men who lived near Micah were called together and overtook the Danites. ²³As they shouted after them, the Danites turned and said to Micah, "What's the matter with you that you called out your men to fight?"
>
> ²⁴He replied, "You took the gods I made, and my priest, and went away. What else do I have? How can you ask, 'What's the matter with you?'"
>
> ²⁵The Danites answered, "Don't argue with us, or some hot-tempered men will attack you, and you and your family will lose your lives." ²⁶So the Danites went their way, and Micah, seeing that they were too strong for him, turned around and went back home.

COMMENTARY

22−26 The Danites' fear of reprisal is not unfounded (see above), as Micah gathers together the surrounding clans to challenge these thieves (18:22). Though the Danites "had gone some distance," because of their accompanying children and livestock Micah's force easily overtakes them. The dramatic narrative in 18:23−25 voices the emotional interchange between the Danites and Micah, one in which the Danites fail to acknowledge the fact that their brazen theft has caused this military encounter (see Notes) and then threaten the lives of Micah and his family. In the end Micah is forced to acknowledge his powerlessness to challenge this greater tribal force.

NOTES

22 נִזְעֲקוּ (nizªqû, "were called together"). The passive Niphal with uncertain subject contributes to the depiction of Micah's helplessness. In contrast, in 18:23 the Danites explicitly identify the subject of this mustering, making Micah responsible for this military confrontation. The Niphal of זעק (zᶜq) is used for mustering a military force in Joshua 8:16; Judges 6:34−35; 1 Samuel 14:20 (cf. its use in the Qal in Jdg 12:2; 18:23; the Hiphil can also be used to summon a militia: Jdg 4:10, 13; 2Sa 20:4−5).

25 אֲנָשִׁים מָרֵי נֶפֶשׁ (ᵃⁿāšîm mārê nepeš, "some hot-tempered men"). The Hebrew phrase here is better, "men bitter of soul," most likely a reference to men hardened by difficult experiences, possibly related to war and death (see esp. 2Sa 17:8; also Eze 27:31; Job 3:20; 21:25; Pr 31:6; cf. 1Sa 15:32; 2Sa 2:26; Am 8:10; Zep 1:14).

g. The Danites Possess Laish and Set Up the Shrine (18:27–31)

²⁷Then they took what Micah had made, and his priest, and went on to Laish, against a peaceful and unsuspecting people. They attacked them with the sword and burned down their city. ²⁸There was no one to rescue them because they lived a long way from Sidon and had no relationship with anyone else. The city was in a valley near Beth Rehob.

The Danites rebuilt the city and settled there. ²⁹They named it Dan after their forefather Dan, who was born to Israel — though the city used to be called Laish. ³⁰There the Danites set up for themselves the idols, and Jonathan son of Gershom, the son of Moses, and his sons were priests for the tribe of Dan until the time of the captivity of the land. ³¹They continued to use the idols Micah had made, all the time the house of God was in Shiloh.

COMMENTARY

27–29 The narrative concludes with a description of the easy victory of the Danites over Laish, resulting in the death of its inhabitants ("attacked them with the sword") and destruction of its buildings ("burned down their city"; 18:27–28a; see further Provan, Long, and Longman, 181–83). The Danites rebuild and rename the city Dan. The illicit character of this Danite action is suggested not only by the fact that they are abandoning the inheritance Yahweh had given them in the south, but also in their violation of the rule of military conduct for distant cities in Deuteronomy 20:10–15, which stipulates that they are to make an offer of peace and, if forced to engage in battle, must only strike the men (see Wong, *Strategy*, 39).

30–31 The closing note explains the import of this story to Israel by revealing that Micah's idols and young Levite formed the foundation of a shrine at Dan that rivaled the tabernacle located in the central region of Israel (in its early phase at Shiloh, as in 1Sa 1–4, and later at Jerusalem; cf. 2Sa 6). This act clearly violates Moses' command in Deuteronomy 12 that Israel worship at one central place. Ironically, the young Levite is now identified as Jonathan son of Gershom, the son of Moses (see Note). Gershom was the firstborn of Moses and Zipporah (Ex 2:22; cf. 1Ch 23:15–16; 26:24).

The mention of the "captivity of the land" (v.30) in a passage related to the establishment of a shrine at Dan has led many to see in this passage a link to a key motif in the book of Kings, namely, Jeroboam's sinful action in setting up golden calves at Bethel and Dan (1Ki 12:25–33). This action is identified as the cause of the defeat of Israel by Assyria and its exile from the land (see esp. 2Ki 17:21–23; cf. 1Ki 15:26, 34; 16:2, 7, 26, 31; 22:52; 2Ki 3:3; 10:29, 31; 13:2, 6, 11, 21; 14:24; 15:9, 18, 24, 28; cf. Mordechai

Cogan, *1 Kings: A New Translation with Introduction and Commentary* [AB 10; New York: Doubleday, 2001], 97, who picks up on Frank M. Cross ["The Themes of the Book of Kings and the Structure of the Deuteronomistic History," in *Reconsidering Israel and Judah: Recent Studies on the Deuteronomistic History* (ed. Gary N. Knoppers and J. Gordon McConville; Winona Lake, Ind.: Eisenbrauns, 2000), 79–94] in arguing that Jeroboam's sin and the promises to David are "pervasive" themes in the book of Kings and shows how they "find their culmination in the actions of Josiah," who will destroy Jeroboam's altar at Bethel; cf. 1Ki 13:2; 2Ki 23).

Other scholars, however, have considered the temporal reference in v.31 to "the time the house of God was in Shiloh" as identifying the "captivity of the land" in v.30 as a reference to an earlier captivity (on Shiloh and its destruction see Provan, Long, and Longman, 184–85), one associated with Israel's defeat under Eli's leadership (1Sa 4) or Saul's leadership (1Sa 31–2Sa 5; see Introduction). The reference to Dan (and possibly even Bethel) and parallels throughout the chapter between Micah and Jeroboam (cf. Jdg 17:5 with 1Ki 12:33; Jdg 18:24 with 1Ki 12:28; Jdg 17:5, 12–13 with 1Ki 13:33; Block, 483; cf. Na'aman), however, suggest the later captivity. The illicit northern (Danite) sanctuary has its roots in acts of thievery and savagery connected with the shady characters of Micah, the young Levite, and the Danites.

NOTE

30 בֶּן־מְנַשֶּׁה (*ben-mᵉnašše*, "son of Moses"). The Codex Leningradis and many medieval Masoretic manuscripts read here "Manasseh," but write the letter נ (*n*) as a superscript between the normal letters מ (*m*) and שׁ (*š*). Many other medieval Masoretic manuscripts write the letter נ normally. Some medieval Masoretic manuscripts read here "Moses" (thus without the suspended נ), a reading that is also reflected in some manuscripts of the Old Greek and Vulgate. It appears that certain scribes were uncomfortable with the association between this young Levite and Moses' clan, and so they opted to connect him to the northern tribe of Manasseh by alluding to that idolatrous southern king Manasseh (2Ki 21), whose behavior caused the exile of the southern kingdom (2Ki 21:10–15; 23:26–27; 24:1–4).

REFLECTION

The account of Micah and the Danites highlights the failure of the judge-deliverers and explicitly states the necessity of appropriate royal rule in Israel. Key to this kind of royal rule is the worship of Yahweh through appropriate means at the designated central shrine. Kings of Yahweh's choosing will be kings who place the worship of Yahweh as their core responsibility, a feature exemplified by David and ultimately by his scion, Jesus the Messiah (see Jn 4).

The Levite here serves as a poignant warning to leaders in all eras of redemptive history. He compromised his calling to accept the handsome support of Micah, only to abandon Micah when the offer from the tribe of Dan was put on the table. This successive compromise ultimately affected not only a household or a tribe, but an entire nation as well.

B. Benjamin's Offense (19:1–21:25)

OVERVIEW

The employment of part of the key refrain used throughout Judges 17–21 in 19:1a ("In those days Israel had no king ... "; cf. 17:6; 18:1; 21:25) signals the end of the first major narrative complex in chs. 17–21 and the beginning of another. The former complex (chs. 17–18) focused on the origins of the illicit cult sanctuary at Dan in northern Israel, while the latter (chs. 19–21) will focus on the immoral behavior of the inhabitants of Gibeah within the tribe of Benjamin. The behavior of the men of Gibeah will threaten the extinction of the Benjamite tribe. That the story begins and ends with a mention of kingship (19:1; 21:25), that Gibeah is the hometown of Saul, the first king of Israel, and that parallels can be discerned between chs. 19–21 and the Saul narratives in Samuel (Lasine; Brettler, "The Book of Judges") suggest that Saul is not being put forward as the ideal king to solve Israel's dilemma. Mention of Bethlehem, the hometown of the story's innocent victim, offered to the Benjamites by the insensitive Ephraimite host and husband, as well as mention of Judah's role in military leadership (20:18), suggest that another innocent Bethlehemite from Judah is the one who will fill the royal vacuum in Israel.

Chapters 19–21 are linked to the previous narrative (chs. 17–18) not only by the continued use of the key refrain (19:1; 21:25; cf. 17:6; 18:1), but also by the presence of similar motifs. Both narratives concern Levites connected with both the hill country of Ephraim and Bethlehem in Judah (cf. 19:1 with 17:7–8), whose lives become intertwined with the violent actions of a different, smaller tribe, a remnant of which is set at six hundred men (cf. 20:47 with 18:11). Both stories begin at the smallest social level within Israel, the household, but soon escalate into a crisis for an entire tribe and ultimately the whole nation (Satterthwaite, "No King in Israel"; O'Connell, 264–65; Sweeney; Block, 474–75, 515, for further connections).

Chapters 19–21, as all of chs. 17–21, are also linked to the first introduction to the book in 1:1–2:5, where tribal identity dominates the description of warfare. In that introduction, wars were conducted externally against the Canaanites, while in chs. 19–21 war is internally focused as civil war tears the nation of Israel apart. In both 1:1–2:5 and chs. 19–21 inquiry is made of Yahweh, who identifies Judah as the tribe that will lead the nation into battle (1:1–2; 20:18; O'Connell, 242, 261; Amit, *Judges*, 353–55).

Chapters 19–21 are structured in three interconnected narratives. This narrative complex begins with the depiction of the brutal death of a Levite's concubine at the hands of the men of Gibeah (19:1–30). This violence serves as the occasioning incident for the narrative that follows in 20:1–48 and depicts the successful military response of the rest of the Israelite tribes against Benjamin. Benjamin's defeat, however, threatens the very existence of that tribe within Israel, a dilemma that prompts the final narrative, in which the rest of the Israelite tribes provide two solutions to Benjamin's impending extinction (21:1–23a).

Judges 21:23b–24 brings closure to the narrative complex of chs. 19–21 as Benjamin and then the rest of Israel return home. Judges 21:25 concludes the entire narrative complex of chs. 17–21 in particular, and the book of Judges as a whole, with the reminder that Israel's lack of a royal leader explained the stark reality that clearly everyone was doing what was right in their own eyes, both in terms of worship as well as ethics.

The repeated refrain throughout chs. 17–21 is that "everyone did as he saw fit," a phrase that highlights by contrast the need for pure worship at the central site of God's choosing (Dt 12:8). That this issue is the key issue in play in chs. 17–18, with its stories about inappropriate means and sites for worship and inquiry, is apparent (see Boda, "Recycling Heaven's Words"). In chs. 19–21 most see a focal shift to ethical rather than religious anarchy, especially related to the treatment of the various women in these chapters (cf. O'Connell, 235, 242). But chs. 19–21 reveal considerable ambiguity over the means and sites for worship and inquiry with references to Bethel, Mizpah, Shiloh, and even Gibeah as places where assemblies were held and inquiries of Yahweh were made during the war against the Benjamites (Brooks, 31). Furthermore, there are ethical elements within chs. 17–18 beyond issues related to worship (Mueller, 126).

The historical context of the events in chs. 19–21 is not delineated clearly at the outset. But later the narrator will provide a passing reference to Aaron's grandson Phinehas's serving before the ark (20:27–28), thus placing these events, as those of chs. 17–18 and 1:1–2:5, in the generation after Joshua's death (contra Brooks, 34–35, who confuses literary with historical connections to post-Saulide Israel).

1. Refrain (19:1a)

> ¹In those days Israel had no king.

COMMENTARY

1a In the transition between his two main narrative complexes in chs. 17–21, once again the narrator inserts part of his key refrain, employed in 17:6 and 21:25 in its full form: "In those days Israel had no king; everyone did as he saw fit" (see comments on 17:6). Only the first half of the refrain appears in 18:1a and here in 19:1a, thus placing the accent on the issue of kingship in the understanding of these stories as well as the book as a whole. The story that follows will reveal the religious and ethical crisis faced by Israel without appropriate leadership. The answer to that royal dilemma is certainly not the delinquent tribe of Benjamin and its depraved city of Gibeah (Saul's hometown), but rather the tribe of Judah (David's tribe), whose leadership is highlighted in the judgment against Benjamin in 20:18 (Brooks, 38–39).

2. The Violent, Shameful Death of a Levite's Concubine in Gibeah (19:1b–30)

OVERVIEW

While several stories to this point in Judges have depicted shocking conditions, this one is the most shocking of all—probably in all of biblical literature (Mieke Bal, "A Body of Writing: Judges 19," in *A Feminist Companion to Judges* [ed. A. Brenner; Sheffield: JSOT, 1993], 209). In this aspect it represents the nadir of despair, which necessitates the rise of a monarchy in line with Deuteronomic values.

a. The Levite, His Concubine, Their Journeys to Bethlehem, and Hospitality of the Concubine's Father (19:1b–10a)

Now a Levite who lived in a remote area in the hill country of Ephraim took a concubine from Bethlehem in Judah. [2]But she was unfaithful to him. She left him and went back to her father's house in Bethlehem, Judah. After she had been there four months, [3]her husband went to her to persuade her to return. He had with him his servant and two donkeys. She took him into her father's house, and when her father saw him, he gladly welcomed him. [4]His father-in-law, the girl's father, prevailed upon him to stay; so he remained with him three days, eating and drinking, and sleeping there.

[5]On the fourth day they got up early and he prepared to leave, but the girl's father said to his son-in-law, "Refresh yourself with something to eat; then you can go." [6]So the two of them sat down to eat and drink together. Afterward the girl's father said, "Please stay tonight and enjoy yourself." [7]And when the man got up to go, his father-in-law persuaded him, so he stayed there that night. [8]On the morning of the fifth day, when he rose to go, the girl's father said, "Refresh yourself. Wait till afternoon!" So the two of them ate together.

[9]Then when the man, with his concubine and his servant, got up to leave, his father-in-law, the girl's father, said, "Now look, it's almost evening. Spend the night here; the day is nearly over. Stay and enjoy yourself. Early tomorrow morning you can get up and be on your way home." [10]But, unwilling to stay another night, the man left.

COMMENTARY

1b–2 The story begins much as ch. 17 did by identifying an individual living in relative obscurity in the hill country of Ephraim. In this case, the individual is left unnamed—a regular feature of the story that unfolds in chs. 19–21 and one that highlights the dehumanizing character of the age it describes (Hudson). Another contrast to the story in ch. 17 is that this individual is not a native member of this region but is living as a temporary alien (see Note). While in ch. 17 the individual was an Ephraimite who took into his household a Levite from Bethlehem in Judah, in ch. 19 the individual is a Levite who takes into his household a concubine from Bethlehem.

This woman's origin in Judah invites a comparison between her and the first woman encountered in Judges, that is, Acsah, the Judahite daughter of Caleb (Schneider, 246–54; McCann, 131). Interestingly, while both women "left their men and returned to their fathers" and both rode on donkeys

(Schneider, 251), Acsah is honored with a name, full marital status, an active voice in the story, and a positive destiny. Contrasts between these two portrayals are indicative of the regressive flow of the book as a whole.

In the ancient world a concubine was a secondary wife taken by a rich male to ensure the continuance of the family line (cf. Ge 25:1, 6; 30:4; 35:22). That in the story of Judges 19 this Levite has a servant and a pair of donkeys suggests that he is of some means. Oddly, no mention is made of a primary wife (Schneider, 248). It may be that concubines were considered within the servant class of the household (cf. Ge 35:22), since the Levite is referred to as the master (ʾādôn) of the servant boy in Judges 19:11–12 as well as of his concubine in 19:26–27. The Levite refers to her as ʾāmâ ("maidservant"; GK 563) in his speech to the old man in 19:19.

Although of secondary status, a concubine was socially bound to her new household and could not be violated by another male (Ge 35:22; 49:4; 2Sa 3:7; 16:20–22; 1Ki 2:13–25; see comments on Jdg 9:1). While in the majority of cases a concubine entered physically into the household of her "husband," Judges 8:31 suggests that Gideon's concubine remained with her family in Shechem.

The narrator informs the reader that the concubine in Judges 19 was unfaithful (znh) to the Levite (see Note), an action elsewhere referring to a female's becoming sexually involved with another man (Ge 38:24; Lev 21:9; Nu 25:1; Dt 22:21; Isa 23:17; Jer 3:1, 6, 8; Eze 16:15–17, 26, 28; 23:3, 5, 19; Hos 2:7; 3:3; 4:13–14; 6:10; Am 7:17) — unacceptable for a woman related to a Levite (Lev 21:15). That such a violation (or accusation of violation) endangered her life (see Ge 38:24; Lev 20:10; 21:9; Dt 22:22; for extrabiblical evidence see Galpaz-Feller, *Samson*, 106–7; Code of Hammurabi §§127, 131) explains her flight to the safety of her father's house in Bethlehem.

For a woman in the ancient world the house of one's father/mother was her only appropriate social network apart from the house of her husband (see Ru 1:8–9). This moral principle is made explicit in the law related to the virginity of a new bride in Deuteronomy 22:13–21, where the father and mother are to defend a daughter's virginity (22:15). Here the narrator may be merely stating the claim of the Levite: "But she had been unfaithful to him." At stake in this situation sociologically is the honor not only of the concubine but also of the Levite, a social dimension that also drives the abuse of the concubine later in the account (see below, Stone, 95–96; cf. idem, *Sex, Honor, and Power in the Deuteronomistic History* [JSOTSup 234; Sheffield: Sheffield Academic, 1996]).

3–4 Because the acquisition of a wife/concubine in the ancient world represented a covenantal agreement between two families/clans, the Levite soon journeys to the house of his concubine's father to bring her back to Ephraim. His four-month wait before journeying may be related to an accusation of "unfaithfulness," four months being the period needed to determine guilt (Schneider, 252–53). The narrator suggests that the Levite has good intentions when he notes that the Levite hopes she might return as a result of his "speaking to her heart" ("persuade her"), most likely an idiom for speaking tenderly (so the NASB; used in Ge 34:3 to refer to a sexual advance and in other contexts to speaking kindly to another [cf. 2Ch 30:22; Ru 2:13; Isa 40:2]).

Ironically, none of the speech of the Levite to the woman is explicitly cited by the narrator, with the focus shifting entirely to the interaction between husband and father, a foreshadowing of similar disregard for this woman in the approaching scene (Bohmbach, 93). It is the concubine who invites him into the house of her father, who then welcomes the Levite into his home. The Levite has with him two donkeys and a helper to facilitate her return.

What follows is an example of ancient Near Eastern hospitality (eating, drinking, sleeping; cf. Ge 18, 24; Jdg 6, 13; cf. Ex 24; Hobbs) as the concubine's father entertains the Levite, most likely hoping to repair the social damage caused by his daughter, though possibly also hoping to ensure that the Levite does not have ill intent. Three days appears to be the length of time the Levite expects to visit his concubine's home (cf. 1Ch 12:39; Jnh 3:3).

5–7 Leaving the concubine's house, however, will prove to be a challenge, as the father seeks to delay the Levite for as long as possible, perhaps, as Laban of old, hoping that the son-in-law would remain (Ge 28–31). On the fourth day the Levite arises to leave on his journey but is delayed by the concubine's father, who offers a piece of bread alongside the promise that the Levite can then depart (v.5). It appears, however, that there is more than just a scrap of bread to be consumed, since they eat and drink (v.6). The meal affords further opportunity for the host to convince the Levite to stay another night, with the promise of the joy that accompanies feasting.

The reason for the father's delay tactics is unclear. Possibly he is hoping to convince the Levite to remain in Bethlehem permanently, or perhaps he is searching for more insight into the Levite's intentions for his daughter. Narratively the delay enhances the motif of hospitality that will be key to the incident in Gibeah (O'Connell, 249; Miller, 110–11; Amit, *Judges*, 344). It also helps to explain why the Levite is caught in a vulnerable situation and is forced to stay in Gibeah overnight (cf. Block, 527).

8–10a The same pattern is repeated on the fifth day. This time the father explicitly mentions staying till afternoon, at which time he then repeats the argument that the day is nearly over and that the Levite should stay the night and enjoy the hospitality. The Levite, however, finally insists on leaving.

NOTES

1 גָּר (*gār*, "lived"). A better translation is "sojourning" or "staying," as this verb means to "dwell as alien and dependent" (*HALOT*, 185).

2 וַתִּזְנֶה (*wattizneh*, "she was unfaithful"). The LXX[a] has ὠργίσθη (*ōrgisthē*; "she became angry"), the LXX[b] has ἐπορεύθη (*eporeuthē*, "she left"), and *Targum Jonathan* has וּבַסָרַת (*ûbasarat*, "she despised"). But *HALOT*, 275, argues that this word is a homonym, זנהII (*znh*), similar to the Akkadian *zenû* ("to be angry, hate"), here "feel repugnance" against (עַל, ᶜl) her husband. In that case, however, here we would see the only use of this root in the OT. Possibly the LXX is relying on a Hebrew text that contained זנח (*znḥ*, "to reject, detest"; cf. Block, 523; Eynikel, 104, n. 6). Stone, 91, argues that ancient Israelite social mores would identify her as "unfaithful" just by taking the initiative as a female to "remove herself from her husband's domain" (cf. Klein, "Structure, Irony and Meaning," 88; Exum, *Fragmented Women*, 178–80; Fewell and Gunn 1993: 133). But if this suggestion is true, here would be the only time this term is used with this sense of being "unfaithful," and if the previous suggestion of the homonym זנהII (*znh*) is true, it also would be the only occurrence of this root in the OT.

Jones-Warsaw (21–22) points to the Torah to understand this verse and notes Leviticus 21:1–15, which stipulates that a Levite must marry a virgin, and Deuteronomy 22:13–21, which stipulates that a girl's parents were to protect her and show evidence of her virginity. This would explain her return home, where she may have been protected by her father. It also may suggest that the unfaithfulness here referred to is merely a claim by the Levite that she was not a virgin and so "had been unfaithful to him." This would make better sense of the behavior of the Levite when he arrives in Bethlehem, as he shows no signs of a vendetta against the girl, possibly because he is sorry for such an accusation.

6 וְיִטַב לִבֶּךָ (weyiṭab libbekâ, "enjoy yourself"), better, "let your heart be glad" (cf. 19:9). This phrase appears elsewhere to refer to the gladness of one's heart (2Ki 25:24; Ecc 7:3; 11:9), which at times is related to the euphoria that follows or accompanies eating and/or drinking (Ru 3:7; 1Ki 21:7). In Judges 19:22 the collocation יטב לב (yṭb lēb, Hiphil) follows a reference to eating and drinking. The phrase טוֹב לֵב (ṭôb lēb, Qal) is the clearer reference to the gladness that accompanies drinking wine (Jdg 16:25; 1Sa 25:36; 2Sa 13:28; Est 1:10).

9 רָפָה הַיּוֹם לַעֲרֹב (rāpâ hayyôm laʿarōb, "the day is nearly over"). This expression is odd in Hebrew. In Exodus 4:26 the verb רפה (rph) denotes "letting go," and in Isaiah 5:24 of hay being "burned up" in a flame. The verb עֲרֹב (ʿrb) means "turn into evening" (cf. Isa 24:11). Thus, here the day is being extinguished by its turning into evening.

חֲנוֹת הַיּוֹם (ḥanôt hayyôm, "the day is coming to an end"). This expression is another odd one in Hebrew. The verb חנה (ḥnh) here is used in Genesis (e.g., Ge 26:17), Exodus (e.g., 13:20), and Numbers (e.g., 9:18) for an individual or group camping for the night.

b. The Levite, His Concubine, and Their Journey to Gibeah (19:10b–15)

[The man] went toward Jebus (that is, Jerusalem), with his two saddled donkeys and his concubine. ¹¹When they were near Jebus and the day was almost gone, the servant said to his master, "Come, let's stop at this city of the Jebusites and spend the night." ¹²His master replied, "No. We won't go into an alien city, whose people are not Israelites. We will go on to Gibeah." ¹³He added, "Come, let's try to reach Gibeah or Ramah and spend the night in one of those places." ¹⁴So they went on, and the sun set as they neared Gibeah in Benjamin. ¹⁵There they stopped to spend the night. They went and sat in the city square, but no one took them into his home for the night.

COMMENTARY

10b–14 The Levite, along with his two donkeys, concubine, and servant, head north out of Bethlehem to begin their journey back to Ephraim. The ancient road takes them by Jerusalem, which lay approximately five and a half miles to the north, and at that time the road was controlled by the group of Canaanites called the Jebusites (Jdg 1:21; cf. Ge 15:21; Ex 3:8, 17; 2Sa 5:6–10; see comments on Jdg 1:21). Passing Jerusalem/Jebus as the sun is setting, the servant suggests stopping for the night at the city. The Levite denies the request out of fear of the foreign population of Jebus and opts instead for Gibeah or Ramah.

This decision is ironic in the light of the violent outcome of his visit to the Benjamite enclave of Gibeah, as noted by Wong (*Strategy*, 207): "a Canaanite group, the Jebusites, is explicitly used as foil to highlight the wickedness of the Gibeathites" (cf. Webb, 188–89; Wong, *Strategy*, 30). Increasing the irony is the fact that Jebus was still under Canaanite control because of the failure of the Benjamites in Judges 1:21 (Schneider, 257). Soon it will be obvious that the Benjamites have adopted the ways of the Canaanites.

Gibeah (if it is modern-day Jaba' instead of Tell el-Ful, it lay about three miles north of Jerusalem; cf. *ABD*, 2:1007) lay five and a half miles to the northeast of Jerusalem, while Ramah lay just over four miles to the north (*ABD*, 5:613). Thus Jerusalem is only the halfway point on the journey, a fact that explains why the sun sets before they even reach Gibeah. The close association between King Saul and this town of Gibeah is evident throughout the books of Samuel (1Sa 10:5; 11:4; 15:34; 22:6; 23:19; 2Sa 21:6). The fact that the innocent victim (concubine) is linked to David's hometown of Bethlehem in a section punctuated by the refrain, "in those days Israel had no king," suggests a polemic contrasting the first two dynastic houses in Israel.

15 Forced to take shelter in what they think will be the safe Israelite town of Gibeah, the small company loiter in the "city square" (*rᵉḥôb*), a term that may refer to "an open plaza in the city set against the inner wall of the gate, or gates" (*HALOT*, 1212), but that in villages and towns refers simply to any open space. Interestingly, reference is made to spending the night in the "city square" in the tragic story of Sodom (Ge 19:2), a story that influences the reading of this text (see further below), but even in Sodom Lot met the visitors at the gate. The open space makes it an ideal place to meet people with the hope that someone will extend hospitality to the Levite and his entourage (see Hobbs).

The narrator carefully notes the lack of hospitality by creating a contrast to the earlier generosity lavished on the Levite by the concubine's father (cf. O'Connell, 249) and suggesting that Gibeah will fail to be the safe haven the Levite assumed it would be in v.12. For the premium on hospitality to strangers and especially Levites in the Torah, see Exodus 22:21; 23:9; Leviticus 19:33–34; and Deuteronomy 16:14; 26:12 (cf. McCann, 129).

c. An Old Man from Ephraim Takes in the Levite and Concubine (19:16–21)

¹⁶That evening an old man from the hill country of Ephraim, who was living in Gibeah (the men of the place were Benjamites), came in from his work in the fields. ¹⁷When he looked and saw the traveler in the city square, the old man asked, "Where are you going? Where did you come from?"

¹⁸He answered, "We are on our way from Bethlehem in Judah to a remote area in the hill country of Ephraim where I live. I have been to Bethlehem in Judah and now I am going to the house of the Lᴏʀᴅ. No one has taken me into his house. ¹⁹We have both straw and fodder for our donkeys and bread and wine for ourselves your servants — me, your maidservant, and the young man with us. We don't need anything."

> ²⁰"You are welcome at my house," the old man said. "Let me supply whatever you need. Only don't spend the night in the square." ²¹So he took him into his house and fed his donkeys. After they had washed their feet, they had something to eat and drink.

COMMENTARY

16–20 Hospitality is finally extended in Gibeah, but not by Benjamites; rather, it is provided by an old man who originally hailed from the Levite's home territory in Ephraim but is sojourning (see Note on v.16) in the town of Gibeah, much as the Levite was doing in Ephraim (*gwr*, v.1). The narrator uses dramatic narrative to depict the dialogue between the old man and the Levite. The Levite emphasizes that he is self-sufficient but had expected to be invited into someone's house. Not surprisingly the Levite reveals nothing about the awkward circumstances that brought him to this southern region and caused this unexpected overnight stay in Gibeah. Instead he creates what is probably a pious excuse ("I am going to the house of the LORD," v.18; see Notes), a trend evident in ch. 20 as this Levite testifies before the tribal council in 20:4–7 (Schneider, 259).

The old man welcomes the Levite into his home and even offers him supplies, while carefully noting that he should not spend the night in the village square. This latter comment may be designed to heighten his offer of hospitality, but it functions narratively to indicate additional caution over the Levite's safety in the town. Even though the old man does extend hospitality to the Levite, there are indications in the text that both he and the Levite violate some of the basic social mores, especially in the old man's intrusive questions in v.17 and the Levite's expression of self-sufficiency (see Matthews, *Judges and Ruth*, 184–85; cf. Matthews, "Hospitality and Hostility in Genesis 19," 13–21).

21–22a The old man follows through on his offer by feeding the Levite's donkeys, washing the guests' feet (see Ge 18:4), and providing food and drink (Ge 18:6–8), which led to gladness of heart (see Note on Jdg 19:6; see esp. Hobbs). This scene parallels the hospitality provided by the concubine's father, but soon this comedy will turn to tragedy.

NOTES

16 וְהִנֵּה (*wᵉhinnēh*, untranslated in NIV). Verse 16 represents an important turn in the narrative with the phrase "now behold," introducing a key character into the narrative.

גָּר (*gār*, "was living"). As in 19:1 above, this term means to "dwell as alien and dependent" (*HALOT*, 185).

18 וְאֶת־בֵּית יְהוָה (*wᵉʾet-bêt yhwh*, "to the house of the LORD"). The NIV follows the MT, which is supported by the Targum, Vulgate, and Syriac. The LXX has here καὶ εἰς τὸν οἶκόν μου (*kai eis ton oikon mou*), suggesting an underlying וְאֶת־בֵּיתִי (*wᵉʾt-byty*, "to my house"). This reading in the LXX probably reflects a scribal change made in the light of the statement by the father-in-law in 19:9 that the Levite was heading to his home (there using the term אֹהֶל, *ʾōhel*; see Schneider, 259; contra Boling, 275; Soggin, 287; O'Connell, 483; Block, 531). The destination of the "house of the LORD" is most likely a pious excuse (see above), but it may also be the Levite's final attempt to test the virginity of his concubine (cf. Nu 5:11–31).

d. The Evil of the Men of Gibeah (19:22–26)

> ²²While they were enjoying themselves, some of the wicked men of the city surrounded the house. Pounding on the door, they shouted to the old man who owned the house, "Bring out the man who came to your house so we can have sex with him."
>
> ²³The owner of the house went outside and said to them, "No, my friends, don't be so vile. Since this man is my guest, don't do this disgraceful thing. ²⁴Look, here is my virgin daughter, and his concubine. I will bring them out to you now, and you can use them and do to them whatever you wish. But to this man, don't do such a disgraceful thing."
>
> ²⁵But the men would not listen to him. So the man took his concubine and sent her outside to them, and they raped her and abused her throughout the night, and at dawn they let her go. ²⁶At daybreak the woman went back to the house where her master was staying, fell down at the door and lay there until daylight.

COMMENTARY

22–24 It is at this point that the reader becomes fully aware of the close associations between this story and what Bach, 13, has called "the mirror of the story" and O'Connell, 243, "a narrative analogue"—that is, Lot and the angels in Sodom in Genesis 19 (cf. Susan Niditch, "The 'Sodomite' Theme in Judges 19–20: Family, Community, and Social Disintegration," *CBQ* 44 [1982]: 365–78; Lasine; Daniel I. Block, "Echo Narrative Technique in Hebrew Literature," *WTJ* 52 [1990]: 325–41; Stone; Wong, *Strategy*, 207–09). This relation is designed to conjure up intense negative associations with this earlier story, which ended in divine judgment. Amit ("Hidden Polemic," 343), however, notes how Gibeah exceeds the evil of Sodom by

carrying out the threatened rape, "resulting in the cruel death of the rape victim."

Greatly wicked men surround the old man's house and begin pounding on the door, demanding that the old man send out the man who was with him (the Levite) in order that they may "know" him, a euphemism for sexual intercourse (see Ge 19:5, 8; cf. Ge 4:1). Such homosexual acts were condemned by the Torah (Lev 18:22; 20:13), which stipulated the penalty of death (contra Stone, 91–93, who sees the issue here as rape, not homosexuality).

The old man is identified as the "owner" (*baʿal*) of the house, a term in Hebrew that not only creates a contrastive play on the word used to describe the evil men (*bᵉlîyaʿal*; see Notes), but also identifies the old man as the one responsible for the protection of the Levite. The old man goes out to reason with his wicked neighbors and identifies their request as evil (r⁽ᶜ⁾) and foolish (nᵉbālâ, "disgraceful"), the latter a term used for deviant sexual acts elsewhere in the OT (see Note on 20:6). The old man appeals to his responsibility as host and offers instead both his own virgin daughter and the Levite's concubine in place of his male guest, the latter because she had been identified by the Levite in 19:19 as "your [the old man's] maidservant" (Matthews, "Hospitality and Hostility in Genesis 19," 9; Eynikel, 107). As Block, 537, notes, "A host's honor is at stake — not justice or morality" (cf. Stone, 95-96, 99-100; Hobbs, 29).

The old man's invitation is for his neighbors to "use them" (see Notes) and "do to them whatever you wish" — the latter a phrase that could be translated, "do to them that which is good in your eyes" (waᶜᵃśû lāhem haṭṭôb bᵉᶜênêkem) — eerily similar to the key refrain in 17:6 and 21:25 that sets the tone for this section of Judges ("everyone did as he saw fit," hayyāšār bᵉᶜênāyw yaᶜᵃśeh) and to the other refrain that dominates Judges 2-16: "Israel did what was evil in the eyes of the Lord" (wayyaᶜᵃśû bᵉnê-yiśrāʾēl ʾet-hāraᶜ bᵉᶜênê yhwh; Eynikel, 114). In this event the evil of Israel has reached its peak.

25-26 While the offer of these two women in place of the Levite is clearly unacceptable to these wicked men of Gibeah, the Levite, in a desperate attempt to protect himself as well as the honor of the old man's daughter, seizes hold of the most vulnerable individual in their midst — his concubine, who was simultaneously an alien, fatherless, and a secondary wife (see Patton, 44) — and sends her out to them. The next time he "seizes" her will be when he cuts her lifeless body into pieces designed to incite Israel to avenge her death (see Note on 19:25).

In the mind of the Levite and/or the narrator this action may have been justified because of the concubine's marital unfaithfulness (19:2; cf. Webb, 188; Jones-Warsaw, 24, n. 12; Exum, "Feminist Criticism," 84; Bach, 4), but regardless, in the light of the Torah it remains a despicable act for all involved. The sexually desirous men take the Levite's bait, "knowing" ("raping") her (see comment on vv.22b-24) in a violent orgy of shameful abuse (see Note on 19:25) that lasted the entire night. The public setting of this violence accentuates its brutality and abhorrence (Bohmbach). As daylight approaches the woman is finally let go and has enough strength to return to the doorway of the old man's house before she collapses.

NOTES

22 אַנְשֵׁי הָעִיר אַנְשֵׁי בְנֵי־בְלִיַּעַל (ʾanšê hāᶜîr ʾanšê bᵉnê-bᵉliyaᶜal, "some of the wicked men of the city"). This dual phrase is better translated "the men of the city, the men of the sons of Beliaᶜal" (cf. 20:13). Its latter component also appears in Deuteronomy 13:13 [14]; 1 Samuel 2:12; 10:27; 23:6; 25:17, 25; 2 Samuel 16:7; 20:1; 1 Kings 21:10, 13; 2 Chronicles 13:7; Proverbs 6:12; 16:27, and refers to greatly evil men, that is, scoundrels (cf. בַּת־בְּלִיָּעַל [bat-bᵉliyāᶜal] in 1Sa 1:16 for an evil woman). This phrase is used to characterize "murderers, rapists, false witnesses, corrupt priests, drunks, boors, ungrateful and selfish folk, rebels, those who lead others into idolatry and who do not know Yahweh" (Block, 535).

In Second Temple Judaism Belial will become associated with the forces of darkness and serve in 2 Corinthians 6:15 (Greek Βελιάρ, Beliar) as a synonym for Satan. Satan, however, is not its meaning in the

OT texts, where it "functions as an emotive term to describe individuals or groups who commit the most heinous crimes against the Israelite religious or social order, as well as their acts" (*DDD*, 169; for possible etymologies of this term see *DDD*, 170; the two leading suggestions treat it as a compound word meaning either "the place from which none ascend [underworld]" or "to be unworthy/of no value").

24 וְעַנּוּ (*weʿannû*, "use them"). This verb "is used to express sexual violation by force" (see Ge 34:2; 2Sa 13:12; Jdg 20:5).

25 וַיַּחֲזֵק הָאִישׁ בְּפִילַגְשׁוֹ (*wayyaḥᵃzēq hāʾîš bᵉpîlagšô*, "the man took his concubine"). The collocation חזק (*ḥzq*) in the Hiphil, with the preposition *bᵉ*, at times in the OT refers to a firm grasp on something (Ex 4:4; Dt 22:25; 25:11; Jdg 7:20; 1Sa 15:27; 17:35; 2Sa 1:11; 2:16; 3:29; 13:11; 1Ki 1:50; 2:28; 2Ki 2:12; 4:27; Isa 4:1; 27:5; Jer 31:22; Zec 8:23; Pr 3:18; 4:13; 7:13; 26:17). The same collocation will appear below in 19:29 to describe the Levite's grasp on the dead body of his concubine as he cuts her into twelve parts.

וַיִּתְעַלְּלוּ-בָהּ (*wayyitʿallᵉlû-bâh*, "and abused her"). The verb עלל (*ʿll*, Hithpael; GK 6618) is used elsewhere for Yahweh's mockery of the Egyptians (Ex 10:2), the donkey's mockery of Balaam (Nu 22:29), Pharaoh's severe treatment of Israel (1Sa 6:6), and the expected abuse of a defeated king after fatal wounding (1Sa 31:4//1Ch 10:4) or capture (Jer 38:19). These uses suggest that the verb has the nuance of shameful abuse of another. The sadistic pleasure of these sexually aroused Gibeathites lies not only in their physical act, but also in the shameful experience of the woman. The same would be true of their intention for the Levite.

e. The Levite Takes His Dead Concubine Home and Alerts the Rest of Israel of the Evil Act of Gibeah (19:27–30)

> ²⁷When her master got up in the morning and opened the door of the house and stepped out to continue on his way, there lay his concubine, fallen in the doorway of the house, with her hands on the threshold. ²⁸He said to her, "Get up; let's go." But there was no answer. Then the man put her on his donkey and set out for home.
>
> ²⁹When he reached home, he took a knife and cut up his concubine, limb by limb, into twelve parts and sent them into all the areas of Israel. ³⁰Everyone who saw it said, "Such a thing has never been seen or done, not since the day the Israelites came up out of Egypt. Think about it! Consider it! Tell us what to do!"

COMMENTARY

27–28 It is evident that the Levite (as well as his host) holds little hope for the survival of the concubine, for no one even takes notice of her return. It is also clear that the Levite has no interest in her well-being (Phyllis Trible, *Texts of Terror: Literary-Feminist Readings of Biblical Narratives* [OBT; Philadelphia: Fortress, 1984], 79; Lasine), as displayed in his two curt commands to her at the outset of v.28 ("Get up; let's go"), which contrast sharply with his earlier "speaking tenderly" in v.3 (see comment). The reference to the Levite as "her master" at the end of v.26 and beginning of v.27 emphasizes not only his authority over her, but more importantly his responsibility for her (see Note). Her wounds from the violent sexual orgy have been fatal (see Note on 19:28), but there is no expression of emotion from the Levite. He simply places her on his donkey and sets out to complete his journey.

29–30 Transporting the body, however, does reveal that the Levite intends to respond in some way. Upon reaching home he grasps his concubine for the final time (see Note on 19:25), then severs her body into twelve pieces to be sent throughout Israel (see Note). The fact that this act takes place in the expected place of safety (the home) is a final reminder of the brutality of this episode (Bohmbach, 96) and the lack of burial a reminder of the tragic disgrace attached to this woman's life (Eynikel, 108; cf. Isa 14:18–19; 55:15–16; Jer 8:1–3; 16:4; 22:19). The use of the number twelve symbolizes the entirety of Israel, traditionally divided into twelve tribes.

In 20:6 the division is explicitly identified as according to the regions of Israel's inheritance, that is, the tribal allotments (a double portion being allotted to Joseph [through Ephraim and Manasseh], but no tribal territory assigned to Levi). Although the verb used here (*nth*, Piel) is elsewhere almost always used for the slaughter of sacrificial animals (1Ki 18:23, 33; cf. Ex 29:17; Lev 1:6, 12;

8:20), it may be that the severing of a body into pieces was an ancient custom for inciting a loosely connected confederacy to war, as was true in Saul's call to arms against Nahash the Ammonite (1Sa 11:7). Block, 546, cites the ancient correspondence of Bahdi-Lim to the Mari King Zimri-Lim: "a prisoner in jail should be killed, his body dismembered, and transported to the area ... in order that the people would fear and gather quickly, and I could make an attempt in accordance with the command which my lord has given, to carry out the campaign quickly" (ARM 2.48). Saul's speech reveals the significance of severing the body: "This is what will be done to the oxen of anyone who does not follow Saul and Samuel." Interestingly, Nahash's threat is also related to the shaming (*ḥerpâ*) of Israelites (1Sa 11:2), which is probably what motivates the Levite even more than the death of his concubine.

The narrator depicts the general response of the people with the dramatic expression of v.30. The arrival of the gruesome body parts in the various tribal allotments prompts a response that not only defines the present moment as the darkest in the history of Israel since the exodus, but also as a time that demands action. The three verbs reveal the proper progression from deep reflection (see Note), to devising plans, to informing the entire group of the plan of action. Having one statement attributed to "everyone who saw it" prepares the way for the next phase of the narrative, in which Israel will finally respond at this moral nadir.

NOTES

27 אֲדֹנֶיהָ (ᵃdōneyhā, "her master"). The term אָדוֹן (ʾādôn; GK 123) is used in descriptions of a wife's relationship to a husband in Genesis 18:12; 1 Kings 1:17; and Amos 4:1, as well as for other family relationships (daughter to father in Ge 31:35; younger to older brother in Ge 32:6). The eldest male in the household possessed authority over all members of the household (bêt-ʾab).

28 וְאֵין עֹנֶה (weʾên ʿōneh, "But there was no answer"). Here the LXX (also Vulgate) contains a further comment, which explains that this lack of answer was due to the fact that she was dead. (The LXX[a] has ἀλλὰ τεθνήκει: [alla tethnēkei], "but she had died" [NETS]; the LXX[b] has ὅτι ἦν νεκρά [hoti ēn nekra], "for she was a corpse" [NETS]). While this difference may reflect the loss of a phrase (כי מתה, ki mth) in the MT's tradition through haplography (homoioteleuton; see Boling, 276), it has been suggested by some that the LXX or its Hebrew Vorlage added the phrase to eliminate the reality that the Levite was the one who dealt the fatal blow, either by placing her on his donkey or by slicing her to pieces (Webb, 191; Exum, "The Centre Cannot Hold," 428; Block, 541; Schneider, 264–65). The phrase "there was no answer," however, suggests that she was dead, the explicit reference being either lost from the text (as Boling) or obvious to the early translators.

29 לַעֲצָמֶיהָ (laʿaṣāmeyhā, "limb by limb"). The English "limb" usually refers to arms and legs, but the Hebrew term here is a more general term for bones or skeletal remains (HALOT, 869). The twelve parts of the woman's body were created by dividing at the joints between sections of the skeletal structure.

30 שִׂימוּ־לָכֶם עָלֶיהָ (śîmû-lākem ʿāleyhā, "Think about it!"). Some Hebrew manuscripts as well as the Targum read here לִבַבְכֶם (lebabkem) instead of לָכֶם (lākem). While לבב/לב (lbb/lb) is often used with שִׂים (śym) to refer to deep reflection on (עַל, ʿl) something (see Hag 1:5, 7; Job 1:8), לבב/לב (lbb/lb) can be omitted (e.g., Isa 41:20), as is the case here in Judges 19:30.

עֻצוּ (ʿuṣû, "Consider it"). This biform of the more common יעץ (yʿṣ) appears elsewhere in the OT only in Isaiah 8:10, with reference there as well to counsel related to a battle.

3. Israel's Punishment of Gibeah and Benjamin (20:1–48)

a. The Gathering of Israel at Mizpah to Investigate the Matter (20:1–11)

[1] Then all the Israelites from Dan to Beersheba and from the land of Gilead came out as one man and assembled before the LORD in Mizpah. [2] The leaders of all the people of the tribes of Israel took their places in the assembly of the people of God, four hundred thousand soldiers armed with swords. [3] (The Benjamites heard that the Israelites had gone up to Mizpah.) Then the Israelites said, "Tell us how this awful thing happened."

[4] So the Levite, the husband of the murdered woman, said, "I and my concubine came to Gibeah in Benjamin to spend the night. [5] During the night the men of Gibeah came after me and surrounded the house, intending to kill me. They raped my concubine, and she died. [6] I took my concubine, cut her into pieces and sent one piece to each region of Israel's inheritance, because they committed this lewd and disgraceful act in Israel. [7] Now, all you Israelites, speak up and give your verdict."

[8] All the people rose as one man, saying, "None of us will go home. No, not one of us will return to his house. [9] But now this is what we'll do to Gibeah: We'll go up against it as the lot directs. [10] We'll take ten men out of every hundred from all the tribes of Israel, and a hundred from a thousand, and a thousand from ten thousand, to get provisions

for the army. Then, when the army arrives at Gibeah in Benjamin, it can give them what they deserve for all this vileness done in Israel." [11]So all the men of Israel got together and united as one man against the city.

COMMENTARY

1 The response of those who received the Levite's gruesome package in 19:30 provokes an assembly of the entire nation, expressed as "all the sons of Israel" ("all the Israelites") in reference to the various tribal units that traced their lineage back to the sons of Jacob. The comprehensive character of this group is accentuated further by the geographic references to "Dan to Beersheba," a merism denoting the farthest inhabitable land to the north (Dan, now a reality after the events of chs. 17–18) and the south (Beersheba, south of which the rainfall levels drops to a level where vegetation for humans or animals can barely survive), and an expression commonly employed in the OT to indicate "all Israel" (1Sa 3:20; 2Sa 3:10; 17:11; 24:2, 15; 1Ki 4:25; 1Ch 21:2; 2Ch 30:5; Am 8:14). Mention of "Dan to Beersheba" constitutes a Cisjordanian reference point and so to it is added "the land of Gilead," a term at times indicating the particular area between the Yarmuk and Arnon rivers, but at others (as here) the entire tribal territory east of the Jordan River (2Ki 10:33; Jer 50:10; Zec 10:10).

The narrator depicts the Israelites as an assembling congregation, as also in Leviticus 8:4; Numbers 17:7; 20:2; Joshua 18:1 and 22:12 (see Note). Strikingly similar is the final incident in which the Cisjordanian tribes gather to punish the Transjordanian tribes for building a rival altar in their region. The explicit reference to their assembling "before the LORD" (ʾel-yhwh) suggests the presence of the ark and pos-

sibly tabernacle on this occasion. Israel's engagement in war is not considered secular activity. It is holy war.

Their gathering point is identified as Mizpah, a Benjamite town that lay at the center of the Cisjordanian territory of Israel, but near the western border of Benjamin as indicated by Joshua 18:13, which draws the line from Luz/Bethel to Ataroth-addar, presumably through Mizpah/Mizpeh (see Note). Scholars identify Mizpah either with Nebi Samwil (five miles north of Jerusalem) or (more likely) Tell en-Nasbeh (eight miles north of Jerusalem; cf. *AEHL* "Mizpeh"; *HBD*, 643). At a later point in Israel's history, Samuel would call all Israelites to Mizpah for an assembly (1Sa 7:5); and after the fall of Jerusalem to the Babylonians, Mizpah would be chosen as the new provincial capital (Jer 40:5–12; see Oded Lipschitz, *The Fall and Rise of Jerusalem: Judah under Babylonian Rule* [Winona Lake, Ind.: Eisenbrauns, 2005]). The link between Mizpah and the assembly "before the LORD" continues the development of the theme of the lack of centralized worship that dominates Judges 17–21 (see comments on 21:25).

Although the assembly takes place in Benjamite territory and although this verse emphasizes the inclusivity ("all ... from Dan to Beersheba") as well as unity ("as one man") of the people, it appears that one tribe, Benjamin, in whose territory Mizpah lay, is not present (see 20:3, 17). Its absence suggests that this assembly is called with ill intent against Benjamin from the beginning.

2–3 What follows in vv.2–11 is a war council among the tribes of Israel. Leaders (see Note) are present in the midst of their warriors, which number four hundred thousand, or four hundred large military units. The war council begins with an investigation of the incident that triggered the assembly. Although the "leaders" are mentioned in v.2, it is "the Israelites" (i.e., "the sons of Israel") as a group who ask for an explanation of the matter, thus giving further evidence of the unity of the other tribes on this issue.

In the midst of this description, however, the narrator makes a clear distinction between "the sons of Israel" ("the Israelites") and "the sons of Benjamin" ("the Benjamites"). This evidence reveals that Benjamin has "heard" (or been informed?) of the gathering at Mizpah but has not responded—an early indication that they will support their clansmen at Gibeah. Judges 21:1–5 will reveal that the responding tribes took two solemn oaths: one that pledged death for those who did not assemble at Mizpah (21:5), and the other that pledged refusal to offer their daughters as wives to the Benjamites (21:1).

4–7 Although the request is directed to the entire group in v.3 ("Tell," masculine plural imperative), it is the Levite from ch. 19 who steps forward to relate his horrific testimony. The Levite rehearses the story in a substantial, dramatic narrative reminding the reader of the hideous character of Gibeah's offense while heightening the tension in the plot. An explicit link is made in this speech between Gibeah and Benjamin, thus implicating Benjamin as a whole in the act.

The Levite says nothing about his own folly in the story, that is, his domestic troubles and inability to extricate himself from his father-in-law's home. He also makes a slight change in the story by claiming that the men of Gibeah surrounded the house with the intent to "kill" him and ended up raping (see Note) and killing his concubine, whereas the narrator had explicitly cited the intention of the men of Gibeah in 19:22 as being to "have sexual relations" (yd^c) with him. This slight shift may be aimed at protecting the honor of the Levite, an underlying theme discerned in ch. 19. Furthermore, the Levite does not reveal "the incriminating act that it was he who had thrown his concubine to the mob in order to save himself" (O'Connell, 263; cf. Schneider, 267; Matthews, *Judges and Ruth*, 193; Eynikel, 110, see 19:25).

The Levite does not merely report the facts in this investigation, but rather evaluates them ("this lewd and disgraceful act," v.6b; see Notes), emphasizing the fact that the act is linked not only to Benjamin but also Israel ("in Israel," v.6b) and then seeking to incite a response from the war council (v.7). The two nouns at the end of v.7 ($d\bar{a}b\bar{a}r$ $w^{e c}\bar{e}\d{s}\hat{a}$, "word and counsel"; NIV "speak up and give your verdict") play off two of the verbs ($^c\hat{u}\d{s}\hat{u}$ $w^e dabb\bar{e}r\hat{u}$, "Consider it! Tell us") that were cited coming from lips of those who saw the body parts in 19:30. The Levite's speech rehearsing the offense is designed to elicit the same response as his original act of sending the body parts to the tribes.

8–11 The response in 20:8–11 to the Levite's testimony and exhortation echoes the people's original response (20:1) to the Levite's bloody call to arms (19:29); that is, they gather "as one man" ($k^{e\flat}\hat{i}\d{s}$ $^\flat eh\bar{a}d$; 20:8, 11). As in 20:3, the people speak as a single character with no mention of the leaders. In a carefully worded speech they lay out a plan:

1. They pledge their commitment to deal with the offense rather than return to their homes (v.8).

2. They declare their commitment to seek the guidance of God through the direction of "the lot" (*gôrāl*; see Note).

3. They lay out a plan for the provision of the army, separating out one-tenth of the force to solicit supplies from the rest of the tribes.

4. They express their commitment to punish "Gibeah in Benjamin" for "all this vileness done in Israel" (v.10b).

Identifying Gibeah "in Benjamin" and their deed as done "in Israel" is the first indication of a belief in corporate solidarity—that is, that the acts committed by Gibeah relay guilt to Benjamin and even to Israel as a whole and so demand some kind of response (cf. Kaminsky; Boda, *Severe Mercy*, 518–19). This belief comes into full view in the Israelite speech to the Benjamites in v.13.

NOTES

1 וַתִּקָּהֵל הָעֵדָה (*wattiqqāhēl hāʿēdâ*, "assembled"). Here קהל (*qhl*; GK 7735) appears in the Niphal, with the addition of הָעֵדָה (*hāʿēdâ*). Closely associated apparently are the verb קהל (*qhl*) in the Hiphil (e.g., 1Ki 12:21), and the noun קָהָל (*qāhāl*, Ge 49:6), both used for the gathering of military forces, but also for the gathering of religious communities (verb קהל, *qhl*, Hiphil, e.g., Dt 4:10; noun קָהָל, *qāhāl*, e.g., Dt 5:19).

מִצְפָּה (*miṣpâ*, "Mizpah"). This name is vocalized as מִצְפֶּה (*miṣpeh*) in Joshua 18:26.

2 פִּנּוֹת (*pinnôt*, "leaders"). This term is most often used in the OT for "corner," either of a structure or of a street (e.g., Job 1:19; Ex 27:2; 38:2; Isa 28:16; Jer 31:40), but in a few places for a leader, as here (1Sa 14:38; Isa 19:13; Zep 3:6; Zec 10:4). Interestingly, 1 Samuel 14:38 also depicts an investigation of a matter by a Benjamite from Gibeah (Saul) concerning another Benjamite from Gibeah (his son Jonathan).

5 עִנּוּ (*ʿinnû*, "raped"). See Note on 19:24.

6 זִמָּה וּנְבָלָה (*zimmâ ûnebālâ*, "lewd and disgraceful act"). The LXX is missing וּ זִמָּה (*zimmâ û*), most likely lost in the Hebrew Vorlage of the LXX when the scribe's eye moved from the final *waw* on עָשׂוּ (*ʿāśû*) to the initial *waw* of וּנְבָלָה (*ûnebālâ*). The first term, זִמָּה (*zimmâ*), describes shameful behavior, especially fornication and incest in priestly literature (Lev 18:17; 19:29; 20:14; Eze 16:27, 43, 58; 22:9, 11; 23:21, 27, 29, 35, 44, 48–49; 24:13; cf. Job 31:11; Jer 13:27). The second term, נְבָלָה (*nebālâ*), was used twice by the old man in Gibeah about the foolish behavior of his fellow citizens in Judges 19:23–24 and is often used for deviant sexual behavior (see Ge 34:7; Dt 22:21; 2Sa 13:12–13; Jer 29:3; Block, 536).

7 עֵצָה (*ʿēṣâ*, "verdict"). This term for advice or counsel is used for advice regarding battle strategy in 2 Samuel 15:31, 34; 16:23; 17:7. For the phrase יהב עֵצָה (*yhb ʿēṣâ*), see 2 Samuel 16:20.

הֲלֹם (*halôm*, untranslated in NIV). The final word of the verse in the Hebrew text should be translated "here," possibly meaning "here and now." Interestingly, the LXX does not translate this term.

9 גּוֹרָל (*gôrāl*, "lot"; GK 1598). Lots were regularly used in a method of discernment throughout the OT (Lev 16:8–10; Nu 26:55–56; Jos 7:14, 16; 14:2; Jdg 1:3; 1Sa 10:20; 14:42; 1Ch 24:5; 25:8; 26:13; Ne 10:34; 11:1; Pr 16:33; 18:18). The actual means used for discernment is never described in the OT, but many suggest that it involved stones of various sizes or shapes and most likely is the function of the Urim and Thummim carried by the high priest (Ex 28:30; Lev 8:8; Nu 27:21; Dt 33:8; 1Sa 28:6; Ezr 2:63//Ne 7:65; possibly 1Sa 14:41, see LXX).

10 עָם (ʿām, "army"). While often translated as "people" in English versions, this term is occasionally used to refer to military personnel (*HALOT*, 838; see 1Sa 14:17; 2Sa 2:26; 10:10; 2Ki 13:7; 18:26//Isa 36:11). לָקַחַת צֵדָה לָעָם לַעֲשׂוֹת לְבוֹאָם לְגֶבַע בִּנְיָמִן (lāqaḥat ṣēdâ lāʿām laʿaśôt lĕbôʾām lĕgebaʿ binyāmin, " ... to get provisions for the army. Then, when the army arrives at Gibeah in Benjamin, it can give them... "). This odd phrase in the MT ("to get provisions for the army in order to act, to go to them, toward Geba in Benjamin") is translated in LXXᵃ as τοῖς εἰσπορευομένοις ἐπιτελέσαι (tois eisporeuomenois epitelesai), suggesting an original reading, לַבָּאִים לַעֲשׂוֹת (labbāʾîm laʿaśôt, "those who are going in to carry out" [*NETS*, 235]). Sense can be made out of the more difficult reading of the MT with the preposition lamed on לְבוֹאָם (lĕbôʾām) functioning temporally (*IBHS* 11.2.10.a), so as to mean "at the time of their entering," that is, when they come against Gibeah (cf. the use of בוֹא [bwʾ] for military action against a place in Job 15:21; Jer 50:26).

לְגֶבַע (lĕgebaʿ, "at Gibeah"). The Hebrew text reads here *Gebaʿ*, a variant of the Gibeah (גִּבְעָה, gibʿâ) of v.9 (cf. 20:33; see Boda, *1–2 Chronicles*).

b. Israel's Proposal to Benjamin Rebuffed (20:12–13)

> ¹²The tribes of Israel sent men throughout the tribe of Benjamin, saying, "What about this awful crime that was committed among you? ¹³Now surrender those wicked men of Gibeah so that we may put them to death and purge the evil from Israel."
> But the Benjamites would not listen to their fellow Israelites.

COMMENTARY

12–13 It is clear that the focus of the war council of 20:8–11 is on the town of Gibeah. For this reason, before engaging in battle against a town within Benjamite territory, they approach the rest of the Benjamites (cf. 20:3a) to ask them to surrender the one clan (Gibeah) in order that they may exact punishment (death) upon it and so "purge the evil from Israel" (20:13). A nearly identical phrase appears regularly throughout Deuteronomy for capital punishment of serious infractions of the Torah (Dt 13:6; 17:7, 12; 19:19; 21:21; 22:21–22, 24; 24:7). Here the evil act is seen as staining the entire community (cf. Kaminsky; Boda, *Severe Mercy*, 518–19), thus necessitating this severe punishment (see Jos 7).

Benjamin, however, which had obviously not dealt with the issue to this point, rejects the proposal of the other tribes. "By siding with Gibeah, it disrupts the unity of all Israel's commitment to the sanctions of Dt. 13:13–19" (O'Connell, 259).

NOTE

13 בְּנֵי־בְלִיַּעַל (*beʿnê-beʿlîyaʿal*, "wicked"). See Note on 19:22.

c. Israel and Benjamin Muster Their Troops (20:14–17)

> ¹⁴From their towns they came together at Gibeah to fight against the Israelites. ¹⁵At once the Benjamites mobilized twenty-six thousand swordsmen from their towns, in addition to seven hundred chosen men from those living in Gibeah. ¹⁶Among all these soldiers there were seven hundred chosen men who were left-handed, each of whom could sling a stone at a hair and not miss.
> ¹⁷Israel, apart from Benjamin, mustered four hundred thousand swordsmen, all of them fighting men.

COMMENTARY

14–16 The implications of Benjamin's rejection of the proposal of the rest of Israel are clear, so the Benjamites immediately muster their troops and assemble at Gibeah from their various towns to protect one of their clans. Benjamin's force, numbering twenty-six thousand (swordsmen), or twenty-six large military units, besides the seven hundred, or seven small military units, from Gibeah, is but a fraction of the rest of Israel. Among the Benjamite units are seven hundred, or seven small military units, of sure-shot left-handed stoneslingers, ironic in light of the meaning of Benjamin's name ("son of the right hand"; see Notes). As the story of Ehud revealed in Judges 3, being left-handed was a valuable trait in ancient warfare; it introduced an element of surprise and placed the enemy at a disadvantage, since war techniques were designed for the dominant right-handers.

17 Having devoted much of the chapter to the military muster of the rest of Israel, the narrator describes Israel's muster in but one verse, repeating the number of four hundred thousand, or four hundred large military units (as seen in 20:2). These troops are all called "swordsmen" and "fighting men" (see Note), that is, infantry well trained for war. The difference in military strength between these two forces is massive, with the rest of Israel outnumbering little Benjamin about fifteen to one.

NOTES

16 אִטֵּר יַד־יְמִינוֹ (*ʾiṭṭēr yad-yeʿmînô*, "left-handed"). This phrase in Hebrew reads as "restricted in his right hand," a phrase that, in light of the number of stoneslingers here, must be an idiom for "left-handed." For the allusion to "left-handed" as a possible mocking parody of the Benjamites, see Miller, 112. See also comments on 3:15–17.

17 אִישׁ מִלְחָמָה (*ʾîš milḥāmâ*, "men of war"). This expression is used elsewhere of seasoned military personnel in Joshua 17:1; 1 Samuel 16:18; 17:33; 2 Samuel 17:8; Isaiah 3:2; Ezekiel 39:20. Compare the similar phrases אִישׁ מִלְחָמוֹת (*ʾîš milḥāmôt*, Isa 42:13; 1Ch 28:3), אַנְשֵׁי (הַ)מִּלְחָמָה (*ʾanšê [ham]milḥāmâ*, Nu 31:28, 49; Dt 2:14, 16; Jos 2:7; 4:9; 5:4, 6; 6:3; 10:24; 1Ki 9:22; 2Ki 25:4; 1Ch 12:39; 2Ch 8:9; 17:13; Jer 38:4; 39:4; 41:3, 16; 49:26; 51:32; 52:7, 25).

d. Civil War: First Battle (20:18–21)

OVERVIEW

The remainder of Judges 20 describes the civil war between Benjamin and the rest of the Israelite tribes. This description is presented in three phases, with each phase containing three basic elements: a description of Israel's inquiring of God (20:18, 23, 26–28), a description of the forces arraying their troops (20:19–20, 22, 29–30), and a description of the ensuing battle (20:21, 24–25, 31–48). The order of the first two elements is reversed in the second phase.

¹⁸The Israelites went up to Bethel and inquired of God. They said, "Who of us shall go first to fight against the Benjamites?"

The LORD replied, "Judah shall go first."

¹⁹The next morning the Israelites got up and pitched camp near Gibeah. ²⁰The men of Israel went out to fight the Benjamites and took up battle positions against them at Gibeah. ²¹The Benjamites came out of Gibeah and cut down twenty-two thousand Israelites on the battlefield that day.

COMMENTARY

18 Though vastly outnumbering the Benjamites, the "Israelites" follow through on the plan articulated in vv.8–11 (see v.9) by inquiring of God (see Notes) at the central sanctuary at Bethel. While it is possible that this designation refers not to the town of Bethel but rather merely the "house of God," that is, the tabernacle, which had been located at Shiloh according to the book of Joshua (Jos 18:1; 19:51; 21:2; 22:9), references to inquiring that took place at different locations (Mizpah, Bethel, Shiloh, Gibeah) throughout Judges 17–21 suggest confusion over the centralization of cultic practice at this point in Israel's history (see Brooks, 31; Boda, "Recycling Heaven's Words").

Bethel "lies between two separable physiographic provinces: the hills of Ephraim to the N, and the plateau of Judea to the S" (*ABD*, 1:711). Through Bethel ran a north–south road from Hebron to Shechem, and just south of Bethel ran also a key east–west road for movement between the Way of the Kings (Transjordanian plateau) and the Way of the Sea (along the Mediterranean coast).

Bethel's position here made it a frontier town (cf. Jos 16:1–2; 18:13; Jdg 1:22–26; see 2Ch 13:19; cf. *ABD*, 1:711). Jacob had encountered God there (Ge 28:10–22), while both Deborah (Jdg 4:5) and Samuel (1Sa 7:16) used the town as a base for dispensing justice. Later, however, it became the site of the rival cult of Jeroboam I and the northern kingdom (1Ki 12:28–33; cf. Am 7:10–13). Bethel lay seven and a half miles north of Gibeah, three and a half miles northeast of Mizpah, and eleven miles north of Jerusalem (*TBD*, 163). Gibeah lay four and a half miles southeast of Mizpah.

The question asked by the Israelites in this inquiry echoes the earlier question they asked at the outset of the book in 1:1: "Who will be the first to go up and fight for us against the Canaanites?" The answer to this inquiry is the same in both cases: Judah.

This connection to the opening inquiry of the book makes for a double emphasis. First, by replacing the Canaanites with Benjamin and directing Israel to advance in battle against them, the answer is suggesting that Benjamin is no better than the Canaanites, who preceded Israel in the land. Links between the behavior of Benjamite Gibeah and the Canaanite city of Sodom in Genesis confirm this connection. Second, by repeating Judah as the answer to the inquiry, these stories highlight the key leadership role expected of Judah among the tribes of Israel. By picturing Judah at the head of the tribes and Benjamin as their enemy, the narrator is emphasizing the leadership of the Judahite Davidic line over that of the Benjamite (Gibeahite) Saulide line (see further Introduction).

19–21 The morning after this inquiry the Israelite army journeys seven and a half miles south to Gibeah from Bethel. At some point they take up offensive battle positions, expecting to defeat the town. But the narrator reveals that the Benjamites emerge from Gibeah and soundly defeat the Israelites. The loss of twenty-two thousand Israelites along with the absence of any report of loss of Benjamites reveals that nearly all the Benjamites defeat one Israelite each. This defeat is a reminder of the decline observed in Judges as a whole. At the outset God's direction is clear and victory is secured (1:2). Here God's direction comes, but without assurance of victory, and defeat is experienced (Exum, "The Centre Cannot Hold," 429; Hudson, 49).

NOTE

18 וַיִּשְׁאֲלוּ בֵאלֹהִים (*wayyiš°alû be°lōhîm*, "and inquired of God"). This collocation (שָׁאַל ב, *š°l b*) is used to refer to consulting the spiritual realm, whether through legitimate (Jdg 1:1; 18:5; 1Sa 10:22; 14:37; 22:10, 13, 15; 23:2, 4; 28:6; 30:8; 2Sa 2:1; 5:19, 23; 1Ch 14:10) or illegitimate means (a medium in 1Ch 10:13; teraphim in Eze 21:26; wooden idols in Hos 4:12).

e. Civil War: Second Battle (20:22–25)

22But the men of Israel encouraged one another and again took up their positions where they had stationed themselves the first day. **23**The Israelites went up and wept before the LORD until evening, and they inquired of the LORD. They said, "Shall we go up again to battle against the Benjamites, our brothers?"

The LORD answered, "Go up against them."

²⁴Then the Israelites drew near to Benjamin the second day. ²⁵This time, when the Benjamites came out from Gibeah to oppose them, they cut down another eighteen thousand Israelites, all of them armed with swords.

COMMENTARY

22 The devastating loss in the first battle, however, does not dissuade the army of Israel, who respond by encouraging one another (cf. 1Sa 4:9) and again arraying themselves in the same offensive battle positions as the previous day.

23 The precise character and timing of v.23 is uncertain. It may refer to the actions of a chosen contingent from the army who proceed to the tabernacle at Bethel (see v.18 above) to inquire of Yahweh while the rest of the army maintains their positions outside Gibeah. It may refer to an event that actually preceded their stationing themselves, in which case vv.22 and 24 refer to the same action, one that followed a second journey to the tabernacle after the defeat on the first day. More likely, however, it refers to an inquiry that takes place not at Bethel, but rather outside Gibeah as they await the battle.

In all these cases, Israel's inquiry is now accompanied by "weeping before" Yahweh that lasts "until evening." Again, the inquiry consists of the simple question of whether they should engage in battle against the Benjamites. The reference to the Benjamites as "our brothers" suggests that there is some questioning within the camp over the legitimacy of the present enterprise (see Satterthwaite, "Narrative Artistry"). The answer from Yahweh, however, is as clear as the first. They are to "go up against them."

24–25 The result is little better on this second day than it was on the first. Again Benjamin soundly defeats Israel, this time killing somewhat fewer of them (eighteen thousand), while still experiencing no losses of their own.

f. Civil War: Third Battle (20:26–48)

²⁶Then the Israelites, all the people, went up to Bethel, and there they sat weeping before the LORD. They fasted that day until evening and presented burnt offerings and fellowship offerings to the LORD. ²⁷And the Israelites inquired of the LORD. (In those days the ark of the covenant of God was there, ²⁸with Phinehas son of Eleazar, the son of Aaron,

ministering before it.) They asked, "Shall we go up again to battle with Benjamin our brother, or not?"

The LORD responded, "Go, for tomorrow I will give them into your hands."

²⁹Then Israel set an ambush around Gibeah. ³⁰They went up against the Benjamites on the third day and took up positions against Gibeah as they had done before. ³¹The Benjamites came out to meet them and were drawn away from the city. They began to inflict casualties on the Israelites as before, so that about thirty men fell in the open field and on the roads — the one leading to Bethel and the other to Gibeah.

³²While the Benjamites were saying, "We are defeating them as before," the Israelites were saying, "Let's retreat and draw them away from the city to the roads."

³³All the men of Israel moved from their places and took up positions at Baal Tamar, and the Israelite ambush charged out of its place on the west of Gibeah. ³⁴Then ten thousand of Israel's finest men made a frontal attack on Gibeah. The fighting was so heavy that the Benjamites did not realize how near disaster was. ³⁵The LORD defeated Benjamin before Israel, and on that day the Israelites struck down 25,100 Benjamites, all armed with swords. ³⁶Then the Benjamites saw that they were beaten.

Now the men of Israel had given way before Benjamin, because they relied on the ambush they had set near Gibeah. ³⁷The men who had been in ambush made a sudden dash into Gibeah, spread out and put the whole city to the sword. ³⁸The men of Israel had arranged with the ambush that they should send up a great cloud of smoke from the city, ³⁹and then the men of Israel would turn in the battle.

The Benjamites had begun to inflict casualties on the men of Israel (about thirty), and they said, "We are defeating them as in the first battle." ⁴⁰But when the column of smoke began to rise from the city, the Benjamites turned and saw the smoke of the whole city going up into the sky. ⁴¹Then the men of Israel turned on them, and the men of Benjamin were terrified, because they realized that disaster had come upon them. ⁴²So they fled before the Israelites in the direction of the desert, but they could not escape the battle. And the men of Israel who came out of the towns cut them down there. ⁴³They surrounded the Benjamites, chased them and easily overran them in the vicinity of Gibeah on the east. ⁴⁴Eighteen thousand Benjamites fell, all of them valiant fighters. ⁴⁵As they turned and fled toward the desert to the rock of Rimmon, the Israelites cut down five thousand men along the roads. They kept pressing after the Benjamites as far as Gidom and struck down two thousand more.

⁴⁶On that day twenty-five thousand Benjamite swordsmen fell, all of them valiant fighters. ⁴⁷But six hundred men turned and fled into the desert to the rock of Rimmon, where they stayed four months. ⁴⁸The men of Israel went back to Benjamin and put all the towns to the sword, including the animals and everything else they found. All the towns they came across they set on fire.

COMMENTARY

26-28 The second unexpected and devastating defeat intensifies the third and final inquiry of Yahweh. In this case the narrator emphasizes that the entire army ("the Israelites, all the people"; better "all the sons of Israel, that is, all the army") returns to Bethel (see v.18), where now they not only weep before Yahweh but also fast and present (burnt and fellowship) offerings to him as they inquire of God. The narrator explicitly notes the presence of the ark (of the covenant of God) and the mediation of Phinehas (son of Eleazar, son of Aaron), two signs of the legitimacy of this inquiry (contrast 18:5-6; see comments). Here is no illicit shrine, as would be true of Bethel at a later stage in Israel's history (see comment on v.20).

The question the Israelites ask of Yahweh is even more explicit than the former ones, beginning as the second inquiry ("Shall we go up again to battle with Benjamin our brother ... "), but then adding the explicit "or not" at the end. The response from Yahweh is the clearest of the three; not only does it command them to engage Benjamin in battle, but now for the first time it also promises the Israelites victory: "I will give them into your hands."

It is difficult to understand the significance of this series of inquiries in Judges 20 (on the progression, see Satterthwaite, "Narrative Artistry," 82). Why would Yahweh send them into battle and yet allow them to face devastating defeat? Possibly the problem may be traced to inquiry at an inappropriate location. Boling, 285, suggested that the Bethel of 20:18 (and supposedly 20:23) is only a shrine ("house of God") located at Mizpah, while the Bethel of 20:26-28 refers to the central shrine housed at the town of Bethel and supervised by Phinehas (son of Eleazer, son of Aaron). While it may be correct that some of the problem may be

linked to the inappropriateness of the location, one cannot make a clear distinction between the "Bethel" in 20:18 and 20:26, for the same terminology is used in both cases.

Another option is to link the problem to inappropriate lines of inquiry. The first inquiry (v.18) does not even leave open the legitimacy of the present enterprise, which from the outset of the war council seems to have been a foregone conclusion (Webb, 193; see above). No attention is given to rites accompanying the inquiry, and reference is only made to seeking the will of God/the gods. This inquiry merely asks who should be the first to go up, and the answer is simply Judah, with no assurance of the success of the venture.

The second inquiry (v.23) does involve accompanying rites (weeping until evening), asks for the first time about the legitimacy of the battle, and specifically speaks of inquiring of Yahweh. The oddity of this inquiry in the way the narrator has arranged the narrative gives the impression that the Israelite army had already convinced themselves of the legitimacy of further battle and had already taken up their positions against Gibeah. The inquiry either took place on the battlefield outside Gibeah, or only a portion of the army went to Bethel for the inquiry. Nevertheless, Yahweh answers with the clear direction to engage Benjamin in battle but does not guarantee success.

It is only in response to the third inquiry—in which the entire army goes to Bethel, participates in substantial accompanying rites (weeping, fasting, sacrifices of burnt and fellowship offerings), avails themselves of the proper means of Yahwistic inquiry (at the ark, mediated by Phinehas), and asks specifically whether they were to engage Benjamin in battle *or not*—that they are given both clear direction ("go") and a guarantee of success ("I will give them into your hands"). The narrative progression that can be traced through these three inquiries, both in terms of the content of Israel's request as well as of Yahweh's answer (Webb, 193), suggests that Israel is learning the importance of proper inquiry.

Moreover, the distinction between the second inquiry (which took place at an undisclosed location, most likely outside Gibeah) and the other inquiries (which took place at Bethel) suggests some confusion over the centralization of worship. These incidents emphasize two concerns often expressed in Deuteronomic literature: the place and means of worship. Yahweh must be worshiped at one central sanctuary through appropriate means. This concern is intricately linked with that refrain in chs. 17–21: "everyone did as he saw fit" (cf. Dt 12:8).

29–30 Not only are the inquiry of Yahweh and Yahweh's response more substantial in the description of this third battle, but as Israel arrays its troops it employs more advanced military tactics, in particular commissioning a smaller force of ten thousand (see v.34) to ambush the town of Gibeah once the Benjamites engaged in battle north of Gibeah. No mention is made in the inquiry of Yahweh of these new techniques, but they appear to be key to Israel's success.

31–36a The description of the battle depicts the wisdom of these military tactics. Seeing the one Israelite force taking up the battle formations used on the previous two days, the Benjamites are enticed to move on the offensive rather than remain on the defensive as before, encouraged along by the ruse of retreat by the Israelite army along the northern road to Bethel (20:31–32). The main army takes up positions at Baal Tamar, most likely a location just north of Gibeah on the road to Bethel. With the Benjamite force drawn away from Gibeah, the smaller Israelite ambush force emerges from their place "west of Gibeah" (see Note) and attacks the now defenseless town of Gibeah (20:33–34a). The Benjamites are so distracted by their battle with the main divisions of the Israelite army that they do not realize at first what has happened on their rear flank (20:34b).

The narrator summarizes the defeat in vv.35–36a, counting 25,100 Benjamites dead out of an original force of 26,000 Benjamites and 700 Gibeathites. The remaining 1,600 "Benjamites" accept defeat. There are links between the battle strategy here and that of Israel against Ai in Joshua 8 (Block, 567; Matthews, *Judges and Ruth*, 196; Wong, *Strategy*, 57–70). There also one finds a battle that follows an initial, devastating defeat. In contrast, however, this battle is against an Israelite tribe rather than a Canaanite town, thus suggesting Benjamin's Canaanization and fracturing of the nation. Furthermore, this battle in Judges will end in mourning (21:1–5), while the earlier battle ended in renewing the covenant (Jos 8:30–35).

36b–48 While earlier scholarship pointed to the repetitive material in vv.36b–48 as evidence of multiples sources (e.g., Charles Fox Burney, *The Book of Judges with Introduction and Notes* [2nd ed.; London: Rivingtons, 1920], 447; Gray, 1988: 379–81; Soggin, 293–94), it has been argued by recent scholars that this repetition is a narrative technique (see Notes). The general summary of the battle in vv.31–36a is followed by a detailed description in vv.36b–48, possibly with an accompanying change in perspective (see Note).

The account in vv.36b–48 begins with the retreat of the main Israelite force (v.36b), which prompts the Israelite ambush force to rush and massacre the town of Gibeah (v.37). The narrator reveals that the Israelites have arranged a signal for relaying the message from the ambush contingents to the main flank of the army that they have taken the town. The column of smoke that rises heavenward not only signals the main flank to turn back against the Benjamite army, but also strikes great fear in the Benjamites so that they now turn in flight to the east toward the wilderness. Not only are the Benjamites caught by the pursuing Israelites, but also the people of any towns into which they flee put them to death.

The general summary of the battle in v.35 notes that 25,100 are slain in this battle and its aftermath. This more detailed description provides a similar number in v.46 (25,000) that is broken down further in vv.44–45 as 18,000 in the main battle, 5,000 along the highways in flight, and 2,000 at Gidom, an unknown location that probably lay in the wilderness region east of Gibeah. As was typical of ancient warfare, loss was never limited to those engaged in battle but also included those now-vulnerable towns and rural areas in the region once protected by the defeated army (v.48).

The impact on Benjamin is depicted as devastating. It appears that the tribe is treated in the same way the Canaanites were to be treated when Israel invaded the land. The implication is that Benjamin has become like the Canaanites and so will now share their fate. But the narrator makes careful note of six hundred soldiers who survive the battle by fleeing to the Rock of Rimmon (meaning "pomegranate rock"). While some have identified the village of Rammun (five and a half miles northeast of Gibeah, if it is modern Jabaᶜ; see Note on 20:33) as the location of the Rock of Rimmon, a location closer to Gibeah (again, if it is modern Jabaᶜ), such as the el-Jaia cave in Wadi es-Swenit, is more likely (*ABD*, 5:774).

This reference to Rimmon prepares the reader for the story of the survival of the tribe of Benjamin in ch. 21. It is not coincidental that another group of six hundred retreating Benjamite soldiers from Gibeah will flee to a place called Rimmon in 1 Samuel 14:2 (cf. 1Sa 13:15), that is, Saul and his force. This allusion to Saul links the first king to this devastating rout of the tribe of Benjamin.

NOTES

33 מִמַּעֲרֵה־גָבַע (*mimmaᶜᵃrēh-gāba*ᶜ, "west of Gibeah"). In the Hebrew text this phrase reads "bare/naked place of Geba" (BDB, 789), possibly a "clearing" (*HALOT*, 615). But the addition of an extra consonant (ב, *b*), possibly lost due to similarity to the ר (*r*), and a slightly different vocalization (מִמַּעֲרַב־הַגָּבַע, *mimmaᶜᵃrab-haggābaᶜ*; *HALOT*, 615) would render "west" (cf. LXXᵃ δυσμῶν τῆς Γαβαα; *dysmōn tēs Gabaa*, "west of Gabaa"; LXXᵇ transliterates into Greek: ἀπὸ Μααραγαβε, *apo Maaragabe*). The town name here is also a problem in the Hebrew text, which cites Geba (גָּבַע, *geba*ᶜ) rather than Gibeah (גִּבְעָה, *gib*ᶜâ). Textual confusion between Geba and Gibeah is common in the OT (Jdg 20:10; 1Sa 13:3, 16; 14:5; Isa 10:29) and is attributable to the use of the *mater lectionis* ה at the end of one of the names. Most likely "Geba" and "Gibeah" refer to the same location, though some have distinguished the two, placing Geba five and a half miles northeast of Jerusalem (associated with the modern village of Jabaᶜ), and Gibeah three miles north of Jerusalem (associated with Tell el-Ful; see *ABD*, 2:1007). See further Boda, *1–2 Chronicles*.

36 Revell, 430, notes how the repetition in vv.36 and 39 of elements in vv.31–32 is a narrative technique that returns the reader to an earlier point in the narrative after a digression; see also Satterthwaite ("Narrative Artistry") and Matthews (*Judges and Ruth*, 196), who leverage this evidence to speak also of shifts in narrative viewpoint, that is, between the Israelite and Benjamite vantage points.

43 מְנוּחָה ($m^e n\hat{u}h\hat{a}$, "easily"). This noun usually means "resting-place, rest." Possibly the preposition מִן (min), to be understood as a privative marker (*IBHS*, 11.2.11.e), has dropped out: "without rest."

4. Wives for the Benjamites (21:1–24)

a. Introductory Inquiry (21:1–5)

OVERVIEW

Having completed the description of the Israelites' absolute victory in 20:48, the narrator now transitions to the dilemma that results from the near annihilation of the tribe of Benjamin. Bracketing the opening verses of ch. 21 (vv.1–5) are two descriptions of oaths sworn by the tribes that had assembled against Benjamin at Mizpah in ch. 20. Although these oaths are not mentioned in the narrative of ch. 20, they are key to the tension of the narrative in ch. 21 and strikingly reminiscent of earlier oaths in the book concerning women — Caleb's vow of Acsah (1:11–15) and especially the rash oath uttered by foolish Jephthah in ch. 11 (Wong, *Strategy*, 132–35; Sjöberg, 62). Interestingly, Israel's harsh treatment of Benjamin echoes the earlier brutality of Jephthah's (and Gideon's) treatment of fellow Israelites (Wong, *Strategy*, 125–31).

At the core of these five opening verses are two inquiries of God conducted by the triumphant Israelites at Bethel, the location of the tabernacle according to 20:26–28. These two inquiries are accompanied by rituals that echo the same language used by the narrator to describe the rituals accompanying the climactic inquiry that secured Israelite victory over Benjamin (20:26). Surely the sitting and weeping are a sign of their mourning over the loss of one of their tribes, similar to their lament and mourning over the catastrophic loss in battle in 20:26.

Such mourning rites, however, are here a prelude to inquiry (cf. Jos 7), since at the heart of lament are those key questions of God: "Why?" and "How long?" (cf. Walter Brueggemann, and Patrick D. Miller, *The Psalms and the Life of Faith* [Minneapolis: Fortress, 1995]; M. J. Boda, "Prayer," in *Dictionary of the Old Testament: Historical Books* [ed. Bill T. Arnold, H. G. M. Williamson, and Daniel G. Reid; Downers Grove, Ill.: InterVarsity Press, 2005], 806–11; idem, "Form Criticism in Transition: Penitential Prayer and Lament, *Sitz im Leben* and Form, in *Seeking the Favor of God*: Vol. 1 — *The Origin of Penitential Prayer in Second Temple Judaism* [ed. Mark J. Boda, Daniel K. Falk, and Rodney A. Werline; SBL Early Judaism and Its Literature 21; Atlanta: Society of Biblical Literature, 2006], 181–92).

20:26	21:2, 4
Then the Israelites, all the people [$h\bar{a}^c\bar{a}m$], went up [$bw^{\flat}$] to Bethel, and there [$\check{s}\bar{a}m$] they sat [$y\check{s}b$] weeping [bkh] before [$lipn\hat{e}$] the LORD. They fasted that day until evening [^cad-$h\bar{a}^c\bar{a}reb$] and presented burnt offerings and fellowship offerings [$wayya^ca l\hat{u}\ ^c\bar{o}l\bar{o}t\ \hat{u}\check{s}^e l\bar{a}m\hat{i}m$] to the LORD.	The people went to [$bw^{\flat}$] Bethel, where [$\check{s}\bar{a}m$] they sat [$y\check{s}b$] before [$lipn\hat{e}$] God until evening [^cad-$h\bar{a}^c ereb$], raising their voices and weeping [bkh] bitterly.... Early the next day the people built an altar and presented burnt offerings and fellowship offerings [$wayya^ca l\hat{u}\ ^c\bar{o}l\bar{o}t\ \hat{u}\check{s}^e l\bar{a}m\hat{i}m$].

Having received an unambiguous answer by employing this set of rituals in 20:26, the people look for similar results at the outset of ch. 21. The first oath (21:1) is directly related to the first ritual and inquiry (21:2–3), while the second oath (21:5b) is directly related to the second ritual and inquiry (21:4), as can been seen in the following structural layout.

A. Description of past oath at Mizpah (21:1)
   not to give daughters to Benjamin
B. Ritual and inquiry at Bethel #1 (21:2–3):
   Why is one tribe missing?
B'. Ritual and inquiry at Bethel #2 (21:4):
   Who did not come to the assembly?
A'. Description of past oath at Mizpah (21:5b)
   to put to death those who did not assemble

¹The men of Israel had taken an oath at Mizpah:"Not one of us will give his daughter in marriage to a Benjamite."

²The people went to Bethel, where they sat before God until evening, raising their voices and weeping bitterly. ³"O Lord, the God of Israel," they cried,"why has this happened to Israel? Why should one tribe be missing from Israel today?"

⁴Early the next day the people built an altar and presented burnt offerings and fellowship offerings.

⁵Then the Israelites asked,"Who from all the tribes of Israel has failed to assemble before the Lord?" For they had taken a solemn oath that anyone who failed to assemble before the Lord at Mizpah should certainly be put to death.

COMMENTARY

1–3 The first grouping (A, B) isolates the core dilemma of this chapter, that is, the impending demise of the entire tribe of Benjamin from Israel, not only because of the victory of the rest of Israel over Benjamin in the war described in ch. 20, but also because of the inability of the surviving Benjamites to reproduce the tribe as a result of the Israelites'

oath not to give their daughters to the Benjamites as wives. That vv.1–3 identify the key problem to be resolved in this chapter is made clear by the fact that the narrator employs a reference to the Israelites' deep sorrow (*nḥm*, Niphal) over the potential loss of the tribe of Benjamin at the outset of the two major sections of ch. 21 (vv.6–14, 15–23a):

21:6	21:15
Now the Israelites grieved [*nḥm*, Niphal] for their brothers, the Benjamites. "Today one tribe is cut off from Israel," they said.	The people grieved [*nḥm*, Niphal] for Benjamin, because the Lord had made a gap in the tribes of Israel.

The vocabulary of raising the voice in weeping before God used in these verses also echoes the response of the people at the outset of the book after receiving the condemnation of the angel of

Yahweh for making a covenant with the Canaanites (Amit, *Judges*, 353; O'Connell, 242; Wong, *Strategy*, 40–42). In both cases such weeping is followed by sacrifice.

2:4-5	21:2, 4
When the angel of the LORD had spoken these things to all the Israelites, the people wept aloud [*wayyiśʾû qôlām wayyibkû*], and they called that place Bokim. There they offered sacrifices to the LORD.	The people went to Bethel, where they sat before God until evening, raising their voices and weeping bitterly [*wayyiśʾû qôlām wayyibkû*].... Early the next day the people built an altar and presented burnt offerings and fellowship offerings.

The resumption of these acts signals to the reader that the story has come full circle. The people are still weeping, now over the Canaanite character of their own community, both Benjamite and Israelite.

4-5 The second grouping (B', A') isolates the initial solution to the core dilemma (A, B). The inquiry seeks to identify any who did not respond to the invitation to assemble at Mizpah to deal with Gibeah's offense at the outset of ch. 20. The related oath stipulated the punishment of death for those who did not respond to the invitation. Jabesh Gilead will ultimately be identified as the offending clan who refused the invitation and so will be punished through death. Not being present at Mizpah meant that Jabesh Gilead was the only clan in Israel in which there would be young women who could be given to the Benjamites. These young women, therefore, would be the only ones spared from the capital punishment stipulated under the oath.

b. Providing Wives from Jabesh-Gilead for Four Hundred Benjamites (21:6-14)

OVERVIEW

The precise relationship between what follows here and what has been described in vv.1-5 is not entirely clear. Possibly vv.1-5 constitute an overview of the inquiries that were made on two successive days at Bethel, and then vv.6-14 provide further details of these inquiries. Verses 6-14 do follow the same bipartite pattern as vv.1-5, beginning with an inquiry regarding the loss of a tribe (v.6b) because of the oath not to give daughters as wives to the Benjamites (v.7), followed by an inquiry regarding the identity of those who did not assemble at Mizpah (v.8a), which leads to carrying out the capital punishment demanded by the oath taken at Mizpah (vv.10-12). This progression matches the narrative technique used for the description of Israel's defeat of Benjamin in Judges 20:31-48, which begins with a general overview of the victory in vv.31-36a before providing a more detailed account in vv.36b-48.

It is also possible, however, that vv.6-14 reflect the Israelites' attempt to resolve their problem based on their own wisdom (so O'Connell, 255). Though many questions are cited in these verses, not once is the voice of Yahweh specifically mentioned, as was seen in the earlier inquiries in 20:18, 23, 28 (Webb, 195). The answer to the question in 21:8 ("Which one of the tribes of Israel failed to assemble before the LORD at Mizpah?") is provided, according to 21:9, "when they counted the people, they found that none of the people of Jabesh Gilead were there"

(O'Connell, 255). Furthermore, according to v.12 the camp of Israel in vv.6–14 was apparently stationed at Shiloh rather than Bethel (cf. 21:2). Even if vv.1–5 represent an overview of the events depicted in detail in vv.6–14, the latter details emphasize a surprising lack of divine response to these inquiries, as Block, 571, notes: "God does not answer, and the people are thrown back on their resources."

---

⁶Now the Israelites grieved for their brothers, the Benjamites. "Today one tribe is cut off from Israel," they said. ⁷"How can we provide wives for those who are left, since we have taken an oath by the LORD not to give them any of our daughters in marriage?" ⁸Then they asked, "Which one of the tribes of Israel failed to assemble before the LORD at Mizpah?" They discovered that no one from Jabesh Gilead had come to the camp for the assembly. ⁹For when they counted the people, they found that none of the people of Jabesh Gilead were there.

¹⁰So the assembly sent twelve thousand fighting men with instructions to go to Jabesh Gilead and put to the sword those living there, including the women and children. ¹¹"This is what you are to do," they said. "Kill every male and every woman who is not a virgin." ¹²They found among the people living in Jabesh Gilead four hundred young women who had never slept with a man, and they took them to the camp at Shiloh in Canaan.

¹³Then the whole assembly sent an offer of peace to the Benjamites at the rock of Rimmon. ¹⁴So the Benjamites returned at that time and were given the women of Jabesh Gilead who had been spared. But there were not enough for all of them.

COMMENTARY

6–7 The narrator begins this detailed account (vv.6–14), as also that of vv.15–23a, with a description of the deep sorrow of the Israelites over the impending demise of Benjamin, the core dilemma of this final chapter of Judges. This dilemma is linked, as was seen in vv.1–3, to the oath they had taken at Mizpah as they were about to enter into battle against the Benjamites, the oath that none of them would allow their daughters to become wives of any surviving male from the tribe of Benjamin.

8–9 As already seen in vv.4–5, the answer to the core dilemma of the loss of Benjamin produced by strict adherence to an oath taken at Mizpah lies in strict adherence to the stipulations of another oath taken at the same time. Accord-

ing to this second oath, any clan that did not join the Israelites at Mizpah was to be put to death. According to vv.8b–9, a count of the people reveals that the town of Jabesh Gilead failed to comply with this order. Jabesh Gilead was situated in the heart of the Transjordanian region of Gilead, about seven miles east of the Jordan River, halfway between the Yarmuk (to the north) and Jabbok (to the south) rivers.

It is interesting that Saul's first military act following his private anointing as king by Samuel and preceding his public affirmation by his compatriots was the rescue of Jabesh Gilead from Ammonite oppression (1Sa 11:1–11). Significant also is the fact that when Saul and his sons were killed and their bodies disgraced by the Philistines on the walls of Beth Shean, it was the men of Jabesh Gilead who retrieved the bodies in order to cremate and bury them (1Sa 31:11–13; cf. 2Sa 2:4–7). Judges 21:8–9 provides the first connection between Benjamin, Gibeah, and Jabesh Gilead by revealing that Benjamites who survived the battle against Gibeah were given wives from Jabesh Gilead. Again a community related to Saul is connected to a devastating defeat (Matthews, *Judges and Ruth*, 199).

10–11 The assembly commissions twelve thousand troops, or twelve large military groups, to carry out the bloody oath. The narrator's description of the assembly's instructions in v.10 mentions the annihilation of "those living there, including the women and children," but the verbal citation in v.11 qualifies this statement slightly: "every male and every woman who is not a virgin." The qualification "who is not a virgin" implies that they are to bring back any woman who is a virgin. By providing someone else's daughters as wives for Benjamin, the Israelites are able to circumvent the oath taken at Mizpah.

12 Four hundred virgins are found and are transported to the main Israelite army camp, which, according to v.12, is located at "Shiloh." Most scholars identify Shiloh with Khirbet Seilun, which lay at the midpoint between Bethel and Shechem (*ABD*, 5:1213; Provan, Long, and Longman, 184–85).

According to Joshua 18:1; 19:51; 21:2; 22:9, Shiloh was established as the cultic center once Israel had conquered Canaan. From Shiloh the land was distributed among the tribes, and Shiloh would be featured as the home of the central sanctuary until Jerusalem with its temple replaced it under Solomon's rule (see 1Sa 1–4; 14:3; cf. Jer 7:12–14; 26:6–9; Ps 78:60).

But throughout this latter part of Judges there has been some confusion over the precise location of this sanctuary (see comment on 21:25). It is most often connected to Bethel (20:18, 26–27; 21:2), but it also appears to be connected to the army at Gibeah (20:23), to the army gathered at Mizpah ("before the LORD," 20:1; 21:5), and to Shiloh (21:19). Bethel is highlighted as the only one of these locations that housed the ark and was administered by the Aaronic priests (see 21:26–27).

13–14 Having now found four hundred women to serve as wives for the male remnant of the tribe of Benjamin, the Israelites make peace with the six hundred Benjamites who have been holed up at the Rock of Rimmon for the past four months (see 20:47) and offer them the surviving young women from Jabesh Gilead in order to secure a future line for the tribe of Benjamin. But the insufficient number of women for all the men prompts a second phase of the solution for restoring the tribe of Benjamin, a phase that unfolds in vv.15–23a.

NOTES

6 נִגְדַּע (*nigdaʿ*, "cut off"). This verb (in the Qal and Niphal) is used for the removal of body limbs (1Sa 2:31; possibly Mal 2:3), animal horns (La 2:3; Jer 48:25), tree limbs (Isa 10:33, possibly Ps 74:5), human hair (Isa 15:2; Jer 48:37), and horns of an altar (Am 3:14). The gory cutting up of the concubine in Judges 19:29, probably intended as a warning to those who would not gather to deal with the evil, has now resulted in an equally gory amputation of one of the limbs (tribes) of Israel.

8 מִי אֶחָד מִשִּׁבְטֵי יִשְׂרָאֵל (*mî ʾeḥād miššibṭê yiśrāʾēl*, "Which one of the tribes of Israel"). This translation in English may suggest that the assembly considered Jabesh Gilead to be a tribe in Israel rather than merely a clan within a tribe (similar to the sociological imprecision of 13:2, where Dan is called a "clan"). The same line of inquiry in 21:5 left this question open: מִי אֲשֶׁר לֹא־עָלָה בַקָּהָל מִכָּל־שִׁבְטֵי יִשְׂרָאֵל אֶל־יְהוָה (*mî ʾăšer lōʾ-ʿālâ baqqāhāl mikkol-šibṭê yiśrāʾēl ʾel-yhwh*). If the construct form אַחַד (*ʾaḥad*) had been used in 21:8, it could be claimed that the query identifies Jabesh Gilead as a tribe (cf. Ge 3:22; Jdg 17:11; 1Sa 9:3; *IBHS*, 9.6.b.). This instance would be similar to cases in which אַחַד (*ʾaḥad*) is used in construct with a plural noun (*IBHS*, 13.8.a.): Genesis 21:15 ("under one of the bushes"), Genesis 22:2 ("on one of the mountains"), 2 Samuel 2:18 ("as one of the wild gazelles"), and 2 Samuel 13:13 ("as one of the wicked fools"). But the use of the absolute form of אֶחָד (*ʾeḥād*) identifies the referent of אֶחָד (*ʾeḥād*) as merely a participant in the referent of the מִן (*min*) clause ("tribes of Israel"), much as in 1 Samuel 1:1 Elkanah is a certain man from the town of Ramathaim and in Judges 13:2 Manoah is a certain man from the town of Zorah from the clan of Dan.

12 נַעֲרָה בְתוּלָה אֲשֶׁר לֹא־יָדְעָה אִישׁ לְמִשְׁכַּב זָכָר (*naʿărâ bᵉtûlâ ʾăšer lōʾ-yādᵉʿâ ʾîš lᵉmiškab zākār*, "young women who had never slept with a man"). Here the Hebrew text piles up descriptors for these potential brides in order to emphasize their suitability for the Benjamites: "a young woman, a virgin who had not known a man in the marriage bed of a male." For the last phrase לְמִשְׁכַּב זָכָר (*lᵉmiškab zākār*) see Numbers 31:17–18, 35 (cf. Ge 49:4; Lev 18:22; 20:13).

13 וַיִּשְׁלְחוּ (*wayyišlᵉḥû*, "sent"). The lack of an explicit object for this verb in the Hebrew text is common with this verb, in which the object is elided (*HALOT*, 1513; e.g., see Ge 31:4; 41:8, 14; Ex 9:27; Jos 24:9). The implied object is most likely the messenger(s) sent.

וַיִּקְרְאוּ לָהֶם שָׁלוֹם (*wayyiqrᵉʾû lāhem šālôm*, "sent an offer of peace"). This phrase could be translated "called to them (with) peace" or "called to them: 'Peace!'" A similar phrase (וְקָרָאתָ אֵלֶיהָ לְשָׁלוֹם, *wᵉqārāʾtā ʾēleyhā lᵉšālôm*) is used in Deuteronomy 20:10 for sending an offer of peace to a city prior to fighting against it. (Many medieval Hebrew manuscripts have לְשָׁלוֹם [*lᵉšālôm*] rather than שָׁלוֹם [*šālôm*] in 21:13.)

c. Providing Wives from Shiloh for the Remaining Two Hundred Benjamites (21:15–23a)

[15]The people grieved for Benjamin, because the LORD had made a gap in the tribes of Israel. [16]And the elders of the assembly said, "With the women of Benjamin destroyed, how shall we provide wives for the men who are left? [17]The Benjamite survivors must have heirs," they said, "so that a tribe of Israel will not be wiped out. [18]We can't give them our daughters as wives, since we Israelites have taken this oath: 'Cursed be anyone who gives a wife to a Benjamite.' [19]But look, there is the annual festival of the LORD in Shiloh, to the north of Bethel, and east of the road that goes from Bethel to Shechem, and to the south of Lebonah."

[20]So they instructed the Benjamites, saying, "Go and hide in the vineyards [21]and watch. When the girls of Shiloh come out to join in the dancing, then rush from the vineyards and each of you seize a wife from the girls of Shiloh and go to the land of Benjamin. [22]When their fathers or brothers complain to us, we will say to them, 'Do us a kindness by helping them, because we did not get wives for them during the war, and you are innocent, since you did not give your daughters to them.'"

> ²³So that is what the Benjamites did. While the girls were dancing, each man caught one and carried her off to be his wife.

COMMENTARY

15 The narrator signals the second phase of the solution for replenishing the tribe of Benjamin by again noting that the Israelites are grieving (*nḥm*, Niphal) for Benjamin (see v.6). Whereas in v.6 the narrator cited the words of the Israelites ("Today one tribe is cut off from Israel"), in v.15 the narrator merely states the reason for their sorrow: "because the LORD had made a gap [*pereṣ*] in the tribes of Israel." While in v.6 the passive form ("is cut off") does not identify the one responsible for the loss, here in v.15 the narrator identifies Yahweh specifically. There is some truth to this assertion in v.15 in the light of Yahweh's explicit direction in 20:28 for Israel to go into battle against Benjamin. But nowhere does Yahweh direct them to eradicate the entire tribe as described in 20:48.

The image used in v.6 is most likely one of amputation of a body part (see Note on 21:6). This time the image used is most likely one drawn from urban defense, since the term "gap" is one often associated with a breach in a city wall (1Ki 11:27; Job 16:14; 30:14; Ne 2:13; 4:1; 6:1; Pss 106:23; 144:14; Isa 30:13; 58:12; Eze 13:5; 22:30; Am 4:3; it is also associated with a place where water bursts out [cf. 2Sa 5:20; 1Ch 14:11], and even where anger bursts out [cf. 2Sa 6:8; 1Ch 13:11]). Here the loss of Benjamin is seen as creating a figurative break in the once completed "wall" of the tribes of Israel. Probably related to this loss is the military threat that such a gap would entail for Israel as a whole.

16–19 As in the previous phase of the solution for Benjamin, in which four hundred women from Jabesh Gilead were found, after noting the sorrow of the Israelites over Benjamin's plight, the people (represented by the elders of the assembly) express several things:

- the present dilemma for Benjamin ("how shall we provide wives for the men who are left?" v.16)
- the general solution ("the Benjamite survivors must have heirs [maintain an inheritance]," v.17; see Notes)
- the present dilemma for the Israelites ("we can't give them our daughters as wives, since we Israelites have taken this oath," v.18)
- the specific solution ("there is the annual festival of the LORD in Shiloh," v.19).

This reference to an annual festival at Shiloh echoes the practice of Elkanah (Hannah's husband) described in 1 Samuel 1:3, 7, thus introducing further ambiguity into the location of Yahweh's sanctuary (see comment on 21:25).

20–23a Whereas in the previous phase (vv.10–11) the Israelites gave instructions to their twelve thousand or twelve large military units of soldiers for finding wives for the Benjamites, in this second phase the Israelites give instructions for finding wives to the remaining two hundred Benjamite men without wives. According to these instructions the Benjamites are to go to Shiloh at the time of what is called "the annual festival of the LORD." According to the Torah, Israelites were required to appear before Yahweh at the central sanctuary three times each year (cf. Ex 23:14, 17; 34:23; Nu 28:26; Dt 16:16–17).

The reference to the Benjamites hiding in the vineyards in 21:20–21 suggests that in view is a festival in the seventh month—the time of year when the grapes, figs, and olives ripened, and during which came the Day of Atonement (tenth day: Lev 16; 23:26–32; Nu 29:7–11) and the required Feast of Tabernacles (fifteenth to twenty-second day: Ex 23:16; 34:22; Lev 23:33–36, 39–43; Nu 29:12–38; Dt 16:13–15, also called Festival of Booths or Feast of Ingathering). It is possible that the Feast of Tabernacles is the "annual festival" in view, though the lack of definition and the reference to only one festival may suggest some confusion over proper Torah practice during this period.

According to the book of Joshua, Shiloh was established as the key central location for the tabernacle (Jos 18:1; 19:51; 21:2; 22:9), a privilege it also enjoyed in the days of Eli and Samuel (1Sa 1–4). First Samuel 1 describes Elkanah's regular practice of worshiping at a festival at Shiloh (1Sa 1:3, 7). While 1 Samuel 1 says nothing about dancing, it does refer to the eating and drinking that followed the festal sacrifice, which may have been accompanied by celebratory dancing. There is no reason to assume that this event was focused on the virgins, but at a later point in the night the young women were allowed to dance. But the reference to these young women as "daughters of Shiloh,"

rather than "daughters of Israel," may suggest that these women were now entering permanently into service at the sanctuary at Shiloh, a service possibly akin to Canaanite cult prostitution (for evidence of both male and female prostitution, see Ge 38; 1Ki 14:23–24; Eze 16:16; 2Ki 23:7; Hos 4:13–14; cf. Block, 581; *ABD* 1:548, 835; 2:649, 792; *NBD*, 164; *AEHL* ["Canaan"] for biblical and ancient Near Eastern evidence).

Taking positions in the vineyards surrounding the festival location, the Benjamite men are to wait until the virgins join in the celebration and then may capture (see Note) a wife. Matthews (*Judges and Ruth*, 199–200) highlights rape-capture laws within the Torah, especially Deuteronomy, which would have ensured that these Benjamites could keep their wives (Dt 22:28–29; cf. Ex 22:16–17). In this way the Israelites leverage the law to circumvent their oath while providing Israelite women for the Benjamites. Technically, they are not breaking the oath "not [to] give daughters to them" since the girls are not "given" to the Benjamites but rather "seized" by the Benjamites themselves. The desperate Benjamites gladly take up the offer. Israel's strategies for rectifying Benjamin's plight, however, "repeat on a mass scale the crimes they found so abhorrent in the men of Gibeah" (Exum, "The Centre Cannot Hold," 430–31; cf. Bach; Eynikel, 113; Niditch, *Judges*, 211).

NOTES

17 יְרֻשַּׁת פְּלֵיטָה לְבִנְיָמִן (*yᵉruššat pᵉlêṭâ lᵉbinyāmin*, "The Benjamite survivors must have heirs"). The term יְרֻשָּׁה (*yᵉruššâ*) is normally used to describe land as inheritance (Dt 2:5, 9, 12, 19; 3:20; Jos 1:15; 12:6–7; Jer 32:8). Most likely, then, the concern here is over how Benjamite territory will now be maintained as part of Israel.

21 וַחֲטַפְתֶּם (*waḥᵃṭaptem*, "seize"). This term is used elsewhere in the OT to depict an oppressor catching the distressed (Ps 10:9), akin to a lion capturing prey; using this term suggests that such an action was an oppressive and violent act toward those captured.

d. Conclusion (21:23b–24)

Then they returned to their inheritance and rebuilt the towns and settled in them. [24]At that time the Israelites left that place and went home to their tribes and clans, each to his own inheritance.

COMMENTARY

23b–24 With the problem solved, the Benjamites return to the tribal allotment they had abandoned after the war with Israel (20:47) and rebuild their towns, which had been destroyed by the Israelites (20:48). With their new wives from Jabesh Gilead and the festival at Shiloh, Benjamin will now be able to restore their tribe once threatened with extinction. This resolution to the dilemma posed at the outset of the chapter releases the rest of the tribes to go home, each to their own inheritance, bringing closure to the book of Judges in the same way the book of Joshua ended (Jos 24:28) and the book of Judges began (Jdg 2:6).

5. Refrain (21:25)

[25]In those days Israel had no king; everyone did as he saw fit.

COMMENTARY

25 The narrator provides here a closing theological comment by repeating the refrain found throughout chs. 17–21 (17:6; 18:1; 19:1). As noted in the introduction to ch. 17, this refrain is an important reminder of the need for a royal house that will unite the Israelite tribes and provide a central place of worship. The problems created by the Benjamite inhabitants of Gibeah cast a dark shadow over Saulide royal legitimacy (Matthews, *Judges and Ruth*, 190), while the offense against the Bethlehemites in the death of the concubine from Bethlehem suggests the innocence of the Davidic line.

Just as chs. 17–18 exposed threats to centralized worship in Israel with the creation of a personal sanctuary by Micah that was coopted by the Danites to form a rival cult center in the far north of Israel, so also chs. 19–21 have revealed similar ambiguity over the centralized cultic location during this period, with references to Bethel, Mizpah, Shiloh, and even Gibeah as places where assemblies were held and inquiries of Yahweh were made during the war against the Benjamites (Brooks, 31; see Boda, "Recycling Heaven's Words"). If the horrendous character of the events and the violent solutions put forward by the Israelites were not enough to convince the reader of the dysfunction of this era of Israelite history, this final theological statement in v.25 articulates clearly the narrator's concern over the events described. For the narrator there is hope, but only in a kingship that puts an end to (lit.) "doing what is right in one's own eyes." It is on that subject that the book of Samuel will focus its attention.

REFLECTION

As with chs. 17–18, so also chs. 19–21 focus on the ideal royal role of sponsoring appropriate worship at the designated central shrine. Here one can discern confusion over the proper method and place of inquiry before Yahweh. Jesus later makes clear to the Samaritan woman in John 4 that this method and place is not on Mount Gerizim and no longer at Jerusalem, but rather through him in spirit and truth. In chs. 19–21 confusion over worship has clear implications for ethics, as exemplified in the Gibeathites, who are depicted as no better than the Canaanites. Thus it is clear that Saulide kingship is disqualified from leadership, and also that worship is foundational to ethics.

The response of Israel to Gibeah's evil in the end may be justified in light of the book of Deuteronomy, but that response is carried out in the midst of considerable confusion over how to hear God's voice. While the evil of the Gibeathites is clear, the Levite is not absolved of guilt, especially in the light of his sacrifice of the woman to the lustful men and his economizing of the truth before the Israelite assembly. The final message of the book creates future expectation for a kind of leadership that will guide and ultimately enable Israel to love the Lord their God with all their heart, soul, and might and to love their neighbor as themselves.

RUTH

GEORGE M. SCHWAB

Introduction

1. RUTH THROUGH TIME

A Tale Long Time Coming

The book of Ruth is for people who, like Naomi, feel empty and abandoned by God. She was a widow who, in a time of famine, had buried both sons. Her husband's heritage was lost, his seed extinct, his life over. Naomi was collateral damage; she expressed with deep-seated bitterness that God caused her plight. What in her life did *not* need restoration? In her hardship she urged her sons' widows to return to their empty gods. The book of Ruth shows how God, gently and (at first) imperceptibly, restores the lost and salves the caustic soul.

The book is also about the Ruths of the world—originally aliens to the promises of God and strangers to his covenant. Orpah returned to her Moabite gods. She failed to comprehend their vanity, and the narrative leaves her unredeemed. But Ruth perceived where *life* was located (certainly not in Moab) and followed Naomi as she returned to the land of promise. And in the story of this little family, the great biblical theme of redemption is put on display.

But did it really happen? When was it written, and how did this family saga capture Israel's imagination? Tradition says that Samuel wrote it. Some scholars more or less agree and date it early; others date it very late (in the postexilic period). But the data are probably best explained as resulting from a process, the story over time being transformed from a domestic tale to a literary work of national prominence—in the end sacred to all Israel.

This process is discussed below using the metaphor of the development of a common chicken egg. At the heart of a fertilized egg is an embryo. As the embryo passes along the oviduct, it draws nourishment from the yolk. The oviduct then surrounds the yolk with nourishing albumen (the egg white). Finally, a hard shell encloses the entire structure.[1] The embryo is analogous to the book of Ruth's beating heart

---

1. I offer thanks to Lieutenant Colonel Carrie G. Benton, DVM, for her help with this terminology.

and lifeblood: unrepeatable historical events, unique individuals taking action in the early Iron Age. The yolk is the circumstance that made these events part of the national consciousness of ancient Israel. At this stage they were not simply history, but history with import. Later, the albumen was layered onto the story: redemption themes were accentuated as it became a chapter of Israel's sacred history, an exemplar of religious virtues. The egg's shell is the final artistic polishing of the postexilic scribes, the last layer when the book hardened into its present form.

Embryonic Provenance: When the Judges Judged

The first word in Hebrew (lit., "and it was") also opens a number of historical works (Joshua, Judges, 1 Samuel, Esther, etc.); "we must presume that the author of Ruth did regard the events that are to unfold as belonging to his past"—i.e., "once upon a time" is *not* an accurate gloss.[2] The Hebrew of Ruth sports numerous (seemingly) older forms that are "hard to explain in a late document."[3] Scholars who propose a late date argue that scribes purposely made the text seem older by faking the language! Thus the use of the paragogic *nun* (*tidbāqîn*; 2:8) is "probably an ancient spelling employed here for archaic stylistic effect";[4] Campbell suggests the *yod* ending of the *Kethiv* form in 3:3 is "archaizing."[5] But Glanzman observes that names in Ruth are found in ninth-eighth century tablets and so are not a later fabrication.[6]

Morris claims the "freshness of the narrative" argues against its treating the "remote past."[7] Obviously, the genealogies admit Boaz as factual; his descendants were known and as real as David (and Jesus!), even if the final form of Ruth reads like a folktale. By explaining the jural details the book intentionally sets the events in history; "that the author clearly intended the legal situation to be credible to his audience may be presupposed from the care which he took to explain the obsolete custom of removing a shoe as a symbol of abdication of interest."[8] Ruth 4:7 claims the custom had ceased, but not so long ago that its purpose was lost to the author.

In sum, the book of Ruth treats true events and people who lived in the actual world, with defined legal customs as integral to a factual genealogy. This is the book's embryonic stage—a family history, orally transmitted. "The setting of the book reflects in a uniform manner the period of the Judges, and however skilled the author, it has to be admitted that such an atmosphere would be very difficult indeed to recapture in the postexilic era."[9]

---

2. Jack Sasson, *Ruth: A New Translation with a Philological Commentary and a Formalist-Folklorist Interpretation* (Baltimore, Md.: Johns Hopkins Univ. Press, 1979), 14–15.
3. Arthur E. Cundall and Leon Morris, *Judges and Ruth* (Downers Grove, Ill.: InterVarsity Press, 1968), 236.
4. Robert L. Hubbard, *The Book of Ruth* (NICOT; Grand Rapids: Eerdmans, 1988), 156.
5. Ed Campbell, *Ruth* (AB; Garden City, N.Y.: Doubleday, 1975), 120.
6. George S. Glanzman, "The Origin and Date of the Book of Ruth," *CBQ* 21 (1959): 206.
7. Cundall and Morris, *Judges and Ruth*, 239.
8. Derek Beattie, "Book of Ruth as Evidence for Israelite Legal Practice," *VT* 24 (1974): 253.
9. R. K. Harrison, *Introduction to the Old Testament* (Grand Rapids: Eerdmans, 1969), 1061–62.

A Yolk-tale: When the Story Captured Israel's Imagination

The extant book of Ruth is customarily grouped with Song of Songs, Lamentations, Ecclesiastes, and Esther (the *Megillôt*), but some of these works were penned long after Ruth's earlier stages. The story could hardly have belonged to a liturgical collection that did not yet exist. Before its inclusion in the *Megillôt*, some form of Ruth probably supplemented Judges (as Lamentations later did Jeremiah). The Septuagint (LXX), followed by all English Bibles, witnesses to this probability.[10] Before Sirach there is no evidence of the Writings—let alone the *Megillôt*—as a separate corpus. The LXX suggests a different arrangement may have predated the formation of the *Megillôt*. Josephus later claimed there were but twenty-two books of the Hebrew Bible (not twenty-four), likely discounting appendices as dependent works.[11] Even Jerome acknowledged the alternative order.[12] Ruth 1:1 sets the story in the period of the Judges, and an early edition once functioned accordingly as the third work of the "Bethlehem Trilogy." The later polished and completed book was adopted into the *Megillôt*.

The observation that "in those days Israel had no king; everyone did as he saw fit" appears in Judges' last two episodes (17:1–18:31; 19:1–21:25). The former contrasts peaceable Bethlehem (ch. 17) with the thieving and threatening Danites (ch. 18); the latter shows Bethlehem's hospitality—but in the territory of Benjamin, scandalous abuse. Israel needed a king—but *what* king? That Saul was a Benjamite raises the possibility of a political motive behind these episodes: "they are included in the sacred record for the purpose of tracing the roots of the Davidic dynasty and justifying its existence in opposition to Saul."[13] In fact, the whole book promotes Judah over against non-Judean judges.[14] Davis suggests that Judges was published during the seven-year civil war between David and the house of Saul as a political tract to promote Judah as better suited to rule than Benjamin.[15]

> The book of Judges in substantially its present form had its *Sitz im Leben* in the period of David's reign over Judah in Hebron; that it constitutes both an apology for a Davidic monarchy and an appeal to the northern tribes—especially Benjamin—to unite under the Davidic kingship; and that the internal data, including the selection of the material itself, betray how suitably this document would fit the period and purpose being suggested.[16]

---

10. See Philippe Guillaume, "From a Post-Monarchical to the Pre-Monarchical Period of the Judges," *BN* 113 (2002): 12–17.

11. Campbell, *Ruth*, 33.

12. See Doug Culver, "Introduction to Old Testament Literature" (unpublished, 2002).

13. Eugene H. Merrill, *Kingdom of Priests: A History of Old Testament Israel* (Grand Rapids: Baker, 1987), 179.

14. Marvin Sweeney, "Davidic Polemics in the Book of Judges," *VT* 47 (1997): 517.

15. Dale R. Davis, "A Proposed Life-Setting for the Book of Judges," Ph.D. diss. (Southern Baptist Theological Seminary, 1978), 24. There was another Benjamite Saul who persecuted God's elect. Sean McDonough ("Small Change: Saul to Paul, Again," *JBL* 125 [2006]: 390–91) links Acts 13:9 and 21 (the only NT mention of OT Saul), thus suggesting the apostle was renamed "Paul" ("small") to identify with David (of modest stature) rather than his namesake.

16. Davis, "A Proposed Life-Setting," 24.

Brettler notes that in Judges Judah's supremacy frames the book (1:1–2; 20:18).[17] He suggests that loyalists to the house of Saul lasted well into Solomon's reign and that Judges is a pro-David answer to this. The period when such propaganda was chiefly needed was when David led from Hebron during the civil war with Saul's son Ishbosheth.[18]

Wright avers "nothing in the book [of Ruth] mirrors in any way the turbulent life" of Judges.[19] But Ruth does reflect the hospitable and peaceable characterization of Bethlehem in Judges' final episodes, with calamity meeting whoever departs from there.[20] Elimelech's flight to Moab may be an indictment of the judges.[21]

Ruth also explicitly points beyond its own time to David (4:17). Its genealogy apparently predates Solomon's fame. Perhaps instructive at this point is a piece of Jewish lore that envisages Doeg the Edomite as questioning David's legitimacy based on Deuteronomy 23:3: "No Ammonite or Moabite shall enter the assembly of Yahweh even to the tenth generation" (b. Yebam. 76–78). The need to explain how David, with his Moabite pedigree, can be king is not a modern one. Ruth can be approached as a political answer to David's hypothetical critics. Ruth is often called "the Moabitess," as though to say, "Remember, this is about a Moabitess!" Thus Elimelech's widow *returned* to Bethlehem from Moab, she did not *originate* there. David is legally descended from Elimelech and Boaz, both native Israelites. And in the end, his grandfather was not called Ruth's child, but Naomi's (4:16)! Having heard the tale, anyone with feeling would admit that it is unassailable and uplifting—a plus and not a minus toward David's kingship.

Thus the "yolk" that raised the story from the status of mere family history to pan-Israel popularization was the need "to soften and make palatable the harmful Moabite tradition which was associated with David's origins."[22] Perhaps it was during the crisis of civil war that the story was most relevant and widely disseminated. It is unknown how similar Ruth was at this stage to the present written work. (Obviously, 4:17 was not later embellished to include Solomon.)

Nourishing Later Spiritual Needs

The family story was propagated and smoothed the way for all twelve tribes to pledge allegiance to David against Ishbosheth, but this development does not explain how it became *sacred* history. Ruth somehow transitioned from political instrument to holy writ. The metaphorical "albumen" layer is its becoming part of the national metanarrative that nurtured Israel's identity as a worshiping community, an essential chapter in the all-encompassing story of redemption. Ruth's story was beloved as surely as that of Judah and Tamar or Rachel and Leah (explicitly mentioned in 4:11–12). It is an exemplary tale worth telling beyond its original setting. Witness Solomon, who later married many foreign women *unlike* Ruth—women who

---

17. Marc Brettler, "The Book of Judges: Literature as Politics," *JBL* 108 (1989): 417.

18. As per Davis, "A Proposed Life-Setting for the Book of Judges."

19. George R. H. Wright, "The Mother-Maid at Bethlehem," *ZAW* (98): 56.

20. Reg Grant, "Literary Structure in the Book of Ruth," *BSac* 149 (1991): 426.

21. Mira Morgenstern, "Ruth and the Sense of Self: Midrash and Difference," *Judaism* 48 (1999): 132–33.

22. Roland Murphy, *Wisdom Literature: Job, Proverbs, Ruth, Canticles, Ecclesiastes, and Esther* (FOTL 13; Grand Rapids: Eerdmans, 1981), 87.

turned his heart to foreign gods. Against their negative influence stands Ruth as a template for intermarrying with positive results.

Redemption is Ruth's *Leitmotif*.[23] What was an apology for David became an apology for Yahweh as Redeemer. Redemption connects Ruth with what is arguably the definitive feature of the Hebrew Bible: the exodus event. God spoke to Moses at the burning bush:

> I am the Lord, and I will bring you out from under the yoke of the Egyptians. I will free you from being slaves to them, and I will *redeem* you with an outstretched arm and with mighty acts of judgment. I will take you as my own people, and I will be your God. Then you will know that I am the Lord your God, who brought you out from under the yoke of the Egyptians. And I will bring you to the land I swore with uplifted hand to give to Abraham, to Isaac and to Jacob. I will give it to you as a possession. I am the Lord. (Ex 6:6–8, emphasis added)

God promises to *redeem* his people from bondage, to adopt them as his people, to be their God, known as Yahweh, to bring them to the Promised Land, and to make it their inheritance. The fulfillment of these promises was experienced in miniature by Ruth and even by Naomi. Although they were not slaves in Moab, they did suffer much and did need redemption. In them the salvation of Israel is personally and immediately recapitulated, as these unfortunate women were caught up in the grand, overarching purposes of God for his people to participate in his redemption of the world.

Israel envisaged the future as bound with David's descendant, who would rule as king (2Sa 7:16). Thus "I will restore David's fallen tent" (Am 9:11), "the Israelites will return ... and seek David their king" (Hos 3:5). Micah 5:1 identifies salvation with Bethlehem—the city of Boaz and Ruth. Frieda Hyman claims, "The theme of *Megillat* Ruth is, unequivocally, Redemption," and she observes that Ruth evokes David and thus Messiah his descendant; a cosmic, messianic redemption that "embraces all of mankind" is its ultimate perspective;[24] "the kinsman-redeemer serves as a Messianic type."[25]

Although the modest little story does not make such grand claims, it is precisely here that it dovetails with the NT. Boaz and Ruth are listed in Matthew 1:5; it is *Jesus* who is David's son, the Messiah, born in Bethlehem to fulfill prophecy, come to redeem the world. The book of Ruth explores the warp and woof of redemption; it invites the reader to come alongside and await with Naomi and Ruth the redemption of everything lost—personally, in community, and cosmically—as Yahweh changes the world to bring food where there was famine, conception where there was barrenness, and life where there was death.

Ruth readily expresses Israel's metanarrative; this is the "albumen" stage of its development, its adoption as a religious work that speaks beyond itself to timeless issues of faith. One undeniable feature of the present book is how amenable it is to folklorist analysis. Sasson's critique is graphically shown in the "Outline: Parsing Ruth" section below, where his symbols representing identified elements of the folklore genre.[26] Often Sasson's equations seem forced to the novice—equations such as Ruth's permission to glean being a "magical agent," the blessedness conferred on Boaz equaling his "being given a new appearance," and the

---

23. Harold Fisch, "Ruth and the Structure of Covenant History," *VT* 32 (1982): 435.

24. Frieda Hyman, "Ruth—Pure Dove of Israel," *Judaism* 38 (1989): 53.

25. Gleason Archer, *A Survey of Old Testament Introduction* (Chicago: Moody Press, 1994), 309.

26. Sasson, *Ruth*, 203–14.

genealogy being the hero "ascending the throne." Key folkloristic elements (e.g., the villain's comeuppance) are absent in Ruth; Sasson also labels key parts of Ruth as mere connectives—such as 2:18–23, the debut of its main theme! Nevertheless, he has shown that Ruth has affinity with the genre of folklore.

Ruth also appears fabulous in that characters' names seem contrived. Despite the fact that such names are attested from antiquity, the (in Hebrew) rhyming names of two sons, "Sickness" and "Destruction," who quickly die, are suspect. Have these names been altered to enhance the plot? And if so, what other details are included (or excluded—e.g., Naomi's employment) to help paint a picture or create a mood? The name "Ruth" is not tied ball-and-chain to the Moabite language. Consider also 4:18–22, which spans the period of Joshua and Judges in a mere four generations—a *stylized* genealogy.[27]

History is one dimension of the book, and its literary quality another; the literary should not swallow up the historical. When engaged in literary analysis, the critic must take care not to exchange "the tangible world of the Bible for a merely abstract construction."[28] The semi-fluid text of Ruth was cast into a legendary form that revealed God's mysterious yet intimate purpose to redeem his people. Over time, Ruth became substantially the story presently extant, as it nourished the community of faith—the way that albumen nourishes life within the egg.

Calcification: Final Stylization and Formatting

Many scholars assert that Ruth originated in the postexilic period to counteract Nehemiah's reforms. Presently, it is grouped with the *Megillôt*—part of the Hagiographa, a collection presumably "canonized" last. (But this placement came late in Ruth's history; an edition apparently once appended Judges—see above.) There are also a number of Aramaisms in Ruth that are easy to explain if the book is postexilic. An Aramaism is either an Aramaic loanword or a Hebrew form suspiciously akin to Aramaic: "Marry" uses the verb for "lift up" (1:4) and stands in contrast to "take" (4:13); Naomi names herself "Mara," ending with *aleph* rather than *he* (1:20); in 4:7 *leqayyēm* looks Aramaic. Scholars who propose an early date argue that these forms are not Aramaisms at all—they just appear to be! This warrants Childs' charge of "an undeniable flavour of special pleading"—a case equally valid against denying the older forms' witness to an early date.[29] Ruth exhibits archaic forms *and* Aramaisms—affinity with both Ugarit and Persia. One may imagine modest editorial activity on a substantially stable text continuing into the Second Temple period.

In the postexilic era, Jews were resettling the land under the rule of Ezra the priest and Nehemiah the governor—and were falling prey to all the temptations of their fathers except outright idolatry. As they rebuilt the temple and the walls of Jerusalem, they needed discipline to forge a community of faith built around the law of Moses. Where some took license, laws were enforced. Nobles were forbidden to charge interest (Ne 5:1–13) and the Sabbath was protected (Ne 13:15–21). Ethnic purity laws also applied, so Tobiah the Ammonite was evicted from the temple (Ne 13:1–9), based on Deuteronomy 23:3, "No Ammonite or Moabite shall enter the assembly of Yahweh." Ezra 9–10 treats the matter of intermarriage

---

27. Derek Beattie, *Jewish Exegesis of the Book of Ruth* (JSOT 2; Sheffield: Sheffield Academic, 1977), 199.
28. Fisch, "Ruth and the Structure of Covenant History," 426.
29. Brevard Childs, *Introduction to the Old Testament as Scripture* (Philadelphia: Fortress, 1979), 563.

between Jew and non-Jew. When Ezra learned that some Jews were marrying aliens (e.g., Moabitesses), he rent his garments, pulled out his beard, and wept while confessing to Yahweh this great breach of covenant. The faithful finally agreed to divorce the outsiders; nonconformists were disenfranchised. In the words of Nehemiah 13:23–27,

> Moreover, in those days I saw men of Judah who had married women from Ashdod, Ammon and Moab. Half of their children spoke the language of Ashdod or the language of one of the other peoples, and did not know how to speak the language of Judah. I rebuked them and called curses down on them. I beat some of the men and pulled out their hair. I made them take an oath in God's name and said: "You are not to give your daughters in marriage to their sons, nor are you to take their daughters in marriage for your sons or for yourselves. Was it not because of marriages like these that Solomon king of Israel sinned? Among the many nations there was no king like him. He was loved by his God, and God made him king over all Israel, but even he was led into sin by foreign women. Must we hear now that you too are doing all this terrible wickedness and are being unfaithful to our God by marrying foreign women?"

To claim that the book of Ruth is in great tension with the ethos of this period would be an understatement (yet it is entirely unaware of the tension). Ruth is so contrary that finding its origins here is scarcely conceivable. Note in Nehemiah's speech above Solomon's exemplary rule — except for his one weakness. This period tends to portray David and Solomon in the best possible light, presumably using past glory as grounds for future hope: David once presided over an assembly like the army of God (1Ch 12:22), and gold was common as stone — let those days come again! Thus the Chronicler records nothing negative about David or Solomon.

Over against this ethos is the book of Ruth, which reads like 2 Samuel in that David is not at all whitewashed; he is inescapably tied with a Moabite heritage. This book is unconcerned with worship at the temple (or even Jerusalem!) and Sabbath-keeping, and it has a modest genealogy (lacking Solomon), unlike the elaborate lists of Ezra, Nehemiah, and 1 Chronicles. In addition, "The absence of polemic or invective makes improbable the view that it was an anti-separatist tract written to counteract the stringent measures of Ezra and Nehemiah."[30]

A postexilic Ruth might have looked like the pseudepigraphical *Joseph and Aseneth*, published around the turn of the millennium (200 BC–AD 200). In Genesis 41:45, the flawless and pure patriarch Joseph married Aseneth, daughter of the priest of the Egyptian god On. *Joseph and Aseneth* imagines how this marriage might have happened — and exposes Joseph's utter distain for idolaters: "It is not fitting for a man who worships God ... to kiss a strange woman who will bless with her mouth dumb idols."[31] Aseneth experienced an emotional conversion and renounced her previous, vain life of devotion to false gods. Only then did Joseph embrace her.

No doubt, this theme is what the book of Ruth would have emphasized had it been composed after the exile. Esther also portrays pagans as vicious and bloodthirsty, at war with Israel and out to destroy her. (The apocryphal additions to Esther accentuate this hostility.) Such enmity is absent in Ruth — the animus

---

30. Harrison, *Introduction*, 1063.
31. C. Burchard, "Joseph and Aseneth," in *Old Testament Pseudepigrapha* (ed. James Charlesworth [New York: Doubleday, 1985]), 2:211–12.

directed instead at Yahweh by an embittered Naomi. Contrast Ruth also with the deuterocanonical Judith, which again portrays Israel as taking arms against idolatrous and corrupt heathens. The amiable and alien-friendly book of Ruth is like a fish out of water in the intertestamental period.

Aside from some dubious Aramaisms, there is little in Ruth that commends its origin to the Second Temple period (see Note on 4:18). Since the book is disinterested in matters preoccupying genuine postexilic works and so contrary to the era's ethos (yet without polemic), it must have won a place among their treasured books in a different setting entirely — much earlier. Being already cherished, the spiritual influence it later had calls for speculation. Might Ruth have been a well-accepted and traditional template for principles of intermarriage? Did the Moabitesses of Nehemiah's day not measure up to Ruth, who "became a model for future proselytes,"[32] and so earn labeling as illegitimate? Nehemiah argues as much: "their children … spoke the language of one of the other peoples, and did not know how to speak the language of Judah" (Ne 13:24). He *first* cites their nonacculturation, and *second* the law. No doubt Ruth reminded the settlers that foreigners were not absolutely taboo.

Some creative development in Ruth should be acknowledged in the postexilic period. The hardening of the text (the "shell" stage) is its final artistic polishing. Later scribes limited themselves to copying, translating, and commenting but formerly were free to shape and format their texts somewhat. This seminal process eventually produced the refined book of Ruth preserved in the Masoretic tradition, including its style and macrostructure (discussed below under "Outline: Parsing Ruth").

2. THE HEBREW TEXT

The typical churchgoing layperson is uninterested in the material above, except perhaps the defense of Ruth's historicity, and remains content simply to assert, "God did it!" Perhaps that is the wisest remark in this commentary. However, a few more comments must be made about the Hebrew text.

This commentary uses *Biblia Hebraica Stuttgartensia* (*BHS*), the critical Hebrew text based on the best and earliest known manuscript (*Codex Leningradensis*). There are other witnesses to the ancient text that at times are cited. For example, in the Second Temple period the entire OT was translated into Greek (called the Septuagint and referred to as the LXX), which occasionally seems to reflect a somewhat different Hebrew text. When an alternative reading impinges on the meaning, I have noted so.

The Masoretes (AD 600–900) even preserved known or suspected errors and placed in the margin their suggested corrections. "What is written" is the *Kethiv*; "what to read" is the *Qere*. This commentary usually follows the *Qere*, but in Ruth some key interpretative issues are related to *Kethiv-Qere* problems. These matters are usually handled in the notes.

Current Hebrew Bibles group Ruth with the *Megillôt*. These five books are read, one each, during the five celebrations in the Jewish calendar. Ruth is read at Pentecost — a two-day festival celebrating God's giving of the law to Israel — when the various harvests have been completed. It is ironic that Ruth is used liturgically for this purpose, since Ruth stands in tension with Moses, as detailed below.

---

32. Sasson, *Ruth*, 13.

3. RUTH AND THE LAW

The Levir and the Gōʾēl

Levirate marriage is one of many aspects of ancient Near Eastern culture that is foreign to modern Westerners, although a form of it is practiced today. Tony Sauder served the Mennonite Central Committee in a village in Chad from 1990–94. In an unpublished letter, he notes that once a woman is married in Chad, she has left her own family and entered her husband's. If he dies, she cannot return to her family of birth but is dependant on her new kin and often marries her dead husband's brother. (Christian women there do not countenance polygamy or marry outside the church, so they are often left destitute.) A similar concept of marriage seems to be regulated by Deuteronomy 25:5–10:

> If brothers are living together and one of them dies without a son, his widow must not marry outside the family. Her husband's brother shall take her and marry her and fulfill the duty of a brother-in-law to her. The first son she bears shall carry on the name of the dead brother so that his name will not be blotted out from Israel.
>
> However, if a man does not want to marry his brother's wife, she shall go to the elders at the town gate and say, "My husband's brother refuses to carry on his brother's name in Israel. He will not fulfill the duty of a brother-in-law to me." Then the elders of his town shall summon him and talk to him. If he persists in saying, "I do not want to marry her," his brother's widow shall go up to him in the presence of the elders, take off one of his sandals, spit in his face and say, "This is what is done to the man who will not build up his brother's family line." That man's line shall be known in Israel as The Family of the Unsandaled.

By definition, a *levir* is a man who marries his brother's widow to engender an heir for his brother. This is presented in Deuteronomy as a familial duty, but not an obligation in the religious sense. There is no need for atonement if the man refuses, but he is shamed. Note the use of the sandal. The widow removes it from him as a symbol of his disgrace. Note also the absence here of the phrase "redeemer" and of land possession as an issue. There is no question of the *levir*'s ownership; presumably land is held in escrow for the future heir.

The story in Genesis 38 exemplifies levirate marriage. Judah's son Er married Tamar, then died. Judah told Onan (another son) to act as *levir* and procreate a son by Tamar; Onan refused, "for he knew the seed would not be his" (Ge 38:9). This refusal offended Yahweh, so Onan also died. Judah then asked Tamar to wait for yet another son (Shelah), not yet grown up (see Ru 1:11–13). Tamar waited, but Judah withheld Shelah for fear that he also would die. She then tricked Judah into donating his own seed. He eventually admitted her deed was justifiable. (The product of this sordid affair was Perez, the ancestor of Boaz named in Ruth 4:18.)

Again, there was no financial benefit to Onan to provide seed, since the land owned by Er would remain separate. But if no heir for Er was born, Onan might well have acquired it. "Levirate marriage is a completely altruistic act.... By fathering his brother's child, the *levir* thus has 'disinherited' himself!"[33]

---

33. Dvora E. Weisberg, "Levirate marriage and the *Halitzah* of the Mishnah," *The Annual of Rabbinic Judaism: Ancient, Medieval, and Modern* 1 (1998): 41.

It was "an institution which could be called … a 'structure of grace.'"[34] The right of inheritance is seen in Numbers 27:8–11:

> If a man dies and leaves no son, turn his inheritance over to his daughter. If he has no daughter, give his inheritance to his brothers. If he has no brothers, give his inheritance to his father's brothers. If his father had no brothers, give his inheritance to the nearest relative in his clan, that he may possess it. This is to be a legal requirement for the Israelites, as the LORD commanded Moses.

"Women view levirate unions as opportunities to ensure family continuity and provide widows with security. Men, in contrast, see levirate unions as a threat to their understanding of paternity and their desire to protect their own interests."[35] The kinsman-redeemer of Ruth 4 evinces a similar reluctance as Onan, Judah, and the Unsandaled—a reluctance to jeopardize his own holdings. In this case, one last piece of legislation seems relevant: Leviticus 25:25–28.

> If one of your countrymen becomes poor and sells some of his property, his nearest relative is to come and *redeem* what his countryman has sold. If, however, a man has no one to *redeem* it for him but he himself prospers and acquires sufficient means to *redeem* it, he is to determine the value for the years since he sold it and refund the balance to the man to whom he sold it; he can then go back to his own property. But if he does not acquire the means to repay him, what he sold will remain in the possession of the buyer until the Year of Jubilee. It will be returned in the Jubilee, and he can then go back to his property. (emphasis added)

Note the absence here of any reference to marriage. Here the word "redeem" comes into play. Redemption involves buying back land; technically it does not apply to the *levir*'s contribution of seed (however necessary a redemptive step). *Gōʾēl* is Hebrew for "redeemer." A *levir* weds the widow; a *gōʾēl* buys the land. The *levir* effects one kind of seed; the *gōʾēl* another.

The problem with the analysis above is that it does not neatly fit the book of Ruth. The *gōʾēl* of Ruth 4 refused without shame and chose a perfectly acceptable option. In fact, the reader does not *want* him to redeem, since Boaz is the hero! The *gōʾēl* removed his sandal not as an embarrassing gesture but to seal the business transaction. (He is not the Unsandaled—he is the Unnamed.) Thompson suggests the shoe symbolizes the right to walk the land (Ps 60:8, "upon Edom I toss my sandal"), and in Deuteronomy, the wife's freedom.[36] But Naomi needed to *sell* the land, not buy it. Ruth resonates to customs otherwise obscure and distinct from Torah. Boaz is neither a *levir* nor a *gōʾēl* in the traditional sense. In fact, the word "act as *levir*" (*yābam*) is not used in Ruth.

"The law of the levirate marriage applies only to brothers and to no other family members."[37] Boaz married not Naomi but her daughter-in-law—and in the genealogy, Obed is *not* Elimelech's son but Boaz's, thus nullifying Boaz's role as *levir*. It seems that the familial distance was great enough that eligible men could refuse without shame, yet close enough to be empowered to act to save Elimelech's place in the

---

34. J. Andrew Dearman, "The Family in the Old Testament," *Int* 52/2 (1998): 122.

35. Dvora E. Weisberg, "The Widow of Our Discontent: Levirate Marriage in the Bible and Ancient Israel," *JSOT* 28 (2004): 405–6.

36. Thomas Thompson, "Some Legal Problems in the Book of Ruth," *VT* 18 (1968): 92–93.

37. Josiah Derby, "A Problem in the Book of Ruth," *JBQ* 22 (1994): 183.

clan. They were not obligated in the sense given in Deuteronomy 25, and even less in the sense of Genesis 38 (where refusal brought death). In Ruth the spirit of the law is fulfilled, if not the letter.

> But when the custom as seen in Ruth is studied in its own right, in the light of specifically Israelite values, we find that it upholds the same values as Deuteronomy does, however different the specific concrete situation presupposed by Deuteronomy might be. Rather than a rule of law, we find in Israel a rule according to values and principles, interpreted by elders and judges who were thought capable of understanding and maintaining the ancient customs.[38]

Although Ruth is cut from the same cultural cloth as the Mosaic books and shares their social milieu, it is not dependant on them. Even though Ruth blurs the roles of *levir* and *gōʾēl* somewhat, they are two distinct agencies that should be kept separate to interpret Ruth with clarity. Even so, there are questions that the modern reader can only speculate in answering. For example, how *exactly* would buying the land have financially harmed the kinsman (4:6)? Would he pour resources into the land only to lose it soon after? Any proposed answer remains conjectural since so little light can be shed on the issue from the law of Moses, other texts, or ancient sources.

Ruth the Moabitess

Another problem with Ruth and the law is her unchallenged and easy integration into Bethlehem's society, despite Deuteronomy 23:2–6:

> No one born of a forbidden marriage nor any of his descendants may enter the assembly of the LORD, even down to the tenth generation.
>
> No Ammonite or Moabite or any of his descendants may enter the assembly of the LORD, even down to the tenth generation. For they did not come to meet you with bread and water on your way when you came out of Egypt, and they hired Balaam son of Beor from Pethor in Aram Naharaim to pronounce a curse on you. However, the LORD your God would not listen to Balaam but turned the curse into a blessing for you, because the LORD your God loves you. Do not seek a treaty of friendship with them as long as you live.

Nehemiah's reforms explicitly utilized this passage (Ne 13:1–3), and Ezra made the people divorce their foreign wives—specifically Moabitesses (Ezr 9:1; 10:19). Why then does Ruth escape this prohibition? After all, intermarriage was a problem in Judges, which "culminates in the story of Samson, who intermarries with the Philistines, and as a result, enables the Philistines to displace the tribe of Dan from its tribal inheritance."[39]

Noted above is the reference to tractate *b. Yebamoth* 76–78, which relates Doeg's accusation of David's illegitimacy. There, rabbis consider legally discriminating between a male and female Moabite—a sex-based loophole in the law. But on what legal basis were Nehemiah and Ezra then working? Obviously, women were at least half the intermarriage problem; the law expresses an early Israelite aversion for all Moabites in particular.

---

38. Thompson, "Some Legal Problems," 89.
39. Sweeney, "Davidic Polemics," 523.

Another resolution is to convert the book of Ruth into a xenophobic "manifesto for ethnoreligious extremism, in direct contrast to the blessing-of-foreigners trajectory in which the narrative is canonically embedded," per *Targum Ruth*, which claims that the original famine was due to Gentile pollution and that Mahlon and Chilion died for their crime of marrying Moabitesses.[40] Thus the Targum makes the book of Ruth assert the exact opposite of what it is about. Besides being artificial, this attempt also fails since the law makes no explicit exceptions, even for converts such as Ruth.

Yet if a resolution is possible, it must be in an unexpressed but implied exception. The law as stated is not qualified in any way — yet it does rest on an historical basis, and it is here that the Moabitess may have found a real loophole, in fulfilling the spirit if not the letter of the law. Irmtraud Fisher observes that the law is a response to the harm Moab caused: "For they did not come to meet you with bread and water on your way when you came out of Egypt" — and they hired Balaam to curse Israel.[41] Fisher compares this failure with Ruth's actions to benefit Naomi: "If the reason no longer applies, the prohibition is no longer justified." Thus the stricture does not apply to one such as Ruth, who did what her own people refused to do by aiding Israelites not only in Moab but also consistently in Bethlehem (and who became a proselyte).

It is a mistake to straightjacket the story of redemption into such a legalistic vice that the principle of God's graciousness is lost. Merrill observes that the genealogy ending Ruth links "the patriarchal and monarchal eras" and almost skips the time period of Moses (see commentary below).[42] The overt connections drawn between Ruth and sacred history are with Leah and Rachel, Tamar and Judah, and Perez (4:11–12). Merrill argues that a link bypassing Moses is forged directly between the Abrahamic and Davidic covenants. "The narrator is writing ... to clarify the fact that the Davidic dynasty is not something which sprang out of the conditional Mosaic Covenant but rather that it has its historical and theological roots in the promises to the patriarchs."[43] Ruth fulfills God's promise to Abraham — a promise that preceded Moses — "I will bless those who bless you, and whoever curses you I will curse; and all peoples on earth will be blessed through you" (Ge 12:3). This assurance of blessing and curse is just as unqualified as Deuteronomy 23:2–6; it does not say, "Those who bless you I will bless *except Moabites* ... through you all peoples *except Moabites* will be blessed." "Those who curse you will be cursed" is the argument of Deuteronomy 23:2–6; "those who bless you will be blessed" is the thesis of Ruth.

Those who bless Abraham are blessed, and the whole world is blessed through him. The inclusion of non-Jews into the kingdom of God is deeply explored in the NT. Acts 10–11 records how Peter was told in a vision to eat unclean food. While pondering this report, some Romans visited; he went with them and preached the gospel, which they gladly accepted. The vision was not about food per se but about their inclusion. Baptizing them created a scandal, for the church assumed Gentile converts would accept circumcision and keep the law. Upon reflection, they recognized that "God has granted even the Gentiles repentance unto life" (Ac 11:18). Grace trumps law. Every non-Jewish Christian who enters God's church

40. Michael S. Moore, "Ruth the Moabitess and the Blessing of Foreigners," *CBQ* 60 (1998): 213–15.
41. Irmtraud Fisher, "The Book of Ruth: A 'Feminist' Commentary on the Torah?' in *The Feminist Companion to the Bible (Second Series)* (ed. Athalya Brenner; Sheffield: Sheffield Academic Press, 1999), 3:36.
42. Eugene H. Merrill, "The Book of Ruth: Narration and Shared Themes," *BSac* 142 (1985): 135
43. Ibid.

through Christ enjoys the special favor that Ruth did; for them also the exclusionary law is set aside. Those who call Jesus blessed will be blessed. Ruth is about Jews and Gentiles finding redemption in the *Gōʾel* whom God provides.

Paul also argues from the Abrahamic covenant in claiming that the later law did not invalidate the promise (Gal 3:17–18). Ruth is numbered with the company of the elect because "the Scripture foresaw that God would justify the Gentiles by faith, and announced the gospel in advance to Abraham: 'All nations will be blessed through you'" (Gal 3:8). She identified with Yahweh, returned to Israel, and found shelter with Boaz, the type of Christ.

The book of Ruth is a narrated story. But the prosaic form is not history for history's sake; it is as theological as Deuteronomy—a holy book conveying divine truth. This truth does not come with a clear "thus says the LORD," but that must be inferred, interpreted, intuited. The tale *is* the qualifier to Deuteronomy 23:2–6; it delineates the weakness and limitation of the law. Rather than read Ruth in the light of the law, we must read the law in the light of Ruth to see when it does not apply. But Ruth as interpretative grid is not limited to one or another legal snippet. Its critique runs deeper, as explored briefly below.

4. RUTH AND NAOMI

Ruth is a story of two women. Even moderns tend to read the story quickly; they rush past the women to the *real* story, which is about Elimelech's inheritance, or David, or Israel, or God. A distinctly female perspective tends to get submerged into these concerns, for usually women are not the central characters in literature or ancient society. But Ruth and Naomi had to act on their own initiative, and so their personalities are revealed. "Women are present in the text in a significant way. Women have their place in the story of faith, they are being brought out of the shadows."[44] Something is lost in the story if this dimension of it is overlooked.

Ruth contrasts with the patriarchal narratives. "In Genesis, whenever women are presented in pairs, conflicts arise."[45] Rachel conceptualized her competition with Leah as warfare (Ge 30:8)—and this troubled home is explicitly cited in Ruth (4:11). But "Ruth's oath (1:16–17), which is often used as a marriage vow in churches, does not tie her to a *man* but to a *woman*."[46] Almost exclusively in the Bible, female solidarity is here revealed as more valuable than male support. "Female companionship is stronger than male companionship, of more worth than the sons and male relatives who know about the woman's misery (cf. 2.11) but do not take initiative to help. A daughter-in-law like Ruth is not only better than *both* her [Naomi's] deceased sons but even better than *seven* sons."[47] Naomi and Ruth must live in a patriarchal society, but they are free to act and choose. Each is shown deciding to value the welfare of the other more than her own. There is a bond between them that helps to overcome the crises of widowhood and famine.

---

44. Johanna W. H. Bos, "Out of the Shadows: Genesis 38; Judges 4:17–22; Ruth 3," *Semeia* 42 (1988): 37.
45. Fisher, "The Book of Ruth," 48.
46. Ibid., 26.
47. Ibid., 32.

Hals argues that the book is about the hidden work of God.[48] But Ruth focuses on the deeds of two women. Might it be about women's participation in accomplishing the work of God, or perhaps women's experience as a people of God? "The Bible represents the viewpoint of high status males, and using it as the only source for information about women's social relationships entails blindness to significant areas of women's behavior patterns. For informal associations of women, the book of Ruth is virtually the only source."[49] In it three men die, the kinsman is an impotent character denied even a personal name, and the elders at the gate are little more than spectators. It is the women who speak for Bethlehem—and for the narrator. When Naomi arrives, the women greet her and name her "Naomi" (1:19). It is they who name "her" son Obed and interpret events for her (and for the reader). They provide the storyteller's perspective (4:14–17). One may read Ruth as being about female initiative, which is as important in fulfilling God's redemptive purposes as male initiative. Ruth's story is not merely a birth narrative that takes a back seat to the more interesting men.

Phyllis Trible claims the opening verses are such that Naomi gradually emerges as a full-orbed individual after Elimelech's death.[50] First, Mahlon and Chilion are called "his sons" (1:2). After his death, they are "her sons." Trible observes that without husband or sons, Naomi is "stripped of all identity." In 1:6 she acts as an individual: "For the first time, she becomes the subject of active verbs. A nonperson inches toward personhood." Once Naomi begins to act, the narrator uses the pronoun "she" rather than her name (1:6–7). "Precisely at the point where third-person narration yields to dialogue … women take over the story (vv.8–14). In this entire first episode, no men are present; women alone act and speak. And furthermore, the solitary widow, who has been stripped of all identity, is now, at the place of poetic speech, given back her name." From this point on the book is *about* women, featuring Ruth and her heroic navigation in a male world to achieve her ambition, namely, finding security for Naomi and herself. "No God promises them blessing; no man rushes to their rescue." Blotz notes that Ruth loses her name in 4:11–12.[51]

Yet in the end the ladies must trust Boaz to achieve their redemption. Although the story until ch. 4 has been "women working out their own salvation with fear and trembling, for it is God who works in them,"[52] their redemption ultimately rests with a male agent. In fact, one may argue that to the extent that Naomi's individuality emerges in the opening verses, other aspects of her personhood fade and are lost. Autonomy for *her* is a tragic vestige of her emptiness. In the Bible, there is a corporate dimension to personality. Through the Moabitess, Naomi inches toward personhood again by belonging afresh to a community. Boaz asks the foreman, "Whose woman is that?" Trible remarks, "Truly a patriarchal question. After all, a young woman must belong to someone; she is a possession, not a person. Thus Boaz does not ask *her*

---

48. Ronald M. Hals, *The Theology of the Book of Ruth* (Philadelphia: Fortress, 1969), 16.

49. Carol L. Meyers, "'Women of the Neighborhood' (Ruth 4.17): Informal Female Networks in Ancient Israel," in *The Feminist Companion to the Bible (Second Series)* (ed. Athalya Brenner; Sheffield: Sheffield Academic Press, 1999), 3:111.

50. Phyllis Trible, *God and the Rhetoric of Sexuality* (Philadelphia: Fortress, 1978), 166–69.

51. Joseph W. Blotz, "Bitterness and Exegesis: A Feminist Exegesis of the Book of Ruth," *CTM* 32 (2005): 53.

52. Trible, *God and the Rhetoric of Sexuality*, 196.

name, but rather the identity of her owner. His question fits his culture, but it does not fit this woman, who is in tension with that culture."[53]

But this is only half the story. It is by sheltering under Boaz's "wing" that Ruth finds a better identity. Naomi lost hers when the men in her life died. While these losses allowed her personality to be revealed in her choices and actions, she remained empty and bitter in this state. She desired redemption, not liberation. Her tragedy is an occasion to explore female loyalty and female society—but also an occasion to show how neither one can redeem. Herein the ladies serve as an allegory: like Ruth and Naomi, people of faith find themselves when they embrace the Redeemer whom God provides. "Whoever finds his life will lose it, and whoever loses his life for my sake will find it" (Mt 10:39).

5. BIBLIOGRAPHY

Bush, Frederic William. "Ruth 4:17: A Semantic Wordplay." Pages 3–14 in *Go to the Land I Will Show You: Studies in Honor of Dwight W. Young*. Edited by Joseph Coleson and Victor Matthews. Winona Lake, Ind.: Eisenbrauns, 1996.

Campbell, Ed. *Ruth*. Anchor Bible Series. Garden City, N.Y.: Doubleday, 1975.

Chertok, Haim. "The Book of Ruth—Complexities within Simplicity." *Judaism* (1986): 290–97.

Collins, C. John. "Ambiguity and Theology in Ruth: Ruth 1:21 and 2:20." *Presbyterion* 19 (1993): 97–102.

De Waard, Jan, and Eugene Nida, *A Translator's Handbook on The Book of Ruth*. New York: UBS, 1992.

Donaldson, Laura E. "The Sign of Orpah: Reading Ruth through Native Eyes." Pages 130–44 in *The Feminist Companion to the Bible (Second Series) 3*. Edited by Athalya Brenner. Sheffield: Sheffield Academic, 1999.

Fewell, Dana, and David Gunn. "'A Son Is Born to Naomi.' Literary Allusions and Interpretation in the Book of Ruth." *Journal for the Study of the Old Testament* 40 (1988): 99–108.

Gordis, Robert. "Personal Names in Ruth: A Note on Biblical Etymologies." *Judaism* 35/3 (1986): 298–99.

Hamlin, E. John. *Surely There Is a Future*. Grand Rapids: Eerdmans, 1996.

Harm, Harry J. "The Function of Double Entendre in Ruth Three." *Journal of Translation and Textlinguistics* 7/1 (1995): 19–27.

Hubbard, Robert L. *The Book of Ruth*. New International Commentary on the Old Testament. Grand Rapids: Eerdmans, 1988.

Hyman, Frieda. "Ruth—Pure Dove of Israel." *Judaism* 38 (1989): 53–62.

Kanyoro, Musimbi. "Biblical Hermeneutics: Ancient Palestine and the Contemporary World." *Review & Expositor* 94 (1997): 363–78.

Loretz, Oswald. "The Theme of the Ruth Story." *Catholic Biblical Quarterly* 22 (1960): 391–99.

Moore, Michael S. "Two Textual Anomalies in Ruth." *Catholic Biblical Quarterly* 59 (1997): 234–43.

Rauber, D. F. "Literary Values in the Bible: The Book of Ruth." *Journal of Biblical Literature* 89 (1970): 27–37.

Richards, Rosa Lee. "Ruth as ᵓEshet Chayil." Th.M. thesis, Trinity Episcopal School for Ministry, 2006.

Sasson, Jack. *Ruth: A New Translation with a Philological Commentary and a Formalist-Folklorist Interpretation*. Baltimore and London: Johns Hopkins University Press, 1979.

Shepherd, David. "Violence in the Fields? Translating, Reading, and Revising in Ruth 2." *Catholic Biblical Quarterly* 63/3 (2001): 444–63.

Trible, Phyllis. *God and the Rhetoric of Sexuality*. Philadelphia: Fortress, 1978.

Wright, George R. H. "The Mother-Maid at Bethlehem." *Zeitschrift für die Alttestamentliche Wissenschaft* 98/1 (1986): 56–72.

---

53. Ibid.

6. OUTLINE: PARSING RUTH

The book of Ruth is divided into four standard chapters. Above I have briefly mentioned Sasson's folk-loristic approach, which subdivides Ruth into elements represented by symbols, each a component of the genre of folklore.[54] Below is a chart depicting some of these elements.

Symbol	Folkloristic Element	Ruth
β^2	intensified absentation, death of parents	1:3–5
↑	the hero leaves home	1:18–22; 2:1–2
§	connective, no plot movement	2:5–7
A^1	something is lacking	3:1
D^2	hero is tested	3:8–9a
>Y	leave taking at a road marker	3:14–15
L	false hero presents unfounded claims	4:1e
W	hero marries and ascends the throne	4:13–15

These elements are shown below in the chart that compares them to a sampling of other creative approaches to Ruth. The book of Ruth exhibits a high degree of literary artistry, and in recent years many interpreters have attempted to discover a more intricate and detailed macrostructure than the simple four chapters. Campbell identifies the use of "lad" in 1:5 and 4:16 as an inclusio, a literary device that *includes* the material it surrounds (see chart below).[55] He then designates the genealogy as an appendix to the book. Hubbard also parses the book into part I (the story, with four sections: A, B, C, and D) and part II, the genealogy.[56]

Ruth exhibits symmetry and interconnectedness, and later sections seem related to earlier ones. Some writers have used this observation as an organizing principle to develop a chiastic form to the book as a whole. A *chiasm* is a symmetrical structure where the first component relates to the last, and the second to the second-to-last, and so on; in Ruth, the second half of the book is seen as a mirror image of the first. Bertman describes all of Ruth as a chiasm; he relates the genealogy with the opening verses, thus demonstrating the book's essential unity. However, some parts do not fit his schema (note the question mark in the table between C 4 and 5). He acknowledges, "Such elements do occur, but their existence would not seem to invalidate the design in which the rest of the book participates."[57] Sasson also is forced to dismiss parts as mere connectives ("§"). The view of Gow is very similar to Bertman's.[58] Luder and Rigsby essentially follow

---

54. Sasson, *Ruth*, 203–12.
55. See Campbell, *Ruth*.
56. See Hubbard, *Ruth*.
57. Stephen Bertman, "Symmetrical Design in the Book of Ruth," *JBL* 84 (1985): 167.
58. Murray D. Gow, "The Significance of Literary Structure for the Translation of the Book of Ruth," *BT* 35 (1984): 309–20.

Campbell's overall design, except they carefully argue for symmetry and find its central focus in 2:18–3:5 (D), even though it overlaps with C and C'.[59]

The standard chapters are shown on the left below. Note that most commentators shown accept these divisions. Rossow considers them the only clear boundaries in Ruth; each references grain or harvest, and a relative.[60] The right-hand column indicates where scholars tend to agree on a division. For Prinsloo to find chs. 2 and 3 each to be chiastic, he must ignore what others recognize as major divisions.[61] To discover a structure intended by the scribes who finalized Ruth, critics must take care not to break up integral units of text, while simultaneously identifying where natural breaks do occur. Thus Hongisto's chiasm is not persuasive, since element A is the whole first chapter, and elements B, C, D, E, and F are 2:1–7, gratuitously divided![62] After a detailed review of prior art, Marjo Korpel concludes that scholars should be able to defend their divisions using syntax, key words, and other markers beyond simply arguing from thematic correspondences; "any structure which is based on content alone is bound to spark … skepticism."[63]

59. Boyd Luder and Richard Rigsby, "An Adjusted Symmetrical Structuring of Ruth," *JETS* 39 (1996): 15–31. Ignoring *maqqeph*, they claim 1:1–5 and 4:13–17 each have 71 words; the true count is 67 and 63. But if *maqqeph* does not signify, other results emerge: Ruth is exactly 2^4 x 3^4 words; its physical center is 2:20, beginning after 40 words in 2:18–23—which is flanked in turn by 40 verses and of 111 words—precisely three times the genealogy's length (4:18–22).

60. Francis C. Rossow, "Literary Artistry in the Book of Ruth and Its Theological Significance," *Concordia* 17 (1991): 12–19.

61. W. S. Prinsloo, "The Theology of the Book of Ruth," *VT* 30 (1980): 330–41.

62. Leif Hongisto, "Literary Structure and Theology in the Book of Ruth," *AUSS* 23 (1985): 19–28.

63. Marjo Korpel, *The Structure of the Book of Ruth* (Assen, Netherlands: Koninklijke van Gorcum, 2001), 29.

Standard chapters	Schwab	Gow	Campbell	Hubbard	Sasson	Bertman	Prinsloo	Sum
	A history	I.A	Intro "lads"	I.A 1 Intro	α	A history	I	
					β^2			
1	B sons	B	journey home, arrival	2 The Return Itself	a	travel		
					B	B1	dialogue starts	
	C Intent				C	2		
	D Identity	C	"barley harvest"		$\uparrow$	travel		
					$[\uparrow]$			
	E grain	II.D	Ruth & Boaz, harvest	B1 2a meeting with Boaz	donor	C1, 2	II.A	
					§	3	B	
2	F 1st meeting	E			D^2			
					E^2			
	G secret provision				$(D^2$	4	C	
					$E^2)$			
	H Gospel	F	"barley & wheat"	b report	F	?	B'	
					G, F, $\downarrow$		A'	
					§	5		
	G' secret provision	III.D'	Ruth & Boaz on threshing floor	C 1 Proposal	$a^{1'}$	C' 1	III.A	
					$B^{1'}, C'$			
3					$\uparrow', D^{2'}$	2		
	F' 2nd meeting	E'			$E^{2'}$	3		
					$F^{9'}$		B	
					>Y	4		
	E' grain	F'	"sit tight and wait"	2 report	G', §			
					O, L	5		
	D' Identity	IV.B'	civil process at gate	D1 legal process	M	B'1	A'	
					N, Q			
4	C' Intent				Ex		IV	
					§, T			
	B' a son	C'	birth, "lad"	2 the son	W	2		
					X			
	A' history	A'	appendix	II.	[a]	A' history	V	

Suggested below is a reasoned chiasm of seven pairs of pericopes with an additional detailed microstructure in the center. Hopefully this organization does justice to the sophistication, beauty, and depth of the book. The commentary uses this outline and provides some argument for the units.

A Generations of Elimelech   (1:1–5)

    B Naomi Is Bereft of Sons, So Each Widow Must *Return* Home   (1:6–14)

       C Ruth's Declaration of Intent/Naomi's Silence   (1:15–19a)

          D Is This Naomi?   (1:19b–22)

             E Ruth Collects Barley in Boaz's Field   (2:1–7)

                F Boaz's and Ruth's First Meeting   (2:8–13)

                   G Boaz Provides with Secret Command   (2:14–17)

                             } 40 verses

            H Ruth Reports Good News to Naomi   (2:18–23)

              1 Ruth brings gleanings home, gives to Naomi

               2 Naomi questions Ruth, blesses benefactor

                3 Ruth reports to Naomi the name of Boaz

                 4 Naomi blesses him through Yahweh

                 4 Naomi recognizes Yahweh's redeemer

                3 Ruth further reports Boaz's offer

               2 Naomi pronounces the situation "good"

              1 Ruth continues to glean, lives with Naomi

                   G' Naomi's Provision with a Secret Command   (3:1–7)

                F' Boaz's and Ruth's Second Meeting   (3:8–13)

             E' Boaz Collects Barley into Ruth's Apron   (3:14–18)

          D' Is This the Redeemer?   (4:1–8)

       C' Boaz's Declaration of Intent/Witnesses' Blessing   (4:9–12)

    B' A Son Is Born to Naomi and Is To Be a *Restorer*   (4:13–17)

A' Generations of Perez   (4:18–22)

                             } 40 verses

Text and Exposition

A: GENERATIONS OF ELIMELECH (1:1–5)

OVERVIEW

The first five verses chronicle the diminution of Elimelech's line, terminating with a one-woman remnant. This information provides the background to the book of Ruth that makes understandable Naomi's move from Moab to Judea. Her "arising" in 1:6 marks the beginning of a new section.

The narrator makes no moral judgments concerning Elimelech's decision to flee the Promised Land. However, sometimes the storyteller's point of view is expressed in how events unfold. In the case of Elimelech, and with the benefit of hindsight (afforded to the reader), his was a bad decision — "This whole migration was riddled with something evil" (Kanyoro, 371). The book leaves the reader to speculate why the choice was poor.

¹In the days when the judges ruled, there was a famine in the land, and a man from Bethlehem in Judah, together with his wife and two sons, went to live for a while in the country of Moab. ²The man's name was Elimelech, his wife's name Naomi, and the names of his two sons were Mahlon and Kilion. They were Ephrathites from Bethlehem, Judah. And they went to Moab and lived there.
³Now Elimelech, Naomi's husband, died, and she was left with her two sons. ⁴They married Moabite women, one named Orpah and the other Ruth. After they had lived there about ten years, ⁵both Mahlon and Kilion also died, and Naomi was left without her two sons and her husband.

COMMENTARY

1 The book of Ruth is set in the era of the judges. The expected order of the world is overturned, and Bethlehem (which means "House of Bread") suffers a famine, while the "fields of Moab" are productive. This situation is temporary and anomalous, but it does last at least a decade. Wright, 60, reads Ruth as a folktale with a mythological past and sees in Moab a figure of the netherworld — a lifeless place across the Salt Sea. Elimelech fled there to sustain life, but death is what he suffered. In the following verses the results of this disastrous decision are specified. Moab, the land of the detestable god Chemosh (1Ki 11:7), brought barrenness, widowhood, more famine, and death. The only thing positive to come from their sojourn was Ruth herself.

2 "Elimelech" means "My God is king," which dovetails with the book of Judges' final verse, "there was no king in Israel." "Naomi," the feminine form of "Naaman," means "sweet" or "pleasant" (Wright, 60). "Mahlon" sounds like "sickness" and "Kilion" means "destruction" (from *kālâ*, "make an end"). "The two names in this sequence mean, therefore, 'sickness and death,' a reference to the all-but-total annihilation of the family who had deserted their native land for greener pastures on Moab" (Gordis, 298). Although the names in Ruth are attested in Ugaritic texts (George S. Glanzman, "The Origin and Date of the Book of Ruth," *CBQ* 21 [1959]: 206), the sons' names might serve a symbolic purpose—to reinforce the true movement of the story, which is not merely geographical. Their names are treated as Naomi treats her own (1:20).

3 With her two sons she "was left"—a term often used in various forms to denote a faithful remnant of Israel (Isa 11:11). Hamlin, 12, sees in Naomi a remnant like Israel who will return to the land.

4 Naomi's sons married Moabite girls. Solomon's wives turned his heart from Yahweh to other gods, including Chemosh (1Ki 11:4–7). Deuteronomy 23:3–4 forbids any children of Moabites from participation in the religious life of Israel because they did not help Israel with food and water in their hour of need. Sasson, 20, posits an etymology of "Orpah" from the Arabic *ġurfa*, "handful of water," and compares this suggested derivation with "Ruth," from the Hebrew *rāwâ*, "saturate, drench." ("Ruth" has become an English word meaning sympathy or pity, usually expressed in the negative with the antonym "ruthless.") Including the toponyms, there are ten names listed in this unit, thus balancing the tenfold genealogy of 4:18–22. Ten years go by without Ruth's or Orpah's bearing children; barrenness has become the new "famine" for this family.

5 Now the remnant of Israel in "exile" has dwindled to a lone woman. Her identity from here on cannot be found in relation to a living man. Naomi must choose for herself the path to take for survival. With the loss of her husband, she is bereft of livelihood (Joyce Hollyday, "'You Shall Not Afflict': A Biblical Perspective on Women and Poverty," *Sojourners* 15/3 [1986]: 26–29, 28). Where can she turn now?

NOTES

1 וַיְהִי (*wayehî*, "And it came about …") also begins such historical books as Joshua, Judges, and 1 Samuel and seems to be an identifier of genre; "we must presume that the author of Ruth did regard the events that are to unfold as belonging to his past" (Sasson, 14, contra Wright, 59). The verb שָׁפַט (*šāpaṭ*) is repeated, once as an infinitive and again as a participle, "in the days of the judging judges."

2 The two boys are referred to here as "his [i.e., Elimelech's] sons"—their identity derived from their father. After his death, in the next verses they are referred to as "her sons" (Trible, 167).

4 There may be a progression implied in the transition from "dwelling as a foreigner" in 1:1 (from גּוּר, *gûr*) to "entering" (from בֹּא, *bōʾ*) the fields of Moab in 1:2, and finally "dwelling" (from יָשַׁב, *yāšab*; GK 3782) there in 1:4. The final status of simply "dwelling" rather than "sojourning" might subtly indicate their spiritual transition from being Israelites to becoming Moabites. The Israelite father died; the sons were losing their identity. Note that the two sons "took" for themselves wives—the women are passive; all the action is done by men.

5 The NIV reads "her two sons," but the Hebrew is יְלָדֶיהָ (*yᵉlādeyhā*), "her lads." It is unusual to employ this term to refer to fully grown and marriageable men. Campbell, 16, considers this word as beginning an inclusio encompassing the material from here through 4:16, where the word occurs again, thus leaving the genealogy as an appendix. If Campbell is correct, might the first four or five verses be considered a prologue?

B: NAOMI IS BEREFT OF SONS, SO EACH WIDOW MUST RETURN HOME (1:6–14)

OVERVIEW

"The males die, they are non-persons; their presence in the story ceases (though their absence continues)" (Trible, 168). The story now treats an autonomous Naomi, her choices, and the choices of her daughters-in-law. Naomi "arose" (from *qôm*) to return, for she heard that Yahweh had visited his people by giving them food. This giving of food is the first of two actions the omniscient narrator ascribes to God. The second and last action is found in 4:13, where Yahweh gives conception to Ruth (Carlos Bovell, "Symmetry, Ruth and Canon," *JSOT* 28 [2003]: 180). These gifts are parallel: God blesses the seed implanted in the fertile land and in fertile Ruth.

Clearly the prominent feature of this pericope is Naomi's lament, especially the refrain, "Return ... return!" "Return" (*šûb*; GK 8740) occurs here in almost every verse, as highlighted with italics in the NIV text below. At issue is the women's decision to return, Naomi to Israel, and Orpah to her own people. Ruth's choice is specified in the next pericope but anticipated in the final three words here: She clung to Naomi.

At issue also is the matter of sons (1:11–12). Naomi has no more sons for them to marry; she is too old to have any more sons; even if by some miracle she were to conceive, the sons would belong to another generation. The matter of Naomi and her hypothetical offspring is not resumed until 4:12–17.

The LXX adds a phrase in 1:14 that indicates a movement of time and breaks the text between 1:14 and 1:15, as shown below in italics.

Hebrew Text (KJV)	Greek Text
And they lifted up their voice,	And they lifted up their voice,
and wept again:	and wept again;
and Orpah kissed her mother-in-law;	and Orpah kissed her mother-in-law
but Ruth clave unto her.	*and returned to her people;*
	but Ruth followed her.

The Greek version clarifies the action by noting that Orpah returned home and Ruth "followed" Naomi; thus, by the end of the pericope only two women are left to the next movement in the story.

> ⁶When she heard in Moab that the LORD had come to the aid of his people by providing food for them, Naomi and her daughters-in-law prepared to *return* home from there. ⁷With her two daughters-in-law she left the place where she had been living and set out on the road that would *take them back* to the land of Judah.
>
> ⁸Then Naomi said to her two daughters-in-law, "*Go back*, each of you, to your mother's home. May the LORD show kindness to you, as you have shown to your dead and to me. ⁹May the LORD grant that each of you will find rest in the home of another husband."
>
> Then she kissed them and they wept aloud ¹⁰and said to her, "We will *go back* with you to your people."
>
> ¹¹But Naomi said, "*Return* home, my daughters. Why would you come with me? Am I going to have any more sons, who could become your husbands? ¹²*Return* home, my daughters; I am too old to have another husband. Even if I thought there was still hope for me — even if I had a husband tonight and then gave birth to sons — ¹³would you wait until they grew up? Would you remain unmarried for them? No, my daughters. It is more bitter for me than for you, because the LORD's hand has gone out against me!"
>
> ¹⁴At this they wept again. Then Orpah kissed her mother-in-law good-by, but Ruth clung to her.

COMMENTARY

6 The first word in this pericope is translated "And-she-arose" (*wattāqām*), highlighting the shift of action from males to females. In the country of Moab Naomi heard that Yahweh had "visited" (*pāqad*) his people by giving them food. Hubbard, 100, sees in this act "the special covenant relationship which bound Yahweh the sovereign to his vassal Israel." (As noted above, this *giving* of food is the first of two direct actions ascribed to Yahweh, the second being noted in 4:13, which uses the same verb: Yahweh *gave* conception to Ruth.) At this point in the story, Moab is revealed as having no advantage over the Promised Land at all.

Naomi arose, resolved to return to the land blessed by Yahweh. Thus Yahweh's action has precipitated the movement of events, has set in motion actions and choices by ordinary women, which ultimately result in the redemption of Israel (Lk 1:68–69).

7 The three women start out together to return to the land of Judah. Both Orpah and Ruth are initially willing to leave Moab. What breaks up the family next is precipitated by Naomi.

8 Naomi urges her daughters-in-law to leave and go home, just as Naomi herself is doing. Her hope is that Yahweh will prove faithful and merciful toward them by doing *ḥesed* (GK 2876) — loyalty and kindness—as the women have done for Naomi and her dead sons. In other words, she blesses them by invoking the name of Yahweh, whom she expects to reward them according to their deeds.

9 The blessing continues: Naomi's wish is that they might find the gift of rest in homes and with husbands Yahweh will provide. It is notable that any blessing, any gift from heaven, any good thing is ascribed to Yahweh and not to any Moabite god such as Chemosh. This scene is an emotional one; it is with much crying, many tears, and kisses that they face the future. Highlighted here is the love and grief of the little sorority. Their lives have been tragic; they do not wish to part, and they mourn the baleful turn of events that have led up to this moment.

10 The Moabite women express their desire to stay with Naomi and to return with her to her people. They are both willing to leave Moab and journey with her into a foreign land. This willingness is the measure of their *ḥesed*, their fidelity.

11–13 But Naomi considers their loyalty to be irrational and ill-conceived. She has become an empty woman. She has no more to offer them; no more sons will be hers. Even if by some miracle she does find a husband and conceives, they will be sons for another generation, not for these women. Naomi's analysis of the situation is analogous to the pseudo-levirate marriage proposed later in the book. (Here Naomi hypothetically considers raising up new sons for the daughters-in-law to marry, thus providing for them. In 4:13–14 Elimelech's family provides for Naomi through a substitute husband for Ruth, who produces a son to take Elimelech's place.)

This long, three-verse monologue is the heart of this pericope underscoring Naomi's lack of sons. It is here that for the first time she names herself "bitter" (*mar*), and she blames her bitterness squarely on the sovereign will of God: "The hand of Yahweh went out against me." She has become a female Job, acutely feeling the enmity of the very LORD she invokes when blessing her daughters. It is Yahweh who blesses women with homes and husbands and sons; it is Yahweh whose hand has been against those whose husband and sons die. This is so, even in a foreign land. Ruth treats the subject of suffering, and as with Job, the ultimate answer to suffering is restoration. Marjo Korpel (*The Structure of the Book of Ruth* [Assen, Netherlands: Koninklijke van Gorcum, 2001], 228) considers the "theodicy problem" to be the central theme of Ruth "only superficially veiled."

14 Orpah heeds Naomi's words and leaves to return to her own people. This is a perfectly fitting and noble action. Her legal connection with Naomi is dissolved; she has no further obligations once Naomi has set her free. Bonnie Miller-McLemore ("Returning to the 'Mother's House': A Feminist Look at Orpah," *ChrCent* 108 [1991]: 428) holds Orpah as an example to follow (as Naomi also does in the next pericope), since she has chosen "not to renounce the 'mother's house.'" In fact, Donaldson, 143, a Cherokee, celebrates Orpah as a heroine who did not "reject her traditions or her sacred ancestors." Orpah's action is what makes Ruth's clinging to Naomi so extraordinary. Ruth's loyalty goes above and beyond societal expectations. She proves herself, both here and throughout the story, to be "better than seven sons" (4:15). Ruth forsakes all, save Naomi.

NOTES

7 "She went out from the place where she was there." This language is vague and general; it is impossible to identify in what actual locale Naomi lived.

8 The *Kethiv* is incompletely vocalized, and of course so also is the *Qere*; both can be read either as a jussive ("May Yahweh do faithfully with you") or a straightforward indicative ("Yahweh will do faithfully with you"). In 1:9, the first verb is followed by an imperative, suggesting Naomi is expressing something stronger than a mere hope: "Yahweh *will give* to you, and you *shall find*...." So here the text also may be read, "Yahweh *will do* faithfully with you"—an unmitigated benediction.

9 Naomi urges them to find מְנוּחָה (*mᵉnûḥâ*, "rest"; GK 4957) with a husband as Yahweh's gift. In 3:1 Naomi assumes the task of securing this מָנוֹחַ (*mānôaḥ*, "rest") for Ruth.

11 The question "Why would you come with me?" is meant in the sense, "You are wrong to go with me; you should not go, there is no point to it" (Ronald Hyman, "Questions and the Book of Ruth," *HS* 24 [1983]: 19).

13 הֲלָהֵן (*hᵃlāhēn*) is a form unique to Ruth 1:13 (where it occurs twice). It is comprised of the interrogative plus "for them," meaning either "would therefore?" or referring to the hypothetical sons (Hubbard, 111). Another unique word here is תֵּעָגֵנָה (*tēʿānēgâ*) from עָגַן (*āgan*; GK 6328), which in the immediate context must signify "wait" or "keep from marriage"; the LXX reads "restrain." מַר (*mar*) is the Qal perfect of מָרַר (*mārar*).

14 The expression Ruth "clung" (from דָּבַק, *dābaq*; GK 1815) to Naomi uses the same verb as that in Genesis 2:24, "a man will leave his father and mother and *be united* to his wife."

C: RUTH'S DECLARATION OF INTENT/NAOMI'S SILENCE (1:15–19A)

OVERVIEW

Sasson, 28, labels this unit "The Pledge." Here the story turns a corner as Naomi compares Ruth to Orpah and Ruth makes her famous oath of loyalty. The obvious main point is Ruth's vow. She will cling to Naomi, and the family will disintegrate no further. This unit is the last part of the text relating action still in Moab; 1:19 repeats the phrase, "they came to Bethlehem," thus forming a seam in the text. (The Greek translator failed to note the seam and edited out the redundancy.) That second "came to Bethlehem" begins with "And it came to pass ...," which marks a new movement in the story. Beginning with 1:19b, the setting has moved permanently to Bethlehem.

Although Ruth's oath carries the pericope, Naomi's response of stony silence has attracted some scholarly attention. Ruth puts into words such feeling of sorority, of loyalty, of love, that she has captured the hearts of the faithful. At times her words are repeated at weddings. But what is Naomi's response? Does Ruth elicit tears from her? Does she spontaneously break down and exclaim what a wonderful daughter-in-law she had? Does Ruth even get a hug? Not according to the text, which tells us only that Naomi stops urging her to go.

Fewell and Gunn, 100, use this silence to speculate Naomi's motivation; they suggest that Naomi is a bigot attempting to rid herself of embarrassing

Moabite family before returning home. Peter Coxon ("Was Naomi a Scold?" *JSOT* 45 [1989]: 27), noting the many tears and heartfelt goodbyes of the women, counterargues that the text highlights a depth of feeling shared among them. After Ruth's declaration of intent, the text does not record any response by Naomi since any words following Ruth's would have been anticlimactic. "It is not the silence of stony resistance but the silence of consent."

It is always precarious to argue from silence, and one must read on to discover what motivated

Naomi. At her core is deep resentment against God for her suffering; perhaps she is indeed ashamed of the Moabitess (Dana Fewell and David Gunn, "Is Coxon a Scold? On Responding to the Book of Ruth," *JSOT* 45 [1989]: 40). By comparison, the witnesses' joyous response to Boaz (4:11) makes Naomi's silent response to Ruth here seem heartless and cold. But once back in Bethlehem Naomi begins to perceive Yahweh's plans to redeem what was lost, and her attitude starts to change.

---

¹⁵"Look," said Naomi, "your sister-in-law is going back to her people and her gods. Go back with her."

¹⁶But Ruth replied, "Don't urge me to leave you or to turn back from you. Where you go I will go, and where you stay I will stay. Your people will be my people and your God my God. ¹⁷Where you die I will die, and there I will be buried. May the LORD deal with me, be it ever so severely, if anything but death separates you and me." ¹⁸When Naomi realized that Ruth was determined to go with her, she stopped urging her.

¹⁹ᵃSo the two women went on until they came to Bethlehem.

COMMENTARY

15 Naomi urges Ruth to follow Orpah's example and reintegrate with Moabite society. It is not only to her mother's house that Orpah has returned—she has also returned to her people and her "gods" (*ʾelōhîm*). To return to the land is to return to that land's gods. On a profound level, for Naomi to return to the land of Israel is to return to Yahweh. In fact, the verb "return" (*šûb*; GK 8740) can be translated "repent" (see Ps 19:7, "The law of the LORD is perfect, *converting* the soul" [KJV]; and Ps 51:13, "I will teach transgressors your ways, and sinners will *turn back* to you" [NIV]). Charles P. Baylis ("Naomi in the Book of Ruth in Light of the Mosaic Covenant," *BSac* 161 [2004]: 427) reads Ruth in the

light of Deuteronomy 30:1–3 and concludes that their "returning" is not merely geographical.

> When all these blessings and curses I have set before you come upon you and you *take them* to heart wherever the LORD your God disperses you among the nations, and when you and your children *return* to the LORD your God and obey him with all your heart and with all your soul according to everything I command you today, then the LORD your God will *restore* your fortunes and have compassion on you and gather you *again* from all the nations where he scattered you. (Dt 30:1–3; where italicized the Heb. verb is *šûb*, "return"; note its fourfold use.)

16 The same designation for Orpah's "gods" is used again in 1:16, where Ruth argues in effect, "your *ʾelōhîm* will be my *ʾelōhîm*." Alastair Hunter ("How Many Gods Had Ruth?" *SJT* 34 [1981]: 428) notes that Naomi desired Ruth to follow Orpah in serving Moabite gods, and therein he sees an implication that Naomi believed the Moabite gods to be just as real as Yahweh, the Israelite God. "Chemosh and Yahweh were hardly to be distinguished; such difference as there was consisting largely in the social and cultural milieu. It is hardly necessary now to labour the point that the god(s) of Moab are as real as the god of Yahweh.... How many gods had Ruth? Surely one only, under whatever name" (435–36)—i.e., where the name of Yahweh is invoked, Chemosh is tacitly so, too. Hunter argues that in this respect the book of Ruth is a counterweight to the strident anti-idolatry polemic found in much of the remainder of Scripture.

This argument, too, is from silence, since throughout the book of Ruth all divine action is Yahweh's. Yahweh blesses Moabite women with home and child (1:8–9); it is he who has made Naomi's life bitter in Moab (1:13, 22). No action at all is ascribed to foreign gods—and it is in Naomi's bitterness of heart that she urges her daughters to return to those gods. How does the book of Ruth agree with the Bible's polemic against the gods of the nations? An embittered lady sends Orpah to her gods. "Go back," she urges in effect. "Go back to your gods." Go back to your famine. Go back to your widowhood. Go back to your barrenness. The gods of Moab are part of this death-complex. When the two sisters-in-law part, one goes to where death prevails, the other to life and Yahweh. Thus the book of Ruth does not "multiculturally" level the divine playing field by considering equal the gods of the nations and the one, true God. It does, in fact, sharply distinguish between them.

17 Ruth understands that her life is in the hands of Yahweh. Her commitment to Naomi is lifelong—until death parts them. Athalya Brenner ("Ruth as a Foreign Worker and the Politics of Exogamy," in *The Feminist Companion to the Bible (Second Series)* [ed. A. Brenner; Sheffield: Sheffield Academic, 1999], 3:160) suggests that this uncompromising and unequivocal oath amounts to a legal contract whereby Ruth willingly becomes Naomi's servant for life. Thus she is a mere sidekick when they return to Bethlehem: "The only one to notice Ruth at the end of ch. 1, the homecoming scene, is the narrator" because "foreign workers are invisible to the dominant culture." Richards, 16, equates Ruth's oath with that of a slave desiring to remain with a master.

18 Naomi stops speaking with Ruth in the sense that she gives up the argument.

19a This half-verse completes the pericope with the arrival of the pair at Bethlehem, the setting of the events in the rest of the story.

NOTES

15 "Sister-in-law" occurs in Ruth only here (twice). Elsewhere, see Deuteronomy 25:7–9 for discussion of the levirate.

16 "Do not urge me" is a gloss of אַל־תִּפְגְּעִי־בִי (*ʾal-tipgeʿî-bî*), the verb being פָּגַע (*pāga*; GK 7003), which elsewhere means "fall upon" or "violently meet" (see 2:22; Ex 5:3, "Lest he *fall upon* us with pestilence or with the sword"). Ruth is saying, "Do not *rage* against me." Naomi's goadings felt like violence.

17 "May Yahweh do to me and more also" is a common oath formula in the early monarchic period (see also 1Sa 3:17; 14:44; 25:22; 2Sa 3:9; 3:25; 1Ki 2:23).

19 This verse can be divided in two. The first part (v.19a) has five words, and the second (v.19b) has ten. The second half begins the next pericope.

D: IS THIS NAOMI? (1:19B–22)

OVERVIEW

This pericope can be organized in a chiastic structure as follows, using a modified NIV translation.

A And it came to pass that they arrived in
   Bethlehem, (1:19bα)

   B And the whole town was stirred because
      of them, and the women exclaimed, "Can
      this be Naomi?" (1:19bβ)

      C "Don't call me Naomi," she told them.
         "Call me Mara, because Shaddai has
         made my life very bitter. (1:20)

         D I went away full, but Yahweh has
            brought me back empty. (1:21a)

      C' Why call me Naomi? Yahweh has wit-
         nessed against me; Shaddai has brought
         misfortune upon me." (1:21b)

   B' So Naomi returned with Ruth the
      Moabitess her daughter-in-law, who
         returned from the fields of Moab, (1:22a)

A' And they arrived in Bethlehem as the barley
   harvest was beginning. (1:22b)

The overriding issue concerns a name: "Is this Naomi?" The answer is an emphatic, "No!" Naomi renames herself "Mara." Naomi declares in effect, "I am not really Naomi, the name does not suit me." Naomi "went out full [*melēʾâ*]" but has been "brought back empty [*rêqām*]" (1:21). "Naomi" belongs with fullness, "Mara" with emptiness. God has, she says, changed her status and thus her name.

> **1:19b**When they arrived in Bethlehem, the whole town was stirred because of them, and the women exclaimed, "Can this be Naomi?"
> **20**"Don't call me Naomi," she told them. "Call me Mara, because the Almighty has made my life very bitter. **21** I went away full, but the LORD has brought me back empty. Why call me Naomi? The LORD has afflicted me; the Almighty has brought misfortune upon me."
> **22**So Naomi returned from Moab accompanied by Ruth the Moabitess, her daughter-in-law, arriving in Bethlehem as the barley harvest was beginning.

COMMENTARY

19b Note that the story gives voice entirely to women. The question concerns Naomi's identity — to which she brings clarity in the next verse.

20 Naomi's name ("sweetness") has been lost. It is not fitting, she says, to call her "Pleasant." Instead, she substitutes "Mara," or "Bitterness" (see 1:13), now her mantra. The "name" is one of the many things in the book of Ruth that needs to be redeemed. Naomi uses two names for God: "Yahweh" and "Shaddai" ("the LORD" and "the Almighty"). Shaddai "has caused bitterness." The outward sign of her change of status is the new name, *mārāʾ*.

21 The NIV reads, "The LORD has afflicted me," following the LXX in reading *ʿanâ* ("answer") as a Piel *ʿinnā* ("afflict"). However, *bî* ("against me") never follows the Piel of *ʿanâ*; thus "the LORD has witnessed against me" (NASB), "the LORD hath testified against me" (KJV). Hubbard, 126, lists no fewer than fifteen texts to show that the grammar is juristic. Naomi does not understand why Yahweh has purposed to harm her (1:13); "she is interpreting her hard circumstances as God's testimony against her sins" (Collins, 99), saying in effect, "This bitterness is the only reality I know or that can be known. This is 'truth,' and by it I will redefine my concept of God" (Reg Grant, "Literary Structure in the Book of Ruth," *BSac* 148 [1991]: 432).

22 The last verse of the pericope anticipates the next movement of the story — the barley harvest. The name "Ruth" is found twelve times in the book and here for the first time Ruth, being a foreigner in Israel, bears the epithet, "Ruth *the Moabitess*." This designation is found five times in Ruth as though to bring it clearly and loudly to the reader's attention. It is her name — but does it suit her?

NOTES

19b The first word of 1:19b is וַיְהִי (*wayehî*) — exactly the same term that begins the book — "And it came to pass that ...," demarking the start of a new pericope. "The town was *stirred*," from הוּם (*hûm*), a rare word denoting loud sound, such as ringing (1Sa 4:5; 1Ki 1:45). B. Jongeling ("HZ'T N'MY (Ruth 1:19)," *VT* 28 [1978]: 476) compares the last two words, הֲזֹאת נָעֳמִי (*hᵃzōʾt nāʿᵒmî*, "Is this Naomi?"), to similar constructions in 1 Kings 18:7, 17, where Obadiah exclaims, "Is it you, Elijah?" and Ahab asks, "Is it you, Israel's troublemaker?" Jongeling concludes that the women of Bethlehem were astonished, quickly passing the word from mouth to mouth.

20 Naomi's word "bitterness" is found (in two forms) three times in Ruth, always as a self-description by Naomi. She uses the verb מָרַר (*mārar*) in 1:13 and 1:20 with the superlative adverb "very"; the employment of the Hiphil stem in 1:20 signifies causality: "Shaddai *has caused* me great bitterness." Also in 1:20, Naomi names herself מָרָא (*mārāʾ*).

21 Moore, 238, suggests that the phrase וַיהוָה עָנָה בִי (*wayhwâ ʿanâ bî*) is deliberately multivalent, denoting emotional pain as well as legal powerlessness. רֵיקָם (*rêqām*, "empty") is seen again in 3:17; Yahweh has rendered Naomi empty, but Boaz will not return Ruth empty. Boaz and Yahweh are juxtaposed in the book, Boaz being God's agent to redeem what is lost and to fill what is lacking.

E: RUTH COLLECTS BARLEY IN BOAZ'S FIELD (2:1–7)

OVERVIEW

Sasson, 38, labels this pericope "A Plan." The story now opens up, and Boaz is introduced. Twice he is identified as being of the clan of Elimelech, and twice Ruth is called a Moabitess. A single verse treats Naomi's and Ruth's conversation about working with grain; four verses record a conversation about Ruth between Boaz and the young man in charge of the gleaners. Once Boaz is informed, he engages her in the first of two conversations.

[1]Now Naomi had a relative on her husband's side, from the clan of Elimelech, a man of standing, whose name was Boaz.

[2]And Ruth the Moabitess said to Naomi, "Let me go to the fields and pick up the leftover grain behind anyone in whose eyes I find favor."

Naomi said to her, "Go ahead, my daughter." [3]So she went out and began to glean in the fields behind the harvesters. As it turned out, she found herself working in a field belonging to Boaz, who was from the clan of Elimelech.

[4]Just then Boaz arrived from Bethlehem and greeted the harvesters, "The LORD be with you!"

"The LORD bless you!" they called back.

[5]Boaz asked the foreman of his harvesters, "Whose young woman is that?"

[6]The foreman replied, "She is the Moabitess who came back from Moab with Naomi. [7]She said, 'Please let me glean and gather among the sheaves behind the harvesters.' She went into the field and has worked steadily from morning till now, except for a short rest in the shelter."

COMMENTARY

1 This verse has four components and is structured as follows:

Now-to-Naomi	is-a–relative	to-her-husband
a-man	(who is) mighty	(and of) standing
from-the-family	of-Elimelech	
and-his-name	is-Boaz	

Boaz, Elimelech's acquaintance and relative, possesses everything that Naomi and Ruth lack.

Naomi has returned empty, but Boaz is abundantly full. The NIV's "standing" is a gloss of *gibbôr ḥayil* (often meaning "strong warrior"); Sasson, 38, glosses "property holder." *Ḥayil* (GK 2657) occurs twice more in Ruth. Boaz calls Ruth a "woman of *ḥayil*," in that context denoting moral and ethical excellence, evidenced by Ruth's having devoted herself to Naomi (3:11). The "woman of *ḥayil*" is described in Proverbs 31:10–31, which in the present Hebrew Bible immediately precedes the book of Ruth, as though Ruth herself is placed as an example of the virtuous woman described in Proverbs.

In 4:11 Yahweh is petitioned to bless Ruth and Boaz for the building up of Israel, which will enhance Boaz's fame (*ḥayil*) in Bethlehem. Thus both Boaz and Ruth embody *ḥayil*. The verse might be arranged in this way:

Now-to-Naomi
    is-a-relative to-her-husband
        a-man (who is) mighty (and of) *ḥayil*
    from-the-family of-Elimelech
and-his-name is-Boaz.

This arrangement highlights the central characteristic of Boaz—his *ḥayil*—and also places Boaz and Naomi parallel to each other. The two seniors represent opposite poles in the book of Ruth: Naomi is the paradigmatic empty one who needs to be filled, and Boaz is the man of potency who is willing and able to redeem. The two never meet; they have intercourse only through Naomi's surrogate, Ruth.

2 After having introduced Boaz, the pericope quickly sets up the circumstances whereby Boaz and Ruth meet. Ruth implores Naomi for permission to glean in the fields, gleaning being an ancient Israelite means of ensuring provision for the poor. For Ruth and Naomi, time is short, since the harvest has already begun. Once the reapers had gleaned the readily available stalks, the leftovers were publicly accessible. Hebrew law legislated that the poor

could gather these leftovers from the harvested fields and keep their gleanings without owing even a percentage of them to the landowner. "Sheaf" (plural "sheaves" in 2:7) is found seven times in the OT, notably in Deuteronomy 24:19, thus forging a verbal connection between Ruth and this law code.

> When you are harvesting in your field and you overlook a sheaf, do not go back to get it. Leave it for the alien, the fatherless and the widow, so that the LORD your God may bless you in all the work of your hands. When you beat the olives from your trees, do not go over the branches a second time. Leave what remains for the alien, the fatherless and the widow. (Dt 24:19–20)
> When you reap the harvest of your land, do not reap to the very edges of your field or gather the gleanings of your harvest. Do not go over your vineyard a second time or pick up the grapes that have fallen. Leave them for the poor and the alien. I am the LORD your God. (Lev 19:9–10)

The first significant impression of Bethlehem society given by the story is that they are a law-abiding, covenant-keeping, hospitable, generous, compassionate people. In the verses to follow, they are also revealed as worshipers of Yahweh, peaceable, and prosperous. This picture accords with the positive presentation of Bethlehem and Judah found in the other two episodes of the Bethlehem trilogy (Jdg 17–18; 19) and stands in antithesis to the northern tribes' (especially Benjamin's) characteristic apostasy and violence in the days of the judges. This distinction likely served to demonstrate the worthiness of kings from Judah over against northern, and especially Benjamite, kings (i.e., Saul's dynasty). In Bethlehem, citizens were happy and safe.

3 Ruth (literally) "chanced her chance to come upon" (from the verb *qārâ* [GK 7936] and its cognate *miqreh* [GK 5247]) Boaz's portion of land. The verb is used in Ecclesiastes 9:11: "time and chance happen [*qrh*] to them all." Although the concept of chance raises theological issues, here it is a literary device (e.g., irony). Imagine Ruth gleaning through random fields, not targeting a particular lot, and finding herself at last grasping the stalks of Boaz. Is Yahweh behind this movement? Keep reading!

4 Both Boaz and Ruth converge at the same place and time in the story. Boaz is trumpeted by the narrator (lit.): "And behold! Boaz came in from Bethlehem!" Boaz greets his employees by Yahweh, and they return with a benediction for Boaz. The text casts the character of Boaz positively — with his first words Boaz is already affiliated with Yahweh. This connection continues throughout as Ruth and Naomi's redemption draws near.

5 The narration immediately leaps to Boaz's query about Ruth, thus giving the impression that Boaz's gaze zeroes in on Ruth; she is instantly recognized as a newcomer. He asks, "To whom is this young woman?" His query concerns her identity — she must belong to someone. What was she doing? Hubbard, 147, suggests that already the story implies Boaz's possible interest in Ruth's marriageability!

6 Her identity is explained: she is a Moabitess who belongs with Naomi. Note that Boaz's knowledge of Ruth is mediated by the young foreman. This is the only place in the narrative where this person is explicitly encountered, but he may be indirectly mentioned again in 3:14b (see comments).

7 Ruth and Boaz have not yet met; she had requested permission from the overseer, who now relates her request to Boaz. This foreman is in the know; Boaz depends on him in the matter concerning Ruth. The pericope ends with a temporal reference ("from morning until now"; "until evening," LXX).

The verse's second half is literally, "and-she-entered and-she-stood from-then the-morning and-until-now this she-has-been-sitting in-the-house a-little." Moore, 239, suggests, "This [field] has been her dwelling. The house has meant little." He argues that Ruth does not begin to glean until after she meets with Boaz and gets permission; the overseer merely passes on the request. Thus she had been waiting (*ʿamad* usually meaning "to stand") for Boaz's response; "and she entered and *waited* from the morning until now; she's been sitting in the house a short time." In 3:18 the women likewise must wait: "Wait [lit., "sit"], my daughter, until you find out what happens." Thus here and in 3:18 Ruth appears to sit, waiting on Boaz.

NOTES

1 The verb *bōʾ* denotes "to go in" and *ʿaz* means "strength"; Gordis, 299, suggests "Boaz" indicates "strength is in him." "Rabbinic commentators ... identify Boaz [בֹּעַז] with Ibzan [אִבְצָן] of Bethlehem (Jdg. 12:8–10)" (Sasson, 15). The NIV glosses "relative," reading the *Qere* (מוֹדַע, *môdaʿ*); the *Kethiv* (מְיֻדָּע, *meyuddāʿ*) is a Pual participle meaning "one-being-known." The *Qere* occurs elsewhere only in Proverbs 7:4: "make Wisdom your מוֹדָע (*môdaʿ*)."

2 Ruth implores Naomi using cohortatives and an intensifying particle, אֵלְכָה־נָּא (*ʾēlkâ-nāʾ*), indicating the urgent need to start. Hubbard, 136, argues that she does not request permission but declares her intention. However, the phraseology parallels Ruth's request of the foreman in 2:7, "Please let me glean."

3 "Field" uses the same word as appears in 1:1 (the NIV glossing "*country* of Moab") and in 1:6, 22 (which the NIV ignores altogether). The "fields" of Moab and Judah seem to denote more than political boundaries; they engender a rural rather than an urban sensibility.

4 The verb "bless" (בָּרַךְ, *bārak*) occurs five times in the book. It is always Boaz (2:4, 19–20) or Ruth (3:10; 4:14), or Yahweh (4:14) who is blessed.

5 The foreman is called נַעַר (*naar*), the masculine form of the word used to refer to Ruth as "young woman." Perhaps this feature subtly highlights the generational affinity between the foreman and Ruth, thus instancing Boaz's remark to her, "You have not pursued the young men" (3:10).

6 Ruth is said to have returned with Naomi "from the field of Moab."

7 Here occurs the first of three embedded quotations. The narrator records the quoting of Ruth by Boaz's servant; the other two quotations appear in the center of the book (2:21) and in 3:17, where Boaz collects grain into Ruth's skirt and which also may contain a tacit reference to Boaz's servant. Some see in the confused Hebrew a chagrined overseer stumbling over words. Michael Carasik ("Ruth 2,7: Why the Overseer Was Embarrassed," *ZAW* 107 [1995]: 493–94) suggests this is so because Ruth had suffered some kind of sexual harassment near the house and was fleeing the property as Boaz entered. This situation would explain why Boaz instantly wondered about Ruth, add weight to the pericope that follows, and underscore Ruth's vulnerability as a foreigner (see also Derek Beattie ["A Midrashic Gloss in Ruth 2:7," *ZAW* 89 (1977): 122–24]).

F: BOAZ'S AND RUTH'S FIRST MEETING (2:8-13)

OVERVIEW

The storyline transitions from the overseer's disclosure to a colloquy between Boaz and Ruth the Moabitess. The new discourse begins (lit.), "Boaz said to Ruth, 'Have you not heard, my daughter?'" This intensity and focus is distinguished from the previous matter-of-fact discourse between employer and employee. The pericope may be diagrammed as follows.

Boaz's overture: Be satisfied here!

Ruth's response: Why do I, an undeserving foreigner, find favor in your eyes?

Boaz's rationale: Yahweh will reward your works; find shelter under his wings!

Ruth's thank you: May I, an undeserving foreigner, find favor in your eyes.

8So Boaz said to Ruth, "My daughter, listen to me. Don't go and glean in another field and don't go away from here. Stay here with my servant girls. **9**Watch the field where the men are harvesting, and follow along after the girls. I have told the men not to touch you. And whenever you are thirsty, go and get a drink from the water jars the men have filled."

¹⁰At this, she bowed down with her face to the ground. She exclaimed, "Why have I found such favor in your eyes that you notice me — a foreigner?"

¹¹Boaz replied, "I've been told all about what you have done for your mother-in-law since the death of your husband — how you left your father and mother and your homeland and came to live with a people you did not know before. ¹²May the LORD repay you for what you have done. May you be richly rewarded by the LORD, the God of Israel, under whose wings you have come to take refuge."

¹³"May I continue to find favor in your eyes, my lord," she said. "You have given me comfort and have spoken kindly to your servant — though I do not have the standing of one of your servant girls."

COMMENTARY

8–9 Boaz promises to Ruth that if she pursues his gleaning in his field alone, she will be satisfied and safe. He implores her to "cling" (*dābaq*) to his maids in language echoing the nuptial embrace of Genesis 2:24. He then says in effect, "Gaze on me and no other." (In Genesis 39:7, Potiphar's wife lustfully "cast her eyes" on Joseph.) Boaz then assures Ruth that the "young men" have been told not to "touch" her. "Touch" (*nāga*; GK 5595) also has sexual connotations; there is more than one way in which to touch a woman (Ge 20:6; Pr 6:29). Here "touch" no doubt includes the sense "molest."

Then Boaz tells Ruth that when she thirsts, she should drink only from his well. The motif of exclusively drinking from a particular well clearly carries a double entendre; compare, for example, Proverbs 5:15–19: "Drink water from your own cistern, flowing water from your own well ... rejoice in the wife of your youth ... be captivated [infatuated, from *rāwâ*] always with her love." Thus by association, in 2:8–9 four sexually suggestive overtones may be discerned. This observation becomes poignant when these two verses are considered alongside the second discourse between this man and

woman — where the erotic atmosphere is unmistakable, even scandalous (3:8–13).

10 Ruth for the first time (but not the last!) positions herself at Boaz's feet. She bows down to the ground and begs to know why a foreigner such as she would deserve such favorable treatment. Here there is a pun in Hebrew: "take notice" is from *nākar* (GK 5795), which shares the same triconsonantal root as *nokrî*, "foreigner." So again the text spotlights Ruth the alien and (through Boaz) reminds the reader of Ruth's extraordinary constancy and worth. Having considered Boaz's response (see next verse), only a heartless partisan would forbid to Ruth full participation in Israelite society. The wings of Yahweh, after all, are Ruth's sanctuary. David's ancestress is thus a positive addition to his résumé as king.

11–12 Boaz notes that Ruth has come to "a people that you did not know before," and he praised her labor on behalf of her mother-in-law. Note Ruth's identity: she is called daughter, wife, daughter-in-law, foreigner, and one belonging to her father and mother. Now she has found shelter "under the wings" of Yahweh. Ruth has been naturalized. Her identity is no longer Moabite, but

Israelite. Boaz foresees satisfying rewards to follow. Greg A. King ("Ruth 2:1–13," *Int* 52 [1998]: 182–83) quips, "There is a redeemer, as Boaz will be later designated, waiting in the wings." The day of Ruth's and Naomi's redemption will soon dawn.

13 The pericope concludes with Ruth's self-denunciation. She claims Boaz has "comforted" (from *nāḥam*; GK 5714) her; after Sarah's death Isaac was *comforted* by espousing Rebekah (Ge 24:67). Literally, Ruth says, "You have spoken to the heart of your maid." Shechem spoke in love to Dinah's heart (Ge 34:3), as the husband of the concubine did to her (Jdg 19:3); again our text hints at more to come. Ruth claims, "I do not have the standing of one of your servant girls." Will she ever become a full participant in the community? Will she judge herself a second-class citizen forever?

NOTES

8 Boaz and Naomi both call Ruth "my daughter," thus suggesting that Boaz and Naomi "were probably contemporaries and, by implication, that a disparity of age separated … [Boaz] from Ruth" (Hubbard, 154).

9 In the sentence, "I have told the men not to touch you," "men" is literally "youths." Apparently there were young, aggressive, ruttish males aplenty in the fields of Boaz. Shepherd, 460, reads נָגַע (*nāgaʿ*, "touch") in the light of 2:22 (פָּגַע, *pāgaʿ*, "harm") and so glosses "harass" or "assault."

10 The verb "bowed down" uses a verb "usually reserved for usage in connection with deities, prophets, kings, and other potentates"; here it seems "an exaggerated display of gratitude" (Sasson, 51). Ruth's bending her body parallels Boaz's contortion in 3:8 — one of the many analogues between their two meetings.

11 The last two words, תְּמוֹל שִׁלְשׁוֹם (*tᵉmôl šilšôm*), literally read "yesterday third" or "day before yesterday." Ruth was fresh to Israel's fields; it "was just like yesterday" when she was in her own land. This comment dovetails with the abrupt 2:2; they arrived just in time to glean, with no leisure first to settle.

12 "Reward" is from מַשְׂכֹּרֶת (*máśkōret*; GK 5382), a rare word found elsewhere only in Genesis 29:15; 31:7, 41 — the first specifically refer to the wages Jacob earned while working for his beloved Rachel. Boaz predicts that Ruth also will earn wages — from God — as payment for her acts of loyalty. Besides in the book of Ruth, finding "refuge" in Yahweh's "wings" occurs only in Psalms 36:8; 57:1–2; 61:4; 91:4 — mostly psalms of David, the second explicitly associated with Saul's persecutions. David and his Moabite precursor find sanctuary under God's pinions, while Saulides oppress God's elect.

G: BOAZ'S PROVISION WITH A SECRET COMMAND (2:14–17)

OVERVIEW

The setting advances to mealtime, and Ruth eats her fill. (This pericope is the first of two in which eating is prominent; the second is 3:1–7, in which Boaz has eaten and drunk and his heart is merry.)

Ruth rests in Boaz's good favor; he personally serves her until she is satisfied to overflowing. More of the same is what Naomi later intrigues to secure, namely, Boaz's conversion from a pseudo-husband to an actual one and Ruth's consummate satisfaction as wife.

Twice in Ruth the reader overhears a command being issued—here by Boaz and in 3:1–7 by Naomi. In both cases the secret instruction is for Ruth's profit (see also 2:9). Here Boaz audaciously orders his men to provide for Ruth; later Naomi audaciously compels her to seek a home with him. Plans are covertly enacted, resulting in Ruth's well-being, and these two scenes flank the central peri-cope, in which the book's chief motif is introduced: redemption.

Ronald Hals (*The Theology of the Book of Ruth* [Philadelphia: Fortress, 1969], 16) considered the book of Ruth to be "a story about the hidden God." God's secret provision is presented in several ways, such as Ruth's seeming to find Boaz's field by chance. Here and in 3:1–7 the invisible character of God's redemption can be discerned: his working and plans are as secret as Boaz's and Naomi's. But Yahweh's actions do not remain obscure forever—the Redeemer is revealed eventually, and this revelation comes to Naomi in the exact center of the book, the next pericope.

---

¹⁴At mealtime Boaz said to her, "Come over here. Have some bread and dip it in the wine vinegar."

When she sat down with the harvesters, he offered her some roasted grain. She ate all she wanted and had some left over. ¹⁵As she got up to glean, Boaz gave orders to his men, "Even if she gathers among the sheaves, don't embarrass her. ¹⁶Rather, pull out some stalks for her from the bundles and leave them for her to pick up, and don't rebuke her."

¹⁷So Ruth gleaned in the field until evening. Then she threshed the barley she had gathered, and it amounted to about an ephah.

COMMENTARY

14 Boaz is not an aloof overseer distantly ensuring through surrogates that Ruth is served. He takes a personal interest and withholds no good thing. This wealthy landowner is close, is concerned, and is present to avail. Her satisfaction "is a foreshadowing of the 'full reward' to come" (Rauber, 32).

15–16 But when the meal is over, behind the scenes and through agents Boaz manipulates events—by commanding the reapers to leave behind extravagantly more than the usual excess. And when she trespasses beyond socially acceptable limits, their new job is not to criticize but is to lighten her task. Boaz anticipates the reapers' offense at Ruth's untoward actions and emphasizes that she is special. Behavior that naturally would be kiboshed is here encouraged and enabled. His is not a simple concern for the poor but is extravagant, even scandalous. Boaz's hidden sovereignty abundantly sustains and secures Ruth and Naomi.

17 The pericope is bounded by two time references—mealtime and evening. Ruth "threshed" or "beat" (from *ḥābaṭ*, a rare word found four times elsewhere [see Jdg 6:11]) the grain. The eyebrow-raising lavishness of Boaz's liberality is not revealed until the last words of the pericope: Ruth was enabled to glean an ephah of grain. This amount borders on too much to carry; it is enough to sus-tain several persons for an extended period of time. Sinclair Ferguson (*Faithful God: An Exposition of the Book of Ruth* [Wales: Bryntirion, 2005], 62) suggests this may be the author's joke, a humorous sight to see the indigent Ruth staggering back to Naomi with so much grain that she can barely carry it.

NOTES

14 The KJV (and LXX) follows the MT's word order by placing "Boaz said" before the time reference. However, "the dramatic effect of Ruth's words ... would be utterly shattered if Boaz's immediate reply to her were [about] ... such mundane matters as eating"; in the end of the last pericope, "she literally leaves Boaz speechless" (Campbell, 102)—"a pregnant pause of unknown duration" between the two scenes (Hubbard, 172). "Food/eat" (root אכל, *ʾkl*) occurs here twice and twice again (3:1–7) to frame the central pericope with Boaz's and Ruth's eating their fill (in contrast with earlier famine motif). The NIV's "offered her" is a gloss of the obscure צָבַט (*ṣābaṭ*). Note the pun with צֶבֶת (*ṣebet*), "bundles of ears," of 2:16. Are these words cognates? Perhaps the reader is meant to equate Boaz's action for Ruth at mealtime with his later instructions to the reapers; they must do as he did.

15 The word translated "embarrass" (Hiphil of כָּלַם, *kālam*; GK 4007) also carries the more demeaning connotation of "humiliate, put to shame."

16 See note on 2:14 on the two hapaxes צָבַט (*ṣābaṭ*) and צֶבֶת (*ṣebet*). Both words denote working with grain; a Ugaritic cognate suggests the use of a tool.

17 A barley harvest occurs elsewhere in the OT only in 2 Samuel 21, which treats David's resolution of Saul's bloodguilt through his sons' hanging, thus lifting a famine—just as in Ruth three men die before Yahweh gives food to his people (see Brian Britt, "Death, Social Conflict, and the Barley Harvest in the Hebrew Bible," *Journal of Hebrew Scriptures* 5/14 [2004–2005]: 1–28). Might this consist in another literary connection between David's and the book of Ruth's repugning of Saulides?

H: RUTH REPORTS THE GOOD NEWS TO NAOMI (2:18–23)

OVERVIEW

If 1:19 is taken as two verses (see Note), then this pericope—the heart of the book—has precisely forty verses before and after it. Here Naomi first hears the "gospel," the good news that Ruth has found favor with Boaz. All along, Yahweh has been working behind the scenes for good! The pericope alternates between Ruth and Naomi and can be organized as shown:

v.1 Ruth brings gleanings home, gives them to Naomi (2:18)

   v.2 Naomi questions Ruth, blesses benefactor (2:19a)

      v.3 Ruth reports to Naomi the name of Boaz (2:19b)

         v.4 Naomi blesses him through Yahweh (2:20a)

         v.4 Naomi recognizes Yahweh's redeemer (2:20b)

      v.3 Ruth further reports Boaz's offer (2:21)

   v.2 Naomi pronounces the situation "good" (2:22)

v.1 Ruth continues to glean, lives with Naomi (2:23)

This microstructure brings the center of the book to a sharp point at 2:20, which contains its first mention of a "redeemer." Although the word "redeem" (from *gāʾal*, often the participle, *gōʾēl*; GK 1457) does not appear in Ruth before 2:20, the root is found twenty-one times in the second half — the main theme has finally and explicitly emerged. (The cognate *geʾullâ* occurs twice more.) The loss of seed, name, land, home, and life — so keenly felt earlier — is not God's last word to Naomi. His agent is revealed, and this knowledge changes her also into an agent of redemption, who in the next pericope offers proactive counsel as important in its own way as Boaz's provision.

[18]She carried it back to town, and her mother-in-law saw how much she had gathered. Ruth also brought out and gave her what she had left over after she had eaten enough.

[19]Her mother-in-law asked her, "Where did you glean today? Where did you work? Blessed be the man who took notice of you!"

Then Ruth told her mother-in-law about the one at whose place she had been working. "The name of the man I worked with today is Boaz," she said.

[20]"The LORD bless him!" Naomi said to her daughter-in-law. "He has not stopped showing his kindness to the living and the dead." She added, "That man is our close relative; he is one of our kinsman-redeemers."

[21]Then Ruth the Moabitess said, "He even said to me, 'Stay with my workers until they finish harvesting all my grain.'"

[22] Naomi said to Ruth her daughter-in-law, "It will be good for you, my daughter, to go with his girls, because in someone else's field you might be harmed."

[23]So Ruth stayed close to the servant girls of Boaz to glean until the barley and wheat harvests were finished. And she lived with her mother-in-law.

COMMENTARY

18–19 Ruth has found satisfaction with Boaz, and this bounty overflows to bless Naomi as well. Obviously, Ruth's success is unexpected. Naomi asks, Who is responsible for this? Ruth replies with the name of Boaz.

20 At Ruth's revelation, "Naomi, who was herself among the dead, now lives again" (Rauber, 33); "with a single stroke, the picture is entirely changed" (Loretz, 394). Naomi is awakening to her new situation—and it is sweet! Below is a translation of this verse.

> And Naomi said to her daughter-in-law,
> "May he be blessed by Yahweh,
> who has not forsaken his *ḥesed*
> to the living or to the dead."
> And Naomi said to her,
> "The man is near to us,
> He is one of our redeemers."

When Naomi says, "May [Boaz] be blessed by Yahweh, who has not forsaken his *ḥesed* [loyalty, fidelity; GK 2876] to the living or the dead," to whom does the relative pronoun "who" refer? Is the antecedent Boaz or Yahweh? Which one did not forsake his *ḥesed* to the living or the dead?

Boaz, not Yahweh, is the subject of the sentence. Basil Rebera ("Yahweh or Boaz: Ruth 2:20 Reconsidered," *BT* 36 [1985]: 317–27) notes that in 1:8 humans display this *ḥesed* and so asserts that Boaz is the antecedent. But W. S. Prinsloo ("The Theology of the Book of Ruth," *VT* 30 [1980]: 336) argues that Yahweh is "indicated by Naomi as the one who bestows *ḥesed*," so God must be the antecedent. Yet Chertok, 295, concludes that the pronoun can refer to either of them!

Ultimately it is impossible to separate Yahweh from his agent, the *gōʾel*. In 1:6 Yahweh gave his people food—found in Boaz's field. Under whose "wings" did Ruth shelter? In 4:13 Yahweh gave Ruth conception—again through Boaz. Yahweh is praised—for providing Naomi with a redeemer (4:14). In the same way, Yahweh's *ḥesed* is actualized through Boaz, the *gōʾel*, in 2:20. Here Yahweh is gracious—through Boaz's graciousness. Thus the ambiguity in the Hebrew wording reflects the spiritual reality that God's actions coincide with his redeemer's; "the redeeming Israelite God and the solidly human Israelite redeemer Boaz are apparently acting together" (Judith McKinley, "A Son Is Born to Naomi: A Harvest for Israel," in *The Feminist Companion to the Bible (Second Series)* [ed. Athalya Brenner; Sheffield: Sheffield Academic Press, 1999], 3:152).

However, at this stage in the story, Boaz has done nothing except to allow Ruth to glean for one day. To pronounce this as "not forsaking his loyalty to the living and to the dead" seems to be saying too much. What inspires Naomi's exclamation is the recognition that Yahweh is working, until now imperceptibly, to redeem her through Boaz. Now she sees what Yahweh is up to.

21–23 These verses mirror 2:18–19 (see above) and together with them focus the book on 2:20. Boaz has invited Ruth to "cling" to his retinue, and Naomi pronounces this development "good." Ruth continues as Boaz's special project throughout the barley and wheat harvests. It is unclear what Naomi does all this time and why she does not also glean. The text is silent about this matter, so the reader can only speculate. Is Naomi perhaps occupied with other necessities of life (one cannot live on barley and wheat alone!)?

But the best analysis asks what effect this silence has on the reader. How would the story be changed if Naomi's daily activities were recounted? Inevitably, Ruth would seem an unnecessary sidekick. The effect of the book's silent bypassing of Naomi's work makes the mother-in-law appear as a dependant, an invalid in need of Ruth's care. In Ruth, Naomi has but one thing to offer—counsel, which the next pericope treats.

NOTES

18 The last word is מִשָּׂבְעָה (*miśśab'āh*, "from her satiation"), highlighting the complete satisfaction the redeemer supplies.

19 Naomi asks, "*Where* did you glean?" Note the pun: "where" (אֵיפֹה, *'ēpōh*) is consonantally "ephah" (2:17). The second "where" uses a different word.

20 "Kinsman-redeemer" translates a participle of the verb גָּאַל (*gā'al*). At this point redemption becomes the main theme in the second half of Ruth. Collins, 100–101, discovers intentional and "irresolvable syntactical ambiguity" here. He proposes two readings—"who has not forsaken his kindness with the living and with the dead," and "whose kindness has not forsaken the living and the dead"—and concludes, "Boaz in the book of Ruth *embodies* aspects of the character of God, most importantly his *ḥesed*" (emphasis his). Hubbard, 187, suggests, "The similarity between Ruth 2 and Genesis 24 suggests that Naomi's remark probably has marriage in mind" (cf. esp. Ge 24:27).

21 Note the embedded quotation—one of three in Ruth, with the other two in complementary pericopes (2:7; 3:17). Here Ruth quotes Boaz, but in a way that yields additional information hitherto unrevealed. Obviously, Ruth is reporting what Boaz actually said and is not embellishing for the sake of Naomi's feelings. This observation guides the reader in analyzing the same phenomenon in 3:17.

22 See the Note on 2:9; sexual harassment is at issue (Shepherd).

23 The pericope ends by referencing an extended period of time; the next scene begins after the last harvest.

REFLECTION

In the NT, of course, Jesus Christ is the Redeemer extraordinaire, whose identity and purposes are one with God's: "It is the Father, living in me, who is doing his work" (Jn 14:10). Often in the NT redemption is framed in legal terms: "Christ has redeemed us from the curse of the law" (Gal 3:13). The book of Ruth, however, explores multifaceted qualities of redemption that inform Christians about what in this life needs saving and restoring. The main thesis of Ruth clearly dovetails with Jesus' gospel—which is also a story of redemption. In the present pericope the message about the redeemer comes by word of mouth; Naomi heard of him through the gospel that Ruth brought home.

G´:NAOMI'S PROVISION WITH A SECRET COMMAND (3:1–7)

OVERVIEW

Naomi wished to convert Boaz from a pseudo-husband to a real one, from kinsman to spouse. Overtly, Boaz had cared for Ruth by allowing her to glean—covertly, by ordering his men to ward her. Naomi now covertly seeks Ruth's "rest" by commanding her how to respond to Boaz's charity.

Both this section and 2:14–17 end with Ruth's acting in the evening or late at night. These two scenes frame the book's center as shown:

Boaz Provides with Secret Command (2:14–17)
    Ruth Reports Good News to Naomi (2:18–23)
Naomi Provides with Secret Command (3:1–7)

Boaz and Naomi both pursue Ruth's welfare. In this pericope it is clear that the right to glean in Boaz's field is not the highest possible blessing. Ruth (and Naomi) can do better, and so they seek to find "rest" with Boaz as husband. They are not content merely with salvation; they want the savior. Simply eating his bread and drinking his wine in

his house are not enough; they wish to know the redeemer in the most profound way possible. This is one aspect of redemption—it is about love, it is about espousal, it is about to whom the redeemed *belong*.

The revelation of the *gōʾēl* is flanked by pericopes treating hidden plans and actions. Redemption is a mystery involving, on the one hand, a deep personal relationship between the Savior and the saved, but on the other hand, an invisible process whereby behind-the-scenes events transpire to save the beloved. Ruth "chanced" upon Boaz's field—for Yahweh has visited his people with food!

¹One day Naomi her mother-in-law said to her, "My daughter, should I not try to find a home for you, where you will be well provided for? ²Is not Boaz, with whose servant girls you have been, a kinsman of ours? Tonight he will be winnowing barley on the threshing floor. ³Wash and perfume yourself, and put on your best clothes. Then go down to the threshing floor, but don't let him know you are there until he has finished eating and drinking. ⁴When he lies down, note the place where he is lying. Then go and uncover his feet and lie down. He will tell you what to do."

⁵"I will do whatever you say," Ruth answered. ⁶So she went down to the threshing floor and did everything her mother-in-law told her to do.

⁷When Boaz had finished eating and drinking and was in good spirits, he went over to lie down at the far end of the grain pile. Ruth approached quietly, uncovered his feet and lay down.

COMMENTARY

1 That Naomi wishes to pursue Ruth's "rest" (*mānôaḥ*; GK 4955) recalls *menûḥâ* of 1:9, "May the LORD grant that each of you will find *rest* in the home of another husband." Naomi is a matchmaker. To find "rest" is to marry. Compare this language with 2:14–17, when Boaz served the seated Ruth.

Was she not resting? But the rest Ruth already enjoyed had not yet been consummated. Deuteronomy 12:9 calls the Promised Land the *mānôaḥ* of God, which Hebrews 4:1–11 connects with the Sabbath—and the gospel, "Now we who have believed enter that rest" (Heb 4:3). This rest is also a quality of redemption; the redeemed are those who have entered God's rest. Naomi might as well have said to Ruth, "Let us, therefore, make every effort to enter that rest" (Heb 4:11).

2 After harvest, Boaz and his people separate the kernels by winnowing and sieving. Meanwhile, Naomi proposes her risky proposition to Ruth. Hosea 9:1 links threshing floors with illicit sex; Naomi scandalously sends Ruth there at night to enchant the man Boaz. "Night is considered to be a time for sinful, not for righteous deeds" (Harm, 19–20). Except for Joseph, "no other biblical man of valor occurs ... who is a champion of sexual restraint" (Chertok, 291). What does Naomi hope will happen?

3 Ruth's grooming parallels Lady Israel's in Ezekiel 16:9–10. Both women bathed, were anointed with oil, and were attractively appareled. In 16:8 Yahweh spreads his "wing" (*kānāp*) over Israel with a marriage vow. However, she was not satisfied (*śābaʿ*) with the food (*leḥem*) Yahweh gave (16:19, 28). Contrast this outcome with that for Ruth: She was satisfied (*śābaʿ*) with the bread (*leḥem*) Boaz fed to her (2:14). In 2:14–17, she rested in Boaz's favor; he personally served her to satiation. Now she responds by preparing as bride, intending to penetrate his domain while he is merry with food and drink. Thus Ruth appears as an Israel that should have been—the embodiment of the response Yahweh vainly looked for in his beloved of Ezekiel 16.

4 Three times this verse employs the verb *šākab* ("lay, sleep"; GK 8886), a word fraught with sexual overtones (see Nu 5:13; 2Sa 12:11; Eze 23:8). The triconsonantal root *ydʿ* denotes "to know" and is found in each verse of 3:2–4: "We know Boaz" (3:2), "do not make yourself known to him" (3:3),

"know where he lays" (3:4). In the OT this verb at times denotes carnal knowledge and thus carries a double entendre (Ge 4:1, 17, 25; Jdg 19:25). Ruth knows Boaz, but Boaz will not *know* she is lying next to him. This situation is reminiscent of Genesis 29:21–25: after much feasting, Jacob unknowingly slept with Leah. Unbeknownst to Judah, Tamar also prepared herself for coitus and seduced him (Ge 38:11–16). The women of Bethlehem later celebrate and compare both these women to Ruth (4:11–12).

What then does it mean for Ruth to "uncover his feet"? "Feet" is also a euphemism for genitalia (Jdg 3:24; SS 5:3; Isa 7:20; Eze 16:25), and "uncover" also suggests sexuality (Eze 16:37; 23:29; Lev 20:11–21). How far up his legs was Naomi counseling the oiled and alluring Ruth to uncover? Naomi assures her that Boaz will explain what to do next.

5–6 Without hesitation or question, Ruth obeys Naomi's "command"—despite the fact that her plan "is not the normal behavior for a widow and ordinarily would be a dangerous course to follow" (Harm, 20).

7 The verse reads literally, "And she went in *secrecy*" (from *lāṭ*; GK 4319), used three times of magicians' arts (Ex 7:22; 8:3; 8:14), of Jael's stealthy approach of Sisera before she killed him (Jdg 4:21), of political intrigue (1Sa 18:22), and of David's surreptitious cutting off of Saul's *kānāp* while he "covered his feet" (1Sa 24:4–5). Naomi's and Ruth's hidden agenda moves events forward—and humanly mirrors God's hidden purposes. In the words "grain pile" (NIV), "a sensitive reader will detect a hidden erotic allusion to the phrase 'heap of wheat' as a description of a lover's body (Cant. 7:2)" (Hamlin, 41).

NOTES

2 The threshing was specifically of the *barley* harvest, which 2:23 suggests had been succeeded by wheat. The Hebrew reads, "Behold, he is winnowing the threshing floor of the barley tonight"; "threshing floor" is the object of "winnowing." Campbell, 117, reads *śeʿārîm* ("gates") for *śeʿōrîm* ("barley"), thus yielding "the threshing floor near the gate." However, the phrase is probably idiomatic; the grain is in fact barley (3:15).

3 The *Qere* reads, "and you will go down," contra the *Kethiv*, "and I will go down."

4 The *Qere* reads, "and you will lie down," contra the *Kethiv*, "and I will lie down." The *Qere* is obviously correct, since only Ruth prepares for the tryst. Cheryl Exum ("'Is This Naomi?': Misreading, Gender Blurring, and the Biblical Story of Ruth," in *The Practice of Cultural Analysis* [ed. Mieke Bal; Palo Alto, Calif.: Stanford Univ. Press, 1999], 201) sees a possible "Freudian slip," with Naomi fancying herself the coseductrix of Boaz!

5 Note the vowels without consonants. The *Qere* is אֵלָי (*ʾēlay*, "I will do whatever you say *to me*"), constituting one of ten places in the OT in which the *Qere* lacks a *Kethiv* (see NIV).

6 Ruth performs what Naomi "commanded" (from צָוָה, *ṣāwâ*), as Boaz's servants obeyed his command (2:9, 15). The older generation orders events to Ruth's benefit.

7 Joanna W. H. Bos ("Out of the Shadows: Genesis 38; Judges 4:17–22; Ruth 3," *Semeia* 42 [1988]: 37, 39) posits a type-scene that connects Jael, Tamar, and Ruth as follows: (1) introduction of a foreign element, (2) woman's initiation of a meeting incorporating a fertility symbol (i.e., threshing floor), (3) use of a ruse, (4) giving of a gift, (5) woman's departure with success. The stories "challenge patriarchy from within patriarchal structures"; the woman initiates the action, through which God's purposes are achieved.

F': BOAZ'S AND RUTH'S SECOND MEETING (3:8–13)

OVERVIEW

The chart below instances many links between Ruth's and Boaz's two dialogues. Of course, both are also pregnant with innuendo.

First encounter (2:8–13)	Second encounter (3:8–13)
v.8 Boaz implores Ruth to stay with him	v.13 Boaz implores Ruth to stay with him
v.9 "cling to my women"	v.10 "you did not go after the men"
v.10 Ruth bows deeply	v.8 Boaz twists himself
v.10 Ruth places herself at Boaz's feet	v.8 Boaz finds Ruth at his feet
v.10 "Why do you favor me?"	v.9 "Who are you?"
v.11 "You came to people you did not know"	v.11 "All the people know you"
v.12 Ruth shelters under Yahweh's wings	v.9 Ruth asks for shelter under Boaz's "wing"
v.13 Ruth lacks the standing of Boaz's girls	v.12 Boaz lacks standing as premier kinsman-redeemer

(The repetition of "lay … until morning" [3:13–14a] forms a seam; see 1:19. Alternatively, the first three Hebrew words of 3:14 may be treated with 3:13. In that case, "And she arose" would begin a new movement, as Naomi's "aris[ing]" in 1:6 begins a pericope.)

In 2:8 Boaz implored Ruth to stay on his plantation—and to spend the night in 3:13. In 2:10 Boaz astonished Ruth—and she surprises him in return in 3:8. In 2:13 Ruth compared herself to Boaz's maids; Boaz compares himself to the kinsman in 3:13. In their first meeting, Boaz's last word was, "May you richly be rewarded by the LORD, the God of Israel, under whose wings [from *kānāp*] you have come to take refuge" (2:12); in their last meeting Ruth's first word is, in effect, "I am Ruth, so shelter me with your *kānāp*, Redeemer" (3:9). Ruth had sheltered under Yahweh's wings. Now she asks Boaz to do for her what Yahweh has done. Here Boaz is in parallel relation to Yahweh as *gō'el*.

But the issue of redemption is presented in the midst of a story that is charged with erotic language. This account of the risky and tension-filled encounter between the woman who desires a covering and the man who would redeem her permits the reader to enter the inner sanctum of the origin of their marriage covenant, sealed with an oath. The answer to Boaz's question, "Who are you?" is simply, "Ruth your maid, so cover me, *Gō'el*."

Redemption is explored elsewhere in the Bible in the image of matrimony. Ruth parallels Israel's preparing for covenanted love (Eze 16). Hosea's purchase of Gomer is an image for the "latter days," when Israel will seek God and David as king (Hos 3:1–5): "I will redeem [*gā'al*; GK 1457] them from death" (Hos 13:14). Paul cites Hosea to describe the glorious final state of the elect (1Co 15:55); in Ephesians 5:25–27 he uses the image of Christ's bride for the same purpose.

> [8]In the middle of the night something startled the man, and he turned and discovered a woman lying at his feet.
>
> [9]"Who are you?" he asked.
>
> "I am your servant Ruth," she said. "Spread the corner of your garment over me, since you are a kinsman-redeemer."
>
> [10]"The LORD bless you, my daughter," he replied. "This kindness is greater than that which you showed earlier: You have not run after the younger men, whether rich or poor. [11]And now, my daughter, don't be afraid. I will do for you all you ask. All my fellow townsmen know that you are a woman of noble character. [12]Although it is true that I am near of kin, there is a kinsman-redeemer nearer than I. [13]Stay here for the night, and in the morning if he wants to redeem, good; let him redeem. But if he is not willing, as surely as the LORD lives I will do it. Lie here until morning."

COMMENTARY

8 "Something startled the man" (NIV) is from *ḥārad*, which always denotes great fear and trem-bling; "the man was afraid" (KJV). "He turned" (NIV) is from *lāpat*, a rare word meaning "grasp, turn oneself." Samson *grasped* the pillars to bring them crashing down (Jdg 16:29). Imagine Boaz's trembling, twisting himself to see what or who was at his feet. The text does not credit cold feet as causing Boaz's sudden arousal.

9 Ruth now throws Boaz's words back at him. On the day of the barley harvest when they first met, Boaz declared that Ruth was safe under Yahweh's plumage (*kānāp*). Now she uses the same word to describe what she wants from Boaz — for him to cover her with his *kānāp* ("corner of your garment"). Boaz *is* Yahweh's wing, God's means of providing Ruth with rest (and Naomi with a son). All the remaining dialogue is from Boaz. But in her one sentence Ruth speaks volumes. Naomi had told her to uncover his feet and then follow his instructions; instead, she tells Boaz what to do, and he agrees to do it. God works his salvation through the initiative of the Moabitess.

10 Boaz recognizes her reference to their prior conversation and explicitly acknowledges Yahweh as the one who ultimately blesses those with *ḥesed*. Her loyalty and worth lie in how her energies and intentions were directed to Naomi and her dead husband. Alternatively, she might have simply walked away from her previous life and gone after available younger men. Boaz's "rich or poor" is a merism, a figure of speech here meaning "anyone" (as "day and night" means "anytime"). Alternatively, Campbell, 124, suggests that Ruth had received various marriage proposals. Boaz says that her proposition — to wed him rather than in her own generation — marks a greater example of *ḥesed* than

returning to Bethlehem with Naomi had been. By pursuing Boaz, Ruth's children will stay in the family of Naomi; Ruth's sons will inherit and work Naomi's land and be responsible for her well-being.

11 Boaz assures Ruth that all will be well. The reason he gives is that the leaders of Bethlehem recognize her worth. Ruth and Boaz trust each other's character in this risky encounter; they both "maintain their righteousness and so demonstrate that the godly can live above their culture" (Harm, 22). Never again does the narrator call Ruth "Moabitess."

12 The marriage proposal is only part of what Ruth is asking for, as is evident in that she clearly makes herself sexually available to Boaz. If this is not an overture to love, what is? But *redemption* involves *property*; so, now that harvesting is done, Ruth asks Boaz to take control of Naomi's estate. Elimelech had left his land to others for a decade. Although his widow had the right to sell it, she lacked the authority to foreclose or manage it (as in 2Ki 8:1-6). Boaz could do so once he bought it from her. Afterwards, in the absence of heirs (brothers or sons) of Elimelech, Boaz could annex it into his own estate. However, there was one unnamed relative with a prior claim who might also be willing to buy the land and hold it in escrow for Elimelech's family.

13 Boaz promises that for Ruth, as Naomi's representative, he will redeem. This statement is a promise to purchase Elimelech's land, as is clearly revealed in the legal proceedings that follow. The text is operating on two levels; redemption of land *and* marriage to Ruth are at issue.

NOTES

8 Campbell, 122, glosses וַיִּלָּפֵת (*wayyillāpēt*), "and groped about," i.e., "for his mantle, to cover himself from the cold."

9 כִּי (*kî*) draws a connection between this marriage and redemption. Ruth pursues him because he is a redeemer, because her intention is to restitute Elimelech's family, not just his land.

10 Sasson, 84, identifies the "former" and the "latter" *ḥesed* as Ruth's two requests: (1) to marry her, and (2) to redeem the land. Hyman, 61, suggests Boaz did not propose earlier because he felt too old for her.

11 Boaz calls her a "woman of חַיִל [*ḥayil*]" (cf. 2:1).

12 The unpointed word אִם (ʾm) is one of eight places in the OT with a *Kethiv* but no *Qere*; thus ignore it.

13 That the verb גָּאַל (gāʾal) is thrice suffixed with the second feminine pronoun—"If he will redeem *you* ... I will redeem *you*"—seems to tie redemption with marriage. But Sasson's gloss, "should he redeem *for you*," limits redemption to the land.

E′: BOAZ COLLECTS BARLEY INTO RUTH'S APRON (3:14-18)

OVERVIEW

As in the discourse above, it is instructive to compare this pericope with its counterpart, 2:1–7. They gird the enclosed material as follows:

E Ruth Collects Barley in Boaz's Field (2:1–7)

  F Boaz's and Ruth's First Meeting (2:8–13)

    ...

    H Ruth Reports Good News to Naomi (2:18–23)

    ...

  F′ Boaz's and Ruth's Second Meeting (3:8–14a)

E′ Boaz Collects Barley into Ruth's Apron (3:14b–18)

In 2:1–7 Ruth left Naomi to go toward Boaz, and in 3:14–18 she leaves Boaz to go home to Naomi.

Reading these pericopes as complementary elements has interpretative implications, delineated below.

At issue is seed, which (metaphorically) highlights another aspect of redemption. Yahweh has visited his people with food (1:6), which Boaz spades into Ruth's apparel. In Genesis 3:15, God set enmity between the seed of the woman and the seed of the serpent with the promise that the serpent would be vanquished by the woman's seed. Yahweh covenanted with Abraham and his seed (Ge 15), which Paul says points to Christ (Gal 3:16), born to redeem God's people, who then cry "Abba, Father!" (4:5–6). Although here in Ruth literal seed is treated, the book concludes with Obed, Boaz's "seed" (4:12), and a genealogy, which continues through time to Jesus (Mt 1:5).

> ¹⁴So she lay at his feet until morning, but got up before anyone could be recognized; and he said, "Don't let it be known that a woman came to the threshing floor."
> ¹⁵He also said, "Bring me the shawl you are wearing and hold it out." When she did so, he poured into it six measures of barley and put it on her. Then he went back to town.
> ¹⁶When Ruth came to her mother-in-law, Naomi asked, "How did it go, my daughter?" Then she told her everything Boaz had done for her ¹⁷and added, "He gave me these six measures of barley, saying, 'Don't go back to your mother-in-law empty-handed.'"

> ¹⁸Then Naomi said, "Wait, my daughter, until you find out what happens. For the man will not rest until the matter is settled today."

COMMENTARY

14 Two scenes begin in the early morning: Ruth was in Boaz's field "from the morning until now" (2:7); and here Ruth arises literally, "before a man can be acquainted with his friend." Boaz then says, "Don't let it be known that a woman came to the threshing floor." To whom is Boaz speaking? "The Midrash regards the utterance as a prayer" (Arthur E. Cundall and Leon Morris, *Judges and Ruth* [Downers Grove, Ill.: InterVarsity Press, 1968], 294). Hubbard, 220, argues, "The following statement is indirect address and hence was not spoken to Ruth (against Vulg.) or to servants (against Targ.)," and he translates, "Now Boaz *thought*, 'No one must know....'" However, when in 2:5–7 Boaz did not recognize Ruth, he queried the foreman, who was in the know. Perhaps here Boaz speaks to this man again, so that at least one of Boaz's clan is entrusted with the secret of what transpired that night.

15 Ruth had gathered Boaz's barley; now Boaz measures barley into her cloak. They depart, Boaz toward Bethlehem and Ruth toward Naomi sporting an "apron bulging with grain" (Rauber, 35), and thus "emblematically anticipating her later conception" (Warren A. Gage, "Ruth upon the Threshing Floor and the Sin of Gibeah: A Biblical-Theological Study," *WTJ* [1989]: 373). In other words, Ruth returns home *symbolically* inseminated, her midriff being pregnant with Boaz's seed. Of course, if coitus had occurred, such imagery would be anticlimactic. Even Freud might admit,

Zuweilen sind Füße nur Füße ("Sometimes feet are only feet").

16 As Boaz asked the foreman in 2:5, "Whose young woman is she?" (the answer being, "Naomi's"), now Naomi asks literally, "My daughter, who are you?" In the words of the late Ray Dillard, "Are you Miss Ruth or Mrs. Boaz?" Redemption is a matter of *belonging*.

17 When Boaz shoveled grain into Ruth's raiment, the text does not record him aver that his mind was on Naomi. Fewell and Gunn argue that Ruth fabricated this claim to cater to Naomi's sensitive feelings. But in the "parallel" embedded quote of 2:7, the foreman did not put words in Ruth's mouth even though he revealed additional data; probably neither does Ruth embellish here. Hamlin, 50, suggests that the six measures of barley foreshadow a consummate seventh, analogous to the sixth day of creation preceding the Sabbath. Of course the seventh measure would consist in another kind of seed altogether.

18 As in 2:7 Ruth sat and waited for Boaz, so here both women sit and wait. The matter is again out of their hands and in his. In this patriarchal culture, the men decide for the women matters of ownership and possession—a good metaphor for the redemption of Israel. Ruth is dependent on God and his *gōʾēl* to determine the manner and circumstance of her redemption; yet her derring-do effectively makes her the coredemptrix.

NOTES

14 "And she arose *beṭerem*" (reading the *Qere*) is usually understood as per the NIV (i.e., Ruth got up before anyone could recognize her), but J. T. Walsh ("Two Notes on Translation and the Syntax of *terem*," *VT* 49 [1999]: 265) glosses, "She got up and, before one person could recognize another, he said, 'It must not be known that the woman came to the threshing floor.'"

15 "But if Boaz has not filled her as a man fills a woman, he does so with food" (Hyman, 61). De Waard and Nida, 57, figure fifty pounds of barley, thus periling the image of pregnancy, since Ruth likely slung it onto her back. The Hebrew says "six of barley," without specifying a "measure." "Six" might be symbolic, the seventh being Obed (4:15–17); see Derek Beattie, *Jewish Exegesis of the Book of Ruth* (JSOTSup 2; Sheffield: JSOT, 1977), 182.

16 The Hebrew of this pericope does not employ Naomi's name, despite the NIV's wording. "Naomi" occurs twenty-one times in Ruth, thus with the same frequency as "redeem/redeemer."

17 As in 3:5, the *Qere* reads "to me" in the absence of any *Kethiv*.

18 In anticipation, Ruth and Naomi sit, waiting to see how matters fall. In the next pericope, "sit" is found six times in the first four verses, possibly as a verbal link tying the scenes.

D′: IS THIS THE REDEEMER? (4:1–8)

OVERVIEW

Loretz, 395, suggests that the theme of the "name" is the "central thread" of the book of Ruth; "Ruth is a book preoccupied with identity" (Richards, 64). Redemption is restoring the *name* of the dead to his inheritance (4:5); the *gōʾēl* raises up the name—at cost to himself.

> The birth of the child and the prospective mention of David form the conclusion of the book. The family of Elimelech, and therefore its "name" has been preserved, and still more, has been found worthy to form the illustrious line of the Davidic ancestry. (Loretz, 398–99)

Jesus made known the Father's name (Jn 17:26), and there is salvation in no other name (Ac 4:12). Similarly, Ruth revealed to Naomi the name of the *gōʾēl* (2:19). Knowing the name of the Redeemer is part and parcel of being numbered among the redeemed. Any whose names are in the Book of Life will be restored and raised (Rev 20:15). Redemption is knowing and being known—by name.

At various places in Ruth the question is asked, "Who are you?" The women called "Naomi" by name, only to be told that her name was unsuitable (1:20): Don't call me that! Call me "Bitter" (from *mar*) instead, for "the LORD has witnessed against me" (NASB). The present pericope also features witnesses in a legal setting—and in question is another appellation. The title of the so-called kinsman-redeemer substitutes for his name; the question is, will the redeemer redeem? Does the title suit him? Or, as with Naomi, will he bear witness that the designation *gōʾēl* is not fitting? Naomi claimed that she "went out full" but has been "brought back empty" (1:21); the kinsman-redeemer fears a similar outcome for himself (4:6). So like Naomi, he denies his identification. She did so with an audible sign ("Mara!"), he does so with a visible sign of "transfer" (root *mûr*)—his sandal (4:7).

In this pericope, redemption occurs in a legal setting—an aspect of redemption deeply explored in the NT. There, however, redemption is from the consequences of sin (Gal 3:13; 4:5; Tit 2:14; Heb 9:15). Here redemption is from the consequence of leaving the Promised Land. What was then lost must be purchased; at personal cost to the Redeemer, the name of the dead must be raised. Only then will legal requirements be satisfied and all that was doomed restored, including the name, seed, inheritance, and family of the dead.

¹Meanwhile Boaz went up to the town gate and sat there. When the kinsman-redeemer he had mentioned came along, Boaz said, "Come over here, my friend, and sit down." So he went over and sat down.

²Boaz took ten of the elders of the town and said, "Sit here," and they did so. ³Then he said to the kinsman-redeemer, "Naomi, who has come back from Moab, is selling the piece of land that belonged to our brother Elimelech. ⁴I thought I should bring the matter to your attention and suggest that you buy it in the presence of these seated here and in the presence of the elders of my people. If you will redeem it, do so. But if you will not, tell me, so I will know. For no one has the right to do it except you, and I am next in line."

"I will redeem it," he said.

⁵Then Boaz said, "On the day you buy the land from Naomi and from Ruth the Moabitess, you acquire the dead man's widow, in order to maintain the name of the dead with his property."

⁶At this, the kinsman-redeemer said, "Then I cannot redeem it because I might endanger my own estate. You redeem it yourself. I cannot do it."

⁷(Now in earlier times in Israel, for the redemption and transfer of property to become final, one party took off his sandal and gave it to the other. This was the method of legalizing transactions in Israel.)

⁸So the kinsman-redeemer said to Boaz, "Buy it yourself." And he removed his sandal.

COMMENTARY

1–2 The legal proceeding begins with the seating of the elders at the city gate. The text bends over backward to keep from mentioning the kinsman-redeemer's name. He is first called "the one of whom Boaz spoke," and then Boaz directly addresses him with *pelōnî ʾalmōnî*, perhaps denoting "such-a-one." The designation is found in 1 Samuel 21:3 and translated "whatever." Hubbard glosses "Mr. So-and-So." "The un-named kinsman acted to secure his name: but it has long since been lost.

Boaz risked the loss of his name; but ... his fame will live on till the end of the world!" (Stephen Dray, "Ruth 3:1–4:22: Living in Grace," *Evangel* 14 [1996]: 36).

3–4 Boaz seems to be a spokesman for Naomi, but in actuality this action is a ploy that reveals the character and motivations of the so-called kinsman-redeemer. Boaz says that Naomi must sell Elimelech's land, but any offspring of hers could reclaim the land. However, Naomi has no sons. Thus this opportunity seems to be quite a deal. The redeemer says simply, "I will redeem."

5–6 Now Boaz unveils the rest of the story. The Hebrew as written says, "On the day that you acquire the field ... *I will acquire* the widow of the dead." (The *Qere* implausibly reads "*you* will acquire," as per the NIV.) Boaz will wed Ruth to sire Elimelech's heir. In other words, the kinsman will hardly own the land before Boaz repossesses it for his/Elimelech's son; "the redeemer suddenly saw the redemption of the field as a profitless exercise" (Derek Beattie, "Book of Ruth as Evidence for Israelite Legal Practice," *VT* 24 [1974]: 264), and he cedes.

Dana Fewell and David Gunn ("Boaz, Pillar of Society: Measures of Worth in the Book of Ruth," *JSOT* 45 [1989]: 45–59) wonder why Boaz is so cagey in this matter and suggest that his "tricky dealing" belies his character. Why does he publicly embarrass his kinsman by disallowing an informed decision from the start? Drawing on his experience under conditions that arguably emulate ancient Bethlehem (Kanyoro, 368), Tony Sauder (see reference to Sauder's unpublished letter in the introduction) recognizes Boaz's logical strategy and explains Boaz's actions as follows. If Boaz had not forced the *gōʾel* to reveal his true motivation, he might later have claimed, "Boaz knew I was unable to buy it then, but it is really mine; he cheated me!" Since he first said yes and then no, he could not make a pretense later. The revelation of his true intentions is also the reason Ruth's nocturnal visit to Boaz had to be kept secret (Derek Beattie, "*Kethibh* and *Qere* in Ruth 4:5," *VT* 21 [1971]: 493).

Of course, the conversation also reveals the kinsman's character to the reader; although the kinsman is not censored for his response, it does stand in contrast with Boaz's willingness to restore what Naomi has lost. In that respect the kinsman and Orpah serve a similar rhetorical purpose: to highlight the extraordinary through comparison with the ordinary.

7 Calum Carmichael ("Ceremonial Crux: Removing a Man's Sandal as a Female Gesture of Contempt," *JBL* 96 [1977]: 321–36) argues that the sandal represented the wife, into whom a man might slip his "foot." However, it probably represents the right to walk the land as owner. This account was written long after the fact (see also Dt 25:7–11).

8 The legal procedure concludes with the response of the kinsman to Boaz's proposal by symbolically removing from his foot his right to the land.

NOTES

1 "Went up to the town gate" is idiomatic for the place of official business, the town hall, so to speak (see Dt 25:7).

3 Boaz calls Elimelech "our brother" in the extended sense. מָכְרָה (*mokrâ*) is not an accomplished act; Naomi "must sell" or "is selling" (see also Boaz's קָנִיתִי [*qānîtay*] in 4:5).

4 The Hebrew idiom is "uncover your ear" ("bring to your attention," NIV).

5 Boaz says the field is sold by Naomi וּמֵאֵת רוּת, (*ûmē'et rût*, "and from Ruth"); the *BHS* suggests, גַּם־אֶת־רוּת (*gam'et-rût*, "also Ruth"). Cyrus Gordon ("WM- 'and' in Eblaite and Hebrew," in *Eblaitica 1* [ed. Cyrus H. Gordon, Gary A. Rendsburg, and Nathan H. Winter; New York: Eisenbrauns, 1987], 29) notes enclitic *mem* and glosses, "But I have acquired Ruth ..."—i.e., they have already married, "cementing their union through one of the three ways in which a man acquires an eligible woman";"no matter what happens to the field, his marriage to Ruth is a *fait accompli*" (Gary A. Rendsburg, "Ù-MA and Hebrew WM-," in *Eblaitica 1* [ed. Cyrus H. Gordon, Gary A. Rendsburg, and Nathan H. Winter; New York: Eisenbrauns, 1987], 39). However, Boaz clearly ties his "acquisition" of Ruth in time to the acquisition of land; thus the state of wedded bliss is not yet theirs. Citing the LXX, Murray D. Gow ("Ruth *quoque*—A Coquette: [Ruth 4:5]," *TynBul* 41 [1990]: 311) needlessly emends to קָנִיתָה (*qnyth*, "you acquire her"), suggesting ה was misread for י. Hubbard, 61, notes unresolved questions with the *Kethiv*, opts for the *Qere*, and argues that the kinsman expected to marry Naomi but was surprised when Boaz swapped her with Ruth!

6 Raymond Dillard and Tremper Longman III (*An Introduction to the Old Testament* [Grand Rapids: Zondervan, 1994], 131) argue that here would have been a perfect opportunity to shame the proponents of Ezra if Ruth were written for that purpose, but the book does not do so. Here also the notion that a *gō'el* must act as *levir* (so-called "widow inheritance") is debunked. "If that was the law, he must certainly have heard about it, for how could a landowner not be familiar with such a basic law?" (Josiah Derby, "A Problem in the Book of Ruth," *JBQ* 22 [1994]: 184).

7 "Transfer" is Hebrew תְּמוּרָה (*t'mûrâ*), a rare word found also in Leviticus 27:10, 33; Job 20:18; 28:17. Compare the shoe as legal symbol with Amos 2:6 and 8:6, "selling the needy for a pair of sandals" (E. A. Speiser, "Of Shoes and Shekels," *BASOR* 77 [1940]: 16).

8 Aharon Pollack ("Notes on Megillat Ruth—Chapter 4," *JBQ* 24 [1996]: 183–85) suggests that throughout, the town knew Boaz would redeem; the drama was a social nicety. However, the text is clear that their betrothal was secret.

C': BOAZ'S DECLARATION OF INTENT/WITNESSES' BLESSING (4:9–12)

OVERVIEW

The kinsman having spoken his last and negotiations concluded, Boaz now declares his intent to marry Ruth and raise up the family of Elimelech—a commitment in defiance of death. Here the (hitherto silent) elders give voice and bless the union. Ruth also had declared her intention to follow Naomi until death did them part (1:16–17); but Naomi responded in bitter silence, in contrast with Bethlehem's exuberant response to Boaz.

9Then Boaz announced to the elders and all the people, "Today you are witnesses that I have bought from Naomi all the property of Elimelech, Kilion and Mahlon. 10I have also acquired Ruth the Moabitess, Mahlon's widow, as my wife, in order to maintain the name of the dead with his property, so that his name will not disappear from among his family or from the town records. Today you are witnesses!"

11Then the elders and all those at the gate said, "We are witnesses. May the LORD make the woman who is coming into your home like Rachel and Leah, who together built up the house of Israel. May you have standing in Ephrathah and be famous in Bethlehem, 12through the offspring the LORD gives you by this young woman, may your family be like that of Perez, whom Tamar bore to Judah."

COMMENTARY

9 Boaz now for the first time addresses the elders and witnesses directly. Redemption occurs in community. This matter is not one that concerns merely a few individuals. In the NT the whole church constitutes the company of the redeemed. The Lord redeems *his people* (Lk 1:68); it is we, ourselves together, who possess redemption (Ro 8:23; Eph 1:7). This transaction of Boaz's typifies Israel's redemption by Yahweh.

10 Boaz puts forward two aspects of redemption. The first is buying and managing the land for Elimelech's heir. The second is marrying the widow of Mahlon to generate this heir. These aspects, discussed rather cryptically on the threshing floor, are here stated clearly (Sasson, 148). What is restored (or more accurately not lost) is threefold: (1) Elimelech's inheritance to his family, (2) Elimelech's family to his clan, and (3) Elimelech's clan to the entire community. These restorations form concentric circles of ever-widening scope.

11 Naomi previously urged Ruth to be like Orpah (1:15). Now Ruth is likened to Rachel and Leah, matriarchs of the twelve tribes. Not only do Naomi and Ruth benefit, not only do the clan and

even the whole town gain *hayil*, but also all Israel is fortified and strengthened! Redemption of an individual has a ripple effect that affects the whole nation; salvation is not about isolated individuals, but individuals in a community of faith. The union of Boaz and Ruth do eventually win fame for Bethlehem through their descendant David — and through their greater descendant Jesus, born in Bethlehem, the "city of David" (Lk 2:4, 11). And in Jesus this redemption extends to the whole world.

12 "Offspring" (NIV) is in Hebrew "seed" (*zeraʿ*), which the elders expect Yahweh will give to Boaz through Ruth, as God did to Judah through Tamar (Ge 38). Tamar's husband died, and his brother Onan refused to impregnate her; so through deception she stole her father-in-law Judah's seed, producing Perez. The elders invoke this cross-generational coupling to bless Boaz! Thus Ruth is compared with both Leah and Tamar, who proactively populated Israel despite uncooperative men, and the once-barren Rachel. This blessing was probably a traditional one pronounced on the betrothed and here recorded for its pertinence (the reader being privy to Ruth's initiative at the threshing floor).

"As we hear the townspeople proclaim a standard benediction, we hear more than they say" (Moshe J. Bernstein, "Two Multivalent Readings in the Ruth Narrative," *JSOT* 50 [1991]: 24).

NOTES

9 The names of Mahlon and Chilion are listed in reverse order compared with 1:2, 5; "the story-teller's use of chiasm ... may be the appropriate explanation" (Campbell, 151).

10 Gene M. Tucker ("Witnesses and 'Dates' in Israelite Contracts," *CBQ* 28 [1966]: 45) compares Boaz's הַיּוֹם (*hayyôm*, "today") with Akkadian notations of date and concludes that it "marked the formal initiation of a legal agreement," forever binding. The verse begins with וְגַם (*wegam*, "and also ..."), delineating a second transaction.

11 Ruth is likened to Rachel, the beloved wife, who died while birthing Benjamin—a tacit anti-Saulide polemic (Eugene H. Merrill, "The Book of Ruth: Narration and Shared Themes," *BSac* 142 [1985]: 133).

12 James Black ("Ruth in the Dark: Folktale, Law, and Creative Ambiguity in the Old Testament," *Journal of Literature and Theology* 5 [1991]: 20) calls Leah's and Tamar's tactics the "bride-in-the-dark or bed-trick stratagem; the device of surprising a man with a bed-partner or of substituting one 'bride' for another"—a maneuver also responsible for Moab (Ge 19:35–37) and yet another link with Ruth (Mira Morgenstern, "Ruth and the Sense of Self: Midrash and Difference," *Judaism* 48 [1999]: 133). Naomi made Ruth a "bride-in-the-dark," but unlike her precursors Ruth does not fox Boaz, but instead reveals her identity.

REFLECTION

In this section of this story, the sting of death is rolled back by the true *gōʾēl* of God, who has not forsaken his *ḥesed* to the living or the dead, whose latter *ḥesed* surpasses the former—who reinstates what death and famine had destroyed. Paul calls the eschatological resurrection of the dead the "redemption of our bodies" (Ro 8:23). Christians groan inwardly, he says, awaiting this adoption as children. Boaz will adopt through natural generation the legal heir of another man and, by this means, redeem from destruction Elimelech and all that is his. After he died and went to see God, apart from his flesh Elimelech might well have said, "I know that my *gōʾēl* lives, at last he will stand up [for me] on the land" (Job 19:25).

B': A SON IS BORN TO NAOMI AND IS TO BE A RESTORER (4:13–17)

OVERVIEW

All that was lacking is finally and fully satisfied at the story's denouement. It is again instructive to set this scene alongside its counterpart and observe matching factors.

B Naomi Is Bereft of Sons so Each Must Return Home (1:6–14)

C Ruth's Declaration of Intent/Naomi's Silence (1:15–19a)

…

C' Boaz's Declaration of Intent/Witnesses' Blessing (4:9–12)

B' A Son Is Born to Naomi Who Is to Be a Restorer (4:13–17)

The chart below instances some links between B and B'.

Naomi is bereft of sons so each must *return home* (1:6–14)	A son is born to Naomi who is to be a *restorer* (4:13–17)
v.6 Yahweh gives food	v.13 Yahweh gives conception
vv.6–8, 10–12 "Return!" (*šûb*)	v.15 The boy is a "restorer" (*šûb*)
v.9 May you find rest with a husband	v.13 Boaz becomes Ruth's husband
v.12 Naomi is too old for a husband	v.15 The boy will sustain Naomi in her old age
v.12 Naomi has no more sons	v.17 Naomi has a son!
v.13 Would you wait until sons grew up?	v.16 Naomi nurses the son
v.13 Yahweh has embittered Naomi	v.14 Yahweh has redeemed Naomi
v.14 Ruth clings to her	v.15 Ruth is better than seven sons

In the book of Ruth, the narration ascribes but two actions to Yahweh. In 1:6 he "visited his people by giving [*nātan*] them food"; and in 4:13 he "gave" (*nātan*) Ruth "conception." "The exegetical importance of this is highlighted by the fact that here … are the only direct references to God as an active agent" (David Lauten, "A Theology of Sovereignty" [unpublished paper, 1989], 5). Only in these pericopes does God act.

The common verb *šûb* (GK 8740) is used fifteen times in Ruth, with all but three instances occurring in 1:6–22 (treating Naomi's return from Moab) and two other times also about her "return from … Moab" (2:6; 4:3). Naomi's lament marks 1:6–14: "Return, return!" Perhaps this feature influenced 4:15 (the centerpiece of this pericope), where Obed is titled "Restorer" (from *šûb*) of life ("renew your life," NIV). Naomi begged her daughters-in-law to *return*; God at last furnishes a *turner* of fortunes.

In 1:12 Naomi's lament, "If I married *tonight* and conceived," is mirrored in 4:14, "Yahweh has not left you without a redeemer *today*"; that is, the night of 1:12 becomes the day of 4:14. Both scenes treat bearing sons; Naomi could not have sons for them (so they must "return"); now Obed is Naomi's son, the "restorer"!

Redemption involves restoring all that has been lost. Everything Naomi lamented has now been answered by Yahweh. The family is restored. Elimelech's seed and name are restored. Naomi's life is now warded. The land is redeemed. Yahweh's people shelter under his wings, thus creating a community of faith wherein the faithful can take risks. But most of all, Yahweh is inseparably identified with the Redeemer he raises up, whose land it is, whose seed it is, whose "wing" protects, whose covenantal fidelity and worth are brought to bear in such a way that not even death itself has the final word. This redemption of one family continues on and eventually produces David, the great king of Israel (4:17). A family story has become a national one in which the character and quality of Yahweh's worshipers are displayed to reveal God's willingness and power to redeem. This is the gospel of Ruth.

> ¹³So Boaz took Ruth and she became his wife. Then he went to her, and the Lord enabled her to conceive, and she gave birth to a son. ¹⁴The women said to Naomi: "Praise be to the Lord, who this day has not left you without a kinsman-redeemer. May he become famous throughout Israel! ¹⁵He will renew your life and sustain you in your old age. For your daughter-in-law, who loves you and who is better to you than seven sons, has given him birth."
> ¹⁶Then Naomi took the child, laid him in her lap and cared for him. ¹⁷The women living there said, "Naomi has a son." And they named him Obed. He was the father of Jesse, the father of David.

COMMENTARY

13–14 The cooperation between Yahweh and the redeemer can be seen no more clearly than here. As Mahlon's wife, Ruth had suffered a barren womb for ten years. Now, older and wedded to Boaz, Yahweh blesses with issue—a development evocative of other special births, such as that of Isaac in Sarah's old age, Samuel by Hannah, and in the NT John and finally Jesus. David's grandfather was born under auspicious circumstances as a gift of Yahweh. This birth is cause to bless God, under whose wings faithful Israelites are secure. Ruth is about the Lord's faithfulness to redeem.

15 Hannah's husband asked, "Don't I mean more to you than ten sons?" (1Sa 1:8) before her heaven-sent pregnancy in the birth narrative about Samuel. Other important figures in the Bible are introduced with birth narratives, such as Moses and Samson. The book of Ruth serves a similar purpose for David. The child Obed is Naomi's redeemer and restorer; this identification is the central part of the pericope (Bush, 6) and

reinforces the theme of the whole book—God is faithful in providing a redeemer. Restoration is not fully accomplished by Boaz but continues on for generations to come.

16–17 Ruth births him, but Naomi nurses him. Through the women, the book interprets this mothering as though Naomi and Ruth were two aspects of one person, as though Naomi had given him birth. This blurring of the two women has led to speculation as to the origin of the book, namely, the suggestion that perhaps at one time there were two independent stories woven together into one (Athalya Brenner, "Naomi and Ruth," *VT* 33 [1983]: 385–97). This speculation highlights the startling identification of Naomi as Obed's mother. Rather than suggesting the book's origin, however, the blurring points to the legal identity of Obed, who was literally born of the Moabitess but was heir to Elimelech's property and thus enjoyed status as Naomi's son. "The narrator regards Naomi's loss of her children at the beginning of the story as reversed—she now once again has acquired a child" (Simon B. Parker, "The Birth Announcement," *Ascribe to the Lord: Biblical and Other Studies in Memory of Peter C. Craigie* [ed. Lyle Eslinger, Peter C. Craigie, and Glen Taylor; JSOTSup 67; Sheffield: JSOT, 1988], 138).

4:17 is composed of two parallel lines, as shown below.

And-called	him	the-women	a name	saying	been-born-a-son	to-Naomi
And-they-called	his-name	Obed	he	the-father-of-Jesse	the-father-of	David

Twice they "call his name." Hubbard ("Ruth 4:17: A New Solution," *VT* 38 [1988]: 300) suggests that the first "calling by name" should be translated, "to proclaim his significance." "What made this newborn infant important was that, under God's providential hand, the old widow Naomi, the one who bitterly despaired of having an heir at all (i 20–21), now held one in her own hands." Bush, 13, takes this thought further and argues that the name "Obed" ("Servant") parallels its meaning: "Naomi has born a son"; that is, he is the one who will serve (provide for) Naomi.

NOTES

13 Yahweh gave הֵרָיוֹן (*hērāyôn*, "conception"), the rare nominative form of הָרָה (*hārâ*; see Hos 9:11). The pericope is bounded by the inclusio "birth a son" (Bush, 4). Boaz "went in" Ruth after the scene at the gate, not the night before.

14 "And-may-be-called his-name in-Israel." Whose name is celebrated, Yahweh's, Obed's, or Boaz's? This ambiguity mirrors that of 2:20; again, one cannot separate God and the redeemer(s) he provides (see Campbell, 163–64).

15 Ruth is "better than seven sons"—note the seventh use of "daughter-in-law." "Old age" uses שֵׂיבָה (*śêbâ*) rather than זָקֵן (*zāken*) to alliterate with מֵשִׁיב (*mēšîb*, "restorer").

16 Naomi and Boaz are again parallel. In 4:13 Boaz "took" (וַיִּקַּח, *wayyiqqaḥ*) Ruth as his wife (וַתְּהִי־לוֹ לְאִשָּׁה, *wattehî lô lᵉiššâ*); here Naomi "took" (וַתִּקַּח, *wattiqqaḥ*) her child (וַתְּהִי־לוֹ לְאֹמֶנֶת, *wattᵉhî-lô lᵉᵓōmenet*). "Nurse" translates the participle of אָמַן (*ᵓāman*; see 2Sa 4:4; Nu 11:12). Campbell, 164, suggests that יֶלֶד (*yeled*) forms an inclusion with 1:5—intentionality that explains its unusual use for adults there.

17 David is as licitly traceable through Naomi as Ruth; is he then truly a scion of Moab?

A′: GENERATIONS OF PEREZ (4:18-22)

OVERVIEW

Ruth's first five verses, which chronicle a significant span of years summarizing a family's demise, are in the last five verses answered with the unbroken line of Perez, thus framing the book with prologue and epilogue. This genealogy sports a number of notable features, commented on below.

> ¹⁸This, then, is the family line of Perez:
>
> Perez was the father of Hezron,
> ¹⁹Hezron the father of Ram,
> Ram the father of Amminadab,
> ²⁰Amminadab the father of Nahshon,
> Nahshon the father of Salmon,
> ²¹Salmon the father of Boaz,
> Boaz the father of Obed,
> ²²Obed the father of Jesse,
> and Jesse the father of David.

COMMENTARY

18 Why begin with Perez? Is the answer perhaps because 4:12 calls Perez Tamar's son (see Ge 38, a story relatable to Ruth)? Or is it that ten names are needed to balance the ten proper names of 1:1–5? Harold Fisch ("Ruth and the Structure of Covenant History," *VT* 32 [1982]: 435) calls 1:1–5 and 4:18–22 "the genealogy at the beginning and end"; Ruth completes the first, David the last. But Sasson, 180–81, persuasively claims these five verses were "tailor made for inclusion as an ending of Ruth," not a stilted, anticlimactic appendix: "Since in Ruth's genealogy Boaz is reckoned as seventh from Perez …

David's line was arranged in order to focus attention on Ruth's protagonist." Indeed, "genealogies were entirely too important to the Hebrew people to be regarded as something extra or nonessential" (De Waard and Nida, 77).

19–20 These verses extend from the patriarchs to the judges. Hezron's grandfather by this list would be Judah. Salmon begot Boaz "in the days of the judges." Obviously, generations are skipped and this is a stylized genealogy (see Lk 3:33). From Perez to David covers eight or nine centuries, represented here in ten generations. The first five lead up to the exodus, the next five follow it.

21 Boaz's father was Salmon. Donaldson, 138, notes that "Ruth's other mother-in-law" was none other than Rahab (Mt 1:5), the non-Israelite harlot who allowed Joshua's spies to escape (Jos 2; 6)! Ruth the Moabitess is identified with many intriguing women in the book named for her, and finally also (by Matthew) with Rahab. Rahab took initiative, forsook her people, identified with Yahweh, and thus saved her (helpless) family.

22 The book has led up to David, whose ancestry is populated with individuals (e.g., Ruth and Boaz) who exemplified covenantal fidelity and enjoyed Yahweh's blessings, such that any Israelite would desire in a king. What of David's Saulide rival? For this history read Judges, especially the last two episodes. Then decide which family should prevail.

NOTES

18 See also 1 Chronicles 2:5–15. Sasson, 186, observes that the author purposely put Boaz in the seventh place and David in the tenth—a pointless design for Chronicles. Thus the list is styled for the book of Ruth, which later influenced the Chronicler.

19–20 Amminadab represents the last generation in Egypt (Ex 6:23). His son Nahshon journeyed in the wilderness (Nu 7:12); Salmon presumably took part in the conquest.

21 For "Salmon," note the variant spellings in 4:20 (שַׂלְמָה, śalmâ) and 4:21 (שַׂלְמוֹן, śalmôn). "Solomon" might be another form from the same root. שַׂלְמָה (śalmâ) begot Boaz; David begot שְׁלֹמֹה (šᵉlōmōh).

22 The genealogy's stopping short of naming Solomon makes unlikely the text's postexilic origin. In fact, it is questionable whether this omission would have been made during any time period after Solomon. Various versions and Matthew 1:6 add, "David *the king*."

REFLECTION

Generations continued on after David until Jesus, whose pedigree is listed in Matthew 1. He also is a king who deserves all Israel's allegiance as the son of David, God's anointed. His is the *ḥesed* and his is the *ḥayil*; he is the Redeemer blessed by the Father. Why follow another, since Jesus is all that one could desire in a King?